MW00334840

1998 ★ 1999
TEXAS
ALMANAC
AND STATE INDUSTRIAL GUIDE

PUBLISHED BY

The Dallas Morning News

The Beautiful Colors of Texas

You will see them all at Dillard's. In our apparel and in our
home fashions, you will find we share the tastes of Texas and
show our colors with pride. Every day of the year we deliver
quality, integrity, value and service in true Texas style.
Shop and see the beautiful things that make
Dillard's a Texas favorite.

Dillard's

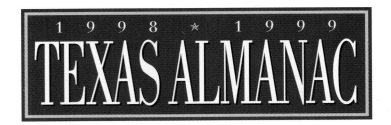

Table of Contents

Mary G. Ramos, Editor
Robert Plocheck, Associate Editor
Brian Morren, Cover Artist

Texas

The Lone Star State

On this and the following page we present a demographic and geographic profile of the second-largest, second-most-populous state in the United States. Look in the index for more detailed information on each subject.

The Government

Capital: Austin
Government: Bicameral Legislature
28th State to enter the Union: Dec. 29, 1845
Present Constitution adopted: 1876
State motto: Friendship (1930)
State symbols:
  Flower: Bluebonnet (1901)
  Bird: Mockingbird (1927)
  Tree: Pecan (1919)
  Song: "Texas, Our Texas" (1929)

Origin of name: Texas, or Tejas, was the Spanish pronunciation of a Caddo Indian word meaning "friends" or "allies."

Nickname: Texas is called the Lone Star State because of the design of the state flag: a broad vertical blue stripe at left centered by a single white star, with horizontal bars of white (uppermost) and red on the right.

The People

Population (1990 U.S. Census) 16,986,510
Population (Jan. 1996 State Data
  Center estimate) 18,898,391
Population (July 1996 U.S. Bureau
  of the Census estimate) 18,378,185

Ethnicity (1990) (Please see explanation of categories on p. 142):
  White 12,775,000
  Black 2,022,000
  Asian 319,000
  American Indian 66,000
  Other 1,804,780

  Hispanic 4,340,000

Population density (1995) . . . . 71.5 per sq. mi.

Voting-age Pop., 1995 13,323,000
(1996 Statistical Abstract of the United States, Bureau of the Census)

On an average day in Texas in 1995:

The **population** increased by **507**.
There were **884** resident **births**.
There were **377** resident **deaths**.
There were **487 marriages**.
There were **266 divorces**.
  (1995 Texas Vital Statistics, Texas Dept. of Health)

Ten largest cities:
  Houston (Harris Co.) 1,749,001
  San Antonio (Bexar Co.) 1,079,207
  Dallas (Dallas Co.) 1,050,698
  El Paso (El Paso Co.) 583,431
  Austin (Travis Co.) 557,532
  Fort Worth (Tarrant Co.) 478,307
  Arlington (Tarrant Co.) 288,227
  Corpus Christi (Nueces Co.) 274,234
  Lubbock (Lubbock Co.) 194,522
  Garland (Dallas Co.) 190,703
(Texas State Data Center estimates, Jan. 1, 1996)

Number of counties 254
Number of incorporated cities 1,186
Number of cities of 100,000 pop. or more 22
Number of cities of 50,000 pop. or more 41
Number of cities of 10,000 pop. or more 200

The Natural Environment

Area (total) . . . . 267,277 sq. miles
  (171,057,280 acres)
Land area . . . . 261,914 sq. miles
  (167,624,960 acres)
Water area . . . . 5,363 sq. miles
  (3,432,320 acres)
Forested area . . . . 22.032 million acres
State forests . . . . 5 (7,609 acres)
National forests . . . . 4 (637,451 acres)

Geographic center: About 15 miles northeast of Brady in northern McCulloch County.
Highest point: Guadalupe Peak (8,749 ft.) in Culberson County in far West Texas.
Lowest point: Gulf of Mexico (sea level).

Normal average annual precipitation range:
  From 58.3 inches at Orange, on the Gulf Coast, to 8.8 inches at El Paso, in West Texas.
109-year average precipitation . . . . **28.10"**

Record highest temperature:
  Seymour, August 12, 1936 . . . . 120°F
  Monahans, June 28, 1994 . . . . 120°F
Record lowest temperature:
  Tulia, Feb. 12, 1899 . . . . -23°F
  Seminole, Feb. 8, 1933 . . . . -23°F

Business

Gross State Product:
  In current dollars (1992) . . . . $417 billion
  In constant (1987) dollars (1992) . . . . . $350 billion
Per Capita Personal Income (1995) $20,654
Civilian Labor Force (average 1995) 9,568,000
(1996 Statistical Abstract of the United States)

Principal products:
  Manufactures: Chemicals and allied products, petroleum and coal products, food and kindred products, transportation equipment.

  Farm products: Cattle, grain sorghums, cotton lint and seed, wheat, rice, dairy products.

  Minerals: Petroleum, natural gas, natural gas liquids.

Finance (as of 12/31/96):
  Number of banks 877
  Total deposits $168,213,664,000
  Number of savings and loan companies 37
  Total assets $54,427,896,000
  Number of savings banks 15
  Total assets $7,872,238,000

Agriculture (1992):
  Number of farms 180,644
  Land in farms (acres) 130,886,608
  Cropland (acres) 28,261,000
  Pastureland (acres) 16,710,000
  Rangeland (acres) 94,155,000
(1996 Statistical Abstract of the United States)

Texas' Rank Among the United States

Texas' rank among the United States in selected categories are given below. Others categories are covered in other chapters in the book; i.e. Agriculture, Business and Transportation, Science and Health.
Source (unless other wise noted): Statistical Abstract of the United States, 1996, Bureau of the Census.

Ten Most Populous States, 1995

Rank		Population est. 1995	%Change 1990-1995
1.	California	31.6 million	6.2
2.	**Texas**	**18.7 million**	**10.2**
3.	New York	18.1 million	0.8
4.	Florida	14.2 million	9.5
5.	Pennsylvania	12.1 million	1.6
6.	Illinois	11.8 million	3.5
7.	Ohio	11.2 million	2.8
8.	Michigan	9.5 million	2.7
9.	New Jersey	7.9 million	2.8
10.	Georgia	7.2 million	11.2
	(United States	262.7 million)	5.6

Ten Most Populous Cities, 1994

Rank	City	Population Est. 1994
1.	New York, NY	7,333,000
2.	Los Angeles, CA	3,449,000
3.	Chicago, IL	2,732,000
4.	**Houston**	**1,702,000**
5.	Philadelphia, PA	1,524,000
6.	San Diego, CA	1,152,000
7.	Phoenix, AZ	1,049,000
8.	**Dallas**	**1,023,000**
9.	**San Antonio**	**999,000**
10.	Detroit, MI	992,000

States with Highest Birth Rates, 1993

Rank	State	Births per 1,000 Pop.
1.	Utah	20.0
2.	California	18.8
3.	Alaska	18.5
4.	District of Columbia	18.4
5.	**Texas**	**17.9**
6.	Arizona	17.5
7.	New Mexico	17.2
8.	Illinois	16.3
9.	Louisiana	16.2
10.	Nevada	16.2
	(United States	15.5)

States with Most Vehicles, 1994

Rank	State	Vehicles	Lic. Drivers
1.	California	22,339,000	20,156,000
2.	**Texas**	**13,626,000**	**12,110,000**
3.	Florida	10,252,000	11,005,000
4.	New York	10,196,000	10,377,000
5.	Ohio	9,664,000	7,142,000
6.	Pennsylvania	8,482,000	8,115,000
7.	Illinois	8,698,000	7,502,000
8.	Michigan	7,574,000	6,602,000
9.	Georgia	5,990,000	4,817,000
10.	New Jersey	5,839,000	5,433,000

Source: Federal Highway Admin., Highway Statistics, annual, and Selected Highway Statistics and Charts, annual.

Miscellaneous Categories

Category	Number	Rank
Gross State Product, 1992	$416.9 billion	3
Per Capita Personal Income, 1995	$20,654	33
Insured Commercial Banks Closed or Assisted by Federal Government, 1995	10	2
Hazardous Waste Sites, 1995	27	14
Violent Crime Rate per 100,000 Pop., 1994	707	16
Child Abuse Cases Reported, 1994	110,742	3
Social Security Recipients, 1994	2,429,000	4
Persons Below Poverty Level, 1994	3,603,000	2
Percent Below Poverty Level, 1994	19.1	5
Public Aid Recipients, 1994	6.3 % of pop.	31

Category	Number	Rank
Public School Teachers' Avg. Salaries, 1995	$31,200	36
Minority College Enrollment, 1994	31.4%	4
Educational Attainment (25 years old or older), 1990: Highest percentage not High School Graduate	27.9%	12
Bachelor's degree or higher	20.4%	22
Per Capita Personal Health Care Expenditures, 1991	$2,345	39
AIDS cases reported: Total, 1981-1995	35,114	4
1995	4,477	4

States with Most Farms, 1992

Rank	State	No. of Farms
1.	**Texas**	**181,000**
2.	Missouri	98,000
3.	Iowa	97,000
4.	Kentucky	90,000
5.	California	78,000
	Illinois	78,000
7.	Minnesota	75,000
	Tennessee	75,000
9.	Ohio	71,000
10.	Wisconsin	68,000

States with Most Land in Farms, 1992

Rank	State	Farm Acreage
1.	**Texas**	**130,900,000**
2.	Montana	59,600,000
3.	New Mexico	46,800,000
4.	Kansas	46,700,000
5.	South Dakota	44,800,000
6.	Nevada	44,400,000
7.	North Dakota	39,400,000
8.	Arizona	35,000,000
9.	Colorado	34,000,000
10.	Wyoming	32,900,000

State Flags and Other Symbols

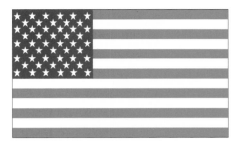

United States, 1845-1861; 1865-Present

Republic, 1836-1845; State, 1845-Present

Spain,
1519-1685
1690-1821

Mexico,
1821-1836

France,
1685-1690

Confederacy,
1861-1865

Texas often is called the **Lone Star State** because of its state flag with a single star. This was also the **flag of the Republic of Texas**. The following information about historic Texas flags, the current flag and other Texas symbols may be supplemented by information available from the **Texas State Library**, Austin.

Six Flags of Texas

Six different flags have flown over Texas during eight changes of sovereignty. The accepted sequence of these flags follows:

Spanish — 1519-1685.
French — 1685-1690.
Spanish — 1690-1821.
Mexican — 1821-1836.
Republic of Texas — 1836-1845.
United States — 1845-1861.
Confederate States — 1861-1865.
United States — 1865 to the present.

Evolution of the Lone Star Flag

The Convention at Washington-on-the-Brazos in March 1836 allegedly adopted a flag for the Republic that was designed by Lorenzo de Zavala. The design of de Zavala's flag is unknown, but the convention journals state that a "Rainbow and star of five points above the western horizon; and a star of six points sinking below" was added to de Zavala's flag. There was a suggestion that the letters "T E X A S" be placed around the star in the flag, but there is no evidence that the Convention ever approved a final flag design. Probably because of the hasty dispersion of the Convention and loss of part of the Convention notes, nothing further was done with the Convention's proposals for a national flag. A so-called "Zavala flag" is sometimes flown in Texas today that consists of a blue field with a white five-pointed star in the center and letters "T E X A S" between the star points, but there is no historical evidence to support this flag's design.

The **first official flag of the Republic**, known as **David G. Burnet's flag**, was adopted on Dec. 10, 1836, as the national standard, "the conformation of which shall be an azure ground with a large golden star central."

The Lone Star Flag

On Jan. 25, 1839, President Mirabeau B. Lamar approved the adoption by Congress of a new national flag. This flag consisted of "a blue perpendicular stripe of the width of one-third of the whole length of the flag, with a white star of five points in the center thereof, and two horizontal stripes of equal breadth, the upper stripe white, the lower red, of the length of two-thirds of the whole flag." This is the **Lone Star Flag**, which later became the state flag. Although Senator William H. Wharton proposed the adoption of the Lone Star Flag in 1844, no one knows who actually designed the flag. The legislature in 1879 inadvertently repealed the law establishing the state flag, but the legislature adopted a new law in 1933 that legally re-established the flag's design.

The state flag's colors represent the same virtues as they do in the national flag: Red means bravery; white, purity; and blue, loyalty.

The Texas Flag Code was first adopted in 1933 and completely revised in 1993. The following is a summary of the rules concerning the proper display of the state flag:

Flown out-of-doors, the Texas flag should not be flown

The State Seal (obverse) is shown above. For information on the development of the design of the seal and a description of the design of the reverse side, as well as the state motto and a listing of other state symbols, see page 380.

earlier than sunrise nor later than sunset unless properly illuminated. It should not be left out in inclement weather unless a weatherproof flag is used. It should be flown with the white stripe uppermost except in case of distress. When the flag is displayed against a wall, the blue field should be at the flag's own right (observer's left). When the flag is displayed vertically, the blue stripe should be uppermost and the white stripe should be to the state flag's right (observer's left). The state flag should be flown on all state holidays and on special occasions of historical significance, and it should fly at every school on regular school days.

If the state and national flags are both carried in a procession, the national flag should be on the marching right (observer's left) and state flag should be on the national flag's left (observer's right). If the state and national flags are displayed from crossed staffs, the state flag should be on the national flag's left (observer's right) and behind the national flag's staff. No flag other than the national flag should be placed above or, if on the same level, to the state flag's right (observer's left). The state flag should be underneath the national flag when the two are flown from the same halyard. When flown from adjacent flagpoles, the national flag and the state flag should be of approximately the same size and on flagpoles of equal height, and the national flag should be on the flag's own right (observer's left). The state flag should neither be flown above the flags of other U.S. states, nations and international organizations on the same flagpole, nor be flown from a higher adjacent flagpole.

The state flag should never be used for any utilitarian or strictly decorative purpose. No advertising should be placed upon the flag or flagstaff, and no picture of the flag should be used in an advertisement. When the state flag is in such condition that it is no longer a suitable emblem for display, it should be destroyed, preferably by burning.

Pledge to the Texas Flag

A pledge to the Texas flag was adopted by the 43rd Legislature. It contained a phrase, "Flag of 1836," which inadvertently referred to the David G. Burnet flag instead of the Lone Star Flag adopted in 1839. In 1965, the 59th Legislature changed the pledge to its current form:

"Honor the Texas flag;
I pledge allegiance to thee,

Texas, one and indivisible."

A person reciting the pledge to the state flag should face the flag, place the right hand over the heart and remove any easily removable hat. The pledge to the Texas flag may be recited at all public and private meetings at which the pledge of allegiance to the national flag is recited and at state historical events and celebrations. The pledge to the Texas flag should be recited after the pledge of allegiance to the United States flag if both are recited.

Other Symbols

State Tree — The **pecan** is the state tree of Texas. The sentiment that led to its official adoption probably grew out of the request of Gov. James Stephen Hogg that a pecan tree be planted at his grave. (Acts of 1919, 36th Legislature, regular session, p. 155; also Acts of 1927, 40th Legislature, p. 234.)

State Flower — The state flower of Texas is the **bluebonnet**, also called **buffalo clover, wolf flower** and *el conejo* (the rabbit). The bluebonnet was adopted as the state flower, on request of the Society of Colonial Dames in Texas, by the 27th Legislature, 1901. (See acts of regular session, p. 232.) The original resolution designated *Lupinus subcarnosus* as the state flower, but a resolution (HCR 44) signed March 8, 1971, by Gov. Preston Smith provided legal status as the state flower of Texas for *"Lupinus Texensis* and any other variety of bluebonnet."

State Bird — The **mockingbird** (*Mimus polyglottos*) is the state bird of Texas, adopted by the Legislature at the request of the Texas Federation of Women's Clubs. (Acts of 1927, 40th Legislature, regular session, p. 486.)

State Song — The state song of Texas is **"Texas, Our Texas."** The music was written by the late William J. Marsh (who died Feb. 1, 1971, in Fort Worth at age 90), and the words by Marsh and Gladys Yoakum Wright, also of Fort Worth. It was the winner of a state song contest sponsored by the legislature and was adopted in 1929. The wording has been changed once: Shortly after Alaska became a state in Jan. 1959, the word "Largest" in the third line was changed by Mr. Marsh to "Boldest." The text follows:

Texas, Our Texas

Texas, our Texas! all hail the mighty State!
Texas, our Texas! So wonderful, so great!
Boldest and grandest, Withstanding ev'ry test;
O Empire wide and glorious, You stand supremely blest.

Chorus
God bless you, Texas!
And keep you brave and strong,
That you may grow in power and worth,
Thro'out the ages long.

Refrain
Texas, O Texas! Your freeborn Single Star,
Sends out its radiance To nations near and far.
Emblem of freedom! It sets our hearts aglow,
With thoughts of San Jacinto And glorious Alamo.

Texas, dear Texas! From tyrant grip now free,
Shines forth in splendor Your Star of Destiny!
Mother of Heroes! We come your children true,
Proclaiming our allegiance, Our Faith, Our Love for you. ☆

Note: For the state motto, a description of the state seal and other state symbols, see page 380.

Texas in Bloom

Bluebonnets and Indian paintbrush dominate this roadside on Texas Highway 71 between Marble Falls and Llano in April. Other species fill out the spring palette, punctuated by live oaks and yucca. Texas Almanac staff photo.

More than 5,000 species of flowering plants are native to Texas. Because Texas covers more than 267,000 square miles and sprawls across many different climate and soil regions, the types of plants range from desert-loving yucca and ocotillo to bog plants such as swamp mallow and spider lily.

March, April and May are the prime months for wildflowers in Texas. From March to early summer, Texas mountain laurel, a tall shrub, perfumes the air from Central Texas to the Chisos and Davis mountains of far West Texas with the intensely grapey scent of its cascading clusters of lavender flowers. Creamy-white dogwood trees are bursting into ethereal bloom in East Texas about the same time.

From March to May, depending on weather conditions, roadsides and meadows in Central and North-Central Texas are blanketed in the blue haze of bluebonnets, the official state flower, as well as the delicate pink of evening primroses, the brilliant red of Indian paintbrush and the rusty-red and yellow of Indian blanket.

In East Texas' Big Thicket, the wild azalea's pink flowers are opening in mid-spring; wild roses adorn rural landscapes in Northeast Texas in mid-May.

From Central Texas to far West Texas, the tough, thorny, forbidding prickly pears display delicate blossoms of yellow, red, red-orange or cream from April to May.

Texas' flower display is not limited to spring, however. Indian blanket continues to spread its cheer through June. From May to July, the long-headed coneflower blooms from East Texas to the Trans-Pecos and the Panhandle, and lemonmint attracts butterflies, bees and hummingbirds to its blossoms across the state from May to September.

Fall brings the lavender spikes of gayfeather, delicate white Queen Anne's lace, goldenrod, and purply-pink wild morning glories.

Lending a helping hand with the wildflower spectacular is the Texas Department of Transportation, which sows tons of wildflower seeds on Texas roadsides each year.

Many Texans think there is a state law forbidding picking wildflowers — or at least bluebonnets. There is no such law, according to the Texas State Law Library.

There is, however, a law forbidding the destruction of state property and another dealing with trespassing on private property. You should not, therefore, pick wildflowers on someone else's property without their permission. And the picking of posies on highway right of way might be interpreted as being the destruction of state property. Since the gorgeous display along Texas roadways belongs to all of us, please leave them for everyone to enjoy — and call the National Wildflower Research Center (see below and page 19) to order their list of native seed and plant suppliers so you can purchase your own to plant at home.

For Further Reading

Native Plant Bibliography for Texas; Clearinghouse, National Wildflower Research Center. A comprehensive list of plant books for the Lone Star State. Each of nine regions of the United States has its own bibliography. Each list costs $2 to members of the center, $3 for nonmembers. Contact the center at 4801 La Crosse Ave., Austin 78739; phone (512) 292-4100.

Texas Wildflowers, A Field Guide by Campbell and Lynn Loughmiller; University of Texas Press, Austin, 1994. Organized by botanical family.

Wildflowers of Texas by Geyata Ajilvsgi; Shearer Publishing, Fredericksburg, 1984. Organized by color of flower. ☆

Flowers (clockwise from top left): Texas mountain laurel, dogwood, claret cup cactus, goldenrod, basket flower, pink phlox, beach morning glory, strawberry cactus, gayfeather, prickly pear, Indian (or Texas) paintbrush, evening primrose (also called buttercup). Directly above, Maximilian sunflower.

Photo credits: Texas mountain laurel courtesy National Wildflower Research Center; gayfeather and goldenrod - Texas Almanac staff photos; sunflower: Martha Sheridan, The Dallas Morning News; all others courtesy Texas Department of Transportation (photographers: J. Griffis Smith - evening primrose, prickly pear; Richard Reynolds - strawberry cactus; Stan A. Williams - basket flower; all others - Jack Lewis).

For information on peak wildflower blooming times:

Texas Department of Transportation, spring prime time only:
800-452-9292

National Wildflower Research Center, from mid-March to the end of May:
(512) 832-4059

For a free brochure **"The Wildflowers of Texas,"** with color photos of 52 commonly seen Texas wildflowers and information on where and when they bloom, call the TXDOT number above.

For a list of **wildflower-related events** around the state: on the Internet, **http://www.traveltex.com**. Click "Search" at the top of the page, then enter "wildflower."

Flowers (clockwise from top left): red phlox, prickly pear, bluebell, yucca, water lily, plains coreopsis, purple gerardia, Indian blanket, wild morning glory, white prickly poppy, eryngo (false purple thistle) and bluebonnet.

Photo credits: Gerardia, wild morning glory and eryngo - Texas Almanac staff photos. All others courtesy Texas Department of Transportation (photographers: Jack Lewis - red phlox, plains coreopsis, prickly pear; J. Griffis Smith - bluebonnet, water lily, yucca; Stan A. Williams - Indian blanket, bluebell; John Suhrstedt - prickly poppies).

National Wildflower Research Center

The National Wildflower Research Center sprawls colorfully over 42 acres of the Central Texas Hill Country just southwest of Austin. Founded in 1982 by Lady Bird Johnson and the late actress Helen Hayes, it is the only national nonprofit organization dedicated to preserving and re-establishing native wildflowers, grasses, vines, shrubs and trees in planned landscapes.

Visitors to the National Wildflower Research Center find a wildflower meadow, a nature trail, a seed court, a formal courtyard landscaped entirely in native plants, and 23 theme gardens showcasing the many uses and adaptations of native plants. The center's grounds also include a research library, a cafe and a gift shop.

One on-going research project of great interest to home gardners is a series of three home comparison gardens. One is a formal garden with a lawn and non-native plants; the second is a formal garden with native landscaping; and the third is an informal, naturalistic garden using native plants. The center's staff continuously monitors water use and the amount of labor, pesticides and fertilizer required by each type of garden. The gathered data is proving that time, money, water and energy can be saved by planting already adapted native plants rather than imported species that need lots of water, fertilizer and pampering.

The center's home on the Edwards Plateau is at the edges of four other ecological regions, as well — the southern extent of the midwestern prairies, the eastern edge of the Chihuahuan desert, the northern extent of the Tamaulipan thorn scrub and the western edge of the southeastern woodlands. Because of the location, more than 500 species of native plants flourish on the grounds of the center.

Flowers fill one of the Center's theme gardens with a riot of color.

Photos courtesy National Wildflower Research Center.

Edwards Aquifer in particular. The aquifer is the underground water formation that underlies the area and provides most of the water for municipal and agricultural users in the region.

The thick stone walls of the buildings provide natural insulation; breezeways between buildings capture the natural cooling power of the wind. Non-polluting solar heat also makes use of a renewable resource, and many materials used at the center are recycled.

The rooftop water-harvesting system, said to be the largest such system in North America, stores up to 68,500 gallons of rainwater for irrigation — water that isn't pumped from the seriously burdened aquifer. The center's irrigation system is linked by computer to the National Weather Service; the computer uses NWS data to direct the water where and when it is needed. During the drought in the summer of 1996, the center irrigated its plants with water harvested during 1995.

Although it is firmly planted in Central Texas, the center is indeed national in scope. Plant experts at the center respond to more than 15,000 requests for information each year, many of them from other states. The center's clearinghouse distributes such educational materials as "fact packs," which include region-specific information on the best native plants for each area of the United States, bibliographies listing books on each region's native plants, and a listing of sources of native plants and seeds.

The center has a very full, active schedule of on-site public programs — seminars, lectures, children's programs, workshops, teacher training and special exhibits. Its annual festival, Wildflower Days, attracts about 10,000 visitors to the center on a weekend in April for a feast of seminars by nationally known experts, gardening demonstrations, arts and crafts, music and food.

In addition to the public offerings, the center's experts also hold classes and seminars for professional landscape architects and teachers from around the country.

The center is closed on Mondays. For more information, the National Wildflower Research Center's address is 4801 La Crosse Ave., Austin 78739; phone (512) 292-4100. On the Internet: http://www.wildflower.org/

The sandstone buildings at the Center reflect 18th-century Spanish mission architecture.

The award-winning design of the center reflects the ethnic diversity of the region. Many of the buildings are of creamy Central Texas limestone, reflecting the architecture brought to the region by German immigrants in the mid-1800s. Others of rusty-brown sandstone are reminiscent of the Spanish missions built 100 years before that.

The placement of the buildings and the center's operating policies also display a sensitity to the environment in general and to the ecologically fragile

La Belle and Fort St. Louis:

Discovering La Salle's Ship and the Site of His Texas Colony

by Mary G. Ramos, editor, Texas Almanac

The royal crest (above) of the Comte de Vermandois, the Admiral of France, graces the three bronze cannons found in the hold of the Belle by archaeologists from the Texas Historical Commission. AP photo by David J. Phillip.

Two bronze cannons (left) are measured by John de Bry before being excavated from the 311-year-old Belle, the ship of French explorer La Salle, in February 1997. The decoration on these two match that on the first cannon discovered in the bottom of Matagorda Bay in July 1995. Finding the first cannon confirmed for archaeologists that they had found La Salle's ship. AP photo by David J. Phillip.

As Chuck Meide ran his hand over the rough, heavy, cylindrical metal object at the bottom of 12 feet of murky water in Matagorda Bay, his heart began to race. Was it a centuries-old cannon? Or was it something mundane and modern?

Unable to see in the muddy water, the Florida State University student archaeologist felt carefully along the cylinder until he found a lump, which he thought might be one of two handles used to lift a cannon. Then his hand found the second lifting handle, which confirmed that it was indeed a cannon, heavily encrusted with marine deposits from long years under water. The jubilant Meide reported his find to the waiting crew in the dive boat above. Carefully they raised the cannon to the deck of a barge and moved it to the Corpus Christi Museum of Science and History for cleaning and further inspection.

Meide was part of a team assembled by the Texas Historical Commission. What they were searching for in the muddy Matagorda in the summer of 1995 was *La Belle*, a ship brought to the Texas coast by French explorer René Robert Cavelier, Sieur de La Salle more than 300 years before.

The lifting handles that Meide had identified by touch were in the shape of gracefully leaping dolphins. Also decorating the barrel in bas-relief were two crests: One was an "L" surmounted by a crown — the crest of King Louis XIV of France; the other was the crest of the Comte de Vermandois. Vermandois was Louis' illegitimate son, who was two years old when Louis appointed him Admiral of France in 1669. These features confirmed to the anxious investigators that they had found

La Salle's ill-fated ship.

The find on July 5, 1995, marked the high point of a 17-year on-and-off search for historic shipwrecks by state marine archaeologist Barto Arnold, who led the team that discovered the shipwreck site. It also marked the beginning of a painstaking, time-consuming effort to excavate what remained of the historic French ship, which had lain encased in muddy silt at the bottom of Matagorda Bay for three centuries. It is, according to many archaeologists, the most important shipwreck discovery in North American waters to date.

Who was La Salle and Why Was He in Texas?

Born in Rouen, France, in 1643, the adventurous La Salle arrived in the French area of Canada in the 1660s, from which the young Frenchman launched several fur-trading and exploration ventures. La Salle was perpetually in debt from his habit of overspending his resources.

In 1682, accompanied by about 50 fellow Frenchmen and American Indians, he canoed down the Mississippi River from a base camp in Illinois to the Gulf of Mexico. Arriving at the mouth of the Mississippi in April, La Salle claimed the entire Mississippi basin in the name of France and King Louis XIV. The drainage basin of the Mississippi includes almost half of today's continental United States. He named the area Louisiana to honor the king, then retraced his steps to Illinois. In November 1683 he returned to France.

The following year La Salle persuaded Louis to finance an expedition to find a sea route to the mouth of the Mississippi with the intention of establishing a per-

The Belle is thought to have looked very much like this drawing. Art courtesy of the Texas Historical Commission.

manent settlement there. Spain considered the Gulf of Mexico to be exclusively Spanish territory, off-limits to all non-Spaniards. Louis welcomed the opportunity to established a French presence there, especially since it was believed to be very near the silver mines of northern Mexico.

La Salle was ill-suited to be a leader. One of the colonists, Henri Joutel, kept a detailed diary of the journey, from which historians have gained substantial understanding of the events of the colonization effort as well as of La Salle himself. Joutel deplored his commander's wild mood swings and erratic behavior, which alienated many of the officers and men. An engineer named Minet, who also journeyed to Texas, described La Salle as brooding, suspicious, secretive, paranoid, headstrong and egotistical. "This is a man who has lost his mind," he wrote in his journal.

Some modern historians believe that La Salle may have been a manic-depressive.

On August 1, 1684, La Salle set sail for the Gulf of Mexico with about 300 people in four ships. *La Belle*, a *barque longue* or light frigate, was a navy ship assigned to La Salle for his exclusive use. She was built at Rochefort in 1683 and had a crew of 27. The *Belle* was accompanied by the 180-ton storeship, *L'Aimable*; a 34-gun man-of-war, *Le Joly*, which was to transport the colonists to their new home, then return to France; and the ketch *Saint-François*, carrying additional supplies.

La Salle's group included supposed artisans and craftsmen, some of whom did not have the skills they claimed to have. Recruited from the human dregs of French port towns were 100 soldiers. There were also six French missionary priests and at least a dozen women and children.

Just before the small fleet made a stop in the West Indies in late September, Spanish pirates seized the *Saint-François*, along with the supplies it carried.

At Cuba's western cape, a sudden squall caused the *Belle* to tangle rigging with the *Aimable*. The *Belle* lost one of her two anchors, a loss that later proved most unfortunate. In late November, the three ships continued their attempt to find the mouth of the Mississippi.

Because he was relying on highly inaccurate maps, La Salle overshot the Mississippi by some 400 miles. On Feb. 18, 1685, the *Belle* entered Matagorda Bay, about halfway between present-day Galveston and Corpus Christi.

Two days later, the *Aimable* ran aground and broke up while attempting to enter the bay through a narrow channel. Many supplies were lost, including arms, medicines, trade goods, numerous casks of wine and brandy, bacon, beef and much of the clothing. The *Joly* returned to France in mid-March as planned; on board were a number of would-be colonists who had taken one look at the Texas coast and wanted no part of it. This left about 200 people to establish the French colony on the Gulf. They constructed a temporary camp on Matagorda Island.

Still believing that he had reached a western arm of the Mississippi, La Salle, accompanied by 52 men in five canoes, left the temporary camp on March 24 to find a site for a colony. He chose a spot on a low hill a league and a half (about four and a half miles) inland from the mouth of Garcitas Creek in today's Victoria County. In April, construction began. In mid-June, 70 settlers arrived at the colony, which La Salle had named Fort St. Louis to honor the French king. La Salle drove them mercilessly on short rations to finish the structures. Felled by diseases, poisonous berries, poisonous snakes and malnutrition, half the colonists were dead by July.

In October, La Salle and 50 men departed in canoes to search for the Mississippi. He ordered the *Belle* again loaded with items that would be needed in the new colony: trade goods for the natives; a forge; hand tools; muskets, cannon and barrels of powder; foods; and even a litter of piglets. Wooden chests packed with clothing, utensils, plates and dishes were stowed in the hold, as well. The *Belle*, with 27 aboard, was to follow La Salle's party. There was no contact between the two groups for a month, while La Salle pursured a band of hostile Indians. In December, La Salle returned to the *Belle*, to find that the pilot and five men had been murdered by Indians while they were sleeping ashore.

In January 1686, La Salle once again left to explore, this time by land. He ordered the crew to stay on board ship until he returned, which was supposed to be in about 10 days. Instead, the group did not return to the coast until two months later, after a long trek which may have taken them far into West Texas. The *Belle* was nowhere to be found.

On May 1, a group of six survivors from the *Belle* arrived at Fort St. Louis, telling a tale of death and destruction. Shortly after La Salle and his party had left, a group of six from the *Belle*, who had gone ashore for water, failed to return, leaving the ship without a boat. The lack of drinking water aboard the *Belle* became critical, but the ship's drunken master refused to move the ship. The unskilled crew, although weak from thirst and disease, tried to sail the *Belle* toward Fort St. Louis. When a stiff north wind came up, the ship, dragging her one remaining anchor, was blown across the bay and driven stern-first into Matagorda Peninsula. Although the crew unloaded as much as they could into a canoe that had drifted across the bay, much of the cargo remained on the ship, some of it submerged. All the crew except the six were dead; the survivors had stayed on the peninsula near the wreck for three months.

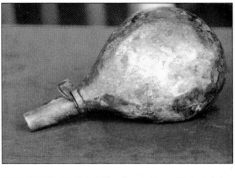

By this time, the colonists numbered fewer than 40. At least four had deserted to live with Indians.

In mid-January 1687, La Salle left with 17 men to find a post on the Illinois River that he had established in 1683 as part of his trading empire. About 20 people, mostly women, children, the sick and misfits, remained behind at Fort St. Louis.

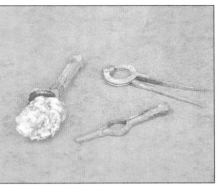

Among the artifacts being conserved at the Conservation Research Laboratory at Texas A&M University are (top to bottom) a brass powder flask, navigational instruments, a ceramic pot, and a pewter plate and pewter porringer. Texas Almanac photos.

Several of the men accompanying La Salle grew mutinous as they made their way slowly to the northeast. On March 17, at a spot probably a short distance west of the Trinity River, three of La Salle's group were murdered by several of their comrades. Two days later, La Salle was lured into an ambush by some of his men and shot dead.

Only five members of the group, including Joutel, finally reached French Canada; some remained behind among the Indians. The piti-

ful remnants of the colony at Fort St. Louis were finished off by Karankawas in January 1688. The Indians took a few children captive; these were later rescued by the Spanish and taken to Mexico. The French threat to Spanish domination of the Gulf of Mexico was temporarily ended by disease, nature, Indians and the French themselves.

The Spanish found the remains of the *Belle* on April 4, 1687. The Spanish pilot Juan Enríquez Barroto's diary describes the ship's condition at the time: The *Belle* was heeled over on her starboard side, with the deck and the prow submerged. Shipworms had cut down the masts. The Spanish carried away several cannons and the anchor, along with tools and rigging. The rest was left to rot.

Although La Salle failed miserably at establishing a French colony at the mouth of the Mississippi, his attempt to do so changed history. When Gen. Alonso de León's expedition found the remains of Fort St. Louis on April 22, 1689, the Spanish government became alarmed at this proof of French intention to lay claim to Spanish territory. The French threat goaded the Spanish to establish missions and settlements in East Texas.

The Search for the *Belle*

Barto Arnold's search for the *Belle* began with careful historical research. In the early 1970s, he read the diaries kept by some of the survivors of La

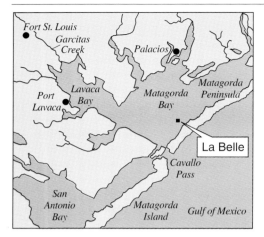

This map locates the sites of the Belle shipwreck and Fort St.
Louis in relation to present-day cities, as well as Matagorda
Bay, Matagorda Peninsula, Lavaca Bay and Garcitas Creek.
Map by The Dallas Morning News.

Salle's expedition, including Henri Joutel, as well as the
journals of Spanish explorers who found the *Belle*
aground. This helped Arnold narrow the area of Matagorda Bay in which he might expect to find what was
left of the ship.

In 1978, the Texas Historical Commission launched
a search, using helicopter, boat and magnetometer. A
magnetometer detects distortions, called anomalies, in
the Earth's magnetic field. A ship that contains large
amounts of iron will distort the magnetic field, producing a detectable anomaly.

While magnetometers can signal the presence of
iron, they cannot identify the ages of the objects. The
muddy Matagorda's shifting sandbars have claimed at
least 200 ships over the years, so searchers often check
out anomalies that turn out to be modern wreckage or
trash.

During his early searching, Arnold found some
interesting old wrecks, but not the *Belle*. The search was
postponed.

By summer 1995, Arnold was able to put together
enough donations from foundations, organizations,
companies and individuals for a two-month project, and
he narrowed his list of promising anomalies to about
three dozen.

Arnold explains that one of the "givens" in archaeology is that you always find the most important artifacts
on the last day of the dig, when you are out of money
and out of time. On the first dive on the first anomaly, a
site designated 41MG86, one diver found a hand-made
wooden plank. The team speculated that it couldn't be
old, because wood exposed to sea water for a long time
would have disintegrated.

The second dive yielded some cast-lead shot, which
could have been made after the Civil War. The third dive
brought up a bronze belt buckle of a type common
before the 1800s.

Then, on the fourth dive, Chuck Meide found the
cannon while groping around in the murky water, doing
what he calls "archaeology by Braille." The cannon was

a bronze, six-foot-long four-pounder, weighing 793
pounds. Even better, the elaborate decorations on the
barrel, Arnold says, "made it seriously old."

And the discovery of this cannon, which would
firmly establish the shipwreck as the *Belle*, adds Arnold
happily, "was before lunch on the first day."

In addition, the divers found and took to the museum
in Corpus Christi a number of ceramic vessels of various
sizes and designs; a stack of 22 pewter plates; hawk
bells and straight pins, possibly intended for trade with
the Indians; several wooden staves from barrels; and
personal objects, including the hand guard from a
sword.

Once the artifacts were positively identified as being
from the *Belle*, the problems of excavating the ship were
considered — and the fund-raising went into high gear.

Because of the low visibility of the waters of the
Matagorda, attempting a complete archaeological excavation by "Braille" is almost impossible. However, those
murky waters are only 12 feet deep at most. The Texas
Historical Commission contracted with marine engineers to build a $1.3 million octagonal, double-walled
cofferdam around the shipwreck in the summer of 1996.

Sixty-foot long, three-foot wide sheets of steel piling
were hammered 40 feet into the floor of the bay to create
the inner octagon. Then a second octagon was built outside the first, creating a structure 148 feet long and 118
feet wide extending about eight feet above the surface of
the water. The space between the two walls was filled
with 10,000 tons of sand, to stabilize the structure and
slow water seepage. The sand was covered by eight
inches of gravel to help support a crane and to provide a
walkway for workers and visitors. Almost 500,000 gallons of water were pumped out of the center of the cofferdam, and a steel canopy was constructed to protect
both workers and artifacts from the relentless sun.

The cofferdam was complete in September 1996,
and the excavation began. The *Belle* team essentially did
dry-land archaeology in their man-made hole in the middle of Matagorda Bay.

The team of archaeologists that came from all over
the United States to excavate the *Belle* operated from a
warehouse in Palacios, about 15 miles, and an hour's
boat ride, from the *Belle* site. There were 16 to 20 at
work on the site at any one time. The project director,
Dr. Jim Bruseth, is deputy state historic preservation
officer with the Texas Historical Commission. The assistant project director is Toni Carrell, on leave from the
Ships of Discovery at the Corpus Christi Museum of
Science and History. The Ships of Discovery organization is involved with the conservation and display of
materials relating to ships of the exploratory period of
North American history.

What The Archaeologists Found

The team found that about two-thirds of the *Belle's*
hull — the part that was above the mud — had disintegrated. The bottom third was still packed with barrels
and chests of 17th-century goods in remarkably good
condition. Because the mud in which the *Belle* was buried is an anaerobic environment, wood, leather, metal
and other substances that would have rotted, rusted or
disintegrated in 300 years of exposure to sand and salt

water have survived in extraordinarily good shape.

The *Belle* is not a "treasure ship" in the common meaning of the word. Her hold contained no precious metals or jewels.

But to archaeologists and historians, her cargo — as well as the remains of the ship itself — was a treasure much more valuable than gold or silver. Since they were not merely passing through, as explorers, but expected to settle in the New World, the colonists brought with them everything that they would need to live. As Bruseth told *The Dallas Morning News'* Bryan Woolley in 1997, "This ship is sort of a colony kit. Many colonies were established in the New World, but the stuff that people brought with them is gone. . . What we have on the *Belle* is a good inventory of what a country in Europe felt was important for establishing a colony in the New World."

Out of the 80 or so barrels and chests in the *Belle's* hull came such everyday items as pewter plates and bowls; cooking pots and utensils; chess and backgammon pieces; buckles from clothing; nested brass pots; clay pipe stems; navigators' instruments; candlesticks; a whisk broom; a shoe last; a brass powder flask; and a stonewware jar still containing traces of grease, perhaps for cooking. Some of the pewter dishes were stamped with a maker's mark and the initials of their owners, making it possible to match some of the items with known colonists.

There were also items that were intended for trade with the natives. Archaeologists found more than half a million tiny Venetian glass beads, as well as bronze hawk bells, brass straight pins, iron ax heads and brass finger rings. They were not merely cheap trinkets: The hawk bells were fine enough to bear makers' marks. The metal items were particularly prized by the Indians of the New World, who had little metal of their own.

Two additional cannons bearing decorations identical to the first one were pulled out of the bottom of the ship's hold in January 1997. The *Belle* carried four bronze cannons in her hold; the fate of the fourth is unknown.

Although dry-land archaeology has its benefits in such muddy waters as Matagorda Bay, there are also problems. Foremost among these is the rapid deterioration of objects suddenly exposed to dry air after several centuries in a watery environment. To keep the artifacts wet, the areas where the archaeologists were working had to be continuously sprinkled with sea water from a garden hose. Exposed areas of the dig were kept covered by wet burlap bags or plastic tarps and sprinkled during periods when they were not being worked.

As the artifacts were extricated from their resting places, the sand and mud that came up with them was put through a fine screen to check for tiny bits that might have escaped the eye. Everything that could be found was excavated, even rat skeletons and cockroach eggs. Except when they were being cleaned or coded, all artifacts were kept immersed in salt water. Most of them were placed in containers of fresh water for their transfer to the conservation lab.

One of the most touching finds was a complete human skeleton. French seamen sometimes stowed their dead below decks until they could be transported to consecrated ground for burial. Investigators say that the unfortunate man, found curled in a fetal position on a coil of rope, must have been in pain from arthritis and a badly abscessed tooth, but the most likely cause of death was dehydration. A pewter porringer with the name "C. Barange" was found next to the skeleton. Dr. Gentry Steele, a forensic anthropologist Texas A&M University, is directing additional research on the skeleton. Initial studies revealed a Caucasian male of about 30 years of age. In addition to the dental problems and arthritis, says Steele, "He had a broken nose and a fracture of the temple area. These were not the cause of death, however. Both wounds showed signs of some healing."

The skull was taken to Texas Scottish Rite Hospital in Dallas for a computerized axial tomography (CT) scan to create a three-dimensional image. Using the scan data, CyberForm, a Richardson company, produced a resin cast of the skull. Dr. Dennis Lee, a forensic prosthetics specialist at the University of Michigan, will use the skull replica to produce facial features, which will give researchers an approximation of the victim's facial appearance.

Additionaly, genetic analysis may be possible using tissue from the bones or from the brain matter that was, amazingly, still preserved in the cranium, leading to the possibility of eventually finding the person's nearest living relative.

Other isolated human bones were also found scattered in the wreckage.

When all the contents were finally removed, the *Belle's* hull was exposed, still resting on its starboard side, as reported by the Spanish pilot Enríquez Barroto in 1687. The *Belle* was surprisingly small: 51 feet long and 14 feet wide — about the size of a modern shrimp boat. The historic ship was carefully dismantled and the timbers were prepared for conservation. Study of the construction of the two-masted ship will be of great value to historians, since shipbuilders of La Salle's era rarely drew plans, and most of the ships of the period have long since disintegrated. Because of the fragile nature of the wood, conservation and stabilization may take eight to 10 years.

The excavation was completed in April 1997.

Glossary

• **anaerobic** - containing no air or free oxygen.

• **DNA** - the abbreviation for deoxyribonucleic acid, a chemical that contains the genetic code for all living beings and through which the hereditary pattern is transmitted. It can be used to determine whether two human beings are related to one another.

• **hawk bells** - small bells attached to the birds' legs in the sport of falconry.

• **porringer** - a small bowl used for porridge or soup.

• **presidio** - a fortified place or military post.

• **shoe last** - a block or form shaped like a person's foot, which is used to make or repair shoes.

Conservation of the Artifacts

The first items to be excavated in 1995 were conserved and prepared for exhibit under the direction of Dr. Donald H. Keith of Ships of Discovery at the Corpus Christi Museum of Science and History. The items excavated in 1996 and 1997 from the *Belle* were taken to the Conservation Research Laboratory at Texas A&M University in College Station, where Dr. Donny Hamilton is the director. There, in a former fire station at a World War II-vintage air field, conservators begin working on each article by carefully cleaning and identifying the item or items. The artifacts are placed in vats of fresh water for several weeks — the amount of time is determined by the type of material — to soak out the salts and to keep them from drying out. Some are further treated with chemicals to keep them from deteriorating when exposed to the air. This step is especially critical for such organic materials as rope and wood. The hundreds of feet of rope brought up from the *Belle* is being treated using two different new techniques: silicone oil polymerization or polyethylene glycol. These substances stabilize the rope and keep it as pliable as it was on the day it was procured for the voyage.

Any number of concretions were excavated. Concretions form around metal objects that are exposed to sea water for a long time. Corrosion of the metal starts a chemical reaction with the seawater that forms a hard, solid covering over the entire surface of the item. Conservators X-ray the concretion to determine whether the object survives inside. If it does, they carefully remove the mineral deposits from the surface. If the item is no longer there, they inject epoxy resin into the natural mold formed by the concretions. When the resin cures and the concretions are removed, they have a duplicate of the original, complete with all surface details. This duplicate can be used for display.

Curtis Tunnell, executive director of the Texas Historical Commission, estimates that it will take three more years to analyze the more than 700,000 artifacts excavated from the *Belle* and write the project's final report. A budget of $5.5 million includes the field work already finished, conservation, analysis of the artifacts and writing the final report, an educational project and an expanded traveling exhibit. A traveling exhibit of the first items recovered, designed and built at the Corpus Christi Museum of Science and History, has toured parts of the state. That tour is scheduled to last through 1998.

Fort St. Louis Found

The site of Fort St. Louis, although documented by both the French and the Spanish at the time, was lost over time.

In 1950, Glen Evans, under the sponsorship of The Texas Memorial Museum in Austin, conducted an investigation at a promising site on the south bank of Garcitas Creek in Victoria County. This site, officially designated site 41VT4, is also known as the Keeran site. Evans' search yielded a large number of European artifacts, including various types of ceramics and metal objects, but did not prove the presence of French colonists.

In 1973, archaeologist Kathleen Gilmore analyzed the objects that had been excavated in the 1950 investigation. Although she determined that some of the artifacts were of French origin, there was not enough evidence to prove actual French occupation of the site. She felt confident that the Keeran site was the site of Fort St. Louis, however, and recommended further investigation, but no further action was taken.

While the *Belle* was being excavated in 1996, a Victoria County ranchhand exploring the Keeran site with a metal detector found an old buried cannon. Searchers from the historical commission dug at the spot and eventually found eight cast-iron cannons — the French cannons that had been found at Fort St. Louis in 1689 by De León's expedition and buried. They are currently undergoing conservation at the lab at A&M, along with the *Belle* artifacts. That the Keeran site was the location of the ill-fated French colony had been proved.

Excavation of Fort St. Louis is expected to begin in 1999 as a two-tiered project. In 1722, the Spanish built the presidio Nuestra Señora de Loreto de la Bahía squarely atop the remains of Fort St. Louis. Today's archaeologists will be excavating two historic sites at once and will have the task of sorting out which objects were associated with Fort St. Louis, which with the presidio, and which were left by indigenous people who had acquired European goods from earlier expeditions.

The *Belle* artifacts, along with the objects excavated at Fort St. Louis, will be installed in a museum eventually for public viewing. At press time, the location had not been determined. ☆

For Further Reading

The French Thorn: Rival Explorers in the Spanish Sea 1682-1762 by Robert S. Weddle; Texas A&M University Press, College Station, 1991.

A Journal of La Salle's Last Voyage by Henri Joutel (written in 1714); Corinth Books, New York, 1962.

"La Salle Shipwreck"; Special Issue of "The Medallion," Texas Historical Commission, Summer, 1996.

La Salle, the Mississippi, and the Gulf: Three Primary Documents; Robert S. Weddle, et al. (eds); Texas A&M University Press, College Station, 1987.

"Sieur de La Salle's fateful landfall" by David Roberts; Smithsonian, April 1997, Vol. 28, No. 1.

"La Salle's Last Voyage" by Lisa Moore LaRoe; National Geographic, May 1997, Vol. 191, No. 5.

On the Internet

For information on the Belle project on the Texas Historical Commission's *Belle* project Website: **http://www.thc.state.tx.us/Belle/index.html**

For information on the conservation of the artifacts at the Conservation Research Laboratory: **http://nautarch.tamu.edu/napcrl.htm**

*The editor wishes to thank the following historians and archaeologists for reviewing this article and offering their corrections and suggestions: **Dr. Barto Arnold, Dr. Jim Bruseth** and **Curtis Tunnell,** Texas Historical Commission; **Toni Carrell,** Ships of Discovery; **Dr. Donny Hamilton,** Conservation Research Laboratory, Texas A&M University; **Robert S. Weddle,** Bonham. Our thanks also go to the **staff of the conservation lab** for their generous hospitality and patient explanations. Any errors are, of course, the author's own.*

After the Great Storm

Galveston's Response to the Hurricane of Sept. 8, 1900

by Mary G. Ramos, editor, Texas Almanac

The ruins of Sacred Heart Church stand in a sea of destruction following the hurricane of 1900. Photo used by permission of the Rosenberg Library, Galveston.

The fact that the city of Galveston exists today is the triumph of imagination, hope and determination over reality. Perched precariously on a sand-barrier island in the Gulf of Mexico, Galveston is subject to the whims of inevitable hurricanes.

One of those hurricanes, dancing its deadly way across the Gulf of Mexico in early September 1900, came very close to dealing the city a fatal blow. An estimated 6,000 residents died, and most structures in the city were destroyed or badly damaged. In terms of human life, it remains the worst natural disaster in United States history.

Galveston's leaders took several major steps to recover from the storm and to prevent a recurrence of the devastation. First, they developed a new form of municipal government, one with strong centralized control to handle the economic recovery of the city. Next, they built a massive seawall to turn back storm-generated waves. Perhaps the most amazing step they took was to raise the level of the entire city, by more than 16 feet in some areas, in order to keep flooding at a minimum.

As we approach the 21st century, we take a look at the storm that struck Galveston as it approached the 20th. And we look at the giant steps the people of Galveston took to make sure the tragedy would never be repeated.

Early History of the Island and the City

Galveston Island, one and one-half to three miles wide and 27 miles long, was part of the Karankawa Indians' territory before Europeans arrived. The first European to see the island was probably Spanish explorer Alonso Alvarez de Pineda, who in 1519 surveyed the entire Gulf Coast from the Florida Keys to Veracruz for the Spanish government.

When Cabeza de Vaca was shipwrecked on a Gulf island that he called Isla de Malhado (Island of Misfortune) in 1528, he may have been on Galveston Island. Other Spanish visitors called it San Luis or Isla de Culebras (Island of Snakes).

In 1785, José Antonio de Evia charted the coastline, naming the bay between island and mainland for Bernardo de Gálvez Gallardo, the viceroy of Mexico. Map makers later also applied the name to the island.

In 1816, Frenchman Louis Michel Aury became the first European to inhabit the island, and he attempted to establish a government. He was displaced by French pirate Jean Lafitte in mid-1817; Lafitte hung around the island until about 1820.

Probably the primary attraction to pirates and to the settlers who followed them was that the eastern end of Galveston Island was the best natural port between New Orleans and Veracruz. The government of Mexico built a small customshouse on the island in 1825 to create a port of entry. The Texas revolutionaries used the port of Galveston during the Texas war for independence from Mexico in 1835-36.

After that war, Michel B. Menard, the French-Canadian for whom Menard County was named, acquired more than 4,000 acres at the harbor for a town. Menard and his associates in the venture called the town "Galveston" and began selling lots on April 20, 1838.

Not surprisingly, Galveston's economy developed around shipping. Its wharves and warehouses moved cotton, sugar, molasses, cattle, pecans and hides from

Galveston surged ahead of other Texas cities in population in the 1870 federal census, with 13,818 residents, and remained on top in 1880, with 22,248.

Texas to the rest of the world via New Orleans, New York and Great Britain. Galveston reported shipment of 82,000 bales of cotton in 1854. The importance of cotton to Galveston increased steadily, with Galveston ranking third among U.S. ports in cotton shipments in 1878.

Before the Civil War, small factories made iron parts, soap, furniture and rope. After the war, cottonseed oil, flour, ice and textiles were manufactured, and cotton compresses operated. There was virtually no major manufacturing at Galveston, however. Investors were reluctant to put their money into an area that was so vulnerable to destructive storms.

Realizing that the economic health of their shipping business depended on railroads to transport goods to and from the port, the City of Galveston financed the construction of a railroad bridge to the mainland in 1860. Shipworms ate much of it, and the remainder blew away in a storm in 1867. A replacement was built in 1868. Another followed in 1877, and a bridge for wagons was constructed in 1893. A third railroad bridge was completed in 1896.

At the outbreak of the Civil War, commerce halted for almost a year. When Union ships began shelling the island city, many residents abandoned their homes and businesses for safer temporary shelter inland.

The Union navy blockaded the port for most of the war. Blockade-runners sneaked through on a regular basis, however, transporting cotton to ports in Mexico and bringing in trade goods and munitions.

The Confederates surrendered at Appomattox Courthouse in Virginia on April 9, 1865. Gen. Gordon Granger, the Union commander in charge of Texas, arrived in Galveston on June 19 to declare, "The people of Texas are informed that in accordance with a proclamation from the Executive of the United States 'all slaves are free.'" Because the news of emancipation did not reach Texas for more than two months past the end

of the war, June 19 (called Juneteenth) is the date on which Texas blacks celebrate the end of slavery.

Recovering from the Civil War, Galveston surged ahead of other Texas cities in population in the 1870 federal census, with 13,818 residents, and remained on top in 1880, with 22,248.

Galveston's port had a chronic sandbar problem first noticed about 1843. In 1845, there were only 11 feet of water over the outer bar; by 1869, there were only eight feet. As ships became larger, they required deeper harbors. At Galveston, large ships had to anchor outside the bar and transfer their cargoes to shallow-draft barges, called "lighters," for transport to the wharves — a slow and expensive process. Since the port was essential to Galveston's economic development, it had to be able to accommodate deeper-draft ships.

When the Reconstruction military officials refused to authorize a city tax for clearing the bar, the city's Board of Harbor Improvements sold city bonds to pay for the project. The firm hired to deepen the harbor sank three rows of cedar piles, which focused the current in a way that washed away the sand. The bar sank to 12 feet below the water's surface by 1873 and continued sinking.

The goal then became a 20-foot depth, but efforts by the U.S. Army Corps of Engineers in 1874 and 1880 only made matters worse.

Led by Col. William L. Moody — a Virginian by birth, a Texan since 1852 — the citizens of Galveston organized a Deep Water Committee in 1881. The DWC gathered information, formulated a plan and presented it to the U.S. Senate, which approved the Galveston Harbor Bill in 1890. The resulting jetties did their work as planned: In October 1896, the largest cargo ship in the world, drawing 21 feet, docked at Galveston wharves.

Imports increased 37 percent. Exports also improved. Before the harbor was deepened, Galveston shipped 22 percent of Texas cotton. In 1897-98, it shipped 64 percent. In 1900, more than 2 million bales of cotton were shipped from the port at Galveston.

By the time the 1900 census count was taken, however, San Antonio, with 53,321 residents, Houston, with 44,633, and Dallas, with 42,638, had left Galveston, with 37,789, in the population dust. The transcontinental railroad lines and growing manufacturing sectors of the three larger Texas cities by-passed hurricane-vulnerable Galveston.

Previous Storms

Hurricanes struck Galveston at least 11 times during the 19th century. In 1818, the entire island was flooded to a depth of four feet, leaving only six buildings habitable.

After a storm inundated the city in 1837, a local carpenter, Joseph Ehlinger, suggested rebuilding the destroyed customshouse on four-foot pilings to raise it above the flood level. After that time, many structures in Galveston, residences included, were built on stilts.

A storm in 1867 tore up all but one of the docks and flooded the business area.

One of the federal government's earliest weather stations was established in Galveston in 1871 for reporting local weather data to the national weather office.

The 1875 hurricane that heavily damaged the port town of Indianola, about 120 crow's-flight miles southwest, also hit Galveston. Following that storm, Galveston asked the state to construct a breakwater. The state refused. In 1878, the city planted salt cedars atop some of the sand dunes, hoping that the trees' root network would hold the dunes in place and create a natural breakwater. A little sand was brought in to raise some areas, but even after that, the highest point in the city was less than nine feet above sea level.

The hurricane that finished off Indianola in 1886 produced more discussions in Galveston of building a seawall, but no action.

The Storm of Sept. 8, 1900

On Sept. 4, 1900, the Galveston weather station received its first notice that a hurricane was moving northward from Cuba.

The barometric pressure at the Galveston weather station at 7:00 a.m. on Sept. 6 was 29.97 inches of mercury and slowly falling. The station's climatologist, Isaac M. Cline, was notified by telegraph that the hurricane had passed over central Florida. On the following day, Cline noted in his journal that the winds at Galveston were becoming stronger and the seas were rough, but he noticed none of the usual warning signs of an imminent hurricane.

On Saturday morning, Sept. 8, in a story datelined "Miami, Fla., Sept. 7," the Galveston News reported, "The tropical hurricane, which has done considerable damage on the islands of Jamaica and Cuba, struck the Florida coast Wednesday morning. No damage was done at Miami. . . Telegraph wires were blown down and this part of the country was shut off from the outside world from Wednesday night until this evening." Telegraph lines were also down on the Louisiana and Mississippi coasts, and Cline could not be notified of the direction of the storm's path.

In Galveston that Saturday morning, rain clouds were building up, the winds were much stronger. The weather forecast in the *Galveston News* for eastern Texas read, "Rain Saturday, with high northerly winds; Sunday rain, follwed by clearing."

Cline noticed that the tide was much higher than usual. When low-lying areas of the city began flooding, Cline became alarmed and hoisted hurricane-warning flags. Numerous times Cline left the weather office in the care of his brother Joseph and a helper to make desperate trips to warn residents closest to the beach that they should find safer shelter. However, many Galvestonians went about their day as usual. They had endured storms in the past, and they were not alarmed by yet another.

The rain gauge blew down from its perch atop the Levy Building about 2:30 p.m. The barometer began a rapid fall during the late afternoon. The anemometer blew away at 5:15 p.m., shortly after recording average wind speeds of 84 miles an hour and gusts of 100 miles per hour. Cline later estimated that the strongest winds were 120 miles per hour. However, many survivors reported seeing slate, timbers, bricks and other heavy debris being blown through the air almost horizontally, which could indicate much stronger winds.

The storm made match sticks out of frame buildings. Even those that had been carefully constructed to withstand the wind and rain of hurricanes were not able to resist battering by bridge trestles and other debris from already collapsed structures. Even "storm-proof" brick buildings fell under the onslaught. The collapsing buildings caught and held victims under water. Others were cut down by wave-tossed or wind-blown debris.

The entire island was covered by a storm surge of up to 15.7 feet of water; the previous record from the 1875 storm was 8.2 feet.

After the Storm

When the wind and rain stopped and the water receded, the survivors emerged from their shelters to a

---

Structures in two-thirds of the city were totally destroyed. In the remaining one-third, most buildings were badly damaged.

---

horrific sight. Bodies lay everywhere. Many victims were buried in the huge piles of rubble that covered the city; they were discovered only as the clean-up progressed. Structures in two-thirds of the city were totally destroyed. In the remaining one-third, most buildings were badly damaged.

The Galveston News published a stark single sheet on Sunday morning, headed, "Galveston News. Sunday Sept. 9, 1900. Following is list of dead as accurately as News men have been able to make it. Those who have lost relatives should report same at News office. This list will be corrected and added to as returns come in." There follows a two-column list of names.

There will probably never be a full accounting of all the people who perished in the 1900 storm. In the semi-tropical climate, the most urgent task was disposing of the remains of the victims for health reasons. Because of the powerful stench of decaying bodies, seacherers wore handkerchiefs saturated with camphor over their noses, and many drank whiskey to dull the horror. When not enough volunteers could be found for this grisly task, men were rounded up at gunpoint or bayonet point to do it.

At first, the remains were transported on barges into the Gulf, weighted with heavy rocks, and dumped overboard. When some of the bodies began to float ashore several days later, funeral pyres were used to cremate the victims.

About 70 victims a day were found during the first month after the storm. The funeral fires burned into November. Not until Feb. 10, 1901, was the last body found. A final list of 4,263 dead was published in the Galveston News in early October, but many bodies were never identified. The best estimates give the number of dead as about 6,000 people in the city, while another 4,000-6,000 died elsewhere on the island and on the nearby mainland.

Besides the human toll, the value of damaged prop-

The seawall was built in alternating sections; concrete was delivered by the machine at left. The granite rip-rap is shown in the foreground. Photo used by permission of the Rosenberg Library, Galveston.

erty was estimated at $30 million, including 3,600 homes destroyed. The wagon bridge had washed away, leaving railroads the only transportation to the mainland.

Recovery Begins

At a mass meeting the day after the storm, citizens elected a committee to direct recovery efforts: Galveston Mayor Walter C. Jones was named chairman of the Central Relief Committee; state senator R.V. Davidson was secretary of the committee; ship agent W.A. McVitie was chairman of relief services; banker John Sealy was in charge of finances; ship agent Daniel Ripley was placed in charge of hospitals; banker and businessman Morris Lasker was in charge of correspondence.

Also on the committee were financier I.H. Kempner; alderman Ben Levy; ship agent Jens Moller; banker Bertrand Adoue; Rabbi Henry Cohen of Congregation B'nai Israel; city recorder and attorney Noah Allen; and editor W.V. McConn.

The relief committee organized quickly to take care of the most urgent needs of the survivors. As the story of the city's tragedy spread, the world responded.

Clara Barton, the 78-year-old founder of the American Red Cross, arrived on Sept. 17 with a group of workers. The Central Relief Committee delegated to them the distribution of food and clothing until the Red Cross group left on Nov. 14.

Donations poured in from cities around the United States and several foreign countries.

Money came from millionaires in New York, from black churches in Georgia, and from a little girl in Chicago, who sent 10 cents.

Donations came from religious groups, labor and fraternal organizations and thousands of individuals. Relief funds were raised by an organ recital in Scranton, Pa., and by a baseball game in Anaconda, Mont. Money was sent by the German Turnverein of St. Louis, Mo., and the Rough and Ready Fire Company of Montrose, Pa. Sunday school classes sent their collections of pennies, nickels and dimes.

In all, donations exceeded $1.25 million. By far the most generous state was New York ($228,055), followed by Texas ($66,790), Illinois ($55,544), Massachusetts ($53,350) and Missouri ($52,116).

Donations also arrived from foreign countries — among them, Canada, Mexico, France, Germany, England and South Africa.

Along with taking care of the immediate needs of clean-up, restoration of utilities, and feeding, clothing and sheltering the survivors of the storm, the Central Relief Committee paid for the building of 483 new houses, plus furnishing partial financial aid for the repair or rebuilding of 1,114 houses.

Long-range Response

A New Form of Municipal Government

As discussion began on what should be done to prevent a recurrence of such a disaster, the old Deep Water Committee resurfaced.

The DWC members were the elite of Galveston's finance and business world. In his book, *Galveston: A History*, David G. McComb says, "Members of the com-

At 28th St. and Avenue P, the houses on the right and the street have been raised. The structures on the left have been lifted and are waiting for sand to be pumped under them. Photo used by permission of the Rosenberg Library, Galveston.

mittee and their associates directed the eight local banks, dominated 62 percent of the corporate capital, and controlled 75 percent of the valuable real estate."

Dissatisfaction with Galveston's municipal government had been building during the preceding several years, especially within the ranks of financial and commercial leaders. The sitting government was guilty not so much of malfeasance as of laxity and procrastination. Fiscal irregularities had been uncovered that were perhaps exacerbated by the fact that the official accountant did not know how to keep books. Galveston's financial situation was bleak.

The city operated under a mayor-council charter, which, since the mid-1890s, provided for 12 councilmen. They were elected at large but were required to live in the wards they represented. Two weeks after the storm, the council began discussing the need for a city government that could lead Galveston through the recovery period. The Deep Water Committee asserted that Galveston needed a stronger, more centralized, more efficient form of government to direct recovery efforts.

The DWC proposed a commission appointed by the governor and composed of a mayor-president and four commissioners. Each commissioner would administer a division of city government: finance and revenue, police and fire, waterworks and sewerage, and streets and public improvements. The committee further suggested that the state exempt Galveston from paying state and county taxes for two years and that the bonded debt be refinanced at a lower rate.

In 1900, any changes in city charters had to be approved by the legislature, so the DWC appealed directly to the state's governing body for enabling legislation for their ground-breaking charter.

The original plan called for all five commission members to be appointed. The legislature approved an amended version providing for the election of two commissioners and the appointment of three.

In 1903, under the threat of court challenges to the constitutionality of the charter, the legislature required that all commissioners be elected. Galveston kept the commission form of city government, with modifications, until 1960.

The Recovery Plan

Recovery was, of course, the highest priority with the new commission, which appointed three engineers to develop a plan to protect Galveston from future storms.

The engineers presented a two-part project: To break the force of the waves, they recommended building a concrete seawall three miles long from the south jetty across the eastern edge of the city and down the beach. To protect the city from flooding, they proposed raising the level of the entire city by picking up most of the structures in the city and filling in beneath them with sand. Cost of the entire project was estimated to be $3.5 million.

The county agreed to pay for the seawall through a bond issue. The state finally agreed to a combination of tax abatement and sales of bonds to finance the grade elevation.

Construction of the Seawall

J.M. O'Rourke and Co. of Denver built the seawall in 50-foot interlocking sections. First, piles were driven 40 to 50 feet deep and set four feet apart. They were protected from undermining on the Gulf side by sheet piling sunk 26 feet into the sea floor. Concrete was poured over the pilings, reinforced with one-and-one-quarter-inch-diameter steel rods inserted every three feet. The crew poured about 100 feet of wall a day. The side of the seawall facing the Gulf was concave, to absorb shock and to turn the waves back on themselves.

Granite riprap three to four feet deep and extending 27 feet out from the wall added protection from erosion.

T. Lindsay Baker, in his book, *Building the Lone Star*, lists the materials used in constructing the seawall: 5,200 railway carloads of crushed granite, 1,800 carloads of sand, 1,000 carloads of cement, 1,200 carloads of round wooden pilings, 4,000 carloads of wooden sheet pilings, 3,700 carloads of stone riprap and five carloads of reinforcing steel.

When the wall was finished, it stood 17 feet above mean low tide, was 15 feet thick at the base, five feet thick at the top, and three-and-one-half miles long. A brick drive extended about 100 feet inland from the top.

The city's portion, begun on Oct. 27, 1902, and completed on July 29, 1904, cost within $326 of the contracted amount. Between December 1904 and October 1905, another section of seawall was built by the federal government to protect Fort Crockett Military Reservation. Additions and modifications to the seawall were made in 1918-1921, 1923, 1926, 1927 and 1950. Today the wall is 10.4 miles long.

Lifting an Entire City

Raising the grade of the city was more complicated.

The work began in December 1903 and was done in quarter-mile-square sections — each about 16 city blocks in size. Each section in turn was enclosed in a dike.

In addition to structures, utility lines within the dike — sewers, water and gas lines, streetcar tracks, fire hydrants and telephone and telegraph poles — had to be lifted. Fences, sidewalks and outbuildings also had to be repositioned.

Some frame structures had been built on stilts because of the city's periodic flooding. Many of them sat high enough to accommodate the increased height in ground level. All buildings that weren't already on stilts — about 2,000 buildings — were raised with jacks. Even the 3,000-ton St. Patrick's Church was lifted five feet with 700 jackscrews.

Sand for the fill was dredged out of an area between the jetties at the entrance to Galveston harbor, which had the benefit of deepening the approach to the harbor.

To transport the fill to the areas being raised, the contractor built a canal 20 feet deep, 200 feet wide and two-and-a-half miles long through the residential district. About 350 houses had to be temporarily relocated so that the canal could be dug.

A slurry of water and fill sand, dug out of the harbor channel by dredges, was sailed down the canal to dis-

charge stations, from which the mixture was pumped into the area to the desired level. The water then drained away, leaving the sand behind. New foundations were constructed for the buildings on top of the fill, and the structures were fastened to their new bases.

While the work was being done, people walked about on catwalks as high as eight to ten feet in the air.

The area immediately behind the seawall was raised just over 16.5 feet, giving the seawall a solid support. The grade decreased one foot for every 1,500 feet west to Galveston Bay, so that the city's streets drained into the bay. A side benefit of the grade raising was that the city's sewer system, which had never worked right, finally had enough slope to enable it to operate properly.

When the job was finished in 1910, 500 city blocks had been raised from a few inches to more than 16 feet by the use of 16.3 million cubic yards of sand.

The Defenses are Tested

The first major test of the seawall came on August 16, 1915, when a large hurricane pushed the tide to three inches higher than in 1900. The storm destroyed 90 percent of the buildings outside the seawall and flooded the downtown area. However, only eight people lost their lives in Galveston, compared with 304 elsewhere.

Tornadoes accompanying Hurricane Carla in 1961 destroyed 120 buildings and killed six people, but the hurricane's wind, rain and tide were not devastating. In 1983, Hurricane Alicia spared the populace but damaged about $300 million worth of property.

Engineering technology appears to have saved Galveston from an encore of the devastation of 1900. But the city has never regained its former place in the shipping industry.

Today Galveston's economy is driven by three paramount areas: tourism, attracting visitors to its beach and its historic districts; the port, which now ranks 7th in shipments among the 13 major Texas ports; and The University of Texas Medical Branch, which has been an important part of the city since 1891. ☆

For Further Reading

Building the Lone Star: An Illustrated Guide to Historic Sites by T. Lindsay Baker; Texas A&M University Press, College Station, 1986.

Galveston: A History, by David G. McComb; University of Texas Press, Austin, 1986.

Galveston in Nineteen Hundred , edited by Clarence Ousley; Wm. C. Chase, Atlanta, 1900.

Report of the Central Relief Committee for Galveston Storm Sufferers; Galveston, May 2, 1902.

"The Galveston Plan of City Government by Commission: The Birth of a Progressive Idea" by Bradley R. Rice; Southwestern Historical Quarterly, Vol. 78, No. 4; Texas State Historical Association, Austin, April 1975.

"The Galveston Storm of 1900" by John Edward Weems; Southwestern Historical Quarterly, Vol. 61, No. 4; Texas State Historical Association, Austin, April 1958.

Texas' All-Woman Supreme Court

by Mary G. Ramos, editor, Texas Almanac

Hattie Henenberg, Hortense Ward and Ruth Brazzil (left to right) constituted the first all-woman Texas Supreme Court. It is believed to have been the first all-woman high court in the United States. Photo courtesy Texas Supreme Court Historical Society.

Three women comprised a special Texas Supreme Court for five months in 1925. It was the first all-woman high court in the United States.

These were not merely honorary appointments. Governor Pat Neff appointed the three women attorneys as a special state supreme court to hear the appeal of a case involving the Woodmen of the World (WOW), a fraternal association. The WOW was an influential political power in Texas, and virtually all elected officials, as well as most lawyers, were members. The association also offered a mutual insurance program with premiums that rose or fell according to the amount of money it had to pay out for insurance claims. Therefore most judges and attorneys in the state had a personal interest in cases having to do with claims against the organization and were ethically required to recuse themselves from cases involving the WOW.

During the five months the all-woman court served, the other business of the court was conducted as usual by the male justices.

In 1924, a lawsuit was appealed to the Texas Supreme Court involving the WOW. Trustees for the WOW were claiming two tracts of land in El Paso under a verbal "secret trust." The supreme court was asked to decide whether it would review the decision of the El Paso Court of Civil Appeals in the case, styled Johnson v. Darr (114 Tex 516). If the high court agreed to review Johnson v. Darr, it then had to decide whether to uphold or to overturn the decision of the El Paso court.

At that time, the Texas Supreme Court was composed of three members: a chief justice and two associate justices. On March 8, 1924, Chief Justice C.M.

Cureton certified to Neff that he and the two associate justices, Thomas B. Greenwood and William Pierson, must excuse themselves from hearing the appeal because of their membership in the WOW. The law provided that the governor should immediately appoint special justices to hear the case. During the following 10 months, Neff evidently attempted to find male attorneys to sit on the special court. However, according to H.L. Clamp, the Deputy Clerk of the Supreme Court from 1902 to 1953, each time Neff offered an appointment to a male attorney, the lawyer responded that he, too, was a member of the WOW, and therefore was disqualified from serving.

Not until Jan. 1, 1925, only a week before the case was scheduled to be heard, did Neff finally appoint the special justices: three women, who could not possibly be members of Woodmen of the World because that organization did not accept women members.

The appointment of three women to the special court was particularly appropriate, since the inauguration of Texas' first woman governor, Miriam A. "Ma" Ferguson, was scheduled for Jan. 20. Women in Texas had gained the right to vote in primary elections only seven years before, the same year that Dr. Annie Webb Blanton became the first woman elected to a statewide office, that of Superintendent of Public Instruction. And it was a mere three years after the first woman was elected to the Texas House of Representatives.

Neff himself had made it his policy to appoint one or more women to all state boards and commissions, starting early in his first term.

The Dallas Morning News reported on Friday, Jan.

2, 1925, "All records were shattered and at least three precedents established on Thursday, when Gov. Neff appointed a special Supreme Court composed entirely of women. It was a healthy New Year gift of recognition to the woman barrister of today. This is the first instance a woman has been appointed to sit on the supreme bench; it is the first time a higher court is to be composed entirely of women and it is the initial case where a majority of the judges will be women."

In the same news item, The Morning News reported that Neff had asked Clamp if the appointment of women to the special supreme court would be legal. Clamp's opinion was that the appointments would be legal if all eligibility rules were observed: a minimum of seven years' practice of law in Texas and being at least 30 years of age.

The first three women appointed to the special tribunal were Nellie Gray Robertson of Granbury, the county attorney of Hood County; Edith E. Wilmans of Dallas, who had been a member of the 38th Legislature; and Hortense Sparks Ward of Houston, an attorney in practice with her husband. Robertson was designated chief justice; the other two women were named associate justices.

On Jan. 5, Wilmans announced that she must resign because she lacked two months having the requisite seven years of law practice in Texas. Neff appointed Hattie Leah Henenberg of Dallas to replace Wilmans. Then Robertson, who had practiced law in Texas for only six years and nine months, also announced her resignation. Only one day before the court was to consider whether it would hear the case, Ruth Virginia Brazzil of Galveston was appointed by the governor to replace Robertson. Ward was named special chief justice.

The three women selected to serve on this history-making court were dedicated practitioners of law:

• Hortense Sparks Ward was the first woman in Texas to pass the state bar exam (1910), and she was the first Texas woman admitted to practice before the U.S. Supreme Court (1915).

Ward was born in Matagorda County to Fred and Marie Louise Sparks in 1875 and attended Nazareth Academy in Victoria. When an early marriage ended in divorce, leaving her with three daughters, she learned stenography in order to become a court reporter. She met Judge W.H. Ward while working at the courthouse, and they married in 1908. Mrs. Ward's growing interest in and study of the law culminated in her passing the bar exam administered by the appellate court in Galveston in 1910.

By 1911, Ward had written a pamphlet, "Property Rights of Married Women in Texas," which spotlighted the dearth of such rights. Ward pointed out, "When a woman in Texas marries today, her husband has the sole management of all her separate property and of all her interest in the community property . . . He may even mortgage or sell every piece of furniture in the home, and she is helpless to prevent, even if her earnings have paid for every piece. He has a right to sell her dresses if he sees fit, and she cannot prevent . . ." With Ward leading the effort, the 33rd Legislature finally passed the Married Woman's Property Rights Law in 1913, allowing women to manage their own property.

Turning her attention to woman suffrage, Ward is credited with drafting the primary-suffrage bill, which passed the Texas Legislature in 1918. As a reward for her leadership in the campaign, Ward was given the privilege of being the first woman in the history of Harris County to register to vote.

Ward was less active politically after her service on the special supreme court, but she continued to practice law with her husband until he died in 1939. Although she was quite outspoken and active in some matters, she never represented a client in the courtroom: She understood that a woman attorney would be at a disadvantage because of the prejudices of the time. Ward died in Houston on Dec. 5, 1944.

• Hattie Leah Henenberg was born in Ennis, Ellis County, Feb. 16, 1893, and she attended public school in Dallas. She graduated from Dallas School of Law and received her license to practice in 1916. For several years she practiced law in association with Albert Walker in Dallas; she then went into general practice alone. She was an attorney in Dallas until 1966.

During World War I, Henenberg served on the Legal Advisory Board, helping men complete their draft registration forms. For six to eight months prior to her appointment to the special Supreme Court, she was in charge of the Free Legal Aid Bureau sponsored by the Dallas Bar Association. Holland's Magazine of March 1925 quoted Henenberg as saying, "From birth to death, the poor man is the prey of petty swindlers . . . Legal aid work consists of giving legal advice and legal assistance gratuitously, if necessary, to all persons who may appear worthy, and who, by reason of poverty, are unable to procure assistance elsewhere. A legal aid society does not give charitable support to needy persons, but only justice and the enforcement of just and honorable claims."

Henenberg was an assistant attorney general of Texas from 1929 to 1931, then served as special assistant U.S. Attorney General in 1934. She was an assistant district attorney in Dallas County from 1941 to 1947.

Henenberg helped raise funds for a variety of social services, among them the legal-aid office and a toy-lending library for poor children in West Dallas. She served on the child welfare committee of the State Bar of Texas and was an organizer and director of the Dallas Bar Association. She died in Dallas on Nov. 28, 1974, at the age of 81.

• Ruth Virginia Brazzil, the third special justice, carefully avoided publicity, so not as much is known about her as about the other two justices. Born in Tyler on Sept. 12, 1889, she attended Wharton public schools. She worked her way through The University of Texas as a "special student" in law, passing the bar exam in 1912.

During her lifetime, she was active in many different occupations, among them dealing in real estate, working for a legislator and managing an abstract company in Wharton. She was assistant treasurer and assistant general manager of American National Life Insurance Company in Galveston.

She had a brief marriage to rice farmer Roy Roome of Louise, Wharton County. Upon their divorce in 1927, she regained her maiden name legally, though she continued to be known as Ruth Roome. Brazzil moved to Bandera in the late 1920s or early 1930s, where she was postmistress. She also lived in Center Point and Kerrville.

Unlike the other two women on the special supreme court, Brazzil is said to have opposed woman suffrage and the advancement of women's rights. When asked to comment on women's place in politics for the article in Holland's Magazine, she said, "In my opinion there is little chance of the majority of our public offices ever being filled by women. There are too many men well qualified for that, and, as a rule, the average woman has more exacting, and, to her, more absorbing duties than those of a political nature."

For the last decade of her life, Brazzil was confined to a wheelchair. At the time of her death in 1976, she was a patient in the Kerrville State Hospital.

The special supreme court met for the first time on Jan. 8, 1925. The occasion was heralded in The New York Times that morning with the headline, "Supreme Court of Women, First Such Body in the Country Meets in Texas Today."

In the consultation room of the Supreme Court, the three women took the oath of special justices administered by Chief Justice Cureton. Attending the ceremony were the other two members of the regular court, Attorney General Dan Moody, Clerk of the Court Fred Connerly and several newspaper correspondents. There were no women observers.

The legally mandated oath of office at the time required each justice to swear, among other things, that she had never fought a duel. That part caused smiles all around.

Cureton explained to Chief Justice Ward three possible dispositions of the case: The tribunal could refuse to grant the writ of error, in effect refusing to hear the appeal; it could affirm the El Paso Court of Civil Appeals' decision, which would also result in not hearing the appeal; or it could grant the writ of error, agreeing to hear the appeal.

After a brief deliberation by the special justices, Ward announced that the writ of error was granted and that they would hear the appeal on Jan. 30.

On Jan. 30, the tribunal met, heard arguments by El Paso attorneys — J.W. Morrow for the plaintiff and Volney Brown for the defendants — and returned to their homes to consider the record.

The case involved a lien on two tracts of land owned by the WOW camp at El Paso. J.M. Darr and others acting as trustees for the WOW at El Paso deeded the two pieces of land to F.P. Jones. The deed was duly recorded. On the same day the deed was executed, Jones signed an agreement to hold the land in trust for the trustees and to deed it back when requested to do so. The agreement was not recorded. Jones' creditors, W.T. Johnson, et al., claimed the property as compensation for past debts. The WOW trustees brought suit to establish the trust agreement and prevent the transfer of the land to Johnson.

The trial court held for the plaintiffs on one piece of land and for the defendants on the other. The Court of Civil Appeals held for the WOW on both tracts. What the Supreme Court had to decide was whether the trust agreement had to be recorded prior to the creditors' claim to protect the WOW interest in the land.

On May 23, 1925, the special tribunal met for the last time to announce its decision. It found for the WOW on both tracts of land, upholding the El Paso Court of Appeals decision. The legal aspects of the case were relatively simple. The court had to decide whether a declaration of trust not placed on record is effective against an attachment for debt. At the time, trust agreements, even "secret" trusts, did not have to be recorded to be legally binding. Ward wrote the majority opinion, with concurring opinions being written by associate justices Henenberg and Brazzil.

With their decision duly handed down, the first all-woman Supreme Court in the land quietly passed into history. ☆

*The author wishes to thank former Supreme Court Justices **Jack Hightower** and **Jack Pope**, Supreme Court Clerk **John Adams**, and **Catherine Harris** of the State Law Library for their review of this article and for their very constructive comments and corrections. Any errors are the author's own.*

National Historic Civil Engineering Landmarks in Texas

Seven engineering projects in Texas have been designated National Historic Civil Engineering Landmarks by the American Society of Civil Engineers:

Acequias of San Antonio - One of the earliest recorded uses of an engineered water supply and irrigation system in the country, the acequias were built starting in 1718 to serve the Spanish missions in the area. Designated in 1968.

El Camino Real (Royal Road), East - A major transportation artery begun in the 16th century, it eventually stretched from the present Republic of Mexico through Texas and east to Florida. Designated in 1986.

Houston Ship Channel - Began with a simple dredged channel in 1839. The modern channel opened in 1914 and has been improved often since

that time. It is an engineering project of major complexity. Designated in 1987.

Denison Dam on the Red River - It was the largest rolled-earth-fill dam in the country when it was completed in 1945. Designated in 1993.

San Jacinto Monument, Houston - The world's tallest free-standing concrete tower at the time of construction in 1936-39. Designated in 1992.

San Antonio's River Walk - Opened in 1939, the River Walk combines flood control with graceful design and respect for the natural beauty of the river. It is an international travel destination, as well. Designated in 1996.

National Bank of Commerce Building, Houston - The foundation design for this building, erected in 1927-28, was the first application of the then-new field of soil mechanics to a building in the Houston region. Designated in 1997. ☆

A Brief Sketch of Texas History

This brief, two-part sketch of Texas' past, from prehistoric times to 1920, is based on "A Concise History of Texas" by former Texas Almanac editor Mike Kingston. Mr. Kingston's history was published in the 1986-87 sesquicentennial edition. Robert Plocheck, associate editor of the Texas Almanac, prepared this excerpt.

Texas: Prehistory to Annexation

Prehistoric Texas

Early Texans were descendants of Asian groups that migrated across the Bering Strait during the Ice Ages of the past 50,000 years.

At intermittent periods, enough water would accumulate in the massive glaciers worldwide to lower the sea level several hundred feet. During these periods, the Bering Strait would become a 1,300-mile-wide land bridge between North America and Asia.

These early adventurers worked their way southward for thousands of years, eventually getting as far as Tierra del Fuego in South America 10,000 years ago.

Biologically they were completely modern homo sapiens. No evidence has been found to indicate that any evolutionary change occurred in the New World.

Four basic stages reflecting cultural advancement of early inhabitants are used by archaeologists in classifying evidence.

These stages are the Paleo-Indian (20,000 years ago to 7,000 years ago); Archaic (7,000 years ago to about the time of Christ); Woodland (time of Christ to 800-1,000 years ago), and Neo-American, or Late Prehistoric (800-1,000 years ago until European contact).

Not all early people advanced through all these stages in Texas. Much cultural change was made in adaptation to changes in climate. The Caddo tribes of East Texas, for example, reached the Neo-American stage before the Spanish and French explorers made contact in the 1500s and 1600s.

Others, such as the Karankawas of the Gulf Coast, advanced no further than the Archaic stage of civilization at the same time. Still others advanced and then regressed in the face of a changing climate.

The earliest confirmed evidence indicates that humans were in Texas between 10,000 and 13,000 years ago.

Paleo-Indians were successful big-game hunters. Artifacts from this period are found across the state but not in great number, indicating they were a small, nomadic population.

As Texas' climate changed at the end of the Ice Age about 7,000 years ago, inhabitants adapted. Apparently the state experienced an extended period of warming and drying and a population increase.

These Texans began to harvest fruits and nuts and, to exploit rivers for food, as indicated by the fresh-water mussel shells in ancient garbage heaps.

The Woodland stage is distinguished by the development of settled societies, and crops and local wild plants provided much of their diet. The bow and arrow came into use, and the first pottery is associated with this period.

Pre-Caddoan tribes in East Texas had formed villages and were building distinctive mounds for burials and for ritual.

The Neo-American period is best exemplified by the highly-civilized Caddoes, who had a complex culture with well-defined social stratification. They were fully agricultural and participated in trade over a wide area of North America.

The Spanish Explorations

Spain's exploration of North America was one of the first acts of a vigorous nation that was emerging from centuries of campaigns to oust the Islamic Moors from the Iberian Peninsula.

In early 1492, the Spanish forces retook the province of Granada, completing the *reconquista* or reconquest. Later in the year, the Catholic royals of the united country, Ferdinand and Isabella, took a major stride toward shaping world history by commissioning Christopher Columbus for the voyage that was to bring Europeans to America.

As early as **1519**, Capt. Alonso Alvarez de Pineda, in the service of the governor of Jamaica, mapped the coast of Texas.

The first recorded exploration of today's Texas was made in the **1530s** by Alvar Núñez Cabeza de Vaca, along with two other Spaniards and a Moorish slave named Estevanico. They were members of an expedition commanded by Panfilo de Narváez that left Cuba in 1528 to explore what is now the southeastern United States.

Ill-fated from the beginning, many members of the expedition lost their lives, and others, including Cabeza de Vaca, were shipwrecked on the Texas coast. Eventually the band wandered into Mexico in 1536.

In **1540**, Francisco Vázquez de Coronado was commissioned to lead an exploration of the American Southwest. The quest took him to the land of the Pueblo Indians in what is now New Mexico. Native Americans, who had learned it was best to keep Europeans away from their homes, would suggest vast riches could be found in other areas. So Coronado pursued a fruitless search for the riches across the **High Plains of Texas**, Oklahoma and Kansas.

While Coronado was investigating Texas from the west, Luis Moscoso de Alvarado approached from the east. He assumed leadership of Hernando de Soto's expedition when the commander died on the banks of the Mississippi River. In **1542**, Moscoso's group ventured as far west as **Central Texas** before returning to the Mississippi.

Forty years passed after the Coronado and Moscoso expeditions before Fray Agustín Rodríguez, a Franciscan missionary, and Francisco Sánchez Chamuscado, a soldier, led an expedition into Texas and New Mexico.

Following the Río Conchos in Mexico to its confluence with the Rio Grande near present-day **Presidio** and then turning northwestward up the great river's valley, the explorers passed through the El Paso area in **1581**.

Juan de Oñate was granted the right to develop this area populated by Pueblo Indians in 1598. He blazed a trail across the desert from Santa Barbara, Chihuahua, to intersect the Rio Grande at the Pass of the North. For the next 200 years, this was the supply route from the interior of Mexico that served the northern colonies.

Texas was attractive to the Spanish in the 1600s. Small expeditions found trade possibilities, and missionaries ventured into the territory. Frays Juan de Salas and Diego López responded to a request by the Jumano Indians for religious instruction in **1629**, and for a brief time priests lived with the Indians near present-day **San Angelo**.

The first permanent settlement in Texas was established in **1681-82** after New Mexico's Indians rebelled and drove Spanish settlers southward. The colonists retreated to the **El Paso** area, where the missions of Corpus Christi de la Isleta and Nuestra Señora del Socorro — each named for a community in New Mexico — were established.

Ysleta pueblo originally was located on the south side of the Rio Grande, but as the river changed course, it ended up on the north bank. Now part of El Paso, the community is considered the oldest European settlement in Texas.

French Exploration

In 1682, **René Robert Cavelier, Sieur de La Salle**, explored the Mississippi River to its mouth at the Gulf of Mexico. La Salle claimed the vast territory drained by the river for France.

Two years later, La Salle returned to the New World with four ships and enough colonists to establish his country's claim. (See related article, pages 29-34.) Guided by erroneous maps, this second expedition overshot the mouth of the Mississippi by 400 miles and ended up on the Texas coast. Though short of supplies because of the loss of two of the ships, the French colonists established Fort Saint Louis on Garcitas Creek several miles inland from Lavaca Bay.

In 1687, La Salle and a group of soldiers began an overland trip to find French outposts on the Mississippi. Somewhere west of the Trinity River, the explorer was murdered by some of his men. His grave has never been found.

In 1689, Spanish authorities sent **Capt. Alonso de León**, governor of Coahuila (which at various times included Texas in its jurisdiction), into Texas to confront the French. He headed eastward from present-day Eagle Pass and found the tattered remains of Fort Saint Louis. Indians had destroyed the settlement and killed many colonists. De León continued tracking survivors of the ill-fated colony into East Texas.

Spanish Rule

Father **Damián Massanet** accompanied de León on this journey. The priest was fascinated with tales about the "Tejas" Indians of the region.

Tejas meant friendly, but at the time the term was considered a tribal name. Actually these Indians were members of the Caddo Confederacy that controlled parts of our present states: Texas, Louisiana, Arkansas and Oklahoma.

The Caddo religion acknowledged one supreme god, and when a Tejas chief asked Father Massanet to stay and instruct his people in his faith, the Spaniards promised to return and establish a mission.

The pledge was redeemed in **1690** when the mission San Francisco de los Tejas was founded near present-day Weches in Houston County.

Twin disasters struck this missionary effort. Spanish government officials quickly lost interest when the French threat at colonization diminished. And as was the case with many New World Indians who had no resistance to European diseases, the Tejas soon were felled by an epidemic. The Indians blamed the new religion and resisted conversion.

The mission languished, and it was hard to supply from other Spanish outposts in northern Mexico. In 1693, the Spanish officials closed the mission effort in **East Texas**.

Although Spain had not made a determined effort to settle Texas, great changes were coming to the territory.

Spain introduced horses into the Southwest. By the late 1600s, Comanches were using the horses to expand their range southward across the plains, displacing the Apaches.

In the 1720s, the Apaches moved onto the lower Texas Plains, taking the traditional hunting grounds of the Jumanos and others. The nomadic Coahuiltecan bands were particularly hard hit.

In 1709, Fray Antonio de San Buenaventura y Olivares had made an initial request to establish a mission at San Pedro Springs (today's San Antonio) to minister to the Coahuiltecans. The request was denied. However, new fears of French movement into East Texas would change that.

Another Franciscan, **Father Francisco Hidalgo**, had served at the missions in East Texas and longed to return. His dream was realized when he, along with **Father Antonio Margil de Jesús**, accompanied **Capt. Diego Ramón** on an expedition in 1716.

In that year, the mission of San Francisco de los Neches was established near the site of the old San Francisco de los Tejas mission. Nuestra Señora de Guadalupe was located at the present-day site of Nacogdoches, and Nuestra Señora de los Dolores was placed near present-day San Augustine.

The East Texas missions did little better on the second try, and supplying the frontier missions remained difficult. It became apparent that a way station between northern Mexico and East Texas was needed.

In **1718**, Spanish officials consented to Fray Olivares' request to found a mission at San Pedro Springs. That mission, called **San Antonio de Valero**, was later to be known as the **Alamo**. Because the Indians of the region often did not get along with each other, other missions were established to serve each group.

These missions flourished and each became an early ranching center. But the large herds of cattle and horses attracted trouble. The San Antonio missions began to face the wrath of the Apaches.

The mission system, which attempted to convert the Indians to Christianity and to "civilize" them, was partially successful in subduing minor tribes but not larger tribes like the Apaches.

The Spanish realized that more stable colonization efforts must be made. Indians from Mexico, such as the Tlascalans who fought with Cortés against the Aztecs, were brought into Texas to serve as examples of "good" Indians for the wayward natives.

In **1731,** Spanish colonists from the Canary Islands were brought to Texas and founded the Villa of San Fernando de Béxar, the first civil jurisdiction in the province and today's **San Antonio.**

In the late 1730s, Spanish officials became concerned over the vulnerability of the large area between the Sierra Madre Oriental and the Gulf Coast in northern Mexico. The area was unsettled, a haven for runaway Indian slaves and marauders, and it was a wide-open pathway for the English or French from the Gulf to the rich silver mines in Durango.

For seven years the search for the right colonizer went on before José de Escandón was selected in 1746. A professional military man and successful administrator, Escandón earned a high reputation by subduing Indians in central Mexico.

On receiving the assignment, he launched a broad land survey of the area running from the mountains to the Gulf and from the Río Pánuco in Tamaulipas, Mexico, to the Nueces River in Texas.

In 1747, he began placing colonists in settlements throughout the area. Tomás Sánchez received a land grant on the Rio Grande in **1755** from which **Laredo** developed. And other small Texas communities along the river sprang up as a result of Escandón's well-executed plan. Many old Hispanic families in Texas hold title of their land based on grants in this period.

In the following decades, a few other Spanish colonists settled around the old missions and frontier forts. Antonio Gil Ybarbo led one group that settled **Nacogdoches** in the **1760s and 1770s.**

The Demise of Spain

Spain's final 60 years of control of the province of Texas were marked with a few successes and a multitude of failures, all of which could be attributed to a breakdown in the administrative system.

Charles III, the fourth of the Bourbon line of kings and generally recognized as an enlightened despot, took the Spanish throne in 1759. He launched a series of reforms in the New World. The king's choice of administrators was excellent. In 1765, José de Gálvez was dispatched to New Spain (an area that then included all of modern Mexico and much of today's American West) with instructions to improve both the economy and the defense.

Gálvez initially toured parts of the vast region, gaining first-hand insight into the practical problems of the colony. There were many that could be traced to Spain's basic concepts of colonial government. Texas, in particular, suffered from the mercantilist economic system that attempted to funnel all colonial trade through ports in Mexico.

But administrative reforms by Gálvez and his nephew, Bernardo Gálvez, namesake of Galveston, were to be followed by ill-advised policies by successors.

Problems with the Comanches, Apaches and "Norteños," as the Spanish called some tribes, continued to plague the province, too.

About the same time, Spain undertook the administration of Louisiana Territory. One of the terms of the cession by France was that the region would enjoy certain trading privileges denied to other Spanish dependencies. So although Texas and Louisiana were neighbors, trade between the two provinces was banned.

The crown further complicated matters by placing the administration of Louisiana under authorities in Cuba, while Texas remained under the authorities in Mexico City.

The death of Charles III in 1788 and the beginning of the French Revolution a year later weakened Spain's hold on the New World dominions. Charles IV was not as good a sovereign as his predecessor, and his choice of ministers was poor. The quality of frontier administrators declined, and relations with Indians soured further.

Charles IV's major blunder, however, was to side with French royalty during the revolution, earning Spain the enmity of Napoleon Bonaparte when he assumed control of the government. Spain also allied with England in an effort to thwart Napoleon, and in this losing cause, the Spanish were forced to cede Louisiana back to France.

In 1803, Napoleon broke a promise to retain the territory and sold it to the United States. Spain's problems in the New World thereby took on an altogether different dimension. Now, Anglo-Americans cast longing eyes on the vast undeveloped territory of Texas.

With certain exceptions for royalists who left the American colonies during the revolution, Spain had maintained a strict prohibition against Anglo or other non-Spanish settlers in their New World territories. But they were unprepared to police the eastern border of Texas after removing the presidios in the 1760s. What had been a provincial line became virtually overnight an international boundary, and an ill-defined one at that.

American Immigrants

Around **1800, Anglo-Americans** began to probe the Spanish frontier. Some settled in East Texas and others crossed the Red River and were tolerated by authorities.

Others, however, were thought to have nefarious designs. Philip Nolan was the first of the American filibusters to test Spanish resolve. Several times he entered Texas to capture wild horses to sell in the United States.

But in 1801, the Spanish perceived an attempted armed uprising by Nolan and his followers. He was killed in a battle near present-day Waco, and his company was taken captive to work in the mines in northern Mexico.

Spanish officials were beginning to realize that the economic potential of Texas must be developed if the Anglo-Americans were to be neutralized.

But Spain's centuries-long role in the history of Texas was almost over.

Resistance to Spanish rule had developed in the New World colonies. Liberal ideas from the American and French revolutions had grown popular, despite the crown's attempts to prevent their dissemination.

In Spain, three sovereigns — the Bourbon Charles IV, Napoleon's brother Joseph Bonaparte, and Ferdinand VII — claimed the throne, often issuing different edicts simultaneously. Since the time of Philip II, Spain had been a tightly centralized monarchy with the crown making most decisions. Now, chaos reigned in the colonies.

As Spain's grip on the New World slipped between 1790 and 1820, Texas was almost forgotten, an internal province of little importance. Colonization was ignored;

the Spanish government had larger problems in Europe and in Mexico.

Spain's mercantile economic policy penalized colonists in the area, charging them high prices for trade goods and paying low prices for products sent to markets in the interior of New Spain. As a result, settlers from central Mexico had no incentives to come to Texas. Indeed, men of ambition in the province often prospered by turning to illegal trade with Louisiana or to smuggling..

On the positive side, however, Indians of the province had been mollified through annual gifts and by developing a dependence on Spain for trade goods.

Ranching flourished. In **1795**, a census found **69 families** living on 45 ranches in the **San Antonio** area. A census in **1803** indicated that there were **100,000 head of cattle** in Texas. But aside from a few additional families in Nacogdoches and La Bahía (near present-day Goliad), the province was thinly populated.

The largest group of early immigrants from the United States was not Anglo, but Indian.

As early as **1818, Cherokees** of the southeastern United States came to Texas, settling north of Nacogdoches on lands between the Trinity and Sabine rivers. The Cherokees had been among the first U.S. Indians to accept the federal government's offers of resettlement. As American pioneers entered the newly-acquired lands of Georgia, Alabama and other areas of the Southeast, the Indians were systematically removed, through legal means or otherwise.

Some of the displaced groups settled on land provided in Arkansas Territory, but others, such as the Cherokees, came to Texas. These Cherokees were among the "Five Civilized Tribes" that had adopted agriculture and many Anglo customs in an unsuccessful attempt to get along with their new neighbors.

Alabama and Coushatta tribes had exercised squatters' rights in present Sabine County in the early 1800s, and soon after the Cherokees arrived, groups of Shawnee, Delaware and Kickapoo Indians came from the United States.

A **second wave of Anglo** immigrants began to arrive in Texas, larger than the first and of a different character. These Anglos were not so interested in agricultural opportunities as in other schemes to quickly recoup their fortunes.

Spain recognized the danger represented by the unregulated colonization by Americans. The Spanish Cortes' colonization law of 1813 attempted to build a buffer between the eastern frontier and northern Mexico. Special permission was required for Americans to settle within 52 miles of the international boundary, although this prohibition often was ignored.

As initially envisioned, Americans would be allowed to settle the interior of Texas. Colonists from Europe and Mexico would be placed along the eastern frontier to limit contact between the Americans and the United States.

Spanish officials felt that the Americans already in Texas illegally would be stable if given a stake in the province through land ownership.

Moses Austin, a former Spanish subject in the vast Louisiana Territory, applied for the first empresario grant from the Spanish government. With the intercession of Barón de Bastrop, a friend of Austin's from Missouri Territory, the request was approved in January **1821.**

Austin agreed to settle **300 families** on land bounded by the Brazos and Colorado rivers on the east and west, by El Camino Real (the old military road running from San Antonio to Nacogdoches) on the north and by the Gulf Coast.

But Austin died in June 1821, leaving the work to his son, **Stephen F. Austin**. Problems began as soon as the first authorized colonists arrived in Texas the following December when it was learned that Mexico had gained independence from Spain.

Mexico, 1821-1836

Mexico's war for independence, 1810-1821, was savage and bloody in the interior provinces, and Texas suffered as well.

In early 1812, Mexican revolutionary José Bernardo Gutiérrez de Lara traveled to Natchitoches, La., where, with the help of U.S. agents, an expedition was organized.

Augustus W. Magee, a West Point graduate, commanded the troop, which entered Texas in August 1812. This "Republican Army of the North" easily took Nacogdoches, where it gathered recruits.

After withstanding a siege at La Bahía, the army took San Antonio and proclaimed the First Republic of Texas in April 1813. A few months later, the republican forces were bloodily subdued at the Battle of Medina River.

Royalist Gen. Joaquín de Arredondo executed a staggering number of more than 300 republicans, including some Americans, at San Antonio, and a young lieutenant, **Antonio López de Santa Anna**, was recognized for valor under fire.

When the war finally ended in Mexico in 1821, little more had been achieved than separation from Spain.

Sensing that liberal reforms in Spain would reduce the authority of royalists in the New World, Mexican conservatives had led the revolt against the mother country.

And they achieved early victories in the debate over the form of government the newly independent Mexico should adopt.

The former royalists won the opening debates, settling Emperor Agustín de Iturbide on the new Mexican throne. But he was overthrown and the Constitution of 1824, a federalist document, was adopted.

The Mexican election of 1828 was a turning point in the history of the country when the legally-elected administration of Manuel Gómez Pedraza was overthrown by supporters of Vicente Guerrero, who in turn was ousted by his own vice president Anastasio Bustamante. Mexico's most chaotic political period followed. Between 1833 and 1855, the Mexican presidency changed hands 36 times.

Texas, 1821-1833

Mexico's **land policy**, like Spain's, differed from the U.S. approach. Whereas the United States sold land directly to settlers or to speculators who dealt with the pioneers, the Mexicans retained tight control of the property transfer until predetermined agreements for development were fulfilled.

But a 4,428-acre *sitio* — a square league — and a 177-acre *labor* could be obtained for only surveying costs and administrative fees as low as $50. The empresario was rewarded with grants of large tracts of land — but only when he fulfilled his quota of families to be brought to the colonies.

Considering the prices the U.S. government charged, Texas' land was indeed a bargain and a major attraction to those Americans looking for a new start.

More than 25 empresarios were commissioned to settle colonists. Empresarios included **Green DeWitt** and **Martín de León**, who in 1824 founded the city of Guadalupe Victoria (present-day Victoria).

By 1830, Texas boasted an estimated population of 15,000, with Anglo-Americans outnumbering Hispanics by a margin of four to one.

Stephen F. Austin was easily the most successful empresario. After his initial success, Austin was authorized in 1825 to bring 900 more families to Texas, and in 1831, he and his partner, **Samuel Williams**, received another concession to bring 800 Mexican and European families.

Through Austin's efforts, 1,540 land titles were issued to settlers.

In the early years of colonization, the settlers busied themselves clearing land, planting crops, building homes and fending off Indian attacks. Many were successful in establishing a subsistence economy.

One weakness of the Mexican colonial policy was that it did not provide the factors for a market economy. While towns were established, credit, banks and good roads were not provided by the government.

Ports were established at Galveston and Matagorda bays after Mexican independence, but the colonists felt they needed more, particularly one at the mouth of the Brazos. And foreign ships were barred from coastwise trade, which posed a particular hardship since Mexico had few merchant ships.

To settle in Texas, pioneers had to become Mexican citizens and to embrace Roman Catholicism. Most of the Americans were Protestants, if they adhered to any religion, and they were fiercely defensive of the right to **religious freedom** enjoyed in the United States.

Although no more than one-fourth of the Americans ever swore allegiance to the Catholic Church, the requirement was a long-standing irritation.

Slavery, too, was a point of contention. Mexico prohibited the introduction of slavery after December 1827. Nevertheless, several efforts were made to evade the government policy. Austin got the state legislature to recognize labor contracts under which slaves were technically free but bound themselves to their masters for life. Often entire families were covered by a single contract.

While many early Anglo colonists were not slaveholders, they were Southerners, and the ownership of slaves was a cultural institution that they supported. The problem was never settled during the colonial period despite the tensions it generated.

Most of the early Anglo-American colonists in Texas intended to fulfill their pledge to become good Mexican citizens. But the political turmoil following the 1828 presidential election raised doubts in the Americans' minds about the ability of Mexico to make representative government function properly.

On a tour of the state in 1827 and 1828, Gen. Manuel Mier y Terán noted that the Texans "carried their constitutions in their pockets." And he feared the Americans' desire for more rights and liberties than the government was prepared to offer would lead to rebellion.

Unrest increased in Texas when Gen. Mier y Terán began reinforcing existing garrisons and establishing new ones.

But a major factor in the discontent of Americans came with the **decree of April 6, 1830**, when the Mexican government in essence banned further American immigration into Texas and tried to control slavery.

Austin protested that the prohibition against American immigration would not stop the flow of Anglos into Texas; it would stop only the stable, prosperous Americans from coming.

Austin's predictions were fulfilled. Illegal immigrants continued to come. By 1836, the estimated number of people in Texas had reached 35,000.

Prelude to Revolution

In the midst of all the turmoil, Texas was prospering. By 1834, some 7,000 bales of cotton with a value of $315,000 were shipped to New Orleans. In the middle of the decade, Texas exports, including cotton and beaver, otter and deer skins, amounted to $500,000.

Trade ratios were out of balance, however, because $630,000 in manufactured goods were imported. And, there was little currency in Texas. Ninety percent of the business transactions were conducted in barter or credit.

In 1833 and 1834, the **Coahuila y Texas** legislature was diligently trying to respond to the complaints of the Texas colonists. The English language was recognized for official purposes. Religious toleration was approved. The court system was revised, providing Texas with an appellate court and trial by jury.

In Mexico City, however, a different scenario was developing. **Santa Anna** assumed supreme authority in April 1834 and began dismantling the federalist government.

Among the most offensive changes dictated by Santa Anna was the reduction of the state militias to one man per each 500 population. The intent was to eliminate possible armed opposition to the emerging centralist government.

But liberals in the state of Zacatecas in central Mexico rebelled. Santa Anna's response was particularly brutal, as he tried to make an example of the rebels. Troops were allowed to sack the state capital after the victory over the insurgents.

Trouble also was brewing closer to the Texans.

In March 1833, the Coahuila y Texas legislature moved the state capital from Saltillo to Monclova. The Monclova legislature in 1834 gave the governor authority to sell 400 sitios — or 1.77 million acres of land — to finance the government and to provide for protection. A year later the lawmakers criticized Santa Anna's reputation on federalism. Seeing a chance to regain lost prestige, Saltillo declared for Santa Anna and set up an opposition government. In the spring of 1835, Santa Anna sent his brother-in-law, Martín Perfecto de Cos, to break up the state government at Monclova.

Texans were appalled by the breakdown in state government, coming on the heels of so many assurances that the political situation was to improve.

Texas politics were polarizing. A "war party" advocated breaking away from Mexico altogether, while a "peace party" urged calm and riding out the political storm. Most of the settlers, however, aligned with neither group.

In January 1835, Santa Anna sent a detachment of soldiers to Anahuac to reinforce the customs office, but duties were being charged irregularly at various ports on the coast. William B. Travis, in an act not supported by all colonists, led a contingent of armed colonists against the Mexican soldiers, who withdrew without a fight.

Although some members of the peace party wrote Mexican Gen. **Martín Perfecto de Cos**, stationed at Matamoros, apologizing for the action, he was not compromising. Cos demanded that the group be arrested and turned over to him. The Texans refused.

The committees of correspondence, organized at the Convention of 1832 (which had asked that Texas be separated from Coahuila), began organizing another meeting. Because the term "convention" aroused visions of revolution in the eyes of Mexican officials, the gathering at Washington-on-the-Brazos in October 1835 was called a "consultation." But with the breakdown of the state government and with Santa Anna's repeal of the Constitution of 1824, the American settlers felt well within their rights to provide a new framework with which to govern Texas.

Fresh from brutally putting down the rebellion in Zacatecas, Santa Anna turned his attention to Texas. Gen. Cos was determined to regarrison the state, and the settlers were equally adamant about keeping soldiers out.

Col. **Domingo de Ugartechea**, headquartered at San Antonio, became concerned about armed rebellion when he heard of the incident at Anahuac. He recalled a six-pound cannon that had been given DeWitt colonists to fight Indians.

Ugartechea ordered Cpl. Casimira de León with five men to Gonzales to retrieve the weapon. No problems were expected, but officials at Gonzales refused to surrender the weapon. When the Mexicans reinforced Cpl. de León's men, a call was sent out for volunteers to help the Gonzales officials. Dozens responded.

On Oct. 2, 1835, the Texans challenged the Mexicans with a **"come-and-take-it"** flag over the cannon. After a brief skirmish, the Mexicans withdrew, but the first rounds in the Texas Revolution had been fired.

Winning Independence

As 1836 opened, Texans felt in control of their destiny, and secure in their land and their liberties. The Mexican army had been driven from their soil.

But tragedy loomed. Easy victories over government forces at Anahuac, Nacogdoches, Goliad, Gonzales and San Antonio in the fall of 1835 had given them a false sense of security.

That independent mood was their undoing, for no government worthy of the name coordinated the defense of Texas. Consequently, as the Mexican counterattack developed, no one was in charge. Sam Houston was titular commander-in-chief of the Texas forces, but he had little authority.

Some even thought the Mexicans would not try to re-enter Texas. Few Texans counted on the energy and

determination of Santa Anna, the dictator of Mexico.

The status of the strongholds along the San Antonio River was of concern to Houston. In mid-January, Houston sent **James Bowie** to San Antonio to determine if the Alamo was defensible. If not, Bowie had orders to destroy it and withdraw the men and artillery to Gonzales and Copano.

On Feb. 8, David Crockett of Tennessee, bringing 12 men with him, arrived to aid the revolutionaries.

On Feb. 12, 1836, Santa Anna's main force crossed the Rio Grande headed for San Antonio. The Mexican battle plan has been debated. But Mexico's national pride had been bruised by the series of defeats the nation's army had suffered in 1835, capped by Gen. Cos's ouster from San Antonio in December.

On Feb. 11, the Consultation's "governor of the government" **Henry Smith**, sent **William B. Travis** to San Antonio. Immediately a split in command at the **Alamo** garrison arose. Most were American volunteers who looked to the Houston-appointed Bowie as their leader. Travis had only a handful of Texas army regulars. So Bowie and Travis agreed to share the command of 150 men.

Arriving at the Alamo on Feb. 23, Santa Anna left no doubt regarding his attitude toward the defenders. He hoisted a blood-red flag, the traditional Mexican symbol of no quarter, no surrender, no mercy. Travis and Bowie defiantly answered the display with a cannon shot.

Immediately the Mexicans began surrounding the Alamo and bombarding it. Throughout the first night and nights to come, Santa Anna kept up a continual din to destroy the defenders' morale.

On Feb. 24, Bowie became ill and relinquished his share of command to Travis. Although the Mexican bombardment of the Alamo continued, none of the defenders was killed. In fact, they conducted several successful forays outside the fortress to burn buildings that were providing cover for the Mexican gunners and to gather firewood.

Messengers also successfully moved through the Mexican lines at will, and 32 reinforcements from Gonzales made it into the Alamo without a loss on March 1.

Historians disagree over which flag flew over the defenders of the Alamo.

Mexican sources have said that Santa Anna was outraged when he saw flying over the fortress a Mexican tricolor, identical to the ones carried by his troops except with the numbers "1 8 2 4" emblazoned upon it.

Texas historians have accepted this version because the defenders of the Alamo could not have known that Texas' independence had been declared on March 2. To the knowledge of the Alamo's defenders, the last official position taken by Texas was in support of the Constitution of 1824, which the flag symbolized. But the only flag found after the battle, according to historian Walter Lord, was one flown by the **New Orleans Greys**.

By March 5, Santa Anna had 4,000 men in camp, a force he felt sufficient to subdue the Alamo.

Historians disagree on the date, but the story goes that on March 3 or 5, Travis called his command together and explained the bleak outlook. He then asked those willing to die for freedom to stay and fight; those not willing could try to get through enemy lines to safety. Even the sick Jim Bowie vowed to stay. Only

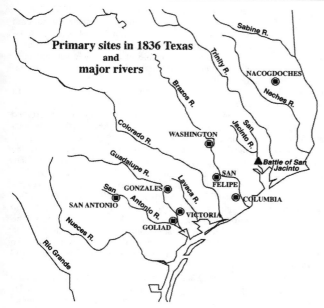

Primary sites in 1836 Texas and major rivers

Louis (Moses) Rose, a veteran of Napoleon's retreat from Moscow slipped out of the Alamo that night.

At dawn March 6, Santa Anna's forces attacked. When the fighting stopped between 8:30 and 9 a.m., all the defenders were dead. Only a few women, children and black slaves survived the assault. **Davy Crockett**'s fate is still debated. Mexican officer Enrique de la Peña held that Crockett was captured with a few other defenders and executed by Santa Anna.

Santa Anna's victory came at the cost of almost one-third his forces killed or wounded. Their deaths in such number set back Santa Anna's timetable. The fall of the Alamo also brutally shook Texans out of their lethargy.

Sam Houston, finally given command of the entire Texas army, left the convention at **Washington-on-the-Brazos** on the day of the fall of the Alamo.

On March 11, he arrived at Gonzales to begin organizing the troops. Two days later, **Mrs. Dickinson**, the wife of one of the victims of the Alamo, and two slaves arrived at Houston's position at Gonzales with the news of the fall of the San Antonio fortress.

Houston then ordered **James Fannin** to abandon the old presidio **La Bahía** at Goliad and to retreat to Victoria. Fannin had arrived at the fort in late January with more than 400 men.

As a former West Pointer, he had a background in military planning. But Fannin had been indecisive. He had refused Travis' pleas for help, and after receiving Houston's orders, Fannin waited for scouting parties to return.

Finally, on March 19, he left, but too late. Forward elements of Gen. José de Urrea's troops caught Fannin's command on an open prairie. After a brief skirmish Fannin surrendered.

Santa Anna was furious when Gen. Urrea appealed for clemency for the captives. The Mexican leader issued orders for their execution. On March 27, a Palm Sunday, most of the prisoners were divided into groups and marched out of Goliad, thinking they were being transferred to other facilities. When the executions began, many escaped. But about 350 were killed.

On March 17, Houston reached the Colorado near the present city of La Grange and began receiving reinforcements. Within a week, the small force of several hundred had become almost respectable, with 1,200-1,400 men in camp.

At the time Houston reached the Colorado, the convention at Washington-on-the-Brazos was completing work. **David Burnet**, a New Jersey native, was named interim president of the new Texas government, and **Lorenzo de Zavala**, a Yucatán native, was named vice president.

On March 27, Houston moved his men to San Felipe on the Brazos. The Texas army was impatient for a fight, and there was talk in the ranks that, if action did not develop soon, a new commander should be elected.

As the army marched farther back toward the San Jacinto River, two Mexican couriers were captured and gave Houston the information he had hoped for. Santa Anna in his haste had led the small Mexican force in front of Houston. Now the Texans had an opportunity to win the war.

Throughout the revolt, Houston's intelligence system had operated efficiently. Scouts, commanded by **Erastus "Deaf" Smith**, kept the Texans informed of Mexican troop movements. **Hendrick Arnold**, a free black, was a valuable spy, posing as a runaway slave to enter Mexican camps to gain information.

Early on April 21, Gen. Cos reinforced Santa Anna's troops with more than 500 men. The new arrivals, who had marched all night, disrupted the camp's routine for a time, but soon all the soldiers and officers settled down for a midday rest.

About 3 p.m., Houston ordered his men to parade and the battle was launched at 4:30 p.m.

A company of Mexican-Texans, commanded by **Juan Seguín**, had served as the rear guard for Houston's army through much of the retreat across Texas and had fought many skirmishes with the Mexican army in the process.

Perhaps fearing the Mexican-Texans would be mistaken for Santa Anna's soldiers, Houston had assigned the company to guard duty as the battle approached. But after the men protested, they fought in the battle of San Jacinto.

Historians disagree widely on the number of troops on each side. Houston probably had about 900 while Santa Anna had between 1,100 and 1,300.

But the Texans had the decided psychological advantage. Two thirds of the fledgling Republic's army were "old Texans" who had family and land to defend. They had an investment of years of toil in building their homes. And they were eager to avenge the massacre of men at the Alamo and Goliad.

In less than 20 minutes they set the Mexican army to

rout. More than 600 Mexicans were killed and hundreds more wounded or captured. Only nine of the Texans died in the fight.

It was not until the following day that Santa Anna was captured. One Texan noticed that a grubby soldier his patrol found in the high grass had a silk shirt under his filthy jacket. Although denying he was an officer, he was taken back to camp, where he was acknowledged with cries of "El Presidente" by other prisoners.

Santa Anna introduced himself when taken to the wounded Houston.

President Burnet took charge of Santa Anna, and on May 14 the dictator signed **two treaties at Velasco**, a public document and a secret one.

The public agreement declared that hostilities would cease, that the Mexican army would withdraw to south of the Rio Grande, that prisoners would be released and that Santa Anna would be shipped to Veracruz as soon as possible.

In the secret treaty, Santa Anna agreed to recognize Texas' independence, to give diplomatic recognition, to negotiate a commercial treaty and to set the **Rio Grande** as the new Republic's boundary.

Republic of Texas, 1836-1845

Sam Houston was easily the most dominant figure through the nearly 10-year history of the Republic of Texas. While he was roundly criticized for the retreat across Texas during the revolution, the victory at San Jacinto endeared him to most of the new nation's inhabitants.

Houston handily defeated Henry Smith and Stephen F. Austin in the election called in September 1836 by the interim government, and he was inaugurated as president on Oct. 22.

The first cabinet appointed by the new president represented an attempt to heal old political wounds. Austin was named secretary of state and Smith was secretary of the treasury. But Texas suffered a major tragedy in late December 1836 when Austin, the acknowledged "**Father of Texas**," died of pneumonia.

A host of problems faced the new government. Gen. Santa Anna was still in custody, and public opinion favored his execution. Texas' leadership wisely kept Santa Anna alive, first to keep from giving the Mexicans an emotional rallying point for launching another invasion. Second, the Texas leaders hoped that the dictator would keep his promise to work for recognition of Texas.

Santa Anna was released in November 1836 and made his way to Washington, D.C. Houston hoped the dictator could persuade U.S. President **Andrew Jackson** to recognize Texas. Jackson refused to see Santa Anna, who returned to Mexico, where he had fallen from power.

Another major challenge was the Texas army. The new commander, Felix Huston, favored an invasion of Mexico, and the troops, made up now mostly of American volunteers who came to Texas after the battle of San Jacinto, were rebellious and ready to fight.

President Houston tried to replace Felix Huston with **Albert Sidney Johnston**, but Huston seriously wounded Johnston in a duel. In May 1837, Huston was asked to the capital in Columbia to discuss the invasion. While Huston was away from the troops, Houston sent

Thomas J. Rusk, the secretary of war, to furlough the army without pay — but with generous land grants. Only 600 men were retained in the army.

The Republic's other problems were less tractable. The economy needed attention; Indians still were a threat; Mexico remained warlike; foreign relations had to be developed; and relations with the United States had to be solidified.

The greatest disappointment in Houston's first term was the failure to have the Republic annexed to the United States. Henry Morfit, President Jackson's agent, toured the new Republic in the summer of 1836. Although impressed, Morfit reported that Texas' best chance at continued independence lay in the "stupidity of the rulers of Mexico and the financial embarrassment of the Mexican government." He recommended that annexation be delayed.

Houston's foreign policy achieved initial success when **J. Pinckney Henderson** negotiated a trade treaty with Great Britain. Although the agreement was short of outright diplomatic recognition, it was progress.

In the next few years, France, Belgium, The Netherlands, and some German states recognized the new Republic.

Under the constitution, Houston's first term lasted only two years, and he could not succeed himself. His successor, **Mirabeau B. Lamar**, had grand visions and was a spendthrift. Houston's first term cost Texas only about $500,000, while President Lamar and the Congress spent $5 million in the next three years.

Early in 1839, Lamar gained recognition as the "**Father of Education**" in Texas when the Congress granted each of the existing 23 counties three leagues of land to be used for education. Fifty leagues of land were set aside for a university.

Despite the lip service paid to education, the government did not have the money for several years to set up a school system. Most education during the Republic was provided by private schools and churches.

Lamar's Indian policies differed greatly from those under Houston. Houston had lived with Cherokees as a youth, was adopted as a member of a tribe and advocated Indian rights long before coming to Texas. Lamar reflected more the frontier attitude toward American Indians. His first experience in public life was as secretary to Gov. George Troup of Georgia, who successfully opposed the federal government's policy of assimilation of Indians at the time. Indians were simply removed from Georgia.

Texans' first tried to negotiate the Cherokees' removal from the region, but in July 1839, the Indians were forcibly ejected from Texas at the **Battle of the Neches River** in Van Zandt County. Houston's close friend, the aging Cherokee chief **Philip Bowles**, was killed in the battle while Houston was visiting former President Jackson in Tennessee. The Cherokees moved on to Arkansas and the Indian Territories.

Houston was returned to the presidency of the Republic in 1841. His second administration was even more frugal than his first; soon income almost matched expenditures.

Houston re-entered negotiations with the Indians in Central Texas in an attempt to quell the raids on settlements. A number of trading posts were opened along the frontier to pacify the Indians.

War fever reached a high pitch in Texas in 1842, and Houston grew increasingly unpopular because he would not launch an offensive war against Mexico.

In March 1842, Gen. **Rafael Vásquez** staged guerrilla raids on San Antonio, Victoria and Goliad, but quickly left the Republic.

A force of 3,500 Texas volunteers gathered at San Antonio demanding that Mexico be punished. Houston urged calm, but the clamor increased when Mexican **Gen. Adrian Woll** captured San Antonio in September. He raised the Mexican flag and declared the reconquest of Texas.

Ranger Capt. **Jack Hays** was camped nearby. Within days 600 volunteers had joined him, eager to drive the Mexican invaders from Texas soil. Gen. Woll withdrew after the **Battle of Salado.**

Alexander Somervell was ordered by Houston to follow with 700 troops and harass the Mexican army. He reached Laredo in December and found no Mexican troops.

Somervell crossed the Rio Grande to find military targets. A few days later, the commander returned home, but 300 soldiers decided to continue the raid under the command of William S. Fisher. On Christmas day, this group attacked the village of **Mier,** only to be defeated by a Mexican force that outnumbered them 10-to-1.

After attempting mass escape, the survivors of the Mier expedition were marched to Mexico City where Santa Anna, again in political power, ordered their execution. When officers refused to carry out the order, it was amended to require execution of one of every 10 Texans. The prisoners drew beans to determine who would be shot; bearers of **black beans** were executed. Texans again were outraged by the treatment of prisoners, but the war fever soon subsided.

As Houston completed his second term, the United States was becoming more interested in annexation. Texas had seriously flirted with Great Britain and France, and the Americans did not want a rival republic with close foreign ties on the North American continent. Houston orchestrated the early stages of the final steps toward annexation. It was left to his successor, **Anson Jones,** to complete the process.

The Republic of Texas' main claim to fame is simply endurance. Its settlers, unlike other Americans who had military help, had cleared a large region of Indians by themselves, had established farms and communities and had persevered through extreme economic hardship.

Adroit political leadership had gained the Republic recognition from many foreign countries. Although dreams of empire may have dimmed, Texans had established an identity on a major portion of the North American continent. The frontier had been pushed to a line running from Corpus Christi through San Antonio and Austin to the Red River.

The U.S. presidential campaign of 1844 was to make Texas a part of the Union. ☆

Texas: Annexation to 1920

Annexation

Annexation to the United States was far from automatic for Texas once independence from Mexico was gained in 1836. Sam Houston noted that Texas "was more coy than forward" as negotiations reached a climax in 1845.

William H. Wharton was Texas' first representative in Washington. His instructions were to gain diplomatic recognition of the new Republic's independence.

After some squabbles, the U.S. Congress appropriated funds for a minister to Texas, and President Andrew Jackson recognized the new country in one of his last acts in office in March 1837.

Texas President **Mirabeau B. Lamar** (1838-41) opposed annexation. He held visions of empire in which Texas would rival the United States for supremacy on the North American continent.

During his administration, Great Britain began a close relationship with Texas and made strenuous efforts to get Mexico to recognize the Republic.

This relationship between Great Britain and Texas raised fears in the United States that Britain might attempt to make Texas part of its empire.

Southerners feared for the future of slavery in Texas, which had renounced the importation of slaves as a concession to get a trade treaty with Great Britain.

And, American newspapers noted that trade with Texas had suffered after the Republic received recognition from European countries.

In Houston's second term in the Texas presidency, he instructed **Isaac Van Zandt,** his minister in Washington, to renew the annexation negotiations.

Although U.S. President **John Tyler** and his cabinet were eager to annex Texas, they were worried about ratification in the U.S. Senate. The annexation question was put off.

In January 1844, Houston again gave Van Zandt instructions to propose annexation talks. This time the United States agreed to Houston's standing stipulation that, for serious negotiations to take place, the United States must provide military protection to Texas. U.S. naval forces were ordered to the Gulf of Mexico and U.S. troops were positioned on the southwest border close to Texas.

On April 11, 1844, Texas and the United States signed a treaty for annexation.

Texas would enter the Union as a territory, not a state, under terms of the treaty. The United States would assume Texas' debt up to $10 million and would negotiate Texas' southwestern boundary with Mexico.

On June 8, 1844, the U.S. Senate rejected the treaty with a vote of 35-16, with much of the opposition coming from the slavery abolition wing of the Whig Party.

But **westward expansion** became a major issue in the U.S. presidential election that year. James K. Polk, the Democratic nominee, was a supporter of expansion, and the party's platform called for adding Oregon and Texas to the Union.

After Polk won the election in November, President Tyler declared that the people had spoken on the issue of annexation, and he resubmitted the matter to Congress.

Several bills were introduced in the U.S. House of Representatives containing various proposals.

In **February 1845**, the U.S. Congress approved a resolution that would bring Texas into the Union as a state. Texas would cede its public property — such as forts and custom houses — to the United States, but it could keep its public lands and must retain its public debt.

The region could be divided into four new states in addition to the original Texas. And the United States would negotiate the Rio Grande boundary claim.

British officials asked the Texas government to delay consideration of the U.S. offer for 90 days to attempt to get Mexico to recognize the Republic. The delay did no good: Texans' minds were made up.

President Anson Jones, who succeeded Houston in 1844, called a convention to write a **state constitution** in Austin on July 4, 1845.

Mexico finally recognized Texas' independence, but the recognition was rejected. **Texas voters overwhelmingly accepted the U.S. proposal** and approved the new constitution in a referendum.

On **Dec. 29, 1845**, the U.S. Congress accepted the state constitution, and Texas became a part of the United States.

1845-1860

The entry of Texas into the Union touched off the **War with Mexico**, a war that some historians now think was planned by President James K. Polk to obtain the vast American Southwest.

Gen. **Zachary Taylor** was sent to Corpus Christi, just above the Nueces River, in July 1845. In February 1846, right after Texas formally entered the Union, the general was ordered to move troops into the disputed area south of the Nueces to the mouth of the Rio Grande. Mexican officials protested the move, claiming the status of the territory was under negotiation.

After Gen. Taylor refused to leave, Mexican President **Mariano Paredes** declared the opening of a defensive war against the United States on April 24, 1846.

After initial encounters at **Palo Alto** and **Resaca de la Palma**, both a few miles north of today's **Brownsville**, the war was fought south of the Rio Grande.

President Polk devised a plan to raise 50,000 volunteers from every section of the United States to fight the war. About 5,000 Texans saw action in Mexico.

Steamboats provided an important supply link for U.S. forces along the Rio Grande. Historical figures such as **Richard King**, founder of the legendary King Ranch, and **Mifflin Kenedy**, another rancher and businessman, first came to the **Lower Rio Grande Valley** as steamboat operators during the war.

Much farther up the Rio Grande, the war was hardly noticed. U.S. forces moved south from Santa Fe, which had been secured in December 1846. After a minor skirmish with Mexican forces north of El Paso, the U.S. military established American jurisdiction in this part of Texas.

Gen. **Winfield Scott** brought the war to a close in March 1847 with the capture of Mexico City.

When the **Treaty of Guadalupe Hidalgo** was signed on Feb. 2, 1848, the United States had acquired the American Southwest for development. And in Texas, the Rio Grande became an international boundary.

Germans, rather than Anglos, were the first whites to push the Texas frontier into west Central Texas after annexation. **John O. Meusebach** became leader of the German immigration movement in Texas, and he led a wagon train of some 120 settlers to the site of **Fredericksburg** in May 1846.

Germans also migrated to the major cities, such as San Antonio and Galveston, and by 1850 there were more people of German birth or parentage in Texas than there were Mexican-Texans.

The eastern part of Texas was flourishing under statehood, as had been expected.

The estimated population of 150,000 at annexation grew to 212,592, including 58,161 slaves, in the first U.S. census count in Texas in 1850.

As the state's population grew, the regions developed distinct population characteristics. The southeast and eastern sections attracted immigrants from the Lower South, the principal slaveholding states. Major plantations developed in these areas.

North Texas got more Upper Southerners and Midwesterners. These immigrants were mostly small farmers and few owned slaves.

Mexican-Texans had difficulty with Anglo immigrants. The **"cart war"** broke out in 1857. Mexican teamsters controlled the transportation of goods from the Gulf coast to San Antonio and could charge lower rates than their competition.

A campaign of terror was launched by Anglo haulers, especially around Goliad, in an attempt to drive the Mexican-Texans out of business. Intervention by the U.S. and Mexican governments finally brought the situation under control, but it stands as an example of the attitudes held by Anglo-Texans toward Mexican-Texans.

Cotton was by far the state's largest money crop, but corn, sweet potatoes, wheat and sugar also were produced. **Saw milling** and grain milling became the major industries, employing 40 percent of the manufacturing workers.

Land disputes and the public-debt issue were settled with the **Compromise of 1850**. Texas gave up claims to territory extending to Santa Fe and beyond in exchange for $10 million from the federal government. That sum was used to pay off the debt of the Republic.

Personalities, especially Sam Houston, dominated elections during early statehood, but, for most Texans, politics were unimportant. Voter turnouts were low in the 1850s until the movement toward secession gained strength.

Secession

Texas' population almost tripled in the decade between 1850 and 1860, when 604,215 people were counted, including 182,921 slaves.

Many of these new settlers came from the Lower South, a region familiar with slavery. Although three-quarters of the Texas population and two-thirds of the farmers did not own slaves, slaveowners controlled 60 or 70 percent of the wealth of the state and dominated the politics.

In 1850, 41 percent of the state's officeholders were from the slaveholding class; a decade later, more than 50 percent of the officeholders had slaves.

In addition to the political power of the slaveholders, they also provided role models for new immigrants to the state. After these newcomers got their first land, they saw slave ownership as another step up the economic ladder, whether they owned slaves or not. Slave ownership was an economic goal.

This attitude prevailed even in areas of Texas where slaveholding was not widespread or even practical.

Against this background were the politics of Texas played and the passions for secession from the Union fanned through the late 1850s.

The appearance of the **Know-Nothing Party**, which based its platform on a pro-American, anti-immigrant foundation, began to move Texas toward party politics. Because of the large number of foreign-born settlers, the party attracted many Anglo voters.

In 1854, the Know-Nothings elected candidates to city offices in San Antonio, and a year later, the mayor of Galveston was elected with the party's backing. Also in 1855, the Know-Nothings elected 20 representatives and five senators to the Legislature.

The successes spurred the **Democrats** to serious party organization for the first time. In 1857, **Hardin Runnels** was nominated for governor at the Democratic convention held in Waco.

Sam Houston sought the governorship as an independent, but he also got Know-Nothing backing. Democrats were organized, however, and Houston was dealt the only election defeat in his political career.

Runnels was a strong states'-rights Democrat who irritated many Texans during his administration by advocating reopening the slave trade. His popularity on the frontier also dropped when Indian raids became more severe.

Most Texans still were ambivalent about secession. The Union was seen as a protector of physical and economic stability. No threats to person or property were perceived in remaining attached to the United States.

In 1859, Houston again challenged Runnels, basing his campaign on Unionism. Combined with Houston's personal popularity, his position on the secession issue apparently satisfied most voters, for they gave him a solid victory over the more radical Runnels. In addition, Unionists **A.J. Hamilton** and **John H. Reagan** won the state's two congressional seats. Texans gave the states'-rights Democrats a sound whipping at the polls.

Within a few months, however, events were to change radically the political atmosphere of the state. On the frontier, the army could not control Indian raids, and with the later refusal of a Republican-controlled Congress to provide essential aid in fighting Indians, the federal government fell into disrepute.

Secessionists played on the growing distrust. Then in the summer of 1860, a series of fires in the cities around the state aroused fears that an abolitionist plot was afoot and that a slave uprising might be at hand — a traditional concern in a slaveholding society.

Vigilantes lynched blacks and Northerners across Texas, and a siege mentality developed.

When **Abraham Lincoln** was elected president (he was not on the ballot in Texas), secessionists went to work in earnest.

Pleas were made to Gov. Houston to call the Legislature into session to consider secession. Houston refused, hoping the passions would cool. They did not. Finally, **Oran M. Roberts** and other secessionist leaders issued a call to the counties to hold elections and send delegates to a convention in Austin. Ninety-two of 122 counties responded, and on Jan. 28, 1861, the meeting convened.

Only eight delegates voted against secession, while 166 supported it. An election was called for Feb. 23, 1861, and the ensuing campaign was marked by intolerance and violence. Opponents of secession were often intimidated — except the governor, who courageously stumped the state opposing withdrawal from the Union. Houston also argued that if Texas did secede it should revert to its status as an independent republic and not join the Confederacy.

Only one-fourth of the state's population had been in Texas during the days of independence, and the argument carried no weight.

On election day, 76 percent of 61,000 voters favored secession.

President Lincoln, who took office within a couple of weeks, reportedly sent the Texas governor a letter offering 50,000 federal troops to keep Texas in the Union. But after a meeting with other Unionists, Houston declined the offer. "I love Texas too well to bring strife and bloodshed upon her," the governor declared.

On March 16, Houston refused to take an oath of loyalty to the Confederacy and was replaced in office by Lt. Gov. **Edward Clark**.

Civil War

Texas did not suffer the devastation of its Southern colleagues in the Civil War. Only on a few occasions did Union troops occupy territory in Texas, except in the El Paso area.

The state's cotton was important to the Confederate war effort because it could be transported from Gulf ports when other Southern shipping lanes were blockaded.

Some goods became difficult to buy, but unlike other states of the Confederacy, Texas still received consumer goods because of the trade that was carried on through Mexico during the war.

Although accurate figures are not available, historians estimate that between 70,000 and 90,000 Texans fought for the South, and between 2,000 and 3,000, including some former slaves, saw service in the Union army.

Texans became disenchanted with the Confederate government early in the war. State taxes were levied for the first time since the Compromise of 1850, and by war's end, the Confederacy had collected more than $37 million from the state.

But most of the complaints about the government centered on Brig. Gen. **Paul O. Hebert**, the Confederate commander of the Department of Texas.

In April 1862, Gen. Hebert declared martial law without notifying state officials. Opposition to the South's new conscription law, which exempted persons owning more than 15 slaves among other categories of exemptions, prompted the action.

In November 1862, the commander prohibited the export of cotton except under government control, and this proved a disastrous policy.

The final blow came when Gen. Hebert failed to

defend **Galveston** and it fell into Union hands in the fall of 1862.

Maj. Gen. **John B. Magruder,** who replaced Hebert, was much more popular. The new commander's first actions were to combat the Union offensive against Texas ports. Sabine Pass had been closed in September 1862 by the Union blockade, and Galveston was in Northern hands.

On Jan. 1, 1863, Magruder retook Galveston with the help of two steamboats lined with cotton bales. Sharpshooters aboard proved devastating in battles against the Union fleet. Three weeks later, Magruder used two other cotton-clad steamboats to break the Union blockade of Sabine Pass, and two of the state's major ports were reopened.

Late in 1863, the Union launched a major offensive against the Texas coast that was partly successful. On Sept. 8, however, Lt. **Dick Dowling** and 42 men fought off a 1,500-man Union invasion force at **Sabine Pass.** In a brief battle, Dowling's command sank two Union gunboats and put the other invasion ships to flight.

Federal forces were more successful at the mouth of the Rio Grande. On Nov. 1, 1863, 7,000 Union troops landed at **Brazos Santiago,** and five days later, Union forces entered Brownsville.

Texas Unionists led by **E.J. Davis** were active in the Valley, moving as far upriver as Rio Grande City. Confederate Col. **John S. "Rip" Ford,** commanding state troops, finally pushed the Union soldiers out of Brownsville in July 1864, reopening the important port for the Confederacy.

Most Texans never saw a Union soldier during the war. The only ones they might have seen were in **prisoner-of-war camps.** The largest, **Camp Ford,** near Tyler, housed 5,000 prisoners. Others operated in Kerr County and at Hempstead.

As the war dragged on, the mood of Texans changed. Those on the homefront began to feel they were sacrificing loved ones and suffering hardship so cotton speculators could profit.

Public order broke down as refugees flocked to Texas. And slaves from other states were sent to Texas for safekeeping. When the war ended, there were an estimated 400,000 slaves in Texas, more than double the number counted in the 1860 census.

Morale was low in Texas in early 1865. Soldiers at Galveston and Houston began to mutiny. At Austin, Confederate soldiers raided the state treasury in March and found only $5,000 in specie. Units broke up, and the army simply dissolved before Gen. **Robert E. Lee** surrendered at **Appomattox** in April 1865.

The last battle of the Civil War was fought at **Palmito Ranch** near Brownsville on May 11, 1865. After the Confederate unit's victory, it learned of the South's defeat.

Reconstruction

On June 19, 1865, **Gen. Gordon Granger,** under the command of Gen. Philip M. Sheridan, arrived in Galveston with 1,800 federal troops to begin the Union occupation of Texas.

Gen. Granger proclaimed the emancipation of the slaves. **A.J. Hamilton,** a Unionist and former congressman from Texas, was named provisional governor by President Andrew Johnson.

Sam Houston   E.J. Davis

Texas was in turmoil. Thousands of the state's men had died in the conflict. Indian raids had caused as much damage as the skirmishes with the Union army, causing the frontier to recede up to 100 miles eastward in some areas.

Even worse, confusion reigned. No one knew what to expect from the conquering forces.

Gen. Granger dispatched troops to the population centers of the state to restore civil authority. But only a handful of the 50,000 federal troops that came to Texas was stationed in the interior. Most were sent to the Rio Grande as a show of force against the French forces in Mexico, and clandestine aid was supplied to Mexican President Benito Juarez in his fight against the French and Mexican royalists.

The **frontier forts,** most of which were built during the early 1850s by the federal government to protect western settlements, had been abandoned by the U.S. Army after secession. These were not remanned, and a prohibition against a militia denied settlers a means of self-defense against Indian raids.

Thousands of freed black slaves migrated to the cities, where they felt the federal soldiers would provide protection. Still others traveled the countryside, seeking family members and loved ones from whom they had been separated during the war.

The **Freedman's Bureau,** authorized by Congress in March 1865, began operation in September 1865 under Gen. E.M. Gregory. It had the responsibility to provide education, relief aid, labor supervision and judicial protection for the newly freed slaves.

The bureau was most successful in opening schools for blacks. Education was a priority because 95 percent of the freed slaves were illiterate.

The agency also was partially successful in getting blacks back to work on plantations under reasonable labor contracts.

Some plantation owners harbored hopes that they would be paid for their property loss when the slaves were freed. In some cases, the slaves were not released from plantations for up to a year.

To add to the confusion, some former slaves had the false notion that the federal government was going to parcel out the plantation lands to them. These blacks simply bided their time, waiting for the division of land.

Under pressure from President Johnson, Gov. Hamilton called for an election of delegates to a **constitutional convention** in January 1866. Hamilton told the gathering what was expected: Former slaves were to be given civil rights; the secession ordinance had to be repealed; Civil War debt had to be repudiated; and slavery was to be abolished with ratification of the Thirteenth Amendment.

Many delegates to the convention were former secessionists, and there was little support for compromise.

J.W. Throckmorton, a Unionist and one of eight men who had opposed secession in the convention of 1861, was elected chairman of the convention. But a coalition of conservative Unionists and Democrats controlled the meeting. As a consequence, Texas took limited steps toward appeasing the victorious North.

Slavery was abolished, and blacks were given some civil rights. But they still could not vote and were barred from testifying in trials against whites.

No action was taken on the Thirteenth Amendment because, the argument went, the amendment already had been ratified.

Otherwise, the constitution that was written followed closely the constitution of 1845. President Johnson in August 1866 accepted the new constitution and declared insurrection over in Texas, the last of the states of the Confederacy so accepted under **Presidential Reconstruction**.

Throckmorton was elected governor in June, along with other state and local officials. However, Texans had not learned a lesson from the war.

When the Legislature met, a series of laws limiting the rights of blacks were passed. In labor disputes, for example, the employers were to be the final arbitrators. The codes also bound an entire family's labor, not just the head of the household, to an employer.

Funding for black education would be limited to what could be provided by black taxpayers. Since few blacks owned land or had jobs, that provision effectively denied education to black children. The thrust of the laws and the attitude of the legislators was clear, however: Blacks simply were not to be considered full citizens.

Many of the laws later were overturned by the Freedman's Bureau or military authorities when, in March 1867, Congress began a **Reconstruction plan** of its own. The Southern states were declared to have no legal government and the former Confederacy was divided into districts to be administered by the military until satisfactory Reconstruction was effected. Texas and Louisiana made up the Fifth Military District under the command of Gen. Philip H. Sheridan.

Gov. Throckmorton clashed often with Gen. Sheridan. The governor thought the state had gone far enough in establishing rights for the newly freed slaves and other matters. Finally in August 1867, Throckmorton and other state officials were removed from office by Sheridan because they were considered an "impediment to the reconstruction." **E.M. Pease**, the former two-term governor and a Unionist, was named provisional governor by the military authorities.

A **new constitutional convention** was called by Gen. Winfield S. Hancock, who replaced Sheridan in November 1867. For the first time, blacks were allowed to participate in the elections that selected delegates. A total of 59,633 whites and 49,497 blacks registered. The delegates that were elected met on June 1. 1868. Deliberations got bogged down on partisan political matters,

however, and the convention spent $200,000, an unheard-of sum.

This constitution of 1869, as it came to be known, granted full rights of citizenship to blacks, created a system of education, delegated broad powers to the governor and generally reflected the views of the state's Unionists.

Gov. Pease, disgusted with the convention and with military authorities, resigned in September 1869. Texas had no chief executive until January 1870, when the newly-elected **E.J. Davis** took office.

Meeting in February 1870, the Legislature created a **state militia** under the governor's control; created a **state police force**, also controlled by the governor; postponed the 1870 general election to 1872; enabled the governor to appoint more than 8,500 local officeholders; and granted subsidized **bonds for railroad construction** at a rate of $10,000 a mile.

For the first time, a **system of public education** was created. The law required compulsory attendance at school for four months a year, set aside one-quarter of the state's annual revenue for education and levied a poll tax to support education. Schools also were to be integrated, which enraged many white Texans.

The Davis administration was the most unpopular in Texas' history. In fairness, historians have noted that Davis did not feel that whites could be trusted to assure the rights of the newly freed blacks.

Violence was rampant in Texas. One study found that between the close of the Civil War and mid-1868, 1,035 people were murdered in Texas, including 486 blacks, mostly victims of white violence.

Gov. Davis argued that he needed broad police powers to restore order. Despite their unpopularity, the state police and militia — blacks made up 40 percent of the police and a majority of the militia — brought the lawlessness under control in many areas.

Democrats, aided by moderate Republicans, regained control of the Legislature in the 1872 elections, and, in 1873, the lawmakers set about stripping the governor of many of his powers.

The political turmoil ended with the gubernatorial election of 1873, when **Richard Coke** easily defeated Davis. Davis tried to get federal authorities to keep him in office, but President Grant refused to intervene.

In January of 1874, Democrats were in control of state government again. The end of Reconstruction concluded the turbulent Civil War era, although the attitudes that developed during the period lasted well into the 20th century.

Capital and Labor

A **constitutional convention** was called in 1875 to rewrite the 1869 constitution, a hated vestige of Radical Republican rule.

Every avenue to cutting spending at any level of government was explored. Salaries of public officials were slashed. The number of offices was reduced. Judgeships, along with most other offices, were made elective rather than appointive.

The state road program was curtailed, and the immigration bureau was eliminated.

Perhaps the worst change was the destruction of the statewide school system. The new charter created a "community system" without a power of taxation, and schools were segregated by race.

Despite the basic reactionary character, the new constitution also was visionary. Following the lead of several other states, the Democrats declared railroads to be common carriers and subject to regulations.

To meet the dual challenge of lawlessness and Indian insurrection, Gov. Coke in 1874 re-established the **Texas Rangers**.

While cowboys and cattle drives are romantic subjects for movies on the Texas of this period, the fact is that the simple cotton farmer was the backbone of the state's economy.

But neither the farmer nor the cattleman prospered throughout the last quarter of the 19th century. At the root of their problems was federal monetary policy and the lingering effects of the Civil War.

Although the issuance of paper money had brought about a business boom in the Union during the war, inflation also increased. Silver was demonetized in 1873. Congress passed the Specie Resumption Act in 1875 that returned the nation to the gold standard in 1879.

Almost immediately a contraction in currency began. Between 1873 and 1891, the amount of national bank notes in circulation declined from $339 million to $168 million.

The reduction in the money supply was devastating in the defeated South. Land values plummeted. In 1870, Texas land was valued at an average of $2.62 an acre, compared with the national average of $18.26 an acre.

With the money supply declining and the national economy growing, farm prices dropped. In 1870, a bushel of wheat brought $1. In the 1890s, wheat was 60 cents a bushel. Except for a brief spurt in the early 1880s, cattle prices followed those of crops.

Between 1880 and 1890, the number of farms in Texas doubled, but the number of tenants tripled. By 1900, almost half the state's farmers were tenants.

The much-criticized crop-lien system was developed following the war to meet credit needs of the small farmers. Merchants would extend credit to farmers through the year in exchange for liens on their crops. But the result of the crop-lien system, particularly when small farmers did not have enough acreage to operate efficiently, was a state of continual debt and despair.

The work ethic held that a man would benefit from his toil. When this apparently failed, farmers looked to the monetary system and the railroads as the causes. Their discontent hence became the source of the agrarian revolt that developed in the 1880s and 1890s.

The entry of the Texas & Pacific and the Missouri-Kansas-Texas **railroads** from the northeast changed trade patterns in the state.

Since the days of the Republic, trade generally had flowed to Gulf ports, primarily Galveston. Jefferson in Northeast Texas served as a gateway to the Mississippi River, but it never carried the volume of trade that was common at Galveston.

The earliest railroad systems in the state also were centered around Houston and Galveston, again directing trade southward. With the T&P and Katy lines, North Texas had direct access to markets in St. Louis and the East.

Problems developed with the railroads, however. In 1882, Jay Gould and Collis P. Huntington, owner of the

James Hogg   Norris Wright Cuney

Southern Pacific, entered into a secret agreement that amounted to creation of a monopoly of rail service in Texas. They agreed to stop competitive track extensions, to divide under a pooling arrangement freight moving from New Orleans and El Paso, to purchase all competing railroads in Texas, and to share the track between Sierra Blanca and El Paso.

The Legislature made weak attempts to regulate railroads, as provided by the state constitution. Gould thwarted an attempt to create a commission to regulate the railroads in 1881 with a visit to the state during the Legislative debate.

The railroad tycoon subdued the lawmakers' interest with thinly disguised threats that capital would abandon Texas if the state interfered with railroad business.

As the 19th century closed, Texas remained an agricultural state. But the industrial base was growing. Between 1870 and 1900, the per capita value of manufactured goods in the United States rose from $109 to $171. In Texas, these per capita values increased from $14 to $39, but manufacturing values in Texas industry still were only one-half of annual agricultural values.

In 1886, a new breed of Texas politician appeared. **James Stephen Hogg** was not a Confederate veteran, and he was not tied to party policies of the past.

As a reform-minded attorney general, Hogg had actively enforced the state's few railroad regulatory laws. With farmers' support, Hogg was elected governor in 1890, and at the same time, a debate on the constitutionality of a **railroad commission** was settled when voters amended the constitution to provide for one.

The reform mood of the state was evident. Voters returned only 22 of the 106 members of the Texas House in 1890.

Despite his reputation as a reformer, Hogg accepted the growing use of **Jim Crow laws** to limit blacks' access to public services. In 1891, the Legislature responded to public demands and required railroads to provide separate accommodations for blacks and whites.

The stage was being set for one of the major political campaigns in Texas history, however. Farmers did not think that Hogg had gone far enough in his reform program, and they were distressed that Hogg had not appointed a farmer to the railroad commission. Many began to look elsewhere for the solutions to their problems. The **People's Party** in Texas was formed in August 1891.

The 1892 general election was one of the most spirited in the state's history. Conservative Democrats, after Gov. Hogg's supporters shut them out of the convention in Houston, bolted and nominated railroad attorney

C.M. "Dad" Joiner (in boots, center) shakes the hand of Dr. A.D. Lloyd, his geologist, at the Daisy Bradford No. 3, discovery well of the East Texas oil field. Second from right is the legendary H.L. Hunt. Ed Laster (right) was the drilling contractor

George Clark for governor.

The People's Party, or **Populists**, for the first time had a presidential candidate, James Weaver, and a gubernatorial candidate, T.L. Nugent.

Texas Republicans also broke ranks. The party's strength centered in the black vote. After the death of former Gov. E.J. Davis in 1883, **Norris Wright Cuney**, a black, was party leader. Cuney was considered one of the most astute politicians of the period, and he controlled federal patronage.

White Republicans revolted against the black leadership, and these "Lily-whites" nominated **Andrew Jackson Houston**, son of Sam Houston, for governor.

Black Republicans recognized that, alone, their strength was limited, and throughout the latter part of the 19th century, they practiced fusion politics, backing candidates of third parties when they deemed it appropriate. Cuney led the Republicans into a coalition with the conservative Democrats in 1892, backing George Clark.

The election also marked the first time major Democratic candidates courted the black vote. Gov. Hogg's supporters organized black voter clubs, and the governor got about one-half the black vote.

Black farmers were in a quandary. Their financial problems were the same as those small farmers who backed the Populists.

White Populists varied in their sympathy with the racial concerns of the blacks. On the local level, some whites showed sympathy with black concerns about education, voting and law enforcement. Black farmers also were reluctant to abandon the Republican Party because it was their only political base in Texas.

Hogg was re-elected in 1892 with a 43 percent plurality in a field of five candidates.

Populists continued to run well in state races until 1898. Historians have placed the beginning of the party's demise in the 1896 presidential election in which national Populists fused with the Democrats and supported **William Jennings Bryan**.

Although the Populist philosophy lived on, the party declined in importance after 1898. Farmers remained active in politics, but most returned to the Democratic Party, which usurped many of the Populists' issues.

Oil

Seldom can a people's history be profoundly changed by a single event on a single day. But Texas' entrance into the industrial age can be linked directly to the discovery of oil at **Spindletop**, three miles from **Beaumont**, on Jan. 10, 1901.

From that day, Texas' progress from a rural, agricultural state to a modern industrial giant was steady.

The presence of oil in **salt domes** along the Gulf Coast had been suspected for many years. **Patillo Higgins** drilled wells near Spindletop for a decade before his resources were exhausted. In 1900, Higgins leased land to **Anthony Lucas** to prospect for oil.

Initial production at Spindletop was estimated between 75,000 and 80,000 barrels of oil per day. Lucas was hardly prepared for the quantity of oil the well produced, and for several days, the oil flowed freely before the drilling crew could bring it under control. Oil was stored in earthen tanks when possible, but much simply was wasted.

Within days, the area was engulfed in the state's first oil boom. Investors and con men from across the nation descended to enrich themselves in the hysterical activity that followed.

Spindletop was not the first oil discovery in Texas. Even before the colonial period, oil from seeps had been used by Indians for medicinal purposes. Early Spanish explorers used it as a lubricant and to caulk boats.

Lyne Barret drilled Texas' first commercial well near **Nacogdoches** in 1866. The well at **Oil Springs** was 106 feet deep and produced 10 barrels of oil a day. The field was abandoned and reopened in 1887, though it was never commercially profitable.

Wells also were made in Brown County in 1878 and in Bexar County in 1886 before the **first major commercial well** was completed at Corsicana in 1894, when oil was struck while the city was drilling a water well.

The first well was abandoned, but others soon were drilled. By 1898, Corsicana had 342 wells producing 500,000 barrels of oil a year.

Joseph S. Cullinan, a former employee of Standard Oil, arrived in Corsicana in 1897 and developed an integrated oil operation. He constructed the **state's first pipeline** to serve the **state's first refinery,** which he also built. Cullinan also was a champion of conservation, supporting an 1899 law that required abandoned wells to be plugged.

With the development of the Corsicana wells, Texas' oil production in 1900 was 836,000 barrels a year, about one-nineteenth of the total U.S. production.

Spindletop exceeded that production within a few days. In its first year of operation, the well produced 3.2 million barrels of oil. But the price also dropped to three cents a barrel.

Desperately needed new markets for oil were soon forthcoming. Railroads were the first to recognize the advantage of the new, inexpensive resource. They began converting locomotives from coal to oil. Steamship lines followed suit, and many industries found great cost-saving advantages in fueling boilers with inexpensive oil rather than more expensive coal. These customers supported the industry until automobiles were in widespread use.

Railroad tank cars at first were used to haul oil, but by January 1902, a pipeline had been completed from Spindletop to the Neches River. Soon lines were constructed to points on the Gulf.

Oil discoveries followed at Sour Lake and Humble, near Houston. Texas' oil production grew steadily until it reached 28 million barrels in 1905 and then declined until 1910. Thereafter the growth resumed.

In October 1930, the gigantic **East Texas field** was discovered by **C.M. "Dad" Joiner**. Joiner's **Daisy Bradford No. 3**, drilled near **Kilgore**, was the first of 1,000 wells drilled in the field in a six-month period. In the first year, the East Texas Field yielded 100 million barrels of oil. When it was finally defined, the gigantic field proved to be 42 miles long, four to eight miles wide and covered 200 square miles.

1900-1920

One of the greatest natural disasters ever to strike the state occurred on Sept. 8, 1900, when a **hurricane devastated Galveston**, killing 6,000 people (see "After the Great Storm" on pages 35-40). In rebuilding from that disaster, Galveston's civic leaders fashioned the **commission form of municipal government**.

Amarillo later refined the system into the **council-manager organization** that is widely used today.

The great Galveston storm also reinforced arguments by Houston's leadership that an inland port should be built for protection against such tragedies and disruptions of trade. The **Houston Ship Channel** was soon a reality.

The reform spirit in government was not dead after the departure of Jim Hogg. In 1901, the Legislature prohibited the issuing of railroad passes to public officials. More than 270,000 passes were issued to officials that year, and farmers claimed that the free rides increased their freight rates and influenced public policy as well.

In 1903, state Sen. **A.W. Terrell** got a major **election reform law** approved, a measure that was further modified two years later. A **primary system** was established to replace a hodgepodge of practices for nominating candidates that had led to charges of irregularities after each election.

Also in the reform spirit, the Legislature in 1903 prohibited abuse of **child labor** and set minimum ages at which children could work in certain industries. The action preceded federal child-labor laws by 13 years.

However, the state, for the first time, imposed the **poll tax** as a requisite for voting. Historians differ on whether the levy was designed to keep blacks or poor whites — or both — from voting. Certainly the poll tax cut election turnouts. Black voter participation dropped from about 100,000 in the 1890s to an estimated 5,000 in 1906.

The Democratic State Executive Committee also recommended that county committees limit participation in primaries to whites only, and most accepted the suggestion.

The election of **Thomas M. Campbell** as governor

in 1906 marked a progressive period in Texas politics. Interest revived in controlling corporate influence.

Under Campbell, the state's **antitrust laws** were strengthened and a **pure food and drug bill** was passed. Life insurance companies were required to invest in Texas 75 percent of their reserves on policies in the state. Less than one percent of the reserves had been invested prior to the law.

Some companies left Texas. But the law was ben-

James E. Ferguson

eficial in the capital-starved economy. In 1904, voters amended the constitution to allow the state to charter **banks** for the first time, and this eased some of the farmers' credit problems. In 1909, the Legislature approved a bank-deposit insurance plan that predated the federal program.

With corporate influence under acceptable control, attention turned to the issue of prohibition of alcohol. Progressives and prohibitionists joined forces against the conservative establishment to exert a major influence in state government for the next two decades.

Prohibitionists had long been active in Texas. They had the **local-option clause** written into the Constitution of 1876, which allowed counties or their subdivisions to be voted dry. But in 1887, a prohibition amendment to the state constitution had been defeated by a two-to-one margin, and public attention had turned to other problems.

In the early 20th century, the prohibition movement gathered strength. Most of Texas already was dry because of local option. When voters rejected a prohibition amendment by a slim margin in 1911, the state had 167 dry counties and 82 wet or partially wet counties. The heavily populated counties, however, were wet. Prohibition continued to be a major issue.

Problems along the U.S.-Mexico border escalated in 1911 as the decade-long **Mexican Revolution** broke out. Soon the revolutionaries controlled some northern Mexican states, including Chihuahua. Juarez and El Paso were major contact points. El Paso residents could stand on rooftops to observe the fighting between revolutionaries and government troops. Some Americans were killed.

After pleas to the federal government got no action, Gov. Oscar Colquitt sent state militia and Texas Rangers into the Valley in 1913 to protect Texans after Matamoros fell to the rebels. Unfortunately, the Rangers killed many innocent Mexican-Texans during the operation. In addition to problems caused by the fighting and raids, thousands of Mexican refugees flooded Texas border towns to escape the violence of the revolution.

In 1914, **James E. Ferguson** entered Texas politics and for the next three decades, "Farmer Jim" was one of the most dominating and colorful figures on the political stage. Ferguson, a banker from Temple, skirted the prohibition issue by pledging to veto any legislation per-

William P. Hobby

taining to alcoholic beverages.

His strength was among farmers, however. Sixty-two percent of Texas' farmers were tenants, and Ferguson pledged to back legislation to limit tenant rents. Ferguson also was a dynamic orator. He easily won the primary and beat out three opponents in the general election.

Ferguson's first administration was successful. The Legislature passed the law limiting tenants' rents, although it was poorly enforced. And, aid to rural schools was improved.

In 1915, the border problems heated up. A Mexican national was arrested in the Lower Rio Grande Valley carrying a so-called **"Plan of San Diego."** The document, named for a small town in South Texas, outlined plans to create a rebellion of Mexican-Americans, Indians, Japanese and blacks in Texas and the Southwest. Once all Anglo males over age 16 were eliminated, a new republic controlled by blacks would be created to serve as a buffer between the United States and Mexico.

Authorship of the plan has never been determined, but whatever its intent, it started a bloodbath in the Valley. Mexican soldiers participated in raids across the Rio Grande, and Gov. Ferguson sent in the Texas Rangers.

Historians differ on the number of people who lost their lives, but a safe assessment would be hundreds. Tensions were raised so high that Gov. Ferguson and Mexican President Venustiano Carranza met at Nuevo Laredo in November 1915 in an attempt to improve relations. The raids continued.

Pancho Villa raided Columbus, N.M., in early 1916, and two small Texas villages in the Big Bend, Glenn Springs and Boquillas, also were attacked. In July, President **Woodrow Wilso**n determined that the hostilities were critical and activated the National Guard.

Soon 1,000 U.S. troops were stationed along the border. **Fort Bliss** in El Paso housed 60,000 men, and **Fort Duncan** near Eagle Pass was home to 16,000 more.

With the exception of Gen. John J. Pershing's pursuit of Villa into Northern Mexico, few U.S. troops crossed into Mexico. But the service along the border gave soldiers basic training that was put to use when the United States entered World War I in 1917.

Ferguson was easily re-elected in 1916, and he worked well with the Legislature the following year. But after the Legislature adjourned, the governor got into a dispute with the board of regents of the **University of Texas**. The disagreement culminated in the governor's vetoing all appropriations for the school.

As the controversy swirled, the Travis County grand jury indicted Ferguson for misappropriation of funds and for embezzlement. In July 1917, Speaker of the Texas House F.O. Fuller called a special session of the Legislature to consider **impeachment** of the governor. The Texas House voted 21 articles of impeachment,

and the Senate in August 1917 convicted Ferguson on 10 of the charges. The Senate's judgment not only removed Ferguson from office, but also barred him from seeking office again. Ferguson resigned the day before the Senate rendered the decision in an attempt to avoid the prohibition against seeking further office.

Texas participated actively in **World War I**. Almost 200,000 young Texans, including 31,000 blacks, volunteered for military service, and 450 Texas women served in the nurses' corps. Five thousand lost their lives overseas, either fighting or in the **influenza pandemic** that swept the globe.

Texas also was a major training ground during the conflict, with 250,000 soldiers getting basic training in the state.

On the negative side, the war frenzy opened a period of intolerance and nativism in the state. German-Texans were suspect because of their ancestry. A law was passed to prohibit speaking against the war effort. Persons who failed to participate in patriotic activities often were punished. Gov. William P. Hobby even vetoed the appropriation for the German department at the University of Texas.

Ferguson's removal from office was a devastating blow to the anti-prohibitionists. Word that the former governor had received a $156,000 loan from members of the brewers' association while in office provided ammunition for the progressives.

In February 1918, a special session of the Legislature prohibited saloons within a 10-mile radius of military posts and ratified the national prohibition amendment, which had been introduced in Congress by Texas Sen. **Morris Sheppard**.

Women also were given the **right to vote in state primaries** at the same session.

Although national prohibition was to become effective in early 1920, the Legislature presented a prohibition amendment to voters in May 1919, and it was approved, bringing prohibition to Texas earlier than to the rest of the nation. At the same time, a woman suffrage amendment was defeated.

Although World War I ended in November 1918, it brought many changes to Texas. Rising prices during the war had increased the militancy of labor unions.

Blacks also became more militant after the war. Discrimination against black soldiers led in 1917 to a riot in Houston in which several people were killed.

With the election of Mexican President Alvaro Obregón in 1920, the fighting along the border subsided.

In 1919, state Rep. J.T. Canales of Brownsville initiated an investigation of the **Texas Rangers'** role in the border problems. As a result of the study, the Rangers' manpower was reduced from 1,000 members to 76, and stringent limitations were placed on the agency's activities. Standards for members of the force also were upgraded.

By 1920, although still a rural state, the face of Texas was changing. Nearly one-third of the population was in the cities. ☆

Environment

Extending from sea level at the Gulf of Mexico to over 8,000 feet in the Guadalupe Mountains of far West Texas and from the semitropical Lower Rio Grande Valley to the High Plains of the Panhandle, Texas has a natural environment best described as "varied." This section discusses the physical features, geology, soils, water, vegetation and wildlife that are found in the Lone Star State.

The Physical State of Texas

Area of Texas

Texas occupies about 7 percent of the total water and land area of the United States. **Second in size** among the states, Texas, according to the 1996 Statistical Abstract of the United States, has a land and water area of 267,277 square miles as compared with Alaska's 615,230 square miles. California, third largest state, has 158,869 square miles. Texas is as large as all of New England, New York, Pennsylvania, Ohio and North Carolina combined.

The **state's area** consists of 261,914 square miles of land and 5,363 square miles of water.

The area given here differs from that given by the State Land Office in the chapter on State Government.

Length and Breadth

The **longest straight-line distance** in a general north-south direction is 801 miles from the northwest corner of the Panhandle to the extreme southern tip of Texas on the Rio Grande below Brownsville. The greatest east-west distance is 773 miles from the extreme eastward bend in the Sabine River in Newton County to the extreme western bulge of the Rio Grande just above El Paso.

The **geographic center** of Texas is southwest of Mercury in the northern portion of McCulloch County.

Texas' Boundary Lines

The boundary of Texas by segments, including only larger river bends and only the great arc of the coastline, is as follows:

Boundary	Miles
Rio Grande	889.0
Coastline	367.0
Sabine River, Lake and Pass	180.0
*Sabine River to Red River	106.5
Red River	480.0
*East Panhandle line	133.6
*North Panhandle line	167.0
*West Panhandle line	310.2
*Along 32nd parallel	209.0
Total	2,842.3

Following the smaller meanderings of the rivers and the tidewater coastline, the following are the boundary measurements:

Rio Grande	1,254
Coastline (tidewater)	624
Sabine River, Lake and Pass	292
Red River	726
*The five unchanged line segments above	926
Total (including segments marked *)	3,822

Latitude and Longitude

The extremes of latitude and longitude are as follows: From Latitude 25° 50' N. at the extreme southern turn of the Rio Grande on the south line of Cameron County to Latitude 36° 30' N. along the north line of the Panhandle, and from Longitude 93° 31' W. at the extreme eastern point on the Sabine River on the east line of Newton County to Longitude 106° 38' W. on the extreme westward point on the Rio Grande above El Paso.

Texas' Highs and Lows

The highest point in the state is **Guadalupe Peak** at **8,749 feet** above sea level. Its twin, **El Capitan**, stands at **8,085** feet and also is located in Culberson county near the New Mexico state line. Both are in the Guadalupe Mountains National Park, which includes scenic McKittrick Canyon. These elevations and the others in this article have been determined by the U. S. Geological Survey, unless otherwise noted.

The named peaks above 8,000 feet and the counties in which they are located are listed below. These elevations may differ from those in earlier editions of the Almanac because of the more accurate measuring methods currently being used by the USGS.

Named Peaks in Texas Above 8,000 Feet

Name, County	Elevation
Guadalupe Peak, Culberson	8,749
Bush Mountain, Culberson	8,631
Shumard Peak, Culberson	8,615
Bartlett Peak, Culberson	8,508
Mount Livermore (Baldy Peak), Jeff Davis	8,378
Hunter Peak (Pine Top Mtn.), Culberson	8,368
El Capitan, Culberson	8,085

Fort Davis in Jeff Davis County is the **highest town** of any size in Texas at 5,050 feet, and the county has the **highest average elevation**. The **highest state highway point** also is in the county at **McDonald Observatory** at the end of a tap from State Highway 118 on **Mount Locke.** The observatory stands at 6,781 feet, as determined by the Texas Department of Transportation.

The **highest railway point** is Paisano Pass, 14 miles east of Marfa on the Southern Pacific in Presidio County.

Sea level is the **lowest elevation** determined in Texas, and it can be found in all the coastal counties. No point in the state has been found by the geological survey to be below sea level. ☆

Physical Regions

NATURAL REGIONS OF TEXAS

A special thanks to Dr. William M. Holmes, chairman of the Department of Geography at the University of North Texas, for his review of this section.

The principal physical regions of Texas are usually listed as follows (see also **Vegetational Areas** and **Soils**.):

The Gulf Coastal Plains

Texas' Gulf Coastal Plains are the western extension of the coastal plain extending from the Atlantic to beyond the Rio Grande. Its characteristic rolling to hilly surface covered with a heavy growth of pine and hardwoods extends into East Texas. In the increasingly arid west, however, its forests become secondary in nature, consisting largely of post oaks and, farther west, prairies and brushlands.

The interior limit of the Gulf Coastal Plains in Texas is the line of the **Balcones Fault and Escarpment.** This geologic fault or shearing of underground strata extends eastward from a point on the Rio Grande near Del Rio. It extends to the northwestern part of Bexar County where it turns northeastward and extends through Comal, Hays and Travis counties, intersecting the Colorado River immediately above Austin. The fault line is a single, definite geologic feature, accompanied by a line of southward- and eastward-facing hills.

The resemblance of the hills to balconies when viewed from the plain below accounts for the Spanish name, *balcones.*

North of Waco, features of the fault zone are sufficiently inconspicuous that the interior boundary of the Coastal Plain follows the traditional geologic contact between upper and lower Cretaceous rocks. This contact is along the western edge of the **Eastern Cross Timbers.**

This fault line is usually accepted as the boundary between lowland and upland Texas. Below the fault line the surface is characteristically coastal plains. Above the Balcones Fault the surface is characteristically interior rolling plains.

Pine Belt or "Piney Woods"

The Pine Belt, called the "Piney Woods," extends into Texas from the east 75 to 125 miles. From north to south it extends from the Red River to within about 25 miles of the Gulf Coast. Interspersed among the pines are some hardwood timbers, usually in valleys of rivers and creeks. This area is the source of practically all of Texas' large commercial timber production (see "Forest Resources" in index). It was settled early in Texas' history and is an older farming area of the state.

This area's soils and climate are adaptable to production of a variety of fruit and vegetable crops. Cattle raising is widespread, accompanied by the development of pastures planted to improved grasses. Lumber production is the principal industry. There is a large iron-and-steel industry near Daingerfield in Morris County based on nearby iron deposits. Iron deposits are also worked in Rusk and one or two other counties.

A great oil field discovered in Gregg, Rusk and Smith counties in 1931 has done more than anything else to contribute to the economic growth of the area. This area has a variety of clays, lignite and other minerals as potentials for development.

Post Oak Belt

The main Post Oak Belt of Texas is wedged between the Pine Belt on the east, Blacklands on the west, and the Coastal Prairies on the south, covering a considerable area in East Central Texas. Principal industry is diversified farming and livestock raising. Throughout, it is spotty in character, with some insular areas of blackland soil and some that closely resemble those of the Pine Belt. There is a small isolated area of pines in Bastrop County known as the "**Lost Pines**." The Post Oak Belt has lignite, commercial clays and some other minerals.

Blackland Belt

The Blackland Belt stretches from the Rio Grande to the Red River, lying just below the line of the **Balcones Fault**, and varying in width from 15 to 70 miles. It is narrowest below the segment of the Balcones Fault from the Rio Grande to Bexar County and gradually widens as it runs northeast to the Red River. Its rolling prairie, easily turned by the plow, developed rapidly as a farming area until the 1930s and was the principal cotton-producing area of Texas. Now, however, other Texas irrigated, mechanized areas lead in farming. Because of the early growth, the Blackland Belt is still the most thickly populated area in the state and contains within it and along its border more of the state's large and middle-sized cities than any other area. Primarily because of this concentration of population, this belt has the most diversified manufacturing industry of the state.

Coastal Prairies

The Texas Coastal Prairies extend westward along the coast from the Sabine River, reaching inland 30 to 60 miles. Between the Sabine and Galveston Bay, the line of demarcation between the prairies and the Pine Belt forests to the north is very distinct. The Coastal Prairie extends along the Gulf from the Sabine to the Lower Rio Grande Valley. The eastern half is covered with a heavy growth of grass; the western half, which is more arid, is covered with short grass and, in some places, with small timber and brush. The soil is heavy clay. Grass supports the densest cattle population in Texas, and cattle ranching is the principal agricultural industry. Rice is a major crop, grown under irrigation from wells and rivers. Cotton, grain sorghum and truck crops are grown.

Coastal Prairie areas have seen the greatest industrial development in Texas history since World War II. Chief concentration has been from Orange and Beaumont to Houston, and much of the development has been in petrochemicals.

Corpus Christi, in the Coastal Bend, and Brownsville, in the Lower Rio Grande Valley, have seaports and agricultural and industrial sections. Cotton, grain, vegetables and citrus fruits are the principal crops. Cattle production is significant, with the famed King Ranch and other large ranches located here.

Lower Rio Grande Valley

The deep alluvial soils and distinctive economy cause the Lower Rio Grande Valley to be classified as a subregion of the Gulf Coastal Plain. The Lower Valley, as it is called locally, is Texas' greatest citrus-winter vegetable area because of the normal absence of freezing weather and the rich delta soils of the Rio Grande. Despite occasional damaging freezes, as in 1951 and 1961, the Lower Valley ranks high among the nation's fruit-and-truck regions. Much of the acreage is irrigated, although dryland farming also is practiced.

Rio Grande Plain

This may be roughly defined as lying south of San Antonio between the Rio Grande and the Gulf Coast. The Rio Grande Plain shows characteristics of both the Texas Gulf Coastal Plain and the North Mexico Plains because there is similarity of topography, climate and plant life all the way from the Balcones Escarpment in Texas to the Sierra Madre Oriental in Mexico, which runs past Monterrey about 160 miles south of Laredo.

The Rio Grande Plain is partly prairie, but much of it is covered with a dense growth of **prickly pear, cactus, mesquite, dwarf oak, catclaw, guajillo, huisache, blackbrush, cenizo** and other wild shrubs. This country is devoted primarily to raising cattle, sheep and goats. The Texas Angora goat and mohair industry centers in this area and on the **Edwards Plateau,** which borders it on the north. San Antonio and Laredo are its chief commercial centers, with San Antonio dominating trade.

There is some farming, and the **Winter Garden,** centering in Dimmit and Zavala counties north of Laredo, is irrigated from wells and streams to produce vegetables in late winter and early spring. Primarily, however, the central and western part of the Rio Grande Plain is devoted to livestock raising. The rainfall is less than 25 inches annually and the hot summers bring heavy evaporation, so that cultivation without irrigation is limited. Over a large area in the central and western parts of the Rio Grande Plain, the growth of **small oaks, mesquite, prickly pear (Opuntia) cactus** and a variety of wild shrubs is very dense and it is often called the **Brush Country**. It is also referred to as the **chaparral** and the **monte**. (Monte is a Spanish word, one meaning of which is dense brush.)

Interior Lowlands

North Central Plains

The North Central Plains of Texas are a southwestern extension into Texas of the interior lowlands that extend northward to the Canadian border, paralleling the Great Plains to the West. The North Central Plains of Texas extend from the Blackland Belt on the east to the Caprock Escarpment on the west. From north to south they extend from the Red River to the Colorado.

West Texas Rolling Plains

The West Texas Rolling Plains, approximately the western two-thirds of the North Central Plains in Texas, rise from east to west in altitude from about 750 feet to 2,000 feet at the base of the **Caprock Escarpment**. Annual rainfall ranges from about 30 inches on the east to 20 on the west. Temperature varies rather widely between summer's heat and winter's cold.

This area still has a large cattle-raising industry with many of the state's largest ranches. However, there is much level, cultivable land.

Grand Prairie

Near the eastern edge of the North Central Plains is the Grand Prairie, extending south from the Red River in an irregular band through Cooke, Montague, Wise, Denton, Tarrant, Parker, Hood, Johnson, Bosque, Coryell and some adjacent counties. It is a limestone-based area, usually treeless except along the numerous streams and adapted primarily to livestock raising and staple-crop growing. Sometimes called the Fort Worth Prairie, it has an agricultural economy and largely rural population, with no large cities except Fort Worth on its eastern boundary.

Eastern and Western Cross Timbers

Hanging over the top of the Grand Prairie and dropping down on each side are the Eastern and Western Cross Timbers. The two southward-extending bands are connected by a narrow strip along the Red River. The Eastern Cross Timbers extend southward from the Red River through eastern Denton County and along the Dallas-Tarrant County boundary, then through Johnson County to the Brazos River and into Hill County. The much larger Western Cross Timbers extend from the Red River south through Clay, Montague, Jack, Wise, Parker, Palo Pinto, Hood, Erath, Eastland, Comanche, Brown and Mills counties to the Colorado River, where they meet the Edwards Plateau. Their soils are adapted to fruit and vegetable crops, which reach considerable commercial production in some areas in Parker, Erath, Eastland and Comanche counties.

Great Plains

The Great Plains which lie to the east of the base of the Rocky Mountains extend into Northwest Texas. This area, which is a vast, flat, high plain covered with thick layers of alluvial material, is known as the **Staked Plains** or the Spanish equivalent, **Llano Estacado**.

Historians differ as to the origin of this name. Some think that it came from the fact that the Coronado expedition, crossing the trackless sea of grass, staked its route so that it would be guided on its return trip. Others think that the "estacado" refers to the palisaded appearance of the Caprock in many places, especially the west-facing escarpment in New Mexico.

The **Caprock Escarpment** is the dividing line between the High Plains and the Lower Rolling Plains of West Texas. Like the Balcones Escarpment, the Caprock Escarpment is a striking physical feature, rising abruptly 200, 500 and in some places almost 1,000 feet above the plains. Unlike the **Balcones Escarpment**, the Caprock was caused by surface erosion. Where rivers issue from the eastern face of the Caprock, there frequently are notable canyons, such as the **Palo Duro Canyon** on the **Prairie Dog Town Fork (main channel) of the Red River** and the breaks along the Canadian as it crosses the Panhandle north of Amarillo.

Along the eastern edge of the Panhandle there is a gradual descent of the earth's surface from high to low plains, but at the Red River the Caprock Escarpment becomes a striking surface feature. It continues as an east-facing wall south through Briscoe, Floyd, Motley, Dickens, Crosby, Garza and Borden counties, gradually decreasing in elevation. South of Borden County the escarpment is less obvious, and the boundary between the High Plains and the Edwards Plateau occurs where the alluvial cover of the High Plains disappears.

Stretching over the largest level plain of its kind in the United States, the **High Plains** rise gradually from about 2,700 feet on the east to more than 4,000 in spots along the New Mexico border.

Chiefly because of climate and the resultant agriculture, subdivisions are called the North Plains and South Plains. The North Plains, from Hale County north, has primarily wheat and grain sorghum farming, but with significant ranching and petroleum developments. Amarillo is the largest city, with Plainview on the south and Borger on the north as important commercial centers. The South Plains, also a leading grain sorghum region, leads Texas in cotton production. Lubbock is the principal city, and Lubbock County is one of the state's largest cotton producers. Irrigation from underground reservoirs, centered around Lubbock and Plainview, waters much of the crop acreage.

Edwards Plateau

Geographers usually consider that the Great Plains at the foot of the Rocky Mountains actually continue southward from the High Plains of Northwest Texas to the Rio Grande and the Balcones Escarpment. This southern and lower extension of the Great Plains in Texas is known as the Edwards Plateau.

It lies between the Rio Grande and the Colorado River. Its southeastern border is the **Balcones Escarpment** from the Rio Grande at Del Rio eastward to San Antonio and thence to Austin on the Colorado. Its upper boundary is the Pecos River, though the **Stockton Plateau** is geologically and topographically classed with the Edwards Plateau. The Edwards Plateau varies from about 750 feet high at its southern and eastern borders to about 2,700 feet in places. Almost the entire surface is a thin, limestone-based soil covered with a medium to thick growth of **cedar, small oak** and **mesquite** with a varying growth of **prickly pear**. Grass for cattle, weeds for sheep and tree foliage for the browsing goats support three industries — cattle, goat and sheep raising — upon which the area's economy depends. It is the **nation's leading Angora goat**

and mohair producing region and one of the nation's leading sheep and wool areas. A few crops are grown.

Toyah Basin

To the northwest of the Edwards and Stockton plateaus is the Toyah Basin, a broad, flat remnant of an old sea floor that occupied the region as recently as Quaternary time. Located in the Pecos River Valley, this region, in relatively recent time, has become important for many agricultural products as a result of irrigation. Additional economic activity is afforded by local oil fields.

The Hill Country

The Hill Country is a popular name for an area of hills and spring-fed streams along the edge of the **Balcones Escarpment**. Notable large springs include **Barton Springs** at Austin, **San Marcos Springs** at San Marcos, **Comal Springs** at New Braunfels, several springs at San Antonio, and a number of others.

The Llano Basin

The Llano Basin lies at the junction of the Colorado and Llano rivers in Burnet and Llano counties. Earlier this was known as the **"Central Mineral Region,"** because of the evidence there of a large number of minerals.

On the Colorado River in this area, a succession of dams impounds two large and five small reservoirs. Uppermost is **Lake Buchanan,** one of the large reservoirs, between Burnet and Llano counties. Below it in the western part of Travis County is **Lake Travis.** Between these two large reservoirs are three smaller ones, **Inks, L. B. Johnson** (formerly Granite Shoals) and **Marble Falls** reservoirs, used primarily for maintaining heads to produce electric power from the overflow from Lake Buchanan. **Lake Austin** is just above the city of Austin. Still another small lake, **Town Lake,** is formed by a low-water dam in Austin. The recreational area around these lakes is called the **Highland Lakes Country.** This is an interesting area with Precambrian and Paleozoic rocks found on the surface.

Basin and Range Province

The Basin and Range province, with its center in Nevada, surrounds the Colorado Plateau on the west and south and enters far West Texas from southern New Mexico. It consists of broad interior drainage, basins interspersed with scattered fault-block mountain ranges. Although this is the only part of Texas regarded as mountainous, these should not be confused with the Rockies. Of all the independent ranges in West Texas, only the Davis Mountains resemble the Rockies and there is much debate about this.

Texas west of the Edwards Plateau, bounded on the north by New Mexico and on the south by the Rio Grande, is distinctive in its physical and economic conditions. Traversed from north to south by an eastern range of the Rockies, it contains all of **Texas' true mountains** and also is very interesting geologically.

Highest of the Trans-Pecos Mountains is the **Guadalupe Range,** which enters the state from New Mexico. It comes to an abrupt end about 20 miles south of the boundary line, where are situated **Guadalupe Peak,** (8,749 feet, highest in Texas) and **El Capitan** (8,085 feet). El Capitan, because of perspective, appears to the observer on the plain below to be higher than Guadalupe. Lying just west of the Guadalupe range and extending to the **Hueco Mountains** a short distance east of El Paso is the **Diablo Plateau** or basin. It has no drainage outlet to the sea. The runoff from the scant rain that falls on its surface drains into a series of salt lakes that lie just west of the Guadalupe Mountains. These lakes are entirely dry during periods of low rainfall, exposing bottoms of solid salt, and for years they were a source of **commercial salt.**

Davis Mountains

The Davis Mountains are principally in Jeff Davis County. The highest peak, **Mount Livermore,** (8,206 feet) is **one of the highest in Texas;** there are several others more than 7,000 feet high. These mountains intercept the moisture-bearing winds and receive more precipitation than elsewhere in the Trans-Pecos, so they have more vegetation than the other Trans-Pecos mountains. Noteworthy are the **San Solomon Springs** at the northern base of these mountains.

Big Bend

South of the Davis Mountains lies the Big Bend country, so called because it is encompassed on three sides by a great southward swing of the Rio Grande. It is a mountainous country of scant rainfall and sparse population. Its principal mountains, the **Chisos**, rise to 7,825 feet in **Mount Emory**. Along the Rio Grande are the **Santa Elena, Mariscal and Boquillas canyons** with rim elevations of 3,500 to 3,775 feet. They are among the noteworthy canyons of the North American continent. Because of its remarkable topography and plant and animal life, the southern part of this region along the Rio Grande is home to the **Big Bend National Park**, with headquarters in a deep valley in the Chisos Mountains. It is a favorite recreation area.

Upper Rio Grande Valley

The Upper Rio Grande (El Paso) Valley is a narrow strip of irrigated land running down the river from El Paso for a distance of 75 miles or more. In this area are the historic towns and missions of **Ysleta, Socorro and San Elizario, oldest in Texas**. Cotton is the chief product of the valley, much of it long-staple variety. This limited area has a dense urban and rural population, in marked contrast to the territory surrounding it. ☆

For Further Reading:
"Texas: A Geography," by Terry G. Jordan with John L. Bean Jr. and William M. Holmes; Westview Press, Boulder and London, 1984.

Geology of Texas

Source: Bureau of Economic Geology, The University of Texas at Austin.

History in the Rocks

Mountains, seas, coastal plains, rocky plateaus, high plains, forests — all this physiographic variety in Texas is controlled by the varied rocks and structures that underlie and crop out in Texas. The fascinating geologic history of Texas is recorded in the rocks — both those exposed at the surface and those penetrated by holes drilled in search of oil and natural gas. The rocks reveal a dynamic, ever-changing earth — ancient mountains, seas, volcanoes, earthquake belts, rivers, hurricanes and winds. Today, the volcanoes and great earthquake belts are no longer active, but rivers and streams, wind and rain, and the slow, inexorable alterations of rocks at or near the surface continue to change the face of Texas. The geologic history of Texas, as documented by the rocks, began more than a billion years ago. Its legacy is the mineral wealth and varied land forms of modern Texas.

Geologic Time Travel

The story preserved in the rocks requires an understanding of the origin of the strata and how they have been deformed. **Stratigraphy** is the study of the composition, sequence and origin of the rocks: what the rocks are made of, how they were formed and the order in which the layers were formed. Structural geology reveals the architecture of the rocks: the locations of the mountains, volcanoes, sedimentary basins and earthquake belts. Above is a map showing where rocks of various geologic ages are visible on the surface of Texas today.

History concerns events through time, but geologic time is such a grandiose concept that most of us find it difficult to comprehend. So, geologists have named the various chapters of earth history.

Precambrian Eon

Precambrian rocks, more than 600 million years old, are exposed at the surface in the Llano Uplift of Central Texas and in scattered outcrops in West Texas, around and north of Van Horn and near El Paso. These rocks, some more than a billion years old, include complexly deformed rocks that were originally formed by cooling from a liquid state as well as rocks that were altered from pre-existing rocks.

Precambrian rocks, often called the "basement complex," are thought to form the foundation of continental masses. Precambrian rocks underlie all of Texas. The outcrop in Central Texas is only the exposed part of the **Texas Craton**, which is primarily buried by younger rocks. (A craton is a stable, almost immovable portion of the earth's crust that forms the nuclear mass of a continent.)

Paleozoic Era

During the early part of the Paleozoic Era (approximately 600 million to 350 million years ago), broad, relatively shallow seas repeatedly inundated the Texas Craton and much of North and West Texas. The evidence for these events is found exposed around the Llano Uplift and in far West Texas near Van Horn and El Paso, and also in the subsurface throughout most of West and North Texas. The evidence includes early Paleozoic rocks — sandstones, shales and limestones, similar to sediments that form in seas today — and the fossils of animals, similar to modern crustaceans — the brachiopods, clams, snails and related organisms that live in modern marine environments.

By **late Paleozoic** (approximately 350 million to 240 million years ago), the Texas Craton was bordered on the east and south by a long, deep marine basin called the Ouachita Trough. Sediments slowly accumulated in this trough until late in the Paleozoic Era. Plate-tectonic theory postulates that the collision of the North American Plate (upon which the Texas Craton is located) with the European and African-South American plates uplifted the thick sediments that had accumulated in the trough to form the Ouachita Mountains. At that time, the Ouachitas extended across Texas. Today, the Texas portion of the old mountain range is entirely buried by younger rocks, and all that remains at the surface of the once-majestic Ouachita Mountain chain is exposed only in southeastern Oklahoma and southwestern Arkansas.

During the **Pennsylvanian Period**, however, the Ouachita Mountains bordered the eastern margin of shallow inland seas that covered most of West Texas. Rivers flowed westward from the mountains to the sea bringing sediment to form deltas along an ever-changing coastline. The sediments were then reworked by the waves and currents of the inland sea. Today, these fluvial, delta and shallow marine deposits compose the late Paleozoic rocks that crop out and underlie the surface of North Central Texas.

Broad marine shelves divided the West Texas seas into several sub-basins, or deeper areas, that received more sediments than accumulated on the limestone shelves. Limestone reefs rimmed the deeper basins. Today, these reef limestones are important **oil reservoirs in West Texas**. These seas gradually withdrew from Texas, and by the late **Permian Period**, all that was left in West Texas were shallow basins and wide tidal flats in which salt, gypsum and red muds accumulated in a hot, arid land. Strata deposited during the Permian Period are exposed today along the edge of the Panhandle, as far east as Wichita Falls and south to Concho County, and in the Trans-Pecos.

Mesozoic Era

Approximately 240 million years ago, the major geologic events in Texas shifted from West Texas to East and Southeast Texas. The European and African-South American plates, which had collided with the North American plate to form the Ouachita Mountains, began to separate from North America. A series of faulted basins, or rifts, extending from Mexico to Nova Scotia were formed. These rifted basins received sediments

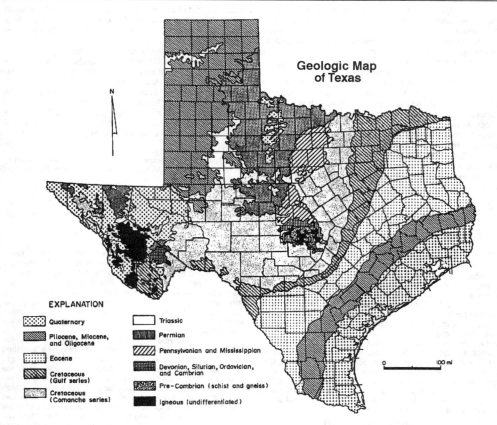

Geologic Map of Texas

N

EXPLANATION

- Quaternary
- Pliocene, Miocene, and Oligocene
- Eocene
- Cretaceous (Gulf series)
- Cretaceous (Comanche series)
- Triassic
- Permian
- Pennsylvanian and Mississippian
- Devonian, Silurian, Ordovician, and Cambrian
- Pre-Cambrian (schist and gneiss)
- Igneous (undifferentiated)

0   100 mi

from adjacent uplifts. As Europe and the southern continents continued to drift away from North America, the Texas basins were eventually buried beneath thick deposits of marine salt within the newly formed East Texas and Gulf Coast basins. **Jurassic** and **Cretaceous** rocks in East and Southeast Texas document a sequence of broad limestone shelves at the edge of the developing Gulf of Mexico. From time to time, the shelves were buried beneath deltaic sandstones and shales, which built the northwestern margin of the widening Gulf of Mexico to the south and southeast. As the underlying salt was buried more deeply by dense sediments, the salt became unstable and moved toward areas of least pressure. As the salt moved, it arched or pierced overlying sediments forming, in some cases, columns known as **"salt domes."** In some cases, these salt domes moved to the surface; others remain beneath a sedimentary overburden. This mobile salt formed numerous structures that would later serve to trap oil and natural gas.

By the early **Cretaceous** (approximately 140 million years ago), the shallow **Mesozoic seas** covered a large part of Texas, eventually extending west to the Trans-Pecos area and north almost to the present-day state boundaries. Today, the limestones deposited in those seas are exposed in the walls of the magnificent **canyons of the Rio Grande** in the Big Bend National Park area and in the canyons and headwaters of streams that drain the Edwards Plateau, as well as in Central Texas from San Antonio to Dallas.

Animals of many types lived in the shallow Mesozoic seas, tidal pools and coastal swamps. Today these lower Cretaceous rocks are some of the most fossiliferous in the state. Tracks of **dinosaurs** occur in several localities, and remains of **terrestrial, aquatic and flying reptiles** have been collected from Cretaceous rocks in many parts of Texas.

During most of the late Cretaceous, much of Texas lay beneath **marine waters** that were deeper than those of the

early Cretaceous seas, except where rivers, deltas and shallow marine shelves existed. River delta and strandline sandstones are the reservoir rocks for the most prolific oil field in Texas. When discovered in 1930, this East Texas oil field contained recoverable reserves estimated at 5.6 billion barrels. The chalky rock that we now call the "Austin Chalk" was deposited when the Texas seas became deeper. Today, the chalk (and other Upper Cretaceous rocks) crops out in a wide band that extends from near Eagle Pass on the Rio Grande, east to San Antonio, north to Dallas and eastward to the Texarkana area. The Austin Chalk and other upper Cretaceous rocks dip southeastward beneath the East Texas and Gulf Coast basins. The late Cretaceous was the time of the last major seaway across Texas, because mountains were forming in the western United States that influenced areas as far away as Texas.

A **chain of volcanoes** formed beneath the late Cretaceous seas in an area roughly parallel to and south and east of the old, buried Ouachita Mountains. The eruptions of these volcanoes were primarily on the sea floor and great clouds of steam and ash likely accompanied them. Between eruptions, invertebrate marine animals built reefs on the shallow volcanic cones. Pilot Knob, located southeast of Austin, is one of these old volcanoes that is now exposed at the surface.

Cenozoic Era

At the dawn of the Cenozoic Era, approximately 65 million years ago, the northern and northwestern margins of the East Texas Basin were sites of deltas fed by rivers. These streams flowed eastward, draining areas to the north and west. Although there were minor incursions of the seas, the Cenozoic rocks principally document extensive seaward building by broad deltas, marshy lagoons, sandy barrier islands and embayments. Thick vegetation covered the levees and areas between the streams. Coastal plains were taking shape, under the same processes still at work today.

The Mesozoic marine salt became buried by thick sediments in the coastal plain area. The salt began to form ridges and domes in the Houston and Rio Grande areas. The heavy load of sand, silt and mud deposited by the deltas eventually caused some areas of the coast to subside and form large fault systems, essentially parallel to the coast. Many of these coastal faults moved slowly and probably generated little earthquake activity. However, movement along the Balcones and Luling-Mexia-Talco zones, a **complex system of faults** along the western and northern edge of the basins, likely generated large earthquakes millions of years ago.

Predecessors of modern animals roamed the Texas Cenozoic coastal plains and woodlands. Bones and teeth of **horses, camels, sloths, giant armadillos, mammoths, mastodons, bats, rats, large cats** and other modern or extinct mammals have been excavated from coastal plain deposits. Vegetation in the area included varieties of plants and trees both similar and dissimilar to modern ones. **Fossil palmwood**, the Texas **"state stone,"** is found in sediments of early Cenozoic age.

The Cenozoic Era in Trans-Pecos Texas was entirely different. There, **extensive volcanic eruptions** formed great calderas and produced copious lava flows. These eruptions ejected great clouds of volcanic ash and rock particles into the air — many times the amount of material ejected by the 1980 eruption of Mount St. Helens. Ash from the eruptions drifted eastward and is found in some of the sand-and-siltstones of the Gulf Coastal Plains. **Lava** flowed over the older Paleozoic and Mesozoic rocks, and igneous intrusions melted their way upward into the crustal rocks. These volcanic and intrusive igneous rocks are well exposed in the arid areas of the Trans-Pecos today.

In the Texas Panhandle, streams originating in the recently elevated southern Rocky Mountains brought floods of gravel and sand into Texas. As the braided streams crisscrossed the area, they formed great **alluvial fans**. These fans, which were deposited on the older **Paleozoic** and **Mesozoic** rocks, occur from northwestern Texas into Nebraska. Between 1 million and 2 million years ago, the streams of the Texas Panhandle were isolated from their Rocky Mountain source, and the eastern edge of this sheet of alluvial material began to retreat westward, forming the **Caprock** of the modern High Plains of Texas.

During the latter part of the Cenozoic Era, a great **Ice Age** descended upon the northern part of the North American continent. For more than 2 million years, there were successive advances and retreats of the thick sheets of glacial ice. Four periods of extensive glaciation were separated by warmer interglacial periods. Although the glaciers never reached as far south as Texas, the state's climate and sea level underwent major changes with each period of glacial advance and retreat. Sea level during times of glacial advance was 300 to 450 feet lower than during the warmer interglacial periods because so much sea water was captured in the ice sheets. The climate was both more humid and cooler than today, and the major Texas rivers carried more water and more sand and gravel to the sea. These deposits underlie the outer 50 miles or more of the Gulf Coastal Plain.

Approximately 3,000 years ago, sea level reached its modern position. The rivers, deltas, lagoons, beaches and barrier islands that we know as coastal Texas have formed since that time. ☆

*Oil and natural gas, as well as nonfuel minerals, are important to the Texas economy. For a more detailed discussion, look for **"Minerals"** in the index.*

Soil Conservation and Use

*Source: **Natural Resources Conservation Service, U. S. Department of Agriculture, Temple, Texas.***

Soil is one of Texas' most important natural resources. The soils of Texas are complex because of the wide diversity of climate, vegetation, geology and landscapes. More than 1,200 different kinds of soil are recognized in the state. Each soil has a specific set of properties that affect its use in some way. The location of each soil and information about its use is in soil survey reports available for most counties. Contact the **Natural Resources Conservation Service** for more information: 101 S. Main St., Temple 76501-7682; phone: 817-298-1228.

The vast expanse of Texas soils encouraged wasteful use of soil and water throughout much of the state's history. About 21 percent of all land area in Texas has been classified as "prime farmland." Settlers were attracted by these rich soils and the abundant water of the eastern half of the region, used them to build an agriculture and agribusiness of vast proportions, then found their abuse had created critical problems.

In the 1930s, interest in soil and water conservation began to mount. In 1935, the Soil Conservation Service, now called the **Natural Resources Conservation Service,** was created in the U. S. Department of Agriculture. In 1939, the **Texas Soil Conservation Law** made it possible for landowners to organize local soil and water conservation districts.

As of April 1997, the state had 214 conservation districts, which manage the conservation functions within the district. A subdivision of state government, each district is governed by a board of five elected landowners. Technical assistance in planning and applying conservation work is provided through the USDA, Natural Resources Conservation Service. State funds for districts are administered through the **Texas State Soil and Water Conservation Board.**

The 1992 National Resources Inventory showed that land use in Texas consisted of about 56 percent rangeland, 17 percent cropland, 10 percent pastureland, 6 percent forestland, 5 percent urban land, 2 percent federal land and 4 percent miscellaneous land. The Inventory also revealed that wind and water erosion removed about 326 million tons of soil annually from Texas cropland.

Soil Subdivisions

Most authorities divide Texas into 19 major subdivisions that have similar or related soils, vegetation, topography, climate and land uses. These are called **Major Land Resource Areas.** Brief descriptions of these subdivisions follow.

1. Trans-Pecos Soils

The 18.7 million acres of the Trans-Pecos, mostly west of the Pecos River, are diverse plains and valleys intermixed with mountains. Surface drainage is slow to rapid. This arid region is used mainly as rangeland. A small amount of irrigated cropland is on the more fertile soils along the Rio Grande and the Pecos River. Vineyards are a more recent use of these soils, as is the disposal of large volumes of municipal wastes.

Upland soils are mostly well-drained, light reddish-brown to brown clay loams, clays and sands (some have a large amount of gypsum or other salts). Many areas have shallow soils and rock outcrops, and sizable areas have deep sands. **Bottomland soils** are deep, well-drained, dark grayish-brown to reddish-brown silt loams, loams, clay loams and clays. Lack of soil moisture and wind erosion are the major soil-management problems. Only irrigated crops can be grown on these soils, and most areas lack an adequate source of good water.

2. High Plains Soils

The High Plains area comprises a vast high plateau of more than 19.4 million acres in northwestern Texas. It lies in the southern part of the Great Plains province that includes large similar areas in Oklahoma and New Mexico. The flat, nearly level treeless plain has few streams to cause local relief. However, several major rivers originate in the High Plains or cross the area. The largest is the **Canadian River,** which has cut a deep valley across the Panhandle section.

Playas, small, intermittent lakes scattered through the area, lie up to 20 feet below the surrounding plains. A 1965 survey counted more than 19,000 playas in 44 counties, occupying some 340,000 acres. They receive most of the runoff from rains, but only 10 to 40 percent of this water percolates back to the aquifer.

Upland soils are mostly well-drained, deep, neutral to alkaline clay loams and sandy loams in shades of brown or red. Sandy soils are in the southern part. Many soils have large amounts of lime at various depths and some are shallow over caliche. Soils of bottomlands are minor in extent.

The area is used mostly for cropland, but significant areas of rangeland are in the southwestern and extreme northern parts. The soils are moderately productive, and the flat surface encourages irrigation and mechanization. Limited soil moisture, constant danger of wind erosion and irrigation water management are the major soil-management problems, but the region is Texas' leading producer of three important crops: **cotton, grain sorghums and wheat**.

3. Rolling Plains Soils

The Rolling Plains include 21.7 million acres east of the High Plains in northwestern Texas. The area lies west of the North Central Prairies and extends from the edge of the Edwards Plateau in Tom Green County northward into Oklahoma. The landscape is nearly level to strongly rolling, and surface drainage is moderate to rapid. Outcrops of red beds geologic materials and associated reddish soils led to use of the name "Red Plains" by some. Limestone underlies the soils in the southeastern part. The eastern part contains large areas of badlands.

Upland soils are mostly deep, pale-brown through reddish-brown to dark grayish-brown, neutral to alkaline sandy loams, clay loams and clays; some are deep sands. Many soils have a large amount of lime in the lower part, and a few others are saline; some are shallow and stony. **Bottomland soils** are mostly reddish-brown and sandy to clayey; some are saline.

This area is used mostly for rangeland, but cotton, grain sorghums and wheat are important crops. The major soil-management problems are brush control, wind erosion, low fertility and lack of soil mosture. Salt spots are a concern in some areas.

4. North Central Prairie Soils

The North Central Prairie occupies about 7 million acres in North Central Texas. Adjacent to this area on the north is the rather small (less than 1 million acres) Rolling Red Prairies area, which extends into Oklahoma and is included here because the soils and land use are similar. This area lies between the Western Cross Timbers and the Rolling Plains. It is dominantly grassland intermixed with small wooded areas. The landscape is undulating with slow to rapid surface drainage.

Upland soils are mostly deep, well-drained, brown or reddish-brown, slightly acid loams over neutral to alkaline, clayey sugbsoils. Some are shallow or moderately deep to shale. Bottomland soils are mostly well-drained, dark-brown or gray loams and clays.

This area is used mostly as rangeland, but wheat, grain sorghums and other crops are grown on the better soils. Brush control, wind and water erosion and limited soil moisture are the major soil-management concerns.

5. Edwards Plateau Soils

The 22.7 million acres of the Edwards Plateau are in southwest Texas east of the Trans-Pecos and west of the Blackland Prairie. Uplands are nearly level to undulating except near large stream valleys where the landscape is hilly with deep canyons and steep slopes. Surface drainage is rapid.

Upland soils are mostly shallow, very stony or gravely, dark alkaline clays and clay loams underlain by limestone. Lighter-colored soils are on the steep sideslopes and deep, less-stony soils are in the valleys. Bottomland soils are mostly deep, dark-gray or brown, alkaline loams and clays.

Raising beef cattle is the main enterprise in this region, but it is also the center of Texas' and the nation's mohair and wool production. The area is a major deer habitat; hunting leases produce income. Cropland is mostly in the valleys on the deeper soils and is used mainly for growing forage crops and hay. The major soil-management concerns are brush control, large stones, low fertility, excess lime and limited soil moisture.

6. Central Basin Soils

The Central Basin, also known as the **Llano Basin**, occupies a relatively small area in Central Texas. It includes parts or all of Llano, Mason, Gillespie and adjoining counties. The total area is about 1.6 million acres of undulating to hilly landscape.

Upland soils are mostly shallow, reddish-brown to brown, mostly gravely and stony, neutral to slightly acid sandy loams over granite, limestone, gneiss and schist bedrock. Large boulders are on the soil surface in some areas. Deeper, less stony sandy-loam soils are in the valleys. Bottomland soils are minor areas of deep, dark-gray or brown loams and clays.

Ranching is the main enterprise, with some farms producing peaches, grain sorghum and wheat. The area provides excellent deer habitat, and hunting leases are a major source of income. Brush control, large stones and limited soil moisture are soil-management concerns.

7. Northern Rio Grande Plain Soils

The Northern Rio Grande Plain comprises about 6.3 million acres in an area of Southern Texas extending from Uvalde to Beeville. The landscape is nearly level to rolling, mostly brush-covered plains with slow to rapid surface drainage.

The major upland soils are deep, reddish-brown or dark grayish-brown, neutral to alkaline loams and clays. Bottomland soils are mostly dark-colored loams.

The area is mostly rangeland with significant areas of cropland. Grain sorghums, cotton, corn and small grains are the major crops. Crops are irrigated in the western part, especially in the Winter Garden area. where vegetables such as spinach, carrots and cabbage are grown. Much of the area is good deer and dove habitat; hunting leases are a major source of income. Brush control, soil fertility, and irrigation-water management are the major soil-management concerns.

8. Western Rio Grande Plain Soils

The Western Rio Grande Plain comprises about 5.3 million acres in an area of Southwestern Texas from Del Rio to Rio Grande City. The landscape is nearly level to undulating except near the Rio Grande where it is hilly. Surface drainage is slow to rapid.

The major soils are mostly deep, brown or gray alkaline clays and loams. Some are saline.

Most of the soils are used for rangeland. Irrigated grain sorghums and vegetables are grown along the Rio Grande. Hunting leases are a major source of income. Brush control and limited soil moisture are the major soil-management problems.

9. Central Rio Grande Plain Soils

The Central Rio Grande Plain comprises about 5.9 million acres in an area of Southern Texas from Live Oak County to Hidalgo County. It Includes the South Texas Sand Sheet, an area of deep, sandy soils and active sand dunes. The landscape is nearly level to gently undulating. Surface drainage is slow to rapid.

Upland soils are mostly deep, light-colored, neutral to alkaline sands and loams. Many are saline or sodic. Bottomland soils are of minor extent.

Most of the area is used for raising beef cattle. A few areas, mostly in the northeast part, are used for growing grain sorghums, cotton and small grains. Hunting leases are a major source of income. Brush control is the major soil-management problem on rangeland; wind erosion and limited soil moisture are major concerns on cropland.

10. Lower Rio Grande Valley Soils

The Lower Rio Grande Valley comprises about 2.1 million acres in extreme southern Texas. The landscape is level to gently sloping with slow surface drainage.

Upland soils are mostly deep, grayish-brown, neutral to alkaline loams; coastal areas are mostly gray, silty clay loam and silty clay; some are saline. Bottomland soils are minor in extent.

Most of the soils are used for growing irrigated vegetables and citrus, along with cotton, grain sorghums and sugar cane. Some areas are used for growing beef cattle. Irrigation water management and wind erosion are the major soil-management problems on cropland; brush control is the major problem on rangeland.

11. Western Cross Timbers Soils

The Western Cross Timbers area comprises about 2.6 million acres. It includes the wooded section west of the Grand Prairie and extends from the Red River southward to the north edge of Brown County. The landscape is undulating and is dissected by many drainageways including the Brazos and Red rivers. Surface drainage is rapid.

Upland soils are mostly deep, grayish-brown, slightly acid loams with loamy and clayey subsoils. Bottomland soils along the major rivers are deep, reddish-brown, neutral to alkaline silt loams and clays.

The area is used mostly for grazing beef and dairy cattle on native range and improved pastures. Crops are peanuts, grain sorghums, small grains, peaches, pecans and vegetables. The major soil-management problems on grazing lands is brush control. Waste management on dairy farms is a more recent concern. Wind and water erosion are the major problems on cropland.

12. Eastern Cross Timbers Soils

The Eastern Cross Timbers area comprises about 1 million acres in a long narrow strip of wooded land that separates the northern parts of the Blackland Prairie and Grand Prairie and extends from the Red River southward to Hill County. The landscape is gently undulating to rolling and is dissected by many streams, including the Red and Trinity rivers. Sandstone-capped hills are prominent in some areas. Surface runoff is moderate to rapid.

The upland soils are mostly deep, light-colored, slightly acid sandy loams and loamy sands with reddish loamy or clayey subsoils. Bottomland soils are reddish-brown to dark gray, slightly acid to alkaline loams or gray clays.

Grassland consisting of native range and improved pastures is the major land use. Peanuts, grain sorghums, small grains, peaches, pecans and vegetables are grown in some areas. Brush control, water erosion and low fertility are the major concerns in soil management.

13. Grand Prairie Soils

The Grand Prairie comprises about 6.3 million acres in North Central Texas. It extends from the Red River to about the Colorado River between the Eastern and Western Cross Timbers in the northern part and just west of the Blackland Prairie in the southern part. The landscape is undulating to hilly and is dissected by many streams including the Red, Trinity and Brazos rivers. Surface drainage is rapid.

Upland soils are mostly dark-gray, alkaline clays; some are shallow over limestone and some are stony. Some areas have light-colored loamy soils over chalky limestone. Bottomland soils along the Red and Brazos rivers are reddish, silty loams and clays. Other bottomlands have dark-gray loams and clays.

Land use is a mixture of rangeland, pastureland and cropland. The area is mainly used for growing beef cattle. Some small grain, grain sorghums, corn and hay are grown. Brush control and water erosion are the major management concerns.

14. Blackland Prairie Soils

The Blackland Prairies consist of about 12.6 million acres of east-central Texas extending southwesterly from the Red River to Bexar County. There are smaller areas to the southeast. The landscape is undulating with few scattered wooded areas that are mostly in the bottomlands. Surface drainage is moderate to rapid.

Both upland and bottomland soils are deep, dark-gray to black alkaline clays. Some soils in the western part are shallow to moderately deep over chalk. Some soils on the eastern edge are neutral to slightly acid, grayish clays and loams over mottled clay subsoils (sometimes called graylands). Blackland soils are known as "cracking clays" because of the large, deep cracks that form in dry weather. This high shrink-swell property can cause serious damage to foundations, highways and other structures and is a safety hazard in pits and trenches.

Land use is divided about equally between cropland and grassland. Cotton, grain sorghums, corn, wheat, oats and hay are grown. Grassland is mostly improved pastures, with native range on the shallower and steeper soils. Water erosion, cotton root rot, soil tallith and brush control are the major management problems.

15. Claypan Area Soils

The Claypan Area consists of about 6.1 million acres in east-central Texas just east of the Blackland Prairie. The landscape is a gently undulating to rolling, moderately dissected woodland also known as the Post Oak Belt or Post Oak Savannah. Surface drainage is moderate.

Upland soils commonly have a thin, light-colored, acid sandy loam surface layer over dense, mottled red, yellow and gray claypan subsoils. Some deep, sandy soils with less clayey subsoils exist. Bottomlands are deep, highly fertile, reddish-brown to dark-gray loamy to clayey soils.

Land use is mainly rangeland. Some areas are in improved pastures. Most cropland is in bottomlands that are protected from flooding. Major crops are cotton, grain sorghums, corn, hay and forage crops, most of which are irrigated. Brush control on rangeland and irrigation water management on cropland are the major management problems. Water erosion is a serious problem on the highly erosive claypan soils, especially where they are overgrazed.

16. East Texas Timberland Soils

The East Texas Timberlands area comprise about 16.1 million acres of the forested eastern part of the state. The landscape is gently undulating to hilly and well dissected by many streams. Surface drainage is moderate to rapid.

This area has many kinds of upland soils but most are deep, light-colored, acid sands and loams over loamy and clayey subsoils. Deep sands are in scattered areas and red clays are in areas of "redlands." Bottomland soils are mostly brown to dark-gray, acid loams and some clays.

The land is used mostly for growing commercial pine timber and for woodland grazing. Improved pastures are scattered throughout and are used for grazing beef and dairy cattle and for hay production. Some commercial hardwoods are in the bottomlands. Woodland management problems include seedling survival, invasion of hardwoods in pine stands, effects of logging on water quality and control of the southern pine beetle. Lime and fertilizers are necessary for productive cropland and pastures.

17. Coast Prairie Soils

The Coast Prairie includes about 8.7 million acres near the Gulf Coast in southeast Texas. It ranges from 30 to 80 miles in width and parallels the coast from the Sabine River in Orange County to Baffin Bay in Kleberg County. The landscape is level to gently undulating with slow surface drainage.

Upland soils are mostly deep, dark-gray, neutral to slightly acid clay loams and clays. Lighter-colored and more-sandy soils are in a strip on the northwestern edge; some soils in the southern part are alkaline; some are saline and sodic. Bottomland soils are mostly deep, dark-colored clays and loams along small streams but are greatly varied along the rivers.

Land use is mainly grazing lands and cropland. Some hardwood timber is in the bottomlands. Many areas are also managed for wetland wildlife habitat. The nearly level topography and productive soils encourage farming. Rice, grain sorghums, cotton, corn and hay are main crops. Brush management on grasslands and removal of excess water on cropland are the major management concerns.

18. Coast Saline Prairies Soils

The Coast Saline Prairies area includes about 3.2 million acres along a narrow strip of wet lowlands adjacent to the coast; it includes the barrier islands that extend from Mexico to Louisiana. The surface is at or only a few feet above sea level with many areas of salt-water marsh. Surface drainage is very slow.

The soils are mostly deep, dark-colored clays and

loams; many are saline and sodic. Light-colored sandy soils are on the barrier islands. The water table is at or near the surface of most soils.

Cattle grazing is the chief economic use of the various salt-tolerant cordgrasses and sedges. Many areas are managed for wetland wildlife. Recreation is popular on the barrier islands. Providing fresh water and access to grazing areas are the major management concerns.

19. Flatwoods Soils

The Flatwoods area includes about 2.5 million acres of woodland in humid southeast Texas just north of the Coast Prairie and extending into Louisiana. The landscape is level to gently undulating. Surface drainage is slow.

Upland soils are mostly deep, light-colored, acid loams with gray, loamy or clayey subsoils. Bottomland soils are deep, dark-colored, acid clays and loams. The water table is near the surface at least part of the year.

The land is mainly used for forest; cattle are grazed in some areas. Woodland management problems include seedling survival, invasion of hardwoods in pine stands, effects of logging on water quality and control of the southern pine beetle. ☆

Water Resources

Beginning in September 1993, regulation of water quality of water resources of the state were placed in the jurisdiction of the **Texas Natural Resource Conservation Commission**. In addition, the **Texas Water Development Board** is responsible for the development of Texas water resources and the financing of facilities, such as dams, that are part of that development. The TWDB furnished the information for this section of the Texas Almanac.

Texas, through its river authorities, municipalities, water districts and state-level agencies, exercises the dominant role in development of municipal and industrial water supplies. Approximately 80 percent of the money invested in the state's water projects has been provided by Texas entities of government.

Ground-water Supplies and Use

Texas has historically relied on its wealth of fresh to slightly saline water that underlies more than 81 percent of the state. Fifty-six percent of the more than 13.5 million acre-feet of water currently being used in Texas is derived from underground sources that occupy nine major and 20 minor aquifers. Approximately 75 percent of the ground water produced is used for irrigating agricultural crops, especially in the Panhandle region. Ground water also supplies about 41 percent of the state's municipal needs.

Major Aquifers (see map on next page):

Ogallala - The Ogallala aquifer extends under 46 counties of the Texas Panhandle and is the southernmost extension of the largest aquifer (High Plains aquifer) in North America. The Ogallala Formation of late Miocene to early Pliocene age consists of heterogeneous sequences of coarse-grained sand and gravel in the lower part grading upward into clay, silt and fine sand. In Texas, the Panhandle is the most extensive region irrigated with ground water. Approximately 95 percent of the water pumped from the Ogallala is used for irrigation. Water-level declines are occurring in part of the aquifer region because of extensive pumping that far exceeds recharge. In 1994, water districts and other water-related entities began developing a regional management plan for achieving aquifer sustainability by more-efficient water use.

Gulf Coast Aquifer -The Gulf Coast aquifer forms an irregularly shaped belt that parallels the Texas coastline and extends through 54 counties from the Rio Grande northeastward to the Louisiana border. The aquifer system is composed of the water-bearing units of the **Catahoula, Oakville, Fleming, Goliad, Willis, Lissie, Bentley, Montgomery** and **Beaumont formations**. This system has been divided into three major water-producing components referred to as the **Chicot, Evangeline,** and **Jasper** aquifers. Municipal uses and irrigation account for about 45 percent each of the total pumage from the aquifer. Water quality is generally good northeast of the San Antonio River basin, but deteriorates to the southwest. Years of heavy pumage have caused significant water-level declines in portions of the aquifer. Some of these declines have resulted in significant **land-surface subsidence** particularly in the Houston-Galveston area.

Edwards (Balcones Fault Zone) - The Edwards (BFZ) aquifer forms a narrow belt extending through nine counties from a ground-water divide in Kinney County through the San Antonio area northeastward to the Leon River in Bell County. A poorly defined ground-water divide in Hays County hydrologically separates the aquifer into the San Antonio and Austin regions. Water in the aquifer occurs in fractures, honeycomb zones and solution channels in the Edwards and associated limestone formations of Cretaceous age. More than 50 percent of the pumage from the aquifer is for municipal use, while irrigation is the principal use in the western segment. San Antonio is one of the largest cities in the world that relies solely on a single ground-water source for its municipal supply. The aquifer also feeds several well-known recreational springs and underlies some of the most environmentally sensitive areas in the state.

Carrizo-Wilcox - Extending from the Rio Grande in South Texas northeastward into Arkansas and Louisiana, the Carrizo-Wilcox aquifer provides water to all or parts of 60 counties. The Wilcox Group and overlying Carrizo Sand form a hydrologically connected system of sand locally interbedded with clay, silt, lignite and gravel. Throughout most of its extent in Texas, the aquifer yields fresh to slightly saline water, which is used primarily for irrigation in the **Winter Garden District** of South Texas and for public supply and industrial use in Central and Northeast Texas. Because of excessive pumping, the water level in the aquifer has been significantly lowered, particularly in the artesian portion of the Winter Garden District of Atascosa, Frio and Zavala counties and in municipal and industrial areas located in Angelina and Smith counties.

Trinity Group - The Trinity aquifer consists of basal Cretaceous-age Trinity Group formations that extend from the Red River in North Texas to the Hill Country of Central Texas. Formations comprising the aquifer include the **Twin Mountains, Glen Rose** and **Paluxy**. Where the Glen Rose thins or is absent, the Twin Mountains and Paluxy formations coalesce to form the **Antlers Formation**. In the southern extent, the Trinity includes the Glen Rose and underlying Travis Peak formations. Water from the Antlers portion of the Trinity is used mainly for irrigation in the outcrop area of North and Central Texas. Elsewhere, water from the Trinity is used primarily for municipal and domestic supply. Extensive development of the Trinity aquifer in the Dallas-Fort Worth and Waco areas has historically resulted in water-level declines of several hundred feet.

Edwards-Trinity (Plateau) - This aquifer underlies the **Edwards Plateau**, extending from the Hill Country of Central Texas westward to the Trans-Pecos region. The aquifer consists of sandstone and limestone formations of theTrinity Group formations and limestones and dolomites of the Edwards and associated limestone formations. Ground-water movement in the aquifer is generally toward the southeast. Near the edge of the plateau, flow is toward the main streams, where the water issues from springs. Irrigation in the northwestern portion of the region accounts for approximately 70 percent of the total aquifer use and has resulted in significant water-level declines in Glasscock and Reagan counties. Elsewhere, the aquifer supplies fresh but hard water for municipal, domestic and livestock use. In 1993, the Edwards Aquifer Authority was created by the legislature regulate pumage from the aquifer for the benefit of all users - agricultural, municipal and environmental. The authority's jurisdiction extends from Uvalde County through a portion of Hays County. Barton Springs-Edwards Aquifer Conservation District provides aquifer management for the remaining portion of Hays and southern Travis counties.

Seymour - This aquifer consists of isolated areas of alluvium found in parts of 22 north-central and Panhandle counties in the upper Red River and Brazos River basins. Eastward-flowing streams during the Quaternary Period deposited discontinuous beds of poorly sorted gravel, sand, silt and clay that were later dissected by erosion, resulting in the isolated remnants of the formation. Individ-

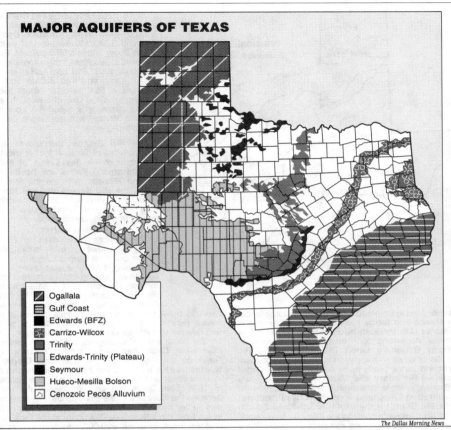

MAJOR AQUIFERS OF TEXAS

Legend:
- Ogallala
- Gulf Coast
- Edwards (BFZ)
- Carrizo-Wilcox
- Trinity
- Edwards-Trinity (Plateau)
- Seymour
- Hueco-Mesilla Bolson
- Cenozoic Pecos Alluvium

The Dallas Morning News

ual accumulations vary greatly in thickness, but most of the Seymour is less than 100 feet. The lower, more permeable part of the aquifer produces the greatest amount of ground water. Irrigation pumpage accounts for 90 percent of the total use. Water quality generally ranges from fresh to slightly saline. However, the salinity has increased in many heavily pumped areas to the point where the water has become unsuitable for domestic and municipal use. Natural salt pollution in the upper reaches of the Red and Brazos River basins precludes the full utilization of these water resources.

Hueco-Mesilla Bolson - These aquifers are located in El Paso and Hudspeth counties in far western Texas and occur in Quaternary basin-fill deposits that extend northward into New Mexico and westward into Mexico. The Hueco Bolson, located on the eastern side of the Franklin Mountains, consists of up to 9,000 feet of clay, silt, sand and gravel and is the principal source of drinking water for both El Paso and Juarez. Located west of the Franklin Mountains, the Mesilla Bolson reaches up to 2,000 feet in thickness and contains three separate water-producing zones. Ground-water depletion of the Hueco Bolson has become a serious problem. Historical large-scale groundwater withdrawals, especially for the municipal uses of El Paso and Juarez, have caused major water-level declines and significntly changed the direction of flow, causing a deterioration of the chemical quality of the ground water in the aquifer.

Cenozoic Pecos Alluvium - Located in the upper Pecos River Valley of West Texas, this aquifer is the principal source of water for irrigation in Reeves and northwestern Pecos counties and for industrial uses, power supply and municipal use elsewhere. Consisting of up to 1,500 feet of alluvial fill, the aquifer occupies two hydrologically separate basins: the Pecos Trough in the west and the Monument Draw Trough in the east. Water from the aquifer is generally hard and contains dissolved-solids concentra-

tions ranging from less than 300 to more than 5,000 parts per milion. Water-level declines in excess of 200 feet have historically occurred in Reeves and Pecos counties, but have moderated since the mid-1970s with the decrease in irrigation pumpage.

Major Rivers

Some **11,247 named streams** are identified in the **U.S. Geological Survey Geographic Names Information System.** Their combined length is about 80,000 miles, and they drain 263,513 square miles within Texas. **Thirteen major rivers** are described below, starting with the southernmost and moving northward:

Rio Grande

The Pueblo Indians called this river **P'osoge,** "river of great water." In 1582, Antonio de Espejo of Nueva Vizcaya, Mexico, followed the course of the **Río Conchos** to its confluence with a great river, which Espejo named **Río del Norte (River of the North).** The name **Rio Grande** was first given the stream apparently by the explorer **Juan de Oñate,** who arrived on its banks near present-day El Paso in 1598.

Thereafter the names were often consolidated, as **Río Grande del Norte.** It was shown also on early Spanish maps as **Río San Buenaventura** and **Río Ganapetuan.** In its lower course it early acquired the name **Río Bravo,** which is its name on most Mexican maps. At times it has also been known as **Río Turbio,** probably because of its muddy appearance during its frequent rises. Some people erroneously call this watercourse the **Rio Grande River.**

From source to mouth, the Rio Grande drops 12,000 feet to sea level as a snow-fed mountain torrent, desert stream and meandering coastal river. Along its banks and in its valley Indian civilizations developed, and Europeans made some of their first North American settlements.

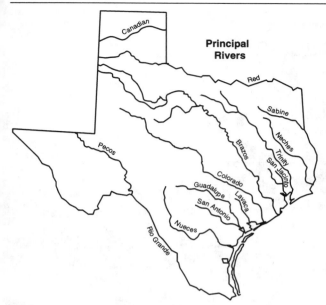

Principal Rivers

This river rises in Colorado, flows the north-south length of New Mexico and **forms the boundary of Texas and international U.S.-Mexican boundary for 889 to 1,254 river miles,** depending upon method of measurement. (See **Texas Boundary Line.)** The length of the Rio Grande, as of other rivers, depends on method of measurement and varies yearly as its course changes. Latest **International Boundary and Water Commission** figure is 1,896 miles, which is considerably below the 2,200-mile figure often used. Depending upon methods of measurement, the Rio Grande is the fourth- or fifth-longest North American river, exceeded only by the Missouri-Mississippi, McKenzie-Peace, St. Lawrence and possibly Yukon. Since all of these except the Missouri-Mississippi are partly in Canada, the Rio Grande is the **second-longest river entirely within or bordering the United States.** It is **Texas' longest river.**

The snow-fed flow of the Rio Grande is used for **irrigation** in Colorado below the San Juan Mountains, where the river rises at the Continental Divide. Turning south, it flows through a canyon in northern New Mexico and again irrigates a broad valley of central New Mexico. This is the oldest irrigated area of the United States, where Spanish missionaries encouraged Indian irrigation in the 1600s. Southern New Mexico impounds Rio Grande waters in Elephant Butte Reservoir for irrigation for 150 miles of valley above and below El Paso. Here is the **oldest irrigated area in Texas** and one of the oldest in the United States. Extensive irrigation practically exhausts the water supply. In this valley are situated the **three oldest towns in Texas — Ysleta, Socorro** and **San Elizario.** At the lower end of the El Paso irrigated valley, the upper Rio Grande virtually ends except in seasons of above-normal flow.

It starts as a perennially flowing stream again where the Río Conchos of Mexico flows into it at Presidio-Ojinaga. Through the **Big Bend** the Rio Grande flows through three successive **canyons,** the **Santa Elena,** the **Mariscal** and the **Boquillas.** The Santa Elena has a river bed elevation of 2,145 feet and a canyon-rim elevation of 3,661. Corresponding figures for Mariscal are 1,925 and 3,625, and for Boquillas, 1,850 and 3,490. The river here flows around the base of the **Chisos Mountains.** For about 100 miles the river is the southern boundary of **Big Bend National Park.** Below the Big Bend, the Rio Grande gradually emerges from mountains onto the Coastal Plains. A 191.2-mile strip on the American shore from Big Bend National Park downstream to the Terrell-Val Verde County line, has federal designation as the **Rio Grande Wild and Scenic River.**

At the confluence of the Rio Grande and the Devils River, the United States and Mexico have built **Amistad Dam,** to impound 3,383,900 acre-feet of water, of which Texas' share is 56.2 percent. **Falcon Reservoir,** also an international project, impounds 2,667,600 acre-feet of water, of which Texas' share in Zapata and Starr counties is 58.6 percent. Where the Rio Grande joins the Gulf of Mexico, has created a fertile delta called the **Lower Rio Grande Valley,** a major vegetable- and fruit-growing area.

The Rio Grande drains over 40,000 square miles of Texas. Principal tributaries flowing from the Texas side of the Rio Grande are the **Pecos** and **Devils** rivers. On the Mexican side are the **Río Conchos,** the **Río Salado** and the **Río San Juan.** About three-fourths of the water running into the Rio Grande below El Paso comes from the Mexican side.

Nueces River

The Nueces River rises in Edwards County and flows 315 miles to Nueces Bay on the Gulf near Corpus Christi.

Draining 17,000 square miles, it is a beautiful, **spring-fed stream** flowing through **canyons** until it issues from the **Balcones Escarpment** onto the Coastal Plain in northern Uvalde County. Alonso de León, in 1689, gave it its name. (Nueces, plural of nuez, means nuts in Spanish.) Much earlier, Cabeza de Vaca had referred to a **Río de las Nueces** in this region, probably the same stream. Its original Indian name seems to have been **Chotilapacquen.** Crossing Texas in 1691, Terán de los Ríos named the river **San Diego.** The Nueces was the boundary line between the Spanish provinces of Texas and Nuevo Santander. After the Revolution of 1836, both Texas and Mexico claimed the territory between the Nueces and the Rio Grande, a dispute which was settled by the **Treaty of Guadalupe Hidalgo** in 1848, which fixed the international boundary at the Rio Grande. Nueces runoff is about 620,000 acre-feet a year in its lower course. Principal water conservation projects are **Lake Corpus Christi** and **Choke Canyon Reservoir.** Principal tributaries of the Nueces are the **Frio** and the **Atascosa.**

San Antonio River

The San Antonio River has its source in **large springs** within and near the city limits of San Antonio. It flows 180 miles across the Coastal Plain to a junction with the **Guadalupe** near the Gulf Coast. Its channel through San Antonio has been developed into a parkway known as the River Walk. Its principal tributaries are the **Medina River** and **Cibolo Creek,** both spring-fed streams and this, with its spring origin, gives it a remarkably steady flow of clear water.

This stream was first named the **León** by Alonso de León in 1689. De León was not naming the stream for himself, but called it "lion" because its channel was filled with a rampaging flood.

Because of its limited and arid drainage area (4,200 square miles) the average runoff of the San Antonio River is relatively small, about 350,000 acre-feet annually near its mouth, but its flow, because of its springs, is one of the steadiest of Texas rivers.

Guadalupe River

The Guadalupe rises in its north and south prongs in the west-central part of Kerr County. A **spring-fed stream,** it flows eastward through the **Hill Country** until it issues from the **Balcones Escarpment** near New Braunfels. It then crosses the Coastal Plain to San Antonio Bay. Its total length is about 250 miles, and its drainage area is about 6,000 square miles. Its principal tributaries are the **San Marcos,** another spring-fed stream, which joins it in Gonzales County; the San Antonio, which joins it just above its mouth on San Antonio Bay; and the Comal, which joins it at New Braunfels. The **Comal River** has its source in large springs within the city limits of New Braunfels and flows only about 2.5 miles to the Guadalupe. It is the **shortest river in Texas** and also the **shortest river in the United States** carrying an equivalent amount of water.

There has been power development on the Guadalupe near Gonzales and Cuero for many years, and there is now power generation at **Canyon Lake.**

Because of its springs, and its considerable drainage area, the Guadalupe has an annual runoff of more than 1 million acre-feet in its lower course.

The name Guadalupe is derived from **Nuestra Señora de Guadalupe,** the name given the stream by Alonso de León.

Lavaca River

The Lavaca is considered a primary stream in the Texas Basin because it flows directly into the Gulf, through Lavaca Bay. Without a spring-water source and with only a small watershed, including that of its principal tributary, the **Navidad,** its flow is intermittent. The Spanish called it the Lavaca (cow) River because of the numerous bison they found. It is the principal stream running to the Gulf between the Guadalupe and the Colorado. The principal lake on the Navidad is **Lake Texana.** Runoff averages about 600,000 acre-feet yearly into the Gulf.

Colorado River

Measured by length and drainage area, the Colorado is the **largest river wholly in Texas.** (The drainage basin of the Brazos River extends into New Mexico.) Rising in Dawson County, the Colorado flows about 600 miles to Matagorda Bay on the Gulf. Its drainage area is 39,900 square miles. Its runoff reaches a volume of more than 2 million acre-feet near the Gulf. Its name is a Spanish word meaning **"reddish."** There is evidence that Spanish explorers originally named the muddy Brazos "Colorado," but Spanish mapmakers later transposed the two names.

The river flows through a rolling, mostly prairie terrain to the vicinity of San Saba County, where it enters the rugged **Hill Country** and **Burnet-Llano Basin.** It passes through a picturesque series of **canyons** until it issues from the **Balcones Escarpment** at Austin and flows across the Coastal Plain to the Gulf. In this area **the most remarkable series of reservoirs in Texas** has been built. There are two large reservoirs, **Lake Buchanan** in Burnet and Llano counties and **Lake Travis** in Travis County. Between these, in Burnet County, are three smaller reservoirs: **Inks, Johnson** (formerly **Granite Shoals**) and **Marble Falls,** built to aid power production from water running over the Buchanan Lake spillway. Below Lake Travis is the older **Lake Austin,** largely filled with silt, whose dam is used to produce power from waters flowing down from the lakes above. **Town Lake** is in the city of Austin. This area is known as **Highland Lakes Country.**

As early as the 1820s, Anglo-Americans settled on the banks of the lower Colorado, and in 1839 the **Capital Commission of the Republic of Texas** chose the picturesque area where the river flows from the **Balcones Escarpment** as the site of a new capital of the Republic — now **Austin,** capital of the state. The early colonists encouraged navigation along the lower channel with some success, and boats occasionally ventured as far upstream as Austin. However, a **natural log "raft"** in the channel near the Gulf blocked river traffic. Conservation and utilization of the waters of the Colorado are under jurisdiction of three agencies created by the state Legislature, the **Lower, Central** and **Upper Colorado River Authorities.**

The principal tributaries of the Colorado are the several prongs of the **Concho River** on its upper course, the **Pecan Bayou** (farthest west **"bayou"** in the United States) and the **Llano, San Saba** and **Pedernales** rivers. All except the Pecan Bayou flow into the Colorado from the **Edwards Plateau** and are spring-fed, perennially flowing. In the numerous mussels found along these streams occasional **pearls** have been found. The Middle Concho was designated on early Spanish maps as **Río de las Perlas.**

Brazos River

The Brazos is the largest river between the Rio Grande and the Red River and is **third in size** of all rivers in Texas. It rises in three upper forks, the **Double Mountain, Salt** and **Clear forks** of the Brazos. The Brazos River proper is considered as beginning where the Double Mountain and Salt Forks flow together in Stonewall County. The Clear Fork joins this main stream in Young County, just above **Possum Kingdom Lake.** The Brazos crosses most of the main physiographic regions of Texas — High Plains, West Texas Lower Rolling Plains, Western Cross Timbers, Grand Prairie and Gulf Coastal Plain.

The total length from the source of its longest upper prong, the Double Mountain Fork, to the mouth of the main stream at the Gulf, was reported to be 923.2 miles in a 1970 study by the Army Corps of Engineers. The drainage area is about 42,800 square miles. It flows directly into the Gulf near Freeport. Its annual runoff at places along its lower channel exceeds 5 million acre-feet.

The original name of this river was **Brazos de Dios,** meaning "Arms of God." There are several legends as to why. One is that the Coronado expedition, wandering on the trackless **Llano Estacado,** exhausted its water and was threatened with death from thirst. Arriving at the bank of the river they gave it the name of Brazos de Dios in thankfulness. Another is that a ship exhausted its water supply and its crew was saved when they found the mouth of the Brazos. Still another story is that miners on the San Saba were forced by drouth to seek water near present-day Waco and in gratitude called it Brazos de Dios.

Much early Anglo-American colonization of Texas took place in the Brazos Valley. Along its channel were **San Felipe de Austin,** capital of Austin's colony, **Washington-on-the-Brazos,** where Texans declared independence, and other historic settlements. There was some **navigation of the lower channel** of the Brazos in this period. Near its mouth it intersects the **Gulf Intracoastal Waterway,** which provides connection with the commerce on the Mississippi.

Most of the Brazos Valley lies within the boundaries of the **Brazos River Authority,** which conducts a multipurpose program for development. A large reservoir on the Brazos is **Whitney Lake** (622,800 acre-feet capacity) on the main channel, where it is the boundary line between Hill and Bosque counties. Another large reservoir is **Possum Kingdom Lake** in Palo Pinto, Stephens, Young and Jack counties. **Waco Lake** on the Bosque and **Belton Lake** on the Leon are among the principal reservoirs on its tributaries. In addition to its three upper forks, other chief tributaries are the **Paluxy, Little** and **Navasota** rivers.

San Jacinto River

A short river with a drainage basin of 3,976 square miles and nearly 2 million acre-feet runoff, the San Jacinto runs directly to the Gulf through Galveston Bay. It is formed by the junction of its East and West forks in the northeastern part of Harris County. Its total length, including the East Fork, is about 85 miles. There are two stories of the origin of its name. One is that when early explorers discovered it, its channel was choked with hyacinth ("jacinto" is the Spanish word for hyacinth). The other is that it was discovered on Aug. 17, St. Hyacinth's Day. Through the lower course of the San Jacinto and its tributary, **Buffalo Bayou,** runs the **Houston Ship Channel** connecting the Port of Houston with the Gulf. On the shore of the San Jacinto was fought the **Battle of San Jacinto,** April 21, 1836, in which Texas won its independence from Mexico. The **San Jacinto State Park and monument** are there. **Lake Conroe** is on the **West Fork,** and **Lake Houston** is located at the junction of the West Fork and the **East Fork.**

Trinity River

The Trinity rises in its East Fork, Elm Fork, West Fork and Clear Fork in Grayson, Montague, Archer and Parker counties, respectively. The main stream begins with the junction of the Elm and West forks at Dallas. Its length is 550 river miles and its drainage area, 17,969 square miles. Because of moderate to heavy rainfall over its drainage area, it has a flow of 5,800,000 acre-feet near its mouth on the Gulf, exceeded only by the Neches, Red and Sabine River basins.

The Trinity derives its name from the Spanish **"Trinidad."** Alonso de León named it **La Santísima Trinidad** (the Most Holy Trinity).

Navigation was developed along its lower course with several riverport towns, such as **Sebastopol** in Trinity

Looking toward Mexico across the Rio Grande near Del Rio. Dallas Morning News file photo.

County. For many years there has been a basin-wide movement for navigation, conservation and utilization of its water. The **Trinity River Authority** is a state agency and the **Trinity Improvement Association** is a publicly supported nonprofit organization advocating its development.

The Trinity has in its valley **more large cities, greater population and more industrial development** than any other river basin in Texas. On the Lower Coastal Plain there is large use of its waters for **rice irrigation**. Largest reservoir on the Elm Fork is **Lewisville Lake** (formerly **Garza-Little Elm** and **Lake Dallas**). There are four reservoirs above Fort Worth — **Lake Worth, Eagle Mountain** and **Bridgeport** on the West Fork and **Benbrook Lake** on the Clear Fork. **Lavon Lake** in southeast Collin County and **Lake Ray Hubbard** in Collin, Dallas, Kaufman and Rockwall counties are on the East Fork. **Livingston Lake** is in Polk, San Jacinto, Trinity and Walker counties. The three major reservoirs below the Dallas-Fort Worth area are **Cedar Creek Reservoir** and **Richland-Chambers Reservoir**.

Neches River

The Neches is in East Texas, with total length of about 416 miles and drainage area of 10,011 square miles. Abundant rainfall all over its entire basin gives it a flow near the Gulf of about 6 million acre-feet a year. The river takes its name from the **Neches Indians** that the early Spanish explorers found living along its banks. Principal tributary of the Neches, and comparable with the Neches in length and flow above their confluence, is the **Angelina River**, so named from **Angelina (Little Angel)**, a Hainai Indian girl who converted to Christianity and played an important role in the early development of this region.

Both the Neches and the Angelina run most of their courses in the **Piney Woods** and there was much settlement along them as early as the 1820s. **Sam Rayburn (McGee Bend) Reservoir**, near Jasper on the Angelina River, was completed and dedicated in 1965.

Reservoirs located on the Neches River include **Lake Palestine** in the upper portion of the basin and **B. A. Steinhagen Lake** located at the junction of the Neches and the Angellina rivers.

Sabine River

The Sabine River is formed by three forks rising in Collin and Hunt counties. From its sources to its mouth on **Sabine Lake**, it flows approximately 360 miles and drains 9,733 square miles. Sabine comes from the **Spanish word for cypress**, as does the name of the **Sabinal River**, which flows into the Frio in Southwest Texas. The Sabine has the largest water discharge (6.8 million acre-feet) at its mouth of any Texas river. Throughout most of Texas history the lower Sabine has been the **eastern Texas boundary line**, though for a while there was doubt as to whether the Sabine or the Arroyo Hondo, east of the Sabine in Louisiana, was the boundary. For a number of years the outlaw-infested **neutral ground** lay between them. There was also a **boundary dispute** in which it was alleged that the Neches was really the Sabine and, there-

fore, the boundary.

Travelers over the **Camino Real**, or **Old San Antonio Road**, crossed the Sabine at the famous **Gaines Ferry**, and there were famous crossings for the **Atascosito Road** and other travel and trade routes of that day.

Two of Texas' larger man-made reservoirs have been created by dams constructed on the Sabine River. The first of these is **Lake Tawakoni**, in Hunt, Rains and Van Zandt counties, with a capacity of 936,200 acre-feet. **Toledo Bend Reservoir** impounds 4,472,900 acre-feet of water on the Sabine in Newton, Panola, Sabine and Shelby counties. This is a joint project of Texas and Louisiana, through the **Sabine River Authority**.

Red River

The Red River (1,360 miles) is **exceeded in length only by the Rio Grande** among rivers associated with Texas. Its original source is water in Curry County, New Mexico, near the Texas boundary, forming a definite channel as it crosses Deaf Smith County, Texas, in tributaries that flow into **Prairie Dog Town Fork of the Red River**. These waters carve the spectacular **Palo Duro Canyon** of the High Plains before the Red River leaves the **Caprock Escarpment**, flowing eastward.

Where the Red River crosses the 100th meridian, the river becomes the **Texas-Oklahoma boundary** and is soon joined by the Salt Fork to form the main channel. Its length across the Panhandle is about 200 miles and, from the Panhandle east, it is the Texas-Oklahoma boundary line for 440 miles and thereafter the **Texas-Arkansas boundary** for 40 miles before it flows into Arkansas, where it swings south to flow through Louisiana. The Red River is a part of the **Mississippi drainage basin**, and at one time it emptied all of its water into the Mississippi. In recent years, however, part of its water, especially at flood stage, has flowed to the Gulf via the **Atchafalaya**.

The Red River takes its name from the red color of the current. This caused every explorer who came to its banks to call it "red" regardless of the language he spoke — **Río Rojo** or **Río Roxo** in Spanish, **Riviere Rouge** in French and **Red River** in English. The Spanish and French names were often found on maps until the middle of the last century when the English came to be generally accepted. At an early date, the river became the axis for French advance from Louisiana northwestward as far as present-day Montague County. There was consistent **early navigation** of the river from its mouth on the Mississippi to Shreveport, above which navigation was blocked by a **natural log raft**. A number of important gateways into Texas from the North were established along the stream such as **Pecan Point** and **Jonesborough** in Red River County, **Colbert's Ferry** and **Preston** in Grayson County and, later, **Doan's Store Crossing** in Wilbarger County. The river was a menace to the early traveler because of both its variable current and its **quicksands**, which brought disaster to many a trail herd cow as well as ox team and covered wagon.

The largest water conservation project on the Red River is **Texoma Lake**, which is the **largest lake** lying wholly or partly in Texas and the **tenth-largest reservoir (in capacity) in the United States**. Its capacity is 5,382,000 acre feet. Texas' share is 2,722,000.

Red River water's high content of salt and other minerals limits its usefulness along its upper reaches. Ten **salt springs** and tributaries in Texas and Oklahoma contribute most of these minerals.

The uppermost tributary of the Red River in Texas is **Tierra Blanca Creek**, which rises in Curry County, N.M., and flows easterly across Deaf Smith and Randall counties to become the **Prairie Dog Town Fork** a few miles east of Canyon. Other principal tributaries in Texas are the **Pease** and the **Wichita** in North Central Texas and the **Sulphur** in Northeast Texas, which flows into the Red River after it has crossed the boundary line into Arkansas. The last major tributary in Northeast Texas is **Cypress Creek**, which flows into Louisiana before joining with the Red River. Major reservoirs on the Northeast Texas tributaries are **Wright Patman Lake, Lake O' the Pines** and

Caddo Lake. From Oklahoma the principal tributary is the **Washita**. The **Ouachita**, a river with the same pronunciation of its name, though spelled differently, is the principal tributary to its lower course.

Canadian River

The Canadian River heads near **Raton Pass** in northern New Mexico near the Colorado boundary line and flows into Texas on the west line of Oldham County. It crosses the Texas Panhandle into Oklahoma and there flows into the Arkansas. Most of its course across the Panhandle is in a deep gorge. A tributary dips into Texas'

northern Panhandle and then flows to a confluence with the main channel in Oklahoma. One of several theories as to how the Canadian got its name is that some early explorers thought it flowed into Canada. **Lake Meredith**, formed by Sanford Dam on the Canadian, provides water for 11 Panhandle cities.

Because of the **deep gorge** and the **quicksand** at many places, the Canadian has been a peculiarly difficult stream to bridge. It is known especially in its lower course in Oklahoma as outstanding among the streams of the country for great amount of quicksand in its channel. ☆

Lakes and Reservoirs

The large increase in the number of reservoirs in Texas during the past half-century has greatly improved water conservation and supplies. As late as 1913, Texas had only eight major reservoirs with a total storage capacity of 376,000 acre-feet. Most of this capacity was in Medina Lake, with 254,000 acre-feet capacity, created by a dam completed in May 1913. (An acre-foot is the amount of water necessary to cover an acre of surface area with water one foot deep.)

By 1920, Texas had 11 major reservoirs with combined storage capacity of 449,710 acre-feet. The state water agency reported 32 reservoirs and 1,284,520 acre-feet capacity in 1930. By 1950, this number had increased to 66 with 9,623,870 acre-feet capacity and to 168 with total capacity of 53,302,400 acre-feet in 1980. By January 1995, Texas had 203 major reservoirs (those with a normal capacity of 5,000 acre-feet or larger) existing or under construction, with a total conservation surface area of 861,381 acres and a conservation storage capacity of 41,822,945 acre-feet.

According to the U.S. Statistical Abstract of 1996, Texas has **4,959 square miles of inland water,** ranking it first in the 48 contiguous states, followed by Minnesota, with 4,780 sq. mi.; Florida, 4,683; and Louisiana, 4,153. There are about **6,736 reservoirs** in Texas with a normal storage capacity of 10 acre-feet or larger.

The following table lists reservoirs in Texas having **more than 5,000 acre-feet capacity**. With few exceptions, the listed reservoirs are those that were completed by Jan. 1, 1997, and in use. An asterisk (*) indicates those that are under construction.

Conservation storage capacity is used in the table below; the surface area used is that area at conservation elevation only. (Different methods of computing capacity area used; detailed information may be obtained from the Texas Water Development Board, Austin; U.S. Army Corps of Engineers; or local sources.) Also, it should be noted that boundary reservoir capacities include water designated for Texas use and non-Texas water, as well.

In the list below, information is given in the following order: (1) Name of lake or reservoir; (2) county or counties in which located; (3) river or creek on which located; (4) location with respect to some city or town; (5) purpose of reservoir; (6) owner of reservoir. Some of these items, when not listed, are not available. For the larger lakes and reservoirs, the dam impounding water to form the lake bears the same name, unless otherwise indicated. Abbreviations in the list below are as follows: L., lake; R., river; Co., county; Cr., creek; (C) conservation; (FC) flood control; (R) recreation; (P) power; (M) municipal; (D) domestic; (Ir.) irrigation; (In.) industry; (Mi.) mining, including oil production; (FH) fish hatchery; USAE, United States Army Corps of Engineers; WC&ID, Water Control and Improvement District; WID, Water Improvement District; USBR, United States Bureau of Reclamation.

Lakes and Reservoirs	Conservation Service Area (Acres)	Conservation Storage Capacity (Acre-Ft.)
Abilene L. — Taylor Co.; Elm Cr.; 6 mi. NW Tuscola; (M-In.-R); City of Abilene	595	7,900
Alcoa L. — Milam Co.; Sandy Cr.; 7 mi. SW Rockdale; (In.-R); Aluminum Co. of America	880	14,750
Alan Henry Reservoir — Garza Co.; Double Mountain Fork Brazos River, 10 mi. E Justiceburg; (M-In.-Ir.); City of Lubbock	3,504	115,937
Amistad Reservoir — Val Verde Co.; Rio Grande, dam between Del Rio and confluence of Rio Grande and Devils River; an international project of the U.S. and Mexico; 12 mi. NWDel Rio; (C-R-Ir.-P-FC); International Boundary and Water Com. (Texas' share of conservation capacity is 56.2 percent.) (Formerly **Diablo R.**)	64,900	3,383,900
Amon G. Carter, L. — Montague Co.; Big Sandy Cr.; 6 mi. S Bowie; (M-In.); City of Bowie	1,540	20,050
Anahuac L. — Chambers Co.; Turtle Bayou; near Anahuac; (Ir.-In.-Mi.); Chambers-Liberty Counties Navigation District.	5,300	35,300
Anzalduas Channel Dam — Hidalgo Co.; Rio Grande; 11 mi. upstream from Hidalgo; (Ir.-FC); United States and Mexico	—	8,400
Aquilla L. — Hill Co.; Aquilla Cr.; 10.2 mi. W of Hillsboro; (FC-M-Ir.-In.-R); USAE-Brazos R. Auth.	3,280	52,400
Arlington L. — Tarrant Co.; Village Cr.; 7 mi. W Arlington; (M-In.); City of Arlington	2,275	45,710
Arrowhead, L. — Clay Co.; Little Wichita R.; 13 mi. SE Wichita Falls; (M); City of Wichita Falls.	16,200	262,100
Athens, L. — Henderson Co.; 8 mi. E Athens; (M-FC-R); Athens Mun. Water Authority (formerly **Flat Creek Reservoir**).	1,520	32,690
Aubrey R. — (see **Ray Roberts L.**)	—	—
Austin, L. — Travis Co.; Colorado R.; W Austin city limits; (M-In.-P); City of Austin, leased to LCRA (impounded by **Tom Miller Dam**).	1,830	21,000
Ballinger L. — Runnels Co.; Valley Creek; 5 mi. W Ballinger; (M); City of Ballinger (also known as **Moonen Lake**).	—	6,850
Balmorhea, L. — Reeves Co.; Sandia Cr.; 3 mi. SE Balmorhea; (Ir.); Reeves Co. WID No. 1	573	6,350
Bardwell L. — Ellis Co.; Waxahachie Cr.; 3 mi. SE Bardwell; (FC-C-R); USAE	3,570	53,580
Barney M. Davis Cooling Reservoir — Nueces Co.; off-channel storage reservoir of Laguna Madre arm of Gulf; 14 mi. SE Corpus Christi; (In.); Central Power & Light Co.	1,100	6,600
Bastrop, L. — Bastrop Co.; Spicer Cr.; 3 mi. NE Bastrop; (In.); LCRA	906	16,590
Baylor Creek L. — Childress Co.; 10 mi. NW Childress; (M-R); City of Childress	610	9,220
Belton L. — Bell-Coryell counties; Leon R.; 3 mi. N. Belton; (M-FC-In.-Ir.); USAE-Brazos R. Auth.	12,300	457,300
Benbrook L. — Tarrant Co.; Clear Fk. Trinity R.; 10 mi. SW Fort Worth; (FC-R); USAE	3,770	88,200

	Acres	Acre-Feet
Big Brown Creek Reservoir — Freestone Co. (see **Fairfield L.**)	—	—
Big Hill Reservoir — Jefferson Co. (see **J. D. Murphree Area Impoundments**)	—	—
Bivins L. — Randall Co.; Palo Duro Cr.; 8 mi. NW Canyon; (M); Amarillo (also known as **Amarillo City Lake**); City of Amarillo	379	5,120
Blackburn Crossing L. — (see **Lake Palestine**)		
Bonham, L. — Fannin Co.; Timber Cr.; 5 mi. NE Bonham; (M); Bonham Mun. Water Auth.	1,020	12,000
Bowie L. — (see **Amon G. Carter, L.**)		
Brady Creek Reservoir — McCulloch Co.; Brady Cr.; 3 mi. W Brady; (M-In.); City of Brady.	2,020	29,110
Brandy Branch Reservoir — Harrison Co.; Brandy Br.; 10 mi. SW Marshall; (In.); Southwestern Electric Power Co.	1,240	29,500
Brazoria Reservoir — Brazoria Co.; off-channel reservoir; 1 mi. NE Brazoria; (In.); Dow Chemical Co.	1,865	21,970
Bridgeport, L. — Wise-Jack counties; W. Fk. of Trinity R.; 4 mi. W Bridgeport; (M-In.-FC-R); Tarrant Co. WC&ID Dist. No. 1	13,000	386,420
Brownwood, L. — Brown Co.; Pecan Bayou; 8 mi. N Brownwood; (M-In.-Ir.); Brown Co. WC&ID No. 1..	7,300	143,400
Brushy Creek Reservoir — (see **Valley L.**)	—	—
Bryan Utilities L. — Brazos Co.; unnamed stream; 6 mi. NW Bryan; (R-In.); City of Bryan	829	15,227
Buchanan, L. — Burnet-Llano-San Saba counties; Colorado R.; 13 mi. W Burnet; (M-Ir.-Mi-P); LCRA	23,060	955,200
Buffalo Springs L. — Lubbock Co.; Double Mtn.Fk. Brazos R.; 9 mi. SE Lubbock; (M-In.-R); Lubbock Co. WC & ID No. 1; (impounded by **W. G. McMillan Sr. Dam**)	200	4,200
Caddo L. — Harrison-Marion counties, Texas and Caddo Parish, La. An original natural lake, whose surface and capacity were increased by construction of dam on Cypress Creek near Mooringsport, La.	25,400	59,800
Calaveras L. — Bexar Co.; Calaveras Cr.; 15 mi. SE San Antonio; (In.); Pub. Svc. Bd. of San Antonio	3,450	61,800
Camp Creek L. — Robertson Co.; 13 mi. E Franklin; (R); Camp Creek Water Co.	750	8,550
Canyon L. — Comal Co.; Guadalupe R.; 12 mi. NW New Braunfels; (M-In.-P-FC); Guadalupe-Blanco R. Authority & USAE	8,240	385,600
Casa Blanca L. — Webb Co.; Chacon Cr.; 3 mi. NE Laredo; (R); Webb County (impounded by **Country Club Dam**)	1,656	20,000
Cedar Bayou Cooling Reservoir — Chambers Co.; Cedar Bayou; 15 mi. SW Anahuac; (In.); Houston Lighting & Power Co.	2,600	20,000
Cedar Creek Reservoir — Henderson-Kaufman counties; Cedar Cr.; 3 mi. NE Trinidad; (also called **Joe B. Hogsett, L.**); (M-R); Tarrant Co. WC&ID No. 1.	33,750	679,200
Cedar Creek Reservoir — Fayette Co.; Cedar Cr.; 8.5 mi. E. La Grange; (In.); LCRA.	2,420	71,400
Champion Creek Reservoir — Mitchell Co.; 7 mi. S. Colorado City; (M-In.); Texas Electric Service Co..	1,560	41,600
Chapman L., Jim — (formerly Cooper Lake) Delta-Hopkins counties; Sulphur R.; 3 mi.SE Cooper; (FC-M-R); USAE.	19,305	310,000
Cherokee L. — Gregg-Rusk counties; Cherokee Bayou; 12 mi. SE Longview; (M-In.-R); Cherokee Water Co.	3,987	46,700
Choke Canyon Reservoir — Live Oak-McMullen counties; Frio R.; 4 mi. W Three Rivers; (M-In.-R-FC); City of Corpus Christi-USBR	26,000	690,400
Cisco, L. — Eastland Co.; Sandy Cr.; 4 mi. N. Cisco; (M); City of Cisco (impounded by **Williamson Dam**)	445	8,800
Cleburne, L. Pat — Johnson Co.; Nolan R.; 4 mi. S. Cleburne; (M); City of Cleburne	1,550	25,300
Clyde, L. — Callahan Co.; N. Prong Pecan Bayou; 6 mi. S. Clyde; (M); City of Clyde and USDA Soil Conservation Service	449	5,748
Coffee Mill L. — Fannin Co.; Coffee Mill Cr.; 12 mi. NW Honey Grove; (R); U.S. Forest Service	650	8,000
Coleman L. — Coleman Co.; Jim Ned Cr.; 14 mi. N. Coleman; (M-In.); City of Coleman	2,000	40,000
Coleto Creek Reservoir — Goliad-Victoria counties; Coleto Cr.; 12 mi. SW Victoria; (In); Guadalupe-Blanco River Auth.	3,100	35,080
Colorado City, L. — Mitchell Co.; Morgan Cr.; 4 mi. SW Colorado City; (M-In.-P); Texas Electric Service Co.	1,612	30,800
Conroe, L. — Montgomery-Walker counties; W. Fk. San Jacinto R.; 7 mi. NW Conroe; (M-In.-Mi.); San Jacinto River Authority, City of Houston and Texas Water Dev. Bd.	20,985	429,900
Cooper L. — (see **Chapman Lake, Jim**)		
Corpus Christi, L. — Live Oak-San Patricio-Jim Wells counties; Nueces R.; 4 mi. SW Mathis; (P-M-In.-Ir.-Mi.-R.); Lower Nueces River WSD (impounded by **Wesley E. Seale Dam**).	19,336	269,900
Crook, L. — Lamar Co.; Pine Cr.; 5 Mi. N. Paris; (M); City of Paris	1,226	9,964
Cypress Springs, L. — Franklin Co.; Big Cypress Cr.; 8 mi. SE Mount Vernon; (In-M); Franklin Co. WD and Texas Water Development Board (formerly **Franklin Co. L.**); impounded by **Franklin Co. Dam**)	3,400	66,800
Dallas, L. — (see **Lewisville L.**)	—	—
Dam B Reservoir — (see **Steinhagen L., B.A.**)	—	—
Daniel, L. — Stephens Co.; Gunsolus Cr.; 7 mi. S Breckenridge; (M-In.); City of Breckenridge; (impounded by **Gunsolus Creek Dam**)	924	9,515
Davis L. — Knox Co.; Double Dutchman Cr.; 5 mi. SE Benjamin; (Ir); League Ranch	585	5,395
Decker L. — (see **Walter E. Long L.**)	—	—
DeCordova Bend Reservoir — (see **Granbury Lake**)		
Delta Lake Res. Units 1 and 2 — Hidalgo Co.; Rio Grande (off channel); 4 mi. N. Monte Alto; (Ir.); Hidalgo-Willacy counties WC&ID No. 1 (formerly **Monte Alto Reservoir**).	2,371	25,000
Diablo Reservoir — (see **Amistad Reservoir**)	—	—
Diversion, L. — Archer-Baylor counties; Wichita R.; 14 mi. W Holliday; (M-In.); City of Wichita Falls and Wichita Co. WID No. 2	3,419	40,000
Dunlap, L. — Guadalupe Co.; Guadalupe R.; 9 mi. NW Seguin; (P); Guadalupe-Blanco R. Auth.; (impounded by **TP-1 Dam**)	410	3,550
Eagle L. — Colorado Co.; Colorado R. (off channel); in Eagle Lake; (Ir.); Lakeside Irrigation Co.	1,200	9,600
Eagle Mountain Lake — Tarrant-Wise counties; W. Fk. Trinity R.; 14 mi. NW Fort Worth; (M-In.-Ir.); Tarrant Co. WC&ID No. 1	9,200	190,300
East L. — (see **Victor Braunig Lake**)	—	—
Eddleman L. — (see **Graham Lake**)	—	—
Edinburg L. — (see **Retama Reservoir**)	—	—
Electra City L. — Wilbarger Co.; Camp Cr. and Beaver Cr.; 7 mi. SW Electra; (In.-M); City of Electra	660	8,055
Ellison Creek Reservoir — Morris Co.; Ellison Cr.; 8 mi. S. Daingerfield; (P-In.); Lone Star Steel	1,516	24,700
Fairfield L. — Freestone Co.; Big Brown Cr.; 11 mi. NE Fairfield; (In.); TP&L, Texas Elec. Service Co., DP&L and Industrial Generating Co. (formerly **Big Brown Creek Reservoir**)	2,350	50,600

Reservoir	Conservation capacity	Surface area
Falcon Reservoir — Starr-Zapata counties; Rio Grande; (International—U.S.-Mexico); 3 mi. W Falcon Heights; (M-In.-Ir.-FC-P-R); International Boundary and Water Com.; (Texas' share of total conservation capacity is 58.6 per cent)	87,210	2,667,600
Farmers Creek Reservoir — Montague Co.; 8 mi. NE Nocona; (M-In.-Mi.) N Montague County Water Supply District (also known as **Lake Nocona**)	1,470	25,400
Ferrell's Bridge Dam Reservoir — (see **Lake O' the Pines**)	—	—
Flat Creek Reservoir — (see **Athens, Lake**)	—	—
Forest Grove Reservoir — Henderson Co.; Caney Cr.; 7 mi. NW Athens; (In.); Texas Utilities Services, Inc., Agent	1,502	20,038
Forney Reservoir — (see **Ray Hubbard, Lake**)	—	—
Fort Phantom Hill, Lake — Jones Co.; Elm Cr.; 5 mi. S. Nugent; (M-R); City of Abilene	4,246	74,300
Franklin County L. — (see **Cypress Springs, Lake**)	—	—
Galveston County Industrial Water Reservoir — Galveston Co.; off-channel storage Dickinson Bayou; 16 mi. S La Porte; (In.-M.); Galveston Co. Water Auth.	812	7,308
Garza-Little Elm — (see **Lewisville L.**)	—	—
Georgetown, L. — Williamson Co.; N. Fk. San Gabriel R.; 3.5 mi. W Georgetown; (FC-M-In.); USAE (formerly **North Fork L.**)	1,310	37,050
Gibbons Creek Reservoir — Grimes Co.; Gibbons Cr.; 9.5 mi NW Anderson; (In.); Texas Mun. Power Agency	2,490	26,824
Gladewater, L. — Upshur Co.; Glade Cr.; in Gladewater; (M-R); City of Gladewater	800	6,950
Graham L. — Young Co.; Flint and Salt Creeks; 2 mi. NW Graham; (M-In.); City of Graham	2,550	45,000
Granbury L. — Hood-Parker counties; Brazos R.; 8 mi. SE Granbury; (M-In.-Ir.-P); Brazos River Authority (impounded by **DeCordova Bend Dam**)	8,700	151,300
Granger L. — Williamson Co.; San Gabriel R.; 10 mi. NE Taylor; (FC-M-In.); USAE (formerly **Laneport L.**)	4,400	64,540
Granite Shoals L. — (see **Johnson L., Lyndon B.**)	—	—
Grapevine L. — Tarrant-Denton counties; Denton Cr.; 2 mi. NE Grapevine; (M-FC-In.-R.); USAE	7,380	187,700
Greenbelt L. — Donley Co.; Salt Fk. Red R.; 5 mi. N Clarendon; (M-In.); Greenbelt M&I Water Auth.	1,990	58,200
H-4 Reservoir — Gonzales Co.; Guadalupe R.; 4.5 mi. SE Belmont; (P); Guadalupe- Blanco R. Auth. (also called **Guadalupe Reservoir H-4**)	696	5,200
Halbert, L. — Navarro Co.; Elm Cr.; 4 mi. SE Corsicana; (M-In-R); City of Corsicana	650	7,420
Harris Reservoir — Brazoria Co.; off-channel between Brazos R. and Oyster Cr.; 8 mi. NW Angleton; (In.); Dow Chemical Co.	1,663	12,000
Hawkins, L. — Wood Co.; Little Sandy Cr.; 3 mi. NW Hawkins; (FC-R); Wood County; (impounded by **Wood Co. Dam No. 3**)	776	11,570
Holbrook L. — Wood Co.; Keys Cr.; 4 mi. NW Mineola; (FC-R); Wood County; (impounded by **Wood Co. Dam No. 2**)	653	7,770
Honea Reservoir — (see **Conroe, Lake**)	—	—
Hords Creek L. — Coleman Co.; Hords Cr.; 5 mi. NW Valera; (M-FC); City of Coleman and USAE	510	8,600
Houston County L. — Houston Co.; Little Elkhart Cr.; 10 mi. NW Crockett; (M-In.); Houston Co. WC&ID No. 1	1,282	19,500
Houston, L. — Harris Co.; San Jacinto R.; 4 mi. N Sheldon; (M-In.-Ir.-Mi.-R); City of Houston; (impounded by **Lake Houston Dam**)	12,240	140,500
Hubbard Creek Reservoir — Stephens Co.; 6 mi. NW Breckenridge; (M-In.-Mi.); West Central Texas Mun. Water Authority	15,250	317,800
Imperial Reservoir — Reeves-Pecos counties; Pecos R.; 35 mi. N Fort Stockton; (Ir.); Pecos County WC&ID No. 2	1,530	6,000
Inks L. — Burnet-Llano counties; Colorado R.; 12 mi. W Burnet; (M-Ir.-Mi.-P); LCRA	803	17,540
Iron Bridge Dam L. — (see **Tawakoni, Lake**)	—	—
Jacksonville, L. — Cherokee Co.; Gum Cr.; 5 mi. SW Jacksonville; (M-R); City of Jacksonville; (impounded by **Buckner Dam**)	1,320	30,500
J. B. Thomas, L. — Scurry-Borden counties; Colorado R.; 16 mi. SW Snyder; (M- In.-R); Colorado River Mun. Water Dist.; (impounded by **Colorado R. Dam**)	7,820	202,300
J. D. Murphree Wildlife Management Area Impoundments — Jefferson Co.; off-channel reservoirs between Big Hill and Taylor Bayous; at Port Acres; (FH-R); TP&WD (formerly **Big Hill Reservoir**)	6,881	13,500
Jim Chapman Lake (see **Chapman Lake, Jim**)	—	—
Joe B. Hogsett, L. — (see **Cedar Creek Reservoir**)	—	—
Joe Pool Reservoir — Dallas-Tarrant-Ellis counties; Mountain Cr.; 14 mi. SW Dallas; (FC-M-R); USAE-Trinity River Auth. (formerly **Lakeview Lake**)	7,470	176,900
Johnson Creek Reservoir — Marion Co.; 13 mi. NW Jefferson; (In.); Southwestern Electric Co.	650	10,100
Kemp, L. — Baylor Co.; Wichita R.; 6 mi. N Mabelle; (M-P-Ir.); City of Wichita Falls; Wichita Co. WID 2	16,540	319,600
Kemp Diversion Dam — (see **Diversion Lake**)	—	—
Kickapoo, L. — Archer Co.; N. Fk. Little Wichita R.; 10 mi. NW Archer City; (M); City of Wichita Falls	6,200	106,000
Kiowa, L. — Cooke Co.; Indian Cr.; 8 mi. SE Gainesville; (R); Lake Kiowa, Inc.	560	7,000
Kirby L. — Taylor Co.; Cedar Cr.; 5 mi. S. Abilene; (M); City of Abilene	740	7,620
Kurth, L. — Angelina Co.; off-channel reservoir; 8 mi. N Lufkin; (In.); Southland Paper Mills, Inc.	770	16,200
Lake Creek L. — McLennan Co.; Manos Cr.; 4 mi. SW Riesel; (In.); Texas P&L Co.	550	8,400
Lake Fork Reservoir — Wood-Rains counties; Lake Fork Cr.; 5 mi. W Quitman; (M-In.); SRA	27,690	635,200
Lake O' the Pines — Marion-Upshur-Harrison-Morris-Camp counties; Cypress Cr.; 9 mi. W Jefferson; (FC-C-R-In.-M); USAE (impounded by **Ferrell's Bridge Dam**)	18,700	252,000
Lakeview L. — (see **Joe Pool Reservoir**)	—	—
Lampasas Reservoir — (see **Stillhouse Hollow Reservoir**)	—	—
Laneport L. — (see **Granger Lake**)	—	—
Lavon L. (Enlargement) — Collin Co.; East Fk. Trinity R.; 2 mi. W Lavon; (M-FC-In.); USAE	21,400	443,800
Leon, Lake — Eastland Co.; Leon R.; 7 mi. S Ranger; (M-In.); Eastland Co. Water Supply Dist.	1,590	26,420
Lewis Creek Reservoir — Montgomery Co.; Lewis Cr.; 10 mi. NW Conroe; (In.); Gulf States Util. Co.	1,010	16,400
Lewisville L. — Denton Co.; Elm Fk. Trinity R.; 2 mi. NE Lewisville; (M-FC-In.-R); USAE; (also called **Lake Dallas** and **Garza-Little Elm**)	23,280	464,500
Limestone, L. — Leon-Limestone-Robertson cos.; Navasota R.; 7 mi. NW Marquez; (M-In.-Ir.); BRA	14,200	225,400
Livingston L. — Polk-San Jacinto-Trinity-Walker counties; Trinity R.; 6 mi. SW Livingston; (M-In.-Ir.); City of Houston and Trinity River Authority	82,600	1,750,000
Loma Alta Lake — Cameron Co.; off-channel Rio Grande; 8 mi. NE Brownsville; (M-In.); Brownsville Navigation Dist.	2,490	26,500
Lone Star Reservoir — (see **Ellison Creek R.**)	—	—
Lost Creek Reservoir — Jack Co.; Lost Cr.; 4 mi. NE Jacksboro; (M); City of Jacksboro	360	11,960

Lyndon B. Johnson L. — Burnet-Llano counties; (formerly Granite Shoals L.); Colorado R.; 5 mi. SW Marble Falls; (P); LCRA; (impounded by **Alvin Wirtz Dam**)	6,375	138,500
McGee Bend Reservoir — (see **Sam Rayburn Reservoir**)	—	—
McQueeney, L. — Guadalupe Co.; Guadalupe R.; 5 mi. W Seguin; (P); Guadalupe-Blanco R. Authority; (impounded by **Abbott Dam**)	396	5,000
Mackenzie Reservoir — Briscoe Co.; Tule Cr.; 9 mi. NW Silverton; (M); Mackenzie Mun. Water Auth.	910	46,250
Marble Falls L. — Burnet County; Colorado R.; (impounded by Max Starcke Dam); 1.25 mi. SE Marble Falls; (P); LCRA	780	8,760
Martin L. — Rusk-Panola counties; Martin Cr.; 17 mi. NE Henderson; (P); Texas Util. Service Co., Inc.	5,020	77,620
Max Starcke Dam — (see **Marble Falls Lake**)	—	—
Medina L. — Medina-Bandera counties; Medina R.; 8 mi. W Rio Medina; (Ir.); Bexar- Medina-Atascosa Co. WID No. 1	5,575	254,000
Meredith, L. — Moore-Potter-Hutchinson counties; Canadian R.; 10 mi. NW Borger; (M-In.- FC-R); cooperative project for municipal water supply by Amarillo, Lubbock and other High Plains cities. Canadian R. Municipal Water Authority-USBR; (impounded by **Sanford Dam**)	16,504	821,300
Mexia, L. — Limestone Co.; Navasota R.; 7 mi. SW Mexia; (M-In); Bistone Mun. Water Dist.; (impounded by **Bistone Dam**)	1,200	10,000
Millers Creek Reservoir — Baylor Co.; Millers Cr.; 9 mi. SE Goree; (M); North Central Texas Mun. Water Auth. and Texas Water Development Board	2,350	30,700
Mineral Wells L. — Parker Co.; Rock Cr.; 4 mi. E Mineral Wells; (M); Palo Pinto Co. Mun. WD No. 1.	646	6,760
Mitchell County Reservoir — Mitchell Co.; Beals Creek; (Mi.-In.); Colorado River MWD.	1,463	27,266
Monte Alto Reservoir — (see **Delta Lake Res. Units 1 and 2**)	—	—
Monticello Reservoir — Titus Co.; Blundell Cr.; 2.5 mi. E. Monticello; (In.); Industrial Generating Co.	2,000	40,100
Moonen L. — Runnels Co. (see **Ballinger L.**)	—	—
Moss L., Hubert H. — Cooke Co.; Fish Cr.; 10 mi. NW Gainesville; (M-In.); City of Gainesville.	1,125	23,210
Mountain Creek L. — Dallas Co.; Mountain Cr.; 4 mi. SE Grand Prairie; (In.); Dallas P&L Co.	2,710	22,840
Mud Creek Dam L. — (see **Tyler Lake, East**)	—	—
Murphree, J. D. Area Impoundments — (see **J. D. Murphree**)	—	—
Murvaul L. — Panola Co.; Murvaul Bayou; 10 mi. W Carthage; (M-In.-R); Panola Co. Fresh Water Supply Dist. No. 1.	3,820	45,815
Mustang Lake East & **Mustang Lake West** — Brazoria co.; Mustang Bayou; 6 mi. S Alvin; (Ir.-In.-R); Chocolate Bayou Land & Water Co.	—	6,451
Nacogdoches, L. — Nacogdoches Co.; Bayo Loco Cr.; 10 mi. W Nacogdoches; (M); City of Nacogdoches	2,210	41,140
Nasworthy, L. — Tom Green Co.; S Concho R.; 6 mi. SW San Angelo; (M-In.-Ir); City of San Angelo.	1,596	12,390
Natural Dam L. — Howard Co.; Sulphur Springs Draw; 8 mi. W Big Spring; (FC); Wilkinson Ranch & Colorado River MWD	—	32,000
Navarro Mills L. — Navarro-Hill counties; Richland Cr.; 16 mi. SW Corsicana; (M-FC); USAE	5,070	60,900
Nocona L. — (see **Farmers Creek Reservoir**)	—	—
North Fk. Buffalo Creek Reservoir — Wichita Co.; 5 mi. NW Iowa Park; (M); Wichita Co. WC&ID No.3 .	1,500	15,400
North Fork L. — (see **L. Georgetown**)	—	—
North L. — Dallas Co.; S. Fork Grapevine Cr.; 2 mi. SE Coppell; (In.); Dallas P&L Co.	800	17,000
Oak Creek Reservoir — Coke Co.; 5 mi. SE Blackwell; (M-In.); City of Sweetwater	2,375	39,360
O. C. Fisher L. — Tom Green Co.; N. Concho R.; 3 mi. NW San Angelo; (M-FC-C- Ir.-R-In.-Mi); USAE —Upper Colo. River Auth. (formerly **San Angelo L.**)	5,440	119,200
O. H. Ivie Reservoir — Coleman-Concho-Runnels counties; 24 mi. SE Ballinger; (M-In.), Colorado R. Mun. Water Dist. (formerly **Stacy Reservoir**)	19,150	554,340
Palestine, L. — Anderson-Cherokee-Henderson-Smith counties; Neches R.; 4 mi. E Frankston; (M-In.-R); Upper Neches R. MWA (impounded by **Blackburn Crossing Dam**)	25,560	411,300
Palmetto Bend Reservoir — (see **Texana, L.**)	—	—
Palo Duro Reservoir — Hansford Co.; Palo Duro Cr.; 12 mi. N Spearman; (M-R); Palo Duro River Auth.	2,410	60,900
Palo Pinto, L. — Palo Pinto Co.; 15 mi. SW Mineral Wells; (M-In.); Palo Pinto Co. Muni. Water Dist. 1	2,661	42,200
Panola L. — (see **Murvaul L.**)	—	—
Pat Mayse L. — Lamar Co.; Sanders Cr.; 2 mi. SW Arthur City; (M-In.-FC); USAE	5,993	124,500
Pinkston Reservoir — Shelby Co.; Sandy Cr.; 12.5 mi. SW Center; (M); City of Center; (formerly **Sandy Creek Reservoir**)	523	7,380
Possum Kingdom L. — Palo Pinto-Young-Stephens-Jack counties; Brazos R.; 11 mi. SW Graford; (M-In.-Ir.-Mi.-P-R); Brazos R. Authority; (impounded by **Morris Sheppard Dam**)	17,700	569,380
Proctor L. — Comanche Co.; Leon R.; 9 mi. NE Comanche; (M-In.-Ir.-FC); USAE- Brazos River Auth.	4,610	59,300
Quitman L. — Wood Co.; Dry Cr.; 4 mi. N Quitman; (FC-R); Wood County (impounded by **Wood Co. Dam No.1**)	814	7,440
Randell, L. — Grayson Co.; Shawnee Cr.; 4 mi. NW Denison; (M); City of Denison.	311	6,290
Raw Water Lake — Calhoun Co. (See **Cox Lake**)	—	—
Ray Hubbard, L. — Collin-Dallas-Kaufman-Rockwall counties; (formerly **Forney Reservoir**); E. Fk. Trinity R.; 15 mi. E Dallas; (M); City of Dallas	22,745	490,000
Ray Roberts, L. — Denton-Cooke-Grayson counties; Elm Fk. Trinity R.; 11 mi. NE Denton; (FC-M-D); City of Denton, Dallas, USAE; (also known as **Aubrey Reservior**)	29,350	799,600
Recycle Lake — Calhoun Co. (see **Cox Lake**)	—	—
Red Bluff Reservoir — Loving-Reeves counties, Texas; and Eddy Co.; N.M.; Pecos R.; 5 mi. N Orla; (Ir.-P); Red Bluff Water Power Control District	11,700	307,000
Red Draw L. — Howard Co.; Red Draw; 5 mi. E Bi Spring; (Mi.-In.); Colorado River MWD	374	8,538
Resacas — Cameron-Hidalgo-Willacy counties; Rio Grande; these reservoirs are primarily for storage of water during periods of normal or above-normal flow in the river for use when the river's water volume is low. Some of these are old loops and bends in the river that have been isolated by the river's changing its channel. They are known by the Spanish ame of resacas. Also a number of reservoirs have been constructed and connected with the main channel of the river by ditches through which the water is either filled by gravity flow or by pumping. This is reserve irrigation water for use during periods of low flow in the river channel. Most of these reservoirs are near the main channel of the river, but some of them are 20 or 25 miles distant.	—	—
Retama Reservoir — Hidalgo Co.; Off-Channel Rio Grande; 5 mi. N Edinburg; (Ir.); Santa Cruz ID #15; (also known as **Edinburg Lake**)	—	5,000
Richland-Chambers Reservoir — Freestone-Navarro counties; Richland Cr.; 20 mi. SE Corsicana; (M); Tarrant Co. WCID No. 1	44,752	1,135,866

Rita Blanca L. — Hartley Co.; Rita Blanca Cr.; 2 mi. S Dalhart; (R) City of Dalhart	524	12,100
River Crest L. — Red River County; off-channel reservoir; 7 mi. SE Bogata; (In.); Texas P&L	555	7,000
Robert Lee Reservoir — (see **Spence Reservoir**)	—	—
Salt Creek L. — (see **Graham L.**)		
Sam Rayburn Reservoir — Jasper-Angelina-Sabine-Nacogdoches-San Augustine counties; Angelina R.; (formerly **McGee Bend Reservoir**); (FC-P-M-In.-Ir.-R); USAE.	114,500	2,876,300
San Angelo L. — (see **O. C. Fisher L.**)	—	—
San Bernard Reservoirs #1, #2, #3 — Brazoria Co.; Off-Channel San Bernard R.; 3 mi. N Sweeney; (In.); Phillips 66 Co.	—	8,610
Sandlin, L. Bob — Titus-Wood-Camp-Franklin counties; Big Cypress Cr.; 5 mi. SW Mount Pleasant; (In.-M-R); Titus Co. FWSD No. 1 (impounded by **Fort Sherman Dam**)	9,460	202,300
Sandow L. — (see **Alcoa Lake**)	—	—
Sandy Creek Reservoir — (see **Pinkston Reservoir**)	—	—
Sanford Reservoir — (see **Meredith, Lake**)	—	—
Santa Rosa L. — Wilbarger Co.; Beaver Cr.; 15 mi. S Vernon; (Mi.); W. T. Waggoner Estate	1,500	11,570
Sheldon Reservoir — Harris Co.; Carpenters Bayou; 2 mi. SW Sheldon; (R-FH); TP&WD.	1,700	5,420
Smithers L. — Fort Bend Co.; Dry Creek; 10 mi. SE Richmond; (In.); Houston Lighting & Power Co.	2,480	18,700
Somerville L. — Burleson-Washington counties; Yegua Cr.; 2 mi. S Somerville; (M-In.-Ir.- FC); USAE-Brazos River Authority.	11,460	160,100
Southland Paper Mills Reservoir — (see **Kurth, Lake**)	—	—
South Texas Project Reservoir — Matagorda Co.; off-channel Colorado R.; 16 mi. S Bay City; (In.); Houston Lighting & Power	7,000	187,000
Spence Reservoir, E. V. — Coke Co.; Colorado R.; 2 mi. W. Robert Lee; (M-In.-Mi); Colorado R. Mun. Water Dist.; (impounded by **Robert Lee Dam**)	14,950	484,800
Squaw Creek Reservoir — Somervell-Hood counties; Squaw Cr.; 4.5 mi. N Glen Rose; (In.); Texas Utilities Services, Inc.	3,228	151,047
Stacy Reservoir — (see **O. H. Ivie Reservoir**)		
Stamford, L. — Haskell Co.; Paint Cr.; 10 mi. SE Haskell; (M-In.); City of Stamford	4,690	52,700
Steinhagen L., B. A. — (Also called **Town Bluff Reservoir** and **Dam B. Reservoir**); Tyler-Jasper counties; Neches R.; 1/2 mi. N Town Bluff; (FC-R-C); (impounded by **Town Bluff Dam**)	13,700	94,200
Stillhouse Hollow L. — Bell Co.; Lampasas R.; 5 mi. SW Belton; (M-In.-Ir.-FC); USAE-BRA; (sometimes called **Lampasas Reservoir**)	6,430	234,900
Striker Creek Reservoir — Rusk-Cherokee counties; Striker Cr.; 18 mi. SW Henderson; (M -In.); Angelina-Nacogdoches WC&ID No. 1	2,400	26,960
Sulphur Springs L. — Hopkins Co.; White Oak Cr.; 2 mi. N Sulphur Springs; (M); Sulphur Springs WD; (impounded by **Lake Sulphur Springs Dam**; formerly called **White Oak Creek Reservoir**)	1,910	17,710
Swauano Creek Reservoir — (see **Welsh Reservoir**)	—	—
Tawakoni, L. — Rains-Van Zandt-Hunt counties; Sabine R.; 9 mi. NE Wills Point; (M-In.-Ir-R); Sabine River Authority; (impounded by **Iron Bridge Dam**)	36,700	936,200
Terrell City L., New — Kaufman Co.; Muddy Cedar Cr.; 6 mi. E Terrell; (M-R); City of Terrell	830	8,712
Texana, L. — Jackson Co.; Navidad R. and Sandy Cr.; 6.8 mi. SE Edna; (M-Ir); USBR, Lavaca-Navidad R. Auth., Texas Water Dev. Bd.; (formerly **Palmetto Bend Reservoir**)	11,000	157,900
Texarkana L. — (see **Wright Patman Lake**)	—	—
Texoma L. — Grayson-Cooke cos., Texas; Bryan-Marshall-Love cos., Okla.; impounded by **Denison Dam** on Red R. short distance below confluence of Red and Washita Rivers; (P-FC-C-R); USAE	89,000	2,722,000
Thomas L. — (see **J. B. Thomas L.**)		
Toledo Bend Reservoir — Newton-Panola-Sabine-Shelby counties; Sabine R.; 14 mi. NE Burkeville; (M-In.-Ir.-PR); Sabine River Authority (Texas' share of capacity is half amount shown)	181,600	4,472,900
Town Bluff Reservoir — (see **Steinhagen, Lake B. A.**)		
Tradinghouse Creek Reservoir — McLennan Co.; Tradinghouse Cr.; 9 mi. E Waco; (In.); Texas P&L	2,010	35,124
Travis, L. — Travis-Burnet counties; Colorado R.; 13 mi. NW Austin; (M-In.-Ir.- Mi.-P-FC-R); LCRA; (impounded by **Mansfield Dam**)	18,930	1,144,100
Trinidad L. — Henderson Co.; off-channel reservoir Trinity R.; 2 mi. S. Trinidad; (P); Texas P&L Co.	740	7,450
Truscott Brine L. — Knox Co.; Bluff Cr.; 26 mi. NNW Knox City; (Chlorine Control); Red River Auth.	2,978	107,000
Turtle Bayou Reservoir — (see **Anahuac Lake**)		
Twin Buttes Reservoir — Tom Green Co.; Concho R.; 8 mi. SW San Angelo; (M-In. -FC-Ir.-R.); City of San Angelo-USBR-Tom Green Co. WC&ID No. 1	9,080	177,800
Twin Oaks Reservoir — Robertson Co.; Duck Cr.; 12 mi. N. Franklin; (In); Texas P&L	2,300	30,319
Tyler L. — Smith Co.; Prairie and Mud Crs.; 12 mi. SE Tyler; (M-In); City of Tyler; impounded by **Whitehouse** and **Mud Creek dams**)	4,800	73,700
Upper Nueces Reservoir — Zavala Co.; Nueces R.; 6 mi. N Crystal City; (Ir.); Zavala-Dimmit Co. WID No. 1	316	7,590
Valley Acres Reservoir — Hidalgo Co.; off-channel Rio Grande; 7 mi. N Mercedes; (Ir-M-FC); Valley Acres Water Dist.	906	7,840
Valley L. — Fannin-Grayson counties; 2.5 mi. N Savoy; (P); TP&L((formerly **Brushy Creek Reservoir**)	1,080	16,400
Victor Braunig L. — Bexar Co.; Arroyo Seco; 15 mi. SE San Antonio; (In.); Pub. Svc. Bd./San Antonio	1,350	26,500
Waco L. — McLennan Co.; Bosque R.; 2 mi. W Waco; (M-FC-C-R); City of Waco- USAE-BRA.	7,270	151,900
*Wallisville L. — Liberty-Chambers counties; Trinity R.; 2 mi. S Wallisville; (M-In.-Ir.); USAE	19,700	58,000
Walter E. Long L. — Travis Co.; Decker Cr.; 9 mi. E of capital, Austin; (M-In.-R); City of Austin (formerly **Decker Lake**)	1,269	33,940
Waxahachie L. — Ellis Co.; S Prong Waxahachie Cr.; 4 mi. SE Waxahachie; (M-In); Ellis County WC&ID No. 1; (impounded by **S. Prong Dam**)	690	13,500
Weatherford L. — Parker Co.; Clear Fork Trinity River; 7 mi. E Weatherford; (M-In.); City of Weatherford.	1,210	19,470
Welsh Reservoir — Titus Co.; Swauano Cr.; 11 mi. SE Mount Pleasant; (R-In.); Southwestern Electric Power Co.; (formerly **Swauano Creek Reservoir**)	1,365	23,587
White Oak Creek Reservoir — (see **Sulphur Springs Lake**)	—	—
White River L. — Crosby Co.; 16 mi. SE Crosbyton; (M-In.-Mi.); White River Municipal Water Dist.	2,020	44,300
White Rock L. — Dallas Co.; White Rock Cr.; within NE Dallas city limits; (R); City of Dallas	1,119	10,740
Whitney L. — Hill-Bosque-Johnson counties; Brazos R.; 5.5 mi. SW Whitney; (FC-P); USAE.	23,560	622,800
Wichita, L. — Wichita Co.; Holliday Cr.; 6 mi. SW Wichita Falls; (M-P-R); City of Wichita Falls.	2,200	9,000
Winnsboro, L. — Wood Co.; Big Sandy Cr.; 6 mi. SW Winnsboro; (FC-R); Wood County; (impounded by **Wood Co. Dam No. 4**)	806	8,100
Winters L. — Runnels Co.; Elm Cr.; 4.5 mi. E. Winters; (M); City of Winters.	640	8,370
Worth, L. — Tarrant Co.; W. Fk. Trinity R.; in NW Fort Worth; (M); City of Fort Worth	3,560	38,130
Wright Patman L. — Bowie-Cass-Morris-Titus-Red River counties; Sulphur R.; 8 mi. SW Texarkana; (FC-M); USAE; (formerly **Texarkana Lake**)	20,300	142,700

Vegetational Areas

(Editor's note: This article was updated for The Texas Almanac by **Stephan L. Hatch, Curator, S.M. Tracy Herbarium and Professor, Dept. of Rangeland Ecology and Management, Texas A&M University.)**

Difference in amount and frequency of rainfall, in soils and in frost-free days gives Texas a great variety of vegetation. From the forests of East Texas to the deserts of West Texas, from the grassy plains of North Texas to the semi-arid brushlands of South Texas, plant species change continuously.

Sideoats grama, which occurs on more different soils in Texas than any other native grass, was officially designated as the **state grass of Texas** by the Texas Legislature in 1971.

The **10 principal plant life areas** of Texas, starting in the east, are:

1. Piney Woods. Most of this area of some 16 million acres ranges from about 50 to 700 feet above sea level and receives 40 to 56 inches of rain yearly. Many rivers, creeks and bayous drain the region. Nearly all of Texas' commercial timber comes from this area. There are three native species of pine, the principal timber.: longleaf, shortleaf and loblolly. An introduced species, the **slash pine**, also is widely grown. Hardwoods include **oaks, elm, hickory, magnolia, sweet** and **black gum, tupelo** and others.

The area is interspersed with **native and improved grasslands.** Cattle are the primary grazing animals. **Deer** and **quail** are abundant in properly managed localities. Primary forage plants, under proper grazing management, include species of the **bluestems, rossettegrass, panicums, paspalums, blackseed needlegrass, Canada and Virginia wildryes, purpletop, broadleaf and spike woodoats, switchcane, lovegrasses, indiangrass** and numerous **legume** species.

Highly disturbed areas have understory and overstory of undesirable woody plants that suppress growth of pine and desirable grasses. The primary forage grasses have been reduced and the grasslands have been invaded by **threeawns, annual grasses, weeds, broomsedge bluestem, red lovegrass** and shrubby woody species.

2. Gulf Prairies and Marshes. The Gulf Prairies and Marshes cover approximately 10 million acres. There are two subunits: (a) the marsh and salt grasses immediately at tidewater, and (b) a little farther inland, a strip of bluestems and tall grasses, with some gramas in the western part. Many of these grasses make excellent grazing. **Oaks, elm** and other hardwoods grow to some extent, especially along streams, and the area has some **post oak** and brushy extensions along its borders. Much of the Gulf Prairies is fertile farmland. The area is well suited for cattle.

Principal grasses of the Gulf Prairies are **tall bunchgrasses,** including **big bluestem, little bluestem, seacoast bluestem, indiangrass, eastern gamagrass, Texas wintergrass, switchgrass** and **gulf cordgrass. Seashore saltgrass** occurs on moist saline sites. Heavy grazing has changed the range vegetation in many cases so that the predominant grasses are the less desirable **broomsedge bluestem, smutgrass, threeawns, tumblegrass** and many other inferior grasses. The other plants that have invaded the productive grasslands include **oak underbrush, Macartney rose, huisache, mesquite, prickly pear, ragweed, bitter sneezeweed, broomweed** and others.

Vegetation of the Gulf Marshes consists primarily of **sedges, bullrush, flat-sedges, beakrush** and other rushes, **smooth cordgrass, marshhay cordgrass, marsh millet** and **maidencane.** The marshes are grazed best during winter.

3. Post Oak Savannah. This secondary forest region, also called the **Post Oak Belt,** covers some 7 million acres. It is immediately west of the primary forest region, with less annual rainfall and a little higher elevation. Principal trees are **post oak, blackjack oak** and **elm.** Pecans, walnuts and other kinds of water-demanding trees grow along streams. The southwestern extension of this belt is often poorly defined, with large areas of prairie.

The upland soils are **sandy and sandy loam,** while the bottomlands are **sandy loams and clays.**

The original vegetation consisted mainly of **little bluestem, big bluestem, indiangrass, switchgrass, purpletop, silver bluestem, Texas wintergrass, spike woodoats, longleaf woodoats, post oak** and **blackjack oak.** The area is still largely native or improved grasslands, with small farms located throughout. Intensive grazing has contributed to dense stands of a woody understory of **yaupon, greenbriar** and **oak** brush. **Mesquite** has become a serious problem. Good forage plants have been replaced by such plants as **splitbeard bluestem, red lovegrass, broomsedge bluestem, broomweed, bullnettle** and **western ragweed.**

4. Blackland Prairies. This area of about 12 million acres,

while called a "prairie," has much timber along the streams, including a variety of **oaks, pecan, elm, horse-apple (bois d'arc)** and **mesquite.** In its native state it was largely a grassy plain — the first native grassland in the westward extension of the Southern Forest Region.

Most of this fertile area has been cultivated, and only small acreages of meadowland remain in original vegetation. In heavily grazed pastures, the tall bunchgrass has been replaced by **buffalograss, Texas grama** and other less productive grasses. **Mesquite, lotebush** and other woody plants have invaded the grasslands.

The original grass vegetation includes **big** and **little bluestem, indiangrass, switchgrass, sideoats grama, hairy grama, tall dropseed, Texas wintergrass** and **buffalograss.** Non-grass vegetation is largely legumes and composites.

5. Cross Timbers and Prairies. Approximately 15 million acres of alternating woodlands, often called the **West Cross Timbers,** and prairies constitute this region. Sharp changes in the vegetational cover are associated with different soils and topography, but the grass composition is rather uniform.

The prairie-type grasses are **big bluestem, little bluestem, indiangrass, switchgrass, Canada wildrye, sideoats grama, hairy grama, tall grama, tall dropseed, Texas wintergrass, blue grama** and **buffalograss.**

On the Cross Timbers soils, the grasses are composed of **big bluestem, little bluestem, hooded windmillgrass, sand lovegrass, indiangrass, switchgrass** and many species of legumes. The woody vegetation includes **shinnery, blackjack, post** and **live oaks.**

The entire area has been invaded heavily by woody brush plants of **oaks, mesquite, juniper** and other unpalatable plants that furnish little forage for livestock.

6. South Texas Plains. South of San Antonio, between the coast and the Rio Grande, are some 21 million acres of subtropical dryland vegetation, consisting of small trees, shrubs, cactus, weeds and grasses. The area is noteworthy for extensive brushlands, known as the **brush country,** or the Spanish equivalents of **chaparral** or **monte.** Principal plants are **mesquite, small live oak, post oak, prickly pear (Opuntia) cactus, catclaw, blackbrush, whitebrush, guajillo, huisache, cenizo** and others which often grow very densely. The original vegetation was mainly perennial warm-season **bunchgrasses** in **post oak, live oak** and **mesquite savannahs.** Other brush species form dense thickets on the ridges and along streams. Long-continued grazing has contributed to the dense cover of brush. Most of the desirable grasses have persisted under the protection of brush and cacti.

There are distinct differences in the original plant communities on various soils. Dominant grasses on the sandy loam soils are **seacoast bluestem, bristlegrass, paspalum, windmillgrass, silver bluestem, big sandbur** and **tanglehead.** Dominant grasses on the clay and clay loams are **silver bluestem, Arizona cottontop, buffalograss, common curlymesquite, bristlegrass, pappusgrass, gramas, plains lovegrass, Texas cupgrass, vinemesquite,** other **panicums** and **Texas wintergrass.** Low saline areas are characterized by **gulf cordgrass, seashore saltgrass, alkali sacaton** and **switchgrass.** In the post oak and live oak savannahs, the grasses are mainly **seacoast bluestem, indiangrass, switchgrass, crinkleawn, paspalums** and **panicums.** Today much of the area has been reseeded to **buffelgrass.**

7. Edwards Plateau. These 25 million acres are rolling to mountainous, with woodlands in the eastern part and grassy prairies in the west. There is a good deal of brushy growth in the central and eastern parts. The combination of grasses, weeds and small trees is ideal for **cattle, sheep, goats, deer** and **wild turkey.**

This limestone-based area is characterized by the large number of **springfed, perennially flowing streams** which originate in its interior and flow across the **Balcones Escarpment,** which bounds it on the south and east. The soils are shallow, ranging from sands to clays and are calcareous in reaction. This area is predominantly rangeland, with cultivation confined to the deeper soils.

In the east-central portion is the well-marked **Central Basin** centering in Mason, Llano and Burnet counties, with a mixture of granitic and sandy soils. The western portion of the area comprises the semi-arid **Stockton Plateau.**

Noteworthy is the growth of **cypress** along the perennially flowing streams. Separated by many miles from cypress growth of the moist Southern Forest Belt, they constitute one of Texas' several **"islands" of vegetation.** These trees, which grow to stately proportions, were commercialized in the past.

The principal grasses of the clay soils are **cane bluestem, silver bluestem, little bluestem, sideoats grama, hairy grama, indiangrass, common curlymesquite, buffalograss,**

fall witchgrass, plains lovegrass, wildryes and Texas wintergrass.

The rocky areas support tall or mid-grasses with an overstory of live oak, shinnery oak, cedar and mesquite. The
heavy clay soils have a mixture of tobosagrass, buffalograss,
sideoats grama and mesquite.

Throughout the Edwards Plateau, live oak, shinnery oak,
mesquite and cedar dominate the woody vegetation. Woody
plants have invaded to the degree that they should be controlled before range forage plants can re-establish.

8. Rolling Plains. This is a region of approximately 24 million acres of alternating woodlands and prairies. The area is
half mesquite woodland and half prairie. Mesquite trees have
steadily invaded and increased in the grasslands for many
years, despite constant control efforts.

Soils range from coarse sands along outwash terraces
adjacent to streams to tight or compact clays on redbed clays
and shales. Rough broken lands on steep slopes are found in
the western portion. About two-thirds of the area is rangeland,
but cultivation is important in certain localities.

The original vegetation includes big, little, sand and silver bluestems, Texas wintergrass, indiangrass, switchgrass, sideoats and blue gramas, wildryes, tobosagrass
and buffalograss on the clay soils.

The sandy soils support tall bunchgrasses, mainly sand
bluestem. Sand shinnery oak, sand sagebrush and mesquite are the dominant woody plants.

Continued heavy grazing contributes to the increase in
woody plants, low-value grasses such as red grama, red
lovegrass, tumblegrass, gummy lovegrass, Texas grama,
sand dropseed, sandbur, western ragweed, croton and
many other weeds. Yucca is a problem plant on certain range-
lands.

9. High Plains. The High Plains, some 19 million treeless
acres, are an extension of the Great Plains to the north. The
level nature and porous soils prevent drainage over wide areas.
The relatively light rainfall flows into the numerous shallow
"playa" lakes or sinks into the ground to feed the great underground aquifer that is the source of water for the countless
wells that irrigate the surface of the plains. A large part of this
area is under irrigated farming, but native grassland remains in
about one-half of the High Plains.

Blue grama and buffalograss comprise the principal vegetation on the clay and clay loam "hardland" soils. Important
grasses on the sandy loam "sandy land" soils are little
bluestem, western wheatgrass, indiangrass, switchgrass
and sand reedgrass. Sand shinnery oak, sand sagebrush,
mesquite and yucca are conspicuous invading brushy plants.

10. Trans-Pecos, Mountains and Basins. With as little as
eight inches of annual rainfall, long hot summers and usually
cloudless skies to encourage evaporation, this 18-million-acre
area produces only drouth-resistant vegetation without irrigation. Grass is usually short and sparse. The principal vegetation consists of lechuguilla, ocotillo, yucca, cenizo and other
arid land plants. In the more arid areas, yeso, chino and
tobosagrass prevail. There is some mesquite. The vegetation
includes creosote-tarbush, desert shrub, grama grassland,
yucca and juniper savannahs, pine oak forest and saline
flats.

The mountains are 3,000 to 8,751 feet in elevation and
support piñon pine, juniper and some ponderosa pine and
other forest vegetation on a few of the higher slopes.

The grass vegetation, especially on the higher mountain
slopes, includes many southwestern and Rocky Mountain
species not present elsewhere in Texas. On the desert flats,
black grama, burrograss and fluffgrass are frequent. More
productive sites have numerous species of grama, muhly, Arizona cottontop, dropseed and perennial threeawn grasses.
At the higher elevations, plains bristlegrass, little bluestem,
Texas bluestem, sideoats grama, chino grama, blue
grama, piñon ricegrass, wolftail and several species of
needlegrass are frequent.

The common invaders on all depleted ranges are woody
plants, burrograss, fluffgrass, hairy erioneuron, ear muhly,
sand muhly, red grama, broom snakeweed, croton, cacti
and several poisonous plants.

Range Uses

More than 100 million acres of Texas are devoted to providing grazing for domestic and wild animals. This is the largest
single use for land in the state. The Piney Woods, primarily
valued for timber, also provide significant grazing. More than 80
percent of the acreage is devoted to range in the Edwards Plateau, Cross Timbers and Prairies, South Texas Plains and
Trans-Pecos Mountains and Basins. Range management
seeks to perpetuate soil stability and water yield through vegetation management while that vegetation is used for animal forage. ☆

For Further Reading

Hatch, S. L., K. N. Gandhi and L. E. Brown, *Checklist of
the Vascular Plants of Texas; MP1655, Texas Agricultural
Experiment Station, College Station, 1990.*

Texas Forest Resources

*Source: Texas Forest Service, The Texas A&M University System, College Station, TX 77843- 2136. On the Internet: http://
agcomwww.tamu.edu/agcom/news/TFShome/tfs.html*

It is a surprise to many people, including life-long Texans, that the state has an abundant and diverse forest
resource. Trees cover roughly 13 percent of the state's
land area. The 22 million acres of forests and woodlands
in Texas is an area larger than the states of Massachusetts, Connecticut, New Hampshire, Rhode Island and
Vermont combined. The principal forest and woodlands
regions are: the East Texas pine-hardwood region often
called the Piney Woods; the Post Oak Belt, which lies
immediately west of the pine-hardwood forest; the Eastern
and Western Cross Timbers areas of North Central Texas;
the Cedar Brakes of Central Texas; the mountain forests of
West Texas; and the coastal forests of the southern Gulf
Coast.

The East Texas Piney Woods

Although Texas contains about 22 million acres of forest and woodlands, detailed forest resource data is available for only the 43-county East Texas timber region. The
Piney Woods, which form the western edge of the southern pine region, extend from Bowie and Red River counties in Northeast Texas, to Jefferson, Harris and Waller
counties in southeast Texas. This region contains 11.9 million acres of forest and is the most economically important
forest area of the state, producing nearly all of the commercial timber. The following discussion summarizes the
findings of the most recent Forest Survey of East Texas,
conducted in 1992 by the USDA Forest Service Southern
Forest Experiment Station.

Timberland Acreage and Ownership

Nearly all (11.8 of 11.9 million acres) of the East Texas
forest is classified as "timberland," which is suitable for
production of timber products and not reserved as parks
or wilderness areas. In contrast to the trends in several
other southern states, Texas timberland acreage is on a
slight upward track. Acreage in timberland increased by 2
percent between 1986 and 1992. Seventy-four percent of
the new timberland acres came from agricultural lands,
such as idle farmland and pasture, which was either inten-
tionally planted with trees or naturally reverted to forest.

Sixty-one percent of 11.8 million acres of East Texas
timberland is owned by approximately 150,000 farmers,
private individuals, families, partnerships and non-wood-
using corporations. Thirty-two percent is owned by forest-
products companies, and only 7 percent is owned by the
government. The following table shows acreage of timberland by ownership:

Ownership Class	Thous. Acres
Non-industrial Private:	
Farmer	1,161.8
Corporate	954.3
Individual	5,106.9
Forest Industry	3,767.4
Public:	
National Forest	576.7
Misc. Federal	91.8
State	68.1
County & Municipal	46.8
Total	11,773.8

There are distinct regional differences in ownership
patterns. Most forest-industry land is found south of
Nacogdoches County, and timberland in some counties,

such as Polk and Hardin, is as much as 75 percent owned by the forest-products industry. North of Nacogdoches, the nonindustrial private landowner predominates, and industry owns a much smaller percent of the timberland.

Forest Types

Six major forest types are found in the East Texas Piney Woods. Two pine forest types are most common. The loblolly-shortleaf and longleaf-slash forest types are dominated by the four species of southern yellow pine. In these forests, pine trees make up at least 50 percent of the trees.

Oak-hickory is the second most common forest type. These are upland hardwood forests in which oaks or hickories make up at least 50 percent of the trees, and pine species are less than 25 percent. Oak-pine is a mixed-forest type in which more than 50 percent of the trees are hardwoods, but pines make up 25 to 49 percent of the trees.

Two forest types, oak-gum-cypress and elm-ash-cottonwood, are bottomland types which are commonly found along creeks, river bottoms, swamps and other wet areas. The oak-gum-cypress forests are typically made up of many species including blackgum, sweetgum, oaks and southern cypress. The elm-ash-cottonwood bottomland forests are dominated by those trees but also contain many other species, such as willows, sycamore, and maple. The following table shows the breakdown in acreage by forest type:

Forest Type Group	Thous. Acres
Southern Pine:	
Loblolly-shortleaf	4,063.7
Longleaf-slash	232.9
Oak-pine	2,503.8
Oak-hickory	3,146.9
Bottomland Hardwood:	
Oak-gum-cypress	1,755.8
Elm-ash-cottonwood	71.0
Total	**11,773.8**

Southern pine plantations, established by tree planting and usually managed intensively to maximize timber production, are an increasingly important source of wood fiber. Texas forests include 1.8 million acres of pine plantations, 72 percent of which are on forest-industry-owned land, 22 percent on nonindustrial private, and 6 percent on public land. Plantation acreage increased 48 percent between 1986 and 1992. Genetically superior tree seedlings, produced at industry and Texas Forest Service nurseries, are usually planted to improve survival and growth.

Timber Volume and Number of Trees

Texas timberland contains 12.9 billion cubic feet of timber "growing-stock" volume. This is enough wood fiber to produce 200 billion copies of National Geographic. The inventory of softwood remained steady at 7.9 billion cubic feet, while the hardwood inventory increased nearly 12 percent to 5.1 billion cubic feet, between 1986 and 1992.

There are more trees in East Texas than there are people living on Earth — an estimated 6.9 billion live trees — according to the 1992 survey. This includes 2 billion softwoods, 4.1 billion hardwoods, and .7 billion trees of noncommercial species. The predominant species are loblolly and shortleaf pine; 1.9 billion trees of these two species are found in East Texas.

Timber Growth and Removals

Between 1986 and 1992, an annual average of 691.6 million cubic feet of timber was removed from the inventory either through harvest or land-use changes. Meanwhile, 728.6 million cubic feet were added to the inventory through growth each year, resulting in a net increase in timber inventory in East Texas.

For pine, however, slightly more is being cut than is being grown. An average 530.5 million cubic feet were removed during those years, while 522.9 million feet were added by growth. For hardwoods, 161.1 million feet were removed, while 205.7 million cubic feet were added by growth.

Texas is fortunate in that the rate of pine over-cutting is small compared to most other Southern states. However, if the 1 percent over-harvest of pine were to continue indefi-

nitely, we could eventually run out of timber. Through increased reforestation and improved management, this short-term trend can be reversed before it becomes a long-term problem.

Other Tree Regions

Compared to commercially important East Texas, relatively little data are available for the other tree regions of Texas. However, these areas are environmentally important with benefits of wildlife habitat, improved water quality, recreation and aesthetics. Following is a brief description of these areas.

• Post Oak Belt: The Post Oak Belt forms a band of wooded savannah mixed with pasture and cropland immediately west of the Piney Woods region. It extends from Lamar and Red River counties southwest as far as Bee and Atascosa counties. Predominant species include post oak, blackjack oak and elm. An interesting area called the "Lost Pines" forms an isolated island of southern-pine forest in Bastrop, Caldwell, Fayette,and Lee counties just a few miles southeast of Austin.

• Eastern and Western Cross Timbers: The Eastern and Western Cross Timbers cover an area of about 3 million acres in North Central Texas. The term "cross timbers" originated with the early settlers who, in their travels from east to west, crossed alternating patches of oak forest and prairies and so affixed the name "cross timbers" to these forests.

• Cedar Brakes: Farther south in the Edwards Plateau region are the cedar brakes, which extend over 3.7 million acres. Cedar, live oak and mesquite dominate these steep slopes and rolling hills. Mesquite is often harvested for cooking wood, knick-knacks and woodworking. Live oak in this region is declining because of the oak wilt disease.

• Mountain Forests: The mountain forests of the Trans-Pecos region of Texas, including Jeff Davis County and the Big Bend, are rugged and picturesque. Several western tree species, including piñon pine, ponderosa pine, southwestern white pine and even Douglas fir are found there, along with aspen and several species of oak.

• Coastal Forests: The coastal forests of the southern Gulf Coast are characterized by a mix of brush and short, scrubby trees. Common species include mesquite, live oak and acacia. Some of these scrub forests are particularly important as migratory bird habitat.

Economic Impact of Timber in Texas

Timber is a major contributor to the state's economy. The forest products industry in Texas manufactures products such as lumber, plywood, oriented-strand board, poles, railroad crossties, wood furniture, pulp, paper and paperboard, and a host of other products from the timber grown in Texas forests. Consider these facts about the Texas forest industry:

• As unbelievable as it may sound, Texas is one of the top producers of forest products in the nation. In 1993, it was the source of 4 percent of lumber, 10 percent of structural panels, and 3 percent of paper and paperboard produced in the U.S.

• In 1993, timber ranked first in East Texas and fifth statewide in the value of agricultural production after beef, cotton, poultry, and milk production. In East Texas, it was the most valuable agricultural commodity. The delivered value of the timber harvest was $744 million.

• In 1992, the forest products industry in Texas produced and sold goods valued at $9.2 billion, 50 percent of which came from the paper sector.

• Forest industry directly employs 67,100 people, ranking first among East Texas manufacturing sectors and ninth statewide.

• Forest industry pays $1.6 billion in wages and salaries each year.

The 1994 Timber Harvest

Total Harvest Volume

East Texas set another new timber-harvest record in 1994 as removals of both pine and hardwood continued a steady climb. The total volume removed from the 43-county region was 867.5 million cubic feet, or 88.7 million cubic feet more than in 1993. Included in total removals is the harvest of timber for industrial use and an estimate of the logging residue and other timber removals.

By species group, removals consisted of 660.1 million cubic feet of pine and 207.4 million cubic feet of hardwood. Hardwood removals increased by 11percent, while removals from the softwood inventory were 12 percent over the 1993 mark.

Eighty-three percent of timber removed, including 87 percent of pine and 67 percent of hardwood, was subsequently utilized in the manufacture of wood products. This portion of total removals, called the industrial roundwood harvest, totaled 576.5 and 139.6 million cubic feet for pine and hardwood, respectively. The pine industrial roundwood harvest was up 13 percent, while harvest of hardwood for industrial use climbed by 15 percent between 1993 and 1994. The combined harvest was up 13 percent to 716.1 million cubic feet.

The harvest of sawlogs for production of lumber and ties was 1,674.2 million board feet and comprised 38 percent of the 1994 timber harvest. Timber cut for the production of structural panels (plywood and oriented strand board) and hardwood veneer represented 30 percent of the timber harvest, or 216.8 million cubic feet. The harvest of timber for the manufacture of pulp and paper products totaled 2.8 million cords, representing 31 percent of the total harvest.

Jasper County continued to lead in timber production with a harvest of 45.7 million cubic feet. Other top producing counties included Angelina, Cass, Shelby, Newton and Tyler.

Total Harvest Value

The value of the East Texas timber harvest surged higher in 1994 due to increasing timber prices and higher harvest volumes. The stumpage value of the timber harvest climbed 43percent to $682.9 million. Pine timber accounted for 95 percent of that total. The value of the timber harvest delivered to the first point of processing (mill or intermediate woodyard) was $932.0 million in 1994, up 25 percent over the previous year's value of $744.0 million.

Primary Forest Products, 1994

Lumber and Ties: Texas sawmills produced 1,536.6 million board feet of lumber and ties in 1994, enough to build 154,000 homes. Production increased 8 percent and was 120.2 million board feet over the mark set in 1993. Production of pine lumber rose nearly 8 percent to 1,340.9 million board feet. This was the sixth consecutive year in which pine-lumber production surpassed the 1 billion board-foot mark. Hardwood lumber production increased by 14 percent, to 195.7 million board feet. Part of the increase is attributable to increases in both pine and hardwood tie output.

Texas Lumber Production, 1984-1994

Year	*Lumber Production		Tie Production	
	Pine	Hardwood	Pine	Hardwood
	(thousand board feet)		(thousand pieces)	
1985	856,157	175,254	101	926
1986	944,465	176,322	120	772
1987	902,987	163,271	112	587
1988	990,118	154,440	61	604
1989	1,067,458	154,726	31	600
1990	1,007,397	148,581	39	591
1991	1,007,801	146,343	60	575
1992	1,092,738	138,874	13	498
1993	1,244,373	171,976	69	725
1994	1,340,882	195,693	66	739

*Includes tie volumes.

Structural Panel Products: Production of structural panels at Texas' eight plywood and four oriented strand board mills continued to increase in 1993. Production rose 8 percent to reach 2,754.9 million square feet (3/8-inch basis). Texas accounted for 10 percent of U.S. panel pro-

duction in 1993.

Texas Structural Panel Production, 1985-1994

Year	Pine (Thd. sq. ft.*)	Year	Pine (Thd. sq. ft.*)
1985	1,985,699	1990	2,422,151
1986	2,082,659	1991	2,203,065
1987	2,250,279	1992	2,557,103
1988	2,343,241	1993	2,754,949
1989	2,130,575	1994	2,632,833

*3/8-inch basis

Paper Products: Paper production at Texas' seven pulp and paper mills posted a slight decline as the industry suffered nationally from overcapacity and reduced product prices. Production of paper and paperboard totaled 2.8 million tons, off 1 percent from the 1992 mark. Paper production increased 3 percent to 1.2 million tons, while output of paperboard was 1.6 million tons, off 4 percent. Market pulp production was also down. Production declined 34 percent to 218 thousand tons.

Texas Pulpwood Production

Year	Roundwood		Chips & Sawdust		Total Pulpwood Production
	Pine	Hardwood	Pine	Hardwood	
	(Thousand cords)				
1985	1,901	716	1,591	462	4,670
1986	1,623	715	1,517	570	4,426
1987	1,650	782	1,456	578	4,466
1988	1,695	819	1,562	492	4,568
1989	1,769	935	1,625	518	4,847
1990	1,695	848	1,662	548	4,753
1991	1,835	950	1,632	568	4,985
1992	1,861	1,038	1,769	605	5,273
1993	1,636	1,099	1,782	674	5,191
1994	1,574	1,213	1,924	795	5,506

Future of Texas' Forest Resources

Because of recent reductions of timber harvests from the vast federal forests of the Pacific Northwest brought about by environmental pressures, most analysts believe that the forest-products industry will continue to expand in the South. Demand for wood products continues to grow both domestically and globally. No other region of the United States has as much potential to fill the void left by the decline of timber harvest in the Pacific Northwest.

However, the South's ability to increase its supply of timber will be a limiting factor for long-term industry growth in the region. In Texas, 95 out of every 100 cubic feet of timber grown annually is harvested. The question is, how can we increase timber supplies to ensure that we can continue to meet wood needs in the future without overharvesting our forests?

Some timberland owners have a good record in reforestation, but others need improvement. The forest-products industry in Texas is doing a credible job in replanting after harvest by maintaining their own tree nurseries, growing and planting 133 million tree seedlings every year. In fact, projections show that timber growth on industry lands may increase by as much as 30 percent as a result of intensive timber-management practices and genetically improved tree seedlings.

Texas' greatest future problem — and opportunity — lies in nonindustrial private forest landowners (NIPF's). These owners are currently replanting only one acre for every nine acres harvested. Thousands of acres in NIPF ownership have been cut-over repeatedly and are not producing the amount of timber they could. Through improved forest management on less productive NIPF forests, and conversion of marginal crop and pastureland to forest, it is estimated that East Texas pine growth could be increased by as much as 40 percent. This would support significant growth of the forest-products industry and provide additional timber income to landowners, while providing environmental benefits such as cleaner air and water, reduced erosion and more wildlife habitat.

Forest Fires

From 1925 through 1996, more than 182,100 forest fires were reported and suppressed in East Texas by the Texas Forest Service. In 1995, TFS crews battled 1,531 East Texas forest fires that scorched 18,877 acres. Major causes were debris burning (54 percent) and arson or incendiary (28 percent). Other causes accounted for roughly 1 percent each, with miscellaneous cause category at 9 percent.

In 1996, TFS crews suppressed 2,622 fires that burned 76,581 acres before being controlled. Primary causes were debris burning (47 percent) and arson (26 percent). In addition as part of the North Texas Fire Response and later North Central Texas Fire Response (the 1996 Texas Fire Siege), TFS personnel took action on 183 fires that burned 153,836 acres.

Forest Pests

In the South, southern pine beetles kill more timber annually than forest fires. The Texas Forest Service coordinates all beetle-control activity in Texas, which includes detecting infestations from the air, notifying landowners, and assisting them in controlling the infestations. The most severe outbreak of southern pine beetles known in Texas occurred in 1985 when more than 15,000 infestations

were detected. That year alone enough trees were killed to build more than 70,000 homes.

Extensive mortality of oaks in the Hill Country of Central Texas is creating increasing public concern. The vascular wilt disease, "oak wilt," is the major cause. A suppression project, which offers affected landowners professional assistance and cost sharing, is administered by the Texas Forest Service. In 1996, the TFS initiated a cooperative project to provide applied research and technical assistance to coop members for control of a variety of forest pests including cone and seed insects, regeneration insects, and Texas leaf-cutting ants.

Urban Forests

No discussion of Texas' forest resources would be complete without a mention of the "urban and community forests" that are an integral part of Texas cities and towns.

Because an estimated 80 percent of Texans live in cities with more than 100,000 population, urban trees and forests play an important part in the lives of many. Trees mitigate the urban heat island effect through shading and evaporative cooling. They also purify the air by absorbing pollutants, slowing the chemical reactions that produce harmful ozone, and filtering dust. Urban forests reduce stormwater runoff and soil erosion. They also buffer against noise, glare and strong winds, while providing habitat for most of the wildlife city dwellers will ever see. Environmental benefits from a single tree may be worth more than $275 each year. Emotional and psychological benefits of urban trees raise the value even higher. ☆

Total Timber Production and Value by County in Texas, 1994

County	Pine	Hardwood	Total	Stumpage Value	Delivered Value
	Cubic feet			Thousand dollars	
Anderson	10,382,944	2,931,989	13,314,933	14,812	19,279
Angelina	34,005,313	2,353,733	36,359,046	38,598	50,902
Bowie	1,487,319	4,927,136	6,414,455	1,894	4,541
Camp	911,880	1,053,474	1,965,354	1,204	1,941
Cass	20,946,422	13,586,509	34,532,931	23,067	36,041
Chambers	2,756,124	777,280	3,533,404	4,350	5,517
Cherokee	22,890,158	5,971,784	28,861,942	29,143	38,954
Franklin	361,862	971,496	1,333,358	598	1,123
Gregg	1,334,462	2,097,560	3,432,022	2,136	3,425
Grimes	4,431,036	310,353	4,741,389	6,102	7,619
Hardin	21,473,098	7,174,731	28,657,829	27,963	37,909
Harris	12,151,334	2,480	12,153,814	18,014	21,734
Harrison	17,234,808	7,002,996	24,237,804	20,836	29,514
Houston	26,010,837	3,960,410	29,971,247	27,175	37,662
Jasper	433,373,436	2,299,565	45,673,001	47,217	62,705
Jefferson	496,388	1,073,218	1,569,606	842	1,439
Leon	697,526	176,399	873,925	810	1,118
Liberty	22,473,316	10,048,580	32,521,896	30,740	42,045
Marion	8,403,709	4,718,413	13,122,122	9,997	14,791
Montgomery	28,887,423	3,163,031	32,050,454	33,139	44,047
Morris	2,270,291	889,219	3,159,510	2,897	4,019
Nacogdoches	26,324,979	3,347,370	29,672,349	33,519	43,384
Newton	29,675,374	4,019,364	33,694,738	33,014	44,579
Orange	4,912,832	3,486,212	8,399,044	7,160	10,187
Panola	19,396,378	6,039,1687	25,435,546	22,449	31,443
Polk	27,825,445	3,992,594	31,819,039	28,415	39,587
Red River	619,845	1,929,080	2,548,925	1,101	2,135
Rusk	15,757,012	6,469,561	22,226,573	20,431	28,196
Sabine	11,593,887	1,749,438	13,343,325	16,400	20,750
San Augustine	21,132,274	2,618,882	23,751,156	29,790	37,493
San Jacinto	11,942,826	2,140,370	14,113,196	12,899	17,852
Shelby	27,384,934	6,443,229	33,838,163	31,733	43,572
Smith	6,682,499	2,564,590	9,247,089	9,208	12,392
Titus	370,148	2,305,192	2,675,340	715	1,830
Trinity	18,837,591	996,364	19,833,956	20,333	27,099
Tyler	29,605,440	4,099,599	33,705,039	28,315	40,268
Upshur	6,038,234	5,725,949	11,784,183	9,486	13,792
Walker	27,257,734	3,409,680	30,667,414	25,164	36,111
Waller	2,635,879	—	2,635,879	3,911	4,716
Wood	2,736,616	1,978,235	4,714,851	3,458	5,207
Other Counties	2,764,230	754,892	3,519,122	3,927	5,111
Totals	**576,503,843**	**139,581,126**	**716,084,969**	**$682,975**	**$932,031**

State Forests

Texas has five state forests, all of which are used primarily for demonstration and research.

The first state forest, now known as the **E.O. Siecke State Forest** in Newton County, was purchased by the state in 1924. It contains 1,722 acres of pine land. An additional 100 acres was obtained by a 99-year lease in 1946.

The **W. Goodrich Jones State Forest**, south of Conroe in Montgomery County, containing 1,725 acres, was purchased in 1926. A 20-acre adjunct was given to the state in 1969.

The **I.D. Fairchild State Forest,** Texas' largest, is located west of Rusk in Cherokee County. This forest was transferred from the state prison system in 1925. An addi-tional 536 acres were added to the original 2,360 acres in 1963 from the Texas State Hospitals and Special Schools, for a total acreage of 2,896.

The 626-acre **John Henry Kirby State Forest** was donated by the late lumberman, John Henry Kirby, in 1929, and later donors. Revenue from this forest is given to the Association of Former Students of Texas A&M University for student-loan purposes.

The newest state forest, the **Paul N. Masterson Memorial Forest** of 520 acres, was donated in the fall of 1984. Mrs. Leonora O'Neal Masterson of Beaumont donated the land in Jasper County in honor of her husband, an active member of the Texas Forestry Association and a tree farmer. ☆

National Forests and Grasslands in Texas

Source: National Forest Service, Lufkin and Albuquerque, NM.

There are four national forests and all or part of five national grasslands in Texas. These federally owned lands are administered by the **U.S. Department of Agriculture-Forest Service**. The national forests cover 755,284 acres in parts of 17 Texas counties.

Supervision of the East Texas forests and North Texas grasslands is by the Forest Supervisor of the division known as the **National Forests and Grasslands in Texas** (701 N. 1st St., Lufkin 75901; (409) 639-8501). The three **National Grasslands in West Texas** (Black Kettle, McClellan Creek and Rita Blanca) are administered by the Forest Supervisor in Albuquerque, New Mexico, as units of the Cibola National Forest. The forests and grasslands are locally administered by district rangers. The following list gives the name of the forest or grassland, the administrative district(s) for each, the acreage in each county and the total acreage:

Angelina National Forest - Angelina Ranger District (Lufkin) - Angelina County, 58,533 acres; Jasper, 21,011; Nacogdoches, 9,238; San Augustine, 64,392. Total, 153,174.

Davy Crockett National Forest - Neches District (Crockett); Trinity District (Apple Springs) - Houston County, 94,683 acres; Trinity, 67,329. Total, 162,012.

Sabine National Forest - Tenaha District (San Augustine); Yellowpine District (Hemphill) - Jasper County, 64 acres; Newton, 1,781; Sabine, 95,409; San Augustine, 4,317; Shelby, 59,037. Total, 160,608.

Sam Houston National Forest - San Jacinto District (Cleveland); Raven District (New Waverly) - Montgomery County, 47,777 acres; San Jacinto, 60,247; Walker, 53,633. Total, 161,657.

Black Kettle National Grassland - Lake Marvin District Ranger in Cheyenne, Okla. - Hemphill County, 576 acres; Roger Mills County, Okla., 31,000 acres. Total, 31,576.

Lyndon B. Johnson and Caddo National Grasslands - District Ranger at Decatur - Fannin County, 17,785 acres; Montague County, 61 acres; Wise, 20,252. Total, 38,098.

McClellan Creek National Grassland - District Ranger at Cheyenne, Okla. - Gray County, 1,449 acres. Total, 1,449.

Rita Blanca National Grassland — District Ranger at Clayton, New Mex. — Dallam County, 78,027 acres; Cimarron County, Okla., 15,736 acres. Total, 93,763.

National Forests

National Forests in Texas were established by invitation of the Texas Legislature by an Act of 1933, authorizing the purchase of lands in Texas for the establishment of national forests. President Franklin D. Roosevelt proclaimed these purchases of national forests on Oct. 15, 1936.

National Grasslands

The submarginal Dust Bowl project lands, purchased by the federal government primarily under the Bankhead-Jones Farm Tenant Act (1937), are today well covered with grasses and native shrubs.

Uses of National Forests and Grasslands

The forests are managed for multiple uses, including production and sales of timber and minerals and programs involving recreation, fish and wildlife, soil and water. The grasslands are administered for uses including range, watershed, recreation and wildlife.

Timber Production

More than 521,000 acres of the National Forests in Texas are suitable for timber production. Sales of sawtimber, pulpwood and other forest products are made at regular intervals.

The estimated net growth is over 200 million board feet per year and is valued at $25 million. About one-third of this growth is removed by cutting. The balance is left to grow. By the year 2000, growth is expected to exceed 200 million board feet per year.

Cattle Grazing

Permits to graze cattle on national forests and national grasslands are granted to the public for an annual fee. Approximately 997 head of cattle are grazed on national forests, and 1,163 head of cattle are grazed on the Caddo-Lyndon B. Johnson National Grasslands annually. On the Rita Blanca NG, 4,000 cattle are grazed each year, most of them in Texas.

Hunting and Fishing

State hunting and fishing laws and regulations apply to all national-forest land. Game-law enforcement is carried out by the Texas Parks and Wildlife Department. The Angelina, Sabine, Neches and San Jacinto rivers, Sam Rayburn and Toledo Bend reservoirs, Lake Conroe and many small streams provide a wide variety of fishing opportunities.

Recreation Facilities

An estimated 3 million people visited the recreational areas in the National Forests and Grasslands in Texas in 1997, primarily for picnicking, swimming, fishing, camping, boating and nature enjoyment. These areas are listed in the Recreation section of the Texas Almanac. ☆

Texas' Threatened and Endangered Species

Strict laws protect species identified as endangered or threatened. Endangered species are those which the Texas Department of Parks and Wildlife has named as being at risk of statewide extinction. Threatened species are those which are likely to become endangered in the future. It is generally unlawful to take, possess, transport, export, process or sell any of the animal species designated as endangered or threatened without a permit. Commerce in threatened and endangered plants and the collection of listed plant species from public land without a permit is prohibited. The following species of Texas flora and fauna are either endangered or threatened as of Jan. 30, 1997, according to the TP&WD. This list varies slightly from the federal list. Any questions about protected species should be directed to the Endangered Resources Branch, Texas Parks and Wildlife Department, 4200 Smith School Road, Austin 78744; (800) 792-1112; Internet: http://www.tpwd.state.tx.us/nature/endang/endang.htm

Threatened Species

Animals:

Mammals: Rafinesque's big-eared, southern yellow and spotted bats; black and Louisiana black bears; white-nosed coati; Atlantic spotted and rough-toothed dolphins; jaguar; margay; Palo Duro mouse; Coues' rice and Texas kangaroo rats; dwarf sperm, false killer, Gervais' beaked, goose-beaked, killer, pygmy killer, pygmy sperm and short-finned pilot whales.

Birds: Rose-throated becard; bald eagle; reddish egret; Arctic peregrine falcon; common black, gray, white-tailed and zone-tailed hawks; white-faced ibis; American swallow-tailed kite; Mexican spotted owl; ferruginous and cactus ferruginous pygmy-owl; tropical parula; piping plover; Bachman's and Botteri's sparrows; wood stork; sooty tern; northern beardless tyrannulet.

Reptiles: Speckled racer; Big Bend blackhead, black-striped, Brazos water, Concho water, indigo, Louisiana pine, northern cat-eyed, smooth green, scarlet and Texas lyre snakes and timber rattlesnake; Texas tortoise; alligator snapping and Chihuahuan mud turtles; loggerhead and green sea turtles; reticulated gecko; mountain short-horned, reticulate collared and Texas horned lizards; black-spotted newt; Blanco blind, Cascade Caverns, Comal blind and San Marcos salamanders; South Texas siren (large form); Mexican burrowing toad; Mexican tree-frog; white-lipped and sheep frogs.

Fishes: Toothless and widemouth blindcats; Rio Grande chub; creek chubsucker; blackside and Rio Grande darters; blotched gambusia; river and blackfin gobies; Devil's River minnow; paddlefish; opossum pipefish; Conchos and Pecos pupfishes; bluehead, bluntnose, Chihuahua and proserpine shiners; Mexican stoneroller; shovelnose sturgeon; blue sucker.

Plants:

Cacti: Bunched cory, Chisos Mountains hedgehog and Lloyd's mariposa cactus.

Trees: Hinckley's Oak.

Wildflowers: McKittrick pennyroyal.

Endangered Species

Animals:

Mammals: Greater long-nosed bat; black-footed ferret; jaguarundi; West Indian manatee; ocelot; black right, blue, finback and sperm whales; gray and red wolves.

Birds: Whooping crane; Eskimo curlew; American peregrine, aplomado and northern aplomado falcons; southwestern willow flycatcher; brown pelican; greater prairie chicken; interior least tern; black-capped vireo; ivory-billed and red-cockaded woodpecker; Bachman's and golden-cheeked warblers.

Reptiles: Atlantic hawksbill, leatherback and Kemp's ridley sea turtles.

Amphibians: Texas blind salamander; Houston toad.

Fishes: Fountain darter; Big Bend, Clear Creek, Pecos and San Marcos gambusias; Rio Grande silvery minnow; Comanche Springs and Leon Springs pupfishes.

Invertebrates: Ouachita rock pocketbook.

Plants:

Cacti: Black lace, Lloyd's hedgehog, Nellie cory, Sneed pincushion, star and Tobusch fishhook cactus; Davis' green pitaya.

Grasses and Grass-like Plants: Little aguja pondweed; Texas wild-rice.

Orchids: Navasota ladies'-tresses.

Trees, Shrubs and Sub-Shrubs: Texas ayenia; Johnston's frankenia; Walker's manioc; Texas snowbells.

Wildflowers: South Texas ambrosia; white bladderpod; Terlingua Creek cat's-eye; ashy dogweed; Texas trailing phlox; Texas poppy-mallow; Texas prairie dawn; slender rush-pea; large-fruited sand verbena. ☆

Nature Conservancy Protects Natural Heritage

The Nature Conservancy of Texas (TNCT) is an affiliate of The Nature Conservancy, a national, private, non-profit organization that uses its resources to preserve unique and significant natural areas. Since 1966, the Texas organization, working closely with government agencies and other private groups, has acquired more than 323,000 acres and has protected 150,000 additional acres through cooperative work with private landowners, for a total of 473,000 acres in Texas. Some of the areas acquired by the conservancy are now managed as state or national parks or wildlife refuges.

Membership in the Nature Conservancy of Texas as of April 1997 was 28,000.

The Nature Conservancy of Texas preserves listed below welcome visitors, but you must call the TNCT office in advance at (210) 224-8774 to arrange your visit.

Clymer Meadow, Hunt County (311 acres) - The spring is the best time to see the wildflowers here. In the fall, the tall native grasses flower. In June, purple coneflower, rosin-weed, blue sage, basketflower, and various species of brown-eyed Susan and gayflower add a colorful contrast to the green backdrop of the meadow.

Clive Runnells Family Mad Island Marsh Preserve, Matagorda County (7,048 acres) - Mid-November through mid-February is the best time to visit primarily because wintering waterfowl, raptors and sandhill cranes are abundant. In late winter alligators are easily spotted sunning themselves on the banks of the sloughs and bayous. October through early November, and also late February until late April, can be a pleasant time to visit and avoid the summer heat of the coast. In the spring, migratory songbirds are abundant. Generally, from the last week of March through the middle of April numerous neotropical birds inhabit the preserve's coastal brush belts. The spring is also usually a good time for sport fishing. From May through September, the weather is hot and the mosquitoes abound. The reward for those that can endure these rigors is optimal sport-fishing opportunities. Several species of wading birds establish a rookery on the preserve during the summer.

Dolan Falls, Val Verde County (4,795 acres) - Fishing and rock art are year-round features here. March and April are optimum wildflower months. Mid-April through end of May are best times for viewing black-capped vireos. Excelent birding opportunities are available spring through mid-fall, but best in spring. Monarch butterflies migrate south through the Devils River corridor in October, and the winter months offer opportunites to see golden eagles.

Lennox Woods, Red River County (366 acres) - This preserve is an undisturbed forest — an old-growth woodland containing shortleaf and loblolly pine and a variety of oaks. It is located about 10 miles north of Clarksville and is open during daylight hours.

Roy E. Larsen Sandyland Sanctuary, Hardin County (2,275 acres) - Village Creek, a major tributary of the Neches River, wanders through the sanctuary, a rare combination of swamp, open-floor forest and southern pine lands. Six miles of nature trails, along which you can view dogwood and wild azaleas blooming from early spring through May, trailing phlox in March and April, and white firewheel and scarlet catchfly July through October.

On the Internet: http://www. tnc.org/. Click on "Domestic" in the table of contents, then click on the Texas outline on the map. ☆

Texas Wildlife

Source: Texas Parks and Wildlife Department, Austin

Texas has many native animals and birds, plus species introduced on game preserves.

More than **540 species of birds** — about three fourths of all different species found in the United States — have been identified in Texas.

Some **142 species of animals**, including some that today are extremely rare, are found in Texas; a list of plant and animal species designated as threatened or endangered by federal or state natural resource officials is found elsewhere in this chapter.

Through efforts of the **Texas Parks and Wildlife Department**, several nonprofit organizations, and many individual landowners involved in conservation, our wildlife should be a permanent resource.

A few of the leading native animals of Texas are described here. Information is provided by the **Nongame and Urban Program**, Texas Parks and Wildlife Department.

Mammals

Armadillo — The **nine-banded armadillo** (Dasypus novemcinctus) is one of Texas' most interesting mammals. It has migrated north and east and is now common as far north and east as Oklahoma and Mississippi. There has been limited commercialization of the armadillo's shell in the manufacture of curios.

Badger — The **badger** (Taxidea taxus) is found throughout West Texas, but in greatly reduced numbers since wholesale eradication of the prairie dog on which the badger preyed. It is a predator, but its pelt is valuable. The range of the badger includes the Texas Panhandle and South Texas, where it is common.

Bat — Thirty-two species of these winged mammals have been found in Texas, more than in any other state in the United States. Of these, 27 species are known residents, though they are seldom seen by the casual observer. The **Mexican free-tailed bat** (Tadarida brasiliensis) and the **cave myotis** (Myotis velifer) constitute most of the cave-dwelling bats of Southwest and West Texas. They have some economic value for their deposits of nitrogen-rich **guano**. Some commercial guano has been produced from **James River Bat Cave**, Mason County; **Beaver Creek Cavern**, Burnet County; and from large deposits in other caves including **Devil's Sinkhole** in Edwards County, **Blowout Cave** in Blanco County and **Bandera Bat Cave**, Bandera County. The largest oncentration of bats in the world is found at **Bracken Cave** in Comal County. The **big brown bat** (Eptesicus fuscus), the **red bat** (Lasiurus borealis) and the **evening bat** (Nycticeius humeralis) are found in East and Southeast Texas. The evening and big brown bats are forest and woodland dwelling mammals. Most of the rarer species of Texas bats have been found along the Rio Grande and in the Trans-Pecos. Bats can be observed at dusk near a water source, and many species may also be found foraging on insects attracted to street lights. Everywhere bats occur, they are the main predators of night-flying insects, including mosquitoes and many crop pests.

Bear — The **black bear** (Ursus americanus) was formerly common throughout most of the state. It is now surviving in the inaccessible river bottoms of eastern Texas and in portions of the Trans-Pecos with potential habitat.

Beaver — Two subspecies of beaver are found in Texas, the **Mexican beaver** (Castor canadensis mexicanus) ranging along the Rio Grande and Devils River and the **Texas beaver** (Castor canadensis texensis) which has been brought back from the verge of extinction to abundance through restocking.

Bighorn — (See **Sheep**.)

Bison — The largest of native terrestrial wild mammals of North America, the **American bison** (Bison bison), commonly called **buffalo**, is found today on a few ranches and in zoos. Deliberate slaughter of this majestic animal for hides and to eliminate the Plains Indians' main food source reached a peak about 1875, and the bison was almost eradicated by 1885. Estimates of the number of buffalo killed vary, but as many as 200,000 hides were sold in Fort Worth at a single two-day sale. Except for the interest of the late **Col. Charles Goodnight** and a few other foresighted men, the bison might be extinct.

Cat — The **jaguar** (Felis onca) is probably now extinct in Texas and, along with the **ocelot, jaguarundi** and **margay**, is listed as rare and endangered by both federal and state wildlife agencies. The **cougar** (Felis concolor), which is also known as **mountain lion, puma, panther** and **Mexican cougar,** is found in many areas of the state, including the broken country of the Edwards Plateau, the Trans-Pecos Mountains and the South Texas brush country. The former panther of the East Texas forest, which was closely related, may be extinct in Texas but still exists in a few areas of Southeastern U.S. The **ocelot** (Felis pardalis), also known as the **leopard cat**, is found usually along the border. The **red-and-gray cat**, or **jaguarundi** (Felis yagouaroundi Geoffroy) is found in extreme South Texas. The **margay** (Felis wiedii) was reported in 1884 near Eagle Pass. There is currently a margay breeding program underway at a wildlife center near Glen Rose with the goal of eventually re-establishing the small cat in the wild. The **bobcat** (Felis rufus) is found over the state in large numbers. The **feral housecat** may have impact on game birds in many parts of Texas.

Chipmunk — The **gray-footed chipmunk** (Tamias canipes) is found at high altitudes in the Guadalupe and Sierra Diablo ranges of the Trans-Pecos (see also **Ground Squirrel**, with which it is often confused in public reference).

Coati — The **coati** (Nasua narica), a relative of the raccoon, is occasionally found in southern Texas. It inhabits woodland areas and feeds both on the ground and in trees. The coati, which is on the list of threatened species, is also found occasionally in Big Bend National Park. There is a captive-breeding project for the coati at a wildlife center near Glen Rose in Somervell County.

Coyote — The **coyote** (Canis latrans), great in num-

White-tailed deer are common in many areas of the state.
Dallas Morning News photo by Ray Sasser.

ber, is the most destructive Texas predator of livestock. On the other hand, it is probably the most valuable predator in the balance of nature. It is a protection to crops and range lands by its control of rodents, rabbits, etc. It is found throughout the state, but is most numerous in the brush country of Southwest Texas.

Deer — The **white-tailed deer** *(Odocoileus virginianus)* is an important Texas game animal. Its number in Texas is estimated at 3 million. It thrives best in the wooded and broken areas of the Edwards Plateau and south of San Antonio where it often competes for feed with domestic and exotic animals. Texas Parks and Wildlife Department has had success in **transplanting deer.** In East Texas, the timbered sections of North Central Texas, and even in the thinly populated areas of Northwest Texas, the white-tailed deer population has increased greatly. The **mule deer** *(Odocoileus heminous)* is found principally in the Trans-Pecos and in smaller numbers in the less thickly settled parts of the Staked Plains. It has increased in number in recent years. The little **Del Carmen deer** (white-tailed subspecies) is found in limited numbers in the high valleys of the Chisos Mountains in the Big Bend. The **American elk** *(Cervus canadensis)*, though not the original subspecies found in Texas, has been introduced into the Guadalupe and Davis mountains.

Ferret — The **black-footed ferret** *(Mustela nigripes)* was formerly found widely ranging through the West Texas country of the prairie dog on which it preyed. It is now considered extinct in Texas. It is of the same genus as the weasel and the mink.

Fox — Most common is the **gray fox** *(Urocyon cinereoargenteus)* found in the forested area of East Texas and throughout most of the state where there is cover, notably in the broken parts of the Edwards Plateau and the rough country at the foot of the Staked Plains. The **kit** or **Swift fox** *(Vulpes velox)* is found in the plains country of Northwest Texas. A second species of **kit fox** *(Vulpes macrotis)* is found in the Trans-Pecos and is fairly numerous in some localities. The **red fox** *(Vulpes vulpes)* is not a native but was introduced for sport.

Gopher — Six species of pocket gophers occur in Texas. The **Botta's pocket gopher** *(Thomomys bottae)* is found in West Texas south of the High Plains, notably along the Rio Grande. The **plains pocket gopher** *(Geomys bursarius)* is found in the Panhandle and throughout North Central and East Texas. The **desert pocket gopher** *(Geomys arenarius)* and the **yellow-faced pocket gopher** *(Pappogeomys castanops)* are found in the Trans-Pecos. The **Texas pocket gopher** *(Geomys personatus)* is found in the sandy soils of the lower coastal region.

Ground Squirrel — Five or more species of ground squirrel live in Texas, mostly in the western part of the state. The **rock squirrel** *(Spermophilus variegatus)* is found throughout the Edwards Plateau and Trans-Pecos. The **Mexican ground squirrel** *(Spermophilus mexicanus)* is found in the Mexican border country from Brownsville to the Davis Mountains. The **spotted ground squirrel** *(Spermophilus spilosoma)* is found generally in favorable localities throughout the western half of the state. The **thirteen-lined ground squirrel** *(Spermophilus tridecemlineatus)* is found in the Panhandle and in a narrow strip from Red River to the Gulf between Dallas and Corpus Christi. The **Texas antelope squirrel** *(Ammospermophilus interpres)* is found along the Rio Grande from El Paso to Val Verde County.

Javelina — The **javelina** or **collared peccary** *(Tayassu tajacu)* is found in South and Southwest Texas. It is fairly numerous. Its meat is edible if properly prepared, and there is limited use of its hide for the manufacture of gloves and other leather articles. A scrappy animal, it is the subject of many tall tales.

Mink — The **mink** *(Mustela vison)* is found in East Texas and along the Coastal Belt, usually in forested river bottoms. It yields a considerable fur crop. It is akin to the otter and weasel. **Mink farming,** partly with native and partly with introduced species, is found on a limited scale, usually in East Texas.

Mole — The **mole** *(Scalopus aquaticus)* is found generally throughout the eastern half of the state.

Muskrat — There are three subspecies of muskrat in Texas: the **muskrat** *(Ondatra zibethica rivalicia)*, which is found in Southeast Texas near Beaumont where it is commercially produced on muskrat ranges; the **Pecos River muskrat** *(Ondatra zibethica ripensis)* of Western Texas; and the **Great Plains muskrat** *(Ondatra zibethica cinnamonia)* of the Panhandle region. The muskrat is one of the most valuable of Texas' fur-bearing animals. Production of pelts comes largely from the coastal area near Beaumont.

Nutria — This introduced species *(Myocastor coypus)* is found in Texas, except the Panhandle and extreme western portions. The fur is not highly valued and, since nutria are in competition with muskrats, their spread is discouraged. They are used widely in Texas as a cure-all for ponds choked with vegetation.

Opossum — A **marsupial,** the **Virginia opossum** *(Didelphis virginiana)* is found in nearly all parts of the state. The opossum has economic value for its pelt, and its meat is considered a delicacy by some. It is one of the chief contributors to the Texas fur crop.

Otter — A few **river otter** *(Lutra canadensis)* are found along East Texas rivers and coastal marshes. Although it is a prized fur-bearing animal, there is no evidence that the river otter can be considered either rare or endangered. The species is numerous in Liberty County where biologists have determined that its numbers have increased in recent years. While excess populations of this species, like other forms of wildlife, can be harvested with no danger to the species, loss of habitat through encroaching civilization presents the most formidable threat to its continued existence.

Porcupine — The **yellow-haired porcupine** *(Erethizon dorsatum)* is found in the higher mountain ranges of the Trans-Pecos and in the western Edwards Plateau. It has recently moved into the eastern portion of the Panhandle along the Caprock.

Prairie Dog — Until recent years probably no sight was so universal in West Texas as the **black-tailed prairie dog** *(Cynomys ludovicianus)* and its burrow. Naturalists estimated its population in the hundreds of millions. Its destruction of range grasses, plus its peculiar susceptibility to eradication (usually by the introduction of the fumes of carbon disulphide into its burrow) have caused a great reduction of its numbers over its past range. However, it is making a comeback. Prairie dog towns often covered many acres with thickly spaced burrows or prairie dog holes. It is being propagated in several public zoos, notably in the **prairie dog town in Mackenzie Park** at Lubbock. It has been honored in Texas by the naming of the **Prairie Dog Town Fork** of the Red River, along one segment of which is located the beautiful **Palo Duro Canyon.**

Pronghorn — The **Pronghorn** *(Antilocapra americana)* is primarily a plains animal. It almost became extinct, but a continuous closed season and a sound management program raised its numbers. There have been limited open seasons since 1944. Specifically, these animals inhabit the plains and basin regions of Brewster, Presidio, Jeff Davis, Culberson and Hudspeth counties. They have also sufficiently increased in numbers in the Permian Basin and Panhandle to permit open seasons in recent years.

Rabbit — The **black-tailed jack rabbit** *(Lepus californicus)* is found throughout Texas except in the East Texas forest area. It breeds rapidly, and its long hind legs make it one of the world's faster-running animals. The **Eastern cottontail** *(Sylvilagus floridanus)* is found throughout Texas except in Trans-Pecos region. The **desert cottontail** *(Sylvilagus auduboni)* is found in South and West Texas, usually on the open range. The **swamp rabbit** *(Sylvilagus aquaticus)* is found in East Texas and the coastal area.

Raccoon — The **raccoon** *(Procyon lotor)* is found throughout Texas, especially along streams and in urban settings.

Rats and Mice — There are 40 or 50 species of rats and mice in Texas of varying characteristics, habitats and economic destructiveness. The **Norway rat** *(Rattus norvegicus)* and the **black rat** *(Rattus rattus)* are probably the most common and the most destructive. Some of the species are native, and others, notably the Norway rat, are invaders. The **common house mouse** *(Mus musculis)* is estimated in the hundreds of millions annually. The rare **Guadalupe Mountain vole** *(Microtus mexicanus guadalupensis)* is found only in the Guadalupe Mountains National Park and just over the border into New Mexico.

Ringtail — The **ringtail** *(Bassariscus astutus)* is found generally in wooded areas west of the Trinity and in the broken sections of the Edwards Plateau. It is a valuable fur-bearing mammal.

Sheep — The **barbary**, or **Aoudad, sheep** *(Ammotragus lervia)*, first introduced to the Palo Duro Canyon area in 1957-58, have become firmly established. Barbary sheep have been introduced into many areas of Texas, but are designated as game animals in only eight counties of the Panhandle surrounding Palo Duro Canyon. Efforts are now under way by the Texas Parks and Wildlife Department to establish the **desert bighorn** *(Ovis canadensis)* in range they formerly occupied. Currently 300 bighorns are free-ranging in West Texas.

Shrew — Three species are found in Texas, the **northern short-tailed shrew** *(Blarina brevicauda)*, the **least shrew** *(Cryptotis parva)* and the **desert shrew** *(Notiosorex crawfordi)*. The first-mentioned is rarer, occurring in the Big Thicket. The least shrew is found generally in South Central and East Texas. The **gray shrew** is found in very limited numbers in the semiarid areas of West Texas and along the border.

Skunk — There are six species of skunk in Texas. The **Eastern spotted skunk** *(Spilogale putorius)* is found throughout North Texas. A small skunk, it is often erroneously called civet cat. This skunk also is found in East Texas and the Gulf area. The **Western spotted skunk** *(Spilogale gracilis)* is found in the central, western and southern parts of the state. The **long-tailed**, or **broad-striped skunk** *(Mephitis mephitis)* is found in many parts of the state, usually along streams or in wooded areas. The **hooded skunk** *(Mephitis macroura)* is found in limited numbers in the Trans-Pecos mountains. The Gulf Coast **hog-nosed skunk** *(Conepatus leuconotus)*, found in the

Brownsville area, ranges southward into Mexico. The **mountain hog-nosed skunk** *(Conepatus mesoleucus)* is found in sparsely timbered areas of Edwards Plateau, Central Texas, Trans-Pecos.

Squirrel — The **fox squirrel** *(Sciurus niger)* is found throughout East, Central and West Central Texas. The **gray**, or **cat, squirrel** *(Sciurus carolinensis)* is found generally in the eastern third of the state. The **flying squirrel** *(Glaucomys volans)* is widely distributed in the Piney Woods and the East Texas Post Oak Belt.

Weasel — The **brindled** or **long-tailed weasel** *(Mustela frenata)*, akin to the mink, is found in the Panhandle-Plains and South Texas.

Wolf — The **red wolf** *(Canis rufus)* was once found over a wide range in Eastern and Central Texas. It is now considered extirpated from the wild, with the only known remnants of the population now in captive propagation. The **gray wolf** *(Canis lupus)* once had a wide range over Central, Southern and Western Texas. It has been reduced almost to extinction. The **red wolf** and **gray wolf** are listed on the federal and state rare and endangered species lists. The few gray wolves which may be encountered in Texas are believed to be occasional individuals crossing over from Mexico.

Reptiles and Arachnids

Most of the more than **100 species and subspecies of snakes** found in Texas are beneficial, as also are other reptiles. There are **16 poisonous species and subspecies.**

Poisonous reptiles include **three species of copperheads** (southern, broad-banded and Trans-Pecos); one kind of **cottonmouth** (western); **11 kinds of rattlesnakes** (canebrake, western massasauga, desert massasauga, western pigmy, western diamondback, timber, banded rock, mottled rock, northern blacktailed, Mojave and prairie); and the **Texas coral snake.**

Also noteworthy are the **horned lizard,** also called **horned toad,** which is on the list of **threatened species;** the **vinegarone,** a type of whip scorpion; **tarantula,** a hairy spider; and **alligator.** ☆

Texas Wildlife Management Areas

Source: Texas Parks and Wildlife Department

The Texas Parks and Wildlife Department (TP&WD) is currently responsible for managing 51 wildlife management areas (WMAs) totaling approximately three quarters of a million acres. Of these, 32 WMAs are owned in fee title, while 19 are managed under license agreements with other agencies.

Long known for exceptional hunting opportunities, the wildlife management areas are multiple-use sites utilized for birdwatching, wildlife viewing and research, hiking, primitive camping, bicycling, horseback riding and fishing, as well, when those activities are compatible with the primary goals for which the WMA was established.

The WMAs also demonstrate the benefits of sound land stewardship practices such as grazing, prescribed burning, brush control and other wildlife habitat management techniques. In addition, WMAs function as living laboratories where research is conducted that provides valuable data about the plants, animals, and natural systems which surround us.

Access to WMAs is provided by six types of permits. A $50 to $100 special permit (selection by drawing) is required to participate in closely supervised hunts where the demand is great. Access for hunting species not so high in demand requiring only a moderate amount of supervision is provided by a permit costing $10 per day. A $40 annual public hunting permit provides unsupervised access to those lands administered under the public hunting program.

A $10 limited public use permit allows an adult unsupervised entry to birdwatch, hike, camp or picnic on designated public hunting lands. The Texas Conservation Passport (Gold $50, Silver $25) provides access at designated times on designated portions of WMAs for nonconsumptive use. Participation in special events is also authorized under the Texas Conservation Passport Program. The Gold Passport also allows entry to state parks. For further information, write to Texas Parks and Wildlife, 4200 Smith School Rd., Austin 78744, or call (512) 792-1112. On the Internet: http://www.tpwd.state.tx.us.

A brief description of some WMAs is given below:

Candy Cain Abshier WMA (Chambers County) is a 207-acre tract managed primarily for nongame wildlife. Located on Smith Point, approximately 25 miles south of Anahuac, the area is popular with bird watchers during the spring and fall. No public facilities available; commercial facilities are nearby.

Alazan Bayou WMA (Nacogdoches County) was purchased in 1991 and consists of 1,973 acres southwest of Nacogdoches on the north shore of the Angelina River. It was purchased primarily to preserve bottomland hardwoods and is managed for waterfowl habitat enhancement. Public hunting allowed by permit for waterfowl, squirrel, woodcock and archery deer. Camping not permitted; camping and other lodging available in the vicinity.

Atkinson Island WMA (Harris County) consists of 151 acres of wading shorebird habitat adjacent to the Houston Ship Channel. Area is accessible only by boat; there are no public use facilities on the island.

Black Gap WMA (Brewster County) is an area of 106,915 acres on the Rio Grande adjacent to Big Bend National Park. Vegetation is typical of Chihuahuan Desert. Wildlife include desert mule deer, javelina, bobcat, coyotes, scaled quail and other desert species. Hunting allowed by special permit for deer and javelina, annual hunting permit for deer (archery), quail, dove and rabbits. Primitive camping allowed during public hunts at designated campgrounds; other facilities nearby.

Walter Buck WMA (Kimble County) includes 2,123 acres on the South Fork of the Llano River about three miles southwest of Junction. The gently rolling terrain is punctuated by canyons with dense stands of ashe juniper, elm and live oak. Wildlife includes white-tailed deer, feral Spanish goats, axis and sika deer, and wild turkey. No camping or fires; camping permitted at South Llano River State Park; commercial facilities available in Junction.

Chaparral WMA (La Salle and Dimmit counties), comprising 15,200 acres eight miles west of Artesia Wells, is in typical South Texas brush country: thorny brush, or "chaparral," includes mesquite, prickly pear cactus, granjeno, blackbrush and leatherstem. The terrain is flat to gently rolling. Wildlife includes deer, javelina and feral hogs, quail and mourning doves. Western diamondback rattlesnakes are common. Has a driving nature trail and two walking trails. Primitive campground available for hunters; commercial facilities nearby.

Dam B WMA (Jasper and Tyler counties) is located on B. A. Steinhagen Lake. Its 13,445 acres of land and water are generally flat with many sloughs separated by low ridges. Knee-high, waterproof footwear recommended. Trees include oaks and hickories, cedar elm, American hornbeam, black and sweet gums, greenbriers, holly, hawthorn, cypress, tupelo, water elm and buttonbush. Wildlife includes white-tailed deer, gray and fox squirrels, cottontail and swamp rabbits and waterfowl. Access by boat only; airboats are prohibited on the Angelina-Neches Scientific Area of the WMA. Permits are required for camping.

James E. Daughtrey WMA (Live Oak and McMullen counties) is located between Three Rivers and Tilden. Approximately 4,000 acres surrounding Choke Canyon Reservoir are available for public hunting. The rolling terrain is covered with thorny brush dominated by mesquite, blackbrush and cacti. Wildlife includes deer, javelina, turkey, quail, mourning dove, waterfowl and feral hogs. Roads are primitive.

Elephant Mountain WMA (Brewster County) consists of 23,347 acres about 26 miles south of Alpine. Vegetation consists of juniper, piñon, Spanish oak, mesquite, sotol,

yucca, lechuguilla and cacti. Wildlife includes deer, pronghorn, javelina, desert bighorn sheep, quail and doves. Primitive camping allowed; water facilities not reliable.

Gus Engeling WMA (Anderson County) comprises 10,941 acres 32 miles southeast of Corsicana. The flat to gently rolling post-oak woodlands, include dense stands of oak-hickory overstory, along with yaupon, greenbrier, dogwood, hawthorn, elm and huckleberry. Wildlife includes numerous deer, feral hogs, squirrels, quail, mourning dove, waterfowl and turkey. Has a driving nature trail and two walking trails.

Granger WMA (Williamson County), three miles southeast of Granger, comprises 11,116 acres of upland grassland with some bottomland hardwoods. Wildlife includes mourning dove, quail, fox squirrel, rabbits, pheasant and migrant waterfowl. Walking nature trail. Only shotguns allowed. No camping on the area; Corps of Engineer campgrounds available at Granger Lake.

Guadalupe Delta WMA (Calhoun County), 6,772 acres of marsh 3.5 miles northeast of Tivoli, is managed primarily for waterfowl and migratory shore birds, alligators and other wetland wildlife.

Gene Howe WMA (Hemphill County) consists of 6,710 acres of rolling sandhills with large natural meadows along the north bank of the Canadian River. Trees and shrubs include sumac, plum, sagebrush, persimmon, cottonwood and buttonbush. Wildlife includes deer, turkey, quail and mourning dove. Four-wheel drive vehicles are recommended.

Keechi Creek WMA (Leon County) consists of 1,500 acres approximately 10 miles south of Oakwood. The terrain is principally bottomland intersected with creek drainages with standing-water sloughs. Vegetation includes willow, water and overcup oaks, elm and sweetgum. Wildlife includes eastern turkey, deer, squirrels, feral hogs and woodland waterfowl. Camping not allowed; commercial facilities nearby.

Kerr WMA (Kerr County), 6,493 acres located on the headwaters of the North Fork of the Guadalupe River 12 miles west of Hunt, has rolling hills, fresh-water springs, dense cedar brakes and live oak-shin oak thickets. Wildlife includes Rio Grande turkey, mourning dove, quail, javelina, armadillo, fox, gray squirrels, black-capped vireo and golden-cheeked warbler. Has driving nature trail. No camping or fires; camp at Kerrville-Schreiner State Park; commercial facilities nearby.

Las Palomas WMA (Cameron, Hidalgo, Starr, Willacy and Presidio counties) comprises 24 units, more than 7,689 acres in all, mostly native brush vegetation with some farmland and some wetlands. Managed primarily for white-winged doves. Other wildlife includes black-bellied tree ducks, chachalacas, mourning doves, javelina, scaled quail, mule deer, ocelot and jaguarundi. Camping is permitted on some units; check Parks and Wildlife Department for details.

Lower Neches WMA (Orange County) consists of 7,998 acres of coastal marsh located on Sabine Lake. Wildlife includes wintering waterfowl, migratory shore birds and alligators. Hunting permitted on specified days. A boat-launching ramp is available near the south end of the area; no other public facilities.

Mad Island WMA (Matagorda County), located five miles west of the town of Matagorda, consists of 7,281 acres of marsh. Wildlife includes puddle and diver ducks, sandhill cranes, snow, Canada and white-fronted geese, alligators, mottled duck, raccoon, river otter, mink, armadillo, white-tailed deer, bobcat, gray fox and cottontail, jack and swamp rabbits.

Matador WMA (Cottle County) consists of 28,184 acres located 7 miles north of Paducah. Wildlife includes bobwhite quail, mule deer, turkey and doves. Not generally open for public use except for hunts. Some special events are scheduled throughout the year.

Old Tunnel WMA (Kendall County) consists of 10.5 acres of Hill Country habitat and includes an abandoned railroad tunnel, which serves as a summer roost site for bats. Bat-flight tours conducted during summer months. No public-use facilities on the area; facilities available at

Comfort.

Pat Mayse WMA (Lamar County), located 12 miles northwest of Paris, consists of 8,925 acres of land and water adjacent to Pat Mayse Reservoir. The terrain is primarily upland oak woodlands as well as bottomland hardwoods including post and blackjack oak, pecan, hackberry, cottonwood and Osage orange.

J.D. Murphree WMA (Jefferson County) is approximately 13,360 acres of marsh along the upper Texas coast, divided into three units. Managed primarily for wintering and resident waterfowl and associated wildlife.

Peach Point WMA (Brazoria County), five miles west of Freeport, contains 10,312 acres of upland hardwood, upland prairie, fresh and saltwater marshes. Vegetation includes live oak, elm, pecan, Chinese tallow, baccharis, sea ox-eye and shortgrass. Wildlife includes waterfowl, rails, gallinules, mourning doves, quail, squirrel, white-tailed deer, cottontail rabbits, armadillo, feral hogs, alligators and various other shore birds. No camping, commercial facilities available nearby.

Playa Lakes WMA (Castro and Donley counties) consists of three tracts in the Panhandle totalling 1,592 acres, managed for waterfowl and other wildlife species associated with playa lakes. Hunting permitted only on Taylor Lakes Unit.

Redhead Pond WMA (Nueces County) is a small tract (37 acres) in Flour Bluff acquired as a sanctuary for wintering waterfowl and other birds. Visitors can view large concentrations of birds within short drive of Corpus Christi.

Richland Creek WMA (Freestone County) consists of 13,800 acres 25 miles southwest of Corsicana. Area used primarily for hunting; annual hunting or limited-use permit required for access. Primitive campgrounds available.

Sierra Diablo WMA (Hudspeth and Culberson counties), located in the mountain range of same name, consists of 11,625 acres approximately 32 miles northwest of Van Horn. Rough, rugged hills and steep canyons make up most of the area, with an average elevation of 6,200 feet, breaking sharply to desert floor to the east. Has well-established desert mule deer population. Used for bighorn sheep broodstock production. Only primitive camping allowed; nearest commercial facilities are one-and-one-half hours away.

Somerville WMA (Burleson and Lee counties), located 12 miles west southwest of Somerville, comprises 3,180 acres of post and blackjack oak, hickory, yaupon, coralberry, American beautyberry, greenbrier and grape. Wildlife includes white-tailed deer, squirrel, rabbit and migrant waterfowl.

Welder Flats Coastal Preserve (Calhoun County) consists of 1,480 acres of submerged coastal wetlands. Numerous species of wading and shore birds use the preserve, the most distinctive being the whooping crane. ☆

National Wildlife Refuges

Source: U.S. Fish and Wildlife Service, U.S. Department of the Interior.

Texas has more than 416,000 acres in **18 national wildlife refuges**. Included in this acreage are two conservation easement refuges, Little Sandy and Moody National Wildlife Refuges, where the Fish and Wildlife Service does not have management responsibility. The other 16 refuges may be visited at different times of the year for bird watching and wildlife viewing, and they are listed on the following pages. Write or call before visiting to check on facilities and to be sure the refuge is open to visitors when you plan to go. Addresses and phone numbers are given at the ends of the descriptions of the 16 refuges.

Anahuac: The more than 34,296 acres of this refuge are located along the upper Gulf Coast in Chambers County. **Fresh and saltwater marshes** and miles of beautiful, sweeping **coastal prairie** provide wintering habitat for large flocks of **geese** and other **waterfowl**. The endangered **peregrine falcon** and **bald eagle** also find protection on the refuge; other species include the **alligator, mottled duck, wood stork** and **least tern**. Fishing, bird watching and waterfowl hunting are available. Address: Box 278, Anahuac 77514. (409) 267-3337.

Aransas: This refuge comprises 114,396 acres in three units on the mainland, with additional acreage on Matagorda Island (see below). The main body of the refuge is located midway between Rockport and Port Lavaca seven miles southeast of Austwell on FM 2040. The three mainland units consist of **oak woodlands, fresh and saltwater marshes** and **coastal grasslands**. Besides providing wintering grounds for the endangered **whooping crane**, the refuge is home to many species of waterfowl and other migratory birds. This refuge has reported the largest number of bird species of any refuge in the country. Bird life abounds from fall through May. **White-tailed deer, javelinas, alligators** and many other species of wildlife can be found. Refuge is open daily sunrise to sunset. Interpretive center is open daily except Thanksgiving and Christmas. Other facilities include a 40-foot observation tower at the edge of a whooping crane marsh, a paved auto-tour loop and six walking trails. Address: Box 100, Austwell 77950. (512) 286-3559.

Attwater Prairie Chicken: Established in 1972 to preserve habitat for the endangered **Attwater's prairie chicken,** the refuge comprises 8,007 acres of **native prairie,** potholes, sandy knolls and some wooded areas. A 5-mile auto-tour route is available year-round, and 350 acres of marsh are accessible for birding. Refuge open sunrise to sunset. Address: Box 519, Eagle Lake 77434. (409) 234-3021.

Balcones Canyonlands: This 14,144-acre refuge was dedicated in 1992. Located in the **Hill Country** northwest of Austin, it was established to protect the nesting habitat of two endangered birds: **black-capped vireo** and **golden-cheeked warbler.** Eventually, the refuge will encompass 46,000 acres of **oak-juniper woodlands** and other habitats. No public facilities are available at this time; viewing must be done from public roadways. Address: 10711 Burnet Rd., #201, Austin 78758. (512) 339-9432.

Big Boggy: This refuge occupies 4,526 acres of **coastal prairie** and **salt marsh** along East Matagorda Bay for the benefit of wintering **waterfowl**, attracting thousands of **ducks and geese** to its ponds and potholes. **The refuge is generally closed,** and visitors are encouraged to visit nearby **San Bernard or Brazoria refuges.** Waterfowl hunting is permitted in season. Address: Box 1088, Angleton 77516. (409) 849-7771.

Brazoria: The 43,338 acres of this refuge, located along the Gulf Coast in Brazoria County, serve as haven for wintering waterfowl and a wide variety of other migratory birds. The refuge also supports many **marsh** and **water birds,** from **roseate spoonbills** and **great blue herons** to **white ibis** and **sandhill cranes.** Brazoria Refuge is within the **Freeport Christmas Bird Count** circle, which frequently achieves the highest number of species seen in a 24-hour period. The first weekend of every month throughout the year, visitors can drive through the refuge to observe coastal wildlife. Fishing is permitted, as well as waterfowl hunting in season; however, access for these activities is by boat only. Address: 1212 North Velasco, #200, Angleton 77516. (409) 849-7771.

Buffalo Lake: Comprising 7,664 acres in Randall County in the Panhandle, this refuge once was a major waterfowl refuge in the **Central Flyway.** Because of changes in rainfall patterns and a decline of underground water supplies, Buffalo Lake is now dry. Ponds and nearby farmlands provide habitat for waterfowl, and semi-arid grasslands and savannahs provide habitat for numerous birds, reptiles, deer and other mammals. Available activities include picnicking, sight-seeing, birding, photography, hiking and camping. Entrance fee. Pheasant hunting allowed by special permit. Address: Box 179, Umbarger 79091. (806) 499-3382.

Hagerman: Hagerman National Wildlife Refuge lies on the Big Mineral arm of Texoma Lake in Grayson County. The 11,320 acres provide a feeding and resting place for migrating **waterfowl.** The refuge includes 3,000 acres of **marsh** and water and 8,000 acres of **farmland, grassland** and **woodlands.** Bird watching and fishing are the most popular activities. Hunting is permitted during limited seasons in designated areas. Address: Rt. 3, Box 123, Sherman 75090-9564. (903) 786-2826.

Laguna Atascosa: Established in 1946 as southernmost waterfowl refuge in the **Central Flyway**, this refuge contains more than 45,187 acres fronting on the **Laguna Madre** in the Lower Rio Grande Valley. Open **lagoons, coastal prairies, salt flats and brushlands** support a wide diversity of wildlife. The United States' largest concentration of **redhead ducks** winters here, along with many other species of **waterfowl** and **shorebirds**. **White-tailed deer, javelina, armadillo** and **Texas tortoise** can be found, along with endangered **ocelot** and **jaguarundi**. Bird watching and nature study are popular, with the abundance of migratory birds in the winter and many **Mexican birds** present year-round. Saltwater fishing is permitted within Adolph Thomae, Jr. County Park. Archery and rifle hunts are held most years for deer and feral hogs. Entrance fee. Address: Box 450, Rio Hondo 78583. (210) 748-3607.

Lower Rio Grande Valley: The U.S. Fish and Wildlife Service is slowly acquiring land in the Lower Rio Grande Valley for a new national refuge, which will encompass some 109,530 acres within Cameron, Hidalgo, Starr and Willacy counties. Area acquired for the refuge will include 11 different habitat types, including **sabal palm forest, tidal flats, coastal brushland, mid-delta thorn forest, woodland potholes and basins, upland thorn scrub, flood forest, barretal, riparian woodland** and **Chihuahuan thorn forest.** At least 100 unique vertebrate species that are listed as endangered, threatened, or which occur at the periphery of their range call the area home. For more information, contact Santa Ana/Lower Rio Grande Valley National Wildlife Refuges, Rt. 2, Box 202A, Alamo 78516. (210) 787-7861.

Matagorda Island: Matagorda Island is jointly owned by the Texas General Land Office and the U.S. Fish and Wildlife Service. The island's 55,694 acres are cooperatively managed by the Matagorda Island National Wildlife Refuge and State Natural Area. Texas Parks and Wildlife manages the habitat and wildlife on the island through the Aransas NWR, and the island's acreage is included with that reported for the Aransas refuge. The island supports a wide variety of migratory birds, some **19 state or federally listed threatened or endangered species,** a large herd of **white-tailed deer, alligators** and other wildlife. Activities include salt-water fishing, hunting (in season), birding, picnicking and historical interpretation. Address: P.O. Box 117, Port O'Connor 77982.

McFaddin: Purchased in 1980, this refuge's 56,180 acres are of great importance to wintering populations of **migratory waterfowl.** The endangered **southern bald eagle** and **peregrine falcon** are rare visitors, but may occasionally be seen during peak fall and spring migrations. One of the densest populations of **alligators** in

Texas is found here. Activities on the refuge include wildlife observation, waterfowl hunting, fishing and crabbing. Address: Box 609, Sabine Pass 77655. (409) 971-2909.

Muleshoe: Oldest of national refuges in Texas, Muleshoe provides winter habitat for **waterfowl** and the continent's largest wintering population of **sandhill cranes.** Comprising 5,809 acres in the High Plains of Bailey County, the refuge contains three **playa lakes, marsh areas, caliche outcroppings** and **native grasslands.** Tour roads are available, as well as a **prairie dog town,** nature trail, campground and picnic area. Address: Box 549, Muleshoe 79347. Phone (806)946-3341.

San Bernard: Located on the Gulf of Mexico near Freeport, this refuge's nearly 27,437 acres attract **migrating waterfowl,** including thousands of **snow geese,** which spend the winter on the refuge. Habitats consist of **coastal prairies, salt/mud flats** and saltwater and freshwater ponds and potholes. Visitors may enjoy photography and bird watching; fishing is permitted, as well as waterfowl hunting in season. A special-permit waterfowl hunt is conducted three days per week. Contact refuge office for details. Address: Box 1088, Angleton 77516. (409) 849-7771.

Santa Ana: Established in 1943 and referred to as **"gem of the National Wildlife Refuge System,"** Santa Ana's more than 2,087 acres of **subtropical forest** and **native brushland** are located on the north bank of the Rio Grande in Hidalgo County. Santa Ana attracts birders from across the United States who can view many species of **Mexican birds** as they reach the northern edge of their ranges in South Texas. Also found at Santa Ana are **ocelot** and **jaguarundi,** endangered members of the cat family. Address: Rt. 2, Box 202A, Alamo 78516. (210) 787-3079.

Texas Point: Texas Point's 8,952 acres are located on the Upper Gulf Coast, where they serve a large wintering population of **waterfowl** as well as migratory birds. The endangered **southern bald eagle** and **peregrine falcon** may occasionally be seen during peak fall and spring migrations. **Alligators** are commonly observed during the spring, summer and fall months. Activities include wildlife observation, waterfowl hunting, fishing and crabbing. Access to the refuge is by boat and on foot only. Address: Box 609, Sabine Pass 77655. (409) 971-2909.

Trinity River: The newest national refuge in Texas was established in 1994 to protect remnant bottomland hardwood forests and associated wetlands. Located in northern Liberty County off State Highway 787 approximately 15 miles east of Cleveland, it provides habitat for wintering, migrating and breeding waterfowl and a variety of other wetland-dependent wildlife. Approximately 4,400 acres of the proposed 20,000-acre refuge have been purchased. Access to the refuge is limited, but tours can be arranged for small groups with advance notice. Address: Box 10015, Liberty 77575 (409) 336-9786. ☆

Wildlife Stamps and Prints

*Source: **Texas Parks and Wildlife Dept.** and **Collectors Covey,** Box 57306, Dallas, TX 75207.*

Since 1981, the Texas Parks and Wildlife Department has funded some of its acquisition, development and management of natural areas with the sale of wildlife stamps and matching art prints designed by wildlife artists. The artists and subjects for the last two years are listed here. For previous artists and subjects, please see the 1996-97 Texas Almanac. Various other stamps are issued and sold by nonprofit organizations for the benefit of wildlife habitat.

Waterfowl Stamp: Commonly called a "Duck Stamp," the waterfowl stamp has been required of all waterfowl hunters since Fiscal Year 1982. Funds from the sale of waterfowl stamps and prints are used for

Nongame Species Stamp for 1997: Golden eagle by artist Joe Hautman.

Texas waterfowl and wetlands conservation. The 1996 waterfowl was gadwalls by artist Daniel Smith; 1997, cinnamon teal, Jim Hautman.

Saltwater Stamp: Funds from the saltwater stamp,

which has been required of all saltwater fishermen since 1986, may be used for coastal fisheries and management. Featured fish for 1996 was sailfish by artist Al Barnes; 1997, dolphin, Don Ray.

Nongame and Endangered Species Stamp: The nongame stamp, was offered for the first time in 1985. Funds from sale of the nongame stamps and art prints are used for conservation of nongame and endangered species. The 1996 nongame subject was the **cardinals** by artist David Drinkard; 1997, golden eagle, Joe Hautman.

Turkey Stamp: The turkey stamp and print were offered for the first time in 1991. Funds from the sale of turkey stamps and prints are used to help finance the largest eastern turkey restoration program ever attempted, restocking birds on 23 million acres of East Texas habitat. The artist for 1996 was Ken Carlson; for 1997, John Dearman. ☆

Calendar For 1998 and 1999

The subsequent calendars were calculated principally from data in the U.S. Naval Observatory's computer program, **MICA for Macintosh, 1990-1999**, and from its publication, **Astronomical Phenomena** for **1998** and **1999**.

Times listed here are **Central Standard Time**, except for the period from 2:00 a.m. on the first Sunday in April until 2:00 a.m. on the last Sunday in October, when **Daylight Saving Time**, which is one hour later than Central Standard Time, is in effect.

All of Texas is in the Central Time Zone except El Paso and Hudspeth counties and the northwest corner of Culberson County, which observe **Mountain Time** (see accompanying map). Mountain Time is one hour earlier than Central Time.

All times are figured for the intersection of 99° 10' west longitude and 31° 23' north latitude, which is about 15 miles northeast of Brady, McCulloch County. This point is the **approximate geographical center of the state**.

To get the time of sunrise or sunset, moonrise or moonset for any point in Texas, apply the following rule: Add four minutes to the time given in this calendar for each degree of longitude that the place lies west of the 99th meridian; subtract four minutes for each degree of longitude the place lies east of the 99th meridian.

At times there will be considerable variation for distances north and south of the line of 31° 23' north latitude, but the rule for calculating it is complicated. The formula given above will get sufficiently close results.

An accompanying map shows the intersection for which all times given here are calculated, with some major Texas cities and their longitudes. These make it convenient to calculate time at any given point.

Planetary Configurations and Phenomena

In the center column of the calendar on pages 96-101 are given the phenomena and planetary configurations of heavens for 1998 and 1999. Below is an explanation of the symbols used in those tables:

⊙ The Sun	● The Earth	♅ Uranus
☽ The Moon	♂ Mars	♆ Neptune
☿ Mercury	♃ Jupiter	♇ Pluto
♀ Venus	♄ Saturn	

Aspects

♂ This symbol appearing before the symbols for heavenly bodies means they are "in conjunction," that is, having the same longitude as applies to the sky and appearing near each other.

♂° This symbol means that the two heavenly bodies are in "opposition," or differ by 180 degrees of longitude.

Common Astronomical Terms

★ **Aphelion** — Point at which a planet's orbit is farthest from the sun.

★ **Perihelion** — Point at which a planet's orbit is nearest the sun.

★ **Apogee** — That point of the moon's orbit farthest from the earth.

★ **Perigee** — That point of the moon's orbit nearest the earth.

★ **Aspect** — Apparent situation of a planet with respect to another body.

Map for Calculating Time of Sunrise, Sunset, Moonrise, Moonset (see text for explanation)

All figures show longitude West except solid line, 31° 23', which is latitude North. Circle marks point used for all time calculations in the Texas Almanac.

The Seasons, 1998 and 1999

1998

The seasons of 1998 begin as follows: **Spring**, March 20, 1:55 p.m. (CST); **Summer**, June 21, 9:03 a.m. (CDT); **Fall**, Sept. 23, 12:37 a.m. (CDT); **Winter**, Dec. 21, 7:56 p.m. (CST).

1999

The seasons of 1999 begin as follows: **Spring**, March 20, 7:46 p.m. (CST); **Summer**, June 21, 2:49 p.m. (CDT); **Fall**, Sept. 23, 6:31 a.m. (CDT); **Winter**, Dec. 22, 1:44 a.m. (CST).

Morning and Evening Stars, 1998 and 1999

Morning Stars, 1998

Venus — Jan. 22 - Sept. 22
Mars — July 10 - Dec. 31
Jupiter — March 9 - Sept. 16
Saturn — May 1 - Oct. 23

Evening Stars, 1998

Venus — Jan. 1 - Jan. 10; Dec. 10 - Dec. 31
Mars — Jan. 1 - March 9
Jupiter — Jan. 1 - Feb. 10; Sept. 16 - Dec. 31
Saturn — Jan. 1 - March 27; Oct. 23 - Dec. 31

Morning Stars, 1999

Venus — Aug. 25 - Dec. 31
Mars — Jan. 1 - April 24
Jupiter — April 15 - Oct. 23
Saturn — May 16 - Nov. 6

Evening Stars, 1999

Jupiter — Jan. 1 - March 18; Oct. 23 - Dec. 31
Saturn — Jan. 1 - April 10; Nov. 6 - Dec. 31
Mars — April 24 - Dec. 31
Venus — Jan. 1 - Aug. 16

Eclipses, 1998 and 1999

Eclipses, 1998

There will be five eclipses during 1998, two of the Sun and three of the Moon, as follows:

Feb. 26 — Total eclipse of the Sun, visible in the Pacific Ocean, extreme southwest and eastern United States, southeast Canada, Mexico, Central America, the northern half of South America, the West Indies, the Atlantic Ocean, the southern tip of Greenland, the extreme western part of Iceland, Portugal and West Africa.
March 13 — Penumbral eclipse of the Moon.
Aug. 8 — Penumbral eclipse of the Moon.
Aug. 21-22 — Annular eclipse of the Sun, visible in the northern Indian Ocean, India, southeast Asia, southern China, Indonesia, Malaysia, the Philippines, southern Japan, Australasia and the South Pacific Ocean.
Sept. 6 — Penumbral eclipse of the Moon.

Eclipses, 1999

There will be four eclipses in 1999, two of the Sun and two of the Moon, as follows:

Jan. 31 — Penumbral eclipse of the Moon.
Feb. 16 — Annular eclipse of the Sun, visible in the southern Atlantic Ocean, southernf Africa, Indian Ocean, Indonesia, Malaysia, southern Philippines, Antarctica, and Australasia.
July 28 — Partial eclipse of the Moon, visible in part of Antarctica; southern and western parts of South America, Central America, western North America except northern Alaska, Pacific Ocean, Australasia, and eastern Asia.
Aug. 11 — Total eclipse of the Sun, visible in the northeastern United States, eastern Canada, northern Atlantic Ocean, Europe, including the British Isles, northern Africa, Asia except the eastern part, and the northern Indian Ocean.

Major Meteor Showers, 1998 and 1999

Note: These dates are not firm. Listen to your local news and weather broadcasts several days before the listed dates to determine peak observation days and hours.

Meteor dates provided by R.L Hawkes, Mount Allison University, Canada.

Meteor Shower	Peak Day 1998	Peak Day 1999
Quadrantids	Jan. 3	Jan. 3
Perseids	August 12	August 13
Leonids	Nov. 17	Nov. 17
Geminids	Dec. 14	Dec. 14

Chronological Eras and Cycles, 1998 and 1999

Chronological Eras, 1998

The year 1998 of the **Christian** era comprises the latter part of the 222nd and the beginning of the 223rd year of the independence of the United States of America, and corresponds to the year 6711 of the Julian period.

All dates in the list below are given in terms of the Gregorian calendar, in which Jan. 14, 1998, corresponds to Jan. 1, 1998, Julian calendar.

Era	Year	Begins
Byzantine	7507	Sept. 14
Jewish (A.M.)*	5759	Sept. 20
Chinese (Wu-Yin)	4535	Jan. 28
Roman (A.U.C.)	2751	Jan. 14
Nabonassar	2747	April 24
Japanese	2658	Jan. 1
Grecian (Seleucidae)	2310	Sept. 14 or Oct. 14
Indian (Saka)	1920	March 22
Diocletian	1715	Sept. 11
Islamic (Hegira)*	1419	April 27

*Year begins at sunset.

Chronological Cycles, 1998

Dominical Letter	D	Julian Period	6711
Epact	2	Roman Indiction	6
Golden Number or Lunar Cycle	IV	Solar Cycle	19

Chronological Eras, 1999

The year 1999 of the **Christian** era comprises the latter part of the 223rd and the beginning of the 224th year of the independence of the United States of America, and corresponds to the year 6712 of the Julian period.

All dates in the list below are given in terms of the Gregorian calendar, in which Jan. 14, 1999, corresponds to Jan. 1, 1999, of the Julian calendar:

Era	Year	Begins
Byzantine	7508	Sept. 14
Jewish (A.M.)*	5760	Sept. 10
Chinese (Ji-mao)	4636	Feb. 16
Roman (A.U.C.)	2752	Jan. 14
Nabonassar	2748	April 24
Japanese	2659	Jan. 1
Grecian (Seleucidae)	2311	Sept. 14 or Oct. 14
Indian (Saka)	1921	March 22
Diocletian	1716	Sept. 12
Islamic (Hegira)*	1420	April 16

*Year begins at sunset.

Chronological Cycles, 1999

Dominical Letter	C	Julian Period	6712
Epact	13	Roman Indiction	7
Golden Number or Lunar Cycle	V	Solar Cycle	20

Holidays, Anniversaries and Festivals, 1998 and 1999

Below are listed the principal federal and state government holidays, Christian, Jewish and Islamic holidays and festivals and special recognition days for 1998 and 1999. Technically, the United States does not observe national holidays. Each state has jurisdiction over its holidays, which are usually designated by its legislature. The list was compiled partially from *Astronomical Phenomena 1998* and *1999*, published by the U.S. Naval Observatory, and from the Texas Government Code. See the footnotes for explanations of the symbols.

1998

*§New Year's Day	Thursday, Jan. 1
Epiphany	Tuesday, Jan. 6
‡Sam Rayburn Day	Tuesday, Jan. 6
*§Martin Luther King's Birthday	Monday, Jan. 19
†**Confederate Heroes Day	Monday, Jan. 19
*§∞Presidents' Day	Monday, Feb. 16
Ash Wednesday	Wednesday, Feb. 25
†Texas Independence Day	Monday, March 2
‡Sam Houston Day	Monday, March 2
‡Texas Flag Day	Monday, March 2
Primary Election Day	Tuesday, March 10
Palm Sunday	Sunday, April 5
‡Former Prisoners of War Recognition Day	Thursday, April 9
§Good Friday	Friday, Apr. 10
¶First Day of Passover (Pesach)	Saturday, Apr. 11
Easter Day	Sunday, Apr. 12
†San Jacinto Day	Tuesday, April 21
§§Islamic New Year (Tabular)	Tuesday, April 28
Mother's Day	Sunday, May 10
Armed Forces Day	Saturday, May 16
Ascension Day	Thursday, May 21
*§Memorial Day	Monday, May 25
¶First Day of Shavuot	Sunday, May 31
Whit Sunday - Pentecost	Sunday, May 31
Trinity Sunday	Sunday, June 7
Flag Day (U.S.)	Sunday, June 14
†Emancipation Day in Texas	Friday, June 19
Father's Day	Sunday, June 21
*§Independence Day	Saturday, July 4
†Lyndon B. Johnson's Birthday	Thursday, Aug. 27
*§Labor Day	Monday, Sept. 7
¶First Day of Rosh Hashanah	Monday, Sept. 21
¶Day of Atonement (Yom Kippur)	Wednesday, Sept. 30
¶First Day of Tabernacles (Sukkot)	Monday, Oct. 5
§‡Columbus Day	Monday, Oct. 12
Halloween	Saturday, Oct. 31
†General Election Day	Tuesday, Nov. 3
‡Father of Texas Day	Tuesday, Nov. 3
*§Veterans Day	Wednesday, Nov. 11
*§††Thanksgiving Day	Thursday, Nov. 26
First Sunday in Advent	Sunday, Nov. 29
¶First Day of Hanukkah	Monday, Dec. 14
§§First Day of Ramadan	Sunday, Dec. 20
*§Christmas Day	Friday, Dec. 25

1999

*§New Year's Day	Friday, Jan. 1
Epiphany	Wednesday, Jan. 6
‡Sam Rayburn Day	Wednesday, Jan. 6
*§Martin Luther King's Birthday	Monday, Jan. 18
†**Confederate Heroes Day	Tuesday, Jan. 19
*§∞Presidents' Day	Monday, Feb. 15
Ash Wednesday	Wednesday, Feb. 17
†Texas Independence Day	Tuesday, March 2
‡Sam Houston Day	Tuesday, March 2
‡Texas Flag Day	Tuesday, March 2
Palm Sunday	Sunday, March 28
¶First Day of Passover (Pesach)	Thursday, Apr. 1
§Good Friday	Friday, Apr. 2
Easter Day	Sunday, Apr. 4
‡Former Prisoners of War Recognition Day	Friday, April 9
§§Islamic New Year (Tabular)	Saturday, Apr. 17
†San Jacinto Day	Wednesday, April 21
Mother's Day	Sunday, May 9
Ascension Day	Thursday, May 13
Armed Forces Day	Saturday, May 15
¶First Day of Shavuot (Feast of Weeks)	Friday, May 21
Whit Sunday - Pentecost	Sunday, May 23
Trinity Sunday	Sunday, May 30
*§Memorial Day	Monday, May 31
Flag Day (U.S.)	Monday, June 14
†Emancipation Day in Texas	Saturday, June 19
Father's Day	Sunday, June 20
*§Independence Day	Sunday, July 4
†Lyndon Baines Johnson Day	Friday, Aug. 27
*§Labor Day	Monday, Sept. 6
¶First Day of Rosh Hashanah	Saturday, Sept. 11
¶Day of Atonement (Yom Kippur)	Monday, Sept. 20
¶First Day of Tabernacles (Sukkot)	Saturday, Sept. 25
§‡Columbus Day	Monday, Oct. 11
Halloween	Sunday, Oct. 31
†General Election Day	Tuesday, Nov. 2
‡Father of Texas Day	Wednesday, Nov. 3
*§Veterans Day	Thursday, Nov. 11
*§††Thanksgiving Day	Thursday, Nov. 25
First Sunday in Advent	Sunday, Nov. 28
¶First Day of Hanukkah	Saturday, Dec. 4
§§First Day of Ramadan (Tabular)	Thursday, Dec. 9
*§Christmas Day	Saturday, Dec. 25

¶ §§ In these tables, the Jewish (¶) and Islamic (§§) dates, are tabular dates, which begin at sunset on the previous evening and end at sunset on the date listed above.

* National holidays observed by state employees.

† State holiday in Texas. For state employees, the Friday after Thanksgiving Day, December 24 and December 26 are also holidays; optional holidays are Rosh Hashanah, Yom Kippur or Good Friday.

‡ State Recognition Days, designated by the Texas Legislature. In addition, the legislature has designated the week of May 22-26 International Trade Awareness Week.

§ Federal legal public holidays.

** Confederate Heroes Day combines the birthdays of Robert E. Lee (Jan. 19) and Jefferson Davis (June 3).

∞ Presidents' Day combines the birthdays of George Washington (Feb. 15) and Abraham Lincoln (Feb. 12).

†† Between 1939 and 1957, Texas observed Thanksgiving Day on the last Thursday in November. As a result, in all Novembers having five Thursdays, Texas celebrated national Thanksgiving on the fourth Thursday and Texas Thanksgiving on the fifth Thursday. In 1957, Texas changed the state observance to coincide in all years with the national holiday. ☆

Calendar for 1998

Times are **Central Standard Time**, except from April 5 to Oct. 25, during which **Daylight Saving Time** is observed. **Boldface times for moonrise and moonset** indicate p.m. Times are figured for the point **99° 10' West and 31° 23' North,** the approximate center of the state. **See page 93 for explanation of how to get the approximate time at any other Texas point.**

1st Month — January 1998 — 31 Days

Moon's Phases — First Qtr., Jan. 5, 8:20 a.m.; Full, Jan. 12, 11:25 a.m.; Last Qtr., Jan. 20, 1:41 p.m.; New, Jan. 28, 12:02 a.m.

Day of Year	Day of Month	Day of Week	Planetary Configurations and Phenomena	*Hour of Sunrise	*Hour of Sunset	*Hour of Moon-rise	*Hour of Moon-set
1	1	Th.	♃ ☌ ☾	7:36	5:45	9:50	**9:12**
2	2	Fr.		7:36	5:46	10:34	**10:17**
3	3	Sa.	☾ at perigee	7:36	5:46	11:16	**11:21**
4	4	Su.	● at perihelion	7:36	5:47	11:56	. . .
5	5	Mo.	♄ ☌ ☾	7:37	5:48	**12:36**	12:24
6	6	Tu.	☿ greatest elong. W.	7:37	5:49	**1:16**	1:27
7	7	We.		7:37	5:50	**1:59**	2:30
8	8	Th.		7:37	5:50	**2:44**	3:32
9	9	Fr.	♀ ☌ ♆	7:37	5:51	**3:32**	4:33
10	10	Sa.		7:37	5:52	**4:24**	5:32
11	11	Su.		7:37	5:53	**5:18**	6:28
12	12	Mo.		7:37	5:54	**6:13**	7:19
13	13	Tu.		7:37	5:55	**7:09**	8:05
14	14	We.		7:36	5:55	**8:04**	8:48
15	15	Th.		7:36	5:56	**8:59**	9:26
16	16	Fr.	♀ inferior	7:36	5:57	**9:52**	10:02
17	17	Sa.		7:36	5:58	**10:44**	10:35
18	18	Su.	☾ at apogee	7:36	5:59	**11:36**	11:08
19	19	Mo.	♆ ☌ ☉	7:35	6:00	. . .	11:41
20	20	Tu.	♂ ☌ ♃	7:35	6:01	12:28	**12:14**
21	21	We.		7:35	6:02	1:21	**12:49**
22	22	Th.		7:34	6:03	2:15	**1:28**
23	23	Fr.		7:34	6:03	3:10	**2:10**
24	24	Sa.		7:34	6:04	4:06	**2:58**
25	25	Su.		7:33	6:05	5:02	**3:50**
26	26	Mo.	☿ ☌ ♀; ♀ ☌ ☾; ☿ ☌ ☾	7:33	6:06	5:58	**4:49**
27	27	Tu.		7:32	6:07	6:51	**5:51**
28	28	We.	♅ ☌ ☉	7:32	6:08	7:42	**6:56**
29	29	Th.	♃ ☌ ☾; ♂ ☌ ☾	7:31	6:09	8:29	**8:03**
30	30	Fr.	☾ at perigee	7:30	6:10	9:13	**9:09**
31	31	Sa.		7:30	6:11	9:55	**10:15**

2nd Month — February 1998 — 28 Days

Moon's Phases — First Qtr., Feb. 3, 4:54 p.m.; Full, Feb. 11, 4:24 a.m.; Last Qtr., Feb. 19, 9:28 a.m.; New, Feb. 26, 11:27 a.m.

Day of Year	Day of Month	Day of Week	Planetary Configurations and Phenomena	*Hour of Sunrise	*Hour of Sunset	*Hour of Moon-rise	*Hour of Moon-set
32	1	Su.	♄ ☌ ☾	7:29	6:12	10:36	**11:20**
33	2	Mo.	☿ ☌ ♆	7:29	6:13	11:17	. . .
34	3	Tu.		7:28	6:13	11:59	12:24
35	4	We.		7:27	6:14	**12:43**	1:26
36	5	Th.	♀ stationary	7:27	6:15	**1:30**	2:27
37	6	Fr.		7:26	6:16	**2:19**	3:26
38	7	Sa.	☿ ☌ ♅	7:25	6:17	**3:11**	4:22
39	8	Su.		7:24	6:18	**4:05**	5:13
40	9	Mo.		7:23	6:19	**5:00**	6:01
41	10	Tu.		7:23	6:20	**5:55**	6:44
42	11	We.		7:22	6:20	**6:50**	7:24
43	12	Th.		7:21	6:21	**7:43**	8:01
44	13	Fr.		7:20	6:22	**8:36**	8:35
45	14	Sa.		7:19	6:23	**9:28**	9:08
46	15	Su.	☾ at apogee	7:18	6:24	**10:20**	9:41
47	16	Mo.		7:17	6:25	**11:12**	10:14
48	17	Tu.		7:16	6:25	. . .	10:48
49	18	We.		7:15	6:26	12:05	11:24
50	19	Th.	♀ greatest brilliancy	7:14	6:27	12:58	**12:04**
51	20	Fr.		7:13	6:28	1:53	**12:48**
52	21	Sa.		7:12	6:29	2:48	**1:37**
53	22	Su.	☿ superior	7:11	6:29	3:42	**2:31**
54	23	Mo.	♃ ☌ ☉; ♀ ☌ ☾	7:10	6:30	4:36	**3:30**
55	24	Tu.	♅ ☌ ☾	7:09	6:31	5:27	**4:33**
56	25	We.		7:08	6:32	6:16	**5:40**
57	26	Th.		7:07	6:33	7:03	**6:48**
58	27	Fr.	☾ at perigee; ♂ ☌ ☾	7:06	6:33	7:47	**7:56**
59	28	Sa.		7:05	6:34	8:30	**9:04**

*See text before January calendar for explanation.

3rd Month — March 1998 — 31 Days

Moon's Phases — First Qtr., March 5, 2:42 a.m.; Full, March 12, 10:35 p.m.; Last Qtr., March 21, 1:38 a.m.; New, March 27, 9:15 p.m.

Day of Year	Day of Month	Day of Week	Planetary Configurations and Phenomena	*Hour of Sunrise	*Hour of Sunset	*Hour of Moon-rise	*Hour of Moon-set
60	1	Su.	♄ ☌ ☾	7:04	6:35	9:13	**10:11**
61	2	Mo.		7:02	6:36	9:56	**11:16**
62	3	Tu.		7:01	6:36	10:41	. . .
63	4	We.		7:00	6:37	11:28	12:20
64	5	Th.		6:59	6:38	**12:17**	1:21
65	6	Fr.		6:58	6:38	**1:08**	2:18
66	7	Sa.	♀ ☌ ♆	6:57	6:39	**2:01**	3:11
67	8	Su.		6:55	6:40	**2:55**	3:59
68	9	Mo.		6:54	6:41	**3:50**	4:43
69	10	Tu.		6:53	6:41	**4:44**	5:24
70	11	We.	☿ ☌ ♂	6:52	6:42	**5:37**	6:01
71	12	Th.	♇ stationary	6:51	6:43	**6:30**	6:36
72	13	Fr.		6:49	6:43	**7:22**	7:09
73	14	Sa.	☾ at apogee	6:48	6:44	**8:14**	7:42
74	15	Su.		6:47	6:45	**9:06**	8:14
75	16	Mo.		6:46	6:45	**9:59**	8:48
76	17	Tu.		6:44	6:46	**10:52**	9:23
77	18	We.		6:43	6:47	**11:45**	10:01
78	19	Th.	♀ ☌ ♅	6:42	6:47	. . .	10:43
79	20	Fr.	Spring begins	6:41	6:48	12:38	**11:28**
80	21	Sa.		6:39	6:49	1:32	**12:19**
81	22	Su.		6:38	6:49	2:24	**1:14**
82	23	Mo.	♆ ☌ ☾	6:37	6:50	3:15	**2:14**
83	24	Tu.	♀ ☌ ☾; ♅ ☌ ☾	6:36	6:51	4:03	**3:17**
84	25	We.		6:34	6:51	4:50	**4:23**
85	26	Th.	♃ ☌ ☾	6:33	6:52	5:35	**5:31**
86	27	Fr.	☿ stationary	6:32	6:53	6:19	**6:39**
87	28	Sa.	☾ at perigee	6:31	6:53	7:02	**7:49**
88	29	Su.	☿ ☌ ♂	6:29	6:54	7:46	**8:57**
89	30	Mo.		6:28	6:55	8:32	**10:04**
90	31	Tu.		6:27	6:55	9:19	**11:09**

4th Month — April 1998 — 30 Days

Moon's Phases - First Qr., April 3, 2:20 p.m.; Full, April 11, 5:24 p.m.; Last Qr., April 19, 2:54 p.m.; New, April 26, 6:43 a.m.

Day of Year	Day of Month	Day of Week	Planetary Configurations and Phenomena	*Hour of Sunrise	*Hour of Sunset	*Hour of Moon-rise	*Hour of Moon-set
91	1	We.		6:25	6:56	10:10	. . .
92	2	Th.		6:24	6:57	11:02	12:10
93	3	Fr.		6:23	6:57	11:56	1:06
94	4	Sa.		6:22	6:58	**12:51**	1:57
95	†5	Su.		7:21	7:59	**2:45**	3:43
96	6	Mo.	☿ inferior	7:19	7:59	**3:39**	4:24
97	7	Tu.		7:18	8:00	**4:33**	5:02
98	8	We.		7:17	8:01	**5:26**	5:37
99	9	Th.		7:16	8:01	**6:18**	6:11
100	10	Fr.	☾ at apogee	7:14	8:02	**7:10**	6:43
101	11	Sa.		7:13	8:03	**8:02**	7:16
102	12	Su.		7:12	8:03	**8:54**	7:49
103	13	Mo.	♄ ☌ ☉	7:11	8:04	**9:47**	8:24
104	14	Tu.		7:10	8:05	**10:40**	9:01
105	15	We.		7:09	8:05	**11:34**	9:41
106	16	Th.		7:07	8:06	. . .	10:25
107	17	Fr.		7:06	8:07	12:27	11:13
108	18	Sa.	☿ stationary	7:05	8:07	1:19	**12:05**
109	19	Su.	♆ ☌ ☾	7:04	8:08	2:09	**1:02**
110	20	Mo.	♅ ☌ ☾	7:03	8:09	2:57	**2:02**
111	21	Tu.		7:02	8:09	3:42	**3:04**
112	22	We.	♀ ☌ ♃	7:01	8:10	4:26	**4:09**
113	23	Th.	♃ ☌ ☾; ♀ ☌ ☾	7:00	8:11	5:09	**5:16**
114	24	Fr.	☿ ☌ ☾	6:59	8:11	5:51	**6:23**
115	25	Sa.	☾ at perigee	6:58	8:12	6:34	**7:32**
116	26	Su.		6:57	8:13	7:19	**8:41**
117	27	Mo.		6:56	8:13	8:06	**9:49**
118	28	Tu.		6:55	8:14	8:56	**10:54**
119	29	We.		6:54	8:15	9:49	**11:54**
120	30	Th.		6:53	8:15	10:44	. . .

†Daylight Saving Time begins at 2:00 a.m.

Calendar for 1998 (Cont'd.)

5th Month — **May 1998** — **31 Days**

Moon's Phases — First Qtr., May 3, 5:05 a.m.; Full, May 11, 9:30 a.m.; Last Qtr., May 18, 11:36 p.m., New, May 25, 2:34 p.m.

Day of Year	Day of Month	Day of Week	Planetary Configurations and Phenomena	*Hour of Sunrise	*Hour of Sunset	*Hour of Moon-rise	*Hour of Moon-set
121	1	Fr.		6:52	8:16	11:41	12:49
122	2	Sa.		6:51	8:17	**12:37**	1:39
123	3	Su.		6:50	8:18	**1:33**	2:23
124	4	Mo.	♆ stationary	6:49	8:18	**2:27**	3:03
125	5	Tu.		6:48	8:19	**3:20**	3:39
126	6	We.		6:47	8:20	**4:13**	4:13
127	7	Th.		6:47	8:20	**5:05**	4:45
128	8	Fr.	☾ at apogee	6:46	8:21	**5:57**	5:18
129	9	Sa.		6:45	8:22	**6:49**	5:50
130	10	Su.		6:44	8:22	**7:42**	6:25
131	11	Mo.		6:43	8:23	**8:36**	7:01
132	12	Tu.	☿ ☌ ♄; ♂ ☌ ☉	6:43	8:24	**9:30**	7:40
133	13	We.		6:42	8:24	**10:24**	8:23
134	14	Th.		6:41	8:25	**11:16**	9:10
135	15	Fr.		6:41	8:26	. . .	10:01
136	16	Sa.		6:40	8:26	12:07	10:56
137	17	Su.	♆ ☌ ☾; ♅ ☌ ☾	6:39	8:27	12:55	11:54
138	18	Mo.		6:39	8:28	1:40	**12:54**
139	19	Tu.		6:38	8:28	2:24	**1:57**
140	20	We.	♃ ☌ ☾	6:38	8:29	3:05	**3:00**
141	21	Th.		6:37	8:30	3:46	**4:05**
142	22	Fr.	♀ ☌ ☾	6:37	8:30	4:27	**5:11**
143	23	Sa.	♄ ☌ ☾; ☾ at perigee	6:36	8:31	5:09	**6:19**
144	24	Su.	☿ ☌ ☾	6:36	8:32	5:54	**7:26**
145	25	Mo.		6:35	8:32	6:42	**8:33**
146	26	Tu.		6:35	8:33	7:33	**9:37**
147	27	We.		6:34	8:33	8:28	**10:36**
148	28	Th.	♀ ☌ ♄	6:34	8:34	9:26	**11:30**
149	29	Fr.		6:34	8:35	10:24	. . .
150	30	Sa.		6:33	8:35	11:21	12:17
151	31	Su.		6:33	8:36	**12:18**	1:00

6th Month — **June 1998** — **30 Days**

Moon's Phases — First Qtr., June 1, 8:46 p.m.; Full, June 9, 11:19 p.m.; Last Qtr., June 17, 5:40 a.m.; New, June 23, 10:52 p.m.

Day of Year	Day of Month	Day of Week	Planetary Configurations and Phenomena	*Hour of Sunrise	*Hour of Sunset	*Hour of Moon-rise	*Hour of Moon-set
152	1	Mo.		6:33	8:36	**1:12**	1:38
153	2	Tu.		6:33	8:37	**2:06**	2:14
154	3	We.		6:32	8:37	**2:58**	2:47
155	4	Th.	☾ at apogee	6:32	8:38	**3:50**	3:19
156	5	Fr.		6:32	8:38	**4:42**	3:52
157	6	Sa.		6:32	8:39	**5:35**	4:25
158	7	Su.		6:32	8:39	**6:29**	5:00
159	8	Mo.		6:32	8:40	**7:23**	5:38
160	9	Tu.		6:32	8:40	**8:18**	6:20
161	10	We.	☿ superior	6:32	8:41	**9:12**	7:06
162	11	Th.		6:32	8:41	**10:04**	7:56
163	12	Fr.		6:32	8:42	**10:54**	8:51
164	13	Sa.	♆ ☌ ☾	6:32	8:42	**11:41**	9:48
165	14	Su.	♅ ☌ ☾	6:32	8:42	. . .	10:48
166	15	Mo.		6:32	8:43	12:24	11:50
167	16	Tu.		6:32	8:43	1:06	**12:52**
168	17	We.	♃ ☌ ☾	6:32	8:43	1:46	**1:55**
169	18	Th.		6:32	8:44	2:25	**2:59**
170	19	Fr.	♄ ☌ ☾	6:32	8:44	3:06	**4:04**
171	20	Sa.	☾ at perigee	6:32	8:44	3:48	**5:10**
172	21	Su.	Summer begins; ♀ ☌ ☾	6:33	8:44	4:33	**6:15**
173	22	Mo.		6:33	8:44	5:21	**7:19**
174	23	Tu.		6:33	8:45	6:14	**8:20**
175	24	We.		6:33	8:45	7:10	**9:17**
176	25	Th.	☿ ☌ ☾	6:34	8:45	8:08	**10:08**
177	26	Fr.		6:34	8:45	9:07	**10:54**
178	27	Sa.		6:34	8:45	10:05	**11:35**
179	28	Su.		6:35	8:45	11:01	. . .
180	29	Mo.		6:35	8:45	11:56	12:12
181	30	Tu.		6:35	8:45	**12:49**	12:47

*See text before January calendar for explanation.

7th Month — **July 1998** — **31 Days**

Moon's Phases — First Qtr., July 1, 1:43 p.m.; Full, July 9, 11:02 a.m.; Last Qtr., July 16, 10:15 a.m.; New, July 23, 8:45 a.m.; First Qtr., July 31, 7:06 a.m.

Day of Year	Day of Month	Day of Week	Planetary Configurations and Phenomena	*Hour of Sunrise	*Hour of Sunset	*Hour of Moon-rise	*Hour of Moon-set
182	1	We.		6:36	8:45	**1:42**	1:20
183	2	Th.	☾ at apogee	6:36	8:45	**2:34**	1:52
184	3	Fr.	● at aphelion	6:37	8:45	**3:26**	2:25
185	4	Sa.		6:37	8:45	**4:19**	2:59
186	5	Su.		6:37	8:45	**5:13**	3:35
187	6	Mo.		6:38	8:45	**6:08**	4:15
188	7	Tu.		6:38	8:45	**7:03**	5:00
189	8	We.		6:39	8:44	**7:57**	5:48
190	9	Th.		6:39	8:44	**8:48**	6:42
191	10	Fr.	♆ ☌ ☾	6:40	8:44	**9:37**	7:39
192	11	Sa.	♅ ☌ ☾	6:40	8:44	**10:23**	8:40
193	12	Su.		6:41	8:43	**11:06**	9:42
194	13	Mo.		6:42	8:43	**11:47**	10:46
195	14	Tu.	♃ ☌ ☾	6:42	8:43	. . .	11:49
196	15	We.		6:43	8:42	12:27	**12:53**
197	16	Th.	☾ at perigee	6:43	8:42	1:07	**1:56**
198	17	Fr.	♄ ☌ ☾	6:44	8:42	1:47	**3:00**
199	18	Sa.	♃ stationary	6:44	8:41	2:30	**4:04**
200	19	Su.		6:45	8:41	3:16	**5:07**
201	20	Mo.		6:46	8:40	4:05	**6:08**
202	21	Tu.	♀ ☌ ☾; ♂ ☌ ☾	6:46	8:40	4:59	**7:06**
203	22	We.		6:47	8:39	5:55	**7:59**
204	23	Th.	♆ ☍	6:47	8:39	6:53	**8:47**
205	24	Fr.		6:48	8:38	7:51	**9:30**
206	25	Sa.	☿ ☌ ☾	6:49	8:37	8:49	**10:09**
207	26	Su.		6:49	8:37	9:45	**10:45**
208	27	Mo.		6:50	8:36	10:39	**11:19**
209	28	Tu.		6:51	8:35	11:32	**11:52**
210	29	We.		6:51	8:35	**12:25**	. . .
211	30	Th.	☿ stationary; ☾ at apogee	6:52	8:34	**1:17**	12:24
212	31	Fr.		6:52	8:33	**2:09**	12:57

8th Month — **August 1998** — **31 Days**

Moon's Phases — Full, Aug. 7, 9:11 p.m.; Last Qtr., Aug. 14, 2:49 p.m.; New, Aug. 21, 9:04 p.m.; First Qtr., Aug. 30, 12:08 a.m.

Day of Year	Day of Month	Day of Week	Planetary Configurations and Phenomena	*Hour of Sunrise	*Hour of Sunset	*Hour of Moon-rise	*Hour of Moon-set
213	1	Sa.		6:53	8:32	**3:03**	1:33
214	2	Su.		6:54	8:32	**3:56**	2:11
215	3	Mo.	♅ ☍	6:54	8:31	**4:51**	2:52
216	4	Tu.	♀ ☌ ♂	6:55	8:30	**5:45**	3:39
217	5	We.		6:56	8:29	**6:38**	4:30
218	6	Th.	♆ ☌ ☾	6:56	8:28	**7:29**	5:26
219	7	Fr.	♅ ☌ ☾	6:57	8:27	**8:17**	6:26
220	8	Sa.		6:58	8:27	**9:02**	7:29
221	9	Su.		6:58	8:26	**9:45**	8:33
222	10	Mo.	♃ ☌ ☾	6:59	8:25	**10:26**	9:39
223	11	Tu.	☾ at perigee	7:00	8:24	**11:07**	10:44
224	12	We.		7:00	8:23	**11:48**	11:49
225	13	Th.	♄ ☌ ☾; ☿ inferior	7:01	8:22	. . .	**12:54**
226	14	Fr.		7:01	8:21	12:30	**1:58**
227	15	Sa.		7:02	8:20	1:15	**3:01**
228	16	Su.	♄ stationary	7:03	8:19	2:02	**4:01**
229	17	Mo.		7:03	8:18	2:54	**4:59**
230	18	Tu.	♇ stationary	7:04	8:17	3:48	**5:53**
231	19	We.	♂ ☌ ☾	7:05	8:15	4:44	**6:42**
232	20	Th.	♀ ☌ ☾	7:05	8:14	5:41	**7:26**
233	21	Fr.		7:06	8:13	6:38	**8:06**
234	22	Sa.		7:06	8:12	7:35	**8:43**
235	23	Su.		7:07	8:11	8:30	**9:18**
236	24	Mo.		7:08	8:10	9:23	**9:51**
237	25	Tu.	☿ ☌ ♀	7:08	8:09	10:16	**10:24**
238	26	We.		7:09	8:08	11:09	**10:57**
239	27	Th.	☾ at apogee	7:09	8:06	**12:01**	**11:31**
240	28	Fr.		7:10	8:05	**12:53**	. . .
241	29	Sa.		7:11	8:04	**1:46**	12:07
242	30	Su.		7:11	8:03	**2:39**	12:47
243	31	Mo.	☿ greatest elong. W.	7:12	8:02	**3:33**	1:30

Calendar for 1998 (Cont'd.)

9th Month — **September 1998** — **30 Days**

Moon's Phases — Full, Sept. 6, 6:23 a.m.; Last Qtr., Sept. 12, 8:59 p.m.; New, Sept. 20, 12:02 p.m.; First Qtr., Sept. 28, 4:12 p.m.

Day of			Planetary Configurations and Phenomena	*Hour of			
Year	Month	Week		Sunrise	Sunset	Moon-rise	Moon-set
244	1	Tu.		7:12	8:00	**4:25**	2:18
245	2	We.		7:13	7:59	**5:16**	3:11
246	3	Th.	♆☌☾; ♅☌☾	7:14	7:58	**6:06**	4:08
247	4	Fr.		7:14	7:57	**6:52**	5:10
248	5	Sa.		7:15	7:55	**7:37**	6:14
249	6	Su.	♃☌☾	7:15	7:54	**8:20**	7:20
250	7	Mo.		7:16	7:53	**9:02**	8:27
251	8	Tu.	☾ at perigee	7:17	7:51	**9:44**	9:35
252	9	We.	♄☌☾	7:17	7:50	**10:27**	10:42
253	10	Th.	☿☌♀	7:18	7:49	**11:12**	11:48
254	11	Fr.		7:18	7:48	...	**12:53**
255	12	Sa.		7:19	7:46	12:01	**1:56**
256	13	Su.		7:20	7:45	12:50	**2:55**
257	14	Mo.		7:20	7:44	1:44	**3:50**
258	15	Tu.	♃☍	7:21	7:42	2:39	**4:40**
259	16	We.		7:21	7:41	3:35	**5:25**
260	17	Th.	♂☌☾	7:22	7:40	4:32	**6:06**
261	18	Fr.		7:22	7:39	5:28	**6:43**
262	19	Sa.		7:23	7:37	6:23	**7:18**
263	20	Su.		7:24	7:36	7:16	**7:51**
264	21	Mo.		7:24	7:35	8:09	**8:24**
265	22	Tu.		7:25	7:33	9:02	**8:57**
266	23	We.	Fall begins; ☾ at apogee	7:25	7:32	9:54	**9:30**
267	24	Th.		7:26	7:31	10:47	**10:06**
268	25	Fr.	☿ superior	7:27	7:29	11:39	**10:43**
269	26	Sa.		7:27	7:28	**12:31**	**11:25**
270	27	Su.		7:28	7:27	**1:24**	...
271	28	Mo.		7:29	7:26	**2:16**	12:10
272	29	Tu.		7:29	7:24	**3:06**	12:59
273	30	We.	♆☌☾	7:30	7:23	**3:55**	1:53

10th Month — **October 1998** — **31 Days**

Moon's Phases — Full, Oct. 5, 3:13 p.m.; Last Qtr., Oct. 12, 6:12 a.m.; New, Oct. 20, 5:10 a.m.; First Qtr., Oct. 28, 5:47 a.m

Day of			Planetary Configurations and Phenomena	*Hour of			
Year	Month	Week		Sunrise	Sunset	Moon-rise	Moon-set
274	1	Th.	♅☌☾	7:30	7:22	**4:42**	2:51
275	2	Fr.		7:31	7:21	**5:26**	3:53
276	3	Sa.		7:32	7:19	**6:10**	4:58
277	4	Su.	♃☌☾	7:32	7:18	**6:52**	6:04
278	5	Mo.		7:33	7:17	**7:35**	7:12
279	6	Tu.	☾ at perigee; ♄☌☾	7:34	7:16	**8:18**	8:21
280	7	We.		7:34	7:14	**9:04**	9:30
281	8	Th.		7:35	7:13	**9:52**	10:38
282	9	Fr.		7:36	7:12	**10:43**	11:45
283	10	Sa.		7:36	7:11	**11:37**	**12:47**
284	11	Su.	♆ stationary	7:37	7:09	...	**1:45**
285	12	Mo.		7:38	7:08	12:33	**2:38**
286	13	Tu.		7:38	7:07	1:30	**3:24**
287	14	We.		7:39	7:06	2:27	**4:06**
288	15	Th.	♂☌☾	7:40	7:05	3:23	**4:45**
289	16	Fr.		7:40	7:04	4:18	**5:20**
290	17	Sa.		7:41	7:03	5:12	**5:53**
291	18	Su.	♅ stationary	7:42	7:01	6:05	**6:26**
292	19	Mo.		7:42	7:00	6:57	**6:58**
293	20	Tu.		7:43	6:59	7:49	**7:31**
294	21	We.	☾ at apogee; ☿☌☾	7:44	6:58	8:42	**8:06**
295	22	Th.		7:45	6:57	9:34	**8:43**
296	23	Fr.	♄☍	7:45	6:56	10:27	**9:22**
297	24	Sa.		7:46	6:55	11:19	**10:06**
298	†25	Su.		6:47	5:54	11:11	**9:53**
299	26	Mo.		6:48	5:53	**12:01**	**10:44**
300	27	Tu.	♆☌☾	6:48	5:52	**12:49**	**11:39**
301	28	We.	♅☌☾	6:49	5:51	**1:35**	...
302	29	Th.	♀ superior	6:50	5:50	**2:19**	12:38
303	30	Fr.		6:51	5:49	**3:01**	1:39
304	31	Sa.	♃☌☾	6:52	5:49	**3:42**	2:42

*See text before January calendar for explanation.
† Daylight Saving Time ends at 2:00 a.m.

11th Month — **November, 1998** — **30 Days**

Moon's Phases — Full, Nov. 3, 11:20 p.m.; Last Qtr., Nov. 10, 6:29 p.m.; New, Nov. 18, 10:28 p.m.; First Qtr., Nov. 26, 6:24 p.m.

Day of			Planetary Configurations and Phenomena	*Hour of			
Year	Month	Week		Sunrise	Sunset	Moon-rise	Moon-set
305	1	Su.		6:52	5:48	**4:24**	3:48
306	2	Mo.		6:53	5:47	**5:06**	4:55
307	3	Tu.	♄☌☾; ☾ at perigee	6:54	5:46	**5:50**	6:04
308	4	We.		6:55	5:45	**6:38**	7:14
309	5	Th.		6:56	5:45	**7:29**	8:24
310	6	Fr.		6:57	5:44	**8:24**	9:31
311	7	Sa.		6:57	5:43	**9:21**	10:33
312	8	Su.		6:58	5:42	**10:20**	11:30
313	9	Mo.		6:59	5:42	**11:19**	**12:21**
314	10	Tu.		7:00	5:41	...	**1:06**
315	11	We.	☿ greatest elong. E.	7:01	5:40	12:17	**1:46**
316	12	Th.		7:02	5:40	1:13	**2:22**
317	13	Fr.	♂☌☾; ♃ stationary	7:02	5:39	2:07	**2:56**
318	14	Sa.		7:03	5:39	3:00	**3:28**
319	15	Su.		7:04	5:38	3:53	**4:00**
320	16	Mo.		7:05	5:38	4:45	**4:33**
321	17	Tu.	☾ at apogee	7:06	5:37	5:37	**5:07**
322	18	We.		7:07	5:37	6:30	**5:43**
323	19	Th.		7:08	5:36	7:23	**6:21**
324	20	Fr.	☿☌☾	7:09	5:36	8:16	**7:04**
325	21	Sa.	☿ stationary	7:09	5:35	9:08	**7:50**
326	22	Su.		7:10	5:35	9:59	**8:40**
327	23	Mo.		7:11	5:35	10:47	**9:33**
328	24	Tu.	♆☌☾; ♅☌☾	7:12	5:35	11:33	**10:30**
329	25	We.		7:13	5:34	**12:17**	**11:28**
330	26	Th.		7:14	5:34	**12:58**	...
331	27	Fr.	♃☌☾	7:15	5:34	**1:38**	12:29
332	28	Sa.		7:15	5:34	**2:18**	1:31
333	29	Su.		7:16	5:34	**2:58**	2:35
334	30	Mo.	♇☌☉; ♄☌☾	7:17	5:34	**3:39**	3:41

12th Month — **December 1998** — **31 Days**

Moon's Phases — Full, Dec. 3, 9:21 a.m.; Last Qtr., Dec. 10, 11:55 a.m.; New, Dec.18, 4:44 p.m.; First Qtr., Dec. 26, 4:47 a.m.

Day of			Planetary Configurations and Phenomena	*Hour of			
Year	Month	Week		Sunrise	Sunset	Moon-rise	Moon-set
335	1	Tu.	☿ inferior	7:18	5:33	**4:24**	4:49
336	2	We.	☾ at perigee	7:19	5:33	**5:12**	5:58
337	3	Th.		7:20	5:33	**6:05**	7:06
338	4	Fr.		7:20	5:33	**7:03**	8:13
339	5	Sa.		7:21	5:33	**8:03**	9:15
340	6	Su.		7:22	5:33	**9:04**	10:10
341	7	Mo.		7:23	5:34	**10:04**	11:00
342	8	Tu.		7:23	5:34	**11:02**	11:43
343	9	We.		7:24	5:34	**11:59**	**12:22**
344	10	Th.		7:25	5:34	...	**12:57**
345	11	Fr.	☿ stationary	7:26	5:34	12:53	**1:30**
346	12	Sa.	♂☌☾	7:26	5:35	1:46	**2:03**
347	13	Su.		7:27	5:35	2:39	**2:35**
348	14	Mo.	☾ at apogee	7:28	5:35	3:31	**3:08**
349	15	Tu.		7:28	5:35	4:24	**3:43**
350	16	We.	☿☌☾	7:29	5:36	5:16	**4:20**
351	17	Th.		7:29	5:36	6:10	**5:01**
352	18	Fr.		7:30	5:37	7:03	**5:46**
353	19	Sa.	☿ greatest elong. W.	7:31	5:37	7:55	**6:36**
354	20	Su.		7:31	5:38	8:45	**7:29**
355	21	Mo.	Winter begins; ♆☌☾	7:32	5:38	9:33	**8:25**
356	22	Tu.	♅☌☾	7:32	5:38	10:18	**9:23**
357	23	We.		7:33	5:39	11:00	**10:22**
358	24	Th.		7:33	5:40	11:39	**11:23**
359	25	Fr.	♃☌☾	7:33	5:40	**12:18**	...
360	26	Sa.		7:34	5:41	**12:56**	12:25
361	27	Su.	♄☌☾	7:34	5:41	**1:35**	1:28
362	28	Mo.		7:35	5:42	**2:16**	2:32
363	29	Tu.		7:35	5:43	**3:01**	3:38
364	30	We.	♄ stationary; ☾ at perigee	7:35	5:43	**3:50**	4:45
365	31	Th.		7:36	5:44	**4:44**	5:51

Calendar for 1999

Times are **Central Standard Time**, except from April 4 to Oct. 31, during which **Daylight Saving Time** is observed. **Boldface times for moonrise and moonset** indicate p.m. Times are figured for the point **99° 10' West and 31° 23' North**, the approximate center of the state. **See page 93 for explanation of how to get the approximate time at any other Texas point**.

1st Month — January 1999 — 31 Days

Moon's Phases — Full, Jan. 1, 8:51 a.m.; Last Qtr., Jan. 9, 8:23 a.m.; New, Jan. 17, 9:47 a.m.; First Qtr., Jan. 24, 1:17 p.m.; Full, Jan. 31, 10:08 a.m.

Day of			Planetary Configurations and Phenomena	*Hour of			
Year	Month	Week		Sunrise	Sunset	Moon-rise	Moon-set
1	1	Fr.		7:36	5:45	**5:42**	6:55
2	2	Sa.		7:36	5:45	**6:43**	7:54
3	3	Su.	● at perihelion	7:36	5:46	**7:45**	8:47
4	4	Mo.		7:36	5:47	**8:46**	9:35
5	5	Tu.	♀ ☌ ♆	7:36	5:48	**9:45**	10:17
6	6	We.		7:37	5:49	**10:42**	10:55
7	7	Th.		7:37	5:49	**11:37**	11:30
8	8	Fr.		7:37	5:50	...	**12:03**
9	9	Sa.	♂ ☌ ☾	7:37	5:51	12:30	**12:35**
10	10	Su.		7:37	5:52	1:23	**1:08**
11	11	Mo.	☾ at apogee	7:37	5:53	2:15	**1:42**
12	12	Tu.		7:37	5:53	3:08	**2:18**
13	13	We.	♀ ☌ ♅	7:37	5:54	4:01	**2:57**
14	14	Th.		7:36	5:55	4:54	**3:41**
15	15	Fr.		7:36	5:56	5:47	**4:29**
16	16	Sa.		7:36	5:57	6:39	**5:21**
17	17	Su.		7:36	5:58	7:28	**6:16**
18	18	Mo.		7:36	5:59	8:15	**7:15**
19	19	Tu.	♀ ☌ ☾	7:35	6:00	8:59	**8:16**
20	20	We.		7:35	6:01	9:40	**9:17**
21	21	Th.	♃ ☌ ☾	7:35	6:01	10:20	**10:19**
22	22	Fr.	♆ ☌ ☉	7:34	6:02	10:58	**11:21**
23	23	Sa.		7:34	6:03	11:36	...
24	24	Su.	♄ ☌ ☾	7:34	6:04	**12:16**	12:24
25	25	Mo.		7:33	6:05	**12:58**	1:28
26	26	Tu.	☾ at perigee	7:33	6:06	**1:44**	2:32
27	27	We.		7:32	6:07	**2:34**	3:37
28	28	Th.		7:32	6:08	**3:28**	4:40
29	29	Fr.		7:31	6:09	**4:27**	5:40
30	30	Sa.		7:31	6:10	**5:27**	6:35
31	31	Su.		7:30	6:11	**6:29**	7:25

2nd Month — February 1999 — 28 Days

Moon's Phases — Last Qtr., Feb. 8, 5:59 a.m.; New, Feb. 16, 12:40 a.m.; First Qtr., Feb. 22, 8:44 p.m.

Day of			Planetary Configurations and Phenomena	*Hour of			
Year	Month	Week		Sunrise	Sunset	Moon-rise	Moon-set
32	1	Mo.	♅ ☌ ☉	7:29	6:11	**7:29**	8:09
33	2	Tu.		7:29	6:12	**8:27**	8:49
34	3	We.		7:28	6:13	**9:24**	9:26
35	4	Th.	☿ superior	7:27	6:14	**10:19**	10:00
36	5	Fr.		7:27	6:15	**11:13**	10:34
37	6	Sa.	♂ ☌ ☾	7:26	6:16	...	11:06
38	7	Su.		7:25	6:17	12:05	11:40
39	8	Mo.	☾ at apogee	7:24	6:18	12:58	**12:15**
40	9	Tu.		7:24	6:18	1:51	**12:53**
41	10	We.		7:23	6:19	2:44	**1:34**
42	11	Th.		7:22	6:20	3:36	**2:19**
43	12	Fr.		7:21	6:21	4:28	**3:09**
44	13	Sa.		7:20	6:22	5:19	**4:04**
45	14	Su.	♆ ☌ ☾	7:19	6:23	6:07	**5:02**
46	15	Mo.		7:18	6:24	6:53	**6:02**
47	16	Tu.		7:17	6:24	7:36	**7:05**
48	17	We.		7:17	6:25	8:17	**8:08**
49	18	Th.	♀ ☌ ☾; ♃ ☌ ☾	7:16	6:26	8:57	**9:12**
50	19	Fr.		7:15	6:27	9:36	**10:17**
51	20	Sa.	☾ at perigee; ♄ ☌ ☾	7:14	6:28	10:16	**11:21**
52	21	Su.		7:13	6:28	10:58	...
53	22	Mo.		7:12	6:29	11:42	12:26
54	23	Tu.	♀ ☌ ♃	7:10	6:30	**12:30**	1:30
55	24	We.		7:09	6:31	**1:22**	2:32
56	25	Th.		7:08	6:32	**2:18**	3:32
57	26	Fr.		7:07	6:32	**3:16**	4:27
58	27	Sa.		7:06	6:33	**4:16**	5:18
59	28	Su.		7:05	6:34	**5:16**	6:04

*See text before January calendar for explanation.

3rd Month — March 1999 — 31 Days

Moon's Phases — Full, March 2, 1:00 a.m.; Last Qtr., March 10, 2:42 a.m.; New, March 17, 12:49 p.m.; First Qtr., March 24, 4:19 a.m.; Full, March 31, 4:50 p.m.

Day of			Planetary Configurations and Phenomena	*Hour of			
Year	Month	Week		Sunrise	Sunset	Moon-rise	Moon-set
60	1	Mo.		7:04	6:35	**6:15**	6:45
61	2	Tu.		7:03	6:35	**7:12**	7:23
62	3	We.	☿ greatest elong. E.	7:02	6:36	**8:07**	7:58
63	4	Th.		7:00	6:37	**9:02**	8:31
64	5	Fr.		6:59	6:38	**9:56**	9:04
65	6	Sa.	♂ ☌ ☾	6:58	6:38	**10:49**	9:38
66	7	Su.	☾ at apogee	6:57	6:39	**11:41**	10:12
67	8	Mo.		6:56	6:40	...	10:49
68	9	Tu.	☿ stationary	6:54	6:40	12:34	11:28
69	10	We.		6:53	6:41	1:26	**12:11**
70	11	Th.		6:52	6:42	2:18	**12:58**
71	12	Fr.		6:51	6:43	3:08	**1:50**
72	13	Sa.	♆ ☌ ☾	6:50	6:43	3:57	**2:45**
73	14	Su.	♅ ☌ ☾; ♇ stationary	6:48	6:44	4:43	**3:44**
74	15	Mo.		6:47	6:45	5:27	**4:46**
75	16	Tu.		6:46	6:45	6:10	**5:50**
76	17	We.		6:45	6:46	6:51	**6:55**
77	18	Th.	♂ stationary; ♃ ☌ ☾	6:43	6:47	7:31	**8:01**
78	19	Fr.	☿ inferior; ☾ at perigee	6:42	6:47	8:12	**9:08**
79	20	Sa.	Spring begins	6:41	6:48	8:54	**10:15**
80	21	Su.		6:40	6:49	9:39	**11:22**
81	22	Mo.		6:38	6:49	10:27	...
82	23	Tu.		6:37	6:50	11:18	12:26
83	24	We.		6:36	6:51	**12:13**	1:28
84	25	Th.		6:35	6:51	**1:11**	2:24
85	26	Fr.		6:33	6:52	**2:10**	3:16
86	27	Sa.		6:32	6:53	**3:09**	4:02
87	28	Su.		6:31	6:53	**4:07**	4:44
88	29	Mo.		6:30	6:54	**5:03**	5:22
89	30	Tu.		6:28	6:55	**5:59**	5:57
90	31	We.		6:27	6:55	**6:54**	6:31

4th Month — April 1999 — 30 Days

Moon's Phases - Last Qtr., April 8, 8:52 p.m.; New., April 15, 11:23 p.m.; 1st Qtr., April 22, 2:03 p.m.; Full, April 30, 9:56 a.m.

Day of			Planetary Configurations and Phenomena	*Hour of			
Year	Month	Week		Sunrise	Sunset	Moon-rise	Moon-set
91	1	Th.	♃ ☌ ☉; ☿ stationary	6:26	6:56	**7:47**	7:04
92	2	Fr.		6:25	6:57	**8:41**	7:37
93	3	Sa.	♂ ☌ ☾	6:23	6:57	**9:34**	8:11
94	†4	Su.	☾ at apogee	7:22	7:58	**11:26**	9:46
95	5	Mo.		7:21	7:58	...	10:25
96	6	Tu.		7:20	7:59	12:19	11:06
97	7	We.		7:18	8:00	1:10	11:51
98	8	Th.		7:17	8:00	2:00	**12:40**
99	9	Fr.		7:16	8:01	2:49	**1:32**
100	10	Sa.	♆ ☌ ☾	7:15	8:02	3:35	**2:28**
101	11	Su.	♅ ☌ ☾	7:14	8:02	4:19	**3:28**
102	12	Mo.		7:12	8:03	5:01	**4:29**
103	13	Tu.	☿ ☌ ☾	7:11	8:04	5:42	**5:33**
104	14	We.		7:10	8:04	6:22	**6:39**
105	15	Th.		7:09	8:05	7:03	**7:47**
106	16	Fr.	☿ greatest elong. W.	7:08	8:06	7:45	**8:55**
107	17	Sa.	☾ at perigee	7:07	8:06	8:29	**10:05**
108	18	Su.	♀ ☌ ☾	7:05	8:07	9:18	**11:13**
109	19	Mo.		7:04	8:08	10:10	...
110	20	Tu.		7:03	8:08	11:05	12:18
111	21	We.		7:02	8:09	**12:04**	1:19
112	22	Th.		7:01	8:10	**1:04**	2:13
113	23	Fr.		7:00	8:10	**2:03**	3:02
114	24	Sa.	♂ ☍	6:59	8:11	**3:02**	3:45
115	25	Su.		6:58	8:12	**3:58**	4:24
116	26	Mo.		6:57	8:13	**4:54**	5:00
117	27	Tu.	♄ ☌ ☉	6:56	8:13	**5:48**	5:33
118	28	We.		6:55	8:14	**6:42**	6:06
119	29	Th.	♂ ☌ ☾	6:54	8:15	**7:35**	6:38
120	30	Fr.		6:53	8:15	**8:28**	7:11

†Daylight Saving Time begins at 2:00 a.m.

Calendar for 1999 (Cont'd.)

5th Month — **May 1999** — **31 Days**

Moon's Phases — Last Qtr., May 8, 12:29 p.m.; New, May 15, 7:06 a.m.; First Qtr., May 22, 12:35 a.m., Full, May 30, 1:41 a.m.

Day of Year	Day of Month	Day of Week	Planetary Configurations and Phenomena	*Hour of Sunrise	*Hour of Sunset	*Hour of Moon-rise	*Hour of Moon-set
121	1	Sa.	☿ ☌ ♃; ♂ closest	6:52	8:16	**9:21**	7:46
122	2	Su.	☾ at apogee	6:51	8:17	**10:14**	8:23
123	3	Mo.		6:50	8:17	**11:06**	9:03
124	4	Tu.		6:49	8:18	**11:56**	9:47
125	5	We.		6:48	8:19	...	10:34
126	6	Th.	♆ stationary	6:48	8:19	12:45	11:24
127	7	Fr.	♆ ☌ ☾	6:47	8:20	1:31	**12:18**
128	8	Sa.	♅ ☌ ☾	6:46	8:21	2:15	**1:15**
129	9	Su.		6:45	8:21	2:57	**2:14**
130	10	Mo.		6:44	8:22	3:36	**3:15**
131	11	Tu.		6:44	8:23	4:15	**4:18**
132	12	We.		6:43	8:24	4:54	**5:23**
133	13	Th.	☿ ☌ ♄	6:42	8:24	5:35	**6:31**
134	14	Fr.		6:41	8:25	6:17	**7:40**
135	15	Sa.	☾ at perigee	6:41	8:26	7:04	**8:51**
136	16	Su.		6:40	8:26	7:55	**10:00**
137	17	Mo.		6:40	8:27	8:50	**11:05**
138	18	Tu.	♀ ☌ ☾	6:39	8:28	9:50	...
139	19	We.		6:38	8:28	10:52	12:05
140	20	Th.		6:38	8:29	11:54	12:58
141	21	Fr.	♅ stationary	6:37	8:30	**12:54**	1:44
142	22	Sa.		6:37	8:30	**1:53**	2:25
143	23	Su.		6:36	8:31	**2:49**	3:02
144	24	Mo.		6:36	8:31	**3:44**	3:36
145	25	Tu.	☿ superior	6:35	8:32	**4:38**	4:09
146	26	We.	♂ ☌ ☾	6:35	8:33	**5:31**	4:41
147	27	Th.		6:35	8:33	**6:23**	5:13
148	28	Fr.		6:34	8:34	**7:16**	5:47
149	29	Sa.	☾ at apogee	6:34	8:35	**8:09**	6:23
150	30	Su.		6:33	8:35	**9:02**	7:02
151	31	Mo.	♇ ☍	6:33	8:36	**9:53**	7:44

6th Month — **June 1999** — **30 Days**

Moon's Phases — Last Qtr., June 6, 11:21 p.m.;New, June 13, 2:04 p.m.; First Qtr., June 20, 1:14 p.m.; Full, June 28, 4:38 p.m.

Day of Year	Day of Month	Day of Week	Planetary Configurations and Phenomena	*Hour of Sunrise	*Hour of Sunset	*Hour of Moon-rise	*Hour of Moon-set
152	1	Tu.		6:33	8:36	**10:43**	8:30
153	2	We.		6:33	8:37	**11:30**	9:20
154	3	Th.	♆ ☌ ☾	6:32	8:37	...	10:13
155	4	Fr.	♅ ☌ ☾	6:32	8:38	12:14	11:08
156	5	Sa.	♂ stationary	6:32	8:38	12:56	**12:05**
157	6	Su.		6:32	8:39	1:36	**1:04**
158	7	Mo.		6:32	8:39	2:13	**2:04**
159	8	Tu.		6:32	8:40	2:51	**3:06**
160	9	We.	♃ ☌ ☾	6:32	8:40	3:29	**4:11**
161	10	Th.	♄ ☌ ☾	6:32	8:41	4:09	**5:17**
162	11	Fr.	♀ greatest elong. E.	6:32	8:41	4:52	**6:26**
163	12	Sa.	☾ at perigee	6:32	8:41	5:40	**7:36**
164	13	Su.		6:32	8:42	6:32	**8:44**
165	14	Mo.		6:32	8:42	7:31	**9:48**
166	15	Tu.	☿ ☌ ☾	6:32	8:43	8:33	**10:46**
167	16	We.	♀ ☌ ☾	6:32	8:43	9:37	**11:37**
168	17	Th.		6:32	8:43	10:40	...
169	18	Fr.		6:32	8:43	11:42	12:22
170	19	Sa.		6:32	8:44	**12:40**	1:01
171	20	Su.		6:32	8:44	**1:37**	1:37
172	21	Mo.	Summer begins	6:33	8:44	**2:32**	2:11
173	22	Tu.	♂ ☌ ☾	6:33	8:44	**3:25**	2:43
174	23	We.		6:33	8:45	**4:18**	3:15
175	24	Th.		6:33	8:45	**5:11**	3:49
176	25	Fr.	☾ at apogee	6:34	8:45	**6:04**	4:24
177	26	Sa.		6:34	8:45	**6:57**	5:01
178	27	Su.		6:34	8:45	**7:49**	5:43
179	28	Mo.	☿ greatest elong. E.	6:35	8:45	**8:40**	6:27
180	29	Tu.		6:35	8:45	**9:28**	7:16
181	30	We.	♆ ☌ ☾	6:35	8:45	**10:14**	8:08

*See text before January calendar for explanation.

7th Month — **July 1999** — **31 Days**

Moon's Phases — Last Qtr., July 6, 6:58 a.m.; New, July 12, 9:25 p.m.; First Qtr., July 20, 4:02 a.m.; Full, July 28, 6:26 a.m.

Day of Year	Day of Month	Day of Week	Planetary Configurations and Phenomena	*Hour of Sunrise	*Hour of Sunset	*Hour of Moon-rise	*Hour of Moon-set
182	1	Th.	♅ ☌ ☾	6:36	8:45	**10:57**	9:03
183	2	Fr.		6:36	8:45	**11:37**	10:00
184	3	Sa.		6:36	8:45	...	10:58
185	4	Su.		6:37	8:45	12:15	11:57
186	5	Mo.		6:37	8:45	12:52	**12:58**
187	6	Tu.	● at aphelion	6:38	8:45	1:28	**1:59**
188	7	We.	♄ ☌ ☾	6:38	8:45	2:06	**3:03**
189	8	Th.		6:39	8:44	2:46	**4:08**
190	9	Fr.		6:39	8:44	3:30	**5:15**
191	10	Sa.		6:40	8:44	4:19	**6:23**
192	11	Su.	☾ at perigee	6:40	8:44	5:13	**7:28**
193	12	Mo.		6:41	8:43	6:13	**8:29**
194	13	Tu.		6:41	8:43	7:16	**9:24**
195	14	We.	☿ ☌ ☾; ♀ greatest brilliancy	6:42	8:43	8:21	**10:13**
196	15	Th.	♀ ☌ ☾	6:43	8:42	9:25	**10:56**
197	16	Fr.		6:43	8:42	10:26	**11:35**
198	17	Sa.		6:44	8:42	11:25	...
199	18	Su.		6:44	8:41	**12:22**	12:10
200	19	Mo.		6:45	8:41	**1:17**	12:43
201	20	Tu.	♂ ☌ ☾	6:45	8:40	**2:11**	1:16
202	21	We.		6:46	8:40	**3:04**	1:49
203	22	Th.		6:47	8:39	**3:57**	2:23
204	23	Fr.	☾ at apogee	6:47	8:39	**4:50**	3:00
205	24	Sa.		6:48	8:38	**5:42**	3:40
206	25	Su.		6:49	8:37	**6:34**	4:23
207	26	Mo.	♆ ☍; ☿ inferior	6:49	8:37	**7:24**	5:11
208	27	Tu.	♀ stationary	6:50	8:36	**8:11**	6:02
209	28	We.	♆ ☌ ☾	6:50	8:36	**8:55**	6:56
210	29	Th.	♅ ☌ ☾	6:51	8:35	**9:37**	7:54
211	30	Fr.		6:52	8:34	**10:16**	8:52
212	31	Sa.		6:52	8:33	**10:54**	9:52

8th Month — **August 1999** — **31 Days**

Moon's Phases — Last Qtr., Aug. 4, 12:28 p.m.; New, Aug. 11, 6:09 a.m.; First Qtr., Aug. 18, 8:48 p.m.; Full, Aug. 26, 6:49 p.m.

Day of Year	Day of Month	Day of Week	Planetary Configurations and Phenomena	*Hour of Sunrise	*Hour of Sunset	*Hour of Moon-rise	*Hour of Moon-set
213	1	Su.		6:53	8:33	**11:30**	10:52
214	2	Mo.		6:54	8:32	...	11:53
215	3	Tu.	♃ ☌ ☾	6:54	8:31	12:07	**12:55**
216	4	We.	♄ ☌ ☾	6:55	8:30	12:46	**1:59**
217	5	Th.	☿ stationary	6:56	8:29	1:27	**3:03**
218	6	Fr.		6:56	8:29	2:12	**4:09**
219	7	Sa.	♅ ☍; ☾ at perigee	6:57	8:28	3:03	**5:13**
220	8	Su.		6:57	8:27	3:58	**6:14**
221	9	Mo.	☿ ☌ ☾	6:58	8:26	4:59	**7:11**
222	10	Tu.		6:59	8:25	6:02	**8:02**
223	11	We.		6:59	8:24	7:06	**8:48**
224	12	Th.		7:00	8:23	8:09	**9:29**
225	13	Fr.		7:01	8:22	9:10	**10:06**
226	14	Sa.	☿ greatest elong. W.	7:01	8:21	10:09	**10:41**
227	15	Su.		7:02	8:20	11:05	**11:14**
228	16	Mo.		7:03	8:19	**12:01**	**11:48**
229	17	Tu.		7:03	8:18	**12:55**	...
230	18	We.	♂ ☌ ☾	7:04	8:17	**1:48**	12:22
231	19	Th.	☾ at apogee	7:04	8:16	**2:41**	12:57
232	20	Fr.	♀ inferior	7:05	8:15	**3:34**	1:36
233	21	Sa.	♇ stationary	7:06	8:14	**4:26**	2:18
234	22	Su.		7:06	8:12	**5:16**	3:03
235	23	Mo.		7:07	8:11	**6:04**	3:53
236	24	Tu.	♆ ☌ ☾	7:08	8:10	**6:50**	4:46
237	25	We.	♃ stationary; ♅ ☌ ☾	7:08	8:09	**7:33**	5:43
238	26	Th.	☿ ☌ ♀	7:09	8:08	**8:14**	6:42
239	27	Fr.		7:09	8:07	**8:53**	7:42
240	28	Sa.		7:10	8:05	**9:30**	8:43
241	29	Su.		7:11	8:04	**10:08**	9:45
242	30	Mo.	♄ stationary	7:11	8:03	**10:46**	10:48
243	31	Tu.	♃ ☌ ☾	7:12	8:02	**11:27**	11:52

Calendar for 1999 (Cont'd.)

9th Month — September 1999 — 30 Days

Moon's Phases — Last Qtr., Sept. 2, 5:18 p.m.; New, Sept. 9, 5:03 p.m.; First Qtr., Sept. 17, 3:07 p.m.; Full, Sept. 25, 5:52 a.m.

Day of Year	Day of Month	Day of Week	Planetary Configurations and Phenomena	*Hour of Sunrise	*Hour of Sunset	*Hour of Moon-rise	*Hour of Moon-set
244	1	We.	♄ ☌ ☾	7:12	8:01	. . .	**12:57**
245	2	Th.	☾ at perigee	7:13	7:59	12:11	**2:01**
246	3	Fr.		7:14	7:58	12:59	**3:05**
247	4	Sa.		7:14	7:57	1:52	**4:06**
248	5	Su.		7:15	7:56	2:49	**5:03**
249	6	Mo.		7:15	7:54	3:50	**5:55**
250	7	Tu.	♀ ☌ ☾	7:16	7:53	4:52	**6:42**
251	8	We.	☿ superior	7:16	7:52	5:54	**7:24**
252	9	Th.	♀ stationary	7:17	7:51	6:55	**8:02**
253	10	Fr.		7:18	7:49	7:55	**8:38**
254	11	Sa.		7:18	7:48	8:53	**9:12**
255	12	Su.		7:19	7:47	9:49	**9:45**
256	13	Mo.		7:19	7:45	10:44	**10:19**
257	14	Tu.		7:20	7:44	11:38	**10:54**
258	15	We.		7:21	7:43	**12:32**	**11:32**
259	16	Th.	♂ ☌ ☾; ☾ at apogee	7:21	7:41	**1:25**	. . .
260	17	Fr.		7:22	7:40	**2:17**	12:12
261	18	Sa.		7:22	7:39	**3:07**	12:56
262	19	Su.		7:23	7:38	**3:56**	1:43
263	20	Mo.	♆ ☌ ☾	7:24	7:36	**4:43**	2:34
264	21	Tu.	♅ ☌ ☾	7:24	7:35	**5:26**	3:29
265	22	We.		7:25	7:34	**6:08**	4:27
266	23	Th.	Fall begins	7:25	7:32	**6:48**	5:27
267	24	Fr.		7:26	7:31	**7:26**	6:28
268	25	Sa.		7:27	7:30	**8:04**	7:31
269	26	Su.	♀ greatest brilliancy	7:27	7:28	**8:43**	8:36
270	27	Mo.	♃ ☌ ☾	7:28	7:27	**9:24**	9:41
271	28	Tu.	♄ ☌ ☾; ☾ at perigee	7:28	7:26	**10:08**	10:47
272	29	We.		7:29	7:25	**10:55**	11:54
273	30	Th.		7:30	7:23	**11:47**	**12:59**

10th Month — October 1999 — 31 Days

Moon's Phases — Last Qtr, Oct. 1, 11:03 p.m.; New, Oct. 9, 6:36 a.m.; First Qtr., Oct. 17, 10:00 a.m.; Full, Oct. 24, 4:04p.m.; Last Qtr., Oct. 31, 6:05 a.m.

Day of Year	Day of Month	Day of Week	Planetary Configurations and Phenomena	*Hour of Sunrise	*Hour of Sunset	*Hour of Moon-rise	*Hour of Moon-set
274	1	Fr.		7:30	7:22	. . .	**2:01**
275	2	Sa.		7:31	7:21	12:44	**3:00**
276	3	Su.		7:31	7:20	1:43	**3:52**
277	4	Mo.		7:32	7:18	2:44	**4:40**
278	5	Tu.	♀ ☌ ☾	7:33	7:17	3:45	**5:22**
279	6	We.		7:33	7:16	4:46	**6:01**
280	7	Th.		7:34	7:15	5:45	**6:36**
281	8	Fr.		7:35	7:13	6:42	**7:10**
282	9	Sa.		7:35	7:12	7:39	**7:44**
283	10	Su.	☿ ☌ ☾	7:36	7:11	8:34	**8:17**
284	11	Mo.		7:37	7:10	9:29	**8:52**
285	12	Tu.		7:37	7:09	10:23	**9:28**
286	13	We.	♆ stationary	7:38	7:07	11:17	**10:07**
287	14	Th.	☾ at apogee	7:39	7:06	**12:09**	**10:49**
288	15	Fr.	♂ ☌ ☾	7:39	7:05	**1:00**	**11:35**
289	16	Sa.		7:40	7:04	**1:49**	. . .
290	17	Su.		7:41	7:03	**2:36**	12:24
291	18	Mo.	♆ ☌ ☾	7:42	7:02	**3:20**	1:17
292	19	Tu.		7:42	7:01	**4:02**	2:12
293	20	We.		7:43	7:00	**4:41**	3:10
294	21	Th.		7:44	6:59	**5:20**	4:10
295	22	Fr.		7:44	6:57	**5:58**	5:12
296	23	Sa.	♅ stationary; ♃ ☍	7:45	6:56	**6:36**	6:16
297	24	Su.	♃ ☌ ☾	7:46	6:55	**7:16**	7:21
298	25	Mo.	♄ ☌ ☾	7:47	6:54	**8:00**	8:29
299	26	Tu.	☾ at perigee	7:47	6:53	**8:47**	9:38
300	27	We.		7:48	6:52	**9:39**	10:47
301	28	Th.		7:49	6:52	**10:36**	11:53
302	29	Fr.		7:50	6:51	**11:36**	**12:54**
303	30	Sa.	♀ greatest elong. W.	7:51	6:50	. . .	**1:50**
304	†31	Su.		6:51	5:49	12:38	**1:40**

*See text before January calendar for explanation.
† Daylight Saving Time ends at 2:00 a.m.

11th Month — November 1999 — 30 Days

Moon's Phases — New, Nov. 7, 9:54 p.m.; First Qtr., Nov. 16, 3:04 a.m.; Full, Nov. 23, 1:05 a.m.; Last Qtr., Nov. 29, 5:19 a.m.

Day of Year	Day of Month	Day of Week	Planetary Configurations and Phenomena	*Hour of Sunrise	*Hour of Sunset	*Hour of Moon-rise	*Hour of Moon-set
305	1	Mo.		6:52	5:48	12:39	**2:23**
306	2	Tu.		6:53	5:47	1:40	**3:02**
307	3	We.	♀ ☌ ☾	6:54	5:46	2:39	**3:38**
308	4	Th.		6:55	5:45	3:36	**4:12**
309	5	Fr.	☿ stationary	6:55	5:45	4:32	**4:45**
310	6	Sa.	♄ ☍	6:56	5:44	5:27	**5:17**
311	7	Su.		6:57	5:43	6:22	**5:51**
312	8	Mo.		6:58	5:42	7:16	**6:27**
313	9	Tu.		6:59	5:42	8:10	**7:04**
314	10	We.		7:00	5:41	9:03	**7:45**
315	11	Th.	☾ at apogee	7:01	5:41	9:55	**8:30**
316	12	Fr.		7:01	5:40	10:45	**9:17**
317	13	Sa.	♂ ☌ ☾	7:02	5:39	11:32	**10:08**
318	14	Su.	♆ ☌ ☾	7:03	5:39	**12:16**	**11:01**
319	15	Mo.	♅ ☌ ☾; ☿ inferior	7:04	5:38	**12:58**	**11:57**
320	16	Tu.		7:05	5:38	**1:37**	. . .
321	17	We.		7:06	5:37	**2:15**	12:54
322	18	Th.		7:07	5:37	**2:51**	1:54
323	19	Fr.		7:07	5:36	**3:28**	2:55
324	20	Sa.	♃ ☌ ☾	7:08	5:36	**4:07**	3:58
325	21	Su.	♄ ☌ ☾	7:09	5:36	**4:48**	5:04
326	22	Mo.		7:10	5:35	**5:33**	6:13
327	23	Tu.	☾ at perigee	7:11	5:35	**6:24**	7:23
328	24	We.	☿ stationary	7:12	5:35	**7:20**	8:33
329	25	Th.		7:13	5:34	**8:21**	9:40
330	26	Fr.		7:13	5:34	**9:25**	10:41
331	27	Sa.		7:14	5:34	**10:29**	11:35
332	28	Su.	♂ ☌ ♆	7:15	5:34	**11:32**	**12:22**
333	29	Mo.		7:16	5:34	. . .	**1:04**
334	30	Tu.		7:17	5:34	12:33	**1:41**

12th Month — December 1999 — 31 Days

Moon's Phases — New, Dec. 7, 4:32 p.m.; First Qtr., Dec. 15, 6:51 p.m.; Full, Dec. 22, 11:33 a.m.; Last Qtr., Dec. 29, 8:05 a.m.

Day of Year	Day of Month	Day of Week	Planetary Configurations and Phenomena	*Hour of Sunrise	*Hour of Sunset	*Hour of Moon-rise	*Hour of Moon-set
335	1	We.		7:18	5:33	1:31	**2:15**
336	2	Th.	☿ greatest elong. W.	7:18	5:33	2:28	**2:48**
337	3	Fr.	♀ ☌ ☾	7:19	5:33	3:23	**3:20**
338	4	Sa.		7:20	5:33	4:17	**3:53**
339	5	Su.	☿ ☌ ☾	7:21	5:33	5:11	**4:27**
340	6	Mo.		7:22	5:33	6:05	**5:04**
341	7	Tu.		7:22	5:34	6:58	**5:44**
342	8	We.	☾ at apogee	7:23	5:34	7:50	**6:27**
343	9	Th.		7:24	5:34	8:41	**7:13**
344	10	Fr.		7:25	5:34	9:30	**8:03**
345	11	Sa.	♆ ☌ ☾	7:25	5:34	10:15	**8:55**
346	12	Su.	♂ ☌ ☾; ♅ ☌ ☾	7:26	5:35	10:57	**9:50**
347	13	Mo.	♂ ☌ ♅	7:27	5:35	11:37	**10:45**
348	14	Tu.		7:27	5:35	**12:14**	**11:42**
349	15	We.		7:28	5:35	**12:50**	. . .
350	16	Th.		7:29	5:36	**1:25**	12:41
351	17	Fr.		7:29	5:36	**2:01**	1:41
352	18	Sa.	♃ ☌ ☾	7:30	5:37	**2:39**	2:43
353	19	Su.	♄ ☌ ☾	7:30	5:37	**3:21**	3:48
354	20	Mo.	♃ stationary	7:31	5:37	**4:07**	4:56
355	21	Tu.		7:32	5:38	**5:00**	6:06
356	22	We.	Winter begins	7:32	5:38	**5:59**	7:16
357	23	Th.		7:33	5:39	**7:03**	8:21
358	24	Fr.		7:33	5:39	**8:10**	9:21
359	25	Sa.		7:33	5:40	**9:16**	10:14
360	26	Su.		7:34	5:41	**10:21**	11:00
361	27	Mo.		7:34	5:41	**11:22**	11:40
362	28	Tu.		7:35	5:42	. . .	**12:16**
363	29	We.		7:35	5:43	12:20	**12:50**
364	30	Th.		7:35	5:43	1:17	**1:23**
365	31	Fr.		7:35	5:44	2:12	**1:55**

201-Year Calendar, A.D. 1894-2094, Inclusive

Using this calendar, you can find the day of the week for any day of the month and year for the period 1894-2094, inclusive. To find any day of the week, first look in the table of common years or leap years for the year required. Under the months are figures that refer to the corresponding figures at the heads of the columns of days below. For example, To know on what day of the week March 2 fell in the year 1918, find 1918 in the table of years. In a parallel line under March is Fig. 5, which directs you to Col. 5 in the table of days, in which it will be seen that March 2 fell on Saturday.

Common Years, 1894 to 2094

											Jan.	Feb.	Mar.	Apr.	May	June	July	Aug.	Sept.	Oct.	Nov.	Dec.
1894	1900	...	...	...	...	...	...	...		...												
1906	1917	1923	1934	1945	1951	1962	1973	1979	1990	...												
2001	2007	2018	2029	2035	2046	2057	2063	2074	2085	2091	1	4	4	7	2	5	7	3	6	1	4	6
1895	...	...	...	...	...	...	...	...		...												
1901	1907	1918	1929	1935	1946	1957	1963	1974	1985	1991												
2002	2013	2019	2030	2041	2047	2058	2069	2075	2086	2097	2	5	5	1	3	6	1	4	7	2	5	7
1897	...	...	...	...	...	...	...	...		...												
1909	1915	1926	1937	1943	1954	1965	1971	1982	1993	1999												
2010	2021	2027	2038	2049	2055	2066	2077	2083	2094	2100	5	1	1	4	6	2	4	7	3	5	1	3
1898	1910	1921	1927	1938	1949	1955	1966	1977	1983	1994												
2005	2011	2022	2033	2039	2050	2061	2067	2078	2089	2095	6	2	2	5	7	3	5	1	4	6	2	4
1899	1905	1911	1922	1933	1939	1950	1961	1967	1978	1989												
1995	2006	2017	2023	2034	2045	2051	2062	2073	2079	2090	7	3	3	6	1	4	6	2	5	7	3	5
1902	1913	1919	1930	1941	1947	1958	1969	1975	1986	1997												
2003	2014	2025	2031	2042	2053	2059	2070	2081	2087	2098	3	6	6	2	4	7	2	5	1	3	6	1
1903	1914	1925	1931	1942	1953	1959	1970	1981	1987	1998												
2009	2015	2026	2037	2043	2054	2065	2071	2082	2093	2099	4	7	7	3	5	1	3	6	2	4	7	2

Leap Years, 1894 to 2094

									29											
...	...	1920	1948	1976	2004	2032	2060	2088	4	7	1	4	6	2	4	7	3	5	1	3
...	...	1924	1952	1980	2008	2036	2064	2092	2	5	6	2	4	7	2	5	1	3	6	1
...	...	1928	1956	1984	2012	2040	2068	2096	7	3	4	7	2	5	7	3	6	1	4	6
...	1904	1932	1960	1988	2016	2044	2072	...	5	1	2	5	7	3	5	1	4	6	2	4
1896	1908	1936	1964	1992	2020	2048	2076	...	3	6	7	3	5	1	3	6	2	4	7	2
...	1912	1940	1968	1996	2024	2052	2080	...	1	4	5	1	3	6	1	4	7	2	5	7
...	1916	1944	1972	2000	2028	2056	2084	...	6	2	3	6	1	4	6	2	5	7	3	5

1		2		3		4		5		6		7	
Mon.	1	Tues.	1	Wed.	1	Thurs.	1	Fri.	1	Sat.	1	SUN.	1
Tues.	2	Wed.	2	Thurs.	2	Fri.	2	Sat.	2	SUN.	2	Mon.	2
Wed.	3	Thurs.	3	Fri.	3	Sat.	3	SUN.	3	Mon.	3	Tues.	3
Thurs.	4	Fri.	4	Sat.	4	SUN.	4	Mon.	4	Tues.	4	Wed.	4
Fri.	5	Sat.	5	SUN.	5	Mon.	5	Tues.	5	Wed.	5	Thurs.	5
Sat.	6	SUN.	6	Mon.	6	Tues.	6	Wed.	6	Thurs.	6	Fri.	6
SUN.	7	Mon.	7	Tues.	7	Wed.	7	Thurs.	7	Fri.	7	Sat.	7
Mon.	8	Tues.	8	Wed.	8	Thurs.	8	Fri.	8	Sat.	8	SUN.	8
Tues.	9	Wed.	9	Thurs.	9	Fri.	9	Sat.	9	SUN.	9	Mon.	9
Wed.	10	Thurs.	10	Fri.	10	Sat.	10	SUN.	10	Mon.	10	Tues.	10
Thurs.	11	Fri.	11	Sat.	11	SUN.	11	Mon.	11	Tues.	11	Wed.	11
Fri.	12	Sat.	12	SUN.	12	Mon.	12	Tues.	12	Wed.	12	Thurs.	12
Sat.	13	SUN.	13	Mon.	13	Tues.	13	Wed.	13	Thurs.	13	Fri.	13
SUN.	14	Mon.	14	Tues.	14	Wed.	14	Thurs.	14	Fri.	14	Sat.	14
Mon.	15	Tues.	15	Wed.	15	Thurs.	15	Fri.	15	Sat.	15	SUN.	15
Tues.	16	Wed.	16	Thurs.	16	Fri.	16	Sat.	16	SUN.	16	Mon.	16
Wed.	17	Thurs.	17	Fri.	17	Sat.	17	SUN.	17	Mon.	17	Tues.	17
Thurs.	18	Fri.	18	Sat.	18	SUN.	18	Mon.	18	Tues.	18	Wed.	18
Fri.	19	Sat.	19	SUN.	19	Mon.	19	Tues.	19	Wed.	19	Thurs.	19
Sat.	20	SUN.	20	Mon.	20	Tues.	20	Wed.	20	Thurs.	20	Fri.	20
SUN.	21	Mon.	21	Tues.	21	Wed.	21	Thurs.	21	Fri.	21	Sat.	21
Mon.	22	Tues.	22	Wed.	22	Thurs.	22	Fri.	22	Sat.	22	SUN.	22
Tues.	23	Wed.	23	Thurs.	23	Fri.	23	Sat.	23	SUN.	23	Mon.	23
Wed.	24	Thurs.	24	Fri.	24	Sat.	24	SUN.	24	Mon.	24	Tues.	24
Thurs.	25	Fri.	25	Sat.	25	SUN.	25	Mon.	25	Tues.	25	Wed.	25
Fri.	26	Sat.	26	SUN.	26	Mon.	26	Tues.	26	Wed.	26	Thurs.	26
Sat.	27	SUN.	27	Mon.	27	Tues.	27	Wed.	27	Thurs.	27	Fri.	27
SUN.	28	Mon.	28	Tues.	28	Wed.	28	Thurs.	28	Fri.	28	Sat.	28
Mon.	29	Tues.	29	Wed.	29	Thurs.	29	Fri.	29	Sat.	29	SUN.	29
Tues.	30	Wed.	30	Thurs.	30	Fri.	30	Sat.	30	SUN.	30	Mon.	30
Wed.	31	Thurs.	31	Fri.	31	Sat.	31	SUN.	31	Mon.	31	Tues.	31

Beginning of the Year

The Athenians began the year in June, the Macedonians in September, the Romans first in March and later in January, the Persians on Aug. 11, and the ancient Mexicans on Feb. 23. The Chinese year, which begins in late January or early February, is similar to the Mohammedan year. Both have 12 months of 29 and 30 days alternating, while in every 19 years, there are seven years that have 13 months. This does not quite fit the planetary movements, hence the Chinese have formed a cycle of 60 years, in which period 22 intercalary months occur.

Weather

Source (unless otherwise noted): John F. Griffiths, Karin Gleason and Brian Belcher, Office of the State Climatologist, Texas A&M University, College Station.

Weather Highlights 1995

January 12: Thunderstorms produced large hail in a strip one mile long and three miles wide west of the city of Mason, Mason Co. Trees were stripped of their leaves, and hail was piled up to 12 inches deep in places. Cars were dented and windows were broken in homes and buildings. Grass and vegetation was reported to have been beaten to the ground in the storm. The thunderstorm moved northeastward, but produced no large hail in Mason.

January 21-22: A combination of an arctic cold-air mass with a lee-side trough and abundant gulf moisture brought heavy snows to the Texas Panhandle. The heaviest snows occurred in Roberts and Gray counties, with reports of five to eight inches, while other areas received four to six inches. The remainder of the Panhandle received one to three inches.

February 13: Warm air overriding cold air, which was spreading into North Texas behind a cold front on the 13th, set the stage for a mixture of wintry precipitation across the northern third of the region. Freezing drizzle, light freezing rain and some sleet resulted in slippery roadways and hundreds of accidents. Numerous people were injured, and at least three deaths resulted indirectly from the icy roadways.

March 25: Severe thunderstorms developed in western North Texas around mid-morning on the 25th, then moved eastward through the late morning. These storms produced hail as large as quarters, reported near Lake Diversion in Baylor County.

April 19: A severe storm developed over West Texas along and ahead of a dryline. There were numerous reports of dime-to golf ball-size hail with these storms, though no significant damage was reported. Two brief tornadoes occurred. The first (technically a landspout) occurred near Lubbock's southern city limits in mid-afternoon. It damaged several signs and a shed and was seen by thousands of citizens in Lubbock, as well as by the tower cameras operated by two local TV stations. The other tornado occurred on ranchland in extreme southern King County and caused no damage.

May 5: Golf ball-size hail 18 inches deep with drifts three feet deep was reported near Annetta, Parker Co. County roads iced over, resulting in accidents and cars sliding into ditches. The area was described as "looking like the dead of winter with vegetation totally stripped from trees and shrubs and the ground white as if covered with snow." Damage in Parker County was estimated at $20 million.

May 28: Extreme winds and giant hail slammed San Angelo, injuring at least 80 people and causing about $120 million in damage. The bulk of the damage occurred in a path that spread from two miles wide at O.C. Fisher Dam to five miles wide at Goodfellow Air Force Base. Sixty-one homes were destroyed, and more than 9,000 were slightly damaged. Near the core of the damage path, hail was six inches deep with drifts to two feet. An additional $8 million in damage was sustained by Goodfellow Air Force Base. This storm was a right-turning supercell that initially formed in Upton County, 75 miles west of San Angelo.

June 25: A cluster of thunderstorms moving to the southeast from southeastern New Mexico formed into a bow echo as it moved into the city of Monahans, Ward Co. Winds of at least 60 mph occurred for up to 25 minutes. An unofficial 84 mph was clocked by a local resident. A small barn was carried by the wind into power lines, resulting in local power outages.

July 28-August 3: On July 27, a weak cyclonic circulation with surface pressure falls of 2.5 millibars (0.73 inches) in 24 hours was indicated by buoy reports in the eastern Gulf of Mexico, while at the upper levels of the atmosphere, a broad quasi-stationary trough extended from the northeastern Gulf through Florida. Based on satellite and surface data, Tropical Depression Four formed about 300 nautical miles southeast of New Orleans at 1:00 p.m. CDT on July 28. The depression moved slowly toward the west-northwest around a well-established high-pressure ridge over the central United States. After some intensification, the depression became Tropical Storm Dean at 1:00 p.m. CDT on July 30 about 60 nautical miles from the Texas coast. The center of Dean crossed the coast near Freeport a few hours later. Two tornadoes briefly touched down, causing minor damage as Dean made landfall. Dean weakened to a tropical depression after landfall and continued on a northwestward track through Texas. The depression became nearly stationary for about 24 to 36 hours over the northwest portion of the state, producing heavy rainfall. Monroe City recorded 16.78 inches of rainfall, and more than 14 inches were recorded near Vernon. Dean dissipated on August 3 as it merged with a frontal zone. There were no reports of injuries or deaths associated with Dean. However, rainfall caused $500,000 in damage.

September 12: A severe thunderstorm in Wilbarger County downed power lines, blew part of the roof off a business, and destroyed outbuildings three miles south of Vernon. Lightning struck, ignited, and destroyed two mobile homes in Henrietta, Clay Co.

Weather Summary - 1995

A warmer-than-normal **January and February** helped balance a cooler-than-normal April and June across the entire state. Overall, temperatures in all regions were either normal or above normal for the year, with departures ranging from 0.0°F to 1.7°F. This is the second year in a row in which temperatures in each climatic division were above normal. Western, central and southern portions of Texas were the warmest in 1995, while temperatures in the Panhandle, northern, and eastern regions of Texas were closer to normal. Precipitation in **March** and **May** was above normal over most divisions, with annual totals below normal in the western and southern regions.

Temperatures in **January and February** were consistently above normal by an average of 3.4°F in each region. Precipitation during this period was above normal in the High Plains, North Central, East Texas and Upper Coast divisions. Precipitation was well below normal in the Southern and Lower Valley regions in January, with only 27 percent and 36 percent of their respective normals. February continued to be dry in the Lower Valley, with only 24 percent of the normal precipitation.

March, April and May were generally wetter than normal across the state. Conversely, temperatures were consistently below normal during this period in the High Plains, Low Rolling Plains and North Central divisions. Departures in temperature for April ranged from 0.8°F below normal in the Southern division to 3.0°F below normal in the High Plains. May showers brought large amounts of precipitation to much of the state as most regions reported totals ranging from 108 to 190 percent

Average Temperatures 1995

	High Plains	Low Plains	North Central	East Texas	Trans-Pecos	Edwards Plateau	South Central	Upper Coast	South Texas	Lower Valley
Jan.	39.5	44.4	47.1	48.2	46.4	48.6	54.0	54.5	56.2	60.2
Feb.	45.7	48.9	51.3	51.8	54.6	53.5	57.9	58.7	61.1	65.7
Mar.	48.1	52.2	54.9	57.8	57.3	56.5	61.2	62.4	64.0	66.5
April	55.5	61.6	63.2	63.5	63.6	65.4	68.4	68.1	72.7	74.0
May	63.6	68.7	71.6	72.8	74.0	74.4	77.0	76.8	81.6	82.2
June	72.7	76.1	77.3	77.8	79.1	77.8	79.3	80.1	82.7	82.8
July	78.7	83.2	83.6	83.0	82.5	83.5	84.3	84.1	86.7	86.1
Aug.	78.4	81.2	83.4	84.3	81.4	83.0	84.2	84.1	86.2	84.6
Sep.	69.0	72.8	75.5	76.6	74.9	76.7	80.3	81.0	82.2	82.6
Oct.	59.4	64.2	66.5	66.3	66.7	66.8	71.2	71.0	73.2	75.5
Nov.	49.3	53.6	54.8	55.2	56.3	56.2	60.8	61.7	63.3	67.1
Dec.	39.7	44.0	47.6	49.2	47.6	49.0	56.0	56.8	58.0	62.4
Ann.	58.3	62.6	64.7	65.5	65.4	66.0	69.6	69.9	72.3	74.1

Precipitation 1995

(Inches)

	High Plains	Low Plains	North Central	East Texas	Trans-Pecos	Edwards Plateau	South Central	Upper Coast	South Texas	Lower Valley
Jan.	0.59	0.78	1.76	6.07	0.28	0.44	1.37	4.68	0.29	0.55
Feb.	0.22	0.56	0.81	2.11	0.52	1.10	1.90	2.56	0.89	0.34
Mar.	0.74	1.34	4.21	4.19	0.27	1.60	3.13	5.08	1.73	1.15
April	0.92	1.66	4.37	6.02	0.57	2.21	2.39	4.34	0.86	1.20
May	4.35	6.38	6.35	4.79	1.25	5.13	5.30	6.32	3.39	1.77
June	2.75	4.60	3.36	3.25	1.99	2.25	3.29	5.35	2.56	2.32
July	2.35	1.84	3.29	3.77	0.58	0.87	1.18	3.88	1.12	0.61
Aug.	1.75	5.62	3.80	2.51	1.00	1.69	3.31	4.08	2.25	5.33
Sep.	4.00	4.78	3.82	3.43	2.66	3.65	2.84	2.38	3.83	2.96
Oct.	0.61	0.84	0.63	1.37	0.43	0.62	2.70	3.58	1.63	5.63
Nov.	0.08	0.70	1.26	1.76	0.34	2.04	2.65	3.85	3.00	3.72
Dec.	0.67	0.56	1.51	4.30	0.36	0.47	1.81	6.99	0.92	1.81
Ann.	19.03	29.66	35.17	43.57	10.25	22.07	31.87	53.09	22.47	26.79

of normal. Exceptions to this were the eastern and extreme southern portions of the state.

June, typically one of the hottest months of the year, was unseasonably cooler than normal as temperatures ranged from 0.2°F in the Lower Valley to 2.7°F below normal in the Low Rolling Plains. Precipitation in June was plentiful in the Low Rolling Plains as well as the Upper Coast and Trans-Pecos regions. Portions of central, eastern and southern Texas experienced below-normal precipitation for the month, ranging from 77 to 85 percent of normal.

Much-below-normal precipitation occurred in the western, central and southern portions of Texas in **July** coupled with above-normal temperatures. Precipitation percentages ranged from 33 percent in the Lower Valley and Trans-Pecos regions to 68 percent in the Southern division. Temperatures were nearly 1°F to 2°F above normal in all divisions except the High Plains and the North Central regions, which were near normal.

August was the warmest month of the year in East Texas (84.3°F) as several climatic divisions experienced temperatures of 1°F to 2°F above normal. In addition to East Texas, the other regions which experienced the warmer-than-normal temperatures in August were the High Plains, Trans-Pecos, Edwards Plateau and Upper Coast. Large amounts of precipitation fell over northern and coastal portions of the state as many regions received more than twice what was expected during August.

As the fall approached, monthly precipitation totals noticeably began to taper off. Unfortunately, no one could tell that this would be the beginning of approximately 10 months of extremely dry conditions across the state. Precipitation percentages throughout this period fell as low as 13 percent in the High Plains during **November** and 18 percent in the North Central division during **October**. Temperatures were slightly above normal in the southern tier of the state during **September and October**, as more northern locations were inevitably battling the onset of winter. 1995 ended on a warm note, as **December** temperatures ranged from nearly 1°F to over 2°F above normal across the state. Warmest conditions were felt in the southern-most regions of Texas as temperatures during the beginning and middle of December topped the 90°F threshold in McAllen and La Joya, both in Hidalgo County, making for a pleasant end to the year.

1995 Weather Extremes

Lowest Temp.: Follett, Lipscomb Co., March 7 . . . . 4°F
Highest Temp.: Heath Canyon, Brewster Co., July 25 . 115°F
24-hour Precip.: Vernon, Wilbarger Co., August 2 . . . . 14.82"
Monthly Precip.: Vernon, Wilbarger Co., August . . . . . . 17.60"
Least Annual Precip.: Fort Hancock, Hudspeth Co. . . . . 3.98"
Greatest Annual Precip.: Orange, Orange Co. . . . . 79.83"

Weather Highlights - 1996

February 21: Anomalously high temperatures were reported over the entire state as Texans experienced heat typical of summer rather than winter. Many records were shattered as the previous records of mid-80 degree F temperatures gave way to temperatures in the high-90s and low-100s. In some regions, temperatures this high had not been observed before the month of May.

April 5: A cold front passing through Texas dumped 18" of snow on Sweetwater, Nolan County, while an all-time 24-hour snowfall record was broken in Abilene when 9.3" fell across the region. Two inches of snow fell in Midland from this system, where it was the first time since 1983 that snow fell in April.

May-June: Drought conditions engulfed Texas as anomalously high temperatures and anomalously low precipitation occurred over the state. Mean monthly temperatures for May were some of the highest ever over Texas, while June and July were also significantly warmer than normal. The hot temperatures caused evaporation to eat away at the available water supplies — supplies which were not replenished by rainfall because of the extremely dry conditions over this period.

Late August: Hurricane Dolly made landfall near Tampico, Mexico, significantly affecting the weather in Texas. Showers and thunderstorms associated with Dolly produced much-needed rain over a large portion of the state. A small tornado during this time destroyed homes and uprooted trees near Brownsville.

December 15-19: An Arctic cold front pushed into Texas, where snow fell as far south as Houston. Blizzard-like conditions covered the Northern Plains, causing interstate highways to become impassable. On the 19th, the lowest temperature of the month (-3°F), as well as of the season, was reported in Dalhart.

Weather Summary - 1996

The main weather issues of 1996 were the drought conditions across Texas, which affected everyone in different ways. Farmers and ranchers were especially hit hard, being forced to sell cattle and watch crops wither in the dry soil. Along with the extremely dry conditions, anomalously warm temperatures, especially in February, May, June and July broke many records statewide and caused 1996 to be warmer than normal across Texas.

The year began on a very dry note. **January** precipitation was almost non-existent in the southern portion of the state, and minimal elsewhere. Mean monthly temperatures were 1 to 2 degrees F above normal over most of Texas.

The beginning of **February** was very cold across most of the state, but this was not characteristic of the remainder of the month. After the first week, when snow and ice were reported as far south as Waco, temperatures began and continued to rise throughout the month; 80s, 90s and 100s were observed over most of the Lone Star State near the latter part of February. In most places, mean monthly temperatures were greater than 4°F above normal, while all regions received less than half of the normal monthly precipitation throughout the state.

The hot trend reversed during **March and April** as temperature anomalies were as far below normal in March as they had been above normal in February. Relatively no relief from the dry conditions occurred during March as all regions in Texas again received significantly below-normal precipitation. April did provide above-normal precipitation for extreme West and East Texas, but other locations were not as lucky. The Panhandle suffered most during April; Amarillo and Lubbock received zero percent and 11 percent of their normal monthly precipitation, respectively.

Extreme heat, even more anomalous than February, returned to Texas during **May**. West Texas observed monthly temperatures greater than 8 degrees F above normal. In other regions of the state, except near the Texas coast, where the water modifies temperature extremes, anomalies of 6 and 7 degrees F above normal were experienced. Drought conditions continued to worsen throughout May. The Southern Panhandle

Average Temperatures 1996

	High Plains	Low Plains	North Central	East Texas	Trans-Pecos	Edwards Plateau	South Central	Upper Coast	South Texas	Lower Valley
Jan.	37.1	41.0	43.3	45.8	46.5	46.4	52.6	53.0	55.5	60.4
Feb.	43.8	48.9	51.6	52.6	54.0	53.2	58.0	57.4	60.8	63.6
Mar.	44.9	49.6	52.1	52.4	53.5	54.1	57.5	57.3	60.8	63.7
April	57.7	62.3	63.4	63.6	64.3	65.8	69.0	67.4	72.2	72.4
May	73.4	78.2	78.3	77.5	79.8	79.7	80.8	79.2	83.7	81.5
June	77.0	80.8	80.9	79.8	82.5	82.8	83.0	81.7	86.4	84.4
July	78.4	83.8	85.3	84.1	82.8	85.4	85.9	84.6	88.0	86.6
Aug.	75.6	80.1	81.3	80.5	78.5	82.1	83.9	82.6	85.6	84.9
Sep.	67.3	71.7	73.9	74.1	73.0	75.3	79.1	79.2	82.1	82.8
Oct.	58.8	63.2	65.9	65.9	64.9	66.3	71.8	71.4	74.3	75.8
Nov.	47.0	51.1	54.6	55.8	55.2	56.7	63.0	64.0	65.9	70.1
Dec.	40.2	46.1	49.1	51.2	48.0	49.3	56.6	58.4	57.7	63.7
Ann.	58.4	63.1	65.0	65.3	65.3	66.4	70.1	69.7	72.8	74.2

Precipitation 1996

(Inches)

	High Plains	Low Plains	North Central	East Texas	Trans-Pecos	Edwards Plateau	South Central	Upper Coast	South Texas	Lower Valley
Jan.	0.09	0.33	0.87	1.60	0.14	0.06	0.08	2.12	0.00	0.04
Feb.	0.11	0.08	0.28	0.53	0.10	0.26	0.38	0.76	0.13	0.09
Mar.	0.16	0.90	1.83	1.73	0.03	0.58	0.89	0.74	0.21	0.30
April	0.21	0.87	2.49	3.55	0.49	1.67	1.69	1.80	0.76	0.86
May	1.57	1.73	1.83	1.68	0.45	2.09	0.55	0.59	0.71	0.44
June	3.05	2.74	2.75	3.85	2.27	1.49	3.78	7.51	1.40	1.51
July	4.70	2.58	3.15	4.19	1.54	1.22	0.91	1.83	1.34	0.10
Aug.	4.48	4.58	5.94	6.85	3.22	4.63	6.07	9.06	4.39	4.29
Sep.	2.93	3.86	4.74	5.37	2.59	4.12	4.78	7.55	2.65	3.98
Oct.	0.66	1.39	3.10	2.79	0.16	2.68	1.02	2.92	0.99	4.91
Nov.	1.10	2.42	5.80	5.63	0.77	2.77	2.46	2.47	0.98	0.64
Dec.	0.20	0.03	1.21	3.47	0.02	0.89	1.88	3.12	0.48	0.47
Ann.	19.26	21.51	33.99	41.24	11.78	22.46	24.49	40.47	14.04	17.63

was the only location in Texas to receive greater than 70 percent of the normal monthly precipitation.

Temperatures remained 2 to 3 degrees F above normal for **June and July.** The intense heat, in combination with the continued devastating lack of rainfall throughout Texas, drew down lakes and reservoirs to minuscule levels. The Palmer Drought Severity Index indicated much of Central and Eastern Texas as being in an "Extreme Drought" while a "Severe Drought" was being experienced in the Panhandle, the Rio Grande Valley and the Texas Coast.

August brought much-needed relief to the state as all locations reported above-normal precipitation. Rain amounts were as much as 400 percent above normal across Central Texas and at least 200 percent above normal in many other regions. The break from dry conditions was caused mainly by the remnants of Hurricane Dolly, which caused numerous showers and thunderstorms to occur. During this welcome relief, monthly temperatures were slightly below normal

As quickly as hopes of escaping the drought were excited in August, they were destroyed in both **September and October.** Except for a tongue of moisture between Dallas and San Angelo, rainfall departures once again reached devastating values in October: 25 percent of normal rainfall was typical for most of Texas.

A line extending across Midland and Waco separated below-normal temperatures to the north from above-normal temperatures to the south in **November.** Except for extreme West and South Texas, precipitation amounts were well above normal across the state. But as learned a few months earlier, Mother Nature can play with our emotions. **December** returned Texas to well-below-normal rainfall conditions, ending a year Texans will not soon forget and hope not to experience again.

1996 Weather Extremes

Lowest Temp.: Perryton, Ochiltree Co., February 3 . . . . -13°F
Highest Temp.: Heath Canyon, Brewster Co., May 23 . . 115°F
  Boquillas Ranger Stn., Brewster Co., May 23 . . 115°F
24-hour Precip: Woodville, Tyler Co., September 27 . . 10.50"
Monthly Precip.: Houston, Harris Co., August . . . . 16.22"
Least Annual Precip.: Candelaria, Presidio Co. . . . . 6.96"
Greatest Annual Precip.: Beaumont, Jefferson Co. . . 62.63"

Extreme Weather Records in Texas

NOAA Environmental Data Service lists the following recorded extremes of weather in Texas:

Temperature

Lowest - Tulia, February 12, 1899 . . . . -23°F
  Seminole, February 8, 1933 . . . . -23°F
Highest - Seymour, August 12, 1936 . . . . 120°F
  Monahans, June 28, 1994 . . . . 120°F
Coldest Winter 1898-1899

Snowfall

Greatest seasonal - Romero 1923-1924 . . . . 65.0 in.
Greatest monthly - Hale Center, Feb. 1956 . . . . 36.0 in.
Greatest single storm - Hale Center, Feb. 2-5, 1956 . . 33.0 in.
Greatest in 24 Hours - Plainview, Feb. 3-4, 1956 . . . . . 24.0 in.
Maximum depth on ground - Hale Center, Feb. 5, 1956 . 33.0 in.

Rainfall

Wettest year - entire state . . . . 1941 . . . 42.62 in.
Driest year - entire state . . . . . 1917 . . . 14.30 in.
Greatest annual - Clarksville . . 1873 . . 109.38 in.
Least annual - Wink . . . . 1956 . . . . 1.76 in.
†Greatest in 24 hours - Thrall,
  Sept. 9-10 , 1921 . . . . 38.20. in

† The greatest 24-hour rainfall ever recorded in Texas at an official observing site occurred at Albany, Shackelford County, on Aug. 4, 1978 - 29.05 inches.

Wind Velocity

Highest sustained wind (fastest mile)
  *Matagorda - Sept. 11, 1961 . . . . .SE, 145 mph
  *Port Lavaca - Sept. 11, 1961 . . . . . . .NE, 145 mph
Highest peak gust (instantaneous velocity)
  *Aransas Pass - Aug. 3, 1970 . . . . . SW, 180 mph
  *Robstown - Aug. 3, 1970 (est.) . . WSW, 180 mph

*These velocities occurred during hurricanes. Theoretically, much higher velocities are possible within the vortex of a tor-*nado, but no measurement with an anemometer has ever been made. The U.S. Weather Bureau's experimental Doppler radar equipment, a device which permits direct measurement of the high speeds in a spinning tornado funnel, received its first big test in the Wichita Falls tornado of April 2, 1958. This was the first tornado tracked by the Doppler radar, and for the first time in history, rotating winds up to 280 mph were clocked.

Destructive Weather

Source: This list of exceptionally destructive weather in Texas since 1766 was compiled from ESSA-Weather Bureau information.

Sept., 4, 1766: Hurricane. Galveston Bay. A Spanish mission destroyed.

Sept. 12, 1818: Hurricane. Galveston Island. Salt water flowed four feet deep. Only six buildings remained habitable. Of the six vessels and two barges in the harbor, even the two not seriously damaged were reduced to dismasted hulks. **Pirate Jean Lafitte** moved to one hulk so his **Red House** might serve as a hospital.

Aug. 6, 1844: Hurricane. Mouth of Rio Grande. All houses destroyed at the mouth of the river and at **Brazos Santiago,** eight miles north; 70 lives lost.

Sept. 19, 1854: Hurricane. After striking near **Matagorda,** the hurricane moved inland northwestward over **Columbus.** The main impact fell in **Matagorda and Lavaca bays.** Almost all buildings in Matagorda were destroyed. Four lives were lost in the town; more lives were lost on the peninsula.

Oct. 3, 1867: Hurricane. This hurricane moved inland **south of Galveston,** but raked the entire Texas coast **from the Rio Grande to the Sabine. Bagdad and Clarksville,** towns at the mouth of the Rio Grande, were destroyed. Much of Galveston was flooded and property damage there was estimated at $1 million.

Sept. 16, 1875: Hurricane. Struck **Indianola,** Calhoun County. Three-fourths of town swept away; 176 lives lost. Flooding from the bay caused nearly all destruction.

Aug. 13, 1880: Hurricane. Center struck **Matamoros, Mexico; lower Texas coast** affected.

Oct. 12-13, 1880: Hurricane. Brownsville. City nearly destroyed, many lives lost.

Aug. 23-24, 1882: Torrential rains caused **flooding** of the **North and South Concho and Bosque rivers** (South Concho reported 45 feet above normal level), destroying **Benficklen,** then county seat of Tom Green County, leaving only the courthouse and the jail. More than 50 persons were reported drowned in **Tom Green and Erath counties,** with property damage at $200,000 and 10,000 to 15,000 head of livestock lost.

Aug. 19-21, 1886: Hurricane. Indianola. Every house destroyed or damaged. Indianola never rebuilt.

Oct. 12, 1886: Hurricane. Sabine, Jefferson County. Hurricane passed over Sabine. The inundation extended 20 miles inland and nearly every house in the vicinity was moved from its foundation; 150 persons were drowned.

April 28, 1893: Tornado. Cisco, Eastland County; 23

killed, 93 injured; damage $400,000.

May 15, 1896: Tornadoes, Sherman, Grayson County; **Justin,** Denton County; **Gribble Springs,** Cooke County; 76 killed; damage $225,000.

Sept. 12, 1897: Hurricane. Many houses in **Port Arthur** were demolished; 13 killed, damage $150,000.

May 1, 1898: Tornado. Mobeetie, Wheeler County. Four killed, several injured; damage $35,000.

June 27-July 1, 1899: Rainstorm. A storm, centered over the **Brazos River watershed,** precipitated an average of 17 inches over an area of 7,000 square miles. At **Hearne** the gage overflowed at 24 inches, and there was an estimated total rainfall of 30 inches. At **Turnersville,** Coryell County, 33 inches were recorded in three days. This rain caused the **worst Brazos River flood on record.** Between 30 and 35 lives were lost. Property damage was estimated at $9 million.

April 5-8, 1900: Rainstorm. This storm began in two centers, over **Val Verde County** on the Rio Grande, and over **Swisher County** on the High Plains, and converged in the vicinity of **Travis County,** causing disastrous floods in the **Colorado, Brazos and Guadalupe rivers.** McDonald Dam on the Colorado River at Austin crumbled suddenly. A wall of water swept through the city taking at least 23 lives. Damage was estimated at $1,250,000.

Sept. 8-9, 1900: Hurricane. Galveston. (See related article on pages 35-40.) The Great Galveston Storm was the **worst natural disaster in U.S. history** in terms of human life. Loss of life at Galveston has been estimated at 6,000 to 8,000, but the exact number has never been exactly determined. The island was completely inundated; not a single structure escaped damage. Most of the loss of life was due to drowning by storm tides that reached 15 feet or more. The anemometer blew away when the wind reached 100 miles per hour at 6:15 p.m. on the 8th. Wind reached an estimated maximum velocity of 120 miles per hour between 7:30 and 8:30 p.m. Property damage has been estimated at $30 to $40 million.

May 18, 1902: Tornado. Goliad. This tornado cut a 250-year-wide path straight through town, turning 150 buildings into rubble. Several churches were destroyed, one of which was holding services; all 40 worshippers were either killed or injured. This tornado killed 114, injured 230, and caused an estimated $200,000 in damages.

April 26, 1906: Tornado. Bellevue, Clay County, demolished; considerable damage done at **Stoneburg,** seven miles east; 17 killed, 20 injured; damage $300,000.

May 6, 1907: Tornado. North of Sulphur Springs, Hopkins County; five killed, 19 injured.

May 13, 1908: Tornado. Linden, Cass County. Four killed, seven injured; damage $75,000.

May 22-25, 1908: Rainstorm; unique because it originated on the Pacific Coast. It moved first into **North Texas** and southern Oklahoma and thence to **Central Texas,** precipitating as much as 10 inches. Heaviest floods were in the upper Trinity basin, but flooding was general as far south as the Nueces. Property damage exceeded $5 million and 11 lives were lost in the Dallas vicinity.

March 23, 1909: Tornado. Slidell, Wise County; 11 killed, 10 injured; damage $30,000.

May 30, 1909: Tornado. Zephyr, Brown County; 28 killed, many injured; damage $90,000.

July 21, 1909: Hurricane. Velasco, Brazoria County. One-half of town destroyed, 41 lives lost; damage $2,000,000.

Dec. 1-5, 1913: Rainstorm. This caused the **second major Brazos River flood,** and caused more deaths than the storm of 1899. It formed over **Central Texas** and spread both southwest and northeast with precipitation of 15 inches at **San Marcos** and 11 inches at **Kaufman.** Floods caused loss of 177 lives and $8,541,000 damage.

April 20-26, 1915: Rainstorm. Originated over Central Texas and spread into North and East Texas with precipitation up to 17 inches, causing floods in **Trinity, Brazos, Colorado, and Guadalupe rivers.** More than 40 lives lost and $2,330,000

Meteorological Data

Source: NOAA, Environmental Data Service, Local Climatological Data.

Additional data for these locations are listed in the table of Texas temperature, freeze, growing season, and precipitation records, by counties.

City	Temperature						Precipitation					Relative Humidity		Wind			Sun
	Record High	Month & Year	Record Low	Month & Year	No. Days Max. 90° and Above	No. Days Min. 32° and Below	Maximum in 24 Hours	Month & Year	Snowfall (Mean Annual)	Max. Snowfall in 24 Hours	Month & Year	6:00 a.m., CST	Noon, CST	Speed, MPH (Mean Annual)	Highest MPH	Month & Year	Percent Possible Sunshine
Abilene	110	7/1978	-9	1/1947	96.6	53.6	6.70	9/1961	4.9	7.5	1/1973	74	51	12.1	54	5/1996	70
Amarillo	108	6/1990	-14	2/1951	63.8	110.7	6.75	5/1951	14.9	13.5	2/1971	73	46	13.6	58	9/1979	73
Austin	109‡	7/1954	-2	1/1949	105.0	21.1	7.22	10/1960	1.1	7.0	1/1944	83	56	9.2	52	9/1987	60
Brownsville	106	3/1984	16	12/1989	117.3	2.2	12.19	9/1967	**	0.0	—	89	60	11.5	51	9/1996	60
Corpus Christi	104	7/1939	13	12/1989	101.9	6.6	8.92	8/1980	0.1	1.1	2/1973	90	62	12.0	55	8/1980	62
Dallas-Fort Worth	113	6/1980	-1	12/1989	96.2	40.9	5.91	10/1959	3.2	12.1	1/1964	82	56	10.9	73	8/1959	64
Del Rio	112	6/1988	10	12/1989	124.2	17.3	7.60	10/1984	0.9	8.6	1/1985	79	54	9.9	60	8/1970	70
El Paso	114	7/1994	-8	1/1962	104.0	65.0	2.63	7/1968	5.4	16.8	12/1987	35	28	8.9	64	1/1996	83
Galveston	101	7/1932	8	2/1999	12.2	3.6	14.35	7/1900	0.2	15.4	2/1995	83	72	11.0	*100	9/1900	62
†Houston	107	8/1980	7	12/1989	94.2	21.2	10.36	5/1989	0.4	2.0	1/1973	90	59	7.8	51	8/1983	56
Lubbock	114	6/1994	-16	1/1963	78.6	94.6	5.82	10/1983	10.5	16.3	1/1983	74	47	12.4	70	3/1952	72
Midland-Odessa	116	6/1994	-11	2/1985	96.2	64.7	5.99	7/1961	4.1	6.8	1/1974	74	43	11.0	67	2/1960	74
Prt. Arthur-Beaumont	107	8/1962	12	12/1989	81.2	16.3	17.16	9/1980	0.4	4.4	2/1960	91	64	9.8	55	6/1986	58
San Angelo	111‡	7/1960	-4	12/1989	106.8	53.9	6.25	9/1980	3.3	7.4	1/1978	78	49	10.4	75	4/1969	73
San Antonio	108	8/1986	0	1/1949	110.8	22.7	7.28	9/1973	0.8	13.2	1/1985	83	55	9.3	48	7/1979	60
Victoria	107	8/1962	9	12/1989	102.7	12.1	9.30	6/1977	0.2	2.1	1/1985	89	60	10.0	99	7/1963	62
Waco	112	8/1969	-5	1/1949	108.5	35.2	7.18	5/1953	1.5	7.0	1/1949	83	57	11.3	69	6/1961	63
Wichita Falls	117	6-80	-8	2/1985	105.9	68.1	6.22	9/1980	6.0	8.1	1/1985	82	51	11.7	60	6/1954	68
§Shreveport, LA	107	8/1962	3	1/1962	89.4	37.3	7.17	4/1953	1.3	5.6	1/1982	87	58	8.4	52	4/1975	63

*100 mph recorded at 6:15 p.m. Sept. 8 just before the anemometer blew away. Maximum velocity was estimated to be 120 mph from the northeast between 7:30 p.m. and 8:30 p.m.

†The official Houston station was moved from near downtown to Intercontinental Airport, located 12 miles north of the old station.

‡ Also recorded on earlier dates, months or years.

§This station is included because it is near the boundary line and its data can be considered representative of the eastern border of Texas.

**Trace, an amount too small to measure.

damage.

Aug. 16-19, 1915: Hurricane. Galveston. Peak wind gusts of 120 miles recorded at Galveston; tide ranged 9.5 to 14.3 feet above mean sea level in the city, and up to 16.1 feet near the causeway. Business section flooded with 5 to 6 feet of water. At least 275 lives lost, damage $56 million. A new seawall prevented a repetition of the 1900 disaster.

Aug. 18, 1916: Hurricane. Corpus Christi. Maximum wind speed 100 miles per hour. 20 Lives lost; damage $1,600,000.

Jan. 10-12, 1918: Blizzard. This was the most severe since that of February, 1899; it was accompanied by zero degree temperature in **North Texas** and temperatures from 7 to 12 below freezing along the **lower coast**.

April 9, 1919: Tornado. Leonard, Ector and Ravenna in Fannin County; 20 killed, 45 injured; damage $125,000.

April 9, 1919: Tornado. Henderson, Van Zandt, Wood, Camp, and Red River counties, 42 killed, 150 injured; damage $450,000.

May 7, 1919: Windstorms. Starr, Hidalgo, Willacy and Cameron counties. Violent thunderstorms with high winds, hail and rain occurred between **Rio Grande City** and the coast, killing 10 persons. Damage to property and crops was $500,000. Seven were killed at **Mission**.

Sept. 14, 1919: Hurricane. Near **Corpus Christi**. Center moved inland south of Corpus Christi; tides 16 feet above normal in that area and 8.8 feet above normal at **Galveston**. Extreme wind at Corpus Christi measured at 110 miles per hour; 284 lives lost; damage $20,272,000.

April 13, 1921: Tornado. Melissa, Collin County, and **Petty**, Lamar County. Melissa was practically destroyed; 12 killed, 80 injured; damage $500,000.

April 15, 1921: Tornado. Wood, Cass and Bowie counties; 10 killed, 50 injured; damage $85,000.

Sept. 8-10, 1921: Rainstorm. Probably the **greatest rainstorm in Texas history**, it entered Mexico as a hurricane from the Gulf. Torrential rains fell as the storm moved northeasterly across Texas. **Record floods** occurred in **Bexar, Travis, Williamson, Bell and Milam counties**, killing 215 persons, with property losses over $19 million. Five to nine feet of water stood in downtown **San Antonio**. A total of 23.98 inches was measured at the U.S. Weather Bureau station at **Taylor** during a period of 35 hours, with a 24-hour maximum of 23.11 on September 9-10. The **greatest rainfall recorded in United States history during 18 consecutive hours fell at Thrall**, Williamson County, 36.40 inches fell on Sept. 9.

April 8, 1922: Tornado. Rowena, Runnels County. Seven killed, 52 injured; damage $55,000.

April 8, 1922: Tornado. Oplin, Callahan County. Five killed, 30 injured; damage $15,000.

April 23-28, 1922: Rainstorm. An exceptional storm that entered Texas from the west and moved from the **Panhandle** to **North Central and East Texas**. Rains up to 12.6 inches over Parker, Tarrant, and Dallas counties caused severe floods in the Upper Trinity at **Fort Worth**; 11 lives were lost; damage was estimated at $1 million.

May 4, 1922: Tornado. Austin, Travis County; 12 killed, 50 injured; damage $500,000.

May 14, 1923: Tornado. Howard and Mitchell counties; 23 killed, 100 injured; damage $50,000.

April 12, 1927: Tornado. Edwards, Real and Uvalde counties; 74 killed, 205 injured; damage $1,230,000. Most of damage was in **Rocksprings** where 72 deaths occurred and town was practically destroyed.

May 9, 1927: Tornado. Garland; eleven killed; damage $100,000.

May 9, 1927: Tornado. Nevada, Collin County; **Wolfe City**, Hunt County; and **Tigertown**, Lamar County; 28 killed, over 200 injured; damage $900,000.

Jan. 4, 1929: Tornado. Near **Bay City**, Matagorda County. Five killed, 14 injured.

April 24, 1929: Tornado. Slocum, Anderson County; seven killed, 20 injured; damage $200,000.

May 24-31, 1929: Rainstorm. Beginning over **Caldwell County**, a storm spread over much of **Central and Coastal Texas** with maximum rainfall of 12.9 inches, causing **floods in**

Texas Annual Average Precipitation, 1888-1996

Year	Inches		Year	Inches
1888	38.61		1943	32.41
1889	34.52		1944	33.38
1890	31.52		1945	29.37
1891	27.49		1946	33.25
1892	26.91		1947	23.73
1893	18.66		1948	20.70
1894	25.37		1949	34.09
1895	30.12		1950	24.98
1896	24.94		1951	20.74
1897	24.94		1952	22.41
1898	25.97		1953	23.64
1899	26.34		1954	18.01
1900	38.54		1955	22.75
1901	20.31		1956	15.52
1902	30.83		1957	37.01
1903	30.16		1958	30.78
1904	27.65		1959	30.33
1905	37.89		1960	31.90
1906	28.90		1961	28.90
1907	30.87		1962	24.32
1908	30.10		1963	19.75
1909	21.50		1964	23.75
1910	19.59		1965	26.82
1911	26.47		1966	26.93
1912	23.89		1967	25.47
1913	32.85		1968	33.20
1914	34.66		1969	29.82
1915	29.33		1970	23.87
1916	22.51		1971	28.39
*1917	14.80		1972	27.06
1918	26.28		1973	35.44
1919	41.95		1974	32.27
1920	31.39		1975	27.30
1921	26.19		1976	30.71
1922	29.88		1977	22.75
1923	36.63		1978	25.87
1924	21.36		1979	31.39
1925	23.66		1980	24.45
1926	33.06		1981	32.69
1927	25.41		1982	26.97
1928	26.54		1983	25.85
1929	28.34		1984	26.19
1930	27.12		1985	30.05
1931	27.43		1986	34.14
1932	32.69		1987	30.56
1933	23.11		1988	21.13
1934	23.04		1989	25.59
1935	34.58		1990	31.77
1936	28.57		1991	37.94
1937	25.16		1992	34.16
1938	24.98		1993	27.60
1939	23.24		1994	29.65
1940	32.09		1995	27.62
**1941	40.94		1996	24.71
1942	30.35			

109-year average: 28.10"
*Driest year
** Wettest year
Source: Office of the State Climatologist

Colorado, Guadalupe, Brazos, Trinity, Neches and Sabine rivers. Much damage at from overflow of bayous. Damage estimated at $6 million.

May 6, 1930: Tornado. Bynum, Irene and Mertens in Hill County; **Ennis**, Ellis County; and **Frost**, Navarro County; 41 killed; damage $2,100,000.

May 6, 1930: Tornado. Kenedy and Runge in Karnes County; **Nordheim**, DeWitt County; 36 killed, 34 injured; damage $127,000.

June 30-July 2, 1932: Rainstorm. Torrential rains fell over the upper watersheds of the **Nueces and Guadalupe rivers**, causing destructive floods. Seven persons drowned; property losses exceeded $500,000.

Aug. 13, 1932: Hurricane. Near **Freeport**, Brazoria County. Wind speed at **East Columbia** estimated at 100 miles per hour; 40 lives lost, 200 injured; damage $7,500,000.

March 30, 1933: Tornado. Angelina, Nacogdoches and San Augustine counties; 10 killed, 56 injured; damage $200,000.

April 26, 1933: Tornado. Bowie County near Texarkana. Five killed, 38 injured; damage $14,000.

July 22-25, 1933: Tropical Storm. One of the greatest U.S. storms in area and general rainfall. The storm reached the vicinity of **Freeport** late on July 22 and moved very slowly overland across eastern Texas, July 22-25. The storm center moved into northern Louisiana on the 25th. Rainfall averaged 12.50 inches over an area of about 25,000 square miles. Twenty inches or more fell in a small area of eastern Texas and western Louisiana surrounding Logansport, La. The 4-day total at Logansport was 22.30 inches. Property damage was estimated at $1,114,790.

July 30, 1933: Tornado. Oak Cliff section of Dallas, Dallas County. Five killed, 30 injured; damage $500,000.

Sept. 4-5, 1933: Hurricane. Near **Brownsville**. Center passed inland a short distance north of Brownsville, where an extreme wind of 106 miles per hour was measured before the anemometer blew away. Peak wind gusts were estimated at 120 to 125 miles per hour. 40 known dead, 500 injured; damage $16,903,100. About 90 percent of the citrus crop in the **Lower Rio Grande Valley** was destroyed.

July 25, 1934: Hurricane. Near **Seadrift**, Calhoun County, 19 lives lost, many minor injuries; damage $4.5 million. About 85 percent of damage was in crops.

Sept. 15-18, 1936: Rainstorm. Excessive rains over the **North Concho and Middle Concho rivers** caused a sharp rise in the Concho River, which overflowed **San Angelo**. Much of the business district and 500 homes were flooded. Four persons drowned and property losses estimated at $5 million. Four-day storm rainfall at San Angelo measured 25.19 inches, of which 11.75 inches fell on the 15th.

June 10, 1938: Tornado. Clyde, Callahan County; 14 killed, 9 injured; damage $85,000.

Sept. 23, 1941: Hurricane. Near **Matagorda.** Center moved inland near Matagorda, and passed over **Houston** about midnight. Extremely high tides along coast in the **Matagorda to Galveston** area. Heaviest property and crop losses were in counties from Matagorda County to the Sabine River. Four lives lost. Damage was $6,503,300.

April 28, 1942: Tornado. Crowell, Foard County; 11 killed, 250 injured; damage $1,500,000.

Aug. 30, 1942: Hurricane. Matagorda Bay. Highest wind estimated 115 miles per hour at **Seadrift.** Tide at **Matagorda,**14.7 feet. Storm moved west-north-westward and finally diminished over the **Edwards Plateau;** eight lives lost, property damage estimated at $11.5 million, and crop damage estimated at $15 million.

May 10, 1943: Tornado. Laird Hill, Rusk County, and **Kilgore,** Gregg County. Four killed, 25 injured; damage $1 million.

July 27, 1943: Hurricane. Near **Galveston.** Center moved inland across **Bolivar Peninsula and Trinity Bay.** A

Texas is Tornado Capital

An **average of 126 tornadoes** touch Texas soil each year. The annual total varies considerably, and certain areas are struck more often than others. Tornadoes occur with **greatest frequency** in the Red River Valley.

Tornadoes may occur in any month and at any hour of the day, but they occur with greatest frequency during the late spring and early summer months, and between the hours of 4:00 p.m. and 8:00 p.m. In the period 1951-1995, nearly 64 percent of all Texas tornadoes occurred within the three-month period of April, May and June. Nearly one-third of the total occurred in May.

Partly because of the state's size, **more tornadoes have been recorded in Texas than in any other state**. Between 1951 and 1995, 5,669 funnel clouds reached the ground, thus becoming tornadoes. In the density of tornadoes, Texas ranks eleventh among the 50 states, with an average of 4.7 tornadoes per 10,000 square miles per year during this period.

The **greatest outbreak of tornadoes on record in Texas** was associated with Hurricane Beulah in September 1967. Within a five-day period, Sept. 19-23, 115 known tornadoes, all in Texas, were spawned by this great hurricane. Sixty-seven occurred on Sept. 20, a **Texas record for a single day**.

In September 1967, Hurricane Beulah produced 124 tornadoes, a **Texas record for a single month**. The **greatest number in Texas in a single year** was 232, also in 1967. The second-highest number in a single year was in 1995, when 223 tornadoes occurred in Texas. In 1982, 123 tornadoes occurred in May, making it the **worst outbreak of spring tornadoes** in Texas.

The table at right, compiled by Environmental Data Service, National Oceanic and Atmospheric Administration, lists tornado occurrences in Texas, by months, for the period 1951-1995.

Number of Tornadoes In Texas,1951-1995

Source: Office of State Climatologist

Year	Jan.	Feb.	March	April	May	June	July	Aug.	Sept.	Oct.	Nov.	Dec.	Annual
1951	0	0	1	1	5	7	1	0	0	0	0	0	15
1952	0	1	3	4	2	1	0	1	0	0	0	1	13
1953	0	2	2	3	6	2	3	5	0	2	1	6	32
1954	0	3	1	23	21	14	5	1	4	5	0	0	77
1955	0	0	7	15	42	32	1	5	2	0	0	0	104
1956	0	3	5	3	17	5	6	4	2	9	2	0	56
1957	0	1	21	69	33	5	0	3	2	6	5	0	145
1958	2	0	7	12	15	13	10	7	0	0	8	0	74
1959	0	0	8	4	32	14	10	3	4	5	6	0	86
1960	4	1	0	8	29	14	3	4	2	11	1	0	77
1961	0	1	21	15	24	30	9	2	12	0	10	0	124
1962	0	4	12	9	25	56	12	15	7	2	0	1	143
1963	0	0	3	9	19	24	8	4	6	4	5	0	82
1964	0	1	6	22	15	11	9	7	3	1	3	0	78
1965	2	5	3	7	43	24	2	9	4	6	0	3	108
1966	0	4	1	21	22	15	3	8	3	0	0	0	77
1967	0	2	11	17	34	22	10	5	124	2	0	5	232
1968	2	1	3	13	47	21	4	8	5	8	11	16	139
1969	0	1	1	16	65	16	6	7	6	8	1	0	127
1970	1	3	5	23	23	9	5	20	9	20	0	3	121
1971	0	20	10	24	27	33	7	20	7	16	4	23	191
1972	1	0	19	13	43	12	19	13	8	9	7	0	144
1973	14	1	29	25	21	24	4	8	5	3	9	4	147
1974	2	1	8	19	18	26	3	9	6	22	2	0	116
1975	5	2	9	12	50	18	10	3	3	3	1	1	117
1976	1	1	8	53	63	11	16	6	13	4	0	0	176
1977	0	0	3	34	50	4	5	5	12	0	6	4	123
1978	0	0	0	34	65	10	13	6	6	1	2	0	137
1979	1	2	24	33	39	14	12	10	4	15	3	0	157
1980	0	2	7	26	44	21	2	34	10	5	0	2	153
1981	0	7	7	9	71	26	5	20	5	23	3	0	176
1982	0	0	6	27	123	36	4	0	3	0	3	1	203
1983	5	7	24	1	62	35	4	22	5	0	7	14	186
1984	0	13	9	18	19	19	0	4	1	5	2	5	95
1985	0	0	5	41	28	5	3	1	3	1	1	2	90
1986	0	12	4	21	50	24	3	5	4	7	1	0	131
1987	1	1	7	0	54	19	11	3	8	0	16	4	124
1988	0	0	0	11	7	7	6	2	42	4	10	0	89
1989	3	0	5	3	70	63	0	6	3	6	1	0	160
1990	3	3	4	56	62	20	5	2	3	0	0	0	158
1991	20	5	2	39	72	36	1	2	3	8	4	0	192
1992	0	5	13	22	43	66	4	4	4	7	21	0	189
1993	1	4	5	17	39	4	4	0	12	23	8	0	117
1994	0	1	1	48	88	2	1	4	3	9	8	0	165
1995	6	0	13	36	66	75	11	3	2	1	0	10	223
Total	74	120	343	916	1,793	945	260	310	368	263	172	105	5,669

wind gust of 104 miles per hour was recorded at **Texas City**; 19 lives lost; damage estimated at $16,550,000.

Aug. 26-27, 1945: Hurricane. Aransas-San Antonio Bay area. At **Port O'Connor**, the wind reached 105 miles per hour when the cups were torn from the anemometer. Peak gusts of 135 miles per hour were estimated at **Seadrift, Port O'Connor and Port Lavaca**; three killed, 25 injured; damage $20,133,000.

Texas Droughts, 1892-1996

The following tables show the **duration and extent of Texas droughts by climatic division, 1892-1996.** For this purpose, droughts are arbitrarily defined as when the division has less than 75 percent of the 1931-1960 average precipitation. The 1931-1960 average precipitation in inches is shown at the bottom of the table for each division. The short table at bottom right shows the frequency of droughts in each area and the total years of droughts in the area.

Year	High Plains	Low Rolling Plains	North Central	East Texas	Trans-Pecos	Edwards Plateau	South Central	Upper Coast	Southern	Lower Valley
1892				68				73		
1893			67	70		49	56	64	53	59
1894				68						
1897							73	72		
1898									69	51
1901		71	70			60	62	70	44	
1902									65	73
1907										65
1909			72	68	67	74	70			
1910	59	59	64	69	43	65	69	74	59	
1911										70
1916		73		74	70		73	69		
1917	58	50	63	59	44	46	42	50	32	48
1920										71
1921				72						73
1922				68						
1924			73	73		71		72		
1925			72					72		
1927								74		74
1933	72					62	68			
1934	66					46	69			
1937								72		
1939							69			72
1943			72							
1948			73	74		62	71	67		
1950							68		74	64
1951						61	53			
1952	68	66		73					56	70
1953	69					49	73			
1954	70	71	68	73		50	50	57	71	
1956	51	57	61	68	44	43	55	62	53	53
1962						68			67	65
1963			63	68		65	61	73		
1964	74			69						63
1970	65	63				72				
1988						67	62	67	68	
1989						72			66	64
1990										73
1994						68				
1996							71		60	70

Normal Annual Rainfall by Region

Listed below is the normal annual rainfall in inches for four 30-year periods in each geographical division. The normals for each division are given in the same order as the divisions which appear in the table above.

Period	Normal Rainfall in Inches									
1931-1960	18.51	22.99	32.93	45.96	12.03	25.91	33.24	46.19	22.33	24.27
1941-1970	18.59	23.18	32.94	45.37	11.57	23.94	33.03	46.43	21.95	23.44
1951-1980	17.73	22.80	32.14	44.65	11.65	23.52	34.03	45.93	22.91	24.73
1961-1990	18.88	23.77	33.99	45.67	13.01	24.00	34.49	47.63	23.47	25.31

Jan. 4, 1946: Tornado. Near **Lufkin**, Angelina County and **Nacogdoches**, Nacogdoches County; 13 killed, 250 injured; damage $2,050,000.

Jan. 4, 1946: Tornado. Near **Palestine**, Anderson County; 15 killed, 60 injured; damage $500,000.

May 18, 1946: Tornado. Clay, Montague and Denton counties. Four killed, damage $112,000.

April 9, 1947: Tornado. White Deer, Carson County; **Glazier**, Hemphill County; and **Higgins**, Lipscomb County; 68 killed, 201 injured; damage $1,550,000. Glazier completely destroyed. **One of the largest tornadoes on record.** Width of path, 1 miles at Higgins; length of path, 221 miles across portions of Texas, Oklahoma and Kansas. This tornado also struck Woodward, Okla.

May 3, 1948: Tornado. McKinney, Collin County; three killed, 43 injured; $2 million damage.

May 15, 1949: Tornado. Amarillo and vicinity; six killed, 83 injured. Total damage from tornado, wind and hail, $5,310,000. Total destruction over one-block by three-block area in southern part of city; airport and 45 airplanes damaged; 28 railroad boxcars blown off track.

Sept. 8-10, 1952: Rainstorm. Heavy rains over the **Colorado and Guadalupe River watersheds** in southwestern Texas caused major flooding. From 23 to 26 inches fell between **Kerrville, Blanco and Boerne.** Highest stages ever known occurred in the **Pedernales River**; five lives lost, three injured; 17 homes destroyed, 454 damaged. Property loss several million dollars.

March 13, 1953: Tornado. Jud and O'Brien, Haskell County; and **Knox City**, Knox County; 17 killed, 25 injured; damage $600,000.

May 11, 1953: Tornado. Near **San Angelo**, Tom Green County; eleven killed, 159 injured; damage $3,239,000.

May 11, 1953: Tornado. Waco, McLennan County; 114 killed, 597 injured; damage $41,150,000. **One of two most disastrous tornadoes**; 150 homes destroyed, 900 homes damaged; 185 other buildings destroyed; 500 other buildings damaged.

April 2, 1957: Tornado. Dallas, Dallas County; 10 killed, 200 injured; damage $4 million. Moving through Oak Cliff and West Dallas, it damaged 574 buildings, largely homes.

April-May, 1957: Torrential Rains. Excessive flooding occurred throughout the area **east of the Pecos River to the Sabine River** during the last 10 days of April; 17 lives were lost, and several hundred homes were destroyed. During May, more than 4,000 persons were evacuated from unprotected lowlands on the **West Fork of the Trinity above Fort Worth** and along creeks in Fort Worth. Twenty-nine houses at **Christoval** were damaged or destroyed and 83 houses and furnishings at **San Angelo** were damaged. Five persons were drowned in floods in **South Central Texas.**

May 15, 1957: Tornado. Silverton, Briscoe County; 21 killed, 80 injured; damage $500,000.

June 27, 1957: Hurricane Audrey. Center crossed the Gulf coast near the Texas-Louisiana line. **Orange** was in the

Drought Frequency

This table shows the number of years of drought and the number of separate droughts. For example, the **High Plains** has had 10 drought years, consisting of five 1-year droughts, one 2-year drought and one 3-year drought, a total of 7 droughts.

Years	High Plains	Low Rolling Plains	North Central	East Texas	Trans-Pecos	Edwards Plateau	South Central	Upper Coast	Southern	Lower Valley
1	5	6	8	6	6	7	12	9	10	14
2	1	1	2	2	4	5	2	2	3	2
3	1	...	...	...	1	...	...	...	...	...
Total Droughts	7	7	10	8	11	12	14	11	13	14
Drght Yrs.	10	8	12	10	17	17	16	13	16	18

western portion of the eye between 9 and 10 a.m. In Texas, nine lives were lost, 450 persons injured; property damage was $8 million. Damage was extensive in **Jefferson and Orange counties,** with less in **Chambers and Galveston counties.** Maximum wind reported in Texas, 85 m.p.h. at **Sabine Pass,** with gusts to 100 m.p.h.

Oct. 28, 1960: Rainstorm. Rains of 7-10 inches fell in **South Central Texas;** 11 died from drowning in flash floods. In **Austin** about 300 families were driven from their homes. Damage in Austin was estimated at $2.5 million.

Sept. 8-14, 1961: Hurricane Carla. Port O'Connor; maximum wind gust at **Port Lavaca** estimated at 175 miles per hour. Highest tide was 18.5 feet at Port Lavaca. Most damage was to **coastal counties between Corpus Christi and Port Arthur** and inland **Jackson, Harris and Wharton counties.** In Texas, 34 persons died; seven in a **tornado** that swept across **Galveston Island;** 465 persons were injured. Property and crop damage conservatively estimated at $300 million. The evacuation of an estimated 250,000 persons kept loss of life low. **Hurricane Carla was the largest hurricane of record.**

Sept. 7, 1962: Rainstorm. Fort Worth. Rains fell over the Big Fossil and Denton Creek watersheds ranging up to 11 inches of fall in three hours. Extensive damage from flash flooding occurred in **Richland Hills and Haltom City.**

Sept. 16-20, 1963: Hurricane Cindy. Rains of 15 to 23.5 inches fell in portions of **Jefferson, Newton and Orange counties** when Hurricane Cindy became stationary west of **Port Arthur.** Flooding from the excessive rainfall resulted in total property damage of $11,600,000 and agricultural losses of $500,000.

April 3, 1964: Tornado. Wichita Falls. Seven killed, 111 injured; damage $15 million; 225 homes destroyed, 50 with major damage, and 200 with minor damage. Sixteen other buildings received major damage.

Sept. 21-23, 1964: Rainstorm. Collin, Dallas and Tarrant counties. Rains of more than 12 inches fell during the first eight hours of the 21st. Flash flooding of tributaries of the Trinity River and smaller creeks and streams resulted in two drownings and an estimated $3 million property damage. Flooding of homes occurred in all sections of **McKinney.** In **Fort Worth,** there was considerable damage to residences along Big Fossil and White Rock creeks. Expensive homes in **North Dallas** were heavily damaged.

Jan. 25, 1965: Dust Storm. West Texas. The worst dust storm since February 1956 developed on the **southern High Plains.** Winds, gusting up to 75 miles per hour at **Lubbock,** sent dust billowing to 31,000 feet in the area **from the Texas-New Mexico border eastward to a line from Tulia to Abilene.** Ground visibility was reduced to about 100 yards in many sections. The worst hit was the **Muleshoe, Seminole, Plains, Morton** area on the South Plains. The rain gage at Reese Air Force Base, Lubbock, contained 3 inches of fine sand.

June 2, 1965: Tornado. Hale Center, Hale County. Four killed, 76 injured; damage $8 million.

June 11, 1965: Rainstorm. Sanderson, Terrell County. Torrential rains of up to eight inches in two hours near Sanderson caused a major flash flood that swept through the town. As a result, 26 persons drowned and property losses were estimated at $2,715,000.

April 22-29, 1966: Flooding. Northeast Texas. Twenty to 26 inches of rain fell in portions of **Wood, Smith, Morris, Upshur, Gregg, Marion and Harrison** counties. Nineteen persons drowned in the rampaging rivers and creeks that swept away bridges, roads and dams, and caused an estimated $12 million damage.

April 28, 1966: Flash flooding. Dallas County. Flash flooding from torrential rains in Dallas County resulted in 14 persons drowned and property losses estimated at $15 million.

Sept. 18-23, 1967: Hurricane Beulah. Near **Brownsville.** The **third largest hurricane of record,** Hurricane Beulah moved inland near the mouth of the Rio Grande on the 20th. Wind gusts of 136 miles per hour were reported during Beulah's passage. Rains 10 to 20 inches over much of the area **south of San Antonio** resulted in record-breaking floods. An unofficial gaging station at **Falfurrias** registered the highest accumulated rainfall, 36 inches. The resultant stream overflow and surface

runoff inundated 1.4 million acres. Beulah spawned 115 tornadoes, all in Texas, the **greatest number of tornadoes on record for any hurricane.** Hurricane Beulah caused 13 deaths and 37 injuries, of which five deaths and 34 injuries were attributed to tornadoes. Property losses were estimated at $100 million and crop losses at $50 million.

April 18, 1970: Tornado. Near **Clarendon,** Donley County. Seventeen killed, 42 injured; damage $2,100,000. Fourteen persons were killed at a resort community at Green Belt Reservoir, 7 miles north of Clarendon.

May 11, 1970: Tornado. Lubbock, Lubbock County. Twenty-six killed, 500 injured; damage $135 million. Fifteen square miles, almost one-quarter of the city of Lubbock, suffered damage.

Aug. 3-5, 1970: Hurricane Celia. Corpus Christi. Hurricane Celia was a unique but severe storm. Measured in dollars, it was **the costliest in the state's history to that time.** Sustained wind speeds reached 130 miles per hour, but it was great bursts of kinetic energy of short duration that appeared to cause the severe damage. Wind gusts of 161 miles per hour were measured at the **Corpus Christi** National Weather Service Office. At **Aransas Pass,** peak wind gusts were estimated as high as 180 miles per hour, after the wind equipment had been blown away. Celia caused 11 deaths in Texas, at least 466 injuries, and total property and crop damage in Texas estimated at $453,773,000. Hurricane Celia crossed the Texas coastline midway between Corpus Christi and Aransas Pass about 3:30 p.m. CST on Aug. 3. Hardest hit was the metropolitan area of **Corpus Christi,** including **Robstown, Aransas Pass, Port Aransas** and small towns on the north side of Corpus Christi Bay.

Feb. 20-22, 1971: Blizzard. Panhandle. Paralyzing blizzard, worst since March 22-25, 1957, storm transformed Panhandle into one vast snowfield as six to 26 inches of snow were whipped by 40 to 60 miles per hour winds into drifts up to 12 feet high. At **Follett,** three-day snowfall was 26 inches. Three persons killed; property and livestock losses were $3.1 million.

Sept. 9-13, 1971: Hurricane Fern. Coastal Bend. Ten to 26 inches of rain resulted in some of worst flooding since Hurricane Beulah in 1967. Two persons killed; losses were $30,231,000.

May 11-12, 1972: Rainstorm. South Central Texas. Seventeen drowned at **New Braunfels,** one at **McQueeney.** New Braunfels and **Seguin** hardest hit. Property damage $17.5 million.

June 12-13, 1973: Rainstorm. Southeastern Texas. Ten drowned. Over $50 million in property and crop damage. From 10-15 inches of rain recorded.

Nov. 23-24, 1974: Flash Flooding. Central Texas. Over $1 million in property damage. Thirteen people killed, ten in **Travis County.**

Jan. 31-Feb. 1, 1975: Flooding. Nacogdoches County. Widespread heavy rain caused flash flooding here, resulting in three deaths; damage over $5.5 million.

May 23, 1975: Rainstorm. Austin area. Heavy rains, high winds and hail resulted in over $5 million property damage; 40 people injured. Four deaths were caused by drowning.

June 15, 1976: Rainstorm. Harris County. Rains in excess of 13 inches caused damage estimated at near $25 million. Eight deaths were storm-related, including three drownings.

Aug. 1-4, 1978: Heavy Rains, Flooding. Edwards Plateau, Low Rolling Plains. Remnants of **Tropical Storm Amelia** caused some of the worst flooding of this century. As much as 30 inches of rain fell near **Albany** in Shackelford County, where six drownings were reported. **Bandera, Kerr, Kendall and Gillespie counties** were hit hard, as 27 people drowned and the damage total was at least $50 million.

Dec. 30-31, 1978: Ice Storm. North Central Texas. Possibly the **worst ice storm in 30 years** hit Dallas County particularly hard. Damage estimates reached $14 million, and six deaths were storm-related.

April 10, 1979: The worst single tornado in Texas' history hit **Wichita Falls.** Earlier on the same day, **several tornadoes** hit farther west. The destruction in Wichita Falls resulted in 42 dead, 1,740 injured, over 3,000 homes destroyed and damage of approximately $400 million. An estimated 20,000 persons were left homeless by this storm. In all, the tornadoes on April 10 killed 53 people, injured 1,812 and caused over $500 million damages.

May 3, 1979: Thunderstorms. Dallas County was hit by a wave of the most destructive thunderstorms in many years; 37 injuries and $5 million in damages resulted.

July 24-25, 1979: Tropical storm Claudette caused over $750 million in property and crop damages, but fortunately only few injuries. Near **Alvin**, 43 inches of rain fell, a new state record for 24 hours.

Aug. 24, 1979: One of the worst **hailstorms** in **West Texas** in the past 100 years; $200 million in crops, mostly cotton, destroyed.

Sept. 18-20, 1979: Coastal flooding from heavy rain, 18 inches in 24 hours at **Aransas Pass**, and 13 inches at **Rockport**.

Aug. 9-11, 1980: Hurricane Allen hit **South Texas** and left three dead, causing $650 million-$750 million in property and crop damages. Over 250,000 coastal residents had to be evacuated. The worst damage occurred along **Padre Island** and in **Corpus Christi**. Over 20 inches of rain fell in **extreme South Texas**, and 29 tornadoes occurred; one of the worst hurricane-related outbreaks.

Summer 1980: One of the hottest summers in Texas history.

Sept. 5-8, 1980: Hurricane Danielle brought **rain and flooding** to both **Southeast and Central Texas.** Seventeen inches of rain fell at **Port Arthur**, and 25 inches near **Junction**.

May 8, 1981: The **most destructive thunderstorm ever in the United States** occurred in **Tarrant, Dallas and surrounding counties. Hail** damage was estimated at $200 million.

May 24-25, 1981: Severe flooding in **Austin** claimed 13 lives, injured about 100 and caused $40 million in damages. Up to 5.5 inches of rain fell in one hour just west of the city.

Oct. 11-14, 1981: Record rains in North Central Texas caused by the remains of **Pacific Hurricane Norma.** Over 20 inches fell in some locations.

April 2, 1982: A tornado outbreak in Northeast Texas. The most severe tornado struck **Paris**; 10 people were killed, 170 injured and 1,000 left homeless. Over $50 million in damages resulted. A total of 7 tornadoes that day left 11 dead and 174 injured.

May 25, 1982: Golf ball-sized **hail** in **Monahans** did $8 million in damages.

May, 1982: Texas recorded **123 tornadoes**, the most ever in May, and one less than the most recorded in any single month in the state. One death and 23 injuries occurred.

Sept. 11, 1982: Tropical Storm Chris. The year's only tropical storm in Texas hit the coast near **Port Arthur** with 55 mph winds. Rainfall was minimal.

Dec. 24, 1982: Rains of up to 15 inches occurred in **Southeast Texas.**

Dec. 1982: Heavy snow. El Paso recorded 18.2 inches of snow, the most in any month there.

Aug. 15-21, 1983: Hurricane Alicia was the first hurricane to make landfall in the continental U.S. in three years (Aug. 18), and **one of the costliest in Texas history** ($3 billion). Alicia caused widespread damage to a large section of **Southeast Texas**, including coastal areas near **Galveston** and the entire **Houston** area. Alicia spawned 22 tornadoes, and highest winds were estimated near 130 mph. In all, 18 people in South Texas were killed and 1,800 injured as a result of the tropical storm.

Jan. 12-13, 1985: A record-breaking snowstorm struck **West and South Central Texas** with up to 15 inches of snow that fell at many locations **between San Antonio and the Rio Grande.** San Antonio recorded 13.2 inches of snow for Jan. 12 (the greatest in a day) and 13.5 inches for the two-day total. **Eagle Pass** reported 14.5 inches of snow.

June 26, 1986: Hurricane Bonnie made landfall between **High Island and Sabine Pass** around 3:45 a.m. The highest

wind measured in the area was a gust to 97 m.p.h., which was recorded at the **Sea Rim State Park.** As much as 13 inches of rain fell in **Ace** in southern Polk County. There were several reports of funnel clouds, but no confirmed tornadoes. While the storm caused no major structural damage, there was widespread minor damage. Numerous injuries were reported.

May 22, 1987: A strong, **multiple-vortex tornado** struck the town of **Saragosa** (Reeves Co.), essentially wiping it off the map. Of the town's 183 inhabitants, 30 were killed and 121 were injured. Eight-five percent of the town's structures were completely destroyed, while total damage topped $1.3 million.

Sept. 16-18, 1988: Hurricane Gilbert stuck 125 miles south of **Brownsville**, Cameron County, bringing tides of three to six feet above average, rainfalls of six inches to 10 inches and at least 29 tornadoes. Total damage associated with Gilbert in Texas was estimated at $3 million-$5 million. The only death attributed to the storm was a woman who was killed by a tornado spawned by remnants of Gilbert in the **San Antonio** area.

Dec. 18-31, 1991: Flooding, entire state. The month of December was one of the wettest in Texas since records began in 1888. Rainfall amounts, from the Hill Country into North Central Texas totaled 12 to 16 inches over the four-day period of Dec. 18-21. Eleven people died as a result of the flooding, and more than $50 million dollars in damages were incurred.

June 20-22, 1993: Tropical Storm Arlene made landfall 5 miles south of **Corpus Christi**; all of eastern Texas was inundated by the remains. **Henderson** (Rusk Co.) received 14,83 inches of rain, and widespread areas reported greater than 7 inches. One person was killed; damage, mostly as a result of tidal flooding, was estimated at $22 million.

October 15-19, 1994: Extreme amounts of rainfall, up to 28.90 inches over a 4-day period, fell throughout southeastern part of the state. Seventeen lives were lost, most of them victims of flash flooding. Many rivers reached record flood levels during this period. **Houston** was cut off from many other parts of the state, as numerous roads, including Interstate 10, were under water. Damage was estimated to be near $700 million; 26 counties were declared disaster areas.

May 28, 1995: A supercell thunderstorm produced extreme winds and giant hail in San Angelo, injuring at least 80 people and causing about $120 million in damage. Sixty-nine homes were destroyed, and more than 9,000 were slightly damaged. In some areas, hail was six inches deep, with drifts to two feet.

February 21, 1996: Anomalously high temperatures were reported over the entire state, breaking records in nearly every region of the state. Temperatures near 100°F shattered previous records by as many as 10°F as Texans experienced heat more characteristic of mid-summer than winter.

May 10, 1996: Forty-eight people were injured and $30 million worth of property damage resulted as hail up to five inches in diameter fell in Howard County. ☆

Is It Normal or Average?

Confusion often occurs when climate summaries refer to the "normal" or "average" of a climate variable. The term "normal" indicates calculations based upon data from the most recent 30-year period ending with a year containing a zero for the last digit. Although 1901-1930 was selected as the first International Standard Period for Normals, the 1961-1990 period is the current 30-year "normal."

The "average" refers to calculations based upon the complete period of record. Usually this is from the first complete year on record to the most recent entire year of record. Therefore, the "normal" and "average" values usually differ to some degree.

How Hot Does It Feel?

In the 40-year period from 1936 to 1975, nearly 20,000 people were killed in the United States by the effects of excessive heat. The overall effect of excessive heat on the body is known as heat stress. Major factors contributing to heat stress are air temperature; humidity; air movement; radiant heat from solar radiation, bright lights, stove or other source; atmospheric pressure; physiological factors which vary among people; physical activity; and clothing.

Of the above factors, temperature and humidity can be controlled by air conditioning. Air movement may be controlled by fans; even a slight breeze is usually effective in reducing heat stress in hot, muggy weather.

However, at very high temperatures (above normal body temperature of about 98.6 F.), winds above 10 miles per hour can increase heat stress in a shaded area by adding more heat to the body, whereas when the body is exposed to direct sunlight the effect of wind is nearly always to reduce heat stress. Radiant heating can be mitigated by shielding or by moving away from the source (for example, seeking shade). Atmospheric pressure is not usually a significant factor. However, at very high elevations, decreased pressure (and therefore decreased air supply) can contribute to heat exhaustion.

General Heat Stress Index

Danger Category	Apparent Temperature (°F)	Heat Syndrome
1. Caution	80°-90°	Fatigue possible with prolonged exposure and physical activity.
2. Extreme Caution	90°-105°	Sunstroke, heat cramps and heat; exhaustion possible with prolonged exposure and physical activity.
3. Danger	105°-130°	Sunstroke, heat cramps or heat exhaustion likely. Heatstroke possible with prolonged exposure and physical activity.
4. Extreme Danger	Greater than 130°	Heatstroke or sunstroke imminent.

Note: Degree of heat stress may vary with age, health and body characteristics.

Heat Discomfort Chart

Actual Thermometer Reading (°F)	Relative Humidity (%)										
	0	10	20	30	40	50	60	70	80	90	100
	Apparent Temperature (°F)										
70	64.8	65.6	66.4	67.3	68.1	68.8	69.6	70.4	71.1	71.8	72.5
75	70.1	71.2	72.1	73.0	73.7	74.6	75.3	76.1	77.1	78.2	79.2
80	75.6	76.6	77.5	78.4	79.4	80.5	81.7	83.0	84.7	86.4	88.3
85	79.9	81.0	82.2	83.6	85.0	86.7	88.7	91.0	93.7	96.8	100.6
90	84.0	85.5	87.1	89.0	91.2	94.1	97.0	101.0	105.4	110.8	
95	88.0	90.0	92.4	95.3	98.4	102.6	107.4	113.9			
100	91.8	94.6	97.8	101.7	106.6	112.7	120.4				

	Relative Humidity (%)										
	0	5	10	15	20	25	30	35	40	45	50
105	95.8	97.5	99.4	101.5	103.8	106.4	109.3	112.4	116.5	121.1	126.0
110	99.7	101.9	104.2	107.0	110.3	113.8	118.0	121.8	128.6		
115	103.6	106.4	109.6	113.3	117.6	122.6	128.4				
120	107.4	111.1	115.2	120.1	125.7	132.2					

How Cold Does It Feel?

Many factors enter into the feeling of coolness or extreme cold, the temperature and wind speed being most important. The following simplified table is based upon more complex "Wind-Chill" indexes available from the National Oceanic and Atmospheric Administration (National Weather Service).

Thermometer readings are listed in the figures across the top of the chart; the wind speeds are shown down the left side. To determine how chilly it really feels, get the proper column for each. Note the figure where they cross.

Thus, a 20-degree temperature with a 20-mile-an-hour wind is equal in chill to 1.8 degrees above zero. A temperature of 10 degrees with a 15 mph wind is equal to 5.3 degrees below.

A chill effect of anything below 25 below zero creates the danger of freezing for persons not properly clothed.

The table below was devised by Dr. Robert G. Steadman, Texas Tech University, and was furnished to the Texas Almanac by the National Oceanic and Atmospheric Administration.

Windchill Chart

Estimated Wind Speed (MPH)	Actual Thermometer Reading (°F)						
	50	40	30	20	10	0	—10
	Apparent Temperature (°F)						
Calm	50	40	30	20	10	0	—10
5	48.3	38.0	27.8	17.5	7.1	- 3.2	- 13.5
10	44.6	33.5	22.5	11.5	0.5	- 10.5	- 21.4
15	41.3	29.6	18.0	6.3	- 5.3	- 16.7	- 28.1
20	38.5	26.2	14.0	1.8	- 10.4	- 22.3	- 34.2
25	36.1	23.3	10.6	- 2.1	- 14.8	- 27.2	- 39.5
30	34.1	20.9	7.8	- 5.3	- 18.3	- 31.0	- 43.7
40	30.9	17.1	3.2	- 10.6	- 24.0	- 37.4	- 50.7

Texas Temperature, Freeze, Growing Season and Precipitation Records by Counties

Data in the table below are from the office of the **State Climatologist for Texas**, College Station. Because of the small change in averages, data are revised only at intervals of 10 years. Data below are the latest compilations, as of Jan. 1, 1993. Table shows temperature, freeze, growing season and precipitation for each county in Texas. Data for counties where a National Weather Service Station has not been maintained long enough to establish a reliable mean are interpolated from isoline charts prepared from mean values from stations with long-established records. **Mean maximum temperature for July** is computed from the sum of the daily maxima. **Mean minimum January** is computed from the sum of the daily minima. For stations where precipitation "Length of Record" are designated with an "N," data are based on the 30-year normal period 1961-90. Stations which have a specified precipitation "Length of Record" are based on data mainly from the period 1931-1993.

County and Station	Temp Length of Record (Yr.)	Mean Max July (F.)	Mean Min January (F.)	Record Highest (F.)	Record Lowest (F.)	Last in Spring Mo.	Last in Spring Day	First in Fall Mo.	First in Fall Day	Growing Season Days	Precip Length of Record (Yr.)	Jan (In.)	Feb (In.)	Mar (In.)	Apr (In.)	May (In.)	Jun (In.)	Jul (In.)	Aug (In.)	Sep (In.)	Oct (In.)	Nov (In.)	Dec (In.)	Annual (In.)
Anderson, Palestine	29	94	36	114	-6	Mar.	8	Nov.	27	264	N	3.1	3.2	3.9	3.9	4.8	4.5	2.3	2.3	3.6	4.4	3.9	3.6	43.3
Andrews, Andrews	N	94	29	113	0	Apr.	6	Nov.	5	213	N	0.4	0.5	0.6	0.9	1.6	2.0	2.5	1.9	2.5	1.5	0.6	0.4	15.4
Angelina, Lufkin	N	93	37	108	7	Mar.	14	Nov.	13	244	N	3.7	2.8	3.2	3.3	4.2	4.2	2.6	2.6	4.0	3.5	3.1	2.3	38.9
Aransas, Rockport	N	91	44	103	9	Feb.	7	Dec.	16	312	N	2.7	2.4	1.4	2.1	4.2	4.7	3.2	3.1	6.2	4.0	2.1	2.7	36.9
Archer, Archer	27	98	29	114	-10	Mar.	31	Nov.	6	220	N	1.0	1.7	2.0	2.6	4.3	3.0	1.7	2.5	4.3	1.7	1.8	1.3	29.3
Armstrong, Claude	28	92	20	108	-7	Apr.	6	Nov.	2	213	N	0.4	0.6	1.1	1.1	2.6	3.7	2.9	3.1	2.4	2.9	0.8	0.4	21.2
Atascosa, Poteet	N	96	38	100	17	Feb.	25	Dec.	5	282	N	1.4	1.7	1.2	2.5	4.0	3.2	1.8	2.6	3.6	2.9	1.8	1.4	28.0
Austin, Sealy	N	94	39	110		Feb.	27	Dec.	5	282	N	3.0	2.9	2.2	2.7	4.1	4.4	2.3	3.2	4.6	3.4	3.6	3.0	40.4
Bailey, Muleshoe	N	92	19	112	-21	Apr.	22	Oct.	20	181	N	0.4	0.5	0.6	0.9	1.9	2.6	2.8	2.9	2.2	1.4	0.8	0.5	16.8
Bandera, Medina*	15	94	31	111	5	Mar.	26	Nov.	16	235	N	1.7	1.8	1.7	3.3	4.5	2.9	2.2	4.7	4.5	3.7	2.3	1.2	35.1
Bastrop, Smithville	N	95	35	111	6	Mar.	7	Nov.	30	268	N	2.6	2.5	2.2	2.2	5.1	3.9	2.8	2.3	4.7	4.0	3.2	2.6	38.3
Baylor, Seymour	N	97	26	116	-14	Apr.	2	Nov.	3	214	N	0.9	1.5	1.6	2.2	3.9	3.4	2.1	2.4	4.1	3.1	1.3	1.2	27.3
Bee, Beeville	N	94	41	109	9	Feb.	22	Dec.	4	285	N	2.0	1.9	1.2	2.3	3.6	3.8	2.8	2.8	4.8	3.1	2.0	1.6	32.1
Bell, Temple	N	95	35	112	-4	Mar.	9	Nov.	24	260	N	1.9	2.7	2.5	2.5	4.6	3.6	2.0	2.5	3.8	3.3	2.3	2.3	34.9
Bexar, San Antonio	27	95	38	108		Mar.	6	Nov.	26	265	N	1.7	1.8	1.5	2.5	4.5	3.8	2.2	2.3	3.4	3.8	1.5	1.4	31.0
Blanco, Blanco	N	94	33	109	-6	Mar.	26	Nov.	15	234	N	1.9	2.4	2.2	2.8	4.5	3.8	2.3	3.0	3.9	3.8	2.3	2.0	34.2
Borden, Gail	N	97	31	113	-1	Apr.	6	Nov.	6	214	N	0.5	0.5	0.4	0.5	1.2	2.2	2.7	2.7	2.9	3.3	0.6	0.5	16.9
Bosque, Lake Whitney*	18	97	33	111	-3	Mar.	23	Nov.	11	243	N	1.9	2.4	1.5	4.1	4.4	3.5	1.6	1.5	3.2	2.7	2.8	2.0	31.6
Bowie, Texarkana*	N	93	35	101	-6	Mar.	21	Nov.	28	235	N	4.5	3.5	4.2	5.1	5.2	3.9	3.5	3.2	3.6	4.0	3.9	4.1	45.3
Brazoria, Angleton	N	92	41	105	10	Mar.	5	Nov.	30	268	N	2.7	2.6	2.6	3.3	4.8	6.3	5.2	2.4	7.3	4.9	4.7	2.8	56.4
Brazos, College Station	29	94	39	110	-2	Mar.	1	Nov.	8	274	N	2.6	2.5	2.6	3.4	4.2	3.7	2.3	2.6	3.3	3.8	3.2	2.8	39.1
Brewster, Alpine	N	89	30	106	-3	Apr.	1	Nov.	9	223	N	0.5	0.5	0.4	0.5	0.6	2.3	3.1	3.0	2.7	1.5	0.6	0.6	16.9
Brewster, Chisos Basin	N	85	35	103		Mar.	31	Nov.	5	223	N	0.6	0.6	0.4	0.6	0.6	2.3	3.6	3.6	2.7	1.9	0.9	0.5	19.2
Briscoe, Silverton	N	91	20	109	9	Apr.	7	Nov.	7	214	N	0.6	0.7	1.1	1.3	3.2	3.2	2.2	3.0	4.9	2.7	1.2	1.1	21.4
Brooks, Falfurrias	N	97	43	110	9	Feb.	10	Dec.	10	303	N	1.3	1.6	0.7	1.6	3.2	3.4	1.7	2.5	4.9	3.4	1.6	1.4	25.9
Brown, Brownwood	N	97	33	111	-6	Mar.	22	Nov.	19	242	N	1.3	1.7	1.9	2.6	3.6	3.6	1.9	2.1	3.2	3.2	2.1	2.8	27.3
Burleson, Somerville*	16	94	37	105		Mar.	1	Dec.	1	275	N	2.7	2.5	2.4	3.9	5.1	3.5	1.9	2.4	4.9	3.5	3.1	1.9	39.1
Burnet, Burnet	N	93	32	108	-4	Mar.	29	Nov.	14	230	N	1.7	2.0	2.1	2.7	4.8	4.4	1.7	2.2	3.5	3.5	2.1	2.4	31.2
Caldwell, Luling	N	96	36	110	11	Feb.	27	Nov.	29	275	N	2.2	2.2	1.9	3.0	4.8	4.4	1.8	3.3	4.4	4.5	3.1	2.7	35.3
Calhoun, Port O'Connor	27	90	46	107		Feb.	19	Dec.	11	300	N	3.1	2.7	1.6	3.0	3.0	3.7	3.7	3.3	6.1	4.5	2.7	2.4	39.4
Callahan, Putnam	N	96	32	110	-8	Mar.	28	Nov.	11	228	N	1.4	1.4	1.7	2.0	4.0	3.0	1.8	2.1	4.0	2.9	1.7	1.1	25.2
Cameron, Brownsville	N	93	50	106	16	Feb.	28	Dec.	12	238	N	1.6	1.1	1.7	1.6	2.6	2.7	1.9	2.2	6.0	3.1	1.5	1.3	26.6
Camp, Pittsburg*	N	94	32	109	-3	Feb.	21	Nov.	25	341	N	2.9	3.3	3.8	5.4	4.8	3.4	2.7	2.2	4.0	3.2	4.0	3.5	43.3
Carson, Panhandle	N	93	22	109	-10	Apr.	17	Oct.	25	191	N	0.5	0.8	1.1	1.3	2.6	3.7	2.3	2.8	2.3	1.7	0.9	0.5	20.8
Cass, Linden	29	93	31	103	8	Mar.	19	Nov.	11	237	22	3.3	3.9	4.9	5.0	4.5	4.8	2.9	2.8	3.2	3.2	3.6	4.5	48.3
Castro, Dimmitt	22	91	19	107	-8	Apr.	17	Oct.	25	193	N	0.4	0.6	0.8	0.8	2.3	3.0	2.3	2.8	2.4	1.5	0.7	0.5	18.0
Chambers, Anahuac	29	92	41	110	8	Mar.	6	Nov.	20	261	N	4.0	2.9	3.0	3.6	4.8	5.8	4.5	4.5	6.2	3.8	4.4	4.2	51.7

Weather Data by County and Station

County and Station	Temp. Length of Record (Yr.)	July Mean Max. (°F)	January Mean Min. (°F)	Record Highest (°F)	Record Lowest (°F)	Last in Spring (Mo.)	(Day)	First in Fall (Mo.)	(Day)	Growing Season (Days)	Precip. Length of Record (Yr.)	Jan (in.)	Feb	Mar	Apr	May	Jun	Jul	Aug	Sep	Oct	Nov	Dec	Annual (in.)
Cherokee, Rusk	N	93	35	107	-1	Mar.	8	Nov.	21	258	N	3.7	3.5	3.6	4.1	4.0	5.1	4.0	2.9	2.2	2.2	4.2	4.2	46.1
Childress, Childress	N	96	26	117	-7	Apr.	3	Nov.	6	217	N	0.5	0.9	1.2	1.5	3.0	3.0	1.9	2.1	2.8	2.0	1.0	0.7	20.7
Clay, Henrietta	N	97	26	116	-8	Mar.	27	Nov.	14	232	N	1.3	2.0	2.5	3.0	3.9	3.9	1.8	2.6	4.2	3.1	1.7	1.6	31.9
Cochran, Morton	27	91	22	110	-12	Apr.	18	Oct.	24	189	N	0.4	0.6	0.6	0.8	1.8	2.7	2.4	3.3	4.2	3.1	0.7	0.5	18.6
Coke, Robert Lee	28	96	28	111	-2	Mar.	31	Nov.	12	226	N	0.8	1.2	1.1	1.8	3.3	2.8	1.6	2.0	3.7	2.8	1.2	0.9	23.2
Coleman, Coleman	N	96	32	114	-4	Mar.	26	Nov.	16	235	N	1.2	1.5	1.6	2.4	4.1	3.3	2.0	2.5	3.8	2.8	1.6	1.2	28.0
Collin, McKinney	N	95	32	118	-7	Mar.	26	Nov.	11	230	N	2.0	2.8	3.5	3.9	5.8	4.0	2.4	2.4	4.6	3.4	3.1	2.3	40.0
Collingsworth, Wellington	N	97	26	113	-6	Apr.	5	Nov.	3	212	N	0.5	0.8	1.3	1.7	3.4	3.2	2.0	2.1	3.0	2.0	1.0	0.6	21.5
Colorado, Columbus	28	95	37	108	4	Mar.	1	Dec.	6	280	28	3.3	2.8	2.5	3.2	5.5	4.1	2.9	2.9	5.0	3.2	3.6	2.9	41.8
Comal, New Braunfels	N	95	37	110	2	Mar.	12	Nov.	25	261	N	1.9	2.2	1.8	2.6	4.6	4.1	2.0	2.5	4.1	3.0	2.8	2.0	34.3
Comanche, Proctor Reservoir	27	95	30	108	-8	Mar.	27	Nov.	20	238	27	1.6	1.9	2.1	3.1	4.6	3.4	1.7	1.9	3.9	2.6	2.0	1.3	30.4
Concho, Paint Rock	N	98	31	111	-1	Mar.	29	Nov.	12	228	N	1.0	1.3	1.4	3.2	3.7	2.9	1.9	2.1	4.0	2.6	1.3	1.1	24.8
Cooke, Gainesville	N	95	27	112	-7	Mar.	25	Nov.	8	226	N	1.7	2.3	3.3	3.2	4.7	3.5	1.9	2.4	4.5	3.1	2.4	1.8	35.8
Coryell, Gatesville	N	96	33	112	-6	Mar.	25	Nov.	12	241	N	1.8	2.3	2.4	3.1	4.3	3.9	2.1	2.2	3.7	3.1	2.3	1.8	32.9
Cottle, Paducah	N	96	25	118	-7	Mar.	31	Nov.	7	219	N	0.7	1.0	1.2	1.5	3.2	3.4	1.8	2.5	3.0	2.1	1.0	0.8	22.3
Crane, Crane	28	97	31	115	3	Mar.	31	Nov.	11	225	28	0.6	0.6	0.4	0.9	1.7	1.7	1.5	1.9	3.1	2.1	0.7	0.5	14.8
Crockett, Ozona	N	94	30	109	4	Mar.	26	Nov.	14	233	N	0.7	0.9	0.9	1.5	2.3	2.0	1.6	2.1	3.3	2.2	1.0	0.6	19.2
Crosby, Crosbyton	N	93	23	113	-6	Apr.	10	Nov.	2	206	N	0.5	0.9	1.2	1.3	2.9	3.0	2.3	2.1	3.6	2.1	1.0	0.6	22.6
Culberson, Van Horn	N	94	28	112	-7	Apr.	2	Oct.	10	224	N	0.5	0.3	0.2	0.3	0.6	1.4	2.1	2.5	2.7	1.3	0.7	0.6	13.1
Dallam, Dalhart	N	92	19	107	-21	Apr.	23	Oct.	18	178	N	0.4	0.5	1.1	1.1	2.6	2.4	3.1	3.1	1.9	1.0	0.7	0.4	17.9
Dallas, Dallas	N	96	35	113	1	Mar.	23	Nov.	13	235	28	1.8	2.3	3.2	3.9	5.0	3.5	2.4	2.3	3.6	3.9	2.4	1.9	36.1
Dawson, Lamesa	N	95	25	114	-12	Apr.	8	Nov.	6	210	N	0.5	0.6	0.8	1.0	2.8	2.8	2.2	1.9	3.5	2.2	0.7	0.5	16.2
De Witt, Yoakum	N	95	39	110	12	Mar.	3	Nov.	29	270	N	2.4	2.3	2.0	3.3	4.3	4.5	2.9	3.0	4.1	3.2	3.0	2.0	37.0
Deaf Smith, Hereford	N	90	20	108	-17	Apr.	16	Oct.	28	195	N	0.4	0.6	0.8	1.0	1.9	3.0	1.9	3.1	2.1	1.4	0.8	0.4	17.2
Delta, Cooper*	N	94	30	110	-1	Mar.	25	Nov.	13	233	N	2.7	2.9	3.6	4.8	5.0	3.9	2.8	2.2	4.8	3.6	3.3	3.4	42.7
Denton, Denton	N	94	30	113	-3	Mar.	27	Nov.	8	226	N	1.8	2.4	3.0	3.7	5.3	3.3	2.2	2.2	4.5	4.0	3.3	2.1	37.3
Dickens, Dickens*	15	94	30	114		Apr.	4	Nov.	7	217	15	0.9	0.6	1.1	1.8	3.3	2.6	2.0	2.5	2.9	1.8	0.7	0.4	20.7
Dimmit, Carrizo Springs	N	95	41	112	10	Feb.	19	Dec.	6	290	N	0.9	0.8	0.8	1.8	3.2	2.6	1.3	2.1	2.9	2.6	1.1	0.9	21.7
Donley, Clarendon	N	95	21	110	-11	Apr.	16	Nov.	8	217	N	0.5	0.7	1.0	1.9	2.7	3.5	3.1	3.3	2.5	1.9	0.7	0.5	22.0
Duval, Freer	N	99	41	109	-8	Feb.	9	Nov.	6	298	N	0.9	1.0	0.8	1.9	2.9	2.6	1.8	2.0	3.6	2.6	1.4	1.3	13.1
Eastland, Rising Star	28	94	29	110	0	Apr.	16	Nov.	1	299	28	1.3	1.7	2.1	2.7	3.8	3.1	2.1	2.1	4.1	3.1	1.7	1.3	24.8
Ector, Penwell	N	96	28	109	9	Mar.	27	Nov.	11	217	N	0.5	0.6	0.5	0.8	1.9	1.6	2.1	2.1	2.9	1.7	0.7	0.6	29.7
Edwards, Carta Valley	27	95	34	110	-8	Apr.	3	Nov.	6	250	27	0.7	1.2	1.0	1.9	2.9	2.7	1.9	2.6	3.0	2.4	1.2	1.0	13.1
El Paso, El Paso	27	95	29	114	-4	Mar.	16	Nov.	12	248	27	0.4	0.4	0.3	0.2	0.3	0.7	1.5	2.0	1.7	0.8	0.4	0.6	8.8
Ellis, Waxahachie	N	96	34	114	-7	Mar.	20	Nov.	21	246	N	1.9	2.8	3.1	3.8	5.1	4.7	1.6	2.0	3.9	3.8	2.7	2.4	36.8
Erath, Dublin	N	94	31	110	-7	Mar.	27	Nov.	18	238	N	1.7	2.1	2.3	3.2	4.6	3.5	2.2	2.1	3.6	3.3	2.1	1.6	32.9
Falls, Marlin	N	96	36	112	-4	Mar.	13	Nov.	25	257	N	2.1	2.4	3.0	3.2	5.2	3.5	2.2	2.1	3.6	3.8	3.2	2.5	36.8
Fannin, Bonham	N	94	29	114	3	Mar.	27	Nov.	25	228	N	2.1	3.1	3.9	3.8	6.1	4.5	3.1	2.3	4.9	4.1	3.4	2.7	44.0
Fayette, Flatonia	N	95	40	114	14	Mar.	23	Nov.	10	277	N	2.5	2.5	1.1	1.9	4.8	4.3	1.9	2.6	5.0	3.2	2.9	2.3	37.1
Fisher, Rotan	N	96	30	116	-9	Mar.	2	Nov.	4	218	N	0.7	1.1	1.0	1.9	2.7	3.6	2.1	2.6	3.0	2.4	1.2	1.0	24.3
Floyd, Floydada	N	92	24	111	-1	Apr.	2	Nov.	6	213	N	0.4	0.7	1.0	1.3	2.8	3.6	2.2	2.6	3.0	1.7	0.9	0.5	20.5
Foard, Crowell*	N	97	41	111	6	Apr.	7	Nov.	7	219	N	0.9	1.1	1.3	2.0	4.1	2.5	2.4	2.6	3.1	2.7	1.2	0.8	23.9
Fort Bend, Sugar Land	18	93	36	106		Feb.	14	Dec.	12	296	18	3.3	2.8	2.7	3.8	5.1	4.9	3.7	4.1	5.6	3.5	4.0	3.3	45.3
Franklin, Mount Vernon*	N	93	33	105	-1	Mar.	23	Nov.	7	234	N	2.8	3.3	4.3	4.4	4.7	4.1	3.4	2.5	5.6	3.5	3.7	4.8	46.8
Freestone, Fairfield	29	95	36	114	2	Mar.	11	Nov.	29	263	29	2.5	3.1	3.2	3.7	4.9	3.5	2.0	2.3	4.0	4.1	3.6	3.0	39.8
Frio, Pearsall	N	97	38	111	9	Feb.	23	Dec.	2	291	N	1.2	1.3	1.0	2.2	3.6	3.3	1.6	2.5	3.0	3.1	1.5	1.1	25.4

County and Station	Temperature — Length of Record (Yr.)	Temperature — Mean Max. July (°F)	Temperature — Mean Min. January (°F)	Temperature — Record Highest (°F)	Temperature — Record Lowest (°F)	Freeze — Last in Spring (Mo.)	Freeze — Last in Spring (Day)	Freeze — First in Fall (Mo.)	Freeze — First in Fall (Day)	Growing Season (Days)	Precip — Length of Record (Yr.)	Jan. (In.)	Feb. (In.)	Mar. (In.)	Apr. (In.)	May (In.)	June (In.)	July (In.)	Aug. (In.)	Sept. (In.)	Oct. (In.)	Nov. (In.)	Dec. (In.)	Annual (In.)
Gaines, Seminole	N	94	25	114	-9	Apr.	8	Nov.	4	210	N	0.5	0.7	0.7	0.9	2.0	2.6	2.0	2.3	2.5	1.4	0.8	0.6	17.5
Galveston, Galveston	N	87	47	101	8	Jan.	24	Dec.	25	335	N	3.3	2.3	2.2	2.4	3.6	4.4	4.0	4.5	5.9	2.8	3.4	3.5	42.3
Garza, Post	28	94	27	115	-1	Apr.	5	Nov.	7	216	N	0.6	0.8	0.9	1.2	2.7	3.6	2.1	2.8	2.9	2.0	0.9	0.7	20.9
Gillespie, Fredericksburg	N	93	35	109	-5	Apr.	1	Nov.	6	219	N	1.3	1.8	1.4	2.5	4.2	3.6	2.2	2.8	3.6	3.6	1.9	1.3	30.0
Glasscock, Garden City	26	95	25	114	0	Apr.	2	Nov.	10	222	N	0.6	0.7	0.7	1.2	2.2	2.0	2.0	2.0	3.3	1.8	0.8	0.6	18.0
Goliad, Goliad	N	94	43	112	7	Feb.	24	Dec.	6	285	N	2.1	2.1	1.4	2.8	4.1	4.5	2.4	3.4	5.0	3.6	2.3	2.0	36.5
Gonzales, Nixon	N	95	40	113	0	Feb.	28	Dec.	1	276	N	2.2	2.1	1.6	2.9	4.0	3.5	1.9	2.6	4.6	3.2	2.4	1.7	32.4
Gray, Pampa	N	92	21	111	3	Apr.	15	Oct.	27	195	N	0.5	0.9	1.4	1.6	2.9	3.6	2.4	2.6	2.4	1.5	1.0	0.5	21.0
Grayson, Sherman	N	95	30	110	-12	Mar.	27	Nov.	9	227	N	1.9	2.7	3.4	3.9	5.8	4.4	2.9	2.8	5.1	4.2	3.1	2.0	40.4
Gregg, Longview	N	93	33	110	-2	Mar.	16	Nov.	15	247	N	3.5	3.6	4.1	4.5	5.1	3.4	2.9	2.8	3.9	3.7	4.3	4.3	47.0
Grimes, Anderson*	9	96	40	110	-7	Mar.	1	Dec.	4	278	9	3.1	3.3	2.8	3.3	4.3	3.4	2.4	2.8	4.1	3.1	3.4	3.4	40.4
Guadalupe, Seguin*	N	96	40	108	4	Mar.	6	Nov.	28	267	N	1.8	2.5	1.8	3.3	3.4	2.9	1.8	2.1	4.1	3.1	2.1	1.7	31.4
Hale, Plainview	N	92	24	110	0	Apr.	10	Nov.	6	211	N	0.5	0.7	0.8	1.1	3.0	3.1	1.7	2.5	2.4	1.6	0.9	0.6	19.8
Hall, Memphis	N	96	24	111	-7	Apr.	4	Nov.	4	213	N	0.5	0.8	1.3	1.7	3.5	3.0	2.1	2.4	2.1	1.8	1.0	0.7	20.5
Hamilton, Hico	N	96	32	111	-7	Mar.	27	Oct.	25	239	N	1.9	2.0	2.4	3.0	4.6	3.0	2.1	2.1	3.4	3.3	2.0	2.2	31.8
Hansford, Spearman	N	95	21	109	-11	Apr.	22	Nov.	7	186	N	0.4	0.7	1.5	1.1	2.9	3.0	2.9	2.4	2.1	1.2	1.0	0.5	19.4
Hardeman, Quanah	22	97	23	119	-15	Mar.	31	Nov.	14	221	N	0.8	1.0	1.5	1.7	3.5	3.2	2.4	2.5	3.6	2.4	1.3	0.9	24.5
Hardin, Evadale	N	93	43	102	12	Feb.	14	Dec.	11	246	N	4.8	3.9	4.0	3.8	5.4	5.0	4.7	3.5	5.3	4.0	3.8	5.1	55.7
Harris, Houston	N	93	32	107	2	Feb.	16	Nov.	17	300	N	3.3	3.0	2.9	3.2	5.2	4.4	3.6	3.5	4.3	3.9	3.7	3.5	46.1
Harrison, Marshall	13	92	27	110	-9	Mar.	22	Oct.	19	245	13	3.8	4.0	4.0	4.4	4.9	5.0	3.0	2.5	3.8	3.9	3.8	4.5	47.7
Hartley, Channing*	N	93	21	108	-6	Apr.	28	Oct.	16	180	N	0.4	0.5	0.7	1.2	2.2	1.9	2.1	2.9	1.9	1.2	0.7	0.2	16.1
Haskell, Haskell	N	96	27	115	-2	Apr.	14	Nov.	28	232	N	0.9	1.4	1.4	1.4	3.6	3.0	2.1	1.8	3.7	2.6	1.3	1.1	26.1
Hays, San Marcos	N	95	36	110	14	Mar.	9	Nov.	23	254	N	2.0	2.3	1.8	2.8	5.0	4.2	2.1	2.3	3.7	3.1	2.5	2.1	34.6
Hemphill, Canadian	N	96	22	112	-14	Apr.	9	Oct.	30	204	39	0.3	0.8	1.3	1.4	3.4	3.1	1.9	1.8	2.6	1.4	1.0	0.5	20.1
Henderson, Athens	N	95	36	110	-2	Mar.	11	Oct.	26	260	N	2.5	3.1	3.6	3.6	5.2	3.8	1.5	2.4	3.8	4.0	3.7	3.3	39.7
Hidalgo, McAllen	N	96	49	110	17	Feb.	7	Nov.	8	327	N	1.4	1.3	0.6	1.3	2.8	2.7	1.7	2.5	4.0	2.6	1.3	1.5	23.4
Hill, Hillsboro	27	95	34	113	7	Mar.	13	Nov.	18	250	N	1.9	2.6	2.6	3.3	4.8	3.9	1.8	2.2	4.4	4.0	2.5	3.3	35.1
Hockley, Levelland	N	92	22	115	-16	Apr.	15	Oct.	28	196	28	0.4	0.7	0.6	0.9	2.0	2.6	2.5	2.2	3.1	2.4	0.7	0.5	19.3
Hood, Granbury*	N	97	33	110	-6	Mar.	26	Nov.	13	232	N	1.9	2.0	1.7	3.9	4.9	3.4	1.8	2.2	2.9	3.2	2.0	1.0	30.9
Hopkins, Sulphur Springs	N	94	30	110	-4	Mar.	23	Nov.	16	238	N	3.5	3.3	4.1	4.7	5.5	3.7	3.0	2.2	4.4	3.9	3.8	3.5	46.0
Houston, Crockett	N	93	34	114	0	Mar.	6	Nov.	26	265	N	3.5	2.9	3.2	4.1	4.4	4.1	2.7	2.0	4.1	3.6	3.8	3.5	42.4
Howard, Big Spring	N	94	28	110	-1	Apr.	4	Nov.	11	217	N	0.6	0.8	0.8	1.3	2.8	2.3	2.3	2.2	2.9	1.9	0.8	0.6	19.2
Hudspeth, Cornudas Ser.	N	95	25	108	-3	Apr.	27	Nov.	13	231	N	0.2	0.3	0.8	0.2	0.5	1.1	1.5	2.0	1.4	0.9	0.4	0.6	10.0
Hunt, Greenville	N	93	29	107	-12	Mar.	21	Oct.	24	237	N	2.2	3.0	3.8	3.9	5.7	3.7	2.7	2.2	4.5	4.1	3.3	2.6	41.6
Hutchinson, Borger	N	95	23	108	-13	Apr.	20	Nov.	14	187	N	0.5	0.9	1.0	1.6	3.2	3.5	2.7	2.2	2.0	1.3	0.8	0.9	20.3
Irion, Mertzon	27	95	32	113	4	Mar.	27	Nov.	27	232	N	0.7	1.3	1.0	1.6	3.1	2.9	2.2	2.2	3.1	2.2	1.0	1.1	21.1
Jack, Jacksboro	N	95	29	113	-7	Apr.	1	Nov.	1	218	N	1.3	1.6	2.1	2.8	4.7	4.6	2.2	2.2	3.1	3.2	2.0	1.5	30.7
Jackson, Edna*	8	94	42	105	7	Feb.	19	Dec.	6	290	26	2.2	2.8	1.7	3.7	5.1	5.3	3.8	3.4	5.7	3.9	2.8	2.6	40.9
Jasper, Jasper	N	93	36	106	17	Feb.	18	Nov.	13	230	N	4.4	4.4	3.2	3.5	5.6	5.6	3.9	4.3	4.5	3.6	4.6	5.3	52.7
Jeff Davis, Mount Locke	22	82	30	104	4	—	—	—	—	—	N	0.5	0.5	0.4	0.5	1.5	2.6	3.9	3.2	2.7	1.2	0.7	0.8	18.5
Jefferson, Port Arthur	N	92	42	107	16	Mar.	11	Nov.	16	250	N	4.8	3.4	3.2	4.1	5.7	5.6	5.4	5.3	6.3	4.1	3.3	4.9	57.2
Jim Hogg, Hebbronville	N	97	42	109	15	Feb.	15	Dec.	15	303	N	1.1	1.3	0.7	1.3	3.2	3.5	1.5	2.0	4.1	2.7	1.6	1.1	22.7
Jim Wells, Alice	N	96	43	111	18	Feb.	18	Nov.	18	289	N	1.3	1.6	0.8	1.6	3.2	3.5	2.5	2.7	3.3	3.3	1.6	1.1	27.8
Johnson, Cleburne	N	97	33	114	-10	Mar.	25	Nov.	14	233	N	1.9	2.2	2.9	3.6	5.4	5.4	2.0	2.1	3.3	2.4	1.6	2.1	34.0
Jones, Anson	N	96	31	114	-5	Mar.	31	Nov.	9	223	22	1.0	1.4	1.3	2.2	3.4	2.9	2.0	2.0	2.6	2.4	1.8	1.1	25.8
Karnes, Kenedy*	18	97	41	112	7	Feb.	24	Dec.	2	281	18	2.3	2.4	1.1	2.2	4.0	4.2	1.2	3.0	3.6	3.6	2.0	1.8	33.2

County and Station	Temperature — Length of Record (Yr.)	July Mean Max. (F.)	January Mean Min. (F.)	Record Highest (F.)	Record Lowest (F.)	Freeze: Last in Spring (Mo.)	Day	First in Fall (Mo.)	Day	Growing Season Days	Freeze Length of Record (Yr.)	Jan.	Feb.	Mar.	Apr.	May	June	July	Aug.	Sep.	Oct.	Nov.	Dec.	Annual
Kaufman, Kaufman	N	95	32	112	-3	Mar.	18	Nov.	21	248	N	2.4	3.0	3.2	3.8	5.0	3.1	2.6	1.8	3.8	3.9	3.3	3.0	38.9
Kendall, Boerne	N	93	33	107	-4	Mar.	25	Nov.	11	236	N	1.7	2.1	2.1	3.1	4.1	3.8	2.2	2.9	4.2	3.6	2.7	1.8	34.2
Kenedy, Armstrong*	14	95	45	110	14	Feb.	2	Dec.	18	319	14	1.2	1.7	0.5	1.1	4.4	3.4	2.1	3.2	6.4	2.9	1.3	1.3	29.7
Kent, Jayton	18	96	25	116	-5	Apr.	4	Nov.	6	216	18	0.7	1.0	1.1	1.6	3.0	2.9	1.8	2.7	2.1	2.1	0.9	0.8	21.8
Kerr, Kerrville*	N	94	32	110	-7	Apr.	6	Nov.	6	216	N	1.6	1.6	2.0	3.1	3.8	2.6	1.7	2.1	4.0	3.6	1.6	1.6	29.8
Kimble, Junction	N	96	31	110	-11	Apr.	3	Nov.	3	213	N	1.0	1.1	1.2	2.1	3.6	2.8	1.7	2.5	3.7	2.4	1.2	1.1	23.8
King, Guthrie	27	98	24	119	-10	Apr.	3	Nov.	8	219	N	0.9	1.1	1.1	1.6	3.5	3.1	1.9	2.7	2.6	2.4	1.1	0.7	23.8
Kinney, Brackettville	23	95	36	109	4	Mar.	1	Nov.	26	270	N	0.8	1.3	0.9	2.3	2.6	4.0	1.6	2.0	4.3	2.7	1.2	0.8	21.7
Kleberg, Kingsville	N	95	45	108	10	Feb.	5	Dec.	16	314	45	1.5	1.8	1.6	2.1	3.4	3.0	2.2	2.6	4.3	2.8	1.4	1.0	27.6
Knox, Munday	N	98	28	117	-9	Apr.	3	Nov.	6	217	N	0.9	1.4	1.6	2.6	3.7	3.0	2.0	2.4	3.3	2.8	1.3	1.0	26.2
La Salle, Fowlerton	N	99	30	111	7	Feb.	20	Dec.	6	288	N	1.1	1.1	0.8	1.8	3.2	2.2	1.5	2.7	3.3	3.0	1.2	1.0	22.5
Lamar, Paris	N	94	30	111	-1	Mar.	25	Nov.	14	235	N	2.2	3.2	4.0	4.0	5.9	3.9	3.6	2.7	4.8	4.6	3.9	3.3	46.1
Lamb, Littlefield	N	91	22	112	-14	Apr.	16	Oct.	27	194	N	0.4	0.6	0.6	1.0	2.3	3.3	2.4	2.8	3.1	1.6	0.7	0.5	18.7
Lampasas, Lampasas	N	95	30	111	-12	Apr.	1	Nov.	10	223	N	1.5	2.0	2.1	2.7	4.1	2.9	1.8	2.5	3.1	3.3	2.0	1.7	29.6
Lavaca, Hallettsville	N	95	41	111	11	Mar.	1	Dec.	6	280	N	2.8	2.4	3.0	3.0	5.3	4.4	2.5	2.7	5.1	3.2	3.0	2.4	39.1
Lee, Lexington	28	94	36	104	-3	Mar.	6	Nov.	29	273	28	2.2	2.5	2.4	2.9	4.8	3.8	1.7	2.4	4.0	3.8	3.0	2.3	35.6
Leon, Centerville	N	93	39	111	7	Mar.	3	Dec.	1	270	N	3.8	3.1	3.1	3.9	4.4	3.5	2.5	2.4	4.0	4.1	3.2	3.1	40.5
Liberty, Liberty	N	93	39	107	7	Mar.	3	Nov.	19	261	N	3.1	3.6	3.4	3.5	4.9	6.1	4.5	4.0	5.7	4.5	5.2	4.8	54.1
Limestone, Mexia	N	95	33	110	-5	Mar.	15	Nov.	26	255	N	3.6	3.1	3.4	3.6	5.4	3.5	1.9	2.3	4.7	4.1	3.4	3.2	40.3
Lipscomb, Follett	N	93	21	110	-12	Apr.	10	Oct.	29	202	N	0.5	1.0	1.9	1.7	3.5	3.4	2.3	3.1	2.1	1.4	0.8	0.7	22.8
Live Oak, George West*	N	95	41	110	-6	Feb.	20	Dec.	6	289	45	1.7	1.6	0.8	1.9	3.3	2.8	1.5	2.9	4.7	3.1	1.2	1.2	27.6
Llano, Llano	N	96	31	113	-6	Mar.	29	Nov.	13	229	N	1.2	1.8	1.6	2.5	3.8	2.8	1.8	2.4	3.0	2.7	1.9	1.2	26.4
Loving, Mentone*	N	96	28	114	-14	Mar.	3	Nov.	8	222	N	0.3	0.3	0.3	0.2	1.1	0.9	1.8	1.4	1.2	1.0	0.3	0.3	9.1
Lubbock, Lubbock	N	92	25	114	-16	Apr.	9	Nov.	3	208	N	0.4	0.7	0.9	1.0	2.4	2.8	2.4	2.5	2.6	1.9	0.8	0.5	18.7
Lynn, Tahoka	N	92	24	111	-5	Apr.	5	Nov.	6	217	N	0.5	0.8	0.9	1.4	2.7	3.0	2.5	2.6	2.6	1.8	0.8	0.7	19.7
Madison, Madisonville	N	96	38	110	-2	Apr.	5	Dec.	2	272	N	3.0	2.8	3.2	3.5	5.0	3.9	2.3	2.6	4.5	4.1	3.7	3.0	41.6
Marion, Jefferson*	24	94	30	109	-5	Mar.	18	Nov.	9	236	24	3.9	3.5	3.2	5.3	4.6	3.4	3.1	2.5	3.6	4.1	3.8	4.1	44.7
Martin, Lenorah*	24	94	30	109	-8	Apr.	6	Nov.	6	215	24	0.6	0.8	0.8	1.2	2.3	1.6	2.4	1.7	2.7	2.0	0.8	0.6	17.2
Mason, Mason	N	95	30	109	5	Mar.	5	Nov.	6	217	N	1.1	1.6	1.5	2.1	3.7	3.3	1.9	2.3	3.2	1.6	1.6	1.1	26.8
Matagorda, Matagorda	N	91	45	102	9	Feb.	17	Dec.	10	296	N	3.6	2.6	1.9	2.6	4.5	4.8	4.0	3.3	6.9	2.8	3.9	2.7	44.7
Maverick, Eagle Pass	28	98	38	115	10	Feb.	21	Dec.	3	285	28	0.7	0.9	0.7	1.9	3.4	3.0	2.3	2.2	2.8	2.4	1.0	0.8	21.5
McCulloch, Brady	N	95	30	110	-7	Mar.	31	Nov.	12	226	N	1.1	1.6	1.4	2.1	3.6	2.9	1.7	2.5	3.6	2.4	1.5	1.1	26.1
McLennan, Waco	N	97	34	112	-5	Mar.	16	Nov.	24	253	N	1.7	2.1	2.3	3.2	4.6	3.3	1.7	1.7	3.5	3.4	2.4	1.9	32.0
McMullen, Tilden	N	98	30	115	5	Feb.	19	Dec.	7	291	N	1.3	2.1	0.9	1.8	3.0	2.9	2.4	2.7	3.1	2.0	1.4	1.1	23.4
Medina, Hondo	N	94	40	109	4	Mar.	6	Nov.	24	263	N	1.4	1.7	1.4	2.6	3.8	3.0	1.6	2.3	2.5	2.0	1.5	1.4	27.3
Menard, Menard	N	94	37	112	-2	Mar.	31	Nov.	6	220	N	1.0	1.5	1.4	3.2	2.8	2.1	1.9	1.9	3.3	1.4	1.2	1.2	24.3
Midland, Midland	N	95	29	109	-11	Apr.	3	Nov.	6	218	N	0.5	0.6	0.5	0.7	2.2	1.4	1.9	1.7	1.4	1.3	0.7	0.3	15.2
Milam, Cameron	24	95	38	116	2	Mar.	13	Nov.	24	256	24	2.2	2.6	2.2	3.3	4.7	2.9	1.6	2.1	4.2	3.2	3.0	1.4	34.2
Mills, Goldthwaite	N	95	34	109	-7	Mar.	31	Nov.	16	230	N	1.3	1.8	1.9	2.4	3.7	3.2	1.7	2.1	3.1	3.1	1.4	0.5	27.6
Mitchell, Colorado City*	24	97	30	112	-7	Apr.	4	Nov.	5	217	24	0.6	0.7	0.9	1.9	2.9	2.2	2.0	2.3	3.0	2.1	1.0	0.7	19.8
Montague, Bowie	N	96	31	112	-11	Mar.	27	Nov.	11	229	N	1.4	2.0	2.6	2.9	4.8	3.4	2.4	3.6	4.1	3.7	2.3	1.6	32.9
Montgomery, Conroe	N	93	38	115	7	Mar.	1	Nov.	26	270	N	3.6	3.2	2.9	3.8	5.4	4.5	2.8	2.7	5.0	3.7	4.2	4.0	47.3
Moore, Dumas	N	92	20	109	-18	Apr.	30	Oct.	22	185	N	0.4	0.7	1.0	1.1	2.7	2.8	2.1	3.3	1.1	1.1	0.8	0.4	17.4
Morris, Daingerfield	N	95	35	109	-5	Mar.	21	Nov.	12	236	25	2.9	3.5	4.4	4.8	4.7	3.6	2.4	2.4	3.7	3.9	4.5	4.1	44.6
Motley, Matador	N	96	36	116	-5	Apr.	3	Nov.	7	218	N	0.6	0.8	1.1	1.3	2.8	3.4	2.8	2.4	3.2	2.0	1.0	0.7	21.2
Nacogdoches, Nacogdoches*	N	94	36	110	0	Mar.	16	Nov.	12	243	N	4.2	3.9	3.7	4.8	5.5	3.9	2.1	2.5	3.8	3.3	3.8	4.7	47.5

County and Station	Temp. Length of Record (Yr.)	July Mean Max. (F.)	January Mean Min. (F.)	Record Highest (F.)	Record Lowest (F.)	Last in Spring Mo.	Last in Spring Day	First in Fall Mo.	First in Fall Day	Growing Season (Days)	Precip. Length of Record (Yr.)	Jan. (In.)	Feb. (In.)	Mar. (In.)	Apr. (In.)	May (In.)	June (In.)	July (In.)	Aug. (In.)	Sept. (In.)	Oct. (In.)	Nov. (In.)	Dec. (In.)	Annual (In.)
Navarro, Corsicana	N	94	33	113	-5	Mar.	10	Nov.	19	253	27	2.2	2.8	3.1	3.6	5.8	3.1	2.1	1.9	3.4	4.2	2.9	2.9	37.9
Newton, Kirbyville Forest Service*	27	93	40	107	-11	Mar.	24	Nov.	9	228	Z	4.8	4.3	4.6	4.6	5.3	4.6	5.3	3.7	5.1	3.8	4.7	6.0	56.0
Nolan, Roscoe	N	94	45	113	13	Apr.	2	Nov.	9	221	Z	1.0	1.2	1.3	1.8	2.9	2.9	2.0	2.4	4.3	2.6	1.2	0.9	24.4
Nueces, Corpus Christi	N	93	17	104	-8	Feb.	9	Dec.	15	309	Z	1.7	2.0	1.8	1.7	3.3	3.4	2.4	3.3	5.5	3.0	1.6	1.3	30.1
Ochiltree, Perryton	26	94	19	110	-17	Apr.	18	Oct.	26	191	Z	0.4	0.7	1.3	1.3	3.3	3.3	2.4	2.4	1.8	1.1	1.1	0.5	19.5
Oldham, Vega*	N	91	39	108	10	Apr.	19	Oct.	21	186	Z	0.5	0.6	0.8	1.1	2.4	2.8	2.8	2.5	1.6	1.2	0.7	0.5	17.4
Orange, Orange	27	91	33	104	3	Mar.	16	Nov.	11	240	27	5.2	3.9	3.4	3.4	5.4	5.6	5.6	4.7	6.2	4.3	4.7	5.5	58.3
Palo Pinto, Mineral Wells	N	96	33	114	1	Mar.	31	Nov.	7	221	Z	1.6	2.0	2.6	3.2	4.5	3.5	2.2	2.4	3.4	3.5	1.9	1.4	32.2
Panola, Carthage	N	94	28	108	-10	Mar.	16	Nov.	11	240	Z	4.0	3.7	3.8	4.0	4.9	4.4	3.2	2.7	4.1	3.9	4.7	4.6	48.0
Parker, Weatherford	N	96	30	119	-15	Mar.	29	Nov.	9	225	Z	1.6	2.2	2.7	3.3	4.5	3.6	2.3	2.4	3.5	3.3	2.0	1.6	32.9
Parmer, Friona	28	90	35	108	3	Apr.	20	Oct.	20	183	28	0.5	0.6	0.4	0.8	1.9	2.8	2.1	2.7	2.2	1.3	0.7	0.5	16.8
Pecos, Fort Stockton	N	95	21	117	-14	Mar.	31	Nov.	10	224	Z	0.5	0.5	1.0	0.7	1.5	1.6	1.3	1.8	2.8	1.6	0.8	0.6	13.9
Polk, Livingston	N	94	26	111	-2	Mar.	11	Nov.	16	250	Z	4.0	3.4	3.7	3.6	5.5	4.7	3.6	3.1	4.5	3.5	4.3	4.7	48.7
Potter, Amarillo	N	92	34	108	4	Apr.	17	Oct.	24	190	Z	0.5	0.6	0.9	1.0	2.5	3.7	2.6	3.2	2.0	1.4	0.7	0.4	19.6
Presidio, Marfa	N	90	31	106	5	Mar.	20	Oct.	13	238	22	0.4	0.4	0.3	0.6	1.2	3.7	2.6	2.9	2.9	1.6	0.6	0.5	15.9
Presidio, Presidio	N	102	23	117	-5	Mar.	20	Nov.	13	238	Z	0.3	0.4	0.3	0.3	0.6	1.7	1.7	1.9	2.0	1.0	0.4	0.5	10.8
Rains, Emory	29	94	28	110	-14	Mar.	21	Nov.	18	242	Z	2.6	3.4	3.7	4.1	5.7	3.5	2.5	2.1	3.7	4.2	3.6	3.3	42.9
Randall, Canyon	N	92	28	107	1	Apr.	15	Oct.	27	195	Z	0.4	0.6	0.9	0.9	2.4	1.8	2.0	3.1	2.0	1.6	1.0	0.8	18.9
Reagan, Big Lake	N	94	28	109	0	Mar.	28	Nov.	12	229	27	0.6	0.9	1.4	1.5	2.4	3.0	2.0	1.9	3.2	2.2	1.0	1.1	19.2
Real, Prade Ranch	27	92	29	107	0	Mar.	26	Nov.	17	236	19	1.2	1.5	4.5	2.3	3.3	3.9	2.6	3.1	3.1	3.5	1.7	3.7	25.7
Red River, Clarksville	19	96	27	109	-5	Mar.	23	Nov.	12	234	Z	2.3	3.2	0.4	4.3	5.5	1.3	2.9	2.1	3.9	4.5	4.2	0.5	44.9
Reeves, Balmorhea	N	96	43	112	-9	Apr.	2	Nov.	11	226	Z	0.5	0.5	1.3	0.6	1.4	1.2	1.8	2.4	3.0	1.3	0.7	0.5	14.3
Reeves, Pecos	N	99	20	118	-9	Mar.	1	Nov.	12	226	Z	0.4	0.4	0.9	0.4	1.0	4.4	1.2	1.7	2.1	1.1	0.5	0.5	11.0
Refugio, Refugio	29	94	37	106	8	Feb.	14	Dec.	15	304	Z	2.2	2.3	1.6	2.3	3.3	3.4	3.6	3.5	6.7	3.9	3.9	1.7	38.0
Roberts, Miami	N	95	33	111	-15	Apr.	16	Oct.	25	192	26	0.5	1.0	1.0	1.3	3.3	2.9	2.3	2.4	2.0	1.6	1.1	0.5	21.6
Robertson, Franklin	26	96	30	110	-1	Mar.	6	Nov.	29	268	Z	2.7	2.8	2.7	3.6	4.5	2.6	2.0	2.3	4.3	4.0	2.9	2.8	37.5
Rockwall, Rockwall*	N	95	36	110	-7	Mar.	23	Nov.	14	236	Z	2.4	2.4	3.1	4.7	5.2	3.1	2.4	2.5	3.8	3.3	2.5	2.4	36.9
Runnels, Ballinger	N	95	35	118	-9	Mar.	30	Nov.	13	228	Z	1.0	1.3	1.2	1.9	3.4	2.6	1.5	2.5	3.1	2.3	1.3	1.0	23.3
Rusk, Henderson	N	93	18	114	-1	Mar.	11	Nov.	16	250	Z	3.6	3.6	3.8	4.0	5.1	4.3	2.8	3.1	3.6	4.0	4.3	3.9	45.6
Sabine, Hemphill*	6	93	43	108	8	Mar.	21	Nov.	12	236	19	5.2	3.2	5.7	4.8	5.1	4.6	3.4	3.1	3.8	4.5	5.0	5.0	52.5
San Augustine, Broaddus	24	93	35	104	9	Mar.	19	Nov.	12	238	24	4.5	3.9	3.9	3.4	4.8	5.5	3.1	3.1	5.7	4.3	4.1	4.7	48.0
San Jacinto, Coldspring	27	93	35	106	9	Mar.	5	Nov.	21	261	25	3.7	3.3	3.5	3.4	5.5	3.5	2.9	2.9	6.1	3.3	2.0	4.7	48.3
San Patricio, Sinton	N	94	43	105	11	Feb.	14	Dec.	14	303	Z	2.0	2.2	1.2	2.1	4.1	2.8	3.4	3.1	6.1	3.8	2.0	3.7	35.0
San Saba, San Saba	N	96	32	107	-1	Apr.	1	Nov.	14	227	Z	1.1	1.7	2.7	2.4	3.6	3.7	1.6	1.8	3.1	2.1	1.0	1.8	26.3
Schleicher, Eldorado*	27	93	31	112	-10	Mar.	28	Nov.	12	229	27	0.7	0.9	1.1	1.7	2.5	2.5	2.0	2.3	3.5	2.4	0.9	0.6	19.0
Scurry, Snyder	15	93	25	115	-8	Apr.	4	Nov.	4	214	Z	0.6	0.8	0.9	1.7	3.2	2.9	2.0	3.0	3.6	2.8	1.7	0.8	22.2
Shackelford, Albany	N	97	31	115	0	Mar.	30	Nov.	9	224	Z	1.2	1.6	0.9	2.6	4.0	3.0	1.9	3.5	4.5	3.9	4.2	1.3	28.6
Shelby, Center	N	94	33	115	-19	Mar.	17	Nov.	12	240	Z	4.3	4.0	4.1	4.0	5.3	4.4	3.3	2.5	3.3	3.3	4.2	4.7	50.2
Sherman, Stratford	N	92	18	108	-15	Apr.	23	Oct.	22	182	Z	0.3	0.5	0.9	1.2	2.7	2.3	2.8	2.5	2.5	0.9	0.9	0.4	17.2
Smith, Tyler*	N	94	33	108	10	Mar.	7	Nov.	21	259	Z	3.0	3.3	3.5	4.2	5.3	3.7	2.2	1.8	4.1	3.3	3.8	3.7	33.3
Somervell, Glen Rose	27	94	30	108	-7	Apr.	25	Nov.	16	236	27	1.7	2.1	2.7	3.2	2.8	2.5	1.4	2.3	3.5	3.4	3.4	1.8	33.1
Starr, Rio Grande City	N	98	43	115	7	Feb.	16	Dec.	7	314	Z	1.0	1.1	0.5	1.5	3.6	3.0	2.0	1.9	5.2	2.1	1.0	1.3	22.3
Stephens, Breckenridge	N	99	29	111	-7	Apr.	1	Nov.	7	222	Z	1.4	1.5	1.8	2.4	2.9	2.4	1.6	3.0	3.6	3.4	1.7	1.3	27.6
Sterling, Sterling City	27	97	31	112	-2	Apr.	31	Nov.	11	224	27	0.8	0.9	0.9	1.9	2.9	3.0	1.6	2.1	3.8	1.7	2.4	0.8	20.3
Stonewall, Aspermont	29	97	27	117	-8	Mar.	31	Nov.	10	220	29	0.8	1.1	1.3	1.9	3.2	2.2	2.1	2.3	3.6	2.4	1.3	0.8	23.3
Sutton, Sonora	N	96	30	109		Mar.	26	Nov.	16	235	Z	0.8	1.0	1.0	1.9	2.6	2.2	2.1	2.7	3.4	2.7	1.2	0.7	22.4

County and Station	Temp. Length of Record (Yr.)	July Mean Max. (°F)	January Mean Min. (°F)	Highest Record (°F)	Lowest Record (°F)	Last in Spring Mo.	Last in Spring Day	First in Fall Mo.	First in Fall Day	Growing Season Days	Precip. Length of Record (Yr.)	Jan. (in.)	Feb. (in.)	Mar. (in.)	Apr. (in.)	May (in.)	June (in.)	July (in.)	Aug. (in.)	Sept. (in.)	Oct. (in.)	Nov. (in.)	Dec. (in.)	Annual (in.)
Swisher, Tulia	N	91	22	110	-10	Apr.	10	Nov.	1	205	N	0.5	0.7	0.9	1.0	2.4	3.9	2.0	2.6	2.5	1.5	0.8	0.6	19.4
Tarrant, Fort Worth*	N	96	35	108	4	Mar.	26	Nov.	11	230	29	2.0	2.2	2.5	3.6	4.6	3.0	1.8	1.7	2.5	2.6	2.5	2.4	31.3
Taylor, Abilene	N	95	31	110	-9	Mar.	31	Nov.	11	225	N	1.0	1.2	1.4	1.9	3.0	2.9	2.1	2.8	3.2	2.5	1.5	1.0	24.4
Terrell, Sanderson	28	92	29	110	2	Mar.	21	Nov.	13	237	N	0.3	0.6	0.4	1.0	1.6	1.8	1.3	1.8	2.7	1.8	0.7	0.5	14.3
Terry, Brownfield	N	93	24	111	-8	Apr.	10	Nov.	6	206	N	0.5	0.7	0.4	0.9	2.7	3.0	2.4	2.4	2.6	1.7	0.7	0.6	19.0
Throckmorton, Throckmorton	N	96	27	114	-11	Mar.	31	Nov.	2	220	N	1.0	1.5	2.0	2.3	3.5	3.1	2.0	2.6	4.2	2.6	1.4	1.3	27.1
Titus, Mount Pleasant	N	94	29	111	-12	Mar.	23	Nov.	12	233	N	2.8	3.7	4.4	4.5	5.1	4.3	3.4	2.4	3.9	4.2	4.5	3.9	46.8
Tom Green, San Angelo	N	96	31	111	-4	Mar.	25	Nov.	15	235	N	0.8	1.1	0.9	1.7	3.0	2.3	1.1	1.9	3.4	2.4	1.1	0.8	20.5
Travis, Austin	23	95	39	109	-4	Mar.	3	Nov.	28	270	N	1.7	2.2	1.9	3.4	4.8	3.7	2.0	3.1	3.4	3.4	2.4	1.9	31.9
Trinity, Groveton	N	94	36	108	2	Mar.	6	Nov.	21	260	23	3.6	3.2	3.6	3.9	4.8	4.5	3.3	3.1	4.1	3.4	3.9	4.1	44.9
Tyler, Warren	N	93	38	106	1	Mar.	17	Nov.	11	241	N	4.5	4.0	3.9	4.8	6.0	5.8	3.8	3.4	4.5	4.0	4.8	5.8	54.3
Upshur, Gilmer	N	93	30	106	6	Mar.	16	Nov.	16	245	N	2.9	3.7	3.6	4.8	4.7	3.6	2.8	2.3	4.0	3.8	4.4	4.0	45.2
Upton, McCamey	N	95	31	113	-4	Mar.	26	Nov.	12	232	N	0.4	0.6	0.4	0.9	1.7	1.5	1.0	1.6	2.8	2.2	0.7	0.6	14.8
Uvalde, Uvalde	N	96	36	111	-2	Mar.	10	Nov.	21	255	N	1.1	1.4	1.1	2.3	3.3	2.8	1.9	2.7	2.8	3.0	1.3	1.1	24.8
Val Verde, Del Rio	N	96	39	112	10	Feb.	12	Dec.	9	300	N	0.6	1.0	0.7	2.0	2.0	2.1	1.9	1.5	2.8	2.2	0.9	0.6	18.2
Van Zandt, Wills Point	N	95	32	113	-2	Mar.	16	Nov.	27	250	N	2.7	3.2	3.6	4.7	5.4	4.2	2.2	2.7	3.9	4.2	3.6	3.3	43.0
Victoria, Victoria	N	94	43	107	2	Feb.	19	Dec.	6	290	N	2.2	2.0	1.6	2.4	4.5	4.9	3.3	3.0	5.6	3.5	3.6	2.0	37.4
Walker, Huntsville	15	94	38	107	9	Mar.	7	Nov.	10	265	15	3.6	3.1	2.1	3.5	5.2	4.2	2.4	3.3	5.0	3.6	4.2	3.8	45.0
Waller, Hempstead*	N	95	38	107	13	Feb.	28	Dec.	4	283	N	2.8	2.9	2.1	3.9	4.7	3.6	2.0	2.4	4.6	4.0	3.2	3.0	38.2
Ward, Monahans	N	96	41	120	-9	Apr.	1	Nov.	10	223	N	0.4	0.6	0.4	0.7	1.8	1.4	1.2	1.4	2.4	1.4	0.6	0.5	12.7
Washington, Brenham	N	96	43	110	1	Mar.	3	Nov.	26	277	N	3.1	2.9	2.1	3.3	5.2	4.3	2.0	2.6	4.8	3.6	3.9	3.2	41.4
Webb, Laredo	27	99	43	110	13	Feb.	7	Dec.	26	322	23	0.8	1.0	0.5	1.6	2.7	3.1	1.4	2.5	3.3	2.5	1.1	0.9	21.4
Wharton, Danevang	N	92	41	108	7	Mar.	5	Nov.	1	266	N	2.8	2.6	2.0	2.5	4.9	4.7	3.6	3.6	5.9	3.9	3.1	2.7	42.3
Wheeler, Shamrock	27	95	22	113	-8	Mar.	7	Nov.	11	208	27	0.4	0.8	1.8	3.0	3.5	3.4	2.0	2.6	2.8	1.8	1.0	0.5	22.1
Wichita, Wichita Falls	N	97	28	117	-8	Mar.	27	Nov.	7	229	N	1.0	1.2	2.2	3.0	4.1	3.5	1.7	2.5	3.6	2.7	1.5	1.3	28.9
Wilbarger, Vernon	N	97	25	119	0	Mar.	31	Nov.	11	221	N	0.9	1.2	1.8	2.3	3.8	2.9	2.0	2.5	3.6	2.6	1.4	0.8	25.7
Willacy, Raymondville	N	96	46	112	14	Feb.	6	Dec.	24	331	N	1.5	1.6	2.3	1.5	3.1	3.3	1.7	3.1	5.8	2.2	1.3	2.1	27.6
Williamson, Taylor	28	96	34	112	-5	Mar.	11	Nov.	1	258	28	2.0	2.5	2.3	2.9	4.7	3.6	2.0	2.3	4.2	3.6	2.7	2.1	34.4
Wilson, Floresville	N	96	36	108	3	Mar.	24	Nov.	8	280	N	1.9	1.9	1.2	2.4	3.4	2.9	1.7	2.3	3.6	2.7	2.0	1.6	29.4
Winkler, Wink	N	97	28	117	-14	Mar.	3	Nov.	6	219	N	0.3	0.4	0.6	0.7	1.0	1.9	2.3	2.0	2.3	1.5	0.6	0.5	12.6
Wise, Bridgeport	14	94	30	115	-8	Mar.	31	Nov.	18	220	14	1.5	1.9	2.6	3.1	5.3	3.5	3.0	2.5	3.6	3.3	2.0	1.5	32.6
Wood, Mineola*	N	91	31	107	-12	Apr.	17	Nov.	1	246	N	3.1	3.0	4.0	4.7	4.9	3.4	2.6	2.3	4.8	4.3	3.7	3.6	45.0
Yoakum, Plains	N	96	26	112	-8	Apr.	15	Oct.	31	199	N	0.4	0.7	0.6	1.0	2.1	2.4	2.1	2.0	2.6	1.3	0.7	1.4	17.7
Young, Graham	N	99	43	112	16	Apr.	2	Nov.	4	216	N	1.3	1.6	1.9	2.8	4.5	3.4	2.1	2.5	4.2	3.1	1.9	0.9	30.6
Zapata, Zapata	27	99	43	112	11	Feb.	14	Dec.	15	304	12	0.8	1.1	0.6	1.4	2.4	2.5	1.6	1.7	4.3	1.6	1.0	0.8	19.7
Zavala, Crystal City	N	97	42	109	11	Feb.	24	Dec.	1	280	N	0.9	1.2	0.8	1.8	2.9	2.8	1.6	1.9	2.7	2.5	1.1	0.8	21.0

Recreation

Information about recreational opportunities in state and national parks and forests and at U.S. Army Corps of Engineers Lakes, a list of a few of the festivals and celebrations in individual towns and communities across the state, as well as information on hunting and fishing opportunities and regulations is found in the following pages. Recreation and special events in each county are also mentioned in the Counties chapter.

Texas' State Parks

Texas' expanding system of state parks offers contrasting attractions — mountains and canyons, arid deserts and lush forests, spring-fed streams, sandy dunes, saltwater surf and fascinating historic sites.

The state park information below was provided by the **Texas Parks and Wildlife Department** (TP&WD). Additional information and brochures on individual parks are available from the Department's Austin headquarters, 4200 Smith School Rd., Austin 78744; 1-800-792-1112. On the Internet: http://www.tpwd.state.tx.us/park/parklist.htm

The TP&WD's **Central Reservation Center** can take reservations for almost all parks that accept reservations. Exceptions are Indian Lodge and the Texas State Railroad and facilities not operated by the TP&WD. Call the center during the usual business hours at (512) 389-8900. The TDD line is (512) 389-8915.

The **Gold Conservation Passport**, currently costing $50 per year, allows free entrance for member and all passengers in member's vehicle to state parks, as well as other benefits. For further information, contact TP&WD at numbers or address above.

Texas State Parklands Passport is a windshield decal granting free or discounted entrance to state parks for senior citizens and disabled veterans. Available at state parks with proper identification. Details can be obtained at numbers or address above.

The following information is a brief glimpse of what each park has to offer. Refer to the chart on pages 124-125 for a more complete list of available activities and facilities. Fees for entrance range from $1 to $5 per person. There are also fees for tours and some activities. Call the central information number listed above before you go. Road abbreviations used in this list are: IH - interstate highway, US - U.S. Highway, TX - state highway, FM - farm-to-market road, RM - ranch-to-market road, PR - park road.

List of State Parks

Abilene State Park, 16 miles southwest of Abilene on FM 89 and PR 32 in Taylor County, consists of 621.4 acres that were deeded by the City of Abilene in 1933. A part of the **official Texas longhorn herd** and a bison are located in the park. Large groves of pecan trees that once shaded bands of Comanches now shade visitors at picnic tables. Activities include camping and hiking; facilities include a swimming pool and screened shelters. In addition to **Lake Abilene, Buffalo Gap**, the original Taylor County seat (1878) and one of the early frontier settlements, is nearby. Buffalo Gap was on the **Western**, or **Goodnight-Loving, Trail**, over which pioneer Texas cattlemen drove herds to railheads in Kansas.

Acton State Historical Park is a .006-acre cemetery plot in Hood County where **Davy Crockett's** second wife, Elizabeth, was buried in 1860. It is six miles east of Granbury on US 77 to FM 208, then 2 miles south on FM 208 to Acton then to FM 1190. Nearby attractions include Cleburne, Dinosaur Valley and Lake Whitney state parks.

Adm. Nimitz Museum and Historical Center is 7 acres in downtown Fredericksburg. First established as a state agency in 1969 by Texas Legislature; transferred to TP&WD in 1981. Named for **Adm. Chester W. Nimitz** of World War II fame, it includes the **Pacific War Museum** in the **Nimitz Steamboat Hotel**; the **Japanese Garden of Peace**, donated by the people of Japan; and the **Historic Walk of the Pacific War**, featuring planes, boats, weapons and equipment from World War II. Nearby is **Kerrville**

State Park.

Atlanta State Park is 1,475 acres located 11 miles northwest of Atlanta on FM 1154 in Cass County; adjacent to **Wright Patman Dam and Reservoir.** Land acquired from the U.S. Army in 1954 by license to 2004 with option to renew to 2054. Camping and hiking in pine forests or water activities, such as boating, fishing, lake swimming. Nearby are historic town of **Jefferson and Caddo Lake and Daingerfield state parks.**

Balmorhea State Park is 45.9 acres four miles southwest of Balmorhea on TX 17 between Balmorhea and Toyahvale in Reeves County. Deeded in 1934-35 by private owners and Reeves Co. Water Imp. Dist. No. 1 and built by the Civilian Conservation Corps (CCC). Swimming pool fed by artesian **San Solomon Springs**; also provides water to **pupfish refuge** in park. Motel rooms available at **San Solomon Springs Courts**. Wildlife includes **deer, javelina, ground squirrel, hawks, barn swallows, roadrunners.** Nearby are city of Pecos, **Fort Davis National Historic Site, Davis Mountains State Park and McDonald Observatory.**

Barton Warnock Environmental Education Center consists of 99.2 acres in Brewster County. Originally built by the Lajitas Foundation in 1982 as the Lajitas Museum Desert Gardens, the TP&WD purchased it in 1990 and renamed it for Texas botanist Dr. Barton Warnock. The center is also the eastern entrance station to **Big Bend Ranch State Park** (see below). Self-guiding museum tour. Bus tours of Big Bend Ranch State Park operate from center.

Bastrop State Park is 3,503.7 acres one mile east of Bastrop on TX 21 or from TX 71. The park was acquired by deeds from the City of Bastrop and private owners in 1933-35; additional acreage acquired in 1979. Site of famous **"Lost Pines,"** isolated region of loblolly pine and hardwoods. **Swimming pool, cabins** and **lodge** are among facilities. Fishing in **Lake Bastrop**. Golf course adjacent to park. **State capitol** at Austin 30 miles away; 13-mile drive through forest leads to **Buescher State Park.**

Battleship Texas State Historic Site (see **San Jacinto Battleground State Historic Site and Battleship Texas**)

Bentsen-Rio Grande Valley State Park, a scenic park, is along the Rio Grande five miles west of Mission off FM 2062 in Hidalgo County. The 587.7 acres of **subtropical resaca woodlands and brushlands** were acquired from private owners in 1944. Park is excellent base from which to tour **Lower Rio Grande Valley** of Texas and adjacent **Mexico;** most attractions within an hour's drive. One hiking trail leads to Rio Grande; another takes you through wilderness. They provide chance to study unique plants, animals and birds of park. Many species of birds unique to southern United States found here, including **pauraque, groove-billed ani, green kingfisher, rose-throated becard and tropical parula.** Park also one of last natural refuges in Texas for cats such as **ocelot** and **jaguarundi.** Trees include **cedar elm, anaqua, ebony** and **Mexican ash.** Nearby are **Santa Ana National Wildlife Refuge** and **Sabal Palm Sanctuary.**

Big Bend Ranch State Park, 269,713.9 acres of **Chihuahuan Desert wilderness** in Brewster and Presidio counties, was purchased from private owners in 1988. The purchase more than doubled the size of the state park system, which comprised at that time 220,000 acres. Eastern entrance at Barton Warnock Environmental Education Center one mile east of Lajitas on FM 170; western entrance is at **Fort Leaton State Historical Park** four miles east of Presidio on FM 170. The area includes **extinct volcanoes**, several **waterfalls**, two **mountain**

ranges, at least **11 rare species of plants and animals,** and **90 major archaeological sites.** There is little development; there is limited vehicular access and wilderness backpacking ahd hiking access. There are scheduled **bus tours** departing from **Barton Warnock Environmental Educational Center** (see above). Call for schedule. Picnicking, fishing and swimming are also allowed. Part of **state longhorn cattle herd** is in park.

Big Spring State Park is 382 acres located on FM 700 within the city limits of Big Spring in Howard County. Both city and park were named for a natural spring that was replaced by an artificial one. The park was deeded by the City of Big Spring in 1934 and 1935. Drive to top of **Scenic Mountain** provides panoramic view of surrounding country and look at **prairie dog colony.** The "big spring," nearby in a city park, provided watering place for herds of bison, antelope and wild horses. Used extensively also as campsite for early Indians, explorers and settlers.

Blanco State Park is 104.6 acres along the Blanco River four blocks south of Blanco's town square in Blanco County. The land was deeded by private owners in 1933. Park area was used as campsite by early explorers and settlers. Fishing for **winter rainbow trout, perch, catfish** and **bass. LBJ Ranch** and **LBJ State Historical Park, Pedernales Falls** and **Guadalupe River** state parks are nearby.

Bonham State Park is a 261-acre park located two miles southeast of Bonham on TX 78, then two miles southeast on FM 271 in Fannin County. It includes a 65-acre lake, **rolling prairies and woodlands.** The land was acquired in 1933 and 1934 from the city of Bonham; originally constructed by CCC. Swimming beach, camping, mountain-bike trail, lighted fishing pier, boating, boat rentals. **Sam Rayburn Memorial Library** in Bonham. **Sam Rayburn Home** and **Valley Lake** nearby.

Brazos Bend State Park in Fort Bend County, seven miles west of Rosharon off FM 1462 on FM 762, approximately 28 miles south of Houston. The 4,897-acre park was purchased from private owners in 1976-77. **George Observatory. Observation platform** for spotting and photographing the **270 species of birds and 23 species of mammals** that frequent the park. Interpretive and educational programs every weekend. Backpacking, camping, hiking, biking, fishing.

Buescher State Park, a scenic area, is 1,016.7 acres 2 miles northwest of Smithville off TX 71 then FM 153 in Bastrop County. Acquired between 1933 and 1936, about one-third deeded by private owner; heirs donated a third; balance from City of Smithville. **El Camino Real (King's Highway)** once ran near park; road connected **San Antonio de Bexar** with **Spanish missions in East Texas.** Parkland was part of **Stephen F. Austin's colonial grant.** Some **250 species of birds** can be seen. **Camping, fishing, hiking.** Scenic park road connects with **Bastrop State Park** through **Lost Pines** area.

Caddo Lake State Park, north of Karnack one mile off TX 43 to FM 2198 in Harrison County, consists of 7,090.23 acres (including adjoining wildlife management area) along **Cypress Bayou,** which runs into Caddo Lake. A scenic area, it was acquired from private owners in 1933-37. Nearby Karnack is childhood home of Mrs. Lyndon B. Johnson. Close by is old city of **Jefferson,** famous as commercial center of Northeast Texas during last half of 19th century. Caddo Indian legend attributes formation of Caddo Lake to **earthquake.** Lake originally only natural lake of any size in state; dam added in 1914 for flood control; new dam replaced old one in 1971. **Cypress trees, American lotus** and **lily pads,** as well as **71 species of fish,** predominate in lake. **Nutria, beaver, mink, squirrel, armadillo, alligator** and **turtle** abound. Originally constructed by CCC. Activities include camping, hiking, swimming, fishing, boating. Screened shelters, cabins.

Caddoan Mounds State Historical Park in Cherokee County six miles southwest of Alto on TX 21. Total of 93.8 acres acquired in 1975 by condemnation. Open for day visits only, park offers exhibits and interpretive trails through reconstructed **Caddo dwellings and ceremonial areas,** including two temple mounds, a burial mound and a village area of people who lived in region for 500 years beginning about A.D. 800. Nearby are **Jim Hogg State**

Water sports are popular on lakes in Texas' state parks, as at Joe Pool Lake in Cedar Hill State Park, pictured here. Dallas Morning News photo by Erich Schlegel.

Historical Park, Mission Tejas State Historical Park and **Texas State Railroad.**

Caprock Canyons State Park, 3.5 miles north of Quitaque off RM 1065 and TX 86 in Briscoe, Floyd and Hall counties, has 15,160.6 acres. Purchased in 1975. Scenic escarpment's **canyons** provided camping areas for **Indians of Folsom culture** more than 10,000 years ago. **Mesquite and cacti in the badlands give way to tall grasses, cottonwood** and **plum thickets** in the bottomlands. Wildlife includes **aoudad sheep, coyote, bobcat, porcupine, ringtail** and **fox.** Activities include scenic drive, camping, hiking, mountain-bike riding, rock climbing, horse riding and horse camping. About half of a planned 64.25-mile rail-to-trail conversion (hike, bike and equestrian trail built on old railroad right of way) is open to public from Quitaque to South Plains.

Casa Navarro State Historical Park, on .6 acre at corner of S. Laredo and W. Nueva streets in downtown San Antonio, was acquired by donation from San Antonio Conservation Society Foundation in 1975. Has furnished **Navarro House** complex built about 1848, home of the statesman, rancher and Texas patriot **José Antonio Navarro.** Guided tours; exhibits.

Cedar Hill State Park is an urban park on 1,810.6 acres 15 miles southwest of Dallas via US 67 and FM 1382 on **Joe Pool Reservoir.** Camping mostly in wooded areas; reservations recommended. Fishing from two lighted jetties and a perch pond for children. Swimming, boating and picnicking popular. Animals include **bobcat, coyote, fox squirrel, armadillo** and **raccoon.** Vegetation includes **mesquite** and **juniper** trees as well as several sections of **tall-grass prairie.** Remnants of **19th-century Penn Farm** house exhibits; monthly guided tours offered.

Choke Canyon State Park consists of two units, South Shore and Calliham, located on 26,000-acre **Choke Canyon Reservoir.** Park acquired in 1981 in a 50-year agreement among Bureau of Reclamation, City of Corpus Christi and Nueces River Authority. Thickets of **mesquite** and **blackbrush acacia** predominate, supporting populations of **javelina, coyote, skunk** and **alligator,** as well as the **crested caracara.** The 385-acre South Shore Unit is located in Live Oak County 3.5 miles west of Three Rivers on TX 72. The Calliham Unit, containing 1,100 acres, is located in McMullen County 12 miles west of Three Rivers, also on TX 72. Fish in the reservoir include several varieties of **sunfish** and **catfish,** along with **bass, carp, drum** and **gar.** Both units offer camping, picnicking, boating, fishing, lake swimming, and baseball and volleyball areas. The Calliham Unit also has a hiking trail, wildlife educational center, screened shelters, rentable **gym and kitchen, sports complex,** including swimming pool and tennis, volleyball, shuffleboard and basketball courts. Equestrian camping area.

Christmas Bay State Park, located on Follet's Island 7 miles northeast of Freeport on San Luis Pass Road, contains 484.8 acres, including 1.5 miles of Gulf frontage and 15,000 feet of water frontage on Christmas and Drum bays. Park, acquired in 1984 by warranty deed and deed of gift, the park preserves **estuarial and coastal marshes** and is home to **migratory and resident waterfowl and shore birds**. Bird watching, swimming, fishing and primitive camping are enjoyed by visitors, but no facilities are provided.

Cleburne State Park is a 528.8-acre park located 10 miles southwest of Cleburne via US 67 and PR 21 in Johnson County with 116-acre spring-fed lake; acquired from the City of Cleburne, Johnson County and private owners in 1935 and 1936. **Oak, elm, mesquite, cedar** and **redbud** cover white rocky hills. Bluebonnets in spring. Nearby are Fossil Rim Wildlife Center and **dinosaur tracks** in Paluxy River at **Dinosaur Valley State Park**.

Colorado Bend State Park, a 5,328.3-acre facility, is located 28 miles west of Lampasas in Lampasas and San Saba counties. Access is from Lampasas to Bend on FM 580 west, then follow signs (access road subject to flooding). Park site was purchased partly in 1984, with balance acquired in 1987. Public use is primitive at this time; primitive camping, river fishing, some hiking, biking and picnicking. Plans include restoration of parts of it to its natural condition. Rare and endangered species here include **golden-cheeked warbler, black-capped vireo** and **bald eagle**. Primitive camping and river fishing. Visit scenic **Gorman Falls** by guided tour arranged in advance.

Confederate Reunion Grounds State Historical Park, located in Limestone County on the Navasota River, is 77.1 acres in size. Acquired 1983 by deed from Joseph E. Johnston Camp No. 94 CSA. Entrance is 6 miles south of Mexia on TX 14, then 2.5 miles west on FM 2705. **Historic buildings**, two **scenic footbridges** span creek; hiking trail. Nearby are **Fort Parker State Park** and **Old Fort Parker State Historical Park**.

Cooper Lake State Park, comprises 3,026 acres three miles southeast of Cooper in Delta and Hopkins counties. Two units, Doctors Creek and South Sulphur, adjoin 19,300-surface-acre Cooper Lake. Fishing, boating, camping, picnicking, swimming. Screened shelters and cabins. Access to Doctors Creek Unit is via TX 24 east from Commerce to Cooper, then east on TX 154 to FM 1529 to Cooper. To South Sulphur Unit, take IH 30 to Exit 122 west of Sulphur Springs to TX 19, then TX 71, then FM 3505.

Copano Bay State Fishing Pier, a 5.9-acre park, is located 5 miles north of Rockport on TX 35 in Aransas County. Acquired by transfer of jurisdiction from state highway department in 1967. Picnicking, saltwater fishing, boating and swimming. Operated by leased concession.

Copper Breaks State Park, 12 miles south of Quanah on TX 6 in Hardeman County, was acquired by purchase from private owner in 1970. Park features rugged scenic beauty on 1,888.7 acres, a 70-acre lake, **grass-covered mesas** and juniper breaks. Nearby **medicine mounds** were important ceremonial sites of Comanche Indians. Nearby **Pease River** was site of 1860 battle in which **Cynthia Ann Parker** was recovered from Comanches. Part of **official Texas longhorn herd** maintained at park. Abundant wildlife. Nature, hiking and equestrian trails; natural and historical exhibits; summer programs; horseback riding; camping, equestrian camping.

Daingerfield State Park, off TX 49 and PR 17 southeast of Daingerfield in Morris County, is a 550.9-acre recreational area that includes an 80-surface-acre lake; deeded in 1935 by private owners. This area is center of iron industry in Texas; nearby is Lone Star Steel Co. In spring, **dogwood, redbuds** and **wisteria** bloom; in fall, brilliant foliage of **sweetgum, oaks** and **maples** contrast with dark green pines. Campsites, lodge and cabins.

Davis Mountains State Park is 2,677.9 acres in Jeff Davis County, 4 miles northwest of town of Fort Davis via TX 118 and PR 3. The scenic area, near **Fort Davis,** was deeded in 1933-1937 by private owners. **First European, Antonio de Espejo**, came to area in 1583. Extremes of altitude produce both **plains grasslands and piñon-juniper-oak woodlands. Montezuma quail**, rare in Texas, visit park. Scenic drives and hiking trails. **Indian Lodge,** built by the Civilian Conservation Corps during the early 1930s, has 39 rooms, restaurant and swimming pool (reservations: 915-426-3254). Four-mile hiking trail leads to **Fort Davis National Historic Site**. Other nearby points of interest include **McDonald Observatory** and 74-mile scenic loop through **Davis Mountains**. **Davis Mountains State Park** located halfway between **Carlsbad Caverns** and **Big Bend National Park**. Nearby are scenic **Limpia, Madera, Musquiz** and **Keesey canyons; Camino del Rio;** ghost town of **Shafter; Big Bend National Park; Big Bend Ranch State Park; Fort Davis National Historic Site;** and **Fort Leaton State Historical Park**.

Devil's River State Natural Area comprises 19,988.6 acres in Val Verde County, 22 miles off US 277, about 65 miles north of Del Rio on graded road. It is an **ecological and archaeological crossroads**. Ecologically, it is in a **transitional area between the Edwards Plateau, the Trans-Pecos desert and the South Texas brush country**. Archaeological studies suggest occupation and/or use by cultures from both east and west. Camping, hiking. Canyon and pictograph-site tours by prearrangement only. Park accessible by reservation only. **Dolan Falls**, owned by The Nature Conservancy of Texas and open only to its members, is nearby.

Devil's Sinkhole State Natural Area, comprising 1,800 acres about 6 miles northeast of Rocksprings in Edwards County, is a **vertical cavern**. The sinkhole, discovered by Anglo settlers in 1867, is a registered **National Natural Landmark**. The cavern opening is about 40 by 60 feet, with a vertical drop of about 140 feet. Minimal development. Picnicking. Bats can be viewed in summer as they exit the cave at dusk. There is no access to the cave itself. Access to the park is made by contacting **Kickapoo Cavern State Park** to arrange a tour.

Dinosaur Valley State Park, located off US 67 just south of Glen Rose in Somervell County, is a 1,524.72-acre scenic park. Land was acquired from private owners in 1969 and 1973. **Dinosaur tracks** in bed of Paluxy River and two full-scale dinosaur models, originally created for New York World's Fair in 1964-65, on display. Part of state **longhorn herd** is in park.

Eisenhower Birthplace State Historical Park is 5.99 acres off US 75 in Denison, Grayson County. The property was acquired in 1958 from the Sid Richardson Foundation. Restoration of home of Pres. Dwight David Eisenhower includes furnishings of period and some personal effects of Gen. Eisenhower, including a crank-type telephone with personal greetings from **"Ike."** Guided tour; call for days and hours available. Town of Denison established on **Butterfield Overland Mail** Route in 1858.

Eisenhower State Park, 457 acres five miles northwest of Denison via US 75 to TX 91N to FM 1310 on the shores of **Lake Texoma** in Grayson County, was acquired by an Army lease in 1954. Named for the **34th U.S. president, Dwight David Eisenhower.** First Anglo settlers came to area in 1835 and 1836; **Fort Johnson** was established in area in 1840; **Colbert's Ferry** established on Red River in 1853 and operated until 1931. Remnants of **tall-grass prairie** exist. Hiking, camping, picnicking, fishing.

Enchanted Rock State Natural Area is 1,643.5 acres on Big Sandy Creek 18 miles north of Fredericksburg on

RM 965 on the line between Gillespie and Llano counties. Acquired in 1978 by The Nature Conservancy of Texas; state acquired from TNCT in 1984. Enchanted Rock is huge **pink granite boulder** rising 425 feet above ground and covering 640 acres. It is **second-largest batholith** (underground rock formation uncovered by erosion) in the United States. Indians believed **ghost fires** flickered at top and were awed by weird creaking and groaning, which geologists say resulted from rock's heating and expanding by day, cooling and contracting at night. Enchanted Rock is a **National Natural Landmark** and is on the **National Register of Historic Places**. Activities include hiking, geological study, technical **rock climbing** and star gazing.

Fairfield Lake State Park is 1,460 acres adjacent to Lake Fairfield, 6 miles northeast of the city of Fairfield off FM 2570 and FM 3285 in Freestone County. It was leased from Texas Utilities in 1971-72. Surrounding, predominantly oak, woods offer sanctuary for many species of birds and wildlife. Extensive schedule of tours, seminars and other activities.

Falcon State Park is 572.6 acres located 15 miles north of Roma off US 83 and FM 2098 at southern end of Falcon Reservoir in Starr and Zapata counties. Park leased from International Boundary and Water Commission in 1949. Gently rolling hills covered by **mesquite, huisache, wild olive, ebony, cactus**. Excellent **birding** and **fishing**. Nearby are **Mexico**, **Fort Ringgold** in Rio Grande City and historic city of **Roma**. **Bentsen-Rio Grande Valley State Park** is 65 miles away.

Fannin Battleground State Historical Park, 9 miles east of Goliad in Goliad County off US 59 to PR 27. The 13.6-acre park was acquired by legislative enactment in 1965. At this site on March 20, 1836, **Col. J. W. Fannin** surrendered to Mexican **Gen. José Urrea** after **Battle of Coleto**; 342 massacred and 28 escaped near what is now **Goliad State Historical Park**. Near Fannin site is **Gen. Zaragoza's Birthplace** and partially restored **Mission Nuestra Señora del Espíritu Santo de Zúñiga**. (See also **Goliad State Historical Park** in this list.)

Fanthorp Inn State Historical Park includes a historic cedar-log structure and 1.4 acres in Anderson, county seat of Grimes County on TX 90. Acquired by purchase in 1977 from Edward Buffington and opened to the public in 1987. Inn records report visits from many prominent civic and military leaders, including **Sam Houston, Anson Jones, Ulysses S. Grant** and generals **Robert E. Lee** and **Stonewall Jackson**. Originally built in 1834, it has been restored to its 1850 use a family home and travelers' hotel. Tours available. Call TP&WD for stagecoach-ride schedule. No dining or overnight facilities.

Fort Griffin State Historical Park is 506.2 acres 15 miles north of Albany off US 283 in Shackelford County. The state was deeded the land by the county in 1935. Portion of **official state longhorn herd** resides in park. On bluff overlooking townsite of **Fort Griffin** and **Clear Fork of Brazos River** valley are partially restored ruins of **Old Fort Griffin**, restored bakery, replicas of enlisted men's huts. Fort constructed in 1867, deactivated 1881. Camping, hiking. Albany annually holds **"Fandangle"** musical show in commemoration of frontier times. Nearby are **Albany** with restored courthouse square, **Abilene and Possum Kingdom State Park**.

Fort Lancaster State Historical Park, 81.6-acres located about 8 miles east of Sheffield on IH 10 then TX 290 and paved access road in Crockett County. Acquired in 1968 by deed from Crockett County; Henry Meadows donated 41 acres in 1975. **Fort Lancaster** established Aug. 20, 1855, to guard San Antonio-El Paso Road and protect movement of supplies and immigrants from Indian hostilities. Site of part of Camel Corps experiment. Fort abandoned March 19, 1861, after Texas seceded from Union. Exhibits on history, natural history and archaeology; nature trail, picnicking. Day use only.

Fort Leaton State Historical Park, 4 miles southeast of Presidio in Presidio County on FM 170, was acquired in 1967 from private owners. Consists of 17.5 acres, 5 of which are on site of **pioneer trading post**. In 1848, **Ben Leaton** built fortified adobe trading post known as Fort Leaton near present Presidio. Ben Leaton died in 1851. Guided tours; exhibits trace history, natural history and

Fort McKavett, built in the 1850s near present-day Menard, welcomes visitors to its partially restored buildings. Photo courtesy Texas Parks &Wildlife Dept.

archaeological history of area. Serves as western entrance to **Big Bend Ranch State Park**.

Fort McKavett State Historical Park, 81.94 acres acquired from 1967 through the mid-1970s from Fort McKavett Restoration, Inc., Menard County and private individuals, is located 23 miles west of Menard off US 190 and RM 864. Originally called **Camp San Saba**, the fort was built by War Department in 1852 to protect frontier settlers and travelers on Upper El Paso Road from Indians. Camp later renamed for **Capt. Henry McKavett**, killed at Battle of Monterrey, Sept. 21, 1846. A **Buffalo Soldier post**. Fort abandoned March 1859; reoccupied April 1, 1868. After Indian hostilities toward white settlers waned, fort no longer needed; abandoned June 30, 1883. Once called by Gen. Wm. T. Sherman, "the prettiest post in Texas." More than 25 restored buildings, ruins of many others. Interpretive exhibits. Day use only.

Fort Parker State Park includes 1,458.8 acres, including 758.78 land acres and 700-acre lake between Mexia and Groesbeck off TX 14 in Limestone County. Named for the former private fort built near present park in 1836, the site was acquired from private owners and the City of Mexia 1935-1937. Boating, fishing, swimming, canoeing, camping, picnicking. Nearby is **Old Fort Parker State Historical Park**.

Fort Richardson State Historical Park, located one-half mile south of Jacksboro off US 281 in Jack County, contains 396.1 acres. Acquired in 1968 from City of Jacksboro. Fort founded in 1866, northernmost of line of federal forts established after Civil War for protection from Indians; originally named **Fort Jacksboro**. In April 1867 it was abandoned for site 20 miles farther north; on Nov. 19, 1867, made permanent post at Jacksboro and named for **Israel Richardson**, who was fatally wounded at Battle of Antietam. Expeditions sent from Fort Richardson arrested Indians responsible for **Salt Creek Massacre** in 1871 and fought Comanches in **Palo Duro Canyon**. Fort abandoned again in May 1878.

Franklin Mountains State Park, created by an act of the legislature in 1979 to protect the mountain range as a wilderness preserve and acquired by TP&WD in 1981, comprises 23,867.2 acres in El Paso County. It is the **largest urban park in the nation**. It includes virtually an entire **Chihuahuan Desert mountain range**, with an elevation of 7,192 feet at the summit. Located completely within the city limits of El Paso, the park is habitat for many Chihuahuan Desert plants including **sotol, lechuguilla, ocotillo, cholla** and **barrel cactus**, as well as **mule deer, fox** and an occasional **cougar**. Contains remnants of one of the few operating **tin mines** in the United States. Pedestrian access for day-use activities such as hiking, nature study and picnicking is permitted. Has multi-use trails. Primitive camping allowed. Most of the site is undeveloped; vehicular traffic is prohibited on dirt roads.

Fulton Mansion State Historic Structure is 3.5 miles north of Rockport off TX 35 in Aransas County. The 2.3 acre-property was acquired by purchase from private

Parks text continues on page 126.

☆ Texas State Parks ☆

Park/†Type of Park/Special Features	NEAREST TOWN	Day Use Only	Historic Site/Museum	Exhibit/Interpretive Center	Restrooms	Showers	Trailer Dump Stn.	††Camping	Screened Shelters	Cabins	Group Facilities	Nature Trail	Hiking Trail	Picnicking	Boat Ramp	Fishing	Swimming	Water Skiing	Miscellaneous
Abilene SP	BUFFALO GAP				★	★	★	18	★		BG		★	★			☆	★	L
Acton SHP (Grave of Davy Crockett's wife)	GRANBURY	★	★																
Admiral Nimitz Museum SHP	FREDERICKSBURG	★	★	★	★									★					
Atlanta SP	ATLANTA				★	★	★	23			DG	★	★	★	★	★	☆	☆	☆	
Balmorhea SP (San Solomon Springs Courts)	BALMORHEA				★	★	★	★	19			DG			★			★		I
Barton Warnock Environmental Education Ctr.	TERLINGUA	★		★	★														
Bastrop SP	BASTROP				★	★	★	19		★	BG		★				☆	★	G
Battleship Texas HS (At San Jacinto Battleground)	DEER PARK	★	★	★															
Bentsen-Rio Grande Valley SP	MISSION				★	★	★	15			BG	★	★	★	★		☆		
Big Bend Ranch SNA (North of Hwy. 170)	PRESIDIO							1			NG	★	★	★					B1, L
Big Bend Ranch SNA (South of Hwy. 170)	PRESIDIO							1						★			☆	☆	
Big Spring SP	BIG SPRING			★	★			2			BG	★		★					
Blanco SP	BLANCO				★	★	★	23	★		DG		★	★			☆	☆	
Bonham SP	BONHAM				★	★	★	19			BG		★	★	★	★	☆		B1
Brazos Bend SP (George Observatory)	RICHMOND			★	★	★	★	4	★		DG	★	★	★		★			B1, B2
Buescher SP	SMITHVILLE				★	★	★	19	★		BG		★	★			☆	☆	
Caddo Lake SP	KARNACK			★	★	★	★	20	★	★	BG	★	★	★	★	★	☆	☆	
Caddoan Mounds SHP	ALTO	★	★	★	★							★							
Caprock Canyons SP	QUITAQUE			★	★	★	★	10			BG	★	★	★	★	★	☆		B1, E
Casa Navarro SHP	SAN ANTONIO	★	★	★	★														
Cedar Hill SP	DALLAS				★	★	★	16			DG		★	★	★	★	★	☆	B1
Choke Canyon SP, Calliham Unit	CALLIHAM				★	★	★	12	★		BG	★		★	★	★	★	☆	
Choke Canyon SP, South Shore Unit	THREE RIVERS				★	★	★	18			DG		★	★	★	★	☆	☆	B1
Christmas Bay SP (Undeveloped Gulf Beach)	LA PORTE							1						☆		☆	☆		
Cleburne SP	CLEBURNE				★	★	★	23	★		BG	★	★	★	★	★	☆		
Colorado Bend SP (Cave Tours)	BEND				★			1				★	★	★	★	★	☆		B1
Confederate Reunion Grounds SHP	MEXIA		★	★	★			1			BG		★	★			☆		
Cooper Lake SP (Doctors Creek Unit)	COOPER				★	★	★	4	★		DG	★	★	★	★	★	★	☆	
Cooper Lake SP (South Sulphur Unit)	SULPHUR SPRINGS				★	★	★	21	★	★	DG	★	★	★	★	★	★	☆	B1, E
Copano Bay SFP ▲	FULTON													★	★	★			
Copper Breaks SP	QUANAH			★	★	★	★	14			BG	★	★	★	★	★	☆		B1, E, L
Daingerfield SP	DAINGERFIELD				★	★	★	20		★	BG	★	★	★	★	★	☆		
Davis Mountains SP (Indian Lodge)	FORT DAVIS		★		★	★	★	13			DG	★	★						I
Devils River SNA (Use by reservation only)	DEL RIO							1			BG								B1
Devil's Sinkhole SNA	ROCKSPRINGS					(No access to cavern. Tours of SNA by special request only.)													
Dinosaur Valley SP (Dinosaur Footprints)	GLEN ROSE			★	★	★	★	17			DG	★	★	★			☆	☆	B1, E, L
Eisenhower SP (Marina)	DENISON				★	★	★	20	★		BG	★	★	★	★	★	☆	☆	B1
Eisenhower Birthplace SHP	DENISON	★	★	★	★														
Enchanted Rock SNA	FREDERICKSBURG			★	★	★		11			DG	★	★	★					R
Fairfield Lake SP	FAIRFIELD				★	★	★	13			DG	★	★	★	★	★	☆	☆	B1
Falcon SP (Airstrip)	ZAPATA				★	★	★	20	★		BG	★		★	★	☆	☆	☆	B1
Fannin Battleground SHP	GOLIAD	★	★	★	★						DG			★					
Fanthorp Inn SHP	ANDERSON	★	★	★	★									★					
Fort Griffin SHP	ALBANY		★		★	★	★	14			BG	★	★	★			☆		L
Fort Lancaster SHP	OZONA	★	★	★	★									☆					
Fort Leaton SHP	PRESIDIO	★	★	★	★									★					
Fort McKavett SHP	FORT McKAVETT	★	★	★	★							★		★					
Fort Parker SP	MEXIA				★	★	★	19	★		BG	★	★	★	★	★	☆		B1
Fort Richardson SHP	JACKSBORO		★		★	★	★	16	★		DG	★		★			☆		
Franklin Mountains SP	EL PASO	★			★			1				★	★	★					B1
Fulton Mansion SHP	FULTON	★	★	★										★					
Galveston Island SP (Summer Theater)	GALVESTON				★	★	★	4	★			★		★			☆	☆	B1
Garner SP	CONCAN				★	★	★	19	★	★	BG	★	★	★			☆	☆	B2
Goliad SHP	GOLIAD	★	★	★	★	★	★	13	★		DG	★	★	★			☆	★	
Goose Island SP	ROCKPORT				★	★	★	19			BG	★	★	★	★	★	☆	☆	
Governor Hogg Shrine SHP	QUITMAN	★	★	★	★						DG	★		★					
Guadalupe River SP	BOERNE				★	★	★	19				★	★	★			☆	☆	
Hill Country SNA	BANDERA							9			NG	★					☆		B1, E
Honey Creek SNA (Guided Tour Only)	BOERNE	★		(Access through Guadalupe SP)					★										
Hueco Tanks SHP (Indian Pictographs)	EL PASO		★		★	★	★	19			DG	★	★	★					R
Huntsville SP	HUNTSVILLE			★	★	★	★	19	★		DG	★	★	★	★	★	☆		B1, B2
Inks Lake SP	BURNET				★	★	★	12	★		BG	★	★	★	★	★	☆	☆	G
Jim Hogg SHP	RUSK	★	★	★	★							★		★					
Kerrville-Schreiner SP	KERRVILLE			★	★	★	★	13	★		BG	★	★	★	★	★	☆		B1

†Types of Parks

SP	State Park
SHP	State Historical Park
SNA	State Natural Area
SFP	State Fishing Pier.

††Type(s) of Camping

1-Primitive; 2-Developed (no utilities); 3-Water at or near site; 4-Water and Electricity; 5-Water, Electricity, Sewage; 6-Equestrian; 7-1, 2 & 4; 8-1, 2, 3 & 4; 9-1, 2 & 6; 10-1, 2, 3, 4 & 6; 11-1 & 3; 12-1, 3 & 4; 13-1, 3, 4 & 5; 14-1, 3, 4 & 6; 15-1, 3 & 5; 16-1 & 4; 17-1, 4 & 6; 18-2, 3 & 4; 19-3 & 4; 20-3, 4 & 5; 21-3, 4 & 6; 22-3 & 5; 23-4 & 5.

☆ Texas State Parks ☆

Park/†Type of Park/Special Features	Nearest Town	Day Use Only	Historic Site/Museum	Exhibit/Interpretive Center	Restrooms	Showers	Trailer Dump Stn.	†Camping	Screened Shelters	Cabins	Group Facilities	Nature Trail	Hiking Trail	Picnicking	Boat Ramp	Fishing	Swimming	Water Skiing	Miscellaneous
Kickapoo Cavern SP (Use by reservation only)	BRACKETTVILLE							1			NG								B1
Lake Arrowhead SP	WICHITA FALLS			★	★	★		14			DG	★		★	★	★	☆	☆	E
Lake Bastrop SP ▲ (Information: 800-776-4272, Ext. 4083)	BASTROP	(For Reservations: 512-321-5408)																	
Lake Bob Sandlin SP	MOUNT PLEASANT				★	★	★	12	★		DG	★	★	★	★		☆	☆	B1
Lake Brownwood SP	BROWNWOOD				★	★	★	20	★	★	BG	★	★	★	★	★	★	☆	
Lake Casa Blanca International SP	LAREDO				★	★	★	19			BG	★	★	☆	★	☆			B1
Lake Colorado City SP	COLORADO CITY				★	★	★	19			DG	★		★	★		☆	☆	
Lake Corpus Christi SP	MATHIS				★	★	★	20	★		DG	★		★	★		☆	☆	
Lake Houston SP	NEW CANEY				★	★		3			BG	★	★	★					B1
Lake Livingston SP	LIVINGSTON				★	★	★	19	★		DG	★	★	★	★	★	☆		B1, B2, E
Lake Mineral Wells SP	MINERAL WELLS				★	★	★	14	★		DG	★	★	★	★	★	☆		B1, E, R
Lake Rita Blanca SP	DALHART	★												★					B1, E
Lake Somerville SP	SOMERVILLE			★	★	★	★	14			BG	★	★	★	★	★	☆	☆	B1, E
Lake Texana SP	EDNA				★	★	★	19			DG	★		★	★		☆	☆	
Lake Whitney SP (Airstrip)	WHITNEY				★	★	★	20	★		BG	★		★	★	☆	☆	☆	B1
Landmark Inn SHP (Hotel Rooms)	CASTROVILLE	★	★	★							DG	★		★			☆		I
Lipantitlan SHP	ORANGE GROVE	★												★					
Lockhart SP	LOCKHART				★	★		23			BG			★			★		G
Longhorn Cavern SP (Cavern Tours) ▲	BURNET	★	★	★	★							★	★	★					
Lost Maples SNA	VANDERPOOL			★	★	★	★	16				★	★	★			☆	☆	
Lubbock Lake Landmark SHP	LUBBOCK	★	★	★	★						DG	★	★						
Lyndon B. Johnson SHP	STONEWALL	★	★	★	★						DG	★		★			☆	★	L
Magoffin Home SHP	EL PASO	★	★	★	★														
Martin Creek Lake SP	TATUM				★	★	★	16	★		DG	★	★	★	★	★	☆	☆	B1
Martin Dies Jr. SP	JASPER				★	★	★	19	★		BG	★	★	★	★	★	☆	☆	B1
Matagorda Island SP (Boat or Air Access Only)	PORT O'CONNOR		★	★	☆	☆		1			NG	★		☆					B1
McKinney Falls SP	AUSTIN			★	★	★	★	18	★		BG	★	★	★			☆	☆	B1, B2
Meridian SP	MERIDIAN				★	★	★	18	★		BG	★	★	★	★	★	☆	☆	
Mission Tejas SHP	WECHES		★		★	★	★	20			BG	★	★	★			☆		
Monahans Sandhills SP	MONAHANS			★	★	★	★	19			DG	★		★					E
Monument Hill/Kreische Brewery SHP	LA GRANGE	★	★	★	★							★		★					
Mother Neff SP	MOODY				★	★	★	12			BG	★	★	★			☆		
Mustang Island SP	PORT ARANSAS				★	★	★	16				★		★			☆	☆	B1
Old Fort Parker SHP	GROESBECK		★	★	★			3						★					
Palmetto SP	LULING				★	★	★	20			DG	★	★	★		★	☆		
Palo Duro Canyon SP (Summer Drama: "Texas")	CANYON			★	★	★	★	10	★			★	★	★					B1, E, L
Pedernales Falls SP	JOHNSON CITY				★	★	★	16			NG	★	★	★			☆	☆	B1, E
Port Isabel Lighthouse SHP	PORT ISABEL	★	★																
Port Lavaca SFP ▲	PORT LAVACA				★									★	★				
Possum Kingdom SP	CADDO				★	★	★	12	★			★	★	★	☆	☆	☆		L
Purtis Creek SP	EUSTACE				★	★	★	16			BG	★	★	★	★	★	☆		P
Ray Roberts Lake SP	PILOT POINT				★	★	★	18	★		BG	★	★	★	★	★	☆	☆	B1, B2, E
Rusk/Palestine SP (Texas State RR Terminals)	RUSK/PALESTINE				★	★	★	20			DG	★	★	★		★			
Sabine Pass Battleground SHP	PORT ARTHUR	★	★		★			16						★	★	☆			
Sam Bell Maxey House SHP	PARIS	★	★	★	★														
San Angelo SP	SAN ANGELO				★	★		8			BG	★	★	★	★	★	☆	☆	B1
San Jacinto Battleground SHP (Battleship Texas)	HOUSTON	★	★	★	★						DG	★		★			☆		
San José Mission SHP ▲	SAN ANTONIO	(See San Antonio Missions National Park)																	
San Marcos SP (John J. Stokes) (No facilities)	SAN MARCOS	★			(No development)													☆	
Sea Rim SP	PORT ARTHUR			★	★	★	★	12				★		★	★	★	☆	★	
Sebastopol SHP	SEGUIN	★	★	★										★					
Seminole Canyon SHP (Indian Pictographs)	LANGTRY		★	★	★	★	★	19				★	★	★					B1
Sheldon Lake SP	HOUSTON	★										★	☆	★	★				
South Llano River SP	JUNCTION			★	★	★	★	12				★	★	★			☆	☆	B1
Starr Family SHP	MARSHALL	★	★	★	★														
Stephen F. Austin SHP	SAN FELIPE	★	★	★	★	★	★	20	★		DG	★	★	★			☆		G
Texas State Railroad SHP (Contact Park for Schedule)	PALESTINE/RUSK	★	★	★	★														
Tyler SP	TYLER				★	★	★	13	★		BG	★	★	★	★	★	★	☆	B1
Varner-Hogg Plantation SHP (Guided Tours)	WEST COLUMBIA	★	★	★	★							★		★					
Village Creek SP	LUMBERTON				★	★	★	12			BG	★	★	★	★	☆	☆		B1
Washington-on-the-Brazos SHP (Anson Jones Home)	WASHINGTON	★	★	★	★						DG	★	★						

Facilities

▲ Facilities not operated by Parks & Wildlife.
★ Facilities or services available for activity.
☆ Facilities or services not provided.

Miscellaneous Codes

B1	Mountain Biking	G	Golf
B2	Surfaced Bike Trail	I	Hotel-Type Facilities
BG	Both Day & Night Group Facilities	L	Texas Longhorn Herd
DG	Day-Use Group Facilities	NG	Overnight Group Facilities
E	Equestrian Trails	R	Rock Climbing

owner in 1976. Three-story wooden structure, built in 1874-1877, was home of **George W. Fulton,** prominent in South Texas for economic and commercial influence; mansion derives significance from its innovative construction and Victorian design. Call ahead for days and hours of guided tours.

Galveston Island State Park, located approximately 6 miles southwest of Galveston on FM 3005, is a 1,950-acre site acquired in 1969 from private owners. Offers camping, birding, nature study and fishing amid **sand dunes and grassland.** Musical productions in **amphitheater** during summer.

Garner State Park is 1,419.8 acres of recreational facilities on US 83 on the Frio River in Uvalde County 10 miles south of Leakey. Named for **John Nance Garner,** U.S. Vice President, 1933-1941, the park was deeded in 1934-36 by private owners. Camping, hiking, picnicking, river recreation, miniature golf, biking, boat rentals. Cabins available. Nearby is **John Nance "Cactus Jack" Garner Museum** in Uvalde. Nearby also are ruins of historic **Mission Nuestra Señora de la Candelaria del Cañon,** founded in 1749; **Camp Sabinal** (a U.S. Cavalry post and later Texas Ranger camp) established 1856; **Fort Inge,** established 1849.

Goliad State Historical Park is 187.3 acres one mile south of Goliad on US 183 and 77. Along the San Antonio River in Goliad County. The land was deeded in 1949 by the City and County of Goliad. Nearby are the sites of several battles in the Texas fight for independence from Mexico. The park includes a replica of **Mission Nuestra Señora del Espíritu Santo de Zúñiga,** originally established 1722 and settled at its present site in 1749. Park unit includes **Gen. Ignacio Zaragoza's Birthplace,** which is located near **Presidio la Bahia.** He was Mexican national hero who led troops against French at historic **Battle of Puebla.** Park property also contains ruins of **Mission Nuestra Señora del Rosario,** established 1754, located four miles west of Goliad on US 59. Other nearby points of historical interest are restored **Presidio Nuestra Señora de Loreto de la Bahía,** established 1722 and settled on site in 1749; it is located short distance south on US 183. Memorial shaft marking common burial site of **Fannin** and victims of **Goliad massacre** (1836) is near **Presidio la Bahía.** Camping, picnicking, historical exhibits, nature trail. (See also **Fannin Battleground State Historical Park,** above.)

Goose Island State Park, 314 acres 10 miles northeast of Rockport on TX 35 and PR 13 on St. Charles and Aransas bays in Aransas County, was deeded by private owners in 1931-1935 plus an additional seven acres donated in the early 1990s by Sun Oil Co. Located here is "Big Tree" estimated to be more than 1,000 years old and listed as the **state champion coastal live oak.** Water activities, picnicking and camping, plus excellent birding. Rare and endangered **whooping cranes** can be viewed during winter just across St. Charles Bay in **Aransas National Wildlife Refuge.**

Gov. Hogg Shrine State Historical Park is a 26.7-acre tract on TX 37 about six blocks south of the Wood County Courthouse at Quitman. Named for **James Stephen Hogg, first native-born governor of Texas,** the park includes museums housing items which belonged to the Hogg and Stinson families. Seventeen acres deeded by the Wood County Old Settlers Reunion Association in 1946; 4.74 acres gift of Miss Ima Hogg in 1970; 3 acres purchased. **Gov. James Stephen Hogg Memorial Shrine** created in 1941. Three museums: Gov. Hogg's wedding held in **Stinson Home; Honeymoon Cottage; Miss Ima Hogg Museum** houses both park headquarters and display of representative history of entire Northeast Texas area.

Guadalupe River State Park comprises 1,938 acres on cypress-shaded Guadalupe River in Kendall and Comal counties, 13 miles east of Boerne on TX 46. Acquired by deed from private owners in 1974. Park has four miles of river frontage with several **white-water rapids** and is located in middle of 9-mile stretch of **Guadalupe River** noted for canoeing, tubing. Picnicking, camping, nature study. Trees include **sycamore, elm, basswood, pecan, walnut, persimmon, willow** and **hackberry.** Rare

golden-cheeked warbler nests here. Animals include **deer, coyote, gray fox, bobcat** and **armadillo.** (see also **Honey Creek State Natural Area,** below).

Hill Country State Natural Area in Bandera and Medina counties, 9 miles west of Bandera on RM 1077. The 5,369.8-acre site acquired by gift and purchase in 1976. Park is located in typical Texas Hill Country on West Verde Creek and contains several **spring-fed streams.** Primitive and equestrian camping, hiking, horseback riding, mountain biking. Group lodge. Access from TX 173 and TX 1077.

Honey Creek State Natural Area consists of 2,293.7 acres adjacent to **Guadalupe River State Park** (above). Entrance is in the park. Acquired from The Nature Conservancy of Texas in 1985 with an addition from private individual in 1988. Diverse plant life includes agarita, Texas persimmon and Ashe juniper in hills, and cedar elm, Spanish oak, pecan, walnut and Mexican buckeye in bottomlands. Abundant wildlife includes ringtail, leopard frog, green kingfisher, golden-cheeked warbler and canyon wren. Open Saturdays only for **guided naturalist tours**; call for details.

Hueco Tanks State Historical Park, located 32 miles northeast of El Paso in El Paso County on RM 2775 just north of US 62-180, was obtained from the county in 1969, with additional 121 acres purchased in 1970. Featured in this 860.3-acre park are large **natural rock basins** that provided water in the arid region for archaic hunters, Plains Indians, Butterfield Overland Mail coach horses and passengers, and other travelers. Indians left behind **pictographs** telling of their adventures. Also in park are **old ranch house** and relocated **ruins of stage station. Rock climbing,** picnicking, camping. Guided tours on weekends. Wildlife includes **gray fox, bobcat, prairie falcons, golden eagles.**

Huntsville State Park is 2,083.2-acre recreational area off IH 45 and PR 40 six miles southeast of Huntsville in Walker County, acquired by deeds from private owners in 1937. Heavily wooded park adjoins **Sam Houston National Forest** and encloses **Lake Raven.** Hiking, camping, fishing, biking, pedal boats, canoeing. **Sam Houston State University** located at nearby Huntsville. **Texas Department of Criminal Justice headquarters** also located in Huntsville as well as old homestead of **Sam Houston (Steamboat House)** and his **grave.** Homestead contains personal effects of Houston. Approximately 50 miles away is **Alabama-Coushatta Indian Reservation** in Polk County.

Inks Lake State Park is 1,201.7 acres of recreational facilities along Inks Lake, 9 miles west of Burnet on the Colorado River off TX 29 on PR 4 in Burnet County. Acquired by deeds from the Lower Colorado River Authority and private owners in 1940. Camping, hiking, fishing, swimming, boating, 9 holes of golf. Nearby are **Longhorn Cavern State Park, LBJ Ranch, LBJ State Historical Park, Pedernales Falls State Park** and **Enchanted Rock State Natural Area. Granite Mountain** and quarry at nearby Marble Falls furnished red granite for **Texas state capitol.** Deer, turkey and other wildlife abundant. **Buchanan Dam,** largest multi-arch dam in world, located 6 miles from park.

Jim Hogg State Historical Park is 178.17 acres of East Texas Piney Woods off US 84 and PR 50 two miles northeast of Rusk in Cherokee County. A memorial to the state's **first native-born governor, James Stephen Hogg,** the property was deeded by the city of Rusk in 1941. Scale replica of birthplace; museum; family cemetery.

Kerrville-Schreiner State Park is a 517.2-acre area 3 miles southeast of Kerrville off TX 173 and PR 19 along the Guadalupe River in Kerr County. Land deeded by City of Kerrville in 1934. Trees include **redbud, sumac, buckeye, pecan, mesquite.** Birding, camping, fishing, picknicking, cycling. Near park is site of **Camp Verde,** scene of an experiment involving use of **camels** for transportation; the camp was active from 1855 to 1869. **Bandera Pass,** 12 miles south of Kerrville, noted gap in chain of mountains through which passed camel caravans, wagon trains, Spanish conquistadores, immigrant trains. In nearby **Fredericksburg** is atmosphere of old country of Germany and famous **Nimitz Hotel** (see **Admiral Nimitz Museum Historical Park).**

Kickapoo Cavern State Park is located about 22 miles north of Brackettville on RM 674 on the Kinney/Edwards county line in the southern Edwards Plateau. **Fifteen known caves** in park, two of which are large enough to be significant: **Kickapoo Cavern,** about 1/4 mile in length, has impressive formations, and **Green Cave,** slightly longer, supports a nursery colony of **Brazilian freetail bats** in summer. Tours of Kickapoo and observation of bats available. Birds include rare species such as **black-capped vireo, varied bunting** and **Montezuma quail.** Reptiles and amphibians include **barking frog, mottled rock rattlesnake,** and **Texas alligator lizard.** Open only by reservation. Group lodge; primitive camping.

Kreische Brewery State Historical Park (see Monument Hill and Kreische Brewery State Historical Park)

Lake Arrowhead State Park consists of 524 acres in Clay County, about 6 miles south of Wichita Falls on US 281 to FM 1954, then 8 miles to park. Acquired in 1970 from the City of Wichita Falls. **Lake Arrowhead** is a reservoir on the Little Wichita River covering approximately 13,500 surface acres, with 106 miles of shoreline. The land surrounding the lake is generally semiarid, gently rolling prairie, much of which has been invaded by mesquite in recent decades. Fishing, camping, lake swimming, picnicking, horseback-riding area.

Lake Bastrop South Shore Park, 773 acres 2 miles northeast of Bastrop off TX 21 and CR 352 in Bastrop County, was made possible through a lease agreement with the Lower Colorado River Authority in 1989. Lake Bastrop is a cooling pond for Sim Gideon Power Plant. Picnicking, camping, swimming, boating and fishing. Near **Bastrop** and **Buescher** state parks.

Lake Bob Sandlin State Park, on the wooded shoreline of 9,400-acre Lake Bob Sandlin, is located 12 miles southwest of Mount Pleasant off FM 21 in Titus County. Activities in the 641-acre park include picnicking, camping, fishing and boating. **Oak, hickory, dogwood, redbud, maple** and **pine** produce spectacular fall color. Reservoir stocked with **largemouth bass, catfish** and **crappie.**

Lake Brownwood State Park in Brown County is 537.5 acres acquired from Brown County Water Improvement District No. 1 in 1934. Park reached from TX 179 to PR 15, 16 miles northwest of Brownwood on Lake Brownwood near **geographical center of Texas.** Water sports, hiking, camping. Cabins available.

Lake Casa Blanca International State Park, located one mile east of Laredo off US 59 on Loop 20, was formerly operated by the City of Laredo and Webb County. **Recreation hall** can be reserved. Camping, picnicking, fishing, ball fields, playgrounds, amphitheater, tennis courts and county-operated golf course.

Lake Colorado City State Park, 500 acres leased for 99 years from a utility company. It is located in Mitchell County 11 miles southwest of Colorado City off IH 20 on FM 2836. Fishing, picnicking, camping, hiking. Mile of **sandy beaches** for lake swimming.

Lake Corpus Christi State Park, a 288 land-acre park located in San Patricio, Jim Wells and Live Oak counties four miles southwest of Mathis off TX 359, was leased from City of Corpus Christi in 1934. Lake noted for **catfish, sunfish, bass** and **crappie.** Camping, picnicking, water sports. Nearby are **Padre Island National Seashore; Mustang Island, Choke Canyon, Golid and Goose Island** state parks; **Aransas National Wildlife Refuge,** and **Fulton Mansion State Historical Park.**

Lake Houston State Park is situated at the confluence of Caney Creek and the East Fork of the San Jacinto River. The 4,912-acre site, purchased from Champion Paper Company in 1981, is northeast of Houston in Harris and Montgomery counties. Camping, birding, hiking, biking, horseback riding are popular activities in the park.

Lake Livingston State Park, in Polk County, six miles southwest of Livingston on FM 3126, contains 635.5 acres along Lake Livingston. Acquired by deed from private landowners in 1971. Near ghost town of **Swartwout,** steamboat landing on Trinity River in 1830s and 1840s. Camping, picnicking, swimming pool, fishing, bicycle camping, guided trail rides.

Lake Mineral Wells State Park, located 4 miles east of Mineral Wells on US 180 in Parker County, consists of 3,010 acres encompassing Lake Mineral Wells. In 1975, the U.S. Government transferred 1,844 acres of Fort Wolters army post to the State of Texas for use as park. The City of Mineral Wells donated 1,057 land acres and the 646-acre lake to TP&WD in 1975. Popular for **rock-climbing/rappelling.** Swimming, fishing, boating, camping; hiking, backpacking and equestrian trails.

More Travel Information

Call the **Texas Department of Transportation's** toll-free number: **1-800-888-8TEX** for:

•The **Texas State Travel Guide, a** free 288-page, full-color publication with a wealth of information about attractions, activities, history and historic sites.

•The official **Texas state highway map.**

On the Internet: **http://www.traveltex.com**

Lake Rita Blanca State Park, the **northernmost state park** in Texas, is located just south of Dalhart off US 385/87 and FM 281 in Hartley County. Consisting of about 1,525 acres, the park was acquired in 1990 through a 101-year lease with Dallam and Hartley counties. Important wintering area for migratory waterfowl, particularly ducks and geese. Other wildlife include scaled quail; bald eagles; mule deer; and swift, gray and red fox. Approved activities are hiking, horseback riding and bicycling on the 9 miles of trails. Day-use only.

Lake Somerville State Park, northwest of Brenham in Lee and Burleson counties, was leased from the federal government in 1969. **Birch Creek Unit** reached off TX 60 and PR 57. **Nails Creek Unit** accessed from US 290 and FM 180. The 5,220-acre park includes miles of hiking-equestrian-mountain bike trails connecting the two units, with equestrian and primitive camp sites, rest benches, shelters and drinking water. Many species of wild game observed at park; **white-tailed deer, fox, coyote, raccoon, rabbit** and **quail** abundant. Various park areas feature sandy or grassy shallow shorelines for wading or swimming.

Lake Texana State Park is 575 acres, 6.5 miles east of Edna on TX 111, half-way between Houston and Corpus Christi in Jackson County, with camping, boating, fishing and picnicking facilities. It was acquired by a 50-year lease agreement with the Bureau of Reclamation in 1977. **Oak/pecan woodlands.** Good **birding. Alligators** found in park coves.

Lake Whitney State Park is 955 acres along the east shore of Lake Whitney west of Hillsboro via TX 22 and FM 1244 in Hill County. Acquired in 1954 by a Department of the Army lease, the state has control until 2003. Located near ruins of **Towash,** early Texas settlement inundated by the lake. Towash Village named for chief of Hainai Indians. Park noted for **bluebonnets** in spring.

Landmark Inn State Historical Park, 4.7 acres in Castroville, about 15 miles west of San Antonio, was acquired through donation by Miss Ruth Lawler in 1974. Castroville, settled in the 1840s by Alsatian farmers, is called **Little Alsace of Texas.** Landmark Inn built about 1844 as residence and store for **Caesar Monad,** mayor of Castroville 1851-1864. Special workshops, tours and events held at inn; grounds may be rented for receptions, family reunions and weddings. **Overnight lodging;** no phones; some rooms air-conditioned.

Lipantitlan State Historical Park is 5 acres 9 miles east of Orange Grove in Nueces County off Texas 359, FM 624 and FM 70. The property was deeded by private owners in 1937. Fort constructed here in 1833 by Mexican government fell to Texas forces in 1835. Only facilities are picnic tables. **Lake Corpus Christi State Park** is nearby.

Lockhart State Park is 263.7 acres 4 miles south of Lockhart via US 183, FM 20 and PR 10 in Caldwell County. The land was deeded by private owners between 1934 and 1937. Camping, picnicking, hiking, fishing, **9-hole golf course. Emanuel Episcopal Church** in Lockhart is **one of oldest Protestant churches** in continuous use in Texas. After Comanche raid at Linnville, **Battle of Plum Creek** (1840) was fought in area.

Longhorn Cavern State Park, off US 281 and PR 4 about 6 miles west and 6 miles south of Burnet in Burnet County, is 639 acres dedicated as a natural landmark in 1971. It was acquired in 1932-1937 from private owners. The cave has been used as a shelter since prehistoric times. Among legends about the cave is that the outlaw **Sam Bass** hid stolen money there. Confederates made gunpowder in the cave during the Civil War. **Nature trail; guided tours** of cave. Cavern operated by concession agreement. **Inks Lake State Park** and **Lyndon B. Johnson Ranch** located nearby.

Lost Maples State Natural Area consists of 2,174.2 scenic acres in Bandera and Real counties, 5 miles north of Vanderpool on RM 187. Acquired by purchase from private owners in 1973. Outstanding example of Edwards Plateau flora and fauna, features isolated stand of uncommon **Uvalde bigtooth maple.** Rare **golden-cheeked warbler, black-capped vireo** and **green kingfisher** nest and feed in park. Fall foliage can be spectacular. Hiking trails, camping, birding. Wildlife includes **gray fox, rock squirrel** and **javelina.**

Lubbock Lake Landmark State Historical Park is a 308.6-acre **archaeological site** and botanical and zoological preserve in **Yellowhouse Draw** on the northwest edge of the city of Lubbock near intersection of Loop 239 and Clovis Road (US 84). The site was leased from the City of Lubbock for 50 years in 1986. **Only known site in North America containing deposits related to all cultures known to have existed on the Southern Plains for the last 12,000 years.** Site is **State Archeological Landmark, National Historic Landmark** and is on the **National Register of Historic Places.** Interpretive center, guded and self-guiding tours of on-going excavation; hiking, fishing, swimming. Day use only.

Lyndon B. Johnson State Historical Park, off US 290 in Gillespie County 14 miles west of Johnson City near Stonewall, contains 732.75 acres. Acquired in 1965 with private donations. **Home of Lyndon B. Johnson** located north bank of **Pedernales River** across Ranch Road 1 from park; portion of **official Texas longhorn herd** maintained at park. Wildlife exhibit includes **turkey, deer** and **bison. Living history demonstrations** at restored **Sauer-Beckmann house.** Reconstruction of **Johnson birthplace** is open to public. Historic structures, swimming pool, tennis courts, baseball field, picnicking. Nearby is family cemetery where former president and relatives are buried. In Johnson City is **boyhood home of President Johnson.** (See also **National Parks.**)

Magoffin Home State Historical Park, in El Paso, is a 19-room territorial-style adobe on a 1.5-acre site. Purchased by the state and City of El Paso in 1976, it is operated by TP&WD. Home was built in 1875 by pioneer El Pasoan **Joseph Magoffin.** Furnished with original family artifacts. Guided tours Wednesday-Sunday.

Martin Creek Lake State Park, 286.9 acres, is located 4 miles south of Tatum off TX 43 and CR 2183 in Rusk County. It was deeded to the TP&WD by Texas Utilities in 1976. Excellent year-round fishing; also camping, picnicking, boating, lake swimming. Roadbed of **Trammel's Trace,** old Indian trail that became major route for settlers moving to Texas from Arkansas, can be seen. **Hardwood and pine** forest shelters abundant wildlife including **swamp rabbits, gophers, nutria, deer** and numerous species of land birds and waterfowl.

Martin Dies Jr. State Park, until 1965 the **Dam B State Park,** is 705 acres in Jasper and Tyler counties on B. A. Steinhagen Reservoir between Woodville and Jasper via US 190. Land leased from Corps of Engineers in 1964. Located at edge of **Big Thicket.** Plant and animal life varied and abundant. Winter **bald eagle census** conducted at reservoir. In spring, **Dogwood Festival** held at Woodville. Park is approximately 30 miles from **Alabama and Coushatta Indian Reservation.**

Matagorda Island State Park and Wildlife Management Area is separated from the mainland by San Antonio and Espiritu Santo bays. Matagorda Island is one of the **barrier islands** that border the Gulf and protect the main-

land from the great tides and strong wave action of the open ocean. About 48,893 acres of park and WMA are managed by the TP&WD. The park occupies abut 7,325 acres of the total. **La Salle** had a camp on the island in 1684. **Lighthouse** was constructed in 1852. Nineteen endangered or threatened species are found here, including **whooping crane, peregrine falcon, brown pelican** and **Ridley sea turtle.** More than **300 species of birds** use island during spring and fall migrations. Camping, birding; scheduled tours. Access only by boat; passenger **ferry operates from Port O'Connor** Thursday-Saturday.

McKinney Falls State Park is 640.6 acres 13 miles southeast of the state capitol in Austin off US 183. Acquired in 1970 by gift from private owners. Named for Thomas F. McKinney, **one of Stephen F. Austin's first 300 colonists,** who built his home here in the mid-1800s on Onion Creek. Ruins of his homestead can be viewed. Hiking, biking, camping, picnicking.

Meridian State Park in Bosque County is a 502.4-acre park including a 73-acre lake. The heavily wooded land was acquired from private owners in 1933-1935. **Tonkawa Indians** lived in surrounding area before coming of Europeans; **Tawakoni Indians** also occupied area prior to 1841. **Texan-Santa Fe expedition** of 1841 passed through Bosque County near present site of park on Bee Creek. **Endangered golden-cheeked warbler** nests here. Camping, picnicking, hiking, lake swimming, birding, bicycling.

Mission Tejas State Historical Park is a 363.3-acre park in Houston County. Situated 12 miles west of Alto in Weches via TX 21 and PR 44, the park was acquired from the Texas Forest Service in 1957. In the park is a replica of **Mission San Francisco de los Tejas,** the first mission in East Texas (1690). It was abandoned, then re-established 1716; abandoned again 1719; re-established again 1721; abandoned for last time in 1730 and moved to San Antonio. Also in park is restored **Rice Family Log House,** built about 1828. Camping, hiking, fishing, picnicking.

Monahans Sandhills State Park consists of 3,840 acres of sand dunes, some up to 70 feet high, in Ward and Winkler counties 5 miles northeast of Monahans on IH 20 to PR 41. Land leased by state from private foundation until 2056. Dunes used as meeting place by raiding Indians. Camping, hiking, picnicking, **sand-surfing.** Scheduled tours. **Odessa meteor crater** is nearby, as is **Balmorhea State Park.**

Monument Hill State Historical Park and **Kreische Brewery State Historical Park** are operated as one park unit. Monument Hill consists of 4 acres one mile south of La Grange on US 77 to Spur Road 92 in Fayette County. The land was acquired in two parcels: monument and tomb area transferred from Board of Control in 1949, the rest from the Archbishop of San Antonio in 1956. The hill bears a memorial shaft dedicated to **Capt. Nicholas Dawson** and his men, who fought at **Salado Creek** in 1842, in Mexican **Gen. Woll's** invasion of Texas, and to the men of the **"black bean lottery"** (1843) of the **Mier Expedition.** Remains were brought to **Monument Hill** for reburial in 1848. Kreische Complex linked to Monument Hill through interpretive trail. **Kreische Brewery State Historical Park** is 36 acres, purchased from private owners. Contains **Kreische Brewery** and stone-and-wood house built between 1850-1855 on Colorado River. One of **first commercial breweries** in state, it closed in 1884. Smokehouse and barn also in complex. Guided tours of brewery and house; call for schedule. Picnicking.

Mother Neff State Park was the **first official state park** in Texas. It originated with 6 acres donated by Mrs. I. E. Neff, mother of **Pat M. Neff,** Governor of Texas from 1921 to 1925. The park, located 8 miles west of Moody on FM 106 and TX 236, now contains 259 acres along the Leon River in Coryell County. The additional land was deeded to the state in 1934 by private owners. Heavily wooded. Camping, picnicking, fishing, hiking.

Mustang Island State Park, 3,703.58 acres on Gulf of Mexico in Nueces County, 14 miles south of Port Aransas on TX 361, was acquired from private owners in 1972. Mustang Island is a barrier island with a complicated ecosystem, dependent upon the sand dune. The foundation plants of the dunes are **sea oats, beach panic grass** and soilbind morning glory. Beach camping; sun, sand and water activities. Excellent birding, especially during spring and fall migrations. **Padre Island National Seashore** 14 miles south.

Old Fort Parker State Historical Park, a 37.5-acre park between Groesbeck and Mexia off TX 14 in Limestone County, was deeded by private owners in 1936. In the park is a replica of **Fort Parker** stockade, a family fort built in 1834, and the site of abduction of **Cynthia Ann Parker** on May 19, 1836, by Comanche and Kiowa Indians. Visitors can explore cabins and blockhouses. Park operated by City of Groesbeck. Nearby is recreational **Fort Parker State Park.**

Palmetto State Park, a scenic park, is 270.3 acres 8 miles southwest of Luling on US 183 and PR 11 along the San Marcos River in Gonzales County. Land deeded in 1934-1937 by private owners and City of Gonzales. Named for **tropical dwarf palmetto** found there. Diverse plant and animal life; excellent birding. Also picnicking, fishing, hiking, swimming. Nearby **Gonzales** and **Ottine** important in early Texas history. Gonzales settled 1825 as center of **Green DeWitt's colonies.**

Palo Duro Canyon State Park consists of 16,402.1 acres 12 miles east of Canyon on TX 217 in Armstrong and Randall counties. The land was deeded by private owners in 1933 and is the scene of the annual summer production of the drama, **"Texas."** Spectacular **scenic canyon** one million years old exposes rocks spanning about 200 million years of geological time. **Coronado** may have visited canyon in 1541. Canyon officially discovered by **Capt. R. B. Marcy** in 1852. Scene of decisive battle in 1874 between Comanche and Kiowa Indians and U.S. Army troops under **Gen. Ranald Mackenzie.** Also scene of ranching enterprise started by **Charles Goodnight** in 1876. Part of **state longhorn herd** is kept here. Camping, horseback and hiking trails, horse rentals.

Pedernales Falls State Park, 5,211.7 acres in Blanco County about 9 miles east of Johnson City on FM 2766 along Pedernales River, was acquired from private owners in 1970. Typical **Edwards Plateau** terrain, with **live oaks, deer, turkey** and **stone hills.** Camping, picnicking, hiking, swimming, tubing. Falls main scenic attraction.

Port Isabel Lighthouse State Historical Park consists of 0.88 acres in Port Isabel, Cameron County. Acquired by purchase from private owners in 1950; site includes **lighthouse** constructed in 1852; near sites of Civil War battle of **Palmito Ranch** (1865), and Mexican War battles of **Palo Alto** and **Resaca de la Palma.** Lighthouse remodeled 1952; visitors can climb to top. Operated by City of Port Isabel. Resort facilities available across causeway at **South Padre Island.**

Port Lavaca State Fishing Pier, a 2-acre recreational area on Lavaca Bay in Calhoun County, was acquired by transfer of authority from state highway department in 1963. The 3,200-foot fishing pier was created from former causeway across the bay. **Port Lavaca City Park,** at base of pier, offers a boat ramp and picnicking facilities. Operated by leased concession.

Possum Kingdom State Park, west of Mineral Wells via US 180 to Caddo then north on PR 33 in Palo Pinto County, is 1,528.7 acres adjacent to **Possum Kingdom Lake,** in **Palo Pinto Mountains** and **Brazos River Valley.** Rugged canyons home to **deer,** other wildlife. Part of **official state longhorn herd** live in park. Acquired from the Brazos River Authority in 1940. Camping, picnicking, swimming, fishing, boating. Cabins available.

Purtis Creek State Park is 1,566 acres in Henderson and Van Zandt counties 3.5 miles north of Eustace on FM 316. Acquired in 1976 from private owners. Fishing for **largemouth bass** on catch-and-release basis only; **catfish and crappie** can be retained. Also camping, hiking and picnicking.

Ray Roberts Lake State Park (Isle du Bois Unit), consists of 1,687 acres on the south side of Ray Roberts Lake on FM 455 between Pilot Point and Sanger in Denton County. **Johnson Branch Unit** contains 1,514 acres on north side of lake in Denton and Cooke counties 7 miles east of IH 30 on FM 3002. Land acquired in 1984 by lease from secretary of Army. Abundant and varied plant and animal life. Fishing, camping, picnicking, swimming,

hiking, biking.

Rusk/Palestine State Park. Rusk unit is 136 acres located adjacent to **Texas State Railroad Rusk Depot** off US 84 in Cherokee County. Palestine unit is 25.8 acres located off US 84 adjacent to **Texas State Railroad Palestine Depot.** Fishing, picnicking, camping, tennis courts, playground. **Train rides** in restored passenger cars (see also **Texas State Railroad State Historical Park).**

Sabine Pass Battleground State Historical Park in Jefferson County 1.5 miles south of Sabine Pass on Dowlen Road, contains 56 acres acquired by deed from Kountze County Trust in 1972. Lt. **Richard W. Dowling,** with small Confederate force, repelled an attempted 1863 invasion of Texas by Union gunboats. **Monument, World War II ammunition bunkers.** Boating, fishing, picnicking, camping. **Sea Rim State Park** nearby.

Sam Bell Maxey House State Historical Park, at the corner of So. Church and Washington streets in Paris, Lamar County, was donated by City of Paris in 1976. Consists of 1.4 acres with 1868 Victorian Italianate-style frame house, plus outbuildings. Most of furnishings accumulated by Maxey family. Maxey served in Mexican and Civil wars and was two-term U.S. Senator. House is on the **National Register of Historic Places.** Open for tours Friday through Sunday.

San Angelo State Park, on **O.C. Fisher Reservoir** adjacent to the city of San Angelo in Tom Green County, contains 7,667 acres of land, most of which will remain undeveloped. Management of the property transferred to TP&WD from the U.S. Corps of Engineers in 1995. Access is from US 87 or 67, then FM 2288. Area gives evidence of **11,000 years of human occupation.** Highly diversified plant and animal life, including **350 species of birds** and 50 species of mammals. Activities include boating, fishing, swimming, hiking, mountain biking, horseback riding, camping, picnicking and wildlife observation. Nearby is **Fort Concho.**

San Jacinto Battleground State Historical Park and **Battleship Texas State Historic Site** are located 22 miles east of downtown Houston off TX 225 East to TX 134 to PR 1836 in east Harris County. The park is 1,002 acres with 570-foot-tall monument erected in honor of Texans who defeated Mexican **Gen. Antonio Lopez de Santa Anna** on April 21, 1836, to win Texas' independence from Mexico. The park is original site of Texan's camp acquired in 1883. Subsequent acquisitions made in 1897 and 1899. Park transferred to TP&WD in 1965. Park registered as **National Historic Landmark.** Elevator ride to observation tower near top of monument; museum. Monument known as **tallest masonry structure in the world.** Interpretive trail around battleground. Adjacent to park is the **U.S.S. Texas,** commissioned in 1914. The battleship is the only survivor of the dreadnought class and the only surviving veteran of two world wars, was donated to people of Texas by U.S. Navy. Ship was moored in the Houston Ship Channel at the **San Jacinto Battleground** on San Jacinto Day, 1948. The ship was dry-docked for major repairs and refurbishing in Dec. 1988; it reopened for visitors in July 1990, but restoration is ongoing.

San José Mission is operated as part of **San Antonio Missions National Historical Park** (see page 132).

San Marcos River State Park (John J. Stokes) , also known as Thompson's Island, is a 5.5-acre site donated by John H. Stokes Sr. and operated by the City of San Marcos. Provides access to river for fishing, canoeing and boating. No facilities; no development; day use only.

Sea Rim State Park in Jefferson County, 20 miles south of Port Arthur, off TX 87, contains 15,094.2 acres of marshland and 5.2 miles of **Gulf beach** shoreline, acquired from private owners in 1972. It is prime wintering area for **waterfowl.** Wetlands also shelter abundant wildlife, including river otter, nutria, alligator, mink, muskrat. Camping, fishing, swimming; **wildlife observation blinds** in marsh; nature trail; boating with canoes or kayaks. **Airboat tours of marsh.** Near **McFaddin National Wildlife Refuge.**

Sebastopol State Historical Park at 704 Zorn Street in Seguin, Guadalupe County, was acquired by purchase in 1976 from Seguin Conservation Society; approximately

2.2 acres. Built about 1856 by **Col. Joshua W. Young** of **limecrete**, concrete made from local gravel and lime, the Greek Revival-style house was restored to its 1880 appearance by the TP&WD and opened to the public in 1989. Tours available Friday through Sunday. Also of interest in the area is historic **Seguin**, founded 1838.

Seminole Canyon State Historical Park in Val Verde County, 9 miles west of Comstock off US 90, contains 2,172.5 acres; acquired by purchase from private owner in 1973. **Fate Bell Shelter** in canyon contains several important **prehistoric Indian pictographs**. Historic interpretive center; guided tours Wednesday through Sunday. Diverse flora and fauna. Hiking, mountain biking, camping.

Sheldon Lake State Park and Wildlife Management Area, 2,503 acres in Harris County on Carpenter's Bayou, lies 20 miles northeast of downtown Houston just north of US 90. Acquired by purchase in 1952 from the City of Houston. Freshwater marsh habitat. Activities include nature study, birding and fishing. Demonstration gardens of native plants.

South Llano River State Park, 5 miles south of Junction in Kimble County off US 377, is a 2,640.8-acre site with 2 miles of river frontage. Land was donated to the TP&WD by private owner in 1977. Wooded bottomland along the winding South Llano River is **largest and oldest winter roosting site for the Rio Grande turkey** in Central Texas. Roosting area closed to visitors October-March. Other animals include **wood ducks, javelina, fox, beaver, bobcat, cottontail** and **armadillo.** Camping, picnicking, tubing, swimming and fishing, hiking, mountain biking.

Starr Family State Historical Park, 3.1 acres at 407 W. Travis in Marshall, Harrison County. Greek Revival-style mansion, **Maplecroft**, was home to five generations of Starr family, powerful and economically influential Texans. Acquired by gift in 1976. Additional land donated in 1982. Tours Friday-Sunday. Special events during year. Grounds feature **azaleas, camellias, dogwoods, roses, wisteria.**

Stephen F. Austin State Historical Park is 667 acres along the Brazos River in San Felipe, Austin County, named for the **"Father of Texas."** The area was deeded by the San Felipe de Austin Corporation and the San Felipe Park Association in 1940. Site of township of **San Felipe** was seat of government where conventions of 1832 and 1833 and Consultation of 1835 held. These led to **Texas Declaration of Independence.** San Felipe was home of **Stephen F. Austin** and other famous early Texans; home of **Texas' first Anglo newspaper (the Texas Gazette)** founded in 1829; postal system of Texas originated here; beginning of **Texas Rangers.** Statue of Austin, museum. Wooded. Camping, picnicking, 18-hole golf course.

Texas State Railroad State Historical Park, in Anderson and Cherokee counties between the cities of Palestine and Rusk, adjacent to US 84, contains 503 acres. Acquired by Legislative Act in 1971. Trains run seasonal schedules on 25.5 miles of track. Call for information and reservations: In Texas (800) 442-8951; outside (903) 683-2561. The railroad was built by the State of Texas to support the **state-owned iron works** at Rusk. Begun in 1896,

and built largely by inmates from the state prison system, the railroad was gradually extended until it reached Palestine in 1909 and established regular rail service between the towns. (See also **Rusk/Palestine State Park.**)

Tyler State Park is 985.5 acres 2 miles north of IH 20 on FM 14 north of Tyler in Smith County. Includes 64-acre lake. The land was deeded by private owners in 1934-1935. Heavily wooded. Camping, hiking, fishing, boating, lake swimming. Nearby Tyler famous as **rose capital of world;** there are located **Tyler Junior College and planetarium, Tyler Rose Garden, Caldwell Children's Zoo** and the **Goodman Museum.** Tyler is home of the **Tyler Rose Festival** each fall. Also Canton First Monday Trade Days, Martin Creek and Purtis Creek state parks.

Varner-Hogg Plantation State Historical Park is 65 acres along Varner Creek 2 miles north of West Columbia on FM 2852 in Brazoria County. The land originally was owned by Martin Varner, a member of Stephen F. Austin's **"Old Three Hundred"** colony; later was home of Texas governor **James Stephen Hogg.** Property was deeded to the state in 1956 by Miss Ima Hogg, former governor's daughter. **First rum distillery** in Texas established in 1829 by Varner. Mansion tours Wednesday-Sunday. Also picnicking.

Village Creek State Park, comprising 1,003.86 heavily forested acres, is located in Lumberton, Hardin County, 10 miles north of Beaumont. Acquired in 1979, the park is full of **cypress, water tupelo, river birch, mayhaw and yaupon** trees. Wildlife includes **snapping turtles,** whitetailed deer, possum, spring-peeper and cricket frogs, bullfrogs, armadillos and occasional alligators; the **200 species of birds** found there include wood ducks, egrets and herons. Activities include fishing, camping, canoeing, swimming, hiking and picnicking. Nearby are **Sea Rim** and **Martin Dies Jr. state parks** and **Big Thicket National Preserve.**

Washington-on-the-Brazos State Historical Park consists of 240 acres 7 miles southwest of Navasota in Washington County on TX 105 and FM 1155. Land acquired by deed from private owners in 1916 and 1976. The land includes the site of the signing on March 2, 1836 of the **Texas Declaration of Independence** from Mexico, as well as the site of the later **signing of the Constitution of the Republic of Texas.** In 1842 and 1845, the land included the **capitol of the Republic.** Daily tours of Barrington, restored **home of Anson Jones, last president of the Republic of Texas. Star of the Republic Museum.** Activities include picnicking and birding.

Future Parks

The following parks were in the development stage when this Texas Almanac went to press: **Bright Leaf SP,** Austin; **Camp Ford SHP,** Tyler; **Chinati Mountains SNA,** Presidio; **Davis Hill SP,** Cleveland; **Eagle Mountain Lake SP,** Fort Worth; **Fort Boggy SP,** Centerville; **Government Canyon SNA,** San Antonio; **Lake Tawakoni SP,** Greenville; **Rancho de las Cabras SHP,** Floresville; and **Resaca de la Palma SP,** Brownsville. ☆

National Parks, Historical Sites, Recreation Areas in Texas

Below are listed the facilities in and the activities that can be enjoyed at the two national parks, a national seashore, a biological preserve, several historic sites, memorials and recreation areas in Texas. They are under supervision of the **U.S. Department of Interior.** In addition, the recreational opportunities in the four national forests in Texas, under the jurisdiction of the **U.S. Department of Agriculture,** are listed at the end of the article.

Alibates Flint Quarries National Monument consists of 1,079 acres in Potter County. For more than 10,000 years, **pre-Columbian Indians** dug agatized limestone from the quarries to make projectile points, knives, scrapers and other tools. The area is presently undeveloped. You may visit the flint quarries on guided walking tours with a park ranger. Tours are at 10:00 a.m. and 2:00 p.m., from Memorial Day to Labor Day. Off-season tours can be arranged by writing to Lake Meredith National Recreation Area, Box 1460, Fritch 79036, or by calling (806) 857-3151.

Amistad National Recreation Area is located on the U.S. side of **Amistad Reservoir,** an international reservoir on the Texas-Mexico border. The recreation area totals 57,292 acres, including 540 miles of shoreline and 43,250 acres of water at normal lake level. Boating, water skiing, fishing, camping and archaeological sites are major attractions. At Panther and Parida caves, accessible only by boat, visitors can see prehistoric pictographs that have been radiocarbon dated to 4,000 years ago. With more than 300 rock art sites in the vicinity, the area is one of the densest concentrations of Archacic rock art in North America. Hunting is allowed in designated areas by permit only. Commercial campgrounds, motels and restaurants are nearby. Full-service marinas located at Diablo East and Rough Canyon. Open year round. (210) 775-7591.

Big Bend National Park, established in 1944, has spectacular **mountain and desert scenery,** a variety of **unusual geological structures.** Located in the great bend of the Rio Grande, the 301,163-acre park is part of the **international boundary** between United States and Mexico. Numerous campsites are located in park, and the **Chisos Mountain Lodge** has accommodations for approximately 345 guests. Write for reservations to National Park Concessions, Inc., Big Bend National Park, Texas 79834. Park open year round. (915) 477-2251.

Big Thicket National Preserve, established in 1974, consists of 86,000 acres of diverse flora and fauna, often nicknamed the **"biological crossroads of North America."** The preserve has been designated an **"International Biosphere Reserve"** by the United Nations Educational, Scientific and Cultural Organization (UNESCO). The visitor information station, which is handicapped accessible, is located on FM 420, approximately seven miles north of Kountze; phone (409) 246-2337. It is open daily from 9:00 a.m. to 5:00 p.m. Naturalist activities are available by reservation only. Reservations can be made through the station. The eight **hiking trails,** ranging in length from one-half mile to 18 miles, visit a variety of forest communities that demonstrate the diversity of the Big Thicket. Parking and detailed maps are available at the trailheads. The two shortest trails are handicapped accessible. The trails are open year round, but keep in mind that some flooding may occur after heavy rains. Bring drinking water, wear comfortable shoes, and don't forget insect repellent during warm weather. Horses are permitted on the **Big Sandy Horse Trail** only. Pets, off-road vehicles and firearms are not permitted on any trails. Back-country camping and hunting are allowed in certain areas by permit only. Fishing is allowed in accordance with state law. Boating and canoeing are popular on preserve corridor units. Park headquarters are located at 3785 Milam, Beaumont 77701; (409) 839-2689.

Chamizal National Memorial, established in 1963 and opened to the public in 1973, stands as a monument to Mexican-American friendship and goodwill. The memorial, on 52 acres, commemorates the peaceful settlement on Aug. 29, 1963, of a 99-year-old boundary dispute between the United States and Mexico. At Chamizal

View from the top of Lost Mine Peak Trail in Big Bend National Park. Photo courtesy National Park Service.

National Memorial, the visual arts, music, dance and the spoken word become cultural bridges between the two nations. It hosts a variety of programs throughout the year, including: the **Border Folk Festival** (first weekend in September) celebrates diverse cultures in music; the **Siglo de Oro** drama festival (early March); the **Oñate Historical Festival** celebrates the First Thanksgiving (April); and **Music Under the Stars** (Sundays June-August). The park has a 1.9-mile trail and picnic areas. (915) 732-7273.

Fort Davis National Historic Site in Jeff Davis County was a key post in the West Texas defense system, guarding immigrants and tradesmen on the San Antonio-El Paso Road. Fort Davis was manned by black troops for many of the years it was active. These troops, called **"Buffalo Soldiers"** because of their curly hair, fought with great distinction in the Indian Wars. **Henry O. Flipper, the first black graduate of West Point,** served at Fort Davis in the early 1880s. The 460-acre historic site is located in the **Davis Mountains,** the second-highest mountain range in the state. The site includes a museum, an auditorium with daily audio-visual programs, restored and refurnished buildings, picnic area and hiking trails. The Friends of Fort Davis NHS Festival is held the Saturday of Labor Day weekend. The site was authorized in 1961 and established in 1963. Lodging is available in the nearby community of Fort Davis. Open year round except Christmas Day.

Guadalupe Mountains National Park, established Sept. 15, 1972, consists of 86,416 acres in Hudspeth and Culberson counties. A mountain mass of Permian limestone, rising abruptly from the surrounding desert, contains one of the most extensive **fossil reefs** on record. Deep **canyons** cut through this exposed fossil reef and provide a rare opportunity for geological study. Special points of interest are **McKittrick Canyon,** a fragile riparian environment, and **Guadalupe Peak,** the highest in Texas. Campground near Pine Springs. Headquarters area has 20 tent sites plus RV parking and is hub for 80 miles of trails. Dog Canyon area located one mile south of Texas-New Mexico state line, at end of NM State Road 137 and County Road 414, contains 18 tent spaces. A comfort station and parking spaces for five self-contained recreational vehicles are also available. Visit the Visitor Center at the headquarters for orientation, free information and natural history exhibits. Also, visit the museum at historic Frijole Ranch. Open year round. Lodging at Van Horn, Texas; White's City or Carlsbad, NM. (915) 828-3251.

Lake Meredith National Recreation Area, about 35

One of the white sand beaches of Padre Island National Seashore. Roddy W. Wilder photo courtesy National Park Service.

miles northeast of Amarillo, consists of a reservoir behind **Sanford Dam** on the Canadian River, in Moore, Hutchinson and Potter counties. Occupies 44,977 acres; popular for water-based activities. Boat ramps, picnic areas, unimproved campsites. Commercial lodging and trailer hookups available in nearby towns. Open year round. Headquarters: 419 E. Broadway, Fritch 79036; (806) 857-3151.

Lyndon B. Johnson National Historical Park includes two separate districts 14 miles apart. The **Johnson City District** comprises the **boyhood home of the 36th President of United States** and the **Johnson Settlement** where his grandparents resided during the late 1800s. The **LBJ Ranch District** can be visited only by taking the National Park Service bus tour (for a nominal fee) starting at the LBJ State Historical Park. The tour includes the reconstructed **LBJ Birthplace**, old school, family cemetery, show barn and a view of the Texas White House. Site in Blanco and Gillespie counties was established in 1969, and contains 673 acres. Open year round except Christmas Day and New Years Day. No camping on site; commercial campgrounds, motels in area. Phone (210) 868-7128.

Padre Island National Seashore consists of a 67.5-mile stretch of a barrier island along the Gulf Coast; noted for it wide sand beaches, excellent fishing and abundant bird and marine life. Contains 130,355 acres in Kleberg, Willacy and Kenedy counties. Open year round. One

paved campground (fee charged) located north of Malaquite Beach, unpaved (primitive) campground area south on beach. Five miles of the beach are accessible by regular vehicles (including motor homes) and are open to camping. Fifty-five miles of beach are accessible only by 4x4 vehicles. All 55 miles of beach are also open to camping. Commercial lodging available outside boundaries of National Seashore. (512) 949-8173.

Palo Alto Battlefield National Historic Site, Brownsville, preserves the site of the **first major battle in the Mexican-American War.** Fought on May 8, 1836, it is recognized for the innovative use of light or "flying" artillery. Participating in the battle were three future presidents: **General Zachary Taylor and Ulysses S. Grant** on the U.S. side, and **Gen. Mariano Arista** on the Mexican. Historical markers are located at the junction of state highways 1847 and 511. There is no site access at press time. For additional information, write 1623 Central Blvd., Ste. 213, Brownsville 78520, or call (210) 541-2785.

Rio Grande Wild and Scenic River is a 191.2-mile strip on the American shore of the Rio Grande in the **Chihuahuan Desert** that protects the river. It begins in Big Bend National Park and continues downstream to the Terrell-Val Verde County line. There are federal facilities in Big Bend National Park only.

San Antonio Missions National Historical Park preserves four Spanish Colonial Missions — **Concepción, San José, San Juan and Espada** — as well as the Espada dam and aqueduct, which are two of the best-preserved remains in the United States of the **Spanish Colonial irrigation system**, and Rancho de Las Cabras, the colonial ranch of Mission Espada. All were crucial elements to Spanish settlement on the Texas frontier. When Franciscan attempts to establish a chain of missions in East Texas in the late 1600s failed, the Spanish Crown ordered three missions transferred to the lush valley of the San Antonio River in 1731, where they flourished until secularization was complete in 1824. The missions are located within the city limits of San Antonio, while Rancho de las Cabras is located 35 miles south in Wilson County near Floresville. The four missions, which are still in use as active parishes, are open to the public from 9:00 a.m. to 5:00 p.m., daily except Thanksgiving, Christmas and New Year's. The visitor center is at San José. For more information, write to 2202 Roosevelt Ave., San Antonio 78210-4919; (210) 534-8833 or (210) 932-1001 (Visitor Center).

Recreation in the National Forests

An estimated 3 million people visited the National Forests in Texas for recreation in 1994. Many of these visitors used established recreation areas primarily for picnicking, swimming, fishing, camping, boating and nature enjoyment. These areas are:

Recreational Visits to National Parks in Texas

This information on daily recreational visits to National Parks in Texas was furnished by the **National Park Service**. Because of rounding, totals may not add up.

Name of Facility	1990	1991	1992	1993	1994	1995	1996
Alibates Flint Quarries National Monument	3,418	3,819	3,419	3,170	3,410	2,770	3,290
Amistad National Recreation Area	1,527,340	1,217,596	1,560,787	1,529,020	1,592,770	1,392,610	1,238,990
Big Bend National Park	257,390	298,834	296,899	326,650	333,380	295,470	203,520
Big Thicket National Preserve	77,950	64,100	59,701	82,940	139,020	115,460	106,620
Chamizal National Memorial	199,000	†	†	257,580	250,670	167,700	185,380
Fort Davis National Historic Site	56,550	66,711	78,037	73,430	69,450	61,040	64,550
Guadalupe Mountains National Park	192,890	200,398	175,125	201,060	203,520	208,980	222,630
Lake Meredith National Recreation Area	1,358,790	1,280,021	1,296,962	1,480,990	1,535,460	1,469,860	1,787,140
Lyndon B. Johnson National Historical Park	193,080	194,220	190,414	184,860	181,570	159,430	136,900
Padre Island National Seashore	593,270	973,825	849,873	766,400	915,630	755,830	444,830
Rio Grande Wild and Scenic River	525	628	962	490	690	510	500
San Antonio Missions National Historical Park	313,450	290,519	950,496*	1,230,560	1,504,530	1,126,230	1,239,970
Total Recreational Visits	4,773,653	4,590,671†	5,462,675*†	6,136,850	6,730,100	5,755,890	5,634,310

In 1992, an electronic method of counting visitors was used at San Antonio Missions National Historical Park for the first time, resulting in an apparent large increase in visitors.
† We were not able to obtain 1991 and 1992 visitation data for Chamizal National Memorial.

Ratcliff Lake, 25 miles west of Lufkin on Highway 7, includes a 45-acre lake and facilities for picnicking, swimming, boating, fishing, camping. There is also a 250-seat campfire theater. Electrical hookups are available. **Double Lake,** 3 miles south of Coldspring on FM Road 2025, has a 30-acre lake and facilities for picnicking, camping, swimming and fishing. **Stubblefield Lake,** 15 miles west-north-west of New Waverly on the shores of Lake Conroe, has facilities for camping, picnicking and fishing. **Scotts Ridge Boat Ramp,** 8 miles west of Willis, provides a boat ramp and parking lot on Lake Conroe. **Boykin Springs,** 15 miles southeast of Zavalla, has a 6-acre lake and facilities for swimming, picnicking, fishing and camping. **Red Hills Lake,** 4 miles north of Milam on Highway 87, has a 17-acre lake and facilities for fishing, swimming, camping and picnicking. Electrical hookups are available. **Bouton Lake,** 7 miles southeast of Zavalla off Texas Highway 63, has a 9-acre natural lake with facilities for camping, picnicking and fishing.

Several areas have been built on the shores of **Sam Rayburn Reservoir,** which has 100 miles of national-forest shoreline. These areas provide camping, picnicking, nature enjoyment, boating and fishing. Recreation areas are: **Sandy Creek** on Forest Service Road 333, 25 miles northwest of Jasper; **Harvey Creek,** 10 miles south of Broaddus on FM 2390; and **Townsend,** 7 miles north of FM 1277. **Caney Creek,** 10 miles southeast of Zavalla off FM 2743, has a 500-seat campfire theater in addition to the usual facilities.

The recreational areas at **Toledo Bend Reservoir** are as follows: **Willow Oak Recreation Area,** 14 miles south of Hemphill off State Highway 87, has facilities for picnicking and camping and a boat ramp; **Indian Mounds Recreation Area,** accessible via FM 83 and FM 3382, a total of 15 miles east of Hemphill, has camping facilities and a boat-launch ramp; **Ragtown,** 25 miles southeast of Center and accessible by State Highways 87 and 139, County Highway 3184 and Forest Service Road 132, has facilities for camping and boat launching; **Lakeview,** a primitive campground 12 miles southeast of Hemphill, can be reached via State Highway 87, County Road 2928 and Forest Service Road 120.

Hiking Trails in National Forests

The Lone Star Hiking Trail, approximately 140 miles long, is located on **Sam Houston National Forest** in Montgomery, Walker and San Jacinto counties. Twenty-six miles of the trail in San Jacinto County has been designated as a **national recreation trail.**

The **4Cs National Recreation Trail** is 19 miles long and goes from Ratcliff Recreation Area to the Neches Bluff overlook on **Davy Crockett National Forest.**

The **Saw Mill Trail** is 5 miles long and goes from the old **Aldrich Sawmill** site to Boykin Springs Recreation Area in the **Angelina National Forest. Trail Between the Lakes** is 26 miles long from Lakeview Recreation Area on Lake Toledo Bend to Highway 96 near Sam Rayburn Reservoir on the **Sabine National Forest.**

Equestrian Trail

The **Piney Creek Horse Trail,** 50 miles long, is located on the **Davy Crockett National Forest** approximately three miles south of Kennard off F.S. Road 525. There is a 30-unit horse camp at this location, but it does not have drinking water available.

Recreation on the National Grasslands

Lake Davy Crockett Recreation Area, 11 miles north of Honey Grove on FM 100, has a boat-launch ramp and camping sites on a 450-acre lake. **Coffee Mill Lake Recreation Area** has camping and picnic facilities on a 750-acre lake. This area is 4 miles west of Lake Davy Crockett Recreation Area. **Black Creek Lake Picnic Area** is located 8 miles southeast of Alvord. It has camping and picnic facilities and a boat-launch ramp on a 30-acre lake.

Lake McClellan in Gray County and **Lake Marvin,** which is part of the **Black Kettle National Grassland** in Hemphill County, receive over 28,000 recreation visitors annually. These areas provide camping, picnicking, fishing and boating facilities. Concessionaires operate facilities at Lake McClellan, and a nominal fee is charged for use of the areas. At the **Rita Blanca National Grassland,** about 4,500 visitors a year enjoy picnicking and hunting. ☆

Recreational Facilities, Corps of Engineers Lakes, 1996

Source: Southwestern Division, Corps of Engineers, Dallas

Reservoir	Swim Areas	Boat Ramps	Picnic Sites	Camp Sites	Rental Units	Visitor Hours, 1996
Addicks*	0	0	721	0	0	6,010,900
Aquilla	0	2	0	0	0	253,600
Bardwell	2	7	29	174	0	1,431,100
Barker*	0	0	50	0	0	3,342,300
Belton	5	21	435	235	10	8,179,100
Benbrook	1	17	115	178	0	3,988,200
Canyon	5	22	411	468	44	7,884,300
Cooper	2	5	98	177	30	364,200
Georgetown	1	3	118	234	0	5,858,400
Granger	2	5	125	133	0	1,337,500
Grapevine	4	17	140	178	0	4,401,200
Hords Creek	1	8	15	140	0	2,312,900
Joe Pool	3	7	315	556	0	10,215,700
Lake O' the Pines	7	25	166	436	0	8,827,900
Lavon	2	19	300	189	0	5,851,100
Lewisville	8	23	324	572	0	9,436,900
Navarro Mills	3	6	16	267	0	4,664,700
O.C. Fisher	0	17	90	61	0	1,511,400
Pat Mayse**	6	11	14	329	0	1,645,400
Proctor	0	6	44	215	0	2,257,600
Ray Roberts	2	9	278	326	0	2,472,700
Sam Rayburn	4	31	36	782	94	12,130,200
Somerville	2	12	241	824	14	15,235,200
Stillhouse Hollow	3	5	91	62	0	1,436,000
Texoma**†	3	27	167	904	233	81,714,700
Town Bluff	2	13	126	344	0	4,532,900
Waco	7	7	90	295	0	3,044,100
Wallisville*	0	0	0	0	0	163,200
Whitney	5	26	46	569	0	6,257,700
Wright Patman	4	10	209	536	0	13,591,600
Totals	84	370	4,810	9,184	425	230,352,700

All above lakes managed by the Fort Worth District, U.S. Army Corps of Engineers, with the following exceptions:
Managed by Galveston District, USACE.
**Managed by Tulsa District, USACE.*
†Figures for facilities on Texas side of lake. Visitation is for entire lake.

Fish and Fishing

Freshwater Fish and Fishing

In Texas, **247 species of freshwater fish** are found. This includes 78 species that are found in areas with low salinity and can be found in rivers entering the Gulf of Mexico. Also included in that total are 18 species that are not native, but were introduced into the state.

The estimated **number of recreational anglers** is 2.6 million, with an economic impact of $1.5 billion annually. The increasing number of fishermen is straining some fishery resources. Catch-and-release fishing has emerged on the Texas scene as the conservation theme of fishermen who desire continued quality fishing.

The **most popular fish** for recreational fishing, all native, are largemouth bass (*Micropterus salmoides*), channel catfish (*Ictalurus punctatus*), blue catfish (*Ictalurus furcatus*), flathead catfish (*Pylodictis olivaris*), white crappie (*Pomoxis annularis*) and black crappie (*Pomoxis* *nigromaculatus).*

The **Texas Parks and Wildlife Department** (TP&WD) operates field stations, fish hatcheries and research facilities to support the conservation and management of fishery resources.

TP&WD has continued its programs of stocking fish in public waters to increase fish numbers and species diversity. The hatcheries operated by TP&WD raise several varieties of bass, as well as rainbow trout, perch, catfish, crappie, sunfish, paddlefish and bluegill.

Texas Freshwater Fisheries Center

The Texas Freshwater Fisheries Center in Athens, about 75 miles southeast of Dallas, is an $18 million hatchery, research laboratory, aquarium and educational center, where visitors can learn about the underwater life in Texas' freshwater streams, ponds and lakes.

The 24,000-square-foot hatchery and research facility concentrates on genetic research and the production of 5 to 6 million Florida largemouth bass for restocking Texas rivers and reservoirs.

The interactive Cox Visitors Center includes aquarium displays of fish in their natural environment. Visitors get an "eye-to-eye" view of three authentically-designed Texas freshwater habitats: a Hill Country stream, an East Texas pond and a reservoir. A marsh exhibit features live American alligators.

Through touch-screen computer exhibits, visitors can learn more about fish habitat and life cycles and the importance of catch-and-release fishing. Films, seminars and demonstrations are also offered.

A casting pond stocked with rainbow trout in the winter and catfish in the summer provides a place for children to learn how to bait a hook, cast a line and land a fish. The center also has an active schedule of special programs and events.

The center is a cooperative effort of the Texas Parks and Wildlife Department, the U.S. Fish and Wildlife Service, the City of Athens and private organizations.

The Texas Freshwater Fisheries Center is open Monday through Sunday, 10:00 a.m. to 5:00 p.m. Admission is charged. It is located four-and-a-half miles east of Athens on FM 2495 at Lake Athens. Address: 5550 Flat Creek Road, Athens 75751, or call (903) 676-2277.

Saltwater Fish and Fishing

Sport Harvest:

There are approximately 1 million saltwater anglers in Texas (6 years old and older) who have a nearly $772.5 million economic impact annually.

The most popular saltwater sport fish in Texas waters are: Atlantic Croaker (*Micropogonias undulatus*), black drum (*Pogonias cromis*), gafftopsail catfish (*Bagre marinus*), groupers (spp.), king mackerel (*Scomberomorus cavalla*), red drum (*Sciaenops ocellatus*), red snapper (*Lutjanus campechanus*), sand seatrout (*Cynoscion arenarius*), sharks (spp.), sheepshead (*Archosargus probatocephalus*), southern flounder (*Paralichthys lethostigma*), spotted seatrout (*Cynoscion nebulosus*), tarpon (*Megalops atlanticus*), yellowfin tuna* (*Thunnus albacares*).
* winter time on headboats

Sea Center Texas

Sea Center Texas is a $13 million marine hatchery, aquarium and educational center located in Lake Jackson, Brazoria County. The center opened in March 1996, featuring interpretive displays and several huge aquariums, where saltwater fish are on display, including Gordon the grouper and several sharks.

The red-drum (redfish) hatchery, said to be the largest in the world, is expected to produce 20 million fingerlings per year for stocking in Texas coastal waters. Although established primarily as a red drum and spotted seatrout hatchery, Sea Center will also serve as a testing ground for production of other marine species, such as flounder and Atlantic croaker.

In 1997, a half-acre youth fishing pond was added, which introduces youngsters to saltwater fishing through scheduled activities. The pond is handicapped accessible and is stocked with a variety of marine fish.

Sea Center Texas is a joint venture of the Texas Parks and Wildlife Department; Dow Chemical Company, Texas Operations; and the Coastal Conservation Association. For more information on Sea Center Texas, call (409) 292-0100.

Commercial Fisheries

Total coastwide landings in 1995 were more than 89 million pounds, valued at more than $182 million. Shrimp accounted for 80 percent of the weight and 88 percent of the value of all seafood landed during calendar year 1995. The approximately 15,000 saltwater commercial fishermen in Texas in 1995 made an economic impact of more than $550 million.

Commercial Landings, 1995†

Species		
Finfish	**Pounds**	**Value**
Drum, Black	2,915,600	$2,506,600
Flounder	274,200	483,900
Sheepshead	54,100	25,800
Snapper	1,244,100	2,424,200
Other	1,979,500	2,575,200
Total Finfish	**6,467,500**	**$8,015,700**
Shellfish		
Shrimp (Heads On):		
Brown and Pink	51,882,400	$119,216,300
White	16,166,000	40,300,200
Other	2,252,500	1,537,000
Crabs	5,786,700	4,062,600
Oysters	4,670,100	8,792,000
Other	145,000	108,100
Total Shellfish	**80,902,700**	**$174,016,200**
Grand Total	**87,370,200**	**$182,031,900**

Source: Trends in Texas Commercial Fishery Landings, 1972-1995, Texas Parks and Wildlife Department Coastal Fisheries Div., Management Data Series No. 127, Austin

National Fish Hatcheries

The **Fish and Wildlife Service** of the U.S. Department of the Interior operates two national fish hatcheries in Texas:

Inks Dam NFH — (Burnet County) Total acreage 84.7. Produces approximately 800,000 channel catfish, largemouth bass and striped bass annually. Visitor hours and facilities are limited; call before visiting. Access is from either Highway 29 or Highway 281 to Park Road 4. Address: Rt. 2 Box 32B, Burnet 78611; phone (512) 793-2474.

Uvalde NFH — (Uvalde County) Total acreage 100P. Produces more than 2 million channel catfish, largemouth bass and striped bass annually. Maintains refugiums for five threatened and endangered fish and plant species. Birding opportunities. Has visitor facilities. Access via U.S. 90 west of Uvalde. Address: Box 708, Uvalde 78802; phone (210) 278-2419; e-mail: R2ffa UV@mail.fws.gov

In addition, the USGS, Biological Resources Div. operates the **San Marcos NFH and Technology Center** — (Hays County) Total acreage 116 acres; fish production is secondary to research. Address: 500 E. McCarty Ln., San Marcos 78666; phone (512) 353-0011. ☆

Hunting, Fishing Licenses

A **hunting license** is required of Texas residents and nonresidents of Texas who hunt any bird or animal. Hunting licenses and stamps are valid during the period September 1 through the following August 31 of each year, except lifetime licenses and licenses issued for a specific number of days. A hunting license (except the nonresident special hunting license and non-resident 5-day special hunting license) is valid for taking all legal species of wildlife in Texas including **deer, turkey, javelina, antelope, aoudad (sheep)** and all **small game and migratory game birds. Special licenses and tags** are required for taking **alligators**, and a **trapper's license** is required to hunt **fur-bearing animals.**

All **sport fishing licenses and stamps** are valid only during the period September 1 through August 31, except lifetime licenses and licenses issued for a specific number of days.

In addition to sports hunting and fishing licenses, **hunting/fishing stamps** are required for special hunting/fishing privileges.

Detailed information concerning licenses, stamps, seasons, regulations and related information can be obtained from **Texas Parks and Wildlife Department, 4200 Smith School Road, Austin 78744; (800) 792-1112 or (512) 389-4800.** Information from the TP&WD on hunting can be accessed on the Internet at **http://www.tpwd.state.tx.us/hunt/hunt.htm**; information on fishing is found at **http://www.tpwd.state.tx.us/fish/fish.htm**

The Texas Parks and Wildlife Department reported revenue of $56.6 million from sales of all licenses during fiscal 1996, a $6.5 million increase over fiscal 1995. More than 4 million licenses were sold.

There were 450,593 **white-tailed deer** killed in the 1995-96 hunting season, compared to 421,423 in 1994-95. The **Wild turkey** harvest was estimated at 28,448, compared to 33,246 in 1994-95. There were 3,845 **mule deer** killed in 1995-96, compared to 5,541 the previous season. The **javelina** harvest was 17,470 in 1995-96 and 19,582 in 1994-95.

The **U.S. Fish and Wildlife Service, Division of Federal Aid**, reports that Texas had the second-largest number of paid **hunting license holders** in 1995, the last year with complete figures, with 1,064,803, at a gross cost to hunters of $19,459,199. Pennsylvania led the way with 1,138,343 paid hunting license holders; Michigan was third with 934,430.

Comparing **fishing-license holders** during 1995 shows Texas second, with 1,755,976, at a gross cost to anglers of $26,592,319. California led with 2,300,463 paid fishing-license holders. ☆

Fairs, Festivals and Special Events

Fairs, festivals and other special events provide year-round recreation in Texas. Some are of national interest, while many attract visitors from across the state. Most of them are primarily of local and regional interest. In addition to those listed here, the recreational paragraphs in the Counties chapter list numerous events. Information was furnished by the event sponsors.

Abilene - West Texas Fair & Rodeo; Sept.; 1700 Hwy. 36 (79602)

Albany - Fort Griffin Fandangle; June; Box 155 (76430)

Alvarado - Pioneers and Old Settlers Reunion; Aug.; Box 217 (76009)

Amarillo - Tri-State Fair; Sept.; Box 31087 (79120)

Angleton - Brazoria County Fair; Oct.; Box 818 (77516)

Aransas Pass - Shrimporee; Oct.; Box 1949 (78335)

Arlington - Texas Scottish Festival and Highland Games; June; Box 151943 (76015)

Athens - Black-Eyed Pea Jamboree; July; Box 2600 (75751)

Athens - Old Fiddlers' Reunion; May; Box 1441 (75751)

Austin - Austin Aqua Festival; July-Aug.; 811 Barton Springs Rd., Ste. 808 (78704)

Austin - Austin-Travis County Livestock Show; March; Box 9876 (78766)

Bay City - Bay City Rice Festival; Oct.; Box 867 (77404)

Bay City - Matagorda County Fair and Livestock Show; March; Box 1803 (77404-1803)

Beaumont - South Texas State Fair; Oct.; Box 3207 (77704)

Big Spring - Howard County Fair; Sept.; Box 2356 (79720)

Boerne - Boerne Berges Fest; June; Box 748 (78006)

Boerne - Kendall County Fair; Aug.-Sept.; Box 954 (78006)

Brownsville - Charro Days Fiesta; Feb.-March; Box 3247 (78523)

Burton - Burton Cotton Gin Festival; April; Box 98 (77835)

Canyon - "Texas" Historical Musical Drama; June-Aug.; Box 268 (79015)

Clute - Great Texas Mosquito Festival; July; Box 997 (77531)

Columbus - Columbus Springtime Festival & Magnolia Homes Tour; May; Box 343 (78934)

Conroe - Montgomery County Fair; March; Box 869 (77305)

Corpus Christi - Bayfest; Sept.; Box 1858 (78403-1858)

Corpus Christi - Texas Jazz Festival; Oct.; Box 424 (78403)

Dalhart - XIT Rodeo & Reunion; Aug.; Box 966 (79022)

Dallas - State Fair of Texas; Sept.-Oct.; Box 150009 (75315)

Decatur - Wise County Old Settlers Reunion; July; Box 203 (76234)

DeLeon - DeLeon Peach & Melon Festival; Aug.; Box 44 (76444)

Denton - North Texas State Fair and Rodeo; Aug.; Box 1695 (76202-1695)

Ennis - National Polka Festival; May; Box 1237 (75120)

Flatonia - Czhilispiel; Oct.; Box 651 (78941)

Fort Worth - Southwestern Exposition & Livestock Show; Jan.-Feb.; Box 150 (76101)

Fredericksburg - Easter Fires Pageant; Easter Eve; Box 526 (78624)

Fredericksburg - Night in Old Fredericksburg; July; 106 N. Adams (78624)

Fredericksburg - Oktoberfest; Oct.; Box 222 (78624)

Giddings - Lee County Junior Livestock Show; March; Box 599 (78942)

Gilmer - East Texas Yamboree; Oct.; Box 854 (75644)

Graham - Wild West Possum Fest; Sept.; Box 299 (76450)

Grand Prairie - National Championship Pow-Wow; Sept.; 2602 Mayfield Rd. (75052)

Greenville - Hunt County Fair; Sept.; Box 1071 (75402)

Hallettsville - Kolache Fest; Sept.; Box 313 (77964)

Hearne - Robertson County Fair; March; Box 246 (77859)

Helotes - Helotes Cornyval; April-May; Box 376 (78023)

Hempstead - Waller County Fair; Sept.-Oct.; Box 911 (77445)

Hico - Hico Old Settlers Reunion; July; Box 93 (76457)

Hidalgo - Border Fest; March; 611 E. Coma (78557)
Hondo - Medina County Fair; Sept.; Box 4 (78861)
Houston - Harris County Fair; Oct.; 1 Abercrombie Dr. (77084)
Houston - Houston Livestock Show & Rodeo; Feb.-March; Box 20070 (77225)
Houston - Houston International Festival; April; 1221 Lamar St. Ste 715 (77010)
Hughes Springs - Wildflower Trails of Texas; April; Box 805 (75656)
Jefferson - Historical Pilgrimage; May; Box 301 (75657)
Johnson City - Blanco County Fair; Aug.; Box 261 (78636)
Kenedy - Bluebonnet Days; April; Box 724 (78119)
Kerrville - Kerr County Fair; Oct.; Box 842 (78029)
Kerrville - Kerrville Folk Festival; May-June; Box 1466 (78029-1466)
Kerrville - Texas State Arts & Crafts Fair; May-June; Box 1527 (78029-1527)
La Grange - Fayette County Country Fair; Aug.-Sept.; Box 544 (78945)
Lamesa - Dawson County Fair; Aug.; Box 1268 (79331)
Laredo - Border Olympics; Feb.-March; 2002 San Bernardo (78040)
Laredo - Laredo International Fair & Exposition; March; Box 1770 (78044)
Laredo - Washington's Birthday Celebration; Feb.; 1819 E. Hillside (78041)
Longview - Gregg County Fair & Expo.; Sept.; Box 1124 (75606)
Lubbock - Panhandle-South Plains Fair; Sept.; Box 208 (79408)
Lufkin - Texas Forest Festival; Sept.; Box 1606 (75901)
Luling - Luling Watermelon Thump; June; Box 710 (78648)
Mercedes - Rio Grande Valley Livestock Show; March; Box 867 (78570)
Mesquite - Mesquite Balloon Festival; July; 703 N. Llano, Fredericksburg (78624)
Mesquite - Mesquite Championship Rodeo; April-Sept.; 1818 Rodeo Dr. (75149)
Mission - Texas Citrus Fiesta; Feb.; Box 407 (78573)
Mount Pleasant - Titus County Fair; Sept.; Box 1232 (75456)
Nacogdoches - Piney Woods Fair; Oct.; 3805 N.W. Stallings Drv. (75961)
Nederland - Nederland Heritage Festival; March; Box 1176 (77627)
New Braunfels - Comal County Fair; Sept.; Box 310223 (78131)
New Braunfels - Wurstfest; Nov.; Box 310309 (78131)
Odessa - Permian Basin Fair & Exposition; Sept.; Box 4812 (79760)
Palestine - Dogwood Trails Festival; March-April; Box 1346 (75801)
Paris - Red River Valley Fair; Aug.-Sept.; Box 964 (75461)
Plantersville - Texas Renaissance Festival; Oct.-Nov.; Rt. 2, Box 650 (77363)
Port Lavaca - Calhoun County Fair; Oct.; Box 42 (77979)
Poteet - Poteet Strawberry Festival; April; Box 227 (78065)
Refugio - Refugio County Fair & Rodeo; March; Box 88 (78377)
Rio Grande City - Starr County Fair; March; Box 841 (78582)
Rosenberg - Fort Bend County Czech Fest; May; Box 1788 (77471)
Salado - Gathering of the Clans; Nov.; Central Texas Area Museum, 1 Main St. (76571)
San Angelo - San Angelo Stock Show & Rodeo; March; 200 W. 43rd (76903)
San Antonio - Fiesta San Antonio; April; 122 Heiman (78205)
San Antonio - Texas Folklife Festival; Aug.; 801 S. Bowie (78205)
Santa Fe - Galveston County Fair & Rodeo; April; Box 889 (77510)
Shamrock - St. Patrick's Day Celebration; March; Box 588 (79079)
Snyder - Scurry County Fair; Sept.; Box 571 (79550)
Stamford - Texas Cowboy Reunion; July; Box 928 (79553)
Sulphur Springs - Hopkins County Fall Festival; Sept.; Box 177 (75483)
Sweetwater - Rattlesnake Roundup; March; Box 1148 (79556)
Texarkana - Four States Fair; Sept.; Box 1915, Texarkana AR (75504)
Tyler - East Texas State Fair; Sept.-Oct.; 2112 W. Front (75702)
Tyler - Texas Rose Festival; Oct.; Box 8224 (75711)
Waco - Brazos River Festival & Cotton Palace Pageant; April; 810 S. 4th St. (76706)
Waco - Heart O'Texas Fair & Rodeo; Oct.; Box 7581 (76714)
Waxahachie - Gingerbread Trail Tour of Homes; June; Box 706 (75165)
Waxahachie - Scarborough Faire; April-June; Box 538 (75165)
Weatherford - Parker County Peach Festival; July; Box 310 (76086)
Wharton - Wharton County Youth Fair; April; Box 266 (77488)
Winnsboro - Autumn Trails Festival; Oct.; 201 W. Broadway (75494)
Yorktown - Western Days; Oct.; Box 488 (78164) ☆

Texas Tourism Facts, 1995

Travel is big business in Texas, according to the Texas Department of Commerce. A study conducted for the agency by D.K. Shifflet & Associates Ltd. during 1995 reported on traveler origins, traveler expenditures, transportation profiles, destination satisfaction ratings and traveler demographics. Below are some of the data from that report.

Texas' 169 million visitors ranked second in the nation behind California (300 million) and ahead of Florida (151 million). The length of time a visitor spent in Texas, measured in "person-days" (one person-day being one person staying in the state for one day), was estimated at 350 million in 1995. That included 215 million person-days spent by Texans traveling within the state and 135 milllion person-days spent by non-Texans. This was an increase over 1994 of 4 percent.

Texas received a 5.9 percent market share of total U.S. person-days, which was estimated at 5.8 billion. This placed Texas third behind California's share of 10.3 percent and Florida's share of 8.5 percent.

Business travel accounted for 32 percent of travel to Texas, while leisure travel accounted for 68 percent..

Texas regions preferred as destinations by non-Texan travelers were Metroplex (31.5 percent), Gulf Coast (19.7 percent), and South (18.2 percent). These three accounted for 70 percent of non-Texan person-days.

The states generating the largest numbers of non-Texan travelers were Oklahoma (11%), Louisiana (10%), California (8%), Illinois (6%), New Mexico (5%), Florida (4%), Missouri (3%) and Arkansas (4%). ☆

Farewell, Southwest Conference; Hello, Big Twelve

By Sam Blair

For much of its 82 years, the Southwest Conference gloried in its distinction as the most tightly knit league in major college sports. Its excitement and energy generated from deep in the heart of Texas.

Ironically, the SWC's original strength became its fatal weakness.

In the '90s, large athletic programs couldn't meet multimillion-dollar budgets, much less thrive, without significant television revenue from football or basketball. The SWC had neither.

By 1994, league members realized a break-up was inevitable.

The SWC was torn and tarnished by football recruiting scandals and NCAA probations, which hit all Texas members except Baylor and Rice in the '80s and saw SMU's program suspended for two years when hit by the NCAA "Death Penalty." The conference was further weakened in 1992 when Arkansas withdrew. A charter member and the SWC's only non-Texas school, Arkansas jumped to the more prosperous, more diverse and more widely-spread Southeastern Conference.

In an earlier era, the SWC and SEC enjoyed similar prestige and success. Now the SEC had left the SWC far behind. It produced national contenders annually and TV paid big money to cover its games. The 9-state SEC, boasting 18 percent of the nation's TV sets, delivered a much larger audience to watch a network's coverage — and its commercials. The all-Texas SWC had only 6.7 percent of the nation's TV sets.

The College Football Association, composed of a majority of major conferences and independents, had given the SWC exposure and revenue through its contracts with ABC and ESPN, but now it was dissolving. The SEC, Atlantic Coast Conference and Big East landed handsome network deals, but the SWC was too small to attract a buyer.

SWC hopes for a merger with the Big Eight to form a 16-team "super conference" died quickly. The Big Eight, composed strictly of state-supported schools in six states with 8.1 percent of America's TV sets, wanted only the SWC's four strongest football members in a new league.

Thus Texas, Texas A&M, Texas Tech and one private institution, Baylor, moved to the Big 12 Conference in the fall of 1996. They joined Oklahoma and Oklahoma State, SWC charter members who left the league during its first decade, in the South Division. Nebraska, Colorado, Missouri, Kansas, Kansas State and Iowa State formed the North Division.

Texas, A&M, Tech and Baylor seemingly fulfilled a best-case scenario. Their four SWC brethren just had to do the best they could.

The three other private schools — SMU, TCU and Rice — joined the far-flung Western Athletic Conference, which expanded to 16 schools for 1996. Although SMU and Rice were based in Dallas and Houston, two of the nation's largest TV markets, their fan support had dwindled to a few thousand loyalists since professional sports first arrived in their cities in 1960. The WAC gambled on turn-arounds at both schools. The Big 12 didn't have to bother.

Houston, a state school also suffering from anemic attendance in a pro-dominated market, joined the new Conference USA. It was a 12-school league with apparently more emphasis on basketball than football. In football, it's a second-tier league with only seven members: Houston, Alabama-Birmingham, Memphis, Tulane, Cincinnati, Southern Mississippi and Louisville. In basketball, it could be a national force.

The SWC's final year of competition was 1995-96, but its demise actually began in 1960 when pro football's arrival first drew fans away from Rice and SMU in the league's largest markets.

Arkansas athletic director Frank Broyles, whose ties with the SWC spanned 46 years before he led the Razorbacks into the SEC in '92, was saddened by his old league's collapse but believed it was inevitable.

"There was no magic formula to turn the tide back to Rice and SMU being the kingpins in attendance like they were in the old days," Broyles said. "There was no way to turn the clock back. How do you get the pride back in a conference with probations and a lack of attendance?"

So the league that sprang from the first organizational meeting in May 1914 at the Oriental Hotel in Dallas ended with the completion of the SWC baseball tournament and track-and-field championships at Lubbock in May 1996. The SWC, like the Oriental Hotel, is now history.

But over the long haul, it's a proud history, gleaming with famous names and achievements.

Football, the premier sport from start to finish, produced seven national champions: SMU, 1935; TCU, 1938; Texas A&M, 1939; Arkansas, 1964; and Texas, 1963, 1969 and 1970. Those three UT national titles were the gems of Darrell Royal's 20 years as Longhorns coach, a career which saw him post the SWC's best winning percentage of .774 (167-47-5).

D.X. Bible, who hired Royal to restore UT's football glory just before he retired as the school's athletic director, also earned a unique place in SWC history. He was the only man who served as head coach at A&M and UT, the league's fiercest rivals. Bible was 72-19-9 in 11 years at A&M (1917, 1919-28) and returned to the SWC after eight years at Nebraska to coach Texas to a 63-31-3 record in 10 years, 1937-46. Bible's 21-year SWC coaching record was .716.

The Heisman Trophy, awarded annually to the nation's outstanding offensive player, was won by five SWC stars: TCU's Davey O'Brien, 1938; SMU's Doak Walker, 1948; A&M's John David Crow, 1957; Texas' Earl Campbell, 1977; and Houston's Andre Ware, 1989. The league also produced five winners of the Outland Trophy, which salutes the nation's outstsanding lineman: Arkansas' Bud Brooks, 1954; Texas' Scott Appleton, 1963; Texas' Tommy Nobis, 1965; Arkansas' Loyd Phillips, 1966; and Texas' Brad Shearer, 1977.

In other sports, SWC schools won a total of 55 national championships. Most notable were Texas' winning the NCAA College World Series four times (1949, 1950, 1975, 1983) and two outstanding women's basketball champions: Texas (34-0) in 1986 and Texas Tech, led by Player of the Year Sheryl Swoopes, in 1993.

The SWC boasted more than 350 first-team all-America athletes in football, basketball and baseball alone. Its track-and-field stars included three historic Olympians. Baylor's Michael Johnson scored the rarest of doubles in 1996, winning both the 200 and 400 at the Atlanta Games to cap a career-best year in which he set world records in both races. In 1984, Houston's Carl Lewis became the first Olympian to win four gold medals in one Games since Jesse Owens in 1936 and added five more golds in the 1988, 1992 and 1996 Olympics. Texas A&M shot putter Randy Matson, the first ever to throw past 70 feet, won the gold in 1968 and held the world record longer than anyone in history.

In the fall of 1996, the final eight SWC members scattered to their new conferences. The football season lacked excellence on all fronts until Texas, winner of a mediocre South Division, faced two-time national champion Nebraska in the Big 12 championship game at St. Louis. The Longhorns, 20-and-one-half-point underdogs, stunned the Cornhuskers with their imaginative, gambling play to win the first Big 12 title, 37-27.

Anyone who remembered the excitement of the SWC at its best sure got their kicks that day. ☆

Sam Blair covered the Southwest Conference and other football conferences, in his 41 years with The Dallas Morning News.

Team National Champions

Source: Southwest Conference Records Book, compiled by SWC Media Relations staff.

Southwest Conference teams won 64 national championships in 17 sports. The championships listed below are limited to those that were won while the teams were in the conference.

Arkansas
Men's Indoor Track - 1984, 1985, 1986, 1987, 1988, 1989, 1990, 1991
Men's Cross Country - 1984, 1986, 1987, 1990
Men's Outdoor Track & Field - 1985
Football - 1964 (UPI)

Houston
Men's Golf - 1977, 1982, 1984, 1985

SMU
Football - 1935 (Eastern College Survey)
Men's Outdoor Track & Field - 1983, 1986
Men's Indoor Track - 1983
Men's Golf - 1954
Women's Golf - 1979

Texas A&M
Women's Softball - 1982 (AIAW), 1983, 1987
Football - 1939 (AP)

TCU
Football - 1935 (Maxwell Survey), 1938 (AP)
Women's Golf - 1983

Texas Tech
Women's Basketball - 1993

University of Texas
Baseball - 1949, 1950, 1975, 1983
Men's Golf - 1971, 1972
Men's Swimming - 1981, 1988, 1989, 1990, 1991, 1996
Football - 1963 (AP), 1969 (AP), 1970 (UPI)
Women's Swimming - 1984, 1985, 1986, 1987, 1988, 1990, 1991
Women's Basketball - 1986
Volleyball - 1981 (AIAW), 1988
Women's Cross Country - 1986
Women's Outdoor Track & Field - 1986
Women's Indoor Track - 1986, 1988, 1990
Women's Tennis - 1993, 1995

National Women's Invitational Tournament:
Arkansas (1987)
Texas A&M (1995)

National Invitational Tournament:
Texas -1978

Women's Intercollegiate Volleyball Champions:
Houston - 1990
Runnerup: **Baylor** - 1993 ☆

Southwest Conference Champions, 1984-1996

Below are listed the winning teams in baseball, basketball, cross-country, football, golf, soccer, swimming and diving, tennis, track & field and volleyball from 1984 through the Southwest Conference's final season in 1996. A list of Southwest Conference champions from its beginnings in 1914 through 1983 can be found in the 1984-1985 Texas Almanac.

In women's basketball, both a regular-season champion and a tournament champion were recognized. This was also the case in men's and women's tennis starting in 1988. In the list below, an asterisk (*) denotes the tournament champion. In cases where the tournament champion was not the regular-season champion or one of the co-champions, the tournament champion's name is in parentheses following the name of the regular-season champion.

In this list, the schools are abbreviated as follows: The University of Texas at Austin-Texas; Texas A&M University-A&M; Baylor University-Baylor; Texas Christian University -TCU; University of Houston-Houston; Rice University-Rice; Texas Technological University -Texas Tech; Southern Methodist University -SMU; University of Arkansas-Arkansas.

Source: Southwest Conference Records Book, compiled by SWC Media Relations staff.

1984
Men's Sports: Baseball - Texas; Basketball - Houston; Cross Country - Arkansas; Football - Houston, SMU (tie); Golf - Houston; Swimming - Texas; Tennis - Arkansas; Indoor Track - Arkansas; Outdoor Track & Field - Arkansas.
Women's Sports: Basketball - *Texas; Cross Country - Houston; Golf - Texas; Swimming - Texas; Tennis - Texas; Indoor Track - Houston; Outdoor Track & Field - Houston; Volleyball - Texas.

1985
Men's Sports: Baseball - Texas; Basketball - Texas Tech; Cross Country - Arkansas; Football - A&M; Golf - Houston; Swimming - Texas; Tennis - SMU; Indoor Track - Arkansas; Outdoor Track & Field - Arkansas.
Women's Sports: Basketball - *Texas; Cross Country - Houston, Texas (tie); Golf - A&M; Swimming - Texas; Tennis - Texas; Indoor Track - Texas; Outdoor Track & Field - Texas; Volleyball - Texas.

1986
Men's Sports: Baseball - Texas (Texas won the regular-season title by defeating A&M three times in three games); Basketball - TCU, Texas, A&M (3-way tie); Cross Country - Arkansas; Football - A&M; Golf - TCU; Swimming - Texas; Tennis - SMU; Indoor Track - Arkansas; Outdoor Track & Field - Texas.
Women's Sports: Basketball - *Texas; Cross Country -

In the finals of the Southwest Conference Championships on May 18, 1996, SMU's Katie Swords (240) wins her third gold medal of the meet, with a time of 4:29.71 in the women's 1,500 meters. AP photo by Eric Gay.

Texas; Golf - SMU; Swimming - Texas; Tennis - A&M; Indoor Track - Texas; Outdoor Track & Field - Texas; Volleyball - Texas.

1987

Men's Sports: Baseball - Texas; Basketball - TCU; Cross Country - Arkansas; Football - A&M; Golf - A&M; Swimming - Texas; Tennis - SMU; Indoor Track - Arkansas; Outdoor Track & Field - Texas.

Women's Sports: Basketball - *Texas; Cross Country - Texas; Golf - Texas; Swimming - Texas; Tennis - Texas; Indoor Track - Texas, Houston (tie); Outdoor Track& Field - Texas; Volleyball - Texas.

1988

Men's Sports: Baseball - Texas; Basketball - SMU; Cross Country - Arkansas; Football - Arkansas; Golf - SMU; Swimming - Texas; Tennis - Arkansas (TCU); Indoor Track - Arkansas; Outdoor Track & Field - Arkansas.

Women's Sports: Basketball - *Texas; Cross Country - Arkansas; Golf - Texas; Swimming - Texas; Tennis - *Texas, SMU (tie); Indoor Track - Texas; Outdoor Track & Field - Texas; Volleyball - Texas.

1989

Men's Sports: Baseball - A&M, Arkansas (tie); Basketball - Arkansas; Cross Country - Arkansas; Football - Arkansas; Golf - Texas; Swimming - Texas; Tennis - Arkansas, *TCU (tie); Indoor Track - Arkansas; Outdoor Track & Field - Arkansas.

Women's Sports: Basketball - *Texas; Cross Country - Texas; Golf - Texas; Swimming - Texas; Tennis - *Texas; Indoor Track - Texas; Outdoor Track & Field - Texas; Volleyball -Texas.

1990

Men's Sports: Baseball - Arkansas; Basketball - Arkansas; Cross Country - Arkansas; Football - Texas; Golf - Texas; Swimming - Texas; Tennis - *Texas; Indoor Track - Arkansas; Outdoor Track & Field - Arkansas.

Women's Sports: Basketball - *Texas, Arkansas (tie); Cross Country - Baylor; Golf - Texas; Swimming - Texas; Tennis - *Texas; Indoor Track - Texas; Outdoor Track & Field - Houston; Volleyball - Texas.

1991

Men's Sports: Baseball - Texas; Basketball - Arkansas; Cross Country - Texas; Football - A&M; Golf - Texas; Swimming - Texas; Tennis - *TCU; Indoor Track - Arkansas; Outdoor Track & Field - Arkansas.

Women's Sports: Basketball - *Arkansas; Cross Country - Baylor; Golf - Texas; Swimming - Texas; Tennis - TCU (Texas); Indoor Track - Texas; Outdoor Track & Field - Texas; Volleyball - Texas.

1992

Men's Sports: Baseball - Texas; Basketball - Houston,

Tournament winner Texas Tech's No. 24, Tony Battie, successfully blocks a Rice player at the Southwest Conference basketball finals on March 8, 1996. Photo by Louis DeLuca, The Dallas Morning News.

Texas (tie); Cross Country - Baylor; Football - A&M; Golf - Texas; Swimming - Texas; Tennis - *TCU; Indoor Track - Texas; Outdoor Track & Field - Texas.

Women's Sports: Basketball - *Texas Tech; Cross Country - Baylor; Golf - SMU; Swimming - Texas; Tennis - *Texas; Indoor Track - Texas; Outdoor Track & Field - Texas; Volleyball - Texas.

1993

Men's Sports: Baseball - A&M; Basketball - SMU; Cross Country - Texas; Football - A&M; Golf - Texas; Swimming - Texas; Tennis - *Texas; Indoor Track - Texas; Outdoor Track & Field - Texas.

Women's Sports: Basketball - *Texas Tech, Texas (tie); Cross Country - Baylor; Golf - Texas; Swimming - Texas; Tennis - *Texas; Indoor Track - Texas; Outdoor Track & Field - Texas; Volleyball - Texas.

1994

Men's Sports: Baseball - TCU; Basketball - Texas; Cross Country - Baylor; Football - Texas, TCU, Rice, Baylor, Texas Tech (5-way tie); Golf - Texas; Swimming - Texas; Tennis - Texas, A&M, *TCU (tie); Indoor Track - Texas; Outdoor Track & Field - Texas.

Women's Sports: Basketball - Texas Tech (Texas); Cross Country - Rice; Golf - Texas; Swimming - Texas; Tennis - *Texas; Indoor Track - Texas; Outdoor Track & Field - Texas; Volleyball - Houston.

1995

Men's Sports: Baseball - Texas Tech; Basketball - Texas, Texas Tech (tie); Cross Country - SMU; Football - Texas; Golf - Texas; Swimming - Texas; Tennis - Texas (TCU); Indoor Track - Rice; Outdoor Track & Field - Texas.

Women's Sports: Basketball - *Texas Tech; Cross Country - SMU; Golf - Texas; Swimming - Texas; Tennis - *Texas; Indoor Track - Texas; Outdoor Track & Field - Texas; Volleyball - Texas; Soccer (1995 only) - SMU.

1996

Men's Sports: Baseball - Texas; Basketball - Texas Tech; Cross Country - Texas; Golf - Texas Tech; Swimming - Texas; Tennis - *TCU; Indoor Track - Baylor; Outdoor Track & Field -Texas.

Women's Sports: Basketball - Texas, Texas Tech (A&M); Golf - Texas; Swimming - Texas; Tennis - *Texas; Indoor Track-Texas; Outdoor Track & Field-Texas. ☆

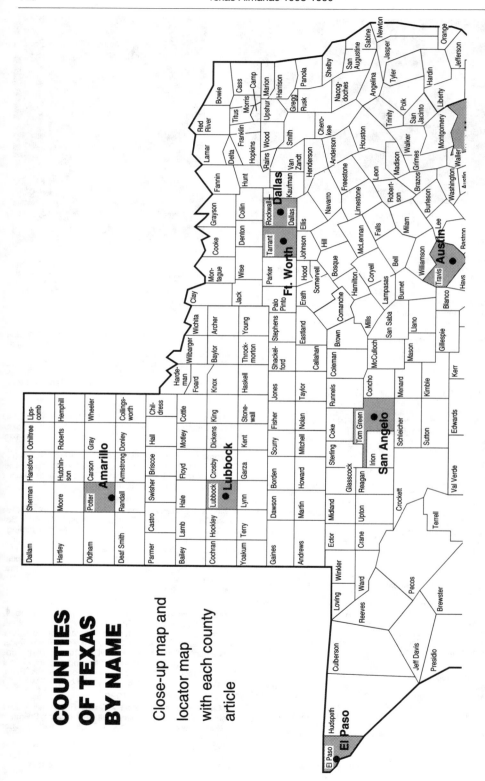

COUNTIES
OF TEXAS
BY NAME

Close-up map and

locator map

with each county

article

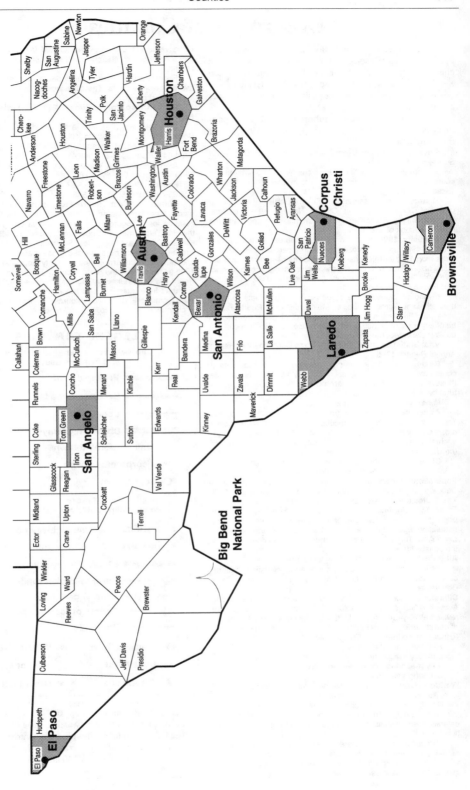

Geography of Counties

These pages describe Texas' 254 counties and hundreds of towns. Descriptions are based on reports from chambers of commerce, Texas Agricultural Extension Service, federal and state agencies, the New Handbook of Texas and other sources. Consult the index for other county information.

County maps are based on those of the Texas Department of Transportation and are copyrighted, 1997, as are the entire contents.

Physical Features: Descriptions are from U.S. Geological Survey and local sources.

Economy: A compilation of local chamber of commerce and county agricultural extension agent information provided to the Texas Almanac.

History: From Texas statutes, Fulmore's History and Geography of Texas as Told in County Names, WPA Historical Records Survey, Texas Centennial Commission Report and the New Handbook of Texas.

Ethnicity, 1990: Based on the U.S. Bureau of the Census count of 1990. In many cases the county percentages will total more than 100, for this reason: In the forms used by the bureau, residents are asked to classify themselves according to race as "White"; "Black"; "American Indian, Eskimo and Aleut"; "Asian and Pacific Islander"; and "Other."

In another question the bureau asks respondents to mark their ethnic background, such as Mexican, Cuban, Puerto Rican, to be classified by the bureau as "Hispanic". Hispanic people can be of any race, thus their numbers are also included in one of the basic racial categories.

Vital Statistics, 1995: From the Texas Department of Health Annual Report, 1995.

Recreation: From information provided by local chambers of commerce and county agents. Attempts were made to note those activities unique to the area or that point to ethnic or cultural heritage.

Minerals: From agricultural agents.

Agriculture: Condensed from information provided to the Texas Almanac by county agricultural agents in 1997. Principal crops and livestock production are listed. Market value of agricultural products sold is from the 1992 Census of Agriculture of the U.S. Department of Commerce for that year.

Cities: The county seat and principal cities are listed.

Sources of Data List

Population: The annual estimate of population from the State Data Center of the Texas Department of Commerce for 1995. The figures are prepared by the Department of Rural Sociology, Texas A&M University. (Also stated in the following line under population is the percentage of increase or decrease from the population in 1990 by the U.S. Bureau of the Census.)

Land Area: The total land area in square miles as determined by the census bureau, 1990.

Altitude (ft.): From the U.S. Geological Survey. Not all of the surface of Texas has been precisely surveyed for elevation; in some cases data are from the Texas Railroad Comission or the Texas Department of Transportation.

Climate: Provided by the National Oceanic and Atmospheric Administration state climatologist, College Station. Data are revised at 10-year intervals. Listed are the latest compilations, as of Jan. 1, 1993, and pertain to a particular site within the county (usually the county seat). The data include:

    Rainfall (annual in inches).

    January mean minimum temperature.

    July mean maximum temperature.

    Growing season (days).

Workforce/Wages: Prepared by the Texas Workforce Commission, Austin, in cooperation with the Bureau of Labor Statistics of the U.S. Department of Labor, for fourth quarter 1995 through third quarter 1996. The data are computed from reports by all establishments subject to the Texas Unemployment Compensation Act.

(Agricultural employers are subject to the act if they employ as many as three workers for 20 weeks or pay cash wages of $6,250 in a quarter. Employers who pay $1,000 in wages in a quarter for domestic services are subject also. Still not mandato-

rily covered are self-employed, unpaid family workers, and those employed by churches and some small nonprofit organizations.)

Federal workers are not included in annual wages and average weekly wage. The data include (with state, lowest and highest county):

Civilian labor force. Texas, 8,242,100; Loving Co., 85; Harris Co., 1,692,905.

Unemployed: (Percentage of workforce): Texas, 5.4; Borden Co., 1.9; Presidio Co., 34.8.

Annual Wages: Texas, $216,510,107,841; Loving Co. $764,647; Harris Co., $51,549,475,128.

Average Weekly Wage: Texas, $529.35; Real Co., $268.15; Carson Co., $770.76.

Federal Wages: Texas, $7,124,529,661; Loving Co., $25,654; Bexar Co., $1,239,543,934.

Agriculture Net Cash Return: From sales, government payments, other farm-related income and Commodity Credit Corporation loans (Source: The 1992 Census of Agriculture of the U.S. Department of Commerce). Texas, $1,485,658,000; Kleberg Co., -$2,341,000; Deaf Smith Co., $52,737,000.

Property Values: The appraised gross market value of real and personal property in each county appraisal district in 1995 as reported to the State Property Tax Board.

Retail Sales: Preliminary figures compiled by the Texas Almanac from quarterly reports for 1996 as reported to the state Comptroller of Public Accounts. The figures are subject to change in the comptroller's final report.

LEGEND FOR MAPS

Following is explanation of signs and symbols used:

▬▬▬ **Principal roads**

▬▬▬ **Secondary roads**

──── **Local roads**

═══ **Divided highways**

○ **Unincorporated towns**

◉ **Incorporated towns**

✪ **County seat**

▨ or ■ **Cities of more than 50,000 population**

═⑩═ **Interstate highway numbers**

■⑲■ **U.S. highway numbers**

■㊱■ **State highway numbers**

▬❨2222❩▬ **Farm-to-Market roads**

──⑫─ **Loop or park road**

─LR─ **County or local roads**

┼┼┼┼┼ **Railroads**

✈ **Civilian airport**   ✈ **Military airport**

🌲 **State parks**   🌲 **National park**

▲ **Historic site**   ◆ **Other features**

A small outline map of Texas counties accompanies each county article. The county is shaded to help locate it within the context of the state. A larger map of Texas with the counties named appears on pages 140 and 141.

Anderson County

Physical Features: Forested, hilly East Texas county, slopes to Trinity and Neches rivers; sandy, clay, black soils; pines, hardwoods.

Economy: Manufacturing, distribution, agribusiness, tourism; hunting and fishing leases; prison units.

History: Comanche, Waco, other tribes. Anglo-American settlers arrived in 1830s. Antebellum slaveholding area. County created from Houston County in 1846; named for K.L. Anderson, last vice president of the Republic of Texas.

Ethnicity, 1990: White, 33,354 (69.5%); Black, 11,143 (23.2%); American Indian, 129 (0.3%); Asian, 125 (0.3%); Other, 3,273 (6.8%). Hispanic, 3,953 (8.2%).

Vital Statistics, 1995: Births, 606; deaths, 497; marriages, 482; divorces, 292.

Recreation: Fishing, hunting, streams, lakes; dogwood trails; historic sites; railroad park; museum. Tourist information at 1890 depot.

Minerals: Oil and gas.

Agriculture: Beef, milk cows, hogs; hay, truck vegetables, grain sorghum, melons, peaches, blackberries. Market value $26 million. Timber sold; Christmas trees.

PALESTINE (17,793) county seat; wholesale meats, auto parts, clothing, metal, wood products; aluminum smelting plant; transportation and agribusiness center; scientific balloon station; library; vocational-technical facilities; hospitals; community college.

Other towns include: **Cayuga** (200); **Elkhart** (1,166); **Frankston** (1,193); **Montalba** (110); **Neches** (175); and **Tennessee Colony** (300) site of state prisons.

Population	51,498
(Change fm '90)	7.2
Land Area (sq. mi.)	1,070.9
Altitude (ft.)	198-624
Rainfall (in.)	43.3
Jan. mean min.	36
July mean max.	94
Growing season (days)	264
Civ. Labor	20,239
Unemployed	5.8
Annual Wages	$356,301,413
Av. Weekly Wage	$414.26
Fed. Wages	$4,801,279
Ag. Net Cash Return	$1,261,000
Prop. Value	$1,666,940,258
Retail Sales	$1,569,176,339

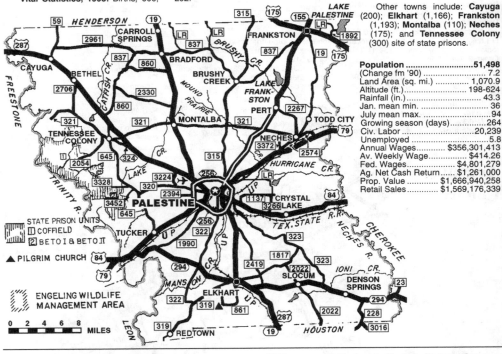

Railroad Abbreviations

AGC	Alamo Gulf Coast Railway Co.
ANR	Angelina & Neches River Railroad Co.
BNSF	Burlington Northern & Santa Fe Railroad Co.
BOP	Border Pacific Railroad Co.
BRG	Brownsville & Rio Grande Int'l Railroad Co.
CYCY	Crystal City Railroad Company
DART	Dallas Area Rapid Transit
DGNO	Dallas, Garland & Northeastern Railroad
ETC	East Texas Central Railroad
FWWR	Fort Worth & Western Railroad Company
GCSR	Gulf, Colorado & San Saba RailwayCorp.
GRR	Georgetown Railroad Co.
GVSR	Galveston Railroad, L.P.
HBT	Houston Belt & Terminal Railway Co.
KCS	Kansas City Southern Railway Co., The
KRR	Kiamichi Railroad Company, Inc.
LHRR	Longhorn Railway Company
LSR	Lone Star Railroad, Inc.
MCSA	Moscow, Camden & San Augustine RR Co.
PCN	Point Comfort & Northern Railway Company
PNR	Panhandle Northern Railroad Company
PTRA	Port Terminal Railroad Association
PVS	Pecos Valley Southern Railway Co., Inc.
RSS	Rockdale, Sandow & Southern Railroad Co.
RV	Rio Valley Railroad
SO	South Orient Railroad Company, LTD
SRN	Sabine River & Northern Railroad Company
SW	Southwestern Railroad
TCT	Texas City Terminal Railway Co.
TM	The Texas Mexican Railway Company
TN	Texas & Northern Railway Co.
TNER	Texas Northeastern Railroad
TNMR	Texas and New Mexico Railroad
TSE	Texas South-Eastern Railroad Company
TXGN	Texas, Gonzales & Northern Railway Co.
TXNW	Texas & North Western Railway Co.
TXOR	Texas and Oklahoma Railroad Company
TXTC	Texas Transportation Company
UP	Union Pacific Railroad Company
WRRC	Western Railroad Co.
WTJR	Wichita, Tillman & Jackson Railway Co.
WTLR	West Texas & Lubbock Railroad Co. Inc.

Andrews County

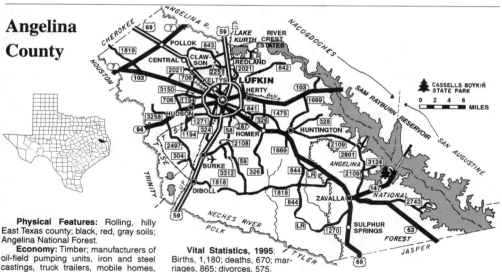

Physical Features: South Plains, drain to playas; grass, mesquite, shin oak; red clay, sandy soils.

Economy: Oil; agribusiness.

History: Apache, Comanche area until U.S. Army campaigns of 1875. Ranching developed around 1900. Oil boom in 1940s. County created 1876 from Bexar Territory; organized 1910; named for Texas Revolutionary soldier Richard Andrews.

Ethnicity, 1990: White, 10,834 (75.6%); Black, 274 (1.9%); American Indian, 82 (0.6%); Asian, 154 (1.1%); Other, 2,994 (20.9%).

Hispanic, 4,552 (31.7%).

Vital Statistics, 1995: Births, 196; deaths, 129; marriages, 132; divorces, 68.

Recreation: Prairie dog town; museum; camper facilities.

Minerals: Oil and gas.

Agriculture: Cattle; cotton, sorghums contribute; grains, corn, hay raised; significant irrigation. Market value $10 million.

ANDREWS (10,223) county seat; amphitheatre; hospital, mental health center; parks.

Population	**14,388**
(Change fm '90)	0.3
Land Area (sq. mi.)	1,500.7
Altitude (ft.)	2,297-2,915
Rainfall (in.)	15.4
Jan. mean min.	29
July mean max.	94
Growing season (days)	213
Civ. Labor	5,470
Unemployed	5.8
Annual Wages	$115,278,894
Av. Weekly Wage	$508.97
Fed. Wages	$1,021,777
Ag. Net Cash Return	$1,748,000
Prop. Value	$1,478,228,630
Retail Sales	$83,273,447

Angelina County

Physical Features: Rolling, hilly East Texas county; black, red, gray soils; Angelina National Forest.

Economy: Timber; manufacturers of oil-field pumping units, iron and steel castings, truck trailers, mobile homes, horse stables; government/services; newsprint, other paper products, wood products, commercial printing; concrete products; cabinet works.

History: Caddoan area. First land deed to Vicente Micheli 1801. Ango-American setters arrived in 1820s. County created 1846 from Nacogdoches County; named for legendary Indian maiden Angelina.

Ethnicity, 1990: White, 54,752 (78.3%); Black, 10,731 (15.4%); American Indian, 153 (0.2%); Asian, 295 (0.4%); Other, 3,953 (5.7%).

Hispanic, 6,072 (8.7%).

Vital Statistics, 1995: Births, 1,180; deaths, 670; marriages, 865; divorces, 575.

Recreation: Sam Rayburn Reservoir; national, state forests, parks; locomotive exhibit; Forest Fest, bike ride in September.

Minerals: Limited output of natural gas and oil.

Agriculture: Beef cattle, poultry, horses; hay, melons. Market value $17.7 million. A leading timber-producing county.

LUFKIN (32,851) county seat; manufacturing; Angelina College; hospitals; U.S., Texas Forest centers; zoo; Museum of East Texas, civic center.

Other towns include: **Burke** (377); **Diboll** (5,636); **Hudson** (2,727); **Huntington** (2,207); **Keltys** (800); **Pollok** (300); **Zavalla** (825).

Population	**76,409**
(Change fm '90)	9.3
Land Area (sq. mi.)	801.6
Altitude (ft.)	139-404
Rainfall (in.)	38.9
Jan. mean min.	37
July mean max.	93
Growing season (days)	244
Civ. Labor	35,108
Unemployed	5.3
Annual Wages	$742,758,296
Av. Weekly Wage	$439.36
Fed. Wages	$15,050,562
Ag. Net Cash Return	$1,417,000
Prop. Value	$2,293,203,796
Retail Sales	$725,098,187

For explanation of sources, abbreviations and symbols, see p. 142.

Aransas County

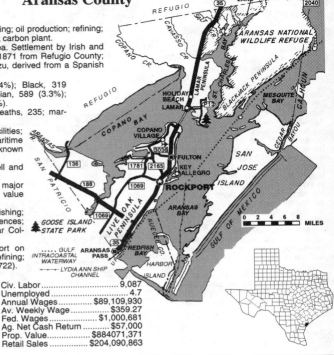

Physical Features: Coastal plains; sandy loam, coastal clays; bays, inlets; mesquites, oaks.

Economy: Tourism, fishing and shrimping; oil production; refining; shipbuilding, offshore equipment fabricated; carbon plant.

History: Karankawa, Coahuiltecan area. Settlement by Irish and Mexicans began in 1829. County created 1871 from Refugio County; named for Rio Nuestra Señora de Aranzazu, derived from a Spanish palace.

Ethnicity, 1990: White, 15,282 (85.4%); Black, 319 (1.8%); American Indian, 111 (0.6%); Asian, 589 (3.3%); Other, 1,591 (8.9%). Hispanic, 3,588 (20.1%).

Vital Statistics, 1995: Births, 220; deaths, 235; marriages, 246; divorces, 127.

Recreation: Fishing, hunting, tourist facilities; Fulton Mansion; state marine lab; Texas Maritime Museum; bird sanctuaries (a nationally known birding hotspot); Rockport Art Center.

Minerals: Oil and gas, also oystershell and sand.

Agriculture: Cow-calf operations; major crops are cotton, sorghum, corn. Market value $357,000. Fishing; redfish hatchery.

ROCKPORT (6,127) county seat; fishing; tourism, retirement and weekend residences; library; clinics; carbon-black plant; Del Mar College program.

Aransas Pass (7,766) deepwater port on Intracoastal Waterway; oil production, refining; industrial plants; tourism; hospital. **Fulton** (722).

Population	19,720
(Change fm '90)	10.2
Land Area (sq. mi.)	252.0
Altitude (ft.)	sea level-24
Rainfall (in.)	36.9
Jan. mean min.	44
July mean max.	91
Growing season (days)	312
Civ. Labor	9,087
Unemployed	4.7
Annual Wages	$89,109,930
Av. Weekly Wage	$359.27
Fed. Wages	$1,000,681
Ag. Net Cash Return	$57,000
Prop. Value	$884071,371
Retail Sales	$204,090,863

Archer County

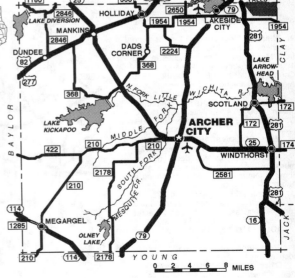

Physical Features: North Central county, rolling to hilly, drained by Wichita River forks; black, red loams, sandy soils; mesquites, post oaks.

Economy: Cattle; oil services. Part of Wichita Falls metropolitan area.

History: Caddo, Comanche, Kiowas and other tribes in area until 1875; Anglo-American settlement developed soon afterward. County created from Fannin Land District, 1858; organized, 1880. Named for Dr. B.T. Archer, Republic commissioner to United States.

Ethnicity, 1990: White, 7,789 (97.7%); Black, 11 (0.1%); American Indian, 36 (0.5%); Asian, 4 (0.1%); Other, 133 (1.7%). Hispanic, 189 (2.4%).

Vital Statistics, 1995: Births, 99; deaths, 70; marriages, 55; divorces, 48.

Recreation: Lakes; hunting of dove, quail, deer, feral hog, coyote.

Minerals: Oil and natural gas.

Agriculture: Dairy, cow/calf, stocker cattle; swine; poultry; wheat, cotton. Market value $52.5 million.

ARCHER CITY (1,878) county seat; cattle, oil field service center; museum; book supply center, some manufacturing; Mayfest.

Other towns include: **Holliday** (1,531) Mayfest in spring; **Lakeside City** (1,061, partly in Wichita County); **Margel** (258); **Scotland** (534, partly in Clay County) **Windthorst** (376, partly in Clay County) biannual German sausage festival (also in Scotland). Part of **Wichita Falls.**

Population	8,439
(Change fm '90)	5.8
Land Area (sq. mi.)	909.8
Altitude (ft.)	934-1,286
Rainfall (in.)	29.3
Jan. mean min.	29
July mean max.	98
Growing season (days)	220
Civ. Labor	4,216
Unemployed	2.9
Annual Wages	$36,220,165
Av. Weekly Wage	$408.42
Fed. Wages	$723,709
Ag. Net Cash Return	$9,862,000
Prop. Value	$474,272,525
Retail Sales	$34,783,567

Armstrong County

Physical Features: Partly on High Plains, broken by Palo Duro Canyon. Chocolate loam, gray soils.

Economy: Agribusiness, tourism.

History: Apache, then Comanche territory until U.S. Army campaigns of 1874-75. Anglo-Americans began ranching soon afterward. County created from Bexar District, 1876; organized 1890; name honors pioneer Texas family.

Ethnicity, 1990: White, 1,976 (97.8%); Black, 0 (0.0%); American Indian, 10 (0.5%); Asian, 7 (0.3%); Other, 28 (1.4%). Hispanic, 55 (2.7%).

Vital Statistics, 1995: Births, 20; deaths, 33; marriages, 18; divorces, 10.

Recreation: Caprock Roundup in July, state park; Goodnight Ranch Home.

Minerals: Sand, gravel.

Agriculture: Stocker cattle, cow-calf operations; wheat, sorghum, cotton and hay; some irrigation. Market value $31 million.

CLAUDE (1,232) county seat; farm, ranch supplies; glass company; medical center; Caprock Roundup.

Other towns include: **Wayside** (35).

Population	**2,114**
(Change fm '90)	4.6
Land Area (sq. mi.)	913.7
Altitude (ft.)	2,829-3,512

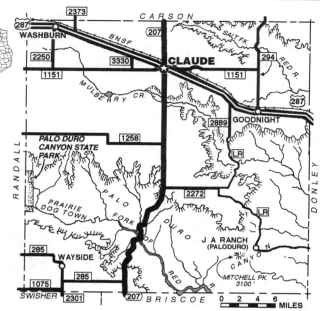

Rainfall (in.)	21..2	Annual Wages	$7,787,674
Jan. mean min.	20	Av. Weekly Wage	$400.51
July mean max.	92	Fed. Wages	$344,498
Growing season (days)	213	Ag. Net Cash Return	$6,175,000
Civ. Labor	988	Prop. Value	$149,711,070
Unemployed	2.9	Retail Sales	$4,835,701

Atascosa County

Physical Features: On grassy prairie south of San Antonio, drained by Atascosa River, tributaries; mesquites, other brush.

Economy: Agribusiness, oil-well supplies, services; coal plant; light manufacturing, shipping.

History: Coahuiltecan Indians; later Apaches, Comanches in area. Families from Mexico established ranches in mid-1700s. Anglo-Americans arrived in 1840s. County created from Bexar District, 1856. Atascosa means boggy in Spanish.

Ethnicity, 1990: White, 25,019 (81.9%); Black, 143 (0.5%); American Indian, 109 (0.4%); Asian, 65 (0.2%); Other, 5,197 (17.0%). Hispanic, 16,064 (52.6%).

Vital Statistics 1995: Births, 497; deaths, 289; marriages, 244; divorces, 126.

Recreation: Quail, deer hunting; museum; river park; theater group; stock show in January; cowboy homecoming in August, Kactus Kick in May.

Minerals: Oil, gas and lignite.

Agriculture: Beef cattle; peanuts, hay, corn, vegetables, sesame; 25,000 acres irrigated. Market value $54.5 million.

JOURDANTON (3,524) county seat; hospital.

Pleasanton (8,555) trading center; hospital.

Other towns include: **Campbellton** (350); **Charlotte** (1,618); **Christine** (472); **Leming** (268); **Lytle** (2,556, partly in Medina, Bexar counties) greenhouse nursery, peanuts processed; **McCoy** (30); **Peggy** (22); **Poteet** (3,568) "strawberry capital".

For explanation of sources, abbreviations and symbols, see p. 142.

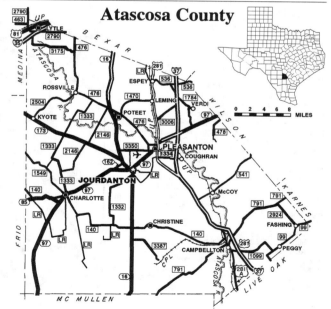

Population	**33,490**
(Change fm '90)	9.7
Land Area (sq. mi.)	1,232.2
Altitude (ft.)	241-725
Rainfall (in.)	28.0
Jan. mean min.	38
July mean max.	96
Growing season (days)	282

Civ. Labor	15,786
Unemployed	4.5
Annual Wages	$138,904,338
Av. Weekly Wage	$372.20
Fed. Wages	$1,798,756
Ag. Net Cash Return	$8,133,000
Prop. Value	$1,307,249,801
Retail Sales	$154,832,024

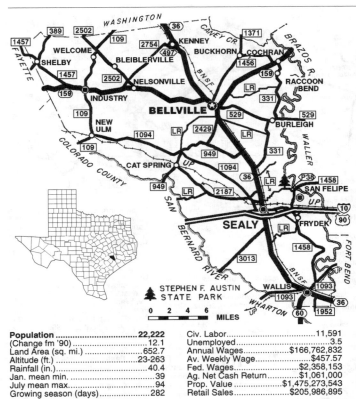

Austin County

Physical Features: Southeast county; level to hilly, drained by San Bernard, Brazos rivers; black prairie to sandy upland soils.

Economy: Agribusiness; steel, other manufacturing, tourism.

History: Tonkawa Indians; reduced by diseases. Birthplace of Anglo-American colonization, 1821, and German mother colony at Industry, 1831. County created 1837; named for Stephen F. Austin, father of Texas.

Ethnicity, 1990: White, 16,244 (81.9%); Black, 2,608 (13.2%); American Indian, 46 (0.2%); Asian, 26 (0.1%); Other, 908 (4.6%). Hispanic, 2,073 (10.5%).

Vital Statistics 1995: Marriages, 165; divorces, 104; births, 267; deaths, 231.

Recreation: Fishing, hunting, state park, Pioneer Trail; Country Livin' festival.

Minerals: Oil and natural gas.

Agriculture: Beef production. Also, hay, pecans, cotton, grain sorghum, corn. Market value $34.9 million.

BELLVILLE (3,760) county seat; varied manufacturing; hospital; oil.

Sealy (5,291) oil-field and military vehicle manufacturing, varied industries.

Other towns include: **Bleiblerville** (71); **Cat Spring** (76); **Frydek** (150); **Industry** (475); **Kenney** (200); **New Ulm** (650); **San Felipe** (723) colonial capital of Texas; **Wallis** (1,137).

Population	22,222	Civ. Labor	11,591
(Change fm '90)	12.1	Unemployed	3.5
Land Area (sq. mi.)	652.7	Annual Wages	$166,762,832
Altitude (ft.)	23-263	Av. Weekly Wage	$457.57
Rainfall (in.)	40.4	Fed. Wages	$2,358,153
Jan. mean min.	39	Ag. Net Cash Return	$1,061,000
July mean max.	94	Prop. Value	$1,475,273,543
Growing season (days)	282	Retail Sales	$205,986,895

Bailey County

Physical Features: High Plains county, san-dy loam soils; mesquite brush; drains to Brazos River, playas.

Economy: Farm supply manufacturing, food-processing plants; muffler manufacturing, medical center.

History: Settlement began after 1900. County created from Bexar 1876, organized 1917. Named for Alamo hero, Peter J. Bailey.

Ethnicity, 1990: White, 6,537 (92.5%); Black, 124 (1.8%); American Indian, 10 (0.1%); Asian, 12 (0.2%); Other, 381 (5.4%). Hispanic, 2,740 (38.8%).

Vital Statistics, 1995: Births, 128; deaths, 52; marriages, 67; divorces, 24.

Recreation: Muleshoe National Wildlife Refuge; "Old Pete," the national mule memorial; historical building park; museum; motorcycle club rally; pheasant hunting.

Minerals: Insignificant.

Agriculture: Feedlot, stocker cattle; cotton, wheat, sorghum, corn, vegetables; 80,000 acres irrigated. Market value $69.9 million.

MULESHOE (4,270) county seat; agribusiness center; feed-corn milling; hospital; livestock show.

Other towns include: **Bula** (35); **Enochs** (80); **Maple** (75).

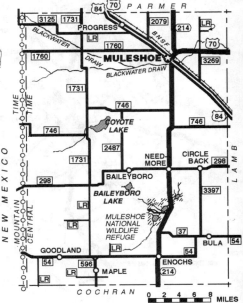

Population	6,690	July mean max.	92	
(Change fm '90)	-5.3	Growing season (days)	181	
Land Area (sq. mi.)	826.7	Civ. Labor	3,700	Fed. Wages	$993,709
Altitude (ft.)	3,790-4,060	Unemployed	5.5	Ag. Net Cash Return	$10,193,000
Rainfall (in.)	16.8	Annual Wages	$40,182,420	Prop. Value	$303,272,620
Jan. mean min.	19	Av. Weekly Wage	$334.82	Retail Sales	$54,662,444

Physical Features: Scenic southwestern county of cedar-covered hills on the Edwards Plateau; Medina River; limestone, sandy soils; species of oaks, walnuts, native cherry and Uvalde maple.

Economy: Tourism, hunting, fishing, ranching supplies, marketing, forest products.

History: Apache, then Comanche territory. White settlement began in early 1850s, including Mormons and Poles. County created from Bexar, Uvalde counties, 1856; named for Bandera (flag) Mountains.

Ethnicity, 1990: White, 10,027 (94.9%); Black, 23 (0.2%); American Indian, 66 (0.6%); Asian, 26 (0.2%); Other, 420 (4.0%). Hispanic, 1,172 (11.1%).

Vital Statistics, 1995: Births, 130; deaths, 108; marriages, 129; divorces, 77.

Recreation: Resort ranches, RV parks; museum; Lost Maples and Hill Country State Natural Areas; race track; Fun-tier Days on Memorial weekend; apple festival in July, Cajun festival in September; Medina Lake.

Agriculture: Beef cattle, sheep, goats; apple production; pecans. Market value $4.7 million.

BANDERA (1,172) county seat; "cowboy capital of the world"; cedar mill, shingle factory; purse factory; spurs, bits manufactured.

Other towns include: **Medina** (515) apple growing; **Pipe Creek** (66); **Tarpley** (30); **Vanderpool** (20).

Also, the community of **Lakehills** (2,786) on Medina Lake.

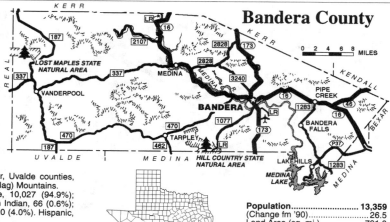

Bandera County

Population............................	**13,359**
(Change fm '90).......................	26.5
Land Area (sq. mi.).................	791.8
Altitude (ft.).....................	1,175-2,185
Rainfall (in.).....................	35.1
Jan. mean min......................	31
July mean max......................	94
Growing season (days).............	235
Civ. Labor........................	6,548
Unemployed........................	3.5
Annual Wages.............	$34,130,230
Av. Weekly Wage..............	$313.87
Fed. Wages.....................	$506,723
Ag. Net Cash Return........	$701,000
Prop. Value.................	$991,660,005
Retail Sales................	$63,582,234

Bastrop County

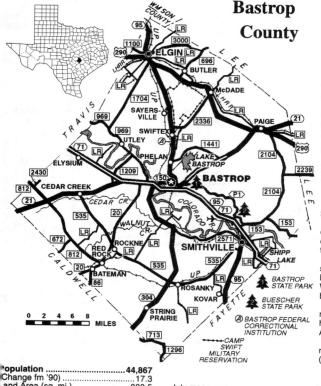

Physical Features: Rolling; alluvial, sandy, loam soils; varied timber, Lost Pines; bisected by Colorado River.

Economy: Government/services; tourism; agribusiness; computer equipment; in Austin metropolitan area.

History: Tonkawa Indian area; Comanches also present. Spanish fort established in 1804. County created 1836; named for Baron de Bastrop, who aided Moses Austin and colonists who settled in 1827.

Ethnicity: White, 29,607 (77.4%); Black, 4,512 (11.8%); American Indian, 181 (0.5%); Asian, 129 (0.3%); Other, 3,834 (10.0%). Hispanic, 6,933 (18.1%).

Vital Statistics, 1995: Births, 672; deaths, 345; marriages, 350; divorces, 280.

Recreation: Fishing, hunting; state parks; Lake Bastrop; historic sites; museum; railroad park.

Minerals: Clay, oil, gas and lignite.

Agriculture: Hay; beef cattle; turfgrasses; horses. Some cotton, wheat. Market value $22.9 million. Pine for lumber, oak for firewood.

BASTROP (5,582) county seat; tourism; oil-well supply, some manufacturing; medical clinic; University of Texas cancer research center; federal correctional center.

Elgin (4,495) computer manufacturing, sausage plants, brick plant; horse, cattle breeding; hospital, medical research; library; Western Days in July, Hogeye festival in October.

Smithville (3,589) rail maintenance, light manufacturing, environmental science park; hospital, model recycling center; jamboree in April.

Other towns include: **McDade** (345) watermelon festival in July; **Paige** (275); **Red Rock** (100); **Rosanky** (210).

Population..............................	44,867
Change fm '90...........................	17.3
Land Area (sq. mi.).....................	888.5
Altitude (ft.)..........................	356-729
Rainfall (in.)..........................	38.3
Jan. mean min...........................	35
July mean max...........................	95
Growing season (days)...................	268
Civ. Labor..............................	24,468
Unemployed..............................	3.4
Annual Wages................	$157,400,931
Av. Weekly Wage....................	$363.28
Fed. Wages.....................	$14,059,195
Ag. Net Cash Return............	-$425,000
Prop. Value.................	$1,509,856,669
Retail Sales................	$373,137,653

Baylor County

Physical Features: North Central county; level to hilly; drains to Brazos, Wichita rivers; sandy, loam, red soils; grassy, mesquites, cedars.

Economy: Agribusiness; retail/service; health services.

History: Comanches, with Wichitas and other tribes; removed in 1874-75. Anglo-Americans settled in the 1870s. County created from Fannin County 1858; organized in 1879. Named for H.W. Baylor, Texas Ranger surgeon.

Ethnicity, 1990: White, 3,962 (90.4%); Black, 180 (4.1%); American Indian, 9 (0.2%); Asian, 13 (0.3%); Other, 221 (5.0%). Hispanic, 334 (7.6%).

Vital Statistics, 1995: Births, 43; deaths, 80; marriages, 34; divorces, 21.

Recreation: Lakes; hunting; park, pavilions; settlers reunion, fish day in spring, autumn leaves festival in October.

Minerals: Oil, gas produced.

Agriculture: Wheat, cotton, hay; stocker cattle, cow-calf operations. Market value $29.6 million.

SEYMOUR (3,198) county seat; agribusiness; hospital; dove hunters' breakfast in September.

Population	4,467
(Change fm '90)	1.9
Land Area (sq. mi.)	870.8
Altitude (ft.)	1,053-1,394
Rainfall (in.)	27.3
Jan. mean min.	26
July mean max.	97
Growing season (days)	214
Civ. Labor	1,833
Unemployed	5.3
Annual Wages	$19,933,734
Av. Weekly Wage	$325.51
Fed. Wages	$791,305
Ag. Net Cash Return	$3,936,000
Prop. Value	$244,978,256
Retail Sales	$27,492,828

Bee County

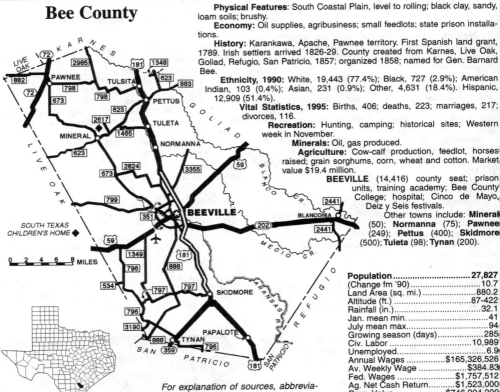

Physical Features: South Coastal Plain, level to rolling; black clay, sandy, loam soils; brushy.

Economy: Oil supplies, agribusiness; small feedlots; state prison installations.

History: Karankawa, Apache, Pawnee territory. First Spanish land grant, 1789. Irish settlers arrived 1826-29. County created from Karnes, Live Oak, Goliad, Refugio, San Patricio, 1857; organized 1858; named for Gen. Barnard Bee.

Ethnicity, 1990: White, 19,443 (77.4%); Black, 727 (2.9%); American Indian, 103 (0.4%); Asian, 231 (0.9%); Other, 4,631 (18.4%). Hispanic, 12,909 (51.4%).

Vital Statistics, 1995: Births, 406; deaths, 223; marriages, 217; divorces, 116.

Recreation: Hunting, camping; historical sites; Western week in November.

Minerals: Oil, gas produced.

Agriculture: Cow-calf production, feedlot, horses raised; grain sorghums, corn, wheat and cotton. Market value $19.4 million.

BEEVILLE (14,416) county seat; prison units, training academy; Bee County College; hospital; Cinco de Mayo, Deiz y Seis festivals.

Other towns include: **Mineral** (50); **Normanna** (75); **Pawnee** (249); **Pettus** (400); **Skidmore** (500); **Tuleta** (98); **Tynan** (200).

Population	27,827
(Change fm '90)	10.7
Land Area (sq. mi.)	880.2
Altitude (ft.)	87-422
Rainfall (in.)	32.1
Jan. mean min.	41
July mean max.	94
Growing season (days)	285
Civ. Labor	10,989
Unemployed	6.9
Annual Wages	$165,326,526
Av. Weekly Wage	$384.83
Fed. Wages	$1,757,512
Ag. Net Cash Return	$1,523,000
Prop. Value	$746,904,200
Retail Sales	$134,636,500

For explanation of sources, abbreviations and symbols, see p. 142.

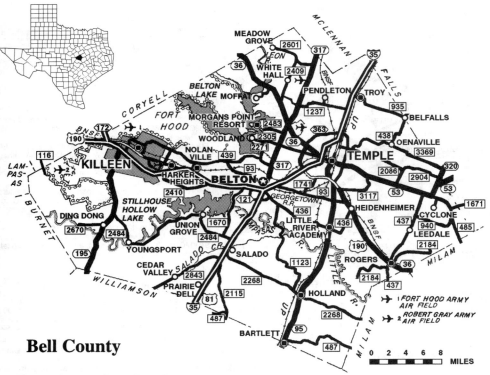

Bell County

Physical Features: Central Texas Blackland, level to hilly; black to light soils in west; mixed timber.

Economy: Fort Hood; diversified manufacturing includes computers, plastic goods, furniture, clothing; agribusiness; distribution center; tourism.

History: Tonkawas, Lipan Apaches; reduced by disease and advancing frontier by 1840s. Comanches raided into 1870s. Settled in 1830s as part of Robertson's colony. A few slaveholders in 1850s. County created from Milam County in 1850; named for Gov. P.H. Bell.

Ethnicity, 1990: White, 136,066 (71.2%); Black, 36,095 (18.9%); American Indian, 944 (0.5%); Asian, 5,531 (2.9%); Other, 12,452 (6.5%). Hispanic, 24,995 (13.1%).

Vital Statistics, 1995: Births, 4,959; deaths, 1,340; marriages, 3,350; divorces, 2,179.

Recreation: Fishing, hunting; lakes; historic sites; exposition center; Salado gathering of Scottish clans in November.

Minerals: Stone, sand, gravel.

Agriculture: Cattle, turkey operations; corn, wheat, sorghums, hay, soybeans. Market value $19.4 million. Cedar posts produced.

BELTON (13,619) county seat; University of Mary Hardin-Baylor; manufactures include school, office furniture, roofing felt, athletic equipment; Central Texas State Fair in September.

Killeen (79,347) Fort Hood; colleges; varied manufacturing; convention facilities; medical center, psychiatric center.

Temple (49,722) rail, market, distribution center; diversified industries; exposition center; junior college; medical centers, VA hospital.

Other towns include: **Harker Heights** (15,420) Founder's Day in October; **Heidenheimer** (144); **Holland** (1,341); **Little River-Academy** (1,672); **Morgan's Point Resort** (2,349); **Nolanville** (2,473); **Pendleton** (60); **Rogers** (1,177); **Salado** (1,357) arts, crafts center, new civic center; **Troy** (1,723).

Also, part of **Bartlett** (1,648) is in Bell County.

Fort Hood has a population of 37,998.

Population	**217,379**
(Change fm '90)	13.8
Land Area (sq. mi.)	1,059.0
Altitude (ft.)	429-1,245
Rainfall (in.)	34.9
Jan. mean min.	35
July mean max.	95
Growing season (days)	260
Civ. Labor	92,108
Unemployed	4.9
Annual Wages	$1,565,585,405
Av. Weekly Wage	$419.07
Fed. Wages	$218,415,178
Ag. Net Cash Return	$1,523,000
Prop. Value	$5,752,391,576
Retail Sales	$2,781,730,065

For explanation of sources, abbreviations and symbols, see p. 142

Bexar County

Physical Features: On edge of Balcones Escarpment, Coastal Plain; heavy black to thin limestone soils; spring-fed streams; underground water; mesquite, other brush.

Economy: Government center with large federal payroll, five military bases; tourism second-largest industry; developing high-tech industrial park, research center; education center with 14 colleges.

History: Coahuiltecan Indian area; also Lipan Apaches and Tonkawas present. Mission San Antonio de Valero (Alamo) founded in 1718. Canary Islanders arrived in 1731. Anglo-American settlers began arriving in late 1820s. County created 1836 from Spanish municipality named for Duke de Bexar; a colonial capital of Texas.

Ethnicity, 1990: White, 878,736 (74.1%); Black, 84,670 (7.1%); American Indian, 4,265 (0.4%); Asian, 15,429 (1.3%); Other, 202,294 (17.1%). Hispanic, 589,180 (49.7%).

Vital Statistics, 1995: Births, 22,564; deaths, 9,215; marriages, 11,122; divorces, 6,911.

Recreation: Historic sites include the Alamo, other missions; River Walk; Seaworld; El Mercado (market), La Villita; Tower of the Americas; Brackenridge Park; zoo; symphony orchestra; HemisFair Plaza; Fiesta Texas; Institute of Texan Cultures; parks, museums; hunting, fishing.

Minerals: Cement, stone, oil, gas, sand and gravel, lime, clays.

Agriculture: Beef cattle; corn, sorghums, vegetables, hay, commercial nursery stock; some irrigation. Market value $45.3 million.

Education: Fourteen colleges including Our Lady of the Lake, St. Mary's University, Trinity University and the University of Texas at San Antonio.

SAN ANTONIO (1,079,207) county seat; Texas' second largest city; varied manufacturing with emphasis on high-tech industries; other products include construction equipment, concrete and dairy products; industrial warehousing.

Other towns include: **Alamo Heights** (7,309); **Balcones Heights** (3,245); **Castle Hills** (4,352); **China Grove** (1,209); **Converse** (10,787); **Elmendorf** (1,033); **Helotes** (1,979); **Kirby** (8,968); **Leon Valley** (10,050); **Live Oak** (10,653); **Olmos Park** (2,269); **St. Hedwig** (1,950); **Selma** (679); **Shavano Park** (2,156); **Somerset** (1,460); **Terrell Hills** (5,131); **Universal City** (14,656); **Windcrest** (5,680).

Population	1,309,550
(Change fm '90)	10.5
Land Area (sq. mi.)	1,246.9
Altitude (ft.)	486-1,892
Rainfall (in.)	31.0
Jan. mean min.	38
July mean max.	95
Growing season (days)	265
Civ. Labor	646,494
Unemployed	4.5
Annual Wages	$12,852,503,679
Av. Weekly Wage	$459.44
Fed. Wages	$1,239,543,934
Ag. Net Cash Return	$6,962,000
Prop. Value	$39,112,772,825
Retail Sales	$13,442,999,632

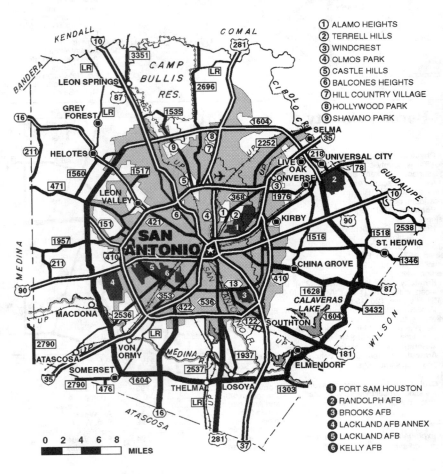

① ALAMO HEIGHTS
② TERRELL HILLS
③ WINDCREST
④ OLMOS PARK
⑤ CASTLE HILLS
⑥ BALCONES HEIGHTS
⑦ HILL COUNTRY VILLAGE
⑧ HOLLYWOOD PARK
⑨ SHAVANO PARK

❶ FORT SAM HOUSTON
❷ RANDOLPH AFB
❸ BROOKS AFB
❹ LACKLAND AFB ANNEX
❺ LACKLAND AFB
❻ KELLY AFB

0 2 4 6 8
MILES

Blanco County

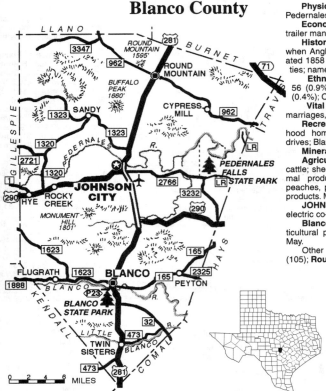

Physical Features: Hill Country county; Blanco, Pedernales rivers; cedars, pecans, other trees.

Economy: Tourism, agribusiness, livestock-trailer manufacturing, ranch supplies, marketing.

History: Lipan Apache area. Comanches present when Anglo-Americans settled in 1850s. County created 1858 from Burnet, Comal, Gillespie, Hays counties; named for Blanco (white) River.

Ethnicity, 1990: White, 5,598 (93.7%); Black, 56 (0.9%); American Indian, 17 (0.3%); Asian, 22 (0.4%); Other, 279 (4.7%). Hispanic, 840 (14.1%).

Vital Statistics, 1995: Births, 95; deaths, 88; marriages, 63; divorces, 39.

Recreation: President Lyndon B. Johnson's boyhood home; state parks; hunting, fishing; scenic drives; Blanco Valley Jamboree in June.

Minerals: Insignificant.

Agriculture: Cow-calf operation, some stocker cattle; sheep, goats, turkeys raised, some exotic animal production; vegetables, wheat, coastal hay, peaches, pecans; limited irrigation for hay and other products. Market value $14.7 million.

JOHNSON CITY (1,156) county seat; tourism; electric co-op; livestock center.

Blanco (1,584) tourism; ranch supply center; horticultural products; nature trail; classic car show in May.

Other towns include: **Cypress Mill** (56); **Hye** (105); **Round Mountain** (232); **Sandy** (25).

Population	7,526
(Change fm '90)	26.0
Land Area (sq. mi.)	711.3
Altitude (ft.)	978-1,888
Rainfall (in.)	34.2
Jan. mean min.	33
July mean max.	94
Growing season (days)	234
Civ. Labor	3,572
Unemployed	2.7
Annual Wages	$37,027,865
Av. Weekly Wage	$375.35
Fed. Wages	$2,523,116
Ag. Net Cash Return	$986,000
Prop. Value	$870,931,968
Retail Sales	$33,541,224

Borden County

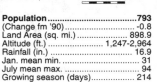

Physical Features: West Texas county of rolling surface, broken by Caprock Escarpment; drains to Colorado River; sandy loam, clay soils.

Economy: Oil, agribusiness.

History: Comanche area. Anglo-Americans settled in 1870s. County created 1876 from Bexar District, organized 1891; named for Gail Borden, patriot, inventor, editor.

Ethnicity, 1990: White, 769 (96.2%); Black, 2 (0.3%); American Indian, 10 (1.3%); Asian, 0 (0.0%); Other, 18 (2.3%). Hispanic, 120 (15.0%).

Vital Statistics, 1995: Births, 5; deaths, 5; marriages, 5; divorces, 2.

Recreation: Fishing, hunting; Lake J.B. Thomas; museum; Coyote Opry in September.

Minerals: Oil, gas, caliche, sand, gravel.

Agriculture: Beef cattle, cotton; also, horses, milo, oats, pecans; some irrigation for cotton. Market value $23.3 million.

GAIL (189) county seat; museum; antique shop, ambulance service; "star" construction atop Gail Mountain.

Population	793
(Change fm '90)	-0.8
Land Area (sq. mi.)	898.9
Altitude (ft.)	1,247-2,964
Rainfall (in.)	16.9
Jan. mean min.	31
July mean max.	94
Growing season (days)	214
Civ. Labor	412
Unemployed	1.5
Annual Wages	$2,517,531
Av. Weekly Wage	$401.54
Fed. Wages	$101,284
Ag. Net Cash Return	$4,091,000
Prop. Value	$291,093,454
Retail Sales	$260,997

For explanation of sources, abbreviations and symbols, see p. 142.

Bosque County

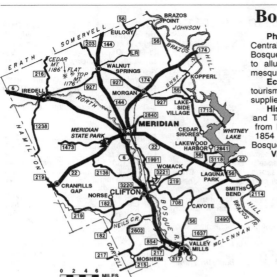

Physical Features: North Central county; hilly, broken by Bosque, Brazos rivers; limestone to alluvial soils; cedars, oaks, mesquites.

Economy: Agribusiness, tourism, small industries; tree supplier.

History: Tonkawa, Waco and Tawakoni Indians. Settlers from England and Norway arrived in 1850s. County created 1854 from Milam District, McLennan County; named for Bosque (woods) River.

Vital Statistics, 1995: Births, 177; deaths, 270; marriages, 107; divorces, 74.

Ethnicity, 1990: White, 14,173 (93.7%); Black, 319 (2.1%); American Indian, 26 (0.2%); Asian, 41 (0.3%); Other, 566 (3.7%). Hispanic, 1,430 (9.5%).

Recreation: Lake, state park, museum at Clifton, conservatory of fine art; fishing, hunting; scenic routes, Norwegian smorgasbord at Norse in November.

Minerals: Limestone.

Agriculture: Beef cow/calf, goats (meat and mohair), sheep, wheat, oats, forage, wildlife, grain sorghum. Market value $38.7 million.

MERIDIAN (1,452) county seat; distribution center; varied manufacturing.

Clifton (3,628) tourism; trade center; light manufacturing; hospital.

Other towns include: **Cranfills Gap** (305); **Iredell** (370); **Kopperl** (225); **Laguna Park** (550); **Morgan** (501); **Valley Mills** (1,157, partly in McLennan County); **Walnut Springs** (814).

Population	16,456		Civ. Labor	6,473
(Change fm '90)	8.8		Unemployed	4.2
Land Area (sq. mi.)	989.3		Annual Wages	$60,798,673
Altitude (ft.)	503-1,221		Av. Weekly Wage	$355.26
Rainfall (in.)	31.6		Fed. Wages	$1,426,562
Jan. mean min.	33		Ag. Net Cash Return	$4,338,000
July mean max.	97		Prop. Value	$846,311,283
Growing season (days)	243		Retail Sales	$65,065,196

Population	84,809		Civ. Labor	40,153
(Change fm '90)	3.8		Unemployed	7.8
Land Area (sq. mi.)	887.9		Annual Wages	$688,985,012
Altitude (ft.)	225-437		Av. Weekly Wage	$417.08
Rainfall (in.)	45.3		Fed. Wages	$88,517,324
Jan. mean min.	35		Ag. Net Cash Return	$4,205,000
July mean max.	93		Prop. Value	$2,469,418,351
Growing season (days)	235		Retail Sales	$911,529,025

Bowie County

Physical Features: Forested hills at northeast corner of state; clay, sandy, alluvial soils; drained by Red and Sulphur rivers.

Economy: Government/services; agribusiness; manufacturing; paper mill.

History: Caddo area, abandoned in 1790s after trouble with Osage tribe. Anglo-Americans began arriving 1815-20. County created 1840 from Red River County; named for Alamo hero, James Bowie.

Vital Statistics, 1995: Births, 1,199; deaths, 955; marriages, 721; divorces, 601.

Ethnicity, 1990: White, 62,878 (77.0%); Black, 17,798 (21.8%); American Indian, 412 (0.5%); Asian, 262 (0.3%); Other, 315 (0.4%). Hispanic, 1,334 (1.6%).

Recreation: Lakes, Crystal Springs beach; hunting, fishing, historic sites; four-states fair in September.

Minerals: Oil, gas, sand, gravel.

Agriculture: Beef, dairy cattle; pine timber, hardwoods, pulpwood harvested; soybeans, wheat, corn, rice, milo, peanuts, blueberries, truck crops. Market value $36.2 million.

BOSTON (200) county seat (but courthouse now located in New Boston).

Texarkana (33,262 in Texas, 22,631 in Arkansas), distribution, manufacturing, regional hospital; tourism; colleges; federal correctional unit; Quadrangle Festival in September, Perot Theatre.

New Boston (5,125) site of courthouse; steel manufactured; agribusiness; lumber mill; state prison unit; Pioneer Days in August.

Other towns include: **De Kalb** (1,941); **Hooks** (2,828); **Leary** (426); **Maud** (1,074); **Nash** (2,372); **Redwater** (857); **Simms** (240); **Wake Village** (5,308).

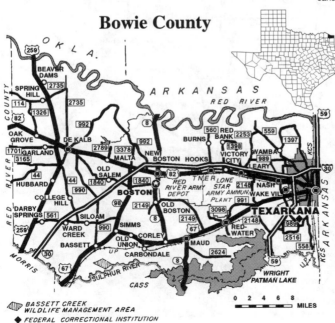

⬛ BASSETT CREEK WILDLIFE MANAGEMENT AREA

◆ FEDERAL CORRECTIONAL INSTITUTION

Brazoria County

Physical Features: Flat Coastal Plain, coastal soils, drained by Brazos and San Bernard rivers.

Economy: Petroleum and chemical industry; fishing; tourism; agribusiness. Part of Houston metropolitan area.

History: Karankawa area. Part of Austin's "Old Three Hundred" colony of families arriving in early 1820s. County created 1836 from Municipality of Brazoria; name derived from Brazos River.

Ethnicity, 1990: White, 154,875 (80.8%); Black, 15,981 (8.3%); American Indian, 812 (0.4%); Asian, 1,961 (1.0%); Other, 18,078 (9.4%). Hispanic, 33,797 (17.6%).

Vital Statistics, 1995: Births, 3,373; deaths, 1,290; marriages, 1,585; divorces, 1,220.

Recreation: Water sports; fishing, hunting; historic sites; state and county parks; replica of the first capitol of the Republic of Texas at West Columbia.

Minerals: Oil, gas, sand gravel.

Agriculture: Rice, hay, greenhouse nurseries, cotton, sorghum, soybeans, corn; beef cattle, hogs, meat goats and ratites; over 32,000 acres of rice irrigated. Market value $43.3 million.

ANGLETON (19,473) county seat; banking, distribution center for oil, chemical, agricultural area; fish-processing plant; hospital.

Brazosport is a community of nine cities; chemical complex; deepwater

For explanation of sources, abbreviations and symbols, see p. 142.

seaport; commercial fishing; tourism; college; hospital; Brazosport cities include **Brazoria** (2,955), **Clute** (9,671), **Freeport** (13,178), **Jones Creek** (2,176), **Lake Jackson** (24,829), **Oyster Creek** (1,061), **Quintana** (62), **Richwood** (2,814), **Surfside Beach** (707).

Alvin (21,005) petrochemical processing; agribusiness; rail, trucking; junior college; hospital; Rice & Crawfest in March; Nolan Ryan museum.

Pearland (25,601, partly in Harris County).

Other towns include: **Bailey's Prairie** (677); **Bonney** (447); **Brookside Village** (1,861); **Damon** (375); **Danbury** (1,682); **Danciger** (357); **Hillcrest Village** (828); **Holiday Lakes** (1,201); **Iowa Colony** (765); **Liverpool** (464); **Manvel** (4,552); **Old Ocean** (915); **Rosharon** (435); **Sweeny** (3,452); **West Columbia** (5,050); tortilla factory, chemical companies; San Jacinto Festival.

Population	**217,318**
(Change fm '90)	13.4
Land Area (sq. mi.)	1,386.9
Altitude (ft.)	sea level-146
Rainfall (in.)	56.4
Jan. mean min.	41
July mean max.	92
Growing season (days)	268
Civ. Labor	105,690
Unemployed	6.7
Annual Wages	$2,104,543,922
Av. Weekly Wage	$585.84
Fed. Wages	$15,730,219
Ag. Net Cash Return	$3,323,000
Prop. Value	$11,924,583,828
Retail Sales	$1,616,938,109

STATE PRISONS
▲ 1 DARRINGTON
▲ 2 RAMSEY
▲ 3 RETRIEVE
▲ 4 CLEMENS
🌲 VARNER-HOGG STATE PARK
🌲 BRYAN BEACH STATE PARK
..... GULF INTRACOASTAL WATERWAY
▨ PEACH POINT WILDLIFE MGMT. AREA

Brazos County

Physical Features: South Central county between Brazos, Navasota rivers; rich bottom soils, sandy, clays on rolling uplands; oak trees.

Economy: Texas A&M University; market and medical center; agribusiness; computers, research and development; government/services; winery; industrial parks; tourism.

History: Bidais and Tonkawas; Comanches hunted in area. Part of Stephen F. Austin's second colony, late 1820s. County created 1841 from Robertson, Washington counties and named Navasota; renamed for Brazos River in 1842, organized 1843.

Ethnicity, 1990: White, 94,866 (77.8%); Black, 13,672 (11.2%); American Indian, 274 (0.2%); Asian, 4,313 (3.5%); Other, 8,737 (7.2%). Hispanic, 16,713 (13.7%).

Vital Statistics, 1995: Births, 1,919; deaths, 612; marriages, 1,341; divorces, 499.

Recreation: Fishing, hunting; raceway; many events related to Texas A&M activities; George Bush Presidential Library and Museum.

Minerals: Sand and gravel, lignite, gas, oil.

Agriculture: Cattle, eggs; cotton, hay, corn, sorghum. Market value $33.3 million.

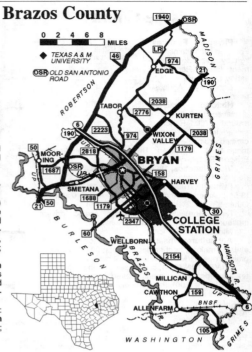

Population	137,057
(Change fm '90)	12.5
Land Area (sq. mi.)	585.8
Altitude (ft.)	197-312
Rainfall (in.)	39.1
Jan. mean min.	39
July mean max.	94
Growing season (days)	274
Civ. Labor	69,463
Unemployed	2.5
Annual Wages	$1,293,117,779
Av. Weekly Wage	$388.99
Fed. Wages	$34,440,550
Ag. Net Cash Return	$3,721,000
Prop. Value	$4,153,541,485
Retail Sales	$1,313,387,827

BRYAN (60,451) county seat; defense electronics, other varied manufacturing; agribusiness center; hospitals, psychiatric facilities; Blinn College extension.
College Station (63,091) home of Texas A&M University, varied high-tech manufacturing; research.

Other towns include: **Kurten** (150); **Millican** (157); **Wellborn** (100); **Wixon Valley** (240).

Brewster County

Physical Features: Largest county, with area slightly less than that of Connecticut plus Rhode Island; mountains, canyons, distinctive geology, plant life, animals.

Economy: Sul Ross State University; ranching; tourism; government/services; retirement developments; hunting leases.

History: Pueblo culture had begun when Spanish explored in 1500s. Mescalero Apaches in Chisos; Comanches raided in area. Ranching developed in northern part 1880s; Mexican agricultural communites along river. County created 1887 from Presidio County; named for Henry P. Brewster, Republic secretary of war.

Ethnicity, 1990: White, 8,300 (95.6%); Black, 85 (1.0%); American Indian, 20 (0.2%); Asian, 52 (0.6%); Other, 224 (2.6%). Hispanic, 3,702 (42.6%).

Vital Statistics, 1995: Births, 119; deaths, 81; marriages, 82; divorces, 34.

Recreation: Big Bend National Park; ghost mining towns; scenic drives; museum; rockhound areas; annual chili cookoff at Terlingua; cavalry post at Lajitas; hunting.

Minerals: Fluorspar, bentonite, perlite.

Agriculture: Beef cattle, sheep, goats, horses; pecans, apples; exotic wildlife; other types of fruit. Market value $12.2 million.

ALPINE (5,993) county seat; ranch trade center; tourism; Sul Ross State University; hospital; varied manufacturing. Other community, **Marathon** (800) ranching center; burro roping in March. Also, **Big Bend National Park** (105) and **Terlingua** (25).

Population	9,453
(Change fm '90)	8.9
Land Area (sq. mi.)	6,193.0
Altitude (ft.)	1,355-7,825
Rainfall (in.)	16.9
Jan. mean min.	30
July mean max.	89
Growing season (days)	223
Civ. Labor	4,891
Unemployed	2.8
Annual Wages	$53,622,283
Av. Weekly Wage	$315.98
Fed. Wages	$5,553,840
Ag. Net Cash Return	$1,866,000
Prop. Value	$386,398,897
Retail Sales	$70,748,505

Briscoe County

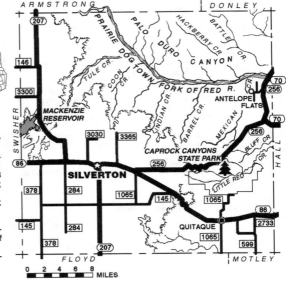

Physical Features: Partly on High Plains, broken by Caprock Escarpment, fork of Red River; sandy, loam soils.

Economy: Agribusiness.

History: Apaches, displaced by Comanches around 1700. Ranchers settled in 1880s. County created from Bexar District, 1876, organized 1892; named for Andrew Briscoe, Republic of Texas soldier.

Vital Statistics, 1995: Births, 26; deaths, 18; marriages, 11; divorces, 12.

Ethnicity, 1990: White, 1,559 (79.1%); Black, 68 (3.5%); American Indian, 5 (0.3%); Asian, 0 (0.0%); Other, 339 (17.2%). Hispanic, 367 (18.6%).

Recreation: Hunting, fishing; scenic drives; museum; state park, Mackenzie Reservoir.

Minerals: Insignificant.

Agriculture: Wheat, sorghums, cotton, corn; vegetables, melons; beef cattle, stockers; 60,000 acres of grains irrigated. Market value $14.9 million.

SILVERTON (814), county seat; agribusiness center; irrigation supplies manufactured; clinics.

Quitaque (500), trade center.

Population.....................2,041		
(Change fm '90) 3.6	July mean max................................91	Av. Weekly Wage $294.75
Land Area (sq. mi.)..................... 900.3	Growing season (days)..................214	Fed. Wages........................... $355,961
Altitude (ft.)......................... 2,174-3,316	Civ. Labor 960	Ag. Net Cash return........... $2,774,000
Rainfall (in.) 21.4	Unemployed.....................................3.1	Prop. Value.................... $106,362,214
Jan. mean min................................... 20	Annual Wages $7,222,677	Retail Sales $5,422,031

Brooks County

Physical Features: On Rio Grande plain near Gulf; level to rolling; brushy; light to dark sandy loam soils.

Economy: Oil, gas, cattle.

History: Coahuiltecan Indians. Spanish land grants date to around 1800. County created from Hidalgo, Starr, Zapata counties, 1911. Named for J.A. Brooks, Texas Ranger and legislator.

Ethnicity, 1990: White, 6,748 (82.3%); Black, 3 (0.0%); American Indian, 13 (0.2%); Asian, 10 (0.1%); Other, 1,430 (17.4%). Hispanic, 7,338 (89.4%).

Vital Statistics, 1995: Births, 158; deaths, 59; marriages, 56; divorces, 2.

Recreation: Hunting, fishing; Heritage Museum, Don Pedrito Shrine; fiestas, May and October.

Minerals: Oil, gas production.

Agriculture: Beef cow-calf operations, stocker; crops include watermelons, grain sorghums, hay. Market value $19 million.

FALFURRIAS (5,815) county seat; market center, government services; oil & gas production; hospital; museum, library.

Other towns include: **Encino** (110).

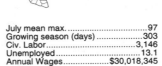

Population 8,396		
(Change fm '90) 2.3	July mean max................................97	Av. Weekly Wage $303.61
Land Area (sq. mi.) 943.3	Growing season (days) 303	Fed. Wages $3,484,521
Altitude (ft.) 46-367	Civ. Labor......................................3,146	Ag. Net Cash Return $1,826,000
Rainfall (in.) 25.9	Unemployed.....................................13.1	Prop. Value.................... $500,135,920
Jan. mean min. 43	Annual Wages...................$30,018,345	Retail Sales $45,276,015

Brown County

Physical Features: Rolling, hilly; drains to Colorado River; varied soils, timber.

Economy: Agribusiness, general manufacturing plants, distribution center.

History: Apaches; displaced by Comanches who were removed by U.S. Army in 1874-75. Anglo-Americans first settled in mid-1850s. County created 1856 from Comanche, Travis counties, organized in 1857. Named for frontiersman Henry S. Brown.

Ethnicity, 1990: White, 30,267 (88.1%); Black, 1,552 (4.5%); American Indian, 131 (0.4%); Asian, 88 (0.3%); Other, 2,333 (6.8%). Hispanic, 3,799 (11.1%).

Vital Statistics, 1995: Births, 509; deaths, 421; marriages, 370; divorces, 184.

Recreation: State park; museum; fishing, hunting.

Minerals: Oil, gas, paving materials, gravel, clays.

Agriculture: Beef cattle, hay, peanuts, pecans, hogs. Market value $31.9 million.

BROWNWOOD (19,254) county seat; retail trade center; varied industries; distribution center; Howard Payne University, MacArthur Academy of Freedom; mental health/mental retardation center; state 4-H Club center; hospitals.

Other towns include: **Bangs** (1,597); **Blanket** (448); **Brookesmith** (61); **Early** (2,652); **May** (285); **Zephyr** (198).

Population	36,899
(Change fm '90)	7.4
Land Area (sq. mi.)	945.0
Altitude (ft.)	1,321-1,894
Rainfall (in.)	27.3
Jan. mean min.	33
July mean max.	97
Growing season (days)	242
Civ. Labor	17,146
Unemployed	6.4

Annual Wages	$284,346,200	Ag. Net Cash Return	$2,561,000
Av. Weekly Wage	$303.55	Prop. Value	$1,186,067,240
Fed. Wages	$3,609,580	Retail Sales	$299,162,853

Burleson County

Physical Features: Rolling to hilly; drains to Brazos, Yegua Creek, Somerville Lake; loam and heavy bottom soils; oaks, other trees.

Economy: Oil and gas; tourism; agribusiness; varied manufacturing; commuters to Texas A&M University.

History: Tonkawas and Caddoes roamed the area. Mexicans and Anglo-Americans settled around fort in 1830. Black freedmen migration increased until 1910. Germans, Czechs, Italians migrated in 1870s-80s. County created 1846 from Milam, Washington counties; named for Edward Burleson, a hero of the Texas Revolution.

Ethnicity, 1990: White, 10,173 (74.7%); Black, 2,430 (17.8%); American Indian, 53 (0.4%); Asian, 18 (0.1%); Other, 951 (7.0%). Hispanic, 1,624 (11.9%).

Vital Statistics, 1995: Births, 207; deaths, 149; marriages, 85; divorces, 86.

Recreation: Fishing, hunting; lake recreation; historic sites; Kolache Festival in September.

Minerals: Oil, gas, sand, gravel.

Agriculture: Beef cattle, hay, cotton, corn, sorghum, oats; some irrigation. Market value $31 million.

CALDWELL (3,909) county seat; agribusiness, oil & gas; manufacturing; tourism; hospital, museum.

Somerville (1,660), tourism, railroad center, some manufacturing.

Other towns include: **Chriesman** (30); **Clay** (61); **Deanville** (130); **Lyons** (360); **Snook** (524).

Population	15,297
(Change fm '90)	12.3
Land Area (sq. mi.)	665.6
Altitude (ft.)	221-417
Rainfall (in.)	39.1
Jan. mean min.	37
July mean max.	94
Growing season (days)	275
Civ. Labor	7,513
Unemployed	4.0
Annual Wages	$68,106,278
Av. Weekly Wage	$397.68
Fed. Wages	$1,312,932
Ag. Net Cash Return	$1,606,000
Prop. Value	$958,891,932
Retail Sales	$86,481,073

For explanation of sources, abbreviations and symbols, see p. 142.

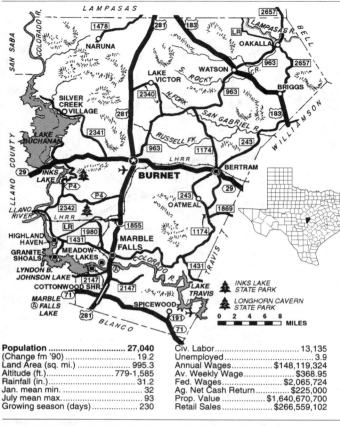

Burnet County

Physical Features: Scenic Hill Country county with lakes; caves; sandy, red, black waxy soils; cedars, other trees.

Economy: Stone processing, manufacturing, agribusinesses, tourism, hunting leases.

History: Tonkawas, Lipan Apaches. Comanches raided in area. Frontier settlers arrived in the late 1840s. County created from Bell, Travis, Williamson counties, 1852; organized 1854; named for David G. Burnet, provisional president of the Republic.

Ethnicity, 1990: White, 20,793 (91.7%); Black, 269 (1.2%); American Indian, 109 (0.5%); Asian, 59 (0.3%); Other, 1,447 (6.4%). Hispanic, 2,440 (10.8%).

Vital Statistics, 1995: Births, 379; deaths, 304; marriages, 284; divorces, 168.

Recreation: Water sports on lakes; sites of historic forts; hunting; state parks.

Minerals: Granite capital of Texas, limestone, graphite.

Agriculture: Cattle, sheep, goats; hay; some grains; 1,400 acres irrigated for pecans. Market value $13.1 million.

BURNET (3,942) tourism; ranching; quarry; light manufacturing; hospital; Bluebonnet festival in April.

Marble Falls (4,762), tourism; ranching; varied manufactured; stone quarry; August drag boat race.

Other towns include: **Bertram** (943) Oatmeal festival on Labor Day; **Briggs** (92); **Cottonwood Shores** (675); **Granite Shoals** (2,278); **Highland Haven** (372); **Meadowlakes** (577); **Spicewood** (110).

Population	27,040	Civ. Labor	13,135
(Change fm '90)	19.2	Unemployed	3.9
Land Area (sq. mi.)	995.3	Annual Wages	$148,119,324
Altitude (ft.)	779-1,585	Av. Weekly Wage	$368.95
Rainfall (in.)	31.2	Fed. Wages	$2,065,724
Jan. mean min.	32	Ag. Net Cash Return	$225,000
July mean max.	93	Prop. Value	$1,640,670,700
Growing season (days)	230	Retail Sales	$266,559,102

Physical Features: Varied soils ranging from black clay to waxy; level, draining to San Marcos River.

Economy: Petroleum, agribusiness, varied manufacturing; part of Austin metro area, also near San Antonio.

History: Tonkawa area. Part of the DeWitt colony, Anglo-Americans settled in the 1830s. Mexican migration increased after 1890. County created from Bas-

Caldwell County

trop, Gonzales counties, 1848; named for frontiersman Mathew Caldwell.

Ethnicity, 1990: White, 18,919 (71.7%); Black, 2,825 (10.7%); American Indian, 65 (0.2%); Asian, 86 (0.3%); Other, 4,497 (17.0%). Hispanic, 9,988 (37.8%).

Vital Statistics, 1995: Births, 432; deaths, 247; marriages, 179; divorces, 141.

Recreation: Fishing; state park; Luling Watermelon Thump; Chisholm Trail roundup at Lockhart; museums; nature trails; rodeo.

Minerals: Oil, gas, sand, gravel.

Agriculture: Beef cattle, turkeys, eggs; cotton, grain sorghums, corn, hay. Market value $30.8 million.

LOCKHART (9,476) county seat, agribusiness center, tourism; hospital, light manufacturing.

Luling (5,236) oil-industry center, oil museum; hospital.

Other towns include: **Dale** (500); **Fentress** (291); **Martindale** (1,061); **Maxwell** (500); **Mustang Ridge** (685, partly in Travis and Bastrop counties); **Niederwald** (257); **Prairie Lea** (255); **Uhland** (388) partly in Hays County.

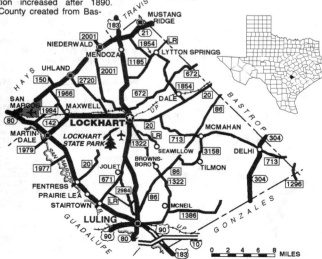

Population	28,636
(Change fm '90)	8.5
Land Area (sq. mi.)	545.8
Altitude (ft.)	388-705
Rainfall (in.)	35.3
Jan. mean min.	36
July mean max.	96
Growing season (days)	275
Civ. Labor	14,676
Unemployed	3.9
Annual Wages	$97,270,883
Av. Weekly Wage	$336.76
Fed. Wages	$1,834,492
Ag. Net Cash Return	$1,654,000
Prop. Value	$767,471,108
Retail Sales	$151,359,523

Calhoun County

Physical Features: Sandy, broken by bays; partly on Matagorda Island.

Economy: Aluminum manufacturing, plastics plant, marine construction, agribusinesses; petroleum; tourism; fish processing.

History: Karankawa area. Empresario Martín De León brought 41 families in 1825. County created from Jackson, Matagorda, Victoria counties, 1846. Named for John C. Calhoun, U.S. statesman.

Ethnicity, 1990: White, 14,819 (77.8%); Black, 556 (2.9%); American Indian, 35 (0.2%); Asian, 556 (2.9%); Other, 3,087 (16.2%). Hispanic, 6,893 (36.2%).

Vital Statistics, 1995: Births, 340; deaths, 149; marriages, 175; divorces, 106.

Recreation: Beaches, fishing, water sports, duck, goose hunting; historic sites, county park; La Salle Days in April.

Minerals: Oil, gas.

Agriculture: Cotton, beef cattle, rice, grain sorghums. Market value $14.2 million. Commercial fishing.

PORT LAVACA (11,532) county seat; commercial seafood operations; offshore drilling operations; tourist center; some manufacturing; convention center; hospital.

Other towns include: **Long Mott** (76); **Point Comfort** (1,137), aluminum, plastic plants, deepwater port; **Port O'Connor** (1,184), tourist center; seafood processing; manufacturing; **Seadrift** (1,496).

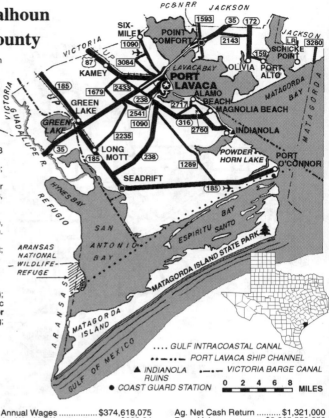

Population................................. 20,057		
(Change fm '90) 5.3		
Land Area (sq. mi.)...................... 512.4		
Altitude (ft.) .... sea level-27		
Rainfall (in.) 39.4		
Jan. mean min................................... 46		
July mean max. 90		
Growing season (days) 300		
Civ. Labor...................................... 9,670		
Unemployed....................................... 7.3		

Annual Wages $374,618,075	Ag. Net Cash Return $1,321,000	
Av. Weekly Wage $680.84	Prop. Value................. $3,265,550,653	
Fed. Wages $1,415,840	Retail Sales $129,952,190	

Callahan County

Physical Features: West Texas county on divide between Brazos, Colorado rivers; level to rolling.

Economy: Feed and fertilizer business; many residents commute to Abilene; 200,000 acres in hunting leases.

History: Comanche territory until 1870s. Anglo-American settlement began around 1860. County created 1858 from Bexar, Bosque, Travis counties; organized 1877. Named for Texas Ranger J.H. Callahan.

Ethnicity, 1990: White, 11,482 (96.8%); Black, 2 (0.0%); American Indian, 44 (0.4%); Asian, 40 (0.3%); Other, 291 (2.5%). Hispanic, 489 (4.1%).

Vital Statistics, 1995: Births, 140; deaths, 148; marriages, 74; divorces, 75.

Recreation: Hunting; museum; lake; Hunters' Supper at deer season.

Minerals: Oil and gas.

Agriculture: Beef cattle; wheat, hay, peanuts, sorghum; goats, horses. Market value $20.2 million.

BAIRD (1,751) county seat; ranching; antique shops; some manufacturing, shipping; hospital.

Clyde (3,405) manufacturing.

Other towns include: **Cross Plains** (1,126), home of creator of Conan the Barbarian; **Putnam** (103).

Population 12,466	Jan. mean min. 32	
(Change fm '90) 5.1	July mean max. 96	
Land Area (sq. mi.) 898.7	Growing season (days).................. 228	
Altitude (ft.)........................1,604-2,204	Civ. Labor 6,555	
Rainfall (in.) 25.2	Unemployed.................................... 4.0	

Annual Wages $34,419,685	
Av. Weekly Wage....................$353.23	
Fed. Wages $1,056,628	
Ag. Net Cash Return $1,799,000	
Prop. Value....................$558,847,768	
Retail Sales $33,114,545	

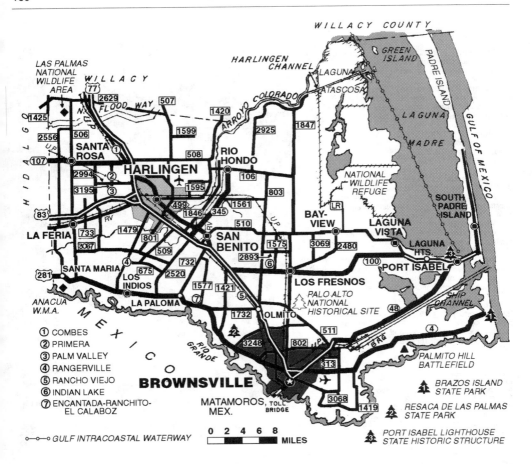

Legend:
① COMBES
② PRIMERA
③ PALM VALLEY
④ RANGERVILLE
⑤ RANCHO VIEJO
⑥ INDIAN LAKE
⑦ ENCANTADA-RANCHITO-EL CALABOZ

o—o—o GULF INTRACOASTAL WATERWAY

0 2 4 6 8 MILES

🐟 BRAZOS ISLAND STATE PARK
🐟 RESACA DE LAS PALMAS STATE PARK
🌲 PORT ISABEL LIGHTHOUSE STATE HISTORIC STRUCTURE

Cameron County

Physical Features: Southernmost county in rich Rio Grande Valley soils; flat landscape; semitropical climate.

Economy: Agribusiness; tourism; seafood processing; shipping, manufacturing; government/services.

History: Coahuiltecan Indian area. Spanish land grants date to 1781. County created from Nueces County, 1848; named for Capt. Ewen Cameron of Mier Expedition.

Ethnicity, 1990: White, 214,424 (82.4%); Black, 825 (0.3%); American Indian, 413 (0.2%); Asian, 750 (0.3%); Other, 43,708 (16.8%). Hispanic, 212,995 (81.9%).

Vital Statistics, 1995: Births, 7,718; deaths, 1,921; marriages, 3,129; divorces, 1,100.

Recreation: South Padre Island: year-round resort; fishing, hunting, water sports; historical sites; gateway to Mexico; state parks; wildlife refuge; recreational vehicle center; Birding Festival in mid-November.

Minerals: Natural gas, oil.

Agriculture: Cotton top crop with grain sorghums, vegetables, and sugar cane raised; wholesale nursery plants raised; small feedlot and cow-calf operations; 200,000 acres irrigated, mostly cotton and grain sorghums. Market value $82.2 million.

BROWNSVILLE (131,524) county seat; varied industries, shipping, college, hospitals, crippled children health center; Gladys Porter Zoo for endangered species; University of Texas at Brownsville.

Harlingen (53,864), medical center; varied manufacturing; construction businesses; agribusiness; college; Riofest in April.

San Benito (22,495), varied manufacturing, bottling; tourism; hospital; recreation facilities.

Other towns include: **Bayview** (295); **Combes** (2,509); **Indian Lake** (426); **La Feria** (5,364); **Laguna Vista** (1,498); **Los Fresnos** (3,196); **Los Indios** (206); **Lozano** (200); **Olmito** (200); **Palm Valley** (1,274).

Also, **Port Isabel** (5,005) tourist center, fishing, Shrimp Cook-Off on Columbus Day, lighthouse; **Primera** (2,628); **Rancho Viejo** (1,107); **Rangerville** (317); **Rio Hondo** (2,328); **Santa Maria** (210); **Santa Rosa** (2,744); **South Padre Island** (2,149).

Population	**304,660**
(Change fm '90)	17.1
Land Area (sq. mi.)	905.6
Altitude (ft.)	sea level-67
Rainfall (in.)	26.6
Jan. mean min.	50
July mean max.	93
Growing season (days)	341
Civ. Labor	124,276
Unemployed	12.6
Annual Wages	$1,697,433,135
Av. Weekly Wage	$355.92
Fed. Wages	$62,622,295
Ag. Net Cash Return	$10,451,000
Prop. Value	$6,706,171,265
Retail Sales	$1,964,916,588

For explanation of sources, abbreviations and symbols, see p. 142.

Camp County

Physical Features: East Texas county with forested hills; drains to Cypress Creek on north; Lake O' the Pines, Lake Bob Sandlin; third smallest county in Texas.

Economy: Agribusiness, chicken processing; timber industries; light manufacturing; retirement center.

History: Caddo area. Anglo-American settlers arrived in late 1830s. Antebellum slaveholding area. County created from Upshur County 1874; named for jurist J.L. Camp.

Ethnicity, 1990: White, 7,130 (72.0%); Black, 2,360 (23.8%); American Indian, 35 (0.4%); Asian, 5 (0.1%); Other, 374 (3.8%). Hispanic, 501 (5.1%).

Vital Statistics, 1995: Births, 178; deaths, 164; marriages, 100; divorces, 41.

Recreation: Water sports, fishing on lakes; Chick Fest in April.

Minerals: Oil, gas, clays, coal.

Agriculture: Beef, dairy cattle; poultry and products important; peaches, hay, blueberries, vegetables. Market value $133.3 million. Forestry.

PITTSBURG (4,418) county seat; agribusiness; timber; tourism; food processing; light manufacturing; community college; Prayer Tower.

Other towns include: **Leesburg** (115) and **Rocky Mound** (57)

Population	10,931
(Change fm '90)	10.4
Land Area (sq. mi.)	197.5
Altitude (ft.)	277-538
Rainfall (in.)	43.3
Jan. mean min.	32
July mean max.	94
Growing season (days)	238
Civ. Labor	5,295
Unemployed	7.9
Annual Wages	$64,797,440
Av. Weekly Wage	$352.11
Fed. Wages	$902,724
Ag. Net Cash Return	$9,964,000
Prop. Value	$382,029,670
Retail Sales	$76,392,046

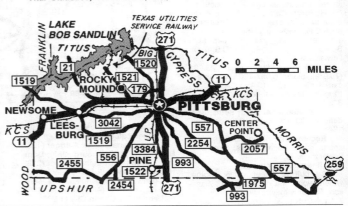

Carson County

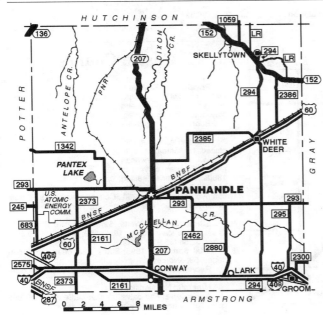

Physical Features: In center of Panhandle on level, some broken land; loam soils.

Economy: Varied manufacturing, Pantex plant (U.S. Atomic Energy Comm.), agribusiness.

History: Apaches, displaced by Comanches. Anglo-American ranchers settled in 1880s. German, Polish farmers arrived around 1910. County created from Bexar District, 1876; organized 1888. Named for Republic secretary of state S.P. Carson.

Ethnicity, 1990: White, 6,315 (96.0%); Black, 11 (0.2%); American Indian, 44 (0.7%); Asian, 9 (0.1%); Other, 197 (3.0%). Hispanic, 354 (5.4%).

Vital Statistics, 1995: Births, 82; deaths, 70; marriages, 45; divorces, 32.

Recreation: Museum, sausage festivals.

Minerals: Oil, gas production.

Agriculture: Beef cattle; wheat, milo, corn, hay; some irrigation. Market value $69.1 million.

PANHANDLE (2,307) county seat; agribusiness, petroleum center; varied manufacturing.

Other towns include: **Groom** (638), **Skellytown** (692), **White Deer** (1,225).

For explanation of sources, abbreviations and symbols, see p. 142.

Population	6,677		Civ. Labor	3,671
(Change fm '90)	1.5		Unemployed	4.2
Land Area (sq. mi.)	923.2		Annual Wages	$184,256,137
Altitude (ft.)	3,204-3,536		Av. Weekly Wage	$770.76
Rainfall (in.)	20.8		Fed. Wages	$12,219,775
Jan. mean min.	22		Ag. Net Cash Return	$7,666,000
July mean max.	93		Prop. Value	$658,851,455
Growing season (days)	191		Retail Sales	$21,461,449

Cass County

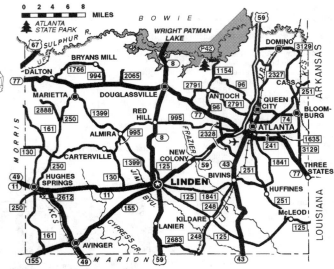

Physical Features: Forested Northeast county rolling to hilly; drained by Cypress Bayou, Sulphur River.

Economy: Government/services; timber; agribusiness; paper production.

History: Caddoes, displaced by other tribes in 1790s. Anglo-Americans arrived in 1830s. Antebellum slaveholding area. County created 1846 from Bowie County; named for U.S. Sen. Lewis Cass.

Ethnicity, 1990: White, 23,651 (78.9%); Black, 6,057 (20.2%); American Indian, 105 (0.4%); Asian, 25 (0.1%); Other, 144 (0.5%). Hispanic, 373 (1.2%).

Vital Statistics, 1995: Births, 387; deaths, 400; marriages, 230; divorces, 184.

Recreation: Fishing, hunting, water sports; state, county parks; lake, wildflower trails.

Minerals: Oil, iron ore.

Agriculture: Beef cattle; forage; watermelons. Market value $18.7 million. Timber is major revenue.

LINDEN (2,369) county seat; woodtreating plants; timber; oldest courthouse still in use as courthouse; hospital.

Atlanta (6,194), varied manufacturing; timber; cattle; two hospitals.

Other towns include: **Avinger** (406); **Bivins** (195); **Bloomburg** (383); **Domino** (106); **Douglassville** (212); **Hughes Springs** (2,100, partly in Morris County), varied manufacturing, warehousing; **Kildare** (49); **Marietta** (170); **McLeod** (230); **Queen City** (1,966).

Population **30,831**
(Change fm '90) 2.8

Land Area (sq. mi.)	937.5
Altitude (ft.)	219-486
Rainfall (in.)	48.3
Jan. mean min.	31
July mean max.	93
Growing season (days)	237
Civ. Labor	15,687
Unemployed	8.6
Annual Wages	$190,100,824
Av. Weekly Wage	$433.25
Fed. Wages	$2,190,489
Ag. Net Cash Return	$1,110,000
Prop. Value	$1,423,578,832
Retail Sales	$193,826,925

Castro County

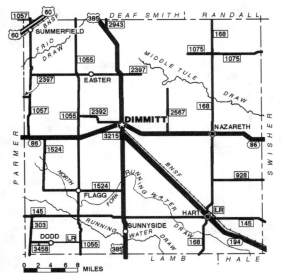

Physical Features: Flat northwest county, drains to creeks, draws and playas; underground water.

Economy: Agribusiness.

History: Apaches, displaced by Comanches in 1720s. Anglo-American ranchers began settling in 1880s. Germans settled after 1900. Mexican migration increased after 1950. County created 1876 from Bexar, organized 1891. Named for Henri Castro, Texas colonizer.

Ethnicity, 1990: White, 5,526 (60.9%); Black, 261 (2.9%); American Indian, 10 (0.1%); Asian, 15 (0.2%); Other, 3,258 (35.9%). Hispanic, 4,187 (46.2%).

Vital Statistics, 1995: Births, 128; deaths, 65; marriages, 59; divorces, 39.

Recreation: Pheasant hunting; Harvest Days celebrated in August.

Minerals: Not significant.

Agriculture: Fed cattle, stocker cattle; crops include corn, cotton and some wheat. Market value $491.5 million.

DIMMITT (4,376) county seat; agribusiness center; library, hospital; Fiestas Patrias in September.

Other towns include: **Hart** (1,198), **Nazareth** (332), **Summerfield** (60).

Population	8,601
(Change fm '90)	-5.2
Land Area (sq. mi.)	898.4
Altitude (ft.)	3,731-3,942
Rainfall (in.)	18.0
Jan. mean min.	19
July mean max.	91
Growing season (days)	193

Civ. Labor	4,134
Unemployed	4.8
Annual Wages	$59,525,273
Av. Weekly Wage	$410.10
Fed. Wages	$1,505,235
Ag. Net Cash Return	$62,246,000
Prop. Value	$428,126,109
Retail Sales	$62,132,346

For explanation of sources, abbreviations and symbols, see. p. 142.

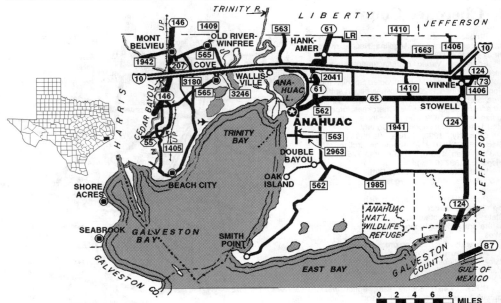

Chambers County

Physical Features: Gulf coastal plain, coastal soils; some forests.

Economy: Petroleum, chemicals, steel plants; agribusinesses; varied manufacturing; fish processing; tourism.

History: Karankawa and other coastal tribes. Nuestra Señora de la Luz Mission established near present Wallisville in 1756. County created 1858 from Liberty, Jefferson counties. Named for Gen. T. J. Chambers, surveyor.

Ethnicity, 1990: White, 16,725 (83.3%); Black, 2,550 (12.7%); American Indian, 53 (0.3%); Asian, 116 (0.6%); Other, 644 (3.2%). Hispanic, 1,195 (5.9%).

Vital Statistics, 1995: Births, 265; deaths, 162; marriages, 138; divorces, 130.

Recreation: Fishing, hunting; water sports; camping; county parks; wildlife refuge; historic sites; Wallisville Heritage Park; Texas Rice Festival, Texas Gatorfest in September.

Minerals: Oil, gas, salt, clays, sand and gravel.

Agriculture: Rice, soybeans; beef cattle; significant irrigation. Market value $14.9 million. Timber important.

ANAHUAC (2,147) county seat; canal connects with Houston Ship Channel; agribusiness; hospital.

Winnie (2,511), Fertilizer manufacturing; wholesale greenhouse; medical center; depot museum.

Other towns include: **Beach City** (1,196); **Cove** (494), **Hankamer** (525), **Monroe City** (90); **Mont Belvieu** (1,540, partly in Liberty County); **Old River-Winfree** (1,396), **Stowell** (1,710) and **Wallisville** (460).

Population	24,165
(Change fm '90)	20.3
Land Area (sq. mi.)	599.4
Altitude (ft.)	sea level-73
Rainfall (in.)	51.7
Jan. mean min.	41
July mean max.	92
Growing season (days)	261
Civ. Labor	10,967
Unemployed	5.3
Annual Wages	$206,900,693
Av. Weekly Wage	$594.25
Fed. Wages	$1,505,235
Ag. Net Cash Return	$665,000
Prop. Value	$3,127,315,897
Retail Sales	$499,959,768

For explanation of sources, abbreviations and symbols, see p. 142.

Fast Growing Counties 1990-96

Rank	County (Largest city)	Percent
1.	Williamson County (Round Rock)	36.3
2.	Collin County (Plano)	35.7
3.	Webb County (Laredo)	32.3
4.	Kendall County (Boerne)	31.5
5.	Fort Bend County (Missouri City)	31.1
6.	Montgomery County (Conroe)	29.6
7.	Comal County (New Braunfels)	28.9
8.	Rockwall County (Rockwall)	28.3
9.	Bandera County (Bandera) Hidalgo County (McAllen)	26.5
11.	Blanco County (Blanco) Childress County (Childress)	26.0
13.	Denton County (Denton)	25.4
14.	Polk County (Livingston)	24.8
15.	Hartley County (Dalhart)	24.7
16.	Lampasas County (Lampasas)	21.3
17.	Starr County (Rio Grande City)	21.1
18.	Hays County (San Marcos) Maverick County (Eagle Pass)	21.0
20.	Chambers County (Winnie)	20.3
21.	Edwards County (Rocksprings)	19.4
22.	Burnet County (Marble Falls) Liberty County (Liberty)	19.2
24.	Medina County (Hondo) Tyler County (Woodville)	19.0
Statewide growth		11.3

Source: State Data Center, Texas Dept. of Commerce (1996 estimates).

Cherokee County

Physical Features: East Texas county; hilly, partly forested; drains to Angelina, Neches rivers; many streams, lakes; sandy, clay soils.

Economy: Varied manufacturing; agribusinesses; tourism.

History: Caddo tribes attracted Spanish missionaries around 1720. Cherokees began settling area around 1820, and soon afterward Anglo-Americans began to arrive. Cherokees forced to Indian Territory 1839. Named for Indian tribe; created 1846 from Nacogdoches County.

Ethnicity, 1990: White, 32,039 (78.1%); Black, 6,931 (16.9%); American Indian, 108 (0.3%); Asian, 196 (0.5%); Other, 1,775 (4.3%). Hispanic, 2,697 (6.6%).

Vital Statistics, 1995: Births, 595; deaths, 493; marriages, 366; divorces, 272.

Recreation: Water sports; fishing, hunting; historical sites; Texas State Railroad; state parks; nature trails through forests; lakes.

Minerals: Oil, gas, iron ore.

Agriculture: Plant nurseries, dairy operations, beef cattle, hay. Market value $83.7 million. Timber income significant.

RUSK (4,461) county seat; agribusiness; tourism, state mental hospital; prison unit; hospital.

Jacksonville (13,289) varied light manufacturing; agribusiness; tourism; retail center; hospital, colleges, Tomato Fest in September.

Other towns include: **Alto** (1,068); **Cuney** (196); **Gallatin** (441); **Maydelle** (250); **New Summerfield** (617); **Reklaw** (263, partly in Rusk County); **Troup** (1,883, mostly in Smith County); **Wells** (775).

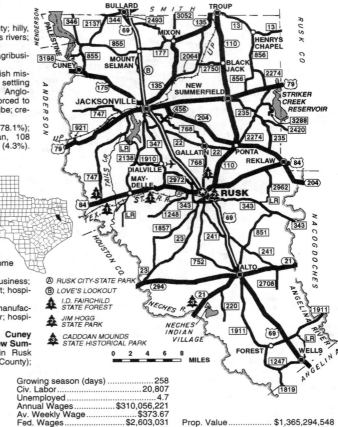

Ⓐ RUSK CITY-STATE PARK
Ⓑ LOVE'S LOOKOUT
🌲 I.D. FAIRCHILD STATE FOREST
🌲 JIM HOGG STATE PARK
🔺 CADDOAN MOUNDS STATE HISTORICAL PARK

Population **43,889**	Growing season (days) 258
(Change fm '90) 6.9	Civ. Labor 20,807
Land Area (sq. mi.) 1,052.3	Unemployed 4.7
Altitude (ft.) 204-708	Annual Wages $310,056,221
Rainfall (in.) 46.1	Av. Weekly Wage $373.67
Jan. mean min. 35	Fed. Wages $2,603,031
July mean max. 93	Ag. Net Cash Return $28,546,000

Prop. Value $1,365,294,548
Retail Sales.................... $290,082,302

Childress County

Physical Features: Rolling prairie, at corner of Panhandle, draining to fork of Red River; mixed soils.

Economy: Cotton; government/services; tourism.

History: Apaches, displaced by Comanches. Ranchers arrived around 1880. County created 1876 from Bexar, Young districts; organized 1887; named for author of Texas Declaration of Independence, George C. Childress.

Ethnicity, 1990: White, 4,969 (83.5%); Black, 321 (5.4%); American Indian, 26 (0.4%); Asian, 17 (0.3%); Other, 620 (10.4%). Hispanic, 853 (14.3%).

Vital Statistics, 1995: Births, 85; deaths, 105; marriages, 86; divorces, 24.

Recreation: Recreation on lakes and creek, fishing, hunting of turkey, quail and wild hog, some deer; parks; county museum.

Agriculture: Cotton, beef cattle, wheat, hay, peanuts, melons; some irrigation. Market value $19.7 million.

CHILDRESS (5,221) county seat; varied manufacturing, hospital, high school all-star football game; settlers reunion; prison unit. Other towns include: **Tell** (63).

Population **7,498**	
(Change fm '90)........................... 26.0	
Land Area (sq. mi.)................... 710.4	
Altitude (ft.) 1,782-1,934	
Rainfall (in.) 20.7	
Jan. mean min. 26	
July mean max. 96	
Growing season (days)............... 217	
Civ. Labor 3,289	
Unemployed 4.7	
Annual Wages $43,248,250	
Av. Weekly Wage $358.93	
Fed. Wages $1,159,048	
Ag. Net Cash Return $5,583,000	
Prop. Value $184,119,212	
Retail Sales $68,879,755	

Clay County

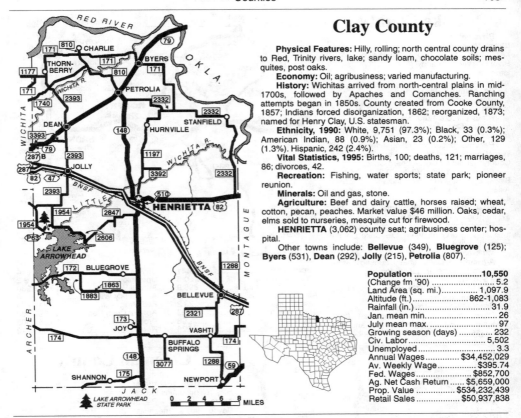

Physical Features: Hilly, rolling; north central county drains to Red, Trinity rivers, lake; sandy loam, chocolate soils; mesquites, post oaks.

Economy: Oil; agribusiness; varied manufacturing.

History: Wichitas arrived from north-central plains in mid-1700s, followed by Apaches and Comanches. Ranching attempts began in 1850s. County created from Cooke County, 1857; Indians forced disorganization, 1862; reorganized, 1873; named for Henry Clay, U.S. statesman.

Ethnicity, 1990: White, 9,751 (97.3%); Black, 33 (0.3%); American Indian, 88 (0.9%); Asian, 23 (0.2%); Other, 129 (1.3%). Hispanic, 242 (2.4%).

Vital Statistics, 1995: Births, 100; deaths, 121; marriages, 86; divorces, 42.

Recreation: Fishing, water sports; state park; pioneer reunion.

Minerals: Oil and gas, stone.

Agriculture: Beef and dairy cattle, horses raised; wheat, cotton, pecan, peaches. Market value $46 million. Oaks, cedar, elms sold to nurseries, mesquite cut for firewood.

HENRIETTA (3,062) county seat; agribusiness center; hospital.

Other towns include: **Bellevue** (349), **Bluegrove** (125); **Byers** (531), **Dean** (292), **Jolly** (215), **Petrolia** (807).

Population	**10,550**
(Change fm '90)	5.2
Land Area (sq. mi.)	1,097.9
Altitude (ft.)	862-1,083
Rainfall (in.)	31.9
Jan. mean min.	26
July mean max.	97
Growing season (days)	232
Civ. Labor	5,502
Unemployed	3.3
Annual Wages	$34,452,029
Av. Weekly Wage	$395.74
Fed. Wages	$852,700
Ag. Net Cash Return	$5,659,000
Prop. Value	$534,232,439
Retail Sales	$50,937,838

Cochran County

Physical Features: South Plains bordering New Mexico with small lakes (playas); underground water; loam, sandy loam soils.

Economy: Agribusiness, oil.

History: Hunting area for various Indian tribes. Ranches operated in 1880s but population in 1900 was still only 25. Farming began in 1920s. County created from Bexar, Young districts, 1876; organized 1924; named for Robert Cochran, who died in the Alamo.

Ethnicity 1990: White, 2,997 (68.5%); Black, 234 (5.3%); American Indian, 13 (0.3%); Asian, 1 (0.0%); Other, 1,132 (25.9%). Hispanic, 1,857 (42.4%).

Vital Statistics, 1995: Births, 57; deaths, 32; marriages, 22; divorces, 15.

Recreation: Rodeo; last frontier days in July; museum.

Minerals: Oil, gas.

Agriculture: Cotton, grain sorghums, wheat, onions; cattle, extensive cattle feeding; 120,500 acres irrigated for cotton, wheat, grain sorghums. Market value $45 million.

MORTON (2,579) county seat; oil, farm center, meat packing; light manufacture; hospital.

Other towns include: **Bledsoe** (125), **Whiteface** (489).

o-o-o (W) MOUNTAIN TIME ZONE
(E) CENTRAL TIME ZONE

Population	**4,306**
(Change fm '90)	-1.6
Land Area (sq. mi.)	775.2
Altitude (ft.)	3,687-3,965
Rainfall (in.)	18.6

Jan. temp. min.	22
July temp. max.	91
Growing season (days)	189
Civ. Labor	1,646
Unemployed	5.5

Annual Wages	$20,493,301
Av. Weekly Wage	$371.58
Fed. Wages	$569,001
Ag. Net Cash Return	$3,675,000
Prop. Value	$467,442,630
Retail Sales	$18,495,303

Coke County

Physical Features: West Texas prairie, hills, Colorado River valley; sandy loam, red soils; reservoir.

Economy: Oil-well supplies, agribusiness, tourism.

History: From 1700 to 1870s, Comanches roamed the area.

Ranches began operating after the Civil War. County created 1889 from Tom Green County; named for Gov. Richard Coke.

Ethnicity, 1990: White, 3,222 (94.1%); Black, 6 (0.2%); American Indian, 17 (0.5%); Asian, 2 (0.1%); Other, 177 (5.2%). Hispanic, 422 (12.3%).

Vital Statistics, 1995: Births, 25; deaths, 57; marriages, 17; divorces, 9.

Recreation: Hunting, fishing; lakes; historic sites, county museum; Ole Coke County Pageant, July 4.

Minerals: Oil, gas.

Agriculture: Cattle; sheep; hunting leases; small grain; some irrigation for hay. Market value $10.8 million.

ROBERT LEE (1,270) county seat; ranching, petroleum center.

Bronte (925); ranching, oil.

Other towns include: **Blackwell** (370, mostly in Nolan County), **Silver** (60) and **Tennyson** (35).

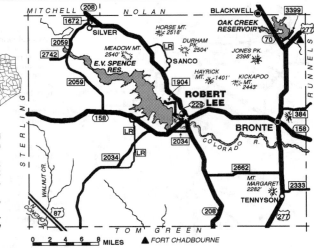

Population	3,441
(Change fm '90)	0.5
Land Area (sq. mi.)	898.9
Altitude (ft.)	1,758-2,608
Rainfall (in.)	23.2
Jan. mean min.	28
July mean max.	96
Growing season (days)	226

Civ. Labor	1,614
Unemployed	2.2
Annual Wages	$19,088,930
Av. Weekly Wage	$366.50
Fed. Wages	$419,770
Ag. Net Cash Return	$1,299,000
Prop. Value	$299,851,905
Retail Sales	$26,367,712

Coleman County

Physical Features: Hilly, rolling; drains to Colorado River, Pecan Bayou; lakes; mesquite, oaks.

Economy: Agribusiness, petroleum, tile plant, varied manufacturing.

History: Presence of Apaches and Comanches brought military outpost, Camp Colorado, before the Civil War. Settlers arrived after organization. County created 1858 from Brown, Travis counties; organization 1864; named for Houston's aide, R.M. Coleman.

Ethnicity, 1990: White, 8,995 (92.6%); Black, 246 (2.5%); American Indian, 29 (0.3%); Asian, 7 (0.1%); Other, 433 (4.5%). Hispanic, 1,139 (11.7%).

Vital Statistics, 1995: Births, 106; deaths, 152; marriages, 89; divorces, 58.

Recreation: Fishing, hunting; water sports; city park, historic sites; lakes; Santa Anna Peak.

Minerals: Oil, gas, stone, clays.

Agriculture: Beef cattle, wheat, sheep, hay, grain sorghums, goats. Market value $19.2 million. Mesquite for firewood and furniture.

COLEMAN (5,374) county seat; clay tile, furniture, other manufacturing; agribusiness center; hospital, museum, bass tournament.

Santa Anna (1,236) agribusiness; some manufacturing; tourism.

Other towns include: **Burkett** (30), **Goldsboro** (30), **Gouldbusk** (70), **Novice** (189), **Rockwood** (80), **Talpa** (127), **Valera** (80), **Voss** (20) and **Whon** (15).

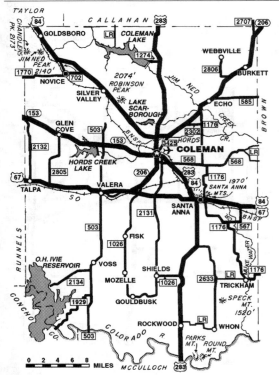

Population	9,926
(Change fm '90)	2.2
Land Area (sq. mi.)	1,272.9
Altitude (ft.)	1,488-2,173
Rainfall (in.)	28.0

Jan. mean min.	32
July mean max.	96
Growing season (days)	235
Civ. Labor	4,010

Unemployed	6.8
Annual Wages	$39,699,763
Av. Weekly Wage	$307.98
Fed. Wages	$1,160,276
Ag. Net Cash Return	$3,386,000
Prop. Value	$448,703,226
Retail Sales	$58,390,405

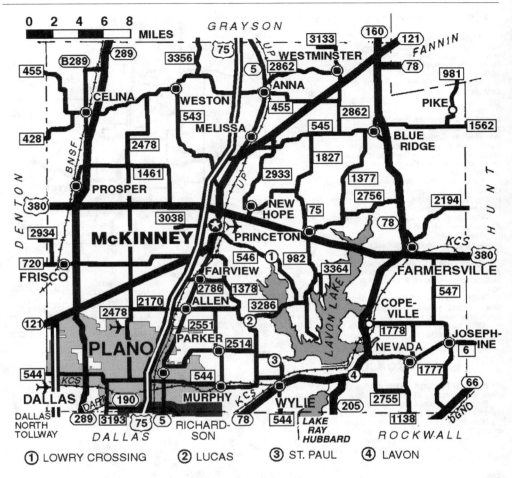

① LOWRY CROSSING   ② LUCAS   ③ ST. PAUL   ④ LAVON

Collin County

Physical Features: North Texas county with heavy, black clay soil; level to rolling; drains to Trinity, Lavon Lake.

Economy: Varied manufacturing plants, agribusinesses, retail and wholesale center; government/services; many residents work in Dallas.

History: Caddo area until 1850s. Settlers of Peters colony arrived in early 1840s. County created from Fannin County 1846. Named for pioneer settler Collin McKinney.

Ethnicity, 1990: White, 235,290 (89.1%); Black, 10,925 (4.1%); American Indian, 1,112 (0.4%); Asian, 7,480 (2.8%); Other, 9,229 (3.5%). Hispanic, 18,158 (6.9%).

Vital Statistics, 1995: Births, 5,829; deaths, 1,318; marriages, 3,086; divorces, 1,854.

Recreation: Fishing, water sports; historic sites; old homes restoration; tours; natural science museum; hot-air balloon festival.

Minerals: Limited stone production.

Agriculture: Wheat, grain sorghum, corn, hay, cotton; beef cattle, horses and sheep raised. Market value $27.9 million.

McKINNEY (30,623) county seat; agribusiness, trade center; varied industry; hospital; museums.

Plano (173,012, partly in Denton County) telecommunications; manufacturing; newspaper printing; medical services; research center; community college; commercial and financial center; hospitals.

Other towns include: **Allen** (25,886); **Anna** (1,115); **Blue Ridge** (580); **Celina** (2,112); **Copeville** (106); **Fairview** (2,295); **Farmersville** (3,213) agribusiness, light industries; **Frisco** (13,076, partly in Denton County) varied manufacturing, community college.

Also, **Josephine** (649); **Lavon** (378); **Lowry Crossing** (1,143); **Lucas** (3,283); **Melissa** (789); **Murphy** (2,358); **Nevada** (597); **New Hope** (611); **Parker** (1,452); **Princeton** (3,273); **Prosper** (1,336); **St. Paul** (558); **Westminster** (497); **Weston** (469); **Wylie** (10,568).

Population	**358,416**
(Change fm '90)	35.7
Land Area (sq. mi.)	847.7
Altitude (ft.)	472-753
Rainfall (in.)	40.0
Jan. mean min.	32
July mean max.	95
Growing season (days)	230
Civ. Labor	215,713
Unemployed	2.7
Annual Wages	$3,990,689,588
Av. Weekly Wage	$635.30
Fed. Wages	$21,856,990
Ag. Net Cash Return	$53,000
Prop. Value	$22,018,314,243
Retail Sales	$3,984,779,740

For explanation of sources, abbreviations and symbols, see p. 142.

Collingsworth County

Physical Features: Panhandle county of rolling, broken terrain, draining to Red River forks; sandy and loam soils.

Economy: Chiefly agribusiness, varied manufacturing.

History: Apaches, displaced by Comanches. Ranchers from England arrived in late 1870s. County created 1876, from Bexar and Young districts, organized 1890. Named for Republic of Texas' first chief justice, James Collinsworth (name misspelled in law).

Ethnicity, 1990: White, 2,977 (83.3%); Black, 230 (6.4%); American Indian, 32 (0.9%); Asian, 3 (0.1%); Other, 331 (9.3%). Hispanic, 561 (15.7%).

Vital Statistics, 1995: Births, 48; deaths, 48; marriages, 57; divorces, 11.

Recreation: Children's camp, county museum, peanut festival; pioneer park.

Minerals: Gas, oil production.

Agriculture: Cotton, peanuts, wheat, alfalfa; cow-calf operation, stocker cattle; 18,000 acres irrigated. Market value $27 million.

WELLINGTON (2,536) county seat; furniture, railroad spikes, mattresses manufactured; agribusiness; hospital.

Other towns include: **Dodson** (113), **Quail** (92), **Samnorwood** (110).

Population	3,657
(Change fm '90)	2.4
Land Area (sq. mi.)	918.8
Altitude (ft.)	1,789-2,389
Rainfall (in.)	21.5
Jan. mean min.	26
July mean max.	97
Growing season (days)	212
Civ. Labor	1,762

Unemployed	3.7
Annual Wages	$14,710,850
Av. Weekly Wage	$319.87
Fed. Wages	$671,548
Ag. Net Cash Return	$2,449,000
Prop. Value	$137,688,430
Retail Sales	$12,392,528

Colorado County

Physical Features: South central county in three soil areas; level to rolling; bisected by Colorado River; oaks.

Economy: Agribusiness; oil-field services and equipment manufacturing; plants process minerals.

History: Karankawa and other tribes. Anglo settlers among Stephen F. Austin's Old Three Hundred families. First German settlers arrived around 1840. Antebellum slaveholding area. County created 1836, organized 1837; named for river.

Ethnicity, 1990: White, 13,352 (72.6%); Black, 3,118 (17.0%); American Indian, 30 (0.2%); Asian, 16 (0.1%); Other, 1,867 (10.2%). Hispanic, 2,833 (15.4%).

Vital Statistics, 1995: Births, 241; deaths, 263; marriages, 143; divorces, 78.

Recreation: Hunting, historic sites; prairie chicken refuge; opera house in Columbus.

Minerals: Gas, oil, uranium.

Agriculture: Rice, corn, soybeans, cotton, peanuts, grain sorghums; cow-calf operations; significant irrigation for rice. Market value $44.9 million. Cedar, pine marketed.

COLUMBUS (3,751) county seat; agribusiness center; oil-field servicing; tourism; hospital; historical sites, homes, walking tour.

Eagle Lake (3,850), rice drying center, wildflower celebration; goose hunting; hospital.

Weimar (2,233), feed mill, light industry, sausage company; hospital; "Gedenke" celebration in May.

Other towns include: **Alleyton** (165), **Altair** (30), **Frelsburg** (75), **Garwood** (975), **Glidden** (255), **Nada** (165), **Oakland** (80), **Rock Island** (160), **Sheridan** (225).

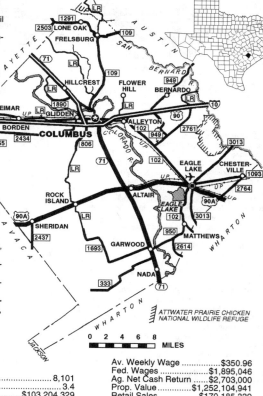

Population	19,473
(Change fm '90)	5.9
Land Area (sq. mi.)	963.0
Altitude (ft.)	151-450
Rainfall (in.)	41.8
Jan. mean min.	37
July mean max.	95
Growing season (days)	280

Civ. Labor	8,101
Unemployed	3.4
Annual Wages	$103,204,329

Av. Weekly Wage	$350.96
Fed. Wages	$1,895,046
Ag. Net Cash Return	$2,703,000
Prop. Value	$1,252,104,941
Retail Sales	$170,185,339

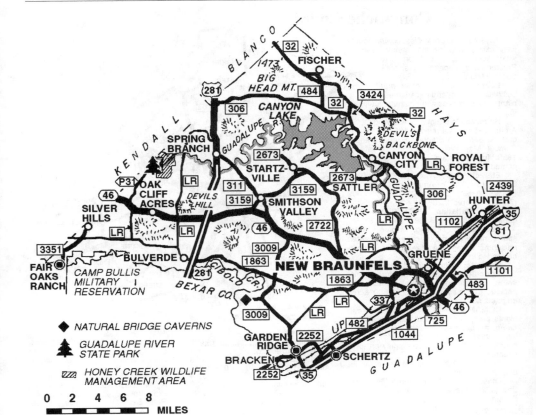

NATURAL BRIDGE CAVERNS

GUADALUPE RIVER STATE PARK

HONEY CREEK WILDLIFE MANAGEMENT AREA

0   2   4   6   8   MILES

Comal County

Physical Features: Scenic Southwest county of hills. Eighty percent above Balcones Escarpment. Spring-fed streams; 2.5-mile-long Comal River, Guadalupe River; Canyon Lake.

Economy: Varied manufacturing; tourism; government/services; county in San Antonio metropolitan area.

History: Tonkawa, Waco Indians. A pioneer German settlement 1845. Mexican migration peaked during Mexican Revolution. County created from Bexar, Gonzales, and Travis counties and organized in 1846; named for river, a name for Spanish earthenware or metal pan used for cooking tortillas.

Ethnicity, 1990: White, 46,821 (90.3%); Black, 443 (0.9%); American Indian, 148 (0.3%); Asian, 164 (0.3%); Other, 4,256 (8.2%). Hispanic, 11,864 (22.9%).

Vital Statistics, 1995: Births, 841; deaths, 592; marriages, 681; divorces, 337.

Recreation: Fishing, hunting; historic sites, Hummel museum; scenic drives; lake facilities; Prince Solms Park, other county parks; Landa Park with 76 species of trees; Gruene historic area; caverns; river resorts; river tubing; Schlitterbahn water park; Wurstfest in October-November.

Minerals: Stone, lime, sand and gravel.

Agriculture: Beef cattle, hogs, goats and sheep; corn, sorghum, hay, wheat. Market value $5 million.

NEW BRAUNFELS (32,724, partly in Guadalupe County) county seat; manufacturing; retail, distribution; one of the most picturesque cities in Texas making it a tourist center; Conservation Plaza; rose garden; hospital; library; mental health and retardation center.

Other towns include: **Bulverde** (NA), **Fair Oaks Ranch** (2,229); **Fischer** (20), **Garden Ridge** (2,174), **Schertz** (12,877); **Spring Branch** (200) and the retirement community area near **Canyon Lake** (11,873).

Population	66,811
(Change fm '90)	28.9
Land Area (sq. mi.)	561.5
Altitude (ft.)	623-1,473
Rainfall (in.)	34.3
Jan. mean min.	37
July mean max.	95
Growing season (days)	261
Civ. Labor	33,727
Unemployed	3.3
Annual Wages	$442,260,584
Av. Weekly Wage	$382.58
Fed. Wages	$5,873,427
Ag. Net Cash Return	-$288,000
Prop. Value	$3,733,201,370
Retail Sales	$2,572,149,246

For explanation of sources, abbreviations and symbols, see p. 142.

Comanche County

Physical Features: West central county with rolling, hilly terrain; sandy, loam, waxy soils; drains to Leon River, Proctor Lake; pecans, oaks, mesquites, cedars.

Economy: Dairies, other agribusiness; Peanut- and pecan-shelling plants; food processing; manufacturing.

History: Comanche area. Anglo-American settlers arrived in 1854 on land granted earlier to Stephen F. Austin and Samuel May Williams. County created 1856 from Bosque, Coryell counties; named for Indian tribe.

Ethnicity, 1990: White, 12,297 (91.9%); Black, 16 (0.1%); American Indian, 51 (0.4%); Asian, 8 (0.1%); Other, 1,009 (7.5%). Hispanic, 2,205 (16.5%).

Vital Statistics, 1995: Births, 141; deaths, 207; marriages, 88; divorces, 61.

Recreation: Hunting, fishing, water sports; museum, parks, community center, museums; Comanche Pow-Wow in September, rodeo in July.

Minerals: Limited gas, oil, stone, clay.

Agriculture: Dairy industry, cattle, swine, sheep and goats; peanuts, hay, pecans, fruit also produced; 38,000 acres irrigated. Market value $101.8 million.

COMANCHE (4,477) county seat; plants process feed, food; varied manufacturing; agribusiness; hospital; Ranger College branch; library; state's oldest courthouse, "Old Cora," on display on town square.

De Leon (2,339) marketing center for peanuts, pecans.

Other towns include: **Energy** (65), **Gustine** (472), **Hasse** (43), **Proctor** (220) and **Sidney** (196).

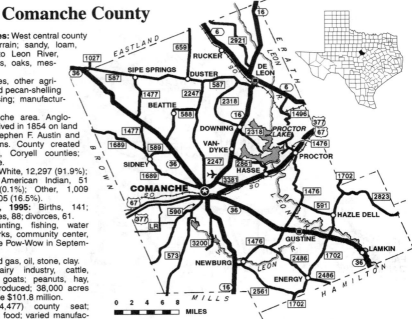

Population............................ **13,975**	Civ. Labor 6,796
(Change fm '90).......................... 4.4	Unemployed 4.3
Land Area (sq. mi.)................... 937.8	Annual Wages $50,949,512
Altitude (ft.)..................... 1,056-1,847	Av. Weekly Wage $331.85
Rainfall (in.) 30.4	Fed. Wages $1,484,400
Jan. mean min............................. 30	Ag. Net Cash Return $23,515,000
July mean max. 95	Prop. Value................ $623,326,403
Growing season (days) 238	Retail Sales $92,697,168

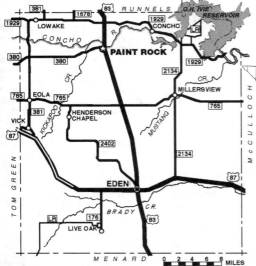

Concho County

Physical Features: West central county on Edwards Plateau, rough, broken to south; level in north; sandy, loam and dark soils; drains to creeks and Colorado River.

Economy: Agribusinesses.

History: Athabascan-speaking Plains Indians, then Jumanos in 1600s, absorbed by Lipan Apaches 1700s. Comanches raided after 1800. Anglo-Americans began ranching around 1850; farming after the Civil War. Mexican-Americans employed on sheep ranches 1920s-30s. County created from Bexar District, 1858, organized 1879; named for river.

Ethnicity, 1990: White, 2,718 (89.3%); Black, 16 (0.5%); American Indian, 5 (0.2%); Asian, 5 (0.2%); Other, 300 (9.9%). Hispanic, 1,194 (39.2%).

Vital Statistics, 1995: Births, 21; deaths, 37; marriages, 20; divorces, 10.

Recreation: Famed for 1,500 Indian pictographs; reservoir.

Minerals: Oil, gas, stone.

Agriculture: Leading sheep-producing area; cattle, goats; wheat, feed grains; 10,000 acres irrigated for cotton. Market value $17.2 million.

PAINT ROCK (215) county seat; named for Indian pictographs nearby; farming, ranching center.

Eden (1,693) steel fabrication, detention center; hospital; fall fest.

Other towns include: **Eola** (218), **Lowake** (40) and **Millersview** (75).

Population............................ **3,163**	
(Change fm '90).......................... 3.9	
Land Area (sq. mi.)................... 991.5	Unemployed.............................. 2.2
Altitude (ft.)..................... 1,631-2,083	Annual Wages $13,201,893
Rainfall (in.) 24.8	Av. Weekly Wage $348.09
Jan. mean min............................. 31	Fed. Wages $443,354
July mean max. 98	Ag. Net Cash Return....... $4,608,000
Growing season (days) 228	Prop. Value................ $306,550,254
Civ. Labor................................ 1,434	Retail Sales................. $16,399,121

For explanation of sources, abbreviations and symbols, see p. 142.

Cooke County

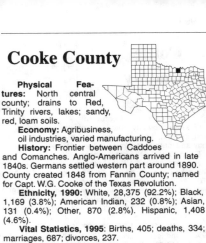

Physical Features: North central county; drains to Red, Trinity rivers, lakes; sandy, red, loam soils.

Economy: Agribusiness, oil industries, varied manufacturing.

History: Frontier between Caddoes and Comanches. Anglo-Americans arrived in late 1840s. Germans settled western part around 1890. County created 1848 from Fannin County; named for Capt. W.G. Cooke of the Texas Revolution.

Ethnicity, 1990: White, 28,375 (92.2%); Black, 1,169 (3.8%); American Indian, 232 (0.8%); Asian, 131 (0.4%); Other, 870 (2.8%). Hispanic, 1,408 (4.6%).

Vital Statistics, 1995: Births, 405; deaths, 334; marriages, 687; divorces, 237.

Recreation: Water sports; hunting, fishing; zoo; museum; park.

Minerals: Oil, gravel, rock.

Agriculture: Beef, dairy operations, wheat, sorghum, corn, soybeans, horses. Market value $39 million.

GAINESVILLE (14,973) county seat; aircraft, steel fabrication, tourism; agribusiness center; zoo; Victorian homes, walking tours; hospital; community college, state school; Camp Sweeney for diabetic children.

Muenster (1,491), dairy center, food processing, oil, varied manufacturing; hospital, Germanfest.

Other towns include: **Callisburg** (425), **Era** (200), **Lindsay** (793), **Myra** (300), **Oak Ridge** (226), **Rosston** (75), **Valley View** (688) and the residential community around **Lake Kiowa** (1,850).

Population 32,899
(Change fm '90) 6.9

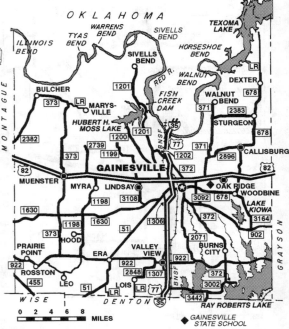

Land Area (sq. mi.)	873.8
Altitude (ft.)	636-1,007
Rainfall (in.)	35.8
Jan. mean min.	27
July mean max.	95
Growing season (days)	226
Civ. Labor	15,883

Unemployed	4.0
Annual Wages	$209,249,592
Av. Weekly Wage	$381.03
Fed. Wages	$2,642,538
Ag. Net Cash Return	$3,460,000
Prop. Value	$1,279,934,901
Retail Sales	$346,765,902

Coryell County

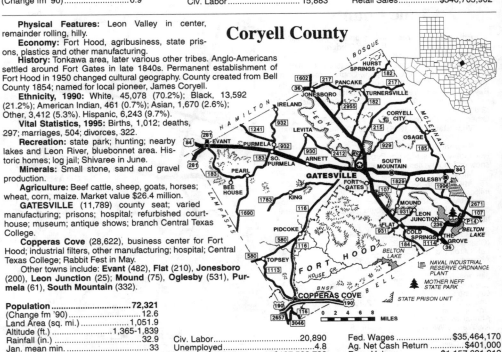

Physical Features: Leon Valley in center, remainder rolling, hilly.

Economy: Fort Hood, agribusiness, state prisons, plastics and other manufacturing.

History: Tonkawa area, later various other tribes. Anglo-Americans settled around Fort Gates in late 1840s. Permanent establishment of Fort Hood in 1950 changed cultural geography. County created from Bell County 1854; named for local pioneer, James Coryell.

Ethnicity, 1990: White, 45,078 (70.2%); Black, 13,592 (21.2%); American Indian, 461 (0.7%); Asian, 1,670 (2.6%); Other, 3,412 (5.3%). Hispanic, 6,243 (9.7%).

Vital Statistics, 1995: Births, 1,012; deaths, 297; marriages, 504; divorces, 322.

Recreation: state park; hunting; nearby lakes and Leon River, bluebonnet area. Historic homes; log jail; Shivaree in June.

Minerals: Small stone, sand and gravel production.

Agriculture: Beef cattle, sheep, goats, horses; wheat, corn, maize. Market value $26.4 million.

GATESVILLE (11,789) county seat; varied manufacturing; prisons; hospital; refurbished courthouse; museum; antique shows; branch Central Texas College.

Copperas Cove (28,622), business center for Fort Hood; industrial filters, other manufacturing; hospital; Central Texas College; Rabbit Fest in May.

Other towns include: **Evant** (482), **Flat** (210), **Jonesboro** (200), **Leon Junction** (25) **Mound** (75), **Oglesby** (531), **Purmela** (61), **South Mountain** (332).

Population 72,321
(Change fm '90) 12.6
Land Area (sq. mi.) 1,051.9
Altitude (ft.) 1,365-1,839
Rainfall (in.) 32.9
Jan. mean min. 33
July mean max. 96
Growing season (days) 241

Civ. Labor	20,890
Unemployed	4.8
Annual Wages	$197,583,728
Av. Weekly Wage	$358.82

Fed. Wages	$35,464,170
Ag. Net Cash Return	$401,000
Prop. Value	$1,157,691,912
Retail Sales	$249,419,922

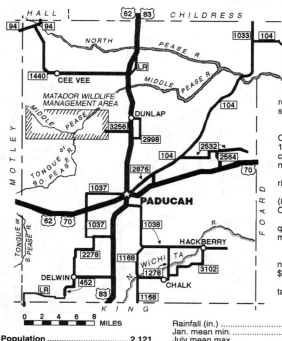

Cottle County

Physical Features: Western county below Caprock, rough in west, level in east; gray, black, sandy and loam soils; drains to Pease River.

Economy: Chiefly agribusiness.

History: Around 1700, Apaches were displaced by Comanches, who in turn were driven out by U.S. Army 1870s. Anglo-American settlers arrived in 1880s. County created 1876 from Fannin County; organized 1892; named for George W. Cottle, Alamo hero.

Vital Statistics, 1995: Births, 27; deaths, 26; marriages, 11; divorces, 5.

Ethnicity, 1990: White, 1,853 (82.5%); Black, 199 (8.9%); American Indian, 4 (0.2%); Asian, 3 (0.1%); Other, 188 (8.4%). Hispanic, 367 (16.3%).

Recreation: Settlers reunion in April; hunting of quail, wild hogs, deer; wildlife management area; museum, courthouse, cotton gins.

Minerals: Oil, natural gas.

Agriculture: Cotton primarily, beef cattle, some peanuts, watermelons; 2,000 acres irrigated. Market value $11.4 million.

PADUCAH (1,682) county seat; agribusiness; hospital.

Other towns include: **Cee Vee** (45).

Population 2,121	Rainfall (in.) 22.3	Annual Wages $9,344,212
(Change from '90) ....-5.6	Jan. mean min. 25	Av. Weekly Wage $330.98
Land Area (sq. mi.) 901.2	July mean max. 96	Fed. Wages $512,099
Altitude (ft.) 1,605-2,149	Growing season (days) 219	Ag. Net Cash Return $2,607,000
	Civ. Labor 875	Prop. Value $125,918,838
	Unemployed 7.3	Retail Sales $11,434,053

Crane County

Physical Features: Rolling prairie, Pecos Valley, some hills; sandy, loam soils; Juan Cordona Lake.

Economy: Oil-based economy.

History: Lipan Apache area. Ranching developed in 1890s. Oil discovered in 1926. County created from Tom Green County 1887, organized 1927; named for Baylor University President W. C. Crane.

Ethnicity, 1990: White, 3,097 (66.6%); Black, 130 (2.8%); American Indian, 11 (0.2%); Asian, 10 (0.2%); Other, 1,404 (30.2%). Hispanic, 1,577 (33.9%).

Vital Statistics, 1995: Births, 72; deaths, 19; marriages, 43; divorces, 25.

Recreation: Sites of pioneer trails and historic Horsehead Crossing on Pecos River; county stock show in January; camping park.

Minerals: Among leaders in oil, gas production.

Agriculture: Cattle ranching. Market value $2.9 million.

CRANE (3,498) county seat; oil-well servicing, production; foundry; steel; surfboard manufacturing; hospital.

Population 4,636	
(Change fm '90) ....-0.3	
Land Area (sq. mi.) 785.6	
Altitude (ft.) 2,475-2,902	
Rainfall (in.) 14.8	
Jan. mean min. 31	
July mean max. 97	
Growing season (days) 225	
Civ. Labor 2,332	
Unemployed 3.5	
Annual Wages $50,088,851	
Av. Weekly Wage $548.18	
Fed. Wages $233,864	
Ag. Net Cash Return $201,000	
Prop. Value $873,250,629	
Retail Sales $31,687,227	

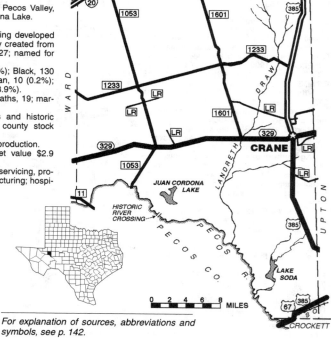

For explanation of sources, abbreviations and symbols, see p. 142.

Crockett County

Physical Features: Level to rough, hilly terrain; drains to Pecos River on south; rocky soils.

Economy: Ranching, oil and gas, hunting leases.

History: Apaches and Tonkawas, displaced by Comanches in 1700s. Fort Lancaster established 1855. Ranching developed during 1880s. County created 1875 from Bexar, organized 1891; named for Alamo hero, Davy Crockett.

Ethnicity, 1990: White, 4,018 (98.5%); Black, 39 (1.0%); American Indian, 9 (0.2%); Asian, 4 (0.1%); Other, 8 (0.2%). Hispanic, 2,021 (49.6%).

Vital Statistics, 1995: Births, 57; deaths, 50; marriages, 42; divorces, 19.

Recreation: Hunting; historic sites, state park; county museum; Davy Crockett statue in park; world championship goat roping in June.

Minerals: Oil, gas production.

Agriculture: A major sheep, Angora goat producing county; income also from beef cattle. Market value $15 million.

OZONA (3,335) county seat; trade center for ranching; hunting leases; tourism; hospital.

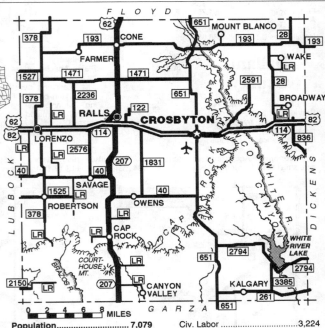

Population	4,479
(Change fm '90)	9.8
Land Area (sq. mi.)	2,807.6
Altitude (ft.)	1,824-3,958
Rainfall (in.)	19.2
Jan. mean min.	30
July mean max.	94
Growing season (days)	233

Civ. Labor	2,019
Unemployed	3.1
Annual Wages	$28,547,344
Av. Weekly Wage	$388.10
Fed. Wages	$293,989
Ag. Net Cash Return	$1,085,000
Prop. Value	$791,277,040
Retail Sales	$27,818,235

Crosby County

Phyical Features: Flat, rich soil above Caprock, broken below; drains into Brazos River forks and playas.

Economy: Agribusiness, tourism, food processing; commuters to Lubbock.

History: Comanches, driven out by U.S. Army in 1870s; ranching developed soon afterward. Quaker colony founded in 1879. County created from Bexar District 1876, organized 1886; named for Texas Land Commissioner Stephen Crosby.

Ethnicity, 1990: White, 5,784 (79.2%); Black, 321 (4.4%); American Indian, 13 (0.2%); Asian, 8 (0.1%); Other, 1,178 (16.1%). Hispanic, 3,111 (42.6%).

Vital Statistics, 1995: Births, 103; deaths, 68; marriages, 52; divorces, 27.

Recreation: Lake; Silver Falls Park; outdoor theater in August.

Minerals: Sand, gravel, oil, gas.

Agriculture: Cotton, beef cattle; sorghum, hay and sunflowers; about 130,000 acres irrigated. Market value $35.5 million.

CROSBYTON (2,021) county seat; agribusiness center; Pioneer Museum, hospital.

Other towns include: **Ralls** (1,995), agribusiness, marketing; museum of Indian artifacts; Cotton Boll Fest in September; **Lorenzo** (1,250).

Population	7,079
(Change fm '90)	-3.1
Land Area (sq. mi.)	899.6
Altitude (ft.)	2,369,3,167
Rainfall (in.)	22.6
Jan. mean min.	23
July mean max.	93
Growing season (days)	206

Civ. Labor	3,224
Unemployed	7.9
Annual Wages	$35,375,049
Av. Weekly Wage	$349.34
Fed. Wages	$676,395
Ag. Net Cash Return	$5,094,000
Prop. Value	$282,073,509
Retail Sales	$53,320,728

Culberson County

Physical Features: Contains Texas' highest mountain; entire county over 3,000 feet in elevation; slopes toward Pecos Valley on east, Diablo Bolson on west; salt lakes; unique vegetation in canyons.

Economy: Agribusiness; tourism; talc mining, processing; oil production; government/services.

History: Apaches arrived about 600 years ago. U.S. military frontier after Civil War. Ranching developed after 1880. Mexican migration increased after 1920. County created from El Paso County 1911, organized 1912; named for D.B. Culberson, Texas congressman.

Vital Statistics, 1995: Births, 56; deaths, 25; marriages, 25; divorces, 14.

Ethnicity, 1990: White, 2,400 (70.4%); Black, 2 (0.1%); American Indian, 16 (0.5%); Asian, 27 (0.8%); Other, 962 (28.2%). Hispanic, 2,419 (71.0%).

Recreation: National park; Guadalupe and El Capitan, twin peaks; scenic canyons and mountains; classic car museum, antique saloon bar; frontier days in June, big buck tournament.

Minerals: Sulfur, talc, marble.

Agriculture: Beef cattle; crops include cotton, vegetables, melons, pecans; 4,000 acres in irrigation. Market value $4.9 million.

VAN HORN (2,150) county seat; tourism; ranching; rock crushing; hospital; airport. Other towns include: **Kent** (60).

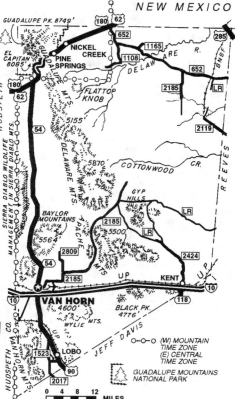

Population	**3,364**
(Change fm '90)	-1.3
Land Area (sq. mi.)	3,812.7
Altitude (ft.)	3,021-8,749
Rainfall (in.)	13.1
Jan. mean min.	28
July mean max.	94
Growing season (days)	224
Civ. Labor.	1,331
Unemployed	9.1
Annual Wages	$21,596,674
Av. Weekly Wage	$384.71
Fed. Wages	$1,757,572
Ag. Net Cash Return	$251,000
Prop. Value	$279,573,864
Retail Sales	$36,681,908

Dallam County

Physical Features: Prairie, over 3,800-foot elevation, broken by creeks; playas; sandy, loam soils; Rita Blanca National Grassland.

Economy: Agribusinesses, tourism, small manufacturing.

History: Earliest Plains Apaches; displaced by Comanches and Kiowas. Ranching developed in late 19th century. Farming began after 1900. County created from Bexar District, 1876, organized 1891. Named for lawyer-editor James W. Dallam.

Ethnicity, 1990: White, 4,600 (84.2%); Black, 112 (2.1%); American Indian, 43 (0.8%); Asian, 14 (0.3%); Other, 692 (12.7%). Hispanic, 1,151 (21.1%).

Vital Statistics, 1995: Births, 118; deaths, 60; marriages, 94; divorces, 38.

Recreation: Interstate Fair in September; XIT Museum; XIT Rodeo and Reunion in August; La Rita Theater in June-August.

Minerals: Not significant.

Agriculture: Beef cattle, feedlots, swine; corn, wheat, grain sorghums, pinto beans, potatoes; substantial irrigation. Market value $282.9 million.

DALHART (6,696, partly in Hartley County) county seat; Frank Phillips College branch, agribusiness center for parts of Texas, New Mexico, Oklahoma; railroad; feedlots; some manufacturing; hospital.

Other towns include: **Kerrick** (60) and **Texline** (446).

Population	**6,119**
(Change fm '90)	12.0
Land Area (sq. mi.)	1,504.8
Altitude (ft.)	3,869-4,693
Rainfall (in.)	17.9
Jan. mean min.	19
July mean max.	92
Growing season (days)	178
Civ. Labor.	3,856
Unemployed	2.6
Annual Wages	$60,334,891
Av. Weekly Wage	$391.67
Fed. Wages	$1,024,891
Ag. Net Cash Return	$50,380,000
Prop. Value	$445,780,020
Retail Sales	$73,336,668

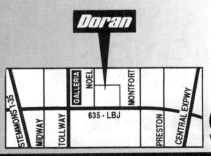

Dallas County

Physical Features: Mostly flat, heavy blackland soils, sandy clays in west; drains to Trinity River.

Economy: A national center for telecommunications, transportation, electronics manufacturing, data processing, conventions and trade shows; foreign-trade zone located at D/FW International Airport, U.S. Customs port of entry; government/services; more than 111 million feet of office space.

History: Caddoan area. Anglo-Americans began arriving in 1840. Antebellum slaveholding area. County created 1846 from Nacogdoches, Robertson counties; named for U.S. Vice President George Mifflin Dallas.

Ethnicity, 1990: White, 1,241,455 (67.0%); Black, 369,597 (19.9%); American Indian, 9,437 (0.5%); Asian, 52,238 (2.8%); Other, 180,083 (9.7%). Hispanic, 315,630 (17.0%).

Vital Statistics, 1995: Births, 36,820; deaths, 13,573; marriages, 17,874; divorces, 10,701.

Recreation: One of the state's top tourist destinations and one of the nation's most popular convention centers.

State Fair, museums, zoo, West End shopping and tourist district, historical sites, including a museum in the old Texas School Book Depository, site of the assassination of President Kennedy.

Other important attractions include the Morton H. Meyerson Symphony Center; performing arts; professional sports; Texas broadcast museum; lakes; theme and amusement parks.

Agriculture: Horticultural crops; corn, wheat, hay; horses, beef cattle, calves, breeder cattle raised. Market value $15.6 million.

Education: Southern Methodist University, University of Dallas, Dallas Baptist College, University of Texas at Dallas, University of Texas Southwestern Medical Center and many other education centers.

DALLAS (1,050,698) county seat; center of state's largest consolidated metropolitan area and third-largest city in Texas; D/FW International Airport is one of the world's busiest in enplanements; headquarters for the U.S. Army and Air Force Exchange Service; Federal Reserve Bank; a leader in fashions and in computer operations; Infomart, a large computer-sales complex; many hotels in downtown area offer adequate accomodations for most conventions (40,000 rooms in greater Dallas area).

Garland (190,703), varied manufacturing; community college branch; hospital; performing arts center.

Irving (169,855), Texas Stadium, home of the Dallas Cowboys; headquarters for the Boy Scouts of America; varied light manufacturing, food processing; distribution center; Northlake College; hospitals.

Other large cities include: **Addison** (10,759) general aviation airport; **Balch**

Springs (18,802); **Carrollton** (99,619, partly in Denton, Collin counties), residential community; distribution center; **Cedar Hill** (24,677, partly in Ellis County), residential community, Northwood University; **Cockrell Hill** (4,239); **Coppell** (23,599) distribution, varied manufacturing; office center; **DeSoto** (34,087), residential community, light industry and distribution; **Duncanville** (37,416), varied manufacturing; residential community; **Farmers Branch** (25,215), varied manufacturing; Brookhaven College; hospital; **Glenn Heights** (5,872); **Grand Prairie** (108,910, partly in Ellis, Tarrant counties), defense industries; distribution center; hospital, Joe Pool Lake; **Highland Park** (9,800); **Hutchins** (2,849), varied manufacturing; **Lancaster** (26,738), residential, industrial, distribution, agricultural center; Cedar Valley College; airport; hospital; **Mesquite** (113,906), residential city with varied industries; hospitals; championship rodeo; Samuel Farm; **Richardson** (87,254), telecommunications, software development; Richland College; hospital; Owens Spring Creek Farm; **Rowlett** (31,818) manufacturing, distribution; hospital; farmers market; **Sachse** (7,288); **Seagoville** (10,293) rural/suburban setting, federal prison; **Sunnyvale** (2,828); **University Park** (22,013); **Wilmer** (2,633).

(Map on following page.)

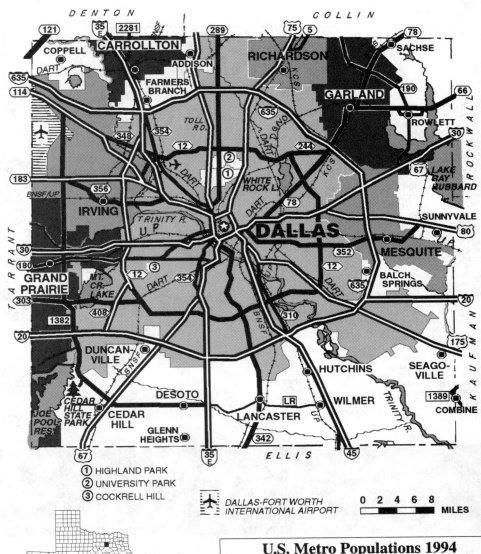

① HIGHLAND PARK
② UNIVERSITY PARK
③ COCKRELL HILL

DALLAS-FORT WORTH
INTERNATIONAL AIRPORT

0 2 4 6 8 MILES

Population 1,989,156
(Change fm '90) 7.4
Land Area (sq. mi.) 879.9
Altitude (ft.)...................................... 382-750
Rainfall (in.)...36.1
Jan. mean min. 35
July mean max...96
Growing season (days) 235
Civ. Labor.......................................1,168,301
Unemployed..4.4
Annual Wages.....................$43,414,854,594
Av. Weekly Wage............................$647.16
Fed. Wages...........................$1,146,657,529
Ag. Net Cash Return....................$1,944,000
Prop. Value $108,664,318,060
Retail Sales..........................$32,695,521,282

U.S. Metro Populations 1994

Rank	Pop. Estimate
1. New York	19.80 million
2. Los Angeles	15.30 million
3. Chicago	8.53 million
4. Washington/Baltimore	7.05 million
5. San Francisco	6.51 million
6. Philadelphia	5.96 million
7. Boston	5.50 million
8. Detroit	5.26 million
9. Dallas/Fort Worth	**4.36 million**
10. Houston	**4.10 million**

Source: U.S. Bureau of the Census

Dawson County

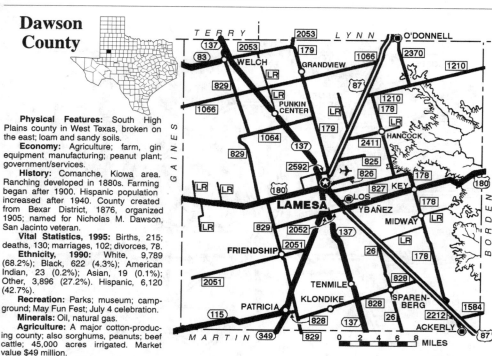

Physical Features: South High Plains county in West Texas, broken on the east; loam and sandy soils.

Economy: Agriculture; farm, gin equipment manufacturing; peanut plant; government/services.

History: Comanche, Kiowa area. Ranching developed in 1880s. Farming began after 1900. Hispanic population increased after 1940. County created from Bexar District, 1876, organized 1905; named for Nicholas M. Dawson, San Jacinto veteran.

Vital Statistics, 1995: Births, 215; deaths, 130; marriages, 102; divorces, 78.

Ethnicity, 1990: White, 9,789 (68.2%); Black, 622 (4.3%); American Indian, 23 (0.2%); Asian, 19 (0.1%); Other, 3,896 (27.2%). Hispanic, 6,120 (42.7%).

Recreation: Parks; museum; campground; May Fun Fest; July 4 celebration.

Minerals: Oil, natural gas.

Agriculture: A major cotton-producing county; also sorghums, peanuts; beef cattle; 45,000 acres irrigated. Market value $49 million.

LAMESA (11,205) county seat; agribusiness; food processing, oil-field services; some manufacturing; computerized cotton-classing office; hospital; campus of Howard College; prison unit.

Other towns include: **Los Ybañez** (86) and **Welch** (110). **Ackerly** (267, partly in Martin County). Part of **O'Donnell** (1,174).

Population	15,223
(Change fm '90)	6.1
Land Area (sq. mi.)	902.1
Altitude (ft.)	2,860-3,095
Rainfall (in.)	16.2
Jan. mean min.	25
July mean max.	95
Growing season (days)	210

Civ. Labor	6,392
Unemployed	6.9
Annual Wages	$90,968,401
Av. Weekly Wage	$359.64
Fed. Wages	$1,910,283
Ag. Net Cash Return	$14,277,000
Prop. Value	$761,352,323
Retail Sales	$102,453,124

Deaf Smith County

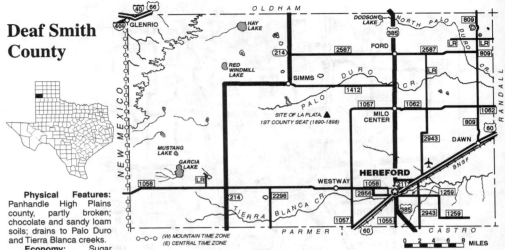

o-o-o-o (W) MOUNTAIN TIME ZONE
(E) CENTRAL TIME ZONE

Physical Features: Panhandle High Plains county, partly broken; chocolate and sandy loam soils; drains to Palo Duro and Tierra Blanca creeks.

Economy: Sugar refinery; meat packers; offset printing; other varied industries, mostly agribusiness.

History: Apaches, displaced by Comanches, Kiowas. Ranching developed after U.S. Army drove out Indians 1874-75. Farming began after 1900. Hispanic settlement increased after 1950. County created 1876, from Bexar District; organized 1890. Named for famed scout in Texas Revolution, Erastus (Deaf) Smith.

Ethnicity, 1990: White, 14,522 (75.8%); Black, 307 (1.6%); American Indian, 49 (0.3%); Asian, 39 (0.2%); Other, 4,236 (22.1%). Hispanic, 9,356 (48.8%).

Vital Statistics, 1995: Births, 359; deaths, 149; marriages, 153; divorces, 69.

Recreation: Museum, tours, POW camp chapel; Cinco de Mayo, Pioneer Day in May.

Minerals: Not significant.

Agriculture: One of leading farm counties; large cattle feedlot operations; crops are sorghums, wheat, oats, barley, beets, corn, cotton, onions, other vegetables, sunflowers; 205,000 acres irrigated. Market value $645 million.

HEREFORD (14,608) county seat; agribusinesses, food processing; varied manufacturing; hospital.

Other towns include: **Dawn** (52).

Population	19,106
(Change fm '90)	-0.2
Land Area (sq. mi.)	1,497.4
Altitude (ft.)	3,789-4,362
Rainfall (in.)	17.2
Jan. mean min.	20
July mean max.	90
Growing season (days)	195
Civ. Labor	8,620
Unemployed	7.5
Annual Wages	$126,417,850
Av. Weekly Wage	$388.54
Fed. Wages	$1,860,114
Ag. Net Cash Return	$52,737,000
Prop. Value	$695,529,050
Retail Sales	$130,064,183

Delta County

Physical Features: Northeast county between two forks of Sulphur River; lake; black, sandy loam soils.

Economy: Agribusiness; tourism; manufacturing.

History: Caddo area, but disease, other tribes caused displacement around 1790. Anglo-Americans arrived in 1820s. County created from Lamar, Hopkins counties 1870. Greek letter delta origin of name, because of shape of the county.

Ethnicity, 1990: White, 4,388 (90.3%); Black, 404 (8.3%); American Indian, 41 (0.8%); Asian, 7 (0.1%); Other, 17 (0.4%). Hispanic, 67 (1.4%).

Vital Statistics, 1995: Births, 68; deaths, 89; marriages, 45; divorces, 19.

Recreation: Fishing, hunting; lakes, state park; Mayfest.

Minerals: Not significant.

Agriculture: Beef, dairy cattle; crops include hay, soybeans, corn, sorghum, cotton, wheat. Market value $8.5 million.

COOPER (2,334) county seat; industrial park, some manufacturing; agribusiness; museum; Chiggerfest in October.

Other towns include: **Ben Franklin** (75), **Enloe** (113), **Klondike** (135), **Lake Creek** (60) and **Pecan Gap** (262, partly in Fannin County).

Population	5,231
(Change fm '90)	7.7
Land Area (sq. mi.)	277.2
Altitude (ft.)	396-536
Rainfall (in.)	42.7
Jan. mean min.	30
July mean max.	94
Growing season (days)	233
Civ. Labor	2,658
Unemployed	4.1
Annual Wages	$17,703,608
Av. Weekly Wage	$311.72
Fed. Wages	$743,614
Ag. Net Cash Return	$614,000
Prop. Value	$148,976,378
Retail Sales	$12,189,048

For explanation of sources, abbreviations and symbols, see p. 142.

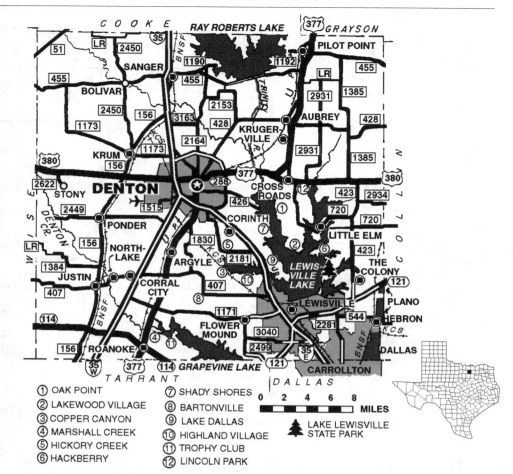

① OAK POINT
② LAKEWOOD VILLAGE
③ COPPER CANYON
④ MARSHALL CREEK
⑤ HICKORY CREEK
⑥ HACKBERRY
⑦ SHADY SHORES
⑧ BARTONVILLE
⑨ LAKE DALLAS
⑩ HIGHLAND VILLAGE
⑪ TROPHY CLUB
⑫ LINCOLN PARK

LAKE LEWISVILLE STATE PARK

Denton County

Physical Features: North Texas county; partly hilly, draining to Trinity River, two lakes; Blackland and Grand Prairie soils and terrain.

Economy: Varied industries; colleges; tourism; government/services; part of Dallas-Fort Worth metropolitan area.

History: Land grant from Texas Congress 1841 for Peters colony. County created out of Fannin County 1846; named for John B. Denton, pioneer Methodist minister.

Ethnicity, 1990: White, 241,982 (88.5%); Black, 13,569 (5.0%); American Indian, 1,416 (0.5%); Asian, 6,870 (2.5%); Other, 9,688 (3.5%). Hispanic, 19,013 (7.0%).

Vital Statistics, 1995: Births, 5,634; deaths, 1,332; marriages, 2,767; divorces, 1,778.

Recreation: Water sports on at Lewisville, Grapevine lakes, seven U.S. Corps of Engineers parks; Ray Roberts lake; universities' cultural, athletic activities, including "Texas Women; A Celebration of History'" exhibit at TWU library; State D.A.R. Museum "First Ladies of Texas" collection of gowns and

memorabilia; Little Chapel in the Woods; Denton Jazzfest in April.

Minerals: Limited output oil, sand, gravel, gas, clay.

Education: University of North Texas and Texas Woman's University.

Agriculture: Horses, hen eggs, beef, slaughter cattle; hay and wheat are the top crops; also grown are sorghum, nursery crops and turfgrass; peanuts, turf irrigated. Market value $43.8 million.

DENTON (73,912) county seat; University of North Texas, Texas Woman's University, Denton State School (for the retarded); plants manufacture a variety of products; hospitals.

Lewisville (58,857), retail center, electronics and varied industries including missile manufacturing; Lewisville Lake, hospital.

Carrollton (99,619, partly in Dallas, Collin counties).

Other towns include: **The Colony** (25,331), on eastern shore of Lewisville Lake, tourism, IBM offices, chili cook-off in June, Las Vegas Night in April; **Flower Mound** (31,227) residential community.

Also, **Argyle** (1,857); **Aubrey** (1,286); **Copper Canyon** (1,279); **Corinth** (5,648); **Corral City** (51); **Cross Roads** (445); **Double Oak**

(2,078); **Hackberry** (238); **Hebron** (1,383); **Hickory Creek** (2,110); **Highland Village** (11,469); **Justin** (1,530); **Krugerville** (971); **Krum** (2,084); **Lake Dallas** (4,314), electronics manufacturing.

Also, **Lakewood Village** (192); **Lincoln Park** (391); **Little Elm** (1,365); **Marshall Creek** (418); **Northlake** (334); **Oak Point** (996); **Pilot Point** (2,910) light manufacturing, agribusinesses, near Lake Ray Roberts, pioneer days in June; **Ponder** (502); **Roanoke** (2,257); **Sanger** (4,129) lake recreation enterprises; **Shady Shores** (1,309); **Trophy Club** (4,689).

Population	343,137
(Change fm '90)	25.4
Land Area (sq. mi.)	888.5
Altitude (ft.)	515-844
Rainfall (in.)	37.3
Jan. mean min.	30
July mean max.	94
Growing season (days)	226
Civ. Labor	211,508
Unemployed	2.8
Annual Wages	$2,143,765,558
Av. Weekly Wage	$462.16
Fed. Wages	$34,659,560
Ag. Net Cash Return	$1,299,000
Prop. Value	$15,356,987,151
Retail Sales	$2,977,955,987

DeWitt County

Physical Features: South central county drained by Guadalupe and tributaries; rolling to level; waxy, loam, sandy soils.

Economy: Wood, furniture plants, textile mill; varied manufacturing; agribusinesses; prison unit.

History: Coahuiltecan area, then Karankawas and other tribes, finally the Comanches. Mexican and Anglo-American settlers arrived in 1820s. County created from Gonzales, Goliad, Victoria counties 1846; named for Green DeWitt, colonizer.

Ethnicity, 1990: White, 14,356 (76.2%); Black, 2,114 (11.2%); American Indian, 22 (0.1%); Asian, 17 (0.1%); Other, 2,331 (12.4%). Hispanic, 4,567 (24.2%).

Vital Statistics, 1995: Births, 215; deaths, 281; marriages, 134; divorces, 99.

Recreation: Hunting, fishing, historic homes; museum.

Minerals: Oil and natural gas.

Agriculture: Cow-calf operations, poultry, swine, dairy products, ratites (emus, ostriches); corn, sorghum, cotton, hay, pecans. Market value $37 million.

CUERO (7,072) county seat; agribusiness, varied manufacturing; food processing; hospital, Turkeyfest in October.

Yorktown (2,307), hospital; museum; oil-well servicing.

Other towns include: **Hochheim** (70), **Meyersville** (110), **Nordheim** (333), **Thomaston** (45), **Westhoff** (410) and **Yoakum** (6,307, mostly in Lavaca County).

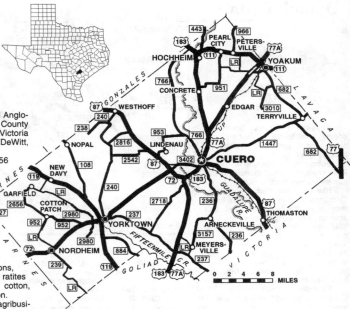

Population **21,060**	Civ. Labor 8,117
(Change fm '90) 11.8	Unemployed 4.5
Land Area (sq. mi.) 909.3	Annual Wages $113,966,522
Altitude (ft.) 163-462	Av. Weekly Wage $368.57
Rainfall (in.) 37.0	Fed. Wages $1,357,768
Jan. mean min. 39	Ag. Net Cash Return $4,476,000
July mean max. 95	Prop. Value $961,527,872
Growing season (days) 270	Retail Sales $114,762,876

Dickens County

Physical Features: West Texas county; broken land, Caprock in northwest; sandy, chocolate, red soils; drains to Croton, Duck creeks.

Economy: Services/prison unit, agribusiness, hunting leases.

History: Comanches driven out by U.S. Army 1874-75. Ranching and some farming began in late 1880s. County created 1876, from Bexar District; organized 1891; named for Alamo hero who is variously listed as James R. Demkins or Dimpkins and J. Dickens.

Ethnicity, 1990: White, 2,193 (85.3%); Black, 113 (4.4%); American Indian, 13 (0.5%); Asian, 1 (0.0%);Other, 251 (9.8%). Hispanic, 479 (18.6%).

Vital Statistics, 1995: Births, 21; deaths, 47; marriages, 14; divorces, 7.

Recreation: Hunting, fishing; Soldiers Mound site, Dickens Springs.

Agriculture: Beef cattle, cotton, sorghum; Spanish goats also raised; hay, wheat, pecans; some irrigation. Market value $12 million.

DICKENS (318) county seat, market for ranching country.

Spur (1,222), agribusiness and shipping center, homecoming in October; state prison

Other towns include: **Afton** (15) and **McAdoo** (75).

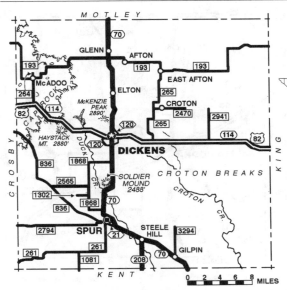

Population **2,497**	Civ. Labor 1,001
(Change fm '90) .... -2.9	Unemployed 6.9
Land Area (sq. mi.) 904.3	Annual Wages $10,298,440
Altitude (ft.) 1,933-2,991	Av. Weekly Wage $352.11
Rainfall (in.) 20.7	Fed. Wages $512,503
Jan. mean min. 26	Ag. Net Cash Return $3,366,000
July mean max. 95	Prop. Value $158,552,820
Growing season (days) 217	Retail Sales $9,075,218

Dimmit County

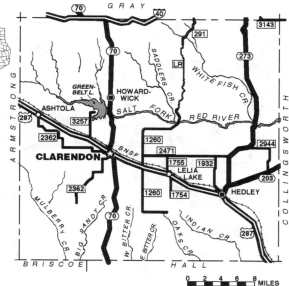

Physical Features: Southwest county; level to rolling; much brush; sandy, loam, red soils; drained by Nueces River.

Economy: Agribusiness; petroleum products; varied manufacturing; tourism; government/services.

History: Coahuiltecan area, later Comanches. John Townsend, a black man from Nacogdoches, led first attempt at settlement before the Civil War. Texas Rangers forced Indians out in 1877. Mexican migration increased after 1910. County created 1858 from Bexar, Maverick, Uvalde, Webb counties; organized 1880. Named for Philip Dimitt of Texas Revolution; law misspelled name.

Ethnicity, 1990: White, 7,599 (72.8%); Black, 60 (0.6%); American Indian, 16 (0.2%); Asian, 12 (0.1%); Other, 2,746 (26.3%). Hispanic, 8,688 (83.3%).

Vital Statistics, 1995: Births, 161; deaths, 69; marriages, 52; divorces, 0.

Recreation: Hunting, fishing, campsites; winter haven for tourist.

Minerals: Oil, gas production.

Agriculture: Cotton, hay, pecans, vegetables; beef cattle raised; among leading irrigated vegetable-growing counties. Market value $14 million.

CARRIZO SPRINGS (5,704) county seat; agribusiness center, feedlot, food processing; oil, gas processing; hunting center; hospitals.

Other towns include: **Asherton** (1,589), **Big Wells** (817) and **Catarina** (45).

Population **10,489**
(Change fm '90) 0.5

Land Area (sq. mi.)	1,331.0
Altitude (ft.)	461-591
Rainfall (in.)	21.7
Jan. mean min.	41
July mean max.	99
Growing season (days)	290
Civ. Labor	3,642
Unemployed	15.4
Annual Wages	$39,060,240
Av. Weekly Wage	$313.60
Fed. Wages	$3,336,705
Ag. Net Cash Return	-$199,000
Prop. Value	$484,312,084
Retail Sales	$42,014,279

Donley County

Physical Features: Northwest county bisected by Red River Salt Fork; rolling to level; clay, loam, sandy soils.

Economy: Agribusinesses; distribution; varied manufacturing.

History: Apaches, displaced by Kiowas and Comanches who were driven out in 1874-75 by U.S. Army. Methodist colony from New York settled in 1878. County created in 1876, organized 1882, out of Bexar District; named for Texas Supreme Court Justice S.P. Donley.

Ethnicity, 1990: White, 3,522 (95.3%); Black, 127 (3.4%); American Indian, 13 (0.4%); Asian, 2 (0.1%); Other, 32 (0.9%). Hispanic, 139 (3.8%).

Vital Statistics, 1995: Births, 41; deaths, 59; marriages, 25; divorces, 13.

Recreation: Lake, hunting, fishing, camping, water sports; museum.

Minerals: Small amount of natural gas.

Agriculture: Cattle top revenue source; cotton important; some wheat, sorghum; 8,500 acres irrigated; peanuts increasing. Market value $54.4 million.

CLARENDON (2,106) county seat; junior college; Saints Roost museum; library; agribusiness, tourism; medical center.

Other towns include: **Hedley** (415), **Howardwick** (215) and **Lelia Lake** (125).

For explanation of sources, abbreviations and symbols, see p. 142.

Population **3,733**
(Change fm 90) 1.0
Land Area (sq. mi.) 929.8
Altitude (ft.) 2,388-3,213
Rainfall (in.) 22.0
Jan. mean min. 21
July mean max. 94
Growing season (days) 206

Civ. Labor	1,615
Unemployed	3.0
Annual Wages	$14,915,406
Av. Weekly Wage	$312.72
Fed. Wages	$540,283
Ag. Net Cash Return	$2,855,000
Prop. Value	$210,075,677
Retail Sales	$17,353,401

Duval County

Physical   Features: Southwestern county; level to hilly, brushy in most areas; varied soils.

Economy: Ranching; petroleum; tourism; government/services.

History: Coahuiltecans, displaced by Comanche bands. Mexican settlement began in 1812. County created from Live Oak, Nueces, Starr counties, 1858, organized 1876; named for B.H. Duval, a victim of Goliad massacre.

Ethnicity, 1990: White, 10,183 (78.8%); Black, 12 (0.1%); American Indian, 12 (0.1%); Asian, 17 (0.1%); Other, 2,694 (20.9%). Hispanic, 11,267 (87.2%).

Vital Statistics, 1995: Births, 222; deaths, 117; marriages, 155; divorces, 56.

Recreation: Hunting, tourist crossroads, rattlesnake roundup.

Minerals: Production of oil, gas, salt, uranium, sand and gravel.

Agriculture: Most income from beef cattle; remainder from grains, cotton, vegetables, hay. Market value $17.9 million.

SAN DIEGO (5,376, partly in Jim Wells County) county seat; ranching, oil field, tourist center; hospital.

Freer (3,395) center of oil and livestock-raising area.

Benavides (1,974) serves truck farming area.

Other towns include: **Concepcion** (25) and **Realitos** (250).

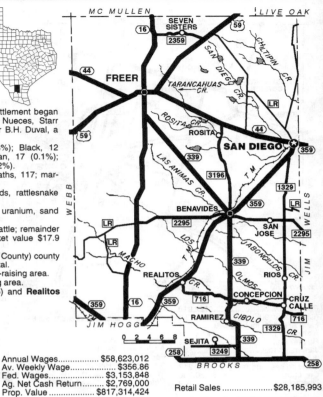

Population	13,631
(Change fm '90)	5.5
Land Area (sq. mi.).......................	1,792.9
Altitude (ft.).................................	244-783
Rainfall (in.).................................	24.8
Jan. mean min..............................	41
July mean max..............................	96
Growing season (days)	298
Civ. Labor....................................	4,656
Unemployed.................................	12.6

Annual Wages.................	$58,623,012
Av. Weekly Wage..................	$356.86
Fed. Wages.....................	$3,153,848
Ag. Net Cash Return.........	$2,769,000
Prop. Value	$817,314,424

Retail Sales $28,185,993

Population	19,547
(Change fm '90)	5.7
Land Area (sq. mi.)	926.1
Altitude (ft.)	1,303-1,882
Rainfall (in.)................................	29.7
Jan. mean min.	29
July mean max.............................	94
Growing season (days)	299
Civ. Labor..................................	8,613
Unemployed................................	4.7
Annual Wages............	$100,329,308
Av. Weekly Wage.................	$340.82

Fed. Wages....................	$2,083,433
Ag. Net Cash Return.....	$7,368,000
Prop. Value	$656,795,625
Retail Sales...............	$136,568,507

For explanation of sources, abbreviations and symbols, see p. 142.

Eastland County

Physical Features: West central county; hilly, rolling; sandy, loam soils; drains to Leon River forks.

Economy: Agribusinesses; education; petroleum industries; varied manufacturing.

History: Plains Indian area. Frank Sánchez among first settlers in 1850s. County created from Bosque, Coryell, Travis counties, 1858, organized 1873; named for W.M. Eastland, Mier Expedition casualty.

Ethnicity, 1990: White, 17,474 (94.5%); Black, 397 (2.1%); American Indian, 52 (0.3%); Asian, 37 (0.2%); Other, 528 (2.9%). Hispanic, 1,404 (7.6%).

Vital Statistics, 1995: Births, 234; deaths, 296; marriages, 169; divorces, 72.

Recreation: Lakes, water sports; fishing, hunting; festivals; historic sites and displays.

Minerals: Production of oil, gas, stone, clays, sand and gravel.

Agriculture: Peanuts; fed beef and goats; hay; greenhouse plants; 20,000 acres irrigated. Market value $29.6 million.

EASTLAND (3,805) county seat; plants make various goods; agribusiness; printing; mental health center; hospital.

Cisco (4,241) agribusiness; plants clothing, windows, molding; Conrad Hilton's first hotel renovated, museum; junior college; hospital; folklife festival; Kendrick Religous Diorama.

Ranger (2,903) oil center, varied manufacturing, junior college, hospital.

Other towns include: **Carbon** (295) livestock equipment manufacturing; **Desdemona** (180); **Gorman** (1,358) peanut processing, agribusiness, hospital; **Olden** (110) and **Rising Star** (876), cap manufacturing.

Ector County

Physical Features: West Texas county; level to rolling, some sand dunes; meteor crater; desert vegetation.

Economy: Center for Permian Basin oil field operations; rubber and plastics.

History: First settlers in late 1880s. Oil boom in 1926. County created from Tom Green County, 1887; organized, 1891; named for jurist M.D. Ector.

Ethnicity, 1990: White, 91,309 (76.8%); Black, 5,557 (4.7%); American Indian, 647 (0.5%); Asian, 662 (0.6%); Other, 20,759 (17.5%). Hispanic, 37,315 (31.4%).

Vital Statistics, 1995: Births, 2,067; deaths, 928; marriages, 1,156; divorces, 772.

Recreation: Globe Theatre replica; presidential museum; art institute; second-largest U.S. meteor crater; antique auto museum; jazz festival in May, oil show in October .

Minerals: More than 2 billion barrels of oil produced since 1926; gas, cement, stone.

Agriculture: Beef cattle, horses are chief producers; pecans, hay raised, also ratites; minor irrigation. Market value $4.7 million.

Education: University of Texas of Permian Basin; Texas Tech University Health Science Center; Odessa (junior) College.

ODESSA (93,495) county seat; oil field services, supplies; petrochemical complex; hosptial; cultural center; fair and expo in September.

Other towns include: **Gardendale** (1,105), **Goldsmith** (292), **Notrees** (338), **Penwell** (74) and **West Odessa** (16,995).

Population............................ 122,910	
(Change fm '90)............................ 3.3	
Land Area (sq. mi.)..................... 901.1	
Altitude (ft.).....................2,817-8,275	
Rainfall (in.) 13.1	
Jan. mean min................................ 28	
July mean max................................. 95	
Growing season (days) 217	
Civ. Labor............................... 60,260	
Unemployed 6.9	

Annual Wages $1,104,580,171	
Av. Weekly Wage $458.96	
Fed. Wages..................... $8,229,391	
Ag. Net Cash Return $780,000	
Prop. Value............. $4,019,931,259	
Retail Sales $1,192,452,989	

Edwards County

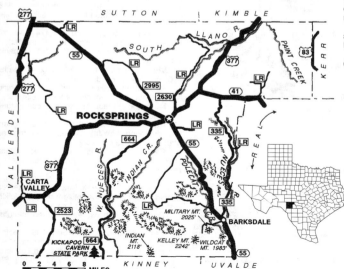

Physical Features: Rolling, hilly; caves; spring-fed streams; rocky, thin soils; drained by Llano, Nueces rivers; varied timber.

Economy: Ranching; hunting leases; tourism; oil, gas production.

History: Apache area. First land sold in 1876. County created from Bexar District, 1858; organized 1883; named for Nacogdoches empresario Hayden Edwards.

Ethnicity, 1990: White, 2,114 (93.3%); Black, 0 (0.0%); American Indian, 4 (0.2%); Asian, 4 (0.2%); Other, 144 (6.4%). Hispanic, 1,182 (52.2%).

Vital Statistics, 1995: Births, 40; deaths, 20; marriages, 8; divorces, 10.

Recreation: Hunting, fishing; scenic drives; state park.

Minerals: Gas.

Agriculture: Center for mohair-wool production; Angora goats, sheep, cattle; some pecans. Market value $9.6 million. Cedar for oil.

ROCKSPRINGS (1,468) county seat; ranching, tourism, Top of the World Festival, July 4.

Other towns include: **Barksdale** (1,081) and **Carta Valley** (12).

Population 2,705	
(Change fm '90) 19.4	
Land Area (sq. mi.) 2,119.9	
Altitude (ft.)..................... 1,507-2,410	
Rainfall (in.)............................. 22.0	
Jan. mean min. 35	
July mean max........................... 95	
Growing season (days).............. 250	
Civ. Labor................................. 932	
Unemployed............................. 5.0	
Annual Wages.............. $6,257,512	
Av. Weekly Wage.......... $302.19	
Fed. Wages.................. $616,883	
Ag. Net Cash Return........ -$400,000	
Prop. Value............ $502,491,633	
Retail Sales.................. $9,299,250	

For explanation of sources, abbreviations and symbols, see p. 142.

Ellis County

Physical Features: North Texas Blackland soils; level to rolling; Chambers Creek, Trinity River.

Economy: Varied manufacturing; agribusinesses; many residents employed in Dallas.

History: Tonkawa area. Part of Peters colony settled in 1843. County created 1849, organized 1850, from Navarro County. Named for Richard Ellis, president of convention that declared Texas' independence.

Ethnicity, 1990: White, 69,049 (81.1%); Black, 8,525 (10.0%); American Indian, 370 (0.4%); Asian, 214 (0.3%); Other, 7,009 (8.2%). Hispanic, 11,243 (13.2%).

Vital Statistics, 1995: Births, 1,517; deaths, 705; marriages, 958; divorces, 389.

Recreation: Medieval theme Scarborough Faire; Gingerbread Trail homes tour, fall festival; lakes, fishing and hunting.

Minerals: Cement, oil, gas.

Agriculture: Beef cattle; crops include cotton, corn, wheat, milo, soybeans, hay. Market value $31.2 million.

WAXAHACHIE (19,049) county seat; varied manufacturing; movie production; tourism; hospital; colleges.

Ennis (14,569), agribusiness; manufacturing; bluebonnet trails, National Polka Festival; tourism; hospital.

Midlothian (5,744), trade zone, cement plant, steel manufacturing; other factories; spring Mad Hatters parade.

Other towns include: **Alma** (240); **Avalon** (130), **Bardwell** (403); **Cedar Hill** (24,677); **Ferris** (2,323); **Forreston** (200), **Garrett** (426); **Italy** (1,895); **Maypearl** (835); **Milford** (799); **Oak Leaf** (1,092); **Ovilla** (2,522); **Palmer** (1,707); **Pecan Hill** (598); **Red Oak** (3,849) and **Telico** (95).

Population	**92,027**
(Change fm '90)	8.1
Land Area (sq. mi.)	940.0
Altitude (ft.)	395-755
Rainfall (in.)	36.8
Jan. mean min.	34
July mean max.	96
Growing season (days)	246
Civ. Labor	49,994
Unemployed	4.4
Annual Wages	$545,697,561
Av. Weekly Wage	$448.20
Fed. Wages	$8,194.433
Ag. Net Cash Return	-$178,000
Prop. Value	$3,846,718,050
Retail Sales	$579,610,956

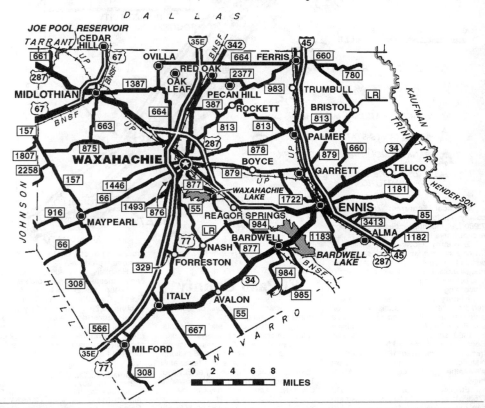

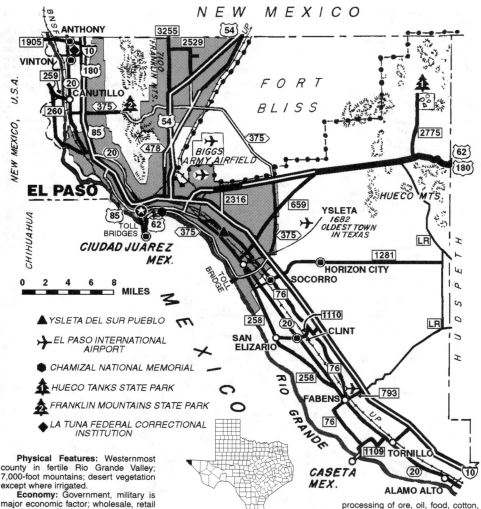

YSLETA DEL SUR PUEBLO

✈ **EL PASO INTERNATIONAL AIRPORT**

⬢ **CHAMIZAL NATIONAL MEMORIAL**

🏔 **HUECO TANKS STATE PARK**

🌲 **FRANKLIN MOUNTAINS STATE PARK**

◆ **LA TUNA FEDERAL CORRECTIONAL INSTITUTION**

Physical Features: Westernmost county in fertile Rio Grande Valley; 7,000-foot mountains; desert vegetation except where irrigated.

Economy: Government, military is major economic factor; wholesale, retail distribution center; education; tourism; maquiladora plants, varied manufacturers; ore smelting, refining, cotton, food processing.

History: Various Indian tribes inhabited the valley before Spanish civilization arrived in late 1650s. Spanish and Tigua and Piro tribes fleeing Santa Fe uprising of 1680 sought refuge at Ysleta and Socorro. County created from Bexar District, 1849; organized 1850; named for historic pass (Paso del Norte), lowest all-weather pass through Rocky Mountains.

Ethnicity, 1990: White, 452,512 (76.5%); Black, 22,110 (3.7%); American Indian, 2,590 (0.4%); Asian, 6,485 (1.1%); Other, 107,913 (18.2%). Hispanic, 411,619 (69.6%).

Vital Statistics, 1995: Births, 15,402; deaths, 3,595; marriages, 7,170; divorces, 2,083.

Recreation: Gateway to Mexico; Chamizal Museum; major tourist center; December Sun Carnival with football game; state parks, missions and other historic sites.

El Paso County

Minerals: Production of cement, stone, sand and gravel.

Agriculture: Dairy and beef cattle; cotton, pecans, onions, forage, peppers also raised; 50,000 acres irrigated, mostly cotton. Market value $88 million.

Education: University of Texas at El Paso; UT School of Nursing at El Paso; Texas Tech University Health Science Center; El Paso Community College.

EL PASO (583,431) county seat; fourth-largest Texas city, largest U.S. city on Mexican border.

A center for government operations. Federal installations include Fort Bliss, William Beaumont General Hospital, La Tuna correctional institution, and headquarters of the U.S. Army Air Defense Command;

Manufactured products include clothing, electronics, auto equipment, plastics; trade and distribution; refining;

processing of ore, oil, food, cotton, and other farm products.

Hospitals; museums; convention center; theater, symphony orchestra,

Other towns include: **Anthony** (3,612); **Canutillo** (4,871); **Clint** (1,112); **Fabens** (5,797); **Horizon City** (2,475); **San Elizario** (4,621); **Socorro** (28,626); **Sparks** (1,406); **Tornillo** (241); **Vinton** (644); **Westway** (2,601) and **Ysleta**, oldest town in Texas (now within El Paso).

Population	**668,358**
(Change fm '90)	13.0
Land Area (sq. mi.)	1,013.1
Altitude (ft.)	3,582-7,192
Rainfall (in.)	8.8
Jan. mean min.	29
July mean max.	96
Growing season (days)	248
Civ. Labor	290,447
Unemployed	11.6
Annual Wages	$4,707,572,898
Av. Weekly Wage	$405.97
Fed. Wages	$306,557,078
Ag. Net Cash Return	$11,285,000
Prop. Value	$16,769,393,471
Retail Sales	$5,116,160,800

Erath County

Physical Features: West central county on Rolling Plains; clay loam, sandy soils; drains to Bosque, Paluxy Rivers.

Economy: Agricultural, industrial and educational enterprises.

History: Caddo and Anadarko Indians moved to Oklahoma in 1860. Anglo-American settlement began 1854-55. County created from Bosque, Coryell counties 1856; named for George B. Erath, Texas Revolution figure.

Ethnicity, 1990: White, 26,413 (94.4%); Black, 195 (0.7%); American Indian, 94 (0.3%); Asian, 115 (0.4%); Other, 1,174 (4.2%). Hispanic, 2,458 (8.8%).

Vital Statistics, 1995: Births, 446; deaths, 289; marriages, 350; divorces, 178.

Recreation: Old courthouse; log cabins; museums; nearby lakes, Bosque River Park; Tarleton State University with fine arts center.

Minerals: Gas, oil.

Agriculture: Leading county in milk production; beef cattle, horses raised; peanuts, the major cash crop, small grains, sorghums; horticulture industry, especially tree growing and greenhouses; some irrigation, mostly peanuts and forage crops. Market value $185.5 million.

STEPHENVILLE (15,923) the county seat; Tarleton State University; various manufacturing plants; hospital, clinics, mental health center; Texas A&M Research and Extension Center.

Dublin (3,634), agribusiness center; food processing; tourism; library; St. Patrick's celebration; old Dr Pepper plant.

Other towns include: **Bluff Dale** (123); **Lingleville** (100); **Morgan Mill** (206); **Thurber**, former coal-mining town.

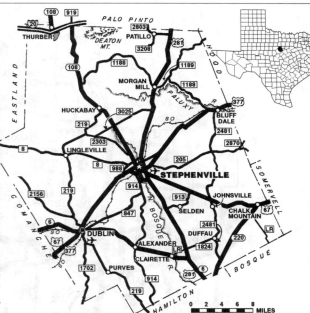

Population	31,344	Civ. Labor	16,206
(Change fm '90)	12.0	Unemployed	2.7
Land Area (sq. mi.)	1,086.4	Annual Wages	$226,750,490
Altitude (ft.)	943-1,558	Av. Weekly Wage	$354.45
Rainfall (in.)	32.9	Fed. Wages	$3,184,460
Jan. mean min.	31	Ag. Net Cash Return	$29,943,000
July mean max.	94	Prop. Value	$1,309,161,662
Growing season (days)	238	Retail Sales	$285,854,446

Falls County

Physical Features: East central county on rolling prairie; bisected by Brazos; blackland, red, sandy loam soils; mineral springs.

Economy: Varied manufacturing; government services; agribusinesses.

History: Wacos, Tawokanis, Anadarkos in conflict with Comanches. Cherokees alone in area 1830 until 1835 when Anglo-American settlement began. County created 1850 from Limestone, Milam counties; named for Brazos River falls.

Ethnicity, 1990: White, 11,390 (64.3%); Black, 4,810 (27.2%); American Indian, 41 (0.2%); Asian, 21 (0.1%); Other, 1,450 (8.2%). Hispanic, 2,072 (11.7%).

Vital Statistics, 1995: Births, 212; deaths, 250; marriages, 104; divorces, 71.

Recreation: Fishing, camping, mineral baths; Highland Mansion and Falls on the Brazos.

Minerals: Gas, stone, some oil.

Agriculture: Stocker cattle, cow-calf operations, swine, sheep, goats raised; corn, grain sorghums, cotton, soybeans; 5,000 acres, mostly cotton, irrigated. Market value $56.5 million.

MARLIN (6,373) county seat; agribusiness, small industries; mineral water and spas; hospital; printing; veterans hospital; tourism; Festival Days in May; prison unit.

Other towns include: **Chilton** (274); **Golinda** (415, partly in McLennan County); **Lott** (871); **Otto** (48); **Perry** (76); **Reagan** (208); **Rosebud** (1,591) feed, fertilizer processing, clothing manufactured; **Satin** (86).

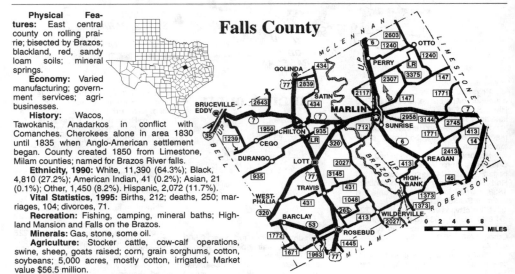

Population	18,176	Civ. Labor	7,738
(Change fm '90)	2.6	Unemployed	3.4
Land Area (sq. mi.)	769.1	Annual Wages	$68,762,696
Altitude (ft.)	314-590	Av. Weekly Wage	$360.72
Rainfall (in.)	36.8	Fed. Wages	$12,600,847
Jan. mean min.	36	Ag. Net Cash Return	$5,404,000
July mean max.	96	Prop. Value	$596,465,760
Growing season (days)	257	Retail Sales	$71,137,792

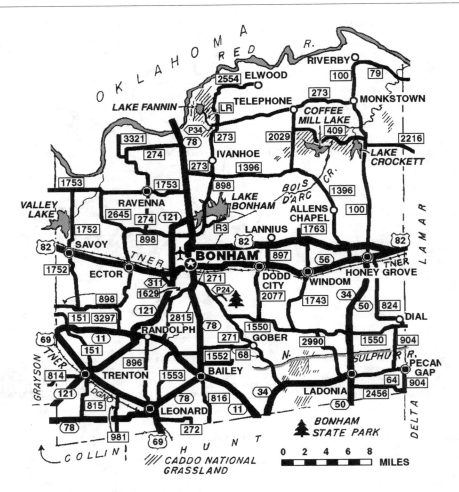

Fannin County

Physical Features: North Texas county of rolling prairie, drained by Red River, Bois d' Arc Creek; mostly blackland soils; national grassland.

Economy: Agribusinesses; government services; distribution, meat packing; tourism.

History: Caddoes who joined with Cherokees. Anglo-American settlement began in 1836. County created from Red River County, 1837, organized, 1838; named for James W. Fannin, a victim of Goliad massacre.

Ethnicity, 1990: White, 22,722 (91.6%); Black, 1,633 (6.6%); American Indian, 182 (0.7%); Asian, 54 (0.2%); Other, 213 (0.9%). Hispanic, 485 (2.0%).

Vital Statistics, 1995: Births, 315; deaths, 345; marriages, 245; divorces, 157.

Recreation: Water activities on lakes; hunting; state park; Ivanhoe Winery; Sam Rayburn home, memorial library.

Minerals: Not significant; some sand produced.

Agriculture: Beef cattle; ratites; goats, sheep hogs; hay, wheat, soybeans, sorghum, corn, turf grass; 2,500 acres irrigated, mainly peanuts. Market value $27.7 million.

BONHAM (6,761) county seat; varied manufacturing; veterans hospital and private hospital; state jail; Bois D'Arc Festival in May.

Other towns include: **Bailey** (210); **Dodd City** (402); **Ector** (506); **Fannin** (359); **Gober** (146); **Honey Grove** (1,782) agribusiness center, varied manufacturing, tourism, historic buildings, Davy Crockett Day in October;

Ivanhoe (110); **Ladonia** (680), restored historical downtown, varied manufacturing; **Leonard** (1,868), varied manufacturing; **Randolph** (70); **Ravenna** (186); **Savoy** (962); **Telephone** (210); **Trenton** (705); **Windom** (295).

Population	**26,937**
Change fm '90	8.6
Land Area (sq. mi.)	891.6
Altitude (ft.)	478-767
Rainfall (in.)	44.0
Jan. mean min.	29
July mean max.	94
Growing season (days)	228
Civ. Labor	12,643
Unemployed	5.6
Annual Wages	$131,503,841
Av. Weekly Wage	$384.00
Fed. Wages	$22,613,476
Ag. Net Cash Returns	$1,567,000
Prop. Value	$856,503,129
Retail Sales	$164,555,838

For explanation of sources, abbreviations and symbols, see p. 142.

Fayette County

Physical Features: Southeast county bisected by Colorado River; rolling to level; sandy loam, black waxy soils.

Economy: Agribusiness; tourism; production of electricity; mineral production; small manufacturing.

History: Lipan Apaches and Tonkawas. Austin's colonists arrived in 1822. Germans and Czechs began arriving in 1840s. County created from Bastrop, Colorado counties, 1837; organized, 1838; named for hero of American Revolution, Marquis de Lafayette.

Vital Statistics, 1995: Births, 276; deaths, 269; marriages, 144; divorces, 53.

Ethnicity, 1990: White, 17,323 (86.2%); Black, 1,686 (8.4%); American Indian, 29 (0.1%); Asian, 15 (0.1%); Other, 1,042 (5.2%). Hispanic, 1,702 (8.5%).

Recreation: Monument Hill State Park, Faison Home Museum, brewery, other historic sites including "Painted Churches"; hunting, fishing, lake; German and Czech ethnic foods; Prazska Pout in August.

Minerals: Oil, gas, sand, gravel.

Agriculture: Beef, dairy cows; corn, sorghums, peanuts, hay, pecans, wheat; some firewood sold. Market value $77.4 million.

LA GRANGE (4,167) county seat; varied manufacturing; food processing; retail trade center; tourism; power generation; hospital; Spring Fling.

Schulenburg (3,024) varied manufacturing; food processing; Bluebonnet Festival.

Round Top (91) music center and **Winedale** (41), historic restorations including Winedale Inn.

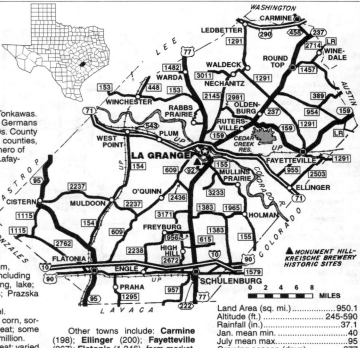

Other towns include: **Carmine** (198); **Ellinger** (200); **Fayetteville** (367); **Flatonia** (1,346), farm market, Czhilispiel in October; **Ledbetter** (76); **Muldoon** (98); **Plum** (95); **Warda** (98); **Warrenton** (65); **West Point** (205) and **Winchester** (50).

Population 21,374
(Change fm '90) 6.4

Land Area (sq. mi.)	950.1
Altitude (ft.)	245-590
Rainfall (in.)	37.1
Jan. mean min.	40
July mean max.	95
Growing season (days)	277
Civ. Labor	10,675
Unemployed	3.2
Annual Wages	$156,396,445
Av. Weekly Wage	$397.99
Fed. Wages	$2,545,537
Ag. Net Cash Return	$5,804,000
Prop. Value	$1,699,434,627
Retail Sales	$241,001,111

Fisher County

Physical Features: West central county on rolling prairie; mesquite; red, sandy loam soils; drains to forks of Brazos River.

Economy: Agribusinesses; electric co-op; oil; gypsum.

History: Lipan Apaches, disrupted by Comanches and other tribes around 1700. Ranching began in 1876. County created from Bexar District, 1876; organized, 1886; named for S.R. Fisher, Republic of Texas secretary of navy.

Vital Statistics, 1995: Births, 54; deaths, 46; marriages, 20; divorces, 20.

Ethnicity, 1990: White, 4,445 (91.8%); Black, 190 (3.9%); American Indian, 19 (0.4%); Asian, 0 (0.0%); Other, 188 (3.9%). Hispanic, 997 (20.6%).

Recreation: Quail, dove, turkey hunting; fair, rodeo in August,

Minerals: Oil, gas, gypsum.

Agriculture: Beef cattle, some swine; crops include cotton, wheat, hay; some irrigation for alfalfa. Market value $27.1 million.

ROBY (574) county seat; agribusiness, cotton gin; hospital between Roby and Rotan.

Rotan (1,791), gypsum plant; oil mill; agribusinesses.

Other towns include: **McCaulley** (96) and **Sylvester** (79). Part of **Hamlin** (2,602).

Population...................................4,574
(Change fm '90) .... -5.5
Land Area (sq. mi.)....................... 901.2
Altitude (ft.) 1,723-2,235
Rainfall (in.) 24.3

Jan. mean min.	30
July mean max.	96
Growing season (days)	218
Civ. Labor	1,884
Unemployed	5.1

Annual Wages	$18,300,683
Av. Weekly Wage	$366.08
Fed. Wages	$863,148
Ag. Net Cash Return	$5,856,000
Prop. Value	$305,169,576
Retail Sales	$10,431,750

Floyd County

Physical Features: Flat High Plains, broken by Caprock on east, by White River on south; many playas; red, black loam soils.

Economy: Cotton; livestock feedlots; farm machinery and oil-field manufacturing; metal products; printing.

History: Plains Apaches and later Comanches. First white settlers arrived in 1884. County created from Bexar District, 1876; organized 1890. Named for Dolphin Ward Floyd, who died at Alamo.

Ethnicity, 1990: White, 5,523 (65.0%); Black, 320 (3.8%); American Indian, 16 (0.2%); Asian, 15 (0.2%); Other, 2,623 (30.9%). Hispanic, 3,381 (39.8%).

Vital Statistics, 1995: Births, 138; deaths, 100; marriages, 60; divorces, 44.

Recreation: Hunting, fishing; Blanco Canyon; Pumpkin Days; museum.

Minerals: Not significant.

Agriculture: Cotton, wheat, sorghum, corn; beef cattle; 260,000 acres irrigated. Market value $109.9 million.

FLOYDADA (3,811) county seat; some manufacturing; meat, vegetable processing; distribution center; Old Settlers Reunion; Texas A&M engineering extension.

Lockney (2,130) agriculture center; manufacturing; hospital.

Other towns include: **Aiken** (57), **Dougherty** (109) and **South Plains** (92).

Population	8,310
(Change fm '90)	-2.2
Land Area (sq. mi.)	992.3
Altitude (ft.)	2,574-3,316
Rainfall (in.)	20.5
Jan. mean min.	22
July mean max.	92
Growing season (days)	213
Civ. Labor	3,525
Unemployed	7.0
Annual Wages	$37,243,291
Av. Weekly Wage	$320.66
Fed. Wages	$1,197,510
Ag. Net Cash Return	$15,551,000
Prop. Value	$333,976,184
Retail Sales	$43,508,404

Foard County

Physical Features: Northwest county drains to North Wichita, Pease rivers; sandy, loam soils, rolling surface.

Economy: Agribusiness, clothes manufacturing, government/service.

History: Comanches, Kiowas ranged the area until driven away in 1870s. Ranching began in 1880. County created out of Cottle, Hardeman, King, Knox counties, 1891; named for Maj. Robert L. Foard of Confederate army.

Ethnicity, 1990: White, 1,552 (86.5%); Black, 88 (4.9%); American Indian, 11 (0.6%); Asian, 4 (0.2%); Other, 139 (7.7%). Hispanic, 233 (13.0%).

Vital Statistics, 1995: Births, 23; deaths, 19; marriages, 13; divorces, 5.

Recreation: Three museums, wild hog cookoff in November.

Minerals: Oil, gas.

Agriculture: Wheat, cotton, hay, alfalfa, peanuts; cow-calf operations, stockers; irrigation for alfalfa. Market value $8.9 million.

CROWELL (1,233) county seat; agriculture center; manufacturing.

Population	1,870
(Change fm '90)	4.2
Land Area (sq. mi.)	706.7
Altitude (ft.)	1,300-1,784
Rainfall (in.)	23.9
Jan. mean min.	24
July mean max.	97
Growing season (days)	219
Civ. Labor	1,133
Unemployed	4.7
Annual Wages	$7,866,115
Av. Weekly Wage	$266.82
Fed. Wages	$364,231
Ag. Net Cash Return	$882,000
Prop. Value	$111,415,939
Retail Sales	$5,472,455

For explanation of sources, abbreviations and symbols, see p. 142.

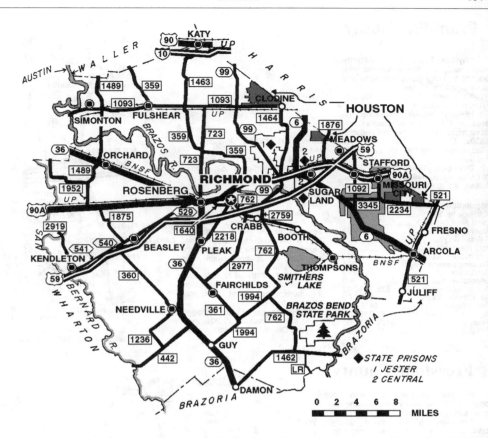

Fort Bend County

Physical Features: On Gulf Coastal Plain; drained by Brazos, San Bernard rivers; level to rolling; rich alluvial soils.

Economy: Agribusiness, petrochemicals, sulfur, sugar refinery; government/service; many residents work in Houston; part of Houston metropolitan area.

History: Karankawas; retreated to Mexico by 1850s. Named for river bend where some of Austin's colonists settled 1824. Antebellum plantations made it one of six Texas counties with black majority in 1850. County created 1837 from Austin County, organized 1838.

Ethnicity, 1990: White, 141,125 (62.6%); Black, 46,593 (20.7%); American Indian, 525 (0.2%); Asian, 14,328 (6.4%); Other, 22,850 (10.1%). Hispanic, 43,892 (19.5%).

Vital Statistics, 1995: Births, 4,128; deaths, 1,139; marriages, 1,434; divorces, 1,100.

Recreation: Many historic sites, museum, memorials; state park with George Observatory; fishing, waterfowl hunting.

Minerals: Oil, gas, sulphur, salt, clays, sand and gravel.

Agriculture: Cotton, grain sorghum, corn, rice, soybeans; cattle, horses; 29,000 acres irrigated, mostly rice. Market value $59.9 million.

RICHMOND (11,825) county seat; foundry, Richmond State School (for mentally retarded).

Rosenberg (26,747), varied industry; annual Czech festival; Wharton County Junior College campus.

Missouri City (50,719, partly in Harris County).

Other towns include: **Arcola** (815); **Beasley** (622); **Fairchilds** (500); **Fresno** (4,119); **Fulshear** (722); **Guy** (60); **Katy** (11,204, part in Harris, Waller counties); **Kendleton** (567); **Meadows** (5,324).

Also, **Needville** (2,864); **Orchard** (476); **Pleak** (872); **Simonton** (930); **Stafford** (11,434); **Sugar Land** (44,009), sugar refinery, prison unit; **Thompsons** (201).

Population	295,480
(Change fm '90)	31.1
Land Area (sq. mi.)	875.0
Altitude (ft.)	46-127
Rainfall (in.)	45.3
Jan. mean min.	41
July mean max.	93
Growing season (days)	296
Civ. Labor	156,488
Unemployed	3.1
Annual Wages	$2,085,191,318
Av. Weekly Wage	$567.64
Fed. Wages	$14,667,106
Ag. Net Cash Return	$12,545,000
Prop. Value	$12,902,831,090
Retail Sales	$1,970,752,105

For explanation of sources, abbreviations and symbols, see p. 142.

Franklin County

Physical Features: Small Northeast county with many wooded hills; drained by numerous streams; alluvial to sandy clay soils; two lakes.

Economy: Agribusiness; tourism, retirement center; oil.

History: Caddoes abandoned the area in 1790s due to disease and other tribes. White settlement began in 1830s. County created 1875 from Titus County; named for jurist B.C. Franklin.

Ethnicity, 1990: White, 7,139 (91.5%); Black, 349 (4.5%); American Indian, 47 (0.6%); Asian, 18 (0.2%);

Other, 249 (3.2%). Hispanic, 357 (4.6%).

Vital Statistics, 1995: Births, 71; deaths, 94; marriages, 52; divorces, 56.

Recreation: Fishing, water sports; Countryfest in October; historic homes.

Minerals: Oil, gas and lignite.

Agriculture: Among top counties in dairy and broiler production; hay is principal crop; blueberries, peaches, Christmas trees, soybeans sorghum, wheat; beef cattle raised. Market value $46.3 million.

MOUNT VERNON (2,401) county seat; distribution center, manufacturing; tourism; dairy, beef cattle; hospital; airport.

Other towns include: **Scroggins** (125) and **Winnsboro** (3,201, mostly in Wood County) commercial center.

Population	**8,423**
(Change fm '90)	8.0
Land Area (sq. mi.)	285.7
Altitude (ft.)	377-493
Rainfall (in.)	46.8
Jan. mean min.	33
July mean max.	93
Growing season (days)	234
Civ. Labor	4,223
Unemployed	6.3
Annual Wages	$35,554,203
Av. Weekly Wage	$371.03
Fed. Wages	$416,243
Ag. Net Cash Return	$7,077,000
Prop. Value	$420,371,200
Retail Sales	$42,686,056

Freestone County

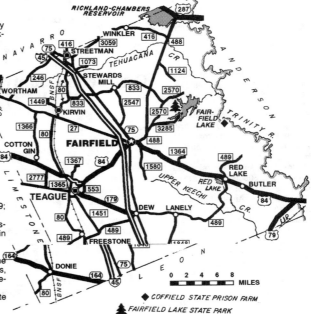

COFFIELD STATE PRISON FARM

FAIRFIELD LAKE STATE PARK

Physical Features: East central county bounded by the Trinity River; rolling Blackland, sandy, loam soils.

Economy: Mining, stone quarry, brick plant; varied manufacturing; agribusinesses; two electricity generating plants.

History: Caddo and Tawakoni area. David G. Burnet received land grant in 1825. Seven Mexican citizens received grants in 1833. In 1860, more than half population was black. County created 1850 from Limestone County, organized 1851. Named for indigenous stone.

Ethnicity, 1990: White, 12,382 (78.3%); Black, 3,013 (19.0%); American Indian, 53 (0.3%); Asian, 37 (0.2%); Other, 333 (2.1%). Hispanic, 619 (3.9%).

Vital Statistics, 1995: Births, 199; deaths, 215; marriages, 134; divorces, 82.

Recreation: Fishing, hunting; lakes; historic sites; coon hunting championship in September.

Minerals: Lignite, oil and gas, sand.

Agriculture: Beef cattle and hay; some peaches, other fruits, vegetables, melons, pecans, corn; hunting; some hardwood, firewood marketed. Market value $18.6 million.

FAIRFIELD (3,349) county seat; lignite mining; GTE telephone operations; trade center; hospital, museum; peach festival on July 4 weekend.

Teague (3,519) nursing homes; oil; manufacturing, railroad museum; prison unit.

Other towns include: **Donie** (206), **Kirvin** (122), **Streetman** (273, partly in Navarro County); **Wortham** (1,038).

Population	**16,927**
(Change fm '90)	7.0
Land Area (sq. mi.)	885.3
Altitude (ft.)	209-608
Rainfall (in.)	39.8
Jan. mean min.	36
July mean max.	95
Growing season (days)	263

Civ. Labor	7,587
Unemployed	5.3
Annual Wages	$93,093,758
Av. Weekly Wage	$441.86
Fed. Wages	$1,225,597
Ag. Net Cash Return	-$251,000
Prop. Value	$1,225,237,946
Retail Sales	$103,950,679

Frio County

Physical Features: South Texas county of rolling terrain with much brush; bisected by Frio River; sandy, red sandy loam soils.

Economy: Agribusinesses; oil-field services.

History: Coahuiltecans; many taken into San Antonio missions. Comanche hunters kept settlers out until after the Civil War. Mexican citizens recruited for labor after 1900. County created 1871 from Atascosa, Bexar, Uvalde counties; named for Frio (cold) River.

Ethnicity, 1990: White, 9,119 (67.7%); Black, 183 (1.4%); American Indian, 23 (0.2%); Asian, 38 (0.3%); Other, 4,109 (30.5%). Hispanic, 9,749 (72.4%).

Vital Statistics, 1995: Births, 243; deaths, 103; marriages, 84; divorces, 43.

Recreation: Hunting; Big Foot Wallace Museum; in Winter Garden area; potato festival.

Minerals: Oil, natural gas, stone.

Agriculture: A leading peanut-producing county; other crops vegetables, grain sorghums, melons, corn, vegetables; cattle, hogs raised. Market value $73.7 million.

PEARSALL (7,692) county seat; oil, ranching center; food processing; shipping; old jail museum; hospital.

Dilley (2,997) shipping center for melons, peanuts.

Other towns include: **Derby** (50); **Moore** (230).

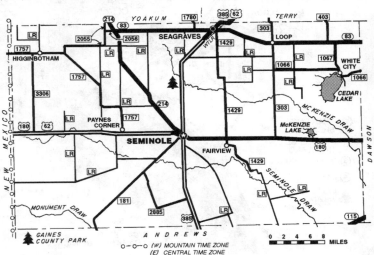

Population	15,600
(Change fm '90)	15.8
Land Area (sq. mi.)	1,133.1
Altitude (ft.)	435-763
Rainfall (in.)	25.4
Jan. mean min.	38
July mean max.	97
Growing season (days)	291

Civ. Labor	6,203
Unemployed	9.6
Annual Wages	$66,301,746
Av. Weekly Wage	$325.91
Fed. Wages	$920,590
Ag. Net Cash Return	$9,372,000
Prop. Value	$588,812,401
Retail Sales	$68,825,448

Gaines County

Physical Features: On South Plains, drains to draws; playas; underground water.

Economy: Oil and gas production, agribusiness.

History: Comanche country until U.S. Army campaigns of 1875. Ranchers arrived in 1880s; farming began around 1900. County created from Bexar District, 1876, organized 1905; named for James Gaines, signer of Texas Declaration of Independence.

Ethnicity, 1990: White, 10,378 (73.5%); Black, 334 (2.4%); American Indian, 38 (0.3%); Asian, 15 (0.1%); Other, 3,358 (23.8%). Hispanic, 4,608 (32.6%).

Vital Statistics, 1995: Births, 288; deaths, 88; marriages, 221; divorces, 55.

Recreation: Cedar Lake one of largest alkali lakes on Texas plains; Ag and Oil Day in September.

Minerals: One of leading oil-producing counties; gas.

Agriculture: A leading cotton and peanut producing county; small grains, vegetables raised; cattle, sheep, hogs; substantial irrigation. Market value $134.3 million.

SEMINOLE (6,558) county seat; market center; hospital.

Seagraves (2,324) market for three-county area; manufacturing, distribution.

Other towns include: **Loop** (315).

Population	14,352
(Change fm '90)	1.6
Land Area (sq. mi.)	1,502.4
Altitude (ft.)	3,039-3,581
Rainfall (in.)	17.5
Jan. mean min.	25
July mean max.	94
Growing season (days)	210
Civ. Labor	6,941
Unemployed	4.1
Annual Wages	$90,736,377
Av. Weekly Wage	$394.16
Fed. Wages	$1,219.411
Ag. Net Cash Return	$29,031,000
Prop. Value	$2,229,844,554
Retail Sales	$76,497,710

For explanation of sources, abbreviations and symbols, see p. 142.

Galveston County

Physical Features: Partly island, partly coastal; flat, artificial drainage; sandy, loam, clay soils; broken by bays.

Economy: Port activities dominate economy; insurance and finance center; petrochemical plants; varied manufacturing; tourism; medical education center; oceanographic research center; ship building; commercial fishing.

History: Karankawa and other tribes roamed the area until 1850. French, Spanish and American settlement began in 1815 and reached 1,000 by 1817. County created from Brazoria County 1838; organized 1839; named for Spanish governor of Louisiana Count Bernardo de Galvez.

Ethnicity, 1990: White, 164,210 (75.5%); Black, 38,154 (17.6%); American Indian, 752 (0.3%); Asian, 3,569 (1.6%); Other, 10,714 (4.9%). Hispanic, 30,962 (14.2%).

Vital Statistics, 1995: Births, 3,526; deaths, 2,116; marriages, 1,395; divorces, 1,390.

Recreation: One of Texas' most historic cities; popular tourist and convention center; fishing, surfing, boating, sailing and other water sports; state park; Historical District tour in spring includes homes, sites; Mardi Gras celebration; Rosenberg Library; museums, drama "Lone Star" presented in outdoor amphitheater in summer; restored sail-

For explanation of sources, abbreviations and symbols, see p. 142.

ing ship, "Elissa," railroad museum; Dickens on the Strand in early December.

Minerals: Production of oil, gas, clays, sand and gravel.

Agriculture: Rice a major crop; substantial irrigation; cattle, horses also raised; other crops soybeans, grain sorghums, corn; aquaculture. Market value $7.8 million.

GALVESTON (63,857) county seat; tourist center; shipyard; other industries; insurance; port container facility; University of Texas Medical Branch; National Maritime Research Center; Texas A&M University at Galveston; Galveston College; hospitals.

Texas City (41,475), refining, petrochemical plants; College of the Mainland; hospitals; Shrimp Boil at end of August.

Other towns include: **Bacliff** (5,163); **Bayou Vista** (1,420); **Clear Lake Shores** (1,191); **Crystal Beach** (787) on Bolivar Peninsula, Fort Travis Seashore Park, shorebird sanctuary; crab festival in May.

Also, **Dickinson** (12,536); **Friendswood** (30,583); **Gilchrist** (750); **High Island** (500); **Hitchcock** (6,228) residential community, tourism, fishing and shrimping, Good Ole Days in August, WWII blimp base.

Also, **Jamaica Beach** (681); **Kemah** (1,477) fishing; **La Marque** (14,299) refining, greyhound racing, Grill-off in March; **League City** (41,331); **Port Bolivar** (1,200); **San Leon** (3,481); **Santa Fe** (9,715); **Tiki Island Village** (681).

Population	**239,292**
(Change fm '90)	10.1
Land Area (sq. mi.)	398.7
Altitude (ft.)	sea level-23
Rainfall (in.)	42.3
Jan. mean min.	47
July mean max.	87
Growing season (days)	335
Civ. Labor	127.275
Unemployed	8.1
Annual Wages	$2,430,842,711
Av. Weekly Wage	$546.54
Fed. Wages	$39,527,799
Ag. Net Cash Return	$338,000
Prop. Value	$17,485,648,676
Retail Sales	$1,722,677,129

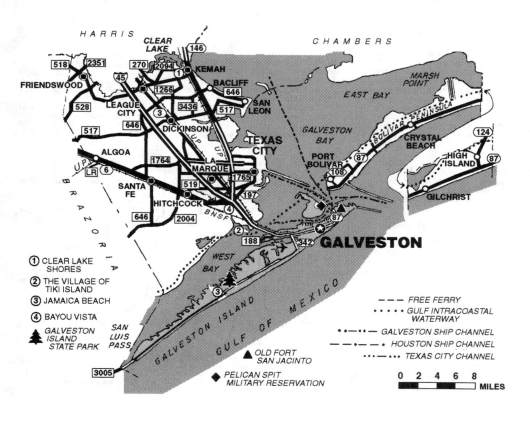

① CLEAR LAKE SHORES
② THE VILLAGE OF TIKI ISLAND
③ JAMAICA BEACH
④ BAYOU VISTA

GALVESTON ISLAND STATE PARK

▲ OLD FORT SAN JACINTO
◆ PELICAN SPIT MILITARY RESERVATION

– – – FREE FERRY
• • • • GULF INTRACOASTAL WATERWAY
• — • • GALVESTON SHIP CHANNEL
— • — • HOUSTON SHIP CHANNEL
• • • — • • • TEXAS CITY CHANNEL

0 2 4 6 8 MILES

Garza County

Physical Features: On edge of Caprock; rough, broken land, with playas, gullies, canyons, Brazos River forks; sandy, loam, clay soils.

Economy: Cotton, oil, tourism.

History: Kiowas and Comanches who yielded to U.S. Army in 1875. Ranching began in 1870s; farming in the 1890s. C.W. Post, the cereal millionaire, established enterprises in 1906. County created from Bexar District, 1876; organized 1907; named for early Texas family.

Ethnicity, 1990: White, 4,588 (89.2%); Black, 328 (6.4%); American Indian, 9 (0.2%); Asian, 21 (0.4%); Other, 197 (3.8%). Hispanic, 1,454 (28.3%).

Vital Statistics, 1995: Births, 72; deaths, 61; marriages, 36; divorces, 19.

Recreation: Post Stampede in August, Indian ceremony for crops, March 22; scenic areas; Post-Garza Museum.

Minerals: Oil and gas.

Agriculture: Cotton is major cash crop; hay, eggs, beef, stocker cattle; 4,000 acres irrigated. Market value $20.6 million.

POST (3,445) county seat; founded by C.W. Post; oil, agribusiness center; hospital.
Other towns include: **Justiceburg** (76).

Population	4,670
(Change fm '90	-9.2
Land Area (sq. mi.)	895.6
Altitude (ft.)	2,176-2,986
Rainfall (in.)	20.9
Jan. mean min.	27
July mean max.	94
Growing season (days)	216
Civ. Labor	2,247
Unemployed	5.6
Annual Wages	$22,618,545
Av. Weekly Wage	$347.06
Fed. Wages	$696,294
Ag. Net Cash Return	$4,618,000
Prop. Value	$418,084,450
Retail Sales	$26,342,982

Gillespie County

Physical Features: Picturesque Edwards Plateau area with hills, broken by spring-fed streams.

Economy: Agribusiness; tourism; food processing; hunting leases; small manufacturing; granite for markers.

History: German settlement founded 1846 in heart of Comanche country. County created 1848 from Bexar, Travis counties; named for Texas Ranger Capt. R.A. Gillespie. Birthplace of President Lyndon B. Johnson and Fleet Admiral Chester W. Nimitz.

Ethnicity, 1990: White, 16,325 (94.9%); Black, 34 (0.2%); American Indian, 60 (0.3%); Asian, 27 (0.2%); Other, 758 (4.4%). Hispanic, 2,426 (14.1%).

Vital Statistics, 1995: Births, 224; deaths, 241; marriages, 161; divorces, 94.

Recreation: Among leading deer-hunting areas; fishing; numerous historic sites and tourist attractions include LBJ Ranch, Nimitz Hotel; Pioneer Museum Complex, Enchanted Rock.

Minerals: Sand, gravel, granite, gypsum, limestone rock.

Agriculture: Most income from beef cattle, turkeys, sheep and goats; a leading peach-producing county; hay, grain sorghums, oats, wheat, grapes also raised. Market value $36.9 million.

FREDERICKSBURG (8,355) county seat; varied manufacturing; wine production; food processing; museum; tourist attractions; hospital; Easter Fires.

Other towns include: **Doss** (75); **Harper** (383); **Luckenbach** (25); **Stonewall** (245) agribusiness, tourism, Peach Jamboree in June, and **Willow City** (75).

Population	19,604
(Change fm '90	14.0
Land Area (sq. mi.)	1,061.2
Altitude (ft.)	1,477-2,244
Rainfall (in.)	30.0
Jan. mean min.	35
July mean max.	93
Growing season (days)	219
Civ. Labor	10,038
Unemployed	1.6
Annual Wages	$112,315,339
Av. Weekly Wage	$334.86
Fed. Wages	$3,053,591
Ag. Net Cash Return	$1,457,000
Prop. Value	$1,626,020,442
Retail Sales	$198,020,852

For explanation of sources, abbreviations and symbols, see p. 142.

Glasscock County

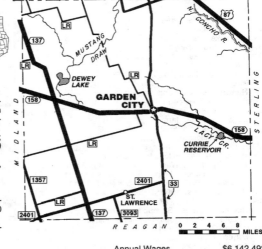

Physical Features: Western county on rolling plains, broken by small streams; sandy, loam soils.

Economy: Farming, ranching, hunting leases, oil and gas.

History: Hunting area for Kickapoos and Lipan Apaches. Anglo-American sheep ranchers and Mexican-American shepherds or *pastores* moved into the area in 1880s. County created 1887, from Tom Green County; organized, 1893; named for Texas pioneer George W. Glasscock.

Ethnicity, 1990: White, 1,156 (79.9%); Black, 0 (0.0%); American Indian, 2 (0.1%); Asian, 0 (0.0%); Other, 289 (20.0%). Hispanic, 424 (29.3%).

Vital Statistics, 1995: Births, 18; deaths, 8; marriages, 11; divorces, 1.

Recreation: Hunting, St. Lawrence Fall Festival.

Minerals: Oil, gas.

Agriculture: Cotton is major crop; grain sorghums; cattle, sheep, swine, meat goats and milk goats raised; 40,000 acres irrigated, mostly cotton. Market value $22.3 million.

GARDEN CITY (293) county seat; serves sparsely settled ranching, oil area.

Population	1,408
(Change fm '90)	-2.7
Land Area (sq. mi.)	900.8
Altitude (ft.)	2,495-2,727
Rainfall (in.)	18.0
Jan. mean min.	25
July mean max.	94
Growing season (days)	222
Civ. Labor	615
Unemployed	2.6
Annual Wages	$6,142,492
Av. Weekly Wage	$365.63
Fed. Wages	$173,790
Ag. Net Cash Return	$7,254,000
Prop. Value	$375,137,940
Retail Sales	$1,932,184

Goliad County

Physical Features: South Texas county; rolling, brushy; bisected by San Antonio River; sandy, loam, alluvial soils.

Economy: Primarily based on oil; agribusiness; tourism, electricity-generating plant.

History: Karankawas, Comanches and other tribes in area in historic period. La Bahía mission established in 1749. County created 1836 from Span-ish municipality, organized 1837; name is anagram of (H)idalgo. Birthplace of Gen. Zaragoza, hero of Battle of Puebla (Mexico).

Ethnicity, 1990: White, 4,953 (82.8%); Black, 407 (6.8%); American Indian, 19 (0.3%); Asian, 5 (0.1%); Other, 596 (10.0%). Hispanic, 2,145 (35.9%).

Vital Statistics, 1995: Births, 67; deaths, 68; marriages, 31; divorces, 22.

Recreation: Missions, restored Presidio La Bahia, Fannin Battleground; Gen. Ignacio Zaragoza statue; Old Market House museum; lake, fishing, hunting, camping.

Minerals: Production of oil, gas.

Agriculture: Beef cattle, stocker operations and fed cattle are top revenue producers; corn, grain sorghums, hay; minor irrigation for pasture, fruit trees. Market value $13.5 million.

GOLIAD (2,203) county seat; one of state's oldest towns; tourism; oil; agriculture; hospital; Christmas in Goliad.

Other towns include: **Berclair** (253), **Fannin** (359) and **Weesatche** (411).

Population	6,439
(Change from '90)	7.7
Land Area (sq. mi.)	853.6
Altitude (ft.)	63-242
Rainfall (in.)	36.5
Jan. mean min.	43
July mean max.	95
Growing season (days)	285
Civ. Labor	2,665
Unemployed	4.8
Annual Wages	$20,287,291
Av. Weekly Wage	$339.19
Fed. Wages	$520,270
Ag. Net Cash Return	$1,199,000
Prop. Value	$654,910,311
Retail Sales	$24,348,566

For explanation of sources, abbreviations and symbols, see p. 142.

Gonzales County

Physical Features: South Texas county; rolling, rich bottom soils along Guadalupe River and its tributaries; some sandy areas; many oaks, pecans.

Economy: Agribusinesses.

History: Coahuiltecan area. Among first Anglo-American settlements; the DeWitt colony late 1820s. County created 1836, organized 1837; named for Coahuila y Texas Gov. Rafael Gonzales.

Ethnicity, 1990: White, 13,025 (75.7%); Black, 1,716 (10.0%); American Indian, 46 (0.3%); Asian, 23 (0.1%); Other, 2,395 (13.9%). Hispanic, 6,142 (35.7%).

Vital Statistics, 1995: Births, 241; deaths, 214; marriages, 132; divorces, 64.

Recreation: Historic sites, 86 officially recognized homes or historical markers; Pioneer Village Living History Center; state park; museums, Independence Park;.

Minerals: Gas, oil, clay, gravel.

Agriculture: Major poultry county; cow-calf operations important; corn, sorghums, watermelon. Market value $190.7 million.

GONZALES (6,323) county seat; first shot in Texas Revolution fired here; shipping, processing center; manufacturing; hospitals, "Come and Take It" festival.

Other towns include: **Bebe** (52); **Belmont** (60); **Cost** (62); **Harwood** (112); **Leesville** (150); **Nixon** (2,100, partly in Wilson County) Feather Fest; **Ottine** (90), crippled children's hospital, Gonzales Warm Springs Foundation Hospital; **Smiley** (487) Settlers Set-To; **Waelder** (766) Guacamole Fest; **Wrightsboro** (76).

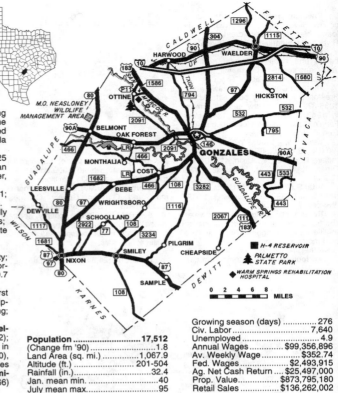

Population	17,512
(Change fm '90)	1.8
Land Area (sq. mi.)	1,067.9
Altitude (ft.)	201-504
Rainfall (in.)	32.4
Jan. mean min.	40
July mean max.	95

Growing season (days)	276
Civ. Labor	7,640
Unemployed	4.9
Annual Wages	$99,356,896
Av. Weekly Wage	$352.74
Fed. Wages	$2,493,915
Ag. Net Cash Return	$25,497,000
Prop. Value	$873,795,180
Retail Sales	$136,262,002

Gray County

Physical Features: Panhandle High Plains, broken by Red River forks, tributaries; sandy loam, waxy soils.

Economy: Petroleum, agriculture, feedlot operations, chemical plant, other manufacturing.

History: Apaches, displaced by Comanches and Kiowas. Ranching began in late 1870s. Farmers arrived around 1900. Oil discovered 1926. County created 1876, from Bexar District; organized, 1902; named for Peter W. Gray, member of first Legislature.

Ethnicity, 1990: White, 21,566 (90.0%); Black, 899 (3.8%); American Indian, 216 (0.9%); Asian, 115 (0.5%); Other, 1,171 (4.9%). Hispanic, 1,895 (7.9%).

Vital Statistics, 1995: Births, 279; deaths, 277; marriages, 171; divorces, 110.

Recreation: Water sports, Lake McClellan National Grassland Park; White Deer Land Museum; barbed-wire museum.

Minerals: Production of oil, gas.

Agriculture: Fed cattle, stocker operations; wheat, grain sorghums, corn, hay and forage raised. Market value $80.7 million.

PAMPA (19,769) county seat; petroleum processing; varied manufacturing; hospital, college.

Other towns include: **Alanreed** (48); **Lefors** (663); **McLean** (779) commercial center for southern part of county.

Population	24,055
(Change fm '90)	0.4
Land Area (sq. mi.)	928.3
Altitude (ft.)	2,558-3,296
Rainfall (in.)	21.0

Jan. mean min.	21
July mean max.	92
Growing season (days)	195
Civ. Labor	10,942
Unemployed	4.5

Annual Wages	$220,673,332
Av. Weekly Wage	$485.71
Fed. Wages	$2,490,701
Ag. Net Cash Return	$12,637,000
Prop. Value	$973,215,040
Retail Sales	$227,471,055

Grayson County

Physical Features: North Texas county; level, some low hills; sandy loam, blackland soils; drains to Red River and tributaries of Trinity River.

Economy: A manufacturing, distribution and trade center for northern Texas and southern Oklahoma; tourism; minerals; agribusiness.

History: Caddo and Tonkawa area. Preston Bend trading post established 1836-37. Peters colony settlers arrived in 1840s. County created 1846 from Fannin County; named for Republic Atty. Gen. Peter W. Grayson.

Ethnicity, 1990: White, 85,553 (90.0%); Black, 6,565 (6.9%); American Indian, 1,046 (1.1%); Asian, 412 (0.4%); Other, 1,445 (1.5%). Hispanic, 2,795 (2.9%).

Vital Statistics, 1995: Births, 1,259; deaths, 1,139; marriages, 1,012; divorces, 740.

Recreation: Lakes; fishing; water sports; state park; cultural activities; wildlife refuge; Pioneer Village; antique boat motor museum.

Minerals: Oil, gas and stone.

Agriculture: Most income from cattle; milk production; swine; hay, grain sorghums, corn, wheat. 4,000 acres irrigated. Market value $34.4 million.

Education: Austin College in Sherman and Grayson County College located between Sherman and Denison.

SHERMAN (32,774) county seat; varied manufacturing; processors, distributors for major companies; Austin College; hospitals.

Denison (21,840) manufacturing; food processing; transportation center; tourism; hospital; Eisenhower birthplace.

Other towns include: **Bells** (959); **Collinsville** (1,152); **Dorchester** (160); **Gordonville** (165); **Gunter** (929); **Howe** (2,182) distribution; varied manufacturing, Founders' Day in May; **Knollwood** (264); **Pottsboro** (1,469); **Sadler** (352); **Southmayd** (759); **Tioga** (648); **Tom Bean** (879); **Van Alstyne** (2,263) window screen, electronics, saddle, tack manufacturing; **Whitesboro** (3,332) agribusiness, tourism, Peanut Festival; **Whitewright** (1,663, partly in Fannin County).

Population	99,236
(Change from '90)	4.4
Land Area (sq. mi.)	933.7
Altitude (ft.)	535-867
Rainfall (in.)	40.4
Jan. mean min.	30
July mean max.	95
Growing season (days)	227
Civ. Labor	49,339
Unemployed	4.8
Annual Wages	$985,373,181
Av. Weekly Wage	$475.82
Fed. Wages	$12,027,138
Ag. Net Cash Return	$3,351,000
Prop. Value	$3,484,090,654
Retail Sales	$1,075,727,411

For explanation of sources, abbreviations and symbols, see p. 142.

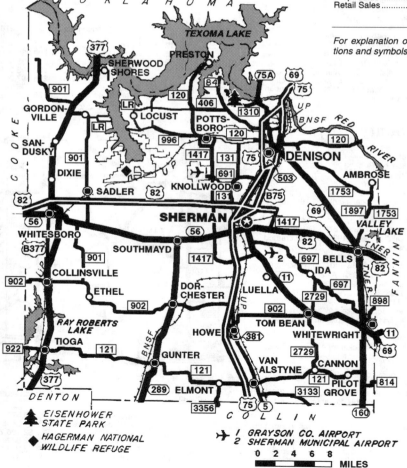

▲ EISENHOWER STATE PARK

◆ HAGERMAN NATIONAL WILDLIFE REFUGE

1 GRAYSON CO. AIRPORT
2 SHERMAN MUNICIPAL AIRPORT

0 2 4 6 8 MILES

Gregg County

Physical Features: A populous, leading petroleum county, heart of the famed East Texas oil field; bisected by the Sabine River; hilly, timbered; with sandy, clay, alluvial soils.

Economy: Oil but with significant other manufacturing; tourism, conventions; agribusinesses and lignite coal production.

History: Caddoes, later Cherokees who were driven out in 1838 by President Lamar. First land grants issued in 1835 by Republic of Mexico. County created and organized in 1873 from Rusk, Upshur counties; named for Confederate Gen. John Gregg. In U.S. censuses 1880-1910, blacks were more numerous than whites. Oil discovered in 1931.

Ethnicity, 1990: White, 81,883 (78.0%); Black, 19,937 (19.0%); American Indian, 478 (0.5%); Asian, 491 (0.5%); Other, 2,159 (2.1%). Hispanic, 3,775 (3.6%).

Vital Statistics, 1995: Births, 1,677; deaths, 1,086; marriages, 1,351; divorces, 662.

Recreation: Water activities on lakes; hunting; varied cultural events; the East Texas Oil Museum, Glory Days in Kilgore in May, Depot Fest Art Festival and Loblolly Festival in October.

Minerals: Leading oil-producing county with more than 3 billion barrels produced since 1931; also, sand and gravel and natural gas.

Agriculture: Timber sales, hay, beef-cattle production. Market value $4.0 million.

LONGVIEW (74,206, partly in Harrison County) county seat; manufacturing, brewery, distribution center; hospitals; LeTourneau University; convention center; balloon race in July.

Kilgore (11,601, partly in Rusk County), oil center; manufacturing; hospital; Kilgore College (junior college); East Texas Treatment Center; Shakespeare festival in summer.

Gladewater (6,185) manufacturing, antique center, oil; Gusher Days in April, Christmas Tyme in Gusherville on Thanksgiving weekend; airport.

Other towns include: **Clarksville City** (820); **Easton** (462); **Judson** (650); **Lakeport** (803); **Liberty City** (1,672); **Warren City** (357); **White Oak** (5,561).

Population	109,772
(Change fm '90)	4.6
Land Area (sq. mi.)	274.1
Altitude (ft.)	289-436
Rainfall (in.)	47.0
Jan. mean min.	33
July mean max.	93
Growing season (days)	247
Civ. Labor	58,350
Unemployed	7.2
Annual Wages	$1,318,235,108
Av. Weekly Wage	$439.49
Fed. Wages	$16,781,259
Ag. Net Cash Return	$112,000
Prop. Value	$5,353,691,194
Retail Sales	$1,720,652,140

For explanation of sources, abbreviations and symbols, see p. 142.

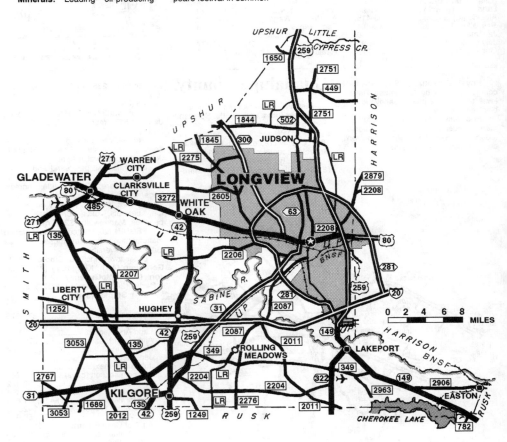

Grimes County

Physical Features: Rich bottom soils along Brazos, Navasota rivers; remainder hilly, partly forested.

Economy: Varied manufacturing; agribusinesses; tourism.

History: Bidais (customs similar to the Caddoes) lived peacefully with Anglo-American settlers who arrived in 1820s, but tribe was removed to Indian Territory. Planter agriculture reflected in 1860 census which listed 77 persons owning 20 or more slaves. County created from Montgomery County 1846; named for Jesse Grimes, who signed Texas Declaration of Independence.

Ethnicity, 1990: White, 12,879 (68.4%); Black, 4,614 (24.5%); American Indian, 52 (0.3%); Asian, 30 (0.2%); Other, 1,253 (6.7%). Hispanic, 2,657 (14.1%).

Vital Statistics, 1995: Births, 283; deaths, 211; marriages, 158; divorces, 74.

Recreation: Hunting, fishing; Gibbons Creek Reservoir; historic sites; fall Renaissance Festival at Plantersville.

Minerals: Lignite coal, oil, gas.

Agriculture: Beef cattle, poultry, some dairy cattle; hay, corn, peaches, pecans, wheat, rye; honey sales significant; some timber sold, Christmas tree farms. Market value $25 million.

ANDERSON (370) county seat; rural center; Fanthorp Inn historical site; Go-Texan weekend.

Navasota (6,887), agribusiness center for parts of three counties; varied manufacturing; food, wood processing; hospital; La Salle statue.

Other towns include: **Bedias** (301); **Iola** (331); **Plantersville** (212); **Richards** (296); **Roans Prairie** (56); **Shiro** (205); **Todd Mission** (65).

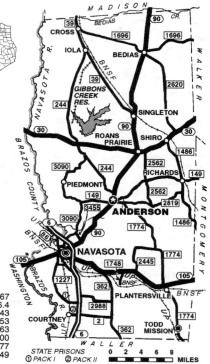

Population 21,275	Civ. Labor...............................8,567
(Change fm '90) 13.0	Unemployed................................6.4
Land Area (sq. mi.) 793.8	Annual Wages $145,192,743
Altitude (ft.) 193-415	Av. Weekly Wage..............$467.53
Rainfall (in.)................................40.4	Fed. Wages $1,377,263
Jan. mean min. 40	Ag. Net Cash Return $2,957,000
July mean max.............................96	Prop. Value $1,166,259,877
Growing season (days) 278	Retail Sales $239,466,249

STATE PRISONS   ① PACK I   ② PACK II   0 2 4 6 8 MILES

Guadalupe County

Physical Features: South central county bisected by Guadalupe River; level to rolling surface; sandy, loam, blackland soils.

Economy: Varied manufacturing; many residents work in San Antonio (county in San Antonio metropolitan area), agribusiness, tourism.

History: Karankawas, Comanches, other tribes until 1850s. Spanish land grant in 1806 to José de la Baume. DeWitt colonists arrived in 1827. County created 1846 from Bexar, Gonzales counties; named for river.

Ethnicity, 1990: White, 52,948 (81.6%); Black, 3,665 (5.6%); American Indian, 235 (0.4%); Asian, 465 (0.7%); Other, 7,560 (11.7%). Hispanic, 19,246 (29.7%).

Vital Statistics, 1995: Births, 946; deaths, 547; marriages, 522; divorces, 348.

Recreation: Fishing, hunting, river floating; historic sites; Freedom Fiesta in July, historic festival in April.

Minerals: Oil, gas, sand and gravel, clays.

Agriculture: Beef cattle, horses, hogs, goats and sheep; grain sorghums, wheat, corn, pecans, nursery crops, cotton, peanuts, oats, Christmas trees, peaches. Market value $27.7 million.

SEGUIN (20,746) county seat; varied manufacturing; hospital, museum; Texas Lutheran University.

Other towns include: **Cibolo** (1,882), **Geronimo** (400), **Kingsbury** (200); **Marion** (983), **McQueeney** (2,117), **New Berlin** (200), **Schertz** (12,877), **Selma** (679), **Staples** (350).

Population 71,875	
(Change fm '90) 10.8	
Land Area (sq. mi.) 711.2	
Altitude (ft.)........................372-726	
Rainfall (in.).................................31.4	
Jan. mean min. 40	
July mean max.............................96	
Growing season (days) 267	
Civ. Labor..............................38,422	
Unemployed................................3.1	
Annual Wages.............. $414,581,864	
Av. Weekly Wage..................$423.40	
Fed. Wages....................$6,258,689	
Ag. Net Cash Return...........$161,000	
Prop. Value $2,684,683,005	
Retail Sales.................$375,489,142	

0 2 4 6 8 MILES

Hale County

Physical Features: High Plains; fertile sandy, loam soils; many playas; large underground water supply.

Economy: Agribusinesses, food-processing plants; manufacturing; government services.

History: Comanche hunters driven out by U.S. Army in 1875. Ranching began in 1880s. First motor-driven irrigation well drilled in 1911. County created from Bexar District, 1876; organized, 1888; named for Lt. J.C. Hale, who died at San Jacinto.

Ethnicity, 1990: White, 23,823 (68.7%); Black, 1,852 (5.3%); American Indian, 148 (0.4%); Asian, 136 (0.4%); Other, 8,712 (25.1%). Hispanic, 14,428 (41.6%).

Vital Statistics, 1994: Births, 637; deaths, 282; marriages, 343; divorces, 210.

Recreation: Llano Estacado Museum; art gallery, antique stores.

Minerals: Production of oil, gas.

Agriculture: One of leading farm-producing counties; 540,000 acres irrigated. Cotton, major crop; corn, sorghum, also produced; fed cattle, stockers raised. Market value $177.4 million.

PLAINVIEW (21,586) county seat; packing plants, distribution center; food processing, other industries; Wayland Baptist University; hospital, mental health center; state prisons.

Hale Center (2,052) commercial center.

Other towns include: **Abernathy** (2,664, partly in Lubbock County), **Cotton Center** (205), **Edmonson** (122), **Petersburg** (1,255), **Seth Ward** (1,560).

Population	35,461
(Change fm '90)	2.3
Land Area (sq. mi.)	1,004.7
Altitude (ft.)	3,501-3,515
Rainfall (in.)	19.8
Jan. mean min.	24
July mean max.	92
Growing season (days)	211
Civ. Labor	17,871
Unemployed	6.4
Annual Wages	$272,400,845
Av. Weekly Wage	$370.97
Fed. Wages	$4,658,625
Ag. Net Cash Return	$11,928,000
Prop. Value	$1,328,597,407
Retail Sales	$2,436,465,915

Hall County

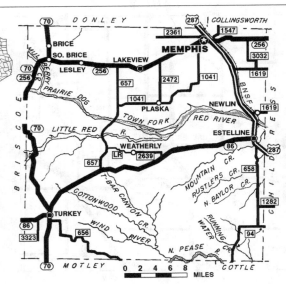

Physical Features: Rolling to hilly, broken by Red River forks, tributaries; red and black sandy loam.

Economy: Grain, cotton processing; farm, ranch supplies, marketing for large rural area.

History: Apaches, displaced by Comanches who were removed to Indian Territory in 1875. Ranching began in 1880s. Farming expanded after 1910. County created 1876 from Bexar, Young districts; organized 1890; named for Republic of Texas secretary of war W.D.C. Hall.

Ethnicity, 1990: White, 2,908 (74.5%); Black, 303 (7.8%); American Indian, 15 (0.4%); Asian, 7 (0.2%); Other, 672 (17.2%). Hispanic, 727 (18.6%).

Vital Statistics, 1995: Births, 63; deaths, 51; marriages, 27; divorces, 20.

Recreation: Fishing, hunting; museum.

Minerals: Not significant.

Agriculture: Most income from crops including cotton, peanuts; also beef cattle, hogs; some irrigation. Market value $21 million.

MEMPHIS (2,428) county seat; foundry; cotton gins; food processing; manufacturing; hospital.

Other towns include: **Estelline** (187), **Lakeview** (227), **Turkey** (531) Bob Wills Day in April.

Population	3,880
(Change fm '90)	- 0.6
Land Area (sq. mi.)	903.1
Altitude (ft.)	2,238-3,315
Rainfall (in.)	20.5
Jan. mean min.	24
July mean max.	96
Growing season (days)	213
Civ. Labor	1,762
Unemployed	7.4
Annual Wages	$13,558,487
Av. Weekly Wage	$282.67
Fed. Wages	$861,332
Ag. Net Cash Return	$4,860,000
Prop. Value	$163,269,608
Retail Sales	$15,604,485

For explanation of sources, abbreviations and symbols, see p. 142.

Hamilton County

Physical Features: Hilly north central county broken by scenic valleys; loam soils.

Economy: Agribusiness; varied manufacturing; hunting leases; tourism; many residents work outside county.

History: Waco and Tawakoni Indian area. Anglo-American settlers arrived in mid-1850s. County created 1842; then re-created, organized 1858, from Bosque, Comanche, Lampasas counties; named for South Carolinian, Gov. James Hamilton, who aided Texas Revolution and Republic.

Ethnicity, 1990: White, 7,389 (95.6%); Black, 2 (0.0%); American Indian, 21 (0.3%); Asian, 24 (0.3%); Other, 297 (3.8%). Hispanic, 403 (5.2%).

Vital Statistics, 1995: Births, 91; deaths, 147; marriages, 77; divorces, 49.

Recreation: Deer, quail, duck hunting; dove festival; July arts and crafts show.

Minerals: Limited gas, oil, gravel.

Agriculture: Dairies, beef cattle top revenue sources. Hay, wheat, oats, sorghums; more land being devoted to pastures. Market value $38.8 million.

HAMILTON (2,997) county seat; dairies, hunting, antique shops, historical homes; varied manufacturing; hospital; library.

Hico (1,515) farm center, Old Settlers Reunion in summer.

Other towns include: **Carlton** (70), **Evant** (482) partly in Coryell County, **Pottsville** (100).

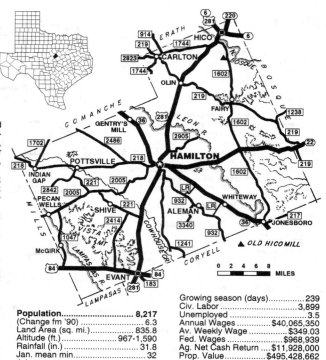

Population	8,217
(Change fm '90)	6.3
Land Area (sq. mi.)	835.8
Altitude (ft.)	967-1,590
Rainfall (in.)	31.8
Jan. mean min.	32
July mean max.	96
Growing season (days)	239
Civ. Labor	3,899
Unemployed	3.5
Annual Wages	$40,065,350
Av. Weekly Wage	$349.03
Fed. Wages	$968,939
Ag. Net Cash Return	$11,928,000
Prop. Value	$495,428,662
Retail Sales	$43,018,135

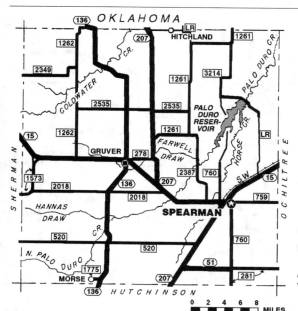

Hansford County

Physical Features: High Plains, many playas, creeks, draws; sandy, loam, black soils; underground water.

Economy: Agribusinesses; mineral operations.

History: Apaches, pushed out by Comanches around 1700. U.S. Army removed Comanches in 1874-75 and ranching began soon afterward. Farmers, including some from Norway, moved in around 1900. County created 1876, from Bexar, Young districts; organized 1889; named for jurist J.M. Hansford.

Ethnicity, 1990: White, 4,821 (82.4%); Black, 0 (0.0%); American Indian, 23 (0.4%); Asian, 14 (0.2%); Other, 990 (16.9%). Hispanic, 1,174 (20.1%).

Vital Statistics, 1995: Births, 65; deaths, 53; marriages, 31; divorces, 15.

Recreation: Stationmasters House Museum; hunting; lake activities.

Minerals: Production of gas, oil, stone, helium.

Agriculture: Large cattle-feeding operations; corn, wheat, sorghums; substantial irrigation. Market value $302.9 million.

SPEARMAN (3,005) county seat; feedlots; grain marketing, storage center; gas processing; hospital; windmill collection.

Other towns include: **Gruver** (1,067) farm-ranch market, Fourth of July Barbecue; **Morse** (150).

Population	5,435
(Change fm '90)	-7.1
Land Area (sq. mi.)	919.9
Altitude (ft.)	2,986-3,237
Rainfall (in.)	19.4
Jan. mean min.	21
July mean max.	95
Growing season (days)	186
Civ. Labor	2,562
Unemployed	3.3
Annual Wages	$44,869,475
Av. Weekly Wage	$456.96
Fed. Wages	$652,188
Ag. Net Cash Return	$29,414,000
Prop. Value	$664,780,620
Retail Sales	$34,257,679

For explanation of sources, abbreviations and symbols, see p. 142.

Hardeman County

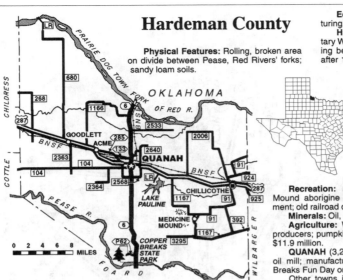

Physical Features: Rolling, broken area on divide between Pease, Red Rivers' forks; sandy loam soils.

Economy: Agribusiness; some manufacturing, tourism.

History: Apaches, later the semi-sedentary Wichitas and Comanche hunters. Ranching began in late 1870s. Farming expanded after 1900. County created 1858 from Fannin County; re-created 1876, organized, 1884; named for pioneer brothers, Bailey and T.J. Hardeman.

Ethnicity, 1990: White, 4,427 (83.8%); Black, 321 (6.1%); American Indian, 26 (0.5%); Asian, 16 (0.3%); Other, 493 (9.3%). Hispanic, 589 (11.1%).

Vital Statistics, 1995: Births, 65; deaths, 74; marriages, 34; divorces, 27.

Recreation: state park; lake activities; Medicine Mound aborigine gathering site; Quanah Parker monument; old railroad depot.

Minerals: Oil, gypsum.

Agriculture: Wheat, cotton, cattle are top revenue producers; pumpkins; some cotton irrigated. Market value $11.9 million.

QUANAH (3,298) county seat; agribusinesses; cotton oil mill; manufacturing; hospital; historical sites; Copper Breaks Fun Day on Memorial Day.

Other towns include: **Chillicothe** (776) farm market center.

Population 5,083	July mean max. 97	Av. Weekly Wage $376.24
(Change fm '90) .... -3.8	Growing season (days) ... 221	Fed. Wages $685,828
Land Area (sq. mi.) ... 695.4	Civ. Labor 2,079	Ag. Net Cash Return ... $1,153,000
Altitude (ft.) ... 1,287-1,749	Unemployed 5.2	Prop. Value $292,935,098
Rainfall (in.) 24.5	Annual Wages ... $28,388,551	Retail Sales $20,756,568
Jan. mean min. 23		

Hardin County

Physical Features: Southeast county; timbered; many streams; sandy, loam soils; Big Thicket covers much of area.

Economy: Paper manufacturing; wood processing; minerals; food processing; county in Beaumont-Port Arthur-Orange metropolitan area.

History: Lorenzo de Zavala received first land grant in 1829. Anglo-American settlers arrived in 1830. County created 1858 from Jefferson, Liberty counties. Named for Texas Revolutionary leader William Hardin.

Ethnicity, 1990: White, 37,485 (90.7%); Black, 3,485 (8.4%); American Indian, 123 (0.3%); Asian, 58 (0.1%); Other, 169 (0.4%). Hispanic, 679 (1.6%).

Vital Statistics, 1995: Births, 660; deaths, 380; marriages, 495; divorces, 340.

Recreation: Big Thicket with rare plant, animal life; national preserve; Red Cloud Water Park; hunting, fishing; state park.

Minerals: Oil, gas, sand, gravel.

Agriculture: Timber provides most income; more than 85 percent of county forested. Beef cattle, hogs raised; eggs marketed; forage, fruit and rice. Market value $2.7 million.

KOUNTZE (2,442) county seat;

For explanation of sources, abbreviations and symbols, see p. 142.

sawmill; some manufacturing; tourism; library.

Silsbee (6,888), trade, manufacturing center; oil, gas processing; pine festival; hospital.

Lumberton (7,410) retail center, tourism, Village Creek Festival in April.

Other towns include: **Batson** (140); **Grayburg** (316); **Rose Hill Acres** (559); **Saratoga** (1,000) Big Thicket Museum; **Sour Lake** (1,749) oil, lumbering; Old Timer's Day in September; **Thicket** (306); **Village Mills** (1,700); **Votaw** (160).

Population 46,178	
(Change fm '90) 11.8	
Land Area (sq. mi.) 894.4	
Altitude (ft.) 29-126	
Rainfall (in.) 55.7	
Jan. mean min. 37	
July mean max. 93	
Growing season (days) ... 246	
Civ. Labor 22,130	
Unemployed 8.2	
Annual Wages ... $193,184,435	
Av. Weekly Wage $386.24	
Fed. Wages $2,302,066	
Ag. Net Cash Return ... $367,000	
Prop. Value ... $1,374,630,988	
Retail Sales ... $331,677,197	

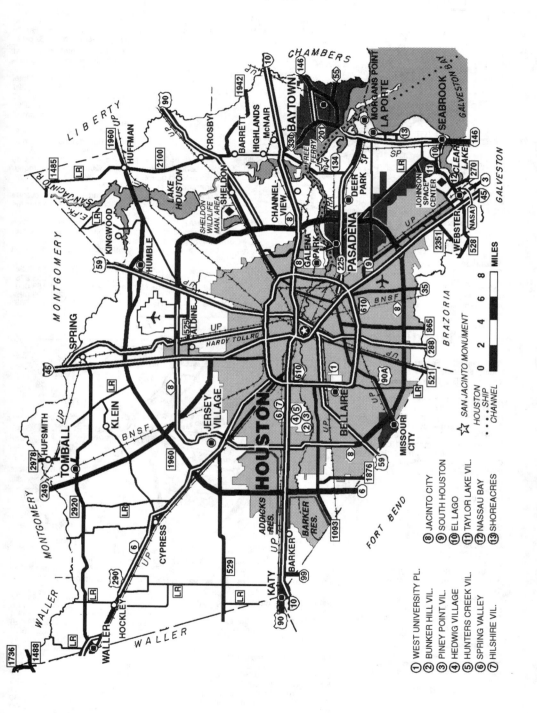

1 WEST UNIVERSITY PL.
2 BUNKER HILL VIL.
3 PINEY POINT VIL.
4 HEDWIG VILLAGE
5 HUNTERS CREEK VIL.
6 SPRING VALLEY
7 HILSHIRE VIL.

8 JACINTO CITY
9 SOUTH HOUSTON
10 EL LAGO
11 TAYLOR LAKE VIL.
12 NASSAU BAY
13 SHOREACRES

Physical Features: Largest county in eastern half of state; level; typically coastal surface and soils; many bayous, lakes, canals for artificial drainage; partly forested.

Economy: Highly industrialized county with largest population; more than 55 foreign governments maintain offices in Houston; corporate management center; nation's largest concentration of petrochemical plants; largest U.S wheat-exporting port, among top U.S. ports in the value of foreign trade and total tonnage.

Petroleum refining, chemicals, food, fabricated metal products, nonelectrical machinery, primary metals, scientific instruments; paper and allied products, printing and publishing; center for energy, space and medical research; center of international business.

History: Orcoquiza villages visited by Spanish authorities in 1746. Pioneer settlers arrived by boat from Louisiana in 1822. Antebellum planters brought black slaves. Mexican migration increased following Mexican Revolution. County created 1836, organized 1837; named for John R. Harris, founder of Harrisburg (now part of Houston) in 1824.

Ethnicity, 1990: White, 1,824,137 (64.7%); Black, 541,180 (19.2%); American Indian, 8,044 (0.3%); Asian, 110,848 (3.9%); Other, 333,990 (11.9%). Hispanic, 644,935 (22.9%).

Vital Statistics, 1995: Births, 57,057; deaths, 18,590; marriages, 29,679; divorces, 16,765.

Recreation: Professional football, baseball, basketball, other activities; Jones Hall for the Performing Arts, Nina Vance Alley Theatre, Houston Theatre Center, Music Hall Coliseum, Convention Center, the Summit, a 17,000-seat sports and entertainment center; Astroworld and WaterWorld amusement parks near the Astrodome.

Sam Houston Park, with restored early Houston homes, church, stores; Museum of Fine Arts, Contemporary Arts Museum, Rice Museum; Wortham Theater for performing arts; museum of natural science, planetarium, zoo in Hermann Park.

San Jacinto Battleground, Battleship Texas; Johnson Space Center; annual livestock show.

Fishing, boating, other freshwater and saltwater activities.

Minerals: Among leading oil, gas, petrochemical areas; production of petroleum, cement, natural gas, liquids, salt, lime, sulfur, sand and gravel, clays, stone.

Harris County

Agriculture: Beef cattle, horses, nursery plants and hay are the major revenue sources. Also, some dairies and ratites. Also harvested are rice, vegetables, corn, peanuts; about 14,700 acres irrigated for rice. Market value $44 million. Substantial income from forest products.

Education: Houston is a major center of higher education, with more than 140,000 students enrolled in 28 colleges and universities in the county. Among these are Rice University, the University of Houston, Texas Southern University, University of St. Thomas, Houston Baptist University.

Medical schools include University of St. Thomas and Houston Baptist University Schools of Nursing, University of Texas Health Science Center, Baylor College of Medicine, Institute of Religion and Human Development, Texas Chiropractic College, Texas Woman's University-Houston Center.

HOUSTON (1,749,001) county seat; largest Texas city; fourth largest in nation.

Ranks first in manufacture of petroleum equipment, agricultural chemicals, fertilizers, pesticides, oil and gas pipeline transmission; a leading scientific center; ranks high in manufacture of machinery, fabricated metals; a major distribution, shipping center; engineering and research center; food processing and textile mills.

Plants make apparel, lumber and wood products; furniture, paper, chemical, petroleum and coal products; publishing center; one of the nation's largest public school systems; prominent corporate center, with more than 200 firms relocating corporate headquarters, divisions or subsidaries to county since 1970.

Pasadena (130,168), residential city with large industrial area manufacturing petrochemicals and other petroleum-related products; civic center; San Jacinto College, Texas Chiropractic College; four hospitals; historical museum; Strawberry Festival.

Baytown (69,004), refining, petrochemical center; Lee College; hospitals; historical homes;

Bellaire (14,955), residential city with several major office buildings.

The **Clear Lake Area** which includes **El Lago** (3,505); **Nassau Bay** (4,615); **Seabrook** (8,558); **Taylor Lake Village** (4,151), Johnson Space Center, University of Houston-Clear Lake; Bayport Industrial Complex includes Port of Bayport; 12 major marinas; two hospitals; **Webster** (5,257).

Other towns include: **Aldine** (11,835); **Bunker Hill Village** (3,462); **Channelview** (27,742); **Crosby** (2,167); **Deer Park** (30,055), ship-channel industries, fall festival; hospital; **Galena Park** (11,021); **Hedwig Village** (3,462); **Highlands** (7,941); **Hilshire Village** (771); **Hockley** (300); **Humble** (14,912), oil-field equipment manufactured, retail center, hospital; **Hunters Creek Village** (4,527); **Jacinto City** (9,459); **Jersey Village** (5,448).

Also, **Katy** (11,204, partly in Fort Bend, Waller counties), varied manufacturing, hospital; rice harvest festival in October, G.I. Joe museum; **Kingwood** (39,997), **La Porte** (31,284), varied manufacturing; Sylvan Beach Festival in April; Galveston Bay; **Missouri City** (50,719), mostly in Fort Bend County); **Morgan's Point** (410); **Piney Point Village** (3,456); **Shoreacres** (1,526); **South Houston** (15,321).

Also, **Southside Place** (1,498); **Spring** (37,730); **Spring Valley** (3,690); **Sheldon** (1,995); **Tomball** (7,252) retail center; regional hospital, sports medical center; museum, parks; **West University Place** (13,645). **Addicks** and **Alief** are now within the city limits of Houston.

Population	3,087,153
(Change fm '90)	9.5
Land Area (sq. mi.)	1,729.0
Altitude (ft.)	sea level-171
Rainfall (in.)	46.1
Jan. mean min.	43
July mean max.	92
Growing season (days)	300
Civ. Labor	1,692,905
Unemployed	5.5
Annual Wages	$51,549,475,128
Av. Weekly Wage	$630.08
Fed. Wages	$1,084,343,880
Ag. Net Cash Return	$7,885,000
Prop. Value	$133,178,613,890
Retail Sales	$36,171,253,016

For explanation of sources, abbreviations and symbols, see p. 142.

Harrison County

Physical Features: East Texas county; hilly, rolling; over half forested; Sabine River; Caddo Lake.

Economy: Oil, gas processing; lumbering; pottery, other varied manufacturing.

History: Agriculturist Caddo Indians whose numbers were reduced by disease. Anglo-Americans arrived in 1830s. In 1850, the county had more slaves than any other in the state. County created 1839, from Shelby County; organized, 1842. Named for eloquent advocate of Texas Revolution, Jonas Harrison.

Ethnicity, 1990: White, 40,387 (70.3%); Black, 16,038 (27.9%); American Indian, 192 (0.3%); Asian, 144 (0.3%); Other, 722 (1.3%). Hispanic, 1,278 (2.2%).

Vital Statistics, 1995: Births, 724; deaths, 608; marriages, 599; divorces, 277.

Recreation: Fishing, other water activities on Caddo and other lakes; hunting; plantation homes, historic sites; Stagecoach Days in May; Old Courthouse Museum; Old World Store; state park, performing arts.

Minerals: Production of oil, gas, coal, clays, sand and gravel.

Agriculture: Cattle, hogs; nursery plants, hay, timber. Market value $11.6 million.

MARSHALL (24,059) county seat; petroleum, lumber processing; varied manufacturing; Wonderland of Lights in December; civic center; historic sites; hospital; Wiley College; East Texas Baptist University.

Other towns include: **Elysian Fields** (300); **Hallsville** (2,872) Western Days in October, museum; **Harleton** (260); **Jonesville** (28); **Karnack** (775); **Nesbitt** (380); **Scottsville** (288); **Uncertain** (215); **Waskom** (1,853); **Woodlawn** (370). Also, part of **Longview**.

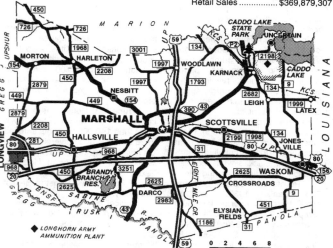

Population	**60,231**
(Change fm '90)	4.8
Land Area (sq. mi.)	898.8
Altitude (ft.)	168-417
Rainfall (in.)	47.7
Jan. mean min.	32
July mean max.	93
Growing season (days)	245
Civ. Labor	28,250
Unemployed	9.6
Annual Wages	$551,770,357
Av. Weekly Wage	$522.69
Fed. Wages	$4,063,097
Ag. Net Cash Return	$8,000
Prop. Value	$3,016,927,270
Retail Sales	$369,879,307

Hartley County

Physical Features: Panhandle High Plains; drains to Canadian River, tributaries; playas; sandy, loam, chocolate soils; lake.

Economy: Agriculture, gas production; varied manufacturing.

History: Apaches, pushed out by Comanches around 1700. U.S. Army removed Indians in 1875. *Pastores* (Hispanic sheepmen) in area until 1880s. Cattle ranching began in 1880s. Farming expanded after 1900. County created 1876 from Bexar, Young districts; organized 1891; named for Texas pioneers O.C. and R.K. Hartley.

Ethnicity, 1990: White, 3,510 (96.6%); Black, 9 (0.2%); American Indian, 30 (0.8%); Asian, 7 (0.2%); Other, 78 (2.1%). Hispanic, 201 (5.5%).

Vital Statistics, 1995: Births, 46; deaths, 36; marriages, 3; divorces, 11.

Recreation: Rita Blanca Lake activities; ranch museum; local events;

XIT Rodeo and Reunion at Dalhart.

Minerals: Natural gas.

Agriculture: Wheat, sorghum, corn; hay; beef cattle; about 120,000 acres irrigated; blue corn, pop corn introduced. Market value $275.2 million.

CHANNING (250) county seat.

Dalhart (6,696 mostly in Dallam County), feedlots; feed, meat processing; other industries. Also, **Hartley** (319).

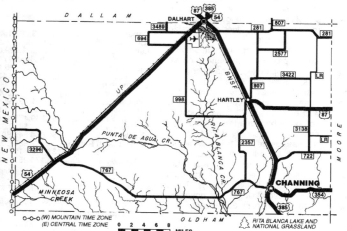

Population	**4,532**
(Change fm '90)	24.7
Land Area (sq. mi.)	1,462.4
Altitude (ft.)	3,439-4,397
Rainfall (in.)	16.1
Jan. mean min.	21
July mean max.	92
Growing season (days)	180
Civ. Labor	2,414
Unemployed	2.5
Annual Wages	$14,856,746
Av. Weekly Wage	$354.21
Fed. Wages	$384,092
Ag. Net Cash Return	$50,102,000
Prop. Value	$428,035,540
Retail Sales	$21,881,161

Haskell County

Physical Features: West central county; rolling; broken areas; drained by Brazos tributaries; lake; sandy loam, gray, black soils.

Economy: Agribusinesses, oil-field operations.

History: Apaches until 1700, then Comanche area. Ranching began in late 1870s after Indians removed. Farming expanded after 1900. County created 1858, from Milam, Fannin counties; re-created 1876; organized 1885; named for Goliad victim C.R. Haskell.

Ethnicity,1990: White, 5,481 (80.4%); Black, 244 (3.6%); American Indian, 17 (0.2%); Asian, 16 (0.2%); Other, 1,062 (15.6%). Hispanic, 1,312 (19.2%).

Vital Statistics, 1995: Births, 68; deaths, 127; marriages, 42; divorces, 23.

Recreation: Lake Stamford activities; bass tournament, arts & crafts show; hunting.

Minerals: Oil and gas.

Agriculture: Most income from cotton, wheat, peanuts; beef cattle raised; 27,000 acres irrigated, mostly peanuts, some cotton, wheat. Market value $37 million.

HASKELL (3,156) county seat; farming center; hospital; city park; Wild Horse Prairie Days in June.

Other towns include: **O'Brien** (163), **Rochester** (507), **Rule** (733), **Sagerton** (115), **Weinert** (253). Also, **Stamford** (3,416, mostly in Jones County),

Population............................. 6,526
(Change fm '90) .... -4.3

Land Area (sq. mi.)	903.0
Altitude (ft.)	1,416-1,681
Rainfall (in.)	26.1
Jan. mean min.	27
July mean max.	96
Growing season (days)..............	232
Civ. Labor	2,868

Unemployed............................	4.1
Annual Wages.............	$26,916,578
Av. Weekly Wage...............	$310.68
Fed. Wages............................	$1,165,855
Ag. Net Cash Return......	$7,150,000
Prop. Value	$354,343,985
Retail Sales	$50,600,860

Hays County

Physical Features: Hilly in west, blackland in east; on edge of Balcones Escarpment.

Economy: Education, tourism, retirement area, some manufacturing; part of Austin metropolitan area.

History: Tonkawa area, also Apache and Comanche presence. Spanish authorities attempted first permanent settlement in 1807. Mexican land grants in early 1830s to Juan Martín Veramendi, Juan Vicente Campos and Thomas Jefferson Chambers. County created 1843 from Travis County; named for Capt. Jack Hays, famous Texas Ranger.

Ethnicity, 1990: White, 55,360 (84.4%); Black, 2,220 (3.4%); American Indian, 230 (0.4%); Asian, 427 (0.7%); Other, 7,377 (11.2%). Hispanic, 18,249 (27.8%).

Vital Statistics, 1995: Births, 1,029; deaths, 425; marriages, 671; divorces, 209.

Recreation: Fishing, hunting; college cultural, athletic events; Cypress Creek and Blanco River resorts, guest ranches.

Minerals: Sand and gravel, cement produced.

Agriculture: Beef cattle, goats, sheep, ratites, some llamas and exotic deer; greenhouse nurseries; corn, sorghum, wheat and hay. Market value $14.3 million.

SAN MARCOS (34,661), county seat; aircraft assemblies, metal stamping; distribution center; 200 stores in two outlet malls; hospital, sports medicine, physical therapy center; Southwest Texas State University, San Marcos Baptist Academy, Gary Job Corps Training Center; Scheib Center for mentally handicapped; Mardi Gras, Cinco de Mayo, Texas Chilympiad in September.

Other towns include: **Buda** (1,922); **Driftwood** (21); **Dripping Springs** (1,070); **Hays** (275); **Kyle** (2,447); **Mountain City** (384); **Niederwald** (257, partly in Caldwell County); **Uhland** (388); **Wimberley** (2,520), retirement community, tourism, artists, concert series; **Woodcreek** (1,018).

Population............................	79,374
(Change fm '90)......................	21.0
Land Area (sq. mi.)..................	677.9
Altitude (ft.)......................	582-1,501
Rainfall (in.)	34.6
Jan. mean min.........................	36
July mean max.	95
Growing season (days)	254
Civ. Labor	45,150
Unemployed.............................	3.1
Annual Wages	$538,853,377
Av. Weekly Wage...............	$366.50
Fed. Wages	$4,664,948
Ag. Net Cash Return	$379,000
Prop. Value.............	$3,280,434,007
Retail Sales	$667,618,576

For explanation of sources, abbreviations and symbols, see p. 142.

Hemphill County

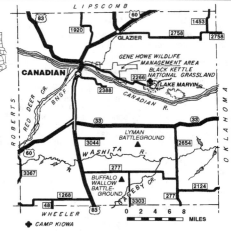

Physical Features: Panhandle county; sloping surface, broken by Canadian, Washita rivers; sandy, red, dark soils.

Economy: Petroleum production and refining, livestock production.

History: Apaches, who were pushed out by Comanches, Kiowas. Tribes removed to Indian Territory in 1875. Ranching began in late 1870s. Farmers began to arrive after 1900. County created from Bexar, Young districts, 1876; organized 1887; named for Republic of Texas Justice John Hemphill.

Ethnicity, 1990: White, 3,503 (94.2%); Black, 7 (0.2%); American Indian, 22 (0.6%); Asian, 5 (0.1%); Other, 183 (4.9%). Hispanic, 412 (11.1%).

Vital Statistics, 1995: Births, 26; deaths, 35; marriages, 44; divorces, 15.

Recreation: Lake Marvin activities; fall foliage tours; hunting, fishing; Buffalo Wallow Indian Battleground, wildlife management area; 4th of July rodeo.

Minerals: Oil, natural gas.

Agriculture: Fed beef, stocker cattle top revenue sources; crops include wheat, sorghum, hay, improved pastures; some irrigation. Market value $82.2 million.

CANADIAN (2,197) county seat; oil, gas production; feedlot; hospital.

Population.................................. 3,527
(Change fm '90) .... -5.2

Land Area (sq. mi.).....................909.7	Unemployed................................2.9
Altitude (ft.) 2,185-2,843	Annual Wages................ $35,422,782
Rainfall (in.) 20.1	Av. Weekly Wage............... $506.60
Jan. mean min. 22	Fed. Wages..................... $512,331
July mean max. 96	Ag. Net Cash Return...... $13,154,000
Growing season (days)..................204	Prop. Value $786,144,162
Civ. Labor.................................1,961	Retail Sales $18,682,060

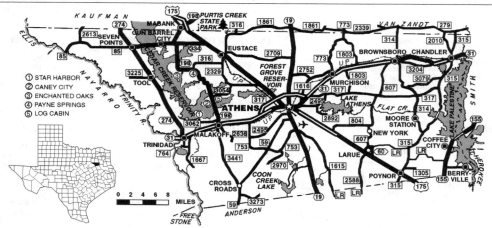

Henderson County

Physical Features: East Texas county bounded by Neches, Trinity rivers; hilly, rolling; one-third forested; sandy, loam, clay soils; commercial timber; Cedar Creek, other lakes.

Economy: Varied manufacturing; agribusinesses; minerals; recreation; tourism.

History: Caddo area. Cherokee, other tribes migrated into the area in 1819-20 ahead of white settlement. Cherokees forced into Indian Territory in 1839. Anglo-American settlers arrived in 1840s. County created 1846 from Nacogdoches, Houston counties and named for Gov. J. Pinckney Henderson.

Ethnicity, 1990: White, 52,216 (89.2%); Black, 4,755 (8.1%); American Indian, 181 (0.3%); Asian, 141 (0.2%); Other, 1,250 (2.1%). Hispanic, 2,368 (4.0%).

Vital Statistics, 1995: Births, 773; deaths, 796; marriages, 589; divorces, 202.

Recreation: Cedar Creek Reservoir, Lake Palestine, and other lakes; Purtis Creek State Park; hunting, fishing; Black-eyed Pea Jamboree, fiddlers' reunion.

Minerals: Oil, gas, clays, lignite, sulphur, sand and gravel.

Agriculture: Most income from cattle, horses, swine, ratites (emu, ostrich, rhea); crops include grain, nursery crops, vegetables, melons; hardwood timber marketed. Market value $36.2 million.

ATHENS (11,530) county seat; agribusiness center; varied manufacturing; tourism; state fish hatchery and museum; hospital, mental health/mental retardation center; Trinity Valley Community College.

Gun Barrel City (4,243) recreation, retirement, retail center.

Malakoff (2,200), brick factory, varied industry, Lakefest.

Other towns include: **Berryville** (894); **Brownsboro** (583); **Caney City** (195); **Chandler** (2,029); **Coffee City** (240); **Enchanted Oaks** (320); **Eustace** (821); **Larue** (160); **Log Cabin** (566); **Moore Station** (298); **Murchison** (588); **Payne Springs** (711); **Poynor** (266); **Seven Points** (804); **Star Harbor** (398); **Tool** (2,014); **Trinidad** (1,123).

Population 64,860
(Change fm '90) 10.8
Land Area (sq. mi.)...................... 874.4
Altitude (ft.) 256-763
Rainfall (in.) 39.7
Jan. mean min............................ 35
July mean max. 95
Growing season (days) 260
Civ. Labor................................ 28,376
Unemployed................................. 5.2
Annual Wages................ $250,784,924
Av. Weekly Wage............... $360.75
Fed. Wages..................... $2,992,052
Ag. Net Cash Return $5,399,000
Prop. Value $2,677,742,053
Retail Sales $497,405,569

Physical Features: Rich alluvial soils along Rio Grande; sandy, loam soils in north; semitropical vegetation.

Economy: Food processing, shipping; other agribusinesses; tourism; mineral operations.

History: Coahuiltecan and Karankawa area. Comanches forced Apaches southward into valley in 1700s; Comanches arrived in valley in 1800s. Spanish settlement occurred 1750-1800. County created 1852 from Cameron, Starr counties; named for leader of Mexico's independence movement, Father Miguel Hidalgo y Costillo.

Ethnicity, 1990: White, 286,858 (74.8%); Black, 806 (0.2%); American Indian, 668 (0.2%); Asian, 1,088 (0.3%); Other, 94,125 (24.5%). Hispanic, 326,972 (85.2%).

Vital Statistics, 1995: Births, 12,882; deaths, 2,467; marriages, 4,843; divorces, 2.

Recreation: Winter resort, retirement area; fishing, hunting; gateway to Mexico; historical sites; Bentsen-Rio Grande Valley State Park; museums; All-Valley Winter Vegetable Show at Pharr.

Minerals: Oil, gas, stone, sand and gravel.

Agriculture: Ninety percent of farm cash receipts from crops, principally from sugar cane, grain, vegetables, citrus, cotton; livestock includes cattle; 270,000 acres irrigated. Market value $202.1 million.

Hidalgo County

EDINBURG (35,773) county seat; vegetable processing, packing; petroleum operations; clothing; tourism, planetarium; the University of Texas-Pan American; hospital; mental health center; museum; Fiesta Hidalgo in February.

McAllen (100,589) Food processing, packing, shipping; foreign trade zone; agriculture; tourism; varied manufacturing; new air terminal; community college; cancer center.

Mercedes (15,174) "boot capital," citrus, vegetable center; food processing; tourism; recreation vehicle show in January, boat show; Rio Grande Valley livestock show.

Pharr (39,843) agriculture, trading center; trucking; tourism; old clock, juke box museums; folklife festival in February.

Other towns include: **Alamo** (10,935) live steam museum; **Alton** (3,308); **Donna** (13,495), citrus center, varied manufacturing; lamb, sheep show; **Edcouch** (3,653); **Elsa** (5,608); **Hargill** (1,349); **Hidalgo** (5,056); **La Blanca** (150); **La Joya** (3,871); **La Villa** (1,712); **Linn** (450); **Los Ebanos** (100).

Also, **Mission** (38,101), Citrus Fiesta; **Monte Alto** (1,769); **Palmhurst** (387); **Palmview** (2,331); **Peñitas** (1,210); **Progreso** (2,717); **Progreso Lakes** (191); **San Juan** (24,324); **Sullivan City** (2,649); **Weslaco** (27,812) Bicultural Museum.

Population	485,332
(Change fm '90)	26.5
Land Area (sq. mi.)	1,569.1
Altitude (ft.)	28-325
Rainfall (in.)	23.4
Jan. mean min.	49
July mean max.	96
Growing season (days)	327
Civ. Labor	189,906
Unemployed	19.0
Annual Wages	$2,395,508,750
Av. Weekly Wage	$351.99
Fed. Wages	$91,039,027
Ag. Net Cash Return	$29,270,000
Prop. Value	$9,898,118,019
Retail Sales	$3,386,635,195

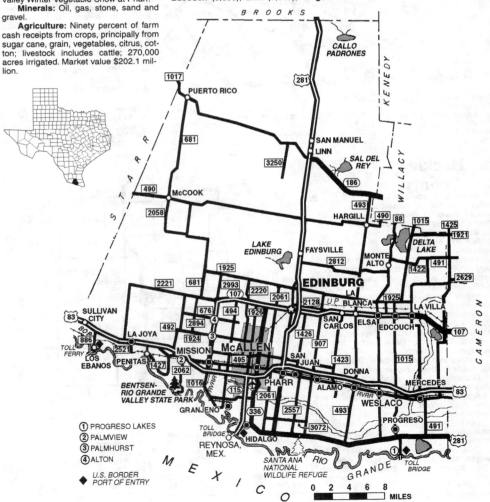

① PROGRESO LAKES
② PALMVIEW
③ PALMHURST
④ ALTON

◆ U.S. BORDER PORT OF ENTRY

0 2 4 6 8 MILES

Hill County

Physical Features: North central county; level to rolling; blackland soils, some sandy loams; drains to Brazos; lakes.

Economy: Agribusiness, varied manufacturing, tourism.

History: Waco and Tawakoni area, later Comanches. Believed to be Indian "council spot," without evidence of raids and a place of safe passage. Anglo-Americans of the Robert-son colony arrived in early 1830s. County created from Navarro County 1853; named for G.W. Hill, Republic of Texas official.

Ethnicity, 1990: White, 23,669 (87.2%); Black, 2,520 (9.3%); American Indian, 80 (0.3%); Asian, 38 (0.1%); Other, 839 (3.1%). Hispanic, 2,230 (8.2%).

Vital Statistics, 1995: Births, 377; deaths, 423; marriages, 282; divorces, 162.

Recreation: Lake activities; excursion boat on Whitney; Confederate Museum, Audie Murphy Gun Museum, historic structures; art festival; motorcycle track.

Minerals: Limestone, gas, oil.

Agriculture: Evenly split between crops, livestock; grain sorghums, wheat, corn, cotton, hay; beef, dairy cattle, horses, swine; dairy products; some firewood. Market value $44.5 million.

HILLSBORO (7,766) county seat; retail center, manufacturing, agribusiness, antique malls, Hill College; hospital; crafts fair.

Whitney (1,683), tourist center; hospital; varied manufacturing. Other towns include: **Abbott** (363); **Aquilla** (164); **Blum** (432); **Brandon** (80); **Bynum** (205); **Carl's Corner** (116); **Covington** (276); **Hubbard** (1,656); **Irene** (160); **Itasca** (1,624); **Malone** (320); **Mertens** (113); **Mount Calm** (322); **Penelope** (217).

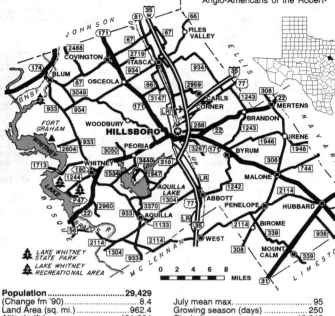

Population	29,429
(Change fm '90)	8.4
Land Area (sq. mi.)	962.4
Altitude (ft.)	481-864
Rainfall (in.)	35.1
Jan. mean min.	34

July mean max.	95
Growing season (days)	250
Civ. Labor	15,045
Unemployed	4.2
Annual Wages	$134,977,720

Av. Weekly Wage	$341.24
Fed. Wages	$2,668,517
Ag. Net Cash Return	$5,442,000
Prop. Value	$1,056,115,530
Retail Sales	$317,900,762

Hockley County

Physical Features: West Texas High Plains, numerous playas, drains to Yellow House River, Lake; loam, sandy loam soils.

Economy: Extensive oil, gas production and services; manufacturing; varied agribusiness.

History: Comanches displaced Apaches in early 1700s. Large ranches of 1880s brought few residents. Homesteaders arrived after 1900. County created 1876, from Bexar, Young districts; organized 1921. Named for Republic of Texas secretary of war Gen. G.W. Hockley.

Ethnicity, 1990: White, 18,937 (78.3%); Black, 1,023 (4.2%); American Indian, 86 (0.4%); Asian, 33 (0.1%); Other, 4,120 (17.0%). Hispanic, 7,650 (31.6%).

Vital Statistics, 1995: Births, 321; deaths, 200; marriages, 136; divorces, 131.

Recreation: Early Settlers' Day in July, Marigolds Arts, Crafts Festival in November.

Minerals: Oil, gas, stone; one of leading oil counties with more than 1 billion barrels produced.

Agriculture: Cotton, grain sorghums are top crops; cattle, hogs raised; substantial irrigation. Market value $59.6 million.

LEVELLAND (14,812) county seat; oil, cotton, cattle center; hospital; South Plains College.

Other towns include: **Anton** (1,257); **Opdyke West** (113); **Pep** (35); **Ropesville** (504); **Smyer** (436); **Sundown** (1,738);

For explanation of sources, abbreviations and symbols, see p. 142.

Population	24,001
(Change fm '90)	-0.8
Land Area (sq. mi.)	908.3
Altitude (ft.)	3,388-3,633
Rainfall (in.)	19.3
Jan. mean min.	22
July mean max.	92
Growing season (days)	196

Civ. Labor	11,164
Unemployed	5.1
Annual Wages	$165,881,480
Av. Weekly Wage	$404.93
Fed. Wages	$1,868,290
Ag. Net Cash Return	$16,934,000
Prop. Value	$2,085,231,570
Retail Sales	$152,469,061

Hood County

Physical Features: Hilly; broken by Paluxy, Brazos rivers; sandy loam soils.

Economy: Agribusinesses; tourism; nuclear power plant.

History: Lipan Apache and Comanche area. Anglo-American settlers arrived in late 1840s. County created, organized 1866 from Johnson County; named for Confederate Gen. John B. Hood.

Ethnicity, 1990: White, 28,054 (96.8%); Black, 52 (0.2%); American Indian, 154 (0.5%); Asian, 177 (0.6%); Other, 544 (1.9%). Hispanic, 1,353 (4.7%).

Vital Statistics, 1995: Births, 381; deaths, 373; marriages, 307; divorces, 235.

Recreation: Lakes, fishing, scenic areas; summer theater; state park; site of grave of Elizabeth Crockett, wife of Davy; Gen. Granbury's Birthday in March.

Minerals: Oil, gas, stone.

Agriculture: Beef, cow-calf operations, stocker cattle top revenue producers; crops include hay, peanuts, pecans; some irrigation. Market value $21.7 million.

GRANBURY (4,974) county seat; agribusiness; tourism; historic downtown area; opera house; hospital; Civil War re-enactment in fall.

Other towns include: **Acton** (1,129), **Cresson** (208), **Lipan** (410), **Paluxy** (76),

Population	32,051
(Change fm '90)	10.6
Land Area (sq. mi.)	421.6
Altitude (ft.)	722-1,230
Rainfall (in.)	30.9
Jan. mean min.	33
July mean max.	97
Growing season (days)	232

Civ. Labor	15,279
Unemployed	4.8
Annual Wages	$151,061,781
Av. Weekly Wage	$380.55
Fed. Wages	$2,712,468
Ag. Net Cash Return	$5,280,000
Prop. Value	$1,412,154,710
Retail Sales	$266,599,552

Hopkins County

Physical Features: Northeast Texas county of varied timber, including pines; drains north to South Sulphur River; Cooper Lake; light, sandy to heavier black soils.

Economy: Dairies, large milk-processing plants; agribusinesses; varied manufacturing.

History: Caddo area, displaced by Cherokees, who in turn were forced out by President Lamar in 1839. First Anglo-American settlement in 1837. County created 1846 from Lamar, Nacogdoches counties; named for pioneer Hopkins family.

Ethnicity, 1990: White, 25,381 (88.0%); Black, 2,476 (8.6%); American Indian, 126(0.4%); Asian, 70 (0.2%); Other, 780 (2.7%). Hispanic, 1,407 (4.9%).

Vital Statistics, 1995: Births, 419; deaths, 340; marriages, 317; divorces, 222.

Recreation: Fishing, hunting; lake activities; stew contest in September; dairy museum; dairy festival in June.

Minerals: Oil, gas and gravel.

Agriculture: Leading dairy county in region; also beef cattle, hay, silage, poultry, sweet potatoes, wheat; some irrigation; firewood and hardwood lumber. Market value $137.1 million.

SULPHUR SPRINGS (15,007) county seat; dairy farming center; food processing, distribution; varied manufacturing; tourism; hospital; library; heritage park; music box gallery; civic center.

Other towns include: **Brashear** (280), **Como** (623), **Cumby** (670), **Dike** (170), **Pickton** (90), **Saltillo** (200), **Sulphur Bluff** (280), **Tira** (293).

Population	30,969
(Change fm '90)	7.4
Land Area (sq. mi.)	784.8
Altitude (ft.)	420-649
Rainfall (in.)	46.0

Jan. mean min.	30
July mean max.	94
Growing season (days)	238
Civ. Labor	16,294
Unemployed	5.5

Annual Wages	$224,139,764
Av. Weekly Wage	$402.30
Fed. Wages	$3,226,199
Ag. Net Cash Return	$27,317,000
Prop. Value	$1,177,160,843
Retail Sales	$364,640,460

Houston County

Physical Features: East Texas county over half forested; rolling terrain, draining to Neches, Trinity rivers; commercial timber production.

Economy: Livestock, timber, manufacturing, tourism.

History: Caddo group attracted mission San Francisco de los Tejas, 1690. Spanish town of Bucareli established in 1774. Both lasted only a few years. Anglo-American settlers arrived in 1820s. County created 1837 from Nacogdoches County by Republic; named for Sam Houston. Cotton plantations before the Civil War had many slaves.

Ethnicity, 1990: White, 14,373 (67.2%); Black, 6,326 (29.6%); American Indian, 32 (0.1%); Asian, 49 (0.2%); Other, 595 (2.8%). Hispanic, 965 (4.5%).

Vital Statistics, 1995: Births, 236; deaths, 289; marriages, 145; divorces, 87.

Recreation: Fishing, hunting; national forest; Mission Tejas State Park; 75 historical markers; Houston County Lake.

Minerals: Oil, gas, sand, gravel.

Agriculture: Cattle and timber are principal income sources; hay, watermelons, cotton, peanuts produced. Market value $29.1 million.

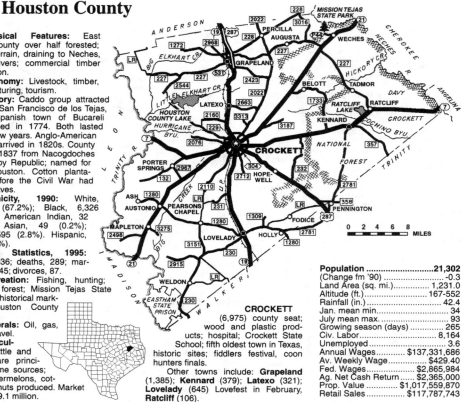

CROCKETT (6,975) county seat; wood and plastic products; hospital; Crockett State School; fifth oldest town in Texas, historic sites; fiddlers festival, coon hunters finals.

Other towns include: **Grapeland** (1,385); **Kennard** (379); **Latexo** (321); **Lovelady** (645) Lovefest in February, **Ratcliff** (106).

Population	21,302
(Change fm '90)	-0.3
Land Area (sq. mi.)	1,231.0
Altitude (ft.)	167-552
Rainfall (in.)	42.4
Jan. mean min.	34
July mean max.	93
Growing season (days)	265
Civ. Labor	8,164
Unemployed	3.6
Annual Wages	$137,331,686
Av. Weekly Wage	$429.40
Fed. Wages	$2,865,984
Ag. Net Cash Return	$2,365,000
Prop. Value	$1,017,559,870
Retail Sales	$117,787,743

Howard County

Physical Features: On edge Llano Estacado; sandy loam soils.

Economy: Oil, gas operations; government/service; agribusinesses; varied manufacturing, including clothing.

History: Pawnee and Comanche area. Anglo-American settlement began in 1870. Oil boom in mid-1920s. County named for V.E. Howard, legislator; created 1876 from Bexar, Young districts; organized 1882.

Ethnicity, 1990: White, 25,282 (78.2%); Black, 1,225 (3.8%); American Indian, 179 (0.6%); Asian, 162 (0.5%); Other, 5,495 (17.0%). Hispanic, 8,607 (26.6%).

Vital Statistics, 1995: Births, 424; deaths, 371; marriages, 290; divorces, 88.

Recreation: Lakes; state park; campground in Comanche Trail Park; Native Plant Trail; museum; historical sites; West Texas agricultural expo in March; Cranefest in February.

Minerals: Oil, gas, sand, gravel and stone.

Agriculture: Principally dry-land cotton; beef, stocker cattle raised. Market value $19.1 million.

BIG SPRING (23,308) county seat; petrochemicals produced; varied manufacturing; Howard College; railroad plaza; hospitals, including a state institution and Veterans Administration hospital; federal prison unit.

Other towns include: **Coahoma** (1,306), **Forsan** (297), **Knott** (685), **Vealmoor** (179), **Vincent** (500).

Population	32,878
(Change fm '90)	1.7
Land Area (sq. mi.)	902.9
Altitude (ft.)	2,271-2,776
Rainfall (in.)	19.2
Jan. mean min.	28
July mean max.	94
Growing season (days)	217
Civ. Labor	13,999
Unemployed	4.1
Annual Wages	$238,051,650
Av. Weekly Wage	$414.64
Fed. Wages	$32,484,472
Ag. Net Cash Return	$2,365,000
Prop. Value	$1,220,911,783
Retail Sales	$259,564,221

For explanation of sources, abbreviations and symbols, see p. 142.

Hudspeth County

Physical Features: Plateau, basin terrain, draining to salt lakes; Rio Grande; mostly rocky, alkaline, clay soils and sandy loam soils, except alluvial along Rio Grande; desert, mountain vegetation. Fertile agricultural valleys.

Economy: Agribusiness, mining, tourism, hunting leases.

History: Mescalero Apache area. Fort Quitman established in 1858 to protect routes to west. Railroad in 1881 brought Anglo-American settlers. Political turmoil in Mexico (1912-29) brought more settlers from Mexico. County named for Texas political leader Claude B. Hudspeth; created 1917 from El Paso County.

Ethnicity, 1990: White, 2,345 (80.4%); Black, 15 (0.5%); American Indian, 9 (0.3%); Asian, 2 (0.1%); Other, 544 (18.7%). Hispanic, 1,935 (66.4%).

Vital Statistics, 1995: Births, 53; deaths, 21; marriages, 30; divorces, 1.

Recreation: Scenic drives; fort ruins; hot springs; salt basin; white sands; hunting; part of Guadalupe Mountains National Park, containing unique plant life, canyons.

Minerals: Talc, stone, gypsum.

Agriculture: Most income from cotton, vegetables, hay-alfalfa; beef cattle raised; 35,000 acres irrigated. Market value $19.2 million.

SIERRA BLANCA (700) county seat; ranching center; tourist stop on interstate highway; 4th of July fair, livestock show in January.

Dell City (779) feedlots; vegetable packing; gypsum processing; clinic; trade center; airport; some of largest water wells in state. Other towns include: **Fort Hancock** (400) and **Salt Flat** (35).

Population	3,422
(Change fm '90)	17.4
Land Area (sq. mi.)	4,571.3
Altitude (ft.)	3,492-7,484
Rainfall (in.)	10.0
Jan. mean min.	25
July mean max.	95
Growing season (days)	231

Civ. Labor	1,639
Unemployed	1.6
Annual Wages	$11,542,189
Av. Weekly Wage	$298.38
Fed. Wages	$3,383,166
Ag. Net Cash Return	$4,616,000
Prop. Value	$280,737,354
Retail Sales	$7,595,226

Largest Counties by Population 1996

Rank	County (Largest city)	Population
1.	Harris County (Houston)	3,087,153
2.	Dallas County (Dallas)	1,989,156
3.	Bexar County (San Antonio)	1,309,550
4.	Tarrant County (Fort Worth)	1,288,261
5.	Travis County (Austin)	678,500
6.	El Paso County (El Paso)	668,358
7.	Hidalgo County (McAllen)	485,332
8.	Collin County (Plano)	358,416
9.	Denton County (Denton)	343,137
10.	Nueces County (Corpus Christi)	309,020
11.	Cameron County (Brownsville)	304,660
12.	Fort Bend County (Missouri City)	295,480
13.	Jefferson County (Beaumont)	245,828
14.	Galveston County (Galveston)	239,392
15.	Montgomery County (Conroe)	236,192
16.	Lubbock County (Lubbock)	233,486
17.	Bell County (Killeen)	217,379
18.	Brazoria County (Brazosport)	217,318
19.	McLennan County (Waco)	202,137
20.	Williamson County (Round Rock)	190,190
21.	Webb County (Laredo)	176,318
22.	Smith County (Tyler)	162,480
23.	Brazos County (College Station)	137,057
24.	Wichita County (Wichita Falls)	127,789
25.	Taylor County (Abilene)	126,805
26.	Ector County (Odessa)	122,910

Source: State Data Center, Texas Dept. of Commerce (Jan. 1, 1996 estimates).

Hunt County

Physical Features: North Texas county; level to rolling surface; Sabine, Sulphur rivers; Lake Tawakoni; mostly heavy Blackland soil, some loam, sandy loams.

Economy: Education, varied manufacturing, agribusiness; several Fortune 500 companies in county; many residents employed in Dallas area.

History: Kiowa Indians who left soon after Anglo-American settlers arrived in 1839. County named for Memucan Hunt, Republic secretary of navy; created 1846 from Fannin, Nacogdoches counties.

Ethnicity, 1990: White, 55,705 (86.6%); Black, 6,802 (10.6%); American Indian, 266 (0.4%); Asian, 351 (0.5%); Other, 1,219 (1.9%). Hispanic, 2,876 (4.5%).

Vital Statistics, 1995: Births, 904; deaths, 707; marriages, 620; divorces, 463.

Recreation: Lake sports; Texas A&M University-Commerce events; museum; Audie Murphy exhibit.

Minerals: Sand and white rock, gas, oil.

Agriculture: Forage, greenhouse nurseries, beef cattle, horses, top revenue sources; wheat, oats, cotton, grain sorghum; some firewood. Market value $23.9 million.

GREENVILLE (24,099) county seat; aircraft electronics; plastics distribution; varied manufacturing; hospitals; branch of Paris Junior College; Cotton Jubilee in October.

Commerce (7,192), Texas A&M University-Commerce; varied manufacturing; tourism; Bois d'Arc Bash in September; hospital.

Other towns include: **Caddo Mills** (1,152); **Campbell** (793); **Celeste** (864); **Lone Oak** (597); **Merit** (215); **Neylandville** (111); **Quinlan** (1,563); **West Tawakoni** (1,158) tourist center, light industry, catfish tournament, Lakefest; **Wolfe City** (1,566).

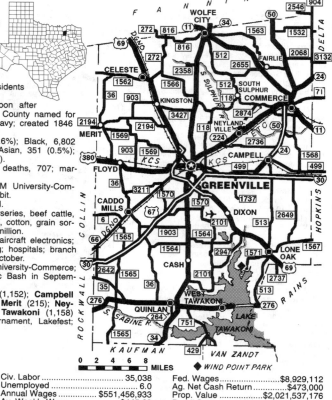

Population	68,571
(Change fm '90)	6.6
Land Area (sq. mi.)	841.2
Altitude (ft.)	688-1,553
Rainfall (in.)	41.6
Jan. mean min.	29
July mean max.	94
Growing season (days)	237

Civ. Labor	35,038	Fed. Wages	$8,929,112
Unemployed	6.0	Ag. Net Cash Return	$473,000
Annual Wages	$551,456,933	Prop. Value	$2,021,537,176
Av. Weekly Wage	$445.69	Retail Sales	$505,877,364

Hutchinson County

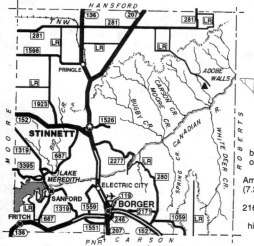

Physical Features: High Plain, broken by Canadian River and tributaries, Lake Meredith; fertile valleys along streams.

Economy: Oil, gas, petrochemicals; agribusiness; varied manufacturing; tourism.

History: Antelope Creek Indian area. Later Comanches were driven out in U.S. cavalry campaigns of 1874-75. Adobe Walls site of two Indian attacks, 1864 and 1874. Ranching began in late 1870s. Oil boom in early 1920s. County created 1876 from Bexar Territory; organized 1901; named for pioneer jurist Anderson Hutchinson.

Ethnicity, 1990: White, 22,661 (88.2%); Black, 677 (2.6%); American Indian, 362 (1.4%); Asian, 105 (0.4%); Other, 1,884 (7.3%). Hispanic, 2,509 (9.8%).

Vital Statistics, 1995: Births, 309; deaths, 247; marriages, 216; divorces, 125.

Recreation: Lake activities; fishing, camping; Adobe Walls, historic Indian battle site; fish fry in June.

Minerals: Gas, oil, sand, gravel.

Agriculture: Corn, wheat, grain sorghums; about 45,000 acres irrigated. Market value $93 million.

STINNETT (2,289) county seat; petroleum refining; farm center.

Borger (15,485) petroleum refining, petrochemicals, carbon-black production, oil-field servicing; varied manufacturing; retail center; Frank Phillips College; hospital.

Other cities include: **Fritch** (2,479), **Sanford** (240).

Population	25,659
(Change fm '90)	-0.1
Land Area (sq. mi.)	887.4
Altitude (ft.)	2,736-3,313
Rainfall (in.)	20.3
Jan. mean min.	23
July mean max.	93
Growing season (days)	187

Civ. Labor	10,141
Unemployed	8.1
Annual Wages	$258,725,993
Av. Weekly Wage	$554.01
Fed. Wages	$2,457,038
Ag. Net Cash Return	$12,337,000
Prop. Value	$1,438,374,864
Retail Sales	$159,465,226

Irion County

Physical Features: West Texas county with hilly surface, broken by Middle Concho, tributaries; clay, sandy soils.

Economy: Ranching; oil, gas production.

History: Tonkawa Indian area. Anglo-American settlement begin in late 1870s. County named for Republic leader R.A. Irion; created 1889 from Tom Green County.

Ethnicity, 1990: White, 1,609 (98.8%); Black, 2 (0.1%); American Indian, 1 (0.1%); Asian, 0 (0.0%); Other, 17 (1.0%). Hispanic, 385 (23.6%).

Vital Statistics, 1995: Births 21; deaths, 7; marriages, 0; divorces, 3.

Recreation: Hunting; historic sites, including Dove Creek battlefield and stagecoach stops, old Sherwood courthouse built 1900.

Minerals: Oil, gas.

Agriculture: Beef cattle, sheep, goats; wheat, cotton. Market value $7.1 million.

MERTZON (697) county seat; farm center; wool warehousing.

Other towns include: **Barnhart** (160).

Population	1,600	Jan. mean min.	32
(Change fm '90)	-1.8	July mean max.	95
Land Area (sq. mi.)	1,051.6	Growing season (days)	232
Altitude (ft.)	2,084-2,725	Civ. Labor	850
Rainfall (in.)	21.1	Unemployed	1.9

Annual Wages	$10,034,047
Av. Weekly Wage	$433.40
Fed. Wages	$252,103
Ag. Net Cash Return	$782,000
Prop. Value	$279,359,560
Retail Sales	$3,401,851

Jack County

Physical Features: Rolling Cross Timbers, broken by West Fork of the Trinity, other streams; sandy, dark brown, loam soils; lakes.

Economy: Petroleum production, oil-field services, livestock, manufacturing, tourism and recreation.

History: Caddo and Comanche borderland. Anglo-American settlers arrived in 1855, part of Peters Colony. County named for brothers, P.C. and W.H. Jack, leaders in Texas' independence effort; created 1856 from Cooke County; organized 1857 with Mesquiteville (orginal name of Jacksboro) as county seat.

Ethnicity,1990: White, 6,748 (96.7%); Black, 51 (0.7%); American Indian, 18 (0.3%); Asian, 10 (0.1%); Other, 154 (2.2%). Hispanic, 232 (3.3%).

Vital Statistics, 1995: Births, 71; deaths, 78; marriages, 57; divorces, 42.

Recreation: Hunting, fishing; Lake activities; Fort Richardson State Historical Park, museum, other historic sites; rattlesnake hunt.

Minerals: Oil, gas, gravel.

Agriculture: Cow-calf operations provide most income; some horses; hay, wheat, pecans; firewood. Market value $14.5 million.

JACKSBORO (3,423) county seat; petroleum production, oil-well servicing; agribusiness; tourism; some manufacturing; hospital; hospice; library; Old Mesquiteville Festival in fall.

Other towns include: **Bryson** (556), **Jermyn** (75), **Perrin** (300).

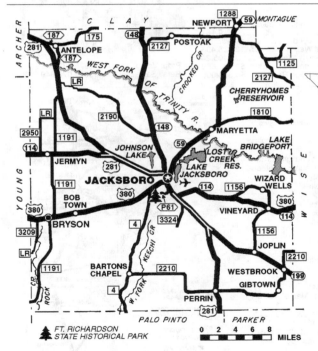

Population	7,274	Civ. Labor	3,386
(Change fm '90)	4.2	Unemployed	3.5
Land Area (sq. mi.)	917.4	Annual Wages	$32,869,957
Altitude (ft.)	976-1,297	Av. Weekly Wage	$379.89
Rainfall (in.)	30.7	Fed. Wages	$636,671
Jan. mean min.	29	Ag. Net Cash Return	$2,224,000
July mean max.	95	Prop. Value	$595,253,920
Growing season (days)	218	Retail Sales	$26,222,023

For explanation of sources, abbreviations and symbols, see p. 142.

Jackson County

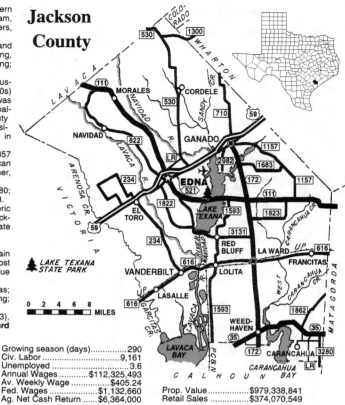

Physical Features: Southeastern county of prairie and motts of trees; loam, clay, black soils; drains to creek, rivers, bays.

Economy: Petroleum production and operation; metal fabrication and tooling, sheet-metal works, plastics manufacturing; agribusinesses; lake recreation.

History: Karankawa area. Six of Austin's Old Three Hundred families (1820s) settled in area. Lipan Apaches and Kiowas arrived in early 1830s. Mexican municipality, created 1835, became original county the following year; named for U.S. President Andrew Jackson. Oil discovered in 1934.

Ethnicity, 1990: White, 10,857 (83.3%); Black, 1,218 (9.3%); American Indian, 41 (0.3%); Asian, 12 (0.1%); Other, 911 (7.0%). Hispanic, 2,772 (21.3%).

Vital Statistics, 1995: Births, 180; deaths, 144; marriages, 111; divorces, 68.

Recreation: Hunting, fishing; historic sites; Texana Museum; Lake Texana, Brackenridge Plantation campground, state park; county fair, rodeo in October.

Minerals: Oil and natural gas.

Agriculture: Corn, cotton, rice, grain sorghums, soybeans; beef cattle; almost 24,000 acres of rice irrigated. Market value $43.4 million.

EDNA (6,383) county seat; oil, gas; tourism; agriculture; varied manufacturing; hospitals; bicycle event in November.

Other towns include: **Francitas** (143), **Ganado** (2,049), **LaSalle** (103), **La Ward** (183), **Lolita** (453), **Vanderbilt** (618).

Population............................. 14,500	Growing season (days)............. 290
(Change fm '90) 11.2	Civ. Labor 9,161
Land Area (sq. mi.)................. 829.5	Unemployed 3.6
Altitude (ft.) .... sea level-109	Annual Wages $112,325,493
Rainfall (in.) 40.9	Av. Weekly Wage $405.24
Jan. mean min.............................. 42	Fed. Wages $1,132,660
July mean max............................... 94	Ag. Net Cash Return $6,364,000

Prop. Value................ $979,338,841
Retail Sales $374,070,549

Jasper County

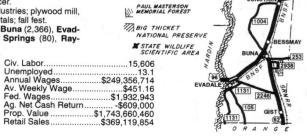

Physical Features: East Texas county; hilly to level; national forests; lakes; Neches River.

Economy: Timber industries; oil; tourism; fishing; agriculture.

History: Caddo and Atakapa Indian area. Land grants to John R. Bevil and Lorenzo de Zavala in 1829. County created 1836, organized 1837, from Mexican municipality; named for Sgt. William Jasper of American Revolution.

Ethnicity, 1990: White, 24,750 (79.6%); Black, 5,868 (18.9%); American Indian, 76 (0.2%); Asian, 38 (0.1%); Other, 370 (1.2%). Hispanic, 594 (1.9%).

Vital Statistics, 1995: Births, 465; deaths, 404; marriages, 363; divorces, 277.

Recreation: Lake activities; hunting; state park; azalea trail.

Minerals: Oil, gas produced.

Agriculture: Cattle, hogs, poultry, horses major revenue source; vegetables, fruit, pecans. Market value $3.7 million. Timber is major income producer.

JASPER (7,604) county seat; wood industries; plywood mill, sawmills; tourism; oil, gas production; hospitals; fall fest.

Other towns include: **Browndell** (222), **Buna** (2,366), **Evadale** (1,709), **Kirbyville** (1,922), **Magnolia Springs** (80), **Rayburn Country** (600).

Population 33,230	Civ. Labor.................................... 15,606
(Change fm '90) 6.8	Unemployed 13.1
Land Area (sq. mi.) 937.5	Annual Wages........... $249,356,714
Altitude (ft.) 68-438	Av. Weekly Wage.................. $451.16
Rainfall (in.)................................. 52.7	Fed. Wages............... $1,932,943
Jan. mean min. 36	Ag. Net Cash Return........... -$609,000
July mean max.................................. 93	Prop. Value $1,743,660,460
Growing season (days)................. 230	Retail Sales.................. $369,119,854

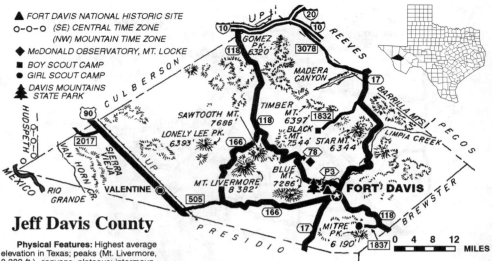

- ▲ FORT DAVIS NATIONAL HISTORIC SITE
- O–O–O (SE) CENTRAL TIME ZONE
  (NW) MOUNTAIN TIME ZONE
- ◆ McDONALD OBSERVATORY, MT. LOCKE
- ■ BOY SCOUT CAMP
- ● GIRL SCOUT CAMP
- ▲ DAVIS MOUNTAINS
  STATE PARK

Jeff Davis County

Physical Features: Highest average elevation in Texas; peaks (Mt. Livermore, 8,382 ft.), canyons, plateaus; intermountain wash, clay, loam soils; cedars, oaks in highlands.

Economy: Tourism; ranching; greenhouse nurseries; small businesses; government; hunting leases.

History: Mescalero Apaches in area when Antonio de Espejo explored in 1583. U.S. Army established Fort Davis in 1854 to protect routes to west. Civilian settlers followed, including Manuel Músquiz, a political refugee from Mexico. County named for Jefferson Davis, U.S. war secretary, Confederate president; created 1887 from Presidio County.

Ethnicity, 1990: White, 1,671 (85.9%); Black, 7 (0.4%); American Indian, 12 (0.6%); Asian, 4 (0.2%); Other, 252 (12.9%). Hispanic, 770 (39.6%).

Vital Statistics, 1995: Births, 20; deaths, 17; marriages, 12; divorces, 9.

Recreation: Scenic drives including scenic loop along Limpia Creek, Mt. Livermore, Blue Mountain; hunting; Fort Davis National Historic Site (with Restoration Festival on Labor Day weekend); state park; McDonald Observatory; solar power park.

Minerals: Not significant.

Agriculture: Beef cattle top cash supplier, greenhouse nuseries; pecans and apples, wine grapes; hunting leases. Market value $10.2 million.

FORT DAVIS (1,179) county seat; ranch center; trade, tourism; government; manufacturing of hats, candles; Harvest Moon fall festival.

Other town, **Valentine** (270).

Population	2,127
(Change fm '90)	9.3
Land Area (sq. mi.)	2,264.6
Altitude (ft.)	3,871-8,382
Rainfall (in.)	20.8
Jan. mean min.	30
July mean max.	82
Growing season (days)	209
Civ. Labor	1,177
Unemployed	2.7
Annual Wages	$10,906,,060
Av. Weekly Wage	$336.55
Fed. Wages	$753,099
Ag. Net Cash Funds	$1,082,000
Prop. Value	$225,466,998
Retail Sales	$7,452,328

Physical Features: Gulf Coast grassy plain, with timber in northwest; beach sands, sandy loams, black clay soils; drains to Neches River, Gulf of Mexico.

Economy: Petrochemical, other chemical plants; shipbuilding; steel mill; port activity; oil-field supplies; government/services.

History: Atakapas and Orcoquizas, whose numbers were reduced by epidemics or migration before Anglo-American settlers arrived in 1820s. Cajuns arrived in 1840s; Europeans in 1850s. Antebellum slaveholding area. County created 1836 from Mexican municipality; organized 1837; named for U.S. President Thomas Jefferson.

Ethnicity, 1990: White, 154,273 (64.4%); Black, 74,412 (31.1%); American Indian, 578 (0.2%); Asian, 5,145 (2.1%); Other, 4,989 (2.1%). Hispanic, 12,629 (5.3%).

Vital Statistics, 1995: Births, 3,548; deaths, 2,486; marriages, 2,481; divorces, 1,470.

Recreation: Beaches, fresh and saltwater fishing; duck, goose hunting; water activities; Dick Dowling Monument and Park; Spindletop site, museums; saltwater lake; wildlife refuge; Lamar University events; historic sites; South Texas Fair.

Jefferson County

Minerals: Large producer of oil, gas, sulfur, salt, sand and gravel.

Agriculture: Rice, soybeans; beef cattle; considerable rice irrigated. Market value $21.6 million.

BEAUMONT (115,521) county seat; petrochemical production; refining; shipbuilding; port activities; rice milling; Lamar University; hospitals; Main Street on the Neches.

Port Arthur (58,196) oil, chemical activities; shipping; drydock; food processing; tourism. **Sabine Pass** is now

(Map on next page.)

within the city limits of Port Arthur.

Other towns include: **Bevil Oaks** (1,493); **China** (1,188); **Fannett** (105); **Groves** (16,672) some manufacturing, government/service; hospital; pecan festival; **Hamshire** (350).

Also, **Nederland** (16,812) marine manufacturing; tourism, Windmill and French museums; hospital; Tex Ritter memorial and park, heritage festival (city founded by Dutch immigrants in 1898); **Nome** (443); **Port Neches** (13,074) chemical and synthetic rubber industry, varied manufacturing, riverfront festival at Christmas.

Population	245,828
(Change fm '90)	2.7
Land Area (sq. mi.)	903.6
Altitude (ft.)	sea level-42
Rainfall (in.)	57.2
Jan. mean min.	42
July mean max.	92
Growing season (days)	250
Civ. Labor	117,391
Unemployed	8.7
Annual Wages	$3,037,309.565
Av. Weekly Wage	$526.72
Fed. Wages	$62,264,297
Ag. Net Cash Return	$1,883,000
Prop. Value	$12,668,685,290
Retail Sales	$2,256,410,920

Jefferson County

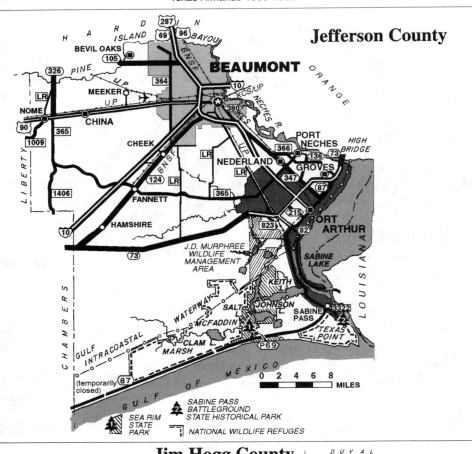

SABINE PASS BATTLEGROUND STATE HISTORICAL PARK

SEA RIM STATE PARK

NATIONAL WILDLIFE REFUGES

Jim Hogg County

Physical Features: South Texas county on rolling plain, with heavy brush cover; white blow sand and sandy loam; hilly, broken.

Economy: Oil, cattle operations.

History: Coahuiltecan area, then Lipan Apache. Spanish land grant in 1805 to Xavier Vela. County named for Gov. James Stephen Hogg; created, organized 1913 from Brooks, Duval counties.

Ethnicity, 1990: White, 4,375 (85.6%); Black, 4 (0.1%); American Indian, 12 (0.2%); Asian, 4 (0.1%); Other, 714 (14.0%). Hispanic, 4,659 (91.2%).

Vital Statistics, 1995: Births, 88; deaths, 58; marriages, 44; divorces, 10.

Recreation: White-tailed deer and bobwhite hunting.

Minerals: Oil and gas.

Agriculture: Cattle, ranching; sorghums; some irrigation. Market value $7 million.

HEBBRONVILLE (4,654) county seat; ranching, oil-field center. Other towns include: **Guerra** (75).

Population	**5,467**
(Change fm '90)	7.0
Land Area (sq. mi.)	1,136.2
Altitude (ft.)	249-742
Rainfall (in.)	22.7
Jan. mean min.	42
July mean max.	97
Growing season (days)	303
Civ. Labor	2,049
Unemployed	8.9
Annual Wages	$19,324,023
Av. Weekly Wage	$310.94
Fed. Wages	$3,348,892
Ag. Net Cash Return	-$384,000
Prop. Value	$400,007,250
Retail Sales	$32,449,622

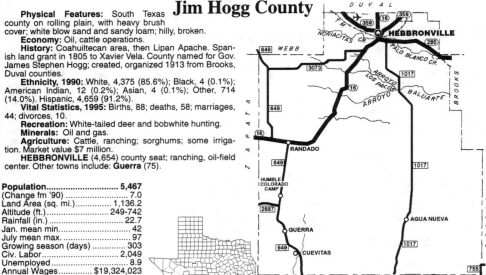

For explanation of sources, abbreviations and symbols, see p. 142.

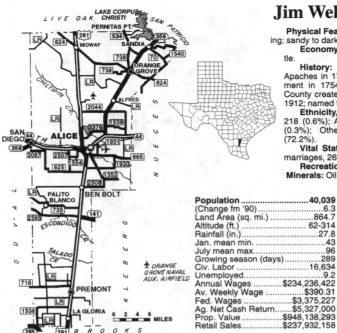

Jim Wells County

Physical Features: South Coastal Plains; level to rolling; sandy to dark soils; grassy with mesquite brush.

Economy: Oil, gas production, sorghum and cattle.

History: Coahuiltecans, driven out by Lipan Apaches in 1775. Tomás Sánchez established settlement in 1754. Anglo-American settlement in 1878. County created 1911 from Nueces County; organized 1912; named for developer J.B. Wells Jr.

Ethnicity, 1990: White, 28,504 (75.6%); Black, 218 (0.6%); American Indian, 82 (0.2%); Asian, 103 (0.3%); Other, 8,772 (23.3%). Hispanic, 27,201 (72.2%).

Vital Statistics, 1995: Births, 598; deaths, 333; marriages, 269; divorces, 103.

Recreation: Hunting; fiestas.

Minerals: Oil, gas, caliche.

Agriculture: Beef cattle primary income source; dairy cattle, hogs raised; sorghums, cotton, wheat, corn, vegetables; some irrigation for coastal Bermuda, vegetables. Market value $43 million.

ALICE (20,252) county seat; oilfield service center; agribusinesses; government/services; hospital; Fiesta Bandana (from original name of city) in May; Bee County College extension.

Other towns include: **Orange Grove** (1,321), **Premont** (2,994); wildflower tour, youth rodeo; **Sandia** (215). Also part of **San Diego** (5,376).

Population	40,039
(Change fm '90)	6.3
Land Area (sq. mi.)	864.7
Altitude (ft.)	62-314
Rainfall (in.)	27.8
Jan. mean min.	43
July mean max.	96
Growing season (days)	289
Civ. Labor	16,634
Unemployed	9.2
Annual Wages	$234,236,422
Av. Weekly Wage	$390.31
Fed. Wages	$3,375,227
Ag. Net Cash Return	$5,327,000
Prop. Value	$948,138,293
Retail Sales	$237,932,158

Johnson County

Physical Features: North central county drained by tributaries of Trinity, Brazos rivers; lake; hilly, rolling, many soil types.

Economy: Agribusiness; railroad shops; manufacturing; distribution; lake activities; residents employed in Fort Worth; part of Fort Worth-Arlington metropolitan area.

History: No permanent Indian villages existed in area. Anglo-American settlers arrived in 1840s. County named for Col. M.T. Johnson of Mexican War, Confederacy; created, organized 1854 out of Ellis, Hill, Navarro counties.

Ethnicity, 1990: White, 90,328 (93.0%); Black, 2,521 (2.6%); American Indian, 419 (0.4%); Asian, 447 (0.5%); Other, 3,450 (3.6%). Hispanic, 7,457 (7.7%).

Vital Statistics, 1995: Births, 1,500; deaths, 900; marriages, 955; divorces, 681.

Recreation: Bird, deer hunting; water activities on Lake Pat Cleburne; state park; museum.

Minerals: Limestone, sand and gravel.

Agriculture: A leading dairy county; 85 percent of annual income from cattle, horses, hogs, and dairy products; crops include hay, silage, sorghum, wheat, corn, cotton. Market value $51.4 million.

CLEBURNE (23,218) county seat; dairy center; rail-shipping terminal; varied manufacturing; hospital; Layland Museum; Hill College, Cleburne campus.

For explanation of sources, abbreviations and symbols, see p. 142.

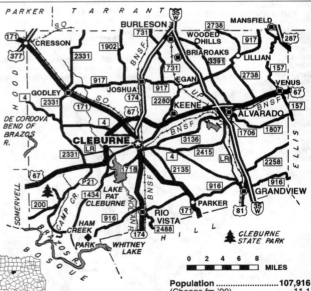

Burleson (19,703, part in Tarrant County) agriculture, retail center; hospital.

Other towns include: **Alvarado** (3,196), County Pioneer Days; **Briaroaks** (636); **Godley** (607); **Grandview** (1,299); **Joshua** (4,544) many residents work in Fort Worth; **Keene** (4,519), Southwestern Adventist College; **Lillian** (105); **Rio Vista** (683), and **Venus** (1,212).

Population	107,916
(Change fm '90)	11.1
Land Area (sq. mi.)	729.4
Altitude (ft.)	651-1,065
Rainfall (in.)	34.0
Jan. mean min.	33
July mean max.	97
Growing season (days)	233
Civ. Labor	55,039
Unemployed	4.5
Annual Wages	$534,195,269
Av. Weekly Wage	$397.55
Fed. Wages	$7,651,553
Ag. Net Cash Return	$2,904,000
Prop. Value	$3,329,639,276
Retail Sales	$680,599,644

Jones County

Physical Features:
West Texas Rolling Plains; drained by Brazos River fork, tributaries; Lake Fort Phantom Hill.

Economy: Agribusiness; varied manufacturing.

History: Comanches and other tribes hunted in area. Military presence began in 1851. Ranching established in 1870s. County named for the last president of the Republic, Anson Jones; created 1858 from Bexar, Bosque counties; re-created 1876; organized 1881.

Ethnicity, 1990: White, 13,786 (83.6%); Black, 666 (4.0%); American Indian, 47 (0.3%); Asian, 31 (0.2%); Other, 1,960 (11.9%). Hispanic, 2,786 (16.9%).

Vital Statistics, 1995: Births, 175; deaths, 228; marriages, 90; divorces, 77.

Recreation: Lake activities; Fort Phantom Hill site, museum; Cowboys Christmas Ball; Cowboy Reunion on July 4 weekend; old courthouse, opera house, museum, art show.

Minerals: Oil, gas, sand and gravel, stone.

Agriculture: Cotton, wheat, sesame and peanuts; beef cattle, stockers, calves; some 10,000 acres irrigated for peanuts and hay. Market value $35 million.

ANSON (2,806) county seat; farming center; boat-trailer factory, Western clothing manufacturing; hospital; historic buildings.

Stamford (3,416) trade center for three counties.

Hamlin (2,602) trade center for farm and oil, gas area; feed mills; hospital; historical festival in June.

Other towns include: Avoca (121), Hawley (667), Lueders (382).

Part of **Abilene** extends into the county.

Population	18,439
(Change fm '90)	11.8
Land Area (sq. mi.)	931.1
Altitude (ft.)	1,560-1,855
Rainfall (in.)	25.8
Jan. mean min.	31
July mean max.	96
Growing season (days)	223

Civ. Labor	10,276
Unemployed	3.2
Annual Wages	$102,763,013
Av. Weekly Wage	$385.04
Fed. Wages	$2,073,375
Ag. Net Cash Return	$2,438,000
Prop. Value	$564,075,352
Retail Sales	$146,533,662

Population	12,526
(Change fm '90)	0.6
Land Area (sq. mi.)	750.3
Altitude (ft.)	225-525
Rainfall (in.)	33.2
Jan. mean min.	41
July mean max.	97
Growing season (days)	281
Civ. Labor	6,118
Unemployed	5.1
Annual Wages	$72,737,858
Av. Weekly Wage	$363.51
Fed. Wages	$1,215,052
Ag. Net Cash Return	$1,726,000
Prop. Value	$606,778,160
Retail Sales	$65,399,695

Karnes County

Physical Features: Sandy loam, dark clay, alluvial soils in rolling terrain; traversed by San Antonio River; mesquite, oak trees.

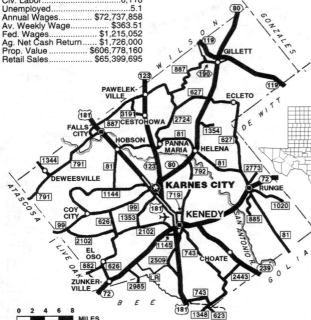

Economy: Agribusiness, mineral production, tourism; varied manufacturing.

History: Coahuiltecan Indian area. Spanish ranching began around 1750. Anglo-Americans arrived in 1840s; Polish in 1850s. County created 1854 from Bexar, Goliad, San Patricio counties; named for Texas Revolutionary figure Henry W. Karnes.

Ethnicity, 1990: White, 9,548 (76.7%); Black, 362 (2.9%); American Indian, 35 (0.3%); Asian, 14 (0.1%); Other, 2,496 (20.0%). Hispanic, 5,916 (47.5%).

Vital Statistics, 1995: Births, 183; deaths, 142; marriages, 78; divorces, 15.

Recreation: Panna Maria, nation's oldest Polish settlement, founded Dec. 24, 1854; Old Helena restored courthouse, museum; bird hunting; bluebonnet days.

Minerals: Oil, gas, stone.

Agriculture: Beef cattle; crops include wheat, corn, sorghum, cotton, sunflowers, peanuts, hay. Market value 17.8 million.

KARNES CITY (3,085) county seat; agribusiness; tourism; processing center; oil-field servicing; varied manufacturing; hospitals; library.

Kenedy (3,606) farm and oil center, dove and quail hunting leases, prison.

Other towns include: Falls City (568) ranching, sausage making, library, city park on river; Gillett (120); Hobson (135); Panna Maria (96); Runge (1,224) farm center.

For explanation of sources, abbreviations and symbols, see p. 142.

Kaufman County

Physical Features: North Blackland prairie, draining to Trinity River, Cedar Creek and Lake.

Economy: varied manufacturing; trade center; government service; antique center; part of Dallas metropolitan area.

History: Caddo and Cherokee Indians; removed by 1840 when Anglo-American settlement began. County created from Henderson County and organized, 1848; named for member of Texas and U.S. Congresses D.S. Kaufman.

Ethnicity, 1990: White, 42,810 (82.0%); Black, 7,295 (14.0%); American Indian, 198 (0.4%); Asian, 229 (0.4%); Other, 1,688 (3.2%). Hispanic, 3,340 (6.4%).

Vital Statistics, 1995: Births, 843; deaths, 561; marriages, 601; divorces, 340.

Recreation: Lake activities; Porter Farm near Terrell is site of origin of U.S.-Texas Agricultural Extension program; antique centers near Forney; historic homes at Terrell.

Minerals: Oil, gas, stone, sand.

Agriculture: Beef cattle, horses, hogs, goats, dairy cattle, sheep; hay, wheat, cotton, corn, sorghum, oats. Market value $26 million.

KAUFMAN (6,490) county seat; varied manufacturing; commuters to Dallas; hospital.

Terrell (13,110) agribusiness, varied manufacturing; outlet center; private hospital, state hospital; community college, Southwestern Christian College.

Other towns include: **Crandall** (2,143); **Combine** (1,781, partly in Dallas County); **Cottonwood** (187); **Elmo** (90); **Forney** (4,697) antiques, light manufacturing, historic homes; **Grays Prairie** (362); **Kemp** (1,351) **Mabank** (1,879, partly in Henderson County) tourism; manufacturing, retail trade; **Oak Grove** (705); **Oak Ridge** (316); **Post Oak Bend** (363); **Rosser** (419); **Scurry** (315).

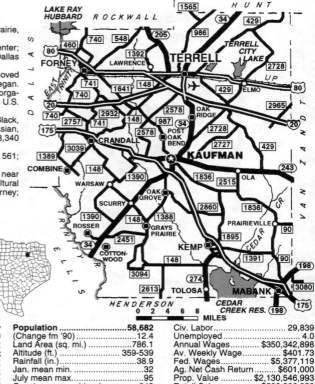

Population	58,682
(Change fm '90)	12.4
Land Area (sq. mi.)	786.1
Altitude (ft.)	359-539
Rainfall (in.)	38.9
Jan. mean min.	32
July mean max.	95
Growing season (days)	248

Civ. Labor	29,839
Unemployed	4.0
Annual Wages	$350,342,898
Av. Weekly Wage	$401.73
Fed. Wages	$5,377,119
Ag. Net Cash Return	$601,000
Prop. Value	$2,130,546,993
Retail Sales	$502,806,823

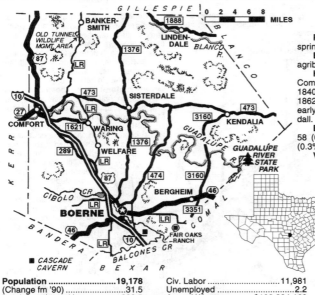

Population	19,178
(Change fm '90)	31.5
Land Area (sq. mi.)	662.5
Altitude (ft.)	1,159-2,011
Rainfall (in.)	34.2
Jan. mean min.	33
July mean max.	93
Growing season (days)	236

Civ. Labor	11,981
Unemployed	2.2
Annual Wages	$108,284,169
Av. Weekly Wage	$375.18
Fed. Wages	$1,641,927
Ag. Net Cash Return	-$279,000
Prop. Value	$1,765,938,408
Retail Sales	$283,065,336

Kendall County

Physical Features: Hill Country, plateau, with springfed streams; caves; scenic drives.

Economy: Tourism, commuters to San Antonio, agribusiness, some manufacturing.

History: Lipan Apaches, Kiowas and Comanches in area when German settlers arrived in 1840s. County created from Blanco, Kerr counties 1862; named for pioneer journalist-sheepman and early contributor to Texas Almanac, George W. Kendall.

Ethnicity, 1990: White, 13,682 (93.8%); Black, 58 (0.4%); American Indian, 71 (0.5%); Asian, (0.3%); Other, 740 (5.1%). Hispanic, 2,392 (16.4%).

Vital Statistics, 1995: Births, 283; deaths, 183; marriages, 235; divorces, 91.

Recreation: Hunting, fishing, state park; tourist center; Cascade Caverns; historic sites.

Minerals: Natural gas.

Agriculture: Cattle, sheep, Angora goats, Spanish goats raised; small grains. Market value $8.7 million.

BOERNE (5,961) county seat; livestock center; tourism; antiques; some manufacturing; village band concerts in summer.

Other towns include: **Bergheim** (22); **Comfort** (1,733) ranching, tourism, has state's only Civil War monument honoring Unionists; **Kendalia** (76); **Sisterdale** (63); **Waring** (73).

For explanation of sources, abbreviations and symbols, see p. 142.

Kenedy County

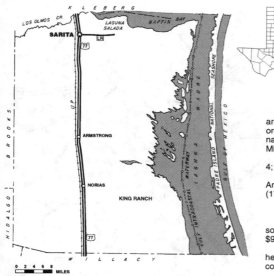

Physical Features: Gulf coastal county; flat, sandy terrain, some loam soils; motts of live oaks.

Economy: Oil, ranching; hunting leases a factor.

History: Coahuiltecan Indians who assimilated or were driven out by Lipan Apaches. Spanish ranching began in 1790s. Anglo-Americans arrived after Mexican War. Among last counties created, organized, 1921, from Cameron, Hidalgo, Willacy counties; named for pioneer steamboat operator and cattleman, Capt. Mifflin Kenedy.

Vital Statistics, 1995: Births, 2; deaths, 3; marriages, 4; divorces, 3.

Ethnicity, 1990: White, 378 (82.2%); Black, 0 (0.0%); American Indian, 0 (0.0%); Asian, 0 (0.0%); Other, 82 (17.8%). Hispanic, 362 (78.7%).

Recreation: Hunting a major enterprise; fishing.

Minerals: Oil, gas.

Agriculture: Cattle, horse production major factors; some watermelons, pasture principal crops. Market value $9.2 million.

SARITA (250) county seat; cattle-shipping point; ranch headquarters; gas processing; one of state's least populous counties. Also, **Armstrong** (20).

Population....................330	Jan. mean min. 45	Av. Weekly Wage $404.08
(Change fm '90)..............-28.3	July mean max...................95	Fed. Wages.....................$49,200
Land Area (sq. mi.)............1,456.9	Growing season (days)..........319	Ag. Net Cash Return $3,256,000
Altitude (ft.)..............sea level-79	Civ. Labor.....................230	Prop. Value....................$400,575,000
Rainfall (in.)..................29.7	Unemployed.....................3.5	Retail Sales $523,331
	Annual Wages..............$5,823,478	

Kerr County

Population 40,908	
(Change fm '90)................12.7	
Land Area (sq. mi.)............1,106.3	
Altitude (ft.) 1,524-2,303	
Rainfall (in.) 29.8	
Jan. mean min. 32	
July mean max..................94	
Growing season (days)..........216	
Civ. Labor 17,421	
Unemployed 2.7	
Annual Wages $249,164,846	
Av. Weekly Wage $367.27	
Fed. Wages $27,835,215	
Ag. Net Cash Return ....-$759,000	
Prop. Value..............$1,836,971,309	
Retail Sales $387,233,948	

Physical Features: Picturesque, hills, spring-fed streams; dams, lakes on Guadalupe River.

Economy: Tourism; medical services; retirement area; agribusiness; manufacturing; hunting leases.

History: Lipan Apaches, Kiowas and Comanches in area. Anglo-American settlers arrived in late 1840s. County created 1856 from Bexar County; named for member of Austin's Colony, James Kerr.

Ethnicity, 1990: White, 32,842 (90.5%); Black, 805 (2.2%); American Indian, 128 (0.4%); Asian, 141 (0.4%); Other, 2,388 (6.6%). Hispanic, 5,994 (16.5%).

Vital Statistics, 1995: Births, 487; deaths, 534; marriages, 376; divorces, 240.

Recreation: Popular area for tourists, hunters, fishermen; private and youth camps; dude ranches; state park; Point theater; camera safari park; wildlife management area; hatchery; Folk Music Festival in Kerrville; experimental aircraft fly-in; Cowboy Artists Museum.

Minerals: Limited sand, gravel.

Agriculture: Cattle, sheep and goats for wool, mohair; crops include apples, hay, pecans; Spanish goats on increase. Market value $8.5 million.

KERRVILLE (20,431) county seat; tourist center; youth camps; agribusiness; aircraft and parts and varied manufacturing; Schreiner College; Kerrville State Hospital; Veterans Administration Medical Center; retirement center; retail trade; state arts, crafts show in May-June; experimental aircraft fly-in during October.

Other towns include: **Camp Verde** (41); **Center Point** (623); **Hunt** (708) youth camps; **Ingram** (1,554) camps, cabins; **Mountain Home** (96).

For explanation of sources, abbreviations and symbols, see p. 142.

Kent County

Physical Features: West central county of rolling, broken terrain; drains to Salt and Double Mountain forks of Brazos River; sandy, loam soils.

Economy: Agribusinesses, oil-field operations, hunting leases.

History: Comanches driven out by U.S. Army in 1870s. Ranching developed in 1880s. County created 1876, from Bexar, Young territories; organized 1892. Name honors Andrew Kent, one of 32 volunteers from Gonzales who died at the Alamo.

Ethnicity, 1990: White, 902 (89.3%); Black, 6 (0.6%); American Indian, 1 (0.1%); Asian, 0 (0.0%); Other, 101 (10.0%). Hispanic, 120 (11.9%).

Vital Statistics, 1995: Births, 4; deaths, 19; marriages, 3; divorces, 0.

Recreation: Hunting; scenic croton breaks and salt flat.

Minerals: Oil, gas.

Agriculture: Cattle, sheep, goats; cotton, wheat, sorghum. Market value $10.7 million.

JAYTON (562) county seat; oil-field services; farming center; fun fest in August.

Other towns include: **Girard** (125).

Population	948		
(Change fm '90)	.........-6.1	July mean max.	96
Land Area (sq. mi.)	.........902.4	Growing season (days)	216
Altitude (ft.)	1,823-2,830	Civ. Labor	444
Rainfall (in.)	.........21.8	Unemployed	.........2.5
Jan. mean min.	25	Annual Wages	.........$4,420,665
		Av. Weekly Wage	.........$337.11

Fed. Wages	.........$266,004
Ag. Net Cash Return	.........$1,383,000
Prop. Value	.........$794,462,139
Retail Sales	.........$11,255,900

Kimble County

Physical Features: Picturesque southwestern county; rugged, broken by numerous streams; drains to Llano River; sandy, gray, chocolate loam soils.

Economy: Livestock production, large goat market, wool, mohair; tourism, hunting, fishing; cedar oil and wood products sold; metal building materials manufactured.

History: Apache, Kiowas and Comanche stronghold until 1870s. Military outposts protected first Anglo-American settlers in 1850s. County created from Bexar County 1858; organized 1876. Named for George C. Kimble, a Gonzales volunteer who died at the Alamo.

Ethnicity, 1990: White, 3,654 (88.6%); Black, 2 (0.0%); American Indian, 5 (0.1%); Asian, 10 (0.2%); Other, 451 (10.9%). Hispanic, 772 (18.7%).

Vital Statistics, 1995: Births, 53; deaths, 56; marriages, 35; divorces, 26.

Recreation: Hunting, fishing in spring-fed streams; among leading deer counties; state park; Kimble Kounty Kow Kick on Labor Day.

Minerals: Limited sand, gravel.

Agriculture: Hunting leases, beef cattle, Angora and Spanish goats, sheep, are primary products; pecans also raised; some irrigation for forage sorghum, coastal Bermuda. Market value $7.8 million. Firewood marketed.

JUNCTION (2,843) county seat; goat auction; cedar oil, wood products; two museums; Texas Tech University center; hospital; library; gun and knife show.

Other towns include: **London** (180); **Roosevelt** (14); **Telegraph** (3).

Population	4,427
(Change fm '90)	.........7.4
Land Area (sq. mi.)	.........1,250.8
Altitude (ft.)	1,783-2,372
Rainfall (in.)	.........23.8
Jan. mean min.	31
July mean max.	96
Growing season (days)	213
Civ. Labor	2,347
Unemployed	.........1.9
Annual Wages	.........$25,669,892
Av. Weekly Wage	.........$335.11
Fed. Wages	.........$669,000
Ag. Net Cash Returns	.........$353,000
Prop. Value	.........$446,807,410
Retail Sales	.........$45,932,691

SOUTH LLANO RIVER STATE PARK & WILDLIFE MANAGEMENT AREA

For explanation of sources, abbreviations and symbols, see p. 142.

King County

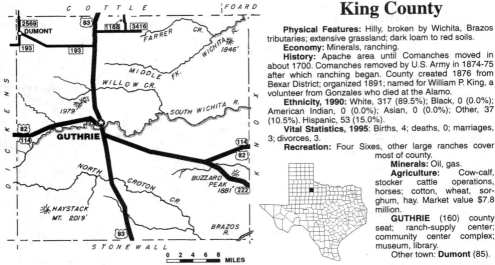

Physical Features: Hilly, broken by Wichita, Brazos tributaries; extensive grassland; dark loam to red soils.

Economy: Minerals, ranching.

History: Apache area until Comanches moved in about 1700. Comanches removed by U.S. Army in 1874-75 after which ranching began. County created 1876 from Bexar District; organized 1891; named for William P. King, a volunteer from Gonzales who died at the Alamo.

Ethnicity, 1990: White, 317 (89.5%); Black, 0 (0.0%); American Indian, 0 (0.0%); Asian, 0 (0.0%); Other, 37 (10.5%). Hispanic, 53 (15.0%).

Vital Statistics, 1995: Births, 4; deaths, 0; marriages, 3; divorces, 3.

Recreation: Four Sixes, other large ranches cover most of county.

Minerals: Oil, gas.

Agriculture: Cow-calf, stocker cattle operations, horses; cotton, wheat, sorghum, hay. Market value $7.8 million.

GUTHRIE (160) county seat; ranch-supply center; community center complex; museum, library.

Other town: **Dumont** (85).

Population		336
(Change fm '90)		-5.1
Land Area (sq. mi.)		912.3
Altitude (ft.)		1,739-2,081
Rainfall (in.)		23.8
Jan. mean min.		24
July mean max.		98
Growing season (days)		219
Civ. Labor		116
Unemployed		6.9
Annual Wages		$3,269,015
Av. Weekly Wage		$455.03
Fed. Wages		$156,176
Ag. Net Cash Return		$1,701,000
Prop. Value		$229,415,687
Retail Sales		$1,538,690

Kinney County

Physical Features: Hilly, broken by Rio Grande tributaries; Anacacho Mountains; Nueces Canyon.

Economy: Agribusinesses, tourism, government service, hunting leases.

History: Coahuiltecans, Apaches, Comanches in area. Spanish Franciscans established settlement in late 1700s. English empresarios John Beales and James Grant established English-speaking colony in 1834. Black Seminoles served as army scouts in 1870s. County created from Bexar County 1850; organized 1874; named for H.L. Kinney, founder of Corpus Christi.

Ethnicity, 1990: White, 2,746 (88.0%); Black, 57 (1.8%); American Indian, 26 (0.8%); Asian, 9 (0.3%); Other, 281 (9.0%). Hispanic, 1,570 (50.3%).

Vital Statistics, 1995: Births, 45; deaths, 28; marriages, 20; divorces, 2.

Recreation: Hunting; replica of Alamo; old Fort Clark Springs; new state park; cowboy poets meeting.

Minerals: Not significant.

Agriculture: Sheep, goats, cattle; cotton, hay, wheat; some irrigation for hay, cotton. Market value $7.8 million.

BRACKETTVILLE (1,883) county seat; tourism, market, retirement center; museum; cowboy cauldron.

Other towns include: **Fort Clark Springs** (1,070); **Spofford** (67).

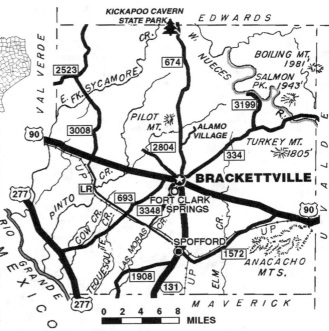

For explanation of sources, abbreviations and symbols, see p. 142.

Population		3,331
(Change fm '90)		6.8
Land Area (sq. mi.)		1,363.5
Altitude (ft.)		909-1,981
Rainfall (in.)		21.7
Jan. mean min.		36
July mean max.		95
Growing season (days)		270
Civ. Labor		1,121
Unemployed		7.3
Annual Wages		$7,875,296
Av. Weekly Wage		$291.15
Fed. Wages		$2,063,278
Ag. Net Cash Return		$290,000
Prop. Value		$284,119,441
Retail Sales		$7,196,868

Physical Features: Coastal plain, broken by bays; sandy, loam, clay soils; tree motts.

Economy: Naval air station; ranch operation; chemicals and plastics; Mexican food products; cotton; Texas A&M University-Kingsville.

History: Coahuiltecan and Ka-

Kleberg County

rankawa area. Spanish land grants date to 1750s. In 1853 Richard King purchased Santa Gerturdis land grant. County created 1913 from Nueces County; named for San Jacinto veteran and rancher, Robert Kleberg.

Ethnicity, 1990: White, 20,650 (68.2%); Black, 998 (3.3%); American Indian, 81 (0.3%); Asian, 414 (1.4%);

Other, 8,131 (26.9%). Hispanic, 18,529 (61.2%).

Vital Statistics, 1995: Births, 537; deaths, 244; marriages, 291; divorces, 152.

Recreation: Fishing, water sports, park on Baffin Bay; wildlife sanctuary; winter bird watching; university events, museum; King Ranch headquarters, tours; La Posada celebration.

Minerals: Oil, gas.

Agriculture: Beef cattle, cotton, grain sorghum, hunting leases. Market value $42.1 million.

KINGSVILLE
(26,557) county seat; oil, gas center; agribusiness; tourism; chemical and plastic plant; university, Bee College branch; hospital. Other towns include: **Riviera** (1,064).

> ✈ KINGSVILLE NAVAL AIR STATION   O—O— GULF INTRACOASTAL WATERWAY
> ◆ KING RANCH HQ.   ///// NATIONAL SEASHORE
> 0 2 4 6 8 MILES

Population	31,453
(Change fm '90)	3.9
Land Area (sq. mi.)	871.1
Altitude (ft.)	sea level-151
Rainfall (in.)	27.6
Jan. mean min.	45

July mean max.	95
Growing season (days)	314
Civ. Labor	13,236
Unemployed	7.0
Annual Wages	$177,122,713

Av. Weekly Wage	$351.41
Fed. Wages	$17,804,625
Ag. Net Cash Return	-$2,341,000
Prop. Value	$1,107,699,894
Retail Sales	$201,142,480

Knox County

Physical Features: Eroded breaks on West Texas Rolling Plains; Brazos, Wichita rivers; sandy, loam soils.

Economy: Agribusiness, government services.

History: Indian conscripts used during Spanish period to mine copper deposits along the Brazos. Ranching, farming developed in 1880s. German colony settled in 1895. County created from Bexar, Young territories 1858; re-created 1876; organized 1886; named for U.S. Secretary of War Henry Knox.

Ethnicity, 1990: White, 3,765 (77.8%); Black, 338 (7.0%); American Indian, 7 (0.1%); Asian, 5 (0.1%); Other, 722 (14.9%). Hispanic, 1,088 (22.5%).

Vital Statistics, 1995: Births, 60; deaths, 55; marriages, 28; divorces, 20.

Recreation: Lake activities, fishing; hunting; watermelon festival in July.

Minerals: Oil, gas.

Agriculture: Stocker calves, beef cattle; wheat, cotton, sorghum, watermelons, peanuts; some dairies; 31,200 acres irrigated. Market value $31.3 million.

BENJAMIN (243) county seat; ranching, farm center; **Munday** (1,544) portable buildings, other manufacturing; Texas A&M Vegetable Research Station; vegetable festival.

Knox City (1,448) agribusiness, petroleum center; USDA Plant Materials Research Center; home of seedless watermelon; hospital.

Other towns include: **Goree** (405); **Rhineland** (100); **Truscott** (50); **Vera** (50).

> 0 2 4 6 8 MILES

Population	4,752
(Change fm '90)	-1.8
Land Area (sq. mi.)	854.2
Altitude (ft.)	1,401-1,646
Rainfall (in.)	26.2
Jan. mean min.	28
July mean max.	98
Growing season (days)	217
Civ. Labor	2,231

Unemployed	5.4
Annual Wages	$25,912,402
Av. Weekly Wage	$347.70
Fed. Wages	$993,692
Ag. Net Cash Return	$3,369,000
Prop. Value	$197,122,888
Retail Sales	$20,011,832

For explanation of sources, abbreviations and symbols, see p. 142.

Lamar County

Physical Features: North Texas county on divide between Red, Sulphur rivers; soils chiefly blackland, except along Red; pines, hardwoods.

Economy: Varied manufacturing; agribusinesses; tourism; government/services.

History: Caddo Indian area. First Anglo-American settlers arrived about 1815. County created 1840 from Red River County; organized 1841; named for second president of Republic, Mirabeau B. Lamar.

Ethnicity, 1990: White, 36,814 (83.8%); Black, 6,397 (14.6%); American Indian, 406 (0.9%); Asian, 153 (0.3%); Other, 179 (0.4%). Hispanic, 475 (1.1%).

Vital Statistics, 1995: Births, 694; deaths, 533; marriages, 562; divorces, 350.

Recreation: Lake activities; Gambill goose refuge; hunting, fishing; state park; Sam Bell Maxey Home; State Sen. A.M. Aikin Archives; other museums; fiddlers contest.

Minerals: Negligible.

Agriculture: Beef, hay, dairies, soybeans, sorghum, wheat, corn, cotton. Market value $34.8 million. Firewood marketed.

PARIS (25,464) county seat; varied manufacturing; food processing; hospitals; junior college; Tour de Paris bicycle rally in July.

Other towns include: **Arthur City** (200), **Blossom** (1,697), **Brookston** (70), **Chicota** (125), **Cunningham** (110), **Deport** (880, partly in Red River County), **Pattonville** (180), **Petty** (100), **Powderly** (185), **Reno** (2,595), **Roxton** (637), **Sumner** (80), **Sun Valley** (78), **Toco** (134).

Population.............................46,104	Civ. Labor...............................22,051
(Change from '90)........................4.9	Unemployed..............................6.2
Land Area (sq. mi.) 917.1	Annual Wages............$418,725,215
Altitude (ft.)....................... 390-602	Av. Weekly Wage.................$427.34
Rainfall (in.)..............................46.1	Fed. Wages....................$4,745,670
Jan. mean min.............................30	Ag. Net Cash Return......$3,839,000
July mean max.............................94	Prop. Value $1,955,410,138
Growing season (days)...............235	Retail Sales $471,167,488

Lamb County

Physical Features: Rich, red, brown soils on West Texas High Plains; some hills; drains to Brazos Double Mountain Fork; numerous playas.

Economy: Agribusiness; distribution center; denim textiles.

History: Apaches, displaced by Comanches around 1700. U.S. Army pushed Comanches into Indian Territory in 1875. Ranching began in 1880s; farming after 1900. County created 1876 from Bexar District; organized 1908; named for Lt. G.A. Lamb, who died in battle of San Jacinto.

Ethnicity, 1990: White, 13,036 (86.5%); Black, 822 (5.5%); American Indian, 88 (0.6%); Asian, 25 (0.2%); Other, 1,101 (7.3%). Hispanic, 5,509 (36.6%).

Vital Statistics, 1995: Births, 253; deaths, 173; marriages, 87; divorces, 59.

Recreation: Pioneer celebration in August.

Minerals: Oil, stone, gas.

Agriculture: Fed cattle, sheep; cotton, wheat, grain sorghum, corn, vegetables, soybeans, hay; 385,000 acres irrigated. Market value $206.5 million.

LITTLEFIELD (6,426) county seat; agribusiness; tourism; varied manufacturing; Denim Festival on Labor Day.

Olton (2,051) agribusiness, commercial center in northwest part of county; Sandhills Celebration in summer.

Other towns include: **Amherst** (757); **Earth** (1,373) farming center, manufacturing, feed lot, supplies; **Fieldton** (126); **Spade** (174); **Springlake** (144); **Sudan** (978) farming center, Pioneer Day in June.

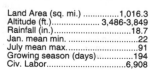

Population 15,102	
(Change fm '90)..........................0.2	
Land Area (sq. mi.) 1,016.3	Unemployed...............................6.0
Altitude (ft.)................... 3,486-3,849	Annual Wages..............$85,426,457
Rainfall (in.).............................18.7	Av. Weekly Wage...............$376.20
Jan. mean min. 22	Fed. Wages...................$1,572,679
July mean max..............................91	Ag. Net Cash Return.....$16,284,000
Growing season (days)...............194	Prop. Value $1,085,782,714
Civ. Labor................................6,908	Retail Sales..................$64,366,481

Lampasas County

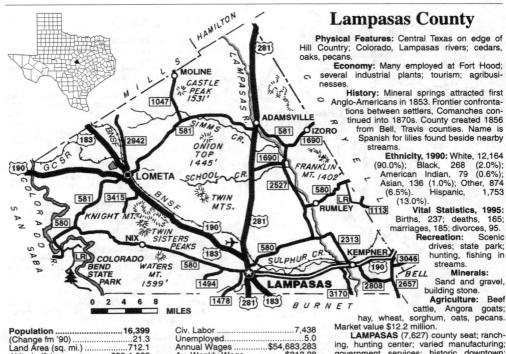

Physical Features: Central Texas on edge of Hill Country; Colorado, Lampasas rivers; cedars, oaks, pecans.

Economy: Many employed at Fort Hood; several industrial plants; tourism; agribusinesses.

History: Mineral springs attracted first Anglo-Americans in 1853. Frontier confrontations between settlers, Comanches continued into 1870s. County created 1856 from Bell, Travis counties. Name is Spanish for lilies found beside nearby streams.

Ethnicity, 1990: White, 12,164 (90.0%); Black, 268 (2.0%); American Indian, 79 (0.6%); Asian, 136 (1.0%); Other, 874 (6.5%). Hispanic, 1,753 (13.0%).

Vital Statistics, 1995: Births, 237; deaths, 165; marriages, 185; divorces, 95.

Recreation: Scenic drives; state park; hunting, fishing in streams.

Minerals: Sand and gravel, building stone.

Agriculture: Beef cattle, Angora goats; hay, wheat, sorghum, oats, pecans. Market value $12.2 million.

LAMPASAS (7,627) county seat; ranching, hunting center; varied manufacturing; government services; historic downtown; hospital; Spring Ho in July.

Other towns include: **Adamsville** (41); **Izoro** (17); **Kempner** (221); **Lometa** (744) market and shipping point.

Population	16,399
(Change fm '90)	21.3
Land Area (sq. mi.)	712.1
Altitude (ft.)	339-1,599
Rainfall (in.)	29.6
Jan. mean min.	30
July mean max.	95
Growing season (days)	223

Civ. Labor	7,438
Unemployed	5.0
Annual Wages	$54,683,283
Av. Weekly Wage	$313.28
Fed. Wages	$1,481,600
Ag. Net Cash Return	$900,000
Prop. Value	$650,723,887
Retail Sales	$84,971,617

La Salle County

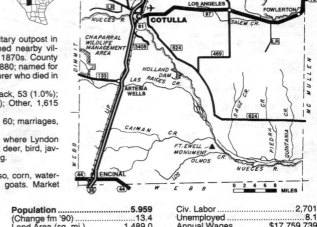

Physical Features: Southwestern county on brushy plain, broken by Nueces, Frio rivers and their tributaries; chocolate, dark gray, sandy loam soils.

Economy: Agribusiness, hunting leases; tourism; government services.

History: Coahuiltecans, squeezed out by migrating Apaches. U.S. military outpost in 1850s; settlers of Mexican descent established nearby village. Anglo-American ranching developed in 1870s. County created from Bexar County 1858; organized 1880; named for Robert Cavalier Sieur de la Salle, French explorer who died in Texas.

Ethnicity, 1990: White, 3,567 (67.9%); Black, 53 (1.0%); American Indian, 9 (0.2%); Asian, 10 (0.2%); Other, 1,615 (30.7%). Hispanic, 4,068 (77.4%).

Vital Statistics, 1995: Births, 82; deaths, 60; marriages, 37; divorces, 5.

Recreation: Nature trails; Cotulla school where Lyndon B. Johnson taught; wildlife management area; deer, bird, javelina hunting; wild hog cookoff in March; fishing.

Minerals: Oil, gas.

Agriculture: Beef cattle and peanuts; also, corn, watermelons, grain sorghum, wheat, vegetables, goats. Market value $11.9 million.

COTULLA (4,330) county seat; livestock, state prison; hunting center; Brush Country museum; Cinco de Mayo celebration.

Other towns include: **Artesia Wells** (35), **Encinal** (637), **Fowlerton** (50).

For explanation of sources, abbreviations and symbols, see p. 142.

Population	5.959
(Change fm '90)	13.4
Land Area (sq. mi.)	1,489.0
Altitude (ft.)	326-588
Rainfall (in.)	22.5
Jan. mean min.	38
July mean max.	99
Growing season (days)	288

Civ. Labor	2,701
Unemployed	8.1
Annual Wages	$17,759,739
Av. Weekly Wage	$322.84
Fed. Wages	$2,110,325
Ag. Net Cash Return	$469,000
Prop. Value	$380,656,516
Retail Sales	$24,445,959

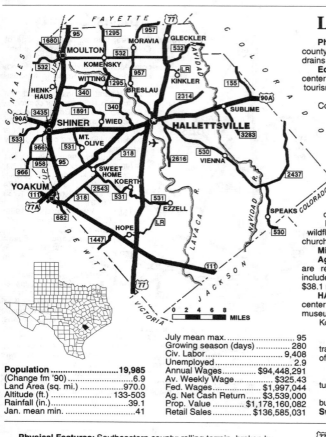

Lavaca County

Physical Features: Southern Coastal Plains county; north rolling; sandy loam, black waxy soils; drains to Lavaca, Navidad rivers.

Economy: Varied manufacturing; leather goods center; agribusinesses; oil and gas production; tourism.

History: Coahuiltecan area; later Comanches until 1850s. Anglo-Americans first settled in 1831. Germans and Czechs arrived 1880-1900. County created 1846 from Colorado, Jackson, Gonzales, Victoria counties. Name is Spanish word for cow, la vaca, from name of river.

Ethnicity, 1990: White, 16,541 (88.5%); Black, 1,342 (7.2%); American Indian, 20 (0.1%); Asian, 14 (0.1%); Other, 773 (4.1%). Hispanic, 1,596 (8.5%);

Vital Statistics, 1995: Births, 231; deaths, 272; marriages, 115; divorces, 52.

Recreation: Deer, other hunting, fishing; wildflower trails, fiddlers frolic; historic sites, churches.

Minerals: Some oil, gas.

Agriculture: Livestock, especially beef cattle, are revenue sources; eggs and poultry; crops include hay, rice, corn, sorghum. Market value $38.1 million.

HALLETTSVILLE (2,772) county seat; retail center; varied manufacturing; agribusiness; museum; hospital; domino, "42" tournaments; Kolache Fest in September.

Yoakum (6,394, partly in DeWitt County); trading center for two counties; hospital; Land of Leather celebration in February.

Shiner (2,317), brewery, varied manufacturing; museum; clinic; Bocktoberfest.

Other towns include: **Moulton** (1,012) agribusiness, clinic; **Speaks** (60); **Sublime** (75); **Sweet Home** (360).

July mean max.	95
Growing season (days)	280
Civ. Labor	9,408
Unemployed	2.9
Annual Wages	$94,448,291
Av. Weekly Wage	$325.43
Fed. Wages	$1,997,044
Ag. Net Cash Return	$3,539,000
Prop. Value	$1,178,160,082
Retail Sales	$136,585,031

Population	**19,985**
(Change fm '90)	6.9
Land Area (sq. mi.)	970.0
Altitude (ft.)	133-503
Rainfall (in.)	39.1
Jan. mean min.	41

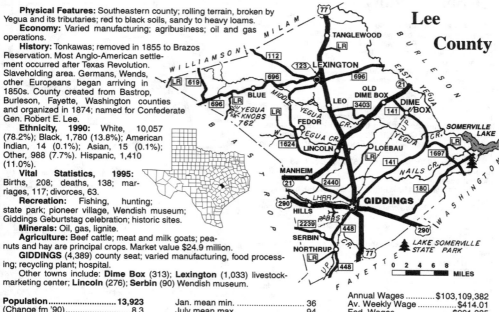

Lee County

Physical Features: Southeastern county; rolling terrain, broken by Yegua and its tributaries; red to black soils, sandy to heavy loams.

Economy: Varied manufacturing; agribusiness; oil and gas operations.

History: Tonkawas; removed in 1855 to Brazos Reservation. Most Anglo-American settlement occurred after Texas Revolution. Slaveholding area. Germans, Wends, other Europeans began arriving in 1850s. County created from Bastrop, Burleson, Fayette, Washington counties and organized in 1874; named for Confederate Gen. Robert E. Lee.

Ethnicity, 1990: White, 10,057 (78.2%); Black, 1,780 (13.8%); American Indian, 14 (0.1%); Asian, 15 (0.1%); Other, 988 (7.7%). Hispanic, 1,410 (11.0%).

Vital Statistics, 1995: Births, 208; deaths, 138; marriages, 117; divorces, 63.

Recreation: Fishing, hunting; state park; pioneer village, Wendish museum; Giddings Geburtstag celebration; historic sites.

Minerals: Oil, gas, lignite.

Agriculture: Beef cattle; meat and milk goats; peanuts and hay are principal crops. Market value $24.9 million.

GIDDINGS (4,389) county seat; varied manufacturing, food processing; recycling plant; hospital.

Other towns include: **Dime Box** (313); **Lexington** (1,033) livestock-marketing center; **Lincoln** (276); **Serbin** (90) Wendish museum.

Population	**13,923**
(Change fm '90)	8.3
Land Area (sq. mi.)	628.6
Altitude (ft.)	238-513
Rainfall (in.)	35.6

Jan. mean min.	36
July mean max.	94
Growing season (days)	273
Civ. Labor	7,061
Unemployed	4.3

Annual Wages	$103,109,382
Av. Weekly Wage	$414.01
Fed. Wages	$991,335
Ag. Net Cash Return	$2,733,000
Prop. Value	$817,652,620
Retail Sales	$127,174,020

Leon County

Physical Features: East central county; hilly, rolling, almost half covered by timber; drains to Navasota, Trinity rivers and tributaries; sandy, dark, alluvial soils.

Economy: Oil, gas production; agribusiness.

History: Bidais band, absorbed into Kickapoos and other groups. Permanent settlement by Anglo-Americans occurred after Texas Revolution; Germans in 1870s. County created 1846 from Robertson County; named for founder of Victoria, Martin de Leon.

Ethnicity, 1990: White, 10,730 (84.7%); Black, 1,615 (12.8%); American Indian, 39(0.3%); Asian, 8 (0.1%); Other, 273 (2.2%). Hispanic, 509 (4.0%).

Vital Statistics, 1995: Births, 168; deaths, 178; marriages, 76; divorces, 86.

Recreation: Hilltop Lakes resort area; sites of Camino Real, Fort Boggy; deer hunting.

Minerals: Oil, gas, iron ore, lignite.

Agriculture: A leading county in cow-calf production; hogs raised; hay, watermelons, vegetables, small grains; Christmas trees. Market value $23.9 million. Forest products sold for cross-ties.

CENTERVILLE (954) county seat; farm center; hunting; tourism; oil, gas; timber.

Buffalo (1,982), farm center; clinic; library; stampede in September.

Other towns include: **Flynn** (81); **Hilltop Lakes** (300) resort, retirement center; **Jewett** (775) electricity-generating plant; civic center, fall frolic; **Leona** (222) candle factory; **Marquez** (275); **Normangee** (694, partly in Madison County) city park; **Oakwood** (604).

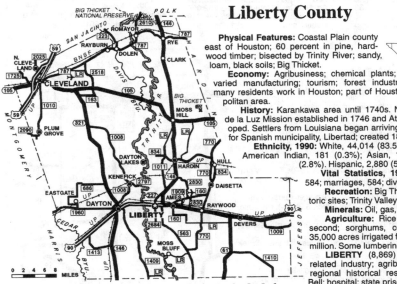

Population	13,446	
(Change fm '90)	6.2	
Land Area (sq. mi.)	1,072.1	
Altitude (ft.)	190-496	
Rainfall (in.)	40.5	
Jan. mean min.	34	
July mean max.	95	
Growing season (days)	270	
Civ. Labor	5,579	
Unemployed	6.8	
Annual Wages	$94,774,466	
Av. Weekly Wage	$522.19	
Fed. Wages	$1,324,186	
Ag. Net Cash Return	-$551,000	
Prop. Value	$1,356,243,325	
Retail Sales	$81,750,489	

Liberty County

Physical Features: Coastal Plain county east of Houston; 60 percent in pine, hardwood timber; bisected by Trinity River; sandy, loam, black soils; Big Thicket.

Economy: Agribusiness; chemical plants; varied manufacturing; tourism; forest industries; many residents work in Houston; part of Houston metropolitan area.

History: Karankawa area until 1740s. Nuestra Señora de la Luz Mission established in 1746 and Atascosito settlement developed. Settlers from Louisiana began arriving in 1810s. County named for Spanish municipality, Libertad; created 1836, organized 1837.

Ethnicity, 1990: White, 44,014 (83.5%); Black, 6,911 (13.1%); American Indian, 181 (0.3%); Asian, 124 (0.2%); Other, 1,496 (2.8%). Hispanic, 2,880 (5.5%).

Vital Statistics, 1995: Births, 922; deaths, 584; marriages, 584; divorces, 349.

Recreation: Big Thicket; hunting, fishing; historic sites; Trinity Valley exposition; Liberty Opry.

Minerals: Oil, gas, sulphur, sand and gravel.

Agriculture: Rice top crop with soybeans second; sorghums, corn; cow-calf operations; 35,000 acres irrigated for rice. Market value $21.6 million. Some lumbering.

LIBERTY (8,869) county seat; petroleum-related industry; agribusiness; library; museum; regional historical resource depository; Liberty Bell; hospital; state prisons.

Cleveland (7,610) forest products processed, shipped; tourism; library; museum; hospital.

Dayton (6,019) rice, oil center.

Other towns include: **Ames** (1,135); **Daisetta** (988); **Dayton Lakes** (226); **Devers** (407); **Hardin** (581); **Hull** (1,800); **Kenefick** (464); **Plum Grove** (562); **Raywood** (231); **Romayor** (96); **Rye** (76).

Population	62,843	
(Change fm '90)	19.2	
Land Area (sq. mi.)	1,159.8	
Altitude (ft.)	23-261	
Rainfall (in.)	54.1	
Jan. mean min.	39	
July mean max.	93	
Growing season (days)	261	
Civ. Labor	26,345	
Unemployed	8.4	
Annual Wages	$304,117,914	
Av. Weekly Wage	$408.56	
Fed. Wages	$4,221,195	
Ag. Net Cash Returns	$1,728,000	
Prop. Value	$2,058,759,938	
Retail Sales	$1,091,137,200	

Limestone County

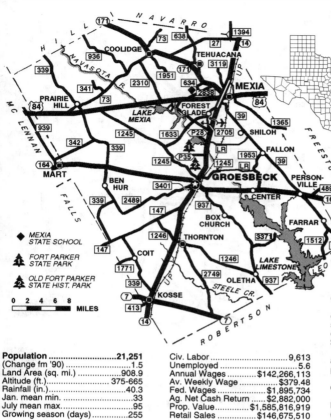

Physical Features: East central county on divide between Brazos and Trinity rivers; borders Blacklands, level to rolling; drained by Navasota and tributaries.

Economy: Varied manufacturing; agribusiness; tourism; mineral operations.

History: Tawakoni (Tehuacana) and Waco area, later Comanche raiders. First Anglo-Americans arrived in 1833. Antebellum slaveholding area. County created from Robertson County and organized 1846; named for indigenous rock.

Ethnicity, 1990: White, 15,695 (74.9%); Black, 4,156 (19.8%); American Indian, 41(0.2%); Asian, 50 (0.2%); Other, 1,004 (4.8%). Hispanic, 1,459 (7.0%).

Vital Statistics, 1995: Births, 260; deaths, 348; marriages, 187; divorces, 132.

Recreation: Fishing, lake activities; Fort Parker; Confederate Reunion Grounds; historic sites; museum; hunting; Christmas at the Fort.

Minerals: Lignite, crushed rock, sand oil, gas.

Agriculture: Cow-calf, stocker cattle operations; dairies, horses, goats, sheep, some exotic animals; crops include hay, corn, cotton, wheat, peaches. Market value $29.6 million.

GROESBECK (3,548) county seat, agribusiness, tourism, hunting, mining, prison, power generating, hospital.

Mexia (6,917), agribusiness, grocery distribution, state school, hospital.

Other towns include: **Coolidge** (740), **Kosse** (509), **Prairie Hill** (150), **Tehuacana** (339), **Thornton** (601).

Population **21,251**	Civ. Labor 9,613
(Change fm '90) 1.5	Unemployed 5.6
Land Area (sq. mi.) 908.9	Annual Wages $142,266,113
Altitude (ft.) 375-665	Av. Weekly Wage $379.48
Rainfall (in.)...............................40.3	Fed. Wages $1,895,734
Jan. mean min. 33	Ag. Net Cash Return $2,882,000
July mean max.............................95	Prop. Value.............$1,585,816,919
Growing season (days)..............255	Retail Sales $146,675,510

Lipscomb County

Physical Features: High Plain, broken in east; drains to tributaries of Canadian, Wolf Creek; sandy loam, black soils.

Economy: Agribusinesses; government/services; oil, gas operations.

History: Apaches, later Kiowas and Comanches who were driven into Indian Territory in 1875. Ranching began in late 1870s. County created 1876 from Bexar District; organized 1887; named for A.S. Lipscomb, Republic of Texas leader.

Ethnicity, 1990: White, 3,092 (98.4%); Black, 1 (0.0%); American Indian, 34 (1.1%); Asian, 13 (0.4%); Other, 3 (0.1%). Hispanic, 379 (12.1%).

Vital Statistics, 1995: Births, 42; deaths, 38; marriages, 39; divorces, 13.

Recreation: Will Rogers Day; Darrouzett festival; Wolf Creek museum.

Minerals: Oil, natural gas.

Agriculture: Stocker, beef cattle, fed beef; alfalfa, wheat, sorghum, corn; 10,000 acres irrigated. Market value $39.8 million.

LIPSCOMB (50) county seat; livestock center.

Booker (1,235, part in Ochiltree County) trade center.

Other towns include: **Darrouzett** (362) **Follett** (459); **Higgins** (481).

For explanation of sources, abbreviations and symbols, see p. 142.

Population **3,241**	Civ. Labor 1,653
(Change fm '90) 3.1	Unemployed 2.4
Land Area (sq. mi.) 932.2	Annual Wages $19,736,248
Altitude (ft.).................. 2,506-2,834	Av. Weekly Wage $406.21
Rainfall (in.)............................. 22.8	Fed. Wages $705,077
Jan. mean min. 20	Ag. Net Cash Value........$2,935,000
July mean max............................93	Prop. Value................$392,423,620
Growing season (days) 202	Retail Sales $10,446,016

Live Oak County

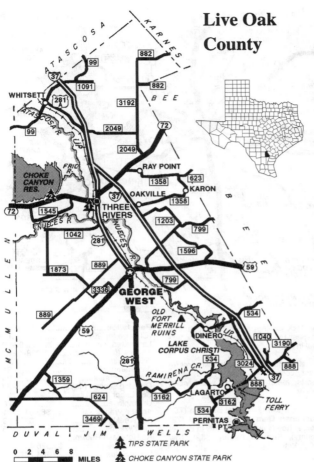

Physical Features: Brushy plains between San Antonio and Corpus Christi, partly broken by Nueces and tributaries; black waxy, gray sandy, other soils.

Economy: Oil, government/services, tourism, agribusinesses.

History: Coahuiltecans squeezed out by Lipan Apaches and Spanish. Spanish ranching started in 1810s. Settlers from Ireland arrived in 1835. County named for predominant tree; created, organized 1856 from Nueces, San Patricio counties.

Ethnicity, 1990: White, 8,316 (87.0%); Black, 10 (0.1%); American Indian, 36 (0.4%); Asian, 31 (0.3%); Other, 1,163 (12.2%). Hispanic, 3,324 (34.8%).

Vital Statistics, 1995: Births, 115; deaths, 92; marriages, 84; divorces, 65.

Recreation: Lakes; water activities; state parks; hunting; historic sites.

Minerals: Oil, gas, sand, gravel.

Agriculture: Cow-calf operations; swine produced; corn, grain sorghums, cotton; some irrigation for hay, coastal Bermuda pastures. Market value $16.3 million.

GEORGE WEST (2,767) county seat, agribusiness, petroleum refineries, Storyfest in November.

Three Rivers (1,996) agribusinesses, refineries, federal prison.

Other towns include: **Dinero** (344), **Oakville** (260), **Pernitas Point** (186), **Whitsett** (200).

Population	10,291
(Change fm '90)	7.7
Land Area (sq. mi.)	1,036.4
Altitude (ft.)	96-479
Rainfall (in.)	27.6
Jan. mean min.	41
July mean max.	95
Growing season (days)	289
Civ. Labor	4,448
Unemployed	3.9
Annual Wages	$48,651,989
Av. Weekly Wage	$400.29
Fed. Wages	$13,554,608
Ag. Net Cash Return	-$529,000
Prop. Value	$959,093,650
Retail Sales	$87,207,007

Armadillos are mostly nocturnal. The armor-plated creatures were designated the state small mammal in 1995. Texas Almanac photo.

Llano County

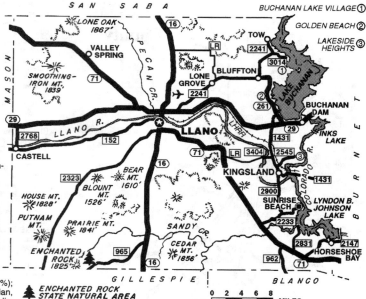

Physical Features: Central county drains to Colorado, Llano rivers; rolling to hilly; Highland lakes.

Economy: Tourism, retirement; ranch trading center; vineyards; granite mined.

History: Tonkawas, later Comanches. Anglo-American and German settlers arrived in 1840s. County name is Spanish for plains; created, organized 1856 from Bexar District, Gillespie County.

Ethnicity, 1990: White, 11,386 (97.9%); Black, 22 (0.2%); American Indian, 39 (0.3%); Asian, 20 (0.2%); Other, 164 (1.4%). Hispanic, 453 (3.9%).

Vital Statistics, 1995: Births, 130; deaths, 235; marriages, 104; divorces, 75.

Recreation: Leading deer-hunting county; fishing; lake activities; major tourist area; Enchanted Rock; bluebonnet festival; hang gliding.

Minerals: Granite, vermiculite, llanite.

Agriculture: Beef cattle; also some swine and sheep raised; hay; peanuts and oats. Market value $11.5 million.

LLANO (3,284) county seat; historic district; tourism; hunting center; livestock trading; some manufacturing; hospital; museum; bluegrass music festival in April.

Kingsland (2,971), tourism, retirement community, fishing and water sports; metal fabrication; wood work; library.

Other towns include: **Bluffton** (75), **Buchanan Dam** (1,155), **Castell** (72) **Horseshoe Bay** (1,712, partly in Burnet County), **Sunrise Beach** (552), **Tow** (305), **Valley Spring** (50).

Population	12,755
(Change fm '90)	9.7
Land Area (sq. mi.)	934.9
Altitude (ft.)	1,038-1,867
Rainfall (in.)	26.4
Jan. mean min.	31
July mean max.	96
Growing season (days)	229
Civ. Labor	4,793
Unemployed	3.6
Annual Wages	$62,614,161
Av. Weekly Wage	$376.09
Fed. Wages	$1,200,765
Ag Net Cash Return	$1,295,000
Prop. Value	$1,375,432,349
Retail Sales	$84,772,774

Loving County

Physical Features: Western county of dry, rolling prairies; slopes to Pecos River; Red Bluff Reservoir; sandy, loam, clay soils.

Economy: Petroleum operations; some cattle.

History: Land developers began operations in late 19th century. Oil discovered in 1925. County created 1887 from Tom Green; organized 1931, last county organized. Named for Oliver Loving, trail driver. Loving is Texas' least populous county.

Ethnicity, 1990: White, 93 (86.9%); Black, 0 (0.0%); American Indian, 0 (0.0%); Asian, 0 (0.0%); Other, 14 (13.1%). Hispanic, 14 (13.1%).

Vital Statistics, 1995: Births, 0; deaths, 0; marriages, 4; divorces, 0.

Recreation: N.A.

Minerals: Oil, gas.

Agriculture: Some cattle. Market value $989,000.

MENTONE (96) county seat, oil-field supply center; only town.

For explanation of sources, abbreviations and symbols, see p. 142.

Population	96
(Change fm '90)	-10.3
Land Area (sq. mi.)	673.1
Altitude (ft.)	2,685-3,311
Rainfall (in.)	9.1
Jan. mean min.	28
July mean max.	96
Growing season (days)	222

Civ. Labor	85
Unemployed	9.4
Annual Wages	$764,647
Av. Weekly Wage	$368.52
Fed. Wages	$25,654
Ag. Net Cash Return	$276,000
Prop. Value	$124,428,180
Retail Sales	$52,385

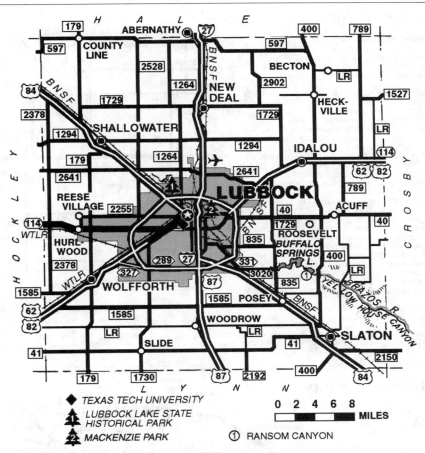

- ◆ TEXAS TECH UNIVERSITY
- ▲1 LUBBOCK LAKE STATE HISTORICAL PARK
- ▲2 MACKENZIE PARK
- ① RANSOM CANYON

0 2 4 6 8 MILES

Physical Features: High Plains of West Texas, broken by 1,500 playas, Yellow House River; rich soils with underground water.

Economy: Among world's largest cottonseed processing centers; a leading agribusiness center; cattle feedlots; manufacturing; higher education center; medical center; government/services.

History: Evidence of human habitation for 12,000 years. In historic period, Apache Indians, followed by Comanche hunters. Sheep raisers from Midwest arrived in late 1870s. Cotton farms brought in Mexican laborers in 1940s-60s. County named for Col. Tom S. Lubbock, an organizer of Confederate Terry's Rangers; county created 1876 from Bexar District; organized 1891.

Ethnicity, 1990: White, 176,037 (79.1%); Black, 17,154 (7.7%); American Indian, 686 (0.3%); Asian, 2,722 (1.2%); Other, 26,037 (11.7%); Hispanic, 51,011 (22.9%).

Vital Statistics, 1995: Births, 3,638; deaths, 1,750; marriages, 2,168; divorces, 1,341.

Recreation: Lubbock Lake State Historical Park and archaeological site; Texas Tech events; civic center, Buddy Holly statue and Walk of Fame, planetarium; Ranching Heritage Center; Panhandle-South Plains Fair; Buffalo Springs Lake.

Lubbock County

Minerals: Oil, gas, stone, sand and gravel.

Agriculture: Fed beef, cow-calf operations; also, swine, sheep, poultry; eggs marketed; cotton major crop, others are grain sorghums, wheat, sunflowers, soybeans, hay, vegetables; more than 230,000 acres irrigated, mostly cotton. Market value $133.2 million.

Education: Texas Tech University with law and medical schools; Lubbock Christian University, South Plains College; Wayland Baptist University off-campus center.

LUBBOCK (194,522) county seat; center for large agricultural area; manufacturing includes electronics, earthmoving equipment, food containers, fireprotection equipment, clothing, other products; distribution center for South Plains; feedlots; psychiatric hospital; museum; hospitals, government/services, state school for retarded.

Other towns include: **Idalou** (2,145); **New Deal** (567); **Ransom Canyon** (868); **Shallowater** (2,039); **Slaton** (6,269) agribusiness, government/services, varied manufacturing, sausage festival in October; **Wolfforth** (2,176).

Population	233,486
(Change fm '90)	4.9
Land Area (sq. mi.)	899.6
Altitude (ft.)	3,015-3,402
Rainfall (in.)	18.7
Jan. mean min.	25
July mean max.	92
Growing season (days)	208
Civ. Labor	122,183
Unemployed	3.9
Annual Wages	$2,325,048,648
Av. Weekly Wage	$425.52
Fed. Wages	$62,164,585
Ag. Net Cash Return	$10,900,000
Prop. Value	$6,796,953,554
Retail Sales	$2,844,499,559

For explanation of sources, abbreviations and symbols, see p. 142.

Lynn County

Physical Features: South High Plains, broken by Caprock Escarpment, playas, draws; sandy loam, black, gray soils.

Economy: Agribusiness.

History: Apaches, ousted by Comanches who were removed to Indian Territory in 1875. Ranching began in 1880s. Farming developed after 1900. County created 1876 from Bexar District; organized 1903; named for Alamo victim, W. Lynn.

Ethnicity,1990: White, 5,214 (77.2%); Black, 223 (3.3%); American Indian, 22 (0.3%); Asian, 11 (0.2%); Other, 1,288 (19.1%). Hispanic, 2,819 (41.7%).

Vital Statistics, 1995: Births, 78; deaths, 68; marriages, 41; divorces, 33.

Recreation: Pioneer museum in Tahoka; Dan Blocker museum in O'Donnell.

Minerals: Oil, natural gas, stone.

Agriculture: Cotton produces largest income; grain sorghums, wheat, cattle raised; 80,000 acres of cotton irrigated. Market value $49.5 million.

TAHOKA (2,757) county seat; agribusiness center; cotton compress; some manufacturing; hospital.

O'Donnell (1,174, partly in Dawson County), commercial center.

Other towns include: **New Home** (205); **Wilson** (560).

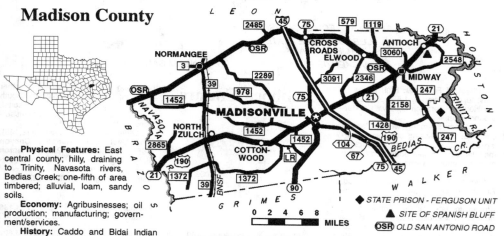

Population	6,660
(Change fm '90)	-1.5
Land Area (sq. mi.)	891.9
Altitude (ft.)	2,881-3,274
Rainfall (in.)	19.7
Jan. mean min.	24
July mean max.	92
Growing season (days)	217
Civ. Labor	3,118
Unemployed	3.9
Annual Wages	$30,754,365
Av. Weekly Wage	$376.64
Fed. Wages	$875,927
Ag. Net Cash Return	$12,818,000
Prop. Value	$349,926,150
Retail Sales	$28,667,346

Madison County

Physical Features: East central county; hilly, draining to Trinity, Navasota rivers, Bedias Creek; one-fifth of area timbered; alluvial, loam, sandy soils.

Economy: Agribusinesses; oil production; manufacturing; government/services.

History: Caddo and Bidai Indian area; Kickapoos migrated from east. Spanish settlements established in 1774 and 1805. Anglo-Americans arrived in 1829. Census of 1860 showed 30 percent of population was black. County named for U.S. President James Madison; created from Grimes, Leon, Walker counties 1853; organized 1854.

Ethnicity, 1990: White, 7,984 (73.0%); Black, 2,575 (23.6%); American Indian, 67 (0.6%); Asian, 13 (0.1%); Other, 292 (2.7%). Hispanic, 1,178 (10.8%).

For explanation of sources, abbreviations and symbols, see p. 142.

Vital Statistics, 1995: Births, 141; deaths, 122; marriages, 113; divorces, 53.

Recreation: Fishing, hunting; Spanish Bluff where survivors of Battle of Medina were executed; other historic sites.

Minerals: Oil, gas, gravel.

Agriculture: Cattle, horses, swine raised; forage for livestock. Market value $42.7 million.

MADISONVILLE (4,100) county seat; farm-trade center; varied manufacturing; hospital, library.

Other towns, **Midway** (313); **Normangee** (694, mostly in Leon County); **North Zulch** (150).

◆ STATE PRISON - FERGUSON UNIT
▲ SITE OF SPANISH BLUFF
OSR OLD SAN ANTONIO ROAD

Population	12,139
(Change fm '90)	11.1
Land Area (sq. mi.)	469.7
Altitude (ft.)	213-364
Rainfall (in.)	41.6
Jan. mean min.	38
July mean max.	96
Growing season (days)	272
Civ. Labor	4,124
Unemployed	3.8
Annual Wages	$66,680,604
Av. Weekly Wage	$373.71
Fed. Wages	$748,610
Ag. Net Cash Return	$5,237,000
Prop. Value	$551,901,767
Retail Sales	$67,950,397

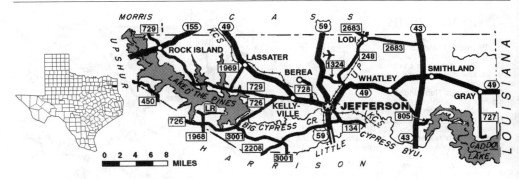

Physical Features: Northeastern county; hilly, three-quarters forested with pines, hardwoods; drains to Caddo Lake, Lake O' the Pines, Cypress Bayou.

Economy: Tourism; timber; food processing.

History: Caddoes forced out in 1790s. Kickapoo in area when settlers arrived from Deep South around 1840. Antebellum slaveholding area. County created 1860 from Cass County; named for Gen. Francis Marion of American Revolution.

Ethnicity, 1990: White, 6,792 (68.0%); Black, 3,100 (31.0%); American Indian, 44 (0.4%); Asian, 7 (0.1%); Other, 41 (0.4%). Hispanic, 147 (1.5%).

Vital Statistics, 1995: Births, 101; deaths, 114; marriages, 105; divorces, 71.

Recreation: Lake activities; hunting;

Excelsior Hotel; 84 medallions on historic sites including Jay Gould railroad car; museum; Mardi Gras; historical pilgrimage in May, founder's day in October.

Minerals: Oil, gas, clays, lignite, gravel.

Agriculture: Beef cattle, horses, hogs, emus, ostriches also raised; coastal Bermuda major crop, hay; also truck crops grown, landscape horticulture plants, peaches, vegetables, blueberries. Market value $$42.7 million. Some forest products produced.

JEFFERSON (2,496) county seat; tourism; paper plant; glass manufacturing; timber; museums; library; historical sites.

Other towns include: **Lodi** (164).

Marion County

Population	10,543
(Change fm '90)	5.6
Land Area (sq. mi.)	381.2
Altitude (ft.)	168-379
Rainfall (in.)	44.7
Jan. mean min.	32
July mean max.	94
Growing season (days)	236
Civ. Labor	4,124
Unemployed	3.8
Annual Wages	$36,688,063
Av. Weekly Wage	$354.95
Fed. Wages	$507,541
Ag. Net Cash Return	$5,237,000
Prop. Value	$383,491,365
Retail Sales	$44,446,496

Martin County

Physical Features: Western county on South Plains; sandy, loam soils, broken by playas, creeks.

Economy: Petroleum production, agribusiness.

History: Apaches ousted by Comanches who in turn were forced out by U.S. Army 1875. Farming began in 1881. County created from Bexar District 1876; organized 1884; named for Wylie Martin, senator of Republic of Texas.

Ethnicity, 1990: White, 3,159 (63.7%); Black, 89 (1.8%); American Indian, 11 (0.2%); Asian, 8 (0.2%); Other, 1,689 (34.1%). Hispanic, 1,960 (39.5%).

Vital Statistics, 1995: Births, 70; deaths, 50; marriages, 48; divorces, 16.

Recreation: Museum, settlers reunion.

Minerals: Oil, gas.

Agriculture: Cotton, hay, sorghum; Beef cattle, sheep, goats, hogs also raised. Market value $30.4 million.

STANTON (2,713) county seat; farm, ranch, oil, center; varied manufacturing; electric co-op; hospital, restored convent, other historic buildings; old sorehead days three times a year.

Other towns include: **Ackerly** (267, partly in Dawson County); **Lenorah** (70); **Tarzan** (80).

For explanation of sources, abbreviations and symbols, see p. 142.

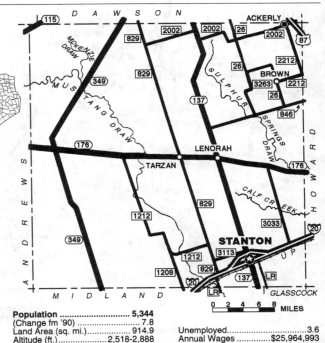

Population	5,344
(Change fm '90)	7.8
Land Area (sq. mi.)	914.9
Altitude (ft.)	2,518-2,888
Rainfall (in.)	17.2
Jan. mean min.	30
July mean max.	94
Growing season (days)	215
Civ. Labor	1,843
Unemployed	3.6
Annual Wages	$25,964,993
Av. Weekly Wage	$428.91
Fed. Wages	$613,313
Ag. Net Cash Return	$8,336,000
Prop. Value	$516,235,076
Retail Sales	$33,400,637

Mason County

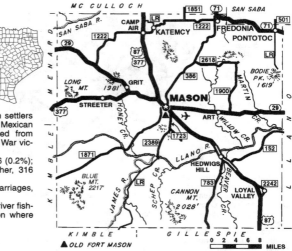

Physical Features: Southwestern county; hilly, draining to Llano, San Saba rivers and tributaries; limestone, red soils; varied timber.

Economy: Ranching; hunting; tourism; soft-drink bottling.

History: Lipan Apaches, driven south by Comanches around 1790. German settlers arrived in mid-1840s, followed by Anglo-Americans. Mexican immigration increased after 1930. County created from Bexar, Gillespie counties 1858; named for Mexican War victim U.S. Army Lt. G.T. Mason.

Ethnicity, 1990: White, 3,084 (90.1%); Black, 6 (0.2%); American Indian, 13 (0.4%); Asian, 4 (0.1%); Other, 316 (9.2%). Hispanic, 671 (19.6%).

Vital Statistics, 1995: Births, 33; deaths, 60; marriages, 26; divorces, 16.

Recreation: Outstanding deer, turkey hunting, river fishing; camping; historic homes of stone; Fort Mason where Robert E. Lee served; wildflower drives in spring.

Minerals: Topaz, granite.

Agriculture: Cattle, goats, sheep; watermelons; some 7,100 acres of peanuts, hay irrigated. Market value $22.5 million.

MASON (2,148) county seat; ranching center; tourism; museum; historical district, homes, rock fences built by German settlers; Tejano festival in September.

Other towns include: **Art** (18), **Fredonia** (50), **Pontotoc** (125).

▲ OLD FORT MASON

Population............................ **3,589**	Civ. Labor............................... 1,609
(Change fm '90) 4.8	Unemployed 2.5
Land Area (sq. mi.)................. 932.1	Annual Wages $13,406,736
Altitude (ft.).................... 1,258-2,260	Av. Weekly Wage $305.25
Rainfall (in.) 26.8	Fed. Wages $387,519
Jan. mean min............................. 31	Ag. Net Cash Return $3,659,000
July mean max. 95	Prop. Value................. $449,106,938
Growing season (days) 217	Retail Sales $15,378,039

Matagorda County

Physical Features: Gulf Coast county; flat, broken by bays; contains part of Matagorda Island; many different soils; drains to Colorado River, creeks, coast.

Economy: Petroleum operations, petrochemicals, agribusiness; varied manufacturing; tourism significant.

History: Karankawa Indian area, Tonkawas later. Anglo-Americans arrived in 1822. Mexican immigration increased after 1920. An original county, created 1836 from Spanish municipality, named for canebrake; organized 1837; settled by Austin colonists.

Ethnicity, 1990: White, 26,622 (72.1%); Black, 5,106 (13.8%); American Indian, 88 (0.2%); Asian, 842 (2.3%); Other, 4,270 (11.6%). Hispanic, 9,088 (24.6%).

Vital Statistics, 1995: Births, 579; deaths, 365; marriages, 337; divorces, 214.

Recreation: Coastal activities, including fishing, water sports, hunting; historic sites, museums; rice festival; boat show.

Minerals: Gas, oil, salt.

Agriculture: Major rice-growing area, nurseries, cotton, grains; beef cattle, cow-calf operations; 49,000 acres irrigated for rice, turf. Market value $44.5 million.

BAY CITY (18,194) county seat; petrochemicals; oil, gas processing; nuclear power plant; commercial fishing; hospital.

Palacios (4,395) tourism; seafood industry; hospital; Marine Education Center; Bay Festival Labor Day; public fishing piers.

Other towns include: **Blessing** (571) historic sites; **Cedar Lane** (85); **Collegeport** (91); **Elmaton** (165); **Markham** (1,349); **Matagorda** (605); **Midfield** (70); **Pledger** (159); **Sargent** (76); **Van Vleck** (1,753), **Wadsworth** (152).

Population **37,541**	
(Change fm '90) 1.7	
Land Area (sq. mi.) 1,114.5	
Altitude (ft.) .... sea level-56	

Rainfall (in.) 44.7	Annual Wages $336,674,996
Jan. mean min............................. 45	Av. Weekly Wage $565.66
July mean max. 91	Fed. Wages $2,638,525
Growing season (days) 296	Ag. Net Cash Return....... $4,772,000
Civ. Labor............................ 16,286	Prop. Value............. $4,450,263,175
Unemployed 13.5	Retail Sales............. $229,028,896

Maverick County

Physical Features: Southwestern county on Rio Grande; broken, rolling surface, with dense brush; clay, sandy, alluvial soils.

Economy: Oil; government/services; agribusinesses; feedlots; tourism.

History: Coahuiltecan Indian area; later Comanches in area. Spanish ranching began in 1760s. First Anglo-Americans arrived in 1834. County named for Sam A. Maverick, whose name is now a synonym for unbranded cattle; created 1856 from Kinney County; organized 1871.

Ethnicity, 1990: White, 23,748 (65.3%); Black, 32 (0.1%); American Indian, 714 (2.0%); Asian, 71 (0.2%); Other, 11,813 (32.5%). Hispanic, 34,024 (93.5%).

Vital Statistics, 1995: Births, 1,147; deaths, 232; marriages, 640; divorces, 120.

Recreation: Tourist gateway to Mexico; white-tailed deer; bird hunting; fishing; historic sites.

Minerals: Oil, gas, sand, gravel.

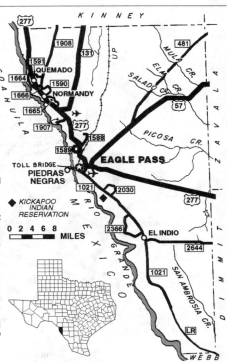

Population............................	44,003
(Change fm '90)	21.0
Land Area (sq. mi.)...............	1,280.2
Altitude (ft.)	703-918
Rainfall (in.)	21.5
Jan. mean min.	38
July mean max.	98
Growing season (days)	285
Civ. Labor..............................	18,186
Unemployed	29.7
Annual Wages...........	$155,436,780
Av. Weekly Wage...............	$325.12
Fed. Wages...........	$13,230,140
Ag. Net Cash Return.....	-$1,379,000
Prop. Value	$836,036,728
Retail Sales	$253,511,910

Agriculture: Cattle feedlots provide most income; oats, sorghums, wheat, pecans, vegetables; some irrigation from Rio Grande. Market value $37 million.

EAGLE PASS (24,806) county seat; varied manufacturing; tourism center; rail, highway entry point to Piedras Negras, Mex.; hospital.

Other towns include: **El Indio** (148); **Quemado** (426).

McCulloch County

Physical Features: Central county; hilly and rolling; drains to Colorado, Brady Creek and Lake, San Saba River; black loams to sandy soils.

Economy: Agribusiness; manufacturing; tourism; hunting leases.

History: Apache area. First Anglo-American settlers arrived in late 1850s, but Comanche raids delayed further settlement until 1870s. County created from Bexar District 1856; organized 1876; named for San Jacinto veteran Gen. Ben McCulloch.

Ethnicity, 1990: White, 7,855 (89.5%); Black, 166 (1.9%); American Indian, 14 (0.2%); Asian, 8 (0.1%); Other, 735 (8.4%). Hispanic, 2,317 (26.4%).

Vital Statistics, 1995: Births, 126; deaths, 126; marriages, 68; divorces, 64.

Recreation: Hunting; lake activities; museum; restored Santa Fe depot, goat cookoff, muzzle-loading rifle association state championship; rodeos; golf, tennis tournaments.

Minerals: Oil, sand, gravel, stone, gas.

Agriculture: Beef cattle provide most income; wheat, hay, cotton, peanuts; some irrigation for peanuts. Market value $21.3 million.

BRADY (5,974) county seat; ranching, tourism; mohair, wool processed; oil-field equipment, other manufacturing; hospital; Central Texas College extension; July Jubilee.

Other towns: **Doole** (74); **Lohn** (149); **Melvin** (170); **Pear Valley** (37); **Rochelle** (163); **Voca** (56).

Population............................	8,733
(Change fm '90)	-0.5
Land Area (sq. mi.)...............	1,069.4
Altitude (ft.)	1,442-2,021
Rainfall (in.)	26.1
Jan. mean min.	30
July mean max.	95
Growing season (days)..............	226
Civ. Labor	3,987
Unemployed................................	4.5
Annual Wages...........	$48,333,543
Av. Weekly Wage...............	$336.78
Fed. Wages.............	$983,641
Ag. Net Cash Return......	$3,393,000
Prop. Value	$479,588,443
Retail Sales	$56,381,363

For explanation of sources, abbreviations and symbols, see p. 142.

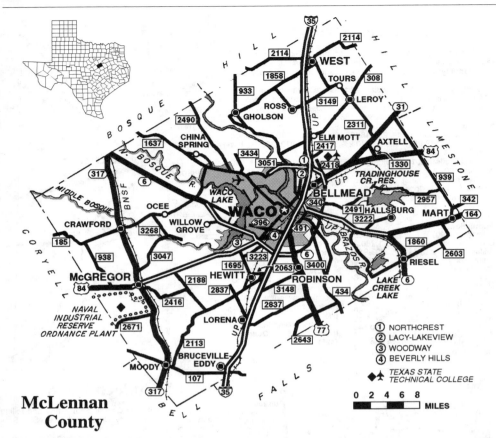

McLennan County

Physical Features: Central Texas county of mostly Blackland prairie, but rolling hills in west; drains to Bosque, Brazos rivers and Lake Waco; heavy, loam, sandy soils.

Economy: A leading distribution, government center for Central Texas; diversified manufacturing; agribusiness; education.

History: Tonkawas, Wichitas and Wacos in area. Anglo-American settlers arrived in 1840s. Indians removed to Brazos reservations in 1854. County created from Milam County in 1850; named for settler, Neil McLennan Sr.

Ethnicity, 1990: White, 146,100 (77.3%); Black, 29,520 (15.6%); American Indian, 563 (0.3%); Asian, 1,384 (0.7%); Other, 11,556 (6.1%). Hispanic, 23,643 (12.5%).

Vital Statistics, 1995: Births, 3,104; deaths, 1,914; marriages, 2,013; divorces, 1,087.

Recreation: Varied metropolitan activies; Fort Fisher Park with camping facilities; Texas Ranger Hall of Fame; Texas Sports Hall of Fame; Dr Pepper Museum; Cameron Park; Brazos River festival; zoo; historic sites, homes; museums; libraries, art center; symphony; civic theater; Baylor University events; Heart o' Texas Fair.

Minerals: Sand and gravel, limestone, oil, gas.

Agriculture: Corn, wheat, hay, grain sorghums, soybeans; beef cattle, also dairy cows; nursery crops; poultry. Market value $68.5 million.

Education: Baylor University; community college; Texas State Technical College.

WACO (108,562) county seat; varied manufacturing; tourism center, conventions; agribusiness; hospitals; Veterans Administration regional office, hospital.

Hewitt (10,837) iron works, other manufacturing; hamburger cookoff.

West (2,835) famous for Czech foods; varied manufacturing; Westfest.

Other towns include: **Axtell** (105); **Bellmead** (8,436); **Beverly Hills** (2,141); **Bruceville-Eddy** (1,270, partly in Falls County); **China Spring** (181); **Crawford** (708); **Elm Mott** (190); **Gholson** (745); **Hallsburg** (535); **Lacy-Lakeview** (4,516); **Leroy** (341); **Lorena** (1,525); **Mart** (2,033); **McGregor** (4,837) farming center, some manufacturing; private telephone museum; Frontier Founders Day in September; **Moody** (1,373); **Northcrest** (1,915); **Riesel** (889); **Robinson** (8,213); **Ross** (222); **Woodway** (9,336).

Population	202,137
(Change fm '90)	6.9
Land Area (sq. mi.)	1,041.9
Altitude (ft.)	381-734
Rainfall (in.)	32.0
Jan. mean min.	34
July mean max.	97
Growing season (days)	253
Civ. Labor.	100,023
Unemployed	4.4
Annual Wages	$1,955,038,617
Av. Weekly Wage	$438.26
Fed. Wages	$111,544,553
Ag. Net Cash Return	$9,589,000
Prop. Value	$5,505,739,446
Retail Sales	$2,048,055,202

McMullen County

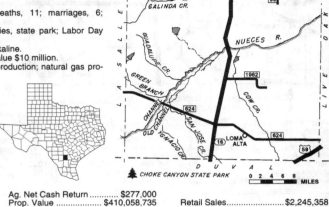

Physical Features: Southern county of brushy plain, sloping to Frio, Nueces rivers and tributaries; saline clay soils.

Economy: Livestock, hunting leases, hay.

History: Coahuiltecans, squeezed out by Lipan Apaches and other tribes. Anglo-American settlers arrived in 1858. Sheep ranching of 1870s attracted Mexican laborers. County created from Atascosa, Bexar, Live Oak counties 1858; organized 1862, reorganized 1877; named for Nueces River pioneer-empresario John McMullen.

Ethnicity, 1990: White, 713 (87.3%); Black, 0 (0.0%); American Indian, 3 (0.4%); Asian, 0 (0.0%); Other, 101 (12.4%). Hispanic, 320 (39.2%).

Vital Statistics, 1995: Births, 7; deaths, 11; marriages, 6; divorces, 4.

Recreation: Deer hunting; lake activities, state park; Labor Day rodeo; Dogtown Day cook-off in October.

Minerals: Gas, oil, lignite coal, zeolite-kaline.

Agriculture: Beef cattle; hay. Market value $10 million.

TILDEN (450) county seat; kitty-litter production; natural gas processing; ranch center; tourism.

Other towns include: **Calliham** (200).

Population	787
(Change from '90)	-3.7
Land Area (sq. mi.)	1,113.1
Altitude (ft.)	230-642
Rainfall (in.)	23.4
Jan. mean min.	40
July mean max.	98
Growing season (days)	291
Civ. Labor	280
Unemployed	2.1
Annual Wages	$4,622,659
Av. Weekly Wage	$399.88
Fed. Wages	$135,086

Ag. Net Cash Return $277,000
Prop. Value .... $410,058,735   Retail Sales $2,245,358

Medina County

Physical Features: Southwestern county with scenic hills in north; south has fertile valleys, rolling surface; Medina River, Lake.

Economy: Agribusinesses; tourism; varied manufacturing; commuters to San Antonio; government/services.

History: Lipan Apaches and Comanches. Settled by Alsatians led by Henri Castro in 1844. Mexican immigration increased after 1900. County created 1848 from Bexar; named for river, probably for Spanish engineer Pedro Medina.

Ethnicity, 1990: White, 23,608 (86.4%); Black, 92 (0.3%); American Indian, 119 (0.4%); Asian, 68 (0.2%); Other, 3,425 (12.5%). Hispanic, 12,134 (44.4%).

Vital Statistics, 1995: Births, 465; deaths, 286; marriages, 228; divorces, 136.

Recreation: A leading deer area; scenic drives; camping, fishing; historic buildings; museum; market trail days most months.

Minerals: Oil, gas, clay, sand, gravel.

Agriculture: Most income from livestock; crops include corn, grains, peanuts, hay, cotton, vegetables; 40,000 acres irrigated. Market value $52.6 million.

HONDO (7,002) county seat; Air Force screening center; aerospace industry; agribusiness; varied manufacturing; hunting leases; hospital; prisons.

Castroville (2,697), farm center; tourism; food processing; light manufacturing; Landmark Inn; St. Louis Day celebration in August.

Devine (4,931) trade center, shipping for truck crop-livestock.

Other towns include: **D'Hanis**

(548); **La Coste** (1,350); **Mico** (98); **Natalia** (1,408); **Riomedina** (53); **Yancey** (202). **Lytle**, which lies partly in Atascosa and Bexar counties, has a population of 2,556.

Population	32,493
(Change fm '90)	19.0
Land Area (sq. mi.)	1,327.9
Altitude (ft.)	635-1,995
Rainfall (in.)	27.3
Jan. mean min.	37
July mean max.	94
Growing season (days)	263
Civ. Labor	15,659
Unemployed	3.1
Annual Wages	$141,839,011
Av. Weekly Wage	$357.87
Fed. Wages	$1,934,203
Ag. Net Cash Return	$5,295,000
Prop. Value	$1,425,938,843
Retail Sales	$212,300,253

Menard County

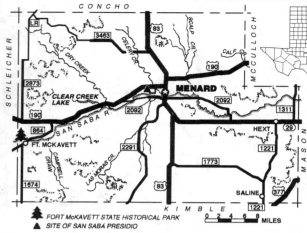

Physical Features: West central county of rolling topography, draining to San Saba River and tributaries; limestone soils.

Economy: Agribusiness; tourism; oil, gas production.

History: Apaches, followed by Comanches in 18th century. Mission Santa Cruz de San Sabá established in 1757. A few Anglo-American and German settlers arrived in 1840s. County created from Bexar County in 1858, organized, 1871; named for Galveston's founder, Michel B. Menard.

Ethnicity, 1990: White, 2,076 (92.2%); Black, 7 (0.3%); American Indian, 5 (0.2%); Asian, 0 (0.0%); Other, 164 (7.3%). Hispanic, 726 (32.2%).

Vital Statistics, 1995: Births, 29; deaths, 40; marriages, 21; divorces, 7.

Recreation: Hunting, fishing; historic sites, including Spanish presidio, mission, state park; museum; Jim Bowie days in June.

Minerals: Oil, gas.

Agriculture: Beef cattle, sheep, goats; crops are pecans, alfalfa, peaches, melons, grapes. Market value $14.7 million.

MENARD (1,631) county seat; hunting, ranching center, hospital. Other towns include: **Fort McKavett** (15); **Hext** (73).

🌲 FORT McKAVETT STATE HISTORICAL PARK
▲ SITE OF SAN SABÁ PRESIDIO

Population **2,396**	Civ. Labor 1,102
(Change fm '90) 6.4	Unemployed 2.6
Land Area (sq. mi.) 902.0	Annual Wages $8,913,984
Altitude (ft.) 1,690-2,346	Av. Weekly Wage $295.67
Rainfall (in.) 24.3	Fed. Wages $288,035
Jan. mean min. 30	Ag. Net Cash Return $990,000
July mean max. 95	Prop. Value $232,358,830
Growing season (days) 220	Retail Sales $9,925,911

Midland County

Physical Features: Flat western county, broken by draws; sandy, loam soils.

Economy: Among leading petroleum-producing counties; distribution, administrative center for oil industry; varied manufacturing; government/services.

History: Comanches in area in 19th century. Sheep ranching developed in 1880s. Permian Basin oil boom began in 1920s. County created from Tom Green County 1885; name came from midway location on railroad between El Paso and Fort Worth.

Ethnicity, 1990: White, 86,977 (81.6%); Black, 8,281 (7.8%); American Indian, 414 (0.4%); Asian, 888 (0.8%); Other, 10,051 (9.4%). Hispanic, 22,780 (21.4%).

Vital Statistics, 1995: Births, 1,841; deaths, 799; marriages, 963; divorces, 635.

Recreation: Permian Basin Petroleum Museum, Library, Hall of Fame; Museum of Southwest; Pliska Aviation Museum; Confederate Air Force and Museum; community theater; metropolitan events; balloon fest in October.

Chihuahua Trail and Emigrant Road were pioneer trails that crossed county.

Minerals: Oil, natural gas.

Agriculture: Horses, beef cattle; cotton top crop, others are alfalfa, pecans; 12,000 acres irrigated. Market value $17.3 million.

MIDLAND (98,251) county seat;

🛩 MIDLAND AIRPORT
2🛩 MIDLAND INTERNATIONAL AIRPORT

petroleum, petrochemical center; varied manufacturing; livestock sale center; hospitals; cultural activities; junior college; Texas League baseball.

Part of **Odessa** city limits extend into Midland County.

Population **116,368**	Rainfall (in.) 15.2
(Change fm '90) 9.2	Jan. mean min. 29
Land Area (sq. mi.) 900.3	July mean max. 95
Altitude (ft.) 2,613-2,936	Growing season (days) 218
	Civ. Labor 59,986
	Unemployed 4.5
	Annual Wages $1,295,363,260
	Av. Weekly Wage $518.94
	Fed. Wages $23,524,440
	Ag. Net Cash Return $3,975,000
	Prop. Value..............$4,060,490,183
	Retail Sales $1,315,530,697

For explanation of sources, abbreviations and symbols, see p. 142.

Milam County

Physical Features: East central county of partly level Blackland; southeast rolling to Post Oak Belt; Brazos, Little rivers.

Economy: Aluminum manufacturing; other varied manufacturing; lignite mining; agribusiness.

History: Lipan Apaches, Tonkawas and Comanches in area. Mission San Francisco Xavier established in 1746. Anglo-American settlers arrived in 1834. County created 1836 from municipality named for Ben Milam, a leader who died at the battle for San Antonio in December 1835; organized 1837.

Ethnicity, 1990: White, 18,603 (81.1%); Black, 2,940 (12.8%); American Indian, 69 (0.3%); Asian, 37 (0.2%); Other, 1,297 (5.7%). Hispanic 3,456 (15.1%).

Vital Statistics, 1995: Births, 356; deaths, 299; marriages, 160; divorces, 121.

Recreation: Fishing, hunting; historic sites include Fort Sullivan, Indian battlegrounds, mission site; museum in old jail at Cameron.

Minerals: Large lignite deposits; limited oil, natural gas production.

Agriculture: Cattle, poultry, some horses; crops are hay, cotton, corn, sorghum, wheat, oats, melons, peanuts. Market value $46.5 million.

CAMERON (5,688) county seat; manufacturing; hospital; library; arts, antique auto fair in October.

Rockdale (5,309) aluminum plant, utility company; agribusiness; hospital; Jubilee Days in June.

Other towns include: **Ben Arnold** (148); **Buckholts** (366); **Burlington** (140); **Davilla** (200); **Gause** (400); **Maysfield** (140); **Milano** (450); **Thorndale** (1,291, partly in Williamson County) market center.

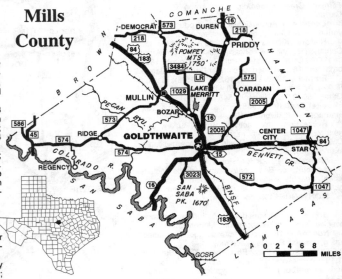

Population	23,415	
(Change fm '90)	2.0	
Land Area (sq. mi.)	1,016.8	
Altitude (ft.)	306-648	
Rainfall (in.)	34.2	
Jan. mean min.	38	
July mean max.	95	
Growing season (days)	256	
Civ. Labor	9,621	
Unemployed	5.4	
Annual Wages	$152,195,489	
Av. Weekly Wage	$473.25	
Fed. Wages	$2,055,493	
Ag. Net Cash Return	$6,522,000	
Prop. Value	$1,200,495,328	
Retail Sales	$130,119,697	

Mills County

Physical Features: West central county of hills, plateau draining to Colorado River; sandy, loam soils.

Economy: Agribusiness, hunting leases.

History: Apache-Comanche area of conflict. Anglo-Americans and a few Germans settled in 1850s. County created 1887 from Brown, Comanche, Hamilton, Lampasas counties; named for pioneer jurist John T. Mills.

Ethnicity, 1990: White, 4,238 (93.5%); Black, 10 (0.2%); American Indian, 4 (0.1%); Asian, 1 (0.0%); Other, 278 (6.1%). Hispanic, 484 (10.7%).

Vital Statistics, 1995: Births, 58; deaths, 66; marriages, 39; divorces, 15.

Recreation: Fishing; deer, dove and turkey hunting; historic suspension bridge; fiddlers' contest; rangeland recreation.

Minerals: Not significant.

Agriculture: Beef cattle; sheep, goats also raised; grain sorghum, hay, dairies; some irrigation for pecans, Bermuda grass pasture. Market value $18.4 million.

GOLDTHWAITE (1,902) county seat; agribusiness; livestock center; light manufacturing; hospital; bike rally, old timers rodeo.

Other towns include: **Mullin** (225); **Priddy** (215); **Star** (85).

For explanation of sources, abbreviations and symbols, see p. 142.

Population	5,076	
(Change fm '90)	12.0	
Land Area (sq. mi.)	748.2	
Altitude (ft.)	1,250-1,762	
Rainfall (in.)	27.6	
Jan. mean min.	34	
July mean max.	95	
Growing season (days)	230	
Civ. Labor	2,349	
Unemployed	3.7	
Annual Wages	$21,919,349	
Av. Weekly Wage	$311.96	
Fed. Wages	$600,783	
Ag. Net Cash Return	$205,000	
Prop. Value	$312,838,588	
Retail Sales	$20,510,589	

Mitchell County

Physical Features: Rolling, draining to Colorado and tributaries; sandy, red, dark soils; Lake Colorado City and Champion Creek Reservoir.

Economy: Agribusiness, oil, some manufacturing.

History: Jumano Indians in area; Comanches arrived about 1780. Anglo-American settlers arrived in late 1870s after Comanches were forced into Indian Territory. County created 1876 from Bexar District; organized 1881; named for pioneer brothers Asa and Eli Mitchell.

Ethnicity, 1990: White, 6,317 (78.8%); Black, 363 (4.5%); American Indian, 14 (0.2%); Asian, 5 (0.1%); Other, 1,317 (16.4%). Hispanic, 2,389 (29.8%).

Vital Statistics, 1995: Births, 87; deaths, 131; marriages, 61; divorces, 50.

Recreation: Lake activities; state park; museum, hunting; railhead arts, crafts show.

Minerals: Oil.

Agriculture: Beef cattle top revenue source, sheep raised; cotton principal crop, grains also produced; some irrigation for cotton, alfalfa. Market value $21.4 million.

COLORADO CITY (5,062) county seat; varied manufacturing; electric service center; hospital.

Other towns include: **Loraine** (755) and **Westbrook** (256), trade centers.

Population......................**8,594**	Jan. mean min..............................30	Annual Wages $42,523,566
(Change fm '90).....................7.2	July mean max...............................97	Av. Weekly Wage $390.58
Land Area (sq. mi.).............910.1	Growing season (days) 217	Fed. Wages $875,148
Altitude (ft.)................2,004-2,616	Civ. Labor.................................3,228	Ag. Net Cash Return..........$4,815,000
Rainfall (in.) 19.8	Unemployed.................................6.8	Prop. Value $501,359,430
		Retail Sales $39,735,053

Montague County

Physical Features: Rolling, draining to tributaries of Trinity, Red rivers; sandy loams, red, black soils; Farmers Creek Reservoir, Lake Amon G. Carter.

Economy: Agribusiness; oil production; varied manufacturing; government/services.

History: Kiowas and Wichitas who allied with Comanches. Anglo-American settlements developed in 1850s. County created from Cooke County 1857, organized 1858; named for pioneer Daniel Montague.

Ethnicity, 1990: White, 16,834 (97.5%); Black, 5 (0.0%); American Indian, 72 (0.4%); Asian, 13 (0.1%); Other, 350 (2.0%). Hispanic, 548 (3.2%).

Vital Statistics, 1995: Births, 200; deaths, 292; marriages, 186; divorces, 109.

Recreation: Lake activities; quail, turkey, deer hunting; scenic drives; museums; historical sites; Chisholm Trail Days, Jim Bowie Days in June; cattleman's roundup.

Minerals: Oil, rock, limestone.

Agriculture: Beef, dairy cattle; crops include wheat, peanuts; watermelons, cantaloupe; some irrigation for peanuts, fruits. Market value $26.8 million.

MONTAGUE (400) county seat.

Bowie (5,429) varied manufacturing, livestock, hospital, library; fall bash; second Monday trade day.

Nocona (3,181) boots, athletic goods manufacturing; hospital; Fun Day each May.

Other towns include: **Forestburg** (200); **Saint Jo** (1,137) farm center; Pioneer Days on Memorial weekend; **Forestburg** (200); **Ringgold** (100); **Sunset** (300).

Population **18,235**	Jan. mean min. 31	
(Change fm '90).....................5.6	July mean max...............................96	Av. Weekly Wage $339.45
Land Area (sq. mi.) 930.7	Growing season (days)................229	Fed. Wages $2,227,169
Altitude (ft.) 766-1,318	Civ. Labor.................................7,790	Ag. Net Cash Return..........$3,312,000
Rainfall (in.) 32.9	Unemployed.................................4.7	Prop. Value $663,664,904
	Annual Wages $75,978,875	Retail Sales...................$127,247,486

Montgomery County

Population	236,192
(Change fm '90)	29.6
Land Area (sq. mi.)	1,044.3
Altitude (ft.)	86-380
Rainfall (in.)	47.3
Jan. mean min.	38
July mean max	94
Growing season (days)	270
Civ. Labor	118,449
Unemployed	4.2
Annual Wages	$1,392,874,473
Av. Weekly Wage	$472.43
Fed. Wages	$15,899,378
Ag. Net Cash Return	-$282,000
Prop. Value	$9,594,726,169
Retail Sales	$2,216,449,156

Physical Features: Rolling, three-fourths timbered; Sam Houston National Forest; loam, sandy, alluvial soils.

Economy: Many residents work in Houston; lumber, oil production; government/services; part of Houston metropolitan area.

History: Orcoquisacs and Bidias, removed from area by 1850s. Anglo-Americans arrived in 1820s as part of Austin's colony. County created 1837 from Washington County; named for Richard Montgomery, American Revolution general.

Ethnicity, 1990: White, 166,107 (91.2%); Black, 7,763 (4.3%); American Indian, 687 (0.4%); Asian, 1,232 (0.7%); Other, 6,412 (3.5%). Hispanic, 13,237 (7.3%).

Vital Statistics, 1995: Births, 3,456; deaths, 1,533; marriages, 2,182; divorces, 1,224.

Recreation: Hunting, fishing; Lake Conroe activities; national and state forests; hiking, boating, horseback riding; historic sites.

Minerals: Oil, gas, sand, gravel.

Agriculture: Timber; beef cattle, horses, ratite birds, swine; Hay and greenhouse nurseries; also blueberries and peaches. Market value $8.9 million.

CONROE (39,387) county seat; residential community with many people working in Houston; some manufacturing; food processing; hospital.

The Woodlands (37,568) planned community.

Other towns include: **Cut and Shoot** (1,090); **Dobbin** (170); **Magnolia** (1,236); **Montgomery** (447) historic buildings, antique stores; **New Caney** (2,771); **Patton Village** (1,311); **Pinehurst** (4,073); **Porter** (2,146); **Roman Forest** (1,261); **Splendora** (845); **Willis** (4,195); **WoodBranch** (1,491); **Woodloch** (369).

① ROMAN FOREST
② PATTON VILLAGE
③ WOODBRANCH
④ WOODLOCH

Moore County

Physical Features: Northern Panhandle county; flat to rolling, broken by creeks; sandy loams; lake.

Economy: Extensive petroleum operations; major natural gas producing county; varied agribusiness.

History: Comanches, removed to Indian Territory in 1874-75; ranching began soon afterward. Farming developed after 1910. Oil boom in 1920s. County created 1876 from Bexar District; organized 1892; named for Republic of Texas navy commander E.W. Moore.

Ethnicity, 1990: White, 12,789 (71.6%); Black, 95 (0.5%); American Indian, 123 (0.7%); Asian, 282 (1.6%); Other, 4,576 (25.6%). Hispanic, 5,693 (31.9%).

Vital Statistics, 1995: Births, 381; deaths, 151; marriages, 227; divorces, 97.

Recreation: Lake Meredith activities; historical museum; arts center; free overnight RV park; dogie days in June.

Minerals: Natural gas, helium and oil.

Agriculture: Fed beef, stocker cattle, cow/calf operations; crops include corn, sorghums, wheat; about 140,000 acres irrigated for wheat, corn, sorghums. Market value $265.2 million.

DUMAS (13,438) county seat; tourist, retail trade center; varied agribusiness; hospital, hospice, retirement complex. Other towns include: **Cactus** (1,864), **Sunray** (1,798).

Population	19,049
(Change fm '90)	6.6
Land Area (sq. mi.)	899.7
Altitude (ft.)	3,221-3,770
Rainfall (in.)	17.4
Jan. mean min.	20
July mean max.	92
Growing season (days)	185
Civ. Labor	9,092
Unemployed	3.7
Annual Wages	$175,760,135
Av. Weekly Wage	$431.90
Fed. Wages	$15,899,378
Ag. Net Cash Return	$34,576,000
Prop. Value	$1,471,387,445
Retail Sales	$113,553,721

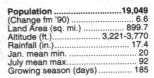

Morris County

Physical Features: East Texas county of forested hills; drains to streams, lakes.

Economy: Varied manufacturing; tourism; livestock, timber.

History: Caddo Indians until 1790s. Kickapoo and other tribes in area 1820s-30s. Anglo-American settlement began in mid-1830s. Antebellum slaveholding area. County named for legislator-jurist W.W. Morris; created from Titus County and organized in 1875.

Ethnicity, 1990: White, 9,770 (74.0%); Black, 3,227 (24.4%); American Indian, 70 (0.5%); Asian, 18 (0.1%); Other, 115 (0.9%). Hispanic, 239 (1.8%).

Vital Statistics, 1995: Births, 195; deaths, 170; marriages, 143; divorces, 91.

Recreation: Activities on Lake O' the Pines, small lakes; fishing, hunting; state park; old courthouse museum in Daingerfield.

Minerals: Iron ore.

Agriculture: Beef cattle, broiler production; pine and hardwood marketed; hay, watermelons; new greenhouse development. Market value $16.2 million.

DAINGERFIELD (2,625) county seat; varied manufacturing; hospital; library; Northeast Texas Community College; Captain Daingerfield Day in October.

Other towns include: **Cason** (173); **Lone Star** (1,608) oil-field equipment manufactured, catfish farming, Starfest in September; **Naples** (1,467) trailer manufacturing, livestock, watermelon festival in July; **Omaha** (960).

Population	**13,101**
(Change fm '90)	-0.8
Land Area (sq. mi.)	254.5
Altitude (ft.)	268-537
Rainfall (in.)	44.6
Jan. mean min.	35
July mean max.	95
Growing season (days)	236
Civ. Labor	6,192
Unemployed	8.0
Annual Wages	$136,729,084
Av. Weekly Wage	$533.96
Fed. Wages	$1,003,404
Ag. Net Cash Return	$2,184,000
Prop. Value	$546,346,340
Retail Sales	$50,099,698

Motley County

Physical Features: Western county just below Caprock; rough terrain, broken by Pease tributaries; sandy to red clay soils.

Economy: Government/services; ranching; cotton; oil production.

History: Comanches, removed to Indian Territory by U.S. Army in 1874-75. Ranching began in late 1870s. County created out of Bexar District 1876; organized 1891; named for Dr. J.W. Mottley, signer of Texas Declaration of Independence (name misspelled in statute).

Ethnicity, 1990: White, 1,362 (88.9%); Black, 68 (4.4%); American Indian, 5 (0.3%); Asian, 4 (0.3%); Other, 93 (6.1%). Hispanic, 136 (8.9%).

Vital Statistics, 1995: Births, 7; deaths, 25; marriages, 12; divorces, 1.

Recreation: Quail, dove, deer hunting; Matador Ranch headquarters; spring-fed pool at Roaring Springs; settlers reunion in August.

Minerals: Oil, gas, sand, gravel.

Agriculture: Beef cattle, cow-calf stocker operations most profitable; cotton, peanuts grown; also hay and wheat; 4,000 acres irrigated. Market value $13.4 million.

MATADOR (719) county seat; farm trade center; pony express days in June.

Other towns include: **Flomot** (181), **Roaring Springs** (228) varied manufacturing.

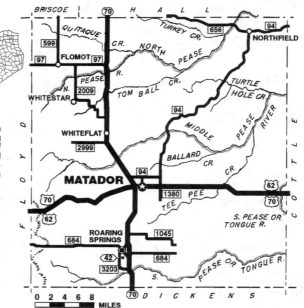

For explanation of sources, abbreviations and symbols, see p. 142.

Population	**1,404**
(Change fm '90)	-8.4
Land Area (sq. mi.)	989.4
Altitude (ft.)	1,928-3,034
Rainfall (in.)	21.2
Jan. mean min.	26
July mean max.	95
Growing season (days)	218
Civ. Labor	675
Unemployed	3.9
Annual Wages	$5,605,291
Av. Weekly Wage	$323.64
Fed. Wages	$370,480
Ag. Net Cash Return	$2,064,000
Prop. Value	$102,926,468
Retail Sales	$4,690,995

Nacogdoches County

Physical Features: East Texas county on divide between streams; hilly; two-thirds forested; red, gray, sandy soils; Sam Rayburn Reservoir.

Economy: Agribusiness; timber; manufacturing; education; tourism.

History: Caddo tribes, joined by displaced Cherokees in 1820s. Indians moved west of Brazos by 1840. Spanish missions established in 1716. Spanish settlers in mid-1700s. Anglo-Americans arrived in 1820s. Original county of Republic 1836, organized 1837.

Ethnicity, 1990: White, 43,772 (79.9%); Black, 9,020 (16.5%); American Indian, 144 (0.3%); Asian, 311 (0.6%); Other, 1,506 (2.8%). Hispanic, 2,788 (5.1%).

Vital Statistics, 1995: Births, 816; deaths, 479; marriages, 582; divorces, 162.

Recreation: Lake, river activities; Stephen F. Austin University events; Angelina National Forest; historic sites major tourist attractions, including Old Stone Fort, pioneer homes, museums, Piney Woods Fair, Blueberry Festival in June.

Minerals: First Texas oil found here, 1866; gas, oil, clay, stone.

Agriculture: A leading poultry-producing county; extensive dairy operations, beef cattle raised. Market value $126.1 million. Substantial timber sold.

NACOGDOCHES (32,358) county seat; varied manufacturing; lumber mills, wood products; trade center; hospitals; Stephen F. Austin University.

Other towns include: **Appleby** (485), **Chireno** (441), **Cushing** (644), **Douglass** (75); **Etoile** (70); **Garrison** (893); **Martinsville** (126); **Sacul** (170); **Woden** (70).

Population	57,805
(Change fm '90)	5.6
Land Area (sq. mi.)	946.8
Altitude (ft.)	182-655
Rainfall (in.)	47.5
Jan. mean min.	36
July mean max.	94
Growing season (days)	243
Civ. Labor	27,951
Unemployed	5.3
Annual Wages	$410,213,718
Av. Weekly Wage	$381.79
Fed. Wages	$6,321,704
Ag. Net Cash Return	$16,667,000
Prop. Value	$1,838,920,758
Retail Sales	$502,323,684

For explanation of sources, abbreviations and symbols, see p. 142.

East Texas is a region of many lakes and forests. In Nacogdoches County some two-thirds of the area is covered with pine and other trees. Texas Almanac photo.

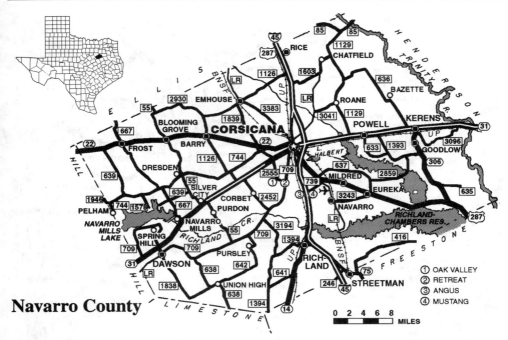

Navarro County

Physical Features: North central county of level Blackland, some rolling; drains to creeks, Trinity River; Navarro Mills Lake, Richland-Chambers Reservoir.

Economy: Diversified manufacturing; agribusinesses; oil-field operations, distribution.

History: Kickapoo and Comanche area. Anglo-Americans settled in late 1830s. Antebellum slaveholding area. County created from Robertson County, organized in 1846; named for Republic of Texas leader Jose Antonio Navarro.

Ethnicity, 1990: White, 30,322 (75.9%); Black, 7,574 (19.0%); American Indian, 127 (0.3%); Asian, 271 (0.7%); Other, 1,632 (4.1%). Hispanic, 2,891 (7.2%).

Vital Statistics, 1995: Births, 640; deaths, 480; marriages, 377; divorces, 289.

Recreation: Lake activities; Pioneer Village; historic buildings; youth exposition, Derrick Days in April.

Minerals: Longest continuous Texas oil flow; more than 200 million barrels produced since 1895; natural gas, sand and gravel also produced.

Agriculture: Beef cattle; hay; also, horses, emus and ostriches raised; crops include cotton, grain sorghums, wheat, herbs, corn. Market value $33 million.

CORSICANA (24,042) county seat; major distribution center; varied manufacturing; agribusiness; hospital; Navarro College; Texas Youth Commission facility.

Other towns include: **Angus** (425); **Barry** (197); **Blooming Grove** (860); **Chatfield** (40); **Dawson** (782); **Emhouse** (232); **Eureka** (292) **Frost** (619); **Goodlow** (373); **Kerens** (1,703), some manufacturing; **Mildred** (207); **Mustang** (45); **Navarro** (254); **Oak Valley** (427); **Powell** (113); **Purdon** (133); **Retreat** (349); **Rice** (634, partly in Ellis County); **Richland** (257).

Population	**42,405**
(Change fm '90)	6.2
Land Area (sq. mi.)	1,071.2
Altitude (ft.)	293-536
Rainfall (in.)	37.9
Jan. mean min.	33
July mean max.	94
Growing season (days)	253
Civ. Labor	21,368
Unemployed	5.6
Annual Wages	$295,748,476
Av. Weekly Wage	$379.63
Fed. Wages	$3,466,060
Ag. Net Cash Return	$3,546,000
Prop. Value	$1,486,439,770
Retail Sales	$350,918,173

Newton County

Physical Features: East Texas county of densely forested hills, valleys; spring-fed streams; Toledo Bend Reservoir; Sabine River; mostly sandy soils.

Economy: Forestry, tourism.

History: Caddo Indian area. Displaced Coushattas moved across area from South. Anglo-American settlement established in 1830s. Antebellum slaveholding area. County created 1846 from Jasper County; named for American Revolutionary soldier John Newton.

Ethnicity, 1990: White, 10,402 (76.7%); Black, 3,039 (22.4%); American Indian, 44 (0.3%); Asian, 11 (0.1%); Other, 73 (0.5%). Hispanic, 153 (1.1%).

Vital Statistics, 1995: Births, 178; deaths, 119; marriages, 142; divorces, 86.

Recreation: Toledo Bend Reservoir; water sports; fishing, hunting;

Newton County

tourism; state forest; Azalea Canyons; spring festival. Belgrade, site of early town.

Minerals: Oil, gas.

Agriculture: Peaches, vegetables raised. Market value $1.2 million. Major forestry area.

NEWTON (1,984) county seat; lumber manufacturing; plywood mill; hospital; private prison unit; clinics; tourist center; airport.

Deweyville (1,420) commercial center for forestry, farming area.

Other towns include: **Bon Wier** (475); **Burkeville** (515); **Call** (170); **Wiergate** (461).

(Map on preceding page.)

Population	14,414
(Change fm '90)	6.2
Land Area (sq. mi.)	932.8
Altitude (ft.)	23-510
Rainfall (in.)	56
Jan. mean min.	40
July mean max.	93
Growing season (days)	228
Civ. Labor	6,097
Unemployed	11.5
Annual Wages	$44,662,120
Av. Weekly Wage	$381.82
Fed. Wages	$699,805
Ag. Net Cash Return	-$724,000
Prop. Value	$755,876,810
Retail Sales	$78,060,100

Nolan County

Physical Features: On divide between Brazos, Colorado watersheds; mostly red sandy loams, some waxy, sandy soils; lakes.

Economy: Varied manufacturing; ranching; oil and gas production.

History: Anglo-American settlement began in late 1870s. County created from Bexar, Young districts 1876; organized 1881; named for adventurer Philip Nolan killed near Waco.

Ethnicity, 1990: White, 12,942 (78.0%); Black, 775 (4.7%); American Indian, 46 (0.3%); Asian, 18 (0.1%); Other, 2,813 (17.0%). Hispanic, 4,246 (25.6%).

Vital Statistics, 1995: Births, 254; deaths, 191; marriages, 158; divorces, 113.

Recreation: Lakes; hunting; rattlesnake roundup; pioneer museum; national junior rodeo finals in summer.

Minerals: Oil, gas, gypsum, limestone, and gravel.

Agriculture: Beef cattle, sheep, Angora goats, hogs; ratites; cotton is the principal crop, sorghums also raised. Market value $44.2 million.

SWEETWATER (12,004) county seat; gypsum plant; varied manufacturing; hospital; Texas State Technical College.

Other towns include: **Blackwell**

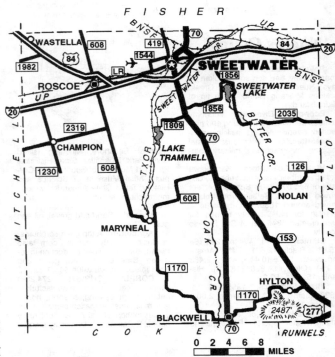

(370, partly in Coke County), Oak Creek Reservoir; **Maryneal** (61); **Nolan** (47); **Roscoe** (1,426).

Population	17,017
(Change fm '90)	2.5
Land Area (sq. mi.)	912.1
Altitude (ft.)	1,990-2,603
Rainfall (in.)	24.4
Jan. mean min.	30
July mean max.	94
Growing season (days)	221
Civ. Labor	7,813
Unemployed	7.3
Annual Wages	$144,400,438
Av. Weekly Wage	$378.37
Fed. Wages	$1,757,120
Ag. Net Cash Return	$6,100,000
Prop. Value	$783,759,299
Retail Sales	$116,148,110

For explanation of sources, abbreviations and symbols, see p. 142.

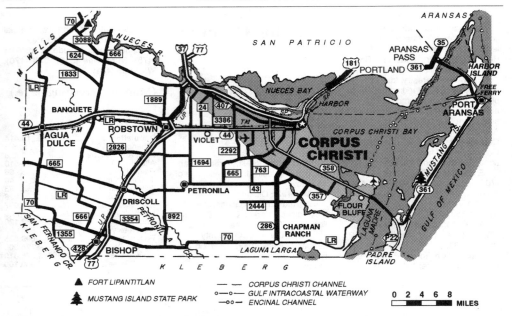

Symbols:
▲ FORT LIPANTITLAN
🌲 MUSTANG ISLAND STATE PARK

— — CORPUS CHRISTI CHANNEL
∘–∘– GULF INTRACOASTAL WATERWAY
–∘∘– ENCINAL CHANNEL

0 2 4 6 8 MILES

Nueces County

Physical Features: Southern Gulf Coast county; flat, rich soils, broken by bays, Nueces River, Petronila Creek; includes Mustang Island, north tip of Padre Island.

Economy: Diversified economy includes petroleum processing and production; deepwater port facilities; agriculture; tourism, conventions; coastal shipping; manufacturing; military complex.

History: Coahuiltecan, Karankawa and other tribes who succumbed to disease or fled by 1840s. Spanish settlers arrived in 1760s. Settlers from Ireland arrived around 1830. County name is Spanish for nuts; county named for river; created 1846 out of San Patricio County.

Ethnicity, 1990: White, 220,168 (75.6%); Black, 12,691 (4.4%); American Indian, 1,175 (0.4%); Asian, 2,483 (0.9%); Other, 54,628 (18.8%). Hispanic, 152,051 (52.2%).

Vital Statistics, 1995: Births, 5,339; deaths, 2,313; marriages, 2,607; divorces, 1,670.

Recreation: Major resort area; fishing, water sports; Padre Island National Seashore; Mustang Island State Park; Lipantitlan State Historical Park; Art Museum of South Texas, Corpus Christi Museum of Science and History; Texas State Aquarium; various metropolitan events; greyhound race track.

Minerals: Sand and gravel, oil and gas.

Agriculture: A top grain sorghums-producing county; cotton, corn also raised; sunflower seed production introduced. Beef cattle, meat goats and hogs raised. Market value $45.9 million.

CORPUS CHRISTI (274,234) county seat; varied manufacturing; petroleum processing; seaport; hospitals; museums; recreation centers; tourist destination; Naval Air Station; Army depot; Texas A&M University-Corpus Christi; Del Mar College; Buccaneer Days; replicas of Columbus' ships on display, U.S.S. Lexington museum.

Port Aransas (2,698) tourism, sea research institute, fishing accomodations, fisheries management, deep sea roundup, birding facility.

Robstown (13,190) market center for oil, farm area; hosptial.

Other towns include: **Agua Dulce** (734); **Banquete** (449); **Bishop** (3,392), petrochemical, pharmaceutical manufacturing, fall carnival; **Chapman Ranch** (100); **Driscoll** (719); **Petronila** (807). **Flour Bluff** now part of Corpus Christi.

Population	**309,020**
(Change fm '90)	6.1
Land Area (sq. mi.)	835.9
Altitude (ft.)	sea level-129
Rainfall (in.)	30.1
Jan. mean min.	45
July mean max.	93
Growing season (days)	309
Civ. Labor	149,987
Unemployed	8.4
Annual Wages	$3,090,225,795
Av. Weekly Wage	$466.26
Fed. Wages	$220,384,288
Ag. Net Cash Return	$4,360,000
Prop. Value	$12,002,130,789
Retail Sales	$3,070,928,743

A beach on North Padre Island. Texas Almanac photo.

Ochiltree County

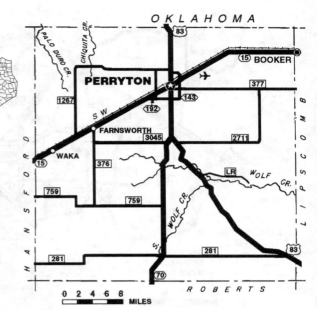

Physical Features: Panhandle county bordering Oklahoma; level, broken by creeks; deep loam, clay soils.

Economy: Oil; agribusiness, center of large feedlot operations, hunting leases.

History: Apaches, pushed out by Comanches in late 1700s. Comanches removed to Indian Territory in 1874-75. Ranching developed in 1880s; farming after 1900. County created from Bexar District 1876, organized 1889; named for Republic of Texas leader W.B. Ochiltree.

Ethnicity, 1990: White, 8,023 (87.9%); Black, 2 (0.0%); American Indian, 105 (1.2%); Asian, 8 (0.1%); Other, 990 (10.8%). Hispanic, 1,641 (18.0%).

Vital Statistics, 1995: Births, 139; deaths, 91; marriages, 100; divorces, 57.

Recreation: Wolf Creek park; Springfest, Wheatheart of the Nation celebration in August; Museum of the Plains; Indian "Buried City" site.

Minerals: Oil, natural gas, caliche, gravel.

Agriculture: Beef cattle, hogs; crops include wheat, grain sorghums, corn, hay; 80,000 acres irrigated for most crops. Market value $123.8 million.

PERRYTON (7,622) county seat; oilfield services, equipment manufacturing; cattle feeding; grain center; hospital; convention center.

Other towns include: **Farnsworth** (130); **Waka** (65). Also, **Booker** (1,235, mostly in Lipscomb County).

Population	9,116	Civ. Labor	4,709
(Change fm '90)	-0.1	Unemployed	3.4
Land Area (sq. mi.)	917.6	Annual Wages	$78,840,409
Altitude (ft.)	2,642-3,007	Av. Weekly Wage	$424.29
Rainfall (in.)	19.5	Fed. Wages	$951,495
Jan. mean min.	17	Ag. Net Cash Return	$18,389,000
July mean max.	94	Prop. Value	$504,866,743
Growing season (days)	191	Retail Sales	$66,772,739

Oldham County

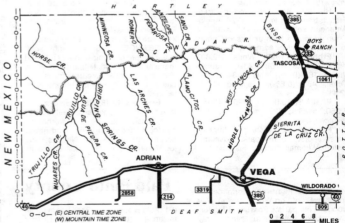

(E) CENTRAL TIME ZONE
(W) MOUNTAIN TIME ZONE

Physical Features: Northwestern Panhandle county; level, broken by Ca-nadian River and tributaries.

Economy: Ranching center.

History: Apaches; followed later by Comanches, Kiowas. U.S. Army removed Indians in 1875. Anglo ranchers and Spanish *pastores* (sheep men) from New Mexico were in area in 1870s. County created 1876 from Bexar District; organized 1880; named for editor-Confederate senator W.S. Oldham.

Ethnicity, 1990: White, 2,112 (92.7%); Black, 9 (0.4%); American Indian, 29 (1.3%); Asian, 18 (0.8%); Other, 110 (4.8%). Hispanic, 200 (8.8%).

Vital Statistics, 1995: Births, 15; deaths, 16; marriages, 22; divorces, 8.

Recreation: Old Tascosa with Boot Hill Cemetery nearby, pioneer town; County Roundup in August; midway point on old Route 66.

Minerals: Sand and gravel, oil, natural gas, stone.

Agriculture: Beef cattle; crops include wheat, grain sorghums. Market value $81.6 million.

VEGA (874) county seat; ranch trade center.

Other towns include: **Adrian** (217); **Wildorado** (180). Cal Farley's Boys Ranch.

Population	2,405	Land Area (sq. mi.)	1,500.7
(Change fm '90)	5.6	Altitude (ft.)	3,238-4,171
		Rainfall (in.)	17.4
		Jan. mean min.	19
		July mean max.	91
		Growing season (days)	186
		Civ. Labor	1,155
		Unemployed	3.9
		Annual Wages	$15,990,164
		Av. Weekly Wage	$368.95
		Fed. Wages	$206,006
		Ag. Net Cash Return	$5,620,000
		Prop. Value	$166,544,290
		Retail Sales	$9,133,218

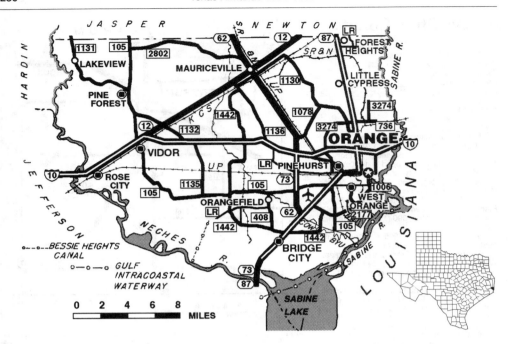

Orange County

Physical Features: In southeastern corner of the state; bounded by Sabine, Neches rivers, Sabine Lake; coastal soils; two-thirds timbered.

Economy: Petrochemicals; shipping; agribusinesses; tourism; lumber processing; county part of Beaumont-Port Arthur metropolitan area.

History: Atakapan Indian area. French traders in area by 1720. Anglo-American settlement began in 1820s. County created from Jefferson County in 1852; named for early orange grove.

Ethnicity, 1990: White, 72,607 (90.2%); Black, 6,768 (8.4%); American Indian, 189 (0.2%); Asian, 484 (0.6%); Other, 461 (0.6%). Hispanic, 1,933 (2.4%).

Vital Statistics, 1995: Births, 1,250; deaths, 722; marriages, 780; divorces, 643.

Recreation: Fishing, hunting; water sports; county park; museums; historical homes; crawfish festivals.

Minerals: Salt, oil, gas, clays, sand and gravel.

Agriculture: Timber. Beef cattle, Christmas trees and rice are top revenue sources; honey a significant revenue producer; other agriculture includes vegetables, horses, hogs; market value $2.9 million. Hunting leases.

ORANGE (20,508) county seat; seaport; petrochemical plants; varied manufacturing; food, timber processing; shipping; hospital; theater, museums; Lamar University branch; gumbo festival in May.

Bridge City (8,525) varied manufacturing; ship repair yard; steel fabrication; fish farming; government/services; library; tall bridge and newer suspension bridge over Neches; stop for Monarch butterfly in fall during its migration to Mexico.

Vidor (12,096) steel processing; railroad-car refinishing; library.

Other towns include: **Mauriceville** (2,417); **Pine Forest** (869); **Pinehurst** (2,831); **Rose City** (690); **West Orange** (4,945).

Population	85,087
(Change fm '90)	5.7
Land Area (sq. mi.)	356.4
Altitude (ft.)	sea level-25
Rainfall (in.)	58.3
Jan. mean min.	39
July mean max.	91
Growing season (days)	240
Civ. Labor	41,400
Unemployed	10.8
Annual Wages	$652,119,997
Av. Weekly Wage	$532.23
Fed. Wages	$4,687,752
Ag. Net Cash Return	$544,000
Prop. Value	$3,732,988,130
Retail Sales	$492,649,980

Palo Pinto County

Physical Features: North central county west of Fort Worth; broken, hilly, wooded in parts; Possum Kingdom Lake, Lake Palo Pinto; sandy, gray, black soils.

Economy: Varied manufacturing; tourism; petroleum; agribusiness.

History: Anglo-American ranchers arrived in 1850s. Conflicts began settlers and numerous Indian tribes who had sought refuge on Brazos resulted in Texas Rangers removing Indians in 1856. County created 1856 from Bosque, Navarro counties; organized 1857; named for creek (in Spanish name means painted stick).

Ethnicity, 1990: White, 22,810 (91.0%); Black, 792 (3.2%); American Indian, 87 (0.3%); Asian, 171 (0.7%); Other, 1,195 (4.8%). Hispanic, 2,301 (9.2%).

Vital Statistics, 1995: Births, 303; deaths, 348; marriages, 229; divorces, 177.

Recreation: Lake activities; hunting, fishing, water sports; state park.

Minerals: Oil, gas, clays, sand and gravel.

Agriculture: Beef cattle, prime revenue producer; wheat and hay; market value $13.1 million. Cedar fence posts marketed.

PALO PINTO (411) county seat; old settlers reunion; government center.

Mineral Wells (14,762) varied manufacturing; tourism; agriculture; hospital; Weatherford College extension; Crazy Water Festival in June; state park east of city in Parker County.

Other towns include: **Gordon** (430), **Graford** (549), **Mingus** (219), **Santo** (445), **Strawn** (646).

(Map on next page.)

For explanation of sources, abbreviations and symbols, see p. 142.

Palo Pinto County

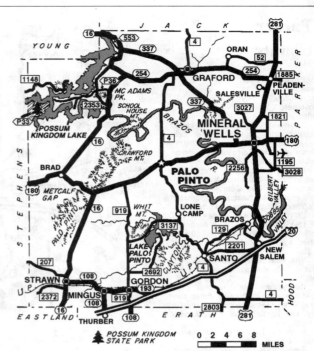

Population	25,119
(Change fm '90)	0.3
Land Area (sq. mi.)	953.0
Altitude (ft.)	782-1,470
Rainfall (in.)	32.2
Jan. mean min.	30
July mean max.	96
Growing season (days)	221
Civ. Labor	12,490
Unemployed	7.6
Annual Wages	$149,295,643
Av. Weekly Wage	$361.87
Fed. Wages	$2,198,233
Ag. Net Cash Return	$687,000
Prop. Value	$1,063,506,573
Retail Sales	$204,871,634

🌲 POSSUM KINGDOM STATE PARK

0 2 4 6 8 MILES

Panola County

Physical Features: East Texas county; sixty percent forested, rolling plain; broken by Sabine, Murvaul Creek and Lake, Toledo Bend Reservoir.

Economy: Gas processing; oil-field operation; agribusinesses; varied manufacturing; forest industries.

History: Caddo area. Anglo-American settlement established in 1833. Antebellum slaveholding area. County name is Indian word for cotton; created from Harrison, Shelby counties 1846.

Ethnicity, 1990: White, 17,702 (80.3%); Black, 4,057 (18.4%); American Indian, 57 (0.3%); Asian, 23 (0.1%); Other, 196 (0.9%). Hispanic, 477 (2.2%).

Vital Statistics, 1995: Births, 234; deaths, 274; marriages, 230; divorces, 132.

Recreation: Lake fishing, other water activities; hunting; scenic drives; Jim Reeves memorial; historic sites, homes; museum.

Minerals: Oil, gas, lignite.

Agriculture: A leading broiler-producing county; beef cattle, dairies, hay, watermelons; market value $32.8 million. Timber sales significant.

CARTHAGE (6,531) county seat; petroleum processing; poultry; sawmills; hospital; junior college.

Other towns include: **Beckville** (766), **Clayton** (79); **DeBerry** (191), **Gary** (276), **Long Branch** (181) **Panola** (296). Also, **Tatum** (1,382) mostly in Rusk County.

Population	22,096
(Change fm '90)	0.3
Land Area (sq. mi.)	801.0
Altitude (ft.)	192-481
Rainfall (in.)	48.0
Jan. mean min.	33
July mean max.	94
Growing season (days)	240
Civ. Labor	8,156
Unemployed	10.6
Annual Wages	$118,766,990
Av. Weekly Wage	$376.42
Fed.Wages	$2,274,368
Ag. Net Cash Return	$2,748,000
Prop. Value	$2,055,557,836
Retail Sales	$114,238,383

0 2 4 6 8 MILES

For explanation of sources, abbreviations and symbols, see p. 142.

Parker County

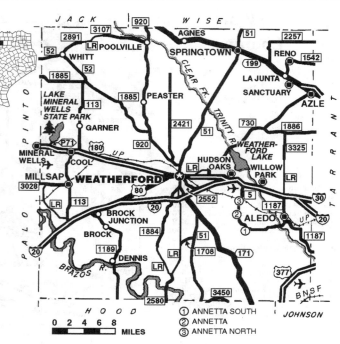

Physical Features: Hilly, broken by Brazos, Trinity tributaries, lakes; varied soils.

Economy: Agribusiness; varied manufacturing; government/services; many residents work in Fort Worth; county part of Fort Worth-Arlington metropolitan area.

History: Comanche and Kiowa area in late 1840s when Anglo-American settlers arrived. County named for pioneer legislator Isaac Parker; created 1855 from Bosque, Navarro counties.

Ethnicity, 1990: White, 62,267 (96.1%); Black, 589 (0.9%); American Indian, 367 (0.6%); Asian, 231 (0.4%); Other, 1,331 (2.1%). Hispanic, 2,697 (4.2%).

Vital Statistics, 1995: Births, 895; deaths, 548; marriages, 640; divorces, 458.

Recreation: Water sports; state park; nature trails; hunting; horse racing at Trinity Meadows; peach festival in July and frontier days; first Monday trade days monthly.

Minerals: Natural gas, oil, stone, sand and gravel, clays.

Agriculture: Hay, beef cattle, horticultural plants, horses, dairies, peaches, peanuts, pecans raised. Market value $41.8 million.

WEATHERFORD (17,711) county seat; varied manufacturing; commuting; agribusiness center; hospital; Weatherford College.

Other towns include: **Aledo** (1,369); **Cool** (259); **Dennis** (86); **Hudson Oaks** (1,189); **Millsap** (534); **Peaster** (80); **Poolville** (230); **Reno**

① ANNETTA SOUTH
② ANNETTA
③ ANNETTA NORTH

(2,595); **Sanctuary** (280); **Springtown** (1,951) government/services, manufacturing; **Whitt** (38); **Willow Park** (2,708). Also, **Azle** (10,670) mostly in Tarrant County, and part of **Mineral Wells.**

Population 72,373
(Change fm '90) 11.7
Land Area (sq. mi.) 903.6
Altitude (ft.) 718-966
Rainfall (in.) 32.9

Jan. mean min. 28
July mean max. 96
Growing season (days) 225
Civ. Labor 37,636
Unemployed 3.6
Annual Wages $290,435,306
Av. Weekly Wage $381.44
Fed. Wages $4,784,193
Ag. Net Cash Return..........$990,000
Prop. Value $2,673,474,1414
Retail Sales.................$656,635,236

Parmer County

(E) CENTRAL TIME ZONE
(W) MOUNTAIN TIME ZONE

Population 10,285
(Change fm '90) 4.3
Land Area (sq. mi.) 881.7
Altitude (ft.) 3,926-4,163
Rainfall (in.) 16.8
Jan. mean min. 21
July mean max. 90
Growing season (days) 183
Civ. Labor 4,436
Unemployed 4.1
Total Wages.................$94,292,631
Av. Weekly Wage $408.13
Fed. Wages $2,103,151
Ag. Net Cash Return..........$40,028,000
Prop. Value $479,336,643
Retail Sales.................$43,547,817

Physical Features: Western High Plains, broken by draws, playas; sandy, clay, loam soils.

Economy: Cattle feeding; grain elevators; meat-packing plant; varied other agribusinesses.

History: Apaches, pushed out in late 1700s by Comanches, Kiowas. U.S. Army removed Indians in 1874-75. Anglo-Americans arrived in 1880s. Mexican migration increased after 1950. County named for Republic figure Martin Parmer; created from Bexar District 1876, organized 1907.

(Map on preceding page.)

Parmer County

Ethnicity, 1990: White, 8,980 (91.0%); Black, 123 (1.2%); American Indian, 29 (0.3%); Asian, 24 (0.2%); Other, 707 (7.2%). Hispanic, 4,096 (41.5%).

Vital Statistics, 1995: Births, 176; deaths, 82; marriages, 197; divorces, 32.

Recreation: Border Town Days.

Minerals: Not significant.

Agriculture: Among leading counties in total farm income. Beef cattle; crops include corn, grain sorghums, wheat, sugar beets, cotton; soybeans and vegetables also raised; 190,000 acres irrigated. Market value $438.8 million.

FARWELL (1,485) county seat; agribusiness center; grain storage; plants make farm equipment.

Friona (3,785) grain elevators, meat packing, feedlots, hospital; Maize Days in September.

Other towns include: **Bovina** (1,766) farm trade center; **Lazbuddie** (248).

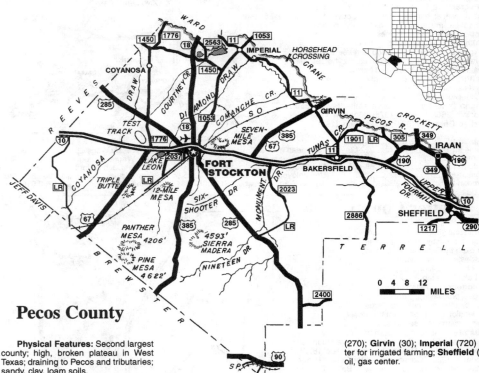

Pecos County

Physical Features: Second largest county; high, broken plateau in West Texas; draining to Pecos and tributaries; sandy, clay, loam soils.

Economy: Agribusiness center; oil, gas chief factors; tourism; government/services.

History: Comanches in area when military outpost established in 1859. Settlement began after Civil War. County created from Presidio 1871; organized 1872; named for Pecos River, name origin uncertain.

Ethnicity, 1990: White, 9,449 (64.4%); Black, 62 (0.4%); American Indian, 45 (0.3%); Asian, 31 (0.2%); Other, 5,088 (34.7%). Hispanic, 4,331 (56.8%).

Vital Statistics, 1995: Births, 214; deaths, 118; marriages, 114; divorces, 55.

Recreation: Old Fort Stockton, Annie Riggs Museum, stagecoach stop; scenic drives; Dinosaur Track Roadside Park; cattle-trail sites; archaeological museum with oil, ranch-heritage collections; Cinco de Mayo.

Minerals: Natural gas, oil.

Agriculture: Most income from vegetables, cotton, pecans and hay; beef cattle. Other crops include large vineyard and other fruits and nuts; 50,000 acres irrigated. Market value $28.3 million.

FORT STOCKTON (9,072) county seat; distribution center for petroleum industry; oil, gas processing; tourism; tire-testing center; varied manufacturing; winery; hospital; historical tours; junior college extension; prison units.

Iraan (1,252) oil, gas center, tourism; ranching, meat processing, hospital, birthplace of Alley Oop comic strip, chili, brisket cookoff.

Other towns include: **Coyanosa** (270); **Girvin** (30); **Imperial** (720) center for irrigated farming; **Sheffield** (600) oil, gas center.

Population	16,144
(Change fm '90)	10.0
Land Area (sq. mi.)	4,764.0
Altitude (ft.)	2,168-4,797
Rainfall (in.)	13.9
Jan. mean min.	30
July mean max.	95
Growing season (days)	224
Civ. Labor	6,993
Unemployed	6.1
Annual Wages	$101,147,839
Av. Weekly Wage	$392.56
Fed. Wages	$1,543,195
Ag. Net Cash Return	$4,793,000
Prop. Value	$2,749,739,897
Retail Sales	$97,053,968

For explanation of sources, abbreviations and symbols, see p. 142.

Polk County

Physical Features: Rolling; densely forested, with Big Thicket, unique plant, animal life; Neches, Trinity rivers, tributaries.

Economy: Timber; lumber production; tourism; manufacturing.

History: Caddo area; Alabama and Coushatta Indians arrived from Louisiana in late 1700s. Anglo-American and Hispanic families received land grants in early 1830s. County named for U.S. President James K. Polk; created from Liberty County, organized 1846.

Ethnicity, 1990: White, 25,100 (81.8%); Black, 3,896 (12.7%); American Indian, 662 (2.2%); Asian, 78 (0.3%); Other, 951 (3.1%). Hispanic, 1,610 (5.2%).

Vital Statistics, 1995: Births, 495; deaths, 472; marriages, 335; divorces, 147.

Recreation: Lake and state park; fishing, other water activities; hunting; Alabama-Coushatta Indian Reservation, museum; Big Thicket; woodlands trails, champion trees; historic homes.

Minerals: Oil, gas, sand, gravel.

Agriculture: Hay, greenhouse nurseries; vegetables raised; income also from beef cattle, horses. Market value $6 million. Timber and hardwood.

LIVINGSTON (7,037) county seat; lumber, tourism, oil center.

Other towns include: **Ace** (40); **Camden** (1,200); **Corrigan** (1,880) plywood plant; **Dallardsville** (350); **Goodrich** (266); **Leggett** (375); **Moscow** (170) historic sites; **Onalaska** (924); **Seven Oaks** (181).

Population...............................38,305	July mean max...............................94	Av. Weekly Wage...................$389.83
(Change fm '90)........................24.8	Growing season (days)................250	Fed. Wages $2,341,351
Land Area (sq. mi.)..................1,057.4	Civ. Labor.................................15,006	Ag. Net Cash Return..............$336,000
Altitude (ft.)..............................68-404	Unemployed....................................5.6	Prop. Value $1,601,354,195
Rainfall (in.)................................48.7	Annual Wages...............$189,267,634	Retail Sales....................$282,016,141
Jan. mean min..............................35		

Potter County

Physical Features: Panhandle county; mostly level, part rolling; broken by Canadian River and tributaries; sandy, sandy loam, chocolate loam, clay soils; Lake Meredith.

Economy: Petrochemicals; gas processing; transportation, distribution hub for large area; feedlot operations, agribusinesses; tourism; government/services.

History: Apaches, pushed out by Comanches in 1700s. Comanches removed to Indian Territory in 1874-75. Ranching began in late 1870s. Oil boom in 1920s. County named for Robert Potter, Republic leader; created 1876 from Bexar District; organized 1887.

Ethnicity, 1990: White, 73,884 (75.5%); Black, 8,673 (8.9%); American Indian, 901 (0.9%); Asian, 2,570 (2.6%); Other, 11,846 (12.1%). Hispanic, 19,246 (19.7%).

Vital Statistics, 1995: Births, 2,074; deaths, 1,150; marriages, 1,800; divorces, 630.

Recreation: Metropolitan activities, events; lake activities; Alibates Flint Quarries National Monument; hunting, fishing; Tri-State Fair.

Minerals: Natural gas, oil.

Agriculture: Beef cattle; wheat, sorghums, corn, sugar beets are chief crops; 6,000 acres irrigated. Market value $22 million.

AMARILLO (168,592, part in Randall County) county seat; hub for northern Panhandle oil, ranching, distribution, marketing center; tourism; varied manufacturing; food processing; hospitals; museum; varied cultural, recreational events; junior college, Texas Tech medical, engineering schools; Texas State Technical College branch; Quarter Horse Heritage Center; "Texas" drama, Cowboy breakfasts during summer.

Other towns include: **Bishop Hills** (250) and **Bushland** (130).

Population...............................106,736	Rainfall (in.).....................................19.6
(Change fm '90)..........................9.1	Jan. mean min...................................21
Land Area (sq. mi.).......................909.4	July mean max...................................92
Altitude (ft.).........................3,047-3,824	Growing season (days)..................190
	Civ. Labor....................................54,045
	Unemployed.....................................4.9
	Annual Wages...............$1,568,102,826
	Av. Weekly Wage....................$437.52
	Fed. Wages.......................$76,061,864
	Ag. Net Cash Return...........$3,194,000
	Prop. Value $3,757,339,775
	Retail Sales.................$1,794,548,279

Presidio County

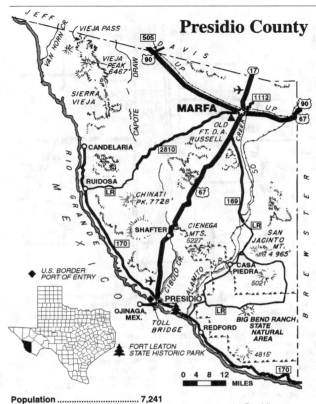

Physical Features: Rugged, some of Texas' tallest mountains; scenic drives; clays, loams, sandy loams on uplands; intermountain wash; timber sparse; Capote Falls, state's highest.

Economy: Ranching; government/services; hunting leases; tourism.

History: Area around Presidio believed to be oldest continuously cultivated farmland in Texas, since 1500 B.C. Jumanos, Apaches and Comanches in area when Spanish arrived in 1680s. Anglo-Americans arrived in 1840s. County created 1850 from Bexar District; organized 1875; named for Spanish Presidio del Norte (fort of the north).

Ethnicity, 1990: White, 5,624 (84.7%); Black, 6 (0.1%); American Indian, 16 (0.2%); Asian, 16 (0.2%); Other, 975 (14.7%). Hispanic, 5,417 (81.6%).

Vital Statistics, 1995: Births, 137; deaths, 51; marriages, 64; divorces, 11.

Recreation: Mild climate and scenic surroundings; hunting; scenic drives along Rio Grande, in mountains; ghost towns, mysterious Marfa Lights; Fort D.A. Russell; Big Bend Ranch State Natural Area; hot springs.

Minerals: Sand and gravel.

Agriculture: Most income from calf sales, breeder and stocker cattle; horses raised; Top crops include onions, hay, cantaloupes, honeydew melons; 5,500 acres irrigated near Rio Grande. Market value $13.7 million.

MARFA (2,496) county seat; ranching supply, Border Patrol sector headquarters; tourist center; gateway to mountainous area; Old Timers Roping in April.

Presidio (3,544), international bridge to Ojinaga, Mex., gateway to Mexico's West Coast by rail; Fort Leaton State Park ; Onion Festival in May.

Other towns include: **Redford** (107); **Shafter** (31) old mining town.

Population 7,241	Jan. mean min. Presidio 34	Annual Wages $19,991,526
(Change fm '90) 9.1	July mean max. Marfa 90	Av. Weekly Wage $296.33
Land Area (sq. mi.) 3,855.8	July mean max. Presidio 102	Fed. Wages $6,674,024
Altitude (ft.) 2,400-7,730	Growing season (days) 238	Ag. Net Cash Return $3,005,000
Rainfall (in.) Marfa 15.9	Civ. Labor 3,418	Prop. Value $260,055,317
Rainfall (in.) Presidio 10.8	Unemployed 34.8	Retail Sales $24,405,701
Jan. mean min. Marfa 26		

Rains County

Physical Features: Northeastern county; rolling; partly Blackland, sandy loams, sandy soils; Sabine River, Lake Tawakoni.

Economy: Oil, tourism, agribusinesses, some manufacturing.

History: Caddo area. In 1700s, Tawakoni Indians entered the area. Anglo-Americans arrived in 1840s. County, county seat named for Emory Rains, Republic leader; created 1870 from Hopkins, Hunt and Wood counties.

Ethnicity, 1990: White, 6,310 (94.0%); Black, 286 (4.3%); American Indian, 29 (0.4%); Asian, 8 (0.1%); Other, 82 (1.2%). Hispanic, 158 (2.4%).

Vital Statistics, 1995: Births, 79; deaths, 98; marriages, 68; divorces, 50.

Recreation: Lake Tawakoni and Lake Fork Reservoir activities; Eagle Fest in January.

Minerals: Gas, oil and coal.

Agriculture: Beef, dairy cattle; crops are vegetables, watermelons, sweet potatoes, hay; greenhouses. Market value $15 million.

EMORY (1,042) county seat; local trade, tourism; some manufacturing.

Other towns include: **East Tawakoni** (741), **Point** (804).

For explanation of sources, abbreviations and symbols, see p. 142.

Population 7,445	Civ. Labor 3,615
(Change fm '90) 10.9	Unemployed 4.5
Land Area (sq. mi.) 232.1	Annual Wages $20,415,880
Altitude (ft.) 406-491	Av. Weekly Wage $338.22
Rainfall (in.) 42.9	Fed. Wages $471,768
Jan. mean min. 31	Ag. Net Cash Return $4,102,000
July mean max. 94	Prop. Value $281,145,934
Growing season (days) 242	Retail Sales $33,692,667

Randall County

Physical Features: Northwestern county; level, but broken by scenic Palo Duro Canyon, Buffalo Lake; silty clay, loam soils.

Economy: Agribusinesses; education; some manufacturing; tourism; part of Amarillo metropolitan area.

History: Comanche Indians removed in mid-1870s; ranching began soon afterward. County created 1876 from Bexar District; organized 1889; named for Confederate Gen. Horace Randal (name misspelled in statute).

Ethnicity, 1990: White, 84,633 (94.4%); Black, 1,115 (1.2%); American Indian, 454 (0.5%); Asian, 646 (0.7%); Other, 2,825 (3.2%). Hispanic, 6,144 (6.9%).

Vital Statistics, 1995: Births, 1,319; deaths, 639; marriages, 335; divorces, 619.

Recreation: Palo Duro Canyon State Park, with "Texas" drama a tourist attraction each summer; Panhandle-Plains Historical Museum; West Texas A&M University events; aoudad sheep, migratory waterfowl hunting in season; Buffalo Lake National Wildlife Refuge.

Minerals: Not significant.

Agriculture: Beef, dairy cattle, horses; wheat, sorghum principal crops; 61,000 acres irrigated. Market value $178.8 million.

CANYON (12,601) county seat; West Texas A&M University, a major economic factor; ranching, feedlot, farm center; light manufacturing; gateway to state park; hospital.

Other towns include: **Lake Tanglewood** (776); **Palisades** (350); **Timbercreek Canyon** (378); **Umbarger** (327). A significant part of **Amarillo** (168,592) lies in the county.

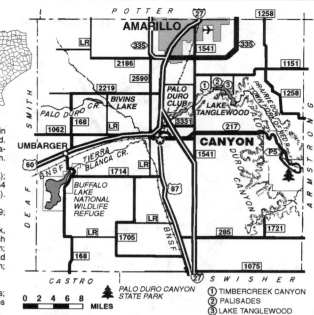

① TIMBERCREEK CANYON
② PALISADES
③ LAKE TANGLEWOOD

Population	98,125
(Change fm '90)	9.4
Land Area (sq. mi.)	914.5
Altitude (ft.)	3,158-3,748
Rainfall (in.)	18.9
Jan. mean min.	23
July mean max.	92
Growing season (days)	195
Civ. Labor	58,362
Unemployed	2.9
Annual Wages	$402,165,524
Av. Weekly Wage	$416.22
Fed. Wages	$2,074,562
Ag. Net Cash Return	$16,567,000
Prop. Value	$3,091,549,185
Retail Sales	$661,722,691

Reagan County

Physical Features: Western county; level to hilly, broken by draws, Big Lake; sandy, loam, clay soils.

Economy: Oil production; natural gas; ranching.

History: Comanches in area until mid-1870s. Ranching began in 1880s. Hispanic migration increased after 1950. County named for Sen. John H. Reagan, first chairman, Texas Railroad Commission; county created 1903 from Tom Green County.

Ethnicity, 1990: White, 3,550 (78.6%); Black, 127 (2.8%); American Indian, 7 (0.2%); Asian, 1 (0.0%); Other, 829 (18.4%). Hispanic, 1,941 (43.0%).

Vital Statistics, 1995: Births, 62; deaths, 32; marriages, 22; divorces, 10.

Recreation: Texon reunion; rodeo; site of 1923 discovery well Santa Rita No. 1 on University of Texas land.

Minerals: Gas, oil.

Agriculture: Cotton, sheep, cattle, goats, sheep; cotton, grains principal crops; 36,000 acres irrigated. Market value $12.3 million.

BIG LAKE (3,486) county seat; center for oil activities, farming, ranching; hospital; Blue Grass Festival in April.

Population	4,382
(Change fm '90)	-2.9
Land Area (sq. mi.)	1,175.4
Altitude (ft.)	2,406-2,953
Rainfall (in.)	19.2
Jan. mean min.	28
July mean max.	94
Growing season (days)	229
Civ. Labor	2,004
Unemployed	3.5
Annual Wages	$27,627,104
Av. Weekly Wage	$436.67
Fed. Wages	$425,946
Ag. Net Cash Return	$2,269,000
Prop. Value	$405,213,810
Retail Sales	$28,424,030

Real County

Physical Features: Hill Country, spring-fed streams, scenic canyons; Frio, Nueces rivers; cedars, pecans, walnuts, many live oaks.

Economy: Tourism, hunting leases; ranch supplies; cedar sales; popular area for artists, recreational "second homes."

History: Tonkawa area; Lipan Apaches arrived in early 1700s; later, Comanche hunters in area. Spanish mission established 1762. Anglo-Americans arrived in 1850s. County created 1913 from Bandera, Edwards, Kerr counties; named for legislator-ranchman Julius Real.

Ethnicity, 1990: White, 2,064 (85.6%); Black, 0 (0.0%); American Indian, 23 (1.0%); Asian, 0 (0.0%); Other, 325 (13.5%). Hispanic, 574 (23.8%).

Vital Statistics, 1995: Births, 40; deaths, 40; marriages, 17; divorces, 11.

Recreation: Tourist, hunting center; many deer killed each season; fishing; camping; scenic drives; state natural area.

Minerals: Not significant.

Agriculture: Beef cattle, sheep, goats produce most income; some oats, grain sorghums. Market value $4.2 million. Cedar posts processed.

LEAKEY (426) county seat; center for ranching, tourism; cedar-oil mill; medical facilities; July Jubilee.

CAMP WOOD (746) San Lorenzo de la Santa Cruz mission site; settlers reunion in August; a tourist, ranching hub for parts of three counties.

Other towns include: **Rio Frio** (50).

Population	**2,674**
(Change fm '90)	10.9
Land Area (sq. mi.)	700.0
Altitude (ft.)	1,494-2,381
Rainfall (in.)	25.7
Jan. mean min.	29
July mean max.	92
Growing season (days)	236

Civ. Labor	1,344
Unemployed	5.1
Annual Wages	$8,163,004
Av. Weekly Wage	$268.15
Fed. Wages	$225,988
Ag. Net Cash Return	$651,000
Prop. Value	$298,404,919
Retail Sales	$10,077,188

Red River County

Physical Features: On Red-Sulphur rivers' divide; 39 different soil types; half timbered.

Economy: Agribusinesses; lumbering; manufacturing.

History: Caddo Indians abandoned area in 1790s. One of the oldest counties; settlers were moving in from the United States in 1810s. Kickapoo and other tribes arrived in 1820s. Antebellum slaveholding area. County created 1836 as original county of the Republic; organized 1837; named for Red River, its northern boundary.

Ethnicity, 1990: White, 11,203 (78.2%); Black, 2,872 (20.1%); American Indian, 75 (0.5%); Asian, 14 (0.1%); Other, 153 (1.1%). Hispanic, 273 (1.9%).

Vital Statistics, 1995: Births, 168; deaths, 203; marriages, 115; divorces, 87.

Recreation: Historical sites include pioneer homes, birthplace of John Nance Garner; water activities; hunting.

Minerals: Small oil flow, gas.

Agriculture: Beef calves, stocker cattle; wheat, soybeans, cotton are principal crops. Market value $37.4 million. Timber sales substantial.

CLARKSVILLE (4,321) county seat; varied manufacturing; hospital; library; century-old courthouse; Historical Society bazaar in October.

Other towns include: **Annona** (363); **Avery** (475); **Bagwell** (150); **Bogata** (1,387) serves farming area; **Detroit** (789) commercial center in west.

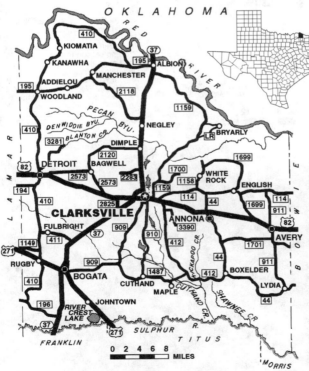

Population	**14,488**
(Change fm '90)	1.2
Land Area (sq. mi.)	1,050.2
Altitude (ft.)	287-525
Rainfall (in.)	44.9
Jan. mean min.	28
July mean max.	92
Growing season (days)	234
Civ. Labor	6,287
Unemployed	7.0
Annual Wages	$59,690,277
Av. Weekly Wage	$317.45

Fed. Wages	$1,418,879
Ag. Net Cash Return	$4,420,000
Prop. Value	$529,819,720
Retail Sales	$70,944,701

For explanation of sources, abbreviations and symbols, p. 142.

Reeves County

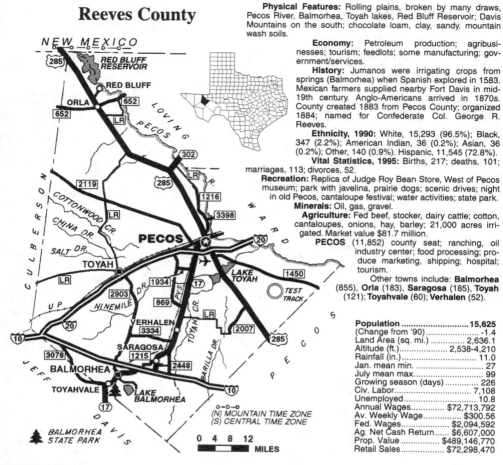

Physical Features: Rolling plains, broken by many draws, Pecos River, Balmorhea, Toyah lakes, Red Bluff Reservoir; Davis Mountains on the south; chocolate loam, clay, sandy, mountain wash soils.

Economy: Petroleum production; agribusinesses; tourism; feedlots; some manufacturing; government/services.

History: Jumanos were irrigating crops from springs (Balmorhea) when Spanish explored in 1583. Mexican farmers supplied nearby Fort Davis in mid-19th century. Anglo-Americans arrived in 1870s. County created 1883 from Pecos County; organized 1884; named for Confederate Col. George R. Reeves.

Ethnicity, 1990: White, 15,293 (96.5%); Black, 347 (2.2%); American Indian, 36 (0.2%); Asian, 36 (0.2%); Other, 140 (0.9%). Hispanic, 11,545 (72.8%).

Vital Statistics, 1995: Births, 217; deaths, 101; marriages, 113; divorces, 52.

Recreation: Replica of Judge Roy Bean Store, West of Pecos museum; park with javelina, prairie dogs; scenic drives; night in old Pecos, cantaloupe festival; water activities; state park.

Minerals: Oil, gas, gravel.

Agriculture: Fed beef, stocker, dairy cattle; cotton, cantaloupes, onions, hay, barley; 21,000 acres irrigated. Market value $81.7 million.

PECOS (11,852) county seat; ranching, oil industry center; food processing; produce marketing, shipping; hospital; tourism.

Other towns include: **Balmorhea** (855), **Orla** (183), **Saragosa** (185), **Toyah** (121); **Toyahvale** (60); **Verhalen** (52).

Population	15,625
(Change from '90)	-1.4
Land Area (sq. mi.)	2,636.1
Altitude (ft.)	2,538-4,210
Rainfall (in.)	11.0
Jan. mean min.	27
July mean max.	99
Growing season (days)	226
Civ. Labor	7,108
Unemployed	10.8
Annual Wages	$72,713,792
Av. Weekly Wage	$300.56
Fed. Wages	$2,094,592
Ag. Net Cash Return	$6,607,000
Prop. Value	$489,146,770
Retail Sales	$72,298,470

Yucca plants in the West Texas landscape. Texas Almanac photo.

Refugio County

Physical Features: Coastal plain, broken by streams, bays; sandy, loam, black soils; mesquite, oak, huisache motts.

Economy: Petroleum, petrochemical production, agribusinesses, tourism.

History: Karankawa area. Spanish mission, for which the county is named, Our Lady of Refuge, established in 1793. Colonists from Ireland and United States arrived in 1830s. Original county of the Republic created 1836, organized 1837.

Ethnicity, 1990: White, 6,201 (77.7%); Black, 645 (8.1%); American Indian, 25 (0.3%); Asian, 5 (0.1%); Other, 1,100 (13.8%). Hispanic, 3,164 (39.7%).

Vital Statistics, 1995: Births, 94; deaths, 79; marriages, 42; divorces, 24.

Recreation: Water activities; hunting, fishing; historic sites; chili cook-off in August; wildlife refuge, home of the whooping crane; Festival of Flags in October.

Minerals: Oil, natural gas.

Agriculture: Cotton, sorghums and corn; beef cattle; hunting leases; soybeans, sunflowers introduced. Market value $21.1 million.

REFUGIO (3,070) county seat; petroleum, agribusiness center; hospital; museum; historic homes.

Other towns include: **Austwell** (200); **Bayside** (445) resorts; **Tivoli** (550); **Woodsboro** (1,811) commercial center.

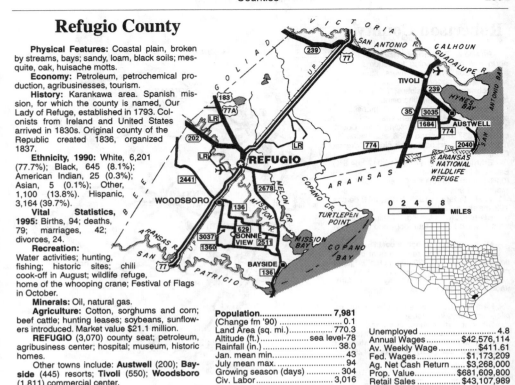

Population	7,981
(Change fm '90)	0.1
Land Area (sq. mi.)	770.3
Altitude (ft.)	sea level-78
Rainfall (in.)	38.0
Jan. mean min.	43
July mean max.	94
Growing season (days)	304
Civ. Labor	3,016
Unemployed	4.8
Annual Wages	$42,576,114
Av. Weekly Wage	$411.61
Fed. Wages	$1,173,209
Ag. Net Cash Return	$3,268,000
Prop. Value	$681,609,800
Retail Sales	$43,107,989

Roberts County

Physical Features: Rolling, broken by Canadian and tributaries; Red Deer Creek; black, sandy loam, alluvial soils.

Economy: Agribusinesses; oil-field operations.

History: Apaches; pushed out by Comanches who were removed in 1874-75 by U.S. Army. Ranching began in late 1870s. County created 1876 from Bexar District; organized 1889; named for Texas leaders John S. Roberts and Gov. O.M. Roberts.

Ethnicity, 1990: White, 1,002 (97.8%); Black, 0 (0.0%); American Indian, 1 (0.1%); Asian, 2 (0.2%); Other, 20 (2.0%). Hispanic, 34 (3.3%).

Vital Statistics, 1995: Births, 5; deaths, 10; marriages, 7; divorces, 3.

Recreation: National cow-calling contest; scenic drives; museum.

Minerals: Production of gas, oil.

Agriculture: Beef cattle top producer; hogs raised; wheat, milo, corn, hay; 9,000 acres irrigated. Market value $20 million.

MIAMI (509) county seat; ranching, oil center; some manufacturing.

Population	855
(Change fm '90)	-16.6
Land Area (sq. mi.)	924.1
Altitude (ft.)	2,467-3,219
Rainfall (in.)	21.6
Jan. mean min.	20
July mean max.	93
Growing season (days)	192
Civ. Labor	533
Unemployed	2.4
Annual Wages	$3,826,258
Av. Weekly Wage	$287.73
Fed. Wages	$348,534
Ag. Net Cash Return	$2,685,000
Prop. Value	$236,406,672
Retail Sales	$1,883,034

For explanation of sources, abbreviations and symbols, see p. 142.

Robertson County

Physical Features: Rolling in north and east, draining to bottoms along Brazos, Navasota rivers; sandy soils, heavy in bottoms.

Economy: Agribusiness; brick manufacturing; power-generating plant.

History: Tawakoni, Waco, Comanche and other tribes. Anglo-Americans arrived in 1820s. Antebellum slaveholding area. County created 1837, organized 1838, subdivided into many others later; named for pioneer Sterling Clack Robertson.

Ethnicity, 1990: White, 10,047 (64.8%); Black, 4,259 (27.5%); American Indian, 36 (0.2%); Asian, 15 (0.1%); Other, 1,154 (7.4%). Hispanic, 1,904 (12.3%).

Vital Statistics, 1995: Births, 241; deaths, 192; marriages, 93; divorces, 66.

Recreation: Hunting; fishing; historic sites; historic-homes tour; dogwood trails, wildlife preserves.

Minerals: Gas, oil, lignite coal.

Agriculture: Most revenue from beef cattle, cotton and hay; 20,000 acres irrigated, mostly cotton. Market value $31.2 million.

FRANKLIN (1,453) county seat; farmtrade center, power plants.

Hearne (4,838), some manufacturing; hospital; Glory Days in October.

Other towns include: **Bremond** (1,164) Polish Days in July; **Calvert** (1,492) tourism, antiques, tour of homes in April; **Mumford** (170); **New Baden** (105); **Wheelock** (125).

Population 15,085	July mean max. 95	Av. Weekly Wage $410.17
(Change fm '90) ....-2.7	Growing season (days)..................268	Fed. Wages $1,420,777
Land Area (sq. mi.) 854.6	Civ. Labor 6,684	Ag. Net Cash Return $3,462,000
Altitude (ft.) 277-491	Unemployed 5.9	Prop. Value.................$1,409,978,970
Rainfall (in.)................................37.5	Annual Wages $72,653,064	Retail Sales $57,428,178
Jan. mean min. 37		

Rockwall County

Physical Features: Rolling prairie, mostly Blackland soil; Lake Ray Hubbard. Texas' smallest county.

Economy: Industrial employment in local plants and in Dallas; in Dallas metropolitan area; tourist and residential development around Lake Ray Hubbard.

History: Caddo area. Cherokees arrived in 1820s. Anglo-American settlers arrived in 1840s. County created 1873 from Kaufman; named for wall-like rock formation.

Ethnicity, 1990: White, 23,991 (93.7%); Black, 855 (3.3%); American Indian, 102 (0.4%); Asian, 164 (0.6%); Other, 492 (1.9%). Hispanic, 1,500 (5.9%).

Vital Statistics, 1995: Births, 475; deaths, 192; marriages, 1,406; divorces, 185.

Recreation: Lake activities; proximity to Dallas; unusual rock outcrop.

Minerals: Not significant.

Agriculture: Most income from cow-calf operations, horses increasing; crops include wheat, grain sorghums, hay; some firewood sold. Market value $2.8 million.

ROCKWALL (13,334) county seat; varied manufacturing; hospital; youth fair in April.

Other towns include: **Fate** (367); **Heath** (2,927); **McLendon-Chisholm** (896); **Mobile City** (209); **Royse City** (2,727, part in Collin County), varied manufacturing, agribusiness, Funfest in October, North Texas Speedway. Part of **Rowlett** (31,818.

Population 32,815	Annual Wages $194,568,330
(Change fm '90) 28.2	Av. Weekly Wage $428.86
Land Area (sq. mi.)................. 128.8	Fed. Wages $2,064,504
Altitude (ft.)........................ 489-588	Ag. Net Cash Return $198,000
Rainfall (in.) 36.9	Prop. Value..............$1,624,465,269
Jan. mean min............................33	Retail Sales $256,836,914
July mean max. 96	
Growing season (days) 236	*For explanation of sources, abbreviations and symbols, see p. 142.*
Civ. Labor............................. 19,114	
Unemployed 2.9	

Runnels County

Physical Features: West central county; level to rolling; bisected by Colorado and tributaries; sandy loam, black waxy soils.

Economy: Agribusiness; oil activity; manufacturing; government/services.

History: Spanish explorers found Jumanos in area in 1650s; later, Apaches and Comanches driven out in 1870s by U.S. military. First Anglo-Americans arrived in 1850s; Germans, Czechs around 1900. County named for planter-legislator H.G. Runnels; created 1858 from Bexar, Travis counties; organized 1880.

Ethnicity, 1990: White, 10,438 (92.4%); Black, 183 (1.6%); American Indian, 16 (0.1%); Asian, 16 (0.1%); Other, 641 (5.7%). Hispanic, 2,740 (24.3%).

Vital Statistics, 1995: Births, 135; deaths, 152; marriages, 84; divorces, 43.

Recreation: Deer and turkey hunting; O.H. Ivie Reservoir; fishing; historical markers in county.

Minerals: Oil, gas, sand, gravel.

Agriculture: Beef and stocker cattle, sheep; crops include cotton, sorghums, wheat. Market value $35.4 million.

BALLINGER (4,170) county seat; varied manufacturing; oil-field services; meat processing; fertilizer produced; Carnegie Library; hospital; Western Texas College extension; The Cross, 100-ft. tall atop hill south of city; Festival of Ethnic Cultures in April.

Other towns include: **Miles** (898); **Norton** (76); **Rowena** (466); **Wingate** (216); **Winters** (2,911), manufacturing, museum; hospital.

Population	11,699
(Change fm '90)	3.6
Land Area (sq. mi.)	1,054.5
Altitude (ft.)	1,628-2,301
Rainfall (in.)	23.3
Jan. mean min.	30
July mean max.	95
Growing season (days)	228
Civ. Labor	5,393
Unemployed	2.9
Annual Wages	$66,622,876
Av. Weekly Wage	$338.63
Fed. Wages	$1,423,015
Ag. Net Cash Return	$3,501,000
Prop. Value	$448,051,917
Retail Sales	$67,629,531

Rusk County

Physical Features: East Texas county on Sabine-Angelina divide; varied deep, sandy soils; over half in pines, hardwoods; lakes.

Economy: Oil, lumbering, agribusiness, government/services, tourism.

History: Caddo area. Cherokees settled in 1820s; removed in 1839. First Anglo-Americans arrived in 1829. Antebellum slaveholding area. County named for Republic, state leader Thomas J. Rusk; created from Nacogdoches County 1843.

Ethnicity, 1990: White, 33,730 (77.1%); Black, 8,984 (20.5%); American Indian, 150 (0.3%); Asian, 51 (0.1%); Other, 820 (1.9%). Hispanic, 1,736 (4.0%).

Vital Statistics, 1995: Births, 552; deaths, 502; marriages, 333; divorces, 244.

Recreation: Water sports, state park; historic homes, sites; scenic drives; marked site of East Texas Field discovery oil well; syrup festival in November.

Minerals: A leading oil county; over 1.5 billion barrels produced since 1930; natural gas, lignite, clays also produced.

Agriculture: Beef cattle top producer; dairy products, poultry, horses raised; timber income substantial; crops include vegetables, nursery plants, hay and watermelons. Market value $21.6 million.

HENDERSON (11,959) county seat; center for agribusiness, oil activities; varied manufacturing; hospital; state jail.

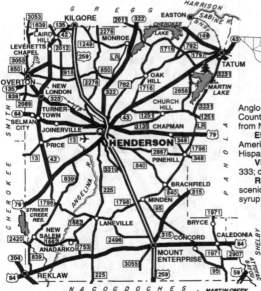

Other towns include: **Joinerville** (140); **Laird Hill** (405); **Laneville** (200); **Minden** (350); **Mount Enterprise** (511); **New London** (983), site of 1937 school explosion that killed 293 students and faculty; **Overton** (2,270) oil, lumbering center, petroleum processing, A&M research center, blue grass festival in July, prison unit; **Price** (275); **Reklaw** (263); **Selman City** (271); **Tatum** (1,382, partly in Panola County). Part of **Kilgore** (11,601).

Population	45,563
(Change fm '90)	4.2
Land Area (sq. mi.)	923.6
Altitude (ft.)	280-662
Rainfall (in.)	45.6
Jan. mean min.	33
July mean max.	93
Growing season (days)	250
Civ. Labor	20,871
Unemployed	6.4
Annual Wages	$282,548,344
Av. Weekly Wage	$467.69
Fed. Wages	$3,043,053
Ag. Net Cash Return	$3,315,000
Prop. Value	$2,031,046,050
Retail Sales	$204,806,768

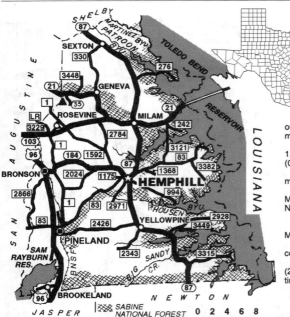

Sabine County

Physical Features: Eighty percent forested; 114,498 acres in national forest; Sabine River, Toledo Bend Reservoir on east; Sam Rayburn Reservoir on southwest.

Economy: Tourism; broilers; timber industries.

History: Caddo area. Spanish land grants in 1790s brought first Spanish and Anglo settlers. An original county, created 1836; organized 1837. Name means cypress in Spanish.

Ethnicity, 1990: White, 8,394 (87.6%); Black, 1,117 (11.7%); American Indian, 10 (0.1%); Asian, 12 (0.1%); Other, 53 (0.6%). Hispanic, 111 (1.2%).

Vital Statistics, 1995: Births, 119; deaths, 150; marriages, 90; divorces, 48.

Recreation: Lake activities; campsites; marinas; McMahan's Chapel, pioneer Protestant church; Sabine National Forest; hunting.

Minerals: Glauconite.

Agriculture: Beef, poultry; vegetables, fruit raised. Market value $6.2 million. Significant timber marketing.

HEMPHILL (1,278) county seat; timber, livestock center; tourism.

Other towns include: **Bronson** (338); **Brookeland** (220); **Geneva** (100); **Milam** (177); **Pineland** (1,047), timber processing.

Population	10,798
(Change fm '90)	12.6
Land Area (sq. mi.)	490.3
Altitude (ft.)	174-590
Rainfall (in.)	52.5
Jan. mean min.	36
July mean max.	93
Growing season (days)	236

Civ. Labor	4,063
Unemployed	9.2
Annual Wages	$47,305,372
Av. Weekly Wage	$410.07
Fed. Wages	$1,791,581
Ag. Net Cash Return	$791,000
Prop. Value	$414,916,109
Retail Sales	$49,345,713

San Augustine County

Physical Features: Hilly East Texas county, 80 percent forested with 66,799 acres in Angelina National Forest, 4,317 in Sabine National Forest; Sam Rayburn Reservoir; varied soils, sandy to black alluvial.

Economy: Lumbering; shipping; varied manufacturing.

History: Presence of Caddoes attracted Spanish mission in 1717. First Anglos and Indians from U.S. southern states arrived around 1800. Antebellum slaveholding area. County ceated and named for Mexican municipality in 1836; an original county; organized 1837.

Ethnicity, 1990: White, 5,663 (70.8%); Black, 2,244 (28.1%); American Indian, 15 (0.2%); Asian, 6 (0.1%); Other, 71 (0.9%). Hispanic, 138 (1.7%).

Vital Statistics, 1995: Births, 105; deaths, 137; marriages, 82; divorces, 24.

Recreation: Lake activities; pine fest, annual tour of homes in April, sassafras festival in October; many historic homes; tourist facilities in national forests.

Minerals: Small amount of oil.

Agriculture: Broilers, cow-calf operation, horses; watermelons, peas, corn, truck crops. Market value $15.1 million. Timber sales significant.

SAN AUGUSTINE (2,433) county seat; tourism; livestock center; varied manufacturing; Deep East Texas Electric Cooperative; lumbering; hospital; Tour of Homes.

Other towns include: **Broaddus** (217).

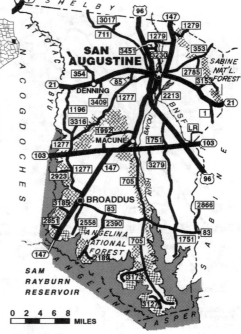

Population	8,096
(Change fm '90)	1.2
Land Area (sq. mi.)	527.9
Altitude (ft.)	156-502
Rainfall (in.)	48.6
Jan. mean min.	35
July mean max.	93
Growing season (days)	238

Civ. Labor	3,488
Unemployed	6.8
Annual Wages	$31,377,574
Av. Weekly Wage	$323.19
Fed. Wages	$743,926
Ag. Net Cash Return	$791,000
Prop. Value	$339,635,622
Retail Sales	$40,650,693

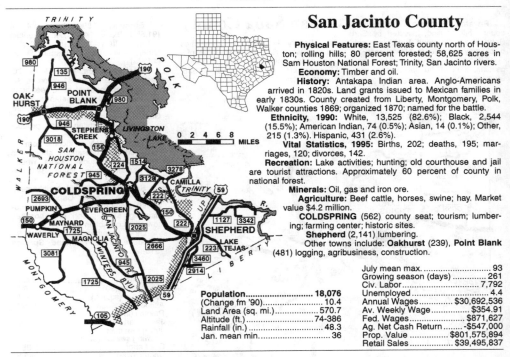

San Jacinto County

Physical Features: East Texas county north of Houston; rolling hills; 80 percent forested; 58,625 acres in Sam Houston National Forest; Trinity, San Jacinto rivers.

Economy: Timber and oil.

History: Antakapa Indian area. Anglo-Americans arrived in 1820s. Land grants issued to Mexican families in early 1830s. County created from Liberty, Montgomery, Polk, Walker counties 1869; organized 1870; named for the battle.

Ethnicity, 1990: White, 13,525 (82.6%); Black, 2,544 (15.5%); American Indian, 74 (0.5%); Asian, 14 (0.1%); Other, 215 (1.3%). Hispanic, 431 (2.6%).

Vital Statistics, 1995: Births, 202; deaths, 195; marriages, 120; divorces, 142.

Recreation: Lake activities; hunting; old courthouse and jail are tourist attractions. Approximately 60 percent of county in national forest.

Minerals: Oil, gas and iron ore.

Agriculture: Beef cattle, horses, swine; hay. Market value $4.2 million.

COLDSPRING (562) county seat; tourism; lumbering; farming center; historic sites.

Shepherd (2,141) lumbering.

Other towns include: **Oakhurst** (239), **Point Blank** (481) logging, agribusiness, construction.

July mean max.	93
Growing season (days)	261
Civ. Labor	7,792
Unemployed	4.4
Annual Wages	$30,692,536
Av. Weekly Wage	$354.91
Fed. Wages	$871,627
Ag. Net Cash Return	-$547,000
Prop. Value	$801,575,894
Retail Sales	$39,495,837

Population	**18,076**
(Change fm '90)	10.4
Land Area (sq. mi.)	570.7
Altitude (ft.)	74-386
Rainfall (in.)	48.3
Jan. mean min.	36

San Patricio County

Population	**65,163**
(Change fm '90)	10.9
Land Area (sq. mi.)	691.8
Altitude (ft.)	sea level-137
Rainfall (in.)	35.0
Jan. mean min.	43
July mean max.	94
Growing season (days)	303
Civ. Labor	28,877
Unemployed	8.4
Annual Wages	$308,992,400
Av. Weekly Wage	$456.42
Fed. Wages	$3,435,296
Ag. Net Cash Return	-$430,000
Prop. Value	$2,344,283,970
Retail Sales	$334,185,118

Physical Features: Grassy, coastal prairie draining to Aransas, Nueces rivers, and to bays; sandy loam, clay, black loam soils; lake.

Economy: Oil, petrochemicals; agribusiness; manufacturing; tourism; Naval base; in Corpus Christi metropolitan area.

History: Karankawa area. Mexican sheep herders in area before colonization. Settled by Irish families in 1830. Created from and named for Spanish municipality in 1836; organized 1837, reorganized 1847.

Ethnicity, 1990: White, 44,834 (76.3%); Black, 968 (1.6%); American Indian, 219 (0.4%); Asian, 163 (0.3%); Other, 12,565 (21.4%). Hispanic, 29,809 (50.7%).

Vital Statistics, 1995: Births, 1,114; deaths, 501; marriages 359; divorces, 303.

Recreation: Water activities; hunting; Corpus Christi Bay; state park; Welder Wildlife Foundation, Park; shrimporee; birdwatching.

Minerals: Production of oil, gas, stone, clays, caliche.

Agriculture: Beef, fed cattle major revenue source; crops include cotton, grain sorghums, corn. Market value $56.4 million. Fisheries income significant.

SINTON (5,837) county seat; oil; agribusiness; tourism; Go Texan Days in October.

Aransas Pass (7,766), shrimping, tourist center; offshore oil-well servicing; aluminum, chemical plants; hospitals.

Portland (13,788), Indian Point pier; many residents work in Corpus Christi.

Other towns include: **Edroy** (200); **Gregory** (2,595); **Ingleside** (6,962) Naval base, chemical and manufacturing plants, ship repair, Navy Days in May; **Ingleside-by-the-Bay** (535); **Lake City** (500); **Lakeside** (330); **Mathis** (5,653); **Odem** (2,686); **San Patricio** (443); **Taft** (3,819), manufacturing, processing; drug rehabilitation center, hospital; Christmas parade.

San Saba County

Physical Features: West central county; hilly, rolling; bisected by San Saba River; Colorado River on east; black, gray sandy loam, alluvial soils.

Economy: Agribusiness; stone processing; tourism; hunting leases; government/services.

History: Apaches and Comanches in area when Spanish explored. Anglo-American settlers arrived in 1850s. County created from Bexar 1856; named for river.

Ethnicity, 1990: White, 4,944 (91.5%); Black, 14 (0.3%); American Indian, 8 (0.1%); Asian, 1 (0.0%); Other, 434 (8.0%). Hispanic, 998 (18.5%).

Vital Statistics, 1995: Births, 70; deaths, 74; marriages, 41; divorces, 32.

Recreation: State park; deer hunting; historic sites; log cabin museum; fishing; scenic drives; wildflower trail; Gorman Falls; pecan festival.

Minerals: Limited stone production.

Agriculture: Most income from fed cattle, cow-calf operations, sheep and goats; crops include pecans, wheat, hay, peanuts. Market value $34.8 million.

SAN SABA (3,296) county seat; claims title "Pecan Capital of the World"; stone processing; varied manufacturing; state prison unit; hospital, cow camp cookoff in May.

Other towns include: **Bend** (115); **Cherokee** (175); **Richland Springs** (318).

Population	5,832
(Change fm '90)	8.0
Land Area (sq. mi.)	1,134.5
Altitude (ft.)	1,110-1,971
Rainfall (in.)	26.3
Jan. mean min.	32
July mean max.	96
Growing season (days)	227
Civ. Labor	2,360
Unemployed	5.8
Annual Wages	$28,678,365
Av. Weekly Wage	$332.10
Fed. Wages	$774,872
Ag. Net Cash Return	$4,651,000
Prop. Value	$495,381,691
Retail Sales	$23,289,478

Schleicher County

Physical Features: Southwestern county on edge of Edwards Plateau, broken by Devils, Concho, San Saba tributaries; part hilly; black soils.

Economy: Oil and ranching.

History: Jumanos in area in 1630s. Later, Apaches and Comanches; removed in 1870s. Ranching began in 1870s. Census of 1890 showed third of population from Mexico. County named for Gustav Schleicher, founder of German colony; county created from Crockett 1887, organized 1901.

Ethnicity, 1990: White, 2,078 (69.5%); Black, 27 (0.9%); American Indian, 3 (0.1%); Asian, 1 (0.0%); Other, 881 (29.5%). Hispanic, 1,062 (35.5%).

Vital Statistics, 1995: Births, 30; deaths, 19; marriages, 27; divorces, 12.

Recreation: Hunting; livestock show in January, youth, open rodeos; playhouse "Way off Broadway".

Minerals: Oil, natural gas.

Agriculture: Sheep, cattle, Angora and meat goats; crops include cotton, milo, hay, small grain. Market value $13.5 million.

ELDORADO (2,071) county seat; center for livestock, woolen mill, mohair marketing; oil activities; medical center.

Population	3,144
(Change fm '90)	5.2
Land Area (sq. mi.)	1,310.7
Altitude (ft.)	2,125-2,467
Rainfall (in.)	19.0
Jan. mean min.	28
July mean max.	93
Growing season (days)	229
Civ. Labor	1,447
Unemployed	4.9
Annual Wages	$17,138,458
Av. Weekly Wage	$419.75
Fed. Wages	$333,054
Ag. Net Cash Return	$1,044,000
Prop. Value	$333,589,190
Retail Sales	$7,985,930

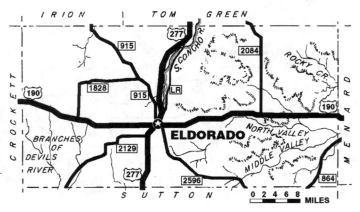

For explanation of sources, abbreviations and symbols, see p. 142.

Scurry County

Physical Features: Plains county below Caprock, some hills; drained by Colorado, Brazos tributaries; lake; sandy, loam soils.

Economy: Oil production; agribusinesses; manufacturing; tourism.

History: Apaches; displaced later by Comanches who were relocated to Indian Territory in 1875. Ranching began in late 1870s. County created from Bexar 1876; organized 1884; named for Confederate Gen. W.R. Scurry.

Ethnicity, 1990: White, 14,113 (75.7%); Black, 879 (4.7%); American Indian, 62 (0.3%); Asian, 35 (0.2%); Other, 3,545 (19.0%). Hispanic, 4,454 (23.9%).

Vital Statistics, 1995: Births, 234; deaths, 162; marriages, 148; divorces, 102.

Recreation: Lake J.B. Thomas water recreation; Sandstone Canyon Indian pictographs; Towle Memorial Park; museums, community theater, white buffalo days.

Minerals: Leading oil-producing county; also gas, stone.

Agriculture: Beef cattle, hogs, dairy cows and sheep; crops are cotton, hay, grain sorghums, silage, wheat, pecans. Market value $20.6 million.

SNYDER (12,203) county seat; oil center; varied manufacturing; Western Texas (Jr.) College; hospital; prison unit: new walking trails along creek in town.

Other towns include: **Dunn** (75); **Fluvanna** (180); **Hermleigh** (200); **Ira** (250).

Population	19,038
(Change fm '90)	2.2
Land Area (sq. mi.)	902.6
Altitude (ft.)	2,129-2,822
Rainfall (in.)	22.2
Jan. mean min.	25
July mean max.	93
Growing season (days)	214

Civ. Labor	7,867
Unemployed	4.4
Annual Wages	$144,019,177
Av. Weekly Wage	$434.49
Fed. Wages	$1,530,959
Ag. Net Cash Return	$4,300,000
Prop. Value	$734,113,034
Retail Sales	$116,408,799

Shackelford County

Physical Features: Rolling, hilly, drained by tributaries of Brazos; sandy and chocolate loam soils; lake.

Economy: Oil and ranching; some manufacturing.

History: Apaches; driven out by Comanches. First Anglo-American settlers arrived soon after establishment of military outpost in 1850s. County created from Bosque County 1858; organized 1874; named for Dr. Jack Shackelford (sometimes referred to as John), Texas Revolutionary hero.

Ethnicity, 1990: White, 3,125 (94.2%); Black, 12 (0.4%); American Indian, 9 (0.3%); Asian, 2 (0.1%); Other, 168 (5.1%). Hispanic, 272 (8.2%).

Vital Statistics, 1995: Births, 39; deaths, 48; marriages, 39; divorces, 16.

Recreation: Fort Griffin State Park, June Fandangle musical production is a major tourist attraction; courthouse historical district; lake activities, hunting.

Minerals: Oil, natural gas.

Agriculture: Beef, stocker cattle, horses, hogs; crops include cotton, wheat. Market value $13.3 million. Mesquite firewood sold.

ALBANY (2,056) county seat; tourism; oil and agriculture center; quarter-horse breeding, training; hospital; historical district.

Other town: **Moran** (292).

Population	3,445
(Change fm '90)	3.9
Land Area (sq. mi.)	914.0
Altitude (ft.)	1,217-1,788
Rainfall (in.)	28.6
Jan. mean min.	31
July mean max.	97
Growing season (days)	224

Civ. Labor	1,494
Unemployed	4.3
Annual Wages	$16,849,038
Av. Weekly Wage	$367.77
Fed. Wages	$353,070
Ag. Net Cash Return	$2,613,000
Prop. Value	$268,866,513
Retail Sales	$11,832,049

Shelby County

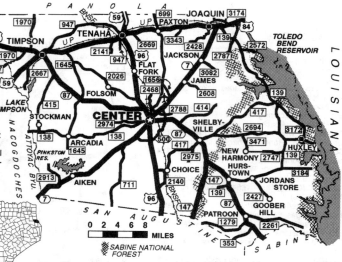

Physical Features: East Texas county; partly hills, much bottomland; well timbered, 67,762 acres in national forest; Attoyac Bayou and Toledo Bend, other streams; sandy, clay, alluvial soils.

Economy: Broiler, egg production; cattle; timber; tourism.

History: Caddo Indian area. First Anglo-Americans settled in 1810s. Antebellum slaveholding area. Original county of Republic, created 1836; organized 1837; named for Isaac Shelby of American Revolution.

Ethnicity, 1990: White, 17,047 (77.4%); Black, 4,727 (21.5%); American Indian, 36 (0.2%); Asian, 31 (0.1%); Other, 193 (0.9%). Hispanic, 539 (2.4%).

Vital Statistics, 1995: Births, 303; deaths, 304; marriages, 226; divorces, 125.

Recreation: Toledo Bend Reservoir activities; Sabine National Forest; hunting, fishing; camping; historic sites; antique show, wolf hunt.

Minerals: Natural gas, oil.

Agriculture: A leader in broiler and egg production; most income from poultry, beef cattle; hay, vegetables, watermelons. Market value $114.4 mil-

lion. Timber sales significant.

CENTER (4,990) county seat; poultry, lumber processing; tourism; hospital; Shelby College Center; Poultry Festival in October; fall fox hunt.

Other towns: **Arcadia** (20); **Huxley** (367); **Joaquin** (919); **Shelbyville** (215); **Tenaha** (1,086); **Timpson** (1,025) timber, poultry, livestock; Frontier Days in July.

Population 22,569
(Change fm '90) 2.4

Land Area (sq. mi.)	794.2
Altitude (ft.)	213-630
Rainfall (in.)	50.2
Jan. mean min.	33
July mean max.	94
Growing season (days)	240
Civ. Labor	9,871
Unemployed	7.2
Annual Wages	$128,415,298
Av. Weekly Wage	$346.52
Fed. Wages	$2,842,808
Ag. Net Cash Return	$15,872,000
Prop. Value	$716,476,185
Retail Sales	$148,553,139

Sherman County

Physical Features: A northernmost Panhandle county; level, broken by creeks, playas; sandy to dark loam soils; underground water.

Economy: Agribusiness.

History: Apaches; pushed out by Comanches in 1700s. Comanches removed to Indian Territory in 1875. Ranching began around 1880; farming after 1900. County named for Texas Gen. Sidney Sherman; created from Bexar District 1876; organized 1889.

Ethnicity, 1990: White, 2,816 (98.5%); Black, 4 (0.1%); American Indian, 12 (0.4%); Asian, 6 (0.2%); Other, 19 (0.7%). Hispanic, 538 (18.8%).

Vital Statistics, 1995: Births, 39; deaths, 26; marriages, 28; divorces, 10.

Recreation: Depot museum; jamboree in September; pheasant hunting.

Minerals: Natural gas, oil.

Agriculture: Beef and stocker cattle important; wheat, corn, grain sorghum; swine; 145,000 acres irrigated. Market value $216.8 million.

STRATFORD (1,928) county seat; agribusiness center; feedlot operations; industrial authority; some manufacturing.

Texhoma (315 in Texas, 746 in Oklahoma), other principal town.

Population 3,087
(Change fm '90) 8.0
Land Area (sq. mi.) 923.1
Altitude (ft.) 3,485-3,743
Rainfall (in.) 17.2

Jan. mean min.	18
July mean max.	92
Growing season (days)	182
Civ. Labor	1,422
Unemployed	2.6
Annual Wages	$15,610,495

Av. Weekly Wage	$374.48
Fed. Wages	$395,933
Ag. Net Cash Return	$35,505,000
Prop. Value	$486,966,309
Retail Sales	$12,221,365

Smith County

Physical Features: Populous East Texas county of rolling hills, many timbered; Sabine, Neches, other streams; Tyler, Palestine lakes; alluvial, gray, sandy loam, clay soils.

Economy: Agribusiness; petroleum production; distribution center; tourism; education; government/services.

History: Caddoes of area reduced by disease and other tribes in 1790s. Cherokees settled in 1820s; removed in 1839. In late 1820s, first Anglo-American settlers arrived. Antebellum slaveholding area. County named for Texas Revolutionary Gen. James Smith; county created 1846 from Nacogdoches.

Ethnicity, 1990: White, 113,676 (75.1%); Black, 31,572 (20.9%); American Indian, 520 (0.3%); Asian, 638 (0.4%); Other, 4,903 (3.2%). Hispanic, 8,986 (5.9%).

Vital Statistics, 1995: Births, 2,466; deaths, 1,627; marriages, 1,727; divorces, 1,014.

Recreation: Activities on Palestine, Tyler lakes and others; famed Rose Garden; Texas Rose Festival in October; Azalea Trail; state park; Goodman Museum; East Texas Fair in September; collegiate events.

Minerals: Oil, gas, clays, sand and gravel, stone.

Agriculture: Horticultural crops and roses; beef cattle important; hay, watermelons, fruits, pecans. Market value $33.7 million. Timber sales substantial; some sawlogs, pulpwood produced.

TYLER (80,204) county seat; claims title, "Rose Capital of the World"; administrative center for oil production; varied manufacturing; University of Texas at Tyler, Tyler Junior College; Texas College, University of Texas Health Center; hospitals, nursing school.

Other towns include: **Arp** (919) Strawberry Festival in April; **Bullard** (1,029, part in Cherokee County); **Flint** (150); **Lindale** (2,633) rose distribution, food processing; Country Fest in October, youth rodeo in August; **New Chapel Hill** (463); **Noonday** (548) Sweet Onion Festival in June; **Troup** (1,883, part in Cherokee County); **Whitehouse** (5,384); **Winona** (575). Part of **Overton** (2,270, mostly in Rusk County) lies in Smith County.

Population	162,480
(Change fm '90)	7.4
Land Area (sq. mi.)	928.5
Altitude (ft.)	52-631
Rainfall (in.)	43.1
Jan. mean min.	33
July mean max.	94
Growing season (days)	259
Civ. Labor.	86,980
Unemployed	6.4
Annual Wages	$1,795,703,201
Av. Weekly Wage	$477.61
Fed. Wages	$33,692,173
Ag. Net Cash Return	$3,552,000
Prop. Value	$5,301,709,376
Retail Sales	$1,950,855,563

For explanation of sources, abbreviations and symbols, see p. 142.

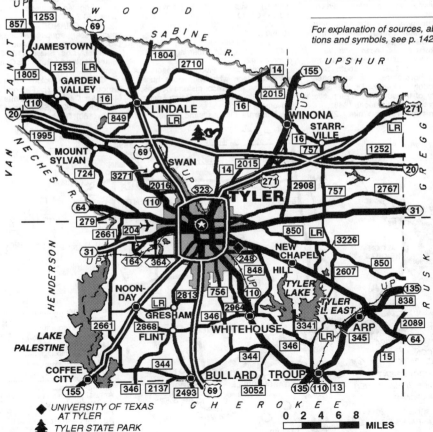

◆ UNIVERSITY OF TEXAS AT TYLER

🌲 TYLER STATE PARK

0 2 4 6 8 MILES

Somervell County

Physical Features: Hilly terrain southwest of Fort Worth; Brazos, Paluxy rivers; gray, dark, alluvial soils.

Economy: Nuclear power plant; tourism, agribusiness.

History: Wichita, Tonkawa area; Comanches later. Anglo-Americans arrived in 1850s. County created as Somerville County 1875 from Hood, Bosque. Spelling changed 1876; named for Republic of Texas Gen. Alexander Somervell.

Ethnicity, 1990: White, 4,849 (90.5%); Black, 10 (0.2%); American Indian, 34 (0.6%); Asian, 22 (0.4%); Other, 445 (8.3%). Hispanic, 749 (14.0%).

Vital Statistics, 1995: Births, 80; deaths, 54; marriages, 63; divorces, 42.

Recreation: Fishing, hunting; unique geological formations; state park; Glen Rose Big Rocks Park; Fossil Rim Wildlife Center; nature trails, museum; exposition center; Celtic festival in April; Passion Play at amphitheatre June-October.

Minerals: Sand, gravel, silica.

Agriculture: Hay, beef cattle, dairy products; also, peanuts, small grains; goats. Market value $2.4 million.

GLEN ROSE (2,188) county seat; tourism, farm trade center; hospital, nuclear power plant.

Other towns include: **Nemo** (56); **Rainbow** (76).

Population	5,765
(Change fm '90)	7.6
Land Area (sq. mi.)	187.2
Altitude (ft.)	627-1,013
Rainfall (in.)	33.3
Jan. mean min.	30
July mean max.	98
Growing season (days)	236

Civ. Labor	2,152
Unemployed	9.2
Annual Wages	$122,367,238
Av. Weekly Wage	$683.47
Fed. Wages	$380,004
Ag. Net Cash Return	$305,000
Prop. Value	$7,979,817,499
Retail Sales	$27,673,665

Starr County

Physical Features: Rolling, some hills; dense brush; clay, loam, sandy soils, alluvial on Rio Grande; Falcon Reservoir.

Economy: Vegetable packing, shipping, other agribusiness; oil processing; tourism; government/services.

History: Coahuiltecan Indian area. Settlers from Spanish villages that were established in 1749 on south bank began to move across river soon afterward. County named for Dr. J.H. Starr, secretary of treasury of the Republic; county created from Nueces 1848.

Ethnicity, 1990: White, 25,067 (61.9%); Black, 25 (0.1%); American Indian, 31 (0.1%); Asian, 25 (0.1%); Other, 15,370 (37.9%). Hispanic, 39,390 (97.2%).

Vital Statistics, 1995: Births, 1,477; deaths, 206; marriages, 680; divorces, 42.

Recreation: Falcon Reservoir activities; deer, white-wing dove hunting; access to Mexico; historic houses; grotto at Rio Grande City; Roma Fest in November.

Minerals: Oil, gas, sand, gravel.

Agriculture: Vegetables, cotton, sorghum; beef and fed cattle; 18,000 acres irrigated for vegetables. Market value $70.3 million.

RIO GRANDE CITY (11,870) county seat; agriculture center; food processing; exports to Mexico; hospital.

ROMA-Los Saenz (10,930) agriculture center; La Purísima Concepcion Visita.

Other towns include: **Delmita** (50); **Escobares** (2,217); **Falcon Heights** (400); **La Casita-Garciasville** (1,423); **La Grulla** (1,828); **Salineno** (175); **San Isidro** (160); **Santa Elena** (64).

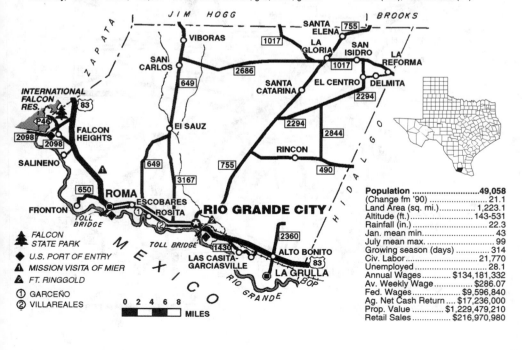

Population	49,058
(Change fm '90)	21.1
Land Area (sq. mi.)	1,223.1
Altitude (ft.)	143-531
Rainfall (in.)	22.3
Jan. mean min.	43
July mean max.	99
Growing season (days)	314
Civ. Labor	21,770
Unemployed	28.1
Annual Wages	$134,181,332
Av. Weekly Wage	$286.07
Fed. Wages	$9,596,840
Ag. Net Cash Return	$17,236,000
Prop. Value	$1,229,479,210
Retail Sales	$216,970,980

Stephens County

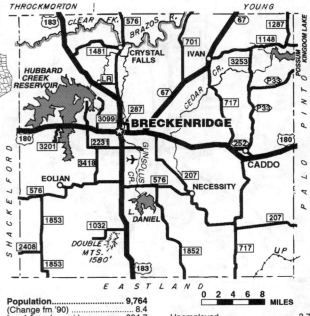

Physical Features: West central county; broken, hilly; Hubbard Creek Reservoir, Possum Kingdom, Daniel lakes; Brazos River; loam, sandy soils.

Economy: Oil, agribusinesses, recreation, some manufacturing.

History: Comanches, Tonkawas in area when Anglo-American settlement began in 1850s. County created as Buchanan 1858 from Bosque; renamed 1861 for Confederate Vice President Alexander H. Stephens; organized 1876.

Ethnicity, 1990: White, 8,187 (90.9%); Black, 252 (2.8%); American Indian, 30 (0.3%); Asian, 28 (0.3%); Other, 513 (5.7%); Hispanic, 767 (8.5%).

Vital Statistics, 1995: Births, 124; deaths, 122; marriages, 97; divorces, 64.

Recreation: Lakes activities; hunting; campsites; historical points; Swenson Museum; Sandefer Oil Museum; aviation museum; Fifties Fun Day in August.

Minerals: Oil, natural gas, stone.

Agriculture: Beef cattle, hogs, goats, sheep; wheat, oats, hay, peanuts, grain sorghums, cotton, pecans. Market value $11.1 million.

BRECKENRIDGE (5,611) county seat; oil and agriculture center; mobil home, aircraft parts manufacturing; petrochemical production; hospital; arts center and library.

Other towns include: **Caddo** (40) gateway to Possum Kingdom State Park.

Population	9,764
(Change fm '90)	8.4
Land Area (sq. mi.)	894.7
Altitude (ft.)	1,127-1,578
Rainfall (in.)	27.6
Jan. mean min.	28
July mean max.	97
Growing season (days)	222
Civ. Labor	4,182

Unemployed	3.7
Annual Wages	$59,338,568
Av. Weekly Wage	$374.61
Fed. Wages	$877,920
Ag. Net Cash Return	$1,323,000
Prop. Value	$514,725,442
Retail Sales	$67,746,237

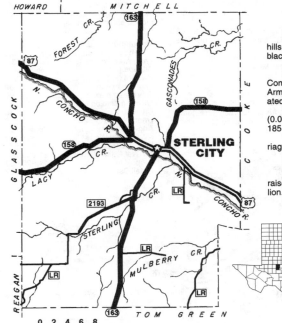

Sterling County

Physical Features: Central prairie, surrounded by hills, broken by Concho River and tributaries; sandy to black soils.

Economy: Oil and ranching; hunting leases.

History: Ranching began in late 1870s after Comanches, Kickapoos and other tribes removed by U.S. Army. County named for buffalo hunter W.S. Sterling; created 1891 from Tom Green County.

Ethnicity, 1990: White, 1,244 (86.5%); Black, 0 (0.0%); American Indian, 9 (0.6%); Asian, 0 (0.0%); Other, 185 (12.9%). Hispanic, 366 (25.5%).

Vital Statistics, 1995: Births, 14; deaths, 8; marriages, 13; divorces, 5.

Recreation: Hunting.

Minerals: Oil, natural gas.

Agriculture: Beef cattle and sheep; some wheat raised; about 1,000 acres irrigated. Market value $8.5 million.

STERLING CITY (943) county seat; farm, ranch trade center; oil-field services; hospital.

Population	1,321
(Change fm '90)	-8.1
Land Area (sq. mi.)	923.4
Altitude (ft.)	2,167-2,623
Rainfall (in.)	20.3
Jan. mean min.	29
July mean max.	96
Growing season (days)	224
Civ. Labor	619
Unemployed	3.9
Annual Wages	$8,751,420
Av. Weekly Wage	$388.56
Fed. Wages	$129,087
Ag. Net Cash Return	$1,076,000
Prop. Value	$336,478,610
Retail Sales	$7,184,338

For explanation of sources, abbreviations and symbols, see p. 142.

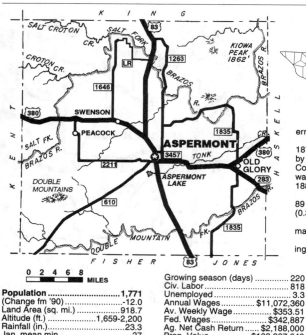

Stonewall County

Physical Features: Western county on rolling plains below Caprock, bisected by Brazos forks; sandy loam, sandy, other soils; some hills.

Economy: Agribusiness, light fabrication, government/services.

History: Anglo-American ranchers arrived in 1870s after Comanches and other tribes removed by U.S. Army. German farmers settled after 1900. County named for Confederate Gen. T.J. (Stonewall) Jackson; created from Bexar 1876, organized 1888.

Ethnicity, 1990: White, 1,898 (94.3%); Black, 89 (4.4%); American Indian, 2 (0.1%); Asian, 7 (0.3%); Other, 17 (0.8%). Hispanic, 237 (11.8%).

Vital Statistics, 1995: Births, 10; deaths, 22; marriages, 12; divorces, 9.

Recreation: Deer, quail, feral hog, turkey hunting; rodeos in June, September; livestock show.

Minerals: Gypsum, gravel, oil.

Agriculture: Beef cattle, wheat, peanuts, hay and cotton. Also, grain sorghum, meat goats and swine. Market value $12.8 million.

ASPERMONT (1,016) county seat; oil field, ranching center; light fabrication; hospital; springfest; livestock show in February.

Other towns include: **Old Glory** (125) farming center; **Peacock** (125); **Swenson** (185).

Population 1,771	Growing season (days) 220
(Change fm '90) ....-12.0	Civ. Labor....................................818
Land Area (sq. mi.) 918.7	Unemployed 3.3
Altitude (ft.) 1,659-2,200	Annual Wages.............$11,072,360
Rainfall (in.)................................23.3	Av. Weekly Wage...............$353.51
Jan. mean min. 27	Fed. Wages...................$342,887
July mean max..............................97	Ag. Net Cash Return $2,188,000
	Prop. Value $103,267,640
	Retail Sales $9,250,343

Sutton County

Physical Features: Southwestern county; level in west, rugged terrain in east, broken by tributaries of Devils, Llano rivers; black, red loam soils.

Economy: Oil and gas; agribusinesses; hunting leases; tourism.

History: Lipan Apaches drove out Tonkawas in 1600s. Comanches, military outpost and disease forced Apaches south. Anglo-Americans settled in 1870s. Mexican immigration increased after 1890. County created from Crockett 1887; organized 1890; named for Confederate officer Col. John S. Sutton.

Ethnicity, 1990: White, 3,125 (75.6%); Black, 2 (0.0%); American Indian, 16 (0.4%); Asian, 6 (0.1%); Other, 986 (23.8%). Hispanic, 1,866 (45.1%).

Vital Statistics, 1995: Births, 68; deaths, 31; marriages, 38; divorces, 22.

Recreation: Among leading hunting counties; Meirs Museum; Caverns of Sonora; goat cookoff; Cinco de Mayo.

Minerals: Oil, natural gas.

Agriculture: Beef cattle, fine-wool sheep, Angora goats, cashmere goats, meat goats. Wheat raised for grazing, hay; minor irrigation. Market value $11.3 million.

SONORA (3,076) county seat; oil field, mohair, wool center; Texas A&M research substation; hospital; wool, mohair show in June.

Population...................................4,574	
(Change fm '90)...........................10.6	
Land Area (sq. mi.) 1,453.9	
Altitude (ft.) 1,942-2,461	
Rainfall (in.) 22.4	
Jan. mean min. 30	
July mean max. 96	
Growing season (days).................235	
Civ. Labor 2,245	
Unemployed 3.8	
Annual Wages $36,845,296	
Av. Weekly Wage $386.19	
Fed. Wages $355,878	
Ag. Net Cash Return $1,035,000	
Prop. Value....................$614,926,683	
Retail Sales $26,689,357	

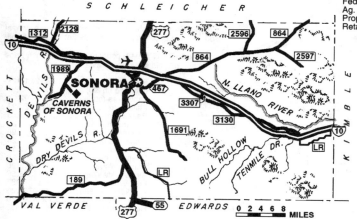

For explanation of sources, abbreviations and symbols, see p. 142.

Swisher County

Physical Features: High Plains county; level, broken by Tule Canyon and Creek; playas; large underground water supply; rich soils.

Economy: Feedlots, grain storage, other agribusinesses; varied manufacturing; tourism; prison unit.

History: Apaches; displaced by Comanches around 1700. U.S. Army removed Comanches in 1874. Ranching began in late 1870s. Farming developed after 1900. County named for J.G. Swisher of Texas Revolution; county created from Bexar, Young territories 1876; organized 1890.

Ethnicity, 1990: White, 5,702 (70.1%); Black, 340 (4.2%); American Indian, 26 (0.3%); Asian, 17 (0.2%); Other, 2,048 (25.2%). Hispanic, 2,496 (30.7%).

Vital Statistics, 1995: Births, 128; deaths, 87; marriages, 64; divorces, 36.

Recreation: Tule Lake activities; museum.

Minerals: Not significant.

Agriculture: A major agricultural county. Cotton, wheat, corn, sorghum raised. Feeder cattle, feed lots. Some 150,000 acres irrigated. Market value $242.3 million.

TULIA (5,229) county seat; farming center; varied manufacturing; grain storage; food processing; hospital; library; museum.

Other towns include: **Happy** (625, part in Randall County), **Kress** (713).

Population	8,685
(Change fm '90)	6.8
Land Area (sq. mi.)	900.5
Altitude (ft.)	3,354-3,604
Rainfall (in.)	19.4
Jan. mean min.	22
July mean max	91
Growing season (days)	205

Civ. Labor	3,867
Unemployed	4.4
Annual Wages	$42,567,858
Av. Weekly Wage	$343.62
Fed. Wages	$1,302,554
Ag. Net Cash Return	$24,655,000
Prop. Value	$359,205,220
Retail Sales	$44,784,825

Tarrant County

Physical Features: Part Blackland, level to rolling; drains to Trinity; Worth, Grapevine, Eagle Mountain, Benbrook lakes.

Economy: Tourism; planes, helicopters, foods, mobile homes, electronic equipment, chemicals, plastics among products of more than 1,000 factories; large federal expenditure; D/FW International Airport; economy closely associated with Dallas urban area.

History: Caddoes in area. Comanches, other tribes arrived about 1700. Anglo-Americans settled in 1840s. Named for Gen. Edward H. Tarrant, who helped drive Indians from area. County created 1849 from Navarro County; organized 1850.

Ethnicity, 1990: White, 917,501 (78.4%); Black, 140,740 (12.0%); American Indian, 5,551 (0.5%); Asian, 29,705 (2.5%); Other, 76,606 (6.5%). Hispanic, 139,879 (12.0%).

Vital Statistics, 1995: Births, 21,685; deaths, 8,402; marriages, 11,807; divorces, 7,723.

Recreation: Scott Theatre; Amon G. Carter Museum; Kimbell Art Museum; Fort Worth Art Museum; Museum of Science and History; Casa Manana; Botanic Gardens; Fort Worth Zoo; Log Cabin Village; Six Flags Over Texas at Arlington; Southwestern Exposition, Stock Show; Convention Center; Stockyards Historical District; Texas Rangers major league baseball at Arlington, other athletic events.

Minerals: Production of cement, sand, gravel, stone, gas.

Agriculture: Beef cattle primarily; some dairies; wheat, hay grain sorghum and corn raised. Market value $21.7 million. Firewood marketed.

Education: Texas Christian University, University of Texas at Arlington, Texas Wesleyan University, Southwestern Baptist Theological Seminary and several other academic centers including a junior college system (three campuses).

FORT WORTH (478,307) county seat; a major mercantile, commercial and financial center; wholesale trade center for much of West Texas; airplane, helicopter and other plants.

A cultural center with renowned art museums; many conventions held in downtown center; agribusiness center for wide area with grain-storage and feed-mill operations; adjacent to D/FW International Airport; hospitals.

ARLINGTON (288,277); industrial and distribution center for automobiles, food products, electronic components, aircraft and parts, rubber and plastic products; medical center, hospitals.

A tourist center with Six Flags Over Texas, the Texas Rangers baseball team, numerous restaurants; educational facilities; Scottish Highland games in June.

Other towns include: **Hurst** (39,741); **Euless** (45,748); **Bedford** (46,179); **North Richland Hills** (50,761); **Azle** (10,670, partly in Parker County), varied industries, Jumpin' Jack Jamboree in October; **Benbrook** (22,947) varied manufacturing; hospitals; **Blue Mound** (2,242); **Colleyville**

(Map on following page.)

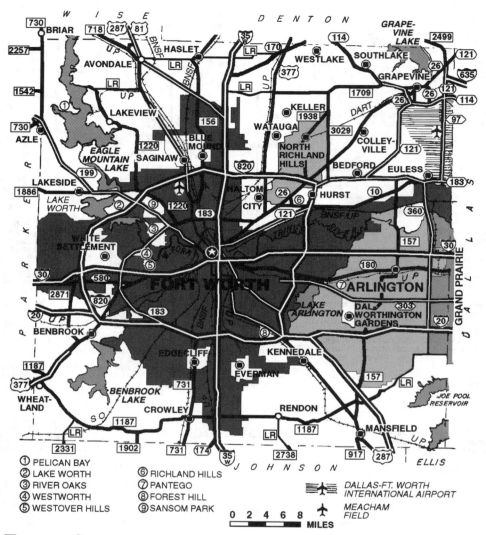

① PELICAN BAY
② LAKE WORTH
③ RIVER OAKS
④ WESTWORTH
⑤ WESTOVER HILLS
⑥ RICHLAND HILLS
⑦ PANTEGO
⑧ FOREST HILL
⑨ SANSOM PARK

DALLAS-FT. WORTH INTERNATIONAL AIRPORT

MEACHAM FIELD

0 2 4 6 8 MILES

Tarrant County (continued)

(15,565) major residential development, some light manufacturing; **Crowley** (7,998, partly in Johnson County), varied manufacturing, hospital; **Dalworthington Gardens** (2,192), **Edgecliff** (3,016); **Everman** (6,520); **Forest Hill** (11,464).

Also, **Grapevine** (38,232, partly in Denton County), varied manufacturing; near D/FW International Airport; tourist center; **Haltom City** (33,906) light manufacturing, food processing, medical center; **Haslet** (956, partly in Denton County); **Keller** (17,017) Bear Creek Park, Wild West Fest.

Also, **Kennedale** (4,986) printing manufacturing; **Lakeside** (979); **Lake Worth** (5,076); **Mansfield** (19,192, partly in Johnson County), varied manufacturing; hospital; Frontier Days, hometown celebration in fall; **Pantego** (2,692); **Pelican Bay** (1,404); **Rendon** (8,414); **Richland Hills** (8,711).

Also, **River Oaks** (7,222); **Saginaw** (9,947); **Sansom Park** (3,859); **Southlake** (8,434) IBM marketing/education center, Heartburn of America chili cookoff; **Watauga** (21,970); **Westlake** (256, partly in Denton County); **Westover Hills** (752); **Westworth Village** (2,334); **White Settlement** (15,283) near aircraft manufacturing, museum, historical sites; hospital; industrial park.

Part of **Grand Prairie** lies in Tarrant County, as does a small part of **Burleson** (19,703, in Johnson County).

Population	1,288,261
(Change fm '90)	10.1
Land Area (sq. mi.)	863.5
Altitude (ft.)	484-864
Rainfall (in.)	31.3
Jan. mean min.	35
July mean max.	96
Growing season (days)	230
Civ. Labor	731,274
Unemployed	3.9
Annual Wages	$16,798,734.514
Av. Weekly Wage	$547.99
Fed. Wages	$582,930,262
Ag. Net Cash Return	$2,467,000
Prop. Value	$54,124,920,512
Retail Sales	$15,124,863,758

For explanation of sources, abbreviations and symbols, see p. 142.

Taylor County

Physical Features: Prairies, with Callahan Divide, draining to Colorado tributaries, Brazos forks; Lakes Abilene, Kirby; mostly loam soils.

Economy: Dyess Air Force Base, feedlots, agribusinesses, diversified manufacturing and education; government/services.

History: Comanches in area about 1700. Anglo-American settlers arrived in 1870s. Named for Alamo heroes Edward, James and George Taylor, brothers; county created from Bexar, Travis 1858; organized 1878.

Ethnicity, 1990: White, 100,237 (83.8%); Black, 7,547 (6.3%); American Indian, 450 (0.4%); Asian, 1,449 (1.2%); Other, 9,972 (8.3%). Hispanic, 17,511 (14.6%).

Vital Statistics, 1995: Births, 1,965; deaths, 1,086; marriages, 1,424; divorces, 931.

Recreation: Abilene State Park; lake activities; Nelson Park Zoo; Texas Cowboy Reunion, West Texas Fair; Fort Phantom Hill; Buffalo Gap historical tour and art festival; rodeo, college events.

Minerals: Oil, natural gas, stone, caliche, clays, sand and gravel.

Agriculture: Beef cattle, wheat, cotton, grain sorghum, hay; also, sheep and goats, sesame introduced. Market value $64.7 million.

Education: Abilene Christian University, Hardin-Simmons University, McMurry University, Cisco Junior College branch.

ABILENE (116,000, part in Jones County) county seat; distribution center; plants make a variety of products; meat, dairy processing; oil-field service center; hospitals; Abilene State School; West Texas Rehabilitation Center.

Other communities include: **Buffalo Gap** (415) historic sites; **Impact** (24); **Lawn** (367); **Merkel** (2,533) agribusiness center, clothing manufacturing, oil-field services; **Ovalo** (225); **Potosi** (1,494); **Trent** (320); **Tuscola** (632); **Tye** (1,173).

Population	126,805
(Change fm '90)	6.0
Land Area (sq. mi.)	915.7
Altitude (ft.)	1,672-2,410
Rainfall (in.)	24.4
Jan. mean min.	31
July mean max.	95
Growing season (days)	225
Civ. Labor	60,528
Unemployed	4.9
Annual Wages	$1,045,204,486
Av. Weekly Wage	$398.33
Fed. Wages	$38,767,379
Ag. Net Cash Return	$8,916,000
Prop. Value	$3,710,253,976
Retail Sales	$1,395,162,563

For explanation of sources, abbreviations and symbols, see p. 142.

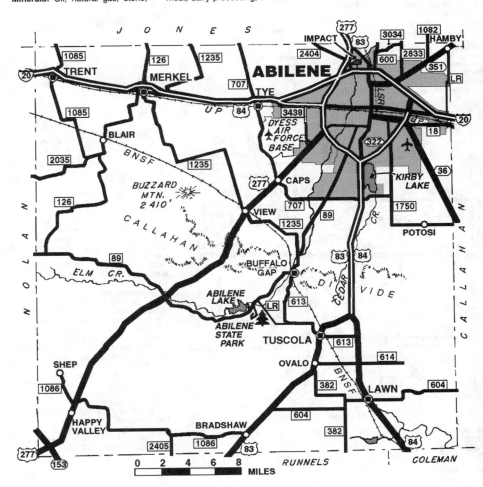

Terrell County

Physical Features: Trans-Pecos southwestern county; semi-mountainous, many canyons; rocky, limestone soils.

Economy: Ranching; some tourism; oil and natural gas exploration; hunting leases.

History: Coahuiltecans, Jumanos, and other tribes left many pictographs in area caves. Sheep ranching began in 1880s. Named for Confederate Gen. A.W. Terrell; county created 1905 from Pecos County.

Ethnicity, 1990: White, 1,189 (84.3%); Black, 1 (0.1%); American Indian, 5 (0.4%); Asian, 2 (0.1%); Other, 213 (15.1%). Hispanic, 751 (53.3%).

Vital Statistics, 1995: Births, 11; deaths, 17; marriages, 5; divorces, 7.

Recreation: Hunting, especially white-tailed, mule deer; lower canyons of Rio Grande accessible by boat; varied wildlife; Cinco de Mayo.

Minerals: Gas, oil, limestone.

Agriculture: Sheep, Angora goats, beef cattle, wool, mohair. Also, pecans and Bermuda grass. Market value $5.9 million.

SANDERSON (979) county seat; ranching, petroleum operations center; rail terminal. Other town: **Dryden** (13).

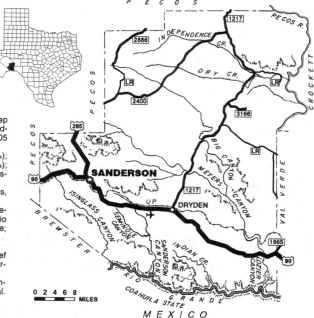

Population		1,292
(Change fm '90)		-8.4
Land Area (sq. mi.)		2,357.9
Altitude (ft.)		1,668-2,792
Rainfall (in.)		14.3
Jan. mean min.		29
July mean max.		92
Growing season (days)		237
Civ. Labor		575
Unemployed		4.2
Annual Wages		$5,472,184
Av. Weekly Wage		$339.34
Fed. Wages		$508,811
Ag. Net Cash Return		-$227,000
Prop. Value		$267,305,662
Retail Sales		$4,438,246

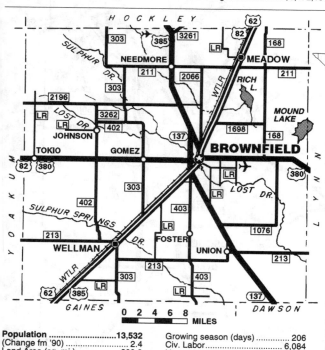

Terry County

Physical Features: Western county on South Plains, broken by draws, playas; sandy, sandy loam, loam soils.

Economy: Agribusiness, petroleum.

History: Comanches removed in 1870s by U.S. Army. Ranching developed in 1890s; farming after 1900. Oil discovered in 1940. County named for head of famed Texas Ranger troop, Col. B.F. Terry. County created from Bexar District 1876; organized 1904.

Ethnicity, 1990: White, 10,202 (77.2%); Black, 449 (3.4%); American Indian, 38 (0.3%); Asian, 28 (0.2%); Other, 2,501 (18.9%). Hispanic, 5,194 (39.3%).

Vital Statistics, 1995: Births, 189; deaths, 119; marriages, 123; divorces, 67.

Recreation: Museum; harvest festival in October; brisket and bean cook-off in April.

Minerals: Oil.

Agriculture: Cotton is principal crop; some sorghum, wheat, peanuts, chili peppers raised; 155,000 acres irrigated. Market value $53.1 million.

BROWNFIELD (9,357) county seat; oilfield services; agribusiness; minerals processed; hospital.

Other towns include: **Meadow** (623); **Tokio** (60); **Wellman** (259).

Population		13,532
(Change fm '90)		2.4
Land Area (sq. mi.)		889.9
Altitude (ft.)		3,183-3,447
Rainfall (in.)		19.0
Jan. mean min.		24
July mean max.		93
Growing season (days)		206
Civ. Labor		6,084
Unemployed		5.8
Annual Wages		$87,385,134
Av. Weekly Wage		$403.04
Fed. Wages		$1,335,049
Ag. Net Cash Return		$11,722,000
Prop. Value		$628,631,547
Retail Sales		$106,768,125

Throckmorton County

Physical Features: North central county southwest of Wichita Falls; rolling, between Brazos forks; red to black soils.

Economy: Oil, agri-business, hunting leases.

History: Site of Comanche Indian Reservation 1854-59. Ranching developed after Civil War. County named for Dr. W.E. Throckmorton, father of Gov. J.W. Throckmorton; county created from Fannin 1858; organized 1879.

Ethnicity, 1990: White, 1,778 (94.6%); Black, 0 (0.0%); American Indian, 4 (0.2%); Asian, 8 (0.4%); Other, 90 (4.8%). Hispanic, 136 (7.2%).

Vital Statistics, 1995: Births, 29; deaths, 26; marriages, 10; divorces, 3.

Recreation: Hunting, fishing; historic sites include Camp Cooper, site of former Comanche reservation; restored ranch home, Miller's Creek Reservoir; Pioneer Day in June.

Minerals: Natural gas, oil.

Agriculture: Beef cattle; crops include wheat, oats, cotton, hay, sorghums. Market value $20.1 million. Mesquite firewood sold.

THROCKMORTON (1,086) county seat; varied manufacturing; oil-field services; hospital.

Other towns include: **Elbert** (150), **Woodson** (252).

Population **1,952**	Jan. mean min. 27	Annual Wages $7,061,497
(Change fm '90) 3.8	July mean max. 96	Av. Weekly Wage...................$304.38
Land Area (sq. mi.) 912.4	Growing season (days)..................220	Fed. Wages.........................$346,887
Altitude (ft.) 1,153-1,583	Civ. Labor 837	Ag. Net Cash Return $3,933,000
Rainfall (in.).................................. 27.1	Unemployed 3.2	Prop. Value....................$209,120,153
		Retail Sales $5,252,675

Titus County

Physical Features: East Texas county; hilly, timbered; drains to Big Cypress Creek, Sulphur River.

Economy: Agribusinesses, varied manufacturing; lignite mining and power generation; tourism.

History: Caddo area. Cherokees and other tribes settled in 1820s. Anglo-American settlers arrived in 1840s. Named for pioneer settler A.J. Titus; county created from Bowie, Red River counties 1846.

Ethnicity, 1990: White, 18,664 (77.7%); Black, 3,229 (13.4%); American Indian, 107 (0.4%); Asian, 27 (0.1%); Other, 1,982 (8.3%). Hispanic, 2,556 (10.6%).

Vital Statistics, 1995: Births, 477; deaths, 296; marriages, 307; divorces, 50.

Recreation: Fishing, hunting; Lake activities; state park; railroad museum; riverboat; flower gardens.

Minerals: Oil, gas, lignite.

Agriculture: Beef cattle, poultry; among leading counties in broilers; crops include corn, watermelons, grain sorghums, hay. Market value $30.7 million.

MOUNT PLEASANT (13,652) county seat; tourism; varied manufacturing; food-processing plants; hospital; Northeast Texas Community College; WranglerFest in October.

Other towns include: **Cookville** (105); **Talco** (615), **Winfield** (348).

Population................................**25,917**	Growing season (days) 233	Prop. Value...................$1,583,581,873
(Change fm '90) 7.9	Civ. Labor...................................12,671	Retail Sales $294,073,271
Land Area (sq. mi.)....................410.6	Unemployed 7.2	
Altitude (ft.)............................301-462	Annual Wages...............$298,455,377	
Rainfall (in.)................................46.8	Av. Weekly Wage...................$432.89	*For explanation of sources, abbreviations and symbols, see p. 142.*
Jan. mean min..................................29	Fed. Wages.......................$4,534,960	
July mean max. 94	Ag. Net Cash Return $3,285,000	

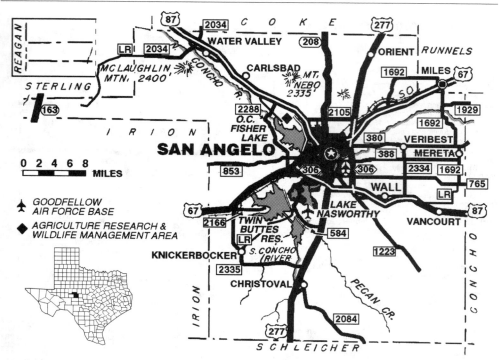

REAGAN

STERLING

163

MCLAUGHLIN MTN. 2400'

LR 2034

87

2034

WATER VALLEY

CARLSBAD

C O K E

208

277

ORIENT | RUNNELS

1692 | MILES 67

MT. NEBO 2335'

0 2 4 6 8 **MILES**

I R I O N

2288 O.C. FISHER LAKE

SAN ANGELO

2105

380 | VERIBEST

1692

388 | MERETA

1929

306

306

2334 | 1692

765

853

WALL

LR

✈ GOODFELLOW AIR FORCE BASE

◆ AGRICULTURE RESEARCH & WILDLIFE MANAGEMENT AREA

67

2166

TWIN BUTTES RES.

LR

KNICKERBOCKER

2335

S. CONCHO RIVER

CHRISTOVAL

LAKE NASWORTHY

✈

584

VANCOURT

87

1223

I R I O N

2084

277

S C H L E I C H E R

C O N C H O

PECAN CR.

Physical Features: West central county of plains, rolling hills, broken by Concho forks; loams in basin, stony hillsides; lakes.

Economy: "Sheep and Wool Capital"; varied agribusinesses, manufacturing; trade center for area, education center, medical center; government/services.

History: Jumano Indians attracted Spanish missionaries around 1630. Comanches controlled area when U.S. military established outposts in 1850s. Anglo-American settlement occurred after Civil War. County created from Bexar District 1874, named for Gen. Tom Green of Texas Revolution; organized 1875; 12 other counties created from this original area.

Ethnicity, 1990: White, 79,533 (80.8%); Black, 4,136 (4.2%); American Indian, 373 (0.4%); Asian, 998

Tom Green County

(1.0%); Other, 13,418 (13.6%). Hispanic, 25,501 (25.9%).

Vital Statistics, 1995: Births, 1,414; deaths, 965; marriages, 1,162; divorces, 660.

Recreation: Water sports; hunting; Fort Concho Museum; urban, collegiate activities; roping fiesta, June Fiesta del Concho; March rodeo.

Minerals: Oil, natural gas.

Agriculture: Cotton, beef cattle, sheep, goats. Also, sorghum, wheat, swine, horses. About 27,000 acres irrigated. Market value $78.6 million.

SAN ANGELO (89,421) county seat; varied agribusiness; plants make a variety of products including medical devices, denim jeans; distribution center; hospitals; Angelo State University,

A&M extension center.

Other towns include: **Carlsbad** (100), **Christoval** (216), **Knickerbocker** (50); **Mereta** (75); **Vancourt** (125); **Veribest** (40); **Wall** (200); **Water Valley** (120).

Population	**104,398**
(Change fm '90)	6.0
Land Area (sq. mi.)	1,522.2
Altitude (ft.)	1,717-2,480
Rainfall (in.)	20.5
Jan. mean min.	31
July mean max.	96
Growing season (days)	235
Civ. Labor	50,776
Unemployed	3.5
Annual Wages	$862,064,174
Av. Weekly Wage	$406.15
Fed. Wages	$37,444,852
Ag. Net Cash Return	$3,745,000
Prop. Value	$2,987,777,860
Retail Sales	$974,070,337

Austin's hike and bike trails on Town Lake offer a convenient respite for the residents and visitors in the downtown area. Texas Almanac photo.

Travis County

Physical Features: Central county of scenic hills, broken by Colorado River and lakes; cedars, pecans, other trees; diverse soils, mineral deposits.

Economy: Education, state government, tourism, research and industry; conventions.

History: Tonkawa and Lipan Apache area; Comanches, Kiowas arrived about 1700. Spanish missions from East Texas temporarily relocated near Barton Springs in 1730 before removing to San Antonio. Anglo-Americans arrived in early 1830s. County created 1840, when Austin became Republic's capital, from Bastrop County; organized 1843; named for Alamo commander Col. William B. Travis; many other counties created from its original area.

Ethnicity, 1990: White, 422,749 (73.3%); Black, 63,173 (11.0%); American Indian, 2,089 (0.4%); Asian, 16,497 (2.9%); Other, 71,899 (12.5%). Hispanic, 121,689 (21.1%).

Vital Statistics, 1995: Births, 11,278; deaths, 3,640; marriages, 7,493; divorces, 3,466.

Recreation: Colorado River lakes; hunting, fishing; McKinney Falls State Park; Austin Aqua Festival; collegiate, metropolitan, governmental events; official buildings and historic sites; museums; Sixth St. restoration area; scenic drives; city parks.

Minerals: Production of lime, stone, sand, gravel, oil and gas.

Agriculture: Beef, dairy cattle, horses, hogs; crops include sorghums, cotton, small grains, pecans. Market value $19.1 million.

Education: University of Texas main campus; St. Edward's University, Maryhill College, Concordia Lutheran College, Huston-Tillotson College, Austin Community College, Episcopal and Presbyterian seminaries; state schools and institutions for blind, deaf, mental illnesses.

AUSTIN (557,532), county seat and state capital; state and federal payrolls; IRS center; a leading convention, tourist city; research, high-tech industries; hospitals, including state institutions; popular retirement area.

Other towns include: **Bee Cave** (274); **Briarcliff** (366); **Creedmoor** (220); **Del Valle** (2,476); **Jonestown** (1,376); **Lago Vista** (2,460); **Lakeway** (4,963); **Manchaca** (2,259); **Manor** (1,186); **McNeil** (70); **Mustang Ridge** (685); **Pflugerville** (7,926) high-tech industries, agriculture, government/services, Deutchenfest in May; **Rollingwood** (1,362); **San Leanna** (393); **Sunset Valley** (395); **West Lake Hills** (2,827).

Population	678,500
(Change fm '90)	17.7
Land Area (sq. mi.)	989.4
Altitude (ft.)	444-1,330
Rainfall (in.)	31.9
Jan. mean min.	39
July mean max.	95
Growing season (days)	270
Civ. Labor	434,302
Unemployed	3.2
Annual Wages	$12,742,314,726
Av. Weekly Wage	$569.02
Fed. Wages	$324,993,781
Ag. Net Cash Return	$4,815,000
Prop. Value	$34,763,742,833
Retail Sales	$8,879,668,907

For explanation of sources, abbreviations and symbols, see p. 142.

Trinity County

Physical Features: Heavily forested East Texas county of hills, between Neches and Trinity (Livingston Lake) rivers; rich alluvial soils, sandy upland; 67,910 acres in national forest.

Economy: Forestry, tourism, cattle; government/services.

History: Caddoes, reduced by disease in late 1700s. Kickapoo, Alabama, Coushatta in area when Anglo-Americans settled in 1840s. Named for river; county created 1850 out of Houston County.

Ethnicity, 1990: White, 9,619 (84.0%); Black, 1,645 (14.4%); American Indian, 24 (0.2%); Asian, 21 (0.2%); Other, 136 (1.2%). Hispanic, 272 (2.4%).

Vital Statistics, 1995: Births, 146; deaths, 184; marriages, 126; divorces, 47.

Recreation: Lake activities; fishing, hiking, hunting; Davy Crockett National Forest; historic sites; Timber Festival in March.

Minerals: Limited oil, gas, lignite, sand and gravel.

Agriculture: Beef cattle, horses, hogs, meat goats; crops include hay, vegetables. Market value $7.7 million. Timber sales significant.

GROVETON (1,145) county seat; gateway to national forest recreation areas; lumber center; petroleum processing.

Trinity (2,845), steel fabrication; hospital; forest-industries center; near Livingston Lake.

Other towns include: **Apple Springs** (185); **Centralia** (53); **Pennington** (67); **Sebastopol** (120) historic town; **Woodlake** (98).

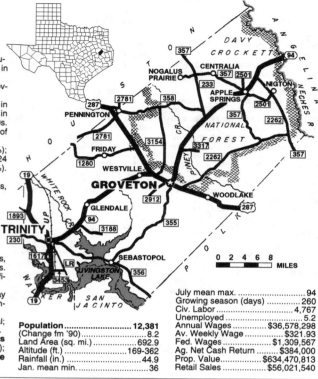

Population	12,381
(Change fm '90)	8.2
Land Area (sq. mi.)	692.9
Altitude (ft.)	169-362
Rainfall (in.)	44.9
Jan. mean min.	36
July mean max.	94
Growing season (days)	260
Civ. Labor	4,767
Unemployed	5.2
Annual Wages	$36,578,298
Av. Weekly Wage	$321.93
Fed. Wages	$1,309,567
Ag. Net Cash Return	$384,000
Prop. Value	$634,470,813
Retail Sales	$56,021,540

Tyler County

Physical Features: Hilly East Texas county; densely timbered; drains to Neches, Angelina rivers; B.A. Steinhagen Lake; Big Thicket is unique plant and animal area.

Economy: Lumbering; government/services, some manufacturing; tourism, hunting leases.

History: Caddoan area. Cherokees, Alabama and Coushatta pushed into area from U.S. South in 1820s. Anglo-Americans settled in 1830s. Named for U.S. President John Tyler; county created 1846 from Liberty.

Ethnicity, 1990: White, 14,550 (87.4%); Black, 1,994 (12.0%); American Indian, 46 (0.3%); Asian, 12 (0.1%); Other, 44 (0.3%). Hispanic, 177 (1.1%).

Vital Statistics, 1995: Births, 210; deaths, 236; marriages, 162; divorces, 103.

Recreation: Big Thicket National Preserve; Heritage Village; lake activities; Allan Shivers Museum; state forest; historic sites; dogwood festival; rodeo, frontier frolics in September; gospel music fest in June.

Minerals: Oil, natural gas.

Agriculture: Beef cattle, hay, blueberries, goats. Market value $3.2 million. Timber sales significant.

WOODVILLE (4,256) county seat; lumber, cattle market; varied manufacturing; tourism; hospital; prison unit.

Other towns include: **Chester** (342), **Colmesneil** (611), **Doucette** (131), **Fred** (239), **Hillister** (200) **Spurger** (472), **Warren** (304).

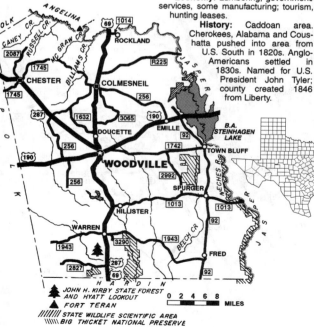

JOHN H. KIRBY STATE FOREST AND HYATT LOOKOUT
FORT TERAN
///////// STATE WILDLIFE SCIENTIFIC AREA
\\\\\\ BIG THICKET NATIONAL PRESERVE

Population	19,815
(Change fm '90)	19.0
Land Area (sq. mi.)	923.0
Altitude (ft.)	109-443
Rainfall (in.)	54.3
Jan. mean min.	38
July mean max.	93
Growing season (days)	241
Civ. Labor	7,223
Unemployed	12.6
Annual Wages	$69,484,777
Av. Weekly Wage	$350.30
Fed. Wages	$1,309,364
Ag. Net Cash Return	-$1,361,000
Prop. Value	$865,210,744
Retail Sales	$89,206,002

Upshur County

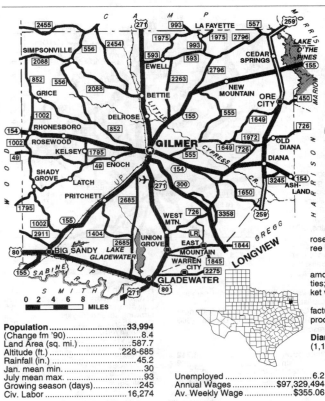

0 2 4 6 8 MILES

Physical Features: East Texas county; rolling to hilly, over half forested; drains to Sabine, Cypress Creek, Lake O' the Pines, Lake Gladewater.

Economy: Manufacturing, agribusinesses, government/services, petroleum products and lumber mill; many residents work at area plants.

History: Caddoes; reduced by epidemics in 1700s. Cherokees in area in 1820s. Anglo-American settlement in mid-1830s. County created from Harrison, Nacogdoches counties 1846; named for U.S. Secretary of State A.P. Upshur.

Ethnicity, 1990: White, 27,076 (86.3%); Black, 3,881 (12.4%); American Indian, 121 (0.4%); Asian, 29 (0.1%); Other, 263 (0.8%). Hispanic, 641 (2.0%).

Vital Statistics, 1995: Births, 426; deaths, 376; marriages, 295; divorces, 197.

Recreation: Scenic trails; hunting, fishing; rose festival, pecan festival, East Texas Yamboree in October.

Minerals: Oil, gas, sand, gravel.

Agriculture: Dairies and beef cattle, poultry; among leading broiler and dairy producing counties; vegetable crops, hay, peaches raised. Market value $41.7 million. Timber a major product.

GILMER (5,406) county seat; varied manufacturing; timber, ceramics produced; vegetable processing; medical center; civic center.

Other towns include: **Big Sandy** (1,293); **Diana** (450); **East Mountain** (907); **Ore City** (1,115); **Union Grove** (303).

Population	33,994
(Change fm '90)	8.4
Land Area (sq. mi.)	587.7
Altitude (ft.)	228-685
Rainfall (in.)	45.2
Jan. mean min.	30
July mean max.	93
Growing season (days)	245
Civ. Labor	16,274

Unemployed	6.2
Annual Wages	$97,329,494
Av. Weekly Wage	$355.06

Fed. Wages	$1,309,364
Ag. Net Cash Return	$5,215,000
Prop. Value	$1,191,171,780
Retail Sales	$174,997,816

Upton County

Physical Features: Western county; north flat, south rolling, hilly; limestone, sandy loam soils, drains to creeks.

Economy: Oil, electric power plant, cotton, ranching.

History: Apache and Comanche area until tribes removed by U.S. Army in 1870s. Sheep and cattle ranching developed in 1880s. Oil discovered in 1925. County created in 1887 from Tom Green County; organized 1910; name honors brothers John and William Upton, Confederate colonels.

Ethnicity, 1990: White, 3,487 (78.4%); Black, 94 (2.1%); American Indian, 20 (0.4%); Asian, 2 (0.0%); Other, 844 (19.0%). Hispanic, 1,666 (37.5%).

Vital Statistics, 1995: Births, 44; deaths, 35; marriages, 36; divorces, 18.

Recreation: Historic sites, Mendoza Trail Museum; scenic areas, chili cookoff in October, Christmas bazaar.

Minerals: Oil, natural gas.

Agriculture: Cotton, pecans, livestock. Market value $8.5 million.

RANKIN (940) county seat, oil, ranching.

McCamey (2,284) oil, ranching; hospital; pecan show. Other town: **Midkiff** (98).

Population	4,149
(Change fm '90)	-6.7
Land Area (sq. mi.)	1,241.8
Altitude (ft.)	2,441-3,141
Rainfall (in.)	14.3
Jan. mean min.	31
July mean max.	95
Growing season (days)	232

Civ. Labor	1,777
Unemployed	3.4
Annual Wages	$34,970,831
Av. Weekly Wage	$505.47
Fed. Wages	$175,312
Ag. Net Cash Return	$1,597,000

Prop. Value	$686,155,767
Retail Sales	$13,626,587

0 2 4 6 8 MILES

For explanation of sources, abbreviations and symbols, see p. 142.

Uvalde County

Physical Features: Edwards Plateau, rolling hills below escarpment; spring-fed Sabinal, Frio, Leona, Nueces rivers; cypress, cedar, other trees; unique maple groves.

Economy: Agribusinesses; light manufacturing; tourism; hunting leases.

History: Spanish mission Nuestra Señora de la Candelaria founded in 1762 for Lipan Apaches near present-day Montell; Comanches harassed mission. U.S. military outpost established in 1849. County created from Bexar 1850; re-created, organized 1856; named for 1778 governor of Coahuila, Juan de Ugalde, with name Anglicized.

Ethnicity, 1990: White, 15,078 (64.6%); Black, 47 (0.2%); American Indian, 49 (0.2%); Asian, 70 (0.3%); Other, 8,096 (34.7%). Hispanic, 14,104 (60.4%).

Vital Statistics, 1995: Births, 451; deaths, 201; marriages, 195; divorces, 95.

Recreation: Deer, turkey hunting area; Garner State Park; water activities on rivers; John Nance Garner Museum; Uvalde Memorial Park; scenic trails; historic sites; recreational homes.

Minerals: Asphalt, stone, sand and gravel.

Agriculture: Beef cattle, goats, sheep; crops include corn, cotton, grain sorghums, hay, wheat; vegetables; substantial irrigation. Market value $61.7 million.

UVALDE (15,823) county seat; varied manufacturing; vegetable, wool, mohair processing; junior college; A&M research center; hospital.

Sabinal (1,677), farm, ranch center; gateway to Frio and Sabinal canyons; tourist, retirement area.

Other towns include: **Concan** (225); **Knippa** (360); **Utopia** (360) resort.

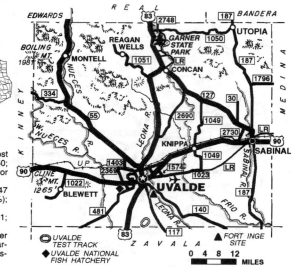

○ UVALDE TEST TRACK
◆ UVALDE NATIONAL FISH HATCHERY
▲ FORT INGE SITE

0 4 8 12 MILES

Population	24,712
(Change fm '90)	5.9
Land Area (sq. mi.)	1,556.6
Altitude (ft.)	699-1,957

Rainfall (in.)	24.8
Jan. mean min.	36
July mean max.	96
Growing season (days)	255
Civ. Labor	11,035
Unemployed	11.4
Annual Wages	$145,636,246
Av. Weekly Wage	$324.86
Fed. Wages	$4,502,806
Ag. Net Cash Return	$10,157,000
Prop. Value	$1,002,325,010
Retail Sales	$192,065,222

Val Verde County

Physical Features: Southwestern county bordering Mexico, rolling, hilly; brushy; Devils, Pecos rivers, Amistad Reservoir; limestone, alluvial soils.

Economy: Agribusiness; tourism; area trade center; large military, other federal expenditures; hunting leases.

History: Apaches, Coahuiltecans, Jumanos present when Spanish explored area 1535. Comanches arrived later. U.S. military outposts established in 1850s to protect settlers. Only county named for Civil War battle; Val Verde means green valley. Created 1885 from Crockett, Kinney, Pecos counties.

Ethnicity, 1990: White, 26,694 (68.9%); Black, 757 (2.0%); American Indian, 126 (0.3%); Asian, 244 (0.6%); Other, 10,900 (28.2%). Hispanic, 27,299 (70.5%).

Vital Statistics, 1995: Births, 885; deaths, 313; marriages, 493; divorces, 189.

Recreation: Gateway to Mexico; deer hunting, fishing; Amistad lake activities; two state parks; Langtry restoration of Judge Roy Bean's saloon; San Felipe Springs; winery.

Minerals: Production sand and gravel, gas, oil.

Agriculture: Sheep, Angora goats, cattle, meat goats; minor irrigation. Market value $14 million.

DEL RIO (34,361) county seat; tourism and trade with Mexico; varied manufacturing; twin plants; hospital; extension colleges; Fiesta de Amistad in October; **Laughlin Air Force Base** (2,892).

Other towns include: **Comstock** (375); **Langtry** (145).

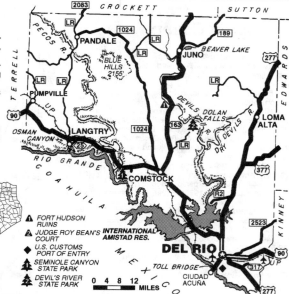

▲ FORT HUDSON RUINS
▲ JUDGE ROY BEAN'S COURT
◆ U.S. CUSTOMS PORT OF ENTRY
▲ SEMINOLE CANYON STATE PARK
▲ DEVIL'S RIVER STATE PARK

0 4 8 12 MILES

Population	43,175
(Change fm '90)	11.5
Land Area (sq. mi.)	3,170.7
Altitude (ft.)	925-2,248
Rainfall (in.)	18.2
Jan. mean min.	39
July mean max.	96
Growing season (days)	300

Civ. Labor	17,990
Unemployed	12.0
Annual Wages	$172,597,905
Av. Weekly Wage	$319.70
Fed. Wages	$49,421,315
Ag. Net Cash Return	$568,000
Prop. Value	$904,824,904
Retail Sales	$300,847,850

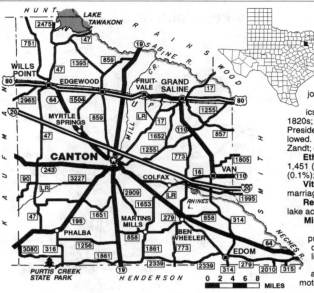

Van Zandt County

Physical Features: Northeastern county in three soil belts; level to rolling; Sabine, Neches rivers; Lake Tawakoni; partly forested.

Economy: Oil, tourism, agribusiness, light manufacturing; many commute to jobs in Dallas.

History: Caddo tribes, reduced by epidemics before settlers arrived. Cherokees settled in 1820s; removed in 1839 under policies of Republic President Lamar; Anglo-American settlement followed. County named for Republic leader Isaac Van Zandt; created from Henderson County 1848.

Ethnicity, 1990: White, 35,351 (93.2%); Black, 1,451 (3.8%); American Indian, 155 (0.4%); Asian, 47 (0.1%); Other, 940 (2.5%). Hispanic, 1,515 (4.0%).

Vital Statistics, 1995: Births, 505; deaths, 498; marriages, 352; divorces, 277.

Recreation: Canton First Monday trades days; lake activities; state park; historic sites.

Minerals: Oil, gas, salt, iron ore, clays.

Agriculture: Nursery plants; beef cattle, dairy products; a major hay and sweet potato producer, also vegetables. Market value $52 million. Some timber, firewood sales.

CANTON (3,417) county seat; tourism; agribusiness; hospice; bluegrass festival; motorcycle rally in June.

Wills Point (3,302) livestock market, some manufacturing, bluebird festival in April.

Other towns include: **Ben Wheeler** (400); **Edgewood** (1,470) heritage square; **Edom** (350) fall art fair; **Fruitvale** (365); **Grand Saline** (2,744), salt plant, manufacturing, hospital, salt palace; **Van** (2,150) oil center, hay, cattle.

Population	41,074	
(Change fm '90)	8.2	
Land Area (sq. mi.)	848.8	
Altitude (ft.)	421-573	
Rainfall (in.)	43.0	
Jan. mean min.	32	
July mean max.	95	
Growing season (days)	250	
Civ. Labor	19,529	
Unemployed	3.9	
Annual Wages	$143,402,592	
Av. Weekly Wage	$361.30	
Fed. Wages	$2,706,596	
Ag. Net Cash Return	$4,865,000	
Prop. Value	$1,566,491,075	
Retail Sales	$224,329,081	

Victoria County

Physical Features: South Central county of rolling prairies, intersected by many streams; sandy loams, clays, alluvial soils.

Economy: Petrochemical plants, government services, oil, manufacturing, agribusiness, tourism.

History: Karankawas, other tribes in area when Spanish explored in 1528.

Comanches, Tawakonis arrived later. French Fort St. Louis on Gracitas Creek 1685-87. Spanish ranching developed in 1750s. Anglo-Americans arrived after 1836. An original county, created 1836 from Mexican municipality named for President Guadalupe Victoria of Mexico.

Ethnicity, 1990: White, 59,251 (79.7%); Black, 4,906 (6.6%); American Indian, 208 (0.3%); Asian, 257 (0.3%); Other, 9,739 (13.1%). Hispanic, 25,372 (34.1%).

Vital Statistics, 1995: Births, 1,276; deaths, 651; marriages, 706; divorces, 408.

Recreation: Fishing, hunting; saltwater activities; historic homes, sites; riverside park, Coleto Creek Reservoir and park; recreational park; zoo; Czech Heritage Festival in October.

Minerals: Oil, gas, sand, gravel.

Agriculture: Corn, beef cattle, grain sorghums, cotton, rice, soybeans. Market value $25.2 million.

VICTORIA (61,320) county seat; tourism, agribusiness center; on barge canal; petrochemicals; foundry equipment; Victoria College, University of Houston at Victoria; community theater, symphony; hospitals.

Other towns include: **Bloomington** (1,938), **Inez** (1,397), **McFaddin** (175), **Nursery** (260), **Placedo** (760), **Telferner** (700).

Population	80,055	
(Change fm '90)	7.7	
Land Area (sq. mi.)	882.6	
Altitude (ft.)	38-205	
Rainfall (in.)	37.4	
Jan. mean min.	43	
July mean max.	94	
Growing season (days)	290	
Civ. Labor	41,909	
Unemployed	5.1	
Annual Wages	$757,086,657	
Av. Weekly Wage	$442.47	
Fed. Wages	$9,077,608	
Ag. Net Cash Return	$2,540,000	
Prop. Value	$3,292,016,820	
Retail Sales	$905,547,898	

Walker County

Physical Features: Southeastern county north of Houston of rolling hills; more than 70 percent forested; national forest; San Jacinto, Trinity rivers.

Economy: State employment in prison system, education; tourism; timber; beef cattle.

History: Coahuiltecans, Bidais in area when Spanish explored around 1690. Later, area became trading ground for many Indian tribes. Anglo-Americans settled in 1830s. Antebellum slaveholding area. County created 1846 from Montgomery County; first named for U.S. Secretary of Treasury R.J. Walker; renamed 1863 for Texas Ranger Capt. S.H. Walker.

Ethnicity, 1990: White, 34,946 (68.6%); Black, 12,334 (24.2%); American Indian, 187 (0.4%); Asian, 323 (0.6%); Other, 3,127 (6.1%). Hispanic, 5,493 (10.8%).

Vital Statistics, 1995: Births, 601; deaths, 334; marriages, 562; divorces, 229.

Recreation: Fishing, hunting; lake activities; Sam Houston Museum, homes, grave; prison museum; other historic sites; state park; Sam Houston National Forest; Cinco de Mayo celebration, Sam Houston folk festival in April.

Minerals: Clays, natural gas, oil, sand and gravel, stone.

Agriculture: Cattle, exotics; nursery plants, hay. Market value $14.2 million. Timber sales substantial; Christmas trees.

HUNTSVILLE (34,594) county seat; Texas Department of Criminal Justice headquarters; Sam Houston State University, museum; varied manufacturing; oil, gas, lignite exploration; hospital.

Other towns include: **Dodge** (150), **New Waverly** (1,065), **Riverside** (514).

Population	55,879
(Change fm '90)	9.7
Land Area (sq. mi.)	787.5
Altitude (ft.)	140-404

Rainfall (in.)	45.0
Jan. mean min.	38
July mean max.	94
Growing season (days)	265
Civ. Labor	22,440

Unemployed	2.6
Annual Wages	$425,794,725
Av. Weekly Wage	$403.52
Fed. Wages	$5,400,803
Ag. Net Cash Return	$3,222,000
Prop. Value	$1,214,183,130
Retail Sales	$354,428,325

STATE PRISONS
❶ WYNNE
❷ GOREE
❸ ELLIS
❹ EASTHAM
🌲 HUNTSVILLE STATE PARK

Waller County

Physical Features: Southeastern county near Houston on rolling prairie; drains to Brazos; alluvial soils; about 20 percent forested.

Economy: Agribusiness, oil, manufacturing, education, county part of Houston metropolitan area.

History: Bidais Indians reduced to about 100 when Anglo-Americans settled in 1820s. Antebellum slaveholding area. County named for Edwin Waller, Republic leader; created 1873 from Austin, Grimes counties.

Ethnicity, 1990: White, 12,987 (55.5%); Black, 8,796 (37.6%); American Indian, 28 (0.1%); Asian, 69 (0.3%); Other, 1,510 (6.5%). Hispanic, 2,592 (11.1%).

Vital Statistics, 1995: Births, 376; deaths, 213; marriages, 201; divorces, 119.

Recreation: Fishing, hunting; historic sites; museum.

Minerals: Oil, gas, sand, gravel.

Agriculture: Beef cattle, hogs, goats, horses; crops include rice, hay, corn, watermelons; 10,000 acres irrigated for rice, commercial vegetables and peanuts. Market value $27.5 million. Some timber marketed.

HEMPSTEAD (3,956) county seat; agribusiness center; varied manufacturing; mental health facility; watermelon fest.

Prairie View (4,105), home of Prairie View A&M University.

Other towns include: **Brookshire** (3,587), **Pattison** (377), **Pine Island** (626), **Waller** (1,831, partly in Harris County). Also, **Katy** (11,204, partly in Harris and Fort Bend Counties).

Population	26,573
(Change fm '90)	13.6
Land Area (sq. mi.)	513.6

Altitude (ft.)	110-249
Rainfall (in.)	38.2
Jan. mean min.	38
July mean max.	95
Growing season (days)	283
Civ. Labor	12,111

Unemployed	4.6
Annual Wages	$181,402,061
Av. Weekly Wage	$417.49
Fed. Wages	$1,713,725
Ag. Net Cash Return	$1,417,000
Prop. Value	$6,379,432,859
Retail Sales	$428,304,460

Ward County

Physical Features: Western county on Pecos River; plain covered by grass, brush; sandy, loam soils.

Economy: Oil, gas; sand and gravel produced.

History: Jumano Indians in area when Spanish explored in 1580s. Comanches arrived later. Railroad stations established in 1880s. Oil discovered in 1920s. County named for Republic leader Thomas W. Ward; county created from Tom Green 1887; organized 1892.

Ethnicity, 1990: White, 9,905 (75.5%); Black, 457 (3.5%); American Indian, 75 (0.6%); Asian, 25 (0.2%); Other, 2,653 (20.2%). Hispanic, 4,830 (36.8%).

Vital Statistics, 1995: Births, 169; deaths, 108; marriages, 87; divorces, 50.

Recreation: Sandhills state park, museum; Pyote Rattlesnake Museum; Million Barrel Museum; county park; freedom fair in July.

Minerals: Oil, gas, sand, gravel.

Agriculture: Beef cattle; horses, hogs and goats also raised; cotton, alfalfa, pecans, hay grown; some irrigation for cotton. Market value $2 million.

MONAHANS (7,844) county seat; center for oil, agribusiness; gasoline plant; pecan shelling; county hospital, nursing home.

Other towns include: **Barstow** (522); **Grandfalls** (632); **Pyote** (379), West Texas Children's Home; **Royalty** (29); **Thorntonville** (767); **Wickett** (541).

Population..............................12,839
(Change fm '90)..............................-2.1
Land Area (sq. mi.)......................835.6

Altitude (ft.)	2,467-2,799
Rainfall (in.)	12.7
Jan. mean min.	27
July mean max.	96
Growing season (days)	223
Civ. Labor	4,473
Unemployed	6.4
Annual Wages	$80,637,646
Av. Weekly Wage	$442.95
Fed. Wages	$817,507
Ag. Net Cash Return	$357,000
Prop. Value	$814,825,378
Retail Sales	$56,693,699

Washington County

Physical Features: Southeastern county in Brazos valley; rolling prairie of sandy loam, alluvial soils.

Economy: Agribusinesses, oil, tourism, manufacturing; government/ services.

Population	**29,213**
(Change fm '90)	11.7
Land Area (sq. mi.)	609.3
Altitude (ft.)	343-460
Rainfall (in.)	41.4
Jan. mean min.	41
July mean max.	96
Growing season (days)	277
Civ. Labor	15,025
Unemployed	2.7
Annual Wages	$254,583,007
Av. Weekly Wage	$399.32
Fed. Wages	$2,393,303
Ag. Net Cash Return	$848,000
Prop. Value	$1,512,345,907
Retail Sales	$237,931,865

History: Coahuiltecan tribes and Tonkawas in area when Anglo-American settlers arrived also in 1821. Antebellum slaveholding area. Germans arrived around 1870. County named for George Washington; an original county, created 1836, organized 1837.

Ethnicity, 1990: White, 19,782 (75.6%); Black, 5,463 (20.9%); American Indian, 46 (0.2%); Asian, 186 (0.7%); Other, 677 (2.6%). Hispanic, 1,158 (4.4%).

Vital Statistics, 1995: Births, 341; deaths, 315; marriages, 225; divorces, 112.

Recreation: Many historic sites; Washington-on-the-Brazos State Park; Texas Baptist Historical Museum; Star of Republic Museum; Somerville Lake; fishing, hunting; antique rose nursery, spring fling.

Minerals: Oil, gas and stone.

Agriculture: Beef cattle, hogs, horses, dairy products, poultry, ratites; crops chiefly cotton, corn, small grains, forage crops. Market value $29.1 million.

BRENHAM (13,873) county seat; cotton processing; varied manufacturing including ceramics, mattresses, computers, Blue Bell creamery; wholesale distribution center; tourism; Blinn College, Brenham State School; Maifest.

Other towns include: **Burton** (338), national landmark cotton gin; **Chappell Hill** (310) historic homes; **Washington** (265) site of signing of Texas Declaration of Independence.

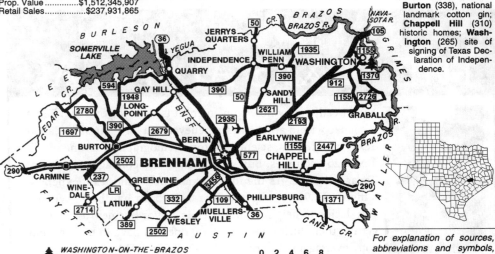

For explanation of sources, abbreviations and symbols, see p. 142.

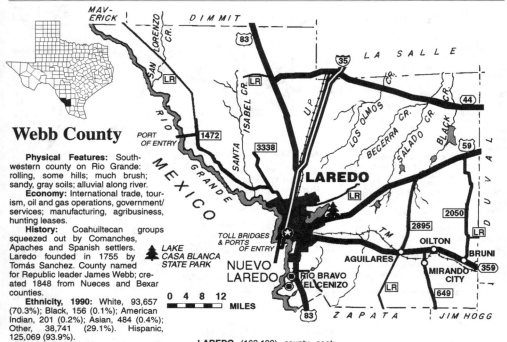

Webb County

Physical Features: Southwestern county on Rio Grande: rolling, some hills; much brush; sandy, gray soils; alluvial along river.

Economy: International trade, tourism, oil and gas operations, government/ services; manufacturing, agribusiness, hunting leases.

History: Coahuiltecan groups squeezed out by Comanches, Apaches and Spanish settlers. Laredo founded in 1755 by Tomás Sanchez. County named for Republic leader James Webb; created 1848 from Nueces and Bexar counties.

Ethnicity, 1990: White, 93,657 (70.3%); Black, 156 (0.1%); American Indian, 201 (0.2%); Asian, 484 (0.4%); Other, 38,741 (29.1%). Hispanic, 125,069 (93.9%).

Vital Statistics, 1995: Births, 4,967; deaths, 820; marriages, 1,982; divorces, 526.

Recreation: Major tourist gateway to Mexico; top hunting, fishing; Lake Casa Blanca State Park, water recreation; art festival; Washington's Birthday celebration; historic sites; museum; Fort McIntosh.

Minerals: Natural gas, oil, coal, caliche, stone, sand and gravel.

Agriculture: Beef cow-calf operations; some stocker production; vegetables, hay, melons; about 4,500 acres irrigated. Market value $22.7 million. Mesquite package wood sales.

LAREDO (162,122) county seat; international trade; retail; tourism; manufacturing; meat packing; rail, highway gateway to Mexico; oil & gas; agribusiness; junior college, Texas A&M International University; mental health center; hospitals.

Other towns include: **Bruni** (581); **El Cenizo** (1,965); **Mirando City** (707); **Oilton** (585); **Rio Bravo** (3,867).

For explanation of sources, abbreviations and symbols, see p. 142.

Population	176,318
(Change fm '90)	32.3
Land Area (sq. mi.)	3,357.0
Altitude (ft.)	372-899
Rainfall (in.)	21.4
Jan. mean min.	43
July mean max.	99
Growing season (days)	322
Civ. Labor	69,188
Unemployed	12.7
Annual Wages	$1,057,849,407
Av. Weekly Wage	$374.18
Fed. Wages	$59,387,545
Ag. Net Cash Return	$4,137,000
Prop. Value	$5,332,935,363
Retail Sales	$1,445,046,726

Wharton County

Population 40,990
(Change fm '90) 2.6
Land Area (sq. mi.) 1,090.2
Altitude (ft.) 71-148
Rainfall (in.) 42.3
Jan. mean min. 41
July mean max. 92
Growing season (days) 266
Civ. Labor 19,205
Unemployed 6.3
Annual Wages $283,453,771
Av. Weekly Wage $390.23
Fed. Wages $3,216,427
Ag. Net Cash Return $21,347,000
Prop. Value $1,824,622,440
Retail Sales $294,156,852

Physical Features: Southeastern county near Houston on prairie; bisected by Colorado River; alluvial, black, sandy loam soils.

Economy: Oil, sulphur, other minerals; agribusiness, hunting leases, varied manufacturing.

History: Karankawas in area until 1840s. Anglo-American colonists settled in 1823. Czechs, Germans arrived in 1880s. Mexican migration increased after 1950. County named for John A. and William H. Wharton, brothers active in the Texas Revolution; created 1846 from Jackson, Matagorda counties.

Ethnicity, 1990: White, 29,127 (72.9%); Black, 6,308 (15.8%); American Indian, 38 (0.1%); Asian, 131 (0.3%); Other, 4,351 (10.9%). Hispanic, 10,103 (25.3%).

Vital Statistics, 1995: Births, 571; deaths, 424; marriages, 281; divorces, 152.

Recreation: Waterfowl hunting, fishing; big-game, art and historical museums; river-front park in Wharton; historic sites; WhartonFest on Colorado.

Minerals: Oil, gas.

Agriculture: Leading rice-producing county; other crops are sorghum, cotton, corn; eggs; turfgrass; beef cattle; hay, soybeans; about 130,000 acres irrigated, mostly rice. Market value $113.4 million.

WHARTON (10,066) county seat; mineral; produce processing; hospitals; Wharton County Junior College.

El Campo (10,798) rice processing, aluminum processing, manufacturing, storage; plastic, styrofoam processing; wholesale nursery; hospital; Texas polka music awards in April.

Other towns include: **Boling-Iago** (1,146); **Danevang** (61); **East Bernard** (1,673), agribusiness, varied manufacturing; **Egypt** (26); **Glen Flora** (210); **Hungerford** (178); **Lane City** (111); **Lissie** (70); **Louise** (310); **Pierce** (49).

Wheeler County

Physical Features: Panhandle county adjoining Oklahoma. Plain, on edge of Caprock; Red River, Sweetwater Creek; some canyons; red sandy loam, black clay soils.

Economy: Oil, agribusinesses, tourism.

History: Apaches, displaced by Kiowas, Comanches around 1700. Military outpost established in 1875 after Indians forced into Oklahoma. Ranching began in late 1870s. Oil boom in 1920s. County named for pioneer jurist R.T. Wheeler; county created from Bexar, Young districts 1876; organized 1879.

Ethnicity, 1990: White, 5,424 (92.3%); Black, 154 (2.6%); American Indian, 42 (0.7%); Asian, 23 (0.4%); Other, 236 (4.0%). Hispanic, 378 (6.4%).

Vital Statistics, 1995: Births, 60; deaths, 99; marriages, 113; divorces, 20.

Recreation: Pioneer West museum at Shamrock; historic sites; Old Mobeetie trading post, Fort Elliott; ostrich depot.

Minerals: Oil, natural gas.

Agriculture: Fed beef, cow-calf and stocker cattle, swine, horses, ostriches; crops include wheat, grain sorghums, cotton. Market value $67 million.

WHEELER (1,384) county seat; agribusiness; petroleum center; tourism; slaughter plant; hospital; library.

Shamrock (2,101) Tourism; agribusiness; hospital; library; St. Patrick's Day event; Octoberfest.

Other towns include: **Allison** (135); **Briscoe** (135); **Mobeetie** (149).

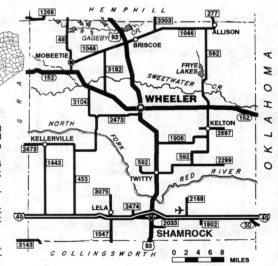

Population 5,602
(Change fm '90) .... -4.7
Land Area (sq. mi.) 914.3
Altitude (ft.) 2,127-2,869
Rainfall (in.) 22.1
Jan. mean min. 22
July mean max. 95
Growing season (days) 208

Civ. Labor 2,893
Unemployed 4.2
Annual Wages $31,765,483
Av. Weekly Wage $341.45
Fed. Wages $837,245
Ag. Net Cash Return $10,593,000
Prop. Value $564,040,886
Retail Sales $38,049,929

Wichita County

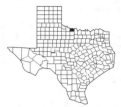

Physical Features: North central county in prairie bordering Oklahoma; drained by Red, Wichita rivers; lakes; sandy, loam soils.

Economy: Retail trade center for large area; air base; government, manufacturing, oil, medical services and agribusiness.

History: Wichitas and other Caddoan tribes in area in 1700s; Comanches, Apaches also present until 1850s. Ango-American settlement increased after 1870. County named for Indian tribe; created from Young Territory 1858; organized 1882.

Ethnicity, 1990: White, 102,427 (83.7%); Black, 11,221 (9.2%); American Indian, 903 (0.7%); Asian, 1,851 (1.5%); Other, 5,976 (4.9%). Hispanic, 10,555 (8.6%).

Vital Statistics, 1995: Births, 1,857; deaths, 1,312; marriages, 2,436; divorces, 945.

Recreation: Metropolitan events; museums; historic Kell House; Oil Bowl football game in August; collegiate activities; water sports on lakes.

Minerals: Oil, natural gas, sand, gravel, stone.

Agriculture: Stocker, cow-calf production important; wheat, cotton; 2,500 acres irrigated for cotton and coastal Bermuda. Market value $20.1 million.

WICHITA FALLS (98,553) county seat; distribution center for large area in Texas, Oklahoma; varied manufacturing; oil-field services; hospitals; Midwestern State University, vocational-technical training center; Wichita Falls State Hospital; major bicycle race in summer; **Sheppard Air Force Base** (3,825).

Other cities include: **Burkburnett** (10,933) some manufacturing; **Electra** (3,253); **Iowa Park** (6,958) some manufacturing, clinic; **Kamay** (642); **Pleasant Valley** (450).

Population	**127,789**
(Change fm '90)	4.4
Land Area (sq. mi.)	627.7
Altitude (ft.)	954-1,225
Rainfall (in.)	28.9
Jan. mean min.	28
July mean max.	97
Growing season (days)	229
Civ. Labor	61,792
Unemployed	4.6
Annual Wages	$1,098,745,445
Av. Weekly Wage	$409.11
Fed. Wages	$75,452,893
Ag. Net Cash Return	$2,370,000
Prop. Value	$3,922,878,764
Retail Sales	$1,221,865,343

For explanation of sources, abbreviations and symbols, see. 142.

Wilbarger County

Physical Features: Gently rolling prairie draining to Red, Pease rivers, tributaries; sandy, loam, waxy soils; Santa Rosa Lake.

Economy: Agribusinesses, oil.

History: Anglo-American settlement developed after removal of Comanches into Indian Territory in 1875. County named for pioneers Josiah and Mathias Wilbarger; created from Bexar District 1858; organized 1881.

Ethnicity, 1990: White, 12,010 (79.4%); Black, 1,349 (8.9%); American Indian, 80 (0.5%); Asian, 82 (0.5%); Other, 1,600 (10.6%). Hispanic, 2,185 (14.5%).

Vital Statistics, 1995: Births, 194; deaths, 197; marriages, 334; divorces, 73.

Recreation: Doan's Crossing, on route of cattle drives; other historic sites; Red River Valley Museum; Santa Rosa roundup in May; hunting, fishing.

Minerals: Oil, natural gas.

Agriculture: Wheat, alfalfa, cotton, peanuts, grain sorghum, beef cattle, watermelons; 25,000 acres irrigated. Market value $32.5 million.

VERNON (12,572) county seat; agribusiness, oil-producing center; varied manufacturing; electricity-generating plant; junior college; mental health center; hospital; downtown antiques, crafts mall.

Other towns include: **Harrold** (320); **Lockett** (200) A&M extension center; **Odell** (131); **Oklaunion** (138).

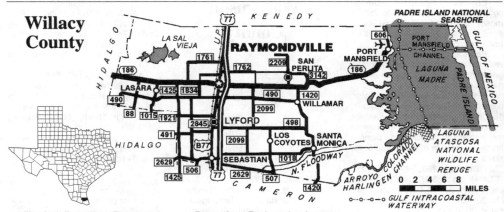

Population	15,855
(Change fm '90)	4.9
Land Area (sq. mi.)	971.1
Altitude (ft.)	1,099-1,361
Rainfall (in.)	25.7
Jan. mean min.	25
July mean max.	97
Growing season (days)	221
Civ. Labor	7,156
Unemployed	4.5

Annual Wages	$111,338,073	Ag. Net Cash Return	$5,486,000
Av. Weekly Wage	$370.08	Prop. Value	$861,494,527
Fed. Wages	$2,462,259	Retail Sales	$92,428,064

Willacy County

Physical Features: Flat coastal prairie sloping toward Gulf; alluvial, sandy, marshy soils; Padre Island; La Sal Vieja, salt lake; wildlife refuge.

Economy: Oil, agribusinesses; tourism; shipping.

History: Coahuiltecan area when Spanish explored in 1500s. Spanish ranching began in 1790s. County named for Texas legislator John G. Willacy; created 1911 from Cameron, Hidalgo counties; reorganized 1921.

Ethnicity, 1990: White, 13,820 (78.1%); Black, 79 (0.4%); American Indian, 29 (0.2%); Asian, 13 (0.1%); Other, 3,764 (21.3%). Hispanic, 14,937 (84.4%).

Vital Statistics, 1995: Births, 379; deaths, 132; marriages, 160; divorces, 164.

Recreation: Fresh and saltwater fishing, hunting; mild climate attracts many winter tourists; Port Mansfield fishing tournament.

Minerals: Oil, natural gas.

Agriculture: Cotton, sorghums, corn, vegetables; livestock includes cattle, hogs, horses, Spanish goats raised; 35,000 acres irrigated. Market value $43.7 million.

RAYMONDVILLE (9,343) county seat; agribusiness, oil center; clothing manufacturing; food processing, shipping; tourist center; museum; hospital; enterprise zone; prison unit.

Other towns include: **Lasara** (100); **Lyford** (1,977); **Port Mansfield** (731) popular fishing port; shrimp processing; **San Perlita** (677); **Sebastian** (1,747).

Population	19,465
(Change fm '90)	9.9
Land Area (sq. mi.)	596.7
Altitude (ft.)	sea level-55
Rainfall (in.)	27.6
Jan. mean min.	46
July mean max.	96
Growing season (days)	331
Civ. Labor	7,697
Unemployed	21.1
Annual Wages	$61,591,038
Av. Weekly Wage	$319.53
Fed. Wages	$1,261,769
Ag. Net Cash Return	$8,518,000
Prop. Value	$683,330,811
Retail Sales	$61,810,755

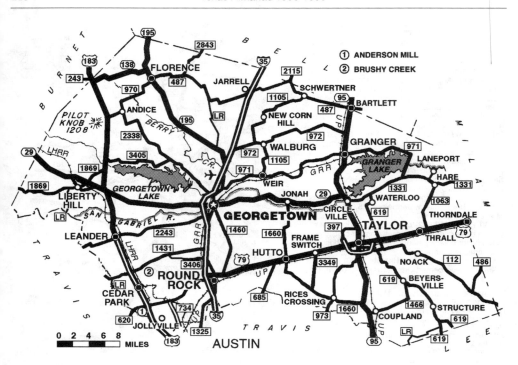

① ANDERSON MILL
② BRUSHY CREEK

Williamson County

Physical Features: Central county near Austin. Level to rolling; mostly Blackland soil, some loam, sand; drained by San Gabriel River and tributaries.

Economy: Agribusinesses, varied manufacturing, education center, government/services; the county is part of Austin metropolitan area.

History: Tonkawa area; later, other tribes. Comanches raided until 1860s. Anglo-American settlement began in late 1830s. County named for Robert M. Williamson, pioneer leader; created from Milam and organized in 1848.

Ethnicity, 1990: White, 121,914 (87.4%); Black, 6,861 (4.9%); American Indian, 508 (0.4%); Asian, 1,846 (1.3%); Other, 8,422 (6.0%). Hispanic, 20,004 (14.3%).

Vital Statistics, 1995: Births, 2,885; deaths, 936; marriages, 1,322; divorces, 868.

Recreation: Lake recreation; Inner Space Cavern; historic sites; hunting, fishing; Gov. Dan Moody Museum at Taylor; San Gabriel Park; old settlers park; walking tours, rattlesnake sacking, barbecue cookoff, frontier days in summer.

Minerals: Building stone, oil, sand and gravel.

Agriculture: Beef cattle, cotton, corn, sorghum, hay. Market value $44.8 million.

GEORGETOWN (20,946) county seat; agribusiness, manufacturing, education, tourism, mining; hospital; Southwestern University; Mayfair; Christmas Stroll.

Round Rock (48,923, partly in Travis County), varied manufacturing; tourism and distribution center; hospital; Texas Baptist Children's Home.

Taylor (13,456), agribusiness, publishing center; varied manufacturing including cottonseed and meat processing; hospital; Temple Junior College extension.

Other towns include: **Bartlett** (1,648, partly in Bell County), first rural electrification in nation in 1933, clinic; library; **Brushy Creek** (6,554); **Cedar Park** (10,371) varied manufacturing, Cedar Chopper festival in June; **Coupland** (135); **Florence** (1,147).

Also, **Granger** (1,346); **Hutto** (740); **Jarrell** (410); **Jollyville** (20,386); **Leander** (5,723); **Liberty Hill** (300) artisans center; **Schwertner** (150); **Thrall** (664); **Walburg** (250); **Weir** (292).

Also, the residential community of **Anderson Mill** (10,600) which extends from Travis County.

Population	190,190
(Change fm '90)	36.3
Land Area (sq. mi.)	1,124.4
Altitude (ft.)	454-1,265
Rainfall (in.)	34.4
Jan. mean min.	34
July mean max.	96
Growing season (days)	258
Civ. Labor	115,538
Unemployed	2.0
Annual Wages	$1,045,654,008
Av. Weekly Wage	$428.23
Fed. Wages	$11,607,426
Ag. Net Cash Return	$3,432,000
Prop. Value	$10,559,670,494
Retail Sales	$1,527,935,760

For explanation of sources, abbreviations and symbols, see p. 142.

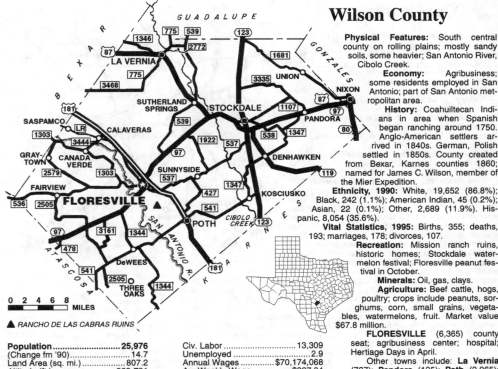

▲ RANCHO DE LAS CABRAS RUINS

Wilson County

Physical Features: South central county on rolling plains; mostly sandy soils, some heavier; San Antonio River, Cibolo Creek.

Economy: Agribusiness; some residents employed in San Antonio; part of San Antonio metropolitan area.

History: Coahuiltecan Indians in area when Spanish began ranching around 1750. Anglo-American settlers arrived in 1840s. German, Polish settled in 1850s. County created from Bexar, Karnes counties 1860; named for James C. Wilson, member of the Mier Expedition.

Ethnicity, 1990: White, 19,652 (86.8%); Black, 242 (1.1%); American Indian, 45 (0.2%); Asian, 22 (0.1%); Other, 2,689 (11.9%). Hispanic, 8,054 (35.6%).

Vital Statistics, 1995: Births, 355; deaths, 193; marriages, 178; divorces, 107.

Recreation: Mission ranch ruins, historic homes; Stockdale watermelon festival; Floresville peanut festival in October.

Minerals: Oil, gas, clays.

Agriculture: Beef cattle, hogs, poultry; crops include peanuts, sorghums, corn, small grains, vegetables, watermelons, fruit. Market value $67.8 million.

FLORESVILLE (6,365) county seat; agribusiness center; hospital; Hertiage Days in April.

Other towns include: **La Vernia** (787); **Pandora** (125); **Poth** (2,065); **Stockdale** (1,369), food processing; medical center; recreation facilities; **Sutherland Springs** (362).

Population **25,976**	Civ. Labor 13,309
(Change fm '90) 14.7	Unemployed 2.9
Land Area (sq. mi.) 807.2	Annual Wages $70,174,068
Altitude (ft.) 362-781	Av. Weekly Wage $327.84
Rainfall (in.) 29.4	Fed. Wages $1,772,393
Jan. mean min. 36	Ag. Net Cash Return $5,232,000
July mean max. 96	Prop. Value $941,897,809
Growing season (days) 280	Retail Sales $90,768,041

Winkler County

Physical Features: Western county adjoining New Mexico on plains, partly sandy hills.

Economy: Oil, natural gas; ranching.

History: Apache area until arrival of Comanches in 1700s. Anglo-Americans began ranching in 1880s. Oil discovered 1926. Mexican migration increased after 1960. County named for Confederate Col. C.M. Winkler; created from Tom Green 1887; organized 1910.

Ethnicity, 1990: White, 6,184 (71.7%); Black, 167 (1.9%); American Indian, 48 (0.6%); Asian, 9 (0.1%); Other, 2,218 (25.7%). Hispanic, 3,172 (36.8%).

Vital Statistics, 1995: Births, 122; deaths, 75; marriages, 68; divorces, 31.

Recreation: Sandhills Park; museum; zoo; wooden oil derrick; Roy Orbison Festival in June at Wink; Wink Sink, large sinkhole.

Minerals: A leading petroleum-producing county; gas, salt also produced.

Agriculture: Cow-calf production, stocker cattle, horses; no crops. Market value $3.2 million.

KERMIT (6,493) county seat, and **Wink** (1,120) are oil-activity centers; hospital.

Population **8,213**	Jan. mean min. 28	Av. Weekly Wage $413.76
(Change fm '90) .... -4.8	July mean max. 97	Fed. Wages $402,621
Land Area (sq. mi.) 841.1	Growing season (days) 219	Ag. Net Cash Return $634,000
Altitude (ft.) 2,671-3,193	Civ. Labor 3,019	Prop. Value $667,950,020
Rainfall (in.) 12.6	Unemployed 7.6	Retail Sales $31,412,387
	Annual Wages $45,283,645	

Wise County

Physical Features: North central county of rolling prairie, some oaks; clay, loam, sandy soils; lakes.

Economy: Agribusiness, petroleum, recreation, hunting leases; many residents work in Fort Worth.

History: Caddo Indian groups. Delaware tribe present when Anglo-Americans arrived in 1850s. County created 1856 from Cooke County; named for Virginian, U.S. Sen. Henry A. Wise, who favored annexation of Texas.

Ethnicity, 1990: White, 32,550 (93.9%); Black, 390 (1.1%); American Indian, 210 (0.6%); Asian, 83 (0.2%); Other, 1,446 (4.2%). Hispanic, 2,663 (7.7%).

Vital Statistics, 1995: Births, 474; deaths, 338; marriages, 328; divorces, 204.

Recreation: Lake activities; hunting; exotic deer preserve; historical sites; Lyndon B. Johnson National Grasslands; Chisholm trail days in June, antique auto swap meet; Butterfield stage days in July; heritage museum, old courthouse.

Minerals: Gas, oil, stone, clays, sand, gravel.

Agriculture: Dairy operations, beef cattle, horses, sheep, goats, ratite birds; a leading dairy county; crops include hay, peanuts, grain sorghums, pecans, wheat and oats. Market value $39.4 million.

DECATUR (4,669) county seat; petroleum center; dairying; cattle marketing; some manufacturing; hospital.

Bridgeport (3,915), trade center for lake resort; oil, gas production; timeshare housing; artistic community; manufacturing.

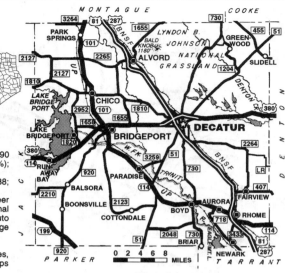

Other towns include: **Alvord** (1,081); **Aurora** (728); **Boyd** (1,163); **Briar** (4,294, partly in Tarrant, Parker counties); **Chico** (910); **Fairview** (237); **Greenwood** (76); **Lake Bridgeport** (355); **Newark** (808); **Paradise** (275); **Rhome** (730); **Slidell** (175).

Population **39,550**
(Change fm '90) 14.0
Land Area (sq. mi.) 904.7

Altitude (ft.) 693-1,180
Rainfall (in.)................................32.6
Jan. mean min. 30
July mean max.................................99
Growing season (days)....................220
Civ. Labor..............................20,646
Unemployed.................................3.4
Annual Wages....................$207,372,520
Av. Weekly Wage $423.88
Fed. Wages....................$3,042,412
Ag. Net Cash Return...........$5,362,000
Prop. Value $1,563,829,597
Retail Sales..................$285,267,943

Wood County

Physical Features: Hilly northeastern county almost half forested; sandy to alluvial soils; drained by Sabine and tributaries; many lakes.

Economy: Oil, natural gas, agribusiness, tourism.

History: Caddo Indians; reduced by disease. Anglo-American settlement developed in 1840s. County created from Van Zandt County 1850; named for Gov. George T. Wood.

Ethnicity, 1990: White, 26,363 (89.7%); Black, 2,402 (8.2%); American Indian, 109 (0.4%); Asian, 40 (0.1%); Other, 466 (1.6%). Hispanic, 788 (2.7%).

Vital Statistics, 1995: Births, 401; deaths, 432; marriages, 317; divorces, 221.

Recreation: Autumn trails; lake activities; hunting; Gov. Hogg Shrine State Park and museum; historic sites; scenic drives; Mineola May Days; railroad heritage days; autumn trails.

Minerals: Natural gas, sand, gravel.

Agriculture: Dairy, poultry, beef cattle, horses, swine; hay, sweet potatoes, ensilage, watermelons, truck crops. Market value $52.4 million. Timber sold.

QUITMAN (1,865) county seat; tourism; food processing; some manufacturing; hospital.

Mineola (4,681), farm, railroad center; food processing; some manufacturing; museum.

Winnsboro (3,201, partly in Franklin County) gas and oil, dairies, tourism; hospital.

Other towns include: **Alba** (519, partly in Rains County); **Golden** (156); **Hawkins** (1,424); **Yantis** (284).

🌲 GOV. HOGG SHRINE STATE PARK

Population **32,031**
(Change fm '90) 9.0
Land Area (sq. mi.) 650.3
Altitude (ft.) 299-630
Rainfall (in.)..............................45.0
Jan. mean min. 31
July mean max.............................94
Growing season (days)...............246

Civ. Labor...............................14,378
Unemployed...............................5.9
Annual Wages...........$143,032,551
Av. Weekly Wage...............$359.19
Fed. Wages....................$3,042,412
Ag. Net Cash Return......$7,237,000
Prop. Value $1,513,691,818
Retail Sales...............$212,332,831

Yoakum County

Physical Features: Western county is level to rolling; playas, draws; sandy, loam, chocolate soils.

Economy: Oil, agriculture.

History: Comanche hunting area. Anglo-Americans began ranching in 1890s. Oil discovered 1936. Mexican migration increased in 1950s. County named for Henderson Yoakum, pioneer historian; created from Bexar District 1876; organized 1907.

Ethnicity, 1990: White, 6,300 (71.7%); Black, 86 (1.0%); American Indian, 31 (0.4%); Asian, 11 (0.1%); Other, 2,358 (26.8%). Hispanic, 3,217 (36.6%).

Vital Statistics, 1995: Births, 126; deaths, 49; marriages, 87; divorces, 43.

Recreation: Tsa Mo Ga Museum at Plains; settlers reunion in August.

Minerals: Oil, natural gas, salt makes this a leading minerals-producing county.

Agriculture: Grains, cotton, sorghums, wheat, peanuts; beef cattle raised; substantial irrigation. Market value $36.4 million.

PLAINS (1,396) county seat; oil, agribusiness center.

Denver City (5,048), center for oil, agriculture activities in two counties; hospital, library.

Population		8,573
(Change fm '90)		-2.4
Land Area (sq. mi.)		799.8
Altitude (ft.)		3,490-3,891
Rainfall (in.)		17.7
Jan. mean min.		22
July mean max.		91
Growing season (days)		199
Civ. Labor		3,745
Unemployed		5.2
Annual Wages		$76,515,124
Av. Weekly Wage		$475.66
Fed. Wages		$601,661
Ag. Net Cash Return		$9,465,000
Prop. Value		$1,477,762,380
Retail Sales		$50,005,936

Young County

Physical Features: Hilly, broken; drained by Brazos and tributaries; Possum Kingdom Lake, Lake Graham.

Economy: Oil, agribusiness, tourism; hunting leases.

History: U.S. military outpost established 1851. Site of Brazos Indian Reservation 1854-59 with Caddoes, Wacos, other tribes. Anglo-American settlers arrived in 1850s. County named for early Texan, Col. W.C. Young; created 1856 from Bosque, Fannin counties; reorganized 1874.

Ethnicity, 1990: White, 17,023 (93.9%); Black, 268 (1.5%); American Indian, 62 (0.3%); Asian, 49 (0.3%); Other, 724 (4.0%). Hispanic, 1,164 (6.4%).

Vital Statistics, 1995: Births, 219; deaths, 243; marriages, 161; divorces, 145.

Recreation: Lake activities; hunting; Fort Belknap restoration; marker at oak tree in Graham where ranchers formed forerunner of Texas and Southwestern Cattle Raisers Association; vintage auto club spring tour; western heritage festival in fall.

Minerals: Oil, gas, sand, gravel.

Agriculture: Beef cattle; wheat chief crop, also hay, cotton, pecans, nursery plants. Market value $22.5 million.

GRAHAM (9,005) county seat; agribusiness, manufacturing; oil-well servicing; hospital, mental health clinic; Ranger Junior College extension; Possom Fest in September.

Other towns include: **Eliasville** (150); **Loving** (300); **Newcastle** (562); **Olney** (3,411) agribusiness center, some manufacturing, hospital, one-arm dove hunt in September; **South Bend** (140).

For explanation of sources, abbreviations and symbols, see p. 142.

Population		17,932
(Change fm '90)		-1.1
Land Area (sq. mi.)		922.4
Altitude (ft.)		1,038-1,389
Rainfall (in.)		30.6
Jan. mean min.		26
July mean max.		96
Growing season (days)		216
Civ. Labor		8,477
Unemployed		6.9
Annual Wages		$125,648,447
Av. Weekly Wage		$400.75
Fed. Wages		$1,800,000
Ag. Net Cash Return		$1,538,000
Prop. Value		$707,015,900
Retail Sales		$123,203,020

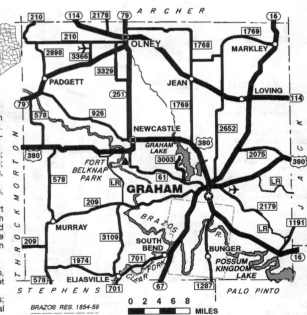

BRAZOS RES. 1854-59

0 2 4 6 8 MILES

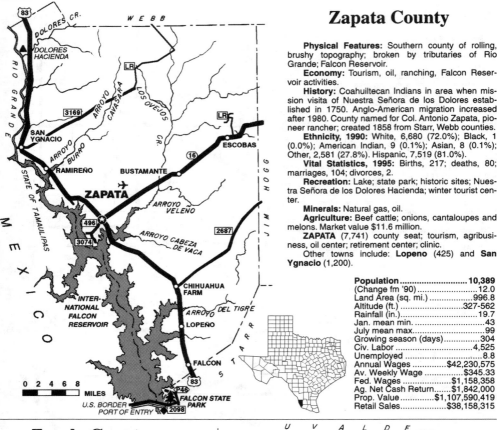

Zapata County

Physical Features: Southern county of rolling, brushy topography; broken by tributaries of Rio Grande; Falcon Reservoir.

Economy: Tourism, oil, ranching, Falcon Reservoir activities.

History: Coahuiltecan Indians in area when mission visita of Nuestra Señora de los Dolores established in 1750. Anglo-American migration increased after 1980. County named for Col. Antonio Zapata, pioneer rancher; created 1858 from Starr, Webb counties.

Ethnicity, 1990: White, 6,680 (72.0%); Black, 1 (0.0%); American Indian, 9 (0.1%); Asian, 8 (0.1%); Other, 2,581 (27.8%). Hispanic, 7,519 (81.0%).

Vital Statistics, 1995: Births, 217; deaths, 80; marriages, 104; divorces, 2.

Recreation: Lake; state park; historic sites; Nuestra Señora de los Dolores Hacienda; winter tourist center.

Minerals: Natural gas, oil.

Agriculture: Beef cattle; onions, cantaloupes and melons. Market value $11.6 million.

ZAPATA (7,741) county seat; tourism, agribusiness, oil center; retirement center; clinic.

Other towns include: **Lopeno** (425) and **San Ygnacio** (1,200).

Population	10,389
(Change fm '90)	12.0
Land Area (sq. mi.)	996.8
Altitude (ft.)	327-562
Rainfall (in.)	19.7
Jan. mean min.	43
July mean max.	99
Growing season (days)	304
Civ. Labor	4,525
Unemployed	8.8
Annual Wages	$42,230,575
Av. Weekly Wage	$345.33
Fed. Wages	$1,158,358
Ag. Net Cash Return	$1,842,000
Prop. Value	$1,107,590,419
Retail Sales	$38,158,315

Zavala County

Physical Features: Southwestern county near Mexican border of rolling plains broken by much brush; Nueces, Leona, other streams.

Economy: Agribusinesses, leading county in Winter Garden truck-farming area; oil, gas, hunting leases.

History: Coahuiltecan area; Apaches, Comanches arrived later. Ranching developed in late 1860s. County created from Maverick, Uvalde counties 1858; organized 1884; named for Texas Revolutionary leader Lorenzo de Zavala.

Ethnicity, 1990: White, 6,443 (53.0%); Black, 296 (2.4%); American Indian, 16 (0.1%); Asian, 3 (0.0%); Other, 5,404 (44.4%). Hispanic, 10,875 (89.4%).

Vital Statistics, 1995: Births, 228; deaths, 91; marriages, 94; divorces, 39.

Recreation: Hunting, fishing; annual spinach festival.

Minerals: Oil, natural gas.

Agriculture: Fed cattle; beef, goats, sheep important; cotton, vegetables, corn, pecans, wheat, grain sorghums; about 40,000 acres irrigated. Market value $37.3 million. Some firewood sold.

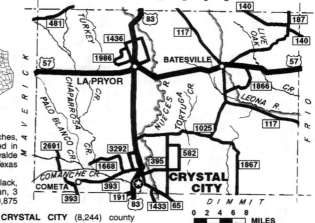

CRYSTAL CITY (8,244) county seat; agribusiness; headquarters for Crystal City railroad; food processing; oil-field services; cotton gin; hospital. Home of Popeye statue.

Other towns include: **Batesville** (1,304), **La Pryor** (1,272).

Population	12,023
(Change fm '90)	-1.1
Land Area (sq. mi.)	1,298.6
Altitude (ft.)	540-956
Rainfall (in.)	21.0
Jan. mean min.	42
July mean max.	97
Growing season (days)	280
Civ. Labor	4,457
Unemployed	23.6
Annual Wages	$36,581,994
Av. Weekly Wage	$293.45
Fed. Wages	$475,015
Ag. Net Cash Return	$5,881,000
Prop. Value	$408,829,477
Retail Sales	$23,886,430

Texas Population Growth Leads Nation

The following article was written by Steve H. Murdock, Md. Nazrul Hoque and Beverly A. Pecotte

The 1990s have witnessed a substantial turnaround in Texas' patterns of population growth from those which existed in the late 1980s. In fact, 1996 estimates of the population of states by the U.S. Bureau of the Census show that Texas increased its population by more than any other state from April 1, 1990 to July 1, 1996.

We examine these statewide patterns and then those which are evident in metropolitan areas, counties and cities in Texas through mid-decade (the most recent period for which Texas State Data Center estimates are available).

Statewide Patterns

Texas' population was 19,128,261 as of July 1, 1996. This represented an increase of 2,141,926 from the 1990 population of 16,986,335 on April 1, 1990. This was slightly larger than the numerical change in the population of California, which is substantially larger with a population estimated at 31,878,234 in 1996.

Florida was the only other state with an increase of more than a million persons, increasing its population by 1,461,914.

Texas' share of national growth has been disproportionate to its size with its 2.1 million increase accounting for 12.9 percent of the nation's growth during the 1990s while its population was only 7.2 percent of the U.S. population total of 265,283,783 in 1996.

The population increase of 12.6 percent for Texas from 1990 to 1996 was the tenth fastest in the nation.

Population Increase 1990-96

Census Estimate

Texas	**2,141,926**
California	2,120,021
Florida	1,461,914
Georgia	875,076
Arizona	762,729
North Carolina	690,422
Washington	666,270
Colorado	528,203
Virginia	486,254
Tennessee	442,451

Total U.S. population July 1, 1996:	**265,283,783**

Source: U.S. Bureau of the Census

The fastest growing state in percentage terms was Nevada with an increase of 33.4 percent, followed by Arizona with an increase of 20.8 percent.

Although nine states showed faster percentage increases in population than Texas, the size of the numerical changes represented by these increases was relatively small compared to Texas' 2.1 million increase and most of the states with faster growth are relatively small states. Thus, the largest numerical increase among other states included among the ten fastest growing states was 875,076 for Georgia.

Texas' rates of growth are dramatically different than those of the middle and late 1980s. For example, Texas' population increased by only 0.3 percent from 1987 to 1988 and during several years in the latter part of the 1980s only a large number of births offset net out-migration from the state so that Texas' population continued to increase.

During that period, Texas' population was growing about one-third as fast as the population of the United States as a whole while, in the 1990s, Texas' rate of growth of 12.6 percent has been more than 88 percent higher than the 6.7 percent rate of growth for the nation.

In the 1990s, among the ten largest states in the nation, Texas' numerical increase was nearly equalled only by California and its percentage increase was exceeded only by Georgia, the eighth largest state.

Many of these large states showed very slow growth. New York increased its population by only 1.1 percent, Pennsylvania increased its population by only 1.5 percent and Illinois, Ohio, and New Jersey all showed increases of between 3 and 4 percent between 1990 and 1996.

During the 1990s, Texas showed average numerical increases of 344,000 per year with an average annual percentage rate of growth of 1.9 percent over the 6.25 years between the 1990 Census and the 1996 estimate. Although Texas' 1995-96 patterns show a slowing of growth compared to the two preceding years, that 1.7 percent was still sufficiently rapid that it would double the state's population in roughly 37 years.

Texas' growth during the 1990s has resulted primarily from natural increase with 1,183,025 persons, or 55.2 percent of all growth from 1990 to 1996, due to natural increase (see Table 2 at end of article).

International immigration accounted for 491,931 new residents, for 23 percent of the growth between 1990 and 1996, and domestic inmigration from other states in the United States accounted for 466,970 or 21.8 percent of population growth from 1990 to 1996. This growth shows a larger proportion of migration than occurred during the 1980s when roughly two-thirds of all growth was due to natural increase.

Patterns of Change in the 1990s

The Council of Governments (COG) regions and metropolitan areas of Texas reflect the overall growth of the state but also display the diversity of Texas. All 24 COG regions have experienced population growth during the 1990s (see Table 1).

The Houston-Galveston region has gained the most

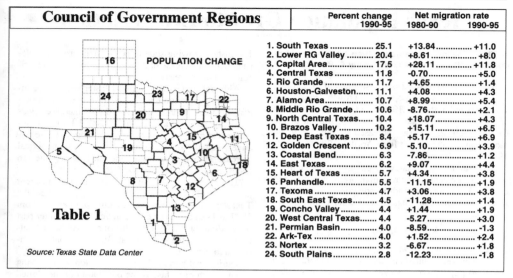

Council of Government Regions	Percent change 1990-95	Net migration rate 1980-90	1990-95
1. South Texas	25.1	+13.84	+11.0
2. Lower RG Valley	20.4	+8.61	+8.0
3. Capital Area	17.5	+28.11	+11.8
4. Central Texas	11.8	-0.70	+5.0
5. Rio Grande	11.7	+4.65	+1.4
6. Houston-Galveston	11.1	+4.08	+4.3
7. Alamo Area	10.7	+8.99	+5.4
8. Middle Rio Grande	10.6	-8.76	+2.1
9. North Central Texas	10.4	+18.07	+4.3
10. Brazos Valley	10.2	+15.11	+6.5
11. Deep East Texas	8.4	+5.17	+6.9
12. Golden Crescent	6.9	-5.10	+3.9
13. Coastal Bend	6.3	-7.86	+1.2
14. East Texas	6.2	+9.07	+4.4
15. Heart of Texas	5.7	+4.34	+3.8
16. Panhandle	5.5	-11.15	+1.9
17. Texoma	4.7	+3.06	+3.8
18. South East Texas	4.5	-11.28	+1.4
19. Concho Valley	4.4	+1.44	+1.9
20. West Central Texas	4.4	-5.27	+3.0
21. Permian Basin	4.0	-8.59	-1.3
22. Ark-Tex	4.0	+1.52	+2.4
23. Nortex	3.2	-6.67	+1.8
24. South Plains	2.8	-12.23	-1.8

POPULATION CHANGE

Table 1

Source: Texas State Data Center

population, followed by the North Central Texas region. The population of the Houston-Galveston increased from 3,897,146 in 1990 to 4,328,105 in 1995. The population of the North Central Texas increased from 4,111,750 in 1990 to 4,540,819 in 1995. The population of the Capital Area region increased from 919,456 in 1990 to 1,080,581 in 1995. In terms of numerical increase, the Houston-Galveston region gained 430,959 persons and the North Central Texas region gained 429,069 persons from 1990 to 1995. The Concho Valley region gained the least population of any region, having gained only 6,304 persons during the 1990s.

In terms of percent population change, the fastest growing regions during the 1990s have been South Texas with a 25.1 percent increase, followed by the Lower Rio Grande Valley with an increase of 20.4 percent, the Capital Area with an increase of 17.5 percent, and the Central Texas region with an 11.8 percent increase.

The slowest growing regions have been the South Plains with a 2.8 percent increase, followed by the Nortex region with an increase of 3.2 percent, and the Ark-Tex and Permian Basin regions with 4.0 percent increases.

In general, then, the fastest growing regions are either along the Texas-Mexico border, in the Houston-Galveston area or in the central corridor of Texas. The slowest growing regions are in the Panhandle and West Texas.

An examination of the data in Table 2 indicates that all but two COG regions have experienced net inmigration during the 1990s. The Permian Basin and South Plains regions are the only regions which have experienced net outmigration during the 1990s.

The regions with the largest number of inmigrants during the 1990s are the North Central Texas region with net inmigration of 174,619 persons, followed by the Houston-Galveston region with net inmigration of 167,294, the Capital Area with net inmigration of 108,887, and the Alamo Area with net inmigration of 79,614. The regions with the largest number of outmigrants during the 1990s have been the South Plains with

net outmigration of 6,627 persons and the Permian Basin with net outmigration of 4,734 persons.

In terms of percent net inmigration in the 1990s, the fastest growing areas are the Capital Area with an inmigration rate of 11.8 percent, followed by South Texas with an inmigration rate of 11.0 percent, the Lower Rio Grande Valley with a rate of 8.0 percent, Deep East Texas with a rate of 6.9 percent, and the Brazos Valley with a rate of 6.5 percent. The outmigration rates for the South Plains and the Permian Basin were -1.8 and -1.3 percent, respectively.

All 27 metropolitan areas (MSAs) have experienced population growth during the 1990s. The largest numerical increases have been in the largest metropolitan areas; Houston increased by 377,960, Dallas increased by 300,661, Austin-San Marcos increased by 152,868, San Antonio increased by 136,596, and Ft. Worth-Arlington increased by 124,400.

In terms of percent population change, the Laredo MSA, with an increase of 28.8 percent during the 1990s, showed the largest gain, followed by the McAllen-Edinburg-Mission MSA with an increase of 24.2 percent, and the Austin-San Marcos MSA which increased by 18.1 percent. The slowest growing MSAs have been Texarkana with an increase of 3.2 percent, Sherman-Denison with an increase of 3.6 percent and Wichita Falls with an increase of 4.0 percent.

Out of 27 metropolitan areas, only Lubbock and Odessa-Midland have experienced net outmigration during the 1990s but the levels of net migration vary widely among the metropolitan areas.

The highest rates of net migration have been in Laredo, Austin-San Marcos, McAllen-Edinburg-Mission, Brazoria, and Bryan-College Station and the lowest in Odessa-Midland, Lubbock, Texarkana, and Corpus-Christi.

Counties and Cities During the 1990s

Texas counties and cities have also shown substantial growth during the 1990s. Although space limitations do not allow us to discuss the patterns for counties and cities in detail, we summarize general patterns for each below. The largest numerical increases in county populations from 1990 to 1995 were in the counties with the largest populations including Harris County with an increase of 251,160, Dallas with an increase of 127,030, Bexar with an increase of 114,092, Tarrant County with an increase of 105,322, and Hidalgo County with an increase of 92,690.

The largest percentage increases were in Collin County with an increase of 31.6 percent, Williamson County with a 31.0 percent increase, Webb County with 28.8 percent, Hartley with 28.0 percent, and Kendall County with an increase of 28.0 percent. In general, the fastest rates of growth were in South Texas, Central Texas and the Gulf Coast areas with slowest rates of growth in West Texas and the Panhandle.

During the 1990s, Collin County has gained the most population due to net inmigration (62,808), followed by Travis County (51,089), Fort Bend County (46,468), and Harris County (42,610). Among the largest counties, Dallas gained the least population due to net inmigration (2,343). Ector and Lubbock were the only two relatively large counties that have experienced net outmigration during the 1990s. Net outmigration for Ector County was 3,398 and for Lubbock County net outmigration was 1,025.

The highest rates of net inmigration were observed in Childress County with 27.7 percent, followed by Hartley County with 26.3 percent, and Polk County with 25.2 percent. Among the counties with net outmigration, the highest rates were in Kenedy with 25.4 percent, Roberts with 14.2 percent, and Castro with a 10.1 percent rate of outmigration.

In general, the data show a relatively dispersed pattern of net inmigration, with counties having higher levels of net immigration being less geographically concentrated than those with higher levels of total population change.

Overall, the 1990s have also brought population growth cities in Texas. From 1990 to 1995, 1,144 of 1,283 cities showed population gains, three cities showed no population change, while the remaining 136 cities lost population. During the 1990s, 1,049 cities gained population due to net inmigration, and 229 places lost population due to net outmigration.

The largest net numerical inmigration was in San Antonio (50,939) followed by Austin (42,738), Plano (29,586), and Laredo (15,705). Houston and Dallas both experienced net outmigration (Dallas lost 18,848 and Houston lost 7,601), as did other relatively large cities and places such as Garland (4,690) and Lubbock (1,887).

In general however, net migration like total population growth was extensive in places in Texas. Towns and cities in Texas have shown rapid population expansion in the 1990s.

Summary and Conclusions

The patterns of population change in Texas from 1990 to 1996 show rapid population growth that is impacting a large majority of the regions, metropolitan areas, counties, and cities of the State. The annual rate of growth is greater than at any time since the early 1980s and a majority of areas are experiencing net inmigration. Growth is extensive and pervasive.

Will such growth continue? It is impossible to predict future patterns with absolute certainty and clearly sharp reversals in population patterns, such as those which appeared during the latter part of the 1980s, are possible.

However, Texas' relatively extensive natural increase coupled with migration should lead to continued growth in the years ahead. In fact, the rates of growth from 1990 to 1996 suggest that there will likely be 20 million Texans in 2000, even if growth slows somewhat in the coming years.

Dr. Murdock is professor and head of the Department of Rural Sociology at Texas A&M University and chief demographer of the Texas State Data Center. Dr. Hoque is an Associate Research Scientist in the department and Ms. Pecotte is a Research Associate.

Table 2: Texas Population Growth by Component of Change

	Population	Births	Deaths	Natural Increase	International Immigration	Net Domestic Migration	Total Change 1990-96
1990	16,986,335	--	--	--	--	--	--
1991*	17,366,958	393,243	154,266	238,977	82,304	59,342	380,623
1992	17,697,419	321,162	128,566	192,596	79,409	58,456	330,461
1993	18,865,397	321,169	131,783	189,386	84,946	93,646	367,978
1994	18,433,735	322,596	136,888	185,708	81,545	101,085	368,338
1995	18,801,380	327,842	136,541	191,301	79,364	96,980	367,645
1996	19,128,261	323,376	138,319	185,057	84,363	57,461	326,881
Total 1990-96	--	2,009,388	826,363	1,183,025	491,931	466,970	2,141,926

Source: Texas State Data Center. * Fifteen months April 1990-July 1991. All others for 12-month periods.

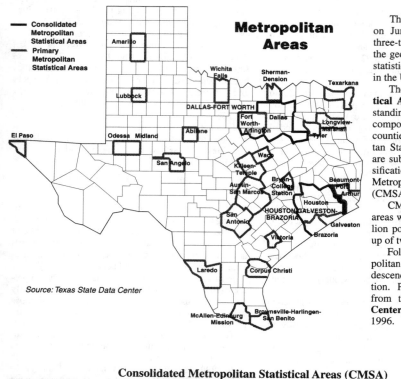

Metropolitan Areas

Source: Texas State Data Center

The federal government on June 30, 1983, began a three-tier system of defining the geographic units to gather statistics in metropolitan areas in the United States.

The **Metropolitan Statistical Areas** (MSA) are free-standing metropolitan areas composed of one or more counties. Primary Metropolitan Statistical Areas (PMSA) are sub-units of a larger classification, the Consolidated Metropolitan Statistical Areas (CMSA).

CMSAs are metropolitan areas with more than one million population and are made up of two or more PMSAs.

Following are the metropolitan areas listed in descending order by population. Population figures are from the Texas **State Data Center** estimates released in 1996.

	Jan. 1, 1996 Population
Consolidated Metropolitan Statistical Areas (CMSA)	
Dallas-Fort Worth (Dallas PMSA and Fort Worth-Arlington PMSA)	4,508,265
Houston-Galveston-Brazoria (Houston PMSA, Galveston PMSA and Brazoria PMSA)	4,189,016

Metropolitan Statistical Areas (MSA) and Primary Metropolitan Statistical Areas (PMSA)

	Jan. 1, 1996 Population
Level A — Population 1,000,000 or More:	
1. Houston (Chambers, Fort Bend, Harris, Liberty, Montgomery and Waller counties)	3,732,406
2. Dallas (Collin, Dallas, Denton, Ellis, Henderson, Hunt, Kaufman and Rockwall counties)	3,007,664
3. Fort Worth-Arlington PMSA (Hood, Johnson, Parker and Tarrant counties)	1,500,601
4. San Antonio MSA (Bexar, Comal, Guadalupe and Wilson counties)	1,474,212
5. Austin-San Marcos MSA (Bastrop, Caldwell, Hays, Travis and Williamson counties)	1,021,567
Level B — Population 250,000 to 1,000,000	
6. El Paso MSA (El Paso County)	668,352
7. McAllen-Edinburg-Mission MSA (Hidalgo County)	485,332
8. Beaumont-Port Arthur MSA (Hardin, Jefferson and Orange counties)	377,093
9. Corpus Christi MSA (Nueces and San Patricio counties)	374,213
10. Brownsville-Harlingen-San Benito MSA (Cameron County)	304,660
11. Killeen-Temple MSA (Bell and Coryell counties)	289,700
Level C — Population 100,000 to 250,000	
12. Galveston-Texas City PMSA (Galveston County)	239,292
13. Odessa-Midland MSA (Ector and Midland County)	239,278
14. Lubbock MSA (Lubbock County)	233,486
15. Brazoria PMSA (Brazoria County)	217,318
16. Amarillo MSA (Potter and Randall counties)	204,861
17. Longview-Marshall MSA (Gregg, Harrison and Upshur counties)	203,997
18. Waco MSA (McLennan County)	202,137
19. Laredo MSA (Webb County)	176,318
20. Tyler MSA (Smith County)	162,480
21. Bryan-College Station MSA (Brazos County)	137,057
22. Wichita Falls MSA (Archer and Wichita counties)	136,228
23. Abilene MSA (Taylor County)	126,805
24. Texarkana MSA (Bowie County, TX, and Miller County, AR)	123,877
25. San Angelo MSA (Tom Green County)	104,398
Level D — Population Under 100,000	
26. Sherman-Denison MSA (Grayson County)	99,236
27. Victoria MSA (Victoria County)	80,055

Places, Towns and Cities

Population: Population figures of **incorporated** cities are Texas State Data Center estimates for Jan. 1, 1996. Names of these incorporated places are in capital letters, e.g., "ABBOTT."

The Census Designated Places (CDPs) are unincorporated towns selected by the U.S. Bureau of the Census for enumeration each decade. The figures here are also 1996 estimates from the state data center. CDPs are designated in the following list by a double dagger symbol (‡).

The population figure given for all other towns is an estimate based on a 1995 Almanac survey of local officials. In some cases, we could not obtain a population estimate; these places show "NA" (Not Available) in place of a population figure.

Location: County in which the town is located immediately follows the name of town. If more than one county is listed, the town is principally in the first-named county, e.g. "AMARILLO, Potter-Randall."

Businesses: The number following the county name indicates the number of business establishments in the town as of Jan. 30, 1997, e.g., "ABBOTT, Hill, 21" means that Abbott in Hill County had 21 businesses that have been given a **credit rating** by Dun & Bradstreet and are not operated out of the personal residence of the principal.

County seats: County seats are marked with a section mark (§).

Post Offices: Places with post offices, as of Jan. 1995, are marked with an asterisk (*) e.g., "*Ace."

Town and County	Pop.	Town and County	Pop.	Town and County	Pop.
A		‡Aldine, Harris	11,835	‡Anderson Mill, Williamson-	
*ABBOTT, Hill, 21	363	*ALEDO, Parker, 203	1,369	Travis	10,600
Aberfoyle, Hunt	35	Aleman, Hamilton	60	Andice, Williamson, 94	NA
*ABERNATHY, Hale-Lubbock,		Alethia, Montgomery	NA	§*ANDREWS, Andrews, 553	10,223
132	2,664	Alexander, Erath	40	§*ANGLETON, Brazoria, 944	19,473
§*ABILENE, Taylor-Jones,		Alexanders Store, Shelby	NA	ANGUS, Navarro	425
5,145	116,000	Aley, Henderson	NA	*ANNA, Collin, 64	1,115
Ables Springs, Kaufman	NA	Alfred, Jim Wells	10	ANNETTA, Parker	821
Abner, Kaufman	NA	Algerita, San Saba, 4	48	ANNETTA NORTH, Parker	286
‡Abram-Perezville, Hidalgo	4,363	Algoa, Galveston	135	ANNETTA SOUTH, Parker	526
Acala, Hudspeth	25	§*ALICE, Jim Wells, 917	20,252	*ANNONA, Red River, 17	363
*Ace, Polk, 2	40	Allamoore, Hudspeth	25	§*ANSON, Jones, 146	2,806
*ACKERLY, Dawson-Martin, 28	267	*ALLEN, Collin, 939	25,886	Antelope, Jack, 1	65
Acme, Hardeman	14	Allendale, Montgomery	NA	Antelope Flats, Briscoe	NA
Acton, Hood	1,129	Allenfarm, Brazos	30	*ANTHONY, El Paso, 78	3,612
Acuff, Lubbock	30	Allenhurst, Matagorda	NA	Antioch, Cass	45
Acworth, Red River	52	Allen's Chapel, Fannin	41	Antioch, Delta	25
Adams Gardens, Cameron	200	Allen's Point, Fannin	76	Antioch, Madison	15
Adams Store, Panola	NA	*Alleyton, Colorado, 7	165	Antioch, Panola	121
Adamsville, Lampasas	41	*Allison, Wheeler, 12	135	Antioch, Shelby	NA
Addielou, Red River	31	Allison, Wise	NA	Antioch, Smith	NA
*ADDISON, Dallas, 140	10,759	Allmon, Floyd	24	*ANTON, Hockley, 49	1,257
Addran, Hopkins	NA	Allred, Yoakum	90	Apache Shores, Travis	NA
Adell, Parker	NA	ALMA, Ellis,	240	APPLEBY, Nacogdoches	485
*Adkins, Bexar, 89	241	Almira, Cass	NA	*Apple Springs, Trinity, 24	185
Admiral, Callahan	18	§*ALPINE, Brewster, 396	5,993	*AQUILLA, Hill, 13	164
Adobes, Presidio	NA	Alsa, Van Zandt	30	*ARANSAS PASS, San Patricio-	
*ADRIAN, Oldham, 15	217	*Altair, Colorado, 12	30	Aransas-Nueces, 466	7,766
Advance, Parker	NA	*ALTO, Cherokee, 73	1,068	Arbala, Hopkins	41
*Afton, Dickens, 7	15	Alto Bonito, Starr	170	*Arcadia, Shelby, 42	NA
Agnes, Parker	NA	Altoga, Collin	367	§*ARCHER CITY, Archer, 79	1,878
*AGUA DULCE, Nueces, 22	734	*ALTON, Hidalgo	3,308	ARCOLA, Fort Bend	815
Agua Nueva, Jim Hogg	20	Alum, Wilson	NA	Arden, Irion	1
Aguilares, Webb	37	Alum Creek, Bastrop	NA	Argo, Titus	200
*Aiken, Floyd, 6	57	*ALVARADO, Johnson, 222	3,196	*ARGYLE, Denton, 124	1,857
Aiken, Shelby	75	*ALVIN, Brazoria, 1,088	21,005	Arkansas Colony, Baylor	NA
Aikin Grove, Red River	26	*ALVORD, Wise, 47	1,081	*ARLINGTON, Tarrant,	
Airport City, Bexar	106	§*AMARILLO, Potter-Randall,		11,864	288,227
Airville, Bell	10	8,521	168,592	Armstrong, Bell	22
Alabama-Coushatta Indian		Ambia, Lamar	20	*Armstrong, Kenedy	20
Reservation, Polk	478	Ambrose, Grayson	90	Arneckeville, DeWitt	50
*ALAMO, Hidalgo, 244	10,935	Ames, Coryell	10	Arnett, Coryell	20
Alamo Alto, El Paso	25	AMES, Liberty	1,135	Arnett, Hockley	10
Alamo Beach, Calhoun	NA	Amherst, Lamar	NA	*ARP, Smith, 69	919
*ALAMO HEIGHTS, Bexar	7,309	*AMHERST, Lamb, 32	757	Arrowhead Shores, Hood	518
*Alanreed, Gray, 3	48	Ammannsville, Fayette	42	Arroyo City, Cameron	NA
Alazan, Nacogdoches	NA	Amphion, Atascosa	26	*Art, Mason, 3	18
*ALBA, Wood-Rains, 64	519	Amsterdam, Brazoria	193	*Artesia Wells, La Salle, 5	35
§*ALBANY, Shackelford, 147	2,056	Anadarko, Rusk	NA	*Arthur City, Lamar, 14	200
Albert, Gillespie, 1	25	§*ANAHUAC, Chambers, 162	2,147	Arvana, Dawson	25
Albion, Red River	50	Ander-Weser-Kilgore, Goliad	322	Asa, McLennan	46
Alderbranch, Anderson	5	§*ANDERSON, Grimes, 47	370	Ash, Houston	19

Town and County	Pop.
Ashby, Matagorda	NA
*ASHERTON, Dimmit, 11	1,589
Ashland, Upshur	20
Ashtola, Donley	25
Ashwood, Matagorda	NA
Asia, Polk	NA
§*ASPERMONT, Stonewall, 78	1,016
*Atascosa, Bexar, 50	300
Ater, Coryell	25
§*ATHENS, Henderson, 924	11,530
*ATLANTA, Cass, 514	6,194
Atlas, Lamar	20
Atoy, Cherokee	NA
Attoyac, Nacogdoches	NA
Atwell, Callahan	8
*AUBREY, Denton, 161	1,286
Auburn, Ellis	12
Augusta, Houston	20
AURORA, Wise	728
§*AUSTIN, Travis-Williamson, 32,467	557,532
Austonio, Houston, 3	37
*AUSTWELL, Refugio, 9	200
Authon, Parker	15
*Avalon, Ellis, 12	130
*AVERY, Red River, 23	475
*AVINGER, Cass, 33	506
*Avoca, Jones, 3	121
Avondale, Tarrant	NA
*Axtell, McLennan, 26	105
*AZLE, Tarrant-Parker, 620	10,670

B

Town and County	Pop.
Back, Gray	14
‡*Bacliff, Galveston, 142	5,163
*Bagwell, Red River, 13	150
*BAILEY, Fannin, 6	210
BAILEY'S PRAIRIE, Brazoria	677
Baileyville, Milam	45
Bainer, Lamb	10
Bainville, Karnes	8
§*BAIRD, Callahan, 102	1,751
Baker, Floyd	46
Bakersfield, Pecos	30
*BALCH SPRINGS, Dallas	18,802
BALCONES HEIGHTS, Bexar	3,245
Bald Hill, Angelina	NA
Bald Prairie, Robertson	31
§*BALLINGER, Runnels, 238	4,170
*BALMORHEA, Reeves, 22	855
Balsora, Wise	50
§*BANDERA, Bandera, 234	1,172
Bandera Falls, Bandera	NA
*BANGS, Brown, 71	1,597
Bankersmith, Kendall	NA
*Banquete, Nueces, 22	449
Barbarosa, Guadalupe	25
Barclay, Falls	58
*BARDWELL, Ellis, 12	403
*Barker, Harris, 37	NA
*Barksdale, Edwards, 14	1,081
Barnes, Polk	NA
*Barnhart, Irion, 5	160
Barnum, Polk, 2	29
‡*Barrett, Harris	3,418
*BARRY, Navarro, 9	197
*BARSTOW, Ward, 10	522
*BARTLETT, Williamson-Bell, 60	1,648
Barton Corners, Lipscomb	4
Bartons Chapel, Jack	NA
BARTONVILLE, Denton	1,039
Barwise, Floyd	16
Bar-X, Brazoria	340
Bascom, Smith	NA

Town and County	Pop.
Basin, Brewster	NA
Bassett, Bowie	373
§*BASTROP, Bastrop, 540	5,582
Bastrop Beach, Brazoria	NA
Bateman, Bastrop	NA
Batesville, Red River	14
‡*Batesville, Zavala, 25	1,304
*Batson, Hardin, 15	140
Battle, McLennan	NA
Baxter, Henderson	20
§*BAY CITY, Matagorda, 880	18,194
Baylor Lake, Childress	27
BAYOU VISTA, Galveston	1,420
*BAYSIDE, Refugio, 7	445
*BAYTOWN, Harris-Chambers, 2,341	69,004
*BAYVIEW, Cameron	295
Bazette, Navarro	30
Beach, Montgomery	NA
BEACH CITY, Chambers	1,196
Beans, Jasper	NA
Bear Creek, Dallas	1,000
*BEASLEY, Fort Bend, 25	622
Beattie, Comanche	50
Beaukiss, Williamson	20
§*BEAUMONT, Jefferson, 5,489	115,521
Beaux Art Gardens, Jefferson	NA
Beaver Dams, Bowie	NA
*Bebe, Gonzales, 1	52
Becker, Kaufman	NA
*BECKVILLE, Panola, 43	766
Becton, Lubbock	125
*BEDFORD, Tarrant, 1,900	46,179
*Bedias, Grimes, 16	301
BEE CAVE, Travis	274
Bee House, Coryell	40
§*BEEVILLE, Bee, 674	14,416
Behrnville, Williamson	30
Belcherville, Montague	34
Belfalls, Bell	20
Belgrade, Newton	NA
Belk, Lamar	55
*BELLAIRE, Harris, 967	14,955
Bell Branch, Ellis	20
*BELLEVUE, Clay, 19	349
*BELLMEAD, McLennan, 174	8,436
*BELLS, Grayson, 60	959
§*BELLVILLE, Austin, 372	3,760
Belmena, Milam	15
*Belmont, Gonzales, 8	60
Belott, Houston	101
§*BELTON, Bell, 716	13,619
*Ben Arnold, Milam, 4	148
*BENAVIDES, Duval, 29	1,974
Ben Bolt, Jim Wells, 2	110
*BENBROOK, Tarrant	22,947
Benchley, Robertson, 1	110
*Bend, San Saba, 4	115
*Ben Franklin, Delta, 6	75
Ben Hur, Limestone	100
§*BENJAMIN, Knox, 15	243
Bennett, Parker	40
Benoit, Runnels	22
Bentonville, Jim Wells	15
*Ben Wheeler, Van Zandt, 66	400
*Berclair, Goliad, 7	253
Berea, Houston	41
Berea, Marion	74
*Bergheim, Kendall, 11	NA
*Bergstrom Air Force Base, Travis	2,945
Berlin, Washington	NA
Bernardo, Colorado	155
Berryhill, Shackelford	5
Berry's Creek, Williamson	50

Town and County	Pop.
BERRYVILLE, Henderson	894
*BERTRAM, Burnet, 70	943
Bessmay, Jasper	NA
Best, Reagan, 8	2
Bethany, Panola	50
Bethel, Anderson	50
Bethel, Ellis	25
Bethel, Henderson	NA
Bethel, Runnels	12
Bethlehem, Upshur	25
Bettie, Upshur	110
Beulah, Limestone	12
*BEVERLY HILLS, McLennan	2,141
BEVIL OAKS, Jefferson	1,493
Bevilport, Jasper	NA
Beyersville, Williamson	75
Biardstown, Lamar	75
*Big Bend National Park, Brewster, 9	105
Big Creek, Burleson	NA
*Bigfoot, Frio, 8	NA
*Biggs Field, El Paso	4,226
Big Hill, Limestone	9
§*BIG LAKE, Reagan, 161	3,486
Big Oaks, Marion	NA
*BIG SANDY, Upshur, 100	1,293
§*BIG SPRING, Howard, 1,122	23,308
Big Square, Castro	3
Big Thicket, Liberty	NA
Big Valley, Mills	35
Big Valley Ranchettes, Coryell	220
*BIG WELLS, Dimmit, 17	817
Bila Hora, Lavaca	NA
Biloxi, Newton	NA
Birch, Burleson	NA
Birome, Hill, 1	31
Birthright, Hopkins	40
Biry, Medina	NA
*BISHOP, Nueces, 111	3,392
BISHOP HILLS, Potter	250
*Bivins, Cass, 9	195
Black, Parmer	100
Blackfoot, Anderson	33
Black Hill, Atascosa	60
Black Hills, Navarro	80
Black Jack, Cherokee	47
Black Jack, Robertson	NA
Blackjack, Smith	NA
Black Oak, Hopkins	NA
*BLACKWELL, Nolan-Coke, 16	370
Blair, Shelby	200
Blair, Taylor	25
Blanchard, Polk	50
*BLANCO, Blanco, 156	1,584
Blanconia, Bee	30
Bland Lake, San Augustine	25
*BLANKET, Brown, 17	448
Blanton, Hill	8
Bleakwood, Newton	300
*Bledsoe, Cochran, 6	125
*Bleiblerville, Austin, 6	71
*Blessing, Matagorda, 32	571
Blevins, Falls	36
Blewett, Uvalde	10
Blodgett, Titus	60
*BLOOMBURG, Cass, 29	383
Bloomdale, Collin	NA
*BLOOMING GROVE, Navarro, 31	860
‡*Bloomington, Victoria, 17	1,938
*BLOSSOM, Lamar, 56	1,697
Blowout, Blanco	NA
Blue, Lee	50
Blueberry Hill, Montgomery	NA
*Bluegrove, Clay, 2	125

Town and County	Pop.	Town and County	Pop.	Town and County	Pop.
Blue Lake Estates, Llano	300	‡Briar, Tarrant-Wise-Parker	4,294	Buffalo Gap, Travis	NA
BLUE MOUND, Tarrant	2,242	BRIARCLIFF, Travis	366	Buffalo Mop, Limestone	21
*BLUE RIDGE, Collin, 38	580	BRIAROAKS, Johnson	636	Buffalo Springs, Clay	51
Bluetown, Cameron	40	Briary, Milam	NA	BUFFALO SPRINGS, Lubbock	415
*Bluff Dale, Erath, 11	123	Brice, Hall	37	Buford, El Paso	NA
Bluff Springs, Travis	50	*BRIDGE CITY, Orange, 306	8,525	Buford, Mitchell	25
*Bluffton, Llano, 4	75	*BRIDGEPORT, Wise, 350	3,915	*Bula, Bailey, 2	35
*BLUM, Hill, 24	432	Bridges Chapel, Titus	90	Bulcher, Cooke	6
Bluntzer, Nueces	150	*Briggs, Burnet, 5	92	*BULLARD, Smith-Cherokee, 119	
Boardhouse, Blanco	NA	Bright Star, Rains	592		1,029
Bobo, Shelby	NA	Brinker, Hopkins	NA	Bull Run, Newton	NA
Bob Town, Jack	NA	*Briscoe, Wheeler, 4	135	*Bulverde, Comal, 136	NA
§*BOERNE, Kendall, 762	5,961	Bristol, Ellis	94	‡*Buna, Jasper, 122	2,366
*BOGATA, Red River, 54	1,387	*BROADDUS, San Augustine, 37	217	Buncombe, Panola	87
Bois d'Arc, Anderson	10	Broadway, Crosby	NA	Bunger, Young	40
Bois d'Arc, Rains	10	Broadway, Lamar	25	Bunker Hill, Jasper	NA
Bold Springs, Polk	100	Brock, Parker	80	Bunker Hill, Lamar	NA
Boldtville, Bexar	NA	Brock Junction, Parker	NA	BUNKER HILL VILLAGE, Harris	3,462
‡*Boling-Iago, Wharton, 46	1,146	Bronco, Yoakum	30	Bunyan, Erath	20
Bolivar, Denton	40	*BRONSON, Sabine, 24	338	*BURKBURNETT, Wichita,	
Bomarton, Baylor	15	*BRONTE, Coke, 33	925	365	10,933
*Bonanza, Hill	NA	*Brookeland, Sabine, 26	220	BURKE, Angelina	377
Bonanza, Hopkins	26	*Brookesmith, Brown, 6	61	*Burkett, Coleman, 6	30
§*BONHAM, Fannin, 414	6,761	Brook Forest, Montgomery	NA	*Burkeville, Newton, 36	515
Bonita, Montague	15	Brooks, Panola	40	Burleigh, Austin	69
Bonnerville, Freestone	NA	*Brooks Air Force Base, Bexar	720	*BURLESON, Johnson-Tarrant,	
BONNEY, Brazoria	441	Brookshier, Runnels	18	1,120	19,703
Bonnie View, Refugio	135	*BROOKSHIRE, Waller, 188	3,587	*Burlington, Milam, 7	140
Bonus, Wharton	42	BROOKSIDE VILLAGE, Brazoria		§*BURNET, Burnet, 369	3,942
*Bon Wier, Newton, 18	475		1,861	Burns, Bowie	NA
*BOOKER, Lipscomb-Ochiltree,		*Brookston, Lamar, 7	70	Burns City, Cooke	60
71	1,235	Broom City, Anderson	20	Burrantown, Houston	70
Boonsville, Wise	52	Broome, Panola	21	Burrow, Hunt	NA
Booth, Fort Bend, 69	NA	Brown, Martin	NA	*BURTON, Washington, 46	338
Borden, Colorado	NA	Brown College, Washington	NA	*Bushland, Potter, 15	130
*BORGER, Hutchinson, 751	15,485	BROWNDELL, Jasper	222	Bustamante, Zapata	15
Bosqueville, McLennan	72	§*BROWNFIELD, Terry, 442	9,357	Busterville, Hockley	6
§*Boston, Bowie, 48	200	Browning, Smith	25	Butler, Bastrop	NA
*BOVINA, Parmer, 46	1,766	Brownsboro, Caldwell	50	Butler, Freestone	67
Bowers, Milam	NA	*BROWNSBORO, Henderson,		*BYERS, Clay, 12	531
Bowers, Polk	NA	72	583	*BYNUM, Hill, 5	205
Bowers City, Gray	26	§*BROWNSVILLE, Cameron,		Byrd, Ellis	15
*BOWIE, Montague, 461	5,429	3,670	131,524	Byrds, Brown	NA
Bowser, San Saba	20	§*BROWNWOOD, Brown,		Byrdtown, Lamar	NA
Box Church, Limestone	45	1,249	19,254		
Boxelder, Red River	258	Broyles Chapel, Anderson	40		
Boxwood, Upshur	NA	*BRUCEVILLE-EDDY,		**C**	
Boyce, Ellis	75	McLennan-Falls, 21	1,270	*CACTUS, Moore, 22	1,864
Boyd, Fannin	40	Brundage, Dimmit	50	*Caddo, Stephens, 6	40
*BOYD, Wise, 138	1,163	*Bruni, Webb, 15	581	*CADDO MILLS, Hunt, 61	1,152
*Boys' Ranch, Oldham, 13	435	Brushie Prairie, Navarro	35	Cade Chapel, Navarro	25
Bozar, Mills	9	Brushy Creek, Anderson	50	Cade Lake, Burleson	NA
Brachfield, Rusk	30	Brushy Creek, Brazos	NA	Cadiz, Bee	15
Bracken, Comal	76	‡Brushy Creek, Williamson	6,554	Cain City, Gillespie	NA
§*BRACKETTVILLE, Kinney,		§*BRYAN, Brazos, 2,760	60,451	Calaveras, Wilson	100
76	1,883	Bryan Beach, Brazoria	14	§*CALDWELL, Burleson, 275	3,909
Brad, Palo Pinto	16	Bryans Mill, Cass	71	Caledonia, Rusk	NA
Bradford, Anderson	30	Bryarly, Red River	5	Calf Creek, McCulloch	23
Bradshaw, Taylor, 2	61	Bryce, Rusk	NA	Calina, Limestone	10
§*BRADY, McCulloch, 346	5,974	*BRYSON, Jack, 14	556	*Call, Newton, 10	170
Brady, Shelby	NA	‡*Buchanan Dam, Llano, 53	1,155	*Calliham, McMullen, 5	200
Branch, Collin	447	Buchanan Lake Village, Llano	NA	CALLISBURG, Cooke	425
Branchville, Milam	200	Buchel, DeWitt	45	Call Junction, Jasper	50
*Brandon, Hill, 4	80	Buck, Polk	NA	*CALVERT, Robertson, 46	1,492
Branom, Hopkins	NA	Buck Creek, Cottle	7	*Camden, Polk, 5	1,200
*Brashear, Hopkins, 20	280	Buckeye, Matagorda	25	§*CAMERON, Milam, 323	5,688
*BRAZORIA, Brazoria, 246	2,955	Buck Hills, Montgomery	NA	‡Cameron Park, Cameron	4,480
Brazos, Palo Pinto	97	*BUCKHOLTS, Milam, 15	366	Camilla, San Jacinto	200
Brazos Point, Bosque	NA	Buckhorn, Austin	20	Camp Air, Mason	15
Brazosport, Brazoria	56,407	Buckhorn, Newton	NA	*CAMPBELL, Hunt, 33	793
§*BRECKENRIDGE, Stephens,		Buckner, Parker	NA	*Campbellton, Atascosa, 10	350
527	5,611	*BUDA, Hays, 260	1,922	Camp Creek Lake, Robertson	241
*BREMOND, Robertson, 44	1,164	Buena Vista, Cameron	NA	Campo Alto, Hidalgo	NA
§*BRENHAM, Washington,		*BUFFALO, Leon, 185	1,982	Camp Ruby, Polk	35
1,116	13,873	Buffalo Camp, Brazoria	1,098	Camp San Saba, McCulloch	36
Breslau, Lavaca	65	*BUFFALO GAP, Taylor, 23	485	Camp Scenic, Kerr	NA
				Camp Seale, Polk	NA

Town and County	Pop.	Town and County	Pop.	Town and County	Pop.
Camp Springs, Scurry	10	Cavazos, Cameron	NA	Cheneyboro, Navarro	100
‡Camp Swift, Bastrop	3,119	Cave Creek, Gillespie	NA	*Cherokee, San Saba, 19	175
Camp Switch, Gregg	70	Caviness, Lamar	80	Cherokee Hill, Smith	NA
Campti, Shelby	NA	Cawthon, Brazos	75	Cherry Spring, Gillespie	75
*Camp Verde, Kerr, 10	41	Cayote, Bosque	75	*CHESTER, Tyler, 13	342
Camp Willow, Guadalupe	NA	*Cayuga, Anderson, 8	200	Chesterville, Colorado	NA
*CAMP WOOD, Real, 43	746	Cedar Bayou, Harris-Chambers	1,287	*CHICO, Wise, 68	910
Camp Worth, San Augustine	NA	*Cedar Creek, Bastrop, 56	145	*Chicota, Lamar, 3	125
Canada Verde, Wilson	123	Cedar Creek, Waller	NA	Chihuahua, Hidalgo	NA
§*CANADIAN, Hemphill, 200	2,197	*CEDAR HILL, Dallas-Ellis, 673	24,677	Chihuahua Farm, Zapata	25
Canary, Leon	NA	Cedar Hill, Floyd	36	§*CHILDRESS, Childress, 310	5,221
Candelaria, Presidio	55	Cedar Lake, Matagorda	148	*CHILLICOTHE, Hardeman, 41	776
Caney, Matagorda	296	*Cedar Lane, Matagorda, 4	85	*Chilton, Falls, 25	274
CANEY CITY, Henderson	195	*CEDAR PARK, Williamson-Travis, 546	10,371	*CHINA, Jefferson, 34	1,188
Cannon, Grayson	50	Cedar Point, Llano	NA	CHINA GROVE, Bexar	1,209
§*CANTON, Van Zandt, 437	3,417	Cedar Shores, Bosque	170	China Grove, Scurry	15
Cantu, Hidalgo	NA	Cedar Springs, Falls	90	*China Spring, McLennan, 69	181
‡*Canutillo, El Paso, 178	4,871	Cedar Springs, Upshur	NA	Chinati, Presidio	NA
Canyon, Lubbock	40	Cedarvale, Kaufman	NA	Chinquapin, Matagorda	NA
§*CANYON, Randall, 484	12,601	Cedar Valley, Bell	4	*CHIRENO, Nacogdoches, 19	441
Canyon City, Comal	100	Cedar Valley, Travis	70	Chita, Trinity	81
‡*Canyon Lake, Comal	11,873	*Cee Vee, Cottle, 3	45	Choate, Karnes	20
Canyon Valley, Crosby	NA	Cego, Falls	42	Chocolate Bayou, Brazoria	60
Capitola, Fisher	NA	Cele, Travis	NA	Choice, Shelby	21
Caplen, Galveston	30	*CELESTE, Hunt, 33	864	*Chriesman, Burleson	30
Capps Corner, Montague	NA	*CELINA, Collin, 126	2,112	*CHRISTINE, Atascosa, 3	472
Cap Rock, Crosby	NA	Center, Limestone	76	*Christoval, Tom Green, 16	216
Caps, Taylor	100	§*CENTER, Shelby, 506	4,990	Church Hill, Rusk	15
Cara Blanca, Baylor	NA	Center City, Mills	15	Churchill, Brazoria	NA
Caradan, Mills	20	Center Grove, Houston	108	*CIBOLO, Guadalupe-Bexar, 112	1,882
Carancahua, Jackson	301	Center Grove, Titus	65	Cipres, Hidalgo	20
*CARBON, Eastland, 19	295	Center Hill, Houston	105	Circle, Cherokee	NA
Carbondale, Bowie	30	Center Line, Burleson	NA	Circle, Lamb	6
Carey, Childress, 1	60	Center Plains, Swisher	NA	Circleback, Bailey	10
Carl, Travis	NA	Center Point, Camp	NA	‡Circle D-KC Estates, Bastrop	1,488
Carlisle, Trinity	68	Center Point, Hunt	NA	Circleville, Travis	NA
Carlos, Grimes	NA	*Center Point, Kerr, 52	623	Circleville, Williamson	42
*Carlsbad, Tom Green, 8	100	Center Point, Panola	NA	*CISCO, Eastland, 204	4,241
CARL'S CORNER, Hill	116	Center Point, Upshur	NA	Cistern, Fayette	75
Carlson, Travis	61	Centerview, Leon	NA	Citrus City, Hidalgo	NA
*Carlton, Hamilton, 5	70	§*CENTERVILLE, Leon, 89	954	Citrus Grove, Matagorda	NA
*CARMINE, Fayette, 24	198	Centerville, Trinity	60	Clairemont, Kent	15
Carmona, Polk	50	Central, Angelina	105	Clairette, Erath	55
Caro, Nacogdoches	113	‡Central Gardens, Jefferson	4,132	Clara, Wichita	100
Carpenter, Wilson	NA	Central Heights, Nacogdoches	NA	Clardy, Lamar	NA
Carricitos, Cameron	25	Central High, Cherokee	NA	§*CLARENDON, Donley, 135	2,106
§*CARRIZO SPRINGS, Dimmit, 216	5,704	*Centralia, Trinity	53	Clareville, Bee	23
Carroll, Smith	60	Cestohowa, Karnes	110	Clark, Liberty	NA
Carroll Springs, Anderson	20	Chaille, Grimes	20	Clarkson, Milam	10
*CARROLLTON, Denton-Dallas-Collin, 4,209	99,619	Chalk, Cottle, 2	17	§*CLARKSVILLE, Red River, 232	4,321
Carson, Fannin	22	Chalk Hill, Rusk	NA	CLARKSVILLE CITY, Gregg-Upshur	820
*Carswell Air Force Base, Tarrant 1	3,162	Chalk Mountain, Erath	25	§*CLAUDE, Armstrong, 76	1,232
*Carta Valley, Edwards	12	Chambersville, Collin	40	Clauene, Hockley	10
Carter Lake, Brazos	NA	Chambliss, Collin	25	Clawson, Angelina	195
Carterville, Cass	39	Champion, Nolan	8	*CLAY, Burleson, 2	61
§*CARTHAGE, Panola, 541	6,531	Champions, Harris	17,125	Clays Corner, Parmer	15
Cartwright, Kaufman	NA	Chances Store, Burleson	NA	*Clayton, Panola, 5	79
Cartwright, Wood	61	*CHANDLER, Henderson, 142	2,029	Claytonville, Swisher	116
Carver, Leon	NA	Chaney, Eastland	35	Clear Creek, Burnet	NA
Carver Park, Bexar	NA	‡*Channelview, Harris, 707	27,742	CLEAR LAKE SHORES, Galveston	1,191
Casa Piedra, Presidio	21	§*CHANNING, Hartley, 15	250	Clear Spring, Guadalupe	200
Casey, El Paso	115	Chapel Hill, Smith	NA	§*CLEBURNE, Johnson, 1,288	23,218
Cash, Hunt	56	Chapman, Rusk	20	Clegg, Live Oak	125
*Cason, Morris, 5	173	*Chapman Ranch, Nueces, 10	100	Clemons, Waller	NA
Cass, Cass	60	Chappel, San Saba	25	Clemville, Matagorda, 1	54
Cassie, Burnet	NA	*Chappell Hill, Washington, 32	310	Cleo, Kimble	3
Cassin, Bexar	NA	Charco, Goliad	96	Cleveland, Austin	78
*Castell, Llano, 4	72	Charleston, Delta	120	*CLEVELAND, Liberty, 684	7,910
*CASTLE HILLS, Bexar	4,352	Charlie, Clay	65	Cliffside, Potter	206
Castolon, Brewster	NA	*CHARLOTTE, Atascosa, 33	1,618	*CLIFTON, Bosque, 260	3,628
*CASTROVILLE, Medina, 159	2,697	CHATEAU WOODS, Montgomery	790	Clifton, Van Zandt	NA
*Catarina, Dimmit, 5	45	*Chatfield, Navarro, 2	40		
*Cat Spring, Austin, 17	76	Cheapside, Gonzales, 12	31		
		Cheek, Jefferson	62		

Town and County	Pop.	Town and County	Pop.	Town and County	Pop.
Climax, Collin	40	Connor, Madison	20	§*CRANE, Crane, 187	3,498
Cline, Uvalde	15	§*CONROE, Montgomery,		*CRANFILLS GAP, Bosque, 21	305
*CLINT, El Paso, 76	1,112	3,033	39,387	*CRAWFORD, McLennan, 39	708
Clinton, Hunt	NA	Content, Bell	25	Creath, Houston	20
*Clodine, Fort Bend	NA	*CONVERSE, Bexar, 300	10,787	Crecy, Trinity	15
Clopton, Franklin	15	Conway, Carson	20	Creechville, Ellis	15
Close City, Garza	94	Cooks Point, Burleson	60	*CREEDMOOR, Travis, 1	220
‡Cloverleaf, Harris	19,619	*Cookville, Titus, 28	105	Crescent Heights, Henderson	NA
*CLUTE, Brazoria, 511	9,671	COOL, Parker	259	*Cresson, Hood-Johnson, 22	208
*CLYDE, Callahan, 186	3,405	*COOLIDGE, Limestone, 28	740	Crestwood, Llano	NA
*COAHOMA, Howard, 46	1,306	§*COOPER, Delta, 133	2,334	Crestwood, Marion	NA
Cobb, Archer	NA	Cooper, Houston	27	Crews, Runnels	40
Cobbs, Kaufman	NA	Copano Village, Aransas	210	§*CROCKETT, Houston, 436	6,975
Coble, Hockley	11	Copeland, Montgomery	NA	‡*Crosby, Harris, 395	2,167
Cochran, Austin	116	Copeland, Smith	NA	§*CROSBYTON, Crosby, 106	2,021
*COCKRELL HILL, Dallas	4,239	Copeland Creek, Marion	NA	Cross, Grimes	49
COFFEE CITY, Henderson	240	*Copeville, Collin, 5	106	Cross, McMullen	60
Coffeeville, Upshur	50	*COPPELL, Dallas-Denton,		Cross Cut, Brown	NA
Cofferville, Lamb	4	654	23,599	‡Cross Mountain, Bexar	1,250
Coit, Limestone	25	*COPPERAS COVE, Coryell-		*CROSS PLAINS, Callahan, 77	1,126
Coke, Wood	105	Lampasas, 651	28,622	Crossroads, Cass	NA
§*COLDSPRING, San Jacinto,		COPPER CANYON, Denton	1,279	Crossroads, Delta	10
96	562	Corbet, Navarro	80	CROSS ROADS, Denton	445
Cold Springs, Coryell	4	Cordele, Jackson	51	Crossroads, Harrison	NA
Coldwater, Dallam	53	CORINTH, Denton	5,648	Cross Roads, Henderson	135
§*COLEMAN, Coleman, 323	5,374	Corinth, Jones	10	Crossroads, Hopkins	NA
Colfax, Van Zandt	35	Corinth, Leon	NA	Cross Roads, Madison	75
Colita, Polk	NA	Corley, Bowie	35	Cross Roads, Milam	35
College Hill, Bowie	116	Cornersville, Hopkins	NA	Cross Roads, Rusk	NA
College Mound, Kaufman	350	Cornett, Cass	30	Cross Timbers, Johnson	245
*Collegeport, Matagorda, 1	91	Cornudas, Hudspeth	19	Croton, Dickens	5
*COLLEGE STATION, Brazos,		§*CORPUS CHRISTI, Nueces-San		Crow, Wood	25
1,897	63,091	Patricio-Kleberg, 10,621	274,234	§*CROWELL, Foard, 70	1,233
*COLLEYVILLE, Tarrant,		Corpus Christi NAS, Nueces		*CROWLEY, Tarrant-Johnson,	
539	15,565		500	316	7,998
*COLLINSVILLE, Grayson,		CORRAL CITY, Denton	51	Crown, Atascosa	10
50	1,152	*CORRIGAN, Polk, 90	1,880	Cruz Calle, Duval	NA
*COLMESNEIL, Tyler, 41	611	§*CORSICANA, Navarro,		Cryer Creek, Navarro	15
Colony, Rains	70	1,197	24,042	*Crystal Beach, Galveston	787
§*COLORADO CITY, Mitchell,		Coryell City, Coryell	125	§*CRYSTAL CITY, Zavala,	
238	5,062	*Cost, Gonzales, 12	62	177	8,244
Colquitt, Kaufman	NA	Cotton Center, Fannin	5	Crystal Falls, Stephens	10
Coltexo, Gray	5	*Cotton Center, Hale, 11	205	Crystal Lake, Anderson	20
Coltharp, Houston	40	Cottondale, Wise	NA	Cuadrilla, El Paso	40
Colton, Travis	50	Cotton Gin, Freestone	28	Cuba, Johnson	NA
Columbia Lakes, Brazoria	646	Cotton Patch, DeWitt	11	§*CUERO, DeWitt, 344	7,072
§*COLUMBUS, Colorado,		Cottonwood, Brazos	NA	Cuevitas, Hidalgo	NA
321	3,751	Cottonwood, Callahan	65	Cuevitas, Jim Hogg	12
Comal, Comal	40	Cottonwood, Erath	23	Culebra, Bexar	NA
§*COMANCHE, Comanche,		COTTONWOOD, Kaufman, 1	187	Culleoka, Collin	NA
313	4,477	Cottonwood, Madison	40	*CUMBY, Hopkins, 44	670
Comanche Cove, Hood	501	Cottonwood, McLennan	NA	Cundiff, Jack	45
Comanche Harbor, Hood	325	Cottonwood, Somervell	24	*CUNEY, Cherokee, 4	196
*COMBES, Cameron, 24	2,509	COTTONWOOD SHORES, Burnet		*Cunningham, Lamar, 5	110
COMBINE, Kaufman-Dallas	1,781		675	Currie, Navarro	25
Cometa, Zavala	10	§*COTULLA, La Salle, 133	4,330	Curtis, Jasper	NA
‡*Comfort, Kendall, 153	1,733	Couch, Karnes	10	*CUSHING, Nacogdoches, 34	644
*COMMERCE, Hunt, 306	7,192	Coughran, Atascosa	20	Cusseta, Cass	30
*COMO, Hopkins, 30	623	County Line, Lubbock	30	*CUT AND SHOOT, Montgomery	
Compton, Harris	NA	County Line, Rains	40		1,090
*Comstock, Val Verde, 9	375	*Coupland, Williamson, 16	135	Cuthand, Red River	116
Comyn, Comanche	27	Courtney, Grimes	55	Cyclone, Bell	45
*Concan, Uvalde, 10	225	COVE, Chambers	494	Cypress, Franklin	20
Concepcion, Duval, 5	25	Cove Springs, Cherokee	NA	*Cypress-Fairbanks, Harris,	
Concho, Concho	NA	*COVINGTON, Hill, 18	276	695	1,310
Concord, Cherokee	NA	Cow Creek, Erath	14	Cypress Creek, Kerr	200
Concord, Hunt	30	Cox, Upshur	NA	*Cypress Mill, Blanco, 16	56
Concord, Johnson	NA	Coxville, Travis	NA	Cyril, Rusk	NA
*Concord, Leon, 5	28	*Coyanosa, Pecos, 10	270		
Concord, Liberty	26	Coy City, Karnes, 1	30	**D**	
Concord, Madison	50	Crabb, Fort Bend	125	Dacosta, Victoria	89
Concord, Rusk	23	Crabbs Prairie, Walker	NA	Dacus, Montgomery	161
Concordia, Nueces	NA	Craft, Cherokee	21	Dads Corner, Archer	NA
Concrete, DeWitt	46	Crafton, Wise	20	Daffan, Travis	NA
Cone, Crosby, 4	110	Craig, Rusk	NA	§*DAINGERFIELD, Morris,	
Conlen, Dallam	69	*CRANDALL, Kaufman, 61	2,143	191	2,625

Town and County	Pop.
*DAISETTA, Liberty, 22	988
Dalby Springs, Bowie	141
*Dale, Caldwell, 19	500
§*DALHART, Dallam-Hartley, 456	6,696
*Dallardsville, Polk, 2	350
§*DALLAS, Dallas-Collin-Denton-Rockwall, 61,903	1,050,698
Dalton, Cass	NA
DALWORTHINGTON GARDENS, Tarrant	2,192
Dam B (Dogwood Station), Tyler	56
*Damon, Brazoria, 40	375
*DANBURY, Brazoria, 60	1,682
*Danciger, Brazoria, 3	357
*Danevang, Wharton, 5	61
Daniels, Panola	NA
Danville, Gregg	NA
Darby Hill, San Jacinto	50
Darco, Harrison	85
Darden, Polk	NA
*DARROUZETT, Lipscomb, 27	362
Datura, Limestone	2
*Davilla, Milam, 4	200
Davis, Atascosa	8
Davis Hill, Liberty	NA
Davis Prairie, Limestone	17
Davisville, Angelina	NA
*Dawn, Deaf Smith, 5	52
*DAWSON, Navarro, 26	782
*DAYTON, Liberty, 368	6,019
DAYTON LAKES, Liberty	226
Deadwood, Panola	106
DEAN, Clay	292
Dean, Hockley	20
*Deanville, Burleson, 9	130
*DeBerry, Panola, 24	191
§*DECATUR, Wise, 444	4,669
Decker Prairie, Montgomery	NA
Deer Haven, Llano	NA
*DEER PARK, Harris, 832	30,055
*DE KALB, Bowie, 136	1,941
*DE LEON, Comanche, 191	2,339
Delhi, Caldwell	300
Delia, Limestone	20
*DELL CITY, Hudspeth, 37	779
*Delmita, Starr, 4	50
Delray, Panola	40
§*DEL RIO, Val Verde, 1,139	34,361
Delrose, Upshur	NA
*Del Valle, Travis, 137	2,476
Delwin, Cottle	12
Demi-John Island, Brazoria	18
Democrat, Mills	8
Denhawken, Wilson	46
*DENISON, Grayson, 1,092	21,840
Denman Crossroads, Van Zandt	NA
Denning, San Augustine	361
*Dennis, Parker, 6	90
Denson Springs, Anderson	100
Denton, Callahan	6
§*DENTON, Denton, 3,009	73,912
*DENVER CITY, Yoakum, 279	5,048
*DEPORT, Lamar-Red River, 29	880
Derby, Frio	50
*Desdemona, Eastland, 10	180
Desert, Collin	25
*DESOTO, Dallas, 1,261	34,087
Dessau, Travis	NA
Detmold, Milam	NA
*DETROIT, Red River, 37	789
*DEVERS, Liberty, 15	407
*DEVINE, Medina, 213	4,931
Dew, Freestone	71
Dewalt, Fort Bend, 4	25

Town and County	Pop.
DeWees, Wilson	35
Deweesville, Karnes	12
‡*Deweyville, Newton, 36	1,420
Dewville, Gonzales	15
Dexter, Cooke	18
Dextra, Nacogdoches	NA
*D'Hanis, Medina, 23	548
Dial, Fannin	76
Dialville, Cherokee, 6	200
*Diana, Upshur, 49	450
*DIBOLL, Angelina, 162	5,636
Dicey, Parker	NA
§*DICKENS, Dickens, 15	318
*DICKINSON, Galveston, 606	12,536
Dies, Tyler	NA
*Dike, Hopkins, 5	170
*DILLEY, Frio, 96	2,997
Dilworth, Gonzales	15
Dilworth, Red River	22
*Dime Box, Lee, 27	313
§*DIMMITT, Castro, 238	4,376
Dimple, Red River	60
*Dinero, Live Oak, 5	344
Ding Dong, Bell	22
Direct, Lamar	70
Dirgin, Rusk	12
Divide, Hopkins	NA
Dixie, Grayson	17
Dixon, Hunt	31
Dixon-Hopewell, Houston	49
Doak Springs, Lee	50
Doans, Wilbarger	20
*Dobbin, Montgomery, 4	170
Dobrowolski, Atascosa	10
Dodd, Castro	15
*DODD CITY, Fannin, 10	402
*Dodge, Walker, 11	150
*DODSON, Collingsworth, 5	113
Dodson Prairie, Palo Pinto	18
Dog Ridge, Bell	125
Dogwood City, Smith	NA
Dolen, Liberty	NA
‡Dominion, Bexar	1,363
DOMINO, Cass	106
*Donie, Freestone, 11	206
*DONNA, Hidalgo, 330	13,495
*Doole, McCulloch, 2	74
DORCHESTER, Grayson, 3	160
Dorras, Stonewall	30
Doss, Cass	NA
*Doss, Gillespie, 6	75
Dot, Falls	17
Dothan, Eastland	20
Dotson, Panola	40
Double Bayou, Chambers	400
Double Diamond Estates, Hutchinson-Moore	175
DOUBLE OAK, Denton	2,078
*Doucette, Tyler, 7	131
*Dougherty, Floyd, 5	109
Dougherty, Rains	342
Douglas, Smith	NA
*Douglass, Nacogdoches, 13	75
*DOUGLASSVILLE, Cass, 13	212
Downing, Comanche	20
Downsville, McLennan	35
Doyle, Limestone	50
Dozier, Collingsworth	30
Drane, Navarro	16
Drasco, Runnels	20
Draw, Lynn	39
Dreka, Shelby	NA
Dresden, Navarro	25
Dreyer, Gonzales	20
*Driftwood, Hays, 30	21

Town and County	Pop.
Driftwood, Henderson	NA
*DRIPPING SPRINGS, Hays, 216	1,070
*DRISCOLL, Nueces, 14	719
*Dryden, Terrell, 1	13
Dubina, Fayette	44
*DUBLIN, Erath, 247	3,634
Dudley, Callahan	25
Duffau, Erath, 3	76
Dugger, Guadalupe	20
§*DUMAS, Moore, 637	13,438
*Dumont, King-Dickens, 2	85
Dunbar, Rains	40
*DUNCANVILLE, Dallas, 1,429	37,416
Dundee, Archer	40
Dunlap, Cottle	10
Dunlap, Travis	80
Dunlay, Medina, 36	119
*Dunn, Scurry, 1	75
Duplex, Fannin	25
Duren, Mills	15
Durango, Falls	54
Duster, Comanche	NA
Duval, Travis	NA
Dye, Montague	NA
*Dyess Air Force Base, Taylor 4	4,676

E

Town and County	Pop.
Eagle, Chambers	50
*EAGLE LAKE, Colorado, 164	3,850
‡Eagle Mountain, Tarrant	6,366
§*EAGLE PASS, Maverick, 953	24,806
*EARLY, Brown	2,652
Earlywine, Washington	NA
*EARTH, Lamb, 63	1,373
East Afton, Dickens	11
‡*East Bernard, Wharton, 114	1,673
East Caney, Hopkins	NA
East Columbia, Brazoria	95
East Delta, Delta	50
East Direct, Lamar	NA
Easter, Castro	30
Easterly, Robertson	61
Eastgate, Liberty	NA
East Hamilton, Shelby	NA
§*EASTLAND, Eastland, 354	3,805
EAST MOUNTAIN, Upshur	907
*EASTON, Gregg-Rusk, 9	462
East Point, Wood	NA
East Sweden, McCulloch	NA
EAST TAWAKONI, Rains	741
East Tempe, Polk	100
Eaton, Robertson	NA
Ebenezer, Camp	55
Ebenezer, Jasper	NA
Echo, Coleman	16
Eckert, Gillespie	NA
Ecleto, Karnes	22
Eclipse, Jasper	NA
*ECTOR, Fannin, 18	506
*EDCOUCH, Hidalgo, 69	3,653
*Eddy, McLennan-Falls, (See Bruceville-Eddy), 31	NA
*EDEN, Concho, 52	1,693
Eden, Nacogdoches	NA
Edgar, DeWitt	8
Edge, Brazos	100
EDGECLIFF, Tarrant	3,016
*EDGEWOOD, Van Zandt, 93	1,470
Edgeworth, Bell	20
Edhube, Fannin	25
§*EDINBURG, Hidalgo, 1,202	35,773

Town and County	Pop.	Town and County	Pop.	Town and County	Pop.
*EDMONSON, Hale, 11	122	*Enloe, Delta, 10	113	Farmers Valley, Wilbarger	50
§*EDNA, Jackson, 331	6,383	*ENNIS, Ellis, 681	14,569	*FARMERSVILLE, Collin, 147	3,213
Edna Hill, Erath	32	Enoch, Upshur	NA	Farmington, Grayson	38
EDOM, Van Zandt, 3	350	*Enochs, Bailey, 3	80	*Farnsworth, Ochiltree, 7	130
*Edroy, San Patricio, 7	200	Enright, Brazos	NA	Farrar, Limestone	51
Egan, Johnson	21	Enterprise, Van Zandt	90	Farrsville, Newton	150
Egypt, Leon	NA	*Eola, Concho, 10	218	§*FARWELL, Parmer, 79	1,485
Egypt, Montgomery	NA	Eolian, Stephens	9	Fashing, Atascosa	35
*Egypt, Wharton, 6	26	*Era, Cooke, 9	200	*FATE, Rockwall, 16	367
Elam Springs, Upshur	NA	Ericksdahl, Jones	35	Faught, Lamar	25
El Arroyo, Starr	500	Erin, Jasper	40	Faulkner, Lamar	48
*Elbert, Throckmorton, 9	150	Ernies Acres, Brazoria	NA	Fawil, Newton	NA
*EL CAMPO, Wharton, 779	10,943	Erwin, Grimes	NA	*FAYETTEVILLE, Fayette, 39	305
El Carro, Jim Wells	NA	‡Escobares, Starr	2,217	Faysville, Hidalgo	300
EL CENIZO, Webb	1,965	Escobas, Zapata	3	Fedor, Lee	76
El Centro, Starr	10	Esperanza, Hudspeth	75	*Fentress, Caldwell, 9	291
§*ELDORADO, Schleicher, 103	2,071	Espey, Atascosa	55	*FERRIS, Ellis, 106	2,323
Eldorado Center, Navarro	20	Estacado, Lubbock	80	Fetzer, Waller	NA
Eldridge, Colorado	NA	*ESTELLINE, Hall, 7	187	Field Schoolhouse, Erath	12
*ELECTRA, Wichita, 150	3,253	Estes, Aransas	50	Fields Store, Waller	NA
Electric City, Hutchinson	350	Ethel, Grayson	40	*Fieldton, Lamb, 1	126
Elevation, Milam	12	*Etoile, Nacogdoches, 17	70	Fife, McCulloch	32
El Gato, Hidalgo	NA	Eula, Callahan	125	Files Valley, Hill	50
*ELGIN, Bastrop, 248	5,495	*EULESS, Tarrant, 1,418	45,748	Fincastle, Henderson	NA
*Eliasville, Young, 1	150	Eulogy, Bosque	45	Finney, Hale	15
*El Indio, Maverick, 3	148	Eunice, Leon	NA	‡First Colony, Fort Bend	23,235
Elk, McLennan	NA	Eureka, Franklin	NA	*Fischer, Comal, 13	20
*ELKHART, Anderson, 82	1,166	EUREKA, Navarro	292	Fisk, Coleman	40
Elkton, Smith	NA	Eureka, Stephens	NA	Five Points, Ellis	10
EL LAGO, Harris	3,505	*EUSTACE, Henderson, 62	821	Flaccus, Karnes	15
*Ellinger, Fayette, 9	200	‡*Evadale, Jasper, 34	1,709	Flagg, Castro	30
Elliott, Robertson	NA	*EVANT, Coryell-Hamilton, 30	482	*Flat, Coryell, 5	210
Elliott, Wilbarger	50	Evergreen, San Jacinto	150	Flat Fork, Shelby	NA
Ellis, Austin	NA	Evergreen Park, Orange	NA	*FLATONIA, Fayette, 107	1,346
*Elmaton, Matagorda, 5	165	*EVERMAN, Tarrant	6,520	Flat Prairie, Trinity	33
Elmdale, Taylor	NA	Ewell, Upshur	100	Flats, Rains	646
*ELMENDORF, Bexar, 67	1,033	Ezzell, Lavaca	55	Flat Top, Stonewall	10
Elm Grove, Cherokee	NA			Flatwoods, Eastland	56
Elm Grove, San Saba	15	**F**		*Flint, Smith, 164	NA
Elm Grove Camp, Guadalupe	150	‡*Fabens, El Paso, 97	5,797	Flo, Leon	20
*Elm Mott, McLennan, 85	190	FAIRCHILDS, Fort Bend	500	*Flomot, Motley, 4	181
*Elmo, Kaufman, 6	90	§*FAIRFIELD, Freestone, 288	3,349	Flora, Hopkins	NA
Elmont, Grayson	15	Fairland, Burnet	NA	*FLORENCE, Williamson, 73	1,147
Elm Ridge, Milam	25	Fairlie, Hunt	80	§*FLORESVILLE, Wilson, 277	6,365
Elmtown, Anderson	5	Fairmount, Sabine	45	Florey, Andrews	25
Eloise, Falls	29	Fair Oaks, Limestone	15	Flowella, Brooks	NA
El Oso, Karnes	35	FAIR OAKS RANCH, Bexar-Comal-Kendall	2,229	Flower Hill, Colorado	NA
§*EL PASO, El Paso, 17,017	583,431	Fair Play, Panola	80	*FLOWER MOUND, Denton, 478	31,227
Elroy, Travis	125	Fairview, Angelina	NA	Floyd, Hunt, 10	220
*ELSA, Hidalgo, 95	5,608	Fairview, Armstrong	75	§*FLOYDADA, Floyd, 192	3,811
El Sauz, Starr, 4	50	Fairview, Brazos	NA	Flugrath, Blanco	NA
El Tacalote, Jim Wells	100	Fairview, Cass	NA	*Fluvanna, Scurry, 6	180
Elton, Dickens	1	FAIRVIEW, Collin	2,295	*Flynn, Leon, 5	81
El Toro, Jackson	126	Fairview, Gaines	NA	Foard City, Foard	10
Elwood, Fannin	31	Fairview, Hockley	10	Fodice, Houston	49
Elwood, Madison	50	Fairview, Hood	30	*FOLLETT, Lipscomb, 34	459
*Elysian Fields, Harrison, 19	300	Fairview, Howard	85	Folsom, Shelby	NA
Elysium, Bastrop	NA	Fairview, Rusk	NA	Footes, Gregg	NA
Emberson, Lamar	80	Fairview, Wilson	322	Ford, Deaf Smith	15
Emblem, Hopkins	52	FAIRVIEW, Wise	237	Fords Corner, San Augustine	NA
Emerald Bay, Smith	NA	Fairy, Hamilton	31	Fordtran, Victoria	18
*EMHOUSE, Navarro	232	Falcon, Zapata	376	Forest, Cherokee	85
Emille, Tyler	NA	*Falcon Heights, Starr, 15	400	*Forestburg, Montague, 11	200
Emmett, Navarro	100	Falcon Village, Starr	25	Forest Chapel, Lamar	NA
§*EMORY, Rains, 127	1,042	§*FALFURRIAS, Brooks, 213	5,815	Forest Glade, Limestone	340
‡Encantada-Ranchito El Calaboz, Cameron	1,339	Fallon, Limestone	100	Forest Grove, Milam	60
Enchanted Forest, Montgomery	NA	*FALLS CITY, Karnes, 33	568	Forest Heights, Orange	250
ENCHANTED OAKS, Henderson	320	Fambrough, Stephens	NA	Forest Hill, Lamar	NA
		Famuliner, Cochran	5	FOREST HILL, Tarrant	11,464
*ENCINAL, La Salle, 12	637	Fannett, Jefferson	105	Forest Hill, Wood	NA
*Encino, Brooks, 12	110	*Fannin, Goliad, 4	359	Forest Hill Estates, Coryell	125
*Energy, Comanche, 1	65	Fargo, Wilbarger	161	Forest Lake, Brazos	NA
Engle, Fayette	106	Farmer, Crosby	NA	Forest Lake, Gregg	NA
English, Red River	92	Farmers Academy, Titus	75	*FORNEY, Kaufman, 318	4,697
		*FARMERS BRANCH, Dallas	25,215	*Forreston, Ellis, 4	200

Town and County	Pop.
*FORSAN, Howard, 14	297
‡*Fort Bliss, El Paso	14,202
Fort Clark Springs, Kinney	1,070
§*Fort Davis, Jeff Davis, 71	1,179
Fort Gates, Coryell	865
Fort Griffin, Shackelford	4
*Fort Hancock, Hudspeth, 14	400
‡*Fort Hood, Bell-Coryell, 95	37,998
*Fort McKavett, Menard, 3	15
Fort Parker, Limestone	2
Fort Parker State Park, Limestone	30
*Fort Sam Houston, Bexar	10,000
Fort Spunky, Hood	15
Fort Stanley Creek, Angelina	NA
§*FORT STOCKTON, Pecos, 423	9,072
§*FORT WORTH, Tarrant-Denton, 26,959	478,307
Foster, Terry	NA
Fostoria, Montgomery	NA
Fouke, Wood	NA
Four Corners, Brazoria	NA
Four Corners, Chambers	18
Four Corners, Montgomery	NA
*Fowlerton, La Salle, 2	50
Frame Switch, Williamson	20
*Francitas, Jackson	143
Frankel City, Andrews	2
Frankell, Stephens	NA
§*FRANKLIN, Robertson, 76	1,453
*FRANKSTON, Anderson, 143	1,198
*Fred, Tyler, 11	239
§*FREDERICKSBURG, Gillespie, 872	8,355
Fredonia, Gregg	NA
*Fredonia, Mason, 4	50
Freedom, Rains	60
Freeneytown, Rusk	NA
*FREEPORT, Brazoria, 729	13,178
*FREER, Duval, 128	3,395
Freestone, Freestone	35
Freheit, Comal	NA
Frelsburg, Colorado	75
Frenstat, Burleson	NA
Fresno, Collingsworth	NA
‡*Fresno, Fort Bend, 52	3,395
Freyburg, Fayette	45
Friday, Trinity	99
Friendly, Van Zandt	NA
Friendship, Dawson	5
Friendship, Leon	NA
Friendship, Smith	NA
Friendship, Upshur	NA
Friendship, Williamson	48
Friendship Village, Bowie	200
*FRIENDSWOOD, Galveston-Harris, 1,213	30,583
Frio, Castro	15
*FRIONA, Parmer, 175	3,785
*FRISCO, Collin-Denton, 462	13,076
*FRITCH, Hutchinson-Moore, 124	2,479
Frog, Kaufman	NA
Frognot, Collin	NA
Front, Panola	NA
Fronton, Starr	110
*FROST, Navarro, 26	619
Fruitland, Montague	20
*FRUITVALE, Van Zandt, 23	365
Frydek, Austin	150
Fulbright, Red River	150
*FULSHEAR, Fort Bend, 54	722
*FULTON, Aransas, 57	812
Funston, Jones	26
Furrh, Panola	40

Town and County	Pop.
G	
Gadston, Lamar	NA
Gafford, Hopkins	NA
§*Gail, Borden, 13	189
§*GAINESVILLE, Cooke, 1,118	14,973
Galena, Smith	NA
*GALENA PARK, Harris, 199	11,021
Galilee, Smith	NA
*GALLATIN, Cherokee, 5	441
Galle, Guadalupe	130
Galleon Bay, Nueces	NA
Galloway, Panola	71
§*GALVESTON, Galveston, 2,481	63,857
*GANADO, Jackson, 99	2,049
Garceño, Starr	100
Garcias, Starr	200
Garciasville, Starr (See La Casita-Garciasville)	
§*Garden City, Glasscock, 101	293
Gardendale, Bexar	NA
‡*Gardendale, Ector, 29	1,105
Gardendale, La Salle	40
GARDEN RIDGE, Comal	2,174
Garden Valley, Smith	150
Garfield, DeWitt	16
‡Garfield, Travis	1,415
Garland, Bowie	NA
*GARLAND, Dallas-Collin-Rockwall, 6,185	190,703
Garner, Parker	196
Garner State Park, Uvalde	50
GARRETT, Ellis	426
Garretts Bluff, Lamar	20
*GARRISON, Nacogdoches, 60	893
*Garwood, Colorado, 43	975
*GARY, Panola, 21	276
Gastonia, Kaufman	30
§*GATESVILLE, Coryell, 411	11,789
*Gause, Milam, 6	400
Gay Hill, Washington	145
Gayle Estates, Brazoria	102
*Geneva, Sabine, 1	100
Geneview, Stonewall	6
Gentrys Mill, Hamilton	17
George's Creek, Somervell	66
§*GEORGETOWN, Williamson, 1,106	20,946
§*GEORGE WEST, Live Oak, 170	2,767
Georgia, Lamar	NA
Germany, Houston	43
*Geronimo, Guadalupe, 13	400
Gethsemane, Marion	NA
GHOLSON, McLennan	743
Gibtown, Jack	NA
§*GIDDINGS, Lee, 455	4,389
*Gilchrist, Galveston, 13	750
*Gillett, Karnes, 5	120
Gilliland, Knox	25
§*GILMER, Upshur, 461	5,406
Gilpin, Dickens	3
Ginger, Rains	96
*Girard, Kent, 4	125
Girlstown USA, Cochran	95
*Girvin, Pecos, 1	30
Gist, Jasper	NA
Givens, Lamar	135
*GLADEWATER, Gregg-Upshur, 348	6,185
Gladys, Montague	NA
Glass, Somervell	NA
Glaze City, Gonzales	10
Glazier, Hemphill	48
Glecker, Lavaca	NA

Town and County	Pop.
Glen Cove, Coleman	40
Glendale, Trinity	175
Glenfawn, Rusk	16
*Glen Flora, Wharton, 23	210
Glenn, Dickens	7
GLENN HEIGHTS, Dallas-Ellis	5,872
Glenn Oaks, Henderson	NA
Glenrio, Deaf Smith	5
§*GLEN ROSE, Somervell, 186	2,188
Glenwood, Upshur	NA
*Glidden, Colorado, 1	255
Globe, Lamar	NA
Glory, Lamar	30
*Gober, Fannin, 5	146
*GODLEY, Johnson, 54	607
*Golden, Wood, 13	156
Golden Beach, Llano	NA
Goldfinch, Frio	NA
*Goldsboro, Coleman, 1	30
*GOLDSMITH, Ector, 25	292
§*GOLDTHWAITE, Mills, 130	1,902
§*GOLIAD, Goliad, 107	2,203
GOLINDA, Falls-McLennan	415
Golly, DeWitt	41
Gomez, Terry	NA
§*GONZALES, Gonzales, 413	6,323
Goober Hill, Shelby	NA
*Goodfellow Air Force Base, Tom Green, 3	345
Goodland, Bailey	10
Goodlett, Hardeman	80
GOODLOW, Navarro	373
Good Neighbor, Hopkins	NA
Goodnight, Armstrong	18
Goodnight, Navarro	25
*GOODRICH, Polk, 31	266
Goodsprings, Rusk	21
Goodwill, Burleson	NA
Goodwin, San Augustine	NA
*GORDON, Palo Pinto, 22	430
*Gordonville, Grayson, 38	165
*GOREE, Knox, 10	405
*GORMAN, Eastland, 62	1,358
Goshen, Walker	NA
Gould, Cherokee	NA
*Gouldbusk, Coleman, 4	70
Gourdneck, Panola	30
Graball, Washington	NA
Grace, King	20
Graceton, Upshur	40
*GRAFORD, Palo Pinto, 79	549
Graham, Garza	139
Graham, Jasper	NA
§*GRAHAM, Young, 771	9,005
§*GRANBURY, Hood, 1,150	4,974
Grand Bluff, Panola	97
*GRANDFALLS, Ward, 15	632
*GRAND PRAIRIE, Dallas-Tarrant-Ellis, 3,696	108,910
*GRAND SALINE, Van Zandt, 167	2,744
Grandview, Dawson	12
Grandview, Gray	13
*GRANDVIEW, Johnson, 169	1,299
*GRANGER, Williamson, 43	1,346
*Grangerland, Montgomery	NA
GRANITE SHOALS, Burnet	2,278
GRANJENO, Hidalgo	NA
Grape Creek, Tom Green	NA
*GRAPELAND, Houston, 115	1,385
Grapetown, Gillespie	NA
*GRAPEVINE, Tarrant-Dallas-Denton, 1,730	38,232
Grassland, Lynn	61
Grassyville, Bastrop	50

Town and County	Pop.	Town and County	Pop.	Town and County	Pop.
Gray, Marion	NA	§*HAMILTON, Hamilton, 248	2,997	Helena, Karnes	35
Grayback, Wilbarger	25	*HAMLIN, Jones-Fisher, 147	2,602	Helmic, Trinity	86
GRAYBURG, Hardin, 2	316	Hammond, Robertson	44	*HELOTES, Bexar, 205	1,979
GRAYS PRAIRIE, Kaufman	362	Hamon, Gonzales	15	§*HEMPHILL, Sabine, 166	1,278
Graytown, Wilson	64	Hampton, Nacogdoches	NA	§*HEMPSTEAD, Waller, 265	3,956
Green, Karnes	35	*Hamshire, Jefferson, 35	350	§*HENDERSON, Rusk, 763	11,959
Green Hill, Titus	150	Hancock, Comal	NA	Henderson Chapel, Concho	NA
Green Lake, Calhoun	51	Hancock, Dawson	30	Hendricks, Hunt	NA
Greenpond, Hopkins	NA	Handy, Milam	NA	Henkhaus, Lavaca	NA
Greens Creek, Erath	75	*Hankamer, Chambers, 13	525	Henly, Hays	55
Greenview, Hopkins	NA	Hannibal, Erath	NA	§*HENRIETTA, Clay, 197	3,062
§*GREENVILLE, Hunt, 1,179	24,099	Hanover, Milam	27	Henry's Chapel, Cherokee	75
Greenvine, Washington	35	*HAPPY, Swisher-Randall, 39	625	§*HEREFORD, Deaf Smith, 684	14,608
Greenway, Bexar	NA	Happy Hill, Johnson	NA	Hermits Cove, Rains	40
Greenwood, Hopkins	35	Happy Union, Hale	15	*Hermleigh, Scurry, 13	200
Greenwood, Midland	2,000	Happy Valley, Taylor	NA	Herty, Angelina	605
Greenwood, Red River	20	Haralson Lakes, Tyler	NA	Hester, Navarro	35
*Greenwood, Wise, 5	76	Harbin, Erath	21	*HEWITT, McLennan, 266	10,837
*GREGORY, San Patricio, 43	2,592	Harborview, Brazoria	NA	*Hext, Menard, 3	73
Gresham, Smith	100	*HARDIN, Liberty, 24	581	HICKORY CREEK, Denton	2,110
*GREY FOREST, Bexar	534	Hardy, Montague	NA	Hickory Creek, Houston	31
Grice, Upshur	20	Hare, Williamson	70	Hickory Creek, Hunt	NA
Griffith, Cochran	12	*Hargill, Hidalgo, 4	1,349	Hickory Forrest, Guadalupe	300
Griffith, Ellis	10	HARKER HEIGHTS, Bell	15,420	Hickory Hollow, Hunt	NA
Grigsby, Shelby	45	Harkeyville, San Saba	12	Hicksbaugh, Tyler	NA
Grit, Mason	30	*Harleton, Harrison, 34	260	Hickston, Gonzales	NA
§*GROESBECK, Limestone, 195	3,584	*HARLINGEN, Cameron, 2,441	53,864	*HICO, Hamilton, 104	1,515
*GROOM, Carson, 48	638	Harlow, Hunt	NA	*HIDALGO, Hidalgo, 273	5,056
Grossville, Mason	NA	Harmon, Lamar	35	Hide-A-Way Lake, Smith	NA
*GROVES, Jefferson, 421	16,672	Harmony, Floyd	42	Hide Away, Brazoria	69
§*GROVETON, Trinity, 107	1,145	Harmony, Grimes	12	Higginbotham, Gaines	NA
Grow, King	70	Harmony, Kent	7	*HIGGINS, Lipscomb, 22	481
Gruenau, DeWitt	18	Harmony, Nacogdoches	NA	High, Lamar	55
*GRUVER, Hansford, 89	1,067	*Harper, Gillespie, 61	383	Highbank, Falls	68
Guadalupe, Victoria	106	Harpersville, Stephens	NA	High Hill, Fayette	116
Guadalupe Station, Culberson	80	Harris Chapel, Panola	180	*High Island, Galveston, 12	500
Gruene, Comal	NA	Harrison, McLennan	25	Highland, Erath	60
*Guerra, Jim Hogg, 1	75	*Harrold, Wilbarger, 7	320	Highland, Smith	NA
Guion, Taylor	18	*HART, Castro, 61	1,198	Highland Addition, Parker	NA
Gum Springs, Cass	NA	Hartburg, Newton	275	Highland Bayou, Galveston	1,209
*GUN BARREL CITY, Henderson	4,243	Hart Camp, Lamb	8	HIGHLAND HAVEN	372
Gunsight, Stephens	6	*Hartley, Hartley, 22	319	HIGHLAND PARK, Dallas	9,800
*GUNTER, Grayson, 31	929	Harvard Switch, Camp	NA	‡*Highlands, Harris, 251	7,941
Gus, Burleson	NA	Harvey, Brazos	310	*HIGHLAND VILLAGE, Denton	11,469
*GUSTINE, Comanche, 24	472	Harwell Point, Burnet	NA	High Point, Grimes	15
*Guthrie, King, 14	160	*Harwood, Gonzales, 17	112	Highsaw, Henderson	NA
*Guy, Fort Bend, 15	60	§*HASKELL, Haskell, 213	3,156	Hightower, Liberty	30
Guys Store, Leon	NA	Haslam, Shelby	101	Hightown, Polk	NA
		*HASLET, Tarrant-Denton, 43	956	*HILL COUNTRY VILLAGE, Bexar	1,320
H		*Hasse, Comanche	43	Hillcrest, Colorado	25
Haciendito, Presidio	NA	Hatchel, Runnels	25	HILLCREST VILLAGE, Brazoria	828
Hackberry, Cottle	30	Hatchetville, Hopkins	NA	*Hillister, Tyler, 7	200
HACKBERRY, Denton	238	Havana, Hidalgo	NA	Hillje, Wharton	51
Hackberry, Edwards	3	*HAWKINS, Wood, 123	1,424	Hills, Lee	20
Hackberry, Garza-Lynn	NA	*HAWLEY, Jones, 57	667	§*HILLSBORO, Hill, 520	7,766
Hackberry, Lavaca	NA	Hawthorne, Shelby	NA	Hills Prairie, Bastrop	35
Hagansport, Franklin	40	Hawthorne, Walker	NA	*Hilltop Lakes, Leon	300
Hagerville, Houston	70	Haynesville, Wichita	60	HILSHIRE VILLAGE, Harris	771
Hail, Fannin	30	Haynie Flat, Travis-Burnet	NA	Hinckley, Lamar	40
Hainesville, Wood	74	HAYS, Hays	275	Hindes, Atascosa	14
*HALE CENTER, Hale, 76	2,052	Hazle Dell, Comanche	NA	Hines, Johnson	NA
Halfway, Hale	58	Headsville, Robertson	NA	Hinkles Ferry, Brazoria	35
Hall, Marion	NA	*HEARNE, Robertson, 212	4,838	Hippie Ridge, Wise	NA
Hall, San Saba	15	*HEATH, Rockwall	2,487	Hiram, Kaufman	34
§*HALLETTSVILLE, Lavaca, 293	2,772	‡§*Hebbronville, Jim Hogg, 162	4,654	*HITCHCOCK, Galveston, 210	6,228
Halls Bluff, Houston	67	HEBRON, Denton	1,383	Hitchland, Hansford	27
HALLSBURG, McLennan	535	Heckville, Lubbock	NA	Hix, Burleson	35
Halls Store, Panola	NA	*HEDLEY, Donley, 10	415	Hoard, Wood	NA
*HALLSVILLE, Harrison, 111	2,872	Hedwigs Hill, Mason	10	Hobbs, Fisher	91
Halsted, Fayette	26	HEDWIG VILLAGE, Harris	3,075	*Hobson, Karnes, 7	135
*HALTOM CITY, Tarrant	33,906	Hefner, Knox	5	*Hochheim, DeWitt, 2	70
Hamby, Taylor	100	Hegar, Waller	NA	*Hockley, Harris, 65	300
		Heidelberg, Hidalgo	NA		
		*Heidenheimer, Bell, 7	144		

Town and County	Pop.	Town and County	Pop.	Town and County	Pop.
Hodges, Jones	150	Hurnville, Clay	15	Jardin, Hunt	22
Hogan Acres, Johnson	NA	*HURST, Tarrant, 1,972	39,741	*Jarrell, Williamson, 41	410
Hogansville, Rains	200	Hurstown, Shelby	NA	§*JASPER, Jasper, 677	7,604
Hogg, Burleson	NA	Hurst Springs, Coryell	8	§*JAYTON, Kent, 32	562
Holiday Beach, Aransas	1,000	*HUTCHINS, Dallas, 145	2,849	Jean, Young	110
HOLIDAY LAKES, Brazoria	1,201	*HUTTO, Williamson, 62	740	Jeddo, Bastrop	75
Holiday Shores, Brazoria	NA	HUXLEY, Shelby	367	§*JEFFERSON, Marion, 324	2,496
*HOLLAND, Bell, 45	1,341	*Hye, Blanco, 5	105	Jenkins, Morris	NA
Holland Quarters, Panola	40	Hylton, Nolan	6	Jennings, Lamar	NA
*HOLLIDAY, Archer, 58	1,531	Hynds City, Montague	NA	Jericho, Shelby	NA
Holly, Houston	112			*Jermyn, Jack, 1	75
Holly Acres, Angelina	NA	**I**		Jerrys Quarters, Washington	NA
Holly Beach, Cameron	NA	Iago, Wharton	56	JERSEY VILLAGE, Harris	5,448
Holly Grove, Polk	NA	Ida, Grayson	30	*JEWETT, Leon, 77	775
Holly Springs, Jasper	50	*IDALOU, Lubbock, 79	2,145	Jiba, Kaufman	NA
*HOLLYWOOD PARK, Bexar	3,103	Ike, Ellis	10	*JOAQUIN, Shelby, 38	919
Holman, Fayette	116	Illinois Bend, Montague	NA	Joe Lee, Bell	2
Homer, Angelina	360	IMPACT, Taylor	24	Johnson, Terry	NA
‡Homestead Meadows, El Paso	5,593	*Imperial, Pecos, 19	720	§*JOHNSON CITY, Blanco, 101	1,156
§*HONDO, Medina, 256	7,002	Imperial Valley, Travis	NA	Johnson Creek, Marion	NA
*HONEY GROVE, Fannin, 103	1,782	Inadale, Scurry	8	Johnston Store, Nacogdoches	NA
Honey Island, Hardin	401	Independence, Washington	140	Johnsville, Erath	25
Hood, Cooke	20	India, Ellis	12	Johntown, Red River	175
Hooker Ridge, Rains	250	Indian Creek, Smith	NA	*Joinerville, Rusk, 2	140
*HOOKS, Bowie, 104	2,828	Indian Gap, Hamilton	36	Joliet, Caldwell	NA
Hoover, Gray	5	Indian Harbor Estates, Hood	2,620	JOLLY, Clay, 1	215
Hoover, Lamar	NA	Indian Hill, Newton	NA	‡Jollyville, Williamson-Travis	20,386
Hope, Lavaca	45	Indian Hills, Llano	NA	Jonah, Williamson, 2	60
Hopewell, Franklin	35	INDIAN LAKE, Cameron	426	Jones, Van Zandt	NA
Hopewell, Houston	22	Indian Lake, Newton	NA	*Jonesboro, Coryell-Hamilton, 14	200
Hopewell, Red River	150	Indianola, Calhoun	200	JONES CREEK, Brazoria	2,176
HORIZON CITY, El Paso	2,475	Indian Rock, Upshur	NA	Jones Prairie, Milam	35
Hornsby Bend, Travis	20	Indian Springs, Polk	NA	*JONESTOWN, Travis	1,376
‡*Horseshoe Bay, Llano-Burnet	1,712	Indio, Presidio	NA	*Jonesville, Harrison, 10	28
Hortense, Polk	25	*INDUSTRY, Austin, 39	475	Joplin, Jack	NA
Horton, Delta	25	‡*Inez, Victoria, 23	1,397	Joppa, Burnet	NA
Horton, Panola	NA	*INGLESIDE, San Patricio, 192	6,962	Jordans Store, Shelby	NA
§*HOUSTON, Harris-Fort Bend-Montgomery, 110,971	1,749,001	INGLESIDE-ON-THE-BAY, San Patricio	535	*JOSEPHINE, Collin-Hunt, 9	649
HOWARDWICK, Donley	215	*INGRAM, Kerr, 153	1,554	*JOSHUA, Johnson, 200	4,544
*HOWE, Grayson, 73	2,182	*Iola, Grimes, 37	331	Josselet, Haskell	NA
Howland, Lamar	90	IOWA COLONY, Brazoria	765	Josserand, Trinity	29
Howth, Waller	65	*IOWA PARK, Wichita, 289	6,958	Jot-Em-Down, Hunt-Delta	10
Hoxie, Williamson	50	*Ira, Scurry, 18	250	§*JOURDANTON, Atascosa, 144	3,524
Hoyte, Milam	20	*IRAAN, Pecos, 68	1,252	Joy, Clay	100
Hub, Parmer	25	Irby, Haskell	NA	Jud, Haskell	40
Hubbard, Bowie	269	*IREDELL, Bosque, 11	370	*Judson, Gregg, 7	650
*HUBBARD, Hill, 74	1,656	Ireland, Coryell	60	Juliff, Fort Bend	NA
Huber, Shelby	NA	*Irene, Hill, 1	160	Jumbo, Castro	3
Huckabay, Erath	150	Ironton, Cherokee	110	Jumbo, Panola	NA
Huddleston, Montague	NA	*IRVING, Dallas, 7,799	169,855	§*JUNCTION, Kimble, 206	2,843
HUDSON, Angelina	2,727	Isla, Sabine	29	Juno, Val Verde	10
Hudson Bend, Travis	NA	Israel, Polk	25	*Justiceburg, Garza	76
HUDSON OAKS, Parker	1,189	*ITALY, Ellis, 48	1,895	*JUSTIN, Denton, 130	1,530
Huff, Archer	NA	*ITASCA, Hill, 68	1,624		
Huffines, Cass	140	Ivan, Stephens	15	**K**	
*Huffman, Harris, 175	250	*Ivanhoe, Fannin, 7	110	Kalgary, Crosby	140
*Hufsmith, Harris, 1	250	Izoro, Lampasas, 1	17	*Kamay, Wichita, 9	642
*HUGHES SPRINGS, Cass-Morris, 123	2,100			Kamey, Calhoun	NA
Hughey, Gregg	NA	**J**		Kanawha, Red River	149
*Hull, Liberty, 25	1,800	*JACINTO CITY, Harris	9,459	*Karnack, Harrison, 43	775
*HUMBLE, Harris, 3,357	14,912	§*JACKSBORO, Jack, 247	3,423	§*KARNES CITY, Karnes, 119	3,085
Humble Colorado Camp, Jim Hogg	NA	Jackson, Marion	NA	Karon, Live Oak	25
*Hungerford, Wharton, 27	178	Jackson, Shelby	NA	Katemcy, Mason, 3	90
*Hunt, Kerr, 41	708	Jackson, Van Zandt	NA	*KATY, Harris-Waller-Fort Bend, 1,876	11,204
Hunter, Comal	30	*JACKSONVILLE, Cherokee, 830	13,289	§*KAUFMAN, Kaufman, 399	6,490
HUNTERS CREEK VILLAGE, Harris	4,527	Jacobia, Hunt	60	Kaufman Estates, Kaufman	240
*HUNTINGTON, Angelina, 97	2,207	Jacobs, Rusk	NA	*Keechi, Leon	67
§*HUNTSVILLE, Walker, 1,308	34,594	Jakes Colony, Guadalupe	60	*KEENE, Johnson, 79	4,519
Hurley, Wood	NA	JAMAICA BEACH, Galveston	681	Keeter, Wise	NA
Hurlwood, Lubbock	115	James, Shelby	NA	Keith, Grimes	NA
		James, Upshur	NA	Keith Lake, Jefferson	NA
		Jamestown, Newton	70	*KELLER, Tarrant, 623	17,017
		Jamestown, Smith	75		

Town and County	Pop.	Town and County	Pop.	Town and County	Pop.
*LA VERNIA, Wilson, 98	787	*Lissie, Wharton, 7	70	147	3,196
*LA VILLA, Hidalgo, 14	1,712	Littig, Travis	37	*LOS INDIOS, Cameron, 1	206
*LAVON, Collin, 7	378	Little Cypress, Orange	1,050	Losoya, Bexar	322
Law, Brazos	NA	*LITTLE ELM, Denton, 83	1,365	‡Lost Creek, Travis	4,366
*LA WARD, Jackson, 8	183	§*LITTLEFIELD, Lamb, 363	6,426	Lost Prairie, Limestone	2
*LAWN, Taylor, 17	367	Little Hope, Wood	NA	LOS YBANEZ, Dawson	86
Lawrence, Kaufman	249	Little Midland, Burnet	NA	*LOTT, Falls, 44	871
Lawsonville, Rusk	NA	Little New York, Gonzales	20	*Louise, Wharton, 50	310
*Lazbuddie, Parmer, 16	248	*LITTLE RIVER-ACADEMY, Bell,		Lovelace, Hill	12
*LEAGUE CITY, Galveston,		23	1,672	*LOVELADY, Houston, 41	645
1,050	41,331	Lively, Kaufman	NA	*Loving, Young, 8	300
Leagueville, Henderson	NA	*LIVE OAK, Bexar	10,653	*Lowake, Concho, 3	40
§*LEAKEY, Real, 76	426	Live Oak, Concho	NA	Lowman, Lamar	NA
*LEANDER, Williamson-Travis,		*LIVERPOOL, Brazoria, 15	464	LOWRY CROSSING, Collin	1,143
543	5,723	§*LIVINGSTON, Polk, 733	7,037	Loyal Valley, Mason	50
*LEARY, Bowie	444	§*LLANO, Llano, 275	3,284	Loyola Beach, Kleberg	NA
*Ledbetter, Fayette, 13	76	Lobo, Culberson	40	*Lozano, Cameron, 4	200
Leedale, Bell	16	Lochridge, Brazoria	NA	§*LUBBOCK, Lubbock,	
*Leesburg, Camp, 13	115	Locker, San Saba	16	9,938	194,522
Lee Spring, Smith	NA	Lockett, Wilbarger	200	LUCAS, Collin	3,283
*Leesville, Gonzales, 5	150	Lockettville, Hockley	20	Luckenbach, Gillespie	25
*LEFORS, Gray, 14	663	§*LOCKHART, Caldwell, 422	9,476	*LUEDERS, Jones-Shackelford,	
*Leggett, Polk, 9	375	*LOCKNEY, Floyd, 76	2,130	14	382
Legion, Kerr	NA	Locust, Grayson	118	Luella, Grayson	639
Lehman, Cochran	8	*Lodi, Marion, 4	164	§*LUFKIN, Angelina, 2,206	32,851
Leigh, Harrison	100	Lodwick, Marion	NA	*LULING, Caldwell, 296	5,236
Leisure Acres, Coryell	25	Loebau, Lee	20	Lull, Hidalgo	NA
Lela, Wheeler	135	Logan, Panola	40	*LUMBERTON, Hardin, 343	7,410
*Lelia Lake, Donley, 6	125	LOG CABIN, Henderson	566	Lumkins, Ellis	20
*Leming, Atascosa, 6	268	*Lohn, McCulloch, 8	149	Lums Chapel, Lamb	6
*Lenorah, Martin, 12	70	Loire, Wilson	50	Lusk, Throckmorton	10
Lenz, Karnes	20	Lois, Cooke	20	Luther, Howard	335
Leo, Cooke	20	*Lolita, Jackson, 14	453	Lutie, Collingsworth	35
Leo, Lee	10	Lollipop, Henderson	NA	Lydia, Red River	109
*LEONA, Leon, 4	222	Loma Alta, McMullen	100	*LYFORD, Willacy, 43	1,977
*LEONARD, Fannin, 81	1,868	Loma Alta, Val Verde	30	Lynn Grove, Grimes	NA
Leona Schroder, Nueces	40	Lomax, Howard	3,554	*Lyons, Burleson, 11	360
Leonidas, Montgomery	NA	*LOMETA, Lampasas, 35	744	*LYTLE, Atascosa-Medina-Bexar,	
*Leon Junction, Coryell	25	*London, Kimble, 5	180	88	2,556
Leon Springs, Bexar	137	London, Rusk	NA	Lytton Springs, Caldwell	500
*LEON VALLEY, Bexar	10,050	Lone Camp, Palo Pinto	110		
*LEROY, McLennan, 12	341	Lone Cedar, Ellis	18	**M**	
Lesley, Hall	45	Lone Elm, Kaufman	NA	*MABANK, Kaufman-Henderson,	
§*LEVELLAND, Hockley,		Lone Grove, Llano	50	539	1,879
721	13,812	Lone Oak, Bexar	NA	Mabelle, Baylor	9
Leverett's Chapel, Rusk	450	Lone Oak, Colorado	NA	Mabry, Red River	60
Levi, McLennan	50	Lone Oak, Erath	NA	*Macdona, Bexar, 4	297
Levita, Coryell	70	*LONE OAK, Hunt, 43	597	Macey, Brazos	NA
*LEWISVILLE, Denton-Dallas,		Lone Pine, Houston	81	Macon, Franklin	NA
3,177	58,857	Lone Star, Cherokee	NA	Macune, San Augustine	100
*LEXINGTON, Lee, 63	1,033	Lone Star, Floyd	42	Madero, Hidalgo	NA
Liberty, Hopkins	NA	Lone Star, Kaufman	NA	§*MADISONVILLE, Madison,	
§*LIBERTY, Liberty, 524	8,869	Lone Star, Lamar	NA	323	4,100
Liberty, Lubbock	10	*LONE STAR, Morris, 75	1,608	Madras, Red River	61
Liberty, Milam	40	*Long Branch, Panola, 4	181	Mae, Jim Wells	NA
Liberty, Newton	NA	Long Hollow, Leon	NA	Magnet, Wharton	42
Liberty Chapel, Johnson	NA	Long Lake, Anderson	15	*MAGNOLIA, Montgomery,	
‡Liberty City, Gregg	1,672	*Long Mott, Calhoun, 3	76	415	1,236
Liberty Hill, Houston	73	Longpoint, Washington	80	Magnolia, San Jacinto	330
Liberty Hill, Milam	25	§*LONGVIEW, Gregg-		Magnolia Beach, Calhoun	NA
*Liberty Hill, Williamson, 68	300	Harrison-Upshur, 4,266	74,206	*Magnolia Springs, Jasper, 3	80
Lilbert, Nacogdoches	NA	Longworth, Fisher	65	Maha, Travis	NA
*Lillian, Johnson, 7	105	Looneyville, Nacogdoches	NA	Mahl, Nacogdoches	NA
*Lincoln, Lee, 15	276	*Loop, Gaines, 21	315	Mahomet, Burnet	47
LINCOLN PARK, Denton	391	*Lopeno, Zapata, 2	425	Mahoney, Hopkins	NA
*LINDALE, Smith, 322	2,633	‡Lopezville, Hidalgo	3,180	Majors, Franklin	NA
§*LINDEN, Cass, 130	2,369	*LORAINE, Mitchell, 22	755	*MALAKOFF, Henderson, 169	2,200
Lindenau, DeWitt	50	*LORENA, McLennan, 140	1,525	Mallard, Montague	NA
Lindendale, Kendall	NA	*LORENZO, Crosby, 49	1,250	*MALONE, Hill, 16	320
*LINDSAY, Cooke, 23	793	Los Angeles, La Salle	20	Malta, Bowie	297
Lingleville, Erath, 5	100	Los Barreras, Starr	75	Malvern, Leon	NA
*Linn, Hidalgo, 11	450	Los Coyotes, Willacy	4	Mambrino, Hood	74
Linn Flat, Nacogdoches	NA	*Los Ebanos, Hidalgo, 2	100	*Manchaca, Travis, 134	2,259
*LIPAN, Hood, 37	410	Los Escondidos, Burnet	NA	Manchester, Red River	185
*Lipscomb, Lipscomb, 3	50	*LOS FRESNOS, Cameron,		Mangum, Eastland	15
				Mangus Corner, Bexar	NA

Town and County	Pop.	Town and County	Pop.	Town and County	Pop.
Manheim, Lee	40	McCoy, Floyd	2	§*MIDLAND, Midland, 6,206	98,251
Mankin, Henderson	NA	McCoy, Kaufman	20	*MIDLOTHIAN, Ellis, 390	5,744
Mankins, Archer	45	McCoy, Panola	NA	Midway, Bell	122
*MANOR, Travis, 134	1,186	McCoy, Red River	175	Midway, Bexar	NA
*MANSFIELD, Tarrant-Johnson-Ellis, 884	19,192	*McDade, Bastrop, 16	345	Midway, Dawson	20
*MANVEL, Brazoria, 177	4,552	McDaniels, Brown	NA	Midway, Fannin	7
*Maple, Bailey, 7	75	*McFaddin, Victoria, 3	175	Midway, Jim Wells	NA
Maple, Red River	30	McGirk, Hamilton	9	Midway, Lavaca	NA
Maple Spring, Titus	25	*McGREGOR, McLennan, 218	4,837	Midway, Limestone	9
Mapleton, Houston	32	§*McKINNEY, Collin, 1,525	30,623	*MIDWAY, Madison, 17	313
*Marathon, Brewster, 32	800	McKinney Acres, Andrews	197	Midway, Montgomery	NA
*MARBLE FALLS, Burnet, 785	4,762	McKnight, Rusk	NA	Midway, Red River	40
§*MARFA, Presidio, 120	2,496	*McLEAN, Gray, 51	861	Midway, Smith	NA
Margaret, Foard	51	McLENDON-CHISHOLM, Rockwall	896	Midway, Titus	110
Marie, Runnels	12	*McLeod, Cass, 5	230	Midway, Upshur	NA
*MARIETTA, Cass, 19	170	McMahan, Caldwell	125	Midway, Van Zandt	31
*MARION, Guadalupe, 74	983	McMillan, San Saba	15	Midyett, Panola	NA
Marion Ferry Park, Angelina	NA	McNair, Harris	2,039	Mikeska, Live Oak	10
‡*Markham, Matagorda, 21	1,349	McNary, Hudspeth	250	‡Mila Doce, Hidalgo	2,340
Markley, Young	50	McNeel, Brazoria	NA	*Milam, Sabine, 19	177
Markout, Kaufman	80	McNeil, Caldwell	200	*MILANO, Milam, 24	450
§*MARLIN, Falls, 261	6,373	*McNeil, Travis, 1	70	Milburn, McCulloch	NA
Marlow, Milam	45	‡*McQueeney, Guadalupe, 41	2,117	MILDRED, Navarro	207
*MARQUEZ, Leon, 21	275	*MEADOW, Terry, 22	623	*MILES, Runnels, 42	898
Mars, Van Zandt	NA	Meadowbrook, Montgomery	NA	*MILFORD, Ellis, 23	799
§*MARSHALL, Harrison, 1,251	24,059	Meadowcreek, Kaufman	240	Mill Creek, Waller	NA
MARSHALL CREEK, Denton	418	Meadow Grove, Bell	10	Mill Creek, Washington	40
Marshall Ford, Travis	NA	Meadow Lake, Guadalupe	450	Miller Grove, Camp	NA
Marshall Northeast, Harrison	1,500	MEADOWLAKES, Burnet	577	Miller Grove, Hopkins	115
Marston, Polk	25	MEADOWS, Fort Bend	5,324	MILLER'S COVE, Titus	89
*MART, McLennan, 80	2,033	Meadowview, Hunt	NA	*Millersview, Concho, 3	75
*MARTINDALE, Caldwell, 25	1,061	Mecca, Madison	48	Millett, La Salle	40
Martinez, Bexar	NA	Medicine Mound, Hardeman	50	Millheim, Austin	150
Martin Prairie, Grimes	75	Medill, Lamar	50	*MILLICAN, Brazos, 5	157
Martins Mills, Van Zandt	125	*Medina, Bandera, 39	515	*MILLSAP, Parker, 37	534
Martin Springs, Hopkins	115	Medina Base, Bexar	NA	Millsville, San Patricio	NA
*Martinsville, Nacogdoches, 3	126	Meeker, Jefferson	NA	Milo Center, Deaf Smith	5
Marvin, Lamar	NA	Meeks, Bell	15	Milton, Lamar	80
Maryetta, Jack	7	*MEGARGEL, Archer, 14	258	Mims, Brazoria	NA
*Maryneal, Nolan, 4	61	Meldrum, Shelby	NA	Mims Chapel, Marion	NA
Marys Creek, Baylor	NA	*MELISSA, Collin, 54	789	*Minden, Rusk, 4	350
Marysville, Cooke	15	Melrose, Nacogdoches	150	*MINEOLA, Wood, 452	4,681
§*MASON, Mason, 140	2,148	*MELVIN, McCulloch, 6	170	*Mineral, Bee, 1	50
Massey Lake, Anderson	NA	§*MEMPHIS, Hall, 154	2,428	*MINERAL WELLS, Palo Pinto-Parker, 813	14,762
Masterson, Moore, 4	15	§*MENARD, Menard, 84	1,631	Minerva, Milam, 16	60
§*MATADOR, Motley, 37	719	Mendoza, Caldwell	100	Mings Chapel, Upshur	NA
*Matagorda, Matagorda, 25	605	Menlow, Hill	10	*MINGUS, Palo Pinto, 18	219
*MATHIS, San Patricio, 227	5,653	§*Mentone, Loving, 3	96	Minter, Lamar	78
Matthews, Colorado	NA	Mentz, Colorado	NA	*Mirando City, Webb, 12	707
*MAUD, Bowie, 43	1,074	*MERCEDES, Hidalgo, 340	15,174	*MISSION, Hidalgo, 1,136	38,101
‡*Mauriceville, Orange, 74	2,417	Mercury, McCulloch	166	‡Mission Bend, Fort Bend	30,272
Maverick, Runnels	31	*Mereta, Tom Green, 3	75	Mission Valley, Victoria	225
Maxdale, Bell	4	§*MERIDIAN, Bosque, 102	1,452	*MISSOURI CITY, Fort Bend-Harris, 1,038	50,719
Maxey, Lamar	55	*Merit, Hunt, 8	215	Mitchell, Eastland	46
*Maxwell, Caldwell, 21	500	*MERKEL, Taylor, 160	2,533	Mitchell Hill, Tyler	NA
*May, Brown, 13	285	Merle, Burleson	NA	Mixon, Cherokee	50
*Maydelle, Cherokee, 4	250	Merriam, Eastland	14	*MOBEETIE, Wheeler, 7	149
Mayfield, Hale	NA	*MERTENS, Hill, 2	113	MOBILE CITY, Rockwall	209
Mayfield, Hill	12	§*MERTZON, Irion, 45	697	Modern, Jim Wells	NA
Mayflower, Newton	100	Mesa, El Paso	50	Moffat, Bell	150
Mayhill, Denton	150	Mesquite, Borden	NA	Moffett, Angelina	NA
Maynard, San Jacinto	150	*MESQUITE, Dallas, 4,072	113,906	Moistown, Cameron	25
*MAYPEARL, Ellis, 31	835	Mesquite Acres Island, San Patricio	NA	Moline, Lampasas	12
*Maysfield, Milam, 1	140	Metcalf Gap, Palo Pinto	6	§*MONAHANS, Ward-Winkler, 394	7,844
*McAdoo, Dickens, 5	75	*MEXIA, Limestone, 398	6,917	Monaville, Waller	180
*McALLEN, Hidalgo, 4,653	100,589	Mexico, Hunt	NA	Monkstown, Fannin	35
*McCAMEY, Upton, 91	2,284	*Meyersville, DeWitt, 6	110	Monroe, Rusk	96
*McCaulley, Fisher, 3	96	§*MIAMI, Roberts, 29	509	*Monroe City, Chambers	90
McClanahan, Falls	42	*Mico, Medina, 4	98	Mont, Lavaca	30
McClelland, Shelby	NA	Midcity, Lamar	NA	§*Montague, Montague, 22	400
McCollum, Montague	NA	Middleton, Leon	26	Montague Village, Coryell	1,410
McCook, Hidalgo	91	*Midfield, Matagorda, 3	70	*Montalba, Anderson, 16	110
*McCoy, Atascosa, 3	30	*Midkiff, Upton, 16	98	*MONT BELVIEU, Chambers-	

Town and County	Pop.
Liberty, 112	1,540
*Monte Alto, Hidalgo	1,769
Monte Grande, Cameron	NA
Montell, Uvalde	20
Monte Robles Park, Bexar	NA
*MONTGOMERY, Montgomery, 431	447
Monthalia, Gonzales	65
Monticello, Titus	20
*MOODY, McLennan, 85	1,373
Moonshine Colony, Baylor	NA
Moore, Brazos	NA
*Moore, Frio, 8	230
Moore Hill, Polk	NA
Moore's Crossing, Travis	25
MOORE STATION, Henderson	298
Mooreville, Falls	96
Mooring, Brazos	80
Morales, Jackson	72
*MORAN, Shackelford, 11	292
Moravia, Lavaca	165
*MORGAN, Bosque, 20	501
Morgan Bluff, Orange	NA
Morgan Creek, Burnet	NA
*Morgan Mill, Erath, 7	206
MORGAN'S POINT, Harris	410
MORGAN'S POINT RESORT, Bell	2,349
Morrill, Cherokee	NA
Morris Ranch, Gillespie	NA
*Morse, Hansford, 12	150
§*MORTON, Cochran, 109	2,579
Morton, Harrison	NA
Morton Valley, Eastland	46
*Moscow, Polk, 5	170
Mosheim, Bosque, 7	75
Moss Bluff, Liberty	65
Moss Hill, Liberty	49
Mosswood, Montgomery	NA
Mossy Grove, Walker	NA
Mostyn, Montgomery	NA
*MOULTON, Lavaca, 60	1,012
*Mound, Coryell, 2	75
Mound City, Anderson-Houston	NA
MOUNTAIN CITY, Hays	384
Mountain Community, Coryell	300
*Mountain Home, Kerr, 24	96
Mountain Peak, Ellis	20
Mountain Springs, Cooke	100
Mountain Top, Eastland	22
Mountain View, Travis	393
Mount Bethel, Panola	62
Mount Blanco, Crosby	NA
*MOUNT CALM, Hill, 13	322
*MOUNT ENTERPRISE, Rusk, 41	511
Mount Haven, Cherokee	NA
Mount Hermon, Shelby	56
Mount Olive, Lavaca	NA
Mount Pleasant, Grimes	12
§*MOUNT PLEASANT, Titus, 908	13,652
Mount Rose, Falls	26
Mount Selman, Cherokee	200
Mount Sylvan, Smith	181
Mount Union, Jasper	NA
§*MOUNT VERNON, Franklin, 174	2,401
Mount Vernon, Houston	43
Mozelle, Coleman	NA
Muddig, Hunt	NA
Mudville, Brazos	NA
Muellersville, Washington	40
*MUENSTER, Cooke, 153	1,491
Mulberry, Fannin	17

Town and County	Pop.
*Muldoon, Fayette, 7	98
§*MULESHOE, Bailey, 299	4,270
*MULLIN, Mills, 28	225
Mullins Prairie, Fayette	52
*Mumford, Robertson, 4	170
*MUNDAY, Knox, 92	1,544
Munger, Limestone	5
Mungerville, Dawson	25
*MURCHISON, Henderson, 44	588
MURPHY, Collin	2,358
Murray, Cameron	NA
Murray, Young	45
Murvaul, Panola	110
Musgrove, Wood	NA
Mustang, Denton	NA
MUSTANG, Navarro	45
Mustang Mott, DeWitt	20
MUSTANG RIDGE, Caldwell-Travis-Bastrop	685
*Myra, Cooke, 2	300
Myrtle Springs, Van Zandt	131

N

Town and County	Pop.
Nacalina, Nacogdoches	NA
§*NACOGDOCHES, Nacogdoches, 1,849	32,358
*Nada, Colorado, 12	165
*NAPLES, Morris, 58	1,467
Naruna, Burnet	45
*NASH, Bowie, 92	2,372
Nash, Ellis	25
NASSAU BAY, Harris	4,615
Nat, Nacogdoches	25
*NATALIA, Medina, 31	1,408
NAVARRO, Navarro	254
Navarro Mills, Navarro	50
*NAVASOTA, Grimes, 466	6,887
Navidad, Jackson	227
Navo, Denton	35
*NAZARETH, Castro, 21	332
Necessity, Stephens	10
Nechanitz, Fayette	21
*Neches, Anderson, 14	175
*NEDERLAND, Jefferson, 826	16,812
Needmore, Bailey	45
Needmore, Terry	NA
*NEEDVILLE, Fort Bend, 172	2,864
Neely Ward, Cochran	5
Negley, Red River	136
Neinda, Jones	21
Nell, Live Oak	60
Nelleva, Brazos	NA
Nelson City, Kendall	NA
Nelsonville, Austin	110
Nelta, Hopkins	36
*Nemo, Somervell, 4	56
NESBITT, Harrison	380
Nesbitt, Robertson	NA
Neuville, Shelby	43
*NEVADA, Collin, 26	597
*NEWARK, Wise-Tarrant, 37	808
*New Baden, Robertson, 4	105
NEW BERLIN, Guadalupe	200
New Bethel, Jefferson	NA
New Bielau, Colorado	NA
New Birthright, Hopkins	NA
New Blox, Jasper	NA
*NEW BOSTON, Bowie, 268	5,125
§*NEW BRAUNFELS, Comal-Guadalupe, 2,303	32,724
New Bremen, Austin	NA
Newburg, Comanche	35
Newby, Leon	40
New Camp Ruby, Polk	NA
*New Caney, Montgomery, 269	2,771
*NEWCASTLE, Young, 13	562

Town and County	Pop.
NEW CHAPEL HILL, Smith	463
New Clarkson, Milam	NA
New Colony, Bell	4
New Colony, Cass	65
New Corn Hill, Williamson	NA
New Davy, DeWitt	20
*NEW DEAL, Lubbock, 13	567
New Fountain, Medina	NA
*Newgulf, Wharton, 4	963
New Harmony, Shelby	NA
New Harmony, Smith	NA
New Harp, Montague	NA
*NEW HOME, Lynn, 20	205
New Hope, Cherokee	NA
NEW HOPE, Collin	611
New Hope, Jones	9
New Hope, San Augustine	NA
New Hope, Smith	NA
New Hope, Wood	NA
Newlin, Hall	31
*NEW LONDON, Rusk, 23	983
New Lynn, Lynn	18
Newman, El Paso	60
New Moore, Lynn	NA
New Mountain, Upshur	NA
Newport, Clay-Jack, 1	70
New Salem, Palo Pinto	89
New Salem, Rusk	31
Newsome, Camp, 1	100
*NEW SUMMERFIELD, Cherokee, 32	617
New Sweden, Travis	60
§*NEWTON, Newton, 126	1,984
*New Ulm, Austin, 40	650
*NEW WAVERLY, Walker, 71	1,065
New Wehdem, Austin	100
New Willard, Polk	160
New York, Henderson	NA
NEYLANDVILLE, Hunt	111
Nickel Creek, Culberson	16
Nickleville, Wise	NA
NIEDERWALD, Hays-Caldwell	257
Nigton, Trinity	87
Nimrod, Eastland	85
Nineveh, Leon	101
Nix, Lampasas	6
*NIXON, Gonzales-Wilson, 74	2,100
Noack, Williamson	60
Nob Hill, Llano	NA
Nobility, Fannin	21
Noble, Lamar	40
Nockenut, Wilson	10
*NOCONA, Montague, 252	3,181
Nogalus Prairie, Trinity	109
*Nolan, Nolan, 4	47
*NOLANVILLE, Bell, 36	2,473
Nolte, Guadalupe	25
*NOME, Jefferson, 21	443
Noodle, Jones	40
NOONDAY, Smith	548
Nopal, DeWitt	25
*NORDHEIM, DeWitt, 15	333
Norias, Kenedy	45
Norman, Williamson	20
Normandy, Maverick	98
*NORMANGEE, Leon-Madison, 56	694
*Normanna, Bee, 2	75
Norse, Bosque	110
North Alamo, Hidalgo	NA
NORTH CLEVELAND, Liberty	196
Northcliff, Guadalupe	2,500
North Cowden, Ector	80
NORTHCREST, McLennan	1,915
Northfield, Motley, 1	15

Town and County	Pop.	Town and County	Pop.	Town and County	Pop.
North Hopkins, Hopkins	NA	50	1,174	**P**	
*North Houston, Harris	NA	Oenaville, Bell, 3	120	Pacio, Delta	15
North Jericho, Shelby	NA	O'Farrell, Cass	20	Padgett, Young	28
NORTHLAKE, Denton	334	Ogburn, Wood	NA	Padre Island, Nueces	NA
North Orange Heights, Orange	NA	*OGLESBY, Coryell, 12	531	§*PADUCAH, Cottle, 80	1,682
*NORTH RICHLAND HILLS,		*Oilton, Webb, 6	585	*Paige, Bastrop, 21	275
Tarrant	50,761	Oklahoma, Montgomery	NA	§*PAINT ROCK, Concho, 15	215
Northrup, Lee	71	Oklahoma Flat, Hockley	8	*PALACIOS, Matagorda, 181	4,395
North San Antonio Hills, Bexar	NA	Oklahoma Lane, Parmer	25	§*PALESTINE, Anderson,	
‡North San Pedro, Nueces	1,090	*Oklaunion, Wilbarger	138	1,054	17,793
North Star, Archer	NA	Okra, Eastland	20	PALISADES	350
*North Zulch, Madison, 11	150	Ola, Kaufman	50	Palito Blanco, Jim Wells	35
*Norton, Runnels, 4	76	Old Boston, Bowie	NA	*PALMER, Ellis, 50	1,707
Notla, Ochiltree	20	Old Bowling, Leon	20	Palm Harbor, Aransas	125
*Notrees, Ector, 4	338	Old Center, Panola	83	PALMHURST, Hidalgo	387
*NOVICE, Coleman, 7	189	Old Diana, Upshur	NA	Palm Park, Bexar	NA
Novice, Lamar	NA	Old Dime Box, Lee	200	PALM VALLEY, Cameron	1,274
Noxville, Kimble	3	*Olden, Eastland, 8	110	PALMVIEW, Hidalgo	2,331
Nubia, Taylor	NA	Oldenburg, Fayette	30	Palo Alto, Nueces	15
Nugent, Jones	41	*Old Glory, Stonewall, 4	125	Palo Alto Park, Bexar	NA
Nunelee, Fannin	25	Oldham, Tyler	NA	Paloduro, Armstrong	10
*Nursery, Victoria, 6	260	Old Midway, Leon	NA	§*Palo Pinto, Palo Pinto, 28	411
		*Old Ocean, Brazoria, 20	915	*Paluxy, Hood, 2	76
O		OLD RIVER-WINFREE,		§*PAMPA, Gray, 1,070	19,769
Oakalla, Burnet	45	Chambers	1,396	Pancake, Coryell	11
Oak Bend, Brazoria	NA	Old Salem, Bowie	NA	Pandale, Val Verde	20
Oak Cliff Acres, Comal	NA	Old Salem, Newton	NA	*Pandora, Wilson, 1	125
Oak Creek, Bexar	NA	Old Union, Bowie	238	§*PANHANDLE, Carson, 118	2,307
Oakdale, Hopkins	NA	Old Union, Limestone	25	*Panna Maria, Karnes, 1	96
Oakdale, Polk	25	Oletha, Limestone	53	*Panola, Panola, 11	296
Oak Flat, Nacogdoches	NA	Olfen, Runnels	50	PANORAMA, Montgomery	1,842
Oak Flats, Rusk	NA	Olin, Hamilton	12	PANTEGO, Tarrant	2,692
Oak Forest, Gonzales	25	Olivia, Calhoun	215	Panther Junction, Brewster	NA
Oak Grove, Bowie	294	Ollie, Polk	NA	Papalote, Bee	70
Oak Grove, Colorado	NA	*Olmito, Cameron, 28	200	*PARADISE, Wise, 41	275
Oak Grove, Ellis	10	Olmos, Guadalupe	75	§*PARIS, Lamar, 1,529	25,464
Oak Grove, Hopkins	NA	*OLMOS PARK, Bexar	2,269	Parita, Bexar	NA
OAK GROVE, Kaufman	705	*OLNEY, Young, 196	3,411	Park, Fayette	47
Oak Grove, Wood	74	*OLTON, Lamb, 107	2,051	Park Community, Navarro	160
Oak Hill, Hood	247	*OMAHA, Morris, 46	960	PARKER, Collin	1,452
Oak Hill, Rusk	24	Omega, Gregg	NA	Parker, Johnson	21
*OAKHURST, San Jacinto, 12	239	Omen, Smith	150	Parks Camp, Stephens	NA
Oak Island, Chambers	255	*ONALASKA, Polk, 95	924	Park Springs, Wise	NA
Oaklake, McLennan	60	‡Onion Creek, Travis	1,596	Parkview Estates, Guadalupe	500
Oakland, Brazoria	NA	Opdyke, Hockley	20	Parsley Hill, Wilbarger	40
Oakland, Cherokee	NA	OPDYKE WEST, Hockley	113	Parvin, Denton	44
*Oakland, Colorado, 2	80	Oplin, Callahan	75	*PASADENA, Harris, 3,826	130,168
Oakland, Jack	NA	O'Quinn, Fayette	25	Patillo, Erath	10
Oakland, Van Zandt	26	Oran, Palo Pinto	61	Patman Switch, Cass	NA
OAK LEAF, Ellis	1,092	§*ORANGE, Orange, 1,293	20,508	Patonia, Polk	NA
Oak Manor, Brazoria	119	Orangedale, Bee	35	Patricia, Dawson, 1	60
Oak Moss, Bexar	NA	*Orangefield, Orange, 24	725	Patrick, McLennan	NA
Oak Park, Travis	NA	*ORANGE GROVE, Jim Wells,		Patroon, Shelby, 3	55
*OAK POINT, Denton	996	80	1,321	*PATTISON, Waller, 13	377
Oak Ridge, Fannin	90	*ORCHARD, Fort Bend, 16	476	Pattonfield, Upshur	NA
Oak Ridge, Grayson	161	*ORE CITY, Upshur, 84	1,115	PATTON VILLAGE, Montgomery	1,311
Oak Ridge, Llano	NA	Orient, Tom Green	40	*Pattonville, Lamar, 8	180
Oak Ridge, Nacogdoches	NA	*Orla, Reeves, 9	183	Pawelekville, Karnes	105
OAK RIDGE, Cooke	226	Osage, Coryell, 1	30	*Pawnee, Bee, 5	249
OAK RIDGE, Kaufman	316	Oscar, Bell	40	Paxton, Shelby	161
OAK RIDGE NORTH,		Osceola, Hill	90	Paynes Corner, Gaines	NA
Montgomery	2,944	Otey, Brazoria	318	PAYNE SPRINGS, Henderson	711
‡Oak Trail Shores, Hood	2,044	Otis Chalk, Howard	79	Payton Colony, Blanco	NA
OAK VALLEY, Navarro	427	*Ottine, Gonzales, 4	90	Peach Creek, Brazos	NA
Oak Village, Bexar	NA	*Otto, Falls, 1	48	Peacock, Stonewall, 1	125
*Oakville, Live Oak, 4	260	*Ovalo, Taylor, 5	225	Peadenville, Palo Pinto	15
*OAKWOOD, Leon, 34	602	*OVERTON, Rusk-Smith, 148	2,270	Pearl, Coryell	125
Oatmeal, Burnet	20	OVILLA, Ellis-Dallas	2,522	*PEARLAND, Brazoria-Harris,	
*O'BRIEN, Haskell, 3	163	Owens, Brown	NA	1,330	25,601
Ocee, McLennan	35	Owens, Crosby	75	Pearl City, DeWitt	4
Odds, Limestone	24	Owensville, Robertson	NA	§*PEARSALL, Frio, 249	7,692
*Odell, Wilbarger, 3	131	Owentown, Smith	NA	Pearson, Medina	NA
*ODEM, San Patricio, 76	2,686	Owl Creek, Bell	45	Pearsons Chapel, Houston	95
§*ODESSA, Ector-Midland,		OYSTER CREEK, Brazoria	1,061	*Pear Valley, McCulloch, 2	4
5,111	93,495	‡§*Ozona, Crockett, 183	3,335	*Peaster, Parker, 4	102
*O'DONNELL, Lynn-Dawson,				‡Pecan Acres, Wise-Tarrant	1,766

Town and County	Pop.	Town and County	Pop.	Town and County	Pop.
Pecan Creek, Tom Green	NA	*PINELAND, Sabine, 43	1,047	‡Porter Heights, Montgomery	1,856
*PECAN GAP, Delta-Fannin, 3	262	Pine Mills, Wood	2	Porter Springs, Houston	50
Pecan Grove, Collin	NA	Pine Prairie, Walker	NA	*PORT ISABEL, Cameron,	
‡Pecan Grove, Fort Bend	12,002	Pine Springs, Culberson	20	442	5,005
PECAN HILL, Ellis	598	Pine Springs, Smith	NA	*PORTLAND, San Patricio-Nueces,	
Pecan Plantation, Hood	3,456	Pineview, Wood	NA	367	13,788
Pecan Wells, Hamilton	7	‡Pinewood Estates, Hardin	1,350	§*PORT LAVACA, Calhoun,	
§*PECOS, Reeves, 434	11,852	Piney, Austin	NA	525	11,532
Peeltown, Kaufman	NA	Piney Point, Montgomery	NA	*Port Mansfield, Willacy, 19	731
Peerless, Hopkins	NA	PINEY POINT VILLAGE,		*PORT NECHES, Jefferson,	
*Peggy, Atascosa, 2	22	Harris	3,456	315	13,074
Pelham, Navarro	75	Pioneer, Eastland	40	*Port O'Connor, Calhoun, 47	1,184
PELICAN BAY, Tarrant	1,404	*Pipe Creek, Bandera, 81	66	Port Sullivan, Milam	15
*Pendleton, Bell, 6	60	Pitner Junction, Rusk	NA	Porvenir, Presidio	NA
*PENELOPE, Hill, 7	217	§*PITTSBURG, Camp, 320	4,418	Posey, Hopkins	NA
*PEÑITAS, Hidalgo, 11	1,210	*Placedo, Victoria, 6	760	Posey, Lubbock	125
*Pennington, Trinity-Houston, 6	67	Placid, McCulloch	32	§*POST, Garza, 245	3,445
*Penwell, Ector, 9	74	Plain, Houston	66	Post Oak, Blanco	NA
Peoria, Hill	81	Plains, Borden	NA	Postoak, Jack	79
*Pep, Hockley, 6	35	§*PLAINS, Yoakum, 63	1,396	Postoak, Lamar	NA
Percilla, Houston	95	§*PLAINVIEW, Hale, 1,052	21,586	Post Oak, Lee	100
PERNITAS POINT, Live Oak-		Plank, Hardin	205	Post Oak, Robertson	NA
Jim Wells	186	*PLANO, Collin-Denton,		POST OAK BEND, Kaufman	363
*Perrin, Jack, 14	300	6,977	173,012	Post Oak Point, Austin	NA
*Perry, Falls, 2	76	*Plantersville, Grimes, 32	212	*POTEET, Atascosa, 86	3,568
§*PERRYTON, Ochiltree, 507	7,622	Plaska, Hall	28	*POTH, Wilson, 44	2,065
Perryville, Wood	52	PLEAK, Fort Bend	872	‡Potosi, Taylor	1,494
Personville, Limestone	50	Pleasant Farms, Ector	NA	*POTTSBORO, Grayson, 164	1,469
Pert, Anderson	20	Pleasant Grove, Bastrop	NA	*Pottsville, Hamilton, 5	100
Peters, Austin	95	Pleasant Grove, Falls	35	*Powderly, Lamar, 45	185
*PETERSBURG, Hale, 47	1,255	Pleasant Grove, Hopkins	NA	*POWELL, Navarro, 9	113
Peter's Prairie, Red River	40	Pleasant Grove, Limestone	20	*POYNOR, Henderson, 9	266
Petersville, DeWitt	38	Pleasant Grove, Upshur	NA	Praesel, Milam	115
*PETROLIA, Clay, 16	807	Pleasant Grove, Wood	NA	Praha, Fayette	25
PETRONILA, Nueces	162	Pleasant Hill, Eastland	15	Prairie Center, Matagorda	NA
Petteway, Robertson	25	Pleasant Hill, Nacogdoches	NA	Prairie Chapel, McLennan	NA
Pettibone, Milam	25	Pleasant Hill, Yoakum	40	Prairie Dell, Bell	12
Pettit, Hockley	26	Pleasant Oaks, Bexar	NA	*Prairie Hill, Limestone, 6	150
*Pettus, Bee, 19	400	*PLEASANTON, Atascosa, 346	8,555	Prairie Hill, Washington	NA
*Petty, Lamar, 3	100	Pleasant Ridge, Leon	NA	*Prairie Lea, Caldwell, 4	255
Petty, Lynn	24	Pleasant Springs, Leon	NA	Prairie Mountain, Llano	NA
Petty's Chapel, Navarro	25	Pleasant Valley, Blanco	NA	Prairie Point, Cooke	40
*PFLUGERVILLE, Travis, 614	7,926	Pleasant Valley, Garza	NA	*PRAIRIE VIEW, Waller, 56	4,105
Phalba, Van Zandt	58	PLEASANT VALLEY, Wichita	450	Prairieville, Kaufman	50
*PHARR, Hidalgo, 1,087	39,843	Pleasure Point, Angelina	NA	*PREMONT, Jim Wells, 109	2,994
Phelan, Bastrop	NA	*Pledger, Matagorda, 6	159	*PRESIDIO, Presidio, 78	3,544
Phelps, Walker	98	Pluck, Polk	NA	Preston, Grayson	325
Phillipsburg, Washington	40	*Plum, Fayette, 7	95	*Price, Rusk, 11	275
Pickens, Henderson	NA	Plum Creek, Freestone	NA	*Priddy, Mills, 11	215
Pickett, Navarro	30	PLUM GROVE, Liberty	562	PRIMERA, Cameron	2,628
*Pickton, Hopkins, 10	90	Pluto, Ellis	15	Primrose, Van Zandt	24
Pidcoke, Coryell	30	Poetry, Kaufman	NA	*PRINCETON, Collin, 168	3,273
Piedmont, Grimes	46	*POINT, Rains, 34	804	Pringle, Hutchinson	40
Piedmont, Upshur	NA	*POINTBLANK, San Jacinto, 25	481	Pritchett, Upshur	125
*Pierce, Wharton, 6	49	*POINT COMFORT, Calhoun, 38		*Proctor, Comanche, 12	220
Pike, Collin	80		1,137	*PROGRESO, Hidalgo, 34	2,717
Pilgrim, Gonzales	60	Point Enterprise, Limestone	200	PROGRESO LAKES, Hidalgo	191
Pilgrim Point, Grimes	12	Point Loma, San Patricio	NA	Progress, Bailey	49
Pilgrim Rest, Rains	72	Point Venture, Travis	NA	Prospect, Rains	40
Pilot Grove, Grayson	48	Polar, Kent	10	*PROSPER, Collin, 64	1,336
Pilot Knob, Travis	NA	*Pollok, Angelina, 40	300	Providence, Floyd	85
*PILOT POINT, Denton, 178	2,910	*PONDER, Denton, 37	502	Providence, Polk	NA
Pinckney, Polk	NA	Ponta, Cherokee, 1	50	Pruitt, Cass	25
Pine, Camp	78	*Pontotoc, Mason, 7	125	Pruitt, Van Zandt	NA
Pine Branch, Red River	NA	Poole, Rains	50	Pueblo, Callahan	1
Pine Forest, Hopkins	51	*Poolville, Parker, 14	520	Pueblo, Eastland	46
PINE FOREST, Orange	869	Port-Au-Prince, Brazoria	NA	Pueblo Nuevo, Webb	377
Pine Grove, Cherokee	NA	Port Alto, Calhoun	NA	Puerto Rico, Hidalgo	91
Pine Grove, Newton	160	*PORT ARANSAS, Nueces, 237		Pullman, Potter	31
Pinehill, Rusk	49		2,698	Pumphrey, Runnels	15
‡*Pinehurst, Montgomery,		*PORT ARTHUR, Jefferson,		Pumpkin, San Jacinto	150
89	4,073	1,547	58,196	Pumpville, Val Verde	21
PINEHURST, Orange	2,831	*Port Bolivar, Galveston, 92	1,200	Punkin Center, Dawson	30
Pine Island, Jefferson	350	Port Brownsville, Cameron	NA	Punkin Center, Eastland	12
PINE ISLAND, Waller	626	*Porter, Montgomery, 389	2,146	*Purdon, Navarro, 12	133

Town and County	Pop.	Town and County	Pop.	Town and County	Pop.
Purley, Franklin	81	Red Hill, Limestone	20	Rita, Burleson	50
*Purmela, Coryell, 5	61	Red Lake, Freestone	NA	River Bend, Newton	NA
Pursley, Navarro	40	Redland, Angelina	NA	Riverbrook, Montgomery	NA
Purves, Erath	50	Redland, Leon	35	Riverby, Fannin	15
*PUTNAM, Callahan, 7	103	Redland, Van Zandt	NA	River Crest Estates, Angelina	NA
*PYOTE, Ward, 10	379	Redlawn, Cherokee	NA	River Hill, Panola	NA
		*RED OAK, Ellis, 441	3,849	River Oaks, Navarro	NA
Q		Red Ranger, Bell	12	*RIVER OAKS, Tarrant	7,222
*Quail, Collingsworth, 4	92	*Red Rock, Bastrop, 12	100	River Plantation, Montgomery	NA
Quail Creek, San Jacinto	50	Red Springs, Baylor, 4	42	Rivers End, Brazoria	NA
§*QUANAH, Hardeman, 194	3,298	Red Springs, Smith	NA	*RIVERSIDE, Walker, 17	514
Quarry, Washington	NA	Redtown, Anderson	30	River Trail, Nueces	NA
Quarterway, Hale	12	Redtown, Angelina	NA	Riverwood, Montgomery	NA
*QUEEN CITY, Cass, 81	1,966	*REDWATER, Bowie, 20	857	*Riviera, Kleberg, 33	1,064
*Quemado, Maverick, 9	426	Redwood, Guadalupe	1,480	Riviera Beach, Kleberg	NA
Quicksand, Newton	NA	Reeds Settlement, Red River	50	Roach, Cass	NA
Quihi, Medina	104	Reedville, Caldwell	NA	Roane, Navarro	120
*QUINLAN, Hunt, 201	1,563	Reese, Cherokee	75	*ROANOKE, Denton, 420	2,257
*QUINTANA, Brazoria	62	‡*Reese Air Force Base, Lubbock		*Roans Prairie, Grimes, 3	56
*QUITAQUE, Briscoe, 28	500	1	1,305	*ROARING SPRINGS, Motley,	
§*QUITMAN, Wood, 249	1,865	Reese Village, Lubbock	2,600	12	228
		Refuge, Houston	27	Robbins, Leon	20
R		§*REFUGIO, Refugio, 201	3,070	*ROBERT LEE, Coke, 64	1,270
Rabb, Nueces	20	Regency, Mills	25	Robertson, Crosby	35
Rabbs Prairie, Fayette	36	Rehburg, Washington	NA	ROBINSON, McLennan	8,213
Raccoon Bend, Austin	NA	Reilly Springs, Hopkins	44	*ROBSTOWN, Nueces, 480	13,190
Rachal, Brooks	36	Rek Hill, Fayette	48	§*ROBY, Fisher, 37	574
Radium, Jones	10	*REKLAW, Cherokee-Rusk, 9	263	*Rochelle, McCulloch, 13	163
Ragtown, Lamar	25	Relampago, Hidalgo	NA	*ROCHESTER, Haskell, 21	507
*Rainbow, Somervell, 10	76	‡Rendon, Tarrant	8,414	Rock Bluff, Burnet	NA
Raisin, Victoria	50	RENO, Lamar	2,353	Rock Creek, McLennan	25
Raleigh, Navarro	40	RENO, Parker	2,595	Rock Creek, Somervell	36
*RALLS, Crosby, 93	1,995	Reservation, Kerr	NA	*ROCKDALE, Milam, 299	5,309
Ramireno, Zapata	25	Retreat, Grimes	NA	Rockett, Ellis	124
Ramirez, Duval	40	RETREAT, Navarro	349	Rockford, Lamar	NA
Rancho Alegre, Jim Wells	1,950	Retta, Johnson	NA	Rock Harbor, Hood	522
Rancho de la Parita, Jim Wells	NA	Reynard, Houston	75	Rockhouse, Austin	NA
RANCHO VIEJO, Cameron	1,107	Rhea, Parmer	98	*Rock Island, Colorado, 4	160
Rand, Kaufman	NA	Rhea Mills, Collin	47	Rock Island, Marion	NA
Randado, Jim Hogg	15	Rhineland, Knox	100	Rockland, Tyler	105
*Randolph, Fannin, 2	70	*RHOME, Wise, 58	730	Rockne, Bastrop	400
*Randolph Air Force Base, Bexar,		Rhonesboro, Upshur	40	§*ROCKPORT, Aransas, 655	6,127
85	3,015	Ricardo, Kleberg	1,641	§*ROCKSPRINGS, Edwards,	
*RANGER, Eastland, 149	2,903	*RICE, Navarro-Ellis, 28	634	48	1,468
RANGERVILLE, Cameron	317	Rices Crossing, Williamson	100	§*ROCKWALL, Rockwall,	
Rankin, Ellis	12	*Richards, Grimes, 13	296	1,066	13,334
§*RANKIN, Upton, 34	940	*RICHARDSON, Dallas-Collin,		*Rockwood, Coleman, 1	80
*RANSOM CANYON, Lubbock,		5,413	87,254	Rocky Branch, Morris	135
13	868	*RICHLAND, Navarro, 9	257	Rocky Creek, Blanco	NA
*Ratcliff, Houston, 5	106	Richland, Rains	100	ROCKY MOUND, Camp	57
Ratibor, Bell	10	Richland, Travis	NA	Rocky Point, Burnet	NA
Rattan, Delta	10	RICHLAND HILLS, Tarrant	8,711	Roddy, Van Zandt	NA
*RAVENNA, Fannin, 13	200	*RICHLAND SPRINGS, San Saba,		Rodney Calm, Navarro	15
Ravenwood, Brazos	NA	15	318	Roeder, Titus	110
Rayburn, Liberty	30	§*RICHMOND, Fort Bend, 675		Roganville, Jasper	100
Rayburn Country, Jasper	600		11,825	*ROGERS, Bell, 36	1,177
Raylake, Angelina	NA	RICHWOOD, Brazoria	2,814	Rogers, Taylor	NA
Rayland, Foard	30	Riderville, Panola	50	Rogers Hill, McLennan	NA
§*RAYMONDVILLE, Willacy,		Ridge, Mills	25	Rogers Plantation, Brazos	NA
272	9,343	Ridge, Robertson	67	Rolling Hills, Potter	1,000
Ray Point, Live Oak	200	Ridgeway, Hopkins	54	Rolling Hills, Waller	NA
*Raywood, Liberty, 16	231	Ridings, Fannin	10	Rolling Hills Shores, Hood	421
Razor, Lamar	15	*RIESEL, McLennan, 36	889	Rolling Meadows, Gregg	346
*Reagan, Falls, 9	208	Rincon, Starr	5	ROLLINGWOOD, Travis	1,362
Reagan Wells, Uvalde	20	*Ringgold, Montague, 5	100	*ROMA-Los Saenz, Starr,	
Reagor Springs, Ellis	45	*RIO BRAVO, Webb	3,867	172	10,930
*Realitos, Duval, 5	250	*Rio Frio, Real, 6	50	ROMAN FOREST, Montgomery	
Red Bank, Bowie	NA	‡§*Rio Grande City, Starr, 390			1,261
Red Bluff, Jackson	35		11,870	*Romayor, Liberty, 4	96
Red Bluff, Reeves	40	Rio Grande Village, Brewster	NA	Romney, Eastland	12
Red Branch, Leon	NA	*RIO HONDO, Cameron, 68	2,328	*Roosevelt, Kimble, 3	14
Red Cut Heights, Bowie	563	*Riomedina, Medina, 5	53	Roosevelt, Lubbock	3,500
Redfield, Nacogdoches	NA	Rios, Duval	75	*ROPESVILLE, Hockley, 23	504
*Redford, Presidio	107	*RIO VISTA, Johnson, 34	683	Rosalie, Red River	100
Red Gate, Hidalgo	NA	*RISING STAR, Eastland, 53	876	*Rosanky, Bastrop, 15	210
Red Hill, Cass	28				

Town and County	Pop.
*ROSCOE, Nolan, 55	1,426
*ROSEBUD, Falls, 83	1,591
ROSE CITY, Orange	690
Rose Hill, San Jacinto	30
ROSE HILL ACRES, Hardin	559
*ROSENBERG, Fort Bend, 921	26,747
Rosevine, Sabine	50
Rosewood, Upshur	100
*Rosharon, Brazoria, 117	435
Rosita, Duval	NA
Rosita, Starr	200
*ROSS, McLennan, 8	222
Ross City, Howard	81
*ROSSER, Kaufman, 4	419
*Rosston, Cooke, 2	75
Rossville, Atascosa	200
*ROTAN, Fisher, 93	1,791
Rough Creek, San Saba	15
Round House, Navarro	40
*ROUND MOUNTAIN, Blanco, 18	232
Round Mountain, Travis	59
Round Prairie, Navarro	40
Round Prairie, Robertson	NA
*ROUND ROCK, Williamson-Travis, 1,776	48,923
Round Timber, Baylor	2
*ROUND TOP, Fayette, 26	91
Roundup, Hockley	20
Rowden, Callahan	30
*Rowena, Runnels, 20	466
Rowland, Montague	NA
*ROWLETT, Dallas-Rockwall, 951	31,818
*ROXTON, Lamar, 15	637
*Royalty, Ward	29
Royal Forest, Comal	NA
Royal View, Bexar	NA
Royder, Brazos	NA
*ROYSE CITY, Rockwall-Collin, 150	2,757
Rucker, Comanche	NA
Rucker's Bridge, Lamar	20
Rugby, Red River	24
Ruidosa, Presidio	43
*RULE, Haskell, 34	733
Rumley, Lampasas	8
RUNAWAY BAY, Wise	873
*RUNGE, Karnes, 35	1,224
Runn, Hidalgo	NA
Rural Shade, Navarro	30
Rushing, Navarro	10
§*RUSK, Cherokee, 199	4,461
Russell, Leon	27
Rutersville, Fayette	52
Ruth Springs, Henderson	NA
*Rye, Liberty, 9	76

S

Town and County	Pop.
Sabanna, Eastland	12
*SABINAL, Uvalde, 71	1,677
Sabine Pass, Jefferson, 46	NA
Sabine Sands, Newton	NA
*SACHSE, Dallas-Collin	7,288
*Sacul, Nacogdoches, 4	170
*SADLER, Grayson, 14	352
*Sagerton, Haskell, 4	115
*SAGINAW, Tarrant, 84	9,947
Saint Elmo, Freestone	NA
St. Francis, Potter	30
*ST. HEDWIG, Bexar, 37	1,950
Saint Holland, Grimes	50
*ST. JO, Montague, 49	1,137
Saint John Colony, Caldwell	150
Saint Lawrence, Glasscock	NA

Town and County	Pop.
ST. PAUL, Collin	558
St. Paul, San Patricio	180
‡*Salado, Bell, 190	1,357
Salem, Cherokee	NA
Salem, Grimes	50
Salem, Newton	85
Salesville, Palo Pinto	88
Saline, Menard	59
*Salineno, Starr, 3	175
Salmon, Anderson	20
*Salt Flat, Hudspeth, 5	35
Salt Gap, McCulloch	25
*Saltillo, Hopkins, 6	200
Samaria, Navarro	90
*Samnorwood, Collingsworth, 2	110
Sample, Gonzales	25
§*SAN ANGELO, Tom Green, 3,550	89,421
§*SAN ANTONIO, Bexar, 37,959	1,079,207
San Antonio Prairie, Burleson	NA
§*SAN AUGUSTINE, San Augustine, 193	2,433
*SAN BENITO, Cameron, 549	22,495
San Carlos, Hidalgo	100
San Carlos, Starr	10
Sanco, Coke	30
SANCTUARY, Parker	280
Sandbranch, Dallas	400
‡§*Sanderson, Terrell, 46	979
Sand Flat, Johnson	NA
Sand Flat, Rains	100
Sand Flat, Smith	NA
Sandhill, Floyd	33
Sand Hill, Upshur	NA
*Sandia, Jim Wells, 29	215
§*SAN DIEGO, Duval-Jim Wells, 93	5,376
Sand Jack, Newton	NA
Sandlin, Stonewall	5
Sandoval, Williamson	50
Sand Springs, Howard	903
Sandusky, Grayson	15
*Sandy, Blanco, 2	25
Sandy, Limestone	5
Sandy Harbor, Llano	85
Sandy Hill, Washington	50
Sandy Hills, Montgomery	NA
Sandy Point, Brazoria	30
‡*San Elizario, El Paso, 33	4,621
*SAN FELIPE, Austin, 12	723
*SANFORD, Hutchinson, 16	240
San Gabriel, Milam, 1	100
*SANGER, Denton, 232	4,129
San Geronimo, Bexar	NA
*San Isidro, Starr, 8	160
San Jose, Duval	15
*SAN JUAN, Hidalgo, 275	24,327
SAN LEANNA, Travis	393
‡*San Leon, Galveston	3,481
San Manuel, Hidalgo	NA
§*SAN MARCOS, Hays-Caldwell, 1,738	34,661
SAN PATRICIO, San Patricio	443
San Pedro, Cameron	NA
*SAN PERLITA, Willacy, 6	677
San Roman, Starr	5
§*SAN SABA, San Saba, 206	3,296
SANSOM PARK, Tarrant	3,859
*SANTA ANNA, Coleman, 62	1,236
Santa Anna, Starr	20
Santa Catarina, Starr	15
*Santa Elena, Starr, 5	64
*SANTA FE, Galveston, 362	9,715
*Santa Maria, Cameron, 8	210

Town and County	Pop.
Santa Monica, Willacy	270
*SANTA ROSA, Cameron, 30	2,744
*Santo, Palo Pinto, 26	445
*San Ygnacio, Zapata, 10	1,200
San Ysidro, El Paso	400
*Saragosa, Reeves, 3	185
*Saratoga, Hardin, 16	1,000
Sarber, Marion	NA
Sarco, Goliad	78
Sardis, Ellis	20
*Sargent, Matagorda	76
§*Sarita, Kenedy, 6	250
Saron, Trinity	5
Saspamco, Wilson	443
*Satin, Falls, 4	86
Sattler, Comal	30
Saturn, Gonzales	15
Sauney Stand, Washington	NA
Savage, Crosby	NA
*SAVOY, Fannin, 27	962
Sayers, Bexar	NA
Sayersville, Bastrop	NA
Scatter Branch, Hunt	NA
Scenic Brook, Travis	NA
Scenic Hills, Guadalupe	170
‡Scenic Oaks, Bexar	2,671
Scharbauer City, Ector	20
*SCHERTZ, Guadalupe-Comal-Bexar, 337	12,877
Schicke Point, Calhoun	NA
School Hill, Erath	22
Schoolland, Gonzales	NA
Schroeder, Goliad	347
*SCHULENBURG, Fayette, 193	3,024
Schumansville, Guadalupe	650
Schwab City, Polk	NA
*Schwertner, Williamson, 5	150
Science Hall, Jasper	NA
‡Scissors, Hidalgo	1,695
*SCOTLAND, Archer-Clay, 7	534
*SCOTTSVILLE, Harrison, 14	288
Scranton, Eastland	40
Scrappin Valley, Newton	NA
*Scroggins, Franklin, 30	125
*Scurry, Kaufman, 35	315
*SEABROOK, Harris-Galveston, 620	8,558
*SEADRIFT, Calhoun, 37	1,496
*SEAGOVILLE, Dallas-Kaufman, 377	10,293
*SEAGRAVES, Gaines, 88	2,324
Seale, Robertson	26
*SEALY, Austin, 415	5,291
Seaton, Bell	60
Seawillow, Caldwell	100
‡*Sebastian, Willacy, 10	1,747
Sebastopol, Trinity	120
Seco Mines, Maverick	NA
Security, Montgomery	24
Sedalia, Collin	25
Segno, Polk	80
Segovia, Kimble, 1	12
§*SEGUIN, Guadalupe, 1,209	20,746
Sejita, Duval	22
Selden, Erath	71
Selfs, Fannin	30
*SELMA, Bexar-Guadalupe-Comal	679
*Selman City, Rusk, 12	271
§*SEMINOLE, Gaines, 389	6,558
Sempronius, Austin	NA
Senior, Bexar	NA
Serbin, Lee	90
‡Serenada, Williamson	3,659

Town and County	Pop.
‡Seth Ward, Hale	1,560
SEVEN OAKS, Polk	181
Seven Pines, Gregg-Upshur	NA
*SEVEN POINTS, Henderson-Kaufman	804
Seven Sisters, Duval	60
Sexton, Sabine	27
Sexton City, Rusk	NA
Seymore, Hopkins	NA
§*SEYMOUR, Baylor, 229	3,198
Seymour Colony, Baylor	NA
Shady Grove, Burnet	NA
Shady Grove, Cherokee	20
Shady Grove, Houston	83
Shady Grove, Panola	NA
Shady Grove, Smith	NA
Shady Grove, Upshur	NA
SHADY SHORES, Denton	1,309
*Shafter, Presidio	31
*SHALLOWATER, Lubbock, 76	2,039
*SHAMROCK, Wheeler, 154	2,101
Shangri La, Burnet	NA
Shankleville, Newton	NA
Shannon, Clay	23
Sharp, Milam	75
*SHAVANO PARK, Bexar	2,159
Shawnee Prairie, Angelina	NA
Shaws Bend, Colorado	NA
*Sheffield, Pecos, 6	600
Shelby, Austin	175
*Shelbyville, Shelby, 28	215
‡Sheldon, Harris	1,995
Shell Camp, Gregg	225
SHENANDOAH, Montgomery	1,970
Shep, Taylor	60
*SHEPHERD, San Jacinto, 96	2,141
*Sheppard Air Force Base, Wichita, 6	3,825
*Sheridan, Colorado, 11	225
§*SHERMAN, Grayson, 1,838	32,774
Sherry, Red River	15
Sherwood, Irion	150
Sherwood Shores, Bell	600
Sherwood Shores, Burnet	NA
Sherwood Shores, Grayson	1,590
Shields, Coleman	13
Shiloh, Bastrop	NA
Shiloh, Lavaca	NA
Shiloh, Leon	NA
Shiloh, Limestone	250
*SHINER, Lavaca, 134	2,317
Shire, Rusk	200
Shirley, Hopkins	NA
Shirley Creek, Nacogdoches	NA
*Shiro, Grimes, 4	205
Shive, Hamilton	61
SHOREACRES, Harris-Chambers	1,526
Short, Shelby	NA
Shovel Mountain, Burnet	NA
*Sidney, Comanche, 3	196
§*Sierra Blanca, Hudspeth, 26	700
Silas, Shelby	NA
Siloam, Bowie	50
*SILSBEE, Hardin, 528	6,888
*Silver, Coke, 6	60
Silver City, Milam	25
Silver City, Montgomery	NA
Silver City, Navarro	100
Silver City, Red River	25
Silver Creek Village, Burnet	NA
Silver Hills, Comal	NA
Silver Lake, Van Zandt	42
Silver Pines, Smith	NA
§*SILVERTON, Briscoe, 56	814

Town and County	Pop.
Silver Valley, Coleman	20
Simmons, Live Oak	65
Simmons Bottom, Liberty	NA
*Simms, Bowie, 13	240
Simms, Deaf Smith	10
*SIMONTON, Fort Bend, 27	930
Simpsonville, Matagorda	NA
Simpsonville, Upshur	100
Sims, Brazos	NA
Simsboro, Freestone	NA
Sinclair City, Smith	NA
Singletary Sites, Newton	NA
Singleton, Grimes	44
§*SINTON, San Patricio, 292	5,837
Sion, Walker	NA
Sipe Springs, Comanche	75
*Sisterdale, Kendall, 14	63
Sivells Bend, Cooke	50
Sixmile, Calhoun	NA
Skeeterville, San Saba	10
*SKELLYTOWN, Carson, 21	692
Skellyville, Travis	NA
*Skidmore, Bee, 25	500
Sky Harbor, Hood	687
Slabtown, Lamar	NA
Slate Shoals, Lamar	NA
*SLATON, Lubbock, 275	6,269
Slayden, Gonzales	15
Sleepy Hollow, Montgomery	NA
Slide, Lubbock	44
*Slidell, Wise, 2	175
Sloan, San Saba	30
Slocum, Anderson, 1	250
Smetana, Brazos	80
*SMILEY, Gonzales, 21	487
*Smithland, Marion	179
Smith Point, Chambers	150
Smiths Bend, Bosque	NA
Smiths Bluff, Jefferson	NA
Smithson Valley, Comal	15
*SMITHVILLE, Bastrop, 206	3,589
Smithwick, Burnet	NA
*SMYER, Hockley, 15	436
Smyrna, Cass	215
Smyrna, Rains	25
*SNOOK, Burleson, 25	524
Snow Hill, Collin	20
Snow Hill, Upshur	NA
Snuff Ridge, Liberty	NA
Snug Harbor, Brazoria	193
§*SNYDER, Scurry, 662	12,203
SOCORRO, El Paso	28,636
Soldier Mound, Dickens	12
Solms, Comal	40
*SOMERSET, Bexar, 57	1,460
*SOMERVILLE, Burleson, 94	1,660
Sommers Mill, Bell	6
§*SONORA, Sutton, 230	3,076
*SOUR LAKE, Hardin, 107	1,749
*South Bend, Young, 3	140
South Bosque, McLennan	80
South Brice, Hall	15
South Camp, King	NA
Southdown, Brazoria	2,427
South Franklin, Franklin	30
*SOUTH HOUSTON, Harris, 628	15,321
*SOUTHLAKE, Tarrant-Denton, 341	8,434
Southland, Garza, 1	157
*SOUTHMAYD, Grayson, 6	759
SOUTH MOUNTAIN, Coryell	332
*SOUTH PADRE ISLAND, Cameron, 224	2,149
*South Plains, Floyd, 5	92
South Purmela, Coryell	3

Town and County	Pop.
Southridge Estates, Guadalupe	125
South San Pedro, Nueces	1,912
South Shore, Bell	40
SOUTHSIDE PLACE, Harris	1,498
South Sulphur, Hunt	60
South Texarkana, Bowie	370
Southton, Bexar	113
*Spade, Lamb, 6	174
Spanish Fort, Montague	50
Spanish Trail, Hood	478
Sparenberg, Dawson	20
Sparks, Bell	30
‡Sparks, El Paso	1,406
*Speaks, Lavaca, 1	60
§*SPEARMAN, Hansford, 240	3,005
Specht Store, Bexar	NA
Speegleville, McLennan	111
Spencer, Montague	NA
*Spicewood, Burnet, 100	110
Spicewood Springs, Travis	NA
Spider Mountain, Burnet	NA
Spillers Store, Leon	NA
*SPLENDORA, Montgomery, 106	845
SPOFFORD, Kinney, 1	67
Spraberry, Midland	46
‡*Spring, Harris, 4,142	37,730
*Spring Branch, Comal, 110	200
Spring Branch, Smith	NA
Spring Creek, Hutchinson	139
Spring Creek, San Saba	20
Spring Creek, Throckmorton	13
Springdale, Cass	55
Springfield, Anderson	30
Springfield, Jim Wells	NA
Spring Forest, Montgomery	NA
Spring Hill, Bowie	209
Spring Hill, Navarro	60
Spring Hill, San Jacinto	38
*SPRINGLAKE, Lamb, 19	144
Springs Hill, Guadalupe	500
*SPRINGTOWN, Parker, 217	1,951
SPRING VALLEY, Harris	3,690
Spring Valley, McLennan	NA
Spring Valley, Travis	NA
Spring Woods, Montgomery	NA
Sprinkle, Travis	NA
*SPUR, Dickens, 114	1,222
*Spurger, Tyler, 22	472
Stacy, McCulloch	20
Staff, Eastland	65
*STAFFORD, Fort Bend-Harris, 1,527	11,434
Stag Creek, Comanche	50
STAGECOACH, Montgomery	480
Stairtown, Caldwell	35
Staley, San Jacinto	55
*STAMFORD, Jones-Haskell, 201	3,416
Stampede, Bell	10
Stamps, Upshur	NA
Stanfield, Clay	15
§*STANTON, Martin, 119	2,713
*Staples, Guadalupe, 4	350
*Star, Mills, 5	85
STAR HARBOR, Henderson	398
Star Route, Cochran	27
Starrville, Smith	75
Startzville, Comal	30
State Line, Culberson	18
Steele Hill, Dickens	6
Steep Creek, San Augustine	NA
Steep Hollow, Brazos	NA
Steiner, Bosque	20
Stephens Creek, San Jacinto	385
§*STEPHENVILLE, Erath, 902	15,923

Town and County	Pop.
Sterley, Floyd	24
§*STERLING CITY, Sterling, 63	943
Sterrett, Ellis	28
Stewards Mill, Freestone	22
Stewart, Rusk	NA
Stiles, Reagan	4
Stillwell Crossing, Brewster	3
§*STINNETT, Hutchinson, 75	2,289
Stith, Jones	50
*STOCKDALE, Wilson, 70	1,369
Stockholm, Hidalgo	50
Stockman, Shelby	52
Stoneburg, Montague	51
Stone City, Brazos	NA
Stoneham, Grimes	12
Stone Point, Van Zandt	32
*Stonewall, Gillespie, 25	245
Stony, Denton	25
Stout, Wood	86
‡*Stowell, Chambers, 14	1,710
Stranger, Falls	27
§*STRATFORD, Sherman, 117	1,928
Stratton, DeWitt	25
*STRAWN, Palo Pinto, 35	646
Streeter, Mason, 4	100
*STREETMAN, Freestone-Navarro, 21	273
String Prairie, Bastrop	75
Stringtown, Hunt	NA
Stringtown, Newton	NA
Strong, Shelby	NA
Structure, Williamson	60
Stuart Place, Cameron	NA
Stubblefield, Houston	15
Stubbs, Kaufman	NA
Study Butte, Brewster	120
Sturgeon, Cooke	10
Styx, Kaufman	NA
*Sublime, Lavaca, 5	75
*SUDAN, Lamb, 47	978
*SUGAR LAND, Fort Bend, 1,955	44,009
Sugar Valley, Matagorda	NA
‡*Sullivan City, Hidalgo, 13	2,649
*Sulphur Bluff, Hopkins, 4	280
Sulphur Springs, Angelina	NA
§*SULPHUR SPRINGS, Hopkins, 917	15,007
Summerall, Henderson	NA
*Summerfield, Castro, 4	60
Summer Hill, Henderson	NA
Summerville, Gonzales	NA
*Sumner, Lamar, 20	80
*SUNDOWN, Hockley, 82	1,738
Sunnyside, Castro	80
Sunnyside, Waller	120
Sunnyside, Wilson	300
SUNNYVALE, Dallas	2,828
*SUNRAY, Moore, 77	1,798
Sunrise, Falls	845
*SUNRISE BEACH, Llano	552
*SUNSET, Montague, 16	300
Sunset Oaks, Burnet	NA
SUNSET VALLEY, Travis	395
SUN VALLEY, Lamar	78
Sunview, Marion	NA
SURFSIDE BEACH, Brazoria	707
Sugar Mill, Brazoria	523
*Sutherland Springs, Wilson, 11	362
Swamp City, Gregg	8
Swan, Smith	150
Swearingen, Collingsworth	NA
*SWEENY, Brazoria, 134	3,452
Sweet Home, Guadalupe	80

Town and County	Pop.
*Sweet Home, Lavaca, 9	360
Sweet Home, Lee	30
Sweet Union, Cherokee	20
§*SWEETWATER, Nolan, 643	12,004
Swenson, Stonewall	185
Swift, Nacogdoches	125
Swiftex, Bastrop	NA
Swinneytown, Smith	NA
Swiss Alp, Fayette	46
Sylvan, Lamar	68
*Sylvester, Fisher, 5	79

T

Town and County	Pop.
Tabor, Brazos	150
Tadmor, Houston	67
*TAFT, San Patricio, 137	3,819
‡Taft Southwest, San Patricio	2,343
§*TAHOKA, Lynn, 104	2,757
Taiton, Wharton	24
*TALCO, Titus, 39	615
*Talpa, Coleman, 7	127
Talty, Kaufman	32
Tamina, Montgomery	NA
Tanglewood, Lee, 2	48
‡Tanglewood Forest, Travis	3,194
Tarkington Prairie, Liberty	NA
*Tarpley, Bandera, 4	30
*Tarzan, Martin, 11	80
Tascosa, Oldham	NA
Tascosa Hills, Potter	90
*TATUM, Rusk-Panola, 53	1,382
*TAYLOR, Williamson, 510	13,456
TAYLOR LAKE VILLAGE, Harris	4,151
Taylorsville, Caldwell	20
Taylor Town, Lamar	40
Tazewell, Hopkins	NA
*TEAGUE, Freestone, 151	3,519
Teaselville, Smith	NA
*TEHUACANA, Limestone, 9	339
*Telegraph, Kimble, 4	3
*Telephone, Fannin, 10	210
*Telferner, Victoria, 15	700
*Telico, Ellis	95
*Tell, Childress, 2	63
*TEMPLE, Bell, 2,201	49,772
Temple Springs, Jasper	NA
*TENAHA, Shelby, 45	1,086
Tenmile, Dawson	30
Tennessee, Shelby	NA
*Tennessee Colony, Anderson, 14	300
*Tennyson, Coke	35
*Terlingua, Brewster, 26	25
Terrace, Bexar	NA
*TERRELL, Kaufman, 789	13,110
*TERRELL HILLS, Bexar	5,131
Terry Chapel, Falls	30
Terryville, DeWitt	40
*TEXARKANA (Texas portion only), Bowie, 2,533	33,262
Including Arkansas Portion (1990 U.S. census count)	54,287
*TEXAS CITY, Galveston, 1,242	41,475
Texas National, Montgomery	NA
TEXHOMA, Sherman	315
*TEXLINE, Dallam, 41	446
Texon, Reagan, 1	12
Thalia, Foard	104
*THE COLONY, Denton	25,331
Thedford, Smith	65
The Divide, Kerr	250
The Grove, Coryell	65
Thelma, Bexar	NA

Town and County	Pop.
Thelma, Limestone	NA
Theon, Williamson	20
Thermo, Hopkins	NA
‡*The Woodlands, Montgomery, 860	37,568
*Thicket, Hardin, 7	306
Thomas, Upshur	NA
*Thomaston, DeWitt, 3	45
*THOMPSONS, Fort Bend, 7	201
Thompsonville, Gonzales	30
Thompsonville, Jim Hogg	NA
Thornberry, Clay	60
*THORNDALE, Milam-Williamson, 51	1,391
*THORNTON, Limestone, 23	601
THORNTONVILLE, Ward	767
Thorp Spring, Hood	184
*THRALL, Williamson, 15	664
Three Oaks, Wilson	150
*THREE RIVERS, Live Oak, 116	1,996
Three States, Cass	45
Three Way, Erath	NA
Thrifty, Brown	NA
§*THROCKMORTON, Throckmorton, 69	1,086
Thurber, Erath	8
Tidwell, Hunt	NA
Tidwell Prairie, Robertson	NA
Tigertown, Lamar	NA
TIKI ISLAND VILLAGE, Galveston	681
§*Tilden, McMullen, 23	450
Tilmon, Caldwell	117
TIMBERCREEK CANYON, Randall	378
‡Timberwood, Bexar	2,997
Timesville, Leon	NA
*TIMPSON, Shelby, 70	1,025
Tin Top, Parker	31
*TIOGA, Grayson, 31	648
TIRA, Hopkins	293
*Tivoli, Refugio, 25	550
Tivy, Kerr	NA
Tobacco Patch, Polk	NA
TOCO, Lamar	134
Todd City, Anderson	10
TODD MISSION, Grimes	65
Tokio, McLennan	NA
*Tokio, Terry, 5	60
*TOLAR, Hood, 25	557
Tolbert, Wilbarger	30
Toledo Village, Newton	NA
Tolette, Lamar	NA
Tolosa, Kaufman	58
*TOMBALL, Harris-Montgomery, 1,086	7,252
*TOM BEAN, Grayson, 27	879
Tomlinson Hill, Falls	64
TOOL, Henderson	2,014
Topsey, Coryell	20
*Tornillo, El Paso, 14	241
Tours, McLennan	100
*Tow, Llano, 21	305
Tower Lake, Wilson	100
Town Bluff, Tyler	26
Townsend, San Augustine	NA
‡Town West, Fort Bend	7,815
*TOYAH, Reeves, 5	121
*Toyahvale, Reeves, 4	60
Travis, Falls	48
Trawick, Nacogdoches	100
Treasure Island, Guadalupe	600
*TRENT, Taylor, 19	320
*TRENTON, Fannin, 40	705

Town and County	Pop.	Town and County	Pop.	Town and County	Pop.
Trickham, Coleman	12	Valley View, Cottle	23	*WAKE VILLAGE, Bowie	5,308
Trimmier, Bell	90	Valley View, Runnels	22	*Walburg, Williamson, 7	250
*TRINIDAD, Henderson, 41	1,123	Valley View, Upshur	NA	Waldeck, Fayette	35
*TRINITY, Trinity, 227	2,845	Valley View, Wichita	200	Walden, Montgomery	NA
TROPHY CLUB, Denton	4,689	Valley Wells, Dimmit	25	Waldrip, McCulloch	NA
*TROUP, Smith-Cherokee, 151	1,883	Val Verde, Hidalgo	NA	Walhalla, Fayette	37
Trout Creek, Newton	NA	Val Verde, Milam	25	*Wall, Tom Green, 11	200
*TROY, Bell, 62	1,723	*VAN, Van Zandt, 102	2,150	Wallace, Van Zandt	NA
Truby, Jones	26	*VAN ALSTYNE, Grayson,		Wallace Prairie, Grimes	75
Trukton, Rusk	NA	111	2,263	*WALLER, Waller-Harris, 201	1,831
Trumbull, Ellis	65	Vance, Real	20	*WALLIS, Austin, 46	1,137
*Truscott, Knox, 4	50	*Vancourt, Tom Green, 3	125	*Wallisville, Chambers, 18	460
Tucker, Anderson	304	Vandalia, Red River	35	Walnut Bend, Cooke	59
*Tuleta, Bee, 11	98	*Vanderbilt, Jackson, 18	618	Walnut Grove, Collin	200
§*TULIA, Swisher, 284	5,229	*Vanderpool, Bandera, 6	20	Walnut Grove, Smith	NA
Tulip, Fannin	10	Vandyke, Comanche	20	Walnut Hills, Potter	60
Tulsita, Bee	25	§*VAN HORN, Culberson,		*WALNUT SPRINGS, Bosque, 21	814
Tundra, Van Zandt	34	123	2,907	Walton, Van Zandt	35
Tunis, Burleson	150	Van Raub, Bexar	NA	Wamba, Bowie	70
*TURKEY, Hall, 18	531	Van Sickle, Hunt	NA	Waneta, Houston	19
Turlington, Freestone	27	‡*Van Vleck, Matagorda, 41	1,753	Waples, Hood	155
Turnbaugh Corner, Ector	NA	Vasco, Delta	20	*Warda, Fayette, 4	98
Turnersville, Coryell	155	Vashti, Clay	80	Ward Creek, Bowie	164
Turnersville, Travis	90	Vattmanville, Kleberg	399	*Waring, Kendall, 1	73
Turnertown, Rusk	76	Vaughan, Hill	70	Warlock, Marion	NA
Turtle Bayou, Chambers	42	Veach, San Augustine	NA	*Warren, Tyler, 31	304
Turtle Cove, Brazoria	50	*Vealmoor, Howard	179	WARREN CITY, Gregg-Upshur	357
*TUSCOLA, Taylor, 52	632	§*VEGA, Oldham, 56	874	*Warrenton, Fayette, 1	65
Tuxedo, Jones	42	*VENUS, Johnson-Ellis, 43	1,212	Warsaw, Kaufman	58
Twin Creek, Bexar	NA	*Vera, Knox, 1	50	Warwick, Smith	NA
Twin Sisters, Blanco	78	Verde Mills, Bexar	NA	Washburn, Armstrong	120
Twitty, Wheeler, 6	12	Verdi, Atascosa	110	*Washington, Washington, 21	265
*TYE, Taylor, 45	1,173	*Verhalen, Reeves	52	*WASKOM, Harrison, 123	1,853
§*TYLER, Smith, 5,444	80,204	*Veribest, Tom Green, 3	40	Wastella, Nolan	4
*Tynan, Bee, 7	200	§*VERNON, Wilbarger, 581	12,572	*WATAUGA, Tarrant	21,970
Type, Williamson	40	Vessey, Red River	14	Waterloo, Williamson	60
		Viboras, Starr	22	Waterman, Shelby	53
U		Vick, Concho	20	*Water Valley, Tom Green, 15	120
UHLAND, Caldwell-Hays	388	Vicksburg, Montgomery	NA	Waterwood, San Jacinto	100
*Umbarger, Randall, 13	327	Victoria, Limestone	25	Watkins, Van Zandt	NA
UNCERTAIN, Harrison	215	§*VICTORIA, Victoria, 2,870	61,320	Watson, Burnet	NA
Union, Brazos	NA	Victory City, Bowie	NA	Watt, Limestone	25
Union, San Augustine	NA	*VIDOR, Orange, 724	12,096	Watterson, Bastrop	NA
Union, Scurry	20	Vienna, Lavaca	40	Watts, Marion	NA
Union, Terry	85	View, Taylor, 1	75	Waverly, San Jacinto	200
Union, Wilson	22	Viewpoint, Lamar	NA	§*WAXAHACHIE, Ellis, 991	19,049
Union Center, Eastland	NA	Vigo Park, Swisher	31	Wayne, Cass	15
Union Grove, Bell	4	*Village Mills, Hardin, 13	1,700	*Wayside, Armstrong, 3	35
Union Grove, Erath	12	Villa Nueva, Cameron	NA	Wayside, Lynn	NA
UNION GROVE, Upshur	303	Villareales, Starr	100	Wayside, Roberts	NA
Union High, Navarro	30	Vincent, Howard	500	Wealthy, Leon	NA
Union Valley, Hunt	25	Vinegarone, Val Verde	NA	§*WEATHERFORD, Parker,	
Unity, Lamar	NA	Vineyard, Jack	37	1,497	17,711
*UNIVERSAL CITY, Bexar,		VINTON, El Paso	644	Weatherly, Hall	20
513	14,656	Violet, Nueces	160	Weaver, Hopkins	35
UNIVERSITY PARK, Dallas	22,013	Vistula, Houston	21	Webb, Shelby	NA
Upper Meyersville, DeWitt	33	Vivian, Foard	NA	Webberville, Travis	50
Upshaw, Nacogdoches	NA	*Voca, McCulloch, 2	56	Webbville, Coleman	50
Upton, Bastrop	25	Volente, Travis	NA	*WEBSTER, Harris, 1,053	5,257
Urbana, San Jacinto	25	Volga, Houston	300	Weches, Houston	26
Utley, Bastrop	30	*Von Ormy, Bexar, 82	264	Weedhaven, Jackson	35
*Utopia, Uvalde, 33	360	Vontress, Haskell	NA	Weeks Settlement, Newton	NA
§*UVALDE, Uvalde, 751	15,823	*Voss, Coleman, 1	20	Weeping Mary, Cherokee	NA
Uz, Montague	NA	*Votaw, Hardin, 3	160	*Weesatche, Goliad, 7	411
		*Voth, Jefferson	NA	*WEIMAR, Colorado, 180	2,233
V		Vsetin, Lavaca	NA	Weinert, Guadalupe	10
*VALENTINE, Jeff Davis, 5	270	Vysehrad, Lavaca	NA	*WEINERT, Haskell, 9	253
*Valera, Coleman, 7	80			Weir, Hopkins	NA
Valley Creek, Fannin	12	**W**		*WEIR, Williamson, 6	292
Valley Grove, Rusk	NA	§*WACO, McLennan, 5,864	108,562	Weiss Bluff, Jasper	NA
Valley Hi, Bexar	NA	*Wadsworth, Matagorda, 13	152	*Welch, Dawson, 24	110
*VALLEY MILLS, Bosque-		*WAELDER, Gonzales, 19	766	Welcome, Austin	150
McLennan, 64	1,157	Wagner, Hunt	NA	Weldon, Houston	131
Valley Ridge, Brazos	NA	*Waka, Ochiltree, 2	65	Welfare, Kendall	36
*Valley Spring, Llano, 4	50	Wake, Crosby	NA	*Wellborn, Brazos, 10	100
*VALLEY VIEW, Cooke, 61	688	Wakefield, Polk	NA		

Town and County	Pop.
§*WELLINGTON, Collingsworth, 186	2,536
*WELLMAN, Terry, 6	259
*WELLS, Cherokee, 26	775
Wells, Lynn	NA
‡Wells Branch, Travis	7,731
Wellswood, San Augustine	NA
Wentworth, Van Zandt	32
Wesco, Gray	7
*WESLACO, Hidalgo, 914	27,812
Wesley, Washington	60
Wesley Grove, Walker	NA
*WEST, McLennan, 224	2,835
West Bluff, Orange	NA
Westbrook, Jack	NA
*WESTBROOK, Mitchell, 13	256
*WEST COLUMBIA, Brazoria, 270	5,050
Westcott, San Jacinto	25
Western Lake, Parker	NA
*Westhoff, DeWitt, 12	410
WESTLAKE, Tarrant-Denton	256
*WEST LAKE HILLS, Travis	2,827
Westlawn, Orange	NA
West Mineola, Wood	NA
*WESTMINSTER, Collin, 5	497
West Mountain, Upshur	445
West Oaks, Travis	NA
‡West Odessa, Ector	16,995
*WESTON, Collin, 4	469
*WEST ORANGE, Orange	4,945
Westover, Baylor	18
WESTOVER HILLS, Tarrant	752
Westphalia, Falls	186
*West Point, Fayette, 5	205
West Point, Lynn	NA
West Sinton, San Patricio	NA
WEST TAWAKONI, Hunt	1,158
WEST UNIVERSITY PLACE, Harris	13,645
Westville, Trinity	46
Westway, Deaf Smith	15
‡Westway, El Paso	2,601
WESTWORTH VILLAGE, Tarrant	2,334
*Wetmore, Bexar, 9	NA
§*WHARTON, Wharton, 509	10,066
Whatley, Marion	NA
Wheatland, Tarrant	175
§*WHEELER, Wheeler, 92	1,384
Wheeler Springs, Houston	NA
*Wheelock, Robertson, 7	125
White City, Gaines	NA
White City, San Augustine	20
White City, Wilbarger	40
*WHITE DEER, Carson, 44	1,225
*WHITEFACE, Cochran, 27	489
Whiteflat, Motley	3
White Hall, Bell	45
White Hall, Grimes	NA
White Hall, Jackson	NA
Whitehall, Kaufman	NA
Whitehead, Hunt	NA
*WHITEHOUSE, Smith, 230	5,384
*WHITE OAK, Gregg, 159	5,561
White Oak, Titus	100
White Oak Junction, Hopkins	NA
White River, Crosby	55
White Rock, Hunt	73
White Rock, Red River	85
White Rock, Robertson	80
White Rock, San Augustine	NA
*WHITESBORO, Grayson, 185	3,332
*WHITE SETTLEMENT, Tarrant	15,283

Town and County	Pop.
Whitestar, Motley	5
Whiteway, Hamilton	10
*WHITEWRIGHT, Grayson-Fannin, 87	1,663
*Whitharral, Hockley, 11	175
Whitman, Washington	25
*WHITNEY, Hill, 221	1,683
*Whitsett, Live Oak, 7	200
Whitson, Coryell	30
*Whitt, Parker, 3	38
Whitton, Van Zandt	NA
*Whon, Coleman	15
Wichita Colony, Baylor	NA
§*WICHITA FALLS, Wichita-Archer, 4,655	98,553
Wicker, Brazos	NA
*WICKETT, Ward, 19	541
Wied, Lavaca	65
Wiedeville, Washington	NA
Wieland, Hunt	NA
*Wiergate, Newton, 6	461
Wigginsville, Montgomery	NA
Wilcox, Burleson	40
Wilcox, Gray	5
Wilderville, Falls	45
Wild Hurst, Cherokee	NA
*Wildorado, Oldham, 14	180
‡Wild Peach, Brazoria	2,545
Wildwood, Bexar	NA
Wilkins, Upshur	NA
Wilkinson, Titus	150
Willamar, Willacy	15
William Penn, Washington	100
Williams, Liberty	NA
Williamsburg, Lavaca	NA
Williamson Settlement, Orange	175
*WILLIS, Montgomery, 367	4,195
*Willow City, Gillespie, 4	75
Willow Grove, McLennan	50
WILLOW PARK, Parker	2,708
Willow Springs, Fayette	35
Willow Springs, Rains	50
*WILLS POINT, Van Zandt, 283	3,302
*WILMER, Dallas, 45	2,633
Wilmeth, Runnels	25
Wilson, Falls	42
Wilson, Kaufman	NA
*WILSON, Lynn, 18	560
‡*Wimberley, Hays, 415	2,520
Winchell, Brown	NA
*Winchester, Fayette, 1	50
*WINDCREST, Bexar	5,780
‡Windemere, Travis	3,474
*WINDOM, Fannin, 8	295
Windsor, McLennan	NA
*WINDTHORST, Archer-Clay, 35	376
Winedale, Fayette	41
*WINFIELD, Titus, 15	348
*Wingate, Runnels, 11	216
*WINK, Winkler, 20	1,120
Winkler, Navarro-Freestone	26
‡*Winnie, Chambers, 199	2,511
*WINNSBORO, Wood-Franklin, 355	3,201
*WINONA, Smith, 49	575
Winterfield, Hopkins	NA
Winter Haven, Dimmit	112
*WINTERS, Runnels, 147	2,911
Wise, Van Zandt	29
Witting, Lavaca	90
WIXON VALLEY, Brazos	240
Wizard Wells, Jack	69
*Woden, Nacogdoches, 6	70
Wokaty, Milam	NA

Town and County	Pop.
*WOLFE CITY, Hunt, 65	1,566
*WOLFFORTH, Lubbock, 117	2,176
Womack, Bosque	25
Wonderland Forest, San Jacinto	40
Woodal Farm, Milam	NA
Woodbine, Cooke	250
WOODBRANCH, Montgomery	1,491
Woodbury, Hill	40
WOODCREEK, Hays	1,018
Wood Creek, Montgomery	NA
Wooded Hills, Johnson	310
Woodhaven, Montgomery	NA
Wood Hi, Victoria	35
Wood Hollow, Montgomery	NA
Woodlake, Brazos	NA
*Woodlake, Trinity, 2	98
Woodland, Bell	NA
Woodland, Red River	128
Woodland Hills, Henderson	NA
*Woodlawn, Harrison, 8	370
Woodlawn, Montgomery	NA
WOODLOCH, Montgomery	369
Woodridge, Orange	1,000
Woodridge Park, Bexar	NA
Woodrow, Lubbock	85
Woods, Panola	65
*WOODSBORO, Refugio, 65	1,811
*WOODSON, Throckmorton, 15	252
Wood Springs, Smith	NA
Woodville, Cherokee	NA
§*WOODVILLE, Tyler, 321	4,256
Woodward, La Salle	10
WOODWAY, McLennan	9,336
Woosley, Rains	47
*WORTHAM, Freestone, 30	1,038
Worthing, Lavaca	55
Wright City, Smith	172
*Wrightsboro, Gonzales, 1	76
‡Wyldwood, Bastrop	2,177
*WYLIE, Collin-Rockwall-Dallas, 539	10,568
Wynne, Van Zandt	175

Y

Town and County	Pop.
*Yancey, Medina, 8	202
*YANTIS, Wood, 34	284
Yard, Anderson	18
Yarrellton, Milam	35
Yellowpine, Sabine	74
*YOAKUM, Lavaca-DeWitt, 300	6,394
*YORKTOWN, DeWitt, 107	2,307
Young, Freestone	27
Youngsport, Bell	40
Yowell, Delta	15
Yowell, Hunt	NA
Ysleta del Sur Pueblo, El Paso	292

Z

Town and County	Pop.
Zabcikville, Bell	38
‡§*Zapata, Zapata, 172	7,741
*ZAVALLA, Angelina, 39	825
*Zephyr, Brown, 9	198
Zimmerscheidt, Colorado	NA
Zion Grove, Rusk	NA
Zion Hill, Guadalupe	30
Zion Hill, Jasper	NA
Zipperlandville, Falls	22
Zippville, Guadalupe	110
Zorn, Guadalupe	60
Zuehl, Guadalupe	150
Zunkerville, Karnes	15

Constitution of Texas

Following is the complete text of the Constitution of Texas. It includes the original document, which was adopted on Feb. 15, 1876, plus the 363 amendments approved through the election of Nov. 7, 1995.

Each amendment is accompanied by a footnote explaining when it was adopted. This text, with footnotes, of the constitution is copyrighted by the A. H. Belo Corporation and may not be reprinted without written permission from the publisher.

Amendment of the Texas Constitution requires a two-thirds favorable vote by both the Texas House of Representatives and the Texas Senate, followed by a majority vote of approval by voters in a statewide election.

Prior to 1973, amendments to the constitution could not be submitted by a special session of the Legislature. But the constitution was amended in 1972 to allow submission of amendments if the special session was opened to the subject by the governor.

Constitutional amendments are not subject to a gubernatorial veto. Once submitted, voters have the final decision on whether to change the constitution as proposed.

The following table lists the total number of amendments submitted to voters by the Texas Legislature and shows the year in which the Legislature approved them for submission to voters; e.g., the Seventieth Legislature in 1987 approved 28 bills proposing amendments to be submitted to voters — 25 in 1987 and three in 1988.

Year	No.	Year	No.	Year	No.
1879	1	1923	2	1965	27
1881	2	1925	4	1967	20
1883	5	1927	8	1969	16
1887	6	1929	7	1971	18
1889	2	1931	9	1973	9
1891	5	1933	12	1975	12
1893	2	1935	13	1977	15
1895	2	1937	7	1978	1
1897	5	1939	4	1979	12
1899	1	1941	5	1981	10
1901	1	1943	3	1982	3
1903	3	1945	8	1983	19
1905	3	1947	9	1985	17
1907	9	1949	10	1986	1
1909	4	1951	7	1987	28
1911	5	1953	11	1989	21
1913	7	1955	9	1990	1
1915	7	1957	12	1991	15
1917	3	1959	4	1993	18
1919	13	1961	14	1995	14
1921	5	1963	7	1997	15

Amendments, 1995

The following 14 amendments were submitted to the voters on **Nov. 7, 1995:**

HJR 31 — Authorizing the exemption from ad valorem taxation of income-producing personal property and mineral interests having a value insufficient to recover the costs of collecting the tax. Passed: 495,144 in favor; 213,178 against.

HJR 34 — Increasing the amount of general obligation bonds authorized for veterans' housing assistance. Passed: 428,484 in favor; 289,690 against.

HJR 35 — Authorizing the governing body of a political subdivision to exempt from ad valorem taxation boats and other equipment used in commercial fishing. Failed: 432,378 against; 267,228 in favor.

HJR 50 — Providing for the issuance of general obligation bonds to finance educational loans to students. Passed: 474,502 in favor; 259,088 against.

HJR 64 — Exempting from ad valorem taxation the residence homestead of the surviving spouse of an elderly person. Passed: 604,604 in favor; 116,888 against.

HJR 68 — To raise the limits of exemption from ad valorem taxation of property owned by disabled veterans or by the surviving spouses and surviving minor children of disabled veterans. Passed: 490,199 in favor; 217,443 against.

HJR 72 — Relating to the ad valorem taxation of open-space land used for wildlife management. Passed: 434,643 in favor; 274,736 against.

HJR 73 — Reducing the amount of general obligation bonds authorized for undertakings related to the superconducting super collider facility. Passed: 558,729 in favor; 155,830 against.

HJR 80 — Abolishing the office of constable in Mills, Reagan and Roberts counties. Passed: 521,933 in favor; 159,233 against.

SJR 1 — Abolishing the office of state treasurer. Passed: 495,181 in favor; 218,473 against.

SJR 7 — Allowing investment of money from the Texas growth fund in a business without requiring the business to disclose investments in or with South Africa or Namibia. Failed: 387,087 against; 324,813 in favor.

SJR 36 — Authorizing the legislature to exempt from ad valorem taxation property of certain organizations chartered by the Congress of the Republic of Texas. Failed: 385,133 against; 333,528 in favor.

SJR 46 — Permitting an encumbrance to be fixed on homestead property for an owelty of partition, including a debt of a spouse resulting from a division or award of a homestead in a divorce proceeding, and for the refinance of a lien against a homestead, including a federal tax lien resulting from the tax debt of the owner. Passed: 368,486 in favor; 347,858 against.

SJR 51 — Allowing the use of existing bond authority of the farm and ranch finance program to include financial assistance for the expansion, development and diversification of production, processing, marketing and export of Texas agricultural products. Passed: 400,968 in favor; 315,880 against.

Amendments, 1997

The following amendment was to be submitted to the voters by the 75th Legislature on **Aug. 9, 1997,** just after this section of the Almanac went to press. **For election results: http://www.sos.state.tx.us/function/elec1/**

HJR 4 — Increasing the amount of the school property tax residence homestead exemption and providing for the continuation and reduction of the school tax limitation on the homesteads of certain persons.

The following 14 amendments were to be submitted to the voters by the 75th Legislature on **Nov. 4, 1997:**

HJR 8 — Extending the full faith and credit of the state to support the Texas tomorrow fund.

HJR 31 — Permitting an encumbrance against homestead property for certain extensions of equity credit.

HJR 55 — Relating to a deadline for supreme court action on a motion for rehearing.

HJR 59 — Limiting debt payable from the general revenue fund.

HJR 83 — Allowing the legislature to prescribe the qualifications of constables.

HJR 96 — Authorizing the legislature to authorize an ad valorem tax of five cents for each $100 of taxable property in rural fire prevention districts in Harris County.

HJR 104 — Eliminating duplicate numbering in and certain obsolete provisions of the Texas Constitution.

SJR 17 — Creating the Texas Water Development Fund II; authorizing the Texas Water Development Board to administer the fund and issue bond relating to it; and regarding repayment of Texas agricultural water conservation bonds.

SJR 19 — Relating to the place at which the Supreme Court of Texas sits to transact business.

SJR 33 — Relating to the purposes for which money in the compensation to victims of crime fund and the compensation to victims of crime auxiliary fund may be used.

SJR 36 — Allowing a municipal court judge to hold more than one civil office of emolument at the same time.

SJR 39 — Allowing the Texas growth fund to continue to invest in businesses without requiring those businesses to disclose investments in South Africa or Namibia.

SJR 43 — Providing for limitations on increases in the appraised value of residence homesteads for ad valorem taxation and for the transfer to a different residence homestead of the school property tax freeze on residence homesteads of the elderly and their spouses.

SJR 45 — Authorizing the legislature to permit a taxing unit to grant an exemption or other relief from ad valorem taxes on property on which a water conservation initiative has been implemented. ☆

Index to the State Constitution

The following index to the Texas State Constitution includes all amendments voted on through the election of Nov. 7, 1995. In some instances, reference may be to a section that has been deleted from the text of the Constitution as carried here. However, these references are included when it is clear, in the note telling that the section has been deleted, that the reference was once a part of the text.

In some instances, an article number is given after the main heading, indicating that most references to the subject are in that article, and most subheadings will have only section numbers. However, there may also be references to other articles with some subheadings. Example: Under the heading "Courts, Art. V" is a subheading, "Impeachment of judges: XV, Secs. 2, 6, 8."

Text of Texas Constitution

The following is a complete text of the Constitution of Texas, containing all amendments adopted through Nov. 7, 1995, with explanatory footnotes:

Preamble

Humbly invoking the blessings of Almighty God, the people of the State of Texas do ordain and establish this Constitution.

Article I — Bill of Rights

That the general, great and essential principles of liberty and free government may be recognized and established, we declare:

Sec. 1. **Texas Free and Independent** — Texas is a free and independent State, subject only to the Constitution of the United States, and the maintenance of our free institutions and the perpetuity of the Union depend upon the preservation of the right of local self-government, unimpaired to all the states.

Sec. 2. **All Political Power Is Inherent in the People** — All political power is inherent in the people, and all free governments are founded on their authority, and instituted for their benefit. The faith of the people of Texas stands pledged to the preservation of a republican form of government, and subject to this limitation only, they have at all times the inalienable right to alter, reform or abolish their government in such manner as they may think expedient.

Sec. 3. **All Free Men Have Equal Rights** — All free men, when they form a social compact, have equal rights, and no man, or set of men, is entitled to exclusive separate public emoluments or privileges but in consideration of public services.

Sec. 3-a. Equality under the law shall not be denied or abridged because of sex, race, color, creed or national origin. This amendment is self-operative.

[Note — Sec. 3-a of Art. I was added to set forth civil rights for all. Submitted by 62nd Legislature (1971) and adopted in election Nov. 7, 1972.]

Sec. 4. **There Shall Be No Religious Test for Office** — No religious test shall ever be required as a qualification to any office or public trust in this State; nor shall anyone be excluded from holding office on account of his religious sentiments, provided he acknowledge the existence of a Supreme Being.

Sec. 5. **How Oaths Shall Be Administered** — No person shall be disqualified to give evidence in any of the courts of this State on account of his religious opinions, or for want of any religious belief; but all oaths or affirmations shall be administered in the mode most binding upon the conscience, and shall be taken subject to the pains and penalties of perjury.

Sec. 6. **Freedom in Religious Worship Guaranteed** — All men have a natural and indefeasible right to worship Almighty God according to the dictates of their own consciences. No man shall be compelled to attend, erect or support any place of worship, or to maintain any ministry against his consent. No human authority ought, in any case whatever, to control or interfere with the rights of conscience in matters of religion, and no preference shall ever be given by law to any religious society or mode of worship. But it shall be the duty of the Legislature to pass such laws as may be necessary to protect equally every religious denomination in the peaceable enjoyment of its own mode of public worship.

Sec. 7. **No Appropriation for Sectarian Purposes** — No money shall be appropriated or drawn from the Treasury for the benefit of any sect, or religious society, theological or religious seminary, nor shall property belonging to the State be appropriated for any such purposes.

Sec. 8. **Liberty of Speech and Press Guaranteed; Libel** — Every person shall be at liberty to speak, write or publish his opinions, on any subject, being responsible for the abuse of that privilege; and no law shall ever be passed curtailing the liberty of speech or of the press. In prosecutions for the publication of papers, investigating the conduct of officers or men in public capacity, or when the matter published is proper for public information, the truth thereof may be given in evidence. And in all indictments for libels, the jury shall have the right to determine the law and the facts, under the direction of the court, as in other cases.

Sec. 9. **No Unreasonable Seizures and Searches Allowed** — The people shall be secure in their persons, houses, papers and possessions from all unreasonable seizures or searches, and no warrant to search any place, or to seize any person or thing, shall issue without describing them as near as may be, or without probable cause, supported by oath or affirmation.

Sec. 10. **Rights of Accused Persons in Criminal Prosecutions** — In all criminal prosecutions the accused shall have a speedy public trial by an impartial jury. He shall have the right to demand the nature and cause of the accusation against him, and to have a copy thereof. He shall not be compelled to give evidence against himself and shall have the right of being heard by himself or counsel, or both; shall be confronted with the witnesses against him and shall have compulsory process for obtaining witnesses in his favor, except that when the witness resides out of the State and the offense charged is a violation of any of the antitrust laws of this State, the defendant and the State shall have the right to produce and have the evidence admitted by deposition, under such rules and laws as the Legislature may here-

Article I (Cont'd.); Articles II and III

after provide; and no person shall be held to answer for a criminal offense, unless on an indictment of a grand jury, except in cases in which the punishment is by fine or imprisonment, otherwise than in the penitentiary; in cases of impeachment and in cases arising in the army or navy, or in the militia, when in actual service in time of war or public danger.

[Note — The foregoing section was amended by the addition of the clause relating to depositions of witnesses resident outside of the State in antitrust suits. Submitted by 35th Legislature (1917) and adopted in election on Nov. 5, 1918.]

Sec. 11. **Bail** — All prisoners shall be bailable by sufficient sureties, unless for capital offenses, when the proof is evident; but this provision shall not be so construed as to prevent bail after indictment found upon examination of the evidence, in such manner as may be prescribed by law.

Sec. 11-a. **Multiple Convictions; Denial of Bail** — (a) Any person (1) accused of a felony less than capital in this State, who has been theretofore twice convicted of a felony, the second conviction being subsequent to the first, both in point of time of commission of the offense and conviction therefor, (2) accused of a felony less than capital in this State, committed while on bail for a prior felony for which he has been indicted, (3) accused of a felony less than capital in this State involving the use of a deadly weapon after being convicted of a prior felony, or (4) accused of a violent or sexual offense committed while under the supervision of a criminal justice agency of the State or a political subdivision of the State for a prior felony, after a hearing, and upon evidence substantially showing the guilt of the accused of the offense in (1) or (3) above, of the offense committed while on bail in (2) above, or of the offense in (4) above committed while under the supervision of a criminal justice agency of the State or a political subdivision of the State for a prior felony, may be denied bail pending trial, by a district judge in this State, if said order denying bail pending trial is issued within seven calendar days subsequent to the time of incarceration of the accused; provided, however, that if the accused is not accorded a trial upon the accusation under (1) or (3) above, the accusation and indictment used under (2) above, or the accusation or indictment used under (4) above within sixty (60) days from the time of his incarceration upon the accusation, the order denying bail shall be automatically set aside, unless a continuance is obtained upon the motion or request of the accused; provided, further, that the right of appeal to the Court of Criminal Appeals of this State is expressly accorded the accused for a review of any judgment or order made hereunder, and said appeal shall be given preference by the Court of Criminal Appeals.

(b) In this section:

(1) "Violent offense" means:

(A) murder;

(B) aggravated assault, if the accused used or exhibited a deadly weapon during the commission of the assault;

(C) aggravated kidnapping; or

(D) aggravated robbery.

(2) "Sexual offense" means:

(A) aggravated sexual assault;

(B) sexual assault; or

(C) indecency with a child.

[Note — Sec. 11-a of Art. I was added to permit denial of bail to a person charged with a felony less than capital who has been theretofore twice convicted of a felony. Submitted by 54th Legislature (1955) and adopted in election Nov. 6, 1956. This section was amended to provide for further denial of bail under circumstances (2) and (3) above, and providing for 60-day limit to that person's incarceration without trial; and providing for that person's right of appeal. Submitted by 65th Legislature (1977) and adopted in election Nov. 8, 1977. It was further amended to permit denial of bail to persons charged with certain violent or sexual offenses while under the supervision of a criminal justice agency or a political subdivision of the state for a prior felony; added were definitions of the terms "violent offense" and "sexual offense." Submitted by the 73rd Legislature (1993) and adopted in election Nov. 2, 1993.]

Sec. 12. **The Writ of Habeas Corpus** — The writ of habeas corpus is a writ of right, and shall never be suspended. The Legislature shall enact laws to render the remedy speedy and effectual.

Sec. 13. **Excessive Bail and Fine and Unusual Punishment Prohibited; Courts Open** — Excessive bail shall not be required, nor excessive fines imposed, nor cruel or unusual punishment inflicted. All courts shall be open, and every person for an injury done him in his lands, goods, person or reputation, shall have due course of law.

Sec. 14. **No Person Shall Be Put Twice in Jeopardy** — No person, for the same offense, shall be twice put in jeopardy of life or liberty, nor shall a person be again put upon trial for the same offense after a verdict of not guilty in a court of competent jurisdiction.

Sec. 15. **Right of Trial by Jury** — The right of trial by jury shall remain inviolate. The Legislature shall pass such laws as may be needed to regulate the same, and to maintain its purity and efficiency. Provided, that the Legislature may provide for the temporary commitment, for observation and/or treatment, of mentally ill persons not charged with a criminal offense, for a period of time not to exceed ninety (90) days, by order of the County Court without the necessity

of a trial by jury.

[Note — Sec. 15 of Art. I was amended by addition of the last sentence. Submitted by 44th Legislature (1935) and adopted in election Aug. 24, 1935.]

Section 15-a. No person shall be committed as a person of unsound mind except on competent medical or psychiatric testimony. The Legislature may enact all laws necessary to provide for the trial, adjudication of insanity and commitment of persons of unsound mind and to provide for a method of appeal from judgments rendered in such cases. Such laws may provide for a waiver of trial by jury. In cases where the person under inquiry has not been charged with the commission of a criminal offense, by the concurrence of the person under inquiry, or his next of kin, and an attorney ad litem appointed by a judge of either the County or Probate Court of the county where the trial is being held, and shall provide for a method of service of notice of such trial upon the person under inquiry and of his right to demand a trial by jury.

[Note — Sec. 15-a of Art. I was added to require medical or psychiatric testimony for commitment of persons of unsound mind and authorizing Legislature to provide for trial and commitment of such persons and for waiver of trial by jury where the person under inquiry has not been charged with commission of a crime. Submitted by 54th Legislature (1955) and adopted in election Nov. 6, 1956.]

Sec. 16. **There Shall Be No Bill of Attainder or Ex-Post Facto Laws** — No bill of attainder or ex post facto law, retroactive law, or any other law impairing the obligation of contracts shall be made.

Sec. 17. **Privileges and Franchises: Eminent Domain** — No person's property shall be taken, damaged or destroyed for or applied to public use without adequate compensation being made, unless by the consent of such person; and when taken, except for the use of the State, such compensation shall be first made or secured by a deposit of money; and no irrevocable or uncontrollable grant of special privileges or immunities shall be made; but all privileges and franchises granted by the Legislature, or created under its authority, shall be subject to the control thereof.

Sec. 18. **No Imprisonment for Debt** — No person shall ever be imprisoned for debt.

Sec. 19. **Due Course of Law** — No citizen of this State shall be deprived of life, liberty, property, privileges or immunities, or in any manner disfranchised, except by the due course of the law of the land.

Sec. 20. **No Outlawry or Deportations** — No citizen shall be outlawed. No person shall be transported out of the State for any offense committed within the same. This section does not prohibit an agreement with another state providing for the confinement of inmates of this State in the penal or correctional facilities of that state.

[Note — Sec. 20 of Art. I was amended to permit state prisoners to be placed in penal facilities of another state pursuant to an interstate agreement. Submitted by 69th Legislature (1985) and adopted in election Nov. 5, 1985.]

Sec. 21. **Corruption of Blood, Forfeiture; Suicide** — No conviction shall work corruption of blood or forfeiture of estate, and the estates of those who destroy their own lives shall descend or vest as in the case of natural death.

Sec. 22. **Treason** — Treason against the State shall consist only in levying war against it, or adhering to its enemies, giving them aid and comfort; and no person shall be convicted of treason except on the testimony of two witnesses to the same overt act or on confession in open court.

Sec. 23. **Right to Bear Arms** — Every citizen shall have the right to keep and bear arms in the lawful defense of himself or the State; but the Legislature shall have power, by law, to regulate the wearing of arms, with a view to prevent crime.

Sec. 24. **Military Subordinate to Civil Authority** — The military shall at all times be subordinate to the civil authority.

Sec. 25. **Quartering Soldiers** — No soldier shall in time of peace be quartered in the house of any citizen without the consent of the owner, nor in time of war but in a manner prescribed by law.

Sec. 26. **Perpetuities; Monopolies; Primogeniture; Entailments** — Perpetuities and monopolies are contrary to the genius of a free government, and shall never be allowed, nor shall the law of primogeniture or entailments ever be in force in this State.

Sec. 27. **Right of Petition Guaranteed** — The citizens shall have the right, in a peaceable manner, to assemble together for their common good and apply to those invested with the powers of government for redress of grievances or other purposes, by petition, address or remonstrance.

Sec. 28. **Power to Suspend Laws** — No power of suspending laws in this State shall be exercised except by the Legislature.

Sec. 29. **"Bill of Rights" Inviolate** — To guard against transgressions of the high powers herein delegated, we declare that everything in this "Bill of Rights" is excepted out of the general powers of government, and shall forever remain inviolate, and all laws contrary thereto, or to the following provisions, shall be void.

Sec. 30. **Rights of Crime Victims** — (a) A crime victim has the following rights:

(1) the right to be treated with fairness and with respect for the victim's dignity and privacy throughout the criminal justice process; and

(2) the right to be reasonably protected from the accused throughout the criminal justice process.

Article I (Cont'd.): Articles II and III

(b) On the request of a crime victim, the crime victim has the following rights:

(1) the right to notification of court proceedings;

(2) the right to be present at all public court proceedings related to the offense, unless the victim is to testify and the court determines that the victim's testimony would be materially affected if the victim hears other testimony at the trial;

(3) the right to confer with a representative of the prosecutor's office;

(4) the right to restitution; and

(5) the right to information about the conviction, sentence, imprisonment, and release of the accused.

(c) The legislature may enact laws to define the term "victim" and to enforce these and other rights of crime victims.

(d) The state, through its prosecuting attorney, has the right to enforce the rights of crime victims.

(e) The legislature may enact laws to provide that a judge, attorney for the state, peace officer, or law enforcement agency is not liable for a failure or inability to provide a right enumerated in this section. The failure or inability of any person to provide a right or service enumerated in this section may not be used by a defendant in a criminal case as a ground for appeal or post-conviction writ of habeas corpus. A victim or guardian or legal representative of a victim has standing to enforce the rights enumerated in this section but does not have standing to participate as a party in a criminal proceeding or to contest the disposition of any charge.

[Note — Sec. 30 of Art. I was added to set forth the rights of crime victims. Submitted by 71st Legislature (1989) and adopted in election Nov. 7, 1989.]

Article II — The Powers of Government

Sec. 1. **Departments of Government to Be Kept Distinct** — The powers of the government of the State of Texas shall be divided into three distinct departments, each of which shall be confined to a separate body of magistracy, to wit: Those which are legislative to one, those which are executive to another, and those which are judicial to another; and no person, or collection of persons, being of one of these departments shall exercise any power properly attached to either of the others, except in the instances herein expressly permitted.

Article III — Legislative Department

Sec. 1. **The Legislature: House and Senate** — The legislative power of this State shall be vested in a Senate and House of Representatives, which together shall be styled "The Legislature of the State of Texas."

Sec. 2. **Number of Members Limited** — The Senate shall consist of thirty-one members, and shall never be increased above this number. The House of Representatives shall consist of ninety-three members until the first apportionment after the adoption of this Constitution, when or at any apportionment thereafter the number of Representatives may be increased by the Legislature, upon the ratio of not more than one Representative for every 15,000 inhabitants; provided, the number of Representatives shall never exceed 150.

Sec. 3. **Election of Senators; New Apportionment** — The Senators shall be chosen by the qualified electors for the term of four years; but a new Senate shall be chosen after every apportionment, and the Senators elected after each apportionment shall be divided by lot into two classes. The seats of the Senators of the first class shall be vacated at the expiration of the first two years, and those of the second class at the expiration of four years, so that one half of the Senators shall be chosen biennially thereafter. Senators shall take office following their election, on the day set by law for the convening of the regular session of the Legislature, and shall serve thereafter for the full term of years to which elected and until their successors shall have been elected and qualified.

[Note — Sec. 3 of Art. III was amended to establish the date on which newly elected members of the Senate shall qualify and take office. Submitted by 59th Legislature (1965) and adopted in election Nov. 8, 1966.]

Sec. 4. **Election of Representatives; Term of Office** — The members of the House of Representatives shall be chosen by the qualified electors for the term of two years. Representatives shall take office following their election, on the day set by law for the convening of the regular session of the Legislature, and shall serve thereafter for the full term of years to which elected and until their successors shall have been elected and qualified.

[Note — Sec. 4 of Art. III was amended to provide for the date on which newly elected members of the House of Representatives shall qualify and take office. Submitted by 59th Legislature (1965) and adopted in election Nov. 8, 1966.]

Sec. 5. **Time of Meeting; Method of Procedure** — The Legislature shall meet every two years at such time as may be provided by law and at other times when convened by the Governor. When convened in regular session, the first thirty days thereof shall be devoted to the introduction of bills and resolutions, acting upon emergency appropriations, passing upon the confirmation of the recess appointees of the Governor and such emergency matters as may be submitted by the Governor in special messages to the Legislature; provided, that during the succeeding thirty days of the regular session of the Legislature the various committees of each house shall hold hearings to consider all bills and resolutions and other matters then pending; and such emergency matters as may be submitted by the Governor; provided, further, that during the following sixty days the Legislature shall act upon such bills and resolutions as may be then pending and upon such emergency matters as may be submitted by the Governor in special messages to the Legislature; provided, however, either house may otherwise determine its order of business by an affirmative vote of four fifths of its membership.

[Note — Sec. 5 of Art. III was amended to provide for a 120-day session. Submitted, together with amendment of Sec. 24 of Art. III, by 41st Legislature (1929) and adopted in election Nov. 4, 1930.]

Sec. 6. **Qualifications of Senators** — No person shall be a Senator unless he be a citizen of the United States, and, at the time of his election, a qualified elector of this State, and shall have been a resident of this State five years next preceding his election and the last year thereof a resident of the district for which he shall be chosen, and shall have attained the age of twenty-six years.

Sec. 7. **Qualifications of Representatives** — No person shall be a Representative unless he be a citizen of the United States, and, at the time of his election, a qualified elector of this State, and shall have been a resident of this State two years preceding his election, the last year thereof a resident of the district for which he shall be chosen, and shall have attained the age of twenty-one years.

Sec. 8. **Each House to Judge Qualifications of Its Own Members** — Each house shall be the judge of the qualifications and election of its own members; but contested elections shall be determined in such manner as shall be provided by law.

Sec. 9. **President Pro Tem of the Senate; Speaker of the House; Officers** — (a) The Senate shall, at the beginning and close of each session, and at such other times as may be necessary, elect one of its members President pro tempore, who shall perform the duties of the Lieutenant Governor in any case of absence or disability of that officer. If the said office of Lieutenant Governor becomes vacant, the President pro tempore of the Senate shall convene the Committee of the Whole Senate within 30 days after the vacancy occurs. The Committee of the Whole shall elect one of its members to perform the duties of the Lieutenant Governor in addition to his duties as Senator until the next general election. If the Senator so elected ceases to be a Senator before the election of a new Lieutenant Governor, another Senator shall be elected in the same manner to perform the duties of the Lieutenant Governor until the next general election. Until the Committee of the Whole elects one of its members for this purpose, the President pro tempore shall perform the duties of the Lieutenant Governor as provided by this subsection.

(b) The House of Representatives shall, when it first assembles, organize temporarily, and thereupon proceed to the election of a Speaker from its own members.

(c) Each House shall choose its other officers.

[Note — Sec. 9 of Art. III was amended to provide for method of filling a vacancy in the office of Lieutenant Governor. Submitted by 68th Legislature (1983) and approved in an election Nov. 6, 1984.]

Sec. 10. **Quorum** — Two thirds of each house shall constitute a quorum to do business, but a smaller number may adjourn from day to day and compel the attendance of absent members, in such manner and under such penalties as each house may provide.

Sec. 11. **Rules: Power to Punish and Expel** — Each house may determine the rules of its own proceedings, punish members for disorderly conduct, and, with the consent of two thirds, expel a member, but not a second time for the same offense.

Sec. 12. **Journal: Yeas and Nays** — Each house shall keep a journal of its proceedings, and publish the same; and the yeas and nays of the members of either house on any question shall, at the desire of any three members present, be entered on the journals.

Sec. 13. **Vacancies, How Filled** — When vacancies occur in either house, the Governor, or the person exercising the power of the Governor, shall issue writs of election to fill such vacancies; and should the Governor fail to issue a writ of election to fill any such vacancy within twenty days after it occurs, the returning officer of the district in which such vacancy may have happened shall be authorized to order an election for that purpose.

Sec. 14. **Members of Legislature Privileged From Arrest** — Senators and Representatives shall, except in cases of treason, felony or breach of the peace, be privileged from arrest during the session of the Legislature, and in going to or returning from the same, allowing one day for every twenty miles such member may reside from the place at which the Legislature is convened.

Sec. 15. **Each House May Punish Disorderly Conduct** — Each house may punish, by imprisonment, during its sessions, any person not a member for disrespectful or disorderly conduct in its presence, or for obstructing any of its proceedings; provided, such imprisonment shall not, at any one time, exceed forty-eight hours.

Sec. 16. **Sessions to Be Open** — The sessions of each house shall be open, except the Senate when in executive session.

Sec. 17. **Adjournments** — Neither house shall, without the consent of the other, adjourn for more than three days, nor to any other place than that where the Legislature may be sitting.

Sec. 18. **Ineligibility of Members to Certain Offices; Not to Be Interested in Contracts** — No Senator or Representative shall, during the term for which he was elected, be eligible to (1) any civil office of profit under this State which shall have been created, or the emoluments of which may have been increased, during such term, or (2) any office or place, the appointment to which may be made, in whole

Article III (Cont'd.)

or in part, by either branch of the Legislature; provided, however, the fact that the term of office of Senators and Representatives does not end precisely on the last day of December but extends a few days into January of the succeeding year shall be considered as de minimis, and the ineligibility herein created shall terminate on the last day in December of the last full calendar year of the term for which he was elected. No member of either House shall vote for any other member for any office whatever, which may be filled by a vote of the Legislature, except in such cases as are in this Constitution provided, nor shall any member of the Legislature be interested, either directly or indirectly, in any contract with the State, or any county thereof, authorized by any law passed during the term for which he was elected.

[Note — Sec. 18 of Art. III was amended to fix the time during which members of Legislature shall be ineligible to hold other office. Submitted by 60th Legislature (1967) and adopted in election Nov. 5, 1968.]

Sec. 19. **What Officers Ineligible to Membership in Legislature** — No judge of any court, Secretary of State, Attorney General, clerk of any court of record, or any person holding a lucrative office under the United States, or this State, or any foreign government, shall, during the term for which he is elected or appointed, be eligible to the Legislature.

Sec. 20. **Receivers or Disbursers of Public Funds Not Eligible to Membership in the Legislature Until Discharge Received** — No person who at any time may have been a collector of taxes or who may have been otherwise entrusted with public money, shall be eligible to the Legislature, or to any office of profit or trust under the State Government, until he shall have obtained a discharge for the amount of such collections, or for all public moneys with which he may have been entrusted.

Sec. 21. **Freedom in Debate** — No member shall be questioned in any other place for words spoken in debate in either house.

Sec. 22. **Personal Interest in Measure or Bill** — A member who has a personal or private interest in any measure or bill, proposed or pending before the Legislature, shall disclose the fact to the house of which he is a member, and shall not vote thereon.

Sec. 23. **Removal Vacates Office** — If any Senator or Representative remove his residence from the district or county for which he was elected, his office shall thereby become vacant, and the vacancy shall be filled as provided in Sec. 13 of this article.

Sec. 23-a. **John Tarleton Contract Validated** — The Legislature is authorized to appropriate so much money as may be necessary, not to exceed seventy-five thousand ($75,000) dollars, to pay claims incurred by John Tarleton Agricultural College for the construction of a building on the campus of such college pursuant to deficiency authorization by the Governor of Texas on Aug. 31, 1937.

[Note — Sec. 23-a. of Art. III was added to provide for payment of a contractor whose contract had been annulled. Submitted by 49th Legislature (1945) and ratified in election Nov. 5, 1946.]

Sec. 24. **Mileage and Per Diem** — (a) Members of the Legislature shall receive from the Public Treasury a salary of Six Hundred Dollars ($600) per month, unless a greater amount is recommended by the Texas Ethics Commission and approved by the voters of this State in which case each member shall also receive a per diem set by the Texas Ethics Commission for each day during each Regular and Special Session of the Legislature.

(b) No Regular Session shall be of longer duration than one hundred and forty (140) days.

(c) In addition to the per diem the Members of each House shall be entitled to mileage at the same rate as prescribed by law for employees of the State of Texas.

[Note — Sec. 24 of Art. III has been amended five times: (1) Raising the per diem and decreasing the mileage. Submitted with amendment of Sec. 5 of Art. III by 41st Legislature (1929); ratified Nov. 4, 1930. (2) To raise per diem to $25 for first 120 days only. Submitted by 53rd Legislature (1953) and adopted in election Nov. 2, 1954. (3) To fix the salary at $4,800 per year and setting the per diem at $12 per day for first 120 days of regular session and 30 days of each special session. Submitted by 56th Legislature (1959) and adopted in election Nov. 8, 1960. (4) To set salaries of members of Legislature at $600 per month and set per diem of $30 per day during legislative sessions and a mileage allowance at the same rate provided by law for state employees. Submitted by 64th Legislature (1975) and adopted in election April 22, 1975. (5) To authorize the Texas Ethics Commission to recommend salaries of the legislature, subject to approval by the voters, and to allow the commission to set the per diem for the legislature. Submitted by 72nd Legislature (1991) and adopted in election Nov. 5, 1991.]

Sec. 24a. (a). **Texas Ethics Commission** — The Texas Ethics Commission is a state agency consisting of the following eight members:

(1) two members of different political parties appointed by the governor from a list of at least 10 names submitted by the members of the house of representatives from each political party required by law to hold a primary;

(2) two members of different political parties appointed by the governor from a list of at least 10 names submitted by the members of the senate from each political party required by law to hold a primary;

(3) two members of different political parties appointed by the

speaker of the house of representatives from a list of at least 10 names submitted by the members of the house from each political party required by law to hold a primary; and

(4) two members of different political parties appointed by the lieutenant governor from a list of at least 10 names submitted by the members of the senate from each political party required by law to hold a primary.

(b) The governor may reject all names on any list submitted under Subsection (a) (1) or (2) of this section and require a new list to be submitted. The members of the commission shall elect annually the chairman of the commission.

(c) With the exception of the initial appointees, commission members serve for four-year terms. Each appointing official will make one initial appointment for a two-year term and one initial appointment for a four-year term. A vacancy on the commission shall be filled for the unexpired portion of the term in the same manner as the original appointment. A member who has served for one term and any part of a second term is not eligible for reappointment.

(d) The commission has the powers and duties provided by law.

(3) The commission may recommend the salary of the members of the legislature and may recommend that the salary of the speaker of the house of representatives and the lieutenant governor be set at an amount higher than that of other members. The commission shall set the per diem of members of the legislature and the lieutenant governor, and the per diem shall reflect reasonable estimates of costs and may be raised or lowered biennially as necessary to pay those costs, but the per diem may not exceed during a calendar year the amount allowed as of January 1 of that year for federal income tax purposes as a deduction for living expenses incurred in a legislative day by a state legislator in connection with the legislator's business as a legislator, disregarding any exception in federal law for legislators residing near the Capitol.

(f) At each general election for state and county officers following a proposed change in salary, the voters shall approve or disapprove the salary recommended by the commission if the commission recommends a change in salary. If the voters disapprove the salary, the salary continues at the amount paid immediately before disapproval until another amount is recommended by the commission and approved by the voters. If the voters approve the salary, the approved salary takes effect January 1 of the next odd-numbered year.

[Note — Section 24a of Article III was added to establish the Texas Ethics Commission, to authorize the commission to recommend salaries of the legislature and the lieutenant governor and to set the per diem for those officials. Submitted by 72nd Legislature (1991) and adopted in election Nov. 5, 1991.]

Sec. 25. **Senatorial Districts, How Apportioned** — The State shall be divided into senatorial districts of contiguous territory according to the number of qualified electors, as nearly as may be, and each district shall be entitled to elect one Senator; and no single county shall be entitled to more than one Senator.

Sec. 26. **Representative Districts, How Apportioned** — The members of the House of Representatives shall be apportioned among the several counties, according to the number of population in each, as nearly as may be, on a ratio obtained by dividing the population of the State, as ascertained by the most recent United States census, by the number of members of which the House is composed; provided that whenever a single county has sufficient population to be entitled to a Representative, such county shall be formed into a separate representative district, and when two or more counties are required to make up the ratio of representation, such counties shall be contiguous to each other; and when any one county has more than sufficient population to be entitled to one or more Representatives, such Representative or Representatives shall be apportioned to such county, and for any surplus of population it may be joined in a representative district with any other contiguous county or counties.

Sec. 26-a. **Redistricting According to Population** — Provided, however, that no county shall be entitled to or have under any apportionment more than seven (7) Representatives unless the population of such county shall exceed seven hundred thousand (700,000) people as ascertained by the most recent United States census, in which event such county shall be entitled to one additional Representative for each one hundred thousand (100,000) population in excess of seven hundred thousand (700,000) population as shown by the latest United States census; nor shall any district be created which would permit any county to have more than seven (7) Representatives except under the conditions set forth above.

[Note — Sec. 26-a of Art. III was added to limit representation of counties with large populations. Submitted by 44th Legislature (1935) and adopted in election Nov. 3, 1936.]

Sec. 27. **Election of Members** — Elections for Senators and Representatives shall be general throughout the State, and shall be regulated by law.

Sec. 28. **Reapportionment After Each Census** — The Legislature shall, at its first regular session after the publication of each United States decennial census, apportion the State into senatorial and representative districts, agreeable to the provisions of Sections 25, 26 and 26-a of this Article. In the event the Legislature shall at any such first regular session following the publication of a United States decennial census, fail to make such apportionment, same shall be done by the Legislative Redistricting Board of Texas, which is hereby created, and shall be composed of five (5) members, as follows: The Lieutenant Governor, the Speaker of the House of Representatives,

Article III (Cont'd.)

the Attorney General, the Comptroller of Public Accounts and the Commissioner of the General Land Office, a majority of whom shall constitute a quorum. Said board shall assemble in the City of Austin within ninety (90) days after the final adjournment of such regular session. The board shall, within sixty (60) days after assembling, apportion the State into senatorial and representative districts, or into senatorial or representative districts, as the failure of action of such Legislature may make necessary. Such apportionment shall be in writing and signed by three (3) or more of the members of the board duly acknowledged as the act and deed of such board, and when so executed and filed with the Secretary of State, shall have force and effect of law. Such apportionment shall become effective at the next succeeding statewide general election. The Supreme Court of Texas shall have jurisdiction to compel such commission to perform its duties in accordance with the provisions of this section by writ of mandamus or other extraordinary writs conformable to the usages of law. The Legislature shall provide necessary funds for clerical and technical aid and for other expenses incidental to the work of the board, and the Lieutenant Governor and the Speaker of the House of Representatives shall be entitled to receive per diem and travel expense during the board's session in the same manner and amount as they would receive while attending a special session of the Legislature. This amendment shall become effective Jan. 1, 1951.

[Note — The foregoing Section 28 of Art. III was amended to provide for the Legislative Redistricting Board of Texas, this action being taken because of failure of past Legislatures to obey the mandate in the original Sec. 28 to redistrict the state after each decennial census. Submitted by 50th Legislature (1947) and adopted in election Nov. 2, 1948.]

Proceedings

Sec. 29. **Enacting Clause** — The enacting clause of all laws shall be: "Be it enacted by the Legislature of the State of Texas."

Sec. 30. **Laws to Be Passed by Bill: Amendments** — No law shall be passed, except by bill, and no bill shall be so amended in its passage through either house as to change its original purpose.

Sec. 31. **Bills May Originate in Either House and May Be Amended or Rejected by the Other House** — Bills may originate in either house, and when passed by such house may be amended, altered or rejected by the other.

Sec. 32. **Bills to Be Read on Three Several Days: Suspension of Rule** — No bill shall have the force of a law until it has been read on three several days in each house, and free discussion allowed thereon; but in cases of imperative public necessity (which necessity shall be stated in a preamble or in the body of the bill) four fifths of the house in which the bill may be pending may suspend this rule, the yeas and nays being taken on the question of suspension and entered upon the journals.

Sec. 33. **Bills for Raising Revenue** — All bills for raising revenue shall originate in the House of Representatives, but the Senate may amend or reject them as other bills.

Sec. 34. **Bill or Resolution Defeated, Not to Be Considered Again** — After a bill has been considered and defeated by either house of the Legislature, no bill containing the same substance shall be passed into a law during the same session. After a resolution has been acted on and defeated, no resolution containing the same substance shall be considered at the same session.

Sec. 35. **Bills to Contain but One Subject, Which Must Be Expressed in Title** — (a) No bill (except general appropriation bills, which may embrace the various subjects and accounts for and on account of which moneys are appropriated) shall contain more than one subject.

(b) The rules of procedure of each house shall require that the subject of each bill be expressed in its title in a manner that gives the Legislature and the public reasonable notice of that subject. The Legislature is solely responsible for determining compliance with the rule.

(c) A law, including a law enacted before the effective date of this subsection, may not be held void on the basis of an insufficient title.

[Note — The foregoing Sec. 35 of Art. III was amended to require each house to include in its rules of procedure a rule that each bill contain title expressing bill's subject. Submitted by 69th Legislature (1985) and adopted in election Nov. 4, 1986.]

Sec. 36. **Reviving or Amending Laws** — No law shall be revived or amended by reference to its title; but in such case the act revived, or the section or sections amended, shall be re-enacted and published at length.

Sec. 37. **Reference to Committees** — No bill shall be considered unless it has been first referred to a committee and reported thereon, and no bill shall be passed which has not been presented and referred to and reported from a committee at least three days before the final adjournment of the Legislature.

Sec. 38. **Signing Bills** — The presiding officer of each house shall, in the presence of the house over which he presides, sign all bills and joint resolutions passed by the Legislature, after their titles have been publicly read before signing, and the fact of signing shall be entered on the journals.

Sec. 39. **When Laws Take Effect** — No law passed by the Legislature, except the general appropriation act, shall take effect or go into force until ninety days after the adjournment of the session at which it was enacted, unless in case of an emergency, which emer-

gency must be expressed in a preamble or in the body of the act, the Legislature shall, by a vote of two thirds of all the members elected to each house, otherwise direct; said vote to be taken by yeas and nays, and entered upon the journals.

Sec. 40. **Business and Duration of Special Sessions** — When the Legislature shall be convened in special session, there shall be no legislation upon subjects other than those designated in the proclamation of the Governor calling such session, or presented to them by the Governor; and no such session shall be of longer duration than thirty days.

Sec. 41. **Elections: Votes, How Taken** — In all elections by the Senate and House of Representatives, jointly or separately, the vote shall be given viva voce, except in the election of their officers.

[Note — Sec. 42 of Art. III, relating to passage of laws, was deleted by constitutional amendment. Submitted by 61st Legislature (1969) and approved in election Aug. 5, 1969.]

Requirements and Limitations

Sec. 43. **Revision and Publication of Laws** — (a) The Legislature shall provide for revising, digesting and publishing the laws, civil and criminal; provided, that in the adoption of and giving effect to any such digest or revision the Legislature shall not be limited by Secs. 35 and 36 of this article.

(b) In this section, "revision" includes a revision of the statutes on a particular subject and any enactment having the purpose, declared in the enactment, of codifying without substantive change statutes that individually relate to different subjects.

[Note — The foregoing Sec. 43 of Art. III was amended to provide for the continuing revision of state laws. Submitted by 69th Legislature (1985) and adopted in election Nov. 4, 1986.]

Sec. 44. **Compensation of Officers: Payment of Claims** — The Legislature shall provide by law for the compensation of all officers, servants, agents and public contractors, not provided for in this Constitution, but shall not grant extra compensation to any officer, agent, servant or public contractors, after such public service shall have been performed or contract entered into for the performance of the same; nor grant, by appropriation or otherwise, any amount of money out of the Treasury of the State, to any individual, on a claim, real or pretended, when the same shall not have been provided for by pre-existing law; nor employ anyone in the name of the State, unless authorized by pre-existing law.

Sec. 45. **Change of Venue** — The power to change the venue in civil and criminal cases shall be vested in the courts, to be exercised in such manner as shall be provided by law; and the Legislature shall pass laws for that purpose.

[Note — Sec. 46 of Art. III, relating to vagrant laws, was deleted by constitutional amendment in election Aug. 5, 1969.]

Sec. 47. Lotteries Shall Be Prohibited Except as Authorized or Operated by State; Bingo Games and Charitable Raffles Permitted; Restrictions — (a) The Legislature shall pass laws prohibiting lotteries and gift enterprises in this State other than those authorized by Subsections (b), (d), and (e) of this section.

(b) The Legislature by law may authorize and regulate bingo games conducted by a church, synagogue, religious society, volunteer fire department, nonprofit veterans organization, fraternal organization, or nonprofit organization supporting medical research or treatment programs. A law enacted under this subsection must permit the qualified voters of any county, justice precinct, or incorporated city or town to determine from time to time by a majority vote of the qualified voters voting on the question at an election whether bingo games may be held in the county, justice precinct, or city or town. The law must also require that:

(1) all proceeds from the games are spent in Texas for charitable purposes of the organizations;

(2) the games are limited to one location as defined by law on property owned or leased by the church, synagogue, religious society, volunteer fire department, nonprofit veterans organization, fraternal organization, or nonprofit organization supporting medical research or treatment programs; and

(3) the games are conducted, promoted, and administered by members of the church, synagogue, religious society, volunteer fire department, nonprofit veterans organization, fraternal organization, or nonprofit organization supporting medical research or treatment programs.

(c) The law enacted by the Legislature authorizing bingo games must include:

(1) a requirement that the entities conducting the games report quarterly to the Comptroller of Public Accounts about the amount of proceeds that the entities collect from the games and the purposes for which the proceeds are spent; and

(2) criminal or civil penalties to enforce the reporting requirement.

(d) The Legislature by general law may permit charitable raffles conducted by a qualified religious society, qualified volunteer fire department, qualified volunteer emergency medical service, or qualified nonprofit organizations under the terms and conditions imposed by general law.

The law must also require that:

(1) all proceeds from the sale of tickets for the raffle must be spent for the charitable purposes of the organizations; and

(2) the charitable raffle is conducted, promoted, and administered exclusively by members of the qualified religious society, qualified

Article III (Cont'd.)

volunteer fire department, qualified volunteer emergency medical service, or qualified nonprofit organization.

(e) The Legislature by general law may authorize the State to operate lotteries and may authorize the State to enter into a contract with one or more legal entities that will operate lotteries on behalf of the State.

[Note — Sec. 47 of Art. III has been amended three times: (1) To authorize bingo games on local option basis if games are conducted by religious society or other charitable society and proceeds are to be spent in Texas for charitable purposes of the organization. Submitted by 66th Legislature (1979) and adopted in election Nov. 4, 1980. (2) Subsection (d) was added to authorize the Legislature to permit and regulate raffles conducted for charitable purposes by certain non-profit organizations. Submitted by 71st Legislature (1989) and adopted in election Nov. 7, 1989. (3) Subsection (a) was amended and Subsection (e) was added to allow for the establishment of a state lottery. Submitted by 72nd Legislature (1991) and adopted in election Nov. 5, 1991.]

[Note — Sec. 48 of Art. III, relating to power to levy taxes, was deleted by constitutional amendment. Submitted by 61st Legislature (1969) and approved in election Aug. 5, 1969.]

[Note — Sec. 48a and Sec. 48b, relating to the Teachers' Retirement Fund and Teachers' Retirement System, respectively, were deleted by constitutional amendment. Submitted by 64th Legislature (975) and approved in election April 22, 1975. See Art. XVI, Sec. 67, which replaces the foregoing sections. (See also note under Art. III, Sec. 51e and Sec. 51f; Art. XVI, Sec. 62 and Sec. 63.)]

Sec. 48-d. Rural Fire Prevention Districts

— The Legislature shall have the power to provide for the establishment and creation of rural fire-prevention districts and to authorize a tax on the ad valorem property situated in said districts not to exceed three (3¢) cents on the one hundred ($100) dollars valuation for the support thereof; provided that no tax shall be levied in support of said districts until approved by vote of the people residing therein.

[Note — Sec. 48-d of Art. III was added for the stated purpose by the 51st Legislature (1949) and ratified in election Nov. 8, 1949. Section 48-c is missing because it was proposed as an amendment but failed to carry.]

Sec. 48-e. Jail Districts

— The legislature, by law, may provide for the creation, operation, and financing of jail districts and may authorize each district to issue bonds and other obligations and to levy an ad valorem tax on property located in the district to pay principal of and interest on the bonds and to pay for operation of the district. An ad valorem tax may not be levied and bonds secured by a property tax may not be issued until approved by the qualified electors of the district voting at an election called and held for that purpose.

[Note — Sec. 48-e of Art. III was added to provide for the creation, operation and financing of jail districts. Submitted by the 70th Legislature (1987) and adopted in election Nov. 3, 1987. (See also note after second Sec. 48-e, below.)]

Sec. 48-e. Emergency Services Districts

— Laws may be enacted to provide for the establishment and creation of special districts to provide emergency services and to authorize the commissioners courts of participating counties to levy a tax on the ad valorem property situated in said districts not to exceed Ten Cents (10¢) on the One Hundred Dollars ($100.00) valuation for the support thereof; provided that no tax shall be levied in support of said districts until approved by a vote of the qualified electors residing therein. Such a district may provide emergency medical services, emergency ambulance services, rural fire prevention and control services, or other emergency services authorized by the Legislature.

[Note — Sec. 48-e of Art. III was added to provide for the creation of emergency medical services districts. Submitted by 70th Legislature (1987) and adopted in election Nov. 3, 1987.]]

[Note — The foregoing two sections of Art. III were both numbered 48-e by 70th Legislature (1987), and they shall remain so designated unless changed by a future Legislature.]

Sec. 49. Purpose for Which Debts May Be Created

— (a) No debt shall be created by or on behalf of the State, except

(1) to supply casual deficiencies of revenue, not to exceed in the aggregate at any one time two hundred thousand dollars;

(2) to repel invasion, suppress insurrection, or defend the State in war;

(3) as otherwise authorized by this constitution; or

(4) as authorized by Subsections (b) through (f) of this section.

(b) The legislature, by joint resolution approved by at least two-thirds of the members of each house, may from time to time call an election and submit to the eligible voters of this State one or more propositions that, if approved by a majority of those voting on the question, authorize the legislature to create State debt for the purposes and subject to the limitations stated in the applicable proposition. Each election and proposition must conform to the requirements of Subsections (c) and (d) of this section.

(c) The legislature may call an election during any regular session of the legislature or during any special session of the legislature in

which the subject of the election is designated in the governor's proclamation for that special session. The election may be held on any date, and notice of the election shall be given for the period and in the manner required for amending this constitution. The election shall be held in each county in the manner provided by law for other statewide elections.

(d) A proposition must clearly describe the amount and purpose for which debt is to be created and must describe the source of payment for the debt. Except as provided by law under Subsection (f) of this section, the amount of debt stated in the proposition may not be exceeded and may not be renewed after the debt has been created unless the right to exceed or renew is stated in the proposition.

(e) The legislature may enact all laws necessary or appropriate to implement the authority granted by a proposition that is approved as provided by Subsection (b) of this section. A law enacted in anticipation of the election is valid if, by its terms, it is subject to the approval of the related proposition.

(f) State debt that is created or issued as provided by Subsection (b) of this section may be refunded in the manner and amount and subject to the conditions provided by law.

(g) State debt that is created or issued as provided by Subsections (b) through (f) of this section and that is approved by the attorney general in accordance with applicable law is incontestable for any reason.

[Note — Article III, Section 49 was amended to authorize the Legislature to submit debt questions to the voters in proposition form. Submitted by 72nd Legislature (1991) and adopted in election Nov. 5, 1991.]

Sec. 49-a. Limiting Appropriations to Anticipated Revenue; Comptroller's Certification Required; Issuance of Certain General Revenue Bonds Authorized

— It shall be the duty of the Comptroller of Public Accounts in advance of each regular session of the Legislature to prepare and submit to the Governor and to the Legislature upon its convening a statement under oath showing fully the financial condition of the State Treasury at the close of the last fiscal period and an estimate of the probable receipts and disbursements for the then current fiscal year. There shall also be contained in said statement an itemized estimate of the anticipated revenue based on the laws then in effect that will be received by and for the State from all sources showing the fund accounts to be credited during the succeeding biennium and said statement shall contain such other information as may be required by law. Supplemental statements shall be submitted at any special session of the Legislature and at such other times as may be necessary to show probable changes.

From and after Jan. 1, 1945, save in the case of emergency and imperative public necessity and with a four-fifths vote of the total membership of each house, no appropriation in excess of the cash and anticipated revenue of the funds from which such appropriation is to be made shall be valid. From and after Jan. 1, 1945, no bill containing an appropriation shall be considered as passed or be sent to the Governor for consideration until and unless the Comptroller of Public Accounts endorses his certificate thereon showing that the amount appropriated is within the amount estimated to be available in the affected funds. When the Comptroller finds an appropriation bill exceeds the estimated revenue he shall endorse such finding thereon and return to the house in which same originated. Such information shall be immediately made known to both the House of Representatives and the Senate, and the necessary steps shall be taken to bring such appropriation to within the revenue, either by providing additional revenue or reducing the appropriation.

For the purpose of financing the outstanding obligations of the general revenue fund of the State and placing its current accounts on a cash basis the Legislature of the State of Texas is hereby authorized to provide for the issuance, sale and retirement of serial bonds equal in principal to the total outstanding, valid and approved obligations owing by said fund on Sept. 1, 1943, provided such bonds shall not draw interest in excess of 2 per cent per annum and shall mature within twenty years from date.

[Note — Sec. 49-a of Art. III was added to provide for Comptroller's estimates of receipts and disbursements and limit legislative appropriations. Submitted by 47th Legislature (1941) and adopted in election Nov. 3, 1942.]

Sec. 49-b. Veterans' Land Board: Bonds Authorized for Creation of Veterans' Land Fund; Purchase of Land by State and Sales to Veterans

— By virtue of prior amendments to this Constitution, there has been created a governmental agency of the State of Texas performing governmental duties which has been designated the Veterans' Land Board. Said Board shall continue to function for the purposes specified in all of the prior Constitutional Amendments except as modified herein. Said Board shall be composed of the Commissioner of the General Land Office and two (2) citizens of the State of Texas, one (1) of whom shall be well versed in veterans' affairs and one (1) of whom shall be well versed in finances. One (1) such citizen member shall, with the advice and consent of the Senate, be appointed biennially by the Governor to serve for a term of four (4) years. In the event of the resignation or death of any such citizen member, the Governor shall appoint a replacement to serve for the unexpired portion of the term to which the deceased or resigning member had been appointed. The compensation for said citizen members shall be as is now or may hereafter be fixed by the Legislature; and each shall make bond in such amount as is now or may hereafter be prescribed by the Legislature.

Article III (Cont'd.)

The Commissioner of the General Land Office shall act as Chairman of said Board and shall be the administrator of the Veterans' Land Program under such terms and restrictions as are now or may hereafter be provided by law. In the absence or illness of said Commissioner, the Chief Clerk of the General Land Office shall be the Acting Chairman of said Board with the same duties and powers that said Commissioner would have if present.

The Veterans' Land Board may provide for, issue and sell not to exceed Nine Hundred and Fifty Million Dollars ($950,000,000) in bonds or obligations of the State of Texas for the purpose of creating a fund to be known as the Veterans' Land Fund, Seven Hundred Million Dollars ($700,000,000) of which have heretofore been authorized. Such bonds or obligations shall be sold for not less than par value and accrued interest; shall be issued in such forms, denominations, and upon such terms as are now or may hereafter be provided by law; shall be issued and sold at such times, at such places, and in such installments as may be determined by said Board; and shall bear a rate or rates of interest as may be fixed by said Board but the weighted average annual interest rate, as that phrase is commonly and ordinarily used and understood in the municipal bond market, of all the bonds issued and sold in any installment of any bonds may not exceed the rate specified in Section 65 of this Article. All bonds or obligations issued and sold hereunder shall, after execution by the Board, approval by the Attorney General of Texas, registration by the Comptroller of Public Accounts of the State of Texas, and delivery to the purchaser or purchasers, be incontestable and shall constitute general obligations of the State of Texas under the Constitution of Texas; and all bonds heretofore issued and sold by said Board are hereby in all respects validated and declared to be general obligations of the State of Texas. In order to prevent default in the payment of principal or interest on any such bonds, the Legislature shall appropriate a sufficient amount to pay the same.

In the sale of any such bonds or obligations, a preferential right of purchase shall be given to the administrators of the various Teacher Retirement Funds, the Permanent University Funds, and the Permanent School Funds.

Said Veterans' Land Fund shall consist of any lands heretofore or hereafter purchased by said Board, until the sale price therefor, together with any interest and penalties due, have been received by said Board (although nothing herein shall be construed to prevent said Board from accepting full payment for a portion of any tract), and of the moneys attributable to any bonds heretofore or hereafter issued and sold by said Board which moneys so attributable shall include but shall not be limited to the proceeds from the issuance and sale of such bonds; the moneys received from the sale or resale of any lands, or rights therein, purchased with such proceeds; the moneys received from the sale or resale of any lands, or rights therein, purchased with other moneys attributable to such bonds; the interest and penalties received from the sale or resale of such lands, or rights therein; the bonuses, income, rents, royalties, and any other pecuniary benefit received by said Board from any such lands; sums received by way of indemnity or forfeiture for the failure of any bidder for the purchase of any such bonds to comply with his bid and accept and pay for such bonds or for the failure of any bidder for the purchase of any lands comprising a part of said Fund to comply with his bid and accept and pay for any such lands; and interest received from investments of any such moneys. The principal and interest on the bonds heretofore and hereafter issued by said Board shall be paid out of the moneys of said Fund in comformance with the Constitutional provisions authorizing such bonds; but the moneys of said Fund which are not immediately committed to the payment of principal and interest on such bonds, the purchase of lands as herein provided, or the payment of expenses as herein provided may be invested as authorized by law until such moneys are needed for such purposes.

All moneys comprising a part of said Fund and not expended for the purposes herein provided shall be a part of said Fund until there are sufficient moneys therein to retire fully all of the bonds heretofore or hereafter issued and sold by said Board, at which time all such moneys remaining in said Fund, except such portion thereof as may be necessary to retire all such bonds which portion shall be set aside and retained in said Fund for the purpose of retiring all such bonds, shall be deposited to the credit of the General Revenue Fund to be appropriated to such purposes as may be prescribed by law. All moneys becoming a part of said Fund thereafter shall likewise be deposited to the credit of the General Revenue Fund.

When a Division of said Fund (each Division consisting of the moneys attributable to the bonds issued and sold pursuant to a single Constitutional authorization and the lands purchased therewith) contains sufficient moneys to retire all of the bonds secured by such Division, the moneys thereof, except such portion as may be needed to retire all of the bonds secured by such Division which portion shall be set aside and remain a part of such Division for the purpose of retiring all such bonds, may be used for the purpose of paying the principal and the interest thereon, together with the expenses herein authorized, of any other bonds heretofore or hereafter issued and sold by said Board. Such use shall be a matter for the discretion and direction of said Board; but there may be no such use of any such moneys contrary to the rights of any holder of any of the bonds issued and sold by said Board or violative of any contract to which said Board is a party.

The Veterans' Land Fund shall be used by said Board for the purpose of purchasing lands situated in the State of Texas owned by the United States or any governmental agency thereof, owned by the Texas Prison System or any other governmental agency of the State of Texas, or owned by any person, firm, or corporation. All lands thus purchased shall be acquired at the lowest price obtainable, to be paid for in cash, and shall be a part of such Fund. Such lands heretofore or hereafter purchased and comprising a part of said Fund are hereby declared to be held for a governmental purpose, although the individual purchasers thereof shall be subject to taxation to the same extent and in the same manner as are purchasers of lands dedicated to the Permanent Free Public School Fund.

The lands of the Veterans' Land Fund shall be sold by said Board in such quantities, on such terms, at such prices, at such rates of interest and under such rules and regulations as are now or may hereafter be provided by law to veterans as they are now or may hereafter be defined by the laws of the State of Texas. The foregoing notwithstanding, any lands in the Veterans' Land Fund which have been first offered for sale to veterans and which have not been sold may be sold or resold to such purchasers, in such quantities, and on such terms, and at such prices and rates of interest, and under such rules and regulations as are now or may hereafter be provided by law.

Said Veterans' Land Fund, to the extent of the moneys attributable to any bonds hereafter issued and sold by said Board may be used by said Board, as is now or may hereafter be provided by law, for the purpose of paying the expenses of surveying, monumenting, road construction, legal fees, recordation fees, advertising and other like costs necessary or incidental to the purchase and sale, or resale, of any lands purchased with any of the moneys attributable to such additional bonds, such expenses to be added to the price of such lands when sold, or resold, by said Board; for the purpose of paying the expenses of issuing, selling, and delivering any such additional bonds; and for the purpose of meeting the expenses of paying the interest or principal due or to become due on any such additional bonds.

All of the moneys attributable to any series of bonds hereafter issued and sold by said Board (a "series of bonds" being all of the bonds issued and sold in a single transaction as a single installment of bonds) may be used for the purchase of lands as herein provided, to be sold as herein provided, for a period ending eight (8) years after the date of sale of such series of bonds; provided, however, that so much of such moneys as may be necessary to pay interest on bonds hereafter issued and sold shall be set aside for that purpose in accordance with the resolution adopted by said Board authorizing the issuance and sale of such series of bonds. After such eight (8) year period, all of such moneys shall be set aside for the retirement of any bonds hereafter issued and sold and to pay interest thereon, together with any expenses as provided herein, in accordance with the resolution or resolutions authorizing the issuance and sale of such additional bonds, until there are sufficient moneys to retire all of the bonds hereafter issued and sold, at which time all such moneys then remaining a part of said Veterans' Land Fund and thereafter becoming a part of said Fund shall be governed as elsewhere provided herein.

This Amendment being intended only to establish a basic framework and not to be a comprehensive treatment of the Veterans' Land Program, there is hereby reposed in the Legislature full power to implement and effectuate the design and objects of this Amendment, including the power to delegate such duties, responsibilities, functions, and authority to the Veterans' Land Board as it believes necessary.

Should the Legislature enact any enabling laws in anticipation of this Amendment, no such law shall be void by reason of its anticipatory nature.

[Note — Sec. 49-b of Art. III has been amended 11 times: (1) To aid war veterans in land purchases. Submitted by 49th Legislature (1945), and ratified in a special election Nov. 7, 1946. (By error, the date was set as Nov. 7 instead of Nov. 5, which was the general election date.) (2) To increase the authorized bond issue from $25,000,000 to $100,000,000 and to make minor changes. Submitted by 52nd Legislature (1951), and ratified in election Nov. 13, 1951. (3) To change membership of the Veterans' Land Board and to raise the total of bonds authorized to $200 million. Submitted by 54th Legislature (1955) and adopted in election Nov. 6, 1956. (4) To fix the rate of interest not to exceed 3 1/2 percent per annum. Submitted by 56th Legislature (1959) and adopted in election Nov. 8, 1960. (5) To provide for offering land in the Veterans' Land Fund to non-veteran purchasers after land has first been offered to veterans. Submitted by 57th Legislature (1961) and adopted in election Nov. 6, 1962. (6) To extend Veterans' Land Program by authorizing sale of bonds to increase Veterans' Land Fund for purchasing land to be sold to Texas veterans who served between Sept. 16, 1940, and date of formal withdrawal of U.S. troops from Vietnam; and providing for additional $200 million in bonds for this program. Submitted by 60th Legislature (1967) and adopted in election Nov. 11, 1967. (7) To provide for additional $100 million in bonds for the Veterans' Land Fund and to make all veterans eligible to participate who served in armed forces after Sept. 16, 1940. Submitted by 63rd Legislature (1973) and adopted in election Nov. 6, 1973. (8) To provide for additional $200 million in bonds for the Veterans' Land Fund and to extend the right to apply to purchase land to unmarried surviving spouses of veterans who meet requirements set out herein. Submitted by 65th Legislature (1977) and adopted in election Nov. 8, 1977. (9) To raise to $950 million the amount of bonds authorized for the Veterans' Land Fund. Submitted by 67th Legislature (1981) and adopted in election Nov. 3, 1981. (10) To define an eligible veteran for purposes of this program. Submitted by 69th Legislature (1985) and adopted in election Nov. 5, 1985. (11) To authorize the Legislature to further clarify the adminis-

Article III (Cont'd.)

tration of the veterans' housing assistance and land programs and to expand the investment authority of the Veterans' Land Board. Submitted by 72nd Legislature (1991) and adopted in election Nov. 5, 1991.]

Sec. 49-b-1. **Bonds Authorized to Finance Veterans' Land Program and Veterans' Housing Assistance Program** — (a) In addition to the general obligation bonds authorized to be issued and to be sold by the Veterans' Land Board by Sec. 49-b of this article, the Veterans' Land Board may provide for, issue, and sell not to exceed $1.3 billion in bonds of the State of Texas, $800 million of which have heretofore been authorized to provide financing to veterans of the state in recognition of their service to their state and country.

(b) For purposes of this section, "veteran" means a person who satisfies the definition of "veteran" as is now or may hereafter be set forth by the laws of the State of Texas.

(c) The bonds shall be sold for not less than par value and accrued interest; shall be issued in such forms and denominations, upon such terms, at such times and places, and in such installments as may be determined by the board; and, notwithstanding the rate of interest specified by any other provision of this Constitution, shall bear a rate or rates of interest fixed by the board. All bonds issued and sold pursuant to Subsections (a) through (f) of this section shall, after execution by the board, approval by the Attorney General of Texas, registration by the Comptroller of Public Accounts of the State of Texas, and delivery to the purchaser or purchasers, be incontestable and shall constitute general obligations of the state under the Constitution of Texas.

(d) Three hundred million dollars of the state bonds authorized by this section shall be used to augment the Veterans' Land Fund. The Veterans' Land Fund shall be used by the board for the purpose of purchasing lands situated in the State of Texas owned by the United States government or any agency thereof, the State of Texas or any subdivision or agency thereof, or any person, firm, or corporation. The lands shall be sold to veterans in such quantities, on such terms, at such prices, at such rates of interest, and under such rules and regulations as may be authorized by law. The expenses of the board in connection with the issuance of the bonds and the purchase and sale of the lands may be paid from money in the fund. The Veterans' Land Fund shall continue to consist of any lands purchased by the board until the sale price therefor, together with any interest and penalties due, have been received by the board (although nothing herein shall prevent the board from accepting full payment for a portion of any tract) and of the money attributable to any bonds issued and sold by the board for the Veterans' Land Fund, which money so attributable shall include but shall not be limited to the proceeds from the issuance and sale of such bonds; the money received from the sale or resale of any lands, or rights therein, purchased from such proceeds; the money received from the sale or resale of any lands, or rights therein, purchased with other money attributable to such bonds; the interest and penalties received from the sale or resale of such lands, or rights therein; the bonuses, income, rents, royalties, and any other pecuniary benefit received by the board from any such lands; sums received by way of indemnity or forfeiture for the failure of any bidder for the purchase of any such bonds to comply with his bid and accept and pay for such bonds or for the failure of any bidder for the purchase of any lands comprising a part of the fund to comply with his bid and accept and pay for any such lands; and interest received from investments of any such money. The principal of and interest on the general obligation bonds previously authorized by Sec. 49-b of this constitution shall be paid out of the money of the fund in conformance with the constitutional provisions authorizing such bonds. The principal of and interest on the general obligation bonds authorized by this section for the benefit of the Veterans' Land Fund shall be paid out of the money of the fund, but the money of the fund which is not immediately committed to the payment of principal and interest on such bonds, the purchase of lands as herein provided, or the payment of expenses as herein provided may be invested as authorized by law until the money is needed for such purposes.

(e) The Veterans' Housing Assistance Fund is created, and $1 billion of the state bonds authorized by this section shall be used for the Veterans' Housing Assistance Fund, $500 million of which have heretofore been authorized. Money in the Veterans' Housing Assistance Fund shall be administered by the Veterans' Land Board and shall be used for the purpose of making home mortgage loans to veterans for housing within the State of Texas in such quantities, on such terms, at such rates of interest, and under such rules and regulations as may be authorized by law. The expenses of the board in connection with the issuance of the bonds and the making of the loans may be paid from money in the fund. The Veterans' Housing Assistance Fund shall consist of any interest of the board in all home mortgage loans made to veterans by the board pursuant to a Veterans' Housing Assistance Program which the legislature may establish by appropriate legislation until, with respect to any such home mortgage loan, the principal amount, together with any interest and penalties due, have been received by the board; the money attributable to any bonds issued and sold by the board to provide money for the fund, which money so attributable shall include but shall not be limited to the proceeds from the issuance and sale of such bonds; income, rents, and any other pecuniary benefit received by the board as a result of making such loans; sums received by way of indemnity or forfeiture for the failure of any bidder for the purchase of any such bonds to comply with his bid and accept and pay for such bonds; and

interest received from investments of any such money. The principal of and interest on the general obligation bonds authorized by this section for the benefit of the Veterans' Housing Assistance Fund shall be paid out of the money of the fund, but the money of the fund which is not immediately committed to the payment of principal and interest on such bonds, the making of home mortgage loans as herein provided, or the payment of expenses as herein provided may be invested as authorized by law until the money is needed for such purposes.

(f) To the extent there is not money in either the Veterans' Land Fund or the Veterans' Housing Assistance Fund, as the case may be, available for payment of principal of and interest on the general obligation bonds authorized by this section to provide money for either of the funds, there is hereby appropriated out of the first money coming into the treasury in each fiscal year, not otherwise appropriated by this Constitution, an amount which is sufficient to pay the principal of and interest on such general obligation bonds that mature or become due during that fiscal year.

(g) Receipt of all kinds of the funds determined by the board not to be required for the payment of principal of and interest on the general obligation bonds herein authorized, heretofore authorized, or hereafter authorized by this Constitution to be issued by the board to provide money for either of the funds may be used by the board, to the extent not inconsistent with the proceedings authorizing such bonds, to pay the principal of and interest on general obligation bonds issued to provide money for the other fund, or to pay the principal of and interest on revenue bonds of the board issued for the purposes of providing funds for the purchasing of lands and making the sale thereof to veterans or making home mortgage loans to veterans as provided by this section. The revenue bonds shall be special obligations and payable only from the receipt of the funds and shall not constitute indebtedness of the state or the Veterans' Land Board. The board is authorized to issue such revenue bonds from time to time which shall not exceed an aggregate principal amount that can be fully retired from the receipts of the funds and other revenues pledged to the retirement of the revenue bonds. The revenue bonds shall be issued in such forms and denominations, upon such terms, at such times and places, and in such installments as may be determined by the board; and, notwithstanding the rate of interest specified by any other provision of the Constitution, shall bear a rate or rates of interest fixed by the board.

(h) This Amendment being intended only to establish a basic framework and not to be a comprehensive treatment of the Veterans' Housing Assistance Program and the Veterans' Land Program, there is hereby reposed in the Legislature full power to implement and effectuate the design and objects of this Amendment, including the power to delegate such duties, responsibilities, functions, and authority to the Veterans' Land Board as it believes necessary.

[Note — Sec. 49-b-1 of Art. III was added to provide financial assistance to veterans and to authorize issuance of bonds to finance the Veterans' Land Program and the Veterans' Housing Assistance Program. Submitted by 68th Legislature (1983) and adopted in election Nov. 8, 1983. It was amended to provide $500 million additional bonding authority for the veterans' housing assistance program and changing definition of veterans eligible to participate in veterans' land and housing assistance programs. Submitted by 69th Legislature (1985) and adopted in election Nov. 5, 1985. Subsections (d) and (e) were amended and Subsection (h) was added to further clarify the administration of the veterans' housing assistance and land programs. Submitted by 72nd Legislature (1991) and adopted in election Nov. 5, 1991.]

Sec. 49-b-2. (a) In addition to the general obligation bonds authorized to be issued and to be sold by the Veterans' Land Board by Sections 49-b and 49-b-1 of this article, the Veterans' Land Board may provide for, issue, and sell general obligation bonds of the state in an amount not to exceed $750 million, to provide financing to veterans of the state in recognition of their service to their state and the United States of America.

(b) Two hundred fifty million dollars of the general obligation bonds authorized by this section shall be used to augment the Veterans' Land Fund. Notwithstanding any provision of Section 49-b or 49-b-1 of this article to the contrary, the Veterans' Land Fund shall be used by the Veterans' Land Board to purchase lands situated in the state owned by the United States government, an agency of the United States government, this state, a political subdivision or agency of this state, or a person, firm, or corporation. Lands purchased and comprising a part of the Veterans' Land Fund are declared to be held for a governmental purpose, but the individual purchasers of those lands shall be subject to taxation to the same extent and in the same manner as are purchasers of lands dedicated to the Permanent Free Public School Fund. The lands shall be sold to veterans in quantities, on terms, at prices, and at fixed, variable, floating, or other rates of interest, determined by the Board and in accordance with rules of the Board. Notwithstanding any provisions of this section to the contrary, lands in the Veterans' Land Fund that are offered for sale to veterans and that are not sold may be sold or resold to the purchasers in quantities, on terms, at prices, and at rates of interest determined by the Board and in accordance with rules of the Board. The expenses of the Board in connection with the issuance of the bonds and the purchase and sale of the lands may be paid from money in the Veterans' Land Fund.

(c) The Veterans' Land Fund shall consist of:
(1) lands heretofore or hereafter purchased by the Board;
(2) money attributable to bonds heretofore or hereafter issued

Article III (Cont'd.)

and sold by the Board for the fund, including proceeds from the issuance and sale of the bonds;

(3) money received from the sale or resale of lands or rights in lands purchased from those proceeds;

(4) money received from the sale or resale of lands or rights in lands purchased with other money attributable to the bonds;

(5) proceeds derived from the sale or other disposition of the Board's interest in contracts for the sale or resale of lands or rights in lands;

(6) interest and penalties received from the sale or resale of lands or rights in lands;

(7) bonuses, income, rents, royalties, and other pecuniary benefits received by the Board from lands;

(8) money received by way of indemnity or forfeiture for the failure of a bidder for the purchase of bonds to comply with the bid and accept and pay for the bonds or for the failure of a bidder for the purchase of lands comprising a part of the Veterans' Land Fund to comply with the bid and accept and pay for the lands;

(9) payments received by the Board under a bond enhancement agreement with respect to the bonds; and

(10) interest received from investments of money in the fund.

(d) The principal of and interest on the general obligation bonds authorized by this section for the benefit of the Veterans' Land Fund, including payments by the Board under a bond enhancement agreement with respect to principal of or interest on the bonds, shall be paid out of the money of the Veterans' Land Fund, but the money in the fund that is not immediately committed to the payment of principal and interest on the bonds, the purchase of lands, or the payment of expenses may be invested as authorized by law until the money is needed for those purposes.

(e) The Veterans' Housing Assistance Fund II is created, and $500 million of the general obligation bonds authorized by this section shall be used for the Veterans' Housing Assistance Fund II. The Veterans' Housing Assistance Fund II is a separate and distinct fund from the Veterans' Housing Assistance Fund established under Section 49-b-1 of this article. Money in the Veterans' Housing Assistance Fund II shall be administered by the Veterans' Land Board and shall be used to make home mortgage loans to veterans for housing within this state in quantities, on terms, and at fixed, variable, floating, or other rates of interest, determined by the Board and in accordance with rules of the Board. The expenses of the Board in connection with the issuance of the bonds and the making of the loans may be paid from money in the Veterans' Housing Assistance Fund II.

(f) The Veterans' Housing Assistance Fund II shall consist of:

(1) the Board's interest in home mortgage loans the Board makes to veterans from money in the fund under the Veterans' Housing Assistance Program established by law;

(2) proceeds derived from the sale or other disposition of the Board's interest in home mortgage loans.

(3) money attributable to bonds issued and sold by the Board to provide money for the fund, including the proceeds from the issuance and sale of bonds;

(4) income, rents, and other pecuniary benefits received by the Board as a result of making loans;

(5) money received by way of indemnity or forfeiture for the failure of a bidder for the purchase of bonds to comply with the bid and accept and pay for the bonds;

(6) payments received by the Board under a bond enhancement agreement with respect to the bonds; and

(7) interest received from investments of money.

(g) The principal of and interest on the general obligation bonds authorized by this section for the benefit of the Veterans' Housing Assistance Fund II, including payments by the Board under a bond enhancement agreement with respect to principal of or interest on the bonds, shall be paid out of the money of the Veterans' Housing Assistance Fund II, but the money in the fund that is not immediately committed to the payment of principal and interest on the bonds, the making of home mortgage loans, or the payment of expenses may be invested as authorized by law until the money is needed for those purposes.

(h) Notwithstanding the provisions of Section 49-b-1 of this article to the contrary, the Veterans' Housing Assistance Fund shall consist of:

(1) the Board's interest in home mortgage loans the Board makes to veterans from the money in the fund under the Veterans' Housing Assistance Program established by law;

(2) proceeds derived from the sale or other disposition of the Board's interest in home mortgage loans;

(3) money attributable to bonds issued and sold by the Board to provide money for the fund, including proceeds from the issuance and sale of bonds;

(4) income, rents, and other pecuniary benefits received by the Board as a result of making loans;

(5) money received by way of indemnity or forfeiture for the failure of a bidder for the purchase of bonds to comply with the bid and accept and pay for the bonds;

(6) payments received by the Board under a bond enhancement agreement with respect to the bonds; and

(7) interest received from investments of money.

(i) The principal of and interest on the general obligation bonds authorized by Section 49-b-1 of this article for the benefit of the Veterans' Housing Assistance Fund, including payments by the Board under a bond enhancement agreement with respect to principal of or

interest on the bonds, shall be paid out of money in the Veterans' Housing Assistance Fund.

(j) If there is not enough money in the Veterans' Land Fund, the Veterans' Housing Assistance Fund, or the Veterans' Housing Assistance Fund II, as the case may be, available to pay the principal of and interest on the general obligation bonds authorized by this section or by Section 49-b or 49-b-1 of this article, including money to make payments by the Board under a bond enhancement agreement with respect to principal of or interest on the bonds, there is appropriated out of the first money coming into the treasury in each fiscal year, not otherwise appropriated by this constitution, an amount that is sufficient to pay the principal of and interest on the general obligation bonds that mature or become due during that fiscal year or to make bond enhancement payments with respect to those bonds.

(k) Notwithstanding any provisions of Section 49-b or 49-b-1 of this article to the contrary, receipts of all kinds of the Veterans' Land Fund, the Veterans' Housing Assistance Fund, or the Veterans' Housing Assistance Fund II that the Board determines are not required for the payment of principal of and interest on the general obligation bonds, including payments by the Board under a bond enhancement agreement with respect to principal of or interest on the bonds, authorized by this section or by Section 49-b or 49-b-1 of this article or otherwise authorized by this constitution to be issued by the Board to provide money for the fund, may be used by the Board, to the extent not inconsistent with the proceedings authorizing the bonds to:

(1) make temporary transfers to another of those funds to avoid a temporary cash deficiency in that fund or make a transfer to another of those funds for the purposes of that fund;

(2) pay the principal of and interest on general obligation bonds issued to provide money for another of those funds or make bond enhancement payments with respect to the bonds; or

(3) pay the principal of and interest on revenue bonds of the Board or make bond enhancement payments with respect to the bonds if the bonds are issued to provide funds to purchase lands and sell lands to veterans or make home mortgage loans to veterans.

(l) If the Board determines that assets from the Veterans' Land Fund, the Veterans' Housing Assistance Fund, or the Veterans' Housing Assistance Fund II are not required for the purposes of the fund, the Board may transfer the assets to another of those funds or use the assets to secure revenue bonds issued by the Board under this section.

(m) The revenue bonds shall be special obligations of the Board and payable only from and secured only by receipts of the funds, assets transferred from the funds, and other revenues and assets as determined by the Board and shall not constitute indebtedness of the state or the Veterans' Land Board. The Board may issue revenue bonds from time to time, which bonds may not exceed an aggregate principal amount that the Board determines can be fully retired from the receipts of the funds, the assets transferred from the funds, and other revenues and assets pledged to the retirement of the revenue bonds. The revenue bonds shall be issued and sold in forms and denominations, in the manner, on terms, at times and places, and in installments the Board determines. Notwithstanding the rate of interest specified by any other provision of this constitution, the revenue bonds shall bear a rate or rates of interest the Board determines. A determination made by the Board under this subsection shall be binding and conclusive as to the matter determined.

(n) Notwithstanding any provisions of Section 49-b or 49-b-1 of this article to the contrary, the bonds authorized to be issued and sold by the Veterans' Land Board by this section or by Sections 49-b and 49-b-1 of this article shall be issued and sold in forms and denominations, on terms, at times, in the manner, at places, and in installments the Board determines. The bonds shall bear a rate or rates of interest the Board determines. The bonds shall be incontestable after execution by the Board, approval by the Attorney General of Texas, and delivery to the purchaser or purchasers of the bonds.

(o) This Amendment being intended only to establish a basic framework and not to be a comprehensive treatment of the Veterans' Housing Assistance Program and the Veteran's Land Program, there is hereby reposed in the Legislature full power to implement and effectuate the design and objects of this Amendment, including the power to delegate such duties, responsibilities, functions, and authority to the Veteran's Land Board as it believes necessary.

(p) In this section, "veteran" has the meaning assigned by Section 49-b-1 of this article.

[Note — Sec. 49-b-2 of Art. III was added to authorize issuance of $750 million in general obligation bonds to augment the Veterans' Land Fund and Veterans' Housing Assistance Fund and to fund the Veterans' Housing Assistance Fund II. Submitted by 73rd Legislature (1993) and adopted in election Nov. 2, 1993]

Sec. 49-b-3. (a) In addition to the general obligation bonds authorized to be issued and to be sold by the Veterans' Land Board by Sections 49-b, 49-b-1, and 49-b-2 of this article, the Veterans' Land Board may provide for, issue, and sell general obligation bonds of the state in an amount not to exceed $500 million to provide housing financing to veterans of the state in recognition of their service to this state and the United States. The Veterans' Land Board may enter into bond enhancement agreements with respect to the bonds. The proceeds from the issuance and sale of the bonds authorized by this section shall be used to augment the Veterans' Housing Assistance Fund II to be administered and invested as provided by law.

(b) The principal of and interest on the general obligation bonds authorized by this section, including payments under bond enhance-

Article III (Cont'd.)

ment agreements with respect to principal of or interest on the bonds, shall be payable from the sources and in the manner provided by Section 49-b-2 of this article for general obligation bonds issued under that section to augment the Veterans' Housing Assistance Fund II.

(c) The general obligation bonds authorized by this section shall be issued and sold in forms and denominations, on terms, at times, in the manner, at places, and in installments the Veterans' Land Board determines. The bonds shall bear a rate or rates of interest the Veterans' Land Board determines. The bonds authorized by this section shall be incontestable after execution by the Veterans' Land Board, approval by the attorney general, and delivery to the purchaser or purchasers of the bonds.

[Note — Sec. 49-b-3 of Art. III was added to increase the amount of bonds authorized for veterans' housing assistance. Submitted by 74th Legislature (1995) and adopted in election Nov. 7, 1996.]

Sec. 49-c. **Texas Water Development Board, Fund; Purpose** — There is hereby created as an agency of the State of Texas the Water Development Board to exercise such powers as necessary under this provision together with such other duties and restrictions as may be prescribed by law. The qualifications, compensation and number of members of said Board shall be determined by law. They shall be appointed by the Governor with the advice and consent of the Senate in the manner and for such terms as may be prescribed by law.

The Texas Water Development Board shall have the authority to provide for, issue and sell general obligation bonds of the State of Texas in an amount not to exceed One Hundred Million Dollars ($100,000,000). The Legislature of Texas, upon two-thirds (2/3) vote of the elected Members of each House, may authorize the Board to issue additional bonds in an amount not exceeding One Hundred Million Dollars ($100,000,000). The bonds authorized herein or permitted to be authorized by the Legislature shall be called "Texas Water Development Bonds," shall be executed in such form, denominations and upon such terms as may be prescribed by law, provided, however, that the bonds shall not bear more than four percent (4%) interest per annum; they may be issued in such installments as the Board finds feasible and practical in accomplishing the purpose set forth herein.

All moneys received from the sale of State bonds shall be deposited in a fund hereby created in the State Treasury to be known as the Texas Water Development Fund to be administered (without further appropriation) by the Texas Water Development Board in such manner as prescribed by law.

Such fund shall be used only for the purpose of aiding or making funds available upon such terms and conditions as the Legislature may prescribe, to the various political subdivisions or bodies politic and corporate of the State of Texas including river authorities, conservation and reclamation districts and districts created or organized or authorized to be created or organized under Article XVI, Section 59 or Article III, Section 52, of this Constitution, interstate compact commissions to which the State of Texas is a party and municipal corporations, in the conservation and development of the water resources of this State, including the control, storing and preservation of its storm and flood waters and the waters of its rivers and streams, for all useful and lawful purposes by the acquisition, improvement, extension, or construction of dams, reservoirs and other water storage projects, including any system necessary for the transportation of water from storage to points of treatment and/or distribution, including facilities for transporting water therefrom to wholesale purchasers, or for any one or more of such purposes or methods.

Any or all financial assistance as provided herein shall be repaid with interest upon such terms, conditions and manner of repayment as may be provided by law.

While any of the bonds authorized by this provision or while any of the bonds that may be authorized by the Legislature under this provision, or any interest on any of such bonds, is outstanding and unpaid, there is hereby appropriated out of the first moneys coming into the Treasury in each fiscal year, not otherwise appropriated by this Constitution, an amount which is sufficient to pay the principal and interest on such bonds that mature or become due during such fiscal year, less the amount in the sinking fund at the close of the prior fiscal year.

The Legislature may provide for the investment of moneys available in the Texas Water Development Fund, and the interest and sinking funds established for the payment of bonds issued by the Texas Water Development Board. Income from such investment shall be used for the purposes prescribed by the Legislature. The Legislature may also make appropriations from the General Revenue Fund for paying administrative expenses of the Board.

From the moneys received by the Texas Water Development Board as repayment of principal for financial assistance or as interest thereon, there shall be deposited in the interest and sinking fund for the bonds authorized by this Section sufficient moneys to pay the interest and principal to become due during the ensuing year and sufficient to establish and maintain a reserve in said fund equal to the average annual principal and interest requirements on all outstanding bonds issued under this Section. If any year prior to December 31, 1982 moneys are received in excess of the foregoing requirements then such excess shall be deposited to the Texas Water Development Fund, and may be used for administrative expenses of the Board and for the same purposes and upon the same terms and con-

ditions prescribed for the proceeds derived from the sale of such State bonds. No grant of financial assistance shall be made under the provisions of this Section after December 31, 1982, and all moneys thereafter received as repayment of principal for financial assistance or as interest thereon shall be deposited in the interest and sinking fund for the State bonds; except that such amount as may be required to meet the administrative expenses of the Board may be annually set aside; and provided, that after all State bonds have been fully paid with interest, or after there are on deposit in the interest and sinking fund sufficient moneys to pay all future maturities of principal and interest, additional moneys so received shall be deposited to the General Revenue Fund.

All bonds issued hereunder shall after approval by the Attorney General, registration by the Comptroller of Public Accounts of the State of Texas, and delivery to the purchasers, be incontestable and shall constitute general obligations of the State of Texas under the Constitution of Texas.

[Note — Sec. 49-c of Art. III was added to create the Texas Water Development Board and Fund and to provide for supervision thereof. Submitted by 55th Legislature (1957) and adopted in election Nov. 5, 1957.]

Sec. 49-d. **Development and Conservation of Public Waters** — It is hereby declared to be the policy of the State of Texas to encourage the optimum development of the limited number of feasible sites available for the construction or enlargement of dams and reservoirs for the conservation of the public waters of the state, which waters are held in trust for the use and benefit of the public, and to encourage the optimum regional development of systems built for the filtration, treatment, and transmission of water and wastewater. The proceeds from the sale of the additional bonds authorized hereunder deposited in the Texas Water Development Fund and the proceeds of bonds previously authorized by Art. III, Sec. 49-c of this Constitution, may be used by the Texas Water Development Board, under such provisions as the Legislature may prescribe by general law, including the requirement of a permit for storage or beneficial use, for the additional purposes of acquiring and developing storage facilities, and any system or works necessary for the filtration, treatment and transportation of water or wastewater, or for any one or more of such purposes or methods, whether or not such a system or works is connected with a reservoir in which the state has a financial interest; provided however, the Texas Water Development Fund or any other state fund provided for water development, transmission, transfer or filtration shall not be used to finance any project which contemplates or results in the removal from the basin of origin of any surface water necessary to supply the reasonably foreseeable future water requirements for the next ensuing fifty-year period within the river basin of origin, except on a temporary, interim basis.

Under such provisions as the Legislature may prescribe by general law the Texas Water Development Fund may be used for the conservation and development of water for useful purposes by construction or reconstruction or enlargement of reservoirs constructed or to be constructed or enlarged within the State of Texas or on any stream constituting a boundary of the State of Texas, together with any system or works necessary for the filtration, treatment and/or transportation of water, by any one or more of the following governmental agencies; by the United States of America or any agency, department or instrumentality thereof; by the State of Texas or any agency, department or instrumentality thereof; by political subdivisions or bodies politic and corporate of the state; by interstate compact commissions to which the State of Texas is a party; and by municipal corporations. The Legislature shall provide terms and conditions under which the Texas Water Development Board may sell, transfer or lease, in whole or in part, any reservoir and associated system or works which the Texas Water Development Board has financed in whole or in part.

Under such provisions as the Legislature may prescribe by general law, the Texas Water Development Board may also execute long-term contracts with the United States or any of its agencies for the acquisition and development of storage facilities in reservoirs constructed or to be constructed by the Federal Government. Such contracts when executed shall constitute general obligations of the State of Texas in the same manner and with the same effect as state bonds issued under the authority of the preceding Sec. 49-c of this Constitution, and the provisions in said Sec. 49-c with respect to payment of principal and interest on state bonds issued shall likewise apply with respect to payment of principal and interest required to be paid by such contracts. If storage facilities are acquired for a term of years, such contracts shall contain provisions for renewal that will protect the state's investment.

The aggregate of the bonds authorized hereunder shall not exceed $200,000,000 and shall be in addition to the aggregate of the bonds previously authorized by said Sec. 49-c of Art. III of this Constitution. The Legislature upon two-thirds (2/3) vote of the elected members of each House, may authorize the board to issue all or any portion of such $200,000,000 in additional bonds herein authorized.

The Legislature shall provide terms and conditions for the Texas Water Development Board to sell, transfer or lease, in whole or in part, any acquired facilities or the right to use such facilities at a price not less than the direct cost of the board in acquiring same; and the Legislature may provide terms and conditions for the board to sell any unappropriated public waters of the state that might be stored in such facilities. As a prerequisite to the purchase of such storage or water, the applicant therefor shall have secured a valid permit from

Article III (Cont'd.)

the Texas Water Commission or its successor authorizing the acquisition of such storage facilities or the water impounded therein. The money received from any sale, transfer or lease of facilities shall be used to pay principal and interest on state bonds issued or contractual obligations incurred by the Texas Water Development Board, provided that when moneys are sufficient to pay the full amount of indebtedness then outstanding and the full amount of interest to accrue thereon, any further sums received from the sale, transfer or lease of such facilities shall be deposited and used as provided by law. Money received from the sale of water, which shall include standby service, may be used for the operation and maintenance of acquired facilities, and for the payment of principal and interest on debt incurred.

Should the Legislature enact enabling laws in anticipation of the adoption of this amendment, such acts shall not be void by reason of their anticipatory character.

[Note — Sec. 49-d of Art. III was added to authorize the Texas Water Development Board to acquire and develop storage facilities in reservoirs and to dispose of such storage facilities and water upon such terms as Legislature shall prescribe. Submitted by 57th Legislature (1961) and adopted in election Nov. 6, 1962. It was further amended to provide for optimum development of water reservoirs and investment of the Texas Water Development Fund. Submitted by 59th Legislature (1965) and adopted in election Nov. 8, 1966. It was again amended to encourage optimum regional development of systems built for filtration, treatment and transmission of water and wastewater. Submitted by 69th Legislature (1985) and adopted in election Nov. 5, 1985.]

Sec. 49-d-1. **Water Development Bonds** — (a) The Texas Water Development Board shall upon direction of the Texas Water Quality Board, or any successor agency designated by the Legislature, issue additional Texas Water Development Bonds up to an additional aggregate principal amount of Two Hundred Million Dollars ($200,000,000) to provide grants, loans, or any combination of grants and loans for water quality enhancement purposes as established by the Legislature. The Texas Water Quality Board or any successor agency designated by the Legislature may make such grants and loans to political subdivisions or bodies politic and corporate of the State of Texas, including municipal corporations, river authorities, conservation and reclamation districts, and districts created or organized or authorized to be created or organized under Art. XVI, Sec. 59, or Art. III, Sec. 52, of this Constitution, State agencies, and interstate agencies and compact commissions to which the State of Texas is a party, and upon such terms and conditions as the Legislature may authorize by general law. The bonds shall be issued for such terms, in such denominations, form and installments, and upon such conditions as the Legislature may authorize.

(b) The proceeds from the sale of such bonds shall be deposited in the Texas Water Development Fund to be invested and administered as prescribed by law.

(c) The bonds authorized in this Sec. 49-d-1 and all bonds authorized by Sections 49-c and 49-d of Art. III shall bear interest at not more than 6 percent per annum and mature as the Texas Water Development Board shall prescribe, subject to the limitations as may be imposed by the Legislature.

(d) The Texas Water Development Fund shall be used for the purposes heretofore permitted by, and subject to the limitations in Sections 49-c, 49-d and 49-d-1; provided, however, that the financial assistance may be made pursuant to the provisions of Sections 49-c, 49-d and 49-d-1 subject only to the availability of funds and without regard to the provisions in Sec. 49-c that such financial assistance shall terminate after Dec. 31, 1982.

(e) Texas Water Development Bonds are secured by the general credit of the State and shall after approval by the Attorney General, registration by the Comptroller of Public Accounts of the State of Texas, and delivery to the purchasers, be incontestable and shall constitute general obligations of the State of Texas under the Constitution of Texas.

(f) Should the Legislature enact enabling laws in anticipation of the adoption of this amendment, such acts shall not be void by reason of their anticipatory character.

[Note — Sec. 49-d-1 was added to provide for an additional $100 million for grants and loans for water improvement; also to raise the interest rate on water bonds to 6 percent. Submitted by 62nd Legislature (1971) and adopted in election May 18, 1971. It was amended to increase to $200 million the amount available for water quality enhancement. Submitted by 64th Legislature (1975) and adopted in election Nov. 2, 1976.]

Sec. 49-d-2. (a) The Texas Water Development Board may issue additional Texas Water Development Bonds up to an additional aggregate principal amount of $980 million. Of the additional bonds authorized to be issued, $590 million of those bonds are dedicated for use for the purposes provided by Sec. 49-c and Sec. 49-d of this article with $400 million of those bonds to be used for state participation in the acquisition and development of facilities for the storage, transmission, transportation, and treatment of water and wastewater as authorized by Sec. 49-d of this article. The Legislature may set limits on the extent of state participation in projects in each fiscal year through the General Appropriations Act or other law, and state participation is limited to 50 percent of the funding for any single project.

Of the additional bonds authorized, $190 million are dedicated for use for the purposes provided by Sec. 49-d-1 of this article and $200 million are dedicated exclusively for flood control projects and may be made available for any acquisition or construction necessary to achieve structural and nonstructural flood control purposes.

(b) The Texas Water Development Board shall issue the additional bonds authorized by this section for the terms, in the denominations, form, and installments, on the conditions, and subject to the limitations provided by Sec. 49-c, Sec. 49-d, and Sec. 49-d-1 of this article and by laws adopted by the Legislature implementing those sections.

(c) Proceeds from the sale of the bonds authorized by this section shall be deposited in the Texas water development fund to be administered and invested as provided by law.

(d) Financial assistance made available for the purposes provided by this section is subject only to availability of funds. The requirement of Sec. 49-c of this article that financial assistance terminate on Dec. 31, 1982, does not apply to financial assistance made available under this section.

(e) Bonds issued under this section shall bear interest as provided by Sec. 65 of this article.

[Note — Sec. 49-d-2 Art. III was added to authorize issuance of an additional $980 million of Texas Water Development Bonds. Submitted by 69th Legislature (1985) and adopted in election Nov. 5, 1985.]

Sec. 49-d-3. (a) The Legislature by law may create one or more special funds in the state treasury for use for or in aid of water conservation, water development, water quality enhancement, flood control, drainage, subsidence control, recharge, chloride control, agricultural soil and water conservation, desalinization or any combination of those purposes, may make money in a special fund available to cities, counties, special governmental districts and authorities, and other political subdivisions of the state for use for the purposes for which the fund was created by grants, loans, or any other means, and may appropriate money to any of the special funds to carry out the purposes of this section.

(b) Money deposited in a special fund created under this section may not be used to finance or aid any project that contemplates or results in the removal from the basin of origin of any surface water necessary to supply the reasonably foreseeable water requirements for the next ensuing 50-year period within the river basin of origin, except on a temporary, interim basis.

[Note — Sec. 49-d-3 of Art. III was added to create special funds for water conservation, development, quality enhancement, flood control, drainage, subsidence control, recharge, chloride control, agricultural soil and water conservation and desalinization of water. Submitted by 69th Legislature (1985) and adopted in election Nov. 5, 1985.]

Sec. 49-d-4. (a) In addition to other programs authorized by this constitution, the Legislature by law may provide for the creation, administration, and implementation of a bond insurance program to which the state pledges its general credit in an amount not to exceed $250 million to insure the payment in whole or in part of the principal of and interest on bonds or other obligations that are issued by cities, counties, special governmental districts and authorities, and other political subdivisions of the state as defined by law for use for or in aid of water conservation, water development, water quality enhancement, flood control, drainage, recharge, chloride control, desalinization, or any combination of those purposes.

(b) The Legislature by law shall designate the state agency to administer the bond insurance program and may authorize that agency to execute insurance contracts that bind the state to pay the principal of and interest on the bonds if the bonds are in default or the bonds are subject to impending default, subject to the limits provided by this section and by law.

(c) The payment by the state of any insurance commitment made under this section must be made from the first money coming into the state treasury that is not otherwise dedicated by this constitution.

(d) Notwithstanding the total amount of bonds insured under this section, the total amount paid and not recovered by the state under this section, excluding the costs of administration, may not exceed $250 million.

(e) Except on a two-thirds vote of the members elected to each house of the Legislature, the ratio of bonds insured to the total liability of the state must be two to one.

(f) Except on a two-thirds vote of the members elected to each house of the Legislature, the state agency administering the bond insurance program may not authorize bond insurance coverage under the program in any state fiscal year that exceeds a total of $100 million.

(g) Unless authorized to continue by a two-thirds vote of the members elected to each house, this section and the bond insurance program authorized by this section expire on the sixth anniversary of the date on which this section becomes a part of the constitution. However, bond insurance issued before the expiration of this section and the program is not affected by the expiration of this section and the program and remains in effect according to its terms, and the state is required to fulfill all of the terms of that previously issued insurance.

[Note — Sec. 49-d-4 of Art. III was added to authorize a bond insurance program. Submitted by 69th Legislature (1985) and adopted in election Nov. 5, 1985.]

Sec. 49-d-5. For the purpose of any program established or autho-

Article III (Cont'd.)

rized by Sec. 49-c, Sec. 49-d, Sec. 49-d-1, Sec. 49-d-2, or Sec. 49-d-4 of this article, the Legislature by law may extend any benefits to nonprofit water supply corporations that it may extend to a district created or organized under Art. XVI, Sec. 59, of this constitution.

[Note — Sec. 49-d-5 of Art. III was added to clarify the purpose for which Texas Water Development Bonds may be issued. Submitted by 69th Legislature (1985) and adopted in election Nov. 5, 1985.]

Sec. 49-d-6. (a) The Texas Water Development Board may issue additional Texas Water Development Bonds up to an additional aggregate principal amount of $400 million. Of the additional bonds authorized to be issued, $200 million of those bonds shall be used for purposes provided by Section 49-c of this article, $150 million of those bonds shall be used for purposes provided by Section 49-d-1 of this article, and $50 million of those bonds shall be used for flood control as provided by law.

(b) The legislature may require review and approval of the issuance of the bonds, of the use of the bond proceeds, or of the rules adopted by an agency to govern use of the bond proceeds. Notwithstanding any other provision of this constitution, any entity created or directed to conduct this review and approval may include members or appointees of members of the executive, legislative, and judicial departments of state government.

(c) The Texas Water Development Board shall issue the additional bonds authorized by this section for the terms, in the denominations, form, and installments, on the conditions, and subject to the limitations provided by Sections 49-c and 49-d-1 of this article and by laws adopted by the legislature implementing this section.

(d) Subsections (c) through (e) of Section 49-d-2 of this article apply to the bonds authorized by this section.

[Note — Sec. 49-d-6 of Art. III was added to authorize the issuance of an additional $400 million of Texas Water Development Bonds for water supply, water quality, and flood control purposes. Submitted by 70th Legislature (1987) and adopted in election Nov. 3, 1987.]

Sec. 49-d-7. (a) The Texas Water Development Board may issue additional Texas water development bonds up to an additional aggregate principal amount of $500 million. Of the additional bonds authorized to be issued, $250 million of those bonds shall be used for purposes provided by Section 49-c of this article, $200 million of those bonds shall be used for purposes provided by Section 49-d-1 of this article, and $50 million of those bonds shall be used for flood control as provided by law.

(b) The Texas Water Development Board may use the proceeds of Texas water development bonds issued for the purposes provided by Section 49-c of this article for the additional purpose of providing financial assistance, on terms and conditions provided by law, to various political subdivisions and bodies politic and corporate of the state and to nonprofit water supply corporations to provide for acquisition, improvement, extension, or construction of water supply projects that involve the distribution of water to points of delivery to wholesale or retail customers.

(c) The legislature may require review and approval of the issuance of the bond, the use of the bond proceeds, or the rules adopted by an agency to govern use of the bond proceeds. Notwithstanding any other provision of this constitution, any entity created or directed to conduct this review and approval may include members or appointees of members of the executive, legislative, and judicial departments of state government.

(d) Except as specifically provided by Subsection (e) of this section, the Texas Water Development Board shall issue the additional bonds authorized by this section for the terms, in the denominations, form, and installments, on the conditions, and subject to the limitations provided by Sections 49-c and 49-d-1 of this article and by laws adopted by the legislature implementing this section.

(e) The legislature may provide by law for subsidized loans and grants from the proceeds of bonds authorized by this section to provide wholesale and retail water and wastewater facilities to economically distressed areas of the state as defined by law, provided, the principal amount of bonds that may be issued for the purposes under this subsection may not exceed 50 percent of the total amount of bonds authorized by this section. Separate accounts shall be established in the water development fund for administering the proceeds of bonds issued for purposes under this subsection, and an interest and sinking fund separate from and not subject to the limitations of the interest and sinking fund created pursuant to Section 49-c for other Texas water development bonds is established in the State Treasury to be used for paying the principal of and interest on bonds for the purposes of this subsection. While any of the bonds authorized for the purposes of this subsection or any of the interest on those bonds is outstanding and unpaid, there is appropriated out of the first money coming into the State Treasury in each fiscal year, not otherwise appropriated by this constitution, and amount that is sufficient to pay the principal of and interest on those bonds issued for the purposes under this subsection that mature or become due during that fiscal year.

(f) Subsections (c) through (e) of Section 49-d-2 of this article apply to the bonds authorized by this section.

[Note — Sec. 49-d-7 of Art. III was added to authorize the issuance of an additional $500 million of Texas water development bonds for water supply, water quality and flood control purposes. Proposed by

71st Legislature (1989) and adopted in election Nov. 7, 1989. Subsection (e) was amended to increased the amount of bonds for water and wastewater facilities that may be issued for economically distressed areas. Submitted by 72nd Legislature (1991) and adopted in election Nov. 5, 1991.]

Sec. 49-e. **Texas Park Development Bonds** — The Parks and Wildlife Department, or its successor vested with the powers, duties, and authority which deals with the operation, maintenance, and improvement of State Parks, shall have the authority to provide for, issue and sell general obligation bonds of the State of Texas in an amount not to exceed Seventy-Five Million Dollars ($75,000,000). The bonds authorized herein shall be called "Texas Park Development Bonds," shall be executed in such form, denominations, and upon such terms as may be prescribed by law, provided, however, that the bonds shall bear a rate or rates of interest as may be fixed by the Parks and Wildlife Department or its successor, but the weighted average annual interest rate, as that phrase is commonly and ordinarily used and understood in the municipal bond market, of all the bonds issued and sold in any installment of any bonds, shall not exceed four and one-half percent (4 1/2%) interest per annum; they may be issued in such installments as said Parks and Wildlife Department, or its said successor, finds feasible and practical in accomplishing the purpose set forth herein.

All moneys received from the sale of said bonds shall be deposited in a fund hereby created with the Comptroller of Public Accounts of the State of Texas to be known as the Texas Park Development Fund to be administered (without further appropriation) by the said Parks and Wildlife Department, or its said successor, in such manner as prescribed by law.

Such fund shall be used by said Parks and Wildlife Department, or its said successor, under such provisions as the Legislature may prescribe by general law, for the purposes of acquiring lands from the United States, or any governmental agency thereof, from any governmental agency of the State of Texas, or from any person, firm, or corporation, for State Park Sites and for developing said sites as State Parks.

While any of the bonds authorized by this provision, or any interest on any such bonds, is outstanding and unpaid, there is hereby appropriated out of the first moneys coming into the Treasury in each fiscal year, not otherwise appropriated by this Constitution, an amount which is sufficient to pay the principal and interest on such bonds that mature or become due during such fiscal year, less the amount in the interest and sinking fund at the close of the prior fiscal year, which includes any receipts derived during the prior fiscal year by said Parks and Wildlife Department, or its said successor, from admission charges to State Parks, as the Legislature may prescribe by general law.

The Legislature may provide for the investment of moneys available in the Texas Park Development Fund and the interest and sinking fund established for the payment of bonds issued by said Parks and Wildlife Department, or its said successor. Income from such investment shall be used for the purposes prescribed by the Legislature.

From the moneys received by said Parks and Wildlife Department, or its said successor, from the sale of the bonds issued hereunder, there shall be deposited in the interest and sinking fund for the bonds authorized by this section sufficient moneys to pay the interest to become due during the State fiscal year in which the bonds were issued. After all bonds have been fully paid with interest, or after there are on deposit in the interest and sinking fund sufficient moneys to pay all future maturities of principal and interest, additional moneys received from admission charges to State Parks shall be deposited to the State Parks Fund, or any successor fund which may be established by the Legislature as a depository for Park revenue earned by said Parks and Wildlife Department, or its said successor.

All bonds issued hereunder shall after approval by the Attorney General, registration by the Comptroller of Public Accounts of the State of Texas, and delivery to the purchasers, be incontestable and shall constitute general obligations of the State of Texas under the Constitution of Texas.

Should the Legislature enact enabling laws in anticipation of the adoption of this amendment, such acts shall not be void by reason of their anticipatory nature.

[Note — Sec. 49-e of Art. III was added to authorize issuance and sale of $75,000,000 in bonds to create the Texas Park Development Fund to acquire lands for State Park sites and to develop State Parks. Submitted by 60th Legislature (1967) and adopted in election Nov. 11, 1967. It was amended to change references to the state treasurer to the state comptroller after the office of state treasurer was eliminated by constitutional amendment. Submitted by 74th Legislature (1995) and adopted in election Nov. 7, 1995.]

Sec. 49-f. (a) The Legislature by general law may provide for the issuance of general obligation bonds of the state, the proceeds of which shall be used to make loans and provide other financing assistance for the purchase of farm and ranch land.

(b) Except as provided by Subsection (g) of this section, all money received from the sale of the bonds shall be deposited in a fund created with the comptroller of public accounts to be known as the farm and ranch finance program fund. This fund shall be administered by the Texas Agricultural Finance Authority in the manner prescribed by law.

(c) Sec. 65(b) of this article applies to the payment of interest on

Article III (Cont'd.)

the bonds.

(d) The principal amount of bonds outstanding at one time may not exceed $500 million.

(e) While any of the bonds authorized by this section or any interest on those bonds is outstanding and unpaid, there is appropriated out of the first money coming into the treasury in each fiscal year not otherwise appropriated by this constitution an amount that is sufficient to pay the principal and interest on the bonds that mature or become due during the fiscal year less the amount in the interest and sinking fund at the close of the prior fiscal year.

(f) The bonds shall be approved by the attorney general and registered with the comptroller of public accounts. The bonds, when approved and registered, are general obligations of the state and are incontestable

(g) Notwithstanding Subsection (a) of this section, the proceeds of $200 million of the bonds authorized by this section may be used for the purposes provided by Section 49-i of this article and for other rural economic development programs, and the proceeds of bonds issued for those purposes under this subsection shall be deposited in the Texas agricultural fund, to be administered in the same manner that proceeds of bonds issued under Section 49-i of this article are administered.

[Note — Sec. 49-f of Art. III was added to authorize the issuance of general obligation bonds to provide financing for purchase of farm and ranch land. Submitted by 69th Legislature (1985) and adopted in election Nov. 5, 1985. It was amended to change references to the state treasurer to the state comptroller after the office of state treasurer was eliminated by constitutional amendment. Submitted by 74th Legislature (1995) and adopted in election Nov. 7, 1995. Subsection (b) was further amended and Subsection (g) was added to change administration of the fund from the Veterans' Land Board to the Texas Agricultural Finance Authority. Also submitted by 74th Legislature (1995) and adopted in election Nov. 7, 1995.]

Sec. 49-g. **Superconducting Super Collider: Bonds Authorized for Facilities** — (See also second Sec. 49-g below, regarding the economic stabilization fund, and the explanatory note which follows it.) (a) The legislature may authorize (1) the appropriate agency to issue up to $250 million in general obligation bonds and to use the proceeds of the bonds (without further appropriation) to establish a superconducting super collider fund to be used in any manner appropriate to fund undertakings related to a superconducting super collider research facility sponsored or authorized by the United States government, and (2) the appropriate agency to grant land or property, whether or not acquired from proceeds of the bonds, to the United States government for undertakings related to a superconducting super collider research facility. The superconducting super collider fund shall contain a project account, an interest and sinking account and such other accounts as may be authorized by the legislature. The fund shall be composed of the proceeds of the bonds authorized by this section, together with any income from investment of money in the fund, amounts received pursuant to Subsection (b) hereof, and any other amounts authorized to be deposited in the fund by the legislature.

(b) Bonds issued under this section constitute a general obligation of the state. While any of the bonds or interest on the bonds is outstanding and unpaid, there is appropriated out of the first money coming into the treasury in each fiscal year, not otherwise appropriated by this constitution, the amount sufficient to pay the principal of and interest on the bonds that mature or become due during the fiscal year, less any amount in the interest and sinking account at the end of the preceding fiscal year that is pledged to payment of the bonds or interest.

(c) The legislature may require review and approval of the issuance of the bonds, of the use of the bond proceeds, or of the rules adopted by an agency to govern use of the bond proceeds. Notwithstanding any other provision of this constitution, any entity created or directed to conduct this review and approval may include members, or appointees of members, of the executive, legislative, and judicial departments of state government.

(d) Should the legislature enact enabling laws in anticipation of the adoption of this section, such acts shall not be void by reason of their anticipatory character.

[Note — Sec. 49-g of Art. III was added to provide for issuance of bonds relating to a superconducting super collider research facility. Submitted by 70th Legislature (1987) and adopted in election Nov. 3, 1987. It was amended to reduce the amount of bonds authorized. Submitted by 74th Legislature (1995) and adopted in election Nov. 7, 1995.]

Sec. 49-g. **Economic Stabilization Fund** — (See also first Sec. 49-g above, regarding the superconducting super collider, and the explanatory note which follows the second Sec. 49-g below.) (a) The economic stabilization fund is established as a special fund in the state treasury.

(b) The comptroller shall, not later than the 90th day of each biennium, transfer to the economic stabilization fund one-half of any unencumbered positive balance of general revenues on the last day of the preceding biennium. If necessary, the comptroller shall reduce the amount transferred in proportion to the other amounts prescribed by this section to prevent the amount in the fund from exceeding the limit in effect for that biennium under Subsection (g) of this section.

(c) Not later than the 90th day of each fiscal year, the comptroller of public accounts shall transfer from general revenue to the economic stabilization fund the amounts prescribed by Subsections (d) and (e) of this section. However, if necessary, the comptroller shall reduce proportionately the amounts transferred to prevent the amount in the fund from exceeding the limit in effect for that biennium under Subsection (g) of this section.

(d) If in the preceding year the state received from oil production taxes a net amount greater than the net amount of oil production taxes received by the state in the fiscal year ending August 31, 1987, the comptroller shall transfer to the economic stabilization fund an amount equal to 75 percent of the difference between those amounts. The comptroller shall retain the remaining 25 percent of the difference as general revenue. In computing the net amount of oil production taxes received, the comptroller may not consider refunds paid as a result of oil overcharge litigation.

(e) If in the preceding year the state received from gas production taxes a net amount greater than the net amount of gas production taxes received by the state in the fiscal year ending August 31, 1987, the comptroller shall transfer to the economic stabilization fund an amount equal to 75 percent of the difference between those amounts. The comptroller shall retain the remaining 25 percent of the difference as general revenue. For the purposes of this subsection, the comptroller shall adjust his computation of revenues to reflect only 12 months of collection.

(f) The legislature may appropriate additional amounts to the economic stabilization fund.

(g) During each fiscal biennium, the amount in the economic stabilization fund may not exceed an amount equal to 10 percent of the total amount, excluding investment income, interest income, and amounts borrowed from special funds, deposited in general revenue during the preceding biennium.

(h) In preparing an estimate of anticipated revenues for a succeeding biennium as required by Article III, Section 49a, of this constitution, the comptroller shall estimate the amount of the transfers that will be made under Subsections (b), (d), and (e) of this section. The comptroller shall deduct that amount from the estimate of anticipated revenues as if the transfers were made on August 31 of that fiscal year.

(i) The comptroller shall credit to general revenue interest due to the economic stabilization fund that would result in an amount in the economic stabilization fund that exceeds the limit in effect under Subsection (g) of this section.

(j) The comptroller may transfer money from the economic stabilization fund to general revenue to prevent or eliminate a temporary cash deficiency in general revenue. The comptroller shall return the amount transferred to the economic stabilization fund as soon as practicable, but not later than August 31 of each odd-numbered year. The comptroller shall allocate the depository interest as if the transfers had not been made. If the comptroller submits a statement to the governor and the legislature under Article III, Section 49a, of this constitution when money from the economic stabilization fund is in general revenue, the comptroller shall state that the transferred money is not available for appropriation from general revenue.

(k) Amounts from the economic stabilization fund may be appropriated during a regular legislative session only for a purpose for which an appropriation from general revenue was made by the preceding legislature and may be appropriated in a special session only for a purpose for which an appropriation from general revenue was made in a preceding legislative session of the same legislature. An appropriation from the economic stabilization fund may be made only if the comptroller certifies that appropriations from general revenue made by the preceding legislature for the current biennium exceed available general revenues and cash balances for the remainder of that biennium. The amount of an appropriation from the economic stabilization fund may not exceed the difference between the comptroller's estimate of general revenue for the current biennium at the time the comptroller receives for certification the bill making the appropriation and the amount of general revenue appropriations for that biennium previously certified by the comptroller. Appropriations from the economic stabilization fund under this subsection may not extend beyond the last day of the current biennium. An appropriation from the economic stabilization fund must be approved by a three-fifths vote of the members present in each house of the legislature.

(l) If an estimate of anticipated revenues for a succeeding biennium prepared by the comptroller pursuant to Article III, Section 49a, of this constitution is less than the revenues that are estimated at the same time by the comptroller to be available for the current biennium, the legislature may, by a three-fifths vote of the members present in each house, appropriate for the succeeding biennium from the economic stabilization fund an amount not to exceed this difference. Following each fiscal year, the actual amount of revenue shall be computed, and if the estimated difference exceeds the actual difference, the comptroller shall transfer the amount necessary from general revenue to the economic stabilization fund so that the actual difference shall not be exceeded. If all or a portion of the difference in revenue from one biennium to the next results, at least in part, from a change in a tax rate or base adopted by the legislature, the computation of revenue difference shall be adjusted to the amount that would have been available had the rate or base not been changed.

(m) In addition to the appropriation authority provided by Subsections (k) and (l) of this section, the legislature may, by a two-thirds vote of the members present in each house, appropriate amounts from the economic stabilization fund at any time and for any purpose.

Article III (Cont'd.)

(n) Money appropriated from the economic stabilization fund is subject to being withheld or transferred, within any limits provided by statute, by any person or entity authorized to exercise the power granted by Article XVI, Section 69, of this constitution.

(o) In this section, "net" means the amount of money that is equal to the difference between gross collections and refunds before the comptroller allocates the receipts as provided by law.

[Note — Sec. 49-g of Art. III was added to establish the economic stabilization fund. Submitted by 70th Legislature and adopted in election Nov. 8, 1988. Subsections (i) and (j) were amended to change references to the state treasurer to the state comptroller after the office of state treasurer was eliminated by constitutional amendment. Submitted by 74th Legislature (1995) and adopted in election Nov. 7, 1995. Please note that the 70th Legislature submitted two different Section 49-g's for Article III: the first, having to do with the superconducting super collider, approved in election Nov. 3, 1987, and the second, having to do with the economic stabilization fund, approved in election Nov. 8, 1988. They are printed here in the order in which they were adopted.]

Sec. 49-h. (a) The legislature may authorize the issuance of up to $500 million in general obligation bonds and the use of the bond proceeds for acquiring, constructing, or equipping new facilities or for major repair or renovation of existing facilities of corrections institutions, including youth corrections institutions, and mental health and mental retardation institutions. The legislature may require the review and approval of the issuance of the bonds and the projects to be financed by the bond proceeds. Notwithstanding any other provision of this constitution, the issuer of the bonds or any entity created or directed to review and approve projects may include members or appointees of members of the executive, legislative, and judicial departments of state government.

(b) Bonds issued under this section constitute a general obligation of the state. While any of the bonds or interest on the bonds is outstanding and unpaid, there is appropriated out of the first money coming into the treasury in each fiscal year, not otherwise appropriated by this constitution, the amount sufficient to pay the principal of and interest on the bonds that mature or become due during the fiscal year, less any amount in any sinking fund at the end of the preceding fiscal year that is pledged to payment of the bonds or interest.

(c) (1) The legislature may authorize the issuance of up to $400 million in general obligation bonds, in addition to the amount authorized by Subsection (a) of this section, and use the proceeds of the bonds for acquiring, constructing, or equipping new corrections institutions, mental health and mental retardation institutions, youth corrections institutions, and statewide law enforcement facilities and for major repair or renovation of existing facilities of those institutions.

(2) The provisions of Subsection (a) of this section relating to the review and approval of bonds and the provisions of Subsection (b) of this section relating to the status of the bonds as a general obligation of the state and to the manner in which the principal and interest on the bonds are paid apply to bonds authorized under this subsection.

(d) (1) The legislature may authorize the issuance of up to $1.1 billion in general obligation bonds, in addition to the amount authorized by Subsections (a) and (c) of this section, and may use the proceeds of the bonds for acquiring, constructing, or equipping new prisons and substance abuse felony punishment facilities to confine criminals, mental health and mental retardation institutions, and Youth corrections institutions, for major repair or renovation of existing facilities of those institutions, and for the acquisition of, major repair to, or renovation of other facilities for use as state prisons or substance abuse felony punishment facilities. Proceeds of general obligation bonds issued under this subdivision may not be appropriated by any session of the legislature other than the 2nd Called Session of the 72nd Legislature or any subsequent session of the legislature.

(2) The provisions of Subsection (a) of this section relating to the review and approval of bonds and the provisions of Subsection (b) of this section relating to the status of the bonds as a general obligation of the state and to the manner in which the principal and interest on the bonds are paid apply to bonds authorized under this subsection.

(e) (1) The legislature may authorize the issuance of up to $1 billion in general obligation bonds, in addition to the amounts authorized by Subsections (a), (c), and (d) of this section, and use the proceeds of the bonds for acquiring, constructing, or equipping new corrections institutions, including youth corrections institutions, and mental health and mental retardation institutions and for major repair or renovation of existing facilities of those corrections and mental health and mental retardation institutions.

(2) The provisions of Subsection (a) of this section relating to the review and approval of bonds and the provisions of Subsection (b) of this section relating to the status of the bonds as a general obligation of the state and to the manner in which the principal and interest on the bonds are paid apply to bonds authorized under this subsection.

[Note — Sec. 49-h of Art. III was added to provide for issuance of general obligation bonds for construction projects for corrections institutions and mental health and mental retardation institutions. Submitted by 70th Legislature and adopted in election Nov. 3, 1987. Subsection (c) was added to provide for the issuance of general obligation bonds for acquiring, constructing or equipping corrections institutions, youth corrections institutions, statewide law enforcement facilities and mental health and mental retardation institutions. Pro-

posed by 71st Legislature (1989) and adopted in election Nov. 7, 1989. Subsection (d) was added to provide for the funding of new prisons, mental health and mental retardation institutions and youth corrections facilities. Submitted by 72nd Legislature (1991) and adopted in election Nov. 5, 1991. Subsection (e) was added to provide for issuance of general obligation bonds for acquiring, constructing, or equipping corrections institutions and mental health and mental retardation institutions and for repair or renovation of existing facilities. Submitted by 73rd Legislature (1993) and adopted in election Nov. 2, 1993.]

Sec. 49-i. (a) The legislature by law may provide for the issuance of general obligation bonds of the state for the purpose of providing money to establish a Texas agricultural fund in the state treasury to be used without further appropriation in the manner provided by law and for the purpose of providing money to establish a rural microenterprise development fund in the state treasury to be used without further appropriation in the manner provided by law. The Texas agricultural fund shall be used only to provide financial assistance to develop, increase, improve, or expand the production, processing, marketing, or export of crops or products grown or produced primarily in this state by agricultural businesses domiciled in the state. The rural microenterprise development fund shall be used only in furtherance of a program established by the legislature to foster and stimulate the creation and expansion of small businesses in rural areas. The financial assistance offered by both funds may include loan guarantees, insurance, coinsurance, loans, and indirect loans or purchases or acceptances of assignments of loans or other obligations.

(b) The principal amount of bonds outstanding at one time may not exceed $25 million for the Texas agricultural fund and $5 million for the rural microenterprise development fund.

(c) The legislature may establish an interest and sinking account and other accounts within the Texas agricultural fund and within the rural microenterprise development fund. The legislature may provide for the investment of bond proceeds and of the interest and sinking accounts. Income from the investment of money in the funds that is not immediately committed to the payment of the principal of and interest on the bonds or the provision of financial assistance shall be used to create new employment and business opportunities in the state through the diversification and expansion of agricultural or rural small businesses, as provided by the legislature.

(d) Bonds authorized under this section constitute a general obligation of the state. While any of the bonds or interest on the bonds is outstanding and unpaid, there is appropriated out of the first money coming into the treasury in each fiscal year, not otherwise appropriated by this constitution, the amount sufficient to pay the principal of and interest on the bonds that mature or become due during the fiscal year, less any amounts in the interest and sinking accounts and the close of the preceding fiscal year that are pledged to payment of the bonds of interest.

[Note — Sec. 49-i of Art. III authorizes the Legislature to provide for issuance of bonds and state financing of development and production of Texas products and businesses. Proposed by 71st Legislature (1989) and adopted in election Nov. 7, 1989.]

Sec. 50. **Credit of State Not to Be Pledged** — The Legislature shall have no power to give or to lend or to authorize the giving or lending of the credit of the State in aid of, or to any person, association or corporation, whether municipal or other, or to pledge the credit of the State in any manner whatsoever, for the payment of the liabilities, present or prospective, of any individual, association of individuals, municipal or other corporation whatsoever.

Sec. 50-a. **State Medical Education Board, Fund; Purpose** — The Legislature shall create a State Medical Education Board to be composed of not more than six (6) members whose qualifications, duties and terms of office shall be prescribed by law. The Legislature shall also establish a State Medical Education Fund and make adequate appropriations therefor to be used by the State Medical Education Board to provide grants, loans or scholarships to students desiring to study medicine and agreeing to practice in the rural areas of this State, upon such terms and conditions as shall be prescribed by law. The term "rural areas" as used in this section shall be defined by law.

[Note — Sec. 50-a of Art. III was added to provide scholarships and to set up a State Medical Education Board. Submitted by 52nd Legislature and adopted in election Nov. 4, 1952.]

Sec. 50-b. **Student Loans** — (a) The Legislature may provide that the Coordinating Board, Texas College and University System, or its successor or successors, shall have the authority to provide for, issue and sell general obligation bonds of the State of Texas in an amount not to exceed Eighty-five Million Dollars ($85,000,000). The bonds authorized herein, shall be called "Texas College Student Loan Bonds," shall be executed in such form, denominations and upon such terms as may be prescribed by law, provided, however, that the bonds shall not bear more than four per cent (4%) interest per annum; they may be issued in such installments as the Board finds feasible and practical in accomplishing the purposes of this section.

(b) All moneys received from the sale of such bonds shall be deposited in a fund hereby created in the State Treasury to be known as the Texas Opportunity Plan Fund to be administered by the Coordinating Board, Texas College and University System, or its successor or successors to make loans to students who have been admitted to attend any institution of higher education within the State of Texas,

Article III (Cont'd.)

public or private, including Junior Colleges, which are recognized or accredited under terms and conditions prescribed by the Legislature, and to pay interest and principal on such bonds and provide a sinking fund therefor under such conditions as the Legislature may prescribe.

(c) While any of the bonds, or interest on said bonds authorized by this section is outstanding and unpaid, there is hereby appropriated out of the first moneys coming into the Treasury in each fiscal year, not otherwise appropriated by this Constitution, an amount sufficient to pay the principal and interest on such bonds that mature or become due during such fiscal year, less the amount in the sinking fund at the close of the prior fiscal year.

(d) The Legislature may provide for the investment of moneys available in the Texas Opportunity Plan Fund, and the interest and sinking funds established for the payment of bonds issued by the Coordinating Board, Texas College and University System, or its successor or successors. Income from such investment shall be used for the purposes prescribed by the Legislature.

(e) All bonds issued hereunder shall, after approval by the Attorney General, registration by the Comptroller of Public Accounts of the State of Texas, and delivery to the purchasers, be incontestable and shall constitute general obligations of the State of Texas under this Constitution.

(f) Should the Legislature enact enabling laws in anticipation of the adoption of this amendment, such acts shall not be void because of their anticipatory nature.

[Note — Sec. 50-b of Art. III was added to provide a system of student loans at institutions of higher education and to provide for creation of the Texas Opportunity Plan Fund. Submitted by 59th Legislature (1965) and adopted in election Nov. 2, 1965.]

Sec. 50-b-1. (a) The Legislature may provide that the Coordinating Board, Texas College and University System, or its successor or successors, shall have authority to provide for, issue and sell general obligation bonds of the State of Texas in an amount not to exceed Two Hundred Million Dollars ($200,000,000) in addition to those heretofore authorized to be issued pursuant to Sec. 50-b of the Constitution. The bonds authorized herein shall be executed in such form, upon such terms and in such denomination as may be prescribed by law and shall bear interest, and be issued in such installments as shall be prescribed by the Board provided that the maximum net effective interest rate to be borne by such bonds may be fixed by law.

(b) The moneys received from the sale of such bonds shall be deposited to the credit of the Texas Opportunity Plan Fund created by Sec. 50-b of the Constitution and shall otherwise be handled as provided in Sec. 50-b of the Constitution and the laws enacted pursuant thereto.

(c) The said bonds shall be general obligations of the state and shall be payable in the same manner and from the same sources as bonds heretofore authorized pursuant to Sec. 50-b.

(d) All bonds issued hereunder shall, after approval by the Attorney General, registration by the Comptroller of Public Accounts of the State of Texas, and delivery to the purchasers, be incontestable and shall constitute general obligations of the State of Texas under this Constitution.

(e) Should the Legislature enact enabling laws in anticipation of the adoption of this amendment such acts shall not be void because of their anticipatory nature.

[Note—Sec. 50-b-1 of Art. III was added to provide for additional loans to students at higher educational institutions under the Texas Opportunity Plan. Submitted by 61st Legislature (1969) and adopted in election Aug. 5, 1969.]

Sec. 50-b-2. **Additional Student Loans** — (a) The legislature by general law may authorize the Texas Higher Education Coordinating Board or its successor or successors to provide for, issue, and sell general obligation bonds of the State of Texas in an amount not to exceed $75 million in addition to those bonds issued under Sections 50-b and 50-b-1 of this constitution. Bonds issued under this section shall be issued as college savings bonds as provided by law.

(b) The bonds shall:

(1) be executed in the form, on the terms, and in the denominations as prescribed by law; and

(2) bear interest and be issued in installments as prescribed by the Texas Higher Education Coordinating Board or its successor or successors.

(c) The maximum net effective interest rate to be borne by bonds issued under this section must be set by law.

(d) The proceeds from the sale of bonds issued under this section shall be credited to the Texas opportunity plan fund created by Section 50-b of this constitution and shall be administered as provided by Section 50-b of this constitution and the law enacted under that constitutional provision.

(e) Bonds issued under this section are payable in the same manner and from the same sources as bonds authorized under Section 50-b of this constitution.

(f) Bonds issued under this section, after approval by the attorney general, registration by the comptroller of public accounts, and delivery to the purchasers, are incontestable and are general obligations of the State of Texas under this constitution.

[Note — Sec. 50-b-2 of Art. III was added to provide for the issu-

ance of general obligation bonds as college savings bonds to provide educational loans to students and to encourage the public to save for a college education. Proposed by 71st Legislature (1989) and adopted in election Nov. 7, 1989.]

Sec. 50-b-3. **Additional Student Loans** — (a) The legislature by general law may authorize the Texas Higher Education Coordinating Board or its successor or successors to issue and sell general obligation bonds of the State of Texas in an amount not to exceed $300 million to finance educational loans to students. The bonds are in addition to those bonds issued under Sections 50b, 50b-1, and 50b-2 of Article III of this constitution.

(b) The bonds shall be executed in the form, on the terms and in the denominations, bear interest, and be issued in installments, as prescribed by the Texas Higher Education Coordinating Board or its successor or successors.

(c) The maximum net effective interest rate to be borne by bonds issued under this section must be set by law.

(d) The legislature may provide for the investment of bond proceeds and may establish and provide for the investment of an interest and sinking fund to pay the bonds. Income from the investment shall be used for the purposes prescribed by the legislature.

(e) While any of the bonds issued under this section or interest on the bonds is outstanding and unpaid, there is appropriated out of the first money coming into the treasury in each fiscal year, not otherwise appropriated by this constitution, the amount sufficient to pay the principal of and interest on the bonds that mature or become due during the fiscal year, less any amount in an interest and sinking fund established under this section at the end of the preceding fiscal year that is pledged to the payment of the bonds or interest.

(f) Bonds issued under this section, after approval by the attorney general, registration by the comptroller of public accounts, and delivery to the purchasers, are incontestable.

[Note — Subsection 50b-3 of Article III was added to provide for issuance of general obligation bonds to provide educational loans to students. Submitted by 72nd Legislature (1991) and adopted in election Nov. 5, 1991.]

Sec. 50b-4. **Additional Student Loans** — (a) The legislature by general law may authorize the Texas Higher Education Coordinating Board or its successor or successors to issue and sell general obligation bonds of the State of Texas in an amount not to exceed $300 million to finance educational loans to students. The bonds are in addition to those bonds issued under Sections 50b, 50b-1, 50b-2, and 50b-3, Article III, Texas Constitution.

(b) The bonds shall be executed in the form, on the terms, and in the denominations, bear interest, and be issued in installments as prescribed by the Texas Higher Education Coordinating Board or its successor or successors.

(c) The maximum net effective interest rate to be borne by bonds issued under this section must be set by law.

(d) The legislature may provide for the investment of bond proceeds and may establish and provide for the investment of an interest and sinking fund to pay the bonds. Income from the investment shall be used for the purposes prescribed by the legislature.

(e) While any of the bonds issued under this section or interest on the bonds is outstanding and unpaid, there is appropriated out of the first money coming into the treasury in each fiscal year, not otherwise appropriated by this constitution, the amount sufficient to pay the principal of and interest on the bonds that mature or become due during the fiscal year, less any amount in an interest and sinking fund established under this section at the end of the preceding fiscal year that is pledged to the payment of the bonds or interest.

(f) Bonds issued under this section, after approval by the attorney general, registration by the comptroller of public accounts, and delivery to the purchasers, are incontestable.

[Note — Sec. 50b-4 was added to provide additional bonds for educational loans to students. Submitted by 74th Legislature (1995) and adopted in election Nov. 7, 1995.]

Sec. 50-c. **Farm and Ranch Loan Security Fund** — (a) The Legislature may provide that the commissioner of agriculture shall have the authority to provide for, issue, and sell general obligation bonds of the State of Texas in an amount not to exceed $10 million. The bonds shall be called "Farm and Ranch Loan Security Bonds" and shall be executed in such form, denominations, and on such terms as may be prescribed by law. The bonds shall bear interest rates fixed by the Legislature of the State of Texas.

(b) All money received from the sale of Farm and Ranch Loan Security Bonds shall be deposited in a fund hereby created with the comptroller of public accounts to be known as the "Farm and Ranch Loan Security Fund." This fund shall be administered without further appropriation by the commissioner of agriculture in the manner prescribed by law.

(c) The Farm and Ranch Loan Security Fund shall be used by the commissioner of agriculture under provisions prescribed by the Legislature for the purpose of guaranteeing loans used for the purchase of farm and ranch real estate, for acquiring real estate mortgages or deeds of trust on lands purchased with guaranteed loans, and to advance to the borrower a percentage of the principal and interest due on those loans; provided that the commissioner shall require at least six percent interest be paid by the borrower on any advance of principal and interest. The Legislature may authorize the commissioner

Article III (Cont'd.)

to sell at foreclosure any land acquired in this manner, and proceeds from that sale shall be deposited in the Farm and Ranch Loan Security Fund.

(d) The Legislature may provide for the investment of money available in the Farm and Ranch Loan Security Fund and the interest and sinking fund established for the payment of bonds issued by the commissioner of agriculture. Income from the investment shall be used for purposes prescribed by the Legislature.

(e) While any of the bonds authorized by this section or any interest on those bonds is outstanding and unpaid, there is hereby appropriated out of the first money coming into the treasury in each fiscal year not otherwise appropriated by this constitution an amount that is sufficient to pay the principal and interest on the bonds that mature or become due during the fiscal year less the amount in the interest and sinking fund at the close of the prior fiscal year.

[Note — Sec. 50-c of Art. III was added to provide for the guarantee of loans for purchase of farm and ranch real estate for qualified borrowers by the sale of general obligation bonds of the State of Texas. Submitted by 66th Legislature (1979) and adopted in election Nov. 6, 1979. Subsection (b)was amended to change references to the state treasurer to the state comptroller after the office of state treasurer was eliminated by constitutional amendment. Submitted by 74th Legislature (1995) and adopted in election Nov. 7, 1995.]

Sec. 50-d. (a) On a two-thirds vote of the members elected to each house of the Legislature, the Texas Water Development Board may issue and sell Texas agricultural water conservation bonds in an amount not to exceed $200 million.

(b) The proceeds from the sale of Texas agricultural water conservation bonds shall be deposited in a fund created in the state treasury to be known as the agricultural water conservation fund.

(c) Texas agricultural water conservation bonds are general obligations of the State of Texas. During the time that Texas agricultural water conservation bonds or any interest on those bonds is outstanding or unpaid, there is appropriated out of the first money coming into the state treasury in each fiscal year, not otherwise appropriated by this constitution, an amount that is sufficient to pay the principal of and interest on those bonds that mature or become due during that fiscal year, less the amount in the sinking fund at the close of the prior fiscal year.

(d) The terms, conditions, provisions, and procedures for issuance and sale and management of proceeds of Texas agricultural water conservation bonds shall be provided by law.

[Note — Sec. 50-d of Art. III was added to authorize issuance and sale of $200 million of Texas agricultural water conservation bonds. Submitted by 69th Legislature (1985) and adopted in election Nov. 5, 1985. Subsection (e) of Sec. 50-d was repealed in order to eliminate certain time limitations relating to the issuance of Texas agricultural water conservation bonds. Repeal proposed by 71st Legislature (1989) and adopted in election Nov. 7, 1989.]

Sec. 50-e. (a) For the purposes of providing surety for the Texas grain warehouse self-insurance fund, the legislature by general law may establish or provide for a guarantee of the fund not to exceed $50 million.

(b) At the beginning of the fiscal year after the fund reaches $5 million, as certified by the comptroller of public accounts, the guarantee of the fund shall cease and this provision shall expire.

(c) Should the legislature enact any enabling laws in anticipation of this amendment, no such law shall be void by reason of its anticipatory nature.

(d) If the provisions of this section conflict with any other provisions of this constitution, the provisions of this section shall prevail.

[Note — Section 50-e was added to establish a self-insurance pool for grain storage facilities. Submitted by 70th Legislature (1987) and adopted in election Nov. 3, 1987.]

Sec. 51. **Tax Levy Authorized for Confederate Soldiers and Sailors and Their Widows** — The Legislature shall have no power to make any grant or authorize the making of any grant of public moneys to any individual, association of individuals, municipal or other corporations whatsoever; provided, however, the Legislature may grant aid to indigent and disabled Confederate soldiers and sailors under such regulations and limitations as may be deemed by the Legislature as expedient, and to their widows in indigent circumstances under such regulations and limitations as may be deemed by the Legislature as expedient; provided that the provisions of this Section shall not be construed so as to prevent the grant of aid in cases of public calamity.

[Note — Sec. 51 of Art. III has been amended nine times (1) Establishing Confederate Home. Submitted by 23rd Legislature (1893) and ratified at election, Nov. 6, 1894, and proclaimed adopted Dec. 21, 1894. (2) Providing for pensions for Confederate veterans from appropriations not to exceed $250,000 annually. Submitted by 25th Legislature (1897), adopted at election, Nov. 1, 1898, and proclaimed Dec. 22, 1898. (3) Raising amount that might be appropriated for Confederate pensions from $250,000 to $500,000 annually. Submitted by 28th Legislature (1903), adopted in election, Nov. 8, 1904, and proclaimed Dec. 29, 1904. (4) Increasing authorized maximum appropriations for Confederate Home from $100,000 to $150,000 annually. Submitted by 31st Legislature (1909), adopted

in election, Nov. 8, 1910, and declared adopted Dec. 31, 1910. (5) Authorizing 5¢ ad valorem tax for Confederate pension fund; also omitting "public calamity" clause. Submitted by 32nd Legislature (1911), adopted Nov. 3, 1912, and proclaimed Dec. 30, 1912. (6) Authorizing 7¢ ad valorem tax for Confederate pension fund and reinstating "public calamity" clause. Submitted by 38th Legislature (1923) and adopted Nov. 4, 1924. (7) Eliminating specific restrictions upon grants of aid to Confederate soldiers, sailors and others with respect to date of removal to Texas, etc., and conferring such authority upon the Legislature. Submitted by 40th Legislature (1927); ratified Nov. 6, 1928; proclaimed Feb. 6, 1929. (8) Cutting tax from 7¢ to 2¢ by addition of Sec. 17 of Art. VII, which was deleted by Constitutional amendment in 1982.

(9) Further amended to provide for abolition of the 2¢ ad valorem tax for this purpose by Dec. 31, 1976, but making provision for aiding these veterans and their widows. (See also Art. VIII, Sec. 1-e.) Submitted by 60th Legislature (1967) and adopted in election Nov. 5, 1968.]

Sec. 51-a — **Assistance and Medical Care to Needy Aged, Needy Blind, Needy Children and Totally Disabled; Limitation on Expenditures for Same** — The Legislature shall have the power, by General Laws, to provide, subject to limitations herein contained, and such other limitations, restrictions and regulations as may be the Legislature be deemed expedient, for assistance grants to dependent children and the caretakers of such children, needy persons who are totally and permanently disabled because of a mental or physical handicap, needy aged persons and needy blind persons.

The Legislature may provide by General Law for medical care, rehabilitation and other similar services for needy persons. The Legislature may prescribe such other eligibility requirements for participation in these programs as it deems appropriate and may make appropriations out of state funds for such purposes. The maximum amount paid out of state funds for assistance grants to or on behalf of needy dependent children and their caretakers shall not exceed the amount of Eighty Million Dollars ($80,000,000) during any fiscal year, except that the limit shall be One Hundred Sixty Million Dollars ($160,000,000) for the two years of the 1982-1983 biennium. For the two years of each subsequent biennium, the maximum amount shall not exceed one percent of the state budget. The Legislature by general statute shall provide for the means for determining the state budget amounts, including state and other funds appropriated by the Legislature, to be used in establishing the biennial limit.

Provided further, that if the limitations and restrictions herein contained are found to be in conflict with the provisions of appropriate federal statutes, as they now are or as they may be amended to the extent that federal matching money is not available to the state for these purposes, then and in that event the Legislature is specifically authorized and empowered to prescribe such limitations and restrictions and enact such laws as may be necessary in order that such federal matching money will be available for assistance and/or medical care for or on behalf of needy persons.

Nothing in this section shall be construed to amend, modify or repeal Sec. 31 of Art. XVI of this Constitution; provided further, however, that such medical care, services or assistance shall also include the employment of objective or subjective means, without the use of drugs, for the purpose of ascertaining and measuring the powers of vision of the human eye, and fitting lenses or prisms to correct or remedy any defect or abnormal condition of vision. Nothing herein shall be construed to permit optometrists to treat the eyes for any defect whatsoever in any manner nor to administer nor to prescribe any drug or physical treatment whatsoever, unless such optometrist is a regularly licensed physician or surgeon under the laws of this state.

[Note — Sec. 51-a of Art. III was first submitted by 49th Legislature and adopted in election Aug. 25, 1945. It supplanted four earlier amendments, as follows: An original Sec. 51-a, which provided for issuance of $20,000,000 in state bonds for relief (the so-called "**Bread bonds**"), this amendment having been submitted by 43rd Legislature and adopted Aug. 26, 1933, and also Secs. 51-b, 51-c and 51-d, which originally provided for old-age pensions and other welfare measures, adopted in elections Aug. 24, 1935 and Aug. 23, 1937. Because of this consolidation, the Constitution did skip from Sec. 51-a to Sec. 51-e until a Sec. 51-b was added in election Nov. 2, 1954, and a Subsection 51-a was added in election Nov. 5, 1957. It was further amended to raise the limit from $35 million to $42 million. Submitted by 53rd Legislature (1953) and adopted in election Nov. 2, 1954. It was again amended to raise the limit from $42 million to $47 million and authorizing legislative appropriations to raise the needed money. Submitted by 55th Legislature (1957) and adopted in election Nov. 5, 1957. It was further amended to raise the total amount of assistance to $52 million per year. Submitted by 57th Legislature (1961) and adopted in election Nov. 6, 1962. It was further amended to combine the former Sections 51-a and 51-b-1 of Art. III into one section to be known as Sec. 51-a; further raising the total amount of assistance to $60 million per year and providing that Legislature shall prescribe the residence requirements. Submitted by 58th Legislature (1963) and adopted in election Nov. 9, 1963. It was further amended to create a new Sec. 51-a, which consolidates the old Sec. 51-a and Subsections 51-a-1 and 51-a-2. The new Sec. 51-a enables the State of Texas to cooperate with the U.S. government in providing assistance and medical care for the needy aged, needy blind, needy children and needy totally disabled; expands age categories of those eligible for blind assistance and of needy children; and extends eligibility for the aged to citizens of the United States or non-citizens who

Article III (Cont'd.)

have resided in the United States for 25 years. Submitted by 59th Legislature (1965) and adopted in election Nov. 2, 1965. It was again amended to raise the limit on amount to be expended from $60 million to $80 million a year. It further provided that certain amounts be allocated out of the Omnibus Tax Clearance Fund for aid to permanently and totally disabled, families with dependent children and for old-age assistance. Submitted by 61st Legislature (1969) and adopted in election Aug. 5, 1969. The regular session of the 67th Legislature (1981) submitted an amendment to raise the amount to be expended on Aid for Dependent Children in the 1982-1983 biennium to a maximum of $160 million and, for each subsequent biennium, the maximum amount would not exceed one percent of the state budget. This proposed amendment inadvertently cut out other needy recipients, and SJR 10 of the Called Session of the 67th Legislature (1982) amended the proposed amendment to include other needy recipients in this fund. Adopted in election Nov. 2, 1982.]

Sec. 51-a-1. (a) The legislature by general law may authorize the use of public money to provide to local fire departments and other public fire-fighting organizations:

(1) loans or other financial assistance to purchase fire-fighting equipment and to aid in providing necessary equipment and facilities to comply with federal and state law; and

(2) scholarships and grants to educate and train the members of local fire departments and other public fire-fighting organizations.

(b) A portion of the money used under this section may be used for the administrative costs of the program. The legislature shall provide for the terms and conditions of scholarships, grants, loans, and other financial assistance to be provided under this section.

[Note — Sec. 51-a-1 of Art. III was added to authorize the state to provide scholarships, grants, loans and other financial assistance to local fire departments and other public fire-fighting organizations. Proposed by 71st Legislature (1989) and adopted in election Nov. 7, 1989.]

[Note — Sec. 51-b of Art. III, creating the State Building Commission and the State Building Fund, was eliminated by a constitutional amendment. Proposed by 65th Legislature and adopted in election Nov. 7, 1978.]

Sec. 51-c. **False Imprisonment** — The Legislature may grant aid and compensation to any person who has heretofore paid a fine or served a sentence in prison, or who may hereafter pay a fine or serve a sentence in prison, under the laws of this State for an offense for which he or she is not guilty, under such regulations and limitations as the Legislature may deem expedient.

[Note — Sec. 51-c of Art. III was added to allow the Legislature to grant aid and compensation to persons who have been fined or imprisoned under laws of this state for offenses of which they are not guilty. Submitted by 54th Legislature (1955) and adopted in election Nov. 6, 1956.]

Sec. 51-d. **Assistance to Survivors of Law Enforcement Officers Killed on Duty** — The Legislature shall have the power, by general law, to provide for the payment of assistance by the State of Texas to the surviving spouse, minor children, and surviving dependent parents, brothers, and sisters of officers, employees and agents, including members of organized volunteer fire departments and members of organized police reserve or auxiliary units with authority to make an arrest, of the state or of any city, county, district, or other political subdivision who, because of the hazardous nature of their duties, suffer death in the course of the performance of those official duties. Should the Legislature enact any enabling laws in anticipation of this amendment, no such law shall be void by reason of its anticipatory nature.

[Note — Sec. 51-d was added to provide assistance for survivors of law enforcement officers killed in performance of their duty. Submitted by 59th Legislature (1965), and adopted in election Nov. 8, 1966. It was amended to provide for assistance to survivors of members of volunteer fire departments and organized police reserve, or auxiliary units with authority to make arrests, of political subdivisions of the state. Submitted by 61st Legislature (1969) and adopted in election Aug. 5, 1969. It was again amended to provide compensation for dependent parents, brothers and sisters of officers killed in performing their duties. Submitted by 68th Legislature (1983) and adopted in election Nov. 6, 1984.]

[Note — Sec. 51e and Sec. 51f, relating to City and Town Pension System and Local Pension Plans, respectively, were deleted by a constitutional amendment. Submitted by 64th Legislature (1975) and approved in election April 22, 1975. See Art. XVI, Sec. 67, which replaces the foregoing Sections. (See also note under Art. III, Sec. 48a and Sec. 48b; Art. XVI, Sec. 62 and Sec. 63.)]

Sec. 51-g. **Social Security Coverage for Municipal Employees** — The Legislature shall have the power to pass such laws as may be necessary to enable the State to enter into agreements with the Federal Government to obtain for proprietary employees of its political subdivisions coverage under the old-age and survivors insurance provisions of Title II of the Federal Social Security Act as amended. The Legislature shall have the power to make appropriations and authorize all obligations necessary to the establishment of such Social

Security coverage program.

[Note — Sec. 51-g of Art. III was added to extend Social Security coverage to municipal employees. Submitted by 53rd Legislature (1953) and adopted in election Nov. 2, 1954.]

Sec. 52. **Counties, Cities, Etc., Not Authorized to Grant Money or Become Stockholders; Exceptions** — (a) Except as otherwise provided by this section, the Legislature shall have no power to authorize any county, city, town or other political corporation or subdivision of the State to lend its credit or to grant public money or thing of value in aid of, or to any individual, association or corporation whatsoever, or to become a stockholder in such corporation, association or company. However, this section does not prohibit the use of public funds or credit for the payment of premiums on nonassessable life, health, or accident insurance policies and annuity contracts issued by a mutual insurance company authorized to do business in this State.

[Note — Sec. 52(a) was amended to allow political subdivisions the opportunity to engage in and transact business with authorized mutual insurance companies in same manner as with other insurance companies. Submitted by 69th Legislature (1985) and adopted in election Nov. 4, 1986.]

(b) Under legislative provision any county, any political subdivision of a county, any number of adjoining counties or any political subdivision of the State or any defined district now or hereafter to be described and defined within the State of Texas, and which may or may not include towns, villages or municipal corporations, upon a vote of a two-thirds majority of the resident property taxpayers voting thereon who are qualified electors of such district or territory, may issue bonds or otherwise lend its credit in any amount not to exceed one fourth of the assessed valuation of the real property of such district or territory, except that the total bonded indebtedness of any city or town shall never exceed the limits imposed by other provisions of this Constitution, and levy and collect taxes to pay the interest thereon and provide a sinking fund for the redemption thereof, as the Legislature may authorize, and in such manner as it may authorize the same, for the following purposes, to wit:

(1) The improvement of rivers, creeks and streams to prevent overflows and to permit of navigation thereof or irrigation thereof, or in aid of such purposes.

(2) The construction and maintenance of pools, lakes, reservoirs, dams, canals and waterways for the purposes of irrigation, drainage or navigation, or in aid thereof.

(3) The construction, maintenance and operation of macadamized, graveled or paved roads and turnpikes or in aid thereof.

(c) Notwithstanding the provisions of Subsection (b) of this section, bonds may be issued by any county in an amount not to exceed one fourth of the assessed valuation of the real property in the county, for the construction, maintenance, and operation of macadamized, graveled, or paved roads and turnpikes, or in aid thereof, upon a vote of a majority of the resident property taxpayers voting thereon who are qualified electors of the county, and without the necessity of further or amendatory legislation. The county may levy and collect taxes to pay the interest on the bonds as it becomes due and to provide a sinking fund for redemption of the bonds.

(d) Any defined district created under this section that is authorized to issue bonds or otherwise lend its credit for the purposes stated in Subdivisions (1) and (2) of Subsection (b) of this section may engage in fire-fighting activities and may issue bonds or otherwise lend its credit for fire-fighting purposes as provided by law and this constitution.

(e) A county, city, town, or other political corporation or subdivision of the state may invest its funds as authorized by law.

[Note — Sec. 52 of Art. III has been amended four times: (1) To authorize formation of districts for issuance of bonds for leveeing, drainage, irrigation, highway construction and other public improvements. Submitted by 28th Legislature (1903), adopted in election, Nov. 8, 1904, and proclaimed Dec. 29, 1904. (2) To permit any county, on vote of a majority of qualified property taxpaying electors, to issue road bonds in an amount not exceeding one-fourth of assessed valuation of the real property in the county. Submitted by 61st Legislature (1969) and adopted in election Nov. 3, 1970. (3) Subsection (d) was added to authorize certain districts to engage in fire-fighting activities and to issue bonds or otherwise lend their credit for fire-fighting purposes. (See also Subsection (f) of Sec. 59, Art. XVI.) Submitted by 65th Legislature (1977) and adopted in election Nov. 7, 1978. (4) Subsection (e) was added to authorize local governments to invest their funds as authorized by law. (See related amendment at Art. XI, Sec. 3.) Proposed by 71st Legislature (1989) and adopted in election Nov. 7, 1989.]

Sec. 52-a. Notwithstanding any other provision of this constitution, the legislature may provide for the creation of programs and the making of loans and grants of public money, other than money otherwise dedicated by this constitution to use for a different purpose, for the public purposes of development and diversification of the economy of the state, the elimination of unemployment or underemployment in the state, the stimulation of agricultural innovation, the fostering of the growth of enterprises based on agriculture, or the development or expansion of transportation or commerce in the state. Any bonds or other obligations of a county, municipality, or other political subdivi-

Article III (Cont'd.)

sion of the state that are issued for the purpose of making loans or grants in connection with a program authorized by the legislature under this section and that are payable from ad valorem taxes must be approved by a vote of the majority of the registered voters of the county, municipality, or political subdivision voting on the issue. An enabling law enacted by the legislature in anticipation of the adoption of this amendment is not void because of its anticipatory character.

[Note — Sec. 52-a of Art. III was added to authorize the Legislature to provide assistance to encourage economic development in the state. Submitted by 70th Legislature (1987) and adopted in election Nov. 3, 1987.]

Sec. 52-b. **Legislature Prohibited to Lend Credit of State in Building or Maintaining Toll Roads and Turnpikes; Exception for Texas Turnpike Authority** — The Legislature shall have no power or authority to in any manner lend the credit of the State or grant any public money to, or assume any indebtedness, present or future, bonded or otherwise, of any individual, person, firm, partnership, association, corporation, public corporation, public agency, or political subdivision of the State, or anyone else, which is now or hereafter authorized to construct, maintain or operate toll roads and turnpikes within this State except that the legislature may authorize the Texas Department of Transportation to expend money, from any source available, for the costs of turnpikes, toll roads, or toll bridges of the Texas Turnpike Authority, or successor agency, provided that any monies expended out of the state highway fund, shall be repaid to the fund from tolls or other turnpike revenue.

[Note — Sec. 52-b of Art. III was added to prohibit Legislature from lending credit of State in building or maintaining toll roads and turnpikes. Submitted by 53rd Legislature (1953) and adopted in election Nov. 2, 1954. It was amended to allow the state to aid turnpikes, toll roads or toll bridges of the Texas Turnpike Authority, provided the money is repaid. Submitted by 72nd Legislature (1991) and adopted in election Nov. 5, 1991.]

Sec. 52-d. **Harris County Road Districts** — Upon the vote of a majority of the resident qualified electors owning rendered taxable property therein so authorizing, a county or road district may collect an annual tax for a period not exceeding five (5) years to create a fund for constructing lasting and permanent roads and bridges or both. No contract involving the expenditure of any of such fund shall be valid unless, when it is made, money shall be on hand in such fund.

At such election, the Commissioners Court shall submit for adoption a road plan and designate the amount of special tax to be levied; the number of years said tax is to be levied; the location, description and character of the roads and bridges; and the estimated cost thereof. The funds raised by such taxes shall not be used for purposes other than those specified in the plan submitted to the voters. Elections may be held from time to time to extend or discontinue said plan or to increase or diminish said tax. The Legislature shall enact laws prescribing the procedure hereunder.

The provisions of this section shall apply only to Harris County and road districts therein.

[Note — Sec. 52-d of Art. III was added to give special local tax powers to Harris County. Proposed by 45th Legislature (1937) and adopted in election Aug. 23, 1937.]

[Note that Sec. 52-c has never existed. The 53rd Legislature (1953) submitted an amendment to be numbered 52-b, and same was adopted in election Nov. 2, 1954. Obviously, the designation, "Sec. 52-d," in Senate Joint Resolution No. 16 of the 45th Legislature resulted from confusion of a new section number with the sequence of paragraphs "a, b and c" under section 52 immediately above. Some published texts of the State Constitution give this as "Paragraph d," under Sec. 52, as it might properly have been designated, but SJR No. 16 of the 53rd Legislature definitely gave it as a separate "Sec. 52-d." Thus 52-b was added in 1954; Sec. 52-a was not added until 1987; and 52-c is still missing.]

Sec. 52-e. **Dallas County Road Bonds** — Bonds to be issued by Dallas County under Sec. 52 of Art. III of this Constitution for the construction, maintenance and operation of macadamized, graveled or paved roads and turnpikes, or in aid thereof, may, without the necessity of further or amendatory legislation, be issued upon a vote of a majority of the resident property taxpayers voting thereon who are qualified electors of said county, and bonds heretofore or hereafter issued under Subsections (a) and (b) of said Sec. 52 shall not be included in determining the debt limit prescribed in said Section.

[Note — Sec. 52-e of Art. III was added to allow Dallas County to issue bonds for construction of roads upon majority vote of resident property taxpayers. Submitted by 60th Legislature (1967) and adopted in election Nov. 5, 1968.]

[Note — As in the case of Sec. 52-d above, this section might more properly have been designated as paragraph "e" under Sec. 52, but the 60th Legislature designated it as Sec. 52-e. As a result, there are two Sections 52-e, since they also designated the section below, relating to payment of medical expenses for county and precinct officials, as Sec. 52-e.]

Sec. 52-e. **Payment of Medical Expenses for County and Pre-** cinct Officials — Each county in the State of Texas is hereby authorized to pay all medical expenses, all doctor bills and all hospital bills for Sheriffs, Deputy Sheriffs, Constables, Deputy Constables and other county and precinct law enforcement officials who are injured in the course of their official duties; providing that while said Sheriff, Deputy Sheriff, Constable, Deputy Constable or other county or precinct law enforcement official is hospitalized or incapacitated that the county shall continue to pay his maximum salary; providing, however, that said payment of salary shall cease on the expiration of the term of office to which such official was elected or appointed. Provided, however, that no provision contained herein shall be construed to amend, modify, repeal or nullify Art. XVI, Sec. 31, of the Constitution of the State of Texas.

[Note — Sec. 52-e of Art. III was added to authorize counties to pay medical bills for county and precinct law enforcement officials who are injured in line of duty; and the county shall continue to pay maximum salary for duration of term to which they were elected or appointed. Submitted by 60th Legislature (1967) and adopted in election Nov. 11, 1967.]

Sec. 52-f. **Private Roads in County** — A county with a population of 5,000 or less, according to the most recent federal census, may construct and maintain private roads if it imposes a reasonable charge for the work. The Legislature by general law may limit this authority. Revenue received from private road work may be used only for the construction, including right-of-way acquisition, or maintenance of public roads.

[Note — Sec. 52-f of Art. III was added to authorize counties with population of 5,000 or less to perform private road work. Submitted by 66th Legislature (1979) and adopted in election Nov. 4, 1980.]

Sec. 53. **No Extra Compensation by Municipal Corporations** — The Legislature shall have no power to grant or to authorize any county or municipal authority to grant any extra compensation, fee or allowance to a public officer, agent, servant or contractor, after service has been rendered or a contract has been entered into and performed in whole or in part; nor pay, nor authorize the payment of any claim created against any county or municipality of the State under any agreement or contract made without authority of law.

Sec. 54. **Liens on Railroads** — The Legislature shall have no power to release or alienate any lien held by the State upon any railroad, or in anywise change the tenor or meaning or pass any act explanatory thereof; but the same shall be enforced in accordance with the original terms upon which it was acquired.

Sec. 55. **Power of Legislature to Release Debt** — The Legislature shall have no power to release or extinguish, or to authorize the releasing or extinguishing, in whole or in part, the indebtedness, liability or obligation of any corporation or individual, to this State or to any county or defined subdivision thereof, or other municipal corporation therein, except delinquent taxes which have been due for a period of at least ten years.

[Note — Sec. 55 of Art. III was amended to add the clause "except delinquent taxes which have been due for a period of at least ten years." Submitted by 42nd Legislature (1931), adopted in election Nov. 8, 1932, and proclaimed Jan. 9, 1933.]

Sec. 56. **Special Laws; Limitations** — The Legislature shall not, except as otherwise provided in this Constitution, pass any local or special law authorizing:

The creation, extension or impairing of liens;

Regulating the affairs of counties, cities, towns, wards or school districts;

Changing the names of persons or places;

Changing the venue in civil or criminal cases;

Authorizing the laying out, opening, altering or maintaining of roads, highways, streets or alleys;

Relating to ferries or bridges, or incorporating ferry or bridge companies, except for the erection of bridges crossing streams which form boundaries between this and any other State;

Vacating roads, town plats, streets or alleys;

Relating to cemeteries, graveyards or public grounds not of the states;

Authorizing the adoption or legitimation of children;

Locating or changing county seats;

Incorporating cities, towns or villages, or changing their charter;

For the opening and conducting of election or fixing or changing the places of voting;

Granting divorces;

Creating offices, or prescribing the powers and duties of officers in counties, cities, towns, election or school districts;

Changing the law of descent or succession;

Regulating the practice or jurisdiction of, or changing the rules of evidence in any judicial proceeding or inquiry before courts, justices of the peace, sheriffs, commissioners, arbitrators or other tribunals, or providing or changing methods for the collection of debts or the enforcing of judgments or prescribing the effect of judicial sales of real estate;

Regulating the fees or extending the powers and duties of aldermen, justices of the peace, magistrates or constables;

Regulating the management of public schools, the building or repairing of schoolhouses, and the raising of money for such purposes;

Fixing the rate of interest;

Affecting the estates of minors or persons under disability;

Article III (Cont'd.)

Remitting fines, penalties and forfeitures and refunding moneys legally paid into the Treasury;

Exempting property from taxation;

Regulating labor, trade, mining and manufacturing;

Declaring any named person of age;

Extending the time for the assessment or collection of taxes, or otherwise relieving any assessor or collector of taxes from the due performance of his official duties or his securities from liability;

Giving effect to informal or invalid wills or deeds;

Summoning or impaneling grand or petit juries;

For limitation of civil or criminal actions;

For incorporating railroads or other works of internal improvements;

And in all other cases where a general law can be made applicable no local or special law shall be enacted; provided, that nothing herein contained shall be construed to prohibit the Legislature from passing special laws for the preservation of the game and fish of this State in certain localities.

Sec. 57. **Notice of Local or Special Laws** — No local or special law shall be passed unless notice of the intention to apply therefor shall have been published in the locality where the matter or thing to be affected may be situated, which notice shall state the substance of the contemplated law, and shall be published at least thirty days prior to the introduction into the Legislature of such bill and in the manner to be provided by law. The evidence of such notice having been published shall be exhibited in the Legislature before such act shall be passed.

Sec. 58. **Sessions to Be Held at Austin, Seat of Government** — The Legislature shall hold its sessions at the City of Austin, which is hereby declared to be the seat of government.

Sec. 59. **Workmen's Compensation for State Employees** — The Legislature shall have power to pass such laws as may be necessary to provide for workmen's compensation insurance for such State employees, as in its judgment is necessary or required; and to provide for the payment of all costs, charges and premiums on such policies of insurance; providing, the state shall never be required to purchase insurance for any employee.

[Note — Sec. 59 of Art. III was added to provide for worker's compensation for state employees. Proposed by 44th Legislature and adopted in election, Nov. 3, 1936.]

Sec. 60. **Workmen's Compensation Insurance for County Employees** — The Legislature shall have the power to pass such laws as may be necessary to enable all counties and other political subdivisions of this State to provide Workmen's Compensation insurance, including the right to provide its own insurance risk, for all employees of the county or political subdivision as in its judgment is necessary or required; and the Legislature shall provide suitable laws for the administration of such insurance in the counties or political subdivisions of this State and for the payment of the costs, charges and premiums on such policies of insurance and the benefits to be paid thereunder.

[Note — Sec. 60 of Art. III was added to provide workmen's compensation insurance for county employees. Submitted by 50th Legislature (1947) and adopted in election Nov. 2, 1948. It was further amended to include all political subdivisions. Submitted by 57th Legislature (1961) and adopted in election Nov. 6, 1962.]

Sec. 61. The Legislature shall have the power to enact laws to enable cities, towns and villages of this state to provide Workmen's Compensation Insurance, including the right to provide their own insurance risk for all employees; and the Legislature shall provide suitable laws for the administration of such insurance in the said municipalities and for payment of the costs, charges, and premiums on policies of insurance and the benefits to be paid thereunder.

[Note — Sec. 61 of Art. III was added to provide workmen's compensation insurance for municipal employees. Submitted by 52nd Legislature and adopted in election Nov. 4, 1952. See also note below regarding second Sec. 61.]

Sec. 61. **Salary of Governor, Attorney General, Comptroller of Public Accounts, Treasurer, Commissioner of General Land Office and Secretary of State** — The Legislature shall not fix the salary of the Governor, Attorney General, Comptroller of Public Accounts, Commissioner of the General Land Office or Secretary of State at a sum less than that fixed for such officials in the Constitution on Jan. 1, 1953.

[Note — Sec. 61 of Art. III was added to fix the salaries of the aforementioned officials. Submitted by 53rd Legislature (1953) and adopted in election Nov. 2, 1954. Please note that there was already a "Section 61" having to do with worker's compensation insurance for municipal employees, as noted above. Unless corrected by the Legislature, they shall both continue to bear that designation. This Section 61 was amended to eliminate reference to the office of state treasurer after that office was eliminated by constitutional amendment. Submitted by 74th Legislature (1995) and adopted in election Nov. 7, 1995.]

Sec. 62. **Continuity of State and Local Governmental Operations** — (a) The Legislature, in order to insure continuity of state and local governmental operations in periods of emergency resulting from disasters caused by enemy attack, shall have the power and the immediate duty to provide for prompt and temporary succession to the powers and duties of public offices, of whatever nature and whether filled by election or appointment, the incumbents of which may become unavailable for carrying on the powers and duties of such offices. Provided, however, that Article I of the Constitution of Texas, known as the "Bill of Rights" shall not be in any manner affected, amended, impaired, suspended, repealed or suspended hereby.

(b) When such a period of emergency or the immediate threat of enemy attack exists, the Legislature may suspend procedural rules imposed by this Constitution that relate to:

(1) the order of business of the Legislature;

(2) the percentage of each house of the Legislature necessary to constitute a quorum;

(3) the requirement that a bill must be read on three days in each house before it has the force of law;

(4) the requirement that a bill must be referred to and reported from committee before its consideration; and

(5) the date on which laws passed by the Legislature take effect.

(c) When such a period of emergency or the immediate threat of enemy attack exists, the Governor, after consulting with the Lieutenant Governor and the Speaker of the House of Representatives, may suspend the constitutional requirement that the Legislature hold its sessions in Austin, the seat of government. When this requirement has been suspended, the Governor shall determine a place other than Austin at which the Legislature will hold its sessions during such period of emergency or immediate threat of enemy attack. The Governor shall notify the Lieutenant Governor and the Speaker of the House of Representatives of the place and time at which the Legislature will meet. The Governor may take security precautions, consistent with the state of emergency, in determining the extent to which that information may be released.

(d) To suspend the constitutional rules specified by Subsection (b) of this section, the Governor must issue a proclamation and the House of Representatives and the Senate must concur in the proclamation as provided by this section.

(e) The Governor's proclamation must declare that a period of emergency resulting from disasters caused by enemy attack exists, or that the immediate threat of enemy attack exists, and that suspension of constitutional rules relating to legislative procedure is necessary to assure continuity of state government. The proclamation must specify the period, not to exceed two years, during which the constitutional rules specified by Subsection (b) of this section are suspended.

(f) The House of Representatives and the Senate, by concurrent resolution approved by the majority of the members present, must concur in the Governor's proclamation. A resolution of the House of Representatives and the Senate concurring in the Governor's proclamation suspends the constitutional rules specified by Subsection (b) of this section for the period of time specified by the Governor's proclamation.

(g) The constitutional rules specified by Subsection (b) of this section may not be suspended for more than two years under a single proclamation. A suspension may be renewed, however, if the Governor issues another proclamation as provided by Subsection (e) of this section and the House of Representatives and the Senate, by concurrent resolution, concur in that proclamation.

[Note — Sec. 62 of Art. III was added to provide for temporary succession to powers and duties of public offices in periods of emergency resulting from disaster caused by enemy attack. Submitted by 57th Legislature (1961) and adopted in election Nov. 6, 1962. It was amended to authorize suspension of certain constitutional rules relating to legislative procedure during disasters or during immediate threat of enemy attack. Submitted by 68th Legislature (1983) and adopted in election Nov. 8, 1983.]

Sec. 63. **Consolidation of Governmental Functions in Counties of 1,200,000 or More Inhabitants** — (1) The Legislature may by statute provide for the consolidation of some functions of government of any one or more political subdivisions comprising or located within any county in this state having one million, two hundred thousand (1,200,000) or more inhabitants. Any such statute shall require an election to be held within the political subdivisions affected thereby with approval by a majority of the voters in each of these political subdivisions, under such terms and conditions as the Legislature may require.

(2) The county government, or any political subdivision(s) comprising or located therein, may contract one with another for the performance of governmental functions required or authorized by this Constitution or the laws of this state, under such terms and conditions as the Legislature may prescribe. The term "governmental functions," as it relates to counties, includes all duties, activities and operations of statewide importance in which the county acts for the state, as well as of local importance, whether required or authorized by this Constitution or the laws of this state.

[Note — Sec. 63 of Art. III was added to provide for consolidation of governmental functions between political subdivisions within counties of 1,200,000 or more inhabitants. Submitted by 59th Legislature (1965) and adopted in election Nov. 8, 1966.]

Sec. 64. **Consolidation of Governmental Offices and Functions in Counties** — (a) The Legislature may by special statute provide for consolidation of governmental offices and functions of government of any one or more political subdivisions comprising or located within any county. Any such statute shall require an election

Article III (Cont'd.); Article IV

to be held within the political subdivisions affected thereby with approval by a majority of the voters in each of these subdivisions, under such terms and conditions as the Legislature may require.

(b) The county government, or any political subdivision(s) comprising or located therein, may contract one with another for the performance of governmental functions required or authorized by this Constitution or the Laws of this State, under such terms and conditions as the Legislature may prescribe. No person acting under a contract made pursuant to this Subsection (b) shall be deemed to hold more than one office of honor, trust or profit or more than one civil office of emolument. The term "governmental functions," as it relates to counties, includes all duties, activities and operations of statewide importance in which the county acts for the State, as well as of local importance, whether required or authorized by this Constitution or the Laws of this State.

[Note — Sec. 64 of Art. III was added to provide for consolidation of governmental functions in El Paso and Tarrant Counties. Submitted by 60th Legislature (1967) and adopted in election Nov. 5, 1968. It was amended to provide for consolidation of governmental functions in any county. Submitted by 61st Legislature (1969) and adopted in election Nov. 3, 1970.]

Sec. 65. **Interest Rate on State Bonds** — (a) Wherever the Constitution authorizes an agency, instrumentality, or subdivision of the State to issue bonds and specifies the maximum rate of interest which may be paid on such bonds issued pursuant to such constitutional authority, such bonds may bear interest at rates not to exceed a weighted average annual interest rate of 12 percent unless otherwise provided by Subsection (b) of this section. All Constitutional provisions specifically setting rates in conflict with this provision are hereby repealed.

(b) Bonds issued by the Veterans' Land Board after the effective date of this subsection bear interest at a rate or rates determined by the board, but the rate or rates may not exceed a net effective interest rate of 10 percent per year unless otherwise provided by law. A statute that is in effect on the effective date of this subsection and that sets as a maximum interest rate payable on bonds issued by the Veterans' Land Board a rate different from the maximum rate provided by this subsection is ineffective unless reenacted by the Legislature after that date.

[Note — Sec. 65 of Art. III was added to set the interest rate on state bonds not to exceed a weighted average annual interest of 6 percent. Submitted by 62nd Legislature (1971) and adopted in election Nov. 7, 1972. The interest rate was raised to 12 percent in an amendment submitted by a special session of 67th Legislature (1982) and adopted in election Nov. 2, 1982.]

Article IV — Executive Department

Sec. 1. **Officers of Executive Department** — The executive department of the State shall consist of a Governor, who shall be the chief executive officer of the State, a Lieutenant Governor, Secretary of State, Comptroller of Public Accounts, Commissioner of the General Land Office and Attorney General.

[Note — Sec. 1 of Art. IV was amended to eliminate reference to the office of state treasurer after that office was eliminated by constitutional amendment. Submitted by 74th Legislature (1995) and adopted in election Nov. 7, 1995.]

Sec. 2. **Election of Executive Officers** — All the above officers of the executive department (except Secretary of State) shall be elected by the qualified voters of the State at the time and places of election for members of the Legislature.

Sec. 3. **Election Results; Ties; Contests** — The returns of every election for said executive officers, until otherwise provided by law, shall be made out, sealed up and transmitted by the returning officers prescribed by law, to the seat of government, directed to the Secretary of State, who shall deliver the same to the Speaker of the House of Representatives as soon as the Speaker shall be chosen, and the said Speaker shall, during the first week of the session of the Legislature, open and publish them in the presence of both houses of the Legislature. The person voted for at said election having the highest number of votes for each of said offices, respectively, and being constitutionally eligible, shall be declared by the Speaker, under sanction of the Legislature, to be elected to said office. But if two or more persons shall have the highest and an equal number of votes for either of said offices, one of them shall be immediately chosen to such office by a joint vote of both houses of the Legislature. Contested elections for either of said offices shall be determined by both houses of the Legislature in joint session.

Sec. 3-a. **Gubernatorial Succession** — If, at the time the Legislature shall canvass the election returns for the offices of Governor and Lieutenant Governor, the person receiving the highest number of votes for the office of Governor, as declared by the Speaker, has died, then the person having the highest number of votes for the office of Lieutenant Governor shall act as Governor until after the next general election. It is further provided that in the event the person with the highest number of votes for the Office of Governor as declared by the Speaker, shall become disabled, or fail to qualify, then the Lieutenant Governor shall act as Governor until a person has qualified for the office of Governor or until after the next general election. Any succession to the governorship not otherwise provided for

in this Constitution may be provided for by law; provided, however, that any person succeeding to the office of Governor shall be qualified as otherwise provided in this Constitution, and shall, during the entire term to which he may succeed, be under all the restrictions and inhibitions imposed in this Constitution on the Governor.

[Note — Sec. 3-a was added to provide for gubernatorial succession. Submitted by 50th Legislature (1947) and adopted in election, Nov. 2, 1948.]

Sec. 4. **Governor, When Installed; Term; Qualifications** — The Governor elected at the general election in 1974, and thereafter, shall be installed on the first Tuesday after the organization of the Legislature, or as soon thereafter as practicable, and shall hold his office for the term of four years, or until his successor shall be duly installed. He shall be at least thirty years of age, a citizen of the United States, and shall have resided in this State at least five years immediately preceding his election.

[Note — Sec. 4 of Art. IV was amended to raise the term of office of Governor to four years. Submitted by 62nd Legislature (1971) and adopted in election Nov. 7, 1972.]

Sec. 5. **Governor's Salary and Mansion** — The Governor shall, at stated times, receive as compensation for his service an annual salary in an amount to be fixed by the Legislature, and shall have the use and occupation of the Governor's Mansion, fixtures and furniture.

[Note — Sec. 5 of Art. IV was first amended to raise Governor's salary from $4,000 to $12,000. Submitted by 44th Legislature (1935) and adopted in election Nov. 3, 1936. It was further amended to give Legislature authority to fix salary. Submitted by 53rd Legislature (1953) and adopted in election Nov. 2, 1954.]

Sec. 6. **Governor to Hold No Other Office, Etc.** — During the time he holds the office of Governor he shall not hold any other office, civil, military or corporate; nor shall he practice any profession or receive compensation, reward, fee or the promise thereof for the same; nor receive any salary, reward or compensation or the promise thereof from any person or corporation for any service rendered or performed during the time he is Governor or to be thereafter rendered or performed.

Sec. 7. **Commander in Chief; May Call Out Militia** — He shall be commander in chief of the military forces of the State, except when they are called into actual service of the United States. He shall have power to call forth the militia to execute the laws of the State, to suppress insurrections, repel invasions and protect the frontier from hostile incursions by Indians or other predatory bands.

Sec. 8. **Governor May Convene Legislature** — The Governor may, on extraordinary occasions, convene the Legislature at the seat of government or at a different place in case that should be in possession of the public enemy, or in case of the prevalence of disease threat. His proclamation therefor shall state specifically the purpose for which the Legislature is convened.

Sec. 9. **Governor's Message; to Account for Moneys; Present Estimates, Etc.** — The Governor shall, at the commencement of each session of the Legislature, and at the close of his term of office, give to the Legislature information, by message, of the condition of the State; and he shall recommend to the Legislature such measures as he may deem expedient. He shall account to the Legislature for all public moneys received and paid out by him from any funds subject to his order, with vouchers; and shall accompany his message with a statement of the same. And at the commencement of each regular session he shall present estimates of the amount of money required to be raised by taxation for all purposes.

Sec. 10. **Governor Shall Cause the Laws to Be Executed; Intercourse With Other States** — He shall cause the laws to be faithfully executed and shall conduct, in person, or in such manner as shall be prescribed by law, all intercourse and business of the State with other States and with the United States.

Sec. 11. **Board of Pardons and Paroles: Advisory Authority to Governor in Granting Reprieves, Paroles, Pardons, Etc.** — (a) The Legislature shall by law establish a Board of Pardons and Paroles and shall require it to keep record of its actions and the reasons for its actions. The Legislature shall have authority to enact parole laws and laws that require or permit courts to inform juries about the effect of good conduct time and eligibility for parole or mandatory supervision on the period of incarceration served by a defendant convicted of a criminal offense.

(b) In all criminal cases, except treason and impeachment the Governor shall have power, after conviction, on the written signed recommendation and advice of the Board of Pardons and Paroles, or a majority thereof, to grant reprieves and commutations of punishment and pardons; and under such rules as the Legislature may prescribe, and upon the written recommendation and advice of a majority of the Board of Pardons and Paroles, he shall have the power to remit fines and forfeitures. The Governor shall have the power to grant one reprieve in any capital case for a period not to exceed thirty (30) days; and he shall have the power to revoke conditional pardons. With the advice and consent of the Legislature, he may grant reprieves, commutations of punishment and pardons in cases of treason.

[Note—Sec. 11 of Art. IV was amended to establish the stated procedure for granting pardons and paroles, which was originally vested exclusively in the Governor's office. Submitted by 44th Legislature (1935) and adopted in election Nov. 3, 1936. It was again amended to make the Board of Pardons and Paroles a statutory agency and to

Article IV (Cont'd.)

give the board power to revoke paroles. Submitted by 68th Legislature (1983) and adopted in election Nov. 8, 1983. It was again amended to authorize jury instructions on good time and eligibility for parole and mandatory supervision. Proposed by 71st Legislature (1989) and adopted in election Nov. 7, 1989.]

Sec. 11A. **Suspension of Sentences; Probation** — The courts of the State of Texas having original jurisdiction of criminal actions shall have the power, after conviction, to suspend the imposition or execution of sentence and to place the defendant upon probation and to reimpose such sentence, under such conditions as the Legislature may prescribe.

[Note — Sec. 11A of Art. IV was added to provide for suspended sentences. Submitted by 44th Legislature (1935) and adopted in election Aug. 24, 1935.]

Sec. 11B. (a) The legislature by law may organize and combine into one or more agencies all agencies of the state that:

(1) have authority over the confinement or supervision of persons convicted of criminal offenses;

(2) set standards or distribute state funds to political subdivisions that have authority over the confinement or supervision of persons convicted of criminal offenses; or

(3) gather information about the administration of criminal justice.

(b) The legislature by law may authorize the appointment of members of more than one department of government to serve on the governing body.

[Note — Sec. 11B of Art. IV was added to authorize the legislature to organize and combine various state agencies that perform criminal justice functions. Proposed by 71st Legislature (1989) and adopted in election Nov. 7, 1989.]

Sec. 12. **Governor to Fill Vacancies in State and District Offices** — (a) All vacancies in State or district offices, except members of the Legislature, shall be filled, unless otherwise provided by law, by appointment of the Governor.

(b) An appointment of the Governor made during a session of the Senate shall be with the advice and consent of two thirds of the Senate present.

(c) In accordance with this section, the Senate may give its advice and consent on an appointment of the Governor made during a recess of the Senate. To be confirmed, the appointment must be with the advice and consent of two-thirds of the Senate present. If an appointment of the Governor is made during the recess of the Senate, the Governor shall nominate the appointee, or some other person to fill the vacancy, to the Senate during the first ten days of its next session following the appointment. If the Senate does not confirm a person under this subsection, the Governor shall nominate in accordance with this section the recess appointee or another person to fill the vacancy during the first ten days of each subsequent session of the Senate until a confirmation occurs. If the Governor does not nominate a person to the Senate during the first ten days of a session of the Senate as required by this subsection, the Senate at that session may consider the recess appointee as if the Governor had nominated the appointee.

(d) If the Senate, at any special session, does not take final action to confirm or reject a previously unconfirmed recess appointee or another person nominated to fill the vacancy for which the appointment was made:

(1) the Governor after the session may appoint another person to fill the vacancy; and

(2) the appointee, if otherwise qualified and if not removed as provided by law, is entitled to continue in office until the earlier of the following occurs:

(A) the Senate rejects the appointee at a subsequent session; or

(B) the Governor appoints another person to fill the vacancy under Subdivision (1) of this subsection.

(e) If the Senate, at a regular session, does not take final action to confirm or reject a previously unconfirmed recess appointee or another person nominated to fill the vacancy for which the appointment was made, the appointee or other person, as appropriate, is considered to be rejected by the Senate when the Senate session ends.

(f) If an appointee is rejected, the office shall immediately become vacant, and the Governor shall, without delay, make further nominations until a confirmation takes place. If a person has been rejected by the Senate to fill a vacancy, the Governor may not appoint the person to fill the vacancy or, during the term of the vacancy for which the person was rejected, to fill another vacancy in the same office or on the same board, commission, or other body.

(g) Appointments to vacancies in offices elective by the people shall only continue until the next general election.

(h) The Legislature by general law may limit the term to be served by a person appointed by the Governor to fill a vacancy in a state or district office to a period that ends before the vacant term otherwise expires or, for an elective office, before the next election at which the vacancy is to be filled. If the appointment is made on or after November 1 preceding the general election for the succeeding term of the office of Governor and the Governor is not elected at that election for the succeeding term.

(i) For purposes of this section, the expiration of a term of office or the creation of a new office constitutes a vacancy.

[Note — Sec. 12(a) was changed and Sec. 12(b) was added to Art. IV to limit the authority of a governor to fill vacancies in state and district offices if the governor is not re-elected. Submitted by 70th Legislature (1987) and adopted in election Nov. 3, 1987. It was further amended to clarify the authority of the Senate to consider certain nominees to state and district offices and to provide to filling vacancies in those offices. Submitted by 71st Legislature (1990) and adopted in election Nov. 6, 1990.]

Sec. 13. **Where Governor Shall Reside** — During the session of the Legislature the Governor shall reside where its sessions are held and at all other times at the seat of government, except when, by act of the Legislature, he may be required or authorized to reside elsewhere.

Sec. 14. **Approval of Bills; Veto Bill Not Returned to Become a Law** — Every bill which shall have passed both houses of the Legislature shall be presented to the Governor for his approval. If he approve, he shall sign it, but if he disapprove it, he shall return it with his objections to the house in which it originated, which house shall enter the objections at large upon its journal, and proceed to reconsider it. If, after such reconsideration, two thirds of the members present agree to pass the bill, it shall be sent, with the objections, to the other house, by which likewise it shall be reconsidered, and if approved by two thirds of the members of that house, it shall become a law; but in such cases the votes of both houses shall be determined by yeas and nays; and the names of the members voting for and against the bill shall be entered on the journal of each house, respectively. If any bill shall not be returned by the Governor with his objections within ten days (Sundays excepted) after it shall have been presented to him, the same shall be a law in like manner as if he had signed it, unless the Legislature, by its adjournment, prevent its return, in which case it shall be a law, unless he shall file the same, with his objections, in the office of the Secretary of State and give notice thereof by public proclamation within twenty days after such adjournment. If any bill presented to the Governor contains several items of appropriation he may object to one or more of such items, and approve the other portion of the bill. In such case he shall append to the bill, at the time of signing it, a statement of the items to which he objects, and no item so objected to shall take effect. If the Legislature be in session he shall transmit to the house in which the bill originated a copy of such statement, and the items objected to shall be separately considered. If, on reconsideration, one or more of such items be approved by two thirds of the members present, of each house, the same shall be part of the law, notwithstanding the objections of the Governor. If any such bill containing several items of appropriation not having been presented to the Governor ten days (Sundays excepted) prior to adjournment, be in the hands of the Governor at the time of adjournment, he shall have twenty days from such adjournment within which to file objections to any items thereof and make proclamation of the same, and such item or items shall not take effect.

Sec. 15. **What to Be Presented for Approval** — Every order, resolution or vote to which the concurrence of both houses of the Legislature may be necessary except on questions of adjournment shall be presented to the Governor, and before it shall take effect shall be approved by him; or, being disapproved, shall be repassed by both houses, and all the rules, provisions and limitations shall apply thereto as prescribed in the last preceding section in the case of a bill.

Sec. 16. **Lieutenant Governor; Election; Term; Powers and Duties** — There shall also be a Lieutenant Governor, who shall be chosen at every election for Governor by the same electors, in the same manner, continue in office for the same time and possess the same qualifications. The electors shall distinguish for whom they vote as Governor and for whom as Lieutenant Governor. The Lieutenant Governor shall, by virtue of his office, be President of the Senate and shall have, when in committee of the whole, a right to debate, and vote on all questions; and when the Senate is equally divided, to give the casting vote. In case of the death, resignation, removal from office, inability or refusal of the Governor to serve, or of his impeachment or absence from the State, the Lieutenant Governor shall exercise the powers and authority appertaining to the office of Governor until another be chosen at the periodical election, and be duly qualified; or until the Governor, impeached, absent or disabled, shall be acquitted, return or his disability be removed.

Sec. 17. **Vacancy in Office; Compensation** — (a) If, during the vacancy in the office of Governor, the Lieutenant Governor should die, resign, refuse to serve or be removed from office or be unable to serve; or if he shall be impeached or absent from the State, the President of the Senate, for the time being, shall, in like manner, administer the government until he shall be superseded by a Governor or Lieutenant Governor.

(b) The Lieutenant Governor shall, while he acts as President of the Senate, receive for his services the same compensation and mileage which shall be allowed to the members of the Senate, and no more unless the Texas Ethics Commission recommends and the voters approve a higher salary in which case the salary is that amount; and during the time he administers the government, as Governor, he shall receive in like manner the same compensation which the Governor would have received had he been employed in the duties of his office, and no more. An increase in the emoluments of the office of Lieutenant Governor does not make a member of the Legislature ineligible to serve in the office of Lieutenant Governor.

(c) The President, for the time being, of the Senate, shall, during the time he administers the Government, receive in like manner the same compensation, which the Governor would have received had

Article IV (Cont'd.): Article V

he been employed in the duties of his office.

[Note — Section 17 Article IV was amended to authorize the Texas Ethics Commission to recommend the salary for the lieutenant governor, subject to approval by voters. Submitted by 72nd Legislature (1992) and adopted in election Nov. 5, 1991.

Sec. 18. **Succession to Governorship** — The Lieutenant Governor, or President of the Senate, succeeding to the office of Governor shall, during the entire terms to which he may succeed, be under all the restrictions and inhibitions imposed in this Constitution on the Governor.

Sec. 19. **Seal of State; Secretary of State to Keep, Etc.** — There shall be a seal of the State which shall be kept by the Secretary of State and used by him officially under the direction of the Governor. The seal of the State shall be a star of five points, encircled by olive and live oak branches, and the words "The State of Texas."

Sec. 20. **Commissions to Be Signed and Sealed** — All commissions shall be in the name and by the authority of the State of Texas, sealed with the State seal, signed by the Governor, and attested by the Secretary of State.

Sec. 21. **Secretary of State; Term; Duties; Compensation** — There shall be a Secretary of State, who shall be appointed by the Governor, by and with the advice and consent of the Senate, and who shall continue in office during the term of service of the Governor. He shall authenticate the publication of the laws and keep a fair register of all official acts and proceedings of the Governor, and shall, when required, lay the same and all papers, minutes and vouchers relative thereto, before the Legislature or either house thereof, and shall perform such other duties as may be required of him by law. He shall receive for his services an annual salary in an amount to be fixed by the Legislature.

[Note — Sec. 21 of Art. IV was amended to raise the salary of the Secretary of State from $2,000 to $6,000 a year. Submitted by 44th Legislature (1935) and adopted in election Nov. 3, 1936. Further amended to give Legislature authority to fix salary. Submitted by 53rd Legislature (1953) and adopted in election Nov. 2, 1954.]

Sec. 22. **Attorney General; Term; Duties; Residence; Salary** — The Attorney General elected at the general election in 1974, and thereafter, shall hold his office for four years and until his successor is duly qualified. He shall represent the State in all suits and pleas in the Supreme Court of the State in which the state may be a party, and shall especially inquire into the charter rights of all private corporations, and from time to time in the name of the State, take such action in the courts as may be proper and necessary to prevent any private corporation from exercising any power or demanding or collecting any species of taxes, tolls, freight or wharfage not authorized by law. He shall whenever sufficient cause exists, seek a judicial forfeiture of such charters, unless otherwise expressly directed by law, and give legal advice in writing to the Governor and other executive officers, when requested by them, and perform such other duties as may be required by law. He shall reside at the seat of government during his continuance in office. He shall receive for his services an annual salary in an amount to be fixed by the Legislature.

[Note — Sec. 22 of Art. IV was amended to raise the Attorney General's salary from $2,000 to $10,000 a year and to eliminate provisions for fees not to exceed $2,000 a year. Submitted by 44th Legislature (1935) and adopted in election Nov. 3, 1936. Further amended to give Legislature authority to fix salary. Submitted by 53rd Legislature (1953) and adopted in election Nov. 2, 1954. It was again amended to lengthen the term of office from two to four years. Submitted by 62nd Legislature (1971) and adopted in election Nov. 7, 1972.]

Sec. 23. **Comptroller and Commissioner of the General Land Office; Terms; Salaries; Residence; Fees** — The Comptroller of Public Account, the Commissioner of the General Land Office and any statutory state officer who is elected by the electorate of Texas at large, unless a term of office is otherwise specifically provided in this Constitution, shall each hold office for the term of four years and until his successor is qualified. The four-year term applies to those officers who are elected at the general election in 1974 or thereafter. Each shall receive an annual salary in an amount to be fixed by Legislature; reside at the capital of the State during his continuance in office, and perform such duties as are or may be required by law. They and the Secretary of State shall not receive to their own use any fees, costs or perquisites of office. All fees that may be payable by law for any service performed by any officer specified in this section, or in his office, shall be paid, when received into the State Treasury.

[Note — Sec. 23 of Art. IV was amended to raise salaries of three state officials mentioned from $2,500 each to $6,000 each annually. Submitted by 44th Legislature, and adopted in election Nov. 3, 1936. Further amended to give Legislature authority to fix salary. Submitted by 53rd Legislature (1953) and adopted in election Nov. 2, 1954. It was further amended to raise the term of office of the above-named officials to four years. Submitted by 62nd Legislature (1971) and adopted in election Nov. 7, 1972. It was further amended to eliminate references to the treasurer after the office of state treasurer was eliminated by constitutional amendment. Submitted by 74th Legislature (1995) and adopted in election Nov. 7, 1995.]

Sec. 24. **Officers to Account to the Governor; Duty of Governor; False Reports** — An account shall be kept by the officers of the executive department and by all officers and managers of State institutions of all moneys and choses in action received and disbursed or otherwise disposed of by them, severally, from all sources, and for every service performed; and a semi-annual report thereof shall be made to the Governor, under oath. The Governor may, at any time, require information in writing from any and all of said officers or managers upon any subject relating to the duties, conditions, management and expenses of their respective offices and institutions, which information shall be required by the Governor under oath, and the Governor may also inspect their books, accounts, vouchers and public funds; and any officer or manager who, at any time shall willfully make a false report or give false information, shall be guilty of perjury and so adjudged and punished accordingly and removed from office.

Sec. 25. **Laws for Investigation of Breaches of Trust** — The Legislature shall pass efficient laws facilitating the investigation of breaches of trust and duty by all custodians of public funds and providing for their suspensions from office on reasonable cause shown, and for the appointment of temporary incumbents of their offices during such suspensions.

Sec. 26. **Notaries Public** — (a) The Secretary of State shall appoint a convenient number of notaries public for the state who shall perform such duties as now are or may be prescribed by law. The qualifications of notaries public shall be prescribed by law.

(b) The terms of office of notaries public shall not be less than two years nor more than four years as provided by law.

[Note — Sec. 26 of Art. IV was amended to give the Secretary of State the authority, formerly held by the Governor, to appoint notaries public, and to include the stated contents of paragraphs (b) and (c). Submitted by 46th Legislature (1939) and adopted in election Nov. 5, 1940. It was further amended to establish terms of notaries public for not less than two years nor more than four years; deleted old sections (b) and (c) and provided for terms of office for notaries. Submitted by 66th Legislature (1979) and adopted in election Nov. 6, 1979.]

Article V — Judicial Department

Sec. 1. **The Several Courts; Criminal Courts** — The judicial power of this State shall be vested in one Supreme Court, in one Court of Criminal Appeals, in Courts of Appeals, in District Courts, in County Courts, in Commissioners' Courts, in courts of Justices of the Peace and in such other courts as may be provided by law.

The Legislature may establish such other courts as it may deem necessary and prescribe the jurisdiction and organization thereof and may conform the jurisdiction of the district and other inferior courts thereto.

[Note — Sec. 1 of Art. V was amended to provide for "Courts of Civil Appeals" and a "Court of Criminal Appeals" in place of the old "Court of Appeals," making minor changes. Submitted by 22nd Legislature (1891), ratified at election Aug. 11, 1891, and declared adopted Sept. 22, 1891. It was again amended to provide for a Court of Criminal Appeals with nine judges and to permit the court to sit in panels of three judges. (See also note under Sec. 4 below.) Submitted by 65th Legislature (1977) and adopted in election Nov. 8, 1977. It was further amended to change Courts of Civil Appeals to Courts of Appeal. Submitted by 66th Legislature (1979) and adopted in election Nov. 4, 1980.]

Sec. 1-a. **Retirement and Compensation of Judges** — (1) Subject to the further provisions of this section, the Legislature shall provide for the retirement and compensation of justices and judges of the Appellate Courts and District and Criminal District Courts on account of length of service, age and disability, and for their reassignment to active duty where and when needed. The office of every such justice and judge shall become needed. The office of every such justice and judge shall become vacant when the incumbent reaches the age of seventy-five (75) years or such earlier age, not less than seventy (70) years, as the Legislature may prescribe; but, in the case of an incumbent whose term of office includes the effective date of this Amendment, this provision shall not prevent him from serving the remainder of said term nor be applicable to him before his period or periods of judicial service shall have reached a total of ten (10) years.

(2) The name of the State Judicial Qualifications Commission is changed to the State Commission on Judicial Conduct. The Commission consists of eleven (11) members, to wit: (i) one (1) Justice of a Court of Appeals; (ii) one (1) District Judge; (iii) two (2) members of the State Bar, who have respectively practiced as such for over ten (10) consecutive years next preceding their selection; (iiii) four (4) citizens, at least thirty (30) years of age, not licensed to practice law nor holding any salaried public office or employment; (v) one (1) Justice of the Peace; (vi) one (1) Judge of a Municipal Court; and, (vii) one (1) Judge of a County Court at Law; provided that no person shall be or remain a member of the Commission, who does not maintain physical residence within this state, or who resides in, or holds a judgeship within or for, the same Supreme Judicial District as another member of the Commission, or who shall have ceased to retain the qualifications above specified for his respective class of membership, except that the Justice of the Peace and the Judges of a Municipal Court and/or a County Court at Law shall be selected at large without regard to whether they reside or hold a judgeship in the same Supreme Judicial District as another member of the Commission. Commissioners of classes (i), (ii), and (vii) above shall be chosen by the Supreme Court with advice and consent of the Senate, those of class (iii) by the Board of Directors of the State Bar under regulations to be

Article V (Cont'd.)

prescribed by the Supreme Court with advice and consent of the Senate, those of class (iiii) by appointment of the Governor with advice and consent of the Senate, and the commissioners of classes (v) and (vi) by appointment of the Supreme Court as provided by law, with the advice and consent of the Senate.

(3) The regular term of office of Commissioners shall be six (6) years; but the initial members of each of classes (i), (ii) and (iii) shall respectively be chosen for terms of four (4) and six (6) years, and the initial members of class (iiii) for respective terms of two (2), four (4) and six (6) years. Interim vacancies shall be filled in the same manner as vacancies due to expiration of a full term, but only for the unexpired portion of the term in question. Commissioners may succeed themselves in office only if having served less than three (3) consecutive years.

(4) Commissioners shall receive no compensation for their services as such. The Legislature shall provide for the payment of the necessary expense for the operation of the Commission.

(5) The Commission may hold its meetings, hearings and other proceedings at such times and places as it shall determine but shall meet at Austin at least once each year. It shall annually select one of its members as chairman. A quorum shall consist of six (6) members. Proceedings shall be by majority vote of those present, except that recommendations for retirement, censure, suspension, or removal of any person holding an office named in paragraph A of Subsection (6) of this section shall be by affirmative vote of at least six (6) members.

(6) A. Any justice or judge of the courts established by this Constitution or created by the Legislature as provided in Sec. 1, Art. V, of this Constitution, may, subject to the other provisions hereof, be removed from office for willful or persistent violation of rules promulgated by the Supreme Court of Texas, incompetence in performing the duties of the office, willful violation of the Code of Judicial Conduct, or willful or persistent conduct that is clearly inconsistent with the proper performance of his duties or casts public discredit upon the judiciary or administration of justice. Any person holding such office may be disciplined or censured, in lieu of removal from office, as provided by this section. Any person holding an office specified in this subsection may be suspended from office with or without pay by the Commission immediately on being indicted by a State or Federal grand jury for a felony offense or charged with a misdemeanor involving official misconduct. On the filing of a sworn complaint charging a person holding such office with willful or persistent violation of rules promulgated by the Supreme Court of Texas, incompetence in performing the duties of the office, willful violation of the Code of Judicial Conduct, or willful and persistent conduct that is clearly inconsistent with the proper performance of his duties or casts public discredit on the judiciary or on the administration of justice, the Commission, after giving the person notice and an opportunity to appear and be heard before the Commission, may recommend to the Supreme Court the suspension of such person from office. The Supreme Court, after considering the record of such appearance and the recommendation of the Commission, may suspend the person from office with or without pay, pending final disposition of the charge.

B. Any person holding an office named in paragraph A of this subsection who is eligible for retirement benefits under the laws of this state providing for judicial retirement may be involuntarily retired, and any person holding an office named in that paragraph who is not eligible for retirement benefits under such laws may be removed from office, for disability seriously interfering with the performance of his duties, which is, or is likely to become, permanent in nature.

C. The law relating to the removal, discipline, suspension, or censure of a Justice or Judge of the courts established by this Constitution or created by the Legislature as provided in this Constitution applies to a master or magistrate appointed as provided by law to serve a trial court of this State and to a retired or former Judge who continues as a judicial officer subject to an assignment to sit on a court of this State. Under the law relating to the removal of an active Justice or Judge, the Commission and the review tribunal may prohibit a retired or former Judge from holding judicial office in the future or from sitting on a court of this State by assignment.

(7) The Commission shall keep itself informed as fully as may be of circumstances relating to the misconduct or disability of particular persons holding an office named in paragraph A of Subsection (6) of this section, receive complaints or reports, formal or informal, from any source in this behalf and make such preliminary investigations as it may determine. Its orders for the attendance or testimony of witnesses or for the production of documents at any hearing or investigation shall be enforceable by contempt proceedings in the District Court or by a Master.

(8) After such investigation as it deems necessary, the Commission may in its discretion issue a private or public admonition, warning, reprimand, or requirement that the person obtain additional training or education, or if the Commission determines that the situation merits such action, it may institute formal proceedings and order a formal hearing to be held before it concerning the public censure, removal, or retirement of a person holding an office or position specified in Subsection (6) of this section, or it may in its discretion request the Supreme Court to appoint an active or retired District Judge or Justice of a Court of Appeals, or retired Judge or Justice of the Court of Criminal Appeals or the Supreme Court, as a Master to hear and take evidence in any such matter, and to report thereon to the Commission. The Master shall have all the power of a District Judge in the enforcement of orders pertaining to witnesses,

evidence, and procedure. If, after formal hearing, or after considering the record and report of a Master, the Commission finds good cause therefor, it shall issue an order of public censure or it shall recommend to a review tribunal the removal or retirement, as the case may be, of the person in question holding an office or position specified in Subsection (6) of this section and shall thereupon file with the tribunal the entire record before the Commission.

(9) A tribunal to review the Commission's recommendation for the removal or retirement of a person holding an office or position specified in Subsection (6) of this section is composed of seven (7) Justices or Judges of the Courts of Appeals who are selected by lot by the Chief Justice of the Supreme Court. Each Court of Appeals shall designate one of its members for inclusion in the list from which the selection is made. Service on the tribunal shall be considered part of the official duties of a judge, and no additional compensation may be paid for such service. The review tribunal shall review the record of the proceedings on the law and facts and in its discretion may, for good cause shown, permit the introduction of additional evidence. Within 90 days after the date on which the record is filed with the review tribunal, it shall order public censure, retirement or removal, as it finds just and proper, or wholly reject the recommendation. A Justice, Judge, Master, or Magistrate may appeal a decision of the review tribunal to the Supreme Court under the substantial evidence rule. Upon an order for involuntary retirement for disability or an order for removal, the office in question shall become vacant. The review tribunal, in an order for involuntary retirement for disability or an order for removal, may prohibit such person from holding judicial office in the future. The rights of an incumbent so retired to retirement benefits shall be the same as if his retirement had been voluntary.

(10) All papers filed with and proceedings before the Commission or a Master shall be confidential, unless otherwise provided by law, and the filing of papers with, and the giving of testimony before the Commission or a Master shall be privileged, unless otherwise provided by law. However, the Commission may issue a public statement through its executive director or its Chairman at any time during any of its proceedings under this Section when sources other than the Commission cause notoriety concerning a Judge or the Commission itself and the Commission determines that the best interests of a Judge or of the public will be served by issuing the statement.

(11) The Supreme Court shall by rule provide for the procedure before the Commission, Masters, review tribunal, and the Supreme Court. Such rule shall provide the right of discovery of evidence to a Justice, Judge, Master, or Magistrate after formal proceedings are instituted and shall afford to any person holding an office or position specified in Subsection (6) of this section, against whom a proceeding is instituted to cause his retirement or removal, due process of law for the procedure before the Commission, Masters, review tribunal, and the Supreme Court in the same manner that any person whose property rights are in jeopardy in an adjudicatory proceeding is entitled to due process of law, regardless of whether or not the interest of the person holding an office or position specified in Subsection (6) of this section in remaining in active status is considered to be a right or a privilege. Due process shall include the right to notice, counsel, hearing, confrontation of his accusers, and all such other incidents of due process as are ordinarily available in proceedings whether or not misfeasance is charged, upon proof of which a penalty may be imposed.

(12) No person holding an office specified in Subsection (6) of this section shall sit as a member of the Commission in any proceeding involving his own suspension, discipline, censure, retirement or removal.

(13) This Sec. 1-a is alternative to and cumulative of, the methods of removal of persons holding an office named in paragraph A of Subsection (6) of this section provided elsewhere in this Constitution.

(14) The Legislature may promulgate laws in furtherance of this Section that are not inconsistent with its provisions.

[Note — Sec. 1-a was added to provide for retirement and compensation of judges. Submitted by 50th Legislature (1947) and adopted in election, Nov. 2, 1948. It was amended to provide for automatic retirement of district and appellate judges for old age; to create the State Judicial Qualifications Commission and defining its functions; and empowering the Supreme Court to remove district and appellate judges for misconduct and to retire such judges in cases of disability. Submitted by 59th Legislature (1965) and adopted in election Nov. 2, 1965. It was further amended to specifically name those offices under the jurisdiction of the Commission and to broaden the Commission's duties and powers. Submitted by 61st Legislature (1969) and adopted in election Nov. 3, 1970. It was further amended to change the name of the State Judicial Qualifications Commission to the State Commission on Judicial Conduct; raise the number of members of the Commission to 11; set out specific qualifications for membership; and provide for the suspension, censure, removal or involuntary retirement of a justice under certain circumstances. Submitted by 65th Legislature (1977) and adopted in election Nov. 8, 1977. It was again amended to specify ways to discipline active judges, certain retired and former judges, and certain masters and magistrates of courts. Submitted by 68th Legislature (1983) and adopted in election Nov. 6, 1984.]

Sec. 2. Supreme Court; Quorum; Qualifications; Election; Salary; Vacancy — The Supreme Court shall consist of the Chief Justice and eight Justices, any five of whom shall constitute a quorum, and the concurrence of five shall be necessary to a decision of a case; provided, that when the business of the court may require, the

Article V (Cont'd.)

court may sit in sections as designated by the court to hear argument of causes and to consider applications for writs of error or other preliminary matters. No person shall be eligible to serve in the office of Chief Justice or Justice of the Supreme Court unless the person is licensed to practice law in this state and is, at the time of election, a citizen of the United States and of this State and has attained the age of thirty-five years and has been a practicing lawyer or a lawyer and judge of a court of record together at least ten years. Said Justices shall be elected (three of them each two years) by the qualified voters of the State at a general election; shall hold their offices six years or until their successors are elected and qualified; and shall each receive such compensation as shall be provided by law. In case of a vacancy in the office of the Chief Justice or any Justice of the Supreme Court, the Governor shall fill the vacancy until the next general election for State officers, and at such general election the vacancy for the unexpired term shall be filled by election by the qualified voters of the State. The Justices of the Supreme Court who may be in office at the time this amendment takes effect shall continue in office until the expiration of their terms of office under the present Constitution and until their successors are elected and qualified.

[Note — Sec. 2 of Art. V has been amended three times: (1) To raise salaries and make minor adjustments. Submitted by 22nd Legislature, ratified in election Aug. 11, 1891, and declared adopted Sept. 22, 1891; (2) To raise the number of justices on the Supreme Court from three to nine and make other adjustments. Submitted by 49th Legislature (1945) and adopted in election Aug. 25, 1945; and (3) To change name of Commission of Appeals and qualifications of Supreme Court Justices. Submitted by 66th Legislature (1979) and adopted in election Nov. 4, 1980.]

Sec. 3. **Jurisdiction; Terms of Court** — The Supreme Court shall exercise the judicial power of the state except as otherwise provided in this Constitution. Its jurisdiction shall be co-extensive with the limits of the State and its determinations shall be final except in criminal law matters. Its appellate jurisdiction shall be final and shall extend to all cases except in criminal law matters and as otherwise provided in this Constitution or by law. The Supreme Court and the Justices thereof shall have power to issue writs of habeas corpus, as may be prescribed by law; and under such regulations as may be prescribed by law, the said courts and the Justices thereof may issue the writs of mandamus, procedendo, certiorari and such other writs as may be necessary to enforce its jurisdiction. The Legislature may confer original jurisdiction on the Supreme Court to issue writs of quo warranto and mandamus in such cases as may be specified, except as against the Governor of the State.

The Supreme Court shall also have power, upon affidavit or otherwise as by the court may be determined to ascertain such matters of fact as may be necessary to the proper exercise of its jurisdiction.

The Supreme Court shall appoint a clerk, who shall give bond in such manner as is now or may hereafter be required by law, and he may hold his office for four years and shall be subject to removal by said court for good cause entered of record on the minutes of said court, who shall receive such compensation as the Legislature may provide.

[Note — Sec. 3 of Art. V has been amended three times: (1) To readjust jurisdiction of the Supreme Court to that of the Courts of Civil Appeals that were established by amendment of the same date, and also to consolidate the original Sec. 4, providing for a clerk of the court, with Sec. 3. Submitted by 22nd Legislature (1891), ratified Aug. 11, 1891, and proclaimed Sept. 22, 1891; (2) To eliminate provisions that the Supreme Court "sit from first Monday in October of each year until the last Saturday in June of the next year," by amendment submitted as part of the amendment that added Sec. 3-a. (See note following that section).(3) To redefine the jurisdiction of the Supreme Court. Submitted by 66th Legislature (1979) and adopted in election Nov. 4, 1980.]

Sec. 3-a. **Time of Sitting** — The Supreme Court may sit at any time during the year at the seat of government for the transaction of business and each term thereof shall begin and end with each calendar year.

[Note — Sec. 3-a of Art. V was added to make the time of sitting of the Supreme Court discretionary with that court. It was substituted for a provision formerly incorporated in Sec. 3. (See note following Sec. 3.) Submitted by 41st Legislature (1929), ratified in election Nov. 4, 1930, and proclaimed Dec. 17, 1930.]

Sec. 3-b. **Direct Appeal** — The Legislature shall have the power to provide by law, for an appeal direct to the Supreme Court of this State from an order of any trial court granting or denying an interlocutory or permanent injunction on the grounds of the constitutionality or unconstitutionality of any statute of this State, or on the validity or invalidity of any administrative order issued by any state agency under any statute of this State.

[Note — Sec. 3-b of Art. V was added to provide for direct appeals. Submitted by 46th Legislature (1939) and adopted in election Nov. 5, 1940.]

Sec. 3-c. (a) The supreme court and the court of criminal appeals have jurisdiction to answer questions of state law certified from a federal appellate court.

(b) The supreme court and the court of criminal appeals shall promulgate rules of procedure relating to the review of those questions.

[Note — Sec. 3-c of Art. V was added to grant the Supreme Court and the Court of Criminals Appeals jurisdiction to answer questions of state law certified from a federal appellate court. Submitted by 69th Legislature (1985) and adopted in election Nov. 5, 1985.]

Sec. 4. **Court of Criminal Appeals** — The Court of Criminal Appeals shall consist of eight Judges and one Presiding Judge. The Judges shall have the same qualifications and receive the same salaries as the Associate Justices of the Supreme Court, and the Presiding Judge shall have the same qualifications and receive the same salary as the Chief Justice of the Supreme Court. The Presiding Judge and the Judges shall be elected by the qualified voters of the state at a general election and shall hold their offices for a term of six years. In case of a vacancy in the office of a Judge of the Court of Criminal Appeals, the Governor shall, with the advice and consent of the Senate, fill said vacancy by appointment until the next succeeding general election.

For the purpose of hearing cases, the Court of Criminal Appeals may sit in panels of three Judges, the designation thereof to be under rules established by the court. In a panel of three Judges, two Judges shall constitute a quorum and the concurrence of two Judges shall be necessary for a decision. The Presiding Judge, under rules established by the court, shall convene the court en banc for the transaction of all other business and may convene the court en banc for the purpose of hearing cases. The court must sit en banc during proceedings involving capital punishment and other cases as required by law. When convened en banc, five Judges shall constitute a quorum and the concurrence of five Judges shall be necessary for a decision. The Court of Criminal Appeals may appoint Commissioners in aid of the Court of Criminal Appeals as provided by law.

[Note — Sec. 4 of Art. V superseded, in part, the original Sec. 5, which provided for the former "Court of Appeals." The original Sec. 4 provided for the appointment of Supreme Court clerks, and was absorbed in the amended Sec. 3. Submitted by 22nd Legislature (1891); ratified Aug. 11, 1891, and adopted Sept. 22, 1891. It was further amended to raise number of judges from three to five and define their terms of office. Submitted by 59th Legislature (1965) and adopted in election Nov. 8, 1966. It was again amended to raise the number of judges from five to nine and to provide that the Court of Criminal Appeals may sit in panels of three judges. Submitted by 65th Legislature (1977) and adopted in election Nov. 8, 1977.]

Sec. 5. **Jurisdiction; Power; Terms; Clerk, Etc.** — The Court of Criminal Appeals shall have final appellate jurisdiction coextensive with the limits of the State and its determinations shall be final in all criminal cases of whatever grade, with such exceptions and under such regulations as may be provided in this Constitution or as prescribed by law.

The appeal of all cases in which the death penalty has been assessed shall be to the Court of Criminal Appeals. The appeal of all other criminal cases shall be to the Courts of Appeal as prescribed by law. In addition, the Court of Criminal Appeals may, on its own motion, review a decision of a Court of Appeals in a criminal case as provided by law. Discretionary review by the Court of Criminal Appeals is not a matter of right, but of sound judicial discretion.

Subject to such regulations as may be prescribed by law, the Court of Criminal Appeals and the Judges thereof shall have the power to issue the writ of habeas corpus, and in criminal law matters, the writs of mandamus, procedendo, prohibition, and certiorari. The court and the judges thereof shall have the power to issue such other writs as may be necessary to protect its jurisdiction or enforce its judgments. The court shall have the power upon affidavit or otherwise to ascertain such matters of fact as may be necessary to the exercise of its jurisdiction.

The Court of Criminal Appeals may sit for the transaction of business at any time during the year and each term shall begin and end with each calendar year. The Court of Criminal Appeals shall appoint a clerk of the court who shall give bond in such manner as is now or may hereafter be required by law, and who shall hold his office for a term of four years unless sooner removed by the court for good cause entered of record on the minutes of said court.

The clerk of the Court of Criminal Appeals who may be in office at the time when this amendment takes effect shall continue in office for the term of his appointment.

[Note — Sec. 5 of Art. V superseded primarily the original Sec. 6, which defined jurisdiction, powers, etc. of the old "Court of Appeals." (See also note following Sec. 6 below.) Submitted by 22nd Legislature (1891); ratified at election Aug. 11, 1891, and declared adopted Sept. 22, 1891. It was further amended to redefine jurisdiction, powers and terms of office. Submitted by 59th Legislature (1965) and adopted in election Nov. 8, 1966. (See note following Sec. 4 above.) It was again amended to enlarge the court's jurisdiction and to redefine its term of office. Submitted by 65th Legislature (1977) and adopted in election Nov. 8, 1977. It was again amended to redefine jurisdiction of Courts of Criminal Appeals. Submitted by 66th Legislature (1979) and adopted in election Nov. 4, 1980.]

Sec. 6. **Supreme Judicial Districts; Courts of Civil Appeals; Jurisdiction; Term; Justices; Election; Salary; Clerk** — The state shall be divided into courts of appeals districts, with each district hav-

Article V (Cont'd.)

ing a Chief Justice, two or more other Justices, and such other officials as may be provided by law. The Justices shall have the qualifications prescribed for Justices of the Supreme Court. The Court of Appeals may sit in sections as authorized by law. The concurrence of a majority of the judges sitting in a section is necessary to decide a case. Said Court of Appeals shall have appellate jurisdiction coextensive with the limits of their respective districts, which shall extend to all cases of which the District Courts or County Courts have original or appellate jurisdiction under such restrictions and regulations as may be prescribed by law. Provided, that the decisions of said courts shall be conclusive on all questions of fact brought before them on appeal or error. Said courts shall have such other jurisdiction, original and appellate, as may be prescribed by law.

Each of said Courts of Appeals shall hold its sessions at a place in its district to be designated by the Legislature and at such time as may be prescribed by law. Said justices shall be elected by the qualified voters of their respective districts at a general election for a term of six years and shall receive for their services the sum provided by law. Each Court of Appeals shall appoint a clerk in the same manner as the clerk of the Supreme Court, which clerk shall receive such compensation as may be fixed by law.

All constitutional and statutory references to the Courts of Civil Appeals shall be construed to mean the Courts of Appeals.

[Note — Sec. 6 of Art. V, establishing the Courts of Civil Appeals, superseded parts of the original Secs. 5 and 6, which provided for the old "Court of Appeals," and defined its jurisdiction, powers, etc. Submitted by 22nd Legislature (1891), ratified in election Aug. 11, 1891, and declared adopted Sept. 22, 1891. It was further amended to increase the number of justices on a Court of Civil Appeals, permitting a Court of Civil Appeals to sit in sections and requiring a concurrence of a majority of justices to decide a case. Submitted by 65th Legislature (1977) and adopted in election Nov. 7, 1978. It was again amended to change the name of the Courts of Civil Appeals to the Courts of Appeal and to redefine the jurisdiction of said courts. Submitted by 66th Legislature (1979) and adopted in election Nov. 4, 1980. It was again amended to redefine the membership and duties of the Courts of Appeals. Submitted by 69th Legislature (1985) and adopted in election Nov. 5, 1985.]

Sec. 7. **Judicial Districts; Judges; Their Qualifications; Residence; Term of Office; Salary; Terms of Court** — The State shall be divided into judicial districts, with each district having one or more Judges as may be provided by law or by this Constitution. Each district judge shall be elected by the qualified voters at a General Election and shall be a citizen of the United States and of this State, who is licensed to practice law in this State and has been a practicing lawyer or a Judge of a Court in this State, or both combined, for four (4) years next preceding his election, who has resided in the district in which he was elected for two (2) years next preceding his election, and who shall reside in his district during his term of office and hold his office for the period of four (4) years, and who shall receive for his services an annual salary to be fixed by the Legislature. The Court shall conduct its proceedings at the county seat of the county in which the case is pending, except as otherwise provided by law. He shall hold the regular terms of his Court at the County Seat of each County in his district in such manner as may be prescribed by law. The Legislature shall have power by General or Special Laws to make such provisions concerning the terms or sessions of each Court as it may deem necessary.

The Legislature shall also provide for the holding of District Court when the Judge thereof is absent, or is from any cause disabled or disqualified from presiding.

[Note — Sec. 7 of Art. V has been amended three times: (1) To eliminate specification that judge must be "twenty-five years of age" and making minor changes. Submitted by 22nd Legislature (1891) and ratified in election Aug. 11, 1891. (2) Providing that the District Court shall conduct its proceedings in the county seat of the county in which the case is pending "except as otherwise provided by law." Submitted by 51st Legislature (1949) and adopted in election Nov. 8, 1949. (3) Redefining the membership and terms of office of the district courts. Submitted by 69th Legislature (1985) and adopted in election Nov. 5, 1985.]

Sec. 7a. (a) The Judicial Districts Board is created to reapportion the judicial districts authorized by Art. V, Sec. 7, of this constitution.

(b) The membership of the board consists of the Chief Justice of the Texas Supreme Court who serves as chairman, the presiding judge of the Texas Court of Criminal Appeals, the presiding judge of each of the administrative judicial districts of the state, the president of the Texas Judicial Council, and one person who is licensed to practice law in this state appointed by the governor with the advice and consent of the senate for a term of four years. In the event of a vacancy in the appointed membership, the vacancy is filled for the unexpired term in the same manner as the original appointment.

(c) A majority of the total membership of the board constitutes a quorum for the transaction of business. The adoption of a reapportionment order requires a majority vote of the total membership of the board.

(d) The reapportionment powers of the board shall be exercised in the interims between regular sessions of the Legislature, except that a reapportionment may not be ordered by the board during an interim immediately following a regular session of the Legislature in which a

valid and subsisting statewide apportionment of judicial districts is enacted by the Legislature. The board has other powers and duties as provided by the Legislature and shall exercise its powers under the policies, rules, standards, and conditions, not inconsistent with this section, that the Legislature provides.

(e) Unless the Legislature enacts a statewide reapportionment of the judicial districts following each federal decennial census, the board shall convene not later than the first Monday of June of the third year following the year in which the federal decennial census is taken to make a statewide reapportionment of the districts. The board shall complete its work on the reapportionment and file its order with the secretary of state not later than Aug. 31 of the same year. If the Judicial Districts Board fails to make a statewide apportionment by that date, the Legislative Redistricting Board established by Art. III, Sec. 28, of this constitution shall make a statewide reapportionment of the judicial districts not later than the 150th day after the final day for the Judicial Districts Board to make the reapportionment.

(f) In addition to the statewide reapportionment, the board may reapportion the judicial districts of the state as the necessity for reapportionment appears by redesignating, in one or more reapportionment orders, the county or counties that comprise the specific judicial districts affected by those reapportionment orders. In modifying any judicial district, no county having a population as large or larger than the population of the judicial district being reapportioned shall be added to the judicial district.

(g) Except as provided by Subsection (i) of this section, this section does not limit the power of the Legislature to reapportion the judicial districts of the state, to increase the number of judicial districts, or to provide for consequent matters on reapportionment. The Legislature may provide for the effect of a reapportionment made by the board on pending cases or the transfer of pending cases, for jurisdiction of a county court where county court jurisdiction has been vested by law in a district court affected by the reapportionment, for terms of the courts upon existing officers and their duties, and for all other matters affected by the reapportionment. The Legislature may delegate any of these powers to the board. The Legislature shall provide for the necessary expenses of the board.

(h) Any judicial reapportionment order adopted by the board must be approved by a record vote of the majority of the membership of both the senate and house of representatives before such order can become effective and binding.

(i) The Legislature, the Judicial Districts Board, or the Legislative Redistricting Board may not redistrict the judicial districts to provide for any judicial district smaller in size than an entire county except as provided by this section. Judicial districts smaller in size than the entire county may be created subsequent to a general election where a majority of the persons voting on the proposition adopt the proposition "to allow the division of _____ County into judicial districts composed of parts of _____ County." No redistricting plan may be proposed or adopted by the Legislature, the Judicial Districts Board, or the Legislative Redistricting Board in anticipation of a future action by the voters of any county.

[Note — Sec. 7a of Art. V was added to create the Judicial Districts Board and to define its membership and duties. Submitted by 69th Legislature (1985) and adopted in election Nov. 5, 1985.]

Sec. 8. **Jurisdiction and Powers of the District Courts** — District Court jurisdiction consists of exclusive, appellate, and original jurisdiction of all actions, proceedings, and remedies, except in cases where exclusive, appellate, or original jurisdiction may be conferred by this Constitution or other law on some other court, tribunal, or administrative body. District Court judges shall have the power to issue writs necessary to enforce their jurisdiction. The District Court shall have appellate jurisdiction and general supervisory control over the County Commissioners' Court with such exceptions and under such regulations as may be prescribed by law.

[Note — Sec. 8 of Art. V was amended to include the words "of contested elections" in the first paragraph and to add the last sentence in the second paragraph. Submitted by 22nd Legislature (1891), ratified in election Aug. 11, 1891, and declared adopted Sept. 22, 1891. It was further amended to give District and County Courts general jurisdiction over probate matters. It further provided that Legislature may increase, diminish or eliminate jurisdiction of District Court or County Court in probate matters and that Legislature may provide that all appeals in such matters be to Courts of Civil Appeals. Submitted by 63rd Legislature (1973) and adopted in election Nov. 6, 1973. It was again amended to define the exact duties of the judges of the district courts. Submitted by 69th Legislature (1985) and adopted in election Nov. 5, 1985.]

Sec. 9. **Clerk of the District Court; Term of Office; How Removed; How Vacancy Is Filled** — There shall be a Clerk for the District Court of each county, who shall be elected by the qualified voters for state and county officers, and who shall hold his office for four years, subject to removal by information, or by indictment of a grand jury and conviction by a petit jury. In case of vacancy the judge of a District Court shall have the power to appoint a Clerk, who shall hold until the office can be filled by election.

[Note — Sec. 9 of Art. V was amended to change the term of office from two to four years. Submitted by 53rd Legislature (1953) and adopted in election Nov. 2, 1954.]

Sec. 10. **Jury Trial; by Whom Fee Is to Be Paid** — In the trial of

Article V (Cont'd.):

all cases in the District Courts, the plaintiff or defendant shall, upon application made in open court, have the right of trial by jury; but no jury shall be impaneled in any civil case unless demanded by a party to the case, and a jury fee be paid by the party demanding a jury, for such sum and with such exceptions as may be prescribed by the Legislature.

Sec. 11. **Disqualification of Judges; Special Judges; Exchange of Districts; Vacancies** — No judge shall sit in any case wherein he may be interested, or where either of the parties may be connected with him either by affinity or consanguinity, within such a degree as may be prescribed by law, or when he shall have been counsel in the case. When the Supreme Court, the Court of Criminal Appeals, the Court of Civil Appeals, or any member of either, shall be thus disqualified to hear and determine any case or cases in said court, the same shall be certified to the Governor of the State, who shall immediately commission the requisite number of persons, learned in the law, for the trial and determination of such cause or causes. When a Judge of the District Court is disqualified by any of the causes above stated, the parties may, by consent, appoint a proper person to try said case; or, upon their failing to do so, a competent person may be appointed to try the same in the county where it is pending in such manner as may be prescribed by law.

And the District Judges may exchange districts or hold courts for each other when they may deem it expedient, and shall do so when required by law. This disqualification of Judges of inferior tribunals shall be remedied, and vacancies in their offices filled, as may be prescribed by law.

[Note — Sec. II of Art. V was amended to use correct references to courts as established in amended Secs. 1, 3, 4, 5 and 6. Submitted by 22nd Legislature (1891), ratified at election Aug. 11, 1891, and declared adopted Sept. 22, 1891.]

Sec. 12. **Judges Conservators of Peace; Style of Writs; Prosecution by State** — (a) All judges of courts of this State, by virtue of their office, are conservators of the peace throughout the State.

(b) An indictment is a written instrument presented to a court by a grand jury charging a person with the commission of an offense. An information is a written instrument presented to a court by an attorney for the State charging a person with the commission of an offense. The practice and procedures relating to the use of indictments and informations, including their contents, amendment, sufficiency, and requisites, are as provided by law. The presentment of an indictment or information to a court invests the court with jurisdiction of the cause.

[Note — Sec. 12 of Art. V was amended to substitute "Courts of the State" for enumeration of kinds of courts contained in original sections and applying to courts before general revision of judiciary in 1891. Submitted by 22nd Legislature (1891), ratified in election Aug. 11, 1891, and declared adopted Sept. 22, 1891. It was further amended to explain the manner in which a person is charged with a criminal offense and certain requirements applicable to state writs and processes. Submitted by 69th Legislature (1985) and adopted in election Nov. 5, 1985.]

Sec. 13. **Jurors, Grand and Petit; Number Required to Return Verdict** — Grand and petit juries in the District Courts shall be composed of twelve men; but nine members of a grand jury shall be a quorum to transact business and present bills. In trials of civil cases and in trials of criminal cases below the grade of felony in the District Courts, nine members of the jury concurring may render a verdict, but when the verdict shall be rendered by less than the whole number, it shall be signed by every member of the jury concurring in it. When, pending the trial of any case, one or more jurors, not exceeding three, may die, or be disabled from sitting, the remainder of the jury shall have the power to render the verdict; provided, that the Legislature may change or modify the rule authorizing less than the whole number of the jury to render a verdict.

[Note — Sec. 14 of Art. V, defining judicial districts and time of holding courts was deleted by constitutional amendment, submitted by 69th Legislature and approved in election Nov. 5, 1985.]

Sec. 15. **County Court; Election; Term of Office of County Judges; Fees** — There shall be established in each county in this State, a County Court, which shall be a court of record; and there shall be elected in each county by the qualified voters a County Judge, who shall be well informed in the law of the state, shall be a conservator of the peace, and shall hold his office for four years and until his successor shall be elected and qualified. He shall receive as compensation for his services such fees and perquisites as may be prescribed by law.

[Note — Sec. 15 of Art. V was amended to change the term of office from two to four years. Submitted by 53rd Legislature (1953) and adopted in election Nov. 2, 1954.]

Sec. 16. **Jurisdiction of County Court; Appeals; Probate Jurisdiction; May Issue Writs; Judge Disqualified, When** — The County Court has jurisdiction as provided by law. The County Judge is the presiding officer of the County Court and has judicial functions as provided by law. County court judges shall have the power to issue writs necessary to enforce their jurisdiction.

County Courts in existence on the effective date of this amendment are continued unless otherwise provided by law. When the Judge of the County Court is disqualified in any case pending in the County Court the parties interested may, by consent, appoint a proper person to try said case, or upon their failing to do so a competent person may be appointed to try the same in the county where it is pending in such manner as may be prescribed by law.

[Note — Sec. 16 of Art. V has been amended four times: (1) To make changes relating to appeals to the county court, relating to disqualification of the judge, and minor changes. Submitted by 22nd Legislature (1891), ratified at election Aug. 11, 1891, and declared adopted Sept. 22, 1891. (2) To extend jurisdiction of Justices of Peace in civil cases. (See also Sec. 19 of Art. V.) Submitted by 65th Legislature (1977) and adopted in election Nov. 7, 1978. (3) To redefine jurisdiction of appellate courts. Submitted by 66th Legislature (1979) and adopted in election Nov. 4, 1980. (4) To define the jurisdiction of the County Judge and his duties. Submitted by 69th Legislature (1985) and adopted in election Nov. 5, 1985.]

[Note — Sec. 16-a of Art. V, providing for probate courts, was deleted by constitutional amendment. Submitted by 69th Legislature (1985) and approved in election Nov. 5, 1985.]

Sec. 17. **Terms of County Court for Criminal Business; Prosecution Commenced by Information; Grand Jury to Inquire Into Misdemeanors; Quashing of Grand Jury Indictments; Jury** — The County Court shall hold terms as provided by law. Prosecutions may be commenced in said court by information filed by the County Attorney, or by affidavit, as may be provided by law. Grand juries empaneled in the District Courts shall inquire into misdemeanors, and all indictments therefor returned into the District Courts shall forthwith be certified to the County Courts, or other inferior courts having jurisdiction to try them, for trial; and if such indictment be quashed in the county, or other inferior court, the person charged shall not be discharged if there is probable cause of guilt, but may be held by such court or magistrate to answer an information or affidavit. A jury in the County Court shall consist of six men; but no jury shall be empaneled to try a civil case, unless demanded by one of the parties, who shall pay such jury fee therefor in advance as may be prescribed by law, unless he makes affidavit that he is unable to pay the same.

[Note — Sec. 17 of Art. V was amended to redefine the terms of office of county judges. Submitted by 69th Legislature (1985) and adopted in election Nov. 5, 1985.]

Sec. 18. **Terms of Justices of the Peace; County Commissioners and Commissioners' Court** — (a) Each county in the state, with a population of 30,000 or more, according to the most recent federal census, from time to time, for the convenience of the people, shall be divided into not less than four and not more than eight precincts. Each county in the State with a population of 18,000 or more but less than 30,000 according to the most recent federal census, from time to time, for the convenience of the people, shall be divided into not less than two and not more than five precincts. Each county in the State with a population of less than 18,000, according to the most recent federal census, from time to time, for the convenience of the people, shall be designated as a single precinct or, if the Commissioners Court determines that the county needs more than one precinct, shall be divided into not more than four precincts. Notwithstanding the population requirements of this subsection, Chambers County, from time to time, for the convenience of the people, shall be divided into not less than two and not more than six precincts. A division or designation under this subsection shall be made by the Commissioners Court provided for by this Constitution. Except as provided by Subsection (e) of this section, in each such precinct there shall be elected one Justice of the Peace and one Constable, each of whom shall hold his office for four years and until his successor shall be elected and qualified; provided that in a county with a population of less than 150,000, according to the most recent federal census, in any precinct in which there may be a city of 18,000 or more inhabitants, there shall be elected two Justices of the Peace, and in a county with a population of 150,000 or more, according to the most recent federal census, each precinct may contain more than one Justice of the Peace Court.

(b) Each county shall, in the manner provided for justice of the peace and constable precincts, be divided into four Commissioners' precincts in each of which there shall be elected by the qualified voters thereof one County Commissioner, who shall hold his office for four years and until his successor shall be elected and qualified. The County Commissioners so chosen, with the County Judge as presiding officer, shall compose the County Commissioners Court, which shall exercise such powers and jurisdiction over all county business as is conferred by this Constitution and the laws of the state, or as may be hereafter prescribed.

(c) When the boundaries of justice of the peace and constable precincts are changed, each Justice and Constable in office on the effective date of the change, or elected to a term of office beginning on or after the effective date of the change, shall serve in the precinct in which the person resides for the term to which each was elected or appointed, even though the change in boundaries places the person's residence outside the precinct for which he was elected or appointed, abolishes the precinct for which he was elected or appointed, or temporarily results in extra Justices or Constables serving in a precinct. When, as a result of a change of precinct boundaries, a vacancy occurs in the office of Justice of the Peace or

Article V (Cont'd.)

Constable, the Commissioners Court shall fill the vacancy by appointment until the next general election.

(d) When the boundaries of commissioners precincts are changed, each commissioner in office on the effective date of the change, or elected to a term of office beginning on or after the effective date of the change, shall serve in the precinct to which each was elected or appointed for the entire term to which each was elected or appointed, even though the change in boundaries places the person's residence outside the precinct for which he was elected or appointed.

(e) The office of Constable in Mills County is abolished. The powers, duties, and records of the office are transferred to the County Sheriff.

(f) The office of Constable in Reagan County and the office of Constable in Roberts County are abolished The functions of the office are transferred to the County Sheriff. However, the office of Constable is abolished under this subsection only if, at the statewide election at which the constitutional amendment providing for the abolition is submitted to the voters, a majority of the voters of Reagan County or Roberts County, as applicable, voting on the question at that election favor the amendment.

[Note — Sec. 18 of Art. V has been amended five times: (1) To change the term of office for Justices of the Peace and Constables from two to four years. Submitted by 53rd Legislature (1953) and adopted in election Nov. 2, 1954. (2) To authorize fewer justice of the peace and constable precincts in counties with populations of less than 30,000 and to provide for continuous service by Justices of Peace, Constables and County Commissioners when precinct boundaries are changed. Submitted by 68th Legislature (1983) and adopted in election Nov. 8, 1983. (3) To allow Chambers County to be divided into two to six precincts. Submitted by 69th Legislature (1985) and adopted in election Nov. 5, 1985. (4) To provide that certain justice precincts may contain more than one justice of the peace court. Submitted by 70th Legislature (1987) and adopted in election Nov. 3, 1987. (5) To abolish the office of Constable in Mills, Reagan and Roberts counties. Submitted by 74th Legislature (1995) and adopted in election Nov. 7, 1995.]

Sec. 19. **Criminal Jurisdiction of Justices of the Peace; Appeals; Justices of the Peace ex-Officio Notaries** — Justice of the peace courts shall have original jurisdiction in criminal matters of misdemeanor cases punishable by fine only, exclusive jurisdiction in civil matters where the amount in controversy is two hundred dollars or less, and such other jurisdiction as may be provided by law. Justices of the peace shall be ex officio notaries public.

[Note — Sec. 19 of Art. V was amended to extend jurisdiction of Justices of Peace and to give them jurisdiction in civil matters involving $200 or less. (See also Sec. 16 of Art. V.) Submitted by 65th Legislature (1977) and adopted in election Nov. 7, 1978. It was again amended to redefine the duties of Justices of the Peace and to make them ex officio notaries public. Submitted by 69th Legislature (1985) and adopted in election Nov. 5, 1985.]

Sec. 20. **County Clerk; Election; Terms; Duties; Vacancies** — There shall be elected for each county, by the qualified voters, a County Clerk, who shall hold his office for four years, who shall be clerk of the County and Commissioners' Courts and recorder of the county, whose duties, perquisites and fees of office shall be prescribed by the Legislature, and a vacancy in whose office shall be filled by the Commissioners' Court until the next general election; provided, that in counties having a population of less than 8,000 persons there may be an election of a single clerk, who shall perform the duties of District and County Clerks.

[Note — Sec. 20 of Art. V was amended to change the term of office from two to four years. Submitted by 53rd Legislature (1953) and adopted in election Nov. 2, 1954.]

Sec. 21. **County and District Attorneys; Duties; Vacancies; Fees** — A County Attorney, for counties in which there is not a resident Criminal District Attorney, shall be elected by the qualified voters of each county, who shall be commissioned by the Governor and hold his office for the term of four years. In case of vacancy the Commissioners' Court of the county shall have power to appoint a County Attorney until the next general election. The County Attorneys shall represent the State in all cases in the District and inferior courts in their respective counties; but if any county shall be included in a district in which there shall be a District Attorney, the respective duties of District Attorneys and County Attorneys shall, in such counties, be regulated by the Legislature. The Legislature may provide for the election of District Attorneys in such districts as may be deemed necessary, and make provisions for the compensation of District Attorneys and County Attorneys. District Attorneys shall hold office for a term of four years, and until their successors have qualified.

[Note — Sec. 21 of Art. V was amended to change the term of office from two to four years; also leaves solely to Legislature provision for annual salary to be paid by State to District and County Attorneys. Submitted by 53rd Legislature (1953) and adopted in election Nov. 2, 1954.]

[Note — Sec. 22 of Art. V, giving Legislature power to change jurisdiction of county courts, was deleted by constitutional amend-

ment. Submitted by 69th Legislature (1985) and adopted in election Nov. 5, 1985.]

Sec. 23. **Sheriff; Term of Office; Vacancy** — There shall be elected by the qualified voters of each county a Sheriff, who shall hold his office for the term of four years, whose duties, qualifications, perquisites, and fees of office shall be prescribed by the Legislature, and vacancies in whose office shall be filled by the Commissioners Court until the next general election.

[Note — Sec. 23 of Art. V was amended to change the term of office from two to four years. Submitted by 53rd Legislature (1953) and adopted in election Nov. 2, 1954. It was further amended to allow the legislature to prescribe the qualifications of sheriffs. Submitted by 73rd Legislature (1993) and adopted in election Nov. 2, 1993.]

Sec. 24. **Certain Officers Removed by District Courts for Drunkenness, Incompetency, Official Misconduct, Etc.** — County Judges, County Attorneys, Clerks of the District and County Courts, Justices of the Peace, Constables and other county officers may be removed by the Judges of the District Courts for incompetency, official misconduct, habitual drunkenness or other causes defined by law, upon the cause therefor being set forth in writing, and the finding of its truth by a jury.

[Note — Sec. 25 of Art. V, giving the Supreme Court power to make rules of procedure, was deleted by constitutional amendment. Submitted by 69th Legislature (1985) and approved in election Nov. 5, 1985.]

Sec. 26. **Limited Right of Appeal by the State in Criminal Cases** — The State is entitled to appeal in criminal cases, as authorized by general law.

[Note — Sec. 26 of Art. V was amended to give the state a limited right to appeal in criminal cases. Submitted by 70th Legislature and adopted in election Nov. 3, 1987.]

Sec. 27. **Transfer of Cases by the Legislature** — The Legislature shall, at its first session provide for the transfer of all business, civil and criminal, pending in District Courts, over which jurisdiction is given by this Constitution to the County Courts or other inferior courts, to such county or inferior courts, and for the trial or disposition of all such causes by such county or other inferior courts.

Sec. 28. **Vacancies in Offices of Judges of Superior Courts to Be Filled by the Governor** — Vacancies in the office of the Judges of the Supreme Court, the Court of Criminal Appeals, the Court of Civil Appeals and District Courts shall be filled by the Governor until the next succeeding general election, and vacancies in the office of County Judge and Justices of the Peace shall be filled by the Commissioners' Court until the next succeeding general election.

[Note — Sec. 28 of Art. V was amended to make names of courts harmonize with names in amended Secs. 1, 3, 4, 5 and 6. Submitted by 22nd Legislature (1891), ratified in election Aug. 11, 1891, and declared adopted Sept. 22, 1891. This section was again amended to provide that appointments to the offices of County Judge and Justice of the Peace should be filled only to the next succeeding general election instead of for the full elected term. Submitted by 55th Legislature (1957) and adopted in election Nov. 4, 1958.]

Sec. 29. **Terms of County Courts; Probate Business; Prosecutions** — The County Court shall hold at least four terms for both civil and criminal business annually, as may be provided by the Legislature, or by the Commissioners' Court of the county under authority of law, and such other terms each year as may be fixed by the Commissioners' Court; provided, the Commissioners' Court of any county having fixed the times and number of terms of the County Court shall not change the same again until the expiration of one year. Said court shall dispose of probate business either in term time or vacation, under such regulations as may be prescribed by law. Prosecutions may be commenced in said courts in such manner as is or may be provided by law, and a jury therein shall consist of six men. Until otherwise provided, the terms of the County Court shall be held on the first Mondays in February, May, August and November, and may remain in session three weeks.

[Note — Sec. 29 of Art. V was added to prescribe county court terms. Submitted by 18th Legislature (1883), ratified in election Aug. 14, 1883, and proclaimed adopted Sept. 25, 1883.]

Sec. 30. **County Judges and Criminal District Attorneys; Terms** — The Judges of all courts of county-wide jurisdiction heretofore or hereafter created by the Legislature of this State, and all Criminal District Attorneys now or hereafter authorized by the laws of this State, shall be elected for a term of four years, and shall serve until their successors have qualified.

[Note — Sec. 30 of Art. V was added to prescribe term of office of county judges and criminal district attorneys. Submitted by 53rd Legislature (1953) and adopted in election Nov. 2, 1954.]

Sec. 31. **Court Administration and Rule-making Authority** — (a) The Supreme Court is responsible for the efficient administration of the judicial branch and shall promulgate rules of administration not inconsistent with the laws of the state as may be necessary for the efficient and uniform administration of justice in the various courts.

(b) The Supreme Court shall promulgate rules of civil procedure for all courts not inconsistent with the laws of the state as may be nec-

Article V (Cont'd.); Articles VI, VII

essary for the efficient and uniform administration of justice in the various courts.

(c) The Legislature may delegate to the Supreme Court or Court of Criminal Appeals the power to promulgate such other rules as may be prescribed by law or this Constitution, subject to such limitations and procedures as may be provided by law.

[Note — Sec. 31 of Art. V was added to provide for the administration and jurisdiction of constitutional courts. Submitted by 69th Legislature (1985) and adopted in election Nov. 5, 1985.]

Article VI. — Suffrage

Sec. 1. Persons Who Cannot Vote — The following classes of persons shall not be allowed to vote in this State, to wit:

*First: Persons under eighteen (18) years of age.

Second: Idiots and lunatics.

Third: All paupers supported by any county.

Fourth: All persons convicted of any felony, subject to such exceptions as the Legislature may make.

[Note — Sec. 1 of Art. VI has been amended twice: (1) To give privilege of ballot to officers and enlisted men of National Guard, National Guard Reserves, Officers Reserve Corps, Organized Reserves and retired officers and enlisted men of Army, Navy and Marine Corps. Submitted by 42nd Legislature (1931) and adopted in election Nov. 8, 1932. Proclaimed Jan. 9, 1933. (2) To remove restrictions against members of the Armed Forces and to repeal the original Sec. 2-a of Art. VI, which provided for poll tax exemption for war veterans. Submitted by 53rd Legislature (1953) and adopted in election Nov. 2, 1954. (See also note under Sec. 2 and new Sec. 2-a.*) Texas on April 27, 1971, became the 21st state to ratify the 26th Amendment to the U.S. Constitution lowering the voting age to 18 from 21. When Ohio ratified the amendment in July 1971, it was the 38th state to do so, the number required to change the voting age. Since the voting age specified in the U.S. Constitution takes precedence over that in the Texas Constitution, Sec. 2 (below) has not been amended by the Legislature to lower the voting age to 18.]

Sec. 2. Annual Registration; Absentee Voting — Every person subject to none of the foregoing disqualifications, who shall have attained the age of *21 years and who shall be a citizen of the United States and who shall have resided in this State one year next preceding an election and the last six months within the district or county in which such person offers to vote, shall be deemed a qualified elector; provided, however, that before offering to vote at an election a voter shall have registered annually, but such requirement for registration shall not be considered a qualification of an elector within the meaning of the term "qualified elector" as used in any other Article of this Constitution in respect to any matter except qualification and eligibility to vote at an election. Any legislation enacted in anticipation of the adoption of this Amendment shall not be invalid because of its anticipatory nature. The Legislature may authorize absentee voting. And this provision of the Constitution shall be self-enacting without the necessity of further legislation.

[Note — Sec. 2 of Art. VI has been amended six times: (1) To provide that declaration of foreigner must be filed at least six months before election to enable him to vote in such election. Submitted by 24th Legislature (1895), ratified in election Nov. 3, 1896, and declared adopted Dec. 18, 1896. (2) To make poll tax receipt the certificate of registration for voting. Submitted by 27th Legislature (1901), ratified in election Nov. 4, 1902, and declared adopted Dec. 26, 1902. (3) To limit suffrage to citizens; allowing husband or wife to pay poll tax for other; authorizing absentee voting. Submitted by 37th Legislature (1921) and ratified in election July 23, 1921. (4) To extend suffrage to members of the Armed Forces of the United States. Submitted by 53rd Legislature (1953) and adopted in election Nov. 2, 1954. (5) To omit the requirement that members of armed services may vote only in county in which they resided at time of entering the service. Submitted by 59th Legislature (1965) and adopted in election Nov. 8, 1966. (6) To repeal the poll tax as a voting requirement and substituting annual registration. Submitted by 59th Legislature (1965) and adopted in election Nov. 8, 1966. (*See also note under Sec. 1 above.)]

Sec. 2-a. Vote for Electors for President and Vice President and Statewide Offices — (a) Notwithstanding any other provision of this Constitution, the Legislature may enact laws and provide a method of registration, including the time of such registration, permitting any person who is qualified to vote in this state except for the residence requirements within a county or district, as set forth in Sec. 2 of this article, to vote for (1) electors for president and vice president of the United States and (2) all offices, questions or propositions to be voted on by all electors throughout this state.

(b) Notwithstanding any other provision of this Constitution, the Legislature may enact laws and provide for a method of registration, including the time for such registration, permitting any person (1) who is qualified to vote in this state except for the residence requirements of Sec. 2 of this article, and (2) who shall have resided anywhere within this state at least thirty (30) days next preceding a general election in a presidential election year, and (3) who shall have been a qualified elector in another state immediately prior to his removal to this state or would have been eligible to vote in such other state had he remained there until such election, to vote for electors for

president and vice president of the United States in that election.

(c) Notwithstanding any other provision of this Constitution, the Legislature may enact laws and provide for a method of registration, including the time for such registration, permitting absentee voting for electors for president and vice president of the United States in this state by former residents of this state (1) who have removed to another state, and (2) who meet all qualifications, except residence requirements, for voting for electors for president and vice president in this state at the time of the election, but the privileges of suffrage so granted shall be only for such period of time as would permit a former resident of this state to meet the residence requirements for voting in his new state of residence, and in no case for more than twenty-four (24) months.

[Note — Sec. 2-a was added to provide for voting on electors for president and vice president and on all statewide offices. Submitted by 59th Legislature (1965) and adopted in election Nov. 8, 1966.]

Sec. 3. Electors in Towns and Cities; Only Property Taxpayers to Vote in Certain Instances — All qualified electors of the State, as herein described, who shall have resided for six months immediately preceding an election within the limits of any city or corporate town, shall have the right to vote for Mayor and all other elective officers; but in all elections to determine expenditure of money or assumption of debt, only those shall be qualified to vote who pay taxes on property in said city or incorporated town; provided, that no poll tax for the payment of debts thus incurred shall be levied upon the persons debarred from voting in relation thereto.

Sec. 3-a. Only Those Who Have Rendered Property for Taxation May Vote in Bond Elections — When an election is held by any county, or any number of counties, or any political subdivision of the State, or any political subdivision of a county, or any defined district now or hereafter to be described and defined within the State and which may or may not include towns, villages or municipal corporations, or any city, town or village, for the purpose of issuing bonds or otherwise lending credit, or expending money or assuming any debt, only qualified electors who own taxable property in the State, county, political subdivision, district, city, town or village where such election is held, and who have duly rendered the same for taxation, shall be qualified to vote and all electors shall vote in the election precinct of their residence.

[Note — Sec. 3-a of Art. VI was added to limit voters participating in bond elections to those who have rendered property for taxation. Submitted by 42nd Legislature (1931) and adopted in election Nov. 8, 1932; proclaimed Jan. 9, 1933.]

Sec. 4. Voter Registration — In all elections by the people the vote shall be by ballot, and the Legislature shall provide for the numbering of tickets and make such other regulations as may be necessary to detect and punish fraud and preserve the purity of the ballot box; and the Legislature shall provide by law for the registration of all voters.

[Note — Sec. 4 of Art. VI has been amended twice: (1) To provide for the registration of voters in cities of 10,000 or more population. Submitted by 22nd Legislature (1891), ratified in election Aug. 11, 1891, and declared adopted Sept. 22, 1891. (2) To delete this provision for registration of voters in cities of 10,000 or more population. (See also note under Sec. 2, Art. VI.) Submitted by 59th Legislature (1965) and adopted in election Nov. 8, 1966.]

Sec. 5. Voters Privileged From Arrest — Voters shall, in all cases except treason, felony or breach of the peace, be privileged from arrest during their attendance at elections and in going to and returning therefrom.

Article VII — Education, The Public Free Schools

Sec. 1. Public Schools to Be Established — A general diffusion of knowledge being essential to the preservation of the liberties and rights of the people, it shall be the duty of the Legislature of the State to establish and make suitable provision for the support and maintenance of an efficient system of public free schools.

Sec. 2. Provisions Governing the Levy and Collection of Taxes for the Support of the Public Free Schools — All funds, lands and other property heretofore set apart and appropriated for the support of public schools, all the alternate sections of land reserved by the State out of grants heretofore made or that may hereafter be made to railroads or other corporations, of any nature whatsoever, one half of the public domain of the State, and all sums of money that may come to the State from the sale of any portion of the same shall constitute a perpetual public school fund.

Sec. 2A. The State of Texas hereby relinquishes and releases any claim of sovereign ownership or title to an undivided one-third interest in and to the lands and minerals within the Shelby, Frazier, and McCormick League (now located in Fort Bend and Austin counties) arising out of the interest in that league originally granted under the Mexican Colonization Law of 1823 to John McCormick on or about July 24, 1824, and subsequently voided by the governing body of Austin's Original Colony on or about December 15, 1830, and title to such interest in the lands and minerals is confirmed to the owners of the remaining interests in such lands and minerals. This section is self-executing.

[Note — Sec. 2A of Art. VII was added to clear certain land titles in Fort Bend and Austin counties. Submitted by 73rd Legislature (1993) and adopted in election Nov. 2, 1993.]

Article VII (Cont'd.)

Sec. 3. **School Taxes** — One fourth of the revenue derived from the State occupation taxes and a poll tax of one ($1.00) dollar on every inhabitant of this State, between the ages of 21 and 60 years, shall be set apart annually for the benefit of the public free schools; and in addition thereto, there shall be levied and collected an annual ad valorem State tax of such an amount not to exceed 35¢ on the one hundred ($100.00) dollars valuation, as, with the available school fund arising from all other sources, will be sufficient to maintain and support the public schools of this State for a period of not less than six months in each year, and it shall be the duty of the State Board of Education to set aside a sufficient amount out of the said tax to provide free textbooks for the use of children attending the public free schools of this State; provided, however, that should the limit of taxation herein named be insufficient the deficit may be met by appropriation from the general funds of the State, and the Legislature may also provide for the formation of school districts by general laws, and all such school districts may embrace parts of two or more counties. And the Legislature shall be authorized to pass laws for the assessment and collection of taxes in all said districts and for the management and control of the public school or schools of such districts, whether such districts are composed of territory wholly within a county or in parts of two or more counties. And the Legislature may authorize an additional ad valorem tax to be levied and collected within all school districts heretofore formed or hereafter formed, for the further maintenance of public free schools, and for the erection and equipment of school buildings therein; provided, that a majority of the qualified property taxpaying voters of the district voting at an election to be held for that purpose shall vote such tax not to exceed in any one year $1 on the $100 valuation of the property subject to taxation in such district, but the limitation upon the amount of school district tax herein authorized shall not apply to incorporated cities or towns constituting separate and independent school districts, nor to independent or common school districts created by general or special law.

[Note — Sec. 3 of Art. VII has been amended six times: (1) To authorize a State ad valorem school tax of not more than 20¢, and further to authorize creation by Legislature of school districts for local taxation not to exceed 20¢. Submitted by 18th Legislature (1883), ratified in election Aug. 14, 1883, and declared adopted Sept. 25, 1883. (2) To authorize maximum tax in school districts of 50¢. Submitted by 30th Legislature (1907), ratified in election Nov. 3, 1908, and declared adopted Feb. 2, 1909. (3) To authorize intercounty school districts and authorizing Legislature to pass laws for management and control of districts. Submitted by 31st Legislature (1909), ratified in election Aug. 3, 1909. See note following 3-a below. (4) To increase maximum tax for State school purposes from 20¢ to 35¢ and provide for free textbooks. Submitted by 35th Legislature (1917) and adopted at election of Nov. 5, 1918. (5) To remove 50¢ limit on school district tax. Submitted by 36th Legislature (1919) and adopted in election of Nov. 2, 1920. (6) To eliminate the provision authorizing the Legislature to create districts by special law. Submitted by 39th Legislature (1925) and ratified in election Nov. 2, 1926, and proclaimed Jan. 20, 1927.]

See Sec. 1-e of Art. VIII for provisions to gradually abolish the ad valorem tax as a source for state school support.

[Note — Sec. 3-a of Art. VII, relating to county line districts, validation, bonds and taxation, was deleted by constitutional amendment. Submitted by 61st Legislature (1969) and approved in election Aug. 5, 1969.]

Sec. 3-b. **County School Districts** — No tax for the maintenance of public free schools voted in any independent school district and no tax for the maintenance of a junior college voted by a junior college district, nor any bonds voted in any such district, but unissued, shall be abrogated, canceled or invalidated by change of any kind in the boundaries thereof. After any change in boundaries, the governing body of any such district, without the necessity of an additional election, shall have the power to assess, levy and collect ad valorem taxes on all taxable property within the boundaries of the district as changed, for the purposes of the maintenance of public free schools or the maintenance of a junior college, as the case may be, and the payment of principal and of interest on all bonded indebtedness outstanding against, or attributable, adjusted or allocated to, such district or any territory therein, in the amount, at the rate, or not to exceed the rate, and in the manner authorized in the district prior to the change in its boundaries, and further in accordance with the laws under which all such bonds, respectively, were voted; and such governing body also shall have the power, without the necessity of an additional election, to sell and deliver any unissued bonds voted in the district prior to any such change in boundaries, and to assess, levy and collect ad valorem taxes on all taxable property in the district as changed, for the payment of principal and of interest on such bonds in the manner permitted by the laws under which such bonds were voted. In those instances where the boundaries of any such independent school district are changed by the annexation of, or consolidation with, one or more whole school districts, the taxes to be levied for the purposes hereinabove authorized may be in the amount or at not to exceed the rate theretofore voted in the district having at the time of such change the greatest scholastic population according to the latest scholastic census and only the unissued bonds of such district voted prior to such change, may be subse-

quently sold and delivered and any voted, but unissued, bonds of other school districts involved in such annexation or consolidation shall not thereafter be issued.

[Note: Sec. 3-b of Art. VII was added to allow independent school districts in Dallas County to work out adjustment of boundaries without abrogating, canceling or invalidating existing tax rates and bonds. Submitted by 57th Legislature (1961) and adopted in election Nov. 6, 1962. It was amended to include school districts in any county of Texas. Submitted by 59th Legislature (1965) and adopted in election Nov. 8, 1966.]

Sec. 4. **Sale of School Lands; No Relief to Purchasers; the Investment of Proceeds** — The lands herein set apart to the Public Free School fund shall be sold under such regulations, at such times and on such terms as may be prescribed by law; and the Legislature shall not have power to grant any relief to purchasers thereof. The proceeds of such sales must be used to acquire other land for the Public Free School fund as provided by law or the proceeds shall be invested by the comptroller of public accounts, as may be directed by the Board of Education herein provided for, in the bonds of the United States, the State of Texas, or counties in said State, or in such other securities and under such restrictions as may be prescribed by law; and the State shall be responsible for all investments.

[Note — Sec. 4 of Art. VII was amended to authorize investment of money from sale of State public school lands in securities other than State and U. S. bonds, as was required by the original section, and to make the State responsible for such investments. Submitted by 18th Legislature (1883), ratified in election Aug. 14, 1883, and declared adopted Sept. 25, 1883. It was again amended to authorize proceeds from sale of land dedicated to permanent school fund to be used to acquire other land for that fund. Submitted by 69th Legislature (1985) and adopted in election Nov. 5, 1985. It was amended to change references to the state treasurer to the state comptroller after the office of state treasurer was eliminated by constitutional amendment. Submitted by 74th Legislature (1995) and adopted in election Nov. 7, 1995.]

Sec. 4A. **Patents Issued for Free Public School Lands** —
(a) On application to the School Land Board, a natural person is entitled to receive a patent to land from the commissioner of the General Land Office if:

(1) the land is surveyed public free school fund land, either surveyed or platted according to records of the General Land Office;

(2) the land was not patentable under the law in effect immediately before adoption of this section;

(3) the person acquired the land without knowledge of the title defect out of the State of Texas or Republic of Texas and held the land under color of title, the chain of which dates from at least as early as January 1, 1941; and

(4) the person, in conjunction with his predecessors in interest:

(A) has a recorded deed on file in the respective county court house and has claimed the land for a continuous period of at least 50 years as of January 1, 1991; and

(B) for at least 50 years has paid taxes on the land together with all interest and penalties associated with any period of delinquency of the taxes; provided, however, that in the event that public records concerning the tax payments on the land are unavailable for any period within the past 50 years, the tax assessors-collectors of the taxing jurisdictions in which the land is located shall provide the School Land Board with a sworn certificate stating that, to the best of their knowledge, all taxes have been paid for the past 50 years and there are no outstanding taxes nor interest or penalties currently due against the property.

(b) The applicant for the patent must submit to the School Land Board certified copies of his chain of title and a survey of the land for which a patent is sought, if requested to do so by the board. The board shall determine the qualifications of the applicant to receive a patent under this section. On a finding by the board that the applicant meets the requirements of Subsection (a) of this section, the commissioner of the General Land Office shall award the applicant a patent. If the applicant is denied a patent, he may file suit against the board in a district court of the county in which the land is situated within 60 days from the date of the denial of the patent under this section. The trial shall be de novo and not subject to the Administrative Procedure and Texas Register Act (Article 6252-13a, Vernon's Texas Civil Statutes), and the burden of proof is on the applicant.

(c) This section does not apply to beach land, submerged or filled land, or islands and may not be used by an applicant to resolve a boundary dispute. This section does not apply to land that, pursuant to an action filed previous to the date of an application for patent thereon, was found by a court of competent jurisdiction to be state owned or to be land on which the state has given a mineral lease that is in effect on the date of an application for patent thereon. A patent under this section for land within five miles of mineral production shall reserve minerals to the state in the same manner provided by law for reservations of minerals in sales to good faith claimants of unsurveyed school land within five miles of production.

(d) Application for a patent under this section must be filed with the School Land Board before January 1, 1993.

(e) This section is self-executing.

[Note — Sec. 4A of Art. VII, above, replaces the original Sec. 4A, which expired on Jan. 1, 1990. The current Sec. 4A authorizes issuance of patents for certain public free school fund land held in good

Article VII (Cont'd.)

faith under color of title for at least 50 years as of Jan. 1, 1991. Submitted by 72nd Legislature (1991) and adopted in election Nov. 5, 1991.]

Sec. 5. Permanent School Fund; Interest; Alienation; Sectarian Schools — (a) The principal of all bonds and other funds, and the principal arising from the sale of the lands hereinbefore set apart to said school fund, shall be the permanent school fund, and all the interest derivable therefrom and the taxes herein authorized and levied shall be the available school fund. The available school fund shall be applied annually to the support of the public free schools. Except as provided by this section, no law shall ever be enacted appropriating any part of the permanent or available school fund to any other purpose whatever; nor shall the same or any part thereof ever be appropriated to or used for the support of any sectarian school; and the available school fund herein provided shall be distributed to the several counties according to their scholastic population and applied in such manner as may be provided by law.

(b) The Legislature by law may provide for using the permanent school fund and the income from the permanent school fund to guarantee bonds issued by school districts or by the state for the purpose of making loans to or purchasing the bonds of school districts for the purpose of acquisition, construction, or improvement of instructional facilities including all furnishings thereto. If any payment is required to be made by the permanent school fund as a result of its guarantee of bonds issued by the state, an amount equal to this payment shall be immediately paid by the state from the treasury to the permanent school fund. An amount owed by the state to the permanent school fund under this section shall be a general obligation of the state until paid. The amount of bonds authorized hereunder shall not exceed $750 million or a higher amount authorized by a two-thirds record vote of both houses of the legislature. If the proceeds of bonds issued by the state are used to provide a loan to a school district and the district becomes delinquent on the loan payments, the amount of the delinquent payments shall be offset against state aid to which the district is otherwise entitled.

[Note — Sec. 5 (b) of Art. VII was amended to provide for using the permanent school fund and its income to guarantee bonds issued by the state for the purpose of aiding school districts. Proposed by 71st Legislature (1989) and adopted in election Nov. 7 1989.]

(c) The Legislature may appropriate part of the available school fund for administration of the permanent school fund or of a bond guarantee program established under this section.

(d) Notwithstanding any other provision of this constitution, in managing the assets of the permanent school fund, the State Board of Education may acquire, exchange, sell, supervise, manage, or retain, through procedures and subject to restrictions it establishes and in amounts it considers appropriate, any kind of investment, including investments in the Texas growth fund created by Article XVI, Section 70, of this constitution, that persons of ordinary prudence, discretion, and intelligence, exercising the judgment and care under the circumstances then prevailing, acquire or retain for their own account in the management of their affairs, not in regard to speculation but in regard to the permanent disposition of their funds, considering the probable income as well as the probable safety of their capital.

[Note — Sec. 5 of Art. VII has been amended four times: (1) To allow Legislature to add not more than 1 percent annually of the total value of the permanent school fund to the available school fund. Submitted by 22nd Legislature (1891), ratified in election Aug. 11, 1891, and declared adopted Sept. 22, 1891. (2) To delete the provision in (1), above. Submitted by 58th Legislature (1963), and adopted in election Nov. 3, 1964. (3) To authorize use of the permanent school fund to guarantee bonds issued by school districts. Submitted by 68th Legislature (1983) and adopted in election Nov. 8, 1983. (4) To authorize the investment of Permanent School Fund monies in the Texas Growth Fund. Submitted by 70th Legislature (1987) and adopted in election Nov. 8, 1988.]

Sec. 6. County School Lands; Limitations; Settlers; Proceeds — All lands heretofore or hereafter granted to the several counties of this State for educational purposes are of right the property of said counties respectively to which they were granted, and title thereto is vested in said counties, and no adverse possession or limitation shall ever be available against the title of any county. Each county may sell or dispose of its lands in whole or in part in manner to be here provided by the Commissioners' Court of the county. Actual settlers residing on said land shall be protected in the prior right of purchasing the same to the extent of their settlement, not to exceed 160 acres, at the price fixed by said court, which price shall not include the value of existing improvements made thereon by such settlers. Said lands, and the proceeds thereof, when sold, shall be held by said counties alone as a trust for the benefit of public schools therein; said proceeds to be invested in bonds of the United States, the State of Texas, or counties in said State, or in such other securities and under such restrictions as may be prescribed by law; and the counties shall be responsible for all investments; the interest thereon and other revenue, except principal, shall be available fund.

[Note — Sec. 6 of Art. VII was amended to authorize the investment of money from sale of county public school lands in securities

other than State and U. S. bonds, as was required in the original section, and making counties responsible for such investments. Submitted by 18th Legislature (1883), ratified in election August 14, 1883, and declared adopted Sept. 25, 1883.]

Sec. 6-a. Taxation of County School Lands — All agriculture or grazing school land mentioned in Sec. 6 of this article owned by any county shall be subject to taxation except for State purposes to the same extent as lands privately owned.

[Note — Sec. 6-a of Art. VII was added to provide for the taxation of lands mentioned in Sec. 6. Submitted by 39th Legislature (1925), ratified in election Nov. 2, 1926, and proclaimed Jan. 20, 1927.]

Sec. 6-b. Notwithstanding the provisions of Sec. 6, Art. VII, Constitution of the State of Texas, any county, acting through the commissioners court, may reduce the county permanent school fund of that county and may distribute the amount of the reduction to the independent and common school districts of the county on a per scholastic basis to be used solely for the purpose of reducing bonded indebtedness of those districts or for making permanent improvements. The commissioners court shall, however, retain a sufficient amount of the corpus of the county permanent school fund to pay ad valorem taxes on school lands or royalty interests owned at the time of the distribution. Nothing in this Section affects financial aid to any school district by the State.

[Note — Sec. 6-b of Art VII was added to allow a county to reduce its county permanent school fund and distribute the money to independent and common school districts on a per capita basis. Submitted by 62nd Legislature (1971) and adopted in election Nov. 7, 1972.]

[Note — Sec. 7 of Art. VII, relating to separate schools for white and colored, was deleted by constitutional amendment. Submitted by 61st Legislature (1969) and adopted in election Aug. 5, 1969.]

Sec. 8. Board of Education; Terms and Duties — The Legislature shall provide by law for a State Board of Education, whose members shall be appointed or elected in such manner and by such authority and shall serve for such terms as the Legislature shall prescribe not to exceed six years. The said board shall perform such duties as may be prescribed by law.

[Note — Sec. 8 of Art. VII was amended to reconstitute the State Board of Education. The original text provided for a Board of Education consisting of Governor, Comptroller and Secretary of State, serving ex officio. Submitted by 40th Legislature (1927); ratified in election Nov. 6, 1928; proclaimed Feb. 6, 1929.]

Asylums

Sec. 9. Lands of Asylums; Sale — All lands heretofore granted for the benefit of the lunatic, blind, deaf and dumb, and orphan asylums, together with such donations as may have been or may hereafter be made to either of them, respectively, as indicated in the several grants, are hereby set apart to provide a permanent fund for the support, maintenance and improvement of said asylums. And the Legislature may provide for the sale of the lands and the investment of the proceeds in the manner as provided for the sale and investment of school lands in Sec. 4 of this article.

University

Sec. 10. University Lands and Funds — The Legislature shall, as soon as practicable, establish, organize and provide for the maintenance, support and direction of a University of the first class, to be located by a vote of the people of this State and styled "The University of Texas," for the promotion of literature and the arts and sciences, including an agricultural, and mechanical department.

Sec. 11. University Funds; How Invested — In order to enable the Legislature to perform the duties set forth in the foregoing section, it is hereby declared all lands and other property heretofore set apart and appropriated for the establishment and maintenance of the University of Texas, together with all the proceeds of sales of the same, heretofore made or hereafter to be made, and all grants, donations and appropriations that may hereafter be made by the State of Texas, or from any other source, except donations limited to specific purposes, shall constitute and become a permanent university fund. And the same as realized and received into the treasury of the State (together with such sums belonging to the fund, as may now be in the treasury) shall be invested in bonds of the United States, State of Texas, or counties of said State, or in school bonds of municipalities or in bonds of any city of this State or in bonds issued under and by virtue of the Federal Farm Loan Act approved by the President of the United States July 17, 1916, and amendments thereto; and the interest accruing thereon shall be subject to appropriation by the Legislature to accomplish the purpose declared in the foregoing section; provided, that the one tenth of the alternate sections of the lands granted to railroads reserved by the State, which were set apart and appropriated to the establishment of the University of Texas by an act of the Legislature of Feb. 11, 1858, entitled "An act to establish the University of Texas" shall not be included in or constitute a part of, the permanent university fund.

[Note — Sec. 11 of Art. VII has been amended twice: (1) To add a clause giving the Board of Regents of the University of Texas latitude in expending part of the permanent fund for buildings. Submitted by 41st Legislature (1929) and adopted in election Nov. 4, 1930. (2) To eliminate this latitude and to restore the original provisions of the Constitution, which limited investments to bonds of the United States,

Article VII (Cont'd.)

State or civil subdivisions. This last amendment also added the clause "except donations limited to specific purposes." Submitted by 42nd Legislature (1931), adopted Nov. 8, 1932 and proclaimed Jan. 9, 1933.]

Sec. 11-a. In addition to the bonds enumerated in Section 11 of Article VII of the Constitution of the State of Texas, the Board of Regents of The University of Texas may invest the Permanent University Fund in securities, bonds or other obligations issued, insured, or guaranteed in any manner by the United States Government, or any of its agencies, and in such bonds, debentures, or obligations, and preferred and common stocks issued by corporations, associations, and other institutions as the Board of Regents of The University of Texas System may deem to be proper investments for said funds; provided, however, that not more than one per cent (1%) of said fund shall be invested in the securities of any one (1) corporation, nor shall more than five per cent (5%) of the voting stock of any one corporation be owned; provided, further, that stocks eligible for purchase shall be restricted to stocks of companies incorporated within the United States which have paid dividends for five (5) consecutive years or longer immediately prior to the date of purchase and which, except for bank stocks and insurance stocks, are listed upon an exchange registered with the Securities and Exchange Commission or its successors.

In making each and all of such investments said Board of Regents shall exercise the judgment and care under the circumstances then prevailing which men of ordinary prudence, discretion, and intelligence exercise in the management of their own affairs, not in regard to speculation but in regard to the permanent disposition of their funds, considering the probable income therefrom as well as the probable safety of their capital.

The interest, dividends and other income accruing from the investments of the Permanent University Fund, except the portion thereof which is appropriated by the operation of Sec. 18 of Art. VII for the payment of principal and interest on bonds or notes issued thereunder, shall be subject to appropriation by the Legislature to accomplish the purposes declared in Sec. 10 of Article VII of this Constitution.

This amendment shall be self-enacting, and shall become effective upon its adoption, provided, however, that the Legislature shall provide by law for full disclosure of all details concerning the investments in corporate stocks and bonds and other investments authorized herein.

[Note — Sec.11-a of Art. VII was added to provide for broader investment of the Permanent University Fund in corporate bonds and stocks under certain conditions and limitations. Submitted by 54th Legislature (1955) and adopted in election Nov. 6, 1956. It was further amended to increase the types of securities available for investment to the Permanent University Fund by allowing securities, bonds or other obligations issued, insured or guaranteed in any manner by the federal government. Submitted by 60th Legislature (1967) and adopted in election Nov. 5, 1968.]

Sec. 11-b. Notwithstanding any other provision of this constitution, in managing the assets of the permanent university fund, the Board of Regents of The University of Texas System may acquire, exchange, sell, supervise, manage, or retain, through procedures and subject to restrictions it establishes and in amounts it considers appropriate, any kind of investment, including investments in the Texas growth fund created by Article XVI, Section 70, of this constitution, that persons of ordinary prudence, discretion, and intelligence, exercising the judgment and care under the circumstances then prevailing, acquire or retain for their own account in the management of their affairs, not in regard to speculation but in regard to the permanent disposition of their funds, considering the probable income as well as the probable safety of their capital. This section does not affect the custodial responsibilities of the comptroller of public accounts for public funds, securities, and other evidences of investment.

[Note — Section 11-b was added to allow the Permanent University Fund to be invested in the Texas Growth Fund. Submitted by 70th Legislature (1987) and adopted in election Nov. 8, 1988. It was amended to change reference to the state treasurer to the state comptroller after the office of state treasurer was eliminated by constitutional amendment. Submitted by 74th Legislature (1995) and adopted in election Nov. 7, 1995.]

Sec. 12. **Lands to Be Sold; No Relief of Purchasers** — The land herein set apart to the university fund shall be sold under such regulations at such times and on such terms as may be provided by law, and the Legislature shall provide for the prompt collection, at maturity, of all debts due on account of university lands heretofore sold, or that may hereafter be sold, and shall in neither event have the power to grant relief to the purchasers.

Sec. 13. **Agricultural and Mechanical College; Appropriations** — The Agricultural and Mechanical College of Texas, established by an act of the Legislature passed April 17, 1871, located in the County of Brazos, is hereby made and constituted a branch of the University of Texas, for instruction in agriculture, the mechanic arts and the natural sciences connected therewith. And the Legislature shall at its next session make an appropriation not to exceed $40,000 for the construction and completion of the buildings and improvements, and

for providing the furniture necessary to put said college in immediate and successful operation.

Sec. 14. Prairie View A&M — Prairie View A&M University in Waller County is an institution of the first class under the direction of the same governing board as Texas A&M University referred to in Article VII, Section 13, of this constitution as the Agricultural and Mechanical College of Texas.

[Note — Sec. 14 of Art. VII was substituted for an earlier Sec. 14 to declare that Prairie View A&M University is an institution of the first class under direction of Texas A&M University governing board. (See also Sections 17 and 18 of Art. VII.) Submitted by 68th Legislature (1983) and adopted in election Nov. 6, 1984.]

Sec. 15. **Land Appropriated for University; How Sold** — In addition to the lands heretofore granted to the University of Texas, there is hereby set apart and appropriated, for the endowment, maintenance and support of said university and its branches, 1,000,000 acres of the unappropriated public domain of the State, to be designated and surveyed as may be provided by law; and said lands shall be sold under the same regulations and the proceeds invested in the same manner as is provided for the sale and investment of the permanent university fund; and the Legislature shall not have the power to grant any relief to the purchasers of said lands.

Sec. 16. **Terms of Office in School Systems** — The Legislature shall fix by law the terms of all offices of the public school system and of the State institutions of higher education, inclusive, and the terms of members of the respective boards, not to exceed six years.

[Note — Sec. 16 of Art. VII is the first of two amendments numbered 16 (See following section and note thereon.). This amendment was added to provide for fixing of terms of office in public school system. Submitted by 40th Legislature (1927); ratified Nov. 6, 1928; proclaimed Feb. 6, 1929.]

Sec. 16 [a.] **Taxation of University Lands** — All land mentioned in Secs. 11, 12 and 15 of Article VII of the Constitution of the State of Texas, now belonging to the University of Texas, shall be subject to the taxation for county purpose to the same extent as lands privately owned; provided, they shall be rendered for taxation upon values fixed by the State Tax Board; and providing, that the State shall remit annually to each of the counties in which said lands are located an amount equal to the tax imposed upon said land for county purposes.

[Note — The foregoing section, which obviously should have been numbered either 16-a or 17, was designated as No. 16 in H.J.R. No. 11 of the 41st Legislature (1929), in which the amendment was submitted. It is customarily printed in legal references as Sec. 16 [a.] This amendment was added to provide for taxation of University of Texas lands. It was ratified in election Nov. 4, 1930; declared adopted Dec. 17, 1930.]

Sec. 17. **Support for Higher Education** — (a) In the fiscal year beginning September 1, 1985, and each fiscal year thereafter, there is hereby appropriated out of the first money coming into the state treasury not otherwise appropriated by the constitution $100 million to be used by eligible agencies and institutions of higher education for the purpose of acquiring land either with or without permanent improvements, constructing and equipping buildings or other permanent improvements, major repair or rehabilitation of buildings or other permanent improvements, acquisition of capital equipment, library books and library materials, and paying for acquiring, constructing, or equipping or for major repair or rehabilitation of buildings, facilities, other permanent improvements, or capital equipment used jointly for educational and general activities and for auxiliary enterprises to the extent of their use for educational and general activities. For the five-year period that begins on September 1, 2000, and for each five-year period that begins after that period, the legislature, during a regular session that is nearest, but preceding, a five-year period, may by two-thirds vote of the membership of each house increase the amount of the constitutional appropriation for the five-year period but may not adjust the appropriation in such a way as to impair any obligation created by the issuance of bonds or notes in accordance with this section.

(b) The funds appropriated under Subsection (a) of this section shall be for the use of the following eligible agencies and institutions of higher education (even though their names may be changed):

(1) East Texas State University including East Texas State University at Texarkana;

(2) Lamar University including Lamar University at Orange and Lamar University at Port Arthur;

(3) Midwestern State University;

(4) University of North Texas;

(5) The University of Texas — Pan American including The University of Texas at Brownsville;

(6) Stephen F. Austin State University;

(7) Texas College of Osteopathic Medicine;

(8) Texas State University System Administration and the following component institutions:

(9) Angelo State University;

(10) Sam Houston State University;

(11) Southwest Texas State University;

(12) Sul Ross State University including Uvalde Study Center;

(13) Texas Southern University;

(14) Texas Tech University;

(15) Texas Tech University Health Sciences Center;

Article VII (Cont'd.)

(16) Texas Woman's University;
(17) University of Houston System Administration and the following component institutions:
(18) University of Houston;
(19) University of Houston — Victoria;
(20) University of Houston — Clear Lake;
(21) University of Houston — Downtown;
(22) Texas A&M University — Corpus Christi;
(23) Texas A&M International University;
(24) Texas A&M University — Kingsville;
(25) West Texas A&M University; and
(26) Texas State Technical College System and its campuses, but not its extension centers or programs.

(c) Pursuant to a two-thirds vote of the membership of each house of the legislature, institutions of higher education may be created at a later date by general law, and, when created, such an institution shall be entitled to participate in the funding provided by this section if it is not created as a part of The University of Texas System or The Texas A&M University System. An institution that is entitled to participate in dedicated funding provided by Article VII, Section 18, of this constitution may not be entitled to participate in the funding provided by this section.

(d) In the year 1985 and every 10 years thereafter, the legislature or an agency designated by the legislature no later than August 31 of such year shall allocate by equitable formula the annual appropriations made under Subsection (a) of this section to the governing boards of eligible agencies and institutions of higher education. The legislature shall review, or provide for a review, of the allocation formula at the end of the fifth year of each 10-year allocation period. At that time adjustments may be made in the allocation formula, but no adjustment that will prevent the payment of outstanding bonds and notes, both principal and interest, may be made.

(d-1) Notwithstanding Subsection (d) of this section, the allocation of the annual appropriation to Texas State Technical College System and its campuses may not exceed 2.2 percent of the total appropriation each fiscal year.

(e) Each governing board authorized to participate in the distribution of money under this section is authorized to expend all money distributed to it for any of the purposes enumerated in Subsection (a). In addition, such governing board may issue bonds and notes for the purposes of refunding bonds or notes issued under this section or prior law, acquiring land either with or without permanent improvements, constructing and equipping buildings or other permanent improvements, acquiring capital equipment, library books, and library materials, paying for acquiring, constructing, or equipping or for major repair or rehabilitation of buildings, facilities, other permanent improvements, or capital equipment used jointly for educational and general activities and for auxiliary enterprises to the extent of their use for educational and general activities, and for major repair and rehabilitation of buildings or other permanent improvements, and may pledge up to 50 percent of the money allocated to such governing board pursuant to this section to secure the payment of the principal and interest of such bonds or notes. Proceeds from the issuance of bonds or notes under this subsection shall be maintained in a local depository selected by the governing board issuing the bonds or notes. The bonds and notes issued under this subsection shall be payable solely out of the money appropriated by this section and shall mature serially or otherwise in not more than 10 years from their respective dates. All bonds issued under this section shall be sold only through competitive bidding and are subject to approval by the attorney general. Bonds approved by the attorney general shall be incontestable. The permanent university fund may be invested in the bonds and notes issued under this section.

(f) The funds appropriated by this section may not be used for the purpose of constructing, equipping, repairing, or rehabilitating buildings or other permanent improvements that are to be used solely for student housing, intercollegiate athletics, or auxiliary enterprises.

(g) The comptroller of public accounts shall make annual transfers of the funds allocated pursuant to Subsection (d) directly to the governing boards of the eligible institutions.

(h) To assure efficient use of construction funds and the orderly development of physical plants to accommodate the state's real need, the legislature may provide for the approval or disapproval of all new construction projects at the eligible agencies and institutions entitled to participate in the funding provided by this section.

(i) The legislature by general law may dedicate portions of the state's revenues to the creation of a dedicated fund ("the higher education fund") for the purposes expressed in Subsection (a) of this section. The legislature shall provide for administration of the fund, which shall be invested in the manner provided for investment of the permanent university fund. The income from the investment of the higher education fund shall be credited to the higher education fund until such time as the fund totals $2 billion. The principal of the higher education fund shall never be expended. At the beginning of the fiscal year after the fund reaches $2 billion, as certified by the comptroller of public accounts, the dedication of general revenue funds provided for in Subsection (a) of this section shall cease. At the beginning of the fiscal year after the fund reaches $2 billion, and each year thereafter, 10 percent of the interest, dividends, and other income accruing from the investments of the higher education fund during the previous fiscal year shall be deposited and become part of the principal of the fund, and out of the remainder of the annual income from the investment of the principal of the fund there shall be

appropriated an annual sum sufficient to pay the principal and interest due on the bonds and notes issued under this section and the balance of the income shall be allocated, distributed, and expended as provided for the appropriations made under Subsection (a).

(j) The state systems and institutions of higher education designated in this section may not receive any additional funds from the general revenue of the state for acquiring land with or without permanent improvements, for constructing or equipping buildings or other permanent improvements, or for major repair and rehabilitation of buildings or other permanent improvements except that:
(1) In the case of fire or natural disaster the legislature may appropriate from the general revenue an amount sufficient to replace the uninsured loss of any building or other permanent improvement; and
(2) the legislature, by two-thirds vote of each house, may, in cases of demonstrated need, which need must be clearly expressed in the body of the act, appropriate additional general revenue funds for acquiring land with or without permanent improvements, for constructing or equipping buildings or other permanent improvements, or for major repair and rehabilitation of buildings or other permanent improvements.

This subsection does not apply to legislative appropriations made prior to the adoption of this amendment.

(k) Without the prior approval of the legislature, appropriations under this section may not be expended for acquiring land with or without permanent improvements, or for constructing and equipping buildings or other permanent improvements, for a branch campus or educational center that is not a separate degree-granting institution created by general law.

(l) This section is self-enacting upon the issuance of the governor's proclamation declaring the adoption of the amendment, and the state comptroller of public accounts shall do all things necessary to effectuate this section. This section does not impair any obligation created by the issuance of any bonds and notes in accordance with prior law, and all outstanding bonds and notes shall be paid in full, both principal and interest, in accordance with their terms. If the provisions of this section conflict with any other provisions of this constitution, then the provisions of this section shall prevail, notwithstanding all such conflicting provisions.

[Note — This Sec. 17 of Art. VII supersedes the old Sec. 17, which provided for a confederate pension fund tax, college building fund tax and reduced the ad valorem ceiling for general purposes. That section was deleted in election Nov. 2, 1982. The above Sec. 17 was added to create from general revenue a special higher education assistance fund for construction and related activities, to restructure the permanent university fund and to increase the number of institutions eligible to benefit from the permanent university fund. (See also Sections 14 and 18 of Art. VII.) Submitted by 68th Legislature (1983) and adopted in election Nov. 6, 1984. Section 17 was amended to adjust the amount and expenditure of certain constitutionally dedicated funds for public institutions of higher education. Submitted by 73rd Legislature (1993) and adopted in election Nov. 2, 1993. Subsection (l) was amended to eliminate the reference to the state treasurer when that office was eliminated. Submitted by 74th Legislature (1995) and adopted in election Nov. 7, 1995.]

Sec. 18. **Building Bonds Authorized for the University of Texas and Texas A&M University; Retired From Income From the Permanent University Fund; Etc.** — (a) The Board of Regents of The Texas A&M University System may issue bonds and notes not to exceed a total amount of 10 percent of the cost value of the investments and other assets of the permanent university fund (exclusive of real estate) at the time of the issuance thereof, and may pledge all or any part of its one-third interest in the available university fund to secure the payment of the principal and interest of those bonds and notes, for the purpose of acquiring land either with or without permanent improvements, constructing and equipping buildings or other permanent improvements, major repair and rehabilitation of buildings and other permanent improvements, acquiring capital equipment and library books and library materials, and refunding bonds or notes issued under this Section or prior law, at or for The Texas A&M University System administration and the following component institutions of the system:
(1) Texas A&M University, including its medical college which the legislature may authorize as a separate medical institution; (2) Prairie View A&M University, including its nursing school in Houston; (3) Tarleton State University; (4) Texas A&M University at Galveston; (5) Texas Forest Service; (6) Texas Agricultural Experiment Stations; (7) Texas Agricultural Extension Service; (8) Texas Engineering Experiment Stations; (9) Texas Transportation Institute; and (10) Texas Engineering Extension Service.

(b) The Board of Regents of The University of Texas System may issue bonds and notes not to exceed a total amount of 20 percent of the cost value of investments and other assets of the permanent university fund (exclusive of real estate) at the time of issuance thereof, and may pledge all or any part of its two-thirds interest in the available university fund to secure the payment of the principal and interest of those bonds and notes, for the purpose of acquiring land either with or without permanent improvements, constructing and equipping buildings or other permanent improvements, major repair and rehabilitation of buildings and other permanent improvements, acquiring capital equipment and library books and library materials, and refunding bonds or notes issued under this section or prior law, at or for The University of Texas System administration and the following component institutions of the system:

Article VII (Cont'd.): Article VIII

(1) The University of Texas at Arlington; (2) The University of Texas at Austin; (3) The University of Texas at Dallas; (4) The University of Texas at El Paso; (5) The University of Texas of the Permian Basin; (6) The University of Texas at San Antonio; (7) The University of Texas at Tyler; (8) The University of Texas Health Science Center at Dallas; (9) The University of Texas Medical Branch at Galveston; (10) The University of Texas Health Science Center at Houston; (11) The University of Texas Health Science Center at San Antonio; (12) The University of Texas System Cancer Center; (13) The University of Texas Health Center at Tyler; and (14) The University of Texas Institute of Texan Cultures at San Antonio.

(c) Pursuant to a two-thirds vote of the membership of each house of the legislature, institutions of higher education may be created at a later date as a part of The University of Texas System or The Texas A&M University System by general law, and, when created, such an institution shall be entitled to participate in the funding provided by this section for the system in which it is created. An institution that is entitled to participate in dedicated funding provided by Article VII, Section 17, of this constitution may not be entitled to participate in the funding provided by this section.

(d) The proceeds of the bonds or notes issued under Subsection (a) or (b) of this section may not be used for the purpose of constructing, equipping, repairing, or rehabilitating buildings or other permanent improvements that are to be used for student housing, intercollegiate athletics, or auxiliary enterprises.

(e) The available university fund consists of the dividends, interest and other income from the permanent university fund (less administrative expenses) including the net income attributable to the surface of permanent university fund land. Out of one-third of the available university fund, there shall be appropriated an annual sum sufficient to pay the principal and interest due on the bonds and notes issued by the Board of Regents of The Texas A&M University System under this section and prior law, and the remainder of that one-third of the available university fund shall be appropriated to the Board of Regents of The Texas A&M University System which shall have the authority and duty in turn to appropriate an equitable portion of the same for the support and maintenance of The Texas A&M University System administration, Texas A&M University, and Prairie View A&M University. The Board of Regents of The Texas A&M University System, in making just and equitable appropriations to Texas A&M University and Prairie View A&M University, shall exercise its discretion with due regard to such criteria as the board may deem appropriate from year to year, taking into account all amounts appropriated from Subsection (f) of this section. Out of the other two-thirds of the available university fund there shall be appropriated an annual sum sufficient to pay the principal and interest due on the bonds and notes issued by the Board of Regents of The University of Texas System under this section and prior law, and the remainder of such two-thirds of the available university fund, shall be appropriated for the support and maintenance of The University of Texas at Austin and The University of Texas System administration.

(f) It is provided, however, that, for 10 years beginning upon the adoption of this amendment, before any other allocation is made of The University of Texas System's two-thirds share of the available university fund, remaining after payment of principal and interest on its bonds and notes issued under this section and prior law, $6 million per year shall be appropriated out of that share to the Board of Regents of The Texas A&M University System for said board's use in making appropriations to Prairie View A&M University. This subsection expires and is deleted from this constitution 10 years from the adoption of this amendment.

(g) The bonds and notes issued under this section shall be payable solely out of the available university fund, mature serially or otherwise in not more than 30 years from their respective dates, and, except for refunding bonds, be sold only through competitive bidding. All of these bonds and notes are subject to approval by the attorney general and when so approved are incontestable. The permanent university fund may be invested in these bonds and notes.

(h) To assure efficient use of construction funds and the orderly development of physical plants to accommodate the state's real need, the legislature may provide for the approval or disapproval of all new construction projects at the eligible agencies and institutions entitled to participate in the funding provided by this section except The University of Texas at Austin, Texas A&M University in College Station, and Prairie View A&M University.

(i) The state systems and institutions of higher education designated in this section may not receive any funds from the general revenue of the state for acquiring land with or without permanent improvements, for constructing or equipping buildings or other permanent improvements, or for major repair and rehabilitation of buildings or other permanent improvements except that:

(1) In the case of fire or natural disaster the legislature may appropriate from the general revenue an amount sufficient to replace the uninsured loss of any building or other permanent improvement; and

(2) The legislature, by two-thirds vote of each house, may, in cases of demonstrated need, which need must be clearly expressed in the body of the act, appropriate general revenue funds for acquiring land with or without permanent improvements, for constructing or equipping buildings or other permanent improvements, or for major repair and rehabilitation of buildings or other permanent improvements.

This subsection does not apply to legislative appropriations made prior to the adoption of this amendment.

(j) This section is self-enacting on the issuance of the governor's proclamation declaring the adoption of this amendment, and the state comptroller of public accounts shall do all things necessary to effectuate this section. This section does not impair any obligation created by the issuance of bonds or notes in accordance with prior law, and all outstanding bonds and notes shall be paid in full, both principal and interest, in accordance with their terms, and the changes herein made in the allocation of the available university fund shall not affect the pledges thereof made in connection with such bonds or notes heretofore issued. If the provisions of this section conflict with any other provision of this constitution, then the provisions of this section shall prevail, notwithstanding any such conflicting provisions.

[Note — Sec. 17 and Sec. 18 of Art. VII were originally added to the Constitution as a single amendment to provide for funding of construction at Texas universities and colleges. Submitted by 50th Legislature (1947) and adopted in election Aug. 23, 1947. It was further amended by 54th Legislature (1956), adopted in election Nov. 6, 1956; and again by 60th Legislature (1967), adopted in election Nov. 8, 1968. Sec. 17 was repealed by 67th Legislature (1981), approved in election Nov. 2, 1982. A new Sec. 17 and Sec. 18 were submitted by 68th Legislature (1983) and adopted in election Nov. 6, 1984. (See also notes under Sec. 14 and Sec. 17.) Subsection (j) was amended to eliminate the reference to state treasurer when that office was eliminated. Submitted by 74th Legislature (1995) and adopted in election Nov. 7, 1995.]

Article VIII — Taxation and Revenue

Sec. 1. **Taxation to Be Equal and Uniform; Occupation and Income Taxes; Exemptions; Limitations Upon Counties, Cities, Etc.** — (a) Taxation shall be equal and uniform.

(b) All real property and tangible personal property in this State, unless exempt as required or permitted by this Constitution, whether owned by natural persons or corporations, other than municipal, shall be taxed in proportion to its value, which shall be ascertained as may be provided by law.

(c) The Legislature may provide for the taxation of intangible property and may also impose occupation taxes, both upon natural persons and upon corporations, other than municipal, doing any business in this State. Subject to the restrictions of Section 24 of this article, it may also tax incomes of both natural persons and corporations other than municipal. Persons engaged in mechanical and agricultural pursuits shall never be required to pay an occupation tax.

[Note — Section 1(c) of Article VIII was amended to add reference to Section 24. Submitted by 73rd Legislature (1993) and adopted in election Nov. 2, 1993.]

(d) The Legislature by general law shall exempt from ad valorem taxation household goods not held or used for production of income and personal effects not held or used for the production of income. The Legislature by general law may exempt from ad valorem taxation: (1) all or part of the personal property homestead of a family or single adult, "personal property homestead" meaning that personal property exempt by law from forced sale for debt; and (2) subject to Subsections (e) and (g) of this section, all other tangible personal property, except structures which are personal property and are used or occupied as residential dwellings and except property held or used for the production of income.

(e) The governing body of a political subdivision, other than a county education district, may provide for the taxation of all property exempt under a law adopted under Subdivision (2) of Subsection (d) of this section and not exempt from ad valorem taxation by any other law. In the manner provided by law, the voters of a county education district at an election held for that purpose may provide for the taxation of all property exempt under a law adopted under Subdivision (2) of Subsection (d) of this section and not exempt from ad valorem taxation by any other law.

(f) The occupation tax levied by any county, city or town for any year, on persons or corporations pursuing any profession or business, shall not exceed one half of the tax levied by the State for the same period on such profession or business.

(g) The Legislature may exempt from ad valorem taxation tangible personal property that is held or used for the production of income and has a taxable value of less than the minimum amount sufficient to recover the costs of the administration of the taxes on the property, as determined by or under the general law granting the exemption.

(h) The Legislature may exempt from ad valorem taxation a mineral interest that has a taxable value of less than the minimum amount sufficient to recover the costs of the administration of the taxes on the interest, as determined by or under the general law granting the exemption.

[Note — Sec. 1 of Art. VIII was amended to provide tax relief for residential homesteads and to provide personal property exemptions. (See also Sec. 1-b, and Sec. 23 of Art. VIII.) Submitted by 65th Legislature, (1977) and adopted in election Nov. 7, 1978. It was further amended to provide exemption from ad valorem taxation for certain tangible personal property located in the state. Submitted by 70th Legislature (1987) and adopted in election Nov. 3, 1987. Sec. 1 (b) was amended to authorize the exemption from ad valorem taxation certain personal property temporarily in the state for certain purposes. (See related amendment at Sec. 1-j, Art. VIII.) Submitted by 71st Legislature (1989) and adopted in election Nov. 7, 1989. Subsection (e) was amended to provide for taxation by a county education district. Submitted by 72nd Legislature and adopted in election Aug. 10, 1991. Subsection (b) was amended and Subsections (g)

Article VIII (Cont'd.)

and (h) were added to authorize exemption from ad valorem taxation personal property and mineral interests having a value insufficient to recover the administrative costs of collecting the taxes. Submitted by 74th Legislature (1995) and adopted in election Nov. 7, 1995.]

Sec. 1-a. **Abolishing Ad Valorem Tax for State's General Fund Purposes; Providing Local Tax Rate, Etc.** — From and after January 1, 1951, no State ad valorem tax shall be levied upon any property within this State for general revenue purposes. From and after January 1, 1951, the several counties of the State are authorized to levy ad valorem taxes upon all property within their respective boundaries for county purposes, except the first three thousand dollars ($3,000) value of residential homesteads of married or unmarried adults, male or female, including those living alone, not to exceed thirty cents (30¢) on each one hundred dollars ($100) valuation, in addition to all other ad valorem taxes authorized by the Constitution of this State, provided the revenue derived therefrom shall be used for construction and maintenance of farm-to-market roads or for flood control, except as herein otherwise provided.

Provided that in those counties or political subdivisions or areas of the State from which tax donations have heretofore been granted, the State Automatic Tax Board shall continue to levy the full amount of the State ad valorem tax for the duration of such donation, or until all legal obligations heretofore authorized by the law granting such donation or donations shall have been fully discharged, whichever shall first occur; provided that if such donation to any such county or political subdivision is for less than the full amount of State ad valorem taxes so levied, the portion of such taxes remaining over and above such donation shall be retained by said county or subdivision.

[Note — Sec. 1-a of Art. VIII was first added and then amended, as follows: (1) Giving homesteads $3,000 exemption from State taxes. Submitted by 42nd Legislature (1931) and adopted in election Nov. 8, 1932. (2) Making more definite the provision for extending the exemption to counties and subdivisions having tax remission as soon as tax remission ceased, whether by expiration of the period designated in the act granting remission or voluntarily by action of local authorities. The original amendment failed to make provision for the latter contingency. Submitted by 43rd Legislature (1933), and adopted in election Aug. 26, 1933. (3) Reducing maximum ad valorem tax for general revenue from 35¢ to 30¢. (4) Abolishing ad valorem tax for state general fund purposes and providing for local taxation as indicated in text of section. (See also Sec. 1-b immediately below and note following.) Submitted by 50th Legislature (1947) and adopted in election Nov. 2, 1948. (5) Extending the $3,000 ad valorem tax exemption to homesteads of unmarried adults. Submitted by 63rd Legislature (1973) and adopted in election Nov. 6, 1973.]

Sec. 1-b. **Homestead Exemption Under State Tax** — (a) Three thousand dollars ($3,000) of the assessed taxable value of all residence homesteads of married or unmarried adults, male or female, including those living alone, shall be exempt from all taxation for all State purposes.

(b) The governing body of any county, city, town, school district, or other political subdivision of the State, other than a county education district, may exempt by its own action not less than Three Thousand Dollars ($3,000) of the market value of residence homesteads of persons, married or unmarried, including those living alone, who are under a disability for purposes of payment of disability insurance benefits under Federal Old-Age, Survivors, and Disability Insurance or its successor or of married or unmarried persons sixty-five (65) years of age or older, including those living alone, from all ad valorem taxes thereafter levied by the political subdivision. As an alternative, upon receipt of a petition signed by twenty percent (20%) of the voters who voted in the last preceding election held by the political subdivision, the governing body of the subdivision shall call an election to determine by majority vote whether an amount not less than Three Thousand Dollars ($3,000) as provided in the petition, of the market value of residence homesteads of disabled persons or of persons sixty-five (65) years of age or over shall be exempt from ad valorem taxes thereafter levied by the political subdivision. In the manner provided by law, the voters of a county education district at an election held for that purpose may exempt an amount not less than Three Thousand Dollars ($3,000), as provided in the petition, of the market value of residence homesteads of disabled persons or of persons sixty-five (65) years of age or over from ad valorem taxes thereafter levied by the county education district. An eligible disabled person who is sixty-five (65) years of age or older may not receive both exemptions from the same political subdivision in the same year but may choose either if the subdivision has adopted both. Where any ad valorem tax has theretofore been pledged for the payment of any debt, the taxing officers of the political subdivision shall have authority to continue to levy and collect the tax against the homestead property at the same rate as the tax so pledged until the debt is discharged, if the cessation of the levy would impair the obligation of the contract by which the debt was created.

An exemption adopted under this subsection based on assessed value is increased, effective January 1, 1979, to an amount that, when converted to market value, provides the same reduction in taxes, except that the market value exemption shall be rounded to the nearest $100.

(c) Five Thousand Dollars ($5,000) of the market value of the residence homestead of a married or unmarried adult, including one living alone, is exempt from ad valorem taxation for general elementary and secondary public school purposes. In addition to this exemption, the Legislature by general law may exempt an amount not to exceed Ten Thousand Dollars ($10,000) of the market value of the residence homestead of a person who is disabled as defined in Subsection (b) of this section and of a person sixty-five (65) years of age or older from ad valorem taxation for general elementary and secondary public school purposes. The Legislature by general law may base the amount of and condition eligibility for the additional exemption authorized by this subsection for disabled persons and for persons sixty-five (65) years of age or older on economic need. An eligible disabled person who is sixty-five (65) years of age or older may not receive both exemptions from a school district but may choose either. An eligible person is entitled to receive both the exemption required by this subsection for all residence homesteads and any exemption adopted pursuant to Subsection (b) of this section, but the Legislature shall provide by general law whether an eligible disabled or elderly person may receive both the additional exemption for the elderly and disabled authorized by this subsection and any exemption for the elderly or disabled adopted pursuant to Subsection (b) of this section. Where ad valorem tax has previously been pledged for the payment of debt, the taxing officers of a school district may continue to levy and collect the tax against the value of homesteads exempted under this subsection until the debt is discharged if the cessation of the levy would impair the obligation of the contract by which the debt was created. The Legislature shall provide for formulas to protect school districts against all or part of the revenue loss incurred by the implementation of Article VIII, Sections 1-b(c), 1-b(d), and 1-d-1, of this constitution. The Legislature by general law may define residence homestead for purposes of this section.

(d) Except as otherwise provided by this subsection, if a person receives the residence homestead exemption prescribed by Subsection (c) of this section for homesteads of persons sixty-five (65) years of age or older, the total amount of ad valorem taxes imposed on that homestead for general elementary and secondary public school purposes may not be increased while it remains the residence homestead of that person or that person's spouse who receives the exemption. If a person sixty-five (65) years of age or older dies in a year in which the person received the exemption, the total amount of ad valorem taxes imposed on the homestead for general elementary and secondary public school purposes may not be increased while it remains the residence homestead of that person's surviving spouse if the spouse is fifty-five (55) years of age or older at the time of the person's death, subject to any exceptions provided by general law. However, taxes otherwise limited by this subsection may be increased to the extent the value of the homestead is increased by improvements other than repairs or improvements made to comply with governmental requirements.

(e) The governing body of a political subdivision, other than a county education district, may exempt from ad valorem taxation a percentage of the market value of the residence homestead of a married or unmarried adult, including one living alone. In the manner provided by law, the voters of a county education district at an election held for that purpose may exempt from ad valorem taxation a percentage of the market value of the residence homestead of a married or unmarried adult, including one living alone. The percentage may not exceed twenty percent. However, the amount of an exemption authorized pursuant to this subsection may not be less than Five Thousand Dollars ($5,000) unless the legislature by general law prescribes other monetary restrictions on the amount of the exemption. An eligible adult is entitled to receive other applicable exemptions provided by law. Where ad valorem tax has previously been pledged for the payment of debt, the governing body of a political subdivision may continue to levy and collect the tax against the value of the homesteads exempted under this subsection until the debt is discharged if the cessation of the levy would impair the obligation of the contract by which the debt was created. The legislature by general law may prescribe procedures for the administration of residence homestead exemptions.

(f) The surviving spouse of a person who received an exemption under Subsection (b) of this section for the residence homestead of a person sixty-five (65) years of age or older is entitled to an exemption for the same property from the same political subdivision in an amount equal to that of the exemption received by the deceased spouse if the deceased spouse died in a year in which the deceased spouse received the exemption, the surviving spouse was fifty-five (55) years of age or older when the deceased spouse died, and the property was the residence homestead of the surviving spouse when the deceased spouse died and remains the residence homestead of the surviving spouse. A person who receives an exemption under Subsection (b) of this section is not entitled to an exemption under this subsection. The legislature by general law may prescribe procedures for the administration of this subsection.

[Note — Sec. 1-b of Art. VIII has been amended seven times: (1) To allow county, city, school district or other political subdivision to exempt not less than $3,000 of the assessed value of residence homesteads of persons 65 years and older from all ad valorem taxes levied by the subdivision. Submitted by 62nd Legislature (1971) and adopted in election Nov. 7, 1972. (See also note under 1-c below.) (2) To extend to unmarried persons
the $3,000 ad valorem exemption on homesteads. Submitted by 63rd Legislature (1973) and adopted in election Nov. 6, 1973. (See also Art. XVI, Secs. 50, 51 and 52.) (3) To give added tax relief to disabled persons and persons over 65 years of age and to provide for admin-

Article VIII (Cont'd.)

istration of property tax. It also added Subsections (c) and (d). (See also Sec. 1, Sec. 21, and Sec. 23 of Art. VIII.) Submitted by 65th Legislature (1977) and adopted in election Nov. 7, 1978. (4) To add Subsection (e) to authorize political subdivisions to provide property tax relief for owners of residence homesteads and changing certain property tax administrative procedures. (See also Sec. 21, Subsection (c) of Art. VIII.) Submitted by 67th Legislature (1981) and adopted in election Nov. 3, 1981. (5) Subsection (d) of Sec. 1-b of Art. VIII was amended to limit school tax increases on the residence homestead of the surviving spouse of an elderly person. Submitted by 70th Legislature (1987) and adopted in election Nov. 3, 1987. (6) Subsections (b) and (e) were amended to clarify the homestead exemptions allowed to be granted by county education districts. Submitted by 72nd Legislature and adopted in election Aug. 10, 1991. (7) Subsection (f) was added to authorize exemption from property tax of the residence homestead of the surviving spouse of an elderly person. Submitted by 74th Legislature (1995) and adopted in election Nov. 7, 1995.]

Sec. 1-b-1. The references to a county education district in Sections 1 and 1-b of this article neither validate nor invalidate county education districts.

[Note — Sec. 1-b-1 of Article VIII was added to clarify the status of county education districts in reference to this article. Submitted by 72nd Legislature, (1991) and adopted in election Aug. 10, 1992.]]

Sec. 1-c. **Optional Provisions Relating to Sec. 1-a and Sec. 1-b** — Provided, however, the terms of this resolution shall not be effective unless House Joint Resolution No. 24 is adopted by the people and in no event shall this resolution go into effect until January 1, 1951.

[Note — Sec. 1-b and Sec. 1-c of Article VIII were added because of an oversight in writing the text of Sec. 1-a (adopted by joint resolution at an earlier date), which would have abolished the $3,000 homestead exemption under the state school tax on adoption of Sec. 1-a by the people. Submitted by 50th Legislature (1947) and adopted in election Nov. 2, 1948.]

Sec. 1-d. **Taxation of Agricultural Land** — (a) All land owned by natural persons which is designated for agricultural use in accordance with the provisions of this section shall be assessed for all tax purposes on the consideration of only those factors relative to such agricultural use. "Agricultural use" means the raising of livestock or growing of crops, fruit, flowers, and other products of the soil under natural conditions as a business venture for profit, which business is the primary occupation and source of income of the owner.

(b) For each assessment year the owner wishes to qualify his land under provisions of this section as designated for agricultural use he shall file with the local tax assessor a sworn statement in writing describing the use to which the land is devoted.

(c) Upon receipt of the sworn statement in writing the local tax assessor shall determine whether or not such land qualifies for the designation as to agricultural use as defined herein and in the event it so qualifies he shall designate such land as being for agricultural use and assess the land accordingly.

(d) Such local tax assessor may inspect the land and require such evidence of use and source of income as may be necessary or useful in determining whether or not the agricultural use provision of this article applies.

(e) No land may qualify for the designation provided for in this act unless for at least three (3) successive years immediately preceding the assessment date the land has been devoted exclusively for agricultural use, or unless the land has been continuously developed for agriculture during such time.

(f) Each year during which the land is designated for agricultural use, the local tax assessor shall note on his records the valuation which would have been made had the land not qualified for such designation under this section. If designated land is subsequently diverted to a purpose other than that of agricultural use, or is sold, the land shall be subject to an additional tax. The additional tax shall equal the difference between taxes paid or payable, hereunder, and the amount of tax payable for the preceding three years had the land been otherwise assessed. Until paid, there shall be a lien for additional taxes and interest on land assessed under the provisions of this section.

(g) The valuation and assessment of any minerals or subsurface rights to minerals shall not come within the provisions of this section.

[Note — Sec. 1-d of Art. VIII was added to provide that all land designated for agricultural use be assessed only as such. Submitted by 59th Legislature (1965) and adopted in election Nov. 8, 1966.]

Sec. 1-d-1. **Open-Space Land Taxation** — (a) To promote the preservation of open-space land, the legislature shall provide by general law for taxation of open-space land devoted to farm, ranch, or wildlife management purposes on the basis of its productive capacity and may provide by general law for taxation of open-space land devoted to timber production on the basis of its productive capacity. The legislature by general law may provide eligibility limitations under this section and may impose sanctions in furtherance of the taxation policy of this section.

(b) If a property owner qualifies his land for designation for agricultural use under Section 1-d of this article, the land is subject to the provisions of Section 1-d for the year in which the designation is effective and is not subject to a law enacted under this Section 1-d-1 in that year.

[Note — Sec. 1-d-1 of Art. VIII was added to promote preservation of open-space land and to provide for taxation of production of timber thereon; also redefines use of open land for agricultural purposes and taxation thereon. Submitted by 65th Legislature (1977) and adopted in election Nov. 7, 1978. Subsection (a) was amended to clarify the taxation of land used for wildlife management. Submitted by 74th Legislature (1995) and adopted in election Nov. 7, 1995.]

Sec. 1-e. **Gradual Abolition of Ad Valorem Tax** — (1) No State ad valorem taxes shall be levied upon any property within this State.

(2) All receipts from previously authorized State ad valorem taxes that are collected on or after the effective date of the 1982 amendment to this section shall be deposited to the credit of the general fund of the county collecting the taxes and may be expended for county purposes. Receipts from taxes collected before that date shall be distributed by the Legislature among institutions eligible to receive distributions under prior law. Those receipts and receipts distributed under prior law may be expended for the purposes provided under prior law or for repair and renovation of existing permanent improvements.

[Note — Sec. 1-e of Art. VIII was added to provide for the gradual abolition of the ad valorem tax for all state purposes except those that were listed under Art. VII, Sec. 17 (which was repealed by constitutional amendment in an election Nov. 2, 1982) for certain institutions of higher education and for pension funds for Confederate veterans and their widows, and for Texas Rangers and their widows. Submitted by 60th Legislature (1967) and adopted in election Nov. 5, 1968. Sec. 1-e was amended to abolish the state property tax and to add Subsection (2), which is self-explanatory. Submitted by Called Session of 67th Legislature (1982) and adopted in election Nov. 2, 1982. (See also Art. III, Sec. 51 and Art. XVI, Sec. 66.)]

Sec. 1-f. **Ad Valorem Tax Relief** — The legislature by law may provide for the preservation of cultural, historical, or natural history resources by:

(1) granting exemptions or other relief from state ad valorem taxes on appropriate property so designated in the manner prescribed by law; and

(2) authorizing political subdivisions to grant exemptions or other relief from ad valorem taxes on appropriate property so designated by the political subdivision in the manner prescribed by general law.

[Note — Sec. 1-f of Art. VIII was added to authorize tax relief to preserve certain cultural, historical or natural history resources. Submitted by 65th Legislature (1977) and adopted in election Nov. 8, 1977.]

Sec. 1-g. **Tax Relief to Encourage Development and Improvement of Property** — (a) The legislature by general law may authorize cities, towns, and other taxing units to grant exemptions or other relief from ad valorem taxes on property located in a reinvestment zone for the purpose of encouraging development or redevelopment and improvement of the property.

(b) The Legislature by general law may authorize an incorporated city or town to issue bonds or notes to finance the development or redevelopment of an unproductive, underdeveloped, or blighted area within the city or town and to pledge for repayment of those bonds or notes increases in ad valorem tax revenues imposed on property in the area by the city or town and other political subdivisions.

[Note — Sec. 1-g of Art. VIII was added to encourage development and improvement of certain areas through tax relief. Submitted by 67th Legislature (1981) and adopted in election Nov. 3, 1981.]

Sec. 1-h — **Validation of Assessment Ratio** — Sec. 26.03, Tax Code, is validated as of January 1, 1980.

[Note — Sec. 1-h of Art. VIII was added to give validation date of Sec. 26.03 of the Tax Code. Submitted by Called Session of 67th Legislature (1982) and adopted in election Nov. 2, 1982.]

Sec. 1-i. — The legislature by general law may provide ad valorem tax relief for mobile marine drilling equipment designed for offshore drilling of oil or gas wells that is being stored while not in use in a county bordering on the Gulf of Mexico or on a bay or other body of water immediately adjacent to the Gulf of Mexico.

[Note — Sec. 1-i of Art. VIII was added to provide ad valorem tax relief for certain offshore drilling equipment that is not in use. Submitted by 70th Legislature (1987) and adopted in election Nov. 3, 1987.]

Sec. 1-j. (a) To promote economic development in the State, goods, wares, merchandise, other tangible personal property, and ores, other than oil, natural gas, and other petroleum products, are exempt from ad valorem taxation if:

(1) the property is acquired in or imported into this State to be forwarded outside this State, whether or not the intention to forward the property outside this State is formed or the destination to which the property is forwarded is specified when the property is acquired in or imported into this State;

(2) the property is detained in this State for assembling, storing, manufacturing, processing, or fabricating purposes by the person who acquired or imported the property; and

(3) the property is transported outside of this State not later than

Article VIII (Cont'd.)

175 days after the date the person acquired or imported the property in this State.

(b) Tangible personal property exempted from taxation in Subsection (a) of this section is subject to the following:

(1) A county, common, or independent school district, junior college district, or municipality, including a home-rule city, may tax such property otherwise exempt, if the governing body of the county, common, or independent school district, junior college district, or municipality takes official action as provided in this section and in the manner provided by law to provide for the taxation of such property.

(2) Any official action to tax such exempt property must be taken before April 1, 1990. If official action is taken to tax such exempt property before January 1, 1990, such property is taxable effective for the tax year 1990. However, if such official action to tax such exempt property is taken prior to April 1, 1990, but after January 1, 1990, the official action shall not become effective to tax such property until the 1991 tax year.

(3) Any of the above-named political subdivisions shall have the authority to exempt from payment of taxation such property located in such above-named political subdivisions for the taxing year 1989. If a governing body exempts the property from 1989 taxes, the governing body shall waive 1989 taxes already imposed and refund 1989 taxes already paid on such property for that year.

(4) The governing body of a county, common, or independent school district, junior college district, or municipality that acts under Subdivision (2) of Subsection (b) of this section to tax the property otherwise exempt by Subsection (a) of this section may subsequently exempt the property from taxation by rescinding its action to tax the property. The exemption applies to each tax year that begins after the date the action is taken and applies to the tax year in which the action is taken if the governing body so provides. A governing body that rescinds its action to tax the property may not take action to tax such property after the rescission.

(c) For purposes of this section:

(1) tangible personal property shall include aircraft and aircraft parts;

(2) property imported into this State shall include property brought into this State;

(3) property forwarded outside this State shall include property transported outside this State or to be affixed to an aircraft to be transported outside this State; and

(4) property detained in this State for assembling, storing, manufacturing, processing, or fabricating purposes shall include property, aircraft, or aircraft parts brought into this State or acquired in this State and used by the person who acquired the property, aircraft, or aircraft parts in or who brought the property, aircraft, or aircraft parts into this State for the purpose of repair or maintenance of aircraft operated by a certificated air carrier.

[Note — Sec. 1-j of Art. VIII was added to authorize the exemption from ad valorem taxation of certain personal property temporarily in the state for certain purposes. (See related amendment in Sec. 1 (a) of Art. VIII.) Proposed by 71st Legislature (1989) and adopted in election Nov. 7, 1989.]

Sec. 1-k. The legislature by general law may exempt from ad valorem taxation property owned by a nonprofit corporation organized to supply water or provide wastewater service that provides in the bylaws of the corporation that on dissolution of the corporation, the assets of the corporation remaining after discharge of the corporation's indebtedness shall be transferred to an entity that provides a water supply or wastewater service, or both, that is exempt from ad valorem taxation, if the property is reasonably necessary for and used in the acquisition, treatment, storage, transportation, sale, or distribution of water or the provision of wastewater service.

[Note — Sec. 1-k was added to Article VIII to exempt from ad valorem taxation property owned by a non-profit water supply or wastewater service corporation. Submitted by 72nd Legislature (1991) and adopted in election Nov. 5, 1991.]

Sec. 1-l. (a) The legislature by general law may exempt from ad valorem taxation all or part of real and personal property used, constructed, acquired, or installed wholly or partly to meet or exceed rules or regulations adopted by any environmental protection agency of the United States, this state, or a political subdivision of this state for the prevention, monitoring, control, or reduction of air, water, or land pollution.

(b) This section applies to real and personal property used as a facility, device, or method for the control of air, water, or land pollution that would otherwise be taxable for the first time on or after January 1, 1994.

(c) This section does not authorize the exemption from ad valorem taxation of real or personal property that was subject to a tax abatement agreement executed before January 1, 1994.

[Note — Sec. 1-l of Art. VIII was added to authorize the exemption from ad valorem taxation of real and personal property used for the control of air, water, or land pollution. Submitted by 73rd Legislature (1993) and adopted in election Nov. 2, 1993.]

Sec. 2. **Occupation Taxes Equal and Uniform; Exemptions Therefrom** — (a) All occupation taxes shall be equal and uniform upon the same class of subjects within the limits of the authority levying the tax; but the Legislature may, by general laws, exempt from taxation public property used for public purposes; actual places of religious worship, also any property owned by a church or by a strictly religious society for the exclusive use as a dwelling place for the ministry of such church or religious society, and which yields no revenue whatever to such church or religious society; provided that such exemption shall not extend to more property than is reasonably necessary for a dwelling place and in no event more than one acre of land; places of burial not held for private or corporate profit; solar or wind-powered energy devices; all buildings used exclusively and owned by persons or associations of persons for school purposes and the necessary furniture of all schools and property used exclusively and reasonably necessary in conducting any association engaged in promoting the religious, educational and physical development of boys, girls, young men or young women operating under a State or National organization of like character; also, the endowment funds of such institutions of learning and religion not used with a view to profit; and when the same are invested in bonds or mortgages, or in land or other property which has been and shall hereafter be bought in by such institutions under foreclosure sales made to satisfy or protect such bonds or mortgages, then such exemption of such land and property shall continue only for two years after the purchase of the same at such sale by such institutions and no longer, and institutions of purely public charity; and all laws exempting property from taxation other than the property mentioned in this Section shall be null and void.

(b) The Legislature may, by general law, exempt property owned by a disabled veteran or by the surviving spouse and surviving minor children of a disabled veteran. A disabled veteran is a veteran of the armed services of the United States who is classified as disabled by the Veterans Administration or by a successor to that agency; or the military service in which he served. A veteran who is certified as having a disability of less than 10 per cent is not entitled to an exemption. A veteran having a disability rating of not less than 10 per cent nor more than 30 per cent may be granted an exemption from taxation for property valued at up to $5,000. A veteran having a disability rating of more than 30 per cent but not more than 50 per cent may be granted an exemption from taxation for property valued at up to $7,500. A veteran having a disability rating of more than 50 per cent but not more than 70 per cent may be granted an exemption from taxation for property valued at up to $10,000. A veteran who has a disability rating of more than 70 per cent, or a veteran who has a disability rating of not less than 10 per cent and has attained the age of 65, or a disabled veteran whose disability consists of the loss or loss of use of one or more limbs, total blindness in one or both eyes, or paraplegia, may be granted an exemption from taxation for property valued at up to $12,000. The spouse and children of any member of the United States Armed Forces who dies while on active duty may be granted an exemption from taxation for property valued at up to $5,000. A deceased disabled veteran's surviving spouse and children may be granted an exemption which is in the aggregate is equal to the exemption to which the veteran was entitled when the veteran died.

(c) The Legislature by general law may exempt from ad valorem taxation property that is owned by a nonprofit organization composed primarily of members or former members of the armed forces of the United States or its allies and chartered or incorporated by the United States Congress.

(d) Unless otherwise provided by general law enacted after January 1, 1995, the amounts of the exemptions from ad valorem taxation to which a person is entitled under Section 11.22, Tax Code, for a tax year that begins on or after the date this subsection takes effect are the maximum amounts permitted under Subsection (b) of this section instead of the amounts specified by Section 11.22, Tax Code. This subsection may be repealed by the Legislature by general law.

[Note — Sec. 2 of Art. VIII has been amended six times: (1) To add clause with reference to endowment fund. Submitted by 29th Legislature (1905); ratified Nov. 6, 1906, and proclaimed adopted Jan. 7, 1907. (2) To permit exemption of ministers' dwellings and certain other property of religious organizations, the original amendment having provided only for exemption for "actual places of worship." Submitted by 40th Legislature (1927); ratified Nov. 6, 1928; proclaimed Feb. 6, 1929. (3) To allow certain tax exemptions to disabled veterans, their surviving spouses and surviving minor children and to survivors of members of the armed forces who lose their lives while on active duty. Submitted by 62nd Legislature (1971) and adopted in election Nov. 7, 1972. (4) To authorize Legislature to exempt from taxation solar- and wind-powered energy devices. Submitted by 65th Legislature (1977) and adopted in election Nov. 7, 1978. (5) To authorize the legislature to exempt from ad valorem taxation certain property of non-profit veterans organizations. Submitted by 71st Legislature (1989) and adopted in election Nov. 7, 1989. (6) To raise the limits of exemption from property taxes of disabled veterans or of property owned by surviving spouses and minor children of disabled veterans. Submitted by 74th Legislature (1995) and adopted in election Nov. 7, 1995.]

Sec. 3. **Taxes to Be Collected for Public Purposes Only** — Taxes shall be levied and collected by general laws and for public purposes only.

Sec. 4. **Power to Tax Corporations Not to Be Surrendered** — The power to tax corporations and corporate property shall not be surrendered or suspended by act of the Legislature, by any contract or grant to which the State shall be a party.

Sec. 5. **Railroad Taxes Due Cities and Towns** — All property of

Article VIII (Cont'd.)

railroad companies, of whatever description lying or being within the limits of any city or incorporated town within this State, shall bear its proportionate share of municipal taxation, and if any such property shall not have been heretofore rendered, the authorities of the city or town within which it lies shall have power to require its rendition and collect the usual municipal tax thereon, as on other property lying within said municipality.

Sec. 6. **Appropriations; How Made and for What Period** — No money shall be drawn from the Treasury but in pursuance of specific appropriations made by law; nor shall any appropriation of money be made for a longer term than two years, except by the First Legislature to assemble under this Constitution, which may make the necessary appropriations to carry on the government until the assembling of the Sixteenth Legislature.

Sec. 7. **Special Funds Not to Be Borrowed or Diverted** — The Legislature shall not have power to borrow, or in any manner divert from its purpose any special fund that may, or ought to, come into the Treasury; and shall make it penal for any person or persons to borrow, withhold or in any manner to divert from its purpose, any special fund or any part thereof.

Sec. 7-a. **Net Motor License Fees and Motor Fuel Tax Revenues Restricted, Except One Fourth of Fuel Taxes to Schools, to Highway Improvement, Policing and Administration** — Subject to legislative appropriation, allocation and direction, all net revenues remaining after payment of all refunds allowed by law and expenses of collection derived from motor vehicle registration fees, and all taxes, except gross production and ad valorem taxes, on motor fuels and lubricants used to propel motor vehicles over public roadways, shall be used for the sole purpose of acquiring rights of way, constructing, maintaining, and policing such public roadways and for the administration of such laws as may be prescribed by the Legislature pertaining to the supervision of traffic and safety on such roads; and for the payment of the principal and interest on county and road district bonds or warrants voted or issued prior to January 2, 1939, and declared eligible prior to January 2, 1945, for payment out of the County and Road District Highway Fund under existing law, provided, however, that one fourth (1/4) of such net revenue from the motor fuel tax shall be allocated to the Available School Fund; and, provided, however, that the net revenue derived by counties from motor vehicle registration fees shall never be less than the maximum amounts allowed to be retained by each county and the percentage allowed to be retained by each county under the laws in effect on January 1, 1945. Nothing contained herein shall be construed as authorizing the pledging of the State's credit for any purpose.

[Note — Sec. 7-a of Art. VIII was added to restrict revenues from motor vehicle registration and motor fuel taxes to the of highway improvement, policing and administration. Submitted by 49th Legislature (1945), ratified in election Nov. 5, 1946.]

Sec. 7-b. All revenues received from the federal government as reimbursement for state expenditures of funds that are themselves dedicated for acquiring rights-of-way and constructing, maintaining, and policing public roadways are also constitutionally dedicated and shall be used only for those purposes.

[Note — Sec. 7-b of Art. VIII was added to provide for the dedication of certain funds for highway purposes. Submitted by 70th Legislature (1987) and adopted in election Nov. 8, 1988.]

Sec. 8. **Railroad Property; How Assessed** — All property of railroad companies shall be assessed, and the taxes collected in the several counties in which said property is situated, including so much of the roadbed and fixtures as shall be in each county. The rolling stock may be assessed in gross in the county where the principal office of the company is located, and the county tax paid upon it shall be apportioned as provided by general law in proportion to the distance such road may run through any such county, among the several counties through which the road passes, as part of their tax assets.

[Note — Sec. 8 of Art. VIII was added to allow Legislature to provide by general law for apportionment of value of railroad rolling stock among counties for purposes of property taxation. Submitted by 69th Legislature (1985) and adopted in election Nov. 4, 1986.]

Sec. 9. **Rate of State and Municipal Taxation** — The State tax on property, exclusive of the tax necessary to pay the public debt, and of the taxes provided for the benefit of the public free school, shall never exceed thirty-five cents (35¢) on the One Hundred Dollars ($100) valuation; and no county, city or town shall levy a tax rate in excess of Eighty Cents (80¢) on the One Hundred Dollars ($100) valuation in any one (1) year for general fund, permanent improvement fund, road and bridge fund and jury fund purposes; provided further that at the time the Commissioners Court meets to levy the annual tax rate for each county it shall levy whatever tax rate may be needed for the four (4) constitutional purposes; namely, general fund, permanent improvement fund, road and bridge fund and jury fund so long as the Court does not impair any outstanding bonds or other obligations and so long as the total of the foregoing tax levies does not exceed Eighty Cents (80¢) on the One Hundred Dollars ($100) valuation in any one (1) year. Once the Court has levied the annual tax rate, the same shall remain in force and effect during that taxable year; and the Legislature may also authorize an additional annual ad valorem tax to be levied and collected for the further maintenance of the public roads; provided that a majority of the qualified property tax-paying voters of the county voting at an election to be held for that purpose shall vote such tax, not to exceed fifteen cents (15¢) on the One Hundred Dollars ($100) valuation of the property subject to taxation in such county. Any county may put all tax money collected by the county into one general fund, without regard to the purpose or source of each tax. And the Legislature may pass local laws for the maintenance of the public roads and highways, without the local notice required for special or local laws. This section shall not be construed as a limitation of powers delegated to counties, cities or towns by any other section or sections of this Constitution.

[Note — Sec. 9 of Art. VIII has been amended seven times: (1) To lower State tax rate from 50¢ to 35¢, a separate State school tax having been provided by companion amendment, Sec. 3 of Art. VII. Submitted by 18th Legislature (1883), ratified in election Aug. 14, 1883, and declared adopted Sept. 25, 1883. (2) To authorize Legislature to provide a 15¢ local road tax. Submitted by 21st Legislature (1889), ratified in election Nov. 3, 1890, and declared adopted Dec. 19, 1890. (3) To authorize 15¢ tax for jurors. Submitted by 29th Legislature (1905), ratified in election Nov. 6, 1906, and declared adopted Jan. 7, 1907. (4) To allow County Commissioners to re-allocate the named county taxes by changing the rates if approved by a majority of the qualified voters, but restricting the period to six years, and restricting total to 80¢ on the $100 valuation. Submitted by 48th Legislature and adopted in election Nov. 7, 1944. (5) To abolish ad valorem tax for State general revenue fund purposes, and making other provisions. (See Sec. 1-a of Art. VIII and note thereon.) Submitted by 50th Legislature (1947) and adopted in election Nov. 2, 1948. (6) To give Commissioners Courts authority to levy taxes for general, permanent improvement, road and bridge and jury fund purposes, so long as total of these tax rates does not exceed 80¢ on the $100 valuation in any one year. Submitted by 54th Legislature (1955) and adopted in election Nov. 6, 1956. (7) To allow counties to put all county taxes into one general fund. Submitted by 60th Legislature (1967) and adopted in election Nov. 11, 1967.]

Sec. 10. **Taxes Not to Be Released Except by Two-Thirds Vote of Each House** — The Legislature shall have no power to release the inhabitants of, or property in, any county, city or town, from the payment of taxes levied for State or county purposes, unless in case of great public calamity in any such county, city or town, when such release may be made by a vote of two-thirds of each house of the Legislature.

Sec. 11. **Where Property Is to Be Assessed** — All property, whether owned by persons or corporations, shall be assessed for taxation and the taxes paid in the county where situated, but the Legislature may by a two-thirds vote authorize the payment of taxes of non-residents of counties to be made at the office of the Comptroller of Public Accounts. And all lands and other property not rendered for taxation by the owner thereof shall be assessed at its fair value by the proper officer.

[Note — Sec. 12 of Art. VIII, relating to unorganized counties, was deleted by constitutional amendment. Submitted by 61st Legislature (1969) and approved in election Aug. 5, 1969.]

Sec. 13. **Tax Sales; Tax Deeds; Redemptions** — (a) Provision shall be made by the Legislature for the sale of a sufficient portion of all lands and other property for the taxes due thereon that have not been paid.

(b) The deed of conveyance to the purchaser for all lands and other property thus sold shall be held to vest a good and perfect title in the purchaser thereof, subject only to redemption as provided by this section or impeachment for actual fraud.

(c) The former owner of a residence homestead sold for unpaid taxes and the former owner of land designated for agricultural use sold for unpaid taxes shall within two years from date of filing for record of the Purchaser's Deed have the right to redeem the property on the following basis:

(1) Within the first year of the redemption period, upon the payment of the amount of money paid for the property, including the Tax Deed Recording Fee and all taxes, penalties, interest, and costs paid plus an amount not exceeding 25 percent of the aggregate total; and

(2) Within the last year of the redemption period, upon the payment of the amount of money paid for the property, including the Tax Deed Recording Fee and all taxes, penalties, interest, and costs paid plus an amount not exceeding 50 percent of the aggregate total.

(d) If the property is sold pursuant to a suit to enforce the collection of the unpaid taxes, the Legislature may limit the application of Subsection (c) of this section to property used as a residence homestead when the suit was filed and to land designated for agricultural use when the suit was filed.

(e) The former owner of real property not covered by Subsection (c) of this section sold for unpaid taxes shall within six months from the date of filing for record of the Purchaser's Deed have the right to redeem the property upon the payment of the amount of money paid for the property, including the Tax Deed Recording Fee and all taxes, penalties, interest, and costs paid plus an amount not exceeding 25 percent of the aggregate total.

TEMPORARY PROVISION. (a) This temporary provision applies to the constitutional amendment proposed by S.J.R. No. 19, 73rd Legislature, Regular Session, 1993, and expires January 1, 1997.

(b) The amendment to Article VIII, Section 13, of this constitution takes effect January 1, 1994.

(c) The amendment applies to redemption of real property sold at

Article VIII (Cont'd.)

a tax sale for which the purchaser's deed is filed for record on or after the effective date of this amendment. Redemption of real property sold at a tax sale for which the purchaser's deed is filed for record before the effective date of this amendment is covered by the former law, and the former law is continued in effect for this purpose.

[Note — Sec. 13 of Art. VIII was amended to insert the provisions for redemption given above for the original clause, which provided for "double the amount of money paid for the land" to be paid by the original owner for redemption. Submitted by 42nd Legislature (1931) and adopted in election Nov. 8, 1932. Proclaimed July 26, 1933. It was further amended to modify the provisions for the redemption of real property sold at a tax sale. Submitted by the 73rd Legislature (1993) and adopted in election Nov. 2, 1993.]

Sec. 14. **County Tax Assessor and Collector** — Except as provided in Sec. 16 of this Article, there shall be elected by the qualified electors of each county an Assessor and Collector of Taxes, who shall hold his office for four years and until his successor is elected and qualified; and such Assessor and Collector of Taxes shall perform all the duties with respect to assessing property for the purpose of taxation and of collecting taxes as may be prescribed by the Legislature.

[Note — Sec. 14 of Art. VIII was amended to consolidate offices of Tax Assessor and Tax Collector. (See also Sec. 16.) Submitted by 42nd Legislature (1931), adopted in election Nov. 8, 1932, proclaimed Jan. 9, 1933. It was again amended to change term of office from two to four years. Submitted by 53rd Legislature (1953) and adopted in election Nov. 2, 1954.]

Sec. 15. **Tax Liens and Sales** — The annual assessment made upon landed property shall be a special lien thereon; and all property, both real and personal, belonging to any delinquent taxpayer shall be liable to seizure and sale for the payment of all the taxes and penalties due by such delinquent, and such property may be sold for the payment of the taxes and penalties due by such delinquent, under such regulations as the Legislature may provide.

Sec. 16. **Sheriff to Be County Tax Assessor-Collector in Some Counties** — The Sheriff of each county, in addition to his other duties, shall be the Assessor and Collector of Taxes therefor. But in counties having ten thousand (10,000) or more inhabitants, to be determined by the last preceding census of the United States, an Assessor and Collector of Taxes shall be elected, as provided in Sec. 14 of this Article and shall hold office for four years and until his successor shall be elected and qualified.

[Note — Sec. 16 of Art. VIII was amended to harmonize with section consolidating offices of Assessor and Collector of Taxes. (See also Sec. 14.) Submitted by 42nd Legislature (1931) and adopted in election Nov. 8, 1932; proclaimed Jan. 9, 1933. It was again amended to change term of office from two to four years. Submitted by 53rd Legislature (1953) and adopted in election Nov. 2, 1954.]

Sec. 16-a. **Assessor-Collector of Taxes in Counties of Less Than Ten Thousand** — In any county having a population of less than ten thousand (10,000) inhabitants, as determined by last preceding census of the United States, the Commissioners' Court may submit to the qualified property taxpaying voters of such county at an election the question of adding an Assessor-Collector of Taxes to the list of authorized county officials. If a majority of such voters voting in such election shall approve of adding an Assessor-Collector of Taxes to such list, then such official shall be elected at the next General Election for such Constitutional term of office as is provided for other Tax Assessor-Collectors in this State.

[Note — Sec. 16-a of Art. VIII was added to provide for a Tax Assessor-Collector in counties of less than 10,000 population. Submitted by 53rd Legislature (1953) and adopted in election Nov. 2, 1954.]

Sec. 17. **Power of Legislature as to Taxes** — The specification of the objects and subjects of taxation shall not deprive the Legislature of the power to require other subjects or objects to be taxed, in such manner as may be consistent with the principles of taxation fixed in this Constitution.

Sec. 18. **Equalization of Taxes** — (a) The Legislature shall provide for equalizing, as near as may be, the valuation of all property subject to or rendered for taxation and may also provide for the classification of all lands with reference to their value in the several counties.

(b) A single appraisal within each county of all property subject to ad valorem taxation by the county and all other taxing units located therein shall be provided by general law. The Legislature, by general law, may authorize appraisals outside a county when political subdivisions are situated in more than one county or when two or more counties elect to consolidate appraisal services.

(c) The Legislature, by general law, shall provide for a single board of equalization for each appraisal entity consisting of qualified persons residing within the territory appraised by that entity. Members of the board of equalization may not be elected officials of the county or of the governing body of a taxing unit.

(d) The Legislature shall prescribe by general law the methods, timing and administrative process for implementing the requirements of this section.

[Note — Sec. 18 of Art. VIII was amended to provide for a single appraisal and a single board of equalization within each county for ad valorem tax purposes. Submitted by 66th Legislature (1979) and adopted in election Nov. 4, 1980.]

Sec. 19. **Farm Products in the Hands of the Producer Exempt From All Taxation** — Farm products, livestock, and poultry in the hands of the producer, and family supplies for home and farm use, are exempt from all taxation until otherwise directed by a two-thirds vote of all the members *elect to both houses of the Legislature.

*Explanatory Note — Expressed thus in official draft of Constitution.

[Note — Sec. 19 of Art. VIII was added to exempt farm products from taxation. Submitted by 16th Legislature (1879), ratified in election Sept. 2, 1879 and declared adopted Oct. 14, 1879. It was amended to change the wording to include livestock and poultry with farm products as exempt from taxation. Submitted by 67th Legislature (1981) and adopted in election Nov. 3, 1981.]

Sec. 19-a. **Farm Implements Exempt From Taxation** — Implements of husbandry that are used in the production of farm or ranch products are exempt from ad valorem taxation.

[Note — Sec. 19-a of Art. VIII was added to exempt implements of farm husbandry from ad valorem taxation. Submitted by Called Session of 67th Legislature (1982) and adopted in election Nov. 2, 1982.]

Sec. 20. Limiting Ad Valorem Tax Assessment; Discount for Prompt Payment of Taxes — No property of any kind in this State shall ever be assessed for ad valorem taxes at a greater value than its fair cash market value nor shall any Board of Equalization of any governmental or political subdivision or taxing district within this State fix the value of any property for tax purposes at more than its fair cash market value; provided, that in order to encourage the prompt payment of taxes, the Legislature shall have the power to provide that the taxpayer shall be allowed by the State and all governmental and political subdivisions and taxing districts of the State a three per cent discount on ad valorem taxes due the State or due any governmental or political subdivision or taxing district of the State if such taxes are paid ninety days before the date when they would otherwise become delinquent; and the taxpayer shall be allowed a two per cent discount on said taxes if paid sixty days before said taxes would become delinquent; and the taxpayer shall be allowed a one per cent discount if said taxes are paid thirty days before they would otherwise become delinquent. This amendment shall be effective Jan. 1, 1939. The Legislature shall pass necessary laws for the proper administration of this Section.

[Note — Sec. 20 of Art. VIII was added (1) to restrict assessed value to true market value, and (2) to provide for stated discounts for prepayment of taxes. Submitted by 45th Legislature (1937) and adopted in election Aug. 23, 1937.]

Sec. 21. **Limitation on Property Taxes** — (a) Subject to any exceptions prescribed by general law, the total amount of property taxes imposed by a political subdivision in any year may not exceed the total amount of property taxes imposed by that subdivision in the preceding year unless the governing body of the subdivision gives notice of its intent to consider an increase in taxes and holds a public hearing on the proposed increase before it increases those total taxes. The legislature shall prescribe by law the form, content, timing, and methods of giving the notice and the rules for the conduct of the hearing.

(b) In calculating the total amount of taxes imposed in the current year for the purposes of Subsection (a) of this section, the taxes on property in territory added to the political subdivision since the preceding year and on new improvements that were not taxable in the preceding year are excluded. In calculating the total amount of taxes imposed in the preceding year for the purposes of Subsection (a) of this section, the taxes imposed on real property that is not taxable by the subdivision in the current year are excluded.

(c) The Legislature by general law shall require that, subject to reasonable exceptions, a property owner be given notice of a revaluation of his property and a reasonable estimate of the amount of taxes that would be imposed on his property if the total amount of property taxes for the subdivision were not increased according to any law enacted pursuant to Subsection (a) of this section. The notice must be given before the procedures required in Subsection (a) are instituted.

[Note — Sec. 21 of Art. VIII was added to limit increases in property revaluation and to prescribe method of giving notice before property revaluated. (See also Sec. 1, Sec. 1-b and Sec. 23 of Art. VIII.) Submitted by 65th Legislature (1977) and adopted in election Nov. 7, 1978. It was further amended to change wording of administrative procedures in notifying property owners. (See also Subsection (e) of Section 1-b of Art. VIII.) Submitted by 67th Legislature (1981) and adopted in election Nov. 3, 1981.]

Sec. 22. **State Tax Revenues** — (a) In no biennium shall the rate of growth of appropriations from state tax revenues not dedicated by this constitution exceed the estimated rate of growth of the state's economy. The Legislature shall provide by general law procedures to implement this subsection.

(b) If the Legislature by adoption of a resolution approved by a record vote of a majority of the members of each house finds that an emergency exists and identifies the nature of the emergency, the

Article VIII (Cont'd.); Article IX

Legislature may provide for appropriations in excess of the amount authorized by Subsection (a) of this section. The excess authorized under this subsection may not exceed the amount specified in the resolution.

(c) In no case shall appropriations exceed revenues as provided in Article III, Sec. 49-a, of this constitution. Nothing in this section shall be construed to alter, amend, or repeal Article III, Sec. 49-a, of this constitution.

[Note — Sec. 22 of Art. VIII was added to limit the rate of growth of appropriations from state tax revenues and to provide for emergency spending by state. (See also Sec. 49-a of Art. III.) Submitted by 65th Legislature (1977) and adopted in election Nov. 7, 1978.]

Sec. 23. **No Statewide Real Property Appraisal** — (a) There shall be no statewide appraisal of real property for ad valorem tax purposes; however, this shall not preclude formula distribution of tax revenues to political subdivisions of the state.

(b) Administrative and judicial enforcement of uniform standards and procedures for appraisal of property for ad valorem tax purposes, as prescribed by general law, shall originate in the county where the tax is imposed, except that the Legislature may provide by general law for political subdivisions with boundaries extending outside the county.

[Note — Sec. 23 of Art. VIII was added to prohibit a statewide appraisal of real property for ad valorem tax purposes while allowing local subdivisions to administer tax rate. (See also Sec. 1, Sec. 1-b, Sec. 21 of Art. VIII.) Submitted by 65th Legislature (1977) and adopted in election Nov. 7, 1978.]

Sec. 24. (a) A general law enacted by the legislature that imposes a tax on the net incomes of natural persons, including a person's share of partnership and unincorporated association income, must provide that the portion of the law imposing the tax not take effect until approved by a majority of the registered voters voting in a statewide referendum held on the question of imposing the tax. The referendum must specify the rate of the tax that will apply to taxable income as defined by law.

(b) A general law enacted by the legislature that increases the rate of the tax, or changes the tax, in a manner that results in an increase in the combined income tax liability of all persons subject to the tax may not take effect until approved by a majority of the registered voters voting in a statewide referendum held on the question of increasing the income tax. A determination of whether a bill proposing a change in the tax would increase the combined income tax liability of all persons subject to the tax must be made by comparing the provisions of the proposed change in law with the provisions of the law for the most recent year in which actual tax collections have been made. A referendum held under this subsection must specify the manner in which the proposed law would increase the combined income tax liability of all persons subject to the tax.

(c) Except as provided by Subsection (b) of this section, the legislature may amend or repeal a tax approved by the voters under this section without submitting the amendment or the repeal to the voters as provided by Subsection (a) of this section.

(d) If the legislature repeals a tax approved by the voters under this section, the legislature may reenact the tax without submitting the reenactment to the voters as provided by Subsection (a) of this section only if the effective date of the reenactment of the tax is before the first anniversary of the effective date of the repeal.

(e) The legislature may provide for the taxation of income in a manner which is consistent with federal law.

(f) In the first year in which a tax described by Subsection (a) is imposed and during the first year of any increase in the tax that is subject to Subsection (b) of this section, not less than two-thirds of all net revenues remaining after payment of all refunds allowed by law and expenses of collection from the tax shall be used to reduce the rate of ad valorem maintenance and operation taxes levied for the support of primary and secondary public education. In subsequent years, not less than two-thirds of all net revenues from the tax shall be used to continue such ad valorem tax relief.

(g) The net revenues remaining after the dedication of money from the tax under Subsection (f) of this section shall be used for support of education, subject to legislative appropriation, allocation, and direction.

(h) The maximum rate at which a school district may impose ad valorem maintenance and operation taxes is reduced by an amount equal to one cent per $100 valuation for each one cent per $100 valuation that the school district's ad valorem maintenance and operation tax is reduced by the minimum amount of money dedicated under Subsection (f) of this section, provided that a school district may subsequently increase the maximum ad valorem maintenance and operation tax rate if the increased maximum rate is approved by a majority of the voters of the school district voting at an election called and held for that purpose. The legislature by general law shall provide for the tax relief that is required by Subsection (f) and this subsection.

(i) Subsections (f) and (h) of this section apply to ad valorem maintenance and operation taxes levied by a school district on or after the first January 1 after the date on which a tax on the net incomes of natural persons, including a person's share of partnership and unincorporated association income, begins to apply to that income, except that if the income tax begins to apply on a January 1,

Subsections (f) and (h) of this section apply to ad valorem maintenance and operation taxes levied on or after that date.

(j) A provision of this section prevails over a conflicting provision of Article VII, Section 3, of this Constitution to the extent of the conflict.

[Note — Sec. 24 of Article VIII was added to prohibit a personal income tax without voter approval and dedicating the proceeds of such a tax to education and property tax relief. Submitted by 73rd Legislature (1993) and adopted in election Nov. 2, 1993.]

Article IX — Counties

Sec. 1. **Creation and Organization of Counties; Changing of County Lines** — The Legislature shall have power to create counties for the convenience of the people, subject to the following provisions:

First. In the territory of the State exterior to all counties now existing, no new counties shall be created with a less area than 900 square miles in a square form, unless prevented by pre-existing boundary lines. Should the State lines render this impracticable in border counties, the area may be less. The territory referred to may, at any time, in whole or in part, be divided into counties in advance of population and attached for judicial and land surveying purposes to the most convenient organized county or counties.

Second. Within the territory of any county or counties now existing, no new county shall be created with a less area than 700 square miles, nor shall any such county now existing be reduced to a less area than 700 square miles. No new counties shall be created so as to approach nearer than twelve miles of the county seat of any county from which it may, in whole or in part, be taken. Counties of a less area than 900, but of 700 or more square miles, within counties now existing, may be created by a two-thirds vote of each house of the Legislature, taken by yeas and nays, and entered on the journals. Any county now existing may be reduced to an area of not less than 700 square miles by a like two-thirds vote. When any part of a county is stricken off and attached to or created into another county, the part stricken off shall be holden for and obliged to pay its proportion of all the liabilities then existing of the county from which it was taken, in such manner as may be prescribed by law.

Third. No part of any existing county shall be detached from it and attached to another existing county until the proposition for such change shall have been submitted, in such manner as may be provided by law, to a vote of the electors of both counties, and shall have received a majority of those voting on the question in each.

Sec. 1-a. **Regulation of Travel on Gulf Coast Beaches** — The Legislature may authorize the governing body of any county bordering on the Gulf of Mexico or the tidewater limits thereof to regulate and restrict the speed, parking and travel of motor vehicles on beaches available to the public by virtue of public right and the littering of such beaches.

Nothing in this amendment shall increase the rights of any riparian or littoral landowner with regard to beaches available to the public by virtue of public right or submerged lands.

The Legislature may enact any laws not inconsistent with this Section which it may deem necessary to permit said counties to implement, enforce and administer the provisions contained herein.

[Note — Sec. 1-a of Art. IX was added to authorize regulation of travel on Gulf Coast beaches open to the public. Submitted by 57th Legislature (1961) and adopted in election Nov. 6, 1962.]

County Seats

Sec. 2. **How County Seats Are Created and Changed** — The Legislature shall pass laws regulating the manner of removing county seats, but no county seat situated within five miles of the geographical center of the county shall be removed except by a vote of two-thirds of all electors voting on the subject. A majority of such electors, however, voting at such election, may remove a county seat from a point more than five miles from a geographical center of the county to a point within five miles of such center, in either case the center to be determined by a certificate from the Commissioner of the General Land Office.

[Note — Sec. 3 of Art. IX, relating to home rule, was deleted by constitutional amendment. Submitted by 61st Legislature and approved in election Aug. 5, 1969.]

Sec. 4. **County-Wide Hospital Districts** — The Legislature may by law authorize the creation of county-wide Hospital Districts in counties having a population in excess of 190,000 and in Galveston County, with power to issue bonds for the purchase, acquisition, construction, maintenance and operation of any county-owned hospital, or where the hospital system is jointly operated by a county and city within the county, and to provide for the transfer to the county-wide hospital district of the title to any land, buildings or equipment, jointly or separately owned, and for the assumption by the district of any outstanding bonded indebtedness theretofore issued by any county or city for the establishment of hospitals or hospital facilities; to levy a tax not to exceed seventy-five (75¢) cents on the One Hundred ($100.00) Dollars valuation of all taxable property within such district, provided, however, that such district shall be approved at an election held for that purpose, and that only qualified, property taxpaying voters in such county shall vote therein; provided further, that such hospital district shall assume full responsibility for providing medical and hospital care to needy inhabitants of the county, and thereafter such county and cities therein shall not levy any other tax for hospital purposes; and provided further that should such hospital district construct, maintain and support a hospital or hospital system, that the

Article IX (Cont'd.)

same shall never become a charge against the State of Texas, nor shall any direct appropriation ever be made by the Legislature for the construction, maintenance or improvement of the said hospital or hospitals. Should the Legislature enact enabling laws in anticipation of the adoption of this amendment, such acts shall not be invalid because of their anticipatory character.

[Note — Sec. 4 of Art. IX was added to provide for county-wide hospital districts. Submitted by 53rd Legislature (1953) and adopted in election Nov. 2, 1954.]

Sec. 5 (a). The Legislature may by law authorize the creation of two hospital districts, one to be coextensive with and have the same boundaries as the incorporated City of Amarillo, as such boundaries now exist or as they may hereafter be lawfully extended, and the other to be coextensive with Wichita County.

If such district or districts are created, they may be authorized to levy a tax not to exceed Seventy-five Cents (75¢) on the One Hundred Dollars ($100.00) valuation of taxable property within the district; provided, however no tax may be levied until approved by a majority vote of the participating resident qualified property taxpaying voters who have duly rendered their property for taxation. The maximum rate of tax may be changed at subsequent elections so long as obligations are not impaired, and not to exceed the maximum limit of Seventy-five Cents (75¢) per One Hundred Dollars ($100.00) valuation, and no election shall be required by subsequent changes in the boundaries of the City of Amarillo.

If such tax is authorized, no political subdivision or municipality within or having the same boundaries as the district may levy a tax for medical or hospital care for needy individuals, nor shall they maintain or erect hospital facilities, but the district shall by resolution assume all such responsibilities and shall assume all of the liabilities and obligations (including bonds and warrants) of such subdivisions or municipalities or both. The maximum tax rate submitted shall be sufficient to discharge such obligations, liabilities, and responsibilities, and to maintain and operate the hospital system, and the Legislature may authorize the district to issue tax bonds for the purpose of the purchase, construction, acquisition, repair or renovation of improvements and initially equipping the same, and such bonds shall be payable from said Seventy-five Cents (75¢) tax. The Legislature shall provide for transfer of title to properties to the District.

(b). The Legislature may by law permit the County of Potter (in which the City of Amarillo is partially located) to render financial aid to that district by paying a part of the expenses of operating and maintaining the system and paying a part of the debts of the district (whether assumed or created by the district) and may authorize the levy of a tax not to exceed Ten Cents (10¢) per One Hundred Dollars ($100.00) valuation (in addition to other taxes permitted by this Constitution) upon all property within the county but without the City of Amarillo at the time such levy is made for such purposes. If such tax is authorized, the district shall by resolution assume the responsibilities, obligations, and liabilities of the county in the manner and to the extent hereinabove provided for political subdivisions having boundaries coextensive with the district, and the county shall not thereafter levy taxes (other than herein provided) for hospital purposes nor for providing hospital care for needy individuals of the county.

(c). The Legislature may by law authorize the creation of a hospital district within Jefferson County, the boundaries of which shall include only the area comprising the Jefferson County Drainage District No. 7 and the Port Arthur Independent School District, as such boundaries existed on the first day of January, 1957, with the power to issue bonds for the sole purpose of purchasing a site for, and the construction and initial equipping of, a hospital system, and with the power to levy a tax of not to exceed Seventy-five Cents (75¢) on the One Hundred Dollars ($100) valuation of property therein for the purpose of paying the principal and interest on such bonds.

The creation of such hospital district shall not be final until approved at an election by a majority of the resident property taxpaying voters voting at said election who have duly rendered their property for taxation upon the tax rolls of either said Drainage or said School District, nor shall such bonds be issued or such tax be levied until so approved by such voters.

The district shall not have the power to levy any tax for maintenance or operation of the hospital or facilities, but shall contract with other political subdivisions of the state or private individuals, associations, or corporations for such purposes.

If the district hereinabove authorized is finally created, no other hospital district may be created embracing any part of the territory within its boundaries, but the Legislature by law may authorize the creation of a hospital district incorporating herein the remainder of Jefferson County, having the powers and duties and with the limitations presently provided by Art. IX, Section 4, of the Constitution of Texas, except that such district shall be confirmed at an election wherein the resident qualified property taxpaying voters who have duly rendered their property within such proposed district for taxation on the county rolls, shall be authorized to vote. A majority of those participating in the election voting in favor of the district shall be necessary for its confirmation and for bonds to be issued.

(d). Should the Legislature enact enabling laws in anticipation of adoption of this amendment, such acts shall not be invalid because of their anticipatory character.

[Note — Sec. 5 of Art. IX was added to provide for the creation of special hospital districts and authorizing the levying of taxes for their support. Submitted by 55th Legislature (1957) and adopted in election Nov. 4, 1958.]

(e). The legislature by law may authorize Randall County to render financial assistance to the Amarillo Hospital District by paying part of the district's operating and maintenance expenses and the debts assumed or created by the district and to levy a tax for that purpose in an amount not to exceed seventy-five cents (75¢) on the One Hundred Dollars ($100.00) valuation on all property in Randall County that is not within the boundaries of the City of Amarillo or the South Randall County Hospital District. This tax is in addition to any other tax authorized by this constitution. If the tax is authorized by the legislature and approved by the voters of the area to be taxed, the Amarillo Hospital District shall, by resolution, assume the responsibilities, obligations, and liabilities of Randall County in accordance with Subsection (a) of this section and, except as provided by this subsection, Randall County may not levy taxes or issue bonds for hospital purposes or for providing hospital care for needy inhabitants of the county. Not later than the end of the first tax year during which taxes are levied under this subsection, Randall County shall deposit in the State Treasury to the credit of the state General Revenue Fund $45,000 to reimburse the state for the cost of publishing the resolution required by this subsection.

(f). Notwithstanding the provisions of Article IX of this constitution, if a hospital district was created or authorized under a constitutional provision that includes a description of the district's boundaries or jurisdiction, the legislature by law may authorize the district to change its boundaries or jurisdiction. The change must be approved by a majority of the qualified voters of the district voting at an election called and held for that purpose.

[Note — Subsection (e) of Sec. 5 of Art. IX was added to expand services provided by the Amarillo Hospital District. Submitted by 70th Legislature (1987) and adopted in election Nov. 3, 1987.]

Sec. 6. **Lamar County Hospital District Abolished** — On the effective date of this Amendment, the Lamar County Hospital District is abolished. The Commissioners Court of Lamar County may provide for the transfer or for the disposition of the assets of the Lamar County Hospital District.

[Note — Sec. 6 of Art. IX was added to authorize creation of a hospital district in Lamar County and authorizing the levying of taxes for its support. Submitted by 56th Legislature (1959) and adopted in election Nov. 8, 1960. It was amended to abolish the hospital district. Submitted by 62nd Legislature (1971) and adopted in election Nov. 7, 1972.]

Sec. 7. **Hidalgo County Hospital District; Creation, Tax Rate** — The Legislature may by law authorize the creation of a Hospital District coextensive with Hidalgo County, having the powers and duties and with the limitations presently provided in Art. IX, Sec. 5 (a), of the Constitution of Texas, as it applies to Hidalgo County, except that the maximum rate of tax that the said Hidalgo County Hospital District may be authorized to levy shall be ten cents (10¢) per One Hundred Dollars ($100) valuation of taxable property within the District subject to district taxation.

[Note — Sec. 7 of Art. IX was added to authorize creation of a hospital district in Hidalgo County and authorizing the levying of taxes for its support. Submitted by 56th Legislature (1959) and adopted in election Nov. 8, 1960.]

Sec. 8. **Comanche County Hospital District; Creation, Tax Rate** — The Legislature may by law authorize the creation of a Hospital District to be coextensive with the limits of County Commissioners Precinct No. 4 of Comanche County, Texas.

If such District is created, it may be authorized to levy a tax not to exceed seventy-five cents (75¢) on the One Hundred Dollar ($100) valuation of taxable property within the District; provided, however, no tax may be levied until approved by a majority vote of the participating resident qualified property taxpaying voters who have duly rendered their property for taxation. The maximum rate of tax may be changed at subsequent elections so long as obligations are not impaired, and not to exceed the maximum limit of seventy-five cents (75¢) per One Hundred Dollar ($100) valuation, and no election shall be required by subsequent changes in the boundaries of the Commissioners Precinct No. 4 of Comanche County.

If such tax is authorized, no political subdivision or municipality within or having the same boundaries as the District may levy a tax for medical or hospital care for needy individuals, nor shall they maintain or erect hospital facilities, but the District shall by resolution assume all responsibilities and shall assume all of the liabilities and obligations (including bonds and warrants) of such subdivisions or municipalities or both. The maximum tax rate submitted shall be sufficient to discharge such obligations, liabilities, and responsibilities and to maintain and operate the hospital system, and the Legislature may authorize the District to issue tax bonds for the purpose of the purchase, construction, acquisition, repair or renovation of improvements and initially equipping the same, and such bonds shall be payable from said seventy-five cents (75¢) tax. The Legislature shall provide for transfer of title to properties to the District.

(b) The Legislature may by law permit the County of Comanche to render financial aid to that District by paying a part of the expenses of operating and maintaining the system and paying a part of the debts of the District (whether assumed or created by the District) and

Article IX (Cont'd.)

may authorize the levy of a tax not to exceed ten cents (10¢) per One Hundred Dollar ($100) valuation (in addition to other taxes permitted by this Constitution) upon all property within the County but without the County Commissioners Precinct No. 4 of Comanche County at the time such levy is made for such purposes. If such tax is authorized, the District shall by resolution assume the responsibilities, obligations and liabilities of the County in the manner and to the extent hereinabove provided for political subdivisions having boundaries coextensive with the District, and the County shall not hereafter levy taxes (other than herein provided) for hospital purposes nor for providing hospital care for needy individuals of the county.

(c) Should the Legislature enact enabling laws in anticipation of the adoption of this amendment, such Acts shall not be invalid because of their anticipatory character.

[Note — Sec. 8 of Art. IX was added to authorize creation of a hospital district in Comanche County and authorizing the levying of taxes for its support. Submitted by 56th Legislature (1959) and adopted in election Nov. 8, 1960.]

Sec. 9. The Legislature may by general or special law provide for the creation, establishment, maintenance and operation of hospital districts composed of one or more counties or all or any part of one or more counties with power to issue bonds for the purchase, construction, acquisition, repair or renovation of buildings and improvements and equipping same, for hospital purposes; providing for the transfer to the hospital district of the title to any land, buildings, improvements and equipment located wholly within the district which may be jointly or separately owned by any city, town or county, providing that any district so created shall assume full responsibility for providing medical and hospital care for its needy inhabitants and assume the outstanding indebtedness incurred by cities, towns and counties for hospital purposes prior to the creation of the district, if same are located wholly within its boundaries, and a pro rata portion of such indebtedness based upon the then last approved tax assessment rolls of the included cities, towns and counties if less than all the territory thereof is included within the district boundaries; providing that after its creation no other municipality or political subdivision shall have the power to levy taxes or issue bonds or other obligations for hospital purposes or for providing medical care within the boundaries of the district; providing for the levy of annual taxes at a rate not to exceed seventy-five cents (75¢) on the one hundred dollar valuation of all taxable property within such district for the purpose of meeting the requirements of the district's bonds, the indebtedness assumed by it and its maintenance and operating expenses, providing that such district shall not be created or such tax authorized unless approved by a majority of the qualified voters thereof voting at an election called for the purpose; and providing further that the support and maintenance of the district's hospital system shall never become a charge against or obligation of the State of Texas nor shall any direct appropriation be made by the Legislature for the construction, maintenance or improvement of any of the facilities of such district.

Provided, however, that no district shall be created by special law except after thirty (30) days' public notice to the district affected, and in no event may the Legislature provide for a district to be created without the affirmative vote of a majority of the qualified voters in the district concerned.

The Legislature may also provide for the dissolution of hospital districts provided that a process is afforded by statute for:

(1) Determining the desire of a majority of the qualified voters within the district to dissolve it;

(2) Disposing of or transferring the assets, if any, of the district; and

(3) Satisfying the debts and bond obligations, if any, of the district, in such manner as to protect the interest of the citizens within the district, including their collective property rights in the assets and property of the district, provided, however, that any grant from federal funds, however dispensed, shall be considered an obligation to be repaid in satisfaction and provided that no election to dissolve shall be held more often than once each year. In such connection, the statute shall provide against disposal or transfer of the assets of the district except for due compensation unless such assets are transferred to another governmental agency, such as a county, embracing such district and using such transferred assets in such a way as to benefit citizens formerly within the district.

[Note — Sec. 9 of Art. IX was added to provide for the creation of special hospital districts and authorizing the levying of taxes for their support. Submitted by 57th Legislature (1961) and adopted in election Nov. 6, 1962. It was further amended to provide method of dissolution of hospital districts. Submitted by 59th Legislature (1965) and adopted in election Nov. 8 1966. It was again amended to authorize the legislature to provide by general or special law for the creation, establishment, maintenance and operation of a hospital district. Submitted by 71st Legislature (1989) and adopted in election Nov. 7, 1989.]

Sec. 9A. The Legislature by law may determine the health care services a hospital district is required to provide, the requirements a resident must meet to qualify for services, and any other relevant provisions necessary to regulate the provision of health care to residents.

[Note — Sec. 9A of Art. IX was added to authorize Legislature to regulate the provision of health care by hospital districts. Submitted by 69th Legislature (1985) and adopted in election Nov. 5, 1985.]

Sec. 9B. The legislature by general or special law may provide for the creation, establishment, maintenance, and operation of hospital districts located wholly in a county with a population of 75,000 or less, according to the most recent federal decennial census, and may authorize the commissioners court to levy a tax on the ad valorem property located in the district for the support and maintenance of the district. A district may not be created or a tax levied unless the creation and tax are approved by a majority of the registered voters who reside in the district. The legislature shall set the maximum tax rate a district may levy. The legislature may provide that the county in which the district is located may issue general obligation bonds for the district and provide other services to the district. The district may provide hospital care, medical care, and other services authorized by the legislature.

[Note — Sec. 9B of Art. XI was added to authorize the legislature to provide for the creation, establishment, maintenance and operation of a hospital district. Submitted by 71st Legislature (1989) and adopted in election Nov. 7, 1989.]

[Note — Sec. 10 of Art. IX is blank.]

Sec. 11. The Legislature may by law authorize the creation of hospital districts in Ochiltree, Castro, Hansford and Hopkins Counties, each district to be coextensive with the limits of such county.

If any such district is created, it may be authorized to levy a tax not to exceed Seventy-five Cents (75¢) on the One Hundred Dollar ($100) valuation of taxable property within the district; provided, however, no tax may be levied until approved by a majority vote of the participating resident qualified property taxpaying voters who have duly rendered their property for taxation. The maximum rate of tax may be changed at subsequent elections so long as obligations are not impaired, and not to exceed the maximum limit of Seventy-five Cents (75¢) per One Hundred Dollar ($100) valuation.

If such tax is authorized, no political subdivision or municipality within or having the same boundaries as the district may levy a tax for medical or hospital care for needy individuals, nor shall they maintain or erect hospital facilities, but the district shall by resolution assume all such responsibilities and shall assume all of the liabilities and obligations (including bonds and warrants) of such subdivisions or municipalities or both. The maximum tax rate submitted shall be sufficient to discharge obligations, liabilities, and responsibilities, and to maintain and operate the hospital system, and the Legislature may authorize the district to issue tax bonds for the purpose of the purchase, construction, acquisition, repair or renovation of improvements and initially equipping the same, and such bonds shall be payable from said Seventy-five Cent (75¢) tax. The Legislature shall provide for transfer of title to properties to the district.

[Note — Sec. 11 of Art. IX was added to provide for the creation of special hospital districts and to authorize the levying of taxes for their support. It is obviously misnumbered, as there is no Sec. 10 of Art. IX. Submitted by 57th Legislature (1961) and adopted in election Nov. 6, 1962.]

Sec. 12. Establishment of Airport Authorities — The Legislature may by law provide for the creation, establishment, maintenance and operation of Airport Authorities composed of one or more counties, with power to issue general obligation bonds, revenue bonds, either or both of them, for the purchase, acquisition by the exercise of the power of eminent domain or otherwise, construction, reconstruction, repair or renovation of any airport or airports, landing fields and runways, airport buildings, hangars, facilities, equipment, fixtures, and any and all property, real or personal, necessary to operate, equip and maintain an airport; shall provide for the option by the governing body of the city or cities whose airport facilities are served by certificated airlines and whose facility or some interest therein, is proposed to be or has been acquired by the authority, to either appoint or elect a board of directors of said authority; if the directors are appointed such appointment shall be made by the County Commissioners Court after consultation with and consent of the governing body or bodies of such city or cities, and if the board of directors is elected they shall be elected by the qualified taxpaying voters of the county which chooses to elect the directors to represent that county, such directors shall serve without compensation for a term fixed by the Legislature not to exceed six (6) years, and shall be selected on the basis of the proportionate population of each county based upon the last preceding federal census, and shall be a resident or residents of such county; provide that no county shall have less than one (1) member on the board of directors; provide for the holding of an election in each county proposing the creation of an authority to be called by the Commissioners Court or Commissioners Courts, as the case may be, upon petition of five percent (5%) of the qualified taxpaying voters within the county or counties, said elections to be held on the same day if more than one county is included, provided that no more than one (1) such election may be called in a county until after the expiration of one (1) year; in the event such an election has failed, and thereafter only upon a petition of ten percent (10%) of the qualified taxpaying voters being presented to the Commissioners Court or Commissioners Courts of the county or counties in which such an election has failed, and in the event that two or more counties vote on the proposition of the creation of an authority therein, the proposition shall not be deemed to carry unless the majority of the qualified tax-paying voters in each county voting thereon vote in favor thereof; provided, however, that an Airport Authority may be created and be composed of the county or counties that vote in favor of its creation if separate propositions are submitted to the voters of each county so that they may vote for a two or more county authority or a single county authority; provide for the appointment by the board of directors of an assessor and collector of taxes in the authority, whether constituted of one or more counties, whose duty it shall be to assess all taxable property, both real and personal, and collect the taxes thereon, based upon the tax rolls approved by the board of directors, the tax to be levied not to exceed seventy-five cents (75¢) per one hundred dollars ($100) assessed valuation of the property, provided, however, that the property of state regulated common carriers required by law to pay a tax upon intangible assets shall not be subject to taxation by the authority, said taxable property shall be assessed on a valuation not to exceed the market value and shall be equal and uniform throughout the authority as is otherwise provided by the Constitution; the Legislature shall authorize the purchase or acquisition by the authority of any existing airport facility publicly owned and financed and served by certificated airlines, in fee or of any interest therein, or to enter into any lease agreement therefor, upon such terms and conditions as may be mutually agreeable to the authority and the owner of such facilities, or authorize the acquisition of same through the exercise of the power of eminent domain, and in the event of such acquisition, if there are any general obligation bonds that the owner of the publicly owned airport facility has outstanding, the same shall be fully assumed by the authority and sufficient taxes levied by the authority to discharge said outstanding indebtedness; and likewise any city or owner that has outstanding revenue bonds where the revenues of the airport have been pledged or said bonds constitute a lien against the airport facilities, the authority shall assume and discharge all the obligations of the city under the ordinances and bond indentures under which said revenue bonds have been issued and sold. Any city which owns airport facilities not serving certificated airlines which are not purchased or acquired or taken over as herein provided by such authority, shall have the power to operate the same under the existing laws or as the same may hereafter be amended. Any such authority when created may be granted the power and authority to promulgate, adopt and enforce appropriate zoning regulations to protect the airport from hazards and obstructions which would interfere with the use of the airport and its facilities for landing and takeoff; an additional county or counties may be added to an existing authority if a petition of five percent (5%) of the qualified taxpaying voters is filed with and an election is called by the Commissioners Court of the county or counties seeking admission to an authority and the vote is favorable, then admission may be granted to such county or counties by the board of directors of the then existing authority upon such terms and conditions as they may agree upon and evidenced by a resolution approved by two-thirds (2/3) of the then existing board of directors, provided, however, the county or counties that may be so added to the then existing authority shall be given representation on the board of directors by adding additional directors in proportion to their population according to the last preceding federal census.

[Note — Sec. 12 was added to provide for the establishment of airport authorities. Submitted by 59th Legislature (1965) and adopted in election Nov. 8, 1966.]

Sec. 13. **Mental Health Services** — Notwithstanding any other section of this article, the Legislature in providing for the creation, establishment, maintenance, and operation of a hospital district, shall not be required to provide that such district shall assume full responsibility for the establishment, maintenance, support or operation of mental health services or mental retardation services including the operation of any community mental health centers, community mental retardation centers or community health and mental retardation centers which may exist or be thereafter established within the boundaries of such district, nor shall the Legislature be required to provide that such district shall assume full responsibility of public health department units and clinics and related public health activities or services, and the Legislature shall not be required to restrict the power of any municipality or political subdivision to levy taxes or issue bonds or other obligations or to expend public moneys for the establishment, maintenance, support, or operation of mental health services, mental retardation services, public health units or clinics or related public health activities or services or the operation of such community mental health or mental retardation centers within the boundaries of the hospital districts; and unless a statute creating a hospital district shall expressly prohibit participation by any entity other than the hospital district in the establishment, maintenance, or support of mental health services, mental retardation services, public health units or clinics or related public health activities within or partly within the boundaries of any hospital district, any municipality or any other political subdivision or state-supported entity within the hospital district may participate in the establishment, maintenance, and support of mental health services, mental retardation services, public health units and clinics and related public health activities and may levy taxes, issue bonds or other obligations, and expend public moneys for such purposes as provided by law.

[Note — Sec. 13 of Art. IX was added to permit municipalities and other political subdivisions within hospital districts to participate in establishment, maintenance, support or operation of mental health, mental retardation or public health services. Submitted by 60th Legislature (1967) and adopted in election Nov. 11, 1967.]

Article X — Railroads

[Note — All of Art. X relating to railroads, except Sec. 2, was deleted by constitutional amendment. Submitted by 61st Legislature and approved in election Aug. 5, 1969.]

Article [Sec.] 2. **Public Highways; Common Carriers; Duty of the Legislature; Fixing Rates** — Railroads heretofore constructed or which may hereafter be constructed in this State are hereby declared public highways and railroad companies common carriers. The Legislature shall pass laws to regulate railroad freight and passenger tariffs to correct abuses, and prevent unjust discrimination and extortion in the rates of freight and passenger tariffs on the different railroads in this State, and enforce the same by adequate penalties; and to the further accomplishments of these objects and purposes may provide and establish all requisite means and agencies invested with such powers as may be deemed adequate and advisable.

[Note — The foregoing "Article [Sec.] 2" of Art. X was amended by addition of the last clause, which permitted establishment of the Railroad Commission of Texas. Submitted by 21st Legislature (1889), ratified in election Nov. 4, 1890, and declared adopted Dec. 19, 1890.]

*Explanatory Note — The legislative resolution submitting this amendment erroneously used the word, "Article," instead of the usual abbreviation, "Sec." Order used above is according to official draft of the Constitution.

Article XI — Municipal Corporations

Sec. 1. **Counties Are Legal Subdivisions of the State** — The several counties of this State are hereby recognized as legal subdivisions of the State.

Sec. 2. **Public Buildings and Roads** — The construction of jails, courthouses and bridges and the establishment of county poorhouses and farms and the laying out, construction and repairing of county roads shall be provided for by general laws.

Sec. 3. **No County or Municipal Corporation Shall Become a Subscriber to the Capital Stock of Any Private Corporation or Make Any Donation to the Same** — No county, city or other municipal corporation shall hereafter become a subscriber to the capital of any private corporation or association, or make any appropriation or donation to the same, or in anywise loan its credit; but this shall not be construed to in any way affect any obligation heretofore undertaken pursuant to law or to prevent a county, city, or other municipal corporation from investing its funds as authorized by law.

[Note — Sec. 3 of Art. XI was amended to authorize local governments to invest their funds as authorized by law. (See related amendment at Art. III, Sec. 52(e).) Proposed by 71st Legislature (1989) and adopted in election Nov. 7, 1989.]

Sec. 4. **Cities and Towns Having a Population of 5,000 or Less Inhabitants to Be Chartered by General Laws; Dues to Be Collected in Current Money** — Cities and towns having a population of 5,000 or less may be chartered alone by general laws. They may levy, assess and collect such taxes as may be authorized by law, but no tax for any purpose shall ever be lawful for any one year which shall exceed 1 1/2 percent of the taxable property of such city; and all taxes shall be collectible only in current money, and all licenses and occupation taxes levied, and all fines, forfeitures and penalties accruing to said cities and towns shall be collectible only in current money.

[Note — Sec. 4 of Art. XI was amended to provide that towns of 5,000 or less (instead of 10,000 or less, as provided by the original section) may be chartered alone by general law. Submitted by 31st Legislature (1909), ratified in election Aug. 3, 1909, and declared adopted Sept. 24, 1909. It was again amended to authorize a maximum tax rate, in towns of 5,000 or less, of 1 1/2 percent of taxable values in lieu of the originally specified maximum of one fourth of 1 percent. Submitted by 36th Legislature (1919) and adopted in election of Nov. 2, 1920.]

Sec. 5. Cities of More Than 5,000 Inhabitants May by a Majority Vote of the Qualified Voters Adopt Their Own Charter; Limitation as to Taxation and Debt — Cities having more than five thousand (5,000) inhabitants may, by a majority vote of the qualified voters of said city, at an election held for that purpose, adopt or amend their charters. If the number of inhabitants of cities that have adopted or amended their charters under this section is reduced to five thousand (5000) or fewer, the cities still may amend their charters by a majority vote of the qualified voters of said city at an election held for that purpose. The adoption or amendment of charters is subject to such limitations as may be prescribed by the Legislature, and no charter or any ordinance passed under said charter shall contain any provision inconsistent with the Constitution of the State or of the general laws enacted by the Legislature of this State. Said cities may levy, assess and collect such taxes as may be authorized by law or by their charters; but no tax for any purpose shall ever be lawful for any one year, which shall exceed two and one-half percent of the taxable property of such city, and no debt shall ever be created by any city, unless at the same time provision be made to assess and collect annually a sufficient sum to pay the interest thereon and creating a sinking fund

Article XI (Cont'd.); Articles XII, XIII, XIV, XV

of at least two percent thereon. Furthermore, no city charter shall be altered, amended or repealed oftener than every two years.

[Note — Sec. 5 of Art. XI has been amended three times: (1) To authorize towns of more than 5,000 population (instead of more than 10,000, as provided in the original section) to be chartered by special act, and allowing in such cities a maximum tax rate of 2 1/2 percent. Submitted by 31st Legislature (1909), ratified in election Aug. 3, 1909, and proclaimed Sept. 24, 1909. (2) To grant home rule to cities of more than 5,000 population. Submitted by 32nd Legislature (1911), adopted in election Nov. 5, 1912, and proclaimed Dec. 30, 1912. (3) To allow home rule cities with populations of 5,000 or fewer to amend their charters. Submitted by 72nd Legislature (1991) and adopted in election Nov. 5, 1991.]

Sec. 6. **Municipal Taxation** — Counties, cities, and towns are authorized, in such mode as may now or may hereafter be provided by law, to levy, assess and collect the taxes necessary to pay the interest and provide a sinking fund to satisfy any indebtedness heretofore legally made and undertaken; but all such taxes shall be assessed and collected separately from that levied, assessed and collected for current expenses of municipal government and shall, when levied, specify in the act of levying the purpose therefor; and such taxes may be paid in the coupons, bonds or other indebtedness for the payment of which such tax may have been levied.

Sec. 7. **Taxation of Seawalls, Etc.; Restrictions and Limitations; Eminent Domain** — All counties and cities bordering on the coast of the Gulf of Mexico are hereby authorized upon a vote of the majority of the resident property taxpayers voting thereon at an election called for such purpose, to levy and collect such tax for construction of seawalls, breakwaters or sanitary purposes, as may now or may hereafter be authorized by law, and may create a debt for such works and issue bonds in evidence thereof. But no debt for any purpose shall ever be incurred in any manner by any city or county unless provision is made at the time of creating the same, for levying and collecting a sufficient tax to pay the interest thereon and provide at least 2 percent as a sinking fund; and the condemnation of the right of way for the erection of such work shall be fully provided for.

[Note — Sec. 7 of Art. XI was amended to simplify language describing electors' qualifications. Submitted by 42nd Legislature (1931), adopted in election Nov. 8, 1932 and proclaimed Jan. 9, 1933. It was further amended to provide that a majority of resident property taxpayers may vote to issue bonds for construction of seawalls and breakwaters. Submitted by 63rd Legislature (1973) and adopted in election Nov. 6, 1973.]

Sec. 8. **State Aid for Seawalls, Etc.** — The counties and cities on the Gulf Coast being subject to calamitous overflows, and a very large proportion of the general revenue being derived from those otherwise prosperous localities.* The Legislature is specially authorized to aid, by donation of such portion of the public domain as may be deemed proper, and in such mode as may be provided by law, the construction of seawalls or breakwaters, such aid to be proportioned to the extent and value of the works constructed, or to be constructed, in any locality.

*Explanatory Note — The starting of a new sentence at this point follows in the official draft of the Constitution, but it is evident that the foregoing phrase ending with "localities" was meant to modify the following sentence.

Sec. 9. **Public Buildings, Etc.** — The property of counties, cities and towns owned and held only for public purposes, such as public buildings and the sites therefor, fire engines and the furniture thereof, and all property used or intended for extinguishing fires, public grounds and all other property devoted exclusively to the use and benefit of the public, shall be exempt from forced sale and from taxation; provided, nothing herein shall prevent the enforcement of the vendor's lien, the mechanic's or builder's lien, or other liens now existing.

[Note — Sec. 10 of Art. XI, relating to special taxes and school districts, was deleted by constitutional amendment. Submitted by 61st Legislature and approved in election Aug. 5, 1969.]

Sec. 11. **Term of Office for City Officials** — A home rule city may provide by charter or charter amendment, and a city, town or village operating under the general laws may provide by majority vote of the qualified voters voting at an election called for that purpose, for a longer term of office than two (2) years for its officers, either elective or appointive, or both, but not to exceed four (4) years; provided, however, that tenure under Civil Service shall not be affected hereby.

Provided, however, if any of such officers, elective or appointive, shall announce their candidacy, or shall in fact become a candidate, in any general, special or primary election, for any office of profit or trust under the laws of this State or the United States other than the office then held, at any time when the unexpired term of the office then held shall exceed one (1) year, such announcement or such candidacy shall constitute an automatic resignation of the office then held, and the vacancy thereby created shall be filled pursuant to law in the same manner as other vacancies for such office are filled.

A municipality so providing a term exceeding two (2) years but not exceeding four (4) years for any of its non-civil service officers must elect all of the members of its governing body by majority vote of the qualified voters in such municipality, and any vacancy or vacancies occurring on such governing body shall not be filled by appointment but must be filled by majority vote of the qualified voters at a special election called for such purpose within one hundred and twenty (120) days after such vacancy or vacancies occur.

[Note — Sec. 11 of Art. XI was added to provide four-year terms for city officials. Submitted by 55th Legislature (1957) and adopted in election Nov. 4, 1958.]

Sec. 12. **Sanitation Sewer Lines** — The Legislature by general law may authorize a city or town to expend public funds for the relocation or replacement of sanitation sewer laterals or water laterals on private property if the relocation or replacement is done in conjunction with or immediately following the replacement or relocation of sanitation sewer mains or water mains serving the property. The law must authorize the city or town to affix, with the consent of the owner of the private property, a lien on the property for the cost of relocating or replacing the sewer laterals on the property and must provide that the cost shall be assessed against the property with repayment by the property owner to be amortized over a period not to exceed five years at a rate of interest to be set as provided by the law. The lien may not be enforced until after five years have expired since the date the lien was affixed.

[Note — Sec. 12 of Art. XI was added to permit a city or town to expend public funds and levy assessments for relocation or replacement of sanitation sewer laterals on private property. Submitted by 68th Legislature (1983) and adopted in election Nov. 8, 1983. It was again amended to allow Legislature to enact laws permitting a city or town to spend public funds for the relocation or replacement of water laterals on private property. Submitted by 69th Legislature (1985) and adopted in election Nov. 5, 1985.]

Sec. 13. **Classification of Municipal Functions** — (a) Notwithstanding any other provision of this constitution, the legislature may by law define for all purposes those functions of a municipality that are to be considered governmental and those that are proprietary, including reclassifying a function's classification assigned under prior statute or common law.

(b) This section applies to laws enacted by the 70th Legislature, Regular Session, 1987, and to all subsequent regular or special sessions of the legislature.

[Note — Sec. 13, Art. XI was added to define the governmental and proprietary functions of a municipality. Submitted by 70th Legislature (1987) and adopted in election Nov. 3, 1987.]

Article XII — Private Corporations

Sec. 1. **Corporations Created by General Laws** — No private corporation shall be created except by general laws.

Sec. 2. **General Laws to be Enacted** — General laws shall be enacted providing for the creation of private corporations, and shall therein provide fully for the adequate protection of the public and of the individual stockholders.

[Note — Sections 3, 4, 5 and 7 of Art. XII, relating to franchises, and wharfage and freight tolls, were deleted by constitutional amendment. Submitted by 61st Legislature and approved in election Aug. 5, 1969. Section 6 of Art. XII, relating to the limitation on the consideration for which stock and bonds of a corporation may be issued, was repealed by amendment. Submitted by 73rd Legislature (1993) and approved in election Nov. 2, 1993.]

Article XIII — Spanish and Mexican Land Titles

[Note — The entire Art. XIII, relating to Spanish and Mexican Land Titles, was deleted by constitutional amendment. Submitted by 61st Legislature (1969) and approved in election Aug. 5, 1969.]

Article XIV — Public Lands and Land Office

Sec. 1. **General Land Office; Grants to Be Registered in; Land Office to Be Self-Sustaining** — There shall be one General Land Office in the State, which shall be at the seat of government, where all land titles which have emanated or may hereafter emanate from the State shall be registered, except those titles the registration of which may be prohibited by this Constitution. It shall be the duty of the Legislature at the earliest practicable time to make the Land Office self-sustaining, and from time to time the Legislature may establish such subordinate offices as may be deemed necessary.

[Note — All of Art. XIV relating to public lands and the Land Office, except Sec. 1, was deleted by constitutional amendment. Submitted by 61st Legislature (1969) and approved in election Aug. 5, 1969.]

Article XV — Impeachment

Sec. 1. **Power of Impeachment Vested in the House of Representatives** — The power of impeachment shall be vested in the House of Representatives.

Sec. 2. **Trial by Senate** — Impeachment of the Governor, Lieutenant Governor, Attorney General, Commissioner of the General Land Office, Comptroller, and the Judges of the Supreme Court, Courts of Appeal and District Courts shall be tried by the Senate.

[Note — Sec. 2 of Art. XV was amended to eliminate the reference

Article XV (Cont'd.); Article XVI

to Treasurer when that office was eliminated. Submitted by 74th Legislature (1995) and adopted in election Nov. 7, 1995.]

Sec. 3. **Oath of Senators** — When the Senate is sitting as a court of impeachment, the Senators shall be on oath, or affirmation, impartially to try the party impeached, and no person shall be convicted without the concurrence of two thirds of the Senators present.

Sec. 4. **Judgment; Party Convicted Subject to Indictment Under the Criminal Laws** — Judgment in cases of impeachment shall extend only to removal from office and disqualification from holding any office of honor, trust or profit under this State. A party convicted on impeachment shall also be subject to indictment, trial and punishment, according to law.

Sec. 5. **Officers Suspended During Pending Proceedings** — All officers against whom articles of impeachment may be preferred shall be suspended from the exercise of the duties of their office during the pendency of such impeachment. The Governor may make a provisional appointment to fill the vacancy occasioned by the suspension of an officer until the decision on the impeachment.

Sec. 6. **Removal of District Judges** — Any Judge of the District Courts of the State who is incompetent to discharge the duties of his office, or who shall be guilty of partiality, or oppression, or other official misconduct, or whose habits and conduct are such as to render him unfit to hold such office or who shall negligently fail to perform his duties as Judge, or who shall fail to execute in a reasonable measure the business in his courts, may be removed by the Supreme Court. The Supreme Court shall have original jurisdiction to hear and determine the causes aforesaid when presented in writing, upon the oaths, taken before some Judge of a court of record, of not less than ten lawyers, practicing in the courts held by such Judge, and licensed to practice in the Supreme Court; said presentment to be founded either upon the knowledge of the persons making it or upon the written oaths as to facts of creditable witnesses. The Supreme Court may issue all needful process and prescribe all needful rules to give effect to this section. Causes of this kind shall have precedence and be tried as soon as practicable.

Sec. 7. **Trial and Removal of Other Officers** — The Legislature shall provide by law for the trial and removal from office of all officers of this State, the modes for which have not been provided in this Constitution.

Address

Sec. 8. **Removal of Judges of Supreme Court and Courts of Appeals and of District Courts** — The Judges of the Supreme Court, Courts of Appeals and District Courts shall be removed by the Governor on the address of two thirds of each house of the Legislature, for willful neglect of duty, incompetency, habitual drunkenness, oppression in office, or other reasonable cause which shall not be sufficient ground for impeachment; provided, however that the cause or causes for which such removal shall be required shall be stated at length in such address and entered on the journals of each house; and provided, further, that the cause or causes shall be notified to the Judge so intended to be removed, and he shall be admitted to a hearing in his own defense before any vote for such address shall pass; and in all such cases the vote shall be taken by yeas and nays and entered on the journals of each house, respectively.

Sec. 9. **Removal of Appointed Officials by Governor; Special Session of Senate for This Purpose** — (a) In addition to the other procedures provided by law for removal of public officers, the governor who appoints an officer may remove the officer with the advice and consent of two-thirds of the members of the senate present.

(b) If the Legislature is not in session when the governor desires to remove an officer, the governor shall call a special session of the senate for consideration of the proposed removal. The session may not exceed two days in duration.

[Note — Sec. 9 of Art. XV was added to authorize the governor to remove appointed officers with the advice and consent of the Senate. Submitted by 66th Legislature (1979) and adopted in election Nov. 4, 1980.]

Article XVI — General Provisions

Sec. 1. **Official Oaths** — (a) Members of the Legislature, and all other elected officers, before they enter upon the duties of their offices, shall take the following Oath or Affirmation:

"I, _____, do solemnly swear (or affirm), that I will faithfully execute the duties of the office of _____ of the State of Texas, and will to the best of my ability preserve, protect, and defend the Constitution and laws of the United States and of this State, so help me God."

(b) Each member of the Legislature and all other elected officers, before taking the Oath or Affirmation of office prescribed by this section and entering upon the duties of office, shall subscribe to the following statement:

"I, _____, do solemnly swear (or affirm) that I have not directly or indirectly paid, offered, promised to pay, contributed, or promised to contribute any money or thing of value, or promised any public office or employment for the giving or withholding of a vote at the election at which I was elected so help me God."

The Secretary of State, and all other appointed officers before they enter upon the duties of their offices, shall take the following Oath or Affirmation:

"I, _____, do solemnly swear (or affirm), that I will faithfully execute the duties of the office of _____ of the State of Texas, and will to the best of my ability preserve, protect, and defend the Constitution and laws of the United States and of this State so help me God."

(d) The Secretary of State, and all other appointed officers, before taking the Oath or Affirmation of office prescribed by this section and entering upon the duties of office, shall subscribe to the following statement:

"I, _____, do solemnly swear (or affirm) that I have not directly or indirectly paid, offered, or promised to pay, contributed, or promised to contribute any money, or valuable thing, or promised any public office or employment, as a reward to secure my appointment or confirmation thereof, so help me God."

(e) Members of the Legislature and all other elected officers shall file the signed statement required by Subsection (b) of this section with the Secretary of State before taking the Oath or Affirmation of office prescribed by Subsection (a) of this section.

(f) The Secretary of State and all other appointed officers shall file the signed statement required by Subsection (d) of this section with the Secretary of State before taking the Oath or Affirmation of office prescribed by Subsection (c) of this section.

[Note — Sec. 1 of Art. XVI has been amended three times: (1) To eliminate that part of the oath stating that the incoming official had not fought a duel or sent or accepted a challenge to a duel or acted as a second in a duel. Submitted by 45th Legislature (1937) and adopted in election Nov. 8, 1938. (2) To change the form of the oath of office to include appointive officers of the State. Submitted by 54th Legislature (1955) and adopted in election Nov. 6, 1956. (3) To change the oath of office prescribed for members of the legislature, the secretary of state and other elected and appointed officers. Proposed by 71st Legislature (1989) and adopted in election Nov. 7, 1989.]

Sec. 2. **Right of Suffrage to Be Protected; Criminals Disfranchised** — Laws shall be made to exclude from office, serving on juries, and from the right of suffrage, those who may have been or shall hereafter be convicted of bribery, perjury, forgery or other high crimes. The privilege of free suffrage shall be protected by laws, regulating elections and prohibiting, under adequate penalties, all undue influence therein from power, bribery, tumult, or other improper practice.

[Note — Sections 3 and 4 of Art. XVI, relating to fines and dueling, were deleted by constitutional amendment. Submitted by 61st Legislature and approved in election Aug. 5, 1969.]

Sec. 5. **Bribery in Elections Disqualification for Holding Office** — Every person shall be disqualified from holding any office of profit or trust in this State who shall have been convicted of having given or offered a bribe to procure his election or appointment.

Sec. 6. Appropriations for Private Purposes Prohibited; Expenditures to Be Published — (a) No appropriation for private or individual purposes shall be made, unless authorized by this Constitution. A regular statement, under oath, and an account of the receipts and expenditures of all public money shall be published annually, in such manner as shall be prescribed by law.

(b) State agencies charged with the responsibility of providing services to those who are blind, crippled, or otherwise physically or mentally handicapped may accept money from private or federal sources, designated by the private or federal source as money to be used in and establishing and equipping facilities for assisting those who are blind, crippled, or otherwise physically or mentally handicapped in becoming gainfully employed, in rehabilitating and restoring the handicapped, and in providing other services determined by the state agency to be essential for the better care and treatment of the handicapped. Money accepted under this subsection is state money. State agencies may spend money accepted under this subsection, and no other money, for specific programs and projects to be conducted by local level or other private, nonsectarian associations, groups, and nonprofit organizations, in establishing and equipping facilities for assisting those who are blind, crippled, or otherwise physically or mentally handicapped in becoming gainfully employed, in rehabilitating and restoring the handicapped, and in providing other services determined by the state agency to be essential for the better care or treatment of the handicapped.

The state agencies may deposit money accepted under this subsection either in the state treasury or in other secure depositories. The money may not be expended for any purpose other than the purpose for which it was given. Notwithstanding any other provision of this Constitution, the state agencies may expend money accepted under this subsection without the necessity of an appropriation, unless the Legislature, by law, requires that the money be expended only on appropriation. The Legislature may prohibit state agencies from accepting money under this subsection or may regulate the amount of money accepted, the way the acceptance and expenditure of the money is administered, and the purposes for which the state agencies may expend the money. Money accepted under this subsection for a purpose prohibited by the Legislature shall be returned to the entity that gave the money.

This subsection does not prohibit state agencies authorized to render services to the handicapped from contracting with privately-owned or local facilities for necessary and essential services, subject

Article XVI (Cont'd.)

to such conditions, standards, and procedures as may be prescribed by law.

[Note — Sec. 6 of Art. XVI was amended to authorize public grants to private groups for assistance to the blind, crippled or otherwise physically and mentally handicapped. Submitted by 59th Legislature (1965) and adopted in election Nov. 8, 1966.]

[Note — Sec. 7 of Art. XVI, relating to paper money, was deleted by constitutional amendment. Submitted by 61st Legislature and approved in election Aug. 5, 1969.]

Sec. 8. Counties May Provide Workhouses, Poorhouses and Farms — Each county in the State may provide, in such manner as may be prescribed by law, a manual labor poorhouse and farm, for taking care of, managing, employing and supplying the wants of its indigent and poor inhabitants.

Sec. 9. Absence on Business of the State or United States Shall Not Forfeit a Residence Once Obtained — Absence on business of the State or of the United States shall not forfeit a residence once obtained, so as to deprive anyone of the right of suffrage, or of being elected or appointed to any office, under the exceptions contained in this Constitution.

Sec. 10. Deductions From Salaries to be Provided for — The Legislature shall provide for deductions from the salaries of public officers who may neglect the performance of any duty that may be assigned them by law.

Sec. 11. Usurious Interest Prohibited — The Legislature shall have authority to classify loans and lenders, license and regulate lenders, define interest and fix maximum rates of interest; provided, however, in the absence of legislation fixing maximum rates of interest all contracts for a greater rate of interest than ten per centum (10%) per annum shall be deemed usurious; provided, further, that in contracts where no rate of interest is agreed upon, the rate shall not exceed six per centum (6%) per annum. Should any regulatory agency, acting under the provisions of this Section, cancel or refuse to grant any permit under any law passed by the Legislature; then such applicant or holder shall have the right of appeal to the courts and granted a trial de novo as that term is used in appealing from the justice of peace court to the county court.

[Note — Sec. 11 of Art. XVI was amended to set 10 percent and 6 percent as interest rates, in place of original provision for 12 percent and 8 percent. Submitted by 22nd Legislature (1891), ratified in election Aug. 11, 1891, and declared adopted Sept. 22, 1891. It was further amended to grant right of appeal from justice of peace court to county court. Submitted by 56th Legislature (1959) and adopted in election Nov. 8, 1960.]

Sec. 12. Officers Not Eligible — No member of Congress, nor person holding or exercising any office of profit or trust under the United States, or either of them, or under any foreign power, shall be eligible as a member of the Legislature or hold or exercise any office of profit or trust under this State.

[Note — Sec. 13 of Art. XVI, relating to arbitration laws, was deleted by constitutional amendment. Submitted by 61st Legislature (1969) and approved in election Aug. 5, 1969.]

Sec. 14. Residence of Officers — All civil officers shall reside within the State, and all district or county officers within their districts or counties, and shall keep their offices at such places as may be required by law; and failure to comply with this condition shall vacate the office so held.

Sec. 15. Community Property of Husband and Wife; Partition Thereof — All Property, both real and personal, of a spouse owned or claimed before marriage, and that acquired afterward by gift, devise or descent, shall be the separate property of that spouse; and laws shall be passed more clearly defining the rights of the spouses, in relation to separate and community property; provided that persons about to marry and spouses, without the intention to defraud pre-existing creditors, may by written instrument from time to time partition between themselves all or part of their property, then existing or to be acquired, or exchange between themselves the community interest of one spouse or future spouse in any property for the community interest of the other spouse or future spouse in other community property then existing or to be acquired, whereupon the portion or interest set aside to each spouse shall be and constitute a part of the separate property and estate of such spouse or future spouse; spouses may also from time to time, by written instrument, agree between themselves that the income or property from all or part of the separate property then owned or which thereafter might be acquired by only one of them, shall be the separate property of that spouse; if one spouse makes a gift of property to the other that gift is presumed to include all the income or property which might arise from that gift of property; and spouses may agree in writing that all or part of their community property becomes the property of the surviving spouse on the death of a spouse.

[Note — Sec. 15 of Art. XVI was amended to provide for partition of community property of husband and wife. Submitted by 50th Legislature (1947) and adopted in election Nov. 2, 1948. It was further

amended to allow spouses to agree that income or property arising from separate property is to be separate property. Submitted by 66th Legislature (1979) and adopted in election Nov. 4, 1980. It was again amended to permit spouses to hold community property with right of survivorship. Submitted by 70th Legislature (1987) and adopted in election Nov. 3, 1987.]

Sec. 16. Banking Corporations — (a) The Legislature shall, by general laws, authorize the incorporation of state banks and savings and loan associations and shall provide for a system of state supervision, regulation and control of such bodies which will adequately protect and secure the depositors and creditors thereof.

No state bank shall be chartered until all of the authorized capital stock has been subscribed and paid in full in cash. Except as may be permitted by the Legislature pursuant to subsections (b), (d), and (e) of this Section 16, a state bank shall not be authorized to engage in business at more than one place, which shall be designated in its charter; however, this restriction shall not apply to any other type of financial institution chartered under the laws of this state.

No foreign corporation, other than the national banks of the United States domiciled in this State, shall be permitted to exercise banking or discounting privileges in this State.

(b) If it finds that the convenience of the public will be served thereby, the Legislature may authorize state and national banks to establish and operate unmanned teller machines within the county or city of their domicile. Such machines may perform all banking functions. Banks which are domiciled within a city lying in two or more counties may be permitted to establish and operate unmanned teller machines within both the city and the county of their domicile. The Legislature shall provide that a bank shall have the right to share in the use of these teller machines, not situated at a banking house, which are located within the county or the city of the bank's domicile, on a reasonable, nondiscriminatory basis, consistent with anti-trust laws. Banks may share the use of such machines within the county or city of their domicile with savings and loan associations and credit unions which are domiciled in the same county or city.

(c) A state bank created by virtue of the power granted by this section, notwithstanding any other provision of this section, has the same rights and privileges that are or may be granted to national banks of the United States domiciled in this State.

Should the Legislature enact legislation in anticipation of the adoption of this amendment, such law shall not be invalid because of its anticipatory character.

(d) The Legislature may authorize a state bank or national bank of the United States domiciled in this State to engage in business at more than one place if it does so through the purchase and assumption of certain assets and liabilities of a failed state bank or a failed national bank of the United States domiciled in this State.

(e) The Legislature may authorize a state bank or national bank of the United States domiciled in this State to establish and operate banking facilities at locations within the county or city of its domicile, subject to limitations the Legislature imposes. The Legislature may permit a bank domiciled within a city located in two or more counties to establish and operate branches within both the city and the county of its domicile, subject to limitations the Legislature imposes.

(f) A bank may not be considered a branch or facility of another bank solely because it is owned or controlled by the same stockholders as the other bank, has common accounting and administrative systems with the other bank, or has a name similar to the other bank's or because of a combination of those factors.

[Note — Sec. 16 of Art. XVI has been amended five times: (1) To eliminate the original provision that "No corporate body shall hereafter be created, renewed or extended with banking or discounting privileges," and making possible the establishment of the present state banking system. Submitted by 28th Legislature (1903), ratified in election Nov. 8, 1904, and declared adopted Dec. 29, 1904. (2) To eliminate a provision, contained in the amendment of 1904, making shareholders of banks liable to the extent of twice the par value of the shares owned. Submitted by 45th Legislature (1937), and adopted in election Aug. 23, 1937. (3) To authorize banks to use unmanned teller machines within the county or city of their domicile on a shared basis. Submitted by 66th Legislature (1979) and adopted in election Nov. 4, 1980. (4) To provide state banks same rights and privileges as national banks. Submitted by 68th Legislature (1983) and adopted in election Nov. 6, 1984. (5) To provide that a bank may offer full service banking at more than one location within the city or county where its principal facility is located, subject to limitations and restrictions provided by law. Submitted by 69th Legislature (1986) and adopted in election Nov. 4, 1986.]

Sec. 17. Officers to Perform Duties Until Successor Qualified — All officers within this State shall continue to perform the duties of their offices until their successors shall be duly qualified.

Sec. 18. Vested Rights — The rights of property and of action, which have been acquired under the Constitution and the laws of the Republic and State, shall not be divested; nor shall any rights or actions, which have been divested, barred or declared null and void by the Constitution of the Republic and State be reinvested, renewed or reinstated by this Constitution; but the same shall remain precisely in the situation which they were before the adoption of this Constitution, unless otherwise herein provided; and provided, further, that no

Article XVI (Cont'd.)

cause of action heretofore barred shall be revived.

Sec. 19. **Qualifications of Jurors** — The Legislature shall prescribe by law the qualifications of grand and petit jurors; provided that neither the right nor the duty to serve on grand and petit juries shall be denied or abridged by reason of sex. Whenever in the Constitution the term "men" is used in reference to grand or petit juries, such term shall include persons of the female as well as the male sex.

[Note — Sec. 19 of Art. XVI was amended to include women jurors. Submitted by 53rd Legislature (1953) and adopted in election Nov. 2, 1954.]

Sec. 20. **Manufacture and Sale of Intoxicants** — (a) The Legislature shall have the power to enact a Mixed Beverage Law regulating the sale of mixed alcoholic beverages on a local option election basis. The Legislature shall also have the power to regulate the manufacture, sale, possession and transportation of intoxicating liquors, including the power to establish a state monopoly on the sale of distilled liquors.

Should the Legislature enact any enabling laws in anticipation of this amendment, no such law shall be void by reason of its anticipatory nature.

(b) The Legislature shall enact a law or laws whereby the qualified voters of any county, justices precinct or incorporated town or city may, by a majority vote of those voting, determine from time to time whether the sale of intoxicating liquors for beverage purposes shall be prohibited or legalized within the prescribed limits; and such laws shall contain provisions for voting on the sale of intoxicating liquors of various types and various alcoholic content.

(c) In all counties, justices precincts or incorporated towns or cities wherein the sale of intoxicating liquors had been prohibited by local option elections held under the laws of the State of Texas in force at the time of the taking effect of Section 20, Article XVI of the Constitution of Texas, it shall continue to be unlawful to manufacture, sell, barter or exchange in any such county, justices precinct or incorporated town or city, any spirituous, vinous or malt liquors or medicated bitters capable of producing intoxication or any other intoxicants whatsoever, for beverage purposes, unless and until a majority of the qualified voters in such county or political subdivision thereof voting in an election held for such purposes shall determine such to be lawful; provided that this subsection shall not prohibit the sale of alcoholic beverages containing not more than 3.2 percent alcohol by weight in cities, counties or political subdivisions thereof in which the qualified voters have voted to legalize such sale under the provisions of Chapter 116, Acts of the Regular Session of the Forty-third Legislature.

[Note — Sec. 20 of Art. XVI, which originally provided only for local option elections in "any county, justices precinct, town or city," has been amended five times: (1) To insert a clause in original section "or such subdivision of a county as may be designated by Commissioners' Court of said county," with reference to local option elections. Submitted by 22nd Legislature (1891), ratified in election Aug. 11, 1891, and declared adopted Sept. 22, 1891. (2) To declare statewide prohibition. Submitted by 36th Legislature (1919), and declared adopted May 24, 1919. (3) To legalize sale of vinous and malt liquors of not more than 3.2 percent alcohol. Submitted by 43rd Legislature (1933), and adopted in election Aug. 26, 1933. (4) To legalize sale of all liquors, as stated in the section printed above. Submitted by 44th Legislature (1935), and adopted in election Aug. 24, 1935. (5) To give Legislature power to enact a Mixed Beverage Law regulating sale of mixed drinks on local option election basis. Submitted by 61st Legislature (1969) and adopted in election Nov. 3, 1970.]

Sec. 21. **Stationery; Public Printing** — All stationery, printing, fuel used in the Legislature and departments of the government other than the judicial department, printing and binding of the laws, journals, and department reports, and all other printing and binding and the repairing and furnishing of the halls and rooms used during meetings of the Legislature and in committees, except proclamations and such products and services as may be done by handicapped individuals employed in nonprofit rehabilitation facilities providing sheltered employment to the handicapped in Texas, shall be performed under contract, to be given to the lowest responsible bidder, below such maximum price and under such regulations as shall be prescribed by law. No member or officer of any department of the government shall in any way have a financial interest in such contracts, and all such contracts or programs involving the state use of the products and services of handicapped individuals shall be subject to such requirements as might be established by the Legislature.

[Note — Sec. 21 of Art. XVI was amended to eliminate reference to the Deaf and Dumb Asylum; to allow certain products and services of handicapped persons to be used by agencies of state government; to require other products and services required for operation of state government be acquired under bids by lowest responsible bidder; and to eliminate requirement that Governor, Secretary of State and Comptroller of Public Accounts be personally involved with such transactions. Submitted by 65th Legislature (1977) and adopted in election Nov. 7, 1978.]

Sec. 22. **Fence Laws** — The Legislature shall have the power to pass such fence laws, applicable to any subdivision of the State or county, as may be needed to meet the wants of the people.

Sec. 23. **Stock Laws** — The Legislature may pass laws for the regulation of livestock and the protection of stock raisers in the stock raising portion of the State, and exempt from the operation of such laws other portions, sections or counties; and shall have power to pass general and special laws for the inspection of cattle, stock and hides, and for the regulation of brands; provided, that any local law thus passed shall be submitted to the freeholders of the section to be affected thereby, and approved by them before it shall go into effect.

Sec. 24. **Roads; Convict Labor** — The Legislature shall make provision for laying out and working public roads, for the building of bridges, and for utilizing fines, forfeitures, and convict labor to all these purposes.

Sec. 25. **Drawbacks and Rebates in Freight Insurance, Transportation, Storage, Etc., Prohibited** — That all drawbacks and rebatement of insurance, freight, transportation, carriage, wharfage, storage, compressing, bailing, repairing, or for any other kind of labor or service of, or to any cotton, grain or any other produce or article of commerce in this State, paid or allowed or contracted for to any common carrier, shipper, merchant, commission merchant, factor, agent or middleman of any kind not the true and absolute owner thereof, are forever prohibited; and it shall be the duty of the Legislature to pass effective laws punishing all persons in this State who pay, receive or contract for or respecting the same.

Sec. 26. **Homicide: Civil Action For** — Every person, corporation or company that may commit a homicide, through willful act or omission or gross neglect, shall be responsible in exemplary damages to the surviving husband, widow, heirs of his or her body, or such of them as there may be, without regard to any criminal proceeding that may or may not be had in relation to the homicide.

Sec. 27. **Vacancies in Offices Filled for Unexpired Term Only** — In all elections to fill vacancies of office in this State, it shall be to fill the unexpired term only.

Sec. 28. **Wages Exempt From Garnishment** — No current wages for personal service shall ever be subject to garnishment, except for the enforcement of court-ordered child support payments.

[Note — Sec. 28 of Art. XVI was amended to provide for additional remedies to enforce court-ordered child support payments. Submitted by 68th Legislature (1983) and adopted in election Nov. 8, 1983.]

[Note — Sec. 29 of Art. XVI, relating to barratry, was deleted by constitutional amendment. Submitted by 61st Legislature (1969) and approved in election Aug. 5, 1969.]

Sec. 30. **Duration of Offices; Term of Railroad Commissioner** — (a) The duration of all offices not fixed by this Constitution shall never exceed two years.

(b) When a Railroad Commission is created by law it shall be composed of three Commissioners, who shall be elected by the people at a general election for state officers, and their term of office shall be six years. Railroad Commissioners first elected after this amendment goes into effect shall hold office as follows: One shall serve two years, and one four years, and one six years; their terms to be decided by lot immediately after they shall have qualified. And one Railroad Commissioner shall be elected every two years thereafter. In case of vacancy in said office the Governor of the State shall fill said vacancy by appointment until the next general election.

(c) The Legislature may provide that members of the governing board of a district or authority created by authority of Art. III, Sec. 52(b) (1) or (2), or Art. XVI, Sec. 59, of this Constitution serve terms not to exceed four years.

(d) The Legislature by general or special law may provide that members of the governing board of a hospital district serve terms not to exceed four years.

[Note — Sec. 30 of Art. XVI was amended to permit six-year terms for the newly created offices of the three-place Railroad Commission of Texas. The original section consisted only of the first clause of the amendment as printed above. Submitted by 23rd Legislature (1893), ratified in election Nov. 6, 1894, and declared adopted Dec. 21, 1894. It was further amended to provide four-year terms for members of governing boards of certain water districts and conservation and reclamation districts. Submitted by 67th Legislature (1981) and adopted in election Nov. 2, 1982. It was again amended by adding Subsection (d) to authorize the members of a hospital district board to serve four-year terms. Proposed by 71st Legislature (1989) and adopted in election Nov. 7, 1989.]

Sec. 30-A. **Board of Regents, Trustees, Managers, Etc.; Term of Office** — The Legislature may provide by law that the members of the Board of Regents of the State University and boards of trustees or managers of the educational, eleemosynary and penal institutions of this State, and such boards as have been or may hereafter be established by law, may hold their respective offices for the term of six (6) years, one third of the members of such boards to be elected or appointed every two years in such manner as the Legislature may determine; vacancies in such offices to be filled as may be provided by law, and the Legislature shall enact suitable laws to give effect to this section.

[Note — Sec. 30-A of Art. XVI was added to give the Legislature authority to provide official terms of more than two years. (See Sec.

Article XVI (Cont'd.)

30 above and accompanying note.) Submitted by 32nd Legislature (1911), ratified at election Nov. 5, 1912, and declared adopted Dec. 30, 1912.]

Sec. 30-B. **Tenure Under Municipal Civil Service** — Wherever by virtue of statute or charter provisions appointive officers of any municipality are placed under the terms and provisions of Civil Service and rules are set up governing appointment to and removal from such offices, the provisions of Article 16, Section 30, of the Texas Constitution limiting the duration of all offices not fixed by the Constitution to two (2) years shall not apply, but the duration of such offices shall be governed by the provisions of the Civil Service law or charter provisions applicable thereto.

[Note — Sec. 30-B of Art. XVI was added to extend to local officials terms under the Civil Service exemption from the two-year restriction in the first clause of Sec. 30. (See Secs. 30 and 30-a and accompanying notes.) Submitted by 46th Legislature; ratified in election Nov. 5, 1940.]

Sec. 31. **Qualifications of Physicians to Be Prescribed** — The Legislature may pass laws prescribing the qualifications of practitioners of medicine in this State, and to punish persons for malpractice, but no preference shall ever be given by law to any schools of medicine.

[Note — Sec. 32 of Art. XVI, relating to Board of Health and Vital Statistics, was deleted by constitutional amendment. Submitted by 61st Legislature (1969) and approved in election Aug. 5, 1969.]

Sec. 33. **Condition Under Which a Person Can Not Receive Compensation From the State** — The accounting officers in this State shall neither draw nor pay a warrant or check on funds of the State of Texas, whether in the treasury or otherwise, to any person for salary or compensation who holds at the same time more than one civil office of emolument, in violation of Sec. 40.

[Note — Sec. 33 of Art. XVI has been amended four times: (1) To release National Guard of Texas, National Guard Reserve and Officers' Reserve Corps and United States Organized Reserves from the prohibition against holding remunerative office. Submitted by 39th Legislature (1925), adopted in election Nov. 2, 1926 and proclaimed Jan. 20, 1927. (2) To add to those released from the prohibition against holding remunerative office all retired officers and enlisted men of the United States Army, Navy and Marine Corps. Submitted by 42nd Legislature (1931), adopted in election Nov. 8, 1932 and proclaimed Jan. 9, 1933. (3) To allow nonelective state officers and employees to serve in other nonelective offices under this state or the United States until Sept. 1, 1969, and thereafter only if authorized by Legislature, if the offices are of benefit to Texas or are required by state or federal law and there is no conflict of interest; prohibiting elected officers from holding any other office under this state; and adding members of Air National Guard, Air National Guard Reserve, Air Force Reserve and retired members of Air Force to list of persons exempted. Submitted by 60th Legislature (1967) and adopted in election Nov. 11, 1967. (4) To delete the old Sec. 33 of Art. XVI and substitute the Sec. 33 above. (See also note under Sec. 40 of Art. XVI.) Submitted by 62nd Legislature (1971) and adopted in election Nov. 7, 1972.]

[Note — Sections 34, 35, 36 and 38 of Art. XVI, relating to military forts, laborers on public works, payments to schoolteachers, and a Commissioner of Insurance, Statistics and History, were deleted by constitutional amendment. Submitted by 61st Legislature (1969) and approved in election Aug. 5, 1969.]

Sec. 37. **Mechanic's Liens to Be Enforced** — Mechanics, artisans and material men of every class shall have a lien upon the buildings and articles made or repaired by them, for the value of their labor done thereon, or material furnished therefor; and the Legislature shall provide by law for the speedy and efficient enforcement of said liens.

Sec. 39. **Memorials of Texas History** — The Legislature may, from time to time, make appropriations for preserving and perpetuating memorials of the history of Texas, by means of monuments, statues, paintings and documents of historical value.

Sec. 40. **Provision Against Holding More Than One Office; Exceptions** — No person shall hold or exercise at the same time, more than one civil office of emolument, except that of Justice of the Peace, County Commissioner, Notary Public and Postmaster, Officer of the National Guard, the National Guard Reserve, and the Officers Reserve Corps of the United States, and enlisted men of the National Guard, the National Guard Reserve, and the Organized Reserves of the United States, and retired officers of the United States Army, Air Force, Navy, Marine Corps, and Coast Guard, and retired warrant officers, and retired enlisted men of the United States Army, Air Force, Navy, Marine Corps, and Coast Guard, and the officers and directors of soil and water conservation districts, unless otherwise specially provided herein. Provided, that nothing in this Constitution shall be construed to prohibit an officer or enlisted man of the National Guard, and the National Guard Reserve, or an officer in the Officers Reserve Corps of the United States, or an enlisted man in the Organized Re-

serves of the United States, or retired officers of the United States Army, Air Force, Navy, Marine Corps, and Coast Guard, and retired warrant officers, and retired enlisted men of the United States Army, Air Force, Navy, Marine Corps, and Coast Guard, and officers of the State soil and water conservation districts, from holding at the same time any other office or position of honor, trust or profit, under this State or the United States, or from voting at any election, general, special or primary in this State when otherwise qualified. State employees or other individuals who receive all or part of their compensation either directly or indirectly from funds of the State of Texas and who are not State officers, shall not be barred from serving as members of the governing bodies of school districts, cities, towns, or other local governmental districts; provided, however, that such State employees or other individuals shall receive no salary for serving as members of such governing bodies. It is further provided that a non-elective State officer may hold other non-elective offices under the State or the United States, if the other office is of benefit to the State of Texas or is required by the State or Federal law, and there is no conflict with the original office for which he receives salary or compensation. No member of the Legislature of this State may hold any other office or position of profit under this State, or the United States, except as a notary public if qualified by law.

[Note — Sec. 40 of Art. XVI has been amended three times: (1) To release National Guard, National Guard Reserve and Officers' Reserve Corps and United States Organized Reserves from the prohibition against holding remunerative office. Submitted by 39th Legislature (1925), adopted in election Nov. 2, 1926 and proclaimed Jan. 20, 1927. (2) To add to those released from the prohibition against holding remunerative office all retired officers and enlisted men of the United States Army, Navy and Marine Corps. Submitted by 42nd Legislature (1931) and adopted in election Nov. 8, 1932. Proclaimed Jan. 9, 1933. (3) To add to those released from the prohibition against holding remunerative office retired officers or enlisted men of the Air Force and Coast Guard; and officers and directors of soil and water conservation districts, unless otherwise specially prohibited; also certain other state employees who are not officers of the state. Submitted by 62nd Legislature (1971) and adopted in election Nov. 7, 1972.]

Sec. 41. **Bribery of Certain Officials to Be Prohibited** — Any person who shall, directly or indirectly, offer, give or promise any money or thing of value, testimonial, privilege or personal advantage to any executive or judicial officer or member of the Legislature, to influence him in the performance of any of his public or official duties, shall be guilty of bribery and be punished in such manner as shall be provided by law. And any member of the Legislature, or executive or judicial officer, who shall solicit, demand or receive, or consent to receive, directly or indirectly, for himself or for another, from any company, corporation or person any money, appointment, employment testimonial, reward, thing of value or employment, or of personal advantage or promise thereof, for his vote or official influence, or for withholding the same, or with any understanding, expressed or implied, that his vote or official action shall be in any way influenced thereby, or who shall solicit, demand and receive any such money or other advantage, matter or thing aforesaid, for another, as the consideration of his vote or official influence, in consideration of the payment or promise of such money, advantage, matter or thing to another, shall be held guilty of bribery within the meaning of the Constitution, and shall incur the disabilities provided for said offenses, with a forfeiture of the office they may hold, and such other additional punishment as is or shall be provided by law.

[Note — Sec. 42 of Art. XVI, relating to an asylum for inebriates, was deleted by constitutional amendment. Submitted by 61st Legislature (1969) and approved in election Aug. 5, 1969.]

Sec. 43. **Exemption From Public Service** — No man or set of men shall ever be exempted, relieved or discharged from the performance of any public duty or service imposed by general law, by any special law. Exemptions from the performance of such public duty or service shall only be made by general law.

Sec. 44. **County Treasurer and Surveyor** — (a) Except as otherwise provided by this section, the Legislature shall prescribe the duties and provide for the election by the qualified voters of each county in this State, of a County Treasurer and a County Surveyor, who shall have an office at the county seat, and hold their office for four years, and until their successors are qualified; and shall have such compensation as may be provided by law.

(b) The office of County Treasurer in the counties of Tarrant and Bee is abolished and all the powers, duties, and functions of the office in each of these counties are transferred to the County Auditor or to the officer who succeeds to the auditor's functions. The office of County Treasurer in the counties of Bexar and Collin are abolished and all the powers, duties, and functions of the office in each of these counties are transferred to the County Clerk. However, the office of County Treasurer shall be abolished in the counties covered by this subsection only after a local election has been held in each county and the proposition "to abolish the elective office of county treasurer" has passed by a majority of those persons voting in said election.

(c) The office of County Treasurer in the counties of Andrews and Gregg is abolished. In Andrews County, the powers, duties, and func-

Article XVI (Cont'd.)

tions of the office are transferred to the County Auditor of the county or to the officer who succeeds to the auditor's functions. In Gregg County, the functions of the office are transferred to an elected official or the County Auditor as designated by the Commissioners Court, and the Commissioners Court may from time to time change its designation as it considers appropriate.

(d) The office of County Treasurer in the counties of El Paso and Fayette is abolished. In El Paso County, the Commissioners Court may employ or contract with a qualified person or may designate another county officer to perform any of the functions that would have been performed by the County Treasurer if the office had not been abolished. In Fayette County, the functions of the abolished office are transferred to the County Auditor or to the officer who succeeds to the auditor's functions. However, the office of County Treasurer in El Paso or Fayette County is abolished under this subsection only if, at the statewide election at which the constitutional amendment providing for the abolition of the office in that county is submitted to the voters, a majority of the voters of that county voting on the question at that election favor the amendment.

(e) The office of County Surveyor in the counties of Denton, Randall, Collin, Dallas, El Paso, McLennan, and Henderson is abolished upon the approval of the abolition by a majority of the qualified voters of the respective county voting on the question at an election that the Commissioners Court of the county may call. If the election is called, the Commissioners Court shall order the ballot at the election to be printed to provide for voting for or against the proposition: "Abolishing the office of county surveyor." Each qualified voter of the county is entitled to vote in the election. If the office of County Surveyor is abolished under this subsection, the maps, field notes, and other records in the custody of the County Surveyor are transferred to the County Clerk of the county. After abolition, the Commissioners Court may employ or contract with a qualified person to perform any of the functions that would have been performed by the County Surveyor if the office had not been abolished.

[Note — Subsection (e) of Art. XVI, Sec. 44 was amended to abolish the office of county surveyor in McLennan County. Submitted by 73rd Legislature (1993) and adopted in election Nov. 2, 1993.]

(f) This subsection applies only to the counties of Cass, Ector, Garza, Smith, Bexar, Harris, and Webb. The office of County Surveyor in the county is abolished on January 1, 1990, if at the statewide election at which the addition to the Constitution of this subsection is submitted to the voters, a majority of the voters of that county voting on the question at that election favor the addition of this subsection. If the office of County Surveyor is abolished in a county under this subsection, the powers, duties, and functions of the office are transferred to the county officer or employee designated by the Commissioners Court of the county in which the office is abolished, and the Commissioners Court may from time to time change its designation as it considers appropriate.

[Note — Subsection (f) of Art. XVI, Sec. 44 was added to abolish the office of county surveyor in designated counties. Proposed by 71st Legislature (1989) and adopted in election Nov. 7, 1989. A previous Subsection (f) relating to abolishing the office of county treasurer in Gregg and Fayette counties had expired on Jan. 2, 1988. It had replaced the previous Subsection (f), which expired Jan. 2, 1986.]

(g) The office of County Treasurer in Nueces County is abolished and all powers, duties, and functions of this office are transferred to the County Clerk. However, the office of County Treasurer in Nueces County is abolished under this subsection only if, at the statewide election at which this amendment is submitted to the voters, a majority of the voters of Nueces County voting on the question at that election favor the amendment. The office of County Treasurer of Nueces County is abolished on January 1, 1988, if the conditions of this subsection are met. If that office in Nueces County is not abolished, this subsection expires on January 1, 1988.

(h) (Ed. note: See also second Subsection (h) below and explanation following) The Commissioners Court of a county may call an election to abolish the office of County Surveyor in the county. The office of County Surveyor in the county is abolished if a majority of the voters of the county voting on the question at that election approve the abolition. If an election is called under this subsection, the Commissioners Court shall order the ballot for the election to be printed to provide for voting for or against the proposition: "Abolishing the office of county surveyor of this county." If the office of County Surveyor is abolished under this subsection, the maps, field notes, and other records in the custody of the County Surveyor are transferred to the county officer or employee designated by the Commissioners Court of the county in which the office is abolished, and the Commissioners Court may from time to time change its designation as it considers appropriate

(h) (Ed. note: See also second Subsection (h) above and explanation at end of Note below) The office of County Surveyor in Jackson County is abolished. The powers, duties, and functions of the office are transferred to the county officer or employee designated by the commissioners court, and the commissioners court may change its designation as it considers appropriate.

[Note — Sec. 44 of Art. XVI has been amended eight times: (1) To raise term of office from two to four years. Submitted by 53rd Legislature (1953) and adopted in election Nov. 2, 1954. (2) To abolish the office of county treasurer in Tarrant and Bee counties. Submitted by 67th Legislature (1981) and adopted in election Nov. 2, 1982. (3) To abolish the office of county treasurer in Bexar and Collin counties. Submitted by 68th Legislature (1983) and adopted in election Nov. 6, 1984. (4) To abolish the office of county treasurer in Andrews and El Paso counties; to abolish the office of county surveyor in Collin, Dallas, Denton, El Paso, Henderson and Randall counties. Submitted by 69th Legislature (1985) and adopted in election Nov. 5, 1985. (5) To abolish the office of county treasurer in Gregg, Fayette and Nueces counties. Submitted by 70th Legislature (1987) and adopted in election Nov. 3, 1987. (6) To abolish the office of county surveyor in Cass, Ector, Garza, Smith, Bexar, Harris and Webb counties. Proposed by 71st Legislature (1989) and adopted in election Nov. 7, 1989. (7) and (8) The 73rd Legislature (1993) approved and submitted to the voters two amendments proposing to add Subsection (h) to Art. XVI, Sec. 44. The first given above permits the voters of a county to decide by election to abolish the office of county surveyor in the county. The second listed above abolishes the office of county surveyor in Jackson County. Both were adopted in election Nov. 2, 1993.]

[Note — Sections 45 and 46 of Art. XVI, relating to records of the history of Texas and organization of a militia, were deleted by constitutional amendment. Submitted by 61st Legislature (1969) and approved in election Aug. 5, 1969.]

Sec. 47. **Scruples Against Bearing Arms** — Any person who conscientiously scruples to bear arms shall not be compelled to do so, but shall pay an equivalent for personal service.

Sec. 48. **Laws to Remain in Force** — All laws and parts of laws now in force in the State of Texas which are not repugnant to the Constitution of the United States or to this Constitution shall continue and remain in force as the laws of this State until they expire by their own limitation or shall be amended or repealed by the Legislature.

Sec. 49. **Exemptions From Forced Sales** — The Legislature shall have power, and it shall be its duty, to protect by law from forced sale a certain portion of the personal property of all heads of families, and also of unmarried adults, male and female.

Sec. 50. **Homestead Exemptions; Encumbrances, Pretended Sales** — The homestead of a family, or of a single adult person, shall be, and is hereby protected from forced sale, for the payment of all debts except for the purchase money thereof, or a part of such purchase money, the taxes due thereon, an owelty of partition imposed against the entirety of the property by a court order or by a written agreement of the parties to the partition, including a debt of one spouse in favor of the other spouse resulting from a division or an award of a family homestead in a divorce proceeding, the refinance of a lien against a homestead, including a federal tax lien resulting from the tax debt of both spouses, if the homestead is a family homestead, or from the tax debt of the owner, or for work and material used in constructing improvements thereon, and in this last case only when the work and material are contracted for in writing, with the consent of both spouses, in the case of a family homestead, given in the same manner as is required in making a sale and conveyance of the homestead; nor may the owner or claimant of the property claimed as homestead, if married, sell or abandon the homestead without the consent of the other spouse, given in such manner as may be prescribed by law. No mortgage, trust deed, or other lien on the homestead shall ever be valid, except for a debt described by this section, whether such mortgage, or trust deed, or other lien, shall have been created by the owner alone, or together with his or her spouse, in case the owner is married. All pretended sales of the homestead involving any condition of defeasance shall be void. A purchaser or lender for value without actual knowledge may conclusively rely on an affidavit that designates other property as the homestead of the affiant and that states that the property to be conveyed or encumbered is not the homestead of the affiant.

[Note — Sec. 50 of Art. XVI was amended to include single persons under the homestead exemption provision; it further made the wife an equal partner under the homestead provision. Submitted by 63rd Legislature (1973) and adopted in election Nov. 6, 1973. It was further amended to permit an encumbrance to be fixed on homestead property for an owelty of partition. Submitted by 74th Legislature (1995) and adopted in election Nov. 7, 1995.]

Sec. 51. **Homestead Defined** — The homestead, not in a town or city, shall consist of not more than two hundred acres of land, which may be in one or more parcels, with the improvements thereon; the homestead in a city, town or village, shall consist of lot or lots amounting to not more than one acre of land, together with any improvements on the land; provided, that the same shall be used for the purposes of a home, or as a place to exercise the calling or business of the homestead claimant, whether a single adult person, or the head of a family; provided also, that any temporary renting of the homestead shall not change the character of the same, when no other homestead has been acquired.

[Note — Sec. 51 was amended to raise the value of lots, exclusive of improvements, from $5,000 to $10,000 when designated as home-

Article XVI (Cont'd.)

steads. Submitted by 61st Legislature (1969) and adopted in election Nov. 3, 1970. It was further amended to provide that family homesteads may not be abandoned except with consent of both spouses. Submitted by 63rd Legislature (1973) and adopted in election Nov. 6, 1973. It was again amended to replace the limitation on the value of an urban homestead with a limitation based on size. Submitted by 68th Legislature (1983) and adopted in election Nov. 8, 1983.]

Sec. 52. **Descent of Homestead** — On the death of the husband or wife, or both, the homestead shall descend and vest in like manner as other real property of the deceased, and shall be governed by the same laws of descent and distribution, but it shall not be partitioned among the heirs of the deceased during the lifetime of the surviving husband or wife, or so long as the survivor may elect to use or occupy the same as a homestead, or so long as the guardian of the minor children of the deceased

may be permitted, under the order of the proper court having jurisdiction, to use and occupy the same.

Sec. 53. **Declaration Validating Process and Writs** — That no inconvenience may arise from the adoption of this Constitution, it is declared that all process and writs of all kinds which have been or may be issued and not returned or executed when this Constitution is adopted shall remain valid, and shall not be in any way affected by the adoption of this Constitution.

[Note — Sections 54 and 55 of Art. XVI, relating to pensions, and the indigent lunatics, were deleted by constitutional amendment. Submitted by 61st Legislature (1969) and approved in election Aug. 5, 1969.]

Sec. 56. **Advertising Texas' Resources** — The Legislature of the State of Texas shall have the power to appropriate money and establish the procedure necessary to expend such money for the purpose of developing information about the historical, natural, agricultural, industrial, educational, marketing, recreational and living resources of Texas, and for the purpose of informing persons and corporations of other states through advertising in periodicals having national circulation, and the dissemination of factual information about the advantages and economic resources offered by the State of Texas; providing, however, that neither the name nor the picture of any living state official shall ever be used in any of said advertising, and providing that the Legislature may require that any sum of money appropriated hereunder shall be matched by an equal sum paid into the State Treasury from private sources before any of said money may be expended.

[Note — Sec. 56 of Art. XVI is substituted for the original Section 56, which prohibited the expenditure of state funds for attracting immigrants. Submitted by 55th Legislature (1957) and adopted in election Nov. 4, 1958.]

[Note — Sections 57, 58 and 60 of Art. XVI, relating to land for state capitol, management of the prison system and the Texas Centennial, were deleted by constitutional amendment. Submitted by 61st Legislature (1969) and approved in election Aug. 5, 1969.]

*Sec. 59-a. **Conservation and Development of Natural Resources** — The conservation and development of all the natural resources of this State, including the control, storing, preservation and distribution of its storm and flood waters, the waters of its rivers and streams, for irrigation, power and all other useful purposes, the reclamation and irrigation of its arid, semi-arid and other lands needing irrigation, the reclamation and drainage

of its overflowed lands, and other lands needing drainage, the conservation and development of its forests, water and hydro-electric power, the navigation of its inland and coastal waters, and the preservation and conservation of all such natural resources of the State are each and all hereby declared public rights and duties; and the Legislature shall pass all such laws as may be appropriate thereto.

*Note — The resolution submitting this amendment was headed "Sec. 59-a," followed by paragraphs "(b)" and "(c)." Obviously, the first heading should have been "Sec. 59 (a)," the parenthetical (a) referring only to the first paragraph.

(b) There may be created within the State of Texas or the State may be divided into, such number of conservation and reclamation districts as may be determined to be essential to the accomplishment of the purposes of this amendment to the Constitution, which districts shall be governmental agencies and bodies politic and corporate with such powers of government and with the authority to exercise such rights, privileges and functions concerning the subject matter of this amendment as may be conferred by law.

(c) The Legislature shall authorize all such indebtedness as may be necessary to provide all improvements and the maintenance thereof requisite to the achievement of the purposes of this amendment, and all such indebtedness may be evidenced by bonds of such conservation and reclamation districts, to be issued under such regulations as may be prescribed by law and shall, also, authorize the levy and collection within such districts of all such taxes, equitably distributed, as may be necessary for the payment of the interest and

the creation of a sinking fund for payment of such bonds; and also for the maintenance of such districts and improvements, and such indebtedness shall be a lien upon the property assessed for the payment thereof; provided, the Legislature shall not authorize the issuance of any bonds or provide for any indebtedness against any reclamation district unless such proposition shall first be submitted to the qualified property taxpaying voters of such district and the proposition adopted.

(d) No law creating a conservation and reclamation district shall be passed unless notice of the intention to introduce such a bill setting forth the general substance of the contemplated law shall have been published at least thirty (30) days and not more than ninety (90) days prior to the introduction thereof in a newspaper or newspapers having general circulation in the county or counties in which said district or any part thereof is or will be located and by delivering a copy of such notice and such bill to the Governor who shall submit such notice and bill to the Texas Water Commission, or its successor, which shall file its recommendation as to such bill with the Governor, Lieutenant Governor and Speaker of the House of Representatives within thirty (30) days from date notice was received by the Texas Water Commission. Such notice and copy of bill shall also be given of the introduction of any bill amending a law creating or governing a particular conservation and reclamation district if such bill (1) adds additional land to the district, (2) alters the taxing authority of the district, (3) alters the authority of the district with respect to the issuance of bonds, or (4) alters the qualifications or terms of office of the members of the governing body of the district.

(e) No law creating a conservation and reclamation district shall be passed unless, at the time notice of the intention to introduce a bill is published as provided in Subsection (d) of this section, a copy of the proposed bill is delivered to the commissioners court of each county in which said district or any part thereof is or will be located and to the governing body of each incorporated city or town in whose jurisdiction said district or any part thereof is or will be located. Each such commissioners court and governing body may file its written consent or opposition to the creation of the proposed district with the governor, lieutenant governor, and speaker of the house of representatives. Each special law creating a conservation and reclamation district shall comply with the provisions of the general laws then in effect relating to consent by political subdivisions to the creation of conservation and reclamation districts and to the inclusion of land within the district.

(f) A conservation and reclamation district created under this section to perform any or all of the purposes of this section may engage in fire-fighting activities and may issue bonds or other indebtedness for fire-fighting purposes as provided by law and this constitution.

[Note — Sec. 59-a, obviously meant to be Sec. 59 (see footnote), was added to establish a conservation policy. Submitted by 35th Legislature (1917), adopted in election of Aug. 21, 1917, and proclaimed Oct. 2, 1917. It has been amended three times: (1) To require notice at both the local and state levels through publication in a newspaper having general circulation in county in which district is to be set up at least 30 days prior to introduction of bill in Legislature. Submitted by 58th Legislature (1963) and adopted in election Nov. 3, 1964. (2) To establish certain requirements relative to enactment of laws creating certain conservation and reclamation districts. Submitted by 63rd Legislature (1973) and adopted in election Nov. 6, 1973. (3) To authorize certain districts to engage in fire-fighting activities and to issue bonds or otherwise lend their credit for fire-fighting purposes. (See also Subsection (d), Sec. 52, Art. III.) Submitted by 65th Legislature (1977) and adopted in election Nov. 7, 1978.]

[Note — See note after Sec. 56 for Sec. 60.]

Sec. 61. **Compensation of District and County Officials** — All district officers in the State of Texas and all county officers in counties having a population of twenty thousand (20,000) or more, according to the then last preceding Federal Census, shall be compensated on a salary basis. In all counties in this State, the Commissioners Courts shall be authorized to determine whether precinct officers shall be compensated on a fee basis or on a salary basis, with the exception that it shall be mandatory upon the Commissioners Courts to compensate all justices of the peace, constables, deputy constables and precinct law enforcement officers on a salary basis beginning January 1, 1973; and in counties having a population of less than twenty thousand (20,000), according to the then last preceding Federal Census, the Commissioners Court shall have the authority to determine whether county officers shall be compensated on a fee basis or on a salary basis, with the exception that it shall be mandatory upon the Commissioners Courts to compensate all sheriffs, deputy sheriffs, county law enforcement officers, including sheriffs who also perform the duties of assessor and collector of taxes, and their deputies, on a salary basis beginning January 1, 1949.

All fees earned by district, county and precinct officers shall be paid into the county treasury where earned for the account of the proper fund, provided that fees incurred by the State, county and any municipality, or in case where a pauper's oath is filed, shall be paid into the county treasury when collected and provided that where any officer is compensated wholly on a fee basis such fees may be retained by such officer or paid into the treasury of the county as the Commissioners Court may direct. All notaries public, county surveyors and

Article XVI (Cont'd.)

public weighers shall continue to be compensated on a fee basis.

[Note — Sec. 61 of Art. XVI has been amended three times: (1) To put all district and county officials in counties of more than 20,000 population on a salary basis, substituting for fee basis, and making it optional with the Commissioners Courts whether precinct officers in counties of less than 20,000 should be on salary or fee basis and optional with reference to county officers in counties of less than 20,000. Submitted by 44th Legislature (1935), and adopted in election Aug. 24, 1935. (2) To make mandatory a salary basis for constables and precinct enforcement officers in counties of more than 20,000 and making it mandatory, in counties of less than 20,000 population, that all sheriffs, deputy sheriffs and other county enforcement officers, be on salary basis. Submitted by 50th Legislature (1947) and adopted in election Nov. 2, 1948. (3) To include justices of the peace within those to be compensated on salary basis beginning Jan. 1, 1973. Submitted by 62nd Legislature (1971) and adopted in election Nov. 7, 1972.]

[Note — Sec. 62 and Sec. 63 of Art. XVI, pertaining to **Retirement, Disability and Death Compensation Funds** and **Teacher and State Employee Retirement System**, respectively, were repealed by constitutional amendment. Submitted by 64th Legislature (1975) and approved in election April 22, 1975. (See also note under Art. III, Sec. 48-a, 48-b, 51-e and 51-f; also see Sec. 67 of Art. XVI, which replaces the foregoing Sections.)]

Sec. 64. **Inspector of Hides and Animals; Elective District, County and Precinct Offices; Terms of Office** — The office of Inspector of Hides and Animals, the elective district, county and precinct offices which have heretofore had terms of two years, shall hereafter have terms of four years; and the holders of such terms shall serve until their successors are qualified.

[Note — Sec. 64 of Art. XVI was added to set term of office for listed officials. Submitted by 53rd Legislature (1953) and adopted in election Nov. 2, 1954.]

Sec. 65. **District and County Officials; Terms of Office** — The following officers elected at the general election in November, 1954, and thereafter, shall serve for the full terms provided in this Constitution.

(a) District Clerks; (b) County Clerks; (c) County Judges; (d) Judges of County Courts-at-Law, County Criminal Courts, County Probate Courts, and County Domestic Relations Courts; (e) County Treasurers; (f) Criminal District Attorneys; (g) County Surveyors; (h) Inspectors of Hides and Animals; (i) County Commissioners for Precincts Two and Four; (j) Justices of the Peace.

Notwithstanding other provisions of this Constitution, the following officers elected at the general election in November, 1954, shall serve only for terms of two years: (a) Sheriffs; (b) Assessors and Collectors of Taxes; (c) District Attorneys; (d) County Attorneys; (e) Public Weighers; (f) County Commissioners for Precincts One and Three; (g) Constables. At subsequent elections, such officers shall be elected for the full terms provided in this Constitution.

In any district, county or precinct where any of the aforementioned offices is of such nature that two or more persons hold such office, with the result that candidates file for "Place No. 1," "Place No. 2," etc., the officers elected at the general election in November, 1954, shall serve for a term of two years if the designation of their office is an uneven number, and for a term of four years, if the designation of their office is an even number. Thereafter, all such officers shall be elected for the term provided in this Constitution.

Provided, however, if any of the officers named herein shall announce their candidacy, or shall in fact become a candidate, in any General, Special or Primary Election, for any office of profit or trust under the laws of this state or the United States other than the office then held, at any time when the unexpired term of the office then held shall exceed one (1) year, such announcement or such candidacy shall constitute an automatic resignation of the office then held, and the vacancy thereby created shall be filled pursuant to law in the same manner as other vacancies for such office are filled.

[Note — Sec. 65 of Art. XVI was added to set the terms of office of the listed officers. Submitted by 53rd Legislature (1953) and adopted in election Nov. 2, 1954. It was further amended to provide that a person must resign his present term of office if same has more than a year to run when he becomes a candidate for another office. Submitted by 55th Legislature (1957) and adopted in election Nov. 4, 1958.]

Sec. 65-A. Notwithstanding Section 65 of this article, the election and term of office of a district attorney serving a judicial district composed entirely of Fort Bend County are governed by the law relating to criminal district attorneys.

[Note — Sec. 65-A of Art. XVI was added relating to the election of a district attorney in Fort Bend County. Proposed by 71st Legislature (1989) and adopted in election Nov. 7, 1989. Subsections (a), (b) and (c), proposed and adopted at the same time, constituted a temporary provision requiring a district attorney serving in a judicial district composed entirely of Fort Bend County to be elected and serve a term in the manner provided by general law for criminal district attorneys.

The temporary provision expired Jan. 2, 1990.]

Sec. 66. **Pensions for Texas Rangers** — The Legislature shall have authority to provide for a system of retirement and disability pensions for retiring Texas Rangers who have not been eligible at any time for membership in the Employees Retirement System of Texas as that retirement system was established by Chapter 352, Acts of the Fiftieth Legislature, Regular Session, 1947, and who have had as much as two (2) years service as a Texas Ranger, and to their widows; providing that no pension shall exceed Eighty Dollars ($80) per month to any such Texas Ranger or his widow, provided that such widow was legally married prior to January 1, 1957, to a Texas Ranger qualifying for such pension.

These pensions may be paid only from the special fund created by *Sec. 17, Art. VII for a payment of pensions for services in the Confederate army and navy, frontier organizations, and the militia of the State of Texas, and for widows of such soldiers serving in said armies, navies, organizations or militia.

*Sec. 17, Art. VII was repealed by amendment submitted by 67th Legislature (1981) and adopted in election Nov. 2, 1982, but no provision has been made for deletion of this reference (See Art. VIII, Sec. 1-e.)

[Note — Sec. 66 of Art. XVI was added to provide for retirement pensions for Texas Rangers and their widows. Submitted by 55th Legislature (1957), adopted in election Nov. 4, 1958. (See also Art. VIII, Sec. 1-e.)]

Sec. 67. **State Retirement Systems** — (a) General Provisions. (1) The Legislature may enact general laws establishing systems and programs of retirement and related disability and death benefits for public employees and officers. Financing of benefits must be based on sound actuarial principles. The assets of a system are held in trust for the benefit of members and may not be diverted.

(2) A person may not receive benefits from more than one system for the same service, but the Legislature may provide by law that a person with service covered by more than one system or program is entitled to a fractional benefit from each system or program based on service rendered under each system or program calculated as to amount upon the benefit formula used in that system or program. Transfer of service credit between the Employees Retirement System of Texas and the Teacher Retirement System of Texas also may be authorized by law.

(3) Each statewide benefit system must have a board of trustees to administer the system and to invest the funds of the system in such securities as the board may consider prudent investments. In making investments, a board shall exercise the judgment and care under the circumstances then prevailing that persons of ordinary prudence, discretion, and intelligence exercise in the management of their own affairs, not in regard to speculation, but in regard to the permanent disposition of their funds, considering the probable income therefrom as well as the probable safety of their capital. The Legislature by law may further restrict the investment discretion of a board.

(4) General laws establishing retirement systems and optional retirement programs for public employees and officers in effect at the time of the adoption of this section remain in effect, subject to the general powers of the Legislature established in this subsection.

(b) **State Retirement Systems.** (1) The Legislature shall establish by law a Teacher Retirement System of Texas to provide benefits for persons employed in the public schools, colleges, and universities supported wholly or partly by the state. Other employees may be included under the system by law.

(2) The Legislature shall establish by law an Employees Retirement System of Texas to provide benefits for officers and employees of the state and such state-compensated officers and employees of appellate courts and judicial districts as may be included under the system by law.

(3) The amount contributed by a person participating in the Employees Retirement System of Texas or the Teacher Retirement System of Texas shall be established by the Legislature but may not be less than six percent of current compensation. The amount contributed by the state may not be less than six percent nor more than 10 percent of the aggregate compensation paid to individuals participating in the system. In an emergency, as determined by the governor, the Legislature may appropriate such additional sums as are actuarially determined to be required to fund benefits authorized by law.

(c) **Local Retirement Systems.** (1) The Legislature shall provide by law for:

(A) The creation by any city or county of a system of benefits for its officers and employees;

(B) A statewide system of benefits for the officers and employees of counties or other political subdivisions of the state in which counties or other political subdivisions may voluntarily participate; and

(C) A statewide system of benefits for officers and employees of cities in which cities may voluntarily participate.

(2) Benefits under these systems must be reasonably related to participant tenure and contributions.

(d) **Judicial Retirement System.** (1) Notwithstanding any other provision of this section, the system of retirement, disability, and survivors' benefits heretofore established in the constitution or by law for justices, judges, and commissioners of the appellate courts and judg-

Article XVI (Cont'd.)

es of the district and criminal district courts is continued in effect. Contributions required and benefits payable are to be as provided by law.

(2) General administration of the Judicial Retirement System of Texas is by the Board of Trustees of the Employees Retirement System of Texas under such regulations as may be provided by law.

(e) Anticipatory Legislation. Legislation enacted in anticipation of this amendment is not void because it is anticipatory.

(f) **Retirement Systems Not Belonging to a Statewide System** —The board of trustees of a system or program that provides retirement and related disability and death benefits for public officers and employees and that does not participate in a statewide public retirement system shall:

(1) administer the system or program of benefits;

(2 hold the assets of the system or program for the exclusive purposes of providing benefits to participants and their beneficiaries and defraying reasonable expenses of administering the system or program; and

(3) select legal counsel and an actuary and adopt sound actuarial assumptions to be used by the system or program.

[Note — Sec. 67 of Art. XVI was added to revise and consolidate provisions relating to state and local retirement systems and programs, and providing for a maximum state contribution to state systems of 10% of aggregate compensation paid to individuals. Submitted by 64th Legislature (1975) and adopted in election April 22, 1975. Subsection (f) was added to clarify duties of trustees of local public pension systems. Submitted by 73rd Legislature (1993) and adopted in election Nov. 2, 1993. See also notes under Art. III, Sections 48-a, 48-b, 51-e and 51-f; and Art. XVI, Sections 62 and 63.]

Sec. 68. **Promoting, Marketing Agricultural Products** — The Legislature may provide for the advancement of food and fiber in this state by providing representative associations of agricultural producers with authority to collect such refundable assessments on their product sales as may be approved by referenda of producers. All revenue collected shall be used solely to finance programs of marketing, promotion, research, and education relating to that commodity.

[Note — Sec. 68 of Art. XVI was added to provide for the advancement of food and fiber production and marketing through research, education and promotion, financed by producers of agricultural products. Submitted by 68th Legislature (1983) and adopted in election Nov. 8, 1983.]

Sec. 69. The Legislature may require, by rider in the General Appropriations Act or by separate statute, the prior approval of the expenditure or the emergency transfer of any funds appropriated by the agencies of state government.

[Note — Sec. 69 of Art. XVI was added to protect public funds by authorizing prior approval of expenditure or emergency transfer of state appropriations. Submitted by 69th Legislature (1985) and adopted in election Nov. 5, 1985.]

Sec. 70. **Texas Growth Fund** — (a) In this section:

(1) "Board of trustees" means the board of trustees of the Texas growth fund.

(2) "Fund" means the Texas growth fund.

(3) "Venture capital investment" means an investment in debt, equity, or a combination of debt and equity that possesses the potential for substantial investment returns, and includes investments in new or small businesses, investments in businesses with rapid growth potential, or investments in applied research and organizational activities leading to business formation and opportunities involving new or improved processes or products.

(b) The Texas growth fund is created as a trust fund. Except as otherwise provided by this section, the fund is subject to the general laws of this state governing private sector trusts. The governing boards of the permanent university fund, the permanent school fund, the Teacher Retirement System of Texas, the Employees Retirement System of Texas, and any other pension system created under this constitution or by statute of this state in their sole discretion may make investments in the fund.

(c) The fund is managed by a board of trustees consisting of four public members appointed by the governor and one member from and elected by the membership of each of the following:

(1) the Board of Regents of The University of Texas System;

(2) the Board of Regents of The Texas A&M University System;

(3) the Board of Trustees of the Teacher Retirement System of Texas;

(4) the Board of Trustees of the Employees Retirement System of Texas; and

(5) the State Board of Education.

(d) Each public member of the board must have demonstrated substantial investment expertise. A public member serves for a six-year term expiring February 1 of an odd-numbered year.

(e) A person filling an elected position on the board of trustees

ceases to be a member of the board of trustees when the person ceases to be a member of the board the person represents or as otherwise provided by procedures adopted by the board the person represents. The governor shall designate a chairman from among the members of the board of trustees who serves a term of two years expiring February 1 of each odd-numbered year. A member may serve more than one term as chairman.

(f) The board of trustees shall manage the investment of the fund, and may:

(1) employ and retain staff, including a chief executive officer;

(2) analyze and structure investments;

(3) set investment policy of the fund;

(4) take any action necessary for the creation, administration, and protection of the fund;

(5) enter into investment contracts with the participating funds or systems;

(6) adopt rules regarding the operation of the fund;

(7) pay expenses of the fund based on an assessment on investor contributions; and

(8) alternatively, or in combination with its own staff, contract for the management of investments under this section with a private investment management firm or with an investing fund or system electing a member of the board of trustees.

(g) In making investments, including venture capital investments, the board of trustees shall exercise the judgment and care under the circumstances then prevailing that persons of ordinary prudence, discretion, and intelligence exercise in the management of their own affairs, not in regard to speculation but in regard to the permanent disposition of their funds, considering the probable income as well as the probable safety of the capital of the fund. All investments of the fund shall be directly related to the creation, retention, or expansion of employment opportunity and economic growth in Texas. In making venture capital investments, all other material matters being equal, the board of trustees shall invest in technological advances that could be expected to result in the greatest increase in employment opportunity and economic growth in Texas.

(h) The board of trustees shall establish and operate the fund to the extent practical under the generally accepted business procedures relating to a mutual fund and shall value the investments for determining the purchase or sales price of participating shares of investing funds or systems participating in the fund consistent with investment contracts. Evidences of participation in the fund shall be held by the comptroller of public accounts in keeping with the custodial responsibilities of that office.

(i) An investing fund or system, without liability at law or in equity to members of the governing board of the fund or system in their personal or official capacities, may cumulatively invest in the Texas growth fund not more than one percent of the book or cost value of the investing fund or system, as determined at the end of each fiscal year.

(j) The board of trustees shall establish criteria for the investment of not more than 10 percent of the fund in venture capital investments. Not more than 25 percent of the funds available for venture capital investments may be used for unilateral investment. Investments of the remainder of the funds available for venture capital investments must be matched at least equally by funds from sources other than the fund, with matching amounts established by the board of trustees. The board of trustees shall also establish criteria for the investment of not less than 50 percent of the fund in equity or debt security, or a combination of equity and debt security, for the initial construction, expansion, or modernization of business or industrial facilities in Texas. The board of trustees may invest in money funds whose underlying investments are consistent and acceptable under the investment policy of the fund.

(k) On a quarterly basis, the amount of income realized on investments under this section shall be distributed to each of the systems and funds investing in the Texas growth fund in proportion to the number of participating shares of each investing system and fund. Capital appreciation becomes a part of the corpus of the Texas growth fund and shall be distributed in accordance with the investment contracts.

(1)The board of trustees shall make arrangements to begin liquidation, phase out investments, and return the principal and capital gains on investments to the investors in the fund not later than the 10th anniversary of the date of the adoption of this section. Except under unusual circumstances where it may be necessary to protect investments previously made, further investments may not be made in or by the fund after the 10th anniversary of the date of the adoption of this section.

(m) At the regular legislative session next preceding the 10th anniversary of the date of the adoption of this section, the legislature, by two-thirds vote of each house, may authorize the creation of Texas growth fund II, which shall operate under this section and under the board of trustees created by this section in the same manner as the Texas growth fund. Funds in Texas growth fund II may not be commingled with funds in the Texas growth fund.

(n) The board of trustees may purchase liability insurance for the coverage of the trustees, employees, and agents of the board.

(o) The legislature shall provide by law for the periodic review of the board of trustees in the same manner and at the same intervals as it

Article XVI (Cont'd.): Article XVII

provides for review of other state agencies, except that the legislature shall provide that the board of trustees is not subject to abolishment as part of the review process.

(p) This section expires September 1, 1998, except that if the legislature authorizes the creation of Texas growth fund II as provided by Subsection (m) of this section, this section expires September 1, 2008.

(q) This section is self-executing and takes effect on its adoption by the voters. All state officials named in this section and the comptroller of public accounts shall take all necessary actions for the implementation of this section. The legislature shall provide by law for full disclosure of all details concerning investments authorized by this section.

(r) The board of trustees may not invest money from the Texas growth fund in a business unless the business has submitted to the board of trustees an affidavit disclosing whether the business has any direct financial investment in or with South Africa or Namibia.

[Note — Sec. 70 of Article XVI was added to establish the Texas growth fund. Submitted by 70th Legislature (1987) and adopted in election Nov. 8, 1988. Subsections (h) and (q) were amended to eliminated references to the state treasurer when that office was eliminated. Submitted by 74th Legislature (1995) and adopted in election Nov. 7, 1995.]

Sec. 71 (a) The Legislature by law may establish a Texas product development fund to be used without further appropriation solely in furtherance of a program established by the legislature to aid in the development and production of new or improved products in this state. The fund shall contain a program account, an interest and sinking account, and other accounts authorized by the legislature. To carry out the program authorized by this subsection, the legislature may authorize loans, loan guarantees, and equity investments using money in the Texas product development fund and the issuance of up to $25 million of general obligation bonds to provide initial funding of the Texas product development fund. The Texas product development fund is composed of the proceeds of the bonds authorized by this subsection, loan repayments, guarantee fees, royalty receipts, dividend income, and other amounts received by the state from loans, loan guarantees, and equity investments made under this subsection and any other amounts required to be deposited in the Texas product development fund by the legislature.

(b) The legislature by law may establish a Texas small business incubator fund to be used without further appropriation solely in furtherance of a program established by the legislature to foster and stimulate the development of small businesses in the state. The fund shall contain a project account, an interest and sinking account, and other accounts authorized by the legislature. A small business incubator operating under the program is exempt from ad valorem taxation in the same manner as an institution of purely public charity under Article VIII, Section 2, of this constitution. To carry out the program authorized by this subsection, the legislature may authorize loans and grants of money in the Texas small business incubator fund and the issuance of up to $20 million of general obligation bonds to provide initial funding of the Texas small business incubator fund. The Texas small business incubator fund is composed of the proceeds of the bonds authorized by this subsection, loan repayments, and other amounts received by the state for loans or grants made under this subsection and any other amounts required to be deposited in the Texas small business incubator fund by the legislature.

(c) The legislature may require review and approval of the issuance of bonds under this section, of the use of the bond proceeds, or of the rules adopted by an agency to govern use of the bond proceeds. Notwithstanding any other provision of this constitution, any entity created or directed to conduct this review and approval may include members, or appointees of members, of the executive, legislative, and judicial departments of state government.

(d) Bonds authorized under this section constitute a general obligation of the state. While any of the bonds or interest on the bonds is outstanding and unpaid, there is appropriated out of the first money coming into the treasury in each fiscal year, not otherwise appropriated by this constitution, the amount sufficient to pay the principal of and interest on the bonds that mature or become due during the fiscal year, less any amount in any interest and sinking account at the end of the preceding fiscal year that is pledged to payment of the bonds or interest.

[Note — Sec. 71 of Art. XVI was added to establish a Texas product development fund to aid in the development and production of new or improved products in this state. Proposed by 71st Legislature (1989) and adopted in election Nov. 7, 1989.]

Article XVII — Mode of Amending the Constitution of This State

Sec. 1. **How the Constitution Is to Be Amended** — The Legislature, at any regular session, or at any special session when the matter is included within the purposes for which the session is convened, may propose amendments revising the Constitution, to be voted upon by the qualified electors for statewide offices and propositions, as defined in the Constitution and statutes of this State. The number of the elections shall be specified by the Legislature. The proposal for submission must be approved by a vote of two-thirds of all the members elected to each House, entered by yeas and nays on the journals.

A brief explanatory statement of the nature of a proposed amendment, together with the date of the election and the wording of the proposition as it is to appear on the ballot, shall be published twice in each newspaper in the State which meets requirements set by the Legislature for the publication of official notices of officers and departments of the state government. The explanatory statement shall be prepared by the Secretary of State and shall be approved by the Attorney General. The Secretary of State shall send a full and complete copy of the proposed amendment or amendments to each county clerk who shall post the same in a public place in the courthouse at least 30 days prior to the election on said amendment. The first notice shall be published not more than 60 days nor less than 50 days before the date of the election, and second notice shall be published on the same day in the succeeding week. The Legislature shall fix the standards for the rate of charge for the publication, which may not be higher than the newspaper's published national rate for advertising per column inch.

The election shall be held in accordance with procedures prescribed by the Legislature, and the returning officer in each county shall make returns to the Secretary of State of the number of legal votes cast at the election for and against each amendment. If it appears from the returns that a majority of the votes cast have been cast in favor of an amendment, it shall become a part of this Constitution, and proclamation thereof shall be made by the Governor.

[Note — Sec. 1 of Art. XVII was amended to revise provisions on time and method of proposing amendments to State Constitution and publishing notice of proposed amendments. Submitted by 62nd Legislature (1971) and adopted in election Nov. 7, 1972.]

Sec. 2. **Rewriting State Constitution** — (a) When the Legislature convenes in regular session in January, 1973, it shall provide by concurrent resolution for the establishment of a constitutional revision commission. The Legislature shall appropriate money to provide an adequate staff, office space, equipment, and supplies for the commission.

(b) The commission shall study the need for constitutional change and shall report its recommendations to the members of the Legislature not later than November 1, 1973.

(c) The members of the Sixty-third Legislature shall be convened as a constitutional convention at noon on the second Tuesday in January, 1974. The Lieutenant Governor shall preside until a chairman of the convention is elected. The convention shall elect other officers it deems necessary, adopt temporary and permanent rules, and publish a journal of its proceedings. A person elected to fill a vacancy in the Sixty-third Legislature before dissolution of the convention becomes a member of the convention on taking office as a member of the Legislature.

(d) Members of the convention shall receive compensation, mileage, per diem as determined by a five-member committee, composed of the Governor, Lieutenant Governor, Speaker of the House, Chief Justice of the Supreme Court, and Chief Justice of the Court of Criminal Appeals. This shall not be held in conflict with Art. XVI, Sec. 33 of the Texas Constitution. The convention may provide for the expenses of its members and for the employment of a staff for the convention, and for these purposes may by resolution appropriate money from the general revenue fund of the State Treasury. Warrants shall be drawn pursuant to vouchers signed by the chairman or by a person authorized by him in writing to sign them.

(e) The convention, by resolution adopted on the vote of at least two-thirds of its members, may submit for a vote of the qualified electors of this State a new Constitution which may contain alternative articles or sections, or may submit revisions of the existing Constitution which may contain alternative articles or sections. Each resolution shall specify the date of the election, the form of the ballots, and the method of publicizing the proposals to be voted on. To be adopted, each proposal must receive the favorable vote of the majority of those voting on the proposal. The conduct of the election, the canvassing of the votes, and the reporting of the returns shall be as provided for elections under Sec. 1 of this article.

(f) The convention may be dissolved by resolution adopted on the vote of at least two thirds of its members; but it is automatically dissolved at 11:59 p.m. on May 31, 1974, unless its duration is extended for a period not to exceed 60 days by resolution adopted on the vote of at least two thirds of its members.

(g) The Bill of Rights of the present Texas Constitution shall be retained in full.

[Note — Sec. 2 of Art. XVII was added to provide for a constitutional convention for the purpose of submitting to the voters a new constitution or revisions of the existing state constitution. Submitted by 62nd Legislature (1971) and adopted in election Nov. 7, 1972.] ☆

State Seal and Other Symbols

The six major flags that have flown over Texas and the design of the front of the state seal, as well as the major state symbols — state tree, flower, bird and song — can be found on pages 11 and 12. The description of the state seal, citizenship designation, motto and other symbols are described below.

The Monarch butterfly, pictured here on a blossom of Mexican bush sage, is the Texas state insect. Almanac staff photo.

State Seal — The design of the obverse (front) of the Great Seal of the State of Texas consists of "a star of five points, encircled by olive and live oak branches, and the words, 'The State of Texas'." (State Constitution, Art. IV, Sec. 19.) This design is a slight modification of the Great Seal of the Republic of Texas, adopted by the Congress of the Republic, Dec. 10, 1836, and readopted with modifications in 1839. An official design for the reverse (back) of the seal was adopted by the 57th Legislature in 1961, but there were discrepancies between the written description and the artistic rendering that was adopted at the same time. To resolve the problems, the 72nd Legislature in 1991 adopted an official design " . . . the design for the reverse side of the Great Seal of Texas shall consist of a shield, the lower half of which is divided into two parts; on the shield's lower left is a depiction of the cannon of the Battle of Gonzales; on the shield's lower right is a depiction of Vince's Bridge; on the upper half of the shield is a depiction of the Alamo; the shield is circled by live oak and olive branches, and the unfurled flags of the Kingdom of France, the Kingdom of Spain, the United Mexican States, the Republic of Texas, the Confederate States of America, and the United States of America; above the shield is emblazoned the motto, "REMEMBER THE ALAMO", and beneath the shield are the words, "TEXAS ONE AND INDIVISIBLE"; over the entire shield, centered between the flags, is a white five-pointed star . . ." Since the description of the design of the reverse of the seal was contained in a concurrent resolution rather than a bill, the design is not a matter of law but can be considered the intent of the Legislature. (CR 159, 72nd Legislature, May 1991).

State Citizenship Designation — The people of Texas usually call themselves **Texans.** However, **Texian** was generally used in the early period of the state's history.

State Motto — The state motto of Texas is **"Friendship."** The word, Texas, or Tejas, was the Spanish pronunciation of a Caddo Indian word meaning "friends" or "allies." (Acts of 1930, fourth called session of the 41st Legislature, p. 105.)

State Air Force — The **Confederate Air Force,** based in Midland at the Midland International Airport, was proclaimed the official air force of Texas by the 71st Legislature in 1989.

State Dinosaur — The **Brachiosaur Sauropod, Pleurocoelus,** was designated the official state dinosaur

by the 75th Legislature in 1997.

State Dish — **Chili** was proclaimed the Texas state dish by the 65th Texas Legislature in 1977.

State Fiber and Fabric - **Cotton** was designated the official state fiber and fabric by the 75th Legislature in 1997.

State Fish — The **Guadalupe bass,** a member of the genus *Micropterus* within the sunfish family, was named the official state fish of Texas by the 71st Legislature in 1989. It is one of a group of fish collectively known as black bass.

State Folk Dance — The **square dance** was designated the official state folk dance by the 72nd Legislature in 1991.

State Fruit — The **Texas red grapefruit** was designated the official state fruit by the 73rd Legislature in 1993.

State Gem — **Texas blue topaz,** the official Texas gem, is found in the Llano uplift area, especially west to northwest of Mason. It was designated by the 61st Legislature in 1969.

State Grass — **Sideoats grama** (*Bouteloua curtipendula*), a native grass found on many different soils, was designated by the 62nd Legislature as the state grass of Texas in 1971.

State Insect — The **Monarch butterfly** (*Danaus plexippus*) was designated the state insect by the 74th Legislature in 1995.

State Mammals — The **armadillo** was designated the state **small mammal**; the **longhorn** was designated the state **large mammal**; and the **Mexican free-tailed bat** was designated the state **flying mammal** by the 74th Legislature in 1995.

State Musical Instrument - The **guitar** was named the official musical instrument of Texas by the 75th Legislature in 1997.

State Native Pepper - The **chiltepin** was named the official state native pepper of Texas by the 75th Legislature in 1997.

State Pepper — The **jalapeño pepper** was designated the official state pepper by the 74th Legislature in 1995.

State Plant — The **prickly pear cactus** was designated the official state plant by the 74th Legislature in 1995.

State Seashell — The **lightning whelk** (*Busycon perversum pulleyi*) was named as the official state seashell by the 70th Legislature in 1987. One of the few shells that open on the left side, the lightning whelk is named for its colored stripes. It is found only on the Gulf Coast.

State Ship — The battleship **Texas** was designated the official state ship by the 74th Legislature in 1995.

State Sport — **Rodeo** was named the official sport of Texas by the 75th Legislature in 1997.

State Stone — **Petrified palmwood,** found in Texas principally in counties near the Texas Gulf Coast, was designated the official state stone by the 61st Legislature in March 1969.

State Vegetable — The **Texas sweet onion** was designated the official state vegetable by the 75th Legislature in 1997. ☆

Republic of Texas

The Declaration of Independence of the Republic of Texas was adopted in general convention at Washington-on-the-Brazos, March 2, 1836.

Richard Ellis, president of the convention, appointed a committee of five to write the declaration for submission to the convention.

However, there is much evidence that George C. Childress, one of the members, wrote the document with little or no help from the other members. Childress is therefore generally accepted as the author.

This is the text, copied from the original. The style of presentation is from broadsides circulated at the time. Following are the names of the signers.

UNANIMOUS

DECLARATION OF INDEPENDENCE,

BY THE

DELEGATES OF THE PEOPLE OF TEXAS,

IN GENERAL CONVENTION,

AT THE TOWN OF WASHINGTON,

ON THE SECOND DAY OF MARCH, 1836.

When a government has ceased to protect the lives, liberty and property of the people from whom its legitimate powers are derived, and for the advancement of whose happiness it was instituted; and so far from being a guarantee for the enjoyment of those inestimable and inalienable rights, becomes an instrument in the hands of evil rulers for their oppression; when the Federal Republican Constitution of their country, which they have sworn to support, no longer has a substantial existence, and the whole nature of their government has been forcibly changed without their consent, from a restricted federative republic, composed of sovereign states, to a consolidated central military despotism, in which every interest is disregarded but that of the army and the priesthood — both the eternal enemies of civil liberty, and the ever-ready minions of power, and the usual instruments of tyrants; When long after the spirit of the Constitution has departed, moderation is at length, so far lost, by those in power that even the semblance of freedom is removed, and the forms, themselves, of the constitution discontinued; and so far from their petitions and remonstrances being regarded, the agents who bear them are thrown into dungeons; and mercenary armies sent forth to force a new government upon them at the point of the bayonet. When in consequence of such acts of malfeasance and abdication, on the part of the government, anarchy prevails, and civil society is dissolved into its original elements: In such a crisis, the first law of nature, the right of self-preservation — the inherent and inalienable right of the people to appeal to first principles and take their political affairs into their own hands in extreme cases — enjoins it as a right towards themselves and a sacred obligation to their posterity, to abolish such government and create another in its stead, calculated to rescue them from impending dangers, and to secure their future welfare and happiness.

Nations, as well as individuals, are amenable for their acts to the public opinion of mankind. A statement of a part of our grievances is, therefore, submitted to an impartial world, in justification of the hazardous but unavoidable step now taken of severing our political connection with the Mexican people, and assuming an independent attitude among the nations of the earth.

The Mexican government, by its colonization laws, invited and induced the Anglo-American population of Texas to colonize its wilderness under the pledged faith of a written constitution, that they should continue to enjoy that constitutional liberty and republican government to which they had been habituated in the land of their birth, the United States of America. In this expectation they have been cruelly disappointed, inasmuch as the Mexican nation has acquiesced in the late changes made in the government by General Antonio Lopez de Santa Anna, who, having overturned the constitution of his country, now offers us the cruel alternative either to abandon our homes, acquired by so many privations, or submit to the most intolerable of all tyranny, the combined despotism of the sword and the priesthood.

It has sacrificed our welfare to the state of Coahuila, by which our interests have been continually depresssed, through a jealous and partial course of legislation carried on at a far distant seat of government, by a hostile majority, in an unknown tongue; and this too, notwithstanding we have petitioned in the humblest terms, for the establishment of a separate state government, and have, in accordance with the provisions of the national constitution, presented the general Congress, a republican constitution which was without just cause contemptuously rejected.

It incarcerated in a dungeon, for a long time, one of our citizens, for no other cause but a zealous endeavor to procure the acceptance of our constitution and the establishment of a state government.

It has failed and refused to secure on a firm basis, the right of trial by jury; that palladium of civil liberty, and only safe guarantee for the life, liberty, and property of the citizen.

It has failed to establish any public system of education, although possessed of almost boundless resources (the public domain) and, although, it is an axiom, in political science, that unless a people are educated and enlightened it is idle to expect the continuance of civil liberty, or the capacity for self-government.

It has suffered the military commandants stationed among us to exercise arbitrary acts of oppression and tyranny; thus trampling upon the most sacred rights of the citizen and rendering the military superior to the civil power.

It has dissolved by force of arms, the state Congress of Coahuila and Texas, and obliged our representatives to fly for their lives from the seat of government; thus depriving us of the fundamental political right of representation.

It has demanded the surrender of a number of our citizens, and ordered military detachments to seize and carry them into the Interior for trial; in contempt of the civil authorities, and in defiance of the laws and constitution.

It has made piratical attacks upon our commerce; by commissioning foreign desperadoes, and authorizing them to seize our vessels, and convey the property of our citizens to far distant ports of confiscation.

It denies us the right of worshipping the Almighty according to the dictates of our own consciences, by the support of a national religion calculated to promote the temporal interests of its human functionaries rather than the glory of the true and living God.

It has demanded us to deliver up our arms; which are essential to our defense, the rightful property of freemen, and formidable only to tyrannical governments.

It has invaded our country, both by sea and by land, with intent to lay waste our territory and drive us from our homes; and has now a large mercenary army advancing to carry on against us a war of extermination.

It has invaded our country, both by sea and by land, with intent to lay waste our territory and drive us from our homes; and has now a large mercenary army advancing to carry on against us a war of extermination.

It has, through its emissaries, incited the merciless savage, with the tomahawk and scalping knife, to massacre the inhabitants of our defenseless frontiers.

It hath been, during the whole time of our connection with it, the contemptible sport and victim of successive military revolutions and hath continually exhibited every characteristic of a weak, corrupt and tyrannical government.

These, and other grievances, were patiently borne by the people of Texas until they reached that point at which forbearance ceases to be a virtue. We then took up arms in defense of the national constitution. We appealed to our Mexican brethren for assistance. Our appeal has been made in vain. Though months have elapsed, no sympathetic response has yet been heard from the Interior. We are, therefore, forced to the melancholy conclusion that the Mexican people have acquiesced in the destruction of their liberty, and the substitution therefor of a military government — that they are unfit to be free and incapable of self-government.

The necessity of self-preservation, therefore, now decrees our eternal political separation.

We, therefore, the delegates, with plenary powers, of the people of Texas, in solemn convention assembled, appealing to a candid world for the necessities of our condition, do hereby resolve and DECLARE that our political connection with the Mexican nation has forever ended; and that the people of Texas do now constitute a FREE, SOVEREIGN and INDEPENDENT REPUBLIC, and are fully invested with all the rights and attributes which properly belong to the independent nations; and, conscious of the rectitude of our intentions, we fearlessly and confidently commit the issue to the decision of the Supreme Arbiter of the destinies of nations.

RICHARD ELLIS, president of the convention and Delegate from Red River.

Charles B. Stewart	Chas. S. Taylor
Thos. Barnet	John S. Roberts
John S.D. Byrom	
Franco. Ruiz	Robert Hamilton
J. Antonio Navarro	Collin McKinney
Jesse B. Badgett	Albert H Latimer
Wm. D. Lacey	James Power
William Menefee	Sam Houston
Jno. Fisher	David Thomas
Mathew Caldwell	Edwd. Conrad
William Mottley	Martin Parmer
Lorenzo de Zavala	Edwin O. LeGrand
Stephen H. Everitt	Stephen W. Blount
Geo W Smyth	Jas. Gaines
Elijah Stapp	Wm. Clark, Jr
Claiborne West	Sydney O. Penington
Wm B Scates	Wm. Carrol Crawford
M.B. Menard	Jno Turner
A.B. Hardin	Benj. Briggs Goodrich
J.W. Bunton	G.M. Barnett
Thos. J. Gazley	James G. Swisher
R M Coleman	Jesse Grimes
Sterling C. Robertson	S. Rhoads. Fisher
Jas Collinsworth	John W. Moore
Edwin Waller	John W. Bower
Asa Brigham	Saml. A Maverick
Geo. C. Childress	(from Bejar)
Bailey Hardeman	Sam P Carson
Rob. Potter	A. Briscoe
Thomas Jefferson Rusk	JB Woods
Test. H.S. Kemble Secretary	

Republicans Continue to Show Strength in Texas

By Carolyn Barta

Texas was the largest state carried by Republican presidential candidate Bob Dole in the 1996 election, signaling Texas' continuing role as a beacon state for the GOP.

It was the second consecutive presidential contest in which Texas went one way and the nation went another to send Democrat Bill Clinton to the White House.

Only 18 other states bucked the national trend to favor Dole, the former senator from Kansas. The largest next to Texas, with less than half as many electoral votes, was North Carolina.

Political analysts said Dole's Texas victory, after a lackluster campaign, demonstrated the growing strength of the Republican party in the state. But there were other signs of GOP muscle.

Sen. Phil Gramm.   Rep. Kay Granger.

• For the first time since Reconstruction, Texans gave Republicans a majority in the Texas Senate.
• For the first time in history, the Republican primary polled more voters than the Democratic primary.
• Republicans swept all 10 statewide offices on the ballot, to give them 20 of 29 statewide offices. Seven years before, Democrats held 22.

The biggest statewide prize was the U.S. Senate seat occupied by Phil Gramm. Gramm was able to retain his seat with 54.8 percent of the vote against storybook candidate Victor Morales. A Mesquite high school civics teacher, Morales unexpectedly won the Democratic primary over more seasoned politicians, beating U.S. Rep. John Bryant, D-Dallas, in a primary runoff.

Gramm had to refocus his attention at home after a $28 million unsuccessful quest for the Republican presidential nomination. He pulled out of the field following dismal showings in the nation's first two caucuses in Louisiana and Iowa.

Morales, meanwhile, captured the attention of national media as the "everyman" candidate who refused contributions from political action committees. His under-funded campaign was symbolized by the little white Nissan pickup he drove across the state.

The state's growing Hispanic population and Morales' candidacy, as the first Hispanic nominee of a major party for U.S. Senate in Texas, boosted Latino voter registration and turnout in 1996. Of 1.6 million registered Hispanics, 400,000 were new voters, according to the San Antonio-based Southwest Voter Research Institute.

The 1996 presidential race drew 5.6 million Texas voters of 10.5 million registered, or 53 percent of those registered, the lowest percentage turnout since 1970. Nearly 1.1 million Latino votes were cast — 69 percent of registered Hispanics.

The Dole-Kemp Republican ticket won 48.8 percent in Texas, compared to 43.8 percent for Clinton-Gore, which was five points below the Democratic ticket's national percentage. Ross Perot, the billionaire industrialist running an outside candidacy for the second time, garnered only 6.7 percent of the vote in his native state, compared to 22 percent in 1992.

Not since 1976 when Jimmy Carter won a scant victory in the Lone Star State has Texas favored a Democrat for president. Yet, political analysts saw 1996 as a prime opportunity for Bill Clinton.

For the first time since 1980, transplanted Texan George Bush was not on the ballot for either vice-president or president. The economy was generally healthy, and Clinton's more centrist persona was thought to have increased appeal in the conservative Texas climate.

But while Clinton was able to win five of the eight largest counties, he lost Harris, Dallas and Tarrant counties, and Dole dominated the non-metropolitan areas.

Democrats said they remained the majority party in the state because they still held 70 percent of offices at the county courthouse level. They also kept control in the Texas House of Representatives. Republicans failed to win the 76 seats for a majority in the 150-member Texas House, despite their "76 in '96" campaign.

Democrat Pete Laney from Hale Center was re-elected House speaker when the 1997 legislative session opened with 82 Democrats and 68 Republicans.

The '96 elections, meanwhile, provided Republicans with all three seats on the Texas Railroad Commission, a 6-3 majority on the Court of Criminal Appeals and a 7-2 edge on the Texas Supreme Court.

Texas' most famous political maverick, Ross Perot, continued his efforts to build a third party under the Reform Party banner after his 1996 presidential finish fell short of his historic independent run four years before. Perot received 8.5 percent of the national vote in 1996, compared to 19 percent in 1992.

His best showings were in Maine and Montana, where he got 14 percent, and Idaho, where he won 12 percent. The Dallas computer magnate blamed his weaker showing on his exclusion from nationally televised debates by the Commission on Presidential Debates.

Building on the organizational work of United We

Stand America, the grass-roots organization started with his supporters in 1994, Perot founded the Reform Party as a vehicle for his candidacy in 1996. He then invited others to compete for the party's nomination, eventually defeating former Colorado Gov. Richard Lamm for the nomination. As his running mate, Perot selected Texas native Pat Choate, a Washington economist and co-author of his 1993 book opposing the North American Free Trade Agreement.

Other political developments in 1996 included the elimination of the state treasurer's office, which had served as a springboard to higher office for two Texas women. Democrat Ann Richards, who served as governor, and Republican Kay Bailey Hutchison, who became a U.S. senator, first won statewide races for treasurer. Democrat Martha Whitehead, however, was elected in 1994 on the promise of eliminating the office of State Treasurer by combining its operations with the state comptroller's office to make state government more efficient and cost-effective.

Voters approved a constitutional amendment to abolish the State Treasurer's office and, at the end of August 1996, its functions were merged with the comptroller's office.

One of Texas' most admired political figures died in 1996, former Congresswoman Barbara Jordan. Ms. Jordan was the first black woman to serve in Congress from the South, and achieved fame with her Judiciary Committee speeches during Watergate hearings.

Another notable Texas political figure, former Sen. Ralph W. Yarborough, died in 1995. He was the only Southern Democrat to vote for the civil rights bill in 1964. Leader of his party's liberal-populist wing, he was defeated by Lloyd Bentsen in the 1970 U.S. Senate primary. Bentsen, meanwhile, retired from public life in 1996 as Secretary of the Treasury in the Clinton administration after serving in the Senate and as running mate to Michael Dukakis on the 1988 Democratic presidential ticket.

Former San Antonio Mayor and Housing Secretary Henry Cisneros quit the Clinton cabinet at the beginning of Clinton's second term, leaving Navy Secretary John Dalton as the highest-ranking Texan in the administration. But other Texans were picking up the mantle as national leaders. Mentioned as potential candidates for future top national office were at least three Texas Republicans: U.S. House Majority Leader Dick Armey, Sen. Kay Bailey Hutchison and Gov. George W. Bush.

After a successful first legislative session marked by bipartisan cooperation, the popular GOP governor began the second half of his 4-year term with an effort to reform the Texas tax system by reducing the property tax and introducing a new business tax.

The highest-ranking Texas Democrat on Capitol Hill was Martin Frost of Dallas, chairman of the Democratic Congressional Campaign Committee, which would try to wrest the U.S. House from Republican control in 1998.

Carolyn Barta is a staff writer of The Dallas Morning News.

Texas Senate Majority Republican: First Time Since Reconstruction

Texas experienced a historical change in power when the Legislature assembled in 1997. For the first time in 125 years, Republicans held a majority in the Texas Senate.

The last time that happened was during the post-Civil War Reconstruction period. U.S. Grant was president, Republican E.J. Davis was governor, and the year was 1871.

While there was no such partisan transfer of power in the Texas congressional delegation, the 1996 elections did produce one of the biggest turnovers in the state's delegation to the U.S. House of Representatives.

When Congress convened in 1997, the 30-member Texas delegation had nine new faces, and a tenth followed after Democratic Rep. Frank Tejeda of San Antonio died, requiring a special election. Ciro Rodriguez, a Democrat and former state legislator from San Antonio, was elected to succeed Mr. Tejeda in a special election runoff April 12.

While much of the turnover came from retirements, redistricting disputes also produced a chaotic election year for congressional seats.

Elections were thrown into turmoil when a panel of federal judges declared one Dallas and two Houston congressional districts racially gerrymandered, a decision upheld by the U.S. Supreme Court.

The federal panel redrew the three districts plus 10 adjoining districts and ordered special elections in the 13 districts. Candidate filings were re-opened, resulting in some multi-candidate fields on Nov. 5. Three districts required runoffs in December to finish the job.

In the state Senate, Republicans were able to pick up one seat in the general election and then won two special elections for seats vacated by Democrats. Sen. John Montford of Lubbock resigned to become chancellor of Texas Tech University, and Sen. Jim Turner of Crockett was elected to Congress.

The 17-14 GOP margin in the Senate — the same as that previously held by the Democrats — enabled Republicans to control the destiny of any bill. But the continuation of Democrat Lt. Gov. Bob Bullock as the body's forceful presiding officer discouraged any hefty display of partisanship. Under his appointments, Democrats kept a majority of committee chairs.

In the congressional delegation, the Democratic majority fell by one member to 17-13.

The only Texas member of Congress to lose re-election in the general election was Rep. Steve Stockman of Friendswood, a freshman Republican criticized for supporting militia groups and pro-gun laws. The one-termer was defeated by Nick Lampson, a former Jefferson county tax assessor, returning the 9th District to the Democratic fold.

Former Democrat Greg Laughlin of West Columbia, who had switched parties, was defeated in the Republican primary in the 14th District by former congressman Ron Paul of Surfside, a physician who was the Libertarian Party's presidential nominee in 1988.

Kay Granger, a former Fort Worth mayor, became the first Republican woman elected to the U.S. House from Texas when she succeeded retiring Democrat Pete Geren in the 12th District. Democrat John Bryant's unsuccessful race for Senate opened up his 5th District for Republican Pete Sessions.

Other retiring Democrats and their successors were: Jim Chapman, 1st District, succeeded by Max Sandlin,

D-Marshall; Charles Wilson, 2nd District, succeeded by Jim Turner, D-Crockett; Kika de la Garza, 15th District, succeeded by Ruben Hinojosa, D-Mercedes; and Ron Coleman, 16th District, succeeded by Silvestre Reyes, D-El Paso.

Retiring Republican Jack Fields was succeeded in the 8th District by Kevin Brady, R-The Woodlands. — *Carolyn Barta.* ☆

General Election, 1996

Below are the voting returns of the general election held November 5, 1996, for all statewide races, and for contested congressional, state senate, courts of appeals and state board of education races. These are official returns as canvassed by the State Canvassing Board. Abbreviations used are (Dem.) Democrat, (Rep.) Republican, (Lib.) Libertarian, (NLP) Natural Law Party and (Ind.) Independent.

President

Bob Dole (Rep.)	2,736,167
Bill Clinton (Dem.)	2,459,683
Ross Perot (Ind.)	378,537
Harry Browne (Lib.)	20,256
Howard Phillips (U.S. Taxpayers)	7,472
Ralph Nader (Write-In)	4,810
John Hagelin (NLP)	4,422
Mary Cal Hollis (Write-In)	297
Total Vote	5,611,644

U.S. Senator

Phil Gramm (Rep.)	3,027,680
Victor M. Morales (Dem.)	2,428,776
Michael Bird (Lib.)	51,516
John Huff (NLP)	19,469
Total Vote	5,527,441

Railroad Commissioner

Carole Keeton Rylander (Rep.)	3,094,273
Hector Uribe (Dem.)	2,071,290
Rick Draheim (Lib.)	102,665
Paul Pigue (NLP)	40,345
Total Vote	5,308,573

Chief Justice, Supreme Court

Tom Phillips (Rep.)	2,954,903
Andrew Jackson Kupper (Dem.)	2,128,234
David Parker (Lib.)	162,396
Total Vote	5,245,533

Justice, Supreme Court, Place 1

John Cornyn (Rep.)	2,686,518
Patrice Barron (Dem.)	2,351,750
Thomas Stults (Lib.)	129,203
Total Vote	5,167,471

Justice, Supreme Court, Place 2

James A. Baker (Rep.)	2,784,192
Gene Kelly (Dem.)	2,212,603
Eileen Flume (Lib.)	188,926
Total Vote	5,185,721

Justice, Supreme Court, Place 3

Greg Abbott (Rep.)	3,201,185
John B. Hawley (Lib.)	604,984
Total Vote	3,806,169

Judge, Court of Criminal Appeals, Place 1

Sue Holland (Rep.)	2,848,961
Bob Perkins (Dem.)	2,287,958
Total Vote	5,136,919

Judge, Court of Criminal Appeals, Place 2

Paul Womack (Rep.)	2,721,048
Charles Holcomb (Dem.)	2,368,192
Total Vote	5,089,240

Judge, Court of Criminal Appeals, Place 3

Tom Price (Rep.)	2,745,701
Frank Maloney (Dem.)	2,358,371
Total Vote	5,104,072

U.S. HOUSE OF REPRESENTATIVES
District 1

Ed Merritt (Rep.)	93,105
Max Sandlin (Dem.)	102,697
Margaret A. Palms (NLP)	3,368
Total Vote	199,170

District 2

Brian Babin (Rep.)	89,838
Jim Turner (Dem.)	102,908
David Constant (Lib.)	1,240
Gary Hardy (NLP)	595
Henry McCullough (Ind.)	2,390
Total Vote	196,971

District 4

Jerry Ray Hall (Rep.)	71,065
Ralph Hall (Dem.)	132,126
Steven Rothacker (Lib.)	3,172
Enos M. Denham Jr. (NLP)	814
Total Vote	207,177

District 10

Teresa Doggett (Rep.)	97,204
Lloyd Doggett (Dem.)	132,066
Gary Johnson (Lib.)	3,950
Steve Klayman (NLP)	1,771
Total Vote	234,991

District 11

Jay Mathis (Rep.)	74,549
Chet Edwards (Dem.)	99,990
Ken Hardin (NLP)	1,396
Total Vote	175,935

District 12

Kay Granger (Rep.)	98,349
Hugh Parmer (Dem.)	69,859
Heather Proffer (NLP)	1,996
Total Vote	170,204

District 13

Mac Thornberry (Rep.)	116,098
Samuel Brown Sliverman (Dem.)	56,066
Don Harkey (NLP)	1,463
Total Vote	173,627

District 14

Ron Paul (Rep.)	99,961
Charles (Lefty) Morris (Dem.)	93,200
Ed Fasanella (NLP)	2,538
Total Vote	195,699

District 15

Tom Haughey (Rep.)	50,914
Ruben Hinojosa (Dem.)	86,347
Rob Wofford (NLP)	1,333
Total Vote	138,594

District 16

Rick Ledesma (Rep.)	35,271
Silvestre Reyes (Dem.)	90,260
Carl Proffer (NLP)	2,253
Total Vote	127,784

District 17

Rudy Izzard (Rep.)	91,429
Charles W. Stenholm (Dem.)	99,678
Richard Caro (NLP)	1,887
Total Vote	192,994

District 19

Larry Combest (Rep.)	156,910
John W. Sawyer (Dem.)	38,316
Total Vote	195,226

District 20
James Walker (Rep.). 47,616
Henry B. Gonzalez (Dem.) 88,190
Alejandro (Alex) De Pena (Lib.). 2,156
Lyndon Felps (NLP) 447
    Total Vote. 138,409

District 21
Lamar Smith (Rep.). 205,830
Gordon H. Wharton (Dem.) 60,338
Randy Rutenbeck (NLP) 3,139
    Total Vote. 269,307

District 23
Henry Bonilla (Rep.) 101,332
Charles P. Jones (Dem.) 59,596
Linda J. Caswell (NLP) 2,911
    Total Vote. 163,839

District 27
Joe Gardner (Rep.) 50,964
Solomon P. Ortiz (Dem.) 97,350
Kevin G. Richardson (NLP) 2,286
    Total Vote. 150,600

District 28
Mark L. Cude (Rep.) 34,191
Frank Tejeda (Dem.) 110,148
Clifford Finley (NLP) 1,796
    Total Vote. 146,135

STATE SENATE
District 2
Bob Reese (Rep.). 75,704
David Cain (Dem.). 82,580
    Total Vote. 158,284

District 3
Drew Nixon (Rep.). 104,222
Jerry K. Johnson (Dem.) 103,835
    Total Vote. 208,057

District 8
Florence Shapiro (Rep.) 189,985
Randal Morgan (Lib.) 21,674
    Total Vote. 211,659

District 14
Gonzalo Barrientos(Dem.) 157,194
Sandra L. BonSell (NLP). 28,013
    Total Vote. 185,207

District 15
Tom Kelly (Rep.) 49,619
John Whitmire (Dem.) 81,134
    Total Vote. 130,753

District 21
James Whitworth (Rep.) 46,698
Judith Zaffirini (Dem.) 91,956
    Total Vote. 138,654

District 24
Troy Fraser (Rep.) 86,828
Rick Rhodes (Dem.) 80,632
    Total Vote 167,460

District 26
Andrew Longaker (Rep.) 41,298
Gregory Luna (Dem.) 85,922
    Total Vote. 127,220

District 29
Randy Berry (Rep.) 32,029
Eloit Shapleigh (Dem.) 89,868
    Total Vote. 121,897

COURTS OF APPEALS
Chief Justice, 1st Court of Appeals
Michael (Mike) Schneider (Rep.). 626,994
Joe Draughn (Dem.) 454,461
    Total Vote. 1,081,455

Chief Justice, Third District
Skeet Des Champ (Rep.) 209,549
Jimmy Carroll (Dem.) 276,975
    Total Vote. 486,524

Chief Justice, Tenth District
Rex Davis (Rep.). 118,844

Joe Cannon (Dem.) 106,385
    Total Vote 225,229

Chief Justice, Fourteenth District
Paul C. Murphy (Rep.) 574,832
Cynthia Owens (Dem.). 507,402
    Total Vote 1,082,234

Justice, First District, Place 1
Sam Nuchia (Rep.). 616,461
George Ellis (Dem.) 496,783
    Total Vote 1,113,244

Justice, First District, Place 2
Jim Gieseke (Rep.). 534,344
Margaret G. Mirabal (Dem.) 545,865
    Total Vote 1,080,209

Justice, Second District, Place 7
Terrie Livingston (Rep.) 341,553
Dick Price (Dem.). 248,111
    Total Vote 589,664

Justice, Fifth District, Place 6
Jim Moseley (Rep.) 410,542
Charles McGarry (Dem.) 301,216
    Total Vote 711,758

Justice, Sixth District
Larry Starr (Rep.) 103,095
Donald R. Ross (Dem.) 109,025
    Total Vote 212,120

Justice, Eleventh District
Jim R. Wright (Rep.) 84,699
Martin L. Peterson (Ind.). 17,316
    Total Vote 102,015

Justice, Thirteenth District
Robert Kern (Rep.). 130,349
J. Bonner Dorsey (Dem.) 197,866
    Total Vote 328,215

Justice, Fourteenth District
Harriet O'Neill (Rep.) .620,267
Dalia Stokes (Dem.). .460,333
    Total Vote 1,080,600

STATE BOARD OF EDUCATION
District 3
Jose Garcia De Lara (Rep.) 68,634
Joe J. Bernal (Dem.) .172,688
Sharon Miller (NLP) 17,968
    Total Vote 259,290

District 4
Earl J. Ehlers (Rep.) 50,012
Alma A. Allen (Dem.) .191,323
    Total Vote 241,335

District 5
Bob Offutt (Rep.) 245,147
Nettie Ruth Bratton (Dem.). 173,695
    Total Vote 418,842

District 6
Jack Christie (Rep.) 283,163
Angela Patton (NLP) 45,357
    Total Vote 328,520

District 7
David Bradley (Rep.) .184,740
Rema Lou Brown (Dem.) 155,226
    Total Vote 339,966

District 10
Charlie Weaver (Rep.) 204,370
Will Davis (Dem.) 221,820
Catherine L. Randolph (NLP). 23,760
    Total Vote 449,950

District 11
Richard Neill (Rep.) 264,380
Robert M. Platt (Dem.) 154,864
    Total Vote 419,244

District 12
Geraldine (Tincy) Miller (Rep.) 271,749
Barbara V. Montgomery (Dem.) 140,477
Brady Byrum (Lib.). 13,426
    Total Vote 425,652

1996 General Election Results by County

Below are the official results by county. Listed are the three candidates who received the most votes for U.S. President and U.S. Senator. The total number of voters who cast ballots in the presidential race, 5,611,644, was 53.2 percent of those eligible to vote. The voting age population was 13,698,284. The statewide turnout in the presidential election of 1992 was 72.9 percent. *Source: Texas Secretary of State.*

County	Registered Voters October 96	President DOLE (Rep.)	President CLINTON (Dem.)	President PEROT (Ind.)	Turnout Percent	U.S. Senator GRAMM (Rep.)	U.S. Senator MORALES (Dem.)	U.S. Senator BIRD (Lib.)
Anderson	23,825	6,458	5,693	1,170	56.2	7,377	5,773	100
Andrews	6,939	2,360	1,181	431	57.7	2,825	1,092	45
Angelina	45,596	11,789	11,346	2,160	55.8	14,293	10,609	235
Aransas	11,677	3,769	2,964	655	63.7	4,485	2,724	94
Archer	5,866	1,974	1,235	437	62.3	2,387	1,168	25
Armstrong	1,374	582	272	75	68.1	670	235	6
Atascosa	18,939	4,102	4,259	813	48.9	4,395	4,739	91
Austin	13,223	4,669	2,719	577	60.5	5,182	2,618	62
Bailey	3,783	1,246	706	109	54.6	1,334	671	12
Bandera	8,821	3,700	1,383	520	64.3	4,154	1,368	83
Bastrop	25,086	6,323	6,773	1,342	58.1	6,976	7,240	191
Baylor	3,221	860	955	262	64.8	1,108	815	27
Bee	16,383	3,611	4,561	539	53.5	4,062	4,534	83
Bell	114,085	30,348	22,638	3,666	50.0	33,728	21,191	421
Bexar	744,645	161,619	180,308	17,822	48.7	172,193	183,426	3,631
Blanco	4,835	1,919	1,028	330	68.6	2,097	1,092	54
Borden	472	194	93	45	70.7	224	92	5
Bosque	9,913	2,840	2,427	739	60.8	3,229	2,585	28
Bowie	52,178	12,750	13,657	2,760	56.1	16,164	12,481	167
Brazoria	120,294	36,392	22,959	5,869	54.6	39,689	24,738	844
Brazos	70,204	22,082	13,968	2,215	55.0	23,212	12,969	422
Brewster	5,590	1,438	1,643	299	61.8	1,628	1,640	64
Briscoe	1,339	416	408	65	66.6	491	374	1
Brooks	6,841	413	2,945	108	51.0	505	2,794	21
Brown	21,280	6,524	4,138	1,081	55.4	7,655	3,915	103
Burleson	8,813	2,174	2,419	347	56.2	2,563	2,271	55
Burnet	16,987	5,744	4,123	1,108	65.0	6,509	4,345	106
Caldwell	15,943	3,239	3,961	545	49.1	3,511	4,028	80
Calhoun	11,978	2,832	2,753	507	51.0	3,236	2,738	69
Callahan	8,101	2,480	1,666	534	58.0	3,055	1,539	37
Cameron	126,888	18,434	34,891	2,760	44.5	20,830	32,562	399
Camp	6,201	1,488	1,912	252	59.1	1,663	1,616	26
Carson	4,338	1,742	742	227	62.9	1,936	750	10
Cass	18,895	4,066	5,691	1,038	57.4	5,573	5,037	74
Castro	4,770	1,231	1,107	144	52.4	1,430	1,010	11
Chambers	14,451	4,101	2,876	818	54.2	4,774	2,804	92
Cherokee	24,049	6,483	5,185	971	52.8	7,476	4,977	106
Childress	3,868	1,072	719	165	50.7	1,220	655	9
Clay	6,968	1,997	1,690	465	59.7	2,506	1,484	23
Cochran	2,387	667	541	127	56.0	751	492	8
Coke	2,446	790	595	157	63.2	963	533	12
Coleman	6,609	1,793	1,488	349	55.2	2,214	1,028	22
Collin	231,160	83,750	37,854	10,443	57.5	91,256	38,708	1,450
Collingsworth	2,335	729	581	118	61.3	796	602	4
Colorado	12,130	3,381	2,795	574	55.9	3,855	2,782	39
Comal	44,428	16,763	7,132	1,903	58.6	18,158	7,303	370
Comanche	8,158	2,123	2,138	511	58.6	2,516	2,115	36
Concho	1,770	488	434	107	58.3	598	398	4
Cooke	20,603	7,320	3,782	1,150	59.7	8,082	4,008	100
Coryell	29,916	7,143	5,300	1,443	46.6	8,596	5,044	141
Cottle	1,615	331	404	77	50.7	378	384	12
Crane	2,804	984	616	201	64.8	1,178	568	18
Crockett	2,788	714	684	147	55.7	830	669	5
Crosby	4,153	968	1,122	189	55.1	1,131	1,038	31
Culberson	2,163	329	804	99	57.4	412	583	14

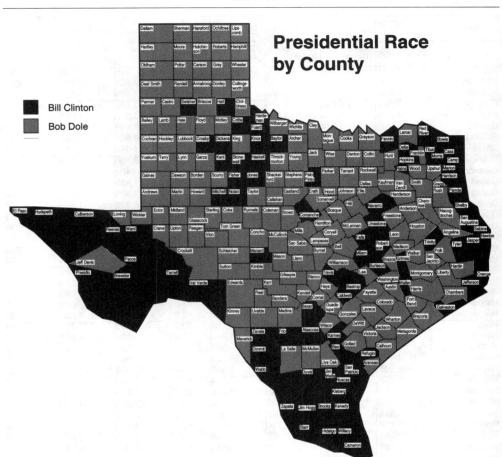

Presidential Race by County

Bill Clinton

Bob Dole

County	Registered Voters	President			Turnout	U.S. Senator		
	October 96	DOLE (Rep.)	CLINTON (Dem.)	PEROT (Ind.)	Percent	GRAMM (Rep.)	MORALES (Dem.)	BIRD (Lib.)
Dallam	2,634	970	483	170	62.0	1,149	424	1
Dallas	1,058,758	260,058	255,766	36,759	52.5	281,797	259,050	5,112
Dawson	8,362	2,319	1,612	232	50.0	2,507	1,482	34
Deaf Smith	9,677	3,051	1,655	310	52.2	3,377	1,568	37
Delta	3,107	744	849	146	56.1	842	837	9
Denton	209,482	65,313	36,138	9,294	53.3	71,393	38,019	1,152
DeWitt	11,383	3,577	2,074	483	54.2	3,906	2,064	34
Dickens	1,774	421	509	117	59.4	506	494	10
Dimmit	8,665	604	2,242	128	34.5	678	2,241	11
Donley	2,518	988	495	97	62.9	1,101	450	5
Duval	10,061	543	3,958	136	46.3	636	3,896	19
Eastland	10,789	3,272	2,594	705	61.1	3,936	2,506	70
Ector	62,123	17,746	12,017	2,511	52.6	21,156	10,707	367
Edwards	1,509	511	437	60	67.1	552	384	8
Ellis	56,749	16,046	10,832	2,750	52.5	17,876	11,371	275
El Paso	296,955	43,255	83,964	6,300	45.4	56,284	76,471	1,371
Erath	16,208	4,750	3,664	1,134	59.2	5,433	3,976	103
Falls	10,177	2,260	3,256	479	59.1	2,685	2,965	27
Fannin	16,143	3,495	4,276	980	54.5	4,231	4,380	80
Fayette	12,620	4,195	3,119	708	63.9	4,693	3,261	56
Fisher	2,945	537	1,142	170	62.8	725	1,069	13
Floyd	4,942	1,530	986	126	53.6	1,681	786	14

County	Registered Voters	President			Turnout	U.S. Senator		
	October 96	DOLE (Rep.)	CLINTON (Dem.)	PEROT (Ind.)	Percent	GRAMM (Rep.)	MORALES (Dem.)	BIRD (Lib.)
Foard	1,153	166	355	52	49.7	236	330	11
Fort Bend	148,169	49,945	38,163	4,363	62.7	53,601	37,794	621
Franklin	5,351	1,575	1,484	386	64.5	1,896	1,387	32
Freestone	10,039	2,888	2,630	568	60.7	3,333	2,665	45
Frio	9,368	1,225	2,593	253	43.7	1,362	2,591	37
Gaines	6,212	1,812	1,012	353	51.4	2,089	1,007	44
Galveston	153,653	35,251	38,458	5,897	52.1	38,991	39,288	871
Garza	2,936	946	703	103	59.7	1,048	615	7
Gillespie	12,082	5,867	1,655	542	67.5	6,198	1,769	117
Glasscock	743	382	70	30	65.1	403	70	2
Goliad	4,308	1,335	1,135	148	61.2	1,459	1,090	25
Gonzales	10,839	2,687	2,110	354	47.8	3,031	2,026	29
Gray	14,935	6,102	2,114	568	59.1	6,856	1,889	64
Grayson	64,046	17,169	14,338	3,745	55.3	20,559	14,227	273
Gregg	73,132	21,611	13,659	2,079	51.2	24,498	12,363	234
Grimes	10,366	2,564	2,584	538	55.0	3,018	2,433	27
Guadalupe	44,843	14,254	8,079	1,811	54.4	15,894	7,892	293
Hale	18,650	5,905	3,204	605	52.3	6,536	2,993	74
Hall	2,551	626	750	94	57.7	732	691	6
Hamilton	4,838	1,493	1,200	323	62.6	1,746	1,221	15
Hansford	3,093	1,493	343	105	62.9	1,639	288	5
Hardeman	2,958	610	750	168	51.8	801	645	8
Hardin	32,010	8,529	7,179	2,112	55.9	10,457	7,032	186
Harris	1,592,569	421,462	386,726	42,364	53.7	439,895	371,937	7,144
Harrison	38,681	9,835	10,307	1,427	56.0	12,285	8,927	107
Hartley	2,560	1,242	463	101	70.7	1,360	422	10
Haskell	4,402	966	1,374	225	58.4	1,204	1,284	10
Hays	48,632	12,865	11,580	1,990	55.2	13,908	12,631	353
Hemphill	2,187	986	344	104	65.8	1,060	361	7
Henderson	40,768	10,345	10,085	2,274	55.9	12,020	10,360	202
Hidalgo	199,246	24,437	56,335	3,536	42.5	27,288	54,317	457
Hill	17,019	4,401	3,988	1,052	55.7	5,167	4,120	85
Hockley	13,187	4,230	2,170	519	52.7	4,783	1,969	96
Hood	23,084	7,575	5,459	1,445	63.0	8,440	5,870	146
Hopkins	17,404	4,341	4,522	1,034	57.1	4,921	4,784	93
Houston	13,729	3,443	3,383	585	54.2	4,090	3,167	48
Howard	17,902	5,007	3,732	1,037	55.1	5,887	3,653	115
Hudspeth	1,584	367	427	92	56.7	422	420	7
Hunt	40,105	10,746	8,801	2,225	54.5	12,272	9,240	199
Hutchinson	16,704	6,350	2,553	864	58.7	7,268	2,424	81
Irion	1,269	386	213	86	54.4	482	193	8
Jack	4,754	1,162	1,019	301	52.3	1,407	1,017	10
Jackson	8,266	2,533	1,785	309	56.1	2,780	1,724	27
Jasper	20,077	4,523	5,039	1,041	53.0	5,377	5,039	105
Jeff Davis	1,524	482	370	99	63.2	540	354	15
Jefferson	160,100	32,821	45,854	5,314	52.7	38,640	43,823	666
Jim Hogg	3,911	307	1,437	64	46.3	375	1,419	6
Jim Wells	25,244	2,989	7,116	430	41.9	3,445	6,943	49
Johnson	61,866	16,246	12,817	3,250	52.5	18,608	13,299	316
Jones	9,840	2,351	2,422	614	55.0	3,013	2,248	72
Karnes	8,037	1,869	2,154	291	53.9	2,156	2,072	38
Kaufman	36,227	8,697	7,383	1,831	49.7	9,903	7,979	173
Kendall	12,671	5,940	2,092	620	69.3	6,544	2,014	125
Kenedy	349	71	133	4	59.6	74	120	0
Kent	809	187	260	67	63.7	243	231	13
Kerr	27,604	11,173	4,192	1,236	60.8	11,981	4,425	207
Kimble	2,737	898	521	131	57.1	1,026	494	7
King	256	97	46	29	71.1	115	59	2
Kinney	2,149	650	503	97	58.4	708	474	16
Kleberg	18,407	3,391	5,136	431	48.9	3,679	5,211	59
Knox	2,805	599	785	149	54.8	740	756	8
Lamar	28,237	6,393	6,075	1,198	48.6	7,298	6,228	96
Lamb	8,564	2,593	1,683	283	53.4	2,973	1,483	25

County	Registered Voters	President			Turnout	U.S. Senator		
	October 96	DOLE (Rep.)	CLINTON (Dem.)	PEROT (Ind.)	Percent	GRAMM (Rep.)	MORALES (Dem.)	BIRD (Lib.)
Lampasas	8,603	3,008	1,819	509	62.3	3,481	1,750	42
LaSalle	4,209	570	1,522	85	51.9	630	1,435	18
Lavaca	11,903	3,697	2,575	551	57.6	3,925	2,753	54
Lee	7,736	2,354	2,008	421	62.9	2,636	1,960	26
Leon	9,710	2,839	2,217	499	57.3	3,344	2,082	41
Liberty	36,648	7,784	6,877	2,011	45.8	9,342	6,974	218
Limestone	12,296	2,691	3,236	693	54.1	3,315	3,199	68
Lipscomb	1,907	869	357	115	70.5	979	308	7
Live Oak	6,888	1,929	1,372	292	52.4	2,152	1,342	27
Llano	10,759	4,290	2,633	762	71.9	4,752	2,901	68
Loving	132	48	14	15	58.3	54	18	0
Lubbock	138,724	47,304	22,786	3,996	53.7	50,861	21,961	769
Lynn	4,041	1,151	903	136	54.4	1,314	810	19
Madison	6,260	1,576	1,470	293	53.5	1,959	1,318	34
Marion	7,617	1,260	2,028	353	48.0	1,622	1,790	17
Martin	3,024	973	643	140	58.6	1,112	555	10
Mason	2,541	949	618	151	68.3	1,074	611	17
Matagorda	21,956	5,876	5,374	1,190	56.9	6,824	5,371	111
Maverick	18,211	1,050	5,307	202	36.2	1,234	5,078	41
McCulloch	5,333	1,465	1,231	296	56.4	1,778	1,111	33
McLennan	117,593	30,666	27,050	5,131	53.6	35,392	26,473	561
McMullen	680	274	117	35	63.2	287	122	4
Medina	18,679	5,710	3,880	715	55.6	6,367	3,869	101
Menard	1,673	443	490	102	62.3	554	447	11
Midland	64,419	25,382	9,513	2,079	57.9	28,064	8,611	377
Milam	13,182	3,019	3,869	657	57.4	3,566	3,848	68
Mills	2,817	1,044	748	230	72.2	1,210	762	12
Mitchell	4,835	949	1,213	232	49.7	1,211	1,105	22
Montague	12,106	3,029	2,718	842	54.7	3,820	2,573	60
Montgomery	138,348	51,011	20,722	6,065	56.5	55,129	21,065	858
Moore	9,184	3,353	1,358	359	55.3	3,729	1,272	42
Morris	9,733	1,449	2,973	402	49.6	1,864	2,819	24
Motley	1,019	380	164	56	59.4	421	164	5
Nacogdoches	34,918	10,361	7,641	1,352	55.7	11,789	7,314	131
Navarro	22,490	5,236	6,078	1,140	55.6	6,263	6,084	92
Newton	9,458	1,409	2,554	474	47.1	1,696	2,609	37
Nolan	10,118	2,166	2,582	613	53.3	2,902	2,346	71
Nueces	182,652	37,470	50,009	5,103	51.0	42,675	48,688	813
Ochiltree	4,832	2,448	467	167	64.0	2,603	436	14
Oldham	1,467	583	213	77	60.1	674	242	4
Orange	52,256	12,560	13,741	2,836	56.1	15,057	13,676	281
Palo Pinto	15,750	3,666	3,938	1,011	55.0	4,208	4,265	79
Panola	14,353	4,008	4,168	777	62.6	5,205	3,636	58
Parker	46,163	14,580	9,447	2,703	58.2	16,199	10,244	222
Parmer	4,508	2,042	676	160	64.1	2,225	685	12
Pecos	8,134	1,730	1,816	369	45.5	2,138	1,706	39
Polk	27,271	6,473	6,360	1,347	52.2	7,641	6,210	129
Potter	50,333	14,995	9,273	1,799	52.1	17,004	8,693	225
Presidio	3,508	383	1,205	111	48.9	479	1,100	8
Rains	4,607	1,123	1,265	335	59.3	1,353	1,272	21
Randall	64,351	28,266	9,177	1,985	61.6	30,401	8,564	252
Reagan	1,985	645	407	101	58.8	746	367	14
Real	2,313	845	414	178	62.6	936	399	17
Red River	8,697	1,783	2,339	433	52.5	2,105	2,251	35
Reeves	7,622	1,007	2,279	245	46.5	1,247	2,217	21
Refugio	5,527	1,376	1,635	222	58.8	1,604	1,567	23
Roberts	808	421	122	40	72.3	474	93	7
Robertson	9,929	1,944	2,912	315	52.1	2,201	2,878	14
Rockwall	21,861	8,319	3,289	1,121	58.5	9,146	3,436	127
Runnels	6,851	1,941	1,417	396	54.9	2,384	1,249	36
Rusk	28,093	8,423	5,988	1,072	55.3	9,817	5,333	95
Sabine	7,888	1,660	1,913	334	49.8	1,974	1,808	31
San Augustine	6,502	1,296	1,924	324	54.8	1,709	1,636	45

County	Registered Voters	President			Turnout	U.S. Senator		
	October 96	DOLE (Rep.)	CLINTON (Dem.)	PEROT (Ind.)	Percent	GRAMM (Rep.)	MORALES (Dem.)	BIRD (Lib.)
San Jacinto	12,157	2,878	2,771	810	53.3	3,446	2,803	72
San Patricio	36,838	7,678	8,132	1,085	46.1	8,721	7,893	147
San Saba	3,276	991	726	194	58.5	1,108	706	9
Schleicher	1,874	587	505	111	64.4	688	466	4
Scurry	10,670	2,929	2,099	813	55.0	3,684	2,014	82
Shackelford	2,281	792	502	169	64.5	956	453	16
Shelby	15,229	3,482	3,720	815	52.8	4,589	3,275	84
Sherman	1,672	809	243	89	68.4	878	228	6
Smith	91,613	32,171	18,265	2,933	58.6	35,360	17,911	357
Somervell	4,486	1,099	993	273	53.0	1,246	1,061	15
Starr	21,843	756	6,312	157	33.2	871	6,065	26
Stephens	5,773	1,714	1,218	336	56.8	2,050	1,167	21
Sterling	1,015	394	186	86	65.9	479	152	7
Stonewall	1,349	323	487	105	68.0	405	448	2
Sutton	2,462	688	508	102	52.9	796	501	7
Swisher	4,802	1,159	1,224	195	54.0	1,381	1,156	12
Tarrant	742,215	208,312	170,431	28,715	55.2	227,519	174,104	3,652
Taylor	71,841	23,682	13,213	2,912	55.7	27,457	12,211	356
Terrell	878	185	278	47	59.1	211	274	5
Terry	7,526	2,013	1,272	269	47.4	2,266	1,175	34
Throckmorton	1,288	360	285	90	57.2	437	264	4
Titus	13,689	3,438	3,725	744	57.9	4,323	3,424	55
Tom Green	58,258	18,112	11,782	2,757	56.3	21,208	10,992	378
Travis	459,115	98,454	128,970	14,008	53.6	104,570	135,246	3,300
Trinity	10,405	2,058	2,774	460	51.0	2,538	2,647	45
Tyler	12,335	2,804	3,340	645	55.3	3,393	3,144	30
Upshur	20,601	5,174	5,032	1,086	54.9	6,289	4,821	89
Upton	2,268	685	424	88	53.1	792	356	5
Uvalde	15,470	3,494	3,397	403	47.4	3,850	3,335	62
Val Verde	19,903	4,357	5,623	548	53.3	4,872	5,492	67
Van Zandt	27,716	7,453	5,752	1,756	54.2	8,581	6,139	116
Victoria	48,447	14,457	8,238	1,197	49.8	15,164	8,182	226
Walker	26,595	7,177	6,088	1,186	54.8	8,503	5,777	122
Waller	17,225	3,559	4,535	499	50.1	3,975	4,456	79
Ward	6,677	1,620	1,644	446	55.9	2,110	1,491	61
Washington	17,122	6,319	3,460	601	60.9	6,946	3,325	53
Webb	68,649	4,712	18,997	936	36.1	6,190	18,206	91
Wharton	21,003	6,163	5,176	871	58.2	7,072	4,999	71
Wheeler	3,826	1,355	750	174	59.8	1,560	661	18
Wichita	74,484	20,495	15,775	3,371	53.6	24,712	14,530	487
Wilbarger	8,602	2,037	1,730	465	49.6	2,591	1,549	30
Willacy	10,233	1,332	3,789	241	52.9	1,658	3,534	45
Williamson	112,140	36,836	24,175	4,931	59.3	39,555	25,585	728
Wilson	17,152	4,530	3,713	760	52.9	5,131	3,720	109
Winkler	4,471	1,009	872	218	47.0	1,308	746	19
Wise	23,685	6,330	5,056	1,516	54.8	7,196	5,508	142
Wood	18,548	6,228	4,711	1,184	65.6	7,199	4,685	129
Yoakum	4,243	1,485	738	218	57.8	1,644	729	40
Young	11,634	3,647	2,394	639	57.6	4,273	2,258	38
Zapata	5,847	521	1,786	131	41.9	623	1,732	15
Zavala	7,890	463	2,629	91	40.5	486	2,567	15
Statewide	10,540,678	2,736,167	2,459,683	378,537	53.2	3,027,680	2,428,776	51,516

VISIT US AT
www.texasalmanac.com

Special Elections, 1996

Below are the voting returns of the special election held November 5, 1996, for 13 congressional races and one state senate race. These are official returns as canvassed by the State Canvassing Board. Abbreviations used are (Dem.) Democrat, (Rep.) Republican, (Lib.) Libertarian, (UST) U.S. Taxpayers and (Ind.) Independent.

U.S. HOUSE OF REPRESENTATIVES

District 3

Lee Cole (Dem.)	47,654
John Davis (Lib.)	5,045
Sam Johnson (Rep.)	142,325
Other	2
Total Vote	195,026

District 5

John Pouland (Dem.)	70,992
Pete Sessions (Rep.)	80,196
Other	1
Total Vote	151,119

District 6

Catherine A. Anderson (Lib.)	14,456
Joe Barton (Rep.)	160,800
Janet Carroll (Skeet) Richardson (Ind.)	26,713
Doug Williams (UST	6,547
Total Vote	208,516

District 7

Bill Archer (Rep.)	152,024
Gene Hsiao (Ind.)	3,896
Al J.K. Siegmund (Dem.)	28,187
Robert R. (Randy) Sims. Jr. (Ind.)	2,724
Total Vote	186,831

District 8

Kevin Brady (Rep.)	80,325
Gene Fontenot (Rep.)	75,399
Robert Musemeche (Dem.)	11,689
Cynthia (CJ) Newman (Dem.)	26,246
Total Vote	193,659

District 9

Nick Lampson (Dem.)	83,782
Geraldine Sam (Dem.)	17,887
Steve Stockman (Rep.)	88,171
Total Vote	189,840

District 18

Jerry Burley (Rep.)	7,877
Mike Lamson (Dem.)	4,412
Sheila Jackson Lee (Dem.)	106,111
Larry White (Rep.)	13,956
George A. Young (Rep.)	5,332
Total Vote	137,688

District 22

Scott Douglas Cunningham (Dem.)	59,030
Tom DeLay (Rep.)	126,056
Total Vote	185,086

District 24

Martin Frost (Dem.)	77,847
Ed Harrison (Rep.)	54,551
Marion Jacob (Dem.)	4,656
Dale Mouton (Ind.)	2,574
Other	9
Total Vote	139,637

District 25

Ken Bentsen (Dem.)	43,701
Beverley Clark (Dem.)	21,699
Dotty Quinn Collins (Rep.)	561
John Devine (Rep.)	9,070
Jerry Freiwirth (Socialist Workers)	270
Ken G. Mathis (Rep.)	3,649
Dolly Madison McKenna (Rep.)	21,898
Ron (RC) Meinke (Rep.)	997
Lloyd W. Oliver (Rep.)	827
Brent Perry (Rep.)	16,737
John M. Sanchez (Rep.)	8,984
Total Vote	128,393

District 26

Dick Armey (Rep.)	163,708
Jerry Frankel (Dem.)	58,623
Other	11
Total Vote	222,342

District 29

Gene Green (Dem.)	61,751
Jack W. Klinger (UST)	1,340
Jack Rodriguez (Rep.)	28,381
Total Vote	91,472

District 30

Marvin E. Crenshaw (Dem.)	7,765
Ada Granado (Ind.)	1,278
Stevan A. Hammond (Ind.)	468
Lisa Hembry (Ind.)	3,501
John Hendry (Rep.)	20,664
Eddie Bernice Johnson (Dem.)	61,723
Lisa Kitterman (Rep.)	7,761
James L. Sweatt (Dem.)	9,909
Other	3
Total Vote	113,072

STATE SENATE
District 28

Dick Bowen (Rep.)	3,938
Robert Duncan (Rep.)	45,106
Monte Hasie (Rep.)	13,303
Tim Lambert (Rep.)	18,885
David R. Langston (Dem.)	36,032
Lorenzo 'Bubba' Sedeno (Dem.)	12,419
Gary L. Watkins (Dem.)	18,652
Total Vote	148,335

Runoff

held December 10, 1996

U.S. HOUSE OF REPRESENTATIVES
District 8

Kevin Brady (Rep.)	30,366
Gene Fontenot (Rep.)	21,004
Total Vote	51,370

District 9

Nick Lampson (Dem.)	59,225
Steve Stockman (Rep.)	52,870
Total Vote	112,095

District 25

Ken Bentsen (Dem.)	29,396
Dolly Madison McKenna (Rep.)	21,892
Total Vote	51,288

STATE SENATE
District 28

Robert Duncan (Rep.)	32,489
David R. Langston (Dem.)	24,686
Total Vote	57,175

TEXAS CONGRESSIONAL DISTRICTS

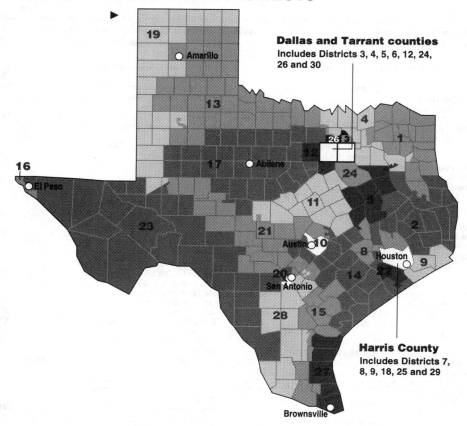

Dallas and Tarrant counties
Includes Districts 3, 4, 5, 6, 12, 24, 26 and 30

Harris County
Includes Districts 7, 8, 9, 18, 25 and 29

Other Special Elections, 1996-97

STATE SENATE
Held May 4, 1996
State Senator, Dist. 16

John Corona	9,419
Jan Erik Fredericksen	3,311
Donna Halstead	7,456
Steve Matthews	3,198
Bob White	294
Write-in	2
Total Vote	23,680

Runoff: Held June 1, 1996
State Senator, Dist. 16

John Corona	10,489
Donna Halstead	7,905
Total Vote	18,394

Below are the voting returns of the special election held January 28, 1997, for one state senate race.

State Senator, Dist. 5

Mary M. Moore (Dem.)	17,062
Steve Ogden (Rep.)	21,245
Total Vote	38,307

U.S. HOUSE OF REPRESENTATIVES

Below are the returns of the special election held March 15, 1997, for the congressional seat that had been held by U.S. Rep. Frank Tejeda, D-San Antonio, who died in office.

District 28

Oliver Lowell Blair (Rep.)	168
Lauro A. Bustamante (Dem.)	818
Robert Cantu (Ind.)	82
Mark Cude (Rep.)	2,452
Jose Julian De La Rocha (Rep.)	53
Michael idrogo (Dem.)	64
John P. Kelly (Rep.)	1,229
Patrick A. Mason (Dem.)	158
Narciso V. Mendoza (Rep.)	621
Mike G. Pacheco (Dem.)	231
Ciro D. Rodriguez (Dem.)	14,018
Phil Ross (Dem.)	376
Juan F. Solis III (Dem.)	8,056
John A. (Drew) Traeger (Dem.)	718
Carlos I. Uresti (Dem.)	1,345
Write-Ins	5
Total Vote	30,394

District 28 Runoff
A runoff election was held on April 12, 1997.

Ciro D. Rodriguez (Dem.)	19,992
Juan F. Solis III (Dem.)	9,990
Total Vote	29,982

Texas Primary Elections, 1996

Below are the official returns for contested races only in the Republican and Democratic Party primaries held March 12, 1996. Included are statewide races and selected district races. The runoffs were held April 9.

Democratic Primary

President
Sal Casamassima	9,648
Bill Clinton	796,041
Ted L. Gunderson	15,550
Heather Harder	28,772
Fred Hudson	32,232
Lyndon H. LaRouche Jr.	28,137
Elvena E. Lloyd-Duffie	10,876
Total Vote	921,256

U.S. Senator
John Bryant	267,545
Jim Chapman	239,427
Victor M. Morales	322,218
John Will Odam	61,433
Total Vote	890,623

Judge, Court of Criminal Appeals, Place 1
Frances Northcutt	362,881
Bob Perkins	388,317
Total Vote	751,198

Judge, Court of Criminal Appeals, Place 2
Winston Cochran	124,799
Charles Holcomb	244,580
Norman Lanford	127,506
Gary Taylor	210,172
Total Vote	707,057

U.S. HOUSE OF REPRESENTATIVES
District 1
Jo Ann Howard	28,962
Tommy Kessler	19,948
Max Sandlin	36,142
Total Vote	85,052

District 2
Edgar J. (Bubba) Groce	15,171
Fred Hudson	16,068
Jim Turner	45,453
Total Vote	76,692

District 5
Wm. A. Foster III	11,510
John Pouland	20,150
Total Vote	31,660

District 6
Terry Jesmore	1,480
Janet Carroll Richardson	7,193
Total Vote	8,673

District 8
Robert W. Musemeche	3,083
C.J. Newman	5,026
Total Vote	8,109

District 9
Rusty Isaac Bertrand	1,766
Jack Cherry	6,741
Nick Lampson	32,161
Mat Safran	815
Geraldine Sam	5,147
Total Vote	46,630

District 13
Aaron Alejandro	16,732
Samuel Brown Silverman	17,931
Total Vote	34,663

District 15
Reynaldo Balli Jr.	1,877
Renato Cuellar	13,832
Tony Dominguez	5,008
Ruben Hinojosa	21,726
Jim Selman	21,138
Total Vote	63,581

District 16
Dolores Briones	11,583
Robert A. (Bob) Levy	610
Tom Petersen	3,095
Silvestre Reyes	22,119
Jose Luis Sanchez	14,698
Total Vote	52,105

District 19
Michael G. Clennan	3,798
John W. Sawyer	8,833
Total Vote	12,631

District 23
Charles P. Jones	17,837
Allen Rindfuss	5,811
Joseph P. (Joe) Sullivan	21,085
Total Vote	44,733

District 27
Mary Helen Berlanga	16,097
Solomon P. Ortiz	37,434
Total Vote	53,531

District 29
Felix Fraga	7,680
Gene Green	13,352
Total Vote	21,032

STATE SENATE
District 3
Jerry K. Johnson	38,913
Dick Swift	18,043
Ralph Wallace	11,191
Total Vote	68,147

District 12
Mike Moncrief	16,932
Nancy Ward	3,369
Total Vote	20,301

District 29
Ray Mancera	8,672
Rene Nunez	5,758
Eliot Shapleigh	17,723
Marie Tarvin-Garland	8,017
Hector Villa	9,722
Total Vote	49,892

STATE BOARD OF EDUCATION
District 3
Vincent R. Alvarado	20,931
Joe J. Bernal	34,632
Total Vote	55,563

District 5
Nettie Ruth Bratton	28,245
Joe (J.B.) Richeson	14,437
Total Vote	42,682

Democratic Runoff

U.S. Senator
John Bryant	235,281
Victor M. Morales	246,614
Total Vote	481,895

Judge, Court of Criminal Appeals, Place 2
Charles Holcomb 206,523
Gary Taylor 187,329
    Total Vote 393,852

U.S. Representative, Dist. 1
Jo Ann Howard 25,063
Max Sandlin 31,659
    Total Vote 56,722

U.S. Representative, Dist. 15
Ruben Hinojosa 24,940
Jim Selman 22,983
    Total Vote 47,923

U.S. Representative, Dist. 16
Silvestre Reyes 21,161
Jose Luis Sanchez 20,157
    Total Vote 41,318

U.S. Representative, Dist. 23
Charles P. Jones 9,384
Joseph P. (Joe) Sullivan 9,131
    Total Vote 18,515

State Senator, Dist. 29
Eliot Shapleigh 24,666
Hector Villa 15,235
    Total Vote 39,901

Republican Primary
President
Lamar Alexander 18,745
Patrick J. (Pat) Buchanan 217,974
Charles E. Collins 633
Bob Dole 567,164
Susan Ducey 1,093
Steve Forbes 130,938
Phil Gramm 18,629
Alan L. Keyes 41,746
Mary (France) LeTulle 650
Richard G. Lugar 2,266
Morry Taylor 458
Uncommitted 19,507
    Total Vote 1,019,803

U.S. Senator
Phil Gramm 838,339
Henry C. (Hank) Grover 72,400
David Young 75,463
    Total Vote 986,202

Railroad Commissioner
Carole Keeton Rylander 541,565
Robert A. (Bob) Wood 316,903
    Total Vote 858,468

Judge, Court of Criminal Appeals, Place 1
Glen Beaman 44,772
James (Daniel) Boone 127,995
Susan Baetz Brown 101,143
Sue Holland 184,163
Jeffrey B. Keck 51,703
Janice Law 84,051
Matthew Paul 111,316
    Total Vote 705,143

Judge, Court of Criminal Appeals, Place 2
Pat Barber 148,764
Mike Keasler 148,175
Ray J. McQuary 76,121
Brad Wiewel 86,614
Paul Womack 214,415
    Total Vote 674,089

Judge, Court of Criminal Appeals, Place 3
John Bradley 204,891

Cheryl A. Johnson 207,979
Tom Price 206,739
J. Gary Trichter 61,493
    Total Vote 681,102

U.S. HOUSE OF REPRESENTATIVES

District 1
Dennis Boerner 6,386
Hamp Hodges 5,150
Ed Merritt 10,133
    Total Vote 21,669

District 2
Brian Babin 7,094
Ben Bius 2,986
Bob Currie 2,348
Jim Hughes 2,401
Donna Peterson 8,047
    Total Vote 22,876

District 4
Jerry Ray Hall 20,024
Jon Newton 17,169
    Total Vote 37,193

District 5
Glenn Box 8,259
Pete Sessions 11,464
    Total Vote 19,723

District 8
Kevin Brady 14,769
Gene Fontenot 24,204
Don Henderson 10,599
Daniel D. New 2,772
Betty Reinbeck 4,800
Fred D. Thornberry 9,786
    Total Vote 66,930

District 11
Jim Broyles 4,459
Dave Jenkins 1,197
Jay Mathis 12,981
Brian Pardo 9,587
    Total Vote 28,224

District 12
Ernest J. Anderson Jr. 6,355
Bill Burch 3,355
Kay Granger 21,774
    Total Vote 31,484

District 14
Ted Bozarth 398
Jim Deats 8,466
Greg Laughlin 14,777
Ron Paul 11,112
    Total Vote 34,753

District 15
Jose Aliseda 3,453
Tom Haughey 7,697
    Total Vote 11,150

District 16
Dick Bowen 5,225
Rick Ledesma 8,329
    Total Vote 13,554

District 20
Kirk K. Colyer 4,771
John Shull 4,872
James Walker 6,274
    Total Vote 15,917

District 22
Tom DeLay 41,874
Greg Pepper 10,464
    Total Vote 52,338

District 24
Olivia Coggin Eudaly 5,305
Ed Harrison 16,078
   Total Vote 21,383

District 25
Bill Brock 5,796
Brent Perry 11,093
   Total Vote 16,889

STATE SENATE
District 2
Richard Harvey 9,566
Bob Reese. 13,568
   Total Vote 23,134

District 7
Jerry Dumas 27,658
Jon Lindsay 29,303
   Total Vote 56,961

District 10
Chris Harris 30,330
Jim Lollar 8,656
   Total Vote 38,986

District 15
Tom Kelly 8,608
David D. Schein 4,105
   Total Vote 12,713

District 24
Bob Barina. 4,204
Troy Fraser. 18,028
   Total Vote 22,232

District 25
Randy Staudt. 24,930
Jef Wentworth 59,476
   Total Vote 84,406

COURTS OF APPEALS
Justice, First District, Place 2
Jim Gieseke. 57,662
Daniel W. Leedy 44,017
Gerald Zimmerer 41,961
   Total Vote 143,640

Justice, Second District, Place 7
Terrie Livingston 51,077
George Petrovich. 31,454
   Total Vote 82,531

Justice, Fourteenth District
Henry L. Burkholder. 31,032
Jack Holland 40,387
Harriet O'Neill 79,137
   Total Vote 150,556

STATE BOARD OF EDUCATION
District 6
Jack Christie 44,087
Terri Leo. 36,254
   Total Vote 80,341

District 10
Don Clark 16,324
Cynthia A. Thornton 24,192
Charlie Weaver 23,019
   Total Vote. 63,535

Republican Runoff

Judge, Court of Criminal Appeals, Place 1
James (Daniel) Boone 74,107
Sue Holland 159,922
   Total Vote. 234,029

Judge, Court of Criminal Appeals, Place 2
Pat Barber. 73,129
Paul Womack 148,135
   Total Vote. 221,264

Judge, Court of Criminal Appeals, Place 3
Cheryl A. Johnson 95,941
Tom Price 128,363
   Total Vote. 224,304

U.S. Representative, Dist. 1
Dennis Boerner. 3,644
Ed Merritt 4,403
   Total Vote 8,047

U.S. Representative, Dist. 2
Brian Babin. 7,405
Donna Peterson 3,675
   Total Vote. 11,080

U.S. Representative, Dist. 8
Kevin Brady. 18,583
Gene Fontenot 16,244
   Total Vote 34,827

U.S. Representative, Dist. 11
Jay Mathis. 10,655
Brian Pardo. 4,520
   Total Vote 15,175

U.S. Representative, Dist. 14
Greg Laughlin. 9,555
Ron Paul. 11,244
   Total Vote 20,799

U.S. Representative, Dist. 20
John Shull. 2,649
James Walker 3,432
   Total Vote 6,081

State Board of Education, Dist. 10
Cynthia A. Thornton 14,802
Charlie Weaver 17,501
   Total Vote. 32,303

Justice, First District, Place 2
Jim Gieseke 43,971
Daniel W. Leedy 22,278
   Total Vote. 66,249

Political Party Organizations

Democratic State Executive Committee

Chairman, Bill White, 3040 Post Oak Ste. 750, Houston 77052; **Vice Chair**, Clara Caldwell, 2118 Endicott Ln., Sugar Land 77478; **Vice Chair for Financial Affairs**, Nancy Brannon, 301 E. Scott, Gainesville 76240; **Secretary**, Walter Hinojosa, 7801 Lowdes Dr., Austin 78745; **Treasurer**, Eliza May, 1605 Sylvan Glade, Austin 78745; **Counsel**, Carroll G. Robinson, 8300 W. Airport Blvd. Apt. 704, Houston 77071; **Co-parliamentarians**, Ed Cogburn, 5002 Doliver, Houston 77056, and Frank Thompson,

6937 Peyton, Houston 77028. **Office Address:** 815 Brazos, Ste. 200, Austin 78701.

National Committee Members: Billie Carr, Houston; Al Edwards, Houston; Hazel Falke-Obey, Austin; Liz Lara-Carreno, Houston; William Leo, La Joya; Mike Lopez, Donna; K. T. McLeaish, Odessa; Ed Miller, Texarkana; Robert Slagle, Sherman; Rosa Walker, Austin.

District — Member and Hometown
1. Patsy Johnson, Sulphur Springs; Leonard Rockwell, Mount Pleasant.

2. Martha Williams, Terrell; Ken Molberg, Dallas.

3. Kathleen Hawkins, Buna; Dennis Teal, Livingston.

4. Mary Kirkwood, Beaumont; Guy Jackson, Anahuac.

5. Melanie Reed, Cameron; Neely Lewis, Bryan.

6. Pat Gandy, Houston; Frumencio Reyes, Houston.

7. Linda Fischer, Spring; Stephen Marak, Houston.

8. Linda Ashton-Smith, Plano; Barry Sprouse, Irving.

9. Lisa Payne, Dallas; Ron Spurlock, Lewisville.

10. Ruby Woolridge, Arlington; Donald Winters, Fort Worth.

11. Ceole Speight, Pasadena; Sam Munn, La Marque.

12. Roy Laverne Brooks, Fort Worth; Grover Swift, Fort Worth.

13. Sue Lovell, Houston; Rodney Griffin, Missouri City.

14. Gwen Foster, Austin; Jeff Heckler, Austin.

15. Etta Crockett, Houston; Clay Sands, Houston.

16. Teresa Daniel, Dallas; Jay Newman, Dallas.

17. Alma Nolen, Pearland; Michael Laster, Houston.

18. Diana Rhodes, Nursery; Marion Garcia, Thompsons.

19. Jo Ann McCall, San Antonio; Gary Woitena, San Antonio.

20. Susie Luna-Saldana, Corpus Christi; William Edwards, Portland.

21. Minnie Dora Bunn Haynes, Laredo; Rene A. Trevino, Carrizo Springs.

22. Teresa Smith, Cleburne; Jesse Sapp, Waco.

23. Ruth Wyrick, Dallas; Charles Rose, Dallas.

24. Alice Anne Wallace, Belton; Morris Bratton, Kingsland.

25. Bennye Frazier, San Antonio; Raul C. Garcia, San Angelo.

26. Jane Velasquez, San Antonio; Darby Riley, San Antonio.

27. Graciela Sanchez, Weslaco; Mike Vega, San Benito.

28. Betty Condra, Lubbock; Daniel Adcock, Lamesa.

29. Iris Burnham, El Paso; Tom Peterson, El Paso.

30. Dorthy Wise, Wichita Falls; Calvin Gambill, Seymour.

31. Linda Shoemaker-Lowrey, Plains; George Dowlen, Amarillo.

Texas Democratic Women: Pres., Cristy Keul, 16127 County Rd. 178, Tyler 75703; Vice Pres., Molly Beth Malcolm, Texarkana.

Coalition of Black Democrats: Bernice G. Conley, Dallas; Gene O. Collins, Odessa.

Non-Urban Caucus: Chair, Lynda Phillips, P.O. Box 591, Gilmer 75644; Vice Chair, Brooks Wm. Conover, Austin.

Tejano Democrats: Mary J. Almendarez, Houston; Thomas Larralde, San Antonio.

Young Democrats: Pres., Gabe Acevedo, 40 N. I35, Apt. 3B1, Austin 78701; Vice Pres., Marisa Schouten, Austin.

County Chair Association: Pres., Ted Lewis, 1245 Dallas Dr., Denton 76205; Vice Pres., Lennie C. Simms, Wellington.

Senate Caucus: Sen. John Montford, Austin.

House Caucus: Rep. Eddie de la Garza, Edinburg.

Republican State Executive Committee

Office Address: 211 E. 7th, Ste. 620, Austin 78701. **Chairman,** Tom Pauken, 10751 Mapleridge Dr., Dallas 75238; **Vice Chairman,** Mrs. Susan Weddington, 217 Halbart Dr., San Antonio 78213; **Secretary,** Mrs. Loyce McCarter, 3943 Gayle, San Antonio 78223; **Treasurer,** Paulette Standefer, 10101 Bettywood Ln., Dallas 75243; **General Counsel**, James W. Walker, 901 Main St., Dallas 75202; **Finance Chairman,** David Hartman, 1717 W. 6th St. Ste. 110; Austin 78768; **Parliamentarian**, Richard Stadelmann, 5538 Spreen Rd. Brenham 77833.

National Committeeman, Tim Lambert, P.O. Box 6621,

Lubbock 79493; **National Committeewoman,** Susan Feldtman, 5 Glendenning Dr., Houston 77024.

District — Member and Hometown

1. Dennis Boerner, Pittsburg; Grace Shore, Longview.

2. Shirley McSpedden, Kemp; John T. Tello, Rockwall.

3. Linda Newton, Jacksonville; Todd Gallaher, Nacogdoches.

4. Lydia Damrel, Vidor; Ralph K. Harrison, The Woodlands.

5. Clara L. Sandstedt, College Station; Barnie O. Henderson Jr., Cameron.

6. Ann Makris, Houston; Doug Johnson, Houston.

7. Linda Dewhurst, Houston; Mark T. Fury, Katy.

8. Dolores C. Hardin, Dallas; Peter Y. Wrench, Dallas.

9. Glenda G. Crenshaw, Lake Dallas; Jim Moseley, Coppell.

10. Olivia Eudaly, Fort Worth; John F. Mauldin, Arlington.

11. Lisa Smith, Pasadena; Kenneth Clark, League City.

12. Mrs. Kerry Lundelius, Fort Worth; James A. Borchert, Fort Worth.

13. Betty Lou Martin, Houston; Ronald C. Meinke, Houston.

14. Kirk Overbey, Austin; Devora Edmondson, Austin.

15. Martha S. Greenlaw, Houston; Louis Butch Davis, Houston.

16. Ms. Jodie Laubenberg, Richardson; Bruce Bishop, Mesquite.

17. Terese A. Raia, Sugar Land; Timothy J. Turner, Bellaire.

18. Robert K. Long, Bastrop; Myrna Patterson McLeroy, Waelder.

19. Mrs. Loyce McCarter, San Antonio; Randy Hurt, Fort Stockton.

20. Richard L. Bowers, Corpus Christi; Patsy Sparkman, Corpus Christi.

21. Dorthy Butler, Seguin; Bob Hurley, Pleasanton.

22. Beverly S. Parks, Hico; Jay P. Mashburn, Granbury.

23. Lawrence J. Phillips, Desoto; Mary E. Mireles, Grand Prairie.

24. Reba Boyd, Abilene; George Dulany, Belton.

25. Rita R. Davis, San Antonio; Randy Staudt, Leander.

26. Shirley O. Thompson, San Antonio; Gene Ryder, San Antonio.

27. Debbie Moutsos, South Padre Island; Tom Wingate, McAllen.

28. Spencer E. Wolfe, Big Spring; Skeet Workman, Lubbock.

29. Donna Yecke, El Paso; Roger O'Dell, El Paso.

30. Patricia C. Peale, Lake Kiowa; Frank Alvarez, Sherman.

31. Rick D. Davis Jr., Midland; Sue Hershey, Amarillo.

Republican State Party Auxiliaries:

Texas Asian Republican Caucus: Chmn., Charles Cho, 13430 Bellaire Blvd., Houston 77083.

Texas Young Republican Federation: Chmn., Robert Eberle, 2400 NASA Rd. 1 A23, Houston 77058-3799.

Black Republican Council of Texas: Chmn., Bill Calhoun, 4200 Montrose No. 480, Houston 77006.

Texas Republican County Chair Assoc.: Chmn., Ann Peden, 1107 28th St., Hondo 78861; Liaison, Meryle G. Barnett.

College Republicans of Texas: Chmn., Suzanne Sanders, P.O. Box 7041, Austin 78713.

Texas Federation of Republican Women: Pres., Dianne H. Thompson, 10038 Johns Rd. Boerne 78006-8811.

Republican Veterans of Texas: Chmn., George R. Leake, 1809 Kensington, Carrollton 75007.

Texas Pachyderms: Chmn., Jack Burton, 1132 Danbury, Houston, 77055. ☆

Texas Vote in Presidential Elections, 1848-1996

Below are the Texas popular vote results for U.S. presidential elections. (Earlier elections listed electors, and often the highest vote recorded by any elector was used as the figure for the presidential candidate.) An asterisk (*) designates the winner of the national election. In the 1860 vote which elected Lincoln president, electors for neither Lincoln nor Stephen Douglas were on the Texas ballot. Texas did not take part in the 1864 and 1868 elections because of the Civil War and Reconstruction.

Election, 1848
Lewis Cass (Democrat) 10,668
*Zachary Taylor (Whig). .4,509
    Total Vote. 15,177

Election, 1852
*Franklin Pierce (Democrat) 13,552
Winfield Scott (Whig) 4,995
    Total Vote. 18,547

Election, 1856
*James C. Buchanan (Democrat). 31,169
Millard Fillmore (Whig) .15,639
    Total Vote. 46,808

Election, 1860
John C Breckinridge (Democrat) 47,548
John Bell (Con. Union) 15,438
    Total Vote. 62,986

CIVIL WAR and RECONSTRUCTION

Election, 1872
Horace Greeley (Democrat) 66,546
*Ulysses S. Grant (Republican) 47,468
Charles O'Conor (Labor-Reform). 2,580
    Total Vote. 116,594

Election, 1876
Samuel J. Tilden (Democrat) 104,755
*Rutherfod B. Hayes (Republican) 44,800
    Total Vote. 149,555

Election, 1880
Winfield S. Hancock (Democrat) 156,428
*James A. Garfield (Republican) 57,893
    Total Vote. 214,321

Election, 1884
*Grover Cleveland (Democrat) 225,309
James G. Blaine (Republican) 93,141
John P. St. John (Prohibitionist) 3,534
Benjamin F. Butler (Greenback) 3,321
    Total Vote. 325,305

Election, 1888
Grover Cleveland (Democrat). 234,883
*Benjamin Harrison (Republican). 88,422
Alson J. Streeter (Union Labor) 29,459
Clinton B. Fisk (Prohibitionist) 4,749
    Total Vote. 357,513

Election, 1892
*Grover Cleveland (Democrat) 239,148
James B. Weaver (Populist) 99,688
Benjamin Harrison (Republican) 81,144
John Bidwell (Prohibitionist). 2.175
    Total Vote. 422,155

Election, 1896
William J. Bryan (Democrat). 234,298
William J. Bryan (Populist) 78,926
*William McKinley (Republican) 167,520

John McA. Palmer (National Democrat) 5,046
Joshua Levering (Prohibitionist) 1,786
    Total Vote 487,576

Election, 1900
William J. Bryan (Democrat) 267,432
*William McKinley (Republican) 130,651
Wharton Barker (Populist). 20,981
John C. Woolley (Prohibitionist). 2,644
Eugene V. Debs (Socialist) 1,846
Joseph F. Malloney (Socialist-Labor). 162
    Total Vote 423,716*

Election, 1904
Alton B. Parker (Democrat) 199,799
*Theodore Roosevelt (Republican) 65,823
Thomas E. Watson (Populist) 8,062
Silas C. Swallow (Prohibitionist) 4,292
Eugene V. Debs (Socialist) 2,791
Charles H. Corregan (Socialist-Labor) 421
    Total Vote 281,188*

*POLL TAX instituted in Texas 1903

Election, 1908
William J. Bryan (Democrat) 224,110
*William H. Taft (Republican). 70,458
Eugene V. Debs (Socialist) 7,870
Eugene W. Chafin (Prohibitionist) 1,634
Thomas E. Watson (Populist) 994
August Gillhaus (Socialist-Labor) 176
Thomas L. Hisgen (Independent) 115
    Total Vote 305,357

Election, 1912
*Woodrow Wilson (Democrat). 222,589
Theodore Roosevelt (Progressive) 28,853
William H. Taft (Republican) 26,755
Eugene V. Debs (Socialist) 25,743
Eugene W. Chafin (Prohibitionist) 1,738
Arthur E. Reimer (Socialist-Labor) 442
    Total Vote 306,120

Election, 1916
*Woodrow Wilson (Democrat) 286,514
Charles E. Hughes (Republican). 64,999
Allan L. Benson (Socialist) 18,969
J. Frank Hanly (Prohibitionist) 1,985
    Total Vote 372,467

Election, 1920
James M. Cox (Democrat). 288,767
*Warren G. Harding (Republican) 114,538
James E. Ferguson (American). 47,968
(Black and Tan Republican). 27,247
Eugene V. Debs (Socialist) 8,121
    Total Vote 486,641

Election, 1924
John W. Davis (Democrat). 484,605
*Calvin Coolidge (Republican) 130,023
Robert M. LaFollette (Progressive) 42,881
    Total Vote 657,509

Election, 1928
*Herbert C. Hoover (Republican) 367,036
Alfred E. Smith (Democrat). 341,032
Norman M. Thomas (Socialist). 722
William Z. Foster (Communist) 209
   Total Vote. 708,999

Election, 1932
*Franklin D. Roosevelt (Democrat) 760,348
Herbert C. Hoover (Republican) 97,959
Norman M. Thomas (Socialist) 4,450
W.H. Harvey (Liberty) 324
William Z. Foster (Communist) 207
(Jacksonian) 104
   Total Vote. 863,392

Election, 1936
*Franklin D. Roosevelt (Democrat) 734,485
Alfred M. Landon (Republican). 103,874
William Lemke (Union) 3,281
Norman M. Thomas (Socialist) 1,075
D. Leigh Colvin (Prohibitionist) 514
Earl R. Browder (Communist). 253
   Total Vote. 843,482

Election, 1940
*Franklin D. Roosevelt (Democrat) 840,151
Wendell L. Willkie (Republican) 199,152
Roger W. Babson (Prohibitionist) 925
Norman M. Thomas (Socialist) 728
Earl R. Browder (Communist). 212
   Total Vote. 1,041,168

Election, 1944
*Franklin D. Roosevelt (Democrat) 821,605
Thomas E. Dewey (Republican) 191,425
‡(Texas Regulars) 135,439
Claude A. Watson (Prohibitionist) 1,017
Norman M. Thomas (Socialist) 594
Gerald L.K. Smith (America First). 251
   Total Vote. 1,150,331

Election, 1948
*Harry S Truman (Democrat) 750,700
Thomas E. Dewey (Republican) 282,240
J. Strom Thurmond (States Rights) 106,909
Henry A. Wallace (Progressive) 3,764
Claude A. Watson (Prohibitionist). 2,758
Norman M. Thomas (Socialist) 874
   Total Vote. 1,147,245

Election, 1952
*Dwight D. Eisenhower (Republican) 1,102,878
Adlai E. Stevenson (Democrat). 969,228
Stuart Hamblen (Prohibitionist) 1,983
Douglas MacArthur (Christian National). 833
Douglas MacArthur (Constitution) 730
Vincent Hallinan (Progressive) 294
   Total Vote. 2,075,946

Election, 1956
*Dwight D. Eisenhower (Republican) 1,080,619
Adlai E. Stevenson (Democrat) 859,958
T. Coleman Andrews (Constitution) 14,591
   Total Vote. 1,955,168

Election, 1960
*John F. Kennedy (Democrat). 1,167,932
Richard M. Nixon (Republican). 1,121,699
Charles L. Sullivan (Constitution) 18,169
Rutherford L. Decker (Prohibitionist). 3,870
   Total Vote. 2,311,670

Election, 1964
*Lyndon B. Johnson (Democrat) 1,663,185
Barry Goldwater (Republican). 958,566
Joseph B. Lightburn (Conservative) 5,060
   Total Vote 2,626,811

Election, 1968
Hubert H. Humphrey (Democrat) 1,266,804
*Richard M. Nixon (Republican) 1,227,844
George C. Wallace (American) 584,269
Write-in 489
   Total Vote 3,079,406

Election, 1972
*Richard M. Nixon (Republican) 2,298,896
George McGovern (Democrat) 1,154,289
Linda Jenness (Socialist) 8,664
John G. Schmitz (American) 6,039
Other. 3,393
   Total Vote 3,371,281

Election, 1976
*Jimmy Carter (Democrat) 2,082,319
Gerald R. Ford (Republican) 1,953,300
Eugene J. McCarthy (Independent) 20,118
Thomas J. Anderson (American). 11,442
Peter Camejo (Socialst Worker) 1,723
Write-in Vote 2,982
   Total Vote 4,071,884

Election, 1980
*Ronald Reagan (Republican) 2,510,705
Jimmy Carter (Democrat) 1,881,147
John Anderson (Independent). 111,613
Ed Clark (Libertarian) 37,643
Write-in Vote 529
   Total Vote 4,541,637

Election, 1984
*Ronald Reagan (Republican) 3,433,428
Walter Mondale (Democrat) 1,949,276
Lyndon Larouche (Independent). 14,613
Other. 254
   Total Vote 5,397,571

Election, 1988
*George Bush (Republican) 3,036,829
Michael S. Dukakis (Democrat). 2,352,748
Ron Paul (Libertarian). .30,355
Other. 7,478
   Total Vote 5,427,410

Election, 1992
George Bush (Republican) 2,496,071
*Bill Clinton (Democrat). 2,281,815
Ross Perot (Independent). 1,354,781
Andre Marrou (Libertarian) 19,699
Other. 1,652
   Total Vote 6,154,018

Election, 1996
Bob Dole (Republican) 2,736,167
*Bill Clinton (Democrat). 2,459,683
Ross Perot (Independent). 378,537
Harry Browne (Libertarian) 20,256
Howard Phillips (U.S. Taxpayers) 7,472
Ralph Nader (Write-In) 4,810
John Hagelin (Natural Law) 4,422
Mary Cal Hollis (Write-In) 297
   Total Vote 5,611,644

State Government

Texas state government is divided into executive, legislative and judicial branches under the Texas Constitution adopted in 1876. The chief executive is the Governor, whose term is for 4 years. Other elected state officials with executive responsibilities include the Lieutenant Governor, Attorney General, Comptroller of Public Accounts, Commissioner of the General Land Office and Commissioner of Agriculture. The terms of those officials are also 4 years. The Secretary of State is appointed by the Governor.

Except for making numerous appointments and calling special sessions of the Legislature, the Governor's powers are limited in comparison with those in most states.

Current state executives and their addresses, phone numbers and proposed salaries for the 1998-99 biennium (the salaries were subject to review at press time in summer, 1997):

Governor: George W. Bush
P.O. Box 12428, Austin 78711
(512) 463-2000
$115,345

Lt. Governor: Bob Bullock
P.O. Box 12068, Austin 78711
(512) 463-0001
For salary, see note* below.

Attorney General: Dan Morales
P.O. Box 12546, Austin 78711
(512) 463-2100
$92,217

Comptroller of Public Accounts: John Sharp
LBJ State Office Building, Austin 78774
(512) 463-4000
$92,217

Commissioner of General Land Office: Garry Mauro
1700 N. Congress, Austin 78701
(512) 463-5256
$92,217

Commissioner of Agriculture: Rick Perry
P.O. Box 12847, Austin 78711
(512) 463-7435
$92,217

Secretary of State: Antonio O. "Tony" Garza Jr.
P.O. Box 12697, Austin 78711
(512) 463-5770
$76,966

*Salary of Lt. Gov. is same as a Senator when serving as Pres. of Senate; same as Gov. when serving as Gov.

Ombudsman Office (Citizens' Advocate): Phil Sims. **Citizens' Assistance Hotline: 1-800-843-5789.**
Part of the Governor's office, the Ombudsman Office receives citizens's comments and complaints over the toll-free assistance hotline and passes them to government officials, as well as referring citizens to sources of assistance.

Texas Legislature

The Texas Legislature has **181 members: 31 in the Senate and 150 in the House of Representatives.** Regular sessions convene on the second Tuesday of January in odd-numbered years, but the governor may call special sessions. Article III of the Texas Constitution deals with the legislative branch.

The following lists are of members of the 75th Legislature, which convened on Jan. 14, 1997.

State Senate

Thirty-one members of the State Senate are elected to **four-year, overlapping terms. Salary:** The salary of all members of the Legislature, both Senators and Representatives, is $600 per month and $95 per diem during legislative sessions; mileage allowance at same rate provided by law for state employees. The per diem payment applies during each regular and special session of the Legislature.

Senatorial Districts include one or more whole counties and some counties have more than one Senator.

The **address of Senators** is Texas Senate, P.O. Box 12068, Austin 78711-2068; phone (512) 463-0001; Fax: (512) 463-0039. Internet: http://www.senate.state.tx.us/

President of the Senate is Lt. Gov. Bob Bullock; **President Pro Tempore**, Bill Ratliff (R-Mt. Pleasant); **Secretary of the Senate**, Betty King; **Sergeant-at-Arms**, Carleton Turner.

Texas State Senators

Dist., Name, Party-Hometown; Year Current Term Ends; Occupation.

1. Bill Ratliff, R-Mt. Pleasant; 1999; consulting engineer.
2. David Cain, D-Dallas; 2001; attorney.
3. Drew Nixon, R-Carthage; 2001; CPA, securities/insurance agency.
4. Michael L. Galloway, R-The Woodlands; 1999; businessman - oil and gas.
5. Steve Ogden, R-Bryan; 1999; oil and gas producer.
6. Mario Gallegos Jr., D-Galena Park; 1999; ret. fire capt.
7. Jon Lindsay, R-Houston; 2001; business consultant.
8. Florence Shapiro, R-Plano; 2001; businesswoman.
9. Jane Nelson, R-Flower Mound; 2001; businesswoman.
10. Chris Harris, R-Arlington; 2001; attorney.
11. Jerry Patterson, R-Pasadena; 1999; health benefits consultant.
12. Mike Moncrief, D-Fort Worth; 2001; businessman.
13. Rodney Ellis, D-Houston; 1999; director, securities firm/attorney.
14. Gonzalo Barrientos, D-Austin; 2001; advertising/public relations.
15. Jonn Whitmire, D-Houston; 2001; attorney.
16. John Carona, R-Dallas; 1999; company CEO.
17. J. E. "Buster" Brown, R-Lake Jackson; 1999; attorney.
18. Kenneth Armbrister, D-Victoria; 1999; businessman.
19. Frank L. Madla, D-San Antonio; 1999; real estate, insurance.
20. Carlos F. Truan, D-Corpus Christi (Dean of the Senate); 1999; life insurance.
21. Judith Zaffirini, D-Laredo; 2001; communications specialist.
22. David Sibley, R-Waco; 1999; attorney.
23. Royce West, D-Dallas; 1999; attorney.
24. Troy Fraser, R-Horseshoe Bay; 2001; businessman.
25. Jeff Wentworth, R-San Antonio; 2001; attorney, realtor.
26. Gregory Luna, D-San Antonio; 2001; attorney.
27. Eddie Lucio Jr., D-Brownsville; 2001; advertising.
28. Robert Duncan, R-Lubbock; 1999; attorney.
29. Eliot Shapleigh, D-El Paso; 2001; attorney.
30. Tom Haywood, R-Wichita Falls; 1999; businessman.
31. Teel Bivins, R-Amarillo; 1999; businessman, cattleman.

House of Representatives

This list on page 403 shows the 150 members of the House of Representatives in the 75th Legislature. They were elected on Nov. 5, 1996, from the districts shown below. Members are elected for two-year terms. Representatives and senators receive the same salary (see State Senate). The **address of all Representatives** is House of Representatives, P.O. Box 2910, Austin, 78768; phone (512) 463-3000; Fax: (512) 463-5896. Internet: http://www.house.state.tx.us/

Speaker: James E. "Pete" Laney (D-Hale Center). **Speaker Pro Tempore**, D.R. "Tom" Uher (D-Bay City). **Chief Clerk**, Sharon Carter. **Sergeant-at-Arms**, Rod Welsh.

Members of Texas House of Representatives
District, Member, Party-Hometown, Occupation

1. Barry B. Telford, D-DeKalb, businessman.
2. Tom Ramsay, D-Mount Vernon; real estate, rancher.
3. L.P. "Pete" Patterson, D-Brookston; farmer/rancher, real estate.
4. Keith Oakley, D-Terrell; rancher, sales representative.
5. Bob Glaze, D-Gilmer; chiropractor, rancher.
6. Ted Kamel, R-Tyler; businessman.
7. Tommy Merritt, R-Longview; businessman.
8. Paul Sadler, D-Henderson; attorney.
9. Wayne Christian, R-Center; investment advisor.
10. Jim Pitts, R-Waxahachie; attorney.
11. Todd Staples, R-Palestine; real-estate appraiser.
12. Clyde H. Alexander, D-Athens; rancher, businessman.
13. Dan Kubiak, D-Rockdale; rancher, real estate, construction.
14. William (Bill) Roman Jr., R-College Station; physician.
15. Thomas Williams, R-The Woodlands; insurance and financial services.
16. Bob Rabuck, R-Conroe; orthodontist.
17. Jim McReynolds, D-Lufkin; landman, rancher.
18. Allen R. Hightower, D-Huntsville; mgr., transit co.
19. Ron E. Lewis, D-Mauriceville; insurance, real estate.
20. Zeb Zbranek, D-Winnie; attorney, engineer.
21. Mark W. Stiles, D-Beaumont; businessman.
22. Albert J. Price, D-Beaumont; retired pilot.
23. Patricia Gray, D-Galveston; attorney.
24. Craig Eiland, D-Galveston; attorney.
25. Dennis H. Bonnen, R-Angleton; insurance.
26. Charlie Howard, R-Sugar Land; real-estate developer.
27. Dora Olivo, D-Rosenberg; attorney.
28. Robert L. "Robby" Cook, D-Eagle Lake; farmer.
29. D.R. "Tom" Uher, D-Bay City; attorney.
30. Steve Holzheauser, R-Victoria; farm & ranch mgmt.
31. Judy Hawley, D-Portland; teacher.
32. Eugene (Gene) J. Seaman, R-Corpus Christi; insurance, real estate.
33. Vilma Luna, D-Corpus Christi; attorney.
34. Hugo Berlanga, D-Corpus Christi; businessman.
35. Irma Rangel, D-Kingsville; attorney.
36. Ismael "Kino" Flores, D-Mission; businessman.
37. Rene O. Oliveira, D-Brownsville; attorney.
38. Jim Solis, D-Harlingen; attorney.
39. Miguel D. "Mike" Wise, D-Weslaco; attorney.
40. Juan Hinojosa, D-McAllen; attorney.
41. Roberto Gutierrez, D-McAllen; petroleum-products distributor.
42. Henry R.Cuellar, D-Laredo; attorney, customs broker.
43. Tracy O. King, D-Uvalde; self-employed.
44. Richard Raymond, D-Benavides; consultant.
45. Edmund Kuempel, R-Seguin; salesman.
46. Alec Rhodes, D-Dripping Springs; businessman.
47. Terry Keel, R-Austin; attorney.
48. Sherri Greenberg, D-Austin; public-finance specialist.
49. Elliott Naishtat, D-Austin; attorney.
50. Dawnna Dukes, D-Austin; consultant.
51. Glen Maxey, D-Austin; data manager.
52. Mike Krusee, R-Round Rock; small-business owner.
53. Harvey Hilderbran, R-Kerrville; businessman.
54. Suzanna Gratia Hupp, R-Lampasas; chiropractor, horse breeder.
55. Dianne Delisi, R-Temple; self-employed.
56. Kip Averitt, R-Waco; manufacturing.
57. Jim Dunnam, D-Moody; attorney.
58. Arlene Wohlgemuth, R-Burleson; flight instructor.
59. Allen Place, D-Gatesville; attorney.
60. James L. (Jim) Keffer, R-Eastland; sales.
61. Ric Williamson, R-Weatherford; small businessman.
62. Ron Clark, R-Sherman; attorney.
63. Mary Denny, R-Denton; businesswoman/rancher.
64. Jim Horn, R-Denton; businessman.
65. Burt Solomons, R-Carrollton; attorney.
66. Brian McCall, R-Plano; insurance executive.
67. Jerry Madden, R-Richardson; insurance.
68. Charles A. Finnell, D-Holliday; small businessman.
69. John Hirschi, D-Wichita Falls; real estate mgmt.
70. David Counts, D-Knox City; insurance, real estate.
71. Bob Hunter, R-Abilene; university administrator.
72. Robert A. "Rob" Junell, D-San Angelo; attorney.

73. Bob Turner, D-Voss; farmer, rancher.
74. Pete P. Gallego, D-Alpine; attorney.
75. Gilbert Serna, D-El Paso; self-employed.
76. Norma Chavez, D-El Paso; businesswoman.
77. Paul Moreno, D-El Paso; attorney.
78. Pat Haggerty, R-El Paso; real-estate broker.
79. Joseph C. Pickett, D-El Paso; real-estate broker.
80. Gary L. Walker, R-Plains; water conservation, landfill consultant.
81. George "Buddy" West, R-Odessa; safety engineer.
82. Tom Craddick, R-Midland; sales representative.
83. Delwin Jones, R-Lubbock; businessman.
84. Carl H. Isett, R-Lubbock; accountant.
85. James E. "Pete" Laney, D-Hale Center; farmer.
86. John T. Smithee, R-Amarillo; attorney.
87. David A. Swinford, R-Dumas; agribusiness.
88. Warren D. Chisum, R-Pampa; oil & gas producer.
89. Sue Palmer, R-Fort Worth; petroleum distributor.
90. Lon Burnam, D-Fort Worth; consultant.
91. Bill G. Carter, R-Fort Worth; insurance agent.
92. Todd Smith, R-Euless; attorney.
93. Toby Goodman, R-Arlington; attorney.
94. Kent Grusendorf, R-Arlington; pres., mfg. co.
95. Glenn Lewis, D-Fort Worth; attorney.
96. Kim Brimer, R-Arlington; Insurance.
97. Anna Mowery, R-Fort Worth; state representative.
98. Nancy Moffat, R-Southlake; marketing representative.
99. Kenny Marchant, R-Coppell; investor.
100. Terri Hodge, D-Dallas; retired.
101. Elvira Reyna, R-Mesquite; state representative.
102. Tony Goolsby, R-Dallas; insurance investment.
103. Steven D. Wolens, D-Dallas; attorney.
104. Domingo Garcia, D-Dallas; attorney.
105. Dale B. Tillery, D-Dallas; attorney.
106. Ray Allen, R-Grand Prairie; publishing.
107. Harryette Ehrhardt, D-Dallas; teacher.
108. Carolyn Galloway, R-Dallas; N.A.
109. Helen Giddings, D-DeSoto; small-business owner.
110. Jesse W. Jones, D-Dallas; educator.
111. Yvonne Davis, D-Dallas; small-business owner.
112. Fred Hill, R-Richardson; businessman.
113. Joe Driver, R-Garland; insurance agent.
114. Will Hartnett, R-Dallas; attorney.
115. Leticia Van de Putte, D-San Antonio; pharmacist.
116. Leo Alvarado Jr., D-San Antonio; attorney.
117. John A. Longoria, D-San Antonio; attorney.
118. Ciro D. Rodriguez, D-San Antonio; educator.
119. Robert Puente, D-San Antonio; attorney.
120. Ruth J. McClendon, D-San Antonio; company pres.
121. Bill Siebert, R-San Antonio; businessman.
122. John H. Shields, R-San Antonio; attorney.
123. Frank J. Corte, Jr., R-San Antonio; businessman.
124. Christine Hernandez, D-San Antonio; education consultant.
125. Arthur C. "Art" Reyna Jr., D-San Antonio; attorney.
126. Peggy Hamric, R-Houston; small-business owner.
127. Joe Crabb, R-Humble; minister, attorney.
128. Fred M. Bosse, R-Houston; attorney.
129. Mike Jackson, R-La Porte; general contractor.
130. John Culberson, R-Houston; attorney.
131. Ron Wilson, D-Houston; attorney.
132. Scott Hochberg, D-Houston; electronics consultant.
133. Joe Nixon, R-Houston; attorney.
134. Kyle Janek, R-Houston; physician.
135. Gary Elkins, R-Houston; businessman, consultant.
136. Beverly Woolley, R-Houston; small-business owner.
137. Debra Danburg, D-Houston; attorney.
138. Ken Yarbrough, D-Houston; executive director.
139. Sylvester Turner, D-Houston; attorney.
140. Kevin Bailey, D-Houston; college teacher.
141. Senfronia Thompson, D-Houston; attorney.
142. Harold V. Dutton Jr., D-Houston; attorney.
143. Gerard Torres, D-Houston; marketing, real estate.
144. Robert E. Talton, R-Pasadena; attorney.
145. Diana Dávila, D-Houston; state representative.
146. Al Edwards, D-Houston; real estate.
147. Garnet Coleman, D-Houston; small-business owner.
148. Jessica Farrar, D-Houston; architect intern.
149. Talmadge L. Heflin, R-Houston; businessman.
150. Paul J. Hilbert, R-Spring; attorney. ☆

Federal and State Courts

The following lists include U.S. district courts in Texas, state higher courts and administrative judicial districts. The lists were compiled from reports of the Texas Judicial Council, clerks of the courts and other sources.

Following this section is a table giving state district courts, court of appeals districts, administratitive judicial districts and U.S. judicial districts for each county and a listing of all state district court judges.

U.S. District Courts In Texas

Texas is divided into four federal judicial districts, each of which is composed of several divisions. Appeal from all Texas federal district courts is to the **Fifth Circuit Court of Appeals**, New Orleans. Judges are appointed for life and receive a salary of $133,600 annually.

Northern Texas District

District Judges — Chief Judge, Jerry Buchmeyer, Dallas. **Senior Judges:** Barefoot Sanders, Dallas; David O. Belew Jr. and Eldon B. Mahon, Fort Worth; Halbert O. Woodard, Lubbock. **Judges:** Mary Lou Robinson, Amarillo; A. Joe Fish, Sidney A. Fitzwater, Jorge A. Solis, Joe Kendall and Robert B. Maloney, Dallas; Sam R. Cummings, Lubbock. **Clerk of District Court:** Nancy Doherty, Dallas. **U.S. Attorney:** Paul Coggins, Dallas. **U.S. Marshal:** W.D. Bransom, Dallas. Court is in continuous session in each division of the Northern Texas District. Following are the different divisions of the Northern District and the counties in each division:

Dallas Division

Dallas, Ellis, Hunt, Johnson, Kaufman, Navarro and Rockwall. **Magistrates:** William F. Sanderson Jr., John B. Tolle, Jane Jackson and Jeff Kaplan, Dallas.

Fort Worth Division

Comanche, Erath, Hood, Jack, Palo Pinto, Parker, Tarrant and Wise. **Magistrate:** Charles Bleil, Fort Worth. **Deputy-in-charge:** Pam Murphy.

Amarillo Division

Armstrong, Briscoe, Carson, Castro, Childress, Collingsworth, Dallam, Deaf Smith, Donley, Gray, Hall, Hansford, Hartley, Hemphill, Hutchinson, Lipscomb, Moore, Ochiltree, Oldham, Parmer, Potter, Randall, Roberts, Sherman, Swisher and Wheeler. **Magistrate:** Clinton E. Averitte, Amarillo. **Deputy-in-charge:** Lynn Sherman.

Abilene Division

Callahan, Eastland, Fisher, Haskell, Howard, Jones, Mitchell, Nolan, Shackelford, Stephens, Stonewall, Taylor and Throckmorton. **Magistrate:** Billy W. Boone, Abilene. **Deputy-in-charge:** Marsha Elliott.

San Angelo Division

Brown, Coke, Coleman, Concho, Crockett, Glasscock, Irion, Menard, Mills, Reagan, Runnels, Schleicher, Sterling, Sutton and Tom Green. Magistrate: Philip R. Lane, San Angelo. **Deputy-in-charge:** Ann Light.

Wichita Falls Division

Archer, Baylor, Clay, Cottle, Foard, Hardeman, King, Knox, Montague, Wichita, Wilbarger and Young. **Magistrate:** R. Kerry Roach, Wichita Falls. **Deputy Clerk:** Allison Terry.

Lubbock Division

Bailey, Borden, Cochran, Crosby, Dawson, Dickens, Floyd, Gaines, Garza, Hale, Hockley, Kent, Lamb, Lubbock, Lynn, Motley, Scurry, Terry and Yoakum. **U.S. District Judge:** Sam R. Cummings, Lubbock. **Magistrate:** J. Q. Warnick Jr., Lubbock. **Deputy-in-charge:** Kristy Weinheimer.

Western Texas District

District Judges — Chief Judge, Harry Lee Hudspeth, El Paso. **Senior Judges:** D. W. Suttle, San Antonio; Lucius D. Bunton III, Midland. **Judges:** Edward C. Prado, H. F. Garcia, Orlando Garcia and Fred Biery, San Antonio; W. Royal Furgeson Jr. and David Briones, El Paso; James R. Nowlin and Sam Sparks, Austin; Walter S. Smith Jr., Waco. **Clerk of District Court:** William G. Putnicki, San Antonio. **Chief Deputy Clerk:** Michael J. Simon. **U.S. Attorney:** J. William (Bill) Blagg, San Antonio. **U.S. Marshal:** Jack Dean, San Antonio. Following are the different divisions of the Western District, and the counties in each division.

San Antonio Division

Atascosa, Bandera, Bexar, Comal, Dimmit, Frio, Gonzales, Guadalupe, Karnes, Kendall, Kerr, Medina, Real and Wilson. **Magistrates:** Robert B. O'Connor, John W. Primomo and Nancy Stein Nowak, San Antonio. **Bankruptcy Judges:** Leif M. Clark and Ronald B. King, San Antonio. **Clerk of Bankruptcy Court:** Larry Bick, San Antonio.

Austin Division

Bastrop, Blanco, Burleson, Burnet, Caldwell, Gillespie, Hays, Kimble, Lampasas, Lee, Llano, Mason, McCulloch, San Saba, Travis, Washington and Williamson. **Magistrates:** Alan D. Albright and Stephen H. Capelle, Austin. **Bankruptcy Judges:** Chief, Larry E. Kelly, and Frank P. Monroe. **District Court Deputy-in-charge:** Robert J. Williams. **Bankruptcy Court Deputy-in-charge:** Tina Warren.

El Paso Division

El Paso County only. **Magistrates:** Michael S. McDonald and Richard P. Mesa, El Paso. **Bankruptcy Judge:** Leif M. Clark, San Antonio. **District Court Deputy-in-charge:** Richard Delgado. **Bankruptcy Court Deputy-in-charge:** Mary Croy.

Waco Division

Bell, Bosque, Coryell, Falls, Freestone, Hamilton, Hill, Leon, Limestone, McLennan, Milam, Robertson and Somervell. **Magistrate:** Dennis Green, Waco. **Bankruptcy Judge:** Larry E. Kelly, Austin. **Deputy-in-charge:** Mark G. Borchardt.

Del Rio Division

Edwards, Kinney, Maverick, Terrell, Uvalde, Val Verde and Zavala. **Magistrates:** Durwood Edwards and Alia Ludlum, Del Rio. **Bankruptcy Judge:** Ronald B. King, San Antonio. **Deputy-in-charge:** Kay West.

Pecos Division

Brewster, Culberson, Hudspeth, Jeff Davis, Loving, Pecos, Presidio, Reeves, Ward and Winkler. **Magistrate:** Katherine H. Baker, Pecos. **Bankruptcy Judge:** Ronald B. King, San Antonio. **Deputy-in-charge:** Karen J. White.

Midland-Odessa Division

Andrews, Crane, Ector, Martin, Midland and Upton. Court for the Midland-Odessa Division is held at Midland, but may, at the discretion of the court, be held in Odessa. **Magistrate:** L. Stuart Platt, Midland. **Bankruptcy Judge:** Ronald B. King, San Antonio. **District Court Deputy-in-charge:** John D. Neil, Midland. **Bankruptcy Court Deputy-in-charge:** Christy L. Carouth.

Eastern Texas District

District Judges — Chief Judge, Richard A. Schell, Beaumont. **Judges:** Joe J. Fisher, Thad Heartfield and Howell Cobb, Beaumont; William M. Steger, John Hannah Jr. and William Wayne Justice, Tyler; Paul N. Brown, Sherman; David J. Folsom, Texarkana. **Clerk of District Court:** David J. Maland, Tyler. **U.S. Attorney:** J. Michael Bradford, Beaumont. **U.S. Marshal:** Norris Batiste, Beaumont. **Chief U.S. Probation Officer:** Kenneth LaBorde, Beaumont. **Judges in Bankruptcy:** C. Houston Abel, Tyler, and Donald R. Sharp, Beaumont. **Federal Public Defender:** G. Patrick Black, Tyler. Following are the different divisions of the Eastern District and the counties in each division:

Tyler Division
Anderson, Cherokee, Gregg, Henderson, Panola, Rains, Rusk, Smith, Van Zandt and Wood. **Magistrates:** Henry W. McKee, Tyler, and Judith Guthrie, Tyler. **Chief Deputy:** Jeanne Henderson.

Beaumont Division
Hardin, Jasper, Jefferson, Liberty, Newton, Orange. **Magistrates:** Earl Hines and J. Michael Bradford, Beaumont. **Chief Deputy:** Kelly Gavagan.

Marshall Division
Camp, Cass, Harrison, Marion, Morris, Upshur. **Deputy-in-charge:** Peggy Anderson.

Sherman Division
Collin, Cooke, Denton and Grayson. **Magistrate:** Roger Sanders. **Deputy-in-charge:** Sandra Southerland.

Texarkana Division
Bowie, Franklin and Titus. **Magistrate:** Charles Attaway. **Deputy-in-charge:** Sue Jordan.

Paris Division
Delta, Fannin, Hopkins, Lamar and Red River.

Lufkin Division
Angelina, Houston, Nacogdoches, Polk, Sabine, San Augustine, Shelby, Trinity, Tyler.

Southern Texas District

District Judges — Chief Judge, George P. Kazen, Laredo. **Senior Judges:** Norman W. Black, Houston; Hugh Gibson, Galveston. **Judges:** Nancy F. Atlas, Kenneth M. Hoyt, Sim Lake, Lynn N. Hughes, David Hittner, John D. Rainey, Melinda Harmon, Vanessa D. Gilmore, Ewing Werlein Jr. and Lee H. Rosenthal, Houston; Hayden W. Head Jr. and Janis Graham Jack, Corpus Christi; Samuel B. Kent, Galveston; Filemon B. Vela, Brownsville; Ricardo H. Hinojosa, McAllen. **Clerk of Court:** Michael N. Milby, Houston. **U. S. Attorney:** Gaynele Griffin Jones, Houston. **U.S. Marshal (Acting):** Frank E. Skroski, Houston. **Bankruptcy Judges:** Chief, Letitia Z. Clark; Manuel D. Leal, R. F. Wheless Jr., William R. Greendyke and Karen K. Brown, Houston; Richard S. Schmidt, Corpus Christi. Following are the different divisions of the Southern District and the counties in each division:

Houston Division
Austin, Brazos, Colorado, Fayette, Fort Bend, Grimes, Harris, Madison, Montgomery, San Jacinto, Walker, Waller and Wharton. **Magistrates:** Calvin Botley, Frances H. Stacy, Nancy Johnson, Marcia A. Crone and Mary Milloy. **Clerk:** Michael N. Milby.

Brownsville Division
Cameron and Willacy. **Magistrates:** Fidencio Garza Jr. and John Wm. Black. **Deputy-in-charge:** Juan Barbosa.

Corpus Christi Division
Aransas, Bee, Brooks, Duval, Jim Wells, Kenedy, Kleberg, Live Oak, Nueces and San Patricio. **Magistrate:** B. Janice Ellington and Jane Cooper-Hill. **Deputy-in-charge:** Monica Seaman. **Bankruptcy Court Deputy-in-charge:** Joyce Bjork.

Galveston Division
Brazoria, Chambers, Galveston and Matagorda. **Magistrate:** John R. Froeschner. **Deputy-in-charge:** Marrianne Gore.

Laredo Division
Jim Hogg, La Salle, McMullen, Webb and Zapata. **Magistrate:** Marcel C. Notzon. **Deputy-in-charge:** Rosie Rodriguez.

Victoria Division
Calhoun, DeWitt, Goliad, Jackson, Lavaca, Refugio and Victoria. **Deputy-in-charge:** Maxine Gammon.

McAllen Division
Hidalgo and Starr. **Magistrate:** Peter E. Ormsby and Dorina Ramos. **Deputy-in-charge:** Ludivina Cervantes.

State Judiciary

The judiciary of the state consists of nine members of the State Supreme Court; nine members of the Court of Criminal Appeals; 80 of the Courts of Appeals; 395 of the State District Courts, including 10 Criminal District Courts; 446 County Courts; 841 Justice of the Peace Courts; and 1,221 Municipal Courts.

In addition to its system of formal courts, the State of Texas has established 13 **Alternative Dispute Resolution Centers**. The centers help ease the caseload of Texas courts by using mediation, arbitration, negotiation and moderated settlement conferences to handle disputes without resorting to more costly, time-consuming court actions. Centers are located in Amarillo, Austin, Beaumont, Conroe, Corpus Christi, Dallas, El Paso, Fort Worth, Houston, Lewisville, Lubbock, Plano and San Antonio. For the fiscal year ending Aug. 31, 1996, the mediation sections of the centers had closed 26,607 cases and had 3,549 cases still pending.

State Higher Courts

The state's higher courts are listed below with corrections to **July 1, 1997**. Notations in parentheses indicate dates of expiration of terms of office. Judges of the Supreme Court, Court of Criminal Appeals and Courts of Appeals are elected to 6-year, overlapping terms. District Court judges are elected to 4-year terms.

The salaries for judges as passed by the 75th Legislature in 1997 were not final at press time. However, the proposed salaries for the 1998-99 biennium are as follows: Chief Justice of the Supreme Court and the Presiding Judge of the Court of Criminal Appeals: each $105,247; Justices, $102,463; Chief Justices of the Courts of Appeals, $97,870; justices, $97,340 from the state. A supplemental amount may be paid by counties, not to exceed $15,000 per year, and total salary must be at least $1,000 less than that received by Supreme Court justices. District Court judges receive $92,217 from the state, plus supplemental pay from various subdivisions. Their total salary must be $1,000 less than that received by justices of the Court of Appeals in which the district court is located.

Below is given information on only the Supreme Court, Court of Criminal Appeals and Courts of Appeals. The information was furnished by each court as of April 1997. Names of county court judges are given by counties on page 447. Names of District Court Judges are given by District number on pages 409-411. To get the District numbers of District Courts in a particular county, look on page 407-409.

Supreme Court
Chief Justice, Thomas R. Phillips (12-31-02). **Justices:** Raul A. Gonzalez (12-31-00); Greg Abbott (12-31-98); Nathan L. Hecht (12-31-00); John Cornyn (12-31-02); James A. Baker (12-31-02); Craig Enoch (12-31-98); Rose Spector (12-31-98); and Priscilla R. Owen (12-31-00). **Clerk of Court,** John T. Adams. Location of court, Austin.

Court of Criminal Appeals
Presiding Judge, Michael J. McCormick (12-31-00). **Judges:** Charles F. Baird (12-31-98); Morris L. Overstreet (12-31-98); Lawrence E. Meyers (12-31-98); Stephen W. Mansfield (12-31-00); Sharon Keller (12-31-00); Tom Price (12-31-02); Sue Holland (12-31-02); Paul Womack (12-31-02). **State's Attorney,** Matthew Paul. **Clerk of Court,** Troy C. Bennett Jr. Location of court, Austin.

Courts of Appeals
These courts have jurisdiction within their respective supreme judicial districts. A constitutional amendment approved in 1978 raised the number of associate justices for Courts of Appeals where needed. Judges are elected from the district for 6-year terms. Another amendment adopted in 1980 changed the name of the old Courts of Civil Ap-

peals to the Courts of Appeals and changed the jurisdiction of the courts. See Art. V, Sec. 6 of the State Constitution.

First District—*Houston. Chief Justice, Michael H. Schneider (12-31-98). **Justices:** Murry B. Cohen (12-31-00); Margaret G. Mirabal (12-31-02); Adele Hedges (12-31-00); Michol O'Connor (12-31-00); Davie L. Wilson (12-31-98); Eric Andell (12-31-00); Tim G. Taft (12-31-00); Sam Nuchia (12-31-00). **Clerk of court,** Margie Thompson. Counties in the First District: Austin, Brazoria, Brazos, Burleson, Chambers, Colorado, Fort Bend, Galveston, Grimes, Harris, Trinity, Walker, Waller, Washington.

Second District—Fort Worth: Chief Justice, John Cayce (12-31-00). **Justices:** Dixon W. Holman (12-31-02); Sam J. Day (12-31-00); Terrie Livingston (12-31-02); Lee Ann Dauphinot (12-31-00); David Richards (12-31-00); and William H. Brigham (12-31-98). **Clerk of court,** Yvonne Palmer. Counties in Second District: Archer, Clay, Cooke, Denton, Hood, Jack, Montague, Parker, Tarrant, Wichita, Wise, Young.

Third District—Austin: Chief Justice, James L. Carroll (12-31-02). **Justices:** John Powers (12-31-98); Marilyn Aboussie (12-31-00); J. Woodfin Jones (12-31-00); Mack Kidd (12-31-00); and Bea Ann Smith (12-31-00). **Clerk of court,** Diane O'Neal. Counties in the Third District: Bastrop, Bell, Blanco, Burnet, Caldwell, Coke, Comal, Concho, Fayette, Hays, Irion, Lampasas, Lee, Llano, McCulloch, Milam, Mills, Runnels, San Saba, Schleicher, Sterling, Tom Green, Travis, Williamson.

Fourth District—San Antonio: Chief Justice, Phil Hardberger (12-31-00). **Justices:** Catherine M. Stone (12-31-00); Tom Rickhoff (12-31-98); Alma L. Lopez (12-31-00); Paul W. Green (12-31-00); Sarah B. Duncan (12-31-00); and Karen Angelini (12-31-00). **Clerk of court,** Herb Schaefer. Counties in the Fourth District: Atascosa, Bandera, Bexar, Brooks, Dimmit, Duval, Edwards, Frio, Gillespie, Guadalupe, Jim Hogg, Jim Wells, Karnes, Kendall, Kerr, Kimble, Kinney, La Salle, McMullen, Mason, Maverick, Medina, Menard, Real, Starr, Sutton, Uvalde, Val Verde, Webb, Wilson, Zapata, Zavala.

Fifth District—Dallas: Chief Justice, Linda Thomas (12-31-00). **Justices:** Deborah Hankinson (12-31-00); Sue Lagarde (12-31-00); Mark Whittington (12-31-02); Ed Kinkeade (12-31-00); John Ovard (12-31-00); Joseph B. Morris (12-31-00); Frances Maloney (12-31-02); Ron Chapman (12-31-98); Joseph Devany (12-31-00); Tom James (12-31-00); Carolyn Wright (12-31-98; David Bridges (12-31-02); and Jim Moseley (12-31-02). **Clerk of Court,** Lisa Rombok. Counties in the Fifth District: Collin, Dallas, Grayson, Hunt, Kaufman, Rockwall, Van Zandt.

Sixth District—Texarkana: Chief Justice, William J. Cornelius (12-31-98). **Justices:** Donald R. Ross (12-31-00) and Ben Z. Grant (12-31-02). **Clerk of court,** Tibby Thomas. Counties in the Sixth District: Bowie, Camp, Cass, Delta, Fannin, Franklin, Gregg, Harrison, Hopkins, Hunt, Lamar, Marion, Morris, Panola, Red River, Rusk, Titus, Upshur, Wood.

Seventh District—Amarillo: Chief Justice, John T. Boyd (12-31-00). **Justices:** Carlton B. Dodson (12-31-98); Brian Quinn (12-31-00) and Don H. Reavis (12-31-98). **Clerk of court,** Peggy Culp. Counties in the Seventh District: Armstrong, Bailey, Briscoe, Carson, Castro, Childress, Cochran, Collingsworth, Cottle, Crosby, Dallam, Deaf Smith, Dickens, Donley, Floyd, Foard, Garza, Gray, Hale, Hall, Hansford, Hardeman, Hartley, Hemphill, Hockley, Hutchinson, Kent, King, Lamb, Lipscomb, Lubbock, Lynn, Moore, Motley, Ochiltree, Oldham, Parmer, Potter, Randall, Roberts, Sherman, Swisher, Terry, Wheeler, Wilbarger, Yoakum.

Eighth District—El Paso: Chief Justice, Richard Barajas (12-31-02). **Justices:** Susan Larsen (12-31-98); Ann Crawford McClure (12-31-00; and David W. Chew (12-31-00). **Clerk of court,** Barbara B. Dorris. Counties in the Eighth District: Andrews, Brewster, Crane, Crockett, Culberson, Ector, El Paso, Gaines, Glasscock, Hudspeth, Jeff Davis, Loving, Martin, Midland, Pecos, Presidio, Reagan, Reeves, Terrell, Upton, Ward, Winkler.

Ninth District—Beaumont: Chief Justice, Ronald L. Walker (12-31-02). **Justices:** Don Burgess (12-31-98) and Earl B. Stover (12-31-00). **Clerk of court,** Carol Anne Flores. Counties in the Ninth District: Angelina, Hardin, Jasper, Jefferson, Liberty, Montgomery, Newton, Orange, Polk, San Jacinto, Tyler.

Tenth District—Waco: Chief Justice, Rex Davis (12-31-00). **Justices:** Bob Cummings (12-31-98) and Bill Vance (12-31-02). **Clerk of court,** Imogene Allen. Counties in the Tenth District: Bosque, Brazos, Coryell, Ellis, Falls, Freestone, Hamilton, Hill, Johnson, Leon, Limestone, McLennan, Madison, Navarro, Robertson, Somervell.

Eleventh District—Eastland: Chief Justice, William G. Arnot (12-31-00). **Justices:** Bob Dickenson (12-31-98) and Jim R. Wright (12-31-02). **Clerk of court,** Sherry Williamson. Counties in the Eleventh District: Baylor, Borden, Brown, Callahan, Coleman, Comanche, Dawson, Eastland, Erath, Fisher, Haskell, Howard, Jones, Knox, Mitchell, Nolan, Palo Pinto, Scurry, Shackelford, Stephens, Stonewall, Taylor, Throckmorton.

Twelfth District—Tyler: Chief Justice, Tom B. Ramey Jr. (12-31-02). **Justices:** Charles R. Holcomb (12-31-98) and Arthur Roby Hadden (12-31-00). **Clerk of court,** Cathy S. Lusk. Counties in the Twelfth District: Anderson, Cherokee, Gregg, Henderson, Hopkins, Houston, Kaufman, Nacogdoches, Panola, Rains, Rusk, Sabine, Smith, San Augustine, Shelby, Smith, Upshur, Van Zandt, Wood.

Thirteenth District—Corpus Christi: Chief Justice, Robert J. Seerden (12-31-00). **Justices:** J. Bonner Dorsey (12-31-02); Federico G. Hinojosa Jr. (12-31-00); Linda Reyna Yañez (12-31-98); Melchor Chavez (12-31-00); and Nelda V. Rodriguez (12-31-00). **Clerk of court,** Cathy Wilborn. Counties in the Thirteenth District: Aransas, Bee, Calhoun, Cameron, DeWitt, Goliad, Gonzales, Hidalgo, Jackson, Kenedy, Kleberg, Lavaca, Live Oak, Matagorda, Nueces, Refugio, San Patricio, Victoria, Wharton, Willacy.

Fourteenth District—Houston†: Chief Justice, Paul C. Murphy (12-31-02). **Justices:** Norman Lee (12-31-98); Leslie Brock Yates (12-31-98); Maurice Amidei (12-31-00); John S. Anderson (12-31-00); J. Harvey Hudson (12-31-00); Wanda McKee Fowler (12-31-00); Harriet O'Niell (12-31-02); and Richard H. Edelman (12-31-00). **Clerk of court,** Mary Jane Smart. Counties in the Fourteenth District: Austin, Brazoria, Brazos, Burleson, Chambers, Colorado, Fort Bend, Galveston, Grimes, Harris, Trinity, Walker, Waller, Washington.

*The location of the First Court of Appeals was changed from Galveston to Houston by the 55th Legislature, with the provision that all cases originated in Galveston County be tried in that city and with the further provision that any case may, at the discretion of the court, be tried in either city.

†Because of the heavy workload of the Houston area Court of Appeals, the 60th Legislature, in 1967, provided for the establishment of a Fourteenth Appeals Court at Houston.

Administrative Judicial Districts of Texas

There are nine administrative judicial districts in the state for administrative purposes. An active or retired district judge or an active or retired appellate judge with judicial experience in a district court serves as the Presiding Judge upon appointment by the Governor. They receive extra compensation of $5,000 paid by counties in the respective administrative districts.

The Presiding Judge convenes an annual conference

of the judges in the administrative district to consult on the state of business in the courts. This conference is empowered to adopt rules for the administration of cases in the district. The Presiding Judge may assign active or retired district judges residing within the administrative district to any of the district courts within the administrative district. The Presiding Judge of one administrative district may request the Presiding Judge of another administrative district to assign a judge from that district to sit in a district court located in the administrative district of the Presiding Judge making the request.

The Chief Justice of the Supreme Court of Texas convenes an annual conference of the nine Presiding Judges to determine the need for assignment of judges and to promote the uniform administration of the assignment of judges. The Chief Justice is empowered to assign judges of one administrative district for service in another whenever such assignments are necessary for the prompt and efficient administration of justice.

First District — Pat McDowell, Dallas: Anderson, Bowie, Camp, Cass, Cherokee, Collin, Dallas, Delta, Ellis, Fannin, Franklin, Grayson, Gregg, Harrison, Henderson, Hopkins, Houston, Hunt, Kaufman, Lamar, Marion, Morris, Nacogdoches, Panola, Rains, Red River, Rockwall, Rusk, Shelby, Smith, Titus, Upshur, Van Zandt and Wood.

Second District — Olen Underwood, Conroe: Angelina, Bastrop, Brazoria, Brazos, Burleson, Chambers, Fort Bend, Freestone, Galveston, Grimes, Hardin, Harris, Jasper, Jefferson, Lee, Leon, Liberty, Limestone, Madison, Matagorda, Montgomery, Newton, Orange, Polk, Robertson, Sabine, San Augustine, San Jacinto, Trinity, Tyler, Walker, Waller, Washington and Wharton.

Third District — B. B. Schraub, Seguin: Austin, Bell, Blanco, Bosque, Burnet, Caldwell, Colorado, Comal, Comanche, Coryell, Falls, Fayette, Gonzales, Guadalupe, Hamilton, Hays, Hill, Johnson, Lampasas, Lavaca, Llano,

McLennan, Mason, Milam, Navarro, San Saba, Somervell, Travis and Williamson.

Fourth District — David Peeples, San Antonio: Aransas, Atascosa, Bee, Bexar, Calhoun, DeWitt, Dimmit, Frio, Goliad, Jackson, Karnes, LaSalle, Live Oak, Maverick, McMullen, Refugio, San Patricio, Victoria, Webb, Wilson, Zapata and Zavala.

Fifth District — Darrell Hester, Brownsville: Brooks, Cameron, Duval, Hidalgo, Jim Hogg, Jim Wells, Kenedy, Kleberg, Nueces, Starr and Willacy.

Sixth District — Stephen B. Ables, Kerrville: Bandera, Brewster, Crockett, Culberson, Edwards, El Paso, Gillespie, Hudspeth, Jeff Davis, Kendall, Kerr, Kimble, Kinney, Medina, Pecos, Presidio, Reagan, Real, Sutton, Terrell, Upton, Uvalde and Val Verde.

Seventh District — Weldon Kirk, Sweetwater: Andrews, Borden, Brown, Callahan, Coke, Coleman, Concho, Crane, Dawson, Ector, Fisher, Gaines, Garza, Glasscock, Haskell, Howard, Irion, Jones, Kent, Loving, Lynn, McCulloch, Martin, Menard, Midland, Mills, Mitchell, Nolan, Reeves, Runnels, Schleicher, Scurry, Shackelford, Sterling, Stonewall, Taylor, Throckmorton, Tom Green, Ward and Winkler.

Eighth — Clyde R. Ashworth, Fort Worth: Archer, Clay, Cooke, Denton, Eastland, Erath, Hood, Jack, Montague, Palo Pinto, Parker, Stephens, Tarrant, Wichita, Wise and Young.

Ninth — Ray D. Anderson, Lubbock: Armstrong, Bailey, Baylor, Briscoe, Carson, Castro, Childress, Cochran, Collingsworth, Cottle, Crosby, Dallam, Deaf Smith, Dickens, Donley, Floyd, Foard, Gray, Hale, Hall, Hansford, Hardeman, Hartley, Hemphill, Hockley, Hutchinson, King, Knox, Lamb, Lipscomb, Lubbock, Moore, Motley, Ochiltree, Oldham, Parmer, Potter, Randall, Roberts, Sherman, Swisher, Terry, Wheeler, Wilbarger and Yoakum. ☆

Texas Courts by County, 1996

Below are listed the state district court or courts, court of appeals district, administrative judicial district and U.S. judicial district for each county in Texas. For the names of the district court judges, see table by district number on pages 409-411. For the names of other judges, see listing on pages 404-407.

County	State Dist. Court(s)	Ct. of App'ls Dist.	Adm. Jud. Dist.	U.S. Jud. Dist.
Anderson	3, 87, 349, 369	12	1	E-Tyler
Andrews	109	8	7	W-Mid.-Od.
Angelina	159, 217	9	2	E-Lufkin
Aransas	36, 156, 343	13	4	S-C.Christi
Archer	97	2	8	N-W. Falls
Armstrong	47	7	9	N-Amarillo
Atascosa	81, 218	4	4	W-San Ant.
Austin	155	1, 14	3	S-Houston
Bailey	287	7	9	N-Lubbock
Bandera	216	4	6	W-San Ant.
Bastrop	21, 335	3	2	W-Austin
Baylor	50	11	9	N-W. Falls
Bee	36, 156, 343	13	4	S-C.Christi
Bell	27, 146, 169, 264	3	3	W-Waco
Bexar	37, 45, 57, 73, 131, 144, 150, 166, 175, 186, 187, 224, 225, 226, 227, 285, 288, 289, 290	4	4	W-San Ant.
Blanco	33	3	3	W-Austin
Borden	132	11	7	N-Lubbock
Bosque	220	10	3	W-Waco
Bowie	5, 102, 202	6	1	E-Texark.
Brazoria	23, 149, 239, 300	1, 14	2	S-Galves.
Brazos	85, 272, 361	1, 10, 14	2	S-Houston
Brewster	394	8	6	W-Pecos
Briscoe	110	7	9	N-Amarillo
Brooks	79	4	5	S-C.Christi
Brown	35	11	7	N-S. Ang.
Burleson	21, 335	1, 14	2	W-Austin
Burnet	33	3	3	W-Austin
Caldwell	22, 207, 274	3	3	W-Austin
Calhoun	24, 135, 267	13	4	S-Victoria
Callahan	42	11	7	N-Abilene
Cameron	103, 107, 138, 197, 357	13	5	S-Brownsville
Camp	76, 276	6	1	E-Marshall
Carson	100	7	9	N-Amarillo
Cass	5	6	1	E-Marshall
Castro	64, 242	7	9	N-Amarillo
Chambers	253, 344	1, 14	2	S-Galves.
Cherokee	2, 369	12	1	E-Tyler
Childress	100	7	9	N-Amarillo
Clay	97	2	8	N-W. Falls
Cochran	286	7	9	N-Lubbock
Coke	51	3	7	N-S. Ang.
Coleman	42	11	7	N-S. Ang.
Collin	199, 219, 296, 366, 380	5	1	E-Sherman
Collingsworth	100	7	9	N-Amarillo
Colorado	25, 2nd 25	1, 14	3	S-Houston
Comal	22, 207, 274	3	3	W-San Ant.
Comanche	220	11	3	N-Ft. Worth

County	State Dist. Court(s)	Ct. of App'ls Dist.	Adm. Jud. Dist.	U.S. Jud. Dist.
Concho	119, 198	3	7	N-S. Ang.
Cooke	235	2	8	E-Sherman
Coryell	52	10	3	W-Waco
Cottle	50	7	9	N-W. Falls
Crane	109	8	7	W-Mid.-Od.
Crockett	112	8	6	N-S. Ang.
Crosby	72	7	9	N-Lubbock
Culberson	205, 394	8	6	W-Pecos
Dallam	69	7	9	N-Amarillo
Dallas	14, 44, 68, 95, 101, 116, 134, 160, 162, 191, 192, 193, 194, 195, 203, 204, 254, 255, 256, 265, 282, 283, 291, 292, 298, 301, 302, 303, 304, 305, 330, 363, Cr.1, Cr.2, Cr 3, Cr.4, Cr.5	5	1	N-Dallas
Dawson	106	11	7	N-Lubbock
DeWitt	24, 135, 267	13	4	S-Victoria
Deaf Smith	222	7	9	N-Amarillo
Delta	8, 62	6	1	E-Paris
Denton	16, 158, 211, 362, 367	2	8	E-Sherman
Dickens	110	7	9	N-Lubbock
Dimmit	293, 365	4	4	W-San Ant.
Donley	100	7	9	N-Amarillo
Duval	229	4	5	S-C.Christi
Eastland	91	11	8	N-Abilene
Ector	70, 161, 244, 358	8	7	W-Mid.-Od.
Edwards	63	4	6	W-Del Rio
El Paso	34, 41, 65, 120, 168, 171, 205, 210, 243, 327, 346, 383, 384	8	6	W-El Paso
Ellis	40, 378	10	1	N-Dallas
Erath	266	11	8	N-Ft. Worth
Falls	82	10	3	W-Waco
Fannin	6, 336	6	1	E-Paris
Fayette	155	3	3	S-Houston
Fisher	32	11	7	N-Abilene
Floyd	110	7	9	N-Lubbock
Foard	46	7	9	N-W. Falls
Fort Bend	240, 268, 328	1, 14	2	S-Houston
Franklin	8, 62	6	1	E-Texark.
Freestone	77, 87	10	2	W-Waco
Frio	81, 218	4	4	W-San Ant.
Gaines	106	8	7	N-Lubbock
Galveston	10, 56, 122, 212, 306	1, 14	2	S-Galves.
Garza	106	7	7	N-Lubbock
Gillespie	216	4	6	W-Austin
Glasscock	118	8	7	N-S. Ang.
Goliad	24, 135, 267	13	4	S-Victoria
Gonzales	25, 2nd25	13	3	W-San Ant.
Gray	31, 223	7	9	N-Amarillo
Grayson	15, 59, 336	5	1	E-Sherman
Gregg	124, 188, 307	6, 12	1	E-Tyler
Grimes	12, 278	1, 14	2	S-Houston
Guadalupe	25, 2nd25, 274	4	3	W-San Ant.
Hale	64, 242	7	9	N-Lubbock
Hall	100	7	9	N-Amarillo
Hamilton	220	10	3	W-Waco
Hansford	84	7	9	N-Amarillo
Hardeman	46	7	9	N-W. Falls
Hardin	88, 356	9	2	E-B'mont.
Harris	11, 55, 61, 80, 113, 125, 127, 129, 133, 151, 152, 157, 164, 165, 174, 176, 177, 178, 179, 180, 182, 183, 184, 185, 189, 190, 208, 209, 215, 228, 230, 232, 234, 245, 246, 247, 248, 257, 262, 263, 269, 270, 280, 281, 295, 308, 309, 310, 311, 312, 313, 314, 315, 333, 334, 337, 338, 339, 351	1, 14	2	S-Houston
Harrison	71	6	1	E-Marshall
Hartley	69	7	9	N-Amarillo
Haskell	39	11	7	N-Abilene
Hays	22, 207, 274	3	3	W-Austin
Hemphill	31	7	9	N-Amarillo
Henderson	3, 173, 392	12	1	E-Tyler
Hidalgo	92, 93, 139, 206, 275, 332, 370	13	5	S-McAllen
Hill	66	10	3	W-Waco
Hockley	286	7	9	N-Lubbock
Hood	355	2	8	N-Ft. Worth
Hopkins	8, 62	6, 12	1	E-Paris
Houston	3, 349	12	1	E-Lufkin
Howard	118	11	7	N-Abilene
Hudspeth	205, 394	8	6	W-Pecos
Hunt	196, 354	5, 6	1	N-Dallas
Hutchinson	84, 316	7	9	N-Amarillo
Irion	51	3	7	N-S. Ang.
Jack	271	2	8	N-Ft. Worth
Jackson	24, 135, 267	13	4	S-Victoria
Jasper	1, 1A	9	2	E-B'mont.
Jeff Davis	394	8	6	W-Pecos
Jefferson	58, 60, 136, 172, 252, 279, 317, Cr.	9	2	E-B'mont.
Jim Hogg	229	4	5	S-Laredo
Jim Wells	79	4	5	S-C.Christi
Johnson	18, 249	10	3	N-Dallas
Jones	259	11	7	N-Abilene
Karnes	81, 218	4	4	W-San Ant.
Kaufman	86	5, 12	1	N-Dallas
Kendall	216	4	6	W-San Ant.
Kenedy	105	13	5	S-C.Christi
Kent	39	7	7	N-Lubbock
Kerr	198, 216	4	6	W-San Ant.
Kimble	198	4	6	W-Austin
King	50	7	9	N-W. Falls
Kinney	63	4	6	W-Del Rio
Kleberg	105	13	5	S-C.Christi
Knox	50	11	9	N-W. Falls
La Salle	81, 218	4	4	S-Laredo
Lamar	6, 62	6	1	E-Paris
Lamb	154	7	9	N-Lubbock
Lampasas	27	3	3	W-Austin
Lavaca	25, 2nd 25	13	3	S-Victoria
Lee	21, 335	3	2	W-Austin
Leon	12, 87, 278	10	2	W-Waco
Liberty	75, 253	9	2	E-B'mont.
Limestone	77, 87	10	2	W-Waco
Lipscomb	31	7	9	N-Amarillo
Live Oak	36, 156, 343	13	4	S-C.Christi
Llano	33	3	3	W-Austin
Loving	143	8	7	W-Pecos
Lubbock	72, 99, 137, 140, 237, 364	7	9	N-Lubbock
Lynn	106	7	7	N-Lubbock
Madison	12, 278	10	2	S-Houston
Marion	115, 276	6	1	E-Marshall
Martin	118	8	7	W-Mid.-Od.
Mason	33	4	3	W-Austin
Matagorda	23, 130	13	2	S-Galves.
Maverick	293, 365	4	4	W-Del Rio
McCulloch	198	3	7	W-Austin
McLennan	19, 54, 74, 170	10	3	W-Waco
McMullen	36, 156, 343	4	4	S-Laredo
Medina	38	4	6	W-San Ant.
Menard	198	4	7	N-S. Ang.
Midland	142, 238, 318, 385	8	7	W-Mid.-Od.
Milam	20	3	3	W-Waco
Mills	35	3	7	N-S. Ang.
Mitchell	32	11	7	N-Abilene
Montague	97	2	8	N-W. Falls
Montgomery	9, 221, 284, 359, 410	9	2	S-Houston
Moore	69	7	9	N-Amarillo
Morris	76, 276	6	1	E-Marshall
Motley	110	7	9	N-Lubbock
Nacogdoches	145	12	1	E-Lufkin
Navarro	13	10	3	N-Dallas
Newton	1, 1A	9	2	E-B'mont.
Nolan	32	11	7	N-Abilene
Nueces	28, 94, 105, 117, 148, 214, 319, 347	13	5	S-C.Christi
Ochiltree	84	7	9	N-Amarillo

County	State Dist. Court(s)	Ct. of App'ls Dist.	Adm. Jud. Dist.	U.S. Jud. Dist.
Oldham	222	7	9	N-Amarillo
Orange	128, 163, 260	9	2	E-B'mont.
Palo Pinto	29	11	8	N-Ft. Worth
Panola	123	6, 12	1	E-Tyler
Parker	43	2	8	N-Ft. Worth
Parmer	287	7	9	N-Amarillo
Pecos	83, 112	8	6	W-Pecos
Polk	258, 411	9	2	E-Lufkin
Potter	47, 108, 181, 251, 320	7	9	N-Amarillo
Presidio	394	8	6	W-Pecos
Rains	8, 354	12	1	E-Tyler
Randall	47, 181, 251	7	9	N-Amarillo
Reagan	83, 112	8	6	N-S. Ang.
Real	38	4	6	W-San Ant.
Red River	6, 102	6	1	E-Paris
Reeves	143	8	7	W-Pecos
Refugio	24, 135, 267	13	4	S-Victoria
Roberts	31	7	9	N-Amarillo
Robertson	82	10	2	W-Waco
Rockwall	382	5	1	N-Dallas
Runnels	119	3	7	N-S. Ang.
Rusk	4	6, 12	1	E-Tyler
Sabine	1, 273	12	2	E-Lufkin
San Augustine	1, 273	12	2	E-Lufkin
San Jacinto	9, 258, 411	9	2	S-Houston
San Patricio	36, 156, 343	13	4	S-C.Christi
San Saba	33	3	3	W-Austin
Schleicher	51	3	7	N-S. Ang.
Scurry	132	11	7	N-Lubbock
Shackelford	259	11	7	N-Abilene
Shelby	123, 273	12	1	E-Lufkin
Sherman	69	7	9	N-Amarillo
Smith	7, 114, 241, 321	12	1	E-Tyler
Somervell	18, 249	10	3	W-Waco
Starr	229, 381	4	5	S-McAllen
Stephens	90	11	8	N-Abilene
Sterling	51	3	7	N-S. Ang.
Stonewall	39	11	7	N-Abilene
Sutton	112	4	6	N-S. Ang.
Swisher	64, 242	7	9	N-Amarillo
Tarrant	17, 48, 67, 96, 141, 153, 213, 231, 233, 236, 297, 322, 323, 324, 325, 342, 348, 352, 360, 371, 372, Cr.1, Cr.2, Cr.3, Cr.4	2	8	N-Ft. Worth
Taylor	42, 104, 326, 350	11	7	N-Abilene
Terrell	63	8	6	W-Del Rio
Terry	121	7	9	N-Lubbock
Throckmorton	39	11	7	N-Abilene
Titus	76, 276	6	1	E-Texark.
Tom Green	51, 119, 340	3	7	N-S. Ang.
Travis	53, 98, 126, 147, 167, 200, 201, 250, 261, 299, 331, 345, 353	3	3	W-Austin
Trinity	258, 411	1, 14	2	E-Lufkin
Tyler	1A, 88	9	2	E-Lufkin
Upshur	115	6, 12	1	E-Marshall
Upton	83, 112	8	6	W-Mid.-Od.
Uvalde	38	4	6	W-Del Rio
Val Verde	63	4	6	W-Del Rio
Van Zandt	294	5, 12	1	E-Tyler
Victoria	24, 135, 267, 377	13	4	S-Victoria
Walker	12, 278	1, 14	2	S-Houston
Waller	9, 155	1, 14	2	S-Houston
Ward	143	8	7	W-Pecos
Washington	21, 335	1, 14	2	W-Austin
Webb	49, 111, 341	4	4	S-Laredo
Wharton	23, 329	13	2	S-Houston
Wheeler	31	7	9	N-Amarillo
Wichita	30, 78, 89	2	8	N-W. Falls
Wilbarger	46	7	9	N-W. Falls
Willacy	103, 107, 138, 197, 357	13	5	S-Brownsville
Williamson	26, 277, 368	3	3	W-Austin
Wilson	81, 218	4	4	W-San Ant.
Winkler	109	8	7	W-Pecos
Wise	271	2	8	N-Ft. Worth
Wood	114, 294	6, 12	1	E-Tyler
Yoakum	121	7	9	N-Lubbock
Young	90	2	8	N-W. Falls
Zapata	49	4	4	S-Laredo
Zavala	293, 365	4	4	W-Del Rio

District Judges in Texas, 1997

Below are the names of all district judges in Texas listed in district court order. To determine which judges have jurisdiction in specific counties, refer to the table on pages 407-409.

Source: Texas Judicial System Directory 1997, Office of Court Administration.

Court	Judge	Court	Judge	Court	Judge
1	Joe Bob Golden	21	John L. Placke	41	Mary Anne Bramblett
1A	Monte D. Lawlis	22	Charles R. Ramsay	42	John Wilson Weeks
2	John Robert Adamson	23	Ben Hardin	43	James O. Mullin
3	James N. Parsons III	24	Joseph P. Kelly	44	Candace G. Tyson
4	J. Clay Gossett	25	Dwight E. Peschel	45	Carol R. Haberman
5	Jack Carter	2nd 25	Gus J. Strauss	46	Tom Neely
6	Jim D. Lovett	26	Billy Ray Stubblefield	47	David Gleason
7	Louis B. Gohmert Jr.	27	Joe Carroll	48	Robert (Bob) McCoy
8	Robert Newsom	28	Nanette Hasette	49	Manuel R. Flores
9	Frederick E. Edwards	29	David Cleveland	50	David Wayne Hajek
10	David E. Garner	30	Robert P. Brotherton	51	Barbara L. Walther
11	Mark Davidson	31	M. Kent Sims	52	Philip H. Zeigler
12	William Lee McAdams	32	Weldon Kirk	53	Mary Pearl Williams
13	John Howard Jackson	33	Guilford L. "Gil" Jones	54	George Allen
14	John McClellan Marshall	34	William E. Moody	55	Kathleen S. Stone
15	James Fry	35	Stephen Ellis	56	Norma Venso
16	John Narsutis	36	Ronald M. Yeager	57	Charles A. Gonzalez
17	Fred W. Davis	37	David Berchelmann Jr.	58	James William Mehaffy Jr.
18	C. C. (Kit) Cooke	38	Mickey Ray Pennington	59	Rayburn M. (Rim) Nall Jr.
19	Bill Logue	39	Charles L. Chapman	60	James Gary Sanderson
20	Charles E. Lance	40	Gene Knize	61	John Donovan

Court	Judge
62	Jim Noble Thompson
63	George M. Thurmond
64	Jack R. Miller
65	Alfredo Chavez
66	F.B. (Bob) McGregor Jr.
67	Jon Barton
68	Gary Hall
69	Ron Enns
70	Jay Gibson
71	Bonnie Leggat
72	J. Blair Cherry Jr.
73	Andy Mireles
74	Alan M. Mayfield
75	J.C. "Zeke" Zbranek
76	Jimmy L. White
77	Horace Dickson Black Jr.
78	John Keith Nelson
79	Terry A. Canales
80	Scott Reiter Link
81	Olin B. Strauss
82	Robert M. Stem
83	Alex R. Gonzalez
84	William D. (Bill) Smith
85	J.D. Langley
86	Glen M. Ashworth
87	Sam Bill Bournias
88	Earl Stover III
89	Juanita Pavlick
90	Stephen O. Crawford
91	Steven R. Herod
92	Ed Aparicio
93	Fernando Mancias
94	Jack E. Hunter
95	Sally Montgomery
96	Jeff Walker
97	Roger E. Towery
98	Jeanne Meurer
99	Mackey K. Hancock
100	David M. McCoy
101	Jay Patterson
102	John F. Miller Jr.
103	Menton Murray Jr.
104	Billy John Edwards
105	J. Manuel Banales
106	George H. Hansard
107	Benjamin Euresti Jr.
108	Abe Lopez
109	James L. Rex
110	Randy Hollums
111	Tony A. Zardenetta
112	Brock Jones Jr.
113	Patricia Hancock
114	Cynthia Stevens Kent
115	Lauren L. Parish
116	Martin Richter
117	Robert Blackmon
118	Robert H. Moore III
119	John E. Sutton
120	Robert Dinsmoor
121	Kelly Glen Moore
122	Frank T. Carmona
123	Guy W. Griffin
124	Alvin G. Khoury
125	Don Wittig
126	Joseph H. Hart
127	Sharolyn P. Wood
128	Patrick Allen Clark
129	Patrick W. Mizell
130	Joseph Ann Ottis
131	John D. Gabriel Jr.
132	Ernie B. Armstrong

Court	Judge
133	Lamar McCorkle
134	Anne Ashby
135	K. Stephen Williams
136	Milton Gunn Shuffield
137	Cecil G. Puryear
138	Robert Garza
139	Leticia Hinojosa
140	Jim Bob Darnell
141	Paul Wendell Enlow
142	George David Gilles
143	Bob Parks
144	Susan D. Reed
145	Jack Pierce
146	Rick Morris
147	Wil Flowers
148	Hilda D. Tagle
149	Robert May
150	Janet P. Littlejohn
151	Carolyn E. Baker
152	Harvey G. Brown Jr.
153	Ken C. Curry
154	Felix Klein
155	Dan R. Beck
156	Joel B. Johnson
157	David M. Medina
158	Phillip Vick
159	Gerald Alton Goodwin
160	David C. Godbey
161	Tryon D. Lewis
162	Bill Rhea
163	David A. Dunn
164	Mary K. (Katie) Kennedy
165	Elizabeth Ray
166	Martha B. Tanner
167	Mike F. Lynch
168	Guadalupe Rivera
169	Oliver Kelley
170	Joe N. Johnson
171	Peter S. Peca Jr.
172	Donald J. Floyd
173	Jack H. Holland
174	George H. Godwin
175	Mary R. Roman
176	James Brian Rains
177	Carol G. Davies
178	William T. Harmon
179	Mike Wilkinson
180	Debbie Mantooth-Stricklin
181	Samuel C. Kiser
182	Jeannie S. Barr
183	Jay W. Burnett
184	Jan Krocker
185	H. Lon Harper
186	Terry McDonald
187	Raymond C. Angelini
188	David Brabham
189	Carolyn Marks Johnson
190	John Phillip Devine
191	David Brooks
192	Merrill L. Hartman
193	Michael J. O'Neill
194	Harold Entz
195	John Nelms
196	Joe M. Leonard
197	Darrell B. Hester
198	Emil Karl Prohl
199	John R. Roach
200	Paul R. Davis Jr.
201	Suzanne Covington
202	Bill Peek

Court	Judge
203	Lana Rolf McDaniel
204	Mark Nancarrow
205	Kathleen H. Olivares
206	Joe B. Evins
207	Jack Hollis Robison
208	Denise Collins
209	Michael Thomas McSpadden
210	Sam M. Paxson
211	Lawrence Dee Shipman
212	Roy Engelke
213	Robert Gill
214	Mike Westergren
215	Dwight Eugene Jefferson
216	Stephen B. Ables
217	David V. Wilson
218	Stella H. Saxon
219	Curt B. Henderson
220	James Edward Morgan
221	Lee G. Alworth
222	David Wesley Gulley
223	Lee Waters
224	David Peeples
225	John J. Specia Jr.
226	Sid L. Harle
227	Mike M. Machado
228	Ted Poe
229	Ricardo H. Garcia
230	(Visiting Judge)
231	Randy Catterton
232	Mary Lou Keel
233	William Wren Harris
234	Scott A. Brister
235	Jerry W. Woodlock
236	Thomas Wilson Lowe III
237	John R. McFall
238	John Hyde
239	J. Ray Gayle III
240	Thomas R. Culver III
241	Diane V. DeVasto
242	Marvin F. Marshall
243	David C. Guaderrama
244	Joe Connally
245	Annette Galik
246	Donald Gene Ritter
247	Bonnie Crane Hellums
248	Werner R. Voigt Jr.
249	Wayne Bridewell
250	John K. Dietz
251	Pat Pirtle
252	Leonard Giblin Jr.
253	W.G. Woods Jr.
254	Dee Miller
255	Don Koons
256	Brenda Garrett Green
257	Linda Motheral
258	Joe Ned Dean
259	Quay Parker
260	Buddie J. Hahn
261	Peter M. Lowry
262	L. Doug Shaver
263	Jim Wallace
264	Martha Jane Trudo
265	Keith Dean
266	Donald R. Jones
267	Whayland W. Kilgore
268	Brady G. Elliott
269	David West
270	John Richard Hall
271	John H. Fostel
272	John M. Delaney

Court	Judge	Court	Judge	Court	Judge
273	John W. Mitchell	315	(Earl) Kent Ellis	357	Rogelio (Roy)Valdez
274	Bill Bender	316	John La Grone	358	Bill McCoy
275	Juan R. Partida	317	Jimmy D. "Skip" Hulett Jr.	359	James H. (Jim) Keeshan
276	William R. (Bill) Porter	318	Dean Rucker	360	V. Sue Koenig
277	John R. Carter	319	Max Bennett	361	Carolyn L. Ruffino
278	Jerry A. Sandel	320	Don Emerson	362	David C. White
279	Robert P. Walker	321	Ruth J. Blake	363	Faith Johnson
280	Tony Lindsay	322	Frank Sullivan	364	Bradley S. Underwood
281	William Franklin Bell	323	Jean Hudson Boyd	365	Amado Abascal III
282	Karen J. Greene	324	Brian A. Carper	366	Nathan E. White Jr.
283	Molly Meredith Francis	325	Judith G. Wells	367	Lee Gabriel
284	Olen Undersood	326	Aleta Hacker	368	Burt Carnes
285	Michael Peden	327	Philip R. (Phil) Martine	369	Bascom W. Bentley III
286	Andy Kupper	328	Tom Stansbury	370	Noe Gonzalez
287	Jack D. Young	329	Daniel R. Sklar	371	James R. Wilson
288	Frank Montalvo	330	Theo Bedard	372	Scott Wisch
289	Carmen Kelsey	331	Bob Perkins	377	Robert C. Cheshire
290	Sharon MacRae	332	Mario E. Ramirez Jr.	378	Roy A. Scoggins Jr.
291	Gerry Meier	333	Joseph "Tad" Halbach Jr.	380	Charles F. Sandoval
292	Mike Keasler	334	Russell Lloyd	381	John A. Pope III
293	Rey Perez	335	H.R. Towslee	382	Sue Pirtle
294	Tommy W. Wallace	336	Ray Felty Grisham	383	Reed W. Leverton
295	Tracy E. Christopher	337	Jim Barr	384	Patrick M. Garcia
296	Betty Ann Caton	338	Mary Bacon	385	Willie Bryan DuBose
297	Everett Young	339	Caprice Cosper	392	Carter W. Tarrance
298	Adolph Canales	340	Dick Alcala	394	Kenneth D. DeHart
299	Jon N. Wisser	341	Elma Teresa Salinas Ender	410	K. Michael Mayes
300	Ogden Bass	342	Bob McGrath	411	Robert Hill Trapp
301	Susan Amanda Rankin	343	Alonzo "Al" T. Rodriguez		
302	Frances A. Harris	344	Carroll E. Wilborn Jr.		
303	Richard Johnson	345	Scott McCown	**Criminal District Courts**	
304	Harold C. "Hal" Gaither	346	Jose J. Baca		
305	Cheryl Lee Shannon	347	Joaquin Villarreal III	Dallas 1	Janice Warder
306	Susan Baker Olsen	348	Dana Womack	Dallas 2	Ed King
307	Robin D. Sage	349	Jerry L. Calhoon	Dallas 3	Robert Francis
308	Georgia Dempster	350	Jesse Aaron Holloway	Dallas 4	John Coleman Creuzot
309	John D. Montgomery	351	Mark Kent Ellis	Dallas 5	Manny D. Alvarez
310	Lisa Ann Millard	352	Bonnie Sudderth	Jefferson	Charles Dana Carver
311	Bill Henderson	353	Margaret A. Cooper	Tarrant 1	Sharen Wilson
312	James Douglas Squier	354	Richard (Rick) Beacom	Tarrant 2	Wayne Francis Salvant
313	Pat Shelton	355	Tom Crum	Tarrant 3	Don Leonard
314	Mary M. Craft	356	Britton Edward Plunk	Tarrant 4	Joe Drago III

State Agencies

On the following pages is information about several of the many state agencies. The agencies themselves supplied this information to the Texas Almanac.

Texas Natural Resource Conservation Commission

Created in 1993, the Texas Natural Resource Conservation Commission (TNRCC), combined the Texas Water Commission, the Texas Air Control Board and several smaller boards and programs into a comprehensive state environmental agency. Along with the responsibilities of the two major agencies, the TNRCC took on the responsibility of dealing with solid waste, drinking water protection, wastewater treatment and performing the functions previously performed by the Water Well Drillers Board and the Board of Irrigators, as well.

One of the TNRCC's primary goals is to protect public health and safety and the environment by reducing the release of pollutants and contaminants, ensuring that waste is properly managed and safely disposed of, and expediting the cleanup of contaminated sites. The agency also manages the state's water resources and enforces compliance with state and federal clean air and water laws.

The agency comprises seven major offices: Water Resource Management, Air Quality, Waste Management, Compliance and Enforcement, Policy and Regulatory Development, Legal Services and Administrative Services. These offices oversee such wide-ranging areas as water runoff from agricultural lands, ozone pollution in highly congested urban areas, leakage from petroleum storage tanks, and water quality in the estuaries of Corpus Christi and Galveston bays.

The executive director of the agency is Dan Pearson. The agency can be contacted at: P.O. Box 13087, Austin 78711-3087; phone (512) 239-1000; fax (512) 463-8317; Internet: http://www.tnrcc.state.tx.us/ The 24-hour pollution-reporting hotline is (512) 463-7727. ☆

The General Land Office

Source: General Land Office of Texas

History of the General Land Office

The **Texas General Land Office** is one of the oldest governmental entities in the state, dating back to the Republic of Texas. The practice of having a commissioner to administer public lands reaches even further back into Texas history, beginning with **Spanish and Mexican land grants.** The earliest Spanish grants in Texas were to missions. The grant to the San José mission in San Antonio, dated 1720, is the oldest surviving Texas land grant. The earliest land grants to settlers were for lands within the limits of San Fernando de Béxar, present-day San Antonio, following the formal establishment of that town in 1731.

Settlement and land distribution in Texas increased dramatically after Mexican independence in 1821. Desiring to enlarge its small population, the state of Coahuila y Texas enacted a colonization law to encourage settlement by Mexicans and foreigners alike through grants of public land at nominal cost.

The Mexican government also began making agreements with contractors, known as **empresarios,** to assist in recruiting and settling colonists. Stephen F. Austin was the most influential and successful of these empresarios. Authority to issue titles, as well as to settle disputes regarding the land grants, rested with commissioners, government officials appointed specifically for this function.

Other features of the Mexican public-land system adopted by Texas after independence, are the homestead laws and the vara as the unit of land measurement.

The sale of public lands was temporarily suspended during the war for Texas independence from Mexico.

The **first General Land Office** was established in the constitution of the Republic of Texas in 1836, and the first Texas Congress enacted the provision into law in 1837. The General Land Office was established to oversee the distribution of public lands, to register titles (called patents) on land grants, and to maintain records. The Mexican system had provided one land commissioner for each colony; the General Land Office established by the Republic was under the direction of a single commissioner. President Sam Houston appointed John P. Borden as the first land commissioner in 1837. Before any applications for titles on land grants could be issued, however, Borden had to locate and gather the land records of the various colonial land offices. Establishing the relative locations of previous grants was essential to ensure that new land grants did not overlap old ones.

During the nine years that the Republic of Texas existed, the government issued a variety of land grants. The congress used land grants to recruit soldiers, to reward military service and to repay loans. To attract immigration, headright grants were issued, depending on the settler's marital status and date of arrival. For example, all heads of households in Texas as of March 2, 1836, were entitled to a league and a labor of land (about 4,605 acres). Single men could claim a third of a league. A board of land commissioners was established in each county to issue headright certificates. In the 10 years Texas existed as a Republic, it allotted 41,570,733 acres to encourage settlement, to reward veterans of the War for Independence, to pay the Republic's debts and to finance its operations.

During negotiations for Texas' entry into the Union in 1844, a proposal that the United States pay $10 million of the Republic's debts and acquire 175 million acres of Texas' public domain was considered. However, opponents to statehood in the U.S. Congress felt that Texas' lands were not worth the assumption of the $10 million debt and refused to make the trade. In the final resolution for annexation, Texas was to keep its public domain and the U.S. was to disclaim any responsibility for Texas' debt. **Texas officially came into the Union on Dec. 29, 1845,** keeping both its debt and its public lands.

In the early years of statehood, Texas established the precedent of using its vast public domain for public benefit. The first use was to sell or trade off land to eliminate the huge debt remaining from the War for Independence and early years of the Republic. A western area of 67 million acres, now part of New Mexico, Colorado, Oklahoma, Kansas and Wyoming, was transferred to the United States by the Texas legislature on Nov. 25, 1850. Texas received $10 million in government bonds. The state had shed all its debts by 1855 and still had over 98 million acres of open domain. Texas gave away land for internal improvements, homesteads, veterans grants, capitol construction, and for settlement of boundary disputes. More than 32 million acres were given away to promote railroad construction. For every acre granted to the railroads, an equal amount was set aside for public use. As a result, 50 million acres were dedicated as an endowment to public schools and colleges.

Perhaps the most visible of these land grants was the appropriation of 3,050,000 acres to build the state capitol. Capitol lands were located across 10 different counties in the Panhandle and formed the basis for the famous XIT Ranch.

The public domain was closed in 1898 when the Texas Supreme Court declared that there was no more vacant and unappropriated land in Texas. Only some small tracts were left, and in 1900, all remaining unappropriated land was set aside by the Texas legislature for the benefit of the public schools.

Today 20.3 million acres are considered to be in the public domain. This includes almost 4 million acres of submerged coastal lands, which are bays, inlets and the area from the Texas shoreline to the three-marine-league line (10.36 miles) in the Gulf of Mexico. In addition, more than one million acres are estimated to make up the state's riverbeds and vacant areas. The **University of Texas System** holds title to 2,109,000 fee acres, and other state agencies or special schools hold title to approximately 2 million acres. Texas owns mineral rights alone in approximately 7.5 million acres covered under the Relinquishment Act, the Free Royalty Act and the various sales acts, and has outright ownership to approximately 784,264 upland acres, mostly west of the Pecos. Texas has liens on 1.5 million acres of land in the active accounts of the **Veterans Land Board** and another 1.7 million acres of excess land that are not calculated into any category.

Tidelands

Perhaps the most valuable segment of the Texas public domain is its **coastal submerged land,** and for some time, there were serious questions about the state's ownership. The Republic of Texas had proclaimed its Gulf boundaries as three marine leagues, recognized by international law as traditional national boundaries. These boundaries were never seriously questioned when Texas joined the Union in 1845, and Texas continued to claim jurisdiction. A congressional resolution in 1930 authorized the U.S. Attorney General to file suit to establish the offshore lands as properties of the federal government.

The legal question was more important to Texas in the 20th century than it would have been upon entering the Union, since offshore oil and gas production had become a source of tremendous income to the state. Gulf of Mexico leases between the three-mile and the three-marine-league limit (the area claimed by the federal government) have brought the state approximately $1.5 billion in revenue since the first oil lease there in 1922. Congress returned the disputed lands to Texas in 1953, and the **Supreme Court finally confirmed Texas' ownership** to the 1,878,394 acres in 1960. (See Tidelands History in 1972-73 Texas Almanac.)

In 1978, the federal government also granted states a "fair and equitable" share of the revenues from offshore federal leases within three miles of the states' outermost boundary. The states did not receive any such revenue until April 1986, when Congress clarified the meaning of "fair and equitable" through additional legislation. Under the 1986 law, coastal states are entitled to 27 percent of all revenues in perpetuity from federal leases within three miles of the state-federal boundary. In addition, Texas received a one-time settlement to cover the 1978 to 1985 period amounting to $426 million in fiscal year 1986 and a deferred payment of $134 million over 15 years.

The General Land Office handles leases and revenue accounting on all lands dedicated to the **Permanent School Fund** and on land owned by various state agencies. The **Land Commissioner**, two members of **The University of Texas Board of Regents** and one **Texas A&M University Board of Regents** member make up the **Board for Lease** of lands dedicated to the **Permanent University Fund**. Revenue accounting for income from Permanent University Lands is processed by The University of Texas. Investment income from the fund is divided approximately two-thirds to one-third between The University of Texas and Texas A&M University, respectively. As of December 1996, the **Permanent University Fund** had reached a book value of more than $5 billion; the **Permanent School Fund** had a book value of more than $10.14 billion.

All activities on state lands are reviewed for their environmental impact, and restrictions are placed in offshore drilling leases where needed to protect resources.

Veterans Programs
Veterans Land Program
In 1946, the Legislature created a bond program to aid veterans in purchasing farm land. Up to $1.5 billion in bonding authority has been authorized over the years in a series of constitutional amendments; as of Jan. 1, 1997, more than $1.26 billion of the bonds had been sold to fund loans.

Loans cannot exceed $40,000, and tracts purchased through the program must be at least five acres. To date, more than 113,000 veterans have participated in the land program, purchasing more than 4.8 million acres of land.

Veterans Housing Assistance Program
The 68th Legislature created the Veterans Housing Assistance Program, which also is funded through bond proceeds. Over the years, the people of Texas have passed constitutional amendments authorizing the selling of $2 billion in bonds to finance this program. To date, $1.245 billion in bonds have been sold to fund housing loans.

Eligible veterans may borrow up to $45,000 toward the purchase of a home; the balance of the purchase price is financed through private-sector lending institutions. When the low-interest veterans loan is combined with private-sector interest rates, monthly payments are significantly reduced. Since the program began operation in January 1984, more than 37,000 veterans have received housing loans.

Veterans Home Improvement Program
In 1986, the Veterans Land Board implemented the Veterans Home Improvement Program, which is funded through the Veterans Housing Assistance Program. This program allows Texas Veterans to borrow up to $25,000 to make substantial home repairs and improvements.

To date, more than 2,800 veterans have received home improvement loans. More than $40 million has been loaned since the program's inception.

All three programs are administered by the **Texas Veterans Land Board**, which is chaired by the Commissioner of the General Land Office. The bonded debt for the programs and all administrative costs are completely financed by the veterans who use the programs; there is no cost to Texas taxpayers. Eligible veterans may participate in each of the three veterans programs once.

Details about the programs may be obtained from the Texas Veterans Land Board by calling toll free 1-800-252-VETS. ☆

Distribution of the Public Lands of Texas

Purpose	Acres
Settlers	**68,027,108**
Spain and Mexico	24,583,923
Spanish and Mexican Grants south of the Nueces River, recognized by Act of Feb. 10, 1852	3,741,241
Headrights	30,360,002
Republic colonies	4,494,806
Pre-emption land	4,847,136
Military	**9,874,262**
Bounty	5,354,250
Battle donations	1,162,240
Veterans donations	1,377,920
Confederate	1,979,852
Improvements	**37,155,714**
Road	27,716
Navigation	4,261,760
Irrigation	584,000
Ships	17,000
Manufacturing	111,360
Railroads	32,153,878
Education	**52,329,168**
University, public school and eleemosynary institutions	52,329,168
Total of distributed lands	**167,386,252**

Texas Department of Commerce

The Texas Department of Commerce is the state's major economic development agency. Its mission is to create a positive business climate that attracts new companies, promotes Texas as a travel destination and trains today's work force for tomorrow's high-skill, high-wage jobs. It disseminates information on international trade, worker-training incentives, tourism and other business matters. The department's three program divisions are:

• The **Business Development Division** endeavors to retain and expand the state's existing business and industrial base while marketing Texas nationally and internationally as the best geographic location and business climate in which to expand or locate a company. This division provides assistance in the areas of research and information; small-business assistance; and Texas Marketplace, an electronic bulletin board and business-referral system.

• The **Tourism Division** promotes Texas as a premiere travel destination and is known for its advertising and media-relations programs.

• The **Business and Fiscal Services Division** works to increase the global competitiveness of Texas businesses by administering incentive programs. This division performs the marketing and administration of the Smart Jobs Fund program, Texas Manufacturing Assistance Center network program and Capital Development program.

Executive director of the department is Brenda F. Arnett. The agency can be contacted at P.O. Box 12728, Austin 78711-2728; phone (512) 936-0100; fax (512) 936-0303; Internet: http://www.tdoc.state.tx.us/ or http://www.traveltex.com ☆

Department of Human Services

Source: Texas Department of Human Services

The **Texas Department of Human Services (DHS)**, administers programs that provide financial and medical assistance and social services to those who are eligible. The department's headquarters are in Austin, but its services are available in all 254 counties.

The **Texas Board of Human Services** is responsible for adoption of most policies, rules and regulations of the department. (See **State Boards and Commissions** for membership.)

Department services are provided through 10 administrative regions, each supervised by a regional administrator. The department's headquarters staff develops program policy and provides support functions, such as legal, personnel, data-processing and fiscal services, that serve all programs.

DHS has two major program divisions: Client Self-support Services and Long-Term Care Services.

Client Self-Support Services

The emphasis in Client Self-support Services (CSS) is providing temporary assistance to low-income families while encouraging the families to become self-sufficient. CSS programs include those that provide assistance to meet basic needs, along with support services to promote economic independence.

• The **Aid to Families with Dependent Children (AFDC)** program is funded through the federal Temporary Assistance for Needy Families block grant. The program provides a small cash grant to needy dependent children and the parents or relatives with whom they live. Financial need must be the result of the absence or disability of a parent or the unemployment of the principal wage-earner parent. Under Texas welfare reform measures, many adults are limited to no more than three years of AFDC grants. The average household of one adult with two children receives a maximum AFDC grant of $188 per month.

The DHS requires heads of AFDC households to adhere to Personal Responsibility Agreements in return for an AFDC grant. The agreement requires that children attend school regularly; children are immunized against preventable diseases; parents provide DHS with information on absent parents who owe child support; parents seek employment as soon as possible and participate in state job-training services. In fiscal year 1996, a monthly average of 690,000 Texans received AFDC.

• The **Food Stamp program** is an entirely federally funded program that provides financial assistance to low-income families to supplement their food-purchasing power and help them to obtain a nutritionally adequate diet. DHS delivers food assistance with the Lone Star debit card under the Electronic Benefit Transfer system. In fiscal year 1996, a monthly average of 2.4 million Texans received food-stamp benefits.

Long-Term Care Services

The DHS provides assistance to Medicaid-eligible clients who are elderly or disabled in community-based programs or nursing facilities. Clients must meet three eligibility criteria to be certified for nursing-facility services: financial need, medical necessity and preadmission screening and annual resident review. DHS also administers the Community Care Services program to help prevent or delay the long-term institutionalization of eligible individuals through community-based services. This program provides in-home services, such as family care, primary home care, electronic monitoring and home-delivered meals. Out-of-home services include day-activity and health services, adult foster-care services and respite services. Residential care is available for those persons who need 24-hour supervision but not daily nursing intervention.

The **DHS Long-Term Care Regulatory** program has responsibility for regulating 1,292 licensed nursing facilities. DHS also licenses personal-care homes, which provide assisted living but not medical care, and adult day health-care facilities.

Other DHS programs include an entirely federally funded **Refugee Resettlement program**. Cash and medical assistance for refugees is limited to their first eight months of residence in the United States.

The **Disaster Assistance program** provides grants to families who are victims of a presidentially declared disaster, such as tornados, floods and hurricanes. Victims are eligible for assistance from this state-administered federal program if they do not have insurance and cannot qualify for low-interest loans from the Small Business Administration.

The **DHS Family Violence program** provides partial funding to 64 state-contracted family-violence shelters, which provided a safe haven to 10,816 women and 14,981 children in fiscal year 1996. The state-funded shelters also provide nonresidential services, which include counseling, legal advocacy, medical care, educational arrangements for children and employment assistance.

DHS provides services to more than 3 million Texans each year. Most department services are provided to people with incomes considerably lower than the federal poverty guidelines.

Costs of Services

Costs of most services are shared by the state and federal governments. Expenditures for fiscal year 1997 are as follows:

Family Income Assistance . . .	$1,008,984,689
Long-term Care Services	2,147,070,427
All other expenditures.	82,953,542
Grand Total	$3,239,008,658

Texas Youth Commission

Source: Texas Youth Commission

The following institutions are under the direction of the **Texas Youth Commission**, the agency that administers the juvenile corrections system of the state. The date of founding of each facility, the superintendent's name and the average daily population are included. In the case of newly constructed schools, where the daily population at press time was far below eventual population, the capacity of the facility is included.

Brownwood State School — Brownwood; 1970; Gaylon Garrison; 274.

Corsicana State Home and School — Corsicana; 1897; Chester Clay Jr.; 145.

Crockett State School — Crockett; 1947 (as **Brady State School for Colored Girls**; changed to **Crockett State School for Girls**; and in 1975 name changed to present form); Rey Gomez; 193.

Evins Regional Juvenile Center — Edinburg; 1990; (Vacancy); 101.

Gainesville State School — Gainesville; 1915; Jerry Day; 366.

Giddings State Home and School — Giddings; 1972; Stan DeGerolami; 325.

J.W. Hamilton Jr. State School — Bryan; 1997; Robert E. Woods; 73 (capacity 696).

Jefferson County State School — Beaumont; 1995; Marie Murdoch; 238.

Marlin Assessment and Orientation Unit — Marlin; 1995; Alan Steen; 355.

San Saba State School — San Saba; 1996; Lydia Barnard; 345.

Texas Youth Commission Bootcamp — Sheffield; 1995; Al Elizondo (commandant); 48.

Victory Field Correctional Academy — Vernon; 1997; Lemuel "Chip" Harrison; 12 (capacity 336).

West Texas State School — Pyote; 1966; Johnny Williams; 244.

In addition, the commission operates nine **half-way houses**, each of which has an average daily population of between 18 and 24 youth. These are located in Austin, Corpus Christi, Dallas, El Paso, Fort Worth, Harlingen, McAllen, Roanoke and San Antonio.

Steve Robinson is executive director of the commission. ☆

Texas Department of Criminal Justice

The Texas Department of Criminal Justice, formed by the Texas Legislature in 1989, is composed of seven divisions. Those most in the public view are:

• The **Institutional Division**, which manages the Department's prisons (more details below).

• The **Pardons and Paroles Division** is responsible for processing offenders for release on parole or mandatory supervision and the subsequent provision of supervision and rehabilitative services for reintegration into the community. In fiscal year 1996, 78,000 adult offenders were under parole or mandatory supervision. More than 27,000 offenders were processed for release from prison and other facilities.

• The **State Jail Division** was established in 1993 to provide community-oriented rehabilitation for property and drug offenders. As of July 15, 1997, there were 17 state jails with a total capacity of 24,261, located in Atascosita, *Austin, *Bartlett, Beaumont, Bonham, *Dallas, Dayton, Edinburg, El Paso, Gatesville, *Henderson, Houston, Hutchins, *Jacksboro, Plainview, *Raymondville, San Antonio, San Diego and Winnsboro. Those marked with an asterisk (*) are operated by private companies. In February 1996, the State Jail Division assumed administrative management of the Substance Abuse Felony Punishment facilities. As of July 15, 1997, there were SAFP facilities in Breckenridge, Brownwood, Burnet, Dayton, Hondo, Plainview, San Diego and Winnsboro, with a total capacity of 4,072.

• The **Community Justice Assistance Division,** which provides punishment, supervision and rehabilitation programs, as well as facilities within communities, for persons under probation supervision. In fiscal 1996, this division provided services to 241,020 adult felony probationers and 188,644 misdemeanor probationers.

The remaining four divisions are primarily internal in scope: **Programs and Services, Operations and Logistics** and **Financial Services.**

Total monies appropriated to the TDCJ by the Texas Legislature for the 1998-99 biennium amounted to $5.46 billion.

The **Texas Board of Criminal Justice** guides the administration and operation of the department in the areas of policy, planning and budgetary matters. For a list of members, see Boards and Commissions list following this article.

Allan B. Polunsky has been board chairman since March 1995. The TDCJ executive director is Wayne Scott.

Institutional Division of the TDCJ

The Institutional Division is responsible for the confinement of adult felony offenders who are sentenced to prison (juvenile offenders are under the jurisdiction of the Texas Youth Commission). The division's headquarters are in Huntsville, with Gary Johnson as director.

The Institutional Division currently consists of 71 major facilities: 57 prisons and 14 transfer facilities, as well as one boot camp, four medical facilities, three psychiatric facilities and two work camps. The **total number of inmates** on hand at the end of fiscal year 1996 was 124,604. This population compares with 18,151 on Aug. 31, 1975.

The **Agriculture Division** operates and manages 138,823 acres located in 35 counties. It employs more than 300 full-time employees and uses 5,800 inmates each year on its 45 different units. They operate prison packing plants, cotton gins and feed mills as well as raising crops and tending livestock.

Texas Correctional Industries operates 44 factories or plants at 36 prison units. These industries utilizing inmate labor produce goods and services for the TDCJ and other tax-supported agencies and governmental entities. Product categories include automobile repairs and products, textile and leather products and metal and wood products. As of August 31, 1996, these industries employed 6,880 inmates and generated sales of more than $96.5 million.

These enterprises help keep the daily costs per inmate to $39.51. This compares with $44.40 in 1995.

In 1969, an **independent school** (Windham School District) was created to offer education in grades 1-12 and special education leading to a GED or high-school diploma. Participation is mandatory for those who cannot read at the sixth-grade level. Participation is voluntary for those deemed literate but who have less than a high- school diploma. In fiscal 1996, more than 63,000 inmates participated in the WSD's programs; 8,296 GED certificates, 7,094 career and technology education certificates and 3,562 vocational certificates were awarded.

Cooperative programs in **higher education** are being implemented on several units at nearby junior colleges, leading to associate degrees. Four-year and graduate degrees can be earned through cooperating senior colleges and universities. In fiscal 1996, 322 associate degrees, 43 baccalaureate degrees and 20 master's degrees were conferred on inmates.

Inmate Profile

Age/Sex/Ethnicity

94 % are male	47 % are black
Average age: 33	28 % are white
	25 % are Hispanic

Sentences/Length of Time Served

Average sentence: 23 years
Average part of sentence served: 25%
More than 50% of inmates have been in prison before.

Education

Average IQ: 92
More than 60% don't have a high school diploma.
Average education achievement score: 7th grade

Rehabilitative programs are also available in the fields of physiological and psychiatric health care, varied recreational programs, legal services, religious activities, inmate self-help groups, work-release programs, job placement services, pre-release programs and support programs in conjunction with other state agencies.

Prison Units

Please note that the town listed is the nearest one to the facility, although the unit may actually be in another county. For instance, the Middleton transfer unit is listed as being near Abilene, which is in Taylor County, but the unit is across the county line in Jones County.

Allred, Wichita Falls, Wichita Co.; **Beto I,** Tennessee Colony, Anderson Co.; **Boyd,** Teague, Freestone Co.; **Briscoe,** Dilley, Frio Co.; **Central,** Sugar Land, Fort Bend Co.; **Clemens,** Brazoria, Brazoria Co.; **Clements,** Amarillo, Potter Co.; **Coffield,** Tennessee Colony, Anderson Co.; **Connally,** Kenedy, Karnes Co.; **Dalhart,** Dalhart, Dallam Co.; **Daniel,** Snyder, Scurry Co.; **Darrington,** Rosharon, Brazoria Co.; **Diagnostic,** Huntsville, Walker Co.; **Eastham,** Lovelady, Houston Co.; **Ellis,** Huntsville, Walker Co.; **Estelle,** Huntsville, Walker Co.; **Ferguson,** Midway, Madison Co.; **Gatesville,** Gatesville, Coryell County (Women's Unit); **Goree,** Huntsville, Walker Co.; **Hightower,** Dayton, Liberty Co.; **Hilltop,** Gatesville, Coryell Co.; **Hobby,** Marlin, Falls Co.; **Hodge,** Rusk, Cherokee Co.; **Hospital Galveston,** Galveston, Galveston Co.; **Hughes,** Gatesville, Coryell Co.; **Huntsville,** Walker Co.; **Jester I, II, III and IV,** Richmond, Fort Bend Co.; **Jordan,** Pampa, Gray Co.; **LeBlanc,** Beaumont, Jefferson Co.; **Lewis,** Woodville, Tyler Co.; **Luther,** Navasota, Grimes Co.; **Lynaugh,** Fort Stockton, Pecos Co.; **McConnell,** Beeville, Bee Co.; **Michael,** Tennessee Colony, Anderson Co.; **Montford,** Lubbock, Lubbock Co.; **Mountain View,** Gatesville, Coryell County (Women's Unit); **Murray,** Gatesville, Coryell Co.; **Neal,** Amarillo, Potter Co.; **Pack,** Navasota, Grimes Co.; **Powledge,** Palestine, Anderson Co.; **Ramsey I, II and III,** Rosharon, Brazoria Co.; **Retrieve,** Angleton, Brazoria Co.; **Roach,** Childress, Childress Co.; **Robertson,** Abilene, Taylor Co.; **Skyview,** at Rusk State Hospital, Cherokee Co.; **Smith,** Lamesa, Dawson Co.; **Stevenson,** Cureo, DeWitt Co.; **Stiles,** Beaumont, Jefferson Co.; **Telford,** New Boston, Bowie Co.; **Terrell,** Livingston, Polk Co.; **Texas City,** Texas City, Galveston Co.; **Torres,** Hondo, Medina Co.; **Wallace,** Colorado City, Mitchell Co.; **Western RMF,** Lubbock, Lubbock Co.; **Wynne,** Huntsville, Walker Co.

Transfer Units

Cotulla, Cotulla, LaSalle Co.; **Diboll,** Diboll, Angelina Co.; **Fort Stockton,** Fort Stockton, Pecos Co.; **Garza East & West,** Beeville, Bee Co.; **Goodman,** Jasper, Jasper Co.; **Gurney,** Tennessee Colony, Anderson Co.; **Holliday,** Huntsville, Walker Co.; **Middleton,** Abilene, Jones Co.; **Moore, C.,** Bonham, Fannin Co.; **Rudd,** Brownfield, Terry Co.; **Segovia,** Edinburg, Hidalgo Co.; **Tulia,** Tulia, Swisher Co.

Parole-ISF: Pampa, Pampa, Gray Co.

Private Prisons

Bridgeport, Wise Co.; Cleveland, Liberty Co.; Diboll, Angelina Co.; Kyle, Hays Co.; Lockhart, Caldwell Co.; Overton, Smith Co.; and Venus, Johnson Co. ☆

Texas State Boards and Commissions

Following is a list of appointees to state boards and commissions, as well as names of other state officials, revised to July 1, 1997. Information includes, where available, (1) date of creation of agency; (2) whether the position is elective or appointive; (3) length of term; (4) number of members; (5) names of appointees, their hometowns and the dates of the terminations of their terms. In some instances the dates of expiration of terms have already passed; in such cases, no new appointment had been made by press time, and the official is continuing to fill the position until a successor can be named. Most positions marked "apptv." are appointed by the Governor. Where otherwise, appointing authority is given. Most advisory boards are not listed. Salaries for commissioners and administrators are those that were authorized by the appropriations bill passed by the 75th Legislature for the 1998-99 biennium; at press time, the salaries had not yet received final approval.

Accountancy, Texas State Board of Public - (1945 with 2-year terms; reorganized 1959 as 9-member board with 6-yr. overlapping terms; number of members increased to 12 in 1979; increased to 15 in 1989); per diem and expenses; 15 members: Nita J. Clyde, Dallas (1/31/99); K. Michael Conaway, Midland (1/31/01); Jerry A. Davis, Houston (1/31/01); April L. Eyeington, College Station (1/31/99); Gwen B. Gilbert, Dallas (1/31/03); Rebecca Beard Junker, Richmond (1/31/03); Wanda Lorenz, Dallas (1/31/99); Frank W. Maresh, Houston (1/31/99); Roel (Roy) Martinez, McAllen (1/31/99); Jimmie L. Mason, Lubbock (1/31/01); Reagan S. McCoy, San Antonio (1/31/03); Lou Miller, San Antonio (1/31/01); Janet F. Parnell, Canadian (1/31/01); Barbara J. Thomas, Houston (1/31/03); I. Lee Wilson, Rockwall (1/31/97); Lorraine J. Yancey, Austin (1/31/99). Exec. Dir., William Treacy ($53,834), 333 Guadalupe, Suite 3-900, Austin 78701-3900.

Acupuncture Examiners, Texas State Board of - (1993); apptv.; 6 yrs.; per diem; 9 members: Rebecca Atchley, Lubbock (1/31/97); Lawrence Woon-Chung Chan, Amarillo (1/31/01); Cheng Ming Chang, San Antonio (1/31/01); Gus L. Garcia, Austin (1/31/97); Nancy M. Land, Crockett (1/31/99); Shen Ping Liang, Houston (1/31/99); Lisa Ping-Hui Lin, Austin (1/31/99); Stephen M. Taylor, Fort Worth (1/31/97); Annette M. Zaharoff, San Antonio (1/31/01).

Ad Valorem Tax Rate, Board to Calculate the - (1907); ex officio; term in other office; 3 members: Governor, State Comptroller of Public Accounts and State Treasurer.

Adjutant General - (1836 by Republic of Texas; present office established 1905); apptv.: Brig. Gen. Daniel James III (2/1/99) ($63,431, plus house and utilities), PO Box 5218, Austin 78763.

Adjutant General - Assistant for Air: Col. Michael B. Smith, PO Box 5218, Austin 78763.

Adjutant General - Assistant for Army: Brig. Gen. Wayne D. Marty, PO Box 5218, Austin 78763.

Administrative Judicial Districts of Texas, Presiding Judges - (Apptv. by Governor); serve terms concurrent with term as District Judge, subject to reappointment if re-elected to bench. No extra compensation. For names of judges, see Administrative Judicial Districts in index.

Aerospace Commission, Texas - (1987; re-established in 1989); apptv.; 6-yr.; 9 members: David W. Carr, Austin (2/1/95); R. Walter Cunningham, Houston (2/1/03); William Earl Juett, Amarillo (2/1/99); Lee L. Kaplan, Houston (2/1/99); Anne H. McNamara, Dallas (2/1/01); James R. Royer, Houston (2/1/99); Bryon D. Sehlke, Austin (2/1/03); T.C. Selman II, Lake Jackson (2/1/01); Norma H. Webb, Midland (2/1/03). Exec. Dir., Larry Griffin, PO Box 12088, Austin 78711-2088.

Aging, Texas Board on - (1965 as Governor's Committee on Aging; name changed in 1981 to present form; due to go out of existence 9-1-97 unless continued operation needed); apptv.; expenses; 9 apptv. members: Nancy S. Bohman, San Antonio (2/1/99); Jack Burton, Cleburne (2/1/01); Miriam Ann Burton, Montgomery (2/1/03); Elena B. Gonzalez, Edinburg (2/1/99); Thomas E. Oliver, Baytown (2/1/03); Jan Patterson, Dallas (2/1/01); Dan Roberts, Fort Worth (2/1/99); William Toler Shaner, Midland (2/1/03); Holly H. Williamson, Houston (2/1/01). Exec. Dir., Mary Sapp ($55,697), PO Box 12786, Austin 78711.

Agricultural Finance Authority, Texas - (1987); expenses; 2-yr.; 6 members: 2 ex officio: Commissioner of Agriculture and director of Institute for International Agribusiness Studies at Prairie View A&M Univ.; 4 apptd. by Governor: Dickie G. Geries, Uvalde (1/1/99); Deborah Herber, Pleasanton (1/1/99); Mark W. Jones, Menard (1/1/99); Charles E. Legg, Dumas (1/1/99).

Agricultural Resources Protection Authority - (1989 with 9 members; changed to 15 members, 1995); 2-yr.; members; 15 members: 9 ex officio: Dir., Texas Agricultural Experiment Station; Dean, College of Agricultural Sciences of Texas Tech University; Dean, University of Texas School of Public Health, Houston; Dir. of Environmental Epidemiology at Texas Department of Health; Chief of Groundwater Conservation section, Texas Natural Resource Conservation Commission; Dir. of Institute for International Agribusiness Studies, Prairie View A&M; Commissioner of Agriculture; Exec. Dir., Texas Structural Pest Control Board; Exec. Dir., State Soil and Water Conservation Board; 6 apptd. by Gov.: Craig Estes, Wichita Falls (2/1/97); L.C. Harrison, Wichita Falls (2/1/97); Gary Johnson, Dalhart (2/1/99); David K. Langford, San Antonio (2/1/97); David M. Nix, Lamesa (2/1/97); Julian H. Treviño, San Antonio (2/1/97).

Aircraft Pooling Board, State - (1979); apptv.; 6-yr.; 5 members — 2 ex officio: representative of State Auditor's Office and representative of General Services Commission; 3 apptv. — one by Gov., one by Speaker and one by Lt. Gov. Gov.'s appointee: Joe B. McShane III, Midland (1/31/01). Exec. Dir., Bob DuLaney ($60,500), 4900 Old Manor Road, Austin 78723.

Alcohol and Drug Abuse, Texas Commission on - (1953 as Texas Commission on Alcoholism; name changed and membership increased to 9 in 1986; members reduced to 6 and term reduced to 2-yr. in 1995); apptv.; 2-yr.; per diem and expenses; 6 members: Rolland Craten Allen, Corpus Christi (2/1/99); Beverly Barron, Odessa (2/1/99); Hector Delgado, El Paso (2/1/97); Dorothy Grasty, Arlington (2/1/97); Norwood W. Knight-Richardson, League City (2/1/97); James C. Oberwetter, Dallas (2/1/97). Exec. Dir., Terry Faye Bleier ($85,000), 9001 N. IH-35 N, Ste. 105, Austin 78753-5233.

Alcoholic Beverage Commission, Texas - (1935 as Liquor Control Board; name changed 1970); apptv.; 6-yr; per diem and expenses; administrator apptd. by commission; 3 members: Martha S. Dickie, Austin (11/15/99); Roy Orr, DeSoto (11/15/97); Allan Shivers Jr., Austin (11/15/01). Admin., Doyne Bailey ($80,761), 5806 Mesa Dr., Austin 78731.

Alzheimer's Disease and Related Disorders, Texas Council on - (1987); 2-yr.; expenses; 17 members: 5 agency heads or their designees: Depts. of Aging, Health, Human Services, Mental Health and Mental Retardation and the Long-Term Care Coordinating Council for the Elderly; plus four apptd. by Lt. Gov.; 4 apptd. by Speaker; 4 apptd. by Gov. as follows: Johnnie B. Elliott, Brownwood (8/31/01); Marian Rowe, Tyler (9/1/93); Margaret Pace Sykes, Fort Worth (8/31/01); Fredericka G. Younger, San Antonio (9/1/94).

Angelina and Neches River Authority, Board of Directors - (1935 as Sabine-Neches Conservation Dist.; reorganized 1950 and name changed to Neches River Conservation Dist.; changed to present name in 1977); apptv.; expenses; 6-yr.; 9 members: Janelle C. Ashley, Nacogdoches (9/5/99); Margie C. Benge, Jacksonville (9/5/97); Susan W. Heckmann, Tyler (9/5/01); Henry H. Holubec Jr., Lufkin (9/5/99); Stewart M. Kenderdine, Palestine (9/5/01); Paul H. (Pete) Smith, Nacogdoches (9/5/97); Roy L. Stark, Palestine (9/5/99); Jack C. Sweeny, Diboll (9/5/01); Herman Wright, Jasper (9/5/97). Gen. Mgr., Gary L. Neighbors, PO Box 387, Lufkin 75902-0387.

Animal Health Commission, Texas - (1893 as Texas Livestock Sanitary Commission; name changed in 1959, membership increased to 9 in 1973; raised to 12 in 1983); apptv.; per diem and expenses; 6-yr.; 12 members: Donald L. Berend, Wichita Falls (9/6/01); Bradley D. Bouma, El Paso (9/6/99); R.A. (Rob) Brown Jr., Throckmorton (9/6/01); Jack R. Gardner, Nacogdoches (9/6/97); H. Tevis Herd, Midland (9/6/01); Joan N. Kelleher, San Antonio (9/6/97); Ernesto A. Morales, Devine (9/6/99); Allan C. Oltjen, Canyon (9/6/93); Charles R. Sherron, Beaumont (9/6/97); Joe w. Templeton, College Station (9/6/01); David W. Winters, Del Rio (9/6/97); Richard W. Winters, Brady (9/6/99). Exec. Dir., Terry Beals, DVM ($72,500), PO Box 12966, Austin 78711-2966.

Appraiser Licensing and Certification Board, Texas - (1991); 2-yr.; apptd.; per diem on duty; 9 members: Exec. Sec. of Veterans' Land Board and 8 apptees: Maria Almanza, El Paso (1/31/98); Ben E. Barnett, Dallas (1/31/98); Leonel Garza Jr., McAllen (1/31/99); Jacqueline G. Humphrey, Amarillo (1/31/98); Eduardo A. Lopez, Corpus Christi (1/31/99); Debra S. Runyan, San Antonio (1/31/98); Robert A. "Pete" Seale Jr., Houston (1/31/99); James Melvin Synatzske, Stephenville (1/31/99). Commissioner, Renil C. Liner, PO Box 12188, Austin 78711-2188.

Architectural Examiners, Texas Board of - (1937 as 3-member board; raised to 6 members in 1951; increased to 9 in

1977); apptv.; 6-yr.; per diem and expenses; 9 members: Maricela R. Barr, Austin (1/31/99); Mary Ann Bryan, Houston (1/31/99); Mary French Cable, Sulphur Springs (1/31/99); Paula C. Day, Fort Worth (1/31/01); Steven Ellinger, Abilene (1/31/03); John Only Greer, Bryan (1/31/01); Chao Chiung Lee, Bellaire (1/31/03); Dorothy Virginia Roberts, Austin (1/31/03); Cleveland Turner III, Amarillo (1/31/01). Exec. Dir., Cathy I. Hendricks, ($53,469), PO Box 12337, Austin 78711-2337.

Arts, Texas Commission on the - (1965 as Texas Fine Arts Commission; name changed to Texas Commission on the Arts and Humanities and membership increased to 18 in 1971; name changed to present form in 1979); apptv.; 6-yr.; expenses; 18 members: Malouf Abraham Jr., Canadian (8/31/01); Doris Alexander, Amarillo (8/31/01); Timothy J. Crowley, College Station (8/31/97); David R. Durham, Abilene (8/31/99); Anne Lamkin Kinder, Houston (8/31/01); Nelda S. Lee, Odessa (8/31/99); Robert R. Lende, San Antonio (8/31/97); Mary Anne McCloud, Eastland (8/31/01); Joan McGuire Mellard, San Antonio (8/31/99); Lurence D. Miller III, Austin (8/31/97); David Montejano, Austin (8/31/97); Alyn Brown Morton, El Paso (8/31/01); Idell G. Rabin, Dallas (8/31/99); Matilda Robinson, Dallas (8/31/97); Kathleen B. Stevens, Fort Worth (8/31/97); Frances Annette Strake, Houston (8/31/93); Jay M. Vogelson, Dallas (8/31/99); Constance M. Ware, Marshall (8/31/01); Gilberto Zepeda Jr., San Juan (8/31/99). Exec. Dir., John Paul Batiste ($55,287), PO Box 13406, Austin 78711-3406.

Athletic Trainers, Advisory Board of - (1971 as Texas Board of Athletic Trainers; name changed and membership increased to 6 in 1975); expenses; 6-yr.; 6 members: Kaye Cosby, San Antonio (1/31/99); John Wesley Harvey, Houston (1/31/03); Susan Leeper Orr, Watauga (1/31/97); Michael D. Saly, Conroe (1/31/01); Natalie Steadman, Lubbock (1/31/03); Michael K. Stephens, Austin (1/31/01); Paul T. Zeek, Nederland (1/31/99). Exec. Secretary, Allen Eggert, Texas Dept. of Health, 1100 W. 49th, Austin 78756-3183.

Attorney, State Prosecuting - apptv.: Matthew Paul ($82,209), PO Box 12405, Austin 78711.

Auditor, State - (1929); apptv. by Legislative Audit Committee, a joint Senate-House committee; 2-yr.: Lawrence F. Alwin, PO Box 12067, Austin 78711-2067.

Banking Commissioner, State - (1923); apptv. by State Finance Commission; 2-yr.: Catherine A. Ghiglieri ($97,072), 2601 N. Lamar Blvd., Austin 78705 (See also Finance Commission of Texas).

Bar of Texas, State - (1939 as administrative arm of Supreme Court); 30 members elected by membership; 3-yr. terms; expenses paid from dues collected from membership. President, president-elect, vice president and immediate past president serve as ex officio members. Exec. Dir., Antonio Alvarado, PO Box 12487, Austin 78711.

Barber Examiners, State Board of - (1929 as 3-member board; membership increased in 1975); apptv.; 6-yr.; per diem and expenses; 6 members: Robert Castro, El Paso (1/31/97); William Kuykendall, Austin (1/31/99); Ernest W. Pack Sr., Waco (1/31/01); Hoye D. Tibbets, Grandview (1/31/99); Janice E. Wiggins, Kingsland (1/31/97); Charles Williams, San Antonio (1/31/01). Exec. Dir., B. Michael Rice ($38,988), 333 Guadalupe, Ste. 2-110, Austin 78701.

Battleship Texas Advisory Board - (1983; superseded Battleship Texas Commission; apptv.; 6-yr.; 9 members: Charles A. Alcorn, Houston (2/1/01); Carol G. Calvert, Waxahachie (2/1/01); Carter Casteel, New Braunfels (2/1/97); Blaine G. Corman, Crosby (2/1/97); Gen. Hugh W. Hardy, Houston (2/1/99); Joshua Hill Sr., Houston (2/1/99); Jerry D. Neel, Friendswood (2/1/99); Thomas J. Perich, Sugar Land (2/1/01); Quinton Rogers, Marshall (2/1/97). Office Address: 3527 Battleground Rd., LaPorte 77571.

Blind and Severely Disabled Persons, Committee on Purchases of Products of - (See **Disabilities, Texas Council on Purchasing from People with**)

Blind and Visually Impaired, Governing Board of Texas School for the - (1979); apptv.; 6-yr.; expenses; 9 members: Mary G. Behnke, Orange (1/31/97); Anita Bonanno, Houston (1/31/01); Michael David Connolly, Nacogdoches (1/31/01); Roseanna Davidson, Lubbock (1/31/99); Kerry L. Goodwin, Dallas (1/31/99); Edward F. Guerro, Austin (1/31/97); Gloria Smith, Lufkin (1/31/97); Mary Sue Staples, Fort Worth (1/31/99); Frankie D. Swift, Miles (1/31/01). Superintendent, Philip H. Hatlen ($68,000), 1100 W. 45th, Austin 78756.

Blind, Texas Commission for the - (1931 as 6-member State Commission for the Blind; raised to 9 members in 1979; name changed in 1985); apptv.; 6-yr.; expenses; 9 members: Dr. James L. Caldwell, Austin (2/1/01); Carolyn Marie Garrett, Houston (2/1/99); C. Robert Keeney Jr., Houston (2/1/01); W. Frank Mullican Jr., Lubbock (2/1/01); Don W. Oates, Nacogdoches (2/1/03); Olivia Sandoval, San Antonio (2/1/99); Olivia Chavez Schonberger, El Paso (2/1/99); Beverly A. Stiles, Freer

(2/1/03); John M. Turner, Dallas (2/1/03). Exec. Dir., Pat D. Westbrook ($65,166), PO Box 12866, Austin 78711.

Board of (Note: In most instances, state boards are alphabetized under key word, as **Accountancy, Texas State Board of Public.**)

Brazos River Authority, Board of Directors - (1929 as Brazos River Conservation and Reclamation Dist.; name changed to present form in 1953); apptv.; 6-yr; expenses; 21 members: Mary E. Ainslie, Sugar Land (2/1/03); Robert Bates Arnot, Breckenridge (2/1/03); Deborah H. Bell, Abilene (2/1/01); Hulen M. Davis, Prairie View (2/1/99); Lynn Elliott, Navasota (2/1/01); C.C. "Jack" Farrar, Hico (2/1/01); Ramiro A. Galindo, Bryan (2/1/01); Rodolfo Garcia, Alvin (2/1/03); Horace R. Grace, Killeen (2/1/99); Shirley M. Herring, Brenham (2/1/03); Everet E. Kennemer III, West Columbia (2/1/99); Lee M. Kidd, Denver City (2/1/99); Ernest M. Koy, Bellville (2/1/03); J. Rodney Lee, Waco (2/1/03); David F. Lengefeld, Hamilton (2/1/99); Linda Kay Lyle, Plainview (2/1/01); Johnoween Smyth Mathis, Hearne (2/1/99); Karen C. Matkin, Waco (2/1/99); Nancy N. Rabb, Round Rock (2/1/03); Ruth Schiermeyer, Lubbock (2/1/01); Judith Vernon, Evant (2/1/01). Gen. Mgr., Roy A. Roberts, P. O. Box 7555, Waco 76714-7555.

Canadian River Compact Commissioner - (1951); apptv.; salary and expenses; (function is to negotiate with other states respecting waters of the Canadian): Xen Harris Oden ($10,767), Lubbock (12/31/97).

Cancer Council, Texas - (1985); 6-yr.; 16 members: 1 State Senator; 1 State Representative; Chmn., Board of Health; Chmn., Board of Human Services; 12 apptd: Joseph Switz Bailes, Dallas (2/1/00); Grover L. Bynum Jr., Austin (2/1/96); Clare Buie Chaney, Dallas (2/1/02); James D. Dannenbaum, Houston (2/1/96); Karen Hausinkveld, Arlington (2/1/96); C. Stratton Hill Jr., Houston (2/1/00); William C. Levin, Galveston (2/1/96); Donald C. Spencer, Austin (2/1/00); Courtney Townsend Jr., Galveston (2/1/98); J. Taylor Wharton, Houston (2/1/98). Exec. Dir., Emily F. Untermeyer ($57,691), PO Box 12097, Austin 78711.

Central Colorado River Authority (See **Colorado River Authority, Central**.)

Chemist, State - (1911); ex officio, indefinite term: George W. Latimer, P. O. Box 3160, College Station 77841-3160.

Childhood Intervention Services, Interagency Council on Early - (1981); apptv.; 2-yr.; (5 members: number raised to 9 in 1993): one each apptd. from Dept. of Health, Comm. on Alcohol and Drug Abuse, Dept. of MHMR, Dept. of Human Services, Dept. of Protective and Regulatory Services and Central Education Agency and three apptd. by Gov.: Claudette W. Bryant, Dallas (2/1/99); Bess Alt-haus Graham, Austin (2/1/01); Tammy H. Tiner, College Station (2/1/97). Exec. Dir., Mary Elder ($61,380), 1100 W. 49th, Austin 78756.

Children's Trust Fund of Texas Council - (1985; became independent agency in 1991); apptv., 6-yr; 9 members: Patricia Aguayo, El Paso (9/1/01); J. Randolph Burton, Spring (9/1/99); Thelma Sanders Clardy, DeSoto (9/1/99); Anne C. Crews, Dallas (9/1/01); Sylvia A. Martinez-Flores, Lubbock (9/1/99); Pauline M. Mouton, Beaumont (9/1/97); Juan M. Parra, San Antonio (9/1/01); Michael Atlee Reilly, Arlington (9/1/97); Peggy B. Smith, Houston (9/1/97). Exec. Dir., Janie D. Fields ($51,840), 8929 Shoal Creek Blvd., #200, Austin 78757-6854.

Chiropractic Examiners, Texas Board of - (1949); apptv.; 6-yr.; expenses; 9 members: Zinetta A. Burney, Houston (8/3/97); Carroll V. Guice, Longview (8/3/97); Keith Hubbard, Fort Worth (2/1/99); Kevin E. Raef, Canyon (2/1/97); William T. Reece, Bay City (8/3/95); Oliver R. Smith Jr., El Paso (2/1/01); Dora Innes Valverde, Mission (2/1/01); Guy L. Watts, Corpus Christi (8/3/99); John C. Weddle, Rockwall (2/1/01); Carolyn Davis Williams, Houston (2/1/99). Exec. Dir., Patte B. Kent ($39,140), 333 Guadalupe, Ste. 3-825, Austin 78701.

Coastal Water Authority, Board of Directors - (1967 as Coastal Industrial Water Authority, Board of Directors of; name changed in 1985); 7 members — 4 apptd. by mayor of Houston with advice and consent of governing body of Houston; 3 apptd. by Gov.; per diem and expenses; 2-yr.; Gov's. apptees: Buster E. French, Dayton (4/1/98); Johnnie G. Jennings, Baytown (4/1/97); Leonard Spearman Sr., Houston (4/1/97). Exec. Dir., Ralph T. Rundle, 1200 Smith St., Ste. 2260, Houston 77002.

College Opportunity Act Committee - (1989); 6-yr.; 9 members: 6 ex officio: Commissioner, General Land Office; Exec. Admin., Texas Water Development Board; Comptroller; State Treasurer; Exec. Dir., Bond Review Board; Commissioner of Higher Education. 3 apptd.: Barbara J. Dugas-Patterson, Houston (2/1/97); Joe Munoz, San Angelo (2/1/01); Linda Perryman, Dallas (2/1/93).

Colorado River Authority, Central, Board of Directors - (1935); apptv.; 6-yr.; per diem on duty; 9 members: Herman B. Cassaday, Talpa (2/1/97); Robert J. Cheaney II, Santa Ana (2/

1/93); Thelbert Elkins, Coleman (2/1/97); Jimmie S. Hobbs, Coleman (2/1/97); Ann Miller Hargett, Coleman (2/1/01); Clifford L. Horn, Talpa (2/1/93); Nicholas J. Knox, Burkett (2/1/93); Nan Knox Markland, Burkett (2/1/01); Ronald W. Owens, Coleman (2/1/01). Operations Mgr., Laneal Maedgen, PO Box 964, Coleman 76834.

Colorado River Authority, Lower, Board of Directors - (1934 as 9-member board; membership increased in 1951 and 1975); apptv.; 6-yr.; per diem on duty; 15 members: Pamela R. Akins, Marble Falls (2/1/03); Richard G. Arellano, Llano (2/1/99); George Cason, Eagle Lake (2/1/99); I.O. Coleman Jr., Wharton (2/1/99); Frederick L. Henneke, Hunt (2/1/01); Pix D. Howell, Austin (2/1/99); Patricia Jean Kirk, San Saba (2/1/03); Hilda C. Kroll, Johnson City (2/1/01); Gale Minzenmeyer Lincke, La Grange (2/1/03); Michael J. Lucksinger, Burnet (2/1/99); Arthur J. Milberger, Bay City (2/1/03); Charles Patrick Oles Jr., Austin (2/1/01); E. Peter Pincoffs, Austin (2/1/09); Steve D. Rivers, Bastrop (2/1/09); John J. Weidner, Brownwood (2/1/03). Gen. Mgr., Mark Rose, P. O. Box 220, Austin 78767-0220.

Colorado River Authority, Upper, Board of Directors - (1935 as 9-member board; reorganized in 1965); apptv.; 6-yr.; per diem and expenses; indefinite number of members: Ray Alderman, Winters (2/1/01); C. Skeete Foster, Sterling City (2/1/99); Ruby N. Gutierrez, San Angelo (2/1/99); Carrol Hill, San Angelo (2/1/97); Ralph E.Hoelscher, Miles (2/1/01); Patricia P. Ivey, Robert Lee (2/1/97); Sara T. Ortiz, Colorado City (2/1/97); Jeffie Harmon Roberts, Robert Lee (2/1/99); Jeffie Roberts, Robert Lee (2/1/99); Dorris Sonnenberg, Bronte (2/1/01). Ellen Groth, Admin. Asst., PO Box 1482, San Angelo 76902-1482.

Commerce Policy Board, Texas Department of - (1987, with 6 apptv. members; changed to present configuration in 1991); apptv.; 6-yr.; 9 members: 3 ex officio: Chmn., State Job Training Coordinating Council; Chmn., International Trade Commission; Chmn., Texas-Mexico Authority; 6 apptv. public members, as follows: Vernon E. Faulconer, Tyler (2/1/95); Murphy George, Lufkin (2/1/97); Gerald Grinstein, Fort Worth (2/1/97); Vidal G. Martinez, Houston (2/1/99); Sonia Perez, McAllen (2/1/99). Exec. Dir., Texas Dept. of Commerce: Brenda F. Arnett (2/1/99); ($79,536), PO Box 12728, Austin 78711-2728.

Commissioner of (See keyword, as **Agriculture, Commissioner of**.)

Concho River Water and Soil Conservation Authority, Lower - (1939); 6-yr.; 9 members: Leroy Paul Beach, Millersview (2/1/93); Howard E. Loveless, Eden (2/1/99); Billy J. Mikeska, Eola (2/1/99); Eugene R. Rogers, Eden (2/1/97); Benjamin O. Sims, Paint Rock (2/1/97); Edwin T. Tickle, Eden (2/1/01); T.E. Wells, Paint Rock (2/1/01); Harvey P. Williams, Eola (2/1/01). Office Address: Rt. 1, PO Box 4, Paint Rock 76866.

Conservatorship Board, State - (1979); apptv.; expenses; 6-yr.; 3 members: Carolyn Gallagher Austin (2/1/01); Byron Tunnell, Bullard (2/1/97); J. Michael Weiss, Lubbock (2/1/99).

Consumer Credit Commissioner - Leslie L. Pettijohn ($76, 915), 2601 N. Lamar, Austin 78705-4207.

Cosmetology Commission, Texas - (1935 as 3-member State Board of Hairdressers and Cosmetologists; name changed and membership increased to 6 apptv. and one ex officio in 1971); apptv.; per diem and expenses; 6-yr.; apptv. members: Comer J. Cottrell Jr., Dallas (12/31/01); Robin D. Crump, Temple (12/31/99); Virginia G. Dillman, Dallas (12/31/99); Lucille C. Garcia, San Antonio (12/31/97); Brian King, Houston (12/31/01); Dianna Mays, Greenville (12/31/97); . Exec. Dir., Dick Strader ($44,558), PO Box 26700, Austin 78755-0700.

Counselors, Texas State Board of Examiners of Professional - (1981); apptv.; 6-yr.; expenses; 9 members: Judy Broussard, Levelland (2/1/01); Joseph D. Dameron, Denton (2/1/01); Graciela Guillen, El Paso (2/1/99); J. Lee Jagers, Richardson (2/1/03); Alice B. Jones, Houston (2/1/99); Mary L. Madison, Stephenville (2/1/03); Susan Moore, San Antonio (2/1/03); Anthony P. Picchioni, Grapevine (2/1/99); Gene Ryder, San Antonio (2/1/01). Exec. Sec., Kathy Craft, 1100 W. 49th, Austin 78756-3183.

Court Reporters Certification Board - (1977 as 9-member Texas Reporters Committee; name changed to present form and membership increased to 12 in 1983); apptv. by State Supreme Court; 6-yr.; expenses Exec. Secy., Peg Liedtke ($40,000), 205 W. 14th St., Ste. 101, Austin 78701.

Credit Union Commission - (1949 as 3-member Credit Union Advisory Commission; name changed and membership increased to 6 in 1969; increased to 9 in 1981); apptv.; 6-yr.; expenses; 9 members: Garold R. Base, Plano (2/15/01); Leon Ewing, San Antonio (2/15/97); Richard Allen Glasco Jr., Austin (2/15/03); Robert S. Hayes, Amarillo (2/15/01); Susan C. Jackson, Houston (2/15/99); L. Gail Mackie, San Antonio (2/15/01); Linda Mann, Bay City (2/15/99); Terry R. Stapleton, Irving (2/15/97); J. Howell "Hal" Thomas, Baytown (2/15/03). Commis-

sioner, Harold E. Feeney ($80,661), 914 E. Anderson Ln., Austin 78752-1699.

Crime Stoppers Advisory Council - (1981); apptv.; 2-yr.; 5 members: Darrell W. Bush, Nederland (9/1/97); Thomas E. Dunn, Lufkin (9/1/97); Susan R. Johnson, Odessa (9/1/97); Carolyn Leyendecker, Laredo (9/1/97); Jane H. Romine, Fort Worth (9/1/97).

Criminal Justice, Texas Board of - (1989: assumed duties of former Texas Board of Corrections and Adult Probation Commission; also oversees Board of Pardons and Paroles Division); apptd; 6-yr.; expenses; 9 members: Patricia A. Day, Dallas (2/1/03); John David Franz, Hidalgo (2/1/01); Gilberto Hinojosa, Corpus Christi (2/1/99); Alfred C. Moran, Arlington (2/1/03); Allan B. Polunsky, San Antonio (2/1/01); Alfred M. "Mac" Stringfellow, San Antonio (2/1/03); Carol S. Vance, Houston (2/1/99); John R. Ward, Gatesville (2/1/99); Carole S. Young, Dallas (2/1/01). Exec. Dir, Dept. of Criminal Justice: Wayne Scott ($120,000), PO Box 13084, Austin 78711. (512) 463-9988.

Criminal Justice Policy Council - (1983); all terms at pleasure of appointor; 11 members: 3 ex officio — Gov., Lt. Gov., Speaker; 2 apptd. by Lt. Gov.; 2 apptd. by Speaker; 4 apptd. by Gov. Gov's apptees: Col. James B. Adams, Austin; John Holmes, Houston; D.L. "Sonny" Keesee, Lubbock; Susan D. Reed, San Antonio. Exec. Dir., Tony Fabelo ($75,000), 205 W. 14th St., Ste. 701, Austin 78701.

Deaf and Hearing Impaired, Governing Board of the Texas School for the - (1979); 6-yr.; expenses; 9 members: Beatrice M. Burke, Big Spring (1/31/01); Johnelle M. Cortner, Houston (1/31/97); Aulby Lawrence (Larry) Gillett, San Angelo (1/31/01); Nancy Ellen Munger, Kyle (1/31/95); Nanci Pagoda-Ciccone, Dallas (1/31/99); Robert E. Parrish, Dallas (1/31/99); Mary Lynch VanManen, Sugar Land (1/31/97); Polly Piercy Walton, Beaumont (1/31/97). Exec. Dir., Marvin B. Sallop ($63,230), P. O. Box 3538, Austin 78764.

Deaf and Hard of Hearing, Texas Commission for the - (1971 as 6-member board; membership raised to 9 in 1979); apptv.; 6-yr.; expenses; 9 members: Douglas L. Bush, Houston (1/31/03); Larry M. Correu, San Antonio (1/31/99); Delores Erlandson, Big Spring (1/31/99); Jean Hale Matney, Fort worth (1/31/01); Timothy B. Rarus, Austin (1/31/01); Robin E. Riccardi, Shallowater (1/31/03); Linda Phillips Thune, Austin (1/31/99); Benna Timperlake, Corpus Christi (1/31/03); Eva Davie Williams, El Lago (1/31/01). Exec. Dir., David W. Myers ($60,000), P. O. Box 12904, Austin 78711.

Dental Examiners, State Board of - (1919 as 6-member board; increased to 9 members in 1971; increased to 12 in 1981; increased to 15 in 1991; sunsetted in 1994; reconstituted with 18 members in 1995); appt.; 6-yr.; per diem while on duty; 18 members: Sheryl Ann Beltrane, San Antonio (2/1/99); Jerry T. Burley, Houston (2/1/99); Tammy R. Fisher, Bedford (2/1/01); J. Hadley Hall, Abilene (2/1/99); Cornelius O. Henry, Tyler (2/1/03); James W. Kenedy, Sugar Land (2/1/03); H. Grant Lappin, Houston (2/1/03); Michael Nogueira, Rancho Viejo (2/1/01); David O. Olson, Bridge City (2/1/01); Miro Pavelka, Dallas (2/1/99); Michael D. Plunk, Dallas (2/1/03); Felipe Reyna, Lorena (2/1/99); Ronald G. Smith, Lubbock (2/1/01); Kent T. Starr, Waco (2/1/99); Patricia Stuart Blackwell, Midland (2/1/01); Marcia Waugh, El Paso (2/1/03); Gail Wilks, Longview (2/1/03); Joe D. Zayas, Brownsville (2/1/01). Exec. Dir., C. Thomas Camp ($54,770), 333 Guadalupe, Ste. 3-800, Austin 78701.

Depository Board, State - (1905); 3 ex officio, term in other office: State Treasurer, Banking Commissioner, Comptroller; one apptd. by Gov. for 2-yr. term: (Vacancy). Office Address: PO Box 12608, Austin 78711.

Developmental Disabilities, Texas Planning Council for - (1971); apptv.; 6-yr.; 27 members — 8 ex offico: Representatives from Dept. of Mental Health and Mental Retardation, Rehabilitation Commission, Dept. of Health, Dept. of Human Services, Texas Dept. on Aging, Texas Education Agency, Texas Commission for the Blind, Texas Commission for the Deaf; 19 apptv. members: David Lee Benson, Houston (2/1/99); Joe Colunga III, Brownsville (2/1/97); Shenikwa Cox, Dallas (2/1/97); Gary D. Day, Austin (2/1/01); Mary M. Durheim, McAllen (2/1/99); Debbie B. Francis, Dallas (2/1/93); Raul Garza Jr., San Benito (2/1/99); Genevieve T. Hearon, Austin (2/1/97); J. Robert Hester Jr., Arlington (2/1/01); Jerijean Houchins, Austin (2/1/01); Theda N. Hoyt, Cypress (2/1/01); Barbara G. Loera, Austin (2/1/97); Federico Marquez, El Paso (2/1/97); Rebecca P. Ratliff, Coppell (2/1/01); Jan Reimann Newsom, Dallas (2/1/01); Margaret Robinson, Amarillo (2/1/97); Hector Saenz, San Antonio (2/1/97); Charley L. Tiggs, Lubbock (2/1/99); Linda Vancil, Ballinger (2/1/01). Exec. Dir., Roger A. Webb, 4900 N. Lamar, Austin 78751.

Diabetes Council, Texas - (1983; with 5 ex officio and 6 public members serving 2-yr. terms; changed in 1987 to 3 ex officio and 8 public members; changed to present configuration in 1991); 4-yr.; 17 members — 5 ex officio; 12 apptv. public members as follows: Maria C. Alen, McAllen (2/1/01); Gene Bell, Lubbock (2/1/00); Stuart Fitts (2/1/01); Victor Hugo Gonzalez, McAllen (2/1/00); Judith Haley, Houston (2/1/00); Richard (Rick) S. Hayley, Corpus Christi (2/1/02); Lawrence B. Harkless, San Antonio (2/1/01); Jacqueline S. Martin, Houston (2/1/94); Thomas R. McCann, Mount Pleasant (2/1/01); Cheryl Jenkins Porter, Midland (2/1/01); Philip L. Ricks II, San Antonio (2/1/01); Rosa M. Valenzuela, El Paso (2/1/98). Address: Texas Dept. of Health, 1100 W. 49th, Austin 78756.

Dietitians, Texas State Board of Examiners of - (1983); apptv.; 6-yr.; per diem and expenses: 9 members: Lucille DiDomenico, Arlington (9/1/99); Maxine B. Freeman, Houston (9/1/97); Ethelind S. Gibson, Nacogdoches (9/1/01); Ada Harden, Austin (9/1/97); Patricia Mayers Krug, Converse (9/1/01); Margarette Leggitt Harden, Lubbock (9/1/99); Helen P. O'Reilly, Plano (9/1/99); Dorothy M. Shafer, Fredericksburg (9/1/01); Janice M. Walker, Houston (9/1/97). Texas Dept. of Health, 1100 W. 49th, Austin 78756.

Disabilities, Governor's Committee on People with - (1991); 16 members: 4 ex officio: Chmn., TEC; Commissioner, Texas Rehabilitation Comm.; Dir., Texas Commission for the Blind; member, Texas Comm. for the Deaf; 12 members apptd. by Governor serve 2-year terms: Mary Ann Board, Houston (2/1/99); James Laurence Caldwell, Austin (2/1/98); Larry Chevallier, Henderson (2/1/99); Victoria Christman, Dallas (2/1/99); Douglas F. Grady Jr., Fort Worth (2/1/98); Peter Grojean, San Antonio (2/1/98); Thomas P. Justis, Fort Worth (2/1/98); Kym I. King, Houston (2/1/98); Debbie H. Morrill, Austin (2/1/99); James G. Olson, Houston (2/1/99); Shirley Ann Pacetti, Houston (2/1/98); Judy Castle Scott, Dallas (2/1/98). Exec. Dir., Virginia Roberts, 4900 N. Lamar, Austin 78751-2613.

Disabilities, Texas Council on Purchasing from People with - (1979 as 10-member Committee on Purchases of Products and Services of Blind and Severely Disabled Persons; name changed and members reduced to 9 in 1995); apptd.; expenses; 6-yr.; 9 members: Rogelio Ibañez Jr., McAllen (1/31/01); John W. Luna, Euless (1/31/97); Eugene F. Matthews, Denton (1/31/99); Gwendolyn C. Morrison, Fort Worth (1/31/99); Margaret Pfluger, San Angelo (1/31/99); Robert A. Swerdlow, Beaumont (1/31/01); Bobbie F. Templeton, Driftwood (1/31/97); Arnold M. Thorner, Spring (1/31/01); Pat A. Wilson, Longview (1/31/97).

East Texas State University, Board of Regents - (1969); apptv.; 6-yr.; 9 members: John R. Armstrong, Bonham (2/15/01); Raymond B. Cameron, Rockwall (2/15/97); Kerry Noble Cammack, Austin (2/15/01); Cynthia A. Gonzalez, Garland (2/15/99); Reuben R. McDaniel III, Duncanville (2/15/97); R. Jay Phillips, Corpus Christi (2/15/01); Eduardo M. Salinas, Lyford (2/15/99); Demetris A. Sampson, Dallas (2/15/97); Nelda Grigsby Strong, Austin (2/15/99). Pres., Dr. Jerry D. Morris, ETSU, Commerce 75429.

Education, Board of Control for Southern Regional - (1969); apptv.; 4-yr.; 5 members: Gov. ex officio, 4 apptd.: Dr. Joann Horton, Houston (6/30/95); Libby Linebarger, Austin (6/30/97); Rene Nuñez, Austin (6/30/98); Carl A. Parker, Austin (6/30/96). Mark E. Musick, Pres., Southern Regional Education Board, 592 10th St. N.W., Atlanta, GA 30318-5790.

Education, Commissioner of - (1866 as Superintendent of Public Instruction; 1949 changed to present name by Gilmer-Aiken Law); apptv. by State Board of Education; 4-yr.: Dr. Michael A. Moses ($156,014) (See also Education, State Board of).

Education, State Board of - (1866; re-created 1928 and reformed by Gilmer-Aikin Act in 1949 to consist of 21 elective members from districts co-extensive with 21 congressional districts at that time; membership increased to 24 with congressional redistricting in 1971, effective 1973; membership increased to 27 with congressional redistricting in 1981, effective 1983; reorganized by special legislative session as 15-member apptv. board in 1984 to become elective board again in 1988; expenses; 4-yr.; 15 members (numerals before names indicate district numbers): (1) Rene Nuñez, El Paso (1/1/99); (2) Mary Helen Berlanga, Corpus Christi (1/1/99); (3) Joe J. Bernal, San Antonio (1/1/01); (4) Dr. Alma A. Allen, Houston (1/1/01); (5) Robert H. Offutt, San Antonio (1/1/01); (6) Jack Christie, Houston (1/1/01); (7) David Brandley, Beaumont (1/1/01); (8) Donna Ballard, The Woodlands (1/1/99); (9) Randy Stevenson, Tyler (1/1/99); (10) Will D. Davis, Austin (1/1/97); (11) Diane Patrick, Arlington (1/1/97); (12) Geraldine "Tincy" Miller, Dallas (1/1/01); (13) Rosie Collins Sorrells, Dallas (1/1/99); (14) Richard Watson, Gorman (1/1/99); (15) Monte Hasie, Lubbock (1/1/99). Commissioner of Education, Dr. Michael A. Moses, Texas Education Agency, 1701 N. Congress Ave., Austin 78701-1494 (see also Education, Commissioner of).

Educator Certification, State Board for - (1995); apptv.; 6-yr.; expenses; 15 members: 3 non-voting - rep. of Comm. of Education; rep of Comm. of Higher Education; 1 dean of a college of education apptd. by Gov.; 12 voting members apptd by Gov.: Virginia S. Collier, Brenham (2/1/99); Peggy O'Neill DeRouen, Kingsville (2/1/99); James D. Harris, Lubbock (2/1/03); Andrew Jackson, Missouri City (2/1/99); Arthur (Art) Lacy, McKinney (2/1/03); Mary Denton Meier, Dallas (2/1/01); James E. Nelson, Odessa (2/1/01); Arturo Pacheco, El Paso (2/1/99); Edward (Ed) Nash Patton Jr., Abilene (2/1/01); Cynthia Tassos Phillips, Austin (2/1/01); James B. (Jim) Price, Cooper (2/1/03); Mary Margaret Rucker, Nassau Bay (2/1/03); Keith Sockwell, Plano (2/1/03).

Egg Marketing Advisory Board - (1957); apptv.; 6-yr.; 11 members — 2 ex officio: Commissioner of Agriculture is chairman; one apptd. by head of Poultry Science Dept., Texas A&M University; 9 apptv.: Leroy Baeza, Fort Davis (9/27/01); Larry J. Berend, Wichita Falls (9/27/97); Gilbert A. Burton, Lufkin (9/27/97); Jack Wilson Evans Jr., Dallas (9/27/93); Charles Jeffrey Hardin, La Grange (9/27/01); Kervin E. Jacob, Houston (9/27/97); James M. (Mike) Robinson, San Antonio (9/27/99); Elias (Alex) Rodgers, Eden (9/27/99); Terry C. Wright, Gilmer (9/27/01). Address: Dept. of Agriculture, PO Box 12847, Austin 78711.

Election Commission, State - (1973); 9 members, ex officio and apptv. as indicated: Chmn. of Democratic State Executive Committee; Chmn. of Republican State Executive Committee; Chief Justice of Supreme Court; Presiding Judge, Court of Criminal Appeals; 2 persons to be named, one a justice of the Court of Appeals apptd. by Chief Justice of Supreme Court, one a District Judge apptd. by presiding judge of Court of Criminal Appeals; 2 county chairmen, one each from Democratic and Republican parties, named by the parties; Secretary of State.

Emergency Communications, Advisory Commission on State - (1985); expenses; 17 members: 5 ex offico: exec. directors of Texas Advisory Commission on Intergovernmental Relations, Depts. of Health, Public Safety, Criminal Justice Policy Council and the major association representing regional planning commissions; 12 public members (6 yr.): 8 apptd. by Gov., 2 by Lt. Gov., 2 by Speaker: Arlene R. Aldridge, San Antonio (9/1/97); Jimmy Burson, Silverton (9/1/01); David Cain, Dallas (9/1/01); Bill Carter, Fort Worth (9/1/01); Patrick A. Craven, Austin (9/1/99); William C. Deere, Arlington (9/1/97); Bradford E. Denton, Round Rock (9/1/97); Ron Harris, McKinney (9/1/99); Laverne H. Hogan, Houston (9/1/95); Terry Keel, Austin (9/1/01); Bill Munn, Dallas (9/1/99); Wayne Whiteaker, Littlefield (9/1/99). Exec. Dir., James D. Goerke ($66,960), 333 Guadalupe St., Ste. 2-212, Austin 78701.

Employment Commission, Texas - (See **Workforce Commission, Texas**)

Engineers, State Board of Registration for Professional - (1937 as 6-member board; membership increased to 9 in 1981); apptv.; per diem and expenses; 6-yr.; 9 members: Linda Yee Chew, El Paso (9/26/97); E.D. Dorchester, Midland (9/26/01); Edmundo R. Gonzalez Jr., Brownsville (9/26/01); Jose I. Guerra, Austin (9/26/99); Derrell E. Johnson, Southlake (9/26/97); Hubert Oxford III, Beaumont (9/26/99); Danny R. Perkins, Houston (9/26/01); Roxanne L. Pillar, Fort Worth (9/26/97); C.H. (Herb) Treat, San Antonio (9/26/99). Exec. Dir., John R. Speed ($68,000), 1917 S. IH-35, Austin 78741.

Ethics Commission, Texas - (1991); apptd.; 4-yr.; 8 members: 2 apptd. by Speaker, 2 apptd. by Lt. Gov, 4 apptd. by Gov.: John E. Clark, San Antonio (11/19/99); Jerome W. Johnson, Amarillo (11/19/99); Norman Lyons, Fort Worth (11/19/99); Louis E. Sturns, Fort Worth (11/19/97). Exec. Dir., Tom Harrison ($85,000), 201 E. 14th St., 10th Fl., Austin 78701.

Evergreen Underground Water Conservation District - (1965); 2-yr.; 5 members — 4 elected: 2 each from Wilson and Atascosa counties; one apptd. by Gov.: Amond Douglas Brownlow, Floresville (2/1/99).

Family Practice Residency Advisory Committee - (1977); 3-yr.; expenses; 12 members apptv. as follows: one practicing physician apptd. by Texas Osteopathic Medical Assn.; 2 apptd. by Assn. of Directors of Family Practice Training Programs; one apptd. by Texas Medical Assn.; 2 administrators of hospitals apptd. by Texas Hospital Assn.; president, Texas Academy of Family Physicians; and 3 public members apptd. by the Gov., as follows: Tamara J. Cowen Brownsville (8/29/97); Dr. Jack L. Eidson, Weatherford (8/29/93); Judith A. Youngs, Dallas (8/29/95).

Finance Commission, State - (1923 as Banking Commission; reorganized as Finance Commission in 1943 with 9 members; membership increased to 12 in 1983; changed back to 9 members in 1989); apptv.; 6-yr.; per diem and traveling expenses; 9 members: Jeff Austin Jr., Jacksonville (2/1/00); James T. Chambers, Stephenville (2/1/98); Kay Glover, Austin (2/1/00); Steven C. Hastings, Southlake (2/1/00); Wilburn D. Hilton Jr., Greenville (2/1/02); Alfred Johnson, Dallas (2/1/98);

Marlene Martin, San Antonio (2/1/02); Manuel J. Mehos, Houston (2/1/02); Victor (Buddy) Puente Jr., Pantego (2/1/98). Banking Commissioner, Catherine A. Ghiglieri ($97,072), 2601 N. Lamar, Austin 78705, appointee of Finance Commission. (See also Banking Commissioner, State.)

Fire Ant Advisory Board - (1987); apptv.; expenses; 6-yr.; 9 members: 3 ex officio: Commissioner of Agriculture, exec. dir. of Parks and Wildlife Dept., engineer-director of Texas Department of Transportation; 6 apptd. — 2 by Commissioner of Agriculture, 4 apptd. by Gov.: Stanley Carter Haddock, Dallas (1/1/99); Juan D. Nichols, Quitman (1/1/97); Wayne R. Snodgrass, Nassau Bay (1/1/95); Davis Whitehurst Jr., Longview (1/1/99).

Fire Fighters' Pension Commissioner - (1937); apptv.; 2-yr.: Helen L. Campbell (7/1/97) ($45,000), PO Box 12577, Austin 78711.

Fire Fighters' Relief and Retirement Fund - (1977); apptv.; expenses; 6-yr.; 9 members: Jennifer S. Armstrong, Mansfield (9/1/99); Robert Barrett, Seminole (9/1/99); Donald A. Eernisse, Alvin (9/1/97); Weir Labatt, San Antonio (9/1/01); Paul V. Loeffler, Alpine (9/1/01); Glenn D. Neutzler, Brenham (9/1/97); Joe Rice, Canyon (9/1/01); Frank Torres, Raymondville (9/1/99); Thomas N. Tourtellotte, Driftwood (9/1/97). Commissioner, Helen L. Campbell, PO Box 12577, Austin 78711.

Fire Protection, Texas Commission on - (1991; formed by consolidation of Fire Dept. Emergency Board and Commission on Fire Protection Personnel Standards and Education); apptv.; 6-yrs.; expenses; 12 members: David Abernathy Pittsburg (2/1/01); Chief Juan J. Adame, Corpus Christi (2/1/97); Elizabeth J. Atchley, Lefors (2/1/99); Capt. Marvin G. Dawson, Brownfield (2/1/99); Gerald K. Hood, Fort Worth (2/1/97); Patrick K. Hughes Sr., Keller (2/1/97); Jon M. Hutchens, Houston (2/1/01); Ronnie E. James, Wichita Falls (2/1/99); Gilbert Robinson, Texas City (2/1/99); Capt. Ricardo Saldana, Mission (2/1/99); Kelley Martin Stalder, Parker (2/1/01); Carl Dewayne Wren, Manchaca (2/1/01). Exec. Dir., Gary L. Warren Sr. ($68,959), 12675 N. Research Blvd., Austin 78759.

Food and Fibers Commission, Texas - (1941 as Cotton Research Committee; name changed in 1971 to Natural Fibers and Food Protein Committee; changed to commission in 1975; changed to present name 1989); 4 members are presidents and chancellor of four major universities (Pres., Texas Woman's University, Denton; Pres., Texas Tech University, Lubbock; Chancellor, Texas A&M University System, College Station; Pres., University of Texas at Austin) serving indefinite terms; and one ex officio member who is director of administrative office in Dallas, apptd. to 2-year term: Exec. Dir., Steve Verett ($60,833), 17360 Coit Rd., Dallas 75252.

Funeral Service Commission, Texas - (1903 as State Board of Embalming; 1935 as State Board of Funeral Directors and Embalmers; 1953 as 6-member board; membership increased to 9 in 1979; name changed to present form in 1987); apptv.; per diem and expenses; 6-yr.; 9 members: Evelyn S. Collins, Texarkana (1/31/99); Robert R. Dixon, West Columbia (1/31/97); Robert G. Duncan, Victoria (1/31/99); Martha Fitzwater, San Antonio (1/31/99); Kenneth Jerry Hughes, Nacogdoches (1/31/99); Patricia Gail Keegan, Rockwall (1/31/01); Charles Richard McNeil, Fort Worth (1/31/01); Leo T. Metcalf III, Conroe (1/31/01); Norberto Salinas Sr., Mission (1/31/97). Exec. Dir., Eliza May ($42,000), 510 S. Congress, Ste. 206, Austin 78704-1716.

General Services Commission - (1919 as Board of Control; name changed to State Purchasing and General Services Commission in 1979; changed to present form and increased to 6 commissioners in 1991); apptv.; 6-yr.; expenses; 6 members: Ofelia de los Santos, Edinburg (1/31/99); Dionicio Vidal (Sonny) Flores, Houston (1/31/01); Ramiro Guzman, El Paso (1/31/99); Alphonso Jackson, Dallas (1/31/01); Barbara N. Rusling, China Spring (1/31/03); Gene Shull, Tyler (1/31/03). Exec. Dir., John Pouland ($78,000), PO Box 13047, Austin 78711-3047.

Growth Fund Board of Trustees, Texas - (1988); apptd.; 6-yr.; 9 members — one member from and elected by membership of each of the following: Board of Regents, University of Texas System; Board of Regents, Texas A&M University System; Board of Trustees, Teacher Retirement System; Board of Trustees, Employees Retirement System; State Board of Education; 4 public members apptd. by Gov.: Daphne Ann Brown, Houston (2/1/99); H. Scott Caven, Houston (2/1/99); Suzanne B. Kriscunas, Dallas (2/1/03); Timothy P. Roth, El Paso (2/1/03).

Guadalupe River Authority, Upper - (1939); apptv.; 6-yr.; 9 members: Georgia H. Christley, Kerrville (2/1/99); Marsha E. Copeland, Kerrville (2/1/01); T. Beck Gipson, Kerrville (2/1/01); Waldean Groff, Kerrville (2/1/97); George G. MacDonald Jr., Kerrville (2/1/01); John R. Mosty, Center Point (2/1/97); Donald C. Oehler, Ingram (2/1/97); Laresa Smith, Kerrville (2/1/99); William H. Williams II, Kerrville (2/1/99). Gen. Mgr., J. T. Brown,

215 W. Water St., Kerrville 78028-4252.

Guadalupe-Blanco River Authority - (1935); apptv.; per diem and expenses on duty; 6-yr.; 9 members: William A. Blackwell, Cuero (2/1/01); Anne Cooper, San Marcos (2/1/01); Marshall Ray Holybee, Bayside (2/1/99); Warren P. Kirksey, Lockhart (2/1/97); Olga Lara, New Braunfels (2/1/99); Catherine Roberts McHaney, Victoria (2/1/97); Wanda Roberts, Port Lavaca (2/1/99); John C. Taylor, McQueeney (2/1/97); Ashley Holmes Turberville, Nixon (2/1/01). Gen. Mgr., W.E. West Jr., 933 E. Court St., Seguin 78155.

Gulf Coast Waste Disposal Authority - (1969); apptv.; 2-yr.; per diem and expenses on duty; 9 members: 3 apptv. by Gov., 3 by County Commissioners Courts of counties in district, 3 by Municipalities Waste Disposal Councils of counties in district. Gov's. apptees: Louis S. Dell'Olio Jr., Galveston (8/31/98); Rafael Ortega, Houston (8/31/97); Shirley U. Seale, Anahuac (8/31/98). Gen. Mgr., Dick Brown, 910 Bay Area Blvd., Houston 77058.

Gulf States Marine Fisheries Commission - (1949); apptv.; 3-yr.; 3 members — 2 ex officio: exec. dir., Texas Parks & Wildlife Dept.; one member of House; one apptd. by Gov.: L. Don Perkins, Houston (3/17/99). Exec. Dir., Larry B. Simpson, PO Box 726, Ocean Springs, MS 30564.

Health, Commissioner of - (1879 as State Health Officer; 1955 changed to Commissioner of Health; 1975 changed to Director, Texas Department of Health Resources; 1977 changed to Commissioner, Texas Department of Health; apptv.; 2-yr.: Dr. William "Reyn" Archer ($148,683), 1100 W. 49th, Austin 78756.

Health and Human Services, Commissioner of - (1991); apptd.; 2-yr.; one commissioner: Michael D. McKinney ($156,014), (2/1/99). 4900 N. Lamar Blvd., Austin 78731.

Health Benefits Purchasing Cooperative, Texas, Board of Trustees - (1993); 6-yr.; apptd.; expenses; 6 members: Maria E. Crowley, Dallas (2/1/95); Matrice Ellis-Kirk, Dallas (2/1/95); Cappy R. McGarr, Dallas (2/1/99); Joseph F. Phillips, Mission (2/1/99); Marvin L. Ragsdale, Georgetown (2/1/97); Philip Patrick Sun, Missouri City (2/1/97).

Health Care Information Council, Texas - (1995); expenses; 18 members: 3 nonvoting ex officio state agency members (commissioner of public health, commissioner of health and human services, commissioner of insurance); 15 apptd. to 6-yr. terms: Cindy S. Basham (9/1/97); Jack Gerhardt Blaz, Dallas (9/1/01); David Cortez, San Antonio (9/1/99); Bobby S. De Rossett, Flint (9/1/97); Dresdene E. Flynn-White, Plano (9/1/99); Arthur Garson, Houston (9/1/97); Norma S. Garza, Brownsville (9/1/01); Jacinto Pablo Juarez, Laredo (9/1/99); Gail Dowdy Neas, Houston (9/1/99); Susan M. Nelson, Plano (9/1/01); Mary Whiting Puckett, San Antonio (9/1/97); Robert E. Schorlemer, San Antonio (9/1/99); D.B. Whittington, Texas City (9/1/97); Nelda P. Wray, Houston (9/1/01).

Health Care Reimbursement Alternatives, Texas Commission on - (1987); term at pleasure of Gov.; apptd., expenses; 18 members — 4 representatives and 3 public members apptd. by Speaker; 4 senators and 3 public members apptd. by Lt. Gov.; 3 public members and chairman apptd. by Gov.; Gov's apptees: Joel T. Allison, Corpus Christi; Lynda Calcote, Abilene; William P. Daves Jr., Dallas; Carol Carlson Dean, Lakeside City.

Health Coordinating Council, Statewide - (1975); apptv.; 2-yr.; membership decreased from 21 to 15 in 1993: 3 health care professionals, 3 from institutions of higher education, 3 consumer advocates, 6 public members; apptv., as follows: Annabel Barker, Big Spring (8/31/95); Joan Wood Biggerstaff, Plano (8/31/97); Nick U. Curry, Fort worth (8/31/95); Dana S. Fitzsimmons, Houston (8/31/97); Barbara Ann Gonzalez, Alice (8/31/99); John P. Howe III, San Antonio (8/31/97); Man-Ja C. Lee, Little Elm (8/31/99); Linda C. Lopez, San Antonio (8/31/95); Polly L. McFadden, El Paso (8/31/99); Betty Fox McLemore, Longview (8/31/99); Shirley McManigal, Lubbock (8/31/99); Therese Ruffing, Austin (8/31/95); Betty J. Shinn, Nacogdoches (8/31/97); deSaussure M. Treviño, Pharr (8/31/95); Francisco J. Velazquez, San Antonio (8/31/97). Exec. Dir., A. Spires, Texas Dept. of Health, 1100 W. 49th, Austin 78756-3199.

Health, Texas Board of - (1903 as State Board of Health; superseded similar department created in 1891; name changed in 1975 to Texas Board of Health Resources and membership increased to 18; name changed in 1977 to present form; membership decreased to 6); apptv.; per diem and expenses on duty; 6-yr.; 6 members: Kent M. Adams, Beaumont (2/1/03); Mario R. Anzaldua, Mission (2/1/03); Mary E. Ceverha, Dallas (2/1/01); David L. Collins, Houston (2/1/99); Ruth F. Stewart, San Antonio (2/1/99); Walter D. Wilkerson Jr., Conroe (2/1/01). Commissioner of Health, Dr. William "Reyn" Archer, 1100 W. 49th, Austin 78756.

Hearing Instruments, State Committee of Examiners in

the **Fitting and Dispensing of** - (1969); apptv.; 6-yr.; expenses; 9 members: Joycie L. Burns, Teague (12/31/97); Max Stanley Chartrand, Gainesville (12/31/01); Larry W. Farris, Universal City (12/31/99); Robert M. Komorn, Houston (12/31/01); Thomas C. Lucenay, Hewitt (12/31/97); Carlos T. Oliveira, Laredo (12/31/01); Andrew Peña, El Paso (12/31/99); Jane W. Porter, Irving (12/31/97); Diane Cecile Shaffer, Beaumont (12/31/97). Exec. Dir., Wanda Stewart ($55,000), 4800 N. Lamar, Ste. 150, Austin 78756.

Higher Education Coordinating Board, Texas - (1953 as temporary board; 1955 as permanent 15-member Texas Commission on Higher Education; increased to 18 members in 1965; name changed to present form in 1987); apptv.; 6-yr.; expenses; 18 members: William C. Atkinson, Bryan (8/31/01); Martin Basaldúa, Kingwood (8/31/97); Dolores H. Carruth, Irving (8/31/01); Joaquin G. Cigarroa Jr., Laredo (8/31/99); Robert I. Fernandez, Fort Worth (8/31/01); Rene Haas, Corpus Christi (8/31/97); Jodie L. Jiles, Houston (8/31/01); Joseph R. Krier, San Antonio (8/31/99); Steve Late, Odessa (8/31/01); Wendy Marsh, Amarillo (8/31/99); Janie S. McGarr, Dallas (8/31/99); Andrew Melontree, Tyler (8/31/97); Martha Miller, Texarkana (8/31/97); Tom C. Nichols, Lubbock (8/31/99); Leonard Rauch, Houston (8/31/01); Robert W. Shepard, Harlingen (8/31/97); Carlos Villa, El Paso (8/31/99); Pamela P. Willeford, Austin (8/31/97). Commissioner of Higher Education, Dr. Kenneth H. Ashworth ($125,106), PO Box 12788, Austin 78711.

Higher Education Tuition Board, Prepaid - (1995); apptv.; expenses; 6-yr.; 7 members: State Comptroller, 2 apptd. by Lt. Gov., 2 apptd. by Gov. Gov.'s apptees: Michael D. Gollob, Tyler (2/1/03); Beth Miller Weakley, San Antonio (2/1/99).

Historical Commission, Texas - (1953); apptv.; expenses; 6-yr.; 18 members: Bruce T. Aiken, Brownsville (2/1/01); Jane Cook Barnhill, Brenham (2/1/01); J.P. Bryan, Houston (2/1/03); Jan Felts Bullock, Austin (2/1/99); Shirley W. Caldwell, Albany (2/1/01); Chris John Carson, San Antonio (2/1/03); T.R. Fehrenbach, San Antonio (2/1/01); Mrs. Willie Lee Glass, Tyler (2/1/99); Betty Elliott Hanna, Breckenridge (2/1/99); Virginia Long, Kilgore (2/1/99); Archie P. McDonald, Nacogdoches (2/1/97); Carl R. McQueary, Salado (2/1/03); Susan Mead, Dallas (2/1/01); John Liston Nau III, Houston (2/1/99); Rose T. Trevino, Laredo (2/1/99); Linda A. Valdez, San Antonio (2/1/03); Clinton P. White, Wharton (2/1/03). Exec. Dir., Curtis Tunnell, P. O. Box 12276, Austin 78711 ($70,000).

Historical Records Advisory Board, Texas - (1976); apptv.; 3-yr.; 9 members: Nancy L. Boothe, Houston (1/23/98); Martha K. Crowley, Richardson (1/23/98); Randal B. Gilbert, Tyler (1/23/98); Diana B. Gonzalez, San Antonio (1/23/97); Chris A. LaPlante, Austin (1/23/91); Gleniece A. Robinson, Dallas (1/23/94); Peggy Thomas, Fort Worth (1/23/99); Wolfram Mateusz Von-Maszewski, Pasadena (1/23/99); Harriette W. Whatley, Fairfield (1/23/99). State Historical Records Coordinator, Chris LaPlante, State Library, PO Box 12927, Austin 78711.

Hospital Licensing Advisory Council - (abolished 1996)

Housing and Community Affairs, Board of Texas Dept. of - (1979 as Texas Housing Agency; merged with Department of Community Affairs and name changed in 1991); apptv.; expenses; 6-yr.; 9 members: Donald R. Bethel, Lamesa (1/31/01); Margie Lee Bingham, Houston (1/31/01); Robert O. Brewer, San Angelo (1/31/01); Harvey Clemons Jr., Houston (1/31/99); C. Kent Conine, Dallas (1/31/03); James Amador Daross, El Paso (1/31/03); Florita Bell Griffin, College Station (1/31/03); Michael E. Jones, Tyler (1/31/99); Paul R. Rodriguez, Mission (1/31/99). Exec. Dir., Larry Paul Manley ($90,177), 507 Sabine, Austin 78701.

Human Rights, State Commission on - (1983); apptv.; 6-yr.; expenses; 6 members: Laura Ayoub Keith, El Paso (9/24/01); Maxine Lee, Austin (9/24/97); Rev. Howard Ransom, Port Arthur (9/24/99); Lynn Ellen Rubinett, Austin (9/24/99); Richard A. Solo, Dallas (9/24/97); Charles W. Taylor Jr., Houston (9/24/01). Exec. Dir., William M. Hale ($54,768), P. O. Box 13493, Austin 78711.

Human Services, Texas Board of - (1941 as State Board of Public Welfare; name changed to present form in 1985); apptv.; 6-yr.; per diem and expenses; 6 members: David Herndon, Austin (1/20/01); Bill Jones, Houston (1/20/03); Anchi H. Ku, Dallas (1/20/99); Elizabeth Darling Seale, San Antonio (1/20/03); Carlela K. Vogel, Fort Worth (1/20/99); Carole A. Woodard, Galveston (1/20/01). Commissioner, Burton F. Raiford ($105,000), PO Box 149030, Austin 78714-9030.

Humanities, Texas Council for the - Kathleen Ford Bay, Austin (12/31/97); Linden Heck Howell, Portland (12/31/98); Wright L. Lassiter Jr., Dallas (12/31/97); J. Landon Short, Houston (12/31/98); Thomas G. West, Irving (12/31/97). Exec. Dir., James F. Veninga, 3809 S. 2nd St., Ste. A100, Austin 78704-7095.

Incentive and Productivity Commission, Texas - (1987 as Productivity and Bonus Commission and Employee Incentive Commission; commissions merged and name changed to present form in 1989); 9 members — 6 state officials (term on commission is term in other office): Gov.; Lt. Gov.; Comptroller; State Treasurer; Administrator, Texas Workforce Comm.; Chmn., Texas Higher Education Coordinating Bd.; 3 apptd. by Gov.: Hattie Hill-Storks, Carrollton (2/1/95); Sherry L. Phelps, Bartonville (2/1/98); Jacob N. Samuel, Galveston (2/1/95). Exec. Dir., M. Elaine Powell ($42,534), PO Box 12482, Austin 78711.

Information Resources, Department of - (1981 as Automated Information and Telecommunications Council; name changed in 1990); 6-yr.; expenses; 3 members recommended by Speaker of House, 3 by Lt. Gov.; 3 by Gov.: 9 members: Ken Armbrister, Austin (2/1/97); Walter A. Bradley III, Dallas (2/1/01); Jim C. Brunjes, Lubbock (2/1/99); R. Dan Burck, Austin (2/1/97); Scott Hochberg, Houston (2/1/99); Robert Junell, Austin (2/1/99); Harry H. Richardson, San Antonio (2/1/01); Jennifer Stamper, Dallas (2/1/01); Dorothy G. Wells, Austin (2/1/97). Exec. Dir., Carolyn Purcell ($90,000), PO Box 13564, Austin 78711.

Insurance, Commissioner of - Elton Bomer (2/1/99); ($150,000), PO Box 149104, Austin 78714.

Insurance, State Board of - Abolished by the 73rd Legislature, eff. Sept. 1, 1994. All members had resigned by Dec. 31, 1993.

International Trade Commission - (1991); apptv.; 6-yr.; 6 members: Robert W. Hsueh, Dallas (2/1/01); José E. Martinez, San Antonio (2/1/99); Robert B. Reeves, Center (2/1/01); Phillip S. Shinoda, Dallas (2/1/97); Patricia J. Smothers, San Antonio (2/1/99). Dir., J. David Bamberger (member), San Antonio (2/1/97), c/o Texas Dept. of Commerce.

Interstate Mining Compact Commission - Melvin Hodgkiss, Austin. Exec. Dir.: Gregory Conrad, 459B Carlisle Drv., Herndon, VA 22070.

Interstate Oil and Gas Compact Commission, Texas Rep. - (1935); ex officio or apptv., according to Gov.'s choice; per diem and expenses. (Approximately 150 other appointees serve on various committees.) Exec. Dir., Christine Hansen, PO Box 53127, Oklahoma City, OK 73152.

Interstate Parole Compact Administrator - (1951); apptv.: Knox Fitzpatrick, Dallas.

Jail Standards, Texas Commission on - (1975); apptv.; 6-yr.; expenses; 9 members: Terry G. Box, McKinney (1/31/03); Marc Cisneros, Premont (1/31/03); Larry T. Craig, Tyler (1/31/01); C.O. Hadnot, Hillister (1/31/99); J.D. Johnson, Fort Worth (1/31/99); Carmella Jones, Claude (1/31/03); Patrick O. Keel, Austin (1/31/01); Manuel Rivera, El Paso (1/31/99); Marcia Saunders, Lake Kiowa (1/31/01). Exec. Dir., Jack E. Crump ($53,634), PO Box 12985, Austin 78711.

Judicial Conduct, State Commission on - (1965 as 9-member Judicial Qualifications Commission; name changed in 1977 to present form and membership raised to 11); expenses; 6-yr.; 11 members: 5 apptd. by Supreme Court; 2 apptd. by State Bar; 4 apptd. by Gov. as follows: Jean Birmingham, Marshall (11/19/99); Carol Jean MacLean, Cleburne (11/19/97); L. Scott Mann, Lubbock (11/19/01); Rosa Walker, Austin (11/19/97). Exec. Dir., Robert C. Flowers ($87,500), PO Box 12265, Austin 78711.

Judicial Council, Texas - (1929 as Texas Civil Judicial Council; name changed in 1975); ex officio terms vary; apptv.; 6-yr. terms; expenses; 19 members — 10 ex officio and 9 apptd. from general public: Stephen B. Ables, Kerrville (2/1/99); Debbie D. Branson, Dallas (6/30/97); Lee Ann Dauphinot, Fort Worth (2/1/99); Algenita Scott Davis, Houston (6/30/99); Judith K. Guthrie, Tyler (6/30/97); Rayleene (Rae) Jackson, Longview (6/30/01); W.T. McDonald, Bryan (6/30/97); Diego J. Peña, San Antonio (6/30/01); Richard P. Richards, Aransas Pass (6/30/01); Cynthia Fay Solls, Dallas (6/30/99); Joe Spurlock II (6/30/99); Blake Tartt, Houston (6/30/93). Exec. Dir., Jerry Benedict, PO Box 12066, Austin 78711.

Judicial Districts Board - (1985); 12 ex officio members (term in other office); one apptv. (4 yrs.); ex officio: Chief Justice of Texas Supreme Court; Presiding Judge, Court of Criminal Appeals; Presiding Judge of each of 9 Administrative Judicial Districts; pres. of Texas Judicial Council.

Judicial Districts of Texas, Admin., Presiding Judges of - (See Administrative Judicial Districts, Presiding Judges).

Juvenile Probation Commission, Texas - (1981); apptv.; 6-yr.; expenses; 9 members — 3 judges of District Courts and 6 private citizens: Eric Andell, Bellaire (8/31/97); Victoria H. Baldwin, Austin (8/31/97); Robert P. Brotherton, Wichita Falls (8/31/01); Raul Garcia, San Angelo (8/31/99); Keith H. Kuttler, College Station (8/31/01); Betsy Lake, Houston (8/31/99); Theresa B. Lyons, Fort Worth (8/31/97); Robert Tejeda, San Antonio (8/31/99); Michael L. Williams, Arlington (8/31/01).

Exec. Dir., Vicki Wright ($70,000), PO Box 13547, Austin 78711.

Lamar University System, Board of Regents - (abolished Sept. 1995 upon the transfer of Lamar University System to the Texas State University System).

Land Board, School - (1939); one ex officio (term in other office); 2 apptd. — one by Atty. Gen. and one by Gov. for 2-yr. term; per diem and expenses; ex officio member: Comm. of General Land Office; Gov's. apptee: C. Louis Renaud, Midland (8/29/97).

Land Surveying, Texas Board of Professional - (1979); formed from consolidation of membership of Board of Examiners of Licensed Land Surveyors, est. 1977, and State Board of Registration for Public Surveyors, est. 1955); apptv.; 6-yr.; 10 members — Commissioner of General Land Office serving by statute; 3 members of general public, 2 licensed land surveyors, 4 registered public surveyors, as follows: Jerry M. Goodson, Lampasas (1/31/01); Betty H. Little, Amarillo (1/31/03); James Noble Johnson, Austin (1/31/99); Paul P. Kwan, Houston (1/31/99); A.W. Osborn, Tyler (1/31/01); Robert Pounds, El Paso (1/31/03); Andrew L. Sikes, Houston (1/31/99); Joan White, Brownsville (1/31/03); Raul Wong Jr., Dallas (1/31/01). Exec. Dir., Sandy Smith ($42,005), 7701 N. Lamar, Ste. 400, Austin 78752.

Lands, Board for Lease of University - (1929 as 3-member board; membership increased to 4 in 1985); ex officio; term in other office; 4 members: Commissioner of General Land Office, 2 members of Board of Regents of University of Texas, 1 member Board of Regents of Texas A&M University.

Lavaca-Navidad River Authority, Board of Directors - (1954 as 7-member Jackson County Flood Control District; reorganized as 9-member board in 1959; name changed to present form in 1969); apptv.; 6-yr.; per diem and expenses; 9 members: Sandra R. Green, LaWard (5/1/01); Harry Lee Hafernick, Edna (5/1/97); Charles M. Hasdorff, Ganado (5/1/01); J.B. Housson, Ganado (5/1/97); Theresa McCaig, Ganado (5/1/97); Michael W. Menefee, Edna (5/1/01); Callaway S. Vance, Edna (5/1/99); Robert J. Whitworth, Edna (5/1/99). Gen. Mgr., Emmett Gloyna, PO Box 429, Edna 77957.

Law Enforcement Officer Standards & Education, Comm. on - (1965); expenses; 14 members — 5 ex officio: Atty. Gen., Directory of Public Safety, Commissioner of Education, Exec. Dir. of Governor's Office Criminal Justice Division, and Commissioner of Higher Education; 9 apptv. members: J.J. Berry Jr., Houston (8/30/97); Claudia Ann Bretz, Odessa (8/30/01); Felipe Garza, Kingsville (8/30/97); Frances A. Kaiser, Kerrville (8/30/01); Onzelo Markum III, League City (8/30/01); Horace L. O'Neal, Lubbock (8/30/99); Benigno Guadalupe Reyna, Brownsville (8/30/97); Joe A. Stivers, Huntsville (8/30/99); Sally Ann Werst, Fort Worth (8/30/99). Exec. Dir., D.C. Jim Dozier ($70,000), 6330 E. Hwy. 290, Ste. 200, Austin 78723.

Law Examiners, Board of - Nine attorneys apptd. by Supreme Court biennially for 2-year terms expiring September 30 of odd-numbered years. Compensation set by Supreme Court not to exceed $20,000 per annum. Exec. Dir., Rachel Martin, PO Box 13486, Austin 78711.

Law Library Board, State - (1971); ex officio; expenses; 3 members: Chief Justice State Supreme Court, Presiding Judge Court of Criminal Appeals and Atty. General. General. Dir., Kay Schlueter ($47,000), PO Box 12367, Austin 78711.

Legislative Budget Board - (1949); 10 members; 6 ex officio members: Lt. Gov.; Speaker of House; Chmn., Senate Finance Comm.; Chmn., Senate State Affairs Comm.; Chmn., House Appropriations Comm.; plus 4 other members of Legislature. Director, John Keel, PO Box 12666, Austin 78711-2666.

Legislative Council, Texas - (1949); 17 ex officio members — 4 senators named by Lt. Gov.; 9 representatives named by Speaker; Chmn., House Administration Committee; Chmn., Senate Administration Committee; Lt. Gov.; and Speaker. Exec. Dir., Robert I. Kelly, PO Box 12128, Austin 78711.

Legislative Redistricting Board - (1948); 5 ex officio members; term in other office: Lt. Gov., Speaker of House, Atty. Gen., Comptroller and Commissioner of General Land Office.

Librarian, State - (Originally est. in 1839; present office est. 1909); apptv., indefinite term: Robert S. Martin ($65,000), PO Box 12927, Austin 78711.

Library and Archives Commission, Texas State - (1909 as 5-member Library and State Historical Commission; number of members increased to 6 in 1953; name changed to present form in 1979); apptv.; per diem and expenses on duty; 6-yr.; 6 members: Carolyn P. Armstrong, San Antonio (9/28/01); Patrick Heath, Boerne (9/28/99); Sandy Melton, Dallas (9/28/01); Sandra J. Pickett, Liberty (9/28/97); Marvin Rich, Houston (9/28/99); Barbara Silberberg, Dallas (9/28/97). Dir. and Librarian Robert S. Martin ($65,000), PO Box 12927, Austin 78711.

Library, State Legislative Reference - (1909); indefinite term; Director: Sally Reynolds. Box 12488, Austin 78711.

Licensing and Regulation, Texas Commission on - (1989); apptv.; 6-yr.; expenses; 6 members: Clara Caldwell, Austin (2/1/99); Mickey Christakos, Allen (2/1/03); William Fowler, Valley Spring (2/1/01); Elliott B. McConnell, Rockport (2/1/03); Ronald Lynn Raspberry, Spring (2/1/99); Earl L. Yeakel III, Austin (2/1/01). Exec. Dir., Tommy V. Smith ($62,494), PO Box 12157, Austin 78711.

Lottery Commission, Texas - (1993); 6-yrs.; apptv.; expenses; 3 members: John L. Hill Jr., Houston (2/1/99); Harriet Ellan Miers, Dallas (2/1/01); Anthony J. Sadberry, Cypress (2/1/97). Exec. Dir., Lawrence Littwin ($110,000), PO Box 16630, Austin 78761-6630.

Lower Colorado River Authority - (See Colorado River Authority, Lower).

Marriage & Family Therapists, Texas State Board of Examiners of - (1991); apptd.; 6 yrs.; per diem and transportation expenses; 9 members: Anna Beth Benningfield, Dallas (2/1/01); Noe Cavazos, Weslaco (2/1/99); Leslie E. Goolishian, Galveston (2/1/97); Ellen Harrison, El Paso (2/1/01); Thomas A. Milholland, Abilene (2/1/97); George P. Pulliam, Dickinson (2/1/01); Harriet N. Roberts, Houston (2/1/99); David A. Talbot Sr., Commerce (2/1/97). Exec. Dir., Bobby D. Schmidt, Dept. of Health, 1100 W. 49th St., Austin 78756-3183.

Medical Examiners District Review Committee: Dist. 1 - (1977); apptv.; 6-hr.; expenses; 20 members — five from each of 4 districts: Jerome L. Armbruster, Pearland (1/15/94); A. David Axelrad, Houston (1/15/00); Robert J. Bacon Sr., Houston (1/15/98); Herman L. Koester, Dickinson (1/15/02); Thomas A. Reiser, Houston (1/15/00). **Dist. 2:** David Baucom, Sulphur Springs (1/15/00); H. Jane Chihal, Carrollton (1/15/02); Allan N. Shulkin, Dallas (1/15/00); B.R. Sienbenlist, Jonesville (1/15/98); Rodney M. Wiseman, Tyler (1/15/00). **Dist. 3:** Robert C. Henderson, Amarillo (1/15/02); Thomas L. Marvelli, Fort Worth (1/15/00); ; Nalin H. Tolia, Odessa (1/15/98)Robert Allan Watson, Fort Worth (1/15/00); Irvin E. Zeitler Jr., San Angelo (1/15/00). **Dist. 4:** Manuel G. Guajardo, Brownsville (1/15/02); Larry Hufford, San Antonio (1/15/00); Julian Gomez III, McAllen (1/15/00); Gladys C. Keene, Laredo (1/15/98); Ann L. Nolen, La Grange (1/15/00).

Medical Examiners, Texas State Board of - (1907 as 12-member board, membership raised to 15 in 1981, raised to 18 in 1993); apptv.; 6-yr.; per diem on duty; 18 members: Penny Angelo, Midland (4/13/01); Marianne Beard, Arlington (4/13/97); Carlos Campos, New Braunfels (4/13/99); Ann Forehand, Texarkana (4/13/99); William H. Fleming III, Houston (4/13/01); Margaret L. Ford, Houston (4/13/01); Catalina E. Garcia, Dallas (4/13/97); Cynthia "Cindy" Jenkins, Stowell (4/13/97); Thomas D. Kirksey, Austin (4/13/01); John M. Lewis, Houston (4/13/97); Paul G. Meyer, Lubbock (4/13/01); Charles W. Monday Jr., Huntsville (4/13/99); Connie Navar-Clark, El Paso (4/13/99); William A. Pollan, Ballinger (4/13/99); Vernon L. Ryan, San Angelo (4/13/01); Ratna Solomon, Dallas (4/13/97); Raymond Russell Thomas, Eagle Lake (4/13/99); Jenat Terhune Turner, Austin (4/13/03). Exec. Dir., Bruce A. Levy ($85,000), PO Box 149134, Austin 78714-9134.

Medical Physicists, Texas Board of Licensure for Professional - (1991); apptv.; 6-yrs.; 9 members: Ralph Blumhardt, San Antonio (2/1/95); Stewart C. Bushong, Houston (2/1/99); Louis H. Deiterman, Temple (2/1/99); Thomas S. Harle, Houston (2/1/97); Paul H. Murphy, Houston (2/1/95); Lester J. Peters, Houston (2/1/97); Wayne A. Wiatgrowski, San Antonio (2/1/95); Ann E. Wright, Houston (2/1/97).

Mental Health and Mental Retardation, Texas Board of - (1965, superseded Board of Texas State Hospitals and Special Schools); apptv.; 6-yr.; per diem and expenses; 9 members: Rodolfo Arredondo Jr., Lubbock (1/31/01); Charles M. Cooper, Dallas (1/31/01); Virginia Eernisse, Alvin (1/31/97); Janelle Smith Jordan, Houston (1/31/99); William A. Lawson, Houston (1/31/97); Rosemary Vivero Neill, El Paso (1/31/99); James I. Perkins, Rusk (1/31/01); Ann K. Utley, Dallas (1/31/97); Edward B. Weyman, Midland (1/31/99). Commissioner of MHMR Don A. Gilbert, PO Box 12668, Austin 78711-2668 ($95,000, plus house and utilities).

Midwestern State University, Board of Regents - (1959); apptv.; 6-yr.; 9 members: Mac Cannedy Jr., Wichita Falls (2/25/00); Margaret F. Darden, Dallas (2/25/98); Barbara Jean Dorman, Plainview (2/25/02); Ervin Garnett, Fort Worth (2/25/98); Elizabeth A. Gifford, Amarillo (2/25/02); Arnold W. Oliver, Wichita Falls (2/25/02); Edward L. Watson, Dallas (2/25/00); Robert G. West, Fort Worth (2/25/98); Kathryn Anne Yeager, Wichita Falls (2/25/00). Pres., Dr. Louis J. Rodriguez, 3400 Taft, Wichita Falls 76308.

Motor Vehicle Board, Texas Department of Transportation - (1971 as 6-member board; membership increased to 9 in 1979; reduced to 6 in 1987; made division of Texas Dept. of

Transportation, name changed to present form and membership increased to 9 in 1992; decreased to 6); apptv.; 6-yr.; per diem and expenses; members: Robert C. Barnes, Odessa (1/31/03); D. Diane Dillard, Houston (1/31/03); N. Scott Jones, Cleburne (1/31/01); Manuel Marrufo, El Paso (1/31/01); Laurie Watson, Austin (1/31/99); Stephen P. Webb, Austin (1/31/99) Division Dir. Brett Bray, PO Box 2293, Austin 78768.

Municipal Retirement System (See Retirement System, Municipal, Board of Trustees).

National Guard Armory Board, Texas - (1935 as 3-member board; reorganized as 6-member board in 1981); 6-yr.; 6 members: Darrel Baker, Austin (4/30/01); Hal Boyd, Big Spring (4/30/97); Lillian Dunlap, San Antonio (4/30/99); Federico Lopez III, Harlingen (4/30/99); David J. Rist, Dallas (4/30/97); Michael G. White, El Paso (4/30/01). Exec. Dir., Michael Huff ($53,469), PO Box 5426, Austin 78763.

National Research Laboratory Commission, Texas - (1986); apptv.; expenses; 6-yr.; 9 members: J. Fred Bucy, Dallas (2/1/01); G.W. Ceverha, Dallas (2/1/01); Charles R. Delgado, Galveston (2/1/99); Peter Flawn, Austin (2/1/97); Rolf R. Haberecht, Dallas (2/1/01); Jerome Johnson, Amarillo (2/1/97); N.B. Jordan, Waxahachie (2/1/99); Thomas D. Williams, Dallas (2/1/99). Exec. Dir., Edward C. Bingler, 2275 N. Highway 77, #100, Waxahachie 75165.

Natural Resource Conservation Commission, Texas - (1913 as State Board of Water Engineers; name changed in 1962 to Texas Water Commission; reorganized and name again changed in 1965 to Water Rights Commission; reorganized and name changed back to Texas Water Commission in 1977 to perform the judicial function for the Texas Dept. of Water Resources; changed to present form Sept. 1, 1993); apptv.; 6-yr.; 3 members full-time at $90,071: John M. Baker Jr., Temple (8/31/01); John L. Hall, Austin (8/31/97); R.B. (Ralph) Marquez, Texas City (8/31/99). Exec. Dir., Dan Pearson ($115,000), PO Box 13087, Austin 78711.

Neches River Municipal Water Authority, Upper - (Est. 1953 as 9-member board; membership changed to 3 in 1959); apptv.; 6-yr.; 3 members: Joe M. Crutcher, Palestine (2/1/01); Edward McCoy Jr., Palestine (2/1/99); Cathy Ann Stark, Palestine (2/1/99). Gen. Mgr., T.G. Mallory, PO Box 1965, Palestine 75802.

Neches Valley Authority, Lower - (1933); apptv.; per diem and expenses on duty; 6-yr.; 9 members: R.C. Aldrich, Nome (7/28/95); F.M. Archer, Woodville (7/28/97); Clyde E. Cole, Silsbee (7/28/99); Gaylyn Cooper, Beaumont (7/28/99); Paul Georgas, Silsbee (7/28/97); Von E. McReynolds, Groves (7/28/97); W.S. Nichols Jr., Woodville (7/28/95); G. Paul Pepper, Beaumont (7/28/01); Thomas A. Thomas, Port Arthur (7/28/99). Gen. Mgr. A. T. Hebert Jr., PO Box 3464, Beaumont 77704.

Nueces River Authority Board of Directors - (1953 as Nueces River Conservation and Reclamation District; name changed in 1971); apptv.; 6-yr.; per diem and expenses; 21 members: Mary B. Autry, Pipe Creek (2/1/97); Madge E. Belcher, Brackettville (2/1/97); Margaret Bowman, Spofford (2/1/99); Cleo Bustamante Jr., Carrizo Springs (2/1/97); Ernestine Carson, Barksdale (2/1/01); William I. Dillard, Uvalde (2/1/01); James F. Dodson, Robstown (2/1/01); George A. Finley III, Corpus Christi (2/1/99); Ariel A. Garcia, Corpus Christi (2/1/01); Hazel R. Graff, Hondo (2/1/01); Susan C. Griffith, Uvalde (2/1/99); Kay Lynn Jasik, Poteet (2/1/01); Robert D. Johanson, Three Rivers (2/1/97); Ted Jones, Ingleside (2/1/97); Beth Reavis Knolle, Sandia (2/1/99); Susan A. Lynch, Rio Frio (2/1/99); Patty Puig Mueller, Corpus Christi (2/1/01); Bob Mullen, Alice (2/1/97); Mary Melissa Ramos, Floresville (2/1/99); Patricia H. Sugarek, Skidmore (2/1/99); Janna Whatley Williams, Odem (2/1/01); Alfredo Zamora Jr., Cotulla (2/1/99). Exec. Dir., Con Mims, PO Box 349, Uvalde 78802-0349.

Nurse Examiners, State Board of - (1909 as 6-member board; reorganized and membership increased to 9 in 1981); apptv.; per diem and expenses; 6-yr.; 9 members: Nancy Boston, Temple (1/31/01); Mary Letrice Brown, Dallas (1/31/01); Rose Marie Caballero, Corpus Christi (1/31/97); Pat Crowe, Fort Worth (1/31/97); Mary V. Fenton, Galveston (1/31/97); Roselyn Holloway, Lubbock (1/31/99); Marcelo Laijas Jr., Floresville (1/31/99); Kenneth W. Lowrance, Clifton (1/31/01); Doris Price-Nealy, Beaumont (1/31/99). Exec. Dir., Katherine A. Thomas ($60,000), 333 Guadalupe, Suite 3-460, Austin 78701.

Nurse Examiners, State Board of Vocational - (1951 as 9-member board; membership increased to 12 in 1981; later increased to 15); apptv.; 6-yr.; 15 members: Ginger M. Brenner, Pittsburg (9/6/01); Lillian K. Brown, San Angelo (9/6/01); Susie Belle Cheney, Pittsburg (9/6/99); Elmer G. Ellis, Tyler (9/6/97); Albert H. Fairweather, Austin (9/6/97); Melba Lee-Hosey, Houston (9/6/97); Carla Sue McCroan, Royse City (9/6/99); Gabriel Perales Jr., San Antonio (9/6/01); Vangie Perez, Needville (9/6/99); Kathleen Gleeson Powell, North Richland Hills (9/

6/01); William H. Rice, Austin (9/6/97); Maria Olivia Rivas, Brownsville (9/6/99); Opal M. Robinson, Lubbock (9/6/97); Betty E. Sims, Victoria (9/6/01); Janet Wood-Yanez, Mercedes (9/6/99). Exec. Dir., Marjorie A. Bronk ($36,000), 333 Guadalupe St., Ste. 3-400, Austin 78701.

Nursing Facility Administrators, Texas Board of - (1993; assumed duties of abolished Texas Board of Licensure for Nursing Home Administrators); 6-yr., transportation expenses; 2 ex officio, nonvoting members (Tx. Dept. on Aging long-term care ombudsman and Comm. of Human Services or designee); 9 apptd. members: Johnnie Lou Avery, Big Spring (2/1/97); Thomas William Gard, Beaumont (2/1/99); Ramona Kennedy, Flower Mound (2/1/01); Cheryl L. Killian, Arlington (2/1/97); Michael O. Sims, Waco (2/1/99); Jack Ray Tinsley, Frisco (2/1/99); Jerry Turner, Hillsboro (2/1/01); Audrey G. Williamson, Elgin (2/1/01). Texas Dept. of Health, 1100 W. 49th, Austin 78756.

Occupational Therapy Examiners, Texas Board of - (1983); apptv.; 6-yr.; per diem and expenses; 6 members: Esperanza J. Brattin, McAllen (2/1/97); M. Judith Lusted, San Antonio (2/1/99); Benny O. McGehee, El Paso (2/1/97); Gwendolyn L.R. Parker, Odessa (2/1/01); Jean E. Polichino, Houston (2/1/99); Charles Paul R. Turco Sr., Beaumont (2/1/01). Exec. Dir., John Maline, 333 Guadalupe St., Ste. 2-510, Austin 78701.

Offenders with Mental Impairments, Texas Council on - (1987); apptv.; expenses; 6-yr.; 27 members: 18 heads of agencies or their designees: Texas Dept. of Criminal Justice, Texas Dept. of MHMR, Board of Pardons and Paroles, Texas Adult Probation Commission, Texas Juvenile Probation Commission, Texas Youth Commission, Texas Rehabilitation Commission, Texas Education Agency, Criminal Justice Policy Council, Mental Health Assn. in Texas, Texas Commission on Alcohol and Drug Abuse, Commission on Law Enforcement Officer Standards and Education, Texas Council of Community MHMR Centers, Commission on Jail Standards, Texas Planning Council for Developmental Disabilities, Texas Assn. for Retarded Citizens, Texas Alliance for the Mentally Ill, and Parent Assn. for the Retarded of Texas; 9 apptd. by Gov. as follows: Michael R. Arambula, San Antonio (2/1/99); Dollie Brathwaite, Houston (2/1/99); James H. Cromwell, Rusk (2/1/01); Betty Hardwick, Baird (2/1/97); Carl Hays, Dallas (2/1/01); Corinne Ann Mason, Richardson (2/1/01); Carol A. Oeller, Houston (2/1/99); Mario E. Ramírez, Edinburg (2/1/97); Jodie E. Stavinoha, Richmond (2/1/97).Exec. Dir., Dee Kifowit, 8610 Shoal Creek Blvd., Austin 78757.

Old San Antonio Road Preservation Commission - (1989); term at pleasure of governor; 9 members: 4 representatives of state agencies: Texas Dept. of Transportation, Texas Historical Commission, Parks and Wildlife, Texas Dept. of Commerce (Tourism Div.); 5 at large recommended by Texas Historical Commission and apptd. by Gov.: Dr. Archie P. McDonald, Nacogdoches; Gen. John R. McGiffert, San Antonio; Ingrid B. Morris, Hemphill; Nan Olsen, Bastrop; Rose T. Treviño, Laredo.

Optometry Board, Texas - (1921 as 6-member State Board of Examiners in Optometry; name changed to present form in 1981 and membership increased to 9); apptv.; per diem; 6-yr.; 9 members: Jimmy Bitner, Kerrville (1/31/01); Carolyn R. Carman-Merrifield, Arlington (1/31/01); Kevin D. DeWolfe, Austin (1/31/01); Katherine M. Garrett, Mineral Wells (1/31/97); Mark A. Latta, Amarillo (1/31/99); Stanley C. Pearle, Dallas (1/31/97); Wesley E. Pittman, Mexia (1/31/97); Susan B. Place, Plano (1/31/99); Donnya Elle Stephens, Nacogdoches (1/31/99). Exec. Dir., Lois Ewald ($39,545), 333 Guadalupe St., Ste. 2-420, Austin 78701.

Pardons and Paroles Division, Board of - (1893 as Board of Pardon Advisers; changed in 1936 to Board of Pardons and Paroles with 3 members; membership increased to 6 in 1983; made a division of the Texas Department of Criminal Justice and membership increased to 18 in 1990); apptv.; 6-yr.; 18 members: Lynn F. Brown, Carrollton (2/1/03); Bennie L. Elmore, Huntsville (2/1/99); John Escobedo, Huntsville (2/1/99); Gerald L. Garrett, Austin (2/1/01); Juanita Maria Gonzalez, Round Rock (2/1/03); Daniel Ray Lang, Houston (2/1/01); Mary Leal, Houston (2/1/99); Thomas W. Moss, Amarillo (2/1/01); Rissie L. Owens, Huntsville (2/1/03); Paul Joseph Prejean, Beaumont (2/1/01); Victor Rodriguez, Brownsville (2/1/01); Brendolyn Rogers-Gardner, Duncanville (2/1/01); Terri Beard Schnorrenberg, Gatesville (2/1/99); Alvin A. Shaw, Austin (2/1/03); Charles A. Shipman, Wichita Falls (2/1/03); Cynthia S. Tauss, League City (2/1/01); Sandie Walker, Bryan (2/1/03); W.G. (Billy) Walker, Tyler (2/1/99).

Parks and Wildlife Commission, Texas - (1963 as 3-member board; membership increased to 6 in 1971; increased to 9 in 1983); apptv.; expenses; 6-yr.; 9 members: Ernest Angelo Jr., Midland (2/1/03); John Avila Jr., Fort Worth (2/1/01); Lee M.

Bass, Fort Worth (2/1/01); Mickey Ruth Burleson, Temple (2/1/99); John Raymond Clymer Jr., Wichita Falls (2/1/99); Carol E. Dinkins, Houston (2/1/03); Richard W. Heath, Dallas (2/1/01); Susan Howard, Fair Oaks Ranch (2/1/99); Nolan Ryan, Alvin (2/1/01). Exec. Dir., Andrew S. Sansom ($105,000), 4200 Smith School Rd., Austin 78744.

Pecos River Compact Commissioner - (1942); apptv.; 2-yr.; expenses: Brad Newton (1/23/99), 103 W. Callaghan, Fort Stockton 79735 ($32,247).

Pension Boards - For old age, blind and dependent children's assistance, see Human Services, State Board of. For retirement pay to state and municipal employees and teachers, see proper category under Retirement.

Pension Review Board, State - (1979); apptv.; 6-yr.; 9 members — one senator apptd. by Lt. Gov., one representative apptd. by Speaker, 7 apptd. by Gov. as follows: Bruce Cox, Fort Worth (1/31/99); Craig S. Goralski Sr., Houston (1/31/03); Ronald L. Haneberg, Rockwall (1/31/01); William Mahomes Jr., Dallas (1/31/03); Don C. Reynolds, Fort Worth (1/31/01); Frederick E. Rowe Jr., Dallas (1/31/03); Shari Ovalline Shivers, Austin (1/31/03). Exec. Dir., Rita Horwitz ($47,786), PO Box 13498, Austin 78711.

Pest Control Board, Texas Structural - (1971 as 7-member board, membership raised to 9 in 1979); apptv.; 6-yr.; expenses; 9 members — 3 ex officio: Commissioner of Agriculture; Commissioner of Health; and head of Entomology Dept., Texas A&M University; 6 apptv. members: Jo-Christy Brown, Austin (2/1/01); Charles G. Coyle, Fresno (2/1/99); Gary L. Gillen, Rosenberg (2/1/01); Pat Graves, Abilene (2/1/97); Les Hoyt, Amarillo (2/1/97); Kathleen St. John, Dallas (2/1/99). Exec. Dir., Benny M. Mathis ($51,493), 1106 Clayton Ln., Ste. 100 LW, Austin 78723-1066.

Pharmacy, State Board of - (1907 as 6-member board; membership increased to 9 in 1981); apptv.; 6-yr.; 9 members: Gilbert P. Acuna, Kingsville (8/31/99); Charlie B. Bethea, Houston (8/31/97); Jeannette H. Coffield, Jasper (8/31/97); Roberta W. High, Haskell (8/31/01); Susan H. Jacobson, El Paso (8/31/99); Ira Wayne McConnell, Houston (8/31/01); Oren M. Peacock Jr., Sachse (8/31/99); Bill C. Pittman, Austin (8/31/97); Marina P. Sifuentes, Austin (8/31/97). Exec. Dir.-Sec., Fred S. Brinkley Jr. ($66,000), 333 Guadalupe St., Ste. 3-600, Austin 78701.

Physical Therapy Examiners, Texas State Board of - (1971); apptv.; 6-yr.; expenses; 9 members: Cecilia G. Akers, San Antonio (1/31/97); Mark G. Cowart, Odessa (1/31/97); Sheila S. Flannery, Rockwall (1/31/99); Martin Infante, Laredo (1/31/99); Penny Butler Patterson, Tyler (1/31/99); Barbara B. Shell, Houston (1/31/97); Susan K. Tripplehorn, Pampa (1/31/01); Ann L. Walker, Dallas (1/31/97); Theodis Ware, Fort Worth (1/31/99). Coordinator Gerard Swain, 333 Guadalupe St., Ste. 3-510, Austin 78701.

Physician Assistant Examiners, Texas State Board of - (1995); apptv.; 6-yr.; per diem; 9 members: Frank Ambriz Jr., Weslaco (2/1/99); Emanuel Bodner, Houston (2/1/99); Dwight M. Deter, El Paso (2/1/01); Glenn S. Forbes, Fort Worth (2/1/97); Tony Gene Hedges, Littlefield (2/1/01); Carlos G. Lopez, Dallas (2/1/01); Joe Mendoza Jr., Seymour (2/1/99); Jane Todd, Center (2/1/97); Myra G. Weaver, Austin (2/1/97).

Plumbing Examiners, State Board of - (1947 as 6-member board; membership increased to 9 in 1981); apptv.; expenses; 6-yr.; 9 members: Stanley J. Briers, Taylor Lake Village (9/5/97); Joe W. Campbell, Houston (9/5/97); José L. Cardenas, Euless (9/5/01); Greg David Contreras, Duncanville (9/5/99); Phillip A. Lord, Pasadena (9/5/97); Nelda Martínez, Corpus Christi (9/5/01); J. DeWitt Morrow Jr., Sugar Land (9/5/99); Fernando Rico Jr., El Paso (9/5/99); Joe Rocha Jr., Blanco (9/5/01). Admin., Gilbert Kissling ($61,909), 929 E. 41st, Austin 78751.

Podiatric Medical Examiners, State Board of - (1923 as 6-member State Board of Chiropody Examiners; name changed in 1967; made 9-member board in 1981); apptv.; 6-yr.; expenses; 9 members: Teresa Barrios-Ogden, San Antonio (7/10/01); C. Stanley Churchill Jr., Carrollton (7/10/01); Alex L. Garcia Jr., Corpus Christi (7/10/01); Thomas S. Garrison, Houston (7/10/97); Preston Goforth, Temple (7/10/99); Mervin E. Perry, Austin (7/10/99); Paul H. Schwarzentraub, Lubbock (7/10/99); J. Michael Valenza, Austin (7/10/97); Barbara G. Young, Bellaire (7/10/97). Exec. Dir., Allen M. Hymans ($36,000), 333 Gadalupe St., Ste. 2-320, Austin 78701.

Polygraph Examiners Board - (1965); apptv.; 6-yr.; 6 members: Janet L. (Jan) Blacklock, Lubbock (6/18/01); Michael C. Gougler, Austin (6/18/99); Horacio Ortiz, Corpus Christi (6/18/01); William H. Quimby, Dallas (6/18/97); Brad Alan Rogers, Killeen (6/18/99); Antonio V. Suarez-Barrio, Killeen (6/18/97). Exec. Officer, Bryan M. Perot ($31,832), PO Box 4087, Austin 78773.

Preservation Board, State - (1983); 2-yr.; 7 members — 4 ex officio: Gov., Lt. Gov., Speaker and Architect of Capitol; 3 apptv.: one apptd. by Gov., one senator apptd. by Lt. Gov. and one representative apptd. by Speaker. Gov's. apptee: Dealey Herndon, Austin (2/1/97). Exec. Dir., Rick Crawford ($77,760), PO Box 13286, Austin 78711.

Prison Board, Texas - (See Criminal Justice, Texas Dept. of).

Private Investigators and Private Security Agencies, Board of - (1969); apptv.; expenses; 6-yr.; 8 members — 2 ex officio: Dir., Dept. of Public Safety and Atty. Gen.; 6 apptd. members: Jim G. Bray Jr., Plano (1/31/03); George B. Craig, Corpus Christi (1/31/03); Joel K. Glenn, Colleyville (1/31/99); Ben C. Nix, Arlington (1/31/99); Jess Ann Thomason, Midland (1/31/01); Matthew Washington, Missouri City (1/31/01). Exec. Dir., Clema D. Sanders ($44,472), PO Box 13509, Austin 78711.

Produce Recovery Fund Board - (1977 as 3-member board; membership increased to 6 in 1981); apptv.; expenses; 6-yr.; 6 members — 2 each from commission merchants, general public and producer representatives. Steven Dexter Jones, Lubbock (1/31/01); Robert B. Lyons, Amarillo (1/31/99); Ly H. Nguyen, Lake Jackson (1/31/03); Joyce Cook Obst, Alamo (1/31/03); David Wayne Smith, Hart (1/31/99); Byron Edward White, Arlington (1/31/01). Admin., Margaret Alvarez, PO Box 12847, Austin 78711.

Protective and Regulatory Services, Board of - (1992); apptv.; 6-yr.; 6 members: Jean P. Beaumont, Bryan (2/1/99); Jon Martin Bradley, Dallas (2/1/03); Maurine Dickey, Dallas (2/1/01); Robert S. Hoffman, Brownsville (2/1/03); Catherine C. Mosbacher, Houston (2/1/03); Bill H. Sheehan, Dumas (2/1/99). Exec. Dir., Janice M. Caldwell ($90,000), PO Box 149030, Austin 78714-9030.

Psychologists, Texas Board of Examiners of - (1969 as 6-member board; membership increased to 9 in 1981); apptv.; 6-yr.; per diem and expenses; 9 members: Susan S. Askanase, Houston (10/31/97); Lorraine E. Breckenridge, Houston (10/31/97); Barry E. Dewlen, San Antonio (10/31/01); Don Goldston, Denton (10/31/99); Jane Halebian, Dallas (10/31/99); Wales H. Madden III, Amarillo (10/31/01); Roberta L. Nutt, Denton (10/31/97); Denise Shade, Dallas (10/31/99); Emily G. Sutter, Friendswood (10/31/01). Exec. Dir., Sherry L. Lee ($42,716), 333 Guadalupe St., Ste. 2-450, Austin 78701.

Public Accountancy, State Board of - (See Accountancy, State Board of Public).

Public Finance Authority, Texas - (1984, assumed duties of Texas Building Authority); apptv.; per diem and expenses; 6-yr.; membership increased from 3 to 6 in 1991: Daniel H. Branch, Dallas (2/1/01); Cheryl D. Creuzot, Houston (2/1/99); Robert B. Davis, Austin (2/1/97); John C. Kerr, San Antonio (2/1/01); Peter Lewis, Dallas (2/1/99); Marc R. Stanley, Dallas (2/1/97). Interim Co-Exec. Dirs., Judith Porras and Lee Deviney ($82,000), 300 W. 15th St., Ste. 411, Austin 78711.

Public Safety Commission - (1935); apptv.; expenses; 6-yr.; 3 members: James B. Francis Jr., Dallas (12/31/99); Robert B. Holt, Midland (12/31/01); Ronald D. Krist, Houston (12/31/97). Dir. of Texas Dept. of Public Safety, Dudley M. Thomas ($90,000), PO Box 4087, Austin 78773-0001.

Public Utility Commission - (1975); apptv.; 6-yr.; 3 members at $90,071: Robert W. Gee, Houston (9/1/97); Judy W. Walsh, Fair Oaks Ranch (9/1/99); Presiding Officer Patrick Henry Wood III, Austin (9/1/01). Exec. Dir., Brenda Jenkins ($74,263), PO Box 13326, Austin 78711-3326.

Racing Commission, Texas - (1986); 6-yr.; per diem and expenses; 8 members — 2 ex officio: Chmn. of Public Safety Commission and Comptroller; 6 apptv.: Larry Jay Christopher, Crockett (2/1/01); Anne Dunigan-Wilson, Abilene (2/1/97); Lukin T. Gilliland Jr., San Antonio (2/1/99); Deorsey E. McGruder Jr., Dallas (l2/1/99); Patricia H. Pangburn, Southlake (2/1/97); James L. Schulze, Conroe (2/1/01). Exec. Secy., David J. Freeman ($77,760), PO Box 12080, Austin 78711.

Radiation Advisory Board - (1961 as 9-member board, membership increased to 18 in 1981); apptv.; 6-yr.; expenses; 18 members: Jimmy L. Barker, Granbury (4/16/01); Susan E. Best, Dallas (4/16/03); Thomas M. Burnette, Plano (4/16/01); Donald S. Butler, Colleyville (4/16/01); Earl P. Erdmann, Midland (4/16/01); Michael S. Ford, Amarillo (4/16/03); David N. Henkes, San Antonio (4/16/99); Walter Kim Howard, Longview (4/16/99); Glen Keith King, Houston (4/16/99); Dale Edward Klein, Austin (4/16/03); Jack S. Krohmer, Georgetown (4/16/99); Justin P. LeVasseur, Wichita Falls (4/16/01); Odis R. Mack, Katy (4/16/01); Troy Marceleno, Dauncanville (4/16/03); Bruce A. Matson, Houston (4/16/03); Connie Rogers, Driftwood (4/16/99); William R. Underdown Jr., George West (4/16/99); Philip M. Wentworth, Plano (4/16/99).

Radioactive Waste Disposal Authority, Texas Low-Level - (1981); apptv.; 6-yr.; expenses; 6 members: James L. Carroll,

El Paso (2/1/97); William L. Fisher, Austin (2/1/99); Milton J. Guiberteau, Houston (2/1/01); Macario Marquez, Sierra Blanca (2/1/99); David Ojeda Jr., Carrizo Springs (2/1/97); John E. Simek, Bryan (2/1/01). Gen. Mgr., Lawrence R. Jacobi Jr. ($76,385), 7701 N. Lamar Blvd., Ste. 300, Austin 78752.

Railroad Commission of Texas - (1891); elective; 6-yr.; 3 members, $92,217 each: Charles Matthews, Dallas (1/1/00); Carole Keeton Rylander, Austin (1/1/03); Barry Williamson, Austin (1/1/99). Exec. Dir., Walt Washington ($88,408), PO Box 12967, Austin 78711.

Real Estate Commission, Texas - (1949 as 6-member board; membership increased to 9 in 1979); apptv.; per diem and expenses; 6-yr.; 9 members: C. Michael Brodie, Richardson (1/31/03); Jay Brummett, Austin (1/31/01); Pete Cantu Sr., Helotes (1/31/99); Christine T. Folmer, El Paso (1/31/01); Maria Gonzalez-Avila, San Antonio (1/31/03); Mitchell Katine, Houston (1/31/99); Hazel W. Lewis, Arlington (1/31/99); Deanna Mayfield, San Angelo (1/31/01); Kay Sutton, Midland (1/31/03). Admin., William H. Kuntz Jr. ($58,932), PO Box 12188, Austin 78711.

Real Estate Research Advisory Committee - (1971); apptv.; 6-yr.; 10 members — one ex officio: representative of Texas Real Estate Commission; 9 apptv. members: Joe Adame, Corpus Christi (1/31/03); Carlos Madrid Jr., San Antonio (1/31/01); Catherine Miller, Arlington (1/31/03); Andrea Lopes Moore, Houston (1/31/99); Marjory Kay Moore, Big Spring (1/31/99); Angela S. Myres, Houston (1/31/01); Jerry L. Schaffner, Lubbock (1/31/03); John P. Schneider Jr., Austin (1/31/99); Gloria Van Zandt, Arlington (1/31/01). Dir., James Christian, Texas A&M, College Station 77843-2115.

Red River Authority, Board of Directors - (1959); apptv.; 6-yr.; per diem and expenses; 9 members: George W. Arrington, Canadian (8/11/01); Paul F. Engler, Amarillo (8/11/99); James P. Fallon, Sherman (8/11/99); Edward L. Lehman Jr., Vernon (8/11/97); Diane Mashburn, Childress (8/11/97); Betty P. Peveto, Gainesville (8/11/01); Edna M. Shepherd, Texarkana (8/11/99); W.F. Smith Jr., Quanah (8/11/01); Judy Warner, Pampa (8/11/97). Gen. Mgr., Ronald J. Glenn, 520 Hamilton Bldg., Wichita Falls 76301.

Red River Compact Commissioner - (1949); apptv.; 4-yr.; (Function of commissioner is to negotiate with other states respecting waters of the Red.): Lowell Cable, Sulphur Springs (2/1/99); ($24,225).

Redistricting Board, Legislative - (See Legislative Redistricting Board).

Rehabilitation Commission, Texas - (1969); apptv.; expenses; 6-yr.; 6 members: Matthew T. Doyle, Texas City (8/31/99); Dr. Dora L. Gonzalez, San Antonio (8/31/97); Jerry Kane, Corpus Christi (8/31/99); Diane M. Novy, Sugar Land (8/31/97); A. Kent Waldrep Jr., Plano (8/31/01); Ray A. Wilkerson, Austin (8/31/01). Commissioner, Vernon M. Arrell ($95,000), 4900 N. Lamar Blvd., Austin 78751-2316.

Retirement System, Municipal, Board of Trustees - (1947); apptv.; 6-yr.; expenses; 6 members: Kathleen Gunn Buehner, Mansfield (2/1/01); Victoria Lee H. LaFollett, Longview (2/1/03); Stephen W. McCullough, Irving (2/1/99); Rick Menchaca, Midland (2/1/01); Isaac Valencia, Corpus Christi (2/1/99); Charles E. Windwehen, Victoria (2/1/03). Exec. Dir., Gary W. Anderson, PO Box 149153, Austin 78714-9153.

Retirement System of Texas, Employees - (1949); apptv.; 6-yr.; 6 members — one apptd. by Gov., one by Chief Justice of State Supreme Court and one by Speaker; 3 are employee members of the system serving 6-yr. overlapping terms: Pamela A. Carley, Austin (8/31/97); Carolyn Gallagher, Austin (8/31/00); Milton Hixson, Austin (8/31/98); Frank J. Smith, Austin (8/31/99); Byron Tunnell, Austin (8/31/96); Janice R. Zitleman, Austin (8/31/01). Exec. Dir., Sheila W. Beckett, PO Box 13207, Austin 78711-3207.

Retirement System, Teacher - (1937 as 6-member board; membership increased to 9 in 1973); expenses; 6-yr.; 9 members — 2 apptd. by State Board of Education, 3 apptd. by Gov. and 4 TRS members apptd. by Gov. after being nominated by popular ballot of members of the retirement system: Frank W. Camp, Brownfield (8/31/97); James P. Cummings, San Angelo (8/31/01); Charlsetta W. Finley, El Paso (8/31/97); James H. Simms, Amarillo (8/31/01); Ronald G. Steinhart, Dallas (8/31/97); Kathryn S. Stream, Denton (8/31/99); Wendell Whittenburg, Sweetwater (8/31/01); Lee R. Williamson, Wichita Falls (8/31/99); Kneeland Youngblood, Dallas (8/31/99). Exec. Dir., Charles Dunlap, 1000 Red River, Austin 78701.

Retirement System, Texas County and District - (1967); apptv.; 6-yr.; 9 members: Giles M. Dalby, Post (12/31/97); Maxine Darst, Terrell (12/31/99); David U. Flores, Georgetown (12/31/97); Martha Gustavsen, Conroe (12/31/99); Kathy Hynson, Rosenberg (12/31/95); Steve Radack, Houston (12/31/95); Sam D. Seale, Port Lavaca (12/31/99); Nelda Wells Spears, Austin (12/31/97); Bill W. Wallis, Tyler (12/31/95) Dir., Terry Hor-

ton, 400 W. 14th, Austin 78701-1688.

Rio Grande Compact Commissioner of Texas - (1929); apptv.; 6-yr.: Jack Hammond, El Paso (6/9/01). Box 1917, El Paso 79950-1917 ($41,195).

Runnels County Water Authority, Board of Directors - (1955); apptv.; 6-yr.; 9 members: Pamela Bauerlein, Ballinger (2/1/97); James D. Condra, Talpa (2/1/95); Dalton E. Crockett, Ballinger (2/1/97); L. Aubrey Faubion Jr., Ballinger (2/1/97); Leon Frerich, Norton (2/1/93); Marvin W. Gerhart, Winters (2/1/95); Werner Harsch, Miles (2/1/93); Elliott J. Kemp, Ballinger (2/1/93); Kenneth H. Slimp, Winters (2/1/95).

Sabine River Authority, Board of Directors - (1949); apptv.; per diem and expenses; 6-yr.; 9 members: Nolton L. Brown, Bridge City (7/6/97); James E. Campbell, Center (7/6/01); Walta Pippen Cooke, Carthage (7/6/99); Karen C. Hampton, Tyler (7/6/01); Joyce Plummer Hugman, Gladewater (7/6/97); Margin Stovall Latham, Sulphur springs (7/6/01); Geraldine J. Nichols, Quitman (7/6/97); Jerry Stallworth, Marshall (7/6/99); Clarence Earl Williams Jr., Orange (7/6/99). Exec. Vice Pres. & Gen. Mgr., Sam F. Collins, PO Box 579, Orange 77630.

Sabine River Compact Commission - (1953); apptv.; 6-yr.; $8,487 each; 5 members — one member and chmn. apptd. by President of United States without a vote; 2 from Texas and 2 from Louisiana. Texas members: Frank Edward Parker, Center (7/12/01); Danny Choate, Orange (7/12/98). Box 579, Orange 77630. ($8,487).

San Antonio River Authority - apptv., 6 yr., 12 members: Ruben Expronceda, San Antonio (1/31/01); Roger V. Gary, San Antonio (1/31/99); Leo J. Gleinser, Goliad (1/31/03); Truett Hunt, Kenedy (1/31/01); W.W. Lorenz, Stockdale (1/31/01); Martha C. McNeel, San Antonio (1/31/01); R.H. Ramsey Jr., Goliad (1/31/01); Louis E. Rowe, San Antonio (1/31/03); H.B. Ruckman III, Karnes City (1/31/03); Nancy Steves, San Antonio (1/31/99); J.C. Turner, Floresville (1/31/03); Otis L. Walker, Goliad (1/31/97); Thomas G. Weaver, San Antonio (1/31/03). Gen. Mgr., Fred. N. Pfeiffer, 100 E. Guenther St., San Antonio 78283-0027.

San Jacinto Historical Advisory Board - (1907 as San Jacinto State Park Commission; changed to San Jacinto Battleground Commission and changed again in 1965 to present name; apptv.; 6-yr.; 5 members — 2 ex officio: Dir., Parks Div., Parks and Wildlife Dept. and pres. of San Jacinto Museum of History Assn.; 3 apptd. by Gov.: Mary C. Burke, Houston (9/1/97); Joel Moore Nash, Bellaire (9/1/95); Frank Calhoun, Houston (9/1/99). Parks Section, Parks and Wildlife Dept., 4200 Smith School Rd., Austin 78744.

San Jacinto River Authority, Board of Directors - (1937); apptv.; expenses while on duty; 6-yr.; 6 members: Henry T. Brooks, Conroe (10/16/99); John H. Choate, Humble (10/16/97); James T. Edmonds, Houston (10/16/99); David L. Mendez, Houston (10/16/97); R. Gary Montgomery, The Woodlands (10/16/95); Walter D. Wilkerson Jr., Conroe (10/16/95). Gen. Mgr., James R. Adams, PO Box 329, Conroe 77305.

Savings and Loan Commissioner - Apptv. by State Finance Commission: James L. Pledger ($89,116), PO Box 1089, Austin 78767.

School Land Board - (See Land Board, School).

Securities Board, State - (Est. 1957, the outgrowth of several amendments to the Texas Securities Act, originally passed 1913); act is administered by the Securities Commissioner, who is appointed by the board members; expenses; 6-yr.; 3 members: Nicholas C. Taylor, Midland (1/20/01); José Adan Treviño, Bellaire (1/21/03); Dan R. Waller, Dallas (1/20/99). Securities Commissioner, Denise Voigt Crawford ($84,000), PO Box 13167, Austin 78711-3167.

Seed and Plant Board, State - (1959); apptv.; 2-yr.; 6 members: A. James Allison, Tulia (10/6/97); Dick L. Auld, Lubbock (10/6/97); Joe M. Crane, Bay City (10/6/98); Charles Leamons, Brenham (10/6/98); Katherine Cave Patrick, Bishop (10/6/98); W. David Worrall, Vernon (10/6/97). Office Address: Texas Dept. of Agriculture, PO Box 12847, Austin 78711.

Sex Offender Treatment, Interagency Council on - (1983); 12 members — 9 ex officio: one each from Texas Dept. of Criminal Justice, Board of Pardons and Paroles, Texas Adult Probation Commission, Texas Juvenile Probation Commission, Texas Dept. of Mental Health and Mental Retardation, Texas Youth Commission, Sam Houston State University, Texas Dept. of Human Services and one member of Gov's. office administering criminal justice planning; 3 apptv. from general public; 6-yr.; expenses; apptv. members: Collier M. Cole, Dickinson (2/1/97); Walter J. Meyer III, Galveston (2/1/95); David L. Cory, Abilene (2/1/99). Exec. Dir., Eliza May ($39,816), PO Box 12546, Austin 78711.

Skill Standards Board, Texas - (1995); 11 members serving terms at pleasure of Gov.; expenses; members: Gary Forrest Blagg, Grapevine; Michael L. Brown, Waxahachie; Ramon

H. Dovalina, Laredo; Roger E. Elliott, Sulphur Springs; Betty Files, Abilene; Beth Ann Graham, Hallsville; John Hamice James, Midland; Denise Laman, Plano; Wayne J. Oswald, Freeport; Billie Conley Pickard, Raymondville; Dick Weinhold, Bedford.

Social Worker Examiners, Texas State Board of - (1993); apptd.; 6-yr.; per diem and travel expenses; 9 members: Ramiro Cabrera, Corpus Christi (2/1/99); Cathy Clancy, Houston (2/1/97); Deborah Hammond, Austin (2/1/01); Marlene LaRoe, Houston (2/1/99); Sgt. Willie McGee, Plainview (2/1/01); Shonna Lynette Olford, Longview (2/1/97); Sylvia S. Ramirez, Portland (2/1/97); Hoye D. Tibbets, Grandview (2/1/99); Gerrianne Waring, El Paso (2/1/01).

Soil and Water Conservation Board, Texas State - (1939); elected by members of individual districts; 2 yrs.; 5 members. Exec. Dir., Robert G. Buckley ($60,000), PO Box 658, Temple 76503.

Speech-Language Pathology and Audiology, State Board of Examiners for - (1983); apptv.; 6-yr.; per diem and expenses; 9 members: John K. Ashby, Abilene (8/31/99); Linda Mora Cano, Corpus Christi (8/31/97); Elsa Cardenas-Hagan, Olmito (8/31/01); George E. Cire, Victoria (8/31/01); Deloris Johnson, Houston (8/31/99); Harvey Komet, San Antonio (8/31/01); Charles K. Kurako, Lubbock (8/31/97); Teri Mata-Pistokache, Edinburg (8/31/99); Jane McConnell, Dallas (8/31/97). Exec. Secy., Dorothy Cawthon, 1100 W. 49th, Austin 78756-3183.

Stephen F. Austin State University, Board of Regents - (1969); apptv.; expenses; 6-yr.; 9 members: Ron Adkison, Henderson (1/31/99); Richard A. Brookshire, Lufkin (1/31/01); Penny H. Butler, Houston (1/31/03); Michael W. Enoch, Mont Belvieu (1/31/03); Pattye Greer, Nacogdoches (1/31/01); Simon Lynn Montes, Lufkin (1/31/99); Jimmy W. Murphy, Houston (1/31/01); Susan Scheumack Roberds, Dallas (1/31/03); Murray Shaw, Austin (1/31/99). Pres., Dr. William J. Brophy, PO Box 6078, SFA Sta., Nacogdoches 75962.

Student Loan Corporation, Texas Guaranteed - (1979); 6-yr.; 11-members — one ex officio; Comptroller of Public Accounts; one apptd. by Commissioner of Higher Education and one apptd. by Chmn. of Coordinating Board; 8 apptd. by Gov. as follows: Ruben E. Esquivel, DeSoto (1/31/03); Jennifer Jen'Nan Ghazal, Wichita Falls (1/31/99); Alfred Jackson, Houston (1/31/03); Jorja L. Kimball, Kingsville (1/31/99); Jerry Don Miller, Canyon (1/31/99); Jane Phipps, San Antonio (1/31/99); Alan V. Rash, El Paso (1/31/01); W. Bruce Robinson, Corsicana (1/31/03); Brent Thompson, Tyler (1/31/01); Charley V. Wootan, College Station (1/31/01). Pres., Milton G. Wright, PO Box 201725, Austin 78720.

Sulphur River Basin Authority, Board of Directors - (1985); apptd.; 6-yr.; per diem and expenses; 6 members: John McCool Howison, Bogata (2/1/99); Mike Huddleston, Wake Village (2/1/97); Patsy R. McClain, Sulphur Springs (2/1/01); Ivory E. Moore, Commerce (2/1/97); Maxine J. Nanze, Atlanta (2/1/99); Robert L. Parker, Paris (2/1/01).

Sunset Advisory Commission - (1977); 10 members: 4 members of House of Representatives, 4 members of Senate, one public member apptd. by Speaker, one public member apptd. by Lt. Gov.; 4-yr.; expenses. Dir., Joey Longley, PO Box 13066, Austin 78711.

Tax Board, State - (1905); ex officio; term in other office; no compensation; 3 members: Comptroller, Secretary of State and State Treasurer.

Tax Professional Examiners, Board of - (1977 as Board of Tax Assessor Examiners; name changed to present form 1983); apptv.; expenses; 6-yr.; 6 members: Carol Autry, Amarillo (3/1/01); Darla P. Doss, Crosbyton (3/1/99); Wayne R. Hawkins, Texarkana (3/1/01); Linda D. Jaynes, Plainview (3/1/03); Foy Mitchell Jr., Plano (3/1/03); Cora D. Viescas, El Paso (3/1/99). Exec. Dir., David E. Montoya ($43,417), 333 Guadalupe, Ste. 2-520 Austin 78701-3942.

Teacher Retirement System - (See Retirement System, Teacher.)

Texas A&M University System - Board of Regents - (1875); apptv.; 6-yr.; expenses; 9 members: Robert H. Allen, Houston (2/1/01); Anne L. Armstrong, Armstrong (2/1/03); Dionel E. Aviles, Houston (2/1/03); John H. Lindsey, Houston (2/1/99); Frederick Donald McClure, Dallas (2/1/01); Erle Allen Nye, Dallas (2/1/03); T. Michael O'Connor, Victoria (2/1/99); Donald E. Powell, Amarillo (2/1/01); M. Guadalupe Lopez Rangel, Corpus Christi (2/1/99). Chancellor, Barry B. Thompson, College Station 77843-1123.

Texas Southern University, Board of Regents - (1947); expenses; 6-yr.; 9 members: Albert C. Black Jr., Rowlett (2/1/01); Enos M. Cabell Jr., Missouri City (2/1/01); Rufus Cormier Jr., Houston (2/1/97); Thomas H. Friedberg, Sugar Land (2/1/03); Jenard M. Gross, Houston (2/1/97); Willard L. Jackson Jr.,

Houston (2/1/99); Anthony D. Lyons, Fort Worth (2/1/99); Gene A. Moore Sr., Houston (2/1/01); Carroll W. Phillips, Houston (2/1/95); Rosie Zamora-Cope, Houston (2/1/99). Pres., Dr. William H. Harris, 3100 Cleburne, Houston 77004.

Texas State Technical College, Board of Regents - (1960 as Board of the Texas State Technical Institute; changed to present name, 1991); apptv.; expenses; 6-yr.; 9 members: Edward B. Adams Sr., Austin (8/31/97); De la Garza, C. "Connie", Harlingen (8/31/01); Jere M. Lawrence, Sweetwater (8/31/01); Nat Lopez, Harlingen (8/31/99); Charles D. Olson, Waco (8/31/99); Jerilyn Kyker Pfeifer, Abilene (8/31/01); Gerald D. Phariss, Garland (8/31/97); Tom L. Ragland, Waco (8/31/99); Thomas L. Whaley Sr., Marshall (8/31/01). Chancellor, Dr. Cecil L. Groves, TSTC System, Waco 76705.

Texas State University System, Board of Regents - (1911 as Board of Regents of State Teachers Colleges; name changed in 1965 to Board of Regents of State Senior Colleges; changed to present form in 1975); apptv.; per diem and expenses; 9 members: John Philip Hageman, Round Rock (2/1/03); Thomas M. Moeller, Beaumont (2/1/01); Elizabeth T. Nash, San Marcos (2/1/99); Nancy R. Neal, Lubbock (2/1/03); Floyd Nickerson, Abilene (2/1/03); Pollyanna A. Stephens, San Angelo (2/1/01); Macedonio Villarreal, Sugar Land (2/1/01); Craig H. Vittitoe, Harlingen (2/1/99); Ray Zapata, Christoval (2/1/01). Chancellor, Lamar G. Urbanovsky, 505 Sam Houston Bldg., Austin 78701.

Texas Tech University, Board of Regents - (1923); apptv.; expenses; 6-yr.; 9 members: J. Robert Brown, El Paso (1/31/01); Dr. Bernard A. Harris Jr., Houston (1/31/99); Patsy W. Martin, Austin (1/31/97); Carl Edward Noe, Dallas (1/31/99); John C. Sims, Lubbock (1/31/97); James E. Sowell, Dallas (1/31/01); Elizabeth (Cissy) Ward, Houston (1/31/97); Edward E. Whitacre Jr., San Antonio (1/31/99); Alan B. White, Lubbock (1/31/01). Chancellor, John T. Montford, PO Box 4039, Lubbock 79409.

Texas Woman's University Board of Regents - (1901); apptv.; expenses; 6-yr.; 9 members: Nan Hutchins Bailey, Flint (2/1/99); Ronald F. Garvey, Dallas (2/1/01); Kay Williams Goodman, Sanger (2/1/01); Richard D. Hayes, Denton (2/1/01); Marie Chapman Martch, Belton (2/1/03); Douglas Bert Myers, Plano (2/1/03); Cynthia Shepard Perry, Houston (2/1/03); Cheryl B. Wattley, Dallas (2/1/99); Sheila Whitaker-Kellagher, Dallas (2/01/99). Pres., Carol D. Surles, PO Box 23925, TWU Sta., Denton 76204-1925.

Texas-Mexico Authority Advisory Board - (1991); apptd.; 6-yr.; 6 members: Santiago F. Cantu, Austin (2/1/97); Marjorie C. Kastman, Lubbock (2/1/95); Mark Langdale, Dallas (2/1/01); William R. Leo, La Joya (2/1/99); William S. Tilney, El Paso (2/1/97).

Transportation Commission, Texas - (1917 as State Highway Commission; merged with Mass Transportation Commission and name changed to State Board of Highways and Public Transportation in 1975; merged with Texas Dept. of Aviation and Texas Motor Vehicle Commission and name changed to present form in 1991); apptv.; 6-yr.; ($15,914); 3 members: David M. Laney, Dallas (2/1/01); Robert Lee Nichols, Jacksonville (2/1/03); Anne S. Wynne, Austin (2/1/99). Exec. Dir., William G. Burnett, P.E. ($115,000), 125 E. 11th St., Austin 78701-2483.

Trinity River Authority, Board of Directors - (1955); apptv.; per diem and expenses; 6-yr.; 24 directors — 3 from Tarrant County, 4 from Dallas County, 2 from area-at-large and one each from 15 other districts: Judi Jones Benestante, Coldspring (3/15/99); Leslie C. Browne, Arlington (3/15/03); Anton B. Brucks, Dallas (3/15/97); Patricia A. Clapp, Dallas (3/15/01); Hector Escamilla Jr., Carrollton (3/15/03); Horace Perry Flatt, Terrell (3/15/99); Benny L. Fogleman, Livingston (3/15/03); Jane M. Fouty, Corsicana (3/15/99); Valerie Freeman, Dallas (3/15/01); Edward Eugene Hargett, Crockett (3/15/03); Michael P. Heiskell, Arlington (3/15/99); William H. Hodges, Huntsville (3/15/01); Jo Ann Jenkins, Waxahachie (3/15/99); John W. Jenkins, Hankamer (3/15/03); William M. Key, Athens (3/15/01); A. Dawn Knight, Madisonville (3/15/99); Maurice L. Locke, Liberty (3/15/01); James W. Porter, Dallas (3/15/99); H. Gene Reynolds Jr., Fairfield (3/15/01); Wanda W. Stovall, Fort Worth (3/15/01); Douglas Lee Sumrall, Palestine (3/15/01); F.L. Thompson, Leona (3/15/99); Jack C. Vaughn Jr., Dallas (3/15/03); Walter C. White, Trinity (3/15/99). Gen. Mgr., Danny F. Vance, PO Box 60, Arlington 76004-0060.

Tuition Board, Prepaid Higher Education - (1996); 6-yr.; 7 members: Comptroller; 4 apptd. by Lt. Gov.; 2 apptd. by Gov.

Tuition Scholarship Foundation Board, Texas Prepaid - (1996); indeterminate terms; 5 members: Comptroller; one apptd. by gov.; 3 apptd. jointly by Comptroller and gov's apptee. Gov's apptee: George H. McShan, Harlingen.

Turnpike Authority, Texas - (incorporated into Texas Dept.

of Transportation eff. Sept. 1, 1997)

Uniform State Laws, Commission on - (1941 as 5-member Commissioners to the National Conference on Uniform State Laws; name changed to present form, membership increased to 6 and term of office raised to 6 years in 1977); apptv.; 6-yr.; 6 members: Patrick C. Guillot, Dallas (9/30/94); Peter K. Munson, Denison (9/30/02); David Peeples, San Antonio (9/30/98); Marilyn E. Phelan, Lubbock (9/30/98); Rodney W. Satterwhite, Midland (9/30/02); Harry L. Tindall, Houston (9/30/02).

University of Houston, Board of Regents - (1963); apptv.; expenses; 6-yr.; 9 members: Eduardo Aguirre Jr., Houston (8/31/01); Zinetta A. Burney, Houston (8/31/97); Philip J. Carroll, Houston (8/31/99); Elyse Lanier, Houston (8/31/97); Charles E. McMahen, Houston (8/31/01); Wilhelmina R. Morian, Houston (8/31/97); John M. O'Quinn, Houston (8/31/99); Gary L. Rosenthal, Houston (8/31/01); Kay Kerr Walker, Victoria (8/31/99). Chancellor/President Arthur K. Smith, 4800 Calhoun, Houston 77004.

University of North Texas Board of Regents - (1949); apptv.; 6-yr.; expenses; 9 members: William D. Bayless Sr., Denison (5/22/97); Jerry S. Farrington, Dallas (5/22/99); Becky Ann Garth, Temple (5/22/89); Nancy S. Halbreich, Dallas (5/22/97); Joe Kirven, Dallas (5/22/95); E. L. Langley, Irving (5/22/95); Lucille G. Murchison, Dallas (5/22/99); Topsy R. Wright, Grand Prairie (5/22/99). Chancellor, Alfred F. Hurley, PO Box 13737, Denton 76203-3737.

University of Texas System, Board of Regents - (1881); apptv.; expenses; 6-yr.; 9 members: Linnet F. Deily, Houston (2/1/01); Donald L. Evans, Midland (2/1/01); Thomas O. Hicks, Dallas (2/1/99); Lowell H. Lebermann, Austin (2/1/99); Thomas G. Loeffler, San Antonio (2/1/01); Patrick C. Oxford, Houston (2/1/03); A.W. Riter Jr., Tyler (2/1/03); A.R. (Tony) Sanchez, Laredo (2/1/03); Martha E. Smiley, Austin (2/1/99). Chancellor, William H. Cummingham, PO Box N, University Sta., Austin 78713-7328.

Veterans Commission, Texas - (1927 as Veterans State Service Office; reorganized as Veterans Affairs Commission in 1947 with 5 members; membership increased to 6 in 1981; name changed to present form in 1985); apptv.; 6-yr.; per diem while on duty and expenses; 6 members: Samuel Bier, Austin (12/31/97); Ralph Lee King, Burkburnett (12/31/97); Herbert W. Odell, Fort Worth (12/31/99); Patsy L. Palmquist, Devine (12/31/99); Brig. Gen. Sue Ilen Turner (Ret.), San Antonio (12/31/01); Alexander Vernon, Killeen (12/31/01). Exec. Dir., Douglas K. Brown ($60,000), PO Box 12277, Austin 78711.

Veterans Land Board - (Est. 1949 as 3-member ex officio board; reorganized 1956); 4-yr.; per diem and expenses; 3 members: one ex officio: Comm. of General Land Office; 2

apptd.: Jesse D. Martin, Lubbock (12/29/96); Darryl Ladd Pattillo, Austin (12/29/98). Exec. Sec., David Gloier (member), 1700 N. Congress Ave., Ste. 836, Austin 78701-1496.

Veterinary Medical Examiners, Texas State Board of - (1911; revised 1953; made 9-member board in 1981); apptv.; expenses on duty; 6-yr.; 9 members: James N. Gomez, Brownsville (8/26/97); Howard Head, Littlefield (8/26/01); Robert I. Hughes, Center (8/26/99); D. Carter King, Roanoke (8/26/01); Sharon O. Matthews, Albany (8/26/99); Michael J. McCulloch, Odessa (8/26/99); Jean McFaddin, Beaumont (8/26/01); Joyce G. Schiff, Dallas (8/26/97); John A. Wood, Lufkin (8/26/97). Exec. Dir., Ron Allen ($53,000), 333 Guadalupe St., Ste. 2-330, Austin 78701-2998.

Water Development Board, Texas - (1957; legislative function for the Texas Dept. of Water Resources, 1977); apptv.; per diem and expenses; 6-yr.; 6 members: Elaine M. Barron, El Paso (12/31/99); Noe Fernandez, McAllen (12/31/01); Charles L. Geren, Fort Worth (12/31/99); Charles W. Jenness, Houston (12/31/97); William B. Madden, Dallas (12/31/01); Diane Elaine Umstead, Houston (12/31/97). Exec. Admin., Craig D. Pedersen ($80,000), PO Box 13231, Austin 78711.

Workers' Compensation Commission, Texas - (1991); 6-yr.; apptv; expenses; 6 members: Jack Abla, Kilgore (2/1/01); Royce Faulkner, Austin (2/1/99); O.D. Kenemore, Lake Jackson (2/1/99); Rebecca F. Olivares, San Antonio (2/1/03); Richard F. Reynolds, Austin (2/1/01); Joel B. (Burt) Terrill, San Angelo (2/1/03). Exec. Dir., Todd K. Brown ($95,000), 4000 S. IH-35, Austin 78704-1287.

Workers' Compensation Insurance Fund Board, Texas - (1991); expenses; 6-yr.; 9 members: Ernesto Ancira Jr., San Antonio (2/1/99); Patricia A. (Pat) Crawford, El Paso (2/1/99); Pat O'Neal, Dallas (2/1/01); Brenda Pejovich, Dallas (2/1/03); James D. Ross, Midland (2/1/03); Tommy G. Salome, Crawford (2/1/01); George Wesch Jr., Lake Hills (2/1/99); Charles Hugh Whiteside, Kilgore (2/1/03); Martin H. Young Jr., The Woodlands (2/1/01).

Workforce Commission, Texas - (1936 as **Texas Employment Commission**; name changed 1995); apptv.; $84,660; 6-yr.; 3 members: Eddie Cavazos, Corpus Christi (2/1/97); Bill Hammond, Austin (2/1/03); Jo Betsy Norton, Austin (2/1/01); David R. Perdue, Arlington (2/1/99). Exec. Dir., Mike Sheridan ($125,000), 101 E. 15th St., Ste. 618 Austin 78778-0001.

Youth Commission, Texas - (1949 as 9-member board; reorganized 1957 and again in 1975); 6-yr.; per diem on duty; 6 apptv. members: Pete C. Alfaro, Baytown (8/31/01); Pete Harrell, Austin (8/31/97); Leonard E. Lawrence, San Antonio (8/31/97); John W. Odam Jr., Houston (8/31/99); Edna L. Tamayo, Harlingen (8/31/99); Lisa C. Teschner, Dallas (8/31/01). Exec. Dir., Steve Robinson ($85,000), PO Box 4260, Austin 78765. ☆

State Government Income and Expenditures

Taxes are the state government's primary source of income. On this and the following pages are summaries of state income and expenditures, tax collections, tax revenue by type of tax, a summary of the state budget for the 1998-99 biennium, Texas Lottery income and expenditures and the amount of federal payments to state agencies.

State Revenues by Source and Expenditures by Function

Amounts (in Millions) and Percent of Total

Revenues by Source	1996	%	1995	%	1994	%	1993	%	1992	%
Tax Collections	$19,763	48.8	$18,859	48.8	$18,106	49.3	$17,011	50.3	$15,849	53.5
Federal Funds	11,658	28.8	11,408	29.5	10,552	28.7	9,853	29.2	8,417	28.4
Licenses, Fees and Permits	3,841	9.5	3,768	9.7	3,151	8.6	2,073	6.1	1,863	6.3
Interest & Other Investment Income	2,076	5.1	1,715	4.4	1,697	4.6	2,155	6.4	1,862	6.3
Land Income	222	0.6	201	0.5	220	0.6	239	0.7	226	0.8
Sales of Goods & Services	198	0.5	173	0.5	141	0.4	128	0.4	41	0.1
Contributions to Employee Benefits	95	0.2	122	0.3	115	0.3	104	0.3	96	0.3
Settlements of Claims	15	0.1	6	0.0	12	0.1	18	0.1	31	0.1
Net Lottery Proceeds	1,718	4.2	1,662	4.3	1,586	4.3	1,113	3.3	312	1.0
Other Revenues	902	2.2	769	2.0	1,126	3.1	1,101	3.2	951	3.2
Total Net Revenues	**$40,488**	**100**	**$38,682**	**100**	**$36,707**	**100**	**$33,975**	**100**	**$29,648**	**100**
Expenditures by Function										
General Government - Total	$1,442	3.6	$1,473	3.7	$1,400	3.9	$1,534	4.6	$1,238	3.6
Executive	1,257	3.2	1,298	3.3	1,238	3.5	1,372	4.1	1,092	3.7
Legislative	81	0.2	83	0.2	72	0.2	77	0.2	67	0.2
Judicial	104	0.2	92	0.2	89	0.2	84	0.3	79	0.3
Education	14,779	37.3	14,510	36.9	13,416	37.6	12,782	38.3	11,910	40.7
Employee Benefits	1,785	4.5	1,732	4.4	1,618	4.5	1,577	4.8	1,320	4.5
Health and Human Services	13,593	34.3	13,540	34.4	12,005	33.7	11,244	33.7	9,548	32.5
Public Safety and Corrections	2,292	5.8	2,260	5.7	1,938	5.4	1,608	4.8	1,374	4.7
Transportation	3,364	8.5	2,741	7.0	2,726	7.7	2,797	8.4	2,368	8.1
Natural Resources and Recreational Services	666	1.7	953	2.4	589	1.7	469	1.4	417	1.4
Lottery Winnings Paid	381	1.0	454	1.2	429	1.2	276	0.8	22	0.1
Regulatory Agencies	171	0.4	166	0.4	169	0.5	171	0.5	165	0.6
Debt Service	526	1.3	463	1.2	348	1.0	317	0.9	370	1.3
Capital Outlay	671	1.7	1,045	2.7	999	2.8	613	1.8	559	1.9
Total Expenditures	**$39,669**	**100**	**$39,337**	**100**	**$35,638**	**100**	**33,389**	**100**	**29,290**	**100**

Amounts rounded.

Source: 1996 Comprehensive Annual Financial Report of the Texas State Comptroller's Office, compiled from State of Texas Financial Statements for Fiscal 1990-1994. This table comprises the following funds: General, Special Revenue, Debt Service and Capital Projects.

State Tax Collections, 1985-1996

Fiscal Year‡	State Tax Collections	Resident Population	Per Capita Tax Collections	Taxes as % of Personal Income
1985	$10,721,208,262	16,242,768	$ 660.06	4.9
1986	10,231,670,211	16.512,533	619.63	4.5
1987	10,266,162,781	16,615,360	617.87	4.5
1988	12,364,618,924	16,669,153	741.77	5.1
1989	12,905,940,817	†16,796,043	†768.39	5.0
1990	13,632,640,459	†17,020,657	†800.95	4.9
1991	14,922,113,980	†17,322,294	†861.44	5.0
1992	15,848,915,148	†17,648,474	†898.03	5.0
1993	17,010,737,258	†18,003,663	†944.85	5.0
1994	18,105,950,594	†18,363,835	†985.96	†5.1
1995	18,858,790,042	*18,685,894	*1,009.25	*5.0
1996	19,762,504,349	*19,005,549	*1,039.83	*4.9

‡ Fiscal years end August 31.
* Estimated
† Revised

Sources: Tax collection data: Texas Comptroller of Public Accounts, Annual Financial Report of various years. Population and personal income figures, 1985 to 1994: U.S. Dept. of Commerce (Bureau of the Census and Bureau of Economic Analysis). 1995 and 1996 population and personal income: Texas Comptroller of Public Accounts estimates.

Tax Revenues, 1995, 1996

Below are listed the major taxes and the amounts each contributed to the state in fiscal years 1995 and 1996.

Type of Tax	FY 1995	FY 1996
Sales	$10,258,652,289	$10,791,471,674
Oil Production	375,213,935	376,975,087
Natural Gas Prod.	512,411,284	447,101,861
Motor Fuels	2,235,343,050	2,321,014,151
Motor Veh. Sales/Rnt*	1,788,449,322	1,965,269,140
Franchise	639,018,651	566,692,013
Cigarette/Tobacco	406,695,645	418,698,170
Alcoholic Bev.	607,974,103	626,644,429
Utility	240,745,676	240,975,016
Inheritance	171,605,722	160,143,199
Hotel/Motel	171,362,399	176,455,623
Other Taxes**	635,851,040	658,692,987
Totals	**$18,858,790,042**	**$19,762,504,350**

*Includes tax on manufactured housing sales and taxes on interstate motor carriers.

**Includes taxes listed at the bottom of the preceding text.

State Government Budget Summary, 1998-99 Biennium

Source: Legislative Budget Board

Article (Govt. Division)	1998-99 Budget (All funds) (in Millions)
Art. I, General Government	$2,111.2
Art. II, Health and Human Services	26,060.7
Art. III, Education	38,110.2
Art. IV, The Judiciary	331.8
Art. V, Public Safety & Criminal Justice	7,036.4
Art. VI, Natural Resources	1,664.0
Art. VII, Business & Economic Dev.	10,267.8
Art. VIII, Regulatory	425.5
Art. IX, General Provisions	701.1
Art. X, The Legislature	246.5
Contingency - Enrollment Growth	165.0
Total	**$87,120.1**

House Bill 1 of the 75th Legislature called for a budget for the operation of state government for the 1998-99 biennium totalling $87,120.1 million from all fund sources. This provides for an increase of 7.7 percent, or $6,242.0 million, in total state funding. In addition to the provisions contained in House Bill 1, the 1998-99 amounts listed here reflect House Bills 4 and 2272, Senate Bill 1898 and the Governor's vetoes. Text of these bills may be obtained on the Texas Legislature's Internet site: http://www.capitol.state.tx.us/

Federal funds for the 1998-99 biennium total $24,623.4 million. This is an increase of $1,732.6 million, or 7.6 percent from the 1996-97 biennium. ☆

Texas Lottery

Source: Texas Lottery Commission

The State Lottery Act was passed by the Legislature in July 1991. The constitutional amendment necessary to approve the lottery was passed in an election on Nov. 5, 1991, by a vote of 1,326,154 to 728,994. The first ticket was purchased on May 29, 1992.

Executive Director of the Texas Lottery is Lawrence Littwin.

Who Plays the Lottery?

The executive director of the Texas Lottery is required to conduct a biennial demographic survey of lottery players in order to determine the income, age, sex, race, education and frequency of participation of players. The information below is from the survey conducted for the Texas Lottery Commission by the Office of Survey Research of The University of Texas at Austin, College of Communication, in Sept. 1996. A total of 1,716 interviews were completed with Texans 18 years of age and older. The margin of error for a sample of 1,716 is approximately plus or minus 2.4 percent.

The percentage of Texans who report purchasing at least one Texas Lottery ticket in the 12 months preceding the survey was 70 percent. Sixty-four percent reported playing Lotto, while 55 percent played scratch games and 16 percent played the daily Pick 3 game. Cash 5 was played by 29 percent.

Age: Seventy-eight percent of Texans between ages 36 and 45 played the lottery, followed by 74 percent of those 26 to 35 and those 46 to 55, 73 percent of those 56 to 66, 63 percent of those 18 to 25 and 53 percent of Texans 67 and older.

Educational Level: Texans with a high school education or some college were more likely to play the lottery (75%) than college graduates (68%) or those with less than a high-school education (60%).

Texas Lottery Financial Data

Starup to August 31, 1996

Period	Value of Prizes Won (billions)	Cost of Product (millions)	Retailer Commissions (millions)	Administration (millions)	To General Rev. Fund* (millions)
Startup through FY 1993	$1.25	$151	$122	$23	$657
FY 1994	1.53	152	138	21	928
FY 1995	1.69	169	152	27	1,020
FY 1996	1.95	195	172	28	1,100

* All figures accrued.

Income Level: Seventy-eight percent of Texans making between $30,000 and $49,999 per year played lottery games, as did 76 percent of those making $20,000 to $29,999, 74 percent of those making $50,000 or more, and 57 percent of those making under $10,000 a year.

Ethnic Background: Seventy-five percent of Hispanic Texans play lottery games, as do 71 percent of blacks and 70 percent of Anglos and other ethnic groups.

Sex: Approximately 75 percent of men play lottery games, and about 65 percent of women play. The gender gap is largest for Lotto Texas players, but much less for other games.

Geography: Of the Texas Lottery's 10 sales districts, the one with the largest percentage of lottery players is Victoria (79%), followed by Abilene (77%), San Antonio (74%), Irving (71%), Houston (70 %), Austin and McAllen (68%), El Paso and Lubbock (64%) and Tyler (63%). ☆

Federal Revenue by State Agency

Source: Comptroller of Public Accounts, Annual Cash Report for the Year Ended August 31, 1996, Vol. 1.

State Agency	1993	1994	1995	1996
Texas Department of Health	$330,465,555	$392,017,505	$4,633,661,477	$4,449,526,194
Department of Human Services	2,554,471,205	1,133,157,941	2,557,890,909	2,582,342,240
Texas Education Agency	1,269,988,544	1,388,325,315	'1,486,163,829	1,624,804,412
Texas Department of Transportation	1,027,793,342	1,107,128,270	1,023,390,309	1,219,992,730
Texas Workforce Commission*	186,009,844	193,716,406	165,214,706	327,895,021
Texas Dept. of Mental Health and Mental Retardation	13,375,473	38,194,074	197,121,513	274,981,524
Department of Protective and Regulatory Services	110,182,069	99,672,547	204,678,631	211,567,471
Texas Rehabilitation Commission	196,668,954	189,171,377	201,608,287	191,143,413
Texas Department of Housing and Community Affairs	94,423,690	117,509,754	136,032,090	153,291,317
All Other Agencies	4,069,315,571	5,893,190,119	802,304,306	623,137,998
Total All Agencies	**$9,852,694,247**	**$10,552,083,308**	**$11,408,108,057**	**$11,657,682,320**

* The 1993-95 numbers represent federal funds of the Texas Employment Commission. The TEC and the Texas Workforce Commission were combined June 1996; the 1996 number represents the funds of both the TEC and the TWC.

Texas' Chief Governmental Officials

On this and following pages are lists of the principal administrative officials who have served the Republic and State of Texas with dates of their tenures of office. In a few instances there are disputes as to the exact dates of tenures. Dates listed here are those that appear the most authentic.

★ ★ ★ ★ ★ ★ ★

Governors and Presidents

*Spanish Royal Governors

Domingo Terán de los Rios	1691-1692
Gregorio de Salinas Varona	1692-1697
Francisco Cuerbo y Valdéz	1698-1702
Mathías de Aguirre	1703-1705
Martín de Alarcón	1705-1708
Simon Padilla y Córdova	1708-1712
Pedro Fermin de Echevers y Subisa	1712-1714
Juan Valdéz	1714-1716
Martín de Alarcón	1716-1719
Joseph de Azlor, Marqués de San Miguel de Aguayo	1719-1722
Fernando Pérez de Almazan	1722-1727
Melchor de Media Villa y Azcona	1727-1730
Juan Antonio Bustillos y Ceballos	1730-1734
Manuel de Sandoval	1734-1736
Carlos Benites Franquis de Lugo	1736-1737
Prudencio de Orobio y Basterra	1737-1741
Tomás Felipe Wintuisen	1741-1743
Justo Boneo y Morales	1743-1744
Francisco García Larios	1744-1748
Pedro del Barrio Junco y Espriella	1748-1751
Jacinto de Barrios y Jauregui	1751-1759
Angel Martos y Navarrete	1759-1766
Hugo Oconór	1767-1770
Baron de Ripperda	1770-1778
Domingo Cabello	1778-1786
Bernardo Bonavia	1786-1786
Rafael Martínez Pacheco	1787-1788

The office of Governor was ordered suppressed and the province put under a presidial captain for a period in ... *1788-1789*

Manuel Muñoz	1790-1798
José Irigoyen	1798-1800
Juan Bautista de Elguezábal	1800-1805
Antonio Cordero y Bustamante	1805-1810
Juan Bautista Casas	1811-1811
Manuel María de Salcedo	1811-1813
Cristóbal Domínguez	1814-1817
Ignacio Pérez	1817-1817
Manuel Pardo	1817-1817
Antonio Martínez	1817-1822

*Some authorities would include Texas under administrations of several earlier Spanish Governors. The late Dr. C. E. Castañeda, Latin-American librarian of The University of Texas and authority on the history of Texas and the Southwest, would include the following four: Francisco de Garay, 1523-26; Pánfilo de Narváez, 1526-28; Nuño de Guzmán, 1528-30; Hernando de Soto, 1538-43.

Governors Under Mexican Rule

The first two Governors under Mexican rule, Trespalacios and García, were of Texas only as Texas was then constituted. Beginning with Gonzáles, 1824, the Governors were for the joint State of Coahuila y Texas.

José Felix Trespalacios	1822-1823
Luciano García	1823-1824
Rafael Gonzáles	1824-1826
Victor Blanco	1826-1827
José María Viesca	1827-1830
Ramón Eca y Músquiz	1830-1831
José María Letona	1831-1832
Ramón Eca y Músquiz	1832-1832
Juan Martín de Veramendi	1832-1833
Juan José de Vidáurri y Villasenor	1833-1834
Juan José Elguezábal	1834-1835
José María Cantú	1835-1835
Agustin M. Viesca	1835-1835
Marciel Borrego	1835-1835
Ramón Eca y Músquiz	1835-1835

Provisional Colonial Governor, Before Independence

Henry Smith (Impeached)	1835

James W. Robinson served as acting Governor just prior to March 2, 1836, after Smith was impeached.

Presidents of the Republic of Texas

David G. Burnet	Mar. 16, 1836-Oct. 22, 1836
Sam Houston	Oct. 22, 1836-Dec. 10, 1838
Mirabeau B. Lamar	Dec. 10, 1838-Dec. 13, 1841
Sam Houston	Dec. 13, 1841-Dec. 9, 1844
Anson Jones	Dec. 9, 1844-Feb. 19, 1846

Governors Since Annexation

J. Pinckney Henderson	Feb. 19, 1846-Dec. 21, 1847

(Albert C. Horton served as acting Governor while Henderson was away in the Mexican War.)

George T. Wood	Dec. 21, 1847-Dec. 21, 1849
Peter Hansbrough Bell	Dec. 21, 1849-Nov. 23, 1853
J. W. Henderson	Nov. 23, 1853-Dec. 21, 1853
Elisha M. Pease	Dec. 21, 1853-Dec. 21, 1857
Hardin R. Runnels	Dec. 21, 1857-Dec. 21, 1859
Sam Houston (*resigned because of state's secession from the Union*)	Dec. 21, 1859-Mar. 16, 1861
Edward Clark	Mar. 16, 1861-Nov. 7, 1861
Francis R. Lubbock (*resigned to enter Confederate Army*)	Nov. 7, 1861-Nov. 5, 1863
Pendleton Murrah (*administration terminated by fall of Confederacy*)	Nov. 5, 1863-June 17, 1865

Fletcher S. Stockdale (*Lt. Gov. performed some duties of office on Murrah's departure, but is sometimes included in list of Governors. Hamilton's appointment was for immediate succession, as shown by the dates.*)

Andrew J. Hamilton (*Provisional, appointed by President Johnson*)	June 17, 1865-Aug. 9, 1866
James W. Throckmorton	Aug. 9, 1866-Aug. 8, 1867
Elisha M. Pease (*appointed July 30, 1867, under martial law*)	Aug. 8, 1867-Sept. 30, 1869

Interregnum

Pease resigned and vacated office Sept. 30, 1869; no successor was named until Jan. 8, 1870. Some historians extend Pease's term until Jan. 8, 1870, but in reality Texas was without a head of its civil government from Sept. 30, 1869, until Jan. 8, 1870.

Edmund J. Davis (*appointed provisional Governor after being elected*)	Jan. 8, 1870-Jan. 15, 1874
Richard Coke (*resigned to enter United States Senate*)	Jan. 15, 1874-Dec. 1, 1876
Richard B. Hubbard	Dec. 1, 1876-Jan. 21, 1879
Oran M. Roberts	Jan. 21, 1879-Jan. 16, 1883
John Ireland	Jan. 16, 1883-Jan. 18, 1887
Lawrence Sullivan Ross	Jan. 18, 1887-Jan. 20, 1891
James Stephen Hogg	Jan. 20, 1891-Jan. 15, 1895
Charles A. Culberson	Jan. 15, 1895-Jan. 17, 1899
Joseph D. Sayers	Jan. 17, 1899-Jan. 20, 1903
S. W. T. Lanham	Jan. 20, 1903-Jan. 15, 1907
Thos. Mitchell Campbell	Jan. 15, 1907-Jan. 17, 1911
Oscar Branch Colquitt	Jan. 17, 1911-Jan. 19, 1915
James E. Ferguson (*impeached*)	Jan. 19, 1915-Aug. 25, 1917

William Pettus Hobby	Aug. 25, 1917-Jan. 18, 1921
Pat Morris Neff	Jan. 18, 1921-Jan. 20, 1925
Miriam A. Ferguson	Jan. 20, 1925-Jan. 17, 1927
Dan Moody	Jan. 17, 1927-Jan. 20, 1931
Ross S. Sterling	Jan. 20, 1931-Jan. 17, 1933
Miriam A. Ferguson	Jan. 17, 1933-Jan. 15, 1935
James V. Allred	Jan. 15, 1935-Jan. 17, 1939
W. Lee O'Daniel (resigned to enter United States Senate)	Jan. 17, 1939-Aug. 4, 1941
Coke R. Stevenson	Aug. 4, 1941-Jan. 21, 1947
Beauford H. Jester	Jan. 21, 1947-July 11, 1949
Allan Shivers (*Lt. Governor succeeded on death of Governor Jester. Elected in 1950 and re-elected in 1952 and 1954*)	July 11, 1949-Jan. 15, 1957
Price Daniel	Jan. 15, 1957-Jan. 15, 1963
John Connally	Jan. 15, 1963-Jan. 21, 1969
Preston Smith	Jan. 21, 1969-Jan. 16, 1973
**Dolph Briscoe	Jan. 16, 1973-Jan. 16, 1979
William P. Clements	Jan. 16, 1979-Jan. 18, 1983
Mark White	Jan. 18, 1983-Jan. 20, 1987
William P. Clements	Jan. 20, 1987-Jan. 15, 1991
Ann W. Richards	Jan. 15, 1991-Jan. 17, 1995
George W. Bush	Jan. 17, 1995 to Present

***Effective in 1975, term of office was raised to 4 years, according to a constitutional amendment approved by Texas voters in 1972. See introduction to State Government chapter in this edition for other state officials whose terms were raised to four years.*

★ ★ ★ ★ ★ ★ ★

Vice Presidents and Lieutenant Governors

Vice Presidents of Republic
Date Elected

Lorenzo de Zavala (*provisional Vice President*)

Mirabeau B. Lamar	Sept. 5, 1836
David G. Burnet	Sept. 3, 1838
Edward Burleson	Sept. 6, 1841
Kenneth L. Anderson	Sept. 2, 1844

Lieutenant Governors

Albert C. Horton	1846-1847
John A. Greer	1847-1851
J. W. Henderson	Aug. 4, 1851
D. C. Dickson	1853-1855
H. R. Runnels	Aug. 6, 1855
F. R. Lubbock	Aug. 4, 1857
Edward Clark	Aug. 1, 1859
John M. Crockett	1861-1863
Fletcher S. Stockdale	1863-1866
George W. Jones	1866
(*Jones was removed by General Sheridan.*)	
J. W. Flanagan	1869
(*Flanagan was appointed U.S. Senator and was never inaugurated as Lt. Gov.*)	
R. B. Hubbard	1873-1876
J. D. Sayers	1878-1880
L. J. Storey	1880-1882
Marion Martin	1882-1884
Barnett Gibbs	1884-1886
T. B. Wheeler	1886-1890
George C. Pendleton	1890-1892
M. M. Crane	Jan. 17, 1893-Jan. 25, 1895
George T. Jester	1895-1898
J. N. Browning	1898-1902
George D. Neal	1902-1906
A. B. Davidson	1906-1912
Will H. Mayes	1912-1914
William Pettus Hobby	1914-1917
W. A. Johnson (*served Hobby's unexpired term and until*	January, 1920)
Lynch Davidson	1920-1922
T. W. Davidson	1922-1924
Barry Miller	1924-1931
Edgar E. Witt	1931-1935
Walter Woodul	1935-1939

Coke R. Stevenson	1939-1941
John Lee Smith	1943-Jan. 21, 1947
Allan Shivers	Jan. 21, 1947-July 11, 1949
(*Shivers succeeded to the governorship on death of Governor Beauford H. Jester.*)	
Ben Ramsey	1951-Sept. 18, 1961
(*Ben Ramsey resigned to become a member of the State Railroad Commission.*)	
Preston Smith	1963-1969
Ben Barnes	1969-1973
William P. Hobby Jr.	1973-1991
Robert D. Bullock	1991-Present

★ ★ ★ ★ ★ ★ ★

Secretaries of State
Republic of Texas

Raines Yearbook for Texas, 1901, gives the following record of Secretaries of State during the era of the Republic of Texas:

Under David G. Burnet — Samuel P. Carson, James Collingsworth and W. H. Jack.

Under Sam Houston (first term) — Stephen F. Austin, 1836. J. Pinckney Henderson and Dr. Robert A. Irion, 1837-38.

Under Mirabeau B. Lamar — Bernard Bee appointed Dec. 16, 1838; James Webb appointed Feb. 6, 1839; D. G. Burnet appointed Acting Secretary of State, May 31, 1839; N. Amory appointed Acting Secretary of State, July 23, 1839; D. G. Burnet appointed Acting Secretary of State, Aug. 5, 1839; Abner S. Lipscomb appointed Secretary of State, Jan. 31, 1840, and resigned Jan. 22, 1841; Joseph Waples appointed Acting Secretary of State, Jan. 23, 1841, and served until Feb. 8, 1841; James S. Mayfield appointed Feb. 8, 1841; Joseph Waples appointed April 30, 1841, and served until May 25, 1841; Samuel A. Roberts appointed May 25, 1841; reappointed Sept. 7, 1841.

Under Sam Houston (second term) — E. Lawrence Stickney, Acting Secretary of State until Anson Jones appointed Dec. 13, 1841. Jones served as Secretary of State throughout this term except during the summer and part of this term of 1842, when Joseph Waples filled the position as Acting Secretary of State.

Under Anson Jones — Ebenezer Allen served from Dec. 10, 1844, until Feb. 5, 1845, when Ashbel Smith became Secretary of State. Allen was again named Acting Secretary of State, March 31, 1845, and later named Secretary of State.

State Secretaries of State

Charles Mariner	Feb. 20, 1846-May 4, 1846
David G. Burnet	May 4, 1846-Jan. 1, 1848
Washington D. Miller	Jan. 1, 1848-Jan. 2, 1850
James Webb	Jan. 2, 1850-Nov. 14, 1851
Thomas H. Duval	Nov. 14, 1851-Dec. 22, 1853
Edward Clark	Dec. 22, 1853-Dec., 1857
T. S. Anderson	Dec. 1857-Dec. 27, 1859
E. W. Cave	Dec. 27, 1859-Mar. 16, 1861
Bird Holland	Mar. 16, 1861-Nov., 1861
Charles West	Nov., 1861-Sept., 1862
Robert J. Townes	Sept., 1862-May 2, 1865
Charles R. Pryor	May 2, 1865-Aug., 1865
James H. Bell	Aug., 1865-Aug., 1866
John A. Green	Aug., 1866-Aug., 1867
D. W. C. Phillips	Aug., 1867-Jan., 1870
J. P. Newcomb	Jan. 1, 1870-Jan. 17, 1874
George Clark	Jan. 17, 1874-Jan. 27, 1874
A. W. DeBerry	Jan. 27, 1874-Dec. 1, 1876
Isham G. Searcy	Dec. 1, 1876-Jan. 23, 1879
J. D. Templeton	Jan. 23, 1879-Jan. 22, 1881
T. H. Bowman	Jan. 22, 1881-Jan. 18, 1883
J. W. Baines	Jan. 18, 1883-Jan. 21, 1887
John M. Moore	Jan. 21, 1887-Jan. 22, 1891
George W. Smith	Jan. 22, 1891-Jan. 17, 1895
Allison Mayfield	Jan. 17, 1895-Jan. 5, 1897
J. W. Madden	Jan. 5, 1897-Jan. 18, 1899

D. H. Hardy .... Jan. 18, 1899-Jan. 19, 1901
John G. Tod .... Jan. 19, 1901-Jan., 1903
J. R. Curl .... Jan., 1903-April, 1905
O. K. Shannon .... April, 1905-Jan., 1907
L. T. Dashiel .... Jan., 1907-Feb., 1908
W. R. Davie .... Feb., 1908-Jan., 1909
W. B. Townsend .... Jan., 1909-Jan., 1911
C. C. McDonald .... Jan., 1911-Dec., 1912
J. T. Bowman .... Dec., 1912-Jan., 1913
John L. Wortham .... Jan., 1913-June, 1913
F. C. Weinert .... June, 1913-Nov., 1914
D. A. Gregg .... Nov., 1914-Jan., 1915
John G. McKay .... Jan., 1915-Dec., 1916
C. J. Bartlett .... Dec., 1916-Nov., 1917
George F. Howard .... Nov., 1917-Nov., 1920
C. D. Mims .... Nov., 1920-Jan., 1921
S. L. Staples .... Jan., 1921-Aug., 1924
J. D. Strickland .... Sept., 1924-Jan. 1, 1925
Henry Hutchings .... Jan. 1, 1925-Jan. 20, 1925
Mrs. Emma G. Meharg .... Jan. 20, 1925-Jan., 1927
Mrs. Jane Y. McCallum .... Jan., 1927-Jan., 1933
W. W. Heath .... Jan., 1933-Jan., 1935
Gerald C. Mann .... Jan., 1935-Aug. 31, 1935
R. B. Stanford .... Aug. 31, 1935-Aug. 25, 1936
B. P. Matocha .... Aug. 25, 1936-Jan. 18, 1937
Edward Clark .... Jan. 18, 1937-Jan., 1939
Tom L. Beauchamp .... Jan., 1939-Oct., 1939
M. O. Flowers .... Oct. 26, 1939-Feb. 25, 1941
William J. Lawson .... Feb. 25, 1941-Jan., 1943
Sidney Latham .... Jan., 1943-Feb., 1945
Claude Isbell .... Feb., 1945-Jan., 1947
Paul H. Brown .... Jan., 1947-Jan. 19, 1949
Ben Ramsey .... Jan. 19, 1949-Feb. 9, 1950
John Ben Shepperd .... Feb. 9, 1950-April 30, 1952
Jack Ross .... April 30, 1952-Jan. 9, 1953
Howard A. Carney .... Jan. 9, 1953-Apr. 30, 1954
C. E. Fulgham .... May 1, 1954-Feb. 15, 1955
Al Muldrow .... Feb. 16, 1955-Nov. 1, 1955
Tom Reavley .... Nov. 1, 1955-Jan. 16, 1957
Zollie Steakley .... Jan. 16, 1957-Jan. 2, 1962
P. Frank Lake .... Jan. 2, 1962-Jan. 15, 1963
Crawford C. Martin .... Jan. 15, 1963-March 12, 1966
John L. Hill .... March 12, 1966-Jan. 22, 1968
Roy Barrera .... March 7, 1968-Jan. 23, 1969
Martin Dies Jr. .... Jan. 23, 1969-Sept. 1, 1971
Robert D. (Bob) Bullock .... Sept. 1, 1971-Jan. 2, 1973
V. Larry Teaver Jr. .... Jan. 2, 1973-Jan. 19, 1973
Mark W. White Jr. .... Jan. 19, 1973-Oct. 27,1977
Steven C. Oaks .... Oct. 27, 1977-Jan. 16, 1979
George W. Strake Jr. .... Jan. 16, 1979-Oct. 6, 1981
David A. Dean .... Oct. 22, 1981-Jan. 18, 1983
John Fainter .... Jan. 18, 1983-July 31, 1984
Myra A. McDaniel .... Sept. 6, 1984-Jan. 26, 1987
Jack Rains .... Jan. 26, 1987-June 15, 1989
George Bayoud Jr. .... June 19, 1989-Jan. 15, 1991
John Hannah Jr. .... Jan. 17, 1991-March 11, 1994
Ronald Kirk .... April 4, 1994 to Jan. 17, 1995
Antonio O. "Tony" Garza Jr. .... Jan. 18, 1995 to Present

★ ★ ★ ★ ★ ★ ★

Attorneys General

Of the Republic

David Thomas and
    Peter W. Grayson .... Mar. 2-Oct. 22, 1836
J. Pinckney Henderson, Peter W. Grayson,
    John Birdsall, A. S. Thurston 1836-1838
J. C. Watrous .... Dec., 1838-June 1, 1840
Joseph Webb and F. A. Morris 1840-1841
George W. Terrell, Ebenezer Allen 1841-1844
Ebenezer Allen 1844-1846

*Of the State

Volney E. Howard .... Feb. 21, 1846-May 7, 1846
John W. Harris .... May 7, 1846-Oct. 31, 1849
Henry P. Brewster .... Oct. 31, 1849-Jan. 15, 1850

A. J. Hamilton .... Jan. 15, 1850-Aug. 5, 1850
Ebenezer Allen .... Aug. 5, 1850-Aug. 2, 1852
Thomas J. Jennings .... Aug. 2, 1852-Aug. 4, 1856
James Willie .... Aug. 4, 1856-Aug. 2, 1858
Malcolm D. Graham .... Aug. 2, 1858-Aug. 6, 1860
George M. Flournoy .... Aug. 6, 1860-Jan. 15, 1862
N. G. Shelley .... Feb. 5, 1862-Aug. 1, 1864
B. E. Tarver .... Aug. 1, 1864-Dec. 11, 1865
Wm. Alexander .... Dec. 11, 1865-June 25, 1866
W. M. Walton .... June 25, 1866-Aug. 27, 1867
Wm. Alexander .... Aug. 27, 1867-Nov. 5, 1867
Ezekiel B. Turner .... Nov. 5, 1867-July 11, 1870
Wm. Alexander .... July 11, 1870-Jan. 27, 1874
George Clark .... Jan. 27, 1874-Apr. 25, 1876
H. H. Boone .... Apr. 25, 1876-Nov. 5, 1878
George McCormick .... Nov. 5, 1878-Nov. 2, 1880
J. H. McLeary .... Nov. 2, 1880-Nov. 7, 1882
John D. Templeton .... Nov. 7, 1882-Nov. 2, 1886
James S. Hogg .... Nov. 2, 1886-Nov. 4, 1890
C. A. Culberson .... Nov. 4, 1890-Nov. 6, 1894
M. M. Crane .... Nov. 6, 1894-Nov. 8, 1898
Thomas S. Smith .... Nov. 8, 1898-Mar. 15,1901
C. K. Bell .... Mar. 20, 1901-Jan., 1904
R. V. Davidson .... Jan., 1904-Dec. 31, 1909
Jewel P. Lightfoot .... Jan. 1, 1910-Aug. 31, 1912
James D. Walthall .... Sept. 1, 1912-Jan. 1, 1913
B. F. Looney .... Jan. 1, 1913-Jan., 1919
C. M. Cureton .... Jan., 1919-Dec., 1921
W. A. Keeling .... Dec., 1921-Jan., 1925
Dan Moody .... Jan., 1925-Jan., 1927
Claude Pollard .... Jan., 1927-Sept., 1929
R. L. Bobbitt (Apptd.) .... Sept., 1929-Jan., 1931
James V. Allred .... Jan., 1931-Jan., 1935
William McCraw .... Jan., 1935-Jan., 1939
Gerald C. Mann (resigned) .... Jan., 1939-Jan., 1944
Grover Sellers .... Jan., 1944-Jan., 1947
Price Daniel .... Jan., 1947-Jan., 1953
John Ben Shepperd .... Jan., 1953-Jan. 1, 1957
Will Wilson .... Jan. 1, 1957-Jan. 15, 1963
Waggoner Carr .... Jan. 15, 1963-Jan. 1, 1967
Crawford C. Martin .... Jan. 1, 1967-Dec. 29, 1972
John Hill .... Jan. 1, 1973-Jan. 16, 1979
Mark White .... Jan. 16, 1979 to Jan. 18, 1983
Jim Mattox .... Jan. 18, 1983 to Jan. 15, 1991
Dan Morales .... Jan. 15, 1991 to Present

The first few Attorneys General held office by appointment of the Governor. The office was made elective in 1850 by constitutional amendment and Ebenezer Allen was the first elected Attorney General.

★ ★ ★ ★ ★ ★ ★

Treasurers

Of the Republic

Asa Brigham 1838-1840
James W. Simmons 1840-1841
Asa Brigham 1841-1844
Moses Johnson 1844-1846

Of the State

James H. Raymond .... Feb. 24, 1846-Aug. 2, 1858
*C. H. Randolph .... Aug. 2, 1858-June, 1865
*Samuel Harris .... Oct. 2, 1865-June 25, 1866
W. M. Royston .... June 25, 1866-Sept. 1, 1867
John Y. Allen .... Sept. 1, 1867-Jan., 1869
†George W. Honey .... Jan., 1869-Jan., 1874
†B. Graham (short term) .... beginning May 27, 1872
A. J. Dorn .... Jan., 1874-Jan., 1879
F. R. Lubbock .... Jan., 1879-Jan., 1891
W. B. Wortham .... Jan., 1891-Jan., 1899
John W. Robbins .... Jan., 1899-Jan., 1907
Sam Sparks .... Jan., 1907-Jan., 1912
J. M. Edwards .... Jan., 1912-Jan., 1919
John W. Baker .... Jan., 1919-Jan., 1921
G. N. Holton .... July, 1921-Nov. 21, 1921
C. V. Terrell .... Nov. 21, 1921-Aug. 15, 1924
S. L. Staples .... Aug. 16, 1924-Jan. 15, 1925

W. Gregory Hatcher	Jan. 16, 1925-Jan. 1, 1931
Charley Lockhart	Jan. 1, 1931-Oct. 25, 1941
Jesse James	Oct. 25, 1941-Sept. 29, 1977
Warren G. Harding	Oct. 7, 1977-Jan. 3, 1983
Ann Richards	Jan. 3, 1983- Jan. 2, 1991
Kay Bailey Hutchison	Jan. 2, 1991 to June 1993
‡Martha Whitehead	June 1993 to Aug. 1996

*Randolph fled to Mexico upon collapse of Confederacy. No exact date is available for his departure from office or for Harris' succession to the post. It is believed Harris took office Oct. 2, 1865.

†Honey was removed from office for a short period in 1872 and B. Graham served in his place.

‡ The office of Treasurer was eliminated by Constitutional amendment in an election Nov. 7, 1995, effective the last day of August 1996.

★ ★ ★ ★ ★ ★ ★

Railroad Commission of Texas

(After the first three names in the following list, each commissioner's name is followed by a surname in parentheses. The name in parentheses is the name of the commissioner whom that commissioner succeeded.)

John H. Reagan	June 10, 1891-Jan. 20, 1903
L. L. Foster	June 10, 1891-April 30, 1895
W. P. McLean	June 10, 1891-Nov. 20, 1894
L. J. Storey (McLean)	Nov. 21, 1894-Mar. 28,1909
N. A. Stedman (Foster)	May 1, 1895-Jan. 4, 1897
Allison Mayfield (Stedman)	Jan. 5, 1897-Jan. 23, 1923
O. B. Colquitt (Reagan)	Jan. 21, 1903-Jan. 17, 1911
William D. Williams (Storey)	April 28, 1909-Oct. 1, 1916
John L. Wortham (Colquitt)	Jan. 21, 1911-Jan. 1, 1913
Earle B. Mayfield (Wortham)	Jan. 2, 1913-March 1, 1923
Charles Hurdleston (Williams)	Oct. 10, 1916-Dec. 31, 1918
Clarence Gilmore (Hurdleston)	Jan. 1, 1919-Jan. 1, 1929
N. A. Nabors (A. Mayfield)	March 1, 1923-Jan. 18, 1925
William Splawn (E. Mayfield)	March 1, 1923-Aug. 1, 1924
C. V. Terrell (Splawn)	Aug. 15, 1924-Jan. 1, 1939
Lon A. Smith (Nabors)	Jan. 29, 1925-Jan. 1, 1941
Pat M. Neff (Gilmore)	Jan. 1, 1929-Jan. 1, 1933
Ernest O. Thompson (Neff)	Jan. 1, 1933-Jan. 8, 1965
G. A. (Jerry) Sadler (Terrell)	Jan. 1, 1939-Jan. 1, 1943
Olin Culberson (Smith)	Jan. 1, 1941-June 22, 1961
Beauford Jester (Sadler)	Jan. 1, 1943-Jan. 21, 1947
William J. Murray Jr. (Jester)	Jan. 21, 1947-Apr. 10, 1963
Ben Ramsey (Culberson)	Sept. 18, 1961-Dec. 31, 1976
Jim C. Langdon (Murray)	May 28, 1963-Dec. 31, 1977
Byron Tunnell (Thompson)	Jan. 11, 1965-Sept. 15, 1973
Mack Wallace (Tunnell)	Sept. 18, 1973-Sept. 22, 1987
Jon Newton (Ramsey)	Jan. 10, 1977-Jan. 4, 1979
John H. Poerner (Langdon)	Jan. 2, 1978-Jan. 1, 1981
James E. (Jim) Nugent (Newton)	Jan. 4, 1979-Jan. 3, 199
Buddy Temple (Poerner)	Jan. 2, 1981-March 2, 1986
Clark Jobe (Temple)	March 3, 1986-Jan. 5, 1987
John Sharp (Jobe)	Jan. 6, 1987-Jan. 2, 1991
Kent Hance (Wallace)	Sept. 23, 1987-Jan. 2, 1991
*Robert Krueger (Hance)	Jan. 3, 1991-Jan. 22, 1993
Lena Guerrero (Sharp)	Jan. 23, 1991-Sept. 25, 1992
James Wallace (Guerrero)	Oct. 2, 1992-Jan. 4, 1993
Barry Williamson (Wallace)	Jan. 5, 1993-Present
Mary Scott Nabers (Krueger)	Feb. 9, 1993-Dec. 9, 1994
Carole Keeton Rylander (Nabers)	Dec. 10, 1994-Present
Charles Matthews (Nugent)	Jan. 3, 1995-Present

* Robert Krueger resigned when Gov. Ann Richards appointed him interim U.S. Senator on the resignation of Sen. Lloyd Bentsen.

★ ★ ★ ★ ★ ★ ★

Comptroller of Public Accounts

Of the Republic

John H. Money	Dec. 30, 1835-Jan. 17, 1836
H. C. Hudson	Jan. 17, 1836-Oct. 22, 1836

E. M. Pease	June, 1837-Dec., 1837
F. R. Lubbock	Dec., 1837-Jan., 1839
Jas. W. Simmons	Jan. 15, 1839-Sept. 30, 1840
Jas. B. Shaw	Sept. 30, 1840-Dec. 24, 1841
F. R. Lubbock	Dec. 24, 1841-Jan. 1, 1842
Jas. B. Shaw	Jan. 1, 1842-Jan. 1, 1846

Of the State

Jas. B. Shaw	Feb. 24, 1846-Aug. 2, 1858
Clement R. Johns	Aug. 2, 1858-Aug. 1, 1864
Willis L. Robards	Aug. 1, 1864-Oct. 12, 1865
Albert H. Latimer	Oct. 12, 1865-Mar. 27, 1866
Robert H. Taylor	Mar. 27, 1866-June 25, 1866
Willis L. Robards	June 25, 1866-Aug. 27, 1867
Morgan C. Hamilton	Aug. 27, 1867-Jan. 8, 1870
A. Bledsoe	Jan. 8, 1870-Jan. 20, 1874
Stephen H. Darden	Jan. 20, 1974-Nov. 2, 1880
W. M. Brown	Nov. 2, 1880-Jan. 16, 1883
W. J. Swain	Jan. 16, 1883-Jan. 18, 1887
John D. McCall	Jan. 18, 1887-Jan. 15, 1895
R. W. Finley	Jan. 15, 1895-Jan. 15, 1901
R. M. Love	Jan. 15, 1901-Jan., 1903
J. W. Stephen	Jan., 1903-Jan., 1911
W. P. Lane	Jan., 1911-Jan., 1915
H. B. Terrell	Jan., 1915-Jan., 1920
M. L. Wiginton	Jan., 1920-Jan., 1921
Lon A. Smith	Jan., 1921-Jan., 1925
S. H. Terrell	Jan., 1925-Jan., 1931
Geo. H. Sheppard	Jan., 1931-Jan. 17, 1949
Robert S. Calvert	Jan. 17, 1949-Jan., 1975
Robert D. (Bob) Bullock	Jan., 1975-Jan. 3, 1991
John Sharp	Jan. 3, 1991 to Present

★ ★ ★ ★ ★ ★ ★

U.S. Senators from Texas

U.S. Senators were selected by the legislatures of the states until the U.S. Constitution was amended in 1913 to require popular elections. In Texas, the first senator chosen by the voters in a general election was Charles A. Culberson in 1916. Because of political pressures, however, the rules of the Democratic Party of Texas were changed in 1904 to require that all candidates for office stand before voters in the primary. Consequently, Texas' senators faced voters in 1906, 1910 and 1912 before the U.S. Constitution was changed.

Following is the succession of Texas representatives in the United States Senate since the annexation of Texas to the Union in 1845:

Houston Succession

Sam Houston	Feb. 21, 1846-Mar. 4, 1859
John Hemphill	Mar. 4, 1859-July 11, 1861

Louis T. Wigfall and W. S. Oldham took their seats in the Confederate Senate, Nov. 16, 1861, and served until the Confederacy collapsed. After that event, the State Legislature on Aug. 21, 1866, elected David G. Burnet and Oran M. Roberts to the United States Senate, anticipating immediate readmission to the Union, but they were not allowed to take their seats.

†Morgan C. Hamilton	Feb. 22, 1870-Mar. 3, 1877
Richard Coke	Mar. 4, 1877-Mar. 3, 1895
Horace Chilton	Mar. 3, 1895-Mar. 3, 1901
Joseph W. Bailey	Mar. 3, 1901-Jan. 8, 1913
Rienzi Melville Johnston	Jan. 8, 1913-Feb. 3, 1913
‡Morris Sheppard (died)	Feb. 13, 1913-Apr. 9, 1941
Andrew J. Houston	June 2-26, 1941
W. Lee O'Daniel	Aug. 4, 1941-Jan. 3, 1949
Lyndon B. Johnson	Jan. 3, 1949-Jan. 20, 1961
William A. Blakley	Jan. 20, 1961-June 15, 1961
†John G. Tower	June 15, 1961-Jan. 21, 1985
†Phil Gramm	Jan. 21, 1985-Present

Rusk Succession

Thomas J. Rusk (died)	Feb 21, 1846-July 29, 1857
J. Pinckney Henderson (died)	Nov. 9, 1857-June 4, 1858
Matthias Ward (appointed	

interim) .... Sept. 29, 1858-Dec. 5, 1859
Louis T. Wigfall .... Dec. 5, 1859-March 23, 1861

Succession was broken by the expulsion of Texas Senators following secession of Texas from Union. See note above under "Houston Succession" on Louis T. Wigfall, W. S. Oldham, Burnet and Roberts.

†James W. Flanagan .... Feb. 22, 1870-Mar. 3, 1875
Samuel B. Maxey .... Mar. 3, 1875-Mar. 3, 1887
John H. Reagan (resigned) ... Mar. 3, 1887-June 10, 1891
Horace Chilton (filled vacancy on
   appointment) .... Dec. 7, 1891-Mar. 30,1892
Roger Q. Mills .... Mar. 30, 1892-Mar. 3, 1899
‡Charles A. Culberson .... Mar. 3, 1899-Mar. 4, 1923
Earle B. Mayfield .... Mar. 4, 1923-Mar. 4, 1929
Tom Connally .... Mar. 4, 1929-Jan. 3, 1953
Price Daniel .... Jan. 3, 1953-Jan. 15, 1957
William A. Blakley .... Jan. 15. 1957-Apr. 27, 1957
Ralph W. Yarborough .... Apr. 27, 1957-Jan. 12, 1971
§Lloyd Bentsen .... Jan. 12, 1971-Jan. 20, 1993
Robert Krueger .... Jan. 20, 1993-June 14, 1993
†Kay Bailey Hutchison .... June 14, 1993-Present

† Republican members
‡ First election to U.S. Senate held in 1916. Prior to that time, senators were appointed by the Legislature.
§ Resigned from Senate when appointed U.S. Secretary of Treasury by Pres. Bill Clinton.

★ ★ ★ ★ ★ ★ ★

Commissioners of the General Land Office

For the Republic

John P. Borden...................... Aug. 23, 1837-Dec. 12, 1840
H. W. Raglin .... Dec. 12, 1840-Jan. 4, 1841
*Thomas William Ward .... Jan. 4, 1841-Mar. 20, 1848

For the State

George W. Smyth..................... Mar. 20, 1848-Aug. 4, 1851
Stephen Crosby .... Aug. 4, 1851-Mar. 1, 1858
Francis M. White .... Mar. 1, 1858-Mar. 1, 1862
Stephen Crosby .... Mar. 1, 1862-Sept. 1, 1865
Francis M. White .... Sept. 1, 1865-Aug. 7, 1866
Stephen Crosby .... Aug. 7, 1866-Aug. 27, 1867
Joseph Spence .... Aug. 27, 1867-Jan. 19, 1870
Jacob Kuechler .... Jan. 19, 1870-Jan. 20, 1874
J. J. Groos .... Jan. 20, 1874-June 15, 1878
W. C. Walsh .... July 30, 1878, Jan. 10, 1887
R. M. Hall .... Jan. 10, 1887-Jan. 16, 1891
W. L. McGaughey ....Jan. 16, 1891-Jan. 26, 1895
A. J. Baker .... Jan. 26, 1895-Jan. 16, 1899
George W. Finger....................Jan. 16, 1899-May 4, 1899
Charles Rogan ....May 11, 1899-Jan. 10, 1903
John J. Terrell......................Jan. 10, 1903-Jan. 11, 1909
J. T. Robison ....Jan, 1909-Sept. 11, 1929
J. H. Walker ....Sept. 11, 1929-Jan., 1937
William H. McDonald .... Jan, 1937-Jan., 1939
Bascom Giles .... Jan., 1939-Jan. 5, 1955
J. Earl Rudder .... Jan. 5, 1955-Feb. 1, 1958
Bill Allcorn .... Feb. 1, 1958-Jan. 1, 1961
Jerry Sadler.........................Jan. 1, 1961-Jan. 1, 1971
Bob Armstrong ....Jan. 1, 1971-Jan. 1, 1983
Garry Mauro ....Jan. 1, 1983-Present
Part of term after annexation.

★ ★ ★ ★ ★ ★ ★

Speaker of the Texas House

The Speaker of the Texas House of Representatives is the presiding officer of the lower chamber of the State Legislature. The official is elected at the beginning of each regular session by a vote of the members of the House.

Speaker, Residence	Year Elected	Legis-lature
William E. Crump, Bellville	1846	1st
William H. Bourland, Paris	1846	1st

James W. Henderson, Houston	1847	2nd
Charles G. Keenan, Huntsville	1849	3rd
David C. Dickson, Anderson	1851	4th
Hardin R. Runnels, Boston	1853	5th
Hamilton P. Bee, Laredo	1855	6th
William S. Taylor, Larissa	1857	7th
Matt F. Locke, Lafayette	1858	7th
Marion DeKalb Taylor, Jefferson	1859	8th
Constantine W. Buckley, Richmond	1861	9th
Nicholas H. Darnell, Dallas	1861	9th
Constantine W. Buckley, Richmond	1863	9th
Marion DeKalb Taylor, Jefferson	1863	10th
Nathaniel M. Burford, Dallas	1866	11th
Ira H. Evans, Corpus Christi	1870	12th
William H. Sinclair, Galveston	1871	12th
Marion DeKalb Taylor, Jefferson	1873	13th
Guy M. Bryan, Galveston	1874	14th
Thomas R. Bonner, Tyler	1876	15th
John H. Cochran, Dallas	1879	16th
George R. Reeves, Pottsboro	1881	17th
Charles R. Gibson, Waxahachie	1883	18th
Lafayette L. Foster, Groesbeck	1885	19th
George C. Pendleton, Belton	1887	20th
Frank P. Alexander, Greenville	1889	21st
Robert T. Milner, Henderson	1891	22nd
John H. Cochran, Dallas	1893	23rd
Thomas Slater Smith, Hillsboro	1895	24th
L. Travis Dashiell, Jewett	1897	25th
J. S. Sherrill, Greenville	1899	26th
Robert E. Prince, Corsicana	1901	27th
Pat M. Neff, Waco	1903	28th
Francis W. Seabury, Rio Grande City	1905	29th
Thomas B. Love, Lancaster	1907	30th
Austin M. Kennedy, Waco	1909	31st
John W. Marshall, Whitesboro	1909	31st
Sam Rayburn, Bonham	1911	32nd
Chester H. Terrell, San Antonio	1913	33rd
John W. Woods, Rotan	1915	34th
Franklin O. Fuller, Coldspring	1917	35th
R. Ewing Thomason, El Paso	1919	36th
Charles G. Thomas, Lewisville	1921	37th
Richard E. Seagler, Palestine	1923	38th
Lee Satterwhite, Amarillo	1925	39th
Robert L. Bobbitt, Laredo	1927	40th
W. S. Barron, Bryan	1929	41st
Fred H. Minor, Denton	1931	42nd
Coke R. Stevenson, Junction	1933	43rd
"	1935	44th
Robert W. Calvert, Hillsboro	1937	45th
R. Emmett Morse, Houston	1939	46th
Homer L. Leonard, McAllen	1941	47th
Price Daniel, Liberty	1943	48th
Claud H. Gilmer, Rocksprings	1945	49th
William O. Reed, Dallas	1947	50th
Durwood Manford, Smiley	1949	51st
Reuben Senterfitt, San Saba	1951	52nd
"	1953	53rd
Jim T. Lindsey, Texarkana	1955	54th
Waggoner Carr, Lubbock	1957	55th
"	1959	56th
James A. Turman, Gober	1961	57th
Byron M. Tunnell, Tyler	1963	58th
Ben Barnes, DeLeon	1965	59th
"	1967	60th
Gus F. Mutscher, Brenham	1969	61st
"	1971	62nd
Rayford Price, Palestine	1972	62nd
Price Daniel Jr., Liberty	1973	63rd
Bill Clayton, Springlake	1975	64th
"	1977	65th
"	1979	66th
"	1981	67th
Gibson D. Lewis, Fort Worth	1983	68th
"	1985	69th
"	1987	70th
"	1989	71st
"	1991	72nd
James M. (Pete) Laney, Hale Center	1993	73rd
"	1995	74th
"	1997	75th

★ ★ ★ ★ ★ ★ ★

Chief Justice of the Supreme Court

Republic of Texas

James Collinsworth .... Dec. 16, 1836-July 23, 1838
John Birdsall .... Nov. 19-Dec. 12, 1838
Thomas J. Rusk .... Dec. 12, 1838-Dec. 5, 1840
John Hemphill .... Dec. 5, 1840-Dec. 29, 1845

Under the Constitutions of 1845 and 1861

John Hemphill .... Mar. 2, 1846-Oct. 10, 1858
Royall T. Wheeler .... Oct. 11, 1858-April 1864
Oran M. Roberts .... Nov. 1, 1864-June 30, 1866

Under the Constitution of 1866
(Presidential Reconstruction)

*George F. Moore .... Aug. 16, 1866-Sept. 10, 1867
*Removed under Congressional Reconstruction by military authorities who appointed members of the next court.

Under the Constitution of 1866
(Congressional Reconstruction)

Amos Morrill .... Sept. 10, 1867-July 5, 1870

Under the Constitution of 1869

Lemuel D. Evans .... July 5, 1870-Aug. 31, 1873
Wesley Ogden .... Aug. 31, 1873-Jan. 29, 1874
Oran M. Roberts .... Jan. 29, 1874-Apr. 18, 1876

Under the Constitution of 1876

Oran M. Roberts .... Apr. 18, 1876-Oct. 1, 1878
George F. Moore .... Nov. 5, 1878-Nov. 1, 1881
Robert S. Gould .... Nov. 1, 1881-Dec. 23, 1882
Asa H. Willie .... Dec. 23, 1882-Mar. 3, 1888
John W. Stayton .... Mar. 3, 1888-July 5, 1894
Reuben R. Gaines .... July 10, 1894-Jan. 5, 1911
Thomas J. Brown .... Jan. 7, 1911-May 26, 1915
Nelson Phillips .... June 1, 1915-Nov. 16, 1921
C. M. Cureton .... Dec. 2, 1921-Apr. 8, 1940
†Hortense Sparks Ward .... Jan. 8, 1925-May 23, 1925
W. F. Moore .... Apr. 17, 1940-Jan. 1, 1941
James P. Alexander .... Jan. 1, 1941-Jan. 1, 1948
J. E. Hickman .... Jan. 5, 1948-Jan. 3, 1961
Robert W. Calvert .... Jan. 3, 1961-Oct. 4, 1972
Joe R. Greenhill .... Oct. 4, 1972-Oct. 25, 1982
Jack Pope .... Nov. 29, 1982-Jan. 5, 1985
John L. Hill Jr. .... Jan. 5, 1985-Jan. 4, 1988
Thomas R. Phillips .... Jan. 4, 1988-Present

†Mrs. Ward served as Chief Justice of a special Supreme Court to hear one case in 1925. (See related article on pages 41-43.)

Presiding Judges, Court of Appeals (1876-1891) and Court of Criminal Appeals (1891-Present)

Mat D. Ector .... May 6, 1876-Oct. 29, 1879
John P. White .... Nov. 9, 1879-Apr. 26, 1892
James M. Hurt .... May 4, 1892-Dec. 31, 1898
W. L. Davidson .... Jan. 2, 1899-June 27, 1913
A. C. Prendergast .... June 27, 1913-Dec. 31, 1916
W. L. Davidson .... Jan. 1, 1917-Jan. 25, 1921
Wright C. Morrow .... Feb. 8, 1921-Oct. 16, 1939
Frank Lee Hawkins .... Oct. 16, 1939-Jan. 2, 1951
Harry N. Graves .... Jan. 2, 1951-Dec. 31, 1954
W. A. Morrison .... Jan. 1, 1955-Jan. 2, 1961
Kenneth K. Woodley .... Jan. 3, 1961-Jan. 4, 1965
W. T. McDonald .... Jan. 4, 1965-June 25, 1966
W. A. Morrison .... June 25, 1966-Jan. 1, 1967
Kenneth K. Woodley .... Jan. 1, 1967-Jan. 1, 1971
John F. Onion Jr. .... Jan. 1, 1971-Jan. 1, 1989
Michael J. McCormick .... Jan. 1, 1989-Present

★ ★ ★ ★ ★ ★ ★

Administrators of Public Education

Superintendents of Public Instruction
Pryor Lea .... Nov. 10, 1866-Sept. 12, 1867

Edwin M. Wheelock .... Sept. 12, 1867-May 6, 1871
Jacob C. DeGress .... May 6, 1871-Jan. 20, 1874
O. H. Hollingsworth .... Jan. 20, 1874-May 6, 1884
B. M. Baker .... May 6, 1884-Jan. 18, 1887
O. H. Cooper .... Jan 18, 1887-Sept. 1, 1890
H. C. Pritchett .... Sept. 1, 1890-Sept. 15, 1891
J. M. Carlisle .... Sept. 15, 1891-Jan. 10, 1899
J. S. Kendall .... Jan. 10, 1899-July 2, 1901
Arthur Lefevre .... July 2, 1901-Jan. 12, 1905
R. B. Cousins .... Jan. 12, 1905-Jan. 1, 1910
F. M. Bralley .... Jan. 1, 1910-Sept. 1, 1913
W. F. Doughty .... Sept. 1, 1913-Jan. 1, 1919
Annie Webb Blanton .... Jan. 1, 1919-Jan. 16, 1923
S. M. N. Marrs .... Jan. 16, 1923-April 28, 1932
C. N. Shaver .... April 28, 1932-Oct. 1, 1932
L. W. Rogers .... Oct. 1, 1932-Jan. 16, 1933
L. A. Woods .... Jan. 16, 1933-*1951

State Commissioner of Education

J. W. Edgar .... May 31, 1951-June 30, 1974
Marlin L. Brockette .... July 1, 1974-Sept. 1, 1979
Alton O. Bowen .... Sept. 1, 1979-June 1, 1981
Raymon Bynum .... June 1, 1981-Oct. 31, 1984
W. N. Kirby .... April 13, 1985-July 1, 1991
Lionel R. Meno .... July 1, 1991-March 1, 1995
Michael A. Moses .... March 9, 1995-Present

*The office of State Superintendent of Public Instruction was abolished by the Gilmer-Aikin act of 1949 and the office of Commissioner of Education created, appointed by a new State Board of Education elected by the people.

First Ladies of Texas

Martha Evans Gindratt Wood 1847-49
†Bell Administration 1849-53
Lucadia Christiana Niles Pease 1853-57; 1867-69
‡Runnels Administration 1857-59
Margaret Moffette Lea Houston 1859-61
Martha Evans Clark 1861
Adele Barron Lubbock 1861-63
Susie Ellen Taylor Murrah 1863-65
Mary Jane Bowen Hamilton 1865-66
Annie Rattan Throckmorton 1866-67
Ann Elizabeth Britton Davis 1870-74
Mary Home Coke 1874-76
Janie Roberts Hubbard 1876-79
Frances Wickliff Edwards Roberts 1879-83
Anne Maria Penn Ireland 1883-87
Elizabeth Dorothy Tinsley Ross 1887-91
Sarah Stinson Hogg 1891-95
Sally Harrison Culberson 1895-99
Orlene Walton Sayers 1899-1903
Sarah Beona Meng Lanham 1903-07
Fannie Brunner Campbell 1907-11
Alice Fuller Murrell Colquitt 1911-15
§Miriam A. Wallace Ferguson 1915-17
Willie Cooper Hobby 1917-21
Myrtle Mainer Neff 1921-25
Mildred Paxton Moody 1927-31
Maud Gage Sterling 1931-33
Jo Betsy Miller Allred 1935-39
Merle Estella Butcher O'Daniel 1939-41
**Fay Wright Stevenson 1941-42
**Edith Will Scott Stevenson 1942-46
Mabel Buchanan Jester 1946-49
Marialice Shary Shivers 1949-57
Jean Houston Baldwin Daniel 1957-63
Idanell Brill Connally 1963-69
Ima Mae Smith 1969-73
Betty Jane Slaughter Briscoe 1973-79
Rita Crocker Bass Clements 1979-83
Linda Gale Thompson White 1983-87
Rita Crocker Bass Clements 1987-91
Laura Welch Bush 1995-Present

†Gov. Peter Hansbrough Bell was not married while in office.
‡Gov. Hardin R. Runnels never married.
**Mrs. Coke R. (Fay Wright) Stevenson, the governor's wife, died in the Governor's Mansion Jan. 3, 1942. His mother, Edith Stevenson, served as Mistress of the Mansion thereafter. ☆

Local Governments

Texas has **254 counties**, a number which has not changed since 1931 when Loving County was organized. Loving had a population of 107 in the 1990 U.S. Census Bureau count, compared with 164 in 1970 and its peak of 285 in 1940. It is the **least-populous county** in Texas. In contrast, Harris County has **the most residents** in Texas, with a population in 1990 of 2,818,199.

Counties range in area from Rockwall's 148.6 square miles to the 6,193.1 square miles in Brewster, which is equal to the combined area of the states of Connecticut and Rhode Island.

The Texas Constitution makes a county a legal subdivision of the state. Each county has a **commissioners court**. It consists of four commissioners, each elected from a commissioner's precinct, and a county judge elected from the entire county. In smaller counties, the county judge retains judicial responsibilities in probate and insanity cases. For names of county and district officials,

see tables on pages 516-530.

Eleven hundred and eighty-six **incorporated Texas municipalities** range in size from 24 residents to Houston's 1,700,672 in the 1996 population estimate by the State Data Center. More than 80 percent of the state's population lives in cities and towns meeting the U.S. Bureau of the Census definition of urban areas.

Texas had **298 municipalities with more than 5,000 population** in the 1990 U.S. census. Under law, these cities may adopt their own charters by a majority vote. Cities of less than 5,000 may be chartered only under the general law. There were **284 home-rule cities** on June 1, 1996, most of them cities with over 5,000 residents. Some of these cities now show fewer than 5,000 residents, because population has declined since they adopted their home-rule charters. Home-rule cities are marked in this list by a single-dagger symbol (†) before the name. ☆

Mayors and City Managers of Texas Cities

The list below was compiled from questionnaires sent out immediately after the municipal elections in May 1997. Included is the name of each city's mayor, as well as the name of the city manager, city administrator, city coordinator or other managing executive of munipalities having that form of government.

An asterisk (*) before the city name indicates that the Almanac received no response to the questionnaire and that the information on city officials is from the most recent information available to us from unofficial sources.

*Abbott .... Robert Lee Tufts
    City Mgr., Harry Frank Holland
Abernathy .... Shane Cunningham
    City Mgr., Frank Russell
†Abilene .... Gary D. McCaleb
    City Mgr., (Vacancy)
*Ackerly .... Jimmie L. Schuelke
*†Addison .... Richard N. Beckert
    City Mgr., Ronald N. Whitehead
Adrian .... Larry W. Loveless
Agua Dulce .... Carl Vajdos
*†Alamo .... Rudolfo "Rudy" Villarreal
    City Mgr., James Pliska
†Alamo Heights (6116 Broadway, San
    Antonio 78209 .... Robert Biechlin
    City Admin., Susan Rash
Alba .... James Reid
    City Mgr., Lindy McCarty
Albany .... Harold G. Cox
    City Mgr., Bobby R. Russell
Aledo .... Robert A. Lewis
*†Alice .... Octavio Figueroa Jr
    City Mgr., Roel G. Valadez
†Allen .... Steve Terrell
    City Mgr., Jon McCarty
Alma (RR 1, Box 109, Ennis
    75119) .... Don Keilers
*†Alpine .... William Sohl
    City Mgr., Jerry Carvajal
Alto .... Sandra H. Wallace
    City Admin., Carol Rozell
Alton (Box 9004, Mission
    78572) .... Salvador Vela
    City Mgr., Israel Sagredo
Alvarado .... Iris Hicks
†Alvin .... Joe Rossano
    City Mgr., Marvin P. Norwood
Alvord .... Edwin Strange
†Amarillo .... Kel Seliger
    City Mgr., John Q. Ward
Ames .... John White
Amherst .... George Thompson
Anahuac .... Ottmar Schimek
Anderson .... John S. Freeman
†Andrews .... Greg Sweeney
    City Mgr., Len L. Wilson
†Angleton .... Gerald Roberts
    City Mgr., Ruth Hertel
*Angus (RR 3, Box 3060, Corsicana
    75110) .... Eben D. Stover
Anna .... Ronald Ferguson
*Annetta (Box 191, Aledo
    76008) .... Bruce Moore
Annetta North (Box 262, Aledo
    76008) .... Edward K. Hensley
*Annetta South (Box 61, Aledo

    76008) .... Doug Koldin
*Annona .... George H. English Sr.
†Anson .... E.M. Spraberry
    City Mgr., Tex Middlebrook
Anthony .... Art Franco
Anton .... Mary E. Grace
*Appleby (RR 10, Box 5186, Nacog-
    doches 75961) .... N. F. Burt
*Aquilla .... Marilyn Pick
†Aransas Pass .... Billy St. Clair
    City Mgr., Rick Ewaniszyk
*Archer City .... Max Wood Sr.
    City Mgr., L. B. Boren Jr.
Arcola .... Alvin Gipson
Argyle .... Yvonne A. Jenkins
†Arlington .... Elzie Odom
    City Mgr., George C. Campbell
Arp .... Vernon L. Bedair
*Asherton .... Sam Galvan Jr.
*Aspermont .... P. C. Carr
†Athens .... Jerry G. King
    City Mgr., Pam Burton
†Atlanta .... Richard Clayton
    City Mgr., Buddy Drake
Aubrey .... Gene King
*Aurora (Box 558, Rhome
    76078) .... Owen J. Landers
†Austin .... Kirk Watson
    City Mgr., Jesús Garza
Austwell .... Dwight L. Mutschler
Avery .... Erby Stinson
Avinger .... David P. Simpson
*†Azle .... Shirley Bradley
    City Mgr., Harry H. Dulin Jr.
Bailey .... Jewel A. Mims (Mr.)
Bailey's Prairie (Box 71, Angleton
    77516) .... J. S. McKinney
Baird .... Jon E. Hardwick
†Balch Springs .... David Haas
    City Mgr., Angie Warner
Balcones Heights (123 Altgelt, San
    Antonio 78201) .... Lucille Wohlfarth
    City Admin., Roy L. Miller
†Ballinger .... R.A. (Rudy) Hoffman
    City Mgr., Tommy New
Balmorhea .... Ishmael Rodriguez
Bandera .... Robert W. Cowan
Bangs .... C.B. Alexander
*Bardwell .... J. Lowry Jr.
Barry .... John W. Braly
*Barstow .... Abram Flores
Bartlett .... Jim Franz
Bartonville .... Lee Lazarus
*Bastrop .... David Lock
    City Mgr., Michael M. Talbot
†Bay City .... Charles Martinez Jr.

*Bayou Vista (2929 Hwy. 6, Ste 100,
    Hitchcock 77563) .... Billie Moore
*Bayside .... Timothy Delaney
†Baytown .... Pete C. Alfaro
    City Mgr., Bobby Rountree
Bayview (RR 3, Box 19A, Los Fresnos
    78566) .... Robert E. Middleton Jr.
*Beach City .... James E. Standridge
Beasley .... James Isbell
†Beaumont .... David W. Moore
    City Mgr., Ray A. Riley
*Beckville .... Thomas R. Adams
†Bedford .... R.D. "Rick" Hurt
    Interim City Mgr., Charles Barnett
Bee Cave (13225 W. Hwy. 71,
    Austin 78738) .... Gene Butler
    City Mgr., Joseph Ventura
†Beeville .... Kenneth Chesshir
    City Mgr., Ford Patton
†Bellaire .... Harold L. Penn
    City Mgr., John L. Pape
Bellevue .... James Broussard
*†Bellmead (3015 Bellmead Dr.,
    Waco 76705) .... Ruth M. Haines
    City Mgr., S.G. Radcliffe
Bells .... Louis Shearer
Bellville .... Jim Bishop
    City Admin., Marcus Johnston
†Belton .... Charley Powell
    City Mgr., Jeff Holberg
*Benavides .... Cynthia Oliveira
*†Benbrook (Box 26569, Fort
    Worth 76126) .... Jerry Dunn
    City Mgr., Cary Conklin
Benjamin .... Mike Sheedy
    City Mgr., Ronnie White
Berryville (Box 908, Frankston
    75763) .... John T. McElvany
Bertram .... Robert Rickelson
*Beverly Hills (3418 Memorial Dr.,
    Waco 76711) .... Betty Gibbs
Bevil Oaks (7390 Sweetgum Rd.,
    Beaumont 77713) .... John Hignett
Big Lake .... H. F. Ritchie
Big Sandy .... David P. Smith
†Big Spring .... Tim Blackshear
    City Mgr., Gary Fuqua
*Big Wells .... Jorge Escobedo
Bishop .... Janie Shafer
    City Admin., Betty Collier
*Bishop Hills (20 Nottingham Rd.,
    Amarillo 79124) .... Wayne Acklin
Blackwell .... Ronald Harris
Blanco .... Tom Gourley
Blanket .... John (Jack) Jones
Bloomburg .... E.M. "Dickey" Davis

*Blooming Grove.................... Boyd Bryant
*Blossom................................ Orville Allen
Blue Mound (301 Blue Mound Rd.,
   Fort Worth 76131)..............Jim Watkins
Blue Ridge.....................Burt Hedrich
   City Mgr., Edie Sims
Blum................................Bernilla F. Gunn
Boerne ....Patrick Heath
   City Mgr., Ron Bowman
Bogata ....Mildred F. Eudy
†Bonham ....Bryan Peeler
   City Mgr., Jim Stiff
Bonney.....................Elmer Cannon Jr.
Booker ....Cynthia Hipskind
   City Mgr., Lois J. Sheets
†Borger .... Judy Flanders
   City Mgr., David Willard
*Bovina ....Galen Hromas
†Bowie .... Gergory Underwood
   City Mgr., James Cantwell
*Boyd ....Steve Cotter
Brackettville..............Carmen M. Berlanga
   City Mgr., David G. Luna
*†Brady ....Dale Harris
   City Mgr., Dennis Smith
Brazoria ....W. V. James
   City Mgr., PeeWee Drake
†Breckenridge...............Virgil E. Moore Jr.
   City Mgr., Gary G. Ernest
*Bremond................................Ricky Swick
†Brenham ....Walter Schwartz
   City Mgr., C.J. Webster
Briarcliff (HCO 1, Box 24, Spice-
   wood 78669)..................V.E. McDaniel
Briaroaks (Box 816, Burleson
   76028).......................... Alan W. Myers
*†Bridge City......................John Dubose
*Bridgeport............William E. Huddleston
Broaddus ....Billie Faye Sanders
Bronte ....Martin Lee
Brookshire.................Keith Allen Woods
Brookside Village ....George D. Carter
*Browndell (Box 430, Brookeland
   75931)...................... Erma L. Garrett
*†Brownfield............................. George Cox
   City Mgr., R.C. Fletcher
Brownsboro .... Bobby Taylor
†Brownsville...................Henry González
   City Mgr., Carlos Rubinstein
†Brownwood .... Bert V. Massey II
   City Mgr., Gary Butts
*Bruceville-Eddy ....Gene McBride
†Bryan ....Lonnie Stabler
   City Mgr., Michael Conduff
Bryson ....Willard Schlittler
Buckholts ....Gwen Hauk
Buda ....W. Grey White
Buffalo................................Byron Ryder
*Buffalo Gap ....John Brolls
*Buffalo Springs (RR 10, Box 500,
   Lubbock 79404) ...........W.B. McMillan
*Bullard.............................S.Ray McCugh
*Bunker Hill Village (11977 Memorial,
   Houston 77024)..............Gene E. Roark
   City Admin., Ruthie P. Sager
†Burkburnett....................Pat Norriss (Mrs.)
   City Mgr., Gary Bean
Burke (RR 3, Box 315, Diboll
   75941) ...................................J.L. Bell
†Burleson .... Rick Roper
   City Mgr., Kay Godbey
*Burnet.......................Howard R. Benton
   City Mgr., Johnny Sartain
Burton ....Peggy Wilford
Byers ............................W.A. Landrum
Bynum ....Jerry Hooker
*Cactus ....Leon W. Graham
   City Mgr., Darrel Read
Caddo Mills ....Joan Bentley
   City Mgr., James Fletcher
Caldwell ....Bernard E. Rychlik
   City Mgr., William L. Broaddus
Callisburg (RR 8 Box 299, Gainesville
   76240)....................Bobby McDaniel
Calvert .... Cooper Wiese
†Cameron ....James E. Lafferty
   City Admin., Lanny C. French
Campbell ....Odis E. Peacock
Camp Wood .... James D. Blakeney

Canadian..........................Jim Pollard
   City Mgr., Dean Looper
Caney City (15241 Barron Rd., Malakoff
   75148)...........................Joe Barron
Canton .... Don Hackney
   City Mgr., Johnny M. Mallory
*†Canyon ....Lois Rice
   City Mgr., Glen Metcalf
Carbon........................Kenneth Knowles
Carl's Corner (RR 3, Box 500, Hillsboro
   76645)..............................Carl Cornelius
   City Mgr., Noe Garcia
Carmine ....Barney A. Eilers
†Carrizo Springs ....Gordon Baehre
   City Mgr., Ricardo Cantu
†Carrollton ....Milburn R. Gravley
   City Mgr., Gary W. Jackson
*†Carthage........................Carson Joines
   City Mgr., Charles Thomas
Castle Hills (6915 West Ave., San
   Antonio 78213)............Marty Rubin
   City Mgr., David R. McLaughlin
Castroville ....Dwight M. Green
   City Admin., Marcie Mora
*†Cedar Hill......................Chris L. Rose
   City Mgr., Gregory Vick
*†Cedar Park ....Dorthey Duckett
   City Mgr., Don Birkner
Celeste ....Elbert Hunter
Celina ....Peggy S. Brown
†Center.......................John D. Windham
   City Mgr., H. Frank Simpson
*Center Point................Charles E. Young
Centerville ....Billy Walters
*Chandler ....Winston Reagan
Channing........................Ethel Hunnicutt
Charlotte ....Mark T. Wilson
Chester ....Bryan Davis
Chico.................................Nobie Tucker
†Childress ....Pat Y. Steed
   City Mgr., David Galligan
Chillicothe ...................E.A. Kennedy Jr.
China.......................William T. Sanders
China Grove (2456 FM 1516, San
   Antonio 78263)........ John H. Vrzalik Sr.
Chireno .............................G.V. Layton
*Christine ....Alvie H. Smith
*Cibolo ....Sam Bauder
   City Admin., Rudy Rene Farias
†Cisco ....Joe Wheatley
   City Mgr., Michael Moore
Clarendon ....Leonard "Tex" Selvidge
Clarksville ....James Mark Lewis
   City Mgr., Wayne Dial
Clarksville City (Box 1209, Glade-
   water 75647)...........Harvey E. Griffin
   City Mgr., Billy F. Silvertooth Jr.
*Claude ....Leon G. James
*Clay (RR 2, Box 70-2, Somerville
   77879) .....................................N.A.
Clear Lake Shores ....Gary Groover
†Cleburne ....Thomas C. Hazlewood
   City Mgr., Joel W. Victory
*†Cleveland ....Lloyd Meadows
   City Mgr., Hector Forestier
Clifton.........................Truman O. Blum
Clint............................G. Michael Goodwin
†Clute..................................Jerry Adkins
   City Mgr., Barbara Hester
Clyde..............................B. M. Warrick
   City Mgr., Tim Powers
Coahoma ....Bill Read
*Cockrell Hill (4125 W. Clarendon,
   Dallas 75211)........ Leo Treviño Landin
*Coffee City (Box 716, Frankston
   75763) ....Michael Warren
Coldspring........................John Benestante
†Coleman .... Woodrow J. Maddox
   City Mgr., David S. Sooter
†College Station................Lynn McIlhaney
   City Mgr., George K. Noe
†Colleyville.....................Richard Newton
   City Mgr., C. Robert Stripling
Collinsville ....Wayne McCorkle
*Colmesneil ....Jackie Brown
†Colorado City ....Jim Baum
   City Mgr., Steve Shutt
Columbus ....Tom B. Hancher
   City Mgr., John Brasher

Comanche.......................Jimmie Warren
*Combes ....Silvestre (Silver) Garcia
*Combine (1233 Davis Rd., Seago-
   ville 75159) .... Charles Stringer
*†Commerce ....John R. Sands
   City Mgr., Roger McKinney
Como.........................Margaret Anderson
†Conroe ....Carter Moore
   City Adminr., Craig Lonon
†Converse ....John W. Steinberg
   City Mgr., Sam Hughes
Cool (R. Rte, Box 150, Weather-
   ford 76086) ....Marsha A. McDonald
Coolidge..............................Bobby Jacobs
Cooper ....Richard Huie
*†Coppell..........................Candy Sheehan
   City Mgr., Jim Witt
†Copperas Cove ...............J.A. Darossett
   City Mgr., Richard Torres
Copper Canyon (400 Woodland Dr.,
   Lewisville 75067) .... Tom Rogers
Corinth (2003 S. Corinth, Denton
   76205) ....Shirley Spellerberg
   City Admin., Richard H. Huckaby
†Corpus Christi .... Samuel Loyd Neal Jr.
   City Mgr., Bill Hennings
Corral City (14007 Corral City Dr.,
   Argyle 76226) .....James "Eddie" Draper
Corrigan .......................R.R. "Bobby" Smiley
   City Mgr., B.K. Johnson
†Corsicana ....Wilson Griffin
   City Mgr., Truitt Gilbreath
*Cottonwood (Box 293, Scurry
   75158) .... Carl Murr
Cottonwood Shores (3915 Cottonwood
   Dr., Marble Falls 78654) ...Dale Pickens
Cotulla ....Pablo Gonzales
*Cove ....Carl Crowder
Covington ....Patti Estes
Crandall.......................Terry Joe Hedrick
   City Mgr., Charlinda D. Gray
Crane ....Terry L. Schul
   City Admin., Bill F. Sanders
Cranfills Gap ....Marc Johnson
Crawford ....Roy A. Jones
*Creedmoor...................Robert Wilhite
†Crockett .... Bill Holcomb
   City Mgr., Ann McNabb
Crosbyton ..............................R.W. Self
*Cross Plains...................Gene Dillard
   City Mgr., Debbie Gosnell
Cross Roads (RR 3, Box 435,
   Aubrey 76227).......... Sheila Alexander
*Cross Timbers (Box 2042, Burleson
   76028)......................Wava McCullough
Crowell ....Robert Kincaid
*Crowley ....Nancy Behrens
   City Admin., Jay Singleton
†Crystal City.................. Jesús E. Guerrero
   City Mgr., Miguel A. Delgado
*†Cuero ....Michael Thamm
   City Mgr., John M. Trayhan
Cumby ....LaVerne Battle
Cuney ....Ethylene King
*Cushing............................Ben G. Baldwin
*Cut and Shoot (Box 7364, Conroe
   77306)....................Donald G. Douget
†Daingerfield ....William L. Thorne
   City Mgr.,Kevin Carruth
Daisetta ....Marvin J. Murray
†Dalhart .... Gene Rahll
   City Mgr., Greg Duggan
†Dallas ....Ronald Kirk
   City Mgr., John Ware
Dalworthington Gardens (2600 Roos-
   evelt, Arlington 76016)..... Albert A. Taub
   City Admin., J. Gregory Shugart
Danbury .... Kenneth Walters Jr.
Darrouzett ....Bob Forgey
   City Mgr., Terry Howard
Dawson ....Bobby Nesmith
†Dayton ....Guy L. Harris
   City Mgr., Robert Ewart
*Dayton Lakes Box 1476, Dayton
   77535) ....MichaelWedgeworth
*Dean (RR 5, Box 516, Wichita Falls
   76031) ....Steve Sicking
Decatur...............................Bobby Wilson
†Deer Park ....Jimmy Burke

City Mgr., Ronald V. Crabtree
De Kalb .... Billy M. Willis
†De Leon .... Norma Jo Locke
*Dell City .... Bill Williams
†Del Rio .... Roberto Chavira
    City Mgr., Gus H. Pappas
†Denison .... Wayne Cabaniss
    City Mgr., Larry Cruise
†Denton .... Jack Miller
    City Mgr., Ted Benavides
*†Denver City .... Royce Hemmeline
    City Mgr., Ray Hohstadt
*Deport .... Charles Foster
†DeSoto .... Richard Rozier
    City Mgr., Jim Baugh
*Detroit .... Hazel Rundles
*Devers .... R.B. Evans
Devine .... Steve A. Lopez
    City Admin., Linda L. Gunn
Diboll .... James P. Simms
    City Mgr., Vernon Cupit
Dickens .... R.L. (Bob) Porter
†Dickinson .... John W. Mitchiner
    CityAdmin., Don Taylor
Dilley .... Mary Ann Obregon
    City Mgr., Catarino Delgado
†Dimmitt .... Wayne Collins
    City Mgr., Don Sheffy
*Dodd City .... Jackie Lackey
*Dodson .... H.M. Riddle
*Domino .... Frank Propps
†Donna .... Hilda R. Adame
    City Mgr., Robert Diaz de Leon
Dorchester (Box 839, Howe
    75059) .... Alice F. Stewart
Double Oak (1100 Cross Timbers Dr.,
    Lewisville 75067) .... Richard Cook
*Douglassville .... Jim Granberry
Dripping Springs .... Terry W. Garnett
Driscoll .... Tony Arredondo Jr.
Dublin .... Katherine Prater
    City Mgr., Thomas W. Winder
†Dumas .... Arlis McBee
    City Mgr., Larry Smith
†Duncanville .... Ed Purcell
    City Mgr., Larry Shaw
Eagle Lake .... David Mann
    City Mgr., Ronald Holland
†Eagle Pass .... Rogelio Flores
    City Mgr., Pete Sepulveda
Early .... Earl W. Rhea
    City Mgr., Kenneth Thomas
Earth .... Raiford R. Daniel Jr.
†Eastland .... Don Griffin
    City Mgr., Paul N. Catoe
*East Mountain (RR. 1, Box 500,
    Gilmer 75644) .... Leldon H . Mathis
Easton .... Leroy Mitchell
East Tawakoni (700 Briggs Blvd., Lone
    Oak 75453) .... James R. Thomas
Ector .... Kenneth Rhudy
*Edcouch .... Joe A. Campos Jr.
    City Admin., Delmira Treviño
Earth .... Raiford R. Daniel Jr.
Eden .... Thomas F. Kelso
Edgecliff Village .... Bill Sherman
Edgewood .... James Holland Valentine
†Edinburg .... Joe Ochoa
    City Mgr., John R. Milford
Edmonson .... Don Ketchum
†Edna .... Joe D. Hermes
    City Mgr., Gerald G. Decker
Edom .... Mary Hornsby Scott
†El Campo .... Kenneth G. Martin
    City Mgr., Terry K. Roberts
*El Cenizo (507 Cadena, Laredo
    78046) .... Noe A. Hernandez
Eldorado .... John Nikolauk
†Electra .... LaJune Lewis
    City Admin., Kandi Waterstreet
†Elgin .... Eric W. Carlson
    Interim City Mgr., Loren Mayfield
Elkhart .... George T. Branch
El Lago .... Roger E. Nylin
*Elmendorf .... Mary Jane Nunez
†El Paso .... Carlos M. Ramirez
†Elsa .... Ramiro Alvarado
*Emhouse (RR 2, Box 1570, Corsicana
    75110) .... Harold Clemens
Emory .... Rubye McKeown

Enchanted Oaks (Box 5019, Gun Barrel
    City 75147) .... Ken Braswell
Encinal .... Tomás C. Flores
    City Mgr., Isaac D. Olivares
†Ennis .... Bill Lewis
    City Mgr., Steve Howerton
*Estelline .... David Walker
†Euless .... Mary Lib Saleh
    City Mgr., Tom Hart
*Eureka (RR6, Box 188A, Corsicana
    75110) .... Barney Thomas
Eustace .... J.W. "Red" York
Evant .... Randall Rigney
†Everman .... Cathey Thurston
    City Mgr., David Hunnicutt
*Fairchilds (8713 Fairchild Rd.,
    Richmond 77469) .... Robert Myska
Fairfield .... Luke Ward Jr.
Fair Oaks Ranch .... E.L. Gaubatz
Fairview (Collin Co.) (Box 551,
    McKinney 75069) .... Don Phillips
    City Mgr., Scott Albert
*Fairview (Wise Co.) (RR 1, Box 26,
    Rhome 76078) .... D. Paulette Layfield
Falfurrias .... J. Michael Guerra
Falls City .... Vi Malone
†Farmers Branch .... Bob Phelps
    City Mgr., Richard Escalante
Farmersville .... George C. Crump
    City Mgr., Alan Hein
Farwell .... Jimmie Mace
*Fate .... Gerry Boren
*Fayetteville .... William Greater
Ferris .... Richard M. Barrett
Flatonia .... Ed Hulsey
    City Mgr., John Hobson
Florence .... Lee Roy Knauth
Floresville .... Raymond M. Ramirez
    City Admin., Gary Pelech
†Flower Mound .... Larry W. Lipscomb
    City Mgr., (Vacancy)
*Floydada .... Hulon Carthel
    City Mgr., Gary Brown
Follett .... Lynn Blau
    City Mgr., Robert Williamson
*†Forest Hill (6800 Forest Hill Dr., Fort
    Worth 76140) .... Esterlene Griffin
    City Mgr., David Vestal
Forney .... Charles Vaught
    City Mgr., James McConnell
Forsan .... Johnny W. Sherman
Fort Stockton .... Howard McKissack
    City Mgr., Jesse "Chuy" Garcia
†Fort Worth .... Kenneth Barr
    City Mgr., Robert Terrell
Franklin .... Charles Ellison
Frankston .... James Gouger
†Fredericksburg .... Linda K. Langerhans
    City Mgr., Gary Neffendorf
†Freeport .... James A. Barnett Jr.
    City Mgr., Gary E. Stone
Freer .... Arnoldo Cantu
†Friendswood .... Harold L. Whitaker
    City Mgr., Ronald E. Cox
*Friona .... Clarence Monroe
    City Mgr., Paula Wilson
†Frisco .... Kathleen A. Seei
    City Mgr., George Purefoy
*Fritch .... J.R. "Bob" Sears
    City Mgr., Deck Shaver
Frost .... J. O. Williams
Fruitvale .... Bea Whisenhunt
Fulshear .... Viola Randle
*Fulton .... Leslie Cole Sr.
†Gainesville .... Kenneth Kaden
    City Mgr., Mike Land
†Galena Park .... R.P. "Bobby" Barrett
    City Admin., John L. Cooper
Gallatin .... Johnnie Grimes
†Galveston .... Henry Freudenburg
    City Mgr., Steve Le Blanc
Ganado .... Dana J. Parks
Garden Ridge .... Jay F. Feibelman
†Garland .... James B. Ratliff
    City Mgr., Jeffrey B. Muzzy
Garrett (208 N. Ferris, Ennis
    75119) .... David Clemons
*Garrison .... M. H. Stoddard
Gary .... Jean L. Heaton

*†Gatesville .... Arthur Dorsey
    City Mgr., Bob Stevens
*†Georgetown .... Leo Wood
    City Mgr., Bob Hart
*†George West .... August Caron Jr.
    City Mgr.,Terri Garza
Gholson (RR 5, Box 495, Waco
    76705) .... H.T. Sexton
†Giddings .... Paul R. Kipp
    City Mgr., D.E. Sosa
†Gilmer .... Everett Dean
    City Mgr., Scott Thompson
†Gladewater .... Jackie D. Wood
    City Mgr., Sharon G. Johnson
†Glenn Heights .... Stephen Pape
    City Mgr., Earl Keaton
Glen Rose .... Helen Leslie Kerwin
Godley .... Larry A. Richeson
Goldsmith .... Bennie V. Cope
*Goldthwaite .... Richard Poss
    City Mgr., Dale Allen
Goliad .... Buddy Zavesky
*Golinda (7021 Golinda Dr.,
    Lorena 76655) .... Ennis Degrate Jr.
†Gonzales .... Bobby O'Neal
    City Mgr., E.T. Gibson
*Goodlow (Box 248, Kerens
    75144) .... Willie H. Washington
*Goodrich .... Shirley Murphy
Gordon .... David Johnson
Goree .... Jimmy Harlan
    City Mgr., Glenda Decker
†Gorman .... Jack Simpson
Graford .... Carl S. Walston
†Graham .... Douglas A. Stroud
    City Mgr., Larry M. Fields
†Granbury .... David Southern
    City Mgr., R.D. Brockman
Grandfalls .... James Norton
    City Admin., Marylyn Thurman
†Grand Prairie .... Charles England
    City Mgr., Gary Gwyn
Grand Saline .... Ray Rucker
Grandview .... Louise Hudson
Granger .... Dollie Hajda
Granite Shoals .... John Adams
Granjeno (RR 4, Box 491, Mission
    78572) .... Vicente Garza
    City Mgr., Jack Parmenter
*Grapeland .... Dick Bridges
*†Grapevine .... William D. Tate
    City Mgr., Trent Petty
*Grayburg (RR9, Box 1034, Sour
    Lake 77659) .... J.W. Floyd
*Grays Prairie (12294 S. FM 148,
    Scurry 75158) .... C.W. Johnson
†Greenville .... Sue Ann Harting
    City Mgr., Ed Thatcher
Gregory .... Luis Galvan
*Grey Forest (18502 Scenic Loop Rd.,
    Helotes 78023) .... Edwin L. Faust
Groesbeck .... Jim Longbotham
Groom .... Joe Homer
†Groves .... Billy Job
    City Mgr., (Vacancy)
Groveton .... P.E. Snyder
Gruver .... Mark Irwin
    City Mgr., A. J. Ratliff
Gun Barrel City .... Joe Agnes
    City Mgr., Tom Donaldson
Gunter .... James H. Donohoe
Gustine .... Roger Oliver
Hackberry (119 Maxwell Rd., Ste. B-7,
    Frisco 75034) .... Chester Thomas
Hale Center .... Bob Stroud
Hallettsville .... Warren Grindeland
*Hallsburg (RR 7, Box 428, Waco
    76705) .... Margie Wilbanks
Hallsville .... T. Bynum Hatley
*†Haltom City .... Gary Larson
    City Mgr., Bill Eisen
Hamilton .... Lambert Little
    City Mgr., Bill Funderburk
Hamlin .... Earl Gregory
Happy .... R.N. McDonald
*Hardin .... Douglas C. Tinkle Jr.
†Harker Heights .... Stewart Meyer
    City Mgr., Steve Carpenter
†Harlingen .... H. Wm. Card Jr.

City Mgr., Natalie Flores Prim
*Hart ....Tony Leibel
Haskell ....Ken Lane
City Mgr., Sam Watson
Haslet.....................I.J. (Blackie) Frazier
Hawkins ....W. C. Maynard
Hawley .... Richard Don Tatum
*Hays (Box 1285, Buda 78610) .Bill Couch
†Hearne ....Ruben Gomez
City Mgr., Kenneth W. Pryor
Heath ....Christopher Cuny
*Hebron (R 2, Box 184, Carrollton
75010) .... Stanley Dozier
Hedley ....Shauna Monroe
Hedwig Village (955 Piney Point Rd.,
Houston 77024)...............Sue V. Speck
Helotes.......................Steven F. Hodges
Hemphill......................Robert Hamilton
Hempstead ....Herbert L. Johnson
City Mgr., James R. Vines
†Henderson ....Wallace Read
City Mgr., Earl Heath
Henrietta...........................Rick Langford
City Mgr., Joe Pence
†Hereford.........Robert D. "Bob" Josserand
City Mgr., Chester R. Nolen
†Hewitt ....Charles D.Turner
City Mgr., Dennis H. Woodard
*Hickory Creek (Box 453, Lake Dallas
75065)...............................John Malloy
Hico.....................................Melton Murff
†Hidalgo.....................John David Franz
City Mgr., Joe Vera III
Higgins ....Hilton Menser
Highland Haven ....John Josefy
†Highland Park (4700 Drexel Dr.,
Dallas 75205) ...... Gifford O. Touchstone
City Mgr., George Patterson
†Highland Village (948 Highland Village
Rd., Lewisville 75067).. Bradley K. Jones
City Mgr., John Klaiber
Hill Country Village (116 Aspen Ln., San
Antonio 78232)... Edward R. McNabb Jr.
City Admin., Terry L. Lively
Hillcrest Village (Box 1172, Alvin
77512) ....Kaye Kubeczka
†Hillsboro...............................Henry Moore
City Mgr., Randy Thomas
Hilshire Village (Box 55233, Houston
77255) ....Steven Tacconelly
†Hitchcock ....Harry W. Robinson
Holiday Lakes (RR 4, Box 747,
Angleton 77515)....................M.A. Berg
Holland.............................Harold Rohde
Holliday .... Marion J. Cummins Jr.
Hollywood Park (2 Mecca Dr., San
Antonio 78232)...............Roy D. Lemons
Hondo ....Jim Barden
City Mgr., Scott Wall
Honey Grove................. Dennis Whitlock
Hooks.........................Michael W. Babb
Horizon City .... Walter C. Lee
*†Houston ....Robert C. Lanier
Howardwick (HC 2 Box 2230,
Clarendon 79226) ....Millie J. Dishong
Howe.................................. Ray Bledsoe
Hubbard ....Steven Weatherby
City Mgr., O.G. (Sonny) Minze
Hudson (201 Mount Carmel Rd., Lufkin
75904)............................M.B. Baker
Hudson Oaks (150 N. Oakridge, Weath-
erford 76087)........ Forrest G. Thompson
City Admin., Mary Jane Holybee
*Hughes Springs............... Reba Simpson
City Mgr., George K. Fite
*†Humble ....Wilson Archer
City Mgr., James P. Baker
Hunters Creek Village (1 Hunters Creek
Pl., Houston 77024) .....Jack W. Howeth
Huntington ....Lamar Tinsley
City Mgr., Robert Walker
†Huntsville ....William B. Green
City Mgr., Gene Pipes
†Hurst ....Bill Souder
City Mgr., Jim D. Starr
Hutchins......................Mary Washington
Hutto .... Glen Pierce
Huxley (RR 1 Box 1410, Shelbyville
75973)..............................Larry Vaughn

Idalou .... Mike Mauldin
City Mgr., Russell Hamilton
Impact (Box 3116, Abilene
79604)............................Dallas Perkins
Indian Lake (62 S. Aztec Cove, Los
Fresnos 78566) .... Mildred B. Gilmore
Industry .... Alan W. Kuehn
†Ingleside.................................C.H. Lewis
City Mgr., Marilyn Hall
Ingleside on the Bay (Box B, Ingleside
78362) .... Alfred D. Robbins
Ingram.................................. Jean Raymer
*Iowa Colony (12003 County Road 65,
Rosharon 77583).. Carolyn Bowen-Lewis
Iowa Park .... Timothy W. Hunter
*Iraan .... Randy Peterson
Iredell ....A. D. Woody Jr.
†Irving.......................... Morris H. Parrish
City Mgr., Steven W. McCullough
Italy ....Dennis Crecelius Jr.
City Admin., Lyall Kirton
*Itasca ....John Merritt
City Admin., Mel Coker
†Jacinto City (10301 Market St. Rd.,
Houston 77029)............. David Gongre
City Mgr., Joann Griggs
Jacksboro.............................Jerry Craft
City Mgr., Michael Webb
*†Jacksonville .... Larry K. Durrett
City Mgr., Jim Anderson
Jamaica Beach (Box 5264, Galveston
77554) .... Paul E. Schmidt
City Admin., Sharon Turnley
†Jasper...................................R.C. Horn
City Mgr., Kerry Lacy
Jayton..............................Travis R. Smith
Jefferson ....Carey B. Heaster Jr.
†Jersey Village (16501 Jersey Dr.,
Houston 77040)...Stephen C. Schneider
City Mgr., Dale Brown
*Jewett .... Herman Hammond
Joaquin .... Steve Hughes
Johnson City .... Kermit A. Roeder
Jolly (RR2, Box 305, Wichita Falls
76301) .... Carroll Vicars
Jones Creek (7207 SFA Rd.,
Freeport 77541)................. Wayne Dubose
City Mgr., Tamie Schmidt
Jonestown ....Sam G. Billings
City Admin., Cindy Lent
Josephine........................ Richard Murray
Joshua ....Kenneth A. Bransom
City Mgr., Les Miles
*Jourdanton............................ Bob Orr
City Mgr., Roy D. Underwood
*Junction .... William Keaton Blackburn
City Admin., Jack L. Smith
Justin.................................Jon Beck
Karnes City ....Don Tymrak
City Admin., David Carrothers
†Katy..........................M.H. Schmidt Jr.
City Admin., Johnny Nelson
†Kaufman............................. Jimmy Wynne
City Mgr., Joseph Portugal
Keene.............................. Gary Heinrich
†Keller................................. Ronald W. Lee
City Mgr., Lyle H. Dresher
*Kemah ....Richard A. Diehl
*Kemp ....James Stroman Jr.
City Mgr., Gary McDaniel
Kendleton ....Carolyn Jones
*Kenedy .... Roy Freeman
City Admin., Joe E. Ponish
Kenefick (RR 5, Box 525A, Dayton
77535) .... Jerry L. Gore Sr.
Kennard ....Bill Thomas
Kennedale ....Robert P. Mundy
City Admin., Ted Rowe
Kerens..............................Tim Crawford
†Kermit ....Ted Westmoreland
City Mgr., Wayne Reynolds
*†Kerrville................Charles P. Johnson
City Mgr., Glenn D. Brown
†Kilgore.................................Bill Wilson
City Mgr., Ronald H. Stephens
†Killeen ....Raúl G. Villaronga
City Mgr.,Talmadge N. Buie
*†Kingsville ..... Filemon "Phil" Esquivel Jr.
City Mgr., Carlos E. Lerma

†Kirby (112 Baumann St., Unit 1, San
Antonio 78219) ....Johnny Duffek
City Mgr., Cindy Fox
Kirbyville ....Fred Herron
City Mgr., Tommy Neal
*Kirvin ..........................J.W. "Billy" Walthall
Knollwood (100 Collins Dr., Sherman
75090) ....Richard Roelke
Knox City ....Tommie (Bud) Reynolds
City Mgr., Robert Patrick
*Kosse ....Walter Graeber
Kountze .... Ann Walters
City Admin., Joe F. Blair
Kress...................................Louise Kirk
Krugerville (Box 770, Aubrey
76227) ....Joel Wingo
Krum ....Floyd Watson
Kyle ....Lee Sturdivant
La Coste ....Andy Keller
Lacy-Lakeview (Box 154549,
Waco 76715) ....Dennis J. Cogliati Jr.
Ladonia ....Leon Hurse
†La Feria ....Paul F. Beechner
City Mgr., Sunny K. Philip
Lago Vista ....Glen Hartman
City Mgr., Dennis Jones
†La Grange ....David R. Noak
City Mgr., Shawn Raborn
*La Grulla (City Hall, Grulla
78548) ....Rene Martínez
Laguna Vista ....Hap Fairhart
La Joya ....Rodolfo "Fito" Farias
City Admin., Oscar Cuellar Jr.
Lake Bridgeport (RR 2, Box 244F, Bridge-
port 76426)............. Jeanita VanDerLee
Lake City (Box 177, Mathis
78368) ....Larry Boyd
Lake Dallas ....Jerry McCutcheon
†Lake Jackson ....Jim Martin
City Mgr., William P. Yenne
Lakeport (Box 7728, Longview
75607)..........................Ricky L. Shelton
*Lakeside (129 Lakewood Dr., Mathis
78368) ....James M. Thomas
*Lakeside (9830 Confederate Park Rd.,
Fort Worth 76108) ..... Raymond E. Beck
City Mgr., William F. Mohr
Lakeside City (Box 4287, Wichita Falls
76308) ....Kenneth Cunningham
City Mgr., Don Sheppard
Lake Tanglewood (RR 8, Box 35-15,
Amarillo 79118) ....................M.L. Ott
Lakeview ....Terry Lindsey
†Lakeway (104 Cross Creek, Austin
78734) ....Jack O'Neill
City Mgr., Dave Benson
*Lakewood Village (100 Highridge Dr.,
Little Elm 75068)..................Greg Page
†Lake Worth ....Walter Bowen
City Mgr., Mark Todd
*†La Marque.................Pete W. Rygaard
City Mgr., Vacant
†Lamesa .... Mike Tyler
City Mgr., Paul Feazelle
†Lampasas ....Jack Calvert
City Mgr., Mike Talbot
†Lancaster ....Joe Tillotson
City Mgr., Steve Norwood
†La Porte ....Norman L. Malone
City Mgr., Robert T. Herrera
*†Laredo.....................Saul N. Ramirez Jr.
City Mgr., Florencio Peña
Latexo ....Billie Jo Bennett
La Vernia ....Charles R. Malloy
*La Villa ....Carlos Perez
City Mgr., Antonio Barco
Lavon ....Chris Wess
La Ward.....................Tillman M. Hunt Sr.
*Lawn ....Johnny B. Hudson
†League City ...... A.T. (Tommy) Frankovich
Leakey ....J. H. Chisum
Leander ....Charles Eaton
City Mgr., Ken Craven
*Leary (RR 5, Box 435, Texarkana
75501) ....Donald McGonigal
Lefors ....Velda Chadwick
*Leona ....Travis J. Oden
Leonard .... Stan Barker
City Admin., Lisa McCasland

*Leon Valley .... Marcus Semmelmann
    City Mgr., Hank Brummett
Leroy .... David Williams
†Levelland .... Raymond O. Dennis
    City Mgr., Greg M. Inghem
†Lewisville .... Bobbie J. Mitchell
    City Mgr., Charles R. Owens
Lexington .... Robert L. Willrich Sr.
†Liberty .... Paul J. Henry
    City Mgr., Norman W. Dykes
*Lincoln Park (RR 1, Box 701, Aubrey
    76227) .... Roger Pock
Lindale .... Bobby McClenny
    City Mgr., Owen Scott
Linden .... Marvin W. Kelly Jr.
Lindsay .... Robert P. Walterscheid
Lipan .... James Reece
Little Elm .... Jim Pelley
†Littlefield .... Howard Head
    City Mgr., Marty Mangum
Little River-Academy (Box 521, Little
    River 76554) .... Ronnie W. White
†Live Oak .... Paula B. Stakes
    City Mgr., Joseph W. Painter
*Liverpool .... Allan F. Moore
Livingston .... Ben R. Ogletree Jr.
    City Mgr., Sam Gordon
Llano .... W.R. Bauman
    City Mgr., Frank Salvato
†Lockhart .... John M. Allred
    City Mgr., Philip G. Cook
*Lockney .... Gary D. Marr
Log Cabin .... Robert Ford
Lometa .... Charles (Chuck) Kelly
Lone Oak .... Noble D. Hiser Sr.
Lone Star .... C.E. "Nick" Nichols
†Longview .... David L. McWhorter
    City Mgr., Ted C. Willis
*Loraine .... Catarino Martínez
Lorena .... Tom Stott
Lorenzo .... Lester C. Bownds
    City Mgr., Jim Norris
Los Fresnos .... Mercedes Cantu
    City Mgr., Don R. Badeaux
*Los Indios .... Tina Bennett
*Los Ybanez (HC 7, Box 52, Lamesa
    79331) .... Mary A. Ybanez
Lott .... John W. (Sonny) Smith
*Lovelady .... Ronald G. LaRue
Lowry Crossing (1405 S. Bridgefarmer,
    McKinney 75069) .... Audie Casey
*†Lubbock .... David R. Langston
    City Mgr., Bob Cass
Lucas (151 Country Club Rd., Allen
    75002 .... David Harvey
    City Admin., John Hubbard
*Lueders .... Robert Wingrove Jr.
†Lufkin .... Louis A. Bronaugh
    City Mgr., C.G. Maclin
†Luling .... John A. Moore
    City Mgr., O. Lamar Schulz
Lumberton .... Jerry Williamson
    City Admin., Norman Reynolds
Lyford .... Rodolfo Suarez Saldaña
*Lytle .... Horace Fincher
Mabank .... Larry R. Teague
    City Admin., Louann Confer
Madisonville .... Kirby H. Woehst
    City Mgr., James K. White
Magnolia .... John Bramlett
*Malakoff .... James Anders
    City Admin., J. Don Hustead
*Malone .... Ray Watson
Manor .... Luis Suarez
*†Mansfield .... Duane Murray
    City Mgr., Clayton Chandler
*Manvel .... Merl Bradley
†Marble Falls .... Richard K. Westerman
    City Mgr., Michael W. Stoldt
Marfa .... C.M. (Fritz) Kahl
    City Admin., Estela Madrid
Marietta .... Roy L. Jones
Marion .... Glenn A. Hild
†Marlin .... Tom Black
    City Mgr., Arthur Douglas
Marquez .... James Kenneth Clary
†Marshall .... Audrey D. Kariel
    City Mgr., Tony N. Williams
Marshall Creek (Box 1080, Roanoke

76262) .... John Murdock
Mart .... Paul S. Thronburg
    City Mgr., David White
*Martindale .... Robby D. Powell
Mason .... R. Clinton Schulze
Matador .... Gary L. Lancaster
Mathis .... Manuel Torres
*Maud .... Edward M. Holley
Maypearl .... David K. Evans
†McAllen .... Leo Montalvo
    City Mgr., Mike R. Perez
McCamey .... Jimmy McClure
†McGregor .... Felix A. Morris
    City Mgr., Bill Dake
*†McKinney .... Don Dozier
    City Mgr., Donald E. Paschal Jr.
McLean .... Charles McClendon
*McLendon-Chisholm (1248 SH 205,
    Rockall 75087) ..... Michael D. Donegan
Meadow .... Dale Wylie
Meadowlakes (167 Broadmoor St.,
    Marble Falls 78654) .... Don E. Reed
Meadows (1 Troyan Dr., Stafford
    77477) .... Jim McDonald
Megargel .... Danny Fails
Melissa .... W.E. "Buck" Weatherby
    City Admin., Susan Bradley
Melvin .... Jessie I. (Jack) Schrier
Memphis .... Ed Hutcherson
Menard .... Max E. Hooten
    City Admin., James F. Cannon
†Mercedes .... Miguel Castillo Jr.
Meridian .... Mervin Spitzer
*Merkel .... Earnest Reynolds
    City Mgr., Robert Harris
Mertens .... Linda Maples
Mertzon .... Patsy Kahlig
    City Co-Admins., David R. & Linda Harris
†Mesquite .... Mike Anderson
    City Mgr., Ted Barron
†Mexia .... William McCullough
    City Mgr.,William P. Cornelius Jr.
Miami .... Gene Hodges
†Midland .... Robert E. Burns
    City Mgr., Fred Michael McGregor
†Midlothian .... Maurice Osborn
    City Mgr., Kim Foutz
Midway .... Patrick H. Wakefield
Milano .... James T. Hartley
*Mildred (RR 6, Box 172A Corsicana
    75110) .... Divana Holland
Miles .... Werner Harsch
Milford .... Morris Killough
*Miller's Cove (RR 3, Box 491, Mount
    Pleasant 75455) .... Wayne Miller
*Millican .... (Vacancy)
Millsap .... Julia Dinda-Weston
Mineola .... Celia Scott Boswell
†Mineral Wells .... Earl L. Medlin
    City Mgr., Lance Howerton
*Mingus .... Robert Bearden
†Mission .... Ricardo A. Pérez
    City Mgr., Pat Townsend Jr.
†Missouri City .... Allen Owen
    City Mgr., James Thurmond
Mobeetie .... Dale Corcoran
Mobile City (824 Lilac Lane, Rockwall
    75087) .... Billie M. Easley
*†Monahans .... David B. Cutbirth
    City Mgr., David Mills
*Mont Belvieu .... Bob Lee
Montgomery .... John Butler
Moody .... Mike Alton
*Moore Station (RR 1, Box 133, Larue
    75770) .... Arthur Earl
Moran .... Marvin Kays
Morgan .... Harold E. Vandiver Jr.
Morgan's Point (Box 839, La
    Porte 77572) .... Russell Applebe
    City Admin., David A. Paulissen
Morgan's Point Resort (8 Morgan's Point
    Blvd, Belton 76513) .... E.W. Berry Jr.
    City Mgr., Stacy Hitchman
Morton .... Ronnie D. Wallace
    City Mgr., (Vacancy)
*Moulton .... Minnie Lee Fisbeck
*Mountain City (116 Cedar, Buda
    78610) .... Beth Smith
Mount Calm .... Gail Souders

Mount Enterprise .... Danny Luis Garcia
†Mount Pleasant .... Jerry Boatner
    City Mgr., Richard E. Chaffin
Mount Vernon .... Mike Edwards
Muenster .... Henry Weinzapfel
    City Admin., Stephen Broyles
†Muleshoe .... Robert Montgomery
    City Mgr., James Fisher
Mullin .... A. R. Whisenhunt
Munday .... Gary Tidwell
    City Mgr., John M. Weeks
Murchison .... David Williams
Murphy (205 N. Murphy Rd., Plano
    75094) .... Roy W. Bentle
*Mustang (Box 325, Corsicana
    75151) .... Glenn Albritton
*Mustang Ridge (12800 Hwy. 138 S.,
    Buda 78610) .... Alfred Vallejo II
†Nacogdoches .... Richard D. Johnson
    City Mgr., Gordon C. Pierce
*Naples .... Ellen Robinson
Nash .... David H. Slaton
    City Admin., Elizabeth A. Lea
†Nassau Bay (1800 NASA Rd. 1,
    Houston 77058) .... Donald C. Matter
    City Mgr., David Stall
Natalia .... Ruberta Vera
Navarro (Box 7502, Corsicana
    75110) .... Yvonne Capehart
†Navasota .... Tony Maddox
    City Mgr., Eugene Daniel
Nazareth .... Ralph Brockman
*†Nederland .... Homer Nagel
    City Mgr., André Wimer
Needville .... Kermit Blezinger
*Nesbitt (RR 5, Box 88, Marshall
    75670) .... Roy A. Nesbitt
Nevada .... Richard Caldwell
Newark .... H.B. "Bill" Malone
*New Berlin (9180 FM 775, La
    Vernia 78121) .... Ferdinand Friederick
New Boston .... Johnny Branson
†New Braunfels .... Jan Kennady
    City Mgr., Mike Shands
Newcastle .... Earline Swarts
*New Chapel Hill (14039 County Rd.
    220, Tyler 75707) .... J. T. Pinkerton
New Deal .... Harry Ford
New Home .... Don Sharp
New Hope (Box 562, McKinney
    75070) .... Johnny Hamm
New London .... M.V. Hudson
New Summerfield .... H.D. Stallings
Newton .... David Hines
    City Admin., Donald H. Meek
New Waverly .... Dan Underwood
Neylandville (General Delivery,
    Greenville 75401) .... Mary I. Miles
Niederwald (13851 Camino Real,
    Kyle 78640) .... Fern B. Howze
Nixon .... Collie L. Murray
    City Mgr., John D. Byrd
Nocona .... Gene E. Fitzgerald
    City Mgr., Joseph M. Gambill Jr.
Nolanville .... Ray Belk
Nome .... David R. Studdert
*Noonday (Box 6425, Tyler
    75711) .... Bennie H. Smith
Nordheim .... Gilbert Pargman
Normangee .... Doug Kule
*North Cleveland (Box 1266,
    Cleveland 77327) .... Woodrow Squier
Northcrest (613 N. Lacy Dr., Waco
    76705) .... Alphonse Straten
Northlake (Box 729, Justin
    76247) .... Michael J. Savoie
†North Richland Hills .... Tommy Brown
    City Mgr., C.A. Sanford
*Novice .... Don Poe
Oak Grove (Box 309, Kaufman
    75142) .... Jim D. Terry
Oakhurst .... Mary Dell Rosier
Oak Leaf .... Wm. D. Forrester
Oak Point (100 Naylor Rd., Little Elm
    75068) .... Eileen Turner
*Oak Ridge (RR 3, Box 325,
    Gainesville 76240) .... Karen Price
Oak Ridge (RR 1, Box 228, Terrell
    75161) .... Humberto (Hue) Arredondo

Oak Ridge North (27326 Robinson#115 Conroe 77385) ....Gary S. North
City Admin., Paul Mendes
Oak Valley (Box 2193, Corsicana 75151) .... Debra Wilson
Oakwood.............................. Dorothy Bell
O'Brien ....Charlene Brothers
*Odem......................Jessie Rodriguez Sr.
†Odessa .... Mike Atkins
City Mgr., Jerry S. McGuire
O'Donnell ....Thomas Woolam
Oglesby .... Kenneth Goodwin
Old River-Winfree (Box 1169, Mont Belvieu 77580) ....Joe Landry
Olmos Park (119 W. El Prado, San Antonio 78212) ....Gerald Z. Dubinski Sr.
City Mgr., Byron E. Hollinger
†Olney .... Phil Jeske II
City Admin., Jack R. Northrup
Olton .... Mike Foskey
City Mgr., Layton Covington
Omaha ....D.D. Tuck
Onalaska............Jeanne Ann Smith-Byrd
Opdyke West (Box 1179, Levelland 79336) ....Wayne Riggins
†Orange ....James D. Gilliam
City Mgr., Charles W. Pinto
Orange Grove .... T.L. Thomas
Orchard..................... Eugene L. Demny
Ore City...............................Angie Edwards
Overton .... Norma Hunter
City Mgr., Joe Cantu Jr.
Ovilla .... Cindy Jones
City Admin., Paul Stevens
Oyster Creek (3210 FM 523, Freeport 77541 .... Richard D. Merriman
Paducah.............................C.D. Dickens
Paint Rock............................. Paul Thorpe
Palacios ......Edward W. Schulze (Pro Tem)
City Admin., Charles R. Winfield
†Palestine ....Joel L. Meyer
City Mgr., Sheyi Ipaye
Palisades (RR7, Box 19-16, Amarillo 79118 ....Randy Hooker
Palmer .... Henry M. Rhoades
Palmhurst (4501 N. Stewart Rd., Mission 78572) ....Elton L. Key
Palm Valley (1313 Stuart Place Rd. Harlingen 78552)....................John Puhl
Palmview (RR 11, Box 1000, Mission 78572) ....Jorge G. Garcia
City Mgr., Jesse Lerma
†Pampa ....Robert L. Neslage
City Mgr., Robert Eskridge
Panhandle............................ Les McNeill
City Mgr., Thomas J. Blazek
Panorama (98 Hiwon Dr., Conroe 77304) ....Howard L. Kravetz
Pantego (1614 S. Bowen Rd., Arlington 76013 ....Robert D. Surratt
City Mgr., Larry W. Smith
Paradise................. E.E. "Sonny" Read Jr.
†Paris.................................. Eric S. Clifford
City Mgr., Michael E. Malone
*Parker (5700 E. Parker Rd., Allen 75002) ....Jack Albritton
City Admin., Betty McMenamy
†Pasadena............................Johnny Isbell
Pattison ....Linda A. Mladenka
Patton Village (16940 Main St., Splendora 77372).....................Ollie Burdett
*Payne Springs (Box 1710, Mabank 75147).....................Lonnie W. Boyers
†Pearland ....Tom Reid
City Mgr., Paul Grohman
†Pearsall...............................Victor Vinton
City Mgr., Tim Gump
†Pecan Gap........................Kevin Royal
Pecan Hill (Box 443, Red Oak 75154) ....Linda White
†Pecos...................................Dot Stafford
City Mgr., Kenneth Neal
Pelican Bay (1300 Pelican Circle, Azle 76020) ....Billy W. Heaton
City Admin., Robert de Saglio
*Penelope ....Malcolm Svacina
Peñitas ....Servando Ramirez
*Pernitas Point (HC 1, Box 1440, Sandia 78383)............... Dorothy Keetch

Perryton .... David Hale
City Mgr., David Landis
Petersburg............................... Jim Fox
City Mgr., Jesse J. Nave
Petrolia................................ Ardell Watson
Petronila (RR 3, Box 317, Robstown 78380) .... William J. Ordner
†Pflugerville ....Haywood L. Ware
City Mgr., Steve Jones
*†Pharr................................Victor Garcia
Acting City Mgr., Ernesto Silva
Pilot Point ....Allen Groff
City Admin., Carolyn Boerner
Pine Forest (Box 1004, Vidor 77670) ....William G. Elliott
*Pinehurst (3640 Mockingbird, Orange 77630) ....Bill Davidson
City Mgr., Curtis Jeanis
Pine Island (RR3 Box 86A, Hempstead 77445) ....Ray Garrett
Pineland ....John O. Booker
Piney Point Village (7721 San Felipe, #100, Houston 77063) ..C. Jim Stewart III
Pittsburg ....D. H. Abernathy
City Mgr., Ned C. Muse
Plains .... T. J. Miller
City Admin., David Brunson
†Plainview ....Lloyd C. Woods
City Mgr., James P. Jeffers
†Plano ....John Longstreet
City Mgr., Thomas H. Muehlenbeck
Pleak (5809 Pleak Rd., Richmond 77469) .... William Poncik
*†Pleasanton........................Bob Hurley
City Mgr., Larry Pippin
Pleasant Valley (4006 Hwy. 287 J, Iowa Park 76367) ....Raymond Haynes
City Mgr., Jeff Watts
Plum Grove (RR 5, Box 322G, Cleveland 77327) .... Noble Enloe
*Point............................. Raymond Clifton
Point Blank ....Lillian Bratton
Point Comfort .... Pam Lambden
*Ponder ....Wayne Futch
†Port Aransas .... James H. Sherrill
City Mgr., Tommy M. Brooks
†Port Arthur ....Robert T. "Bob" Morgan
City Mgr., Steve Fitzgibbons
*†Port Isabel ....Quirino Martinez
City Mgr., Manuel Hinojosa
†Portland .............................A.R. Moser
City Mgr., Michael A. Tanner
†Port Lavaca ....Tiney Browning
City Mgr., Barbara Gibson
†Port Neches ....Frances Monk
City Mgr., Randy Kimler
Post ....Jim Jackson
City Mgr., Rick L. Hanna
Post Oak Bend (RR4, Box 87, Kaufman 75142)..........Wayne Rebholz
Poteet ....Diana M. Martinez
Poth ....Richard Pollok
Pottsboro ....Steve Atkins
*Powell ....Royce Bancroft
*Poynor ....Dannie Smith
Prairie View .... Ronald Leverett
Premont ....Lee Rodriguez
Presidio ....Locho Nichols
City Mgr., Arturo J. Ochoa
Primera ....José J. Ramirez
Princeton ....Bill Caldwell
Progreso ....Arturo Valdez
Progreso Lakes (Box 511, Progreso 78579) ....Karen L. Evans
*Prosper.......................Stephen Coffman
*Putnam ....Winford Fry
*Pyote ....Randy Earnest
†Quanah ....Jess W. (Bud) Adkins
City Admin., Dena Daniel
Queen City ....James McCormack
Quinlan...............................Lois Cagle
City Admin., Rick Voorhies
Quintana (814 N. Lamar, Freeport 77541) ....Debbie Alongis
Quitaque .... James M. Davidson
City Admin., Clyde Dudley
Quitman .... Bill Medlin
Ralls .... David A. Prewitt
Rancho Viejo .........................B.D. Cummins

†Ranger .... Billy E. Guess
*Rangerville (RR 4, Box 77, San Benito 78586) ....Wayne Halbert
Rankin ....Cora Gaynelle McFadden
Ransom Canyon ....Lee Kitchens
Ravenna .... Lyndon Hale
*†Raymondville .... C. M. Crowell
City Mgr., José L. López
Red Oak ....Dennis R. Brown
City Mgr., Ken Pfeifer
Redwater ....James B. Stokes
Refugio ....James Shelve
Reklaw .... Harlan Crawford
Reno (Lamar Co.) (165 Bybee St., Paris 75462) ....Weldon M. Coston
City Admin., Shannon Barrentine
*Reno (Parker Co.) (174 W. Reno Rd., Azle 76020) ....Loyd Bailey
Retreat (RR 3, Box 2050, Corsicana 75110) ....Betty Carpenter
Rhome..........................William Troxell
Rice ....Roger A. Wear
†Richardson ....Gary A. Slagel
City Mgr., Bill Keffler
Richland ....Dolores Baldwin
†Richland Hills (3200 Diana Dr., Fort Worth 76118).......................C.F. Kelley
City Mgr., James W. Quin
*Richland Springs ....Dale McKinnerney
Richmond ....Hilmar G. Moore
City Mgr., R. Glen Gilmore
Richwood (215 Halbert St., Clute 77531).......................James M. Vera
Riesel ....Mike Posey
Rio Bravo (1419 Centeno Ln., Laredo 78046) ....Feliciano Garcia Jr.
Rio Grande City...............Baldemar Garza
Rio Hondo ....Alejandro Chavez Jr.
Rio Vista ....Sam Bigham
*Rising Star ....Jerrell Bible
†River Oaks (4900 River Oaks Blvd., Fort Worth 76114) ....Jack Adkison
Riverside ....Randell L. Vincent
*Roanoke ....Jewell W. "Joe" Grace
*Roaring Springs ....Joe Thacker
City Mgr., Rickey Lawrence
Robert Lee ....Kelly S. Nichols
*Robinson (111 W. Lyndale, Waco 76706) .... Diane Rendon
†Robstown ....Rene DeAlejandro
Roby ....Cecil J. King
City Mgr., Jimmy C. Price
Rochester...........................Rod Townsend
City Mgr., Danny Bass
†Rockdale ....Bill T. Avrett
City Mgr., Sue Foster
†Rockport...........................Glenda Burdick
City Mgr., M.H. Gildon
Rocksprings ....Charles W. Carson III
†Rockwall ....George Hatfield
City Mgr., Julie Couch
*Rocky Mound (Box 795, Pittsburg 75686) ....Noble T. Smith
City Mgr., Brenda Evans
Rogers................................Billy Ray Crow
*Rollingwood (403 Nixon Dr., Austin 78746) ....Mark Whitehouse
City Admin., Cindy Selman
Roma...........................Fernando Peña
Roman Forest (2430 Roman Forest Blvd., New Caney 77357) ....James D. Walters
*Ropesville ....Victor Marrett
Roscoe ....Tom Griffith
*Rosebud ....Heriberto C. Hernandez
City Mgr., Dick Gillespie
*Rose City (370 S. Rose City Dr., Vidor 77662) ....Ruth Dubuisson
*Rose Hill Acres (Box 8285, Lumberton 77711) ....Rayedene Graves
†Rosenberg................Dorothy W. Ryan
City Mgr., Jeff D. Braun
Ross.................................James L. Jaska
*Rosser ....Albert Davis
Rotan.................................Jerry Marshall
City Mgr., Harold Sanders
Round Mountain....................... E. B. Seals
†Round Rock ....Charles Culpepper
City Mgr., Robert L. Bennett Jr.
Round Top ....Dave Nagel

†Rowlett.....................H.K. "Buddy" Wall
   City Mgr., Mike Gibson
Roxton..............................Luther Smith
Royse City.................................Paul Fisk
Rule ....Malcolm Herttenberger
Runaway Bay (101 Runaway Bay Dr.,
   Bridgeport 76426) ....Clay Dent
   City Coordinator, Mike Evans
Runge ....Jack Roberson
†Rusk.................Emmett H. Whitehead
   City Mgr., Mike Murray
*Sabinal ....Reynaldo Rodriguez
*†Sachse ....Larry Holden
   City Mgr., Lloyd Henderson
*Sadler..............................Virginia Reese
†Saginaw ....Monte Nichols
   City Mgr., Pat Moffatt
St. Hedwig ....Albert Strzelczyk
Saint Jo.........................Earl R. Garrison
Saint Paul (2505 Butschers Block,
   Wylie 75098) ....Joyce Pockrus
†San Angelo ....Johnny Fender
   City Mgr., Thomas L. Adams
†San Antonio ....Howard W. Peak
   City Mgr., Alexander E. Briseno
San Augustine ....Gertrude Lane
   City Mgr., Alton Shaw
†San Benito.................Cesar Gonzalez
   City Mgr., John Vidaurri
Sanctuary (1920 Ash Creek Dr. S., Azle
   76020) ....Floyd Galloway
San Diego ....Alfredo E. Cardenas
San Felipe ....Mark Miller
Sanford ....Ronald Kirby
Sanger ....John W. Coker III
   City Admin., Larry Keesler
†San Juan.................Roberto F. Loredo
   City Mgr., Jorge A. Arcaute
San Leanna (Box 1107, Manchaca
   78652) ....James E. Payne
†San Marcos.......................Billy G. Moore
   City Mgr., Larry D. Gilley
San Patricio (RR 2, Box 45, Mathis
   78368) ....Lonnie Glasscock III
*San Perlita.......................Oscar de Luna
San Saba ....Marcus D. Amthor
   City Mgr., Joe Ragsdale
Sansom Park (5500 Buchanan St., Fort
   Worth 76114)..............Merle Easterling
Santa Anna ....Karen Morris
†Santa Fe ....Robert Cheek
   City Mgr., Joe Dickson
Santa Rosa.................Ruben Ochoa Jr.
Savoy ....Clete Stogsdill
†Schertz ....Harold D. "Hal" Baldwin
   City Mgr., Kerry R. Sweatt
Schulenburg..............Connie Koopmann
   City Mgr., Ronald Brossmann
Scotland...............................Mike Carlton
Scottsville.............John P. "Jack" Verhalen
†Seabrook ....Jan Bosone
   City Mgr., Ron Wicker
Seadrift ....Mark Daniel
†Seagoville ....Calvin Travers
   City Mgr.,Larry Graves
*Seagraves ....Pat McAdoo
†Sealy................................Betty Reinbeck
   Interim City Mgr., John Maresh
†Seguin ....Mark Stautzenberger
   City Mgr., Jack S. Hamlett
Selma.......................Harold Friesenhahn
   City Mgr., Margie Lubianski
†Seminole............................Wayne Mixon
   City Mgr., Tommy Phillips
Seven Oaks (RR 1, Box 833,
   Livingston 77351).....Barbara A. Shirley
Seven Points.........................Marian Hill
Seymour ....Dick Wirz
   City Admin., John F. Caussey
Shady Shores (Box 362, Lake
   Dallas 75065) ....Olive Stephens
Shallowater ....Moe Dozier
Shamrock ..............................R.L. Roberts
   City Mgr., Johnny Rhodes
Shavano Park (99 Saddletree Rd.,
   San Antonio 78231) ....Tommy Peyton
   City Mgr., Michael C. Cernech
Shenandoah (29811 IH-45,
   Spring 77381)............ David J. Vetter Jr.

City Admin., Ron Bourbeau
Shepherd ....Lee Ainsworth
†Sherman ....Julie Ellis Starr
   City Mgr., Jim Andrews
Shiner.............................Arthur T. Ward
Shoreacres ....Wayne Gamble
†Silsbee ....Dean T. Robinson
Silverton ....John Bowman
   City Mgr., Jerry Patton
Simonton ....Jim Gammill
†Sinton...............Fernando Hernandez Jr.
   City Mgr., (Vacancy)
Skellytown ....Ralph Tice
†Slaton ....Don Kendrick
   City Mgr., Mitch Grant
Smiley ....Donald R. Janicek
Smithville ....Vernon Richards
   City Mgr., Robert (Bob) Miller
Smyer.........................Mary Beth Sims
Snook....................................John See III
†Snyder.....................................David Holt
   City Mgr., John Gayle
*Socorro ....Rogelio Lozoya
Somerset............................Paul G. Cuellar
Somerville ....Donald L. Strickland
   City Admin., Lloyd A. Behm
Sonora....................Margaret Cascadden
*Sour Lake ....Bruce Robinson
   City Mgr., Kyle J. Jung
South Houston ....Cipriano Romero
†Southlake ....Rick Stacy
   City Mgr., Curtis E. Hawk
Southmayd ....Billy Kerr
*South Mountain (RR 2, Box 298A,
   Gatesville 76528).......Lester Blanchard
*South Padre Island Edmond Cyganiewicz
   City Mgr., James V. Chisholm
Southside Place (6309 Edloe,
   Houston 77005) ....Ben M. Hurst III
   City Mgr., Seth Young
Spearman ....Burl Buchanan
Splendora.........................Wayne Carley
*Spofford ....J. B. Herndon
Springlake .......................P.A. Washington
Springtown ....Thomas Gentry
   City Mgr., (Vacancy)
*Spring Valley (1025 Campbell Rd.,
   Houston 77055) ....Louise Richman
   City Admin., Richard Rockenbaugh
Spur ....Grady Joe Harrison
Stafford ....Leonard Scarcella
Stagecoach (Box 364, Tomball
   77377) ....Daniel K. Donnelly
†Stamford......................Louis E. Johnson
   City Mgr., Ken Roberson
Stanton ....Lester Baker
   City Mgr., Danny Fryar
Star Harbor (Box 949, Malakoff
   75148) ....Jack Ferguson
†Stephenville......................John Pollan
   City Mgr., Donald B. Davis
Sterling City.................Clyde Ross Foster
*Stinnett ......................J.F. (Buck) Formby
   City Admin., Mike Weatherford
Stockdale ....Hubert Tomerlin
   City Mgr., Carl R. Lambeck
*Stratford ....David Brown
   City Mgr., E.R. Bell
*Strawn..................Paul L. Stephen II
Streetman ....James M. Compton
Sudan.............................Freddie Maxwell
†Sugar Land ....Dean Hrbacek
   City Mgr., David Neeley
*†Sulphur Springs.................Stacy Cody
   City Mgr., Marc Maxwell
Sundown ....Ronnie Popejoy
   City Mgr., Brad Stafford
Sunnyvale (537 Long Creek Rd.,
   Mesquite 75182)...................Jim Wade
   City Mgr., Robert Ewalt
Sunray ....Dow Brewer
   City Mgr., Greg Smith
Sunrise Beach Village ....Dolores Smith
*Sunset ....Ron Whitson
Sunset Valley (2 Lone Oak Trail,
   Austin 78745) ....Michael C. Francis
*Sun Valley (RR 2, Box 800, Paris
   75462) ....Maria Z. Wagnon

*Surfside Beach (1304 Monument Dr.,
   Freeport 77541) ....Larry Davison
Sweeny................................Larry G. Piper
   City Mgr., Tim Moss
†Sweetwater ....Jay Lawrence
   City Mgr., David Maddox
Taft......................................J.D. Mayo
   City Mgr., Mike Rhea
Tahoka.............................Mike Mensch
   City Mgr., Jerry W. Webster
Talco ..........................K.M. (Mike) Sloan
Tatum..........................Walter N. Mullins Jr.
†Taylor ....Donald R. Hill
   City Mgr., Kenneth A. Taylor
Taylor Lake Village.........Einar H. Goerland
Teague..........................Blelve Bridges
   City Mgr., David N. Moss
Tehuacana ....E. B. Trotter
†Temple.................................J.W. Perry
   City Mgr., David R. Taylor
Tenaha ....George N. Bowers
†Terrell.............................Don L. Lindsey
   Interim City Mgr., Linda Seabolt
†Terrell Hills (5100 N. New Braunfels, San
   Antonio 78209) ......Barbara B. Christian
   City Mgr., Cal D. Johnson
*†Texarkana.........................John Jarvis
   City Mgr., George T. Shackleford
†Texas City.....................Charles T. Doyle
*Texhoma.......................Garland K. Dahl
*Texline ....Doug Antwiler
   City Mgr., Bernard Eads
*†The Colony ....Mary Watts
   City Mgr., Lanny Lambert
Thompsons ......................G.W. Longserre
Thorndale ....Garry Williams
   City Mgr., Keith Kiesling
Thornton..........................J. Wayne Marks
*Thorntonville (2414 W. 2nd, Monahans
   79756)......................Don McKenzie
Thrall ....James Dvorak
Three Rivers...............Jimmie M. Dewberry
   City Admin., Marian R. Forehand
Throckmorton ....John O. Kunkel
Timbercreek Canyon (RR 7, Box 4-5,
   Amarillo 79118)..................Ed Tunnicliff
Timpson.........................Ross Graves Jr.
*Tioga ....Bobby Gray
*Tira (RR 7, Box 220, Sulphur
   Springs 75482) ....Coy O. Vicars
Toco (2103 Chestnut, Brookston
   75421)........ Hugh D. (Rocky) Thompson
*Todd Mission (390 N. Millcreek Dr.,
   Plantersville 77363) ......George Coulam
Tolar.............................Thomas D. Furlow
†Tomball .........................H.G. Harrington
   City Mgr., Warren Driver
Tom Bean ....James Yowell
Tool (RR 6, Box 843, Kemp
   75143)..........................Aden J. Phillips
Toyah ....Charlotte H. Waight
Trent ....James Wallis
Trenton ....Donald Withrow
Trinidad..............................J.C. Airheart
   City Admin., Nelda Cartlidge
Trinity ....Lyle Stubbs
Trophy Club ....Jim Carter
   City Mgr., Donna Welsh
Troup ....Steve Patterson
   City Mgr., Jyl Moose
Troy................................Thomas R. Vanderveer
†Tulia.................................John C. Emmitt
   City Mgr., Bryan Easum
*Turkey...............................George Colvin
Tuscola ....Mark Young
Tye ....Luanne Goodgion
†Tyler..................................Kevin P. Eltife
   City Mgr., Pinkney L. Butler
Uhland.............................Dan T. Sorrels
*Uncertain ....Bill Mauthe
*Union Grove (RR 2, Box 196, Glade-
   water 75647)............Randy Lee Simcox
†Universal City ....Wesley D. Becken
   City Mgr., Marion E. Thorpe
†University Park (Box 8005, Dallas
   75205).................F.B. Pete Goldman
   City Mgr., Bob Livingston
*†Uvalde ....George Horner
   City Mgr., H.G. (Bert) Lumbreras

*Valentine......................Jesús Calderon
Valley Mills ....Howard Hillin
Valley View......................John Kubicek
Van...............................E.L. Raulston
Van Alstyne................Teddie Ann Salmon
*Van Horn ....Okey D. Lucas
Vega......................Mark J. Groneman
Venus......................James A. Flatt
   City Mgr., John Daniel
†Vernon ....Kelly Couch
   City Mgr., Jim Murray
†Victoria ....Gary Middleton
   City Mgr., Denny L. Arnold
†Vidor ....Lamech N. Wright
   City Mgr., Dan Graves
Village of Tiki Island (802 Tiki Dr. , Gal-
   veston 77554) ....Ralph H. Miller
Vinton (436 Vinton Rd., Canutillo
   79835) ....Samuel Monrreal
†Waco......................Michael D. Morrison
   City Mgr., James N. Holgersson
Waelder ....Roy Tovar
Wake Village ....Mike Huddleston
   City Mgr., Bob Long
Waller......................Danny Marburger
Wallis ....Tony I. Salazar Jr.
*Walnut Springs...............Roberta Hilliard
Warren City (3004 George Richey Rd.,
   Gladewater 75647)... H.L. Hearnsberger
Waskom ....Jesse Moore
†Watauga ....Hector F. Garcia
   City Mgr., Lee Maness
†Waxahachie ....Charles "Chuck" Beatty
   City Mgr., Robert W. Sokoll
†Weatherford......................Tom McLaughlin
   City Mgr., Kenneth Reneau
†Webster ....Floyd Myers
   City Mgr., Francis E. Parks
Weimar ....Bennie Kosler
*Weinert...............................Todd Herricks
Weir ....Mervin Walker
Wellington......................Gary Brewer
   City Mgr., Jon Sessions
Wellman ....Lynn Hudson Sr.
Wells ....William M. Bailey

†Weslaco ....Gene A. Braught
   City Mgr., Frank Castellanos
West...............................Russell D. Willsey
Westbrook......................John Leslie Rees
West Columbia......................M.A. Brooks
   City Mgr., (Vacancy)
Westlake (3 Village Cr. #207, Roanoke
   76262) ....(In dispute at press time)
West Lake Hills (911 Westlake Dr.,
   Austin 78746) ....Dwight Thompson
   City Mgr., Daniel E. Sowada
*Westminster...................Richard J. Davis
*Weston......................Kenneth Cowan
†West Orange (2700 Austin Ave.,
   Orange 77630) ....Roy McDonald
Westover Hills (5824 Merrymount, Fort
   Worth 76107).........Earle A. Shields Jr.
West Tawakoni (RR 1, Box 354,
   Quinlan 75474).............Harold Bedwell
†West University Place (3800 Uni-
   versity Blvd., Houston
   77005) ....Teresa W. Fogler
   City Mgr., Robert (Sherman) Yehl
*Westworth Village (311 Burton Hill Rd.,
   Ft. Worth 76114)...................Betty Sarlls
†Wharton ....Dennis M. Voulgaris
   City Mgr., Andres Garza Jr.
Wheeler......................Wanda Herd
White Deer ...............................R.T. Laurie
Whiteface......................Mack Ashmore
   City Mgr., Syd Albus
Whitehouse ....Dale E. Moran
   City Mgr., (Vacancy)
†White Oak ....Tim Vaughn
   City Mgr., Ralph Weaver
Whitesboro......................Alfred C. Miller
   City Mgr., Charles Whitecotton
†White Settlement......................James Herring
   City Mgr., Richard J. Mills
Whitewright ....Bill Goodson
Whitney......................Harold Lehmann
†Wichita Falls...............Kathryn A. Yeager
   City Mgr., Jim Berzina
Wickett ....Harold Ferguson
Willis......................Ruth Castleschouldt

Willow Park (101 Stagecoach Trail,
   Weatherford 76087).............Les Cooley
   City Admin., C. Guy Natale
Wills Point......................Bobby E. Mitchell
   City Mgr., C.C. Girdley
Wilmer...............................Eugene Lowe
Wilson...............................Jackie Bishop
Windcrest (8601 Midcrown Dr., San
   Antonio 78239) ....Joe D. Cochran
Windom...............................Bill Roberts
Windthorst......................Donald J. Frerich
Winfield...............................Mark Rigney
*Wink...............................Edith A. Jones
Winnsboro......................Dayne Redding
   City Mgr., Jim Blanchard
Winona......................Carl W. Granberry
Winters ....Dawson McGuffin
   City Mgr., Aref Hassan
Wixon Valley (Box 105, Kurten
   77862)...................Ruby Tice Andrews
Wolfe City ....Benny Richards
Wolfforth ....Bob Tate
   City Admin., Frankie Pittman
Woodbranch Village (Box 804, New
   Caney 77357) ....Timothy B. McCrary
Woodcreek (Box 1570, Wimberley
   78676)......................Kenneth E. Jacobs
Woodloch (Box 1379, Conroe
   77305)......................Diane L. Lincoln
Woodsboro......................Joseph Hernandez
Woodson......................Bobby Mathiews
Woodville......................Larry A. Phillips
   City Mgr., Donald W. Shaw
†Woodway (Box 20937, Waco
   76702)......................Donald J. Baker
   City Mgr., Mark L. McDaniel
Wortham......................John W. Vineyard
†Wylie......................James Swartz
   City Mgr., Mike Collins
Yantis...............................Colleen Nolen
†Yoakum......................M. W. Harbus Jr.
   City Mgr., A.J. Veselka
Yorktown......................George F. Klein
   City Mgr., Milton Ledwig
Zavalla...............................Opal C. Gant

Texas Main Street Program

To encourage Texas cities to rehabilitate and reuse existing historic buildings, the Texas Historical Commission established the Texas Main Street Program in 1981.

Each year, several towns, or neighborhoods within large cities, are designated Main Street cities.

Each designated city/neighborhood hires a Main Street manager to coordinate its project. The Texas Main Street Program office provides architectural-design assistance, as well as supervision for the Main Street manager.

Each city receives a three-day visit by a team of professional consultants, who provide immediate and long-term suggestions for the community's revitalization. Other state agencies, including the Texas Department of Commerce, the Texas Department of Housing and Community Affairs and the Governor's Office, provide additional assistance.

Cities that are not officially designated, but wish to begin a revitalization program on their own following Main Street guidelines, are called self-initiated cities.

Georgetown received national recognition in 1997 for its Main Street Program.
Photo courtesy Georgetown C&VB.

Following is a list of Texas Main Street cities/neighborhoods as of spring 1997, grouped by year of designation. An asterisk before the name denotes a city no longer active in the program. Self-initiated cities are listed last.

1981: *Eagle Pass, Hillsboro, *Navasota, Plainview, Seguin. 1982: *Gainesville, *Georgetown, *Kingsville, *Marshall, *McKinney. 1983: *Brenham, Harlingen, Lufkin, *Stamford, *Waxahachie. 1984: *Belton, *Brownwood, *Ennis, Goliad, *Paris.

1985: Corsicana, *Cuero, Lampasas, *Mineral Wells, *Sweetwater. 1986: *Greenville, *Palestine, *Pampa, Pittsburg, San Marcos. 1987: *Kilgore, Post, *Terrell, Weatherford, *Wharton. 1988: *Center, *Daingerfield, Gonzales, Henderson, *Longview, Temple. 1989: Denison, Fort Stockton, Mineola, *Sulphur Springs, *Yoakum.

1990: *Athens, Denton, *El Campo, Elgin, Jasper, Tyler. 1991: *Abilene, Angleton, *Glen Rose, *Jefferson Avenue/Dallas, Market Square/Houston, New Braunfels, Odessa. 1992: Bay City, Cleburne, McGregor, Mission, Mount Vernon. 1993: Dallas City Center, Littlefield, Mount Pleasant, Sherman, Van Alstyne. 1994: Decatur, Graham, Lancaster, Marlin, Sonora and Martin Luther King Boulevard/Dallas. 1995: Alpine, Bonham, Clifton, Kerrville and Rusk, plus Irving's commercial district. 1996: Duncanville, Fairfield, La Grange, Olton, Quanah. 1997: Bowie, Breckenridge, Celina, Ferris, Weslaco.

Self-initiated cities for 1997 include Cooper, Monahans, Amarillo City Center and Garland. ☆

Regional Councils of Government

The concept of regional planning and cooperation, fostered by enabling legislation in 1965, has spread across Texas since organization of the **North Central Texas Council of Governments** in 1966.

Regional councils are voluntary associations of local governments that deal with problems and planning needs that cross the boundaries of individual local governments or that require regional attention. These concerns may include criminal justice, emergency communications, job-training programs, solid-waste management, transportation needs, and water-quality management. The councils make recommendations to member governments and may assist in implementing the plans.

The **Texas Association of Regional Councils** is at 508 W. 12th, Austin 78701; (512) 478-4715; Fax (512) 463-1880. Financing is provided by the local governments, the state and the federal government.

A list of the **24 regional councils**, the **counties served** and the **executive director** as of September 1996, follows (map on page 294):

Alamo Area Council of Governments: Counties — Atascosa, Bandera, Bexar, Comal, Frio, Gillespie, Guadalupe, Karnes, Kendall, Kerr, Medina and Wilson. Al J. Notzon III, 118 Broadway, Ste. 400, San Antonio 78205.

Ark-Tex Council of Governments: Bowie, Cass, Delta, Franklin, Hopkins, Lamar, Morris, Red River, Titus, and Miller County, Ark. James C. Fisher, PO Box 5307, Texarkana, Texas 75505-5307.

Brazos Valley Development Council: Brazos, Burleson, Grimes, Leon, Madison, Robertson and Washington. Tom M. Wilkinson Jr., PO Box 4128, Bryan 77805-4128.

Capital Area Planning Council: Bastrop, Blanco, Burnet, Caldwell, Fayette, Hays, Lee, Llano, Travis and Williamson. Betty Voights, 2520 S. IH 35 South, Ste. 100, Austin 78704.

Central Texas Council of Governments: Bell, Coryell, Hamilton, Lampasas, Milam, Mills and San Saba. A. C. Johnson, PO Box 729, Belton 76513-0729.

Coastal Bend Council of Governments: Aransas, Bee, Brooks, Duval, Jim Wells, Kenedy, Kleberg, Live Oak, McMullen, Nueces, Refugio and San Patricio. John Buckner, PO Box 9909, Corpus Christi 78469-9909.

Concho Valley Council of Governments: Coke, Concho, Crockett, Irion, Kimble, Mason, McCulloch, Menard, Reagan, Schleicher, Sterling, Sutton and Tom Green. Bob Weaver, Box 60050, San Angelo 76906-0050.

Deep East Texas Council of Governments: Angelina, Houston, Jasper, Nacogdoches, Newton, Polk, Sabine, San Augustine, San Jacinto, Shelby, Trinity and Tyler. Walter G. Diggles, 274 E. Lamar, Jasper 75951.

East Texas Council of Governments: Anderson, Camp, Cherokee, Gregg, Harrison, Henderson, Marion, Panola, Rains, Rusk, Smith, Upshur, Van Zandt and Wood. Glynn Knight, 3800 Stone Rd., Kilgore 75662.

Golden Crescent Regional Planning Commission: Calhoun, De Witt, Goliad, Gonzales, Jackson, Lavaca and Victoria. Patrick J. Kennedy, PO Box 2028, Victoria 77902-2028.

Heart of Texas Council of Governments: Bosque, Falls, Freestone, Hill, Limestone and McLennan. Leon Wilhite, 300 Franklin Ave., Waco 76701-2244.

Houston-Galveston Area Council: Austin, Brazoria, Chambers, Colorado, Fort Bend, Galveston, Harris, Liberty, Matagorda, Montgomery, Walker, Waller and Wharton. Jack Steele, PO Box 22777, Houston 77227.

Lower Rio Grande Valley Development Council: Cameron, Hidalgo and Willacy. Ken Jones, 311 N. 15th, McAllen 78501-4705.

Middle Rio Grande Development Council: Dimmit, Edwards, Kinney, La Salle, Maverick, Real, Uvalde, Val Verde and Zavala. Leodoro Martinez Jr., PO Box 1199, Carrizo Springs 78834-1199.

Nortex Regional Planning Commission: Archer, Baylor, Clay, Cottle, Foard, Hardeman, Jack, Montague, Wichita, Wilbarger and Young. Dennis Wilde, PO Box 5144, Wichita Falls 76307-5144.

North Central Texas Council of Governments: Collin, Dallas, Denton, Ellis, Erath, Hood, Hunt, Johnson, Kaufman, Navarro, Palo Pinto, Parker, Rockwall, Somervell, Tarrant and Wise. Mike Eastland, PO Box 5888, Arlington 76005-5888.

Panhandle Regional Planning Commission: Armstrong, Briscoe, Carson, Castro, Childress, Collingsworth, Dallam, Deaf Smith, Donley, Gray, Hall, Hansford, Hartley, Hemphill, Hutchinson, Lipscomb, Moore, Ochiltree, Oldham, Parmer, Potter, Randall, Roberts, Sherman, Swisher and Wheeler. Gary Pitner, PO Box 9257, Amarillo 79105.

Permian Basin Regional Planning Commission: Andrews, Borden, Crane, Dawson, Ector, Gaines, Glasscock, Howard, Loving, Martin, Midland, Pecos, Reeves, Terrell, Upton, Ward and Winkler. Ernie Crawford, PO Box 60660, Midland 79711-0660.

Rio Grande Council of Governments: Brewster, Culberson, El Paso, Hudspeth, Jeff Davis, Presidio and Doña Ana Co., New Mexico. Justin Ormsby, 1100 N. Stanton, Ste. 610, El Paso 79902.

South East Texas Regional Planning Commission: Hardin, Jefferson and Orange. Don Kelly, PO Box 1387, Nederland 77627-1387.

South Plains Association of Governments: Bailey, Cochran, Crosby, Dickens, Floyd, Garza, Hale, Hockley, King, Lamb, Lubbock, Lynn, Motley, Terry and Yoakum. Jerry Casstevens, PO Box 3730, Lubbock 79452-3730.

South Texas Development Council: Jim Hogg, Starr, Webb and Zapata. Amando Garza, PO Box 2187, Laredo 78044-2187.

Texoma Regional Planning Commission: Cooke, Fannin and Grayson. Ms. Francis Pelley, 3201 Texoma Pkwy., Ste. 200, Sherman 75090-1974.

West Central Texas Council of Governments: Brown, Callahan, Coleman, Comanche, Eastland, Fisher, Haskell, Jones, Kent, Knox, Mitchell, Nolan, Runnels, Scurry, Shackelford, Stephens, Stonewall, Taylor and Throckmorton. Brad Helbert, Box 3195, Abilene 79604. ☆

County Tax Appraisers

The following list of Chief Appraisers for Texas counties was furnished by the **State Property Tax Division of the State Comptroller's** *office. It includes the mailing address for each appraiser and is current to May 30, 1997.*

Anderson—R. Cliff Wooten, PO Box 279, Palestine 75802
Andrews—Mickey Green, 600 N. Main, Andrews 79714
Angelina—John Whitley (Interim), PO Box 2357, Lufkin 75902
Aransas—Jad Smith, 601 S. Church, Rockport 78382
Archer—Edward H. Trigg III, PO Box 1141, Archer City 76351
Armstrong—Ron Patterson, Drawer 835, Claude 79019
Atascosa—Curtis Stewart, PO Box 139, Poteet 78065
Austin—Glen Whitehead, 906 E. Amelia St., Bellville 77418
Bailey—Kaye Elliott, 302 Main St., Muleshoe 79347
Bandera—P. H. Coates IV, PO Box 1119, Bandera 78003
Bastrop—Dana Ripley, Drawer 578, Bastrop 78602
Baylor—Ronnie Hargrove, 411 W. Idaho, Seymour 76380
Bee—Blaine Luthringer, PO Box 1262, Beeville 78104
Bell—Carl Moore, PO Box 390, Belton 76513
Bexar—John Gaines, PO Box 830248, San Antonio 78283
Blanco—Ms. Hollis Boatright, PO Box 338, Johnson City 78636
Borden—Royal D. Lewis, PO Box 298, Gail 79738
Bosque—F. Janice Henry, PO Box 393, Meridian 76665
Bowie—Wayne Hawkins, PO Box 6527, Texarkana 75505

Brazoria—Cheryl Evans, 500 N. Chenango, Angleton 77515
Brazos—Gerald L. Winn, 1673 Briarcrest Dr., #A-101, Bryan 77802
Brewster—Jerry Ratcliff, PO Box 1231, Alpine 79831
Briscoe—Carlye Fleming, PO Box 728, Silverton 79257
Brooks—Humberto Rivera, Drawer A, Falfurrias 78355
Brown—Doran E. Lemke, 403 Fisk, Brownwood 76801
Burleson—Elizabeth Plagens, PO Box 1000, Caldwell 77836
Burnet—Stan Hemphill, Drawer E, Burnet 78611
Caldwell—Russell Sanders, PO Box 59, Lockhart 78644
Calhoun—Andrew J. Hahn, PO Box 48, Port Lavaca 77979
Callahan—Rodney Lewallen, PO Box 806, Baird 79504
Cameron—Mike Amezquita, PO Box 1010, San Benito 78586
Camp—Vaudeane Bennett, PO Box 739, Pittsburg 75686
Carson—Donita Davis, PO Box 970, Panhandle 79068
Cass—Janelle Clements, PO Box 1150, Linden 75563
Castro—Jerry Heller, 204 S.E. 3rd (Rear), Dimmitt 79027
Chambers—Michael Fregia, PO Box 1520, Anahuac 77514
Cherokee—Sid R. Danner, PO Box 494, Rusk 75785

Childress—Nadine Parr, PO Box 13, Childress 79201
Clay—A. G. Reis, 101 E. Omega, Henrietta 76365
Cochran—H. Loy Kern, 109 S.E. 1st, Morton 79346
Coke—Patsy N. Dunn, PO Box 2, Robert Lee 76945
Coleman—Bill W. Jones, PO Box 914, Coleman 76834
Collin—Jimmie Honea, 1024 S. Greenville, #120, Allen 75002
Collingsworth—Ann Wauer, 800 W. Ave., Rm. 4, Wellington 79095
Colorado—William T. Youens Jr., PO Box 10, Columbus 78934
Comal—Lynn E. Rodgers, PO Box 311222, New Braunfels 78131
Comanche—Clay Fowler, PO Box 6, Comanche 76442
Concho—Eugene Dillard, PO Box 68, Paint Rock 76866
Cooke—Will Presson, 200 W. California, Gainesville 76240
Coryell—Darrell Lisenbe, PO Box 142, Gatesville 76528
Cottle—Rue Young, PO Box 459, Paducah 79248
Crane—Peggy Dickson, 511 W. 8th, Crane 79731
Crockett—W. Tom Stokes, Drawer H, Ozona 76943
Crosby—Darla Doss, PO Box 479, Crosbyton 79322
Culberson—Sally Carrasco, PO Box 550, Van Horn 79855
Dallam—Huie V. Stanley, PO Box 592, Dalhart 79022
Dallas—Foy Mitchell Jr., 2949 N. Stemmons Fwy., Dallas 75247
Dawson—Tom Anderson, PO Box 797, Lamesa 79331
Deaf Smith—Fred Fox, PO Box 2298, Hereford 79045
Delta—Toyce Phillips, PO Box 47, Cooper 75432
Denton—Joe Rogers, PO Box 2816, Denton 76202
DeWitt—John Haliburton, PO Box 4, Cuero 77954
Dickens—Dexter Clay, PO Box 119, Dickens 79229
Dimmit—Rufino Lozano, 402 N. 7th, Carrizo Springs 78834
Donley—Paula Lowrie, PO Box 1220, Clarendon 79226
Duval—Ernesto Molina Jr., PO Box 809, San Diego 78384
Eastland—Steve Thomas, PO Box 914, Eastland 76448
Ector—James Goodwin, 1301 E. 8th, Odessa 79761
Edwards—Wiley Rudasill, PO Box 858, Rocksprings 78880
Ellis—Kathy Rodrigue, PO Box 878, Waxahachie 75165
El Paso—Cora Viescas, 5801 Trowbridge, El Paso 79925
Erath—Jerry Lee, PO Box 94, Stephenville 76401
Falls—Joyce Collier, Drawer 430, Marlin 76661
Fannin—Carrol Garrison, 920 N. Center, Bonham 75418
Fayette—Kathleen Giovannini, PO Box 836, La Grange 78945
Fisher—Betty Mize, PO Box 516, Roby 79543
Floyd—Sheila Faulkenberry, PO Box 249, Floydada 79235
Foard—Jo Ann Vecera, PO Box 419, Crowell 79227
Fort Bend—Gene Brewer, 2801 B.F. Terry Blvd., Rosenberg 77471
Franklin—Mike McKibben, PO Box 720, Mount Vernon 75457
Freestone—Bud Black, 218 N. Mount, Fairfield 75840
Frio—Irma Gonzalez, PO Box 1129, Pearsall 78061
Gaines—Betty Caudle, PO Box 490, Seminole 79360
Galveston—Ken Wright, PO Box 3647, Texas City 77592
Garza—Billie Windham, Drawer F, Post 79356
Gillespie—Bob Drury, PO Box 429, Fredericksburg 78624
Glasscock—Royce Pruit, PO Box 89, Garden City 79739
Goliad—E. J. Bammert, PO Box 34, Goliad 77963
Gonzales—Glenda Strackbein, PO Box 867, Gonzales 78629
Gray—W. Pat Bagley, PO Box 836, Pampa 79066
Grayson—Robert Tollison, 205 N. Travis, Sherman 75090
Gregg—Marvin Hahn, 1333 Harrison Rd., Longview 75604
Grimes—Bill Sullivan, PO Box 489, Anderson 77830
Guadalupe—Pat Fox, 3000 N. Austin, Seguin 78155
Hale—Linda Jaynes, PO Box 29, Plainview 79073
Hall—Jack Scott, 721 Robertson, Memphis 79245
Hamilton—Doyle Roberts, 119 E. Henry, Hamilton 76531
Hansford—Alice Peddy, PO Box 519, Spearman 79081
Hardeman—Twila Butler, PO Box 388, Quanah 79252
Hardin—Amador Reyna, PO Box 670, Kountze 77625
Harris—Jim Robinson, PO Box 920975, Houston 77292
Harrison—David Whitmire, PO Box 818, Marshall 75671
Hartley—Donna Bryant, PO Box 405, Hartley 79044
Haskell—Jamie Weaver, PO Box 467, Haskell 79521
Hays—Pete Islas, 21001 N. IH-35, Kyle 78640
Hemphill—William D. Lanier, PO Box 65, Canadian 79014
Henderson—Bill Jackson, PO Box 430, Athens 75751
Hidalgo—Daniel Boone, PO Box 632, Pharr 78577
Hill—Shirley Holub, PO Box 416, Hillsboro 76645
Hockley—Nick Williams, PO Box 1090, Levelland 79336
Hood—Harold Chestnut, PO Box 819, Granbury 76048
Hopkins—William Sherman, 109 College St., Sulphur Springs 75482
Houston—Kathryn Keith, PO Box 112, Crockett 75835
Howard—Keith Toomire, PO Box 1151, Big Spring 79721
Hudspeth—John Ferrell, PO Box 429, Sierra Blanca 79851
Hunt—Mildred Compton, PO Box 1339, Greenville 75403
Hutchinson—George Nies, PO Box 5065, Borger 79008
Irion—Frances Grice, PO Box 980, Mertzon 76941
Jack—Gary Zeitler, PO Box 958, Jacksboro 76458
Jackson—Tommy Watson, 411 N. Wells, Rm. 109, Edna 77957
Jasper—David Luther, PO Box 1300, Jasper 75951
Jeff Davis—John Ferrell, PO Box 373, Fort Davis 79734

Jefferson—Roland Bieber, PO Box 1470, Groves 77619
Jim Hogg—Arnoldo Gonzalez, PO Box 459, Hebbronville 78361
Jim Wells—Sidney Vela, PO Box 607, Alice 78333
Johnson—Don Gilmore, 109 N. Main, Cleburne 76031
Jones—Susan Holloway, PO Box 348, Anson 79501
Karnes—Oscar Caballero, 915 S. Panna Maria, Karnes City 78118
Kaufman—Jackie Self, PO Box 819, Kaufman 75142
Kendall—Leta Schlinke, PO Box 788, Boerne 78006
Kenedy—Clyde Hamilton Jr., PO Box 705, Bastrop 78602
Kent—Garth Gregory, PO Box 68, Jayton 79528
Kerr—David Oehler, PO Box 1885, Kerrville 78029
Kimble—Elaine Chaney, PO Box 307, Junction 76849
King—Sandy Burkett, PO Box 117, Guthrie 79236
Kinney—Joyce Fuentes, PO Box 1377, Brackettville 78832
Kleberg—Tina Loera, PO Box 1027, Kingsville 78364
Knox—Stanton Brown, PO Box 47, Benjamin 79505
Lamar—Joe Welch, PO Box 400, Paris 75461
Lamb—Vaughn McKee, PO Box 950, Littlefield 79339
Lampasas—Katrina Perry, PO Box 175, Lampasas 76550
La Salle—Juanita Lozano, Drawer O, Cotulla 78014
Lavaca—Diane Munson, PO Box 386, Hallettsville 77964
Lee—Roy Holcomb, 218 E. Richmond, Giddings 78942
Leon—Jeff Beshears, PO Box 536, Centerville 76050
Liberty—Alan Conner, PO Box 10016, Liberty 77575
Limestone—Karen Wietzikoski, Drawer 831, Groesbeck 76642
Lipscomb—Jerry Reynolds, PO Box 128, Darrouzett 79024
Live Oak—Robert Dirks, PO Box MM, George West 78022
Llano—Gary Eldridge, 103 E. Sandstone, Llano 78643
Loving—J. W. Busby, PO Box 352, Mentone 79754
Lubbock—Dave Kimbrough, PO Box 10542, Lubbock 79408
Lynn—Dovie Miller, PO Box 789, Tahoka 79373
Madison—David Bailey, PO Box 1328, Madisonville 77864
Marion—Brenda Keith, PO Box 690, Jefferson 75657
Martin—Delbert Dickinson, PO Box 1349, Stanton 79782
Mason—Deborah Geistweidt, Drawer 1119, Mason 76856
Matagorda—Vince Maloney, PO Box 179, Bay City 77404
Maverick—Victor Perry, PO Box 2628, Eagle Pass 78853
McCulloch—Orlando Rubio, 104 N. College, Brady 76825
McLennan—Charles Gauer, PO Box 2297, Waco 76703
McMullen—Jesse Bryan, PO Box 38, Tilden 78072
Medina—James Garcia, 1410 Ave. K, Hondo 78861
Menard—Margaret Cannon, PO Box 1058, Menard 76859
Midland—Ron Stegall, PO Box 908002, Midland 79708
Milam—Patricia Moraw, PO Box 769, Cameron 76520
Mills—Bill Presley, PO Box 565, Goldthwaite 76844
Mitchell—Kaye Cornutt, PO Box 358, Colorado City 79512
Montague—June Deaton, PO Box 121, Montague 76251
Montgomery—Jimmy Foreman, PO Box 2233, Conroe 77305
Moore—Joyce Cearley, PO Box 717, Dumas 79029
Morris—Rhonda Hall, PO Box 563, Daingerfield 75638
Motley—Brenda Osborn, PO Box 779, Matador 79244
Nacogdoches—Gary Woods, 216 W. Hospital, Nacogdoches 75961
Navarro—Harry Hudson, PO Box 3118, Corsicana 75151
Newton—Margie Herrin, Drawer X, Newton 75966
Nolan—Patricia Davis, PO Box 1256, Sweetwater 79556
Nueces—George Moff, 201 N. Chaparral, Corpus Christi 78401
Ochiltree—Terry Symons, 825 S. Main, #100, Perryton 79070
Oldham—Jen Carter, Drawer 310, Vega 79092
Orange—Ms. Pat Sanderson, PO Box 457, Orange 77630
Palo Pinto—Carol Holmes, PO Box 250, Palo Pinto 76484
Panola—Louis Wall, 2 Ball Park Rd., Carthage 75633
Parker—Larry Hammonds, 118 W. Columbia, Weatherford 76086
Parmer—Ron Proctor, PO Box 56, Bovina 79009
Pecos—Ann Stapp, PO Box 237, Fort Stockton 79735
Polk—Clyde Arrendell, 312 N. Washington, Livingston 77351
Potter—Jim Childers, PO Box 7190, Amarillo 79114
Presidio—Irma Salgado, PO Box 879, Marfa 79843
Rains—Terry Green, PO Box 70, Emory 75440
Randall—Jim Childers, PO Box 7190, Amarillo 79114
Reagan—Byron Bitner, PO Box 8, Big Lake 76932
Real—Ruth Sanderlin, PO Box 158, Leakey 78873
Red River—Jan Raulston, PO Box 461, Clarksville 75426
Reeves—Carol King Markham, PO Box 1229, Pecos 79772
Refugio—Bettye Kret, PO Box 156, Refugio 78377
Roberts—Carol Billingsley, PO Box 458, Miami 79059
Robertson—Dan Brewer, PO Box 998, Franklin 77856
Rockwall—Ray Helm, 106 N. San Jacinto, Rockwall 75087
Runnels—Gene Stewart, PO Box 524, Ballinger 76821
Rusk—Melvin Cooper, PO Box 7, Henderson 75653
Sabine—Jim Nethery, PO Box 137, Hemphill 75948
San Augustine—Jamie Doherty, 122 N. Harrison, San Augustine 75972
San Jacinto—Mac Ridley, PO Box 1170, Coldspring 77331
San Patricio—Kathryn Vermillion, PO Box 938, Sinton 78387
San Saba—Henry J. Warren, 423 E. Wallace, San Saba 76877
Schleicher—Ray Ballew, PO Box 936, Eldorado 76936

Scurry—L.R. Peveler, 2612 College Ave., Snyder 79549
Shackelford—Bruce Bailey, PO Box 565, Albany 76430
Shelby—Keith Kraemer, 5907 Loop 500, Center 75935
Sherman—Teresa Edmond, PO Box 239, Stratford 79084
Smith—Michael Barnett, 245 South S.E. Loop 323, Tyler 75702
Somervell—Sandra Montgomery, 112 Allen Dr., Glen Rose 76043
Starr—José Jaime Treviño, PO Box 137, Rio Grande City 78582
Stephens—Troy Sloan, PO Box 351, Breckenridge 76424
Sterling—Linda Low, PO Box 28, Sterling City 76951
Stonewall—Ozella E. Warner, PO Box 308, Aspermont 79502
Sutton—Rex Ann Friess, 300 E. Oak, Sonora 76950
Swisher—Rose Lee Powell, PO Box 8, Tulia 79088
Tarrant—John Marshall, 2315 Gravel Rd., Fort Worth 76118
Taylor—Richard Petree, PO Box 1800, Abilene 79604
Terrell—Blain Chriesman, PO Box 747, Sanderson 79848
Terry—Ronny Burran, PO Box 426, Brownfield 79316
Throckmorton—Linda Carrington, PO Box 788, Throckmorton 76483-0788
Titus—Burt Lively, PO Box 528, Mount Pleasant 75456
Tom Green—Elvin Field, PO Box 3307, San Angelo 76902
Travis—Art Cory, PO Box 149012, Austin 78714
Trinity—Allen McKinley, PO Box 950, Groveton 75845
Tyler—Travis Chalmers, Drawer 9, Woodville 75979
Upshur—Louise Stracener, PO Box 280, Gilmer 75644

Upton—Jo Beth Wright, PO Box 1110, McCamey 79752
Uvalde—Brownie Jones, 209 N. High, Uvalde 78801
Val Verde—Buster Vernor, PO Box 1059, Del Rio 78841
Van Zandt—Chris Becker, PO Box 926, Canton 75103
Victoria—Terry Turner, 1611 E. North, Victoria 77901
Walker—Grover Cook, PO Box 1798, Huntsville 77342
Waller—David Piwonka, PO Box 159, Katy 77492
Ward—Arlice Wittie, PO Box 905, Monahans 79756
Washington—Charles Gaskamp, PO Box 681, Brenham 77834
Webb—Sergio Delgado, PO Box 719, Laredo 78042
Wharton—Larry Holub, PO Box 1068, Wharton 77488
Wheeler—Larry Schoenhals, PO Box 1200, Wheeler 79096
Wichita—Lanier Wilson, PO Box 5172, Wichita Falls 76307
Wilbarger—Doyle Graham Sr., PO Box 1519, Vernon 76384
Willacy—Augustin Colchado, Rt. 2, Box 256, Raymondville 78580
Williamson—Bill Carroll, PO Box 1120, Georgetown 78627
Wilson—Carlton R. Pape (Interim), Box 849, Floresville 78114
Winkler—Helen Oldham, PO Box 1219, Kermit 79745
Wise—Mickey Hand, 206 S. State, Decatur 76234
Wood—Carson Wages, PO Box 518, Quitman 75783
Yoakum—Saundra Stephens, PO Box 748, Plains 79355
Young—Pat Butler, PO Box 337, Graham 76450
Zapata—Rosalva Guerra, PO Box 2315, Zapata 78076
Zavala—Alberto Mireles, 323 W. Zavala, Crystal City 78839 ☆

Wet-Dry Counties

When approved in local-option elections in "wet" precincts of counties, sale of **liquor by the drink** is permitted in Texas. This resulted from adoption of an amendment to the Texas Constitution in 1970 and subsequent legislation, followed by local-option elections. This amendment marked the first time in 50 years that the sale of liquor by the drink was legal in Texas.

The list below shows the wet-or-dry status of counties in Texas as of Aug 31, 1996. A dagger (†) indicates counties in which the sale of mixed beverages is legal in all or part of the county (97). An asterisk (*) indicates counties wholly wet (37). All others are dry in part (79).

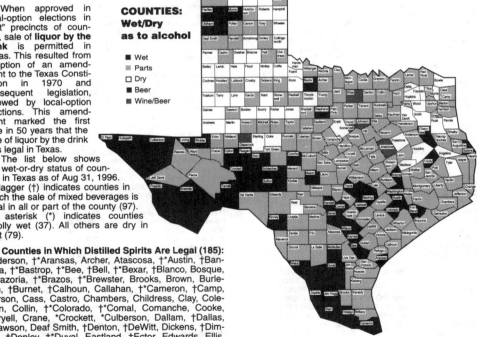

COUNTIES: Wet/Dry as to alcohol

- ■ Wet
- ▨ Parts
- ☐ Dry
- ■ Beer
- ▨ Wine/Beer

Counties in Which Distilled Spirits Are Legal (185): Anderson, †*Aransas, Archer, Atascosa, †*Austin, †Bandera, †*Bastrop, †*Bee, †Bell, †*Bexar, †Blanco, Bosque, †Brazoria, †*Brazos, †*Brewster, Brooks, Brown, Burleson, †Burnet, †Calhoun, Callahan, †*Cameron, †Camp, Carson, Cass, Castro, Chambers, Childress, Clay, Coleman, Collin, †*Colorado, †*Comal, Comanche, Cooke, Coryell, Crane, *Crockett, *Culberson, Dallam, †Dallas, †Dawson, Deaf Smith, †Denton, †DeWitt, Dickens, †Dimmit, †Donley, †*Duval, Eastland, †Ector, Edwards, Ellis, †*El Paso, †Falls, Fannin, Fayette, †*Fort Bend, †Frio, †Galveston, †Garza, †Gillespie, †Goliad, Gonzales, Gray, Grayson, Gregg, †Grimes, †Guadalupe, Hall, Hamilton, Hardin, †Harris, Harrison, Haskell, †Hays, †Henderson, †*Hidalgo, †Hill, †Hockley, Hood, †Howard, †*Hudspeth, Hunt, Hutchinson, Jack, †Jackson, †Jasper, Jeff Davis.

Also †Jefferson, †*Jim Hogg, †Jim Wells, *Karnes, Kaufman, †*Kendall, Kenedy, †Kerr, Kimble, King, †*Kinney, †Kleberg, †Lamar, Lampasas, †La Salle, †Lavaca, †Lee, Leon, Liberty, Lipscomb, Live Oak, †Llano, †*Loving, †Lubbock, Marion, †Matagorda, †Maverick, †McCulloch, †McLennan, †Medina, Menard, †Midland, Milam, Mills, Mitchell, Montague, †Montgomery, †*Moore, Nacogdoches, †Navarro, Newton, Nolan, †Nueces.

Also, †Orange, Palo Pinto, Parker, Pecos, †Polk, †Potter, †*Presidio, Rains, †Randall, *Reagan, Red River, †Reeves, Refugio, Robertson, †Rockwall, Runnels, San Augustine, San Jacinto, †San Patricio, San Saba, *Schleicher, Shackelford, Shelby, †*Starr, Stonewall, †*Sutton, †Tarrant, †Taylor, *Terrell, †Titus, †Tom Green, †*Travis, *Trinity, Upshur, *Upton, Uvalde, †Val Verde, †Victoria, †Walker, †Waller, Ward, †Washington, †*Webb, †Wharton, †Wichita, Wilbarger, †Willacy, †Williamson, †*Wilson, *Winkler, Young, †*Zapata, †Zavala.

Counties in Which Only 4 Percent Beer Is Legal (11): Baylor, Caldwell, Cherokee, Concho, Hartley, Irion, Mason, McMullen, Oldham, Sabine, Stephens.

Counties in Which 14 Percent or Less Alcoholic Beverages Are Legal (5): Glasscock, Johnson, Limestone, Somervell, Wise.

Counties Wholly Dry (53): Andrews, Angelina, Armstrong, Bailey, Borden, Bowie, Briscoe, Cochran, Coke, Collingsworth, Cottle, Crosby, Delta, Erath, Fisher, Floyd, Foard, Franklin, Freestone, Gaines, Hale, Hansford, Hardeman, Hemphill, Hopkins, Houston, Jones, Kent, Knox, Lamb, Lynn, Madison, Martin, Morris, Motley, Ochiltree, Panola, Parmer, Real, Roberts, Rusk, Scurry, Sherman, Smith, Sterling, Swisher, Terry, Throckmorton, Tyler, Van Zandt, Wheeler, Wood, Yoakum. ☆

County Courts

Below are listed county courts, including county courts at law, probate courts, juvenile/domestic relations courts, criminal courts and criminal courts of appeals as reported by the county clerks as of May 1997. Other courts with jurisdiction in each county can be found in the list on pages 407-409. Other county and district officials can be found on pages 448-458.

Anderson County Court at Law: J. Christopher Kolstad.

Angelina County Courts at Law: No. 1, Joe E. Martin; No. 2, Holly Perkins-Meyers.

Austin County Court at Law: Gladys M. Oakley.

Bastrop County Court at Law: Benton Eskew.

Bell County Courts at Law: No. 1, Edward S. Johnson; No. 2, John Barina.

Bexar County Courts at Law: No. 1, Anthony J. Ferro; No. 2, H. Paul Canales; No. 3, Shay Gebhardt; No. 4, Sarah Garrahan-Moulder; No. 5, Timothy F. Johnson; No. 6, Ray Harris Adams; No. 7, Bill C. White; No. 8, Karen Crouch; No. 9, Wayne A. Christian II. **County Probate Courts:** No. 1, Polly Jackson Spencer; No. 2, Sandee Bryan Marion.

Brazoria County Courts at Law: No. 1, Jerri Lee Mills; No. 2, Garvin Germany Jr.; No. 3, James Blackstock.

Brazos County Courts at Law: No. 1, Steve Smith; No. 2, Sarah Ryan.

Caldwell County Court at Law: Edward L. Jarrett.

Calhoun County Court at Law: Michael M. Fricke.

Cameron County Courts at Law: No. 1, Everardo Garcia; No. 2, Migdalia Lopez.

Cherokee County Court at Law: A. LeRue Dixon

Collin County Courts at Law: No. 1, Weldon Copeland; No. 2, Jerry Lewis; No. 3, John O'Keefe Barry; No. 4, Mark Rusch.

Comal County Court at Law: Fred Clark.

Coryell County Court at Law: Susan Stephens.

* **Dallas County Courts at Law:** No. 1, David W. Evans; No. 2, Carlos Lopez; No. 3, Victoria Welcome; No. 4, Bruce Woody; No. 5, Charles Stokes. **County Criminal Courts:** No. 1, Henry M. Wade Jr.; No. 2, Jim Pruitt; No. 3, Mike Schwille; No. 4, Ralph Taite; No. 5, Tom Fuller; No. 6, Phil Barker; No. 7, Elizabeth Crowder; No. 8, Vic Cunningham; No. 9, Keith Anderson; No. 10, Marshall W. Gandy. **County Probate Courts:** No. 1, Nikki DeShazo; No. 2, Robert E. Price; No. 3, Joe H. Loving Jr. **County Criminal Courts of Appeals:** No. 1, Kenneth Vaughan; No. 2, Lynn Burson.

* **Denton County Courts at Law:** No. 1, Darlene Whitten. **County Criminal Court No. 1:** Jim E. Crouch; **No. 2:** Virgil Vahlenkamp. **Probate Court:** Don Windle.

Ector County Courts at Law: No. 1, J. A. (Jim) Bobo; No. 2, Mark D. Owens.

Ellis County Court at Law: Bob Carroll.

El Paso County Courts at Law: No. 1, Ricardo Herrera; No. 2, John L. Fashing; No. 3, Javier Alvarez; No. 4, Kitty Schild; No. 5, Herbert Cooper. **County Probate Court:** Max Higgs. **Domestic Relations/Juvenile Court:** Phil Martinez.

Erath County Court at Law: Bart McDougal.

Fort Bend County Courts at Law: No. 1, Larry Wagenbach; No. 2, Walter S. McMeans; No. 3, Susan G. Lowery.

Galveston County Courts at Law: No. 1, Mary Nell Crapitto; No. 2, C.G. Dibrell III; **County Probate Court:** Jerome Jones.

Grayson County Courts at Law: No. 1, Donald L. Jarvis; No. 2, Kenneth D. Daniel.

Gregg County Court at Law: John Sharp; **Domestic Relations Court,** Robin D. Sage.

Guadalupe County Court at Law: Linda Z. Jones.

Harris County Courts at Law: No. 1, Eugene Chambers; No. 2, Tom Sullivan; No. 3, Lynn Bradshaw-Hull; No. 4, Cynthia Crowe. **County Criminal Courts at Law:** No. 1, Reagan C. Helm; No. 2, Michael A. Peters; No. 3, Donald W. Jackson; No. 4, James Anderson; No. 5, Hannah Chow; No. 6, J.R. Musslewhite; No. 7, Shelly P. Hancock; No. 8, Neel Richardson; No. 9, Analia Wilkerson; No. 10, Sherman Ross; No. 11, Diane Bull; No. 12, Robin Brown; No. 13, Mark Atkinson; No. 14, Jim Barkley; No. 15, Jean Spradling Hughes. **County Probate Courts:** No. 1, Russell Austin; No. 2, Mike Wood; No. 3, Jim Scanlan; No. 4, William C. McCulloch.

Harrison County Court at Law: Jim Ammerman II.

Hays County Courts at Law: No. 1, Howard S. Warner; No. 2, Linda A. Rodriguez.

Henderson County Court at Law: D. Matt Livingston.

* **Hidalgo County Courts at Law:** No. 1, Rodolfo Delgado; No. 2, G. Jaime Garza; No. 3, Homero Garza; No. 4, Federico Garza.

* **Hopkins County Court at Law:** Amy Smith.

Houston County Court at Law: Lynn Markham.

Hunt County Court at Law: Steve Shipp.

Jefferson County Courts at Law: No. 1, Alfred S. Gerson; No. 2, Harold Plessala; No. 3, John Paul Davis.

Johnson County Courts at Law: No. 1, Tommy Altaras; No. 2, William R. Anderson Jr.

Kaufman County Court at Law: Joe M. Parnell.

Kerr County Court at Law: Spencer W. Brown.

Kleberg County Court at Law: Martin J. Chiuminatto Jr.

Liberty County Court at Law: Chap B. Cain III.

Lubbock County Courts at Law: No. 1, Sam Medina; No. 2, G. Thomas Cannon; No. 3, Paula Lanehart.

McLennan County Courts at Law: No. 1, David Hodges; No. 2, Mike Gassaway

Medina County Court at Law: Watt Murrah.

Midland County Courts at Law: No. 1, Al Walvoord; No. 2, Marvin L. Moore.

Montgomery County Courts at Law: No. 1, Suzanne Stovall; No. 2, Jerry Winfree; No. 3, Mason Martin.

Moore County Court at Law: Delwin T. McGee.

Nacogdoches County Court at Law: J. Jack Yarbrough.

Nolan County Court at Law: Glen Harrison.

Nueces County Courts at Law: No. 1, Robert J. Vargas; No. 2, Hector de Peña Jr.; No. 3, Marisela Saldaña; No. 4, James E. Klager. **Juvenile Court:** Cynthia Morales.

Orange County Court at Law: Michael W. Shuff.

Panola County Court at Law: Rick McPherson.

Parker County Court at Law: Graham Quisenberry.

Polk County Court at Law: Stephen Phillips.

Potter County Courts at Law: No. 1, W. F. "Corky" Roberts; No. 2, Richard P. Dambold.

Randall County Court at Law: Darrell R. Carey.

Reeves County Court at Law: Lee S. Green.

Rusk County Court at Law: Darrell Hyatt.

San Patricio County Court at Law: Michael E. Welborn.

Smith County Courts at Law: No. 1, Thomas A. Dunn; No. 2, Randall L. Rogers.

Starr County Court at Law: Alex W. Gabert.

Tarrant County Courts at Law: No. 1, R. Brent Keis; No. 2, Steve Wallace; No. 3, Vincent G. Sprinkle. **County Criminal Courts at Law:** No. 1, Sherry Hill; No. 2, Michael D. Mitchell; No. 3, Billy D. Mills; No. 4, Wallace Bowman; No. 6, Rufus J. Adcock; No. 7, Cheril Hardy; No. 8, Daryl Coffee; No. 9, Brent A. Carr; No. 10, Phil Sorrels. **County Criminal Court of Appeals:** Mamie Bush Johnson. **Probate Courts:** No. 1, Steve M. King; No. 2, Patrick Ferchill.

Taylor County Courts at Law: No. 1, Jack Grant; No. 2, Barbara Rollins. **Domestic Relations Court:** Aleta Hacker.

Tom Green County Court at Law: No. 1, Ronald L. Blann; No. 2, Penney Roberts.

Travis County Courts at Law: No. 1, J. David Phillips; No. 2, Orlinda Naranjo; No. 3, David Crain; No. 5, Wilfred Aguilar; No. 6, David Puryear; No. 7, Brenda Kennedy. **Probate Court:** Guy Herman;

Val Verde County Court at Law: James M. Simmonds.

Victoria County Courts at Law: No. 1, Laura A. Weiser; No. 2, Juan Velasquez III.

Walker County Court at Law: Barbara Hale.

Waller County Court at Law: June Jackson.

Washington County Court at Law: Matthew Reue.

Webb County Courts at Law: No. 1, Raul Vasquez; No. 2, Jesús Garza.

Wichita County Courts at Law: No. 1, Jim Hogan; No. 2, Tom Bacus.

* **Williamson County Courts at Law:** No. 1, Kevin D. Henderson; No. 2, Robert "Skip" Morse.

Wise County Court at Law: Melton D. Cude. ☆

* Incomplete information received from county clerk. This information is taken from the Texas Judicial System Directory, 1997, Office of Court Administration.

Texas County and District Officials — Table No. 1

County Seats, County Judges, County Clerks, County Attorneys, County Treasurers, Tax Assessors-Collectors and Sheriffs.

See Table No. 2 on pages following this table for District Clerks, District Attorneys and County Commissioners. Judges in county courts at law, as well as probate courts, juvenile/domestic relations courts, county criminal courts and county criminal courts of appeal, can be found on page 447. The officials listed here are elected by popular vote. Names preceded by an asterisk (*) were not furnished to us by the county clerk; the name here is from most recent unofficial sources available to us.

County	County Seat	County Judge	County Clerk	County Attorney	County Treasurer	Assessor-Collector	Sheriff
Anderson	Palestine	Jack W. Rogers	Lena Smith		Sharon Peterson	Connie Rose	Mickey Hubert
Andrews	Andrews	Gary W. Gaston	F. Wm. Hoermann	Katrina Jackson	Office abolished 11-5-85.	Royce Underwood	Wayne Farmer
Angelina	Lufkin	Joe Berry	JoAnn Chastain	Ed Jones	Joann Denby	Bill Shanklin	Kent Henson
Aransas	Rockport	Agnes A. "Tony" Harden	Peggy L. Friebele	James L. Anderson Jr.	Marvine Wix	Jeri D. Cox	David L. Petrusaitis
Archer	Archer City	Paul O. Wylie Jr.	Jane Ham	R.B. Morris	Betty Tarno	Teresa Martin	Melvin Brown
Armstrong	Claude	Hugh Reed	Joe Reck		Ray C. Minkley	Ronald Patterson	Carmella Jones
Atascosa	Jourdanton	Deborah Herber	Laquita Hayden	R. Thomas Franklin	Gloria P. Smith	Barbara Schorsch	Tommy Williams
Austin	Bellville	Carolyn Bilski	Carrie Gregor	Carissa Cleavinger	Betty Krueger	Joyce Kokemor	R. DeWayne Burger
Bailey	Muleshoe	Marilyn Cox	Billie R. Downing	K. H. Schneider	Dorothy Turner	Kathleen Hayes	Jerry N. Hicks
Bandera	Bandera	Richard A. Evans	Bernice Bates		Kay Welch	Jean Stevens	James MacMillan
Bastrop	Bastrop	Peggy Walicek	Shirley Wilhelm		Doris Oldfield	Barbara Brinkmeyer	Richard Hernandez
Baylor	Seymour	Robin R. Smajstrla	Doris S. Rushing	Lee Price Fernon	Mary Benge	Jeanette Holub	Luke Griffin
Bee	Beeville	Jimmy Martinez	Julia V. Torres	Mike Knight	Office abolished 11-2-82.	Andrea W. Gibbud	Robert L. Horn
Bell	Belton	John Garth	Vada Sutton	Rick Miller	Charles Jones	Janelle Burson	Dan Smith
Bexar	San Antonio	Cyndi Taylor Krier	Gerry Rickhoff		Office abolished 11-6-84.	Sylvia S. Romo	Ralph Lopez
Blanco	Johnson City	George E. Byars Jr.	Dorothy Uecker	Dean C. Myane	Doris Cage	Hollis Boatright	William R. "Bill" Elsbury
Borden	Gail	Van L. York	Joyce Herridge		Kenneth P. Bennett	Royale D. Lewis	Royale D. Lewis
Bosque	Meridian	Bobby Jo Conrad	Jane H. (Janie) Staley	Patricia Ferguson	Randy Pullin	Denise E. Wallace	Tim S. Gage
Bowie	Boston	James M. Carlow	Marylene Megason		Pansy Baird	Toni Barron	Mary Choate
Brazoria	Angleton	John Willy	Dolly Bailey		Sharon L. Reynolds	Ray M. Cornett	E. J. "Joe" King
Brazos	Bryan	Al Jones	Mary Ann Ward	Jim Kuboviak	Kay Hamilton	Gerald "Buddy" Winn	Chris Kirk
Brewster	Alpine	Val Clark Beard	Berta Rios Martinez	Steve Houston	Hortencia Ramos	Jerry Ratcliff	Steve Whitley
Briscoe	Silverton	Jimmy Burson	Bess McWilliams	William P. (Bill) Smith	Janice S. Hill	Betty Ann Stephens	Jerry D. Beck
Brooks	Falfurrias	Joe B. Garcia	Ruben Castellano	David T. Garcia	Gilberto Vela	Balde Lozano	Balde Lozano
Brown	Brownwood	E. Ray West III	Margaret Woods		Judy Stirman	Linda Lewis Parker	Glen Smith
Burleson	Caldwell	Paul J. Batista	Evelyn M. Henry	Joseph J. Skrivanek III	Beth Andrews Bills	Sandra Faust	Thomas E. Barber
Burnet	Burnet	Martin McLean	Janet Parker	Robert Klaeger	Katy Gilmore	Sherri Frazier	Joe Pollock
Caldwell	Lockhart	Rebecca M. Hawener	Nina S. Sells		Amelia G. Rizzuto	Mary Smith	Mike Bading
Calhoun	Port Lavaca	Howard G. Hartzog	Marlene Paul	Allen Wright	Sharron Marek	Annette Baker	B.B. Browning
Callahan	Baird	Bill Johnson	Darlene Walker		Dora Hounshell	Bun Barry	Eddie G. Curtis
Cameron	Brownsville	Gilberto Hinojosa	Joe G. Rivera	Douglas Wright	Eddie A. Gonzalez	Tony Yzaguirre Jr.	Omar Lucio
Camp	Pittsburg	Preston Combest	Elaine Young	James W. Wallace	LaJuana Leftwich	Brenda Irby	Alan D. McCandless
Carson	Panhandle	Jay Robert Roselius	Barbara S. White	Scott Sherwood	Jeannie Cunningham	Roslyn Watson	Loren Brand
Cass	Linden	Charles L. McMichael	Jannis Mitchell	Randal Lee	Jo Ellen Whatley	Bobbie Derrick	Paul W. Boone
Castro	Dimmitt	Irene Miller	Joyce M. Thomas		Janice Shelton	Billy Hackelman	C. D. Fitzgearld
Chambers	Anahuac	Oscar Nelson	Norma W. Rowland	Charles Brack	Carren Sparks	Margie Henry	Philip Burkhalter
Cherokee	Rusk	Harry Tilley	Fairy Upshaw	Robert (Bob) McNatt	Diann Norton	Linda Beard	James Campbell
Childress	Childress	Dean Decker	Nancy Garrison	Greg Buckley	Office abolished 11-5-85.	Juanell Halford	Kevin Overstreet
Clay	Henrietta	Kenneth J. Liggett	Kay Hutchison	Eddy Atkins	Liz Kitchens	Linda Wood Overstreet	Paul Bevering
Cochran	Morton	Robert J. Yeary	Rita Tyson	J. C. Adams Jr.	Sue Sims Brock	Betty Akin	Wallace Stalcup
Coke	Robert Lee	Jackie Walker	Ettie Hubbard	Lane Arthur	Jean Abbe	D. Kristeen Roe	Michael L. (Mike) Harris
Coleman	Coleman	Sherrill Radsdale	JoAnn Hale	Joe Dan LeMay	Kay LeMay	Donna Seymore	Wade Turner
Collin	McKinney	Ron Harris	Helen Starnes		Office abolished 11-5-85.	Kenneth L. Maun	Terry G. Box
Collingsworth	Wellington	Jim Forrester	Karen Coleman	Charles W. Darter	Yvonne Brewer	Rose Mary Throne	Dale Tarver
Colorado	Columbus	Vince Slominski	Darlene Hayek	John (Julian) Moore	Joyce M. Stancik	Mary Jane Poenitzsch	R.H. "Curley" Wied
Comal	New Braunfels	Carter Casteel	Joy Streater	Bill M. Reimer	R. A. "Bart" Bartholomew	Gloria K. Clennan	Bob Holder
Comanche	Comanche	John M. Weaver	Betty Conway	C. H. (Terry) McCall	Billy Ruth Rust	Gay Horton	Billy J. Works

County	County Seat	County Judge	County Clerk	County Attorney	County Treasurer	Assessor-Collector	Sheriff
Concho	Paint Rock	Allen Amos	Barbara K. Hoffman	Bill Campbell	Dorothy Kirkpatrick	William J. "Bill" Fiveash	William J. "Bill" Fiveash
Cooke	Gainesville	Paul F. Hesse	Evelyn Walterscheid	Tanya McDaniel Davis	Janet Johnson	Billy Jean Knight	Michael E. Compton
Coryell	Gatesville	John A. Hull	Barbara Simpson	Edwin E. Powell Jr.	Donna Medford	Barbara Sue McKamie	Gerald Kitchens
Cottle	Paducah	Billy J. Gilbert	Beckey J. Tucker	John H. Richards	Atha Prater	Rue Young	Roy LeHew
Crane	Crane	Arlen White	Maxine Willis	Gene Clack	Gayla Phillips	Rebecca M. Gonzales	Danny Simmons
Crockett	Ozona	Jeffrey K. Sutton	Debbi Puckett	William S. Mason	Burl J. Myers	Tom Stokes	Shane Fenton
Crosby	Crosbyton	Jerry Robertson	Betty J. Pierce	C. Michael Ward	Joyce M. Whitehead	Anna R. Rodriguez	Lavoice "Red" Riley
Culberson	Van Horn	John Conoly	Linda McDonald	Stephen L. Mitchell	Norma Hernandez	Amalia Hernandez	Glenn A. Humphries
Dallam	Dalhart	David D. Field	LuAnn Taylor	Greg Oelke	Wes Ritchey	Patricia Radford	E. H. Little
Dallas	Dallas	Lee Jackson	Earl Bullock		Bill Melton	David Childs	Jim Bowles
Dawson	Lamesa	Charles C. Arthur	Gloria Vera	Steven B. Payson	Gene DeFee	Diane Hogg	J. Terry Brown
Deaf Smith	Hereford	Tom Simons	David Ruland		Nan Rogers	Margaret del Toro	Joe C. Brown Jr.
Delta	Cooper	John I. Hickman	Patsy P. Barton	Frank D. Moore	Glynana Stockton	Dawn Curtis	Benny Fisher
Denton	Denton	Jeff Moseley	Tim Hodges		Claudia Mulkey	Mary Horn	Weldon Lucas
DeWitt	Cuero	Ben E. Prause	Ann Drehr	Raymond H. Reese	Peggy Ledbetter	Susie Dreyer	Clifton G. Foulds
Dickens	Dickens	Woodie McArthur Jr.	Yvonne (Tookie) Cash	Robert Heald	Druline Rape	Dexter Z. Perez	*Ken Brendle
Dimmit	Carrizo Springs	Charles D. Johnson	Mario Z. Garcia	James B. Davis	Elisa G. Duran	Esther Z. Perez	Candido R. DeAnda Jr.
Donley	Clarendon	W. R. Christal	Fay Vargas	Stuart Messer (pro tem)	Wanda Smith	Wilma Lindley	William J. Thompson
Duval	San Diego	Edmundo B. Garcia Jr.	Oscar Garcia Jr.	José Ramón Falcón	Daniel S. Lopez Jr.	Zaragosa Gutierrez III	Santiago Barrera Jr.
Eastland	Eastland	Scott Bailey	Joann Johnson	Tracey Bright	Ruth Pugliese Hart	Sandra S. Cagle	Wayne Bradford
Ector	Odessa	Jim T. Jordan	Barbara Bedford	Allen Ray Moody	Carolyn Bowen	Lea Taylor	Reginald Yearwood
Edwards	Rocksprings	Neville G. Smart Jr.	Dorothy R. Hatley	Joe F. Grubbs	Lupe Sifuentes-Enriquez	Teresa Sweeten	Don G. Letsinger
Ellis	Waxahachie	Al Cornelius	Cindy Polley		Mark Price	Carol Calvert	Ray Stewart
El Paso	El Paso	Charles W. Mattox	Hector Enriquez Jr.	José Rodriguez	Office abolished 1-1-86.	Victor Flores	Leo Samaniego
Erath	Stephenville	Tab Thompson	Nelda Crockett	William H. Oxford	Donna Kelley	Jennifer Schlicke	Tommy Bryant
Falls	Marlin	Robert B. Cunningham	Bryant L. Hinson	Thomas B. Sehon	Marilyn Ejem	Kate Vande Veegaete	John F. Trousdale
Fannin	Bonham	Derrell Hall	Margaret Gilbert	James S. Moss	Florence Keahey	Earlene Wix	Talmage Moore
Fayette	La Grange	Edward F. Janecka	Carolyn Kubos Roberts	John W. Wied	Office abolished 11-3-87.	Carol Johnson	Rick Vandel
Fisher	Roby	Marshal Bennett	Bettie Rivers	Robie Robinson	Martha Williamson	Betty Mize	Gene Pack
Floyd	Floydada	William D. Hardin	Margaret Collier		Mary Shurbet	Penny Golightly	Bily R. (Royce) Gilmore
Foard	Crowell	Charlie Bell	Sherry Weatherred	Daryl Halencak	Esther Kajs	Bobby D. Bond	Bobby D. Bond
Fort Bend	Richmond	Michael D. Rozell	Dianne Wilson	Ben W. "Bud" Childers	Kathy Hynson	Marsha P. Gaines	Milton Wright
Franklin	Mount Vernon	Wayne Foster	Tammie Dickson	Walt Sears Jr.	Marla Carrell	Marjorie Jaggers	Charles J. (Chuck) White
Freestone	Fairfield	Joel E. Lane	Mary Lynn White	Robert W. "Bob" Gage	Patricia Robinson	Carolyn Varley	Carl H. Burris
Frio	Pearsall	Carlos A. Garcia	Gloria Leal Cubriel	James W. Smith Jr.	Anna Luna Hernandez	Ysabela C. Peña	Jon Key
Gaines	Seminole	Max Townsend	Pat Lacy	Sterling Harmon	Linda Clark	Edith Renfroe	Bruce Jordan
Galveston	Galveston	James D. Yarbrough	Patricia Ritchie	Harvey Bazaman	Gerald Burks	Charles E. Wilson	Joe Max Taylor
Garza	Post	Giles W. Dalby	Sonny Gossett	Leslie C. Acker	Ruth Ann Young	Laura "Chita" Hataway	Kenneth Ratke
Gillespie	Fredericksburg	Mark Stroeher	Doris Lange	Jay Weinheimer	Jeanie Bel Crenwelge	Leola Brodbeck	Milton E. Jung
Glasscock	Garden City	Wilburn E. Bednar	Betty Pate	Hardy Wilkerson	Alan Dierschke	Royce Pruit	Royce Pruit
Goliad	Goliad	Steven G. Paulsgrove	Gail M. Turley	Brenda J. Heinold	Deborah Bego	Anna Lopez	J. K. McMahan
Gonzales	Gonzales	Henry H. Vollentine	Sonny Sievers	Robert B. Scheske	Marie Scoggins	Norma Jean DuBose	D. J. Brzozowski
Gray	Pampa	Richard D. Peet	Wanda Carter	Todd L. Alvey	Scott B. Hahn	Sammie Morris	Don Copeland
Grayson	Sherman	Horace A. Groff	Sara Jackson	Robert T. Jarvis	Virginia Hughes	John W. Ramsey	J. Keith Gary
Gregg	Longview	Mickey D. Smith	Laurie Woloszyn		Office abolished 1-1-88.	William Kirk Shields	Bobby Weaver
Grimes	Anderson	Ira E. (Bud) Haynie	David Pasket	Joe S. Falco Jr.	Phillis Allen	Connie Perry	Bill Foster
Guadalupe	Seguin	James E. Sagebiel	Lizzie M. Lorenz	Bob Covington	Larry Jones	Betty Boyd	Melvin L. Harborth
Hale	Plainview	Bill Hollars	Diane Williams	John M. Deaver II	Evelyn Carroll	Kemp Hinch	David B. Mull
Hall	Memphis	Kenneth E. Dale	Raye Bailey	Thomas E. White	Marion Bownds	Pat Floyd	Jarrett L. Wilde
Hamilton	Hamilton	Charles Garrett	Virginia Lovell	John L. Hutchison	Karen S. Tyson	Cynthia Roberts	W.R. "Randy" Murphree
Hansford	Spearman	Jim D. Brown	Kim V. Vera	Stanley K. Watson	Norma Jean Mackie	Helen Dry	R. L. McFarlin Jr.
Hardeman	Quanah	K. D. McNabb	Judy Cokendolpher	David Sheffield	Mary Ann Naylor	Darlene Gamble	Randy L. Akers
Hardin	Kountze	Tom Mayfield	Dee Hatton		Eddie Doggett	Billy Bruce Caraway	Ed Cain

County	County Seat	County Judge	County Clerk	County Attorney	County Treasurer	Assessor-Collector	Sheriff
Harris	Houston	Robert A. Eckels	Beverly B. Kaufman	Michael Fleming	Don Sumners	Carl S. Smith	Tommy Thomas
Harrison	Marshall	Rodney Gilstrap	Martha Dieste		Jamie Noland	Betty Wright	Bob Green
Hartley	Channing	Ronnie Gordon	Diane Thompson	William A. Cunningham	Dinkie Parman	John E. Williams Jr.	John E. Williams Jr.
Haskell	Haskell	David Davis	Rhonda Moeller	L. W. (Bill) Jones III	Willie Faye Tidrow	Bobbye Collins	Johnny Mills
Hays	San Marcos	Eddy A. Etheredge	Margie T. Villalpando		Michelle Tuttle	Luanne Caraway	Don Montague
Hemphill	Canadian	Bob Gober	Davene Hendershot		Claudette Hand	Gladene Woodside	Billy V. Bowen
Henderson	Athens	Tommy G. Smith	Gwen Moffeit	Charles Kessie	Carolyn Herrington	Milburn Chaney	H. B. Alfred
Hidalgo	Edinburg	Renato Cuellar	José Eloy Pulido	Lawrence E. Heffington	Norma Gonzalez	Armando Barrera	Enrique Escalon
Hill	Hillsboro	Tommy J. Walker	Ruth Pelham	Mark F. Pratt	Jewel Burton	Thomas J. Davis	Brent Button
Hockley	Levelland	Larry D. Sprowls	Mary K. Walker	J. M. "Pat" Phelan	Jo Beth Hittson	Christy Clevenger	Donald Caddell
Hood	Granbury	Don Cleveland	Anjanette Ables	R. Kelton Conner	Peggy Moreno	Sandra Tidwell	Allen Hardin
Hopkins	Sulphur Springs	Joe B. Minter	Debbie Shirley	VaLinda Hathcox	"Betty Moore	Jo Ruth Hodge	Charles "Butch" Adams
Houston	Crockett	R.C. "Chris" von Doenhoff	Nancy Huff	Donna Gordon Weesner	Dianne Rhone	Joan Lucas	Jimbo Rains
Howard	Big Spring	Ben Lockhart	Margaret Ray	C.E. (Mike) Thomas III	Bonnie Franklin	Kathy A. Sayles	W.B. "Bill" Jennings
Hudspeth	Sierra Blanca	James Peace	Patricia Bramblett	Thomas Chellis	Pilar R. West	Kay Scarbrough	Jerry Kresta
Hunt	Greenville	Joe Bobbitt	Linda Brooks	Peter Morgan	Louise Walker	Joyce Barrow	Don Anderson
Hutchinson	Stinnett	Jack L. Worsham	Carol Ann Herbst	Michael D. Milner	Kathy Sargent	Mary Lou Henderson	Michael L. Blackmon
Irion	Mertzon	Sidney Mabry	Reba Criner		Linda Pierce	Joyce Gray	Jimmy Martin
Jack	Jacksboro	Mitchell G. Davenport	Patsy Ramzy	Michael G. Mask	Floyd Easter	Sarah Pruit	Danny R. Nash
Jackson	Edna	Harrison Stafford II	Kenneth W. McElveen		Marcell Maresh Jr.	Donna Atzenhoffer	Kelly R. Janica
Jasper	Jasper	Joe Bobbitt	Evelyn Stott		Mary Jane Hancock	Robert C. Pace Jr.	Billy Rowles
Jeff Davis	Fort Davis	Peggy Robertson	Sue Blackley	Joseph James	Geen Parrott	Steve Bailey	Steve Bailey
Jefferson	Beaumont	Carl Griffith Jr.	Sandy Wilson	Tom Maness	Linda P. Robinson	Miriam K. Johnson	Mitch Woods
Jim Hogg	Hebbronville	Horacio S. Ramirez	Gloria Diana Rodriguez		Linda Jo G. Soliz	Marina Vasquez	Gilberto Ybañez
Jim Wells	Alice	L. Arnoldo Saenz	Arnoldo Gonzalez	Jesusa Sanchez-Vera	Pearlie Jo Valadez	Lucila Reynolds	Oscar Lopez
Johnson	Cleburne	Roger Harmon	Curtis H. Douglas	Bill Moore	Barbara Robinson-Cole	W.E. "Ed" Carroll	Bob L. Alford
Jones	Anson	Brad Rowland	Margaret Jones	Dwade R. King	Irene Hudson	Tom Isbell	Robby Wedeking
Karnes	Karnes City	Alfred Pawelek	Elizabeth Swize	John Wilson Berry	Sandra Garza	Phillis Pawelek	Bobby Mutz
Kaufman	Kaufman	Maxine Darst	Crissy Gann		Linda Spencer	Donna Sprague	Robert Harris
Kendall	Boerne	James W. (Bill) Gooden	Darlene Herrin	Pamela K. McKay	Barbara J. Schwope	James A. Hudson Jr.	Henry B. Hodge
Kenedy	Sarita	J.A. Garcia Jr.	Barbara B. Turcotte	Roy C. Turcotte	John W. Turcotte	Eleuteria S. Gonzalez	Rafael M. Cuellar Jr.
Kent	Jayton	Tommy Stanaland	Cornelia Cheyne	Howard Freemyer	Linda McCurry	Charles C. Alderman	Charles C. Alderman
Kerr	Kerrville	Robert A. Denson	Patricia Dye	David Motley	Barbara Nemec	Paula Rector	Frances A. Kaiser
Kimble	Junction	Delbert R. Roberts	Elaine Carpenter	Callan Graham	Sheila D'Spain	Michael Chapman	Michael Chapman
King	Guthrie	Royce McLaury	Tavia Vinson	Bobby Burnett	Mary Lee Hurt	Sadie Mote	Jim Waller
Kinney	Brackettville	Tommy Seargeant	Dora Elia Sandoval	Tully Shahan	Janis Floyd	Martha Peña-Hooten	L.K. (Buddy) Burgess
Kleberg	Kingsville	Pete de la Garza	Sam D. Deanda	Delma Rios	Elaine Maca	Melissa Treviño	Tony Gonzalez
Knox	Benjamin	David N. Perdue	Danny Speck	Bobby D. Burnett	Judie Whitten	Stanton Brown	Michael L. Carlson
Lamar	Paris	M.C. Superville	Kathy Lou Poole	J. Kerye Ashmore	Latricia Miller	Peggy Noble	Billy Joe McCoy
Lamb	Littlefield	Wayne Whiteaker	Bill Johnson	Mark Yarbrough	Janice B. Wells	Linda G. Charlton	Jerry Collins
Lampasas	Lampasas	Tommy Honeycutt	Connie Hartmann	Larry W. Allison	Patsy Young	Glenda Henderson	Gordon Morris
La Salle	Cotulla	Jimmy P. Patterson	Nora Mae Tyler	Edward Hargrove	Joel Rodriguez Jr.	Elida A. Linares	Luis Rene Benavidez
Lavaca	Hallettsville	Charles J. Rother	Henry J. Sitka	James W. Carr	Thomas M. Grahmann	Margaret M. Kallus	Robert E. Wurm
Lee	Giddings	E. W. Kraus	Carol Dismukes	Ted Weems	Joyce Mitschke	Virginia Jackson	Joe G. Goodson
Leon	Centerville	Donald "Gene" Douget	Carla N. McEachern	Tom Holleman	William D. Lemons	Louise Wilson	L.T. Watson
Liberty	Liberty	Lloyd Kirkham	Della Sellers	A.J. Hartel III	Winn Skidmore	Mark McClelland	O.J. Stewart
Limestone	Groesbeck	Elenor Holmes	Sue Lown	Don Cantrell	Imogene Archibald	Barbara Rader	Doyle Coslin
Lipscomb	Lipscomb	Willis V. Smith	Coeta Sperry	Randy M. Phillips	Pat Wyatt	Ann Word	James Robertson
Live Oak	George West	Jim Huff	Mildred James	J.R. "Rob" Schneider	Violet Person	Larry R. Busby	Larry R. Busby
Llano	Llano	J.P. Dodgen	Bette Sue Hoy	Cheryll Mabray	Ma'Joyce Swope	Anna Henderson	Nathan Garrett
Loving	Mentone	Donald C. Creager	Lenell Chandler		Ann Blair	Richard Putnam	Richard Putnam
Lubbock	Lubbock	Don McBeath	Ann Davidson		Connie H. Nicholson	Stephen P. Watt	D.L. "Sonny" Keesee
Lynn	Tahoka	J.F. Brandon	Ima Robinson	Jimmy B. Wright	Janet Porterfield	Sherry Pearce	Charlie Smith

County	County Seat	County Judge	County Clerk	County Attorney	County Treasurer	Assessor-Collector	Sheriff
Madison	Madisonville	Cecil N. Neely	Joyce M. Coleman	David Hammit	Judy Weathers	Judy Nickerson	Dan Douget
Marion	Jefferson	Gene S. Terry	Clairece Ford	James L. Finstrom	Dorothy T. Whatley	Mary Alice Biggs	Eugene H. Tefteller
Martin	Stanton	Bob Deavenport	Susie Hull	James L. McGilvray	H.D. Howard	Kathy Hull	Mike Welling
Mason	Mason	Tommy Reardon	Beatrice Langehennig	Rob Hoffman	Rita P. McMillan	Melvin James Metzger	Melvin James Metzger
Matagorda	Bay City	Loy E. Sneary	Sarah Vaughn	Jill Cornelius	Suzanne S. Kucera	William B. Wiginton	James Mitchell
Maverick	Eagle Pass	Rogelio Escobedo	Sara Montemayor	Ernesto G. Mireles	Manuel Reyes Jr.	Esteban Luna	Salvador Rios
McCulloch	Brady	Randy Young	Tina A. Smith	Jim Oglesby	Donna Robinett	Deena G. Moore	Clyde "Earl" Howell
McLennan	Waco	Jim Lewis	J.A. (Andy) Harwell		Bill Helton	A. F. "Buddy" Skeen	Jack Harwell
McMullen	Tilden	Elaine Franklin	Nell Hodgin		Donald Haynes Jr.	Mary K. Edwards	W. I. "Tito" Potts
Medina	Hondo	David F. Montgomery	Anna Van De Walle	Ralph Bernsen	Rita L. Moos	Loraine Neuman	Wesley Scott
Menard	Menard	Charles "Tim" Childers	Elsie Maserang	Ben Neel	Robert Bean	Brent Bratton	Bruce Hough
Midland	Midland	Jeff Norwood	Alice Brown	Russell Malm	Julie Fry	Kathy Hodge Reeves	Gary Painter
Milam	Cameron	Roger Hashem	La Verne Soefje	Hollis C. Lewis Jr.	Grover C. "Pete" York Jr.	Frances R. Price	Charles L. West
Mills	Goldthwaite	Randy Wright	Beulah L. Roberts	Tommy M. Adams	Patsy E. Miller	Darwin R. Odom	Darwin R. Odom
Mitchell	Colorado City	Ray Mayo	Debby Carlock	Mark Piland	Ann Hallmark	Faye Lee	Patrick Toombs
Montague	Montague	Cleve E. Steed	Gayle Edwards	Jeb McNew	James M. (Mike) Johnson	Lyndall (Lindy) Ritchie	Chris Hamilton
Montgomery	Conroe	Alan B. Sadler	Mark Turnbull	Frank Bass	Martha Gustavsen	J. R. Moore Jr.	Guy Williams
Moore	Dumas	Billie Faye Schumacher	Rhonnie C. Mayer	Rayford A. Ratliff	Phyllis Holmes	Joy Robertson	H.T. "Ted" Montgomery
Morris	Daingerfield	Vanoy Boozer	Doris McNatt	Richard Townsend	Peggy Campbell	Jerry L. Chambliss	Charles R. Blackburn
Motley	Matador	Laverna M. Price	Lucretia Campbell		Joe E. Campbell	Elaine Hart	James Berry Meador
Nacogdoches	Nacogdoches	Ocie L. Westmoreland	Carol Wilson	Bryan H. Davis	Kay Watkins	Janie Weatherly	Joe Evans
Navarro	Corsicana	James P. Bagnell	James F. Doolen	Patrick Batchelor	Joe Graves	Peggy Blackwell-Moore	Leslie Cotten
Newton	Newton	Lon M. Sharver	Mary Cobb	Edward Tracy	Ruth Dickerson	Beatrice Westbrook	Wayne Powell
Nolan	Sweetwater	Jack Aycock	Elsie Pierce	Lisa L. Peterson	Gayle Biggerstaff	Fonda Holman	Donnie Rannefeld
Nueces	Corpus Christi	Richard M. Borchard	Ernest M. Briones	Carl Lewis	Office abolished 11-3-87.	Ramiro "Ronnie" Canales	Larry Olivarez
Ochiltree	Perryton	Kenneth R. Donahue	Jane Hammerbeck	Bruce Roberson	Ginger Hays	Helen Bates	Joe Hataway
Oldham	Vega	Don R. Alfred	Becky Groneman	Donald L. Davis	Charlotte Cook	Cynthia Artho	David T. Medlin
Orange	Orange	Carl Thibodeaux	Karen Jo Vance	John Kimbrough	Vergie Moreland	Linda Gunstream	Mike White
Palo Pinto	Palo Pinto	Mickey D. West	Bobbie Smith	Phil Garrett	Tanya Fallin	Max Wheeler	Larry L. Watson
Panola	Carthage	John Cordray	Sue Grafton		Gloria Portman	Jean Whiteside	Jack Ellett
Parker	Weatherford	Ben Long	Jeane Brunson	Glen Wilson	Jim Thorp	Marjorie King	Jay Brown
Parmer	Farwell	Bonnie J. Clayton	Bonnie Warren	Charles Aycock	Anne G. Norton	Doris Herington	Rex Williams
Pecos	Fort Stockton	Fredie Capers	Judy Deerfield	Kriste Burnett	Barry McCallister	Santa Acosta	Bruce Wilson
Polk	Livingston	John P. Thompson	Barbara Middleton		Cheryl Tamez	Marion A. "Bid" Smith	Billy Ray Nelson
Potter	Amarillo	Arthur Ware	Sue Daniel	Sonya Letson	Judy Messer	L. R. (Bob) Roberts	Jimmy Don Boydston
Presidio	Presidio	Jake Brisbin Jr.	Ramona Lara	Teresa Todd	Mario S. Rivera	Melissa Catano	Danny Dominguez
Rains	Emory	Diana Fleming	Mary Sheppard	Victor Sellars	Teresa Northcutt	Richard Wilson	Richard Wilson
Randall	Canyon	Theodore "Ted" Wood	LeRoy Hutton		Geneva Bagwell	Carol Autry	Harold Hooks
Reagan	Big Lake	Mike Elkins	Billie Havis	J. Russell Ash	Nancy L. Ratliff	Sue Turner	Efrain "Frank" Gonzales
Real	Leakey	G. W. Twiligear Jr.	Bella A. Rubio	John A. Daniel	Kathy Brooks	Donna Brice	James Earl Brice
Red River	Clarksville	L. D. Williamson	Mary Hausler	Jack O. Herrington	Beverly White	Leslie Nix	Robert (Bob) Edrington
Reeves	Pecos	Jimmy B. Galindo	Dianne O. Florez	Walter M. Holcombe	Linda Clark	Elfida Zuniga	Arnulfo "Andy" Gomez
Refugio	Refugio	Charles S. Stone	Janelle Morgan	Robert P. McGuill	Betty Greebon	Veronica Rocha	Jim Hodges
Roberts	Miami	Vernon H. Cook	Donna L. Goodman	Richard J. Roach	Billie J. Lansford	Carol S. Billingsley	Bill Britton
Robertson	Franklin	Billy Lee Stellbauer	Mary B. Reagan	John C. Paschall	Jacqueline Vann	Charlene Bush	Gerald Yezak
Rockwall	Rockwall	William B. Lofland	Paulette Burks		Scott Self	Kathryn Feldpausch	Jacques I. Kiere
Runnels	Ballinger	Marilyn Egan	Linda Bruchmiller	John W. McGregor	Margarette Smith	Robin Burgess	William A. Baird
Rusk	Henderson	Sandra Hodges	Frank Hudson	Kyle Freeman	Nora Rousseau	Matt B. Johnson	James Stroud
Sabine	Hemphill	Jack Leath	Janice McDaniel	R. Earl Lord	Ollie Faye Sparks	Tammy Reeves	Thomas Phillips
San Augustine	San Augustine	Curt Goetz	Geraldine Smith	Michael J. Adams	Carol W. Vaughn	Deborah Woods	John Cartwright
San Jacinto	Coldspring	Robert E. Smith	Joyce Hogue		Charlene Everitt	Barbara Shelly	Lacy Rogers
San Patricio	Sinton	Josephine W. Miller	Dottie Maley	David Aken	Judy Burr	Thelma Kelley	Leroy Moody
San Saba	San Saba	Harlen Barker	Kim Wells	David M. Williams	Gayla Hawkins	John Benner	John Benner

County	County Seat	County Judge	County Clerk	County Attorney	County Treasurer	Assessor-Collector	Sheriff
Schleicher	Eldorado	Johnny F. Griffin	Peggy Williams	Marian Overstreet	Karen Henderson	Lou Ann Turner	David R. Doran
Scurry	Snyder	Ricky Fritz	Joan Bunch	Michael Hartman	Charlie Bell	Rona Sikes	Darren Jackson
Shackelford	Albany	Ross Montgomery	Frances Wheeler	Gary M. Brown (pro tem)	Sherry Enloe	Larry V. Bonner	Larry V. Bonner
Shelby	Center	Floyd A. Watson	Peaches Conway	Gary W. Rholes	Lamerle Davis	Janie Ruth Graves	Carl N. Shofner
Sherman	Stratford	W.C. Fesler	Mary Lou (M.L.) Albert	Kimberly Allen	Linda R. Keener	Valerie McAlister	Jack Haile
Smith	Tyler	Larry Craig	Mary Morris		Joyce Woodward Smith	Kay M. Smith	J. B. Smith
Somervell	Glen Rose	Dale McPherson	Lovella Williams	Ronald D. Hankins	Vicki Crisp	Dorothy Keller	Mac Yocham
Starr	Rio Grande City	José M. Martinez Jr.	Omar J. Garza	Romero Molina	David D. Porras	Carmen A. Peña	Eugenio (Gene) Falcón
Stephens	Breckenridge	Gary L. Fuller	Helen Haddock	Gary D. Trammel	Nancy Clary	Terry Sullivan	James D. "Jim" Reeves
Sterling	Sterling City	Robert L. Browne	Diane A. Haar	Robert Herring Jr.	Beth Kilpatrick	Joy Manning	Don Howard
Stonewall	Aspermont	Bobby F. McGough	Betty L. Smith	Norman Arnett	Linda Messick	Joyce Y. McNutt	Bill Mullen
Sutton	Sonora	Carla Garner	Bobbie Smith	David W. Wallace	Joyce H. Chalk	Peggy W. Sharp	W. W. "Bill" Webster
Swisher	Tulia	Harold Keeter	Brenda Hudson	J. Michael Criswell	Lanelle Dovel	Shirley Whitehead	Larry P. Stewart
Tarrant	Fort Worth	Tom Vandergriff	Suzanne Henderson		Office abolished 4-2-83.	June Garrison	David Williams
Taylor	Abilene	Lee Hamilton	Janice Lyons		Laura Browder	Lavena Cheek	Jack Dieken
Terrell	Sanderson	S.D. "Dudley" Harrison	Martha Allen	Marsha Monroe	Sherry Hall	Y. E. "Chel" Duarte	Y. E. "Chel" Duarte
Terry	Brownfield	Douglas Ryburn	Ann Willis	G. Dwayne Pruitt	Bobbye Jo Floyd	Redelle Davis-Cox	Jerry L. Johnson
Throckmorton	Throckmorton	Trey Carrington	Cathey Mitchell	R. David Helton	Brenda Rankin	Greg Dunlap	Greg Dunlap
Titus	Mt. Pleasant	Danny P. Crooks	Sherry Jo Mars	Tim R. Taylor	Cynthia Agan	June Roach	Ricky W. Poole
Tom Green	San Angelo	Michael D. Brown	Judith Hawkins	Thomas M. Goff	Donna Long	Cindy Jetton	Dan Gray
Travis	Austin	Bill Aleshire	Dana DeBeauvoir	Ken Oden	Delores Ortega-Carter	Nelda Wells Spears	Margo Frasier
Trinity	Groveton	Mark Evans	Elaine I. Lockhart	Joe Warner Bell	Frances Worsham	Charlene Carr	Brent Phillips
Tyler	Woodville	Jerome P. Owens Jr.	Donece Gregory		Tina Bump	Sandra H. Crittenden	Gary Hennigan
Upshur	Gilmer	Charles L. Still	Rex A. Shaw		Myra Harris	Michael L. Smith	R. D. "Buck" Cross
Upton	Rankin	Vikki Bradley	Phyllis Stephens	Roy L. Scott	Nancy P. Poage	Dan W. Brown	Dan W. Brown
Uvalde	Uvalde	William R. Mitchell	Lucille C. Hutcherson	Pete Nieto	Joni Deorsam	Margarita Del Toro	Beaumont Watkins
Val Verde	Del Rio	Ray M. Kirkpatrick	Maria Elena Cardenas	Ana Markowski Smith	Morris L. Taylor	Wayne H. Hyde	D'Wayne Jernigan
Van Zandt	Canton	Richard Lawrence	Elizabeth Everitt	Leslie Poynter Dixon	Shirley Morgan	Joyce Fugate	Jeryl Cockerham
Victoria	Victoria	Helen R. Walker	Val D. Huvar		Cathy Bailey	Rena Scherer	Michael Ratcliff
Walker	Huntsville	Charles H. Wagamon	James D. Patton		Barbara T. McGilberry	Allan D. Rushing	Victor Graham
Waller	Hempstead	Freddie R. Zach	Cheryl Peters	Kevin D. Acker	Susan Winfree	Ellen C. Shelburne	Randy Smith
Ward	Monahans	Sam G. Massey	Pat V. Finley	Renee Ann Mueller	Nell Berry	Dolores Hannah Fine	Ben Keele
Washington	Brenham	Dorothy Morgan	Beth Ann Rothermel	Homero Ramirez	Norman Draehn	Candy Arth	J. W. Jankowski
Webb	Laredo	Mercurio Martinez Jr.	Henry Flores		William N. Hall Jr.	Patricia Ann Barrera	Juan Garza
Wharton	Wharton	Lawrence E. Naiser	Sandra K. Sanders	Karen H. Meinardus	Gus Wessels Jr.	Patrick L. Kubala	Jess Howell
Wheeler	Wheeler	Wendell Morgan	Margaret Dorman	Steven R. Emmert	Jerrie Moore	Jerry Dan Hefley	Jimmy Adams
Wichita	Wichita Falls	Nick Gipson	Vernon Cannon		Marsha Watson	Lou H. Murdock	Thomas J. Callahan
Wilbarger	Vernon	Gary Streit	Frances McGee	Mike Baskerville	Joann Carter	JoAnn Bourland	David Quisenberry
Willacy	Raymondville	Simon Salinas	Terry Flores	Juan Angel Guerra	Dolores Duron	LaQuita Garza	Larry G. Spence
Williamson	Georgetown	John C. Doerfler	Elaine Bizzell	Eugene Taylor	Vivian Wood	Deborah Hunt	Ed Richards
Wilson	Floresville	Martha B. Schnabel	Eva S. Martinez	Russell Wilson	Carolyn Orth	Anna D. Gonzales	Joe D. Tackitt Jr.
Winkler	Kermit	Bonnie Leck	Sonja Fullen	Thomas A. Cameron	Dawn McLennan	Patti Franks	Robert L. Roberts Jr.
Wise	Decatur	L. B. McDonald	Sherry Parker	Todd Durden	Emma Ray	* Pat Younger	Phil Ryan
Wood	Quitman	Lee E. Williams	Brenda Taylor		June Robinson	Fred Morrow	Bill Skinner
Yoakum	Plains	Dallas Brewer	Deborah L. Rushing		Toni Jones	Wanda Smith	Jimmie Rice
Young	Graham	Ken Andrews	Shirley Choate	Boyd L. Richie	Charlotte Farmer	Tim Moreland	Carey W. Pettus
Zapata	Zapata	Norma V. Ramirez	Consuelo R. Villarreal	José A. López	Alejandro R. Ramirez	Rosalva D. Guerra	Sigifredo Gonzalez Jr.
Zavala	Crystal City	Pablo Avila	Teresa P. Flores	Joe W. Taylor	Susie Perez	Florinda Perez	Eusebio Salinas

Texas County and District Officials — Table No. 2

District Clerks, District Attorneys and County Commissioners

See Table No. 1 on preceding pages for County Seats, County Judges, County Clerks, County Attorneys, County Treasurers, Tax Assessors-Collectors and Sheriffs.

County	District Clerk	District Attorney*	Comm. Precinct 1	Comm. Precinct 2	Comm. Precinct 3	Comm. Precinct 4
Anderson	Maxine Barnette	Jeff Herrington	Joe W. Chaffin	Arthur Sherrod	T. L. Beard	J. T. Davis
Andrews	Imogene Tate	Katrina Jackson	Barney Fowler	John Hogue	Jerry McPherson	Willard Snow
Angelina	Jimmie Robinson	Clyde Herrington	Clayton Richardson	I.D. Henderson	Jim Risinger	James Stanley
Aransas	Bobbie Rogers	Thomas Bridges	Oscar Piña	Ray Longino	Glenn D. Guillory	Larry Barnebey
Archer	Jane Ham	Tim Cole	Richard Shelley	James R. Wolf	Ben Buerger	D. W. Stone
Armstrong	Joe Reck	Rebecca King	Dee Aduddell	Thomas G. Fulgham	Tim Bagwell	C. M. Bryant
Atascosa	Jerome T. Brite	Lynn Ellison	Tommy Shearrer	Alfred Korus	Freddie Ogden	Weldon P. Cude
Austin	Marie Meyer	Travis J. Koehn	Harlan Schrader	Mark C. Wittner	James Bubba Duke	Royce Burger
Bailey	Elaine Parker	Johnny Actkinson	Floyd J. Vandiver	C. E. Grant Jr.	Joey R. Kindle	Bennie Claunch
Bandera	Bernice Bates	E. Bruce Curry	James Mormando Jr.	Dan C. Alanis III	Ralph Chancy	Nancy J. Thompson
Bastrop	LaNelle Hibbs	Charles Penick	Johnny Sanders	Charles McKeown	G. L. Hanna	Lee Dildy
Baylor	Doris Rushing	Bill Neal	Don Matus	Jack Brown	Jerry Pruitt	Billy Joe Carlock
Bee	Sandra Clark	George P. Morrill II	Adan V. Gonzales	Susan Stasny	Toribio M. Ortiz	Curtis H. Roberts
Bell	Sheila Norman	Arthur C. Eads	Richard Cortese	Tim Brown	Leroy Schiller	Royce Matkin
Bexar	David J. Garcia	Steven C. Hilbig	Robert Tejeda	Paul Elizondo	Lyle T. Larson	Mike Novak
Blanco	Dorothy Uecker	Sam Oatman	Dorsey L. Smith	Robert Riddell	Robert "Bob" Mauck	Paul Granberg
Borden	Joyce Herridge	Dana W. Cooley	Doug Isaacs	Larry D. Smith	Vernon Wolf	Hurston Lemons Jr.
Bosque	Sandra L. Woosley	B.J. Shepherd	Rick Kelley	David H. Jones	Gary Arnold	Carl Smith Jr.
Bowie	Billy Fox Branson	Bobby Lockhart	Jack Stone	John Addington	Dale Barrett	Paul Fannin
Brazoria	Jerry Deere	Jerome Aldrich	David Head	James D. "Jim" Clawson	Jack Harris	Jack Patterson
Brazos	Marc Hamlin	Bill Turner	Tony Jones	Sandie Walker	Randy Sims	Carey Cauley Jr.
Brewster	Jo Ann Salgado	Albert G. Valadez	Asa "Cookie" Stone	J.W. "Red" Pattillo	Emilio Salmon	Abelardo Leyva
Briscoe	Bess McWilliams	Becky McPherson	Terry Grimland	J. L. Chandler	L. B. Garvin Jr.	Gary Weaks
Brooks	Pete Martinez	Joe Frank Garza	Gloria Garza	Ramon Navarro Jr.	Raul Ramirez	Salvador Gonzalez
Brown	Jan Brown	Lee Haney	Steve Adams	Wayne Worley	Richard Gist	Vernon Moore
Burleson	Doris H. Brewer	Charles J. Sebesta Jr.	Frank W. Kristof	Don L. Groce	W. J. Stracener	Bobby E. Schoppe
Burnet	Modena Curington	Sam Oatman	James Holbrook	Carroll McCoy	George DeSpain	Craig Seward
Caldwell	Emma Jean Schulle	Charles R. Kimbrough	Morris Alexander	Charles Bullock	Ronnie Duesterheft	Joe Ivan Roland
Calhoun	Pamela Martin-Hartgrove	John D. Whitlow	Leroy Belk	Franklin Jurek	W.H. Floyd	Kenneth W. Finster
Callahan	Cubelle Harris	Allen Wright	Harold Hicks	Bryan Farmer	Tommy Holland	Charlie Grider
Cameron	Aurora de la Garza	Yolanda de Leon	Pedro "Pete" Benavides	Carlos H. Cascos	James R. Matz	Hector Peña
Camp	Deloria Bradshaw	Charles C. Bailey	Jack Eturd	Larry Shelton	Hervy Hiner	Curtis Wall
Carson	Barbara S. White	Randall C. Sims	Mike Britten	C. F. "Choc" Smith	Jerry Strawn	Kevin Howell
Cass	Becky Wilbanks	Randal Lee	William Taylor Duncan	H.B. Frost	Robert Buzbee	Freddie Tyson
Castro	Joyce M. Thomas	Jerry Matthews	Newlon Rowland	Larry Gonzales	W.A. Baldridge	Dan Schmucker
Chambers	R. B. Scherer	Mike Little	Mark Huddleston	Sidney Desormeaux	Jimmy Sylvia	Paul Lott
Cherokee	Marlys Mason	James (Jim) Cromwell	E. R. (Bob) Gregg	Alton Hicks	F. E. Hassell	Billy McCutcheon
Childress	Nancy Garrison	Randall C. Sims	David Hill	Dan Imhof	Lyall Foster	Jack Burrus
Clay	Dan Slagle	Tim Cole	R.L. "Lindy" Choate	Harlan Hicks	Wilson Scaling	Brice Jackson
Cochran	Rita Tyson	Gary Goff	Gerald Ramsey	J.B. Allen	Stacey Dunn	Jimmy Mullinax
Coke	Ettie Hubbard	Stephen R. Lupton	William Paul Burns	Melvin Royce Lee	Patrick K. (Pat) Percifull	James Arnold Tidwell
Coleman	Jo Chapman	Ross L. Jones	Jim Porter	Billy Don McCrary	John Kenneth Puckett	Alan Davis
Collin	Hannah Kunkle	Tom O'Connell	Phyllis Cole	Jerry Hoagland	Joe Jaynes	Jack Hatchell

County	District Clerk	District Attorney*	Comm. Precinct 1	Comm. Precinct 2	Comm. Precinct 3	Comm. Precinct 4
Collingsworth	Karen Coleman	Randall C. Sims	Glen Taylor	Zeb Roberson	Joe Tipton	Dudley Coleman
Colorado	Harvey Vornsand	W. C. (Bud) Kirkendall	Richard Charles Seifert	Johnnie Elstner	Tommy Hahn	Leon "Sonny" Spanihel
Comal	Margaret Herbrich	Dib Waldrip	Jack Dawson	Danny Scheel	Christina Zamora	Morris "Moe" Schwab
Comanche	LaNell S. Williams	B.J. Shepherd	Garry Steele	Chris Biggs	Mark Pinson	Clyde Brinson
Concho	Barbara K. Hoffman	Stephen H. Smith (119th) Ronald L. Sutton (198th)	R.M. Kingston	John Hruska	Frankie Wotjek	John B. "Son" Williams
Cooke	Patricia A. Payne	Janelle M. Haverkamp	Phil Young	Richard Brown	Jerry Lewis	Virgil Hess
Coryell	Carolyn Pollard	Riley Simpson	Jack Wall	Don Thompson	Hiram Davidson	Kyle Pruitt
Cottle	Beckey J. Tucker	Bill Neal	Paul Whitener	John Shavor	Manuel Cruz Jr.	D.N. Gregory Jr.
Crane	Maxine Willis	Michael Fostel	Gordon Hooper	John D. Daniell	Ellis Lane	Weldon J. McCutchen
Crockett	Debbi Puckett	Ori T. White	Frank Tambunga	Fred Deaton	Freddie Nicks	Rudy Martinez
Crosby	Billie Jo Freeman	C. Michael Ward	Gary V. Jordan	William M. Odom	Larry Wampler	James A. Boydstun
Culberson	Linda McDonald	Jaime Esparza	Cornelio Garibay	Joel U. Sanchez	John Jones	Lupe Escajeda
Dallam	LuAnn Taylor	Barry Blackwell	Bob Sheets	Oscar Przlas	Don Bowers	Eulan Sheets
Dallas	Bill Long	John Vance	Jim Jackson	Mike Cantrell	John Wiley Price	Kenneth A. Mayfield
Dawson	Carolyn Turner	Ricky B. Smith	Delmar Moore	Bill Meares	Troy Howard	Guy Kinnison
Deaf Smith	Lola Faye Veazey	Roland Saul	Wayne Betzen	Lupe Chavez	Troy Don Moore	Johnny Latham
Delta	Patsy P. Barton	Frank L. Long	C. D. (Mickey) Goforth	David Max Moody	James Campbell	Ted Carrington
Denton	Tracy Kunkel	Bruce Isaacks	Jeff Krueger	Sandy Jacobs	Scott Armey	Don Hill
DeWitt	Tabeth Ruschhaupt	Michael A. Sheppard	Wallace W. Beck	Billy E. Moore	John C. Oliver	Alfred Rangnow
Dickens	Yvonne (Tookie) Cash	Becky B. McPherson	John D. Foreman	Billy G. Drennan	Doc Edwards	Duane (Slim) Durham
Dimmit	Agustine G. Martinez Jr.	Roberto Serna	Larry Speer	Joaquin Salgado	Oscar Alvarado	Rodrigo Jaime
Donley	Fay Vargas	Randall C. Sims	Randy White	C.W. Cornell	Ronny Hill	William R. Chamberlain
Duval	Richard M. Barton	Heriberto Silva	Alejo C. Garcia	Rene M. Perez	Nestor Garza Jr.	Gilberto Uribe Jr.
Eastland	Bill Miears	Mike Siebert	Ken Lyerla	Calvin Ainsworth	L. T. Owen	Reggie Pittman
Ector	Jackie Sue Barnes	John W. Smith	Freddie Gardner	Mike Patton	Tom Todd	Bob Bryant
Edwards	Dorothy R. Hatley	Thomas F. Lee	Nicholas Gallegos	L.A. Field Sr.	James (Epp) Epperson	Robert Perez
Ellis	Billie Fuller	Joe F. Grubbs	Hallie Robinson	Jerry Holland	Charles Waller	Ron Brown
El Paso	Edie Rubalcaba	Jaime Esparza	Charles C. Hooten	Carlos Aguilar	Miguel Teran	Daniel R. Haggerty
Erath	Thomas Pack	John Terrill	Jerry Martin	Don Stone	Douglas Eberhart	Tommy Shelton
Falls	Larry R. Hoelscher	Thomas B. Sehon	Milton A. Albright	Bishop W. Williams	Tony Lynn Hoelscher	James Phillips
Fannin	Tommie Eaton	James Moss	Jerry L. Jenkins	Lloyd Flanagan	Dewayne Strickland	Pat Hilliard
Fayette	Virginia Wied	John W. Wied	Lawrence Adamcik	Ronnie Stork	Wilbert L. Gross	Tom Muras
Fisher	Bettie Hargrove	Mark Edwards	Charles Meek	Billy Henderson	Perry Thomson	Gene Terry
Floyd	Barbara Edwards	Becky McPherson	Ray Nell Bearden	Leonard Gilroy	George Taylor	Jon Jones
Foard	Sherry Weatherred	Dan Mike Bird	Rick Hammonds	Johnny Urquizo	Larry Wright	Edward Crosby
Fort Bend	Glory Hopkins	John Healey	R. L. "Bud" O'Shieles	Grady Prestage	Andy Meyers	Bob Lutts
Franklin	Tammie Dickson	Frank Long	Jearl Cooper	Bobby R. Elbert	Deryl W. Carr	Charles Davis
Freestone	Janet Chappell	Robert W. Gage	Luke Ward Sr.	W. R. McSwane	Stanley Gregory	John B. Massey
Frio	Ramona B. Rodriguez	Lynn Ellison	Jesús Salinas	Jesse M. Lindsey III	Adolfo Alvarez	Humberto Berrones
Gaines	Virginia Stewart	Ricky B. Smith	Robert Wood	Joe Rowlett	Ray Garrett	Charlie Lopez
Galveston	Evelyn Wells Robinson	Michael J. Guarino II	Eddie Barr	Eddie Janek	Wayne Johnson III	Ed Stuart
Garza	Sonny Gossett	Ricky Smith	Lee Norman	Mason McClellan	John Valdez	Royce Josey
Gillespie	Barbara Meyer	E. Bruce Curry	Dayton E. Weidenfeller	William A. Roeder	James J. Knopp	Eldon Ray Feller
Glasscock	Betty Pate	Hardy Wilkerson	Jimmy Strube	Ervin Wooten	Hugh Schafer	Michael Hoch
Goliad	Gail M. Turley	Michael Sheppard	Tony Garcia	Jerry Rodriguez	Louis Fromme Jr.	W. Wayne Key
Gonzales	Patricia Heinemeyer	William Kirkendall	E. R. Breitschopf	Truman DuPree	David Kuntschik	Welly Gibson
Gray	Yvonne Moler	John Mann	Joe Wheeley	Jim Greene	Gerald L. Wright	James L. Hefley

County	District Clerk	District Attorney*	Comm. Precinct 1	Comm. Precinct 2	Comm. Precinct 3	Comm. Precinct 4
Grayson	Cyndi Spencer	Robert T. Jarvis	Doug Walker	Johnnie "Butch" McCraw	Carol Shea	Gene Short
Gregg	Ruby Cooper	William Jennings	Charles Davis	Darryl Primo	David McBride	James Johnson
Grimes	Wayne Rucker	Tuck McLain	Doug Morris	Thomas Kitkoski	Zac H. Falkenbury	Marcus Mallard
Guadalupe	James Behrendt	W. C. Kirkendall	Shirley Hester	Casareo Guadarrama III	Jim O. Wolverton	Wyatt L. "Butch" Kunde
Hale	Anna Evans	Terry McEachern	E.E. McDonough	Mario Martinez	Roy Borchardt	Benny Cantwell
Hall	Raye Bailey	Randall C. Sims	Larry Don Maddox	Joe N. Berry	Buddy C. Logsdon	U. F. Coker Jr.
Hamilton	LaJuan Mizell	B.J. Shepherd	Jim Boatwright	Ora Dell Tyson	Jon Bonner	Loyd Crownover
Hansford	Kim V. Vera	Clay Ballman	Worley J. Smith	Joe T. Venneman	Kent Guthrie	Danny Henson
Hardeman	Judy Cokendolpher	Dan Mike Bird	Charles McSpadden	James Rine	Charles Taylor	Van D. Foster
Hardin	Vicki Johnson	Charles Roach	Bob Burgess	John Golden	Ken Pelt	John D. Brown
Harris	Charles Bacarisse	John B. Holmes Jr.	El Franco Lee	Jim Fonteno	Steve Radack	Jerry Eversole
Harrison	Sherry Griffis	Rick Berry	James D. Mooney	Charles Bennett	Glen Hobbs	Jeff Thompson
Hartley	Diane Thompson	Barry E. Blackwell	David Vincent	Ron Sherman	James Yoder	R.B. Reynolds
Haskell	Carolyn Reynolds	John Fouts	Billy Wayne Hester	Ronnie Chapman	Kenny Thompson	Bud Turnbow
Hays	Cecelia Adair	Marcos Hernandez	Debbie Gonzales Ingalsbe	Jeff W. Barton	William "Bill" Burnett	Russ G. Molenaar
Hemphill	Davene Hendershot	John Mann	Joe Schaef	Ed Culver	John Ramp	Lee Young
Henderson	Betty Ramsey	Donna Bennett	Bill Faulk	Harold Hammer	Cleburn Shavor	Jerry West
Hidalgo	Pauline Gonzalez	Rene Guerra	Sylvia Handy	Lalo Arcaute	Juan Rosel	Guadalupe Garces
Hill	Charlotte Barr	Dan V. Dent	J.K. Lane	Kenneth Reid	Bobbie Brustrom	John W. Erwin
Hockley	Dennis Price	Gary A. Goff	Jack Ayers	El Lea Hensley	J.R. Stanley	Billy W. Thetford
Hood	Tonna Trumble	Richard Hattox	Bob Anderson	Cliff Moody	Ron Cullers	Kennith Umphress
Hopkins	Patricia Dorner	Frank Long	Beth B. Wisenbaker	H.W. Halcomb	Don Patterson	Calvin Prince
Houston	Pam Pugh Crouch	Cindy Maria Garner	George "Buzzy" Bush	Gene Musick	Burtis Wooten	Billy Ray Duren
Howard	Glenda Brasel	Hardy Wilkerson	Emma Puga Brown	Jerry Kilgore	W. B. "Bill" Crooker	John M. (Sonny) Choate
Hudspeth	Patricia Bramblett	Jaime Esparza	Wayne R. West	Curtis Carr	Jim Kiehne	Larry Brewton
Hunt	Ann Prince	F. Duncan Thomas	Kenneth Thornton	Ralph Green	Jim Walker	Allen Lynn Martin
Hutchinson	Sharron Orr	Clay Ballman	R. D. Cornellison	J. C. Berry	S.T. "Red" Isbell	John E. Bayless
Irion	Reba Criner	Stephen Lupton	E. Wayne Smith	Orlie Wolfenbarger	John Nanny	Barbara Searcy
Jack	Lelia Vene Cozart	Larry Green	Lewis Kirk	Jerry M. Adams	James L. Cozart	Milton R. Pruitt
Jackson	Sharon Whittley	Robert E. Bell	Miller Rutledge	Erwin Skalicky	Priscilla Hurta	W. O. Walker
Jasper	Neil Powers	Guy James Gray	Edgar W. Lewis	Cecil "Buddy" Ellis	James E. Smith	Mack Rose
Jeff Davis	Sue Blackley	Albert Valadez	Billy Cotton	Joe Dominguez	Billie Weston	Bill Gearhart
Jefferson	John S. Appleman	Tom Maness	Jimmie P. Cokinos	Mark L. Domingue	Waymon D. Hallmark	Edward C. Moore
Jim Hogg	Gloria Diana Rodriguez	Heriberto Silva	Francisco X. Escobedo	Oscar O. Gonzalez	Alberto Benavides Jr.	Ruben Rodriguez
Jim Wells	Olga Villarreal	Joe Frank Garza	Zenaida Sanchez	C. L. Cornelius	Oswald Alanis	Xavier Garcia
Johnson	Jeaniv Johnson	Dale Hanna	R. C. McFall	Ron Harmon	Mark Carpenter	Troy Thompson
Jones	Nona Carter	Gary M. Brown	James Clawson	Mike Polk	J.L. Wylie	Steve Lollar
Karnes	Patricia "Pat" Brysch	Lynn Ellison	Darrel Blaschke	Carl E. Beam	Juan Martinez	Isidro "Stormy" Rossett
Kaufman	Sandra Featherston	Louis W. Conradt Jr.	Charles Rhea Fox	Rod Kinkaid	Ivan Johnson	Jerry Brewer
Kendall	Shirley R. Stehling	E. Bruce Curry	John C. Kight	L.M. Holman	Darrel L. Lux	Victor King
Kenedy	Barbara B. Turcotte	Carlos Valdez	Leonard May	Louis E. Turcotte Jr.	Tobin Armstrong	Gus A. Puente
Kent	Cornelia Cheyne	John Fouts	Bob E. Hamilton	Don Long	Michael W. Owen	Don Trammel
Kerr	Linda Uecker	Ronald L. Sutton (198th) E. Bruce Curry (216th)	H.A. "Buster" Baldwin	T. H. "Butch" Lackey	Jonathan A. Letz	Bruce Oehler
Kimble	Elaine Carpenter	Ronald L. Sutton	Ray Jacoby	Ilee Simon	George Wright	Victor Herbst
King	Tavia Vinson	Bill Neal	Billy Paul Vinson	Sam Fulton	Bob Tidmore	Darwood Marshall
Kinney	Dora Elia Sandoval	Thomas F. Lee	Freddie Frerich	Joe Montalvo	Joe (Boy) Williams	Paul D. O'Rourke
Kleberg	Martha I. Soliz	Carlos Valdez	David Rosse	Tony R. Barbour	Dewey Hubert	Romeo Lomas

County	District Clerk	District Attorney*	Comm. Precinct 1	Comm. Precinct 2	Comm. Precinct 3	Comm. Precinct 4
Knox	Danny Speck	Bill Neal	Weldon Skiles	Jerry Parker	Jimmy Urbanczyk	Johnny Birkenfeld
Lamar	Marvin A. Patterson	Kerye Ashmore	Mike R. Blackburn	Carl L. Steffey	Rodney C. Pollard	Alan R. Weatherford
Lamb	Teresa McGaa	Mark Yarbrough	Willie Gene Green	Thurman Lewis	Emil Macha	Leonard Pierce
Lampasas	Terri Cox	Larry Allison	Robert L. Vincent Jr.	Edd Barefoot	Travis Herring	Tommy Harkey
La Salle	Nora Mae Tyler	Lynn Ellison	Raymond A. Landrum Jr.	Roberto F. Aldaco	Arcenio A. Garcia	Carlos B. Gonzalez
Lavaca	Calvin J. Albrecht	W. C. "Bud" Kirkendall	Maxie P. Brocker	Eddie Vrana	Daniel Peters	Glen Blundell
Lee	Adeline Melcher	Ted Weems	Maurice Pitts Jr.	Otto Becker Jr.	O. B. "Butch" Johnson	Larry Wachsmann
Leon	Gloria McCarty	Ray Montgomery	Joseph D. Sullivan	F. G. Lipsey	Jim Miles	Burel Biddle
Liberty	Joy Kay McManus	Michael Little	Harry D. Hylton	Lee Groce	Melvin Hunt	Bobby Payne
Limestone	Mary D. Budde	Don Cantrell	Keith Eaves	Billy Waldrop	G. Z. (Peaches) Stone	Don Ford
Lipscomb	Coeta Sperry	John A. Mann	Garner Schoenhals	F.R. Loesch	Marvin V. Born	John D. Fritzlen
Live Oak	Lois Shannon	George P. Morrill II	J.J. "Bucky" Houdmann	Hilbert Kopplin	Jimmy Strause	Emilio Garza
Llano	Debbie Honig	Sam Oatman	Randy C. Leifeste	Keith Faulkner	Duane Stueven	Marc Miller
Loving	Lenell Chandler	Randall Reynolds	Harlan Hopper	Joe R. Renteria	Skeet L. Jones	Royce Creager
Lubbock	Jean Anne Stratton	William C. Sowder	Kenny Maines	James Kitten	Gilbert Flores	Gary Schwantz
Lynn	Sandra Laws	Ricky B. Smith	Don Morton	Mike Braddock	Sandra (Sandy) Cox	J. T. Miller
Madison	Joyce Batson	Ray Montgomery	Reed Reynolds	Walton Reynolds	David Callaham	Bob Grisham
Marion	Janie McCay	James P. Finstrom	R. M. (Ric) Blevins	T.W. (Sam) Smith	Eugene R. Robinson	C.W. (Charlie) Treadwell
Martin	Susie Hull	Hardy L. Wilkinson	Doyle Hale	Homer Henson	Eldon A. Welch	C.W. Turner
Mason	Beatrice Langehennig	Sam Oatman	Rolly D. Lumpkins	T.J. Webster	Drew Tallent	Billy Kothmann
Matagorda	Becky Denn	Steven E. Reis	Michael J. Pruett	George W. Deshotels	Leonard Lamar	E. R. Vacek
Maverick	Diamantina Treviño	Roberto Serna	Johnny E. Martinez	Guillermo Mancha	David R. Saucedo	Roberto Ruiz
McCulloch	Mackye Johnson	Ronald Sutton	Joe H. Johnson	Jackie Behrens	Kenneth Adams	Jerry Tedder
McLennan	Joe Johnson	John Segrest	Wayne Davis	Lester Gibson	Joe Mashek	Ray Meadows
McMullen	Neil Hodgin	George P. Morrill II	Asa M. Farrer Jr.	Rodney Swaim Jr.	Paul M. Koonce	Maximo G. Quintanilla Jr.
Medina	Jean Marty	Mickey Pennington	Royce R. Hartmann	Stanley Keller Jr.	Enrique G. Santos	Kelly Carroll
Menard	Elsie Maserang	Ronald Sutton	Rudy Gonzales	Richard Cordes	Bart Wilkinson	Donald Kothmann
Midland	Vivian Wood	Al Schorre	Henry Goulet	Guy McCrary	Louisa Valencia	James Brezina
Milam	Leola L. Komar	Hollis C. Lewis Jr.	V. W. Hauk	Troy Mode	C. Dale Jaecks	Burke Bauerschlag
Mills	Beulah L. (Patty) Roberts	G. Lee Haney	Joe Karnes	Carroll Bunting	Dale Henry	Hawley B. Jernigan
Mitchell	Sharon Hammond	Mark Edwards	Edward B. Roach	Carl Guelker	Wyndell (Wendy) Inman	Billy H. Preston
Montague	Condell Lowrie	Tim Cole	Jon A. Kernek	Jerry Clement	Tommy L. Sparks	Tommie Sappington
Montgomery	Barbara Adamick	Michael McDougal	Mike Meadors	Ed Chance	Malcolm Purvis	Jim Simmons
Moore	June Mills	Barry E. Blackwell	Jerrie Howe	Louis Dubuque	Keith Christie	Lynn Cartrite
Morris	Welton Walker	Richard Townsend	Coy Lee Roney	Dearl Quarles	James Settles	Gary Camp
Motley	Lucretia Campbell	John R. Hollums	John M. Russell	Donald Hughes	Franklin Jameson	J. N. Fletcher
Nacogdoches	Shelby Solomon	Tim James	Jimmy Daniels	Norman Henderson	Alvin Stanaland	George Self
Navarro	Marilyn Greer	Patrick C. Batchelor	Paul Slaughter	Olin Nickelberry	William Baldwin	Betty Armstrong
Newton	Abbie N. Stark	Charles Mitchell	Weldon R. Wilkinson	Anderson White	Melton G. Jarrell	Ricky Odom
Nolan	Vera Holloman	Mark Edwards	Edsel Bankhead	Harold Ware	Tommy White	Dalton Owens
Nueces	Oscar Soliz	Carlos Valdez	Frank L. Schwing Jr.	Roy O. Hinojosa	Oscar O. Ortiz	Joe McComb
Ochiltree	Shawn Rogers	Bruce Roberson	Jack Kile	Tom O'Dell	James W. Clark	Larry Hardy
Oldham	Becky Groneman	Donald Davis	Quincy Tylor	Donnie Knox	Roger Morris	Grady Skaggs
Orange	Stella Winter	John Kimbrough	Claude Wimberley	Marlin Shelton	Flo Edgerly	Sherry Smith
Palo Pinto	Helen Slemmons	Jerry Ray	David Lee	Robert Murray	George Nowak	Earnest Pechacek
Panola	Sandra King	Danny Buck Davidson	Ronnie LaGrone	Buddy Harris	Joe Harris	Jimmy E. Davis
Parker	Lana Tibbitts	Don Schnebly	Danny Choate	Mack Dobbs	Charlie Horton	Rena Peden

County	District Clerk	District Attorney*	Comm. Precinct 1	Comm. Precinct 2	Comm. Precinct 3	Comm. Precinct 4
Parmer	Sandra Warren	Johnny Actkinson	John W. Tannahill	Thomas Ware	Jerry L. Davis	Raymond McGehee
Pecos	Janice Stockburger	Albert Valadez(83rd) / Ori T. White (112th)	Gregg McKenzie	Tony Villarreal	Linda McKenzie Webb	Paul Valenzuela
Polk	Nell Lowe	John S. Holleman	B. E. "Slim" Speights	Bobby Smith	James J. "Buddy" Purvis	R. R. "Dick" Hubert
Potter	Cindy Groomer	Rebecca King	John Stradley	Manuel Perez Villasenor	Strick Watkins	Will C. Thirkill
Presidio	Ramona Lara	Albert Valadez	Felipe A. Cordero	Juan José Muñiz	Jaime Ramirez	Jack W. Brunson
Rains	Mary Sheppard	Frank Long	Virgil McEnturff	William Potts	Gary Bishop	Rayford Briggs
Randall	LaQuitta Polvadore	James Farren	John J. Currie Jr.	Jan Reid	George "Skip" Huskey	John M. Dodson
Reagan	Billie Havis	Albert Valadez. (83rd) / Ori T. White (112th)	Jim O'Bryan	Michael Fisher	Bill Schneemann	Thomas Strube
Real	Bella A. Rubio	Anton E. (Tony) Hackebeil	W. B. Sansom Jr.	Kenneth B. Shackelford	Castulo San Miguel	Milburn Wooldridge
Red River	Clara Gaddis	Jack O. Herrington	Ricky Daniels	Ronnie James	Elmer Caton	Lane Duncan
Reeves	Juana Jaquez	Randall W. Reynolds	Felipe Arredondo	Won Joo Bang	Herman S. Tarin	Bernardo Martinez
Refugio	Ruby Garcia	Michael A. Sheppard	Valentin R. "Val" Ortega	Ronald K. Hicks	James R. Henry	Richard Martinez
Roberts	Donna L. Goodman	John A. Mann	William H. Clark	Ken Gill	Kelly Flowers	James F. Duvall Jr.
Robertson	Cornelia A. Starkey	John C. Paschall	John Anderson	Bobby Ray Madden	Michael Byer	Marie Abraham
Rockwall	Kay McDaniel	Ray Sumrow	Jerry Wimpee	Dale Troutt	Bruce Beaty	Trey Chaney
Runnels	Loretta Michalewicz	Stephen Smith	Skipper Wheeless	Keith Collom	James Thurman Self	Richard W. Strube
Rusk	Linda J. Smith	Kyle Freeman	Bill Hale	Harold Kuykendall	Dan Cates	Kimble Harris
Sabine	Tanya Walker	Charles Mitchell	Keith C. Clark	S. Lynn Smith	Doyle Dickerson	Will Smith Sr.
San Augustine	Jean Steptoe	Charles R. Mitchell	Tommy Hunter	Edward Wilson	Joey Lee Holloway	Bill T. Langford
San Jacinto	Marilyn Nettles	Scott Rosekrans	Norman Street	Weaver Stripling	Thomas Bonds	Will Copeland Jr.
San Patricio	Patricia Norton	Tom Bridges	Nina Treviño	Fred P. Nardini	Pedro G. Rodriguez	Gordon Porter
San Saba	Kim Wells	Sam Oatman	Roger Crockett	Hollis Lord	Wayland Perry	Jackie Brister
Schleicher	Peggy Williams	Stephen Lupton	Johnny Mayo Jr.	Kerry Joy	Steve Minor	William Ross Whitten
Scurry	Elois Pruitt	Dana Cooley	Ralph Trevey	Roy Idom	Howard Limmer	Jerry Gannaway
Shackelford	Frances Wheeler	Gary M. Brown	James Tabor	R. P. Mitchell	Jimmy T. Brooks	James Waddington
Shelby	Marsha Singletary	Karren E. Price	Donnie Borders	O. K. Hagler	Spencer Hamilton	Larry Moreland
Sherman	Mary Lou Albert	Barry E. Blackwell	Wayne Cummings	Wayland Brown	David Hass	Tommy Asher
Smith	R. Brad Burger	Jack Skeen Jr.	Sharon Emmett	Gus Ramirez	Derrell Cooper	Andrew R. Melontree
Somervell	Lovella Williams	Dale Hanna	Larry Hulsey	Foy Edwards	Randy Whitworth	Jim Gartrell
Starr	Juan Erasmo Saenz	Heriberto Silva	José Maria Alvarez	Adrian Gonzalez	Eloy Garza	Abel N. Gonzalez Jr.
Stephens	Shirley Parker	Stephen Bristow	Jerry Toland	D. C. "Button" Sikes	Ozell Devenport	Carter Fore
Sterling	Diane A. Haar	Stephen Lupton	Billy Joe Blair	Edward J. Michulka Jr.	Patsy Bynum	Melvin Foster
Stonewall	Betty L. Smith	John Fouts	Mike Hill	Pat Cumbie	Larry Dickerson	Dickey Parker
Sutton	Bobbie Smith	Ori White	Miguel (Mike) Villanueva	John Wade	Bill Keel	Bella Castaneda
Swisher	Brenda Hudson	Terry McEachern	Lloyd Rahlfs	A. G. House	Billy Settle	W. C. Weatherred
Tarrant	Tom Wilder	Tim Curry	Dionne Bagsby	Marti VanRavenswaay	Glenn Whitley	J. D. Johnson
Taylor	JoAnn Lackey	James Eidson	Jack Turner	Don Dudley	Stan Egger	Neil Fry
Terrell	Martha Allen	Thomas F. Lee	Thelma Calzada	Santiago Flores	Lloyd Goldwire	Hudson Kerr
Terry	Paige Lindsey	G. Dwayne Pruitt	Earl J. Brown Jr.	Bill Keesee	Don Robertson	John Franks
Throckmorton	Cathey Mitchell	John Fouts	Doyle Wells	John Jones	Carlton Sullivan	George Seedig
Titus	Bobby LaPrade	Charles Bailey	Mike Price	Mike Fields	Billy Jack Thompson	Thomas E. Hockaday
Tom Green	Sue Bramhall	Steve Lupton (51st) / Stephen H. Smith (119th)	Clayton Friend	Karl Bookter	Jodie Weeks	Tim Weatherby
Travis	Amalia Rodriguez-Mendoza	Ronald Earle	Sam Biscoe	Karen Sonleitner	Valarie Bristol	Margaret Gomez
Trinity	Cheryl Cartwright	Joe L. Price	Grover "Tiger" Worsham	Dean Price	Cecil Webb	Sam O. Blair
Tyler	Patricia Brown	James A. Clark	Maxie Riley	Arthur M. (Pete) Barnes	Joe Marshall	Henry Earl Sawyer

County	District Clerk	District Attorney*	Comm. Precinct 1	Comm. Precinct 2	Comm. Precinct 3	Comm. Precinct 4
Upshur	Horace A. Ray	Tim Cone	Gaddis Lindsey	Tommy L. Stanley	Rickey Jackson	Charles K. Thompson
Upton	Phyllis Stephens	Albert G. Valadez (83rd) Ori White (112th)	Morris E. "Mack" McKenzie	Tommy Owens	W.M. "Willie" Martinez	Leon Patrick
Uvalde	Lydia Steele	Anton E. Hackebeil	Randy Scheide	Gilbert Torres	Jerry W. Bates	Jesse R. Moreno
Val Verde	Martha Germany	Thomas E. Lee	Bradley R. Birch	Gary Leonard	John M. Cody	John F. Qualia
Van Zandt	Nancy Young	Leslie Poynter Dixon	O. D. Hazel	Cary Hilliard	Leonard M. Morris	Loy D. Hutchins
Victoria	Mary Elizabeth Jimenez	George J. Filley III	Chris Rivera	Jerry Nobles	John J. Hammack	Rex L. Easley
Walker	Bernice Coleman	David P. Weeks	B.J. Gaines Jr.	Robert Earl Autery	James C. "Buddy" Reynolds	Joe Malak Jr.
Waller	Beverly A. Kluna	Sherry L. Robinson	Leroy Singleton	Frank Pokluda	Frank D. Jackson	Eddie Neuman
Ward	Jo Ann Roark	Randall (Randy) Reynolds	Julian Florez	Bill Welch	Larry Hunt	Don Creech
Washington	Blondean Kuecker	Charles Sebesta	David Simpson	Robert Mikeska	Alfred Boeker Jr.	Paul Pipes
Webb	Manuel Gutierrez	Joe Rubio	Jorge O. de la Garza	Roque Vela	Rick Reyes	David Cortez
Wharton	Evelyn Kramer	Josh McCown	Mickey Reynolds	D. C. "Chris" King	Philip Miller	Catherine Drapela
Wheeler	Sherri Jones	John Mann	Kenneth Childress	Tommy Puryear	Hubert C. Moore	Boyd Hittbrunner
Wichita	Dorsey Trapp	Barry L. Macha	Woodrow W. Gossom Jr.	Weldon Nix	Gordon Griffith	Harold White
Wilbarger	Wilda Byers	Dan Mike Bird	John A. Milner Jr.	Freddie Streit	Glen Turner	Lenville Morris
Willacy	Santiago "Chago" Fonseca	Juan Angel Guerra	Israel Tamez	Gene McGee	Alfredo Serrato	Pedro Garcia
Williamson	Bonnie Wolbrueck	Ken Anderson	Michael Heiligenstein	Greg Boatright	David Hays	Jerry Mehevec
Wilson	Shirley Polasek	Lynn Ellison	Roger A. Lopez	Albert Pruski	Bobby Lynn	Wayne Stroud
Winkler	Virginia Healy	Michael L. Fostel	Tommy R. Smith	James A. Winn	Randy Neal	Benito Davila
Wise	Lawana Snider	Barry Green	Jerry Flusche	James A. Hubbard	Farley Bridges	Paul Wood
Wood	Jo Anna Nelson	Marcus D. Taylor	Glenn Bevill	Kenneth Wilson	Roger Pace	Roger Tinney
Yoakum	Mae Barnett	Richard Clark	Woody Lindsey	F.R. Slentz	Jim Barron	Macky McWhirter
Young	George C. Birdwell	Stephen E. Bristow	Duane Downey	John C. Bullock	John Hawkins	R.L. Spivey
Zapata	Consuelo R. Villarreal	José A. Rubio	José Luis Flores	Angel Garza	Adolfo Gonzalez Jr.	Amaro Bustamante
Zavala	Frankie G. Mancha	Roberto Serna	Jesús M. Vasquez	Miguel (Mike) Acosta	David Lopez	Matthew McHazlett Jr.

* If more than one District Attorney is listed for a county, the district court number is noted in parentheses after each attorney's name. If no District Attorney is listed, the County Attorney, whose name can be found in Table No. 1, assumes the duties of that office.

Texans in Congress

Besides the two members of the U.S. Senate allocated to each state, Texas is allocated 30 members in the U.S. House of Representatives. The term of office for members of the House is two years; the terms of all members will expire on Jan. 1, 1999. Senators serve six-year terms. Sen. Kay Bailey Hutchison's will end in 2001. Sen. Phil Gramm's term will end in 2003.

Addresses and phone numbers of the lawmakers' Washington and district offices are given below, as well as the committees on which they serve. Washington **zip codes** are **20515** for members of the House and **20510** for senators. The telephone **area code** for Washington is **202**. See map of congressional districts on p. 394.

U.S. Senate

GRAMM, Phil. Republican (Home: College Station); Washington Office: 370 RSOB, Washington, D.C. 20510-4302; (202) 224-2934, Fax 228-2856.

Texas Offices: 222 E. Van Buren Ste. 404, **Harlingen** 78550, (512) 423-6118; 712 Main Ste. 1704, **Houston** 77002, (713) 718-4000; 1205 Texas Ave. Ste. 1205, **Lubbock** 79401, (806) 743-7533; 2323 Bryan Ste. 2150, **Dallas** 75201, (214) 767-3000; 310 N. Mesa Ste. 1004, **El Paso** 79901, (915) 534-6897; 100 E. Ferguson Ste. 1004, **Tyler** 75702, (903) 593-0902; 402 E. Ramsey Rd. Ste. 200, **San Antonio** 78216, (210) 366-9494. **Committees**: the Budget; Finance; Banking, Housing and Urban Affairs.

HUTCHISON, Kay Bailey. Republican (Home: Dallas); Washington Office: 284 RSOB, Washington, D.C. 20510-4304; (202) 224-5922, Fax 224-0776.

Texas Offices: 961 Federal Bldg., 300 E. 8th St., **Austin** 78703, (512) 482-5834; 500 Chestnut St. Ste. 1570, **Abilene** 79602, (915) 676-2937; 10440 N. Central Expy. Ste. 1160, **Dallas** 75231, (214) 361-3500; 1919 Smith St. Ste 800, **Houston** 77002, (713) 653-3456; 8023 Vantage Dr. Ste. 460, **San Antonio** 78230, (210) 340-2885. **Committees**: Commerce, Science and Transportation; Appropriations; Rules and Administration.

U.S. House of Representatives

ARCHER, Bill, R-Houston, District 7; Washington Office: 1236 LHOB; (202) 225-2571, Fax 225-4381; **District Office**: 10000 Memorial Dr., Suite 620, Houston 77024-3490, (713) 682-8828. **Committees**: Ways and Means (chairman).

ARMEY, Richard, R-Irving, District 26; Washington Office: 301 CHOB; (202) 225-7772, Fax 225-7614; **District Office**: 9901 Valley Ranch Parkway East, Suite 3050, Irving 75063, (214) 556-2500. **House Majority Leader**.

BARTON, Joe, R-Ennis, District 6; Washington Office: 2264 RHOB; (202) 225-2002. Fax 225-3052; **District Offices**: 4521 S. Hulen, Ste. 210, Fort Worth 76109, (817) 543-1000; 303 West Knox, Suite 101, Ennis 75119-3942, (817) 543-1000; 105F Washington St., Arlington 76011, (817) 543-1000. **Committees**: Commerce, Science.

BENTSEN, Ken, D-Houston, District 25; Washington Office: 128 CHOB; (202) 225-7508, Fax 225-2947; **District Offices**: 515 Rusk, Ste. 12102, Houston 77002-2667; (713) 718-4100, Fax 475-7823; 1001 E. Southmore Ste. 810, Pasadena 77502-1296, (713) 473-4334, Fax 475-8887; 1300 Rollingbrook Ste. 517, Baytown 77521, (281) 837-8225. **Committees**: Banking and Financial Services, Budget.

BONILLA, Henry, R-San Antonio, District 23; Washington Office: 1427 LHOB; (202) 225-4511, Fax 225-2237; **District Offices**: 11120 Wurzbach Ste. 300, San Antonio 78230, (210) 697-9055; 1300 Matamoros Ste. 113B, Laredo 78040, (210) 726-4682; 111 E. Broadway Ste. 101, Del Rio 78840, (210) 774-6547; 4400 N. Big Spring Ste. 211, Midland 79705, (915) 686-8833. **Committee**: Appropriations.

BRADY, Kevin, R-The Woodlands, District 8; Washington Office: 1531 LHOB; (202) 225-4901. **Committees**: International Relations, Resources, Science.

COMBEST, Larry, R-Lubbock, District 19; Washington Office: 1026 LHOB; (202) 225-4005, Fax (202) 225-9615; **District Office**: 5809 S. Western, No. 205, Amarillo 79110, (806) 353-3945; 1205 Texas Avenue, Room 810, Lubbock, 79401, (806) 763-1611; 3800 East 42nd, No. 205, Odessa 79762, (915) 550-0743. **Committees**: Agriculture, Small Business.

DeLAY, Tom, R-Sugar Land, District 22; Washington Office: 341 CHOB; (202) 225-5951, Fax 225-5241; **District Office:** 10707 Corporate Dr., No. 130, Stafford 77477, (713) 240-3700. **House Majority Whip. Committee**: Appropriations.

DOGGETT, Lloyd, D-Austin, District 10; Washington Office: 126 CHOB; (202) 225-4865, Fax 225-3073; **District Office**: 300 8th St. No. 763, Austin 78701, (512) 916-5921. **Committees**: Budget, Resources.

EDWARDS, Chet, D-Waco, District 11; Washington Office: 2459 RHOB; (202) 225-6105, Fax 225-0350; **District Offices**: 116 Southeast, Belton 76513, (817) 933-2904; 710 Clifton-Robinson Tower, 700 S. University Parks Dr., Waco 76706, (817) 752-9600, Fax 752-7769. **Committee**: Appropriations.

**FROST, Martin, D-Dallas, District 24; Washing-

1995 Medal of Freedom Honors Texas Activist

William C. "Willie" Velásquez.

William C. "Willie" Velásquez, founder of the Southwest Voter Registration Education Project in San Antonio, was awarded the nation's highest civilian honor in 1995 with a Medal of Freedom from President Bill Clinton.

Velásquez, who died from kidney cancer in 1988, was recognized posthumously for his civil rights work. His widow, Jane, accepted the award from President Clinton who said "his appeal to the Hispanic community was simple, passionate and direct — *su voto es su voz* — your vote is your voice."

The Southwest Voter Registration Education Project defines its work since 1974 as being "committed to increasing the participation of Latinos and other minority group members in the American democratic process."

William C. Velásquez was born on May 9, 1944, to William and Mary Louise Velásquez, in Orlando, Florida, where the elder Velásquez was stationed during World War II.

The young Velásquez graduated from Central Catholic High School in San Antonio. He received a B.A. in political science from St. Mary's University in 1966.

While pursuing graduate studies in economics at the San Antonio university he was appointed assistant to the executive director of the U.S. Catholic bishops' Committee for the Spanish Speaking.

During his tenure with the bishops' committee, Velásquez was one of the founders and charter members of the Mexican American Youth Organization (MAYO), a Chicano youth group.

His involvement with the Chicano movement of the 1960s and early 1970s eventually brought him to become one of the founders of La Raza Unida Party, but he soon left the party over differences about tactics. Velásquez was also involved with the United Farm Workers strike in the Rio Grande Valley.

In 1984, a sister group to the Registration Project, the Southwest Voter Research Institute, was founded by Velásquez to conduct surveys and analyze public policy affecting Hispanics in the Southwest. He was described as the most respected Hispanic pollster in the United States at the time of his death at age 44. Besides his wife, he was survived by three children.

Velásquez was among 12 persons honored by President Clinton in 1995. Others included Peggy Charren and Joan Ganz Cooney for their work in children's television; former Wisconsin Sen. Gaylord Nelson, founder of Earth Day; John Hope Franklin, a black historian; and urban designer James Rouse.

The Medal of Freedom was established in 1945 by President Harry Truman.

Other Texans who have received the honor include Barbara Jordan, Dr. Michael DeBakey, Lady Bird Johnson and J. Frank Dobie.

Also, several astronauts and NASA officials serving in Houston have received the award, as well as national figures who have spent part of their professional lives in Texas, including writer James Michener, now associated with UT-Austin, and artist Georgia O'Keeffe, who was attracted to the openness of the Southwest while teaching in public schools in the Panhandle. ☆

---

ton Office: 2256 RHOB; (202) 225-3605, Fax 225-4951; **District Offices**: 400 South Zang, Dallas 75208, (214) 948-3401; 3020 S.E. Loop 820, Fort Worth 76140, (817) 293-9231; 100 N. Main Ste. 534, Corsicana (903) 874-0760. **Committee**: Rules.

GONZALEZ, Henry B., D-San-Antonio, District 20; Washington Office: 2413 RHOB; (202) 225-3236, Fax 225-1915; **District Office**: 124-B Federal Building, 727 East Durango, San Antonio 78206, (210) 472-6192.

Committee: Banking and Financial Services (ranking minority member).

GRANGER, Kay, R-Fort Worth, District 12; Washington Office: 515 CHOB; (202) 225-5071; **District Office**: P.O. Box 413, Fort Worth 76101, (817) 496-1460. **Committee**: Budget, House Oversight, Transportation and Infrastructure.

GREEN, Gene, D-Houston, District 29; Washington Office: 2429 RHOB; (202) 225-1688, Fax 225-

9903; **District Office**: 5502 Lawndale, Houston 77023, (713) 923-9961; 420 W. 19th St. Houston 77008, (713) 880-4364. **Committee**: Commerce.

HALL, Ralph M., D-Rockwall, District 4; Washington Office: 2221 RHOB; (202) 225-6673, Fax (202) 225-3332; **District Office**: 104 N. San Jacinto, 119 Federal Building, Rockwall 75087, (972) 771-9118. **Committees**: Commerce, Science.

HINOJOSA, Rubén, D-Mercedes, District 15; Washington Office: 1032 LHOB; (202) 225-2531; **District Office**: P.O. Box 415, Mercedes 78570, (210) 565-6363. **Committee**: Education and the Workforce.

JOHNSON, Eddie Bernice, D-Dallas, District 30; Washington Office: 1123 LHOB; (202) 225-8885, Fax 226-1477; **District Office**: 2515 McKinney Ave., No. 1565, Dallas 75201, (214) 922-8885; 1634B W. Irving Blvd, Irving 75061, (972) 253-8885. **Committees**: Science, Transportation and Infrastructure.

JOHNSON, Sam, R-Dallas, District 3; Washington Office: 1030 LHOB; (202) 225-4201, Fax 225-1485; **District Office**: 801 E. Campbell Rd., Ste. 425, Richardson 75081, (972) 470-0892, Fax 470-9973. **Committees**: Education and the Workforce, Ways and Means.

LAMPSON, Nick, D-Beaumont, District 9; Washington Office: 417 CHOB; (202) 225-6565. **Committees**: Science, Transportation and Infrastructure.

LEE, Sheila Jackson, D-Houston, District 18; Washington Office: 1520 LHOB; (202) 225-3816, Fax 225-3317; **District Offices**: 1919 Smith St., No. 1180, Houston 77002, (713) 655-0050, Fax 665-1612; 6719 W. Montgomery Rd, Rm. 204, Houston 7709,1 (713) 691-4882; 420 W. 19th St., Houston 77008, (713) 861-4070. **Committees**: Judiciary, Science.

ORTIZ, Solomon P., D-Corpus Christi, District 27; Washington Office: 2136 RHOB; (202) 225-7742, Fax 226-1134; **District Offices**: 3649 Leopard, Suite 510, Corpus Christi 78408, (512) 883-5868; 3505 Boca Chica Blvd., Brownsville 78521, (210) 541-1242. **Committees**: National Security, Resources.

PAUL, Ron, R-Surfside, District 14, Washington Office: 203 CHOB; (202) 225-2831; **District Offices**: 200 W. Second Ste. 210, Freeport, (409) 230-0000; 312 S. Main, Victoria 77901, (512) 576-1231; 301 Guadalupe Ste. 105, San Marcos 78665, (512) 396-1400. **Committees**: Banking and Financial Services, Education and the Workforce.

REYES, Silvestre, D-El Paso, District 16; Washington Office: 514 CHOB; (202) 225-4831; **District Office**: 310 N. Mesa Ste. 400, El Paso 79901, (915) 534-4400. **Committees**: National Security, Veterans' Affairs.

RODRIGUEZ, Ciro D., D-San Antonio, District

28; **Washington Office**: 323 CHOB (202) 225-1640; **District Offices**: 1313 SE Military Hwy. Ste. 115, San Antonio 78214, (210) 924-7383; 202 E. St. Joseph Ste. 5, San Diego 78384, (512) 279-3097. **Committee**: National Security.

SANDLIN, Max, D-Marshall, District 1; Washington Office: 214 CHOB; (202) 225-3035; **District Offices**: 1300 E. Pinecrest Ste. 30, Marshall 75670, (903) 938-8386, Fax 935-5772; P.O. Box 248, New Boston 75570, (903) 628-5594, Fax 628-3155; P.O Box 538, Sulphur Springs 75483, (903) 885-8682, Fax 885-2976. **Committee**: Transportation and Infrastructure.

SESSIONS, Pete, R-Dallas, District 5; Washington Office: 1318 LHOB; (202) 225-2231, Fax 225-5878; **District Offices**: 10677 E. Northwest Hwy. Ste. 410, Dallas 75238, (214) 349-9996, Fax 349-0738; 104 E. Corsicana St., Athens 75751, (903) 675-8288, Fax 675-8351. **Committees**: Banking and Financial Services, Government Reform and Oversight, Science.

SMITH, Lamar S., R-San Antonio, District 21; Washington Office: 2231 RHOB; (202) 225-4236, Fax 225-8628; **District Offices:** 1100 NE Loop 410, Suite 640, San Antonio 78216, (210) 821-5024; 4305 N. Garfield Ste. 228B, Midland 79701, (915) 653-3971; 33 East Twohig, Site. 302, San Angelo 76903, (915) 653-3971; 1006 Junction Highway, Kerrville 78028, (210) 895-1414; 221 East Main, Suite 318, Round Rock 78664, (512) 218-4221. **Committees**: Budget, Judiciary.

STENHOLM, Charles, D-Stamford, District 17, Washington Office: 1211 LHOB; (202) 225-6605, Fax 225-2234; **District Offices**: P. O. Box 1237, Stamford 79553, (915) 773-3623, Fax 773-2833; 241 Pine St. Ste. 4A, Abilene 79601, (915) 673-7221, Fax 676-9547; 33 E. Twohig Ave., No. 318, San Angelo 76903, (915) 655-7994, Fax 548-2798. **Committee**: Agriculture.

THORNBERRY, William M. (Mac), R-Clarendon, District 13; Washington Office: 412 CHOB; (202) 225-3706, Fax 225-3486; **District Offices**: 724 S. Polk, No. 400, Amarillo 79101, (806) 371-8844; and 811 6th St., No. 130, Wichita Falls 76301, (817) 767-0541. **Committees**: National Security, Resources.

TURNER, Jim, D-Crockett, District 2; Washington Office: 1508 LHOB; (202) 225-2401; **District Office**: P.O. Box 780, Crockett 75835, (409) 544-3100. **Committees**: Government Reform and Oversight, National Security. ☆

Congressional leadership

Carolyn Barta, staff writer for *The Dallas Morning News*, provides an explanation and analysis of the leadership role of Texans in the current Congress. See the Elections section beginning on page 384.

Major Military Installations

Below are listed the major military installations in Texas in 1997. Data are taken from U.S. Defense Department sources. The base closings or re-arrangements being implemented in mid-1997 may alter the list. Some bases may be closed altogether; others may be assigned alternate roles; some units may be reassigned; and numbers of personnel may change.

U.S. Army

Fort Bliss
Location: Northeast El Paso.
Address: Fort Bliss, Texas 79916-0058
Main phone number: (915) 568-2121
Personnel: 15,551 active-duty; 2,107 civilians.
Major units: Army Air Defense Artillery Center and School; Army Sergeants Major Academy; 11th Air Defense Artillery Brigade; 31st Air Defense Artillery Brigade; 6th Air Defense Artillery Brigade.

Fort Hood
Location: In Killeen.
Address: Fort Hood, Texas 76544-5066
Main phone number: (817) 287-1110
Personnel: 43,328 active-duty; 4,031 civilians.
Major units: III Armored Corps; 1st Cavalry Div.; 4th Infantry Div.; 3rd Armored Cavalry Reg.; 13th Corps Support Command; 3rd Signal Brigade; 6th Cavalry Brigade; 89th Military Police Brigade; 504th Military Intelligence Brigade; Combat Aviation Training Brigade, Third Personnel Group; 13th Finance Group; 3rd Weather Squadron; Test and Experimentation Command.

Fort Sam Houston
Location: In San Antonio.
Address: Fort Sam Houston, Texas 78234-5000
Main phone number: (210) 221-1211
Personnel: 8,588 active-duty; 3,946 civilians.
Major units: U.S. Army Garrison; 5th U.S. Army; Army Medical Command; Army Medical Dept. Center and School; Brooke Army Medical Center.

U.S. Air Force

Brooks Air Force Base
Location: In San Antonio.
Address: Brooks AFB, Texas 78235-5304
Main phone number: (210) 536-1110
Personnel: 2,010 active-duty; 1,985 civilians.
Major units: Headquarters, Human Systems Center; Air Force School of Aerospace Medicine; Armstrong Laboratory; Air Force Center for Environmental Excellence; 70th Air Base Group.

Dyess AFB
Location: On west side of Abilene.
Address: Dyess AFB, Texas 79607-1960
Main phone number: (915) 696-0212
Personnel: 4,823 active-duty; 455 civilians.
Major units: 7th Bomb Wing (Air Combat Command); 9th Bomb Squadron; 28th Bomb Squadrons; 317th Airlift Group; 39th Airlift Squadron; 40th Airlift Squadron.

Goodfellow AFB
Location: On southwest side of San Angelo.
Address: Goodfellow AFB, San Angelo, Texas 76908-5000
Main phone number: (915) 654-3231
Personnel: 1,816 active-duty; 469 civilians.
Major units: 17th Training Group; 17th Support Group; 17th Medical Group; 344th Military Intelligence Battalion; Naval Technical Training Center Detachment; Marine Corps Detachment.

Kelly AFB
Location: Five miles southwest of San Antonio.
Address: Kelly AFB, Texas 78241-5842
Main phone number: (210) 925-1110
Personnel: 4,668 active-duty; 13,609 civilians.
Major units: San Antonio Air Logistics Center; Headquarters, Air Intelligence Agency; 76th Air Base Wing; 433rd Airlift Wing-Reserve; 149th Airlift Wing (Texas Air National Guard).

Lackland AFB
Location: Eight miles southwest of San Antonio.
Address: Lackland AFB, Texas 78236-5110
Main phone number: (210) 671-1110
Personnel: 13,817 active-duty; 3,023 civilians.
Major units: 37th Training Wing; Defense Language Institute English Language Center, Inter-American Air Forces Academy; 59th Medical Wing-Wilford Hall Medical Center.

Laughlin AFB
Location: Six miles east of Del Rio.
Address: Laughlin AFB, Texas 78843-5000
Main phone number: (210) 298-3511
Personnel: 1,230 active-duty; 470 civilians.
Major units: 47th Flying Training Wing.

Randolph AFB
Location: In Universal City, about 13 miles northeast of San Antonio.
Address: Randolph AFB, Texas 78150-4562
Personnel: 4,417 active-duty; 3,270 civilians.
Major units: Headquarters, Air Education and Training Command; Air Force Military Personnel Center; Headquarters, 19th Air Force; 12th Flying Training Wing; U.S. Air Force Recruiting Service.

Reese AFB

Location: 10 miles west of Lubbock.

Personnel: Closed 1997.

Sheppard AFB

Location: Five miles north of Wichita Falls.

Address: Sheppard AFB, Texas 76311-2943

Main phone number: (817) 676-2511

Personnel: 5,898 active-duty; 1,490 civilians.

Major units: 82nd Training Wing; 364th Training Squadron; 782nd Training Group; 82nd Mission Support Squadron; 882nd Training Group; 80th Flying Training Wing.

U.S. Navy

Corpus Christi Naval Air Station

Location: 12 miles east of Corpus Christi.

Address: NAS Corpus Christi, 11001 D St., #143, Corpus Christi 78419-5021

Main phone number: (512) 939-2383

Personnel: 1,892 active-duty; 4,428 civilians.

Major units: Headquarters, Naval Air Training Command; Training Air Wing 4; Commander of Mine Warfare Command; Coast Guard Air Group; Corpus Christi Army Depot.

Dallas Naval Air Station

Location: 10 miles west of downtown Dallas.

Address: NAS, Dallas, Texas 75211-9501

Main phone number: (972) 266-6111

Personnel: Reduced to closing personnel. Scheduled to close in 1998.

Naval Air Station-Joint Reserve Base, Fort Worth
(Carswell Field)

Location: westside Fort Worth.

Address: NAS-JRB, 1215 Depot Ave., Fort Worth 76127-5000.

Main phone number: (817) 782-7815

Personnel: 1,835 active-duty; 1,498 civilians.

Major units: Fighter Squadron 201, Marine Air Group 41; 14th Marines; Fleet Support Squadron 59; Army Reserve; Coast Guard Reserve; and Texas Air Guard.

Ingleside Naval Station

Location: In Ingleside.

Address: 1455 Ticonderoga Rd., #W123, Ingleside 78362-5001

Main phone number: (512) 776-4200.

Personnel: 2,200 active-duty; 150 civilians.

Major units: Mine Countermeasures Groups 1, 2, and 3; Shore Intermediate Maintenance Activity; 14 mine countermeasures ships.

Kingsville NAS

Location: In Kingsville.

Address: NAS Kingsville, Texas 78363-5000

Main phone number: (512) 595-6136

Personnel: 900 active-duty; 1,260 civilians.

Major units: Naval Auxiliary Landing Field Orange Grove; Squadrons: VT-21, VT-22; Training Air Wing 2; and McMullen Target Range, Escondido Ranch. ☆

A ship of the U.S. Navy receives maintenance in Galveston. Texas Almanac photo.

Federal Funds to Texas by County, 1996

The first figure represents total **direct expenditures to the county** for fiscal year 1996 in thousands of dollars. Texas received $86.8 billion; Anderson Co. received $185.6 million, etc. The second figure is that part of the total that went directly to individuals, primarily in **retirement and disability benefits** such as Social Security. *For a more complete explanation, see end of chart. Source: Consolidated Federal Funds Report 1996, U.S. Commerce Dept.*

County	Total (thousands)	To indiv. (thousands)
Texas	$86,782,754	$46,389,523
Anderson	$185,608	$140,981
Andrews	42,100	31,650
Angelina	287,000	219,073
Aransas	83,699	68,798
Archer	45,895	37,650
Armstrong	11,531	6,222
Atascosa	104,034	77,815
Austin	240,393	76,773
Bailey	34,157	18,119
Bandera	57,212	47,063
Bastrop	148,718	111,430
Baylor	23,886	18,507
Bee	113,594	87,382
Bell	2,453,565	562,425
Bexar	7,984,699	3,765,253
Blanco	50,964	45,839
Borden	1,940	848
Bosque	68,632	59,233
Bowie	622,609	310,824
Brazoria	551,363	398,101
Brazos	432,262	220,026
Brewster	39,040	25,171
Briscoe	13,970	9,910
Brooks	38,284	24,708
Brown	156,489	127,598
Burleson	56,398	46,598
Burnet	108,331	93,721
Caldwell	93,148	74,221
Calhoun	68,091	45,314
Callahan	47,603	39,585
Cameron	1,104,124	648,775
Camp	46,262	39,760
Carson	43,221	17,389
Cass	133,363	107,719
Castro	33,883	17,210
Chambers	78,728	41,521
Cherokee	170,984	122,295
Childress	29,948	21,373
Clay	31,671	26,009
Cochran	18,384	10,692
Coke	15,016	12,045
Coleman	58,988	46,046
Collin	917,243	421,286
Collingsworth	19,431	12,460
Colorado	82,051	60,870
Comal	246,367	211,553
Comanche	59,568	49,316
Concho	15,485	9,850
Cooke	114,022	94,797
Coryell	176,706	137,148
Cottle	11,925	7,611
Crane	12,043	9,706
Crockett	12,776	8,639
Crosby	35,978	24,642

County	Total (thousands)	To indiv. (thousands)
Culberson	$10,512	$6,308
Dallam	32,992	21,163
Dallas	7,992,522	3,902,287
Dawson	70,655	46,038
Deaf Smith	69,021	42,461
Delta	24,088	17,853
Denton	864,480	388,341
DeWitt	76,081	59,109
Dickens	17,633	12,645
Dimmit	43,815	25,809
Donley	22,209	14,495
Duval	60,265	41,216
Eastland	91,394	74,628
Ector	378,233	285,683
Edwards	12,603	8,981
Ellis	265,414	205,705
El Paso	3,104,055	1,531,790
Erath	103,702	83,502
Falls	84,665	58,082
Fannin	136,110	95,421
Fayette	85,160	72,740
Fisher	23,096	15,656
Floyd	38,284	22,755
Foard	10,710	6,548
Fort Bend	433,862	319,229
Franklin	31,519	26,511
Freestone	60,511	45,541
Frio	48,456	31,658
Gaines	46,437	27,345
Galveston	1,003,314	595,157
Garza	21,450	15,342
Gillespie	84,958	73,144
Glasscock	7,542	1,488
Goliad	22,497	18,435
Gonzales	75,005	54,912
Gray	100,837	83,289
Grayson	382,857	319,035
Gregg	419,367	336,066
Grimes	64,614	51,850
Guadalupe	244,830	205,152
Hale	139,363	95,152
Hall	22,304	14,902
Hamilton	38,195	33,169
Hansford	20,741	12,974
Hardeman	26,991	18,844
Hardin	145,094	121,535
Harris	12,060,476	5,418,724
Harrison	221,333	154,652
Hartley	8,019	2,835
Haskell	34,262	24,762
Hays	225,649	149,183
Hemphill	9,877	7,922
Henderson	212,468	172,191
Hidalgo	1,611,332	945,099
Hill	126,304	101,666

County	Total (thousands)	To indiv. (thousands)
Hockley	$82,700	$57,272
Hood	136,672	122,235
Hopkins	113,415	86,850
Houston	100,980	76,416
Howard	185,650	114,418
Hudspeth	13,684	5,357
Hunt	522,859	200,540
Hutchinson	84,467	70,193
Irion	5,708	4,107
Jack	25,100	20,864
Jackson	56,973	40,477
Jasper	147,472	110,380
Jeff Davis	7,753	5,826
Jefferson	1,188,345	794,492
Jim Hogg	25,471	15,521
Jim Wells	162,851	111,071
Johnson	323,268	269,785
Jones	74,363	56,255
Karnes	55,512	40,802
Kaufman	261,077	218,811
Kendall	84,873	76,582
Kenedy	967	648
Kent	5,419	3,091
Kerr	225,316	187,252
Kimble	20,650	13,878
King	1,389	418
Kinney	17,763	12,747
Kleberg	193,163	97,252
Knox	24,156	16,701
Lamar	182,350	144,456
Lamb	69,294	45,885
Lampasas	77,533	67,291
La Salle	28,168	13,607
Lavaca	88,904	74,940
Lee	37,436	31,525
Leon	67,372	57,353
Liberty	233,598	172,634
Limestone	83,316	66,874
Lipscomb	12,712	8,470
Live Oak	56,343	24,808
Llano	75,303	70,149
Loving	445	201
Lubbock	887,816	602,206
Lynn	28,785	18,377
Madison	35,183	27,625
Marion	43,540	33,934
Martin	19,452	10,951
Mason	16,543	13,350
Matagorda	130,661	89,331
Maverick	157,790	94,205
McCulloch	40,537	31,909
McLennan	983,200	574,789
McMullen	2,308	1,626
Medina	108,909	86,881
Menard	11,558	9,014

County	Total (thousands)	To indiv. (thousands)	County	Total (thousands)	To indiv. (thousands)	County	Total (thousands)	To indiv. (thousands)
Midland	$316,310	$233,898	Reeves	$51,587	$30,304	Titus	$91,543	$70,549
Milam	87,398	70,979	Refugio	32,725	25,916	Tom Green	487,299	280,047
Mills	22,483	18,035	Roberts	3,165	2,399	Travis	4,476,105	1,265,372
Mitchell	38,647	27,850	Robertson	62,557	48,973	Trinity	65,456	54,433
Montague	81,747	69,822	Rockwall	67,064	54,368	Tyler	79,724	67,283
Montgomery	574,021	459,732	Runnels	51,297	38,059	Upshur	119,704	98,611
Moore	75,041	33,113	Rusk	140,218	114,322	Upton	12,269	9,433
Morris	60,466	50,048	Sabine	61,746	53,747	Uvalde	92,799	61,943
Motley	8,387	5,648	S. Augustine	38,026	31,041	Val Verde	245,528	98,759
Nacogdoches	206,009	152,092	San Jacinto	61,087	49,432	Van Zandt	166,092	135,031
Navarro	161,488	124,963	San Patricio	328,290	161,233	Victoria	269,431	195.156
Newton	49,031	38,636	San Saba	28,945	20,342	Walker	133,266	102,956
Nolan	73,652	53,884	Schleicher	10,932	7,346	Waller	91,614	57,883
Nueces	1,594,445	791,043	Scurry	62,654	47,065	Ward	36,514	29,275
Ochiltree	26,895	17,704	Shackelford	13,240	10,904	Washington	94,284	80,404
Oldham	20,835	5,585	Shelby	103,600	81,135	Webb	565,388	290,711
Orange	315,410	241,760	Sherman	15,291	6,826	Wharton	147,471	107,520
Palo Pinto	108,288	84,891	Smith	623,868	461,612	Wheeler	28,901	22,028
Panola	81,656	64,510	Somervell	16,835	13,750	Wichita	780,358	402,770
Parker	202,744	172,581	Starr	152,984	84,082	Wilbarger	61,753	48,940
Parmer	36,913	20,036	Stephens	36,591	30,534	Willacy	71,221	41,923
Pecos	46,394	28,512	Sterling	4,051	2,705	Williamson	348,452	274,536
Polk	219,416	184,807	Stonewall	9,102	6,402	Wilson	74,601	60,094
Potter	947,516	416,996	Sutton	11,968	8,091	Winkler	28,074	23,345
Presidio	29,582	17,371	Swisher	40,480	23,892	Wise	101,308	84,175
Rains	25,603	21,072	Tarrant	7,357,726	2,598,123	Wood	147,065	126,230
Randall	98,143	73,613	Taylor	783,895	348,252	Yoakum	25,233	15,976
Reagan	9,549	6,012	Terrell	5,732	3,892	Young	74,372	61,551
Real	13,933	11,651	Terry	55,331	36,643	Zapata	40,273	28,483
Red River	73,218	54,446	Throckmorton	8,742	6,614	Zavala	45,702	27,407

*Total federal government expenditures include the categories: grants, salaries and wages (Postal Service, Dept. of Defense, etc.), procurement, direct payments for individuals, other direct payments, direct loans, insured loans and insurance.

Retirement and disability programs include Federal employee retirement and disability benefits, Social Security payments of all types, selected Veterans Administration programs and military retirees.

Direct payments for individuals also includes earned income tax credit payments, Higher Education Act Insured Loans interest subsidies and federal housing assistance programs.

Source: Consolidated Federal Funds Report, Fiscal Year 1996, U.S. Department of Commerce, Bureau of the Census.

U.S. Tax Collections in Texas

Source: Internal Revenue Service

Fiscal Year	Individual Income and Employment Taxes	Corporation Income Taxes	Estate Taxes	Gift Taxes	Excise Taxes	Total U.S. Taxes Collected in Texas
1996	$76,863,689,000	$12,393,992,000	$733,282,000	$158,237,000	$10,418,847,000	$101,079,028,000
1995	69,706,333,000	10,677,881,000	869,528,000	152,683,000	11,135,857,000	92,342,282,000
1994	63,916,496,000	9,698,069,000	624,354,000	347,900,000	9,528,449,000	84,086,676,000
1993	59,962,756,000	7,211,968,000	618,469,000	111,896,000	7,552,247,000	75,457,335,000
1992	57,367,765,000	6,338,621,000	598,918,000	121,164,000	7,558,642,000	71,985,109,000
1991	55,520,001,000	8,761,621,000	588,298,000	87,739,000	6,647,312,000	71,604,791,000
1990	52,795,489,000	6,983,762,000	521,811,000	196,003,000	5,694,006,000	66,191,071,000
1989	50,855,904,000	8,675,006,000	458,106,000	96,699,000	5,766,594,000	66,052,309,000
1988	45,080,428,000	6,058,172,000	444,349,000	39,137,000	5,957,085,000	57,579,171,000
1987	43,165,241,000	4,124,164,000	443,947,000	27,342,000	3,908,826,000	51,669,519,000
1986	44,090,929,000	4,808,703,000	493,405,000	35,355,000	4,169,857,000	53,598,248,000
1985	41,497,114,000	5,637,148,000	528,106,000	41,560,000	6,058,110,000	53,762,038,000
1984	37,416,203,000	4,750,079,000	494,431,000	19,844,000	5,553,491,000	48,234,047,000
1983	36,072,975,000	6,574,940,000	624,559,000	6,789,000	6,880,102,000	50,159,365,000
1982	31,692,219,000	7,526,687,000	526,420,000	31,473,000	8,623,799,000	48,400,598,000
1981	25,707,514,000	7,232,486,000	453,830,000	23,722,000	4,122,538,000	37,540,089,000

Fine Arts Organizations Across State

The following information on the fine arts in Texas was prepared for the Texas Almanac *by the staff of the Texas Commission on the Arts.*

Culture in Texas, as in any market, is a mixture of activity generated by both the commercial and the non-profit sectors.

The commercial sector encompasses Texas-based profit-making businesses including commercial recording artists (such as the legendary Willie Nelson), night-clubs, record companies, private galleries, assorted boutiques that carry fine art collectibles and private dance and music halls. In addition, Texas is becoming an important media center, with Texas-based publications, television and film companies gaining national recognition.

Texas also has extensive cultural resources offered by nonprofit organizations that are engaged in charitable, educational and/or humanitarian activities.

The Texas Legislature has authorized six state agencies to administer cultural services and funds for the public good. The agencies, listed below, fall under the auspices of the Texas Legislature's Cultural and Historical Resources Committee.

They are: **State Antiquities Committee**, Box 12276, Austin 78711; **Texas Commission on the Arts**, Box 13406, Capitol Sta., Austin 78711; **Texas Film Commission, the Governor's office**, Box 12428, Austin 78711; **Texas Historical Commission**, Box 12276, Austin 78711; **Texas State Library and Archives Commission**, Box 12927, Austin 78711; and the **State Preservation Board**, Box 13286, Austin 78711.

Although not a state agency, another organization that provides cultural services to the citizens of Texas is the **Texas Committee for the Humanities**, 1604 Nueces, Austin 78701.

The Texas Commission on the Arts was established in 1965 to develop a receptive climate for the arts in Texas and to serve as a source of arts information to state government and Texas at large. The commission achieves these objectives by providing financial, informational and technical assistance.

The commission's assistance programs serve as a financial catalyst to assist individuals and organizations in opening doors to local resources. Its clientele includes theaters (professional, civic, children's, ethnic), media (radio, television, film, publications), festivals, music (folk, symphonic, chamber, choral, jazz, opera, and new music), visual arts (sculpture, crafts, photography, painting, environmental), dance (modern, ballet, folkloric), schools, presenters of cultural events, and service organizations.

In 1993, the Texas Legislature created the Texas Cultural Endowment Fund as a public/private funding source to enhance the performing, visual and literary arts and education. Goals of the Texas Cultural Endowment Fund are to: 1) create financial self-sufficiency for the Texas Commission on the Arts by providing a stable and predictable base of funding no longer dependent on tax-based legislative support; 2) enhance arts education, encourage economic development, and cultivate a higher quality of life in communities throughout Texas;

3) demonstrate leadership by encouraging public and private partnerships, ensuring public access to the arts for all communities statewide; and 4) diversify revenue sources, and increase the state's capacity to introduce the arts to future generations, to build audiences, and to create supporters.

The Texas Commission on the Arts seeks support for the Texas Cultural Endowment Fund and is responsible for the management of the fund. The commission is also ultimately responsible for the distribution of the fund to artists, arts, cultural and educational projects and organizations throughout Texas. For more information about the services of the commission, call toll-free (800) 252-9415.

Some of Texas' major nonprofit arts institutions — orchestras, museums, dance companies, theaters and cultural centers — are listed below.

Addison — Addison Centre Theatre, Box 933, (75001).

Amarillo — Amarillo Symphony Orchestra, Box 2552 (79105); Lone Star Ballet, Box 1133 (79178).

Austin — Austin Symphony Orchestra, 1101 Red River (78701); Ballet Austin, 3002 Guadalupe (78705); Laguna Gloria Art Museum, Box 5568 (78763); Paramount Theatre for the Performing Arts, Box 1205 (78767).

Beaumont — Beaumont Art Museum, 1111 9th St. (77702).

Corpus Christi — Art Museum of South Texas, 1902 N. Shoreline Dr. (78401); Corpus Christi Ballet, 5610 Everhart (78469).

Corsicana — Community Playhouse, Box 2224 (75110).

Dallas — Ballet Dallas, 309 S. Pearl (75201); Dallas Opera, 1925 Elm (75201); Dallas Museum of Art, 1717 N. Harwood (75201); Dallas Symphony Orchestra, Box 26207 (75226); Dallas Theatre Center, 3636 Turtle Creek Blvd. (75219); Shakespeare Festival, 3630 Harry Hines (75210); Teatro Dallas, 2204 Commerce (75201); Theatre Three, 2800 Routh (75201).

El Paso — Museum Of Arts, 1211 Montana Ave. (79902); El Paso Symphony Orchestra, Box 180 (79942).

Fort Worth — Amon Carter Museum Of Western Art, Box 2365 (76101); Museum of Modern Art, 1309 Montgomery (76107); Fort Worth Ballet Assn., 6845 Green Oaks Rd. (76116); Fort Worth Opera, 3505 W. Lancaster (76107); Fort Worth Symphony Orchestra, 4401 Trail Lake Dr. (76109); Kimbell Art Museum, Box 9440 (76107); Stage West, Box 2587 (76113); Van Cliburn Foundation, 2525 Ridgmar Blvd. (76116).

Houston — Alley Theatre, 615 Texas (77002); Contemporary Arts Museum, 5216 Montrose Blvd. (77006); Houston Ballet Foundation, Box 130487 (77219); Houston Grand Opera, 510 Preston, #500 (77002); Houston Museum of Fine Arts, Box 6826 (77265); Houston Symphony Orchestra, 615 Louisiana (77002); Texas Opera Theatre, 510 Preston, #440 (77002); Theatre Under the Stars, 4235 San Felipe (77027).

Midland/Odessa — Midland/Odessa Symphony and Chorale, Box 60658 (79711).

Round Top — James Dick Foundation for the Performing Arts, Box 89 (78954).

San Antonio — Carver Cultural Center, 226 N. Hackberry (78202); Guadalupe Cultural Arts Center, 1300 Guadalupe (78207); McNay Art Institute, Box 6069 (78209); San Antonio Art Institute, Box 6069 (78209); San Antonio Museum Association, Box 2601 (78299-2601); San Antonio Performing Arts Assn., 110 Broadway, Ste. 230 (78205); San Antonio Symphony Orchestra, 109 Lexington Ave., Ste. 207 (78205); Southwest Craft Center, 300 Augusta (78205).

The Texas Alliance for Education and the Arts , 3939 Bee Caves Rd., Ste. 203, Austin 78746, promotes, develops and supports local arts agencies. Listed below are the some of the members as of mid-1997.

Abilene — Abilene Cultural Affairs Council, 1101 N. First St. (79604).

Albany — The Old Jail Art Center, Rt. 1, Box 1 (76430).

Amarillo — Chamber Arts Committee, Box 9480 (79105).

Andrews — Andrews Cultural Affairs Committee, 700 West Broadway (79714).

Arlington — Arlington Arts Council, 629 Crowley Rd. (76012).

Athens — Henderson County Arts Council, P.O. Box 2633 (75751).

Austin — Cultural Arts Division — City of Austin, PARD, Box 1088 (78767).

Bastrop — Bastrop Assn. for the Arts, 807 Main (78602).

Bay City — Bay City Cultural Assn., P.O. Box 419(77414).

Beaumont, Orange and Port Arthur — Southeast Texas Arts Council, Box 3925, Beaumont (77704).

Belton — Bell Fine Arts Assoc., P.O. Box 624 (76513).

Big Bend — Big Bend Arts Alliance, 505 W. San Antonio, Marfa (79843).

Big Spring — Big Spring Cultural Affairs Council, Box 1391 (79720). West Texas Center for the Arts, Box 1810 (79720).

Borger — Magic Plains Arts Council, 601 W. 3rd (79007).

Beckenridge — Breckenridge Fine Arts Center, Box 549 (76424).

Brenham — Arts Council of Washington County, 701 Milroy Dr. (77833).

Brownfield — Brownfield Arts Assn., 1103 W. Main (79316).

Brownwood — Community Cultural Affairs Commission, P.O Box 880 (76804).

Buchanan Dam — Highland Lakes Art Council, Rt. 1 Box 118, (78605).

Carrizo Springs — Arts Council of Dimmit County, 412 Pena (78834).

Clifton — Bosque Co. Conservatory of Fine Arts, Box 373 (76634).

Coleman — Fine Arts League, Box 376 (76834).

College Station — Arts Council of Brazos Valley, 310 University Dr. East (77840).

Columbus — Live Oak Art Center, 1014 Milam (78934).

Conroe — Montgomery County Performing Arts Society, Box 1714 (77305).

Corpus Christi — Municipal Arts Commission, PARD, Box 9277 (78401).

Corsicana — Navarro Council of the Arts, Box 2224 (75151).

Crockett — Piney Woods Fine Arts Assn., Box 1213 (75835).

Cuero — Oscar Scott Memorial Foundation, 203 E. Church (77954).

Cuney — Cuney Cultural Committee, Box 92 (75759).

Dalhart — Dalhart Area Fine Arts Assn., 1022 Oak (79022).

Dallas — Office of Cultural Affairs, 1925 Elm, Ste. 500 (75201).

Del Rio — Del Rio Council for the Arts, 120 East Garfield (78840).

Denison — Denison Arts Council, P.O. Box 325 (75020).

Denton — Greater Denton Arts Council, 207 S. Bell (76201).

DeSoto — DeSoto Council of Cultural Arts, 624 Bentcreek Dr. (75115).

Dumas — Moore County Arts Assn., Crabb Art Center P.O. Box 74 (79029).

Duncanville — Duncanville Regional Arts Assn., Box 381014 (76138).

Eagle Pass — Arts Council of Eagle Pass, Box 2929 (78853).

El Paso — El Paso Arts Resources Department, City of El Paso, 2 Civic Center Plaza (79901).

Fort Worth — Arts Council of Fort Worth & Tarrant County, 508 Main (76102).

Gainesville — Cooke County Arts Council, Box 194 (76241).

Garland — Garland Center for the Performing Arts, Box 469002 (75046).

Gilmer — Upshur County Arts Council, Box 854 (75644).

Grand Prairie — Grand Prairie Arts Council, Box 531613 (75053).

Harlingen — Harlingen Arts Council, Box 531105 (78553).

Hondo — Art League of Hondo, 1160 26th, (78861).

Houston — Cultural Arts Council of Houston, 3201 Allen Parkway (77019).

Huntsville — Huntsville Arts Commission, 1212 Ave. M (77340).

Ingram — The Point Visual & Performing Arts Center, P.O. Box 169 (78025).

Irving — Irving Arts Center, 3333 N. McArthur, Ste. 300 (75062); Irving Cultural Affairs Council, same address.

Killeen — Vive les Artes Society, Box 10657 (76547).

Lake Jackson — Brazosport Fine Arts Council, 400 College Dr. (77566).

Lampasas — Keystone Art Alliance, Box 1013 (76550).

Laredo — Laredo Center for the Arts, 500 San Agustin (78040).

Lubbock — Lubbock Arts Alliance, Inc., 2109 Broadway (79401).

Marble Falls — Highland Lakes Arts Guild, 318 Main (78654).

Marfa — Big Bend Arts Alliance, Alliance, 505 W. San Antonio (78654).

Marshall — Marshall Regional Arts Council, Box C (75671).

Mesquite — Mesquite Arts Council, 1515 North Galloway (75149).

Midland — Midland Arts Assembly, Box 3494 (79702).

Missouri City — Fort Bend Cultural Arts Council, 8314 Bee Meadow (77489).

Mount Vernon — Franklin County Arts Assoc., P.O. Box 1276 (75457).

New Braunfels — Greater New Braunfels Arts Council, Box 311171 (78131).

Odessa — Odessa Cultural Council, Box 7195 (79760).

Pampa — Pampa Fine Arts Assn., Box 818 (79065).

Paris — Paris Area Arts Alliance, P.O. Box 6085 (75461).

Pasadena — Pasadena Cultural Affairs Committee, 4334 Fairmont Parkway (77504).

Pecos — Pecos Arts Coalition, Box 2399 (79772).

Pittsburg — Pittsburg/Camp County Arts Council, Box 72 (75686).

Plains — Yoakum County Art Assn., Box 38 (79355).

Plainview — Plainview Cultural Council, 1900 W. Seventh (79702).

Plano — Art Center of Plano, Box 861011 (75086).

Point Aransas — Island Art Assoc., P.O. Box 1871 (78373).

Point Comfort — Calhoun County Arts Council, P.O. Box 268 (77978).

Post — Caprock Cultural Assn., Box 37 (79356).

Richardson — Richardson Arts Commission, Box 830309 (75083).

Rockport — Rockport Center for the Arts, 902 Navigation Circle (78382).

San Angelo — San Angelo Cultural Affairs Council, Box 2477 (76902).

San Antonio — City of San Antonio Arts and Cultural Affairs, 222 E. Houston, Ste. 500 (78205).

San Marcos — Performing Arts Assn., Box 651 (78666).

Schulenburg — Backstage Inc. Fine Arts Council, Box 66 (78956).

Seagoville — Seagoville Fine Arts Council, 2403 Seagoville Rd. (75159).

Sherman — Council for the Arts and Humanities, Box 1029 (75091).

Silsbee — Performing and Visual Arts Council, Rt. 1, Box 150 (77656).

South Padre Island — Area Funds Foundation, Box 2326 (78597).

Stephenville — Cross Timbers Fine Arts Council, Box 1172 (76401).

Temple — Temple Cultural Activities Center, 3011 N. Third (76501).

Texarkana — Texarkana Regional Arts and Humanities Council Inc., Box 1171 (75504).

The Woodlands — The Woodlands Living Arts Council, Box 7411 (77387).

Tomball — Regional Arts Center, Box 1321 (77377).

Uvalde — Uvalde Arts Council, 104 W. North (78801).

Vernon — Vernon Council of the Arts, Box 222 (76384).

Victoria — Cultural Council of Victoria, Box 1758 (77902).

Waco — Greater Waco Council for the Arts, 3115 Pine, Ste. 202 (76708).

Waxahachie — Waxahachie Arts Council, 311 Olive (75165).

Wichita Falls — Wichita Falls Arts Commission, 607 Tenth (76301).

Wimberly — Wimberley Institute of Cultures, Box 167 (78676). ☆

Cormac McCarthy was honored by the Texas Institute of Letters in its most recent awards for lifetime achievement. Mr. McCarthy of El Paso is the author of All the Pretty Horses *and* The Crossing *and other works. Marion Ettlinger photo.*

Texas Institute of Letters
Awards

Each year since 1939, the **Texas Institute of Letters** has chosen outstanding literature and journalism that are either by Texans or about Texas subjects. Awards have been made for fiction, nonfiction, Southwest history, general information, magazine and newspaper journalism, children's books, poetry and book design. The awards for recent years are listed below:

Writer/Designer: Title

1996
Sandra Scofield: *A Chance to See Egypt*
Nolan Porterfield: *Last Cavalier: The Life and Times of John A Lomax*
Kathleen Cambor: *The Book of Mercy*
Rick Bass: *The Book of Yaak*
Isabel Nathaniel: "The Dominion of Light'"
Daniel Stern: "The Passion According to St. John by J.S. Bach"
Debbie Nathan: "The Death of Jane Roe"
Mike Tolson: "When Hope Dies"
D.J. Stout: *Heaven of Animals*
Thomas Taylor and Barbara Whitehead: *Trading in Santa Fe*
J.A. Benner: *Uncle Comanche*
Lon Tinkle Award: Cormac McCarthy

1995
Paul Scott Malone: *In an Arid Land: Thirteen Stories of Texas*
Mary Karr: *The Liars' Club: A Memoir*
Jewel Mogan: *Beyond Telling*
Ben Huseman: *Wild River, Timeless Canyon*
Paul Christensen: "Water"

Rick Bass: "The Fires Next Time'
Mike Tolson: "Race to the Future"
Dick Gerdes: *The Fourth World* (trans.)
Ellen McKie: *Codex Telleriano-Remensis*
Diane Stevens: *Liza's Blue Moon*
Lon Tinkle Award: William Humphrey

1994
Reginald Gibbons: *Sweetbitter*
Lawrence Wright: *Remembering Satan*
Ron Tyler: *Prints of the West*
Pattiann Rogers: *Firekeeper*
Donley Watt: *Can You Get THere From Here?*
William J. Cobb: " White Circles"
Mimi Swartz: "Promised Land"
Dr. Bertie Acker: *Iphigenia* (trans.)
Florence George Graves: "The Other Woman"
W. Thomas Taylor: *The War Between the United States and Mexico*
Barbara Elmore: *Breathing Room*
Lon Tinkle Award: Américo Paredes

1993
Dagoberto Gilb: *The Magic of Blood*
Howard Swindle: *Deliberate Indifference*
William H. Goetzmann: *Sam Chamberlain's Mexican War: The San Jacinto Museum Paintings*
Jack Myers: *Blindsided*
Lee Merrill Byrd: *My Sister Disappears*
Dagoberto Gilb: "Nancy Flores"
Elizabeth Franklin: "The Quest of a Projects Kid"
Denise Gamino: "The Lost Children"
W. Thomas Taylor: *Audubon's Great National Work: The Royal Octavo Edition of The Birds of America*
Dee Stuart: *The Astonishing Armadillo*
Lon Tinkle Award: Horton Foote

1992
Cormac McCarthy: *All the Pretty Horses*
David Weber: *The Spanish Frontier in North America*
Joel Barna: *The See-Through Years: Creation and Destruction in Texas Architecture*
Susan Wood: *Campo Santo*
Christopher Middleton and Letitia Garza-Falcon: *The Andalusian Poems* (trans.)
William Cobb: "The Atmosphere of Venus"
Dudley Althaus: "The New Awakening: Breaking the Chain of Conquest in Latin America"
Dudley Althaus: *Prayers, Death and Angels: A Day in Baidoa*
Sherry Garland: *Song of the Buffalo Boy*
D. J. Stout: *Mojo*
Lon Tinkle Award: Vassar Miller

1991
Sarah Bird: *The Mommy Club*
Max Oelschlaeger: *The Idea of Wilderness*
Robert S. Weddle: *The French Thorn*
Andrew Hudgins: *The Never-Ending*
Lee Merrill Byrd: "Major Six Pockets"
Lawrence Wright: "The Sensual Christian"
Mike Cochran: "Profile of Pinkie Roden"
Charlotte Baker Montgomery: *The Trail North*
W. Thomas Taylor: *Self-Portrait With Birds*
Lon Tinkle Award: Margaret Cousins

1990
Lionel G. Garcia: *Hardscrub*
Virginia Stem Owens: *If You Do Love Old Men*
Nicolas Kanellos: *A History of Hispanic Theatre in the United States: Origins to 1940*
Daryl Jones: *Someone Going Home Late*
Frances M. Lopez-Morillas: *Behind the Curtains* (trans.)
Rick Bass: "The Legend of the Pig-Eye"
Bryan Woolley: "A Family Nightmare"

Scott McCartney: "S & Ls on Main Street"
Zinita Fowler: *The Last Innocent Summer*
Lon Tinkle Award: Marshall Terry

1989

James Magnuson: *Ghost Dancing*
Ernestine Sewell Linck and Joyce Gibson Roach: *Eats: A Folk History of Texas Foods*
Randolph B. Campbell: *An Empire for Slavery: The Peculiar Institution in Texas*
Pattiann Rogers: *Splitting and Binding*
James Hoggard: "The Scapegoat"
Lance Bertelsen: "San Pietro and the 'Art' of War"
Ilo Hiller: *Introducing Birds to Young Naturalists*
George Lennox: *Epitaphs for the Living: Words and Images in the Time of AIDS*
Lon Tinkle Award: John Edward Weems

1988

William Hauptman: *Good Rockin' Tonight*
William Hauptman: "Moon Walking"
Lawrence Wright: *In the New World: Growing Up with America, 1960-1984*
Emily Fourmy Cutrer: *The Art of the Woman: The Life and Work of Elisabet Ney*
William Olsen: *The Hand of God and a Few Bright Flowers*
Evan Moore: "Cult of Terror"
Ronnie Dugger: "Voting by Computer"
David Price: *The Song of Things Begun*
Lon Tinkle Award: C. L. Sonnichsen

1987

Beverly Lowry: *The Perfect Sonya*
Kenneth B. Ragsdale: *The Year America Discovered Texas: Centennial '36*
David Montejano: *Anglos and Mexicans in the Making of Texas 1836-1986*
Walter McDonald: *The Flying Dutchman*
Steve Barthelme: "Zorro"
Mike Cochran: "Texas Fugitives"
Robert Sherrill: "Can Miami Save Itself?"
Ruby C. Tolliver: *Muddy Banks*
Walter Horton: "Texas Wildflower Portraits"
Lon Tinkle Award: A. C. Greene

1986

William H. and William N. Goetzmann: *The West of the Imagination*
Rosalind Wright: *Veracruz*
Alfred W. Crosby: *Ecological Imperialism: The Biological Expansion of Europe, 900-1900*

Gail Galloway Adams: "Inside Dope"
Edward Hirsch: *Wild Gratitude*
Brenda Bell: "Life After Death"
George Lenox and Omega Clay: *The Panoramic Photography of Eugene O. Goldbeck*
Lon Tinkle Award: Elmer Kelton

1985

Elizabeth W. and Robert A. Fernea: *The Arab World: Personal Encounters*
Larry McMurtry: Lonesome Dove
Darwin Payne: *Owen Wister: Chronicler of the West*
Reginald Gibbons: "Mr. Walsh's Mare"
Paula G. Paul: *Sarah, Sissy Weed and the Ships of the Desert*
C. W. Smith: "Uncle Dad"
Andrew Hudgins: *Saints and Strangers*
Walter McDonald: *Witching on Hardscrabble*
Doug Swanson: Woodrow Wilson High School (Dallas) series
Walter Horton: *Dallas Architecture, 1936-1986*
Lon Tinkle Award: Don Barthelme

1984

Max Apple: *Free Agents*
Celia Morris Eckhardt: *Fanny Wright*
John Bloom and Jim Atkinson: *Evidence of Love*
William Roger Louis: *The British Empire in the Middle East, 1945-1951*
Rosemary Catacalos: *Again for the First Time*
Beverly Lowry: "So Far from the Road, So Long Until Morning"
Judith Alter: *Luke and the Van Zandt County War*
Jeff Unger: *Huck at 100*
John Davidson: "The Man Who Dreamed Luckenbach"
Drew Jubera: "To Find a Mockingbird"
George Lenox: *The Other Texas Frontier*
Lon Tinkle Award: Larry McMurtry

1983

Joe Coomer: *The Decatur Road*
Michael Mewshaw: *Short Circuit*
Lawrence C. Kelly: *The Assault on Assimilation*
Albert Goldbarth: Original Light: New and Selected Poems, 1973-1983
Bryan Woolley: "Where Texas Meets the Sea"
Jack Kent: *Silly Goose*
Tim Zigal: "Curios"
Barbara and Fred Whitehead: *Clem Maverick*
Lon Tinkle Award: William Owens
Special Citation: The Texas Almanac ☆

Van Cliburn Competition Recognizes Top Pianists

The Van Cliburn International Piano Competition was initiated in 1962 by music teachers and community leaders in Fort Worth. The event is held every four years. It commemorated Van Cliburn's victory in the Tchaikovsky International Piano Competition in Moscow in 1958.

Gold medalists receive cash prizes, tour engagements and free management for two years.

Past gold medalists are as follows:

Jon Nakamatsu holds the winning trophy as winner of the 1997 Fort Worth competition. The Dallas Morning News *photo.*

1962	Ralph Votapek, USA
1966	Radu Lupu, Romania
1969	Christina Ortiz, Brazil
1973	Vladimir Viardo, USSR
1977	Steven De Groote, South Africa
1981	André-Michel Schub, USA
1985	José Feghali, Brazil
1989	Alexei Sultanov, USSR
1993	Simone Pedroni, Italy
1997	Jon Nakamatsu, USA

Public Libraries

The following information on Texas Public Libraries was furnished by Patty Davis of the Library Development Division of the Texas State Library, Austin.

Public libraries continue to strive to meet the education and information needs of Texans by providing library services and materials in print format, in audio-visual format, in programs, and in electronic format such as CD-ROM and the Internet. Each year, services provided by public libraries to the citizens of Texas increase, with more visits to public libraries and higher attendance in library programs.

In 1995, the latest year for which data has been received, the public libraries in Texas served 16,313,265 people, and answered 16,368,226 reference questions, both in person and on the phone. During the same reporting period, there were 45,788,985 visits to Texas public libraries, amounting to 2.81 visits per capita. 3,512,805 people attended programs at Texas public libraries, including 1,932,217 children who attended library-sponsored juvenile programs such as story hours and summer reading programs.

The total number of books and other materials checked out of Texas public libraries was 70,161,608, a total of 4.30 circulations per capita, and this number does not include the information printed or downloaded by patrons from electronic sources in public libraries.

Library income per capita increased 6.5% from 1994 to 1995, from $11.45 to $12.20; $11.53 of this amount was from local governments. The remaining income came from federal, state, contributions, gifts, and foundation and corporate grants funds. According to preliminary findings of a nationwide survey, Texas ranked 39th in local government income.

The challenges facing the public libraries in Texas are varied. The costs for providing electronic and on-line sources, in addition to traditional library services, are growing faster than library budgets. Urban libraries are trying to serve growing populations, while libraries in rural areas are trying to serve remote populations and provide distance learning, most at inadequate levels of support.

More than 1.3 million Texans are not served by a local library, an increase from 1.2 million in 1993. There are eight counties where there is no public library. Of the 504 public libraries reporting statistics in 1995, 26 were unable to meet the minimum standards for accreditation by the Texas State Library, and there are more than 300 public libraries serving a population of 2,231,803, that do not have professionally trained librarians. In order to fill the growing information needs of Texans, there is a continuing need for funding, materials, and staff in Texasí public libraries.

These and other statistics on public libraries are available on the Texas State Library's web page at: **http://www.tsl.state.tx.us/LD/LDhome.html**.

The following table lists Texas public libraries by city mailing address. Many of these libraries and branches are establishing web pages on the Internet. To visit your local library's web page, call the library for the web address or find a list of libraries with addresses on the Texas State Electronic Library at **http://link.tsl.state.tx.us/t/texlibs2.html**. Check the changing area codes in your city.

Libraries by City

LIBRARY	ADDRESS	CITY	ZIP	AC	PHONE
Abernathy Public	P.O. Box 686	Abernathy	79311-0686	806	298-2546
Abilene Public	202 Cedar Street	Abilene	79601-5793	915	676-6328
Lalo Arcaute Public	502 Duranta St.	Alamo	78516	210	787-6160
Shackelford County	P.O. Box 445	Albany	76430-0445	915	762-2672
East Parker County	P.O. Box 275	Aledo	76008-0275	817	441-6545
Alice Public	401 East Third Street	Alice	78332-4798	512	664-9506
Allen Public	Two Allen Civic Plaza	Allen	75013-2559	972	727-0190
Alpine Public	203 North 7th Street	Alpine	79830-4693	915	837-2621
Stella Hill Memorial	Route 1 Box 724	Alto	75925-9791	409	858-4343
Alvarado Public	200 N. Spears	Alvarado	76009-3873	817	783-7323
Alvin Branch	105 S. Gordon St.	Alvin	77511-2332	281	388-4300
Alvord Public	P.O. Box 323	Alvord	76225-0323	817	427-2842
Amarillo Public	P.O. Box 2171	Amarillo	79189-2171	806	378-3050
Lake Tanglewood Public	Rt. 8, Box 35-15	Amarillo	79118-9430	806	622-1242
Chambers County System	P.O. Box 520	Anahuac	77514-0520	409	267-8261
Andrews County	208 NW 2nd Street	Andrews	79714-6396	915	524-1432
Brazoria County System	412 N. Front Street	Angleton	77515-4428	409	849-5711
Anna Community	Rt 1 Box 280A	Anna	75003	214	924-2456
Anson Public	P.O. Box 528	Anson	79501-0528	915	823-2711
Ed & Hazel Richmond Public	110 North Lamont Street	Aransas Pass	78336-3698	512	758-2350
Archer Public	P.O. Box 957	Archer City	76351-0957	817	574-4954
Arlington Public System	101 E. Abram Street	Arlington	76010-1183	817	459-6901
Stonewall County	P.O. Box H	Aspermont	79502-0907	817	989-2730
Henderson Co. Murchison	121 South Prairieville St.	Athens	75751-2595	903	677-6350
Atlanta Public	101 West Hiram Street	Atlanta	75551-2509	903	796-2112
Aubrey Area	109 S. Main Street	Aubrey	76227-9164	817	365-9162

LIBRARY	ADDRESS	CITY	ZIP	AC	PHONE
Lake Travis Community	3322 Ranch Road 620 South	Austin	78734-6801	512	263-2885
Westbank Community	1309 Westbank Drive	Austin	78746-6565	512	327-3045
Austin Public	P.O. Box 2287	Austin	78768-2287	512	499-7300
Austin History Center	810 Guadalupe	Austin	78701-2314	512	499-7480
Azle Public	609 SE Parkway Street	Azle	76020-3654	817	444-7114
Callahan County	"100 W. 4th, B-1"	Baird	79504-5305	915	854-1718
Balch Springs	4301 Pioneer Road	Balch Springs	75180-4001	972	286-8856
Carnegie of Ballinger	204 8th Street	Ballinger	76821	915	365-3616
Bandera County	P.O. Box 1568	Bandera	78003-1568	210	796-4213
Nueces Canyon Public	P.O. Box 58	Barksdale	78828-0058	210	234-3173
Ward County Barstow	P.O. Box 74	Barstow	79719-0074		
Teinert Memorial Public	Box 12	Bartlett	76511-0012	817	527-3208
Bastrop Public	P.O. Box 670	Bastrop	78602-0670	512	321-5441
Bay City Public	1100 Seventh Street	Bay City	77414-4915	409	245-6931
Sterling Municipal	Mary Elizabeth Wilbanks Ave.	Baytown	77520	281	427-7331
Jefferson County	2748 Viterbo Road - Box 7	Beaumont	77705-9554	409	727-2735
Beaumont Public System	P.O. Box 3827	Beaumont	77704-3827	409	838-6606
Bedford Public	1805 L. Don Dodson Drive	Bedford	76021-1897	817	952-2160
Bee County Public	210 E. Corpus Christi Street	Beeville	78102-4812	512	358-5541
Bellaire City	5111 Jessamine	Bellaire	77401-4498	713	662-8160
Bellville Public	12 W. Palm Street	Bellville	77418-1446	409	865-3731
Mary Ruth Briggs	7 Morgan's Point Blvd.	Belton	76513-6438		
Belton City	301 East First Avenue	Belton	76513-3168	817	933-5832
Benbrook Public	101-C Del Rio Street	Benbrook	76126-2557	817	249-6632
Bertram Free	P.O. Box 243	Bertram	78605-0243	512	355-2113
Reagan County	County Courthouse	Big Lake	76932	915	884-2854
Holly Community	Route 1, Box 799	Big Sandy	75755-9600	903	769-5142
Howard County	312 Scurry Street	Big Spring	79720-2559	915	264-2260
Williams Memorial	P.O. Box 489	Blanco	78606-0489	210	833-4280
Blessing	P.O. Box 210	Blessing	77419-0210	512	588-7717
Boerne Public	210 N. Main Street	Boerne	78006-2036	210	249-3053
Kendall County System	210 N. Main Street	Boerne	78006	210	249-3053
Bonham Public	305 East 5th Street	Bonham	75418-4002	903	583-3128
Booker School/Public	Drawer 288	Booker	79005-0288	806	658-9323
Hutchinson County	625 N. Weatherly Street	Borger	79007-3621	806	273-0126
Bowie Public	315 W. Walnut Street	Bowie	76230-4828	817	872-2681
Boyd Public	733 East Rock Island Avenue	Boyd	76023-3001	817	433-5580
Kinney County Public	P.O. Box 975	Brackettville	78832-0975	210	563-2884
F.M. (Buck) Richards Memorial	1106 South Blackburn Street	Brady	76825-6222	915	597-2617
Brazoria Branch	620 S. Brooks St.	Brazoria	77422-9022	409	798-2372
Breckenridge	207 N. Breckenridge Avenue	Breckenridge	76424-3503	817	559-5505
Nancy Carol Roberts Memorial	100 West Academy Street	Brenham	77833-3107	409	277-1271
Bridge City Public	101 Parkside Drive	Bridge City	77611-2442	409	735-4242
Bridgeport Public	2159 Tenth Street	Bridgeport	76426-2071	817	683-4412
Waller County Brookshire	P.O. Box 790	Brookshire	77423-0790	409	934-3516
Kendrick Memorial	301 West Tate	Brownfield	79316-4329	806	637-3848
Brownsville Public	2600 Central Blvd.	Brownsville	78520-8824	210	548-1055
Brownwood Public	600 Carnegie Boulevard	Brownwood	76801-7097	915	646-0155
Bryan/Coll. St. Public System	201 East 26th Street	Bryan	77803-5389	409	361-3715
College Station Public	2551 South Texas Ave., Ste E-1	Bryan	77802-2330	409	764-3416
Lakeshore Branch	Lakeshore Drive	Buchanan Dam	78609	915	379-1174
Moreau Memorial	P.O. Box 608	Buda	78610-0608	512	295-5899
Buffalo Public	P.O. Drawer 1290	Buffalo	75831-1290	903	322-4146
Bullard Community	P.O. Box 368	Bullard	75757-0368	903	894-6125
Bulverde Public	P.O. Box 207	Bulverde	78163-0207	210	438-3666
Buna Public	P.O. Box 1571	Buna	77612-1571	409	994-5501
Burkburnett	215 East 4th Street	Burkburnett	76354-3446	817	569-2991
Burleson Public	248 SW Johnson Avenue	Burleson	76028-4765	817	295-6131
Burnet County System	100 E. Washington Street	Burnet	78611-3114	512	756-2328
Harrie P. Woodson Memorial	704 West Highway 21	Caldwell	77836-1198	409	567-4111
Cameron Public	304 E. Third Street	Cameron	76520-3350	817	697-2401
Camp Wood Public	P.O. Box 108	Camp Wood	78833-0108	210	597-3208
Hemphill County	5th & Main Street	Canadian	79014	806	323-5282
Van Zandt County	317 First Monday Lane	Canton	75103-1052	903	567-4276
Canyon Public	301 16th Street	Canyon	79015-2828	806	655-5015

LIBRARY	ADDRESS	CITY	ZIP	AC	PHONE
Tye Preston Memorial	1321 Highway 2673	Canyon Lake	78133-5301	210	964-3744
Dimmit County Public	200 N. 9th Street	Carrizo Springs	78834-3704	210	876-5788
Carrollton Public	2001 Jackson Road	Carrollton	75006-1743	972	466-3360
Sammy Brown	522 West College Street	Carthage	75633-1408	903	693-6741
Castroville Public	P.O. Box 532	Castroville	78009-0532	210	538-2656
Zula B. Wylie	225 Cedar Street	Cedar Hill	75104-2655	972	291-7323
Cedar Park Public	550 Discovery Blvd.	Cedar Park	78613-2200	512	259-5353
Celina Community	P.O. Box 188	Celina	75009-0188	972	382-3750
Fannie Brown Booth Memorial	619 Tenaha Street	Center	75935-3535	409	598-5522
Leon County	P.O. Box 567	Centerville	75833-0567		
Henderson County East	P.O. Box 301	Chandler	75758-0301	903	849-4122
Charlotte Public	P.O. Box 757	Charlotte	78011-0757	210	277-1212
Chico Public	P.O. Box 707	Chico	76431-0707	817	644-2330
Childress Public	117 Avenue B, NE	Childress	79201-4509	817	937-8421
Cisco Public	600 Avenue G	Cisco	76437-3039	817	442-1020
G.B. Burton Memorial	Box 783	Clarendon	79226-0783	806	874-3641
Red River County Public	P.O. Box 508	Clarksville	75426-0508	903	427-3991
Claude Public	P.O. Box 109	Claude	79019-0109	806	226-7881
Cleburne Municipal	302 W. Henderson Street	Cleburne	76031-5494	817	645-0935
Austin Memorial	220 S. Bonham Street	Cleveland	77327-4591	281	592-3920
Nellie Pederson Civic	P.O. Box 231	Clifton	76634	817	675-6495
Clint Public	P.O. Box 779	Clint	79836-0779	915	851-2344
Clute Branch	215 N. Shanks St.	Clute	77531-4122	409	265-4582
Clyde Public	P.O. Box 679	Clyde	79510-0679	915	893-5315
Cockrell Hill Public	4125 West Clarendon Drive	Cockrell Hill	75211-4919	214	330-9935
"Coldspring Area Public , Inc."	P.O. Box 1756	Coldspring	77331-1756	409	653-3104
Coleman Public	402 Commercial Avenue	Coleman	76834-4202	915	625-3043
Mitchell County Public	340 Oak Street	Colorado City	79512-6214	915	728-3968
Nesbitt Memorial	529 Washington Street	Columbus	78934-2326	409	732-3392
Comanche Public	P.O. Box 411	Comanche	76442-0411	915	356-2122
Comfort Public	P.O. Box 536	Comfort	78013-0536	210	995-2398
Commerce Public	P.O. Box 308	Commerce	75429-0308	903	886-6858
Montgomery County	P.O. Box 579	Conroe	77305-0579	409	788-8377
Converse Area Public	502 Station Street	Converse	78109-1300	210	659-4160
Delta County Public	300 W. Dallas Avenue	Cooper	75432-1632	903	395-4575
William T. Cozby Public	P.O. Box 478	Coppell	75019-0478	972	304-3655
Copperas Cove Public	602 South Main Street	Copperas Cove	76522-2997	817	547-3826
Corpus Christi Public Libraries	805 Comanche Street	Corpus Christi	78401-2798	512	880-7070
Mickey Reily Public	604 South Mathews Street	Corrigan	75939-2645	409	398-4156
Corsicana Public	100 North 12th Street	Corsicana	75110-5205	903	654-4810
Alexander Memorial	201 South Center Street	Cotulla	78014-2255	210	879-2601
Crane County	701 South Alford Street	Crane	79731-2521	915	558-3142
J.H. Wootters-Crockett Public	P.O. Box 1226	Crockett	75835-1226	409	544-3089
Crosby Branch	135 Hare Road	Crosby	77532-8895	281	328-3535
Crosby County	114 West Aspen Street	Crosbyton	79322-2502	806	675-2673
Cross Plains Public	P.O. Box 333	Cross Plains	76443-0333	817	725-7722
Foard County	P.O. Box 317	Crowell	79227-0317	817	684-1250
Crowley Public	Box 747	Crowley	76036-0747	817	297-6707
Crystal City Memorial	101 E. Dimmit Street	Crystal City	78839-3505	210	374-3477
Cuero Public	207 East Main Street	Cuero	77954-3048	512	275-2864
Cushing Community	P.O. Box 421	Cushing	75760-0421	409	326-4608
Northwest Branch	11355 Regency Green Drive	Cypress	77429-4705	281	890-2665
Daingerfield Public	207 Jefferson Street	Daingerfield	75638-1713	903	645-2823
Dallam-Hartley County	420 Denrock Avenue	Dalhart	79022-2628	806	249-2761
Highland Park	4700 Drexel Drive	Dallas	75205-3199	214	559-9400
Martin Luther King, Jr. /LC	2922 MLK Jr. Blvd.	Dallas	75215-2395	214	670-0344
Dallas Public	1515 Young Street	Dallas	75201-5499	214	670-1400
Edmund E. & Nida Smith Jones	307 West Houston	Dayton	77535-2537	409	258-7060
Decatur Public	1700 Highway 51 South	Decatur	76234-9292	817	627-5512
Deer Park Public	3009 Center Street	Deer Park	77536-5099	281	478-7208
Val Verde County	300 Spring Street	Del Rio	78840-5199	210	774-7595
Elroy Community	13512 F.M. 812	Del Valle	78617-	512	243-1981
DeLeon Public	105 South Texas Street	DeLeon	76444-1862	817	893-2417
Grace Grebing Public/School	P.O. Box 37	Dell City	79837-0037	915	964-2468
Denison Public	300 West Gandy	Denison	75020-3153	903	465-1797

LIBRARY	ADDRESS	CITY	ZIP	AC	PHONE
Denton Public	502 Oakland St.	Denton	76201-3102	817	566-8566
Yoakum County/Cecil Bickley	P.O. Box 900	Denver City	79323-0900	806	592-2754
DeSoto Public	211 E. Pleasant Run Rd., Ste C	DeSoto	75115-3939	972	230-9656
Driscoll Public	P.O. Box 619	Devine	78016-0619	210	663-2993
TLL Temple Memorial	300 Park Street	Diboll	75941-1633	409	829-5497
Mares Memorial	4324 Highway 3	Dickinson	77539-6801	281	534-3812
Rhoads Memorial	103 SW 2nd	Dimmitt	79027-2501	806	647-3532
Donna Public	301 South Main Street	Donna	78537-3288	210	464-2221
Dripping Springs Community	P.O. Box 279	Dripping Springs	78620-0279	512	858-7825
Dublin Public	206 West Blackjack Street	Dublin	76446-2204	817	445-4141
Killgore Memorial	124 S. Bliss Avenue	Dumas	79029-3804	806	935-4941
Duncanville Public	103 E. Wheatland Road	Duncanville	75116-4899	972	780-5050
Eula & David Wintermann	101 N. Walnut Avenue	Eagle Lake	77434-2326	409	234-5411
Eagle Pass Public	589 Main Street	Eagle Pass	78852	210	773-2516
Springlake-Earth Community	P.O. Box 259	Earth	79031-0259	806	257-3357
East Bernard Branch	P.O. Box 516	East Bernard	77435	409	335-6142
Centennial Memorial	210 South Lamar Street	Eastland	76448-2794	817	629-2281
Eden Public	P.O. Box 896	Eden	76837-0896	915	869-7761
Edinburg Public	401 East Cano	Edinburg	78539-4596	210	383-6246
Jackson County Memorial	411 North Wells Street	Edna	77957-2734	512	782-2162
El Campo Branch	409 E. Hillje St.	El Campo	77437-4503	409	543-2362
El Paso Public	501 North Oregon Street	El Paso	79901-1195	915	543-5413
Schleicher County Public	P.O. Box 611	Eldorado	76936-0611	915	853-3767
Electra Public	401 North Waggoner Street	Electra	76360-2134	817	495-2208
Elgin Public	404 N. Main Street	Elgin	78621-2625	512	281-5678
Elsa Public	P.O. Box 1447	Elsa	78543-1447	210	262-3061
Rains County Public	P.O. Box 189	Emory	75440-0189	903	473-2221
Ennis Public	501 W. Ennis Avenue	Ennis	75119-3803	972	875-5360
Euless Public	201 N. Ector Drive	Euless	76039-3595	817	685-1482
Everman Public	212 Race Street	Everman	76140-3297	817	551-0726
El Paso County	P.O. Drawer 788	Fabens	79838-0788	915	764-3635
Fairfield	350 W. Main Street	Fairfield	75840-3028	903	389-3574
Ed Rachal Memorial	203 S. Henry Street	Falfurrias	78355-4321	512	325-2144
Falls City Public	P.O. Box 220	Falls City	78113-0220	210	254-3361
Farmers Branch Manske Public	13613 Webb Chapel	Farmers Branch	75234-3799	972	247-2511
Charles J. Rike Memorial	P.O. Box 50	Farmersville	75442-0050	972	782-6681
Ferris Public	514 S. Mable Street	Ferris	75125-3028	972	544-3696
Flatonia Public	P.O. Box 656	Flatonia	78941-0656	512	865-3920
Florence Public	P.O. Box 430	Florence	76527-0430	817	793-2672
Sam Fore Jr. Wilson Co. Public	One Lane	Floresville	78114-2239	210	393-2886
Flower Mound Public	2121 Cross Timbers Rd.	Flower Mound	75028-2602	972	539-0120
Floyd County	Floyd County Courthouse	Floydada	79235-2749	806	983-4922
Forest Hill Public	6619 Forest Hill Drive	Forest Hill	76140-1260	817	483-9811
West Memorial	811 South Bois D'Arc	Forney	75126-	972	552-9555
Jeff Davis County	Box 1054	Fort Davis	79734-1054	915	426-3802
Ft. Hancock/Hudspeth Public	P.O. Box 98	Fort Hancock	79839-0098	915	769-3868
Fort Stockton Public	500 North Water	Fort Stockton	79735-5634	915	336-3374
Blue Mound Community	1600 Bell Avenue	Fort Worth	76131-1002	817	232-0662
River Oaks Public	4900 River Oaks Boulevard	Fort Worth	76114-3007	817	624-7344
Fort Worth Public	300 Taylor Street	Fort Worth	76102-7333	817	871-7703
Robertson County	P.O. Box 1027	Franklin	77856-1027	409	828-4331
Frankston Depot	P.O. Box 639	Frankston	75763-0639	903	876-4463
Pioneer Memorial	115 West Main Street	Fredericksburg	78624-3751	210	997-6513
Freeport Branch	410 Brazosport Blvd.	Freeport	77541-	409	233-3622
Friendswood Public	416 S. Friendswood	Friendswood	77546-3906	281	482-7135
Friona Public	109 W. 7th Street	Friona	79035-2548	806	247-3200
Frisco Public	8750 McKinney Road, Ste. 200	Frisco	75034-3000	972	335-5510
Hutchinson County - Fritch	P.O. Box 430	Fritch	79036-0430	806	857-3752
Cooke County	200 S. Weaver Street	Gainesville	76240-4790	817	665-2401
Galena Park Branch	100 Main Street	Galena Park	77547	713	674-2245
Rosenberg	2310 Sealy Avenue	Galveston	77550-2296	409	763-8854
Galveston County System	2310 Sealy Avenue	Galveston	77550-2296	409	763-8854
Nicholson Memorial System	625 Austin Street	Garland	75040-6365	972	205-2543
Veterans Memorial	P.O. Box 275	Garwood	77442		
Gatesville Public	811 Main Street	Gatesville	76528-1432	817	865-5367

LIBRARY	ADDRESS	CITY	ZIP	AC	PHONE
Live Oak County	P.O. Box 698	George West	78022-0698	512	449-1124
Georgetown Public	808 Martin Luther King Street	Georgetown	78626-5527	512	930-3551
Rufus Young King	177 South Madison Street	Giddings	78942-3317	409	542-2716
Upshur County	702 West Tyler Street	Gilmer	75644-2198	903	843-5001
Lee Public	P.O. Box 791	Gladewater	75647-0791	903	845-2640
Somervell County	108 Allen Street	Glen Rose	76043-4526	817	897-4582
Jennie Trent Dew .	P.O. Box 101	Goldthwaite	76844-0101	915	648-2447
Goliad County	P.O. Box 789	Goliad	77963-0789	512	645-2291
Gonzales County System	P.O. Box 220	Gonzales	78629	210	672-6315
Charlie Garrett Memorial	P.O. Box 219	Gorman	76454-0219		
Graham	910 Cherry Street	Graham	76450-3547	817	549-0600
Hood County Public	222 N. Travis Street	Granbury	76048-2164	817	573-3569
Grand Prairie Memorial	901 Conover Drive	Grand Prairie	75051-1590	972	264-9536
Grand Saline Public	201 E. Pacific Street	Grand Saline	75140-1934	903	962-5516
Ward County Grandfalls	P.O. Box 186	Grandfalls	79742-0186	915	547-2861
Grapevine Public	1201 S. Main Street	Grapevine	76051-5545	817	481-0341
W. Walworth Harrison Public	3716 Lee Street	Greenville	75401-3999	903	457-2992
Maffett Memorial	601 W. Yeagua Street	Groesbeck	76642-1658	817	729-3667
Groom Branch	Box 308	Groom	79039-0308	806	248-7353
Groves Public	5600 West Washington Street	Groves	77619-3629	409	962-6281
Groveton Public	P.O. Box 399	Groveton	75845-0399	409	642-2483
Gruver City	Box 701	Gruver	79040-0701	806	733-2191
King County Public	Box 1	Guthrie	79236-0001	806	596-4385
Hale Center Public , Inc.	P.O. Box 214	Hale Center	79041-0214	806	839-2055
Friench Simpson Memorial	P.O. Drawer 269	Hallettsville	77964-0269	512	798-3243
Haltom City Public	P.O. Box 14277	Haltom City	76117-0277	817	831-6431
Hamilton Public	201 N. Pecan Street	Hamilton	76531-1925	817	386-3474
Harker Heights Public	100 East Beeline Lane	Harker Heights	76543-1262	817	699-5008
Harlingen Public	410 '76 Drive	Harlingen	78550	210	430-6650
Haskell County	300 North Avenue E	Haskell	79521-4924	817	864-2747
Allen Memorial Public	Drawer 329	Hawkins	75765-0329	903	769-2241
Smith-Welch Memorial	114 W. 4th Street	Hearne	77859-2506	409	279-5191
Jim Hogg County Public	210 North Smith Avenue	Hebbronville	78361-2899	512	527-3421
J.R. Huffman Public	P.O. Box 1036	Hemphill	75948-1036	409	787-4829
Waller County	2331 11th Street	Hempstead	77445-6799	409	826-8335
Rusk County	106 East Main Street	Henderson	75652-3117	903	657-8557
Edwards Public	P.O. Drawer 529	Henrietta	76365-0529	817	538-4791
Deaf Smith County	211 East 4th Street	Hereford	79045-5521	806	364-1206
Hewitt Community	107 Hewitt Drive	Hewitt	76643	817	666-2442
Higgins Public	P.O. Box 250	Higgins	79046-0250	806	852-2214
Stratford Branch	509 Stratford Street	Highlands	77562-2547	281	426-3521
Hillsboro City	118 South Waco Street	Hillsboro	76645-7708	817	582-7385
Genevieve Miller/Hitchcock	8005 Barry Avenue	Hitchcock	77563-3238	409	986-7814
Hondo Public	1011 19th Street	Hondo	78861-2431	210	426-5333
Bertha Voyer Memorial	P.O. Box 47	Honey Grove	75446-0047	903	378-2206
Hooks Public	P.O. Box 1540	Hooks	75561-1540	903	547-3365
Houston Public	500 McKinney Street	Houston	77002-2534	713	247-2700
Harris County Public	8080 El Rio Street	Houston	77054-4195	713	749-9000
Howe Community	Box 960	Howe	75059-0960	903	532-5519
Octavia Fields Branch	111 West Higgins Street	Humble	77338-4304	281	446-3377
Baldwin Boettcher Branch	22248 Aldine Westfield Road	Humble	77338-1080	281	821-1320
Huntsville Public	1216 14th Street	Huntsville	77340-4507	409	291-5472
Hurst Public	901 Precinct Line Road	Hurst	76053	817	788-7300
Hutchins-Atwell Public	P.O. Box 888	Hutchins	75141-0888	972	225-4711
Idalou Public	P.O. Box 108	Idalou	79329-0108	806	892-2114
Imperial Public	P.O. Box 307	Imperial	79743-0307	915	536-2236
West End	P.O. Box 179	Industry	78944-0179	409	357-4434
Ingleside Public	P.O. Drawer 400	Ingleside	78362-0400	512	776-2517
Tom Burnett Memorial	400 West Alameda	Iowa Park	76367-1616	817	592-4981
Iraan Public	P.O. Box 638	Iraan	79744-0638	915	639-2235
Irving Public	P.O. Box 152288	Irving	75015-2288	972	721-2639
S.M. Dunlap	Box A	Italy	76651	214	483-6481
Gladys Johnson Ritchie Public	626 West College Street	Jacksboro	76458-1655	817	567-2240
Jacksonville Public	502 South Jackson Street	Jacksonville	75766-2415	903	586-7664
Jasper Public	175 East Water Street	Jasper	75951-4438	409	384-3791

LIBRARY	ADDRESS	CITY	ZIP	AC	PHONE
Kent County	Box 28	Jayton	79528-0028	806	237-3287
Jefferson Carnegie	301 W. Lafayette St.	Jefferson	75657	903	665-8911
Jewett Public	P.O. Box 926	Jewett	75846	903	626-4202
Johnson City	Box 332	Johnson City	78636-0332	210	868-4469
Jonestown Community	P.O. Box 5023	Jonestown	78645-0002	512	267-7511
Joshua Community	909 S. Broadway	Joshua	76058-	817	641-2285
Jourdanton Community	1220 Simmons Avenue	Jourdanton	78026-2896	210	769-3087
Kimble County	208 North 10th Street	Junction	76849	915	446-2342
Justin Community	P.O. Box 877	Justin	76247-0877	817	648-3649
Karnes City Public	302 S. Panna Maria Avenue	Karnes City	78118-3240	210	780-2539
Katy	5702 Second Street	Katy	77493-2417	281	391-3509
Maud Smith Marks	1815 Westgreen Blvd.	Katy	77450-5370	281	492-8592
Kaufman County	3790 S. Houston Street	Kaufman	75142-3714	972	932-6222
Keller Public	640 Johnson Road	Keller	76248-4136	817	431-3919
Henderson County West	101 Causeway Beach	Kemp	75143-9234	903	431-4185
Kendalia Public	P.O. Box 399	Kendalia	78027-0399	210	336-2002
Karnes County System HQ	303 W. Main Street	Kenedy	78119-2795	210	583-3313
The Kennedale	P.O. Box 213	Kennedale	76060-0213	817	478-7876
Winkler County	307 South Poplar	Kermit	79745-4300	915	586-3841
Butt-Holdsworth Memorial	505 Water Street	Kerrville	78028-5393	210	257-8422
Kilgore Public	301 N. Henderson Blvd.	Kilgore	75662-2799	903	984-1529
Killeen Public	711 N. Gray Street	Killeen	76541-4898	817	526-8379
Kingsland Branch	125 W. Polk St.	Kingsland	78639-5908	915	288-3170
Robert J. Kleberg Public	220 North 4th Street	Kingsville	78363-4410	512	592-6381
Kingwood Branch	4102 Rustic Woods Drive	Kingwood	77345-1350	281	360-6804
Kirbyville Public	P.O. Box 567	Kirbyville	75956-0567	409	423-4653
Kountze Public	Drawer 39	Kountze	77625-0039	409	246-2826
Krum Public	P.O. Box 780	Krum	76249-0780	817	482-3455
Kyle Community	P.O. Box 366	Kyle	78640-0366	512	268-7411
Bailey H. Dunlap Memorial	Box 5804	La Feria	78559-2580	210	797-1242
Fayette Public	855 South Jefferson	La Grange	78945-3230	409	968-3765
La Joya Municipal	P.O. Box H	La Joya	78560-	210	581-7002
La Marque Public	1011 Bayou Road	La Marque	77568-4195	409	938-9270
La Porte Branch	526 San Jacinto	La Porte	77571-5498	281	471-4022
La Vernia Branch	P.O. Box 667	La Vernia	78121-0667	210	779-2239
Lago Vista Community	P.O. Box 4967	Lago Vista	78645-0009	512	267-3868
Laguna Vista Public	122 Fernandez Street	Laguna Vista	78578	210	943-1793
Lake Cities	P.O. Box 775	Lake Dallas	75065-0775	817	497-3566
Lake Jackson Branch	250 Circle Way	Lake Jackson	77566-5203	409	297-1271
Mary Lou Reddick Public	3801 Adam Grubb Street	Lake Worth	76135-3509	817	237-9681
Dawson County	P.O. Box 1264	Lamesa	79331-1264	806	872-6502
Lampasas Public	P.O. Box 308	Lampasas	76550-0308	512	556-3251
Lancaster Veterans Memorial	220 West Main Street	Lancaster	75146-3116	972	227-1080
Laredo Public	1120 San Bernardo Ave.	Laredo	78040-4489	210	722-2435
Helen Hall	100 West Walker	League City	77573-3899	281	338-4864
Real County Public	P.O. Box 108	Leakey	78873-0108	210	232-5199
Leander Public	P.O. Box 410	Leander	78641-0410	512	259-5259
Leonard Public	Box 264	Leonard	75452-0264	903	587-2391
Hockley County Memorial	Courthouse Box 8	Levelland	79336-4594	806	894-6750
Lewisville Public	P.O. Box 299002	Lewisville	75029-9002	972	219-3570
Liberty Municipal	1710 Sam Houston St.	Liberty	77575-4796	409	336-8901
Lindale	P.O. Box 1535	Lindale	75771-1535	903	882-1900
Lamb County	232 Phelps Avenue	Littlefield	79339-3428	806	385-5223
Murphy Memorial	601 West Church Street	Livingston	77351-3199	409	327-4252
Llano County System	102 E. Haynie	Llano	78643-2072	915	247-5248
Dr. Eugene Clark	P.O. Box 209	Lockhart	78644-0209	512	398-3223
Floyd County Branch	224 S. Main	Lockney	79241	806	652-3561
Longview Public	222 West Cotton Street	Longview	75601-6348	903	237-1340
Lorenzo	Box 426	Lorenzo	79343-0426	806	634-5639
Ethel L. Whipple Memorial	402 W. Ocean Blvd.	Los Fresnos	78566-3650	210	233-5330
Louise Branch	P.O. Box 36	Louise	77455	409	646-2018
Lubbock City-County	1306 9th Street	Lubbock	79401-2798	806	767-2834
Kurth Memorial	101 N. Cotton Square	Lufkin	75901-2997	409	634-7617
Luling Public	215 S. Pecan Avenue	Luling	78648-2607	210	875-2813
Lumberton Public	P.O. Box 8733	Lumberton	77711-0733	409	755-7400

LIBRARY	ADDRESS	CITY	ZIP	AC	PHONE
Lytle Public	P.O. Box 841	Lytle	78052-0841	210	772-3142
Tri-County /Family Resource	P.O. Box 1770	Mabank	75147-1770	903	887-9622
Madison County	605 S. May Street	Madisonville	77864-2561	409	348-6118
Magnolia Branch	31350 Industrial Lane	Magnolia	77355-2603	281	259-8324
Red Waller Community	P.O. Box 1177	Malakoff	75148-1177	903	489-1818
Mansfield Public	110 South Main Street	Mansfield	76063-3101	817	473-4391
Manvel Branch	7402 Masters Road	Manvel	77578-4814	281	489-7596
Marathon Public	P.O. Box 264	Marathon	79842-0264		
Marble Falls	801 4th Street	Marble Falls	78654-5430	210	693-3023
Marfa Public	P.O. Drawer U	Marfa	79843-0609	915	729-4631
Marion Community	P.O. Box 619	Marion	78124-0619	210	914-4268
Marlin Public	301 Winter Street	Marlin	76661-2806	817	883-6602
Marshall Public	300 S. Alamo Blvd.	Marshall	75670-4273	903	935-4465
Mason County/Eckert Memorial	Drawer 780	Mason	76856-0780	915	347-5446
Motley County	Box 557	Matador	79244-0557	806	347-2717
Matagorda Branch	800 Fisher Street	Matagorda	77457	409	863-7925
Mathis Public	103 Lamar Street	Mathis	78368-2441	512	547-6201
Maud Public	P.O. Box 306	Maud	75567-0306	903	585-5255
McAllen Memorial	601 North Main Street	McAllen	78501-4666	210	682-4531
Hidalgo County System	4305 North 10th St., Ste E	McAllen	78504-3095	210	682-6397
Upton County Public	Drawer L	McCamey	79752-1112	915	652-8718
McGinley Memorial	317 South Main Street	McGregor	76657-1608	817	840-3732
McKinney Memorial Public	220 North Kentucky Street	McKinney	75069-3807	972	542-4461
Lovett Memorial	P.O. Box 8	McLean	79057-0008	806	779-2851
Melissa Public	P.O. Box 325	Melissa	75454-0325	972	837-4540
Memphis Public	303 S. 8th	Memphis	79245-3211	806	259-2062
Menard Public	P.O. Box 404	Menard	76859-0404	915	396-2717
Mercedes Memorial	434 S. Ohio	Mercedes	78570-3196	210	565-2371
Irion County	P.O. Box 766	Mertzon	76941-0766	915	835-2704
Mesquite Public	300 West Grubb Drive	Mesquite	75149-3492	972	216-6220
Gibbs Memorial	305 East Rusk Street	Mexia	76667-2398	817	562-3231
Roberts County	Box 143	Miami	79059-0143	806	868-3721
Midkiff Public	P.O. Box 160	Midkiff	79755-0160	915	535-2311
Midland County Public	301 W. Missouri Ave.	Midland	79701-5108	915	688-8991-23
A.H. Meadows	925 South Ninth Street	Midlothian	76065-3636	972	775-3417
Mineola Memorial	301 North Pacific Street	Mineola	75773-1799	903	569-2767
Boyce Ditto Public	2300 SE 7th Street	Mineral Wells	76067-5763	817	328-1383
Mirando City	P.O. Box 509	Mirando City	78369	512	586-4626
Speer Memorial	801 E. 12th Street	Mission	78572-4493	210	580-8750
Missouri City Branch	1530 Texas Parkway	Missouri City	77489-2170	281	499-4100
Ward County	409 S. Dwight Street	Monahans	79756-4609	915	943-3332
West Chambers County Branch	P.O. Box 1289	Mont Belvieu	77580-1289	281	576-2243
West Branch	51 Western Hills Plaza	Montgomery	77356	409	788-8314
Cochran County/Love Memorial	318 S. Main	Morton	79346-3006	806	266-5051
Mount Calm Regional	P.O. Box 84	Mount Calm	76673	817	993-2761
Morrow Branch	P.O. Box 360	Mt. Enterprise	75681-0360	903	822-3532
Mt. Pleasant Public	213 N. Madison Ave.	Mt. Pleasant	75455-3944	903	572-2705
Franklin County	P.O. Box 579	Mt. Vernon	75457-0579	903	537-4916
Muenster Public	P.O. Drawer E	Muenster	76252-0140	817	759-4291
Muleshoe Area Public	322 W. 2nd Street	Muleshoe	79347-3633	806	272-4707
City-County	Box 268	Munday	76371-0268	817	422-4877
Nacogdoches Public	206 E. Main St.	Nacogdoches	75961-5212	409	569-8281
Navasota Public	1411 East Washington Avenue	Navasota	77868-3240	409	825-6744
D. Bob Henson Memorial	1903 Atlanta Avenue	Nederland	77627-5099	409	722-1255
Albert George Branch	9230 Gene Street	Needville	77461-8313	409	793-4270
New Boston Public	127 N. Ellis Street	New Boston	75570-2905	903	628-5414
Dittlinger Memorial	373 Magazine Avenue	New Braunfels	78130-5689	210	608-2150
R.B. Tullis Branch	Route 2, Box 1035 K	New Caney	77357-9045	281	354-6152
New Waverly Public	P.O. Box 843	New Waverly	77358-0843	409	344-2198
Newark Public	P.O. Box 1219	Newark	76071-1219	817	489-2224
Newton County Public	P.O. Box 657	Newton	75966-0657	409	379-8300
Nixon Public	108 W. Third	Nixon	78140	512	582-1913
Nocona Public	10 Cooke Street	Nocona	76255-2148	817	825-6373
North Richland Hills Public	6720 NE Loop 820	N. Richland Hills	76180-7901	817	581-5700
Della Mae Baylor Public	P.O. Box 636	Odem	78370-0636	512	368-2831

LIBRARY	ADDRESS	CITY	ZIP	AC	PHONE
Ector County	321 W. 5th Street	Odessa	79761-5066	915	332-0633-30
Olney Community-Arts Center	Box 67	Olney	76374-0067	817	564-5513
Olton Branch	Box 675	Olton	79064-0675	806	285-7772
Orange Public	220 N. Fifth Street	Orange	77630-5796	409	883-1086
Orange Grove School/Public	P.O. Box 534	Orange Grove	78372-0534	512	384-2461
McMillan Memorial	302 South Street	Overton	75684-1818	903	834-6318
Crockett County Public	Box 3030	Ozona	76943-3030	915	392-3565
Bicentennial City-County	Drawer AD	Paducah	79248-1197	806	492-2006
Harry Benge Crozier Memorial	P.O. Box 173	Paint Rock	76866-0173		
Palacios Inc.	326 Main Street	Palacios	77465-5499	512	972-3234
Palestine Public	1101 N. Cedar Street	Palestine	75801-7697	903	729-4121
Lovett Memorial	P.O. Box 342	Pampa	79066-0342	806	669-5780
Carson County Public	Box 339	Panhandle	79068-0339	806	537-3742
Paris Public	326 South Main Street	Paris	75460-5825	903	785-8531
Pasadena Public	1201 Jeff Ginn Memorial Dr.	Pasadena	77506-4895	713	477-0276
Fairmont Branch	4330 Fairmont Pkwy.	Pasadena	77504-3306	713	998-1095
Pearland Branch	3523 Liberty Drive	Pearland	77581	281	485-4876
Pearsall Public	200 East Trinity Street	Pearsall	78061-3351	210	334-9367
Reeves County	505 S. Park Street	Pecos	79772	915	445-5340
Perry Memorial	22 SE 5th Avenue	Perryton	79070-3112	806	435-5801
Petersburg Public	Box 65	Petersburg	79250-0065	806	667-3657
Pflugerville Community	P.O. Box 307	Pflugerville	78691-0307	512	251-9185
Pharr Memorial	200 S. Athol Street	Pharr	78577-4892	210	787-3966
Pilot Point Community	P.O. Box 969	Pilot Point	76258-0969	817	686-5004
"Arthur Temple, Sr. Memorial "	P.O. Box 296	Pineland	75968-0296	409	584-2546
Pittsburg-Camp County	613 Quitman Street	Pittsburg	75686-9028	903	856-3302
Yoakum County	Box 419	Plains	79355-0419	806	456-8725
Unger Memorial	825 Austin Street	Plainview	79072-7235	806	296-1148
Gladys Harrington	1501 E. 18th Street	Plano	75074-6099	972	578-7175
L.E.R. Schimelpfenig	5024 Custer Road	Plano	75023-5199	972	964-4200
Plano Public System	P.O. Box 860356	Plano	75086-0356	972	964-4208
"W.O. Haggard, Jr. "	2501 Coit Road	Plano	75075-3892	972	964-4250
Pleasanton Public	321 North Main Street	Pleasanton	78064-3596	210	569-3622
Point Comfort Branch	P.O. Box 382	Point Comfort	77978-0382	512	987-2954
Ellis Memorial	700 West Avenue A	Port Aransas	78373-4128	512	749-4116
Port Arthur Public	3601 Cultural Center Drive	Port Arthur	77642-5799	409	985-8838
Port Isabel Public	213 N. Yturria St.	Port Isabel	78578-4602	210	943-1822
Calhoun County	200 W. Mahan Street	Port Lavaca	77979-3368	512	552-7323
Effie & Wilton Hebert Public	2025 Merriman Street	Port Neches	77651-3797	409	722-4554
Port O'Connor Branch	P.O. Box 424	Port O'Connor	77982-0424	512	983-4365
Bell/Whittington Public	2400 Memorial Parkway	Portland	78374-3208	512	643-6501
Post Public	105 East Main St.	Post	79356-3229	806	495-2149
Poteet Public	P.O. Box 380	Poteet	78065-0380	210	742-8917
Pottsboro Area Public	P.O. Box 477	Pottsboro	75076-0477	214	786-8274
Premont Public	P.O. Box 829	Premont	78375-0829	512	348-3815
City of Presidio	P.O. Box K	Presidio	79845-1231	915	229-3317
Thompson-Sawyer Public	403 West Third Street	Quanah	79252-3825	817	663-2654
Quemado Public	P.O. Drawer 210	Quemado	78877-0210	210	757-1313
Tawakoni Area Public	"Rt. 1, Box 178-A11"	Quinlan	75474-9759	903	447-3445
Caprock Public	P.O. Box 487	Quitaque	79255-0487	806	455-1225
Quitman Public	P.O. Box 77	Quitman	75783-0077	903	763-4191
Ralls	Box 608	Ralls	79357-0608	806	253-2755
Ranger Community	P.O. Box 93	Ranger	76470	817	647-3522
Rankin Public	P.O. Box 6	Rankin	79778-0006	915	693-2881
Reber Memorial	193 North Fourth Street	Raymondville	78580-1994	210	689-2930
Refugio County Public	815 S. Commerce Street	Refugio	78377-3107	512	526-2608
Rhome Public	P.O. Box 57	Rhome	76078-0057	817	636-2767
Richardson Public	900 Civic Center Drive	Richardson	75080-5298	972	238-4000
Richland Hills Public	6724 Rena Drive	Richland Hills	76118-6273	817	595-6630
Fort Bend County Law	401 Jackson Street, Room 302	Richmond	77469-3110	281	341-3718
Fort Bend County Libraries	1001 Golfview Drive	Richmond	77469-5199	281	342-4455
Starr County Public	600 N. Garza St.	Rio Grande City	78582-3538	210	487-4389
Rio Hondo Public	P.O. Box 740	Rio Hondo	78583-0740	210	748-3322
Rising Star Public	P.O. Box 303	Rising Star	76471-0303	817	643-6823
Roanoke Public	308 Walnut Street	Roanoke	76262-8635	817	491-2691

LIBRARY	ADDRESS	CITY	ZIP	AC	PHONE
Coke County	P.O. Box 637	Robert Lee	76945-0637	915	453-2495
Nueces County	Nueces County Bldg.	Robstown	78380	512	387-1032
Lucy Hill Patterson Memorial	201 Ackerman Street	Rockdale	76567-2901	512	446-3410
Aransas County Public	701 East Mimosa St.	Rockport	78382-4150	512	790-0153
Edwards County Memorial	P.O. Box 262	Rocksprings	78880-0262	210	683-6171
Rockwall County	105 S. First Street	Rockwall	75087-3649	972	771-2272
Ropes Branch	P.O. Box 96	Ropesville	79358-0096	806	562-3531
Rotan Public	404 E. Snyder Ave.	Rotan	79546-3820	915	735-3362
Round Rock Public	216 E. Main Ave.	Round Rock	78664-5245	512	218-7005
Rowlett Public	P.O. Box 1017	Rowlett	75030-1017	972	412-6161
Runge Public	P.O. Box 37	Runge	78151-0037	210	239-4192
Singletary Memorial	207 E. 6th Street	Rusk	75785-1103	903	683-5916
Sabinal Public	P.O. Box 61	Sabinal	78881-0061	210	988-2911
Sabine Pass Branch	5030 S. Gulfway Dr.	Sabine Pass	77655-	409	971-2944
Sachse Public	3033 Sixth Street	Sachse	75048-3118	972	530-8966
Saginaw Public	P.O. Drawer 79070	Saginaw	76179-0070	817	232-2100
Salado Public	P.O. Box 706	Salado	76571-0706	817	947-9191
Tom Green County System	113 West Beauregard Ave.	San Angelo	76903-5887	915	655-7321
San Antonio Public	600 Soledad St.	San Antonio	78205-1200	210	207-2500
Leon Valley Public	6425 Evers Road	San Antonio	78238-1453	210	684-0720
San Augustine Public	413 E. Columbia Street	San Augustine	75972-2111	409	275-5367
San Benito Public	101 West Rose Street	San Benito	78586-5169	210	361-3860
Duval County/San Diego Public	404 S. Mier St.	San Diego	78384-	512	279-8201
San Juan Public	506 S. Standard	San Juan	78589	512	787-0943
San Marcos Public	625 E. Hopkins Street	San Marcos	78667-6313	512	393-8200
Rylander Memorial	103 S. Live Oak St.	San Saba	76877-4799	915	372-3079
Terrell County Public	P.O. Box 692	Sanderson	79848-0692	915	345-2294
Sanger Public	P.O. Box 578	Sanger	76266-0578	817	458-3257
Santa Anna	Rt. 1 Box 299	Santa Anna	76878-9520	915	348-3395
Mae S. Bruce	P.O. Box 950	Santa Fe	77510-0950	409	925-5540
Sargent Branch	P.O. Box 4007	Sargent	77404-4007	409	245-3032
Schertz Public	608 Schertz Parkway	Schertz	78154-1911	210	658-6011
Schulenburg Public	700 Bohlmann Avenue	Schulenburg	78956-1316	409	743-3345
Evelyn Meador Branch	2400 N. Meyer Rd.	Seabrook	77586-2964	281	474-9142
Seadrift Branch	P.O. Box 567	Seadrift	77983-0567	512	785-4241
Seagoville Public	702 N. Highway 175	Seagoville	75159-1799	972	287-7720
Gaines County Seagraves Br.	P.O. Box 366	Seagraves	79359-0366	806	546-2480
Virgil & Josephine Gordon	917 North Circle St.	Sealy	77474-3333	409	885-7469
Seguin-Guadalupe Co. Public	707 E. College Street	Seguin	78155-3299	210	379-1531
Gaines County	704 Hobbs Hwy.	Seminole	79360-3402	915	758-4007
Baylor County Free	101 South Washington Street	Seymour	76380-2558	817	888-2662
Shamrock Public	415 East First Street	Shamrock	79079-2401	806	256-3921
Shepherd Public	P.O. Box 585	Shepherd	77371-0585	409	628-3515
Sheridan Memorial	Box 274	Sheridan	77475-0274		
Sherman Public	421 N. Travis Street	Sherman	75090-5975	903	892-7240
Shiner Public	P.O. Box 1602	Shiner	77984-1602	512	594-3044
Sierra Blanca	P.O. Box 308	Sierra Blanca	79851	915	369-2781
Silsbee Public	Santa Fe Park	Silsbee	77656-4000	409	385-4831
Silverton Public	Box 69	Silverton	79257-0069		
Simonton/Fulshear Mini-Branch	P.O. Drawer A	Simonton	77476-1001	281	533-9809
Sinton Public	212 E. Sinton Street	Sinton	78387-2655	512	364-4545
Skellytown Branch	Box 92	Skellytown	79080-0092	806	848-2551
Slaton City	200 West Lynn St.	Slaton	79364-4136	806	828-2008
Stella Ellis Hart Public	P.O. Box 88	Smiley	78159-0088	210	587-6101
Smithville Public	101 NW Sixth Street	Smithville	78957-1461	512	237-2707
Scurry County	1916 23rd Street	Snyder	79549-1910	915	573-5572
Sutton County	212 S. Concho Ave.	Sonora	76950-3729	915	387-2111
Alma M. Carpenter Public	P.O. Box 536	Sour Lake	77659-0536	409	287-3592
South Houston Branch	607 Avenue A	South Houston	77587-3659	713	941-2385
Hansford County	122 Main Street	Spearman	79081-2064	806	659-2231
"McCracken Public , Inc."	P.O. Drawer 1937	Splendora	77372-1937	713	689-0044
Cypress Creek Branch	6815 Cypresswood Drive	Spring	77379-7705	281	376-4610
Springtown Public	P.O. Box 428	Springtown	76082-0428	817	523-5862
Dickens County-Spur Public	P.O. Box 282	Spur	79370-0282	806	271-3714

LIBRARY	ADDRESS	CITY	ZIP	AC	PHONE
Mamie George Branch	320 Dulles Avenue	Stafford	77477-4799	281	491-8086
Stamford Carnegie	600 East McHarg Street	Stamford	79553	915	773-2532
Martin County	Box 1187	Stanton	79782-1187	915	756-2472
Stephenville Public	174 North Columbia St.	Stephenville	76401-3421	817	965-5665
Sterling County Public	P.O. Box 1130	Sterling City	76951-1130	915	378-2212
Hutchinson Co. - Stinnett	P.O. Box 478	Stinnett	79083-0478	806	878-4013
Sherman County Public	P.O. Box 46	Stratford	79084-0046	806	396-2200
First Colony Branch	2121 Austin Parkway	Sugar Land	77479-1219	281	265-4444
Sulphur Springs Public	201 Davis St. N	Sulphur Springs	75482-2636	903	885-4926
Sundown Branch	Box 600	Sundown	79372-0600	806	229-3131
Sunnyvale Public	402 Tower Place	Sunnyvale	75182-9278	972	226-4491
Britain Memorial	P.O. Box 180	Sunray	79086-0180	806	948-5501
Sweeny Branch	205 W. Ashley Wilson Road	Sweeny	77480-1023	409	548-2567
County-City	206 Elm Street	Sweetwater	79556-4596	915	235-4978
Taft Public	P.O. Box 416	Taft	78390-0416	512	528-3512
City-County	Box 1018	Tahoka	79373-1018	806	998-4050
Tatum Public	P.O. Box 1087	Tatum	75691-1087	903	947-2211
Taylor Public	721 Vance Street	Taylor	76574-3266	512	352-3434
Teague Public	400 Main Street	Teague	75860-1641	817	739-3311
Temple Public	101 North Main Street	Temple	76501-7641	817	770-5556
Terrell Public	301 N. Rockwall St.	Terrell	75160-2618	972	551-6663
Texarkana Public	600 West Third Street	Texarkana	75501-5054	903	794-2149
Moore Memorial Public	1701 9th Avenue North	Texas City	77590-5496	409	643-5979
Texline Public	P.O. Box 356	Texline	79087-0356	806	362-4849
The Colony Public	5151 N. Colony Blvd.	The Colony	75056-1219	972	625-1900
South Regional Branch	2101 Lake Robbins Dr.	The Woodlands	77380-1152	281	298-9110
Live Oak County Branch	P.O. Box 869	Three Rivers	78071-0869	512	786-3037
Tivoli Public	Oleander Street	Tivoli	77990		
Tomball Branch	701 James Street	Tomball	77375-4506	281	351-7269
Blanche K. Werner Public	P.O. Box 1168	Trinity	75862-1168	409	594-2087
Troup Municipal	P.O. Box 721	Troup	75789-0721	903	842-3101
Swisher County	127 SW 2nd Street	Tulia	79088-2747	806	995-3447
Turkey Public	"Route 1, Johnson Avenue"	Turkey	79261-9801	806	423-1034
Tyler Public	201 S. College Avenue	Tyler	75702-7381	903	531-1317
Universal City Public	100 Northview Drive	Universal City	78148-4150	210	659-7048
Utopia Memorial	P.O. Box 461	Utopia	78884-0461	210	966-3448
El Progreso Memorial	129 West Nopal St.	Uvalde	78801-5284	210	278-2017
Valley Mills Public	P.O. Box 914	Valley Mills	76689-0025	817	932-6370
Van Alstyne Public	P.O. Box 629	Van Alstyne	75495-0629	903	482-5991
Van Horn City-County	Box 129	Van Horn	79855-0129	915	283-2855
Oldham County	P.O. Box 640	Vega	79092-0640	806	267-2635
Venus School & Community	P.O. Box 364	Venus	76084-0364	972	366-8353
Carnegie City-County	2810 Wilbarger Street	Vernon	76384-4597	817	552-2462
Victoria Public	302 N. Main	Victoria	77901-6592	512	572-2704
Vidor Public	440 East Bolivar St.	Vidor	77662-5098	409	769-7148
Wildwood Heritage	P.O. Box 774	Village Mills	77663-0774	409	834-2261
Waco-McLennan County	1717 Austin Avenue	Waco	76701-1794	817	750-5941
Wadsworth Branch	Wadsworth Community Building	Wadsworth	77483-	409	245-3447
Waelder Public	P.O. Box 428	Waelder	78959-0428	512	665-7331
Melanie Smith	P.O. Box 192	Waller	77484	409	372-3961
Austin County System	P.O. Box 519	Wallis	77485-0519	409	478-6813
Fayette County Bookmobile	P.O. Box 13	Warrenton	78961		
Watauga Public	7109 Whitley Road	Watauga	76148-2024	817	428-9412
Nicholas P. Sims & Lyceum	515 W. Main	Waxahachie	75165-3235	972	937-2671
Weatherford Public	1214 Charles Street	Weatherford	76086-5098	817	598-4150
Weimar Public	#1 Jackson Square	Weimar	78962-2019	409	725-6608
Collingsworth Public	711 15th Street	Wellington	79095-3605	806	447-2116
Rube Sessions Memorial	P.O. Box 120	Wells	75976-0120	409	867-4757
Weslaco Public	525 South Kansas Avenue	Weslaco	78596-6215	210	968-4533
West Public	P.O. Box 513	West	76691-0513	817	826-3070
West Columbia Branch	518 E. Brazos	West Columbia	77486-2944	409	345-3394
Wharton County	1017 N. Alabama Road	Wharton	77488-4299	409	532-8080
Wheeler Public	Box 676	Wheeler	79096-0676	806	826-5977
White Deer Branch	Box 85	White Deer	79097-0085	806	883-7121
White Settlement Public	8215 White Settlement Road	White Settlement	76108-1604	817	367-0166

LIBRARY	ADDRESS	CITY	ZIP	AC	PHONE
Whitehouse Community	107 Bascom Road	Whitehouse	75791-3230	903	839-2949
Whitesboro Public	308 West Main St.	Whitesboro	76273-1639	903	564-5432
Whitewright Public	Box 128	Whitewright	75491-0128	903	364-2955
Lake Whitney	P.O. Box 1669	Whitney	76692-1669	817	694-4639
Kemp Public	1300 Lamar Street	Wichita Falls	76301-7096	817	761-8800
Meador Branch	709 W. Montgomery Street	Willis	77378-8682	409	856-4411
Gilliam Memorial Public	205 East Beltline Road	Wilmer	75172-1127	972	441-3713
The Village	P.O. Box 1240	Wimberley	78676-1240	512	847-2188
Wink Branch	P.O. Box 457	Wink	79789-0457	915	527-3691
Juanita Hargraves Branch	P.O. Box 597	Winnie	77665-0597	409	296-8245
Gilbreath Memorial	916 N. Main Street	Winnsboro	75494-2120	903	342-6866
Winters Public	120 N. Main St.	Winters	79567-5108	915	754-4251
Wolfe City Public	P.O. Box 109	Wolfe City	75496-0109	903	496-7311
City of Wollforth	P.O. Box 36	Wolfforth	79382-0036	806	866-9280
Allan Shivers & Museum	302 N. Charlton St.	Woodville	75979-4899	409	283-3709
Rita & Truett Smith Public	800 Thomas Street	Wylie	75098-3872	972	442-7566
Carl & Mary Welhausen	810 Front Street	Yoakum	77995-3058	512	293-5001
Yorktown Public	P.O. Box 308	Yorktown	78164-0308	512	564-3232
Zapata County Public	Box 2806	Zapata	78076-2806	210	765-5351

Bill Moyers, above, and Arturo Madrid. The Dallas Morning News *photos.*

National Endowment for Humanities Honors Two Texans in 1996

Source: National Endowment for the Humanities.

The Charles Frankel Prize, originated by the National Endowment for the Humanities in 1989, honors individuals who have made outstanding contributions to the public's understanding of history, literature, philosophy and other humanities disciplines.

The award goes to each of up to five Americans selected annually for their achievements in stimulating public reflection about ideas and themes in the humanities through museum, library or classroom programs, scholarship, documentary filmmaking and philanthropy.

The 1996 recipients include two Texans: Arturo Madrid and Bill Moyers.

Dr. Madrid is a scholar of Latino literature who as founding president of the Tomás Rivera Center at Trinity University in San Antonio helped develop the field of Latino studies in the United States. He is also on the board of directors of the A.H. Belo Corporation. (See his biography on page 533 of this Texas Almanac.)

Mr. Moyers was raised in Marshall. The television journalist has produced for public television numerous documentary explorations of ideas and issues in contemporary American life.

The three other 1996 recipients were: Doris Kearns Goodwin, presidential historian; Rita Dove, playwright; and Daniel Kemmis, political philosopher.

The National Endowment for the Humanities is an independent federal agency created by Congress in 1965 to promote knowledge of human history and culture. The award commemorates Charles Frankel (1917-1979), who was a professor of philosophy at Columbia University, beginning in 1939. He served as assistant secretary of state for educational and cultural affairs in the administration of President Lyndon Johnson.

Past recipients include CBS correspondent Charles Kuralt and writer-journalist Richard Rodriguez

Other Texans previously honored include Américo Paredes of San Antonio and Louise Cowan of Dallas. ☆

Film and Multimedia Work in Texas

Source: Texas Film Commission, a division of the Office of the Governor.

The year 1995 was Texas' best year ever for dollars spent in the state on film and television production. Texas hosted 69 major projects, including feature films, television movies, television miniseries and music videos. Those projects, along with an estimated $40 million in commercial television production, brought Texas' total production dollars for 1995 to a record high of $327.8 million. The previous record was set in 1994.

Typically, half of a project's budget is spent "on location," so 1995 saw $164 million spent in Texas on such diverse goods and services as salaries for locally-hired technicians, actors and extras, location fees, hotel rooms, fuel, hardware, lumber, dry cleaning, security services and many others.

In 1996, an estimated $138.5 was spent in Texas on location. Among high-profile Texas projects in 1996 were 10 feature films including: **Michael**, directed by Nora Ephron and starring John Travolta, William Hurt and Andie MacDowell, filmed in the Austin area. **The Only Thrill**, directed by Peter Masterson and including Sam Shepard and Diane Keaton in the cast, also filmed in the Austin area. And **Home Fries**, starring Robin Williams and Drew Barrymore, filmed at Bastrop and Austin.

Among the 1996's 22 television projects were the hit CBS series, **Walker, Texas Ranger**, starring Chuck Norris, filmed in the Dallas area, and the miniseries **Rough Riders** and **True Women**. Texas is also the permanent home of the tremendously popular PBS children's series **Barney & Friends**, which is made at the Studios at Las Colinas in Irving.

Highlights from 1995 included the feature films: **The Evening Star**, starring Shirley MacLaine, made in the Houston/Galveston area; **Courage Under Fire**, with Denzel Washington, Meg Ryan and Lou Diamond Phillips, filmed in El Paso and the Austin area; **Tin Cup**, with Kevin Cosner, made in Houston; and **Powder**, starring Sean Patrick Flanery, Jeff Goldblum and Mary Steenburgen, filmed in Wharton and the Galveston/Houston area.

Texas remains a popular choice for filmmakers because of its diverse locations; a large labor pool of experienced technicians, actors and suppliers; readily available technical equipment; moderate climate; and low costs of doing business. ☆

Below is a table showing the number of major productions shot at least partially in the state since the Texas Film Commission was established in 1971. Also listed are the gross budgets of those projects.

Year(s)	Projects	Gross Budgets
1971-79	119	$178,200,000
1980	22	99,500,000
1981	18	55,000,000
1982	13	45,700,000
1983	30	114,400,000
1984	30	89,900,000
1985	27	56,700,000
1986	27	102,100,000
1987	24	66,300,000
1988	24	93,900,000
1989	32	117,100,000
1990	31	42,100,000
1991	44	120,454,000
1992	28	143,207,800
1993	44	180,400,000
1994	41	191,500,000
1995	69	327,782,000
1996	65	$277,161,000
Total	669	$2,301,434,800

Texas Multimedia Office

Created as a division of the Texas Film Commission in the Office of the Governor in 1993, the mission of the Texas Multimedia Program is to foster growth in Texas' multimedia industry, including game development, enhanced CD and CD-ROM technology, and the Internet and World Wide Web.

A statewide directory lists multimedia-related businesses, free-lance personnel and services.

The Multimedia Program, in conjunction with the Texas Internet Service Providers Association (TISPA) is working on a survey of ISPs available to Texans. The goal is to provide the people of Texas with accurate, up-to date information on all of their options for Internet access. The survey will also provide the basis for a permanent directory of Texas' ISPs, which will be searchable and accessible at TISPA's web site, **http://www.tispa.org**. ☆

Film Commissions

In addition to the following film commissions operating in Texas as of summer 1997, many chambers of commerce and convention and visitors' bureaus have employees who specialize in assisting film companies:

Texas Film Commission
Office of Music, Film, Television and Multimedia
Box 13246
Austin 78711
(512) 463-9200
Fax (512) 463-4114
Amarillo Film Office
P.O. Box 9480
Amarillo 79105
(806) 374-1497 or
(800) 692-1338

Austin Film Office
P.O. Box 1088
Austin 78767
(512) 404-4562
Fax (512) 404-4564
Brownsville Area Film Commission
P.O. Box 4697
Brownsville 78523
(210) 546-3721
(800) 626-2639
Dallas/Fort Worth Regional Film Commission
P.O. Box 160246
DFW Airport 75261
(800) 234-5699 (outside Texas)
(972) 621-0400
Fax (972) 912-0916
El Paso Film Commission
1 Civic Center Plaza
El Paso 79901

(915) 534-0686
Fax (915) 534-0686
Houston Film Commission
801 Congress
Houston 77002
(713) 227-3100
(800) 365-7575
Fax (713) 227-6336
Irving Texas Film Commission
1 Dallas Communications Complex
LB 119
6309 N. O'Connor
Irving 75039-3510
(800) 2-IRVING
Fax (214) 869-4609
San Antonio Film Commission
P.O. Box 2277
San Antonio 78298
(800) 447-3372
FAX (210) 270-8782

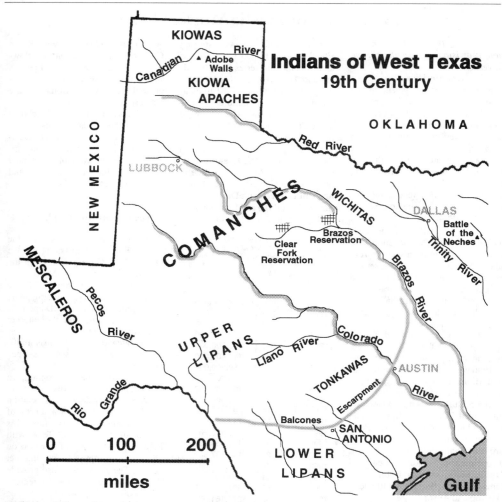

The Comanches were the predominant influence in 19th-century West Texas. (Based on map in Indians of Texas, Newcomb.)

American Indians of Texas: Powwows Mark Revival

In 1900, the U.S. census counted only 470 American Indians in Texas. In 1990, there were 65,877.

The statistics belie the fact that there is a much longer history of Indians in Texas. The state is filled with Indian names, as evidence — Cherokee County, cities like Waxahachie, Anahuac and Nacogdoches, and places like Caddo Lake and Comanche Peak.

Obviously, the 20th century has seen the return of a culture to Texas.

Before 1900, historians have estimated, more than 50 Indian "nations" roamed the prairies, or had more permanent settlements, in what is now the state of Texas. Tribes, clans, families, bands, alliances, confederations: all these terms have been used to describe the various indigenous groupings that populated this region. Some, like the Karankawas and Jumanos, show up only briefly in modern history, having disappeared about the time of the first European settlement.

Often, two named "tribes" encountered by adventurers were actually the same tribe but labeled differently by French and Spanish.

In prehistoric times — as far back as 37,000 years ago, anthropologists estimate — primitive peoples who are the ancestors of modern American Indians existed in Texas.

A burial site in the Permian Basin, dated to 12,000 years ago, was discovered in 1953 and the skeletal remains labeled "Midland Minnie." Lubbock Lake state park is at the site of a primitive civilization dated to 12,000 years ago, as well.

These early migrants arrived here by crossing over the land bridge between Alaska and Asia and moving south. Scholars say that in 1492 nearly 10 million natives inhabited North America, but by the middle of the 19th century this population had dwindled by 90 percent. In 1830, according to Walter Prescott Webb, there were "more Anglo-Americans in Texas than there were Mexicans and Indians combined."

It should be kept in mind that all these figures on "Indians" do not include descendants of the indigenous people who were enculturated or Christianized and mixed into *la raza*. The Institute of Texan Cultures puts it well: "It is almost forgotten that through many Texas families there runs a strong strain of Indian blood. Texans of Mexican heritage are descended from the proud peoples who created great civilizations south of the Rio Grande long before the Spaniards came," says *The Indian Texans*, a booklet published by the institute.

Never static, the aboriginal populations pushed and shoved each other from territory to territory. By the time Europeans arrived, there was never simply one frontier of European and Indian. It was much more complex. It was more a matter of Spanish-Anglo-French-Comanche-Caddo-Apache etc., frontiers.

Major players in the drama of 19th-century Texas were definitely the Comanches who at this time swept down from the cool highlands of the southern Rockies, and, mounted on horses, drove other tribes from West Texas. Lipan Apaches were principal victims in this new arrangement.

To a lesser extent, Tonkawas and Wichitas were caught in the battle over territory above the Balcones Escarpment, where the Texas Hill Country begins.

The only other group to have inhabited western Texas, the Mescalero Apaches, left for Mexico or for the New Mexico reservation in the 1870s. In January 1881, a band of Mescaleros raided a stagecoach in Quitman Canyon in Hudspeth County. "Texas Rangers pursued, killed eight, and dispersed the rest. This was the last Indian fight on Texas soil." (*The Indian Texans*).

About a quarter century before the 1900 census count, the last major military campaign against Indians occurred following the Battle of Adobe Walls in the Panhandle. On June 27, 1874, a Kiowa and Comanche war party led by Quanah Parker attacked buffalo hunters encamped in the abandoned trading post on the Canadian River. At the end of the encounter, three hunters were dead and 13 Indians killed. This battle spurred the military action of 1875 that forced the last Indians living east of the Pecos River into the Oklahoma territory.

This kind of forced migration into Oklahoma had occurred decades earlier in East Texas in another historic moment — the Battle of the Neches in Van Zandt and Henderson counties, near present-day Chandler. Here, in 1839, it was the armed forces of the Republic of Texas against the Cherokee people led by Chief Bowles, also called Duwali. These Cherokees had been pushed into Texas from the southeastern United States

after the War of 1812 by the U.S. government. At the same time, a policy of welcome from Spanish officials, who wanted a buffer to Anglo-American migration, drew the Cherokees to land northeast of the Trinity River.

Despite the conciliatory influence of Sam Houston, Texas President Mirabeau B. Lamar was able to enforce his hostile Indian policy and drive the Cherokee farmers north across the Red River.

In the decades between this East Texas battle of 1839 and the Adobe Walls battle of 1874, few public lands were reserved for Indians. Unlike other states in the U.S. West, the federal government did not have public land in Texas to give to the Indians.

The Texas legislature made 53,000 acres of land near the Brazos River available for two reservations in 1854. However, Clear Fork Reservation and Brazos Reservation near Fort Belknap soon encountered suspicion and hostility from white settlers in the area.

Powwows involving dancing and other events are held at various Texas locations throughout the year. This one, at Grand Prairie, occurs in early September. Texas Almanac photo.

In 1859, the Comanche remnant at Clear Fork and the Tonkawas, Wichitas and the Caddo remnant at the Brazos Reservation were forced north across the Red River into Indian Territory.

Long before Anglo-Americans and these Plains Indians of West Texas encountered each other, the Spanish missions of South and East Texas impacted other groups of natives, most prominently the Caddoes.

In 1690, the Caddo confederation of East Texas became the focus of the missionary zeal of Franciscan friars.

These Indians were part of the mound cultures that surround the Gulf of Mexico from the Yucatan to the less-developed groups of the southeastern United States. The Caddoes were a sedentary, planter people.

One of the Caddoan tribes, called Tejas by the Spanish, is the origin for the name Texas.

Coahuiltecans in South Texas were the impetus for the San Antonio missions. The European diseases to which they were not immune diminished their number. Comanches and Apaches killed many more. And the rest were absorbed into the Mexican people.

Other Indians such as the Tlaxcalans were brought up from Mexico by the Spanish Franciscans to help establish the missions. These Indians are a primary example of those who became enculturated, and their descendants still live in South Texas.

There are three reservations in Texas today. The oldest is the Alabama-Coushatta Indian Reservation in Polk County in southeast Texas, where some 650 live. These Creek remnants were forced into Texas from the southern United States and later allied with the cause of Texas independence from Mexico.

They were the only group ever able to have Republic, state, and federal governments sustain guarantees to certain land.

The two other tribes — both along the Rio Grande — received state legal recognition only since 1960. These two groups arrived in Texas after the arrival of Europeans.

The Tiguas, who moved down from the area around present-day Albuquerque, live on trust land in El Paso County, and, in 1994, tribal rolls listed 1,463 members of one-eighth blood quantum or greater.

The Kickapoos, originally from the Great Lakes region, received land in 1985 for a reservation south of Eagle Pass, but the semi-nomadic people continue to move each year from Mexico to the southwestern United States as hired farmworkers. They spend the winter months at the small reservation. There are about 650.

Starting in the 1950s and until 1980, the federal government resettled as many as 40,000 Indians in the Dallas-Fort Worth area in a program of integration into the wider American culture.

For many of these Indians, the program was only a brief experiment in urban life. Most chose to return to their reservations in other states, but many stayed and provided the core for the resurgence of American Indians in Texas.

Today there are about 20,000 urban Indians in the Dallas-Fort Worth area, and the majority of the other Indians in Texas are living and working in urban environments, although most counties number a few American Indians among their citizens.

American Indian culture is celebrated in many different powwows and other festivals. The powwows are gatherings where participants dance to the beat of drums accompanied by chants.

Chandler, the site of the Battle of the Neches, has an annual Duwali Hoop the last weekend in September. It includes Indian food, archery competition and tours of historic Native American locations.

More than 5,000 meet every year at the Texas Red Nations Powwow in **Dallas**. The event is held in November.

Grand Prairie stages the National Championship Powwow at Traders Village in early September.

In **Crowley**, south of Fort Worth, the annual Texas Kiowa Tia-Pia powwow is held in early May.

The Inter-Tribal Council of **Houston** has its annual powwow in May.

Laredo is the site of an annual powwow the last Sunday in May.

San Antonio plays host to a powwow in July.

In **Corpus Christi**, the Coastal Bend Council of Native Americans holds its annual powwow in the early fall.

The Texas A&M University Native American Student Association sponsors a powwow at the **College Station** campus each February.

In November, the **Austin** Independent School District sponsors a celebration the first Saturday of November.

The Alabama-Coushatta Indian Reservation between **Livingston** and **Woodville** stages an annual powwow the first weekend in June.

Other cultural events around the state include the St. Anthony Festival in **El Paso**. The Tiguas, for whom the Ysleta del Sur Pueblo was established in 1681 and one of the oldest ethnic groups in Texas, honor their patron saint with ceremonies, authentic dances and ethnic foods.

Visitors are also welcome at the Tigua and Alabama-Coushatta reservations all year.

Palo Duro Canyon State Park near **Canyon** is the site of the Kwahadi Indian Summer Ceremonials in early October.

In **Post**, the annual Indian ceremony for crops is in late March. A Plains Indian dance is performed at sunrise the day after the first day of spring. The wind's direction at sunrise determines success of the coming year. There is a traditional ceremony and early-morning breakfast.

Indian arts and crafts are celebrated at two North Texas events each year. Downtown **Dallas** is the site of the annual American Indian ArtFestival & Market in October.

And in **Fort Worth**, the Museum of Science and History hosts the annual Shared Worlds: Native American Day each October. ☆

FOR FURTHER READING

England, Nelson, "Urban Indians: Trails of Hope," *Texas Highways*, October 1995.

Institute staff, *The Indians of Texas*, Institute of Texan Cultures, San Antonio, 1970.

Newcomb, W.W. Jr., *The Indians of Texas*, University of Texas Press, 1961 (Fourth Paperback Printing 1978).

Utley, Robert M., *The Indian Frontier of the American West 1846-1890*, University of New Mexico Press, 1984.

Highland Games Celebrate Scottish Heritage in Texas

Sam Houston. You can start there when naming the Texans with ancestors from Scotland.

Even Chief Bowles, the revered Texas Cherokee leader killed at the Battle of the Neches in 1839, was of mixed Scot and Indian heritage. His father was William Augustus Bowles. The chief was described as "decidedly Gaelic in appearance, having light eyes, red hair and somewhat freckled."

You can go on to name Stephen F. Austin, Davy Crockett, Jim Bowie, Jim Hogg, J. Frank Dobie, and, of less fame, Neil McLennan, John and Ewen Cameron, Edmund D. Montgomery, Jesse Chisholm — and John Wesley Hardin.

Most of these figures would mention "Scotch-Irish" as a distinction, but, just the same, the Celtic blood line goes back to the land of plaid kilts and "Mc" clans.

Scotch-Irish are those Scots who moved to Northern Ireland in the 1600s and moved on to other lands in the 1700s when they would not succumb to the "Anglican ascendancy" or mix with "papish Catholics" in Ireland.   More than 250,000 of these Scotch-Irish emigrated to the American colonies between 1717 and the American Revolutionary War. These Presbyterian "Scotch-Irish" were the majority of settlers who first moved over the Appalachians. Men such as Daniel Boone. And they kept moving. To Kentucky. To Tennessee. To Missouri. And, eventually into Texas.

During their continual migration, their formal religious ties dissolved into the individualistic, churchless American milieu of the early 1800s, and many would be born-again as Baptists or converted by the Methodist itinerant preachers of the frontier.

These are the Scotch-Irish whose numbers get mixed up with ambiguous references to "British" colonists, and "Irish" ancestors, and "Anglo-American" settlers.

Later, especially when ranching came to define Texas in the late 1800s, eager and ambitious Scots came directly from Edinburgh and Aberdeen to raise cattle and build railroads — and make money.

The 1990 U.S. Census, 5.4 million Americans claimed Scottish ancestry; one third of them lived in the South. Another 5.6 million respondents identified Scotch-Irish ancestry, almost half of whom lived in the South. This was in a four-region division of South-Northeast-Midwest-West.

In the same 1990 census, the massive impact of Americans of Scotch-Irish descent continued to be obscured. The census found that Southerners comprise one third of the 39 million Americans identifying "Irish" ancestors. And, then there were the 1.1 million of "British" ancestry. These broad labels probably conceal many Scottish anscestors. This Southern stock is the core group of "Anglo-American" Texans.

Rarely coming or settling in groups, 100-proof Scot-Texans have begun to celebrate their ethnic heritage only in the last part of the 20th century with annual "highland games" and festivals in various parts of the state.

The Hamilton Pipe and Drum Band of Houston performs. The band competed in the bagpipe contest at the Texas Scottish Festival and Highland Games in Arlington in 1997. Arlington Morning News *photo.*

The Scottish festivals involve not only athletic competition but also feature music, especially piping and drumming, as well as dance and food.

The longest running and probably best-known are the Scottish Games in **Salado**. The 38th annual fete, sponsored by the Central Texas Area Museum, will be in early November in 1998. In 1999, the games will also be in November.

The Glen of Roses Celtic Festival in **Glen Rose** is held in early April.

The Texas Scottish Festival and Highland Games at the University of Texas in **Arlington** will be in early June in 1998 and 1999.

The Mo-Ranch Day of the Scots in **Hunt** will be in September.

The state's largest city, **Houston**, holds its annual British Sports Festival and Scottish Highland Games annually in the spring.

The West Texas Scottish Heritage Society in **Lubbock** will stage a festival in 1998 in early October.

The Institute of Texan Cultures' annual Folklife Festival in **San Antonio** includes the Scottish legacy in its August celebrations. ☆

FOR FURTHER READING

Burton, Morris S., "The Cherokee War 1839," *Chronicles of Smith County.*

De Bruhl, Marshall, *Sword of San Jacinto*, Random House, 1993.

Fehrenbach, T.R., *Lone Star*, MacMillan, 1968.

Flannery, John Brendan, *The Irish Texans*, Institute of Texan Cultures, 1980.

Leslie, Candace, "Scottish Texans — A Feisty Bunch," *Texas Highways*, June 1992.

State Has Religious Diversity

Religion has played an important part in Texas history from pre-Columbian times to the present day. Spanish Catholic missionaries led the initial European contact. The state's earliest inhabitants practiced their own religion, and hundreds of years before the Spanish arrived, proselytizers from the Toltec culture of central Mexico visited the El Paso area.

Even when Texas was a Mexican state and Roman Catholicism was the state religion, Protestant ministers conducted clandestine — and some open — services. In the years immediately preceeding Texas' independence, Mexican officials often looked the other way when Protestants preached, as long as they did not stir up trouble.

Protestantism was spread by circuit preachers sponsored by specific denominations, like the Methodists and Baptists, and by itinerant ministers representing no specific denominations.

Religion played a major role in the social life of the settlers in rural areas. Institutions like camp meetings developed, which attracted people for several days of preaching, praying and singing, accompanied by communal meals.

Often these were the only real social events in thinly populated areas and were popular for both their spiritual and social benefits. The Bloys Camp Meeting, begun in 1890 by Presbyterian minister W.B. Bloys and still held each summer near Fort Davis in West Texas, is a remnant of that period.

Perhaps because of its great size, Texas has more churches than any other state, with almost 17,000. This is almost 2,500 more than second-place California. Texas also has the most members with 5,282,341. Texas has long been considered a strong link in the Bible Belt that was thought to run westward from North Carolina through Texas.

Dale Jones, a Church of the Nazarene researcher, sees Texas more as a pivot. Mr. Jones believes that Texas stands at the intersection of two swaths of high church-membership areas. One runs from North Carolina into Texas, and the other extends between North Dakota and Texas.

Rural counties still maintain higher church membership and participation than the metropolitan and urban areas.

The study from which the numbers presented here were taken was published by the Glenmary Research Center, a Catholic agency, of Atlanta, Ga., and the figures have been reprinted here by permission of the center.

The Church of the Nazarene International Headquarters in Kansas City, Mo., collected the data and prepared the information.

The data were compiled from reports from 133 church bodies. The study was sponsored by the Association of Statisticians of American Religious Bodies.

"**Members**" in this study includes only communicant, confirmed members with full membership status.

"**Adherents**" are defined as all members, including regular participants who are not considered as communicant . . . (but) "the baptized."

Roman Catholics are the largest group in Texas with 3.6 million adherents.

The largest Protestant group is the Southern Baptist Convention with 3.3 million adherents.

The Jewish estimate in the study was made by Jewish Federations in local communities.

This study encompasses only Judeo-Christian denominations and religions. With the influx of immigrants from Asia, particularly since the Vietnam War, Eastern religions have flourished in Texas as in the rest of the United States. But such religious groups as Buddhists, Muslims and Hindus were not counted.

Black Baptist churches were included in the study for the first time in 1990, registering 635,179 members, or 4.8 percent of the state total. The specific number of Black Baptist churches was not reported.

A listing by county follows showing the percentage of the total population that is associated with organized religious groups, i.e. "adherents."

(For more information on the methodology employed in the Glenmary Research Center study, see the report, "Churches and Church Membership in the United States, 1990.")

Religious Groups in Texas	Members	Adherents
Advent Christian Church	172	221
African Methodist Episcopal Zion	1,842	2,191
American Baptist Churches in the USA	10,046	12,905
Apostolic Christian Churches of America	8	13
Assemblies of God	146,688	202,082
Baptist General Conference	218	278
Baptist Missionary Association of America	98,509	125,323
Beachy Amish Mennonite Churches	56	70
Brethren In Christ Church	53	73
Catholic Church	NA	3,574,728
Christ Catholic Church	3	3
Christian & Missionary Alliance, The	1,605	3,082
Christian Church (Disciples of Christ)	74,098	105,495
Christian Churches & Churches of Christ	26,012	33,766
Christian Reformed Church	528	866
Church of Christ, Scientist	NR	NR
Church of God General Conference, Abrahamic Faith	71	93
Church of God (Anderson, Ind.)	4,218	5,854

Religious Groups in Texas	Members	Adherents
Church of God (Cleveland, Tenn.)	21,728	27,828
Church of God (Seventh Day) Denver, Col., The	1,243	1,743
Church of God in Christ (Mennonite)	406	522
Church of God of Prophecy	2,251	2,918
Church of Jesus Christ of Latter -Day Saints (Mormon)	NA	111,276
Church of the Brethren	235	302
Church of the Lutheran Brethren of America	36	71
Church of the Lutheran Confession	107	144
Church of the Nazarene	31,163	45,097
Churches of Christ	292,585	380,948
Congregational Christian Churches, National Association of	556	721
Congregational Christian Churches (Not part of any national CCC body)	18	23
Conservative Baptist Association of America	NR	NR
Conservative Congregational Christian Conference	81	104
Cumberland Presbyterian Church	9,177	10,373
Episcopal Church, The	127,315	169,112
Evangelical Free Church of America, The	2,772	5,463
Evangelical Lutheran Church in America	120,004	155,276
Evangelical Lutheran Synod	119	146
Evangelical Bible Churches, Fellowship of (was Ev. Mennonite Bre., Inc.)	18	20
Evangelical Methodist Church	1,154	1,482
Evangelical Presbyterian Church	473	490
Free Lutheran Congregations, The Association of	115	144
Free Methodist Church of North America	549	886
Free Will Baptist, National Association of, Inc.	3,883	4,936
Friends (Quakers)	1,853	2,548
General Conference of Mennonite Brethren Churches	236	329
Greek Orthodox Archdiocese of North and South America	NR	NR
Holy Apostolic Catholic Assyrian Church of the East	70	282
Independent Fundamental Churches of America	NR	NR
International Church of the Foursquare Gospel	3,286	4,278
Interstate & Foreign Landmark Missionary Baptists Association	59	76
Lutheran Church—Missouri Synod, The	99,974	134,280
Mennonite Church	673	1,012
Eastern Pennsylvania Mennonite Church	30	39
Mennonite Church, The General Conference	172	216
North American Baptist Conference	1,262	1,634
Old Order Amish Church	NA	400
Open Bible Standard Churches, Inc.	NR	NR
Orthodox Church in America	NR	NR
Pentecostal Church of God	6,477	12,296
Pentecostal Holiness Church, Inc.	4,221	5,517
Christian (Plymouth) Brethren	4,225	6,766
Presbyterian Church (USA)	156,155	200,969
Presbyterian Church in America	4,221	5,445
Primitive Baptists Associations	1,977	2,544
Reformed Church in America	760	1,592
Reformed Episcopal Church	71	115
Romanian Orthodox Episcopate of America	NR	NR
Salvation Army, The	5,257	5,676
Seventh-Day Adventists	31,985	41,470
Seventh Day Baptist General Conference	190	242
Southern Baptist Convention	2,538,245	3,259,395
Syrian Orthodox Church of Antioch (Archdiocese of the USA and Canada)	NA	1,800
Two-Seed-in-the-Spirit Predestinarian Baptists	42	53
Unitarian Universalist Association	4,440	5,843
United Church of Christ	16,321	20,950
United Methodist Church, The	781,389	1,004,318
Wesleyan Church, The	329	892
Wisconsin Evangelical Lutheran Synod	3,117	4,463
Jewish Estimate	NA	107,980
Black Baptists Estimate	635,179	815,771
Independent, Charismatic Churches	NA	127,850
Independent Non-Charismatic Churches	NA	132,292
Statewide Totals	**5,282,341**	**10,896,401**

Source: Glenmary Research Center, Atlanta, Ga.

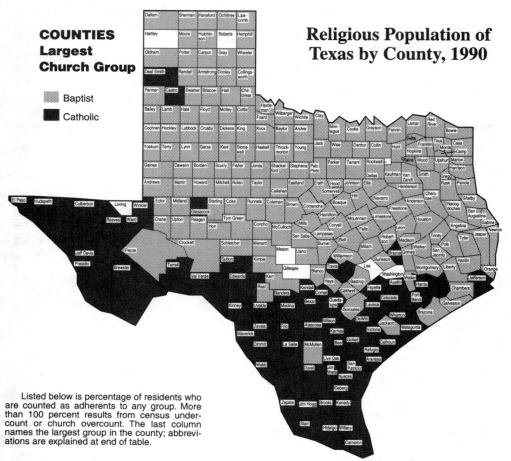

COUNTIES Largest Church Group

- Baptist
- Catholic

Religious Population of Texas by County, 1990

Listed below is percentage of residents who are counted as adherents to any group. More than 100 percent results from census undercount or church overcount. The last column names the largest group in the county; abbreviations are explained at end of table.

County	% of total pop.	Largest group
Anderson	54.8	S.BAPT.
Andrews	76.6	S.BAPT.
Angelina	68.3	S.BAPT.
Aransas	43.7	R.C.
Archer	78.0	S.BAPT.
Armstrong	78.0	S.BAPT.
Atascosa	65.3	R.C.
Austin	71.8	R.C.
Bailey	74.7	S.BAPT.
Bandera	49.2	R.C.
Bastrop	46.1	S.BAPT.
Baylor	106.0	S.BAPT.
Bee	64.3	R.C.
Bell	49.7	S.BAPT.
Bexar	64.9	R.C.
Blanco	59.2	S.BAPT.
Borden	26.9	S.BAPT.
Bosque	74.0	S.BAPT.
Bowie	68.3	S.BAPT.
Brazoria	62.0	S.BAPT.
Brazos	49.6	R.C.
Brewster	91.4	R.C.

County	% of total pop.	Largest group
Briscoe	82.0	S.BAPT.
Brooks	76.7	R.C.
Brown	73.0	S.BAPT.
Burleson	60.2	S.BAPT.
Burnet	57.2	S.BAPT.
Caldwell	52.1	S.BAPT.
Calhoun	98.7	R.C.
Callahan	67.6	S.BAPT.
Cameron	95.5	R.C.
Camp	82.1	S.BAPT.
Carson	93.8	S.BAPT.
Cass	71.0	S.BAPT.
Castro	112.5	R.C.
Chambers	59.4	S.BAPT.
Cherokee	64.7	S.BAPT.
Childress	96.0	S.BAPT.
Clay	76.9	S.BAPT.
Cochran	109.7	S.BAPT.
Coke	84.0	S.BAPT.
Coleman	67.7	S.BAPT.
Collin	45.0	S.BAPT.
Collingsworth	81.4	S.BAPT.

County	% of total pop.	Largest group
Colorado	103.7	R.C.
Comal	58.6	R.C.
Comanche	63.8	S.BAPT.
Concho	58.5	S.BAPT.
Cooke	68.1	S.BAPT.
Coryell	46.9	S.BAPT.
Cottle	125.1	S.BAPT.
Crane	70.1	S.BAPT.
Crockett	82.7	S.BAPT.
Crosby	75.4	S.BAPT.
Culberson	101.1	R.C.
Dallam	118.7	S.BAPT.
Dallas	60.3	S.BAPT.
Dawson	100.3	S.BAPT.
Deaf Smith	84.4	R.C.
Delta	76.1	S.BAPT.
Denton	37.7	S.BAPT.
DeWitt	80.9	R.C.
Dickens	110.0	S.BAPT.
Dimmit	81.0	R.C.
Donley	77.0	S.BAPT.
Duval	75.3	R.C.

County	% of total pop.	Largest group	County	% of total pop.	Largest group	County	% of total pop.	Largest group
Eastland	81.2	S.BAPT.	Kent	95.7	S.BAPT.	Roberts	141.6	CHR/CH
Ector	64.2	S.BAPT.	Kerr	49.3	S.BAPT.	Robertson	68.6	S.BAPT.
Edwards	97.5	R.C.	Kimble	65.5	S.BAPT.	Rockwall	67.7	Ind. CHA.
Ellis	67.3	S.BAPT.	King	68.4	S.BAPT.	Runnels	86.1	S.BAPT.
El Paso	82.3	R.C.	Kinney	69.6	R.C.	Rusk	61.0	S.BAPT.
Erath	68.0	S.BAPT.	Kleberg	82.2	R.C.	Sabine	49.0	S.BAPT.
Falls	73.8	S.BAPT.	Knox	110.8	S.BAPT.	San Augustine	58.6	S.BAPT.
Fannin	75.7	S.BAPT.	Lamar	69.1	S.BAPT.	San Jacinto	31.7	S.BAPT.
Fayette	91.5	R.C.	Lamb	88.0	S.BAPT.	San Patricio	80.7	R.C.
Fisher	90.3	S.BAPT.	Lampasas	76.6	S.BAPT.	San Saba	81.1	S.BAPT.
Floyd	124.3	S.BAPT.	La Salle	110.7	R.C.	Schleicher	75.4	S.BAPT.
Foard	102.4	S.BAPT.	Lavaca	85.5	R.C.	Scurry	73.5	S.BAPT.
Fort Bend	44.5	R.C.	Lee	69.3	LUTH.	Shackelford	85.0	S.BAPT.
Franklin	78.1	S.BAPT.	Leon	70.3	S.BAPT.	Shelby	59.2	S.BAPT.
Freestone	68.1	S.BAPT.	Liberty	70.9	S.BAPT.	Sherman	80.8	S.BAPT.
Frio	84.9	R.C.	Limestone	62.1	S.BAPT.	Smith	70.2	S.BAPT.
Gaines	87.2	S.BAPT.	Lipscomb	98.4	S.BAPT.	Somervell	57.1	S.BAPT.
Galveston	51.1	S.BAPT.	Live Oak	81.9	R.C.	Starr	85.6	R.C.
Garza	65.7	S.BAPT.	Llano	62.3	S.BAPT.	Stephens	77.3	S.BAPT.
Gillespie	66.9	LUTH.	Loving	0	0	Sterling	80.9	S.BAPT.
Glasscock	61.5	R.C.	Lubbock	65.8	S.BAPT.	Stonewall	79.6	S.BAPT.
Goliad	72.2	R.C.	Lynn	93.3	S.BAPT.	Sutton	75.0	R.C.
Gonzales	71.4	S.BAPT.	McCulloch	70.0	S.BAPT.	Swisher	99.7	S.BAPT.
Gray	86.9	S.BAPT.	McLennan	73.6	S.BAPT.	Tarrant	56.1	S.BAPT.
Grayson	72.3	S.BAPT.	McMullen	47.0	S.BAPT.	Taylor	72.5	S.BAPT.
Gregg	83.4	S.BAPT.	Madison	62.5	S.BAPT.	Terrell	80.3	R.C.
Grimes	63.0	S.BAPT.	Marion	61.3	S.BAPT.	Terry	70.3	S.BAPT.
Guadalupe	48.0	R.C.	Martin	71.5	S.BAPT.	Throckmorton	128.0	S.BAPT.
Hale	94.4	S.BAPT.	Mason	70.8	METH.	Titus	69.8	S.BAPT.
Hall	112.3	S.BAPT.	Matagorda	74.7	R.C.	Tom Green	63.2	S.BAPT.
Hamilton	72.5	S.BAPT.	Maverick	84.5	R.C.	Travis	48.4	R.C.
Hansford	88.0	S.BAPT.	Medina	75.2	R.C.	Trinity	57.7	S.BAPT.
Hardeman	89.3	S.BAPT.	Menard	94.3	S.BAPT.	Tyler	74.0	S.BAPT.
Hardin	69.4	S.BAPT.	Midland	70.0	S.BAPT.	Upshur	64.7	S.BAPT.
Harris	58.3	R.C.	Milam	66.6	S.BAPT.	Upton	108.9	S.BAPT.
Harrison	61.6	S.BAPT.	Mills	82.7	S.BAPT.	Uvalde	72.5	R.C.
Hartley	44.6	METH.	Mitchell	78.9	S.BAPT.	Val Verde	35.2	R.C.
Haskell	109.5	S.BAPT.	Montague	66.8	S.BAPT.	Van Zandt	66.8	S.BAPT.
Hays	42.7	S.BAPT.	Montgomery	47.9	S.BAPT.	Victoria	83.0	R.C.
Hemphill	78.5	S.BAPT.	Moore	65.4	S.BAPT.	Walker	49.5	S.BAPT.
Henderson	48.0	S.BAPT.	Morris	69.4	S.BAPT.	Waller	51.2	S.BAPT.
Hidalgo	94.1	R.C.	Motley	94.3	S.BAPT.	Ward	133.5	R.C.
Hill	65.6	S.BAPT.	Nacogdoches	52.6	S.BAPT.	Washington	68.7	LUTH.
Hockley	75.6	S.BAPT.	Navarro	68.5	S.BAPT.	Webb	80.6	R.C.
Hood	50.5	S.BAPT.	Newton	47.9	S.BAPT.	Wharton	79.3	R.C.
Hopkins	74.8	S.BAPT.	Nolan	90.0	S.BAPT.	Wheeler	90.3	S.BAPT.
Houston	68.9	S.BAPT.	Nueces	74.6	R.C.	Wichita	75.8	S.BAPT.
Howard	82.3	S.BAPT.	Ochiltree	69.1	S.BAPT.	Wilbarger	87.6	S.BAPT.
Hudspeth	84.6	R.C.	Oldham	71.6	S.BAPT.	Willacy	104.7	R.C.
Hunt	62.6	S.BAPT.	Orange	75.2	S.BAPT.	Williamson	46.9	S.BAPT.
Hutchinson	83.0	S.BAPT.	Palo Pinto	69.3	S.BAPT.	Wilson	61.3	R.C.
Irion	74.4	S.BAPT.	Panola	56.4	S.BAPT.	Winkler	139.6	R.C.
Jack	87.2	S.BAPT.	Parker	54.9	S.BAPT.	Wise	52.3	S.BAPT
Jackson	72.1	S.BAPT.	Parmer	65.6	S.BAPT.	Wood	73.4	S.BAPT.
Jasper	71.9	S.BAPT.	Pecos	55.1	S.BAPT.	Yoakum	86.6	S.BAPT.
Jeff Davis	109.0	R.C.	Polk	60.7	S.BAPT.	Young	85.0	S.BAPT.
Jefferson	78.5	R.C.	Potter	100.6	S.BAPT.	Zapata	38.5	R.C.
Jim Hogg	90.8	R.C.	Presidio	80.0	R.C.	Zavala	83.6	R.C.
Jim Wells	84.5	R.C.	Rains	59.8	S.BAPT.			
Johnson	57.9	S.BAPT.	Randall	40.8	S.BAPT.			
Jones	78.9	S.BAPT.	Reagan	70.6	S.BAPT.			
Karnes	91.3	R.C.	Real	78.6	S.BAPT.			
Kaufman	63.4	S.BAPT.	Red River	57.4	S.BAPT.			
Kendall	65.6	R.C.	Reeves	127.5	R.C.			
Kenedy	95.7	R.C.	Refugio	100.2	R.C.			

S.BAPT. Southern Baptist; R.C., Catholic, METH., Methodist; LUTH., Lutheran; CHR/CH, Church of Christ; Ind. CHA., Independent Charismatic. Source: **"Churches and Church Membership in the United States 1990,"** published by Glenmary Research Center, Atlanta. Reprinted with permission.

International Prizes Recognize Texas Scientists

Robert F. Curl Jr., left, and Richard E. Smalley of Rice University in Houston were awarded the 1996 Nobel Prize in chemistry for discovering of fullerenes, a family of soccer ball-shaped carbon molecules. The Dallas Morning News photo.

Henry M. Beachell of the Alvin-based RiceTec Inc. was awarded the World Food Prize for his research in rice production. The World Food Prize was established in 1987 and was the idea of 1970 Nobel Peace Prize laureate Norman E. Borlaug. It has been sponsored since 1990 by The John Ruan Foundation of Des Moines. Associated Press photo.

Hospital Care in Texas

Source: Chiefly the Texas Hospital Association.

As our population increases and technological advances continue, this field of essential services is greatly expanding in Texas. Houston, Dallas and other Texas cities are internationally known for their medical centers.

However, many small communities of the state have no hospital or access to professional medical care. As our population ages, access to health care becomes a greater concern for many Texans, as evidenced by the coverage of health-care issues in the Texas media.

Hospitals

In 1995, Texas hospitals employed 280,617 full-time equivalent people (FTEs) with a payroll, including benefits, of more than $10.3 billion.

These employees were reported by the 498 hospitals, with approximately 71,000 beds, registered with the American Hospital Association. One of every 12.6 U.S. hospitals is located in Texas.

The average length of stay in the 416 community hospitals was 5.6 days in 1995, compared to 6.8 days in 1975.

The average length of stay in Texas community hospitals was one day less than the U.S. average, and the average cost per admission in Texas was $5,879, which was 5.4 percent less than the U.S. average of $6,215.

Admissions to Texas community hospitals totaled 2,029,050, or 90.5 percent of the total admissions to all Texas hospitals.

There were 28,595,321 out-patient visits in 1995, of which 22,656,995 or 79 percent were provided by community hospitals.

Psychiatric admissions of 55,195 represented 2.5 percent of total admissions in 1995.

Of the total 3,833,132 births in U.S. hospitals in 1995, 323,210 were in Texas hospitals.

There were 62,605 Registered Nurse FTEs, 16,794 Licensed Vocational Nurse FTEs, and 5,370 FTE health-care professions trainees working in Texas hospitals in 1995.

Allied Health Training

Hospitals are the leading source of allied health education in Texas.

All allied health personnel are either completely or partially educated in a hospital, clinical, internship or residency program.

Texas continues to experience a need for rehabilitation workers in health-care fields. There is still a demand for physical therapists, occupational therapists, respiratory therapists, medical technologists, radiologic technologists and pharmacists.

The Texas Health Careers Program, sponsored by the THA Hospital Education and Research Foundation, P.O. Box 15587, Austin, Texas 78761, collects information on nursing, allied health and other medical and dental education programs, and provides free information to anyone interested in a career in the health field.

Nursing

For nursing professionals, the Texas Organization of Nurse Executives and the Texas Society of Infection Control Practitioners offer opportunities for continuing education and networking with others in the profession.

They also serve as advocates for nursing and provide representatives to regulatory agency committees, legislative study groups and other related nursing organizations.

These societies are affiliated with the Texas Hospital Association, the principal organization for health-care providers. ☆

Texans in the National Academy of the Sciences

Source: National Academy of Sciences.

The National Academy of Sciences is a private organization of scientists and engineers dedicated to the furtherance of science and its use for the general welfare.

Established by congressional acts of incorporation, which were signed by Abraham Lincoln in 1863, the science academy acts as official adviser to the federal government in matters of science or technology.

Added to the membership in 1997 were three Texas scientists.

Robert **Curl**, who also received a Nobel Prize last year (see previous page) was named.

Another new member was Ferid **Murad** of the University of Texas Health Science Center in Houston. Dr. Murad was recognized for his studies of guanylyl cyclases which "permit understanding of molecular mechanisms of action of many hormones, autacoids, toxins and drugs."

In 1996, the Academy elected to membership Karl W. **Butzer** of the University of Texas at Austin. Dr. Butzer's citation said he has made "important theoretical contributions to understanding the spread of early hominids, the origins of anatomically-modern people in sub-Saharan Africa, and the co-evolution of early agricultural lifeways with their biotic resources."

Election to membership in the Academy is one of the highest honors that can be accorded a U.S. scientist or engineer.

As of July 1, 1996, the total number of active members was 1,743.

In addition, 306 scientists with citizenship outside the United States were nonvoting foreign associates.

In 1997, Johann **Deisenhofer** of the Universtiy of Texas Southwestern Medical Center at Dallas was named as a nonvoting foreign associate.

In 1948, Karl Folkers of The University of Texas at Austin became the first Texan elected to the academy.

In July 1997, 50 scientists affiliated with Texas institutions when they were elected were full, voting members.

Academy Member	Affiliation*	Yr. Elected
Perry L. Adkisson	A&M	1979
Abram Amsel	UT-Austin	1992
Neal R. Amundon	U of H	1992
Charles J. Arntzen	A&M	1983
Allen J. Bard	UT-Austin	1982
Brian J.L. Berry	UT-Dallas	1975
Norman E. Borlaug	A&M	1968
Michael S. Brown	UTSWMC	1980
Karl W. Butzer	UT-Austin	1996
C. Thomas Caskey	Baylor Med.	1993
Joseph W. Chamberlain	Rice	1965
C.W. Chu	U of H	1989
F. Albert Cotton	A&M	1967
Robert F. Curl	Rice	1997
Gerard H. de Vaucouleurs	UT-Austin	1986
Bryce DeWitt	UT-Austin	1990
Ronald W. Estabrook	UTSWMC	1979
Karl Folkers	UT-Austin	1948
Marye Anne Fox	UT-Austin	1994
David L. Garbers	UTSWMC	1993
Alfred G. Gilman	UTSWMC	1985
Joseph L. Goldstein	UTSWMC	1980
William E. Gordon	Rice	1968
Verne E. Grant	UT-Austin	1968
Norman Hackerman	Welch	1971
A. James Hudspeth	UTSWMC	1991
James L. Kinsey	Rice	1991
Ernst Knobil	UTHSC-Houston	1986
Jay K. Kochi	U of H	1982
John L. Margrave	Rice	1974
S.M. McCann	UTSWMC	1983
Ferid Murad	UTHSC-Houston	1997
Jack Myers	UT-Austin	1975
Bert W. O'Malley	Baylor Med.	1992
Kenneth L. Pike	SIL	1985
Lester J. Reed	UT-Austin	1973
Richard E. Smalley	Rice	1990
Esmond E. Snell	UT-Austin	1955
Richard C. Starr	UT-Austin	1976
Max D. Summers	A&M	1989
Harry L. Swinney	UT-Austin	1992
John T. Tate	UT-Austin	1969
Karen K. Uhlenbeck	UT-Austin	1986
Jonathan W. Uhr	UTSWMC	1984
Roger H. Unger	UTSWMC	1986
Ellen S. Vitetta	UTSWMC	1994
Salih J. Wakil	Baylor Med.	1990
Steven Weinberg	UT-Austin	1972
D. Fred Wendorf	SMU	1987
Jean D. Wilson	UTSWMC	1983

Source: National Academy of Sciences

* A&M - Texas A&M University
UT-Austin - The University of Texas at Austin
U of H - University of Houston
UT-Dallas - The University of Texas at Dallas
UTSWMC - The University of Texas Southwestern Medical Center at Dallas
Baylor Med. - Baylor College of Medicine
Rice - Rice University
Welch - Robert A. Welch Foundation
UTHSC - Houston - The University of Texas Health Science Center at Houston
SIL - Summer Institute of Linguistics
SMU - Southern Methodist University

In addition to the above full members, **D.H.R. Barton** was elected as a Foreign Associate in 1970 from Texas A&M University, and **Cecil H. Green** of Texas Instruments, Inc., was awarded a Public Welfare Medal in 1979. ☆

Persons without health insurance

State rank	Percent of population
1. Texas	**24.2**
2. New Mexico	23.1
3. California	21.1
4. Arizona	20.2
5. Louisiana	19.2
Alabama	19.2
7. Oklahoma	17.8
Mississippi	17.8
9. Arkansas	17.4
10. Florida	17.2

Source: Statistical Abstract of the United States 1996, U.S. Bureau of the Census.

Death, Birth Rates Continue Trends in Public Health Statistics

Heart disease and cancer remained the major causes of death in 1995, the latest year for which statistics are available from the Bureau of Vital Statistics, Texas Department of Health.

Heart disease claimed 41,630 victims, and cancer caused 31,571 deaths during the year.

Human Immunodeficiency Virus (HIV), which entered the list of top ten killers in Texas in 1990, totaled 2,764 in 1995.

The other leading causes of death in Texas were as follows:

- •Cerebrovascular diseases — 9,788
- •Accidents — 6,402
- •Chronic Obstructive Pulmonary Diseases and Allied Conditions — 6,232
- •Diabetes Mellitus — 4,569
- •Pneumonia and Influenza — 3,827

- •Suicide — 2,229
- •Liver Disease — 1,867

The death rate for the state in both 1994 and 1995 stood at 7.4 percent per 1,000 estimated population, down from 7.5 percent in 1993. There were 137,549 deaths in Texas in 1995.

While there was a record number of babies born to Texas' mothers in 1995 (322,669), the state's birth rate continued to decline from 18.6 per 1,000 population in 1990 to 17.3. In 1961, that figure was 24.8

Infant deaths also declined. The state's infant mortality rate fell to 6.5 per 1,000 births in 1995, an all-time low for the category. In 1961, that figure was 26.7.

Induced terminations of pregnancy (abortions) continued to decline slightly since 1990, with 87,501 in 1995. Abortions were induced in an estimated 20 percent of the state's pregnancies.

Health Care and Deaths in Texas Counties

County	Patient Care, 1995				Leading Causes of Death by County, 1995											Misc., 1995	
	Doctors	Nurses	Hospital Beds	Ambulances	Total Deaths	Heart Disease	Cancer	Cerebrovascular	Accidents	Pulmonary	Diabetes	Pneumonia	HIV	Suicides	Liver Disease	Pregnancy Rate*	Abortions
Anderson	65	206	213	5	497	133	123	47	30	22	15	16	0	3	3	111.4	324
Andrews	9	52	89	3	120	49	18	13	4	5	5	2	0	5	2	66.4	24
Angelina	92	371	361	7	670	192	144	89	28	27	20	28	3	6	9	85.5	154
Aransas	9	30	0	3	235	68	64	20	12	15	1	7	3	1	4	85.9	81
Archer	0	14	0	1	70	23	20	5	4	5	1	2	0	1	1	67.5	13
Armstrong	0	10	0	3	33	9	7	2	7	1	1	1	0	0	2	65.7	3
Atascosa	14	36	65	10	289	62	59	35	10	15	10	11	2	10	2	78.2	83
Austin	10	40	32	8	231	88	45	21	12	10	4	7	0	2	0	76.2	39
Bailey	3	21	31	3	52	21	9	5	2	0	4	1	0	0	1	98.1	14
Bandera	1	16	0	8	108	31	33	8	4	2	4	4	1	2	3	72.5	36
Bastrop	16	65	35	5	345	96	89	19	23	11	15	7	5	7	7	79.8	100
Baylor	2	21	49	2	80	28	14	11	6	1	3	6	0	1	1	92.9	21
Bee	12	47	70	5	223	53	59	13	10	14	11	2	5	3	4	84.2	79
Bell	375	1,290	997	31	1,340	517	276	62	82	43	23	34	19	27	20	127.4	1,005
Bexar	2,096	7,742	5,427	165	9,215	2,754	2,016	665	394	368	342	248	193	175	177	95.9	6,508
Blanco	3	13	0	5	88	19	16	18	4	2	3	1	1	4	0	90.6	19
Borden	0	0	0	2	5	0	3	0	1	0	0	0	0	0	0	50.8	2
Bosque	13	49	72	6	270	90	59	21	8	15	8	8	1	3	2	79.4	34
Bowie	198	490	681	23	995	287	214	70	38	30	40	30	6	8	6	69.6	44
Brazoria	131	647	364	43	1,290	423	334	77	53	51	44	20	9	29	18	82.4	492
Brazos	195	417	304	12	612	177	156	49	30	12	14	16	4	8	4	71.5	554
Brewster	9	28	50	6	81	19	14	11	8	7	3	2	1	5	2	63.6	29
Briscoe	0	1	0	4	18	3	5	1	1	1	0	0	0	0	1	114.3	10
Brooks	3	14	31	8	59	25	11	1	3	2	1	2	0	0	1	103.8	22
Brown	52	136	218	8	421	137	80	38	21	26	14	11	2	3	2	86.6	63
Burleson	4	16	37	3	149	51	35	10	7	5	9	5	0	0	0	80.7	20
Burnet	18	65	42	11	304	79	76	17	11	16	14	9	0	5	5	90.3	60
Caldwell	11	46	30	4	247	71	49	7	18	11	17	4	4	5	4	80.3	89
Calhoun	15	43	75	8	149	47	39	12	8	4	3	1	2	3	4	90.9	27
Callahan	4	26	0	5	148	60	27	10	3	8	9	5	1	7	0	67.6	13
Cameron	277	797	948	21	1,921	438	385	120	100	86	104	56	14	20	46	125.4	969
Camp	6	27	49	3	164	53	41	14	10	3	11	4	0	2	0	96.0	15
Carson	0	16	0	4	70	18	18	6	3	8	0	1	1	1	0	66.0	5
Cass	15	82	162	9	400	132	79	36	23	13	5	13	3	2	1	68.4	16
Castro	4	15	46	3	65	21	13	3	5	4	1	4	1	1	2	75.9	21
Chambers	5	44	106	7	162	46	42	8	5	8	8	5	0	3	2	66.5	34
Cherokee	59	175	197	4	493	172	117	41	29	13	23	14	1	7	3	81.7	69
Childress	6	23	75	1	105	33	18	11	2	6	5	4	0	2	0	83.5	4
Clay	3	16	32	0	121	50	29	15	2	5	3	1	0	0	0	57.9	10
Cochran	2	5	30	3	32	12	7	2	1	3	2	1	1	0	0	62.1	2
Coke	0	8	0	3	57	11	15	3	1	2	0	4	0	3	1	43.3	1
Coleman	4	13	46	1	152	49	37	14	4	7	9	4	0	1	2	73.3	9

Health Care and Deaths in Texas Counties

County	Patient Care, 1995				Leading Causes of Death by County, 1995											Misc., 1995	
	Doctors	Nurses	Hospital Beds	Ambulances	Total Deaths	Heart Disease	Cancer	Cerebrovascular	Accidents	Pulmonary	Diabetes	Pneumonia	HIV	Suicides	Liver Disease	Pregnancy Rate*	Abortions
Collin	466	1,250	718	14	1,318	349	373	114	86	53	45	25	16	34	11	78.0	957
Collingswth	3	9	25	4	48	19	8	3	3	2	3	2	0	0	0	88.8	7
Colorado	13	61	125	9	263	94	53	23	6	13	9	15	4	3	2	82.8	32
Comal	49	166	116	11	592	163	150	56	31	25	23	11	2	14	7	77.9	151
Comanche	9	38	65	5	207	75	49	14	31	8	6	2	0	5	3	79.9	29
Concho	3	11	20	3	37	13	6	4	1	1	0	1	1	1	0	43.7	0
Cooke	19	156	106	4	334	105	81	26	15	15	9	11	3	4	7	74.7	55
Coryell	24	115	55	14	297	111	75	11	14	14	7	4	2	3	4	73.3	196
Cottle	1	3	0	2	26	15	5	0	1	2	1	2	0	0	0	98.6	8
Crane	2	8	28	3	19	4	5	0	0	1	1	1	0	0	1	83.7	16
Crockett	2	5	20	3	50	13	14	5	2	4	2	4	0	0	1	78.6	7
Crosby	3	7	50	4	68	18	18	7	4	1	5	1	0	2	1	80.8	15
Culberson	3	7	25	2	25	6	6	2	2	0	4	1	0	0	1	72.3	3
Dallam	3	20	0	4	60	16	12	6	4	3	1	2	0	0	1	123.1	20
Dallas	3,678	12,267	8,545	213	13,573	3,952	3,133	933	659	593	377	317	562	234	168	98.9	12,505
Dawson	5	25	44	3	130	34	29	8	7	10	10	6	1	1	0	82.0	17
Deaf Smith	10	41	40	3	149	44	36	6	6	6	5	8	1	1	3	95.4	35
Delta	1	13	0	2	89	33	19	9	2	4	5	0	1	1	2	96.8	15
Denton	216	880	698	25	1,332	453	306	69	68	78	35	35	29	33	11	73.4	1,259
DeWitt	7	37	49	8	281	115	46	34	8	11	6	6	2	3	1	69.7	34
Dickens	0	4	0	2	47	16	8	5	4	2	3	1	0	0	0	64.5	7
Dimmit	7	16	49	2	69	11	16	4	2	1	7	5	1	0	2	79.9	26
Donley	1	8	0	2	59	23	19	6	2	3	1	0	0	1	0	85.7	11
Duval	0	8	0	5	117	37	32	6	8	4	8	5	0	2	1	94.2	45
Eastland	10	35	85	8	296	124	58	23	7	17	10	8	0	2	1	87.7	45
Ector	138	534	496	13	928	275	206	55	47	65	28	45	14	18	10	84.2	381
Edwards	1	2	0	2	20	8	2	1	2	0	0	2	0	1	0	88.5	3
Ellis	56	233	125	9	705	222	157	55	44	34	27	17	7	9	5	73.1	211
El Paso	643	2,364	1,980	45	3,595	959	805	215	190	166	213	81	60	55	118	108.5	2,500
Erath	29	110	98	5	289	86	74	24	15	12	2	10	0	2	3	83.0	125
Falls	8	71	68	7	250	99	52	10	8	15	14	13	0	1	1	75.2	29
Fannin	18	95	65	6	345	142	65	25	24	17	7	13	0	1	5	76.0	28
Fayette	16	34	60	5	269	88	65	27	15	9	6	9	0	2	5	84.1	24
Fisher	2	11	30	3	46	14	7	5	2	4	4	0	0	0	0	77.4	12
Floyd	4	17	27	3	100	35	24	8	3	1	3	3	0	1	1	90.8	14
Foard	0	3	0	2	19	8	4	1	2	0	1	3	0	1	0	100.0	6
Fort Bend	177	904	368	16	1,139	307	257	88	61	51	48	27	23	32	17	68.7	904
Franklin	7	30	51	2	94	31	17	5	9	5	1	8	0	1	1	61.2	17
Freestone	6	34	48	5	215	65	37	18	17	9	8	7	3	6	0	76.4	32
Frio	5	27	22	4	103	39	25	3	3	3	5	3	0	0	0	89.4	30
Gaines	6	23	49	6	88	33	16	9	7	5	4	1	0	1	1	97.0	19
Galveston	253	1,949	1,637	22	2,116	633	558	137	79	95	77	33	49	40	21	84.3	861
Garza	3	8	26	2	61	18	10	4	0	8	4	4	0	1	2	77.6	7
Gillespie	34	81	61	6	241	77	55	23	13	9	5	8	0	3	2	80.7	22
Glasscock	0	2	0	3	8	2	1	0	1	0	1	0	0	1	0	72.1	4
Goliad	1	13	24	2	68	24	11	7	1	0	4	0	0	2	0	61.2	9
Gonzales	9	41	110	5	214	75	55	14	14	4	5	5	0	2	0	81.0	35
Gray	28	93	110	7	277	92	65	17	4	20	8	9	2	4	0	72.4	27
Grayson	160	679	618	20	1,139	405	251	58	47	49	37	57	11	19	6	72.8	226
Gregg	186	643	489	15	1,086	319	264	82	49	62	31	39	10	15	7	75.4	96
Grimes	8	25	57	1	211	64	54	13	13	5	7	3	2	5	4	87.0	37
Guadalupe	39	152	75	11	547	163	144	20	26	30	17	16	2	11	7	68.5	162
Hale	39	77	140	13	282	100	43	38	15	9	3	6	2	7	1	95.5	54
Hall	2	11	42	4	51	24	8	3	0	2	2	1	0	1	1	110.2	6
Hamilton	6	21	49	6	147	59	34	11	4	8	3	4	0	4	0	84.7	13
Hansford	2	17	28	4	52	33	8	3	5	4	0	3	0	0	0	62.5	6
Hardeman	5	16	63	3	74	24	9	5	3	2	6	0	0	1	1	80.4	9
Hardin	19	98	69	17	380	119	98	24	23	18	10	22	2	2	9	82.8	99
Harris	5,430	17,862	16,277	384	18,590	5,314	4,348	1,316	728	695	542	411	844	330	283	103.8	22,062
Harrison	46	125	141	6	608	205	131	50	35	26	13	18	2	7	7	57.0	37
Hartley	0	0	23	4	36	8	13	1	3	4	0	2	0	1	0	87.3	14
Haskell	3	16	30	2	127	58	23	9	0	5	8	1	0	1	0	65.6	4
Hays	81	198	109	9	425	102	103	35	22	18	11	16	9	9	3	67.4	404
Hemphill	4	12	26	3	35	16	5	3	1	2	0	1	0	2	0	43.8	6
Henderson	36	139	115	0	796	235	207	66	35	37	19	33	10	5	11	74.8	118
Hidalgo	341	895	975	38	2,467	697	518	156	161	123	127	86	15	23	56	129.2	1,079
Hill	13	67	164	9	423	158	87	39	13	19	8	7	0	3	3	85.2	63

Health Care and Deaths in Texas Counties

County	Patient Care, 1995				Leading Causes of Death by County, 1995											Misc., 1995	
	Doctors	Nurses	Hospital Beds	Ambulances	Total Deaths	Heart Disease	Cancer	Cerebrovascular	Accidents	Pulmonary	Diabetes	Pneumonia	HIV	Suicides	Liver Disease	Pregnancy Rate*	Abortions
Hockley	13	57	78	6	200	70	40	17	4	9	7	0	1	2	6	67.7	46
Hood	25	121	56	6	373	86	106	23	16	18	14	11	1	5	2	74.4	115
Hopkins	18	95	100	5	340	102	82	20	22	18	10	11	1	5	2	81.4	55
Houston	13	64	93	2	289	88	65	21	18	7	7	10	4	3	3	68.9	27
Howard	42	210	153	6	371	108	86	13	19	14	11	11	7	5	6	82.8	79
Hudspeth	0	3	0	7	21	3	5	2	2	0	2	1	1	0	0	100.6	9
Hunt	50	179	178	0	707	227	178	37	28	36	22	33	5	9	7	72.9	176
Hutchinson	18	64	99	10	247	79	62	12	12	20	9	4	1	7	2	64.3	23
Irion	1	0	0	2	7	1	3	0	0	1	0	1	0	0	1	74.1	3
Jack	4	16	49	6	78	27	18	9	4	2	5	1	0	0	1	75.9	23
Jackson	5	26	35	7	144	50	33	12	4	7	5	6	0	1	0	89.0	47
Jasper	25	90	144	16	404	148	84	29	26	15	11	16	1	7	2	88.5	80
Jeff Davis	1	3	0	2	17	6	4	1	0	0	1	0	1	0	0	65.0	4
Jefferson	484	1,681	1,842	56	2,486	705	632	185	88	95	89	86	42	28	30	83.0	759
Jim Hogg	2	4	0	1	58	16	7	2	4	2	4	5	0	0	2	89.3	17
Jim Wells	19	52	131	8	333	130	65	23	12	10	21	4	1	4	9	88.4	127
Johnson	70	326	112	10	900	301	191	78	37	47	26	32	5	14	8	65.3	264
Jones	6	36	144	6	288	95	53	10	7	4	12	10	0	4	2	68.1	38
Karnes	3	21	46	2	142	52	32	12	6	3	6	1	1	1	1	82.0	22
Kaufman	62	262	194	4	561	156	136	37	22	32	23	26	2	12	3	70.9	145
Kendall	15	53	0	5	183	58	34	17	10	10	9	8	2	1	2	98.1	44
Kenedy	0	0	0	0	3	0	0	0	1	0	0	0	0	0	1	30.9	1
Kent	0	4	0	2	19	13	3	0	1	0	1	0	0	0	0	24.5	0
Kerr	78	281	200	5	534	155	139	37	24	21	23	20	2	10	7	83.6	83
Kimble	3	13	18	4	56	19	10	5	2	4	1	2	0	0	3	89.8	8
King	0	0	0	0	0	0	0	0	0	0	0	0	0	0	0	72.3	2
Kinney	1	5	0	2	28	7	7	2	2	0	2	0	0	0	0	93.3	5
Kleberg	20	70	100	5	244	86	45	18	6	3	15	4	3	4	8	92.4	163
Knox	4	13	28	4	55	26	11	2	0	4	5	2	0	0	0	77.2	4
Lamar	87	300	410	6	533	183	120	48	11	25	9	13	4	9	3	91.5	102
Lamb	6	34	75	10	173	64	40	16	7	8	7	4	0	2	1	97.1	18
Lampasas	4	45	0	3	165	71	38	3	7	13	6	2	1	5	1	101.0	37
La Salle	3	6	0	1	60	23	11	7	5	1	0	4	0	1	0	85.5	13
Lavaca	15	45	79	6	272	107	51	14	13	10	8	8	0	3	3	75.9	20
Lee	2	24	0	5	138	44	30	11	9	4	1	3	0	3	3	89.7	34
Leon	4	26	0	10	178	67	39	12	16	11	5	4	0	2	1	71.3	24
Liberty	31	112	153	15	584	193	151	40	36	29	14	10	5	2	8	87.3	115
Limestone	12	80	115	5	348	96	77	37	13	14	15	14	2	5	4	74.0	48
Lipscomb	1	6	0	8	38	13	9	4	1	1	0	3	0	3	0	75.7	1
Live Oak	3	8	0	3	92	24	29	8	3	3	3	1	0	3	0	80.7	34
Llano	13	36	30	5	235	57	70	20	5	23	5	12	0	4	3	102.4	24
Loving	0	0	0	0	0	0	0	0	0	0	0	0	0	0	0	45.5	1
Lubbock	499	1,776	1,819	33	1,750	535	403	129	84	91	55	33	18	33	23	82.1	891
Lynn	2	15	24	3	68	19	15	5	2	4	2	4	0	2	0	63.6	8
Marion	5	16	0	0	114	49	19	6	6	8	1	1	1	2	0	66.6	16
Martin	3	6	26	4	50	18	12	5	3	4	1	0	0	1	2	125.9	63
Mason	1	7	0	2	60	20	11	6	2	3	1	4	0	0	0	69.5	5
Matagorda	29	105	117	13	365	92	87	29	12	19	22	16	8	6	6	80.5	67
Maverick	20	42	77	5	232	60	51	11	18	4	20	8	3	1	3	120.8	18
McCulloch	5	19	49	3	126	40	31	8	4	6	4	4	2	0	1	82.0	4
McLennan	259	1,011	589	20	1,914	665	428	138	78	77	51	52	20	30	14	87.0	694
McMullen	0	1	0	1	11	6	2	1	0	0	1	0	0	0	0	72.5	3
Medina	12	49	34	7	286	81	63	15	31	11	12	15	0	6	3	87.8	79
Menard	0	7	0	3	40	7	11	6	1	42	4	31	0	0	0	108.0	8
Midland	126	518	455	17	799	227	180	37	35	42	20	31	12	18	14	76.6	353
Milam	9	51	91	6	299	100	48	30	10	9	14	2	1	2	5	88.4	36
Mills	3	21	0	3	66	26	13	4	4	2	1	3	0	1	1	87.7	7
Mitchell	3	14	39	3	131	41	38	7	2	7	1	4	0	2	1	65.1	7
Montague	11	60	96	7	292	97	66	30	22	10	5	6	5	3	2	78.5	23
Montgomery	199	520	694	15	1,533	459	389	80	95	85	42	41	21	26	19	83.8	613
Moore	10	46	60	5	151	43	28	10	4	10	7	4	0	6	0	105.0	28
Morris	4	32	0	4	170	58	47	12	12	10	5	7	3	3	3	83.4	15
Motley	1	5	0	2	25	9	6	8	12	10	1	6	0	3	0	48.0	5
Nacogdoches	88	309	334	8	479	135	108	26	37	22	14	13	7	10	1	65.2	127
Navarro	43	180	185	1	480	130	100	45	31	22	22	17	3	6	4	87.3	99
Newton	2	12	0	2	119	31	36	6	8	4	5	4	0	2	3	71.2	24
Nolan	10	45	85	5	191	63	29	14	14	6	7	7	0	3	1	87.9	36

Health Care and Deaths in Texas Counties

County	Patient Care, 1995				Leading Causes of Death by County, 1995											Misc., 1995	
	Doctors	Nurses	Hospital Beds	Ambulances	Total Deaths	Heart Disease	Cancer	Cerebrovascular	Accidents	Pulmonary	Diabetes	Pneumonia	HIV	Suicides	Liver Disease	Pregnancy Rate*	Abortions
Nueces	536	1,550	2,009	24	2,313	669	544	151	12	112	95	54	28	39	46	100.0	1,665
Ochiltree	4	25	65	2	91	31	20	7	4	7	3	3	0	2	2	81.7	22
Oldham	0	3	0	3	16	9	2	1	4	1	3	1	0	2	0	47.7	4
Orange	46	225	167	6	722	241	188	30	41	43	21	22	6	11	9	81.2	209
Palo Pinto	22	73	99	12	348	137	81	20	11	17	8	11	0	9	2	71.9	59
Panola	8	46	91	0	274	67	82	30	11	10	11	3	1	4	2	50.9	12
Parker	33	157	97	6	548	185	113	52	27	40	26	8	4	8	4	63.6	221
Parmer	4	20	34	6	82	24	20	4	8	6	2	3	0	3	0	94.6	14
Pecos	7	36	51	9	118	28	25	5	12	8	6	2	1	3	1	75.4	30
Polk	9	71	45	1	472	175	128	30	22	13	11	9	6	5	7	96.6	56
Potter	343	1,593	1,032	12	1,150	373	231	72	51	75	22	34	20	21	17	103.3	327
Presidio	0	8	0	4	51	14	11	1	1	1	3	3	0	1	0	90.4	3
Rains	1	7	0	0	98	23	25	11	5	8	0	1	1	0	0	62.9	7
Randall	9	77	49	8	639	202	142	37	34	46	9	12	6	21	3	65.7	276
Reagan	2	9	20	2	32	9	6	5	0	3	1	2	0	0	1	60.4	4
Real	0	2	0	3	40	19	12	1	0	1	1	0	1	0	2	103.1	3
Red River	6	38	52	0	203	86	42	10	8	6	3	15	0	3	0	72.5	20
Reeves	8	20	62	8	101	30	31	3	8	6	4	5	1	0	2	69.8	19
Refugio	2	24	49	3	79	32	16	9	4	1	4	1	0	1	1	72.0	22
Roberts	0	1	0	2	10	3	3	2	0	0	4	0	0	0	0	29.3	1
Robertson	4	18	0	6	192	64	54	8	9	7	3	9	1	4	3	88.4	39
Rockwall	23	74	92	5	192	66	37	18	9	7	6	7	1	3	2	71.7	66
Runnels	7	24	55	6	152	48	30	12	6	13	8	4	0	2	4	69.5	6
Rusk	23	98	163	7	502	166	108	38	19	21	22	21	4	3	3	65.2	33
Sabine	3	16	36	3	150	56	37	15	5	8	2	3	0	3	0	84.8	9
S. Augustine	3	15	48	0	137	60	37	5	8	7	7	3	1	1	0	82.2	5
San Jacinto	1	7	0	1	195	60	46	14	10	15	9	1	1	7	3	64.0	17
SanPatricio	33	107	75	10	501	149	120	24	21	25	25	10	10	7	9	94.1	178
San Saba	1	8	0	3	74	30	14	3	1	1	1	6	0	1	0	89.4	13
Schleicher	3	12	16	2	19	5	7	0	2	1	0	1	0	0	0	59.2	7
Scurry	13	47	99	4	162	42	40	17	7	9	5	6	0	1	3	71.3	39
Shackelford	3	7	24	2	48	24	10	6	0	2	3	0	0	0	0	73.7	5
Shelby	11	41	60	10	304	91	62	29	24	18	13	5	3	2	2	74.4	4
Sherman	2	3	0	2	26	5	10	2	1	2	0	1	0	0	0	89.1	9
Smith	365	1,191	1,044	62	1,627	500	391	118	78	78	39	64	16	23	10	78.5	369
Somervell	3	12	16	4	54	14	16	5	2	1	1	1	0	1	0	82.3	23
Starr	7	29	44	3	206	61	38	18	14	7	16	3	3	2	1	125.8	58
Stephens	5	18	40	2	122	33	32	7	6	9	2	4	0	0	0	90.5	23
Sterling	0	3	0	3	8	2	1	2	1	1	0	0	0	0	0	46.0	1
Stonewall	2	7	25	1	22	10	5	1	1	0	0	0	0	0	0	31.0	1
Sutton	1	7	21	3	31	7	7	3	3	3	1	0	1	0	0	81.9	7
Swisher	4	16	30	4	87	29	14	8	7	3	1	3	0	2	2	91.8	12
Tarrant	1,938	6,986	5,494	121	8,402	2,531	1,928	632	406	471	240	241	167	152	106	87.9	8,403
Taylor	202	765	616	15	1,086	384	222	75	42	55	36	35	13	23	10	75.4	190
Terrell	0	1	0	2	17	7	3	0	2	1	1	0	0	1	0	80.0	11
Terry	7	21	97	3	119	27	29	7	3	7	5	6	0	3	3	78.5	24
Throckmortn	1	8	30	2	26	10	2	1	4	2	1	0	0	1	0	129.3	12
Titus	36	125	165	6	296	104	64	24	8	11	9	10	3	3	3	107.0	55
Tom Green	180	667	689	12	965	262	201	89	35	59	27	31	4	16	12	68.3	288
Travis	1,276	4,015	1,830	40	3,640	895	836	249	215	165	106	90	223	72	62	97.2	4,098
Trinity	3	22	30	4	184	55	39	12	12	14	12	7	2	0	1	80.2	19
Tyler	10	34	49	0	236	90	66	14	11	14	5	3	2	3	2	98.4	82
Upshur	14	67	46	3	376	108	86	29	33	21	11	9	2	4	2	67.3	18
Upton	3	12	36	5	35	12	9	1	3	1	3	1	0	1	1	47.2	2
Uvalde	17	64	62	7	201	60	43	20	6	5	12	11	3	3	4	96.3	54
Val Verde	21	103	93	6	313	89	78	20	15	11	17	14	0	2	6	109.9	102
Van Zandt	16	66	52	4	498	169	118	30	24	36	17	21	1	2	4	75.2	56
Victoria	163	485	732	11	651	222	165	54	30	25	18	8	5	9	10	83.0	179
Walker	48	172	144	26	334	108	73	30	6	14	12	7	4	2	3	69.5	202
Waller	3	28	0	7	213	76	51	15	12	8	7	10	0	1	1	80.4	128
Ward	5	31	49	4	108	28	38	9	1	5	4	1	0	2	2	68.8	24
Washington	33	104	60	4	315	107	72	33	10	11	8	20	0	5	2	70.1	72
Webb	117	305	418	15	820	225	168	55	41	19	42	36	15	7	27	153.2	822
Wharton	53	163	221	9	424	151	89	30	16	16	16	18	2	5	5	75.5	55
Wheeler	4	27	83	4	99	32	26	7	5	4	1	2	0	0	0	69.1	11
Wichita	214	721	644	10	1,312	429	305	109	29	60	42	44	7	18	17	77.4	360
Wilbarger	21	68	98	4	197	65	36	32	5	7	5	3	0	2	1	79.2	32

Health Care and Deaths in Texas Counties

County	Patient Care, 1995				Leading Causes of Death by County, 1995											Misc., 1995	
	Doctors	Nurses	Hospital Beds	Ambulances	Total Deaths	Heart Disease	Cancer	Cerebrovascular	Accidents	Pulmonary	Diabetes	Pneumonia	HIV	Suicides	Liver Disease	Pregnancy Rate*	Abortions
Willacy	10	15	0	5	132	29	33	12	5	5	7	6	1	1	3	101.0	51
Williamson	116	356	206	12	936	252	217	64	57	39	18	40	16	17	13	76.6	592
Wilson	6	43	44	7	193	73	49	16	4	5	4	4	2	2	3	69.1	42
Winkler	4	16	85	3	75	21	16	3	1	9	2	4	2	2	0	71.5	12
Wise	10	63	50	6	338	121	70	35	19	13	14	12	0	5	3	70.1	88
Wood	23	87	80	5	432	150	103	24	15	25	16	18	0	7	2	79.8	36
Yoakum	2	15	24	4	49	21	10	2	3	5	1	0	1	1	0	73.0	19
Young	14	68	92	7	243	77	44	12	12	20	6	14	1	1	3	71.7	18
Zapata	0	4	0	4	80	28	20	3	6	3	2	6	0	1	1	99.6	21
Zavala	4	5	0	3	91	24	19	10	9	1	3	4	0	4	5	90.9	26
Statewide Total	25,025	86,943			137,549	41,630	31,571	9,788	6,402	6,232	4,569	3,827	2,764	2,229	1,867	92.9	87,501*

Sources: Bureau of State Health Data and Policy Analysis, May 1995, and Texas Vital Statistics, 1995, of the Texas Department of Health (by county of residence).
Broader definition of patient care terms: Doctors - Direct Patient Care Physicians; Nurses - registered nurses (RNs); Hospital Beds - Acute Care Hospital Beds Licensed; Ambulances - Ambulances Licensed.
Broader definition of categories of death include: Heart - Diseases of the Heart; Cancer - Malignant Neoplasms; Cerebrovascular - Cerebrovascular diseases; Accidents - Accidents and adverse effects; Pulmonary - Chronic Obstructive Pulmonary Diseases & Allied Conditions; Diabetes - Diabetes Mellitus; Pneumonia - Pneumonia and Influenza; HIV - Human Immunodeficiency Virus; Suicide - Suicide; Liver Disease - Liver Disease and Cirrhosis.
*Pregnancy Rate figured per 1,000 women age 15-44.
*Abortion total statewide includes abortions performed in Texas plus abortions obtained in other states by Texas residents.

State Institutions for Mental Health Services

Source: Texas Department of Mental Health and Mental Retardation.

The mission of the Texas Department of Mental Health and Mental Retardation (TXMHMR) is to offer an array of services that respond to the needs of people with mental illness and mental retardation and that enable them to make choices that result in lives of dignity and increased independence.

The agency administers state **hospitals** for persons with mental illness, state **schools** for persons with mental retardation, and state **centers** for persons with mental illness and/or mental retardation.

Two special components, Vernon State Hospital and Waco Center for Youth, serve the entire state. The adult unit of Vernon is a maximum security facility which treats individuals who are incompetent to stand trial, not guilty by reason of insanity or manifestly dangerous. The hospital also operates an inpatient program for adolescents with mental illness and chemical dependency. Waco Center for Youth serves severely emotionally disturbed youth ages 10 through 17.

El Paso and Rio Grande centers provide residential services to individuals with mental retardation.

Since January 1996, the department's central office oversees 13 state-operated community MHMR services (SOCS) organizations. In 142 counties, individuals access services through the authority for their county, which links people with appropriate service providers. Services range from 24-hour crisis care to supported housing and in-home assistance.

Additionally, TXMHMR contracts with 35 community MHMR centers to provide services. Community MHMR centers are the local mental health authority (MHA) and/or mental retardation authority (MRA) for the counties they serve.

For areas not served by a community MHMR center, the SOCS or state center is the local MHA/MRA. Services are obtained through local MHAs/MRAs.

The mailing address for the TXMHMR central office is P.O. Box 12668, Austin 78711-2668; phone (512) 454-3761.

Information in the list below includes the city where the facility is located, the facility name, the date the facility was established and the name of the executive in charge of the facility.

The number of patients or individuals served for state hospitals and schools is the average daily census for Fiscal Year 1996, separated into mental health and mental retardation categories. The figures for state centers and community MHMR centers are the total numbers of individuals served during Fiscal Year 1996.

During Fiscal Year 1996, a total of 171,567 persons received services from MHMR facilities: 132,969 received mental health services and 41,438 received mental retardation services.

Hospitals for Persons With Mental Illness

Austin State Hospital — Austin; 1857; Diane Faucher, superintendent; 303 patients.

Big Spring State Hospital — Big Spring; 1937; Ed Moughon, superintendent; 249 patients.

Kerrville State Hospital — Kerrville; 1950; Gloria P. Olsen, Ph.D., superintendent; 185 patients.

Rusk State Hospital — Rusk; 1919; Harold Parrish, superintendent; 352 patients.

San Antonio State Hospital — San Antonio; 1892; Robert C. Arizpe, superintendent; 390 patients.

Terrell State Hospital — Terrell; 1885; Beatrice Butler, superintendent; 355 patients.

Vernon State Hospital — Vernon; 1969; James E. Smith, superintendent; 345 patients.

Waco Center for Youth — Waco; 1979; Stephen Anfinson, superintendent; 73 patients.

Wichita Falls State Hospital — Wichita Falls; 1922; James E. Smith, superintendent; 349 patients.

Schools for Persons with Mental Retardation

Abilene State School — Abilene; 1901; Bill Waddill, superintendent; 635 individuals.

Austin State School — Austin; 1917; James G. Armstrong, Ph.D., superintendent; 442 individuals.

Brenham State School — Brenham; 1974; Stephen L. Fletcher, superintendent; 516 individuals.

Corpus Christi State School — Corpus Christi; 1970; Aurelio Valdez Jr., superintendent; 394 individuals.

Denton State School — Denton; 1960; Pat Jessee, superintendent; 664 individuals.

Lubbock State School — Lubbock; 1969; Lonnie H. Willis, superintendent; 391 individuals.

Lufkin State School — Lufkin; 1962; Sandra Cain, superintendent; 484 individuals.

Mexia State School — Mexia; 1946; William H. Lowry, Ph. D., superintendent; 616 individuals.

Richmond State School — Richmond; 1968; Barbara Dawson, M.S., superintendent; 676 individuals.

San Angelo State School — Carlsbad; 1969; R. Allen Williams, superintendent; 344 individuals.

San Antonio State School — San Antonio; 1978; Dean Lasley, superintendent; 302 individuals.

State Centers

El Paso State Center — El Paso; 1974; John Mark Friedmann, director; 50 (MH); 117 (MR).

Rio Grande State Center — Harlingen; 1962; Sonia Hernandez, M.S.W., director; 50 (MH); 90 (MR).

State-Operated Community Services

(The persons whose names appear in the list below are the executive directors of the centers, unless otherwise specified.)

Amarillo State Center — Amarillo; 1967; Richard D. Browder.

Beaumont State Center — Beaumont; 1968; Gary Hidalgo.

Big Bend SOCS — Alpine; 1996; Dick Ancell.

Blackland SOCS — Mexia; 1996; Jack Leath.

Camino Real SOCS — San Antonio; Terresa Stallworth, M.D., director

Capital Area SOCS — Austin; 1996; Booth O'Quinn.

Central Gulf SOCS — Richmond; 1996; Jeff Enzinna.

Coastal Plain SOCS — Corpus Christi; 1996; Charles Sportsman.

Hill Country SOCS — Austin; 1996; Janis Beck.

Laredo State Center — Laredo; 1969; Javier Ramirez, director.

The Lakes Regional SOCS — Terrell; 1996; Robert Evans, director.

Rolling Plains SOCS — Wichita Falls; 1996; Raymond Atkins.

West Texas SOCS — Big Spring; 1996; Martha King.

Community Mental Health and Mental Retardation Centers

(The persons whose names appear in the list below are the executive directors of the centers, unless otherwise specified.)

Abilene — Abilene Regional MHMR Center; 1971; Don Teeler; 984 (MH); 562 (MR).

Amarillo — Texas Panhandle Mental Health Authority; 1968; Sanford Skelton; 2,822 (MH).

Austin — Austin-Travis County MHMR Center; 1967; David L. Evans; 5,580 (MH); 1,434 (MR).

Beaumont — Life Resource; 1967; N. Charles Harris; 4,696 (MH).

Brownwood — Central Texas MHMR Center; 1969; Roy A. Cronenberg; 855 (MH); 409 (MR).

Bryan-College Station — MHMR Authority of Brazos Valley; 1972; Jack Leon Bawcom; 1,564 (MH); 556 (MR).

Cleburne — Johnson-Navarro County MHMR Center; 1985; Joseph P. Mirisciotti; 2,289 (MH); 362 (MR).

Conroe — Tri-County MHMR Services; 1983; Cynthia Sill; 2,931 (MH); 816 (MR).

Corpus Christi — Nueces County MHMR Community Center; 1970; Wallace E. Whitworth Jr.; 2,159 (MH); 969 (MR).

Dallas — Dallas County MHMR Center; 1967; Barry Waller, interim exec. dir.; 13,350 (MH); 2,895 (MR).

Denison — MHMR Services of Texoma; 1974; Anthony Mattox; 1,264 (MH); 420 (MR).

Denton — Denton County MHMR Center; 1987; Bill Drybread; 1,361 (MH); 473 (MR).

Edinburg — Tropical Texas Center for MHMR; 1967; Leroy Torres; 4,696 (MH); 1,425 (MR).

El Paso — Life Management Center; 1968; C. Edward Coleman; 3,286 (MH); 1,019 (MR).

Fort Worth — Tarrant County MHMR Services; 1969; Jim McDermott, Ph.D.; 7,766 (MH); 2,329 (MR).

Galveston — Gulf Coast Center; 1969; G. Michael Winburn; 3,311 (MH); 565 (MR).

Greenville — Hunt County Family Services Center; 1971; Rick Davis, Ph.D.; 1,062 (MH); 375 (MR).

Houston — MHMR Authority of Harris County; 1965; Steven Schnee, Ph.D.; 20,822 (MH); 5,095 (MR).

Jacksonville — Anderson-Cherokee Community Enrichment Services; 1995; John D. Gill; 1,329 (MH); 397 (MR).

Longview — Sabine Valley Center; 1970; Inman White; 3,611 (MH); 945 (MR).

Lubbock — Lubbock Regional MHMR Center; 1969; Gene Menefee; 1,918 (MH); 883 (MR).

Lufkin — Burke Center; 1975; Susan Rushing; 3,145 (MH); 1,125 (MR).

McKinney — Collin County MHMR Center; 1986; Randy Routon, Ph.D.; 1,263 (MH); 637 (MR).

Midland/Odessa — Permian Basin Community Centers for MHMR; 1969; Larry Carroll; 2,106 (MH); 627 (MR).

Plainview — Central Plains Center for MHMR and Substance Abuse; 1969; Ron Trusler; 917 (MH); 360 (MR).

San Angelo — MHMR Services for the Concho Valley; 1969; John Brubaker; 898 (MH); 330 (MR).

San Antonio — The Center for Health Care Services; 1966; Ron Morales; 5,364 (MH); 2,180 (MR).

Stephenville — Pecan Valley MHMR Region; 1977; Theresa B. Mulloy, Ed.D.; 1,437 (MH); 422 (MR).

Temple — Central Counties Center for MHMR Services; 1967; Eldon Tietje; 2,017 (MH); 1,024 (MR).

Texarkana — Northeast Texas MHMR Center; 1974; Joe Bob Hall; 808 (MH); 206 (MR).

Tyler — Andrews Center; 1970; Richard DeSanto; 3,046 (MH); 768 (MR).

Victoria — Gulf Bend MHMR Center; 1970; Bill Dillard; 1,600 (MH); 248 (MR).

Waco — Heart of Texas Region MHMR Center; 1969; Dean Maberry; 2,365 (MH); 715 (MR).

Wharton — Riceland Regional Mental Health Authority; 1988; Charlie Boone; 2,460 (MH).

Wichita Falls — Helen Farabee Center; 1969; William I. Ivey; 1,553 (MH); 253 (MR). ☆

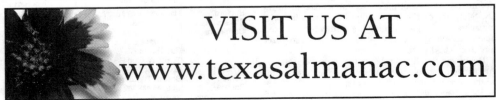

Texans Lead National Academic Decathlon in First-Place Honors

Source: United States Academic Decathlon

Texas high school teams have won more top honors than those of any other state since the National Academic Decathlon competition began in 1982.

The academic decathlon began in California about 1970 as a local contest. In 1981, it expanded to include teams from across the United States. In the 16 national competitions that have been held, **Texas teams have won first place ten times**, with California teams winning six times. J.J. Pearce High School in Richardson won five of those gold medals. In addition, Texas teams have taken two second places and two thirds.

The academic decathlon was begun by Dr. Robert Peterson, former superintendent of schools in Orange County, Calif. He hoped to encourage academic excellence through competition and recognition.

He developed a 10-event scholastic competition for nine-member teams of high school juniors and seniors: three members are A or "Honor" students, three are B or "Scholastic" students and three are C or "Varsity" students. Each student competes in all 10 events, which include economics, essay, fine arts, interview, language and literature, math, science, social science, speech and the Super Quiz. The winning teams advance through local, regional and state contests, with each participating state sending one team to the national finals each April.

The decathlon is sponsored by the United States Academic Association. In 1996, schools in 40 states participated.

The Texas teams that have won gold, silver or bronze medals in the National Academic Decathlon are:

J.J. Pearce High School, Richardson
First Place in 1984, 1985, 1986, 1988 and 1991
Frank Dobie High School, Pasadena
First Place in 1992 and 1996
Lake Highlands High School, Richardson
First Place in 1990
Plano East Senior High School, Plano
First Place in 1993
Deer Park High School, Deer Park
Second Place in 1989
John Foster Dulles High School, Sugar Land
Second Place in 1987
James E. Taylor High School, Katy
First Place in 1997; third Place in 1995
Oliver Wendell Holmes High School, San Antonio
Third Place in 1994 ☆

Texas Blue Ribbon Schools

Source: U.S. Department of Education

The U.S. Department of Education's Blue Ribbon Schools program has presented **201 awards to 194 Texas schools** since the program began in 1982. Seven of the schools were named Blue Ribbon Schools twice.

The program gives national recognition to schools that are unusually effective in meeting local, state and national educational goals. Selected schools must have high academic standards and a rigorous curriculum; a disciplined, supportive, safe and drug-free environment; a strong partnership among the family, the school and the community; excellent teaching; low dropout rates; and documented student achievement. The competition is open to public and private schools in the 50 states, District of Columbia, Puerto Rico, the Virgin Islands and schools run by the Bureau of Indian Affairs and the Department of Defense.

Public schools are nominated by the chief state school officers; the Council for American Private Education nominates private schools; and officials of the Bureau of Indian Affairs and the Department of Defense nominate schools in their jurisdictions.

Nominations are reviewed by a panel consisting of 100 outstanding public- and private-school educators, college and university staffs, state and local government officials, school-board members, parents, the education press, medical professionals, business representatives and the general public. Site visits at the most promising schools are conducted to verify the accuracy of information provided by the school and to gather additional information. The panel makes recommendations to the U.S. Secretary of Education, who announces the winning schools. The program honors elementary and secondary schools in alternate years, and has recognized more than 3,000 since its inception.

Below are the Texas schools that have been named Blue Ribbon Schools, the cities where they are located and the year or years of their honors.

Abbreviations used in this list are: Acad.: Academy; ES: Elementary School; HS: High School; IS: Intermediate School; JHS: Junior High School; MS: Middle School; Sch.: School; SHS: Senior High School.

City	School	Year of Award(s)
Amarillo	Crockett MS	1994-96
Anna	Anna MS	1992-93
Arlington	Pope ES	1985-86
Austin	Canyon Vista MS	1990-91
	Daniel F. Ortega ES	1993-94
	Eanes ES	1996-97
	Forest Trail ES	1989-90
	Highland Park ES	1991-92
	Hill Country MS	1990-91
	Hill ES	1993-94
	James Bowie HS	1992-93
	Laurel Mountain ES	1991-92
	Live Oak ES	1991-92
	L.L. Campbell ES	1996-97
	Lorenzo de Zavala ES	1996-97
	Noel Grisham MS	1994-96
	North Oaks ES	1993-94
	Pond Springs ES	1996-97
	Robert E. Lee ES	1991-92
	Smith ES	1996-97
	Stephen F. Austin H	1982-83
	T.A. Brown ES	1996-97
	Valley View ES	1996-97
	Walnut Creek ES	1996-97
	Westlake HS	1988-89
	West Ridge MS	1992-93
	Westwood HS	1994-96
Beaumont	Monsignor Kelly HS	1984-85, 1990-91
Bedford	Harwood JHS	1986-87
Bellaire	Bellaire SHS	1983-84
Carrollton	Charles M. Blalack JHS	1992-93
	E.L. Kent ES	1993-94
	R.L. Turner HS	1990-91
Clute	Terrell W. Ogg ES	1996-97
Colleyville	O.C. Taylor ES	1996-97
Conroe	Booker T. Washington JHS	1992-93
Coppell	Coppell MS West	1994-96
Corpus Christi	Incarnate Word Acad.	1984-85

City	School	Year of Award(s)
	Los Encinos Special Emph. Sch.	1987-88
	Lozano Special Emphasis Sch..	1985-86
	Mirabeau B. Lamar ES	1991-92
	Rose Shaw Special Emph. Sch..	1985-86
	St. James Episcopal Sch.	1991-92
	St. Patrick Sch.	1985-86, 1996-97
Dallas	Akiba Acad. of Dallas	1985-86
	Arch H. McCulloch MS	1990-91
	Bishop Lynch HS	1990-91
	Booker T. Washington HS for ....Performing and Visual Arts	1994-96
	Brentfield ES.	1993-94
	Christ the King Catholic Sch.	1993-94
	Forest Meadow JHS	1994-96
	Good Shepherd Episcopal Sch	1991-92
	Greenhill Sch.	1984-85
	Hamilton Park Pacesetter Sch.	1985-86
	Highland Park HS	1984-85
	Jesuit College Preparatory Sch	1990-91
	John S. Armstrong ES	1985-86
	John S. Bradfield ES.	1989-90
	Merriman Park ES	1989-90
	Moss Haven ES	1993-94
	Parkhill JHS	1992-93
	Prestonwood ES.	1996-97
	Robert S. Hyer ES	1991-92
	St. Elizabeth Catholic Sch.	1987-88
	St. Mark's Sch. of Texas	1986-87
	St. Thomas Aquinas Catholic Sch.	1996-97
	Sidney Lanier Vanguard School	1987-88
	The Lamplighter Sch.	1993-94
	The Parish Day Sch.	1993-94
	University Park ES	1987-88
	Ursuline Acad. of Dallas	1992-93
	William H. Atwell Fund. Acad.	1986-87
Denton	Strickland MS	1994-96
El Paso	Crockett Elemen.-Intermed. School	1985-86
	Desert View MS	1983-84
	North Loop ES	1987-88
	St. Clement's Episcopal Parish Sch	1996-97
	Schuster ES	1987-88
	Socorro HS	1994-96
Farmers Branch	L.P. Montgomery ES	1991-92
	Vivian Field JHS	1992-93
Flower Mound	Edward S. Marcus HS.	1994-96
	Flower Mound ES	1993-94
Fort Worth	Tanglewood ES.	1991-92
Garland	Austin Acad. for Excellence	1992-93
	Big Springs ES	1987-88
	Charlie Richard Lyles MS	1992-93
	Kimberlin Acad. for Excellence	1991-92
	Walnut Glen Acad. for Excellence	1996-97
Georgetown	Georgetown HS	1994-96
Grand Prairie	Immaculate Conception Sch.	1985-86
Grapevine	Grapevine MS	1994-96
Greenville	Travis ES.	1987-88
Groesbeck	Groesbeck MS	1994-96
Houston	Arnold JHS	1990-91
	Bear Creek ES	1987-88
	Bleyl JHS	1983-84, 1990-91
	Bunker Hill ES.	1991-92
	Clear Lake HS	1986-87
	Clear Lake IS	1986-87
	Corpus Christi Catholic Sch..	1989-90
	Duchesne Acad. of Sacred Heart	1992-93
	Eisenhower HS.	1988-89
	Fiest ES	1993-94
	Francone ES.	1991-92
	Frostwood ES	1989-90
	Grace Sch.	1996-97
	Hunters Creek ES.	1993-94
	John Paul II Catholic Sch.	1996-97
	Labay JHS	1988-89, 1992-93
	Langham Creek HS	1990-91
	Lowery ES	1991-92
	Mayde Creek ES.	1989-90
	Mayde Creek HS	1994-96
	Memorial HS.	1988-89
	Memorial JHS.	1988-89
	Memorial Drive ES	1996-97
	Michael Kennedy ES	1996-97
	Northbrook MS.	1994-96
	Northbrook SHS	1988-89
	Nottingham ES	1991-92
	Olle MS.	1990-91
	River Oaks Baptist Sch.	1991-92
	Rummel Creek ES	1985-86
	Saint Agnes Acad.	1983-84, 1988-89
	St. Thomas More Parish Sch..	1993-94
	Scarborough SHS	1986-87
	Spring Forest MS	1994-96
	Spring Oaks MS	1994-96
	Spring Shadows ES	1996-97
	Stratford HS	1983-84
	T. H. Rogers Sch.	1991-92
	Thomas J. Stovall JHS	1990-91
	V.W. Miller IS.	1988-89
	Wilchester ES.	1989-90
Hurst	Lawrence D. Bell HS.	1994-96
Irving	Holy Family of Nazareth Sch.	1989-90
	Las Colinas ES.	1993-94
Katy	Hazel S. Pattison ES.	1993-94
	James E. Taylor HS	1994-96
Kingwood	Kingwood HS	1984-85
	Pines Montessori Sch.	1985-86
Klein	Strack IS	1990-91
La Joya	E.B. Reyna ES	1993-94
Lewisville	Christa McAuliffe ES.	1991-92
	Highland Village ES	1993-94
	Lina Milliken MS	1992-93
Longview	Forest Park MS.	1994-96
	Pine Tree HS	1988-89, 1992-93
	Pine Tree JHS.	1990-91
	Pine Tree MS	1996-97
	Pine Tree Middle 6/7 Sch.	1992-93
Lubbock	All Saints Episcopal Sch.	1991-92
	Lubbock HS	1994-96
McAllen	Ben Milam ES.	1989-90
	Juan N. Seguin ES	1985-86
	Travis MS	1994-96
McKinney	Valley Creek ES	1996-97
Mesquite	Dr. Joey Pirrung ES	1996-97
Muenster	Sacred Heart Sch.	1993-94
Palacios	East Side ES	1989-90
Pharr	Raul Longoria ES.	1987-88
Plano	A.H. Meadows ES.	1996-97
	Armstrong MS	1992-93
	Clark HS.	1992-93
	Davis ES.	1993-94
	Dooley ES.	1989-90
	Forman ES	1993-94
	H.B. Carlisle ES	1987-88
	Hedgcoxe ES	1993-94
	Huffman ES	1991-92
	Maureen Connolly Brinker ES..	1996-97
	Plano East SHS	1992-93
	Plano SHS	1984-85, 1994-96
	Renner MS.	1994-96
	R.W. Carpenter MS	1992-93
	Saigling ES.	1991-92
	St. Mark the Evangelist Cath. Sch.	1991-92
	Schimelpfenig MS.	1988-89
	Shepard ES	1991-92
	W.H.L. Wells ES	1991-92
	Wilson MS	1988-89
Port Arthur	Booker T. Washington ES	1987-88
Port Lavaca	Travis MS	1983-84
Richardson	Dartmouth ES.	1989-90
	J.J. Pearce HS	1988-89
	L.V. Berkner HS	1988-89
	Richardson HS	1983-84
	Richardson JHS	1990-91

City	School	Year of Award(s)
Rockdale	Rockdale HS	1984-85
Round Rock. . .	Chisholm Trail MS	1992-93
San Antonio. . .	Bradley MS	1986-87
	Castle Hills ES	1987-88
	Coke R. Stevenson MS	1990-91
	Douglas MacArthur HS	1988-89
	Dwight D. Eisenhower MS.	1988-89
	Fort Sam Houston ES.	1993-94
	Holy Cross HS	1983-84
	John Marshall HS	1992-93
	Lackland Junior-Senior HS	1994-96
	Mary Hull ES.	1996-97
	Northside Health Careers HS . . .	1990-91
	Robert G. Cole Jr./Sr. HS	1986-87, 1990-91
	St. Peter Prince of Apostles Sch.	1985-86

City	School	Year of Award(s)
	Winston Churchill HS	1982-83
Southlake	Carroll ES	1993-94
	Carroll HS	1994-96
	Carroll MS	1994-96
	Florence ES	1993-94
	Jack D. Johnson ES	1993-94
Spring	Anderson ES.	1989-90
	Klein Oak HS	1994-96
	Spring HS	1992-93
Sugar Land . . .	John Foster Dulles HS	1984-85
Taylor.	T.H. Johnson ES	1985-86
Temple.	Meridith Magnet Sch.	1987-88
Waco.	Woodway ES.	1985-86
Wake Village . .	Wake Village Sch.	1985-86
Wylie	T.F. Birmingham ES.	1991-92

Private Schools on the Border 100 Years Ago

The Colegio Altamirano class of 1898. Photo from E.E. Mireles & Jovita González de Mireles Papers, special Collections & Archives, Texas A&M University-Corpus Christi Bell Library.

Around the turn of the century, the Anglo-dominated public school systems in Texas often neglected Mexican-American children, believing that they did not need more than the most basic schooling. The educational emphasis was on training for menial domestic work and manual labor. Many school systems expected Tejano children to deny their ethnic culture and become totally absorbed into the Anglo way of life.

Tejanos who could afford it often sent their children to parochial schools affiliated with their churches. However, there were also a number of private non-sectarian schools established in the border counties for children of less-affluent Mexican-American families. In addition to fundamental academic subjects, these schools emphasized the values and culture of Mexico.

In his book *Mexican-Americans in Texas*, historian Arnoldo de León lists a school near Ysleta in the El Paso area established in 1871; the Aoy School, 1887 in El Paso; the Colegio Altamirano, Hebbronville, 1897; the Colegio Preparatorio, Laredo, 1906; the Escuela Particular, Zapata County, 1909; and another such school in Laredo in 1911.

The Aoy School was established by Olives Villanueva Aoy, a Spaniard who came to El Paso about 1887 after spending time in Cuba, Mexico, Utah and New Mexico. Aoy, who went by the initials O.V., is said to have lived with the Mayas in Yucatan and had helped translate the Book of Mormon into Spanish.

Although the first public school in El Paso opened in 1883, no Spanish surnames appeared on the rolls. Using his own money, Aoy rented space in an old building on San Francisco Street in 1887, equipping his school for poor Tejano children with chairs, blackboards and books. Besides English and other fundamental subjects, he taught his young charges music, calisthenics, manners and patriotism.

By 1890, he was broke, having spent all his savings on the school. The school board took over the school and named it the Mexican Preparatory School. Aoy was hired to teach English to Mexican children to prepare them to enter regular classrooms. After Aoy's death in 1895, the school board built a new building, named it for Aoy, and continued his work.

The Colegio Altamirano was started in Hebbronville by Dionicio Peña, Francisco Barrera Guerra, Tomás Barrera, José Angel Garza and Ascención Martínez in 1897, with Rosendo Barrera as its first professor. According to a Jim Hogg County chamber of commerce publication, the school emphasized Spanish culture, art, music, discipline and social graces, along with reading, writing and math. After attending this school, many of the students graduated from Hebbronville public schools and went on to institutions of higher learning. The Colegio Altamirano closed in 1958. ☆

Public Schools

Source: Texas Education Agency

Public school enrollment in Texas reached a peak of 3,837,096 in 1996-97, according to the **Texas Education Agency.** Enrollment in 1995-96 was 3,748,167.

The **seven largest districts** (listed in descending order by average daily attendance), Houston, Dallas, Austin, Fort Worth, El Paso, San Antonio and Northside (Bexar Co.).

Texas has **two types of school districts,** independent and common, each administering local affairs through a board of trustees. Independent school districts deal directly with Texas Education Agency; common districts are supervised by elected county school superintendents and county trustees. In 1996, there were six common districts and 1,038 independent districts.

History of Public Education

Public education was one of the primary goals of the early settlers of Texas, who listed the failure to provide education as one of their grievances in the **Texas Declaration of Independence** from Mexico.

As early as 1838, **President Mirabeau B. Lamar's** message to the Republic of Texas Congress advocated setting aside public domain for public schools. His interest caused him to be called the **"Father of Education in Texas."** In 1839 Congress designated three leagues of land to support public schools for each Texas county and 50 leagues for a state university. In 1840 each county was allocated one more league of land.

The Republic, however, did not establish a public school system or a university. The 1845 State Constitution advocated public education, instructing the Legislature to designate at least 10 percent of the tax revenue for schools. Further delay occurred until **Gov. Elisha M. Pease,** on Jan. 31, 1854, signed the bill setting up the **Texas public school system.**

The public school system was made possible by setting aside $2 million out of $10 million Texas received for relinquishing its claim to land to the north and west of its present boundaries in the Compromise of 1850.

During 1854, legislation provided for state apportionment of funds based upon an annual census and required railroads that were granted land to survey alternate sections to be set aside for public school financing. The **first school census** that year showed 65,463 students; state fund apportionment was 62¢ per student.

When adopted in 1876, the present Texas Constitution provided: "All funds, lands and other property heretofore set apart and appropriated for the support of public schools; all the alternate sections of land reserved by the state of grants heretofore made or that may hereafter be made to railroads, or other corporations, of any nature whatsoever; one half of the public domain of the state, and all sums of money that may come to the state from the sale of any portion of the same shall constitute a **perpetual public school fund."**

Over 52 million acres of the Texas **public domain** were allotted for school purposes. (See table, **Distribution of**

the **Public Lands of Texas** on page 413.)

The Constitution also provided for one-fourth of occupation taxes and a poll tax of one dollar for school support and made provisions for local taxation. No provision was made for direct ad valorem taxation for maintenance of an **available school fund,** but a maximum 20¢ state ad valorem school tax was adopted in 1883, and raised to 35¢ in connection with provision of **free textbooks** in the amendment of 1918.

In 1949, the **Gilmer-Aikin Laws** reorganized the state system of public schools by making sweeping changes in administration and financing. The Texas Education Agency, heded by the governor-appointed Commissioner of Education, administers the public school system. The policy-making body for public education is the 15-member State Board of Education, which is elected from separate districts for overlapping four-year terms. Current membership of the board may be found in the State Government section of this Almanac.

School Reform

Members of the 68th Legislature passed a historic education-reform bill in the summer of 1984. House Bill 72 came in response to growing concern over deteriorating literacy in Texas' schoolchildren over two decades, reflected in Texas students' scores on standardized tests.

Provisions of HB 72 raised teachers' salaries, but tied those raises to teacher performance. It also introduced more stringent teacher certification and initiated competency testing for teachers.

Academic achievement was set as a priority in public education with stricter attendance rules, adoption of a **no-pass, no-play rule** prohibiting students who were failing courses from participating in sports and other extracurricular activities for a six-week period, and national norm testing through the grades to assure parents of individual schools' performance through a common frame of reference.

The 74th Legislature passed the **Public Schools Reform Act of 1995,** which increased local control of public schools by limiting the Texas Education Agency to recommending and reporting on educational goals; granting, modifying and revoking campus charters; managing the permanent, foundation and available school funds; setting standards for graduation and curriculum; administering an accountability system; recommending educator appraisal and counselor evaluation instruments; and developing plans for special, bilingual, compensatory, gifted and talented, vocational, and technology education.

Each school district may choose to operate as either an independent school district subject to general law requirements of the Education Code; a special-purpose district, such as Boys Home Ranch, that now have special status; or a home-rule district with a charter approved by the district's voters that must comply with graduation requirements, accountability, no-pass, no-play, federal law and court orders, compulsory attendance, pre-kindergarten, bilingual education, and information-reporting requirements; teacher certification and a few other basic matters. As of July 15, 1997, none of the state's school districts had sought home-rule status.

Charter schools may be granted by school districts free of all local board instructional rules and policies, subject only to pre-kindergarten, bilingual education and graduation requirements, no pass-no play, reporting requirements and accountability. The number of charters that may be granted are limited by the Legislature. As of the end of the 1996-97 school year, there were 20 open-enrollment charter schools operating in Texas or planning to open by fall of 1997: seven in Houston; three in Dallas; two each in Austin, Corpus Christi, Irving and San Antonio; and one each in Mission and Waco.

Other action by the 74th Legislature required proficiency in a foundation curriculum including English language arts, mathematics, science and social studies and

---

Enrollment

(Refined Average Daily Attendance)

1996-97	3,837,096	1991-92	3,173,143
1995-96	3,748,167	1990-91	3,073,966
1994-95	3,677,171	1989-90	3,151,659
1993-94	3,608,262	1988-89	3,098,092
1992-93	3,541,769	1987-88	3,057,147

High School Graduates

1995-96	171,983	1989-90	172,480
1994-95	170,406	1988-89	176,951
1993-94	163,310	1987-88	171,436
1992-93	160,546	1986-87	168,430
1991-92	176,209	1985-86	161,150
1990-91	185,013	1984-85	159,343

Texas School Personnel, Salaries

Year/ Personnel Type	Personnel (Full-Time Equivalent)*	Average Base Salaries†
1994-95 All Personnel	**450,582.2**	**$ 24,639**
Teachers	234,424.5	29,494
Support Staff*	29,964.8	36,871
Administrators	15,332.7	50,114
Total Professional	279,722.0	31,415
Educational Aides	41,609.7	11,290
Auxiliary Staff	129,250.6	14,272
1995-96 All Personnel	**462,981.7**	**$ 25,843**
Teachers	240,592.2	31,413
Support Staff*	30,868.6	38,195
Administrators	15,636.4	51,762
Total Professional	287,097.2	33,251
Educational Aides	43,319.7	11,598
Auxiliary Staff	132,564.8	14,457
1996-97 Personnel	**440,809.2**	**$ 28,025**
Teachers	247,885.5	32,425
Support Staff*	32,666.4	39,617
Administrators	16,111.1	53,156
Total Professional	296,663.0	34,342
Educational Aides	43,032.4	12,010
Auxiliary Staff	101,113.8	16,307

*Support staff includes supervisors, counselors, educational diagnosticians, librarians, nurses/physicians, therapists and psychologists.

†Supplements for non-teaching duties and career-ladder supplements are not included in this figure.

Permanent School Fund

Year	Total Investment Fund*	Total Income Earned by P.S.F.
1854	$ 2,000,000.00	...
1880	3,542,126.00	...
1900	9,102,872.75	$ 783,142.08
1910	16,752,406.93	1,970,526.52
1920	25,698,281.74	2,888,555.44
1930	38,718,106.35	2,769,547.05
1940	68,299,081.91	3,331,874.12
1950	161,179,979.24	3,985,973.60
1960	425,821,600.53	12,594,000.28
1970	842,217,721.05	34,762,955.32
1980	2,464,579,397.00	163,000,000.00
1985	5,095,802,979.00	417,080,383.00
1988	6,493,070,622.00	572,665,253.00
1989	6,873,610,771.00	614,786,823.00
1990	7,328,172,096.00	674,634,994.00
1991	10,227,777,535.00	661,744,804.00
1992	10,944,944,872.00	704,993,826.00
1993	11,822,465,497.00	714,021,754.00
1994	11,330,590,652.00	716,972,115.00
1995	12,273,168,900.00	737,008,244.00
1996	12,995,820,070.00	739,996,574.00

*Includes cash — bonds at par and stocks at book value.

an enrichment curriculum of other languages, fine arts, and health, physical, career and technology education for graduation from high school.

No pass-no play now requires only a three-week suspension for failing a course grade, during which time the student can continue to practice, but not participate in competition.

High-school graduation requires passing either current exit-level TAAS (Texas Assessment of Academic Skills) exams or end-of-course exams in algebra and English and biology or history.

A teacher may remove a disruptive student from class and, subject to review by a campus committee, veto the student's return to class. The district must provide alternative education for students removed from class. A student must be placed in alternative education for assault, selling drugs or alcohol, substance abuse or public lewdness. A student must be expelled and referred to the appropriate court for serious offenses, such as murder or aggravated assault.

In 1997, the 75th Legislature passed House Bill 318, which allows the State Board of Education to award up to 100 new open-enrollment charters during 1998 and 1999. More than the limit may be awarded if the proposed school documents that its initial enrollment will be at least 75 percent recovered drop-outs or students at risk of dropping out and maintains that minimum percentage in its student body each year it operates. ☆

Scholastic Population, Apportionment, 1854-1996

The Texas public school system was established and the permanent fund set up by the Fifth Legislature, Jan. 31, 1854. The first apportionment by the state to public schools was for the school year 1854-55.
Source: **Texas Education Agency**

Years	Amount of P.S.F. Distributed to Schools	No. of Students	Per Capita
1854-55	...	65,463	$ 0.62
1880-81	$ 679,317	266,439	3.00
1900-01	3,002,820	706,546	4.25
1910-11	5,931,287	949,006	6.25
1920-21	18,431,716	1,271,157	14.50
1930-31	27,342,473	1,562,427	17.50
1940-41	34,580,475	1,536,910	22.50
1950-51	93,996,600	1,566,610	60.00
1960-61	164,188,461	2,249,157	73.00
1970-71	287,159,758	2,800,500	119.45
1980-81	3,042,476	*	397.00
1985-86	807,680,617	*	280.00
1988-89	882,999,623	*	295.00
1989-90	917,608,395	*	303.00
1990-91	700,276,846	*	227.69
1991-92	739,200,044	*	240.19
1992-93	739,494,967	*	232.94
1993-94	737,677,545	*	227.83
1994-95	737,008,244	*	218,85
1995-96	739,996,574	*	215.25

*See enrollment figures for these years in separate table.

School District Profiles by County, 1995-96

The following public school district information includes ratings of academic excellence, student population and ethnicity, and financial data for the state's 1,044 school districts for the 1995-96 school year, the last full school year for which the information was available at the time this edition of the Almanac went to press. Data for subsequent years will be posted on the Texas Education Agency's Internet site: http://www.tea.state.tx.us/

The information is listed by county, with the county name and the number of school districts within the county in bold-face type. Indented under the county name are the school districts within the county.

The **district ratings** are determined by the Texas Education Agency by using the following criteria:

EX: Exemplary. At least 90 percent of all students in each student group (Black, Hispanic, White and economiclly disadvantaged) must pass each section of the Texas Assessment of Academic Skills (TAAS) test. The dropout rate must be one percent or less for all students and each student group, and the attendance rate must be 94 percent or more. In the 1995-96 school year, 37 districts, whose names are in bold-faced type in the table below, received this highest rating.

RE: Recognized. At least 70 percent of all students and those in each student group must pass each section of the TAAS; the dropout rate must be 3.5 percent or less; and the attendance rate must be 94 percent or higher. If fewer than 80 percent of all students and those in each student group pass any section of the TAAS, the improvement between 1995 and 1996 must meet or exceed the change needed to reach a 90 percent passing mark within 5 years. In 1995-96, 209 districts received this rating.

AA: Academically Acceptable. At least 30 percent of all students and those in each student group must pass the TAAS; the dropout rate must be 6 percent or less; and the attendance rate must be 94 percent or higher. In 1995-96, 789 districts received this rating.

AU: Academically Unacceptable. Those districts falling below the Academically Acceptable rating are rated Academically Unacceptable. In 1995-96, 9 districts received this lowest rating.

Types of School Districts: The abbrebviation "Cons." in the name of the district indicates a consolidated school district. The six districts marked by an asterisk (*) are common school districts, which are supervised by elected county school superintendents and county trustees. The other 1,038 are independent school districts, which deal directly with the Texas Education Agency.

Ethnicity in this table was determined by the Texas Education Agency. Percentages may not total 100% because of rounding.

Source: Texas Education Agency.

County/Dist.	District Rating	Number of Students	% Black	% Asian	% Hispanic	% Amer. Ind.	% White	Total Revenue	% Local	% Other	% State	% Federal	Total Spending	Spending Per Student
Texas State Totals			14.3	2.3	36.7	0.3	46.4							
Anderson - 7			20.7	0.3	9.0	0.1	69.8							
Cayuga	RE	640	12.3	0.3	2.8	0.5	84.1	$ 3,630,692	58.1	1.7	40.1	0.0	$ 3,392,674	$ 5,301
Elkhart	RE	1,085	8.0	0.0	2.2	0.1	89.7	6,310,397	20.5	3.0	76.4	0.0	5,675,824	5,231
Frankston	AA	781	12.1	1.0	2.5	0.0	84.3	4,459,758	34.7	0.8	64.3	0.0	3,777,186	4,836
Neches	AA	318	12.6	0.0	1.6	0.0	85.8	2,157,934	31.9	1.2	66.9	0.0	1,831,932	5,761
Palestine	AA	3,808	32.2	0.4	16.2	0.1	51.1	16,892,963	41.0	1.5	57.2	0.1	17,393,299	4,568
Slocum	RE	335	3.3	0.0	4.8	0.0	91.9	1,827,348	35.5	1.5	62.8	0.0	1,681,888	5,021
Westwood	AA	1,799	15.6	0.2	5.2	0.3	78.8	7,443,708	31.6	3.1	65.1	0.0	6,715,306	3,733
Andrews - 1			1.8	0.9	46.3	0.4	50.7							
Andrews	AA	3,638	1.8	0.9	46.3	0.4	50.7	20,719,012	91.7	2.4	5.7	0.0	20,580,433	5,657
Angelina - 6			20.0	0.6	15.9	0.1	63.4							
Central	AA	1,453	2.9	0.0	5.5	0.3	91.3	7,737,117	16.2	1.0	82.6	0.1	6,284,302	4,325
Diboll	AA	2,046	18.8	0.1	38.0	0.0	43.0	12,233,011	23.2	1.8	74.7	0.0	10,540,598	5,152
Hudson	AA	2,051	3.7	0.3	12.9	0.1	82.9	9,383,328	15.3	1.2	83.3	0.0	7,790,148	3,798
Huntington	AA	1,622	5.6	0.1	1.4	0.0	92.9	7,412,927	16.2	3.7	80.0	0.0	6,642,228	4,095
Lufkin	AU	8,053	31.4	0.9	16.6	0.2	50.8	37,739,757	47.5	2.3	49.9	0.1	34,454,417	4,278
Zavalla	AA	389	0.0	0.0	1.0	0.0	99.0	2,598,517	21.0	4.6	74.3	0.0	2,041,688	5,249
Aransas - 1			2.2	8.3	28.3	0.1	61.1							
Aransas County	AA	3,320	2.2	8.3	28.3	0.1	61.1	18,654,621	63.1	2.3	33.5	0.8	17,869,792	5,382
Archer - 4			0.4	0.2	4.7	0.1	94.8							
Archer City	RE	583	0.3	0.0	1.2	0.0	98.5	3,322,959	39.3	2.4	58.2	0.0	3,280,739	5,627
Holliday	AA	947	0.3	0.0	4.3	0.1	95.3	4,511,934	32.4	2.7	64.8	0.0	4,435,003	4,683
Megargel	AA	72	0.0	4.2	6.9	0.0	88.9	563,839	62.0	2.0	35.9	0.0	551,942	7,666
Windthorst	RE	374	0.5	0.0	10.4	0.0	89.0	1,935,440	20.7	1.8	77.4	0.0	1,882,638	5,034
Armstrong - 1			0.2	0.7	3.3	0.0	95.7							
Claude	RE	418	0.2	0.7	3.3	0.0	95.7	2,482,567	33.9	2.1	63.8	0.0	2,138,223	5,115
Atascosa - 5			0.4	0.2	63.9	0.1	35.4							
Charlotte	AA	508	0.0	0.0	84.1	0.0	15.9	3,310,326	14.9	3.0	81.9	0.0	2,860,903	5,632
Jourdanton	AA	1,203	0.3	0.2	53.1	0.2	46.1	6,607,108	71.6	3.1	25.2	0.0	6,258,426	5,202
Lytle	AA	1,205	0.2	0.1	65.0	0.0	34.7	6,934,325	13.4	1.3	84.4	0.7	5,753,977	4,775
Pleasanton	AA	3,426	0.8	0.2	56.5	0.1	42.4	18,143,554	25.7	3.4	70.6	0.1	16,858,785	4,921
Poteet	AA	1,595	0.0	0.0	80.8	0.1	19.1	8,313,270	14.2	1.7	84.0	0.0	7,327,240	4,594
Austin - 3			14.5	0.1	19.3	0.1	66.0							
Bellville	AA	2,048	14.0	0.1	10.6	0.1	75.2	9,724,111	46.5	2.6	50.8	0.0	8,685,673	4,241
Sealy	AA	2,165	14.8	0.2	25.1	0.0	59.9	11,253,098	36.1	1.9	61.9	0.0	9,827,935	4,539
Wallis-Orchard	AA	904	15.1	0.0	25.0	0.3	59.6	5,054,568	44.5	0.5	54.7	0.1	5,035,823	5,571

County/Dist.	District Rating	Number of Students	% Black	% Asian	% Hispanic	% Amer. Ind.	% White	Total Revenue	% Local	% Other	% State	% Federal	Total Spending	Spending Per Student
Bailey - 2			2.0	0.2	58.1	0.0	39.7							
Muleshoe	AA	1,498	2.1	0.3	58.6	0.0	39.0	8,540,877	27.9	1.9	70.1	0.0	8,368,071	5,586
Three Way	AA	113	0.0	0.0	51.3	0.0	48.7	1,324,862	43.2	5.9	50.7	0.0	1,340,790	11,865
Bandera - 2			0.3	0.0	15.6	0.1	84.0							
Bandera	AA	2,101	0.3	0.0	16.3	0.1	83.3	10,225,608	59.9	0.8	39.1	0.1	8,793,570	4,185
Medina	RE	361	0.6	0.0	11.4	0.0	88.1	2,419,632	30.1	2.7	66.9	0.0	2,133,469	5,910
Bastrop - 4			12.1	0.4	26.3	0.5	60.6							
Bastrop	AA	5,338	10.1	0.4	24.4	0.8	64.3	30,412,873	26.4	1.4	71.8	0.2	26,028,753	4,876
Elgin	AA	2,551	16.1	0.6	35.7	0.3	47.4	13,579,671	23.7	1.2	75.0	0.0	11,704,644	4,588
McDade	AA	138	4.3	0.7	25.4	0.0	69.6	764,014	44.0	1.1	54.7	0.0	651,833	4,723
Smithville	AA	1,624	13.3	0.2	17.9	0.2	68.5	8,898,418	28.1	2.1	69.5	0.1	7,362,295	4,533
Baylor - 1			7.2	0.2	16.3	0.1	76.2							
Seymour	AA	806	7.2	0.2	16.3	0.1	76.2	4,998,359	28.1	1.0	70.8	0.0	4,532,587	5,624
Bee - 4			2.8	0.4	64.1	0.1	32.6							
Beeville	AA	4,305	3.5	0.6	68.1	0.1	27.7	23,568,246	15.4	1.6	82.4	0.5	20,884,302	4,851
Pawnee	RE	118	1.7	0.0	62.7	0.0	35.6	983,955	78.9	0.5	20.4	0.0	847,745	7,184
Pettus	AA	475	0.2	0.2	40.6	0.0	58.9	2,751,296	37.8	2.4	59.6	0.0	2,679,963	5,642
Skidmore-Tynan	AA	703	0.7	0.0	55.5	0.0	43.8	3,510,660	24.7	1.5	73.6	0.0	3,541,913	5,038
Bell - 9			27.7	3.0	17.4	0.5	51.5							
Academy	RE	965	0.8	0.3	10.5	0.2	88.1	4,819,501	15.1	2.8	81.9	0.0	4,233,312	4,387
Bartlett	AA	565	18.6	0.2	36.8	0.2	44.2	2,841,494	16.5	1.9	81.5	0.0	2,430,836	4,302
Belton	AA	6,180	5.3	0.5	20.7	0.5	73.0	31,951,939	17.7	2.1	79.8	0.2	28,170,093	4,558
Holland	AA	465	7.1	0.9	15.2	0.2	76.7	3,735,203	15.4	0.6	83.8	0.0	3,009,300	6,472
Killeen	AA	27,892	37.3	4.6	15.7	0.5	41.9	148,489,506	16.6	1.2	73.2	8.9	122,120,315	4,378
Rogers	AA	843	2.6	0.1	15.1	0.2	82.0	4,561,858	14.3	2.3	83.2	0.0	4,775,257	5,665
Salado	AA	724	1.0	0.6	10.9	0.1	87.4	4,115,671	46.6	2.2	51.0	0.0	3,535,908	4,884
Temple	AA	8,852	26.0	1.2	20.3	0.4	52.2	48,163,093	51.6	2.3	45.6	0.2	44,675,449	5,047
Troy	AA	1,194	1.5	0.5	19.0	0.2	78.8	6,072,064	17.2	2.5	80.2	0.0	5,339,240	4,472
Bexar - 15			8.3	1.2	61.4	0.1	29.0							
Alamo Heights	AA	4,054	2.3	0.6	23.7	0.2	73.1	24,037,635	88.1	6.1	5.7	0.0	21,422,328	5,284
East Central	AA	6,673	12.4	0.4	37.9	0.1	49.2	37,058,943	27.9	2.8	68.9	0.2	31,168,728	4,671
Edgewood	AA	14,587	2.0	0.1	95.7	0.1	2.0	84,060,179	9.3	1.3	88.8	0.5	82,648,609	5,666
Fort Sam Houston	AA	1,185	35.4	3.2	15.8	0.4	45.2	7,668,325	0.0	5.5	66.4	27.9	8,490,498	7,165
Harlandale	AA	14,847	0.4	0.2	91.9	0.1	7.5	89,298,735	12.2	2.0	85.5	0.2	85,069,173	5,730
Judson	AA	15,049	21.4	2.8	29.3	0.2	46.3	77,747,310	32.5	1.7	64.7	0.9	66,328,848	4,408
Lackland	RE	887	20.5	2.9	16.7	0.5	59.5	13,804,531	0.0	2.4	67.0	30.5	6,659,674	7,508
North East	AA	44,447	8.6	2.3	33.1	0.1	55.9	232,760,975	67.3	2.5	29.6	0.4	220,067,351	4,951
Northside	AA	57,409	6.9	2.0	49.9	0.2	41.0	237,071,320	44.3	2.1	53.3	0.1	260,756,699	4,542
Randolph Field	RE	1,002	17.0	4.3	11.1	1.0	66.7	7,054,743	0.0	3.2	64.3	32.3	6,761,111	6,748
San Antonio	AA	60,794	10.9	0.3	83.1	0.1	5.6	342,614,285	28.9	2.0	68.6	0.3	324,196,792	5,333
Somerset	AA	2,263	0.1	0.2	76.3	0.2	23.3	12,744,025	6.7	0.5	92.5	0.1	9,990,170	4,415
South San Antonio	AA	10,314	1.9	0.2	92.7	0.0	5.1	59,150,151	12.6	1.6	85.6	0.0	58,729,464	5,694
Southside	AA	3,400	0.8	0.1	79.9	0.2	19.0	19,008,095	7.6	6.7	85.6	0.0	17,974,489	5,287
Southwest	AA	9,036	4.8	0.5	79.2	0.1	15.4	50,278,228	6.2	3.5	89.9	0.2	44,611,599	4,937
Blanco - 2			1.2	0.3	22.6	0.3	75.6							
Blanco	AA	855	2.1	0.2	26.2	0.2	71.2	4,620,862	32.2	2.3	65.3	0.0	4,198,275	4,910
Johnson City	AA	599	0.0	0.3	17.6	0.3	81.8	3,663,537	45.4	2.3	52.2	0.0	3,160,966	5,277
Borden - 1			1.0	0.0	20.4	1.5	77.1							
Borden County	RE	201	1.0	0.0	20.4	1.5	77.1	2,784,079	88.8	9.1	1.9	0.0	2,290,616	11,396
Bosque - 8			3.8	0.2	16.7	0.1	79.3							
Clifton	AA	1,224	5.1	0.1	16.7	0.0	78.2	6,061,815	36.1	1.0	62.8	0.0	5,198,558	4,247
Cranfills Gap	AA	157	0.6	0.0	14.6	0.0	84.8	929,716	37.0	1.5	61.4	0.0	827,936	5,273
Iredell	AA	118	0.0	0.0	16.9	0.0	83.1	923,584	34.1	4.0	61.8	0.0	944,759	8,006
Kopperl	RE	305	0.0	0.0	4.6	0.0	95.4	1,650,033	26.7	0.9	72.2	0.0	1,555,114	5,099
Meridian	AA	496	5.6	0.6	23.1	0.4	70.3	2,884,152	22.0	1.2	76.6	0.0	2,446,922	4,933
Morgan	AA	174	0.0	0.0	33.7	0.0	66.3	1,129,407	32.6	0.7	66.6	0.0	1,053,547	6,055
Valley Mills	RE	497	6.0	0.2	8.2	0.2	85.3	4,275,870	23.8	1.1	74.9	0.0	3,429,309	6,900
Walnut Springs	AA	207	0.0	0.0	26.1	0.5	73.4	1,015,214	16.6	4.6	78.7	0.0	992,398	4,794
Bowie - 13			30.3	0.5	1.7	0.3	67.1							
DeKalb	AA	1,045	32.9	0.2	1.7	0.1	65.1	6,042,148	19.9	4.9	74.5	0.6	5,392,752	5,161
Hooks	AA	1,142	21.7	0.4	1.3	0.1	76.4	6,602,999	13.8	5.5	80.5	0.0	5,286,137	4,629
Hubbard	AA	71	0.0	0.0	4.2	0.0	95.8	358,770	24.7	1.7	73.5	0.0	380,578	5,360
Leary	RE	119	5.0	0.0	0.0	0.0	95.0	628,167	23.7	2.0	74.2	0.0	608,476	5,113
Liberty-Eylau	AA	2,712	41.5	0.4	0.8	0.1	57.2	13,680,360	24.0	2.8	72.7	0.3	12,753,548	4,703
Malta	AA	102	1.0	0.0	0.0	0.0	99.0	460,938	22.0	4.2	73.7	0.0	502,635	4,928
Maud	AA	445	17.3	0.0	1.3	0.0	81.3	2,633,338	8.5	2.1	89.2	0.0	2,405,127	5,405
New Boston	AA	1,525	21.6	0.3	0.6	0.5	77.0	8,985,376	19.4	2.6	76.1	1.6	8,030,726	5,266
Pleasant Grove	EX	1,879	5.5	1.4	2.3	0.3	90.5	9,095,853	38.5	2.2	59.2	0.0	7,733,833	4,116

County/Dist.	District Rating	Number of Students	% Black	% Asian	% Hispanic	% Amer. Ind.	% White	Total Revenue	% Local	% Other	% State	% Federal	Total Spending	Spending Per Student
Red Lick	RE	322	3.1	0.6	2.2	1.2	92.9	1,331,033	29.7	2.4	67.7	0.0	1,060,703	3,294
Redwater	RE	1,154	5.0	0.0	1.4	0.4	93.2	4,844,445	12.3	2.9	84.6	0.0	4,700,136	4,073
Simms	AA	488	0.2	0.0	1.8	0.8	97.1	2,464,075	16.5	1.5	81.9	0.0	2,270,420	4,653
Texarkana	AA	5,535	49.1	0.7	2.4	0.4	47.4	27,208,576	54.0	2.7	42.1	1.1	24,401,904	4,409
Brazoria - 8			8.5	1.6	24.8	0.2	64.9							
Alvin	AA	10,790	2.7	1.5	29.1	0.2	66.5	49,621,663	30.4	3.3	66.1	0.0	46,908,630	4,347
Angleton	AA	6,589	14.2	0.9	24.4	0.2	60.3	32,725,575	75.0	1.4	23.5	0.0	28,140,257	4,271
Brazosport	RE	12,629	8.5	1.3	31.2	0.2	58.9	63,122,459	92.3	0.8	6.8	0.0	57,905,391	4,585
Columbia-Brazoria	AA	3,662	16.5	0.2	13.9	0.1	69.4	17,757,464	39.5	3.4	57.0	0.0	16,312,312	4,454
Damon	RE	154	0.0	0.0	22.6	0.0	77.4	925,515	43.6	2.2	53.7	0.3	878,037	5,702
Danbury	RE	689	1.2	0.3	13.2	0.3	85.1	3,674,552	24.8	1.0	74.0	0.0	3,399,265	4,934
Pearland	AA	8,411	5.2	3.7	19.9	0.1	71.1	42,801,448	42.4	1.6	55.9	0.0	37,932,983	4,510
Sweeny	AA	2,304	21.4	0.2	11.1	0.3	66.9	12,774,204	91.0	2.0	6.8	0.0	11,505,592	4,994
Brazos - 2			19.7	2.7	22.1	0.1	55.4							
Bryan	AA	12,969	23.7	0.5	29.1	0.1	46.6	69,523,295	38.0	2.3	59.5	0.0	66,130,765	5,099
College Station	AA	6,545	11.9	6.9	8.3	0.0	72.9	35,835,289	86.2	2.3	11.3	0.0	28,699,972	4,385
Brewster - 4			0.5	0.2	57.9	0.1	41.2							
Alpine	AA	1,285	0.6	0.2	55.5	0.2	43.5	7,626,894	28.4	1.4	69.9	0.0	6,694,124	5,209
Marathon	AA	121	0.0	0.0	79.3	0.0	20.7	860,555	45.8	1.6	52.5	0.0	826,543	6,831
San Vicente	AA	23	0.0	0.0	56.5	0.0	43.5	380,900	13.3	6.5	72.2	7.8	380,771	16,555
Terlingua*	AA	101	0.0	0.0	63.4	0.0	36.6	607,188	64.5	1.1	32.6	1.6	598,149	5,922
Briscoe - 1			3.8	0.0	26.9	0.3	68.9							
Silverton	RE	285	3.8	0.0	26.9	0.3	68.9	1,745,290	29.8	1.3	68.7	0.0	1,630,878	5,722
Brooks - 1			0.1	0.1	92.9	0.3	6.6							
Brooks	AA	1,984	0.1	0.1	92.9	0.3	6.6	10,376,429	52.0	1.6	46.2	0.0	10,308,694	5,196
Brown - 7			5.7	0.4	18.0	0.4	75.5							
Bangs	RE	994	7.3	0.0	10.6	0.4	81.7	5,241,184	27.2	1.9	70.8	0.0	4,728,873	4,757
Blanket	AA	220	1.4	0.0	18.2	0.0	80.5	1,460,750	12.8	2.5	84.6	0.0	1,172,483	5,329
Brookesmith	AA	200	0.0	0.0	8.0	2.5	89.5	1,386,949	16.7	1.6	81.6	0.0	1,118,709	5,594
Brownwood	AA	4,126	7.8	0.4	24.3	0.2	67.3	21,366,292	38.7	2.7	58.2	0.2	20,032,619	4,855
Early	RE	1,183	0.4	1.2	8.4	0.4	89.6	6,460,879	17.3	2.6	80.0	0.0	5,286,390	4,469
May	RE	265	0.0	0.0	3.4	3.0	93.6	1,483,702	43.1	1.7	55.1	0.0	1,411,817	5,328
Zephyr	AA	174	0.0	0.0	8.6	0.0	91.4	997,120	16.8	3.3	79.8	0.0	905,270	5,203
Burleson - 3			23.2	0.2	17.2	0.1	59.3							
Caldwell	AA	1,871	15.1	0.3	18.4	0.0	66.2	9,993,806	51.5	1.8	46.6	0.0	9,767,518	5,220
Snook	AA	557	43.1	0.0	15.1	0.4	41.5	2,946,634	63.2	0.0	36.7	0.0	2,742,259	4,923
Somerville	AA	844	28.0	0.2	16.1	0.0	55.7	4,865,373	38.8	1.4	59.6	0.0	4,536,556	5,375
Burnet - 2			2.1	0.3	19.8	0.2	77.5							
Burnet Cons.	AA	2,456	2.1	0.3	16.7	0.1	80.8	14,388,499	42.0	3.1	54.7	0.0	12,551,194	5,110
Marble Falls	AA	3,211	2.1	0.3	22.2	0.3	75.0	16,923,624	54.7	3.5	41.5	0.2	14,483,633	4,511
Caldwell - 3			9.3	0.2	44.8	0.3	45.4							
Lockhart	AA	3,972	8.9	0.2	44.5	0.4	46.0	21,226,425	15.8	2.3	81.1	0.6	19,554,521	4,923
Luling	AA	1,603	9.9	0.2	45.6	0.1	44.1	7,013,210	16.8	2.2	80.5	0.3	6,474,903	4,039
Prairie Lea	AA	161	10.9	0.0	44.2	0.0	44.8	1,174,007	34.9	0.9	64.0	0.0	1,175,754	7,303
Calhoun - 1			3.1	4.6	47.0	0.0	45.3							
Calhoun County	AA	4,269	3.1	4.6	47.0	0.0	45.3	24,244,121	78.4	11.6	9.5	0.3	21,841,623	5,116
Callahan - 4			0.1	0.2	7.0	0.3	92.4							
Baird	AA	478	0.0	1.0	14.4	0.2	84.3	2,643,323	27.5	2.0	70.4	0.0	2,726,245	5,703
Clyde Cons.	RE	1,546	0.2	0.1	5.9	0.4	93.4	9,083,583	18.5	1.8	79.6	0.0	7,027,086	4,545
Cross Plains	AA	442	0.0	0.0	3.2	0.0	96.8	2,496,421	23.5	2.1	74.3	0.0	2,152,637	4,870
Eula	AA	571	0.0	0.0	7.0	0.2	92.8	3,607,894	29.5	2.3	68.1	0.0	2,896,164	5,072
Cameron - 10			0.2	0.3	92.5	0.1	6.9							
Brownsville	AA	40,270	0.1	0.2	96.7	0.0	2.9	234,175,128	9.9	1.5	88.3	0.1	215,138,233	5,342
Harlingen Cons.	AA	15,801	0.6	0.6	84.4	0.0	14.4	88,273,111	20.8	1.7	77.2	0.1	78,110,394	4,943
La Feria	AA	2,589	0.2	0.2	87.4	0.0	12.2	14,574,126	7.0	1.4	91.3	0.1	12,710,669	4,909
Los Fresnos Cons.	RE	5,718	0.4	0.2	89.5	0.3	9.7	33,818,864	10.2	0.6	88.6	0.3	27,664,075	4,838
Point Isabel	RE	2,251	0.1	0.2	82.4	0.0	17.1	12,653,777	81.5	8.6	8.0	1.7	11,167,999	4,961
Rio Hondo	AA	2,001	0.0	0.0	93.6	0.1	6.2	11,453,362	12.6	5.2	76.9	5.1	10,237,952	5,116
San Benito Cons.	RE	8,336	0.1	0.1	96.5	0.0	3.3	50,219,460	8.2	1.3	90.2	0.1	41,934,960	5,031
Santa Maria	AA	494	0.0	0.0	99.4	0.2	0.4	4,072,038	6.6	1.2	86.7	5.3	3,777,143	7,646
Santa Rosa	AA	1,145	0.1	0.1	97.6	0.2	2.2	7,337,787	5.4	1.0	88.5	5.0	6,172,855	5,391
South Texas	RE	1,987	0.7	2.5	74.9	0.2	21.8	16,359,768	33.9	1.1	64.9	0.0	14,863,465	7,480
Camp - 1			26.4	0.1	12.3	0.0	61.1							
Pittsburg	RE	2,093	26.4	0.1	12.3	0.0	61.1	9,473,032	42.4	3.6	53.7	0.0	9,194,836	4,393
Carson - 3			0.1	0.1	7.2	0.1	92.4							
Groom	RE	208	0.0	0.0	5.7	0.5	93.8	1,368,479	55.0	5.6	39.3	0.0	1,301,645	6,258
Panhandle	RE	715	0.0	0.3	9.1	0.0	90.6	4,364,674	82.2	2.1	15.5	0.0	4,179,674	5,846
White Deer	RE	503	0.4	0.0	5.2	0.0	94.2	3,133,933	91.4	2.3	6.2	0.0	3,107,293	6,178

County/Dist.	District Rating	Number of Students	Ethnicity of Student Population					Total Revenue	Sources of Revenue				Total Spending	Spending Per Student
			% Black	% Asian	% Hispanic	% Amer. Ind.	% White		% Local	% Other	% State	% Federal		
Cass - 8			25.6	0.2	1.1	0.2	72.9							
Atlanta	AA	2,007	36.1	0.0	0.4	0.0	63.3	10,367,927	39.3	1.8	58.7	0.0	9,684,181	4,825
Avinger	AA	190	28.4	0.0	3.2	0.0	68.4	1,194,402	26.9	3.5	69.5	0.0	1,307,642	6,882
Bloomburg	AA	237	7.6	0.0	2.1	1.3	89.0	1,554,656	10.6	2.3	87.0	0.0	1,285,502	5,424
Hughes Springs	AA	1,007	17.2	0.1	3.8	0.3	78.6	5,326,999	30.7	2.0	66.7	0.4	4,819,143	4,786
Linden-Kildare Cons.	AA	1,160	26.8	0.3	0.6	0.1	72.2	5,481,151	22.7	1.7	75.4	0.0	5,758,031	4,964
Marietta	AA	36	44.4	0.0	0.0	0.0	55.6	300,905	58.4	5.8	35.6	0.0	300,405	8,345
McLeod	RE	324	4.9	0.0	0.6	0.0	94.5	1,841,653	17.2	1.2	81.4	0.0	1,487,633	4,591
Queen City	AA	1,352	22.2	0.4	0.3	0.4	76.7	7,108,606	66.1	0.8	33.0	0.0	6,560,750	4,853
Castro - 3			3.4	0.0	64.9	0.1	31.6							
Dimmitt	AA	1,567	4.0	0.1	70.3	0.1	25.5	8,403,470	33.5	2.6	63.5	0.2	7,975,630	5,090
Hart	AA	479	3.3	0.0	79.2	0.0	17.6	3,231,111	22.9	2.7	74.1	0.1	3,117,234	6,508
Nazareth	RE	260	0.0	0.0	5.4	0.0	94.6	2,120,968	12.3	2.2	85.3	0.0	1,596,138	6,139
Chambers - 3			11.4	0.9	11.5	0.1	76.1							
Anahuac	AA	1,437	21.7	2.0	16.0	0.0	60.4	7,537,734	54.2	8.2	37.5	0.0	7,317,207	5,092
Barbers Hill	RE	2,184	2.7	0.3	9.2	0.2	87.6	16,167,610	85.1	5.6	9.1	0.0	12,241,903	5,605
East Chambers	AA	1,054	15.3	0.4	10.3	0.2	73.8	8,134,510	35.8	10.4	53.7	0.0	6,658,689	6,318
Cherokee - 5			23.0	0.2	13.5	0.2	63.1							
Alto	AA	667	38.9	0.0	6.1	0.0	54.9	4,607,035	24.8	2.8	72.2	0.0	3,881,207	5,819
Jacksonville	AA	4,459	23.6	0.3	16.0	0.2	59.9	21,283,509	33.2	3.3	63.2	0.1	19,939,951	4,472
New Summerfield	AA	315	18.3	0.0	47.8	0.0	33.9	2,057,402	11.5	1.8	86.6	0.0	1,731,638	5,497
Rusk	AA	1,831	17.9	0.4	6.1	0.2	75.4	10,042,086	26.9	1.7	70.9	0.3	9,006,923	4,919
Wells	AA	302	14.2	0.0	2.3	0.0	83.4	1,689,806	18.1	2.1	79.7	0.0	1,639,615	5,429
Childress - 1			7.6	0.8	27.4	0.6	63.6							
Childress	AA	1,297	7.6	0.8	27.4	0.6	63.6	6,630,067	23.7	1.2	74.8	0.1	6,374,528	4,915
Clay - 5			0.5	0.2	4.7	0.7	93.9							
Bellevue	**EX**	165	0.0	0.0	0.6	0.0	99.4	1,044,458	32.2	2.5	65.2	0.0	1,051,658	6,374
Byers	RE	153	0.0	0.0	7.1	0.0	92.9	926,589	15.0	2.0	82.9	0.0	726,512	4,748
Henrietta	RE	1,054	0.9	0.4	3.5	1.4	93.8	5,711,194	30.2	2.0	67.6	0.0	5,239,819	4,971
Midway	RE	184	0.5	0.0	4.9	0.0	94.6	1,112,542	58.8	2.1	39.0	0.0	1,140,849	6,200
Petrolia	AA	457	0.0	0.0	8.0	0.0	92.0	2,695,851	13.4	0.9	85.5	0.0	2,179,397	4,769
Cochran - 3			6.1	0.1	53.9	0.1	39.8							
Bledsoe	**EX**	20	0.0	0.0	50.0	0.0	50.0	301,885	82.4	9.5	3.4	4.5	502,645	25,132
Morton	AA	716	8.4	0.0	64.1	0.0	27.5	5,689,921	19.0	9.4	71.5	0.0	5,403,697	7,547
Whiteface Cons.	AA	524	3.2	0.2	40.1	0.2	56.3	3,418,531	86.7	8.9	4.3	0.0	3,219,231	6,144
Coke - 2			6.1	0.1	21.7	0.1	71.9							
Bronte	**RE**	395	11.6	0.3	18.9	0.0	69.2	2,911,063	24.9	2.4	72.5	0.0	2,650,418	6,710
Robert Lee	RE	371	0.3	0.0	24.7	0.3	74.7	2,287,280	67.4	1.6	30.9	0.0	2,164,220	5,833
Coleman - 4			4.6	0.3	19.3	0.1	75.8							
Coleman	AA	1,201	4.9	0.3	21.5	0.1	73.2	7,230,575	11.9	1.7	86.3	0.0	6,484,136	5,399
Novice	RE	99	0.0	0.0	8.1	0.0	91.9	954,819	44.4	1.7	53.8	0.0	915,811	9,251
Panther Creek Cons.	RE	237	0.0	0.4	9.6	0.0	90.0	2,217,238	23.2	3.4	73.2	0.0	1,689,800	7,130
Santa Anna	AA	332	8.1	0.0	21.6	0.3	70.0	2,267,238	23.6	1.2	75.0	0.0	2,067,927	6,229
Collin - 14			5.2	5.3	9.0	0.3	80.1							
Allen	RE	7,452	4.0	1.6	5.2	0.6	88.5	39,390,414	31.7	19.7	48.5	0.0	31,430,314	4,218
Anna	AA	864	0.2	0.0	13.4	0.0	86.2	4,761,559	13.9	5.9	80.0	0.0	3,952,821	4,575
Blue Ridge	AA	432	0.5	0.0	5.1	0.2	94.2	2,698,259	25.2	4.0	70.7	0.0	2,564,278	5,936
Celina	AA	863	9.2	0.1	10.4	0.7	79.6	4,833,546	29.1	14.2	56.5	0.0	4,013,095	4,650
Community	AA	921	2.5	0.2	7.2	0.3	89.8	5,394,992	15.6	2.9	81.4	0.0	4,823,052	5,237
Farmersville	AA	1,105	8.7	0.0	13.1	0.0	78.2	5,951,072	20.6	2.0	77.3	0.0	5,088,524	4,605
Frisco	AA	2,692	2.8	0.7	21.8	0.6	74.2	13,941,045	63.4	2.8	33.7	0.0	11,008,749	4,089
Lovejoy	**EX**	551	1.6	0.4	0.9	0.5	96.6	3,823,148	94.1	1.0	4.8	0.0	3,523,916	6,395
McKinney	AA	7,086	10.4	0.4	19.3	0.3	69.3	40,512,469	51.7	2.5	45.7	0.0	33,947,959	4,791
Melissa	AA	308	0.0	0.3	7.5	0.6	91.6	2,050,291	43.1	3.9	52.9	0.0	1,124,306	3,650
Plano	AA	38,429	5.4	8.7	7.0	0.2	78.7	225,043,307	87.1	4.7	8.1	0.0	200,480,939	5,217
Princeton	AA	1,874	1.8	0.1	7.7	0.7	89.7	8,883,605	13.1	2.1	84.7	0.0	7,723,550	4,121
Prosper	AA	729	0.3	0.5	16.6	0.1	82.4	4,323,981	30.8	1.5	67.6	0.0	3,252,659	4,462
Wylie	AA	3,407	1.2	0.5	7.3	0.7	90.3	19,031,265	42.8	1.7	55.3	0.1	15,350,791	4,506
Collingsworth - 2			8.4	0.2	32.9	0.6	57.9							
Samnorwood	AA	113	3.5	0.0	22.6	0.0	73.9	884,080	37.3	0.4	62.1	0.0	822,485	7,279
Wellington	RE	711	9.1	0.3	34.6	0.7	55.3	4,028,018	16.0	1.8	81.9	0.1	3,838,930	5,399
Colorado - 3			20.7	0.1	25.0	0.0	54.1							
Columbus	AA	1,693	15.9	0.2	16.2	0.0	67.7	7,269,937	10.7	39.8	49.1	0.2	6,811,094	4,023
Rice Cons.	AA	1,427	25.6	0.0	38.8	0.1	35.5	9,456,002	47.7	1.8	50.2	0.1	8,361,235	5,859
Weimar	AA	600	22.7	0.0	17.6	0.0	59.7	3,887,206	35.2	1.9	62.8	0.0	3,002,324	5,004
Comal - 2			1.2	0.4	28.8	0.1	69.5							
Comal	AA	8,586	1.1	0.4	18.6	0.1	79.9	44,973,746	69.7	1.2	28.8	0.2	38,080,839	4,435
New Braunfels	AA	5,698	1.4	0.4	44.2	0.1	53.9	28,324,251	40.8	2.4	56.5	0.1	24,352,525	4,274

County/Dist.	District Rating	Number of Students	Ethnicity of Student Population					Total Revenue	Sources of Revenue				Total Spending	Spending Per Student
			% Black	% Asian	% Hispanic	% Amer. Ind.	% White		% Local	% Other	% State	% Federal		
Comanche - 4			0.2	0.1	31.4	0.3	68.0							
Comanche	AA	1,280	0.3	0.2	33.7	0.2	65.6	5,668,596	25.4	2.8	71.7	0.0	4,915,805	3,840
De Leon	RE	757	0.0	0.0	31.1	0.1	68.8	4,178,979	34.2	2.6	62.6	0.4	3,993,657	5,276
Gustine	AA	206	0.0	0.0	30.1	0.5	69.4	1,392,758	23.6	1.4	74.9	0.0	1,263,489	6,133
Sidney	RE	160	0.0	0.0	16.3	1.3	82.5	927,014	15.8	4.4	79.7	0.0	867,197	5,420
Concho - 2			0.0	0.2	45.8	0.2	53.8							
Eden Cons.	AA	395	0.0	0.0	48.7	0.3	51.0	2,267,963	69.1	1.8	28.9	0.0	2,528,678	6,402
Paint Rock	RE	176	0.0	0.6	39.2	0.0	60.2	1,127,177	34.7	5.5	59.6	0.1	1,112,528	6,321
Cooke - 8			5.1	0.8	9.6	0.6	83.9							
Callisburg	AA	973	0.2	0.4	2.5	1.0	95.9	5,445,873	40.9	1.6	57.2	0.2	4,957,776	5,095
Era	RE	406	0.0	0.5	3.7	0.0	95.8	2,171,762	18.6	3.4	77.9	0.0	2,132,817	5,253
Gainesville	AU	2,724	10.5	0.7	17.0	0.6	71.2	15,593,252	40.8	1.7	57.3	0.0	13,696,234	5,028
Lindsay	RE	518	0.2	2.7	1.0	0.6	95.6	2,243,874	25.6	4.5	69.7	0.0	2,024,105	3,908
Muenster	EX	424	0.5	0.5	0.9	0.2	97.9	2,074,749	45.9	3.0	51.0	0.0	1,828,764	4,313
Sivells Bend	EX	77	0.0	0.0	5.2	0.0	94.8	408,790	72.3	2.6	25.0	0.0	409,432	5,317
Valley View	AA	602	0.0	0.3	7.0	0.7	92.0	3,100,985	22.0	2.6	75.2	0.1	2,824,000	4,691
Walnut Bend	AA	50	2.0	0.0	2.0	0.0	96.0	334,755	38.5	5.7	55.7	0.0	344,750	6,895
Coryell - 5			18.5	2.9	10.3	0.6	67.7							
Copperas Cove	AA	7,586	24.4	4.0	10.2	0.6	60.7	33,376,132	20.7	1.8	77.4	0.0	34,313,834	4,523
Evant	RE	292	0.0	0.0	17.1	0.0	82.9	1,461,843	25.9	4.1	69.9	0.0	1,301,703	4,458
Gatesville	AA	2,423	5.2	0.2	10.0	0.3	84.3	11,436,665	23.7	2.2	73.9	0.0	9,707,052	4,006
Jonesboro	AA	223	0.0	0.0	2.7	0.4	96.9	1,351,185	22.7	1.9	75.2	0.0	1,280,036	5,740
Oglesby	AA	143	0.0	0.0	21.0	1.4	77.6	1,279,497	18.7	4.9	76.3	0.0	816,338	5,709
Cottle - 1			14.7	0.0	26.1	0.0	59.2							
Paducah	AA	401	14.7	0.0	26.1	0.0	59.2	2,781,875	28.8	1.5	69.3	0.2	2,501,236	6,237
Crane - 1			4.5	0.0	47.4	0.3	47.9							
Crane	AA	1,191	4.5	0.0	47.4	0.3	47.9	12,782,859	94.0	2.8	3.0	0.0	8,102,029	6,803
Crockett - 1			0.6	0.3	59.9	0.0	39.2							
Crockett County Cons.*	AA	965	0.6	0.3	59.9	0.0	39.2	6,438,364	89.8	3.2	6.8	0.0	6,281,675	6,510
Crosby - 3			5.0	0.2	62.9	0.0	32.0							
Crosbyton	AA	581	7.7	0.3	55.8	0.0	36.1	4,668,300	21.6	0.5	77.7	0.0	4,050,367	6,971
Lorenzo	AA	437	7.8	0.2	63.7	0.0	28.3	3,267,348	27.4	1.7	70.8	0.0	3,599,098	8,236
Ralls	AA	758	1.2	0.0	67.8	0.0	31.0	4,812,705	20.5	1.3	77.8	0.2	4,219,408	5,567
Culberson - 1			0.0	0.6	79.1	0.3	20.0							
Culberson Co.-Allamoor	AA	794	0.0	0.6	79.1	0.3	20.0	4,558,820	59.1	2.6	38.2	0.0	4,287,149	5,399
Dallam - 2			2.2	0.6	27.3	0.3	69.6							
Dalhart	AA	1,563	2.4	0.6	27.6	0.4	69.0	8,017,416	40.4	1.6	57.8	0.0	7,297,127	4,669
Texline	AA	185	0.0	0.0	25.3	0.0	74.7	1,239,412	59.1	2.1	36.6	2.0	1,165,746	6,301
Dallas - 15			27.3	4.0	29.1	0.5	39.1							
Carrollton-F'rmersBranch	AA	20,343	7.5	11.2	24.0	0.5	56.8	117,055,759	87.1	2.9	9.8	0.0	97,304,388	4,783
Cedar Hill	AA	5,615	28.4	2.1	11.0	0.7	57.9	26,771,184	43.3	2.0	54.5	0.0	21,505,136	3,830
Coppell	EX	6,357	2.6	8.4	6.7	0.8	81.5	34,768,753	91.0	2.5	6.3	0.0	29,380,567	4,622
Dallas	AA	148,839	42.6	1.7	43.4	0.5	11.9	691,109,331	78.2	1.4	20.1	0.0	683,566,057	4,593
DeSoto	AA	6,558	37.6	1.3	7.5	0.1	53.5	32,298,368	51.5	2.3	45.8	0.2	27,084,829	4,130
Duncanville	AA	10,126	31.5	2.9	12.5	0.3	52.8	51,536,807	62.8	2.2	34.9	0.0	46,479,014	4,590
Garland	AA	43,553	14.3	5.3	19.9	0.6	59.8	208,170,106	42.7	1.5	55.6	0.0	175,945,383	4,040
Grand Prairie	AA	17,934	12.6	3.7	37.7	0.8	45.2	84,667,193	34.6	1.2	63.9	0.1	74,442,292	4,151
Highland Park	EX	5,222	0.1	1.0	1.3	0.2	97.5	29,883,342	91.3	3.7	4.8	0.0	25,674,564	4,917
Irving	AA	26,459	13.7	6.0	33.1	0.6	46.5	133,734,368	68.1	4.5	27.2	0.1	122,680,410	4,637
Lancaster	AA	4,042	52.9	0.5	11.5	0.4	34.8	20,683,477	51.7	2.4	45.5	0.2	16,879,122	4,176
Mesquite	AA	29,242	10.8	3.5	12.6	0.4	72.7	144,627,889	28.6	3.5	67.7	0.1	124,319,008	4,251
Richardson	AA	33,984	18.7	8.7	12.8	0.3	59.4	197,141,646	88.1	2.4	9.4	0.0	169,861,923	4,998
Sunnyvale	RE	367	0.3	0.0	3.8	0.8	95.1	2,103,027	91.0	0.9	8.0	0.0	1,889,190	5,148
Wilmer-Hutchins	AA	3,837	78.3	0.1	14.6	0.3	6.6	20,332,283	27.0	1.3	71.3	0.3	19,347,264	5,042
Dawson - 4			4.2	0.0	58.6	0.1	37.0							
Dawson	RE	198	0.0	0.0	48.0	0.0	52.0	1,757,099	91.2	5.4	3.2	0.0	1,678,526	8,477
Klondike	EX	258	0.0	0.0	25.6	0.4	74.0	1,978,783	89.5	2.8	7.6	0.0	2,046,991	7,934
Lamesa	AA	2,626	5.3	0.0	63.9	0.0	30.7	13,826,564	32.2	3.6	64.1	0.0	13,261,983	5,050
Sands	RE	202	0.0	0.0	43.1	0.0	56.9	15,547,746	80.7	3.8	15.4	0.0	1,496,108	7,406
Deaf Smith - 2			2.4	0.3	70.1	0.1	27.1							
Hereford	AA	4,501	2.4	0.3	70.9	0.1	26.2	19,882,907	29.6	2.2	68.0	0.0	21,192,587	4,708
Walcott	RE	94	0.0	0.0	29.8	0.0	70.2	643,000	44.7	1.4	53.0	0.6	599,734	6,380
Delta - 2			17.6	0.4	2.4	0.7	78.9							
Cooper	AA	877	13.8	0.0	1.9	0.6	83.7	4,397,955	23.6	2.0	74.2	0.0	4,246,038	4,842
Fannindel	AA	242	31.4	1.7	4.1	1.2	61.6	1,602,290	15.1	2.3	82.4	0.0	1,583,339	6,543
Denton - 11			5.8	1.8	9.6	0.6	82.3							
Argyle	RE	555	0.7	0.0	3.4	0.5	95.3	3,888,641	61.0	22.4	16.5	0.0	3,507,830	6,320
Aubrey	AA	848	0.1	0.4	5.3	0.6	93.6	4,990,632	27.0	2.0	70.8	0.0	4,283,385	5,051

County/Dist.	District Rating	Number of Students	Ethnicity of Student Population					Total Revenue	Sources of Revenue				Total Spending	Spending Per Student
			% Black	% Asian	% Hispanic	% Amer. Ind.	% White		% Local	% Other	% State	% Federal		
Denton	AA	12,035	11.8	1.5	14.7	0.4	71.5	64,857,017	59.7	2.7	37.3	0.1	55,205,901	4,587
Krum	AA	872	1.3	0.3	5.7	0.0	92.7	5,121,242	21.9	1.2	76.8	0.0	4,494,815	5,155
Lake Dallas	RE	2,226	2.3	1.3	5.9	1.1	89.4	10,553,867	42.9	1.7	54.2	1.0	8,949,511	4,020
Lewisville	AA	28,320	5.2	2.4	8.3	0.6	83.4	135,697,342	60.6	2.8	36.5	0.0	123,689,687	4,368
Little Elm	AA	1,265	0.4	0.2	21.6	0.2	77.6	7,850,002	22.7	2.1	74.9	0.1	6,513,481	5,149
Northwest	AA	4,265	0.7	1.1	6.7	0.8	90.6	22,785,278	59.8	3.9	36.0	0.0	20,584,689	4,826
Pilot Point	AA	1,060	5.8	0.1	8.7	0.9	84.4	6,073,077	31.0	3.0	65.9	0.0	5,180,325	4,887
Ponder	AA	489	0.0	0.6	5.5	0.6	93.3	2,612,430	25.0	1.1	73.7	0.0	2,293,099	4,689
Sanger	RE	1,779	2.0	0.1	6.1	0.7	91.2	9,189,581	23.5	3.1	73.3	0.0	8,507,848	4,782
DeWitt - 6			12.2	0.1	33.2	0.0	54.4							
Cuero	AA	1,991	16.1	0.2	35.6	0.1	48.0	11,674,696	21.8	5.6	72.4	0.1	10,611,980	5,330
Meyersville	EX	143	0.0	0.7	9.1	0.7	89.5	812,594	51.3	6.8	41.8	0.0	982,000	6,867
Nordheim	AA	101	1.0	0.0	41.6	0.0	57.4	795,515	63.3	2.1	34.4	0.0	842,475	8,341
Westhoff	EX	77	7.8	0.0	23.4	0.0	68.8	512,673	27.0	1.2	71.7	0.0	452,333	5,874
Yoakum	AA	1,579	14.5	0.0	31.1	0.0	54.4	8,398,681	31.7	2.4	65.5	0.1	8,767,549	5,553
Yorktown	AA	784	1.8	0.0	35.8	0.0	62.4	4,437,570	24.4	2.1	73.4	0.0	4,267,055	5,443
Dickens - 2			5.1	0.6	33.2	0.6	60.5							
Patton Springs	RE	128	0.0	0.0	34.4	2.3	63.3	1,097,646	25.5	2.6	67.9	3.8	1,162,751	9,084
Spur	AA	384	6.8	0.8	32.8	0.0	59.6	2,837,826	30.8	11.6	57.4	0.0	2,345,184	6,107
Dimmit - 2			1.1	0.4	88.1	0.0	10.4							
Asherton	AA	388	0.8	0.0	98.7	0.0	0.5	3,546,043	6.6	0.3	93.0	0.0	2,768,247	7,135
Carrizo Springs Cons.	AA	2,291	1.2	0.5	86.3	0.0	12.0	14,597,398	19.5	3.7	76.0	0.6	13,167,417	5,747
Donley - 2			11.1	0.3	7.1	0.1	81.3							
Clarendon	RE	512	14.6	0.4	7.4	0.2	77.4	3,304,953	34.1	2.1	63.7	0.0	3,036,283	5,930
Hedley	AA	162	0.0	0.0	6.2	0.0	93.8	959,397	29.3	1.3	69.3	0.0	961,656	5,936
Duval - 4			0.1	0.1	92.2	0.2	7.4							
Benavides	AA	590	0.0	0.0	98.3	0.0	1.7	5,000,000	47.9	0.9	48.2	2.9	4,540,120	7,695
Freer	AA	1,022	0.3	0.3	78.3	0.1	21.0	6,792,668	54.4	3.5	42.0	0.0	6,428,809	6,290
Ramirez*	AU	29	0.0	0.0	93.1	0.0	6.9	403,584	87.2	0.3	12.4	0.0	391,557	13,502
San Diego	AA	1,683	0.1	0.0	98.7	0.4	0.8	9,512,605	23.6	0.0	76.3	0.0	10,019,908	5,954
Eastland - 5			1.5	0.5	14.2	0.3	83.5							
Cisco	RE	997	2.5	0.1	9.2	0.4	87.8	4,893,148	25.3	1.0	73.5	0.0	4,581,672	4,595
Eastland	AA	1,244	1.0	0.9	11.9	0.2	86.0	5,887,865	35.6	1.5	62.8	0.0	5,833,737	4,689
Gorman	RE	436	0.0	0.9	26.6	0.0	72.5	2,749,427	18.9	1.5	79.5	0.0	2,869,465	6,581
Ranger	AA	594	2.5	0.5	18.7	0.5	77.8	3,400,546	20.1	1.8	77.9	0.0	3,083,312	5,191
Rising Star	AA	248	0.0	0.0	12.5	0.0	87.5	1,359,456	23.5	3.1	73.3	0.0	1,373,026	5,536
Ector - 1			5.1	0.7	48.9	0.3	45.0							
Ector County	AA	28,528	5.1	0.7	48.9	0.3	45.0	127,481,778	41.5	6.7	51.6	0.0	119,500,015	4,189
Edwards - 2			0.1	0.3	51.9	0.2	47.4							
Nueces Canyon Cons.	AA	387	0.0	0.0	24.8	0.5	74.7	2,464,722	37.5	1.0	61.4	0.0	2,219,176	5,734
Rocksprings	AA	469	0.2	0.6	74.1	0.0	25.1	3,398,405	47.4	1.8	47.5	3.2	3,058,923	6,522
Ellis - 10			11.4	0.3	20.6	0.2	67.4							
Avalon	AA	201	3.0	0.0	43.3	1.5	52.2	1,179,812	19.9	2.2	77.7	0.0	1,143,667	5,690
Ennis	AA	4,392	17.6	0.3	33.2	0.2	48.8	21,389,778	36.2	3.1	60.5	0.0	19,557,659	4,453
Ferris	AA	1,685	15.7	0.1	30.1	0.4	53.8	8,767,349	16.5	0.9	82.4	0.0	8,304,665	4,929
Italy	AA	624	23.8	0.0	13.7	0.0	62.5	4,270,238	14.5	1.5	83.9	0.0	3,261,669	5,227
Maypearl	AA	637	2.4	0.5	18.8	0.0	78.4	3,651,877	12.3	1.7	85.9	0.0	3,212,274	5,043
Midlothian	AA	3,427	2.5	0.5	9.8	0.2	87.0	18,011,449	67.9	1.6	30.4	0.0	14,493,560	4,229
Milford	AA	192	29.9	0.0	13.4	0.0	56.2	1,680,697	13.7	3.1	83.1	0.0	1,309,622	6,821
Palmer	AA	860	0.3	0.2	24.7	1.2	73.6	4,253,906	20.6	1.9	77.3	0.0	3,876,594	4,508
Red Oak	AA	3,688	4.2	0.3	11.4	0.4	83.8	17,661,141	28.2	2.2	69.5	0.0	15,441,028	4,187
Waxahachie	AA	5,083	17.1	0.2	20.5	0.1	62.1	25,234,468	46.0	2.4	51.5	0.0	22,016,016	4,331
El Paso - 9			3.0	0.7	82.3	0.2	13.7							
Anthony	RE	810	0.2	0.1	94.7	0.0	4.9	4,559,688	30.0	1.5	68.1	0.2	4,164,393	5,141
Canutillo	AA	4,206	0.5	0.0	92.1	0.1	7.3	24,894,355	15.6	0.5	83.3	0.4	22,407,712	5,328
Clint	AA	6,064	0.6	0.2	90.7	0.2	8.4	30,819,964	9.3	0.0	90.5	0.0	27,317,910	4,505
El Paso	AA	64,260	4.5	1.0	75.7	0.1	18.7	340,906,132	34.8	2.5	61.5	1.0	299,413,598	4,659
Fabens	AA	2,681	0.1	0.0	96.7	0.3	2.8	14,579,164	6.6	1.6	85.0	6.7	13,413,018	5,003
San Elizario	AA	3,315	0.0	0.0	98.9	0.2	0.9	19,398,539	2.8	0.4	96.5	0.1	15,369,608	4,636
Socorro	AA	20,115	1.3	0.3	88.3	0.1	10.0	103,701,361	15.3	1.0	83.2	0.3	94,017,521	4,674
Tornillo	AA	616	1.0	0.0	97.2	0.2	1.6	3,998,543	4.5	0.1	95.2	0.0	3,639,731	5,909
Ysleta	AA	47,144	2.8	0.5	84.6	0.5	11.6	262,232,214	23.1	1.5	74.2	1.1	232,670,420	4,935
Erath - 7			0.7	0.4	20.3	0.4	78.2							
Bluff Dale	RE	88	3.4	0.0	3.4	1.1	92.0	400,744	45.4	1.4	53.0	0.0	427,594	4,859
Dublin	AA	1,426	0.2	0.3	32.2	0.8	66.5	6,535,371	21.8	2.0	76.0	0.0	5,903,693	4,140
Huckabay	AA	229	0.4	0.9	24.9	0.0	73.8	1,314,896	34.5	1.6	63.7	0.0	1,156,745	5,051
Lingleville	RE	206	0.0	0.0	41.5	0.0	58.5	1,412,291	26.6	2.6	70.6	0.0	1,217,186	5,909
Morgan Mill	RE	74	0.0	0.0	8.1	0.0	91.9	395.390	53.3	2.7	41.9	0.0	459,932	6,215

County/Dist.	District Rating	Number of Students	% Black	% Asian	% Hispanic	% Amer. Ind.	% White	Total Revenue	% Local	% Other	% State	% Federal	Total Spending	Spending Per Student
Stephenville	AA	3,353	1.0	0.5	13.8	0.3	84.4	15,144,510	41.1	2.4	56.4	0.0	14,208,809	4,238
Three Way	RE	61	0.0	0.0	44.3	0.0	55.7	322,392	46.7	1.1	52.1	0.0	284,240	4,660
Falls - 4			36.5	0.1	18.4	0.0	45.0							
Chilton	AA	375	24.8	0.0	33.1	0.0	42.1	2,256,333	18.9	1.5	79.1	0.4	2,202,899	5,874
Marlin	AA	1,764	52.2	0.1	16.7	0.0	31.1	9,164,682	20.8	3.0	76.0	0.0	8,907,787	5,050
Rosebud-Lott	AA	1,033	17.5	0.0	17.5	0.0	65.0	6,034,518	17.7	4.7	76.9	0.4	5,881,741	5,694
Westphalia	EX	98	0.0	0.0	3.1	0.0	96.9	473,079	21.3	2.6	76.0	0.0	507,557	5,179
Fannin - 8			7.6	0.3	3.4	0.9	87.8							
Bonham	AA	2,057	9.9	0.4	3.7	1.2	84.9	10,647,015	31.3	2.2	66.3	0.0	8,677,003	4,218
Dodd City	AA	239	0.8	0.8	0.0	0.0	98.3	1,544,834	11.8	3.2	84.9	0.0	1,309,934	5,481
Ector	AA	187	0.0	1.6	1.6	3.2	93.7	1,074,257	15.3	1.3	83.3	0.0	877,623	4,693
Honey Grove Cons.	AA	689	16.7	0.0	4.3	0.0	79.0	3,802,620	22.4	2.1	75.1	0.2	3,611,837	5,242
Leonard	AA	747	5.4	0.0	2.9	0.8	90.9	3,873,375	11.1	3.9	84.9	0.0	3,411,666	4,567
Sam Rayburn	AA	344	1.7	0.0	2.3	1.7	94.2	2,123,858	17.3	3.6	79.0	0.0	1,846,394	5,367
Savoy	AA	293	0.0	1.4	2.7	0.0	95.9	1,985,729	55.6	2.7	41.6	0.0	1,455,503	4,968
Trenton	AA	372	2.2	0.0	5.1	0.8	91.9	2,129,798	14.8	1.3	83.7	0.0	1,870,268	5,028
Fayette - 5			10.5	0.2	16.6	0.1	72.6							
Fayetteville	RE	242	2.9	0.0	0.0	0.0	97.1	1,396,239	51.7	4.5	43.7	0.0	1,207,112	4,988
Flatonia	AA	551	8.3	0.9	34.1	0.0	56.6	2,847,894	47.2	0.8	51.9	0.0	2,647,616	4,805
La Grange	AA	1,931	10.3	0.1	16.8	0.0	72.9	10,092,816	91.3	2.7	5.9	0.0	9,076,555	4,700
Round Top-Carmine	RE	224	8.9	0.0	3.1	0.0	87.9	1,422,172	85.3	4.7	9.9	0.0	1,501,460	6,703
Schulenburg	AA	726	15.9	0.0	12.5	0.3	71.3	4,526,367	37.0	2.6	60.3	0.0	3,988,454	5,494
Fisher - 2			5.4	0.0	31.0	0.1	63.4							
Roby Cons.	AA	325	2.8	0.0	22.8	0.0	74.5	2,306,227	31.9	10.7	57.2	0.0	2,115,354	6,509
Rotan	RE	452	7.3	0.0	36.9	0.2	55.5	3,142,439	26.3	2.4	71.2	0.0	2,933,195	6,489
Floyd - 2			4.2	0.2	60.5	0.0	35.1							
Floydada	AA	1,217	5.4	0.2	62.2	0.0	32.2	8,042,869	27.4	0.8	71.7	0.0	7,341,259	6,032
Lockney	AA	869	2.5	0.3	58.0	0.0	39.1	4,832,453	21.6	1.8	76.5	0.0	4,220,780	4,857
Foard - 1			4.5	0.5	28.5	0.0	66.5							
Crowell	AA	397	4.5	0.5	28.5	0.0	66.5	2,475,580	26.7	4.4	68.7	0.0	2,256,940	5,685
Fort Bend - 5			22.8	10.0	23.3	0.1	43.7							
Fort Bend	AA	40,280	27.2	13.5	14.6	0.1	44.6	223,874,226	45.8	1.6	52.4	0.0	194,628,294	4,839
Kendleton	AA	110	65.5	0.0	33.6	0.0	0.9	1,362,274	25.0	1.6	73.2	0.0	1,211,109	11,010
Lamar Cons.	AA	13,774	13.4	0.8	46.5	0.1	39.2	73,000,434	59.9	2.5	37.4	0.0	70,797,974	5,140
Needville	AA	2,259	7.3	0.4	22.5	0.2	69.6	10,300,643	26.0	2.0	71.8	0.0	9,183,821	4,065
Stafford Mun.	AA	2,263	15.5	13.7	37.7	0.4	32.7	13,778,266	85.9	1.3	12.6	0.0	10,527,433	4,652
Franklin - 1			7.4	0.2	10.3	0.4	81.7							
Mount Vernon	RE	1,433	7.4	0.2	10.3	0.4	81.7	7,089,248	51.1	2.9	45.8	0.0	6,792,513	4,740
Freestone - 4			20.9	0.2	7.2	0.2	71.5							
Dew	RE	77	6.5	0.0	0.0	0.0	93.5	444,139	79.9	0.9	19.1	0.0	416,030	5,403
Fairfield	AA	1,583	22.9	0.3	6.3	0.4	70.1	8,575,614	83.1	2.4	14.3	0.1	8,910,519	5,629
Teague	AA	1,170	18.3	0.1	10.5	0.1	71.0	5,600,509	91.8	2.4	5.5	0.0	5,111,214	4,369
Wortham	AA	373	23.3	0.0	1.9	0.0	74.8	2,374,884	21.6	0.9	77.3	0.0	2,386,178	6,397
Frio - 2			0.2	0.1	85.3	0.0	14.4							
Dilley	AA	955	0.1	0.0	83.2	0.0	16.7	5,577,183	22.6	3.5	73.6	0.1	5,195,811	5,441
Pearsall	AA	2,369	0.2	0.1	86.2	0.0	13.5	12,866,222	26.1	3.3	70.3	0.2	12,452,148	5,256
Gaines - 3			3.7	0.1	46.3	0.0	49.9							
Loop	AA	156	0.0	0.0	52.6	0.0	47.4	2,827,375	73.8	18.6	5.6	1.8	1,818,158	11,655
Seagraves	AA	734	8.7	0.0	63.9	0.1	27.2	7,908,624	16.8	44.8	38.2	0.0	6,103,646	8,316
Seminole	AA	2,391	0.4	0.1	40.5	0.0	57.0	14,861,541	55.0	35.7	9.1	0.0	14,108,079	5,900
Galveston - 9			17.0	4.4	15.6	0.2	62.8							
Clear Creek	AA	26,563	6.6	7.9	10.6	0.3	74.6	118,033,193	86.0	3.1	10.7	0.0	109,087,494	4,107
Dickinson	AA	5,898	12.8	4.1	22.1	0.2	60.8	32,368,065	58.0	1.6	40.3	0.0	27,940,396	4,737
Friendswood	EX	4,306	1.1	2.5	4.5	0.2	91.8	22,101,063	60.3	3.1	36.5	0.0	19,942,011	4,631
Galveston	AA	9,910	38.6	2.5	29.7	0.2	29.1	51,323,277	61.3	2.5	35.7	0.4	51,192,470	5,166
High Island	AA	303	1.0	0.0	4.9	0.0	94.1	1,954,657	43.2	4.2	52.5	0.0	1,928,294	6,364
Hitchcock	AA	1,352	40.6	0.5	18.2	0.3	40.4	9,650,977	32.4	1.9	65.6	0.0	8,396,566	6,210
La Marque	AA	4,435	61.5	0.6	9.5	0.0	28.3	25,541,430	82.2	0.9	16.7	0.0	22,957,247	5,176
Santa Fe	AA	4,349	0.1	0.2	10.4	0.1	89.1	19,473,471	26.9	2.4	70.4	0.0	18,079,765	4,157
Texas City	AA	5,906	17.9	0.9	23.9	0.3	57.0	35,885,055	89.0	1.8	8.8	0.2	31,994,459	5,417
Garza - 2			8.0	0.1	44.1	0.0	47.8							
Post	AA	1,018	8.9	0.1	41.9	0.0	49.1	5,633,880	73.3	3.5	23.1	0.0	5,498,339	5,401
Southland	AA	176	2.8	0.0	56.8	0.0	40.3	1,202,186	36.6	3.8	59.4	0.0	1,245,416	7,076
Gillespie - 3			0.6	0.5	28.0	0.2	70.8							
Doss Cons. *	RE	19	0.0	0.0	15.8	0.0	84.2	142,918	91.9	3.5	4.5	0.0	144,878	7,625
Fredericksburg	AA	2,790	0.6	0.5	30.3	0.2	68.4	14,244,780	65.0	4.9	30.0	0.0	12,400,679	4,445
Harper	AA	335	0.9	0.0	9.5	0.0	89.6	2,248,918	52.9	2.1	44.9	0.0	1,922,833	5,740

County/Dist.	District Rating	Number of Students	Ethnicity of Student Population					Total Revenue	Sources of Revenue				Total Spending	Spending Per Student
			% Black	% Asian	% Hispanic	% Amer. Ind.	% White		% Local	% Other	% State	% Federal		
Glasscock - 1			0.0	0.0	34.4	0.0	65.6							
Glasscock County	AA	406	0.0	0.0	34.4	0.0	65.6	3,426,706	90.0	3.8	6.1	0.0	3,137,006	7,727
Goliad-1			5.7	0.1	39.7	0.1	54.4							
Goliad	AA	1,437	5.7	0.1	39.7	0.1	54.4	7,560,916	72.3	2.6	25.0	0.0	7,326,885	5,099
Gonzales - 3			11.5	0.2	49.7	0.0	38.6							
Gonzales	AA	2,648	13.7	0.3	44.6	0.0	41.4	12,532,710	29.0	3.1	67.7	0.0	12,454,963	4,704
Nixon-Smiley Cons.	AA	997	1.9	0.0	58.9	0.0	39.2	5,345,166	21.9	1.4	76.5	0.0	5,106,976	5,122
Waelder	AA	257	26.1	0.0	66.5	0.0	7.4	1,838,005	25.8	1.3	72.8	0.0	1,712,827	6,665
Gray - 4			4.5	0.8	15.3	1.1	78.2							
Grandview-Hopkins	EX	31	3.2	0.0	6.5	0.0	90.3	304,826	91.7	5.6	2.5	0.0	351,007	11,323
Lefors	RE	130	0.8	0.0	3.8	0.8	94.6	989,522	93.4	2.6	3.9	0.0	1,029,291	7,918
McLean	AA	214	2.3	0.0	7.0	0.9	89.7	1,495,890	69.4	3.1	27.4	0.0	1,458,150	6,814
Pampa	RE	3,990	4.7	0.9	16.2	1.2	77.0	19,237,388	59.6	4.3	35.8	0.1	18,559,658	4,652
Grayson - 13			9.0	0.5	5.3	1.0	84.1							
Bells	RE	764	0.4	0.0	1.0	0.1	98.4	4,314,226	12.5	0.9	86.4	0.0	3,570,139	4,673
Collinsville	RE	456	0.0	0.0	7.7	0.7	91.7	2,607,545	15.8	2.1	82.0	0.0	2,221,386	4,871
Denison	AA	4,632	11.1	0.5	3.6	1.6	83.2	24,051,601	38.2	1.5	60.1	0.0	22,097,269	4,771
Gunter	RE	476	0.2	0.2	20.8	0.8	77.9	4,794,343	9.3	4.2	86.4	0.0	3,829,921	8,046
Howe	AA	928	0.0	0.3	3.6	1.5	94.6	5,185,009	14.9	4.2	80.8	0.0	4,570,259	4,925
Pottsboro	RE	1,226	0.1	0.3	0.6	0.6	98.5	6,288,600	42.5	4.2	52.9	0.3	5,514,598	4,498
S and S Cons.	RE	807	0.2	0.4	1.4	1.2	96.8	4,883,185	31.4	7.7	60.7	0.0	4,130,245	5,118
Sherman	AA	5,964	18.2	0.8	8.6	0.9	71.5	33,999,617	60.1	3.0	36.8	0.0	27,625,344	4,632
Tioga	RE	137	0.7	0.0	12.4	0.7	86.1	874,100	25.5	0.9	70.9	2.5	787,136	5,746
Tom Bean	RE	752	0.7	0.8	0.5	1.3	96.7	4,004,884	12.9	2.7	84.3	0.0	3,506,419	4,663
Van Alstyne	RE	873	2.7	0.5	5.4	0.5	91.0	4,507,974	20.7	1.6	77.6	0.0	4,057,479	4,648
Whitesboro	RE	1,347	0.3	0.3	2.8	0.9	95.6	6,485,114	31.7	1.6	65.3	1.2	5,606,665	4,162
Whitewright	RE	630	13.2	0.0	4.1	0.2	82.5	3,725,372	18.3	2.1	79.4	0.0	3,040,548	4,826
Gregg - 7			25.4	0.7	6.8	0.2	66.9							
Gladewater	AA	2,120	20.0	0.2	3.2	0.1	76.5	11,759,167	48.0	2.4	49.5	0.0	10,321,009	4,868
Kilgore	AA	3,637	21.1	0.3	5.6	0.2	72.8	16,898,172	43.8	3.4	52.6	0.0	15,025,290	4,131
Longview	AA	8,261	50.7	0.8	8.6	0.1	39.9	42,757,695	63.5	2.1	34.1	0.1	39,426,777	4,773
Pine Tree	AA	5,030	6.3	1.6	9.5	0.3	82.4	23,831,600	79.3	2.3	18.2	0.0	21,688,582	4,312
Sabine	RE	1,324	12.0	0.6	2.7	0.5	84.2	6,842,364	32.4	2.6	64.8	0.0	6,616,640	4,997
Spring Hill	RE	1,605	2.3	0.2	4.5	0.1	92.8	6,678,116	55.7	2.7	41.4	0.0	6,563,160	4,089
White Oak	AA	1,385	3.2	0.2	1.4	0.8	94.5	6,127,239	85.2	4.0	10.6	0.0	6,414,567	4,631
Grimes - 4			25.2	0.1	20.4	0.2	54.1							
Anderson-Shiro Cons.	AA	525	19.8	0.0	7.2	1.3	71.7	2,809,734	44.3	6.7	48.9	0.0	2,541,016	4,840
Iola	AA	450	3.3	0.0	12.2	0.2	84.3	2,536,599	18.2	10.3	71.4	0.0	2,187,971	4,862
Navasota	AA	3,036	29.1	0.1	24.6	0.1	46.2	16,260,967	31.5	3.0	65.4	0.0	14,744,394	4,857
Richards	AA	117	32.5	0.0	4.3	0.0	63.2	1,019,076	47.4	5.3	47.2	0.0	996,063	8,513
Guadalupe - 4			6.2	0.8	39.0	0.1	53.9							
Marion	AA	1,092	2.2	0.7	22.9	0.0	74.2	6,454,562	19.1	0.7	80.1	0.0	5,227,679	4,787
Navarro	AA	777	1.5	0.5	33.8	0.3	63.9	4,537,744	47.0	1.3	51.6	0.0	3,961,168	5,098
Schertz-Cibolo-Univ. City	AA	4,831	4.9	1.2	23.8	0.2	69.9	24,525,935	30.9	3.4	64.8	0.8	21,902,805	4,534
Seguin	AA	7,192	8.2	0.6	52.1	0.1	38.9	40,596,315	34.0	1.5	64.2	0.1	35,558,652	4,944
Hale - 5			5.9	0.2	59.8	0.3	33.9							
Abernathy	AA	884	3.4	0.0	50.1	0.2	46.3	5,274,349	41.2	0.5	58.0	0.0	5,281,484	5,975
Cotton Center	AA	186	0.0	0.5	50.5	0.5	48.4	1,130,714	46.5	5.7	47.4	0.2	1,098,685	5,907
Hale Center	AA	756	5.2	0.0	66.7	0.1	28.0	3,916,062	20.6	1.7	77.3	0.2	3,728,530	4,932
Petersburg	AA	435	2.1	0.0	66.2	0.5	31.3	2,647,710	23.2	0.5	76.2	0.0	2,754,266	6,332
Plainview	AA	6,265	6.8	0.3	60.1	0.3	32.6	29,635,528	34.0	2.4	63.3	0.1	29,151,544	4,653
Hall - 3			11.1	0.1	44.5	0.0	44.3							
Lakeview	AA	74	0.0	0.0	85.5	0.0	14.5	632,421	35.0	1.6	63.3	0.0	620,526	8,385
Memphis	AA	544	16.9	0.2	38.2	0.0	44.8	3,165,885	31.7	1.5	66.7	0.0	3,207,745	5,897
Turkey-Quitaque	AA	287	3.4	0.0	45.6	0.0	51.0	1,648,511	22.8	2.8	74.2	0.0	1,679,168	5,851
Hamilton - 2			0.1	0.3	10.4	0.1	89.3							
Hamilton	AA	927	0.1	0.4	6.3	0.0	93.1	6,199,560	31.2	2.5	66.2	0.0	5,388,472	5,813
Hico	AA	603	0.0	0.0	16.6	0.0	83.4	1,482,530	58.9	5.7	35.1	0.1	2,979,124	4,941
Hansford - 3			0.1	0.0	36.5	0.0	63.3							
Gruver	RE	467	0.2	0.0	37.8	0.0	62.0	3,327,957	86.0	5.8	8.1	0.0	3,232,881	6,923
Pringle-Morse Cons.	AA	85	0.0	0.0	34.1	0.0	65.9	1,150,320	93.6	4.1	2.2	0.0	878,543	10,336
Spearman	RE	804	0.1	0.0	36.1	0.0	63.8	4,404,986	75.5	2.6	21.6	0.0	4,129,401	5,136
Hardeman - 2			7.7	0.1	22.9	0.3	69.0							
Chillicothe	AA	318	8.6	0.3	27.6	0.6	62.9	1,730,223	66.7	1.2	31.9	0.1	1,568,923	4,934
Quanah	AA	767	7.3	0.0	20.9	0.0	71.7	5,588,700	35.5	2.1	62.2	0.0	5,420,004	7,066
Hardin - 5			11.8	0.2	1.5	0.0	86.5							
Hardin-Jefferson	AA	2,366	13.7	0.1	2.5	0.0	83.8	10,989,918	35.7	2.7	61.4	0.0	10,336,800	4,369
Kountze	AA	1,328	16.3	0.0	1.2	0.0	82.3	6,905,553	23.2	1.2	75.3	0.1	5,791,686	4,361

County/Dist.	District Rating	Number of Students	Ethnicity of Student Population					Total Revenue	Sources of Revenue				Total Spending	Spending Per Student
			% Black	% Asian	% Hispanic	% Amer. Ind.	% White		% Local	% Other	% State	% Federal		
Lumberton	AA	3,120	0.1	0.3	1.4	0.1	98.1	13,685,813	21.5	1.8	75.8	0.7	12,635,782	4,050
Silsbee	AA	3,639	21.1	0.2	1.1	0.0	77.5	17,249,948	25.6	2.1	72.1	0.0	18,817,082	5,171
W. Hardin County Cons.	AA	694	0.1	0.0	0.7	0.0	99.1	3,636,676	31.4	0.8	67.7	0.0	3,537,145	5,097
Harris - 20			23.6	4.7	35.5	0.1	36.1							
Aldine	AA	45,139	35.3	4.0	40.4	0.1	20.2	236,414,260	35.9	1.9	62.0	0.0	228,486,806	5,062
Alief	AA	36,587	32.6	19.2	27.6	0.1	20.4	192,419,439	36.6	1.0	62.0	0.2	170,373,262	4,657
Channelview	AA	5,698	10.2	2.0	32.7	0.1	55.0	31,103,485	53.8	1.5	44.5	0.0	27,214,401	4,776
Crosby	AA	3,791	24.8	0.5	8.6	0.3	65.7	19,550,900	43.7	1.1	55.1	0.0	18,125,396	4,781
Cypress-Fairbanks	AA	50,817	8.9	7.3	16.4	0.2	67.3	261,520,159	59.9	1.8	38.2	0.0	234,348,319	4,612
Deer Park	AA	11,352	1.1	1.8	20.9	0.3	76.1	66,811,835	87.4	3.9	8.7	0.0	58,025,491	5,111
Galena Park	AA	17,439	19.9	2.4	50.0	0.1	27.6	85,163,057	43.5	1.4	54.9	0.0	78,210,217	4,485
Goose Creek	AA	17,876	17.0	0.8	34.0	0.2	48.1	101,559,522	82.2	3.5	14.0	0.1	88,474,471	4,949
Houston	AA	206,704	34.9	2.7	50.8	0.1	11.5	1,055,989,182	62.5	2.2	33.5	1.6	1,061,961,746	5,138
Huffman	AA	2,230	0.0	0.4	4.6	0.3	94.7	11,998,780	28.3	0.5	71.1	0.0	11,214,311	5,029
Humble	AA	22,159	7.6	2.6	9.0	0.2	80.7	122,479,731	52.7	1.7	45.4	0.0	106,301,781	4,797
Katy	AA	25,231	4.7	4.0	11.5	0.1	79.7	135,492,711	60.0	3.4	36.5	0.0	110,895,520	4,395
Klein	AA	29,324	11.4	6.8	12.8	0.3	68.7	156,899,058	44.4	1.3	54.1	0.0	138,747,803	4,732
La Porte	AA	7,444	8.3	1.2	18.8	0.3	71.3	42,642,274	91.7	2.1	6.0	0.0	37,263,386	5,006
North Forest	AA	13,450	85.6	0.1	13.2	0.0	1.1	70,741,853	13.4	0.6	85.8	0.1	65,278,788	4,853
Pasadena	AA	40,053	5.4	3.6	51.3	0.3	39.5	191,693,368	39.2	4.5	56.1	0.0	179,628,086	4,485
Sheldon	AA	3,917	22.5	1.4	22.7	0.1	53.3	22,501,260	89.9	2.6	7.4	0.0	19,535,119	4,987
Spring	AA	20,246	19.8	5.7	18.0	0.3	56.1	110,743,537	52.2	1.9	45.8	0.0	99,478,387	4,913
Spring Branch	AA	29,543	7.4	8.1	43.1	0.1	41.4	173,472,664	86.4	3.6	9.6	0.2	155,566,173	5,266
Tomball	AA	5,862	3.6	0.9	8.0	0.2	87.4	32,245,001	86.3	3.1	10.4	0.0	28,488,705	4,860
Harrison - 6			31.1	0.2	4.1	0.2	64.4							
Elysian Fields	AA	1,007	22.3	0.5	2.8	0.1	74.3	4,609,712	54.9	2.7	42.3	0.0	4,614,067	4,582
Hallsville	AA	3,557	6.1	0.2	2.2	0.4	91.1	17,815,784	98.2	1.7	0.0	0.0	15,386,086	4,326
Harleton	RE	535	9.3	0.0	0.0	0.2	90.5	3,228,593	29.6	5.2	65.1	0.0	2,948,738	5,512
Karnack	AA	435	63.0	0.0	1.8	0.0	35.2	3,001,265	33.4	1.0	65.5	0.0	2,589,745	5,953
Marshall	AA	6,299	46.8	0.3	5.6	0.1	47.2	26,356,676	57.4	4.2	38.1	0.0	27,251,196	4,326
Waskom	AA	819	26.4	0.1	5.9	0.1	67.5	4,315,745	46.9	1.6	51.4	0.0	3,907,805	4,771
Hartley - 2			0.7	0.0	12.2	0.0	87.2							
Channing	RE	124	0.0	0.0	14.5	0.0	85.5	1,017,668	86.8	8.5	4.6	0.0	1,088,638	8,779
Hartley	AA	172	1.2	0.0	10.5	0.0	88.4	1,200,675	58.4	2.3	39.2	0.0	1,084,692	6,306
Haskell - 4			5.2	0.3	30.2	0.2	64.0							
Haskell	AA	749	6.4	0.5	33.5	0.4	59.2	4,485,587	22.8	2.8	74.3	0.0	4,221,334	5,636
Paint Creek	AA	132	0.0	0.0	9.1	0.0	90.9	980,930	48.9	3.3	47.6	0.0	962,323	7,290
Rochester	RE	169	8.3	0.0	36.7	0.0	55.0	1,179,375	27.1	12.1	60.7	0.0	1,089,793	6,448
Rule	RE	185	1.1	0.0	26.3	0.0	72.6	1,376,917	33.1	9.4	57.3	0.0	1,209,128	6,536
Hays - 4			2.8	0.4	40.8	0.3	55.8							
Dripping Springs	RE	2,432	0.7	0.2	8.5	0.6	90.1	13,363,279	48.3	2.4	49.1	0.0	10,415,192	4,283
Hays Cons.	AA	5,444	2.3	0.3	39.0	0.1	58.2	31,246,208	21.1	0.7	77.7	0.0	27,480,298	5,048
San Marcos Cons.	AA	6,649	4.3	0.6	61.7	0.2	33.3	36,760,331	42.0	2.9	54.5	0.4	33,685,677	5,066
Wimberley	RE	1,401	1.1	0.3	4.6	0.6	93.4	8,244,030	66.8	1.4	31.7	0.0	6,731,284	4,805
Hemphill - 1			3.1	0.1	24.1	0.2	72.5							
Canadian	RE	878	3.1	0.1	24.1	0.2	72.5	5,903,802	93.8	1.5	4.6	0.0	5,790,471	6,595
Henderson - 8			12.0	0.3	7.6	0.2	79.9							
Athens	AA	3,448	18.1	0.3	14.8	0.1	66.7	16,552,928	43.0	2.4	54.4	0.0	14,438,315	4,187
Brownsboro	RE	2,316	9.4	0.2	4.4	0.2	85.8	12,170,977	33.0	2.9	64.0	0.0	11,448,411	4,943
Cross Roads	RE	596	0.7	0.8	1.8	0.7	96.0	3,237,809	42.0	1.7	56.2	0.0	2,716,836	4,558
Eustace	AA	1,314	1.7	0.3	2.7	0.3	95.0	7,992,936	38.0	2.5	59.4	0.0	5,376,083	4,091
LaPoynor	AA	460	12.6	0.0	2.2	0.0	85.2	2,563,967	90.3	5.3	4.2	0.0	2,498,953	5,433
Malakoff	AA	1,140	16.1	0.7	4.5	0.5	78.2	5,710,785	68.8	1.9	29.1	0.0	5,246,893	4,603
Murchison	RE	131	0.0	0.0	0.8	0.0	99.2	876,585	38.5	0.0	61.4	0.0	786,335	6,003
Trinidad	AA	286	17.5	0.0	4.5	0.0	78.0	1,642,205	28.0	1.6	70.4	0.0	1,519,067	5,311
Hidalgo - 15			0.1	0.3	94.9	0.0	4.6							
Donna	AA	9,391	0.1	0.0	98.2	0.1	1.6	52,337,837	7.5	2.1	83.4	6.9	48,114,282	5,123
Edcouch-Elsa	AA	4,464	0.1	0.0	98.9	0.1	0.9	25,196,351	4.3	1.2	88.0	6.4	22,690,347	5,083
Edinburg Cons.	AA	18,710	0.1	0.2	95.0	0.1	4.5	103,052,693	19.1	2.2	78.3	0.3	92,367,407	4,937
Hidalgo	AA	2,571	0.0	0.0	99.3	0.0	0.7	14,649,978	11.0	1.8	79.9	7.2	13,981,607	5,438
La Joya	AA	13,545	0.0	0.0	99.3	0.0	0.6	78,651,427	10.3	1.6	88.0	0.0	64,191,647	4,739
La Villa	RE	747	0.0	0.0	99.3	0.1	0.5	6,349,376	7.1	1.1	91.6	0.1	4,780,833	6,400
McAllen	AA	21,830	0.4	1.4	86.7	0.1	11.5	121,523,686	30.0	2.5	67.2	0.1	108,617,392	4,976
Mercedes	AA	5,103	0.1	0.0	98.2	0.0	1.6	27,766,326	8.0	2.0	89.4	0.4	26,092,010	5,113
Mission Cons.	AA	11,746	0.1	0.1	95.7	0.0	4.1	65,829,340	10.2	1.8	87.7	0.1	59,431,119	5,060
Monte Alto	AA	467	0.0	0.0	97.9	0.0	2.1	3,723,011	10.3	1.4	87.5	0.6	3,397,327	7,275
Pharr-San Juan-Alamo	AA	20,299	0.1	0.1	98.1	0.0	1.8	118,139,479	9.9	0.8	89.0	0.1	106,254,087	5,234
Progreso	AA	1,788	0.0	0.0	99.4	0.2	0.3	12,866,584	3.9	1.4	88.8	5.8	9,582,599	5,359

County/Dist.	District Rating	Number of Students	Ethnicity of Student Population					Total Revenue	Sources of Revenue				Total Spending	Spending Per Student
			% Black	% Asian	% Hispanic	% Amer. Ind.	% White		% Local	% Other	% State	% Federal		
Sharyland	RE	4,298	0.1	0.5	77.3	0.1	22.0	22,155,859	20.5	2.5	76.8	0.0	19,030,195	4,428
Valley View	AA	1,711	0.0	0.0	99.9	0.0	0.1	9,908,745	9.0	0.2	90.6	0.1	8,188,285	4,786
Weslaco	AA	12,814	0.1	0.1	96.4	0.0	3.3	79,935,901	9.0	1.5	89.2	0.2	70,239,381	5,481
Hill - 12			12.0	0.1	14.9	0.2	72.9							
Abbott	RE	276	2.2	0.0	7.2	0.4	90.2	1,548,741	20.9	2.2	76.8	0.0	1,367,077	4,953
Aquilla	RE	149	4.0	0.0	4.7	0.0	91.3	1,086,946	30.9	2.4	66.3	0.2	894,050	6,000
Blum	AA	267	2.6	0.0	8.6	0.0	88.8	1,786,128	19.4	2.1	78.3	0.0	1,571,987	5,888
Bynum	RE	191	9.9	0.0	6.3	0.0	83.9	1,210,054	23.3	1.2	75.4	0.0	1,083,169	5,671
Covington	RE	303	0.3	0.0	8.8	0.3	90.5	2,027,790	7.0	1.9	91.0	0.0	1,280,779	4,227
Hillsboro	AA	1,636	19.7	0.1	27.2	0.1	52.9	10,053,066	40.1	1.6	58.1	0.0	9,248,665	5,653
Hubbard	AA	506	23.9	0.2	2.2	0.0	73.7	3,098,039	15.1	2.2	82.5	0.0	3,022,891	5,974
Itasca	AA	529	18.9	0.0	26.3	0.2	54.6	3,255,039	16.5	1.8	81.6	0.0	2,983,601	5,640
Malone	AA	61	24.6	0.0	14.8	0.0	60.7	461,200	26.7	4.2	68.7	0.1	437,470	7,172
Mount Calm	AA	82	13.3	0.0	10.8	0.0	75.9	941,946	30.2	0.2	69.4	0.0	900,929	10,987
Penelope	RE	136	0.0	0.0	12.5	0.0	87.5	758,323	19.6	1.1	79.2	0.0	753,809	5,543
Whitney	AA	1,369	3.8	0.2	7.2	0.3	88.5	6,704,750	29.4	1.3	69.1	0.1	5,180,041	3,784
Hockley - 6			5.0	0.1	46.5	0.2	48.3							
Anton	AA	375	5.6	0.0	50.9	0.0	43.5	2,112,974	22.4	4.1	73.3	0.0	2,218,412	5,916
Levelland	AA	3,596	6.4	0.1	46.7	0.2	46.7	22,370,134	63.7	5.0	31.2	0.0	21,421,863	5,957
Ropes	AA	353	2.0	0.0	54.4	0.3	43.3	2,645,205	28.4	11.8	59.5	0.1	2,028,644	5,747
Smyer	AA	393	2.0	0.0	30.0	0.0	67.9	2,192,578	33.5	1.4	65.0	0.0	1,749,139	4,451
Sundown	EX	579	0.9	0.0	49.4	1.0	48.7	5,374,608	88.4	6.1	5.3	0.0	5,185,436	8,956
Whitharral	AA	211	2.4	0.5	43.1	0.0	54.0	1,354,814	28.7	3.7	67.5	0.0	1,299,680	6,160
Hood - 3			0.5	0.5	7.5	0.6	90.9							
Granbury	AA	5,816	0.6	0.5	7.8	0.7	90.5	28,381,877	46.7	3.0	50.1	0.0	23,545,674	4,048
Lipan	AA	309	0.0	0.3	4.9	0.6	94.2	1,858,526	26.4	1.3	72.1	0.0	1,594,124	5,159
Tolar	AA	425	0.0	0.5	5.6	0.2	93.7	2,372,648	22.0	3.2	74.7	0.0	2,218,106	5,219
Hopkins - 7			10.4	0.5	8.1	0.1	80.9							
Como-Pickton	AA	692	5.3	0.1	18.6	0.6	75.3	3,524,434	23.5	1.7	74.7	0.0	2,695,646	3,895
Cumby	RE	254	0.4	1.2	7.5	0.4	90.6	1,475,769	24.6	1.3	73.9	0.0	1,204,357	4,742
Miller Grove	AA	213	0.0	0.0	7.0	0.5	92.5	1,134,220	30.0	0.8	69.1	0.0	1,051,549	4,937
North Hopkins	AA	380	3.2	1.1	2.1	0.0	93.7	2,035,028	22.6	1.5	75.8	0.0	1,740,066	4,579
Saltillo	AA	234	0.9	0.0	6.4	0.0	92.7	1,153,839	20.0	1.3	78.6	0.0	1,097,101	4,688
Sulphur Bluff	RE	226	0.9	0.4	10.6	0.0	88.1	1,228,827	25.0	1.7	73.2	0.0	1,196,008	5,292
Sulphur Springs	AA	3,909	14.4	0.5	6.8	0.1	78.2	18,624,998	44.6	3.1	52.2	0.0	17,970,315	4,597
Houston - 5			39.1	0.3	4.8	0.1	55.7							
Crockett	AA	1,934	59.5	0.2	7.2	0.1	33.0	9,358,842	29.1	4.9	65.0	0.9	9,064,405	4,687
Grapeland	AA	788	30.3	0.5	1.0	0.0	68.2	3,903,004	38.0	2.0	58.2	1.6	3,843,492	4,878
Kennard	AA	405	32.6	0.2	0.2	0.0	66.9	2,662,240	25.5	2.0	67.8	4.4	2,487,919	6,143
Latexo	RE	457	2.6	0.4	6.3	0.0	90.6	2,419,472	36.7	2.3	60.1	0.8	1,997,328	4,371
Lovelady	RE	509	13.4	0.2	3.3	0.2	82.9	3,058,963	34.8	1.6	59.0	4.3	2,585,313	5,079
Howard - 3			4.4	0.4	38.1	0.2	57.0							
Big Spring	AA	4,480	5.9	0.5	45.9	0.2	47.6	20,904,811	47.4	2.6	49.8	0.0	20,434,667	4,561
Coahoma	AA	975	0.1	0.1	21.1	0.4	78.3	5,788,236	41.0	1.5	57.3	0.0	5,328,632	5,465
Forsan	AA	685	0.1	0.0	11.5	0.0	88.3	3,759,075	78.6	2.0	19.2	0.0	3,547,117	5,178
Hudspeth - 3			0.4	0.0	80.5	0.4	18.8							
Dell City	AA	211	0.0	0.0	64.5	1.4	34.1	2,006,692	24.5	7.2	59.0	9.2	1,754,169	8,314
Fort Hancock	AA	470	0.6	0.0	93.4	0.0	6.0	3,005,285	28.3	1.9	69.7	0.0	2,572,681	5,474
Sierra Blanca	AA	144	0.0	0.0	62.5	0.0	37.5	2,633,599	43.5	2.2	52.7	1.5	2,389,802	16,596
Hunt - 10			14.5	0.6	7.5	0.4	77.0							
Bland	AA	433	0.0	0.7	4.8	0.0	94.5	2,371,554	15.5	1.5	82.9	0.0	2,028,482	4,685
Boles	AA	388	1.3	0.5	5.2	0.5	92.5	3,031,959	2.2	0.6	97.0	0.0	1,796,894	4,631
Caddo Mills	RE	810	4.8	0.0	2.3	0.4	92.5	4,012,774	20.4	6.6	72.8	0.0	3,518,720	4,344
Campbell	AA	330	0.6	0.3	3.6	0.0	95.5	2,487,751	17.0	0.3	82.6	0.0	2,004,711	6,075
Celeste	RE	445	2.5	0.2	2.2	0.4	94.6	2,687,029	14.0	4.7	81.1	0.0	2,527,626	5,680
Commerce	AA	1,681	23.6	1.9	4.3	0.3	69.9	9,589,798	27.7	1.4	70.7	0.0	8,676,341	5,161
Greenville	AA	5,372	26.2	0.8	12.0	0.1	60.9	26,461,226	43.1	2.0	54.6	0.0	24,456,534	4,553
Lone Oak	RE	644	1.9	0.2	4.3	1.1	92.5	4,040,000	12.8	3.8	83.2	0.0	3,057,911	4,748
Quinlan	AA	2,649	0.3	0.1	5.9	0.6	93.1	12,147,074	22.4	1.9	75.4	0.0	9,794,555	3,697
Wolfe City	RE	577	9.0	0.0	2.8	0.9	87.3	2,786,617	20.7	2.1	77.0	0.0	2,572,048	4,458
Hutchinson - 4			2.8	0.3	16.6	0.7	79.6							
Borger	AA	3,318	4.2	0.3	22.4	0.4	72.7	15,856,330	40.5	3.4	55.7	0.1	14,613,460	4,404
Plemons-Stin.-Phil. Cons.	AA	817	0.2	0.2	13.3	2.1	84.1	6,063,877	91.9	3.4	4.5	0.0	5,236,067	6,409
Sanford	AA	1,272	0.6	0.3	4.1	0.6	94.4	6,535,680	25.2	2.6	72.0	0.0	6,248,261	4,912
Spring Creek	EX	91	2.2	0.0	9.9	0.0	87.9	914,845	38.3	19.3	42.3	0.0	731,553	8,039
Irion - 1			0.5	0.0	28.4	0.0	71.1							
Irion County	AA	390	0.5	0.0	28.4	0.0	71.1	3,187,316	90.4	3.4	6.1	0.0	2,918,442	7,483

County/Dist.	District Ratings	Total Number of Students	Ethnicity of Student Population†					Total Revenue	Sources of Revenue				Total Spending	Spending Per Student
			% Black	% Asian	% Hispanic	% Amer. Indian	% White		% Local	% Other	% State	% Federal		
Jack - 3			0.9	0.4	8.6	0.1	89.9							
Bryson	RE	248	0.8	0.0	6.0	0.0	93.1	1,502,493	49.7	4.3	45.8	0.0	1,322,050	5,331
Jacksboro	AA	1,144	1.1	0.7	10.9	0.2	87.1	5,973,778	49.4	3.2	47.3	0.0	5,855,266	5,118
Perrin-Whitt Cons.	AA	406	0.2	0.0	3.9	0.0	95.8	2,572,505	34.0	1.8	64.1	0.0	2,287,204	5,634
Jackson - 3			8.1	0.1	27.2	0.1	64.5							
Edna	AA	1,754	12.9	0.3	30.5	0.0	56.4	8,254,738	34.8	2.0	63.0	0.0	8,073,565	4,603
Ganado	RE	689	3.9	0.0	34.1	0.3	61.7	3,511,000	29.5	1.3	69.1	0.0	3,267,833	4,743
Industrial	AA	911	2.0	0.0	15.7	0.0	82.3	8,200,086	37.4	9.5	52.9	0.0	5,654,725	6,207
Jasper - 5			24.7	0.2	3.1	0.2	71.9							
Brookeland	AA	308	14.9	0.3	0.6	0.0	84.1	2,182,093	70.4	12.7	13.7	3.0	1,791,593	5,817
Buna	AA	1,697	4.9	0.1	1.2	0.4	93.5	9,321,696	23.6	4.8	71.4	0.0	7,959,246	4,690
Evadale	AA	415	0.0	0.0	0.0	0.0	100.0	4,378,887	92.9	4.4	2.6	0.0	3,084,087	7,432
Jasper	AA	3,540	41.7	0.3	4.9	0.1	53.0	19,817,479	24.9	4.4	70.4	0.0	17,945,490	5,069
Kirbyville	AA	1,593	16.5	0.0	2.2	0.2	81.2	7,835,368	18.4	1.2	80.2	0.0	7,075,454	4,442
Jeff Davis - 2			3.4	0.0	37.7	2.5	56.4							
Fort Davis	AA	340	4.1	0.0	35.6	2.9	57.4	2,267,799	37.1	2.9	59.9	0.0	2,101,711	6,182
Valentine	RE	68	0.0	0.0	48.5	0.0	51.5	646,725	31.7	0.0	68.2	0.0	669,342	9,843
Jefferson - 6			44.7	4.0	7.5	0.1	43.7							
Beaumont	AA	19,938	64.7	2.5	5.8	0.2	26.9	110,905,274	81.4	1.6	16.9	0.0	101,871,248	5,109
Hamshire-Fannett	AA	2,067	6.5	0.7	4.5	0.1	88.2	10,074,494	44.5	6.5	48.8	0.0	9,147,394	4,425
Nederland	RE	5,381	1.2	2.2	3.9	0.0	92.6	24,646,309	50.3	1.6	47.9	0.0	24,217,284	4,501
Port Arthur	AA	11,719	58.3	9.2	13.8	0.1	18.5	61,126,240	63.7	2.1	34.0	0.0	61,698,453	5,265
Port Neches-Groves	AA	5,414	0.4	1.3	5.0	0.1	93.2	26,344,803	77.1	2.0	20.8	0.0	25,747,459	4,756
Sabine Pass	AA	187	5.9	1.1	0.5	0.0	92.5	1,184,887	96.4	1.0	2.4	0.0	1,783,398	9,537
Jim Hogg - 1			0.1	0.0	94.9	0.2	4.8							
Jim Hogg County	AA	1,300	0.1	0.0	94.9	0.2	4.8	8,080,762	38.2	1.6	60.1	0.0	7,209,384	5,546
Jim Wells - 5			0.5	0.3	79.9	0.1	19.2							
Alice	AA	5,959	0.7	0.4	82.2	0.1	16.7	33,193,730	19.1	1.8	78.7	0.2	29,870,059	5,013
Ben Bolt-Palito Blanco	AA	526	0.0	0.2	93.0	0.0	6.8	3,296,227	21.5	13.9	64.4	0.0	2,839,641	5,399
La Gloria	RE	85	0.0	0.0	71.8	0.0	28.2	601,122	76.0	0.8	23.1	0.0	605,744	7,126
Orange Grove	AA	1,336	0.3	0.0	59.6	0.1	40.0	6,851,272	12.8	1.6	85.5	0.0	6,227,271	4,661
Premont	AA	1,019	0.0	0.2	87.3	0.0	12.5	5,664,170	31.9	1.2	66.7	0.0	5,248,049	5,150
Johnson - 9			3.1	0.8	10.9	0.3	84.9							
Alvarado	RE	2,637	4.6	0.1	11.5	0.6	83.2	12,213,303	22.1	4.1	73.3	0.3	10,455,067	3,965
Burleson	RE	5,853	0.7	0.5	4.6	0.2	94.0	26,717,232	43.6	1.6	54.6	0.1	23,896,258	4,083
Cleburne	AA	5,720	6.0	0.6	17.6	0.3	75.5	26,989,544	37.2	5.9	56.7	0.0	23,327,031	4,078
Godley	RE	795	0.6	0.1	7.4	0.6	91.2	4,169,589	17.2	2.1	80.6	0.0	3,772,759	4,746
Grandview	AA	923	4.4	0.0	8.0	0.1	87.4	6,156,282	17.8	1.9	80.2	0.0	5,228,663	5,665
Joshua	AA	3,614	0.6	0.2	6.8	0.2	92.2	17,783,210	24.6	2.1	72.8	0.4	16,259,160	4,499
Keene	AA	714	16.5	4.3	28.6	0.3	50.3	5,160,671	14.4	0.8	84.6	0.0	4,398,500	6,160
Rio Vista	AA	816	0.1	0.0	4.0	0.0	95.8	5,385,261	11.8	2.3	85.8	0.0	4,147,849	5,083
Venus	AA	1,090	0.3	5.5	20.3	0.6	73.2	6,754,978	7.3	1.2	91.3	0.0	5,475,152	5,023
Jones - 5			6.1	0.2	23.3	0.1	70.3							
Anson	RE	803	1.9	0.0	35.6	0.0	62.5	4,771,611	22.2	3.1	74.6	0.0	4,387,355	5,464
Hamlin	AA	659	10.9	0.6	23.1	0.2	65.3	4,347,738	22.4	3.4	74.0	0.0	3,764,749	5,713
Hawley	AA	806	0.4	0.2	5.7	0.0	93.7	4,082,651	16.0	2.1	81.8	0.0	3,780,896	4,691
Lueders-Avoca	AA	168	0.0	0.0	6.5	0.6	92.9	1,326,415	27.2	10.3	62.4	0.0	1,223,556	7,283
Stamford	AA	842	12.9	0.0	31.9	0.2	54.9	6,193,940	16.6	10.0	73.3	0.0	5,733,305	6,809
Karnes - 4			2.9	0.2	60.9	0.0	36.0							
Falls City	RE	337	0.0	0.0	14.2	0.0	85.8	1,906,280	29.4	2.1	68.4	0.0	1,666,730	4,946
Karnes City	AA	1,106	4.3	0.0	57.3	0.0	38.4	6,081,388	33.4	1.6	64.7	0.1	5,340,016	4,828
Kenedy	AA	1,170	2.7	0.5	73.4	0.0	23.3	7,892,629	15.2	2.7	81.5	0.3	6,835,221	5,842
Runge	AA	314	1.3	0.0	77.4	0.3	21.0	2,192,571	24.0	2.6	73.1	0.2	2,032,652	6,473
Kaufman - 7			13.0	0.4	9.4	0.2	76.9							
Crandall	RE	1,469	5.8	0.1	4.6	0.1	89.5	7,510,346	22.0	2.7	75.1	0.0	6,834,713	4,653
Forney	RE	2,013	5.2	0.5	5.5	0.2	88.5	10,908,123	31.2	2.1	66.5	0.0	9,044,673	4,493
Kaufman	AA	2,889	9.3	0.2	20.2	0.1	70.2	13,001,294	25.9	2.3	71.6	0.0	11,141,617	3,857
Kemp	AA	1,608	3.7	0.2	4.8	0.5	90.8	9,333,294	17.3	1.7	80.1	0.8	8,209,127	5,105
Mabank	AA	2,773	2.5	0.2	3.7	0.4	93.1	13,677,102	38.0	1.8	60.0	0.0	12,095,951	4,362
Scurry-Rosser	AA	711	5.8	0.0	4.1	0.3	89.9	4,122,742	16.9	1.7	81.3	0.0	3,766,957	5,298
Terrell	AA	3,839	35.5	1.1	12.3	0.1	50.9	21,134,096	34.0	2.7	62.6	0.5	18,626,383	4,852
Kendall - 2			0.6	0.3	22.0	0.1	77.1							
Boerne	AA	3,947	0.5	0.3	17.3	0.1	81.7	18,575,922	59.4	2.1	38.2	0.1	15,936,500	4,038
Comfort	AU	916	0.7	0.1	42.0	0.0	57.2	5,590,534	32.4	1.1	66.3	0.0	5,168,270	5,642
Kenedy - 1			0.0	0.0	94.0	0.0	6.0							
Kenedy County Wide*	EX	50	0.0	0.0	94.0	0.0	6.0	654,228	92.4	2.3	5.2	0.0	962,803	19,256

County/Dist.	District Ratings	Total Number of Students	Ethnicity of Student Population†					Total Revenue	Sources of Revenue				Total Spending	Spending Per Student
			% Black	% Asian	% Hispanic	% Amer. Indian	% White		% Local	% Other	% State	% Federal		
Kent - 1			3.1	0.0	15.9	0.5	80.5							
Jayton-Girard	EX	195	3.1	0.0	15.9	0.5	80.5	2,299,118	85.2	9.6	5.0	0.0	2,201,028	11,287
Kerr - 5			2.8	0.6	28.2	0.3	68.1							
Center Point	AA	635	1.1	0.0	21.1	0.5	77.3	3,299,874	19.4	2.5	77.9	0.0	2,979,844	4,693
Divide	EX	16	0.0	0.0	15.0	20.0	65.0	98,041	87.3	6.2	6.4	0.0	125,491	7,843
Hunt	EX	142	0.0	0.7	29.6	0.7	69.0	1,087,848	94.3	2.6	3.0	0.0	1,033,956	7,281
Ingram	AA	1,239	1.3	0.2	16.2	0.3	81.9	7,459,910	28.5	4.4	66.7	0.1	7,295,257	5,888
Kerrville	AA	4,637	3.5	0.8	32.3	0.2	63.2	22,283,466	58.5	2.4	38.8	0.0	19,207,337	4,142
Kimble - 1			0.0	0.1	30.7	0.0	69.1							
Junction	AA	774	0.0	0.1	30.7	0.0	69.1	4,467,348	26.4	1.9	71.6	0.0	4,445,945	5,744
King - 1			0.0	0.0	14.8	0.0	85.2							
Guthrie*	EX	81	0.0	0.0	14.8	0.0	85.2	1,303,274	94.3	3.2	1.9	0.3	1,271,344	15,696
Kinney - 1			3.6	0.0	60.8	0.5	35.1							
Brackett	AA	615	3.6	0.0	60.8	0.5	35.1	4,424,625	25.5	2.6	71.6	0.1	3,841,876	6,247
Kleberg - 4			3.8	0.9	72.5	0.1	22.7							
Kingsville	AA	5,136	4.8	1.1	73.3	0.2	20.6	27,477,608	24.7	4.0	70.7	0.5	26,732,551	5,205
Ricardo	AA	648	0.3	0.0	75.0	0.0	24.7	3,837,092	19.4	2.7	77.8	0.0	3,364,905	5,193
Riviera	AA	625	0.2	0.0	64.6	0.2	35.0	3,861,566	57.5	8.0	34.3	0.0	3,871,320	6,194
Santa Gertrudis	AA	217	0.0	0.0	69.6	0.0	30.4	2,449,624	93.2	1.2	5.5	0.0	2,399,918	11,060
Knox - 4			9.0	0.3	38.7	0.1	51.9							
Benjamin	RE	104	0.0	0.0	22.2	0.0	77.8	1,012,397	26.2	20.7	53.0	0.0	863,621	8,304
Goree	AA	80	11.3	0.0	65.0	0.0	23.8	782,922	24.0	60.3	15.7	0.0	837,528	10,469
Knox City-O'Brien	AA	396	7.8	0.8	40.2	0.3	51.0	3,229,723	24.0	6.4	69.4	0.1	3,111,871	7,858
Munday	AA	460	11.7	0.0	36.7	0.0	51.5	2,505,105	12.6	1.2	86.1	0.0	2,537,917	5,517
Lamar - 5			20.8	0.4	1.5	1.1	76.3							
Chisum	AA	783	11.9	0.3	0.3	1.0	86.6	3,990,272	82.0	3.4	14.5	0.0	3,527,385	4,505
North Lamar	AA	2,937	5.1	0.2	0.8	1.2	92.7	14,551,756	41.2	1.2	57.4	0.0	12,240,333	4,168
Paris	AA	3,860	39.0	0.6	2.2	1.1	57.1	20,655,031	36.1	2.5	61.2	0.0	19,537,592	5,062
Prairiland	AA	990	1.2	0.1	1.2	1.0	96.5	5,013,384	22.5	1.6	75.8	0.0	4,678,663	4,726
Roxton	AA	234	29.5	0.0	2.1	0.0	68.4	1,556,964	17.4	2.6	79.8	0.0	1,197,387	5,117
Lamb - 6			7.1	0.1	54.8	0.1	38.0							
Amherst	AA	202	16.8	0.0	35.6	0.0	47.5	1,169,723	32.9	1.5	65.5	0.0	1,485,474	7,354
Littlefield	AA	1,662	10.5	0.2	54.3	0.1	34.9	7,748,587	28.5	1.1	70.2	0.0	7,255,262	4,365
Olton	AA	835	1.2	0.0	69.1	0.0	29.7	4,473,842	28.6	1.8	69.2	0.2	4,757,471	5,698
Spade	AA	114	0.0	0.0	49.1	0.0	50.9	948,627	25.0	2.6	72.3	0.0	961,908	8,438
Springlake-Earth	RE	480	2.5	0.0	54.8	0.0	42.8	3,317,457	29.0	2.9	67.7	0.3	2,306,291	4,805
Sudan	AA	388	7.5	0.0	37.5	0.5	54.5	3,232,329	95.4	0.7	3.8	0.0	3,496,729	9,012
Lampasas - 2			4.0	0.6	17.2	0.5	77.6							
Lampasas	AA	3,159	3.9	0.7	15.8	0.6	79.0	16,297,580	27.2	1.5	71.1	0.0	13,201,269	4,179
Lometa	AA	325	5.5	0.0	30.5	0.0	64.0	1,656,510	19.3	3.0	77.3	0.2	1,619,471	4,983
La Salle - 1			0.7	0.1	85.4	0.0	13.7							
Cotulla	AA	1,388	0.7	0.1	85.4	0.0	13.7	8,202,075	24.7	6.2	68.8	0.1	7,527,873	5,424
Lavaca - 6			10.0	0.2	9.5	0.0	80.3							
Ezzell	EX	86	0.0	0.0	1.1	0.0	98.9	542,355	93.6	1.6	4.7	0.0	531,723	6,183
Hallettsville	AA	1,079	11.8	0.0	8.4	0.0	79.7	5,302,958	61.3	3.5	35.1	0.0	5,000,925	4,635
Moulton	RE	374	1.3	0.5	14.9	0.0	83.3	1,967,478	24.7	1.0	74.1	0.0	1,766,155	4,722
Shiner	AA	544	17.1	0.6	11.6	0.0	70.8	3,339,541	34.9	2.1	62.8	0.0	2,995,894	5,507
Sweet Home	AA	88	0.0	0.0	1.1	0.0	98.9	388,350	50.2	1.1	48.6	0.0	399,604	4,541
Vysehrad	EX	78	0.0	0.0	2.5	0.0	97.5	499,306	88.7	6.4	4.8	0.0	521,434	6,685
Lee - 3			15.7	0.2	22.4	0.1	61.6							
Dime Box	AA	240	19.6	0.0	21.7	0.0	58.8	1,388,080	56.1	2.1	41.4	0.2	1,617,801	6,741
Giddings	AA	1,753	15.8	0.1	30.4	0.1	53.6	10,775,954	50.8	4.3	44.7	0.0	9,334,245	5,325
Lexington	AA	904	14.6	0.3	6.7	0.3	78.0	4,833,900	23.4	2.8	73.7	0.0	4,469,788	4,944
Leon - 5			14.0	0.3	7.4	0.2	78.1							
Buffalo	AA	829	16.0	0.5	11.4	0.1	71.9	4,050,814	27.2	2.0	70.6	0.0	3,609,257	4,354
Centerville	AA	645	15.3	0.2	2.0	0.3	82.3	4,114,781	68.8	1.3	29.7	0.0	4,013,797	6,223
Leon	AA	695	4.0	0.4	11.1	0.1	84.3	4,375,801	87.1	2.6	10.1	0.0	3,823,930	5,502
Normangee	AA	501	8.9	0.0	4.0	0.6	86.5	2,634,922	59.7	1.7	38.5	0.0	2,352,700	4,696
Oakwood	RE	277	39.0	0.4	4.7	0.0	56.0	1,891,219	42.0	1.6	56.2	0.0	1,681,815	6,072
Liberty - 7			14.1	0.2	9.2	0.2	76.3							
Cleveland	AA	2,857	21.8	0.4	16.5	0.3	61.1	13,947,810	29.0	5.9	64.8	0.1	13,564,196	4,748
Dayton	AA	3,947	9.6	0.3	6.6	0.1	83.4	16,639,502	29.1	4.2	66.7	0.0	16,183,846	4,100
Devers	EX	130	21.5	0.0	20.0	0.0	58.5	1,323,425	90.5	6.7	2.5	0.1	1,159,181	8,917
Hardin	AA	1,216	4.4	0.2	6.5	0.2	88.7	6,644,926	26.4	1.3	72.2	0.0	6,235,398	5,128
Hull-Daisetta	AA	795	24.2	0.1	2.0	0.4	73.3	4,639,768	36.5	1.3	62.0	0.0	4,328,468	5,445
Liberty	AA	2,464	21.7	0.3	11.9	0.2	65.9	14,632,808	36.7	8.3	54.8	0.0	13,367,746	5,425
Tarkington	AA	1,570	1.5	0.0	3.1	0.2	95.2	6,900,286	29.6	2.8	67.3	0.1	6,118,940	3,897

County/Dist.	District Ratings	Total Number of Students	Ethnicity of Student Population†					Total Revenue	Sources of Revenue				Total Spending	Spending Per Student
			% Black	% Asian	% Hispanic	% Amer. Indian	% White		% Local	% Other	% State	% Federal		
Limestone - 3			26.5	0.1	12.7	0.3	60.4							
Coolidge	RE	246	37.0	0.0	22.4	0.0	40.7	2,230,727	10.4	64.2	25.3	0.0	2,506,170	10,188
Groesbeck	AA	1,674	17.1	0.2	10.3	0.3	72.2	10,260,519	91.4	3.9	4.4	0.0	8,458,419	5,053
Mexia	AA	2,228	32.4	0.1	13.5	0.3	53.7	12,209,051	19.2	1.5	79.1	0.0	11,620,325	5,216
Lipscomb - 4			0.1	0.5	24.6	0.8	73.9							
Booker	AA	428	0.2	0.9	40.0	1.2	57.6	3,020,205	45.7	5.3	48.8	0.0	2,346,494	5,482
Darrouzett	EX	38	0.0	0.0	2.6	0.0	97.4	762,981	90.0	5.0	4.8	0.0	724,603	19,069
Follett	RE	164	0.0	0.0	5.5	0.0	94.5	1,224,521	93.6	2.4	3.8	0.0	1,194,420	7,283
Higgins	AA	117	0.0	0.0	1.7	0.9	97.4	870,159	85.1	2.4	12.3	0.0	964,022	8,240
Live Oak - 2			0.2	0.2	47.6	0.1	51.8							
George West	AA	1,372	0.1	0.1	47.1	0.1	52.6	6,869,022	62.4	2.8	34.6	0.0	6,547,864	4,772
Three Rivers	AA	808	0.5	0.2	48.5	0.2	50.5	5,524,911	79.4	2.7	17.8	0.0	4,778,994	5,915
Llano - 1			0.3	0.1	9.2	0.1	90.4							
Llano	RE	1,457	0.3	0.1	9.2	0.1	90.4	8,600,245	87.1	3.7	9.1	0.0	7,789,752	5,346
Loving - 0			No School Districts in Loving County. See Winkler Co.											
Lubbock - 8			11.1	0.9	36.7	0.2	51.1							
Frenship	AA	5,323	5.6	1.0	22.5	0.1	70.8	26,594,533	21.6	1.8	75.7	0.7	22,212,232	4,173
Idalou	AA	850	0.9	0.5	48.4	0.0	50.2	4,754,347	26.7	1.4	71.7	0.0	4,076,463	4,796
Lubbock	AA	30,317	13.8	1.1	39.1	0.2	45.8	160,977,122	46.1	1.5	52.0	0.2	145,883,545	4,812
Lubbock-Cooper	AA	1,724	1.0	0.1	27.3	0.2	71.4	8,938,630	27.9	1.5	70.5	0.0	7,365,313	4,272
New Deal	AA	672	0.9	0.0	38.4	0.0	60.7	4,186,219	29.8	1.6	68.6	0.0	3,490,621	5,194
Roosevelt	AA	1,426	6.0	0.0	33.9	0.5	59.6	8,067,256	19.7	2.4	77.7	0.1	7,051,563	4,945
Shallowater	AA	1,112	0.7	0.0	27.0	0.0	72.3	5,903,832	12.8	1.5	85.6	0.0	5,125,357	4,609
Slaton	AA	1,623	9.5	0.3	50.9	0.0	39.4	10,600,386	28.3	3.1	68.2	0.3	10,855,036	6,688
Lynn - 4			3.4	0.2	55.6	0.0	40.7							
New Home	RE	209	0.5	0.0	53.6	0.0	45.9	1,200,660	43.1	1.6	55.2	0.0	1,405,655	6,726
O'Donnell	AA	432	1.4	0.0	65.5	0.0	33.1	3,622,344	20.2	12.6	63.3	3.7	2,829,336	6,549
Tahoka	AA	787	6.4	0.5	50.3	0.0	42.8	4,871,146	21.8	1.5	76.5	0.0	4,100,719	5,211
Wilson	AA	227	0.0	0.0	57.3	0.0	42.7	1,696,968	31.2	3.1	65.6	0.0	1,442,616	6,355
Madison - 2			22.1	0.3	13.4	0.3	64.0							
Madisonville Cons.	AU	1,935	25.1	0.3	14.9	0.2	59.5	9,099,527	32.1	1.6	66.1	0.0	9,188,162	4,748
North Zulch	AA	281	1.1	0.0	2.8	1.4	94.7	2,337,423	29.2	14.3	56.4	0.0	1,938,923	6,900
Marion - 1			45.5	0.1	0.8	0.1	53.5							
Jefferson	AA	1,670	45.5	0.1	0.8	0.1	53.5	9,202,731	34.1	2.7	62.7	0.3	8,245,084	4,937
Martin - 2			2.1	0.0	52.9	0.2	44.8							
Grady	AA	226	0.0	0.0	44.7	0.0	55.3	1,714,469	91.0	4.9	4.0	0.0	1,638,993	7,252
Stanton	AA	867	2.7	0.0	55.0	0.2	42.1	6,065,899	32.6	2.8	64.4	0.0	5,709,786	6,586
Mason - 1			0.4	0.1	30.4	0.1	68.9							
Mason	AU	689	0.4	0.1	30.4	0.1	68.9	4,590,326	36.8	2.1	61.0	0.0	4,024,892	5,842
Matagorda - 5			14.9	3.5	34.6	0.1	46.9							
Bay City	AA	4,827	19.3	0.9	34.9	0.1	44.8	23,120,337	44.5	2.5	52.8	0.0	21,660,729	4,487
Matagorda	RE	102	2.0	0.0	12.7	0.0	85.3	837,652	91.8	4.2	3.8	0.0	824,353	8,082
Palacios	AA	1,811	3.4	14.8	45.5	0.4	35.9	10,138,060	82.2	11.6	6.1	0.0	10,537,957	5,819
Tidehaven	AA	997	6.4	0.0	34.8	0.0	58.8	4,803,696	55.0	1.3	43.6	0.0	4,639,323	4,653
Van Vleck	AA	1,038	23.6	0.0	16.4	0.0	60.1	5,507,711	44.6	1.1	54.2	0.0	5,430,583	5,232
Maverick - 1			0.1	0.3	96.9	0.8	1.8							
Eagle Pass	AA	11,585	0.1	0.3	96.9	0.8	1.8	60,401,347	12.7	2.6	84.6	0.0	55,049,377	4,752
McCulloch - 3			2.1	0.1	33.9	0.2	63.7							
Brady	AA	1,491	2.6	0.1	35.3	0.1	61.9	8,673,960	24.3	2.7	72.8	0.1	8,021,141	5,380
Lohn	EX	109	0.0	0.0	33.0	0.0	67.0	763,842	24.5	3.0	72.4	0.0	805,048	7,386
Rochelle	AA	228	0.0	0.0	25.0	0.9	74.1	1,484,656	21.6	2.8	75.5	0.0	1,437,965	6,307
McLennan - 18			21.6	0.6	20.7	0.2	56.9							
Axtell	AA	692	6.6	0.0	6.1	0.3	87.0	2,633,342	19.8	0.3	79.8	0.0	2,376,399	3,434
Bosqueville	AA	412	6.6	0.0	14.3	0.0	79.1	2,194,001	28.3	3.0	68.6	0.0	1,986,688	4,822
Bruceville-Eddy	AA	800	2.4	0.3	15.6	0.0	81.8	11,534,559	13.9	0.4	85.6	0.0	10,241,750	12,802
China Spring	RE	1,304	0.5	0.1	4.1	0.1	95.2	6,157,326	19.9	1.1	78.9	0.0	5,074,872	3,892
Connally	AA	2,510	12.6	1.1	13.1	0.3	72.8	12,643,066	20.8	2.0	76.6	0.4	11,771,963	4,690
Crawford	EX	519	1.5	0.0	9.8	0.2	88.4	2,964,669	11.8	3.8	84.3	0.0	2,301,890	4,435
Gholson	AA	145	8.2	0.0	4.1	0.7	87.1	814,806	17.4	1.4	81.1	0.0	934,484	6,445
Hallsburg	RE	97	3.1	0.0	6.2	0.0	90.7	846,549	96.3	0.6	3.0	0.0	704,294	7,261
La Vega	AA	2,454	19.0	0.1	21.7	0.4	58.8	12,667,292	23.9	2.1	73.8	0.0	12,980,043	5,289
Lorena	RE	1,298	1.4	0.2	6.9	0.5	91.1	6,463,712	15.3	1.1	83.5	0.0	5,066,447	3,903
Mart	AA	705	28.8	0.0	4.0	0.0	67.2	3,578,998	17.5	4.1	78.3	0.0	3,365,883	4,774
McGregor	AA	1,194	14.2	0.0	30.6	0.1	55.2	7,154,438	16.2	2.6	81.1	0.0	6,161,625	5,160
Midway	RE	5,593	4.5	2.1	6.9	0.4	86.1	26,660,122	68.8	1.6	29.3	0.1	22,115,161	3,954
Moody	AA	762	9.3	0.0	16.7	0.3	73.8	4,742,611	14.8	2.2	82.9	0.0	3,440,329	4,515
Riesel	AA	542	7.2	0.9	9.0	0.2	82.7	2,714,491	21.6	4.6	73.6	0.0	2,155,003	3,976

County/Dist.	District Ratings	Total Number of Students	Ethnicity of Student Population†					Total Revenue	Sources of Revenue				Total Spending	Spending Per Student
			% Black	% Asian	% Hispanic	% Amer. Indian	% White		% Local	% Other	% State	% Federal		
Robinson	AA	1,901	4.7	0.2	9.6	0.1	85.3	10,017,126	19.3	1.6	78.7	0.2	8,740,281	4,598
Waco	AA	15,973	40.6	0.5	33.8	0.0	25.1	89,735,689	33.8	1.3	64.5	0.2	81,246,017	5,086
West	RE	1,518	4.1	0.1	7.7	0.1	87.9	6,512,439	24.2	1.9	73.8	0.0	5,865,762	3,864
McMullen - 1			0.0	0.0	42.4	0.0	57.6							
McMullen County	AA	191	0.0	0.0	42.4	0.0	57.6	2,147,953	94.4	3.1	2.5	0.0	1,792,563	9,385
Medina - 5			0.7	0.2	52.7	0.2	46.2							
Devine	AA	1,811	0.4	0.2	46.4	0.1	52.9	8,267,430	20.8	2.8	76.2	0.0	7,525,042	4,155
D'Hanis	AA	269	0.0	0.0	47.6	0.0	52.4	1,779,309	24.6	3.0	72.2	0.0	1,415,704	5,263
Hondo	AA	2,071	1.2	0.0	61.1	0.2	37.5	11,220,518	24.6	1.8	73.5	0.0	9,682,258	4,675
Medina Valley	AA	2,544	0.5	0.6	44.5	0.4	54.0	11,003,983	29.3	2.4	68.1	0.0	9,189,778	3,612
Natalia	AA	976	0.7	0.0	69.1	0.1	30.1	5,573,153	13.1	1.0	85.8	0.0	4,896,342	5,017
Menard - 1			0.7	0.0	53.2	0.0	46.1							
Menard	RE	445	0.7	0.0	53.2	0.0	46.1	4,056,566	31.8	3.8	64.4	0.0	3,541,986	7,960
Midland - 2			9.5	0.9	34.4	0.3	54.9							
Greenwood	AA	1,543	0.3	0.2	18.5	0.1	80.9	8,568,872	32.8	2.2	64.9	0.0	6,675,147	4,326
Midland	AA	23,159	10.1	0.9	35.5	0.3	53.2	106,169,736	47.9	1.7	50.2	0.0	96,514,675	4,167
Milam - 6			14.0	0.2	24.7	0.1	61.0							
Buckholts	AA	141	0.0	0.0	44.8	0.0	55.2	1,097,430	17.8	2.7	79.3	0.0	1,018,478	7,223
Cameron	AA	1,744	19.5	0.1	31.1	0.1	49.3	8,761,840	24.4	1.5	73.9	0.0	7,776,104	4,459
Gause	RE	168	6.0	0.0	8.9	0.0	85.1	810,475	18.4	1.1	80.4	0.0	762,246	4,537
Milano	AA	335	12.2	0.0	8.3	0.0	79.5	2,058,368	24.4	1.2	74.2	0.1	1,999,744	5,969
Rockdale	AA	1,893	12.7	0.3	23.2	0.0	63.7	8,991,367	79.2	3.0	17.7	0.0	8,513,693	4,497
Thorndale	RE	445	6.5	0.0	17.7	1.1	74.7	2,647,429	26.8	2.7	70.3	0.0	2,469,313	5,549
Mills - 4			1.0	0.0	16.8	0.2	81.9							
Goldthwaite	RE	623	1.3	0.0	17.9	0.0	80.8	3,545,289	20.7	5.9	73.2	0.1	3,491,136	5,604
Mullin	AA	159	0.0	0.0	10.7	0.0	89.3	1,083,038	30.5	2.7	66.6	0.0	879,573	5,532
Priddy	AA	94	1.1	0.0	14.9	2.1	81.9	773,795	17.6	3.4	78.9	0.0	729,665	7,762
Star	AA	108	0.9	0.0	21.3	0.0	77.8	1,160,056	13.7	2.1	84.1	0.0	1,273,600	11,793
Mitchell - 3			5.1	0.2	39.2	0.1	55.4							
Colorado	AA	1,214	5.8	0.2	39.1	0.1	54.8	8,526,751	47.1	4.2	48.5	0.0	7,864,185	6,478
Loraine	AA	213	5.6	0.0	55.4	0.0	39.0	1,439,894	24.9	1.7	73.3	0.0	1,384,204	6,499
Westbrook	AA	192	0.0	1.0	21.4	0.0	77.6	1,686,920	93.4	4.0	2.5	0.0	1,623,788	8,457
Montague - 7			0.0	0.3	8.1	0.1	91.4							
Bowie	AA	1,701	0.1	0.4	5.8	0.2	93.5	7,863,396	34.7	2.0	63.1	0.0	7,156,152	4,207
Forestburg	AA	144	0.0	0.0	5.6	0.0	94.4	1,061,820	26.8	2.7	70.4	0.0	979,201	6,800
Gold Burg	RE	121	0.0	0.0	3.3	0.0	96.7	1,025,130	32.5	4.8	62.6	0.0	920,455	7,607
Montague	RE	86	0.0	0.0	10.5	0.0	89.5	479,174	23.7	3.1	73.1	0.0	462,984	5,384
Nocona	AA	788	0.0	0.3	15.6	0.0	84.1	5,646,700	24.7	1.8	73.2	0.0	5,107,991	6,482
Prairie Valley	RE	125	0.0	0.0	3.2	0.0	96.8	902,523	44.4	3.0	52.5	0.0	830,152	6,641
Saint Jo	RE	358	0.0	0.6	6.4	0.0	93.0	2,371,293	29.2	2.2	68.4	0.0	2,048,178	5,721
Montgomery - 6			5.1	0.9	11.6	0.2	82.3							
Conroe	AA	28,573	5.7	1.4	13.1	0.1	79.6	152,445,209	53.7	1.2	44.9	0.0	137,113,210	4,799
Magnolia	AA	4,599	2.4	0.2	10.6	0.2	86.7	27,672,458	27.7	3.6	68.6	0.0	20,748,708	4,512
Montgomery	AA	2,658	8.9	0.4	4.9	0.1	85.7	15,148,200	84.6	3.0	12.0	0.1	13,221,933	4,974
New Caney	AA	5,470	1.6	0.3	10.0	0.1	88.0	28,544,180	28.1	1.7	69.8	0.2	26,204,762	4,791
Splendora	AA	2,556	0.3	0.2	6.8	0.1	92.7	15,046,556	10.6	7.2	82.0	0.0	11,901,224	4,656
Willis	AA	3,785	9.4	0.2	11.1	0.3	78.9	21,466,828	49.3	1.2	49.3	0.0	18,478,959	4,882
Moore - 2			0.5	1.3	52.3	0.3	45.6							
Dumas	AA	3,954	0.5	1.5	54.0	0.2	43.7	19,076,053	87.4	2.3	10.2	0.0	17,502,123	4,426
Sunray	AA	595	0.2	0.0	40.8	0.8	58.2	3,404,582	85.6	3.1	11.1	0.0	3,115,842	5,237
Morris - 2			32.9	0.1	3.9	0.2	62.9							
Daingerfield-Lone Star	AA	1,888	35.3	0.1	4.2	0.3	60.2	10,967,398	85.5	4.0	10.3	0.0	10,590,410	5,609
Pewitt	AA	1,013	28.5	0.1	3.3	0.0	68.1	5,937,937	22.8	2.7	74.4	0.0	5,584,843	5,513
Motley - 1			5.4	0.0	21.1	0.8	72.8							
Motley Co.	AA	261	5.4	0.0	21.1	0.8	72.8	1,972,591	40.1	1.6	58.2	0.0	1,903,659	7,294
Nacogdoches - 9			24.2	0.5	12.1	0.1	63.1							
Central Heights	RE	617	10.7	0.3	1.9	0.0	87.0	3,458,054	11.6	2.0	86.2	0.0	2,902,913	4,705
Chireno	RE	305	14.8	0.0	4.9	0.0	80.3	1,737,233	16.3	1.6	81.6	0.3	1,681,070	5,512
Cushing	AA	543	8.3	0.0	3.3	0.2	88.2	2,604,071	67.5	0.9	31.3	0.0	2,352,756	4,333
Douglass	EX	298	7.0	0.7	4.0	0.7	87.6	1,446,397	29.4	0.4	70.1	0.0	1,224,351	4,109
Etoile	RE	155	0.0	0.0	0.6	0.0	99.4	1,001,711	27.5	1.4	70.6	0.3	762,406	4,919
Garrison	AA	716	29.5	0.0	2.9	0.0	67.6	3,589,472	20.2	4.3	75.3	0.0	3,387,973	4,732
Martinsville	RE	272	5.1	0.0	5.5	0.0	89.3	1,505,957	16.4	0.1	83.4	0.0	1,376,179	5,059
Nacogdoches	AU	6,134	31.9	0.7	17.5	0.1	49.9	30,481,598	42.5	2.1	55.1	0.1	27,742,879	4,523
Woden	RE	753	1.5	0.5	1.9	0.0	96.1	4,840,857	13.1	5.1	81.4	0.2	4,347,141	5,773
Navarro - 7			24.3	0.6	12.2	0.3	62.7							
Blooming Grove	AA	750	5.5	0.3	6.5	0.0	87.8	4,189,007	17.3	3.7	78.8	0.0	3,734,864	4,980

County/Dist.	District Ratings	Total Number of Students	Ethnicity of Student Population†					Total Revenue	Sources of Revenue				Total Spending	Spending Per Student
			% Black	% Asian	% Hispanic	% Amer. Indian	% White		% Local	% Other	% State	% Federal		
Corsicana	AA	4,966	31.1	0.8	15.3	0.2	52.6	25,197,653	39.2	1.6	59.1	0.0	23,195,940	4,671
Dawson	AA	490	13.5	0.4	8.2	0.0	78.0	2,778,520	13.0	1.9	84.9	0.0	2,368,999	4,835
Frost	RE	384	6.3	0.0	11.2	0.0	82.6	2,357,808	10.4	1.1	88.4	0.0	1,990,737	5,184
Kerens	AA	696	33.3	0.4	4.6	0.0	61.6	4,495,199	17.7	2.7	79.4	0.0	3,794,422	5,452
Mildred	RE	439	4.3	0.0	5.0	0.0	89.7	5,322,077	47.8	1.5	50.6	0.0	2,135,992	4,866
Rice	AA	322	8.4	0.0	10.9	1.6	79.2	1,661,017	15.9	2.3	81.7	0.0	1,426,106	4,429
Newton - 3			29.6	0.0	1.2	0.1	69.1							
Burkeville	AA	431	42.5	0.0	4.2	0.0	53.4	2,258,419	85.9	2.1	11.9	0.0	2,736,354	6,349
Deweyville	RE	766	0.0	0.0	0.8	0.4	98.8	3,982,984	30.9	0.8	68.2	0.0	3,720,600	4,857
Newton	AA	1,553	40.7	0.0	0.6	0.0	58.7	9,289,578	24.0	0.8	74.9	0.2	8,542,009	5,500
Nolan - 4			6.9	0.1	37.5	0.3	55.3							
Blackwell Cons.	RE	187	0.0	0.0	25.5	1.1	73.4	1,514,081	77.6	3.1	19.2	0.0	1,449,330	7,750
Highland	RE	199	1.5	0.0	13.1	2.0	83.4	1,562,307	55.7	1.5	42.7	0.0	1,292,538	6,495
Roscoe	AA	440	0.0	0.0	47.7	0.2	52.0	2,926,242	21.1	1.3	77.5	0.0	2,480,064	5,637
Sweetwater	AA	2,851	8.8	0.1	38.4	0.1	52.6	15,103,586	37.3	1.9	60.7	0.0	15,031,101	5,272
Nueces - 12			4.8	0.9	62.4	0.3	31.6							
Agua Dulce	AA	342	0.0	0.0	67.5	1.5	31.0	2,561,316	38.8	1.6	59.4	0.0	2,307,229	6,746
Banquete	AA	882	0.2	0.0	73.5	0.0	26.3	5,527,642	33.0	2.4	64.5	0.0	4,605,288	5,221
Bishop Cons.	AA	1,445	2.3	0.0	66.9	0.1	30.8	8,676,173	92.0	2.6	5.3	0.0	8,203,076	5,677
Calallen	AA	4,767	1.7	0.4	30.6	0.2	67.0	24,642,859	52.4	2.0	45.5	0.0	20,676,982	4,338
Corpus Christi	AA	41,624	5.7	0.8	67.7	0.4	25.5	207,424,275	40.7	2.1	56.5	0.5	192,743,763	4,631
Driscoll	AA	280	0.0	0.0	75.0	0.4	24.6	1,830,044	61.3	2.2	33.1	3.3	1,537,580	5,491
Flour Bluff	AA	5,402	5.2	3.9	20.2	0.6	70.1	26,657,639	38.0	2.6	57.9	1.3	25,141,082	4,654
London	RE	166	0.0	0.6	33.1	0.0	66.3	1,202,953	59.2	7.7	32.8	0.1	1,126,027	6,783
Port Aransas	AA	479	0.0	0.8	6.9	0.4	91.9	3,580,008	88.2	3.7	7.9	0.0	3,214,622	6,711
Robstown	AA	4,437	1.1	0.0	97.6	0.1	1.3	27,059,420	7.6	1.4	90.4	0.4	23,046,129	5,194
Tuloso-Midway	AA	2,884	1.3	0.3	52.5	0.2	45.7	17,134,568	93.3	0.7	5.8	0.0	14,781,743	5,125
West Oso	AA	1,949	14.1	0.1	82.8	0.2	2.9	11,096,132	32.7	1.2	65.9	0.0	9,897,291	5,078
Ochiltree - 1			0.0	0.2	32.0	0.2	67.6							
Perryton	AA	2,053	0.0	0.2	32.0	0.2	67.6	9,715,383	63.8	2.1	34.0	0.0	9,471,358	4,613
Oldham - 4			3.4	0.5	15.3	1.0	79.8							
Adrian	EX	102	0.0	0.0	22.5	0.0	77.5	985,501	36.4	1.5	61.9	0.0	947,101	9,285
Boys Ranch	RE	386	7.5	0.5	9.8	0.8	81.3	4,419,785	0.0	41.0	58.8	0.1	3,898,164	10,099
Vega	AA	329	0.0	0.3	19.8	1.8	78.1	2,341,758	26.7	3.4	69.8	0.0	2,356,103	7,161
Wildorado	AA	57	1.7	1.7	13.8	0.0	82.8	460,637	58.9	3.2	37.7	0.0	488,902	8,577
Orange - 5			11.2	0.8	2.7	0.2	85.1							
Bridge City	RE	2,845	0.2	2.5	3.2	0.3	93.7	14,699,200	47.7	1.4	50.7	0.0	12,909,182	4,537
Little Cypress-Maur'ville	RE	3,714	4.8	0.8	3.2	0.3	90.8	17,426,032	39.0	2.3	58.6	0.0	17,529,027	4,720
Orangefield	RE	1,521	0.1	2.4	2.1	0.3	95.1	8,055,678	32.7	1.8	65.4	0.0	7,178,052	4,719
Vidor	RE	5,709	0.4	0.1	2.1	0.1	97.3	27,926,198	26.3	0.9	72.4	0.2	26,117,235	4,575
West Orange-Cove Cons	AA	3,703	46.9	0.2	2.7	0.1	50.1	25,157,155	90.4	3.6	5.5	0.4	23,257,370	6,281
Palo Pinto - 6			3.9	0.7	15.0	0.6	79.9							
Gordon	RE	201	0.0	0.5	5.0	0.5	94.0	1,339,141	44.5	6.0	49.3	0.0	1,271,679	6,327
Graford	AA	374	0.3	0.5	8.3	2.1	88.8	2,320,204	78.0	3.4	18.5	0.0	2,261,534	6,047
Mineral Wells	RE	3,553	5.1	0.7	17.1	0.4	76.6	17,352,926	28.3	1.0	70.5	0.1	16,500,436	4,644
Palo Pinto	AA	43	4.7	0.0	9.3	0.0	86.0	525,721	92.7	3.9	3.3	0.0	451,967	10,511
Santo	AA	383	0.3	0.5	6.0	0.0	93.2	1,825,039	80.8	2.5	16.6	0.0	2,089,255	5,455
Strawn	RE	194	0.0	0.0	18.6	1.5	79.9	1,394,883	40.7	2.3	56.9	0.0	1,090,500	5,621
Panola - 3			24.1	0.3	3.4	0.1	72.2							
Beckville	AA	459	16.3	1.5	2.8	0.0	79.3	3,579,465	91.0	4.5	4.4	0.0	3,403,365	7,415
Carthage	AA	3,366	27.1	0.1	3.4	0.1	69.3	18,055,654	90.3	3.1	6.4	0.0	17,270,433	5,131
Gary	AA	272	0.0	0.0	4.8	0.0	95.2	1,325,618	49.6	1.7	48.5	0.0	1,365,002	5,018
Parker - 8			1.1	0.4	6.2	0.4	91.9							
Aledo	RE	2,175	0.3	0.8	2.9	0.4	95.6	10,142,927	45.2	2.3	52.4	0.0	8,282,403	3,808
Brock	RE	498	0.4	0.0	2.4	0.8	96.4	2,854,550	22.8	2.4	74.7	0.0	2,637,244	5,296
Garner	AA	195	0.0	0.0	1.0	0.0	99.0	1,312,434	40.9	6.4	52.6	0.0	1,100,679	5,645
Millsap	RE	637	0.6	0.0	6.1	0.0	93.3	3,382,703	25.4	3.6	70.9	0.0	3,043,514	4,778
Peaster	RE	665	0.8	0.0	2.0	0.2	97.1	3,725,812	11.0	3.6	85.2	0.0	2,772,222	4,169
Poolville	AA	307	0.0	0.0	2.3	0.0	97.7	1,787,791	26.7	2.0	71.2	0.0	1,683,765	5,485
Springtown	AA	2,856	0.3	0.2	4.1	0.4	94.9	13,821,960	18.0	2.6	79.2	0.0	12,505,472	4,379
Weatherford	AA	6,069	2.0	0.4	9.6	0.4	87.6	28,334,669	35.9	4.5	59.5	0.0	23,555,377	3,881
Parmer - 4			0.9	0.2	59.9	0.0	39.0							
Bovina	AU	578	0.8	0.0	77.3	0.0	21.8	2,992,764	19.8	2.2	77.6	0.2	2,714,515	4,696
Farwell	RE	536	0.2	0.2	39.1	0.2	60.4	3,093,296	21.7	1.2	76.9	0.0	2,896,456	5,404
Friona	AA	1,261	1.3	0.3	65.4	0.0	32.9	6,769,997	30.9	3.4	65.6	0.0	6,286,342	4,985
Lazbuddie	AA	246	0.0	0.0	35.4	0.0	64.6	1,681,834	40.7	2.3	56.7	0.1	1,634,183	6,643

County/Dist.	District Ratings	Total Number of Students	Ethnicity of Student Population†					Total Revenue	Sources of Revenue				Total Spending	Spending Per Student
			% Black	% Asian	% Hispanic	% Amer. Indian	% White		% Local	% Other	% State	% Federal		
Pecos - 3			1.1	0.3	67.2	0.2	31.2							
Buena Vista	AA	143	0.0	0.0	42.1	0.0	57.9	1,210,995	93.1	3.4	3.3	0.0	1,162,573	8,130
Fort Stockton	AA	2,949	0.7	0.4	74.3	0.1	24.5	17,652,572	91.7	3.0	5.1	0.1	17,810,412	6,039
Iraan-Sheffield	AA	620	3.7	0.0	39.0	0.5	56.8	20,005,850	82.7	12.0	5.1	0.0	4,864,214	7,846
Polk - 6			16.0	0.3	10.5	1.8	71.3							
Big Sandy	RE	378	0.5	0.0	1.6	21.2	76.7	3,446,884	57.9	1.3	40.6	0.0	2,184,039	5,778
Corrigan-Camden	AA	1,195	29.4	0.1	25.0	0.1	45.4	7,242,946	29.3	5.0	65.6	0.0	6,651,268	5,566
Goodrich	AA	313	33.9	0.6	16.3	1.0	48.2	1,960,097	46.7	1.3	51.8	0.0	1,706,925	5,453
Leggett	AA	214	24.3	0.0	12.1	0.9	62.6	1,637,656	40.9	2.1	56.8	0.0	1,511,810	7,065
Livingston	AA	3,860	13.1	0.3	7.4	0.8	78.4	20,277,103	32.3	4.6	63.0	0.0	18,093,427	4,687
Onalaska	AA	491	3.4	1.0	2.4	0.4	92.7	2,832,930	81.0	0.8	18.1	0.0	2,553,678	5,201
Potter - 4			9.0	2.7	26.3	0.4	61.6							
Amarillo	AA	29,958	9.6	2.9	27.7	0.4	59.4	144,951,623	35.1	3.1	61.3	0.4	127,092,957	4,242
Bushland	RE	416	0.0	0.0	7.6	1.4	91.0	2,688,485	92.9	2.5	4.5	0.0	2,402,891	5,776
Highland Park	AA	749	5.1	1.7	17.4	0.9	74.8	4,885,137	94.1	0.9	4.9	0.0	4,209,958	5,621
River Road	AA	1,343	0.1	0.4	6.8	0.4	92.3	6,834,939	30.7	1.7	67.5	0.0	6,308,713	4,697
Presidio - 2			0.0	0.1	94.4	0.2	5.3							
Marfa	AA	447	0.0	0.2	83.4	0.0	16.3	2,842,571	31.4	0.4	68.1	0.0	2,757,547	6,169
Presidio	AA	1,243	0.0	0.1	98.4	0.2	1.3	6,933,213	8.1	1.8	89.5	0.4	6,501,762	5,231
Rains - 1			4.9	0.1	4.2	0.5	90.4							
Rains	AA	1,332	4.9	0.1	4.2	0.5	90.4	7,183,989	34.8	6.3	58.8	0.0	6,119,471	4,594
Randall - 1			1.4	0.8	9.7	0.4	87.8							
Canyon	AA	6,874	1.4	0.8	9.7	0.4	87.8	30,350,551	35.2	2.0	62.7	0.0	26,540,354	3,861
Reagan - 1			3.6	0.0	55.7	0.1	40.7							
Reagan County	AA	1,121	3.6	0.0	55.7	0.1	40.7	7,073,112	65.9	5.6	28.4	0.0	6,486,324	5,786
Real - 1			0.4	0.0	23.9	0.0	75.7							
Leakey	AA	268	0.4	0.0	23.9	0.0	75.7	1,666,145	57.3	1.9	40.7	0.0	1,661,755	6,201
Red River - 4			28.6	0.1	3.9	0.6	66.7							
Avery	AA	344	7.6	0.0	4.9	0.6	86.9	2,210,506	11.4	3.1	84.9	0.4	2,167,007	6,299
Clarksville	AA	1,336	49.7	0.1	4.3	0.9	44.9	7,833,761	26.4	2.3	71.0	0.1	7,917,045	5,926
Detroit	AA	431	13.7	0.2	0.5	0.0	85.6	3,241,962	17.1	3.0	79.8	0.0	3,257,819	7,559
Talco-Bogata Cons.	AA	737	9.0	0.0	4.6	0.5	85.9	3,409,207	25.7	1.5	72.7	0.0	3,504,460	4,755
Reeves - 2			2.0	0.2	84.1	0.1	13.6							
Balmorhea	AA	221	0.5	0.0	81.0	0.0	18.6	1,938,549	13.7	1.8	84.2	0.1	1,974,593	8,935
Pecos-Barstow-Toyah	RE	3,205	2.1	0.2	84.3	0.1	13.3	17,110,328	34.2	3.4	62.1	0.0	16,645,966	5,194
Refugio - 3			8.7	0.1	50.4	0.1	40.7							
Austwell-Tivoli	AA	217	0.9	0.0	70.0	0.0	29.0	1,573,945	86.4	4.7	8.8	0.0	1,759,623	8,109
Refugio	AA	843	14.1	0.0	46.6	0.2	39.0	5,370,456	83.5	2.9	13.5	0.0	5,186,451	6,152
Woodsboro	AA	601	4.0	0.2	48.6	0.0	47.3	3,915,071	32.6	11.3	55.9	0.0	3,835,342	6,382
Roberts - 1			0.5	1.1	4.3	0.0	94.1							
Miami	RE	186	0.5	1.1	4.3	0.0	94.1	1,373,250	86.6	4.2	9.1	0.0	1,561,392	8,395
Robertson - 5			37.8	0.0	17.6	0.1	44.5							
Bremond	RE	346	23.1	0.0	3.8	0.3	72.8	3,298,847	92.0	3.3	4.6	0.0	2,409,957	6,965
Calvert	AA	337	77.9	0.0	11.5	0.0	10.6	1,651,443	3.0	2.0	94.9	0.0	2,137,203	6,342
Franklin	AA	896	9.2	0.0	8.5	0.0	82.4	5,101,068	54.8	0.0	45.1	0.0	4,487,943	5,009
Hearne	AA	1,502	51.0	0.0	25.0	0.1	24.0	8,712,561	23.9	2.8	73.2	0.0	8,627,308	5,744
Mumford	AA	149	20.1	0.0	45.0	0.0	34.9	735,710	21.9	3.6	74.3	0.0	637,795	4,281
Rockwall - 2			4.0	0.9	10.2	0.2	84.6							
Rockwall	AA	6,007	3.7	1.0	7.9	0.2	87.1	31,592,495	57.1	1.6	41.2	0.0	25,358,651	4,222
Royse City	AA	1,526	5.4	0.6	19.3	0.1	74.6	7,639,333	14.5	1.8	83.6	0.0	6,624,323	4,341
Runnels - 4			1.9	0.1	36.6	0.1	61.3							
Ballinger	AA	1,238	2.8	0.0	34.6	0.0	62.6	7,629,351	22.1	2.3	75.4	0.0	6,148,536	4,967
Miles	RE	467	0.2	0.0	30.1	0.2	69.4	3,611,403	11.2	0.8	87.8	0.0	2,431,826	5,207
Olfen	AA	90	2.2	0.0	23.3	0.0	74.4	474,166	11.1	0.4	88.4	0.0	466,975	5,189
Winters	AA	880	1.6	0.2	44.2	0.1	53.9	5,162,281	21.0	1.4	77.5	0.0	4,509,240	5,124
Rusk - 8			24.8	0.2	8.2	0.1	66.6							
Carlisle	AA	456	13.6	0.2	11.6	0.9	73.7	2,388,124	23.3	2.5	74.1	0.0	2,436,563	5,343
Henderson	AA	3,718	25.3	0.4	7.3	0.0	66.9	19,004,444	42.8	3.3	53.7	0.0	17,179,814	4,621
Laneville	AA	283	64.0	0.4	13.4	0.0	22.3	1,730,926	20.9	3.2	75.8	0.0	2,033,025	7,184
Leveretts Chapel	AA	226	16.2	0.0	5.7	0.0	78.1	1,568,308	20.1	2.2	77.5	0.0	1,525,930	6,752
Mount Enterprise	AA	350	31.7	0.0	0.9	0.0	67.4	2,376,130	17.4	3.4	79.0	0.0	2,544,088	7,269
Overton	AA	464	13.1	0.4	1.9	0.6	83.8	2,938,175	15.6	3.0	81.2	0.0	2,647,207	5,705
Tatum	AA	1,230	23.8	0.0	14.3	0.2	61.7	7,615,753	89.1	2.7	8.1	0.0	7,761,097	6,310
West Rusk	AA	995	23.1	0.0	7.1	0.1	69.6	6,080,864	52.9	2.4	44.6	0.0	5,943,814	5,974
Sabine - 2			17.0	0.1	1.7	0.1	81.2							
Hemphill	AA	977	19.2	0.0	2.2	0.0	78.5	5,672,380	43.1	6.5	50.2	0.0	4,971,867	5,089
West Sabine	AA	644	13.6	0.2	0.8	0.2	85.3	3,489,120	25.9	2.4	71.5	0.0	3,007,900	4,671

County/Dist.	District Ratings	Total Number of Students	Ethnicity of Student Population†					Total Revenue	Sources of Revenue				Total Spending	Spending Per Student
			% Black	% Asian	% Hispanic	% Amer. Indian	% White		% Local	% Other	% State	% Federal		
San Augustine - 2			42.4	0.0	3.1	0.1	54.4							
Broaddus	AA	432	9.5	0.0	2.9	0.2	87.4	2,704,112	33.0	1.3	61.7	3.9	2,396,053	5,546
San Augustine	AA	1,158	55.3	0.0	3.2	0.0	41.5	6,583,440	20.3	0.3	79.2	0.0	6,284,116	5,427
San Jacinto - 2			22.6	0.1	4.8	0.2	72.3							
Coldspring-Oak'st Cons.	AA	1,778	33.0	0.0	3.4	0.2	63.4	9,189,054	61.2	3.2	34.5	0.9	8,557,301	4,813
Shepherd	AA	1,648	11.5	0.2	6.3	0.1	81.9	8,232,770	21.1	1.2	77.4	0.2	7,747,431	4,701
San Patricio - 7			2.2	0.6	58.1	0.2	38.9							
Aransas Pass	AA	2,226	4.7	0.5	44.3	0.3	50.2	12,480,472	24.8	2.9	72.2	0.0	11,534,987	5,182
Gregory-Portland	AA	4,223	1.4	1.0	39.1	0.2	58.3	19,893,688	41.3	1.9	56.5	0.0	18,470,737	4,374
Ingleside	AA	1,786	2.7	1.5	32.6	0.3	62.9	8,351,005	95.0	0.9	3.9	0.1	8,514,124	4,767
Mathis	AA	2,201	1.0	0.1	84.0	0.0	14.9	13,160,287	16.9	1.6	81.4	0.0	10,905,542	4,955
Odem-Edroy	AA	1,238	0.1	0.2	73.3	0.0	26.4	6,615,762	19.4	2.1	78.1	0.1	6,112,757	4,938
Sinton	AA	2,218	2.3	0.3	76.6	0.2	20.6	11,786,998	27.1	1.3	71.3	0.1	11,769,703	5,306
Taft	AA	1,490	3.4	0.1	83.4	0.1	13.0	8,528,846	23.4	1.6	74.9	0.0	8,131,375	5,457
San Saba - 3			0.9	0.0	28.2	0.3	70.6							
Cherokee	AA	172	4.1	0.0	19.2	1.2	75.6	1,222,213	24.4	2.9	72.6	0.0	1,130,478	6,573
Richland Springs	AA	187	0.0	0.0	16.5	0.0	83.5	1,478,330	27.7	0.9	71.3	0.0	1,213,136	6,487
San Saba	AA	823	0.5	0.0	32.8	0.1	66.6	4,799,280	24.8	3.1	71.9	0.0	4,481,154	5,445
Schleicher - 1			0.9	0.0	53.6	0.0	45.5							
Schleicher	RE	769	0.9	0.0	53.6	0.0	45.5	4,676,207	49.6	3.3	47.0	0.0	4,295,705	5,586
Scurry - 3			4.2	0.2	35.3	0.3	60.0							
Hermleigh	AA	162	0.0	0.0	35.2	0.0	64.8	1,231,318	35.8	3.0	61.1	0.0	1,219,908	7,530
Ira	RE	183	0.0	0.0	12.0	0.0	88.0	1,293,049	85.1	9.8	5.0	0.0	1,340,838	7,327
Snyder	AA	3,398	4.6	0.3	36.6	0.3	58.2	16,772,719	47.4	2.1	50.4	0.0	16,103,324	4,739
Shackelford - 2			0.4	0.4	12.7	0.1	86.2							
Albany	EX	579	0.5	0.5	12.8	0.2	86.0	3,096,530	39.3	2.1	58.5	0.0	2,967,851	5,126
Moran	EX	97	0.0	0.0	12.4	0.0	87.6	928,962	35.5	2.6	61.9	0.0	875,302	9,024
Shelby - 6			27.7	0.2	6.6	0.1	65.4							
Center	AA	2,368	28.6	0.3	9.8	0.2	61.1	11,253,509	22.4	3.1	73.4	0.9	10,115,037	4,272
Excelsior	AA	74	0.0	0.0	0.0	0.0	100.0	552,386	14.8	5.4	79.7	0.0	525,665	7,104
Joaquin	AA	651	8.1	0.0	0.5	0.0	91.4	3,074,475	27.2	3.4	68.3	0.9	2,893,715	4,445
Shelbyville	AA	725	33.2	0.0	2.9	0.0	63.9	3,921,102	14.4	2.4	81.0	2.0	3,774,591	5,206
Tenaha	AA	372	38.2	0.0	10.2	0.3	51.3	2,416,605	14.6	3.5	81.1	0.6	2,407,988	6,473
Timpson	AA	660	34.8	0.2	4.1	0.2	60.8	4,338,087	14.8	2.1	82.6	0.3	4,175,254	6,326
Sherman - 2			0.1	0.0	28.0	0.1	71.8							
Stratford	AA	529	0.2	0.0	33.5	0.2	66.2	3,210,822	81.5	2.0	16.4	0.0	3,139,045	5,934
Texhoma	RE	308	0.0	0.0	18.5	0.0	81.5	694,923	94.1	2.3	3.5	0.0	691,395	2,245
Smith - 8			27.1	0.7	12.3	0.2	59.7							
Arp	AA	819	29.1	0.7	2.2	0.0	68.0	4,466,501	22.3	0.7	76.9	0.0	4,320,449	5,275
Bullard	AA	1,174	6.5	0.3	2.6	0.6	89.9	5,357,519	42.9	2.1	54.9	0.0	4,545,704	3,872
Chapel Hill	AA	3,294	27.0	0.0	8.9	0.5	63.2	13,361,436	29.9	1.2	68.8	0.0	14,618,400	4,438
Lindale	AA	2,485	8.8	0.9	3.1	0.6	86.6	11,054,773	32.5	2.7	64.7	0.0	9,610,330	3,867
Troup	AA	917	19.6	0.0	5.0	0.0	75.4	5,110,589	21.9	2.6	75.3	0.0	4,683,860	5,108
Tyler	AA	16,534	35.9	0.7	18.5	0.1	44.7	83,381,930	58.2	1.8	39.8	0.0	78,186,588	4,729
Whitehouse	AA	3,609	8.7	0.9	2.7	0.2	87.5	16,755,541	35.2	1.8	62.9	0.0	14,857,463	4,117
Winona	AA	905	21.2	0.2	4.0	0.1	74.5	5,038,336	36.5	1.3	62.0	0.0	4,223,354	4,667
Somervell - 1			0.2	0.2	16.5	0.7	82.4							
Glen Rose	AA	1,492	0.2	0.2	16.5	0.7	82.4	11,657,794	77.6	14.6	7.7	0.0	10,586,514	7,096
Starr - 3			0.0	0.0	99.6	0.0	0.4							
Rio Grande City	AA	7,944	0.0	0.1	99.5	0.0	0.4	45,304,843	12.9	1.8	78.3	6.9	42,290,687	5,324
Roma	AA	5,917	0.1	0.0	99.7	0.0	0.2	34,970,436	9.4	4.0	81.8	4.6	27,329,366	4,619
San Isidro	RE	333	0.0	0.0	97.6	0.0	2.4	2,731,450	66.4	11.9	21.5	0.0	2,457,147	7,379
Stephens - 1			2.7	0.7	19.3	0.5	76.9							
Breckenridge	AA	2,024	2.7	0.7	19.3	0.5	76.9	9,372,378	55.4	1.9	42.6	0.0	8,589,090	4,244
Sterling - 1			0.3	0.0	34.0	0.0	65.8							
Sterling City	AA	373	0.3	0.0	34.0	0.0	65.8	3,396,997	94.0	1.8	4.0	0.0	2,378,140	6,376
Stonewall - 1			6.4	0.3	19.4	0.3	73.7							
Aspermont	AA	376	6.4	0.3	19.4	0.3	73.7	2,331,492	75.3	3.7	20.9	0.0	2,423,352	6,445
Sutton - 1			0.3	0.1	53.3	0.2	46.2							
Sonora	AA	1,095	0.3	0.1	53.3	0.2	46.2	6,250,692	88.4	3.3	8.2	0.0	6,393,970	5,839
Swisher - 3			7.0	0.0	45.8	0.2	47.0							
Happy	RE	253	0.4	0.0	13.8	0.4	85.4	2,058,382	28.4	1.5	69.9	0.0	1,950,885	7,711
Kress	AA	366	6.0	0.0	50.5	0.3	43.2	2,261,822	32.3	2.4	65.1	0.0	2,286,746	6,248
Tulia	AA	1,467	8.4	0.1	50.1	0.1	41.3	8,828,492	18.0	2.6	79.3	0.0	7,455,217	5,082
Tarrant - 17			16.9	3.8	19.2	0.4	59.6							
Arlington	AA	51,960	15.9	6.3	15.6	0.6	61.5	231,966,738	68.2	2.6	28.8	0.2	199,664,919	3,843
Azle	RE	5,591	0.8	0.3	4.0	0.5	94.4	24,402,869	28.4	1.8	69.5	0.0	22,174,173	3,966

County/Dist.	District Ratings	Total Number of Students	Ethnicity of Student Population†					Total Revenue	Sources of Revenue				Total Spending	Spending Per Student
			% Black	% Asian	% Hispanic	% Amer. Indian	% White		% Local	% Other	% State	% Federal		
Birdville	AA	20,129	2.6	4.8	10.4	0.2	81.9	101,415,302	51.1	3.3	45.3	0.1	89,989,384	4,471
Carroll	EX	4,142	1.0	0.9	2.1	0.2	95.7	23,097,405	86.5	1.5	11.9	0.0	19,216,149	4,639
Castleberry	AA	3,138	1.2	1.1	24.9	0.2	72.6	16,090,355	27.4	1.7	70.8	0.0	14,957,890	4,767
Crowley	AA	7,149	12.5	3.5	9.7	0.6	73.6	37,196,818	48.1	2.9	48.8	0.0	32,978,869	4,613
Eagle Mt.-Saginaw	AA	5,468	1.9	5.4	13.1	0.3	79.4	25,892,090	63.1	2.9	33.9	0.0	21,505,902	3,933
Everman	AA	3,290	55.8	1.0	14.0	0.3	28.9	18,009,321	39.6	1.2	59.1	0.0	16,793,345	5,104
Fort Worth	AA	74,021	34.0	2.5	36.4	0.2	27.0	378,378,646	48.4	2.2	48.7	0.5	349,815,657	4,726
Grapevine-Colleyville	AA	11,623	1.9	2.1	5.5	0.5	90.0	68,528,010	88.9	4.4	6.5	0.0	56,685,708	4,877
Hurst-Euless-Bedford	AA	19,243	6.0	6.1	9.1	0.8	78.0	100,795,567	75.0	2.2	22.7	0.0	89,894,498	4,672
Keller	AA	11,880	3.2	3.8	5.8	0.3	86.8	52,309,085	43.4	1.4	55.1	0.0	42,190,486	3,551
Kennedale	AA	2,290	8.1	1.4	9.2	0.3	81.0	10,451,521	44.5	2.3	52.8	0.3	9,688,830	4,231
Lake Worth	AA	1,634	5.1	0.7	31.7	0.5	61.9	8,788,442	31.7	2.2	65.8	.02	7,852,178	4,805
Mansfield	AA	10,202	7.3	2.5	10.1	0.5	79.6	49,498,865	48.1	2.6	49.0	0.1	41,543,895	4,072
Masonic Home	RE	109	0.0	2.8	16.5	2.8	78.0	841,601	0.0	97.0	2.9	0.0	837,950	7,688
White Settlement	RE	4,301	6.6	2.5	11.1	0.6	79.2	19,325,025	34.3	1.5	63.7	0.3	17,809,502	4,141
Taylor - 5			8.6	1.4	22.2	0.3	67.6							
Abilene	AA	19,649	10.4	1.6	25.9	0.4	61.7	100,916,815	28.3	1.5	68.9	1.0	95,828,755	4,877
Jim Ned Cons.	AA	899	0.6	0.0	6.5	0.2	92.7	5,377,873	20.7	1.2	78.1	0.0	4,635,178	5,156
Merkel	AA	1,405	1.4	0.2	14.7	0.1	83.6	7,379,648	17.3	2.1	80.5	0.0	6,282,720	4,472
Trent	AA	157	1.9	0.0	10.2	0.0	87.9	1,133,997	49.2	3.2	47.5	0.0	1,104,811	7,037
Wylie	RE	2,562	1.5	1.2	3.5	0.1	93.8	11,878,450	43.9	2.3	53.6	0.0	9,241,168	3,607
Terrell - 1			0.8	0.8	58.5	1.2	38.6							
Terrell Co.	EX	246	0.8	0.8	58.5	1.2	38.6	2,576,792	73.6	23.3	3.0	0.0	2,307,068	9,378
Terry - 4			4.5	0.4	57.2	0.3	37.7							
Brownfield	AA	2,485	5.6	0.4	58.2	0.3	35.5	13,608,159	44.4	4.4	51.1	0.0	13,169,555	5,300
Meadow	AA	290	0.0	0.0	61.7	0.0	38.3	1,870,795	41.3	2.9	55.6	0.0	1,693,928	5,841
Union	AA	151	0.0	0.0	68.2	0.7	31.1	887,900	60.6	3.4	35.9	0.0	887,266	5,876
Wellman	EX	179	0.6	1.1	25.7	0.0	72.6	1,267,425	77.3	6.2	16.4	0.0	1,377,715	7,697
Throckmorton - 2			0.0	0.0	9.8	0.3	89.9							
Throckmorton	RE	241	0.0	0.0	9.1	0.4	90.5	1,546,487	60.4	4.0	35.3	0.1	1,533,511	6,363
Woodson	AA	144	0.0	0.0	11.1	0.0	88.9	1,029,897	32.6	3.5	63.7	0.0	947,580	6,580
Titus - 4			15.4	0.2	27.7	0.4	56.3							
Chapel Hill	RE	466	3.2	0.2	11.6	0.6	84.3	3,097,723	13.2	0.6	86.0	0.0	1,935,295	4,153
Harts Bluff	RE	418	1.0	0.5	12.4	0.5	85.6	1,904,560	28.7	1.4	69.8	0.0	1,488,396	3,561
Mount Pleasant	AA	4,290	18.6	0.2	31.2	0.4	49.7	21,956,943	57.4	4.7	37.7	0.0	19,669,866	4,585
Winfield	RE	141	0.0	0.0	19.9	0.0	80.1	973,290	91.6	3.3	5.0	0.0	896,623	6,359
Tom Green - 6			5.2	0.9	39.2	0.2	54.5							
Christoval	AA	358	0.6	0.3	17.5	0.0	81.6	2,096,533	43.0	2.3	54.6	0.0	1,954,249	5,459
Grape Creek-Pulliam	RE	738	0.5	0.3	21.0	0.1	78.0	3,548,030	31.7	1.4	65.7	1.0	3,563,544	4,829
San Angelo	AA	17,489	5.9	1.0	42.0	0.1	50.9	75,415,336	33.2	5.2	61.1	0.4	72,012,593	4,118
Veribest	RE	164	0.0	0.6	25.6	0.0	73.8	1,018,351	54.8	0.9	44.2	0.0	836,343	5,100
Wall	AA	850	0.2	0.1	21.5	0.4	77.8	9,372,069	25.2	2.6	72.1	0.0	7,901,906	9,296
Water Valley	AA	398	0.0	0.0	13.6	3.5	82.9	2,146,326	39.4	3.6	56.8	0.0	2,183,696	5,487
Travis - 7			15.6	2.6	35.2	0.3	46.2							
Austin	AA	74,772	18.3	2.2	40.3	0.3	38.9	375,021,452	84.8	2.2	12.8	0.1	345,089,537	4,615
Del Valle	AA	4,745	12.3	1.3	53.2	0.7	32.6	24,998,468	54.9	1.6	43.4	0.0	21,955,142	4,627
Eanes	EX	6,865	0.5	4.3	3.7	0.5	90.9	44,610,569	90.5	4.5	4.9	0.0	34,387,886	5,009
Lago Vista	AA	656	0.9	2.0	5.3	0.2	91.6	4,212,854	92.2	1.8	5.9	0.0	3,795,944	5,787
Lake Travis	EX	2,649	0.3	0.4	9.8	0.3	89.1	16,459,347	88.3	5.8	5.5	0.2	12,834,614	4,845
Manor	AA	1,903	20.5	0.4	36.8	0.4	41.9	12,926,784	66.0	2.0	31.7	0.1	9,913,850	5,210
Pflugerville	AA	9,689	11.6	6.2	18.6	0.5	63.1	46,251,052	38.9	2.1	58.8	0.0	37,073,721	3,826
Trinity - 4			19.9	0.3	5.6	0.0	74.2							
Apple Springs	RE	197	24.4	0.0	1.5	0.0	74.1	1,848,942	24.9	0.8	71.5	2.6	1,362,484	6,916
Centerville	RE	165	3.6	0.0	3.6	0.0	92.7	1,163,833	16.6	4.7	75.2	3.3	1,044,094	6,328
Groveton	AA	710	14.0	0.1	5.0	0.0	80.8	5,054,114	30.2	2.2	65.5	2.0	4,863,519	6,850
Trinity	AA	1,289	24.5	0.4	6.8	0.1	68.2	6,157,636	36.2	1.1	62.1	0.5	5,586,251	4,334
Tyler - 5			17.4	0.1	1.3	1.3	80.0							
Chester	AA	251	23.5	0.0	2.8	0.4	73.3	1,577,327	41.3	1.7	56.9	0.0	1,483,747	5,911
Colmesneil	AA	467	7.1	0.0	0.4	0.0	92.5	2,795,193	27.6	1.7	70.6	0.0	2,735,785	5,858
Spurger	AA	401	3.2	0.0	0.2	0.2	96.3	2,292,301	18.6	0.9	80.4	0.0	2,115,503	5,276
Warren	AA	1,066	3.5	0.1	1.3	0.0	95.1	5,083,936	38.3	1.3	60.2	0.0	5,354,423	5,023
Woodville	AA	1,682	31.5	0.1	1.5	3.0	64.0	9,359,436	33.4	1.6	64.7	0.1	8,692,090	5,168
Upshur - 7			13.3	0.0	3.3	0.4	83.1							
Big Sandy	AA	736	16.8	0.0	2.8	0.0	80.4	3,847,520	24.6	2.1	73.2	0.0	3,657,936	4,970
Gilmer	AA	2,414	19.8	0.0	2.8	0.6	76.7	11,127,820	43.3	6.4	46.8	3.3	10,231,027	4,238
Harmony	AA	849	0.0	0.0	6.6	0.1	93.3	4,417,201	39.6	2.0	58.3	0.0	4,006,711	4,719
New Diana	AA	836	11.7	0.0	2.6	0.8	84.8	4,465,016	11.8	1.9	86.2	0.0	3,820,540	4,570

County/Dist.	District Ratings	Total Number of Students	Ethnicity of Student Population†					Total Revenue	Sources of Revenue				Total Spending	Spending Per Student
			% Black	% Asian	% Hispanic	% Amer. Indian	% White		% Local	% Other	% State	% Federal		
Ore City	AA	844	12.1	0.1	3.8	0.0	84.0	4,393,388	19.4	1.7	78.8	0.0	4,345,856	5,149
Union Grove	AA	723	0.6	0.0	1.4	0.1	97.9	3,725,848	24.7	2.0	73.1	0.0	3,636,013	5,029
Union Hill	AA	279	28.7	0.0	3.6	0.0	67.7	1,787,361	17.1	1.6	81.2	0.0	1,581,801	5,670
Upton - 2			1.6	0.0	50.0	0.4	48.0							
McCamey	AA	699	1.6	0.0	53.5	0.4	44.5	5,537,763	92.3	3.1	4.5	0.0	5,309,262	7,596
Rankin	AA	390	1.8	0.0	43.6	0.3	54.3	3,352,126	88.7	4.3	6.9	0.0	3,161,078	8,105
Uvalde - 4			0.3	0.3	73.9	0.1	25.4							
Knippa	AA	240	0.0	0.0	55.8	0.0	44.2	1,223,270	22.3	3.7	73.8	0.0	1,128,284	4,701
Sabinal	AA	488	0.2	0.4	62.7	0.2	36.5	3,467,151	22.9	1.9	74.9	0.1	3,106,411	6,366
Utopia	AA	201	0.0	0.5	10.0	0.0	89.6	1,164,057	66.6	1.1	32.1	0.0	978,095	4,866
Uvalde Cons.	AA	5,371	0.3	0.3	78.1	0.1	21.2	29,372,681	18.2	1.9	79.7	0.1	25,294,245	4,709
Val Verde - 2			1.2	0.4	84.0	0.1	14.3							
Comstock	AA	131	0.0	0.8	51.1	2.3	45.8	968,957	79.9	1.2	18.7	0.0	1,003,691	7,662
San Felipe-Del Rio Cons.	AA	10,202	1.2	0.3	84.4	0.1	13.9	48,643,413	17.8	1.6	79.4	0.9	46,736,280	4,581
Van Zandt - 7			4.7	0.1	6.5	0.2	88.4							
Canton	RE	1,723	3.5	0.2	2.9	0.2	93.1	7,879,324	35.8	1.4	62.7	0.0	6,877,035	3,991
Edgewood	RE	824	7.0	0.0	4.9	0.0	88.1	3,972,031	32.3	3.3	64.3	0.0	3,577,207	4,341
Fruitvale	AA	337	0.0	0.0	5.9	0.3	93.8	1,855,862	27.0	1.6	71.3	0.0	1,747,369	5,185
Grand Saline	AA	1,108	0.4	0.0	11.6	0.1	87.9	5,994,730	22.4	2.4	75.0	0.0	5,475,438	4,942
Martins Mill	RE	364	4.1	0.0	10.2	0.0	85.7	2,648,327	17.0	2.1	80.8	0.0	2,112,866	5,805
Van	AA	1,990	3.7	0.3	6.2	0.3	89.5	9,048,930	39.7	2.1	58.1	0.0	8,503,347	4,273
Wills Point	AA	2,443	8.2	0.2	7.1	0.2	84.3	11,127,362	23.8	2.5	73.5	0.0	10,263,104	4,201
Victoria - 3			7.6	0.6	48.9	0.1	42.8							
Bloomington	AA	928	3.8	0.0	71.3	0.0	25.0	5,351,859	26.3	0.9	72.7	0.0	5,197,214	5,600
Nursery	RE	103	0.0	0.0	14.6	0.0	85.4	610,776	87.5	3.0	9.3	0.0	619,061	6,010
Victoria	AA	14,668	7.9	0.7	47.7	0.1	43.6	67,802,961	54.3	2.1	43.4	0.0	68,931,978	4,699
Walker - 2			28.5	0.6	14.3	0.1	56.5							
Huntsville	AA	6,848	28.1	0.6	14.6	0.1	56.5	33,952,153	30.5	1.4	67.7	0.2	30,876,540	4,509
New Waverly	AA	837	31.5	0.0	11.7	0.1	56.7	4,332,430	23.6	2.9	73.3	0.1	4,696,430	5,611
Waller - 3			29.7	0.7	22.3	0.2	47.2							
Hempstead	AA	1,364	42.4	0.0	23.4	0.1	34.1	6,929,389	32.5	2.2	65.2	0.0	6,335,087	4,644
Royal	AU	1,433	40.8	0.6	32.2	0.0	26.4	7,196,338	44.7	1.0	54.2	0.0	6,709,989	4,682
Waller	AA	3,321	19.7	1.1	17.5	0.2	61.5	117,369,777	41.1	0.7	58.1	0.0	15,160,370	4,565
Ward - 2			4.9	0.5	46.2	0.0	48.4							
Grandfalls-Royalty	AA	180	1.1	0.0	58.3	0.0	40.6	1,272,996	82.2	1.5	16.1	0.0	1,254,319	6,968
Monahans-Wick.-Pyote	AA	2,526	5.1	0.5	45.4	0.0	48.9	12,187,217	80.5	2.2	17.1	0.0	13,409,995	5,309
Washington - 2			30.5	1.7	7.8	0.0	60.0							
Brenham	AA	4,782	30.9	1.8	8.1	0.0	59.2	26,381,045	40.7	2.0	57.1	0.0	21,575,827	4,512
Burton	AA	437	26.7	0.7	4.1	0.0	68.5	2,114,634	69.9	2.5	27.4	0.0	2,317,023	5,302
Webb - 4			0.1	0.4	96.2	0.1	3.4							
Laredo	AA	23,434	0.1	0.1	98.1	0.0	1.7	125,476,626	11.4	2.4	85.7	0.2	118,676,228	5,064
Mirando City	AA	63	0.0	0.0	93.7	0.0	6.3	1,176,500	47.9	1.5	50.5	0.0	970,281	15,401
United	AA	19,765	0.1	0.6	94.0	0.1	5.1	105,595,889	30.1	8.9	60.7	0.1	92,397,333	4,675
Webb Cons.	AA	397	0.0	0.0	87.8	0.3	12.0	6,086,832	94.8	3.0	2.0	0.0	4,987,103	12,562
Wharton - 5			19.9	0.2	36.1	0.0	43.8							
Boling	AA	983	21.2	0.0	33.0	0.0	45.9	5,712,561	34.1	1.2	64.5	0.0	5,084,870	5,173
East Bernard	AA	821	10.1	0.0	19.4	0.0	70.5	4,742,817	38.0	2.1	59.7	0.0	4,333,777	5,279
El Campo	AA	3,629	14.3	0.4	42.3	0.0	43.1	16,261,504	54.2	1.9	43.8	0.0	15,872,563	4,374
Louise	AA	534	3.6	0.0	38.5	0.2	57.8	2,821,478	42.1	1.8	56.0	0.0	2,449,832	4,588
Wharton	AA	2,793	32.9	0.2	33.4	0.1	33.4	14,709,369	48.3	2.1	49.3	0.1	13,854,498	4,960
Wheeler - 5			5.4	0.6	13.4	0.5	80.1							
Allison	RE	66	0.0	0.0	0.0	0.0	100.0	955,290	94.0	3.7	2.2	0.0	951,340	14,414
Fort Elliott Cons.	RE	108	0.0	0.0	0.9	0.0	99.1	1,280,118	93.8	3.4	2.7	0.0	1,294,187	11,983
Kelton	AA	41	4.9	0.0	24.4	0.0	70.7	611,256	87.5	9.3	3.1	0.0	516,796	12,605
Shamrock	AA	443	12.0	1.1	14.7	0.2	72.0	3,032,460	34.5	3.1	62.2	0.0	3,098,322	6,994
Wheeler	RE	358	0.0	0.3	16.8	1.1	81.8	2,647,667	45.1	2.5	52.2	0.0	2,403,578	6,714
Wichita - 5			13.0	2.1	12.8	0.4	71.5							
Burkburnett	RE	3,764	8.7	1.5	5.3	0.4	84.1	17,684,555	33.1	1.4	61.4	4.0	16,523,624	4,390
City View	RE	753	9.0	4.6	10.2	1.2	74.9	3,783,037	30.5	1.8	67.6	0.0	3,422,060	4,545
Electra	AA	715	7.8	0.0	10.1	0.0	82.1	3,974,716	35.6	2.2	61.9	0.2	3,847,397	5,381
Iowa Park Cons.	AA	2,139	0.2	0.3	3.2	1.1	95.1	8,926,635	36.1	4.1	59.6	0.0	8,274,595	3,868
Wichita Falls	AA	15,805	16.2	2.5	16.2	0.3	64.7	81,362,962	41.3	2.7	55.1	0.8	73,626,483	4,658
Wilbarger - 3			9.8	0.4	26.8	0.4	62.6							
Harrold	AA	119	2.5	0.0	8.4	0.0	89.1	766,446	32.5	1.5	65.8	0.0	715,276	6,011
Northside	AA	130	6.2	1.5	23.1	0.8	68.5	881,093	18.4	7.0	74.4	0.0	957,459	7,365
Vernon	AA	2,690	10.3	0.4	27.8	0.4	61.2	12,897,025	69.0	1.6	29.3	0.0	11,453,875	4,258

County/Dist.	District Ratings	Total Number of Students	% Black	% Asian	% Hispanic	% Amer. Indian	% White	Total Revenue	% Local	% Other	% State	% Federal	Total Spending	Spending Per Student
Willacy - 4			0.4	0.1	93.3	0.1	6.1							
Lasara	AA	263	0.0	0.0	95.6	0.0	4.4	1,996,172	13.4	2.1	83.9	0.5	1,832,719	6,969
Lyford	AA	1,687	0.1	0.0	94.7	0.1	5.1	10,027,732	18.2	2.7	78.8	0.2	9,268,271	5,494
Raymondville	AA	2,925	0.6	0.1	93.7	0.0	5.5	16,572,592	15.2	1.4	83.0	0.2	15,599,512	5,333
San Perlita	AA	261	0.0	0.0	77.8	0.8	21.5	1,946,861	31.1	1.7	66.7	0.2	1,799,881	6,896
Williamson - 11			5.5	2.7	16.1	0.3	75.3							
Coupland	EX	94	0.0	0.0	5.3	0.0	94.7	666,541	49.5	2.2	48.1	0.0	597,810	6,360
Florence	AA	773	0.4	0.3	10.4	0.9	88.0	4,688,167	11.5	1.4	86.9	0.0	4,042,177	5,229
Georgetown	AA	6,283	3.4	0.4	19.2	0.3	76.8	32,684,708	45.3	2.7	51.7	0.1	28,685,293	4,566
Granger	AA	396	8.7	0.0	28.5	0.2	62.6	2,137,780	23.5	2.1	73.8	0.4	1,945,871	4,914
Hutto	RE	768	4.8	0.8	14.3	0.7	79.4	4,629,485	32.4	1.6	65.8	0.0	3,843,231	5,004
Jarrell	AA	533	1.5	0.0	29.3	0.2	69.0	3,058,282	16.8	1.8	81.3	0.0	2,339,110	4,389
Leander	AA	8,932	2.6	1.6	11.4	0.4	83.9	47,127,459	51.6	1.5	46.8	0.0	37,775,230	4,229
Liberty Hill	AA	1,161	2.3	0.2	16.3	0.3	80.9	8,449,948	20.4	4.6	74.8	0.0	7,310,922	6,297
Round Rock	AA	25,087	5.9	4.4	14.3	0.3	75.1	141,928,986	57.6	1.6	40.6	0.1	116,367,084	4,639
Taylor	AA	2,702	19.4	0.1	37.8	0.4	42.2	16,064,959	28.6	2.4	68.8	0.0	14,205,287	5,257
Thrall	RE	465	7.7	0.2	20.2	0.2	71.6	2,455,927	26.3	3.6	70.0	0.0	2,346,222	5,046
Wilson - 4			1.4	0.1	39.8	0.1	58.7							
Floresville	AA	2,942	1.5	0.1	54.1	0.0	44.3	15,624,392	25.6	2.0	72.3	0.0	12,593,988	4,281
La Vernia	AA	1,740	1.8	0.3	14.0	0.1	83.8	7,742,960	16.6	1.7	81.6	0.0	6,703,087	3,852
Poth	AA	773	0.1	0.0	42.9	0.1	56.8	3,155,776	24.8	2.1	73.0	0.0	3,262,492	4,221
Stockdale	AA	731	1.2	0.0	40.1	0.3	58.4	3,231,168	24.2	1.6	74.0	0.0	3,119,578	4,268
Winkler - 2			1.6	0.2	50.5	0.0	47.7							
Kermit	AA	1,585	1.6	0.2	57.6	0.0	40.6	11,309,740	42.7	7.6	49.6	0.0	8,375,857	5,284
Wink-Loving	RE	383	1.6	0.0	20.9	0.0	77.5	4,478,131	96.3	1.2	2.4	0.0	3,842,641	10,033
Wise - 7			1.0	0.2	14.3	0.5	84.0							
Alvord	AA	449	0.4	0.0	10.2	0.4	88.9	2,532,842	29.9	1.1	68.1	0.8	2,603,743	5,799
Boyd	AA	1,094	0.8	0.3	6.9	1.0	91.0	5,827,332	23.4	3.1	73.4	0.0	5,072,748	4,637
Bridgeport	AA	1,899	0.2	0.2	19.4	0.4	79.8	9,542,765	43.3	4.0	52.6	0.0	8,563,933	4,510
Chico	AA	637	0.2	0.0	5.8	0.3	93.7	3,105,937	46.9	1.2	51.8	0.0	2,884,465	4,528
Decatur	AA	2,036	2.7	0.2	21.6	0.0	75.3	11,273,240	47.8	3.2	48.8	0.0	10,011,732	4,917
Paradise	AA	717	0.0	0.3	5.3	1.0	93.4	4,405,704	28.0	1.4	70.5	0.0	3,527,041	4,919
Slidell	AA	261	0.0	0.0	4.2	0.4	95.4	1,528,640	23.3	0.8	75.8	0.0	1,326,572	5,083
Wood - 6			8.2	0.2	6.0	0.3	85.2							
Alba-Golden	RE	669	0.0	0.0	3.3	1.2	95.5	3,693,509	26.3	2.4	69.1	2.1	3,312,475	4,951
Hawkins	AA	854	18.3	0.0	0.8	0.0	80.8	5,235,600	81.6	2.1	16.1	0.0	4,924,300	5,766
Mineola	AA	1,595	13.2	0.4	9.6	0.4	76.4	8,493,635	34.6	1.9	63.3	0.0	6,828,286	4,281
Quitman	AA	1,205	6.6	0.2	5.9	0.1	87.2	6,542,030	52.1	2.6	45.2	0.0	6,508,929	5,402
Winnsboro	AA	1,410	3.8	0.4	5.0	0.1	90.7	6,487,067	34.4	4.2	61.3	0.0	5,910,154	4,192
Yantis	AA	356	0.0	0.0	11.8	0.6	87.6	1,965,441	46.3	0.8	52.8	0.0	1,684,034	4,730
Yoakum - 2			1.6	0.0	51.7	0.1	46.5							
Denver City	AA	1,804	2.0	0.1	51.2	0.1	46.6	11,958,277	88.8	2.8	8.3	0.0	10,860,669	6,020
Plains	RE	530	0.2	0.0	53.4	0.2	46.2	5,036,995	87.7	3.0	6.5	2.6	4,742,245	8,948
Young - 3			1.7	0.6	13.5	0.4	83.8							
Graham	AA	2,637	1.8	0.8	12.2	0.4	84.8	11,453,351	39.5	1.2	59.2	0.0	11,002,264	4,172
Newcastle	AA	201	0.5	0.0	6.5	0.5	92.5	1,357,540	32.6	1.2	66.1	0.0	1,170,037	5,821
Olney	AA	864	1.6	0.3	18.8	0.5	78.7	5,024,224	21.4	2.1	76.2	0.1	5,080,519	5,880
Zapata - 1			0.1	0.0	93.7	0.1	6.1							
Zapata Co.	AA	2,894	0.1	0.0	93.7	0.1	6.1	16,474,102	90.9	1.8	7.2	0.0	15,721,302	5,432
Zavala - 2			0.5	0.0	96.1	0.2	3.2							
Crystal City	AA	2,026	0.5	0.0	98.3	0.1	1.1	10,800,013	20.9	1.3	77.2	0.4	10,496,617	5,181
La Pryor	AA	463	0.2	0.2	86.5	0.9	12.3	3,998,171	11.4	2.7	85.7	0.0	3,690,391	7,971

Texas' Rank in Public Education

Source: Statistical Abstract of the United States, 1996, U.S. Dept. of Commerce, Bureau of the Census.

Enrollment, Fall, 1993		**Teachers, 1995**		**Expenditures, 1995**	
1. California	5,328,000	1. Texas	234,200	1. California	$28,176,000,000
2. Texas	3,608,000	2. California	221,700	2. New York	$25,945,000,000
3. New York	2,734,000	3. New York	190,400	3. Texas	$21,120,000,000

Texas Higher Education

Source: Texas Higher Education Coordinating Board.

The $86.2 billion 1998-99 state budget approved by the 75th Legislature included $10.8 billion for higher education, a 10.1 percent increase in all-funds appropriations over the previous biennium. General-revenue appropriations were increased by 8.4 percent to $7.4 billion.

Enrollment

Enrollment in Texas' public and independent colleges and universities in fall 1996 was 926,827, an increase of 5,387 students, or .6 percent from fall 1995.

Enrollment in the 35 public universities decreased by 3,340 (.8%). Seventeen public universities reported combined net increases of 2,694 students, while 18 reported a combined net decrease of 6,212 students.

The state's public community-college districts reported fall 1996 enrollments totaling 407,556 students, up 6,507 students (1.6%) from fall 1995. The Texas State Technical College System's three campuses reported a fall 1996 enrollment of 8,008 students, an increase of 451 (6%) from the previous fall.

Enrollments at 38 independent senior colleges and universities increased to 96,685 students, up 1,409 (1.5%) from fall 1995. The state's three independent junior colleges reported 751 students, an increase of 83 (12.4%) over the previous fall.

Public medical, dental, nursing and allied-health schools reported enrollments totaling 15,378 students in fall 1996, an increase of 264 (1.8%) from fall 1995. Enrollment at independent medical and health-related institutions increased to 1,156 students, up 13 (1.1%) from the previous fall. The Texas Higher Education Coordinating Board (THECB) forecasts that higher-education enrollments in Texas will increase by 131,000 students annually by the year 2010.

Hopwood v. Texas Ruling

In the court case *Hopwood v. Texas*, the 5th U.S. Circuit Court of Appeals ruled in March 1996 that The University of Texas at Austin School of Law could no longer legally consider race or ethnicity in admissions decisions. In an interpretive opinion issued in February 1997, Texas Attorney General Dan Morales stated that the *Hopwood* ruling applies to admissions and financial-aid decisions at all Texas public higher-education institutions: No Texas public higher-education institution can consider race or ethnicity in deciding whom to admit or who shall receive financial aid.

The 75th Texas Legislature, concerned by the subsequent decrease in Texas university admissions applications from black and Hispanic students, required universities that are not open-admissions institutions to admit automatically students who rank in the top 10 percent of their high-school graduating classes. In addition, those universities have the option of automatically admitting students who rank in the top 25 percent in high school. Other admissions must be based on race-neutral criteria, such as academic record and family income.

The Legislature also required students who receive athletic scholarships to meet the same minimum grade-point average standards as nonathletes at the same institutions; required the THECB to monitor admission of minority students in Texas public higher-education institutions; and provided $10 million over the 1998-99 biennium to pay college costs for students who maintained a "B" average in high school and perform community service while in college.

Changes in the Texas Academic Skills Program

Changes in the Texas Academic Skills Program (TASP) were made by the Legislature to help ensure that the program encourages and helps students complete higher education. The program is designed to identify students who have not yet developed the reading, writing and math skills needed to succeed in college, then help them get those skills.

With the changes approved by the Legislature, students must take the TASP Test or an alternative test before enrolling in college courses. Students who do not have adequate skills, as determined by one of those assessments, must enroll in developmental education. Students who earn the grade of "B" or better in certain freshman-level credit courses in the subject matter for which the developmental education was required can proceed through college. Students who do not earn at least the grade of "B" in those freshman-level courses must pass the TASP test before enrolling in upper-division courses beyond 60 semester credit hours.

The Legislature also directed the THECB to develop a method for providing additional funding to higher-education institutions for each student who successfully completes developmental education.

Core Curriculum

To improve the transfer of course credit between higher education institutions, the 75th Legislature required the THECB to develop a core curriculum of at least 42 semester credit hours. A student who successfully completes core-curriculum courses at one institution may transfer those courses to any other Texas institution. The THECB will also develop field-of-study curricula for bachelor's-degree programs. Credit for courses in the field-of-study curricula may be transferred to another institution and substituted for that institutions' lower-division requirements for a bachelor's degree in the same field.

Tuition and Fees Combined

The 75th Legislature redesignated the building-use fee as "tuition." Since building-use fees vary among institutions, public universities in Texas will not have identical tuition rates beginning in fall 1997.

Graduation Incentives

In an effort to encourage students to earn bachelor's degrees in a reasonable amount of time, the Legislature limited institutional funding to 170 hours for undergraduate students beginning with the fall 1999 semester. A university will be able to charge additional tuition, up to the non-resident tuition rate, to a student with more than 170 undergraduate hours. Excluded are students enrolled in a double-degree or double-major program or a health professional-degree program. Also excluded are degreed students returning to school after more than one year or remedial courses.

The bill also creates a tuition rebate of $1,000 for resident students who receive their bachelor's degrees and have attempted no more than three hours above the hours required in their degree plan. Students who enter a bachelor's-degree program on or after Sept. 1, 1997, will be eligible for the rebate.

Distance Learning

Texas higher-education institutions will be able to offer courses over the Internet, and other computer-based courses, statewide if the course is within the curriculum approved for the institution by the THECB. The THECB will maintain an on-line repository of information, called Texas Colleges On-Line, about these courses.

The Internet address for the Higher Education Coordinating Board is **http://www.thecb.state.tx.us/** ☆

Performance Evaluation of Tenured Faculty

In an effort to ensure accountability among faculty, the Legislature required the governing boards of each Texas public higher-education institution to adopt rules for periodic performance review for all tenured faculty at the institution. Evaluations must be conducted at least once every six years after the faculty member receives tenure and or received an academic promotion at the institution.

Tuition Revenue Bonds

To help universities construct new buildings and related facilities, the Legislature authorized $638 million in tuition revenue bonds to be issued by institutions. ☆

Brief History of Higher Education in Texas

While there were earlier efforts toward higher education, the first permanent institutions established were church-supported schools: **Rutersville University**, established in 1840 by Methodist minister Martin Ruter in Fayette County, predecessor of **Southwestern University**, Georgetown, established in 1843; Baylor University, now at Waco, but established in 1845 at Independence, Washington County, by the Texas Union Baptist Association; and **Austin College**, now at Sherman, but founded in 1849 at Huntsville by the Brazos Presbytery of the Old School Presbyterian Church.

Other historic Texas schools of collegiate rank included: **Larissa College**, 1848, at Larissa, Cherokee County; **McKenzie College**, 1841, Clarksville; **Chappell Hill Male and Female Institute**, 1850, Chappell Hill; **Soule University**, 1855, Chappell Hill; **Johnson Institute**, 1852, Driftwood, Hays County; **Nacogdoches University**, 1845, Nacogdoches; **Salado College**, 1859, Salado, Bell County. **Add-Ran College**, established at Thorp Spring, Hood County, in 1873, was the predecessor of present **Texas Christian University**, Fort Worth.

Texas A&M and University of Texas

(See special history feature below.)

First College for Women

In 1901, the 27th Legislature established the **Girls Industrial College**, which began classes at its campus in Denton in 1903. A campaign to establish a state industrial college for women was led by the State Grange and Patrons of Husbandry. A bill was signed into law on April 6, 1901, creating the college. It was charged with a dual mission, which continues to guide the university today — to provide a liberal education and to prepare young women with a specialized education "for the practical industries of the age." In 1905 the name of the college was changed to the **College of Industrial Arts**; in 1934, it was changed to **Texas State College for Women**. Since 1957 the name of the institution, which is now the largest university principally for women in the United States, has been the **Texas Woman's University**.

Historic, Primarily Black Colleges

A number of Texas schools were established primarily for blacks, although collegiate racial integration is now complete in the state. The black-oriented institutions include state-supported **Prairie View A&M University** (originally established as **Alta Vista Agricultural College** in 1876), Prairie View; **Texas Southern University**, Houston; and privately supported **Huston-Tillotson College**, Austin; **Jarvis Christian College**, Hawkins; **Wiley College**, Marshall; **Paul Quinn College**, originally located in Waco, now in Dallas; and **Texas College**, Tyler. Predominantly black colleges that are important in the history of higher education in Texas, but that have ceased operations, include **Bishop College**, established in Marshall in 1881, then moved to Dallas; **Mary Allen College**, established in Crockett in 1886; and **Butler College**, originally named the **Texas Baptist Academy**, in 1905 in Tyler. ☆

The Beginnings of The University of Texas and Texas A&M

On Jan. 14, 1839, the Congress of the Republic of Texas provided for the selection of a site for the seat of government, to be named Austin. Included in the legislation were provisions for sites for a capitol, an arsenal, a magazine, an academy, churches, a common school, a hospital, a penitentiary and "all other necessary public buildings and purposes." A 40-acre site named College Hill was also set aside for a university, but no plans for construction were made at the time. Congress also set aside 50 square leagues of land, approximately 221,420 acres, to endow two universities.

A bill establishing The University of Texas passed the Legislature in 1858, including a provision that the sum of $100,000 in U.S. bonds be set aside in the State Treasury for the development of the university. The Civil War postponed further action.

The 50 sections of land previously set aside for the two universities was augmented by a grant of one section of land for every 10 sections that were granted to the railroads.

The Morrill Land-Grant Bill, passed by the U.S. Congress in 1862, granted Texas 180,000 acres of land to establish an agricultural and mechanical college. The offer was accepted in 1866, but again there was a delay. The Legislature finally provided for the establishment of a land-grant college in April 1871. Three commissioners were appointed to locate and build the college within three months, an impossible task.

The commissioners were wooed by officials of several communities, including Bryan in Brazos County, Kellum Springs and Piedmont Springs in Grimes County, and Bellville in Austin County. Officials in Bryan successfully courted the commissioners with talk of contributions of $20,000-30,000 if the college located there.

Bryan businessmen aggressively promoted the town through land give-aways. To the Agricultural and Mechanical College, they made a total grant of 2,416 acres. Those acres have been described as a "wild, bleak prairie, barren of trees and shrubs . . .except for one small mesquite tree." Wolves were abundant: One early student was attacked by wolves during the day in full sight of the main building. Another was attacked at night when he fell off a porch.

Early plans for the college were clouded in factional disputes, at least partly because they were proposed by a Radical Republican administration. With the legislative session of 1873, the future of A&M College improved. The main building was completed by the end of 1874 and additional buildings were constructed. In 1875, the Legislature separated the administrations of A&M and The University of Texas, the latter of which still existed only on paper. The Agricultural and Mechanical College formally opened on Oct. 4, 1876.

The Constitution of 1876 provided that a "university of the first class" be established at a site selected by a vote of the people and that it be called "The University of Texas." The Agricultural and Mechanical College was to be a branch of the main university. The university's million-acre land endowment was carved out of arid West Texas. Another million acres, equally arid, were added to the endowment in 1883.

Finally, on March 30, 1881, the Legislature passed a law providing for the organization of The University of Texas. On Sept. 6, 1881, voters selected Austin — over sites at Waco, Tyler, Thorp Spring, Lampasas, Williams Ranch, Albany, Graham, Matagorda and Caddo Grove and Peak — for the main university and Galveston for its medical branch. Men and women were to be accepted as students on equal terms, and no religious qualifications for either students or faculty were to be required.

The cornerstone for the west wing of the main building was laid on Nov. 17, 1882, on the site originally designated for the university in 1839. At the ceremony, Ashbel Smith, president of the board of regents, made an unwittingly prophetic speech, in which he declared, "Smite the rocks with the rod of knowledge, and fountains of unstinted wealth will gush forth." The unstinted wealth gushed forth in 1923, when the Texon Oil and Land Company struck oil on its lease on university lands in Reagan County. The Santa Rita No. 1, discovery well of the Big Lake oil field, was named at the request of a group of Catholic women investors from New York in honor of the patron saint of the impossible and hopeless.

The university formally opened on Sept. 15, 1883, with a ceremony in the unfinished west wing of the main building. Classes were held in the temporary capitol at the corner of Congress Avenue and Eleventh Street until the building was finished in December.

The University Co-Op, almost as old as the university

itself, began operations in 1896 in a space 10 feet by 20 feet under the stairway of the second floor of the Main Building. It is now housed in spacious quarters across Guadalupe Street from the main campus. To generations of University of Texas students, it has been a fixture of university life. ☆

Universities and Colleges

Source: Texas Higher Education Coordinating Board and institutions. In some cases, dates of establishment differ from those given in the preceding discussion because schools use the date when authorization was given, rather than actual date of first classwork. For explanation of type of institution and other symbols, see notes at end of table.

Name of Institution; Location; (Type* - Ownership, if private sectarian institution); Date of Founding; President (unless otherwise noted)	Number in Faculty†	Enrollment		
		Fall Term 1996	Summer Session 1996	Extension or Continuing Ed.
Abilene Christian University—Abilene; (3 - Church of Christ); 1906 (as **Childers Classical Institute**; became **Abilene Christian College** by 1914; became university in 1976); Dr. Royce Money	348	4,397	1,892	NA
ALAMO COMMUNITY COLLEGE DISTRICT (9) — Robert Ramsay, Chancellor				
Northwest Vista College — San Antonio; (7); 1995; Dr. Robert W. Ramsay, Interim Pres.	**	840	40	NA
Palo Alto College—San Antonio; (7); 1985; Dr. Ernest A. Martinez, Interim President	348	7,607	3,232	751
St. Philip's College—San Antonio; (7); 1898; Dr. Charles A. Taylor.	522	7,867	NA	5,216
‡ **San Antonio College**—San Antonio; (7); 1925; Dr. Ruth Burgos-Sasscer	930	20,729	12,550	2,581
Alvin Community College—Alvin; (7); 1949; Dr. A. Rodney Allbright	228	3,872	2,788	598
Amarillo College—Amarillo; (7); 1929; Dr. Luther "Bud" Joyner.	220	7,000	2,800	NA
Amber University—Garland; (3); 1971; Dr. Douglas W. Warner	45	1,500	1,400	NA
Angelina College—Lufkin; (7); 1968; Dr. Larry Phillips	**	3,900	**	**
Angelo State University—San Angelo (See **Texas State University System**)				
Arlington Baptist College—Arlington; (3 - Baptist); 1939 (as **Bible Baptist Seminary**; changed to present name in 1965); Dr. David Bryant	25	212	45	NA
Austin College—Sherman; (3 - Presbyterian USA); 1849; Dr. Oscar C. Page	97	1,184	130	465
‡ **Austin Community College**—Austin; (7); 1972; Dr. Bill Segura	1,797	25,276	20,678	7,481
Austin Presbyterian Theological Seminary—Austin; Presbyterian; 3-yr; 1902 (successor to **Austin School of Theology**, est. 1884); Dr.Robert M. Shelton, Acting President	29	316	130	73
Baptist Missionary Association Theological Seminary—Jacksonville; Baptist Missionary, 3-yr.; 1955; Dr. Philip R. Bryan	13	61	15	NA
Baylor College of Dentistry—(see **Texas A&M University System**)				
Baylor College of Medicine—Houston; (5 - Baptist until 1969); 1903 (Dallas; moved to Houston, 1943); Ralph D. Feigin, M.D.	¶¶3,212	2,444	NA	NA
Baylor University—Waco; (3 - So. Baptist); 1845 (at Independence; merged with **Waco University** in 1887 and moved to Waco); Dr. Robert B. Sloan Jr.	606	12,311	5,187	1,134
Bee County College—Beeville; (7); 1966; Dr. Norman E. Wallace.	200	3,000	854	261
Blinn College—Brenham; (7); 1883 (as academy; jr. college, 1927); Dr. Donald E. Voelter.	376	9,731	§8,851	NA
Brazosport College—Lake Jackson; (7); 1967; Dr. Millicent M. Valek	168	3,426	2,590	2,928
Brookhaven College—Farmers Branch (See **Dallas County Community College District**)				
Cedar Valley College—Lancaster (See **Dallas County Community College District**)				
Central Texas College—Killeen; (7); 1965; Dr. James R. Anderson, Chancellor	534	7,387	5,277	1,176
Cisco Junior College—Cisco; (7); 1909 (as private institution; became state school in 1939); Dr. Roger C. Schustereit	65	2,573	1,313	205
Clarendon College—Clarendon; (7); 1898 (as church school; became state school in 1927); Dr. Scott Elliott	50	800	650	100
College of the Mainland—Texas City; (7); 1967; Larry L. Stanley	370	3,744	2,819	5,451
College of St. Thomas More—Fort Worth; (**); (3-Roman Catholic); 1981 (as **St. Thomas More Inst.**; became college 1989; accredited as 2-year college 1994); James A. Patrick, Provost	6	55	15	0
Collin County Community College—McKinney; (7); 1985; Dr. John H. Anthony	**	10,580	7,827	3,897
Concordia University—Austin; (3 - Mo. Lutheran); 1926 (as **Concordia Lutheran College**; name changed in 1995); Dr. David Zersen	47	728	**	NA
Cooke County College—Gainesville (See **North Central Texas College**)	85	4,150	1,600	3,500
Corpus Christi State University—(See **Texas A&M University-Corpus Christi** listing under **Texas A&M University System**)				
Dallas Baptist University—Dallas; (3 - Southern Baptist).; 1898 (as **Decatur Baptist College**; moved to Dallas and name changed in 1965); Dr. Gary Cook.	231	3,283	1,742	NA
Dallas Christian College—Dallas; (3 - Christian); 1950; Dr. Keith Ray	35	250	100	50
DALLAS COUNTY COMMUNITY COLLEGE DISTRICT (9) —J. William Wenrich, Chancellor				
Brookhaven College—Farmers Branch; (7); 1978; **	500	7,000	5,000	14,000
Cedar Valley College—Lancaster; (7); 1977; Dr. Carol J. Spencer	141	2,851	1,114	2,000
Eastfield College—Mesquite; (7); 1970; Dr. Rodger Pool	600	8,056	§5,059	4,498
El Centro College—Dallas; (7); 1966; Dr. Wright L. Lassiter Jr.	572	4,252	2,364	3,500
Mountain View College—Dallas; (7); 1970; Dr. Monique Amerman	69	5,569	2,426	3,176
‡ **North Lake College**—Irving; (7); 1977; Angie Runnels, Interim President	65	6,835	4,040	4,406
Richland College—Dallas; (7); 1972; Dr. Stephen K. Mittelstet	538	12,898	§9,704	8,341
Dallas Theological Seminary—Dallas; private, graduate; 1924; Dr. Charles R. Swindoll	80	1,514	789	331
Del Mar College—Corpus Christi; (7); 1935; Dr. Terry L. Dicianna	700	10,682	0	17,500
Eastfield College—Mesquite (See **Dallas County Community College District**)				
East Texas Baptist University—Marshall; (3 - Baptist); 1913 (as **College of Marshall**; became **East Texas Baptist Coll.**, 1944; became university in 1984); Dr. Bob E. Riley	67	1,300	§403	NA
East Texas State University (see **Texas A&M University-Commerce** in **Texas A&M System** listing)				
East Texas State University at Texarkana (see **Texas A&M University-Texarkana** in **Texas A&M System** listing)				

Name of Institution; Location; (Type* - Ownership, if private sectarian institution); Date of Founding; President (unless otherwise noted)	Number in Faculty†	Enrollment		
		Fall Term 1996	Summer Session 1996	Extension or Continuing Ed.
El Centro College—Dallas (See Dallas County Community College District)				
El Paso Community College District—El Paso; (7); 1969; three campuses: Rio Grande, TransMountain and Valle Verde; Dr. Adriana D. Barrera	††2,000	19,000	19,800	2,000
Episcopal Theological Seminary of the Southwest—Austin; Episcopal; Graduate-level; 1952; Very Rev. Durstan R. McDonald, Dean	19	79	18	NA
Frank Phillips College—Borger; (7); 1948; Dr. William A. Griffin Jr.	64	1,026	755	533
Galveston College—Galveston; (7); 1967; Dr. C.B. Rathburn	76	2,041	1,700	3,000
Grayson County College—Denison; (7); 1963; Dr. Alan Scheibmeir	118	3,221	1,400	1,688
Hardin-Simmons University—Abilene; (3 - So. Baptist); 1891 (as Simmons College; changed to Simmons University, 1925; changed to present name, 1934); Dr. Lanny Hall	179	2,279	1,374	450
Hill College—Hillsboro; (7); 1923 (as Hillsboro Junior College; name changed, 1962); Dr. William R. Auvenshine	80	2,500	500	200
Houston Baptist University—Houston; (3 - Baptist); 1960; Dr. E. D. Hodo	110	2,200	2,200	285
‡ ‡‡HOUSTON COMMUNITY COLLEGE SYSTEM—Houston; (9); 1971; Dr. James Harding, Interim Chancellor. System consists of following colleges (president): Central College (James P. Engle); College Without Walls (Baltazar Acevedo Jr.); Northeast College (Elaine P. Adams); Northwest College (Zach Hodges); Southeast College (Sylvia Ramos); Southwest College (Sue Cox).	2,352	42,757	25,210	11,860
‡‡ Howard County Junior College District—Big Spring; (7); 1945; includes Howard College and Southwest Collegiate Institute for the Deaf; Dr. Cheryl T. Sparks	110	2,107	1,281	1,103
Howard Payne University—Brownwood; (3 - Baptist); 1889; Dr. Don Newbury	124	1,468	NA	130
Huston-Tillotson College—Austin; (3 - Methodist/Church of Christ); 1875 (Tillotson College, 1875, Samuel Huston College, 1876; merged 1952); Dr. Joseph T. McMillan Jr.	50	701	168	0
International Bible College—San Antonio; (3); 1944; Rev. David W. Cook	16	120	NA	NA
Jacksonville College—Jacksonville; (8 - Missionary Baptist); 1899; Dr. Edwin Crank	28	345	119	0
Jarvis Christian College—Hawkins; (3); 1912; Dr. Sebetha Jenkins	44	557	22	NA
Kilgore College—Kilgore; (7); 1935; Dr. William M. Holda	157	4,312	§2,107	2,576
Lamar University and all branches (see Texas State University System)				
Laredo Community College—Laredo; (7); 1946; Dr. Ramon H. Dovalina	303	7,208	§4,400	3,000
LeTourneau University—Longview; (3); 1946 (as LeTourneau Technical Institute; became 4-yr. college in 1961); Dr. Alvin O. Austin	305	2,056	219	800
‡ Lee College—Baytown; (7); 1934; Dr. Jackson N. Sasser	326	5,628	4,011	2,703
Lon Morris College—Jacksonville; (8 - Methodist); 1854 (as Danville Academy; changed in 1873 to Alexander Inst.; present name, 1923); Dr. Clifford M. Lee	44	363	NA	NA
Lubbock Christian University—Lubbock; (3 - Church of Christ); 1957; Dr. L. Ken Jones	99	1,124	495	NA
McLennan Community College—Waco; (7); 1965; Dr. Dennis Michaelis	320	6,000	5,500	9,500
McMurry University—Abilene; (3 - Methodist); 1923; Dr. Robert E. Shimp	115	1,400	§703	NA
Midland College—Midland; (7); 1972; Dr. David E. Daniel	215	4,076	1,633	4,400
Midwestern State University—Wichita Falls; (2); 1922; Dr. Louis J. Rodriguez	181	5,643	§3,859	1,460
Mountain View College—Dallas (See Dallas County Community College District)				
Navarro College—Corsicana; (7); 1946; Dr. Gerald E. Burson	213	3,421	1,500	998
North Central Texas College—Gainesville; (7); 1924 (as Gainesville Jr. College; Cooke County College, 1960; present name, 1994); Dr. Ronnie Glasscock	237	4,158	1,100	1,403
Northeast Texas Community College—Mount Pleasant; (7); 1984; Dr. Charles B. Florio	49	1,992	§1,575	NA
‡ NORTH HARRIS MONTGOMERY COMMUNITY COLLEGE DISTRICT (9)— John Pickelman, Chancellor. Includes these colleges, location (president): Kingwood College, Kingwood (Stephen Head); Montgomery College, Conroe (William D. Law); North Harris College, Houston (Sanford Shugart); Tomball College, Tomball (Diane Troyer)	1,117	19,299	10,026	8,400
North Lake College—Irving (See Dallas County Community College District)				
Northwest Vista College (see Alamo Community College District)				
Northwood Institute—Cedar Hill; private; 1966; Donald B. Tallman, Provost	35	1,050	276	NA
Oblate School of Theology—San Antonio; Rom. Catholic, 4-yr.; 1903 (formerly DeMazenod Scholasticate); Rev. J. William Morell, O.M.I.	35	323	57	2,930
Odessa College—Odessa; (7); 1946; Dr. Vance W. Gipson	214	4,894	2,832	NA
Our Lady of the Lake University of San Antonio—San Antonio; (3 - Catholic); 1895 (as acad. for girls; sr. college, 1911; university, in 1975); Sister Elizabeth Anne Sueltenfuss	217	3,468	702	380
Palo Alto College—San Antonio (See Alamo Community College District)				
Panola College—Carthage; (7); 1947 (as Panola Junior College; name changed, 1988); Dr. William F. Edmonson	65	1,777	1,143	282
Paris Junior College—Paris; (7); 1924; Bobby R. Walters	81	2,917	1,085	1,312
‡ Paul Quinn College—Dallas; (3); 1872 (in Waco; Dallas, 1990); Dr. Lee E. Monroe	43	667	NA	NA
Prairie View A&M University—Prairie View (See Texas A&M University System)				
‡ Ranger College—Ranger; (7); 1926; Dr. Joe Mills	122	829	590	65
Rice University (William Marsh)—Houston; (3); chartered 1891, opened 1912 (as Rice Institute; name changed in 1960); Dr. S. Malcolm Gillis	598	4,187	866	4,123
Richland College—Dallas (See Dallas County Community College District)				
St. Edward's University—Austin; (3 - Roman Catholic); 1885; Dr. Patricia A. Hayes	130	3,082	**	NA
St. Mary's University of San Antonio—San Antonio; (3 - Catholic); 1852; Rev. John Moder	†††180	4,096	2,341	150
St. Philip's College—San Antonio (See Alamo Community College District)				
Sam Houston State University—Huntsville (See Texas State University System)				
San Antonio College—San Antonio (See Alamo Community College District)				
SAN JACINTO COLLEGE DISTRICT (9) —Dr. Dr. Jim Horton, Chancellor				
‡ Central Campus—Pasadena; (7); 1961; Dr. Monte Blue	532	10,264	6,285	3,353
North Campus —Houston; (7); 1974; Dr. Edwin E. Lehr	107	4,081	2,021	1,170

Name of Institution; Location; (Type* - Ownership, if private sectarian institution); Date of Founding; President (unless otherwise noted)	Number in Faculty†	Enrollment		
		Fall Term 1996	Summer Session 1996	Extension or Continuing Ed.
‡ South Campus —Houston; (7); 1979; Dr. Parker Williams	200	5,157	3,025	1,354
Schreiner College—Kerrville; (3 - Presbyterian); 1923; Dr. J. Thompson Biggers	¶64	654	107	68
South Plains College—Levelland; (7); 1957; Dr. Gary D. McDaniel.	310	5,843	2,661	1,239
South Texas College of Law—Houston; private, 3-yr.; 1923; Tom Read, Dean and Pres.	100	1,217	489	NA
South Texas Community College—McAllen; (7); NA; Dr. Shirley A. Reed	400	5,432	4,219	1,033
‡ Southern Methodist University—Dallas; (3 - Methodist); 1911; Dr. R. Gerald Turner	648	9,014	3,652	***3,131
Southwest Collegiate Institute for the Deaf — Big Spring (See Howard County Junior College District)				
Southwestern Adventist University—Keene; (3 - Seventh-Day Adventist); 1893 (as Keene Industrial Acad.; named Southwestern Jr. College in 1916; changed to Southwestern Union College in 1963, then to Southwestern Adventist College in 1980; became university in 1996); Dr. Marvin Anderson	110	1,030	NA	NA
Southwestern Assemblies of God University—Waxahachie; (3 - Assemblies of God); 1927 (in Enid, Okla., as Southwestern Bible School; moved to Fort Worth and merged with South Central Bible Institute in 1941; moved to Waxahachie as Southwestern Bible Institute in 1943; changed to Southwestern Assemblies of God College,1963; university since 1996); Dr. Delmer R. Guynes	60	1,343	238	0
Southwestern Baptist Theological Seminary—Fort Worth; Southern Baptist, 4-yr.; 1908; Dr. Ken Hemphill.	**	3,077	**	**
Southwestern Christian College—Terrell; (3 - Church of Christ); 1948 (as Southern Bible Inst. in Fort Worth; moved to Terrell, changed name to present, 1950); Dr. Jack Evans	30	200	25	NA
Southwestern University—Georgetown; (3 - Methodist); 1840 (Southwestern University was a merger of Rutersville (1840), Wesleyan (1846) and McKenzie (1841) colleges and Soule University (1855). First named Texas University; chartered under present name in 1875); Dr. Roy B. Shilling Jr.	152	1,226	256	NA
Southwest Texas Junior College—Uvalde; (7); 1946; Dr. Billy Word	185	3,273	1,436	309
Southwest Texas State University—San Marcos (see Texas State University System)				
Stephen F. Austin State University—Nacogdoches; (2); 1921; Dr. Dan Angel.	609	11,690	6,110	500
Sul Ross State University—Alpine (See Texas State University System)				
Sul Ross State University-Rio Grande College—Uvalde (See Texas State University System)				
Tarleton State University—Stephenville (See Texas A&M University System)				
Tarrant County Junior College District—Fort Worth; (7); 1965; four campuses: Northeast (Hurst), Northwest (Fort Worth), South (Fort Worth) and Southeast (Arlington); Dr. Leonardo de la Garza, Chancellor	1,038	25,174	§18,275	18,633
Temple College—Temple; (7); 1926; Dr. Marc A. Nigliazzo	165	2,801	1,755	2,542
Texarkana College—Texarkana; (7); 1927; Dr. Carl M. Nelson	110	3,669	1,862	9,256
Texas A&I University—Kingsville (See Texas A&M University-Kingsville listing under Texas A&M University System)				
TEXAS A&M UNIVERSITY SYSTEM (1) —Dr. Barry B. Thompson, Chancellor				
Baylor College of Dentistry—Dallas; (5); 1905 (transferred to Texas A&M system 1995); Dr. Dominick P. DePaola, President	††300	495	104	500
Prairie View A&M University—Prairie View; (2); 1876 (as Alta Vista Agricultural College; changed to Prairie View State Normal Institute in 1879; later Prairie View Normal and Industrial College; in 1947 changed to Prairie View A&M College as branch of Texas A&M University System; present name since 1973); Dr. Charles A. Hines	358	6,167	2,590	NA
Tarleton State University—Stephenville; (2); 1899 (as John Tarleton College; taken over by state in 1917 as John Tarleton Agricultural College; changed 1949 to Tarleton State College; present name since 1973); Dr. Dennis McCabe	352	6,370	2,790	NA
Texas A&M International University-Laredo; (2); 1970 (as Laredo State University; name changed to present form 1993); Dr. J. Charles Jennett	117	2,677	§2,527	NA
Texas A&M University—College Station; (2); 1876 (as Agricultural and Mechanical College of Texas; present name since 1963; includes College of Veterinary Medicine and College of Medicine at College Station); Dr. Ray M. Bowen	2,500	43,031	§34,000	NA
‡Texas A&M University - Commerce—Commerce; (2); 1889 (as East Texas Normal College; renamed East Texas State Teachers College in 1923; "Teachers" dropped, 1957; university status conferred and named changed to East Texas State University, 1965; transferred to Texas A&M system 1995; includes ETSUMetroplex Commuter Facility, Mesquite); Dr. Jerry D. Morris	383	7,952	6,794	333
Texas A&M University-Corpus Christi —Corpus Christi; (2); 1973 (as upper-level Corpus Christi State Univ.; present name since 1993; 4-year in 1994); Dr. Robert R. Furgason	251	5,686	§5,037	1,830
Texas A&M University at Galveston—Galveston; (2); 1962 (as Texas Maritime Academy; changed to Moody College of Marine Sciences and Maritime Resources and became 4-yr. college in 1971); Dr. Vi Flores, Interim VP and CEO.	385	1,122	858	NA
Texas A&M University-Kingsville—Kingsville; (2); 1925 (as South Texas State Teachers College; name changed to Texas College of Arts and Industries in 1929, to Texas A&I University in 1967; made part of Univ. of South Texas System in 1977; entered A&M system in 1993); Dr. Manuel L. Ibañez	380	6,117	2,875	NA
‡Texas A&M University - Texarkana—Texarkana; (2 - upper-level); 1971 (as East Texas State University at Texarkana, transferred to Texas A&M system and name changed, 1995); Dr. Stephen Hensley	29	1,210	NA	NA
West Texas A&M University—Canyon; (2); 1910 (as West Texas State Normal College; became West Texas State Teachers College in 1923; West Texas State College, 1949; changed to West Texas State Univ., 1949; present name, 1993); Dr. Russell C. Long	340	6,483	4,147	803
Texas Baptist Institute-Seminary—Henderson; (3 - Calvary Baptist); 1948; Dr. Ray O. Brooks.	13	58	49	25
Texas Christian University—Fort Worth; (3 - Disciples of Christ); 1873 (as Add- Ran College at Thorp Spring; name changed to Add-Ran Christian Univ. 1890; moved to Waco 1895; present name, 1902; moved to Fort Worth 1910); Dr. William E. Tucker	†††347	6,830	2,286	131

Name of Institution; Location; (Type* - Ownership, if private sectarian institution); Date of Founding; President (unless otherwise noted)	Number in Faculty†	Enrollment		
		Fall Term 1996	Summer Session 1996	Extension or Continuing Ed.
Texas College—Tyler; (3 - C.M.E.); 1894; Dr. Haywood L. Strickland	37	293	NA	NA
Texas College of Osteopathic Medicine—Fort Worth (See University of North Texas Health Science Center at Fort Worth)	152	416	NA	NA
Texas Lutheran University —Seguin; (3 - Lutheran); 1891 (in Brenham as Evangelical Lutheran College; moved to Seguin, 1912 and renamed Lutheran College of Seguin; renamed Texas Lutheran College, 1932; changed to university, 1996); Dr. Jon N. Moline	107	1,234	659	350
‡Texas Southern University—Houston; (2); 1926 (as Houston Colored Junior Coll.; upper level added, name changed to Houston College for Negroes in mid-1930s; became Texas State University for Negroes, 1947; present name, 1951); Dr. James Douglas . .	514	9,441	1.903	NA
Texas Southmost College—Brownsville (see The University of Texas at Brownsville under University of Texas System listing)				
‡‡TEXAS STATE TECHNICAL COLLEGE SYSTEM (6) — Ralph T. Strother, Chancellor	370	8,013	5,859	2,430
Texas State Technical College-Harlingen—Harlingen; (7); 1967; Dr. J. Gilbert Leal, Campus President				
Texas State Technical College-Sweetwater—Sweetwater; (7); 1901; Dr. Clay G. Johnson, Campus President				
Texas State Technical College- Waco—Waco; (7); 1965 (as James Connally Technical Inst.; name changed in 1969); Dr. Fred Williams, Campus President (The system also includes extension centers in Abilene, Breckenridge, Brownwood and Marshall.)				
TEXAS STATE UNIVERSITY SYSTEM (1)—Dr. Lamar G. Urbanovsky, Chancellor				
Angelo State University—San Angelo; (2); 1928; Dr. E. James Hindman.	232	6,198	4,102	958
Lamar University - Beaumont—Beaumont; (2); 1923 (as South Park Junior Coll.; name changed to Lamar Coll., 1932; name changed to Lamar State Coll. of Technology, 1951; present name, 1971; transferred from Lamar Univ. System, 1995); Dr. Rex Cottle	414	8,417	4,398	936
Lamar University - Orange—Orange; (10); 1969 (transferred from Lamar University System, Sept. 1995); Dr. J. Michael Shahan	71	1,513	818	26
Lamar University - Port Arthur—Port Arthur; (10); 1909 (as Port Arthur College; became part of Lamar Univ. in 1975; became part of TSU system, 1995); Dr. W. Sam Monroe . . .	135	2,475	1,824	31
Lamar University Institute of Technology—Beaumont; (10); (part of TSU system, 1995); Dr. Robert D. Krienke	92	1,613	978	NA
Sam Houston State University—Huntsville; (2); 1879; Dr. Bobby K. Marks	516	12,564	9,204	5,325
Southwest Texas State University—San Marcos; (2); 1903 (as Southwest Texas Normal School; changed1918 to Southwest Texas State Normal College, in 1923 to Southwest Texas State Teachers College, in 1959 to Southwest Texas State College, and in 1969 to present form); Dr. Jerome H. Supple	931	20,776	9,683	NA
Sul Ross State University-Rio Grande College—Uvalde; (2 - upper-level); 1973 (name changed from Sul Ross State University, Uvalde Center 1995); Frank Abbott, Dean	35	866	720	NA
Sul Ross State University—Alpine; (2); 1917 (as Sul Ross State Normal Coll.; changed to Sul Ross State Teachers Coll., 1923; to Sul Ross State Coll., 1949; present name since 1969); Dr. Vic Morgan	129	2,518	§2,194	NA
TEXAS TECH UNIVERSITY (1) — John T. Montford, Chancellor				
Texas Tech University—Lubbock; (2); 1923 (as Texas Technological College; present name since 1969); Dr. Donald R. Haragan	3,000	24,717	8,923	40,000
Texas Tech University Health Sciences Center—Lubbock; (4); 1972; David R. Smith, M.D.	1,634	1,514	597	814
Texas Wesleyan University—Fort Worth; (3 - United Methodist); 1891 (as college; present name since 1989); Dr. Jake B. Schrum.	245	2,966	1,127	NA
Texas Woman's University—Denton; (2); 1901 (as Coll. of Industrial Arts; name changed to Texas State Coll. for Women, 1934; present name, 1957); Dr.Carol D. Surles.	††500	9,786	§6,400	4,185
Trinity University—San Antonio; (3 - Presbyterian); 1869 (at Tehuacana; moved to Waxahachie, 1902; to San Antonio, 1942); Dr. Ronald K. Calgaard	220	2,495	337	NA
Trinity Valley Community College—Athens; also campus at Terrell; (7); 1946 (originally Henderson County Junior College); Dr. Ronald C. Baugh	113	4,995	§2,734	2,500
Tyler Junior College—Tyler; (7); 1926; Dr. William R. Crowe	450	7,800	NA	5,000
University of Central Texas—Killeen; (3); 1973 (originally American Technological University; name changed, 1989); Dr. Pauline S. Moseley	50	988	1,041	NA
University of Dallas—Irving; (3 - Catholic); 1956; Msgr. Milam J. Joseph	180	2,600	††200	250
UNIVERSITY OF HOUSTON SYSTEM (1) — Arthur K. Smith, Chancellor				
University of Houston—Houston; (2); 1927; Arthur K. Smith	1,927	30,774	14,275	1,285
University of Houston-Clear Lake—Houston; (2 - upper level and grad.); 1974; Dr. William A. Staples	443	6,968	3,957	3,000
University of Houston-Downtown—Houston; (2); 1948 (as South Texas College; became part of University of Houston in 1974) ; Dr. Max Castillo	394	7,947	4,572	NA
University of Houston-Victoria—Victoria; (2 - upper-level); 1973; Dr. Karen S. Haynes . . .	91	1,809	NA	NA
University of the Incarnate Word—San Antonio; (3 - Catholic); 1881 (as Incarnate Word College; name changed 1996; Dr. Louis Agnese Jr.	268	3,276	1,060	NA
University of Mary Hardin-Baylor—Belton; (3 - So. Baptist); 1845; Dr. Jerry G. Bawcom . .	184	2,265	§1,231	NA
University of North Texas—Denton; (2); 1890 (as North Texas Normal College; name changed 1923 to North Texas State Teachers Coll.e; in 1949 to North Texas State Coll.; became university, 1961; present name since 1988); Dr. Alfred F. Hurley, Chancellor	2,638	25,000	20,610	6,136
University of North Texas Health Science Center at Fort Worth—Fort Worth; (4);1966 (as private college; came under direction of North Texas State University in 1975; present name since 1993); Dr. David M. Richards.	170	569	NA	NA
University of St. Thomas—Houston; (3); 1947; Dr. Joseph M. McFadden	204	2,504	1,433	NA

Name of Institution; Location; (Type* - Ownership, if private sectarian institution); Date of Founding; President (unless otherwise noted)	Number in Faculty†	Enrollment		
		Fall Term 1996	Summer Session 1996	Extension or Continuing Ed.
UNIVERSITY OF TEXAS SYSTEM (1) —William H. Cunningham, Chancellor				
University of Texas at Arlington, The—Arlington; (2); 1895 (as **Arlington Coll.**; became state inst. in 1917 and renamed **Grubbs Vocational Coll.**; 1923 became **North Texas Agricultural and Mechanical Coll.**; became **Arlington State Coll.**, 1949; present name since 1967); Dr. Robert E. Witt	1,315	20,544	10,118	5,500
University of Texas at Austin, The—Austin; (2); 1883; Dr. Peter Flawn, Interim President	7,388	48,008	18,879	56,171
University of Texas at Brownsville, The (2 - upper-level); 1973 (as branch of **Pan American Coll.**; changed to **Univ. of Texas-Pan American - Brownsville**; present name, 1991) and **Texas Southmost College** (7); 1926 (as **Brownsville Jr. Coll.**; name changed, 1949) — Brownsville; Dr.Juliet V. Garcia.	202	8,359	6,159	476
University of Texas at Dallas, The—Richardson; (2); 1961 (as **Graduate Research Center of the Southwest**; changed to **Southwest Center for Advanced Studies** in 1967; joined U.T. System and present name, 1969; full undergraduate program, 1975); Dr. Franklyn G. Jenifer.	426	9,417	NA	NA
University of Texas at El Paso, The—El Paso; (2); 1913 (as **Texas Coll. of Mines and Metallurgy**; changed to **Texas Western Coll.** of U.T., 1949; present name, 1967); Dr. Diana S. Natalicio.	792	15,386	7,475	6,249
University of Texas-Pan American, The—Edinburg; (2); 1927 (as **Edinburg Junior Coll.**; changed to **Pan American College** and made 4-yr., 1952; became **Pan American University** in 1971; present name since 1991); Dr. Miguel A. Nevárez.	612	12,692	7,497	1,940
University of Texas of the Permian Basin, The—Odessa; (2); 1969 (as 2-yr. upper- level institution; expanded to 4-yr., Sept. 1991); Dr. Charles A. Sorber	128	2,193	1,181	**
University of Texas at San Antonio—San Antonio; (2); 1969; Dr. Samuel Kirkpatrick	2,555	17,547	8,633	507
University of Texas at Tyler—Tyler; (2 - upper-level); 1971 (as **Tyler State Coll.**; became **Texas Eastern University**, 1975; joined U.T. System, 1979); Dr. George F. Hamm	155	3,463	2,624	NA
UNIVERSITY OF TEXAS HEALTH SCIENCE CENTER AT HOUSTON (4) — Dr. M. David Low. Established 1972; consists of following divisions (year of founding): **Dental Branch** (1905); **Graduate School of Biomedical Sciences** (1963); **Medical School** (1970); **School of Allied Health Sciences** (1973); **School of Nursing** (1972); **School of Public Health** (1967); **Division of Continuing Education** (1958).	1,144	3,117	NA	NA
UNIVERSITY OF TEXAS HEALTH SCIENCE CENTER AT SAN ANTONIO (4) —Dr. John P. Howe III. Established 1968; consists of following divisions (year of founding): **Dental School** (1970); **Graduate School of Biomedical Sciences** (1970); **Health Science Center** (1972); **Medical School** (1959 as **South Texas Medical School** of UT; present name, 1966); **School of Allied Health Sciences** (1976); **School of Nursing** (1969).	1,342	2,722	NA	NA
UNIVERSITY OF TEXAS MEDICAL BRANCH AT GALVESTON (4) — Dr. Thomas N. James. Established 1891; consists of following divisions (year of founding): **Graduate School of Biomedical Sciences** (1952); **Medical School** (1891); **School of Allied Health Sciences** (1968); **School of Nursing** (1890).	***2,022	2,780	NA	NA
UNIVERSITY OF TEXAS SOUTHWESTERN MEDICAL CENTER AT DALLAS (4) — Dr. Kern Wildenthal. Established 1943 (as private institution; became **Southwestern Medical Coll.** of UT 1948; became **UT Southwestern Medical School at Dallas**, 1967; made part of **UT Health Science Center at Dallas**, 1972); consists of following divisions (year of founding): **Graduate School of Biomedical Sciences** (1947); **School of Allied Health Sciences** (1968); **Southwestern Medical School** (1943).	†††1,193	1,714	NA	NA
Vernon Regional Junior College—Vernon; (7); 1970; Dr. Wade Kirk	56	1,721	§1,697	1,709
Victoria College, The —Victoria; (7); 1925; Dr. Jimmy Goodson	††125	3,598	2,221	NA
Wayland Baptist University—Plainview; (3 -Southern Baptist); 1910; Dr. Wallace Davis Jr.	83	4,034	6,058	NA
Weatherford College—Weatherford; (7); 1869 (as branch of **Southwestern Univ.**; 1922, became denominational junior college; became muni. jr. college, 1949); **	200	2,500	746	1,500
Western Texas College—Snyder; (7); 1969; Dr. Harry Krenek	45	1,032	784	281
Wharton County Junior College—Wharton; (7); 1946; Dr. Frank Robert Vivelo	225	3,958	§2,656	1,203
‡**Wiley College**—Marshall; (3 - Methodist); 1873; Dr. Lamore J. Carter.	35	589	152	NA

*Type: (1) Public University System
(2) Public University
(3) Independent Senior College or University
(4) Public Medical School or Health Science Center
(5) Independent Medical or Dental School
(6) Public Technical College System
(7) Public Community College
(8) Independent Junior College
(9) Public Community College System
(10) Public Lower-Level Institutions

† Unless otherwise noted, faculty count includes professors, associate professors, adjunct professors, instructors and tutors, but does not include voluntary instructors.
‡ No reply received to questionnaire. Information repeated from 1996-97 Texas Almanac.
§ Includes all students in two summer sessions.
¶ Does not include part-time, vocational nursing or continuing education instructors.
** Information not supplied by institution.
†† Approximate count.
‡‡ Includes faculty and enrollment at all branches or divisions.
§§ Includes students enrolled in extension and continuing-education courses, fall semester of 1996.
¶¶ Includes voluntary and emeritus faculty.
*** Includes voluntary faculty.
††† Full-time faculty only.
NA - Not applicable

Belo Growing with Texas

A.H. Belo Corporation, a Dallas-based media concern, has a history parallel to that of Texas itself. Pioneered in 1842 as the one-page *Galveston News*, Belo has grown to become a leading diversified media company, encompassing newspaper publishing and network-affiliated television broadcasting operations across the country. The Texas Almanac is published by Belo's flagship newspaper, *The Dallas Morning News*.

The Early Days

A.H. Belo Corporation is the oldest continuously operating business in Texas. Founded by Samuel Bangs, a transplanted publisher from Boston, the company was in the publishing business three years before the Republic of Texas achieved statehood. Bangs sold the business within a year of its founding to Wilbur F. Cherry and Michael Cronican, and Cherry soon acquired sole ownership.

Another Massachusetts émigré, Willard Richardson, became editor of the paper a few years later. He campaigned editorially for annexation, fiscal responsibility and railroads. In 1857, Richardson conceived and founded the Texas Almanac, which he hoped would help attract settlers to the new state. Eight years later, he hired A.H. Belo, for whom the company was eventually named.

A.H. Belo, a former Confederate colonel from North Carolina, joined the company as bookkeeper. He was made a full partner in the growing company after only three months and carved out a new life for himself in the Southwest.

Nine years later, George Bannerman Dealey, a 15-year-old English emigrant, was hired as an office boy. Dealey, too, quickly moved up in the company. Working tirelessly, Dealey made his way from office boy to business manager and then to publisher of *The Dallas Morning News*. It was Dealey who chose the then-small settlement of Dallas as a site for a sister publication. Dealey and several other members of the *Galveston News'* staff relocated to Dallas, and the company prospered and grew.

Belo Was a Radio Broadcasting Pioneer

On June 26, 1922, Belo began operating a 50-watt radio station, WFAA-AM, which was the first network station in the state. The company sold its radio properties in 1987.

The Publishing Division

The Dallas Morning News began publication on October 1, 1885, with a circulation of 5,000 subscribers. After being in operation only two months, *The Dallas Morning News* acquired its first competitor, the *Dallas Herald* (not to be confused with the *Dallas Times Herald* that closed in December 1991). Rather than compete with each other for subscribers, the two newspapers combined, keeping the name of *The Dallas Morning News*, but dating itself with the volume number of the former *Dallas Herald*.

In 1906, on the 21st anniversary of *The Dallas Morning News*, Dealey gave a speech that became the motto for the company: "Build The News upon the rock of truth and righteousness. Conduct it always upon the lines of fairness and integrity. Acknowledge the right of the people to get from the newspaper both sides of every important question." Today these words are carved in a three-story-high space above the entrance to *The Dallas Morning News*. The *News* building, a long-standing dream of Dealey's, was completed in 1949, three years after his death.

While Belo has become one of the nation's largest diversified media companies, *The Dallas Morning News* remains the flagship of its newspaper business. *The Morning News* now has a total circulation of 524,000 daily and 800,000 Sunday.

On December 26, 1995, Belo purchased *The Bryan-College Station Eagle*, a daily newspaper serving Bryan-College Station, Texas. On January 5, 1996, Belo acquired the assets of the *Messenger-Inquirer*, a daily newspaper in Owensboro, Ky. In the spring of 1996, Belo launched the *Arlington Morning News* to serve readers and advertisers in Arlington, Texas. The newspaper, which was originally distributed Wednesday through Saturday, increased publication to seven days a week in July 1996.

In January 1997, Belo held a 38.45 percent interest in *The Press-Enterprise*, a daily newspaper serving Riverside County and the inland Southern California area. In July 1997, the company purchased the remaining interest in the Press-Enter-

prise Company.

Through the acquisition of The Providence Journal Company on February 28, 1997, Belo acquired the *Providence Journal-Bulletin*, the leading newspaper in Rhode Island and southeastern Massachusetts. The *Journal-Bulletin*, founded in 1829, is America's oldest major daily newspaper of general circulation in continuous publication.

On March 31, 1997, Belo acquired the assets of the Gleaner and Journal Publishing Company of Henderson, Kentucky. Those assets included *The Gleaner*, a daily newspaper in Henderson, Ky.; seven weekly newspapers; printing operations; and an AM radio station.

The Broadcast Division

Belo entered the television broadcasting business in 1950 with the acquisition of its flagship station, ABC affiliate WFAA-TV in Dallas-Fort Worth. In 1983, in the nation's largest broadcast acquisition to date, Belo acquired KHOU-TV (CBS) in Houston, Texas; KXTV (ABC) in Sacramento-Stockton-Modesto, Calif.; WVEC (ABC) in Hampton-Norfolk, Va.; and KOTV (CBS) in Tulsa, Okla. In June 1994, Belo acquired WWL-TV (CBS) in New Orleans, La., and in September 1994, the company acquired KIRO-TV in Seattle-Tacoma, Wash.

When Belo acquired The Providence Journal Company in February 1997 in the largest transaction in the company's 155-year history, the acquisition included five NBC affiliates (KING-TV, Seattle-Tacoma, Wash.; KGW-TV, Portland, Ore.; WCNC-TV, Charlotte, N.C.; KHNL-TV, Honolulu, Hawaii; and KTVB-TV, Boise, Idaho); one ABC affiliate (WHAS-TV, Louisville, Ky.); one CBS affiliate (KREM-TV, Spokane, Washington); two FOX affiliates (KASA-TV, Albuquerque-Santa Fe, N.M. and KMSB-TV, Tucson, Ariz.); and NorthWest Cable News in Seattle-Tacoma. Belo also assumed the management of four television stations through local marketing agreements and became the managing general partner of the Television Food Network in New York, N.Y.

In connection with the acquisition of the Providence Journal Company, Belo agreed to exchange KIRO-TV for a station in another market to comply with Federal Communications Commission regulations, which prohibit a company from owning multiple television stations in a market. The agreement resulted in Belo's acquisition of KMOV-TV (CBS) in St. Louis, Mo., on June 2, 1997.

In early 1997, the company opened its Capital Bureau in Washington, D.C., which houses Washington-based journalists representing the company's 16 network-affiliated television stations as well as *The Dallas Morning News* and the *Providence Journal-Bulletin*.

Belo also owns Belo Productions, Inc., in Seattle-Tacoma, Wash.

Today, Belo's Broadcast Division reaches 13.5 percent of all U.S. television households and is ranked 8th in revenue and 10th in audience reach.

Officers and Directors

Officers of A.H. Belo Corporation are Robert W. Decherd, chairman of the board, president and chief executive officer; Ward L. Huey Jr., vice chairman of the board, president/Broadcast Division; Burl Osborne president/Publishing Division and publisher, *The Dallas Morning News*; Michael J. McCarthy, senior corporate vice president/general counsel and secretary; Michael D. Perry, senior corporate vice president/chief financial officer; Dunia A. Shive, senior vice president/corporate operations; Harold F. Gaar Jr., vice president/public affairs; A. Jeff Lamb, vice president/administration; Brenda C. Maddox, vice president/treasurer; William E. Nolen, vice president/internal audit; Marian Spitzberg, vice president/deputy general counsel; and Vicky C. Teherani, vice president/controller.

The following are members of Belo's Board of Directors: John W. Bassett Jr.; Henry P. Becton Jr.; Fanchon M. Burnham; Judith L. Craven, M.D., M.P.H.; Robert W. Decherd; Roger A. Enrico; Peter B. Freeman; Stephen Hamblett; Dealey D. Herndon; Ward L. Huey Jr.; Lester A. Levy; Arturo Madrid, Ph.D.; James M. Moroney Jr.; Burl Osborne; Hugh G. Robinson; William T. Solomon; Thomas B. Walker Jr.; and J.

McDonald Williams.

Officers of Belo's Publishing Division include Robert W. Mong Jr., executive vice president. Officers of the The Dallas Morning News are Jeremy L. Halbreich, president and general manager; Ralph Langer, executive vice president/editor; Gilbert Bailon, executive editor; Stuart Wilk, managing editor; Rena Pederson, vice president/editorial page editor; J. William Cox, senior vice president/operations and administration; W. Richard Starks, senior vice president/sales and marketing; Barry T. Peckham, senior vice president/circulation; Sergio H. Salinas, vice president/advertising; Barbara van Pelt, vice president/marketing; Harry A. Greaves Jr., vice president/ finance; Frank Tyler, vice president/production; Grover D. Livingston, vice president/information management; Ellen Silva Wilson, vice president/human resources; and Nancy Barry, vice president/community services. Stephen Hamblett is chairman, chief executive officer and publisher of The Providence Journal Company. Officers and senior managers of the Providence Journal-Bulletin are Howard G. Sutton, president and general manager; Joel P. Rawson, senior vice president and executive editor; Carol Young, deputy executive editor; Joel N. Stark, senior vice president; Sandra J. Radcliffe, vice president, finance; Mark T. Ryan, vice president, legal and administration; Robert A. Shadrick, vice president, operations; Donald J. Ross, vice president, advertising; and Michael J. Dooley, vice president, circulation. Officers of The Press-Enterprise are Howard H Hays Jr., chairman; Marcia McQuern, editor and publisher; Jonathan F. Hays, executive vice president. Officers and senior managers of the Owensboro Messenger-Inquirer include T. Edward Riney, publisher; Robert Ashley, editor; Frank Leto, advertising director; Tony Maddox, circulation/packaging director; Sue Trautwein, human resources director; Doug Robinson, controller; Mike Weafer, production manager; Terri Kenitzer, information systems manager; Lynda Bebrowsky, marketing/community relations manager; John Hager, publisher emeritus. Officers and senior managers of The Bryan-College Station Eagle include Donnis G. Baggett, publisher and editor; Rod Armstrong, finance director; Dwight McKenzie, advertising director; Joe Michael Feist, managing editor; Carol Herrington, marketing director; Lyle Parker, production director; Lorenzo Vigliante, circulation director. Officers and senior managers of The Gleaner include Steve Austin, publisher; Ron Jenkins, editor; and David Dixon, managing editor. Bureau chiefs Carl P. Leubsdorf and David M. Cassidy head Belo's Capital Bureau in Washington D.C.

. Officers of Belo's Broadcast Division include James M. Moroney III, president/ Television Group; Jack Sander, executive vice president/Television Group; H. Martin Haag, senior vice president/news; Lee R. Salzberger, senior vice president/ administration; Glenn C. Wright, senior vice president/Television Group; Cathleen A. Creany, senior vice president/Television Group; and R. Paul Fry, vice president/Cable and Program Development. Officers of Belo's 16 television stations are Kathy Clements-Hill, vice president and general manager, WFAA-TV; Peter Diaz, vice president and general manager, KHOU-TV; Dennis Williamson, president and general manager, KING-TV; Allan E. Howard, president and general manager, KXTV; Allan Cohen, president and general manager, KMOV-TV; Michael D. Grant, vice president and general manager, KGW-TV; Richard J. Keilty, president and general manager, WCNC-TV; Mario A. Hewitt, vice president and general manager, WVEC-TV; J. Michael Early, president and general manager, WWL-TV; Erick Steffens, president and general manager, KASA-TV; Joseph Goleniowski, president and general manager, WHAS-TV; Ronald S. Longinotti, vice president and general manager, KOTV; John Fink, president and general manager, KHNL-TV; Barry Barth, president and general manager, KREM-TV; Kenneth Middleton, president and general manager, KMSB-TV; and Douglas Armstrong, president and general manager, KTVB-TV. Erica Gruen is president and chief executive officer of the Television Food Network; Craig Marrs is president and general manager of NorthWest Cable News; and Matt Chan is president and general manager, Belo Productions, Inc.

Robert W. Decherd

Robert W. Decherd has worked for Belo or its principal newspaper subsidary, The Dallas Morning News, since his graduation from Harvard College in 1973.

Decherd graduated cum laude from Harvard, where he was president of the Harvard Crimson, recipient of an Honorary Freshman Scholarship, winner of the David McCord Award for literary contributions and class orator for the Class of 1973.

Decherd began his career with Belo in a management training program at The Dallas Morning News. Following three years in that program, Decherd was appointed assistant to the executive editor of The Dallas Morning News. In 1978, he became the company's first corporate staff executive. Between 1978 and 1981, Decherd led Belo's preparation to become publicly held and devised its initial corporate management structure. During the 1980s, he served as vice president, executive vice president, chief operating officer and president of the company. In January 1987, he was elected chairman and chief executive officer and in 1993, reassumed the title of president.

In addition to his executive role, Decherd is Belo's largest shareholder. He was elected to the company's board of directors in 1976, and also serves as a director of Kimberly-Clark Corporation and CCBG, Inc., one of the largest privately held Coca-Cola bottlers in the United States.

Decherd is a past president of the Dallas Society of Professional Journalists and the Freedom of Information Foundation of Texas, Inc. He has served as a director and member of the executive committee of the Newspaper Association of America (NAA) and chaired NAA's Public Policy Committee. He has served on committees of the American Newspaper Publishers Association, the Southern Newspaper Publishers Association and as a director of the Newspaper Advertising Bureau.

In civic affairs, Decherd is currently chair of a $29 million capital and endowment campaign for Paul Quinn College, the only historically black college in North Texas. He is also a trustee and former executive committee member of the Tomás Rivera Policy Institute and is a founding member of the Dallas Together Forum.

Decherd has received a variety of industry and civic awards over the past two decades, including a citation of honor from the American Institution of Architects (1981); American Newspaper Executive of the Year (1985); the James Madison Award from the Freedom of Information Foundation of Texas, Inc. (1989); and, the Henry Cohn Humanitarian Award from the Anti-Defamation League (1991). In 1995, he became the youngest inductee ever to the Texas Business Hall of Fame.

Ward L. Huey Jr.

Ward L. Huey Jr. has worked for Belo and played a role in the company's broadcast operations since 1960.

A 1960 graduate of Southern Methodist University, Huey worked as a copywriter and an account executive for Glenn Advertising in Dallas before joining Belo as part of WFAA-TV's production department. In 1961, Huey became the sales service manager, and over the next 10 years served in a variety of sales and marketing positions at WFAA including account executive, regional sales manager and general sales manager.

Huey was promoted to station manager of WFAA in 1972 and became a vice president in 1973. In 1975, he was named vice president and general manager of Belo's broadcast properties. He was elected a director of Belo in 1982 and vice chairman of the board in 1987. Huey was named president of Belo's Broadcast Division in 1987 and also serves on Belo's five-member Management Committee. In addition to his primary executive responsibilities, Huey is a trustee of the A.H. Belo Corporation Foundation.

Currently, Huey serves on the board of Maximum Service Television and has recently completed a four-year term on the board of the Television Bureau of Advertising. Huey is a past chairman of both the ABC Television Affiliates board of governors and the Television Operators Caucus board of directors.

In civic affairs, Huey currently serves as a trustee of Southern Methodist University and is on the boards of Meadows School of the Arts of Southern Methodist University, the Dallas Foundation, and the State Fair of Texas, where he serves on its executive committee. He is a past president of the Salesmanship Club of Dallas and has served as a trustee of Children's Medical Foundation of Texas. He has also served on the boards of the Association of Broadcast Executives of Texas, the Dallas Advertising League, the SMU Alumni Association and Goodwill Industries of Texas.

Burl Osborne

Burl Osborne joined Belo in 1980 following a 20-year career with The Associated Press.

In 1960, Osborne graduated from Marshall University in Huntington, W. Va., with a degree in journalism. He earned a master's degree in business administration from Long Island University in 1984 and is a graduate of the Harvard Business School Advanced Management Program.

Osborne joined *The Dallas Morning News* as executive editor in 1980. In 1981, he became vice president and executive editor, and was promoted to senior vice president and editor in 1983. He was named president and editor in 1985 and became publisher in 1991. Osborne was elected a director of Belo in 1987 and was named president of Belo's Publishing Division in November 1995. He also serves on Belo's five-member Management Committee. In addition to Osborne's primary executive responsibilities, he is president of the A.H. Belo Corporation Foundation.

During his tenure at Belo, Osborne has served as a member and co-chairman of the Pulitzer Prize Board, president of the American Society of Newspaper Editors, chairman of the Foundation for American Communications, chairman of the American Press Institute, president and chairman of the Texas Daily Newspaper Association, trustee of the Southern Newspaper Publishers Association Foundation and chairman of the Presstime Advisory Committee of the Newspaper Association of America.

Currently, Osborne is a member of the executive committee of the board of The Associated Press and serves on the boards of the Newspaper Association of America and the Southern Newspaper Publishers Association. He is also a trustee of Paul Quinn College and serves on the Journalism Advisory Committee of the Knight Foundation and the Advisory Committee for the Neiman Foundation at Harvard University.

In 1992, Osborne received the National Press Foundation George David Beveridge Jr. Award for Editor of the Year, and was awarded the Pat Taggart Texas Newspaper Leader of the Year Award in 1993.

James M. Moroney Jr.

James M. Moroney Jr. is the son of the late James M. Moroney and the late Maidie Dealey Moroney. He was born in Dallas, attended Highland Park School and St. John's Military Academy in Delafield, Wis. He graduated from The University of Texas at Austin in 1943. During summer vacations, he worked part-time at radio and television stations WFAA and *The Dallas Morning News.*

During World War II, he entered the U.S. Navy, rising to the rank of lieutenant (jg). He was released from active duty in 1946.

Moroney joined *The News* as a reporter, served as an advertising salesman and worked in the promotion and circulation departments before becoming assistant to the business manager in 1950. He also spent a year at the radio and television stations.

He progressed to assistant treasurer of the corporation and was elected to the board of directors in 1952. In 1955, he was named treasurer, elevated to vice president and treasurer in 1960 and became executive vice president in 1970. In 1973, Moroney was named president and chief executive officer of Belo Broadcasting Corporation and in 1974 became chairman of the board of that corporation.

In 1980, he was elected president and chief executive officer of *The Dallas Morning News* and president and chief operating officer of Belo.

He was promoted to the position of president and chief executive officer of Belo January 1983. In April 1984, he was elected chairman of the board. In January 1985, he relinquished the title of president.

Moroney retired as an active operating officer of Belo on December 31, 1986.

John W. Bassett Jr.

John W. Bassett Jr. was elected a director of Belo in 1979.

In 1960, Bassett graduated from Stanford University with a degree in economics. He graduated with honors from The University of Texas School of Law in 1964 and became associate editor of The Texas Law Review. Following his graduation, he passed the Texas and New Mexico Bar examinations and practiced law in Roswell.

In 1966, Bassett was selected as a White House Fellow and served a year in Washington, D.C., as a special assistant to the Attorney General of the United States. He then returned to Roswell to practice law with the firm of Atwood, Malone, Mann & Turner, P.A., of which he was a shareholder-partner from 1967-1995. In October 1995, he formed a law firm known as Bassett & Copple, LLP. Through his law firm, Bassett represents numerous large corporations and educational and governmental entities.

A native of Roswell, Bassett is a former member of the Board of Education for the State of New Mexico. He is a Rotarian and a member of several boards of directors of local charitable institutions in Roswell.

Henry P. Beton Jr.

Henry P. Becton Jr. was elected a director of Belo in 1997.

In 1965, Becton graduated magna cum laude from Yale University, where he majored in American Studies, was elected to Phi Beta Kappa and was chairman of the Yale Broadcasting Corporation. He began his filmmaking career while studying at Harvard Law School, and in 1968 received his J.D. degree cum laude from Harvard. He is a member of the Massachusetts Bar.

In 1970, Becton joined the staff of the WGBH Educational Foundation as a producer. In 1974 he became program manager for Cultural Affairs, and he was appointed vice president and general manager in 1978. He was elected president and general manager in February of 1984.

In addition to WGHB's national programming, educational publishing and access technology activities, Becton supervises a 1,000-member staff, oversees the $135 million budget and is responsible for Channels 2 and 44 and WGBH-FM, 89.7 in Boston and Channel 57 in Springfield. Under Becton's direction, WGBH has received every major award for broadcasting excellence including National and International Emmy Awards, the George Foster Peabody Award, the George Polk Award and the duPont-Columbia School of Journalism Award.

Becton has served on various public broadcasting policy committees, is a member of the PBS board of directors and a founding director of the independent production company which produces the American Playhouse and P.O.V. series.

Fanchon M. (Monty) Burnham

Fanchon M. (Monty) Burnham was elected a director of Belo in 1997.

Burnham holds a degree in English from Vassar College (1966) and a Masters of Science in Accounting from Georgetown University (1982).

Burnham is an independent accountant in Washington, D.C., with her own practice, F.M. Burnham & Associates. She began her career in finance with Donaldson, Lufkin & Jenrette, Inc. (NYC) working in their Personal Resource Management Group, a financial counseling service. F.M. Burnham & Associates provides accounting, bookkeeping and financial analysis services for a wide variety of small businesses.

In April 1992, Burnham was elected a director of The Providence Journal Company. During both her first and second terms she has been a member of the audit committee and has served on the nominating committee during her second term. In addition, she is a trustee of the Providence Journal Charitable Foundation.

Burnham has also been active in community service in Washington, D.C. Since 1984, she has been an at-large member of the finance committee of the Washington National Cathedral (Protestant Episcopal Cathedral Foundation) and a member of the board of trustees of Family & Child Services, Inc. since 1978, and has also served as treasurer. Burnham completed two consecutive terms as president of the board in January 1996 and continues to servce on the board and its finance committee.

Born in Providence, R.I., Burnham is the eldest child of Helen D. Buchanan, a major stockholder in The Providence Journal Company, and John C.A. Watkins, chairman emeritus of The Providence Journal Company.

Judith L. Craven, M.D., M.P.H.

Judith L. Craven was elected a director of Belo in 1992.

Craven holds a bachelor of science degree from Bowling Green University, a doctor of medicine from Baylor College of Medicine and a master of public health from The University of Texas School of Public Health. She also completed a program for senior managers in government at the John F. Kennedy School of government at Harvard University.

A Houston resident, Craven has served as president of the United Way of the Texas Gulf Coast since July 1992. Prior to 1992, Craven served nine years as dean of the School of Allied Health Sciences at The University of Texas Health Science Center at Houston, and five years concurrently as vice president of multicultural affairs for The University of Texas Health Science Center.

Craven has held numerous offices with local, state and national boards and committees, including president of United Way of Texas. She has served on three gubernatorial commissions in Texas. She has received many awards recognizing her achievements, and she is the second female and the first African American to serve as president in the 71-year history of the United Way of the Texas Gulf Coast.

Roger A. Enrico

Roger A. Enrico was elected a director of Belo in 1995.

A native of Minnesota, Enrico is a graduate of Babson College with a bachelor's degree in finance and holds an honorary doctorate of law from Babson.

Enrico is vice chairman of the board and chief executive officer of PepsiCo, Inc. He has played a major role in PepsiCo's development throughout his 26-year career with the corporation.

Enrico assumed his position as chief executive officer April 1, 1996. He was appointed vice chairman in 1994. Since the end of 1994, he has served as chairman and chief executive officer of PepsiCo Worldwide Restaurants. From 1991 to 1993, Enrico served in PepsiCo's snack food business first as chairman and chief executive officer of Frito-Lay, the corporation's U.S. snack-food business, then as chairman and chief executive officer of PepsiCo Worldwide Foods, the corporation's worldwide snack-food business. He was elected to the PepsiCo board of directors in 1987.

He serves on the boards of directors of Dayton Hudson Corporation, The Prudential Insurance Company of America, Inc. and the United Negro College Fund. He is a member of the Babson College Corporation and the executive board of the Dallas Symphony Association.

Peter B. Freeman

Peter B. Freeman was elected a director of Belo in 1997.

Freeman graduated from Yale University in 1954 with a bachelor of arts degree in economics. He earned a master's degree in business administration from New York University's Graduate School of Business Administration in 1961.

Freeman, a corporate director and trustee, has focused his career on banking and investment management. From 1977 to 1979, he was president of Fields Point Management Company. From 1971 to 1977, he was president of Goelet Estate Company in New York. For ten years prior to 1971, Freeman was vice president of Scudder, Stevens & Clark and is now a trustee for various investment companies managed by the firm.

Freeman is currently a director of Amica Mutual Life Insurance Company, as well as a trustee of Eastern Utilities Associates. He is also a member of the board of advisors of Hospital Trust National Bank and serves as a consultant for Point Gammon Corporation. From 1981 until 1997, Freeman served as a director of The Providence Journal Company, having also served as chairman of the Audit Committee. His civic activities include work with the Rhode Island School of Design, the Preservation Society and the Providence Public Library, Rhode Island Hospital, the Bradley Hospital, Rhode Island Renal Institute, Greater Providence YMCA and the Providence Public Library.

Stephen Hamblett

Stephen Hamblett was elected a director of Belo in 1997.

Following his graduation from Harvard College in 1957, Hamblett joined the advertising department of The Providence Journal Company.

In 1969, he was named assistant vice president for administration. In 1974, he became vice president-marketing and five years later was named vice president-marketing and corporate development. He served as such until 1983, when he was named executive vice president and assistant publisher. In April 1985, he was named president and chief operating officer of the The Providence Journal Company. In September, 1987, he was named chairman of the board, chief executive officer and publisher of The Providence Journal Company, a title he holds today.

Hamblett serves on the boards of the Newspaper Association of America, the Associated Press, the American Press Institute and the Inter American Press Association.

In Rhode Island, he is presently on the board of trustees of Trinity Repertory Company, Providence Performance Arts Center, and the Rhode Island School of Design. He is a trustee of Save the Bay and serves on the advisory board of the University of Rhode Island Marine Programs and Graduate School of Oceanography.

He also serves on the boards of the National Conference, Rhode Island Hospital Trust National Bank, and the Providence Foundation.

Dealey D. Herndon

Dealey D. Herndon was elected a director of Belo in 1986.

A Dallas native, Herndon is the daughter of the late H. Ben Decherd and Isabelle Thomason Decherd. She is an honors graduate of Hockaday School and The University of Texas at Austin.

Herndon is currently president of Herndon, Stauch & Associates, a Texas project and construction management firm in Austin, Texas. Prior to opening her firm, Herndon had overall responsibility for the Capitol Preservation and Extension Project, which she directed from 1988 to its completion in 1995. She also served as administrator of Friends of the Governor's Mansion from 1983 to 1984.

Prior to 1991, Herndon served as a community volunteer in a wide range of projects in Dallas and Austin, with a primary focus on historic preservation, finance and fund-raising. She served as president of the Seton Hospital development board, the Austin Historic Center Association, and Friends of the Governor's Mansion, and served as treasurer of several organizations including St. Andrews School. She served as one of the six members of the State Preservation Board from 1987 to 1991. Herndon currently serves as chair of the board of St. Edward's University and as a board member of the Capitol Area United Way, the Just For the Kids Foundation and the National Trust for Historic Preservation. She is president and a director of the Friends of the Governor's Mansion in Austin, and the executive director of the State Preservation Board of the State of Texas.

Lester A. Levy

Lester A. Levy was elected a director of Belo 1985.

Levy, a native of Dallas, attended The University of Texas at Austin until early 1943, at which time he entered the Air Force. He received his license to practice law during 1943 while in the service. After an honorable discharge in 1946, he joined his father's company, now known as NCH Corporation, while awaiting a semester change in order to take refresher courses at The University of Texas. His father's untimely death caused him to remain with the company, where he is presently chairman of the board of directors.

He has served on the boards of the University of Dallas, Greenhill School, Baylor College of Dentistry, the Lamplighter School, and was co-founder and director of the Winston School. He has also served as a trustee for Temple Emanu-El, Golden Acres Home for the Aged and Special Care and Career Center (formerly Special Care School for Handicapped Children).

Arturo Madrid, Ph.D.

Dr. Arturo Madrid was elected a director of Belo in January 1994.

Madrid is the Norine R. and T. Frank Murchison Distinguished Professor of the Humanities at Trinity University in San Antonio. A native of New Mexico and a leading scholar in Latino history and culture, Madrid served as the founding president of the Tomas Rivera Center for Policy Studies, the nation's first institute for policy studies on Latino issues, from 1984 to 1993. In addition to holding academic and administrative appointments at Dartmouth College, The University of California, San Diego, and the University of Minnesota, he also served as director of the Fund for the Improvement of Post-Secondary Education (FIPSE), U.S. Department of Education and of the Ford Foundation's Graduate Fellowships Program.

In 1996, Madrid was awarded the Charles Frankel Prize, the highest honor bestowed by the National Endowment for the Humanities. The Frankel Prize recognizes outstanding contributions to the public's understanding of history, literature, philosophy and other humanities disciplines.

Over the past two decades, Madrid has served on the

boards of some of the country's most prominent organizations, including The College Board, the Association for the Advancement of Higher Education and others. Madrid holds honorary doctorates from New England College and The California State University, Hayward, and is an elected fellow of the Council on Foreign Relations, the nation's premier foreign-policy association, and the National Academy for Public Administration, which honors persons with distinguished records in public administration.

Hugh G. Robinson

Hugh G. Robinson was elected a director of Belo in 1989. Robinson was born in Washington, D.C., and graduated from the U.S. Military Academy, West Point, in 1954. He earned a master's degree in civil engineering from Massachusetts Institute of Technology in 1959, and he holds an honorary doctor of laws degree from Williams College.

He entered the U.S. Army in 1954, following his graduation from West Point, and served until his retirement in 1983 with the rank of major general.

He is currently chief executive officer of The Tetra Group, a construction management firm. For more than five years prior to that, Robinson was president of Cityplace Development Corporation, a real estate development subsidiary of The Southland Corporation, and vice president of The Southland Corporation.

Robinson received numerous military awards, including the Distinguished Service Medal. He is a former member of the board of directors of the Federal Reserve Bank of Dallas, and he is currently a member of the boards of directors of Lomas Financial Corporation, Guaranty Federal Savings Bank and TU Electric Company, among others.

William T. Solomon

William T. Solomon was elected a director of Belo in 1983.

Born and reared in Dallas, Solomon holds a civil engineering degree from Southern Methodist University and an M.B.A. from Harvard Graduate School of Business.

Solomon is chairman, president and chief executive officer of Austin Industries Inc., which is the largest general contractor in Dallas and one of the five largest contractors in the southern half of the United States. Austin Industries is the only major contractor in its markets that is completely employee owned. Solomon joined Austin Industries, Inc., full-time in

1967 and became president and chief executive officer in 1970. In 1987, the title of chairman was added.

A 1996 inductee into the Texas Business Hall of Fame, Solomon is a former member of the board of directors of Fidelity Union Life Insurance Company and served on the board of trustees of Southern Methodist University. He is a past chairman of the Dallas Chamber of Commerce and currently serves on the boards of directors of numerous other civic and community organizations.

Thomas B. Walker Jr.

Thomas B. Walker Jr. was elected a director of Belo in 1982.

Walker is a native of Nashville, Tenn., and is a Phi Beta Kappa graduate of Vanderbilt University. Since 1968, he has been a partner, either general or limited, in Goldman, Sachs & Co., investment bankers, since 1968.

During World War II, he served as a lieutenant in the U.S. Navy operating in the Mediterranean, Atlantic and South Pacific areas.

After the war, Walker joined the Equitable Securities Corporation and moved to Dallas in 1950. He served as senior vice president and director of Equitable Securities (American Express Company) until 1968.

He is also a member of the boards of directors of NCH Corporation, SYSCO Corporation and Central and Southwest Corporation, and he is a former member of the Kleinwort Benson International Equity Fund board.

J. McDonald Williams

J. McDonald (Don) Williams was elected a director of Belo in 1985.

A native of Roswell, N.M., Williams graduated from Abilene Christian University in 1963 and from George Washington University Law School in 1966, both with honors.

He practiced law in Dallas seven years until he joined the Trammell Crow Company in May 1973. He entered the firm as the partner responsible for overseas development and then was named managing partner in 1977. He was named chairman in 1994.

Williams is also a former member of the board of directors of Fidelity Union Life Insurance Company. He currently serves on the boards of Abilene Christian University, George Washington University, Pepperdine University and Southwestern Christian College. ☆

Texas Newspapers, Radio and Television Stations

In the list of print and broadcast media below, frequency of publication of newspapers is indicated after the names by the following codes: (D), daily; (S), semiweekly; (BW), biweekly; (SM), semimonthly; (M), monthly; all others are weeklies. The radio and television stations are those with valid operating licenses as of the dates noted at the end of the list. Not included are those with only construction permits or with applications pending. Sources: Newspapers: 1997 Texas Newspaper Directory, Texas Press Association; Broadcast media: Federal Communications Commission; TV data as of Feb. 25, 1995; FM data as of Jan. 31, 1995; AM data as of March 27, 1995.

Abernathy — Newspaper: Weekly Review.

Abilene — Newspaper: Reporter-News (D). **Radio-AM:** KEAN,1280 Khz; KYYD, 1340; KNTS, 1470; KBBA, 1560. **Radio-FM:** KGNZ, 88.1 MHz; KACU, 89.7; KORQ, 100.7; KEAN, 105.1; KHXS, 106.3; KEYJ, 107.9. **TV:** KRBC-Ch. 9; KTAB-Ch. 32.

Alamo — **Radio-FM:** KJAV, 104.9 MHz.

Alamo Heights — **Radio-AM:** KDRY, 1100 Khz.

Albany — Newspaper: News.

Aledo — Newspaper: Community News.

Alice — Newspaper: Echo-News (D). **Radio-AM:** KOPY, 1070 Khz. **Radio-FM:** KOPY, 92.1 MHz; KNDA, 102.9.

Allen — Newspaper: American (S).

Alpine — Newspaper: Avalanche. **Radio-FM:** KALP, 92.7 MHz.

Alvarado — Newspaper: Post.

Alvin — Newspaper: Sun (S). **Radio-AM:** KTEK, 1110 Khz. **Radio-FM:** KACC, 89.7 MHz. **TV:** KHSH-Ch. 67.

Alvord — Newspaper: Gazette.

Amarillo — Newspapers: Globe-News (D); Southwest Stockman. **Radio-AM:** KGNC, 710 Khz; KIXZ, 940; KTMZ, 1010; KZIP, 1310; KDJW, 1360; KPUR, 1440. **Radio-FM:** KJRT, 88.3 MHz; KLMN, 89.1; KACV, 89.9; KYFA, 91.9; KQIZ, 93.1; KBUY, 94.1; KMML, 96.9; KGNC, 97.9; KQAC, 98.7; KLLR, 99.7; KATP, 101.9; KRGN, 103.1; KAEZ, 105.7. **TV:** KACV-Ch. 2; KAMR-Ch. 4; KVII-Ch. 7; KFDA-Ch. 10; KCIT-Ch. 14.

Amherst — Newspaper: Press (SM).

Anahuac — Newspaper: The Progress.

Andrews — Newspaper: Andrews County News (S). **Radio-AM:** KACT, 1360 Khz. **Radio-FM:** KACT, 105.5 MHz.

Angleton — Newspaper: Times (S).

Anson — Newspaper: Western Observer. **Radio-FM:** KKHR, 98.1 MHz.

Aransas Pass — Newspaper: Progress.

Archer City — Newspaper: Archer County News.

Arlington — Newspaper: Morning News (D). **Radio-FM:** KSNN, 94.9 MHz.

Aspermont — Newspaper: Stonewall County Courier.

Athens — Newspaper: Daily Review (D). **Radio-AM:** KWRD, 1410 Khz.

Atlanta — Newspaper: Citizens Journal (S). **Radio-AM:** KALT, 900 Khz. **Radio-FM:** KPYN, 100.1 MHz.

Austin — Newspapers: American-Statesman (D); Austin Business Journal; Lake Travis View; Texas Observer (BW); Texas Weekly; Westlake Picayune. **Radio-AM:** KVET, 590 Khz; KVET, 1300; KFON, 1490. **Radio-FM:** KAZI, 88.7 MHz; KMFA, 89.5; KUT, 90.5; KVRZ, 91.7; KLBJ, 93.7; KKMJ, 95.5; KVET, 98.1; KASE, 100.7; KPEZ, 102.3. **TV:** KTBC-Ch. 7; KLRU-Ch. 18; KVUE-Ch. 24; KXAN-Ch. 36; KEYE-Ch. 42; KNVA-Ch. 54.

Azle — Newspaper: News.

Baird — Newspaper: Callahan County Star.

Balch Springs — Newspaper: Suburban Tribune. **Radio-AM:** KSKY, 660 Khz.

Ballinger — Newspaper: Ledger. **Radio-AM:** KRUN, 1400 Khz. **Radio-FM:** KCSE, 103.1 MHz.

Bandera — Newspaper: Bulletin. **Radio-FM:** KEEP, 98.3 MHz.

Bartlett — Newspaper: Tribune-Progress.

Bastrop — Newspaper: Advertiser (S) **Radio-FM:** KGSR,

107.1 MHz.

Bay City — **Newspaper:** Daily Tribune (D). **Radio-AM:** KFCC, 1270 Khz. **Radio-FM:** KXGJ, 101.7 MHz; KMKS, 102.5.

Baytown — **Newspaper:** Sun (D). **Radio-AM:** KWWJ, 1360 Khz. **TV:** KVVV-Ch. 57.

Beaumont — **Newspaper:** Enterprise (D). **Radio-AM:** KLVI, 560 Khz; KZZB, 990; KJUS, 1380; KAYD, 1450. **Radio-FM:** KTXB, 89.7 MHz; KVLU, 91.3; KQXY, 94.1; KYKR, 95.1; KAYD, 97.5; KTCX, 102.5; KXTJ, 107.9. **TV:** KFDM-Ch. 6; KBMT-Ch. 12; KITU-Ch. 34.

Bedford/Hurst — **Newspaper:** Mid-Cities News (S).

Beeville — **Newspaper:** Bee-Picayune (D). **Radio-AM:** KIBL, 1490 Khz. **Radio-FM:** KYTX, 97.9 MHz; KTKO, 105.7.

Bellville — **Newspaper:** Times. **Radio-AM:** KFRD, 1090 Khz.

Belton — **Newspaper:** Journal. **Radio-AM:** KTON, 940 Khz. **Radio-FM:** KOOC, 106.3 MHz. **TV:** KNCT-Ch. 46.

Big Lake — **Newspaper:** Wildcat. **Radio-AM:** KWGH, 1290 Khz. **Radio-FM:** KBAU, 90.7 MHz.

Big Sandy — **Newspaper:** Big Sandy-Hawkins Journal.

Big Spring — **Newspaper:** Herald (D). **Radio-AM:** KBYG, 1400; KBST, 1490. **Radio-FM:** KBST, 95.9 MHz. **TV:** KWAB-Ch. 4.

Bishop — **Radio-FM:** KFLZ, 106.9 MHz.

Blanco — **Newspaper:** Blanco County News.

Bloomington — **Radio-FM:** KLUB, 106.9 MHz.

Blossom — **Newspaper:** Times.

Boerne — **Newspapers:** Hill Country Recorder; Star (S). **Radio-AM:** KBRN, 1500 Khz.

Bogata — **Newspaper:** News.

Bonham — **Newspaper:** Daily Favorite (D). **Radio-AM:** KFYN, 1420 Khz. **Radio-FM:** KFYZ, 98.3 MHz.

Booker — **Newspaper:** News.

Borger — **Newspaper:** News-Herald (D). **Radio-AM:** KQTY, 1490 Khz; KBBB, 1600. **Radio-FM:** KQFZ, 104.3 MHz.

Bovina — **Newspaper:** Blade.

Bowie — **Newspaper:** News (S). **Radio-AM:** KRJT, 1410 Khz. **Radio-FM:** KRJT, 100.7 Mhz.

Brackettville — **Newspaper:** Brackett News.

Brady — **Newspapers:** Herald; Standard. **Radio-AM:** KNEL, 1490 Khz. **Radio-FM:** KNEL, 95.3 MHz.

Breckenridge — **Newspaper:** American (S). **Radio-AM:** KBIL, 1430 Khz. **Radio-FM:** KROO, 93.5 MHz.

Bremond — **Newspaper:** Press.

Brenham — **Newspaper:** Banner-Press (D). **Radio-AM:** KWHI, 1280 Khz. **Radio-FM:** KULF, 94.1 Mhz; KTTX, 106.1.

Bridgeport — **Newspaper:** Index. **Radio-FM:** KBOC, 96.7 MHz.

Brookshire — **Newspaper:** Times Tribune.

Brownfield — **Newspaper:** News (S). **Radio-AM:** KKUB, 1300 Khz. **Radio-FM:** KLZK, 103.9 MHz.

Brownsboro — **Newspaper:** Chandler and Brownsboro Statesman.

Brownsville — **Newspaper:** Herald (D). **Radio-AM:** KBOR, 1600 Khz. **Radio-FM:** KBNR, 88.3 MHz; KKPS, 99.5; KTEX, 100.3. **TV:** KVEO-Ch. 23.

Brownwood — **Newspaper:** Bulletin (D). **Radio-AM:** KXYL, 1240 Khz; KBWD, 1380. **Radio-FM:** KBUB, 90.3 MHz; KPSM, 99.3; KOXE, 101.5; KXYL, 104.1.

Bryan — **Newspaper:** Bryan-College Station Eagle (D). **Radio-AM:** KTAM, 1240 Khz; KAGC, 1510. **Radio-FM:** KORA, 98.3 MHz; KKYS, 104.7. **TV:** KBTX-Ch. 3; KYLE-Ch. 28.

Buda — **Newspaper:** Free Press.

Buffalo — **Newspaper:** Press.

Buna — **Newspaper:** Beacon.

Burkburnett — **Newspaper:** Informer Star. **Radio-FM:** KYYI, 104.7 MHz.

Burleson — **Newspaper:** Star (S).

Burnet — **Newspapers:** Bulletin; Citizens Gazette. **Radio-AM:** KHLB, 1340 Khz. **Radio-FM:** KBLK, 92.5 MHz; KHLB, 106.9.

Caldwell — **Newspaper:** Burleson County Citizen-Tribune.

Calvert — **Newspaper:** Tribune.

Cameron — **Newspaper:** Herald. **Radio-AM:** KMIL, 1330 Khz. **Radio-FM:** KHLR, 103.9 MHz.

Canadian — **Newspaper:** Record. **Radio-FM:** KYEG, 103.1 MHz.

Canton — **Newspaper:** Herald.

Canyon — **Newspaper:** News (S). **Radio-AM:** KZRK, 1550 Khz. **Radio-FM:** KWTS, 91.1 MHz; KPUR, 107.1; KZRK, 107.9.

Canyon Lake — **Newspaper:** Times Guardian and Comal County Chronicle.

Carrizo Springs — **Newspaper:** Javelin. **Radio-AM:** KBEN, 1450 Khz. **Radio-FM:** KCZO, 92.1 MHz.

Carthage — **Newspaper:** Panola Watchman (S). **Radio-AM:** KGAS, 1590 Khz. **Radio-FM:** KTUX, 98.9 MHz.

Castroville — **Newspaper:** News Bulletin.

Cedar Hill — **Newspaper:** Today.

Celina — **Newspaper:** Record.

Center — **Newspaper:** Light & Champion (S). **Radio-AM:** KDET, 930 Khz. **Radio-FM:** KDET, 102.3 MHz.

Centerville — **Newspaper:** News.

Chico — **Newspaper:** Texan.

Childress — **Newspaper:** Index (S). **Radio-AM:** KCTX, 1510 Khz. **Radio-FM:** KSRW, 96.1 MHz.

Chillicothe — **Newspaper:** Valley News.

Cisco — **Newspaper:** Press (S).

Clarendon — **Newspaper:** Enterprise.

Clarksville — **Newspaper:** Times. **Radio-AM:** KCAR, 1350 Khz. **Radio-FM:** KGAP, 98.5 MHz.

Claude — **Newspaper:** News. **Radio-FM:** KARX, 95.7 MHz.

Clear Lake — **Newspaper:** Citizen.

Cleburne — **Newspaper:** Times-Review (D). **Radio-AM:** KCLE, 1120 Khz.

Cleveland — **Newspaper:** Advocate. **Radio-FM:** KOND, 97.1 MHz.

Clifton — **Newspaper:** Record (S). **Radio-FM:** KWOW, 103.3 MHz.

Clute — **Newspaper:** Brazosport Facts (D).

Clyde — **Newspaper:** Journal.

Cockrell Hill — **Radio-AM:** KRVA, 1600 Khz.

Coleman — **Newspaper:** Chronicle & Democrat-Voice (S). **Radio-AM:** KSTA, 1000 Khz. **Radio-FM:** KSTA, 107.1 MHz.

College Station — **Newspaper:** Battalion (D). **Radio-AM:** WTAW, 1150 Khz. **Radio-FM:** KEOS, 89.1 MHz; KAMU, 90.9; KTSR, 92.1. **TV:** KAMU-Ch. 15.

Colleyville — **Newspaper:** News & Times.

Colorado City — **Newspaper:** Record. **Radio-AM:** KVMC, 1320 Khz. **Radio-FM:** KAUM, 106.3 MHz.

Columbus — **Newspapers:** Banner Press; Colorado County Citizen. **Radio-FM:** KULM, 98.3 MHz.

Comanche — **Newspaper:** Chief. **Radio-AM:** KCOM, 1550 Khz.

Comfort — **Newspaper:** News. **Radio-FM:** KRNH, 95.1 MHz.

Commerce — **Newspaper:** Journal (S) **Radio-FM:** KETR, 88.9 MHz; KEMM, 92.1.

Conroe — **Newspaper:** Courier (D). **Radio-AM:** KJOJ, 880 Khz; KCHC, 1140. **Radio-FM:** KKHT, 106.9 MHz. **TV:** KTFH-Ch. 49.

Cooper — **Newspaper:** Review.

Coppell — **Newspaper:** Citizens' Advocate.

Copperas Cove — **Newspaper:** Leader Press. **Radio-FM:** KOOV, 103.1 MHz.

Corpus Christi — **Newspapers:** Caller-Times (D); Coastal Bend Legal & Business News (D); South Texas Catholic (BW). **Radio-AM:** KCTA, 1030 Khz; KCCT, 1150; KSIX, 1230; KRYS, 1360; KUNO, 1400; KEYS, 1440. **Radio-FM:** KFGG, 88.7 MHz; KEDT, 90.3; KBNJ, 91.7; KMXR, 93.9; KBSO, 94.7; KZFM, 95.5; KLTG, 96.5; KRYS, 99.1. **TV:** KIII-Ch. 3; KRIS-Ch. 6; KZTV-Ch. 10; KEDT-Ch. 16; KORO-Ch. 28.

Corrigan — **Newspaper:** Times.

Corsicana — **Newspaper:** Daily Sun (D). **Radio-AM:** KAND, 1340 Khz. **Radio-FM:** KICI, 107.9 MHz.

Crane — **Newspaper:** News. **Radio-AM:** KXOI, 810 Khz. **Radio FM:** KXXL, 101.3 MHz.

Creedmoor — **Radio AM:** KWTR, 1530 Khz.

Crockett — **Newspaper:** Houston County Courier (S). **Radio-AM:** KIVY, 1290 Khz. **Radio-FM:** KIVY, 92.7 MHz; KBHT, 93.5.

Crosbyton — **Newspaper:** Crosby County News & Chronicle.

Cross Plains — **Newspaper:** Review.

Crowell — **Newspaper:** Foard County News.

Crowley — **Newspaper:** Star Review.

Crystal Beach — **Radio FM:** KSTB, 101.5 MHz.

Crystal City — **Newspaper:** Zavala County Sentinel. **Radio-FM:** KHER, 94.3 MHz.

Cuero — **Newspaper:** Record. **Radio-AM:** KTXC, 1600 Khz. **Radio-FM:** KVCQ, 97.7 MHz.

Cypress — **Radio-AM:** KYND, 1520 Khz.

Daingerfield — **Newspaper:** Bee. **Radio-AM:** KEGG, 1560 Khz. **Radio-FM:** KWSK, 106.9 MHz.

Dalhart — **Newspaper:** Daily Texan (D). **Radio-AM:** KXIT, 1240 Khz. **Radio-FM:** KXIT, 95.9 MHz.

Dallas — **Newspapers:** The Dallas Morning News (D); Business Journal; Commercial Record (D); Dallas/Oak Cliff Tribune (BW); Park Cities News; Park Cities People; Texas Jewish Post; White Rocker. **Radio-AM:** KLIF, 570 Khz; KGGR, 1040; KRLD, 1080; KOOO, 1190; KSCR, 1310; KMRT, 1480. **Radio-FM:** KNON, 89.3 HMz; KERA, 90.1; KCBI, 90.9; KVTT, 91.7; KZPS, 92.5; KRSM, 93.3; KRRW, 97.9; KLUV, 98.7; KRBV, 100.3; WRR, 101.1; KDMX, 102.9; KKDA, 104.5; KYNG, 105.3. **TV:** KDFW-Ch. 4; WFAA-Ch. 8;

KERA-Ch. 13; KDFI-Ch. 27; KDAF-Ch. 33; KXTX-Ch. 39; KDTX-Ch. 58.

Decatur — Newspaper: Wise County Messenger (S).

Deer Park — Newspaper: Progress.

De Kalb — Newspaper: News.

De Leon — Newspapers: Free Press; Monitor.

Dell City — Newspaper: Hudspeth County Herald.

Del Rio — Newspaper: News-Herald (D). **Radio-AM:** KDLK, 1230 Khz; KWMC, 1490. **Radio-FM:** KDLK, 94.3 MHz; KTDR, 96.3.

Del Valle — Radio-AM: KIXL, 970 Khz.

Denison — Radio-AM: KDSX, 950 Khz. **Radio-FM:** KTCY, 104.9 MHz; KDVE, 101.7.

Denton — Newspaper: Record-Chronicle (D). **Radio-AM:** KINF, 1440 Khz. **Radio-FM:** KNTU, 88.1 MHz; KDZR, 99.1; KHKS, 106.1. **TV:** KDTN-Ch. 2.

Denver City — Newspaper: Press (S).

Deport — Newspaper: Times.

DeSoto — Newspapers: Best Southwest Focus (S); Today.

Detroit — Newspaper: Weekly.

Devine — Newspaper: News. **Radio-FM:** KTXX, 92.1 MHz.

Diboll — Newspaper: Free Press. **Radio-AM:** KSML, 1260 Khz. **Radio-FM:** KAFX, 95.5 MHz.

Dimmitt — Newspaper: Castro County News. **Radio-AM:** KDHN, 1470 Khz.

Dripping Springs — Newspaper: Dispatch.

Dublin — Newspaper: Citizen.

Dumas — Newspaper: Moore County News-Press (S). **Radio-AM:** KDDD, 800 Khz. **Radio-FM:** KMRE, 95.3 MHz.

Duncanville — Newspaper: Today.

Eagle Lake — Newspaper: Headlight.

Eagle Pass — Newspapers: News Gram; News-Guide (S). **Radio-AM:** KEPS, 1270 Khz. **Radio-FM:** KEPI, 88.7 MHz; KEPX, 89.5; KINL, 92.7. **TV:** KVAW-Ch. 16.

East Bernard — Newspaper: Tribune.

Eastland — Newspaper: Telegram (S). **Radio-AM:** KEAS, 1590 Khz. **Radio-FM:** KVMX, 96.7 MHz; KEAS, 97.7.

Eden — Newspaper: Echo.

Edgewood — Newspaper: Enterprise.

Edinburg — Newspaper: Daily Review (D). **Radio-AM:** KURV, 710 Khz. **Radio-FM:** KOIR, 88.5 MHz; KBFM, 104.1; KVLY, 107.9.

Edna — Newspaper: Jackson County Herald/Tribune. **Radio-AM:** KTMR, 1130 Khz.

El Campo — Newspaper: Leader-News (S). **Radio-AM:** KULP, 1390 Khz. **Radio-FM:** KIOX, 96.9 MHz.

Eldorado — Newspaper: Success.

Electra — Newspaper: Star-News.

Elgin — Newspaper: Courier. **Radio-AM:** KELG, 1440 Khz. **Radio-FM:** KKLB, 92.5 MHz.

El Paso — Newspapers: Herald-Post (D); Times (D). **Radio-AM:** KROD, 600 Khz; KHEY, 690; KAMA, 750; KBNA, 920; KFNA, 1060; KSVE, 1150; KVIV, 1340; KTSM, 1380; KELP, 1590. **Radio-FM:** KTEP, 88.5 MHz; KXCR; 89.5; KVER, 91.1; KOFX, 92.3; KSII, 93.1; KINT, 93.9; KSET, 94.7; KLAQ, 95.5; KHEY, 96.3; KBNA, 97.5; KTSM, 99.9; KPRR, 102.1. **TV:** KDBC-Ch. 4; KVIA-Ch. 7; KTSM-Ch. 9; KCOS-Ch. 13; KFOX-Ch. 14; KINT-Ch. 26; KSCE-Ch. 38; KJLF-Ch. 65.

Emory — Newspaper: Rains County Leader.

Ennis — Newspapers: Daily News (D); The Press.

Everman — Newspaper: Times.

Fabens — Radio-FM: KPAS, 103.1 MHz.

Fairfield — Newspaper: Recorder. **Radio-FM:** KNES, 92.1 MHz.

Falfurrias — Newspaper: Facts. **Radio-AM:** KPSO, 1260 Khz. **Radio-FM:** KPSO, 106.3 MHz.

Farmersville — Newspaper: Times.

Farwell — Newspaper: State Line Tribune. **Radio-AM:** KIJN, 1060 Khz. **Radio-FM:** KIJN, 92.3 MHz; KICA, 98.3.

Ferris — Newspaper: Ellis County Press. **Radio-AM:** KDFT, 540 Khz.

Flatonia — Newspaper: Argus.

Floresville — Newspaper: Chronicle-Journal; Wilson County News. **Radio-FM:** KWCB, 89.7 MHz; KRIO, 94.1.

Flower Mound — Newspaper: FlowerPlex PipeLine.

Floydada — Newspaper: Floyd County Hesperian-Beacon. **Radio-FM:** KFLL, 95.3 MHz.

Follett — Newspaper: The Golden Spread.

Forney — Newspaper: Messenger.

Fort Davis — Newspaper: Jeff Davis County Mountain Dispatch.

Fort Stockton — Newspaper: Pioneer. **Radio-AM:** KFST, 860 Khz. **Radio-FM:** KFST, 94.3 MHz.

Fort Worth — Newspapers: Business Press; Commercial Recorder (D); Star-Telegram (D); Times-Record; Weekly Livestock Reporter. **Radio-AM:** WBAP, 820 Khz; KFJZ, 870; KHVN, 970; KESS, 1270; KAHZ, 1360; KTMO, 1540; KRVA,

1600. **Radio-FM:** KTCU, 88.7 MHz; KLTY, 94.1; KSCS, 96.3; KEGL, 97.1; KPLX, 99.5; KOAI, 107.5; KTXQ, 102.1. **TV:** KXAS-Ch. 5; KTVT-Ch. 11; KTXA-Ch. 21; KFWD-Ch. 52.

Franklin — Newspapers: Advocate; News Weekly. **Radio FM:** KZTR, 101.9 MHz.

Frankston — Newspaper: Citizen.

Fredericksburg — Newspaper: Standard/Radio Post. **Radio-AM:** KNAF, 910 Khz. **Radio-FM:** KONO, 101.1 MHz.

Freeport — Radio-AM: KBRZ, 1460 Khz. **Radio-FM:** KJOJ, 103.3 MHz.

Freer — Newspaper: Press. **Radio-FM:** KBRA, 95.9 MHz.

Friendswood — Newspapers: Journal; Reporter News.

Friona — Newspaper: Star. **Radio FM:** KGRW, 94.7 MHz.

Frisco — Newspaper: Enterprise.

Fritch — Newspaper: Eagle Press.

Gail — Newspaper: Borden Star.

Gainesville — Newspaper: Register (D). **Radio-AM:** KGAF, 1580 Khz. **Radio-FM:** KDGE, 94.5 MHz.

Galveston — Newspaper: Galveston County Daily News (D). **Radio-AM:** KHCB, 1400 Khz; KGBC, 1540. **Radio-FM:** KLTP, 104.9 MHz; KQQK, 106.5. **TV:** KLTJ-Ch. 22; KTMD-Ch. 48.

Garland — Newspaper: News (S). **Radio-AM:** KPBC, 770 Khz. **TV:** KUVN-Ch. 23.

Garrison — Newspaper: In the News.

Gatesville — Newspaper: Messenger and Star (S). **Radio-FM:** KRYL, 98.3 MHz.

Georgetown — Newspapers: Sunday Sun; Williamson County Sun. **Radio-FM:** KHFI, 96.7 MHz; KNNC, 107.7.

Giddings — Newspaper: Times & News. **Radio-FM:** KROX, 101.5 MHz.

Gilmer — Newspaper: Mirror (S). **Radio-AM:** KBNB, 1060 Khz. **Radio-FM:** KFRO, 95.3 MHz.

Gladewater — Newspaper: Mirror. **Radio-AM:** KEES, 1430 Khz.

Glen Rose — Newspaper: Reporter. **Radio-FM:** KCLE, 92.1 MHz.

Goldthwaite — Newspaper: Eagle.

Goliad — Newspaper: Texan Express. **Radio FM:** KHMC, 95.9 MHz.

Gonzales — Newspaper: Inquirer (S). **Radio-AM:** KCTI, 1450 Khz. **Radio-FM:** KCII, 106.3 MHz.

Gorman — Newspaper: Progress.

Graham — Newspaper: Leader (S). **Radio-AM:** KSWA, 1330 Khz. **Radio-FM:** KWKQ, 107.1 MHz.

Granbury — Newspaper: Hood County News (S). **Radio-AM:** KPAR, 1420 Khz. **Radio-FM:** KMRT, 106.7 MHz.

Grand Prairie — Newspaper: News (S). **Radio-AM:** KKDA, 730 Khz.

Grand Saline — Newspaper: Sun.

Grandview — Newspaper: Tribune.

Granger — Newspaper: News.

Grapeland — Newspaper: Messenger.

Greenville — Newspaper: Herald-Banner (D). **Radio-AM:** KGVL,1400 Khz. **Radio-FM:** KIKT, 93.5 MHz. **TV:** KTAQ-Ch. 47.

Greenwood — Newspaper: Ranger.

Groesbeck — Newspaper: Journal.

Groom — Newspaper: Groom/McLean News.

Groves — Radio-FM: KTFA, 92.5 MHz.

Groveton — Newspaper: News.

Gun Barrel City — Newspaper: Cedar Creek Pilot (S).

Hale Center — Newspaper: American.

Hallettsville — Newspaper: Tribune-Herald (S). **Radio-AM:** KHLT, 1520 Khz.

Hallsville — Newspaper: Herald.

Haltom City — Radio FM: KKZN, 93.3 MHz.

Hamilton — Newspaper: Herald-News. **Radio-AM:** KCLW, 900 Khz.

Hamlin — Newspaper: Herald. **Radio-FM:** KCDD, 103.7 MHz.

Harker Heights — Radio-FM: KNRV, 105.5 MHz.

Harlingen — Newspaper: Valley Morning Star (D). **Radio-AM:** KGBT, 1530 Khz. **Radio-FM:** KMBH, 88.9 MHz; KFRQ, 94.5; KIWW, 96.1. **TV:** KGBT-Ch. 4; KLUJ-Ch. 44; KMBH-Ch. 60.

Harper — Newspaper: Herald.

Hart — Newspaper: Beat.

Haskell — Newspaper: Free Press. **Radio-FM:** KVRP, 95.5 MHz.

Hearne — Newspaper: Democrat. **Radio-FM:** KHRN, 94.3 MHz.

Hebbronville — Newspapers: Jim Hogg County Enterprise; View.

Hemphill — Newspaper: Sabine County Reporter. **Radio-AM:** KAWS, 1240 Khz.

Hempstead — Newspaper: Waller County News-Citizen.

Henderson — **Newspaper:** Daily News (D). **Radio-AM:** KWRD, 1470 Khz. **Radio-FM:** KGRI, 99.9 MHz.

Henrietta — **Newspaper:** Clay County Leader.

Hereford — **Newspaper:** Brand (D). **Radio-AM:** KPAN, 860 Khz. **Radio-FM:** KPAN, 106.3 MHz.

Hico — **Newspaper:** News Review.

Highland Park — **Radio-AM:** KDMM, 1150 Khz. **Radio-FM:** KVIL, 103.7 MHz.

Highlands — **Newspaper:** Star/Crosby Courier.

Hillsboro — **Newspaper:** Reporter (S). **Radio-AM:** KHBR, 1560 Khz. **Radio-FM:** KBRQ, 102.5 MHz.

Hondo — **Newspaper:** Anvil Herald. **Radio-AM:** KCWM, 1460 Khz.

Honey Grove — **Newspaper:** Signal-Citizen.

Hooks — **Radio-FM:** KLLI, 95.9 MHz.

Hornsby — **Radio FM:** KOOP, 91.7 MHz.

Houston — **Newspapers:** Business Journal; Chronicle (D); Daily Court Review (D); Forward Times; Informer and Texas Freeman; Jewish Herald-Voice; Post (D); Texas Catholic Herald (BW). **Radio-AM:** KILT, 610 Khz; KTRH, 740; KKBQ, 790; KEYH, 850; KPRC, 950; KLAT, 1010; KENR, 1070; KNUZ, 1230; KXYZ, 1320; KCOH, 1430; KYOK, 1590. **Radio-FM:** KUHF, 88.7 MHz; KPFT, 90.1; KTSU, 90.9; KTRU, 91.7; KKRW, 93.7; KLDE, 94.5; KIKK, 95.7; KHMX, 96.5; KBXX, 97.9; KODA, 99.1; KILT, 100.3; KLOL, 101.1; KMJQ, 102.1; KQUE, 102.9; KRBE, 104.1; KHCB, 105.7. **TV:** KPRC-Ch. 2; KUHT-Ch. 8; KHOU-Ch. 11; KTRK-Ch. 13; KETH-Ch. 14; KTXH-Ch. 20; KRIV-Ch. 26; KHTV-Ch. 39; KZJL-Ch. 61.

Howe — **Newspaper:** Enterprise. **Radio-FM:** KHYI, 95.3 MHz.

Hubbard — **Newspaper:** City News.

Humble — **Radio-AM:** KGOL, 1180 Khz. **Radio-FM:** KSBJ, 89.3 MHz.

Huntington — **Radio-FM:** KYBI, 101.9 MHz.

Huntsville — **Newspaper:** Item (D).**Radio-AM:** KYLR, 1400 Khz; KSAM, 1490. **Radio-FM:** KSHU, 90.5 MHz; KSAM, 101.7.

Hutto — **Radio-FM:** KIKY, 92.1 MHz.

Idalou — **Newspaper:** Beacon.

Ingleside — **Newspaper:** Index. **Radio FM:** KAHX, 107.3 MHz.

Iowa Park — **Newspaper:** Leader.

Iraan — **Newspaper:** News.

Irving — **Newspaper:** News (S). **TV:** KHSX-Ch. 49.

Jacksboro — **Newspapers:** Gazette-News; Jack County Herald.

Jacksonville — **Newspaper:** Daily Progress (D). **Radio-AM:** KEBE, 1400 Khz. **Radio-FM:** KBJS, 90.3 MHz; KSIZ, 102.3; KOOI, 106.5. **TV:** KETK-Ch. 56.

Jasper — **Newspaper:** News-Boy. **Radio-AM:** KTXJ, 1350 Khz. **Radio-FM:** KRTX, 100.9 MHz; KWYX, 102.3; KJAS, 107.3.

Jefferson — **Newspaper:** Jimplecute. **Radio-FM:** KJTX, 104.5 MHz.

Jewett — **Newspaper:** Messenger.

Johnson City — **Newspaper:** Record-Courier. **Radio-FM:** KFAN, 107.9 MHz.

Joshua — **Newspaper:** Star Tribune.

Junction — **Newspaper:** Eagle. **Radio-AM:** KMBL, 1450 Khz.

Karnes City — **Newspaper:** Karnes Citation. **Radio-AM:** KAML, 990 Khz.

Katy — **Newspaper:** Times (S). **TV:** KNWS-Ch. 51.

Kaufman — **Newspaper:** Herald.

Keene — **Newspaper:** Star Reporter. **Radio-AM:** KJCR; 88.3 MHz.

Kenedy — **Newspaper:** Advance-Times. **Radio-AM:** KAML, 990 Khz. **Radio-FM:** KTNR, 92.1 MHz.

Kennedale — **Newspaper:** News.

Kerens — **Newspaper:** Tribune.

Kermit — **Newspaper:** Winkler County News. **Radio-AM:** KERB, 600 Khz. **Radio-FM:** KERB, 106.3 MHz.

Kerrville — **Newspapers:** Daily Times (D); Mountain Sun. **Radio-AM:** KERV, 1230 Khz. **Radio-FM:** KITE, 92.3 MHz; KRVL, 94.3. **TV:** KRRT-Ch. 35.

Kilgore — **Newspaper:** News Herald (D). **Radio-AM:** KKTX, 1240 Khz. **Radio-FM:** KTPB, 88.7 Mhz; KKTX, 96.1.

Killeen — **Newspaper:** Daily Herald (D). **Radio-AM:** KRMY, 1050 Khz. **Radio-FM:** KNCT, 91.3 MHz; KIIZ, 92.3; KAJZ, 93.3.

Kingsville — **Newspaper:** Record (S). **Radio-AM:** KINE, 1330 Khz. **Radio-FM:** KTAI, 91.1 MHz; KKBA, 92.7; KFTX, 97.5.

Kirbyville — **Newspaper:** East Texas Banner.

Knox City — **Newspaper:** Knox County News.

Kress — **Newspaper:** Chronicle.

Ladonia — **Newspaper:** News.

La Feria — **Newspaper:** News.

La Grange — **Newspaper:** Fayette County Record (S). **Radio-AM:** KVLG, 1570 Khz. **Radio-FM:** KBUK, 104.9 MHz.

Lake Dallas — **Newspaper:** Lake Cities Sun. **TV:** KLDT-Ch. 55.

Lake Jackson — **Newspaper:** Brazorian News. **Radio-FM:** KYBJ, 91.1 MHz; KTBZ, 107.5.

La Marque — **Newspaper:** Times.

Lamesa — **Newspaper:** Press Reporter (S). **Radio-AM:** KPET, 690 Khz. **Radio-FM:** KMMX, 100.3 MHz; KIOL, 104.7.

Lampasas — **Newspaper:** Dispatch Record (S). **Radio-AM:** KCYL, 1450 Khz. **Radio-FM:** KJFK, 98.9 MHz.

Lancaster — **Newspaper:** Today.

La Porte — **Newspaper:** Bayshore Sun (S).

Laredo — **Newspaper:** Morning Times (D). **Radio-AM:** KVOZ, 890 Khz; KLAR, 1300; KDOS, 1490. **Radio-FM:** KHOY, 88.1 MHz; KBNL, 89.9; KJBZ, 92.7; KOYE, 94.9; KRRG, 98.1; KZTQ, 106.1. **TV:** KGNS-Ch. 8; KVTV-Ch. 13; KLDO-Ch. 27.

La Vernia — **Newspaper:** News.

Leakey — **Newspaper:** Real American.

Leonard — **Newspaper:** Graphic.

Levelland — **Newspaper:** Hockley County News-Press (S). **Radio-AM:** KLVT, 1230 Khz. **Radio-FM:** KLVT, 105.5 MHz.

Liberty — **Newspaper:** Vindicator (S). **Radio-AM:** KPXE, 1050 Khz. **Radio-FM:** KSHN, 99.9 MHz.

Lindale — **Newspapers:** News and Times.

Linden — **Newspaper:** Cass County Sun.

Little Elm — **Newspaper:** Journal.

Littlefield — **Newspaper:** Lamb County Leader-News (S). **Radio-AM:** KZZN, 1490 Khz.

Livingston — **Newspaper:** Polk County Enterprise (S). **Radio-AM:** KETX, 1140 Khz. **Radio-FM:** KETX, 92.3 MHz.

Llano — **Newspaper:** News. **Radio-FM:** KBAE, 104.7 MHz. **TV:** KXAM-Ch. 14.

Lockhart — **Newspaper:** Post-Register. **Radio-AM:** KFIT, 1060 Khz.

Longview — **Newspaper:** News-Journal (D). **Radio-AM:** KARW, 1280 Khz; KFRO, 1370. **Radio-FM:** KYKX, 105.7 MHz. **TV:** KFXK-Ch. 51.

Lorenzo — **Newspaper:** Examiner. **Radio-FM:** KKCL, 98.1 MHz.

Los Ybanez — **Radio-FM:** KYMI, 107.9 Mhz.

Lubbock — **Newspaper:** Avalanche-Journal (D). **Radio-AM:** KRFE, 580 Khz; KFYO, 790; KXTQ, 950; KKAM, 1340; KLFB, 1420; KBZO, 1460; KLLL, 1590. **Radio-FM:** KTXT, 88.1 MHz; KOHM, 89.1; KAMY, 90.1; KYFT, 90.9; KXTQ, 93.7; KFMX, 94.5; KLLL, 96.3; KJBX, 99.5; KONE, 101.1; KZII, 102.5; KEJS, 106.5. **TV:** KTXT-Ch. 5; KCBD-Ch. 11; KLBK-Ch. 13; KAMC-Ch. 28; KJTV- Ch. 34.

Lufkin — **Newspaper:** Daily News (D). **Radio-AM:** KRBA, 1340 Khz. **Radio-FM:** KLDN, 88.9 Mhz; KSWP, 90.9; KUEZ, 99.3; KYKS, 105.1. **TV:** KTRE-Ch. 9.

Luling — **Newspaper:** Newsboy & Signal. **Radio-FM:** KAMX, 94.7 MHz.

Lytle — **Newspaper:** Medina Valley Times. **Radio-FM:** KXPZ, 91.3 MHz.

Mabank — **Newspaper:** Monitor (S).

Madisonville — **Newspaper:** Meteor. **Radio-AM:** KMVL, 1220 Khz. **Radio-FM:** KAGG, 96.1 MHz; KMVL, 100.5.

Malakoff — **Newspaper:** News. **Radio-FM:** KCKL, 95.9 MHz.

Mansfield — **Newspaper:** News-Mirror (S).

Marble Falls — **Newspapers:** Highlander (S); River Cities Tribune.

Marfa — **Newspaper:** Big Bend Sentinel.

Marion — **Radio-AM:** KBIB, 1000 Khz.

Marlin — **Newspaper:** Democrat. **Radio-FM:** KEYR, 92.9 MHz.

Marshall — **Newspaper:** News Messenger (D). **Radio-AM:** KCUL, 1410 Khz; KMHT, 1450. **Radio-FM:** KBWC, 91.1 MHz; KCUL, 92.3; KZEY, 103.9.

Mart — **Newspaper:** Texan.

Mason — **Newspaper:** Mason County News.

Matador — **Newspaper:** Motley County Tribune.

Mathis — **Newspaper:** News.

McAllen — **Newspapers:** Monitor (D); News Journal. **Radio-AM:** KRIO, 910 Khz. **Radio-FM:** KHID, 88.1 MHz; KVMV, 96.9; KGBT, 98.5. **TV:** KNVO-Ch. 48.

McCamey — **Newspaper:** News.

McGregor — **Newspaper:** Mirror and Crawford.

McKinney — **Newspaper:** Courier-Gazette (D). **Radio-FM:** KRVA, 106.9 MHz.

Memphis — **Newspaper:** Democrat. **Radio-AM:** KLSR, 1130 Khz. **Radio-FM:** KLSR, 105.3 MHz.

Menard — **Newspaper:** News and Messenger.

Mercedes — **Newspaper:** Enterprise. **Radio-FM:** KTJN, 106.3 MHz.

Meridian — **Newspaper:** Bosque County News.
Merkel — **Newspaper:** Mail. **Radio-AM:** KMXO, 1500 Khz. **Radio-FM:** KCWS, 102.7 MHz.
Mesquite — **Radio-FM:** KEOM, 88.5 MHz.
Mexia — **Newspaper:** Daily News (D). **Radio-AM:** KRQX, 1590 Khz. **Radio-FM:** KYCX, 104.9 MHz.
Miami — **Newspaper:** Chief.
Midland — **Newspaper:** Reporter-Telegram (D). **Radio-AM:** KCRS, 550 Khz; KWEL, 1070; KJBC, 1150; KMND, 1510. **Radio-FM:** KNFM, 92.3 MHz; KBAT, 93.3; KQRX, 95.1; KCRS, 103.3; KCHX, 106.7. **TV:** KMID-Ch. 2.
Midlothian — **Newspapers:** Mirror; Today.
Miles — **Newspaper:** Messenger.
Mineola — **Newspaper:** Monitor. **Radio-AM:** KVCI, 1510 Khz. **Radio-FM:** KMOO, 96.7 MHz.
Mineral Wells — **Newspaper:** Index (D). **Radio-AM:** KJSA, 1140 Khz. **Radio-FM:** KYXS, 95.9 MHz.
Mirando City — **Radio-FM:** KBDR, 100.5 MHz.
Mission — **Newspaper:** Progress-Times. **Radio-AM:** KIRT, 1580 Khz. **Radio-FM:** KTJX, 105.5 MHz.
Monahans — **Newspaper:** News. **Radio-AM:** KLBO, 1330 Khz. **Radio-FM:** KGEE, 99.9 MHz; KCDQ, 102.1.
Moody — **Newspaper:** Courier.
Morton — **Newspaper:** Tribune.
Moulton — **Newspaper:** Eagle.
Mount Pleasant — **Newspaper:** Daily Tribune (D). **Radio-AM:** KIMP, 960 Khz. **Radio-FM:** KPXI, 100.7 MHz.
Mount Vernon — **Newspaper:** Optic-Herald.
Muenster — **Newspaper:** Enterprise. **Radio-FM:** KXGM, 106.5 MHz.
Muleshoe — **Newspapers:** Bailey County Journal; Journal. **Radio-AM:** KMUL, 1380 Khz. **Radio-FM:** KKYC, 103.1 MHz.
Munday — **Newspaper:** Courier.
Nacogdoches — **Newspaper:** Daily Sentinel (D). **Radio-AM:** KSFA, 860 Khz; KEEE, 1230. **Radio-FM:** KSAU, 90.1 MHz; KJCS, 103.3; KTBQ, 107.7. **TV:** KLSB-Ch. 19.
Naples — **Newspaper:** Monitor.
Navasota — **Newspaper:** Examiner. **Radio-AM:** KWBC, 1550 Khz. **Radio-FM:** KMBV, 92.5 MHz.
Nederland — **Radio-AM:** KQHN, 1510 Khz.
Needville — **Newspaper:** Gulf Coast Tribune.
New Boston — **Newspaper:** Bowie County Citizens Tribune (S). **Radio-AM:** KNBO, 1530 Khz. **Radio-FM:** KZRB, 103.5 Mhz.
New Braunfels — **Newspaper:** Herald-Zeitung (D). **Radio-AM:** KGNB, 1420 Khz. **Radio-FM:** KNBT, 92.1 MHz.
Newton — **Newspaper:** Newton County News.
New Ulm — **Newspaper:** Enterprise.
Nixon — **Newspaper:** Cow Country Courier.
Nocona — **Newspaper:** News.
Nolanville — **Radio FM:** KLFX, 107.3 MHz.
Normangee — **Newspaper:** Star.
Odem — **Newspaper:** Odem-Edroy Times. **Radio-FM:** KLHB, 98.3 MHz.
Odessa — **Newspaper:** American (D). **Radio-AM:** KENT, 920 Khz; KOZA, 1230; KOYL, 1310; KRIL, 1410. **Radio-FM:** KENT, 90.5 MHz; KOCV, 91.3; KMRK, 96.1; KQIP, 96.9; KODM, 97.9; KKKK, 99.1. **TV:** KOSA-Ch. 7; KWES -Ch. 9; KPEJ-Ch. 24; KOCV-Ch. 36; KMLM-Ch. 42.
O'Donnell — **Newspaper:** Index-Press.
Olney — **Newspaper:** Enterprise.
Olton — **Newspaper:** Enterprise.
Orange — **Newspaper:** Leader (D). **Radio-AM:** KOGT, 1600 Khz. **Radio-FM:** KKMY, 104.5 MHz; KIOC, 106.1.
Overton — **Newspaper:** Press.
Ozona — **Newspaper:** Stockman. **Radio-FM:** KYXX, 94.3 MHz.
Paducah — **Newspaper:** Post.
Paint Rock — **Newspaper:** Concho Herald.
Palacios — **Newspaper:** Beacon.
Palestine — **Newspaper:** Herald Press (D). **Radio-AM:** KNET, 1450 Khz. **Radio-FM:** KLIS, 96.7 MHz; KYYK, 98.3.
Pampa — **Newspaper:** News (D). **Radio-AM:** KGRO, 1230 Khz; KPDN, 1340. **Radio-FM:** KOMX, 100.3 MHz.
Panhandle — **Newspaper:** Herald.
Paris — **Newspaper:** News (D). **Radio-AM:** KGDD, 1250 Khz; KPLT, 1490. **Radio-FM:** KOYN, 93.9 MHz; KBUS, 101.9; KPLT, 107.7.
Pasadena — **Newspaper:** Citizen (D). **Radio-AM:** KIKK, 650 Khz; KLVL, 1480. **Radio-FM:** KFTG, 88.1 MHz; KKBQ, 92.9.
Pearland — **Newspapers:** Journal; Reporter News.
Pearsall — **Newspaper:** Frio-Nueces Current. **Radio-AM:** KVWG, 1280 Khz. **Radio-FM:** KVWG, 95.3 MHz.
Pecos — **Newspaper:** Enterprise (D). **Radio-AM:** KIUN, 1400 Khz. **Radio-FM:** KPTX, 98.3 MHz.
Perryton — **Newspaper:** Herald (S). **Radio-AM:** KEYE, 1400 Khz. **Radio-FM:** KEYE, 95.9 MHz.

Petersburg — **Newspaper:** Post.
Pflugerville — **Newspaper:** Pflag.
Pharr — **Newspaper:** Pharr/San Juan/Alamo Advance News Journal. **Radio-AM:** KVJY, 840 Khz.
Pilot Point — **Newspaper:** Post-Signal.
Pittsburg — **Newspaper:** Gazette. **Radio-FM:** KXAL, 103.1 MHz.
Plains — **Radio-FM:** KPHS, 90.3 MHz.
Plainview — **Newspaper:** Daily Herald (D). **Radio-AM:** KKYN, 1090 Khz; KVOP, 1400. **Radio-FM:** KWLD, 91.5 MHz; KVOP, 97.3; KKYN, 103.9.
Plano — **Newspaper:** Star Courier (D). **Radio AM:** KAAM, 620 Khz.
Pleasanton — **Newspaper:** Express. **Radio-AM:** KBOP, 1380 Khz. **Radio-FM:** KBUC, 98.3 MHz.
Port Aransas — **Newspaper:** South Jetty.
Port Arthur — **Newspaper:** News (D). **Radio-AM:** KALO, 1250 Khz; KOLE, 1340. **Radio-FM:** KLTN, 93.3 MHz; KHYS, 98.5. **TV:** KJAC-Ch. 4.
Port Isabel — **Newspaper:** Port Isabel/South Padre Press (S). **Radio-FM:** KVPA, 101.1 MHz.
Portland — **Newspaper:** News. **Radio-FM:** KRAD, 105.5 MHz.
Port Lavaca — **Newspaper:** Wave (S). **Radio-AM:** KILE, 1560 Khz. **Radio-FM:** KPLV, 93.3 MHz.
Port Neches — **Radio-AM:** KUHD, 1150 Khz.
Post — **Newspaper:** Dispatch. **Radio-AM:** KPOS, 1370 Khz. **Radio-FM:** KPOS, 107.3 MHz.
Pottsboro — **Newspaper:** Press.
Prairie View — **Radio-FM:** KPVU, 91.3 MHz.
Premont — **Radio-FM:** KMFM, 104.9 MHz.
Presidio — **Newspaper:** The International.
Princeton — **Newspaper:** Herald.
Quanah — **Newspaper:** Tribune-Chief (S). **Radio-AM:** KVDL, 1150 Khz. **Radio-FM:** KIXC, 100.9 MHz.
Quinlan — **Newspaper:** Tawakoni News.
Quitaque — **Newspaper:** Valley Tribune.
Quitman — **Newspaper:** Wood County Democrat.
Ralls — **Radio-AM:** KCLR, 1530 Khz.
Ranger — **Newspaper:** Times (S).
Rankin — **Newspaper:** News.
Raymondville — **Newspaper:** Chronicle and Willacy County News. **Radio-AM:** KSOX, 1240 Khz. **Radio-FM:** KSOX, 102.1 MHz.
Red Oak — **Newspapers:** North Ellis County Chronicle.
Refugio — **Newspaper:** County Advantage Press. **Radio-FM:** KZTX, 106.3 MHz.
Richardson — **Newspaper:** News (S).
Riesel — **Newspaper:** Rustler.
Rio Grande City — **Newspaper:** Rio Grande Herald. **Radio-FM:** KCTM, 103.1 MHz.
Rising Star — **Newspaper:** Rising Star.
Robert Lee — **Newspaper:** Observer/Enterprise.
Robstown — **Newspaper:** Nueces County Record-Star. **Radio-AM:** KGLF, 1510 Khz. **Radio-FM:** KLUX, 89.5 MHz; KSAB, 99.9; KMIQ, 105.1.
Rochester — **Newspaper:** Twin Cities News.
Rockdale — **Newspaper:** Reporter and Messenger. **Radio-FM:** KRXT, 98.5 MHz.
Rockport — **Newspapers:** Herald; Pilot (S). **Radio-FM:** KXCC, 102.3 MHz.
Rocksprings — **Newspaper:** Texas Mohair Weekly.
Rockwall — **Newspapers:** Chronicle; Texas Success (S).
Rollingwood — **Radio-AM:** KJCE, 1370 Khz.
Roma — **Newspaper:** South Texas Reporter. **Radio-FM:** KBMI, 97.7 MHz.
Rosebud — **Newspaper:** News.
Rosenberg — **Newspaper:** Herald-Coaster (D). **Radio-AM:** KMPQ, 980 Khz. **Radio-FM:** KLTO, 104.9 Mhz. **TV:** KXLN-Ch. 45.
Rotan — **Newspaper:** Advance-Star-Record.
Round Rock — **Newspaper:** Leader (S). **Radio-FM:** KNLE, 88.1 MHz.
Rowena — **Newspaper:** Press.
Rowlett — **Newspaper:** Lakeshore Times.
Royse City — **Newspaper:** News.
Rusk — **Newspaper:** Cherokeean/Herald. **Radio-AM:** KTLU, 1580 Khz. **Radio-FM:** KWRW, 97.7 Mhz.
Saint Jo — **Newspaper:** Tribune.
San Angelo — **Newspaper:** Standard-Times (D). **Radio-AM:** KGKL, 960 Khz; KKSA, 1260; KCRN, 1340. **Radio-FM:** KUTX, 90.1 MHz; KDCD, 92.9; KDCD, 92.9; KCRN, 93.9; KIXY, 94.7; KGKL, 97.5; KELI, 98.7; KSJT, 107.5. **TV:** KACB-Ch. 3; KIDY-Ch. 6; KLST-Ch. 8.
San Antonio — **Newspapers:** Business Journal; Commercial Recorder (D); Express-News (D); North San Antonio Times; Today's Catholic (BW). **Radio-AM:** KTSA, 550 Khz; KSLR,

630; KKYX, 680; KTKR, 760; KONO, 860; KENS, 1160; WOAI, 1200; KZDC, 1250; KXTN, 1310; KCOR, 1350; KCHL, 1480; KEDA, 1540. **Radio-FM:** KPAC, 88.3 MHz; KSTX, 89.1; KSYM, 90.1; KYFS, 90.9; KRTU, 91.7; KROM, 92.9; KSJL, 96.1; KAJA, 97.3; KISS, 99.5; KCYY, 100.3; KQXT, 101.9; KTFM, 102.7; KZEP, 104.5; KXTN, 107.5. **TV:** KMOL-Ch. 4; KENS-Ch. 5; KLRN-Ch. 9; KSAT-Ch. 12; KHCE-Ch. 23; KABB-Ch. 29; KWEX-Ch. 41; KVDA-Ch. 60.

San Augustine — Newspaper: Tribune. **Radio-FM:** KCOT, 92.5 MHz.

San Benito — Newspaper: News (S).

Sanderson — Newspaper: Times.

San Diego — Newspaper: Duval County Picture. **Radio-FM:** KUKA, 105.9 MHz.

Sanger — Newspaper: Courier.

San Juan — Radio-AM: KUBR, 1210 Khz.

San Marcos — Newspaper: Daily Record (D). **Radio-AM:** KUOL, 1470 Khz. **Radio-FM:** KTSW, 89.9 MHz; KEYI, 103.5.

San Saba — Newspaper: News & Star. **Radio-AM:** KBAL, 1410 Khz.

Santa Anna — Newspaper: News.

Santa Fe — Radio-FM: KJIC, 90.5 MHz.

Schulenburg — Newspaper: Sticker.

Seabrook — Radio-FM: KRTS, 92.1 MHz.

Seagoville — Newspaper: Suburbia News.

Seagraves — Newspaper: Gaines County News.

Sealy — Newspaper: News (S).

Seguin — Newspaper: Gazette-Enterprise (D). **Radio-AM:** KWED, 1580 Khz. **Radio-FM:** KSMG, 105.3 MHz.

Seminole — Newspaper: Sentinel (S). **Radio-AM:** KIKZ, 1250 Khz. **Radio-FM:** KSEM, 106.3 MHz.

Seymour — Newspaper: Baylor County Banner. **Radio-AM:** KSEY, 1230 Khz. **Radio-FM:** KSEY, 94.3 MHz.

Shamrock — Newspaper: Texan.

Shepherd — Newspaper: San Jacinto News-Times.

Sherman — Newspaper: Herald Democrat (D). **Radio-AM:** KXEB, 910 Khz; KJIM, 1500. **Radio-FM:** KIKM, 96.7 MHz; KIXL, 104.1. **TV:** KXII-Ch. 12.

Shiner — Newspaper: Gazette.

Silsbee — Newspaper: Bee. **Radio-AM:** KKAS, 1300 Khz. **Radio-FM:** KWDX, 101.7 MHz.

Silverton — Newspaper: Briscoe County News.

Sinton — Newspaper: San Patricio County News. **Radio-AM:** KDAE, 1590 Khz. **Radio-FM:** KNCN, 101.3 MHz; KOUL, 103.7.

Slaton — Newspaper: Slatonite. **Radio-FM:** KJAK, 92.7 MHz.

Smithville — Newspaper: Times.

Snyder — Newspaper: Daily News (D). **Radio-AM:** KSNY, 1450 Khz. **Radio-FM:** KSNY, 101.7 MHz.

Somerset — Radio-AM: KCHG, 810 Khz.

Sonora — Newspaper: Devil's River News. **Radio-AM:** KHOS, 980 Khz. **Radio-FM:** KHOS, 92.1 MHz.

South Padre Island — Radio-FM: KESO, 92.7 MHz; KZSP, 95.3.

Spearman — Newspaper: Hansford County Reporter-Statesman. **Radio-FM:** KRDF, 98.3 MHz.

Springtown — Newspaper: Epigraph. **Radio-FM:** KMQX, 89.1 MHz.

Spur — Newspaper: Texas Spur.

Stamford — Newspaper: American. **Radio-AM:** KVRP, 1400 Khz.

Stanton — Newspaper: Martin County Messenger.

Stephenville — Newspaper: Empire-Tribune (D). **Radio-AM:** KSTV, 1510 Khz. **Radio-FM:** KCUB, 98.3 MHz; KRNB, 105.7.

Sterling City — Newspaper: News-Record.

Stinnett — Newspaper: Post

Stratford — Newspaper: Star.

Sudan — Newspaper: Beacon-News.

Sugar Land — Newspaper: Fort Bend Mirror.

Sulphur Springs — Newspaper: News-Telegram (D). **Radio-AM:** KSST, 1230 Khz. **Radio-FM:** KDXE, 95.9 MHz.

Sweetwater — Newspaper: Reporter (D). **Radio-AM:** KXOX, 1240 Khz. **Radio-FM:** KXOX, 96.7 MHz. **TV:** KTXS-Ch. 12.

Taft — Newspaper: Tribune.

Tahoka — Newspaper: Lynn County News.

Talco — Newspaper: Times.

Tatum — Newspaper: Trammel Trace Tribune.

Taylor — Newspaper: Daily Press (D). **Radio-AM:** KTAE, 1260 Khz.

Teague — Newspaper: Chronicle.

Temple — Newspaper: Daily Telegram (D). **Radio-AM:** KTEM, 1400 Khz. **Radio-FM:** KLTD, 101.7 MHz; KKIK, 104.3. **TV:** KCEN-Ch. 6.

Terrell — Newspaper: Tribune (D). **Radio-AM:** KPYK, 1570 Khz. **Radio-FM:** KTLR, 107.1 MHz.

Terrell Hills — Radio-AM: KLUP, 930 Khz. **Radio-FM:** KCJZ, 106.7 MHz.

Texarkana — Newspaper: Gazette (D). **Radio-AM:** KCMC, 740 Khz; KTFS, 940; KHSP, 1400. **Radio-FM:** KTXK, 91.5 MHz; KTAL, 98.1; KKYR, 102.5. **TV:** KTAL-Ch. 6.

Texas City — Newspaper: Sun (D). **Radio-AM:** KYST, 920 Khz.

Thorndale — Newspaper: Champion.

Three Rivers — Newspaper: Progress.

Throckmorton — Newspaper: Tribune.

Timpson — Newspaper: Timpson & Tenaha News.

Tomball — Radio-AM: KSEV, 700 Khz.

Trenton — Newspaper: Tribune.

Trinity — Newspaper: Standard.

Tulia — Newspaper: Herald; Sentinel. **Radio-AM:** KTUE, 1260 Khz. **Radio-FM:** KJMX, 104.9 Mhz.

Tuscola — Newspaper: Journal.

Tye — Radio-FM: KBCY, 99.7 MHz.

Tyler — Newspapers: Morning Telegraph (D); Catholic East Texas (BW). **Radio-AM:** KTBB, 600 Khz; KZEY, 690; KGLD, 1330; KYZS, 1490. **Radio-FM:** KVNE, 89.5 MHz; KGLY, 91.3; KDOK, 92.1; KTYL, 93.1; KNUE, 101.5; KKUS, 104.1. **TV:** KLTV-Ch. 7.

Universal City — Radio-AM: KSAH, 720 Khz.

Uvalde — Newspaper: Leader-News (S). **Radio-AM:** KVOU, 1400 Khz. **Radio-FM:** KBNU, 93.7 MHz; KUVA, 102.3; KYUF, 104.9.

Valley Mills — Newspaper: Progress.

Van Alstyne — Newspaper: Leader.

Van Horn — Newspaper: Advocate.

Vega — Newspaper: Enterprise.

Vernon — Newspaper: Daily Record (D). **Radio-AM:** KVWC, 1490 Khz. **Radio-FM:** KVWC, 102.3 MHz.

Victoria — Newspaper: Advocate (D). **Radio-AM:** KAMG, 1340 Khz; KNAL, 1410. **Radio-FM:** KXBJ, 89.3 MHz; KVRT, 90.7; KVLT, 92.3; KVIC, 95.1; KTXN, 98.7; KEPG, 100.9; KIXS, 107.9. **TV:** KVCT-Ch. 19; KAVU-Ch. 25.

Vidor — Newspaper: Vidorian.

Waco — Newspapers: Citizen (S); Tribune-Herald (D). **Radio-AM:** KBBW, 1010; KWTX, 1230 Khz; KKTK, 1460; KRZI, 1580. **Radio-FM:** KCKR, 95.5 MHz; KWTX, 97.5; WACO, 99.9; KWBU, 107.1. **TV:** KWTX-Ch. 10; KXXV-Ch. 25; KCTF-Ch. 34; KWKT-Ch. 44.

Wallis — Newspaper: News-Review.

Waskom — Newspaper: Review.

Waxahachie — Newspaper: Daily Light (D). **Radio-AM:** KBEC, 1390 Khz.

Weatherford — Newspapers: Democrat (D); Community News. **Radio-AM:** KZEE, 1220 Khz. **Radio-FM:** KYQX, 89.5 MHz.

Weimar — Newspaper: Mercury.

Wellington — Newspaper: Leader.

Weslaco — Radio-AM: KRGE, 1290 Khz. **TV:** KRGV-Ch. 5.

West — Newspaper: News.

West Lake Hills — Radio-AM: KTXZ, 1560 Khz.

Wharton — Newspaper: Journal-Spectator (S). **Radio-AM:** KANI, 1500 Khz.

Wheeler — Newspaper: Times. **Radio-FM:** KPDR, 90.5 MHz.

White Deer — Newspaper: News.

Whitehouse — Newspaper: Tri County Leader. **Radio-FM:** KISX, 107.3 MHz.

White Oak — Newspaper: Independent.

Whitesboro — Newspaper: News-Record.

Whitewright — Newspaper: Sun.

Whitney — Newspapers: Messenger; Lake Whitney View (M).

Wichita Falls — Newspaper: Times-Record-News (D). **Radio-AM:** KWFT, 990; KWFS, 1290. **Radio-FM:** KMOC, 89.5 MHz; KTEQ, 90.5; KNIN, 92.9; KLUR, 99.9; KQXC, 102.5; KWFS, 103.3; KTLT, 106.3. **TV:** KFDX-Ch. 3; KAUZ-Ch. 6; KJTL-Ch. 18.

Willis — Radio FM: KVST, 103.7 MHz.

Wills Point — Newspapers: Chronicle; Van Zandt News.

Wimberley — Newspaper: View.

Winfield — Radio-FM: KALK, 97.7 MHz.

Winnie — Newspaper: Hometown Press. **Radio FM:** KRTX, 100.7 MHz.

Winnsboro — Newspapers: News; Tribune. **Radio-FM:** KWNS, 104.9 MHz.

Winters — Newspaper: Enterprise.

Wolfe City — Newspaper: Mirror.

Woodville — Newspaper: Tyler County Booster. **Radio-AM:** KVLL, 1490 Khz. **Radio-FM:** KVLL, 94.7 MHz.

Wylie — Newspaper: News.

Yoakum — Newspaper: Herald-Times Four Star Reporter. **Radio-FM:** KYKM, 92.5 MHz.

Yorktown — Newspapers: DeWitt County View; News.

Zapata — Newspapers: Zapata County News. ☆

The Texas Economy: Still Building

Source: State of Texas Annual Cash Report 1996, Comptroller of Public Accounts

For the fourth straight year, the Texas economy added more than 200,000 jobs. Yet, despite this gain, a somewhat slower national economy caused the state's rate of job growth to fall below 3 percent for the first time since fiscal 1992.

Texas relinquished the top spot in the number of new jobs added to a resurgent California. Despite shifting out of overdrive, the Texas economy remains strong and healthy, having added 220,000 jobs, a 2.7 percent increase, which exceeded the national employment growth rate of 2.1 percent by more than one-half percentage point. Over the last four years, Texas has added 1 million jobs and accounted for 9 percent of the nation's total job growth. Among the 50 states, Texas continues to rank 10th in the rate of employment growth, behind mostly mountain states with relatively small populations.

In one sense, Texas' economic emphasis during fiscal 1996 shifted from job growth to income growth. Based on state income data from the U.S. Bureau of Economic Analysis, Texas' total personal income grew faster than might be expected from job growth in fiscal 1996.

Total personal income growth (at 7 percent) exceeded the nation's by 2 percentage points in fiscal 1996. Data from the winter of 1996 indicate that the state's total personal income in the durable-goods industry advanced by more than 12 percent in a year, with strong showings in retail trade (up 10.6 percent), construction (9.8 percent), and services (9.7 percent).

The only sector in which total income declined during the fiscal year was in the military sector, where ongoing defense cuts have reduced total military income in Texas by 3 percent.

In per capita terms, Texas' personal income grew by 5.1 percent, well above the 2.8 percent inflation rate.

Services Recapture the Limelight

During most of the 1980s and early 1990s, the state's fastest-growing industry was the amalgam of jobs classified as services, particularly health services. After trailing construction in fiscal 1994 and 1995, services edged ahead in fiscal 1996 to recapture the top spot. Services added 94,000 jobs, for a growth rate of 4.4 percent, during fiscal 1996. Services comprise the largest major sector of the Texas economy, with more than 2.2 million jobs, employing 27 percent of Texas employees, compared with 21 percent only 10 years ago.

During fiscal 1996, the growth was uneven among service-industry subsectors. Business services added 39,300 jobs, for a booming 8.1 percent increase, largely because of out-sourcing from manufacturers of such tasks as payroll and advertising.

Agricultural services added 7.4 percent, amusement parks and motion-picture services grew by 6.5 percent, and repair services saw healthy job growth of 5.3 percent. The largest service subsector, health services, jumped 4.9 percent, for 29,900 additional jobs. The slowest-growing subsector was legal services, which grew at about 1.7 percent.

Services, as defined by the standard industrial classification, is only one component of the larger mix of service-producing industries. Service-producing industries include all sectors not engaged in producing goods, including wholesale and retail trade; finance, insurance and real estate; transportation, communications and public utilities; business, health and other services (the component discussed above); and government.

Combined, service-producing industries now represent more than 80 percent of Texas' total nonfarm employment. During fiscal 1996, the combined service-producing sectors accounted for 87 percent of job growth in the state.

Energy Declines for the Fifth Straight Year

The oil-and-gas industry experienced another declining year in fiscal 1996. Although oil and natural-gas prices rose strongly during the fiscal year, they lost much of their gains as the year progressed, and they remained below the level needed to stimulate domestic drilling activity. However, offshore and overseas drilling activity increased, so the loss of 3,350 jobs was less than half of the 7,200 net jobs lost statewide in fiscal 1995.

Mining employment, which is 95 percent oil and gas in Texas, fell by 2.1 percent in fiscal 1996, to stand at its lowest level since 1977. Oil and gas now comprises only 10 percent of Texas' total gross state product. The silver lining in the decline is that, since the economic cycles for the oil and gas industry are highly unstable and politically volatile, the state is less susceptible to economic shocks than in the past.

Construction — 18,000 More Jobs

Construction remained a strong segment of the state economy in fiscal 1996, after two years of leading the state in the rate of job growth. Over the past three years, construction has taken advantage of a renewed Texas real-estate market and relatively attractive mortgage rates to lead other industries in the rate of job growth. Although relinquishing the top spot to services in fiscal 1996, total construction employment in Texas was up 18,000 jobs, or 4.3 percent.

Mortgage rates dropped about half a point during the first half of the fiscal year, boosting housing permits by 15 percent. The 119,000 new housing starts in fiscal 1996 was the highest number in 10 years, and was nearly two-and-a-half times the starts in 1989. Apartment construction was also strong, to the point that concerns about oversupply led to some curtailments in multifamily housing construction in the latter half of the fiscal year.

Nonresidential construction also held onto the double-digit growth rates of 1994 and 1995, driven mainly by large gains in industrial and retail space. During the 1996 fiscal year, about 93 million square feet of nonresidential construction space was put in place, up from about 66 million four years ago and roughly equal to 1995's pace.

Manufacturing Varies by Industry

In Texas manufacturing the durable-goods subsector significantly outperformed nondurables. Durable-goods manufacturing, dominated by electronics, computers and building materials, collectively added jobs at a rate of 2.8 percent, while nondurable manufacturing lost 0.5 percent of its jobs.

Jobs in the durable-goods sector increased by 16,700 jobs, while nondurables declined by roughly 2,000 jobs. Total personal income in durable-goods manufacturing rose faster than in all of the state's major industries. Income from nondurable-goods manufacturing hardly increased at all.

Among the durable-goods industries, electronics added the most new manufacturing jobs (up 6,400, or 5.6 percent). Three-fourths of the increase occurred in the first half of the fiscal year, but slowed as optimism for continued explosive growth in the world semiconductor industry faded.

Electrical machinery, including computers, jumped 3.3 percent, with the addition of 4,200 jobs. Building materials (including lumber, wood, glass and concrete products) collectively added 3,300 jobs, for a 4 percent increase. Much of the fabricated-metals industry also owes its 4.8 percent growth (4,500 jobs) to the construction industry's demand for metal products such as frames and girders.

On the weaker side of Texas' durable-goods industry were furniture and fixtures, which lost 600 jobs, and transportation equipment, which was impacted by the nation's defense cutbacks. The manufacturing of transportation equipment fell by 1,800 jobs (or 2.5 percent) during the fiscal year.

Weakness in the nondurable sector mostly reflected losses in apparel manufacturing and food processing. The apparel and textile industry, which is centered largely in El Paso and South Texas, experienced its

Service-producing industries now represent more than 80 percent of Texas' total non-farm employment

worst year since 1986, having cut back 5.2 percent of its workforce (3,300 jobs) during the fiscal year.

Apparel sales have been particularly weak for men's and boys' clothing, which comprise the largest components of the Texas apparel-manufacturing industry. Weak clothing retail and exports, coupled with increasing worker productivity from technology changes, have coalesced to drive down Texas' apparel-manufacturing employment.

Given the strength of durable goods manufacturing, it is not surprising that the greatest number of new jobs added in nondurable goods was in the plastics industry.

Texas has long sent its petrochemical raw materials to other states for processing into various forms of plastics, but the addition of 1,500 jobs in plastics manufacturing (up 3.0 percent) attests to the state's potential for plastics production and fabrication. Small gains were experienced in the printing and publishing industry, as well as petrochemicals, which reversed two years of losses.

Overall, Texas manufacturers added about 9,000 jobs during fiscal 1996, for an increase of just under 1 percent. Despite the slowdown of growth relative to fiscal 1995, the increase was in the face of national manufacturing losses of about 1 percent. Further, since technological advancements allow more productivity from each manufacturing worker, Texas' real gross state product in manufacturing grew at almost twice the rate of job growth.

Transportation, Communications, Utilities

In many respects, the boom industry of fiscal 1996 in Texas was communications, propelled by a robust market for telecommunications and Internet-related services. Overall communications employment grew by 6.1 percent in Texas, making the industry a leader in Texas job growth. Communications employment increased by 6,300 jobs, to reach 109,100 statewide.

The transportation industry (rail, air and trucking) added jobs in fiscal 1996, with the strongest gains in trucking and air transportation, which combined for a gain of 13,300 jobs (4.7 percent). Abundant fuel at relatively low prices, increased tonnage due to trucking deregulation, and growing international trade combined to spur trucking employment growth. Rail transportation, on the other hand, dropped 1,000 jobs, or about 6 percent.

While transportation and communications together grew much faster than the state's overall growth, public utilities remained weak. Public utilities lost 2,500 jobs, or 3.4 percent, due to cost-containment layoffs and increasing productivity arising from technological change. Overall, TCPU added 14,500 jobs during the fiscal year, for an increase of 3.0 percent.

Trade Grows Faster than Overall Economy

In most years, employment growth in wholesale and retail trade is slightly slower than that of the overall economy. But wholesale- and retail-trade jobs in Texas grew by 2.9 percent in fiscal 1996, compared to 2.7 percent in all industries.

During the first three-quarters of the fiscal year, automobile sales were particularly strong — up 22 percent over the same period in fiscal 1995 — and generated 4 percent employment growth in automotive trade. Even faster employment growth, however, was in the building-materials sector, where a 21 percent increase in housing permits spawned employment growth of 8.8 percent, the fastest of any subsector tracked by the Comptroller's office.

This represented an increase of 4,600 jobs, to a total of 56,700, in the state's building-materials sector. As might be expected, job growth in home furnishings and furniture followed the lead of strong housing construction, with employment gains of 7.2 percent.

All retail-trade sectors in Texas showed growth, with the exception of apparel and accessories. Employment in the retail apparel industry has been eroding by about 2 percent a year over the last 10 years, following a national trend toward lower expenditures on clothing. At the end of fiscal 1996 clothing retailers employed 5,000 fewer employees, for a decline of 6.6 percent during the year.

Except for apparel, each of the state's retail sectors experienced healthy gains. Overall, wholesale trade added 10,800 jobs, for a growth of 2.3 percent, while retail-trade employment grew by 49,200, an increase of 3.3 percent.

Finance, Insurance and Real Estate

All sectors of the Texas finance industry grew during the fiscal year, taking advantage of continued net migration to Texas. During the year, 140,000 more people moved to Texas than moved away. Fiscal 1996 was only the second year in the last 10 in which all three sectors of banking/finance, insurance and real estate added jobs.

Banking, which has hemorrhaged more than 20 percent of its jobs over the past decade because of mergers, consolidations and automation, was the fastest-growing sector over the past year. Favorable interest rates joined with higher fee and trading-activity revenues to help banks and savings institutions add 3,100 jobs, for 2.7 percent growth. Insurance added 1,100 jobs, or 0.7 percent over the past year, while real estate, benefiting from house purchasing by new migrants, added 3,400 jobs, a gain of 1.9 percent.

Government Adds Jobs

For the first time since 1990, all three levels of government — federal, state and local — added jobs in the fiscal year. The federal government sector, in which statewide employment had shrunk by about 16,000 jobs from 1990 to 1995, eked out a gain of 200 jobs in fiscal 1996, due largely to Postal Service hiring. The number of military personnel at bases across the state has been declining since 1985.

The state- and local-government sectors continued to grow, with state government adding 9,000 jobs. State-government employment continued to rise in response to staffing needs associated with the massive prison-construction program, although the hiring tapered off in the latter half of the fiscal year.

Local government, after seven consecutive years of adding more than 3 percent employment annually, slowed to 1.9 percent growth, but still added 17,100 jobs. At the local level, most job increases are in school districts, but public concern over property-tax rates is starting to be reflected in reduced growth.

In Summary: A Healthy State Economy

Stronger real gross state product growth led to statewide job growth of 2.7 percent during the fiscal year, real per capita wages increased, and net migration continued to fuel the economic engine during fiscal 1996. Toward the end of the fiscal year, consumer confidence in the West South Central states reached its highest level since fiscal 1983, which was reflected in strong sales of automobiles, housing and house furnishings.

The 13 percent rise in confidence brought the level to 124 (1985=100), compared to a recent low of 58 during fiscal 1993. Texas exports, which have more than tripled over the past decade, continued to grow at double-digit rates, posting a 14.8 percent gain in calendar 1995. While overall economic growth moderated a bit from last year because of the cooling of U.S. economic activity, the overall Texas economy was growing and healthy in fiscal 1996.

Major Metro Areas in Review

The **Austin-San Marcos** metro area's increasingly diversified economy has been bolstered by moderate mortgage rates, lower vacancy rates in the real estate markets and continued growth in the high-tech manufacturing and service industries.

In fiscal 1996, employment in the Austin-San Marcos MSA (Bastrop, Caldwell, Hays, Travis and Williamson counties) grew by 3.7 percent, or 19,200 jobs to stand at 541,900. Unemployment in the metro area dipped to 3.1 percent in August 1996.

Employment growth, which was concentrated in the trade, services and government sectors, accounted for 74 percent of the total job growth for the year, adding a total of 14,200 jobs.

The services industry, Austin's largest employment sector, added 4,000 jobs during fiscal 1996 to stand at 146,000, or 26.9 percent of the area's economy. Service employment continues to expand, driven by rapid population growth.

The wholesale and retail trade sector employs 119,500, slightly more than 22 percent of the area's total employment. Trade employment increased by 7,400 jobs, or 6.6 percent during the year.

The government sector accounted for 131,400 of the Austin-San Marcos area's jobs in August 1996, or 24.2 of all jobs, despite the recent shutdown of Bergstrom Air Force Base and the loss of 1,300 jobs. State government employment, concentrated in state-agency operations and The University of Texas, is a mainstay in the government sector of the Austin economy. Government employment increased by 2,800 during fiscal 1996.

Despite recent consolidation efforts by some of the metro area's largest employers, Austin's manufacturing sector added 1,900 jobs during the year. Employment in the area's manufacturing sector increased to 71,700 in August 1996, which was 13.2 percent of total employment. Most of the area's largest manufacturers — IBM, Motorola, Advanced Micro Devices and Texas Instruments — are technology intensive. Austin's newest addition to the manufacturing sector — Samsung Electronics — announced the construction of a $1.3 billion semiconductor facility that will add 1,000 new jobs by 1998.

Employment gains were realized in construction (1,200), finance, insurance and real estate (900), transportation and public utilities (900) and mining (100), as well.

In 1995, *Fortune* magazine listed Austin as 7th in its list of best U.S. cities for business, citing Austin as home to 825 high-tech firms and a leader in research and development in the computer industry.

The 1990s have been a period of continued employment growth for the **Dallas** MSA (Collin, Dallas, Denton, Ellis, Henderson, Hunt, Kaufman and Rockwall counties). Almost all industry sectors experienced employment growth during fiscal 1996; the mining and finance, insurance and real estate sectors experienced declines, however. During this period, employment grew by 3.4 percent, or 55,600 jobs, to 1.67 million. Dallas' unemployment rate dropped to 4.1 percent in August 1996.

The service industry, Dallas' largest employment sector with more than 29 percent of total employment, grew by 19,800 jobs, or 4.2 percent, in the past year. Substantial gains in business and health services contributed to the jobs growth.

Trade, representing 25.3 percent of the metro's total job base, boasted impressive employment gains and grew to 422,300, adding 14,500 jobs for a 3.6 percent increase. Government employment increased by 6,100 jobs to a total of 197,700.

Manufacturing, which represents 14.1 percent of total Dallas employment, is experiencing modest employment gains, with growth concentrated in the manufacturing of fabricated-metal products, industrial machinery and equipment and electronics. Employment in the manufacturing sector rose 2.3 percent to 235,700, adding 5,300 jobs in the past year, while the transportation industry increased by 5,900 jobs, or 5.6 percent, to 110,500.

The construction sector posted job gains as well, with increased residential and nonresidential demand. During fiscal 1996, construction employment rose by 5,000 jobs, or 7.4 percent, to 72,700.

The finance, insurance and real estate sector continues to recover from the problems of the late 1980s. While jobs in nondepository credit institutions like credit unions and mortgage companies have increased, the growth has not been sufficient to offset the job losses in the still-restructuring banking industry. Finance, insurance and real estate employment declined by 500 jobs to 130,900 in August 1996. Mining employment fell to 11,500, losing 500 jobs during the year.

The long-lasting effects of the peso devaluation have plagued **El Paso** during the past year. El Paso's economic base had a difficult year, losing 1,900 jobs during fiscal 1996 to stand at 233,300. Employment in the El Paso metro area is concentrated in trade, services and government, which comprise 67 percent of the total job base. Unemployment in the metro area increased to 13.1 percent.

While the government and manufacturing sectors continue to be the foundation of the El Paso economy, the services and finance, insurance and real estate sectors recorded growth over the 12-month period, while all other industry sectors saw a decline in employment.

El Paso's service sector added 400 jobs during fiscal 1996 to stand at 51,300. Representing 22 percent of the metro area's economic base, employment growth in this sector is concentrated in business, health and social services.

Modest employment gains were also realized by the finance, insurance and real estate sector, which added 100 jobs to a total of 8,800.

El Paso's trade sector has been hardest hit by the peso devaluation and changing retail trends. Trade-sector employment fell by 1,200 jobs to 55,000 jobs in August 1996. Trade-sector employment makes up 23.6 percent of the metro area's jobs base. In December 1995, the City of El Paso announced an expected $4 million shortfall in sales tax because border shoppers,

feeling the pinch of a devalued peso, have cut back on purchases from the United States.

Government employment in El Paso declined by 200 during fiscal 1996, and now stands at 49,800. Construction employment fell to 9,900 in August 1996, losing 400 workers, while the transportation and public utilities sector fell 1.6 percent to 12,400.

During the last 12 months, manufacturing employment decreased by 400, or 0.9 percent. Employment in El Paso's apparel industry has declined during the year

---

The boom industry was communications, propelled by a robust market for telecommunications and Internet-related services

---

after almost a decade of growth. While apparel and copper production remain local manufacturing mainstays, electronics, auto parts and plastics continue to gain importance.

Implementation of the North American Free Trade Agreement (NAFTA) has increased interest in and concern about air pollution and the development and improvement of the El Paso/Juarez border's public infrastructure. Thus, bi-national projects have been undertaken to increase monitoring of the area's air pollution and improve wastewater collection and treatment plants, roads and international bridges.

The **Fort Worth-Arlington** MSA (Tarrant, Parker, Hood and Johnson counties) posted healthy increases in employment during fiscal 1996. During the past year, employment jumped by 20,900 jobs, a 3.2 percent increase, to stand at 678,200. It was the area's fifth straight year of employment growth. The unemployment rate dipped to 4.2 percent.

Fort Worth's service and trade sectors led all other industries in employment growth. Strong employment gains in these sectors, however, were offset by slight declines in transportation and public utilities and mining.

The service industry grew by 10,500 jobs, or 6.1 percent, to 182,300 in August 1996. Strong gains in business, health and engineering and management services have led this sector's growth. Growing by 3.3 percent, the trade sector added 5,600 of the 20,900 new jobs in the area. Trade employment stands at 173,700.

Construction saw an increase of 2,400 jobs, up 8.5 percent from September 1995, while government added 2,700 jobs to 90,000. Jobs in the metro area's finance, insurance and real estate sector increased by 1,400 during the year to stand at 30,500. The manufacturing sector gained a modest 400 jobs during fiscal 1996. Fort Worth's manufacturing sector has largely recovered from dramatic losses in defense manufacturing. Manufacturing employment jumped to 106,100 in August 1996.

Employment increased in nearly all of Fort Worth's other industries during fiscal 1996. However, the mining and transportation and public utilities sectors lost a combined 2,100 jobs to stand at 4,400 jobs and 60,500 jobs, respectively. The transportation sector lost 2,000 jobs during the year, with most of the decrease occurring in railroad, water and pipeline (except natural gas) transportation. Air transportation and transportation services experienced small declines during the year as well. However, employment has stabilized and is now increasing.

Fort Worth's commitment to a diversified economy that is less dependent on the defense industry should push employment even higher as the nation's economy continues to grow.

The **Houston** metropolitan area's economy, once the nearly exclusive province of the oil and gas industry, continues to diversify. The Houston metro area (Chambers, Fort Bend, Harris, Liberty, Montgomery and Waller counties) experienced modest growth during the past year, rising from 1.77 million in September 1995 to 1.81 million in August 1996, a 2.1 percent increase.

Job increases were concentrated in services (15,200), trade (10,100), manufacturing (4,400), government (3,700), transportation and public utilities (2,100), construction (1,800) and mining (800).

The finance, insurance and real estate sector posted an employment decrease, losing 400 jobs. The unemployment rate in the metro area stood at 5.5 percent in August 1996, down from 5.7 percent in September 1995.

Houston remains home to many oil-and-gas extraction and production companies like Exxon, Shell and Lyondell Petrochemical. Restructuring continues in many parts of the industry as Tenneco moves its headquarters out of the Houston area to Connecticut.

The service and trade sectors comprise the largest percentages of total employment, 29.6 percent and 23.6 percent respectively. Service-sector employment rose to 536,300 during the year, a 2.9 percent increase. Employment in wholesale and retail trade experienced a 2.4 percent increase to reach 426,800 in August 1996.

Government currently employs 246,000, concentrated in education and city services, and accounts for 13.6 percent of total employment. The transportation and public utilities sector employs 126,100, and is anticipated to continue to increase with NAFTA.

Houston's industrial real estate market has spurred healthy increases in construction employment during the year. Construction jobs stood at 123,300, or 6.8 percent of the total job base, in August 1996. Developers are planning more than a dozen projects that will add over a million square feet to the local industrial sector. Much of this new space will be occupied by expansions from existing companies.

Last year, Houston was cited by *Fortune* magazine as 9th in best cities for business because of its affordable office-rental rates. Houston is recognized for its abundance of world-class academic and governmental research centers, namely NASA's Johnson Space Center, the Houston Advanced Research Center and the Texas Medical Center.

The **San Antonio** metro area's job base grew by 2.1 percent, or 13,400 jobs, to stand at 639,600 in August 1996. Unemployment in the metro area (Bexar, Comal, Guadalupe and Wilson counties) stood at 4.7 percent in August 1996.

All industry sectors experienced employment growth during the year, except mining, which remained unchanged. Employment growth in the metro area was concentrated in the trade, services and government sectors, adding a total of 9,800 jobs to the economy, 73 percent of total job growth during the year.

The services industry, San Antonio's largest employment sector, added 5,500 jobs during fiscal 1996 to stand at 190,600, or 29.8 percent of the metro area's economy.

The wholesale and retail trade sector employs 158,000, 24.7 percent of the area's total employment. Trade employment increased by 1.3 percent during the year, adding 2,100 jobs.

The government sector employs 132,800 in the San Antonio metro area, 20.8 percent of all jobs. Employment increased by 2,200 during fiscal 1996.

Employment in the metro area's manufacturing sector continues to increase, standing at 49,700 in August 1996, 7.8 percent of total employment.

Employment gains were also realized in construction (1,700), manufacturing (700), finance, insurance and real estate (600), and transportation and public utilities (600). Employment in the mining sector remained unchanged at 1,900. ☆

Texas and NAFTA

By Richard Alm

No state has more at stake in the North American Free Trade Agreement than Texas.

NAFTA was designed to eliminate barriers to trade among the United States, Mexico and Canada. With major rail and road transfer points at Laredo and El Paso, Texas tops all other states in trade with Mexico, reaching $27.4 billion in exports and a bare minimum of $16.5 billion in imports in 1996.

On both sides of Texas' 1,200-mile border with Mexico, moreover, a daily commingling of companies, workers and consumers has created an interdependent economic zone reaching hundreds of miles north and south of the Rio Grande. The South Texas economy often reacts more readily to trends in Mexico than to those in the United States.

The Mexican market takes more than a third of Texas' exports. Over the past decade, growth has been strong, averaging an inflation-adjusted 14 percent a year, largely because reforms opening Mexico's market began in the mid-1980s. The leading industries in sales to Mexico are electronics and electrical gear, transportation equipment, industrial machinery and computer supplies. Taken together, these products make up more than half the state's Mexican business and indicate that the Mexican market supports high-paying jobs.

When NAFTA came up for ratification in 1993, it touched off a divisive war of words. Proponents argued that chopping away commercial barriers among the United States, Mexico and Canada would increase trade, create jobs and raise incomes in all three countries.

Opponents worried that encouraging imports from a low-wage country would — to borrow Dallas billionaire Ross Perot's famous phrase — create a "giant sucking sound" of American jobs fleeing south to Mexico.

Once NAFTA went into effect on Jan. 1, 1994, the bickering moved off center stage; trade with Mexico was no longer a hot-button political issue.

Yet, the far-reaching agreement is still very much part of the state's future, and it will be at work over the next decade or so to alter the economic relationship between Texas and Mexico.

Although NAFTA is first and foremost a trade agreement, it touches on several other aspects of Texas' relations with Mexico. Among the most significant are cross-border pollution, illegal immigration and drugs.

As with trade, NAFTA supporters contend the agreement will help remedy these problems by speeding up Mexico's economic development. NAFTA's opponents disagree, arguing that making the border more porous will only worsen pollution and illegal activities.

The straightforward goal of NAFTA is to eliminate tariffs, quotas and other barriers to trade in North America. In practice, getting there is a intricate process. The trade accord stretches to more than 2,000 pages, chock full of lawyerly details prescribing how each of the three nations will open its markets.

Just a few years into the NAFTA era, it's too early to render a final verdict on the trade agreement's impact on Texas. One reason is NAFTA itself. By design, it's a long-term process, phased in over 15 years.

Although duties on many industrial products quickly dropped to zero, trade restraints on such industries as automobiles, energy and financial services come off more gradually. Tariffs on the most sensitive agricultural products won't reach zero until the year 2010.

Another reason is the complexity of the economic forces that influence trade. A year after NAFTA went into effect, a currency crisis eroded the purchasing power of the Mexican peso and plunged the country into a sharp economic downturn.

The Mexican recession cut demand for U.S. exports, and a weakened peso made American exports more expensive for Mexican consumers. For the United States as a whole, the peso crisis had large reverbera-

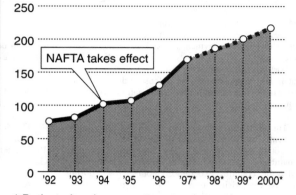

ECONOMIC GROWING PAINS

Bilateral trade between the United States and Mexico and projections through 2000, in billions of U.S. dollars at the end of each year:

* Projected under current economic trends

SOURCES: U.S. Department of Commerce, Mexico's Ministry of Commerce and Industrial Development, Dr. Rafael Rubio and Dr. Sidney Weintraub, *Dallas Morning News* research

tions in trade with Mexico, swinging a $1.3 billion surplus in 1994 to a $16.2 billion deficit in 1995.

Texas' trade suffered, too, although the state, unlike the nation, maintained its strong trade surplus with Mexico. Prior to enactment of the trade agreement, Mexico had much higher trade barriers than the United States. As the impediments came down, Texas' Mexico business figured to build on several years of healthy increases.

The first year NAFTA did just that, but the state's exports to Mexico dropped at a sharp 37 percent annual rate in the first six months of 1995. The culprit was the peso crisis.

Using sophisticated analysis, economists at the Federal Reserve Bank of Dallas separated NAFTA from macroeconomic forces. They conclude that NAFTA has been positive, increasing Texas' inflation-adjusted exports to Mexico by 6 percent since January 1994.

The Dallas Fed didn't find any evidence that NAFTA added much to Texas' imports from Mexico, a conclusion consistent with the state's already high level of economic integration with its neighbor.

The peso crisis overwhelmed NAFTA's trade-expanding impetus. According to the Fed economists, Texas' exports to Mexico would have been 31 percent higher in 1996 if there had been no economic crisis in Mexico. Imports increased slightly.

The Dallas Fed figures the peso problems will prove temporary. Mexico's economy began to recover in the second half of 1995, and so prospects for the state's exports are likely to improve as Mexico continues to open its market.

Texas exports did in fact begin to rebound in 1996, although it wasn't until late 1996 that sales to Mexico recovered to levels reached before the peso's plunge.

Although the faltering Mexican economy put a damper on cross-border trade, it didn't crimp Texas' overall economy. While Mexican trade declined in 1995, Texas' economy boomed, and total employment rose by 433,000 jobs in the first three years NAFTA was in force.

The strong U.S. economy helped Texas weather the peso crisis, as did success in finding other export markets. While Mexico was in the doldrums, Texas increased its exports to Asia, Europe and Latin America, with total exports rising to a record $74.2 billion in 1996.

Another expanding market was the third NAFTA country — Canada. Texas' sales to Canada rose from $4.3 billion in 1993 to $7.4 billion in 1996.

Another part of the story of Texas' trade with Mexico centers on the maquiladora factories in the border cities from Matamoros to El Paso. (The word "maquiladora" is derived from the Spanish term for the portion of grain that is returned to a farmer after his corn is ground.)

These plants, many of them owned by General Motors, Sony and other large multinational companies, have since the 1960s benefited from duty-free status for assembling finished and semi-finished goods from imported components, taking advantage of Mexico's low wages.

At the end of 1996, there were 2,411 maquiladoras along the length of the U.S.-Mexico border, a majority of them across the Rio Grande from Texas. This number is an increase from 2,114 in 1993.

What's important for Texas' economy is that maquiladoras tend to offset the effects of a trade shock. When exports to Mexico decline due to a tumble in the peso's value, for example, the maquiladora business picks up because Mexican labor costs fall relative to U.S. wages. Texas provides an overwhelming proportion of the inputs that go into maquiladora production, and therefore sees a gain in exports when the rest of Mexico's economy slips into recession.

How will NAFTA affect the maquiladoras? When the agreement has eliminated nearly all trade barriers, the advantage of duty-free import of components will extend to any factory in the country.

What's more, the influx of factories over the past two decades has created congestion and rising wages in the border region, creating incentives to relocate production deeper into Mexico. The advantages of cheap labor and being on the doorstep of the huge U.S. market remain, but growth of the maquiladora industry may slow as NAFTA creates a more open North American market.

Along the U.S.-Mexican border, pollution and poverty have worsened for decades. If it did nothing else, the debate over NAFTA focused a spotlight on the border region's problems. To help overcome U.S. opposition to NAFTA, the United States and Mexico signed side agreements, including one on the environment aimed at cleaning up the border region.

A result was the creation of the San Antonio-based North American Development Bank, with the capacity for $3 billion in loans. Funded jointly by the United States and Mexican governments, the NADBank took more than two years to get up and running. By February 1997, it had funded just four projects, including a $1.1 million sewage plant at a Matamoros, Mex., industrial park and a $4.1 million expansion of a sewage-treatment plant in Mercedes, Texas.

NADBank officials expect the pace of loans for infrastructure projects to pick up over the next few years. Even so, NAFTA's promises for environmental protection and economic development will take decades to realize.

Implementation of NAFTA hasn't always been smooth. In both Mexico and the United States, companies and workers worried about being hurt by provisions of the trade agreement pressed their governments to delay the market-opening process.

Trade disputes arose over alcoholic beverages, package delivery, avocados, tomatoes, brooms and cement. Friction also resulted from new trucking rules that would have allowed trucks to travel in the border states after December 1995.

Responding to protests by U.S. truckers, Washington refused to allow the provision to go into effect, citing concerns about the safety of Mexican vehicles. The United States insists it will live up to its NAFTA obligations and open its market to Mexican truckers, probably in 1997.

NAFTA's biggest selling point was the prospect of jobs in Texas' export industries. Among low-wage workers, however, competition from Mexico has cost the state jobs.

No place has been hit harder than El Paso, where by late 1996 at least 7,000 workers in apparel and other industries had qualified for federal NAFTA-related job-retraining programs.

No sooner had NAFTA gone into effect than the United States, Mexico, Canada and their Latin American allies began discussing expansion of the trade agreement.

At the Summit of the Americas in December 1994, Chile emerged as the leading candidate to become the trade pact's fourth member. The ultimate goal is a regional pact by 2004. Foes, worried about the adverse effects on jobs and the environment, have slowed the negotiating process, but President Clinton renewed his pledge to Chile's accession in February 1997.

Texas' political and corporate establishment has lined up in favor of bringing additional countries under the NAFTA umbrella. No Latin American country besides Mexico offers Texas a large, nearby market, but the state figures to be competitive in the market. Exports to Latin America outside Mexico have grown at double-digit annual rates in the 1990s.

Before NAFTA came into being, nearly every economic analysis suggested that Texas would benefit more than any other state from the opening of Mexico's market.

The peso crisis marred NAFTA's second and third years, but the recovery of the Mexican economy is likely to rekindle demand for Texas exports. The United States, Mexico and Canada remain committed to NAFTA — and its expansion into the rest of Latin America — and Texas' future will in part be shaped by the free-trade agreement. ☆

Richard Alm is a staff writer of The Dallas Morning News.

Employment in Texas by Industry

Source: Texas Workforce Commission. Additional information available at web site: www.twc.state.tx.us.

Employment in Texas increased to 8,322,700 in February 1997, up from 8,256,500 in February 1996.

The following table shows Texas Workforce Commission estimates of the nonagricultural labor force by industry for Feb. 1996 and 1997. The final column shows the change in the number employed.

(in thousands)

Industry	1997	1996	Chng.
MANUFACTURING	1,059.5	1,041.6	17.9
Durable Goods	620.2	607.0	13.2
Lumber & Wood Products	43.2	40.7	2.5
Logging Camps, Sawmills, Planing Mills	7.6	7.2	0.4
Furniture & Fixtures	18.3	18.4	-0.1
Stone, Clay & Glass Products	40.2	39.0	1.2
Concrete, Gypsum & Plaster - Prod.	18.5	17.7	0.8
Primary Metal Industries	30.0	29.4	0.6
Fabricated Metal Industries	96.3	93.5	2.8
Fabr. Structural Metal Prod.	48.9	47.0	1.9
Industrial Machinery & Equipment	136.8	133.4	3.4
Oil & Gas Field Machinery	26.8	25.1	1.7
Electronic & Other Electrical Equipment	118.5	117.1	1.4
Transportation Equipment	75.7	74.1	1.6
Aircraft & Parts	44.1	42.8	1.3
Instruments & Related Products	42.4	42.5	-0.1
Misc. Manufacturing Industries	18.8	18.9	-0.1
Non-Durable Goods	439.3	434.6	4.7
Food & Kindred Products	99.3	97.8	1.5
Meat Products	32.5	32.2	0.3
Dairy Products	5.0	4.9	0.1
Bakery Products	9.7	9.7	0.0
Malt Beverages	2.9	2.7	0.2
Textile Mill Products	3.7	3.6	0.1
Apparel & Other Finished Textile Prod.	60.3	60.2	0.1
Paper & Allied Products	29.9	29.4	0.5
Printing & Publishing	74.9	73.1	1.8
Newspapers, Periodicals, Books, Misc.	34.7	33.2	1.5
Chemicals & Allied Products	83.2	83.6	-0.4
Petroleum & Coal Products	27.0	28.0	-1.0
Petroleum Refining	23.8	24.7	-0.9
Rubber & Misc. Plastic Prod.	53.1	50.6	2.5
Leather & Leather Products	7.7	8.1	-0.4
TOTAL NON-MANUFACTURING			
Mining	159.8	154.1	5.7
Oil & Gas Extraction	151.6	145.9	5.7
Construction	441.6	415.7	25.9
Transportation & Public Utilities	490.4	481.1	9.3
Railroad Transportation	16.4	17.0	-0.6
Transportation by Air	103.1	102.6	0.5
Communications	114.9	106.4	8.5
Electric, Gas & Sanitary Services	70.9	72.6	-1.7
Electric Services	31.4	32.7	-1.3
Gas Production & Distribution	24.1	25.0	-0.9
Wholesale & Retail Trade	1,992.6	1,933.2	59.4
Wholesale Trade	479.7	466.8	12.9
Retail Trade	1,512.9	1,466.4	46.5
Building Materials & Garden Supplies	54.9	51.5	3.4
General Mercha. Stores	198.9	198.1	0.8
Food Stores	253.0	246.0	7.0
Automotive Dealers & Service Stations	158.0	155.2	2.8
Apparel & Accessory Stores	70.5	72.4	-1.9
Eating & Dining Places	545.6	520.1	25.5
Other Retail Trade	232.0	223.1	8.9
Finance, Insurance & Real Estate	445.7	436.6	9.1
Depository Insts., incl. Banks	116.6	113.8	2.8
Insurance Carriers, Agents & Brokers	148.2	146.6	1.6
Other Finance, Insurance & Real Estate	180.9	176.2	4.7
Services	2,243.7	2,150.6	93.1
Hotels & Other Lodging Places	83.6	83.5	0.1
Personal Services	88.3	89.0	-0.7
Business Services	526.5	492.9	33.6
Auto Repair Services	79.2	75.2	4.0
Misc. Repair Services	29.6	27.4	2.2
Amusement, including Motion Pictures	100.4	98.2	2.2
Health Services	645.1	617.5	27.6
Educational Services	97.0	95.4	1.6
Engineering & Mgmt Services	201.7	190.1	11.6
Other Services & Misc.	257.2	248.3	8.9
Total Government	1,489.4	1,467.4	22.0
Federal Government	185.8	186.9	-1.1
State Government	319.8	319.7	0.1
Local Government	983.8	960.8	23.0

Average Hours and Earnings

The following table shows the average weekly hours worked, weekly earnings and hourly wage for selected industries in 1997. Figures are provided by the Texas Workforce Commission in cooperation with the U. S. Bureau of Labor Statistics.

Industry	Earnings	Hours	Wage
MANUFACTURING	$519.26	43.2	$12.02
Durable Goods	520.21	44.5	11.69
Lumber & Wood Products	395.25	42.5	9.30
Furniture & Fixtures	354.21	39.4	8.99
Stone, Clay & Glass	506.38	46.8	10.82
Primary Metals Industries	579.14	46.0	12.59
Fabricated Metal Products	519.83	45.8	11.35
Industrial Machinery	522.26	45.1	11.58
Oil Field Machinery	636.02	49.0	12.98
Electronic & Other Electrical Equipment	529.25	44.4	11.92
Transportation Equipment	687.96	44.1	15.60
Instruments & Related Prodcts	510.14	42.3	12.06
Misc. Manufacturing	337.30	41.9	8.05
Non-Durable Goods	516.67	41.4	12.48
Food & Kindred Products	401.53	40.6	9.89
Meat Products	360.64	44.8	8.05
Malt Beverages	1117.03	47.9	23.32
Textile Mill Products	441.53	45.1	9.79
Apparel & Finished Textiles	283.73	36.8	7.71
Paper & Allied Products	591.11	43.4	13.62
Printing & Publishing	484.81	40.3	12.03
Chemicals & Allied Products	847.71	44.9	18.88
Petroleum & Coal Products	774.84	38.8	19.97
Petroleum Refining	804.67	38.1	21.12
Rubber & Misc. Plastics	477.16	45.1	10.58
Leather & Leather Products	270.66	38.5	7.03
NON-MANUFACTURING			
Mining	$740.37	46.1	$16.06
Oil & Gas Extraction	680.89	43.9	15.51
Communications	655.16	44.0	14.89
Electric, Gas & Sanitary	281.66	32.3	8.72
Wholesale & Retail Trade	487.22	40.1	12.15
Wholesale Trade	222.60	30.0	7.42
Retail Trade	236.00	31.3	7.54
Gen. Merchandise Stores	332.79	35.9	9.27

Selected Metro Areas

DALLAS			
Manufacturing	$534.82	44.2	$12.10
Durable Goods	550.03	44.9	12.25
Non-Durable Goods	507.83	43.0	11.81
FORT WORTH-ARLINGTON			
Manufacturing	551.18	43.4	12.70
Durable Goods	581.24	43.9	13.24
Non-Durable	490.68	42.3	11.60
HOUSTON			
Manufacturing	610.13	44.6	13.68
Durable Goods	554.67	46.3	11.98
Non-Durable	692.16	42.0	16.48
SAN ANTONIO			
Manufacturing	396.76	41.2	9.63
Durable Goods	405.96	40.8	9.95
Non-Durable Goods	386.88	41.6	9.30

Construction Industry

Contract awards for construction in 1996 totaled $4,383,336,574. Although the number of contracts stayed strong, dollar value was considerably lower than the record volume of 1993: $5,394,342,718, as shown in the Analysis of Awards tables below. Another table shows the approved Texas construction for 1997. These data were compiled by editors of **Texas Contractor** from official sources.

Comparison of Construction Awards by Years, 1956-1996

Source: Texas Contractor

Year	Total Awards	Year	Total Awards	Year	Total Awards
1996	$4,383,336,574	1982	3,453,784,388	1967	1,316,872,998
1995	4,771,332,413	1981	3,700,112,809	1966	1,421,312,029
1994	4,396,199,988	1980	3,543,117,615	1965	1,254,638,051
1993	5,394,342,718	1979	3,353,243,234	1964	1,351,656,302
1992	4,747,666,912	1978	2,684,743,190	1963	1,154,624,634
1991	3,926,799,801	1977	2,270,788,842	1962	1,132,607,006
1990	3,922,781,630	1976	1,966,553,804	1961	988,848,239
1989	4,176,355,929	1975	1,737,036,682	1960	1,047,943,630
1988	3,562,336,666	1974	2,396,488,520	1959	1,122,290,957
1987	4,607,051,270	1973	1,926,778,365	1958	1,142,138,674
1986	4,636,310,266	1972	1,650,897,233	1957	1,164,240,546
1985	4,806,998,065	1971	1,751,331,262	1956	1,220,831,984
1984	3,424,721,025	1970	1,458,708,492	1955	949,213,349
1983	4,074,910,947	1969	1,477,125,397	1954	861,623,224
		1968	1,363,629,304	1953	1,180,320,174

Approved Texas Construction, 1997

The following is a recapitulation of all approved Texas construction. The data were compiled by the editors of **Texas Contractor** from official sources.

Federal:

General Services Administration	$38,000,000
Federal Aviation Administration	92,000,000
Veterans Administration	42,000,000
NASA	14,000,000
Department of Defense	186,851,000
Rural Utilities Service	80,000,000
U.S. Department of Agriculture	100,000,000
Soil Conservation Service	4,200,000
Federal Highway Administration	1,295,825,481
Total Federal	**$1,852,876,481**

State:

Texas Dept. of Transportation	$1,676,960,400
State Agencies	382,494,414
State Colleges and Universities	309,623,000
Total State	**$2,369,077,814**

Water Projects:

Corps of Engineers	$54,952,000
Bureau of Reclamation	26,100,000
River Authorities	330,000,000
Total Water Projects	**$411,052,000**

Cities:

Schools, Colleges	$333,322,962
Streets, Bridges	354,848,221
Waterworks, Sewers	641,571,782
Apartments, Residences	1,197,363,802
Commercial	1,342,018,509
City Buildings	229,261,408
Total Cities	**$4,098,386,684**

Counties:

New Roads-County Funds	$55,004,524
Road Maintenance	192,338,984
Machinery Purchases	86,417,100
County Buildings	249,200,000
Miscellaneous	4,016,340
Total Counties	**$586,976,948**
Grand Total 1997 Approved Construction	**$9,318,369,927**

Analysis of Awards

The following table analyzes and classifies awards in Texas for the year 1996, as compared with 1995, as reported by **Texas Contractor**.

Category	1996		1995	
	No.	Amount	No.	Amount
Engineering Awards	1,749	$2,333,224,039	1,970	$2,907,009,874
Non-Residential Awards	1,091	2,050,112,535	1,085	1,864,322,539
Total	**2,840**	**$4,383,336,574**	**3,055**	**$4,771,332,413**

ENGINEERING AWARDS

Type of Project	1996		1995	
	No.	Amount	No.	Amount
Highways, Streets, Airports	1,178	$1,836,398,671	1,442	$2,365,113,304
Waterworks, Sewers, etc.	518	473,352,032	479	517,831,970
Irrigation, Drainage, etc.	53	23,473,336	49	24,064,600
Misc.	0	0	0	0
Total	**1,749**	**$2,333,224,039**	**1,970**	**$2,907,009,874**

NON-RESIDENTIAL CONSTRUCTION AWARDS

Type of Project	1996		1995	
	No.	Amount	No.	Amount
Educational Bldgs	341	$990,439,619	329	$998,791,200
Churches, Theaters, etc.	23	24,027,810	10	9,747,531
Hospitals, Hotels, Motels	62	116,105,162	71	86,523,629
Public Bldgs	327	641,463,413	350	579,732,310
Commercial/Industrial	338	278,076,531	325	189,527,869
Misc.	0	0	0	0
Total	**1,091**	**$2,050,112,535**	**1,085**	**$1,864,322,539**

Deposits and Assets of Insured Commercial Banks by County

Source: Federal Reserve Bank of Dallas as of Dec. 31, 1996

(in thousands of dollars)

COUNTY	Banks	Deposits	Assets
Anderson	4	$270,638	$308,463
Andrews	2	94,312	102,904
Angelina	3	370,977	410,227
Archer	1	23,689	25,990
Armstrong	1	21,539	23,723
Atascosa	4	159,641	184,012
Austin	5	367,564	414,595
Bailey	2	141,389	154,465
Bandera	2	71,097	95,159
Bastrop	4	267,378	300,909
Baylor	2	54,590	61,271
Bee	3	184,341	208,718
Bell	9	811,324	926,200
Bexar	14	6,766,631	7,673,254
Blanco	3	116,538	129,417
Bosque	3	104,384	117,320
Bowie	5	846,933	957,506
Brazoria	10	713,575	810,154
Brazos	2	231,752	254,136
Brewster	1	65,563	72,519
Briscoe	2	39,801	45,126
Brooks	2	53,916	66,033
Brown	2	173,539	202,984
Burleson	3	149,693	167,988
Burnet	3	158,653	179,291
Caldwell	3	157,098	178,507
Calhoun	2	142,976	161,408
Callahan	3	145,310	163,790
Cameron	9	1,776,632	2,085,888
Camp	1	79,035	97,187
Carson	1	12,191	14,028
Cass	4	147,392	163,419
Castro	1	154,780	170,973
Chambers	4	128,045	153,812
Cherokee	4	373,271	519,255
Childress	1	39,002	43,239
Clay	1	35,916	40,374
Cochran	1	44,161	48,921
Coke	2	49,368	58,115
Coleman	3	103,147	115,308
Collin	9	664,754	723,623
Collingsworth	2	92,799	102,120
Colorado	4	248,762	300,449
Comanche	3	150,823	171,054
Concho	2	34,607	39,644
Cooke	3	322,607	362,377
Coryell	4	295,744	334,013
Cottle	1	30,765	36,615
Crockett	2	139,593	157,816
Crosby	3	75,929	84,504
Culberson	1	15,202	19,730
Dallam	2	43,591	48,291
Dallas	50	55,914,996	75,309,665
Dawson	2	255,554	285,688
Deaf Smith	1	73,189	80,757
Delta	3	48,260	54,998
Denton	7	767,573	849,252
DeWitt	2	142,387	164,153
Dickens	1	23,036	25,225
Dimmit	1	20,560	22,333
Donley	2	62,190	70,466

COUNTY	Banks	Deposits	Assets
Duval	2	$57,086	$64,425
Eastland	2	78,780	92,229
Ector	3	330,660	375,875
Edwards	1	25,458	29,575
Ellis	8	445,779	495,442
El Paso	7	2,197,740	2,539,635
Erath	4	182,760	202,019
Falls	1	19,122	22,344
Fannin	5	176,939	206,367
Fayette	7	283,968	330,259
Fisher	1	63,600	71,308
Floyd	2	132,281	149,561
Foard	1	19,162	21,232
Fort Bend	4	311,578	354,957
Franklin	2	83,092	100,584
Freestone	2	72,171	79,741
Frio	2	146,962	205,064
Gaines	2	96,833	105,330
Galveston	10	943,471	1,083,554
Gillespie	2	286,972	322,244
Goliad	1	26,249	28,940
Gonzales	3	103,924	114,995
Gray	2	55,860	65,676
Grayson	7	594,733	650,872
Gregg	10	1,260,051	1,419,049
Grimes	3	123,956	138,331
Guadalupe	4	325,664	381,317
Hale	4	238,936	258,401
Hall	2	57,404	63,705
Hamilton	2	41,007	45,319
Hansford	3	138,839	156,514
Hardeman	3	80,272	88,461
Hardin	3	188,270	208,408
Harris	62	36,937,405	45,220,133
Harrison	5	389,394	439,032
Haskell	4	119,154	130,898
Hemphill	1	50,472	55,902
Henderson	5	552,674	613,899
Hidalgo	11	1,998,698	2,216,664
Hill	5	131,574	154,219
Hockley	3	105,239	115,239
Hood	4	393,903	434,710
Hopkins	4	479,713	524,857
Houston	6	217,774	242,967
Howard	3	368,163	406,401
Hudspeth	1	10,575	11,756
Hunt	4	121,632	138,131
Hutchinson	1	16,124	18,212
Irion	1	78,928	89,533
Jack	3	115,169	127,948
Jackson	1	32,564	35,156
Jasper	2	222,603	248,849
Jeff Davis	1	17,144	18,924
Jefferson	3	742,960	830,639
Jim Hogg	2	76,117	91,005
Jim Wells	4	254,285	283,389
Johnson	7	525,625	583,869
Jones	2	81,082	94,995
Karnes	3	119,973	134,380
Kaufman	4	545,744	604,230
Kendall	1	43,990	50,970
Kent	1	10,083	11,024
Kerr	1	207,782	230,774

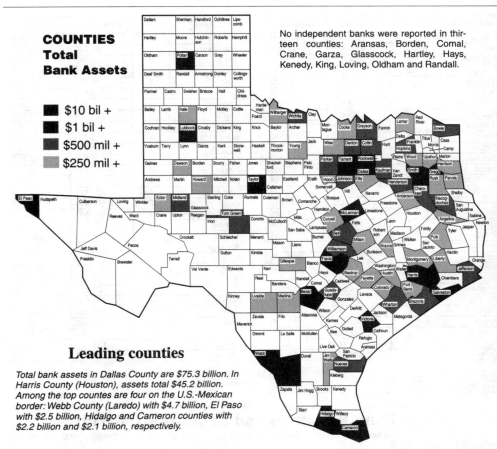

**COUNTIES
Total
Bank Assets**

No independent banks were reported in thirteen counties: Aransas, Borden, Comal, Crane, Garza, Glasscock, Hartley, Hays, Kenedy, King, Loving, Oldham and Randall.

- ■ $10 bil +
- ■ $1 bil +
- ▨ $500 mil +
- ░ $250 mil +

Leading counties

Total bank assets in Dallas County are $75.3 billion. In Harris County (Houston), assets total $45.2 billion. Among the top countes are four on the U.S.-Mexican border: Webb County (Laredo) with $4.7 billion, El Paso with $2.5 billion, Hidalgo and Cameron counties with $2.2 billion and $2.1 billion, respectively.

COUNTY	Banks	Deposits	Assets
Kimble	2	$49,259	$55,573
Kinney	1	12,727	14,022
Kleberg	2	182,486	205,912
Knox	2	60,143	68,102
Lamar	5	392,541	454,219
Lamb	4	99,113	111,294
Lampasas	1	79,534	90,943
La Salle	1	22,354	25,079
Lavaca	3	181,143	207,250
Lee	2	88,374	102,644
Leon	4	107,189	123,622
Liberty	6	278,487	319,554
Limestone	4	144,356	160,896
Lipscomb	1	28,208	32,218
Live Oak	2	96,739	115,253
Llano	3	169,457	193,505
Lubbock	13	3,469,775	4,981,668
Lynn	3	111,225	128,301
Madison	2	131,223	146,706
Marion	2	49,370	57,050
Martin	1	35,918	43,741
Mason	2	45,234	52,465
Matagorda	2	151,912	174,917
Maverick	1	155,623	173,557
McCulloch	2	104,244	118,584
McLennan	15	1,380,761	1,551,404
McMullen	1	25,711	29,058

COUNTY	Banks	Deposits	Assets
Medina	7	$232,922	$257,030
Menard	2	30,030	34,801
Midland	3	633,251	698,568
Milam	5	312,716	360,758
Mills	2	115,606	128,400
Mitchell	2	81,506	92,365
Montague	3	193,743	219,736
Montgomery	1	79,614	87,853
Moore	1	86,399	93,805
Morris	3	106,062	117,578
Motley	1	9,724	10,673
Nacogdoches	3	478,639	538,837
Navarro	6	218,648	247,631
Newton	1	82,710	90,300
Nolan	3	163,249	181,812
Nueces	8	764,640	860,550
Ochiltree	1	46,270	52,436
Orange	3	177,016	197,868
Palo Pinto	4	145,311	162,705
Panola	3	234,446	280,907
Parker	3	512,089	603,729
Parmer	2	131,729	160,664
Pecos	3	113,675	128,891
Polk	4	335,679	378,633
Potter	4	2,367,004	3,015,624
Presidio	2	41,309	47,523
Rains	1	48,323	52,812

COUNTY	Banks	Deposits	Assets
Reagan	1	$29,516	$32,391
Real	1	19,744	22,266
Red River	1	16,070	17,741
Reeves	2	104,144	121,231
Refugio	2	72,229	88,443
Roberts	1	13,659	15,303
Robertson	3	162,763	191,033
Rockwall	2	73,421	81,831
Runnels	4	76,325	84,481
Rusk	4	445,033	496,373
Sabine	2	113,729	128,743
San Augustine	1	45,592	52,322
San Jacinto	2	47,002	50,990
San Patricio	2	74,247	85,754
San Saba	1	33,774	40,176
Schleicher	1	29,222	35,014
Scurry	2	168,170	191,025
Shackelford	1	144,765	165,038
Shelby	3	159,030	179,881
Sherman	1	102,610	115,281
Smith	7	870,581	1,003,279
Somervell	1	24,952	27,882
Starr	1	40,515	48,710
Stephens	1	51,648	57,659
Sterling	1	26,598	32,939
Stonewall	1	23,941	32,603
Sutton	2	71,479	79,132
Swisher	2	81,069	88,289
Tarrant	31	3,823,768	4,313,212
Taylor	5	1,024,286	1,119,156
Terrell	1	15,284	16,953
Terry	1	107,328	122,725
Throckmorton	1	20,157	22,160

COUNTY	Banks	Deposits	Assets
Titus	3	$227,536	$249,797
Tom Green	3	360,539	414,851
Travis	6	909,341	1,019,660
Trinity	3	69,605	77,546
Tyler	2	88,844	98,403
Upshur	4	279,421	326,491
Upton	2	77,342	86,261
Uvalde	2	232,574	289,272
Val Verde	2	205,718	229,593
Van Zandt	7	209,859	234,594
Victoria	3	2,228,636	2,625,056
Walker	2	171,729	190,245
Waller	2	72,275	80,396
Ward	2	97,122	108,885
Washington	4	205,125	228,176
Webb	6	3,869,404	4,732,397
Wharton	7	840,847	929,739
Wheeler	3	56,410	62,849
Wichita	7	804,150	894,134
Wilbarger	3	229,949	272,000
Willacy	1	57,522	63,509
Williamson	12	553,657	621,022
Wilson	2	135,962	151,774
Winkler	2	67,929	78,480
Wise	4	376,961	411,916
Wood	6	275,092	314,979
Yoakum	2	26,260	29,106
Young	5	229,664	261,599
Zapata	2	125,026	146,950
Zavala	1	37,428	40,658
TOTALS:	877	$165,856,818	$205,050,179

Texas Bank Resources and Deposits—1905-1996

On Dec. 31, 1994, Texas had a total of 983 national and state banks with total deposits of $153,403,984,000 and total resources of $188,144,234,000.

Source: **Federal Reserve Bank of Dallas.**

Date	National Banks			State Banks			Combined Total		
	No. Banks	Total Resources (add 000)	Deposits (add 000)	No. Banks	Total Resources (add 000)	Deposits (add 000)	No. Banks	Total Resources (add 000)	Deposits (add 000)
Sept. 30, 1905	440	$189,484	$101,285	29	$4,341	$2,213	469	$193,825	$103,498
Oct. 31, 1906	483	221,574	116,331	136	19,322	13,585	619	240,896	129,916
Dec. 3, 1907	521	261,724	141,803	309	34,734	20,478	830	296,458	162,281
Nov. 27, 1908	535	243,240	115,843	340	40,981	27,014	875	284,221	142,857
Dec. 31, 1909	523	273,473	139,024	515	72,947	51,472	1,038	346,420	190,496
Nov. 10, 1910	516	293,245	145,249	621	88,103	59,766	1,137	381,348	205,015
Dec. 5, 1911	513	313,685	156,083	688	98,814	63,708	1,201	412,499	219,791
Nov. 26, 1912	515	352,796	179,736	744	138,856	101,258	1,259	491,652	280,994
Oct. 21, 1913	517	359,732	183,623	832	151,620	101,081	1,349	511,352	284,704
Dec. 31, 1914	533	377,516	216,953	849	129,053	73,965	1,382	506,569	290,648
Dec. 31, 1915	534	418,094	273,509	831	149,773	101,483	1,365	567,867	374,992
Dec. 27, 1916	530	567,809	430,302	836	206,396	160,416	1,366	774,205	590,718
Dec. 31, 1917	539	679,316	531,066	874	268,382	215,906	1,413	947,698	746,972
Dec. 31, 1918	543	631,978	431,612	884	259,881	191,500	1,427	891,859	623,112
Dec. 31, 1919	552	965,855	777,942	948	405,130	336,018	1,500	1,370,985	1,113,960
Dec. 29, 1920	556	780,246	564,135	1,031	391,127	280,429	1,587	1,171,373	844,564
Dec. 31, 1921	551	691,087	501,493	1,004	334,907	237,848	1,555	1,025,994	739,341
Dec. 29, 1922	557	823,254	634,408	970	338,693	262,478	1,527	1,161,947	896,886
Sept. 14, 1923	569	860,173	648,954	950	376,775	306,372	1,519	1,236,948	955,326
Dec. 31, 1924	572	999,981	820,676	933	391,040	322,392	1,505	1,391,021	1,143,068
Dec. 31, 1925	656	1,020,124	832,425	834	336,966	268,586	1,490	1,357,090	1,101,011
Dec. 31, 1926	656	1,020,113	820,778	782	290,554	228,741	1,438	1,310,667	1,049,519
Dec. 31, 1927	643	1,134,595	938,129	748	328,574	267,559	1,391	1,463,168	1,205,688
Dec. 31, 1928	632	1,230,469	1,017,168	713	334,870	276,875	1,345	1,565,339	1,294,043
Dec. 31, 1929	609	1,124,369	897,538	699	332,534	264,013	1,308	1,456,903	1,161,551

Date	National Banks			State Banks			Combined Total		
	No. Banks	Total Resources (add 000)	Deposits (add 000)	No. Banks	Total Resources (add 000)	Deposits (add 000)	No. Banks	Total Resources (add 000)	Deposits (add 000)
Dec. 31, 1930	560	1,028,420	826,723	655	299,012	231,909	1,215	1,327,432	1,058,632
Dec. 31, 1931	508	865,910	677,307	594	235,681	172,806	1,102	1,101,591	850,113
Dec. 31, 1932	483	822,857	625,586	540	208,142	148,070	1,023	1,030,999	773,653
Dec. 30, 1933	445	900,810	733,810	489	185,476	132,389	934	1,086,286	866,199
Dec. 31, 1934	456	1,063,453	892,264	460	197,969	148,333	916	1,261,422	1,040,597
Dec. 31, 1935	454	1,145,488	1,099,172	442	205,729	162,926	896	1,351,217	1,172,098
June 30, 1936	456	1,192,845	1,054,284	426	228,877	169,652	882	1,421,722	1,223,936
Dec. 31, 1937	453	1,343,076	1,194,463	415	217,355	177,514	868	1,560,431	1,371,977
Sept. 28, 1938	449	1,359,719	1,206,882	406	217,944	170,286	855	1,577,663	1,377,168
Dec. 31, 1939	445	1,565,108	1,409,821	395	235,467	201,620	840	1,800,575	1,611,441
Dec. 31, 1940	446	1,695,662	1,534,702	393	227,866	179,027	839	1,923,528	1,713,729
Dec. 31, 1941	444	1,975,022	1,805,773	391	312,861	269,505	835	2,287,883	2,075,278
Dec. 31, 1942	439	2,696,768	2,525,299	391	417,058	353,109	830	3,113,826	2,878,408
Dec. 31, 1943	439	3,281,853	3,099,964	391	574,463	536,327	830	3,856,316	3,636,291
Dec. 31, 1944	436	4,092,473	3,891,999	398	780,910	738,779	834	4,873,383	4,630,778
Dec. 31, 1945	434	5,166,434	4,934,773	409	998,355	952,258	843	6,164,789	5,887,031
Dec. 31, 1946	434	4,883,558	4,609,538	418	1,019,369	964,938	852	5,902,927	5,574,476
Dec. 31, 1947	437	5,334,309	5,039,963	436	1,149,887	1,087,347	873	6,484,196	6,127,310
Dec. 31, 1948	437	5,507,823	5,191,334	444	1,208,884	1,137,259	881	6,716,707	6,328,593
Dec. 31, 1949	440	5,797,407	5,454,118	446	1,283,139	1,203,244	886	7,080,546	6,657,362
Dec. 31, 1950	442	6,467,275	6,076,006	449	1,427,680	1,338,540	891	7,894,955	7,414,546
Dec. 31, 1951	443	6,951,836	6,501,307	453	1,571,823	1,473,569	896	8,523,659	7,974,876
Dec. 31, 1952	444	7,388,030	6,882,623	457	1,742,270	1,631,757	901	9,130,300	8,514,380
Dec. 31, 1953	443	7,751,667	7,211,162	460	1,813,034	1,696,297	903	9,564,701	8,907,459
Dec. 31, 1954	441	8,295,686	7,698,690	465	1,981,483	1,851,724	906	10,277,169	9,550,414
Dec. 31, 1955	446	8,640,239	7,983,681	472	2,087,066	1,941,706	918	10,727,305	9,925,387
Dec. 31, 1956	452	8,986,456	8,241,159	480	2,231,497	2,067,927	932	11,217,953	10,309,086
Dec. 31, 1957	457	8,975,321	8,170,271	486	2,349,935	2,169,898	943	11,325,256	10,340,169
Dec. 31, 1958	458	9,887,737	9,049,580	499	2,662,270	2,449,474	957	12,550,007	11,499,054
Dec. 31, 1959	466	10,011,949	9,033,495	511	2,813,006	2,581,404	977	12,824,955	11,614,899
Dec. 31, 1960	468	10,520,690	9,560,668	532	2,997,609	2,735,726	1,000	13,518,299	12,296,394
Dec. 30, 1961	473	11,466,767	10,426,812	538	3,297,588	3,009,499	1,011	14,764,355	13,436,311
Dec. 28, 1962	486	12,070,803	10,712,253	551	3,646,404	3,307,714	1,037	15,717,207	14,019,967
Dec. 30, 1963	519	12,682,674	11,193,194	570	4,021,033	3,637,559	1,089	16,703,707	14,830,753
Dec. 31, 1964	539	14,015,957	12,539,142	581	4,495,074	4,099,543	1,120	18,511,031	16,638,685
Dec. 31, 1965	545	14,944,319	13,315,367	585	4,966,947	4,530,675	1,130	19,911,266	17,846,042
Dec. 31, 1966	546	15,647,346	13,864,727	591	5,332,385	4,859,906	1,137	20,979,731	18,724,633
Dec. 31, 1967	542	17,201,752	15,253,496	597	6,112,900	5,574,735	1,139	23,314,652	20,828,231
Dec. 31, 1968	535	19,395,045	16,963,003	609	7,107,310	6,489,357	1,144	26,502,355	23,452,360
Dec. 31, 1969	529	19,937,396	16,687,720	637	7,931,966	7,069,822	1,166	27,869,362	23,757,542
Dec. 31, 1970	530	22,087,890	18,384,922	653	8,907,039	7,958,133	1,183	30,994,929	26,343,055
Dec. 31, 1971	530	25,137,269	20,820,519	677	10,273,200	9,179,451	1,207	35,410,469	29,999,970
Dec. 31, 1972	538	29,106,654	23,892,660	700	12,101,749	10,804,827	1,238	41,208,403	34,697,487
Dec. 31, 1973	550	32,791,219	26,156,659	716	14,092,134	12,417,693	1,266	46,883,353	38,574,352
Dec. 31, 1974	569	35,079,218	28,772,284	744	15,654,983	13,758,147	1,313	50,734,201	42,530,431
Dec. 31, 1975	584	39,138,322	31,631,199	752	17,740,669	15,650,933	1,336	56,878,991	47,282,132
Dec. 31, 1976	596	43,534,570	35,164,285	761	19,846,695	17,835,078	1,357	63,381,265	52,999,363
Dec. 31, 1977	604	49,091,503	39,828,475	773	22,668,498	20,447,012	1,377	71,760,001	60,275,487
Dec. 31,1978	609	56,489,274	44,749,491	786	25,987,616	23,190,869	1,395	82,476,890	67,940,360
Dec. 31,1979	615	65,190,891	50,754,782	807	30,408,232	26,975,854	1,422	95,599,123	77,730,636
Dec. 31,1980	641	75,540,334	58,378,669	825	35,186,113	31,055,648	1,466	110,726,447	89,434,317
Dec. 31, 1981	694	91,811,510	68,750,678	829	42,071,043	36,611,555	1,523	133,882,553	105,362,233
Dec. 31, 1982	758	104,580,333	78,424,478	841	48,336,463	41,940,277	1,599	152,916,796	120,364,755
Dec. 31, 1983	880	126,914,841	98,104,893	848	55,008,329	47,653,797	1,728	181,923,170	145,758,690
Dec. 31, 1984	999	137,565,365	105,862,656	855	60,361,504	52,855,584	1,854	197,926,869	158,718,240
Dec. 31, 1985	1,058	144,674,908	111,903,178	878	64,349,869	56,392,634	1,936	209,024,777	168,295,812
Dec. 31, 1986	1,077	141,397,037	106,973,189	895	65,989,944	57,739,091	1,972	207,386,981	164,712,280
Dec. 31, 1987	953	135,690,678	103,930,262	812	54,361,514	47,283,855	1,765	190,052,192	151,214,117
Dec. 31, 1988	802	130,310,243	106,740,461	690	40,791,310	36,655,253	1,492	171,101,553	143,395,714
Dec. 31, 1989	687	133,163,016	104,091,836	626	40,893,848	36,652,675	1,313	174,056,864	140,744,511
Dec. 31, 1990	605	125,808,263	103,573,445	578	45,021,304	40,116,662	1,183	170,829,567	143,690,107
Dec. 31, 1991	579	123,022,314	106,153,441	546	46,279,752	41,315,420	1,125	169,302,066	147,468,861
Dec. 31, 1992	562	135,507,244	112,468,203	529	40,088,963	35,767,858	1,091	175,596,207	148,236,061
Dec. 31, 1993	502	139,409,250	111,993,205	510	44,566,815	39,190,373	1,012	183,976,065	151,183,578
Dec. 31, 1994	481	140,374,540	111,881,041	502	47,769,694	41,522,943	983	188,144,234	153,403,984
Dec. 31, 1995	456	152,750,093	112,557,468	479	49,967,946	42,728,454	935	202,718,039	155,285,922
Dec. 31, 1996	432	$152,299,695	$122,242,990	445	$52,868,263	$45,970,674	877	$205,167,958	$168,213,664

Leading Commercial Banks Ranked by Deposits
Source: Federal Reserve Bank of Dallas, Dec. 31, 1996
Abbreviations: Bk-Bank; St-State; NB-National Bank; B&TC-Bank and Trust Company; NA-National Association

(in thousands of dollars)

Rank	Name, Location	Deposits
1	Nationsbank of Tx NA, Dallas	$27,517,993
2	Texas Cmrc Bk NA, Houston	17,317,138
3	Bank One Tx NA, Dallas	15,738,687
4	Wells Fargo Bk (Tx) NA, Houston	6,929,763
5	Bank of America Tx NA, Irving	5,640,788
6	Compass Bk, Houston	4,179,132
7	Frost NB, San Antonio	4,160,993
8	Comerica Bk-Tx, Dallas	2,730,481
9	International Bk of Cmrc, Laredo	2,151,885
10	Norwest Bk Tx S Cntrl, Victoria	1,778,033
11	Laredo NB, Laredo	1,339,366
12	Norwest Bk Tx NA, Lubbock	1,306,144
13	Boatmens First NA, Amarillo	1,219,787
14	Texas St Bk, McAllen	1,105,399
15	Central B&TC, Fort Worth	1,014,008
16	Norwest Bk El Paso NA, El Paso	1,001,252
17	Southwest Bk of Tx NA, Houston	833,624
18	Amarillo NB, Amarillo	786,724
19	Broadway NB, San Antonio	778,678
20	Sterling Bk, Houston	719,296
21	Prime Bk, Channelview	695,804
22	Plains NB of West Texas, Denton	694,076
23	Mercantile Bk NA, Brownsville	670,710
24	Overton B&T, Fort Worth	645,839
25	American St Bk, Lubbock	603,535
26	First St Bk of Tx, Denton	541,170
27	First NB, Abilene	494,396
28	Sunwest Bk, El Paso	487,234
29	Norwest Bk Tx South NA, San Antonio	466,144
30	First St Bk, Austin	444,410
31	Merchants Bk, Houston	440,323
32	Southside Bk, Tyler	426,311
33	First Valley Bk, Harlingen	406,244
34	American NB of Tx, Terrell	404,352
35	North Dallas B&TC, Dallas	403,669
36	Norwest Bk Tx Midland NA, Midland	397,465
37	Texarkana NB, Texarkana	385,752
38	First Victoria NB, Victoria	383,016
39	Metrobank NA, Houston	382,572
40	Community Bk of Tx, Beaumont	369,693
41	American Bk of Tx, Sherman	343,107
42	Norwest Bk Tx NA, Wichita Falls	340,053
43	Northern Trust Bk of Tx NA, Dallas	339,670
44	First Bk SW NA, Amarillo	336,229
45	Plano B&TC, Plano	322,405
46	International Bk of Cmrc, Brownsville	307,200
47	Norwest Bk Tx Waco NA, Waco	304,895
48	Citizens NB, Henderson	300,171
49	Texas Bk, Weatherford	299,932
50	First B&TC, Groves	297,464
51	Fidelity Bk NA, University Park	290,505
52	Alliance Bank, Sulphur Springs	290,437
53	Woodforest NB, Houston	279,438
54	First Bk, Katy	278,892
55	Riverway Bk, Houston	275,780
56	Longview B&TC, Longview	273,138
57	First Prosperity Bk, El Campo	270,978
58	First NB, Edinburg	269,427
59	Inwood NB, Dallas	264,019
60	First Svc Bk, Gladewater	257,821
61	Jefferson St Bk, San Antonio	257,025

Rank	Name, Location	Deposits
62	First NB, Temple	$256,466
63	Klein Bk, Klein	256,085
64	Moody NB, Galveston	254,119
65	Heritage Bk, Wharton	247,479
66	Security St B&TC, Fredericksburg	246,629
67	Bank of the West, El Paso	244,304
68	Citizens B&TC of Baytown, Baytown	243,785
69	Texas First NB, Houston	242,898
70	Citizens NB of Tx, Houston	238,327
71	American Bk NA, Corpus Christi	234,491
72	BankTexas NA, Houston	233,709
73	CaminoReal Bk NA, San Antonio	229,631
74	Security St Bk, Abilene	227,381
75	First NB, Marshall	222,456
76	Fredonia St Bk, Nacogdoches	217,312
77	First St Bk, Uvalde	211,194
78	Central NB, Waco	210,272
79	Tyler B&TC, Tyler	208,267
80	Pinemont Bk, Houston	207,988
81	Norwest Bk Tx Kerrville NA, Kerrville	207,782
82	First NB, Athens	206,917
83	NorwestBkTxBigSpring NA, B. Spring	206,777
84	First NB of Park Cities, Dallas	204,347
85	University Bk, Houston	201,170
86	Texas Independent Bk, Irving	200,813
87	American Bk Cmrc, Wolfforth	200,377
88	Texas NB, Waco	195,082
89	First NB, Grapevine	193,482
90	First St Bk, Athens	192,516
91	Citizen St Bk, Corpus Christi	191,899
92	First St Bk Na, Abilene	189,904
93	First St Bk, Rio Vista	188,249
94	Citizens Bk, Kilgore	187,626
95	NorwestBkTxKellyFld NA SanAntonio	186,503
96	Harrisburg Bk Houston Tx, Houston	183,984
97	Texas Gulf Bk NA, Freeport	183,793
98	National Bk, Gatesville	183,535
99	First NB of South Tx, San Antonio	183,050
100	First NB, Killeen	181,017
101	Citizens 1st Bk, Rusk	179,901
102	Hartland Bk NA, Austin	179,146
103	First NB, Decatur	179,130
104	Guaranty Bk, Mount Pleasant	178,142
105	Midland Amer Bk, Midland	175,283
106	First NB, Bryan	174,470
107	Bayshore NB, La Porte	173,377
108	Lubbock NB, Lubbock	171,032
109	Summit NB, Fort Worth	169,912
110	Southwest Bk, Fort Worth	166,345
111	First B&TC East Tx, Diboll	165,963
112	Texas Bk, Odessa	165,740
113	First St B&TC, Carthage	165,250
114	First Bk of Tx, Tomball	164,783
115	First NB, Bowie	164,728
116	Hale Cnty St Bk, Plainview	161,669
117	TxComrcBk-SanAngeloNA S.Angelo	161,446
118	State First NB, Texarkana	159,453
119	First St Bk, Gainsville	157,233
120	Surety Bk NA, Midlothian	156,447
121	NBC Bk-Eagle Pass NA, Eagle Pass	155,623
122	Montwood NB, El Paso	154,784
123	First United Bk, Dimmitt	154,780
124	South Tx Bk, Laredo	154,452

Rank	Name, Location	Deposits
125	Harlingen NB, Harlingen	$153,864
126	Provident Bk, Dallas	153,593
127	Kleberg First NB, Kingsville	152,694
128	American NB, Wichita Falls	152,383
129	Lamesa NB, Lamesa	151,592
130	First NB, Granbury	150,544
131	Community Bk, Granbury	150,090
132	Southern NB of Tx, Sugar Land	149,095
133	Western NB, Odessa	148,413
134	Liberty NB, Paris	148,088
135	Stone Fort NB, Nacogdoches	146,965
136	State B&T, Seguin	146,393
137	FirstBank, Texarkana	145,259

Rank	Name, Location	Deposits
138	Norwest Bk Tx, Alice	$145,207
139	First NBAlbanyBreckenridge, Albany	144,765
140	First St Bk, Livingston	142,910
141	Inter NB, McAllen	142,346
142	Security NB, San Antonio	140,938
143	Weatherford NB, Weatherford	140,917
144	American Bk, Houston	140,014
145	Bank of Houston, Houston	139,681
146	Longview NB, Longview	139,504
147	Community B&T, Waco	137,848
148	First NB, Jasper	136,353
149	Lone Star NB, Pharr	133,792
150	United States NB, Galveston	133,311

Texas State Banks

Consolidated Statement, Foreign and Domestic
Offices, as of Dec. 31, 1996
Source: **Federal Reserve Bank of Dallas**

Number of Banks 445

(All figures in thousand dollars)

Assets

Cash and due from banks:
Non-interest-bearing balances and currency
and coin $3,177,480
Interest-bearing balances 362,327
Held-to-maturity securities 6,969,446
Available-for sale securities 11,961,557
Federal funds sold 2,545,939
Securities purchased under agreement to resell .. 1,090
Loans and lease financing receivables:
Loans and leases, net of unearned income: 25,950,711
Less: allowance for loan and lease losses 377,996
Less: allocated transfer risk reserve 0
Loans and leases, net 25,572,715
Assets held in trading accounts 1,402
Premises and fixed assets 1,098,486
Other real estate owned..................... 74,074
Investments in unconsolidated subsidiaries
and associated companies 4,906
Customers liability on acceptances outstanding 239
Intangible assets.......................... 300,696
Other assets 797,914
    Total Assets **$52,868,263**

Liabilities

Deposits:
In domestic offices $45,970,674
Non-interest-bearing 10,190,765
Interest-bearing 35,779,908
In foreign offices, edge & agreement subsidiaries
& IBF's.................................
Non-interest-bearing ....
Interest-bearing.........................
Federal funds purchased 577,560
Securities sold under agreements to repurchase 319,495
Demand notes issued to the U.S. Treasury 235,716
Trading Liabilities 1
With original maturity of one year or less.......... 335,438
With original maturity of more than one year 213,539
Mortgage indebtedness and obligations
under capitalized leases 5,139
Banks' liability on acceptances executed
and outstanding 239
Notes and debentures subordinated to deposits ... 5,800
Other liabilities 429,753
    Total Liabilities **$48,093,352**

Equity Capital

Limited-life preferred stock 0
Perpetual preferred stock.................... 6,320
Common stock............................ 521,834
Surplus (exclude surplus related to preferred stock) 2,314,971
Undivided profits and capital reserves 1,926,900
Less: Net unrealized loss on marketable
equity securities 4,886
Cumulative foreign currency translation adjustments
    Total Equity Capital..................... **$4,774,911**
Total liabilities, limited-life preferred
    stock and equity capital **$52,868,263**

Texas National Banks

Consolidated Statement, Foreign and Domestic
Offices, as of Dec. 31, 1996
Source: **Federal Reserve Bank of Dallas**

Number of Banks 432

(All figures in thousand dollars)

Assets

Cash and due from banks:
Non-interest-bearing balances and cur-
rency and coin........................ $14,060,548
Interest-bearing balances 7,520,651
Held-to-maturity securities 7,330,230
Available-for-sale securities 26,003,536
Federal funds sold 9,009,845
Securities purchased under agreement to resell 241,054
Loans and lease financing receivables:
Loans and leases, net of unearned income 80,593,578
Less: allowance for loan and lease losses 1,212,727
Less: allocated transfer risk reserve 0
Loans and leases, net.................... 79,380,852
Assets held in trading accounts 218,145
Premises and fixed assets 2,737,039
Other real estate owned................... 91,757
Investments in unconsolidated subsidiaries
and associated companies 3,561
Customers liability on acceptances outstanding 233,594
Intangible assets 2,490,799
Other assets............................ 2,978,250
    Total Assets..................... **$152,299,695**

Liabilities

Deposits:
In domestic offices 119,886,144
Non-interest-bearing 36,098,434
Interest-bearing 83,787,709
In foreign offices, edge & agreement
subsidiaries & IBF's.................... 2,356,846
Non-interest-bearing 0
Interest-bearing...................... 2,356,846
Federal funds purchased 5,092,341
Securities sold under agreement to re-
purchase 2,786,235
Demand notes issued to the U.S. Treasury 1,540,694
Trading Liabilities 58,934
With original maturity of one year or less........ 2,011,228
With original maturity of more than one year 1,871,879
Mortgage indebtedness and obligations
under capitalized leases 421,492
Banks' liability on acceptances executed
and outstanding 233,594
Notes and debentures subordinated to deposits 1,359,600
Other liabilities 2,205,888
    Total Liabilities **$139,824,880**

Equity Capital

Limited-life preferred stock................... 100
Perpetual preferred stock................... 48,959
Common stock.......................... 2,113,868
Surplus................................ 5,981,373
Undivided profits and capital reserves 4,299,253
Less: Net unrealized loss on marketable
equity securities 31,278
Cumulative foreign currency translation
adjustments .... -16
    Total Equity Capital..................... **12,474,715**
Total liabilities, limited preferred stock
    and equity capital................... **$152,299,695**

Savings Institutions

The state savings bank charter was approved by the Legislature in 1993 and the first state savings bank in Texas was chartered in January 1994. Savings banks have existed for many years, primarily in the Northeast and, in fact, are among the oldest types of financial-institution charters in the country. Savings banks operate similarly to savings and loans associations in that they are housing-oriented lenders.

Under federal law a state savings bank is categorized as a commercial bank and not a thrift. Therefore savings-bank information is also reported with state and national-bank information.

Texas Savings Banks

Year	No. Assn./Banks	Total Assets	*Mortgage Loans	†Cash	†Investment Securities	Savings Capital	FHLB Advances and other Borrowed Money	‡Net Worth
					Thousands of Dollars			
Dec. 31, 1996	15	$7,872,238	$6,227,811	$856,970	...	$5,329,919	$1,930,378	$611,941
Dec. 31, 1995	13	7,348,647	5,644,591	1,106,557	...	4,603,026	2,225,793	519,827
Dec. 31, 1994	8	6,347,505	2,825,012	3,139,573	...	3,227,886	2,628,847	352,363

Texas Savings and Loan Associations

Year	No. Assn./Banks	Total Assets	*Mortgage Loans	†Cash	†Investment Securities	Savings Capital	FHLB Advances and other Borrowed Money	‡Net Worth
Dec. 31, 1996	37	$54,427,896	$27,514,639	$5,112,995	...	$28,053,292	$20,210,616	$4,345,257
Dec. 31, 1995	45	$52,292,519	$27,509,933	$5,971,364	...	$28,635,799	$15,837,632	$3,827,249
Dec. 31, 1994	50	$50,014,102	$24,148,760	$6,790,416	...	$29,394,433	$15,973,056	$3,447,110
Dec. 31, 1993	62	$42,983,595	$14,784,215	$10,769,889	...	$25,503,656	$13,356,018	$2,968,840
Dec. 31, 1992	64	$47,565,516	$14,137,191	$14,527,573	...	$33,299,278	$10,490,144	$2,917,881
Dec. 31, 1991	80	53,500,091	15,417,895	11,422,071	...	41,985,117	8,189,800	2,257,329
Dec. 31, 1990§	131	72,041,456	27,475,664	20,569,770	...	56,994,387	17,738,041	-$4,566,656
Conservatorship	51	14,952,402	6,397,466	2,188,820	...	16,581,525	4,304,033	-6,637,882
Privately Owned	80	57,089,054	21,078,198	18,380,950	...	40,412,862	13,434,008	2,071,226
Dec. 31, 1989§	196	90,606,100	37,793,043	21,218,130	...	70,823,464	27,158,238	-9,356,209
Conservatorship	81	22,159,752	11,793,445	2,605,080	...	25,381,494	7,103,657	-10,866,213
Privately Owned	115	68,446,348	25,999,598	18,613,050	...	45,441,970	20,054,581	1,510,004
Dec. 31, 1988	204	110,499,276	50,920,006	26,181,917	...	83,950,314	28,381,573	-4,088,355
Dec. 31, 1987	279	99,613,666	56,884,564	12,559,154	...	85,324,796	19,235,506	-6,677,338
Dec. 31, 1986	281	96,919,775	61,489,463	9,989,918	...	80,429,758	14,528,311	109,807
Dec. 31, 1985	273	91,798,890	60,866,666	10,426,464	...	72,806,067	13,194,147	3,903,611
Dec. 31, 1984	273	77,544,202	45,859,408	10,424,113	...	61,943,815	10,984,467	2,938,044
Dec. 31, 1983	273	56,684,508	36,243,290	6,678,808	...	46,224,429	6,317,947	2,386,551
Dec. 31, 1982	288	42,505,924	28,539,378	4,713,742	...	34,526,483	5,168,343	1,631,139
Dec. 31, 1981	311	38,343,703	30,013,805	3,294,327	...	30,075,258	4,846,153	1,493,795
Dec. 31, 1980	318	34,954,129	27,717,383	3,066,791	...	28,439,210	3,187,638	1,711,201
Dec. 31, 1979	310	31,280,006	25,238,483	2,512,797	...	25,197,598	2,969,838	1,640,049
Dec. 31, 1978	318	27,933,526	22,830,872	142,721	$1,876,882	22,848,519	2,251,631	1,444,607
Dec. 31, 1975	303	16,540,181	13,367,569	167,385	1,000,095	13,876,780	919,404	914,502
Dec. 31, 1970	271	7,706,639	6,450,730	122,420	509,482	6,335,582	559,953	531,733
Dec. 31, 1965	267	5,351,064	4,534,073	228,994	230,628	4,631,999	286,497	333,948
Dec. 31, 1960	233	2,508,872	2,083,066	110,028	157,154	2,238,080	48,834	166,927

* Beginning in 1982, net of loans in process.
† Beginning in 1979, cash and investment securities data combined.
‡ Net worth includes permanent stock and paid-in surplus general reserves, surplus and undivided profits.
§ In 1989 and 1990, the Office of Thrift Supervision, U.S. Department of the Treasury, separated data on savings and loans (thrifts) into two categories: those under the supervision of the Office of Thrift Supervision (Conservatorship Thrifts) and those still under private management (Privately Owned).
Details in the table above were supplied by the Dallas District of the Office of Thrift Supervision of the U.S. Department of the Treasury and the Texas Savings and Loan Department.

Texas Credit Unions

Membership in Texas' **798** credit unions has grown by approximately 185,000 each year during the past decade.

Nationally, there are 11,562 credit unions representing more than $337.3 billion in assets. There are 5,492,253 credit union members in Texas. That is, **one Texan of every four** belongs to a credit union.

In **1996** at mid-year, share (savings) accounts stood at $21.2 billion, and loans amounted to $15.4 billion.

Credit unions are chartered at federal and state levels. The **National Credit Union Administration** (NCUA) is the regulatory agency for the federal chartered credit unions in Texas. The **Texas Credit Union Department**, Austin, is the regulatory agency for the state-chartered credit unions.

The **Texas Credit Union League** and Affilliates at 4455 LBJ Freeway, Farmers Branch 75244-5998, has been the state association for federal and state chartered credit unions since October 1934. ☆

Source: Texas Credit Union League.

International Trade a Major Target

Since its days as an independent republic, Texas has attracted attention from foreign countries. With a gross state product larger than many nations in the world, the state is an attractive trading partner.

As the world economy further embraces that of the United States and Texas, channels of communications between nations become more important.

In 1857, the Texas Almanac reported that 17 foreign consuls and commercial agents from 16 countries were in Texas. Among the countries represented were France, Great Britian, Mexico, Prussia, Switzerland, Uruguay, Austria and the Netherlands. All but three lived in Galveston. (The others lived in Indianola and Brownsville).

As the world economy of the 21st century develops, the State of Texas Department of Commerce keeps private businesses informed about the possibilities in foreign trade. Through the Office of International Marketing, the state provides basic and advanced export counseling; distributes leads for trade and matches foreign needs with producers in Texas; and displays the state's wares at overseas trade shows and promotional events organized by the Office of International Marketing.

The office is divided into three groups: one for Mexico; another for Europe; and a third for Asia-Pacific-Canada.

Information on the services provided can be obtained by writing the Office of International Marketing, P.O. Box 12047, Austin 78711. The street address is 410 East 5th St., Austin. The telephone number is (512) 472-5059 and the Fax number is (512) 320-9424.

Foreign Trade Zones in Texas

Foreign-trade-zone status endows a domestic site with certain customs privileges, causing it to be considered to be outside customs territory and therefore available for activities that might otherwise be carried on overseas. Operated as public utilities for qualified corporations, the zones are established under grants of authority from the Foreign Trade Zones board, which is chaired by the Secretary of Commerce.

Zone facilities are available for operations involving storage, repacking, inspection, exhibition, assembly, manufacturing and other processing. A foreign-trade zone is especially suitable for export processing or manufacturing operations when foreign components or materials with a high U.S. duty are needed to make the end product competitive in markets abroad.

Additional information on the zones is available from each zone manager; from U.S. customs offices; from the executive secretary of the Foreign Trade Zones Board, Dept. of Commerce, Washington, D.C., or from the nearest Dept. of Commerce district office.

Source: The International Trade Reporter, *copyright 1979 by the Bureau of National Affairs, Inc., Washington, D.C.*

Source Texas Department of Commerce.

There are 25 Foreign Trade Zones in Texas as of August 31, 1996.

McAllen, FTZ No. 12
McAllen E.D.C.
6401 South 33rd Street
McAllen, Texas 78501

Galveston, FTZ No. 36
Port of Galveston
P.O. Box 328
Galveston, Texas 77553

Dallas/Ft.Worth, FTZ No. 39
D/FW International Airport Board
P.O. Drawer 619428
D/FW Airport, Texas 75261-9428

Brownsville, FTZ No. 62
Brownsville Navigation District
Port of Brownsville
P.O. Box 3070
Brownsville, Texas 78523-3070

El Paso, FTZ No. 68
5B Butterfield Trail Blvd.
El Paso, Texas 79906-4945

San Antonio, FTZ No. 80
City of San Antonio
P.O. Box 839966
San Antonio, Texas 78283-3966

Harris County, FTZ No. 84
Port of Houston Authority

111 East Loop North
Houston, Texas 77029

Laredo, FTZ No. 94
Laredo International Airport
518 Flightline, Building 132
Laredo, Texas 78041

Starr County, FTZ No. 95
Starr County Industrial Foundation
P.O. 502
Rio Grande City, Texas 78582

Eagle Pass, FTZ No. 96
Maverick Company Development Corp.
P.O. Box 3693
Eagle Pass, Texas 78853

Del Rio, FTZ No. 97
City of Del Rio
114 West Martin Street
Del Rio, Texas 78841

Ellis County, FTZ No. 113
Trade Zone Operations, Inc.
1500 North Service Road, Highway 67
P.O. Box 788
Midlothian, Texas 76065

Beaumont, FTZ No. 115;
Port Arthur, FTZ No. 116
Orange, FTZ No. 117
FTZ of Southeast Texas, Inc.
2748 Viterbo Rd., Box 9
Beaumont, Texas 77705

Corpus Christi, FTZ 122
Port of Corpus Christi
P.O. Box 1541
Corpus Christi, Texas 78403

Freeport, FTZ No. 149
Brazos River Harbor Navigation District
Box 615
Freeport, Texas 77541

El Paso, FTZ No. 150
Westport E.D.C.
P.O. Box 9368
El Paso, Texas 79984

Calhoun/Victoria Counties
FTZ No. 155
Calhoun-Victoria FTZ, Inc.
P.O. Drawer 397
Point Comfort, Texas 77978

Weslaco, FTZ No. 156
City of Weslaco
500 South Kansas
Weslaco, Texas 78596

Midland, FTZ No. 165
Midland International Airport
P.O. Box 60305
Midland, Texas 79711

Dallas/Fort Worth, FTZ No. 168
FTZ Co. of Texas
P.O. Box 742916
Dallas, Texas 75374-2916

Liberty County, FTZ No. 171
Liberty County Economic Development Corp.
P.O. Box 857
Liberty, Texas 77575

Presidio, FTZ No. 178
Presidio E.D.C.
P.O. Box 1414
Presidio, Texas 79845

Austin, FTZ No. 183
Georgetown Industrial Foundation
P.O. Box 114
Georgetown, Texas 78627

Fort Worth, FTZ No. 196
Alliance Corridor, Inc.
2421 Westport Pkwy, Suite 200
Fort Worth, Texas 76177

Texas City, FTZ No. 199
City of Texas City
1801 9th Ave. North
Texas City, Texas 77590

Note: El Paso contains two Foreign Trade Zones.

Foreign and Domestic Commerce Through Major Ports

Data in table below represent receipts and shipments for only the 13 major Texas ports in 1995. Total receipts and shipments for these ports amounted to 360,659,000 tons. Total receipts and shipments for all Texas ports in 1995 was 371,021,000 tons. Note: "0" means tonnage reported was less than 500 tons, a "-" indicates no tonnage was reported.
Source: U.S. Army Corps of Engineers

(All figures in short tons)

Port	Total	Foreign		Domestic				Local
				Coastwise		Internal		
		Imports	Exports	Receipts	Shipments	Receipts	Shipments	
Sabine Pass	231,000	-	-	-	-	105,000	126,000	-
Orange	693,000	-	74,000	3,000	-	513,000	102,000	-
Beaumont	20,937,000	4,026,000	1,988,000	518,000	2,706,000	5,128,000	5,979,000	594,000
Port Arthur	49,800,000	36,865,000	6,171,000	46,000	639,000	2,323,000	3,584,000	171,000
Houston	135,231,000	42,860,000	28,677,000	3,438,000	9,590,000	22,748,000	15,384,000	12,534,000
Texas City	50,403,000	29,980,000	1,209,000	206,000	4,211,000	7,379,000	6,954,000	463,000
Galveston	10,465,000	1,986,000	4,664,000	102,000	1,734,000	1,490,000	465,000	25,000
Freeport	19,662,000	12,271,000	1,915,000	295,000	441,000	2,633,000	1,916,000	192,000
Corpus Christi	70,218,000	38,422,000	5,945,000	690,000	10,824,000	3,216,000	8,513,000	2,610,000
Port Isabel	129,000	-	-	-	-	129,000	-	-
Brownsville	2,656,000	497,000	1,116,000	35,000	55,000	833,000	118,000	1,000
Port Aransas (Harbor Island)	214,000	203,000	1,000	-	-	7,000	3,000	-
Port Mansfield	20,000	-	-	-	-	20,000	0	-
Grand Total	360,659,000	167,110,000	51,759,000	5,333,000	30,200,000	46,524,000	43,144,000	16,590,000

Tonnage Handled by Ports, 1988-1995

Source: Corps of Engineers, U.S. Army
Table below gives consolidated tonnage handled by ports. All figures are in short tons (2,000 lbs.).

Ports	1995	1994	1993	1992	1991	1990	1989	1988
Brownsville	2,656,000	3,396,000	1,734,526	1,594,222	1,610,295	1,371,606	1,360,964	1,237,027
Port Isabel	129,000	206,000	239,370	234,401	247,455	269,174	263,335	318,466
Corpus Christi	70,218,000	76,060,000	58,408,549	58,678,726	56,973,650	60,165,497	58,440,714	56,310,445
Freeport	19,662,000	17,450,000	14,024,604	14,952,599	15,665,993	14,526,096	15,176,018	15,137,891
Galveston	10,465,000	10,257,000	9,755,324	12,317,599	10,858,221	9,619,891	11,837,611	12,354,709
Houston	135,231,000	143,663,000	141,476,979	137,663,612	131,513,521	126,177,627	125,583,156	124,886,883
Texas City	50,403,000	44,351,000	53,652,781	43,104,101	43,289,659	48,052,157	41,272,401	42,746,698
Sabine	231,000	296,000	393,547	418,927	499,817	631,157	726,141	1,248,308
Port Arthur	49,800,000	45,586,000	38,326,902	33,525,819	29,835,115	30,680,942	31,127,913	23,801,409
Beaumont	20,937,000	21,201,000	25,409,757	22,701,500	22,383,039	26,728,664	31,668,257	31,947,319
Orange	693,000	686,000	579,062	552,504	849,307	709,940	727,454	657,627
Port Lavaca	-	-	5,892,656	5,899,832	6,266,244	6,097,107	4,715,349	5,061,695
Anahuac	-	0	0	0	0	0	21,399	3,033
Moss Bluff	-	-	0	0	0	0	294,125	0
Channel to Liberty	-	0	0	2,800	20,987	0	4,791	4,433
Double Bayou	-	0	0	240	0	0	0	2,850
Cedar Bayou	473,000	321,000	349,680	302,824	217,692	219,206	308,807	275,458
Colorado River	576,000	639,000	536,811	505,198	577,379	476,300	618,147	682,328
Sweeny	-	-	718,118	684,274	477,370	534,406	529,648	480,519
Palacios	-	0	0	0	0	0	0	0
Dickinson	657,000	556,000	423,368	449,336	532,184	555,523	475,275	722,645
Aransas Pass	181,000	45,000	25,226	13,398	16,851	169,020	1,893	84,325
Port Mansfield	20,000	10,000	3,781	2,657	120	102	88	3,909
Harlingen	-	-	898,132	786,994	795,305	764,577	728,954	753,937
Channel to Victoria	4,624,000	4,567,000	3,937,400	4,265,228	3,407,884	3,740,374	3,142,614	3,562,336
Chocolate Byu.	3,480,000	3,757,000	3,715,107	3,343,072	3,469,030	3,462,762	3,278,422	3,526,758
Johnsons Bayou	585,000	613,000	515,957	567,298	596,247	715,917	765,454	839,594
Rockport	-	3,000	0	0	0	0	643,563	2,336
Clear Creek	-	5,000	66	0	0	0	0	0
Other Ports	0	0	0	0	0	0	0	0
TOTAL	371,021,000	373,668,000	361,017,695	390,567,161	330,103,365	335,311,608	330,068,930	326,652,938

Foreign Consulates in Texas

In the list below, the following abbreviations appear in parentheses after the name of the city: (CG) Consulate General; (C) Consulate; (VC) Vice Consulate. The letter "H" before the designation indicates honorary status. Compiled from "Foreign Consular Offices in the United States," U.S. Dept. of State, Fall/Winter 1996. Note: Changes occur frequently, especially with area codes.

Albania: Houston (HC); 10738 Villa Lea, 77071. (713) 790-1341.

Argentina: Houston (CG); 1990 S. Post Oak Rd., Ste. 770, 77056. (713) 871-8935.

Australia: Houston (CG); 1990 S. Post Oak Rd., Ste. 800, 77056. (713) 629-9131.

Austria: Houston (HCG); 6575 West Loop South, Ste. 493, Bellaire, 77401. (713) 723-9979.

Barbados: Houston (HC); 25226 Sandi Lane, Katy, 77494. (281) 392-9794.

Belgium: Houston (HCG); 2929 Allen Pkwy., Ste. 2222, 77019. (713) 224-8000.
Dallas (HC); 8350 N. Central Expy., Ste. 2000, 75206. (214) 750-2554.
San Antonio (HC); 105 S. St. Mary's St., No. 2115, 78205. (210) 225-1951.

Belize: Dallas (HC); 1315 19th St., Ste. 2A, Plano, 75074. (972) 579-0070.
Houston (HC); 7101 Breen, 77086. (713) 999-4484.

Bolivia: Houston (HCG); 1880 Dairy Ashford, Ste. 691, 77077. (713) 497-4068.

Botswana: Houston (HC); 4615 Post Oak Pl., Ste. 104, 77027. (713) 622-1900.

Brazil: Houston (CG); 1700 W. Loop S., Ste. 1450, 77027. (713) 961-3063.

Cameroon: Houston (HC); 2711 Weslayan, 77027. (713) 499-3502.

Canada: Dallas (CG); 750 N. Saint Paul, Ste. 1700, 75201. (214) 922-9806.

Chile: Houston (CG);1360 Post Oak Blvd., Ste. 2330, 77056; (713) 621-5853.
Dallas (HC); 3500 Oak Lawn, Apt. 200, 75219-4343. (214) 528-2731.

China: Houston (CG); 3417 Montrose, 77006. (713) 524-0780.

Colombia: Houston (CG); 2990 Richmond Ave., Ste. 544, 77098; (713) 527-8919.

Costa Rica: Houston (CG); 2901 Wilcrest, Ste. 347, 77042. (713) 266-1527.
San Antonio (CG); 6836 San Pedro, Ste. 206-B, 78216. (210) 308-8623.
Austin (C); 1730 E. Oltorf, Unit 320, 78741. (512) 445-0023.

Cyprus: Houston (HCG); 320 S. 66th St., 77011. (713) 928-2264.

Czech Republic: Dallas (HC); 3239 Oradell Lane, 75220. (214) 350-6871.
Houston (HC); 2323 S. Shepherd, Ste. 1400, 77019. (713) 523-3030.

Denmark: Corpus Christi (HC); 22 Townhouse Lane (P.O. Box 4585), 78408. (512) 991-3012.
Dallas (HC); 3200 Trammell Crow Center, 2001 Ross Ave., 75201. (214) 979-6200.
Houston (HC); 5 Post Oak Park, Ste. 2370, 77027. (713) 622-9018.

Dominican Republic: Houston (C); 3300 S. Gessner, Ste. 113, 77024. (713) 467-4372.
Dallas (HC); 12127 Ridgelake Dr., 75218. (214) 341-3250.
El Paso (HC); 67977 Granero Dr., 79912.

Ecuador: Houston (CG); 4200 Westheimer, Ste. 218, 77027. (713) 622-1787.

Egypt: Houston (CG); 3 Post Oak Central, 1990 Post Oak Blvd., Ste. 2180, 77056. (713) 961-4915.

El Salvador: Dallas (CG); 1555 W. Mockingbird Lane, Ste. 216, 75235.

Houston (CG); 6420 Hillcroft, Ste. 100, 77081. (713) 270-6239.

Finland: Dallas (HC); 1445 Ross Ave., Ste. 3200, 75202. (214) 855-4715.
Houston (HC); 2190 North Loop W., Ste. 410, 77018. (713) 680-2727.

France: Houston (CG); 2777 Allen Pkwy., Ste. 650, 77019. (713) 528-2181. **Trade Commission:** 5847 San Felipe, Ste. 1600, 77056. (713) 266-6595.
Austin (HC); 2300 Interfirst Tower, Ste. 976, 78701. (512) 480-5605.
Dallas (HC); 750 N. St. Paul, Ste. 220, 75201. (214) 855-5495.
San Antonio (HC); Route 1, 78109. Box 229, 78109. (210) 659-3101.

Germany: Houston (CG); 1330 Post Oak Blvd., Ste. 1850, 77056. (713) 627-7770.
Corpus Christi (HC); 5440 Old Brownsville Rd., 78469. (512) 289-2416.
Dallas (HC); 5580 Peterson Lane, Ste. 150, 75240. (214) 239-0788.
San Antonio (HC); 1500 Alamo Bldg., 105 S. St. Mary's St., 78205. (210) 224-4455.

Ghana: Houston; 3434 Locke Lane, 77027. (713) 960-8806.

Greece: Houston (CG); Cigna Tower, 1360 Post Oak Blvd., Ste. 2480, 77056. (713) 840-7522.

Guatemala: Houston (CG); 3600 S. Gessner Rd., Ste 200, 77063. (713) 953-9531.
San Antonio (HC); 4840 Whirlwind, 78217.

Haiti: Houston (HC); 3535 Sage Rd., 77027.

Honduras: Houston (CG); 4151 Southwest Fwy., Ste. 700, 77027. (713) 622-4572.

Hungary: Houston (HC); 50 Briar Hollow Lane, Ste. 515W, 77027. (713) 961-3333.

Iceland: Dallas (HC); 3205 Seaside, Irving, 75062. (972) 699-5417.
Houston (HC); 2348 W. Settler's Way, The Woodlands, 77380. (713) 367-2777.

India: Houston (CG); 1990 Post Oak Blvd., Ste 600, 77056. (713) 626-2148.

Indonesia: Houston (CG); 10900 Richmond Ave., 77042.

Ireland: Houston (HC); 1900 W. Loop S., Suite 850, 77027.

Israel: Houston (CG); Weslayan Tower, 24 Greenway Plz., Ste. 1500, 77046. (713) 627-3780.

Italy: Houston (CG); 1300 Post Oak Blvd., Ste. 660, 77056. (713) 850-7520.
Dallas (HVC); 6255 W. Northwest Hwy., Apt. 304, 75225. (214) 368-4113.

Jamaica: Houston (HC); 7737 Southwest Fwy., Suite 580, 77074. (713) 774-2229.

Japan: Houston (CG);1000 Louisiana, Ste. 5300, 77002. (713) 652-2977.
Dallas (HCG); 1601 Elm St., 40th Floor, 75201.

Jordan: Houston (HC); 723 Main St., Ste. 408, 77002. (713) 224-2911.

Korea: Houston (CG); 1990 Post Oak Blvd., Ste. 1250, 77056. (713) 961-0186.
Dallas (HC); 13111 N. Central Expy., 75243. (214) 454-1112.

Lesotho: Austin (HC); 7400 Valburn Dr., 78731.

Liberia: Houston (HCG); 3300 S. Gessner, 77063.

Luxembourg: Fort Worth/Dallas (HC); 301 Commerce St., Ste 600, Fort Worth, 76102. (817) 878-8000.

Madagascar: Houston (HC); 18010 Widcombe Dr.,

77084. (713) 550-2559.
Malta: Houston (HCG); 654 N. Belt E., Ste. 400, 77060. (713) 999-1812.
Mexico: Austin (CG); Littlefield Bldg., 200 E. 6th St., Ste. 200, 78701.
    Brownsville (C); 724 E. Elizabeth 78520. (210) 542-4431.
    Corpus Christi (C); 800 N. Shoreline, Ste. 410, 78401.
    Dallas (CG); 8855 Stemmons Fwy, 75247. (214) 522-9740.
    Del Rio (C); 300 East Losoya, 78840. (210) 775-2352.
    Eagle Pass (C); 140 Adams St., 78852. (210) 773-9255.
    El Paso (CG); 910 E. San Antonio St., 79901. (915) 533-3644.
    Fort Worth (HC); 1 N. Commerce St., 76102. (817) 870-2270.
    Houston (CG); 3015 Richmond Ave., Ste. 100, 77098. (713) 524-2300. **Tourism Office:** 2707 N. Loop, Ste. 450, 77008.
    Laredo (C); 1612 Farragut St., 78040. (210) 723-6369.
    McAllen (C); 600 S. Broadway, 78501. (210) 686-0243.
    Midland (C); 511 W. Ohio St., Ste. 121, 79701.
    San Antonio (CG); 127 Navarro St., 78205. (210) 227-9145. **Commercial Affairs Office**: 1100 NW Loop 410, Ste. 754, 78213.
Monaco: Dallas (HC); 4700 St. Johns Dr., 75205. (214) 521-1058.
Morocco: Houston (HC); 5555 Del Monte, No. 2405, 77056. (713) 963-9110.
Netherlands: Houston (CG); 2200 Post Oak Blvd., Ste. 610, 77056. (713) 622-8000.
New Zealand: Houston (HC); 2248 Robinhood St., 77005. (713) 526-9325.
Nicaragua: Houston (CG); 6300 Hillcroft, Ste. 312, 77081. (713) 272-9628.
Norway: Houston (CG); 2777 Allen Parkway, 77019. (713) 521-2900.
    Dallas (HC); 4605 Live Oak St., 75204. (214) 826-5231.
Panama: Houston (CG); 24 Greenway Plaza, Ste. 1307, 77046. (713) 493-5997.

Paraguay: Houston (HC); 14770 Cindywood, 77079.
Peru: Houston (CG); 5847 San Felipe Ave., Ste. 1481, 77056. (713) 781-5000.
    San Antonio (HC); 28055 Ruffian Drive., 78006.
Portugal: Houston (HC); 700 Louisiana, Ste. 4800, 77002. (713) 759-1188.
Saint Kitts/Nevis: Dallas (HC); 6336 Greenville Ave., 75206.
Saint Lucia: Dallas (HC); Dallas City Hall, 1500 Marilla, 75201. (214) 670-3319.
Saudi Arabia: Houston (CG); 5718 Westheimer, Ste. 1500, 77057. (713) 785-5577.
Senegal: Houston (HCG); 3602 S. McGregor, 77021. (713) 748-5016.
Slovenia: Houston (HC); 2925 Briarpark, 7 Floor, 77042. (713) 430-7350.
Spain: Houston (CG); 1800 Bering Dr., Ste. 660, 77057. (713) 783-6200.
    Dallas (HC); Lee Park Place, 3141 Hood St., 75219. (214) 520-1717.
    El Paso (HC); 420 Golden Springs Dr., 79912. (915) 534-0677.
    San Antonio (HC); 8350 Delphian, 78148.
Sweden: Houston (HCG); 2401 Fountainview Dr., Ste 510, 77057. (713) 953-1417.
    Dallas: (HC); 1341 W. Mockingbird Lane, Ste. 500, 75225; (214) 363-0800.
Switzerland: Houston (CG); 1000 Louisiana, Ste. 5670, 77002. (713) 650-0000.
    Dallas (HC); 2651 N. Harwood, Ste. 455, 75201. (214) 965-1025.
Syria: Houston (HCG); 5433 Westheimer Rd., Ste. 1020, 77056. (713) 622-8860.
Thailand: Dallas (HCG); 1717 Main St., Ste. 4100, 75201.
    El Paso (HCG); 4401 N. Mesa, Ste. 204, 79902. (915) 533-5757.
Turkey: Houston (CG); **1990** Post Oak Central, 77056. (713) 622-5849.
United Kingdom: Houston (CG); 1000 Louisiana St., Ste. 1900, 77002. (713) 659-6270.
    Dallas (C); 2911 Turtle Creek, Ste. 940, 75219. (214) 637-3600.
Venezuela : Houston (CG); 2700 S. Post Oak Blvd., Ste. 1500, 77056. (713) 961-5141.

Number of Foreign-Affiliated Establishments in Texas*

Texas is a major recipient of foreign direct investment. More than 2,300 foreign companies hold assets or employ more than 300,000 workers in Texas and have invested a cumulative value of $64.7 billion in the state.

Canada, France, Germany and Australia all have concentrated larger investment holdings in Texas than in any other state. Texas is also the leading state for Latin American and Middle Eastern investment.

Year	All	Canada	Europe						Latin America	Africa	Middle East	Pacific			Other
			Total	France	Germany	Nether-lands	Switzer-land	U.K.				Total	Australia	Japan	
1987	1,777	198	977	113	209	68	126	271	177	15	88	313	33	217	9
1988	1,879	208	1,015	121	224	68	128	279	181	16	92	357	37	252	10
1989	2,082	223	1,111	144	240	75	136	302	197	12	99	427	43	303	13
1990	2,241	234	1,183	155	246	87	145	327	219	13	97	483	46	335	12
1991	2,344	247	1,217	153	248	89	148	328	226	13	104	527	45	364	10
1992p	2,233	236	1,128	153	218	98	138	297	231	10	82	537	39	383	9
1993p	2,321	243	1,164	154	247	95	134	304	249	10	86	560	40	397	9

Source: U.S. Bureau of Economic Analysis. *Defined as the number of foreign affiliates in Texas with (1) property, plant and equipment or (2) employment. Firms are listed by the country of ultimate beneficial owner. **Foreign affiliation is defined as an ownership interest of 10 percent or greater.** Data for 1992-92 is preliminary (p).

Oil & Gas Exploration in Texas

Source: Texas Railroad Commission

Year(s)	Wells Completed	Oil Wells	Gas Wells	Stratigraphic & Core Tests	Service Wells	Dry Holes	Percent Dry
1889-1900*	97	71	2			24	24.7
1901-1910*	692	462	9			221	32.0
1911-1920*	2,451	1,682	66			703	28.7
1921-1930*	6,352	3,745	306			2,301	36.2
1931-1940*	9,915	7,404	288	...	...	2,224	22.9
1941-1950*	9,147	5,767	457	...	44	2,901	32.5
1951-1960*	18,439	10,838	814	...	155	6,632	36.0
1961-1970*	11,595	5,798	1,115	367	393	4,121	35.8
1971	7,728	3,880	810	8	449	2,581	33.4
1972	8,088	3,963	943	8	414	2,760	34.1
1973	8,494	3,686	1,475	34	362	2,937	34.6
1974	9,808	4,402	1,843	19	260	3,284	33.5
1975	12,483	6,074	2,135	36	361	3,877	31.1
1976	12,740	5,779	2,443	45	285	4,188	32.9
1977	14,759	6,533	3,064	37	443	4,682	31.7
1978	15,037	6,086	3,292	26	415	5,218	34.7
1979	16,149	6,765	3,609	35	515	5,225	32.4

Year(s)	Wells Completed	Oil Wells	Gas Wells	Stratigraphic & Core Tests	Service Wells	Dry Holes	Percent Dry
1980	19,253	9,668	3,684	10	546	5,345	27.8
1981	23,940	13,052	3,807	2	368	6,711	28.0
1982	26,849	13,851	4,345	4	692	7,957	29.6
1983	24,616	13,102	3,317	...	652	7,545	30.6
1984	26,134	14,591	3,242	17	678	7,606	29.1
1985	18,882	11,206	2,215	...	666	5,461	28.9
1986	11,425	6,141	1,326	2	345	3,958	34.6
1987	10,797	5,504	1,589	...	365	3,704	34.3
1988	9,106	6,441	2,665	...	...	3,155	...
1989	8,590	4,003	1,758	...	528	2,380	...
1990	9,821	4,704	1,925	...	525	2,744	27.5
1991	9,848	5,051	1,786	...	543	2,515	25.5
1992	8,065	4,154	1,615	...	409	1,930	23.9
1993	8,277	3,724	2,220	...	365	2,028	24.5
1994	7,571	3,058	2,527	...	287	1,784	23.6
1995	8,483	4,334	3,778	...	371	1,673	19.7
1996	8,544	4,061	2,527	...	423	1,626	19.0

*Annual Averages.

A History of Fuel Minerals in Texas

Oil and natural gas are the most valuable minerals produced in Texas, contributing 23 percent of the oil production and 24 percent of the gas production in the United States in 1993.

Oil and gas have been produced from most areas of Texas and from rocks of all geologic eras except the Precambrian.

All of the major sedimentary basins of Texas have produced some oil or gas.

The well-known Permian Basin of West Texas has yielded large quantities of oil since 1921. It is an area of considerable promise for future production as well.

Although large quantities of petroleum have been produced from rocks of Permian age, production in the area also occurs from older Paleozoic rocks. Production from rocks of Paleozoic age occurs primarily from North Central Texas westward to New Mexico and southwestward to the Rio Grande, but there is also significant Paleozoic production in North Texas in Tarrant, Grayson and Cooke counties.

Mesozoic rocks are the primary hydrocarbon reservoirs of the East Texas Basin and the area south and east of the Balcones Fault Zone. Cenozoic sandstones are the main reservoirs along the Gulf Coast and offshore state waters.

Coal and lignite occur in rocks of Pennsylvanian, Cretaceous and Tertiary ages. Coal was produced in Texas from about 1850 to the 1940s, when petroleum became the common fuel.

Significant production of coal did not resume until the mid-1970s. Most of the pre-1940 production was **bituminous coal** from North Central Texas, an area near Eagle Pass or from near Laredo.

North Central Texas production was from Pennsylvanian rocks. Thurber, Newcastle and Bridgeport all had viable coal industries in the early 1900s. As early as 1850, soldiers from Fort Duncan near Eagle Pass are reported to have mined coal from the Cretaceous rocks.

Commercial mining of coal from Eocene rocks near Laredo began in 1881. In addition to the commercial mining, small amounts of coal occurring in the Trans-Pecos were used to roast the ore in mercury mining districts in the Big Bend.

Small amounts of "brown coal" or **lignite** have been produced throughout the history of the state. It was mined by many early settlers for family and small industry use. It was also used to generate "coal gas" or "producer gas" for Texas cities around the turn of the century.

Today, Texas ranks sixth nationally in coal production, and lignite accounts for most of this. Almost all of the lignite is consumed by mine-mouth electrical generating plants. Approximately 20 percent of the electricity generated in the state in 1990 was from plants fired by Texas lignite.

Uranium occurs in several widely separated Texas localities, but production has been limited to the Cenozoic sandstones along the coastal plains of south-central Texas, roughly from Karnes County southwest to Webb County.

The surface mines, active from 1959 to the mid-1970s, have largely been abandoned and reclaimed, and production today is all from in-situ leaching. This requires the injection of a leaching fluid into the uranium-bearing strata, reaction of the fluid with the uranium ore and return of the fluid to the surface for stripping of the uranium. The fluid is then re-used.

Crude Oil

Indians found oil seeping from the soils of Texas long before the first Europeans arrived. They told explorers that the fluid had medicinal values. The first record of Europeans using crude oil, however, was the caulking of boats in 1543 by survivors of the **DeSoto**

expedition near Sabine Pass.

Melrose, in Nacogdoches County, was the site in 1866 of the **first drilled well to produce oil** in Texas. The driller was **Lyne T. Barret** (whose name has been spelled several ways by historians). Barret used an auger, fastened to a pipe and rotated by a cogwheel driven by a steam engine — a basic principle of rotary drilling that has been used since, although with much improvement.

In 1867 **Amory (Emory) Starr** and **Peyton F. Edwards** brought in a well at **Oil Springs,** in the same area. Other wells followed and **Nacogdoches County** was the site of Texas' **first commercial oil field, pipeline and effort to refine crude.** Several thousand barrels of oil were produced there during these years.

Other oil was found in crudely dug wells in Texas, principally in Bexar County, in the latter years of the 19th century. But it was not until June 9, 1894, that Texas had a **major discovery.** This occurred in the drilling of a water well for the City of Corsicana. Oil caused that well to be abandoned, but a company formed in 1895 drilled several producing wells.

The first well-equipped refinery in Texas was built, and this plant usually is called the state's **first refinery,** despite the earlier effort at Nacogdoches. Discovery of the **Powell Field** near Corsicana followed in 1900.

Spindletop, 1901

Jan. 10, 1901, is the most famous date in Texas petroleum history. This is the date that the great gusher erupted in the oil well being drilled at **Spindletop,** near Beaumont, by a mining engineer, **Capt. A. F. Lucas.** Thousands of barrels of oil flowed before the well could be capped. This was the **first salt dome oil discovery.**

It created a sensation throughout the world, and encouraged exploration and drilling in Texas that has continued since.

Texas oil production increased from 836,039 barrels in 1900 to 4,393,658 in 1901; and in 1902 Spindletop alone produced 17,421,000 barrels, or 94 percent of the state's production. Prices dropped to 3c a barrel, an all-time low.

A water-well drilling outfit on the W. T. Waggoner Ranch in Wichita County hit oil, bringing in the **Electra Field** in 1911. In 1917, came the discovery of the **Ranger Field** in Eastland County. The **Burkburnett Field** in Wichita County was discovered in 1919.

Oil discoveries brought a short era of swindling with oil stock promotion and selling on a nationwide scale. It ended after a series of trials in a federal court.

The **Mexia Field** in Limestone County was discovered in 1920, and the **second Powell Field** in Navarro County in 1924.

Another great area opened in 1921 with discovery of oil in the **Panhandle,** a field which developed rapidly with sensational oil and gas discoveries in Hutchinson and contiguous counties and the booming of **Borger.**

The **Luling Field** was opened in 1922 and 1925 saw the comeback of Spindletop with a production larger than that of the original field. Other fields opened in this period included **Big Lake,** 1923; **Wortham,** 1924-25 and **Yates,** 1926.

In 1925 **Howard County** was opened for production. **Winkler** in West Texas and **Raccoon Bend,** Austin County, were opened in 1927. **Sugar Land** was the most important Texas oil development in 1928.

The **Darst Creek Field** was opened in 1929. In the same year, new records of productive sand thickness were set for the industry at **Van,** Van Zandt County. **Pettus** was another contribution of 1929 in Bee County.

East Texas Field

The **East Texas field,** biggest of them all, was discovered near Turnertown and Joinerville, Rusk County, by veteran wildcatter **C. M. (Dad) Joiner,** in October 1930. The success of this well — drilled on land condemned many times by geologists of the major companies — was followed by the biggest leasing campaign in history. The field soon was extended to Kilgore, Longview and northward. The East Texas field brought overproduction and a rapid sinking of the price. Private attempts were made to prorate production, but without much success.

On Aug. 17, 1931, **Gov. Ross S. Sterling** ordered the National Guard into the field, which he placed under **martial law.** This drastic action was taken after the **Texas Railroad Commission** had been enjoined from enforcing production restrictions. After the complete shutdown, the Texas Legislature enacted legal **proration,** the system of regulation still utilized.

The most significant subsequent oil discoveries in Texas were those in **West Texas,** following a discovery well in Scurry County, Nov. 21, 1948, and later major developments in that region. Many of the leading Texas counties in minerals value are in that section.

Major Fields

Texas fields with estimated ultimate recovery of 100 million barrels of oil or more are in the following list, which gives the name of the field, county and discovery date.

Data furnished by the **Oil and Gas Journal.**

Panhandle, Carson-Collingsworth-Gray-Hutchinson-Moore-Potter-Wheeler, 1910; **Thompson** (all fields), Fort Bend, 1921; **Howard-Glasscock,** Howard, 1925; **Iatan East,** Howard, 1926; **Yates,** Pecos, 1926; **Waddell,** Crane, 1927; **Van,** Van Zandt, 1929; **Ward Estes North,** Ward, 1929; **Cowden North,** Ector, 1930; **East Texas,** Gregg-Rusk, 1930; **Sand Hills,** Crane, 1930; **Conroe,** Montgomery, 1931; **Tom O'Connor,** Refugio, 1931; **Cowden South,** Ector, 1932; **Greta** (all fields), Refugio, 1933; **Tomball,** Harris, 1933; **Means** (all fields), **Andrews-Gaines,** 1934; **Anahuac,** Chambers, 1935; **Goldsmith** (all fields), Ector, 1935; **Hastings,** Brazoria, 1935; **Magnet Withers** (all fields), Wharton, 1936; **Seminole** (all fields), Gaines, 1936; **Webster,** Harris, 1936; **Jordan,** Crane-Ector, 1937; **Slaughter,** Cochran, 1937; **Wasson** (all fields), Gaines, 1937; **Dune,** Crane, 1938; **West Ranch,** Jackson, 1938; **Keystone,** Winkler, 1939; **Diamond M,** Scurry, 1940; **Hawkins,** Wood, 1940; **Fullerton** (all fields), Andrews, 1941; **McElroy,** Crane, 1941; **Oyster Bayou,** Chambers, 1941; **Welch,** Dawson, 1941; **Quitman** (all fields), Wood, 1942; **Anton-Irish,** Hale, 1944; **TXL** (all fields), Ector, 1944; **Block 31,** Crane, 1945; **Levelland,** Cochran-Hockley, 1945; **Midland Farms** (all fields), Andrews; 1945; **Andector,** Ector, 1946; **Dollarhide,** Andrews, 1947; **Kelly-Snyder,** Scurry, 1948; **Cogdell Area,** Scurry, 1949; **Prentice,** Yoakum, 1950; **Salt Creek,** Kent, 1950; **Spraberry Trend,** Glasscock-Midland, 1952; **Lake Pasture,** Refugio, 1953; **Neches,** Anderson-Cherokee, 1953; **Fairway,** Anderson-Henderson, 1960; **Giddings,** Lee-Fayette-Burleson, 1971.

Texas Oil Production History

The table shows the year of oil or gas discovery in each county, oil production in 1995 and 1996 and total oil production from date of discovery to Jan. 1, 1997. The 21 counties omitted have not produced oil.

The table has been compiled by the Texas Almanac from information provided in past years by theTexas Mid-Continent Oil & Gas Assoc. Since 1970, production figures have been compiled from records of the Railroad Commission of Texas. In prior years, U.S. Bureau of Mines and State Comptroller reports were the basis of these compilations. The figures in the final column are cumulative of all previously published figures. The change in sources, due to different techniques, may create some discrepancies in year-to-year comparisons among counties.

County	Year of Discovery	Production in Barrels*		Total Production to Jan. 1, 1997
		1995	1996	
Anderson	1929	1,364,148	1,262,639	291,427,272
Andrews	1930	31,489,675	30,898424	2,570,440,073
Angelina	1936	2,913	34,735	484,660
Aransas	1936	653,433	547,891	82,112,695
Archer	1911	2,143,794	2,036,227	482,682,694
Atascosa	1917	792,206	761,177	144,103,468
Austin	1915	459,844	458,438	112,062,349
Bandera	1995	3,439	2,657	6,096
Bastrop	1913	273,716	246,486	15,199,448
Baylor	1924	251,463	238,725	56,746,201
Bee	1930	579,413	582,138	102,949,652
Bell	1980	0	0	446
Bexar	1889	250,806	237,514	34,566,883
Borden	1949	4,531,563	4,612,752	368,097,518
Bowie	1944	249,457	292,263	4,778,488
Brazoria	1902	3,548,556	3,503,097	1,248,742,163
Brazos	1942	5,396,539	3,746,844	117,130,765
Brewster	1969	0	0	56
Briscoe	1982	0	0	3,554
Brooks	1936	970,351	979,760	159,072,020
Brown	1917	229,384	211,746	52,177,814
Burleson	1938	6,839,336	6,899,122	161,233,821
Caldwell	1922	1,137,231	1,047,797	274,136,434
Calhoun	1935	914,141	900,272	98,935,055
Callahan	1923	510,866	447,516	83,557,802
Cameron	1944	3,023	2,564	451,360
Camp	1940	434,938	384,412	25,487,865
Carson	1921	560,426	568,307	176,626,372
Cass	1935	722,456	752,583	110,395,290
Chambers	1916	2,233,325	2,133,748	893,827,738
Cherokee	1926	479,972	458,636	68,167,621
Childress	1961	10,440	10,281	1,392,416
Clay	1902	1,306,390	1,272,465	196,699,592
Cochran	1936	5,833,675	5,812,184	466,431,219
Coke	1942	1,277,689	1,265,651	216,794,952
Coleman	1902	468,444	414,618	91,912,783
Collin	1963	0	0	53,000
Collingsworth	1936	6,004	5,762	1,212,670
Colorado	1932	724,837	809,959	35,965,610
Comanche	1918	12,444	13,212	5,874,051
Concho	1940	986,575	907,453	19,069,724
Cooke	1926	2,097,767	2,250,330	374,679,313
Coryell	1964	0	0	1,100
Cottle	1955	84,691	76,766	3,830,312
Crane	1926	15,042,642	14,453,323	1,648,841,801
Crockett	1925	3,527,416	3,531,478	333,938,241
Crosby	1955	747,670	824,322	18,582,053
Culberson	1953	293,188	210,029	23,690,554
Dallas	1986	0	0	231
Dawson	1937	6,397,342	6,834,436	332,431,479
Delta	1984	0	0	64,058
Denton	1937	18,926	15,874	3,437,638
DeWitt	1930	384,666	357,471	64,245,491

County	Year of Discovery	Production in Barrels*		Total Production to Jan. 1, 1997
		1995	1996	
Dickens	1953	532,752	519,325	8,531,585
Dimmit	1943	1,090,956	1,130,953	99,698,066
Duval	1905	2,216,931	2,068,227	573,203,495
Eastland	1917	600,019	510,452	153,548,705
Ector	1926	27,496,069	26,768,650	2,911,407,935
Edwards	1946	7,264	11,417	454,331
Ellis	1953	4,064	5,402	826,548
Erath	1917	9,039	8,953	2,050,511
Falls	1937	8,602	7,716	810,381
Fannin	1980	0	0	13,281
Fayette	1943	8,579,187	6,847,997	123,976,031
Fisher	1928	1,484,557	1,339,258	240,638,097
Floyd	1952	2,328	2,052	142,471
Foard	1929	266,401	219,159	22,608,853
Fort Bend	1919	2,837,739	3,181,176	666,142,903
Franklin	1936	620,881	640,412	172,751,118
Freestone	1916	318,065	280,479	42,759,377
Frio	1934	1,997,179	1,600,009	139,233,020
Gaines	1936	37,805,487	37,649,434	1,908,619,774
Galveston	1922	1,165,185	1,332,920	438,023,748
Garza	1926	6,695,058	6,558,131	291,829,716
Glasscock	1925	5,634,845	6,236,406	224,359,834
Goliad	1930	436,614	554,720	77,136,760
Gonzales	1902	733,710	707,108	39,815,952
Gray	1925	2,355,847	2,392,074	657,577,916
Grayson	1930	1,725,960	1,760,661	243,071,554
Gregg	1931	21,644,787	19,357,671	3,227,006,847
Grimes	1952	3,186,694	2,313,446	14,519,000
Guadalupe	1922	1,369,491	1,261,752	195,380,988
Hale	1946	1,073,817	1,019,110	154,599,127
Hamilton	1938	2,568	1,628	141,508
Hansford	1937	374,460	358,099	37,204,743
Hardeman	1944	2,705,852	2,799,723	63,907,449
Hardin	1893	1,633,222	1,524,254	423,277,902
Harris	1905	4,218,830	4,139,397	1,351,953,394
Harrison	1928	994,987	970,069	81,737,868
Hartley	1937	288,322	303,952	4,682,095
Haskell	1929	747,596	747,016	111,976,970
Hays	1956	0	0	296
Hemphill	1955	516,751	510,614	32,099,397
Henderson	1934	1,930,584	1,802,748	167,822,328
Hidalgo	1934	2,976,025	3,039,937	79,803,748
Hill	1949	2,290	629	68,094
Hockley	1937	26,048,913	25,947,241	1,447,249,000
Hood	1958	1,953	2,391	103,812
Hopkins	1936	591,101	538,563	86,501,108
Houston	1934	778,164	766,229	49,921,203
Howard	1925	9,391,760	9,118,618	752,220,900
Hunt	1942	18,746	10,936	2,012,651
Hutchinson	1923	1,598,377	1,921,101	521,185,106
Irion	1928	3,188,487	2,866,401	85,491,765
Jack	1923	1,247,241	1,129,920	196,320,950
Jackson	1934	1,897,074	1,771,968	670,066,459
Jasper	1928	1,827,969	1,872,578	28,467,219

County	Year of Discovery	Production in Barrels* 1995	Production in Barrels* 1996	Total Production to Jan. 1, 1997
Jeff Davis	1980	0	0	20,866
Jefferson	1901	2,352,217	3,340,086	514,755,034
Jim Hogg	1922	327,315	362,822	108,972,654
Jim Wells	1933	444,053	440,824	460,377,118
Johnson	1962	0	0	194,000
Jones	1926	1,162,719	1,160,016	213,626,687
Karnes	1930	450,342	434,846	105,150,371
Kaufman	1948	152,770	127250	23,948,209
Kenedy	1947	467,854	536,523	35,002,323
Kent	1946	10,958,549	10,826,358	509,435,476
Kerr	1982	996	2,614	73,382
Kimble	1939	759	742	92,821
King	1943	4,479,549	4,118,004	153,741,612
Kinney	1960	0	0	402
Kleberg	1926	773,961	682,306	330,363,641
Knox	1946	427,564	418,886	59,447,571
Lamb	1945	488,208	582,241	30,703,153
Lampasas	1985	0	0	111
La Salle	1940	437,287	409,526	25,339,846
Lavaca	1941	779,289	723,443	25,734,938
Lee	1939	5,752,890	4,255,179	115,881,477
Leon	1936	1,969,606	1,498,078	53,848,373
Liberty	1905	2,243,888	1,994,586	510,526,351
Limestone	1920	334,658	284,375	117,852,096
Lipscomb	1956	942,419	852,374	55,212,218
Live Oak	1931	1,184,561	998,749	77,878,415
Llano	1978	0	0	647
Loving	1925	1,449,977	1,428,486	99,867,843
Lubbock	1941	1,972,359	1,867,400	54,787,185
Lynn	1950	268,213	269,428	17,322,720
Madison	1946	520,715	642,190	28,123,145
Marion	1910	263,290	266,961	53,847,095
Martin	1945	6,088,001	5,714,544	268,327,999
Matagorda	1904	1,084,131	884,894	267,927,963
Maverick	1929	1,084,131	1,011,802	43,535,587
McCulloch	1938	381,113	176,234	917,958
McLennan	1902	2,721	1,968	323,722
McMullen	1919	1,810,440	1,832,134	92,456,598
Medina	1901	121,746	116,935	10,019,488
Menard	1941	76,134	71,971	6,304,803
Midland	1945	12,341,350	12,493,733	522,095,936
Milam	1921	221,316	878,572	13,795,552
Mills	1982	0	0	28,122
Mitchell	1920	3,677,607	3,597,599	200,577,388
Montague	1924	1,691,920	1,637,738	278,509,094
Montgomery	1931	1,975,015	2,051,479	763,950,029
Moore	1936	477,546	436,213	27,359,596
Motley	1957	149,313	119,184	10,443,862
Nacogdoches	1866	47,024	51,956	3,176,667
Navarro	1895	370,425	351,147	215,610,386
Newton	1937	2,329,166	2,164,399	56,222,463
Nolan	1939	2,035,775	2,140,125	183,996,962
Nueces	1930	1,664,551	1,566,884	550,317,859
Ochiltree	1951	1,168,679	1,169,406	152,336,985
Oldham	1957	181,922	153,876	13,021,468
Orange	1913	2,312,305	2,219,998	147,399,799
Palo Pinto	1902	635,549	477,558	20,249,233
Panola	1917	1,757,817	2,035,497	75,464,014
Parker	1942	18,223	20,585	2,771,537
Parmer	1963	0	0	144,000
Pecos	1926	22,899,777	21,282,411	1,639,686,414
Polk	1930	2,231,594	3,043,221	106,448,323
Potter	1925	372,476	350,372	8,153,472
Presidio	1980	0	0	1,873
Rains	1955	0	120	148,886

County	Year of Discovery	Production in Barrels* 1995	Production in Barrels* 1996	Total Production to Jan. 1, 1997
Reagan	1923	5,634,452	6,534,611	457,300,351
Red River	1951	499,244	569,086	4,384,095
Reeves	1939	1,027,422	958,213	71,440,768
Refugio	1928	5,668,504	5,198,791	1,284,277,226
Roberts	1945	469,248	428,529	43,012,916
Robertson	1944	999,463	1,648,942	5,714,344
Runnels	1927	996,353	937,635	142,012,107
Rusk	1930	4,924,031	4,724,829	1,800,379,110
Sabine	1981	698,242	584,294	4,357,603
San Augustine	1947	657,023	403,178	2,046,770
San Jacinto	1940	318,165	321,428	23,889,716
San Patricio	1930	1,225,929	1,097,588	476,804,895
San Saba	1982	0	0	32,362
Schleicher	1937	660,047	627,815	83,418,578
Scurry	1923	7,582,948	7,294,264	1,963,236,577
Shackelford	1910	1,458,092	1,296,170	174,004,040
Shelby	1917	64,290	67,487	2,075,973
Sherman	1938	307,793	322,476	7,738,607
Smith	1931	2,043,331	2,002,093	252,878,391
Somervell	1978	0	0	119
Starr	1929	1,518,220	1,556,770	275,608,909
Stephens	1916	4,257,449	3,951,955	314,836,906
Sterling	1947	1,661,455	1,607,765	78,527,076
Stonewall	1938	2,744,758	2,631,397	248,707,512
Sutton	1948	97,824	84,135	7,054,983
Swisher	1981	0	0	6
Tarrant	1969	0	0	53
Taylor	1929	819,191	934,786	138,649,027
Terrell	1952	580,116	631,534	5,099,708
Terry	1940	5,595,658	5,504,944	399,794,637
Throckmorton	1924	1,612,474	1,561,459	210,277,829
Titus	1936	675,952	673,671	206,790,452
Tom Green	1940	1,177,693	948,850	87,698,789
Travis	1934	2,735	2,725	727,959
Trinity	1946	48,133	45,457	530,787
Tyler	1937	512,582	563,119	37,042,391
Upshur	1931	767,782	926,805	281,452,369
Upton	1925	11,625,630	11,132,993	748,284,074
Uvalde	1950	0	0	1,814
Val Verde	1935	1,137	1,992	122,055
Van Zandt	1929	2,116,625	1,833,374	536,553,735
Victoria	1931	1,157,187	1,059,455	245,214032
Walker	1934	7,967	7,137	439,307
Waller	1934	57,687	46,379	19,902,373
Ward	1928	5,910,536	6,284,350	709,611,485
Washington	1915	1,207,712	933,825	25,724,907
Webb	1921	2,520,111	2,618,875	144,227,464
Wharton	1925	2,494,556	2,861,384	321,498,873
Wheeler	1921	737,628	732,953	95,712,658
Wichita	1910	3,235,442	3,109,535	808,333,627
Wilbarger	1915	889,162	930,029	257,880,798
Willacy	1936	652,515	657,659	108,312,197
Williamson	1915	14,179	14,731	9,467,448
Wilson	1941	846,479	666,919	45,374,899
Winkler	1926	4,676,801	5,109,088	1,037,667,026
Wise	1942	983,299	885,774	94,224,092
Wood	1941	7,857,924	6,982,529	1,151,556,176
Yoakum	1936	30,020,368	29,918,987	1,849,451,796
Young	1917	2,211,962	2,035,589	295,430,167
Zapata	1919	289,198	259,256	45,020,768
Zavala	1937	943,491	727,770	42,814,050

*Total includes condensate production.
State totals: (1995), 548,801,956; (1996), 533,773,714.
Source: Railroad Commission, 1995-96 production reports.

Oil and Gas Production by County 1996

Source: Texas Railroad Commission.
BBL refers to barrels and MCF to thousand cubic feet.

County	Gas Well Gas MCF	Condensate BBL	Crude Oil BBL	Casinghead MCF
Anderson	4,849,414	72,307	1,190,332	3,285,178
Andrews	1,561,409	8,801	30,889,623	38,936,389
Angelina	900,255	10,247	24,488	7,489
Aransas	10,301,661	210,384	337,507	955,926
Archer	20,761	320	2,035,907	566,874
Atascosa	19,294,397	51,620	709,557	317,358
Austin	1,843,017	26,069	432,369	169,608
Bandera	0	0	2,657	0
Bastrop	612,689	14,099	232,387	585,417
Baylor	0	0	238,725	272
Bee	15,766,568	109,442	472,696	1,017,633
Bexar	21,666	0	237,514	1,545
Borden	0	0	4,612,752	3,513,608
Bowie	132,436	10,270	281,993	113,428
Brazoria	66,495,867	1,010,182	2,492,915	2,531,046
Brazos	42,776,502	788,767	2,958,077	12,277,895
Brooks	46,671,936	697,209	282,551	598,958
Brown	1,708,949	2,809	208,937	498,095
Burleson	6,384,802	158,940	6,740,182	27,435,197
Caldwell	29,013	151	1,047,646	825,824
Calhoun	13,747,560	148,580	751,692	1,052,134
Callahan	1,291,393	4,061	443,455	710,701
Cameron	1,062,334	1,180	1,384	1,081
Camp	1,610,428	2	384,410	47,963
Carson	32,866,609	9	568,298	3,747,646
Cass	12,534,190	68,426	684,157	619,849
Chambers	55,160,656	275,382	1,858,366	4,867,034
Cherokee	14,456,980	72,702	385,934	539,844
Childress	0	0	10,281	220
Clay	495,705	13,243	1,259,222	1,205,623
Cochran	549,638	4,162	5,808,022	4,364,409
Coke	1,782,032	5,976	1,259,675	4,114,298
Coleman	1,823,943	7,227	407,391	1,091,402
Collingswth	1,910,699	0	5,762	50,323
Colorado	30,216,781	337,254	472,705	1,321,476
Comanche	876,684	1,586	11,626	178,738
Concho	1,742,879	3,839	903,614	2,820,420
Cooke	193,142	1,315	2,249,015	858,730
Cottle	2,774,578	27,503	49,263	214,849
Crane	16,292,318	57,687	14,395,636	100,315,752
Crockett	138,534,376	336,871	3,194,607	6,345,458
Crosby	0	0	824,322	108,400
Culberson	255,861	1	210,028	202,532
Dallam	21,558	0	0	0
Dawson	0	0	6,834,436	5,467,735
Denton	9,930,179	2,691	13,183	19,389
DeWitt	12,436,415	142,593	214,878	353,149
Dickens	0	0	519,325	15,374
Dimmit	1,038,975	5,499	1,125,454	1,286,376
Donley	26,468	0	0	0
Duval	65,755,986	206,639	1,861,588	1,587,824
Eastland	5,887,933	26,105	484,347	1,457,493
Ector	47,780,704	25,181	26,743,469	27,012,749

County	Gas Well Gas MCF	Condensate BBL	Crude Oil BBL	Casinghead MCF
Edwards	16,234,038	8,743	2,674	2,140
Ellis	0	0	5,402	24
Erath	2,892,379	2,369	6,584	10,487
Falls	22,561	60	7,656	115
Fayette	56,336,708	2,085,109	4,762,888	30,014,896
Fisher	112,313	1,160	1,338,098	1,715,207
Floyd	0	0	2,052	23
Foard	171,084	0	219,159	22,151
Fort Bend	20,774,013	312,182	2,868,994	1,437,243
Franklin	7,866,959	76,758	563,654	121,335
Freestone	52,801,563	140,170	140,579	143,324
Frio	682,639	503	1,599,596	1,066,134
Gaines	3,183,500	3,513	37,645,921	45,973,583
Galveston	17,508,544	176,414	1,156,506	1,755,278
Garza	0	0	6,558,131	1,562,592
Glasscock	2,199,366	27,952	6,208,454	16,055,232
Goliad	24,056,717	210,882	343,838	901,501
Gonzales	1,454,048	15,491	691,617	280,129
Gray	14,044,688	1,329	2,390,745	5,676,275
Grayson	2,896,148	13,435	1,747,226	3,527,749
Gregg	61,988,980	351,126	19,006,561	8,462,367
Grimes	106,463,202	1,757,841	555,605	2,862,241
Guadalupe	0	0	1,261,752	325,910
Hale	0	0	1,019,110	228,835
Hamilton	61,988	0	1,628	6
Hansford	31,276,888	35,590	322,509	1,076,898
Hardeman	0	0	2,799,723	1,015,235
Hardin	2,537,787	85,349	1,438,905	1,355,136
Harris	57,650,791	633,982	3,505,415	41,498,730
Harrison	55,087,336	295,784	674,285	2,258,679
Hartley	4,097,686	0	303,952	12
Haskell	109,645	461	746,555	252,651
Hemphill	81,311,801	354,376	156,238	3,280,624
Henderson	24,102,474	38,126	1,764,622	11,602,332
Hidalgo	224,062,582	2,900,938	138,999	415,482
Hill	0	0	629	11
Hockley	188,048	1,948	25,945,293	36,997,424
Hood	1,845,221	2,391	0	0
Hopkins	440,173	8,389	530,174	381,381
Houston	4,875,224	68,057	698,172	351,026
Howard	270,575	1,753	9,116,865	7,521,206
Hunt	0	0	10,936	3,059
Hutchinson	13,246,287	16,840	1,904,261	8,601,382
Irion	4,800,937	35,675	2,830,726	17,804,261
Jack	13,035,465	68,164	1,061,756	5,056,302
Jackson	18,304,108	151,147	1,620,821	1,622,757
Jasper	20,853,488	998,544	874,034	4,362,002
Jefferson	30,062,117	1,745,201	1,594,885	1,768,687
Jim Hogg	16,540,591	196,219	166,603	777,288
Jim Wells	20,978,976	169,395	271,439	1,130,263
Jones	46,486	0	1,160,016	730,178
Karnes	9,759,384	116,511	318,437	925,946
Kaufman	0	0	127,250	5,182
Kenedy	22,904,271	176,557	359,966	493,332
Kent	0	0	10,826,358	39,318,639

County	Gas Well Gas MCF	Conden-sate BBL	Crude Oil BBL	Casinghead MCF
Kerr	0	0	2,614	0
Kimble	70,934	0	742	472
King	1,132,079	3,816	4,114,188	429,663
Kleberg	652,805	259,878	422,428	723,074
Knox	0	0	418,886	19,484
Lamb	0	0	582,241	64,727
La Salle	506,884	61,529	347,997	841,665
Lavaca	478,294	412,679	310,764	735,621
Lee	839,100	200,808	4,054,371	20,983,483
Leon	977,698	92,074	1,406,004	1,815,644
Liberty	230,728	271,618	1,722,968	1,221,462
Limestone	589,955	141,329	143,046	141
Lipscomb	155,776	148,034	704,340	5,454,172
Live Oak	922,690	577,869	420,880	414,156
Loving	138,992	5,253	1,423,233	3,804,039
Lubbock	0	0	1,867,400	103,656
Lynn	0	0	269,428	114,269
McCulloch	132,095	0	176,234	181,586
McLennan	0	0	1,968	128
McMullen	689,736	439,116	1,393,018	5,426,064
Madison	509,608	60,342	581,848	751,592
Marion	570,756	56,293	210,668	271,100
Martin	110,887	1,737	5,712,807	12,107,534
Matagorda	489,760	194,653	690,241	1,141,641
Maverick	894,222	14,551	997,251	372,861
Medina	4,440	0	116,935	1,774
Menard	111,555	0	71,971	6,365
Midland	095,334	458,976	12,034,757	34,613,361
Milam	30,847	356	878,216	340,454
Mitchell	1,801	1	3,597,598	1,279,104
Montague	321,041	1,948	1,635,790	1,474,044
Montgomery	16,358,062	485,303	1,566,176	7,785,174
Moore	66,999,795	4,802	431,411	4,229,074
Motley	0	0	119,184	3,998
Nacogdches	22,185,180	36,140	15,816	336,864
Navarro	413,576	4,115	347,032	57,690
Newton	16,018,154	1,471,966	692,433	3,063,926
Nolan	791,436	2,466	2,137,659	4,027,979
Nueces	42,542,680	483,264	1,083,620	1,867,458
Ochiltree	30,063,282	112,827	1,056,579	4,597,112
Oldham	488,505	0	153,876	23,818
Orange	18,411,497	887,519	1,332,479	2,150,704
Palo Pinto	15,958,745	69,874	407,684	2,878,733
Panola	252,744,947	1,224,593	810,904	4,786,487
Parker	9,221,483	12,093	8,492	89,270
Pecos	204,621,655	179,198	21,103,213	50,513,428
Polk	43,744,680	2,470,335	572,886	451,411
Potter	28,683,011	136	350,236	683,374
Rains	9,804,944	120	0	0
Reagan	3,888,667	145,518	6,389,093	28,367,414
Red River	0	0	569,086	29
Reeves	31,240,750	42,425	915,788	2,043,895
Refugio	20,217,601	35,885	5,162,906	20,713,440
Roberts	24,036,918	162,126	266,403	3,193,192
Robertson	22,926,572	491	1,648,451	822,673
Runnels	398,632	1,154	936,481	1,806,433
Rusk	62,363,372	264,025	4,460,804	2,844,579

County	Gas Well Gas MCF	Conden-sate BBL	Crude Oil BBL	Casinghead MCF
Sabine	1,091,399	150,539	433,755	2,477,773
S.Augustine	191,532	7,327	395,851	2,229,892
San Jacinto	7,001,917	281,686	39,742	18,548
San Patricio	17,273,779	244,127	853,461	2,070,642
Schleicher	13,838,011	62,896	564,919	1,739,844
Scurry	0	0	7,294,264	26,540,453
Shackelford	4,539,076	29,608	1,266,562	2,225,020
Shelby	9,744,908	28,016	39,471	149,525
Sherman	35,383,201	29,320	293,156	367,092
Smith	10,730,377	142,991	1,859,102	3,548,932
Somervell	24,653	0	0	0
Starr	184,269,277	1,148,178	408,592	1,560,120
Stephens	7,956,463	40,520	3,911,435	3,099,247
Sterling	13,695,703	129,794	1,477,971	19,793,185
Stonewall	0	0	2,631,397	788,231
Sutton	65,386,755	61,433	22,702	28,322
Tarrant	182,458	0	0	0
Taylor	75,096	754	934,032	477,730
Terrell	69,431,293	563,849	67,685	937,366
Terry	588,166	0	5,504,944	2,328,784
Throckmrton	804,926	2,297	1,559,162	2,023,029
Titus	488,143	12,222	661,449	5,585
Tom Green	1,215,121	9,467	939,383	5,472,520
Travis	0	0	2,725	23
Trinity	133,015	1,110	44,347	800,969
Tyler	1,571,042	69,279	493,840	1,151,321
Upshur	65,158,288	726,927	199,878	69,250
Upton	29,130,615	297,717	10,835,276	35,674,738
Val Verde	11,331,270	1,464	528	0
Van Zandt	14,145,662	57,143	1,776,231	2,625,054
Victoria	13,690,190	72,365	987,090	1,206,294
Walker	707,470	3,291	3,846	40,278
Waller	10,725,685	1,476	44,903	18,578
Ward	49,925,682	167,200	6,117,150	14,944,122
Washington	86,620,538	272,102	661,723	3,807,002
Webb	298,950,673	2,325,241	293,634	276,970
Wharton	55,745,460	1,009,158	1,852,226	1,649,132
Wheeler	40,608,606	159,520	573,433	1,188,264
Wichita	0	0	3,109,535	180,961
Wilbarger	7,204	0	930,029	94,064
Willacy	48,412,074	31,632	626,027	410,032
Williamson	120,702	92	14,639	72
Wilson	130,566	2,844	663,919	100,334
Winkler	55,026,169	90,160	5,018,928	13,629,636
Wise	60,242,995	158,831	726,943	9,025,794
Wood	14,079,491	59,078	6,923,451	25,180,050
Yoakum	0	0	29,918,987	79,612,333
Young	2,385,505	21,342	2,014,247	2,757,696
Zapata	298,538,090	186,818	72,438	80,258
Zavala	4,032,023	2,927	724,843	768,944

Business and Transportation data

There are additional data on each county's total wages, average weekly wage, civilian labor force, unemployment and retail trade and other economic factors on pages 142-292.

Nonfuel Mineral Production and Value, 1994, 1995 and 1996

Source: U.S. Dept. of the Interior, Bureau of Mines (Production measured by mine shipments, sales or marketable production, including consumption by producer.)

Mineral	1994		1995		1996*	
	Production	Value (add 000)	Production	Value (add 000)	Production	Value (add 000)
Cement:						
Masonry (thous. metric tons). . . .	258	$18,232	202	$17,634	228	$19,891
Portland (thous. metric tons).	8,624	455,951	8,091	498,914	8,367	515,892
††**Clays** (thous. metric tons)	2,194	13,675	2,453	26,027	2,491	17,954
Gemstones	†	448	†	353	†	**
Gypsum (thous. metric tons).	1,874	10,105	1,882	16,237	1,870	16,575
Helium, crude (million cu. meters)	7	7,046	5	4,725	**	**
Lime (thous. metric tons).	1,211	76,179	1,369	85,838	1,405	88,080
Salt (thous. metric tons).	8,764	76,489	9,107	84,953	8,974	76,124
Sand and gravel:						
Construction (thous. metric tons)	56,705	241,791	61,089	270,908	72,000	342,000
Industrial (thous. metric tons)	1,567	37,927	1,596	40,341	1,575	39,282
Stone:						
Crushed (thous. metric tons).	76,132	300,449	81,123	309,923	86,000	335,400
Dimension (thous. metric tons) . . .	**	**	53,955	13,265	51,801	12,614
Sulfur (Frasch) (thous. metric tons). tons	**	**	**	**	**	**
Talc and pyrophyllite (metric tons)	224,827	5,862	293,533	5,838	235,868	4,577
‡**Combined value**	. . .	294,936	. . .	301,159	. . .	313,888
‡‡**Total Texas Values**	. . .	**$1,539,090**	. . .	**$1,676,115**	. . .	**$1,782,277**

*Estimated. † Not available.
‡Includes clays (ball, bentonite, fuller's earth, kaolin), fluorspar (1993-94), helium (grade A), iron ore, magnesium compounds, magnesium metal, sodium sulfate (natural) and values indicated by symbol **.
**Data withheld to avoid disclosing proprietary data; value included with "Combined value."
††Excludes certain clays; kind and value included in "Combined value."
‡‡Data do not add to total shown because of independent rounding.

Nonpetroleum Minerals

The nonpetroleum minerals that occur in Texas constitute a long list. Some are currently mined; some may have a potential for future development; some are minor occurrences only. Although overshadowed by the petroleum, natural gas and natural gas liquids that are produced in the state, many of the nonpetroleum minerals are, nonetheless, important to the economy. In 1995, they were valued at approximately $1.68 billion. Texas is annually **among the nation's leading states in value of non-petroleum mineral production.** In 1995, **Texas ranked sixth nationally** in total mineral output.

The **Bureau of Economic Geology**, which functions as the state geological survey of Texas, revised the following information about nonpetroleum minerals for this edition of the Texas Almanac. Publications of the bureau, on file in many libraries, contain more detailed information. Among the items available are a map, "Mineral Resources of Texas," showing locations of resource access of many nonpetroleum minerals, and a computer-generated list of Texas nonpetroleum mineral producers.

A catalog of Bureau publications is also available free on request from the Bureau Publications Sales, University Station, Box X, Austin, TX 78713-7508; (512) 471-7144.

Texas' nonpetroleum minerals are as follows:

ALUMINUM — No aluminum ores are mined in Texas, but three Texas plants process aluminum materials in one or more ways. Plants in San Patricio and Calhoun counties produce **aluminum oxide (alumina)** from imported raw ore (**bauxite**), and a plant in Milam County reduces the oxide to aluminum.

ASBESTOS — Small occurrences of amphibole-type asbestos have been found in the state. In West Texas, **richterite**, a white, long-fibered amphibole, is associated with **talc deposits** northwest of **Allamoore** in Hudspeth County. Another type, **tremolite**, has been found in the **Llano Uplift** of Central Texas where it is associated with **serpentinite** in eastern Gillespie and western Blanco County. No asbestos is mined in Texas.

ASPHALT (Native) — Asphalt-bearing Cretaceous lime-stones crop out in Burnet, Kinney, Pecos, Reeves, Uvalde and other counties. The most significant deposit is in southwestern Uvalde County where asphalt occurs naturally in the pore spaces of the Anacacho Limestone. The material is quarried and used extensively as **road-paving material**. Asphalt-bearing sandstones occur in Anderson, Angelina, Cooke, Jasper, Maverick, Montague, Nacogdoches, Uvalde, Zavala and other counties.

BARITE — Deposits of a heavy, nonmetallic mineral, barite (barium sulphate), have been found in many localities, including Baylor, Brown, Brewster, Culberson, Gillespie, Howard, Hudspeth, Jeff Davis, Kinney, Llano, Live Oak, Taylor, Val Verde and Webb counties. During the 1960s, there was small, intermittent production in the **Seven Heart Gap** area of the **Apache Mountains** in Culberson County, where barite was mined from open pits. Most of the deposits are known to be relatively small, but the Webb County deposit has not been evaluated. Grinding plants, which prepare barite mined outside of Texas for use chiefly as a **weighting agent** in well-drilling muds and as a **filler**, are located in Brownsville, Corpus Christi, El Paso, Galena Park, Galveston, and Houston.

BASALT (TRAP ROCK) — Masses of basalt — a hard, dark-colored, fine-grained igneous rock — crop out in Kinney, Travis, Uvalde and several other counties along the **Balcones Fault Zone**, and also in the Trans-Pecos area of West Texas. Basalt is quarried near Knippa in Uvalde County for use as **road-building material, railroad ballast and other aggregate.**

BENTONITE (see **CLAYS**).

BERYLLIUM — Occurrences of beryllium minerals at several Trans-Pecos localities have been recognized for several years. Evaluation and development of a beryllium prospect near **Sierra Blanca** in Hudspeth County, a portion of which is on state-owned land, is now underway. **Behoite** and other beryllium minerals are associated with **fluorspar** at this site.

BRINE (see also **SALT, SODIUM SULPHATE**) — Many wells in Texas produce brine by solution mining of subsurface salt deposits, mostly in West Texas counties such as Andrews, Crane, Ector, Loving, Midland, Pecos, Reeves, Ward and others. These wells in the Permian Basin dissolve salt from the **Salado Formation,** an enormous salt deposit that extends in the subsurface from north of the Big Bend northward to Kansas, has an east-west width of 150 to 200 miles, and may have several hundred feet of net salt thickness. The majority of the brine is used in the **petroleum industry,** but it also is used in **water softening, the chemical industry** and other uses. Three Gulf Coast counties, Fort Bend, Duval and Jefferson, have brine stations that produce from **salt domes.**

BUILDING STONE (DIMENSION STONE) — Granite and **limestone** currently are quarried for use as dimension stone. The granite quarries are located in Burnet, Gillespie, Llano and Mason counties; the limestone quarries are in Shackelford and Williamson counties. Past production of limestone for use as dimension stone has been reported in Burnet, Gillespie, Jones, Tarrant, Travis and several other counties. There has also been production of **sandstone** in various counties for use as dimension stone.

CEMENT MATERIALS — Cement is currently manufactured at 13 plants in Bexar, Comal, Dallas, Ector, Ellis, Hays, McLennan, Nolan, and Potter counties. Many of these plants utilize Cretaceous limestones and shales or clays as raw materials for the cement. On the Texas High Plains, a cement plant near Amarillo uses impure **caliche** as the chief raw material. **Iron oxide,** also a constituent of cement, is available from the iron ore deposits of East Texas and from smelter slag. **Gypsum,** added to the cement as a retarder, is found chiefly in North Central Texas, Central Texas and the Trans-Pecos areas.

CHROMIUM — Chromite-bearing rock has been found in several small deposits around the margin of the Coal Creek **serpentinite** mass in northeastern Gillespie County and northwestern Blanco County. Exploration has not revealed significant deposits.

CLAYS — Texas has an abundance and variety of ceramic and non-ceramic clays and is one of the country's leading producers of clay products.

Almost any kind of clay, ranging from common clay used to make ordinary brick and tile to clays suitable for manufacture of specialty whitewares, can be used for ceramic purposes. **Fire clay** suitable for use as **refractories** occurs chiefly in East and North Central Texas; **ball clay,** a high-quality plastic ceramic clay, is found locally in East Texas.

Ceramic clay suitable for quality structural clay products such as **structural building brick, paving brick and drain tile** is especially abundant in East and North Central Texas. Common clay suitable for use in the manufacture of cement and ordinary brick is found in most counties of the state. Many of the Texas clays will expand or bloat upon rapid firing and are suitable for the manufacture of lightweight aggregate, which is used mainly in concrete blocks and highway surfacing.

Nonceramic clays are utilized without firing. They are used primarily as **bleaching and adsorbent clays, fillers, coaters, additives, bonding clays, drilling muds, catalysts** and potentially as sources of alumina. Most of the nonceramic clays in Texas are **bentonites and fuller's earth.** These occur extensively in the Coastal Plain and locally in the High Plains and Big Bend areas. **Kaolin clays** in parts of East Texas are potential sources of such nonceramic products as **paper coaters and fillers, rubber fillers and drilling agents.** Relatively high in alumina, these clays also are a potential source of metallic aluminum.

COAL (see also LIGNITE) — **Bituminous coal,** which occurs in North Central, South and West Texas, was a significant energy source in Texas prior to the large-scale development of oil and gas. During the period from 1895 to 1943, Texas mines produced more than 25 million tons of coal. The mines were inactive for many years, but the renewed interest in coal as a major energy source prompted a revaluation of Texas' coal deposits. In the late 1970s, bituminous coal production resumed in the state on a limited scale when mines were opened in Coleman, Erath and Webb counties.

Much of the state's bituminous coal occurs in North Central Texas. Deposits are found there in Pennsylvanian rocks within a large area that includes Coleman, Eastland, Erath, Jack, McCulloch, Montague, Palo Pinto, Parker, Throckmorton, Wise, Young and other counties. Before the general availability of oil and gas, underground coal mines near **Thurber, Bridgeport, Newcastle, Strawn** and other points annually produced significant coal tonnages. Preliminary evaluations indicate substantial amounts of coal may remain in the North Central Texas area. The coal seams there are generally no more than 30 inches thick and are commonly covered by well-consolidated overburden. Ash and sulphur content are high. Beginning in 1979, two bituminous coal mine operations in North Central Texas — one in southern Coleman County and one in northwestern Erath County — produced coal to be used as fuel by the cement industry. Neither mine is currently operating.

In South Texas, bituminous coal occurs in the Eagle Pass district of Maverick County, and bituminous **cannel coal** is present in the **Santo Tomas district** of Webb County. The Eagle Pass area was a leading coal-producing district in Texas during the late 1800s and early 1900s. The bituminous coal in that area, which occurs in the Upper Cretaceous Olmos Formation, has a high ash content and a moderate moisture and sulfur content. According to reports, Maverick County coal beds range from four to seven feet thick.

The **cannel coals** of western Webb County occur near the Rio Grande in middle Eocene strata. They were mined for more than 50 years and used primarily as a boiler fuel. Mining ceased from 1939 until 1978, when a surface mine was opened 30 miles northwest of Laredo to produce cannel coal for use as fuel in the cement industry and for export. An additional mine has since been opened in that county. Tests show that the coals of the Webb County Santo Tomas district have a high hydrogen content and yield significant amounts of gas and oil when distilled. They also have a high sulfur content. A potential use might be as a source of various petrochemical products.

Coal deposits in the Trans-Pecos country of West Texas include those in the Cretaceous rocks of the Terlingua area of Brewster County, the Eagle Spring area of Hudspeth County and the **San Carlos** area of Presidio County. The coal deposits in these areas are believed to have relatively little potential for development as a fuel. They have been sold in the past as a soil amendment (see **LEONARDITE**).

COPPER — Copper minerals have been found in the **Trans-Pecos** area of West Texas, in the **Llano Uplift** area of Central Texas and in redbed deposits of North Texas. No copper has been mined in Texas during recent years, and the total copper produced in the state has been relatively small. Past attempts to mine the North Texas and Llano Uplift copper deposits resulted in small shipments, but practically all the copper production in the state has been from the **Van Horn-Allamoore** district of Culberson and Hudspeth Counties in the Trans-Pecos area. Chief output was from the **Hazel copper-silver mine** of Culberson County that yielded over 1 million pounds of copper during 1891-1947. Copper ores and concentrates from outside of Texas are processed at **smelters** in El Paso and Amarillo.

CRUSHED STONE — Texas is among the leading states in the production of crushed stone. Most production consists of **limestone;** other kinds of crushed stone produced in the state include **basalt (trap rock), dolomite, granite, marble, rhyolite, sandstone and serpentinite.** Large tonnages of crushed stone are used as **aggregate** in concrete, as **road material** and in the manufacture of cement and lime. Some is used as **riprap, terrazzo, roofing chips, filter material, fillers** and for other purposes.

DIATOMITE (DIATOMACEOUS EARTH) — Diatomite is a very lightweight siliceous material consisting of the remains of microscopic aquatic plants (diatoms). It is used chiefly as a **filter and filler;** other uses are for **thermal insulation,** as an **abrasive,** as an **insecticide carrier** and as a **lightweight aggregate,** and for other purposes. The diatomite was deposited in shallow fresh-water lakes that were present in the High Plains during portions of the Pliocene and Pleistocene epochs. Deposits have been found in Armstrong, Crosby, Dickens, Ector, Hartley and Lamb counties. No diatomite is mined in Texas.

DOLOMITE ROCK — Dolomite rock, which consists

largely of the mineral dolomite (calcium-magnesium carbonate), commonly is associated with limestone in Texas. Areas in which dolomite rock occurs include Central Texas, the Callahan Divide and parts of the Edwards Plateau, High Plains and West Texas. Some of the principal deposits of dolomite rock are found in Bell, Brown, Burnet, Comanche, Edwards, El Paso, Gillespie, Lampasas, Mills, Nolan, Taylor and Williamson counties. Dolomite rock can be used as crushed stone (although much of Texas dolomite is soft and not a good aggregate material), in the manufacture of lime and as a source of **magnesium**.

FELDSPAR — Large crystals and crystal fragments of feldspar minerals occur in the Precambrian pegmatite rocks that crop out in the **Llano Uplift** area of Central Texas — including Blanco, Burnet, Gillespie, Llano and Mason counties — and in the **Van Horn area** of Culberson and Hudspeth Counties in West Texas. Feldspar has been mined in Llano County for use as **roofing granules** and as a **ceramic material**, but is not currently mined anywhere within the state.

FLUORSPAR — The mineral fluorite (calcium fluoride), which is known commercially as fluorspar, occurs in both Central and West Texas. In Central Texas, the deposits that have been found in Burnet, Gillespie and Mason counties are not considered adequate to sustain mining operations. In West Texas, deposits have been found in Brewster, El Paso, Hudspeth, Jeff Davis and Presidio counties. Fluorspar has been mined in the **Christmas Mountains** of Brewster County and processed in Marathon. Former West Texas mining activity in the **Eagle Mountains** district of Hudspeth County resulted in the production of approximately 15,000 short tons of fluorspar during the peak years of 1942-1950. No production has been reported in Hudspeth County since that period. Imported fluorspar is processed in Brownsville, Eagle Pass, El Paso and Houston. Fluorspar is used in the **steel, chemical, aluminum, magnesium, ceramics and glass industries** and for various other purposes.

FULLER'S EARTH (see CLAY).

GOLD — No major deposits of gold are known in Texas. Small amounts have been found in the **Llano Uplift** region of Central Texas and in West Texas; minor occurrences have been reported on the **Edwards Plateau** and the **Gulf Coastal Plain** of Texas. Nearly all of the gold produced in the state came as a by-product of silver and lead mining at **Presidio mine**, near **Shafter**, in Presidio County. Additional small quantities were produced as a by-product of copper mining in Culberson County and from residual soils developed from gold-bearing quartz stringers in metamorphic rocks in Llano County. No gold mining has been reported in Texas since 1952. Total **gold production** in the state, 1889-1952, amounted to more than 8,419 troy ounces according to U.S. Bureau of Mines figures. Most of the production — at least 73 percent and probably more — came from the Presidio mine.

GRANITE — Granites in shades of red and gray and related intrusive igneous rocks occur in the **Llano Uplift** of Central Texas and in the **Trans-Pecos** country of West Texas. Deposits are found in Blanco, Brewster, Burnet, El Paso, Gillespie, Hudspeth, Llano, McCulloch, Mason, Presidio and other counties. Quarries in Burnet, Gillespie, Llano and Mason counties produce Precambrian granite for a variety of uses as **dimension stone and crushed stone**.

GRAPHITE — Graphite, a soft, dark-gray mineral, is a form of very high-grade carbon. It occurs in Precambrian schist rocks of the **Llano Uplift** of Central Texas, notably in Burnet and Llano counties. Crystalline-flake graphite ore formerly was mined from open pits in the **Clear Creek area** of western Burnet County and processed at a plant near the mine. The mill now occasionally grinds imported material. Uses of natural crystalline graphite are in **refractories, steel production, pencil leads, lubricants, foundry facings and crucibles** and for other purposes.

GRINDING PEBBLES (ABRASIVE STONES) — Flint pebbles, suitable for use in **tube-mill grinding**, are found in the **Gulf Coastal Plain** where they occur in gravel deposits along rivers and in upland areas. Grinding pebbles are produced from **Frio River terrace** deposits near the McMullen-Live Oak county line, but the area is now part of the Choke Canyon Reservoir area.

GYPSUM — Gypsum is widely distributed in Texas. Chief deposits are bedded gypsum in the area east of the **High Plains**, in the **Trans-Pecos** country and in **Central Texas**. It also occurs in **salt-dome caprocks** of the Gulf Coast. The massive, granular variety known as rock gypsum is the kind most commonly used by industry. Other varieties include **alabaster, satin spar and selenite**.

Gypsum is one of the important industrial minerals in Texas. Bedded gypsum is produced from surface mines in Culberson, Fisher, Gillespie, Hardeman, Hudspeth, Kimble, Nolan and Stonewall counties. Gypsum was formerly mined at **Gyp Hill salt dome** in Brooks County and at **Hockley salt dome** in Harris County. Most of the gypsum is calcined and used in the manufacture of **gypsum wallboard, plaster, joint compounds** and other construction products. Crude gypsum is used chiefly as a **retarder in portland cement** and as a **soil conditioner**.

HELIUM — Texas is a leading producer of this very light, non-flammable, chemically inert gas. Helium is extracted from natural gas of the **Panhandle area** at the **U.S. Bureau of Mines Exell plant** near Masterson in Moore County and at two privately owned plants in Moore and Hansford counties. As a conservation measure, the Bureau of Mines injects the helium that is not sold when the gas is produced into the **Cliffside gas field** near Amarillo for storage. Helium is used in **cryogenics, welding, pressurizing and purging, leak detection, synthetic breathing mixtures** and for other purposes.

IRON — Iron oxide (**limonite, goethite and hematite**) and **iron carbonate (siderite)** deposits occur widely in East Texas, notably in Cass, Cherokee, Marion and Morris counties, and also in Anderson, Camp, Harrison, Henderson, Nacogdoches, Smith, Upshur and other counties. **Magnetite (magnetic, black iron oxide)** occurs in Central Texas, including a deposit at **Iron Mountain** in Llano County. Hematite occurs in the **Trans-Pecos** area and in the **Llano Uplift** of Central Texas. The extensive deposits of **glauconite** (a complex silicate containing iron) that occur in East Texas and the hematitic and goethitic Cambrian sandstone that crops out in the northwestern Llano Uplift region are potential sources of low-grade iron ore.

Limonite and other East Texas iron ores are mined from open pits in Cherokee and Henderson counties for use in the preparation of **portland cement**, as a **weighting agent in well-drilling fluids**, as an **animal feed supplement** and for other purposes. East Texas iron ores also were mined in the past for use in the iron-steel industry.

KAOLIN (see CLAY).

LEAD AND ZINC — The lead mineral **galena (lead sulfide)** commonly is associated with zinc and silver. It formerly was produced as a by-product of West Texas silver mining, chiefly from the **Presidio mine at Shafter** in Presidio County, although lesser amounts were obtained at several other mines and prospects. Deposits of galena also are known to occur in Blanco, Brewster, Burnet, Gillespie and Hudspeth counties.

Zinc, primarily from the mineral **sphalerite (zinc sulphide)**, was produced chiefly from the **Bonanza** and **Alice Ray** mines in the **Quitman Mountains** of Hudspeth County. In addition, small production was reported from several other areas, including the **Chinati** and **Montezuma mines** of Presidio County and the **Buck Prospect** in the **Apache Mountains** of Culberson County. Zinc mineralization also occurs in association with the lead deposits in Cambrian rocks of Central Texas.

LEONARDITE — Deposits of weathered (oxidized) low-Btu value bituminous coals, generally referred to as "leonardite," occur in Brewster County. The name leonardite is used for a mixture of chemical compounds that is high in humic acids. In the past, material from these deposits was sold as **soil conditioner**. Other uses of leonardite include **modification of viscosity of drill fluids and as sorbants in water-treatment**.

LIGHTWEIGHT AGGREGATE (see CLAY, DIATOMITE, PERLITE, VERMICULITE).

LIGNITE — Lignite, a low-rank coal, is found in belts of Tertiary Eocene strata that extend across the Texas Gulf Coastal Plain from the Rio Grande in South Texas to the Arkansas and Louisiana borders in East Texas. The largest resources and best grades (approximately 6,500 BTU/pound) of lignite occur in the Wilcox Group of strata north of the Colorado River in East and Central Texas.

The near-surface lignite resources, occurring at depths of less than 200 feet in seams of three feet or thicker, are estimated at 23 billion short tons. **Recoverable reserves of strippable lignite** — those that can be economically mined under current conditions of price and technology — are estimated to be 9 billion to 11 billion short tons.

Additional lignite resources of the Texas Gulf Coastal Plain occur as deep-basin deposits. Deep-basin resources, those that occur at depths of 200 to 2,000 feet in seams of five feet or thicker, are comparable in magnitude to near-surface resources. The deep-basin lignites are a potential energy resource that conceivably could be utilized by *in situ* (in place) recovery methods such as underground gasification.

As with bituminous coal, lignite production was significant prior to the general availability of oil and gas. Remnants of old underground mines are common throughout the area of lignite occurrence. Large reserves of strippable lignite have again attracted the attention of energy suppliers, and Texas is now the nation's **6th leading producer of coal,** 99 percent of it lignite. Eleven large strip mines are now producing lignite that is burned for **mine-mouth electric-power generation,** and additional mines are planned. One of the currently operating mines is located in Milam County, where part of the electric power is used for **alumina reduction.** Other mines are in Atascosa, Bastrop, Freestone, Grimes, Harrison, Limestone, Rusk, Panola, Titus and Hopkins counties, where the electricity generated supplies municipal, domestic and industrial needs. Another Harrison County strip mine produces lignite that is used to make **activated carbon.**

LIME MATERIAL — Limestones, which are abundant in some areas of Texas, are heated to produce lime (calcium oxide) at a number of plants in the state. High-magnesium limestone and dolomite are used to prepare lime at a plant in Burnet County. Other lime plants are located in Bexar, Bosque, Comal, Hill, Johnson and Travis counties. Lime production captive to the kiln's operator occurs in several Texas counties. Lime is used in **soil stabilization, water purification, paper and pulp manufacture, metallurgy, sugar refining, agriculture, construction, removal of sulfur from stack gases** and for many other purposes.

LIMESTONE (see also **BUILDING STONE**) — Texas is one of the nation's leading producers of limestone, which is quarried in more than 60 counties. Limestone occurs in nearly all areas of the state with the exception of most of the Gulf Coastal Plain and High Plains. Although some of the limestone is quarried for use as **dimension stone,** most of the output is crushed for uses such as **bulk building materials (crushed stone, road base, concrete aggregate), chemical raw materials, fillers or extenders, lime and portland cement raw materials, agricultural limestone and removal of sulfur from stack gases.**

MAGNESITE — Small deposits of magnesite (natural magnesium carbonate) have been found in Precambrian rocks in Llano and Mason counties of Central Texas. At one time there was small-scale mining of magnesite in the area; some of the material was used as **agricultural stone** and as **terrazzo chips.** Magnesite also can be calcined to form **magnesia,** which is used in **metallurgical furnace refractories** and other products.

MAGNESIUM — On the Texas Gulf Coast in Brazoria County, magnesium chloride is **extracted from sea water** at a plant in Freeport and used to produce **magnesium compounds and magnesium metal.** During World War II, high-magnesium Ellenburger dolomite rock from Burnet County was used as magnesium ore at a plant near Austin.

MANGANESE — Deposits of manganese minerals, such as **braunite, hollandite and pyrolusite,** have been found in several areas, including Jeff Davis, Llano, Mason, Presidio and Val Verde counties. Known deposits are not large. Small shipments have been made from Jeff Davis, Mason and Val Verde counties, but no manganese mining has been reported in Texas since 1954.

MARBLE — Metamorphic and sedimentary marbles suitable for **monument and building stone** are found in the **Llano Uplift** and nearby areas of Central Texas and the **Trans-Pecos** area of West Texas. Gray, white, black, greenish black, light green, brown and cream-colored marbles occur in Central Texas in Burnet, Gillespie, Llano and Mason counties. West Texas metamorphic marbles include the bluish-white and the black marbles found southwest of Alpine in Brewster County and the white marble from **Marble Canyon** north of Van Horn in Culberson County. Marble can be used as **dimension stone, terrazzo and roofing aggregate** and for other purposes.

MERCURY (QUICKSILVER) — Mercury minerals, chiefly **cinnabar,** occur in the **Terlingua district** and nearby districts of southern Brewster and southeastern Presidio counties. Mining began there about 1894, and from 1905 to 1935, Texas was one of the nation's leading producers of quicksilver. Following World War II, a sharp drop in demand and price, along with depletion of developed ore reserves, caused abandonment of all the Texas mercury mines.

With a rise in the price, sporadic mining took place between 1951-1960. In 1965, when the price of mercury moved to a record high, renewed interest in the Texas mercury districts resulted in the reopening of several mines and the discovery of new ore reserves. By April 1972, however, the price had declined and the mines have reported no production since 1973.

MICA — Large crystals of flexible, transparent mica minerals in igneous pegmatite rocks and mica flakes in metamorphic schist rocks are found in the **Llano area** of Central Texas and the **Van Horn area** of West Texas. Most Central Texas deposits do not meet specifications for sheet mica, and although several attempts have been made to produce West Texas sheet mica in Culberson and Hudspeth counties, sustained production has not been achieved. A mica quarry operated for a short time in the early 1980s in the Van Horn Mountains of Culberson and Hudspeth counties to mine mica schist for use as an **additive in rotary drilling fluids.**

MOLYBDENUM — Small occurrences of molybdenite have been found in Burnet and Llano counties, and **wulfenite,** another molybdenum mineral, has been noted in rocks in the **Quitman Mountains** of Hudspeth County. Molybdenum minerals also occur at **Cave Peak** north of Van Horn in Culberson County, in the **Altuda Mountain area** of northwestern Brewster County and in association with uranium ores off the Gulf Coastal Plain.

PEAT — This spongy organic substance forms in bogs from plant remains. It has been found in the **Gulf Coastal Plain** in several localities including Gonzales, Guadalupe, Lee, Milam, Polk and San Jacinto counties. There has been intermittent, small-scale production of some of the peat for use as a **soil conditioner.**

PERLITE — Perlite, a glassy igneous rock, expands to a lightweight, porous mass when heated. It can be used as a **lightweight aggregate, filter aid, horticultural aggregate** and for other purposes. Perlite occurs in Presidio County, where it has been mined in the **Pinto Canyon area** north of the **Chinati Mountains.** No perlite is currently mined in Texas, but perlite mined outside of Texas is expanded at plants in Bexar, Dallas, El Paso, Guadalupe, Harris and Nolan counties.

PHOSPHATE — Rock phosphate is present in Paleozoic rocks in several areas of Brewster and Presidio counties in West Texas and in Central Texas, but the known deposits are not large. In Northeast Texas, sedimentary rock phosphate occurs in thin conglomeratic lenses in Upper Cretaceous and Tertiary rock units; possibly some of these low-grade phosphorites could be processed on a small scale for local use as a **fertilizer.** Imported phosphate rock is processed at a plant in Brownsville.

POTASH — The potassium mineral **polyhalite** is widely distributed in the subsurface Permian Basin of West Texas and has been found in many wells in that area. During 1927-1931, the federal government drilled a series of potash-test wells in Crane, Crockett, Ector, Glasscock, Loving, Reagan, Upton and Winkler counties. In addition to polyhalite, which was found in all of the counties, these wells revealed the presence of the potassium minerals **carnallite and sylvite** in Loving County and carnallite in Winkler County. The known Texas potash deposits are not as rich as those in the New Mexico portion of the Permian Basin and have not been developed.

PUMICITE (VOLCANIC ASH) — Deposits of volcanic ash occur in Brazos, Fayette, Gonzales, Karnes, Polk, Starr and other counties of the Texas Coastal Plain. Deposits also have been found in the Trans-Pecos area, High Plains and in several counties east of the High Plains. Volcanic ash is used to prepare **pozzolan cement, cleansing and scouring compounds and soaps and sweeping compounds**; as a **carrier for insecticides**, and for other purposes. It has been mined in Dickens, Lynn, Scurry, Starr and other counties.

QUICKSILVER (see **MERCURY**).

RARE-EARTH ELEMENTS AND METALS — The term, "rare-earth elements," is commonly applied to elements of the **lanthanide** group (atomic numbers 57 through 71) plus **yttrium**. Yttrium, atomic number 39 and not a member of the lanthanide group, is included as a rare-earth element because it has similar properties to members of that group and usually occurs in nature with them. The metals **thorium and scandium** are sometimes termed "rare metals" because their occurence is often associated with the rare-earth elements.

The majority of rare-earth elements are consumed as **catalysts** in petroleum cracking and other chemical industries. Rare earths are widely used in the **glass industry for tableware, specialty glasses, optics and fiber optics**. Cerium oxide has growing use as a **polishing compound** for glass, gem stones, cathode-ray tube faceplates, and other polishing. Rare earths are alloyed with various metals to produce materials used in the **aeronautic, space and electronics** industries. Addition of rare-earth elements may improve resistance to metal fatigue at high temperatures, reduce potential for corrosion, and selectively increase conductivity and magnetism of the metal.

Various members of this group, including **thorium**, have anomalous concentrations in the **rhyolitic and related igneous rocks** of the **Quitman Mountains** and the **Sierra Blanca area** of Trans-Pecos.

SALT (SODIUM CHLORIDE) (see also **BRINES**) — Salt resources of Texas are virtually inexhaustible. Enormous deposits occur in the subsurface **Permian Basin** of West Texas and in the **salt domes of the Gulf Coastal Plain**. Salt also is found in the alkali **playa lakes** of the High Plains, the **alkali flats or salt lakes in the Salt Basin** of Culberson and Hudspeth counties and along some of the bays and lagoons of the South Texas **Gulf Coast**.

Texas is one of the leading salt-producing states. **Rock salt** is obtained from underground mines in **salt domes at Grand Saline** in Van Zandt County. Approximately one-third of the salt produced in the state is from rock salt; most of the salt is produced by solution mining as brines from wells drilled into the underground salt deposits.

SAND, INDUSTRIAL — Sands used for special purposes, due to **high silica content** or to unique physical properties, command higher prices than common sand. Industrial sands in Texas occur mainly in the **Central Gulf Coastal Plain** and in **North Central Texas**. They include **abrasive, blast, chemical, engine, filtration, foundry, glass, hydraulic-fracturing (propant), molding and pottery sands**. Recent production of industrial sands has been from Atascosa, Colorado, Hardin, Harris, Liberty, Limestone, McCulloch, Newton, Smith, Somervell and Upshur counties.

SAND AND GRAVEL (CONSTRUCTION) — Sand and gravel are among the most extensively utilized resources in Texas. Principal occurrence is along the major streams and in stream terraces. Sand and gravel are important **bulk construction materials, used as railroad ballast, base materials** and for other purposes.

SANDSTONE — Sandstones of a variety of colors and textures are widely distributed in a number of geologic formations in Texas. Some of the sandstones have been quarried for use as **dimension stone** in El Paso, Parker, Terrell, Ward and other counties. **Crushed sandstone** is produced in Freestone, Gaines, Jasper, McMullen, Motley and other counties for use as **road-building material, terrazzo stone and aggregate**.

SERPENTINITE — Several masses of serpentinite, which formed from the alteration of basic igneous rocks, are associated with other Precambrian metamorphic rocks of the **Llano Uplift**. The largest deposit is the **Coal Creek serpentinite mass** in northern Blanco and Gillespie counties from which **terrazzo chips** have been produced. Other deposits are present in Gillespie and Llano counties. (The features that are associated with surface and subsurface Cretaceous rocks in several counties in or near the **Balcones Fault Zone** and that are commonly known as **"serpentine plugs"** are not serpentine at all, but are altered igneous volcanic necks and pipes and mounds of altered volcanic ash — **palagonite** — that accumulated around the former **submarine volcanic pipes**.)

SHELL — Oyster shells and other shells in shallow coastal waters and in deposits along the **Texas Gulf Coast** have been produced in the past chiefly by dredging. They were used to a limited extent as raw material in the **manufacture of cement, as concrete aggregate and road base**, and for other purposes. No shell has been produced in Texas since 1981.

SILVER — During the period 1885-1952, the production of silver in Texas, as reported by the U.S. Bureau of Mines, totaled about **33 million troy ounces**. For about 70 years, silver was the most consistently produced metal in Texas, although always in moderate quantities. All of the production came from the **Trans-Pecos country** of West Texas, where the silver was mined in Brewster County (**Altuda Mountain**), Culberson and Hudspeth counties (**Van Horn Mountains and Van Horn-Allamoore district**), Hudspeth County (**Quitman Mountains and Eagle Mountains**) and Presidio County (**Chinati Mountains area, Loma Plata mine and Shafter district**).

Chief producer was the **Presidio mine in the Shafter district**, which began operations in the late 1800s, and, through September 1942, produced more than 30 million ounces of silver — more than 92 percent of Texas' total silver production. Water in the lower mine levels, lean ores and low price of silver resulted in the closing of the mine in 1942. Another important silver producer was the **Hazel copper-silver mine** in the **Van Horn-Allamoore district** in Culberson County, which accounted for more than 2 million ounces.

An increase in the price of silver in the late 1970s stimulated prospecting for new reserves, and exploration began near the old **Presidio mine**, near the old **Plata Verde mine** in the Van Horn Mountains district, at the **Bonanza mine** in the **Quitman Mountains** district and at the old **Hazel mine**. A decline in the price of silver in the early 1980s, however, resulted in reduction of exploration and mine development in the region. There is no current exploration in these areas.

SOAPSTONE (see **TALC AND SOAPSTONE**).

SODIUM SULFATE (SALT CAKE) — Sodium sulfate minerals occur in salt beds and brines of the alkali **playa lakes** of the High Plains in West Texas. In some lakes, the sodium sulfate minerals are present in deposits a few feet beneath the lakebeds. Sodium sulfate also is found in underground brines in the Permian Basin. Current production is from brines and dry salt beds at alkali lakes in Gaines and Terry counties. Past production was reported in Lynn and Ward counties. Sodium sulfate is used chiefly by the **detergent and paper and pulp industries**. Other uses are in the **preparation of glass and other products**.

STONE (see **BUILDING STONE** and **CRUSHED STONE**).

STRONTIUM — Deposits of the mineral **celestite (strontium sulfate)** have been found in a number of places, including localities in Brown, Coke, Comanche, Fisher, Lampasas, Mills, Nolan, Real, Taylor, Travis and Williamson counties. Most of the occurrences are very minor, and no strontium is currently produced in the state.

SULFUR — Texas is **one of the world's principal sulfur-producing areas**. The sulfur is mined from deposits of native sulfur, and it is extracted from sour (sulfur-bearing) natural gas and petroleum. **Recovered sulfur** is a growing industry and accounted for approximately 60 percent of all 1987 sulfur production in the United States, but only approximately 40 percent of Texas production. Native sulfur is found in large deposits in the caprock of some of the **salt domes** along the Texas Gulf Coast and in some of the surface and subsurface Permian strata of West Texas, notably in Culberson and Pecos counties.

Native sulfur obtained from the underground deposits is known as **Frasch sulfur**, so-called because of Herman Frasch, the chemist who devised the method of drilling wells into the deposits, melting the sulfur with superheated water and forcing the molten sulfur to the surface. Most of the production now goes to the users in molten form.

Frasch sulfur is produced from only one Gulf Coast salt dome in Wharton County and from West Texas underground Permian strata in Culberson County. Operations at several Gulf

Coast domes have been closed in recent years. During the 1940s, acidic sulfur earth was produced in the **Rustler Springs district** in Culberson County for use as a **fertilizer and soil conditioner.** Sulfur is recovered from sour natural gas and petroleum at plants in numerous Texas counties.

Sulfur is used in the preparation of **fertilizers and organic and inorganic chemicals, in petroleum refining** and for many other purposes.

TALC AND SOAPSTONE — Deposits of talc are found in the Precambrian metamorphic rocks of the **Allamoore area** of eastern Hudspeth and western Culberson counties. Soapstone, containing talc, occurs in the Precambrian metamorphic rocks of the **Llano Uplift** area, notably in Blanco, Gillespie and Llano counties. Current production is from surface mines in the **Allamoore area.** Talc is used in **ceramic, roofing, paint, paper, plastic, synthetic rubber** and other products.

TIN — Tin minerals have been found in El Paso and Mason counties. Small quantities were produced during the early 1900s in the Franklin Mountains north of El Paso. **Cassiterite (tin dioxide)** occurrences in Mason County are believed to be very minor. The **only tin smelter in the United States,** built at **Texas City** by the federal government during World War II and later sold to a private company, processes tin concentrates from ores mined outside of Texas, tin residues and secondary tin-bearing materials.

TITANIUM — The titanium mineral **rutile** has been found in small amounts at the **Mueller prospect** in Jeff Davis County. Another titanium mineral, **ilmenite,** occurs in sandstones in Burleson, Fayette, Lee, Starr and several other counties. Deposits that would be considered commercial under present conditions have not been found.

TRAP ROCK (see **BASALT**).

TUNGSTEN — The tungsten mineral **scheelite** has been found in small deposits in Gillespie and Llano counties and in the **Quitman Mountains** in Hudspeth County. Small deposits of other tungsten minerals have been prospected in the **Cave Peak area** north of Van Horn in Culberson County.

URANIUM — Uranium deposits were discovered in the **Texas Coastal Plain** in 1954 when abnormal radioactivity was detected in the Karnes County area. A number of uranium deposits have since been discovered within a belt of strata extending more than 250 miles from the middle Coastal Plain southwestward to the Rio Grande.

Various uranium minerals also have been found in other areas of Texas, including the **Trans-Pecos,** the **Llano Uplift** and the **High Plains.** With the exception of small shipments from the High Plains during the 1950s, all the uranium production in Texas has been from the Coastal Plain. Uranium has been obtained from surface mines extending from northern Live Oak County, southeastern Atascosa County, across northern Karnes County and into southern Gonzales County.

All mines are now reclaimed. All current uranium production is by **in-situ leaching,** brought to the surface through wells, and stripped from the solution at several Coastal Plain recovery operations. Decreased demand and price of uranium since 1980 has brought a sharp decline in operations in Texas.

VERMICULITE — Vermiculite, a mica-like mineral that expands when heated, occurs in Burnet, Gillespie, Llano, Mason and other counties in the **Llano region.** It has been produced at a surface mine in Llano County. Vermiculite, mined outside of Texas, is exfoliated (expanded) at plants in Dallas, Houston and San Antonio. Exfoliated vermiculite is used for **lightweight concrete aggregate, horticulture, insulation** and other purposes.

VOLCANIC ASH (see **PUMICITE**).

ZEOLITES — The zeolite minerals **clinoptilolite** and **analcime** occur in Tertiary lavas and tuffs in Brewster, Jeff Davis and Presidio counties, in West Texas. Clinoptilolite also is found associated with Tertiary tuffs in the southern Texas Coastal Plain, including deposits in Karnes, McMullen and Webb counties, and currently is produced in McMullen County. Zeolites, sometimes called **"molecular sieves,"** can be used in **ion-exchange processes to reduce pollution,** as a catalyst in **oil cracking,** in obtaining **high-purity oxygen and nitrogen** from air, in **water purification** and for many other purposes.

ZINC (see **LEAD AND ZINC**). ☆

Insurance in Texas

The **State Board of Insurance** reported that on Aug. 31, 1996, there were **2,668** firms licensed to handle insurance business in Texas, including **809** Texas firms and **1,859** out-of-state companies.

Annual premium income of firms operating in Texas caused Dallas and some other cities to rank among the nation's major insurance centers.

The former **Robertson Law,** enacted in 1907 and repealed in 1963, encouraged the establishment of many Texas insurance firms.

It required life insurance companies operating in the state to invest in Texas three-fourths of all reserves held for payment of policies written in the state.

Many out-of-state firms withdrew from Texas. Later many companies re-entered Texas and the law was liberalized and then repealed.

The State Board of Insurance administers legislation relating to the insurance business. This agency was established in 1957, following discovery of irregularities in some firms.

It succeeded two previous regulatory groups, established in 1913 and changed in 1927.

The governor appoints the three-member board, which, in turn, appoints the **State Commissioner of Insurance.**

The commissioner serves as chief administrator of the agency and has other powers with which to regulate the insurance industry. In 1991, the legislature moved to revise the operation of the commission.

Companies in Texas

The following table shows the number and kinds of insurance companies licensed in Texas on Aug. 31, 1996:

Type of Insurance	Texas	Out-of-State	Total
Stock Life...................	168	594	762
Mutual Life.................	2	73	75
Stipulated Premium Life.........	53	...	53
Non-profit Life	...	1	1
Stock Fire..................	1	5	6
Stock Fire and Casualty.........	109	647	756
Mutual Fire and Casualty........	7	60	67
Stock Casualty...............	8	85	93
Mexican Casualty	...	9	9
Lloyds	68	...	68
Reciprocal Exchanges..........	13	15	28
Fraternal Benefit Societies.......	10	27	37
Titles......................	5	18	23
Non-profit Legal Services	2	...	2
Health Maintenance............	59	3	62
Risk Retention Groups..........	1	...	1
Multiple Employers Welfare Arrang.	9	2	11
Joint Underwriting Associations...	...	6	6
Third Party Administrators.......	201	312	513
Continuing Care Retirement Communities.................	17	2	19
Total	**733**	**1,859**	**2,592**
Statewide Mutual Assessment....	1	0	1
Local Mutual Aid Associations....	13	0	13
Burial Associations	3	0	3
Exempt Associations	12	0	12
Non-profit Hospital Service	3	0	3
County Mutual Fire	24	0	24
Farm Mutual Fire..............	20	0	20
Total	**76**		**76**
Grand Total	**809**	**1,859**	**2,668**

Public Utilities: Telecommunications Lead Growth

By Jennifer Files

Telecommunications is one of Texas' fastest-growing industries, employing more than 100,000 workers, up from 81,000 in 1988.

Texas is home to the nation's two largest local telephone companies, dozens of other large service providers and manufacturers, and hundreds of smaller supplier companies.

Vast legal reforms, intense competition and technological uncertainties have accompanied the growth, making the 1990s a turbulent decade for telecommunications.

Three out of four Texas telephone customers — and nearly all of the state's big-city residents — buy local phone service from Southwestern Bell, a local phone unit of San Antonio-based SBC Communications. Southwestern Bell has **8.1 million** Texas access lines.

Formerly a part of AT&T, SBC became the nation's largest local phone company in 1997, when it completed the $16.5 billion acquisition of Pacific Telesis. Now, it has revenue of $23.5 billion and 25 percent of the local phone market in the United States.

Besides Texas, Southwestern Bell serves Arkansas, Kansas, Missouri and Oklahoma, while Pacific Telesis dominates the California and Nevada markets.

GTE Corp. provides local phone service to 16 percent of Texans, with 1.6 million access lines, mainly in suburbs or rural markets. GTE announced in 1997 that it would move its headquarters from Stamford, Conn., to the Las Colinas suburb of Dallas, where its telecommunications operations were already located.

Nearly 60 other companies provide residential local telephone service in Texas. Most have fewer than 5,000 access lines, but together they cover 40 percent of the state's land. The largest of these providers include Border to Border Communications, with 186,401 access lines; Central Telephone of Texas, with 177,179 lines; United Telephone Company of Texas, with 134,447 lines; and, Lufkin-Conroe Telephone Exchange, with 79,859 lines.

Until recently, business and the government believed a telephone system would operate most efficiently if only one company provided the service, saving billions of dollars in costs of building duplicate networks. As technology improved, telecommunications businesses saw opportunities to sell to customers outside their traditional service areas.

Telephone companies started trying to find ways to transmit information fast enough to provide television services. They also wanted to jump into the already competitive long-distance industry, while long-distance businesses were interested in a piece of the local phone markets. At the same time, cable companies, whose expensive networks already passed millions of homes in Texas, began testing ways those cable lines could carry telephone service.

Leaders across all sectors of the industry laid vast plans for becoming not just bigger phone or cable companies, but full-scale telecommunications companies able to sell all those services and more.

Companies saw deregulation as a way to sell a variety of new services to their existing customers. Customers liked the idea of doing business with just one company and getting a single phone bill for all their telecommunications purchases.

The Texas Public Utility Regulatory Act of 1995, effective Sept. 1995, proposed to open the state's phone markets to competition. Big long distance companies would have had to build their own local phone networks, however, and they complained that would be prohibitively expensive.

The federal Telecommunications Act of 1996, signed by President Clinton in Feb. 1996, set different terms for competition.

It ordered AT&T's former local phone divisions, known as the Baby Bells, to open their local phone territories to competition before they could sell long-distance services there.

One exception: GTE was allowed to enter the long-distance market immediately because it did not already dominate large U.S. regions. GTE's lucrative head start over its Baby Bell competitors allowed it to reach 1 million long distance customers within about one year after the law passed.

Competition has been slow in coming. Major local and long-distance companies have argued in private negotiations, arbitration hearings and courtrooms over how to structure the financial deals. Once deals are reached, technical problems, including how to transfer customers to a new company, cause further delays in true local phone competition.

By mid-1997, Texas local phone competition exists only in a few cases, usually with highly profitable business customers.

Crossing over between telephone and cable industries has proved even harder to achieve. Southwestern Bell discontinued a trial of cable TV services in Richardson, and most of its competitors have also scaled back such plans or put them on hold.

The 1997 legislative session brought no reforms to

Telephones in Texas

Source: Southwestern Bell. The table refers to access lines.

City	1994	1997
Abilene	64,625	66,862
Amarillo	107,078	110,871
Arlington	128,143	134,176
Austin (Metro)	526,434	550,237
Bay City	12,758	14,300
Beaumont	71,920	75,041
Brownsville-Harlingen	90,733	94,428
Cleburne	21,409	22,476
Corpus Christi (Metro)	147,532	153,022
Corsicana	14,431	14,854
Dallas (Metro)	1,149,379	1,226,721
El Paso	274,209	271,756
Fort Worth	553,600	586,208
Galveston	38,267	39,043
Greenville	15,568	16,051
Houston	1,746,992	1,802,024
Laredo	65,342	68,512
Longview	59,036	61,407
Lubbock	131,305	137,106
McAllen-Edinburg	74,585	81,367
McKinney	19,672	22,853
Midland	70,739	72,361
Mineral Wells	9,244	9,468
Odessa	62,447	64,526
Paris	20,974	21,664
Port Arthur	33,276	33,438
San Antonio (Metro)	689,409	725,910
Temple	32,064	34,196
Texas City	15,951	16,249
Tyler	70,530	74,030
Vernon	6,906	6,997
Victoria	39,627	40,864
Waco	103,414	105,798
Wichita Falls	58,119	60,041

rival the landmark legislation of the previous two years, but some new laws will affect consumers and companies.

— Senate Bill 1581 forced telemarketing firms that claim to represent charities to register with the state Attorney General's office, and to disclose what percentage of receipts will go toward the firm's fees and profits.

— Under House Bill 2128, telemarketers may not block caller ID information.

— Possibly the highest-impact new law is Senate Bill 253, which gives the Public Utility Commission stronger powers to stop "slamming" or switching a person's long-distance provider without their permission. Companies that can't prove a customer consented to the change must refund the customer any overcharges, repay the former long-distance provider for the cost of calls made while the customer was switched, and switch the customer back for free. When companies repeat slamming violations, the commission may fine them or suspend their license to do business in Texas.

Improved technology has driven change and heightened competition in other telecommunications services sectors, including wireless telephone and paging services, cable and the Internet. Until recently, pagers and wireless phones were niche services for doctors, stockbrokers or real estate agents. Computer modems were so slow that words crawled across the screens, and the few dial-up databases that existed required complex codes for finding information that most consumers didn't bother to learn.

Families either had cable or they didn't; the monopoly companies had no competition.

Today's pagers can transmit headline news, stock quotes or voice messages. Cell phones have shrunk, with better call quality. Modems are speedier, and, with the Internet and online services such as America Online and CompuServe, the information customers can find via computer turned immensely more interesting. And new digital satellite service has become the fastest-growing consumer product in history, challenging an entrenched cable sector to improve service or lose customers.

Like more traditional phone companies, many of the businesses that sell new telecommunications services picked Texas for their home. Dallas and Plano are home to so many large paging operations that North Texas has been dubbed the "Paging Prairie."

Three of the nation's biggest paging companies are based in North Texas: Paging Network, the largest paging provider, has 9.5 million subscribers, while PageMart and ProNet have 2.0 million and 1.3 million, respectively. A fourth paging company, MobileMedia, owns a customer service center employing 1,000 in the Red Bird area of southern Dallas. A victim of its own growth, MobileMedia is operating under Chapter 11 bankruptcy protection.

Paging companies introduced several new products in 1996 and 1997. Two-way messaging allows customers to reply to messages, usually by selecting a predetermined code. Voice paging works like a tiny answering machine, sending short messages that users can play, rewind or store.

So far, customer response has been mixed. Paging investors are generally more skeptical about the industry, which spent billions on networks and has never been profitable except in small niches. Paging stocks have fallen sharply, and analysts say some companies will probably not survive over the long term.

Competition is also increasing in the wireless telephone industry, as the the federal goverment auctioned off new licenses to broadcast phone signals.

Older companies provide traditional cellular phone service, either through analog systems, which transmit speech through the air in waves, or through updated digital systems, which send the signals in groups of zeros and ones.

Newer wireless providers sell a new kind of system called Personal Communications Services. PCS, a digital system, offers clearer voice quality and less static, though calls can still be disconnected suddenly when signals get too weak. And unlike cellular networks, which generally work across most of the United States, PCS customers can make calls only in certain cities where companies have built networks.

Higher demand for new products has been a boon to equipment makers, concentrated in Richardson's Telecom Corridor, which increased sales as their telephone company customers install new networks or improve existing ones in the United States and other nations. The area includes the U.S. headquarters or major operations from some of the world's biggest telecommunications manufacturers, including Alcatel, DSC Communications, Ericcson, Fujitsu, Lucent, Northern Telecom, Philips Consumer Electronics and Samsung.

So many smaller companies have sprouted up to sell technology or services to these telecommunications giants that some businesses are complaining of a shortage of workers, leading community colleges to partner with corporations to develop courses that will do a better job of training students for telecom work.

A 1996 report by the North Texas Commission said the sector, combined with other communications and information industry business, is the third-largest industry in the Dallas-Fort Worth area, behind health care and the convention/tourism industry. The companies spent $22.9 billion, and paid wages and salaries of $6.2 billion.

By the mid-1990s, so many Texans bought new telecommunications services that the state's biggest cities literally ran out of telephone numbers.

Areas around Dallas, Houston, Fort Worth and San Antonio all received, or soon will, new area codes, forcing residents of the cities to dial 10 digits to make local calls for the first time. New codes include:

• In Houston, a new 281 area surrounds the city, which remains 713.

• Dallas' 214 area split so that most of the city keeps 214 while the suburbs switch to 972.

• The 817 area code divided into three: 940 for Denton and Wichita Falls, 254 for Waco and 817 for the Fort Worth metropolitan area.

• And, the 210 area broke into three area codes in July, with 830 serving Kerrville, Fredericksburg and Uvalde, 956 in Laredo and Brownsville, and San Antonio keeping 210.

The Public Utility Commission says Texas' biggest cities will need more new area codes before the turn of the century. ☆

Jennifer Files is a staff writer of The Dallas Morning News.

The Public Utility Commission of Texas, the Federal Reserve Bank of Dallas, the North Texas Commission and Southwestern Bell provided background information for this article. For more details on telecommunications competition in Texas, see the Public Utility Commission's Report to the Seventy-Fifth Texas Legislature on the Scope of Competition in Telecommunications Markets.

Electric Industry

Source: Texas Business Review, *Bureau of Business Research, UT-Austin.*

Texas is served by **ten** investor-owned electric utilities, **nineteen** municipal utilities (including San Antonio and Austin), **86** electric cooperatives and four river authorities.

These utilities provide electric services to about **7** million households and businesses, employ more than **40,000** workers, and earn annual revenues of about **$15** billion.

Texas Utilities Electric Company, serving the Dallas-Fort Worth metroplex and Central Texas, and Houston Lighting & Power Company are the two largest electric utilities in Texas. ☆

Electric Cooperatives

Source: The Texas Electric Cooperatives.

Electric cooperatives are nonprofit, consumer-owned utilities providing electric service primarily in rural areas.

They were organized in the 1930s and 1940s when investor-owned utilities neglected or refused to serve farms and rural communities.

By the end of 1996, there were **75** electric-distribution cooperatives serving over **1.2** million meters in **244** of the 254 counties in Texas.

There are also **11** generation and transmission cooperatives (G&Ts) that are owned by local distribution cooperatives. Three of the G&Ts generate power while the others represent their member distribution systems in wholesale power supply arrangements. The systems operate more than **260,000** miles of line with an average density of fewer than **5** meters per mile of line.

The distribution systems and G&Ts employ more than 5,500 persons. ☆

Gas Utilities

Approximately **211** investor-owned gas companies in Texas are classified as gas utilities and come under the regulatory jurisdiction of the Texas Railroad Commission. Approximately **135** of these companies reported gas operating revenue of **$5.1** billion in 1995, with operating expenses of **$5** billion.

In 1995, fixed investment for distribution facilities in Texas was **$2.2** billion and for transmission facilities, **$4.9** billion. Investment in Texas plants in service totaled **$8.77** billion. There were **34** investor-owned and **85** municipally owned distribution systems in operation in 1995 serving **1,017** Texas cities.

The **eight** largest distribution systems — six private and two municipal — served **97** percent of all residential customers. In 1995, there were approximately **3.4** million residential customers, **295,788** small commercial and industrial users, **232** large industrial customers and **10,994** other gas- utility customers. The breakdown of distribution sales to these customers was: **58** Mcf (thousand cubic feet) per residential customer, **496** Mcf per commercial customer, **192,063** Mcf per industrial customer and **3,082** Mcf for customers in the "other" category. Distribution sales amounted to **404.2** billion cubic feet in 1995.

In addition to industrial sales made by distribution companies, transmission companies reported pipeline-to-industry sales of **1.3** trillion cubic feet and revenue from these sales of **$3.6** billion.

In 1995, the average annual residential gas bill in the United States was **$533**. The average annual bill in Texas for the same year was **$340**, down **$20** from the previous year. The State of Texas collected **$4.9** million in gas-utility taxes from gas utilities in fiscal year 1996.

Texas had a total of **123,525** miles of natural-gas pipelines in operation in 1995, including **9,957** miles of field and gathering lines, **39,021** miles of transmission lines and **74,547** miles of distribution lines. ☆

Texas Transportation System

Texas is a leader among the states in a number of transportation indicators, including total road and street mileage, total railroad mileage and total number of airports. Texas ranks second behind California in motor-vehicle registrations and in number of general-aviation aircraft.

The Texas transportation system includes more than 220,000 miles of municipal and rural highways, more than 13,000 miles of **railroad line**, approximately 1,600 **landing facilities** and 13 major **Gulf Coast ports**. Texans own and operate almost 15 million motor vehicles and about 21,000 aircraft.

The transportation industry is a major employer in Texas. Texas Employment Commission statistics indicate that transportation employs more than 300,000 Texans.

The largest group, 108,637, is employed in trucking and warehousing. Railroads employ 11,400, air transportation 77,492 and water transportation 16,030.

The largest state government agency involved in transportation, the **Texas Department of Transportation**, is responsible for highways, motor vehicles and aviation. The **Railroad Commission** has intrastate authority over railroad safety, truck lines, buses and pipelines.

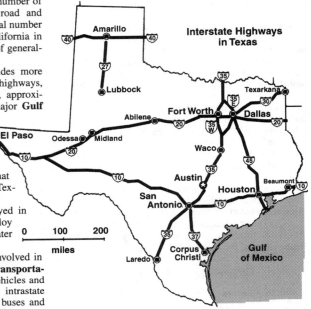

Vehicles, Highway Miles, Construction, Maintenance, 1996

The following mileage, maintenance and construction figures refer only to roads that are maintained by the state: Interstates, U.S. highways, state highways, farm-to-market roads and some loops around urban areas. Not included are city- or county-maintained streets and roads. A lane mile is one lane for one mile; i.e., one mile of four-lane highway equals four lane miles. Source: Texas Dept. of Transportation.

County	Vehicles Registered	Lane Miles of Highways	Vehicle Miles Driven Daily	County Maintenance Expenditures	State Construction Expenditures	Vehicle Registration Fees	County Net Receipts	State Net Receipts
Anderson	37,933	942	991,035	$3,424,003	$5,409,925	$2,101,937	$871,926	$1,230,011
Andrews	12,708	540	401,463	1,970,433	1,664,727	754,386	422,379	332,006
Angelina	67,669	911	1,741,340	6,376,681	6,508,709	3,996,212	1,180,180	2,816,033
Aransas	16,319	161	312,959	918,752	3,135,730	822,317	415,990	406,328
Archer	9,337	524	343,470	2,479,594	266,087	457,385	353,276	104,109
Armstrong	2,396	372	255,796	986,883	146,514	135,046	133,603	1,443
Atascosa	24,695	1010	1,003,397	3,709,460	7,595,874	1,362,699	684,013	678,686
Austin	23,334	607	890,143	2,136,137	8,974,837	1,435,893	714,480	721,413
Bailey	6,021	473	188,509	3,518,796	2,734,312	389,590	355,303	34,288
Bandera	14,520	393	269,194	1,358,169	16,785	766,887	565,192	201,695
Bastrop	43,080	776	1,184,334	1,710,973	2,719,860	2,452,967	1,160,136	1,292,832
Baylor	5,081	434	173,403	2,359,254	1,431,195	296,895	270,541	26,354
Bee	17,878	639	459,256	2,808,094	2,057,499	1,037,119	625,508	411,612
Bell	179,712	1383	3,994,436	5,884,461	20,792,438	10,582,778	3,557,987	7,024,791
Bexar	961,425	2937	17,579,506	15,650,889	113,772,500	59,623,582	17,728,550	41,895,032
Blanco	8,182	451	367,057	1,319,902	286,616	485,505	357,223	128,282
Borden	937	344	51,944	981,176	16970	44,113	43,716	397
Bosque	15,640	695	417,009	2,237,030	1,104,529	849,157	571,858	277,300
Bowie	76,305	1157	2,233,296	8,254,458	21,796,447	4,396,392	1,636,668	2,759,725
Brazoria	193,880	1175	3,476,354	5,749,369	32,351,155	10,343,451	2,648,190	7,695,260
Brazos	90,968	762	1,808,481	4,758,323	30,391,574	5,476,348	1,955,324	3,521,024
Brewster	7,265	588	238,492	1,899,465	7,488,786	385,131	302,004	83,127
Briscoe	2,083	328	52,743	1,079,450	144,492	120,610	120,609	1,626
Brooks	5,501	264	337,668	939,044	114,672	253,422	202,377	51,045
Brown	35,578	742	617,038	2,234,079	3,504,252	1,818,647	735,561	1,083,087
Burleson	14,849	517	578,225	2,767,113	8,059,696	840,362	537,192	303,170
Burnet	31,202	793	756,857	1,441,673	1,849,613	1,847,243	808,472	1,038,771
Caldwell	21,662	602	627,559	1,896,445	2,407,985	1,219,260	639,142	580,118
Calhoun	17,652	382	410,330	1,511,344	2,151,162	904,425	441,712	462,714
Callahan	14,383	743	708,783	1,846,786	4,599,125	778,116	568,022	210,094
Cameron	177,460	1519	3,597,218	6,193,629	39,549,739	10,230,905	3,090,387	7,140,518
Camp	10,739	267	228,242	765,999	686,710	723,077	414,171	308,906

County	Vehicles Registered	Lane Miles of Highways	Vehicle Miles Driven Daily	County Maintenance Expenditures	State Construction Expenditures	Vehicle Registration Fees	County Net Receipts	State Net Receipts
Carson	6,402	776	621,683	2,583,060	4,704,867	349,731	317,484	32,246
Cass	28,438	974	831,630	4,336,795	9,693,563	1,434,801	679,647	755,154
Castro	7,842	529	242,542	1,370,796	2,052,471	506,075	416,571	89,504
Chambers	24,202	700	1,510,551	2,917,656	3,320,173	1,318,865	569,553	749,312
Cherokee	34,767	1113	1,010,459	4,038,023	5,490,000	2,044,037	920,065	1,123,971
Childress	6,376	477	272,048	1,973,804	4,351,334	339,755	327,210	12,546
Clay	10,625	789	673,382	3,600,223	1,138,557	587,928	481,363	106,565
Cochran	3,465	470	98,798	2,524,192	716,332	193,147	190,777	2,369
Coke	4,536	357	171,827	1,183,550	28,865	236,393	232,600	3,794
Coleman	10,028	738	308,247	1,884,250	1,578,909	531,808	448,337	83,472
Collin	311,138	1244	3,605,871	8,797,316	31,686,969	18,671,301	5,992,532	12,678,769
Collingsworth	3,426	445	86,582	800,657	0	183,284	180,451	2,832
Colorado	19,929	761	1,108,224	2,680,335	6,710,474	1,224,107	644,309	579,798
Comal	68,241	604	1,807,732	2,282,938	12,280,105	4,161,977	1,460,772	2,701,205
Comanche	14,008	726	407,184	1,768,805	630,077	795,621	579,006	216,615
Concho	3,087	422	248,896	1,448,430	622,132	155,766	153,354	2,413
Cooke	31,859	842	1,068,153	3,560,986	5,837,745	1,835,939	831,782	1,004,156
Coryell	37,295	682	770,261	3,125,835	5,100,818	2,050,788	925,350	1,125,438
Cottle	1,976	391	80,126	1,007,424	1,450,862	100,454	98,783	1,671
Crane	5,389	319	169,876	652,245	1,010,476	365,285	255,081	110,204
Crockett	4,101	782	402,681	1,317,230	610,809	215,085	212,482	2,604
Crosby	6,200	569	178,398	1,690,308	12,193	314,599	299,647	14,953
Culberson	2,311	744	518,318	1,748,430	1,098,019	114,735	112,964	1,771
Dallam	5,478	603	316,694	1,308,433	308,291	362,830	322,653	40,176
Dallas	1,587,355	2902	27,663,252	23,018,112	202,189,579	101,090,783	31,597,704	69,493,079
Dawson	12,140	710	332,039	2,397,761	2,146,470	746,749	531,328	215,422
Deaf Smith	17,086	601	324,675	2,967,007	995,296	1,169,782	638,639	531,143
Delta	5,066	342	147,746	2,210,830	989,050	265,050	244,875	20,176
Denton	265,373	1238	5,120,882	8,120,987	33,896,771	15,759,340	4,763,272	10,996,068
De Witt	16,016	641	373,446	1,882,891	2,674,387	902,029	597,438	304,591
Dickens	2,463	460	81,289	1,091,130	0	112,393	110,766	1,628
Dimmit	6,829	504	238,373	1,158,991	1,063,586	388,320	331,397	56,923
Donley	3,524	455	384,571	911,183	1,634,851	192,309	189,320	2,989
Duval	8,460	630	407,544	1,306,699	1,350,864	493,312	397,321	95,991
Eastland	19,117	1025	914,918	3,164,578	8,253,585	1,080,666	608,975	471,691
Ector	110,119	927	1,322,546	3,162,692	3,635,117	6,539,626	1,729,087	4,810,539
Edwards	2,137	500	77,227	1,026,874	31,780	111,208	109,557	1,650
Ellis	93,313	1422	2,752,623	5,353,133	28,158,827	5,900,055	1,723,656	4,176,399
El Paso	400,250	1429	6,940,625	8,152,723	64,527,100	23,242,001	6,647,755	16,594,246
Erath	28,456	784	864,422	2,239,447	6,716,412	1,617,486	774,674	842,811
Falls	13,037	706	504,886	3,425,677	3,271,718	716,561	542,369	174,192
Fannin	26,519	906	491,168	5,890,019	5,729,126	1,450,613	768,669	681,945
Fayette	23,417	981	1,100,524	2,217,908	2,018,933	1,334,704	657,539	677,165
Fisher	4,353	553	148,308	1,436,617	0	225,853	222,540	3,313
Floyd	8,261	668	168,592	3,543,675	111,464	490,641	427,516	63,125
Foard	1,550	299	61,855	812,359	0	86,613	85,351	1,262
Fort Bend	215,290	942	3,618,347	8,608,825	23,447,674	12,695,997	3,914,633	8,781,364
Franklin	7,555	334	318,842	4,293,750	2,567,240	372,228	291,960	80,268
Freestone	16,424	822	1,052,638	3,738,046	3,242,523	804,458	554,014	250,444
Frio	9,217	758	659,093	2,553,375	5,053,993	572,370	451,388	120,983
Gaines	11,969	668	389,585	3,853,973	0	703,849	413,875	289,973
Galveston	176,536	956	3,787,322	6,952,945	25,522,788	10,252,722	3,219,278	7,033,444
Garza	4,189	460	334,511	1,756,612	7,438,841	230,285	218,812	11,473
Gillespie	20,366	703	542,347	2,362,674	3,060,480	1,155,755	670,343	485,413
Glasscock	2,252	274	165,759	638,739	1,672,989	156,904	154,035	2,869
Goliad	5,922	500	246,407	1,827,224	571,711	271,912	259,966	11,946
Gonzales	16,121	876	792,113	2,755,073	803,716	886,558	513,821	372,738
Gray	25,378	770	542,439	2,630,006	1,018,759	1,407,187	537,301	869,886
Grayson	96,783	1173	2,092,257	7,971,412	9,388,959	5,569,261	1,999,318	3,569,943
Gregg	118,458	741	2,178,362	3,006,424	10,374,647	7,577,582	2,599,610	4,977,972
Grimes	17,764	610	585,940	4,534,000	2,865,065	994,167	629,272	364,895
Guadalupe	65,573	912	1,811,948	3,349,171	5,881,754	3,825,354	1,422,706	2,402,648
Hale	29,503	1054	677,978	2,453,408	3,671,065	1,768,291	798,638	969,626
Hall	3,252	449	173,649	887,425	3,755,354	183,944	181,176	2,769
Hamilton	7,993	575	252,911	2,258,683	955,680	457,868	398,230	59,638
Hansford	6,287	509	114,720	1,346,842	1,913,104	400,487	363,794	36,694
Hardeman	4,521	466	279,533	2,124,675	67,159	247,533	243,901	3,632
Hardin	44,045	531	1,031,240	2,123,219	5,672,316	2,505,296	1,145,399	1,359,897
Harris	2,436,352	4051	38,962,025	32,935,434	548,051,292	157,158,141	51,765,871	105,392,270
Harrison	49,181	1154	1,878,334	4,714,306	16,865,651	2,864,815	1,114,620	1,750,195
Hartley	4,929	508	285,726	3,070,247	4,126,609	314,304	282,426	31,877
Haskell	7,106	646	200,867	1,504,366	397,808	387,260	376,314	10,946
Hays	63,579	634	2,177,255	2,325,224	6,490,417	3,629,556	1,436,474	2,193,081
Hemphill	4,654	384	117,496	783,578	2,981,388	267,940	250,751	17,189
Henderson	63,487	933	1,357,638	3,898,936	14,979,140	3,516,823	1,238,735	2,278,089
Hildago	257,001	1902	5,361,663	8,749,280	38,997,889	15,867,649	4,665,223	11,202,426
Hill	29,470	1086	1,603,963	4,658,835	4,223,786	1,631,458	843,184	788,273
Hockley	20,794	750	508,803	2,254,398	203,526	1,261,499	566,990	694,510
Hood	37,620	375	681,744	2,044,030	251,529	1,953,163	829,007	1,124,157

County	Vehicles Registered	Lane Miles of Highways	Vehicle Miles Driven Daily	County Maintenance Expenditures	State Construction Expenditures	Vehicle Registration Fees	County Net Receipts	State Net Receipts
Hopkins	31,574	952	1,135,373	2,613,452	3,333,753	2,001,971	926,339	1,075,632
Houston	19,055	835	515,373	3,955,260	1,622,235	1,070,178	642,808	427,369
Howard	29,549	837	812,876	3,193,315	6,401,788	1,741,641	817,957	923,684
Hudspeth	2,335	818	787,994	2,652,925	774,772	107,489	106,111	1,377
Hunt	62,937	1279	1,796,009	7,402,648	23,496,501	3,165,555	1,022,422	2,143,133
Hutchinson	29,487	475	331,852	2,398,091	602,007	1,697,961	678,406	1,019,555
Irion	2,255	247	96,946	405,663	0	137,014	135,297	1,716
Jack	8,128	571	278,946	3,217,958	1,416,727	493,437	390,421	103,016
Jackson	13,293	636	620,494	3,655,247	194,054	707,209	504,323	202,885
Jasper	33,011	682	1,018,103	3,201,846	6,116,025	1,773,311	763,153	1,010,158
Jeff Davis	2,126	469	160,253	1,945,682	3,019,987	128,404	113,360	15,043
Jefferson	196,078	992	3,732,440	5,767,485	40,970,851	11,733,630	3,616,902	8,116,728
Jim Hogg	3,638	288	110,533	766,043	98,038	200,959	164,931	36,029
Jim Wells	27,472	633	788,117	3,226,166	5,958,337	1,734,847	710,359	1,024,478
Johnson	98,570	881	1,977,828	5,093,586	29,189,123	5,611,559	1,312,813	3,698,747
Jones	15,756	978	439,489	2,904,960	4,674,288	1,038,415	622,507	415,909
Karnes	9,864	691	313,963	2,960,962	4,066,108	559,122	460,289	98,833
Kaufman	57,322	1191	2,474,809	4,774,836	7,408,769	3,072,696	1,236,730	1,835,967
Kendall	25,229	443	565,649	1,295,844	1,857,430	1,435,378	835,898	599,479
Kenedy	392	187	324,084	416,218	0	16,252	15,988	264
Kent	1,545	326	49,153	1,637,098	112,541	66,270	65,405	866
Kerr	38,177	702	848,558	2,184,386	3,476,215	2,163,807	931,374	1,232,432
Kimble	5,003	687	425,009	914,930	6,319,135	238,020	226,065	11,956
King	460	199	60,943	1,060,615	2,247,582	27,918	27,674	244
Kinney	2,611	407	161,690	1,357,780	46,182	143,040	131,387	11,653
Kleberg	22,178	363	547,010	2,327,807	4,521,841	1,293,574	615,584	677,990
Knox	3,819	434	118,950	1,413,105	2,139,010	244,787	241,698	3,090
Lamar	43,913	991	910,868	5,175,644	7,361,772	2,553,712	1,044,970	1,508,742
Lamb	13,471	809	388,716	2,277,275	621,616	775,946	562,850	213,096
Lampasas	15,731	476	337,500	1,648,231	2,495,786	849,322	594,024	255,298
La Salle	3,280	648	426,877	1,115,548	7,361,772	204,346	201,442	2,905
Lavaca	20,154	639	418,411	1,614,905	3,115,684	1,183,450	638,579	544,871
Lee	15,230	514	501,649	1,340,562	134,744	959,064	559,081	399,983
Leon	13,381	834	974,928	3,912,808	5,316,631	711,460	518,432	193,029
Liberty	52,571	805	1,371,560	3,961,009	2,333,648	3,235,192	1,210,423	2,024,770
Limestone	18,721	769	543,669	2,940,441	4,104,656	907,496	528,158	379,337
Lipscomb	3,454	447	66,209	762,713	709,435	255,576	252,971	2,604
Live Oak	9,932	947	928,539	3,555,931	9,337,369	593,738	489,340	104,399
Llano	16,085	498	339,937	1,116,576	32,804	848,073	573,276	274,798
Loving	297	67	11,263	186,179	0	15,785	15,324	462
Lubbock	197,088	1627	2,609,421	5,369,579	18,373,348	11,916,249	3,806,652	8,109,597
Lynn	5,849	708	266,860	4,732,348	811,128	318,022	312,356	5,667
Madison	10,594	569	640,835	1,816,535	3,894,780	570,124	447,282	122,842
Marion	8,568	316	269,121	1,178,816	5,094,235	440,702	371,323	69,379
Martin	5,228	572	345,514	1,458,737	1,388,850	299,934	270,894	29,040
Mason	3,941	416	137,316	1,397,083	0	187,239	184,928	2,311
Matagorda	30,643	681	724,088	3,825,991	13,118,317	1,713,439	760,382	953,056
Maverick	20,978	447	426,203	1,990,393	4,983,643	1,304,389	557,348	747,040
McCulloch	9,043	608	254,555	1,988,666	801,616	462,589	392,522	70,068
McLennan	169,723	1593	4,128,993	5,347,498	18,904,138	10,588,357	2,928,486	7,659,872
McMullen	1,453	317	95,127	2,439,902	455,296	140,250	135,500	4,750
Medina	30,248	727	796,320	2,157,703	5,456,720	1,613,468	755,962	857,507
Menard	4,071	346	128,056	709,820	1,373,992	686,067	250,158	435,909
Midland	105,311	930	1,444,301	3,175,931	19,357,699	6,561,879	2,122,911	4,438,969
Milam	21,234	685	669,776	6,171,625	8,149,627	1,129,331	612,893	516,438
Mills	5,584	424	176,194	1,508,517	2,479,624	280,225	275,926	4,298
Mitchell	6,732	657	421,726	2,443,794	2,772,368	339,108	312,877	26,232
Montague	19,316	825	628,752	3,379,490	2,251,920	1,113,106	628,301	484,805
Montgomery	208,762	1047	4,491,036	5,920,421	28,209,309	12,342,780	3,864,105	8,478,675
Moore	17,520	469	420,213	2,027,384	60,737	1,139,170	549,164	590,006
Morris	12,836	357	393,277	1,692,371	937,165	731,949	434,063	297,887
Motley	1,592	331	59,205	777,100	0	82,252	81,043	1,209
Nacogdoches	43,218	908	1,389,365	4,533,705	7,922,978	2,539,324	1,070,411	1,468,913
Navarro	36,223	1154	1,409,368	4,140,226	14,253,089	2,084,560	943,782	1,140,778
Newton	10,941	547	423,560	2,499,498	1,750,069	566,578	439,962	126,727
Nolan	14,601	690	686,735	2,881,692	3,261,470	854,683	584,956	269,727
Nueces	228,917	1356	4,124,122	6,494,967	52,833,761	14,130,802	4,494,996	9,635,806
Ochiltree	9,819	428	171,866	1,004,717	1,603,963	650,156	512,661	137,494
Oldham	2,141	462	582,326	1,009,245	8,752,645	134,701	132,880	1,821
Orange	73,119	576	1,916,928	3,308,059	8,315,155	4,050,772	1,389,058	2,661,714
Palo Pinto	24,668	829	744,899	3,545,912	2,948,024	1,445,252	739,270	705,982
Panola	21,776	746	777,401	3,980,182	9,578,759	1,042,885	482,495	560,390
Parker	76,589	855	2,049,449	3,146,881	6,210,717	4,299,884	1,617,865	2,682,019
Parmer	9,515	539	349,504	1,582,696	27,332	595,001	482,702	112,299
Pecos	12,015	1658	775,931	3,793,078	777,373	629,678	413,171	222,507
Polk	38,649	833	1,260,320	3,735,333	14,828,370	2,452,659	972,894	1,479,494
Potter	96,790	860	1,985,422	4,398,115	16,924,381	5,935,412	2,112,601	3,822,811
Presidio	4,924	545	165,912	1,381,971	2,032,236	254,021	249,838	4,183
Rains	8,188	270	210,965	1,856,493	3,854,991	394,768	307,118	87,650

County	Vehicles Registered	Lane Miles of Highways	Vehicle Miles Driven Daily	County Maintenance Expenditures	State Construction Expenditures	Vehicle Registration Fees	County Net Receipts	State Net Receipts
Randall	92,427	878	939,192	3,200,037	3,382,189	5,506,407	2,002,219	3,504,187
Reagan	3,716	320	105,495	405,902	1,236,817	247,658	216,023	31,635
Real	2,775	297	67,819	1,934,299	28,457	153,279	151,091	2,187
Red River	12,623	748	354,944	5,633,636	2,962,915	654,418	523,064	131,354
Reeves	9,145	1170	666,124	2,717,343	5,938,201	517,214	430,263	86,951
Refugio	6,793	464	518,358	2,823,124	10,691	411,089	318,700	92,388
Roberts	1,219	241	64,499	889,146	2,753,827	58,984	58,164	821
Robertson	13,081	625	526,733	2,016,816	2,142,457	652,311	493,326	158,985
Rockwall	31,227	317	844,348	1,251,132	2,659,063	1,897,713	667,502	1,230,211
Runnels	11,994	735	319,773	1,599,143	29,481	710,259	531,233	179,027
Rusk	36,841	1143	1,111,388	5,214,480	5,742,019	2,157,306	872,741	1,284,564
Sabine	10,106	454	271,270	3,073,858	2,094,960	560,074	460,789	99,285
San Augustine	7,834	516	260,610	3,895,720	1,555,535	459,596	404,973	54,623
San Jacinto	16,245	506	540,502	2,002,457	1,697,197	870,834	463,170	407,663
San Patricio	49,574	880	1,425,318	4,199,194	4,402,312	2,824,155	1,066,419	1,757,710
San Saba	6,332	427	135,550	1,434,060	1,808,501	343,747	338,689	5,059
Schleicher	3,562	362	128,468	1,301,547	50,882	160,337	158,678	1,659
Scurry	17,868	660	474,839	3,695,918	2,542,595	1,126,768	615,991	510,778
Shackelford	3,731	353	141,545	1,294,546	499,217	212,592	209,859	2,733
Shelby	22,919	857	626,837	3,228,731	6,373,320	1,430,763	726,613	704,149
Sherman	3,078	429	196,664	1,334,346	1,832,750	190,259	187,813	2,446
Smith	156,412	1500	3,802,064	6,044,514	24,487,897	9,194,330	3,171,523	6,022,808
Somervell	5,693	184	168,279	1,192,840	35,521	262,104	194,347	67,757
Starr	24,205	463	671,873	2,861,815	7,693,072	1,425,186	703,878	721,308
Stephens	9,815	553	210,761	2,608,776	1,026,424	515,984	410,188	105,796
Sterling	1,708	240	159,146	514,115	679,192	84,383	83,294	1,088
Stonewall	2,277	329	86,678	990,884	62,984	139,119	137,699	1,420
Sutton	5,935	592	435,121	1,230,437	649,317	373,554	262,867	110,687
Swisher	7,193	808	321,022	1,382,073	1,330,865	425,527	383,181	42,346
Tarrant	1,062,496	2780	20,853,946	16,442,943	142,809,299	65,169,745	19,238,747	45,930,999
Taylor	114,508	1151	1,700,095	4,073,429	13,438,464	7,114,032	2,396,631	4,717,400
Terrell	1,190	343	87,013	1,697,456	60,014	59,444	58,617	828
Terry	12,686	631	357,765	2,126,615	95,022	819,426	564,527	254,899
Throckmorton	2,007	341	68,283	2,116,824	1,431,630	104,649	103,320	1,329
Titus	24,515	540	785,776	1,609,662	3,455,245	1,341,361	651,116	690,245
Tom Green	92,564	948	1,197,752	2,256,100	18,456,197	5,401,646	1,948,212	3,453,434
Travis	546,780	1562	10,126,198	11,797,040	103,518,569	33,194,270	10,511,895	22,682,376
Trinity	12,050	429	305,841	2,430,622	3,030,451	644,236	441,207	203,030
Tyler	16,113	510	502,265	3,304,954	3,062,979	841,347	512,986	328,360
Upshur	29,622	744	749,861	2,775,074	2,042,457	1,447,672	632,222	815,450
Upton	3,539	388	134,055	983,750	465,411	187,382	184,930	2,453
Uvalde	19,143	719	533,748	1,780,342	3,160,494	1,202,434	600,311	602,122
Val Verde	32,577	665	414,621	3,818,417	2,434,078	1,800,370	743,598	1,056,772
Van Zandt	45,212	1153	1,651,390	4,961,567	1,387,341	2,410,333	1,055,932	1,381,401
Victoria	73,353	716	1,394,513	3,593,317	13,027,633	4,040,776	1,263,672	2,777,105
Walker	34,954	783	1,599,753	6,918,372	7,124,508	2,077,947	966,552	1,111,396
Waller	31,778	550	1,064,165	2,182,210	7,569,892	1,833,010	221,617	611,394
Ward	11,041	672	359,083	1,545,478	3,245,856	612,943	383,706	229,237
Washington	28,639	627	783,410	3,151,040	6,325,911	1,804,891	814,871	990,020
Webb	89,765	898	1,509,319	5,717,894	27,894,837	6,228,693	1,696,351	4,532,342
Wharton	37,134	883	1,200,762	5,080,243	1,495,203	2,304,029	876,188	1,427,841
Wheeler	5,926	670	483,211	1,437,206	435,860	296,782	292,738	4,043
Wichita	112,848	1059	1,750,630	3,790,502	11,170,647	6,085,457	1,684,406	4,401,051
Wilbarger	13,768	723	536,316	2,603,134	1,949,247	749,711	560,331	189,381
Willacy	12,191	478	330,651	1,354,025	1,162,550	703,677	518,700	184,977
Williamson	166,137	1395	3,584,438	4,698,343	34,106,475	9,703,200	3,063,679	6,639,521
Wilson	22,686	724	540,587	2,943,034	907,408	1,219,452	677,091	542,361
Winkler	7,124	295	140,955	728,951	67,451	424,282	324,925	99,356
Wise	51,766	841	1,571,882	3,189,250	9,056,488	3,306,085	1,281,666	2,024,420
Wood	35,008	890	698,230	2,910,378	5,885,823	1,747,833	687,931	1,059,902
Yoakum	8,630	427	181,625	767,429	2,507,676	583,466	446,098	137,368
Young	19,259	711	346,303	2,555,717	954,994	1,192,790	634,645	558,145
Zapata	6,583	250	336,553	649,936	546,567	364,408	260,674	103,735
Zavala	5,819	556	214,250	1,828,063	138,476	348,624	277,582	71,041
Totals	15,274,164	183,335	327,944,663	$791,170,423	$2,576,320,941	$923,486,600	$333,144,056	$598,464,807

Motor Vehicle Accidents, Losses

| Year | No. Killed | †No. Injured | Accidents by Kinds | | | | ‡Vehicle Miles Traveled | | |
			No. Fatal	†No. Involving Injury	†No. Non-Injury	†Total	*Number	Deaths per 100 million Miles	§Economic Loss
1960	2,254	127,980	1,842	71,100	239,300	312,242	46,352,734,855	4.9	$350,022,500
1961	2,314	132,570	1,899	73,650	248,600	324,149	47,937,315,761	4.8	356,112,000
1962	2,421	144,943	2,002	80,524	277,680	360,206	49,882,977,516	4.9	387,843,000

Year	No. Killed	†No. Injured	No. Fatal	†No. Involving Injury	†No. Non-injury	†Total	*Number	Deaths per 100 million Miles	§Economic Loss
			Accidents by Kinds				‡Vehicle Miles Traveled		
1963	2,729	161,543	2,251	89,746	307,920	399,917	52,324,589,656	5.2	432,715,000
1964	3,006	182,081	2,486	101,156	351,120	454,762	55,677,488,273	5.4	486,846,000
1965	3,028	186,062	2,460	103,368	365,160	470,988	*52,163,239,027	5.8	498,087,000
1966	3,406	208,310	2,784	115,728	406,460	524,972	55,260,849,798	6.2	557,414,000
1967	3,367	205,308	2,778	114,060	768,430	885,268	58,123,603,943	5.8	793,094,000
1968	3,481	216,972	2,902	120,540	816,830	940,272	62,794,494,339	5.5	836,802,000
1969	3,551	223,000	2,913	124,000	850,000	976,913	67,742,000,000	5.2	955,300,000
1970	3,560	223,000	2,965	124,000	886,000	1,012,965	‡68,031,000,000	5.2	1,042,200,000
1971	3,594	224,000	2,993	124,000	890,000	1,016,993	70,709,000,000	5.1	1,045,000,000
1972	3,688	128,158	3,099	83,607	346,292	432,998	76,690,000,000	4.8	1,035,000,000
1973	3,692	132,635	3,074	87,631	373,521	464,226	80,615,000,000	4.6	1,035,000,000
1974	3,046	123,611	2,626	83,341	348,227	434,194	78,290,000,000	3.9	1,095,000,000
1975	3,429	138,962	2,945	92,510	373,141	468,596	84,575,000,000	4.1	1,440,000,000
1976	3,230	145,282	2,780	96,348	380,075	479,203	91,279,000,000	3.5	1,485,000,000
1977	3,698	161,635	3,230	106,923	393,848	504,001	96,998,000,000	3.8	1,960,000,000
1978	¶3,980	178,228	3,468	117,998	**304,830	**426,296	102,624,000,000	3.9	2,430,000,000
1979	4,229	184,550	3,685	122,793	322,336	448,814	101,909,000,000	4.1	2,580,000,000
1980	4,424	185,964	3,863	123,577	305,500	432,940	103,255,000,000	4.3	3,010,000,000
1981	4,701	206,196	4,137	136,396	317,484	458,017	111,036,000,000	4.2	3,430,000,000
1982	4,271	204,666	3,752	135,859	312,159	451,770	††124,910,000,000	3.4	3,375,000,000
1983	3,823	208,157	‡‡3,328	137,695	302,876	443,899	129,309,000,000	3.0	3,440,000,000
1984	3,913	220,720	3,466	145,543	293,285	442,294	137,280,000,000	2.9	3,795,000,000
1985	3,682	231,009	3,270	151,657	300,531	452,188	143,500,000,000	2.6	3,755,000,000
1986	3,568	234,120	3,121	154,514	298,079	452,593	150,474,000,000	2.4	3,782,000,000
1987	3,261	226,895	2,881	146,913	246,175	395,969	151,221,000,000	2.2	3,913,000,000
1988	3,395	238,845	3,004	152,004	237,703	392,711	152,819,000,000	2.2	4,515,000,000
1989	3,361	243,030	2,926	153,356	233,967	390,249	159,679,000,000	2.1	4,873,000,000
1990	3,243	262,576	2,882	162,424	216,140	381,446	163,103,000,000	2.0	4,994,000,000
1991	3,079	263,430	2,690	161,470	207,288	371,448	162,780,000,000	1.9	5,604,000,000
1992	3,057	282,025	2,690	170,513	209,152	382,355	162,769,000,000	1.9	6,725,000,000
1993	3,037	298,891	2,690	178,194	209,533	390,417	167,988,000,000	1.8	11,784,000,000
1994	3,142	326,837	2,710	192,014	219,890	414,614	172,976,000,000	1.8	12,505,000,000
1995	3,172	334,259	2,790	196,093	152,190	351,073	183,103,000,000	1.7	13,005,000,000
1996§§	3,738	350,397	3,247	204,635	90,261	298,143	187,064,000,000	2.0	$7,766,000,000

*Vehicle miles traveled since 1964 were estimated on the basis of new data furnished by U.S. Bureau of Public Roads through National Safety Council. Vehicle miles and deaths per 100 million vehicle miles after 1964 cannot, therefore, be compared with previous years.

†In August 1967, amended estimating formula received from National Safety Council. Starting with 1972, actual reported injuries are listed rather than estimates.

‡Vehicle miles traveled estimated by Texas Highway Department starting with 1970. Method of calculation varies from that used for prior years. Vehicle miles and deaths per 100,000,000 vehicle miles for 1969 and before cannot be compared to subsequent years.

§Economic loss formula last changed 1984.

¶Change in counting fatalities. Counted when injury results in death within 90 days of vehicle accident in which the injury occurred.

**Total accidents and non-injury accidents for 1978 and after cannot be compared with years prior to 1978 due to changes in reporting laws.

††Method of calculating vehicle miles traveled revised for 1982 by the Texas State Department of Highways and Public Transportation. Vehicle miles and deaths per 100,000,000 miles cannot be compared to prior years.

‡‡Change in counting fatalities. Counted when injury results in death within 30 days of vehicle accident in which injury occurred.

§§Beginning in July 1995, only property damage accidents having at least one vehicle towed due to damages is tabulated. Therefore, total accidents and non-injury accidents cannot be compared to prior years.

Source: Analysis Section, Accident Records Bureau of the **Texas Department of Public Safety**, Austin.

Drivers' Licenses Issued

The following report from the Texas Department of Public Safety shows the number of drivers' licenses issued during the fiscal year and number of valid licenses at the end of each fiscal year.

Fiscal Year Ending Aug. 31:	*Licenses Issued During Year	Valid Licenses at Year's End
1996	4,876,793	14,103,325
1995	4,373,019	13,785,992
1994	4,459,076	13,293,255
1993	4,484,179	13,293,255
1992	4,411,473	13,140,171
1991	3,998,300	13,011,502
1990	4,205,385	11,738,602
1989	4,397,140	11,672,696
1988	4,130,447	11,641,984
1987	3,886,622	11,550,219
1986	4,325,742	11,436,780
1985	4,677,788	11,241,367
1984	4,498,902	11,009,567
1983	4,090,602	10,805,539
1982	4,281,652	10,463,962
1981	3,818,303	9,909,721
1980	3,699,543	9,551,683
1979	3,616,754	9,189,198
1978	3,529,926	8,805,604
1977	3,418,606	8,420,678
1976	3,233,610	8,127,188
1975	2,980,024	7,806,703
1974	2,887,456	7,588,372
1973	2,807,828	7,334,913
1972	2,573,010	7,098,425
1971	2,418,170	6,768,319
1970	2,321,416	6,420,602
1969	3,403,122	6,035,944
1968	3,603,082	5,849,126
1967	3,516,794	5,772,852
1966	3,505,108	5,587,709

*Includes renewals during year.

Amtrak Passengers On/Off at Texas Stations, 1988-1996

City	1996	1995	1994	1993	1992	1991	1990	1989	1988
Alpine	2,284	2,503	2,746	2,873	2,312	1,718	1,754	2,008	1,720
Austin	10,112	10,449	13,211	20,290	19,633	22,795	18,913	11,973	15,621
Beaumont	2,483	2,578	2,362	2,671	2,945	3,026	3,677	4,058	5,010
Cleburne	616	669	859	1,865	2,350	2,845	3,579	1,939	2,302
College Stat.-Bryan	—	—	4,287	10,603	10,687	10,582	8,370	7,090	—
Corsicana	—	—	889	1,985	2,110	2,141	2,380	3,143	—
Dallas	23,301	36,673	46,139	74,680	69,062	76,695	64,350	54,982	33,035
Del Rio	1,207	1,383	1,444	1,245	1,122	1,136	1,235	1,745	1,598
El Paso	14,977	17,729	22,099	22,193	19,300	18,591	19,676	22,656	26,516
Fort Worth	9,643	10,064	12,577	21,773	22,607	23,926	23,623	14,049	15,565
Hearne	—	—	289	374	—	—	—	—	—
Houston	21,453	32,186	35,274	50,332	48,480	55,297	47,514	45,370	22,151
Longview	18,297	7,442	7,556	11,429	10,426	11,431	9,519	7,069	6,759
Marshall	3,274	4,147	4,870	7,985	8,389	8,349	6,901	4,537	4,203
McGregor	1,301	1,278	1,692	3,203	2,670	3,202	3,099	1,955	2,308
Mineola	1,312	—	—	—	—	—	—	—	—
San Antonio	32,202	33,443	38,839	51,730	46,217	48,667	43,186	22,691	31,272
San Marcos	793	869	1,264	2,067	1,805	2,541	2,211	1,621	2,652
Sanderson	—	—	365	313	297	380	413	952	665
Taylor	1,351	1,439	1,617	3,317	3,214	4,596	4,626	3,723	4,732
Temple	2,738	2,985	4,033	8,155	6,994	7,478	7,495	5,191	5,958
Texarkana	—	—	5,843	8,334	—	—	—	—	—
Totals	**147,944**	**170,183**	**208,255**	**307,417**	**280,620**	**305,396**	**272,521**	**216,752**	**182,067**

Source: Texas Railroad Commission, 1997.

Amtrak operates two long-distance trains through Texas — the Sunset Limited (a tri-weekly Miami-New Orleans-San Antonio-Los Angeles route); and the Texas Eagle (a tri-weekly Chicago-St. Louis-Dallas-San Antonio route).

Amtrak expended $1.9 million for goods and services in Texas during fiscal year 1995 and $2.19 million in 1996. As of December 1996, Amtrak employed 120 Texas residents who earned approximately $3.4 million. Source: National Railroad Passenger Corp.

The 'Railroads' in the Railroad Commission

Source: The Texas Railroad Commission.

Within a very short period of time after its creation, the Railroad Commission cut the rates railroads were allowed to charge. Almost immediately, the Commission was taken to court and placed under injunction. It was not until 1894, when the United States Supreme Court ruled that the act creating the Railroad Commission was constitutional, that the lower rates were put into effect.

In the meantime, in 1892, the railroads made an unsuccessful run at having the legislature abolish the Commission. In 1893, the Commission was granted statutory authority to regulate issuance of railroad stocks and bonds. In 1894, the constitution was amended to change the office of the three Commissioners from appointive to elective, with six-year staggered terms.

The Commission's responsibilities included: 1) Administration of laws relating to the railroads of Texas. 2) Determination of passenger fares, freight rates, and charges for all classes of common carriers in Texas. 3) Holding public hearings. 4) Receiving of reports, making investigations, and keeping of records regarding fiscal structure, valuation, revenues and expenses, and train, terminal, and traffic service of Texas railroads.

The legal focus of the Commission was on intrastate passenger and freight activities within the borders of Texas. Interstate moves fell under the jurisdiction of the U. S. Interstate Commerce Commission.

John H. Reagan, first chairman of the Railroad Commission, had been instrumental in the creation of the federal commission in 1887 while he was serving as U.S. Senator from Texas.

When the Commission was founded in 1891, there were some 8,700 miles of track. When the railroads reached their peak in Texas in 1930, there were 17,500 miles. Following World War II, increasingly goods began to travel by truck and people by buses and cars and the miles of track began to shrink.

Over recent decades, the role of the Railroad Commission in the regulation of railroads has changed, moving from economic regulation to safety regulation. The Federal Railroad Safety Act of 1970 vested rail safety responsibilities in the Federal Railroad Administration. In 1983, the Railroad Commission began a cooperative process with the federal government, implementing a rail safety program.

The Rail Safety and Planning section of the Transportation/Gas Utilities Division monitors the state's rail lines, inspecting railroad equipment, operations, and track. This section also maintains the state's rail planning program and oversees the use of federal funds for track rehabilitation projects.

Under provisions of the 1980 Federal Staggers Rail Act, the Railroad Commission recognized that it could hold only a passive role in rate setting. In 1984, the Railroad Commission ceased its historic role in economic regulation of the Texas rail industry. ☆

Statistical History of Railroad Operation in Texas, 1939-1995

The table below shows development and trends of railroad line operations, freight tonnage, operating revenues and expenses in Texas since the Railroad Commission's first report.

Year	Average Miles Operated Including Trackage Rights	Tons Revenue Freight	Railway Operating Revenues	Railway Operating Expenses	Operating Ratio	*Net Revenue From Railway Operations	Amounts per mile operated			Freight Revenue Per Ton Mile
							Freight Revenue	Passenger Revenue	Net From Operations	
1995	10,804	298,544,547	$2,355,731,000	$1,928,125,000	78.30	$427,606,000	$206,809.00	...	$33,267.00	$.0245
1994	10,543	296,607,281	2,313,085,000	1,741,625,620	83.35	571,459,380	201,497.00	...	47,908.00	.0243
1993	10,430	283,533,150	2,265,753,000	1,793,032,000	80.93	472,721,000	201,524.00	...	39,667.00	.0260
1992	10,522	270,172,326	2,213,517,000	1,786,709,000	87.60	426,808,000	188,872.00	...	30,633.00	.0276
1991	11,396	262,484,463	2,110,479,000	1,886,405,000	89.40	223,975,000	162,630.00	...	8,700.00	.0260
1990	11,541	253,778,285	2,061,579,000	1,709,369,000	89.00	352,210,000	161,178.00	...	22,984.00	.0270
1989	12,225	265,583,737	2,098,829,000	1,801,451,000	89.30	297,378,000	157,927.00	...	22,547.00	.0270
1988	12,337	315,073,199	2,111,522,843	1,678,802,000	82.90	415,169,412	143,882.00	...	23,999.00	.0270
1987	12,683	299,473,842	1,908,188,000	1,528,948,000	82.70	379,334,000	141.430.00	...	27,820.00	.0250
1986	12,774	207,679,132	1,827,330,000	1,736,580,000	96.90	90,750,000	134,532.00	...	7,834.00	.0298
1985	12,860	217,096,477	2,026,001,000	1,713,245,620	83.90	312,755,380	148,040.00	...	26,816.00	.0300
1984	13,071	263,846,292	2,204,659,000	1,848,500,000	83.90	357,197,000	161,980.00	...	33,005.00	.0298
1983	12,942	245,502,145	2,032,792,000	1,705,625,000	83.80	327,167,000	147,548.00	...	25,824.00	.0296
1982	13,017	242,451,128	2,138,768,000	1,883,375,000	85.20	225,393,000	145,147.00	...	23,178.00	.0324
1981	13,051	274,576,260	2,400,252,000	2,055,057,000	81.78	345,195,000	169,528.00	...	32,585.00	.0320
†1980	13,075	268,445,039	2,064,108,000	1,761,650,000	85.34	304,742,000	151,918.00	...	23,310.00	.0268
†1979	13,075	239,943,773	1,718,912,000	1,469,238,000	85.47	249,674,000	126,819.00	...	19,096.00	.0243
‡1978	13,923	241,386,721	1,445,104,000	1,265,949,000	87.60	166,937,000	100,110.00	...	11,990.00	.0216
1977	14,554	242,267,810	1,314,952,036	993,342,280	75.54	321,609,756	86,994.26	...	22,097.69	.0213
1976	14,679	206,130,425	1,158,004,603	874,250,182	75.50	283,754,421	75,737.76	...	19,330.64	.0224
1975	14,717	230,120,781	1,073,029,254	792,786,773	73.88	280,242,481	69,982.79	...	19,042.09	.0196
1974	14,712	247,320,696	1,048,980,920	794,249,941	75.72	254,730,979	67,805.72	...	17,314.50	.0175
1973	14,830	253,365,741	928,419,976	699,019,572	75.29	229,400,404	59,512.05	0.15	15,468.67	.0147
1972	14,800	222,303,703	784,815,674	614,035,456	78.24	170,780,218	50,884.46	0.20	11,539.20	.0149
1971	14,909	208,878,010	725,469,372	554,682,694	76.46	170,786,678	46,429.13	38.81	11,455.27	.0145
1970	14,683	211,069,076	655,638,834	504,146,691	76.89	151,492,143	42,245.42	170.71	10,317.52	.0134
1969	15,019	201,455,133	599,461,296	465,795,906	77.70	133,665,390	37,570.23	206.72	8,899.75	.0130
1968	15,039	193,822,546	560,178,714	446,936,382	79.78	113,242,332	34,672.47	291.82	7,529.91	.0126
1967	15,128	183,742,685	517,617,077	411,306,768	79.46	106,310,309	31,432.83	400.93	7,027.39	.0124
1966	15,295	197,208,761	543,803,770	408,281,725	75.08	135,522,045	32,349.45	522.40	8,860.55	.0117
1965	15,214	181,553,163	502,191,485	380,412,080	75.75	121,779,405	29,754.73	605.40	8,004.43	.0118
1964	15,254	173,074,704	462,053,638	366,103,656	79.23	95,949,982	26,875.78	712.94	6,290.15	.0115
1963	15,279	158,750,736	445,048,337	348,210,665	78.24	96,837,672	25,635.01	791.81	6,337.96	.0120
1962	15,389	155,728,821	439,606,758	351,277,249	79.91	88,329,509	24,948.34	871.95	5,739.78	.0120
1961	15,622	157,700,142	429,983,796	344,217,323	80.05	85,766,473	23,915.32	892.94	5,490.11	.0126
1960	15,445	149,360,161	438,531,081	347,353,628	79.21	91,177,453	26,149.41	937.69	5,903.36	.0121
1959	15,600	162,985,000	460,813,237	355,981,564	77.25	104,831,673	25,889.59	924.41	6,719.98	.0127
1958	15,853	152,687,265	449,909,607	338,708,662	75.28	111,200,945	24,908.93	904.14	7,014.50	.0134
1957	16,003	156,218,472	455,449,879	349,842,282	76.81	105,607,597	24,923.21	1,002.17	6,599.24	.0136
1956	16,078	163,448,004	451,785,741	354,734,911	78.52	97,050,830	24,502.50	1,089.91	6,036.25	.0131
1955	16,151	166,742,660	450,865,455	341,963,345	75.85	108,902,110	24,482.83	1,085.84	6,742.75	.0134
1954	16,254	151,639,475	426,223,548	326,373,490	76.57	99,850,058	22,758.67	1,161.88	6,143.11	.0140
1953	16,248	163,120,436	474,112,360	359,553,092	75.84	114,559,268	25,489.81	1,238.52	7,050.67	.0147
1952	16,249	171,536,799	480,598,102	353,835,324	73.62	126,762,778	25,554.16	1,471.58	7,801.27	.0140
1951	16,268	171,974,878	458,070,697	351,407,963	76.71	106,662,734	24,025.44	1,582.08	6,556.60	.0131
1950	16,296	155,970,914	420,864,968	310,731,697	73.83	210,133,271	22,021.66	1,366.76	6,758.30	.0132
1949	16,327	147,769,627	389,948,675	298,378,439	76.52	91,570,236	20,461.53	1,390.79	5,608.63	.0131
1948	16,345	172,717,282	436,136,267	330,029,402	75.67	106,106,865	22,907.44	1,626.45	6,491.81	.0120
1947	16,346	163,222,681	372,282,426	280,421,729	75.32	91,860,697	19,005.06	1,727.19	5,619.86	.0079
1946	16,366	140,735,375	321,208,561	261,245,259	81.33	59,963,302	15,183.86	2,634.56	3,663.98	.0094
1945	16,376	159,795,571	390,672,459	263,883,854	67.54	126,788,605	17,635.26	4,370.32	7,742.36	.0102
1944	16,413	165,921,126	412,831,093	251,675,821	60.96	161,155,272	18,411.51	4,933.33	9,818.66	.0101
1943	16,524	164,970,686	379,659,061	222,135,959	58.51	157,523,102	16,671.20	4,615.05	9,532.94	.0100
1942	16,775	141,223,552	283,433,884	169,494,082	59.80	113,939,802	13,187.93	2,440.20	6,792.27	.0100
1941	17,016	91,780,832	180,368,515	127,218,178	70.53	53,150,337	8,859.09	1,205.19	3,123.55	.0100
1940	17,057	69,107,695	144,124,269	110,626,057	76.76	33,498,212	7,028.74	944.72	1,963.85	.0106
1939	17,102	66,975,729	145,213,331	109,379,297	75.32	35,834,034	7,071.15	929.94	2,095.35	.0111

*Net revenue before interest, taxes. †No data available for Rock Island. ‡Beginning in 1978, no data for Class II and III carriers.

Aviation in Texas

Source: Texas Transportation Institute.

Air transportation is a vital and vigorous part of the Texas economy, and Texans are major users of air transportation.

The state's airport system ranks as one of the busiest and largest in the nation.

The State of Texas has long been committed to providing air transportation to the public. In 1945 the Texas Aeronautics Commission (TAC) was created and directed by the Legislature to encourage, foster, and assist in the development of aeronautics within the state, and to encourage the establishment of airports and air navigational facilities.

The Commission's first annual report of December 31, 1946, stated that Texas had 592 designated airports and 7,756 civilian aircraft.

The commitment to providing air transportation was strengthened in October 18, 1989, when the TAC became the Texas Department of Aviation (TDA). This commitment was further strengthened on September 1, 1991, when the Texas Department of Transportation was created and the TDA became the Aviation Division within the Department.

TxDOT Aviation Division reports that in 1995 Texas airports with scheduled passenger service enplaned more than 57.7 million passengers; scheduled carriers served 28 Texas airports in 25 cities; and more than 91 percent of the state's population lived within 50 miles of an airport with scheduled air passenger service.

Dallas/Fort Worth International, Dallas Love Field, Houston Intercontinental, and Houston's William P. Hobby together accounted for 77 percent of these enplanements.

Texas leads the nation in the number of landing facilities, 1,671 as of December 1994, followed by California with 946.

One of TxDOT's goals is to develop a statewide system of airports that will provide adequate air access to the population and economic centers and will rank as one of the finest in the United States.

TxDOT has identified 307 airports in the Texas Aeronautical System Plan as needed to meet the forecast aviation demand for the state and to maximize access by aircraft to the state's population, business activity, and agricultural production and mineral production value. Of these 307 sites, 27 are commercial service airports, 24 are reliever airports, 66 are transport airports, 127 are general utility airports, and 63 are basic utility airports.

Commercial service airports provide scheduled pas-

Passengers by Airport 1995

Source: Quarterly Aviation Activity Report, Texas Department of Transportation, Division of Aviation

City	Enplanements
Abilene	69,555
Amarillo	454,536
Austin	2,658,039
Beaumont-Port Arthur	108,520
Brownwood	2,015
College Station	85,331
Corpus Christi	511,841
Dallas-Fort Worth Intl.	27,013,761
Dallas Love Field	3,355,238
El Paso	1,835,162
Harlingen	489,082
Houston Intercont.	10,165,671
Houston Hobby	4,111,175
Houston Ellington	1,870,552
Killeen	59,126
Laredo	59,948
Longview	33,761
Lubbock	602,680
McAllen	313,082
Midland	566,904
San Angelo	52,674
San Antonio	3,058,274
Temple	15,976
Texarkana	45,242
Tyler	78,524
Victoria	19,517
Waco	55,824
Wichita Falls	59,275
Total	**57,751,285**

Airline Markets: Leading U.S. Routes, 1994

Rank, Route	Passengers
1. New York to-from Chicago	2.97 million
2. NY to-from Los Angeles	2.95 million
3. NY to-from Miami	2.68 million
4. NY to-from Boston	2.62 million
5. **Dallas/Fort Worth to-from Houston**	2.27 million
6. NY to-from Washington	2.23 million
7. LA to-from San Francisco	2.14 million
8. NY to-from Orlando	2.07 million
9. NY to-from San Francisco	2.02 million
10. NY to-from Atlanta	1.84 million

Source: Air Transport Assoc. of America, Washington, D.C., Air Transport 1995.

Aircraft Departures, 1994

Rank, State	Takeoffs
1. **Texas**	809,167
2. California	705,484
3. Illinois	489,225
4. Florida	471,589
5. New York	350,623
6. Georgia	347,153
7. Missouri	292,822
8. Pennsylvania	282,778
9. Ohio	255,714
10. North Carolina	253,554

Source: Statistical Handbook of Aviation, U.S. Dept. of Transportation..

senger service. The reliever airports provide alternative landing facilities in metropolitan areas separate from the commercial service airports and, together with the transport airports, provide access for business and executive turbine-powered aircraft.

The general and basic utility airports provide access for single- and multi-engined piston-powered aircraft to smaller communities throughout the state.

TxDOT is charged by the Legislature with planning, programming, and implementing improvement projects at approximately 256 general aviation airports. In carrying out these responsibilities, TxDOT channels the Airport Improvement Program (AIP) funds provided by the Federal Aviation Administration (FAA) for all general aviation airports in Texas.

Since 1993 TxDOT has participated in the FAA's state block grant demonstration program. Under this program TxDOT assumes most of FAA's responsibility for the administration of the AIP funds for general aviation airports.

The Aviation Facilities Development Program oversees planning and research, assists with engineering and technical services, and provides financial assistance through state grantsand loans to public bodies operating airports for the purpose of establishing, constructing, reconstructing, enlarging, or repairing airports, airstrips, or navigational facilities.

To implement and administer the Aviation Facilities Development Program, the 74th Legislature appropriated $8 million for the 1996-1997 biennium.

The Aeronautical Services and Information Section provides specialized training programs, aeronautical publications, and safety information to individuals and groups throughout the state who are involved or interested in aviation.

Scheduled passenger traffic (air carriers and commuters) experienced moderate growth during 1995. Scheduled passenger enplanements in Texas increased by 1.67 million or 3 percent over 1994 figures.

According to Federal Aviation Administration data, Texas leads the United States in aircraft departures and ranks second after California in passengers enplaned by scheduled air carriers.

Air Traffic History
Source: FAA
Airline passenger traffic enplaned in Texas by scheduled certificated carriers.

Year	Total Passengers
1957	2,808,558
1973	12,230,861
1974	13,209,568
1975	13,182,957
1976	14,485,340
1977	15,871,147
1978	18,241,029
1979	21,546,794
1980	25,303,214
1981	27,449,480
1982	29,541,788
1983	30,853,297
1984	35,130,762
1985	38,913,027
1986	39,957,392
1987	41,493,225
1988	42,655,971
1989	45,348,326
1990	46,435,641
1991	45,825,027
1992	48,869,034
1993	50,594,658
1994	55,633,180
1995	57,751,285

The size of the general aviation fleet has declined slightly since 1980 and is expected to remain stable during the 1990s.

The proportion of the general aviation fleet consisting of single-engine airplanes, planes associated with personal or pleasure flying, is decreasing, while the proportion of multi-engine airplanes, planes associated with business and executive transportation, is increasing. Business continues to increase its use of general aviation aircraft.

The state's 47,331 active pilots represent 7.7 percent of the nation's pilots. ☆

Top Ten Texas Cities — 1995
Source: Quarterly Aviation Activity Report, Texas Dept. of Transportation, Division of Aviation.

City Rank (by Passengers)	Operations Performed	Percent Total	Enplaned Passengers	Percent Total
1. Dallas-Fort Worth	1,062,143	27	30,368,999	53
2. Houston	692,613	18	16,147,398	28
3. San Antonio	238,638	6	3,058,274	5
4. Austin	206,483	5	2,658,039	5
5. El Paso	150,217	4	1,835,162	3
6. Lubbock	99,703	3	602,680	1
7. Midland-Odessa	100,117	3	566,904	1
8. Corpus Christi	128,193	3	511,841	1
9. Brownsville-Harlingen-San Benito	192,415	5	489,082	1
10. Amarillo-Borger	74,911	2	454,530	1
Texas Totals of All Airports	**3,929,340**		**57,751,285**	

Crime in Texas, 1996

Source: Texas Department of Public Safety, Austin

The number of violent crimes reported in Texas decreased in 1996, but a rise in the number of property crimes accounted for an overall crime increase of 2.6 percent compared with 1995. The total estimated number of index crimes reported for 1996 was 1,091,878.

The crime rate is tabulated on seven major offenses designated by the Federal Bureau of Investigation as Index Crimes. These seven categories include four violent offenses (murder, rape, robbery and aggravated assault) and three nonviolent crimes (burglary, larceny and auto theft.) In Texas, these figures are collected by the Texas Department of Public Safety and are provided to the FBI.

Although all Texas counties except Loving County suffered from some major crimes in 1996, most of the incidents are confined to the urban areas. In the list of the 10 counties with the highest crime rates, four are urban counties with populations more than 500,000, and five are metro counties with populations between 75,000 and 500,000.

Except for a slight increase in the number of aggravated assaults, all categories of violent crime were down nearly one percent in 1996. The violent crime rate was 644.2 in 1996 compared to 663.7 the year before, a decrease of 2.9 percent.

Nonviolent crimes rose 3 percent. The value of property stolen during the commission of index crimes in 1996 was more than $1.3 billion. The value of stolen property recovered by Texas law-enforcement agencies in 1996 was more than $547 million. ☆

Texas Crime History 1975-1996

Year	Murder	Rape	Robbery	Aggra-vated Assault	Burglary	Larceny	Car Theft	Rate Per 100,000 Popula-tion
1975	1,639	3,430	20,076	22,658	203,821	362,665	47,386	5,407.2
1976	1,519	3,666	17,352	21,885	193,208	400,767	43,871	5,464.4
1977	1,705	4,338	19,552	26,714	205,672	383,451	51,018	5,397.1
1978	1,853	4,927	21,395	28,475	209,770	398,923	57,821	5,556.8
1979	2,226	6,028	25,636	33,909	239,263	411,555	72,687	5,911.7
1980	2,389	6,694	29,532	39,251	262,332	450,209	79,032	6,135.7
1981	2,438	6,816	28,516	40,673	275,652	454,210	83,244	6,042.4
1982	2,463	6,814	33,603	45,221	285,757	501,312	87,090	6,297.5
1983	2,238	6,334	29,769	42,195	262,214	503,555	82,522	5,907.1
1984	2,091	7,340	28,537	42,764	266,032	529,469	87,781	6,029.2
1985	2,124	8,367	31,693	47,868	289,913	596,130	99,561	6,570.9
1986	2,255	8,605	40,018	59,002	341,560	664,832	119,095	7,408.2
1987	1,960	8,068	38,049	57,903	355,732	711,739	123,378	7,724.3
1988	2,021	8,122	39,307	60,084	362,099	739,784	134,271	8,019.6
1989	2,029	7,953	37,910	63,978	342,360	741,642	150,974	7,926.8
1990	2,388	8,746	44,316	73,860	314,346	730,926	154,387	7,823.7
1991	2,651	9,265	49,698	84,104	312,719	734,177	163,837	7,818.6
1992	2,240	9,368	44,582	86,067	268,864	689,515	145,039	7,055.1
1993	2,149	9,923	40,464	84,892	233,944	664,738	124,822	6,438.5
1994	2,023	9,101	37,639	81,079	214,698	624,048	110,772	5,873.1
1995	1,694	8,526	33,666	80,377	202,637	632,523	104,939	5,684.5
1996	1,476	8,374	32,796	80,572	204,335	659,397	104,928	5,064.1

Source: Texas Department of Public Safety, Austin, and the Federal Bureau of Investigation, Washington. Population figures used to determine crime rate per 100,000 population based on U.S. Bureau of Census. The population figure used in determining the crime rate for 1996 in Texas was 19,128,000.

Top 10 County Crime Rates Per 100,000 Population in 1996

1. Potter.....13,491
2. Nueces.....10,249
3. Dallas.....7,813
4. McLennan.....7,568
5. Bexar.....7,566
6. Gregg.....7,534
7. Lamar.....7,234
8. El Paso.....7,227
9. Jefferson.....7,183
10. Travis.....7,158

Family Violence Still on the Increase in Texas in 1996

Family violence is defined in the Texas Family Code as an act by a member of a family or household against another member that is intended to result in physical harm, bodily injury, assault or a threat that reasonably places the member in fear of imminent physical harm.

By definition, "family" includes individuals related by blood or affinity, marriage or former marriage, biological parents of the same child, foster children, foster parents and members or former members of the same household, including roommates.

In 1996, 187,005 offenders were involved in reported incidents of family violence against 190,945 victims. In 58.35 percent of the incidents, the relationship of victim to offender was marital: 28 percent of those victims were wives, and 17.83 percent were common-law wives.

Of the remaining offenses, 15.06 percent involved parents against children or children against parents. Other family/household relationships, such as grandparents or grandchildren, siblings, step-siblings, roommates or in-laws were involved in 26.59 percent.

There are six general categories of family violence: assaults, homicides, kidnapping and abductions, robberies, forcible sex offenses and nonforcible sex offenses. Assaults accounted for 98 percent of all offenses in 1996.

In 1995, there were 172,476 incidents of family violence reported, committed by 181,246 offenders. There were 184,926 victims.

Investigation of reports of domestic violence can be hazardous to police officers. During 1996, 813 Texas law officers were assaulted while investigating such reports. ☆

Crime Profile of Texas Counties, 1996

County	Agencies	Commissioned Personnel †	Murder	Rape	Robbery	Assault	Burglary	Larceny	Auto Theft	Total Index Crimes (see page 585 for definition)	*Crime Rate Per 100,000
Anderson	3	59	5	26	40	252	496	1,280	77	2,176	4,225
Andrews	2	28	2	3	1	22	103	415	17	563	3,913
Angelina	4	125	9	19	75	204	607	2,123	155	3,192	4,178
Aransas	2	54	1	14	8	28	198	538	45	832	4,219
Archer	2	7	0	5	0	7	42	35	8	97	1,149
Armstrong	1	3	0	0	0	1	16	33	1	51	2,412
Atascosa	5	51	4	3	5	39	198	466	30	745	2,225
Austin	4	47	0	4	8	42	111	340	17	522	2,349
Bailey	2	9	0	6	1	23	52	184	9	275	4,111
Bandera	1	15	0	3	0	2	114	214	6	339	2,538
Bastrop	4	58	7	4	14	140	433	886	76	1,560	3,477
Baylor	2	10	0	0	0	25	25	89	7	146	3,268
Bee	2	38	1	7	3	84	282	649	21	1,047	3,763
Bell	10	391	6	135	252	696	2,053	8,093	652	11,887	5,468
Bexar	28	3,212	126	703	2,479	2,447	15,697	68,115	9,520	99,087	7,566
Blanco	3	12	0	0	0	13	62	72	6	153	2,033
Borden	1	2	1	0	0	1	3	2	2	9	1,135
Bosque	3	15	0	1	3	15	111	206	7	343	2,084
Bowie	6	144	10	34	86	337	969	2,613	213	4,262	5,025
Brazoria	17	420	10	64	73	474	1,439	4,320	420	6,800	3,129
Brazos	4	284	7	77	121	455	1,546	5,836	433	8,475	6,184
Brewster	3	23	0	2	3	21	83	160	12	281	2,973
Briscoe	1	2	0	0	0	3	11	16	1	31	1,519
Brooks	2	21	1	0	0	9	77	92	5	184	2,192
Brown	4	57	3	17	17	153	520	1,500	78	2,288	6,201
Burleson	3	26	1	5	7	47	117	225	17	419	2,739
Burnet	6	65	0	10	3	51	285	540	55	944	3,491
Caldwell	4	42	1	15	14	131	208	589	29	987	3,447
Calhoun	4	33	1	3	8	80	293	582	59	1,026	5,115
Callahan	2	9	2	0	0	4	32	24	8	70	562
Cameron	13	485	19	33	337	1,375	3,738	12,895	908	19,305	6,337
Camp	2	14	2	11	8	26	110	226	26	409	3,742
Carson	2	9	0	2	0	19	11	73	3	108	1,617
Cass	2	24	2	23	9	73	169	272	28	576	1,868
Castro	3	19	0	1	2	17	74	140	14	248	2,883
Chambers	2	29	3	11	11	25	140	533	60	783	3,240
Cherokee	6	60	5	14	19	119	492	880	63	1,592	3,627
Childress	2	15	1	1	1	25	52	201	7	288	3,841
Clay	1	9	0	2	0	6	49	119	17	193	1,829
Cochran	1	8	0	0	0	8	37	65	1	111	2,578
Coke	1	4	0	0	0	1	16	37	0	54	1,569
Coleman	3	15	3	0	0	19	64	105	5	196	1,975
Collin	11	475	2	96	140	689	2,282	8,870	607	12,686	3,539
Collingsworth	1	7	2	0	1	12	28	41	3	87	2,379
Colorado	4	33	0	4	7	85	116	351	19	582	2,989
Comal	2	102	7	32	29	124	660	2,079	95	3,026	4,529
Comanche	3	19	2	5	4	16	78	164	14	283	2,025
Concho	2	6	0	0	0	116	7	5	2	130	4,110
Cooke	2	45	1	8	10	51	187	576	59	892	2,711
Coryell	3	71	0	10	16	76	361	1,064	76	1,603	2,217
Cottle	1	2	0	0	0	3	17	5	0	25	1,130
Crane	2	13	0	2	0	3	25	87	7	124	2,675
Crockett	1	9	0	1	1	7	17	36	6	68	1,518
Crosby	1	7	0	0	0	2	16	15	0	33	466
Culberson	1	6	1	1	2	5	1	19	1	30	892
Dallam	2	15	1	0	3	50	40	151	12	257	4,200
Dallas	33	5,196	269	1,048	7,116	12,731	26,697	85,463	22,090	155,414	7,813
Dawson	2	23	0	2	3	94	127	277	15	518	3,403
Deaf Smith	2	43	0	4	7	58	126	537	20	752	3,936
Delta	1	6	0	1	0	10	30	41	1	83	1,587
Denton	16	473	4	78	147	447	1,819	7,482	603	10,580	3,083
DeWitt	3	22	0	4	3	28	137	173	21	366	1,738
Dickens	2	5	0	2	0	10	33	46	2	93	3,724
Dimmit	1	11	1	2	0	72	66	67	2	210	2,002
Donley	1	5	0	5	0	9	25	51	0	90	2,411
Duval	3	23	1	3	4	64	124	181	21	398	2,920
Eastland	5	29	1	3	4	64	140	421	24	657	3,361
Ector	3	277	15	45	142	946	1,496	4,946	369	7,959	6,475
Edwards	1	5	2	0	0	6	33	9	2	52	1,922

County	Agencies	Commissioned Personnel †	Murder	Rape	Robbery	Assault	Burglary	Larceny	Auto Theft	Total Index Crimes (see page 585 for definition)	*Crime Rate Per 100,000
Ellis	7	144	6	35	59	240	805	2,036	166	3,347	3,637
El Paso	6	1,239	37	319	1245	4,013	4,532	33,555	4,602	48,303	7,227
Erath	4	65	1	6	4	35	171	778	42	1,037	3,308
Falls	3	20	5	15	15	43	148	298	19	543	2,987
Fannin	2	28	0	9	3	45	166	401	40	664	2,465
Fayette	3	22	0	0	1	13	68	155	5	242	1,132
Fisher	1	5	0	0	0	7	36	30	4	77	1,683
Floyd	3	14	0	1	0	7	37	92	4	141	1,697
Foard	1	3	0	0	0	2	1	4	1	8	428
Fort Bend	10	485	20	78	263	556	2,169	5,553	586	9,225	3,122
Franklin	1	16	0	1	2	18	48	97	6	172	2,042
Freestone	3	27	2	3	4	41	179	211	15	455	2,688
Frio	3	24	0	2	0	70	168	221	17	478	3,064
Gaines	3	18	0	2	0	27	112	234	20	395	2,752
Galveston	15	734	21	141	453	1,531	3,584	9,717	1,430	16,877	7,053
Garza	1	8	0	4	2	17	31	60	8	122	2,612
Gillespie	2	28	0	5	1	34	67	328	5	440	2,244
Glasscock	1	2	0	0	0	0	1	9	0	10	710
Goliad	1	8	0	0	0	17	26	26	1	70	1,087
Gonzales	2	27	2	7	1	47	73	140	13	283	1,616
Gray	2	51	1	5	18	64	209	739	51	1,087	4,519
Grayson	7	173	5	69	100	323	1,011	3,732	247	5,487	5,529
Gregg	5	268	12	84	206	465	1,352	5,434	717	8,270	7,534
Grimes	2	26	0	1	2	51	237	527	44	862	4,052
Guadalupe	3	93	4	29	46	315	736	1,941	120	3,191	4,440
Hale	4	87	1	12	12	113	391	970	30	1,529	4,312
Hall	2	6	0	0	0	12	24	41	3	80	2,062
Hamilton	2	12	0	0	2	11	44	86	1	144	1,752
Hansford	3	10	0	0	1	16	40	85	7	149	2,741
Hardeman	2	8	1	0	1	2	12	18	6	40	787
Hardin	5	61	0	7	7	47	247	643	84	1,035	2,241
Harris	38	9,012	337	1,519	10,061	18,575	38,038	98,713	29,634	196,877	6,377
Harrison	2	79	9	25	61	183	714	1,859	249	3,100	5,147
Hartley	1	2	1	0	0	1	14	8	6	30	662
Haskell	3	8	1	1	0	5	33	65	2	107	1,640
Hays	4	159	1	37	34	170	655	1,943	145	2,985	3,761
Hemphill	1	9	0	0	0	1	7	43	1	52	1,474
Henderson	8	84	4	16	13	151	714	1,384	107	2,389	3,683
Hidalgo	16	713	36	151	519	1,806	7,334	18,825	2,790	31,461	6,482
Hill	5	48	1	9	16	65	407	714	47	1,259	4,278
Hockley	4	32	3	7	0	14	104	480	29	637	2,654
Hood	2	40	0	7	3	44	274	842	34	1,204	3,757
Hopkins	2	55	2	7	15	92	210	584	66	976	3,152
Houston	3	24	1	9	3	64	134	345	32	588	2,760
Howard	2	38	3	13	11	113	285	861	62	1,348	4,100
Hudspeth	1	8	0	1	1	11	19	21	8	61	1,783
Hunt	8	103	2	33	86	312	1,076	2,487	184	4,180	6,096
Hutchinson	3	42	0	7	11	48	137	544	40	787	3,067
Irion	1	4	0	1	0	1	12	22	1	37	2,313
Jack	2	17	0	4	0	14	62	88	5	173	2,378
Jackson	2	21	0	5	8	21	81	180	13	308	2,124
Jasper	3	37	3	3	9	58	273	468	36	850	2,558
Jeff Davis	1	3	0	0	0	2	2	4	3	11	517
Jefferson	7	519	21	252	613	1,124	3,603	10,663	1,383	17,659	7,183
Jim Hogg	1	15	0	0	0	12	14	27	2	55	1,006
Jim Wells	4	56	5	9	11	149	408	897	105	1,584	3,956
Johnson	6	166	4	35	20	188	800	2,509	155	3,711	3,439
Jones	5	24	3	4	0	45	135	186	13	386	2,093
Karnes	2	13	1	1	1	20	55	50	2	130	1,038
Kaufman	5	86	1	13	35	140	656	1,452	173	2,470	4,209
Kendall	2	31	2	1	0	20	77	325	19	444	2,315
Kenedy	1	8	0	0	0	3	3	1	2	9	2,727
Kent	1	3	0	0	0	2	1	6	5	14	1,477
Kerr	3	80	3	16	21	85	254	926	53	1,358	3,320
Kimble	2	9	0	0	0	6	17	31	3	57	1,288
King	1	1	0	0	0	1	1	8	1	11	3,274
Kinney	1	4	0	1	0	2	2	1	1	7	210
Kleberg	3	88	5	13	12	110	359	1,344	57	1,900	6,041
Knox	3	8	0	3	0	19	17	39	1	79	1,662
Lamar	3	76	4	10	38	503	562	2,106	112	3,335	7,234
Lamb	4	25	2	1	1	42	72	185	13	316	2,092

County	Agencies	Commissioned Personnel †	Murder	Rape	Robbery	Assault	Burglary	Larceny	Auto Theft	Total Index Crimes (see page 585 for definition)	*Crime Rate Per 100,000
Lampasas	2	22	2	0	1	26	103	372	16	520	3,171
La Salle	1	8	0	1	0	32	65	40	15	153	2,568
Lavaca	3	24	0	1	3	25	96	282	13	420	2,102
Lee	3	19	1	3	3	29	84	221	11	352	2,528
Leon	1	9	0	2	2	7	75	56	3	145	1,078
Liberty	4	85	4	14	31	113	736	1,152	134	2,184	3,475
Limestone	3	40	3	11	8	81	188	452	28	771	3,628
Lipscomb	1	4	0	1	0	3	21	24	0	49	1,512
Live Oak	2	20	1	2	1	5	32	57	9	107	1,040
Llano	2	22	0	1	0	19	85	145	12	262	2,054
Loving	1	2	0	0	0	0	0	0	0	0	0
Lubbock	10	515	15	140	288	1,773	2,762	8,732	1,025	14,735	6,311
Lynn	2	10	1	4	1	6	40	67	4	123	1,847
Madison	2	15	0	3	1	33	119	330	13	499	4,111
Marion	2	15	4	5	5	47	126	185	23	395	3,747
Martin	2	8	0	0	0	1	36	28	0	65	1,216
Mason	1	1	0	0	0	1	1	5	0	7	195
Matagorda	3	87	0	16	46	212	506	1,374	106	2,260	6,020
Maverick	2	69	0	3	6	88	583	1,396	84	2,160	4,909
McCulloch	2	14	0	1	0	27	61	180	5	274	3,138
McLennan	18	477	16	110	439	1,056	2,844	9,352	1,480	15,297	7,568
McMullen	1	3	0	0	0	0	1	1	0	2	254
Medina	3	37	2	13	4	86	253	531	41	930	2,862
Menard	1	4	0	0	0	2	4	7	0	13	543
Midland	3	260	4	77	85	276	1175	3,842	320	5,779	4,966
Milam	3	30	3	10	6	76	186	490	32	803	3,429
Mills	1	5	0	0	0	6	10	13	2	31	611
Mitchell	2	12	0	3	0	6	39	153	11	212	2,467
Montague	4	27	1	1	6	32	150	317	14	521	2,857
Montgomery	7	366	9	70	133	722	1,986	5,309	647	8,876	3,758
Moore	2	40	1	10	6	39	53	364	20	493	2,588
Morris	4	17	0	6	6	38	70	169	19	308	2,351
Motley	1	2	0	0	0	1	8	0	0	9	641
Nacogdoches	3	96	4	15	37	317	365	1,078	70	1,886	3,263
Navarro	2	91	2	32	45	104	467	1,432	109	2,191	5,167
Newton	1	13	2	2	3	19	72	60	10	168	1,166
Nolan	3	32	2	6	7	55	143	414	23	650	3,820
Nueces	6	524	20	289	498	2,353	4,126	22,650	1,734	31,670	10,249
Ochiltree	2	15	0	1	0	21	32	130	7	191	2,095
Oldham	1	5	2	0	1	4	15	26	5	53	2,204
Orange	7	150	6	28	95	318	945	2,650	231	4,273	5,022
Palo Pinto	2	47	2	9	2	95	249	681	44	1,082	4,307
Panola	2	39	2	6	6	80	159	356	21	630	2,851
Parker	4	80	4	23	11	95	444	1,108	91	1,776	2,454
Parmer	4	15	0	2	1	6	54	87	4	154	1,497
Pecos	2	35	1	4	2	56	88	414	22	587	3,636
Polk	4	50	3	6	19	74	346	696	59	1,203	3,141
Potter	5	340	12	72	336	1,034	2,189	10,039	718	14,400	13,491
Presidio	2	9	0	1	15	9	34	25	6	90	1,243
Rains	1	10	0	1	0	14	77	110	13	215	2,888
Randall	3	87	0	9	6	36	105	470	24	650	662
Reagan	1	6	0	1	0	19	22	31	8	81	1,848
Real	1	3	3	0	0	0	13	8	3	27	1,010
Red River	2	18	1	4	3	44	127	183	16	378	2,609
Reeves	2	32	1	1	3	35	127	290	14	471	3,014
Refugio	2	19	0	0	2	23	53	147	3	228	2,857
Roberts	1	3	0	0	0	2	1	6	0	9	1,053
Robertson	2	20	1	4	2	49	181	207	22	466	3,089
Rockwall	4	54	0	12	9	57	152	546	41	817	2,490
Runnels	3	19	0	4	1	12	63	190	7	277	2,368
Rusk	4	63	1	21	30	286	401	1,200	136	2,075	4,554
Sabine	2	11	0	2	1	18	84	126	13	244	2,260
San Augustine	2	10	0	3	6	32	52	130	4	227	2,804
San Jacinto	1	14	1	4	4	24	192	288	26	539	2,982
San Patricio	7	86	3	10	12	150	525	1,161	77	1,938	2,974
San Saba	1	4	0	4	1	10	30	34	5	84	1,440
Schleicher	1	4	0	1	0	2	29	49	2	83	2,640
Scurry	2	25	1	5	1	32	100	388	18	545	2,863
Shackelford	1	4	0	1	1	1	11	21	1	36	1,045
Shelby	2	22	2	7	12	70	220	368	34	713	3,159
Sherman	2	7	0	2	0	0	9	39	4	54	1,749

County	Agencies	Commissioned Personnel †	Murder	Rape	Robbery	Assault	Burglary	Larceny	Auto Theft	Total Index Crimes (see page 585 for definition)	*Crime Rate Per 100,000
Smith	10	265	15	114	210	611	1,657	6,147	535	9,289	5,717
Somervell	1	18	0	0	0	4	35	109	1	149	2,585
Starr	3	67	0	9	12	209	554	735	91	1,610	3,282
Stephens	2	15	0	0	0	9	75	149	1	234	2,397
Sterling	1	3	0	0	0	2	6	10	2	20	1,514
Stonewall	1	2	1	1	0	2	8	14	0	26	1,468
Sutton	2	10	0	0	0	19	23	144	7	193	4,220
Swisher	3	16	0	5	8	21	50	182	8	274	3,155
Tarrant	38	3,306	97	673	2,630	5,823	15,224	49,487	8,168	82,102	6,373
Taylor	5	251	8	74	128	438	1,252	4,224	250	6,374	5,027
Terrell	1	3	0	0	0	4	11	5	1	21	1,625
Terry	2	25	3	3	5	67	76	182	8	344	2,542
Throckmorton	1	1	0	0	0	1	4	2	1	8	410
Titus	2	38	2	6	10	182	171	638	65	1,074	4,144
Tom Green	4	221	3	53	43	518	826	4,116	170	5,729	5,488
Travis	12	1,519	45	311	1,452	2,436	8,988	31,329	4,008	48,569	7,158
Trinity	2	12	2	3	4	60	164	193	29	455	3,675
Tyler	2	19	1	5	4	41	172	182	20	425	2,145
Upshur	4	35	2	11	5	41	264	447	54	824	2,424
Upton	1	9	0	2	0	13	22	49	5	91	2,193
Uvalde	3	38	2	2	3	91	274	592	27	991	4,010
Val Verde	2	84	1	0	37	141	487	1,433	99	2,198	5,091
Van Zandt	6	56	2	6	9	129	371	586	89	1,192	2,902
Victoria	2	203	2	42	70	548	940	2,712	209	4,523	5,650
Walker	2	61	1	10	48	236	452	1,207	98	2,052	3,672
Waller	5	65	0	16	10	78	267	643	85	1,099	4,136
Ward	2	27	0	6	2	19	83	224	9	343	2,672
Washington	2	62	2	26	14	230	278	767	45	1,362	4,662
Webb	5	437	11	30	249	810	1,855	7,786	1,082	11,823	6,705
Wharton	3	79	2	28	40	154	570	1,213	87	2,094	5,109
Wheeler	2	7	0	2	3	15	22	51	8	101	1,803
Wichita	6	241	11	83	154	684	1,216	4,890	397	7,435	5,818
Wilbarger	2	29	0	0	8	27	122	235	16	408	2,573
Willacy	2	35	1	3	9	102	249	348	23	735	3,776
Williamson	11	304	1	44	61	309	1,351	3,658	272	5,696	2,995
Wilson	3	30	1	0	1	62	169	385	3	621	2,391
Winkler	2	17	0	4	0	8	23	82	3	120	1,461
Wise	3	47	0	5	6	41	236	581	29	898	2,271
Wood	5	50	1	28	3	111	274	505	58	980	3,060
Yoakum	2	17	1	2	1	14	46	164	4	232	2,706
Young	3	33	0	1	1	43	131	400	22	598	3,335
Zapata	1	26	0	0	0	1	71	129	10	211	2,031
Zavala	2	17	0	2	4	54	108	165	7	340	2,828

* County population figures used for calculation of crime rate are the State Data Center estimates for Jan. 1, 1996.
† The commissioned officers listed here are those employed by sheriffs' offices and the police departments of municipalities, universities and colleges, transit systems, park departments and medical facilities. In addition, the Texas Department of Public Safety has 2,797 commissioned personnel stationed statewide.

Crime Rates by States, 1994

(Index Crimes per 100,000 population)

1.	Washington, D.C.	11,085
2.	Florida	8,250
3.	Arizona	7,925
4.	Hawaii	6,681
5.	Nevada	6,677
6.	Louisiana	6,671
7.	Oregon	6,296
8.	New Mexico	6,188
9.	California	6,174
10.	Maryland	6,123
11.	Washington	6,028
12.	Georgia	6,010
13.	South Carolina	6,001
14.	**Texas**	**5,872**
	(United States	**5,374**

Source: Statistical Abstract of the United States, 1996.

Agriculture in Texas

Source: Texas Agricultural Extension Service.

Agribusiness, the combined phases of food and fiber production, processing, transporting and marketing, is a leading Texas industry. Most of the following discussion is devoted to the phase of production on farms and ranches.

Information was provided by Agricultural Extension Service specialists, Texas Agricultural Statistics Service, U.S. Department of Agriculture, and U.S. Department of Commerce. It was coordinated by Carl G. Anderson, Extension Marketing Economist, Texas A&M University. All references are to Texas unless otherwise specified.

Agriculture is one of the most important industries in Texas. Many businesses, financial institutions, and individuals are involved in providing supplies, credit, and services to farmers and ranchers and in processing and marketing agricultural commodities.

Including all its agribusiness phases, agriculture added about $44 billion in 1996 to the economic activity of the state.

The estimated value of farm assets in Texas--the land, buildings, livestock, machinery, crops, inventory on farms, household goods, and farm financial assets-- totaled approximately $80 billion at the beginning of 1996.

Texas agriculture is a strong industry. Receipts from farm and ranch marketings in 1996 were estimated at $13.3 billion. In 1984, this figure stood at $9.7 billion.

The potential for further growth is great. With the increasing demand for food and fiber throughout the world, and because of the importance of agricultural exports to this nation's trade balance, agriculture in Texas is destined to play an even greater role in the future.

Major efforts of research and educational programs by the Texas A&M University System are directed toward developing the state's agricultural industry to its fullest potential.

The goal is to capitalize on natural advantages that agriculture has in Texas because of the relatively warm climate, productive soils, and availability of excellent export and transportation facilities.

The number and nature of farms have changed over time. The number of farms in Texas has decreased from 418,000 in 1940 to 205,000 in 1996 with an average size of 620 acres. Average value per farm of all farm assets, including land and buildings, has increased from $20,100 in 1950 to $350,920 in 1996.

Mechanization of farming continues as new and larger machines replace manpower. Even though machinery price tags are high relative to times past, machines are technologically advanced and productive.

Tractors, mechanical harvesters, and numerous cropping machines have virtually eliminated menial tasks that for many years were traditional to farming.

Revolutionary agricultural chemicals have appeared along with improved plants and animals and methods of

Balance Sheet of Texas Farms and Ranches
Jan. 1, 1986-1995

Table below shows the financial status of Texas farms and ranches as of Jan. 1 of the years 1986-95.

Item	1986	‡1987	1988	1989	1990	1991	1992	1993	1994	§1995
ASSETS:					Million dollars					
Physical Assets:										
Real estate	$73,101	$73,264	$68,467	$58,853	$57,673	$55,355	$55,719	$57,204	$62,382	$63,459
Non-real estate:										
Livestock and poultry	4,761	6,621	7,514	7,929	8,570	8,343	8,983	8,986	8,703	6,417
Machinery and motor vehicles	5,384	5,330	5,437	5,411	5,503	5,590	5,554	5,675	5,845	5,814
*Crops stored on and off farms	721	810	794	841	562	598	618	531	628	702
Purchased Inputs	136	349	317	222	134	111	157	147	169	109
†Household equipment and furnishings	1,861	3,347	3,482	—	—	—	—	—	—	—
Financial assets:										
‡Investments in co-ops	1,538	—	—	—	—	—	—	—	—	—
‡Other financial	3,286	—	—	—	—	—	—	—	—	—
‡Financial	—	5,104	5,121	2,746	2,929	3,136	3,406	3,788	3,921	3,933
Total Assets.	90,789	94,824	91,131	76,003	75,371	73,133	74,437	76,331	81,649	80,434
LIABILITIES:										
**Real estate debt	6,071	5,678	5,143	4,560	4,604	4,589	4,489	4,521	4,523	4,679
***Non-real estate debt:										
****Excluding CCC loans . .	5,878	5,763	5,576	5,104	4,876	5,059	4,811	5,153	5,386	5,469
Total Liabilities	11,949	11,441	10,718	9,663	9,479	9,648	9,300	9,674	9,909	10,149
Owners' equities	78,840	83,383	80,412	66,339	65,892	63,485	65,137	66,657	71,740	70,285
TOTAL CLAIMS	$90,789	$94,824	$91,131	$76,003	$75,371	$73,133	$74,437	$76,331	$81,649	$80,434

*All crops held on farms including value above loan rates for crops held under CCC.
**Includes CCC storage and drying facilities loans.
***Includes debt owed to institutional lender and to noninstitutional or miscellaneous lenders.
****Nonrecourse CCC loans secured by crops owned by farmers. These crops are included as assets in this balance sheet.
†As of 1993, Household equipment and furnishings not reported.
‡As of 1987, Investments in Co-ops and Other Financial reported as Financial.
§Preliminary.
Source: **"Economic indicators of the Farm Sector: State Financial Summary 1985,"** USDA, ERS, January 1987, p.229.; 1988, 1989, 1991, 1993, p. 136 (including operator households). Farm Business Economics Report, Aug. 1996; Farm Business Sheet, April 1997.

handling them. Many of the natural hazards of farming and ranching were reduced by better use of weather information, machinery and other improvements; but rising costs, labor availability, and high energy costs have added to concerns of farmers and ranchers.

Among the major changes in Texas agriculture since World War II are these:

Farms have become fewer, larger, specialized, and much more expensive to own and operate, but far more productive.

Irrigation has become an important factor in crop production.

Crops and livestock have made major changes in production areas, as in the concentration of cotton on the High Plains and livestock increases in Central and Eastern Texas.

Pest and disease control methods have greatly improved. Herbicides are relied upon for weed control.

Ranchers and farmers are better educated and informed, more science- and business-oriented.

Feedlot finishing, commercial broiler production, artificial insemination, improved pastures and brush control, reduced feed requirements, and other changes have greatly increased livestock and poultry efficiency. Bio-technology and genetic engineering promise new breakthroughs in reaching even higher levels of productivity.

Horticultural plant and nursery businesses have expanded. Improved wildlife management has increased deer, turkey and other wildlife populations.

Cooperation among farmers in marketing, promotion, and other fields has increased.

Agricultural producers have become increasingly dependent on off-the-farm services to supply production inputs such as feeds, chemicals, credit, and other essentials.

Texas 1995 Crop Production

*Rank Among States	Crop	Planted Acres (000)	Harvested Acres (000)	Yield Per Acre	Production (000)
1	Upland Cotton	6,400.00	5,750.00	376.00	4,500
1	All Cotton	6,436.00	5,783.00	378.00	4,551
1	All Other Hay	.	3,600.00	2.10	7,560
2	Sorghum for Grain	2,700.00	2,400.00	54.00	129,600
2	Peanuts for Nuts	275.00	270.00	2,050.00	553,500
2	Blackeye (peas) Beans	11.10	10.10	1,200.00	121
2	Pecans	.	.	.	60,000
3	Sorghum for Silage	.	45.00	14.00	630
3	Amer-Pima Cotton	36.00	33.00	742.00	51
3	All Hay	.	3,760.00	2.16	8,136
3	Mid & Navel Oranges	.	5.99	159.00	950
3	All Oranges	.	6.97	151.00	1,055
3	All Grapefruit	.	14.96	311.00	4,650
4	All Rice	320.00	318.00	5,600.00	17,802
4	Sugarcane for Sugar	.	41.30	33.40	1,381
4	Sugarcane for Seed	.	1.00	23.00	23
4	All Sugarcane	.	42.30	33.20	1,404
4	Valencia Oranges	.	0.98	107.00	105
4	Summer Potatoes	7.30	7.00	235.00	1,645
5	Other Dry Edible Beans	11.50	10.60	760.00	81
5	Spring Potatoes	5.20	5.00	185.00	925
6	Winter Wheat	5,800.00	2,800.00	27.00	75,600
6	Sweet Potatoes	5.60	5.20	130.00	676
7	Sunflower Seed, Oil	21.00	18.00	1,000.00	18,000
7	Sunflower Seed, Non-oil	23.00	22.00	820.00	18,040
7	All Sunflowers	44.00	40.00	901.00	36,040
10	All Wheat	5,800.00	2,800.00	27.00	75,600
10	Corn for Grain	2,100.00	1,900.00	114.00	216,600
11	Oats	650.00	120.00	42.00	5,040
11	Sugarbeets	20.20	19.30	18.20	351
11	Freestone Peaches	.	.	.	24,000
12	Rye	150.00	20.00	19.00	380
13	All Dry Edible Beans	25.00	23.00	980.00	225
14	Pinto Beans	2.40	2.30	1,000.00	23
15	Corn for Silage	.	70.00	22.00	1,540
19	All Potatoes	12.50	12.00	214.00	2,570
22	Barley	15.00	7.00	46.00	322
24	Soybeans for Beans	250.00	240.00	25.00	6,000
28	Alfalfa Hay	.	160.00	3.60	576

*Based on production. Source: U.S. and Texas Departments of Agriculture.

Agribusiness

Texas farmers and ranchers have developed considerable dependence upon agribusiness. With many producers specializing in the production of certain crops and livestock, they look beyond the farm and ranch for supplies and services. On the input side, they rely on suppliers of production needs and services and, on the output side, they need assemblers, processors, and distributors. The impact of production agriculture and related businesses on the Texas economy is about $44 billion annually.

Since 1940, the proportion of Texans whose livelihood is linked to agriculture has changed greatly.

In 1940, about 23 percent were producers on farms and ranches, and about 17 percent were suppliers or were engaged in assembly, processing, and distribution of agricultural products.

The agribusiness alignment in 1996 was less than 2 percent on farms and ranches with about 17 percent of the labor force providing production or marketing supplies and services and retailing food and fiber products.

Cash Receipts

Farm and ranch cash receipts in 1995 totaled $13.287 billion. With estimates of $642.9 million for government payments, $797.6 million of noncash income, and $943.1 million of other farm-related income included, realized gross farm income totaled $15.706 billion. With farm production expenses of $13.288 billion, net farm income totaled $2.419 billion. The value of inventory adjustment was $35.0 million.

Farm and Ranch Assets

Farm and ranch assets totaled $80.4 billion on January 1, 1996. This was down from the 1994 level of $81.6 billion. Value of real estate increased almost 2 percent to $63.5 billion. Liabilities totaled $10.1 billion, up slightly from $9.9 billion in 1994.

Percent of Income From Products

Livestock and livestock products accounted for 63.6 percent of the $13.3 billion cash receipts from farm marketings in 1995 with the remaining 36.4 percent from crops.

Receipts from livestock have trended up largely because of reduced crop acreage associated with farm programs and low prices. However, these relationships change because of variations in commodity prices and volume of marketings.

Meat animals (cattle, hogs and sheep) accounted for 48.4 percent of total cash receipts received by Texas farmers and ranchers in 1995. Most of these receipts were from cattle and calf sales.

Dairy products made up 6.0 percent of receipts,

poultry and eggs 7.3 percent, and miscellaneous livestock 1.9 percent.

Cotton accounted for 12.5 percent of total receipts, feed crops 8.2 percent, food grains 3.1 percent, vegetables 3.4 percent, greenhouse/nursery products 6.0 percent, oil crops 1.5 percent, fruits and nuts 0.8 percent, and other crops 6.8 percent.

Texas Rank Among States

Measured by cash receipts for farm and ranch marketings, Texas ranked second in 1995. California ranked first and Iowa third.

Texas normally leads all other states in numbers of farms and ranches and farm and ranch land, cattle slaughtered, cattle on feed, calf births, sheep and lambs slaughtered, goats, cash receipts from livestock marketings, cattle and calves, beef cows, sheep and lambs, wool production, mohair production, and exports of lard and tallow. The state also usually leads in production of cotton.

Texas Agricultural Exports

The value of Texas' share of agricultural exports in fiscal year 1996 was $3.566 billion. Cotton accounted for $760.3 million of the exports; feed grains, $529.9 million; wheat and flour, $217.5 million; rice, $106.4 million; fats, oil, and greases, $99.0 million; cottonseed and products, $28.1 million; hides and skins, $247.7 million; meats and meat products, $745.3 million; fruits, $43.2 million; peanuts and products, $46.5 million; soybeans and products, $21.8 million; vegetables, $46.0 million; poultry and products, $136.9 million; dairy products, $21.4 million; and miscellaneous and other products, $502.3 million.

Texas' 1996 exports of $3.566 billion of farm and ranch products compares with $3.452 billion in 1995 and $3.022 billion in 1994.

Hunting

The management of wildlife as an economic enterprise through leasing for hunting makes a significant contribution to the economy of many counties. Leasing the right of ingress on a farm or ranch for the purpose of hunting is the service marketed. After the leasing, the consumer--the hunter--goes onto the land to seek the harvest of the wildlife commodity. Hunting lease income to farmers and ranchers in 1996 was estimated at $221 million.

The demand for hunting opportunities is growing while the land capable of producing huntable wildlife is decreasing. As a result, farmers and ranchers are placing more emphasis on wildlife management practices to help meet requests for hunting leases.

Irrigation

Texas farmers irrigate approximately 6.3 million acres of land (third in the nation behind California and Nebraska). Although some irrigation is practiced in nearly every county of the state, about 60 percent of the total irrigated acreage is on the High Plains of Texas.

Other concentrated areas of irrigation are the Gulf Coast rice producing area, the Lower Rio Grande Valley, the Winter Garden district of South Texas, the Trans-Pecos area of West Texas, and the peanut producing area in North Central Texas centered around Erath, Eastland, and Comanche Counties. Sprinkler irrigation

*Realized Gross Income and Net Income from Farming, Texas, 1960-1995

Year	**Realized Gross Farm Income	Farm Production Expenses	Net Change In Farm Inventories	***Total Net Farm Income	***Total Net Income Per Farm
	— Million Dollars —				Dollars
1960	2,547.0	1,751.5	43.2	838.7	3,396.0
1970	4,026.5	3,232.5	106.8	900.8	4,249.0
1980	§9,611.4	9,081.1	-542.5	530.4	2,806.3
1982	11,372.7	9,581.5	-124.3	1,791.2	9,527.7
1983	11,129.2	9,387.9	-590.7	1,741.4	9,312.3
1984	12,058.8	9,762.8	168.8	2,296.0	11,835.0
1985	11,272.7	9,226.3	-9.0	2,046.4	10,658.3
1986	10,282.0	9,459.5	-349.0	1,012.3	5,327.9
1987	11,155.6	9,945.5	-563.2	2,328.1	12,383.5
1988	12,133.0	10,363.9	-62.1	2,280.6	12,195.7
1989	12,873.3	10,658.7	-637.6	2,214.6	11,906.0
1990	14,356.0	11,366.0	311.9	2,990.0	15,904.0
1991	14,336.9	11,344.6	69.1	2,992.4	16,175.0
1992	14,181.4	10,982.0	299.0	3,199.5	17,484.0
1993	15,724.7	11,626.7	310.7	4,098.0	22,151.0
1994	15,347.1	11,610.0	109.9	3,737.1	18,685.5
1995	15,706.3	13,287.2	35.0	2,419.0	11,975.2

*Details for items may not add to totals because of rounding. Series revised, September, 1981.
**Cash receipts from farm marketings, government payments, value of home consumption and gross rental value of farm dwellings.
***Farm income of farm operators.
§Starting in 1977, farms with production of $1,000 or more used to figure income.
Source: "Economic Indicators of the Farm Sector, State Financial Summary, 1985," 1987," 1989,: 1993"; USDA/ERS; "Texas Agricultural Cash Receipts and Price Statistics," USDA/NASS/ Agricultural Statistician, Texas Agricultural Statistics Service, Bulletin 252, Nov. 1994. Farm Business Economics Report, Aug. 1996; Farm Business Sheet, April 1997.

was used on about 44 percent of the total irrigated acreage with surface irrigation methods, primarily furrow and surge methods, being used on the remaining irrigated area.

Drip, or trickle, irrigation has attracted much attention in recent years for use on tree crops such as citrus, pecans, avocados, peaches, and apples, or for irrigating vegetables under plastic mulch.

Some drip irrigation of cotton and forages is being practiced in West Texas. The use of drip irrigation is increasing with present acreage estimated to be 75,000 acres.

Approximately 81 percent of the state's irrigated acreage is supplied with water pumped from wells. Surface water sources supply the remaining area. Declining groundwater levels in several of the major aquifers is a serious problem. As the water level declines, well yields decrease and pumping costs increase.

Irrigation is an important factor in the productivity of Texas agriculture. The value of crop production from irrigated acreage is 50 to 60 percent of the total value of all crop production, although only about 30 percent of the state's total harvested cropland acreage is irrigated.

The percentage of total crop production which comes from irrigated lands varies from year to year, depending primarily upon the amount of rainfall

Export Shares of Commodities

Commodity*	1993	1994	1995	1996	1996 % of U.S. Total
	— million dollars —				
Rice	100.5	85.8	125.7	106.4	11.60
Cotton.	313.9	736.8	879.9	760.3	25.11
Fats, Oils & Greases	73.2	75.0	123.8	99.0	14.68
Hides & Skins	191.4	218.6	273.1	247.7	14.77
Meats other than Poultry . . .	527.2	585.1	722.3	745.3	13.34
Feed Grains	353.4	372.0	357.6	529.9	4.86
Poultry Products	66.2	87.2	111.0	136.9	5.02
Fruits	32.8	35.7	37.7	43.2	1.33
Vegetables	39.7	36.8	51.9	46.0	1.22
Wheat & Flour . .	223.4	170.7	144.5	217.5	3.06
Soybeans	35.9	11.7	20.1	21.8	0.28
Cottonseed & Prod.	20.9	40.2	42.4	28.1	26.71
Peanuts	41.6	35.6	49.8	46.5	15.59
Tree Nuts	18.2	8.4	9.8	13.6	0.99
Dairy Products . .	25.5	23.3	26.8	21.4	2.91
†All Other	400.5	432.4	476.0	502.3	5.16
TOTAL	**2,464.3**	**2,955.3**	**3,452.4**	**3,565.9**	**5.96**

Totals may not add because of rounding.
† Mainly confectionary, nursery and greenhouse, essential oils, sunflower seed oil, beverages, and other miscellaneous animal and vegetable products.
*Commodity and related preparations.
*Source: **Foreign Agricultural Trade of the United States**, various issues, 1994, 1995 and 1997.*

Value of Cotton and Cottonseed

Crop Year	Cotton Production (Bales)	Cotton Value	Cottonseed Production (Tons)	Cottonseed Value
	(All Figures in Thousands)			
1900	3,438	$157,306	1,531	$20,898
1910	3,047	210,260	1,356	31,050
1920	4,345	376,080	1,934	41,350
1930	4,037	194,080	1,798	40,820
1940	3,234	162,140	1,318	31,852
1950	2,946	574,689	1,232	111,989
1960	4,346	612,224	1,821	75,207
1970	3,191	314,913	1,242	68,310
*1980	3,320	1,091,616	1,361	161,959
1981	5,645	1,259,964	2,438	207,230
1982	2,700	664,848	1,122	90,882
1983	2,380	677,443	1,002	162,324
1984	3,680	927,360	1,563	157,863
1985	3,910	968,429	1,634	102,156
1986	2,535	560,945	1,053	82,118
1987	4,635	1,325,981	1,915	157,971
1988	5,215	1,291,651	2,131	238,672
1989	2,870	812,784	1,189	141,491
1990	4,965	1,506,182	1,943	225,388
1991	4,710	1,211,789	1,903	134,162
1992	3,265	769,495	1,346	145,368
1993	5,095	1,308,396	2,147	255,493
1994	4,915	1,639,644	2,111	213,211
1995	4,460	1,597,037	1,828	201,080
1996	4,350	1,394,784	1,833	238,290

*Beginning in 1971, the basis for cotton prices was changed from 500-pound gross weight to 480-pound net weight bale. To compute comparable prices for previous years, multiply price times 1.04167.
Source: "Texas Agricultural Facts," Feb., 1997, and "1995 Texas Crop Statistics," Texas Agricultural Statistics Service, Austin for recent statistics.
This table was compiled by Texas Cottonseed Crushers from their historical records and reports of the U.S.Department of Commerce and U.S. Department of Agriculture.

received. In good rainfall years, the proportion of irrigated crop production to total crop production is somewhat less.

However, in years of below average rainfall, the percentage of the total crop production which comes from irrigated lands increases.

Thus, irrigation provides a stabilizing influence upon Texas agriculture, enabling Texas farmers to produce a more dependable supply of food and fiber products without total dependence upon natural rainfall.

I. Principal Crops

In most recent years the value of crop production in Texas is less than half of the total value of the state's agricultural output. Cash receipts from farm sales of crops are reduced somewhat because some grain and roughage is fed to livestock on farms where produced.

Receipts from all Texas crops totaled $4.8 billion in 1995; $4.8 billion in 1994; and $4.5 billion in 1993.

Cotton, corn, and grain sorghum account for a large part of the total crop receipts. In 1995, cotton contributed about 34.5 percent of the crop total; corn, 12.5 percent; sorghum grain, 7.3 percent; and wheat, 5.9 percent. Hay, vegetables, rice, cottonseed, peanuts and soybeans are other important cash crops.

Cotton

Cotton has been a major crop in Texas for more than a century. Since 1880, Texas has led all states in cotton production in most years, and today the annual Texas cotton harvest amounts to approximately a fourth of total production in the United States.

The annual cotton crop has averaged 4.45 million bales since 1986.

Total value of upland and Pima lint cotton produced in Texas in 1996 was $1.421 billion. Cottonseed value in 1996 was $238,290,000 -- making the total value of the Texas crop around $1.660 billion.

Since 1880, Texas has led all states in cotton production in most years. Texas Almanac photo.

Upland cotton was harvested from 4.1 million acres in 1996 and American-Pima from 36,000 acres, for a total of 4.136 million acres. Yield for upland cotton in 1996 was 509 pounds per acre, with American-Pima yielding 801 pounds per acre.

Cotton acreage harvested in 1995 totaled 5.783 million, with a yield of 372 pounds per acre for upland cotton and 756 pounds per acre for American-Pima. Total cotton production amounted to 4.405 million bales in 1996 and 4.512 million in 1995. Counties leading in production of upland cotton in 1995 included Gaines, Lubbock, Hale, Terry, and Hockley.

Cotton is the raw material for processing operations at gins, oil mills, compresses, and a small number of textile mills in Texas. Less than 10 percent of the raw cotton is processed within the state.

Cotton in Texas is machine harvested. Growers in the 1994/95 season used stripper harvesters to gather 85 percent of the crop and spindle pickers to harvest the remaining 15 percent. Field storage of harvested seed cotton is gaining in popularity as gins decline in number. In 1994/95, 91 percent of the cotton was ginned from modules and 9 percent from trailers. Much of the Texas cotton crop is exported. Japan, South Korea, and Mexico are major buyers.

With the development of open-end spinning and the improved strength of cotton, more utilization of cotton by mills within the state may develop in the future. Unlike the conventional ring spinning method, open-end spinning techniques can efficiently produce high-quality yarn from relatively strong, short staple cotton with fine mature fiber.

The state's major cotton-producing areas are tied together by an electronic marketing system. This system is a computer network that links producers through terminals that are usually located at gins to a relatively large number of buyers. The network provides farmers with a centralized market that allows many sellers and buyers to trade with each other on a regular basis.

The first high volume instrument cotton classing office in the nation was opened at Lamesa, Texas in 1980.

Grain Sorghum

Grain sorghum in 1996 ranked fourth in dollar value. Much of the grain is exported, as well as being used in livestock and poultry feed throughout the state.

Total production of grain sorghum in 1996 was 102,144,000 hundredweight (cwt), with an average 2,688 pounds per acre. With an average price of $5.89 per cwt., the total value reached $601,920,000. In 1995, 2.40 million acres of grain sorghum were harvested, yielding an average of 3,024 pounds per acre for a total production of 72,576,000 cwt.

It was valued at $5.18 per cwt, for a total value of $375,840,000. In 1994, 2.6 million acres were harvested with an average of 3,304 pounds per acre, or 85,904,000 cwt. The season's price was $3.88 per cwt. for a total value of $332,878,000.

Although grown to some extent in all counties where crops are important, the largest concentrations are in the High Plains, Rolling Plains, Blackland Prairie, Coastal Bend, and Lower Rio Grande Valley areas. Counties leading in production in 1995 were Nueces, Wharton, San Patricio, Hidalgo, Williamson, and Cameron.

Research to develop high-yielding hybrids resistant to diseases and insect damage continues. A leader in this development, J. Roy Quinby is principal author of a history of grain sorghums which appeared in the 1972-73 edition of the Texas Almanac.

Rice

Rice, which is grown in about 20 counties on the Coast Prairie of Texas, ranked third in value among

Texas crops for a number of years. However, in recent years, cotton, grain sorghum, wheat, corn, peanuts and hay have outranked rice.

Farms are highly mechanized, producing rice through irrigation and using airplanes for much of the planting, fertilizing, and application of insecticides and herbicides.

Texas farmers grow long- and medium-grain rice only. The Texas rice industry, which has grown from 110 acres in 1850 to a high of 642,000 acres in 1954, has been marked by significant yield increases and improved varieties.

Record production was in 1981, with 27,239,000 hundredweights harvested. Highest yield was 6,250 pounds per acre in 1986.

Several different types of rice milling procedures are in use today. The simplest and oldest method produces a product known as regular milled white rice, the most prevalent on the market today.

During this process, rice grains are subjected to additional cleaning to remove chaff, dust, foreign seed, etc., and then husks are removed from the grains. This results in a product which is the whole unpolished grain of rice with only the outer hull and a small amount of bran removed.

This product is called brown rice and is sometimes sold without further treatment other than grading. It has a delightful nutlike flavor and a slightly chewy texture.

When additional layers of the bran are removed, the rice becomes white in color and begins to appear as it is normally recognized at retail level. The removal of the bran layer from the grain is performed in a number of steps using two or three types of machines.

After the bran is removed, the product is ready for classification as to size. Rice is more valuable if the grains are not broken. In many cases, additional vitamins are added to the grains to produce what is called "enriched rice."

Another process may be used in rice milling to produce a product called parboiled rice. In this process, the rice is subjected to a combination of steam and pressure prior to the time it is milled in the manner described above. This process gelatinizes the starch in the grain, the treatment aiding in the retention of much of the natural vitamin and mineral content. After cooking, parboiled rice tends to be fluffy, more separate, and plump.

Still another type of rice is precooked rice, which is actually milled rice that, after milling, has been cooked. Then the moisture is removed through a dehydration process. Precooked rice requires a minimum of preparation time since it needs merely to have the moisture restored to it.

The United States produces only a small part of the world's total rice, but it is one of the leading exporters. American rice is popular abroad and is exported to more than 100 foreign countries.

Rice production in 1996 totaled 18,465,000 cwt. from 298,000 harvested acres, with a yield of 6,200 pounds per acre. The crop value totaled $192,036,000. Rice production was 17,802,000 in 1995 on 318,000 harvested acres, yielding 5,600 pounds per acre.

Total value in 1995 was $173,213,000. Rice production was 21,252,000 cwt. in 1994 on 354,000 harvested acres. Production in 1994 was valued at $151,314,000, with a yield of 6,000 pounds per acre. Counties leading in production in 1995 included Wharton, Colorado, Matagordo, Jackson, Brazoria, and Jefferson.

Wheat

Wheat for grain is one of the state's most valuable cash crops. In 1996, wheat was exceeded in value by cotton, hay, corn, and grain sorghum. Wheat pastures also provide considerable winter forage for cattle which is reflected in value of livestock produced.

Texas wheat production totaled 75,400,000 bushels in 1996 as yield averaged only 26.0 bushels per acre. Planted acreage totaled 6,000,000 acres and 2,900,000 acres were harvested.

With an average price of $5.05 per bushel, the 1996 wheat value totaled $380,770,000. In 1995, Texas wheat growers planted 5,800,000 acres and harvested 2,800,000 acres.

The yield was 27.0 bushels per acre for 1995 with total production of 75,600,000 bushels at $4.19 per bushel valued at $316,764,000.

Texas wheat growers planted 6,000,000 acres in 1994 and harvested grain from 2,900,000 acres. The yield was 26.0 bushels per acre for a total production of 75,400,000 bushels valued at $242,788,000.

Leading wheat-producing counties, based on production in 1995, were Dallam, Deaf Smith, Moore, Hansford, Castro, and Hartley. The leading counties, based on acreage planted in 1995, were Hansford, Ochiltree, Deaf Smith, Swisher, and Dallam.

Wheat was first grown commercially in Texas near Sherman about 1833. The acreage expanded greatly in North Central Texas after 1850 because of rapid settlement of the state and introduction of the well-adapted Mediterranean strain of wheat. A major family flour industry was developed in the Fort Worth/Dallas/Sherman area between 1875 and 1900.

Now, around half of the state acreage is planted on the High Plains and about a third of this is irrigated. Most of the Texas wheat acreage is of the hard red winter class.

Because of the recent development of varieties with improved disease resistance and the use of wheat for winter pasture, there has been a sizable expansion of acreage in Central and South Texas.

Most all wheat harvested for grain is used in some phase of the milling industry. The better-quality hard red winter wheat is used in the production of commercial bakery flour. Lower grades and varieties of soft red winter wheat are used in family flours. By-products of milled wheat are used for feed.

Corn

Interest in corn production throughout the state has increased since the 1970s as yields improved with new varieties. Once the principal grain crop, corn acreage declined as plantings of grain sorghum increased. Only 500,000 acres were harvested annually until the mid-1970's when development of new hybrids occurred.

Harvested acreage was 1,800,000 in 1996; 1,900,000 in 1995; and 2,040,000 in 1994. Yields for the corresponding years (1996-1994) were 112, 114, and 117 bushels per acre, respectively.

Most of the acreage and yield increase has occurred

in the Central and South Texas. In 1996, corn ranked third in value among the state's crops. It was valued at $655,200,000 in 1996; $690,954,000 in 1995; and $599,087,000 in 1994. The grain is largely used for livestock feed, but other important uses are in food products.

The leading counties in production for 1995 were Dallam, Castro, Parmer, Hartley, and Moore.

Rye

Rye is grown mainly on the Northern and Southern High Plains, the Northern Low Plains, Cross Timbers, Blacklands, and East Texas areas. Minor acreages are seeded in South Central Texas, the Edwards Plateau, and the Upper Coast. Rye is grown primarily as a cover crop and for grazing during the fall, winter, and early spring.

Rye production in 1996 totaled 190,000 bushels valued at $836,000. Of the 120,000 acres planted, 10,000 were harvested, yielding an average of 19.0 bushels per acre. In 1995, 20,000 of the 150,000 acres planted were harvested, with an average yield per acre of 19.0 bushels.

Value of production for the 380,000 bushels was $1,178,000. In 1994, 120,000 acres were planted to rye with 15,000 acres harvested, averaging 29.0 bushels per acre. The crop value was estimated at $1,414,000 or $3.25 per bushel.

Oats

Oats are grown extensively in Texas for winter pasture, hay, silage, and greenchop feeding, and some acreage is harvested for grain.

Of the 650,000 acres planted to oats in 1996, 100,000 acres were harvested. The average yield was 34.0 bushels per acre. Production totaled 3,400,000 bushels with a value of $11,900,000. In 1995, 650,000 acres were planted.

From the plantings, 120,000 acres were harvested, with an average yield of 42 bushels per acre for a total production of 5,040,000 bushels. Average price per bushel was $2.19 and total production value was $11,038,000.

Texas farmers planted 600,000 acres of oats in 1994. They harvested 130,000 acres which averaged 40.0 bushels per acre for a total production of 5,200,000 bushels at an average price of $1.83 per bushel with an estimated value of $9,516,000. Most of the acreage was used for grazing.

Almost all oat grain produced in Texas is utilized as feed for livestock within the state. A small acreage is grown exclusively for planting seed.

Leading oat grain-producing counties in 1995 were McLennan, Hamilton, Uvalde, Medina, and Cooke.

Barley

Texas barley acreage and production falls far below that of wheat and oats. In 1996, barley was harvested from 11,000 of the 16,000 acres planted. Production totaled 374,000 bushels and was valued at $1,403,000, with a yield of 34 bushels per acre.

In 1995, farmers harvested 7,000 of the 15,000 acres planted to barley. Yields averaged 46.0 bushels per acre for total production of 322,000 bushels. Value of production was $902,000 with an average price of $2.80 per bushel. In 1994, farmers planted 17,000

acres and harvested 8,000 acres which averaged 33.0 bushels per acre for a total production of 264,000 bushels. With price averaging $2.78 per bushel, the estimated value totaled $734,000.

Sugarbeets

Sugarbeets have been grown on a commercial scale in Texas since 1964 when the first beet sugar factory was built by Holly Sugar Company in Hereford.

Sugarbeet production in 1996 totaled 242,000 tons from 12,600 harvested acres, yielding 19.2 tons per acre. In 1995, 20,200 acres were planted and 19,300 were harvested. Average yield was 18.2 tons per acre and total production was 351,000 tons. In 1994, 25,400 acres were planted with 24,500 harvested. The yield averaged 20.3 tons per acre for total production of 494,000 tons.

Sugarcane

Sugarcane is grown from seed cane planted in late summer or fall. It is harvested 12 months later and milled to produce raw sugar and molasses. Raw sugar requires additional refining before it is in final form and can be offered to consumers.

The sugarcane grinding mill operated at Santa Rosa, Cameron County, is considered as one of the most modern mills in the United States. Texas sugarcane-producing counties are Hidalgo, Cameron, and Willacy.

At a yield of 26.7 tons per acre, sugarcane production in 1996 totaled 920,000 tons from 34,500 harvested acres. In 1995, 42,300 acres were harvested for total production of 1,364,000 tons valued at $36,282,000, or $26.60 per ton. The yield was 32.2 tons per acre.

In 1994, 43,500 acres were harvested from which 1,356,000 tons of sugarcane were milled. The yield averaged 31.2 tons per acre. The price averaged $29.90 per ton for a total value of $40,544,000.

Hay, Silage, and Other Forage Crops

A large proportion of Texas' agricultural land is devoted to forage crop production. This acreage produces forage needs and provides essentially the total feed requirements for most of the state's large domestic livestock population as well as game animals.

Approximately 80 million acres of native rangeland which are primarily in the western half of Texas provide grazing for beef cattle, sheep, goats, horses, and game animals.

An additional 20 million acres are devoted to introducing forage species. Of this total, approximately 16 million acres are established to introduce improved perennial grasses and legumes and are harvested by grazing animals.

The average annual acreage of crops grown for hay, silage, and other forms of machine-harvested forage is close to 4 million acres with an estimated value in excess of $600 million.

Hay accounts for a large amount of this production with some corn and sorghum silage being produced. The most important hay crops are annual and perennial grasses and alfalfa.

Production in 1996 totaled 7,815,000 tons of hay from 4,350,000 harvested acres at a yield of 1.8 tons per acre. Value of hay was $707,865,000, or $99.50 per

Cash Receipts for Commodities, 1991-1995

Commodity	1991	1992	1993	1994	1995	Percentage of '95 Commodities
			— Value in $1,000 —			
All Commodities:	$12,216,219	$11,461,101	$12,616,905	$12,929,651	$13,287,680	100.00 percent
Livestock and products	7,880,901	7,524,215	8,342,222	8,112,253	8,453,836	63.62 percent
Crops, Fruits and others	4,335,318	3,936,886	4,274,683	4,817,398	4,833,844	36.38 percent
Livestock and products:						
Cattle and calves .	6,115,818	5,644,620	6,353,371	5,882,207	6,295,596	47.38 percent
Milk.	683,260	760,213	780,710	830,800	791,570	5.96 percent
Broilers	508,939	553,784	608,700	659,453	646,316	4.86 percent
Eggs	203,038	181,755	202,541	198,147	218,238	1.64 percent
Hogs	95,156	75,505	88,270	76,838	76,963	0.58 percent
Sheep and lambs .	64,461	74,495	62,097	63,917	64,082	0.48 percent
Mohair	19,388	12,354	11,197	30,602	20,940	0.16 percent
Wool	13,861	16,896	11,050	15,582	15,488	0.12 percent
†Other Livestock .	166,243	195,352	215,968	354,707	324,643	2.44 percent
Crops:						
Cotton lint	1,505,831	827,012	1,136,596	1,645,296	1,486,066	11.18 percent
Corn	422,261	465,373	519,031	610,281	603,356	4.54 percent
Sorghum, grain. . .	413,197	465,995	437,998	334,084	351,136	2.64 percent
Wheat	230,934	367,504	329,550	225,344	284,715	2.14 percent
Cottonseed	128,105	124,490	207,659	191,843	180,355	1.36 percent
Peanuts	191,100	182,960	156,250	172,587	154,980	1.17 percent
Hay	127,870	121,825	113,801	133,340	127,234	0.96 percent
Onions	72,619	64,921	90,306	64,813	81,001	0.61 percent
Rice	152,323	153,279	90,042	173,231	129,553	0.97 percent
Watermelons	72,038	29,304	42,336	60,060	67,165	0.51 percent
Cabbage.	31,460	31,536	37,191	30,666	54,570	0.41 percent
Soybeans	25,496	59,187	35,224	26,454	38,651	0.29 percent
Sugar cane	27,750	33,731	34,731	40,544	41,980	0.32 percent
Cantaloupes	65,828	24,123	31,738	52,348	54,659	0.41 percent
Potatoes	28,690	30,839	30,433	34,293	28,270	0.21 percent
Sugar beets	20,600	28,911	28,359	18,290	12,917	0.10 percent
Peppers, Green . .	21,870	28,277	19,488	29,753	30,215	0.23 percent
Sweet potatoes. . .	10,791	10,560	14,449	11,558	8,569	0.06 percent
Cucumbers	15,783	18,522	14,296	19,938	15,105	0.11 percent
Celery	7,409	5,363	12,463	6,916	8,280	0.06 percent
Spinach	5,832	11,693	11,428	7,819	10,708	0.08 percent
Carrots	14,331	11,744	11,163	12,839	18,303	0.14 percent
Beans, Dry	5,387	6,339	9,089	6,508	3,495	0.03 percent
Honeydew melons	20,215	12,096	8,944	14,760	21,156	0.16 percent
Oats	4,995	6,028	7,345	6,251	5,857	0.04 percent
Sunflowers	3,114	5,961	5,122	3,777	4,198	0.03 percent
Broccoli.	6,251	8,259	4,067	4,281	7,600	0.06 percent
Corn, sweet	1,568	1,118	1,350	1,555	2,720	0.02 percent
Tomatoes	2,075	2,191	1,105	4,277	8,064	0.06 percent
Cauliflower	564	515	905	1,933	1,382	0.01 percent
Lettuce	1,680	862	880	NA	NA	0.00 percent
Rye	379	569	738	1,028	861	0.01 percent
Barley	578	525	532	534	736	0.01 percent
††Other crops. . . .	67,488	73,226	65,702	77,746	94,892	0.71 percent
Fruits and Nuts						
Pecans	66,000	87,300	48,000	48,800	68,110	0.51 percent
Grapefruit	963	3,304	9,786	13,486	19,673	0.15 percent
Oranges	285	1,709	2,572	3,353	8,832	0.07 percent
Peaches	8,772	7,696	8,136	5,811	6,480	0.05 percent
Other Farm Income:						
Greenhouse and nursery	556,000	628,000	701,000	721,001	792,000	5.96 percent

†Includes milkfat, turkey eggs, bees, equine, goats, goat milk and other poultry and livestock.
††Miscellaneous vegetables, field crops, fruits and nuts.
Includes only sales from farms but excluded in cash receipts for all farm commodities.
Source: "Farm Business Economic Report," August 1996. "Economic Indicators of the Farm Sector, State Financial Summary,," various years.

ton. In 1995, 8,136,000 tons of hay were produced from 3,760,000 harvested acres at a yield of 2.16 tons per acre. The value in 1995 was $517,212,000, or $72.00 per ton. In 1994, the production of hay was 8,455,000 tons from 3,590,000 harvested acres with a value of $511,475,000, or $69.00 per ton, at a yield of 2.36 tons per acre.

Alfalfa hay production in 1996 totaled 675,000 tons with 150,000 acres harvested with a yield of 4.5 tons per acre. At a value of $139.00 per ton, total value was $93,825,000. In 1995, 576,000 tons of alfalfa hay were harvested from 160,000 acres at a yield of 3.6 tons per acre.

Value was $67,392,000, or $117.00 per ton. Alfalfa hay was harvested from 90,000 acres in 1994, producing an average of 4.5 tons per acre for total production of 405,000 tons valued at $48,600,000.

An additional sizable acreage of annual forage crops

such as sudan and millet is grazed as well as much of the small grain acreage. Alfalfa, sweet corn, vetch, arrowleaf clover, grasses, and other forage plants also provide income as seed crops.

Peanuts

Peanuts are grown on approximately 300,000 acres in Texas. Well over half of the crop annually produced is on acreage that is irrigated. Texas ranked second nationally in production of peanuts in 1995. Among Texas crops, peanuts rank about seventh in value.

Until 1973, essentially all of the Texas acreage was planted to the Spanish type which was favored because of its earlier maturity and better drought tolerance than other types. The Spanish variety is also preferred for some uses due to its distinctive flavor.

The Florunner variety, a runner market type, is now planted on a sizable proportion of the acreage where soil moisture is favorable. The variety is later maturing but better yielding than Spanish varieties under good-growing conditions. Florunner peanuts have acceptable quality to compete with the Spanish variety in most products.

In 1996, peanut production totaled 679,200,000 pounds from 283,000 harvested acres, yielding 2,400 pounds per acre. At 24.5¢ per pound, value of the crop was estimated at $166,404,000.

In 1995, peanut production amounted to 540,000,000 pounds from 275,000 acres planted and 270,000 harvested. Average yield of 2,000 pounds per acre and average price of 28.7¢ per pound combined for a 1995 value of $154,980,000.

Production in 1994 amounted to 605,570,000 pounds of peanuts from 295,000 acres planted and 287,000 acres harvested, or an average of 2,110 pounds per harvested acre valued at 28.5¢ per pound for a $172,587,000 value.

Leading counties in peanut production in 1995 included Gaines, Comanche, Frio, Atascosa, Eastland, and Haskell.

Soybeans

Production is largely in the areas of the Upper Coast, irrigated High Plains, and Red River Valley of Northeast Texas. Soybeans are adapted to the same general soil climate conditions as corn, cotton, or grain sorghum--provided moisture, disease, and insects are not limiting factors. The major counties in soybean production in 1995 were Lamar, Liberty, Victoria, Fannin, Delta, and Hale.

In low-rainfall areas, yields have been too low or inconsistent for profitable production under dryland conditions. Soybeans' need for moisture in late summer minimizes economic crop possibilities in the Blacklands and Rolling Plains.

In the Blacklands, cotton root rot seriously hinders soybean production. Limited moisture at critical growth stages may occasionally prevent economical yields, even in high-rainfall areas of Northeast Texas and the Coast Prairie.

Because of day length sensitivity, soybeans should be planted in Texas during the long days of May and June to obtain sufficient vegetative growth for optimum yields. Varieties planted during this period usually cease vegetative development and initiate reproductive processes during the hot, usually dry months of July and August. When moisture is insufficient during the blooming and fruiting period, yields are drastically reduced. In most areas of the state, July and August rainfall is insufficient to permit economical dryland production.

The risk of dryland soybean production in the Coast Prairie and Northeast Texas is considerably less when compared to other dryland areas because moisture is available more often during the critical fruiting period.

The 1996 soybean crop totaled 7,020,000 bushels and was valued at $47,736,000, or $6.80 per bushel. Of the 290,000 acres planted, 270,000 were harvested with an average yield of 26 bushels per acre.

In 1995, the Texas soybean crop averaged 25.0 bushels per acre from 240,000 acres harvested. Total production of 6,000,000 bushels was valued at $39,120,000, or $6.52 per bushel.

In 1994, the Texas soybean crop average 33.5 bushels per acre from 210,000 acres harvested. Total production of 7,035,000 bushels was valued at $35,175,000, or $5.00 per bushel. Soybeans were planted on acreage that had been planted to cotton but was lost to adverse weather.

Sunflowers

Sunflowers constitute one of the most important annual oilseed crops in the world. The cultivated types, which are thought to be descendants of the common wild sunflower native to Texas, have been successfully grown in several countries including Russia, Argentina, Romania, Bulgaria, Uruguay, Western Canada, and portions of the northern United States.

Extensive trial plantings conducted in the Cotton Belt states since 1968 showed sunflowers have considerable potential as an oilseed crop in much of this area including Texas. This crop exhibits good cold and drought tolerance, is adapted to a wide range of soil and climate conditions, and tolerates higher levels of hail, wind, and sand abrasion than other crops normally grown in the state.

In 1996, sunflower production totaled 32,200,000 pounds and was harvested from 28,000 acres at a yield of 1,150 pounds per acre. With an average price of $14.00 per pound, the crop was valued at $4,508,000.

In 1995, 40,000 of the 44,000 acres planted to sunflowers were harvested with an average yield of 901 pounds per acre. Total production of 36,040,000 pounds was valued at $4,506,000, or $12.50 per pound.

In 1994, of 34,000 acres planted to sunflowers, 33,000 acres were harvested, yielding 1,100 pounds per acre for a total yield of 36,300,000 pounds valued at $3,839,000, or $10.60 per pound. The leading counties in production in 1995 were Hale, Briscoe, Carson, Jim Wells, and Lubbock.

Reasons for growing sunflowers include the need for an additional cash crop with low water and plant nutrient requirements, the development of sunflower hybrids, and interest by food processors in Texas sunflower oil which has a high oleic acid content.

Commercial users have found many advantages in this high oleic oil, including excellent cooking stability particularly for use as a deep frying medium for potato chips, corn chips, and similar products.

Sunflower meal is a high-quality protein source free

of nutritional toxins that can be included in rations for swine, poultry, and ruminants. The hulls constitute a source of roughage which can also be included in livestock rations.

Flaxseed

Earliest flax planting was at Victoria in 1900. Since the first planting, Texas flax acreage has fluctuated depending on market, winterkill, and drought. Flax acreage has dropped in recent years and estimates were discontinued in 1980.

Forest Products

The 1994 harvest of timber from East Texas' 11.8 million acres of timberland was valued at $932.0 million (measured as the value delivered to the first point of processing). This represents a 25 percent increase over the previous year's value of $744.0 million.

An estimated 53 percent of the timber harvest came from nonindustrial private lands, 41 percent came from forest-industry lands and the remaining 6 percent form public lands. The volume harvested totaled 867.5 million cubic feet, including 660.1 million cubic feet of pine and 207.4 million cubic feet of hardwood.

The stumpage value of the 1994 harvest, which is the value of the timber before cutting, was $682.9 million.

In addition to these timber products, Texas' forests produce other benefits as well. Over 400,000 Christmas trees, grown primarily in East Texas but found throughout the state, were sold in the Texas market.

In Central Texas, some timber is harvested for fuelwood, lumber, veneer, crossties, posts, and cedar oil. The forests of Texas provide a multitude of additional benefits such as wildlife habitat, watershed protection, livestock grazing, and opportunities for outdoor recreation. Minor products include pine straw, edible berries and nuts, wild honey, and decorative plants such as mistletoe.

For information on the Texas forest resource, refer to the section titled, *Texas Forest Resources*.

Horticultural Specialty Crops

The trend to increase production of horticulture specialty crops continues to rise as transportation costs on long-distance hauling increases.

This has resulted in a marked increase in the production of container-grown plants within the state. This increase is noted especially in the production of bedding plants, foliage plants, sod, and the woody landscape plants.

Plant rental services have become a multimillion dollar business. This relatively new service provides the plants and maintains them in office buildings, shopping malls, public buildings, and even in some homes for a fee. The response has been good as evidenced by the growth of companies providing these services.

The interest in plants for interior landscapes is confined to no specific age group as both retail nurseries and florist shops report that people of all ages are buy-

Texas 1995 Vegetable Production

*Rank Among States	Crop	Planted Acres (000)	Harvested Acres (000)	Yield Per Acre	Production (000)
1	Spinach Proces-Tons	8.20	7.90	8.00	67
2	Honeydew Fresh-Cwt	4.60	4.30	200.00	860
3	Cabbage Frsh-Cwt	10.30	9.70	375.00	3,638
3	Celery Frsh-Cwt	1.10	1.00	600.00	600
3	Cucumbers Proc-Tons	13.00	12.60	5.00	57
3	Cantaloups Frsh-Cwt	12.90	12.40	190.00	2,356
3	Watermelons Frsh-Cwt	52.80	47.50	140.00	6,650
3	Spinach Frsh-Cwt	2.70	2.50	80.00	200
4	Broccoli Dual-Cwt	3.30	3.20	73.00	234
4	Carrots Frsh-Cwt	5.20	5.00	150.00	750
4	Carrots Proc-Tons	5.30	5.10	10.00	51,000
4	Bell Peppers Dual-Cwt	4.90	4.60	145.00	667
6	Cauliflower Dual-Cwt	0.80	0.80	85.00	68
6	Onions, All Frsh-Cwt	18.00	17.00	260.00	4,421
8	Cucumbers Frsh-Cwt	2.40	2.10	110.00	231
13	Tomatoes Frsh-Cwt	3.80	3.60	80.00	288
18	Sweet Corn Frsh-Cwt	3.70	3.40	50.00	170

*Based on production. Source: U.S. and Texas Departments of Agriculture.

ing their plants--from the elderly in retirement homes to high school and college students in dormitory rooms and apartments.

Extension specialists estimated cash receipts from horticultural specialty crops in Texas to be around $858 million in 1996. Texans are creating colorful and green surroundings by improving their landscape plantings.

II. Truck Crops

Some market vegetables are produced in almost all Texas counties, but most of the commercial crop comes from about 200 counties. Hidalgo County is the leading Texas county in vegetable acres harvested, followed by Starr and Cameron Counties. Other leading producing counties are: Frio, Uvalde, Duval, Webb, Hale, and Zavala.

Texas is one of the five leading states in the production of fresh market vegetables.

Nationally, in 1996, Texas ranked fifth in harvested acreage, exceeded by California, Florida, Georgia, and Arizona; and ranked fourth in production and in value of fresh-market vegetables, exceeded by California, Florida, and Arizona. Texas had 6.1 percent of the harvested acreage, 6.0 percent of the production, and 3.8 percent of the value of fresh-market vegetables produced. Texas ranked first in the production of spinach for processing.

Onions were the number one cash crop with watermelons second. Other vegetables leading in value of production usually are cantaloupes, cabbage, Irish potatoes, bell peppers, and carrots.

In 1996, total vegetable production of 27,811,000 cwt. was valued at $286,929,000 from 145,100 acres harvested. In 1995, Texas growers harvested total commercial vegetable crops valued at $389,249,000 from 152,400 acres with a production of 25,492,000 cwt. Texas growers harvested 28,054,000 cwt. of commercial vegetable crops from 160,800 acres, valued at $317,754,000 in 1994.

Onions

Onion production in 1996 totaled 4,954,000 cwt. from 17,200 harvested acres and was valued at $50,930,000, at a yield of 288 cwt. per acre. In 1995, 4,633,000 cwt. of onions were harvested from 17,900 acres and valued at $83,821,000, at a yield of 259 cwt. per acre. A total of 5,541,000 cwt. of onions were produced from 19,900 harvested acres and valued at $64,813,000 in 1994, yielding 278 cwt. per acre.

Carrots

Carrot production in 1996 totaled 907,000 cwt. from 4,900,000 harvested acres at a yield of 185 cwt. per acre. Production was valued at $13,877,000. In 1995, carrots were harvested from 5,000 acres with a value of $14,850,000.

At a yield of 150 cwt. per acre, 1995 production was 750,000 cwt. Carrot production was valued at $10,143,000 in 1994 from 5,500 acres harvested. Production was 882,000 cwt. at a yield of 160 cwt. per acre.

The winter carrot production from South Texas accounts for about three-fourths of total production during the winter season.

Irish Potatoes

In 1996, Irish potatoes were harvested from 16,000 acres with production of 3,385,000 cwt. valued at $34,687,000 at a yield of 212 cwt. per acre. Irish potatoes were harvested from 12,000 acres with production of 2,570,000 cwt. valued at $28,302,000 in 1995, yielding 214 cwt. per acre.

This compares with 13,000 acres harvested valued at $35,315,000 in 1994 with production of 2,900,000 cwt. and a yield of 223 cwt. per acre.

Cantaloupes - Honeydews

Cantaloupe production in 1996 totaled 2,520,000 cwt. from 12,000,000 harvested acres and was valued at $47,124,000 at a yield of 210 cwt. per acre. In 1995, cantaloupes were harvested from 12,400 acres for total production of 2,356,000 cwt. valued at $54,659,000, yielding 190 cwt. per acre. Of the 13,100 harvested acres in 1994, 2,358,000 cwt. cantaloupes were produced at a yield of 180 cwt. per acre and were valued at $52,348,000.

Honeydew production totaled 640,000 cwt. and was valued at $12,352,000 at a yield of 200 cwt. per acre in 1996. In 1995, 860,000 cwt. of honeydew melons were harvested from 4,300 acres for total value of $21,156,000, yielding 200 cwt. per acre. Honeydew melons valued at $14,760,000 were harvested on 4,500 acres, producing a yield of 200 cwt. per acre for a total production of 900,000 cwt. in 1994.

Cabbage

In 1996, 10,900 acres were harvested and yielded total production of 4,033,000 cwt. which was valued at $40,330,000. Yield was 370 cwt. per acre. In 1995, 9,700 acres of cabbage were harvested yielding total production of 3,638,000 cwt., or 375 cwt. per acre, valued at $54,570,000. The 11,200 acres of cabbage harvested in Texas in 1994 brought a value of $30,666,000.

At a yield of 370 cwt. per acre, total production was 4,144,000 cwt.

Cauliflower

Production of cauliflower in 1996 was 56,000 cwt. on 700 acres at a value of $1,404,000. Yield equaled 80 cwt. per acre. Cauliflower production in 1995 was 68,000 cwt. and valued at $1,382,000, at a yield of 85 cwt. per acre. A total of 99,000 cwt. cauliflower was harvested from 900 acres at a yield of 110 cwt. per acre and valued at $1,933,000 in 1994.

Broccoli

Broccoli production in 1996 totaled 93,000 cwt. from 1,500 harvested acres for a value of $2,270,000 with a yield of 62 cwt. per acre. In 1995, at a yield of 73 cwt. per acre, broccoli production totaled 234,000 cwt. from 3,200 harvested acres and valued at $7,600,000. Broccoli in 1994 was produced on 3,700 harvested acres with a value of $4,281,000. Total production in 1994 was 229,000 cwt. or a yield of 62 cwt. per acre.

Broccoli is primarily a South Texas crop.

Watermelons

Watermelon production in 1996 was 8,800,000 cwt. from 44,000 acres with a value of $48,136,000, yielding 200 cwt. per acre. In 1995, at a yield of 140 cwt. per acre, 6,650,000 cwt. watermelons were harvested from 47,500 acres and valued at $67,165,000. Watermelon production was 7,800,000 cwt. from 52,000 acres in 1994, with a value of $60,060,000 at a yield of 150 cwt. per acre.

Tomatoes

Commercial tomatoes are marketed throughout the year from Texas partly as a result of recent increases in greenhouse production during the winter.

In 1996, 3,900 harvested acres of tomatoes at a yield of 110 cwt. per acre produced 429,000 cwt. of tomatoes with a value of $7,722,000. In 1995, 3,600 acres of tomatoes were harvested, producing 288,000 cwt. at a yield of 80 cwt. per acre for a value of $8,064,000.

The tomato crop in 1994 was valued at $4,277,000 from 3,300 harvested acres. Tomato production was 198,000 cwt. at a yield of 60 cwt. per acre.

Bell Peppers

Bell pepper production in 1996 of 702,000 cwt. from 5,200 harvested acres was valued at $22,604,000 with a yield of 135 cwt. per acre. In 1995, bell peppers were harvested from 4,600 acres valued at $30,215,000. At a yield of 145 cwt. per acre, 667,000 cwt. were produced. Bell peppers in 1994 were harvested from 4,600 acres valued at $29,753,000. Production of bell peppers was 644,000 cwt. with a yield of 140 cwt. per acre.

Sweet Potatoes

In 1996, 1,045,000 cwt. sweet potatoes were harvested from 5,500 acres for a value of $17,452,000 at a yield of 190 cwt. per acre. Sweet potatoes in 1995 produced 650,000 cwt. from 5,200 harvested acres with a value of $8,255,000. Yield was 125 cwt. per acre. This compared with 837,000 cwt. produced at a yield of 155 cwt. from 5,400 harvested acres valued at $10,463,000 in 1994.

Spinach

Spinach production is primarily concentrated in the Winter Garden area of South Texas.

The 1996 production value of spinach was estimated at $3,758,000. Production of 154,000 cwt. was harvested from 2,800 acres with a yield of 55 cwt. per acre. In 1995, 2,600 acres were harvested with a value of $5,944,000. At a yield of 90 cwt. per acre, production was 234,000 cwt. The 2,300 acres harvested in 1994 produced 115,000 cwt. at a yield of 50 cwt. per acre and valued at $2,829,000.

Cucumbers

In 1996, 1,600 acres of cucumbers were harvested. Production totaled 112,000 cwt. and was valued at $1,512,000. The 1996 yield was 70 cwt. per acre. In 1995, 2,100 acres of cucumbers were harvested with a value of $2,518,000. Production was 231,000 cwt. with a yield of 110 cwt. per acre. At a yield of 110 cwt. per acre, the 242,000 cwt. cucumber crop in Texas during 1994 was harvested from 2,200 acres and valued at $3,630,000.

Sweet Corn

In 1996, 112,000 cwt. of sweet corn was harvested from 2,800 acres. Value of production was estimated at $1,120,000 with a yield of 40 cwt. per acre. In 1995, 170,000 cwt. sweet corn was produced from 3,400 harvested acres at a yield of 50 cwt. per acre and valued at $2,720,000. Sweet corn was harvested in Texas from 3,200 acres valued at $1,555,000 in 1994. Production was 144,000 cwt. at a yield of 45 cwt. per acre.

Vegetables for Processing

In 1996, 3,649,000 cwt. of cucumbers, snap beans, tomatoes, and spinach for processing were harvested from 33,400 acres and valued at $29,045,000. In 1995, 34,300 acres were harvested and valued at $26,304,000 with a production of 4,113,000 cwt. In 1994, 33,100 acres were harvested and valued at $29,790,000, producing 4,030,000 cwt.

III. Fruits and Nuts

Texas is noted for producing a wide variety of fruits. The pecan is the only commercial nut crop in the state. The pecan is native to most of the state's river valleys and is the Texas state tree.

Citrus is produced in the three southernmost counties in the Lower Rio Grande Valley. Production has continued to increase since the severe freeze several years ago. Some new orchards have been planted.

Peaches represent the next most important Texas fruit crop, yet there is a considerable amount of interest in growing apples.

Citrus

Prior to the 1989 freeze, Texas ranked with Florida, California and Arizona as leading states in the production of citrus. Most of the Texas production is in Cameron, Hidalgo, and Willacy Counties of the Lower Rio Grande Valley. In 1996/97, grapefruit production was estimated at 5,300,000 boxes. At a yield of 257 boxes per acre, grapefruit production in 1995/96 was 4,550,000 boxes at $4.67 per box for a total of $21,257,000.

Production in 1994/95 was 4,650,000 boxes at $3.34 with a value of $15,539,000 and a yield of 311 boxes per acre. Production of oranges in 1996/97 was 1,450,000 boxes; and, in 1995/96, 940,000 boxes at $7.78 per box for a total of $7,310,000 with a yield of 120 boxes per acre. Production reached 1,055,000 boxes in 1994/95 at $4.58 for a value of $4,828,000 and a yield of 151 boxes per acre.

Peaches

Primary production areas are East Texas, the Hill Country, and the West Cross Timbers. Production varies substantially due to adverse weather conditions. Recently, peach production has spread to South and West Texas. Low-chilling varieties for early marketings are being grown in Atascosa, Frio, Webb, Karnes, and Duval Counties.

The Texas peach crop totaled 5,200,000 pounds in 1996 for a value of $3,848,000 or 74¢ per pound and a yield of 500 pounds per acre.

In 1996, the peach crop was severely damaged by a late freeze. In 1995, 18,000,000 pounds were produced at a yield of 2,000 pounds per acre that was valued at $6,480,000 or 36¢ per pound. The 1994 crop totaled 14,900,000 pounds and was valued at $5,811,000 or 39¢ per pound and a yield of 1,670 pounds per acre.

The demand for high-quality Texas peaches greatly exceeds the supply. Texas ranked 14th nationally in peach production in 1996. Leading Texas counties in production are Gillespie, Parker, Montague, Comanche, Limestone, and Eastland.

Apples

Small acreages of apples, usually marketed in the state, are grown in a number of counties. The leading counties in production are Montague and Gillespie.

Other counties which have apples include: Callahan, Collingsworth, Clay, Cass, Donley, Eastland, Hudspeth, Jeff Davis, Lampasas, Parker, San Saba, and Young. The crop is harvested and marketed from July to October.

A considerable number of apple trees have been planted in the Hill Country. Most of the trees are new varieties of Red and Golden Delicious types on semi-dwarfing rootstocks. Trees are established in high-density plantings of 100 to 200 trees per acre. Most of the apples are sold at roadside stands or go to nearby markets.

Pears

Well adapted for home and small orchard production, the pear is not commercially significant in Texas. Comanche, Parker, Lampasas, Cooke, McCulloch, and Eastland counties lead in trees. Usually the fruit goes for home consumption or to nearby market.

Apricots

Not a commercial crop, apricots are grown chiefly in Comanche, Denton, Wilbarger, Parker and Collingsworth counties. Others reporting apricots include: Martin, Clay, Young, Lampasas, Gillespie, Anderson, Erath, Wichita, and Eastland counties.

Plums

Plum production is scattered over a wide area of the state with the heaviest production in East and Central Texas. The leading counties in production are Smith,

Gillespie, and Knox. Most of the production goes to nearby markets or to processors.

Blackberries

Smith County is a blackberry center with the Tyler-Lindale area having processed the crop since 1890. Other counties with blackberry acreage include Wood, Van Zandt, and Henderson. The Brazos blackberry is grown as a local market or "pick-your-own" fruit in many sections of the state. Dewberries grow wild in Central and East Texas and are gathered for home use and local sale in May and June.

Strawberries

Atascosa County is the leading commercial area, although strawberries are grown for local markets in Wood, Van Zandt, and Smith Counties in East Texas. The most concentrated production occurs in the Poteet area below San Antonio.

Avocados

Avocados grow on a small acreage in the Lower Rio Grande Valley. Interest in this crop is increasing and production is expected to expand. Lulu is the principal variety.

Pecans

The pecan, the state tree, is one of the most widely distributed trees in Texas. It is native to over 150 counties and is grown commercially in some 30 additional counties. The pecan is also widely used as a dual-purpose yard tree. The commercial plantings of pecans have greatly accelerated in Central and West Texas with many of the new orchards being irrigated. Many new pecan plantings are being established under trickle-irrigation systems. The development and use of the new USDA pecan varieties have greatly helped to increase quality and yields.

In 1996, pecan production totaled 45,000,000 pounds and was valued at $37,250,000 or 83¢ per pound. In 1995, 75,000,000 pounds were produced. Total value was estimated at $68,110,000 as price averaged 91¢ per pound. The 1994 crop totaled 40,000,000 pounds valued at $48,800,000 or $1.22 per pound. In 1993, the crop totaled 75,000,000 pounds valued at $48,000,000 or 64¢ per pound.

Nationally, Texas ranked second behind Georgia in pecan production in 1996. Leading Texas counties in pecan production are Hood, El Paso, Pecos, San Saba, Mills, Comanche, Wharton, and Gonzales.

IV. Livestock and Their Products

Livestock and their products usually account for about two-thirds of the agricultural cash receipts in Texas. The state ranks first nationally in all cattle, beef cattle, cattle on feed, sheep and lambs, wool, goats, and mohair.

Meat animals normally account for around 80 percent of total cash receipts from marketings of livestock and their products. Sales of livestock and products in 1995 totaled $8.454 billion, up from $8.112 billion in 1994.

Cattle dominate livestock production in Texas, contributing more than 70 percent of cash receipts from livestock and products each year. The January 1, 1997 inventory of all cattle and calves in Texas totaled 14,100,000 head, valued at $6.204 billion, compared to 15,000,000 as of January 1, 1996, valued at $6.225 billion.

On January 1, 1997, the sheep and lamb inventory stood at 1,400,000 head, valued at $100,800,000, compared with 1,650,000 head as of January 1, 1996, valued at $108,900,000. Sheep and lambs numbered 3,214,000 on January 1, 1973, down from a high of 10,829,000 in 1943.

Sheep and lamb production fell from 148,295,000 pounds in 1973 to 68,718,000 pounds on January 1, 1997. Wool production decreased from 26,352,000 pounds valued at $23,190,000 in 1973 to 9,900,000 pounds valued at $8,316,000 in 1996. Production was 13,468,000 pounds in 1995 valued at $15,488,000. The price of wool per pound was 88¢ in 1973, $1.15 in 1995, and 84¢ in 1996.

Lamb prices averaged $87.80 per cwt. in 1996, $78.50 per cwt. in 1995, and $64.80 per cwt. in 1994. The average value per head of sheep stock was $72.00 as of January 1, 1997, $66.00 in 1996, and $59.00 in 1995.

Mohair production in Texas has dropped from a 1965 high of 31,584,000 pounds to 7,490,000 pounds in 1996. Production was valued at $14,606,000 or $1.95 per pound. In 1995, production was 11,319,000 pounds valued at $20,940,000 or $1.85 per pound. Mohair production in 1994 was 11,680,000 pounds valued at $30,602,000 or $2.62 per pound.

Texas Cattle Marketed, 1965-1996 by Size of Feedlot

Year	Feedlot Capacity (head)						Total
	Under 1,000	1,000-1,999	2000-3,999	4,000-7,999	8,000-15,999	16,000-& Over	
	Cattle Marketed — 1,000 head —						
1965	104	108	205	324	107	246	1,094
1970	98	53	112	281	727	1,867	3,138
1975	50	22	51	134	485	2,325	3,067
1976	60	33	62	170	583	3,039	3,947
1977	146	22	38	206	604	3,211	4,227
1978	80	20	50	242	697	3,826	4,915
1979	54	19	46	227	556	3,543	4,445
1980	51	18	47	226	533	3,285	4,160
1981	50	20	50	220	510	3,110	3,960
1982	55	20	60	210	540	3,190	4,075
1983	100	20	80	130	490	3,580	4,400
1984	60	20	180	150	540	4,140	5,090
1985	70	10	20	170	620	4,140	5,030
1986	90	10	40	180	550	4,390	5,260
1987	90	20	35	170	625	4,375	5,255
1988	30	15	35	185	650	4,120	5,035
1989	40	15	40	165	675	3,810	4,745
1990	35	24	56	180	605	3,940	4,840
1991	35	25	45	225	500	4,250	5,080
1992	50	10	25	140	505	4,065	4,795
1993	30	20	70	160	640	4,370	5,290
1994	14	13	55	173	725	4,680	5,660
1995	12	24	43	166	630	4,665	5,540
1996	NA	17	43	180	460	4,800	5,500

Number of feedlots with 1,000 head or more capacity is number of lots operating any time during the year. Number under 1,000 head capacity and total number of all feedlots is number at end of year.
Source: "Texas Agricultural Facts," Texas Agricultural Statistics Service, 1996. Numbers for 1986-1992, "1993 Texas Livestock Statistics," Bulletin 252, August 1994. ¹Cattle on Feed annual summary, USDA/NASS, Feb. 1997.

Beef Cattle

Raising beef cattle is the most extensive agricultural operation in Texas. In 1995, 47.4 percent of total cash receipts from farm and ranch marketings--$6,295,596 of $13,287,680--came from cattle and calves, compared with $5,882,207 of $12,929,651 in 1994 (45.5%) and $6,188,563 of $12,730,745 in 1993 (48.6%). The next leading commodity is cotton.

Nearly all of the 254 counties in Texas derive more revenue from cattle than from any other agricultural commodity, and those that don't usually rank cattle second in importance.

Within the boundaries of Texas are 14 percent of all the cattle in the U.S., as are 16 percent of the beef breeding cows, and 13 percent of the calf crop as of January 1, 1997 inventory.

The number of all cattle in Texas on January 1, 1997 totaled 14,100,000, compared with 15,000,000 on January 1, 1996; and 15,100,000 in 1995.

Calves born on Texas farms and ranches in 1996 totaled 5,250,000, compared with 5,550,000 in 1995; and 5,600,000 in 1994.

Sale of cattle and calves at approximately 149 livestock auctions inspected by Texas Animal Health Commission totaled 6,351,000 head in 1996; 5,719,000 head in 1995; and 5,825,000 in 1994. The number of cattle and calves shipped into Texas totaled 2,704,154 head in 1996; 3,976,436 head in 1995 and 2,960,901 head in 1994.

Livestock Industries

A large portion of Texas livestock is sold through local auction markets. In 1996, 147 livestock auctions were reported by the Texas Animal Health Commission. Auctions sold 6,351,000 head of cattle and calves; 168,000 hogs; and 1,558,000 sheep and lambs in 1996. This compared with 5,719,000 cattle and calves; 199,000 hogs; 1,417,000 sheep and lambs in 1995. Figures for 1994 were 5,825,000 cattle and calves; 238,000 hogs; 1,834,000 sheep and goats.

During 1996, the Commission reported 1,654,560 cattle and calves shipped from Texas to other states and 2,704,154 shipped in, compared with 1,451,943 shipped out and 3,976,436 shipped in during 1995, and 1,705,000 shipped out and 2,961,000 shipped in during 1994. (Figures exclude cattle shipped direct to slaughter where no health certificates are required.)

Texas, during 1996, shipped out 452,073 sheep and lambs and shipped in 78,221, compared with 410,913 shipped out and 67,242 shipped in during 1995; and 1,022,000 shipped out in 1994 and 99,000 shipped in.

Feedlot fattening of livestock, mainly cattle, is a major industry in Texas. Annual fed cattle marketings totaled 5,500,000 for 1,000 and over feedlot capacity (head) in 1996.

Texas lots marketed a total of 5,540,000 head (including under 1,000 feedlot capacity) of grain-fed cattle in 1995, compared with 5,660,000 in 1994; and 5,290,000 in 1993. In recent years, more cattle have been fed in Texas than any other state in the United States.

During 1996, there were 150 feedlots in Texas with capacity of 1,000 animals or more. This compared with 135 in 1995, 137 in 1994, and 138 in 1993.

Federally-inspected slaughter plants in Texas num-

Hog Production
1960-1996

Year	Production (1,000 Pounds)	Avg. Market Wt. (Pounds)	Avg. Price Per Cwt. (Dollars)	Gross Income (1,000 Dollars)
1960	288,844	228	$14.70	$44,634
1970	385,502	241	22.50	75,288
1980	315,827	259	35.90	111,700
1981	264,693	256	41.70	121,054
1982	205,656	256	49.60	112,726
1983	209,621	256	45.20	95,343
1984	189,620	262	45.50	95,657
1985	168,950	266	43.40	72,512
1986	176,660	269	47.30	82,855
1987	216,834	NA	50.60	103,983
1988	236,658	NA	41.30	100,029
1989	224,229	NA	39.90	93,178
1990	196,225	NA	48.20	92,222
1991	207,023	NA	45.10	97,398
1992	213,604	NA	36.40	76,433
1993	214,080	NA	39.90	89.464
1994	224,397	NA	35.10	78,394
1995	221,323	NA	35.50	81,509
1996	205,331	NA	45.90	94,962

Source: "1985 Texas Livestock, Dairy and Poultry Statistics," USDA, Bulletin 235, June 1986, pp. 32, 46; "Texas Livestock Statistics"; USDA, "Meat Animals - Prod., Dips., & Income," 1993; "1993 'Texas Livestock Statistics," Bulletin 252, Texas Agricultural Statistics Service, 1994. Texas Agricultural Facts, Sept. 1996.

bered 42 in 1996. This compared with 43 in 1995 and 43 in 1994. In 1996, the number of cattle slaughtered in Texas totaled 6,725,500 cattle; 166,000 hogs; and 37,600 calves. This compared with 6,391,800 cattle; 164,200 hogs; 29,300 calves in 1995; and 6,150,000 cattle; 178,000 hogs; and 21,000 calves in 1994.

Feeding of cattle in commercial feedlots is a major economic development that has stimulated the establishment and expansion of beef slaughtering plants. Most of this development is in the Panhandle-Plains area of Northwest Texas.

This area alone accounts for over 80 percent of the cattle fed in the state in 1995.

Feedlots with capacities of 1,000 head or more accounted for more than 99 percent of the cattle fed in Texas in 1996. Total feedlot marketings represented about 25 percent of total U.S. fed cattle marketings in 1995. Large amounts of capital are required for feedlot operations. This has forced many lots to become custom feeding facilities.

Feedlots are concentrated on the High Plains largely because of extensive supplies of sorghum and other feed. Beef breeding herds have increased most in East Texas, where grazing is abundant.

Dairying

Ninety-five percent of the state's dairy industry is located east of the line from Wichita Falls to Brownwood, to San Antonio to Corpus Christi. As of January 1, 1996 inventory, leading counties in milk production are Erath, Hopkins, Comanche and Johnson, which combined, produce 46.6 percent of the milk in the state, with Erath producing over 20 percent of the total.

Angora Goats and Mohair
1900-1996

Year	Goats		Mohair	
	*Number	Farm Value	Produc-tion (lbs)	Value
1900	627,333	$923,777	961,328	$267,864
1910	1,135,000	2,514,000	1,998,000	468,000
1920	1,753,000	9,967,000	6,786,000	1,816,000
1930	2,965,000	14,528,000	14,800,000	4,995,000
1940	3,300,000	10,560,000	18,250,000	9,308,000
1950	2,295,000	13,082,000	12,643,000	9,735,000
1960	3,339,000	29,383,000	23,750,000	21,375,000
1970	2,572,000	19,033,000	17,985,000	7,032,000
1980	1,400,000	64,400,000	8,800,000	30,800,000
1981	1,380,000	53,130,000	10,100,000	35,350,000
1982	1,410,000	57,810,000	10,000,000	25,500,000
1983	1,420,000	53,250,000	10,600,000	42,930,000
1984	1,450,000	82,215,000	10,600,000	48,160,000
1985	1,590,000	76,797,000	13,300,000	45,885,000
1986	1,770,000	70,997,000	16,000,000	40,160,000
1987	1,780,000	82,592,000	16,200,000	42,606,000
1988	1,800,000	108,180,000	15,400,000	29,876,000
1989	1,850,000	100,270,000	15,400,000	24,794,000
†1990	1,900,000	93,100,000	14,500,000	13,775,000
1991	1,830,000	73,200,000	14,800,000	19,388,000
1992	2,000,000	84,000,000	14,200,000	12,354,000
1993	1,960,000	84,280,000	13,490,000	11,197,000
1994	1,960,000	74,480,000	11,680,000	30,602,000
1995	1,850,000	81,400,000	11,319,000	20,940,000
1996	1,900,000	89,300,000	7,500,000	14,600,000

*Goat number includes all goats, not just Angora goats.
Source: "1985 Texas Livestock, Dairy and Poultry Statistics," USDA Bulletin 235, June 1986, p. 25. "Texas Agricultural Facts," Crop and Livestock Reporting Service, various years; "1993 Texas Livestock Statistics," Texas Agricultural Statistics Service, Bulletin 252, August 1994. Texas Agricultural Statistics, Sept. 1996.

All the milk sold by Texas dairy farmers is marketed under the terms of Federal Marketing Orders. Most Texas dairymen are members of one of four marketing cooperatives. Associate Milk Producers, Inc. is the largest, representing the majority of the state's producers.

Texas dairy farmers received an average price for milk of $15.10 per hundred pounds in 1996, $13.00 in 1995, and $13.40 in 1994.

A total of 6.098 billion pounds of milk was sold to plants and dealers in 1996, bringing in cash receipts from milk to dairy farmers of $920,798,000. This compared with 6.089 billion pounds sold in 1995 that brought in $791,570,000 in cash receipts. In 1994, Texas dairymen sold 6.200 billion pounds of milk, which brought in cash receipts of $830,800,000.

The annual average number of milk cows in Texas was 390,000 head as of January 1, 1997 inventory. This compared with 400,000 head as of January 1, 1996 and 400,000 as of January 1, 1995.

Average production per cow in the state has increased steadily over the past several decades. The average production per cow in 1996 was 15,377 pounds. Milk per cow in 1995 was 15,244 pounds. In 1994, milk per cow was 15,485 pounds.

Total milk production in Texas was 6.12 billion pounds in 1996, 6.113 billion pounds in 1995, and 6.225 billion pounds in 1994.

There were 3,000 operations reporting milk cows in Texas in 1996. In 1995, 3,700 operations reported milk cows and in 1994, 4,200 operations reported milk cows in Texas.

Dairy Manufacturing

The major dairy products manufactured in Texas include condensed, evaporated and dry milk, creamery butter, and cheese. However, this data is not available because of the small number of manufacturing plants producing these products.

Frozen Desserts

Production of frozen desserts in Texas totaled 99,228,000 gallons in 1996. The 1995 production amounted to 119,394,000 gallons and 119,045,000 in 1994.

Ice cream production in Texas in 1996 amounted to 47,783,000 gallons, compared to 50,982,000 in 1995 and 47,711,000 gallons in 1994. Ice cream mix produced in Texas in 1996 amounted to 27,018,000 gallons; 28,014,000 in 1995; and 27,038,000 gallons in 1994.

Milk sherbet mix in Texas totaled 1,294,000 gallons in 1996 and 1,292,000 gallons in 1995. Milk sherbet production in 1996 totaled 2,069,000 gallons. This compared with 1995 milk sherbet production of 2,035,000 gallons and 1994 production of 1,885,000 gallons.

Swine

Texas had 500,000 head of swine on hand, December 1, 1996 -- only 9 percent of the U.S. swine herd. Swine producers in the state usually produce about one-fifth of the pork consumed by the state's population, or about 826,000 head marketed annually.

Although the number of farms producing hogs has steadily decreased, the size of production units has increased substantially. There is favorable potential for increased production.

In 1996, 826,000 head of hogs were marketed in Texas, producing 205,331,000 pounds of pork valued at $45.90 per 100 pounds, or $94,246,929. In 1995, 900,000 head of hogs were marketed, producing 221,323,000 pounds of pork valued at $78,569,665, or $35.50 per 100 pounds. Comparable figures for 1994 were 816,000 head marketed, and 224,397,000 pounds of pork produced with a value of $78,763,347, or $35.10 per 100 pounds.

Goats and Mohair

Goats in Texas numbered 1,650,000 on January 1, 1997. This compares with 1,900,000 on January 1, 1996 and 1,850,000 on January 1, 1995. They had a value of $70,950,000 or $43.00 per head in 1997; $89,300,000 or $47.00 per head in 1996; and $81,400,000 or $44.00 per head as of January 1, 1995.

The goat herd largely consists of Angora goats for mohair production. Angora goats totaled 1,000,000 as of January 1, 1997; 1,250,000 as of 1996; and 1,250,000 as of January 1, 1995.

Spanish goats and others numbered 650,000 as of January 1, 1997; 650,000 as of 1996; and 600,000 as of January 1, 1995.

Mohair production during 1996 totaled 7,490,000 pounds. This compares with 11,319,000 in 1995 and 11,680,000 in 1994. Average price per pound in 1996 was $1.95 from 1,070,000 goats clipped for a total value of $14,605,500.

In 1995, producers received $1.85 per pound from 1,470,000 goats clipped for a total value of

$20,940,000. In 1994, producers received $2.62 per pound from 1,600,000 goats for a total value of $30,602,000.

Nearly half of the world's mohair and 92 percent of the U.S. clip are produced in Texas. The leading Texas counties in Angora goats are: Edwards, Val Verde, Uvalde, Sutton, Crockett, Mills, Kinney, Kimble, Gillespie, and Tom Green as of January 1, 1996.

Sheep and Wool

The sheep herd continues to decline. Sheep and lambs in Texas numbered 1,400,000 head on January 1, 1997, down from 1,650,000 as of 1996; and 1,700,000 as of January 1, 1995. All sheep were valued at $100,800,000 or $72.00 per head on January 1, 1997, compared with $108,900,000 or $66.00 per head as of 1996 and $100,300,000 or $59.00 per head as of January 1, 1995.

Breeding ewes one year old and over numbered 980,000 in January 1, 1997; 1,080,000 as of 1996; and 1,100,000 as of January 1,1995. Replacement lambs totaled 130,000 head as of January 1, 1997; 170,000 as of 1996; and 195,000 as of January 1, 1995.

Sheep operations in Texas were estimated to be 7,000 as of January 1, 1997; 7,300 as of 1996; and 7,600 as of January 1, 1995.

Texas wool production in 1996 was 9,900,000 pounds from 1,320,000 sheep.

Texas Sheep and Wool Production, 1850-1996

Year	Sheep		Wool	
	*Number	Value	Produc-tion (lbs)	Value
1850	100,530	N A	131,917	N A
1860	753,363	N A	1,493,363	N A
1870	1,223,000	$2,079,000	N A	N A
1880	6,024,000	12,048,000	N A	N A
1890	4,752,000	7,128,000	N A	N A
1900	2,416,000	4,590,000	9,630,000	N A
1910	1,909,000	5,536,000	8,943,000	$1,699,170
1920	3,360,000	33,600,000	22,813,000	5,019,000
1930	6,304,000	44,758,000	48,262,000	10,135,000
1940	10,069,000	49,413,000	79,900,000	23,171,000
1950	6,756,000	103,877,000	51,480,000	32,947,000
1960	5,938,000	85,801,000	51,980,000	21,832,000
1970	3,708,000	73,602,000	30,784,000	11,082,000
1980	2,400,000	138,000,000	18,300,000	17,751,000
1981	2,360,000	116,820,000	20,500,000	24,600,000
1982	2,400,000	100,800,000	19,300,000	16,212,000
1983	2,225,000	86,775,000	18,600,000	15,438,000
1984	1,970,000	76,830,000	17,500,000	16,100,000
1985	1,930,000	110,975,000	16,200,000	13,284,000
1986	1,850,000	107,300,000	16,400,000	13,284,000
1987	2,050,000	133,250,000	16,400,000	19,844,000
1988	2,040,000	155,040,000	18,200,000	35,854,000
1989	1,870,000	133,445,000	18,000,000	27,180,000
1990	2,090,000	133,760,000	17,400,000	19,662,000
1991	2,000,000	108,000,000	16,700,000	13,861,000
1992	2,140,000	111,280,000	17,600,000	16,896,000
1993	2,220,000	118,320,000	17,000,000	11,050,000
1994	1,895,000	106,120,000	14,840,000	15,582,000
1995	1,700,000	100,300,000	13,468,000	15,488,000
1996	1,650,000	108,900,000	9,900,000	8,300,000

*Number given here represents all sheep on farms as of Jan. 1; number clipped will vary because of spring and fall clipping.
Source: "1985 Texas Livestock, Dairy and Poultry Statistics," USDA Bulletin 235, June 1986, pp. 24-25. "Texas Agricultural Facts," Crop and Livestock Reporting Service, various years; "1993 Texas Livestock Statistics," Texas Agricultural Statistics Service, Bulletin 252, August 1994. Texas Agricultural Statistics, Sept. 1996.

Value totaled $8,316,000 or 84¢ per pound. This compared with 13,468,000 pounds of wool valued at $15,488,000 or $1.15 per pound in 1995; and 14,840,000 pounds from 2,120,000 sheep valued at $15,582,000 or $1.05 per pound in 1994.

Most sheep in Texas are concentrated in the Edwards Plateau area of West Central Texas and nearby counties. In 1995, the ten leading counties are: Val Verde, Crockett, Tom Green, Pecos, Gillespie, Schleicher, Concho, Menard, Sterling, and Coke. Sheep production is largely dual purpose, for both wool and lamb production.

San Angelo long has been the largest sheep and wool market in the nation and the center for wool and mohair warehouses, scouring plants and slaughterhouses.

Horses

Nationally, Texas ranks as one of the leading states in horse numbers and is the headquarters for many national horse organizations. The largest single breed registry in America, the American Quarter Horse Association, has its headquarters in Amarillo. The National Cutting Horse Association and the American Paint Horse Association are both located in Fort Worth.

In addition to these national associations, Texas also has active state associations that include Palominos, Arabians, Thoroughbreds, Appaloosa, and Ponies.

Horses are still used to support the state's giant beef cattle and sheep industries. However, the largest horse numbers within the state are near urban and suburban areas where they are mostly used for recreation activities.

Horses are most abundant in the heavily populated areas of the state. State participation activities consist of horse shows, trail rides, play days, rodeos, polo and horse racing. Residential subdivisions have been developed within the state to provide facilities for urban and suburban horse owners.

Poultry and Eggs

Poultry and eggs annually contribute about 6 percent to the average yearly cash receipts of Texas farmers.

In 1995, Texas ranked 6th among the states in broilers produced, 7th in eggs produced and 7th in hens.

In 1996, cash receipts to Texas producers from the production of poultry and eggs totaled $1.019 billion. This compares with $865,317,000 in 1995 and $900,060,000 in 1994.

Gross income from eggs was $290,646,000 in 1996. This compares with $216,691,000 in 1995 and $198,147,000 in 1994.

Eggs produced in 1996 totaled 3.99 billion eggs, compared with 3.92 billion in 1995 and 3.86 billion in 1994. The average price received per dozen in 1996 was 87.5¢, compared with 66.3¢ in 1995, and 61.6¢ in 1994.

Broiler production in 1996 totaled 419,200,000 birds, compared with 395,200,000 in 1995 and 371,000,000 in 1994.

Value of production from broilers totaled $726,264,000 in 1996; $646,316,000 in 1995; and $659,453,000 in 1994. Price per pound averaged 38.5¢ in 1996, 37.0¢ in 1995, and 39.5¢ in 1994. ☆

Statewide Civic Organizations

Listed below are privately supported civic, commercial and other nonprofit Texas organizations. Listing is alphabetical by the keyword in the title; i.e., Texas Egg Council is found under "Egg." All addresses are in Texas unless otherwise noted.

Advertising & Magazine Publishing, Texas Council of — 1104 West Ave., Ste. 101, Austin 78701-2046.

AFL-CIO, Texas — PO Box 12727, Austin 78711-2727.

Agricultural Cooperative Council, Texas — Box 9527, Austin 78766.

Ag Teachers Asso. of Texas, Vocational — 614 E. 12th St., Austin 78701-1908.

Anesthesiologists, Texas Society of — 401 W. 15th, Ste. 990, Austin 78701-1665.

Archaeological Organizations

Archeological Society, Central Texas — 4229 Mitchell Rd., Waco 76710-2139.

Archeological Society, El Paso — PO Box 4345, El Paso 79914-4345.

Archeological Society, Houston — PO Box 6751, Houston 77265-6751.

Archaeology, Institute of Nautical — PO Box HG, College Station 77841-5137.

Architects, American Inst. (Dallas Chapter) — 2811 McKinney LB 104, Dallas 75204-2587.

Arts, Texans for the — 6757 Arapaho Rd., Ste. 711-278, Dallas 75248.

Assessing Officers, Texas Assn. of — 7501 E. Hwy 290, Austin 78723.

Association Executives, Texas Society of — 2550 S. I H 35, Ste. 200, Austin 78704-5749.

Austin College Alumni Assn. — 900 N. Grand Ave., Ste. 6G, Sherman 75090-4440.

Automotive Service Assn. — PO Box 929, Bedford 76095-0929.

Bank Counsel, Texas Assn. of — 203 W. 10th St., Austin 78701-2388.

Bankers Assn. of Texas, Independent — 408 W. 14th St., Austin 78701-1619.

Bankers Assn., Texas — 203 W. 10th St., Austin 78701-2388.

Baptist General Convention of Texas — 333 N. Washington, Dallas 75246-1798.

Bar of Texas, State — PO Box 12487, Austin 78711-2487.

Baylor Alumni Assn. — PO Box 97116, Waco 76796-7116.

Big Bend Natural History Assn. — PO Box 196, Big Bend National Park 79834-0196.

Blindness, Texas Society to Prevent (Dallas Branch) — 3610 Fairmount St., Dallas 75219-4709.

Blueberry Growers Assn. — Texas, PO Box 891, Georgetown 78627-0891.

Boating Trades Assn. of Texas — 3811 Turtle Creek Blvd., Ste. 950, Dallas 75219-4442.

Book Publishers of Texas — 1629 Junior Drive, Dallas 75208.

Bowling Proprietors' Assn. of America — PO Box 5802, Arlington 76005-5802.

Brahman Breeders Assn., American — 1313 La Concha Ln., Houston 77054-1890.

Brangus Assn., American Red — 3995 E. Hwy 290, Dripping Springs 78620-4205.

Broiler Council, Texas — PO Box 9589, Austin 78766-9589.

Business, Texas Assn. of & Chambers of Commerce — PO Box 2989, Austin 78768-2989.

Cattle Raisers Assn., Inc., Texas and Southwestern — 1301 W. 7th St., Fort Worth 76102-2665.

Chamber Professionals of East Texas — Kilgore Chamber of Commerce, PO Box 1582, Kilgore 75663-1582.

Chili Appreciation Society International (CASI) — 1516 Prairie Dr., El Paso 79925-2543.

Churches, Texas Conference of — 1033 La Posada, Ste. 225, Austin 78752.

Communication Assn., International — PO Box 9589, Austin 78766-9589.

Contractors, AG of Texas, Highway, Heavy, Utility & Industrial Branch — PO Box 2185, Austin 78768-2185.

Convention and Visitor Bureaus, Texas Assn. of — PO Box 1264, Fredericksburg 78624-1264.

Cotton Growers Co-operative Assn., Texas — PO Box 391, Taylor 76574-0391.

Cotton Growers, Inc., Plains — 4510 Englewood Ave., Lubbock 79414-1227.

Counseling Assn., Texas — 316 W. 12th St., Ste. 402, Austin 78701-1840.

Counties, Texas Assn. of — 1204 San Antonio St., Austin 78701.

Credit Union League, Texas — PO Box 655147, Dallas 75265-5147.

Dancing, Texas Assn. of Teachers of — 7811 Zilonis Court, Houston 77040-1351.

Daughters Organizations

Daughters of American Colonists, Texas Society — 410 Mantooth Ave., Lufkin 75904-3013.

Daughters of Colonial Wars, Texas Society — 6408 Dovenshire Terrace, Fort Worth 76112-3213.

Daughters of the Republic of Texas — 501 E. Anderson Ln., Austin 78752-1237.

Dermatological Society, Texas — 401 W. 15th St., Austin 78701-1680.

Dietetic Assn., Texas — 1033 La Posada Dr., Ste. 220, Austin 78752-3880.

Donkey and Mule Society, Inc., American — 2901 N. Elm St., Denton 76201-7631.

Earth Scientists, Society of Independent Professional — 4925 Greenville Ave., Ste. 1106, Dallas 75206.

East Texas Tourism Assn. — PO Box 1592, Longview 75606-1592.

Educational Secretaries Assn., Texas — PO Box 1565, Austin 78767-1575.

Egg Council, Texas — PO Box 9589, Austin 78766-9589.

Electric Cooperatives, Inc., Texas — PO Box 9589, Austin 78766-9589.

Electronics Assn., Inc., Texas — 823 Congress Ave., Ste. 1300, Austin 78701.

Engineers Council of Texas, Consulting — 400 W. 15th St., Ste. 820, Austin 78701-1646.

Engineers, Texas Society of Professional — PO Box 2145, Austin 78768-2145.

Fair Organizations

Fair Assn., East Texas State — 2112 W. Front St., Tyler 75702-6828.

Fair of Texas, State — PO Box 150009, Dallas 75315-0009.

Fairs and Expositions, Texas Assn. of — PO Box 577, Santa Rosa 78593-0577.

Family & Consumer Sciences, Texas Assn. of — PO Box 831, Hurst 76053-0831.

Farm and Ranch Club, East Texas — 2112 W. Front St., Tyler 75702-6828.

Fashion Assn., Inc., American — PO Box 586454, Ste. 1A11, Dallas 75258-6454.

Folklore Society, Texas — PO Box 13007, Nacogdoches 75962-3007.

Food Processors Assn., Texas — PO Box 341, College Station 77841-0341.

Forage and Grassland Council, Texas — PO Box 891, Georgetown 78627-0891.

Foresters, Texas Society of American — PO Box 150555, Lufkin 75915-0555.

Forestry Assn., Texas — PO Box 1488, Lufkin 75902-1488.

Fruit Growers Assn., Texas — PO Drawer CC, College Station 77841.

Future Farmers of America (FFA) Asso., Texas — PO Box 13064, Austin 78711-3064.

Gastroenterology and Endoscopy, Texas Society for — 401 W. 15th St., Austin 78701-1680.

Genealogical Society, Texas State — 3219 Meadow Oaks Circle, Temple 76502-1752.

General Agents and Managers Assn., Texas — 1920 S. I H 35, Austin 78704-3628.

Geriatrics Society, Texas — 401 W. 15th St., Austin 78701-1680.

German-American Heritage Society — PO Box 684171, Austin 78768-4171.

Grange, Texas State — 2738 Oak Island Dr. Ste. 4, San Antonio 78264.

Grocers Assn., D/FW — 3001 LBJ Fwy, Ste. 133, Dallas 75234-7756.

Healthcare Environmental Services, Texas Society for — PO Box 15587, Austin 78761-5587.

Health, Physical Education, Recreation & Dance, Texas Assn. for — 6300 La Calma Dr., Ste. 100, Austin 78752-3890.

Heart Assn., American, Texas Affiliate — PO Box 15186, Austin 78761-5186.**Healthcare Environmental Services, Texas Society for** — PO Box 15587, Austin 78761-5587.

History Organizations

Historical Society, Texas Baptist — PO Box 22000, Fort Worth 76122-2490.

Historical Society, Texas Catholic — 1625 Rutherford Ln., Bldg. D, Austin 78754-5105.

Historical Assn., East Texas — PO Box 6223, Nacogdoches 75962-6223.

Historical Foundation, Texas — PO Box 50314, Austin 77863-0314.

Historical Society, Texas Jewish — PO Box 10193, Austin 78766-0193.

History Assn., Texas Oral — PO Box 97271, Waco 76798-7271.

Historical Society, Panhandle Plains — WTAMU Box 967, Canyon 79015.

Historical Society, Permian — 4901 E. University, Odessa 79762-0001.

Historical Assn., Texas State — 2.306 Sid Richardson Hall, Austin 78712.

Historical Assn., West Texas — PO Box 16172, Abilene 79698-6172.

Horse Club, Texas Appaloosa — PO Box 557, Cedar Hill 75106-0557.

Horse Assn., National Cutting — 4704 Hwy. 377 S., Fort Worth 76116-8805.

Horse Assn., American Quarter — PO Box 200, Amarillo 79168-0200.

Hospital Assn., Texas — PO Box 15587, Austin 78761-5587.

Hospital Auxiliaries, Texas Assn. of — PO Box 15587, Austin 78761-5587.

Insurance Agents, Texas Assn. of — PO Box 684487, Austin 78768-9960.

Insurance Organization, Texas — PO Box 15, Austin 78767-0015.

Interior Designers, Texas Chapter of American Society of — 1909 Hi Line Dr., Ste. C, Dallas 75207-3345.

Internal Medicine, Texas Society of — 401 W. 15th St., Austin 78701-1680.

Jewish Women International (formerly B'nai B'rith Women) — 8323 Southwest Fwy, Ste. 385, Houston 77074-1616.

Keep Texas Beautiful, Inc. — PO Box 2251, Austin 78768-2251.

Knights of the Order of San Jacinto — 1717 8th St., Bay City 77414.

Lawyers Assn., Texas Young — PO Box 12487, Austin 78711-2487.

Letters, Texas Institute of — PO Box 9032, Wichita Falls 76308-9032.

Libertarian Party of Texas — PO Box 56426, Houston 77256-6426.

Life Underwriters, Texas Assn. of — 1920 S. I H 35, Austin 78704-3695.

Llama Assn., South Central — PO Box 163654, Austin 78716-3654.

Lung Assn. of Texas, American — PO Box 26460, Austin 78755-0460.

Lupus Foundation of America, Inc., North Texas Chapter — 14465 Webb Chapel, Ste. 206, Farmers Branch 75234-3678.

Manufactured Housing Assn., Texas — PO Box 14428, Austin 78761-4428.

Medical Assistants, Texas Society of — 401 W. 15th St., Austin 78701-1680.

Medical Assn., Texas — 401 W. 15th, Austin 78701-1680.

Medical Assn. Alliance, Texas — 401 W. 15th St., Austin 78701-1680.

Mental Health Assn. in Texas — 8401 Shoal Creek Blvd., Austin 78757-7597.

Municipal Advisory Council of Texas — PO Box 2177, Austin 78768-2177.

Municipal Clerks Assn., Texas — PO Box 5065, Denton 76203-5065.

National Guard Assn. of Texas — PO Box 10045, Austin 78766-1045.

Nature Conservancy of Texas, The — PO Box 1440, San Antonio 78295-1440.

Neurological Society, Texas — 401 W. 15th St., Austin 78701-1680.

Newspaper Assn., Texas Daily — 816 Congress Ave., Ste. 960, Austin 78701-2443.

Nuclear Medicine, Texas Asso. of Physicians in — 401 W. 15th St., Austin 78701-1680.

Nurse Executives, Texas Organization of — PO Box 15587, Austin 78761-5587.

Nurserymen, Texas Assn. of — 7730 S. I H 35, Austin 78745-6698.

Nursing, Texas League for — PO Box 80110, Austin 78708-0110.

Obstetricians and Gynecologists, Texas Assn. of — 401 W. 15th St., Austin 78701-1680.

Oncology, Texas Society of Medical — 401 W. 15th St., Austin 78701-1680.

Ophthalmological Assn., Texas — 401 W. 15th, Ste. 825, Austin 78701.

Paper & Sanitary Supply Assn., Southwest — PO Box 140046, Austin 78714-0046.

Pathologists, Texas Society of — 401 W. 15th St., Austin 78701-1680.

Peanut Growers' Assn., Southwest — PO Box 338, Gorman 76454-0338.

Pecan Growers Assn., Texas — PO Box CC, College Station 77841.

Pharmacy Asso., Texas — PO Box 14709, Austin 78761-4709.

Philosophical Society of Texas — 2.306 Sid Richardson Hall, Austin 78712.

Plastic Surgeons, Texas Society of — 401 W. 15th St., Austin 78701-1680.

Police Assn., Texas — PO Box 4247, Austin 78765-4247.

Poultry Organizations

Poultry Assn., Texas Allied — PO Box 9589, Austin 78766-9589.

Poultry Federation, Texas — PO Box 9589, Austin 78766-9589.

Poultry Improvement Assn., Texas — PO Box 9589,

Austin 78766-9589.

Prairies Assn. of Texas, Native — 3503 Lafayette Ave., Austin 78722-1807.

Press Assn., Texas — 718 W. 5th St., Austin 78701-2799.

Press Assn., West Texas — 2502 Ivanhoe, Abilene 79605-6216.

Produce Asso., Texas — 901 Business Park Dr., Ste. 500, Mission 78572-6007.

Producers & Royalty Owners Assn., Texas Independent (TIPRO) — 515 Congress Ave., Ste. 1910, Austin 78701-3566.

Property Tax Professionals, Texas Assn. of — 1033 La Posada Dr., Ste. 220, Austin 78752-3880.

Public Employees Assn., Texas — PO Box 12217, Austin 78711-2217.

Radiological Society, Texas — 401 W. 15th St., Austin 78701-1680.

Ranching Heritage Assn. — PO Box 43201, Lubbock 79409-3201.

Range Management, Texas Section of Society for — PO Box 918, Sonora 76950-0918.

Realtors, Texas Assn. of — PO Box 2246, Austin 78768-2246.

Retailers Assn., Texas — 504 W. 12th St., Austin 78701-1898.

Savings and Community Bankers Assn., Texas — 910 Congress Ave., Floor 2, Austin 78701-2422.

School Boards, Texas Assn. of — 7703 N. Lamar Blvd., Austin 78752.

Sheep Breeders Assn., American Rambouillet — 2709 Sherwood Way, San Angelo 76901-3040.

Sheriffs' Assn. of Texas, Inc. — PO Box 4488, Austin 78765-4488.

Shrine Assn., Texas — PO Box 670627, Dallas 75367.

Socialist Party of Texas — PO Box 2640, Austin 78768-2640.

Social Workers, Texas Chapter of Nat'l. Assn. — 810 W. 11th St., Austin 78701-2096.

Sons Organizations

Sons of Confederate Veterans (Texas Division) — PO Box 619, Hillsboro 76645-0619.

Sons of Hermann in the State of Texas, Grand Lodge, Order of the — PO Box 1941, San Antonio 78297.

Sons of the Republic of Texas — 1717 8th St., Bay City 77414.

Sons of the Revolution in the State of Texas — 12 Woodland Drive East, Mineola 74773-9725.

TCU Alumni Assn. — TCU Box 297430, Fort Worth 76129.

Teachers Organizations

Teachers Asso., Texas Classroom — PO Box 1489, Austin 78767-1489.

Teachers, Texas Assn. of College — 9513 Burnet Rd., Ste. 206, Austin 78758-5248.

Teachers, Texas Community College — 901 So. MoPac, Ste. 1-410, Austin 78746-5747.

Teachers, Texas Federation of — 3000 S. I H 35, Ste. 175, Austin 78704-6536.

Teachers Assn., Texas State — 316 W. 12th St., Austin 78701-1892.

Texas Rangers Assn., Former — 3805 Broadway, San Antonio 78209.

Theatres, Inc., Texas Non-profit — 3505 W. Lancaster Ave. , Fort Worth 76107-3002.

Thoracic Society, Texas — PO Box 26460, Austin 78755-0460.

Trailer Manufacturers, Nat'l. Assn. of — 1033 La Posada Dr., #220, Austin 78752-3880.

Transplantation Society, Texas — 401 W. 15th St., Austin 78701-1680.

Turkey Federation, Texas — PO Box 9589, Austin 78766-9589.

United Way of Texas — 823 Congress Ave., Ste. 1103, Austin 78701.

University Presidents & Chancellors, Council of Public — 2609 Coatbridge Drive, Austin 78745-3423.

Urological Society, Texas — 401 W. 15th St., Austin 78701-1680.

Veterans of Foreign Wars, Texas — 8503 N. I H 35, Austin 78753-5758.

Veterinary Medical Assn., Texas — 6633 Hwy. 290 E, Ste. 201, Austin 78723-1157.

Water Conservation Assn., Texas — 221 E. 9th St., Ste. 206, Austin 78701-2513.

Wheat Producers Assn., Texas — 2201 Civic Circle, Ste. 803, Amarillo 79109-1853.

Wholesale Distributors, Texas Assn. of — 7320 N. MoPac Expy., Ste. 209, Austin 78731-2309.

Wine and Grape Growers Assn., Texas — One Liberty Park Plaza, Grapevine 76051-5374.

Women Voters of Texas, League of — 1212 Guadalupe, Ste. 107, Austin 78701-1800.

Women's Clubs, Texas Federation of — 2312 San Gabriel St., Austin 78705-5014.

Writers Assn., Texas Outdoor — 1415 Northridge Dr., Austin 78723-1824. ✭

Texas Pronunciation Guide

Texas' rich cultural diversity is reflected nowhere better than in the names of places. Standard pronunciation is used in many cases, but purely colloquial pronunciation often is used, too.

In the late 1940s, George Mitchel Stokes, a graduate student at Baylor University, developed a list of pronunciations of 2,300 place names across the state.

Stokes earned his doctorate and eventually served as director of the speech division in the Communications Studies Department at Baylor University. He retired in 1983.

In the following list based on Stokes longer list, pronunciation is by respelling and diacritical marking. Respelling is employed as follows: "ah" as in the exclamation, ah, or the "o" in tot; "ee" as in meet; "oo" as in moot; "yoo" as in use; "ow" as in cow; "oi" as in oil; "uh" as in mud.

Note that ah, uh and the apostrophe(') are used for varying degrees of neutral vowel sounds, the apostrophe being used where the vowel is barely sounded. Diacritical markings are used as follows: bāle, băd, lĕt, rīse, rĭll, ōak, brōŏd, fŏŏt.

The stressed syllable is capitalized. Secondary stress is indicated by an underline as in Atascosa—ăt uhs KŌ suh.

A

Abbott— Ă buht
Abernathy—Ă ber nă thĭ
Abilene—ĂB uh leen
Acala—uh KĂ luh
Ackerly—ĂK er lĭ
Acme—ĂK mĭ
Acton—ĂK t'n
Acuff—Ă kuhf
Adamsville—Ă d'mz vĭl
Addicks—Ă dĭks
Addielou—ă dĭ LŌŌ
Addison—A di s'n
Adkins—ĂT kĭnz
Adrian—Ă drĭ uhn
Afton—ĂF t'n
Agua Dulce—ah wuh DŌŌL sĭ
Agua Nueva—ah wuh nyōō Ā vuh
Aiken—Ā kĭn
Alamo—ĂL uh mō
Alamo Heights—ăl uh mō HĬTS
Alanreed—ĂL uhn reed
Alba—ĂL buh
Albany—AWL buh nĭ
Albert—ĂL bert
Aledo—uh LEE dō
Alexander—ĕl ĭg ZĂN der
Alfred—ĂL frĕd
Algoa—ăl GŌ uh
Alice—Ă lĭs
Alief—Ā leef
Allen—Ă lĭn
Allenfarm—ălĭn FAHRM
Alleyton—Ă lĭ t'n
Allison—ĂL uh s'n
Alma—AHL muh
Alpine—ĂL pīn
Altair—awl TĂR
Alta Loma—ăl tuh LŎ muh
Alto—ĂL tō
Altoga—ăl TŌ guh
Alvarado—ăl vuh RĂ dō
Alvin—ĂL vĭn
Alvord—ĂL vord
Amarillo—ăm uh RĬL ŏ
Amherst—AM herst
Ammannsville—ĂM 'nz vĭl
Anahuac—ĂN uh wăk
Anderson—ĂN der s'n

Andice—ĂN dĭs
Andrews—ĂN drōōz
Angelina—ăn juh LEE nuh
Angleton—ĂNG g'l t'n
Anna—ĂN uh
Annona—ă NŌ nuh
Anson—ĂN s'n
Antelope—ĂNT uh lōp
Anton—ĂNT n
Appleby—Ă p'l bi
Apple Springs—ă p'l SPRĬNGZ
Aquilla—uh KWĬL uh
Aransas—uh RĂN zuhs
Aransas Pass—uh răn zuhs PĂS
Arbala—ahr BĂ luh
Arcadia—ahr KĂ dĭ uh
Archer—AHR cher
Archer City—ahr cher SĬT ĭ
Arcola—ahr KŌ luh
Argo—AHR gō
Argyle—ahr GĬL
Arlington—AHR lĭng t'n
Arneckeville—AHR nĭ kĭ vĭl
Arnett—AHR nĭt
Arp—ahrp
Artesia Wells—ahr tee zh' WĔLZ
Arthur City—ahr ther SĬT ĭ
Asherton—ĂSH er t'n
Aspermont—ĂS per mahnt
Atascosa—ăt uhs KŌ suh
Athens—Ă thĕnz
Atlanta—ăt LĂN tuh
Atlas—ĂT l's
Attoyac—AT uh yăk
Aubrey—AW brĭ
Augusta—aw GUHS tuh
Austin—AWS t'n
Austonio—aws TŌ nĭ ŏ
Austwell—AWS wĕl
Avalon—ĂV uhl n
Avery—Ā vuh rĭ
Avinger—Ă vĭn jer
Avoca—uh VŌ kuh
Axtell—ĂKS t'l
Azle—Ā z'l

B

Bagwell—BĂG w'l
Bailey—BĂ li

Baileyboro—BĂ lĭ ber ruh
Baileyville—BĂ lĭ vĭl
Baird—bărd
Bakersfield—BĂ kers feeld
Ballinger—BĂL ĭn jer
Balmorhea—băl muh RĂ
Bandera—băn DĔR uh
Bangs—băngz
Banquete—băn KĔ tĭ
Barclay—BAHRK lĭ
Bardwell—BAHRD w'l
Barker—BAHR ker
Barksdale—BAHRKS dăl
Barnhart—BAHRN hahrt
Barnum—BAHR n'm
Barry—BĂ rĭ
Barstow—BAHRS tō
Bartlett—BAHRT lĭt
Bassett—BĂ sĭt
Bastrop—BĂS trahp
Batesville—BĂTS v'l
Batson—BĂT s'n
Baxter—BĂKS ter
Bay City—ba SĬT ĭ
Baylor—BĂ ler
Bayside—BĂ sĭd
Baytown—BĂ town
Beasley—BEEZ lĭ
Beaukiss—bō KĬS
Beaumont—BŌ mahnt
Bebe—bāb
Beckville—BĔK v'l
Becton—BĔK t'n
Bedias—BEE dĭs
Bee—bee
Beehouse—BEE hows
Beeville—BEE vĭl
Belcherville—BĔL cher vĭl
Bell—bĕl
Bellaire—bĕl ĂR
Bellevue—BĔL vyōō
Bellmead—bĕl MEED
Bells—bĕlz
Bellville—BĔL vĭl
Belmont—BĔL mahnt
Belton—BĔL t'n
Benarnold—bĕn AHR n'ld
Benavides—bĕn uh VEE d's
Ben Bolt—bĕn BŌLT

Benbrook—BĬN brŏŏk
Benchley—BĔNCH lĭ
Bend—bĕnd
Ben Franklin—bĕn FRĂNGk lĭn
Ben Hur—bĕn HER
Benjamin—BĔN juh m'n
Bennett—BĔN ĭt
Bentonville—BĔNT n vĭl
Ben Wheeler—bĭn HWEE ler
Berclair—ber KLĂR
Bertram—BERT r'm
Bessmay—bĕs MĂ
Best—bĕst
Bettie—BĔT ĭ
Bexar—BA är
Beyersville—BĬRZ vĭl
Biardstown—BĂRDZ t'n
Bigfoot—BĬG fŏŏt
Big Lake—bĭg LĂK
Big Sandy—bĭg SĂN dĭ
Big Spring—bĭg SPRĬNG
Bigwells—bĭg WĔLZ
Birdville—BERD vĭl
Birome—bĭ RŌM
Birthright—BERTH rĭt
Bishop—BĬ sh'p
Bivins—BĬ vĭnz
Black—blăk
Blackfoot—BLĂK fŏŏt
Blackwell—BLĂK w'l
Blair—blär
Blanchard—BLĂN cherd
Blanco—BLĂNG kō
Blanket—BLĂNG kĭt
Bleakwood—BLEEK wŏŏd
Bledsoe—BLĔD sō
Blessing—BLĔ sĭng
Blewett—BLŌŌ ĭt
Blooming Grove—blŏŏ mĭng GRŌV
Bloomington—BLŌŌM ĭng t'n
Blossom—BLAH s'm
Blue Grove—blŏŏ GRŌV
Blue Ridge—blŏŏ RĬJ
Bluff Dale—BLUHF dāl
Bluffton—BLUHF t'n
Blum—bluhm
Boerne—BER nĭ
Bogata—buh GŌ duh
Boling—BŌL ĭng
Bolivar—BAH lĭ ver
Bomarton—BŌ mer t'n
Bonham—BAH n'm
Bonita—bō NEE tuh
Bonney—BAH nĭ
Bonus—BŌ n's
Bon Wier—bahn WEER
Booker—BŌŌ ker
Boonsville—BŌŌNZ vĭl
Booth—bŏŏth
Borden—BAWRD n
Borger—BŌR ger
Bosque—BAHS kĭ
Boston—BAWS t'n
Bovina—bō VEE nuh
Bowie—BŌŌ ĭ
Box Elder—bahks ĔL der
Boyce—bawis
Boyd—boid
Brachfield—BRĂCH feeld

Bracken—BRĂ kĭn
Brackettville—BRĂ kĭt vĭl
Bradford—BRĂD ferd
Bradshaw—BRĂD shaw
Brady—BRĂ dĭ
Brandon—BRĂN d'n
Brashear—bruh SHĬR
Brazoria—bruh ZŌ rĭ uh
Brazos—BRĂZ uhs
Breckenridge—BRĔK uhn rĭj
Bremond—bree MAHND
Brenham—BRĔ n'm
Brewster—BRŌŌ ster
Brice—brĭs
Bridgeport—BRĬJ pōrt
Briggs—brĭgz
Briscoe—BRĬS kō
Britton—BRĬT n
Broaddus—BRAW d's
Brock—brahk
Bronson—BRAHN s'n
Bronte—brahnt
Brookeland—BRŌŌK l'nd
Brookesmith—BRŌŌK smith
Brooks—brŏŏks
Brookshire—BRŌŌK sher
Brookston—BRŌŌKS t'n
Brown—brown
Browndel—brown DĔL
Brownfield—BROWN feeld
Brownsboro—BROWNZ buh ruh
Brownsville—BROWNZ vĭl
Brownwood—BROWN wŏŏd
Bruceville—BRŌŌS v'l
Brundage—BRUHN dĭj
Bruni—BRŌŌ nĭ
Brushy Creek—bruh shĭ KREEK
Bryan—BRĬ uhn
Bryans Mill—brĭ 'nz MĬL
Bryarly—BRĬ er lĭ
Bryson—BRĬ s'n
Buchanan Dam—buhk hăn uhn DĂM
Buckholts—BUHK hŏlts
Buckhorn—BUHK hawrn
Buda—BYŌŌ duh
Buena Vista—bwă nuh VEES tuh
Buffalo—BUHF uh lō
Buffalo Gap—buhf uh lō GĂP
Buffalo Springs—buhf uh lō SPRĬNGZ
Bula—BYŌŌ luh
Bullard—BŌŌL erd
Bulverde—bŏŏl VER dĭ
Buna—BYŌŌ nuh
Burkburnett—berk ber NET
Burkett—BER kĭt
Burkeville—BERK vĭl
Burleson—BER luh s'n
Burlington—BER lĭng t'n
Burnet—BER nĕt
Burton—BERT n
Bushland—BŌŌSH l'nd
Bustamante—buhs tuh MAHN tĭ
Butler—BUHT ler
Byers—BĬ erz
Bynum—BĬ n'm
Byrd—berd

C

Cactus—KĂK t's
Caddo Mills—kă dō MĬLZ
Calallen—kăl ĂL ĭn
Calaveras—kăl uh VĔR's
Caldwell—KAHL wĕl
Calhoun—kăl HŌŌN
Call—kawl
Calliham—KĂL uh hăm
Callisburg—KĂ lĭs berg
Call Junction—kawl JUHNGK sh'n
Calvert—KĂL vert
Camden—KĂM dĭn
Cameron—KĂM uh r'n
Camilla—kuh MEEL yuh
Camp—kămp
Campbell—KĂM uhl
Campbellton—KĂM uhl t'n
Camp Wood—kămp WŌŌD
Canadian—kuh NĂ dĭ uhn
Candelaria—kăn duh LĔ rĭ uh
Canton—KĂNT n
Canyon—KĂN y'n
Caplen—KĂP lĭn
Caps—kăps
Caradan—KĂR uh dăn
Carbon—KAHR b'n
Carey—KĂ rĭ
Carlisle—KAHR lĭl
Carlsbad—KAHR uhlz bad
Carlton—KAHR uhl t'n
Carmine—kahr MEEN
Carmona—kahr MŌ nuh
Caro—KAH rō
Carrizo Springs—kuh ree zuh SPRĬNGZ
Carrollton—KĂR 'l t'n
Carson—KAHR s'n
Carthage—KAHR thĭj
Cash—kăsh
Cason—KĂ s'n
Cass—kăs
Castell—kăs TĔL
Castro—KĂS trō
Castroville—KĂS tro vĭl
Catarina—kăt uh REE nuh
Cat Spring—kăt SPRĬNG
Caviness—KĂ vĭ nĕs
Cayuga—kā YŌŌ guh
Cedar Bayou—see der BĬ ō
Cedar Creek—see der KREEK
Cedar Hill—see der HĬL
Cedar Lake—see der LĂK
Cedar Lane—see der LĂN
Cedar Park—see der PAHRK
Cedar Valley—see der VA lĭ
Cee Vee—see VEE
Celeste—suh LĔST
Celina—suh LĬ nuh
Center—SENT er
Center City—sĕn ter SĬT ĭ
Center Point—sĕn ter POINT
Centerville—sĕn ter vĭl
Centralia—sĕn TRĂL yuh
Chalk—chawlk
Chalk Mountain—chawlk MOWNT n
Chambers—CHĂM berz
Chandler—CHĂND ler
Channelview—chăn uhl VYŌŌ

Channing—CHĂN ĭng
Chapman Ranch—chăp m'n RĂNCH
Chappell Hill—chă p'l HĬL
Charco—CHAHR kō
Charleston—CHAHR uhls t'n
Charlie—CHAHR lĭ
Charlotte—SHAHR l't
Chatfield—CHĂT feeld
Cheapside—CHEEP sīd
Cheek—cheek
Cherokee—CHĔR uh k<u>ee</u>
Chester—CHĔS ter
Chico—CHEE kō
Chicota—chĭ KŌ tuh
Childress—CHĬL drĕs
Chillicothe—<u>chĭl</u> ĭ KAH thĭ
Chilton—CHĬL t'n
China—CHĪ nuh
China Spring—chī nuh SPRĬNG
Chireno—sh' REE nō
Chisholm—CHĬZ uhm
Chita—CHEE tuh
Chocolate Bayou—<u>chah</u> kuh lĭt BĪ ō
Choice—chois
Chriesman—KRĬS m'n
Christine—krĭs TEEN
Christoval—krĭs TŌ v'l
Cibolo—SEE bō lō
Circle Back—SER k'l băk
Circleville—SER k'l vĭl
Cisco—SĬS kō
Cistern—SĬS tern
Clairemont—KLĂR mahnt
Clairette—klăr ĭ ĔT
Clarendon—KLĂR ĭn d'n
Clareville—KLĂR vĭl
Clarksville—KLAHRKS vĭl
Clarkwood—KLAHRK wōōd
Claude—klawd
Clawson—KLAW s'n
Clay—klā
Clayton—KLĀT n
Clear Lake—KLĬR lăk
Clear Spring—klĭr SPRĬNG
Cleburne—KLEE bern
Clemville—KLĔM vĭl
Cleveland—KLEEV l'nd
Clifton—KLĬF t'n
Cline—klīn
Clint—klĭnt
Clodine—klaw DEEN
Clute—klōōt
Clyde—klīd
Coahoma—kuh HŌ muh
Cockrell Hill—kahk ruhl HĬL
Coke—kōk
Coldspring—KŌLD sprĭng
Coleman—KŌL m'n
Colfax—KAHL făks
Collegeport—kah lĭj PŌRT
College Station—<u>kah</u> lĭj STĀ sh'n
Collin—KAH lĭn
Collingsworth—KAH lĭnz werth
Collinsville—KAH lĭnz vĭl
Colmesneil—KŌL m's neel
Colorado—<u>kahl</u> uh RAH dō
Colorado City—kah luh r<u>ă</u> duh SĬT ĭ
Columbus—kuh LUHM b's
Comal—KŌ măl

Comanche—kuh MĂN chĭ
Combes—kōmz
Comfort—KUHM fert
Commerce—KAH mers
Como—KŌ mō
Comstock—KAHM stahk
Concan—KAHN kăn
Concepcion—kuhn sep sĭ ŌN
Concho—KAHN chō
Concord—KAHN kawrd
Concrete—kahn KREET
Cone—kōn
Conlen—KAHN lĭn
Conroe—KAHN rō
Converse—KAHN vers
Conway—KAHN wā
Cooke—kōōk
Cookville—KŌŌK vĭl
Coolidge—KŌŌ lĭj
Cooper—KŌŌ per
Copeville—KŌP v'l
Coppell—kuh PĔL
Copperas Cove—kahp ruhs KŌV
Corbett—KAWR bĭt
Cordele—kawr DĔL
Corinth—KAH rĭnth
Corley—KAWR lĭ
Corpus Christi—<u>kawr</u> p's KRĬS tĭ
Corrigan—KAWR uh g'n
Corsicana—<u>kawr</u> sĭ KĂN uh
Coryell—kō rĭ ĔL
Cost—kawst
Cottle—KAH t'l
Cotton Center—<u>kaht</u> n SĔNT er
Cotton Gin—KAHT n jĭn
Cottonwood—KAHT n wōōd
Cotulla—kuh TŌŌ luh
Coupland—KŌP l'n
Courtney—KŌRT nĭ
Covington—KUHV ĭng t'n
Coy City—koi SĬT ĭ
Craft—krăft
Crafton—KRĂF t'n
Crandall—KRĂN d'l
Crane—krān
Cranfills Gap—krăn f'lz GĂP
Crawford—KRAW ferd
Creedmore—KREED mōr
Cresson—KRĔ s'n
Crisp—krĭsp
Crockett—KRAH kĭt
Crosby—KRAWZ bĭ
Crosbyton—KRAWZ bĭ t'n
Cross—kraws
Cross Cut—KRAWS kuht
Cross Plains—kraws PLĂNZ
Cross Roads—KRAWS rōdz
Crow—krō
Crowell—KRŌ uhl
Crowley—KROW li
Crystal City—krĭs t'l SĬT ĭ
Crystal Falls—krĭs t'l FAWLZ
Cuero—KWĔR o
Culberson—KUHL ber s'n
Cumby—KUHM bĭ
Cuney—KYŌŌ nĭ
Cunningham—KUHN ĭng hăm
Currie—KER rĭ
Cushing—KŌŌ shĭng

Cuthand—KUHT hănd
Cyclone—SĪ klōn
Cypress—SĪ prĕs

D

Dabney—DĂB nĭ
Dacosta—duh KAHS tuh
Dacus—DĂ k's
Daingerfield—DĂN jer feeld
Daisetta—dā ZĔT uh
Dalby Springs—dĂl bĭ SPRĬNGZ
Dale—dāl
Dalhart—DĂL hahrt
Dallam—DĂL uhm
Dallas—DĂ luhs
Damon—DĂ m'n
Danbury—DĂN bĕrĭ
Danciger—DĂN sĭ ger
Danevang—DĂN uh văng
Darrouzett—dăr uh ZĔT
Davilla—duh VĬL uh
Dawn—dawn
Dawson—DAW s'n
Dayton—DĀT n
Deadwood—DĔD wōōd
Deaf Smith—dĕf SMĬTH
Deanville—DEEN vĭl
De Berry—duh BĔ rĭ
Decatur—<u>dee</u> KĂT er
Deer Park—dĭr PAHRK
De Kalb—dĭ KĂB
De Leon—da lee AHN
Del Rio—dĕl REE o
Delta—DĔL tuh
Delvalle—dĕl VĂ lĭ
Delwin—DĔl wĭn
Denhawken—DĬN haw kĭn
Denison—DĔN uh s'n
Denning—DĔN ĭng
Dennis—DĔ nĭs
Denton—DĔNT n
Denver City—<u>dĕn</u> ver SĬT ĭ
Deport—dĭ PŌRT
Derby—DER bĭ
Desdemona—<u>dĕz</u> dĭ MŌ nuh
DeSoto—dĭ SŌ tuh
Detroit—dee TROIT
Devers—DĔ vers
Devine—duh VĬN
Dew—dyōō
Deweyville—DYŌŌ ĭ vĭl
DeWitt—dĭ WĬT
Dewville—DYŌŌ vĭl
Dexter—DĔKS ter
D'Hanis—duh HĂ nĭs
Dialville—DĪ uhl vil
Diboll—DĬ bawl
Dickens—DĬK ĭnz
Dickinson—DĬK ĭn s'n
Dike—dĭk
Dilley—DĬL i
Dilworth—DĬL <u>werth</u>
Dimebox—dīm BAHKS
Dimmit—DĬM ĭt
Dinero—dĭ NĔ rō
Direct—duh RĔKT
Dixon—DĬK s'n
Dobbin—DAH bĭn
Dobrowolski—<u>dah</u> bruh WAHL skĭ

Dodd City—dahd SĬT ĭ
Dodge—DAH j
Dodson—DAHD s'n
Donie—DŌ nĭ
Donley—DAHN ĭĭ
Donna—dah nuh
Doole—DOO ĭĭ
Dorchester—dawr CHĔS ter
Doss—daws
Doucette—DŌŌ sĕt
Dougherty—DAHR tĭ
Douglass—DUHG l's
Douglassville—DUHG ĭĭs vĭĭ
Downing—DOWN ĭng
Downsville—DOWNZ vĭĭ
Dozier—DŌ zher
Draw—draw
Driftwood—DRĬFT wŏŏd
Dripping Springs—drĭp ĭng SPRĬNGZ
Driscoll—DRĬS k'l
Dryden—DRĬD n
Dublin—DUHB lĭn
Duffau—DUHF ō
Dumas—DŌŌ m's
Dumont—DYŌŌ mahnt
Dundee—DUHN dĭ
Dunlap—DUHN lăp
Dunlay—DUHN ĭĭ
Dunn—duhn
Durango—duh RĂNG go
Duval—DŌŌ vawl

E

Eagle—EE g'l
Eagle Lake—ee g'l LĀK
Eagle Pass—ee g'l PĂS
Earth—erth
East Bernard—eest ber NAHRD
Easterly—EES ter lĭ
Eastland—EEST l'nd
Easton—EES t'n
Ector—ĔK ter
Edcouch—ĕd KOWCH
Eddy—E di
Eden—EED n
Edge—ĕj
Edgewood—ĔJ wŏŏd
Edinburg—ĔD n berg
Edmonson—ĔD m'n s'n
Edna—ED nuh
Edom—EE d'm
Edroy—ĔD roi
Edwards—ĔD werdz
Egan—EE g'n
Egypt—EE juhpt
Elbert—ĔL bert
El Campo—ĕl KĂM pō
Eldorado—ĕl duh RĂ duh
Electra—ĭ LĔK truh
Elgin—ĔL gĭn
Eliasville—ee LĪ uhs vĭĭ
El Indio—ĕl ĬN dĭ ō
Elkhart—ĔLK hahrt
Ellinger—ĔL ĭn jer
Elliott—ĔL ĭ 't
Ellis—ĔL uhs
Elmendorf—ĔLM 'n dawrf
Elm Mott—ĕl MAHT
Elmo—ĔL mō

Eloise—ĔL o eez
El Paso—ĕl PĂS ō
Elsa—ĔL suh
Elysian Fields—uh lee zh'n FEELDZ
Emhouse—ĔM hows
Emory—ĔM uh rĭ
Encinal—ĕn suh NAHL
Encino—ĕn SEE nō
Energy—ĔN er jĭ
Engle—ĔN g'l
English—ĬNG glĭsh
Enloe—ĔN lō
Ennis—ĔN ĭs
Enochs—EE nuhks
Eola—ee Ō luh
Era—EE ruh
Erath—EE răth
Esperanza—ĕs per RĂN zuh
Estelline—ĔS tuh leen
Etoile—ĭ TOIL
Etter—ĔT er
Eula—YŌŌ luh
Euless—YŌŌ lis
Eureka—yōō REE kuh
Eustace—YŌŌS t's
Evadale—EE vuh dāl
Evant—EE vănt
Evergreen—Ĕ ver green
Everman—Ĕ ver m'n

F

Fabens—FĀ b'nz
Fairbanks—FĂR bangks
Fairfield—FĂR feeld
Fairlie—FĂR lee
Fair Play—făr PLĀ
Fairview—FĂR vyōō
Fairy—FĀ rĭ
Falfurrias—făl FYŌŌ rĭ uhs
Falls—fawlz
Falls City—fawlz SĬT ĭ
Fannett—fă NĔT
Fannin—FĂN ĭn
Fargo—FAHR gō
Farmers Branch—fahr merz
BRĂNCH
Farmersville—FAHRM erz vĭĭ
Farnsworth—FAHRNZ werth
Farrar—FĂR uh
Farrsville—FAHRZ vĭĭ
Farwell—FAHR w'l
Fashing—FĂ shĭng
Fate—fāt
Fayette—fă ĔT
Fayetteville—FĂ uht vĭĭ
Fentress—FĔN trĭs
Ferris—FĔR ĭs
Field Creek—feeld KREEK
Fieldton—FEEL t'n
Fife—fīf
Fisher—FĬSH er
Fischer—fĭ sher
Fisk—fĭsk
Flagg—flăg
Flat—flăt
Flatonia—flă TŌN yuh
Flint—flĭnt
Flomot—FLŌ maht
Florence—FLAH ruhns

Floresville—FLŌRZ vil
Florey—FLŌ ri
Floyd—floid
Floydada—floi DĂ duh
Fluvanna—flōō VĂN uh
Flynn—flĭn
Foard—fōrd
Foard City—fōrd SĬT ĭ
Fodice—FŌ dĭs
Follett—fah LĔT
Fordtran—fōrd TRĂN
Forest—FAW rĕst
Forestburg—FAW rĕst berg
Forney—FAWR nĭ
Forreston—FAW rĕs t'n
Forsan—FŌR săn
Fort Bend—fōrt BĔND
Fort Chadbourne—fōrt CHĂD bern
Fort Davis—fōrt DĂ vĭs
Fort Griffin—fōrt GRĬF ĭn
Fort Hancock—fōrt HĂN kahk
Fort McKavett—fōrt muh KĂ vet
Fort Stockton—fōrt STAHK t'n
Fort Worth—fōrt WERTH
Fowlerton—FOW ler t'n
Francitas—frăn SEE t's
Franklin—FRĂNGK lĭn
Frankston—FRĂNGS t'n
Fred—frĕd
Fredericksburg—FRĔD er rĭks berg
Fredonia—free DŌN yuh
Freeport—FREE pōrt
Freer—FREE er
Freestone—FREE stōn
Frelsburg—FRĔLZ berg
Fresno—FRĔZ nō
Friday—FRĪ dĭ
Friendswood—FRĔNZ wŏŏd
Frio—FREE ō
Friona—free O nuh
Frisco—FRĬS ko
Fritch—frĭch
Frost—frawst
Fruitland—FRŌŌT lănd
Fruitvale—FRŌŌT vāl
Frydek—FRĪ dĕk
Fulbright—FŌŌL brīt
Fulshear—FUHL sher
Fulton—FŌŌL t'n

G

Gail—gāl
Gaines—gănz
Gainesville—GĂNZ vuhl
Galena Park—guh lee nuh PAHRK
Gallatin—GĂL uh t'n
Galveston—GĂL vĕs t'n
Ganado—guh NĂ dō
Garceno—gahr SĂ nō
Garciasville—gahr SEE uhs vĭĭ
Garden City—GAHRD n sĭt ĭ
Gardendale—GAHRD n dāl
Garden Valley—gahrd n VĂ ĭĭ
Garland—GAHR l'nd
Garner—GAHR ner
Garrett—GĂR ĭt
Garrison—GĂ rĭ s'n
Garwood—GAHR wŏŏd
Gary—GĔ rĭ

Garza—GAHR zuh
Gatesville—GĀTS vil
Gause—gawz
Gay Hill—gā HĬL
Geneva—juh NEE vuh
Georgetown—JAWRJ town
George West—jawrj WĚST
Geronimo—juh RAH nǐ mō
Giddings—GĬD ĭngz
Gillespie—guh LĚS pĭ
Gillett—juh LĚT
Gilliland—GĬL ĭ l'nd
Gilmer—GĬL mer
Ginger—JĬN jer
Girard—juh RAHRD
Girvin—GER vĭn
Gladewater—GLĀD wah ter
Glasscock—GLĂS kahk
Glazier—GLĀ zher
Glen Cove—glĕn KŌV
Glendale—GLĚN dāl
Glenfawn—glĕn FAWN
Glen Flora—glĕn FLŌ ruh
Glenn—glĕn
Glen Rose—GLĚN rōz
Glidden—GLĬD n
Gober—GŌ ber
Godley—GAHD lĭ
Golden—GŌL d'n
Goldfinch—GŌLD fĭnch
Goldsboro—GŌLZ buh ruh
Goldsmith—GŌL smith
Goldthwaite—GŌLTH wāt
Goliad—GŌ lĭ ăd
Golindo—gō LĬN duh
Gonzales—guhn ZAH l's
Goodland—GŌŌD l'n
Goodlett—GŌŌD lĕt
Goodnight—GŌŌD nīt
Goodrich—GŌŌD rĭch
Gordon—GAWRD n
Gordonville—GAWRD n vĭl
Goree—GŌ ree
Gorman—GAWR m'n
Gouldbusk—GŌŌLD buhsk
Graford—GRĀ ferd
Graham—GRĀ 'm
Granbury—GRĂN bĕ rĭ
Grandfalls—gränd FAWLZ
Grand Saline—grän suh LEEN
Grandview—GRĂN vyōō
Granger—GRĂN jer
Grapeland—GRĀP l'nd
Grapevine—GRĀP vĭn
Grassland—GRĂS l'nd
Grassyville—GRĀ sĭ vĭl
Gray—grā
Grayburg—GRĀ berg
Grayson—GRĀ s'n
Green—green
Greenville—GREEN v'l
Greenwood—GREEN wŏŏd
Gregg—grĕg
Gregory—GRĚG uh rĭ
Grimes—grīmz
Groesbeck—GRŌZ bĕk
Groom—grōōm
Groveton—GRŌV t'n
Grow—grō

Gruene—green
Grulla—GRŌŌL yuh
Gruver—GRŌŌ ver
Guadalupe—gwah duh LŌŌ pĭ
Guerra—GWĚ ruh
Gunter—GUHN ter
Gustine—GUHS teen
Guthrie—GUHTH rĭ
Guy—gī

H

Hackberry—HĂK bĕ rĭ
Hagansport—HĀ gĭnz pōrt
Hainesville—HĀNZ v'l
Hale—hāl
Hale Center—hāl SĚNT er
Hall—hawl
Hallettsville—HĂL ĕts vĭl
Hallsville—HAWLZ vĭl
Hamilton—HĂM uhl t'n
Hamlin—HĂM lĭn
Hammond—HĂM 'nd
Hamon—HĂ m'n
Hamshire—HĂM sher
Handley—HĂND lĭ
Hankamer—HĂN kăm er
Hansford—HĂNZ ferd
Happy—HĂ pĭ
Hardeman—HAHR duh m'n
Hardin—HAHRD n
Hare—hăr
Hargill—HAHR gĭl
Harleton—HAHR uhl t'n
Harlingen—HAHR lĭn juhn
Harper—HAHR per
Harris—HĂ rĭs
Harrison—HĂ rĭ s'n
Harrold—HĂR 'ld
Hart—hahrt
Hartburg—HAHRT berg
Hartley—HAHRT lĭ
Harwood—HAHR wŏŏd
Haskell—HĂS k'l
Haslam—HĂZ l'm
Haslet—HĂS lĕt
Hasse—HĂ sĭ
Hatchell—HĂ ch'l
Hawkins—HAW kĭnz
Hawley—HAW lĭ
Hays—hāz
Hearne—hern
Heath—heeth
Hebbronville—HĚB r'n vĭl
Hebron—HEE br'n
Hedley—HĚD lĭ
Heidenheimer—HĪD n hīmer
Helena—HĚL uh nuh
Helotes—hĕl Ō tĭs
Hemphill—HĚMP hĭl
Hempstead—HĚM stĕd
Henderson—HĚN der s'n
Henly—HĚN lĭ
Henrietta—hĕn rĭ Ě tuh
Hereford—HER ferd
Hermleigh—HER muh lee
Hewitt—HYŌŌ ĭt
Hicks—hĭks
Hico—HĪ kō
Hidalgo—hĭ DĂL gō

Higgins—HĬ gĭnz
High—hī
Highbank—HĬ băngk
High Island—hī Ī l'nd
Highlands—HĬ l'ndz
Hightower—HĬ tow er
Hill—hĭl
Hillister—HĬL ĭs ter
Hillsboro—HĬLZ buh ruh
Hindes—hĭndz
Hiram—HĪ r'm
Hitchcock—HĬCH kahk
Hitchland—HĬCH l'nd
Hobson—HAHB s'n
Hochheim—HŌ hīm
Hockley—HAHK lĭ
Holland—HAHL 'nd
Holliday—HAH luh dā
Hondo—HAHN dō
Honey Grove—HUHN ĭ grŏv
Honey Island—huhn Ī Ī l'nd
Honey Springs—huhn ĭ SPRĬNGZ
Hood—hŏŏd
Hooks—hŏŏks
Hopkins—HAHP kĭnz
Houston—HYŌŌS t'n or YŌŌS t'n
Howard—HOW erd
Howe—how
Howland—HOW l'nd
Hubbard—HUH berd
Huckabay—HUHK uh bĭ
Hudspeth—HUHD sp'th
Huffman—HUHF m'n
Hufsmith—HUHF smĭth
Hughes Springs—hyōōz SPRĬNGZ
Hull—huhl
Humble—HUHM b'l
Hungerford—HUHNG ger ferd
Hunt—huhnt
Hunter—HUHNT er
Huntington—HUHNT ĭng t'n
Huntsville—HUHNTS v'l
Hurlwood—HERL wŏŏd
Hutchins—HUH chĭnz
Hutchinson—HUH chĭn s'n
Hutto—HUH tō
Hye—hī
Hylton—HĬL t'n

I

Iago—ĭ Ā gō
Idalou—Ī duh lōō
Imperial—ĭm PĬR ĭ uhl
Inadale—Ī nuh dāl
Independence—ĭn duh PĚN d'ns
Indian Creek—ĭn dĭ uhn KREEK
Indian Gap—ĭn dĭ uhn GĂP
Industry—ĬN duhs trĭ
Inez—ĭ NĚZ
Ingleside—ĬNG g'l sīd
Ingram—ĬNG gr'm
Iola—ĭ Ō luh
Iowa Park—ĭ uh wuh PAHRK
Ira—Ī ruh
Iraan—ĭ ruh ĂN
Iredell—Ī ruh dĕl
Ireland—Ī rĭ l'nd
Irene—ĭ REEN
Irion—ĬR ĭ uhn

Ironton—ĬRN t'n
Irving—ER vĭng
Italy—ĬT uh lĭ
Itasca—ī TĂS kuh
Ivan—Ī v'n
Ivanhoe—Ī v'n hō

J

Jack—jăk
Jacksboro—JĂKS buh ruh
Jackson—JĂK s'n
Jacksonville—JĂK s'n vĭl
Jamestown—JĂMZ town
Jardin—JAHRD n
Jarrell—JĂR uhl
Jasper—JĂS per
Jayton—JĂT n
Jean—jeen
Jeddo—JĔ dō
Jeff Davis—jĕf DA vĭs
Jefferson—JĔF er s'n
Jericho—JĔ rĭ kō
Jermyn—JER m'n
Jewett—JŌŌ ĭt
Jiba—HEE buh
Jim Hogg—jĭm HAWG
Jim Wells—jĭm WĔLZ
Joaquin—waw KEEN
Johnson—JAHN s'n
Johnson City—jahn s'n SĬT ĭ
Johntown—JAHN town
Johnsville—JAHNZ vĭl
Joinerville—JOI ner vĭl
Jolly—JAH lĭ
Jollyville—JAH lĭ vĭl
Jonah—JŌ nuh
Jones—jōnz
Jonesboro—JŌNZ buh ruh
Jonesville—JŌNZ vĭl
Josephine—JŌ suh feen
Joshua—JAH sh' wa
Jourdanton—JERD n t'n
Joy—joi
Joyce—jawĭs
Juliff—JŌŌ lĭf
Junction—JUHNGK sh'n
Juno—JŌŌ nō
Justiceburg—JUHS tĭs berg
Justin—JUHS tĭn

K

Kalgary—KĂL gĕ rĭ
Kamay—KĀ ĭm ā
Kanawha—KAHN uh wah
Karnack—KAHR năk
Karnes—kahrnz
Karnes City—kahrnz SĬT ĭ
Katemcy—kuh TĔM sĭ
Katy—KĀ tĭ
Kaufman—KAWF m'n
Keechi—KEE chĭ
Keene—keen
Kellerville—KĔL er vĭl
Kemah—KEE muh
Kemp—kĕmp
Kemp City—kĕmp SĬT ĭ
Kempner—KĔMP ner
Kendalia—kĔn DĀL yuh
Kenedy—KĔN uh dĭ

Kennard—kuh NAHRD
Kennedale—KĔN uh dāl
Kent—kĕnt
Kerens—KER 'nz
Kermit—KER mit
Kerr—ker
Kerrville—KER vĭl
Kildare—KĬL dăr
Kilgore—KĬL gōr
Killeen—kuh LEEN
Kimble—KĬM b'l
King—kĭng
Kingsbury—KĬNGZ bĕ rĭ
Kingsland—KĬNGZ l'nd
Kingsmill—kĭngz MĬL
Kingston—KĬNGZ t'n
Kingsville—KĬNGZ vĭl
Kinney—KĬN ĭ
Kirby—KER bĭ
Kirbyville—KER bĭ vĭl
Kirkland—KERK l'nd
Kirvin—KER vĭn
Kleberg—KLĀ berg
Klondike—KLAHN dīk
Knickerbocker—NĬK uh bah ker
Knippa—kuh NĬP uh
Knott—naht
Knox—nahks
Knox City—nahks SĬT ĭ
Kosciusko—kuh SHŌŌS kō
Kosse—KAH sĭ
Kountze—kōōntz
Kress—kres
Krum—kruhm
Kurten—KER t'n
Kyle—kīl

L

La Blanca—lah BLAHN kuh
Lacoste—luh KAWST
Ladonia—luh DŌN yuh
LaFayette—lah fĭ ĔT
Laferia—luh FĔ rĭ uh
Lagarto—luh GAHR tō
La Gloria—lah GLŌ rĭ uh
La Grange—luh GRĂNJ
Laguna—luh GŌŌ nuh
Laird Hill—lărd HĬL
La Joya—luh HŌ yuh
Lake Creek—lāk KREEK
Lake Dallas—lāk DĂL uhs
Lake Jackson—lāk JĂK s'n
Laketon—LĀK t'n
Lake Victor—lāk VĬK ter
Lakeview—LĂK vyōō
Lamar—luh MAHR
Lamarque—luh MAHRK
Lamasco—luh MĂS kō
Lamb—lăm
Lamesa—luh MEE suh
Lamkin—LĂM kĭn
Lampasas—lăm PĂ s's
Lancaster—LĂNG k's ter
Land City—lăn SĬT ĭ
Laneville—LĀN vĭl
Langtry—LĂNG trĭ
Lanier—luh NĬR
La Paloma—lah puh LŌ muh
La Porte—luh PŌRT

La Pryor—luh PRĪ er
Laredo—luh RĀ dō
Lariat—LĂ ri uht
La Rue—luh RŌŌ
LaSalle—luh SĂL
Lasara—luh SĔ ruh
Lassater—LĂ sĭ ter
Latch—lĂch
Latexo—luh TĔKS ō
Lavaca—luh VĂ kuh
La Vernia—luh VER nĭ uh
La Villa—lah VĬL uh
Lavon—luh VAHN
La Ward—luh WAWRD
Lawn—lawn
Lawrence—LAH r'ns
Lazbuddie—LĂZ buh dĭ
League City—leeg SĬT ĭ
Leakey—LĀ kĭ
Leander—lee ĂN der
Leary—LĬ er ĭ
Ledbetter—LĔD bĕt er
Lee—lee
Leesburg—LEEZ berg
Leesville—LEEZ vĭl
Lefors—lĭ FŌRZ
Leggett—LĔ gĭt
Leigh—lee
Lela—lee
Lelia Lake—leel yuh LĀK
Leming—LĔ mĭng
Lenorah—lĕ NŌ ruh
Leo—LEE ō
Leon—lee AHN
Leona—lee Ō nuh
Leonard—LĔN erd
Leon Springs—lee ahn SPRĬNGZ
Leroy—LEE roi
Levelland—LĔ v'l lănd
Levita—luh VĬ tuh
Lewisville—LŌŌ ĭs vĭl
Lexington—LĔKS ĭng t'n
Liberty—LĬB er tĭ
Liberty Hill—lĭ ber tĭ HĬL
Lillian—LĬL yuhn
Limestone—LĬM stōn
Lincoln—LĬNG k'n
Lindale—LĬN dāl
Linden—LĬN d'n
Lindenau—lĭn duh NOW
Lindsay—LĬN zĭ
Lingleville—LĬNG g'l vĭl
Linn—lĭn
Lipan—lĭ PĂN
Lipscomb—LĬPS k'm
Lissie—LĬ sĭ
Little Elm—lĭt l ĔLM
Littlefield—LĬT uhl feeld
Little River—lĭt uhl RĬV er
Live Oak—lĭV ōk
Liverpool—LĬ ver pōōl
Livingston—LĬV ĭngz t'n
Llano—LĂ nō
Locker—LAH ker
Lockett—LAH kĭt
Lockhart—LAHK hahrt
Lockney—LAHK nĭ
Lodi—LŌ dĭ
Lohn—lahn

Lolita—lō LEE tuh
Loma Alto—lō muh ĂL tō
Lometa—lō MEE tuh
London—LUHN d'n
Lone Grove—lōn GRŌV
Lone Oak—LŌN ōk
Long Branch—lawng BRĂNCH
Long Mott—lawng MAHT
Longview—LAWNG vyōō
Longworth—LAWNG werth
Loop—lōōp
Lopeno—lō PEE nō
Loraine—lō RĂN
Lorena—lō REE nuh
Los Angeles—laws AN juh l's
Los Ebanos—lōs ĔB uh nōs
Los Fresnos—lōs FRĔZ nōs
Los Indios—lōs ĬN dĭ ōs
Losoya—luh SAW yuh
Lott—laht
Louise—LŌŌ eez
Lovelady—LUHV lā dĭ
Loving—LUH vĭng
Lubbock—LUH b'k
Lueders—LŌŌ derz
Luella—lōō ĔL uh
Lufkin—LUHF kĭn
Luling—LŌŌ lĭng
Lund—luhnd
Lutie—LŌŌ tĭ
Lyford—LĪ ferd
Lynn—lĭn
Lyons—LĪ 'nz
Lytton Springs—lĭt n SPRĬNGZ

M

McAdoo—MĂK uh dōō
McAllen—măk ĂL ĭn
McCamey—muh KĂ mĭ
McCaulley—muh KAW lĭ
McCoy—muh KOI
McCulloch—muh KUH luhk
McFaddin—măk FĂD n
McGregor—muh GRĔ ger
McKinney—muh KĬN ĭ
McLean—muh KLĂN
McLennan—muhk LĔN uhn
McLeod—măk LOWD
McMahan—măk MĂN
McMullen—măk MUHL ĭn
McNary—măk NĂ rĭ
McNeil—măk NEEL
McQueeney—muh KWEE nĭ
Mabank—MĂ băngk
Macune—muh KŌŌN
Madison—MĂ dĭ s'n
Madisonville—MĂ duh s'n vĭl
Magnolia—măg NŌL yuh
Magnolia Springs—măg nol yuh SPRINGZ
Malakoff—MĂL uh kawf
Malone—muh LŌN
Malta—MAWL tuh
Manchaca—MĂN shăk
Manchester—MĂN chĕs ter
Manheim—MĂN hīm
Mankins—MĂN kĭnz
Manor—MĂ ner
Mansfield—MĂNZ feeld

Manvel—MĂN v'l
Maple—MĂ puhl
Marathon—MĂR uh th'n
Marble Falls—mahr b'l FAWLZ
Marfa—MAHR fuh
Margaret—MAHR guh rit
Marietta—mĕ rĭ Ĕ tuh
Marion—MĔ rĭ uhn
Markham—MAHR k'm
Marlin—MAHR lĭn
Marquez—mahr KĂ
Marshall—MAHR sh'l
Mart—mahrt
Martin—MAHRT n
Martindale—MAHRT n dāl
Martinsville—MAHRT nz vĭl
Maryneal—mā rĭ NEEL
Marysville—MĂ rĭz vĭl
Mason—MĂ s'n
Matador—MĂT uh dōr
Matagorda—măt uh GAWR duh
Mathis—MĂ thĭs
Maud—mawd
Mauriceville—maw REES vĭl
Maverick—MĂV rĭk
Maxey—MĂKS ĭ
Maxwell—MĂKS w'l
May—mā
Maydell—MĂ dĕl
Maypearl—mā PERL
Maysfield—MĂZ feeld
Meadow—MĔ dō
Medicine Mound—mĕd uhs n MOWND
Medill—mĕ DĬL
Medina—muh DEE nuh
Megargel—muh GAHR g'l
Melissa—muh LĬS uh
Melrose—MĔL rōz
Melvin—MĔL vĭn
Memphis—MĔM fĭs
Menard—muh NAHRD
Mendoza—mĕn DŌ zuh
Mentone—mĕn TON
Mercedes—mer SĂ deez
Mercury—MER kyuh ri
Mereta—muh RĔT uh
Meridian—muh RĬ dĭ uhn
Merit—MĔR ĭt
Merkel—MER k'l
Mertens—mer TĔNZ
Mertzon—MERTS n
Mesquite—muhs KEET
Mexia—muh HĂ uh
Meyersville—MĬRZ vĭl
Miami—mĭ ĂM ĭ
Mico—MEE kō
Middleton—MĬD uhl t'n
Midfields—MĬD feeldz
Midland—MĬD l'nd
Midlothian—mĭd LŌ thĭ n
Midway—MĬD wā
Milam—MĪ l'm
Milano—mĭ LĂ nō
Mildred—MĬL drĕd
Miles—mīlz
Milford—MĬL ferd
Miller Grove—mĭl er GRŌV
Millersview—MĬL erz vyōō

Millett—MĬL ĭt
Millheim—MĬL hĭm
Millican—MĬL uh kuhn
Mills—mīlz
Millsap—MĬL săp
Minden—MĬN d'n
Mineola—mĭn ĭ Ō luh
Mineral—MĬN er uhl
Mineral Wells—mĭn er uhl WĔLZ
Minerva—mĭ NER vuh
Mingus—MĬNG guhs
Minter—MĬNT er
Mirando City—mĭ răn duh SĬT ĭ
Mission—MĬSH uhn
Mission Valley—mĭsh uhn VĂ lĭ
Missouri City—muh zŏŏr uh SĬT ĭ
Mitchell—MĬ ch'l
Mobeetie—mō BEE tĭ
Moline—mō LEEN
Monahans—MAH nuh hănz
Monaville—MŌ nuh vĭl
Monkstown—MUHNGKS town
Monroe—MAHN rō
Monroe City—mahn rō SĬT ĭ
Montague—mahn TĂG
Montalba—mahnt ĂL buh
Mont Belvieu—mahnt BĔL vyōō
Montell—mahn TĔL
Montgomery—mahnt GUHM er ĭ
Monthalia—mahn THĂL yuh
Moody—MŌŌ dĭ
Moore—mor
Morales—muh RAH lĕs
Moran—mō RĂN
Morgan—MAWR g'n
Morgan Mill—mawr g'n MĬL
Morse—mawrs
Morton—MAWRT n
Moscow—MAHS kow
Mosheim—MŌ shĭm
Moss Bluff—maws BLUHF
Motley—MAHT lĭ
Moulton—MŌL t'n
Mound—mownd
Mountain Home—mownt n HŌM
Mount Calm—mownt KAHM
Mount Enterprise—mownt ĔN ter prīz
Mount Pleasant—mownt PLĔ z'nt
Mount Selman—mownt SĔL m'n
Mount Sylvan—mownt SĬL v'n
Mount Vernon—mownt VER n'n
Muenster—MYŌŌNS ter
Muldoon—muhl DŌŌN
Muleshoe—MYŌŌL shōō
Mullin—MUHL ĭn
Mumford—MUHM ferd
Munday—MUHN dĭ
Murchison—MER kuh s'n
Murphy—MER fĭ
Mykawa—mĭ KAH wuh
Myra—MĪ ruh
Myrtle Springs—mert l SPRĬNGZ

N

Nacogdoches—năk uh DŌ chĭs
Nada—NĂ duh
Naples—NĂ p'lz
Nash—năsh

Natalia—nuh TĂL yuh
Navarro—nuh VĂ rō
Navasota—năv uh SŌ tuh
Nazareth—NĂZ uh r'th
Neches—NĂ chĭs
Nederland—NEE der l'nd
Needville—NEED vĭl
Nelsonville—NĔL s'n vĭl
Neuville—NYOO v'l
Nevada—nuh VĂ duh
Newark—NOO erk
New Baden—nyoo BĂD n
New Berlin—nyoo BER lin
New Boston—nyoo BAWS t'n
New Braunfels—nyoo BROWN fĕlz
Newby—NYOO bĭ
New Caney—nyoo KĂ nĭ
Newcastle—NYOO kăs uhl
New Gulf—nyoo GUHLF
New Home—NYOO hōm
New Hope—nyoo HŌP
Newlin—NYOO lĭn
New London—nyoo LUHN d'n
Newman—NYOO m'n
Newport—NYOO pōrt
New Salem—nyoo SĂ l'm
Newsome—NYOO s'm
New Summerfield—nyoo SUHM er
feeld
Newton—NYOOT n
New Ulm—nyoo UHLM
New Waverly—nyoo WĂ ver lĭ
New Willard—nyoo WĬL erd
Nimrod—NĬM rahd
Nineveh—NĬN uh vuh
Nixon—NĬKS uhn
Nocona—nō KŌ nuh
Nolan—NŌ l'n
Nolanville—NŌ l'n vĭl
Nome—nōm
Noonday—NOON dā
Nopal—NŌ păl
Nordheim—NAWRD hīm
Normandy—NAWR m'n dĭ
Normangee—NAWR m'n jee
Normanna—nawr MĂN uh
Northrup—NAWR thr'p
North Zulch—nawrth ZOOLCH
Norton—NAWRT n
Novice—NAH vĭs
Nueces—nyoo Ă sĭs
Nugent—NYOO j'nt
Nursery—NER suh rĭ

O

Oakalla—ō KĂL uh
Oak Grove—ōk GRŌV
Oak Hill—ōk HĬL
Oakhurst—ŌK herst
Oakland—ŌK l'nd
Oakville—ŌK vĭl
Oakwood—ŌK wŏŏd
O'Brien—ō BRĪ uhn
Ochiltree—AH k'l tree
Odell—ō DĔL
Odem—Ō d'm
Odessa—ō DĔS uh
O'Donnell—ō DAH n'l
Oenaville—ō EEN uh v'l

Oglesby—Ō g'lz bĭ
Oilton—OIL t'n
Oklaunion—ōk luh YOON y'n
Olden—ŌL d'n
Oldenburg—ŌL dĭn berg
Oldham—ŌL d'm
Old Glory—ōld GLŌ rĭ
Olivia—ō LĬV ĭ uh
Olmito—awl MEE tuh
Olmos Park—ahl m's PAHRK
Olney—AHL ni
Olton—ŌL t'n
Omaha—Ō muh haw
Omen—Ō mĭn
Onalaska—uhn uh LĂS kuh
Oplin—AHP lĭn
Orange—AHR ĭnj
Orangefield—AHR ĭnj feeld
Orange Grove—AHR ĭnj GRŌV
Orchard—AWR cherd
Ore City—ōr SĬT ĭ
Osceola—ō sĭ Ō luh
Otey—Ō tĭ
Otis Chalk—ō tĭs CHAWLK
Ottine—ah TEEN
Otto—AH tō
Ovalo—ō VĂL uh
Overton—Ō ver t'n
Owens—Ō ĭnz
Ozona—ō ZŌ nuh

P

Paducah—puh DYOO kuh
Paige—pāj
Paint Rock—pānt RAHK
Palacios—puh LĂ sh's
Palestine—PAL uhs teen
Palito Blanco—p' lee to BLAHNG kō
Palmer—PAH mer
Palo Pinto—pă lō PĬN tō
Paluxy—puh LUHK sĭ
Pampa—PĂM puh
Pandora—păn DŌR uh
Panhandle—PĂN hăn d'l
Panna Maria—păn uh muh REE uh
Papalote—pah puh LŌ tĭ
Paradise—PĂR uh dīs
Paris—PĂ rĭs
Parker—PAHR ker
Parmer—PAH mer
Parnell—pahr NĔL
Parsley Hill—pahrs lĭ HĬL
Pasadena—păs uh DEE nuh
Patricia—puh TRĬ shuh
Patroon—puh TROON
Pattison—PĂT uh s'n
Pattonville—PĂT n vĭl
Pawnee—paw NEE
Paxton—PĂKS t'n
Peacock—PEE kahk
Pearl—perl
Pearland—PĂR lănd
Pearsall—PEER sawl
Peaster—PEES ter
Pecan Gap—pĭ kahn GAP
Pecos—PĂ k's
Penelope—puh NĔL uh pĭ
Penitas—puh NEE t's
Pennington—PĔN ĭng t'n

Penwell—PĬN wĕl
Peoria—pee Ō rĭ uh
Percilla—per SĬL uh
Perrin—PĔR ĭn
Perry—PĔ rĭ
Perryton—PĔ rĭ t'n
Peters—PEET erz
Petersburg—PEET erz berg
Petrolia—puh TRŌL yuh
Petteway—PĔT uh wā
Pettit—PĔT ĭt
Pettus—PĔT uhs
Petty—PĔT ĭ
Pflugerville—FLOO ger vĭl
Pharr—fahr
Phelps—fĕlps
Phillips—FĬL uhps
Pickton—PĬK t'n
Pidcoke—PĬD kŏk
Piedmont—PEED mahnt
Pierce—PĬ ers
Pilot Point—pī l't POINT
Pine Forest—pĭn FAW rĕst
Pine Hill—pĭn HĬL
Pinehurst—PĬN herst
Pineland—PĬN land
Pine Mills—pĭn MĬLZ
Pine Springs—pĭn SPRĬNGZ
Pioneer—pī uh NĬR
Pipecreek—pīp KREEK
Pittsburg—PĬTS berg
Placedo—PLĂS ĭ dō
Placid—PLĂ sĭd
Plains—plānz
Plainview—PLĂN vyoo
Plano—PLĂ nō
Plantersville—PLĂN terz vĭl
Plaska—PLĂS kuh
Plateau—plă TŌ
Pleasant Grove—plĕ z'nt GRŌV
Pleasanton—PLĔZ uhn t'n
Pledger—PLĔ jer
Plum—pluhm
Point—point
Pointblank—pint BLĂNGK
Polk—pōlk
Pollock—PAHL uhk
Ponder—PAHN der
Ponta—pahn TĂ
Pontotoc—PAHNT uh tahk
Poolville—POOL vĭl
Port Aransas—pōrt uh RĂN zuhs
Port Arthur—pōrt AHR ther
Port Bolivar—pōrt BAH lĭ ver
Porter Springs—pōr ter SPRĬNGZ
Port Isabel—pōrt ĬZ uh bĕl
Portland—PŌRT l'nd
Port Lavaca—pōrt luh VĂ kuh
Port Neches—pōrt NĂ chĬs
Port O'Connor—pōrt ō KAH ner
Posey—PŌ zĭ
Post—pōst
Postoak—PŌST ōk
Poteet—pō TEET
Poth—pōth
Potosi—puh TŌ sĭ
Potter—PAHT er
Pottsboro—PAHTS buh ruh
Pottsville—PAHTS vĭl

Powderly—POW der li
Powell—POW w'l
Poynor—POI ner
Prairie Dell—prĕr ĭ DĔL
Prairie Hill—prĕr ĭ HĬL
Prairie Lea—prĕr ĭ LEE
Prairie View—prĕr ĭ VYŌO
Prairieville—PRĔR ĭ vĭl
Premont—PREE mahnt
Presidio—pruh SĬ dĭ ō
Priddy—PRĬ dĭ
Primera—pree MĔ ruh
Princeton—PRĬNS t'n
Pritchett—PRĬ chĭt
Proctor—PRAHK ter
Progreso—prō GRĔ sō
Prosper—PRAHS per
Purdon—PERD n
Purley—PER lĭ
Purmela—per MEE luh
Putnam—PUHT n'm
Pyote—PĬ ŏt

Q

Quail—kwāl
Quanah—KWAH nuh
Queen City—kween SĬT ĭ
Quemado—kuh MAH dō
Quihi—KWEE hee
Quinlan—KWĬN l'n
Quintana—kwĭn TAH nuh
Quitaque—KĬT uh kwa
Quitman—KWĬT m'n

R

Rainbow—RĀN bō
Rains—rānz
Ralls—rahlz
Randall—RĂN d'l
Randolph—RĂN dahlf
Ranger—RĂN jer
Rangerville—RĂN jer vĭl
Rankin—RĂNG kĭn
Ratcliff—RĂT klĭf
Ravenna—rĭ VĔN uh
Rayburn—RĀ bern
Raymondville—RĀ m'nd vĭl
Raywood—RĀ wŏŏd
Reagan—RĀ g'n
Real—REE awl
Realitos—ree uh LEE t's
Redford—RĔD ferd
Red Oak—RĔD ōk
Red River—rĕd RĬ ver
Red Rock—rĕd RAHK
Red Springs—rĕd SPRĬNGZ
Red Water—RĔD wah ter
Reeves—reevz
Refugio—rĕ FYŌO rĭ ō
Reilly Springs—rĭ lĭ SPRĬNGZ
Reklaw—RĔK law
Reno—REE nō
Rhineland—RĬN l'nd
Rhome—rōm
Rhonesboro—RŌNZ buh ruh
Ricardo—rĭ KAHR dō
Rice—rīs
Richards—RĬCH erdz
Richardson—RĬCH erd s'n

Richland—RĬCH l'nd
Richland Springs—rĭch l'nd SPRĬNGZ
Richmond—RĬCH m'nd
Ridge—rĭj
Ridgeway—RĬJ wā
Riesel—REE s'l
Ringgold—RĬNG gōld
Rio Frio—ree ō FREE ō
Rio Grande City—ree ō grahn dĭ SĬT ĭ
Rio Hondo—ree ō HAHN dō
Riomedina—ree ō muh DEE nuh
Rios—REE ōs
Rio Vista—ree ō VĬS tuh
Rising Star—rĭ zĭng STAHR
River Oaks—rĭ ver ŌKS
Riverside—RĬ ver sĭd
Riviera—ruh VĬR uh
Roane—rōn
Roanoke—RŌN ōk
Roans Prairie—rōnz PRĔR ĭ
Roaring Springs—rōr ĭng SPRĬNGZ
Robert Lee—rah bert LEE
Roberts—RAH berts
Robertson—RAH bert s'n
Robinson—RAH bĭn s'n
Robstown—RAHBZ town
Roby—RŌ bĭ
Rochelle—rō SHĔL
Rochester—RAH chĕs ter
Rockdale—RAHK dāl
Rock Island—rahk Ĭ l'nd
Rockland—RAHK l'nd
Rockport—rahk PŌRT
Rocksprings—rahk SPRĬNGZ
Rockwall—rahk WAWL
Rockwood—RAHK wŏŏd
Roganville—RŌ g'n vĭl
Rogers—RAH jerz
Roma—RŌ muh
Romayor—rō MĀ er
Roosevelt—RŌO suh v'lt
Ropesville—RŌPS vĭl
Rosanky—rō ZĂNG kĭ
Roscoe—RAHS kō
Rosebud—RŌZ b'd
Rose Hill—rōz HĬL
Rosenberg—RŌZ n berg
Rosenthal—RŌZ uhn thawl
Rosewood—RŌZ wŏŏd
Rosharon—rō SHĔ r'n
Rosita—rō SEE tuh
Ross—raws
Rosser—RAW ser
Rosston—RAWS t'n
Rossville—RAWS vĭl
Roswell—RAHZ w'l
Rotan—rō TĂN
Round Rock—ROWND rahk
Round Top—ROWN tahp
Rowena—rō EE nuh
Rowlett—ROW lĭt
Roxton—RAHKS t'n
Royalty—ROI uhl tĭ
Royse City—roi SĬT ĭ
Royston—ROIS t'n
Rugby—RUHG bĭ
Ruidosa—ree uh DŌ suh
Rule—rōol

Runge—RUHNG ĭ
Runnels—RUHN 'lz
Rural Shade—rŏōr uhl SHĀD
Rusk—ruhsk
Rutersville—RŌO ter vĭl
Rye—rī

S

Sabinal—SĂB uh năl
Sabine—suh BEEN
Sabine Pass—suh been PĂS
Sabinetown—suh been TOWN
Sachse—SĂK sĭ
Sacul—SĂ k'l
Sadler—SĂD ler
Sagerton—SĂ ger t'n
Saginaw—SĂ guh naw
Saint Jo—sănt JŌ
Saint Paul—sănt PAWL
Salado—suh LĀ dō
Salesville—SĂLZ vĭl
Salineno—suh LEEN yō
Salmon—SĂL m'n
Salt Gap—sawlt GĂP
Saltillo—săl TĬL ō
Samfordyce—săm FOR dis
Sample—SĂM p'l
Samnorwood—săm NAWR wŏŏd
San Angelo—săn ĂN juh lō
San Antonio—săn ăn TŌ nĭ ō
Sanatorium—săn uh TŌ rĭ uhm
San Augustine—săn AW g's teen
San Benito—săn buh NEE tuh
Sanderson—SĂN der s'n
Sandia—săn DEE uh
San Diego—săn dĭ Ā gō
Sandy Point—săn dĭ POINT
San Felipe—săn fuh LEEP
Sanford—SĂN ferd
San Gabriel—săn GĀ brĭ uhl
Sanger—SĂNG er
San Jacinto—săn juh SĬN tuh
San Juan—săn WAHN
San Marcos—săn MAHR k's
San Patricio—săn puh TRĬSH ĭ ō
San Perlita—săn per LEE tuh
San Saba—săn SĂ buh
Santa Anna—săn tuh ĂN uh
Santa Elena—săn tuh LEE nuh
Santa Maria—săn tuh muh REE uh
Santa Rosa—săn tuh RŌ suh
Santo—SĂN tō
San Ygnacio—săn ĭg NAH sĭ ō
Saragosa—sĕ ruh GŌ suh
Saratoga—sĕ ruh TŌ guh
Sargent—SAHR juhnt
Sarita—suh REE tuh
Saspamco—suh SPĂM kō
Satin—SĂT n
Savoy—suh VOI
Schattel—SHĂT uhl
Schertz—sherts
Schleicher—SHLĬ ker
Schroeder—SHRĀ der
Schulenburg—SHŌO lĭn berg
Schwertner—SWERT ner
Scotland—SKAHT l'nd
Scottsville—SKAHTS vĭl

Scranton—SKRĂNT n
Scurry—SKUH rĭ
Scyene—sī EEN
Seabrook—SEE brŏŏk
Seadrift—SEE drĭft
Seagoville—SEE gō vĭl
Seagraves—SEE grāvz
Seale—seel
Sealy—SEE lĭ
Sebastian—suh BĂS tĭ 'n
Security—sĭ KYŌŌR ĭ tĭ
Segno—SĔG nō
Segovia—sĭ GŌ vĭ uh
Seguin—sĭ GEEN
Selfs—sĕlfs
Selma—SĔL muh
Seminole—SĔM uh nōl
Seymour—SEE mōr
Shackelford—SHĂK uhl ferd
Shady Grove—shā dĭ GRŌV
Shafter—SHĂF ter
Shallowater—SHĂL uh wah ter
Shamrock—SHĂM rahk
Shannon—SHĂN uhn
Sharp—shahrp
Sheffield—SHĔ feeld
Shelby—SHĔL bĭ
Shelbyville—SHĔL bĭ vĭl
Sheldon—SHĔL d'n
Shepherd—SHĔ perd
Sherman—SHER m'n
Sherwood—SHER wood
Shiner—SHĪ ner
Shiro—SHĪ rō
Shive—shĭv
Sidney—SĬD nĭ
Sierra Blanca—sĭer ruh BLĂNG kuh
Siloam—suh LŌM
Silsbee—SĬLZ bĭ
Silver Lake—sĭl ver LĀK
Silverton—SĬL ver t'n
Silver Valley—sĭl ver VĂ lĭ
Simms—sĭmz
Simonton—SĪ m'n t'n
Singleton—SĬNG g'l t'n
Sinton—SĬNT n
Sipe Springs—SEEP sprĭngz
Sisterdale—SĬS ter dāl
Sivells Bend—sĭ v'lz BĔND
Skellytown—SKĔ lĭ town
Skidmore—SKĬD mōr
Slaton—SLĀT n
Slayden—SLĀD n
Slidell—slī DĔL
Slocum—SLŌ k'm
Smiley—SMĪ lĭ
Smith—smĭth
Smithfield—SMĬTH feeld
Smithland—SMĬTH l'nd
Smithson Valley—smĭth s'n VĂ lĭ
Smithville—SMĬTH vĭl
Smyer—SMĪ er
Snook—snŏŏk
Snyder—SNĪ der
Somerset—SUH mer sĕt
Somervell—SUH mer vĕl
Somerville—SUH mer vĭl
Sonora—suh NŌ ruh
Sour Lake—sowr LĀK

South Bend—sowth BĔND
South Bosque—sowth BAHS kĭ
South Houston—sowth HY S t'n
Southland—SOWTH l'nd
Southmayd—sowth MĀD
South Plains—sowth PLĀNZ
Spade—spād
Spanish Fort—spă nĭsh FŌRT
Sparenberg—SPĂR ĭn berg
Speaks—speeks
Spearman—SPĬR m'n
Spicewood—SPĪS wŏŏd
Splendora—splĕn DŌ ruh
Spofford—SPAH ferd
Spring—sprĭng
Springdale—SPRĬNG dāl
Spring Lake—sprĭng LĀK
Springtown—SPRĬNG town
Spur—sper
Spurger—SPER ger
Stacy—STĀ sĭ
Stafford—STĂ ferd
Stamford—STĂM ferd
Stanton—STĂNT n
Staples—STĀ p'lz
Starr—stahr
Stephens—STEE vĕnz
Stephenville—STEEV n vĭl
Sterley—STER lĭ
Sterling—STER lĭng
Sterling City—ster lĭng SĬT ĭ
Stiles—stīlz
Stinnett—stĭ NĔT
Stockdale—STAHK dāl
Stoneburg—STŌN berg
Stoneham—STŌN uhm
Stone Point—stōn POINT
Stonewall—STŌN wawl
Stout—stowt
Stowell—STO w'l
Stranger—STRĂN jer
Stratford—STRĂT ferd
Strawn—strawn
Streeter—STREET er
Streetman—STREET m'n
Study Butte—styŏŏ dĭ BYŌŌT
Sublime—s'b LĪM
Sudan—SŌŌ dăn
Sugar Land—SHŌŌ ger lănd
Sullivan City—suh luh v'n SĬT ĭ
Sulphur Bluff—suhl fer BLUHF
Sulpher Springs—suhl fer SPRĬNGZ
Summerfield—SUHM er feeld
Sumner—SUHM ner
Sundown—SUHN down
Suniland—SUH nĭ lănd
Sunny Side—SUH nĭ sīd
Sunray—SUHN rā
Sunset—SUHN sĕt
Sutherland Springs—suh ther l'nd
SPRĬNGZ
Sutton—SUHT n
Swan—swahn
Sweeny—SWEE nĭ
Sweethome—sweet HŌM
Sweetwater—SWEET wah ter
Swenson—SWĔN s'n
Swift—swĭft
Swisher—SWĪ sher

Sylvester— sil VES ter

T

Taft—tăft
Tahoka—tuh HŌ kuh
Talco—TĂL kō
Talpa—TĂL puh
Tanglewood—TĂNG g'l wŏŏd
Tankersley—TĂNG kers lĭ
Tarrant—TAR uhnt
Tarzan—TAHR z'n
Tascosa—tăs KŌ suh
Tatum—TĂ t'm
Tavener—TĂV uh ner
Taylor—TĂ ler
Teague—teeg
Tehuacana—tuh WAW kuh nuh
Telephone—TĔL uh fōn
Telferner—TĔLF ner
Tell—tĕl
Temple—TĔM p'l
Tenaha—TĔN uh haw
Tennyson—TĔN uh s'n
Terlingua—TER lĭng guh
Terrell—TĔR uhl
Terrell Hills—ter uhl HILZ
Terry—TĔR ĭ
Texarkana—tĕks ahr KĂN uh
Texas City—tĕks ĕz SĬT ĭ
Texhoma—tĕks Ō muh
Texline—TĔKS līn
Texon—tĕks AHN
Thalia—THĂL yuh
The Grove—th' GRŌV
Thicket—THĬ kĭt
Thomaston—TAHM uhs t'n
Thompsons—TAHMP s'nz
Thorndale—THAWRN dāl
Thornton—THAWRN t'n
Thorp Spring—thawrp SPRING
Thrall—thrawl
Three Rivers—three RĬ verz
Throckmorton—THRAHK mawrt n
Thurber—THER ber
Tilden—TĬL d'n
Timpson—TĬM s'n
Tioga—tĭ Ō guh
Titus—TĬT uhs
Tivoli—tĭ VŌ luh
Tokio—TŌ kĭ ō
Tolar—TŌ ler
Tolbert—TAHL bert
Tolosa—tuh LŌ suh
Tomball—TAHM bawl
Tom Bean—tahm BEEN
Tom Green—tahm GREEN
Tool—tool
Topsey—TAHP sĭ
Tornillo—tawr NEE yō
Tow—tow
Toyah—TOI yuh
Toyahvale—TOI yuh văl
Trawick—TRĂ wĭk
Travis—TRĂ vĭs
Trent—trĕnt
Trenton—TRĔNT n
Trickham—TRĬK uhm
Trinidad—TRĬN uh dăd
Trinity—TRĬN ĭ tĭ

Troup—trōōp
Troy—TRAW ĭ
Truby—TRŌŌ bĭ
Trumbull—TRUHM b'l
Truscott—TRUHS k't
Tucker—TUHK er
Tuleta—tōō LEE tuh
Tulia—TŌŌL yuh
Tulsita—tuhl SEE tuh
Tundra—TUHN druh
Tunis—TŌŌ nĭs
Turkey—TER kĭ
Turlington—TER lĭng t'n
Turnersville—TER nerz vĭl
Turnertown—TER ner town
Turney—TER nĭ
Tuscola—tuhs KŌ luh
Tuxedo—TUHKS ĭ dō
Twin Sisters—twĭn SĬS terz
Twitty—TWĬ tĭ
Tye—tī
Tyler—TĪ ler
Tynan—TĪ nuhn

U

Uhland—YŌŌ l'nd
Umbarger—UHM bahr ger
Union—YŌŌN y'n
Upshur—UHP sher
Upton—UHP t'n
Urbana—er BĀ nuh
Utley—YŌŌT lĭ
Utopia—yōō TŌ pĭ uh
Uvalde—yōō VĂL dĭ

V

Valdasta—văl DĂS tuh
Valentine—VĂL uhn tīn
Valera—vuh LĬ ruh
Valley Mills—vă lĭ MĬLZ
Valley Spring—vă lĭ SPRĬNG
Valleyview—vă lĭ VYŌŌ
Van—văn
Van Alstyne—văn AWLZ teen
Vancourt—VĂN kŏrt
Vanderbilt—VĂN der bĭlt
Vanderpool—VĂN der pōōl
Van Horn—văn HAWRN
Van Vleck—văn VLĔK
Van Zandt—văn ZĂNT
Vashti—VĂSH tī
Vaughan—vawn
Vega—VĀ guh
Velasco—vuh LĂS kō
Venus—VEE n's
Vera—VĬ ruh
Veribest—VĔR ĭ bĕst
Vernon—VER n'n
Vickery—VĬK er ĭ
Victoria—vĭk TŌ rĭ uh
Vidor—VĪ der
Vienna—vee ĔN uh
View—vyōō
Village Mills—vĭl ĭj MĬLZ
Vincent—VĬN s'nt
Vinegarone—vĭn er guh RŌN
Vineyard—VĬN yerd
Violet—VĪ ō lĕt
Voca—VŌ kuh

Von Ormy—vahn AHR mĭ
Voss—vaws
Votaw—VŌ taw

W

Waco—WĀ kō
Wadsworth—WAHDZ werth
Waelder—WĔL der
Waka—WAH kuh
Walberg—WAWL berg
Waldeck—WAWL dĕk
Walker—WAWL ker
Wall—wawl
Waller—WAW ler
Wallis—WAH lĭs
Wallisville—WAH lĭs vĭl
Walnut Springs—wawl n't SPRĬNGZ
Walton—WAWL t'n
Warda—WAWR duh
Ward—wawrd
Waring—WĂR ĭng
Warren—WAW rĭn
Warrenton—WAW rĭn t'n
Washburn—WAHSH bern
Washington—WAHSH ĭng t'n
Waskom—WAHS k'm
Wastella—wahs TĔL uh
Watauga—wuh TAW guh
Water Valley—wah ter VĂ lĭ
Waxahachie—wawks uh HĂ chĭ
Wayland—WĀ l'nd
Weatherford—WĔ ther ferd
Weaver—WEE ver
Webb—wĕb
Webberville—WĔ ber vĭl
Webster—WĔBS ter
Weches—WEE chĭz
Weesatche—WEE săch
Weimar—WĪ mer
Weinert—WĪ nert
Weir—weer
Welch—wĕlch
Welcome—WĔL k'm
Weldon—WĔL d'n
Wellborn—WĔL bern
Wellington—WĔL ĭng t'n
Wellman—WĔL m'n
Wells—wĕlz
Weser—WEE zer
Weslaco—WĔS luh kō
West—wĕst
Westbrook—WĔST brŏŏk
Westfield—WĔST feeld
Westhoff—WĔS tawf
Westminster—
wĕst MĬN ster
Weston—WĔS t'n
Westover—WĔS tō ver
Westphalia—wĕst FĀL yuh
West Point—wĕst POINT
Wetmore—WĔT mŏr
Wharton—WHAWRT n
Wheeler—HWEE ler
Wheelock—HWEE lahk
White Deer—HWĬT Deer
Whiteface—HWĬT făs
Whiteflat—hwĭt FLĂT
Whitehouse—HWĬT hows
Whitesboro—HWĬTS buh ruh

Whitewright—HWĬT rīt
Whitharral—HWĬT hăr uhl
Whitney—HWĬT nĭ
Whitsett—HWĬT sĭt
Whitson—HWĬT s'n
Whitt—hwĭt
Whon—hwahn
Wichita—WĬCH ĭ taw
Wichita Falls—
wĭch ĭ taw FAWLZ
Wickett—WĬ kĭt
Wiergate—WEER găt
Wilbarger—WĬL bahr ger
Wildorado—wĭl duh RĀ dō
Willacy—WĬL uh s'l
Williamson—WĬL yuhm s'n
Willis—WĬ lĭs
Wills Point—wĭlz POINT
Wilmer—WĬL mer
Wilson—WĬL s'n
Wimberley—WĬM ber lĭ
Winchester—WĬN ches ter
Windom—WĬN d'm
Windthorst—WĬN thr'st
Winfield—WĬN feeld
Wingate—WĬN găt
Wink—wĭngk
Winkler—WĬNGK ler
Winnie—WĬ nĭ
Winnsboro—WĬNZ buh ruh
Winona—wĭ NŌ nuh
Winterhaven—WĬN ter hă v'n
Winters—WĬN terz
Wise—wīz
Wizard Wells—wĭ zerd WĔLZ
Woden—WŌD n
Wolfe City—wŏŏlf SĬT ĭ
Wolfforth—WŎŎL forth
Wood—wŏŏd
Woodbine—WŎŎD bīn
Woodlake—wŏŏd LĀK
Woodland—WŎŎD l'nd
Woodlawn—wŏŏd LAWN
Woodrow—WŎŎD rō
Woodsboro—WŎŎDZ buh ruh
Woodson—WŎŎD s'n
Woodville—WŎŎD v'l
Wortham—WERTH uhm
Wright City—rīt SĬT ĭ
Wrightsboro—RĪTS buh ruh
Wylie—WĪ lĭ

Y

Yancey—YĂN sĭ
Yantis—YĂN tĭs
Yoakum—YŌ k'm
Yorktown—YAWRK town
Young—yuhng
Youngsport—YUHNGZ pŏrt
Ysleta—īs LĔT uh

Z

Zapata—zuh PAH tuh
Zavalla—zuh VĂL uh
Zephyr—ZĔF er
Zuehl—ZEE uhl

Zip Codes for Texas Towns

The following list shows Zip Code number for towns in Texas. The county in which each town is located follows the name of the town. Towns whose names are preceded by an asterisk (*) have more than one Zip Code. The local postmasters of those towns can supply individual Zip Code directories.

On the Internet, you can obtain Zip Codes for individual addresses, as well as Zip + 4 codes, at this address: http://www.usps.gov/ncsc/lookups/lookup_zip+4.html

Abbott, Hill 76621
Abernathy, Hall 79311
*ABILENE, Taylor.................... 79604
Ace, Polk 77326
Ackerly, Dawson 79713
Addison, Dallas...................... 75001
Adkins, Bexar......................... 78101
Adrian, Oldam........................ 79001
Afton, Dickens........................ 79220
Agua Dulce, Nueces.............. 78330
Aiken, Floyd 79221
Alamo, Hidalgo 78516
Alanreed, Gray....................... 79002
Alba, Rains 75410
Albany, Shackelford 76430
Albert, Stonewall.................... 78671
Aledo, Parker 76008
*ALICE, Jim Wells.................. 78332
Alief, Harris 77411
Allen, Collin 75002
Alleyton, Colorado 78935
Allison, Wheeler..................... 79003
*ALPINE, Brewster 79830
Altair, Colorado 77412
Alta Loma, Galveston 77510
Alto, Cherokee 75925
Alvarado, Johnson 76009
*ALVIN, Brazoria.................... 77511
Alvord, Wise 76225
*AMARILLO, Potter................ 79105
Ames, Liberty......................... 77575
Amherst, Lamb 79312
Anahuac, Chambers............... 77514
Anderson, Grimes.................. 77830
Andice, Williamson 78628
Andrews, Andrews................. 79714
*ANGLETON, Brazoria 77515
Anna, Collin 75409
Annona, Red River 75550
Anson, Jones......................... 79501
Anthony, El Paso.................... 79821
Anton, Hockley....................... 79313
Appleby, Nacogdoches 75961
Apple Springs, Trinity 75926
Aquilla, Hill............................. 76622
*ARANSAS PASS, San Patricio
.... 78336
Arcadia, Shelby...................... 77517
Archer City, Archer................. 76351
Argyle, Denton 76226
*ARLINGTON, Tarrant 76010
Armstrong, Kenedy 78338
Arp, Smith 75750
Art, Mason 76820
Artesia Wells, LaSalle 78001
Arthur City, Lamar.................. 75411
Asherton, Dimmit................... 78827
Aspermont, Stonewall............ 79502
Atascosa, Bexar..................... 78002
Athens, Henderson 75751
Atlanta, Cass 75551

Aubrey, Denton 76227
*AUSTIN, Travis 78767
Austinio, Houston................... 75835
Austwell, Refugio 77950
Avalon, Ellis 76623
Avery, Red River 75554
Avinger, Cass......................... 75630
Avoca, Jones 79503
Axtell, McLennan 76624
*AZLE, Parker........................ 76020
Bacliff, Galveston 77518
Bagwell, Red River 75412
Bailey, Fannin........................ 75413
Baird, Callahan 79504
Balch Springs, Dallas............. 75180
Balcones Heights, Bexar........ 78201
Ballinger, Runnels.................. 76821
Balmorhea, Reeves 79718
Bandera, Bandera 78003
Bangs, Brown 76823
Banquete, Nueces 78339
Bardwell, Ellis 75101
Barker, Harris......................... 77413
Barksdale, Edwards 78828
Barnhart, Irion........................ 76930
Barnum, Polk 75939
Barrett, Harris......................... 77532
Barry, Navarro........................ 75102
Barstow, Ward 79719
Bartlett, Bell 76511
Bastrop, Bastrop 78602
Batesville, Zavala................... 78829
Batson, Hardin 77519
*BAY CITY, Matagorda........... 77414
Bayside, Refugio 78340
*BAYTOWN, Harris 77520
Beasley, Fort Bend................. 77417
*BEAUMONT, Jefferson 77704
Bebe, Gonzales 78603
Beckville, Panola.................... 75631
*BEDFORD, Tarrant 76021
Bedias, Grimes....................... 77831
Bee House, Coryell 76525
*BEEVILLE, Bee 78102
*BELLAIRE, Harris 77401
Bellevue, Clay 76228
Bellmead, McLennan.............. 76705
Bells, Grayson........................ 75414
Bellville, Austin....................... 77418
Belmont, Gonzales 78604
Belton, Bell............................. 76513
Ben Arnold, Milam.................. 76517
Benavides, Duval 78341
Ben Bolt, Jim Wells................ 78342
Bend, San Saba..................... 76824
Ben Franklin, Delta 75415
Benjamin, Knox...................... 79505
Ben Wheeler, Van Zandt 75754
Berclair, Goliad 78107
Bergheim, Kendall 78004
Bertram, Burnet 78605

Best, Reagan 76932
Beverly Hills, McLennan 76711
Big Bend National Park,
  Brewster 79834
Bigfoot, Frio........................... 78005
Biggs Field, El Paso............... 79908
Big Lake, Reagan 76932
Big Sandy, Upshur 75755
*BIG SPRING, Howard 79720
Big Wells, Dimmit................... 78830
Birome, Hill............................. 76673
Bishop, Nueces...................... 78343
Bivins, Cass 75555
Black, Parmer 79035
Blackwell, Nolan..................... 79506
Blanco, Blanco 78606
Blanket, Brown....................... 76432
Bledsoe, Cochran 79314
Bleiblerville, Austin................. 78931
Blessing, Matagorda 77419
Bloomburg, Cass 75556
Blooming Grove, Navarro....... 76626
Bloomington, Victoria 77951
Blossom, Lamar 75416
Bluegrove, Clay 76352
Blue Ridge, Collin 75424
Bluff Dale, Erath..................... 76433
Bluffton, Llano 78607
Blum, Hill................................ 76627
Boerne, Kendall 78006
Bogata, Red River.................. 75417
Boling, Wharton...................... 77420
Bonanza, Hill.......................... 76692
Bonham, Fannin 75418
Bon Wier, Newton 75928
Booker, Lipscomb 79005
Booth, Fort Bend.................... 77469
*BORGER, Hutchinson 79007
Boston, Bowie 75570
Bovina, Parmer 79009
Bowie, Montague 76230
Boyd, Wise 76023
Boys Ranch, Oldham 79010
Brackettville, Kinney............... 78832
Brady, McCulloch 76825
Brandon, Hill.......................... 76628
Brashear, Hopkins 75420
Brazoria, Brazoria 77422
Breckenridge, Stephens......... 76424
Bremond, Robertson.............. 76629
*BRENHAM, Washington....... 77833
Bridge City, Orange................ 77611
Bridgeport, Wise 76426
Briggs, Burnet 78608
Briscoe, Wheeler.................... 79011
Broaddus, San Augustine 75929
Bronson, Sabine 75930
Bronte, Coke 76933
Brookeland, Sabine................ 75931
Brookesmith, Brown............... 76827
Brookshire, Waller.................. 77423

Lavon, Collin 75166
La Ward, Jackson 77970
Lawn, Taylor 79530
Lazbuddie, Parmer 79053
*LEAGUE CITY, Galveston 77573
Leakey, Real 78873
*LEANDER, Williamson 78641
Leary, Bowie 75561
Ledbetter, Fayette 78946
Leesburg, Camp 75451
Leesville, Gonzales 78122
Lefors, Gray 79054
Leggett, Polk 77350
Leilia Lake, Donley 79240
Leming, Atascosa 78050
Lenorah, Martin 79749
Leona, Leon 75850
Leonard Fannin 75452
Leon Junction, Coryell 76552
Leroy, McLennan 76654
*LEVELLAND, Hockley 79336
*LEWISVILLE, Denton 75067
Lexington, Lee 78947
Liberty, Liberty 77575
Liberty Hill, Williamson 78642
Lillian, Johnson 76061
Lincoln, Lee 78948
Lindale, Smith 75771
Linden, Cass 75563
Lindsay, Cooke 76250
Lingleville, Erath 76461
Linn, Hidalgo 78563
Lipan, Hood 76462
Lipscomb, Lipscomb 79056
Lissie, Wharton 77454
Little Elm, Denton 75068
Littlefield, Lamb 79339
Little River, Bell 76554
Live Oak, Bexar 78233
Liverpool, Brazoria 77577
Livingston, Polk 77351
Llano, Llano 78643
Lockhart, Caldwell 78644
Lockney, Floyd 79241
Lodi, Marion 75564
Lohn, McCulloch 76852
Lolita, Jackson 77971
Lometa, Lampasas 76853
London, Kimble 76854
Lone Oak, Hunt 75453
Lone Star, Morris 75668
Long Branch, Panola 75669
Long Mott, Calhoun 77972
*LONGVIEW, Gregg 75601
Loop, Gaines 79342
Lopeno, Zapata 78564
Loraine, Mitchell 79532
Lorena, McLennan 76655
Lorenzo, Crosby 79343
Los Ebanos, Hidalgo 78565
Los Fresnos, Cameron 78566
Los Indios, Cameron 78567
Lott, Falls 76656
Louise, Wharton 77455
Lovelady, Houston 75851
Loving, Young 76460
Lowake, Concho 76855
Lozano, Cameron 78568
*LUBBOCK, Lubbock 79408
Lueders, Jones 79533

*LUFKIN, Angelina 75901
Luling, Caldwell 78648
Lumberton, Hardin 77711
Lyford, Willacy 78569
Lyons, Burleson 77863
Lytle, Atascosa 78052
Mabank, Kaufman 75147
Macdona, Bexar 78054
Madisonville, Madison 77864
Magnolia, Montgomery 77355
Magnolia Springs, Jasper 75957
Malakoff, Henderson 75148
Malone, Hill 76660
Manchca, Travis 78652
Manor, Travis 78653
Mansfield, Tarrant 76063
Manvel, Brazoria 77578
Maple, Bailey 79344
Marathon, Brewster 79842
Marble Falls, Burnet 78654
Marfa, Presidio 79843
Marietta, Cass 75566
Marion, Guadalupe 78124
Markham, Matagorda 77456
Marlin, Falls 76661
Marquez, Leon 77865
*MARSHALL, Harrison 75670
Mart, McLennan 76664
Martindale, Caldwell 78655
Martinsville, Nacogdoches 75958
Maryneal, Nolan 79535
Mason, Mason 76856
Masterson, Moore 79058
Matador, Motley 79244
Matagorda, Matagorda 77457
Mathis, San Patricio 78368
Maud, Bowie 75567
Mauriceville, Orange 77626
Maxwell, Caldwell 78656
May, Brown 76857
Maydelle, Cherokee 75772
Maypearl, Ellis 76064
Maysfield, Milam 76555
McAdoo, Dickens 79243
*McALLEN, Hidalgo 78501
McCamey, Upton 79752
McCaulley, Fisher 79534
McCoy, Atascosa 78053
McDade, Bastrop 78650
McFaddin, Victoria 77973
McGregor, McLennan 76657
*McKINNEY, Collin 75069
McLean, Gray 79057
McLeod, Cass 75565
McNeil, Travis 78651
McQueeney, Guadalupe 78123
Meadow, Terry 79345
Medina, Bandera 78055
Megargel, Archer 76370
Melissa, Collin 75454
Melvin, McCulloch 76858
Memphis, Hall 79245
Menard, Menard 76859
Mentone, Loving 79754
Mercedes, Hidalgo 78570
Mereta, Tom Green 76940
Meridian, Bosque 76665
Merit, Hunt 75458
Merkel, Taylor 79536
Mertens, Hill 76666

Mertzon, Irion 76941
*MESQUITE, Dallas 75149
Mexia, Limestone 76667
Meyersville, DeWitt 77974
Miami, Roberts 79059
Mico, Medina 78056
Midfield, Matagorda 77458
Midkiff, Upton 79755
*MIDLAND, Midland 79702
Midlothian, Ellis 76065
Midway, Madison 75852
Milam, Sabine 75959
Milano, Milam 76556
Miles, Runnels 76861
Milford, Ellis 76670
Millersview, Concho 76862
Millican, Brazos 77866
Millsap, Parker 76066
Minden, Rusk 75680
Mineola, Wood 75773
Mineral, Bee 78125
*MINERAL WELLS, Palo Pinto
.... 76067
Mingus, Palo Pinto 76463
Mirando City, Webb 78369
*MISSION, Hidalgo 78572
*MISSOURI CITY, Fort Bend
.... 77459
Mobeetie, Wheeler 79061
Monahans, Ward 79756
Monroe City, Chambers 77514
Montague, Montague 76251
Montalba, Anderson 75853
Mont Belvieu, Chambers 77580
Monte Alto, Hidalgo 78538
Montgomery, Montgomery 77356
Moody, McLennan 76557
Moore, Frio 78057
Moran, Shackelford 76464
Morgan, Bosque 76671
Morgan Mill, Erath 76465
Morse, Hansford 79062
Morton, Cochran 79346
Moscow, Polk 75960
Moulton, Lavaca 77975
Mound, Coryell 76558
Mountain Home, Kerr 78058
Mount Calm, Hill 76673
Mount Enterprise, Rusk 75681
Mount Pleasant, Franklin 75455
Mount Selman, Cherokee 75757
Mount Sylvan, Smith 75771
Mount Vernon, Franklin 75457
Muenster, Cooke 76252
Muldoon, Fayette 78949
Muleshoe, Bailey 79347
Mullin, Mills 76864
Mumford, Robertson 77867
Munday, Knox 76371
Murchison, Henderson 75778
Murphy, Collin 75094
Myra, Cooke 76253
*NACOGDOCHES, Nacogdoches
.... 75961
Nada, Colorado 77460
Naples, Morris 75568
Nash, Bowie 75569
Natalia, Medina 78059
Navasota, Grimes 77868
Nazareth, Castro 79063

Ringgold, Montague.............. 76261
Rio Bravo, Webb 78043
Rio Frio, Real 78879
Rio Grande City, Starr.......... 78582
Rio Hondo, Cameron 78583
Riomedina, Medina............... 78066
Rio Vista, Johnson 76093
Rising Star, Eastland 76471
Riverside, Walker 77367
Riviera, Kleberg 78379
Roanoke, Denton 76262
Roans Prairie, Grimes 77875
Roaring Springs, Motley 79256
Robert Lee, Coke................. 76945
Robinson Plaza, McLennan
.... 76716
Robstown, Nueces............... 78380
Roby, Fisher........................ 79543
Rochelle, McCulloch 76872
Rochester, Haskell 79544
Rockdale, Milam 76567
Rock Island, Colorado........... 77470
Rockland, Tyler 75938
*ROCKPORT, Aransas 78382
Rocksprings, Edwards 78880
Rockwall, Rockwall 75087
Rockwood, Coleman............. 76873
Roganville, Jasper 75956
Rogers, Bell 76569
Roma, Starr 78584
Romayor, Liberty.................. 77368
Roosevelt, Kimble 76874
Ropesville, Hockley 79358
Rosanky, Bastrop................. 78953
Roscoe, Nolan 79545
Rosebud, Falls 76570
Rosenberg, Fort Bend 77471
Rosharon, Brazoria............... 77583
Ross, McLennan 76684
Rosser, Kaufman 75157
Rosston, Cooke 76263
Rotan, Fisher 79546
Round Mountain, Blanco 78663
*ROUND ROCK, Williamson
.... 78664
Round Top, Fayette 78954
Rowena, Runnels 76875
*ROWLETT, Dallas 75088
Roxton, Lamar 75477
Royalty, Ward 79779
Royse City, Rockwall............. 75189
Rule, Haskell....................... 79547
Runge, Karnes..................... 78151
Rusk, Cherokee 75785
Rye, Liberty........................ 77369
Sabinal, Uvalde.................... 78881
Sabine Pass, Jefferson 77655
Sachse, Dallas 75048
Sacul, Nacogdoches............. 75788
Sadler, Grayson 76264
Sagerton, Haskell 79548
Saginaw, Tarrant 76179
Saint Hedwig, Bexar 78152
Saint Jo, Montague............... 76265
Salado, Bell........................ 76571
Salineno, Starr 78585
Salt Flat, Hudspeth 79847
Saltillo, Hopkins 75478
Samnorwood, Collingsworth
.... 79077

Sam Rayburn, Jasper 75951
*SAN ANGELO, Tom Green
.... 76902
*SAN ANTONIO, Bexar.......... 78205
San Augustine, San Augustine
.... 75972
San Benito, Cameron............ 78586
Sanderson, Terrell 79848
Sandia, Jim Wells 78383
San Diego, Duval 78384
Sandy, Blanco 78665
San Elizario, El Paso 79849
San Felipe, Austin................ 77473
Sanford, Hutchinson 79078
Sanger, Denton 76266
San Isidro, Starr 78588
San Juan, Hidalgo 78589
San Leon, Galveston 77539
*SAN MARCOS, Hays 78666
San Perlita, Willacy 78590
San Saba, San Saba 76877
Santa Anna, Coleman............ 76878
Santa Elena, Starr 78591
*SANTA FE, Galveston 77510
Santa Maria, Cameron........... 78592
Santa Rosa, Cameron 78593
Santo, Palo Pinto 76472
San Ygnacio, Zapata............. 78067
Saragosa, Reeves 79780
Saratoga, Hardin.................. 77585
Sargent, Matagorda 77404
Sarita, Kenedy 78385
Satin, Falls 76685
Savoy, Fannin 75479
Schertz, Guadalupe.............. 78154
Schulenburg, Fayette 78956
Schwertner, Williamson 76573
Scotland, Archer 76379
Scottsville, Harrison 75688
Scroggins, Franklin 75480
Scurry, Kaufman 75158
Seabrook, Harris.................. 77586
Seadrift, Calhoun 77983
Seagoville, Dallas 75159
Seagraves, Gaines 79359
Sealy, Austin 77474
Sebastian, Willacy................ 78594
Segno, Polk........................ 77351
*SEGUIN, Guadalupe............ 78155
Selma, Bexar 78154
Selman City, Rusk................ 75689
Seminole, Gaines 79360
Seven Points, Henderson 75143
Seymour, Baylor 76380
Shafter, Presidio 79850
Shallowater, Lubbock............ 79363
Shamrock, Wheeler 79079
Shavano Park, Bexar 78231
Sheffield, Pecos 79781
Shelbyville, Shelby............... 75973
Shepherd, San Jacinto 77371
Sheridan, Colorado............... 77475
*SHERMAN, Grayson 75090
Shiner, Lavaca 77984
Shiro, Grimes 77876
Shoreacres, Harris............... 77571
Sidney, Comanche 76474
Sierra Blanca, Hudspeth........ 79851
Silsbee, Hardin 77656
Silver, Coke........................ 76949

Silverton, Briscoe................. 79257
Simms, Bowie 75574
Simonton, Fort Bend............. 77476
Singleton, Grimes 77831
Sinton, San Patricio 78387
Sisterdale, Kendall 78006
Skellytown, Carson 79080
Skidmore, Bee 78389
Slaton, Lubbock 79364
Slidell, Wise 76267
Slocum, Anderson 75839
Smiley, Gonzales 78159
Smithland, Jefferson 75657
Smithville, Bastrop 78957
Smyer, Hockley 79367
Snook, Burleson 77878
*SYNDER, Scurry 79549
Somerset, Bexar 78069
Somerville, Burleson 77879
Sonora, Sutton 76950
Sour Lake, Hardin 77659
South Bend, Young 76481
South Houston, Harris 77587
Southland, Garza 79364
Southmayd, Grayson 76268
South Padre Island, Cameron
.... 78597
South Plains, Floyd 79258
Spade, Lamb 79369
Speaks, Lavaca 77985
Spearman, Hansford............. 79081
Spicewood, Burnet................ 78669
Splendora, Montgomery 77372
Spofford, Kinney 78877
*SPRING, Harris................... 77373
Spring Branch, Comal............ 78070
Springlake, Lamb 79082
Springtown, Parker 76082
Spur, Dickens 79370
Spurger, Tyler 77660
*STAFFORD, Fort Bend......... 77477
Stamford, Jones 79553
Stanton, Martin 79782
Staples, Guadalupe 78670
Star, Mills 76880
Stephenville, Erath............... 76401
Sterling City, Sterling 76951
Stillhouse, Bell 76542
Stinnett, Hutchinson.............. 79083
Stockdale, Wilson 78160
Stonewall, Gillespie 78671
Stowell, Chambers................ 77661
Stratford, Sherman 79084
Strawn, Palo Pinto 76475
Streetman, Freestone 75859
Sublime, Lavaca 77986
Sudan, Lamb 79371
*SUGAR LAND, Fort Bend
.... 77478
Sullivan City, Hidalgo 78595
Sulphur Bluff, Hopkins 75481
*SULPHUR SPRINGS, Hopkins
.... 75482
Summerfield, Castro 79085
Sumner, Lamar 75486
Sundown, Hockley 79372
Sunray, Moore 79086
Sunrise Beach, Llano 78643
Sunset, Montague................. 76270
Sutherland Springs, Wilson

Town, County	Zip
....	78161
Sweeny, Brazoria	77480
Sweet Home, Lavaca	77987
Sweetwater, Nolan	79556
Sylvester, Fisher	79560
Taft, San Patricio	78390
Tahoka, Lynn	79373
Talco, Franklin	75487
Talpa, Coleman	76882
Tarpley, Bandera	78883
Tarzan, Martin	79783
Tatum, Rusk	75691
Taylor, Williamson	76574
Taylor Lake Village, Harris	77586
Teague, Freestone	75860
Tehuacana, Limestone	76686
Telegraph, Kimble	76883
Telephone, Fannin	75488
Telferner, Victoria	77988
Telico, Ellis	75119
Tell, Childress	79259
*TEMPLE, Bell	76501
Tenaha, Shelby	75974
Tennessee Colony, Anderson	75861
Tennyson, Coke	76953
Terlingua, Brewster	79852
Terrell, Kaufman	75160
Terrell Hills, Bexar	78209
*TEXARKANA, Bowie	75501
*TEXAS CITY, Galveston	77590
Texline, Dallam	79087
Texon, Reagan	76932
The Colony, Denton	75056
The Grove, Coryell	76576
The Woodlands, Montgomery	77387
Thicket, Hardin	77374
Thomaston, DeWitt	77989
Thompsons, Fort Bend	77481
Thorndale, Milam	76577
Thornton, Limestone	76687
Thrall, Williamson	76578
Three Rivers, Live Oak	78071
Throckmorton, Throckmorton	76483
Tilden, McMullen	78072
Timpson, Shelby	75975
Tioga, Grayson	76271
Tivoli, Refugio	77990
Tokio, Terry	79376
Tolar, Hood	76476
*TOMBALL, Harris	77375
Tom Bean, Grayson	75489
Tornillo, El Paso	79853
Tow, Llano	78672
Toyah, Reeves	79785
Toyahvale, Reeves	79786
Trent, Taylor	79561
Trenton, Fannin	75490
Trinidad, Henderson	75163
Trinity, Trinity	75862
Trophy Club, Denton	76262
Troup, Smith	75789
Troy, Bell	76579
Truscott, Knox	79260
Tuleta, Bee	78162
Tulia, Swisher	79088
Turkey, Hall	79261
Turnersville, Coryell	76528
Turnertown, Rusk	75689
Tuscola, Taylor	79562
Twitty, Wheeler	79079
Tye, Taylor	79563
*TYLER, Smith	75702
Tynan, Bee	78391
Uhland, Caldwell	78640
Umbarger, Randall	79091
Universal City, Bexar	78148
Utopia, Uvalde	78884
*UVALDE, Uvalde	78801
Valentine, Jeff Davis	79854
Valera, Coleman	76884
Valley Mills, Bosque	76689
Valley Spring, Llano	76885
Valley View, Cooke	76272
Van, Van Zandt	75790
Van Alstyne, Grayson	75495
Vancourt, Tom Green	76955
Vanderbilt, Jackson	77991
Vanderpool, Bandera	78885
Van Horn, Culberson	79855
Van Vleck, Matagorda	77482
Vealmoor, Howard	79720
Vega, Oldham	79092
Venus, Johnson	76084
Vera, Knox	76383
Verhalen, Reeves	79772
Veribest, Tom Green	76886
*VERNON, Wilbarger	76384
Vickery, Dallas	75231
*VICTORIA, Victoria	77901
*VIDOR, Orange	77662
Vigo Park, Swisher	79088
Village Mills, Hardin	77663
Voca, McCulloch	76887
Von Ormy, Bexar	78073
Voss, Coleman	76888
Votaw, Hardin	77376
Voth, Jefferson	77709
*WACO, McLennan	76703
Wadsworth, Matagorda	77483
Waelder, Gonzales	78959
Waka, Ochiltree	79093
Wake Village, Bowie	75501
Walburg, Williamson	78673
Wall, Tom Green	76957
Waller, Waller	77484
Wallis, Austin	77485
Wallisville, Chambers	77597
Walnut Springs, Bosque	76690
Warda, Fayette	78960
Waring, Kendall	78074
Warren, Tyler	77664
Warrenton, Fayette	78961
Washington, Washington	77880
Waskom, Harrison	75692
Watauga, Tarrant	76148
Water Valley, Tom Green	76958
Waxahachie, Ellis	75165
Wayside, Armstrong	79094
*WEATHERFORD, Parker	76086
Webster, Harris	77598
Weesatche, Goliad	77993
Weimar, Colorado	78962
Weinert, Haskell	76388
Weir, Williamson	78674
Welch, Dawson	79377
Wellborn, Brazos	77881
Wellington, Collingsworth	79095
Wellman, Terry	79378
Wells, Cherokee	75976
*WESLACO, Hidalgo	78596
West, McLennan	76691
Westbrook, Mitchell	79565
West Columbia, Brazoria	77486
Westhoff, DeWitt	77994
Westminster, Collin	75096
West Odessa, Ector	79764
Weston, Collin	75097
West Orange, Orange	77630
West Point, Fayette	78963
Wetmore, Bexar	78163
Wharton, Wharton	77488
Wheeler, Wheeler	79096
Wheelock, Robertson	77882
White Deer, Carson	79097
Whiteface, Cochran	79379
Whitehouse, Smith	75791
White Oak, Gregg	75693
Whitesboro, Grayson	76273
White Settlement, Tarrant	76108
Whitewright, Grayson	75491
Whitharral, Hockley	79380
Whitney, Hill	76692
Whitsett, Live Oak	78075
Whitt, Parker	76490
Whon, Coleman	76889
*WICHITA FALLS, Wichita	76307
Wickett, Ward	79788
Wiergate, Newton	75977
Wildorado, Oldham	79098
Willis, Montgomery	77378
Willow City, Gillespie	78675
Wills Point, Van Zandt	75169
Wilmer, Dallas	75172
Wilson, Lynn	79381
Wimberley, Hays	78676
Winchester, Fayette	78964
Windcrest, Bexar	78239
Windom, Fannin	75492
Windthorst, Archer	76389
Winfield, Titus	75493
Wingate, Runnels	79566
Wink, Winkler	79789
Winnie, Chambers	77665
Winnsboro, Wood	75494
Winona, Smith	75792
Winters, Runnels	79567
Woden, Nacogdoches	75978
Wolfe City, Hunt	75496
Wolfforth, Lubbock	79382
Woodlake, Trinity	75865
Woodlawn, Harrison	75694
Woodsboro, Refugio	78393
Woodson, Throckmorton	76491
Woodville, Tyler	75979
Wortham, Freestone	76693
Wrightsboro, Gonzales	78677
Wylie, Collin	75098
Yancey, Medina	78886
Yantis, Wood	75497
Yoakum, Lavaca	77995
Yorktown, DeWitt	78164
Zapata, Zapata	78076
Zavalla, Angelina	75980
Zephyr, Brown	76890

Obituaries 1995-1997

Adamcik, Charlie F., 81; longtime leader of Czech community in Dallas; state director of the Czech Catholic Union of Texas for more than 20 years and honorary state director until his death; in Dallas, Oct. 8, 1996.

Anderson, Pat, 63; co-founder of Half Price Books, one of the largest used-book chains in the United States; in Dallas, Oct. 6, 1995.

Andujar, Elizabeth R. "Betty," 84; former state senator from Fort Worth and matriarch of the Tarrant County Republican Party; in Fort Worth, June 8, 1997.

Applewhite, Marshall H., 65; Spur native and Texas minister's son who led Heaven's Gate cult into suicides in California; March 26, 1997, buried in San Antonio.

Aston, James W., 83; Dallas business leader pivotal in building Dallas/Fort Worth International Airport and UT Southwestern Medical Center; in Dallas, Oct. 2, 1995.

Bell, Ray Howard, 71; former Fort Worth NAACP president who helped guide city through school desegregation; in Fort Worth, June 11, 1997.

Besser, Saul, 62; rabbi at Temple Shalom in Dallas for 20 years, catalyst for Jewish-Christian dialogue in city; in Tampa, Fla., Aug. 30, 1996.

Bradshaw, A.G., 65; labor leader and United Way worker; former president of Dallas Council of the AFL-CIO; in Garland, Jan. 16, 1997.

Braubach, John H. 80; longtime San Antonio civic leader; helped form the San Antonio Tennis Association and Alamo Boys' Ranch; in San Antonio; Aug. 9, 1996.

Bruner, Millie, 61; served Grand Prairie in a variety of Democratic Party positions; political strategist at state and national level; in Arlington, Aug. 2, 1997.

Burleson, T.E. Sr., 88; started honey-packing business in 1929 in Waxahachie where he later served as mayor; in Waxahachie, Sept. 14, 1996.

Bybee, Faith P., 96; former president of the Texas Historical Foundation and art patron in Houston, Round Top and Dallas; in Houston, Oct. 26, 1996.

Carruth, Allen H. "Buddy," 77; Houston business and civic leader, former president of the Wortham Foundation, one of the city's largest philanthropic organizations; in Houston, Sept. 12, 1996.

Carter, Minnie Meacham, 93; wife of former Fort Worth Star-Telegram publisher Amon Carter Sr.; active in opera and garden associations; father was mayor of Fort Worth; in

Fort Worth, Jan. 27, 1996.

Castillo, Ed, 80; columnist who worked at the San Antonio Light for more than 25 years, helped open way for younger Hispanic journalists; in San Ramon, Calif., Sept. 28, 1996.

Cecil, Andrew R., 85; ethicist, distinguished scholar in residence at UT-Dallas, former president of the Southwestern Legal Foundation; in Dallas, Sept. 16, 1996.

Chandler, Mable, 81; spent 39 years as teacher and guidance counselor in Dallas schools; in Dallas, Jan. 13, 1997.

Cheever, Elizabeth Daley, 100; matriarch of San Antonio banking family and benefactor of the University of the Incarnate Word; in San Antonio, April 22, 1997.

Cisneros Jose, 65; an electrician and mechanic who was lead plantiff in a 1968 lawsuit which desegregated the Corpus Chrisit schools; in Corpus Christi, Aug. 4, 1996.

Condon, Richard, 81; author of The Manchurian Candidate and Prizzi's Honor; in Dallas, April 10, 1996.

Conn, Fred, 89; former publisher of the San Angelo Standard-Times; in San Angelo, June 18, 1997.

Cook, Ben H., 70; Longview business and industrial leader; in Longview, Dec. 29, 1996.

Copeland, Johnny, 60; Grammy-winning blues guitarist known as the "Texas Twister," formed his first band in Houston in 1954; in New York, July 3, 1997.

Corrigan, Douglas, 88; internationally-known as pilot "Wrong Way Corrigan." The Galveston native died in Orange, Calif., Dec. 9, 1995.

Cousins, Margaret, 91; former managing editor of McCall's and Good Housekeeping magazines, senior editor at Doubleday, writer of children's books; in San Antonio, July 30, 1996.

Creighton, Tom, 70; former state senator from North Texas, served in Legislature for 19 years; in Mineral Wells, April 28, 1997.

Cuellar, Kathleen, 87; Troup native who helped establish the Cuellar family's El Chico Restaurants, Inc.; in Dallas, Jan. 1, 1996.

Daffan, Ted, 84; country-Western songwriter who wrote Born to Lose in early 1940s; in Houston, Oct. 6, 1996.

Dale, Allan, 84; dean of San Antonio talk radio and one of founders of nationwide phenomenon in the 1950s; in Florida, Jan. 14, 1997.

Daniel, Neil, 67; professor of English at Texas Christian University for 30 years; community leader in Fort

Worth's Ryan Place neighborhood; in Fort Worth, Sept. 21, 1996.

Daniels, King David, 83; teacher for 36 years and civic leader in Grand Prairie; Dec. 18, 1996.

Davis, Lyle, 91; musician and pianist who arranged music for some of Walt Disney's earliest films; in Dallas, March 28, 1996.

Dealey, Trudie Lewellen, 91; widow of former Dallas Morning News publisher E.M. "Ted" Dealey. The Mount Pleasant native died in Dallas, Aug. 13, 1995.

Dillard, Katherine, 85; journalist, women's editor of The Dallas Morning News from late 1940s until she retired in 1976; in Albuquerque, N.M., March 7, 1997.

Dixon, Ernest, 73; a retired leader of the United Methodist Church in San Antonio. Bishop Dixon was president of the church's Council of Bishops 1988-89; in San Antonio, June 29, 1996.

Drossos, Angelo, 68; brought professional basketball to San Antonio as owner of the Spurs for 15 years; in San Antonio, Jan. 9, 1997.

Evans, Jack W. Sr., 74; Tom Thumb grocery executive and banker who served as mayor of Dallas 1981-83; June 5, 1997.

Felty, L.T., 81; longtime teacher and coach known as "Mr. Waxahachie;" helped woo filmmakers to area; in Waxahachie, March 17, 1996.

Gaido, Maureen Schwertferger, 78; civic leader and wife of the founder of the landmark Gaido's Seafood Restaurant in Galveston; in Galveston, Aug. 19, 1995.

García, Héctor P., 82; physician and noted civil rights leader in South Texas, called "Martin Luther King of Hispanics;" founder of American GI Forum; in Corpus Christi, Aug. 26, 1996.

Garson, Greer, 92; Oscar-winning actress who lived in Dallas off and on since 1949 when she married Texas oilman E.E. "Buddy" Fogelson; in Dallas, April 6, 1996.

Gilvin, L.P. "Pete," 93; Amarillo contractor and philanthropist, pushed for creation of Palo Duro Canyon State Park; in Amarillo, May 30, 1997.

Ginsburg, Marcus, 81; Fort Worth attorney and civic leader; former vice president of the Children's Museum of Fort Worth and the American Jewish Congress; in Fort Worth, Sept. 5, 1996.

Gordone, Charles, 70; the first black playwright to win the Pulitzer Prize (in 1970); in College Station, Nov. 17, 1995.

Grimes, Johnnie-Marie, 91; chief advisor to former Southern Methodist University president Willis

Tate 1955-75; in Dallas, Jan. 29, 1997.

Gronouski, John A, 76; former postmaster general and ambassador to Poland; retired in 1989 as professor at the Lyndon B. Johnson School of Public Affairs at the Universtiy of Texas in Austin; in Green Bay, Wis., Jan. 7, 1996.

Guerra, Joe A. Jr., 79; San Antonio businessman and activist with Republican Party and the League of United Latin American Citizens; in San Antonio, Oct. 31, 1996.

Hackler, Loyd, 70; former aide to Lyndon Johnson and Lloyd Bentsen, editor at various newspapers in Texas; at his Hope, N.M., cattle ranch, Dec. 21, 1996.

Haley, J. Evetts, 94; archconservative writer and historian of the Texas frontier; in Midland, Oct. 9, 1995.

Hammond, Ulysses, 76; one of first African-Americans in the nation to serve as a Boy Scout area director (1946-71 in East Texas); in Dallas, Oct. 25, 1995.

Hancock, T.S., 81; educator, superintendent at Cypress-Fairbanks schools 1954 to 1968; in Houston, Dec. 14, 1996.

Hardin, Ross, 84; Texas legislator of the 1930s and '40s who helped create the first pension for Texas' elderly; in Kaufman, Feb. 4, 1996.

Hawn, C.F., 89; East Texas businessman for whom a Dallas freeway is named; served on state Highway Commission in 1950s and '60s; in Athens, Oct. 9, 1996.

Herman, Robert, 82; scientist and Big Bang theorist who taught at UT-Austin; in Austin, Feb. 13, 1997.

Hines, John, 87; bishop of the Episcopal Diocese of Texas 1956-64; presided over the Episcopal Church in the late 1960s; in Austin, July 19, 1997.

Hitt, Dick, 63; former *Dallas Times Herald* columnist, author, TV anchor and radio host; in Tyler June 27, 1996.

Hobby, Oveta Culp, 90; organized Women's Army Auxiliary Corps during World War II, secretary of Health, Education and Welfare in Eisenhower Cabinet and led media empire that included *The Houston Post*; in Houston, Aug. 16, 1995.

Hogan, Ben, 84; golfing great who won all four major championships; in Fort Worth, July 25, 1997.

Hyatt, Walter, 47; country songwriter whose Uncle Walt's Band influenced many musicians in Austin's 1970s cosmic cowboy era; in an airliner crash, May 11, 1996.

Jernigan, James, 81; educator, former president of Texas A&I University in Kingsville; in Richardson, Aug. 10, 1996.

Johnson, E.J. "Jack," 89; between 1931 and 1951 served Irving as mayor, councilman, policeman, school board member and fire fighter; in Irving, Nov. 16, 1996.

Johnson, George S., 83; former executive of the *Dallas Times Herald* where he worked from 1953 until his retirement in 1978; in Stuart, Fla., April 27, 1997.

Jonsson, J. Erik, 93; former mayor of Dallas 1964-71, whose impact as civic leader preceded and followed those years; former chairman of Texas Instruments; in Dallas, Aug. 31, 1995.

Jordan, Barbara, 59; elected to Congress from Houston in 1972, becoming first black woman member from a Southern state; first black woman in Texas Senate 1966-1972; professor at the LBJ School of Public Affairs at UT-Austin 1979 until her death; in Austin, Jan. 17, 1996.

Junkins, Jerry R, 58; chairman and CEO of Texas Instruments Inc., the global electronic giant, Dallas civic leader; of a heart attack in Stuttgart, Germany, May 29, 1996.

Kemp, Harris A., 84; architect who designed Dallas Memorial Auditorium and other downtown landmarks; in Dallas, Oct. 24, 1996.

Kreigel, Henry, 88; served in Houston as city treasurer for 17 years and eight as Harris County treasurer; in Beaumont, July 18, 1996.

Kronkosky, Albert Jr., 87; heir and former owner of the Gebhardt Chili Powder Co.; in San Antonio, Oct. 23, 1995.

Landes, James H., 84; former Hardin-Simmons University president and former executive director of Baptist General Convention of Texas; in Waco, Dec. 28, 1996.

Leachman, Robert, 68; led the surgical team that performed the first heart catheterization in 1964 at St. Luke's Hospital in Houston; in Houston, April 1, 1996.

Linthicum, Virginia Murchison, 83; philanthropist and arts patron, was wife of oilman Clint Murchison Sr. and rancher Edward B. Linthicum; in Dallas, Dec. 25, 1996.

Luna, Earl, 74; politically active lawyer; in 1963 as president of school board cast deciding vote to desegregate Garland schools; in Dallas, Aug. 15, 1996.

Macdonald, H. Malcolm, 83; professor of government at The University of Texas for more than 30 years; in Austin, July 5, 1997.

Maddux, Elizabeth Huth Coates, 86; descendant of a Castroville founder and noted San Antonio philanthropist; in San Antonio, May 12, 1996.

Mantle, Mickey, 63; famed baseball player for the New York Yankees. The Oklahoma native had been a Dallas resident since 1957; in Dallas, Aug. 13, 1995.

Masterson, Harris III, 82; Houston investor and art patron; in Houston, April 7, 1997.

Matthews, Watt, 98; legendary West Texas cattleman of the Reynolds-Matthews ranching clan; at his Lambshead Ranch near Albany, April 13, 1997.

Matz, Eleanor, 81; one of Harlingen's best-known civic activists; in Harlingen, Dec. 25, 1995.

McCann, Thomas, 80; construction contractor who served as Fort Worth mayor in late 1950s; in Fort Worth, Aug. 1, 1996.

McConn, Jim, 68; businessman who served as Houston's mayor during the boom years 1978-82; from 1989 until his death, director of the Greater Houston Convention and Visitors Bureau; in Houston, March 14, 1997.

McCulloch, Robert, 92; Scottish machinist who was a cornerstone of what became LTV Corp.; in Dallas, Nov. 30, 1995.

McKinley, DeWitt, 91; former foundry worker and Fuller Brush salesman who became Fort Worth's mayor in the late 1960s; in Fort Worth, April 9, 1997.

McKnight, Peyton, 71; former state legislator and oilman; in Tyler, Dec. 21, 1995.

Mecom, Mary Elizabeth, 86; widow of Houston oilman John W. Mecom, active in her husband's enterprises; in Houston, May 4, 1996.

Meyer, June, 79; San Antonio business leader and mentor to professional women; in San Antonio, May 13, 1997.

Miller, Dale, 87; veteran lobbyist in Washington for many Texas interests; from 1932-40 edited in Dallas *The Southwestern Banker* and *Texas Weekly*; in Washington, April 23, 1997.

Miller, J.D., 73; El Campo native, country songwriter (*It Wasn't God Who Made Honky-Tonk Angels*); in Lafayette, La., March 23, 1996.

Moody, Shearn Jr., 63; son of wealthy Galveston family, supported various projects including Moody Gardens and restoration of Opera House; in Galveston, June 26, 1996.

Morales, Francisco "Pancho," 78; credited with inventing the margarita in Ciudad Juarez in 1942; in El Paso, Jan. 2, 1997.

Nelson, George "Pop," 92; Houston barber who was a key civil rights leader there starting in the 1940s; in Houston, March 13, 1997.

Neumann, Charles, 74; former president of St. Mary's University who taught theology there for 28 years; in San Antonio, May 9, 1997.

O'Connor, Tom Jr., 81; prominent South Texas rancher, oilman and banker; in Victoria, Aug. 7, 1996.

Overcash, Clifton Sr., 75; businessman and former Fort Worth mayor; in Fort Worth, Jan. 5, 1997.

Page, Minnie Goodlow, 81; Dallas schoolteacher and community leader who served 13 years as president of Dallas Metro Section of the National Council of Negro Women; in Dallas, March 6, 1996.

Passe, Loel, 82; broadcasting voice of Houston baseball for 25 years, first with the Houston Buffs and finally with the Astros; in Houston, July 15, 1997.

Peabody, Elizabeth, 75; art and drama patron, former State Fair of Texas creative arts director; in Dallas, Dec. 25, 1996.

Pearce, J.J., 88; former superintendent of Richardson schools from 1946-70, guiding it from one rural campus to 44 schools; in Richardson, Sept. 10, 1995.

Perez, Eloy N., 72; Tejano saxophonist and composer who formed the Latinaires in Rosenberg, a top band of the 1950s and '60s; in Houston, March 19, 1996.

Pierce, Robert J., 66; physician who served Irving as mayor, school board president and city council member; in Irving, May 31, 1997.

Powell, Boone Sr., 84; chief executive officer of Baylor University Medical Center in Dallas, 1948-1974; in Dallas, Sept. 15, 1996.

Rhodes, Mary, 49; registered nurse who served three terms as Corpus Christi mayor; of cancer in Corpus Christi, June 4, 1997.

Rhodes, Robert, 69; retired executive editor of *Corpus Christi Caller-Times* and former president of the Associated Press Managing Editors; in Corpus Christi, Dec. 30, 1996.

Richardson, George L. "Skeet," 66; state legislator, Tarrant County commissioner and mayor of Keller; advocate of UT-Arlington as four-year school; in Dallas, July 28, 1996.

Richardson, Thelma Page, 85; retired teacher whose lawsuit in the 1940s forced Dallas schools to use equal pay scale for black and white teachers; in La Mirada, Calif., Sept. 14, 1996.

Riddle, Charles, 60; operated Sonny Bryan's Smokehouse from 1989; named one of four greatest "pitmasters" in America by *Parade* magazine in 1995; in Irving, Dec. 30,1996.

Roach, Walter, 82; devoted 39 years to Texas Christian University as football player, coach and director of the placement office; in Fort Worth, Sept. 25, 1996.

Safir, Nathan, 83; developed Spanish-language radio and television stations in the 1940s and '50s; in San Antonio, Sept. 7, 1996.

Sanchez, Ricardo, 54; Chicano poet

and educator who grew up in El Paso's El Barrio del Diablo; in El Paso, Sept. 3, 1995.

Sandoval, Ruben, 55; civil rights lawyer and activist; in San Antonio, June 19, 1996.

Scarlett, Harold Thomas, 70; pioneering environmental reporter for *The Houston Post* in the 1970s; in Houston, Oct. 21, 1996.

Schorre, Charles, 71; artist and important figure in Houston art community; in Houston, July 20, 1996.

Semenova, Tatiana, 76; first artistic director of the Houston Ballet in the 1950s; in Houston, Sept. 23, 1996.

Sewell, James, 91; oilman and former Texas A&M alumni association president; in Dallas, Sept. 3, 1995.

Shahan, James Tullis "Happy," 80; rancher who built the movie set for *The Alamo* and helped launch the Texas film industry; in Brackettville, Jan. 31, 1996.

Shankle, Perry, 93; a founder of the San Antonio Livestock Show and former San Antonio Chamber of Commerce president; in San Antonio, June 22, 1996.

Sharpe, Ernest A., 80; University of Texas journalism professor for 40 years until 1982, wrote biography of *Dallas Morning News* founder George B. Dealey; in Austin, May 1, 1996.

Shearer, Bill, 45; led one of Texas' best-known publishing companies; the Shearer company printed the first in a series of state atlases, *The Roads of Texas*; of cancer, March 13, 1996.

Shelton, A.B. "Stormy," 82; publisher of *Abilene Reporter-News* from 1964, becoming board chairman in 1995; in Abilene, Jan. 16, 1997.

Shivers, Marialice Shary, 86; widow of former Gov. Allan Shivers; she served on the board of regents of Pan American University 1965-78; in Austin, Sept. 29, 1996.

Slater, O. Eugene, 90; retired Methodist bishop of San Antonio and bishop-in-residence-emeritus for Perkins School of Theology at SMU; in Dallas, March 11, 1997.

Southern, Terry, 71; Dallas-reared author and screenwriter, including *Dr. Stranglove* and *The Loved One*; in New York, Oct. 25, 1995.

Spears, Franklin Scott, 64; former Texas Supreme Court justice and state legislator; in San Antonio, April 10, 1996.

Stovall, R.M. "Sharkey," 79; former Fort Worth mayor who played major role in creation of Dallas/Fort Worth International Airport; in Fort Worth, March 22, 1996.

Tejeda, Frank, 51; Democratic member of Congress for South Texas, decorated Marine veteran,

served 16 years in Legislature; in San Antonio, of cancer, Jan. 30, 1997.

Thornberry, Homer, 86; Democratic congressman from Austin 1948-63; federal judge from 1963 until his death; in Austin, Dec. 12, 1995.

Tichenor, McHenry, 98; built a radio empire of all-Spanish radio to the United States and spread Tejano music; in La Feria, Oct. 24, 1996.

Trigg, Charles, 93, and **Mary Katherine "Kitty,"** 87; benefactors of Southern Methodist University including $10 million in 1985; in San Angelo, he on Dec. 30, 1996, she on Aug. 2, 1997.

Van Zandt, Townes, 52; noted country-folk songwriter, Fort Worth native; in Smyrna, Tenn., Jan. 1, 1997.

Watson, Johnny "Guitar," 61; rhythm and blues musician; Houston native's recordings included *Mercy, Mercy, Mercy*; on tour in Japan, May 17, 1996.

Weirus, Richard "Buck," 76; headed Texas A&M University former students association 1964-79; in College Station, May 8, 1997.

Wells, Marshall F., 78; served 37 years as grants coordinator for Houston Endowment, the charitable trust; in Houston, Nov. 5, 1996.

Wentworth, Margaret Stafford, 75; leader of the Republican Party in Bexar County; in San Antonio, May 2, 1996.

Wilkerson, Floyd F., 89; Dallas educator, journalist and civic leader; in DeSoto, Nov. 18, 1996.

Whiteaker, Mildred, 75; journalist who pioneered coverage of women's issues in the *San Antonio Express-News* where she worked for 32 years; in Alamo Heights, July 8, 1996.

Williams, Clarence, 69; longtime civic leader in East Side San Antonio; in San Antonio, Aug. 24, 1996.

Wyvell-Dickson, Dorothy, 83; one of the first medical specialists in Midland in the late 1940s, conservative political activist who ran for Congress in 1960; in Midland, May 20, 1997.

Yancy, James Weldon II, 84; former Paul Quinn College president 1939-42 and a recognized African Methodist Episcopal Church historian; in Forrest City, Ark., Sept. 10, 1995.

Yarborough, Ralph, 92; longtime leading political liberal of Texas; from 1957-70, the Chandler native served in the U.S. Senate where he sponsored the Cold War GI Bill; in Austin, Jan. 27, 1996.

Zimmerman, Brian, 24; former "boy mayor" of Crabb who attracted worldwide attention at age 11; of a heart attack in Houston, Sept. 20, 1996. ☆

Advertisers' Index

General Index

For towns not listed in the index, see complete list of towns on pages 288-311.

For towns not listed in the index, see complete list of towns on pages 288-311.

For towns not listed in the index, see complete list of towns on pages 288-311.

For towns not listed in the index, see complete list of towns on pages 288-311.

For towns not listed in the index, see complete list of towns on pages 288-311.

For towns not listed in the index, see complete list of towns on pages 288-311.

For towns not listed in the index, see complete list of towns on pages 288-311.

For towns not listed in the index, see complete list of towns on pages 288-311.

For towns not listed in the index, see complete list of towns on pages 288-311.

For towns not listed in the index, see complete list of towns on pages 288-311.

For towns not listed in the index, see complete list of towns on pages 288-311.

Index 665

For towns not listed in the index, see complete list of towns on pages 288-311.

For towns not listed in the index, see complete list of towns on pages 288-311.

For towns not listed in the index, see complete list of towns on pages 288-311.

For towns not listed in the index, see complete list of towns on pages 288-311.